INDEX TO THE
ROLL OF HONOR

INDEX
TO THE
ROLL
OF
HONOR

Compiled by
Martha & William Reamy

With a Foreword and an
Index to Burial Sites
by Mark Hughes

GENEALOGICAL · PUBLISHING Co., Inc.

Foreword

By Mark Hughes

he American Civil War caused unprecedented losses on both sides. In 1870 the U.S. Army's Surgeon General reported a total of 303,504 deaths of Union soldiers. About 95,000 of these soldiers were either killed in action or died of wounds. Over 185,000 died of disease. The records did not list a cause of death for over 24,000 men. By contrast, a total of only 1,733 United States soldiers had died during the Mexican War (1846–48). Most of the bodies of soldiers killed in the Mexican War were never recovered. The few that were recovered had to be buried as unknowns in a soon forgotten cemetery in Mexico City. To prevent this from happening again, on September 11, 1861 the War Department issued General Order #75. This order made the commanding officer of military departments and corps responsible for the burial of dead soldiers.

Soldiers who died in hospitals in the rear were often buried in civilian cemeteries. As these filled up new cemeteries were started near the hospital. Soldiers who were killed in battle were normally buried near where they died. Sometimes the graves were well marked by wooden headboards, but more often they were not. Standard practice was to bury the bodies of the unknown casualties in trenches. At Spotsylvania Court House, only a few bodies were buried before both armies moved toward Richmond. Not until a year later were any arrangements made to bury the Union dead, and by then only about 700 of the over 4,100 Union dead could be identified.

On July 17, 1862 President Lincoln signed an omnibus act that empowered the president ". . . to purchase cemetery grounds . . . to be used as a national cemetery. . . ." Twelve cemeteries were established in 1862 pursuant to the provisions of this legislation:

Alexandria National Cemetery (Virginia)
Annapolis National Cemetery (Maryland)
Camp Butler National Cemetery (Illinois)
Cypress Hills National Cemetery (Long Island, New York)
Danville National Cemetery (Kentucky)
Fort Leavenworth National Cemetery (Kansas)
Fort Scott National Cemetery (Kansas)
Keokuk National Cemetery (Iowa)
Loudon Park National Cemetery (Maryland)
Military Asylum National Cemetery (Washington, DC)
Mill Springs National Cemetery (Kentucky)
New Albany National Cemetery (Indiana)

Of these twelve original national cemeteries only Mill Springs (also known as Logan's Crossroads) was at the site of a battle. Fort Scott and Fort Leavenworth were supply depots located far from most of the fighting. Their existing post cemeteries were expanded. Cypress Hills was started to bury Confederate POWs and their guards who were killed in a train wreck. The other cemeteries were located near training camps, large supply depots, or in cities with large hospitals.

Most of the soldiers who died near Washington were buried in either the Military Asylum National Cemetery or in the Alexandria National Cemetery in Virginia. The first burials in the Military Asylum National Cemetery were made about August 1, 1861. By the time the cemetery was closed to further burials on May 12 or 13, 1864, a total of 5,211 Union soldiers had been interred. Arlington National Cemetery, located on Mrs. Robert E. Lee's estate, opened May 13, 1864. By June 30, 1865, a total of 5,003 burials had been made in Arlington. By 1871 a total of 11,276 Union soldiers (7,199 known) had been buried there; 4,276 "others" were also buried in the cemetery. Some were cemetery employees. A few were "citizens," civilians held by military authorities without trial. Three hundred forty-seven

Confederate POWs were buried in Arlington. Before becoming a cemetery for Union soldiers, part of Arlington had served as a camp for ex-slaves. By 1871, a total of 3,235 of these refugees (or contrabands as Union officers often called them) had been buried on the grounds.

The responsibility for overseeing the burial of Union soldiers fell to the Quartermaster General's Office. During the war the Quartermaster's Office was more concerned with supplying living Union soldiers with food, weapons, and clothing than starting cemeteries. Burying the dead was not a priority.

After the war, Quartermaster General Montgomery C. Meigs assigned much of the early work of reburying the Union dead to Captain James M. Moore. Moore had charge of burials in the District of Columbia in 1864 and 1865. Later, Captain (later Brevet Lieutenant Colonel) Moore commanded burial parties sent to the Wilderness and Spotsylvania Court House battlefields and the Andersonville POW camp.

One of Captain Moore's duties was answering letters from parents and wives of soldiers who did not return from the war. In order for "surviving comrades and friends" to locate the graves of deceased Union soldiers, the Quartermaster General's Office published a series of 27 volumes of burial rosters of various cemeteries. This series, published in paperback, became known as the *Roll of Honor*, although the title of a few volumes varies slightly. By 1868 the Quartermaster's Department had received reports of burials in 72 national cemeteries and 320 post and local cemeteries. A total of 316,233 soldiers had been buried. Of these, 175,764, or about 55.5%, were identified. The *Roll of Honor* series contains most of these burial lists.

Two volumes of the series were published in 1865. Volume 1, which "listed" the names of most Union soldiers buried in Washington and in the Arlington National Cemetery, was published on June 15, 1865. Volume 2, published on October 6, 1865, listed names of soldiers buried by Captain Moore at the Wilderness and Spotsylvania Court House battlefields.

Moore's report of his trip to rebury the dead at Andersonville (printed in volume 3 of the *Roll of Honor*) fails to acknowledge two of the members of his party, Clara Barton and Dorence

Atwater. Atwater, a former prisoner at Andersonville, had served as Andersonville's "Clerk of the Dead." He secretly made a copy of the original burial roster, but after the war he had been forced to sell his copy of the burial roster to the War Department.

Atwater apparently mistrusted the War Department's intentions, and he refused to turn over his copy of the burial roster. He was quickly court-martialed and sent to prison. Clara Barton, Horace Greeley, and others pushed for his release, and after two months at hard labor he was freed. Because the list of names of the Union dead at Andersonville had not been published, Atwater made arrangements with Greeley to publish his list. On February 14, 1866 the Tribune Publishing Company published the Atwater list. The War Department was publicly embarrassed. Three days later, Acting Quartermaster General D. H. Rucker (Quartermaster General Meigs was on leave) wrote Moore asking when he had sent the manuscript for volume 3 of the *Roll of Honor* to the "public printing office." According to Moore's reply the manuscript would ". . . be completed in a few days . . ." (words every editor has heard).

Apparently this embarrassment spurred the Quartermaster General's Office to quick action. Eight more volumes of the series were published in 1866.

Volume 14 of the series, the first of four volumes released in 1868, contained the names of 10,959 Union prisoners who died during the war. Volume 3 of the series had listed 12,912 POWs buried at Andersonville. Volume 19 added 2,797 burials at Florence, South Carolina. A total of 3,504 burials (only three unknown) at Salisbury, North Carolina, were recorded in volume 14, although the unknown writer of the short description of the cemetery claimed ". . . over five thousand fell victim . . ." And in 1871 Col. Oscar Mack, the Inspector of National Cemeteries, claimed although ". . . no records have been found . . .," some 11,700 Union prisoners died at "this golgotha." Mack forgot that just three years earlier the War Department had published volume 14 of the *Roll of Honor* which contained the list of names of 3,504 soldiers buried at Salisbury. (For a more complete analysis of the burials at Salisbury see this author's *Bivouac of the Dead*.)

Volume 14 of the *Roll of Honor* was the first volume of the series not completed under the direction of Col. Moore. The remaining volumes were completed under the direction of Brevet Brigadier General Alexander J. Perry. However, the real work on volumes 14 to 24 was done by Brevet Colonel Charles W. Folsom, Assistant Quartermaster–U.S. Volunteers. Col. Folsom remained in service after the war to oversee the completion of much of the work of burying Union soldiers. He served as Inspector of National Cemeteries in 1868. By the time he returned to civilian life, most bodies of Union soldiers had been reburied in 74 national cemeteries. Folsom moved to Massachusetts where he owned a landscaping business. However, he retained his interest in national cemeteries, sometimes writing magazine articles or writing the Quartermaster General about reports of unburied bodies being found.

In the March 25, 1869 issue of *Nation* he wrote about the problems of identifying the bodies of Union soldiers who had died years before: "Every pains was taken to preserve all memorials of identity, from the scrap of a letter hastily pinned on the breast or buried in a can or bottle with the remains, up to the rudely-ornamented headboard which comrades provided were more time was allowed." (sic) Volume 2 of the series reprints extracts from a report of Chaplain William Earnshaw who was in charge of disinterring Union soldiers and removing the bodies to the new national cemetery at Stone's River, Tennessee. According to Earnshaw, the troops under his command saw their duty as a "holy cause."

But not everyone who had charge of burying Union troops took such care. In 1866, Brevet Major E.B. Whitman, Army Quartermaster, wrote:

> Doubtless, in many instances, the mortuary records were neglected or left incomplete from the influence of circumstances beyond the control of the officer in charge; but oftener from inexperience and want of forethought, and sometimes, unquestionably, from culpable and inexcusable neglect.

> In several cases a large number of interments were made by contractors, and the records and gravemarks were the work of illiterate or careless employees. Frequently the

> lists kept by hospital stewards and quartermasters' clerks, intended to be correct, have been rendered of comparatively little value from barbarous spelling and bad or careless penmanship.

(After attempting to read some of these records in the National Archives it appears to the author that many clerks used the plan: "If in doubt – scribble.")

Whitman continued:

> Many burials have been made by troops on detached service or on the march. The regimental returns alone will show any official record of these; and the only source of information within reach is to be found in the inscriptions or marks at the grave itself—sometimes a half-obliterated penciling upon a rough board, or a rude carving upon a neighboring tree.

According to a report Col. Folsom wrote in May 1868, there were many errors in the various volumes of the *Roll of Honor*. He proposed that a consolidated report be produced with the dead listed alphabetically by state. That would save searching through some 300 cemetery burial lists in 27 volumes.

Folsom realized that state adjutant general records and other records would need to be consulted to produce "a record . . . worthy of the nation, and which will gratify many generations of the brave men therein commemorated." Folsom proposed that "a zealous and conscientious officer be detailed, so long as needed for . . . republication of these lists. . . ." But the War Department failed to act on Folsom's recommendations. In that same year, 1868, the Quartermaster General's Office published an *Alphabetical Index to Places of Interment of Deceased Union Soldiers*. This was designed to assist in locating cemeteries by state, but only the first thirteen volumes of the series were covered. Then in 1868/69 the Quartermaster General's Office published the so-called *Final Disposition* (included in the Genealogical Publishing Company's 1994 reprint edition of the *Roll of Honor*, as is the *Alphabetical Index to Places of Interment*). These four slim volumes identify the original places of burial from which bodies had been removed and name the national cemeteries where those bodies were deposited. A total of 197,000

reinterments were recorded, but the *Final Disposition* listed reinterments in only 55 of the 74 national cemeteries active in 1871, so it, too, is far from complete. This present publication is, in fact, the first to provide a comprehensive place index to the *Roll of Honor* (by state) and is the only alphabetical name index to the *Roll* ever attempted.

In 1871, Col. Mack, the Inspector of National Cemeteries, reported a revised total of the burial of 305,492 Union soldiers:

white soldiers — known	151,237
white soldiers — unknown	117,678
colored soldiers — known	13,176
colored soldiers — unknown	20,043
unknown and unclassified*	3,358
	305,492

Col. Mack's report incorrectly lists 12,112 burials at Salisbury, North Carolina. However, he does not count soldiers who died in western states and territories because "their deaths were not incidental to the rebellion." Even though Col. Mack's figure of about 305,000 Union burials is about 9,000 too high, it compares favorably with the Union Surgeon General's 1870 report listing 303,504 deaths. Col. Mack's figure is 11,000 less than Col. Folsom's 1868 report. An unknown number (Col. Folsom estimated 40,000) who were wounded or "took sick" were sent home to recuperate, only to die there. Perhaps this accounts for the discrepancy in the figures. Very few of the burials who died "at home" were reported in the *Roll of Honor*.

This index contains a total of 228,639 names. However, an undetermined number of them are either duplications of names in earlier volumes or corrected names. Volume 14, for example, records a total of 685 burials at Lawton, Georgia. Volume 17 repeats those names. In 1868 those bodies were moved to the Beaufort (South Carolina) National Cemetery. Volume 27 of the series, which lists the Beaufort cemetery, repeats those names again. It appears that about 20% of the names are duplications.

---

*Most of these burials were at Port Hudson, Louisiana.

A few names were apparently corrected by comparing burial lists with other records.

Although the *Roll of Honor* was supposed to list all Union deaths, it does not. It fails to list the one known soldier buried at the Ball's Bluff (Virginia) National Cemetery. Nor does it list the 1,262 burials at Grafton (West Virginia) National Cemetery. The *Roll* even missed the 200-odd burials at Saint Elizabeth's Hospital in Washington!

One reason for these names being omitted from the *Roll of Honor* appears to be the utter chaos in the Quartermaster General's cemetery records. Although the records were supposed to be in some form of alphabetical order, the records that remain in the National Archives are in utter disarray. As one archivist put it: "As you know, the material on national cemeteries before 1920 is incomprehensible." In 1885 Quartermaster General Samuel Holabird wrote: "No published reports on this subject (the history of national cemeteries) are now reliable or accurate. . . ." Holabird admitted: ". . . we have not at hand the necessary data upon which to base such [history]."

One example of this lack of data is the soldiers' lot at Carlisle, Pennsylvania. Volume 7 of the *Roll of Honor* lists thirty-five Union cavalrymen buried at Carlisle. However, other data in the Quartermaster General's files list 70 burials at Carlisle. By 1878 a total of 313 soldiers were believed to have been buried at Carlisle. An 1890 report stated that 41 soldiers were buried in Carlisle's Ashland Cemetery. According to current Department of Veterans Affairs records, a total of 523 soldiers are buried in 24 grave sites.

Today, the Union graves in the Ashland Cemetery Soldiers' Lot are marked by a bronze tablet. The tablet's inscription reads: "500 US SOLDIERS OF THE CIVIL WAR ARE HERE INTERRED." The tablet then lists the thirty-five names found in volume 7 of the *Roll of Honor*. The inscription concludes: "THE REST ARE KNOWN BUT TO GOD."

The War Department didn't even know what cemeteries they owned. Volume 18 of the *Roll of Honor* listed a total of 655 burials in the Spring Grove National Cemetery in Cincinnati, Ohio. According to the *Roll of Honor*, two of the lots were donated to

the federal government by the State of Ohio. However, when Col. Mack completed his 1871 report, he could not determine if the land had been deeded to the United States. The Spring Grove Cemetery believes the federal government owns the land but cannot determine when the title was transferred. Today the Department of Veterans Affairs does not list Spring Grove as either a national cemetery or a soldiers' lot. The War Department did not mark the graves at Spring Grove. That means the Department of Veterans Affairs has no record of the soldiers buried there.

A similar problem occurs with the Rose Hill Cemetery near Chicago. Volume 9 of the series lists 159 burials "at Chicago." Volume 18 adds 317 burials in Chicago's Rose Hill Cemetery. Although several reports state that the lots in Rose Hill Cemetery were owned by the federal government, today the VA has no record of burials in the cemetery because the graves were not marked when the graves in national cemeteries were.

Although there are errors in the *Roll of Honor*, it remains the only record of burials of many of the Union soldiers who died during the Civil War. Most of the graves listed in the *Roll of Honor* were not permanently marked until headstones were placed in national cemeteries in 1873. The Department of Veterans Affairs uses copies of the orders for headstones to determine if a soldier is buried in a national cemetery. If a wooden headboard had been destroyed before a permanent headstone was ordered, the VA will have no record of the burial. Burials in most post cemeteries were not marked until 1885. Often the *Roll of Honor* is the only record of the burial of Union soldiers.

The VA turned its copy of the *Roll of Honor* over to the National Archives in the early 1970s. As a VA spokesman explained: "As you know there is no index of names for the *Roll of Honor*. It's just too hard to search through all those books for a name. Anyway, many of those bodies were moved and we have no record of where they are now." Martha and William Reamy, along with the Genealogical Publishing Company, have solved those problems with this volume. After more than 125 years we finally have the means of accessing the only official memorial to the Union dead ever published.

BIBLIOGRAPHY

National Archives Record Groups

RG92-576. "General Correspondence and Reports Relating to National and Post Cemeteries." 1865–1890

RG92-582. "Requests for Information Relating to Missing Soldiers, Received by James Moore, Quartermaster." 1863–1867.

RG92-587. "Correspondence Relating to the Administration of National Cemeteries." 1907–1919.

RG92-682. "Abstracts of Officer's Reports Relating to Burial Places of Soldiers, Available Records, and Recommendations." 1866.

RG92-683. "Descriptive List of National Cemeteries." 1867–1870.

Government Publications

Quartermaster General's Department

Folsom, Col. C.W. *Report of the Inspector General of the National Cemeteries.* 1868.

Mack, Col. Oscar A. *Report of the Inspector General of the National Cemeteries for the Years 1870 and 1871.*

Mack, Col. Oscar A. *Report of the Inspector General of the National Cemeteries.* 1874.

Roll of Honor: Names of Soldiers Who Died in Defense of the American Union, Interred in the National Cemeteries. 27 vols. (1865–1871), repr. in 10 vols. Baltimore, 1994.

Other Government Sources

Medical and Surgical History of the War of the Rebellion. 6 vols. U.S. Surgeon-General's Office. 1866–88.

Official Records of the Union and Confederate Armies in the War of the Rebellion. U.S. War Department. 1880–1901.

"Station Data Sheets." Department of Veterans Affairs and National Park Service.

Other Sources

Booth, B.F. *Dark Days of the Rebellion.* Indianola, Ind., 1897.

Hughes, Mark. *Bivouac of the Dead: Burial Sites of United States Soldiers 1861–1865.* Bowie, Md., 1995.

Roberts, Robert. *Encyclopedia of Historic Forts.* New York, 1987.

Steere, Edward. "Origins of the National Cemetery System," *The Quartermaster Review* (1953).

Weigley, Russell. *Quartermaster General of the Army: M.C. Meigs.* New York, 1959.

INDEX TO BURIAL SITES

Bodies Buried by Friends

Location	Volume	Page
Buried at unknown locations	14	332
Buried by friends (colored)	1	192
Delivered to friends	10	12
Delivered to friends (colored)	10	24
Died aboard ships	14	331
Died aboard ships	14	333
Exchanged POWs who died	14	333

Bodies Buried in Alabama

Location	Volume	Page
Cabawha (a misspelling of Cahaba)	14	313
Moved to Marietta (Ga) National Cemetery		
Demopolis	14	318
Huntsville	14	318
Moved to Chattanooga (Tenn) National Cemetery		
Mobile National Cemetery	14	318
Mobile	25	267
Montgomery	14	320
Moved to Marietta (Ga) National Cemetery		
Moulton	14	326

Bodies Buried in Arizona

Location	Volume	Page
Camp Lincoln	12	172
Fort McDowell	12	173

Camp McDowell 19 324
    Moved to San Francisco National Cemetery
Camp McKee 12 168
El Picacho 8 119
Fort Bowie 12 172
    Moved to San Francisco National Cemetery
Fort Goodwin 12 169
Fort Grant 12 173
    Moved to San Francisco National Cemetery
Fort Mason 12 171
    Moved to San Francisco National Cemetery
Fort Mojare 12 173
    Moved to San Francisco National Cemetery
Fort Wallen 12 170
    Moved to San Francisco National Cemetery
Tucson 8 119

Bodies Buried in Arkansas

Location	Volume	Page
Arkansas Post	12	164

Moved to either Memphis National Cemetery or Pine Bluff (Ark). If moved to Pine Bluff, the bodies were later moved to Little Rock National Cemetery.

Batesville	7	72

Moved to Fort Smith National Cemetery

Camden	8	59
Camden (colored)	8	59

Moved to Baton Rouge (La) National Cemetery

De Vall's Bluff	8	70
De Vall's Bluff (colored)	8	76

Moved to Little Rock National Cemetery

Fayetteville National Cemetery	10	179
Fayetteville	14	330
Fayetteville	18	170
Fayetteville	26	203
Fort Smith National Cemetery	18	186
Fort Smith	26	209
Helena	8	44

Helena (colored)   8   58
    Moved to Memphis National Cemetery
Jacksonport   7   71
    Moved to Little Rock National Cemetery
Little Rock National Cemetery   8   7
Little Rock   14   330
Little Rock   18   118
Little Rock   26   147
Little Rock (colored)   8   37
Ozark Hospital   14   330
Pea Ridge   10   192
    Moved to both Springfield (Mo) and Fayetteville
    National Cemeteries
Pine Bluff   8   61
Pine Bluff (colored)   8   69
    Moved to Little Rock National Cemetery
Prairie Grove   10   185
    Moved to Fayetteville National Cemetery

Bodies Buried in California

Location	Volume	Page
Alcatraces Island (sic)	12	168
A misspelling of Alcatraz Island. Possibly moved to		
San Francisco National Cemetery		
Benicia Barracks	8	60
Benicia Barracks	12	169
Today a US Army post cemetery		
Camp Anderson	12	168
Camp Babbitt	12	172
Camp Bidwell	12	173
Camp Cameron	12	173
Camp Independence	8	60
Camp Independence	12	173
Moved to San Francisco National Cemetery		
Camp Joqua (sic)	12	170
A misspelling of Camp Jaqua		
Camp Wright	12	171
Moved to San Francisco National Cemetery		

Drum Barracks	12	172
Fort Bidwell	8	60
Fort Cook	12	173
Fort Gaston	12	171
Fort Humboldt	12	170
Fort Point	12	168
Fort Wright	8	60
Moved to San Francisco National Cemetery		
Fort Yuma	12	169
Moved to San Francisco National Cemetery		
Locations not designated	12	173
Monterey Barracks	12	171
Today a US Army post cemetery		
New San Diego	8	60
New San Diego	12	170
Became Fort Rosecrans National Cemetery		
Presidio—San Francisco	12	167
Became San Francisco National Cemetery		

Bodies Buried in Colorado

Location	Volume	Page
Camp Collins	7	138
Denver	8	119
Denver	13	134
Three bodies from the Denver area were moved to Fort Leavenworth National Cemetery		
Fort Garland	19	324
Moved to Fort Leavenworth National Cemetery		
Fort Lyon	19	325
Moved to Fort Leavenworth National Cemetery		
Fort Morgan	19	324
Fort Sedgwick	7	12
Moved to Fort McPherson National Cemetery		

Bodies Buried in Connecticut

Location	Volume	Page
Hartford	9	15

| New Haven | 9 | 11 |
| New Haven (colored) | 9 | 15 |

Some bodies from New Haven were moved to
Cypress Hills National Cemetery

Bodies Buried in the Dakota Territory

Location	Volume	Page
Fort Abercrombie	9	244
Fort Abercrombie	19	317
Moved to Custer Battlefield National Cemetery		
Fort Buford	19	327
Moved to Custer Battlefield National Cemetery		
Fort Casper	10	212
Fort Dakota	19	327
Fort David A. Russell	19	338
Fort Laramie	9	239
Fort Laramie	19	336
Fort Phil Kearney	19	328
Moved to Custer Battlefield National Cemetery		
Fort Randall	9	244
Fort Randall	19	331
Moved to Fort Leavenworth National Cemetery		
Fort Reno	9	244
Fort Reno	19	333
Moved to Custer Battlefield National Cemetery		
Fort Rice	9	242
Fort Rice	19	325
Moved to Custer Battlefield National Cemetery		
Fort Scully	19	327
Moved to Fort Leavenworth National Cemetery		
Fort Thompson	19	328
Fort Wadsworth	19	339
Yankton	9	239

Bodies Buried in the District of Columbia

Location	Volume	Page
Battleground National Cemetery	1	103

Harmony	1	93
Harmony	1	96
Moved to Arlington National Cemetery		
Military Asylum	1	9
Now called Soldiers' Home National Cemetery		

Bodies Buried in Delaware

Location	Volume	Page
Wilmington	7	14
Wilmington	7	15

Bodies Buried in Florida

Location	Volume	Page
Apalachicola	9	158
Apalachicola (colored)	9	159
Moved to Barrancas National Cemetery		
Baldwin	14	327
Barrancas National Cemetery	7	73
Barrancas	25	291
Barrancas (colored)	7	77
Chattahoochee	7	82
Fort Jefferson	9	159
Fort Jefferson (colored)	9	160
Jacksonville	9	160
Jacksonville	14	327
Jacksonville (colored)	9	161
Moved to Beaufort National Cemetery		
Key West	9	156
Key West (colored)	9	157
Moved to Barrancas National Cemetery		
Lake City	9	158
Lake City (colored)	9	158
Pensacola	7	79
Pensacola	14	328
Now Barrancas National Cemetery		
Quincy (colored)	7	82

Santa Rosa Island   7   81
    Most bodies moved to Barrancas National
    Cemetery; however, bodies of yellow fever
    victims were left
Tallahassee   9   162
Tallahassee (colored)   9   162

Bodies Buried in Georgia

Location	Volume	Page
Andersonville National Cemetery	3	9
Andersonville	3	223
Andersonville	14	267
Andersonville	17	493
Atlanta	14	264
Augusta	14	277
Moved to Marietta National Cemetery		
Cassville	14	267
Covington	14	267
Moved to Andersonville National Cemetery		
Lawton	17	466
Moved to Beaufort National Cemetery		
Macon	14	279
First move to Lawton National Cemetery, then moved to Beaufort National Cemetery		
Madison	14	286
Moved to Andersonville National Cemetery		
Marietta National Cemetery	14	287
Marietta	23	9
Millen	14	293
AKA Lawton National Cemetery. Moved to Beaufort National Cemetery		
Savannah	14	313
Moved to Beaufort National Cemetery		

Bodies Buried in the Idaho Territory

Location	Volume	Page
Camp Lyon	8	120

Camp Winthrop	19	340
Fort Boise	8	120
Fort Boise	19	340
Fort Loproai (sic)	8	120
A misspelling of Fort Lapwai		

Bodies Buried in Illinois

Location	Volume	Page
Alton National Cemetery	9	71
Alton	12	139
Alton	13	60
Cairo	9	74
Cairo (colored)	9	95
Moved to Mound City National Cemetery		
Camp Butler National Cemetery	9	47
Camp Butler (colored)	9	65
Carlinville	13	60
Chicago	9	65
Chicago	18	273
Dixon	18	271
Dundee	18	270
Elgin	18	271
Joliet	18	272
Mound City National Cemetery	9	74
Mound City	18	226
Mound City	26	7
Mound City (colored)	9	95
Quincy	9	95
Quincy (colored)	9	100
Became Quincy National Cemetery in 1882		
Rock Island National Cemetery	9	68
Rock Island (colored)	9	70
Rockford	18	270
Springfield	9	100
Springfield	9	101
St. Charles	18	270

Bodies Buried in the Indian Territory

Location	Volume	Page
Fort Gibson National Cemetery	25	331

Bodies Buried in Indiana

Location	Volume	Page
Evansville	8	102
Evansville (colored)	8	112
Indianapolis	8	78
Indianapolis (colored)	8	99
Indianapolis	18	203
Now Crown Hill National Cemetery		
Jeffersonville	17	431
Jeffersonville	17	438
Moved to New Albany National Cemetery		
Madison	8	100
Madison	17	458
Apparently moved to New Albany National Cemetery		
New Albany National Cemetery	17	414
New Albany	24	149
Various Sites **	18	213

Bodies Buried in Iowa

Location	Volume	Page
Davenport	12	160
Davenport	12	163
Davenport	12	164
Davenport (colored)	12	163
159 bodies moved to Rock Island National Cemetery; however, 76 bodies remain in Oakdale Soldiers' Lot		
Des Moines	10	26
Keokuk National Cemetery	12	150
Keokuk (colored)	12	160
Sioux City	9	239
Various Sites **	18	390

Bodies Buried in Kansas

Location	Volume	Page
Barnesville	18	465
Apparently moved to Fort Riley Post Cemetery		
Fort Aubrey	9	233
Fort Dodge	9	233
Fort Dodge	10	210
Fort Dodge	18	425
Moved to Fort Leavenworth National Cemetery		
Fort Ellsworth	9	234
Fort Ellsworth	10	211
Moved to Fort Leavenworth National Cemetery		
Fort Fletcher	9	234
Fort Fletcher	10	210
Fort Harker	18	429
Moved to Fort Leavenworth National Cemetery		
Fort Hays	18	433
Moved to Fort Leavenworth National Cemetery		
Fort Larned	9	234
Fort Larned	9	241
Fort Larned	18	423
Fort Larned (colored)	9	241
Moved to Fort Leavenworth National Cemetery		
Fort Leavenworth National Cemetery	9	235
Fort Leavenworth	9	238
Fort Leavenworth	18	410
Fort Leavenworth	26	215
Fort Leavenworth (colored)	9	238
Fort Riley	9	235
Fort Riley	18	419
At least two bodies moved to Fort Leavenworth National Cemetery; however, most were left in the post cemetery		
Fort Scott National Cemetery	10	204
Fort Scott (colored)	10	208
Fort Scott	18	405
Fort Wallace	18	439
Moved to Fort Leavenworth National Cemetery		

Geneva	10	210
Geneva	18	453
Iola	10	211
Iola	18	455
Lawrence	10	209
Lawrence	18	443
Marmaton City	18	457
Monument Station	10	210
Monument Station	18	437
Mound City Soldiers' Lot	10	211
Mound City	18	459
Olathe	10	211
Olathe	18	449
Ossawatamie (sic)	18	445

Moved to Fort Riley Post Cemetery

Ottumwa (sic)	18	451
Paola	10	211
Paola	18	463
Spring Hill	18	461
Topeka	10	210
Topeka	18	447

Moved to Fort Leavenworth National Cemetery

Various locations **	18	467

Bodies from the Mine Creek Battlefield were moved
to Mound City Soldiers' Lot

Bodies Buried in Kentucky

Location	Volume	Page
Camp Nelson National Cemetery	17	142
Covington	17	386

Moved to Camp Nelson National Cemetery

Location	Volume	Page
Danville National Cemetery	17	312
Frankfort	17	306

Moved to Camp Nelson National Cemetery

Location	Volume	Page
Lebanon National Cemetery	17	270
Lexington National Cemetery	17	230
London	17	334

Moved to Camp Nelson National Cemetery

Louisville	17	12
Now Cave Hill National Cemetery		
Louisville (colored)	17	126
Moved to New Albany National Cemetery		
Mill Springs National Cemetery	17	198
Perryville	17	345
Moved to Camp Nelson National Cemetery		
Richmond	17	325
Moved to Camp Nelson National Cemetery		
Tompkinsville	17	408
Moved to Nashville National Cemetery		

Bodies Buried in Louisiana

Location	Volume	Page
Alexandria National Cemetery	9	163
Alexandria	14	328
Alexandria	25	315
Alexandria (colored)	9	164
Baton Rouge National Cemetery	9	167
Baton Rouge	19	223
Baton Rouge (colored)	9	199
Brasher City	7	83
Brasher City (colored)	7	84
Moved to Chalmette National Cemetery		
Chalmette National Cemetery	21	293
Fort Livingston	7	82
Fort Livingston (colored)	7	82
Fort Macomb	9	212
Fort Macomb (colored)	9	213
Moved to Chalmette National Cemetery		
Fort St. Phillip	19	295
Moved to Chalmette National Cemetery		
Grand Terre Island	7	82
Grand Terre Island (colored)	7	82
Monroe	14	328
New Orleans	7	84
New Orleans	21	293
New Orleans (colored)	7	116

New Orleans (colored)	14	329
Now called Chalmette National Cemetery		
Pettus Farilla	14	329
Port Hudson National Cemetery	9	203
Port Hudson	18	62
Port Hudson (colored)	9	205

Bodies Buried in Maine

Location	Volume	Page
Augusta	7	8
Augusta (colored)	7	9
Now Mount Pleasant Cemetery Soldiers' Lot		
Danville	7	7
Fort Preble	7	7
Portland	7	7
Wallingford	7	7

Bodies Buried in Maryland

Location	Volume	Page
Annapolis National Cemetery	7	18
Annapolis	7	47
Annapolis	7	55
Annapolis	7	62
Annapolis	14	1
Annapolis (colored)	7	47
Antietam National Cemetery	15	1
Baltimore	7	9
Baltimore	19	1
Now Loudon Park National Cemetery		
Baltimore (colored)	7	10
Baltimore (colored)	19	44
Moved to Loudon Park National Cemetery		
Camp Casey	1	193
Roberts' *Encyclopedia of Historic Forts* lists Camp Casey under Maryland.		
Camp Parole	14	1
Moved to Annapolis National Cemetery		

Fort Washington	10	26
Frederick City	12	61
Moved to Antietam National Cemetery		
Point Lookout	9	107
Point Lookout (colored)	9	114
Moved to Arlington National Cemetery		

Bodies Buried in Massachusetts

Location	Volume	Page
Brookline	9	9
Brookline	16	1
Cambridge	9	9
Cambridge	16	2
Chelsea	9	10
Chelsea	16	4
Dedham	9	8
Dedham (colored)	9	9
Galloup's Island	9	10
Galloup's Island (colored)	9	10
Readville	9	10
Roxbury	9	9
Worcester	9	10
Worcester	16	6
Worcester	16	8
Worcester	16	9

Bodies Buried in Michigan

Location	Volume	Page
Corunna	18	331
Detroit	8	112
Detroit	18	322
Detroit (colored)	8	116
Flint	18	331
Fort Wayne	18	325
Grand Rapids	18	326
Jackson	8	116
Jackson	18	329

Jackson (colored)	8	117
Kalamazoo	18	331
Niles	18	332
Ypsilanti	18	331

Bodies Buried in Minnesota

Location	Volume	Page
Alexandria	7	9
Fort Ridgely	8	117
Fort Ridgeley (sic)	19	315
Apparently a typo		
Fort Ripley	19	316
Fort Snelling	9	239
Fort Snelling	9	241
Fort Snelling	19	316
Became National Cemetery in 1939		
Pomme de Terre	7	18
Sauk Centre	7	9

Bodies Buried in Mississippi

Location	Volume	Page
Corinth National Cemetery	20	1
Grenada	14	330
Moved to Vicksburg National Cemetery		
Jackson	7	73
Jackson	14	331
Natchez National Cemetery	27	139
Oxford	14	331
Moved to Corinth National Cemetery		
Ship Island	9	213
Ship Island (colored)	9	217
Moved to Chalmette National Cemetery		
Starkville	14	331
Moved to Vicksburg National Cemetery		
Vicksburg National Cemetery	14	331
Vicksburg	24	7
Vicksburg	27	157

Bodies Buried in Missouri

Location	Volume	Page
Bloomfield	13	130
Bodies from this area were moved to both Jefferson Barracks and Springfield National Cemeteries		
Brunswick	10	36
Moved to Jefferson City National Cemetery		
Cape Girardeau	9	229
Moved to Jefferson Barracks National Cemetery		
Cassville	9	226
Bodies from this area were moved to both Fayetteville and Springfield National Cemeteries		
Dallas	13	130
Moved to Jefferson Barracks National Cemetery		
Four Miles	13	131
Moved to Jefferson Barracks National Cemetery		
Franklin	12	140
Moved to Jefferson Barracks National Cemetery		
Fredericktown	12	140
Glasgow	10	34
Moved to Jefferson City National Cemetery		
Greenville	13	132
Huntsville	10	32
Moved to Jefferson Barracks National Cemetery		
Independence	12	145
Moved to Fort Leavenworth National Cemetery		
Ironton	12	141
Moved to Jefferson Barracks National Cemetery		
Jackson	13	130
Moved to Jefferson Barracks National Cemetery		
Jefferson Barracks National Cemt.	20	195
Jefferson Barracks (colored)	20	399
Jefferson City National Cemetery	10	26
Jefferson City	19	298
Kansas City	10	34
Lebanon	9	228
Moved to Springfield National Cemetery		
Lexington	12	148
Moved to Fort Leavenworth National Cemetery		

Mexico   10   37
        Moved to Jefferson Barracks National Cemetery
Newtonia   12   148
        Moved to Springfield National Cemetery
Otterville   12   147
        Moved to Jefferson City National Cemetery
Patterson   13   132
Patterson   13   133
        Moved to Jefferson Barracks National Cemetery
Reeve's Station   13   131
Reeve's Station   13   132
        Moved to Jefferson Barracks National Cemetery
Sedalia   12   147
        Moved to Jefferson City National Cemetery
Springfield National Cemetery   9   217
Springfield   18   360
St. Louis   10   38
St. Louis   10   89
St. Louis   10   94
St. Louis   10   100
St. Louis (colored)   10   98
        Moved to Jefferson Barracks National Cemetery
Tipton   10   32
        Moved to Jefferson Barracks National Cemetery
Warrensburg   12   146
        Moved to either Jefferson City or Jefferson Barracks
        National Cemetery
Warrenton   12   149
Waynesville   12   140
        Moved to Jefferson Barracks National Cemetery
Weston   12   149
        Moved to Fort Leavenworth National Cemetery

Bodies Buried in the Montana Territory

Location	Volume	Page
Camp Cooke	19	342
Fort Shaw	19	344
Moved to Custer Battlefield National Cemetery		

Bodies Buried in Nebraska

Location	Volume	Page
Fort Kearney	7	10
Moved to Fort McPherson National Cemetery		
Fort McPherson National Cemetery	7	13
Became a national cemetery in 1873		
Omaha	7	13
Now Forest Lawn Soldiers' Lot		

Bodies Buried in Nevada

Location	Volume	Page
Camp Mc Dermot	12	171
Dun Glen	12	173
Fort Churchill	12	169
Moved to Camp Dun Glen		
Fort Ruby	8	118
Fort Ruby	12	170
Moved to San Francisco National Cemetery		

Bodies Buried in New Hampshire

Location	Volume	Page
Concord	9	8
Manchester	9	7

Bodies Buried in New Jersey

Location	Volume	Page
Beverly National Cemetery	12	7
Beverly (colored)	12	10
Bridgeton	12	10
Newark	9	15
Newark (colored)	9	17

Bodies Buried in New Mexico

Location	Volume	Page
Albuquerque	8	120
Albuquerque	19	319
Apache Canon (sic)	19	321
Fort Bascom	8	123
Fort Bascom	19	319
Moved to Fort Leavenworth National Cemetery		
Fort Bayard	19	320
Moved to both Fort Leavenworth and San Antonio National Cemeteries		
Fort Craig	8	121
Fort Craig	19	317
Moved to Santa Fe National Cemetery		
Fort Cummings	19	321
Moved to Fort Leavenworth National Cemetery		
Fort Marcy	8	124
Fort Marcy	19	323
Moved to Santa Fe National Cemetery		
Fort McRae	8	124
Fort McRae	19	319
Moved to Santa Fe National Cemetery		
Fort Selden	8	125
Fort Selden	19	321
Moved to Fort Leavenworth National Cemetery		
Fort Stanton	8	125
Fort Stanton	12	61
Fort Stanton	19	320
Moved to Santa Fe National Cemetery		
Fort Sumner	8	123
Fort Sumner	19	320
Moved to Santa Fe National Cemetery		
Fort Union	19	322
Moved to both the Santa Fe and Fort Leavenworth National Cemeteries		
Fort Wingate	8	123
Fort Wingate	19	319
Possibly moved to Fort Leavenworth National Cemetery		

Kozlowske's Ranch	19	323
Moved to Santa Fe National Cemetery		
Los Pinos	8	125
Los Pinos	19	320
Moved to Santa Fe National Cemetery		
Santa Fe National Cemetery	8	125

Bodies Buried in New York

Location	Volume	Page
Albany	10	7
Albany Rural Cemetery Soldiers' Lot		
Buffalo	16	10
Buffalo	16	12
Buffalo	16	14
Chautauqua County	16	16
Cherry Creek	16	16
Cypress Hills National Cemetery	13	7
Cypress Hills	16	18
Cypress Hill (colored)	13	56
David's Island	10	9
David's Island (colored)	10	10
Elmira	7	15
Elmira (colored)	7	17
Became Woodlawn National Cemetery in 1877		
Fort Columbus	10	8
Moved to Cypress Hills National Cemetery		
Fort Hamilton	10	10
Fort Niagara	16	64
Lansingburg	10	10
Lockport	16	66
Lodi	16	68
Madison Barracks	7	13
Madison Barracks	16	70
Plattsburg Barracks	16	72
Rochester	16	74
Sandy Hook	10	9
Seneca Falls	12	7
Willett's Point	10	9

Bodies Buried in North Carolina

Location	Volume	Page
Carolina City	10	155
Moved to Newberne National Cemetery		
Charlotte	10	151
Charlotte	10	178
Moved to Salisbury National Cemetery		
Goldsboro	10	151
Goldsboro	14	133
Bodies from this area were moved to both		
Raleigh and Newberne National Cemeteries		
Greensboro	10	152
Moved to Raleigh National Cemetery		
Morehead City	10	153
Morehead City (colored)	10	154
Moved to Newberne National Cemetery		
Morgantown	10	151
Newberne National Cemetery	10	156
Newberne	10	170
New Berne (sic)	19	144
Newberne (colored)	10	169
Newberne (colored)	10	175
Raleigh National Cemetery	10	146
Raleigh	14	133
Raleigh	18	43
Raleigh (colored)	10	150
Salisbury National Cemetery	10	146
Salisbury	14	134
Washington	10	144
Washington	10	145
Moved to Newberne National Cemetery		
Weldon	14	237
Wilmington National Cemetery	18	22
Wilmington	14	235
Wilson	14	237

Bodies Buried in Ohio

Location	Volume	Page
Camp Dennison	18	289

Moved to Spring Grove Cemetery in
Cincinnati

Location	Volume	Page
Cincinnati	9	17
Cincinnati	18	300
Cincinnati	26	89
Cincinnati (colored)	9	31

See the introduction for information on the status of
Spring Grove Cemetery

Location	Volume	Page
Cleveland	9	31
Cleveland	26	137
Cleveland (colored)	9	40

Woodlawn Cemetery is a Soldiers' Lot with only 48
burials. No record of the other burials has been
located

Location	Volume	Page
Columbus	9	41
Columbus	26	119
Columbus (colored)	9	46
Dayton	26	143

These burials were in Woodlawn Cemetery, they
were never moved to Dayton National Cemetery

Location	Volume	Page
Gallipolis	18	283
Gallipolis	26	133
Johnson's Island	9	47
Johnson's Island (Sandusky)	26	141

Bodies Buried in Oregon

Location	Volume	Page
Camp C.F. Smith	19	341
Camp Warner	19	341
Camp Watson	9	107
Fort Dalles	9	107

Moved to Fort Vancouver Post Cemetery

Location	Volume	Page
Fort Klamath	9	107

Moved to San Francisco National Cemetery

Bodies Buried in Pennsylvania

Location	Volume	Page
Bristol	12	54
Moved to Philadelphia National Cemetery		
Bristol (colored)	12	56
Carlisle	7	63
Ashland Cemetery Soldiers' Lot, also listed by the US Army as Carlisle Barracks Post Cemetery		
Chambersburg	10	25
Chester	12	53
Fort Mifflin	12	56
Gettysburg National Cemetery	16	76
Gettysburg	16	151
Gettysburg	16	153
The 66 soldiers buried in Gettysburg's Evergreen Cemetery were not moved to the Gettysburg National Cemetery		
Harrisburg	12	56
Harrisburg (colored)	12	57
Lebanon	12	56
Mercersburg	16	155
Philadelphia	12	11
Philadelphia	16	159
Philadelphia	16	161
Philadelphia (colored)	12	47
Most of these bodies were moved to the Philadelphia National Cemetery when it was established in 1885; however, the bodies of the 401 soldiers buried in Mount Moriah Soldiers' Lot were not moved.		
Pittsburgh	7	64
Pittsburgh	7	65
Pittsburgh	7	66
Pittsburgh (colored)	7	66
Now Allegheny Soldiers' Lot		
Reading	16	157
Spring Mills	12	56
Tamaqua	16	163
Upton	16	163
York	12	58

York	12	60
York	16	153
Now Prospect Hills Soldiers' Lot		

Bodies Buried in Rhode Island

Location	Volume	Page
Portsmouth Grove	7	66
Portsmouth Grove (colored)	7	71
Moved to Cypress Hills National Cemetery		

Bodies Buried in South Carolina

Location	Volume	Page
Anderson	9	155
Beaufort National Cemetery	9	115
Beaufort	27	7
Beaufort (colored)	9	128
Charleston	14	238
These bodies, of prisoners, were moved to Beaufort National Cemetery. Burials of Union occupation troops (not listed in the *Roll of Honor*) were reinterred in Florence National Cemetery.		
Columbia	14	250
It appears these bodies were moved to Florence National Cemetery		
Florence National Cemetery	14	252
Florence	19	222
Hilton Head	9	138
Hilton Head	14	261
Hilton Head (colored)	9	153
Moved to Beaufort National Cemetery		
Orangeburg	9	155
Orangeburg (colored)	9	155
Some of these bodies were moved to Florence National Cemetery in 1879.		
Sumter	9	138

Bodies Buried in Tennessee

Location	Volume	Page
Bear station	14	262
Chattanooga National Cemetery	11	14
Chattanooga	14	262
Chattanooga	23	249
Elliott's Hospital	14	262
Fort Donelson National Cemetery	23	239
Greenville	14	262
Moved to Knoxville National Cemetery		
Knoxville	11	380
Knoxville	14	262
Knoxville	23	300
Memphis National Cemetery	14	263
Memphis	21	8
Nashville National Cemetery	14	263
Nashville	22	7
Nashville	22	397
Shiloh National Cemetery	20	119
Shiloh	20	174
Shiloh	27	160
Stone's River National Cemetery	11	230
Stone's River	11	438
Stone's River	23	275

Bodies Buried in Texas

Location	Volume	Page
Austin	9	217
Moved to San Antonio National Cemetery		
Brazos Santiago	6	22
Brazos Santiago (colored)	6	23
Moved to Brownsville National Cemetery		
Brownsville National Cemetery	6	14
Brownsville	6	20
Brownsville (colored)	6	14
Brownsville (colored)	6	22

Brownsville   18   75
   In 1911 the entire cemetery (3,007 bodies) was moved
   to Alexandria (La) National Cemetery
Camp Ford   6   29
Camp Ford   12   166
Camp Ford   14   329
   Moved to Alexandria (La) National Cemetery
Camp Verde   14   329
   Moved to San Antonio National Cemetery
Corpus Christi (colored)   6   35
Edinburgh (colored)   6   27
   Moved to Brownsville National Cemetery
Fort Bliss   18   117
   Became National Cemetery in 1939
Galveston   6   7
Galveston (colored)   6   8
Galveston   18   106
   Apparently moved to Brownsville National Cemetery
Green Lake   6   11
Hempstead   6   7
Houston   6   7
Houston   14   329
   Moved to Galveston National Cemetery
Indianola   6   9
Indianola (colored)   6   11
Indianola (colored)   6   13
   Moved to Brownsville National Cemetery
Jasper   6   7
Lavaca   6   11
   Moved to Galveston National Cemetery
Matagorda   6   13
Matagorda (colored)   6   14
Powderhorn Bayou (colored)   6   14
Ringgold Barracks   6   28
   Apparently moved to Brownsville National
   Cemetery, in any case moved to Alexandria
   National Cemetery in 1911
Roma   6   28
San Antonio National Cemetery   6   8

San Antonio	18	101
Victoria	6	9
Victoria	6	10
Victoria	6	11

Moved to Brownsville National Cemetery

Bodies Buried in the Utah Territory

Location	Volume	Page
Camp Douglas	13	134
Camp Douglas	19	345
Fort Bridger	19	347
Fort Bridges (sic)	12	167

Apparently a typo, really Fort Bridger. This fort was located in what today is Wyoming.

Bodies Buried in Vermont

Location	Volume	Page
Battleboro	16	165

Now Prospect Hill Cemetery Soldiers' Lot

Montpelier	16	165

Now Green Mountain Cemetery Soldiers' Lot

Bodies Buried in Virginia

According to page 276 of Volume 15, bodies from the areas identified by the symbol # were moved to either Yorktown National Cemetery or Poplar Grove National Cemetery.

Location	Volume	Page
Alexandria National Cemetery	4	7
Alexandria (colored)	4	64
Arlington National Cemetery	1	107
Arlington	1	187
Arlington	15	100
Arlington (colored)	1	191
Belle Island	12	91

Moved to Richmond National Cemetery

Burkesville #   15   364
    Moved to Poplar Grove National Cemetery
Camp Casey   1   193
    Roberts' *Encyclopedia of Historic Forts* lists Camp
    Casey under Maryland.
Charlottesville   14   1
City Point National Cemetery   13   103
City Point   13   124
City Point   13   126
City Point   16   167
City Point (colored)   13   128
Cold Harbor National Cemetery   15   149
Cold Harbor   26   247
Culpeper Court House   14   1
Culpeper Court House   15   116
Culpeper Court House   26   249
    Now Culpeper National Cemetery
Danville National Cemetery   13   82
Danville   14   2
Danville   16   265
Danville (colored)   13   103
Dinwiddie County #   15   354
    Moved to Poplar Grove National Cemetery
Fords of the Rapiden River   12   121
    Moved to Culpeper National Cemetery
Fort Harrison National Cemetery   18   11
Fort Pocahontas   12   97
Fortress Monroe   5   49
Fortress Monroe   5   55
    Moved to Hampton National Cemetery
Fredericksburg National Cemetery   25   9
Front Royal #   15   347
    Moved to Winchester National Cemetery
Glendale National Cemetery   16   276
Gloucester Point #   15   349
Gordonsville   14   25
Gordonsville   15   363
    Bodies from this area were moved to both
    Culpeper and Richmond National Cemeteries

Hampton National Cemetery   5   7
Hampton   25   131
Hampton   26   243
Hampton (colored)   5   35
Harrison's Landing #   15   351
    Bodies from this area were moved to both Glendale
    and Popular Grove National Cemeteries
Harrisonburg   14   26
    Moved to Staunton National Cemetery
Liberty   15   363
Lynchburg   12   94
Lynchburg   14   27
Lynchburg #   15   357
Lynchburg (colored)   12   97
    Moved to Poplar Grove National Cemetery
Mount Jackson   14   27
New Kent County #   15   347
Nottoway County #   15   363
Orange and Alexandria Railroad   12   121
    Moved to Arlington National Cemetery
Orange Court House   14   28
    Bodies from this area were moved to both Arlington
    and Culpeper National Cemeteries
Petersburg   13   61
Petersburg   13   76
Petersburg   13   77
Petersburg   13   78
Petersburg   13   79
Petersburg   13   80
Petersburg   13   82
Petersburg   14   28
Petersburg   26   235
Petersburg #   15   283
    Now known as Poplar Grove National Cemetery
Poplar Grove National Cemetery   19   51
Portsmouth   12   80
    Moved to Hampton National Cemetery

Rappahannock County #	15	349
Bodies from this area were moved to both Arlington and Culpeper National Cemeteries		
Richmond National Cemetery	12	81
Richmond	12	85
Richmond	12	91
Richmond	14	31
Richmond	16	286
Richmond	16	360a
Richmond (colored)	12	85
Robinson's Tavern	14	129
Seven Pines National Cemetery	12	98
Seven Pines	15	366
Southampton Court House	14	129
Moved to Fredericksburg National Cemetery		
Spotsylvania Court House	2	7
Moved to Fredericksburg National Cemetery		
Staunton National Cemetery	14	130
Staunton	15	257
Suffolk #	15	277
Moved to Hampton National Cemetery		
Wilderness	2	7
Moved to Fredericksburg National Cemetery		
Williamsburg #	15	350
Moved to Yorktown National Cemetery		
Wilson's Landing	12	97
Wilson's Landing #	15	356
Wilson's Landing (colored)	12	98
Moved to Glendale National Cemetery		
Winchester National Cemetery	14	132
Winchester	15	179
Winchester	26	245
Yorktown National Cemetery	15	338
Yorktown	16	361

Bodies Buried in Washington State

Location	Volume	Page
Camp Steele	19	348

Fort Colville   19   348
    Moved to San Francisco National Cemetery
Fort Steilacoom   19   349
    Some bodies from this post were moved to San
    Francisco National Cemetery
Fort Vancouver   8   126
Fort Vancouver   19   349
    Now a US Army Post Cemetery
Fort Walla Walla   19   349

Bodies Buried in West Virginia

Location	Volume	Page
Parkersburg	13	129
Parkersburg (colored)	13	130
Moved to Grafton National Cemetery		
Wheeling	13	128
Wheeling (colored)	13	129
Moved to Grafton National Cemetery		

Bodies Buried in Wisconsin

Location	Volume	Page
Fond du Lac	18	352
Green Bay	18	356
Janesville	18	343
Kenosha	18	348
Madison	9	101
Madison	18	336
Now Forest Hill Cemetery Soldiers' Lot		
Milwaukee	9	105
Milwaukee	18	333
Now Forest Home Cemetery Soldiers' Lot		
Oshkosh	18	354
Prairie du Chien	10	7
Prairie du Chien	18	358
Now Fort Crawford Cemetery Soldiers' Lot		
Racine	18	345
Now Mound Cemetery Soldiers' Lot		
Ripon	18	350

INDEX TO THE
ROLL OF HONOR

A

A---, --- 23:284; 25:134; 26:204
A---, A. 25:134
A---, A. J. 11:235
A---, A. L. B. 20:91
A---, A. S. 20:153
A---, B. 23:201, 312
A---, B. A. 25:134
A---, B. D. 12:148
A---, B. J. 15:180
A---, C. 9:48; 11:297; 15:28; 20:86
A---, D. 17:296
A---, D. C. 20:196
A---, E. M. 18:228; 26:9
A---, F. 25:12; 26:149; 27:8
A---, Frederick 11:102
A---, G. 11:235; 15:28
A---, G. B. 13:61
A---, H. 19:299; 22:349
A---, H. B. 20:153
A---, H. F. 11:338
A---, I. K. P. 16:362
A---, Ira I. 15:28
A---, J. 8:44; 18:228; 20:54; 23:245, 259; 25:316
A---, J. A. 20:54
A---, J. C. 24:11
A---, J. D. 23:292
A---, J. M. 14:267
A---, J. W. 11:338
A---, James A. 16:168
A---, John 13:61
A---, L. F. 15:62
A---, L. H. 21:165
A---, L. S. 15:180; 23:245
A---, Louis 18:411
A---, M. 18:12, 63; 19:234
A---, M. P. 8:44
A---, M. W. 17:216
A---, N. W. 11:297
A---, P. 18:23; 24:108
A---, Patrick 19:145
A---, R. 20:153
A---, S. A. 15:289
A---, S. H. 17:346
A---, S. K. 24:34
A---, T. A. 19:296
A---, T. B. 20:153
A---, U. 18:361
A---, W. 21:207; 26:149
A---, W. B. 24:11
A---, W. D. 15:171
A---, William 20:54

A----, H. 22:174
A---g, C. 11:235
A---ger, William 20:196
A., J. 26:9
Aabin, John 14:333
Aalferson, J. W. 14:31
Aaron, John 9:164
Aaron, N. 20:196
Aaron, Nathaniel 10:38
Aaron, T. 23:266
Aaron, Thomas 3:9
Aaron, William 7:116
Aarons, Charles 21:294
Aarons, Henry E. 19:328
Abarr, W. R. 17:433
Abarr, William R. 24:163
Abb, Peter 22:511
Abbatt, S. P. 20:120
Abbe, C. B. 12:11
Abbe---, John 23:201
Abbeny, William 13:56
Abbey, Albert S. 19:265
Abbey, Isaac 25:283
Abbey, James 22:507
Abbey, John 22:174
Abbey, O. 1:107; 3:9
Abbey, R. B. 22:471
Abbey, W. H. 3:9
Abbey, William H. 24:47
Abbie, William 12:11
Abbington, Jordan 21:145
Abbitt, Robert F. 22:62
Abbitt, Thomas 17:201
Abbitt, Thomas M. 17:278
Abbitts, George 9:47
Abble, Thomas 17:169
Abbord, Joseph 16:286
Abbot, A. 14:4
Abbot, Amos W. 11:285
Abbot, Daniel 9:115
Abbot, David P. 15:25
Abbot, E. H. 9:115
Abbot, James E. 9:115
Abbot, L. A. 15:62
Abbot, Nash 9:115
Abboth, Charles 11:409
Abbots, Henry 11:189
Abbott, --- 26:149
Abbott, A. 3:9
Abbott, A. M. 15:287; 19:52
Abbott, Abiel J. N. 15:79
Abbott, Abner 14:31, 135
Abbott, B. G. 7:84
Abbott, Barnett 15:101
Abbott, C. 3:9; 13:131; 20:196; 25:316
Abbott, C. H. 16:168
Abbott, C. M. 3:9
Abbott, Charles 1:108; 26:149

Abbott, Charles A. 15:89
Abbott, Charles B. 17:158
Abbott, Charles H. 2:7; 25:12
Abbott, Charles P. 13:7
Abbott, Cyrus 27:10
Abbott, D. E. 3:9
Abbott, Daniel 21:263; 27:10
Abbott, David 7:7; 19:145
Abbott, E. 6:29
Abbott, E. H. 27:9
Abbott, Edward 19:225
Abbott, Edward M. 5:7
Abbott, Elon 17:287
Abbott, Frank J. 4:7
Abbott, Frederick 23:130
Abbott, G. A. 7:18; 9:167
Abbott, G. W. 13:82; 16:265
Abbott, George 1:108; 15:277; 17:93; 22:160; 25:134
Abbott, George M. 18:361
Abbott, George N. 10:12
Abbott, H. 25:12
Abbott, H. M. 14:31
Abbott, Henry 10:38; 20:196
Abbott, Hiram 2:7
Abbott, Israel P. 23:251
Abbott, J. 1:12; 9:47; 19:52
Abbott, J. A. 7:73; 25:292
Abbott, J. C. 15:314
Abbott, J. H. 8:61
Abbott, J. J. 1:108
Abbott, J. P. 17:146
Abbott, J. S. 1:11
Abbott, J. W. 11:409; 17:146; 23:17
Abbott, Jacob M. 22:471
Abbott, James 7:18; 14:135, 253; 16:19; 20:120; 27:11
Abbott, James G. 13:7
Abbott, James M. 10:100; 20:196
Abbott, James W. 19:234; 22:174
Abbott, Jasino C. 27:9
Abbott, Jesse 23:84
Abbott, John 17:93; 18:227; 20:196; 26:9
Abbott, Jonathan L. 2:7
Abbott, Joseph 4:7; 18:460
Abbott, Lafayette 17:16
Abbott, Levi C. 21:294
Abbott, Lewis 21:219
Abbott, Lucius 17:309

Abbott, M. 14:294;
   17:475; 27:10
Abbott, Nash 27:10
Abbott, Nathaniel 14:267
Abbott, Nelson 19:52
Abbott, Nelson F. 17:62
Abbott, Oscar 17:28
Abbott, Peter 17:450;
   24:176
Abbott, Phildrick R.
   19:145
Abbott, Richard 10:38;
   20:196
Abbott, Robert I. 12:58
Abbott, S. 1:12; 7:73;
   25:292
Abbott, S. M. 11:21
Abbott, S. W. 16:168
Abbott, Samuel W.
   10:100; 20:196
Abbott, Sandhope 22:239
Abbott, Tho. J. 20:196
Abbott, Thomas 17:346;
   21:294
Abbott, Thomas A.
   23:127
Abbott, Thomas J. 10:38
Abbott, W. 14:31; 20:196
Abbott, William 1:11;
   9:95; 10:38; 11:50;
   22:415
Abbott, William H. 12:54
Abbott, William M. 11:50
Abby, D. 25:134
Abby, Henry 18:204
Abby, Jason M. 23:130
Abdile, Joseph 1:108
Abe, Henry 8:37; 26:148
Abe, William 22:329
Abee, J. L. 27:9
Abee, John 8:7
Abeel, J. H. 12:7
Abel, --- 25:12
Abel, Harlow 14:135
Abel, Henry 20:120
Abel, John 7:18
Abel, Joseph 17:69
Abel, Luke 11:297
Abel, Robert 22:17
Abel, S. A. J. 22:62
Abel, Wallace 21:62
Abel, William 21:263
Abell, Burton 19:2
Abell, C. 3:9
Abell, J. A. 16:168
Abell, L. L. 9:138
Abelon, H. 16:19
Abels, John B. 8:7;
   18:119
Abels, Theodore 10:38
Abendroth, Jacob 27:9

Abendroth, Lewis 13:7
Abent, William 15:351
Aber, A. 3:9
Aber, Eben L. 19:52
Aber, Harrison 4:7
Aber, John 18:119
Aber, William 9:17;
   18:320
Aber, William B. 24:72
Abercrombie, W. H. 3:9
Abercrombie, Young
   11:20
Aberiams, Joseph 26:120
Abermathie, Sterling
   10:98
Abernathy, A. B. 23:105
Abernathy, Batty 22:164
Abernathy, David 8:78
Abernathy, Elijah 23:17
Abernathy, Frank 23:290
Abernathy, Giles 11:335
Abernathy, Jacob 23:84
Abernathy, James 22:62
Abernathy, Martin 22:287
Abernathy, Nathan 21:294
Abernathy, William
   18:227; 26:9
Aberndths, T. J. 18:63
Abers, Henry V. 22:275
Abes, William F. 20:45
Abets---, John 24:64
Abily, John 13:76
Abinger, J. 9:167
Abinson, E. A. 15:297
Abka, Gotlieb 21:15
Able, B. H. 11:293
Able, Christian 24:64
Able, Datus E. 10:38;
   20:196
Able, Frank 1:192
Able, J. 3:9
Able, J. P. 17:199
Able, John 22:459
Able, John B. 10:100;
   20:196
Able, Jonathan 11:325
Able, Joseph 10:34
Able, Moses 11:325
Able, Walter 23:17
Able, William 10:12
Ablee, H. F. 27:8
Ables, Henry A. 8:44;
   21:133
Ables, Theodore 20:196
Ables, W. E. 1:108
Ables, William 23:183
Ables, William J. 9:32
Abling, Charles 18:440
Abner, Elisha 22:115
Abner, J. 14:279

Abner, Jesse 10:100;
   20:196
Abner, John R. 20:185
Abner, John W. 22:115
Abner, Joseph 17:258
Abner, W. W. 21:184
Abney, Aaron F. 17:351
Abney, Elbert P. 17:351
Abney, H. C. 21:15
Abney, James W. 22:399
Abney, John K. 23:96
Abney, L. 9:47
Abola, M. 12:7
Abor, J. 3:9
Aborms, F. 25:134
Abos, Theodore 19:145
Abott, S. W. 15:297
Abraham, Ezekiel 20:196
Abraham, Frank 9:128;
   27:9
Abraham, Freight 7:116
Abraham, George 8:78
Abraham, J. 18:23
Abraham, James L. 26:8
Abraham, John 25:283
Abraham, M. 16:168
Abraham, Robert 1:11
Abraham, William H. 1:11
Abrahams, Andrew
   25:316
Abrahams, Danford J. 5:7
Abrahams, George 9:107
Abrahams, Joseph C.
   15:351
Abrahams, Peter 26:9
Abrahams, Thomas
   16:362
Abrahamson, Keurdt
   18:119
Abrahumson, Kundt 8:7
Abrain, G. 3:9
Abrams, --- 17:337
Abrams, Albert 8:112
Abrams, Andrew J. 6:29
Abrams, Charles A. 27:11
Abrams, Charles G. 8:78
Abrams, Elijah 10:38;
   20:196
Abrams, G. W. 7:18
Abrams, James 9:167;
   13:7; 16:19
Abrams, Joseph 10:170;
   16:277; 19:145
Abrams, L. 25:134
Abrams, R. 25:134
Abrams, Robert 5:7
Abrams, Samuel 11:21
Abrams, W. M. 4:7
Abrams, William H. 17:73
Abrams, William N. 1:12
Abrane, Robert 19:145

Abs, Harry 11:50
Abselon, H. 13:7
Absent, Elijah 7:82
Abshire, John 22:62
Abshire, John R. 21:219
Abshure, Jackson 8:78
Abstance, Booker 23:270
Aby, John 26:8
Acaman, J. B. 25:134
Acberhooft, Benedict 8:7
Acby, Sidney 14:135
Accoo, J. 6:14
Accor, J. 18:76
Aceashure, --- 15:180
Acelis, E. 21:184
Acers, Francis P. 22:115
Acers, W. D. 12:11
Acerton, T. C. 9:47
Achanbush, --- 12:169
Achart, Samuel 9:156
Achenbach, Samuel 14:137
Achenback, Lewis 13:7
Achens, Green 18:227; 26:9
Acher, S. A. 12:94
Acher, Washington 21:219
Acherhartl, Burdict 18:119
Acherman, H. 25:12
Achers, Nicholas 26:91
Achert, Henry 17:74
Aches, T. J. 3:9
Achinson, John 9:32
Achlart, Christian 18:204
Achley, A. 16:362
Achmer, P. 14:31
Achols, W. J. 23:17
Achron, Lindsley M. 11:21
Ack, H. 16:362
Ackely, Charles 12:150
Ackens, J. 25:134
Ackeny, Samuel W. 22:174
Acker, Adam 13:7
Acker, B. F. 15:180
Acker, C. S. 21:15
Acker, George 17:387
Acker, Henry C. 11:133
Acker, J. 3:9
Acker, John 13:76; 17:74
Acker, L. 15:180; 20:131
Acker, Nicholas 9:17
Acker, T. 1:107; 9:47
Ackerley, A. M. 27:8
Ackerly, William 18:12
Ackerman, Abraham 7:84
Ackerman, C. 3:9
Ackerman, Carl 9:11

Ackerman, David 11:123
Ackerman, David J. 9:239
Ackerman, E. 19:145
Ackerman, George 11:114
Ackerman, Gordon 4:7
Ackerman, J. B. 22:135
Ackerman, J. F. 13:61
Ackerman, Jacob 10:38; 20:196
Ackerman, James B. 5:49
Ackerman, John 16:137; 19:52; 23:111
Ackerman, John A. 24:47
Ackerman, John E. 18:102
Ackerman, Joseph 9:105
Ackerman, M. 10:209
Ackerman, M. A. 22:8
Ackerman, Mathias 22:8
Ackerman, O. I. 15:180
Ackerman, Peter 12:58
Ackerman, Samuel 3:9; 13:103
Ackerman, Stephen 4:7
Ackerman, W. B. 25:316
Ackerman, W. F. 27:11
Ackerman, William 9:217; 16:131
Ackerman, William H. 16:89
Ackers, Nicholas 18:301
Ackers, William C. 2:7
Ackerson, John 12:66; 15:26
Ackert, George 12:11
Ackey, Jerm 17:478; 27:10
Ackford, George 14:130
Ackford, S. 15:273
Ackhart, David 3:9
Ackinger, Elijah 11:50
Ackland, George 7:84
Ackland, James 13:103
Ackleck, Anton 18:107
Acklee, C. 13:82
Acklen, B. 11:83
Acklen, Jasper N. 18:227; 26:9
Ackler, W. 3:9
Ackles, F. 15:28
Ackles, Franklin 12:66
Ackles, James 1:108
Ackley, C. 1:107
Ackley, Carlton 13:7
Ackley, Casander 12:66
Ackley, Cassander 15:21
Ackley, E. H. 15:117
Ackley, G. 21:294
Ackley, G. B. 3:9
Ackley, George 12:53
Ackley, Henry 13:7; 16:19
Ackley, Henry T. 13:7

Ackley, J. 11:285; 13:82
Ackley, John 13:7
Ackley, Joseph 22:287
Ackley, Lewis 15:338
Ackley, Maurice 12:173
Ackley, Obed 23:130
Ackley, Oliver 11:399
Ackley, Price P. 17:75
Ackley, Reuben 1:11
Ackley, S. M. 4:7
Ackley, Samuel P. 4:7
Ackley, Wesley 15:52
Ackley, William 13:7
Ackly, Edmund 16:362
Ackney, Jerm 14:294
Ackrill, R. B. 24:169
Acktill, R. B. 17:446
Aclage, William 26:149
Acliar, S. W. 14:135
Acola, George 8:7; 18:119
Acome, John 14:135
Acor, James 10:156
Acord, John 14:135
Acordier, Christian 22:174
Acosia, --- 8:125
Acquire, Joseph 4:7
Acree, William A. 11:89
Acres, A. 20:196
Acres, C. B. 16:286
Acres, Joshua 21:47
Acru, James L. 22:239
Acters, John T. 27:9
Action, F. 15:338
Acton, F. 16:362
Acton, John W. 22:399
Acton, Lot 19:2
Acton, Philip 21:133
Acton, Sidney 22:174
Acton, Thomas 16:115
Actwise, --- 15:180
Acuff, George 22:62
Acuff, Robert D. 17:214
Acuin, Charles Lyon 25:134
Adair, --- 15:28
Adair, Benjamin 10:100; 20:196
Adair, Charles 18:227; 26:9
Adair, F. M. 21:294
Adair, G. 17:28
Adair, George A. 23:130
Adair, Harvey 8:7; 18:119
Adair, Hiram 22:62
Adair, J. 11:230
Adair, Jacob 11:235
Adair, James 9:162; 27:11
Adair, James D. 22:472
Adair, John 8:44; 15:28; 21:96

Adair, John B. 13:7
Adair, Joseph 11:49
Adair, Mathias 17:322
Adair, William 21:47
Adaire, H. C. 7:84
Adall, Martin L. 9:167
Adam, W. R. 14:327
Adamier, Benjour 11:117
Adams, --- 8:70; 11:21,
    325; 15:15; 16:168;
    17:505
Adams, A. 3:10; 14:31,
    294; 16:362; 18:227;
    25:134; 26:9
Adams, A. B. 1:107;
    16:19
Adams, A. F. 3:9
Adams, A. H. 9:167;
    19:225
Adams, A. J. 1:108; 9:47;
    13:103
Adams, A. V. 4:7
Adams, A. W. 11:50
Adams, Aaron 17:453;
    24:185
Adams, Albert 16:19
Adams, Albert E. 14:31
Adams, Albert F. 22:164
Adams, Albert W. 26:149
Adams, Alfred 22:287
Adams, Allision 18:119
Adams, Allison 8:7
Adams, Alphonso 20:120
Adams, Andrew 5:7
Adams, Appleton 4:7
Adams, B. 18:76
Adams, B. F. 18:63
Adams, B. N. 11:50
Adams, Benjamin 6:11;
    7:116; 11:383;
    21:294; 22:115
Adams, Benjamin F.
    17:146, 425; 24:176
Adams, C. 9:107; 10:185;
    15:293; 18:12, 171;
    21:294; 26:149
Adams, C. A. 11:99
Adams, C. E. 15:329
Adams, C. P. 11:235
Adams, C. W. 1:12
Adams, Charles 1:12;
    7:116; 8:76; 12:7;
    15:171; 17:388;
    18:187, 411; 21:294;
    25:134
Adams, Charles E. 1:12;
    19:52
Adams, Charles F. 9:95;
    12:63; 23:130
Adams, Charles H. 1:11;
    22:135

Adams, Charles P. 9:47
Adams, Charles R. 15:180
Adams, Chester 13:7
Adams, Clifton 16:168
Adams, Cyrus 17:278
Adams, D. 9:138
Adams, D. J. 9:217;
    18:361
Adams, Daniel 3:9;
    17:358; 18:426;
    27:10
Adams, David 6:29;
    10:38; 20:196; 21:15;
    25:316
Adams, David S. 22:415
Adams, E. 3:9; 9:138;
    13:61; 19:52
Adams, E. B. 18:424
Adams, E. F. 21:294
Adams, E. O. 21:294
Adams, E. P. 25:134
Adams, Edward 13:103;
    21:294; 22:116;
    25:268
Adams, Edward P. 5:7
Adams, Edwin P. 7:84
Adams, Eld 11:235
Adams, Eli A. 1:12
Adams, Ephraim M.
    24:165
Adams, Erastus 27:9
Adams, Eri G. 17:320
Adams, F. 14:31
Adams, F. J. 15:117
Adams, F. W. 20:153
Adams, Francis 9:32;
    17:69
Adams, Frank 6:11
Adams, G. 3:9
Adams, G. W. 7:18
Adams, George 1:11; 8:7;
    9:138; 10:12; 12:63,
    171; 15:15, 171;
    18:119, 320; 22:174,
    447; 23:130; 27:9
Adams, George G. 23:262
Adams, George L. 8:102
Adams, George R. 10:100;
    17:241; 20:196
Adams, George S. 11:21
Adams, George W. 16:19,
    113; 22:62, 115
Adams, Guy C. 23:118
Adams, H. 3:9; 12:164;
    13:82; 14:3, 31;
    19:273; 26:149
Adams, H. A. 8:70
Adams, H. B. 11:399
Adams, H. C. 11:50;
    13:80
Adams, H. E. 9:128; 27:9

Adams, H. F. 19:52
Adams, H. H. 5:7
Adams, H. L. 9:47
Adams, H. T. 3:9
Adams, H. V. 20:131
Adams, Harvey 9:167
Adams, Harvey J. 21:117
Adams, Henry 11:21;
    12:11; 21:210, 294
Adams, Henry L. 9:47
Adams, Henry W. 11:235
Adams, Hiram 7:116
Adams, Hosey J. 10:38
Adams, Howard 6:14;
    18:76
Adams, I. A. 9:138
Adams, I. N. 21:118
Adams, I. P. 14:135
Adams, Ira 21:133
Adams, Ira J. 5:7; 25:134
Adams, Isaac 9:128;
    13:103; 27:9
Adams, Isaac H. 11:21
Adams, J. 1:96, 107; 3:9;
    12:173; 16:168;
    21:15; 25:134, 292,
    310
Adams, J. A. 3:9; 26:8
Adams, J. A. T. 3:9
Adams, J. B. 3:9; 9:47;
    10:100
Adams, J. B. J. 9:217
Adams, J. D. 3:9
Adams, J. F. 14:31
Adams, J. G. 1:107
Adams, J. H. 11:256; 27:8
Adams, J. I. C. 21:84
Adams, J. L. 3:9
Adams, J. M. 25:134
Adams, J. N. E. 12:11
Adams, J. P. 27:9
Adams, J. Q. 1:107;
    15:262; 23:118;
    25:134
Adams, J. R. 25:277
Adams, J. T. 19:52;
    26:236
Adams, J. W. 2:7; 16:168;
    21:15; 24:98; 25:12
Adams, Jack 6:11; 18:76
Adams, Jacob 22:111
Adams, James 1:108;
    9:205; 10:100;
    11:383; 14:31;
    15:101; 17:16, 424;
    18:63; 19:234;
    20:196; 21:13, 207;
    23:15, 287; 24:176
Adams, James A. 9:74;
    10:100; 20:196
Adams, James C. 13:103

Adams, James R. 22:62
Adams, James V. 17:258
Adams, Jesse 10:38;
   20:196
Adams, Jesse A. 21:245
Adams, John 5:35; 7:55;
   8:7, 37; 11:21, 132,
   133, 319, 399; 13:7,
   103; 17:348; 18:23,
   63, 119, 284; 19:145,
   316; 21:294; 22:17,
   116; 26:134, 148
Adams, John A. 17:318
Adams, John B. 24:71
Adams, John C. 12:11;
   18:44
Adams, John D. 9:239
Adams, John E. 18:355
Adams, John H. 11:89
Adams, John N. 22:174
Adams, John P. 22:414
Adams, John Q. 7:116;
   9:65; 15:180;
   17:252; 21:238; 27:8
Adams, John Quincy
   10:156; 19:145
Adams, John R. 22:17, 62
Adams, John S. 9:74; 26:8
Adams, John W. 4:7;
   21:15
Adams, Jonathan 21:134
Adams, Joseph 9:138;
   10:38; 15:62;
   20:196; 23:130; 27:8
Adams, Joseph E. 10:146;
   18:44
Adams, Joseph Q. 22:399
Adams, L. 23:17
Adams, L. B. 15:338;
   16:362
Adams, L. D. 11:21
Adams, Leonard 10:7
Adams, Levi 5:7; 18:12;
   21:12
Adams, Lewis 8:76
Adams, Martin 4:7; 9:17;
   15:10
Adams, Merit 17:212
Adams, Mortimer 18:301;
   26:91
Adams, Moses 23:58
Adams, N. 1:12, 108
Adams, Nathaniel 7:18
Adams, O. 3:9; 11:285
Adams, O. E. 12:7
Adams, Oregon 23:130
Adams, Osker G. 22:17
Adams, P. 11:418; 25:285
Adams, P. B. J. 18:361
Adams, Patrick 9:107
Adams, Perry 9:17; 22:62

Adams, Peter 7:84; 10:89;
   18:227; 26:9
Adams, Philip 7:47
Adams, Porter 20:196
Adams, Preston 18:23
Adams, Q. 10:185; 18:171
Adams, R. 14:287;
   17:475; 23:17; 27:11
Adams, R. A. 24:11
Adams, R. B. 21:15
Adams, R. C. 14:294;
   17:481; 27:10
Adams, R. W. 7:55
Adams, Reuben 11:196
Adams, Richard 17:215,
   454; 22:17; 24:187
Adams, Robert 8:61
Adams, Robert W. 8:61
Adams, S. 3:9
Adams, S. B. 3:9; 22:239
Adams, S. D. 14:320;
   23:127
Adams, S. E. O. 21:294
Adams, Samuel 10:38;
   17:204; 20:196;
   21:294; 23:58;
   25:271
Adams, Sanford P. 11:21
Adams, Seth 22:62
Adams, Silas W. 22:459
Adams, Simpson 17:47
Adams, Smith 4:64
Adams, Step 19:145
Adams, Stephen 10:175;
   21:47
Adams, T. 1:107; 21:145
Adams, T. J. 9:226; 14:31;
   18:361
Adams, T. R. 3:9
Adams, Taylor 17:234
Adams, Thomas 4:7; 7:14,
   84; 12:11; 17:17;
   18:12; 19:145;
   22:287, 415
Adams, Thomas K. 11:50
Adams, W. 2:7; 13:82;
   14:3, 31; 15:180
Adams, W. B. 11:409
Adams, W. E. 21:294
Adams, W. H. 18:102
Adams, W. J. 1:12;
   15:323
Adams, W. R. 9:160
Adams, W. R. M. 27:11
Adams, Warren B. 22:17
Adams, Wentworth E.
   9:212
Adams, Wilham 9:32
Adams, William 4:7; 6:14;
   8:37, 44; 9:18, 41;
   10:156; 12:11, 54;

Adams, William 15:15;
   17:234, 336; 18:76,
   290, 301; 19:44, 145;
   21:263, 294; 23:284;
   24:11; 25:13; 26:91,
   120, 148
Adams, William F. 23:130
Adams, William H. 9:217;
   20:94; 22:469
Adams, William J. 1:11
Adams, William R. 9:47
Adams, William S. 17:257
Adams, Wyatt 17:169
Adams, Zimri 11:407
Adamson, Charles 6:7
Adamson, Isaac 17:161
Adamson, J. 8:70
Adamson, John W. 23:58
Adamson, Robert 15:52
Adamson, S. 1:12
Adamson, Simon 22:239
Adamson, William 3:10;
   11:132
Adanapper, Herbert
   22:287
Adare, J. 8:70
Adcock, --- 11:235
Adcock, Cabel 21:184
Adcock, J. 11:235
Adcock, James 3:10;
   14:31
Adcock, John A. 22:116
Adcock, John E. 17:47
Adcock, Nathan 18:227
Addamis, C. 16:168
Addams, P. 3:10
Adder, W. 3:10; 14:135
Adderton, W. 1:12
Addington, Henry 22:62
Addington, James 23:186
Addington, Joseph C.
   17:46
Addington, Nason 22:414
Addington, William B.
   11:284
Addis, B. D. 22:174
Addison, Hamilton K.
   12:11
Addison, I. T. 9:138
Addison, I. W. 9:153
Addison, Israel T. 10:100;
   20:196
Addison, J. S. 27:8
Addison, J. W. 27:9
Addison, James 25:134
Addison, John 9:157;
   19:322
Addison, Mark 1:191
Addison, O. 15:180
Addison, P. 13:82
Addison, Thomas 9:167

Addison, W. B. 24:108
Addison, Wilson 18:346
Addleman, Andrew J. 18:213
Addleman, Joseph O. 18:213
Addleman, Riley 21:184
Addleman, T. Jacob O. 18:213
Addlesparger, T. 11:132
Addley, A. 3:10
Addy, Jabez 22:174
Addy, John 10:12
Addy, Thomas 14:135
Ade, Henry 13:7
Adee, William 22:135
Adeferson, J. W. 14:31
Adell, James H. 21:214
Adelsberger, John 27:11
Adelsperger, John 14:327
Adelsperyer, John 9:160
Aden, James 15:101
Aderhold, August 22:275
Aderick, Frederick 7:84
Aderick, Joseph H. 9:157
Aderson, George 11:50
Aderson, H. 12:150
Aderson, Nath 19:52
Aderton, J. M. 1:12
Ades, Edward 3:10
Adeson, Luke 17:241
Adgate, F. A. 8:44
Adiler, A. 3:10
Adin, Charles 11:180
Adis, Robert 11:133
Adkins, --- 8:78
Adkins, A. 25:134
Adkins, Bartlett 17:47
Adkins, Benton 25:275
Adkins, C. F. 13:82
Adkins, Elijah 22:62
Adkins, George 3:10; 21:263
Adkins, Hawkins 17:258
Adkins, Ira 25:281
Adkins, Isaac 11:195
Adkins, J. 16:168
Adkins, J. H. 8:61
Adkins, J. W. 18:361; 23:17
Adkins, James 22:116
Adkins, James H. 26:149
Adkins, James J. 21:240
Adkins, John 1:108; 8:78; 9:167
Adkins, John W. 9:217
Adkins, Joseph W. 21:96
Adkins, Luke 11:383
Adkins, M. P. 15:164
Adkins, Nelson 22:62
Adkins, Owens 17:47

Adkins, R. 14:31
Adkins, R. C. 26:149
Adkins, Rachel S. 22:349
Adkins, Reuben C. 8:61
Adkins, Richard 24:187
Adkins, Robert 6:20; 18:76
Adkins, Stanton 14:135
Adkins, T. W. 25:277
Adkins, Thomas 9:217; 18:361
Adkins, W. 15:180
Adkins, William 10:170; 19:145; 22:415
Adkins, William H. 21:62
Adkinson, Alexander 22:287
Adkinson, David E. 8:102
Adkinson, J. C. 22:231
Adkinson, John A. 19:145
Adkinson, Syke 11:196
Adkinson, William 8:7
Adkison, E. R. 20:3
Adle, Cornelius 4:7
Adlefang, Peter 26:149
Adleman, --- 15:157
Adleman, J. O. 15:6
Adler, Ambrose J. 15:62
Adler, Ambrose S. 12:61
Adler, Anthony T. 4:7
Adler, Earnest 8:78
Adler, Henry 1:12
Adler, L. V. 21:294
Adler, Philip 21:134
Adler, S. 11:256
Adlerhast, V. 14:3
Adleshot, J. 13:82
Adlet, John 3:10
Adlington, Francis 27:8
Adlington, H. L. 14:135
Adlington, James 27:8
Admil, John H. 20:54
Adms, Ephraim 12:58
Admure, Thomas 9:65
Adner, Thomas 22:62
Adny, F. 3:10
Adolph, Balsier 22:471
Adolph, G. 9:74
Adolph, Gust 26:8
Adolph, P. 14:31
Adony, M. C. 14:31
Adrain, F. 21:118
Adrian, --- 15:267
Adrian, F. 3:10
Adrick, L. 17:93
Ads, Goltlerb 19:2
Adsa, John 14:31
Adsit, James E. 15:28
Adsit, Martin W. 7:84
Adsit, W. W. 1:107
Adtkins, James 17:252

Aduddlle, J. 11:235
Aduhault, Frederick 12:66
Adveson, Patrick 16:362
Adwood, Ezra 18:337
Ady, N. 15:180
Adyers, James F. 9:115
Aeberly, Tac 19:52
Aebi, Jacob 4:7
Aeby, Frederick 13:7
Aefan, John 15:89
Aeg, Henry 12:173
Aegon, Michael 17:204
Aehansen, Brown 10:38
Aeinshield, Louis 19:145
Ael, Aug 27:8
Aelimang, Jacob 13:7
Aely, Frederick 16:19
Aeres, A. 9:229
Aeres, Lewis 9:205
Aerl, Enos 20:120
Aernes, David 12:11
Aernshield, Louis 10:170
Aeson, A. J. 20:196
Aeson, Andrew J. 10:38
Aetell, Charles 9:115
Affemran, H. 18:23
Afferman, M. 14:31
Afflerk, T. 3:10
Affold, Frederick 11:297
Affolder, John 26:148
Affolter, John 19:2
Afiner, John 19:289
Afland, W. 11:235
Agan, James 14:135
Agan, John 25:12
Agan, Joseph 21:241
Agan, Patrick O. 13:7
Agan, S. 1:12
Agan, Samuel 18:227; 26:9
Agan, Timothy 1:11
Agan, William 14:135
Agar, Mathew S. 13:7
Agar, Matthew S. 16:19
Agar, T. 1:108
Agard, Morgan B. 8:78
Agart, William 16:19
Agdell, Andrew H. 9:32
Age, Jacob 17:205
Agee, Ambrose 8:44; 21:96
Agee, Benjamin F. 17:278
Agee, Charles F. 12:11
Agee, Charles H. B. 20:197
Agee, James I. 8:7
Agee, James J. 18:119
Agee, John M. 21:96
Agen, A. 13:103
Agener, J. J. 1:108

Ager, Alfred 18:290;
  26:91
Ager, Charles H. B.
  10:100
Ager, G. 20:197
Ager, Gabriel 10:38
Ager, William 10:38, 100
Agerly, H. F. 25:134
Agers, George W. 12:11
Agerter, D. 20:38
Aggart, William 13:7
Aggee, W. 20:197
Agin, James 16:146
Agin, Thomas 25:278
Aginer, John 9:167
Agins, Christian 18:290
Agle, J. 14:31
Agle, John 17:336
Agler, C. W. 24:11
Agler, Peter 10:89
Agleston, M. 14:31
Aglor, Peter 20:197
Agne, George 26:120
Agne, H. 11:297
Agner, William J. 20:197
Agnew, F. 10:144; 14:31;
  19:145
Agnew, Jacob 15:338;
  16:362
Agnew, James R. 7:18
Agnew, John 15:351;
  16:277; 21:294;
  22:329
Agnew, John R. 21:240
Agnew, Perry 7:116
Agnew, Samuel J. 26:216
Agnew, Thomas 22:17
Agnew, W. 14:31
Agnew, William 14:135;
  25:277
Agnew, William J. 10:38
Agnis, Christian 26:91
Agras, --- 18:187
Agretius, Charles G. 12:53
Agu, Nathaniel 18:119
Ague, Nathaniel 8:7
Ahas, Charles 20:197
Ahearn, Daniel 3:10
Ahem, D. 16:168
Ahem, Patrick 12:169
Ahenn, Joseph 4:7
Ahern, C. A. 15:336;
  16:168
Ahern, D. 25:134
Aherns, Nicholas 1:11
Ahill, James H. 10:38
Ahit, Michael 15:331
Ahl, William H. 14:135
Ahlis, Christian 20:120
Ahrendt, Lewis 22:164
Ahrens, A. 15:101

Ahrens, Deitrich 8:7
Ahrens, Frederick 5:49
Ahrens, Matis 14:135
Ahreotergeshig, O. 1:107
Ahrers, Dutrick 18:119
Ahues, L. 1:107
Aichel, Philip 20:197
Aichell, Philip 10:38
Aigain, John 21:96
Aigle, John 16:131
Aiken, Alexander 9:32;
  16:83
Aiken, David 19:287
Aiken, David M. 11:297
Aiken, E. 11:21
Aiken, George L. 8:112
Aiken, George W. 3:10
Aiken, H. A. 13:103
Aiken, H. L. 11:235
Aiken, Henry 10:12
Aiken, Isham 27:9
Aiken, J. J. 9:68
Aiken, J. W. 3:10
Aiken, Jack 9:153
Aiken, James 9:74; 26:148
Aiken, Jesse 11:195
Aiken, John 20:197;
  26:216
Aiken, Joseph 7:116
Aiken, Peter 7:73; 25:292
Aiken, Philip 21:294
Aiken, Therom 11:189
Aiken, W. A. 3:10
Aiken, William A. 22:415
Aiken, William P. 22:399
Aikens, A. 3:10
Aikens, Adam 22:231
Aikens, Ezra L. 24:11
Aikens, J. W. 17:28
Aikens, John W. 22:415
Aikens, M. 22:8
Aikens, Marshall 22:17
Aikens, Samuel 22:511
Aikens, William R. 12:11
Aikerman, Frederick
  19:328
Aikey, Robert 20:120
Aikin, Henry 25:285
Aikin, J. 26:8
Aikin, James 8:37; 18:119
Aikin, John 20:197
Aikin, Joshua 9:128
Aikin, Thomas 9:128
Aikin, William 3:10
Aikins, George W. 26:149
Aikins, J. F. 25:134
Aikler, John 16:168
Aikles, Frank 21:263
Aikman, James 21:47
Aikman, Michael E. 8:7;
  18:119

Ailand, C. 3:10
Aile, George M. 11:117
Ailes, John 4:7
Ailes, T. G. 3:10
Ailey, Henry 22:239
Ailey, Herman 9:47
Aimes, Joseph 1:11
Aine, Willis 9:41
Aines, A. G. 1:107
Aines, F. 21:294
Ainsworth, C. H. 17:289
Ainsworth, Francis M.
  21:15
Ainsworth, G. W. 17:289
Ainsworth, George 8:100;
  17:463
Ainsworth, George W.
  21:249; 22:160
Ainsworth, Henry M.
  21:206
Ainsworth, J. 22:329
Ainsworth, J. L. 9:167;
  19:234
Ainsworth, James 4:7
Ainsworth, James E.
  20:28
Ainsworth, James H.
  21:96
Ainsworth, John 11:293
Ainsworth, M. 8:44;
  20:197
Ainsworth, Mahlon 10:38
Ainsworth, Marvel 21:134
Ainsworth, N. 14:239
Ainsworth, O. E. 9:167
Ainsworth, R. 14:31
Ainsworth, W. 27:11
Ainsworth, W. W. 20:47
Aird, James 23:177
Airhart, William 21:219
Airtaugh, Leonard 9:41
Airy, N. R. 18:63
Ait, M. 3:10
Aitken, William 10:144
Aitkin, William 19:145
Aitor, John 26:9
Aitton, James F. 11:26
Akais, Charles 22:287
Akan, R. J. 16:115
Ake, George Z. 11:49
Akedangol, Pitsmon
  23:308
Akehorst, James L. 5:7;
  25:134
Aken, John 10:38
Aken, S. 25:12
Aken, Samuel 2:7
Akens, Alfred 24:187
Akens, Russell 10:38
Akenson, A. 3:10
Akent, William 10:12

Aker, G. W. 25:134
Aker, Jacob B. 20:94
Aker, John 4:7; 16:115, 168
Aker, John W. 17:28
Aker, Joseph F. 17:28
Aker, L. A. 15:357
Aker, Robert 7:116
Akere, Alexander 15:180
Akere, Charles 14:31
Akerly, P. 19:246
Akerman, M. 3:10
Akers, A. A. 3:10
Akers, Alfred 17:127
Akers, George 3:10
Akers, George C. 23:84
Akers, H. H. 3:10
Akers, Harvey 20:197
Akers, J. D. 19:52
Akers, J. W. 3:10
Akers, James R. 23:96
Akers, John 10:100; 20:197
Akers, R. 20:197
Akers, Thomas 17:258
Akers, William 21:294; 23:58
Akers, William C. 25:13
Akers, William E. 8:7; 18:119
Akerson, James 21:238
Akiman, Martin 11:275
Akin, Alex 18:290
Akin, Andrew 25:13
Akin, C. R. 5:7; 25:134
Akin, John 10:100
Akin, Levi 6:23
Akin, M. R. 8:7; 18:119
Akin, R. 13:82; 14:3
Akin, Thomas 27:9
Akins, Alexander 26:91
Akins, Amos P. 23:118
Akins, C. F. 14:3
Akins, Harrison 26:9
Akins, J. F. 3:10
Akins, James 8:7
Akins, John 24:64
Akins, W. 13:82; 14:3
Akins, William O. 23:118
Akler, C. 16:265
Akley, C. 14:3
Akley, Charles W. 4:7
Akley, J. 14:3
Akman, James 17:146
Akom, Samuel 23:130
Akroyd, W. 1:108
Al---, I. 17:271
Alabaugh, Charles 23:130
Aladid, Jose 8:125
Aladrid, Jose 12:61
Alaes, Peter 9:199

Alaksen, Torger 21:249
Alamson, Samuel 8:7
Alan, Eugene 27:11
Alar, Eugene 14:294; 17:469
Alb, Conrad 11:133
Alback, H. 25:134
Alban, James S. 20:191
Alban, W. 14:267
Alban, William H. 21:249
Albany, D. 3:10
Albarty, E. F. 18:119
Albaugh, Henry F. 23:130
Albaugh, Isaac 22:8
Albaugh, L. 15:62
Albaugh, Levi 12:66
Albee, Albert C. 20:197
Albee, Jesoph H. 19:145
Alber, Albert C. 10:100
Alber, Edwin 7:18
Alber, J. 17:13
Alber, S. 3:10
Alberding, Frederick 23:58
Alberger, Charles 15:157
Albers, Albert 10:100; 20:197
Albers, Henry 22:17
Albers, Joseph 9:15
Alberson, Alfred 10:100
Alberson, L. 3:10
Alberson, Solomon 10:100; 20:197
Albert, --- 16:265
Albert, Benjamin 17:348
Albert, C. 14:31
Albert, Charles 22:174
Albert, Dennis 10:100; 20:197
Albert, F. 14:31
Albert, Frank 22:415; 25:271
Albert, Frans 14:318
Albert, Frederick 11:50
Albert, G. 1:96
Albert, George 13:7
Albert, Heckman 24:34
Albert, Henry B. 12:11
Albert, Henry C. 13:7
Albert, J. 1:11, 107
Albert, Jack 9:128
Albert, Jacob 27:9
Albert, James 10:156; 19:145
Albert, John 1:11; 17:17; 18:117; 19:2
Albert, John G. 10:12
Albert, Joseph 11:217
Albert, Levi 22:164
Albert, Louis R. 11:49
Albert, Marion 21:84

Albert, Paul 12:11
Albert, Richard 17:169
Albert, Thomas 11:196
Albert, Toney 8:76
Albert, William 3:10; 13:82; 14:3; 25:134
Alberti, Frank 27:8
Albertis, Jacob 20:176
Alberton, A. 14:31
Alberton, J. E. 25:292
Alberton, Stephen W. 17:75
Alberton, Thomas J. 18:227; 26:9
Alberts, Quincy 11:21
Alberts, R. 8:44
Alberts, Rinehart 21:15
Albertson, Alfred 20:197
Albertson, Gabriel 9:115
Albertson, Henley 22:62
Albertson, John 21:62
Albertson, Lewis 21:294
Albertson, Samuel 17:448; 24:173
Albertson, W. G. 27:8
Albertson, W. K. 25:134
Albertson, William 10:100; 20:197
Albertson, William H. 8:102
Albertus, Arthur F. 22:275
Albertuty, Albertes 10:38
Alberty, E. F. 8:7
Alberty, Nelson 21:249
Albett, Christian 16:146
Albey, Charles 27:8
Albice, Frederick 12:66
Albin, Benjamin F. 7:84
Albin, George 22:62
Albin, I. 3:10
Albin, James R. 22:447
Albinger, J. 19:246
Albinger, John 11:133
Albiough, J. 18:23
Alborn, --- 15:180
Albough, G. 25:283
Albough, William H. 5:7
Albrasham, A. 27:10
Albratton, G. 27:9
Albraugh, John 14:135
Albrecht, --- 8:124
Albrecht, Henry 24:64
Albred, William H. 16:19
Albricht, Charles 21:96
Albridge, John 10:12
Albriel, Henry B. 12:11
Albright, A. D. 14:31
Albright, Adam 13:103
Albright, Amos 11:319
Albright, C. 3:10
Albright, Charles 22:472

Albright, Daniel 22:174
Albright, David 14:135
Albright, Ferdinand 10:100; 20:197
Albright, Franklin 14:32
Albright, Frederick 19:2
Albright, George S. 17:89
Albright, Gideon W. 22:414
Albright, H. 19:52
Albright, Henry 19:52
Albright, Henry E. 26:216
Albright, Henry Ernest 9:235
Albright, Isaac 13:7
Albright, J. 14:32; 27:11
Albright, Jacob 8:78
Albright, Joel 21:47
Albright, John 16:113
Albright, Joseph N. 22:414
Albright, M. 15:180
Albright, Samuel W. 27:11
Albright, William C. 19:145
Albrin, James 27:10
Albrin, Joseph 14:294; 17:475
Albring, J. 1:108
Albro, Charles 12:58
Albro, G. W. 1:11
Albro, James H. 10:156; 19:145
Albro, John 10:38; 20:197
Albro, Philon R. 15:150
Albro, William 13:7
Albrough, W. H. 25:134
Albus, Henry 1:108
Albus, John 13:103
Alcarro, Esano 7:116
Alcarve, E. 21:294
Alcock, Frank 18:227; 26:9
Alcock, J. 1:108
Alcock, John B. 22:135
Alcock, Nathan 26:9
Alcock, Thornton 18:227; 26:9
Alcom, John 17:146
Alcom, S. W. 3:10
Alcorn, A. P. 16:151
Alcorn, George W. 3:10
Alcorn, John 17:215
Alcorn, Thomas 27:157
Alcorn, W. W. 4:7
Alcott, Burritt 22:507
Alcott, Henry 22:17
Aldas, Henry 13:7
Alde, Adolphas 18:301
Alde, Adolphus 26:91

Aldeed, N. 14:3
Alden, A. P. 16:362
Alden, Charles 23:118
Alden, Edward M. 25:134
Alden, F. 9:47
Alden, G. G. 9:41
Alden, H. H. 19:52
Alden, Isaac S. 27:9
Alden, Leonard G. 9:138
Alden, Reuben M. 5:7
Alden, William D. 12:11
Alden, William P. 18:274
Aldended, James 15:117
Alder, Anderson C. 17:234
Alder, I. S. 9:138
Alder, James 24:73
Alderdice, James 13:104
Alderding, Henry 24:175
Alderich, James M. 17:287
Alderling, Henry 17:449
Alderman, Alexander 9:239
Alderman, Demetrius F. 17:75
Alderman, F. 3:10
Alderman, Henry 7:55; 21:84
Alderman, James A. 18:337
Alderman, John 20:178
Alderman, Theron W. 23:118
Alderman, W. W. 3:10
Alderon, John 6:10
Alderson, Buford 23:17
Alderson, William 10:94
Aldin, A. P. 15:338
Aldin, Henry 16:168
Aldinger, Ed 11:335
Aldinger, Edward 17:253
Aldiss, Henry 15:293
Aldoes, Henry 27:8
Aldrap, Henry 18:227
Aldred, N. 13:82
Aldric, Edward 18:76
Aldrich, A. 17:73
Aldrich, A. H. 14:135
Aldrich, Ambrose E. 18:361
Aldrich, Arunnah K. 13:7
Aldrich, Asa 13:104
Aldrich, D. 21:15
Aldrich, Franklin 24:11
Aldrich, G. W. 13:104
Aldrich, H. 3:10; 21:15
Aldrich, H. B. 3:10
Aldrich, H. W. 3:10
Aldrich, Harrison G. 10:156; 19:145

Aldrich, Henry 19:2
Aldrich, Hiram B. 7:15
Aldrich, Isaac T. 17:417; 24:155
Aldrich, J. 26:149
Aldrich, James 19:2
Aldrich, James E. 22:135
Aldrich, Jarvis 11:132
Aldrich, Jesse 18:361
Aldrich, John H. 13:7
Aldrich, John J. 24:90
Aldrich, L. 20:178
Aldrich, Lafayette 11:297
Aldrich, M. 1:107
Aldrich, M. A. 14:32
Aldrich, P. 11:235
Aldrich, Peter 11:21
Aldrich, Silas 22:135
Aldrich, Theodore M. 22:399
Aldrich, Thomas B. 23:17
Aldrich, Timothy 1:108
Aldrich, William C. 22:286
Aldrick, Ambrose 9:226
Aldrick, Jesse 9:217
Aldrick, S. 18:76
Aldridge, Bradley 22:116
Aldridge, C. W. 3:10
Aldridge, David 22:62
Aldridge, George 16:286
Aldridge, Gum 8:76
Aldridge, James 11:256
Aldridge, James J. 20:197
Aldridge, John 23:290
Aldridge, John G. 19:2
Aldridge, Joseph L. 10:38
Aldridge, Perry 26:149
Aldridge, Simon 23:290
Aldridge, V. 11:383
Aldridge, W. J. 20:197
Aldridge, William 22:239
Aldridge, William J. 10:100
Aldrige, James E. 21:294
Aldrige, Madison 17:233
Aldrige, Thomas 26:210
Aldrigo, Henry 11:50
Aldringer, Christian 1:12
Aldritch, Henry 15:2
Aldrop, Henry 26:8
Aleander, R. 16:265
Alebaugh, Henry 8:117
Alen, --- 27:10
Alen, D. 3:10
Alenson, Gabriel 27:10
Aleny, F. 3:10
Aler, B. 3:10
Alesher, John 7:18
Aleshure, Jackson 18:204
Aleson, Andrew 9:32

Alespear, William 27:8
Alex---, Chester W.
    16:138
Alexander, --- 25:332
Alexander, A. 11:278
Alexander, A. C. 23:130;
    27:11
Alexander, A. D. 1:12
Alexander, Adam 21:263
Alexander, Alex. David
    27:8
Alexander, Alfred R.
    21:219
Alexander, Anderson
    7:116; 11:195
Alexander, Andrew
    11:383; 22:415
Alexander, Anson 23:105
Alexander, B. 3:10
Alexander, B. F. 11:21
Alexander, Benjamin
    1:11; 17:127; 24:187
Alexander, Benson 7:116
Alexander, C. 1:12; 9:18;
    18:301; 26:91
Alexander, C. E. 8:61
Alexander, C. H. 21:184,
    214
Alexander, Charles
    13:126; 15:288;
    17:127, 169; 19:52;
    22:329; 24:187
Alexander, Charles C.
    10:38; 20:197
Alexander, Charles E.
    26:149
Alexander, Charles G
    22:471
Alexander, Christ 20:197
Alexander, Christian
    10:38
Alexander, D. W. 1:108
Alexander, Daniel A.
    22:399
Alexander, E. 14:267, 279
Alexander, E. B. 7:18
Alexander, E. H. 14:32
Alexander, Edward 17:62
Alexander, Edwin 18:213;
    21:219
Alexander, Ephraim
    14:135
Alexander, F. 11:297
Alexander, Freeman
    17:422
Alexander, G. 17:98;
    18:361; 21:294
Alexander, G. W. 23:17
Alexander, George 17:318
Alexander, George F.
    26:149

Alexander, George G.
    9:217
Alexander, George T. 8:61
Alexander, George W.
    20:131; 23:111
Alexander, Gilbert 21:16
Alexander, Grand H.
    22:239
Alexander, H. 15:164;
    25:292
Alexander, Henry 7:79;
    10:98; 11:196; 12:47;
    17:75
Alexander, Hiram P.
    22:17
Alexander, Isaac 11:383
Alexander, J. 1:12, 107;
    3:10; 16:286; 24:73;
    25:134
Alexander, J. D. 3:10
Alexander, J. M. 20:197;
    25:13
Alexander, J. W. 10:192;
    18:171
Alexander, Jackson
    23:197
Alexander, Jacob 17:75;
    22:287
Alexander, James 6:22;
    11:196; 17:169;
    21:96, 294; 22:62,
    287
Alexander, James H.
    20:120
Alexander, James M.
    10:38
Alexander, Jeremiah 8:7;
    18:119; 21:88
Alexander, Jerry 17:267;
    22:63
Alexander, Jesse 7:116
Alexander, John 5:35; 9:9;
    10:100; 15:89; 16:19;
    18:420; 20:197;
    21:62; 22:287; 24:73
Alexander, John A. 22:17
Alexander, John C.
    21:206
Alexander, John D. 21:47
Alexander, John H. 7:18;
    20:185
Alexander, John L. 24:47
Alexander, John S. 25:13
Alexander, John T. 17:211
Alexander, John W.
    9:100; 20:3; 22:447
Alexander, Joseph 5:35
Alexander, Joseph J. 13:7
Alexander, King 22:287
Alexander, L. F. 16:168
Alexander, Lacey 22:287

Alexander, Little 25:332
Alexander, Lockwood
    21:16
Alexander, Loren 1:108
Alexander, M. 3:10
Alexander, M. H. 9:47
Alexander, Mary B.
    25:134
Alexander, N. 20:197
Alexander, Nathan 22:239
Alexander, Nicholas 9:18
Alexander, P. S. 3:10
Alexander, Peter 21:134
Alexander, Pielman 8:37
Alexander, Pillman
    26:148
Alexander, R. 16:168;
    23:130
Alexander, Reuben 1:108
Alexander, Robert 4:7;
    9:65; 11:380
Alexander, S. 3:10; 14:32
Alexander, S. A. 7:84
Alexander, S. H. 8:44
Alexander, S. K. 8:44
Alexander, Samuel 8:78;
    12:86; 16:286;
    22:287
Alexander, Samuel H.
    21:96
Alexander, Samuel M.
    10:100; 20:197
Alexander, T. 22:287
Alexander, T. J. 22:511
Alexander, Than 22:498
Alexander, Thomas 9:167;
    17:75; 19:273; 20:54;
    22:63, 174; 24:47
Alexander, Thompson
    14:294; 17:471
Alexander, Tobias 8:37;
    26:148
Alexander, W. 1:108;
    3:10; 10:38
Alexander, W. A. 10:175
Alexander, W. C. 10:38;
    20:197
Alexander, W. E. 9:226
Alexander, W. S. 3:10
Alexander, W. T. 17:28
Alexander, Wesley 8:99
Alexander, William 1:108;
    4:7; 7:116; 11:196,
    230, 325; 18:23, 76;
    19:145; 20:3; 21:63
Alexander, William B.
    15:6
Alexander, William E.
    21:219
Alexander, William F.
    23:278

Alexander, William H.
21:96; 22:287
Alexander, William J.
23:84
Alexander, William M.
13:56
Alexander, William P.
22:116
Alexander, William T.
17:278
Alexander, William W.
21:219
Alexandre, Paul 21:294
Alexandria, J. 25:135
Alexandria, James 14:135
Alexy, Philip 11:132
Aley, John 20:34
Alf, H. 3:10
Alfers, H. 23:255
Alfka, H. 3:10
Alfont, John 18:213
Alford, A. P. 11:256
Alford, B. C. 3:10
Alford, E. 1:13
Alford, G. W. 9:167
Alford, George 3:10;
14:130
Alford, H. 14:32
Alford, Harvey 17:17
Alford, Isaac L. 10:38;
20:197
Alford, James L. 21:13
Alford, John R. 22:116
Alford, Jonas 22:116
Alford, W. I. 3:10
Alford, William 17:205
Alfred, G. W. 19:272
Alfred, Isaac 22:288
Alfred, J. 16:168
Alfred, John 7:116
Alfred, Joshua 11:49
Alfred, Peter 10:169
Alfred, R. 21:108
Alfrey, Lewis 22:63
Alfrod, Isaac W. 24:11
Algar, William 1:108
Alger, Abner 10:100;
20:197
Alger, Abraham 10:100;
20:197
Alger, Alfred 13:7
Alger, Augustus G.
10:100
Alger, Charles 23:118
Alger, Charles S. 23:282
Alger, Chester 7:18
Alger, D. B. 25:13
Alger, Daniel E. 27:8
Alger, E. L. 25:135
Alger, Eugene 7:18
Alger, G. W. 17:309

Alger, J. J. 23:17
Alger, Leonard 8:78
Alger, N. E. 17:210
Alger, Samuel G. 23:105
Alger, Thomas 8:44;
21:134; 22:507
Alger, W. A. 3:11
Algers, George M. 12:11
Algert, H. K. 3:11
Alges, G. W. 7:18
Algier, Horace 17:392
Algier, James H. 26:10
Algier, William 19:2
Algot, A. 14:32
Alherall, William 18:204
Alherus, Victor F. 19:145
Aliber, William 9:199;
19:289
Alice, F. 15:28
Alice, Francis 17:446
Alies, Francis 24:169
Aliff, F. H. 10:26; 19:299
Aliff, T. W. 8:44
Alin, C. 1:109
Alinger, Louis 22:415
Alingert, D. 3:11
Alinson, Robert C. 22:399
Alison, Andrew C. 9:167
Alison, J. 13:82; 14:3
Alison, Jeremiah 9:47
Alison, Noah 15:157
Alistock, J. D. 9:242
Alkanus, George 16:19
Alkiel, Mahlon 7:47
Alkinback, Christopher
22:135
Alkire, William 22:17
Alkman, B. F. 26:9
Alkness, George 13:7
All, Robert 21:210
Allabaugh, R. R. 23:17
Allan, T. C. 20:197
Allard, Asa 7:81; 25:292
Allard, Charles 15:180
Allard, Charles W. 7:84
Allard, G. 16:362
Allard, Gabriel 17:62
Allard, J. W. 25:135
Allard, Jacob 25:135
Allard, W. C. 1:12
Allard, W. O. 7:84
Allason, W. 26:9
Allbeck, G. B. 3:11
Allbot, Simon 17:246
Allbridge, Edwin W.
21:294
Allbright, M. W. 25:135
Allbritten, Wade 6:23
Allbrook, C. W. 3:11
Allcock, Joseph 21:294
Allcock, Nathan 17:151

Allcome, Hanson 21:295
Allcorn, Thomas 8:78
Allcot, Harmon 15:80
Allcott, William 14:135
Alldridge, John H. 21:295
Alleck, Frederick 9:239
Allee, John W. 23:58
Allemange, W. W. 13:82
Allemore, Elisha G.
18:290
Allen, --- 5:49; 8:44;
23:301; 25:135
Allen, A. 1:12, 107; 3:11;
9:217; 13:82; 14:3,
239; 18:361; 25:12,
279; 27:11
Allen, A. A. 3:11
Allen, A. B. 3:11; 8:61;
14:135; 26:149
Allen, A. C. 22:175
Allen, A. J. 9:48; 11:275;
18:227, 391; 20:143;
21:295; 26:9
Allen, A. S. A. 21:202
Allen, A. T. 1:107
Allen, A. W. 3:11
Allen, Aaron 6:9; 7:85;
18:107; 23:197
Allen, Aaron B. 26:144
Allen, Abner 4:7
Allen, Acumari 18:274
Allen, Addison D. 21:134
Allen, Adoniram 21:47
Allen, Albert 11:295;
20:197; 21:295
Allen, Alexander 4:64;
7:116
Allen, Alfred 6:20; 9:161;
21:263
Allen, Alonzo A. 20:105
Allen, Alonzo E. 22:17
Allen, Alonzo O. 21:63
Allen, Alonzo W. 21:88
Allen, Alva 13:61; 16:168
Allen, Alvin 23:105
Allen, Alvin K. 24:90
Allen, Ancel 20:103
Allen, Andrew 20:105
Allen, Andrew J. 4:7
Allen, August G. 20:197
Allen, B. 24:108
Allen, B. F. 1:96
Allen, B. W. 21:295
Allen, Ben J. 14:135
Allen, Benjamin 7:85;
12:11, 94; 15:357;
17:165, 396; 21:241
Allen, Benjamin F.
19:340; 22:135;
27:10
Allen, Benjamin L. 21:129

Allen, Benjamin R. 21:165
Allen, Benjamin W. 22:414
Allen, Bernard 19:2
Allen, Berry 12:160
Allen, C. 3:11; 10:25; 11:297; 16:168
Allen, C. B. 1:12, 107; 3:11
Allen, C. M. 22:17
Allen, C. P. 25:12
Allen, C. W. 5:7; 25:135
Allen, Caleb M. 12:11
Allen, Carbin 8:112
Allen, Caswell 17:201
Allen, Charles 3:11; 7:55; 9:9; 10:8, 13, 170, 171; 17:13; 18:213, 434; 19:2, 145; 26:8; 27:10
Allen, Charles A. 7:85; 21:295
Allen, Charles B. 9:74
Allen, Charles H. 9:217; 18:204, 361
Allen, Charles J. 20:33
Allen, Charles R. 18:444
Allen, Charles W. 7:85; 25:135
Allen, Christ 6:12; 18:76
Allen, Cineas 1:108
Allen, D. 1:107; 21:295
Allen, D. B. 3:11
Allen, D. M. 17:28
Allen, D. N. 22:471
Allen, D. W. 14:32
Allen, Daniel 11:195; 17:262; 22:175; 27:142
Allen, Daniel M. 18:301; 26:91
Allen, Daniel W. 9:18; 10:38; 20:197
Allen, David 8:70, 112; 9:48; 15:171; 17:62; 18:323
Allen, David C. 23:118
Allen, Decatur 21:263
Allen, DeLanson T. 18:357
Allen, Dock 11:196
Allen, Doctor 21:248
Allen, E. 7:55; 21:16; 22:239
Allen, E. A. 16:115
Allen, E. B. 10:179; 18:171
Allen, E. D. 26:204
Allen, E. J. 13:82
Allen, E. P. 19:279

Allen, E. R. 4:7
Allen, E. S. 1:12; 3:11
Allen, E. T. 14:32
Allen, E. W. 25:12
Allen, Eben S. 16:77
Allen, Eber N. 22:170
Allen, Edward 4:7; 7:12; 9:167; 19:246; 22:63, 275, 507
Allen, Edward F. 22:459
Allen, Edwin Y. 11:230
Allen, Elijah 22:511
Allen, Elisha 16:89
Allen, Ellis 7:116
Allen, Elwood 11:285
Allen, Ethan 1:11
Allen, Ezra J. 9:167
Allen, F. 14:294; 17:480; 27:10
Allen, F. A. 20:197
Allen, F. C. 23:17
Allen, F. P. 9:74
Allen, F. T. 21:163
Allen, Fayette L. 8:7; 18:119
Allen, Francis 3:11; 9:242
Allen, Francis A. 10:38
Allen, Francis M. 22:116; 23:58
Allen, Frank 26:144
Allen, Franklin P. 22:471
Allen, Fred 9:18
Allen, Frederick 14:135
Allen, Frederick A. 12:53
Allen, G. 18:44; 27:8
Allen, G. B. 5:49
Allen, G. G. 26:120
Allen, G. H. 3:11; 16:115
Allen, G. P. 19:2
Allen, G. W. 1:107; 3:11; 17:62
Allen, George 5:7; 7:7; 10:38, 100; 15:28; 19:2; 20:197; 21:263; 24:64; 25:135
Allen, George A. 1:12; 4:7
Allen, George E. 15:351; 16:277
Allen, George F. 10:156; 19:145
Allen, George H. 11:284; 21:295
Allen, George M. 13:7
Allen, George N. 9:167; 19:234; 22:399
Allen, George W. 10:210; 11:102; 18:63
Allen, Gideon 17:322
Allen, Gilbert 9:95; 21:295
Allen, Gordon 24:90

Allen, Gustave 11:21
Allen, Gustavus 1:191
Allen, H. 13:76; 16:168; 19:2; 25:13; 27:8
Allen, H. H. 1:107; 14:32; 25:135
Allen, H. M. 16:19
Allen, H. W. 19:145
Allen, Hamilton 2:7; 20:399
Allen, Harrison 10:147; 12:11; 18:44
Allen, Haub. T. 21:244
Allen, Hen 18:187
Allen, Henry 7:116; 9:74, 205; 10:152; 11:196; 12:11; 13:7; 18:44; 21:145; 22:135, 288; 27:142
Allen, Henry A. 5:7
Allen, Henry B. 7:85
Allen, Henry C. 17:47
Allen, Henry I. 8:7
Allen, Henry J. 18:119
Allen, Henry T. 25:135
Allen, Henry W. 9:100; 10:156; 20:176
Allen, Hezekiah 11:180
Allen, Hiram 12:11; 21:238; 26:9
Allen, Horace 21:295; 23:251
Allen, Horatio W. 22:472
Allen, Horian 9:74
Allen, I. 1:11; 21:87
Allen, Ira T. 2:7; 25:13
Allen, Isa 9:74
Allen, Isaac 10:38, 98
Allen, J. 3:11; 11:297; 12:98; 15:180; 18:44; 20:198; 21:295; 27:8
Allen, J. A. 13:7; 25:292
Allen, J. B. 9:18; 18:301; 26:91
Allen, J. C. 14:136; 20:198
Allen, J. E. 1:11; 21:295
Allen, J. H. 1:108; 9:48; 11:324; 20:84
Allen, J. L. 3:11
Allen, J. N. 14:32
Allen, J. O. 25:135
Allen, J. P. C. 12:47
Allen, J. T. 3:11
Allen, J. W. 1:108; 3:11; 6:10; 14:32; 18:76
Allen, Jacob C. 21:63
Allen, James 9:9, 235; 10:7; 14:135, 253; 15:180; 16:168; 18:107, 284; 19:2;

Allen, James 21:145;
22:239; 25:135; 26:8,
134, 216; 27:9
Allen, James B. 18:44;
22:116
Allen, James C. 3:11
Allen, James F. 22:399
Allen, James H. 21:295
Allen, James M. C.
21:219
Allen, James P. 22:498
Allen, James S. 19:324
Allen, James W. 3:11;
11:331
Allen, Jefferson 9:205
Allen, Jeremiah 22:175;
25:135
Allen, Jeremiah B. 23:84
Allen, Jerome 17:62
Allen, Jerome B. 20:38
Allen, Jerry 17:169
Allen, Jesse 3:11
Allen, Jesse K. 14:136
Allen, John 1:12; 6:11;
7:17; 8:76; 9:95,
205; 10:38; 11:195,
256; 12:161; 13:104;
14:32, 136, 253;
15:293; 16:89, 168;
17:234; 18:76; 20:47,
153, 198; 21:129,
295; 22:288, 447
Allen, John B. 10:100;
20:198
Allen, John C. 10:38;
27:10
Allen, John D. 10:89
Allen, John E. 9:65
Allen, John J. 4:7
Allen, John K. 12:150
Allen, John L. 20:198
Allen, John O. 5:7
Allen, John P. 9:138;
22:239
Allen, John R. 7:85; 24:88
Allen, John S. 21:295
Allen, John W. 22:498
Allen, Jonathan C. 24:11
Allen, Joseph 12:11;
21:238; 22:239, 399;
25:135
Allen, Joseph C. 21:129;
23:103
Allen, Joshua 17:348;
23:58
Allen, Jules B. 16:83
Allen, Julius 25:268
Allen, L. 21:295
Allen, L. F. 21:295
Allen, L. J. 13:82; 14:3
Allen, Lafayette 25:135

Allen, Lawson 13:7
Allen, Leonidas 17:75
Allen, Leroy 23:282
Allen, Levi 9:235; 23:17;
26:216
Allen, Levi C. 25:13
Allen, Levi H. 18:391
Allen, Lewis 15:324;
19:52; 20:94; 27:10
Allen, Lewis C. 9:138
Allen, Louis 9:213
Allen, Louis C. 27:8
Allen, M. 9:226; 11:235;
18:361
Allen, M. A. D. L. 11:89
Allen, Margaret 25:292
Allen, Marion 11:117
Allen, Mark 18:227; 26:9
Allen, Martin 11:196;
22:288, 471
Allen, Martin V. 23:17
Allen, Merrick 20:3
Allen, Merritt 17:241
Allen, Michael 17:427;
24:182
Allen, Miles 7:85; 8:44;
11:102; 21:89;
26:149
Allen, Milo 8:61
Allen, Milton 22:135
Allen, Morgan L. 16:89
Allen, Morris 22:329
Allen, N. 3:11; 13:82;
14:3
Allen, N. G. 1:107
Allen, Nathan 13:104, 130
Allen, Nathan H. 21:295
Allen, Nathaniel 11:50;
13:79; 16:168
Allen, Nathaniel P. 22:17
Allen, Nelson A. 16:138
Allen, Newell B. 16:5
Allen, Noax 10:13
Allen, O. J. 23:17
Allen, O. P. 20:151; 21:16
Allen, Obadiah T. 21:47
Allen, Orman 10:169
Allen, Orville 1:11
Allen, Oscar C. 12:11
Allen, Oscar D. 16:80
Allen, Otis D. 17:28
Allen, P. B. 19:222
Allen, P. S. 25:13
Allen, Peter 23:312;
25:316
Allen, R. 14:294; 17:191,
481; 18:23; 27:11
Allen, R. C. 3:11
Allen, R. D. 17:403
Allen, R. F. 16:19
Allen, R. G. 13:104

Allen, Richard 12:47
Allen, Richard W. 22:415
Allen, Robert 7:18; 8:37;
11:420; 13:7; 20:102;
21:16, 118, 295;
22:288; 26:148
Allen, Robert C. 20:198
Allen, Robert G. 16:19
Allen, Robert H. 16:19
Allen, Robert J. 12:11
Allen, S. 3:11; 14:32, 136,
253; 25:279
Allen, S. B. 25:135
Allen, S. C. 22:498
Allen, S. D. 1:107
Allen, S. E. 8:102
Allen, S. H. 1:12
Allen, S. J. 25:12
Allen, S. S. 21:108
Allen, Samuel 7:84;
10:210; 13:7; 20:141;
21:9; 25:135
Allen, Samuel B. 21:295
Allen, Samuel L. 24:73
Allen, Samuel R. 21:134
Allen, Samuel S. 3:11
Allen, Sidney 7:18
Allen, Silas 17:320;
25:135
Allen, Silas W. 22:116,
459
Allen, Simon 17:169
Allen, Simon E. 4:7
Allen, Smith P. 27:10
Allen, Stephen 7:116
Allen, Sterling 11:196
Allen, Sylvester 20:20
Allen, T. 3:11; 13:82;
14:3; 15:329; 19:52,
246
Allen, T. C. 10:38
Allen, Thomas 8:78, 102;
9:167; 12:11; 15:157;
19:279
Allen, Thomas D. 16:115
Allen, Thomas H. 21:63
Allen, Thomas S. 7:85
Allen, Thomas W. 7:18
Allen, Tibbett 25:135
Allen, Timothy 9:167
Allen, True W. 9:115
Allen, Trueman 25:135
Allen, Truman 19:2
Allen, U. D. 21:165
Allen, W. 1:12; 3:11;
11:297; 15:28;
18:187; 24:73
Allen, W. B. 7:85; 26:149
Allen, W. F. 11:293
Allen, W. G. G. 18:23
Allen, W. H. 3:11; 25:135

Allen, W. J. 25:292
Allen, W. K. 16:151
Allen, W. M. 22:349
Allen, W. N. 5:7; 25:135
Allen, W. S. 13:61; 19:52
Allen, W. T. 17:294
Allen, Walter 23:118
Allen, Washington 17:169
Allen, William 3:11; 6:12;
    7:116; 8:78; 9:47, 70,
    74; 11:132, 324, 325,
    338; 12:11, 47, 91,
    160; 13:7; 14:32,
    136; 16:286; 17:46,
    191, 234; 18:76;
    22:116, 239, 414;
    23:267, 312; 25:13,
    316; 26:8, 148
Allen, William A. 7:79;
    14:32; 25:292
Allen, William B. 15:171
Allen, William C. 22:415
Allen, William F. 17:494;
    21:295; 23:58
Allen, William H. 10:38,
    100; 13:104; 18:274;
    20:198; 23:58, 105
Allen, William J. 17:395;
    21:219
Allen, William L. 22:415
Allen, William M. 14:32
Allen, William N. 20:143
Allen, William S. 22:170,
    471
Allen, William T. 23:130
Allen, Wilson M. 22:63
Allen, Zachariah 27:10
Allen, Zuke 9:48
Allenback, Frank 15:302;
    16:168
Allenberger, J. 3:11
Allenburg, T. 9:138
Allenden, Samuel S.
    20:38
Allender, B. 13:82
Allender, William 19:145
Allender, William H.
    10:100; 20:198
Allendorf, J. W. 15:157
Allenpot, G. W. 17:264
Allensder, James 11:296
Allenton, Francis M. 16:8
Allenworth, Washington
    22:288
Allerdist, W. 1:12
Allers, Peter 26:8
Allerton, A. O. 11:297
Allery, Albert 21:295
Alleson, Abraham 8:37
Alleson, Kenard 23:186
Alley, Amos H. 24:34

Alley, Charles H. 20:47
Alley, Enoch M. 19:324
Alley, George 19:2
Alley, George W. 22:415
Alley, Huston 22:239
Alley, J. T. 14:32
Alley, Jacob H. 1:11
Alley, James 20:191
Alley, John H. 7:18
Alley, Leonard 8:44;
    21:134
Alley, O. 14:32
Alley, Samuel 14:313
Alley, Samuel D. 23:58
Alley, W. L. 1:108
Alley, William 8:44;
    24:34
Alley, William H. 10:38
Alleymanny, W. W. 14:3
Alleyn, George W. 22:135
Allgood, Iredell 24:34
Allicon, B. 18:107
Alliger, H. 9:138
Allin, W. 18:76
Alling, G. I. 15:180
Alling, George A. 15:347
Allinger, L. 3:11
Allington, Eagan 13:77
Allington, William H.
    22:170
Allinson, John 21:134
Allinson, William 5:7
Alliott, G. 17:17
Allis, Hiram 17:28;
    18:213
Allis, I. J. 1:12
Allis, J. D. 10:13
Allis, Lucius 25:278
Allis, P. 26:210
Allis, R. F. 25:316
Allis, R. S. 9:163
Allis, Sandy 17:127;
    24:187
Allis, Stephen 9:167
Allis, T. C. 27:11
Allis, William 11:297
Allishouse, Amos 14:32
Allision, Watson 17:271
Allison, A. 12:61
Allison, A. C. 19:279
Allison, A. P. 26:144
Allison, Abraham 26:148
Allison, Alexander 15:89
Allison, B. 9:138
Allison, B. F. 3:11
Allison, C. D. 26:9
Allison, Charles 19:285
Allison, Cyrus 7:116
Allison, D. B. 3:11
Allison, Daniel 23:17
Allison, Daniel W. 22:17

Allison, David 23:17
Allison, E. 3:11; 20:198
Allison, Eagle 11:189
Allison, F. S. 13:7
Allison, G. 3:11
Allison, G. G. 12:7
Allison, George W. 8:102
Allison, Henry 17:158;
    22:288
Allison, J. 1:108
Allison, J. D. 18:227
Allison, J. K. 14:32
Allison, J. S. 16:151
Allison, J. W. 13:104
Allison, Jacob 9:115;
    18:117; 27:9
Allison, James 8:37;
    14:32; 16:286; 21:16;
    26:148
Allison, James C. 22:174
Allison, James R. 17:17
Allison, John 4:7
Allison, John D. 9:71
Allison, John M. 8:78
Allison, Joseph 12:121;
    15:117; 18:420
Allison, Joseph J. 12:11
Allison, L. F. 3:11
Allison, P. 27:9
Allison, Robert 13:7
Allison, Robert O. 11:19
Allison, Rufus A. 11:235
Allison, S. 23:284
Allison, Thomas 18:227;
    23:130; 26:9
Allison, Thomas G. 13:7
Allison, W. 18:227
Allison, W. J. 7:18
Allison, Walter S. 22:415
Allison, William 8:78;
    9:162; 18:227;
    25:135; 26:9; 27:11
Allison, William M. 24:34
Alliston, William 9:199
Allitterson, J. F. 22:239
Allman, Charles 3:11
Allman, George W.
    22:111
Allman, H. C. 23:130
Allman, John 22:415
Allman, John W. 7:84
Allman, N. J. 21:295
Allonan, E. 19:52
Allor, Joseph 21:241
Alloway, William R.
    22:239
Allowey, Peter O. 4:7
Allridge, Enos 8:61
Allridge, J. 14:136
Allridge, P. 8:61
Alls, William 20:150

Allsarer, Peter 14:136
Allsbrook, M. 9:48
Allshire, D. L. 9:242
Allshouse, L. 14:32
Allsop, Joseph 4:64
Allsop, M. P. 7:84
Allspaugh, Robert 22:175
Allstetter, Herman 23:130
Allston, James 21:295
Allston, William 9:9
Allum, James 12:98
Allumis, Henry 13:104
Allwise, J. R. 3:11
Allwood, George W. 24:11
Allwood, John B. 10:38
Ally, James 8:102
Allyer, Smith 21:295
Allyn, D. 3:11
Allyn, Edwin W. 11:380
Allyn, Henry A. 15:90
Alman, L. 18:44
Alman, Robert 8:78
Alman, Thomas B. 8:78
Almas, --- 16:138
Alme, Michael M. 8:78
Almmer, Fitz 4:7
Almon, John 17:246
Almond, A. 3:11
Almond, Baker 9:18; 18:301; 26:91
Almond, James W. 23:240
Almond, John 17:391
Almond, Louis 11:101
Almonds, Henry 7:116
Almut, James P. 21:245
Almy, Thomas 16:160
Alney, Aaron 8:78
Alno, A. 8:44
Aloes, Nicholas 9:48
Alonso, O. Limber 9:101
Alonzo, A. 13:104
Aloord, Allen 11:21
Alory, William 11:50
Alp, Joseph 25:279
Alpen, R. 1:107
Alphards, Paton 9:217
Alphin, Luke P. 20:54
Alphord, J. 3:11
Alphord, Paton 18:361
Alpie, Augustus 17:28
Alpin, John 16:286
Alrey, John 8:78
Alright, William C. 10:156
Alsapp, Andrew 24:187
Alsasser, Lawrence 26:120
Alsaver, S. 3:11
Alsen, Hans 8:117
Alshouse, J. 25:135

Alsoft, William 15:302
Alson, John 14:136
Alsons, Hans 21:16
Alsop, George 1:13
Alsop, John 1:11; 21:47
Alsop, M. P. 21:295
Alsope, William 11:49
Alspach, David J. 7:66
Alspaugh, D. D. 11:297
Alspaugh, Jacob 22:175
Alspaugh, Joseph 18:23
Alspaugh, Reuben 21:219
Alspaugh, Sanford 21:219
Alsten, William 4:7
Alston, Alonzo 27:9
Alston, George 21:145, 210
Alston, Henry 9:128
Alston, John 14:239
Alston, O. 8:7; 18:119
Alston, Sampson 9:128; 27:9
Alston, Washington 17:169
Alston, William 19:289
Alsup, J. 22:329
Alsworth, Reuben 21:263
Alt, Charles 1:12
Alt, Christopher 22:63
Alt, Frederick 10:171
Altan, John 12:66
Alteem, Alfred A. 11:50
Altefoght, Rudolph 9:74
Altefogt, R. 26:8
Alteman, Joseph 23:84
Altemire, Fred 23:130
Altenberg, F. 27:8
Altenbrend, E. 3:11
Altenbury, James A. 9:74
Alter, J. A. 1:108
Alter, John 20:94
Alter, John A. 24:11
Alterniger, Frederick 23:130
Alters, John S. 9:115
Althof, William 16:168
Althons, William K. 22:17
Althouse, Henry 8:61
Althouse, J. 18:411
Althouse, Lyman 22:459
Altick, C. 13:82
Altizer, Moses 21:219
Altman, G. W. 1:107
Altman, Martin 11:409
Altman, William 4:7
Altmensberger, Henry 10:38
Altmus, William 3:11
Altmyer, Peter 23:10
Altoft, William 11:123
Alton, Charles P. 24:11

Alton, J. E. 15:52
Alton, James 20:198
Alton, Jason 13:7
Alton, John 11:50
Alton, Joseph 10:38
Alton, S. 3:11
Alton, W. 23:312
Altop, Ephraim 22:472
Altor, John 18:227
Altsman, Samuel 10:100; 20:198
Altsmenberger, H. 20:198
Altson, John 27:11
Altson, Peter 11:196
Altwood, Abraham 3:11
Alvason, William 18:346
Alvato, Looker 19:2
Alven, John 3:11
Alverson, C. C. 14:136, 253
Alverson, David 11:102
Alverson, H. 18:44
Alverson, James 25:135
Alverson, James V. 10:210
Alverson, William 22:459
Alves, James 21:295
Alvey, John 23:243
Alvey, Luke 22:63
Alvey, Nicholas 22:63
Alvian, Estevan 8:121
Alville, William F. 8:78
Alvin, Robert 8:37; 26:148
Alvior, Estephen 19:317
Alvis, D. 16:168
Alvis, John 8:61; 26:149
Alvis, Joseph 22:17
Alvis, Marcus A. 22:498
Alvis, Wesley 7:116
Alvison, M. 22:288
Alvon, I. 15:180
Alvord, A. 3:11
Alvord, A. O. 9:11
Alvord, Eli 17:262
Alvord, J. C. 11:235
Alvord, James 14:32
Alvord, Seymour F. 24:61
Alvord, Wayne 20:94
Alvord, William 22:135
Alward, A. 3:11
Alward, James 8:79
Alwayra, Richard 16:138
Always, Thomas 21:295
Alwine, J. 13:80; 16:168
Alwis, Henry 21:203
Alwood, John B. 20:198
Alwood, Josiah 10:100; 20:198
Alwood, Leonard 7:47
Alworth, Eugene 11:133

Aly, John 9:74
Alyea, E. C. 8:7; 18:119
Alyey, Aaron A. 24:35
Alynn, John 18:63
Amable, William H.
25:135
Amach, William M.
25:135
Amack, R. W. 12:161
Amadon, H. D. 16:168
Amagas, Eli 3:11
Amalard, Leo 13:104
Aman, William 16:277
Amand, Joseph K. 10:94
Amas, Andrew 20:87
Amas, James L. 11:133
Amas, John 11:133
Amas, L. 10:179; 26:204
Amass, W. T. 21:47
Amavine, Valentine 8:79
Ambenster, A. 11:21
Amberson, Thomas
19:328
Amble, Abner C. 22:116
Ambler, Ambram 22:329
Ambler, C. 3:11
Ambler, Frederick 3:11
Ambler, George 11:50
Ambler, William 8:44;
21:134
Ambler, William H. 16:89
Amborg, Michael 22:164
Ambroder, Hermon
11:427
Ambros, Julius 17:278
Ambrose, Celestin 9:205
Ambrose, Charles 9:18;
18:301; 26:91
Ambrose, D. 21:184
Ambrose, H. 16:135
Ambrose, Isaac 27:11
Ambrose, Jacob 3:11
Ambrose, James 23:130
Ambrose, Levi P. 20:3
Ambrose, Marcus T.
15:85
Ambrose, Robert P. 25:12
Ambrose, Sanford 1:108
Ambrose, Thomas 7:85
Ambrose, W. 14:32
Amburg, J. Van 26:149
Amburg, T. H. 15:305
Ambuster, F. 11:123
Amdinson, Arm 10:10
Amdon, C. S. 19:52
Amee, Jacob 27:8
Ameigh, W. J. 1:108
Amel, C. 25:135
Amel, Charles 5:7
Amen, John 21:219

Amen, P. Q. R. S. Q.
25:135
Ament, Anson G. 21:16
Ament, John 7:18
Amer, James 20:153
Amercon, John H. 22:239
Americo, --- 17:399
Amerinan, H. H. 24:35
Amerman, Joseph 22:288
Amerman, Oakley 16:168
Ameron, A. 17:469; 27:10
Ameron, Simeon 9:32
Amerson, A. 14:294
Ames, --- 25:12
Ames, A. C. 18:411
Ames, Ambrose C. 23:266
Ames, Andrew J. 12:66
Ames, Asa D. 8:79
Ames, Charles 6:23; 19:52
Ames, Charles W. 17:62
Ames, E. M. 16:362
Ames, E. T. 1:107
Ames, Edward 16:362
Ames, F. J. 1:107
Ames, Fisher 9:100
Ames, Foster 17:287
Ames, Frank 10:10
Ames, Franklin 22:175
Ames, George 3:12; 6:35
Ames, George H. 16:277
Ames, George W. 1:12
Ames, Gotlieb 16:19
Ames, H. 3:12
Ames, H. A. 1:12
Ames, Hartland G. 14:294
Ames, Hartland S. 17:474;
27:10
Ames, Henry 3:12; 11:133
Ames, Henry C. 22:116
Ames, Horatio W. 5:49
Ames, Ira L. 20:110
Ames, J. C. 9:138; 27:9
Ames, J. E. 19:145
Ames, J. R. 3:12
Ames, J. S. 22:175
Ames, Jacob S. 15:164
Ames, James 9:101
Ames, Jesse 25:135
Ames, John C. 4:8
Ames, John G. 3:11
Ames, M. 11:256
Ames, M. A. 14:268
Ames, M. L. 3:12
Ames, Martin 12:66;
15:28
Ames, Moses 15:180
Ames, Nathaniel 21:295
Ames, Nelson A. 15:349
Ames, Newton 25:13
Ames, O. H. 9:167

Ames, O. W. 19:244
Ames, Richard 18:23
Ames, Robert 7:85; 9:167;
15:180; 19:234
Ames, Rollan 21:214
Ames, Russell M. 17:73
Ames, S. B. 9:18
Ames, Simeon C. 20:3
Ames, Stephen W. 17:13
Ames, T. G. 18:63
Ames, W. H. 25:135
Ames, William 5:35;
25:135
Ames, William H. 5:7
Ameslenigh, J. 20:198
Ameston, George 25:135
Amesworth, O. E. 19:265
Amet--, --- 20:54
Ametims, Carlton 11:50
Amey, Alfred 22:288
Amey, Peter 14:294;
17:475; 27:10
Amey, Reuben 25:283
Amey, William P. 4:8
Amhurst, George 14:32
Amias, Hilliard 7:116
Amick, William M. 5:7
Amidon, E. H. 7:18
Amidon, George W.
22:275
Amidon, Henry 11:256
Amidon, John 25:135
Amidon, R. 15:308
Amidona, Malcom 27:11
Amie, J. 14:3; 16:265
Amiel, Charles 9:205
Amiet, Charles V. 16:75
Amigent, Emil 10:100;
20:198
Amily, William 3:12
Amiot, John B. 20:120
Amis, Charles 10:100;
20:198
Amlin, Alfred 11:133
Ammarn, John 24:73
Ammerman, D. A. 16:115
Ammerman, H. H. 3:12
Ammerman, J. 14:136
Ammerman, John E.
17:394
Ammerman, John J.
17:234
Ammerman, O. 15:289
Ammerman, W. 1:107
Ammidon, Edward 1:12
Ammidon, William 19:2
Ammin, Charles 18:23
Ammon, Fred 9:107
Ammond, Alex 9:107
Ammondson, Giermund
22:160

Ammons, Albert 11:49
Ammons, Henry 10:38; 20:198
Ammons, W. 9:138
Ammounon, M. G. 14:32
Amnan, Walter A. 9:128
Amob, John 14:3
Amol, J. 16:265
Amon, J. 1:107
Amon, William 12:97
Amon, Williams 15:356
Amonce, Carlos 21:295
Amond, Israel 4:8
Amonder, Conrad 7:85
Amons, Henry 8:37; 14:32; 26:148
Amorgan, T. 18:187
Amos, Creed H. 21:63
Amos, David 16:19
Amos, H. 25:135
Amos, H. T. 24:164
Amos, H. W. 25:135
Amos, Henry 5:35
Amos, Henry M. 13:7
Amos, Henry S. 17:403
Amos, Ira A. 10:38; 20:198
Amos, J. 3:12
Amos, John 17:348
Amos, L. 18:171
Amos, Perry G. 17:481; 27:11
Amos, Perry H. 14:294
Amos, Peter 22:288
Amos, T. G. 3:12
Amos, William 10:7; 15:180
Amour, W. H. 14:33
Amous, James 22:63
Ampaugh, Lewis 8:102
Ampfer, Lewis 22:447
Ample, Jerry 11:383
Amps, C. 3:12
Ampy, William 8:99
Amrig, Godfrey 21:247
Amrine, Amos 17:75
Amsbaugh, Robert 22:175
Amsbury, Horace 17:231
Amsdell, A. D. 21:295
Amsden, E. H. 21:295
Amsden, E. P 19:234
Amsden, E. P. 9:167
Amsden, J. E. 19:234
Amsden, Jacob E. 9:167
Amsden, Marcus 23:186
Amsley, James 16:115
Amstead, William 21:263
Amsworth, J. R. 16:265
Amundsen, Ingebret 21:249
Amundson, Amund 27:10

Amus, Rollin 21:118
Amven, John 4:8
Amwoy, A. 12:161
Amy, David 18:63
Amy, G. 3:12
Amy, George 4:8
Amy, James 19:2
Amy, John 9:107
Amy, Samuel C. 21:134
Amyx, Andrew 25:316
Amyx, J. N. 17:216
Amzen, John Henry 17:47
Analla, Bernardo 8:123
Anberg, C. 14:136
Anbris, W. 26:149
Anchler, C. 16:169
Andees, William 10:171
Andeman, George 21:16
Anderhold, Frederick 15:62
Anderlin, --- 18:411
Anderly, Fran 21:96
Anders, Ignatius 15:90
Anders, Job J. 23:262
Anders, John 7:9
Anders, Lewis 24:151
Anders, William 19:145
Anders, William R. 20:198
Anders, Y. 23:17
Anderson, --- 10:185; 11:230; 15:62, 258, 338; 26:149, 210
Anderson, A. 1:11, 108; 3:12; 14:294; 16:169, 286; 18:76; 19:52; 21:16; 25:316
Anderson, A. B. 21:203
Anderson, A. C. Nathan 21:295
Anderson, A. M. 12:150
Anderson, A. W. 18:44
Anderson, Aaron 21:219
Anderson, Adam 4:8
Anderson, Albert A. 21:165
Anderson, Albert D. 9:158
Anderson, Alexander 7:18; 18:107
Anderson, Allen W. 10:147
Anderson, Alpheus 8:44
Anderson, Ambrose 23:130
Anderson, Amos 23:58
Anderson, Andrew 1:108; 6:10; 8:7; 9:239; 11:114; 12:150; 15:101; 18:119; 20:3; 22:275; 23:186; 25:135

Anderson, Aug 26:149
Anderson, Augustus 8:70
Anderson, B. 21:108; 25:135
Anderson, B. C. 17:480; 27:11
Anderson, Bailey 11:21
Anderson, Belvin 17:127; 24:187
Anderson, Benjamin 13:8; 15:277; 18:12
Anderson, Benjamin M. 22:17
Anderson, C. 1:12; 18:337; 25:136
Anderson, C. C. 8:44; 22:135
Anderson, C. M. 23:267
Anderson, C. S. 3:12
Anderson, Carl 21:89
Anderson, Carter 23:312
Anderson, Charles 3:12; 5:35; 7:77, 116; 10:98; 16:362; 18:444; 22:17; 25:292; 26:8
Anderson, Charles F. 21:193; 22:17
Anderson, Charles O. C. 21:63
Anderson, Christian 10:153; 19:146
Anderson, Christopher 21:134
Anderson, Christopher H. 22:399
Anderson, Clinton T. C. 7:18
Anderson, Cornelius 4:8
Anderson, D. 3:12; 9:138; 14:33; 16:169; 21:145; 25:136; 27:8
Anderson, Danford N. 22:63
Anderson, Daniel 7:116; 12:54; 15:164; 19:52
Anderson, Daniel W. B. 10:100; 20:198
Anderson, David 5:35; 10:100; 11:195; 18:76; 20:198; 21:210; 23:17
Anderson, David S. 9:68
Anderson, Demmick 11:427
Anderson, E. 9:74; 10:26; 11:89; 15:180; 19:299; 24:73; 25:136
Anderson, E. C. 19:234
Anderson, E. I. 15:180

Anderson, Ebenezer 9:167
Anderson, Edward 12:7;
  18:227; 21:295;
  22:288; 26:9
Anderson, Elias 9:74;
  26:8
Anderson, Elisha 9:235;
  21:295
Anderson, Erank 26:9
Anderson, Eric 17:98
Anderson, Erich 26:8
Anderson, Erick 20:198
Anderson, Erwin 7:116
Anderson, Ever 8:102
Anderson, F. 3:12; 27:11
Anderson, Ferge 22:239
Anderson, Finley 20:135
Anderson, Florian 9:74
Anderson, Fortune 9:153
Anderson, Francis 17:396
Anderson, Francis A.
  23:240
Anderson, Frank 16:138;
  17:161; 18:227
Anderson, G. 24:73;
  25:136
Anderson, G. A. 18:171
Anderson, G. D. 25:136
Anderson, G. H. 11:383
Anderson, G. Hatfield
  24:73
Anderson, G. M. 10:192
Anderson, G. N. 26:204
Anderson, G. P. 24:11
Anderson, G. W. 8:7;
  11:235; 14:136;
  18:119
Anderson, Galac 23:186
Anderson, George 3:12;
  7:85; 9:18, 41;
  18:337; 19:246;
  22:239
Anderson, George A.
  23:276
Anderson, George D. 5:35
Anderson, George H.
  12:11
Anderson, George T.
  9:167
Anderson, George W.
  11:49, 383; 22:471
Anderson, Gilbert 25:283
Anderson, Gulick 25:136
Anderson, Gustavous
  9:239
Anderson, H. 1:12; 3:12;
  8:7; 12:81; 17:169;
  23:17
Anderson, H. A. 15:26;
  25:316
Anderson, H. B. 27:11

Anderson, H. M. 6:29
Anderson, H. W. 21:90
Anderson, H. William
  11:123
Anderson, Halvor 21:249
Anderson, Hans 21:206
Anderson, Harrison
  21:295
Anderson, Hendrick 27:8
Anderson, Henry 7:116;
  8:79, 112; 10:26;
  11:196; 16:143;
  22:275; 27:142
Anderson, Henry A.
  12:66; 17:265
Anderson, Hurd 27:11
Anderson, I. A. 11:230
Anderson, Isaac 7:116;
  18:227; 22:175, 447;
  23:130; 26:10
Anderson, Isom 18:76
Anderson, Ison 6:14
Anderson, J. 1:108, 109;
  3:12; 10:94; 11:89,
  296; 13:82, 103;
  14:33; 16:265;
  17:435; 18:76, 361;
  21:295; 23:130;
  24:181; 26:149;
  27:11
Anderson, J. A. 17:75
Anderson, J. B. 1:107
Anderson, J. C. 9:18
Anderson, J. E. 26:8
Anderson, J. K. 25:136
Anderson, J. M. 24:73
Anderson, J. N. 3:12
Anderson, J. P. 9:217;
  18:361
Anderson, J. R. 5:49; 15:6
Anderson, J. T. 17:161;
  18:23
Anderson, J. V. 17:363
Anderson, J. W. 20:176
Anderson, Jackson 4:64;
  8:79
Anderson, James 7:47, 83,
  85; 8:7, 79; 9:74,
  217; 10:13, 38;
  11:196, 235, 256,
  338; 12:11; 13:126;
  17:146; 18:119;
  20:198; 21:16; 23:10,
  131; 25:12, 271;
  26:8; 27:8
Anderson, James H.
  21:295
Anderson, James K. 21:47
Anderson, James M.
  18:284; 22:498;
  23:58; 26:134

Anderson, James N. 23:58
Anderson, James T. 22:17
Anderson, James W.
  10:89; 20:198;
  22:239
Anderson, Jasper 10:89;
  20:198
Anderson, Jeff 17:169
Anderson, Jefferson 23:17
Anderson, Jerry B. 24:64
Anderson, Jesse 21:47
Anderson, John 1:108;
  3:12; 4:64; 7:13, 55,
  83, 116; 8:7, 58;
  9:217; 10:38, 100,
  211; 11:133, 256;
  13:8, 56; 14:33, 136;
  15:52, 62, 325;
  17:47, 71; 18:119,
  361, 450; 19:2, 52,
  146; 20:198; 21:96,
  146, 295, 296; 22:63,
  288, 329, 517;
  23:186
Anderson, John A. 24:11
Anderson, John B. 17:28
Anderson, John C. 14:33,
  136; 18:391
Anderson, John D. 6:14;
  18:76
Anderson, John K. 9:41;
  26:120
Anderson, John M. 18:119
Anderson, John R.
  17:409; 22:63
Anderson, John S. 8:79;
  15:52
Anderson, John V. 22:517
Anderson, John W. 8:7
Anderson, Johnson 20:198
Anderson, Joseph 9:32;
  15:80; 17:28; 22:135
Anderson, Joseph R.
  16:19
Anderson, Joshua 11:196
Anderson, Josiah 22:18
Anderson, K. 8:44; 26:148
Anderson, Knud 9:115;
  27:10
Anderson, L. 3:12;
  14:264, 287; 16:169;
  18:450; 20:15;
  25:292
Anderson, L. C. 10:100;
  20:199
Anderson, L. H. 9:74
Anderson, Leroy 16:19
Anderson, Lewis 7:77;
  9:128; 17:439;
  20:110, 199; 23:186;
  27:9

Anderson, Louis 10:38; 13:134; 19:346
Anderson, M. 11:21; 14:250; 18:119, 227; 25:136; 26:9
Anderson, Mathew 20:143
Anderson, Matthew 12:11
Anderson, Matthias 9:167; 19:273; 21:134
Anderson, Michael 7:116; 23:270
Anderson, Mitchell 11:195
Anderson, Myron 23:17
Anderson, N. 16:169; 19:52
Anderson, N. C. 9:47
Anderson, Nathaniel N. 17:358
Anderson, Nelson D. 17:200
Anderson, Niles 16:7
Anderson, O. 1:107; 13:82; 14:3; 22:329
Anderson, P. B. 11:338
Anderson, P. J. 18:187
Anderson, P. S. 16:169
Anderson, Perry 17:234, 396
Anderson, Peter 10:100; 17:322; 20:199; 22:18; 24:63
Anderson, Pleasant 23:306
Anderson, R. 3:12; 9:18; 12:47; 16:169; 17:478; 27:11
Anderson, R. D. P. 21:296
Anderson, R. J. 15:262
Anderson, Randolph 16:3
Anderson, Richard 4:64; 22:288, 498
Anderson, Richard P. 10:100; 20:199
Anderson, Robert 8:37; 9:9; 10:100, 147; 11:196; 12:11; 14:136; 17:47; 18:44; 20:199; 26:148; 27:11
Anderson, Robert B. 22:18
Anderson, Roy 19:340
Anderson, S. 3:12; 7:85; 14:136; 25:136, 310
Anderson, S. J. 21:108
Anderson, Sam 8:7
Anderson, Samuel 5:7; 6:14; 8:37, 61; 9:32, 161; 12:47; 14:136; 18:76, 117, 119, 290;

Anderson, Samuel 20:103; 22:447; 26:91, 148
Anderson, Samuel B. 16:277
Anderson, Samuel T. 11:21
Anderson, Sanford 17:258
Anderson, Shelton 22:116
Anderson, Sidney M. 10:156
Anderson, Simeon 7:77
Anderson, Simon 18:227; 25:292; 26:9
Anderson, Simon A. 18:290; 26:91
Anderson, Solomon 11:102
Anderson, Solomon S. 17:46
Anderson, Soon 18:119
Anderson, Stephen 26:8
Anderson, Stillman 7:66
Anderson, Strother 23:58
Anderson, Swen 21:90
Anderson, T. 3:12
Anderson, T. L. 1:11
Anderson, T. V. 22:349
Anderson, Thomas 9:167; 11:83; 12:11; 19:246; 21:296; 22:18, 63; 25:12; 26:8
Anderson, Thomas C. 20:4
Anderson, Thomas H. 23:131
Anderson, Thomas J. 22:164
Anderson, Thomas S. 18:434
Anderson, W. 1:12, 93; 3:12; 10:154; 13:82; 15:150; 16:169; 19:146; 25:136
Anderson, W. A. 11:409
Anderson, W. B. 4:8; 18:290; 23:111
Anderson, W. C. 7:85; 26:142
Anderson, W. F. 14:318; 25:282
Anderson, W. H. 1:11; 8:44; 15:2
Anderson, W. M. 23:17
Anderson, W. P. 23:17
Anderson, W. R. 14:268; 23:17; 26:149
Anderson, W. T. 7:85
Anderson, W. W. 1:108
Anderson, Wesley 18:391

Anderson, William 1:108; 3:12; 4:8; 5:35; 6:24; 7:116; 9:48, 128; 10:38, 100; 11:133; 13:82; 14:3; 16:169; 17:165; 18:187; 19:296; 20:199; 21:219; 22:18, 288, 415; 23:131, 266, 284; 25:136; 27:9
Anderson, William A. 9:74; 26:8
Anderson, William B. 9:32; 26:91
Anderson, William C. 5:7
Anderson, William D. 23:58
Anderson, William E. 21:47
Anderson, William F. 9:18
Anderson, William H. 9:128; 10:100; 12:66; 20:199; 21:63; 22:239, 414; 27:9
Anderson, William M. 20:47
Anderson, William P. 10:100; 20:199
Anderson, William S. 4:8; 11:132; 17:47
Anderson, William T. 20:4
Anderson, William W. 25:136
Anderson, Wilsey 11:189
Anderton, T. B. 14:136
Andes, Alexander C. 11:325
Andes, J. H. 11:325
Andes, John 1:11
Andes, John M. 9:48
Andgrave, Francis 22:63
Andien, John 9:205
Andis, John 6:29; 25:316
Andis, L. 7:18
Andor, W. M. 1:12
Andove, Charles A. 19:246
Andre, James 7:116
Andre, John 25:136
Andre, William 8:70
Andreas, George 11:235
Andree, William 22:507
Andreson, Anton 21:249
Andress, David 25:136
Andress, Davis 15:277
Andrew, Adam W. 22:175
Andrew, Charles 12:94; 15:357; 22:414
Andrew, D. E. 1:107
Andrew, D. M. 21:118

Andrew, E. 13:82
Andrew, G. 19:52
Andrew, G. H. 11:297
Andrew, George 11:133
Andrew, J. 15:305
Andrew, J. A. 11:21
Andrew, Joseph 10:38;
    20:199
Andrew, Richard 18:391;
    21:249
Andrew, S. E. 21:296
Andrew, Wesley 22:472
Andrews, --- 11:50;
    12:147; 26:8
Andrews, A. 14:33;
    15:180, 267; 17:346;
    25:12, 136
Andrews, Adam 5:7
Andrews, Add. E. 11:133
Andrews, Albert 9:159
Andrews, Alphonso M.
    20:199
Andrews, Alphonzo M.
    10:100
Andrews, B. F. H. 14:33
Andrews, B. H. 9:48
Andrews, Benjamin
    10:171; 19:146
Andrews, C. 15:338;
    16:362; 25:136
Andrews, C. H. 1:108
Andrews, C. M. 1:12
Andrews, C. R. 9:48
Andrews, C. S. 1:13
Andrews, C. W. 19:52
Andrews, Calvin 7:116
Andrews, Carlos 11:101
Andrews, Charles 4:8;
    9:212; 13:7; 19:52;
    21:296
Andrews, Charles B. 5:7
Andrews, Charles C.
    21:63
Andrews, Chauncey 8:79
Andrews, Clark N. 22:399
Andrews, D. 18:44; 20:21
Andrews, D. C. 14:33
Andrews, Daniel 20:178;
    23:118
Andrews, David 24:73
Andrews, Dewitt C. 24:11
Andrews, E. 14:33
Andrews, E. A. 14:3
Andrews, E. B. 17:13
Andrews, E. L. 3:12
Andrews, E. S. 20:28
Andrews, Eben 7:8
Andrews, Edmund 18:23
Andrews, Edwin L.
    21:249

Andrews, Eli M. N.
    21:296
Andrews, Elisha 18:411
Andrews, Ephraim 7:8
Andrews, F. 25:12;
    26:149
Andrews, F. H. 11:102;
    21:296
Andrews, F. W. 13:8
Andrews, Flavius 10:100;
    20:199
Andrews, Franklin M.
    26:144
Andrews, G. 15:310
Andrews, G. E. 1:108
Andrews, G. G. 1:108
Andrews, George 16:89;
    23:131
Andrews, George H.
    26:148
Andrews, George N. 10:9
Andrews, Green 22:511
Andrews, H. 1:13; 17:403
Andrews, H. A. 23:17
Andrews, H. B. 14:136
Andrews, Harvey 22:175
Andrews, Henry 18:76
Andrews, Henry F. 17:17
Andrews, Henry N.
    10:100; 20:199
Andrews, Hugh 10:208
Andrews, Hugh C. 20:21
Andrews, Ira 8:61
Andrews, Ira A. 26:149
Andrews, Israel D. 10:38
Andrews, J. 11:50;
    15:180; 19:52;
    21:296; 24:73;
    25:136
Andrews, J. D. 20:199
Andrews, J. H. 9:213
Andrews, J. R. 3:12
Andrews, J. W. 18:391
Andrews, Jack 22:511
Andrews, Jacob 22:231
Andrews, Jacob B. 13:7
Andrews, James 5:7;
    20:91
Andrews, James P.
    18:290; 26:91
Andrews, James S. 19:2
Andrews, Jefferson 10:38;
    20:199
Andrews, John 9:71;
    11:189; 13:7; 17:265;
    22:472; 24:90
Andrews, John A. 11:133
Andrews, John C. 22:414
Andrews, John F. 21:249
Andrews, John H. 11:195;
    23:17

Andrews, John T. 10:171;
    19:146
Andrews, Jones E. 23:131
Andrews, Joseph 3:12;
    13:7; 16:286; 23:284
Andrews, Joseph Said
    7:18
Andrews, L. 14:136, 253
Andrews, L. B. 7:85
Andrews, Lars 18:119
Andrews, Lavs 8:7
Andrews, Leroy 13:8
Andrews, Lucas 13:8
Andrews, Luerrin 16:19
Andrews, M. 1:12; 21:296
Andrews, Mary Bell
    26:216
Andrews, Mayten E.
    21:134
Andrews, Michael 7:85;
    22:8
Andrews, Miletus 10:151
Andrews, Militue 10:178
Andrews, Mort 25:136
Andrews, Morton 20:199
Andrews, Moses 21:193
Andrews, Nelson C. 8:7;
    18:119
Andrews, Newton 9:18;
    18:301; 26:91
Andrews, Noble 14:33
Andrews, O. A. 16:277
Andrews, O. P. 26:8
Andrews, Oliver G. 19:2
Andrews, Oliver P. 9:74
Andrews, R. R. 9:95
Andrews, Randolph
    26:216
Andrews, Robert 8:7;
    17:75; 18:120
Andrews, Royal G. 13:8
Andrews, Russell 8:79
Andrews, S. A. 11:324;
    15:171
Andrews, S. B. 26:8
Andrews, S. C. 1:96
Andrews, S. H. 19:146
Andrews, Samuel 2:7;
    7:116; 17:271;
    22:135; 25:13
Andrews, Samuel D. 1.11
Andrews, Solomon
    21:263
Andrews, Sylvester 9:115;
    27:10
Andrews, T. 1:107; 27:8
Andrews, T. F. 8:44;
    21:165
Andrews, T. P. 15:180
Andrews, Thomas 20:120

Andrews, Valentine 15:180
Andrews, W. 3:12; 11:49; 23:17
Andrews, W. H. 18:227; 20:143; 26:10, 120; 27:11
Andrews, W. L. 11:21; 20:199
Andrews, W. N. 16:169
Andrews, W. S. 14:318
Andrews, W. W. 5:49
Andrews, Walter B. 16:5
Andrews, Wesley 17:307
Andrews, William 4:8; 14:136; 22:135; 24:165
Andrews, William G. 19:52
Andrews, William H. 19:2
Andrews, William L. 10:38
Andrews, William W. 22:18
Andrews, Winslow B. 21:87
Andrews, Z. G. 21:296
Andri, James 14:136
Andrick, Jacob 7:55; 22:63
Andrum, Samuel 3:12
Andrus, Edson 22:135
Andrus, Hezekiah 21:241
Andry, John 21:47
Andson, George 12:47
Andson, S. 3:12
Andy, John 17:169
Ane, Jacob 22:472
Ane, Philip 11:420
Aneerson, C. B. 15:181
Anesmeir, Fred 20:199
Aney, Benjamin 18:12
Anfield, Londridge 11:409
Anga, Ozoda 9:101
Angel, A. 15:338; 16:362
Angel, Charles A. 23:127
Angel, D. W. 22:471
Angel, Elias 11:399
Angel, Franklin V. 22:276
Angel, George W. 11:297; 22:275; 24:169
Angel, O. E. 25:13
Angel, Thomas 22:288
Angel, William 1:12
Angeler, DeLos 25:275
Angeline, Michael 10:7
Angelist, Henry D. 20:199
Angell, A. S. 5:7; 25:136
Angell, C. R. 20:34
Angell, Charles 11:50

Angell, Daniel 7:66
Angell, George W. 17:446
Angell, H. 17:69
Angell, H. N. 9:217; 18:361
Angell, Jesse W. 15:181
Angell, O. E. 2:7
Angell, W. H. 15:351
Angell, William H. 16:277
Angells, David J. 20:84
Angelsberg, Nicholas 22:160
Anger, Andrew J. 17:358
Anger, George 9:167; 19:246; 22:18
Angerman, Frederick 23:58
Angermeiar, John 4:8
Angersoll, C. 21:296
Angier, Leander 21:184
Anglan, J. 3:12
Angle, David 9:32
Angle, Eli D. 15:101
Angle, Frank 18:44
Angle, H. 9:138
Angle, Hiram 22:175
Angle, Jacob 22:175
Angle, James 22:471
Angle, John 22:116
Angle, John A. 17:287
Angle, T. L. 12:11
Angle, William B. 7:14
Anglebrak, Charles 20:153
Angleist, Henry D. 10:101
Angleman, James 17:28
Angleman, Robert 24:187
Anglemeyer, J. H. 17:336
Angles, Valentine 9:226; 18:361
Anglesmyer, E. 22:135
Angless, J. J. 22:231
Anglestin, William 11:428
Anglin, John 22:18
Anglius, Richard 18:227; 26:9
Anglon, William 3:12
Angst, Gebhard 22:164
Anguany, A. 16:362
Anguary, A. 15:338
Anguish, Horace 16:89
Angus, Charles 15:28
Angus, Levy 25:136
Angus, W. H. 9:41; 26:120
Angus, William G. 11:133
Anible, Edward 18:227; 26:10
Anidon, R. 15:354
Aning, John A. 19:269

Aniscow, Charles 10:171; 19:146
Anisley, George 5:7
Ankeny, Jacob 19:2
Ankeny, Peter 19:3
Anker, George 3:12
Ankerbrand, John 20:151
Ankerbrand, M. 20:191
Ankerman, Abraham 27:10
Ankerson, A. 13:79
Ankey, Henry 22:8
Ankies, A. 16:169
Ankles, Henry 7:15
Ankney, Adam 23:131
Ankony, Solomon 23:131
Ankrom, Jos. 19:146
Ankrom, William J. 17:75
Anlaslino, --- 3:12
Anlenback, James 9:107
Anlerkobler, Albert 7:55
Anlin, Richard 14:136
Anlman, Peter 20:199
Anmoon, H. 27:8
Ann, A. 14:33
Ann, Willis 23:197
Annable, George M. 25:13
Annais, Hilliard 21:296
Annden, H. D. 15:297
Annen, Mathias 23:131
Annette, Elijah 11:380
Annhult, J. H. 3:12
Annie, J. 13:103
Annis, A. H. 15:338; 16:362
Annis, Francis 24:47
Annis, George 15:117, 349
Annis, George M. 21:90
Annis, Ira P. 4:8
Annis, John B. 24:11
Annis, Myron 15:29
Annis, Stillman L. 15:15
Annis, Stilman L. 12:66
Annoe, Samuel F. 22:471
Annoine, William 22:239
Annon, Alfred 6:23
Annsis, Duane 10:101; 20:199
Annway, Edwin 22:459
Ano, John 23:17
Anorson, John 3:12
Anrold, George 10:101
Anschutz, Thomas 11:256
Ansel, J. R. 17:101
Ansel, Richard 13:124
Ansen, J. E. 19:246
Anshutz, Andrew 11:256
Anshutz, Bradford 22:175
Ansing, John A. 9:167

Ansirmus, Charles H. 21:214
Ansley, Edward F. 22:239
Anson, James 19:53
Anson, N. F. 25:136
Anson, Nelson F. 5:7
Anson, Robert 3:12
Anson, S. E. 9:167
Ansoret, --- 18:63
Anspach, Moses 22:399
Anspoker, John 21:203
Anstod, Frank 10:101; 20:199
Anstolt, Jacob 14:136
Ansum, Christian 4:8
Answell, J. 3:12
Anterville, W. 3:12
Anthis, Amasa 9:71
Anthoine, E. 18:12
Anthon, Huller 17:17
Anthon, William 1:108
Anthonie, John 11:21
Anthony, --- 12:86; 16:169, 286
Anthony, Abraham 20:94
Anthony, C. 25:136
Anthony, Charles C. 18:227; 26:9
Anthony, Cornelius M. 23:186
Anthony, Cyrus 5:7
Anthony, D. 22:175
Anthony, Dan 21:16
Anthony, E. 3:12
Anthony, Edward 14:33
Anthony, G. 25:136
Anthony, George 5:35; 10:101; 20:199
Anthony, George W. 17:13
Anthony, Gould 7:85
Anthony, H. 1:107
Anthony, H. C. 11:275
Anthony, James 12:150
Anthony, James M. 18:120
Anthony, James W. 22:447
Anthony, John 15:62; 25:136
Anthony, Jordan 23:244
Anthony, Joseph 12:167; 19:347
Anthony, Lewis 15:29
Anthony, Mark 17:169; 23:111
Anthony, Mildred E. 22:349
Anthony, P. 13:61
Anthony, Philip 11:196
Anthony, Richard 20:110

Anthony, S. 25:13
Anthony, Samuel 8:79
Anthony, Stephen 2:7
Anthony, W. 18:187
Anthony, W. M. 8:44
Anthony, William 10:156; 19:146; 21:47
Anthony, William A. 21:63
Anthony, William W. 8:79
Antibus, Jacob 18:120
Anticliff, Joseph 17:287
Antill, I. 3:12
Antill, William 24:73
Antioch, Stephen 22:471
Antis, Henry 25:136
Antisdal, George 3:12
Antler, F. 3:12
Antman, Peter 10:101
Antoine, Abram 24:90
Antol, Catol 24:11
Anton, Joseph 1:12
Anton, Long 11:117
Antone, C. 3:12
Antonie, August 7:116
Antonie, B. 9:48
Antonie, Lewis 12:150
Antonio, J. 1:107
Antonio, P. 3:12
Antony, H. D. 21:296
Antony, W. W. 20:199
Antrem, Knox 12:161
Antrim, James T. 22:414
Antrim, L. C. 16:135
Antrim, Samuel 22:8
Antrope, Theo 4:8
Antry, John L. 18:227
Antry, W. 25:136
Antwine, Henry S. 19:146
Anty, Peter 16:169
Anviden, P. 16:362
Anzer, Charles W. 1:11
Aons, Peter 8:7
Aork, J. 21:219
Apel, Adam 21:63
Apel, Henry 1:108
Apel, Mich 19:53
Aperson, Joseph 17:127
Apetz, Gustav 4:8
Apgar, J. H. 1:12
Aphott, J. P. 8:70
Apitz, A. 23:17
Apker, Jacob O. 5:7
Apker, John 21:214; 25:271
Apker, S. S. 25:136
Apkoe, Samuel S. 5:7
Apland, J. 14:33
Apley, A. 7:47
Aplin, H. S. 16:169
Aplin, John 15:26

Apodaces, Jose 12:169
Apodaces, Jose Rafel 12:169
Appel, Charles 19:331
Appel, J. H. 25:136
Appel, Oscar 13:56; 16:19
Appelton, D. 14:287
Appenzeller, Wesley 26:144
Apperson, Andrew 21:146
Apperson, Verge 21:146
Apple, Andrew 18:120
Apple, Andrew B. 8:7
Apple, Anthony 11:14
Apple, August 24:151
Apple, C. 8:7; 18:120
Apple, D. H. 1:96
Apple, Eli 11:383
Apple, George 11:383
Apple, George S. 22:415
Apple, H. 11:256
Apple, Henry 10:38; 20:199
Apple, M. 11:383; 12:7
Apple, Samuel 8:79
Applebee, Jonas 20:38
Applebee, Simeon 13:8
Appleberry, J. 11:132
Applebury, J. W. 17:165
Applebury, William 17:165
Appleby, Albert 21:296
Appleby, S. W. 3:13
Appleby, Simon 16:19
Appleby, T. M. 3:13
Appleby, W. 9:138; 27:9
Appledom, W. V. 11:399
Appleford, John 15:181
Applegate, A. 20:143
Applegate, Cyrus 22:175
Applegate, F. H. 14:3
Applegate, Henry 11:297
Applegate, Hezekiah 11:50
Applegate, J. M. 26:8
Applegate, James M. 9:74
Applegate, Polk 9:199; 19:289
Applegate, Randolph 11:380
Applegate, Robert 22:18
Applegate, T. F. 15:181
Applegate, T. M. 13:82
Applegate, Thomas F. 21:219
Applegate, Thomas M. 9:18
Applegate, William 17:13
Appleget, D. C. 8:121
Appleman, Henry B. 15:117

Appleman, L. B. 16:362
Appleton, C. 15:181
Appleton, Charles M. 10:13
Appleton, D. 23:187
Appleton, David 14:264
Appleton, F. 14:237
Appleton, Jonathan B. 18:117
Appley, G. 11:123
Appley, Gilbert 22:170
Applin, A. F. 12:66
Applin, H. S. 13:61; 16:169
Applin, W. F. 15:29
Apply, Albert 16:286
April, I. 9:153
April, John 27:9
Apsley, William B. 15:181
Aptell, L. D. 25:136
Apthorp, Thomas 4:8
Apthorpe, S. 14:136
Ar--en, --- 24:47
Arain, M. L. 24:47
Arant, Isaac 21:264
Arants, William H. 15:26
Arb, Simon 3:13
Arbaugh, James 23:58
Arbaugh, Joseph 11:409
Arbaugh, Josiah 1:108
Arbaugh, W. 11:133
Arbie, Thomas 3:13
Arble, T. P. 19:322
Arbogart, G. W. 15:258
Arbogast, M. 7:55
Arbogast, W. 3:13
Arbogust, Henry 5:35
Arbooch, William 26:148
Arbouch, William 8:37
Arbrough, Scott 8:76
Arbucke, Thomas 14:136
Arbuckle, Benjamin T. 21:90
Arbuckle, C. P. 10:101; 20:199
Arbuckle, James 1:12
Arbuckle, Thomas 7:85
Arbuthnod, Alexander 23:10
Arbuthnot, James 20:182
Arbuthnot, John 23:278
Arch, A. 1:12
Arch, Darwin 11:407
Arch, J. 20:143, 178
Arch, J. R. 1:12
Archanbault, Euclid 7:18
Archard, Asbury 26:8
Archart, H. 3:13
Archcraft, Harvey 21:16
Archcroft, Jonathan 8:7

Archedphol, Albert 14:136
Archer, Albert M. 4:8
Archer, Andrew 1:108
Archer, Ben 14:287; 23:201
Archer, Benjamin 20:188; 22:498
Archer, Berry 14:264
Archer, Charles 16:169
Archer, Cyrus 9:205; 18:63
Archer, David C. 1:12
Archer, Dick 15:181
Archer, E. 17:290
Archer, Edward 23:131
Archer, George 20:143
Archer, George T. 19:3
Archer, H. 1:107; 3:13
Archer, Henry 22:175
Archer, Henry H. 23:84
Archer, Hiram 13:126
Archer, Isaac 22:471
Archer, J. E. 1:107
Archer, J. O. 24:73
Archer, James 10:204
Archer, John 10:38, 101; 20:199
Archer, Joseph 14:235
Archer, Lewis 23:17
Archer, Moses 25:136
Archer, N. 1:107
Archer, Newton O. 21:129
Archer, Nicholas 22:18
Archer, Pem 20:54
Archer, Richard C. 16:81
Archer, Robert 12:58
Archer, William 2:7; 11:256; 20:191; 25:13
Archer, William A. 7:15
Arches, Joseph L. 3:13
Archeson, John 6:8
Archey, Turner 9:128; 27:9
Archibald, A. 11:235; 14:33
Archibald, Andrew 11:123
Archibald, Edward 1:11; 16:19
Archibald, F. A. 16:89
Archibald, John 8:70; 9:107; 21:117
Archibald, John W. 20:199
Archibald, Robert 11:235
Archibald, T. 25:136
Archible, Thomas 5:7
Archie, Hugh 17:417; 24:155
Archie, John 21:264

Archley, A. 16:362
Archord, Ashbury 9:74
Archuleta, --- 19:322
Archy, J. 3:13
Arckenoe, Carl 22:63
Arckenoe, T. H. 15:181
Arcroft, Jonathan 18:120
Ard, James 20:16
Ardell, Lucius 9:167
Arden, Wil 17:494
Ardley, Charles 8:7
Ardray, A. F. 3:13
Ardrey, Marion 12:66
Ardvay, Hiram 15:10
Arebaugh, Leonard 26:120
Arehef, Charles 13:61
Arenett, D. 21:184
Arenhamer, C. 14:287; 23:201
Arensten, Henry 21:16
Arent, William 16:277
Arer, John M. 18:204
Arey, Charles D. 13:8
Arey, J. S. 25:292
Arey, Josiah S. 7:73
Arey, Marquis 9:48
Arf, Adolph 23:131
Arford, John J. 23:84
Argabright, Franklin 11:319
Argabright, John W. 17:265
Argant, G. 13:61
Arge, James 15:21
Argenringer, Albert 13:8
Argerbright, Abraham 21:219
Argetsinger, M. C. 21:296
Argetsinger, Philip 7:85
Argnette, Gilbert 22:175
Argo, Andrew 10:151, 178
Argo, Comodore 11:89
Argo, John 22:397
Argo, William I. 23:17
Argt, C. 3:13
Arguetle, Alexander 20:105
Argur, Reuben 11:21
Argy, William I. 1:11
Arhie, L. 18:171
Arington, J. F. 10:147; 18:44
Arington, Robert A. 22:239
Arington, William 1:108
Arison, Joseph 17:107
Arivett, J. 9:48
Ark, C. 11:297
Arkenburg, Giles 19:246

Arkensburg, Giles 9:167
Arker, Thomas 19:3
Arker, William 15:62
Arkes, William 12:66
Arkey, John 10:13
Arley, Robert 8:61
Arlhart, H. 25:136
Arlinghouse, Harmon
  9:74; 26:9
Arlman, John 14:33
Arm, J. E. 20:54
Armand, Abner 16:19
Armand, J. J. 9:167
Armand, William 19:53
Armbruster, Victor 23:187
Armbuster, Samuel 10:25
Armentront, Moses
  20:199
Armentrout, Daniel R.
  20:135
Armentrout, J. L. 21:207
Armentrout, Moses 10:39
Armentrout, William R.
  8:79
Armer, J. R. 15:62
Armer, Robert A. 16:19
Armes, Alfred G. 16:89
Armes, Micajah 17:47
Armes, Vivian D. 17:47
Armes, W. E. 18:430
Armgust, A. W. 1:11
Armibrish, A. 3:13
Armick, W. 3:13
Armick, William S. 11:14
Armidon, John 19:146
Armidon, R. 19:53
Armidona, Malcolm
  14:239
Armidster, M. 3:13
Armin, Charles 3:13
Armington, H. 3:13
Armitage, Cas 11:297
Armitage, David 20:182
Armitage, Hiram 23:131
Armitage, James 16:65
Armitage, John 18:327
Armitage, Thomas
  14:294; 17:474;
  27:10
Armond, F. 1:107
Armond, Patterson 6:20
Armond, William 3:13
Armontrant, G. W. 26:8
Armontsant, G. W. 18:228
Armor, Alfred 17:258
Armor, C. D. 21:296;
  23:131
Armor, J. 20:38
Armour, Andrew 7:85
Armour, John 5:55; 23:17
Armour, Samuel S. 21:16

Arms, Benjamin 7:116
Arms, James 17:258
Armsby, Frank 14:137
Armsby, Jeremiah 11:256
Armstage, --- 17:307
Armstead, --- 25:316
Armstead, A. 26:149
Armstead, Carey 7:116
Armstead, Charles 9:205;
  18:63
Armstead, Henry 21:296
Armstead, John 8:58
Armstead, John W. 8:44
Armsted, A. 8:77
Armsten, A. E. 19:146
Armsting, E. 15:181
Armstrng, Andrew 14:313
Armstrog, William H.
  25:12
Armstrong, --- 12:47;
  15:95; 19:322;
  21:296
Armstrong, A. 3:13; 7:18;
  25:136, 137
Armstrong, A. J. 10:94
Armstrong, A. M. 14:33;
  17:403
Armstrong, A. W. 17:262
Armstrong, Alex 17:93
Armstrong, B. 25:137
Armstrong, B. C. P. 8:7;
  18:120
Armstrong, Benjamin 19:3
Armstrong, C. 17:346;
  25:137
Armstrong, C. W. 20:199
Armstrong, Charles 2:7;
  3:13; 5:35; 7:55;
  9:213; 14:1; 19:53;
  21:296; 25:12
Armstrong, Clinton J.
  21:219
Armstrong, Cuylar 20:199
Armstrong, Cuyler 10:101
Armstrong, Daniel 7:85;
  18:23
Armstrong, David 13:104;
  21:296; 22:18
Armstrong, Dennis G.
  23:131
Armstrong, Doug 17:446
Armstrong, Douglass
  24:169
Armstrong, E. 11:50, 297;
  16:169
Armstrong, Ed 17:62
Armstrong, Edward
  22:288
Armstrong, Edward A.
  14:137
Armstrong, F. G. 13:124

Armstrong, G. 3:13;
  20:199
Armstrong, G. A. 5:7
Armstrong, G. B. 3:13
Armstrong, George 3:13;
  14:33; 22:18
Armstrong, George D.
  20:110
Armstrong, George M.
  10:39; 20:199
Armstrong, Gottleib 10:39
Armstrong, H. 3:13
Armstrong, Henry 13:8;
  16:19; 17:127;
  21:264; 23:118;
  24:187
Armstrong, Henry H.
  12:11
Armstrong, Henry W.
  23:84
Armstrong, I. 9:138
Armstrong, I. D. 14:132
Armstrong, Ira 20:28
Armstrong, J. 1:107, 108;
  3:13; 5:35; 7:85;
  9:48; 16:160; 24:11;
  25:137; 27:9
Armstrong, J. A. 25:137
Armstrong, J. F. 16:19
Armstrong, J. H. 10:101;
  20:199
Armstrong, J. L. 26:120
Armstrong, J. M. 9:32
Armstrong, J. T. 13:8
Armstrong, J. W. 21:12
Armstrong, Jacob 19:3
Armstrong, James 1:11;
  4:64; 6:24; 10:101,
  208; 11:399; 13:61;
  17:153; 18:228, 344;
  19:53; 20:27, 199;
  22:523; 25:285; 26:8
Armstrong, James C.
  22:18
Armstrong, James D.
  8:102
Armstrong, James H. 22:8
Armstrong, James W.
  17:17
Armstrong, John 8:119;
  10:156; 16:158;
  18:228; 19:3; 22:135,
  175; 26:10
Armstrong, John A. 8:79;
  15:319
Armstrong, John F. 11:50;
  22:414
Armstrong, John H. 19:53
Armstrong, John W.
  11:21; 15:52; 17:417

Armstrong, John Willey 24:155
Armstrong, Joseph 4:8; 17:75; 21:63
Armstrong, Joshua 15:52
Armstrong, Josiah 8:102
Armstrong, Laut 7:18
Armstrong, Lee 12:11
Armstrong, Luther 4:8
Armstrong, M. 7:18; 13:82; 16:169
Armstrong, Madison S. 22:399
Armstrong, Marvin L. 21:215
Armstrong, Merion M. 16:19
Armstrong, Milton 22:471
Armstrong, Miron M. 13:8
Armstrong, N. 14:33
Armstrong, Newele 8:79
Armstrong, P. 9:218; 18:361
Armstrong, Philip 19:319
Armstrong, Quanton 18:171; 26:204
Armstrong, Quinston 10:179
Armstrong, R. 3:13; 16:169; 25:137
Armstrong, Richard 22:511
Armstrong, Robert 5:35; 12:53; 18:284; 19:337; 26:134
Armstrong, Robert W. 11:383
Armstrong, S. 1:107; 15:117; 22:288; 25:137; 26:8
Armstrong, S. K. 19:53
Armstrong, Samuel 10:39; 17:421; 20:199; 22:240, 511; 24:165
Armstrong, Samuel F. 22:18
Armstrong, Samuel P. 7:55
Armstrong, Sylvester 9:74
Armstrong, T. 1:11
Armstrong, T. J. 15:297
Armstrong, T. W. 22:472
Armstrong, Theodore 20:28
Armstrong, Thomas 11:133; 12:11; 13:8, 132; 22:135, 239; 25:12
Armstrong, Thomas N. 22:63

Armstrong, Thompson 9:18; 18:301; 26:91
Armstrong, W. 3:13
Armstrong, W. S. 1:12
Armstrong, Washington 7:85
Armstrong, William 7:55, 66; 10:101; 14:33; 18:213, 434; 22:111; 23:111, 251; 25:12
Armstrong, William A. 5:7
Armstrong, William B. 22:18
Armstrong, William C. 22:415
Armstrong, William H. 18:213; 23:281
Armstrong, William H. E. 19:3
Armstrong, William J. 22:447
Armstrong, William K. 23:131
Armstrong, Wilson T. 17:28
Armsworth, George 5:8
Arnald, Frank 19:146
Arnald, J. 17:471
Arnand, J. J. 19:246
Arnass, G. 1:108
Arnat, Samuel 18:227
Arnault, Victor 6:7
Arndh, Jacob 17:13
Arndst, Earnest 11:102
Arndt, Henry 22:415
Arndt, John 25:137
Arndt, W. H. 1:12
Arne, A. 1:12
Arne, J. 3:13
Arnenda, M. 1:11
Arner, A. 18:227
Arner, Robert A. 13:8
Arnes, Gotleib 13:8
Arnes, Wilson 1:108
Arneson, Lawrence 23:187
Arnet, Ray 19:53
Arnett, Abijah 22:135
Arnett, George 20:28
Arnett, H. S. 3:13
Arnett, Herman 13:8
Arnett, Hiram 16:20
Arnett, J. 14:33
Arnett, James J. 20:199
Arnett, James P. 22:18
Arnett, Ray 15:364
Arnett, S. 23:131
Arnett, T. 3:13
Arnett, Thomas 11:21
Arnett, W. J. 14:33

Arney, Charles 23:303
Arney, J. B. 9:74
Arney, James M. 11:420
Arney, James W. 11:319
Arney, Obadiah 17:29
Arney, William H. 22:415
Arnick, W. 14:137
Arnn, William 23:187
Arnob, John 13:82
Arnold, --- 5:49; 22:18
Arnold, A. 8:7; 11:438; 18:120; 25:13
Arnold, A. F. 20:120
Arnold, A. N. 15:117
Arnold, A. P. 13:82
Arnold, A. W. 26:148
Arnold, Amassa 15:15
Arnold, Andrew 11:49
Arnold, Angnes 15:181
Arnold, B. 9:199
Arnold, B. B. 5:49
Arnold, Benjamin 14:137
Arnold, C. 15:339; 16:362
Arnold, Charles 3:13; 9:95, 235; 15:52; 23:10; 26:216
Arnold, Conrad 10:101; 20:199
Arnold, D. 21:146
Arnold, D. E. 22:18
Arnold, D. P. 19:234
Arnold, Daniel 3:13; 13:104
Arnold, Daniel P. 9:167
Arnold, David 17:108
Arnold, E. 2:7
Arnold, E. W. 3:13
Arnold, F. 18:44
Arnold, Fordeau 19:289
Arnold, Francis 27:9
Arnold, Francis M. 10:39; 20:200
Arnold, Frank 9:128; 21:16
Arnold, Franklin D. 21:206
Arnold, G. 17:153; 18:76
Arnold, G. H. 14:294; 17:475; 27:10
Arnold, G. P. 26:148
Arnold, George 11:196; 18:23; 20:200
Arnold, George C. 13:104
Arnold, George H. 17:313
Arnold, George W. 9:115
Arnold, Gideon 17:161
Arnold, H. 3:13; 22:507
Arnold, H. M. 23:17
Arnold, Head 9:205
Arnold, Henry 14:33; 15:181; 22:18, 175

Arnold, Hollis F. 16:77
Arnold, I. D. 1:108
Arnold, Isaac 8:7; 17:313; 18:120
Arnold, J. 1:109; 14:294; 25:137; 27:10
Arnold, J. A. 20:120
Arnold, J. E. 14:33
Arnold, J. H. 10:37; 20:200; 21:16
Arnold, J. S. 21:16
Arnold, J. W. 1:12; 7:85
Arnold, Jacob 5:35
Arnold, James 17:17, 158; 20:200
Arnold, James B. 10:101; 20:200
Arnold, James H. 22:240
Arnold, James K. 21:249
Arnold, Jaques 16:20
Arnold, Jerry 21:242
Arnold, Jesse 21:16
Arnold, John 1:108; 11:14, 383; 13:8; 14:137; 21:16; 22:63, 175; 25:137
Arnold, John E. 17:453; 24:185
Arnold, John R. 20:34
Arnold, John S. 23:18
Arnold, John W. 26:144; 27:10
Arnold, Jordan 9:167
Arnold, Joseph 1:107; 10:39; 23:127
Arnold, L. 3:13
Arnold, L. E. 21:296
Arnold, L. S. 25:137
Arnold, Lewis I. 5:8
Arnold, Lighter 18:468
Arnold, Luke M. 9:156
Arnold, Lyman S. 17:241
Arnold, Marcus 17:241
Arnold, Michael 8:7; 18:120; 22:329
Arnold, Moses 21:47
Arnold, O. 16:169
Arnold, Oscola 9:205
Arnold, P. 14:33
Arnold, P. B. 25:137
Arnold, Peter 1:11; 21:296
Arnold, Philip 9:95
Arnold, R. 20:200
Arnold, R. B. 3:13
Arnold, Robert 8:7; 9:159; 11:195; 18:120
Arnold, Robert R. 9:218
Arnold, Rudolph 11:133
Arnold, Samuel 7:116; 11:383; 13:104

Arnold, Samuel H. 13:8
Arnold, Spencer 21:146
Arnold, Stephen 16:169
Arnold, Sylvanus 4:8
Arnold, T. H. 18:187
Arnold, Thomas 8:121
Arnold, Tileton 8:70
Arnold, W. 1:12; 20:153
Arnold, W. H. 7:47
Arnold, W. John 21:96
Arnold, W. W. 1:11
Arnold, William 8:44; 10:101; 12:94, 150; 15:357; 20:200; 21:249; 25:268; 26:138
Arnold, William A. 13:8
Arnold, Willis 19:331
Arnolds, D. C. 11:235
Arnot, --- 5:49
Arnot, B. 25:137
Arnot, Daniel 22:18
Arnot, Jacob 5:49; 25:137
Arnot, Samuel 26:9
Arnoti, James R. 21:96
Arnott, B. 20:178
Arnott, C. 3:13
Arnott, James 10:101
Arnott, Peter 17:169
Arnott, Thomas 18:464
Arnow, Andrew 21:296
Arns, Peter 18:120
Arnsby, George 26:148
Arnsen, Peter 11:331
Arnson, Arne 17:98
Arnst, Franklin 23:131
Arnsting, Thomas S. 16:169
Arnsworth, G. 25:137
Arnt, Edwin 8:7; 26:148
Arnts, R. M. 14:137
Arnum, Walter A. 27:9
Arny, J. 19:53
Aroff, C. 14:33
Aron, J. L. 21:193
Aron, W. 3:13
Aronld, John H. 21:219
Arqueringer, Albert 16:19
Arrance, J. 13:61; 19:53
Arrance, William 4:8
Arrant, Joseph 8:37; 26:148
Arrasmith, Willis 23:84
Arrel, Willis 26:120
Arrent, A. 13:61
Arrenze, Charles 4:8
Arreux, Nuna 24:108
Arrick, C. 9:74
Arrick, John C. 18:120
Arrison, John 11:196
Arroll, Henry 9:68

Arron, Moses 7:77; 25:292
Arron, Thomas 9:68
Arronsmith, William F. 9:74
Arrowhead, N. 8:44
Arrowhood, Nelson 21:63
Arrowood, James 3:13
Arrowood, Wesley 22:240
Arrowsmith, E. 14:137
Arrowsmith, W. R. 3:13
Arscher, J. M. 11:297
Arsnott, W. 3:13
Arson, Richard 27:11
Art, Casper 25:137
Arte, Philip 7:18
Arter, F. 12:121; 15:117
Arter, Nathan B. 21:13
Arterberry, Benjamin 9:74
Arterberry, Wesley 20:103
Arterberry, William H. 17:278; 24:155
Arterbery, William H. 17:442
Arterbery, William T. 22:496
Arth, Frank 17:425; 24:176
Arthe---, May 24:187
Arther, D. 14:137
Arther, M. 20:200
Artherington, John S. 23:18
Arthor, J. C. 3:13
Arthur, A. 25:310
Arthur, Alexander 11:256
Arthur, D. 3:13; 25:137
Arthur, Daniel 21:296
Arthur, George 3:13
Arthur, J. 3:13
Arthur, James 21:296
Arthur, James A. 22:415
Arthur, James H. 11:256
Arthur, James V. 17:275
Arthur, James W. 18:361
Arthur, John 18:228; 26:9
Arthur, John M. 22:135
Arthur, John W. 23:10
Arthur, Levi 11:297
Arthur, M. 1:107
Arthur, M. H. 1:93
Arthur, Malachi 10:89
Arthur, Patrick 26:148
Arthur, Samuel 24:11
Arthur, Thomas 22:400
Arthur, W. 17:169
Arthur, W. T. 11:235
Arthur, William A. 23:131
Arthur, William B. 17:395
Arthur, William H. 11:49

Arthur, William James 9:218

Arthurs, Asa A. 19:53

Arthurs, David 5:35

Arthurs, E. H. 11:132

Arthurs, George W. 17:354

Arthurs, Joseph H. 24:73

Arthurs, Nehemiah 22:414

Artis, Isham 9:100

Artis, Mathew 8:116

Artist, Asbury 10:175; 19:146

Artiste, Moses 4:64

Artley, Asher D. 16:138

Artman, H. B. 17:17

Artman, Lewis 22:231

Arton, A. 11:297

Artudge, Richard 15:90

Artus, Frank 13:61

Artwell, H. T. 12:11

Aruts, William 12:66

Arver, L. G. 1:108

Arviden, Lewis P. 20:110

Arvin, Denzil 23:59

Arvin, William F. 12:150

Arwin, William 15:181

Arwine, J. 10:192

Arwood, John 22:240

Arwor, John 18:23

Ary, Barton 13:56

Ary, Wesley 20:4

As---, J. G. 12:98

Asb, D. 16:286

Asbery, Anderson 3:13

Asborn, Charles R. 9:74; 26:8

Asborn, Sylvester 11:99

Asbshire, Thomas H. 21:47

Asburg, Thomas 10:101

Asbury, A. M. 1:108

Asbury, Christopher 23:270

Asbury, George 19:3

Asbury, Thomas 20:200

Asbury, W. 20:200

Asby, David 9:18

Aschee, Ugeal B. 8:112

Ascherin, August 10:101; 20:200

Aschinger, Gotlieb 22:329

Asdell, Andrew A. 13:8

Aseltine, M. 15:181

Asetue, --- 19:266

Asgood, H. P. 18:337

Ash, Alfred A. 7:116

Ash, Alonzo 8:100; 17:459; 24:155

Ash, Antoine 16:81

Ash, Benjamin 1:11

Ash, Charles A. 21:296

Ash, Charles N. 21:296

Ash, Elias 26:120

Ash, George 20:120

Ash, George W. 22:116

Ash, J. W. 22:471

Ash, Jonas 20:120

Ash, Joshua G. 17:47

Ash, Maj 19:146

Ash, Moses 16:169

Ash, N. 16:169

Ash, Peter H. 18:274

Ash, Robert 18:434

Ash, Samuel 5:49

Ash, Valentine 22:471

Ash, W. T. 7:117

Ash, William 23:243

Ashba, Benjamin A. 22:63

Ashbaugh, Andrew 17:290

Ashbaugh, George 12:11

Ashbaugh, Henry C. 13:60

Ashbell, Henry 23:312

Ashber, Jesse 19:337

Ashberg, Abram 22:414

Ashberry, Henry 10:208

Ashberry, James W. 23:18

Ashborn, J. C. 22:329

Ashbough, A. 1:103

Ashbrook, Andrew 6:20

Ashbrook, H. P. 20:88

Ashbrook, J. 13:82; 14:3; 24:73

Ashbrook, N. 16:169

Ashbrook, N. R. 13:82; 14:3

Ashbrook, William 9:48

Ashburn, C. 10:212

Ashburn, Mills 6:24

Ashbury, S. R. 8:61

Ashby, Alexander 7:117

Ashby, Daniel 18:301; 26:91

Ashby, David C. 9:71

Ashby, Francis H. 13:8

Ashby, J. 22:517

Ashby, J. F. 3:13

Ashby, J. M. 17:199

Ashby, L. 14:33

Ashby, Thomas G. 11:254

Ashby, W. C. 11:278

Ashby, William 22:63, 288

Ashcott, Robert 16:20

Ashcraft, Elijah 24:163

Ashcraft, J. L. 9:74; 26:8

Ashcraft, Robert H. 22:116

Ashcroft, James L. 23:131

Ashcroft, Joseph 17:29

Ashcroft, S. 20:34

Ashdown, James 21:242

Ashe, Amos D. 16:135

Ashe, Benjamin F. 24:8

Ashel, W. L. 20:200

Ashel, William L. 10:39

Asheland, Jacob 14:137

Ashen, W. H. 25:137

Ashenfelter, John M. 22:63

Ashenhurst, James D. 11:88

Asher, A. 11:275

Asher, C. 14:33

Asher, F. 18:228; 26:9

Asher, H. 21:47

Asher, Hamilton 22:63

Asher, J. 16:169, 286

Asher, John 10:39; 20:200

Asher, Joseph 12:91

Asher, Milton 21:47

Asher, Richard 16:169

Asher, William 5:35; 10:39; 20:200

Asherwood, J. 1:107

Ashfert, Elijah 17:444

Ashford, A. W. 3:13

Ashford, B. 11:324

Ashford, J. 12:91; 14:33; 16:286

Ashford, J. C. 11:217

Ashford, Jesse 20:177

Ashford, S. G. 12:121; 14:25; 15:117, 363

Ashford, William H. 20:185

Ashforth, G. E. 13:104

Ashing, James W. 23:59

Ashkettle, Horace 20:120

Ashlee, David B. 16:20

Ashley, --- 3:13

Ashley, A. 9:128

Ashley, Baxton 9:32

Ashley, Benjamin 5:35

Ashley, Benjamin F. 7:85

Ashley, C. G. 3:13

Ashley, Charles 9:199; 19:289; 21:210

Ashley, Charles C. 21:9

Ashley, Chauncey 22:135

Ashley, Chauncy C. 21:296

Ashley, D. B. 3:13

Ashley, Edward 22:447

Ashley, Eldred 22:63

Ashley, Ephraim 25:137

Ashley, F. 16:169

Ashley, F. B. 1:12

Ashley, Francis H. 16:20

Ashley, Francis M. 22:400

Ashley, Henry 8:37; 26:148

Ashley, Hiram 22:511
Ashley, J. 12:7; 21:146
Ashley, J. M. 3:13
Ashley, J. W. 14:137
Ashley, John 6:22; 8:37;
    18:76; 21:210
Ashley, John E. 10:208
Ashley, Joseph 12:11;
    16:81
Ashley, Josiah 7:18
Ashley, Morris 7:18
Ashley, N. 17:450; 24:176
Ashley, Nelson 27:9
Ashley, P. B. 19:247
Ashley, Philo B. 9:167
Ashley, Russell D. 19:3
Ashley, Samuel 8:37;
    26:148
Ashley, Thomas 11:89
Ashley, Thomas W.
    11:230
Ashley, W. H. 18:337
Ashley, William 18:228;
    26:10
Ashley, William H. 7:18
Ashlock, J. B. 20:84
Ashly, B. 25:137
Ashman, A. J. 11:21
Ashman, D. H. 18:213
Ashman, James 5:8
Ashmead, Oliver G. 10:13
Ashmond, J. 25:137
Ashmore, A. W. 11:420
Ashmore, J. W. 18:187
Ashmore, James W. 22:18
Ashmore, John 20:120
Ashren, Charles 14:239
Ashtan, --- 3:13
Ashten, Henry 9:115
Ashton, Edward G.
    19:146
Ashton, Henry 27:10
Ashton, Joseph 10:39;
    20:200
Ashton, Philip N. 23:200
Ashton, Theodore 9:48
Ashton, Thomas 13:8
Ashton, W. J. 23:18
Ashton, William 4:8;
    8:44; 21:63
Ashurst, F. M. 18:228;
    26:9
Ashurst, J. J. 21:16
Ashwood, John 18:23
Ashwood, Troy 27:142
Ashworth, George 9:11
Ashworth, John 20:135
Ashworth, Richard 1:108;
    10:39; 20:200
Ashworth, Shadrick
    22:240

Ashworth, Thomas 27:10
Ashworth, William 17:266
Ask, Elias 9:41
Ask, J. 26:149
Askem, John 18:456
Asken, D. G. 8:7
Asken, George 21:296
Asken, J. C. 5:8
Asken, Thomas 24:100
Askew, D. 15:164
Askew, D. G. 18:120
Askew, David 10:101
Askew, George W. 22:18
Askew, Thomas 21:296
Askey, James 6:29;
    25:316
Askey, Thomas 6:14;
    18:76
Askin, J. H. 11:133
Askin, M. 9:107
Askin, William 1:12
Askingburg, J. 13:82
Askins, Aaron 18:228;
    26:8
Askins, Armstedt 5:35
Askins, E. P. 11:50
Askins, G. 24:73
Askins, George 13:8
Askins, George W. 22:18
Askins, James 11:132
Askins, John 6:14; 18:76
Askins, Lewis 10:175;
    19:146
Askins, William 22:18,
    400
Askler, W. I. 1:108
Askley, Lucien 8:44
Askma, John W. 20:103
Askren, John C. 11:49
Aslage, William 8:70
Aslasken, Halver 22:276
Aslee, David B. 13:8
Aslet, O. 14:287; 23:187
Asley, Andrew J. 17:318
Asley, John 25:137
Aslin, O. 14:264
Asnew, W. M. 16:286
Asnew, William M. 12:85
Asp, John 24:108
Aspeler, A. 13:82; 14:3
Aspell, Samuel 8:60
Aspell, Samuel H. 12:170
Aspenwall, J. 25:137
Asper, Abram 17:316
Aspery, John 21:219
Aspinwall, Robert 17:161
Aspinwall, S. 10:13
Aspinwall, Samuel 23:18
Aspinwall, Theodore H.
    11:409
Aspray, W. 3:13

Asptenfeller, G. W.
    22:175
Asque, Armstead 25:137
Assan, John 12:91
Assar, John 16:286
Assasmith, P. 9:229
Assay, T. 14:3
Asselmeyer, H. 23:131
Asseltyne, Mariott B. 4:8
Assey, J. 13:82
Assmitson, Peter 20:200
Ast, William T. 21:296
Astell, Anthony 4:8
Aster, Henry 22:288
Aster, Sam 24:11
Asterberry, James 22:18
Asterburn, Theo 22:400
Asthoff, J. 1:108
Astings, --- 27:142
Astion, Joel 17:15
Astle, Thomas 1:108
Astley, J. 19:53
Astley, John 10:101;
    20:200
Astridge, E. 14:33
Atberry, E. 18:361
Atcherson, John 17:29
Atcherson, William H.
    17:391
Atcheson, M. C. 18:23
Atchier, George 11:420
Atchinson, M. 14:33
Atchinson, Robert 11:256
Atchinson, Samuel P.
    18:120
Atchinson, W. P. 3:13
Atchinson, William
    18:228; 26:9
Atchison, Anthony 22:63
Atchison, J. M. 15:356;
    16:277
Atchison, James M.
    12:168
Atchison, N. D. 23:18
Atchison, W. P. 14:137
Atchison, William 12:11
Atchison, Willis 17:127;
    24:187
Atchley, A. 3:13
Atchley, S. 14:33
Aten, J. C. 25:137
Aten, Peter 5:8
Atencio, Pedro 8:123
Ater, Levi 11:256
Ater, Thornton 22:175
Ater, Z. 23:18
Aterick, L. E. 3:13
Ates, Thomas 12:47
Atfield, A. 14:294;
    17:472; 27:10
Atha, Calvin H. 21:63

Atham, Isaac 17:144
Atheam, E. 9:138
Atheam, John H. 10:89;
    20:200
Athearn, E. 27:9
Athearn, M. C. 23:18
Atherly, Robert 11:407
Atheron, Samuel D.
    18:337
Atherson, J. 16:169
Atherton, A. H. 13:61
Atherton, Alex 19:53
Atherton, Charles E. 24:8
Atherton, E. R. 1:11
Atherton, John S. 19:53
Atherton, Joseph 7:18
Atherton, R. F. 22:175
Atherton, Samuel 18:337
Atherton, W. 20:143
Atherton, Warren W.
    15:157
Atherton, William 16:286
Atherton, Zora 17:346
Athery, Edmond 9:218
Athey, A. J. 18:120
Athey, Austin 16:169
Athey, J. 1:12
Athey, John 23:131
Athington, Edgar 9:11
Athon, John W. 14:318;
    23:18; 25:274
Atichkinson, J. C. 1:107
Atin, P. 25:137
Atk, Oli 24:108
Atkerson, Daniel 9:218
Atkin, G. A. 16:89
Atkin, Orin E. 23:59
Atkins, --- 10:211; 18:464
Atkins, A. 3:14
Atkins, A. W. 23:131
Atkins, Alfred 17:153
Atkins, Benjamin F. 16:89
Atkins, Calvin 11:195
Atkins, David 4:8; 7:18
Atkins, E. 3:14
Atkins, Elijah 1:11
Atkins, Francis 18:107
Atkins, Harrison 18:228
Atkins, Homer E. 22:286,
    459
Atkins, Isaac N. 21:16
Atkins, J. 14:239; 19:247;
    23:131; 25:137;
    27:11
Atkins, J. H. 3:14
Atkins, J. L. 17:278
Atkins, J. W. 11:49;
    26:148
Atkins, James 7:85; 8:37;
    21:296
Atkins, James F. 22:116

Atkins, James R. 21:219
Atkins, John 4:8; 5:35;
    9:167; 10:169;
    15:352; 16:277;
    18:187; 19:247;
    20:200; 26:148
Atkins, Joseph 10:39;
    17:93; 24:164
Atkins, L. 3:14
Atkins, Leonidas 26:148
Atkins, Lester 13:8
Atkins, Lewis 22:63
Atkins, Loren 24:64
Atkins, Martin 22:18
Atkins, Mathew 22:288
Atkins, Parker 14:137
Atkins, R. M. G. 1:108
Atkins, Ralph 9:100
Atkins, Samuel 21:96;
    22:18; 23:250
Atkins, Stephen 8:37;
    26:148
Atkins, T. W. 14:318
Atkins, Thomas 10:101;
    13:76; 16:169;
    20:200
Atkins, Thomas L. 14:263
Atkins, William 1:11
Atkins, William C. 20:94
Atkins, William D. 1:11
Atkins, William H. 12:11
Atkins, William O. D.
    1:12
Atkins, William S. 15:85
Atkinson, A. P. 15:322
Atkinson, Albert 22:18
Atkinson, B. A. 25:12
Atkinson, Bob 6:22
Atkinson, C. M. 16:169
Atkinson, C. S. 4:8
Atkinson, Cephas 21:247
Atkinson, D. 16:169;
    21:118
Atkinson, D. H. 11:102
Atkinson, Daniel 18:361
Atkinson, David 23:187
Atkinson, Eli 8:44; 21:16
Atkinson, Elisha 7:85
Atkinson, Eph 26:148
Atkinson, Eph. 8:37
Atkinson, G. P. 20:200
Atkinson, George 3:14;
    10:147; 18:44;
    25:137
Atkinson, H. 21:16
Atkinson, Henry 10:98;
    22:472
Atkinson, Henry C. 19:3
Atkinson, J. 16:169
Atkinson, J. H. 8:44;
    27:11

Atkinson, J. M. 9:107;
    12:97
Atkinson, J. T. 11:21
Atkinson, Jacob 19:3
Atkinson, James 1:11; 8:8;
    18:120; 21:47
Atkinson, James W.
    9:229; 20:200
Atkinson, John 3:14;
    21:297
Atkinson, John H. 27:142
Atkinson, Joseph 10:39;
    17:425; 20:200;
    24:176
Atkinson, Joseph B. 20:94
Atkinson, L. L. 24:98
Atkinson, Lyon H. 22:240
Atkinson, M. B. A. 9:41
Atkinson, P. 3:13
Atkinson, R. 25:13
Atkinson, R. W. 27:10
Atkinson, Ralph N.
    17:212
Atkinson, Robert 2:7
Atkinson, S. 1:12
Atkinson, Thomas 14:137;
    17:127; 24:187;
    26:148
Atkinson, W. 1:13; 27:9
Atkinson, W. T. 16:169
Atkinson, William 10:204;
    18:120; 21:193
Atkinson, William K.
    17:452; 24:182
Atkinson, William M.
    10:101; 20:200
Atkinson, Wilson 6:14;
    18:76
Atland, P. G. 25:316
Atland, Robert 22:288
Atler, P. 27:9
Atley, Samuel 21:249
Atmore, C. 3:14
Atmore, G. W. 3:14
Atno, A. 21:165
Ato, J. 24:35
Atonbough, A. 20:200
Atrick, --- --- 15:258
Atridge, Thomas 11:189
Att, Joseph 23:255
Atter, Daniel 21:129
Atterberry, Amos 24:11
Atterberry, Charles H.
    17:71
Atterberry, David 17:17
Atterbury, D. J. 26:148
Atterbury, David 8:44
Atterbury, W. H. 26:120
Attey, Albert J. 9:167
Attic, A. 16:266
Attic, C. 14:3

Attig, William 20:200
Atting, William 10:39
Attinger, Michael 21:220
Attlebury, Charles 16:20
Attlebury, W. H. 9:41
Attu, --- 11:338
Attwell, J. R. 13:124
Attwood, B. F. 27:9
Attwood, L. J. 13:61
Atuston, Clarke 15:90
Atward, H. M. 11:256
Atwater, Benjamin 8:70
Atwater, Franklin B.
     10:13
Atwater, Henry 1:11
Atwater, John S. 19:3
Atwater, Julius 7:19
Atwater, William A.
     16:169
Atwell, --- 17:278
Atwell, A. D. 1:11
Atwell, Albert 21:16
Atwell, Chauncey 12:11
Atwell, George 17:127;
     24:187
Atwell, John B. 24:64
Atwell, L. H. 20:200
Atwell, Louis H. 10:39
Atwell, Thomas 3:14
Atwell, W. B. 23:131
Atwich, F. I. 16:20
Atwood, --- 15:181
Atwood, A. 3:14; 21:297
Atwood, A. A. 9:74; 26:8
Atwood, A. E. 25:13
Atwood, A. L. 10:39;
     20:200
Atwood, Albert 15:297
Atwood, B. 1:107
Atwood, Bradley V. 10:89
Atwood, Brady 20:200
Atwood, C. 2:7; 25:12
Atwood, Charles E.
     22:400
Atwood, Charles H. 13:8
Atwood, Chester L.
     23:240
Atwood, Daniel L. 19:296
Atwood, Eli 22:415
Atwood, Ezra 9:101
Atwood, F. 9:138
Atwood, G. C. 13:8
Atwood, G. H. 7:85
Atwood, G. S. 3:14
Atwood, George B. 7:73;
     25:292
Atwood, George W.
     10:89; 15:90
Atwood, H. 15:181
Atwood, Henry C. 16:20
Atwood, J. H. 1:109

Atwood, James 10:171;
     19:146
Atwood, James H. 15:101
Atwood, James W. 23:84
Atwood, John 10:39;
     17:205; 20:201
Atwood, John F. 4:8
Atwood, L. D. 1:108
Atwood, Lowell 10:39;
     20:201
Atwood, M. W. 1:109
Atwood, Nathan 23:131
Atwood, Robert 16:169
Atwood, S. M. 15:181
Atwood, Thomas 6:29;
     25:316
Atwood, W. 1:93
Atwood, W. H. 23:245
Atwood, William 15:297;
     16:169; 17:69;
     22:459
Atwood, William C. 24:47
Atwood, William F. 1:11
Atwood, William T.
     19:146
Atzenger, F. 20:201
Atzinger, Frederick 10:39
Atzinger, Jacob 12:11
Aubel, George 10:13
Auberry, George H.
     17:233
Auberry, Philip F. 17:234
Auberton, Alewise 7:19
Aubin, John 7:19
Auborn, Cornelius 17:29
Aubrey, K. 3:14
Aubry, F. 21:118
Auburg, Milton 10:154
Aubury, Milton 19:146
Auch, Charles C. 17:417
Auchenbach, William
     16:20
Auchenback, --- 13:8
Auchinclass, James
     19:324
Auchmuty, --- 9:65
Aucott, Joseph 7:19
Auders, John 19:3
Audhart, Fred 11:101
Audley, Charles 18:120
Aufance, S. 11:285
Aufderheid, John H. F.
     20:201
Aufderheid, John H. T.
     10:101
Aufdermaner, Martin 4:8
Augabright, James C. 20:4
Auge, Marcel 23:84
Augenete, Charles 11:133
Auger, A. 3:14
Auger, B. F. 8:79

Auger, G. 3:14
Auger, George 9:41
Auger, J. 13:124
Auger, W. 3:14
Augers, William 22:231
Augh, --- 9:159
Aughe, Darlington 23:59
Aughenbaugh, John 12:11
Auglin, J. A. 3:14
Augstead, John 17:75
Augtin, Seth J. 11:99
Augur, Charles 10:156
Augur, Marshall C.
     10:156
August, --- 27:9
August, Carl 1:12
August, Charles 16:151
August, Eugene 7:117
August, J. 27:9
August, John 23:131
August, Will 11:297
Augusta, C. L. 1:108
Augustin, Noel 18:63
Augustine, August 25:287
Augustine, J. 3:14
Augustine, Noel 9:205
Augustine, Virgil 22:400
Augustine, William 9:159
Augustus, C. H. 25:137
Augustus, Charles H. 5:35
Augustus, Clark 19:146
Augustus, Clarkson
     10:176
Augustus, F. 3:14
Augustus, Frederick 13:8
Augustus, George 12:47
Augustus, P. 14:137
Augustus, Peter 11:21
Auhenbaugh, Jacob
     21:220
Auit, J. P. 21:63
Auker, Edwin 15:52
Auker, L. J. 11:21
Aukney, David 11:133
Aukron, Joseph 10:156
Aul, James 1:108
Auld, John G. 22:63
Auld, Samuel R. 20:201
Auld, Thomas 17:404
Auld, W. H. 24:99
Auld, William 15:181
Auldman, W. 27:8
Aule, D. 25:13
Aulger, George 3:14
Ault, Andrew J. 22:240
Ault, Charles 7:85; 23:59
Ault, George 10:101;
     20:201
Ault, Henry 15:85
Ault, J. W. 3:14
Ault, James L. 3:14

Ault, John 22:276
Ault, Loren 22:63
Ault, Lyman 11:132
Ault, Philip 24:73
Ault, Solomon 26:120
Aultz, Samuel 23:272
Aultz, Solomon 9:41
Aumack, John H. 8:8;
  18:120
Auman, D. K. 1:108
Aumiller, Jacob 22:8
Auncock, Elijah 22:164
Aungstedt, --- 3:12
Aunnick, D. 1:107
Aunty, G. 21:297
Aurand, Abner 13:8
Aurand, George M. 13:61;
  19:53
Aurell, J. 16:169
Auric, H. 27:8
Ausbach, George 17:89
Ausberry, Alex 9:48
Ausburn, David 11:420
Ausburn, H. 21:297
Ausburn, John F. 17:75
Ausden, Thomas O.
  19:146
Aushurn, W. A. 14:287;
  23:18
Ausley, Noah 19:146
Ausmeier, Frederick 10:89
Ausment, Isaac 7:85
Ausnoe, John 14:279
Aussky, Joseph 19:53
Austen, Daniel B. 10:39
Austen, George 14:137
Austin, --- 9:226
Austin, A. 1:107; 3:14;
  12:61, 141; 15:52;
  17:47; 25:137; 27:8
Austin, A. B. 14:279
Austin, A. M. 15:101
Austin, Aaron 16:131
Austin, Abraham 5:8
Austin, Albert H. 7:66
Austin, Alden K. 10:156;
  19:146
Austin, Alexander 5:8
Austin, Anderson 14:313
Austin, Anton 21:90
Austin, B. 13:82
Austin, B. K. 2:7; 25:12
Austin, C. 8:70; 26:149
Austin, C. H. 15:15
Austin, Caswell 21:264
Austin, Charles 8:37, 60,
  112; 9:70; 21:249;
  23:131; 26:148
Austin, Charles E. 12:58;
  21:297

Austin, Charles H.
  10:156; 19:146
Austin, Clark 12:61
Austin, Cornelius 22:288
Austin, Costal 15:62
Austin, D. 1:108; 3:14;
  25:137
Austin, D. B. 3:14
Austin, D. K. 15:286;
  19:53
Austin, Daniel 8:112
Austin, David 10:101;
  20:201
Austin, E. 1:11; 16:170
Austin, E. A. 19:247
Austin, E. E. 11:133
Austin, E. W. 9:167
Austin, Edmund 23:105
Austin, Edwin 20:16
Austin, Edwin S. 22:18
Austin, Elijah W. 22:276
Austin, Elliah 18:187
Austin, Ephraim A.
  22:135
Austin, Ezra B. 20:191
Austin, F. 14:33
Austin, Freeman 13:8;
  21:240
Austin, G. 19:146
Austin, G. B. 18:391
Austin, G. E. 18:102
Austin, G. W. 13:126
Austin, George 11:133;
  12:173; 13:8; 21:146,
  264
Austin, George E. 15:181
Austin, Grafton 21:297
Austin, H. 1:107
Austin, H. A. 9:167;
  19:247
Austin, H. D. 19:247
Austin, H. G. 9:18;
  18:301; 26:9
Austin, H. R. W. 10:13
Austin, Harris 4:8; 8:102
Austin, Harrison 7:117
Austin, Henry D. 9:167
Austin, Humphrey 8:79
Austin, I. 12:164
Austin, I. M. 21:12
Austin, Ira 23:105
Austin, Ira F. 24:169
Austin, Ira T. 17:422
Austin, Isaac 3:14; 9:205;
  22:288
Austin, J. 3:14; 9:167;
  14:137; 26:149
Austin, J. A. 3:14
Austin, J. B. 10:94
Austin, J. F. 14:3
Austin, J. M. 1:11; 21:297

Austin, J. P. 23:18
Austin, J. R. 11:132
Austin, J. T. 13:82
Austin, Jacob 25:137
Austin, James 3:14; 9:18;
  17:98; 23:292;
  25:278
Austin, James H. 26:91
Austin, James W. 18:301
Austin, John 9:205; 22:18;
  27:10
Austin, John F. 10:39;
  20:201
Austin, John G. 22:116
Austin, John H. 11:196
Austin, John S. 17:241
Austin, John W. 11:123;
  22:116
Austin, Joshua 1:12
Austin, L. 18:361
Austin, Levi 22:135
Austin, Lockwood 22:170
Austin, M. G. 19:3
Austin, Marion 8:70;
  26:149
Austin, Merritt F. 22:18
Austin, Miles W. 17:205
Austin, Monroe 13:8
Austin, Nathan 11:196
Austin, Nathan R. 8:8;
  18:120
Austin, Norman P. 23:105
Austin, O. 23:261
Austin, Oliver 22:175
Austin, Otis 22:135
Austin, P. M. 21:193
Austin, Philip 21:220
Austin, Philip A. 9:218
Austin, Phillip A. 18:361
Austin, Porter 15:29
Austin, R. 25:292
Austin, R. C. 24:73
Austin, R. S. 18:63
Austin, Rauel 7:73
Austin, Richard 17:494
Austin, Robert L. 22:400
Austin, S. 9:48; 12:7;
  18:228; 26:9
Austin, S. C. 17:354
Austin, S. J. 1:12; 22:231
Austin, S. P. 23:187
Austin, Samuel 22:175
Austin, Single 9:205
Austin, Stephen 7:19
Austin, T. 13:129
Austin, Thomas 16:20;
  17:335; 21:16
Austin, Thomas C. 22:240
Austin, Thomas J. 13:8
Austin, W. 3:14
Austin, W. A. 13:104

Austin, W. F. 1:109
Austin, W. H. 1:93
Austin, W. H. H. 8:79
Austin, W. J. 18:228; 26:9
Austin, W. S. 1:108
Austin, Warren 21:297
Austin, William 7:66;
    11:285; 21:297
Austin, William S. 20:191
Austin, Zena W. 24:212
Austindalph, I. 3:14
Austine, T. 3:14
Austins, George 4:8
Auston, C. O. 1:12
Auston, J. 19:273
Auston, John 14:294;
    17:481
Auston, Tar 18:187
Austrat, Adolph 8:8;
    18:120
Autcliffe, Joseph 11:102
Autem, Daniel B. 20:199
Autherbuck, John 13:104
Authurs, Asa A. 15:286
Autibus, Jacob 8:8
Autle, James 11:50
Autney, John 22:399
Auton, Charles 19:3
Auton, D. 15:6
Autry, Dergin 19:3
Autry, James 21:63
Autry, John L. 26:8
Auttman, Manuel 6:35
Auvandt, J. 3:14
Avant, Isaac 21:264
Avars, Frederick 11:133
Avary, Samuel H. 23:59
Aveline, F. H. 18:213
Aveline, William C. 8:44;
    24:109
Avely, J. 16:362
Avenle, J. K. 27:8
Aveny, William C. 22:116
Avera, Warren 4:8
Averall, George 13:104
Averett, John 10:210
Averett, John J. 9:234
Averette, J. 25:137
Averhill, W. H. 21:297
Averill, Edwin 13:8
Averill, Emerson M.
    22:135
Averill, F. 15:29
Averill, F. E. 3:14
Averill, Henry 1:11
Averill, J. 19:225
Averill, J. E. 1:107
Averill, Lyman H. 22:459
Averill, Miles W. 7:85
Averill, William 8:102

Averill, William C.
    18:120
Averill, William H. 19:53
Averin, E. 1:107
Averon, Calb 1:11
Avers, John 14:33
Avery, A. C. 16:170
Avery, Alfred A. 17:246
Avery, Alonzo 9:18;
    18:301; 26:91
Avery, Alonzo E. 24:11
Avery, Amos 22:276
Avery, Amos B. 10:101;
    20:201
Avery, Arthur M. 9:11
Avery, B. M. 1:11
Avery, C. 1:107
Avery, Charles 4:8; 14:33
Avery, Charles S. 7:55;
    14:1
Avery, Charlse G. 9:11
Avery, D. 1:12
Avery, E. 7:19
Avery, Edward 10:171;
    19:146
Avery, Edwin 10:13
Avery, G. R. 25:137
Avery, G. W. 5:8; 25:137
Avery, George F. 9:11
Avery, George H. 11:102
Avery, George R. 5:8
Avery, George W. 21:297
Avery, H. O. 18:301;
    26:91
Avery, Henry 22:63
Avery, Henry H. 22:116
Avery, J. 1:12, 96; 3:14;
    12:141; 13:82
Avery, J. C. 12:97
Avery, Jacob 21:297
Avery, James 2:7; 25:12
Avery, James C. 15:356;
    16:277
Avery, Joel 7:85
Avery, John 9:115; 22:175
Avery, John A. 10:13
Avery, John T. 17:388;
    27:8, 9
Avery, John W. 3:14
Avery, L. H. 15:181
Avery, Luther 10:39;
    20:201
Avery, Lyman 19:3
Avery, M. 25:310
Avery, Miron E. 11:383
Avery, O. 9:18
Avery, Philow 17:216
Avery, S. 21:297
Avery, S. S. 10:39; 20:201
Avery, Squire 1:11
Avery, Stephen 10:13

Avery, Sylvester 5:8
Avery, T. 20:54
Avery, T. W. 4:8
Avery, Thomas 17:168
Avery, W. 14:33
Avery, W. H. 17:450;
    24:176
Avery, Walter 14:137
Avery, William 15:29
Avery, William L. 22:116
Avey, J. 14:3
Avidson, Avil 16:20
Avins, Nicholas 23:183
Avirill, William H. 15:331
Avis, Caleb R. 1:12
Avis, Edward 17:445;
    24:165
Avis, Isaac 1:11
Avis, James 24:72
Avis, S. 21:47
Avison, William 11:133
Avlon, William 8:8
Avoy, O. C. 1:12
Avrell, William C. 8:8
Avy, Barton 16:20
Awbro, Christopher
    18:361
Awehall, James 18:23
Awood, Charles 18:23
Axe, Alias J. 11:49
Axe, Charles 1:11
Axe, John 17:435; 24:176
Axford, K. 1:12
Axir, H. 11:21
Axit, Conrad 14:33
Axley, A. C. 11:21
Axley, Martin 1:108
Axline, Joseph 9:32
Axom, John 27:9
Axon, John 9:128
Axson, James 7:85
Axtel, Samuel A. 18:301;
    26:91
Axtell, A. R. 19:53
Axtell, Charles 27:10
Axtell, Daniel M. 23:59
Axtell, F. H. 14:130
Axtell, G. 16:362
Axtell, Hubbard 11:114
Axtell, James 17:406
Axtell, Lorenzo 5:8
Axtell, Samuel A. 9:18
Axtell, William O. 25:12
Ay, B. N. 17:246
Ayars, Jonathan D. 24:47
Aycork, James M. 9:48
Aydelott, Joseph 22:63
Aydelott, Joseph W.
    22:415
Aydoan, C. 21:63
Aye, E. 1:107

Ayer, A. J. 1:12
Ayer, Alfred 9:32
Ayer, Allen 11:235
Ayer, Christ 9:32
Ayer, E. L. 15:328
Ayer, Oliver 1:12
Ayer, T. P. 21:297
Ayers, --- 15:181; 17:335
Ayers, A. 16:362
Ayers, Anthony 6:29
Ayers, Burton 21:63
Ayers, D. 22:288
Ayers, Dana 7:9; 19:3
Ayers, E. 13:82; 14:4,
    137; 15:297
Ayers, Edward 18:228;
    26:9
Ayers, Elisha 18:228
Ayers, Ezra 16:170
Ayers, G. B. B. 25:137
Ayers, G. R. 20:151
Ayers, G. S. 3:14
Ayers, George W. 7:55;
    14:137; 25:12
Ayers, H. 22:135
Ayers, Hiram 15:181
Ayers, J. 7:19
Ayers, J. R. 13:77; 16:170
Ayers, Jacob 22:175
Ayers, James 21:16
Ayers, James D. 25:137
Ayers, James F. 27:8
Ayers, James P. 20:135
Ayers, John 18:327;
    19:247; 23:117
Ayers, John E. 22:472
Ayers, Joseph 22:240
Ayers, M. H. 22:471
Ayers, Martin 11:123
Ayers, Matson 22:175
Ayers, Oscar F. 20:120
Ayers, Reed 22:459
Ayers, Richard 11:297
Ayers, T. B. 13:104
Ayers, T. C. 17:144
Ayers, W. 11:235
Ayers, Wesley 20:201
Ayerson, James 15:283;
    19:53
AyKroid, Albert 19:53
Aykroyd, A. 13:61
Ayler, Fred 16:362
Ayler, Frederick 15:347
Ayler, William 18:120
Ayles, T. 25:137
Ayles, Thomas 5:8
Ayless, M. 20:153
Aylesworth, Edward G.
    16:89
Aylesworth, O. I. 15:181

Ayleworth, Jason H.
    21:242
Ayling, Edward 11:102
Ayling, Edwin 11:102
Aylmer, Edw. P. 7:85
Aylor, Daniel 20:178
Aylsworth, W. W. 17:246
Aylward, Richard 16:138
Ayotte, Dennis 22:18
Ayrast, F. 11:21
Ayre, William 4:8
Ayres, A. 15:339
Ayres, Anthony 25:316
Ayres, Austin 5:8
Ayres, Benjamin F.
    17:241
Ayres, Caleb B. 21:220
Ayres, Charles A. 20:47
Ayres, D. 25:137
Ayres, Elisha 26:9
Ayres, G. A. 14:33
Ayres, George A. 14:1
Ayres, Green 20:4
Ayres, J. L. 21:47
Ayres, J. M. 20:201
Ayres, James H. 20:4
Ayres, John 1:108; 9:167
Ayres, John B. 21:129
Ayres, John S. 4:8
Ayres, Joseph 17:29
Ayres, Martin 7:85
Ayres, Oliver C. 23:84
Ayres, P. 16:89
Ayres, Peter 21:242
Ayres, Robert C. 7:138
Ayres, S. 3:14
Ayres, S. Y. 3:14
Ayres, W. S. 17:322
Ayres, Wesley 10:101
Ayres, William 9:205
Ayrs, David 5:35
Aysoaner, David 18:120
Azbell, Joseph 10:101;
    20:201
Azbill, Sylvester 22:175
Aznall, Henry 9:74
Azwell, Henry 26:8

B

B---, --- 15:273; 16:170,
    287; 24:11; 25:137;
    27:23
B---, --iley 20:45
B---, A. 11:257; 18:23;
    19:299; 20:201;
    22:349; 24:109;
    27:12
B---, A. A. 19:152
B---, A. F. 16:365

B---, A. H. 20:201
B---, A. M. 11:298
B---, A. O. 14:320
B---, B--- 26:134
B---, B. 18:284; 24:109;
    25:137
B---, B. H. 20:201
B---, B. Williams 12:98
B---, C. 16:365; 18:23;
    23:96
B---, C. E. 24:109
B---, C. H. 25:19
B---, C. P. 11:53; 25:15
B---, C. V. B. 26:217
B---, Charles 23:312
B---, Christian 20:201
B---, D. 12:140; 18:231;
    19:152; 23:18, 255;
    26:16
B---, D. B. 20:201
B---, D. C. 17:363
B---, D. H. 23:201
B---, E. 11:83
B---, E. A. 26:153
B---, E. B. 22:349
B---, E. F. 21:207
B---, E. G. 25:310
B---, E. H. 11:236
B---, E. M. 26:153
B---, E. W. 21:207
B---, F. 20:201
B---, F. G. 25:292
B---, F. M. H. B. 23:292
B---, F. O. 15:6
B---, Fred 25:17
B---, G. 15:29; 18:23;
    23:201
B---, G. I. 18:78
B---, G. J. 15:297
B---, G. P. 23:96
B---, George W. 15:187
B---, H. 10:26; 11:339;
    14:268; 15:29;
    19:299; 23:267;
    27:9
B---, H. A. 11:331
B---, H. B. 27:11
B---, H. D. 25:318
B---, H. J. 10:192
B---, H. M. 22:349
B---, H. S. 16:135
B---, H. Y. 19:59
B---, Henry 20:55
B---, I. 11:428; 18:171
B---, I. N. 11:236
B---, I. S. 11:395
B---, I. W. 19:299
B---, Isaac 25:14
B---, J. 9:213; 10:192;
    11:236, 257, 339;
    12:141; 14:268;

B---, J. 15:187; 16:113; 17:216, 363; 18:231; 20:201; 21:146; 23:201, 242; 24:109, 213; 25:17, 318; 26:16; 27:13
B---, J. A. 19:299; 20:201
B---, J. B. 17:216; 25:15
B---, J. C. 18:23
B---, J. D. 16:89; 17:94; 18:231; 24:109; 26:13
B---, J. F. 20:55
B---, J. H. 9:229; 11:321; 20:201; 25:271
B---, J. K. 20:201
B---, J. M. 8:61; 17:109; 23:59; 24:109; 26:153
B---, J. P. 17:363
B---, J. S. 11:297; 26:153
B---, J. T. 23:262
B---, J. V. 11:256
B---, J. W. 12:147; 15:187; 16:287; 20:201; 21:207; 24:109
B---, James 1:14
B---, James H. 18:13
B---, John 22:400
B---, John H. 11:279
B---, K--- 8:46
B---, K. C. 25:15
B---, L. 15:292; 18:13
B---, L. A. 25:16
B---, L. D. 14:268
B---, M. 11:53; 12:98; 20:50, 144, 201; 21:207; 23:18; 26:153
B---, M. E. 20:153
B---, Miles H. 15:187
B---, N. 11:331, 339; 15:101; 18:231; 19:152; 26:17
B---, N. E. 11:236
B---, N. H. 12:166
B---, N. I. 18:171
B---, N. P. 20:91
B---, O. M. 19:59
B---, P. 17:216; 18:23; 19:152; 23:201
B---, Q. M. 25:15
B---, R--- 26:134
B---, R. 18:284; 21:165
B---, R. A. 22:349
B---, R. O. 23:187
B---, R. R. 19:152
B---, Richard 20:33
B---, S. 15:187; 23:312; 27:142

B---, S. H. 11:294
B---, S. J. 19:152
B---, S. M. 20:153
B---, S. P. 26:153
B---, S. W. 21:165
B---, Samuel P. 15:102
B---, So-es--- A. 25:17
B---, T. 10:26; 17:278
B---, T. H. 16:365
B---, T. W. 17:272
B---, Thomas 15:187
B---, W. 10:26; 11:339; 13:130; 15:187, 262; 17:327; 18:464; 19:299; 21:146, 207; 23:59, 262; 27:13
B---, W. C. 17:216
B---, W. G. 21:207
B---, W. H. 19:152
B---, W. J. 20:201
B---, W. M. 24:11
B---, W. R. 23:201
B---, W. S. 20:38; 23:201
B---, W. W. P. H. 17:337
B---, William 18:231, 284; 26:16, 134
B---, William B. 15:366
B---, William O. 17:363
B---, Wo--- R--- 15:171
B---, Y. W. 23:59
B----, C. M. 22:175
B-----, George F. 8:10
B---eo, Joel 25:15
B---er, I. 18:102
B---m, G. 15:171
B---man, Jacob 9:213
B---scher, August 23:201
B---w, O. H. B. 24:109
B--ggs, Nelson 8:37
B-o--y, J. 23:18
B--oney, --- 19:152
B-ewer, Alexander 8:37
B-iles, Moses 8:37
Ba---, Abraham 17:296
Ba---ws, Levi 16:170
Ba-ke, Frederick 23:187
Baader, John 19:146
Babb, Alpheus 23:284
Babb, Benjamin 11:83
Babb, Daniel 7:19
Babb, David H. 24:99
Babb, G. W. 3:14; 22:116
Babb, George 22:417
Babb, Horatio 8:61
Babb, J. 13:104
Babb, J. P. 2:7; 25:19
Babb, James 3:14
Babb, James H. 21:96
Babb, James K. 17:93
Babb, John 10:101; 20:201

Babb, John W. 18:204
Babb, M. 1:19
Babb, Richard 22:288
Babb, Sampson 22:231
Babb, Samuel 3:14
Babb, Scott 11:197
Babb, Stephen 10:39; 20:201
Babb, W. 3:14
Babb, William 1:13
Babb, Y. 9:48
Babbett, A. 1:110; 13:82
Babbett, F. C. 8:70
Babbington, Mitchell 27:23
Babbit, Stephen A. 11:22
Babbit, William 14:137
Babbitt, Absalom 21:47
Babbitt, Charles F. 23:118
Babbitt, E. 14:33
Babbitt, F. C. 26:153
Babbitt, Harrison 12:11; 21:47
Babbitt, J. W. 18:301; 26:92
Babbitt, John 3:14
Babbitt, W. H. 3:14
Babbitt, William 8:100; 17:459; 24:151
Babbock, Samuel 26:11
Babbs, A. 23:18
Babbs, Albert 21:16
Babbs, J. W. 25:138
Babbs, John N. 5:8
Babbs, Thomas 25:138
Babcock, --- 15:347
Babcock, A. J. 20:174
Babcock, Aaron 20:201
Babcock, Adelbert 21:206
Babcock, Albert 22:135
Babcock, Albert C. 9:11
Babcock, Allen K. 20:21
Babcock, Alonzo J. 16:83
Babcock, Alvin 12:58
Babcock, Ans'n. E. 1:13
Babcock, Benjamin 14:137
Babcock, C. 1:112; 13:79; 18:44
Babcock, C. C. 12:66; 15:10
Babcock, C. L. 21:90
Babcock, Charles 11:335
Babcock, Charles H. 18:346
Babcock, Charles M. 11:103
Babcock, D. 1:110
Babcock, D. G. W. 20:110
Babcock, Daniel 5:8; 7:19; 25:138

Babcock, David 17:153
Babcock, E. 21:16
Babcock, E. G. 9:235; 26:216
Babcock, E. J. 25:278
Babcock, Edwin 23:266
Babcock, Elias 5:8
Babcock, Elisha 1:15
Babcock, Elmer F. 19:53
Babcock, F. 1:14; 3:14
Babcock, G. 13:82
Babcock, G. H. 16:89
Babcock, G. L. 8:44
Babcock, G. M. 9:138
Babcock, Gilbert R. 13:8
Babcock, H. J. 22:175
Babcock, Henry 20:191; 22:19
Babcock, Hiram 17:74
Babcock, Hiram V. 20:105
Babcock, Hubert 4:8
Babcock, Ira 11:137
Babcock, Isaac 7:117
Babcock, J. 3:14; 14:137
Babcock, J. A. 14:33
Babcock, J. C. 15:181
Babcock, J. H. 1:116
Babcock, J. M. 3:14
Babcock, J. S. 3:14
Babcock, Jeremiah 14:137
Babcock, Jesse 24:73
Babcock, Job 12:11
Babcock, John 1:13; 15:181; 17:29
Babcock, John W. 1:14
Babcock, Kinsley A. 18:301; 26:93
Babcock, L. A. 3:14; 15:181
Babcock, L. E. 15:325
Babcock, L. J. 1:114
Babcock, Lemuel 22:63
Babcock, Merritt 11:230
Babcock, N. 3:14
Babcock, N. R. 11:134
Babcock, Nathan 21:90
Babcock, Norman 17:153
Babcock, O. 17:153
Babcock, Oliver H. P. 19:146
Babcock, P. H. 11:137
Babcock, R. 1:110; 3:14; 19:53
Babcock, R. A. 9:18
Babcock, R. F. 13:82
Babcock, Robert 6:14; 18:76
Babcock, S. 1:18
Babcock, Samuel 9:74; 18:120; 21:242

Babcock, Samuel I. 8:8
Babcock, Silas 13:104
Babcock, T. 3:14
Babcock, V. E. 7:65
Babcock, W. C. 20:201
Babcock, W. E. 24:11
Babcock, W. F. 9:48
Babcock, W. H. 15:101; 17:153
Babcock, W. M. 21:16
Babcock, W. N. 3:14
Babcock, Washington O. 17:442; 24:156
Babcock, William 12:81; 16:287
Babcock, William C. 1:15; 10:89
Babcock, William P. 12:150
Babcock, William W. 8:44; 21:96
Babel, Isaac H. 9:41
Baber, George W. 17:205
Baber, John 11:383
Babesck, G. M. 27:13
Babin, Joseph 18:63
Babins, Joseph 9:205
Babkirk, W. D. 1:111
Bable, H. H. 27:18
Bable, Isaac H. 26:121
Babman, C. 21:17
Babo, Adam 8:8
Babor, W. J. 19:299
Babson, Sylvanus B. 2:7
Babst, F. 1:19
Babst, M. 3:15
Babston, J. 11:410
Babston, P. 18:228; 26:14
Babswood, David 5:35
Babter, D. 17:108
Babtist, John 18:23
Baburk, Horace 14:137
Baca, Jesus 12:61
Bacchus, A. 3:15
Baccon, A. 16:170
Baccus, S. 18:228
Baccus, William T. 10:101; 20:201
Baceno, S. 26:13
Bach, E. 8:44
Bach, Eddil 11:103
Bach, Henry 18:424; 22:8
Bach, John N. 17:13
Bachand, Frank 18:63
Bachdel, David 11:53
Bachdol, William H. 18:213
Bache, Charles 17:231
Bache, Henry 12:94
Bachelder, B. F. 3:15
Bachelder, Benjamin 3:15

Bachelder, Benjamin L. 21:63
Bachelder, George W. 14:137
Bachelder, James 9:213
Bachelder, John 22:19
Bachelder, Justin S. 15:277
Bachelder, William 17:153
Bacheler, G. A. 19:222
Bacheler, George 19:3
Bachellor, J. R. 3:15
Bachelor, A. 15:181
Bachelor, C. P. 1:113
Bachelor, James 1:17
Bachelor, Joseph 17:151
Bacher, J. R. 6:29
Bachle, Frank 22:175
Bachman, Benjamin 4:8
Bachman, Boxer Z. 22:349
Bachman, D. 9:138; 27:16
Bachman, David 12:11
Bachman, Felix 12:11
Bachman, J. 13:82; 25:138
Bachman, Robert 12:11
Bachtel, David 12:12
Bachtel, John 1:18
Bachtel, Samuel E. 5:8
Bachtol, S. E. 25:138
Bachtold, Samuel 10:39, 89; 20:201
Bachus, C. 11:257
Bachus, E. R. 3:15
Bachus, F. E. 13:128
Bachus, Isaac 17:17
Bachus, Lewis 7:19
Bachus, Michael 22:19
Bacil, Andw. 8:79
Back, G. 21:197
Back, Jackson 25:274
Back, Samuel M. 23:96
Back, Solomon 24:165
Back, W. L. 20:153
Backer, B. 17:169
Backer, B. B. 8:61
Backer, Henry 8:61; 10:39; 20:201
Backer, James M. 8:61
Backer, John 7:85; 9:168; 22:460
Backer, John T. 5:35
Backer, P. 14:294; 17:475
Backer, Peter 23:84
Backer, Thomas 8:8
Backer, U. H. 9:48
Backer, Valentine 20:94
Backers, W. H. 21:297
Backet, N. T. 13:82

Backett, Hiram F. 22:63
Backett, William 13:104
Backhouse, George W. 4:8
Backinson, J. C. 9:48
Backley, C. 3:15
Backley, George 18:107
Backley, J. F. 3:15
Backlow, John H. 10:13
Backman, Isaac 22:19
Backman, J. 19:279
Backman, John 9:199; 10:156; 26:13
Backman, John H. 12:56
Backmer, John 15:357
Backnet, Charles 5:35
Backos, Wallace 21:63
Backstone, Benjamin 19:279
Backus, C. H. 7:19
Backus, C. T. 18:424
Backus, Charles B. 9:241
Backus, Charles E. 11:123
Backus, Cyrus 21:134
Backus, Daniel 22:111
Backus, E. H. 13:8; 16:20
Backus, G. H. 24:87
Backus, George W. 13:8
Backus, J. K. 16:151
Backus, William 1:114; 5:8; 14:129; 23:127; 25:138
Bacon, A. L. 27:157
Bacon, A. W. 3:15
Bacon, Aaron 7:117
Bacon, Albert G. 17:307
Bacon, Arthur 16:170
Bacon, B. C. 25:138
Bacon, Bowman W. 22:19
Bacon, C. S. 15:181
Bacon, Cerrel B. 22:472
Bacon, Charles 7:55; 10:39; 17:153; 20:201
Bacon, Charles C. 22:175
Bacon, Clinton 22:175
Bacon, Clinton D. 21:63
Bacon, Curtis 13:8; 16:20
Bacon, Daniel 20:191
Bacon, E. P. 3:15
Bacon, Edmond 7:19
Bacon, Elijah 10:39; 20:201
Bacon, Emory 20:4
Bacon, Emory C. 21:184
Bacon, Eugene 7:79; 8:8; 18:120; 25:292
Bacon, Fernando 9:107
Bacon, Frederick A. 18:440

Bacon, Freedus C. 21:249
Bacon, G. 15:181
Bacon, George 4:8
Bacon, George H. 17:390
Bacon, George L. 17:262
Bacon, Henry 15:53; 17:262
Bacon, Horace A. 14:137
Bacon, Isaiah H. 27:13
Bacon, Israel 7:77; 25:292
Bacon, J. E. 13:8
Bacon, Jacob 17:151; 22:499
Bacon, James 15:332; 16:67; 19:53
Bacon, Jeremiah 22:240
Bacon, Joel M. 22:63
Bacon, John 9:74; 15:29; 26:11
Bacon, L. 14:33
Bacon, L. L. 1:13
Bacon, Leander 13:8
Bacon, Lewellen 17:396
Bacon, Melvin C. 22:135
Bacon, Oscar E. 19:3
Bacon, P. 14:137
Bacon, Roswell 25:283
Bacon, S. 27:15
Bacon, Samuel 9:203; 14:286
Bacon, William B. 7:19; 14:336
Bacon, William F. 23:276
Bacus, George S. 22:63
Bad, Elias 8:8
Badagan, John 20:201
Badagen, John 10:39
Badd, P. 11:138
Badder, Abraham 17:62
Badder, William 20:201
Baddorf, P. 1:110
Baden, Albert 22:329
Baden, Augustus 15:29
Baden, William 8:8; 18:120
Badenborough, John 17:75
Badenschwartz, B. 16:170
Badenshritz, B. 13:61
Bader, Alonzo 13:104
Bader, Henry 15:357; 19:53
Bader, Marion C. 13:104
Bader, Mathew 19:317
Bader, William 10:39
Badfield, I. 15:181
Badge, O. 15:53
Badgel, G. H. 12:150
Badger, H. 1:14
Badger, Henry 27:22
Badger, Hiram S. 17:17

Badger, J. C. 5:8; 25:138
Badger, John 21:297
Badger, L. B. 1:116
Badger, Oliver 12:66
Badger, P. 3:15
Badger, R. J. 1:114
Badger, Richon 9:157
Badger, Robert 9:218; 18:361
Badger, W. H. H. 25:15
Badger, Willard F. 11:99
Badger, William 14:34
Badger, Z. 14:28
Badgers, S. 19:285
Badgers, William W. 24:90
Badgert, S. 9:168
Badgett, C. 14:34
Badgley, D. 20:201
Badgley, George W. 12:12
Badgley, John 8:79
Badgley, Joseph 22:63
Badgley, William David 24:11
Badgley, William H. 7:85
Badgly, Josiah 17:278
Badgly, Newton 10:101; 20:201
Badgly, Robert 21:242
Badigan, John 14:137
Badin, N. C. L. 26:236
Badine, Sebastian 25:13
Badiner, --- 24:165
Badley, Erastus C. 16:20
Badley, Simon 9:74
Badley, Zach 18:391
Badman, William 4:8
Badsford, William H. 4:8
Baduine, Florence 19:222
Badwell, James 23:276
Bady, P. 25:14
Bady, Peter 2:7
Baeger, Conrad 21:134
Bael, E. S. 24:181
Baen, James 14:137
Baensan, P. A. 1:20
Baer, Franklin 11:23
Baerick, John F. 26:93
Baert, J. L. 1:20
Baetheman, Thomas 9:41
Baetman, Henry 16:277
Bagan, Joseph 13:8
Bagard, William D. 18:301
Bagby, John 20:4
Bagby, Peter 20:202
Bagby, W. 24:11
Bage, G. 13:79
Bagely, Daniel C. 11:53
Bagely, Frank 22:175
Bagely, J. W. 21:17

Bager, A. 1:18
Bagett, George W. 20:120
Bagg, Sheppard 11:115
Bagg, Wilford A. 11:319
Bagg, William J. 13:8
Baggaly, T. 3:15
Bagger, H. 20:55
Baggess, G. W. 11:22
Bagget, Campbell 22:499
Bagget, John 21:215
Baggewell, A. J. 9:115
Baggs, John C. 25:316
Bagle, Sanford 17:234
Bagles, Henry 11:123
Bagles, John 22:63
Bagley, A. 14:137
Bagley, A. J. 25:138
Bagley, Bernard 1:114
Bagley, C. 25:138
Bagley, Clement 21:297
Bagley, Francis 1:114
Bagley, George 22:329
Bagley, George F. 22:170
Bagley, George H. 7:73
Bagley, H. 3:15
Bagley, J. 16:287
Bagley, J. H. 25:292
Bagley, J. J. 19:53
Bagley, Jefferson 8:112
Bagley, Jeremiah 9:218;
    18:361
Bagley, John W. 4:8
Bagley, Lawrence 4:8
Bagley, Orlando 10:101;
    20:202
Bagley, Richard 1:114
Baglor, William 14:34
Bagnall, William 7:85
Bagnerd, S. F. 14:137
Bags, J. 16:138
Bagsby, John 12:47
Bagsley, A. M. 9:18
Bagten, J. W. 20:120
Bagunier, Fisher 15:13
Baguss, William 17:17
Bagwell, John 6:14; 18:76
Bagwell, Wiley 22:63
Bahen, F. 11:88
Bahill, J. Z. 11:298
Bahinger, George 16:20
Bahme, Henry 18:213
Bahn, Isaac 16:170
Bahn, William 3:15
Bahringer, George 13:8
Bai, H. B. 9:115
Baiard, Clinton L. 19:146
Baid, Benjamin F. 20:202
Baier, A. 2:8
Bail, Charles A. 25:14
Bail, F. 1:109
Bail, W. M. 1:111

Bailean, J. 14:4
Bailel, J. B. 22:350
Bailer, W. H. 14:137, 253
Bailes, Alexander 17:29
Bailes, John 10:13
Bailes, John B. 24:165
Bailess, William H. 22:63
Bailey, --- 18:187; 25:14
Bailey, --- H. G. 23:187
Bailey, A. 3:15; 13:104;
    21:297
Bailey, A. C. 18:228
Bailey, A. D. 3:15
Bailey, A. F. 2:8
Bailey, A. G. 19:225
Bailey, A. H. 16:362
Bailey, A. J. 1:113; 14:34;
    21:17; 22:473
Bailey, A. J. M. 1:115
Bailey, A. W. 3:15
Bailey, Addison D. 7:66
Bailey, Alanson 22:460
Bailey, Alfred 12:66;
    15:5; 17:234; 24:64
Bailey, Alonzo 7:117
Bailey, Amos 21:297
Bailey, Andrew 3:15;
    16:170
Bailey, Anson E. 21:250
Bailey, Auburn 14:137
Bailey, Augustus 11:291
Bailey, B. 12:81; 16:287
Bailey, B. C. 13:8
Bailey, Barney 11:410
Bailey, Barton 11:399
Bailey, Benjamin 13:56;
    14:137; 16:20;
    23:131
Bailey, Butler D. 10:39
Bailey, Buttor D. 20:202
Bailey, C. 1:111; 3:15;
    12:86; 16:287;
    20:144; 21:47
Bailey, C. C. 18:23
Bailey, C. E. 14:34
Bailey, C. M. 25:138
Bailey, Calvin G. 18:391
Bailey, Calvin S. 19:3
Bailey, Calwell 18:391
Bailey, Chaplin 17:421
Bailey, Charles 11:399;
    17:75, 404
Bailey, Charles H. 13:8;
    21:134
Bailey, D. 1:112
Bailey, D. F. 15:181
Bailey, D. W. 25:292
Bailey, Daniel W. 7:81
Bailey, David 7:85; 19:53
Bailey, David C. 10:101;
    20:202; 26:121

Bailey, David E. 9:41
Bailey, David M. 23:131
Bailey, Dick 6:22
Bailey, Dobson 22:349
Bailey, E. 1:17; 9:138;
    27:14
Bailey, E. M. 12:141;
    20:202
Bailey, E. S. 1:116
Bailey, E. W. 9:18
Bailey, Ed 17:267
Bailey, Edward 1:114
Bailey, Eleven 16:170
Bailey, Eli 23:284
Bailey, Enoch L. 20:110
Bailey, Enos D. 25:274
Bailey, Ezra 23:18
Bailey, F. 1:110; 3:15;
    21:297
Bailey, F. A. 1:110
Bailey, F. C. 17:392
Bailey, F. M. 3:15
Bailey, F. R. 20:202
Bailey, Francis A. 21:250
Bailey, Francis S. 22:19
Bailey, Frank 18:351
Bailey, G. 22:350; 24:169
Bailey, G. W. 1:115; 3:15;
    7:85; 12:150; 14:34;
    16:20, 170
Bailey, George 3:15; 13:8;
    16:20, 83; 17:434;
    21:297; 27:12
Bailey, George H. 10:7
Bailey, George S. 13:104
Bailey, George W. 13:8;
    15:171; 21:297
Bailey, Gilbert 10:101;
    20:202
Bailey, H. 15:29
Bailey, H. G. 22:469
Bailey, H. H. 15:157
Bailey, H. N. 15:150
Bailey, H. W. 12:141
Bailey, Harrison 20:202
Bailey, Henry 6:28
Bailey, Henry J. 20:202
Bailey, Hignac L. 22:240
Bailey, Horace 15:157
Bailey, Hugh 13:8
Bailey, I. A. 11:421
Bailey, Ira K. 4:8
Bailey, Isaac C. 8:79
Bailey, Isaac E. 11:123
Bailey, Isaiah 19:3
Bailey, J. 1:20, 116; 3:15;
    8:45; 13:103; 14:34;
    16:170; 23:312;
    25:138
Bailey, J. E. 1:112; 9:74;
    16:89; 19:53

Bailey, J. F. 3:15; 15:302
Bailey, J. J. 3:15
Bailey, J. L. 1:111
Bailey, J. M. 14:34; 24:73
Bailey, J. R. 9:107
Bailey, J. V. 11:339
Bailey, J. W. 10:26;
    19:299
Bailey, Jackson 11:196
Bailey, Jacob 17:47
Bailey, James 1:16; 3:15;
    5:35, 49; 7:19, 117;
    8:79; 9:128; 10:39;
    15:267; 20:202;
    22:231, 240; 23:59;
    25:287; 27:17
Bailey, James C. 22:19
Bailey, James D. 18:76
Bailey, James E. 17:348
Bailey, James H. 1:13;
    8:79; 23:18
Bailey, James M. 22:400
Bailey, John 1:18; 3:15;
    4:8; 9:11; 16:170;
    18:430; 22:63;
    25:138
Bailey, John A. 21:297
Bailey, John C. 4:8
Bailey, John D. 22:240
Bailey, John F. 4:8;
    16:170
Bailey, John P. 21:297
Bailey, John W. 13:8
Bailey, Jonathan 8:45;
    21:250
Bailey, Joseph 1:115;
    8:79; 9:115; 16:130;
    23:59; 25:138
Bailey, Joseph N. 23:131
Bailey, Joseph W. 27:11
Bailey, Joshua 17:392
Bailey, Joshua M. 27:12
Bailey, Judson D. 10:39;
    20:202
Bailey, L. 3:15
Bailey, Larey 11:409
Bailey, Leander J. 24:90
Bailey, Lucian 25:138
Bailey, Lucien 5:49
Bailey, Marion 17:47
Bailey, Marshall 11:197
Bailey, Martin I. 7:85
Bailey, Martin V. 23:131
Bailey, McConnell 8:79
Bailey, Minor D. 23:118
Bailey, Monroe 17:127;
    24:188
Bailey, Moses 17:191
Bailey, N. J. 26:204
Bailey, Nathanial 19:3

Bailey, Nelson 10:39;
    20:202
Bailey, Norman 17:241
Bailey, O. F. 25:13
Bailey, Orson H. 10:204
Bailey, P. 3:15; 11:299
Bailey, P. D. 15:181
Bailey, Palmer A. 21:220
Bailey, Perry T. 11:52
Bailey, Peter 7:117
Bailey, Philander 9:18;
    18:301; 26:92
Bailey, R. 3:15; 11:257;
    16:170
Bailey, R. H. 11:421
Bailey, R. J. 14:34
Bailey, Ransom 11:103
Bailey, Reuben 13:61;
    16:170
Bailey, Reuben E. 20:94
Bailey, Richard 6:15;
    11:197, 383; 17:108;
    18:76; 22:240
Bailey, Robert 9:205;
    10:101; 14:137;
    20:202
Bailey, Romangs J. E.
    17:62
Bailey, Rowland S.
    16:287
Bailey, S. 26:10
Bailey, S. M. 14:34
Bailey, S. T. 3:15
Bailey, S. W. 19:272
Bailey, Samuel A. 21:297
Bailey, Samuel M. 8:8;
    18:120
Bailey, Stephen 9:74;
    14:137
Bailey, Stephen A. 4:8;
    10:13
Bailey, Sylvester 23:131
Bailey, T. 25:14
Bailey, Thaddeus L. 21:15
Bailey, Thomas 8:77, 79;
    15:157; 21:297;
    26:216
Bailey, Thomas A. 21:220
Bailey, Thomas M. 26:217
Bailey, Tilsford 21:297
Bailey, W. 1:112; 3:15;
    9:68
Bailey, W. H. 4:8; 22:472;
    25:138
Bailey, W. L. 18:102
Bailey, W. S. 9:41
Bailey, William 11:421;
    15:90, 101; 16:20,
    131; 17:191, 258;
    20:4; 22:240
Bailey, William A. 1:17

Bailey, William B. 22:240
Bailey, William H. 12:80;
    17:234; 22:116;
    26:217
Bailey, William L. 14:34
Bailey, William S. 9:168
Bailey, William W.
    14:137
Bailiey, Samuel 15:181
Bailiff, Henry H. 23:59
Bailling, James 11:420
Bails, William 22:240
Baily, C. 16:287
Baily, Edwin 1:16
Baily, Gaines 22:288
Baily, James 22:288
Baily, James C. 14:336
Baily, James E. 7:14
Baily, John 3:15
Baily, Stiles M. 22:116
Baimon, James 7:19
Bain, A. 21:203
Bain, A. F. 19:247
Bain, Andrew F. 9:168
Bain, D. F. M. 21:17
Bain, F. 15:297
Bain, Feston 18:76
Bain, Foster 6:15
Bain, G. 3:15
Bain, George F. 23:59
Bain, H. W. 21:17
Bain, Henry 14:294;
    17:480; 27:21
Bain, J. A. 14:137
Bain, J. W. 18:417
Bain, John 9:74; 10:39;
    12:171; 18:391;
    26:11
Bain, Joshua 12:121;
    15:117
Bain, R. I. 26:92
Bain, R. J. 9:18; 18:301
Bain, Sylvester 18:391
Bain, William 16:131;
    19:3
Bain, William J. 19:53
Bainbridge, J. 1:17;
    16:116
Bainbridge, John 22:63
Baine, E. 14:34
Baine, Enoch F. 24:47
Baine, F. 16:170
Baine, H. 1:111; 3:15
Baine, James 18:23
Baine, John 18:23
Baine, Patrick 18:107
Bainer, D. W. 17:275
Baines, Henry 21:250
Baines, John 18:301
Baines, Samuel 6:24
Baines, Thomas H. 12:58

Baines, William 14:137
Bainford, Luke 10:39;
    20:202
Bainhart, Martin 19:3
Bainly, William M. 20:4
Bains, James A. 23:18
Bains, R. 14:137
Bainter, Philip 22:175
Bair, Abraham K. 23:84
Bair, Cyrus H. 24:35
Bair, Finley 17:29
Bair, Joel S. 24:73
Bair, John 25:138
Bair, John G. 3:15
Bair, N. T. 4:8
Baird, Abel 22:400
Baird, Andrew 4:8
Baird, B. F. 10:101
Baird, Charles H. 17:161
Baird, Charles R. 20:142
Baird, Clinton L. 10:171
Baird, Curtis 11:24
Baird, D. 14:34
Baird, D. W. 23:131
Baird, Elias 11:50
Baird, Emery C. 11:285
Baird, Felix W. 23:131
Baird, Francis 5:8
Baird, G. 11:230
Baird, George C. 16:362
Baird, Henry 6:29; 25:316
Baird, J. 1:16; 3:15
Baird, J. F. 21:203
Baird, J. W. 26:150
Baird, James 14:138
Baird, James A. 11:53
Baird, John 15:333;
    18:361; 19:53;
    22:474
Baird, John P. 22:400
Baird, John W. 9:48
Baird, L. L. 16:81
Baird, M. E. 14:294;
    17:480; 27:20
Baird, Maurice B. 11:123
Baird, Miles 22:447
Baird, Robert B. 10:13
Baird, Samuel 8:45;
    11:285
Baird, Smith 14:314, 320
Baird, Smith H. 23:131
Baird, T. 19:53
Baird, Thomas 23:187
Baird, Thomas R. 23:18
Baird, Warren 8:8; 18:120
Baird, William 11:134;
    21:129; 22:135
Baird, William E. 8:8
Bairden, William 11:52
Bais, Mack 8:37; 26:150

Baisaubler, Martin J.
    16:65
Baise, John 22:507
Baisinger, Reuben 11:52
Baisley, A. 14:34
Baisley, Ash 14:27
Baisly, William D. 22:19
Baisor, John 15:325;
    19:53
Baiston, --- 8:45
Baite, John 8:102
Baiter, G. 3:15
Baites, Robert 14:138
Baithwait, Charles B.
    11:189
Baize, --- 16:170
Baizer, Fred 6:29
Bakann, Samuel S. 21:63
Bakcman, John 18:228
Bake, Horace O. 12:98
Bake, W. H. 14:138
Bakell, G. H. 18:187
Bakeman, A. 13:126
Bakeman, Charles 13:61
Bakeman, J. 1:18
Baken, J. 3:16
Baker, --- 11:278; 15:21,
    181; 16:287; 18:23,
    102; 19:3, 53; 24:109
Baker, A. 1:110; 3:15, 16;
    11:102; 14:138, 253;
    15:325; 17:153, 278;
    19:53; 24:11; 27:11
Baker, A. B. 4:9
Baker, A. S. 14:34
Baker, A. T. 21:297
Baker, A. W. 3:15
Baker, Able 8:79
Baker, Abner 12:12
Baker, Abraham N.
    21:297
Baker, Albert 8:8; 11:103;
    15:62; 18:120
Baker, Albert M. 18:12
Baker, Albert T. 9:212
Baker, Alfred 17:127
Baker, Allen 12:47; 17:17
Baker, Alonzo 11:53
Baker, Alred 25:138
Baker, Alvah 19:53
Baker, Alverton 20:188
Baker, Amos 4:9; 9:74;
    19:3; 26:11
Baker, Anderson 4:9
Baker, Andrew 4:9; 10:39,
    101; 14:138; 20:202;
    22:288
Baker, Anthony 21:264
Baker, Anton 7:85
Baker, Artem 13:8
Baker, Arthur 16:170

Baker, Artist 18:76
Baker, Asa T. 17:287
Baker, Ashton 11:14
Baker, August 1:15
Baker, B. 1:112; 14:34
Baker, B. A. 1:17
Baker, B. B. 26:152
Baker, B. H. 3:16
Baker, B. L. 9:74; 26:10
Baker, Benjamin I. 20:202
Baker, Benjamin J. 10:39
Baker, Benjamin R.
    18:411
Baker, C. 14:4; 18:102;
    25:138
Baker, C. C. 8:45; 10:204
Baker, C. G. 23:201
Baker, C. H. 11:21; 27:23
Baker, C. M. 9:107
Baker, C. W. 14:34, 132,
    263
Baker, Carlo 18:12
Baker, Cato 7:117
Baker, Channcy 18:337
Baker, Charles 3:15; 5:8;
    8:79; 9:115; 11:136,
    383; 12:47; 15:101,
    181, 262; 16:145;
    20:50, 144; 21:297;
    27:19
Baker, Charles C. 23:187
Baker, Charles H. 8:79,
    112; 17:98; 22:135
Baker, Charles I. 23:244
Baker, Charles O. 17:75
Baker, Charles P. 9:74;
    26:12
Baker, Charles S. 13:8
Baker, Chauncey 9:101
Baker, Chauncy C. 7:66
Baker, Christian 21:220
Baker, Christopher C.
    21:250
Baker, Cladius 9:115
Baker, Clark 17:169
Baker, Claudius 27:19
Baker, Columbus 22:416
Baker, Cornelius 6:15;
    18:77
Baker, Curtis L. 21:17
Baker, Cyrus 9:101;
    18:337; 20:202
Baker, Cyrus C. 14:138
Baker, D. 11:51; 22:289
Baker, D. B. 1:19; 9:139
Baker, D. D. 25:310
Baker, D. H. 7:19
Baker, D. J. 14:34
Baker, Daniel D. 23:177
Baker, Daniel W. 11:384

Baker, David 8:45, 79, 112; 9:18; 12:12; 18:301; 21:17; 22:19, 64, 288; 23:243; 26:92
Baker, David A. 23:59
Baker, David C. 20:182; 21:63; 24:73
Baker, David E. 8:45
Baker, David H. 17:75
Baker, Decane 14:336
Baker, DeW. 1:110
Baker, Dowling 23:131
Baker, E. 3:15; 10:26, 39; 14:28, 34; 19:235; 20:202; 21:297; 23:201; 25:138
Baker, E. E. 3:16
Baker, Edmund C. 20:103
Baker, Edward 5:8; 10:156; 15:171; 19:3, 146; 21:297
Baker, Edward M. 20:47
Baker, Eli 23:131
Baker, Eli S. 5:8
Baker, Elijah 3:15; 10:101; 20:202
Baker, Elijah M. 22:64
Baker, Ephraim M. 24:11
Baker, Ephriam 16:287
Baker, Ernest 9:74
Baker, F. 3:15; 7:19; 21:297
Baker, F. H. 17:337
Baker, Fieman 11:136
Baker, Francis 4:9
Baker, Francis M. 11:399; 15:181; 22:19
Baker, Frank 3:15; 17:169; 26:144
Baker, Frank H. K. 8:79
Baker, Frank N. 17:358
Baker, Fred 19:53; 24:165
Baker, Frederic 11:89
Baker, Frederick 6:22; 22:473
Baker, Frederick W. 19:3
Baker, Freeman 24:11
Baker, G. 8:45; 13:83; 16:170; 18:361, 424; 26:153; 27:16
Baker, G. W. 10:39; 15:181; 17:153; 20:202
Baker, George 9:139, 218; 14:138; 15:181; 16:89, 170; 17:17; 19:3; 20:94; 21:118; 22:511; 23:105; 25:138; 27:13

Baker, George A. 9:115; 22:176; 27:19
Baker, George B. 1:17
Baker, George M. 4:9; 14:34
Baker, George Q. 21:297
Baker, George S. 20:4
Baker, George W. 8:79; 9:115; 26:210; 27:19
Baker, Gilford D. 16:20
Baker, Girard 23:187
Baker, H. 17:62; 27:23
Baker, H. A. 15:334; 19:53
Baker, H. C. 21:17
Baker, H. F. 15:157
Baker, H. H. 16:170; 25:138
Baker, H. I. 27:16
Baker, H. J. 9:139
Baker, H. L. 11:137, 189
Baker, H. S. 27:13
Baker, Haden 17:127; 24:189
Baker, Hamilton G. 21:220
Baker, Harris 15:29
Baker, Harry 19:147
Baker, Harward A. 16:20
Baker, Hazel 22:64
Baker, Henry 1:14, 113; 3:15; 10:145, 156; 16:287; 17:98; 19:147; 22:64, 135, 175; 23:59, 262; 26:151
Baker, Henry C. 20:102
Baker, Henry J. 11:51
Baker, Henry L. 11:410
Baker, Henry M. 23:59
Baker, Herman 9:115; 27:11
Baker, Horace A. 13:8
Baker, I. W. 3:16
Baker, Inston C. 8:8
Baker, Ira 3:16
Baker, Isaac 1:13; 3:15, 16
Baker, Isaac N. 23:59
Baker, Isaac P. 22:176
Baker, Isaac S. 17:346
Baker, J. 1:116; 3:15, 16; 10:192; 12:98; 13:61; 14:138; 15:5, 101; 16:170; 17:435; 19:247; 21:118; 23:245, 281; 24:176; 25:138
Baker, J. A. 27:13, 15
Baker, J. B. 8:70; 27:16, 23

Baker, J. C. 5:8; 25:138
Baker, J. D. 3:15
Baker, J. G. 3:16
Baker, J. M. 14:294; 17:480; 27:21
Baker, J. N. 14:277
Baker, J. P. 9:18
Baker, J. R. 22:175
Baker, J. S. 14:287; 15:80
Baker, J. W. 8:79; 11:83; 23:261
Baker, Jacob 15:83; 21:297; 24:11; 25:138
Baker, James 3:16; 8:70; 9:46; 14:138; 18:391; 19:328; 20:144, 202; 21:200; 22:176; 26:121
Baker, James A. 1:18
Baker, James B. 10:39; 11:53
Baker, James C. 8:8; 18:120
Baker, James H. 22:63; 26:152
Baker, James M. 11:180
Baker, James R. 10:156; 19:147
Baker, Jason C. 23:131
Baker, Jerry 11:197
Baker, Jesse W. 22:240
Baker, John 1:13, 16; 3:15, 16; 5:8; 9:157; 10:156; 11:102, 237, 384; 12:66; 14:138, 264; 15:53, 62; 17:47; 19:147; 21:63, 297; 22:135, 175, 288; 24:11; 25:15, 138
Baker, John A. 10:101; 20:202
Baker, John C. 10:101; 15:181; 20:202
Baker, John D. 21:63
Baker, John E. 13:134; 19:346
Baker, John G. 6:14; 18:77
Baker, John H. 15:181; 22:474
Baker, John J. 23:119
Baker, John Julius 25:310
Baker, John S. 12:61; 23:95
Baker, John W. 7:85; 14:34; 18:213; 19:3
Baker, Joseph 5:35; 9:138; 11:136; 13:8; 18:228; 19:3, 147;

Baker, Joseph 21:96; 22:240; 23:131; 27:14
Baker, Joshua 10:101; 20:202
Baker, Josiah 19:3
Baker, Julson C. 18:121
Baker, L. 1:13; 14:34; 18:228; 26:15
Baker, L. D. 6:29; 25:316
Baker, L. F. 1:96, 113
Baker, L. M. 14:138
Baker, Levi 11:90
Baker, Lewis 8:79; 11:133
Baker, Lewis A. 17:316
Baker, Lewis J. 22:64
Baker, Lewis L. 12:12
Baker, M. 3:16; 6:29; 12:61; 13:61; 15:62, 157
Baker, M. A. 3:16
Baker, M. G. 12:85; 16:287
Baker, Marion M. 15:62
Baker, Martin 17:231; 18:228; 26:16
Baker, Michael 17:254
Baker, Milan 11:136
Baker, Milford 8:102
Baker, Milo 20:91
Baker, Milton 26:236
Baker, Monroe J. 13:104
Baker, Moses W. 7:55
Baker, N. 14:320; 22:176
Baker, N. S. 14:4
Baker, Narus S. 11:24
Baker, Nathaniel 8:79
Baker, Nerson 16:170
Baker, Newell 10:152; 18:44
Baker, Nicholas 12:63; 17:161, 399
Baker, Noah 14:314; 19:3
Baker, O. G. 14:250
Baker, O. S. 26:121
Baker, Orin 9:101
Baker, Orington L. 4:9
Baker, Oscar 9:18; 18:301; 26:92
Baker, Othello S. 9:41
Baker, Owen 21:47
Baker, P. 1:19; 7:85; 27:20
Baker, P. H. 11:299
Baker, P. R. 14:239; 27:24
Baker, P. S. 19:247
Baker, Peter 9:157; 10:13; 22:176, 276; 23:131, 308; 27:22
Baker, Peter S. 9:168

Baker, Peter W. 22:111
Baker, Philip 7:85; 8:45; 24:11
Baker, Philo S. 23:177
Baker, Porter 22:289
Baker, Prescott 12:12
Baker, R. 1:96; 15:289; 16:170; 23:132
Baker, R. H. 26:10
Baker, R. W. 9:229; 20:202
Baker, Reuben W. 9:11
Baker, Richard 7:55; 14:1; 17:358
Baker, Richard T. 22:276
Baker, Robert 8:117; 9:168; 13:129; 17:144; 19:273; 20:4
Baker, Robert H. 9:74
Baker, Robert W. 1:16
Baker, Roger 11:51
Baker, Roland T. 10:156; 19:147
Baker, Rufus 26:151
Baker, Runnell 18:12
Baker, S. 17:295; 21:118, 207
Baker, S. B. 21:207
Baker, S. M. 25:18
Baker, Samuel 10:13; 20:4; 23:177
Baker, Sandy 9:128; 27:17
Baker, Sarah A. 1:96
Baker, Solomon 7:55; 18:420
Baker, Stephen 11:52; 13:61; 15:53
Baker, Sylvester 24:109
Baker, T. 14:294; 17:475; 27:21
Baker, T. B. 23:258
Baker, T. W. 3:15
Baker, Theodore 21:165
Baker, Thomas 3:15; 4:9; 8:61; 22:63, 240
Baker, Thomas B. 9:74; 26:10
Baker, Thomas P. 11:134
Baker, Thomas S. F. 7:85
Baker, Thomas W. 17:409; 22:19
Baker, Tim Brock 11:399
Baker, U. 23:18
Baker, Uriah 9:218; 18:361
Baker, V. 14:138, 253
Baker, W. 1:14; 10:185; 13:61; 14:138; 16:170; 18:24, 171; 19:147
Baker, W. A. 1:20

Baker, W. C. 3:16
Baker, W. F. 19:3
Baker, W. G. 18:337
Baker, W. H. 18:24; 27:19
Baker, W. L. 9:68; 22:240
Baker, W. M. 14:34
Baker, W. R. 25:278
Baker, W. W. 14:138
Baker, Walter 22:400
Baker, Walton 22:507
Baker, Warren 4:9
Baker, Wiley 23:59
Baker, Willard 15:181
Baker, William 1:116; 3:15, 16; 7:85; 9:11, 41, 168; 11:198, 428; 13:8; 14:138; 16:170; 20:202; 21:9, 63, 297; 22:64, 135, 176; 26:121; 27:22
Baker, William C. 22:116
Baker, William D. 10:89
Baker, William E. 17:278
Baker, William H. 8:8; 9:115; 18:121; 22:288
Baker, William M. 22:64
Baker, William R. 17:246; 27:21
Baker, William S. 22:164
Baker, William W. 24:64
Baker, Willis 18:301; 26:93
Baker, Wincen 8:8
Baker, Wineed 18:121
Baker, Z. 3:16
Baker, Zachariah 8:8; 22:64
Baker, Zackamial 18:121
Bakers, Joseph P. 3:16
Bakes, William 21:297
Baket, Rufus 8:37
Bakewell, G. 11:278
Bakke, Ole O. 24:90
Bakley, A. 17:127; 24:187
Bal, Christian 26:216
Bal, Samuel 16:171
Balander, James 16:171
Balaney, August 6:12
Balb, Horatio 26:151
Balbridge, David 13:9
Balby, F. C. 16:171
Balby, Simon P. 11:23
Balcan, D. 3:16
Balch, A. 7:66
Balch, Alex. H. 24:11
Balch, Columbus 10:101; 20:202
Balch, Edward W. 17:266
Balch, Ezra W. 1:15
Balch, John E. 10:94

Balch, John F. 23:240
Balch, Judson 13:9
Balch, Myron 11:102
Balch, Samuel 10:39; 20:202
Balch, Young M. 21:250
Balciger, Christopher 11:297
Balcolm, Justus A. 22:135
Balcom, A. S. 15:2
Balcom, Barney H. 10:147; 18:44
Balcom, George 24:91
Balcom, H. H. 23:132
Balcom, Hiram G. 26:149
Balcom, Marton S. 10:13
Balcomb, --- 3:16
Balcon, Hiram G. 8:8
Balcors, Anson S. 12:66
Bald, J. H. 14:34
Baldan, S. 5:8
Baldaux, John 7:85
Baldeck, David W. 21:96
Balden, Francis 12:66; 15:80
Balden, Samuel 12:12
Balder, Christian 16:146
Balder, Joseph 19:269
Balders, Jacob 10:39; 20:202
Balderson, R. 26:152
Balderson, Robert 8:61
Baldes, Joaquin 12:171
Baldey, Edgar A. 17:241
Balding, Jackson 9:32
Baldman, L. 14:138
Baldman, S. 14:253
Baldock, John T. 17:47
Baldree, Richard 10:156; 19:147
Baldridge, Ebenezer 10:101; 20:203
Baldridge, Holmes 22:19
Baldridge, Robert H. 21:96
Baldridge, Samuel 21:63
Baldridge, Samuel R. 22:19
Baldrie, L. 19:147
Baldt, Henry 10:101; 20:203
Baldwin, --- 9:153
Baldwin, A. 1:112; 3:16; 13:83; 24:109
Baldwin, A. D. 14:34
Baldwin, A. G. 19:147
Baldwin, A. H. 3:16; 20:203
Baldwin, A. W. 14:138
Baldwin, Abraham 21:146, 210

Baldwin, Alexander T. 22:496
Baldwin, Alfred 22:136
Baldwin, Alfred A. 10:39
Baldwin, Amos 21:47
Baldwin, B. B. 13:8
Baldwin, Benedict 6:15; 18:77
Baldwin, Bruce 9:139; 27:14
Baldwin, Byron 11:399
Baldwin, C. 3:16; 19:53
Baldwin, C. E. 19:147
Baldwin, C. W. 21:297
Baldwin, Charles 8:102; 15:181; 18:63, 187, 228; 25:13; 26:14
Baldwin, Charles K. 11:83
Baldwin, Chauncy 10:156
Baldwin, D. 8:45
Baldwin, Daniel 22:400
Baldwin, David 10:39; 20:203
Baldwin, E. 5:35; 25:138
Baldwin, E. T. 13:104
Baldwin, Elisha 21:297
Baldwin, Ervine S. 22:136
Baldwin, Franklin 22:447, 472
Baldwin, G. 3:16
Baldwin, G. M. 23:18
Baldwin, George 3:16; 21:298; 22:64; 25:138
Baldwin, George L. 16:81
Baldwin, George S. 5:8
Baldwin, George W. 19:3, 147
Baldwin, H. 1:110
Baldwin, H. C. 17:165
Baldwin, H. G. 1:19
Baldwin, Ira 10:13
Baldwin, J. 1:110; 13:83; 14:4; 25:138
Baldwin, J. A. 4:9
Baldwin, J. B. 14:138, 253
Baldwin, J. C. 2:7; 24:99
Baldwin, J. M. 8:61; 22:176
Baldwin, J. S. 4:9
Baldwin, J. W. 3:16; 19:273
Baldwin, James 5:8; 6:29; 8:102; 20:203; 21:63; 24:47; 25:316
Baldwin, James A. 22:518
Baldwin, James H. 9:164; 13:134; 19:346
Baldwin, James R. 17:442; 24:156

Baldwin, Jason 8:45; 21:134
Baldwin, Jerome 13:8
Baldwin, Jesse 22:472
Baldwin, John 10:101; 11:257; 15:182; 20:203; 22:64
Baldwin, John C. 22:240
Baldwin, John W. 9:168
Baldwin, Joseph 1:15; 10:39; 12:98; 20:203
Baldwin, Julian 27:15
Baldwin, Kipps 23:18
Baldwin, L. A. 3:16
Baldwin, L. J. 9:235; 26:216
Baldwin, Louis M. 10:13
Baldwin, Lucas M. 23:84
Baldwin, Luserne 16:20
Baldwin, Luzerne 13:8
Baldwin, M. 14:34; 21:184; 24:35; 26:216
Baldwin, M. L. 17:336
Baldwin, Moses P. 16:81
Baldwin, N. 3:16
Baldwin, O. 1:109
Baldwin, P. 14:138
Baldwin, R. C. 11:122
Baldwin, R. L. 13:104
Baldwin, Randall 21:264
Baldwin, Reuben W. 17:358
Baldwin, Richard W. 5:8
Baldwin, Samuel 7:138
Baldwin, Stephen 13:8; 16:89
Baldwin, T. 18:77
Baldwin, T. H. 21:203
Baldwin, T. P. 8:102
Baldwin, Thomas 3:16; 10:94; 11:138; 19:3
Baldwin, Thomas H. 6:10
Baldwin, Thomas J. 20:203
Baldwin, Tracy 22:136
Baldwin, V. B. 26:12
Baldwin, Vincent 22:289
Baldwin, W. 3:16; 11:331
Baldwin, William 21:298; 22:240, 400
Baldwin, William F. 16:83
Baldwin, William H. 1:116
Baldwin, Willis A. 7:19
Bale, J. G. 15:80
Bale, John 17:17
Bale, Lewis 8:59; 19:277
Bale, Reuben V. 17:351
Bale, W. 9:48
Bale, W. H. 7:73

Bale, William 18:391
Baleham, Milton 21:298
Balem, E. 15:182
Balen, James W. 11:50
Balenbaugh, John 11:136
Balenger, David 17:442
Balenger, John B. 24:35
Balentine, A. J. 19:54;
    26:236
Balentine, James 20:21
Balerawter, James 14:138
Bales, Amer J. 22:64
Bales, Curtis 18:391
Bales, D. G. 11:133
Bales, F. 14:138
Bales, Franklin 8:79
Bales, G. W. 3:16
Bales, George 11:420;
    16:135
Bales, Harvey 22:240
Bales, Henry 3:16
Bales, Isaac 11:420;
    22:417
Bales, J. 11:399
Bales, Jacob 11:325
Bales, James W. 23:18
Bales, John 11:134
Bales, John W. 14:138
Bales, Lee 8:8
Bales, Noah 22:19
Bales, P. 3:16
Bales, Thomas L. 14:286
Bales, Toliver 22:240
Baley, Cornelius S.
    16:151
Baley, E. 3:16
Baley, Edward 11:197
Baley, George 21:220
Baley, J. 14:4; 16:266
Baley, J. W. 12:85;
    16:287
Baley, James 18:24;
    21:264
Baley, James A. 15:117
Baley, James W. 24:107
Baley, John W. 16:277
Baley, Joseph 25:18
Baley, Silas 19:337
Baley, Stephen 22:135
Balf, Hugh 14:34
Balf, Malcom C. 21:298
Balfour, Harrison M.
    22:460
Balfour, J. 20:55
Balger, J. 22:116
Balgreat, B. 9:107
Balhill, Isaac 8:79
Baliff, Eugene 13:9; 16:20
Balinear, David 24:156
Baling, Christian 10:34
Baling, James 14:286

Baliorn, B. 9:139
Balis, Thomas 3:16
Balis, W. H. 19:54
Balis, W. H. H. 15:291
Balistri, Louis 22:240
Balka, Earnest 26:10
Balke, H. 13:79; 16:171
Balke, Henry L. 12:7
Balkey, Joseph 9:205
Ball, --- 11:236
Ball, A. 9:168; 17:246;
    21:165; 23:201;
    25:138
Ball, A. J. 1:113
Ball, Aaron 9:74; 12:161;
    26:11
Ball, Alexander 8:102
Ball, Andrew 5:8
Ball, Anthony 21:146
Ball, Augustus 1:114
Ball, Azra M. 23:18
Ball, Charles 16:171
Ball, Charles A. 15:182
Ball, Charles J. 17:246
Ball, Charles M. 19:54
Ball, D. M. 20:203
Ball, Daniel 3:16; 9:115;
    27:18
Ball, E. W. 13:104
Ball, Edward 12:47;
    23:119
Ball, Elias 18:121
Ball, Enoch 10:101;
    20:203
Ball, F. M. 19:235
Ball, George 12:47
Ball, Green B. 20:120
Ball, Gustavus 22:330
Ball, H. 3:16
Ball, H. A. 3:16
Ball, H. H. 25:138
Ball, Henry C. 16:83
Ball, Henry H. 5:35
Ball, Herman 24:90
Ball, Hiram 23:15
Ball, Isaac 7:19; 11:325;
    14:333; 21:220
Ball, Isaac M. 7:19
Ball, J. 3:16; 18:362
Ball, J. A. 24:73
Ball, J. H. 18:44
Ball, J. M. 3:16
Ball, Jabez B. 15:85
Ball, James 19:316
Ball, Jasper 9:218
Ball, John 1:17; 9:74;
    13:8; 22:64
Ball, John C. 15:53
Ball, John D. 23:59
Ball, John E. 7:85
Ball, John G. 15:182

Ball, John W. 22:517
Ball, Joseph 26:10
Ball, L. 3:16
Ball, L. H. 21:298
Ball, Levi 19:147
Ball, Martin V. 17:93
Ball, Morgan 21:264
Ball, Newton 17:275
Ball, P. 3:16
Ball, Peter 1:18
Ball, S. A. 8:112
Ball, S. O. 9:48
Ball, Samuel 11:197
Ball, Shadrack 7:85
Ball, Sylvester B. 13:83
Ball, Thomas 7:85; 9:18;
    18:301; 26:92; 27:21
Ball, W. 3:16; 22:176
Ball, W. H. 25:292
Ball, William 15:150;
    20:16; 21:298;
    22:350
Ball, William B. 12:58
Ball, Z. M. 18:274
Ball, Zack 15:182
Ball, Zephaniah 22:116
Ballad, Evan 4:9
Ballantine, D. 1:115
Ballantine, Robert 3:16
Ballard, Absalom 8:79
Ballard, Albert 8:8;
    16:171; 26:149
Ballard, Alvin 11:22
Ballard, Arthur M. 10:171
Ballard, B. F. 1:116
Ballard, Benjamin F.
    22:417
Ballard, C. B. 1:113
Ballard, Charles 16:138
Ballard, Charles W.
    17:262
Ballard, Daniel 9:128;
    27:17
Ballard, David J. 20:177
Ballard, E. L. 13:61;
    19:54
Ballard, E. N. 9:168;
    19:247
Ballard, Frank 19:54
Ballard, Franklin 15:53
Ballard, George 17:169;
    22:240
Ballard, George W.
    22:240
Ballard, H. 11:19
Ballard, Hudson 17:169
Ballard, J. 12:94; 15:357;
    17:153; 19:54
Ballard, James 22:64;
    25:13
Ballard, James H. 23:255

Ballard, James M. 17:93
Ballard, Jeff 4:64
Ballard, Joel 22:19
Ballard, John 18:187;
   21:63
Ballard, John H. 14:314
Ballard, Joseph 10:39;
   20:203
Ballard, Luther 11:135
Ballard, Martin H. 10:94
Ballard, Orrin 4:9
Ballard, R. B. 3:16
Ballard, Robert 13:9
Ballard, S. A. 5:49;
   25:138
Ballard, S. T. 25:14
Ballard, Simder 25:17
Ballard, Smith 17:191
Ballard, Thomas 24:88
Ballard, V. W. 1:13
Ballard, W. 8:45; 11:339;
   25:138
Ballard, Willard 21:250
Ballard, William 5:35;
   8:77; 11:258; 14:34
Ballard, William G. 22:64
Ballaw, Ambrose 22:64
Balldock, George 20:103
Balle, A. 19:243
Balled, Mose 17:454;
   24:189
Ballegas, Pedro 8:125
Ballegos, --- 12:61
Ballely, Edmund S. 9:115
Ballen, A. G. 14:34
Ballen, Morris 17:169
Ballengell, Andrew D.
   19:3
Ballenger, Burrough
   21:184
Ballenger, E. 21:203
Ballenger, Israel 17:313
Ballenger, James 18:284;
   26:134
Ballenger, James C. 8:102
Ballentine, Samuel 22:64
Ballentine, Thomas 24:73
Balleony, John 15:62
Baller, Frank 21:298
Ballett, C. 19:289
Ballett, J. 3:16
Balletton, William 21:47
Ballew, Jacob S. 23:112
Ballew, Joseph 9:168
Ballew, Preston 17:47
Balley, Daniel 7:117
Ballhausen, J. C. E. 1:15
Ballhole, Christian 1:114
Ballhover, L. 27:16
Ballieu, J. 13:83
Balling, Michael 21:220

Ballinger, --- 19:54
Ballinger, A. 13:61
Ballinger, B. 1:112
Ballinger, Benjamin 13:9
Ballinger, David 26:12
Ballinger, Ebenezer 22:64
Ballinger, George 3:16
Ballinger, J. 16:171
Ballinger, John H. R.
   10:39; 20:203
Ballinger, John R. 12:12
Ballinger, Robert 3:16;
   22:473
Ballinger, William 22:64
Ballinger, William T.
   22:64
Ballingtane, Henry 22:499
Ballis, Moses 26:150
Balliss, David 14:35
Ballman, Christopher 8:79
Balloff, Christy 1:113
Ballon, Farnam 19:247
Ballon, George 21:298
Ballon, O. G. 12:86;
   16:287
Ballord, Eugene C. 19:325
Ballot, John 11:407
Ballou, D. M. 1:114
Ballou, David 9:41
Ballou, Edward B. 20:191
Ballou, George 7:83
Ballou, Henry H. 16:87
Ballou, R. 18:77
Ballou, S. W. 22:330
Ballou, William A. 19:3
Ballow, D. G. 14:250
Ballow, F. D. 7:55
Ballow, G. E. 1:115
Ballow, Joseph 24:73
Balls, Benjamin 16:20
Bally, Edward 22:289
Balmer, August 11:299
Balmer, Levi S. 12:58
Balmer, M. V. 14:35
Balmes, Joseph 16:143
Balmet, J. 3:16
Balmut, Ambrose 23:132
Balock, Sam 14:138
Balon, James A. 26:152
Balonfield, J. W. 14:35
Balsch, Judson 16:20
Balser, C. 20:131
Balser, Richard 20:203
Balser, Solomon 8:79
Balser, Thomas J. 20:94
Balsh, C. C. 27:11
Balsh, E. C. 1:113
Balsh, Eddy 27:15
Balshar, B. 9:168
Balshaw, B. 19:279
Balsinger, John 4:9

Balsley, Julius 1:115
Balsley, William 3:16
Balsmeyer, Henry 10:101;
   20:203
Balson, George W. 17:153
Balson, Henry 19:54
Balson, L. 3:16
Balst, Jacob 21:184
Balston, James 25:19
Balston, William 21:184
Balstrom, I. 14:138
Balstron, J. 3:16
Balter, J. 1:109
Balthropt, J. 22:289
Baltimore, William
   15:182
Baltin, John 22:176
Baltner, David F. 19:3
Balton, J. 16:266
Balton, M. 9:74
Balton, Nathan 8:102
Balturst, Aulis 8:79
Baltus, --- 18:462
Baltz, Peter 15:339
Baltzell, A. P. 20:182
Baltzell, J. L. 27:142
Baltzell, William B.
   18:362
Baltzer, J. A. 23:18
Balver, Riley 6:12
Baly, John M. 17:442;
   24:156
Balzar, William 7:19
Balzell, W. 27:142
Balzer, Richard 10:39
Bamaler, Charles 10:101
Bamat, J. 1:20
Bambeck, John 26:12
Bamberger, Joseph 11:117
Bambill, Benjamin 6:12
Bambrick, William 1:15
Bame, Isaac 17:93
Bamer, August 22:330
Bamer, Elijah 11:420
Bamer, Louis 22:289
Bamer, W. 16:266
Bames, N. R. 14:4
Bames, Tho. 20:203
Bamey, William 21:210
Bamhart, Robert M.
   10:39; 20:203
Bamhart, Samuel 7:66
Bamhill, Hamill J. 21:215
Bamhisell, M. J. 1:16
Bamis, Bantis 11:394
Bammon, J. 19:54
Bamrick, Patrick 1:16
Bams, --- 9:115
Bams, J. H. 20:203
Bamster, John 6:12
Bana, E. 25:316

Banaler, Charles 20:203
Banall, John 21:298
Banar, Ernest 21:298
Banard, --- 22:116
Banard, A. 14:35
Banbann, J. 27:15
Banbaugh, William 25:138
Banbria, Gabrill 16:171
Bance, Jacob H. 12:66
Bance, John H. 9:74; 26:11
Banchart, A. 16:266
Bancher, Henry 27:19
Bancho, William 12:12
Bancleaw, H. 9:48
Bancon, William A. 21:248
Bancourt, C. 1:16
Bancroft, --- 15:157
Bancroft, A. 20:203
Bancroft, A. H. 3:17
Bancroft, A. J. 15:62
Bancroft, Algernon 10:39
Bancroft, C. 14:35
Bancroft, C. H. 13:104
Bancroft, Charles 13:9
Bancroft, Conrad 5:8
Bancroft, Daniel 4:9
Bancroft, Edwin 12:150
Bancroft, F. 21:298
Bancroft, Henry 17:75
Bancroft, J. 1:93
Bancroft, J. H. 27:16
Bancroft, John 4:9
Bancroft, John H. 9:128
Bancroft, O. D. 10:192; 18:171
Bancroft, W. 1:14
Bancroft, William 19:54
Bancry, A. P. 13:61
Bancy, Jacob 17:108
Band, Harrison 19:247
Banden, Henry 19:147
Banden, William 21:200
Bander, John 7:117
Bander, William 21:9
Banders, Frank 9:71
Banderson, Jacob 11:52
Bandike, Simmean 9:218
Bandin, L. 15:182
Bandis, John C. 7:83
Bandley, A. C. 14:35
Bandole, Henry 17:358
Bandy, C. 16:171
Bandy, E. 14:138
Bandy, George 21:298
Bandy, Henry 6:20
Bandy, Yancy D. 17:47
Bane, A. J. 18:228; 26:15
Bane, George 24:11

Bane, Henry C. 14:138
Bane, S. 3:16; 15:63
Bane, W. M. 23:18
Bane, William B. 25:15
Baneard, J. 14:138
Baner, E. 16:113
Baner, George 1:20; 22:176
Baner, Jacob 11:133; 19:54
Baner, Louis 21:134
Baner, Martin 22:330
Baner, Solomon 9:115
Baner, Tobias 12:12
Banersfield, C. 22:8
Banes, A. 3:17
Banes, A. N. 21:17
Banes, E. H. 19:273
Banes, John 9:168; 19:269
Banes, R. D. 20:153
Banes, W. T. 23:18
Banetorn, David 23:105
Baney, Elias 11:135
Baney, George 3:17
Baney, Henry 3:17
Baney, J. 3:17
Banfield, T. C. 12:141
Banfield, William 17:234
Banfill, T. 1:110
Bang, Elias 10:101; 20:203
Bangarden, --- 16:266
Bangardner, B. 3:17
Bange, Henry 20:203
Bangerson, G. 25:316
Bangham, J. B. 1:19
Bangham, Zachariah M. 21:63
Banghart, J. 3:16
Bangle, J. 16:266
Bangle, Lewis 4:9
Bangs, Charles W. 17:241
Bangs, L. H. 1:17
Bangs, Luther W. 21:250
Bangs, R. 25:139
Bangs, William 10:39; 20:203
Bangs, William W. 13:104
Bangsley, A. 23:127
Bangson, C. 1:19
Banham, John W. 6:22
Banhard, David 17:153
Banhard, Joseph 24:12
Banin, L. 15:182
Banington, James 23:132
Baniser, L. 23:18
Banister, --- 18:77
Banister, Charles 4:9
Banister, D. F. 25:139
Banister, Daniel S. 5:8
Banister, Horatio 20:203

Banister, Nimrod 10:101; 20:203
Banister, Robert 22:517
Banister, William 8:70
Bank, George N. 15:63
Bank, Nathan 24:189
Bank, S. 26:14
Bank, Wilson 9:205
Banke, Benjamin 15:182
Banker, A. D. 13:61
Banker, D. 16:171
Banker, E. 27:13
Banker, J. M. 3:17
Banker, John 13:104
Banker, Thomas 9:101
Bankers, John 7:19
Bankert, William 14:138
Bankes, I. H. 1:109
Bankhard, J. 13:104
Bankhard, J. M. 16:171
Bankhead, George 7:117
Bankhead, H. C. (Mrs.) 18:440
Bankhead, Samuel 22:289
Bankman, Charles K. 19:4
Banks, Albert 16:171
Banks, Alfred 10:156; 19:147
Banks, Amos 13:56
Banks, Andrew 22:116
Banks, Andrew J. 22:64
Banks, Benton 21:184
Banks, Caesar 9:128; 27:17
Banks, Charles 7:117
Banks, David 23:10
Banks, E. E. 3:17
Banks, Edward A. 23:242
Banks, Elias H. 10:13
Banks, George 9:168; 19:273
Banks, George A. 10:39; 20:203
Banks, George W. 17:47; 20:94
Banks, Gordon 19:337
Banks, Henry 6:35; 9:205
Banks, Hugh 17:29
Banks, J. 8:45; 14:277; 23:103; 25:139
Banks, J. W. 1:15; 21:86
Banks, Jackson 21:264
Banks, James 16:171; 17:169
Banks, James L. 27:20
Banks, Jenkins 18:107
Banks, Jeremiah 14:139; 21:96
Banks, Jesse 10:101; 20:203

Banks, John 5:35; 18:228; 25:139; 26:13
Banks, John D. 22:64
Banks, John M. 20:120
Banks, Joseph S. 24:35
Banks, L. H. 1:18
Banks, Lewis 6:15, 22; 18:77
Banks, M. 21:146
Banks, Michael 9:74; 26:11
Banks, P. 16:171
Banks, P. W. 26:151
Banks, Philip 16:20
Banks, Robert E. 23:267
Banks, Spencer H. 20:105
Banks, Stephen 7:73; 24:100; 25:292
Banks, Uriah 17:161
Banks, W. 1:109
Banks, W. H. 22:64
Banks, Walter 9:128; 27:17
Banks, Wesley 17:271
Banks, William 15:339; 16:363; 22:240; 27:18
Banks, William C. 17:29
Bankston, James 18:121
Bankstone, James 8:8
Bankstone, John 8:8; 18:121
Bankstone, Robert 7:85
Banman, A. 10:40; 20:203
Banman, Anthony 10:39; 20:203
Banman, James 25:18
Banman, Lewis 20:203
Banman, Louis 10:40
Banman, Mathew 22:19
Bannahee, B. 18:204
Bannakendorf, B. 14:35
Bannam, H. 3:17
Bannders, --- 15:354
Bannen, M. 14:35
Bannenger, James M. 18:391
Banner, Frank 7:117
Banner, George 7:14
Banner, Henry 17:165
Banner, J. 3:17
Banner, James 4:64
Banner, M. 3:17
Banner, Walter 6:24
Bannes, James N. 12:171
Bannett, John 24:8
Bannett, T. 27:15
Banney, John 5:8; 25:139
Bannin, Daniel 17:75
Banning, Alex 9:48
Banning, Andrew 21:17

Banning, J. F. 3:17
Banning, John 6:22; 18:77
Banning, John L. 10:39; 20:203
Banning, Pinkney A. 22:164
Banninger, A. A. 21:17
Banninger, Andrew 10:39
Bannister, A. J. 14:35
Bannister, Charles 18:107
Bannister, E. W. 9:107
Bannister, Horatio 10:89
Bannister, James 22:330
Bannister, William 10:101; 20:203
Bannon, Edward 1:115
Bannon, Rufus 26:16
Bannon, Shadrach 4:64
Bannon, T. B. 20:132
Bannyer, F. 3:17
Banock, William H. 18:301
Banous, Samuel 14:139
Banrall, J. 3:17
Bans, James 4:9
Banschooter, Oliver W. 22:472
Bansell, Philip 16:89
Bansham, Thomas M. 17:47
Bansman, James 17:17
Banson, G. W. 24:12
Banta, A. E. 16:151
Banta, Albert 17:417; 24:156
Banta, Henry K. 21:63
Banta, John 17:348
Banta, Marcus L. 23:278
Banta, Samuel 4:9
Banta, W. H. 24:12
Banta, Warren 20:182
Banta, Washington A. 23:59
Banta, William A. 17:348
Banta, William H. 8:79
Bantas, Gibbon 15:79
Banten, Henry 24:91
Banter, Alexander 1:115
Banter, John 9:101
Banth, Harman 17:29
Banther, Robert 12:7
Bantle, John 24:47
Banton, James 14:264
Bants, John 17:29
Bantum, Thomas 21:298
Banty, D. 25:139
Banty, J. W. 14:327
Bantz, George F. 18:121
Banval, Philip 1:115
Banway, Charles 15:262
Banyard, G. 27:12

Banyber, Venbit 9:95
Banyer, J. S. 3:17
Baok, --- 11:335
Bapman, F. 14:35
Bappler, George 12:12
Bapter, G. 14:139
Baptist, Edward 4:9
Baptist, John 12:47
Baptiste, John 21:298
Baquet, F. D. 1:14
Bar, Henry 13:104
Barabo, John 1:114
Barace, W. 15:262
Baram, William 17:127; 24:188
Barbar, Henry 9:70
Barbecker, Jacob 15:101
Barbee, Elias W. 22:241
Barbee, George E. 17:48
Barbee, Smith 24:189
Barbens, C. 22:8
Barber, A. 13:61; 14:35; 19:54
Barber, A. B. 13:61
Barber, A. E. 11:123; 25:18
Barber, A. F. 27:13
Barber, A. H. 18:274
Barber, A. J. 16:151; 24:12
Barber, A. P. 1:110
Barber, Albert 11:198
Barber, Albert H. 19:3
Barber, Alexander C. 22:176
Barber, Alfred 9:229; 20:203
Barber, Alfred C. 11:236
Barber, Andrew 1:15
Barber, Armer 17:241
Barber, B. 3:18
Barber, Benjamin 21:298
Barber, Bower 27:12
Barber, Byron 17:319
Barber, C. 3:18; 11:102; 14:139; 16:171
Barber, C. F. 3:18
Barber, C. S. 15:182
Barber, Charles 10:171; 12:169; 22:65
Barber, Charles H. 9:101; 23:18
Barber, Charles W. 18:337
Barber, Clark 17:75
Barber, D. E. 17:62
Barber, Daniel 8:8
Barber, David 18:121
Barber, E. J. 25:139
Barber, Edward R. 17:428; 24:185

Barber, Emmet 20:182
Barber, Ephraim 9:128; 27:18
Barber, Frank J. 9:168; 19:273
Barber, Garland 1:191
Barber, George 17:73; 18:63
Barber, George E. 17:108
Barber, H. 3:18; 10:152
Barber, H. W. 1:110; 11:14; 25:139
Barber, Hallet 21:47
Barber, Henry 8:120; 15:277; 21:298
Barber, Henry C. 20:33
Barber, Ira 13:83; 14:4
Barber, Isaac 27:21
Barber, Israel E. 4:9
Barber, J. 9:75; 15:317; 25:139; 26:12
Barber, J. D. 27:12
Barber, J. M. 3:18
Barber, J. R. 20:203
Barber, J. S. 20:120
Barber, Jack 9:205
Barber, James 3:18; 5:8
Barber, James A. 11:137; 16:20
Barber, James E. 21:298; 22:19
Barber, James L. 22:416
Barber, James M. 21:185
Barber, Jesse 8:8
Barber, Joe. 22:117
Barber, John M. 20:38
Barber, John W. 16:138
Barber, Joseph 1:17; 6:24; 17:63; 23:105
Barber, L. 18:187; 22:350
Barber, Luther 22:276
Barber, M. 17:191; 25:16
Barber, Martin V. 11:114
Barber, Oren A. 22:136
Barber, Orrin 21:47
Barber, Royal H. 4:9
Barber, S. 7:65
Barber, S. V. 19:4
Barber, Samuel F. 12:12
Barber, Spencer T. 22:460
Barber, Stephen 25:139
Barber, Sylvester 10:40; 20:203
Barber, T. 3:18; 15:182
Barber, Thomas A. 22:64
Barber, Thomas M. 10:89
Barber, W. B. 1:110
Barber, W. H. 3:18
Barber, W. T. 24:12
Barber, Warren 19:4
Barber, Washington 19:44

Barber, William 12:150; 14:139; 17:48; 18:337; 22:417
Barber, William P. 22:241
Barber, Zack 12:12
Barbie, George 22:176
Barbier, P. M. 22:231
Barbo, --- 8:8; 18:121
Barbon, Marson R. 17:446
Barbon, Mason R. 24:169
Barbor, H. S. 25:19
Barbor, J. S. 18:24
Barbour, Charles E. 24:72
Barbour, Colbert 12:47
Barbour, Frank 16:138
Barbour, Hiram C. 2:7
Barbour, John 8:121
Barbour, L. E. 25:17
Barbour, Owen 21:298
Barbour, William 12:121; 15:117
Barbours, James 26:216
Barbright, Ransom 1:15
Barbur, J. 19:54
Barcas, E. L. 27:12
Barce, H. 1:116
Barcer, Cottleb 25:18
Barchfield, Eli 3:18
Barchis, George 19:147
Barclay, John K. 16:131
Barclay, P. 3:18
Barclay, Robert 26:121
Barclay, Uriah 14:139
Barclay, W. H. 11:384
Barclay, William 4:64
Barclow, John H. 22:417
Barcock, C. 16:171
Barcum, James 11:395
Barcus, George 22:474
Barcus, Henry 21:63
Barcus, John L. 10:171; 19:147
Barcus, Levi 11:136
Barcus, Lewis 13:104
Barcus, N. S. 17:271
Bard, Benjamin F. 21:63
Bard, C. 27:12
Bard, Charles 23:18
Bard, Daniel 24:187
Bard, G. L. 5:49
Bard, George 5:49; 25:139
Bard, Henry 7:47
Bard, Isaac 4:9; 20:4
Bard, John 9:228
Bard, John W. 17:417
Bard, W. F. 3:17
Bard, W. H. 22:176
Bardeck, J. 18:24
Bardeen, Floyd 11:115
Bardell, Conrad 9:15
Barden, Charles L. 3:17

Barden, Hiram 24:91
Barden, Issa T. 10:40
Barden, J. P. 19:54
Barden, J. W. 1:113
Barden, M. 13:9
Barden, Michael 21:298
Barden, Orman 11:102
Barden, W. 13:83
Bardett, Lindsey 18:204
Bardin, A. B. 11:165
Barditt, S. J. 1:16
Bardley, Oscar F. 22:170
Bardlow, H. 14:35
Bardlow, William 21:17
Bardoe, James 12:47
Bardon, Ira 6:29; 25:316
Bardon, Michael 7:86
Bardry, S. 21:185
Bardsell, F. C. 12:150
Bardsley, Joseph 16:83
Bardwell, Dwight W. 10:157
Bardwell, Oliver 18:274
Bardy, Henry 18:307
Bare, David H. 22:496
Bare, Elias 22:176
Bare, George W. 22:64
Bare, John H. 17:275
Bare, Manassas 23:59
Bare, Richard 11:136
Bare, Urias 13:9
Barefryer, T. H. 9:48
Barell, Joseph 17:246
Bareman, Edward 19:54
Baren, Benjamin F. 8:102
Barer, John W. 18:454
Barer, Joseph N. 11:186
Barere, T. J. 3:18
Bares, Henry 22:416
Bareter, David C. 11:275
Barfied, Alfred 11:275
Barfield, Alexander 18:213
Barfield, Robert 7:117
Barfield, Samuel 27:143
Barflet, Samuel 16:171
Bargan, William 1:15
Barge, Henry 3:17
Bargenhault, James 21:63
Barger, Absalom 24:91
Barger, David S. 10:101; 20:203
Barger, G. H. 16:130
Barger, George 3:18
Barger, George W. 22:65
Barger, H. 3:17
Barger, I. 11:133
Barger, I. S. 18:228
Barger, Jacob 7:66
Barger, John 22:176
Barger, John W. 20:95

Barger, L. D. 14:277
Barger, Oliver G. 23:96
Barger, Samuel H. 20:203
Barger, W. 17:89
Barges, J. S. 26:13
Barges, L. D. 23:119
Bargess, Thomas 21:63
Bargis, George 11:257
Bargour, --- 15:182
Bargus, Thomas 17:18
Barham, Henry 9:71
Barham, J. 22:19
Barhan, Eli 10:101;
    20:203
Barhurz, J. 15:182
Bari, Alexander 10:13
Barich, Noah 17:417
Barick, George F. 16:171
Baricklow, James 21:17
Bariea, Raymans 25:310
Barille, Reiff 8:45
Baring, J. F. 13:80
Baringer, Andrew 20:203
Baris, E. 11:118
Bark, John 20:16; 25:274
Bark, Simeon 12:66
Barkehurt, --- 25:19
Barkel, Frederick 22:231
Barkely, John S. 22:447
Barker, --- 15:117; 19:54
Barker, A. 16:171;
    20:399; 22:289
Barker, A. W. 9:18
Barker, Albert 15:10
Barker, Alfred 12:63
Barker, Ancill C. W.
    12:12
Barker, Anson B. 22:19
Barker, Benjamin F. 21:63
Barker, Bethel 20:4
Barker, C. 14:35
Barker, Caleb 11:198
Barker, Charles G. 26:12
Barker, Charles J. 9:75
Barker, Clinton 18:44
Barker, D. W. 25:292
Barker, Daniel W. 7:73
Barker, David 6:15;
    16:171; 18:77
Barker, David B. 4:9
Barker, E. 4:9; 23:201
Barker, Edmund V.
    18:271
Barker, Edward 17:108;
    21:298; 24:8
Barker, Edwin 9:95;
    22:472
Barker, Eli 20:144
Barker, F. 3:18
Barker, F. J. 24:12
Barker, F. R. 20:203

Barker, Fitch R. 10:40
Barker, Francis M. 11:133
Barker, G. 25:139
Barker, G. D. 11:285
Barker, G. H. 17:403
Barker, George 3:18;
    9:164; 14:35; 24:12
Barker, George E. 12:12
Barker, H. C. 23:18
Barker, H. L. 12:56
Barker, Harvey 17:146
Barker, Henry 4:9;
    16:171; 17:421
Barker, J. 1:111; 3:17;
    11:299; 22:176;
    24:73
Barker, J. A. 13:61
Barker, J. E. 13:104;
    15:293
Barker, J. W. 25:139
Barker, Jacob N. 11:299
Barker, James E. 22:400
Barker, Jesse 18:121
Barker, John 5:49; 7:64;
    11:88, 180; 12:61,
    94; 15:13, 357;
    19:54, 147; 23:301;
    24:35; 25:139, 310
Barker, John A. 12:12
Barker, John D. 12:66
Barker, John R. 11:399
Barker, John W. 5:8;
    22:64
Barker, John W. W.
    11:298
Barker, Joseph 26:10
Barker, L. C. 14:279
Barker, Leander 23:312
Barker, Levi 11:384
Barker, Lucius 20:191
Barker, Marquis 22:507
Barker, Martin 11:196
Barker, N. 22:472
Barker, Owen 1:114
Barker, P. 21:119
Barker, P. W. 25:16
Barker, Paul 22:499
Barker, R. C. 13:9
Barker, R. F. 8:45
Barker, Richard H. 11:51
Barker, Robert R. 11:298
Barker, S. 13:61
Barker, S. G. 15:334;
    19:54
Barker, S. M. 20:203
Barker, Samuel 7:79
Barker, Sewell 25:292
Barker, Stephen 19:54
Barker, Stephen M. 10:40
Barker, T. 7:19; 16:171

Barker, T. W. 10:101;
    20:204
Barker, Thomas 15:339;
    18:121
Barker, Thomas A. 4:9
Barker, Thomas H. 10:13
Barker, Timothy 12:12
Barker, Truman 1:114
Barker, Verlin 10:101;
    20:204
Barker, W. 14:277
Barker, W. W. 18:301;
    26:92
Barker, Walter 12:63
Barker, Willard C. 9:168;
    19:266
Barker, William 1:115;
    14:264; 18:24; 23:85
Barker, William H. 17:290
Barker, William W.
    22:136
Barker, Wilson 22:64
Barkersterger, Frederick
    16:287
Barkes, John 23:132
Barket, Benjamin 22:447
Barkfield, J. Barney 23:96
Barkheart, Z. 14:264
Barkhurst, Robert 22:65
Barkins, T. 21:17
Barklett, H. 3:18
Barkley, A. S. 25:16
Barkley, Frank 12:47
Barkley, Gardner 22:65
Barkley, J. 21:17
Barkley, J. C. 25:18
Barkley, John S. 24:12
Barkley, R. C. 26:12
Barkley, Robert C. 9:75
Barkley, William 11:257
Barkly, Henry 11:117
Barkman, Henry F. 11:53
Barkman, Robert 18:187
Barkman, William M.
    21:47
Barkon, Peley 25:139
Barks, Charles 12:47
Barks, Henry T. 25:274
Barksdale, George 11:185
Barksdale, J. A. 25:19
Barksdale, W. S. 25:14
Barkshire, Edward H.
    22:65
Barlama, H. 14:35
Barlean, Ephraim 21:63
Barleon, August 22:474
Barlets, Peter B. 5:8
Barlett, Charles 17:494
Barlett, Ephraim 25:139
Barlett, W. W. 13:77
Barley, A. C. 26:13

Barley, Anthony 4:9
Barley, George 17:169
Barley, J. 13:104
Barley, Jacob 7:117
Barley, L. H. 10:40
Barley, Phileter S. 12:12
Barley, Rensler 4:9
Barley, Richard 22:289
Barley, Robert M. 22:160
Barley, Samuel 15:182
Barley, Simpson 22:289
Barley, W. R. 27:13
Barley, William B. 13:9
Barley, William S. 19:247
Barlne, Edwin M. 22:19
Barlors, Levi 19:147
Barlow, Andrew J. 11:53
Barlow, E. W. 15:182
Barlow, Elijah S. 13:9
Barlow, F. R. 13:9
Barlow, George W. 5:8;
    22:176; 23:132
Barlow, Henry 10:101;
    20:204
Barlow, Herbert S. 16:1
Barlow, I. 15:339
Barlow, Isaac 21:298
Barlow, J. 16:363; 25:139
Barlow, J. H. 1:18
Barlow, Jesse 17:258
Barlow, Job 17:351
Barlow, John 4:9; 5:8;
    23:127
Barlow, Joseph C. 20:95
Barlow, O. L. 3:18
Barlow, T. 7:55
Barlow, T. H. 8:103
Barlow, William 11:197
Barlta, W. 25:17
Barltell, J. 15:337
Barly, R. 14:35
Barman, Elias 4:9
Barman, Rufus 9:75
Barmanceltoo, John 26:11
Barmbs, J. 25:18
Barmeat, Daniel 22:241
Barment, J. 11:230
Barmer, Joseph 9:199
Barmer, R. 16:363
Barmer, Robert 9:218;
    18:362
Barmer, William 22:473
Barmhart, J. 14:4
Barmose, H. 18:391
Barmradt, Albert 9:107
Barn, D. C. 15:150
Barn, Freeborn 7:117
Barn, Samuel 7:117
Barnaby, G. W. 8:61
Barnaby, Thomas 14:139
Barnagan, W. 9:139

Barnam, Hiram 17:494
Barnard, --- 15:182;
    18:187
Barnard, Alonzo 12:12
Barnard, C. P. 7:47
Barnard, Calvin 11:258
Barnard, Edward L. 16:8
Barnard, Fernando 24:35
Barnard, Frank 23:267
Barnard, G. 3:18
Barnard, George 12:66;
    15:2
Barnard, George E. 19:54
Barnard, George P.
    21:134
Barnard, H. A. 3:18
Barnard, Henry A. 22:136
Barnard, Isaac 21:298
Barnard, James 21:298
Barnard, Jesse 8:79
Barnard, John 7:55
Barnard, John W. 22:64
Barnard, M. 9:159
Barnard, Oliver 15:157
Barnard, Richard 21:47
Barnard, S. 1:109
Barnard, Samuel 21:298;
    22:64
Barnard, Thomas G.
    10:156; 19:147
Barnard, W. 3:18; 12:91;
    14:35; 16:287
Barnard, William 16:363
Barnard, William N. 3:17
Barncroft, C. 25:139
Barnd, Elijah 11:319
Barne, Eugene 11:136
Barneg, William 14:139
Barnell, George 11:196
Barnellan, Henry 6:24
Barnelt, Samuel 16:116
Barnencatto, John 9:75
Barner, A. B. 22:241
Barner, Henry 21:220
Barnes, --- 18:187; 27:12
Barnes, A. 9:218; 14:35;
    17:48; 18:362;
    25:139
Barnes, A. C. 3:17
Barnes, A. E. 9:139; 27:14
Barnes, A. O. 18:337
Barnes, A. S. 7:86
Barnes, Aaron 21:298
Barnes, Albert 21:298
Barnes, Alberty 25:14
Barnes, Alex 16:171
Barnes, Alfred C. 9:101
Barnes, Allen J. 21:134
Barnes, Alvin T. 23:15
Barnes, Amos P. 10:156;
    19:147

Barnes, B. 14:35
Barnes, B. E. 16:277
Barnes, B. H. 3:17
Barnes, B. O. 9:68
Barnes, B. T. 24:109
Barnes, Benjamin 4:9
Barnes, C. 1:18, 111
Barnes, C. A. 13:83
Barnes, C. C. 21:17
Barnes, C. E. 25:18
Barnes, C. F. 12:66;
    26:217
Barnes, Calder 19:4
Barnes, Calet 22:473
Barnes, Calvin 9:217;
    17:448; 24:173
Barnes, Charles 11:103;
    14:139; 15:101;
    23:260; 24:12
Barnes, Charles G. 13:9
Barnes, Charles W. 17:63
Barnes, Cyrus 10:39;
    20:204
Barnes, D. 9:75, 139;
    14:35; 24:64
Barnes, Daniel R. 22:117
Barnes, David 7:19;
    11:136; 13:129;
    15:13; 20:120;
    24:151
Barnes, Davier 17:415
Barnes, Dewitt 24:188
Barnes, Dick 7:117
Barnes, Doctor 7:117
Barnes, E. 1:109; 13:83;
    14:4
Barnes, E. H. 3:17; 14:139
Barnes, Edward 16:171
Barnes, Edward H. 9:168
Barnes, Edwin 1:115
Barnes, Elijah W. 14:139
Barnes, Elisha 10:39;
    20:204
Barnes, Emma 12:12
Barnes, Eugene L. 21:298
Barnes, F. B. 3:17
Barnes, Francis 4:64;
    18:107
Barnes, Frank 6:7; 9:32;
    18:290; 26:94
Barnes, G. 3:17
Barnes, G. C. 1:111
Barnes, G. F. 14:35
Barnes, G. W. 21:298
Barnes, G. W. L. 10:40
Barnes, Gabriel F. 24:156
Barnes, George 1:15;
    10:89; 11:23; 16:171;
    17:278; 20:188, 204;
    21:264; 23:132

Barnes, George C. 10:102; 20:204; 22:136
Barnes, George F. 11:23
Barnes, George H. 22:136
Barnes, George S. 5:8; 25:139
Barnes, George W. 22:400
Barnes, H. 13:77; 22:400
Barnes, H. A. 1:111
Barnes, H. L. 15:262
Barnes, H. M. 22:65
Barnes, H. O. 25:139
Barnes, Harvey W. 20:142
Barnes, Hay 16:171
Barnes, Henry 12:66; 13:104; 15:29; 21:146; 22:289
Barnes, Henry B. 19:4
Barnes, Henry M. 23:18
Barnes, Hiram 19:54
Barnes, Hiram S. 9:7
Barnes, Ho. 15:182
Barnes, Hollis J. 12:54
Barnes, Horace 1:15; 23:119
Barnes, Horace G. 15:317; 19:54
Barnes, Horatio N. 4:9
Barnes, Houston M. 4:9
Barnes, Hugh 15:6
Barnes, Hughram 17:278
Barnes, I. 14:35
Barnes, I. P. 15:182
Barnes, J. 3:17; 16:363; 25:139
Barnes, J. A. 1:114; 19:247
Barnes, J. B. 1:16; 6:11
Barnes, J. C. 20:139
Barnes, J. J. 14:35
Barnes, J. M. 25:292
Barnes, J. N. 4:9; 22:176
Barnes, J. P. 25:14
Barnes, J. R. 18:107
Barnes, J. S. 3:17
Barnes, J. W. 13:61
Barnes, James 5:8; 7:19; 9:75; 10:89, 101; 14:279; 16:20, 171, 287; 17:494; 19:54; 20:204; 23:304
Barnes, James A. 15:63
Barnes, James F. 13:9; 22:276
Barnes, James M. 7:79; 22:117
Barnes, James R. 17:205
Barnes, James S. 20:88
Barnes, Jedethen W. 19:54
Barnes, Jesse 16:363

Barnes, John 1:19; 5:35; 8:8; 9:18, 32; 11:135; 13:129; 14:35, 139; 15:10; 16:171; 18:44, 77, 121, 187, 290; 19:54; 21:298; 22:176; 26:92, 93
Barnes, John A. 8:77
Barnes, John D. 10:156; 19:147
Barnes, John G. 10:39; 20:204
Barnes, John H. 10:40
Barnes, John J. 21:250
Barnes, John S. 9:41; 26:121
Barnes, Jonas S. 13:79
Barnes, Joseph 11:384; 22:19; 27:22
Barnes, Joshua 7:86; 25:274
Barnes, Joshua L. 15:53
Barnes, Josiah 8:79
Barnes, Julius 5:35
Barnes, L. A. 3:17
Barnes, L. H. 7:47
Barnes, L. W. 23:132
Barnes, Lawrence 20:28
Barnes, Leroy H. 17:296
Barnes, Levi 12:66; 15:6
Barnes, Lewis C. 22:176
Barnes, Lorenzo D. 23:105
Barnes, Lorin 5:49; 25:139
Barnes, Luther 11:51
Barnes, Lyman 17:390
Barnes, M. 3:17; 16:171
Barnes, Marin 22:116
Barnes, Marion 17:409
Barnes, Martin A. 8:102
Barnes, Matthew 17:48
Barnes, Michael 9:32; 18:290; 26:94
Barnes, Monroe 13:104
Barnes, Nathan 22:289
Barnes, Nathaniel 23:127
Barnes, P. 1:110; 16:171
Barnes, P. H. 14:139
Barnes, Peter 13:9
Barnes, R. 5:49
Barnes, R. A. 1:115
Barnes, R. W. 3:17
Barnes, Reuben 23:19
Barnes, Richard 21:146
Barnes, Robert 14:139; 21:298
Barnes, Russel 9:164
Barnes, S. 14:35
Barnes, S. J. 9:139; 27:14
Barnes, S. T. 14:28

Barnes, S. W. 21:298
Barnes, Samuel 11:297; 15:182; 18:107; 21:298
Barnes, Samuel G. 21:115
Barnes, Samuel H. 12:12
Barnes, Selden 7:79
Barnes, Seldon 25:292
Barnes, Sherman W. 10:102; 20:204
Barnes, Squire 17:169
Barnes, Stephen 8:102; 12:150; 17:257
Barnes, Stephen C. 10:94
Barnes, T. M. 3:17
Barnes, T. S. 3:17
Barnes, Thomas 3:17
Barnes, Thomas W. 4:9
Barnes, Thorton S. 11:299
Barnes, U. L. 3:17
Barnes, Uri 7:85
Barnes, W. 3:17
Barnes, W. C. 27:22
Barnes, W. E. 15:182; 24:91
Barnes, W. H. 5:8; 11:331; 14:35; 19:147
Barnes, W. J. 26:151
Barnes, W. L. 9:218; 18:362
Barnes, W. R. 13:83
Barnes, Walker L. 11:88
Barnes, Walter W. 21:299
Barnes, Wesley 13:56
Barnes, Willard 23:132
Barnes, William 1:16; 3:17; 7:19; 10:40, 156; 11:279; 12:12; 13:104; 14:139, 334; 17:89, 127; 19:147; 21:193; 24:189; 27:21
Barnes, William A. 18:121
Barnes, William C. 9:101
Barnes, William E. 13:104
Barnes, William H. 11:258; 15:29
Barnesley, J. 13:83
Barnesly, I. 14:4
Barnest, J. 11:258
Barneswort, John 9:75
Barnet, Charles 17:127; 24:188
Barnet, D. 24:73
Barnet, Daniel 13:104
Barnet, George W. 21:221
Barnet, Nathan 20:204
Barnett, --- 24:100
Barnett, A. 3:18

Barnett, A. C. 14:35
Barnett, A. G. 23:132
Barnett, Albertine 22:176
Barnett, Andrew 16:20
Barnett, Anson A. 4:9
Barnett, Charles F. 17:48
Barnett, Charles R. 11:257
Barnett, D. 13:83; 14:4
Barnett, D. W. 21:17
Barnett, David 22:64
Barnett, Ducat 22:289
Barnett, E. T. 3:17
Barnett, Francis 11:51
Barnett, G. W. 3:18
Barnett, George 11:196
Barnett, George M.
  17:435; 24:177
Barnett, George W.
  22:518
Barnett, Granville 18:411
Barnett, H. H. 22:176
Barnett, H. L. 14:130
Barnett, Henry F. 26:144
Barnett, Isaac 17:422;
  24:165
Barnett, Israel 8:79
Barnett, J. 1:113; 3:17,
  18; 14:35; 15:63
Barnett, J. T. 25:139
Barnett, James 3:17;
  10:40; 20:204;
  22:289
Barnett, James L. 17:48
Barnett, James M. 21:47
Barnett, Jesse 10:102;
  20:204
Barnett, John 11:25;
  23:251
Barnett, John E. 22:117
Barnett, John M. 22:19
Barnett, John W. 22:447
Barnett, L. 25:139
Barnett, Lauder 9:41
Barnett, Leander 26:121
Barnett, Lewis 7:55;
  11:394
Barnett, M. 3:18; 14:35
Barnett, Madison 22:289
Barnett, Mills 11:197
Barnett, N. 22:289
Barnett, Nathan 10:102
Barnett, Oscar M. 23:59
Barnett, P. 13:83
Barnett, P. S. 11:114
Barnett, R. 13:83
Barnett, Robert 24:156
Barnett, Robert T. 17:316
Barnett, S. L. 19:269
Barnett, Samuel 7:117;
  10:102; 23:132
Barnett, Simon 22:241

Barnett, Sylvester 4:9
Barnett, T. 3:18
Barnett, Thomas 14:139;
  15:85
Barnett, W. F. E. 23:132
Barnett, W. P. 1:19
Barnett, William 4:9;
  21:185
Barnett, William A.
  17:146
Barnett, Zachariah T.
  24:58
Barney, --- 24:189
Barney, A. 16:171
Barney, A. E. 11:236
Barney, Aaron 9:115
Barney, Andrew 5:8
Barney, George 14:139,
  250
Barney, George W.
  20:110
Barney, H. 3:18
Barney, H. S. 22:473
Barney, Israel 11:410
Barney, J. 15:277; 25:139
Barney, J. J. 24:91
Barney, J. P. 12:94; 19:54
Barney, J. R. 1:115
Barney, James 7:19
Barney, James S. 9:75;
  26:10
Barney, Jeremiah 14:139
Barney, John 7:63; 12:12;
  21:299; 25:139
Barney, Jonathan 22:19
Barney, Lorenzo 16:360a
Barney, M. 16:363
Barney, P. 20:204
Barney, Perry 8:37;
  26:150; 27:21
Barney, Philo L. 11:136
Barney, Redmond 13:9
Barney, Samuel 26:151
Barney, T. J. 22:330
Barney, W. 1:20; 21:146
Barney, W. H. 9:168;
  19:235
Barney, William 9:65;
  17:75
Barney, William H.
  22:111
Barney, Z. E. 25:139
Barney, Zebet E. 15:277
Barngrover, J. A. 3:18
Barnham, F. 3:18
Barnham, John 26:149
Barnhard, John 22:176
Barnhardt, Bigelow 13:9
Barnhardt, Christ 11:135
Barnhardt, Daniel 27:21
Barnhardt, Jacob 21:197

Barnhardt, Lewis 10:102;
  20:204
Barnhardt, Z. 1:116
Barnhart, Aaron 10:40;
  20:204
Barnhart, Ambrose 23:132
Barnhart, Amos L. 21:63
Barnhart, C. C. 1:16
Barnhart, D. F. 3:18
Barnhart, D. W. 23:132
Barnhart, E. 14:139
Barnhart, Edward 12:150
Barnhart, Ezra 21:220
Barnhart, G. 3:18
Barnhart, George 25:139
Barnhart, H. 1:109
Barnhart, Henry 11:123
Barnhart, I. 9:139
Barnhart, J. 27:13
Barnhart, James 14:139
Barnhart, John 8:102;
  11:418; 12:12
Barnhart, M. H. 15:182
Barnhart, R. 1:112
Barnhart, William 23:59
Barnhause, William
  12:150
Barnheart, A. 14:4
Barnheart, Andrew 22:176
Barnheisel, George 24:185
Barnhesel, George 17:428
Barnhill, B. 18:77
Barnhill, Daniel 11:198
Barnhill, Elmore 11:380
Barnhill, F. M. 24:74
Barnhill, J. H. 21:17
Barnhill, John 22:136
Barnhill, Margaret E.
  26:217
Barnhill, R. 25:139
Barnhill, Rigdon S. 23:19
Barnhill, Robert 5:8
Barnhill, Samuel 7:85
Barnhisel, B. F. 11:299
Barnhizer, Jacob 22:64
Barnholt, Thomas 8:102
Barnhouse, Patrick 20:95
Barnille, E. Layan 26:151
Barnitt, William 6:29
Barnlem, Noah 9:18
Barnoby, N. 23:287
Barnold, Charles 19:54
Barns, --- 27:19
Barns, A. C. 3:17
Barns, D. 27:13
Barns, DeWitt 17:127
Barns, J. 3:17
Barns, James E. 21:193
Barns, Oscar 21:88
Barns, Samuel 15:63
Barns, T. L. 14:35

Barns, Thomas R. 15:182
Barns, Walter 16:363
Barns, William 20:204
Barns, Winston 11:196
Barnse, Edmund F. 27:13
Barnsky, Charles 9:168
Barnsley, R. W. 11:257
Barnson, O. 7:83
Barnstead, G. T. 1:110
Barnswell, F. A. 21:299
Barnswill, Reuben 21:299
Barnsworth, John 26:11
Barnthouse, Joseph
  21:220
Barnton, Frederick J.
  27:14
Barnum, Amos W. 24:12
Barnum, C. E. 10:209
Barnum, C. F. 1:114
Barnum, David 11:399
Barnum, Dwight 21:242
Barnum, E. H. 9:168;
  19:244
Barnum, Eliakim 16:20
Barnum, G. 1:14
Barnum, H. 3:18; 14:279
Barnum, H. V. 17:390
Barnum, Henry E. 12:12
Barnum, Isaac 4:9
Barnum, J. 12:94; 15:357
Barnum, James 18:274
Barnum, James A. 9:18;
  18:320
Barnum, K. 22:511
Barnum, Levi 4:9
Barnum, Noah 18:301;
  26:92
Barnum, Oliver S. 4:9
Barnum, Pius 24:12
Barnum, Richard 27:22
Barnum, T. J. 26:16
Barnum, Washington
  24:47
Barnum, William 7:19
Barnum, William H.
  16:143
Barnus, Joseph 18:24
Barnwell, Ethelred
  10:102; 20:204
Barnwell, J. 25:139
Barnwell, J. H. 21:203
Barny, J. P. 15:357
Baron, L. 9:139
Baron, Lewis 15:304
Baron, S. La 27:22
Barpell, Daniel 11:409
Barper, C. A. 13:104
Barr, --- 1:112; 15:63;
  16:116
Barr, --- S. 7:66
Barr, A. 11:218

Barr, Alexander 23:177
Barr, Amos 17:246
Barr, Augustus A. 3:17
Barr, Bankhead B. 4:9
Barr, Benjamin F. 21:63
Barr, C. W. 25:15
Barr, Charles 6:15;
  10:102; 18:77;
  20:204
Barr, Charles E. 22:136
Barr, Charles W. 2:8
Barr, D. 24:74
Barr, David C. 11:102
Barr, E. 3:17
Barr, F. 11:24
Barr, George F. 21:299
Barr, H. 26:152
Barr, Hardy 23:290
Barr, Henry M. 10:102;
  20:204
Barr, Henson 27:17
Barr, J. C. 21:129
Barr, J. J. 1:113
Barr, J. T. 3:17
Barr, Jacob 20:204
Barr, Jacob W. 15:63
Barr, James 1:19; 11:136;
  27:13
Barr, James A. 4:9; 20:95
Barr, James C. 14:327
Barr, James E. 9:160;
  27:23
Barr, John 11:279;
  12:150; 13:9
Barr, John D. 18:171
Barr, John M. 22:19
Barr, John W. 22:176
Barr, Lewis J. 13:9
Barr, M. 12:121
Barr, Martin 22:350
Barr, O. 9:107
Barr, R. 20:176
Barr, R. H. 23:132
Barr, Richard L. 22:400
Barr, Robert 13:9; 15:13
Barr, S. 3:17
Barr, S. P. 16:363
Barr, Samuel R. 12:167
Barr, Stephen V. 23:132
Barr, T. 2:8; 25:19
Barr, Titus 18:284; 26:134
Barr, W. 3:17
Barr, W. B. 3:17
Barr, W. H. 1:19
Barr, W. W. 10:102;
  20:204
Barr, William 4:8; 16:158;
  19:334; 21:220, 299
Barr, William C. 22:496
Barr, William H. 17:497
Barr, Ziba H. 20:21

Barra, John 3:17
Barrack, James C. 22:19
Barrack, John F. 18:290
Barrack, W. H. 26:94
Barracks, Ephraim 22:518
Barracks, John 9:157
Barradough, Theodore
  19:54
Barrager, J. K. 1:109
Barrager, Sidney 21:134
Barran, Joseph 20:28
Barranne, A. 21:299
Barrant, D. B. 15:337
Barrass, David 24:35
Barrat, George 9:128
Barrato, Cleto 27:19
Barrats, Clato 9:115
Barratt, A. G. 26:153
Barratt, D. 14:35
Barratt, Elijah 15:182
Barratt, George 3:18;
  16:171
Barratt, John 23:96
Barratt, Stephen 24:58
Barraws, Jacob J. 12:150
Barre, Alexander F. 16:3
Barre, Charles 7:117
Barreclough, J. H. 1:18
Barrel, P. 25:17
Barrell, A. W. 12:12
Barrell, C. S. 1:18
Barrell, George W. 4:9
Barrell, H. 25:139
Barrell, Thomas J. 11:22
Barrell, Washington 9:199
Barren, James 4:9
Barren, T. 16:171
Barren, Thomas 16:89
Barrenger, A. C. 18:391
Barrer, --- 23:288
Barres, H. A. 15:292
Barret, Francis M. 12:150
Barret, Henry 20:142
Barret, J. 23:119
Barret, John G. 7:19
Barret, Mary J. 15:182
Barret, W. 17:500
Barrett, --- 8:119; 13:61
Barrett, A. 3:17; 4:9
Barrett, A. B. 10:40;
  20:204
Barrett, Abner 12:150
Barrett, Almond 11:256
Barrett, Alonys 21:299
Barrett, Alonzo 9:213
Barrett, Andrew 18:391
Barrett, Arthur 21:210,
  264
Barrett, Ben 6:22
Barrett, Benjamin 7:19;
  13:9; 16:21; 18:77

Barrett, Benton 22:65
Barrett, C. F. 14:139
Barrett, Charles 4:9;
    12:147; 15:182
Barrett, D. 3:17; 25:13
Barrett, Daniel 4:64;
    10:13, 102; 20:204
Barrett, David 2:8; 17:231
Barrett, E. 3:17; 13:80;
    16:171
Barrett, E. C. 1:103
Barrett, E. M. 21:17
Barrett, E. R. 17:158
Barrett, Ebenezer 16:171
Barrett, Ed 1:19
Barrett, Edward 10:154;
    19:147
Barrett, Edwin 13:104
Barrett, Elisha 23:19
Barrett, Francis M. 23:59
Barrett, Frank 10:156;
    19:147
Barrett, Franklin 1:114
Barrett, G. Y. 1:17
Barrett, George 6:7; 7:19;
    9:32; 18:107; 27:16
Barrett, Green 13:9
Barrett, Henry 19:4, 147
Barrett, Hiram E. 20:28
Barrett, I. 3:17
Barrett, J. 3:17
Barrett, J. B. 14:130;
    15:262
Barrett, J. F. 15:29
Barrett, J. Frank 15:182
Barrett, J. L. 12:12
Barrett, J. S. 11:53
Barrett, Jackson 23:105
Barrett, Jacob 16:171
Barrett, James 6:22;
    11:138; 12:66; 13:9;
    18:77; 22:276; 23:10
Barrett, James E. 20:204
Barrett, James P. 22:417
Barrett, Jesse 9:168;
    19:273
Barrett, John 7:83; 8:79;
    9:235; 17:169;
    18:420
Barrett, John D. 23:187
Barrett, John H. 8:103
Barrett, John T. 22:417
Barrett, John W. 22:176,
    507
Barrett, Joseph 1:16;
    16:131
Barrett, L. 19:233
Barrett, Lew 9:168
Barrett, Michael 12:12
Barrett, Nathaniel 11:123
Barrett, Oliver 11:88

Barrett, Patrick 24:213
Barrett, Peter 20:120
Barrett, R. H. 15:29
Barrett, R. S. 8:125;
    19:323
Barrett, Richard 18:107
Barrett, Robert 19:54
Barrett, S. C. 3:17
Barrett, Sylvester W.
    22:65
Barrett, Thomas 11:53;
    12:12
Barrett, Thomas H.
    14:294; 17:477;
    27:21
Barrett, Tilman H. 20:204
Barrett, Tilman K. 10:40
Barrett, W. 1:116; 27:22
Barrett, W. H. 14:294;
    17:475; 18:77; 27:21
Barrett, W. O. K. 22:231
Barrett, Wesley 21:193
Barrett, William 8:70;
    9:71; 12:53; 16:21;
    25:316
Barrett, William A. 18:12
Barrett, William D. 12:12
Barrett, William H.
    11:395
Barretts, William 13:9
Barrey, John 16:89
Barrey, Pleasant A. 20:2
Barrick, Eli 21:47
Barrick, John F. 9:32
Barrick, L. 22:176
Barrick, S. 3:18
Barrick, W. H. 9:18
Barricklow, A. 1:19
Barricklow, J. 1:18
Barricks, Andrew J. 17:29
Barricks, H. 17:17
Barrie, Joshua 11:133
Barrier, John 17:29
Barrigan, A. 3:18
Barrigan, J. 1:19
Barrigan, William 14:334
Barringer, F. 1:112
Barringer, Frederic 11:135
Barringer, Kernie 10:7
Barringer, L. 18:44
Barringer, R. P. 16:171
Barrington, --- 16:146
Barrington, A. 16:171
Barrington, Henry 15:25
Barrington, J. 1:19
Barrington, Jacob H.
    27:23
Barrington, John C. 16:5
Barrington, Richard 4:9
Barrington, T. 16:171

Barrington, William
    11:137
Barris, Abram 22:397
Barris, Christian 21:134
Barriskman, Allen 9:18
Barrister, O. 1:111
Barrister, William 10:171;
    19:147
Barrit, Sylvester 11:285
Barritt, A. G. 8:70
Barritt, Henry 10:171
Barritt, P. 21:17
Barrix, George 17:234
Barroff, A. J. 12:66
Barron, Aaron 21:299
Barron, J. J. 27:24
Barron, James 7:10; 27:17
Barron, John 21:17
Barron, John W. 22:19
Barron, Lawrence 27:13
Barron, P. 15:117
Barron, Reuben 8:37
Barron, Robert 20:110
Barrott, G. M. 3:17
Barrott, George 22:289
Barrow, C. S. 3:18
Barrow, Charles E. 12:12
Barrow, Henry H. 22:400
Barrow, J. 14:139
Barrow, J. J. 14:239
Barrow, J. L. 26:14
Barrow, James 9:107, 128
Barrow, James P. W.
    22:447
Barrow, John 14:250
Barrow, John H. 20:120
Barrow, L. T. 20:55
Barrow, Lewis 16:171
Barrow, R. M. 22:19
Barrow, Reuben 26:151
Barrows, A. C. 20:204
Barrows, Artemus C.
    10:40
Barrows, B. Franklin
    16:21
Barrows, C. C. 11:319
Barrows, E. S. G. 10:40;
    20:204
Barrows, George T.
    19:316
Barrows, H. 3:18
Barrows, J. 3:18
Barrows, J. L. 18:228
Barrows, Joshua 22:176,
    474
Barrows, Levi 15:293
Barrows, Luther 21:90
Barrows, R. B. 18:171
Barrows, Richmond H.
    21:90
Barrows, Samuel 24:47

Barrows, Thomas 11:83
Barrows, William E.
   16:77
Barrowson, Alfred 18:274
Barrum, Eliakim 13:9
Barrush, John 3:18
Barry, A. H. 5:8; 25:139
Barry, Amos 7:19
Barry, Brin 15:182
Barry, Charles 5:8;
   21:185; 25:139
Barry, Charles E. 13:9
Barry, D. W. 15:349
Barry, Dennis 1:17
Barry, E. 16:83
Barry, E. P. 9:48
Barry, G. S. 3:18
Barry, Garrett 23:10
Barry, George 9:205;
   16:172
Barry, Henry 17:127;
   22:136; 24:188
Barry, J. 25:14, 139
Barry, J. J. 21:299
Barry, J. M. 14:139
Barry, J. W. 22:176; 27:13
Barry, James 2:8; 13:104;
   27:22
Barry, Jeremiah 16:89
Barry, John 5:8; 15:182;
   16:287; 22:19; 23:19
Barry, John D. 10:40
Barry, John M. 22:474
Barry, Joseph 25:139
Barry, L. 11:298
Barry, M. 9:48
Barry, Patrick 4:9; 9:168;
   10:157; 15:15;
   19:147
Barry, Samuel 8:37
Barry, T. C. 15:336
Barry, Thimothy 16:172
Barry, Thomas 1:114;
   12:12; 21:299
Barry, Thomas L. 22:136
Barry, Timothy 13:61
Barry, W. 3:18; 15:150
Barry, William 15:101;
   18:420; 21:96
Bars, Edwin L. 4:9
Bars, M. 9:65
Barsard, Henry 17:450
Barse, Horace 16:138
Barselton, Winfield S.
   22:400
Barsher, Johnson O. 4:9
Barslar, Henry 6:29
Barsler, Henry 25:316
Barslow, D. 15:306
Barsole, Henry E. 15:183
Barson, S. P. 25:19

Barsto, Miron 8:45
Barston, S. R. 19:54
Barstow, J. 3:18
Barstow, Joseph 7:7
Barstow, Myron 21:250
Barstow, Nathaniel
   10:157
Bart, Eli 7:19
Bart, H. 22:240
Bart, John 9:48
Bart, Kenyer 19:4
Bart, Sebastin 19:4
Bartaille, Frederick
   26:150
Bartch, Christopher 12:12
Bartche, C. P. 3:17
Bartcher, Henry 5:8
Bartel, P. 18:44
Bartelette, --- 10:13
Bartelheim, Frederick
   21:127
Barteline, Peter 10:102;
   20:204
Bartell, A. R. 1:13
Bartell, Charles 1:15
Bartell, Horace 9:18
Bartell, Victor M. 10:40
Bartell, W. R. 1:111
Bartells, J. 9:139
Bartelman, John 19:54
Bartels, Carl 14:139
Bartels, Ehrich 19:55
Bartels, P. B. 25:139
Bartels, William 14:139
Barteman, James 22:136
Bartens, Herman 24:109
Bartenstein, George 1:114
Barter, E. 26:236
Barter, Elem 19:55
Barter, Franklin 22:19
Barter, J. A. 14:139, 253
Barter, James A. 13:9
Bartersho, Joseph 15:183
Bartges, J. M. 11:134
Barth, Adam 9:115; 27:19
Barth, Anthony 4:9
Barth, Benjamin 24:99
Barth, Jacob 14:35
Barth, John 27:23
Barth, Phillip 18:107
Bartha, C. 13:83; 14:4
Barthalf, James H. 25:18
Barthals, Christian 26:150
Barthaner, William 12:12
Barthe, Benjamin 24:8
Barthelow, George 4:9
Barthick, C. C. 13:83
Barthilaw, F. 9:163
Barthlow, Richard 9:168
Bartholaman, C. M.
   15:183

Bartholemew, Charles L.
   11:298
Bartholemew, F. L. 27:23
Bartholemew, Thomas
   26:121
Bartholmew, W. 12:85
Bartholomew, A. 1:111
Bartholomew, Abner
   10:102; 20:205
Bartholomew, Abraham
   21:250
Bartholomew, Albert
   10:102; 20:205
Bartholomew, B. 1:110
Bartholomew, B. F.
   24:169
Bartholomew, Benjamin
   24:74
Bartholomew, Benjamin
   F. 17:434
Bartholomew, Chester
   23:132
Bartholomew, David
   23:132
Bartholomew, E. 3:18;
   9:31; 19:247
Bartholomew, Erastus
   9:168
Bartholomew, Frank 8:70;
   26:153
Bartholomew, George W.
   22:276
Bartholomew, Green
   20:34
Bartholomew, Isaac
   10:204
Bartholomew, J. 3:18;
   11:285
Bartholomew, J. L. 14:139
Bartholomew, J. O. 3:18
Bartholomew, John N.
   20:188
Bartholomew, L. 1:20
Bartholomew, Lewis
   22:416
Bartholomew, M. 14:35
Bartholomew, M. H.
   17:290
Bartholomew, Nathaniel
   S. 9:115; 27:19
Bartholomew, Stephen 9:9
Bartholomew, Theodore
   H. 21:63
Bartholomew, W. 16:287
Bartholomew, Walter D.
   22:64
Bartholomew, William
   22:460
Bartill, R. 3:18
Bartin, Charles 14:139
Bartin, Martin 7:19

Bartis, Daniel C. 9:101
Bartlebough, Henry 5:8
Bartleman, August 23:19
Bartleman, John 15:334
Bartlen, James 9:160
Bartles, H. 8:61
Bartles, J. 27:16
Bartlet, Milton 9:95
Bartlett, --- 12:12
Bartlett, A. 13:83
Bartlett, A. W. 9:115; 27:19
Bartlett, Abram 9:115; 27:18
Bartlett, Alonzo 8:8; 18:121
Bartlett, Andrew 22:461; 25:15
Bartlett, Benjamin 17:63
Bartlett, C. 10:102; 20:205
Bartlett, C. A. 1:13
Bartlett, Charles 14:35
Bartlett, Charles H. 11:291; 21:299
Bartlett, D. 19:225
Bartlett, Daniel 9:168
Bartlett, David 18:24
Bartlett, E. A. 14:35
Bartlett, E. G. 22:473
Bartlett, E. K. 3:18
Bartlett, Ebenezer N. 7:86
Bartlett, Edward W. 21:299
Bartlett, Eliza 22:64
Bartlett, Estus 21:299
Bartlett, F. M. 14:250
Bartlett, G. W. 15:157
Bartlett, George 10:147; 11:24; 18:44
Bartlett, George J. 9:168
Bartlett, George L. 12:66; 15:63
Bartlett, George T. 22:160
Bartlett, George W. 22:136
Bartlett, H. D. 14:139
Bartlett, H. H. 13:83
Bartlett, Henry 20:4
Bartlett, Hiram 4:9
Bartlett, Horace 18:301; 26:92
Bartlett, Horace W. 11:103
Bartlett, Isaac H. 5:8
Bartlett, J. 3:18; 14:35; 15:312; 16:77; 19:55
Bartlett, J. H. 25:139
Bartlett, J. J. 1:16
Bartlett, J. W. 22:160

Bartlett, James 14:327; 27:142
Bartlett, John 1:13
Bartlett, John E. 19:147
Bartlett, John W. 15:309; 19:55
Bartlett, Johnson 9:115; 27:19
Bartlett, Joseph 12:150
Bartlett, Julius 18:24
Bartlett, K. S. 15:118
Bartlett, L. 3:18
Bartlett, Lafayette 11:285
Bartlett, Levi H. 7:85
Bartlett, M. 14:250
Bartlett, M. H. 12:66; 15:83; 17:158
Bartlett, Marcus C. 15:10
Bartlett, Meriam 8:117
Bartlett, Morriss 23:119
Bartlett, N. 16:287
Bartlett, N. P. 19:235, 279
Bartlett, Napoleon B. 24:12
Bartlett, Nat. 12:91
Bartlett, Nathaniel 9:168
Bartlett, O. 13:83
Bartlett, Olivia S. 26:217
Bartlett, P. 17:169
Bartlett, Palmer 10:144; 19:147
Bartlett, Phineas 10:156; 19:147
Bartlett, R. P. 20:55
Bartlett, R. S. 12:121
Bartlett, Richard 20:21
Bartlett, Rufus 8:45
Bartlett, S. H. 27:14
Bartlett, Simeon 9:128; 27:17
Bartlett, T. 21:119
Bartlett, Thomas 21:215; 23:96
Bartlett, Thomas H. 13:9
Bartlett, V. A. 14:139
Bartlett, W. 14:139; 15:273
Bartlett, William 22:136
Bartlett, William H. 14:139; 22:176
Bartlett, William W. 16:172
Bartlett, Zenos L. 20:21
Bartlette, Welcome 1:115
Bartley, Alfred 9:32
Bartley, Amos 14:268
Bartley, Arnold 7:19
Bartley, C. 25:139
Bartley, Cornelius 22:8
Bartley, G. W. 1:111
Bartley, George 20:4

Bartley, H. 25:277
Bartley, Henry 22:65
Bartley, J. 1:110
Bartley, J. J. 14:35
Bartley, J. L. 19:55
Bartley, John 21:299; 23:59
Bartley, Marion J. 8:79
Bartley, Martin J. 18:204
Bartley, Robert 21:299
Bartley, S. 3:18
Bartley, William 26:11
Bartlop, William 15:183
Bartlow, D. D. 22:176
Bartlow, John 15:183
Bartlow, Richard 19:244
Bartlow, Robert 17:89
Bartman, Blackman 9:203
Bartman, Fred 15:164
Bartnall, Charles 15:305
Barto, A. B. 16:363
Barto, A. S. 15:339
Barto, David 1:116
Barto, Francis 12:12
Barto, Frank 11:137
Barto, Peter N. 10:102
Bartoe, Daniel 24:177
Bartoll, W. H. 1:111
Barton, --- 25:292
Barton, A. 15:183; 19:147
Barton, A. F. 12:12
Barton, A. G. W. 22:8
Barton, Albert 5:35
Barton, Alonzo D. 17:320
Barton, Andrew F. 21:299
Barton, Anson 4:9
Barton, Asa 22:231
Barton, Augustus 13:9
Barton, B. F. 1:14
Barton, C. W. 14:139
Barton, Charles 10:102; 20:205
Barton, D. 3:18; 15:157
Barton, Daniel 26:121
Barton, E. 3:18
Barton, E. W. 1:116
Barton, Edward 1:114
Barton, Elezar 26:14
Barton, Elizar 18:228
Barton, F. 14:139
Barton, Felix 21:210
Barton, Francis A. 10:102; 20:205
Barton, Frank 9:168
Barton, G. 9:139
Barton, G. H. 25:16, 310
Barton, George 3:18
Barton, George W. 10:40; 20:205
Barton, Granberry 17:246

Barton, Henry 10:13; 16:21
Barton, Herbert 10:102
Barton, Hezekiah A. 8:8; 18:121
Barton, Hubert 20:205
Barton, I. W. 7:19
Barton, Isaac 10:13
Barton, Isaac J. 17:13
Barton, Israel 23:270
Barton, J. C. 1:113
Barton, J. E. 1:20
Barton, J. J. 14:35
Barton, J. N. 17:429; 24:186
Barton, J. T. 3:18
Barton, J. W. 22:176
Barton, James 1:19; 3:18; 9:18; 11:51; 18:301; 22:241; 26:92
Barton, Jason H. 10:13
Barton, Jasper W. 16:363
Barton, John 12:12; 23:85
Barton, John P. 23:19
Barton, Johnson 23:19
Barton, Joseph 12:12
Barton, Joshua 8:79; 24:12
Barton, Lorenzo J. 14:139
Barton, N. 25:292
Barton, Nathan 20:182
Barton, Pelee 14:139
Barton, Peter H. 20:205
Barton, R. G. 7:19
Barton, S. 1:113; 10:26; 19:299; 23:19, 132
Barton, S. J. 15:101
Barton, Samuel 25:140
Barton, T. F. 3:18
Barton, Thomas 16:143
Barton, V. R. 22:160
Barton, W. 3:18
Barton, W. G. 16:172
Barton, W. H. 4:9
Barton, William 3:18; 13:9
Barton, William E. 4:9
Barton, William H. 16:21
Bartons, Clarke 4:9
Bartonwaper, L. 17:293
Bartow, F. 19:247
Bartow, R. G. 7:19
Bartow, Sylvester 23:187
Bartram, G. 27:16
Bartram, Henry 9:32
Bartren, Wills 17:271
Bartruff, Henry 13:124
Barts, August 20:205
Barts, Daniel C. 18:337
Barttley, H. 14:279
Bartton, Samuel 14:139

Barty, John 11:22
Bartz, August 10:40
Bartz, John 7:85
Bartzam, D. D. 18:187
Baruff, James 12:12
Barus, John 20:204
Barusky, Charles 19:224
Barwell, J. H. 21:247
Barwell, James 22:417
Barwell, P. F. 14:35
Bary, W. H. 3:19
Bary, William 3:18
Barycraft, Tim 24:151
Barycroft, Tim 17:439
Barzman, Green 8:45
Basart, Pedro 10:157
Basborough, Charles 19:244
Basby, T. 25:140
Bascard, M. D. 16:172
Basche, Fred 20:205
Basche, Frederick 10:40
Bascom, --- 19:317
Bascom, George H. 17:402
Bascom, John A. 9:75
Bascomb, H. H. 9:205
Bascomb, Orwin N. 22:160
Bascouner, M. 16:363
Bascour, J. 26:12
Base, --- 10:209
Base, H. 22:160
Base, Henry 22:160
Baselgria, J. 18:44
Basell, John 16:21
Baset, George L. 11:103
Basey, John 16:172
Basford, B. D. 1:14
Basford, J. 3:19
Basford, Shilo 17:318
Bash, J. J. 17:289
Bash, Jonathan 19:4
Bash, Moses 10:102; 20:205
Bash, Samuel 13:56
Bash, Thomas 8:70
Bash, William 19:4
Basham, J. 23:201
Basham, John 8:8; 17:48
Basham, Solomon 3:19
Basham, Thomas M. 22:117
Basham, W. 1:96
Bashan, Levy 8:70
Bashars, Perkins 20:121
Bashave, J. L. 18:391
Bashford, Riley 7:86
Bashlor, Conrad 21:200
Bashore, Frank 14:139
Bashun, S. 15:103

Basick, B. H. 14:264
Basil, Conard 7:19
Basil, F. 11:439
Basil, George 9:128; 27:16
Basil, J. W. 1:115
Basil, T. 19:55
Basinger, William 21:220
Basins, William 22:177
Basket, --- 21:193
Basket, Benjamin 21:193, 220
Basket, George 17:127; 24:187
Basket, Reuben 22:241
Baskill, B. O. 26:152
Baskill, R. M. 8:70
Baskin, Alexander 9:205
Baskins, George W. 18:391; 21:63
Baskins, S. C. 2:8
Baskins, T. M. 18:63
Baskville, John 10:102; 20:205
Basler, Henry 25:17
Basley, Charles W. 9:18
Basley, Chesley 22:289
Baslow, M. 1:16
Basom, J. J. 11:299
Basom, John 21:215
Bason, Daniel 23:10
Basquis, Antoine 6:14; 18:77
Bass, Albert 9:203
Bass, Albert P. 18:468; 26:216
Bass, Alphens 12:12
Bass, Andrew J. 1:15
Bass, Burrell 23:19
Bass, Charles 3:19
Bass, Edmonds 7:81
Bass, Emmons 25:292
Bass, Enoch L. 17:429
Bass, G. 3:19
Bass, George A. 10:147; 18:44
Bass, George L. 16:83
Bass, Gibson 22:19
Bass, Hardy 23:290
Bass, Henry 19:4; 21:264; 23:19
Bass, J. 3:19; 21:96
Bass, James 27:157
Bass, James W. 21:17
Bass, Jethro 16:21
Bass, John 22:350
Bass, John B. 19:4
Bass, Lion P. 18:213
Bass, Nathan 14:35
Bass, Samuel J. 9:168; 19:247

Bass, W. B. 16:172
Bass, Willard H. 23:132
Bass---, J. 24:109
Bassamunson, E. 16:83
Bassan, Dennis 14:139
Bassar, Jacob 25:13
Bassard, Francis 8:126
Bassard, Henry 24:176
Bassardet, F. P. 12:12
Bassardo, Fredric 19:4
Basse, Henry 22:8
Bassel, Christian 22:330
Bassel, Winfield S. 15:85
Bassell, Adam 22:177
Bassell, C. 22:65
Bassender, George 15:183
Bassenger, H. 3:19
Basset, George 22:350
Basset, George S. 22:160
Basset, Louis 17:29
Bassett, A. C. 23:19
Bassett, A. F. 15:286; 19:55
Bassett, Austin C. 7:55
Bassett, B. C. 3:19
Bassett, Brit 17:169
Bassett, Caesar 7:117
Bassett, Corydon C. 22:416
Bassett, D. W. 1:109
Bassett, Delos A. 20:47
Bassett, Elisha 22:19
Bassett, George 24:12
Bassett, Griffith 18:228; 26:15
Bassett, Henry 7:117; 19:4
Bassett, Henry G. 24:74
Bassett, I. 15:339
Bassett, J. 9:41; 14:294; 16:363; 17:469; 27:20
Bassett, J. R. 3:19
Bassett, Jesse A. 20:38
Bassett, John 19:4
Bassett, Joseph 4:10
Bassett, L. K. 9:18
Bassett, L. R. 18:302; 26:91
Bassett, Marcellus 10:146
Bassett, Martin 20:110
Bassett, N. W. 22:518
Bassett, Nathan 17:127; 24:188
Bassett, Nelson 25:140
Bassett, R. H. 23:105
Bassett, Robert 14:35
Bassett, S. J. 21:299
Bassett, Samuel 23:59
Bassett, W. 13:83
Bassett, W. H. 1:111
Bassey, J. 17:127; 24:187

Bassford, E. 22:177
Bassford, Wesley 21:299
Basshammer, Conrad 22:472
Bassill, L. 25:140
Bassinger, George 21:96
Bassitt, Ellis 27:23
Bassitt, J. W. 25:140
Bassler, M. 1:17
Basso, William J. 7:86
Basston, G. H. 3:19
Bast, A. 20:144
Bast, John 18:204
Bastan, Tho. 20:205
Bastard, A. A. 17:161
Baster, Elisha 23:96
Baster, Solomon 18:204
Bastian, H. M. 14:36
Bastian, J. D. 1:112
Bastick, Joseph 16:21
Bastin, H. 14:4
Bastin, Thomas B. 21:220
Basting, C. 3:19
Bastion, B. B. 20:132
Basto, G. M. 11:123
Basto, Robert 11:383
Baston, George 6:24
Baston, Joseph 12:47
Baston, Thomas 10:40
Bastorough, Charles 9:168
Bastwick, George L. 18:362
Basurline, Jacob 19:147
Baswell, Elijah 22:65
Basye, Isaac N. 22:507
Bat, I. 20:205
Bata, A. 26:150
Batch, Charles 21:299
Batch, John 21:64
Batch, O. 3:19
Batcham, Eli D. 15:90
Batchel, Daniel 3:19
Batchel, N. J. 20:205
Batchelder, A. 19:235
Batchelder, C. H. 7:73
Batchelder, C. M. 25:292
Batchelder, Enos 26:153
Batchelder, George 12:12
Batchelder, George F. 23:85
Batchelder, J. 3:19
Batchelder, J. S. 25:140
Batchelder, James 21:299
Batchelder, Josiah H. 16:5
Batchelder, Martin 15:118
Batchelder, Stephen 13:9
Batchelder, William 16:153
Batcheldor, C. P. 1:112
Batcheldor, Charles R. 20:110

Batcheldor, William H. 12:58
Batchelet, J. 10:102
Batchelor, A. 9:168
Batchelor, Albert 1:17
Batchelor, Andrew J. 24:35
Batchelor, Fred. T. 23:187
Batchelor, George W. 16:135
Batchelor, John L. 21:299
Batchelor, P. 3:19
Batchelor, V. 23:19
Batcher, J. R. 25:316
Batcher, James 18:213
Batchett, Franklin 9:163; 25:316
Batcock, Jerome 17:319
Batdorf, M. 3:19
Batdorf, Peter 9:218; 18:362
Bate, Thomas H. 23:187
Batehouse, Henry 7:64
Bateman, Abraham 8:8; 18:121
Bateman, B. W. 25:140
Bateman, D. P. 3:19
Bateman, George 15:339
Bateman, James G. 22:460
Bateman, John P. 21:250
Bateman, L. M. 22:474
Bateman, Levi 8:8; 18:121
Bateman, Milton 7:86
Bateman, P. 1:112
Bateman, R. 1:13
Bateman, Richard W. 5:8
Bateman, Walter 10:40; 20:205
Baterece, W. 21:108
Baters, W. 3:19
Bates, --- 9:168; 19:147
Bates, A. 13:60
Bates, Abraham 1:14
Bates, Albert E. 12:12
Bates, Alex. L. 20:110
Bates, Andrew J. 10:13
Bates, Austin 8:103; 20:105
Bates, B. 12:86; 16:287
Bates, B. E. 14:140
Bates, B. L. 21:17
Bates, B. O. 20:205
Bates, Benjamin 12:66; 15:26, 85
Bates, Bushrod 10:208
Bates, C. 17:127; 20:205; 24:187
Bates, C. C. 22:350
Bates, C. E. 9:168; 19:235
Bates, C. H. 22:474
Bates, C. W. 25:140

Bates, Calvin 10:40
Bates, Charles 10:102;
    20:205; 24:91
Bates, Charles E. 19:4
Bates, Charles H. 15:102
Bates, Charles S. 13:9;
    16:21
Bates, Christopher 11:137
Bates, Claiborn 11:197
Bates, Clinton 9:168
Bates, Cyrus 23:119
Bates, D. B. 9:139; 27:24
Bates, Daniel 24:165
Bates, Daniel W. 11:23
Bates, David L. 9:218;
    18:362
Bates, David W. 13:76;
    16:172
Bates, E. C. 9:107
Bates, E. L. 3:19
Bates, E. Smith 12:66
Bates, E. W. 22:473
Bates, Elijah S. 12:12
Bates, F. E. 3:19
Bates, F. M. 25:271
Bates, Frederick 23:282
Bates, Frederick M. 8:8;
    18:121
Bates, G. 3:19
Bates, George 15:83;
    22:289
Bates, George D. 11:102;
    21:299
Bates, George H. 21:134
Bates, George W. 11:237
Bates, H. 13:83
Bates, Harvey 17:316
Bates, Henry 22:177
Bates, Henry C. 1:15
Bates, Henry J. 17:258
Bates, Herman 23:132
Bates, Hugh 15:339;
    16:363
Bates, Ira 17:153
Bates, Isaac 9:75; 11:197;
    26:11
Bates, J. 15:102; 18:24;
    21:146; 23:132
Bates, J. D. 1:96
Bates, J. E. 19:235
Bates, J. F. 22:177
Bates, J. W. 1:115; 14:140
Bates, Jackson 21:210
Bates, James 17:48
Bates, James H. 22:241
Bates, John 1:15; 3:19;
    10:153, 208; 14:36;
    27:142, 157
Bates, John A. 4:10
Bates, John S. 7:8

Bates, John W. 10:40;
    20:205
Bates, Joseph P. 12:12
Bates, Joshua E. 9:168
Bates, L. B. 3:19
Bates, Lester 3:19
Bates, Levi 4:10; 18:121
Bates, Lewis 17:127;
    24:188
Bates, M. 15:118
Bates, M. C. 18:102
Bates, M. G. 12:66
Bates, Martin 7:117
Bates, N. 18:228; 26:14
Bates, R. S. 21:299
Bates, Reuben S. 7:86
Bates, Richard 10:40;
    20:205
Bates, Richard M. 11:51
Bates, Rufus 12:150
Bates, S. 11:298; 15:26;
    19:235
Bates, S. N. 9:75; 26:11
Bates, S. T. 7:19
Bates, S. W. 13:77;
    16:172
Bates, Samuel 10:7;
    22:241
Bates, Samuel A. 18:121
Bates, Samuel N. 8:8
Bates, Selon 21:299
Bates, Solon 7:83
Bates, Stephen 11:399
Bates, Sylvester 4:10
Bates, T. S. 1:96
Bates, Thomas 22:473
Bates, W. 15:118
Bates, W. C. 6:8
Bates, W. F. 14:36
Bates, W. P. 14:36
Bates, W. R. 23:19
Bates, Walter B. 7:86
Bates, William 7:86;
    11:136; 22:65
Bates, William H. 10:40;
    16:287; 20:205;
    23:187
Bates, William W. 19:147
Bates, Zachariah 10:102;
    20:205
Batesil, G. W. 19:325
Batey, A. 26:150
Batey, John 14:140;
    22:177
Bath, Augustus 19:147
Bath, Charles 13:9
Bathe, John 10:40
Bathe, John C. 20:205
Bathelder, G. H. 19:235
Bathgate, James 13:9
Bathman, John 10:153

Batho, Ira A. 20:205
Bathrick, Andrew 21:90
Bathrick, J. 3:19
Batkin, William W. 11:22
Batkins, A. S. 3:19
Batley, Davis 15:2
Batley, William 21:242
Batlon, A. F. 18:274
Batman, Alexander 20:16
Batman, George 16:363
Batman, Jonathan 10:102;
    20:205
Batoon, G. H. 11:285
Batram, Francis 17:201
Bats, Henry 17:254
Batson, Henry 18:228;
    26:15
Batson, J. T. 23:132
Batt, A. R. 7:19
Batt, C. 14:36
Batt, Charles 16:21
Batt, H. 22:289
Batt, M. 3:19
Batt, W. H. 3:19
Batt, William 18:229;
    26:13
Battaff, Daniel C. 12:150
Batte, Antilichus C. 22:65
Batte, Isaac 16:172
Battee, A. J. 24:74
Battee, Philip 23:132
Battel, H. 19:299
Battel, Joseph 16:89
Battell, James 19:147
Batten, J. 16:363
Batten, John C. 16:21
Batten, Richard 11:230
Batten, S. 11:335
Batten, William 8:117
Battenfield, D. S. 11:299
Battenger, Asa 19:55
Battens, George W.
    18:274
Batter, Punman 9:168
Batter, W. W. 9:168
Batterbury, John 13:9
Batterman, Henry 20:205
Batterman, J. 18:229;
    26:14
Battersly, William 1:113
Batterson, D. 3:19
Batterson, L. 3:19
Batterton, Henry 20:121
Batterton, Jeremiah
    22:418
Battey, Andrew J. 10:210
Battey, Hiram 9:18;
    18:302
Batthrie, N. Z. 1:111
Battice, John L. 21:299
Batticks, Robert 22:289

Battie, David 15:53
Battin, Samuel 22:472
Batting, Isaac 3:19
Battis, John 25:285
Battise, Fountain 7:117
Battishill, William 11:399
Battiste, Samuel 21:299
Battit, John 27:23
Battle, Charles 21:299
Battle, Edwin 17:415
Battle, H. W. 19:147
Battle, Martin 11:197
Battle, R. 22:289
Battle, Timothy 23:119
Battle, William 22:511
Battles, Edwin 24:151
Battles, John L. 24:100
Battles, John S. 22:447
Battles, Thomas 21:299
Battleson, Sidney 14:294;
    17:478; 27:21
Battner, W. F. 18:121
Batton, Isaac 7:117
Batton, J. 11:237
Batton, J. M. 8:70
Batton, John C. 13:9
Batton, Noah 7:117
Batton, William 17:290
Battons, Lorenzo D.
    10:171
Batts, Andrew J. 9:128;
    27:17
Batts, John 21:9
Batts, Nilear 17:396
Batts, R. 23:59
Batts, Richard A. 23:59
Batty, Charles A. 22:19
Batty, F. 1:13
Batty, Hiram 26:93
Batty, Isaac 13:79
Battz, Peter 16:363
Baty, A. 3:19
Baty, John 3:19
Baty, Mich 9:158
Baty, Michael 27:23
Baty, Nicholas 22:499
Baty, Rice 9:203
Batyel, Jacob 25:15
Batz, Isaac H. 20:205
Bauch, John 18:302;
    26:93
Baucher, Chris 18:302
Baucher, Christian 9:18;
    26:93
Baucher, Henry 9:116
Baucher, John 15:118
Bauchman, A. 24:109
Bauchman, J. 14:4
Bauden, Henry 10:154
Bauer, Andreas 22:160
Bauer, Christian 22:117

Bauer, Francis 22:117
Bauer, George 18:302
Bauer, Gustave A. 19:328
Bauer, Jacob 24:47
Bauer, John 23:112
Bauer, Joseph 1:115
Bauer, Peter 22:19
Bauermister, Carl 11:123
Bauers, F. I. 15:183
Bauge, Henry 10:40
Baugh, --- 21:17
Baugh, A. C. 25:283
Baugh, Amos 23:96
Baugh, Charles 7:19
Baugh, Elliott 17:351
Baugh, G. H. 19:299
Baugh, Henry 20:95
Baugh, I. O. 25:282
Baugh, Jesse 23:251
Baugh, Joseph G. 10:40
Baugh, Marshall 10:40
Baugh, Noah 18:24
Baugh, Wilson 11:137
Baugham, H. 18:229
Baugham, John R. 18:229
Baughan, Lystra 20:95
Baugher, F. A. 23:243
Baugher, Solomon 17:75
Baughfinan, T. 3:19
Baughman, E. I. 17:13
Baughman, F. S. 22:350
Baughman, G. W. 18:44
Baughman, George F.
    11:180
Baughman, H. 26:13
Baughman, Harman 12:53
Baughman, I. H. 17:478
Baughman, J. 18:44
Baughman, J. H. 14:140,
    294; 27:20
Baughman, John J. 11:299
Baughman, John R. 26:15
Baughman, Levi 9:32;
    18:290; 26:93
Baughman, Paul 8:100;
    17:462
Baughman, Samuel
    16:131
Baughman, T. W. 22:472
Baughn, Charles 24:47
Baughnan, Paul 24:177
Baughs, Andrew J. 11:197
Baughue, Delos H. 8:103
Baugles, M. 9:168
Baukamp, Clark 8:45
Bauker, Albert 11:257
Baulding, William F.
    17:48
Baulglee, Maurice 19:269
Baulig, Sebastian 22:160
Bault, W. A. 11:279

Baulton, Samuel 12:150
Baulton, William 15:29
Baulus, Samuel 15:63
Baum, C. 1:116
Baum, James L. 18:213
Baum, John 18:213
Baum, Thomas 7:86
Baum, William 17:199
Bauman, Babtist 16:363
Bauman, F. 1:111
Bauman, J. R. 25:140
Bauman, Jacob 11:123
Bauman, John 22:65
Bauman, L. 23:276
Bauman, Lewis 12:12
Baumann, Babtist 15:339
Baumann, John 21:96
Baumert, J. 8:61
Baumgaitner, Matthias
    9:168
Baumgardna, --- 9:71
Baumgardner, E. A.
    14:140
Baumgardner, F. 22:177
Baumgarten, Alexan
    20:205
Baumgarten, Alexander
    10:102
Baumgratte, C. 3:19
Baumhauer, Joseph
    19:287
Baumheofener, August
    10:102
Baumhoefener, August
    20:205
Baumhoffer, F. 23:132
Baun, Barkley 20:4
Baun, George 23:85;
    24:12
Baunte, --- 19:55
Bauntress, --- 15:311
Baur, Jacob 10:40
Baur, R. 20:38
Bause, John 22:415
Bautg, David 5:35
Bautman, C. 27:22
Bautz, Daniel 13:129
Baux, James 9:11
Bavard, Frank 1:14
Bavart, J. 1:20
Baverstock, Barney A. 5:8
Bavett, E. S. 1:103
Bavi, Samuel 22:240
Bavi, William 22:136
Bavid, Samuel 22:240
Baviea, Nelson 22:231
Baville, Henry 9:160
Bavvitt, E. 14:36
Baw, William 7:86
Bawaroes, N. 14:36
Bawen, John 26:10

Bawer, George 26:93
Bawer, Jacob 15:315
Bawers, H. G. 12:150
Bawers, William 12:66
Bawers, William H. 5:8
Bawhart, J. 21:17
Bawkard, E. 14:36
Bawks, Jenkins 6:8
Bawles, C. 14:36
Bawman, John 11:123
Bawment, J. 26:151
Bawser, S. 25:140
Baxler, Richard S. 16:172
Baxter, A. C. 23:103
Baxter, Alfred 16:21
Baxter, Andrew 23:187
Baxter, B. 15:63
Baxter, B. M. 7:86
Baxter, C. H. 22:19
Baxter, Charles 25:285
Baxter, Cyrus 17:75
Baxter, E. 16:172
Baxter, Eli 11:103
Baxter, Elwood 10:102;
    20:205
Baxter, Frank 16:130
Baxter, G. H. 19:147
Baxter, George 17:48;
    18:77
Baxter, H. 27:15
Baxter, H. B. 1:18
Baxter, Harrison 8:77
Baxter, Henry 7:117
Baxter, Isaac W. 22:417
Baxter, J. B. 17:29
Baxter, J. M. 12:66; 15:85
Baxter, J. W. 14:253
Baxter, Jackson 23:19
Baxter, James 10:40;
    11:189; 18:121;
    20:205
Baxter, John 13:56;
    23:119
Baxter, Joseph 11:235;
    24:189
Baxter, Julius 17:169
Baxter, L. 14:295; 17:475;
    27:21
Baxter, Lewis 15:356;
    16:277; 24:189
Baxter, Lindsey 7:117
Baxter, Morris 11:134
Baxter, Orville 19:148
Baxter, P. 3:19; 25:140
Baxter, P. D. 3:19
Baxter, Parter 5:8
Baxter, Perry 22:499
Baxter, R. S. 15:302
Baxter, Richard 9:205
Baxter, S. 3:19

Baxter, Samuel 10:13;
    12:12; 26:12
Baxter, T. B. 11:399
Baxter, W. H. 1:109
Baxter, W. W. 15:183
Baxter, Westerfield 22:65
Baxter, William 9:235;
    11:189; 13:104;
    16:172; 17:170;
    26:216
Baxter, William A. 20:121
Baxter, William O. 13:9
Baxton, Absalom 12:54
Baxton, H. 3:19
Baxton, James A. 17:258
Baxton, Leonard 16:172
Baxton, Thomas 2:8
Bay, Constantine 12:140
Bay, D. P. 6:29; 25:316
Bay, David 18:302; 26:92
Bay, Hugh 22:65
Bay, L. 12:47
Bay, Martin 10:40; 20:205
Bay, S. 14:287, 289;
    23:96
Bay, Stansberry 10:102
Bay, Stansbury 20:205
Bay, Thomas 13:56
Bay, W. W. 9:75; 26:11
Bayall, William 15:183
Bayan, W. G. 24:64
Bayard, A. 9:153; 27:24
Bayard, C. 15:26
Bayard, William 6:23
Baybourn, J. R. 21:197
Bayce, W. H. 21:185
Bayday, M. 16:363
Baye, Simeon 23:308
Bayer, Daniel 9:139
Bayer, F. 3:19
Bayer, F. C. 19:247
Bayer, M. 9:139
Bayer, Martin 27:14
Bayes, John 9:71
Bayhmer, S. G. 3:19
Bayil, Jeff 26:150
Bayle, D. 25:140
Bayle, William 3:19
Bayler, W. H. 20:205;
    27:15
Bayles, Aaron 19:269
Bayles, Christopher
    17:234
Bayles, David 9:235
Bayles, G. L. 25:292
Bayles, G. W. 24:74
Bayles, Leveritt E. 11:399
Bayles, Peter M. 18:391
Bayles, Thomas D. 21:96
Bayless, C. W. I. 23:283
Bayless, David 21:185

Bayless, James M. 11:115
Bayless, R. 3:19
Bayless, William 18:362;
    20:121; 21:15
Bayley, A. 9:168
Bayley, A. J. 9:168
Bayley, Alvin 9:168
Bayley, C. H. 25:140
Bayley, Charles 5:8; 9:107
Bayley, E. 21:17
Bayley, Frank 3:19
Bayley, George W. 10:94
Bayley, Hanson 10:40
Bayley, Isaiah 7:9
Bayley, S. C. 14:36
Bayley, Stephen 9:168
Bayley, T. 3:19
Baylie, J. 1:18
Baylie, William H. 10:40
Baylis, Edgar L. 25:140
Bayliss, Jacob 9:71
Bayliss, William 9:218
Baylor, Elias 22:65
Baylor, John 15:258
Baylor, Stephen 12:12
Bayman, Thomas 10:176;
    19:148
Baymont, Ch. 21:146
Bayn, Harrison 11:339
Baynard, --- 16:172
Baynard, William 3:19
Bayne, C. 21:299
Bayne, Donald 3:223;
    17:501
Bayne, Frederick 19:55
Bayne, John 17:351
Bayne, Philip 20:132
Bayne, Reuben T. 4:10
Bayne, Robert 22:117
Bayne, Saul 14:36
Baynes, Joseph 18:102
Baynton, H. K. 1:19
Baynton, Henry 3:19
Bayou, John E. 11:103
Bays, David T. 17:75
Bays, James 15:183
Bays, Joshua 21:193
Bays, Josiah J. 22:65
Bays, William 17:389
Bayse, Robert 17:258
Baysinger, James 22:65
Baytis, Isaac 22:330
Bayton, James G. 1:13
Baywell, A. J. 27:19
Baywood, J. 3:19
Baza, James S. 13:56
Bazarth, Joseph S. 11:83
Baze, Andrew 19:148
Bazel, Samuel C. 24:163
Bazen, Andrew 10:157
Bazer, S. 1:93

Bazetti, Felix 27:19
Bazier, Fred 25:316
Bazil, Jeff 8:37
Bazin, C. P. 9:139; 27:16
Bazin, Elijah 22:400
Bazin, Joulious 7:19
Bazor, Henry 6:35
Bazzard, H. 22:289
Bazzetti, Felix 9:116
Bazzle, Azzle 22:241
Be---ge-, John H. 23:187
Bea, Henry 23:127
Beablehuner, L. 13:61
Beach, A. 13:61; 19:55;
  25:140
Beach, Addison H. 7:86
Beach, Allen 4:10
Beach, Amos 22:136
Beach, Amos T. 13:9
Beach, Anthony 9:128;
  27:17
Beach, Benjamin J. 15:2
Beach, C. 25:140
Beach, Calvin 9:41
Beach, Charles 5:8; 13:61;
  19:55; 24:107
Beach, Cyrus T. 13:9
Beach, Daniel F. 10:13
Beach, David M. 10:144;
  19:148
Beach, E. 1:17
Beach, E. L. 10:102;
  17:63; 20:205
Beach, F. 11:331
Beach, F. A. 24:12
Beach, G. M. 1:17
Beach, G. W. 26:93
Beach, Gabrel 25:140
Beach, George 22:136
Beach, George
  Washington 18:302
Beach, H. 13:104
Beach, Henry 22:136
Beach, Henry S. 9:116
Beach, Horace 17:423
Beach, Horace M. 24:172
Beach, Horates 24:72
Beach, J. 1:96; 3:19
Beach, J. F. 3:20
Beach, J. P. 14:140
Beach, James 27:21
Beach, James A. 15:277;
  25:140
Beach, Jerome 24:47
Beach, John 4:10; 13:9
Beach, John R. 15:337
Beach, Josephus 8:103
Beach, Levi 4:10
Beach, Lyman A. 19:148
Beach, Marshall 22:136
Beach, Martin L. 1:15

Beach, Marvin 12:12
Beach, Michael 25:140
Beach, Milton 22:136
Beach, Oliver 17:241
Beach, R. 1:20
Beach, Samuel E. 22:446
Beach, Thomas A. 22:241
Beach, Upton 11:331
Beach, William H.
  10:144; 19:148
Beacham, David 7:117;
  21:299
Beacham, Zachariah
  20:121
Beachem, John 12:47
Beachenberger, Henry
  11:136
Beachiol, J. 10:147
Beachlol, J. 18:44
Beachner, J. M. 14:27
Beacht, Jacob 12:12
Beachtel, Nelson 20:205
Beachum, G. 25:292
Beachum, J. 7:73
Beacie, James 25:255
Beacken, W. P. 4:10
Beacon, Charles 1:17
Beacon, Elijah 12:47
Beacon, Jacob 18:204
Beacon, Wesley 21:264
Beacraft, D. 15:336
Beacraft, Dubois 19:55
Beadd, J. M. 11:257
Beadis, Joseph P. 22:241
Beadle, Charles 24:61
Beadle, Charles M. 12:12
Beadle, Frank 24:63
Beadle, George R. 26:16
Beadle, H. H. 3:20
Beadle, Henry 14:268
Beadle, Isaiah 17:275
Beadle, J. F. 9:239
Beadle, O. H. 7:66
Beadle, Pinkney 22:511
Beadle, Robert 12:12
Beadles, Nathan R.
  17:348
Beadleston, John J.
  20:110
Beadman, James L. 23:96
Beady, William 3:20
Beagle, Anson 22:19
Beagle, J. K. 16:138
Beagler, A. 3:19
Beagy, J. M. 13:9
Beahler, H. 20:205
Beais, C. J. 18:24
Beaker, A. 1:112
Beakman, H. 11:236
Beal, Andrew J. 9:32
Beal, B. W. 1:109

Beal, Calvin H. 21:94
Beal, Charles L. 15:297
Beal, D. S. 13:104
Beal, Edward 8:100;
  17:461; 19:299;
  24:169
Beal, George 22:19
Beal, George E. 21:299
Beal, H. B. 10:40; 20:205
Beal, J. 18:44
Beal, J. K. 23:132
Beal, James M. 12:66
Beal, James P. 22:416
Beal, John 3:20
Beal, Joseph 16:83
Beal, Joseph A. 22:241
Beal, Joseph H. 10:157
Beal, Mathias 9:18
Beal, Peleg H. 15:258
Beal, R. 17:435
Beal, Robert 24:176
Beal, S. A. 27:21
Beal, William 21:299
Bealder, A. 16:172
Beale, Archibald 22:400
Beale, John A. 22:473
Beale, Martin 22:19
Beale, Peleg H. 14:130
Beale, R. 3:20
Bealer, A. 26:217
Beales, G. W. 22:447
Bealey, Robert 12:150
Bealinster, A. 23:21
Beall, Byron A. 22:8
Beall, James 9:75; 21:64
Beall, James N. 17:313
Beall, Josiah 22:19
Beall, Sivas H. 17:290
Beall, William 22:400
Bealor, Andrew 9:235
Beals, C. H. 19:148
Beals, Daniel 17:29
Beals, Daniel M. 18:274
Beals, Eli 21:64
Beals, H. F. 1:110
Beals, James E. 16:116
Beals, James M. 15:83
Beals, Jed 8:103
Beals, John 9:168; 19:279
Beals, John H. 14:36
Beals, Joseph 4:10
Beals, Joseph S. 19:148
Bealter, James W. 26:10
Bealty, Reuben 22:19
Bealty, Stephen 11:338
Beam, C. F. 18:44
Beam, C. J. 9:213
Beam, D. 3:20
Beam, Frederick 15:53
Beam, G. D. 9:15
Beam, G. F. 15:171

Beam, G. W. 1:19
Beam, J. 14:295; 17:477; 27:21
Beam, Jacob 18:45
Beam, Jeremiah 27:19
Beam, John 8:45
Beam, John H. 15:164
Beam, Joseph 14:36
Beam, Nelson 22:473
Beam, Perry A. 26:12
Beam, Scabbard 11:52
Beaman, Alvin 20:95
Beaman, Azar 27:21
Beaman, Daniel 22:111
Beaman, Henry S. 7:55
Beaman, M. 16:266
Beamer, Jacob E. 21:17
Beamer, Samuel 17:90
Beames, James 21:264
Beamis, Ezra D. 22:177
Beamis, James 22:177
Beamish, John W. 15:157
Beamish, R. D. 20:151
Beamont, Joel 9:41
Beams, George 21:193, 220
Beams, George W. 26:11
Beams, Henry 22:177
Bean, A. 17:262
Bean, A. A. 21:119
Bean, Abram 1:14
Bean, Albert 15:83
Bean, Amos P. 21:299
Bean, Ashberry 22:19
Bean, C. S. 3:20
Bean, C. T. 14:36
Bean, Charles 18:77
Bean, Columbus 9:32; 18:290; 26:93
Bean, D. A. 25:140
Bean, D. B. 7:86
Bean, Daniel A. 5:8
Bean, E. H. 14:140
Bean, E. W. 1:109
Bean, Eben 1:17
Bean, Edward 17:29
Bean, F. 15:10
Bean, G. W. 3:20
Bean, George 14:279; 16:172; 21:299
Bean, George P. 7:66
Bean, George W. 19:225; 26:152
Bean, H. S. 1:16
Bean, H. T. 3:20
Bean, Henry 18:107
Bean, Horatio 1:16
Bean, I. R. 21:119
Bean, J. 13:61, 83; 14:28, 36
Bean, J. A. 21:299

Bean, J. W. 3:20
Bean, James 9:162; 14:140; 27:23
Bean, James Otis 15:63
Bean, Jeremiah 9:116
Bean, Joe 14:140
Bean, John 3:20; 9:168; 11:22; 22:523; 25:280
Bean, John C. 9:168; 19:235
Bean, John S. 10:13
Bean, Levi L. 20:21
Bean, Lewis 15:183
Bean, M. M. 19:225
Bean, Merrill M. 9:168
Bean, O. A. 16:172
Bean, Peter 17:205
Bean, Pleasant M. 21:90
Bean, R. 21:299
Bean, Rosca 15:10
Bean, Solomon 8:79; 22:65
Bean, T. 26:11
Bean, Theo 9:75
Bean, W. 16:172
Bean, W. C. 22:241
Bean, Wash 17:170
Bean, William 7:86; 27:23
Bean, William D. 10:211
Bean, William F. 13:61; 16:172
Bean, William H. 9:32
Bean, William S. 1:19
Beane, John 19:269
Beaneham, R. 18:229
Beaner, H. 14:36
Beaner, Robert 17:29
Beaney, John 12:66
Beanham, R. 26:15
Beanmister, A. 21:299
Beannian, William 3:20
Beanony, Charles 12:7
Beans, Charles H. 12:63; 15:10
Beans, Harmony Y. 19:4
Beans, J. 14:4
Beans, John R. 23:19
Beans, John W. 9:75
Beans, William 20:105
Beany, J. 15:26
Bear, A. 1:19; 14:36
Bear, Andrew H. 11:410
Bear, Benson 11:257
Bear, Charles 6:27; 21:96
Bear, Christopher R. 22:177
Bear, D. 3:20
Bear, E. 3:20
Bear, George 14:279

Bear, George M. 9:168; 19:225
Bear, George W. 12:164
Bear, H. H. 7:55
Bear, J. 26:12
Bear, J. W. 20:87
Bear, Jackson 9:75
Bear, Jacob 14:140; 15:118
Bear, John 3:20
Bear, Joseph 6:27
Bear, M. 14:140
Bear, R. D. 14:140
Bear, Robert 11:197; 14:140
Bear, S. 16:266
Bear, Samuel 3:20; 6:27
Bear, Thomas 11:384
Bear, William 21:64
Bear, William S. 20:182
Beararch, Henry 17:417
Bearcroft, William 4:10
Beard, --- 11:133
Beard, A. 12:86; 14:36; 16:287
Beard, A. C. 17:214
Beard, Albert 21:299
Beard, Alex 13:9
Beard, Alexander 8:8; 18:121
Beard, Alexander W. 23:59
Beard, Allen B. 11:237
Beard, Andrew 22:418
Beard, Arthur 21:299
Beard, C. J. 9:48
Beard, Charles 20:121
Beard, Cyrus 23:59
Beard, D. 23:19
Beard, Daniel 22:177
Beard, Dexter 11:103
Beard, Edmund B. 20:205
Beard, G. 16:172; 19:55
Beard, G. G. 25:140
Beard, George H. 11:51
Beard, Henry 22:330
Beard, Hiram 22:8
Beard, Howard 11:180
Beard, J. 3:20; 14:27, 133
Beard, J. C. 3:20
Beard, J. H. 9:75; 26:11
Beard, J. O. 16:21
Beard, J. R. 3:19
Beard, J. W. 22:473
Beard, James 11:134; 12:94; 15:357; 17:29; 19:55; 23:132
Beard, John 11:103; 16:172
Beard, John A. 20:185
Beard, John B. 8:79

Beard, John C. 22:65
Beard, John M. 10:102; 20:205
Beard, John S. 20:4
Beard, Joseph 10:40; 20:206
Beard, L. 14:140
Beard, M. M. 22:460
Beard, M. V. 20:206
Beard, Marion 12:12
Beard, Martin 26:152
Beard, Martin V. 10:40
Beard, Miles C. 18:229; 26:16
Beard, Minor 22:289
Beard, Nelson 9:70
Beard, O. 3:19
Beard, Robert 22:241
Beard, Samuel 10:98
Beard, Samuel J. 3:19
Beard, Samuel W. 23:19
Beard, Thornton 22:289
Beard, Uriah 12:12
Beard, W. H. 26:93
Beard, Wesley 23:132
Beard, William 9:48; 10:102; 16:87; 18:107; 20:206; 21:129, 264
Beard, William E. 18:121
Beard, William G. 10:102; 20:206
Beard, William H. 2:8; 18:290
Beard, William J. 22:400
Beard, William M. 20:50
Bearden, Isaac H. 22:241
Bearden, J. J. 26:13
Bearden, James 10:102; 20:206
Beardey, Harvey 9:107
Beardman, John 10:40
Beardmore, Charles 21:299
Beardmore, Thomas 16:363
Beardslee, B. 1:19
Beardslee, M. A. 3:20
Beardsley, --- 18:337
Beardsley, A. 12:91; 16:287
Beardsley, Andrew 4:10
Beardsley, Beach 4:10
Beardsley, Benjamin P. 20:91
Beardsley, C. S. 23:132
Beardsley, Charles 17:63; 18:24
Beardsley, E. C. 19:148
Beardsley, H. C. 15:339; 16:363

Beardsley, H. D. 9:242
Beardsley, J. G. 10:40; 20:206
Beardsley, John G. 12:94
Beardsley, Levi 22:8
Beardsley, R. B. 26:14
Beardsley, R. S. 18:229
Beardsley, William 25:140
Beardsly, C. D. 7:86
Beardsly, J. G. 15:357
Beardy, John 22:447
Beare, --- 16:172
Beare, A. 15:183
Beare, Jacob 4:10
Beare, Thomas 20:206
Beare, Townsend 24:63
Bearen, James 12:47
Bearer, Henry 17:404
Bearer, James 17:392
Bearer, John 9:48
Bearer, W. C. 18:187
Beares, M. E. 1:20
Bearfield, Benjamin 4:10
Beari, Thomas 10:102
Bearmaster, Lewis 23:19
Bearor, David 20:206
Bears, F. S. 25:19
Bears, Frank S. 2:8
Bearson, --- 19:55
Bearss, E. F. 22:276
Beart, Jacob 22:231
Bearters, Henry W. 7:15
Bearts, Samuel 12:56
Beary, Mark 16:116
Beary, Milton 17:445; 24:165
Beasaug, C. 3:20
Beasby, S. M. 11:297
Beasel, E. 25:140
Beasel, Erasmus 5:35
Beaseley, George B. 14:36
Beaseley, Richard 9:128
Beasely, Richard 19:4
Beaseman, F. 14:36
Beasin, D. H. 21:185
Beaskard, Thomas H. 20:34
Beasler, Henry 1:114
Beasley, E. 16:172
Beasley, Edward 22:289
Beasley, Elijah 27:22
Beasley, George 23:132
Beasley, H. 11:438
Beasley, H. G. 21:300
Beasley, J. S. 17:170
Beasley, Jacob 25:316
Beasley, Jasper 8:8; 18:121
Beasley, Jesse 10:170; 19:148

Beasley, Jochlan 6:29
Beasley, M. 21:165
Beasley, Milton 1:114
Beasley, P. 3:20
Beasley, Peter 22:289
Beasley, Richard 23:59; 27:17
Beasley, Thomas 22:289
Beasley, William 22:241
Beasly, Josiah 10:40
Beasly, William 25:268
Beasly, Zach 11:197
Beasmer, Dewitt C. 22:170
Beason, Benjamin 3:19; 22:241
Beason, George W. 22:177
Beason, Henry H. 24:47
Beason, John S. 17:205
Beason, Lewis 9:199
Beason, Louis 19:279
Beason, Thomas 10:40
Beason, W. 25:140
Beason, William 22:178
Beat, John 16:172
Beatel, John 12:56
Beath, G. 15:53
Beath, Granville 12:66
Beath, J. L. 13:83; 14:4
Beathey, James 11:103
Beatic, Robert 3:20
Beatle, John 14:140
Beatley, Richard 9:205
Beatly, H. L. 27:23
Beatly, John 17:191
Beatly, Robert 13:9
Beaton, A. F. 13:9
Beaton, John 4:10
Beatson, Boswell 16:287
Beatson, Robert J. 15:183
Beatter, Charles 14:36
Beattey, H. S. 9:160
Beattie, Alfred 22:289
Beattie, John 2:7
Beattie, William 1:17
Beatton, John 11:428
Beatty, Clelland 22:117
Beatty, D. 3:19
Beatty, D. W. 1:18
Beatty, Daniel 21:200
Beatty, E. 1:109
Beatty, Edgar 17:13
Beatty, G. W. 26:13
Beatty, George 12:12
Beatty, H. L. 14:327
Beatty, Henry 15:63
Beatty, J. 25:310
Beatty, J. H. 14:36
Beatty, James H. 9:18
Beatty, John 25:140

Beatty, John A. 8:45
Beatty, John H. 25:14
Beatty, Madison 22:65
Beatty, P. 17:212
Beatty, Payden 21:146
Beatty, R. 3:19
Beatty, Richard 21:300
Beatty, Robert 10:157; 19:148
Beatty, Robert M. 19:4
Beatty, Thomas 3:19
Beatty, William 18:391; 22:177; 25:15
Beaty, Adam 1:115
Beaty, D. N. 11:134
Beaty, Frank 1:114
Beaty, G. W. 18:229
Beaty, John 10:40; 15:322; 19:55; 20:206
Beaty, Mason 23:59
Beaty, S. 11:297; 23:132
Beaty, W. 13:83; 14:4
Beaty, W. C. 20:206
Beaty, William C. 10:40
Beauchamp, Clark W. 21:64
Beaufman, M. Q. 9:75
Beauford, J. D. 12:81
Beaufort, J. D. 16:287
Beauland, A. C. 25:140
Beauliean, Harrison H. 23:187
Beauline, Mercer 22:400
Beaumaaa, Felix 18:63
Beauman, Zeonhart 19:299
Beaumer, William I. 10:40
Beaumont, Isaac 11:198
Beaumont, James 1:16
Beaumont, John 19:55
Beaumont, Samuel 11:197
Beaumont, William 16:116
Beauregard, Adam 6:7; 18:107
Beauregard, Colodomer 4:10
Beaven, Thomas W. 26:217
Beaver, --- 15:183
Beaver, Ben 11:22
Beaver, Benjamin F. 18:229; 26:13
Beaver, David 10:40
Beaver, Ezekiel 17:75
Beaver, G. S. 1:116
Beaver, George 3:19
Beaver, H. A. 9:168
Beaver, Jacob 25:140
Beaver, James 6:29

Beaver, James A. 21:64
Beaver, John 9:235
Beaver, John F. 11:137
Beaver, John M. 12:12
Beaver, L. F. 17:29
Beaver, M. 3:19
Beaver, M. S. 11:236
Beaver, Nicholas 21:17
Beaver, P. 3:19
Beaver, Peter 11:137; 16:21
Beaver, Robert 11:256
Beaver, Thomas 4:10
Beaver, Thomas W. 9:235
Beaver, William 4:10; 15:29
Beaver, William H. 11:137; 16:116
Beaverly, J. A. 17:17
Beavers, John 17:93
Beavers, Martin 17:271
Beavers, Norman 15:63
Beavey, H. Y. 3:20
Beavins, Louis 21:300
Beavins, William A. 24:88
Beavro, Henry 17:454; 24:186
Beazley, William 4:10
Bebb, S. S. 21:17
Bebbell, E. 21:300
Bebee, Chester 18:391
Bebeler, William C. 17:205
Beber, J. 10:102
Beberstine, David 26:93
Bebount, William 16:172
Bebout, Andrew G. 13:9
Beby, Abram 7:19
Beccum, Isaac 11:335
Becer, Alvin 9:218
Bech, George 21:220
Bechdell, Mathias R. 17:29
Becher, Jesse 14:235
Becher, William 26:216
Bechman, Albert C. 9:95
Bechman, Ezeriah D. 11:278
Bechstedt, Frederick 5:9
Bechtel, Abraham 22:417
Bechtel, Benjamin 26:121
Bechtel, I. 5:8
Bechtel, J. 25:140
Bechtel, R. 24:74
Bechtel, W. H. 19:4
Bechtel, William 23:112
Bechter, Aug 25:140
Bechtold, C. H. 21:200
Beck, --- 16:65, 138
Beck, Abram H. 8:8
Beck, Andrew 14:140

Beck, Charles 18:107
Beck, Charles F. 10:40; 20:206
Beck, Christopher 23:132
Beck, Clark 18:391
Beck, D. 1:14; 23:59
Beck, Daniel 27:21
Beck, Daniel R. 17:316
Beck, David 21:17
Beck, E. G. 25:140
Beck, Edward 7:86; 10:13; 16:21
Beck, F. H. 11:138
Beck, Frank 4:10; 22:177
Beck, Frederick 25:140
Beck, G. 3:20
Beck, G. William 22:177
Beck, George 20:91; 21:64
Beck, George W. 22:177; 23:19
Beck, Gottlieb 22:276
Beck, Gustav 18:337
Beck, Henry 7:77; 17:17; 21:96; 25:293
Beck, I. 15:63
Beck, I. W. 18:171
Beck, J. 1:112; 7:19
Beck, J. G. 12:81
Beck, J. J. 16:89
Beck, J. M. 10:185
Beck, Jacob 9:163; 20:47; 25:316
Beck, James 6:9; 12:170; 18:77
Beck, Jo. W. 18:171
Beck, Joel F. 22:177
Beck, John 3:20; 9:239; 15:102; 17:48; 19:247; 22:8, 330
Beck, John E. 10:89
Beck, John H. 22:65
Beck, John P. 22:177
Beck, Lewis 9:168
Beck, Louis 7:117
Beck, M. 7:65
Beck, McHenryell 9:75
Beck, Medad 1:116
Beck, Michael 12:13; 14:140
Beck, N. 15:293
Beck, Nicholas J. 24:35
Beck, Thomas H. 12:12
Beck, Uherie 15:293
Beck, Uhlrice 16:172
Beck, V. 1:112
Beck, W. S. 23:201
Beck, Washington 5:49; 22:8

Beck, William 8:8; 17:251, 390; 18:102; 24:61
Beck, William H. 17:275, 425; 24:177
Beck, William J. 7:86
Beck, William M. 24:35
Beck, William T. 24:35
Beckall, Edward 26:150
Beckbach, S. 15:29
Becke, --- 3:20
Beckel, John 9:41
Becken, Ferdinand 14:140
Becken, Thomas 22:511
Beckenbaugh, George 9:48
Becker, Bernard 21:300
Becker, C. 22:177
Becker, Charles 19:4
Becker, Christian 13:60
Becker, Conrad 19:55
Becker, D. L. 20:38
Becker, Emenzo F. 20:91
Becker, Francis 24:58
Becker, Fred 19:55
Becker, Frederick 22:65
Becker, G. 3:20
Becker, George 23:10
Becker, George W. 21:250
Becker, Gerardus 22:136
Becker, H. J. 20:206
Becker, J. 2:8; 25:13
Becker, J. B. 19:247
Becker, Jacob 18:406; 22:507; 25:16
Becker, Jacob C. 20:121
Becker, James 15:350; 16:363
Becker, John 17:309; 21:300; 23:187
Becker, John A. 25:140
Becker, John T. 25:140
Becker, John W. 10:40; 20:206
Becker, Joseph 7:86
Becker, Joseph J. 11:136
Becker, Josiah 24:156
Becker, Louis 24:156
Becker, Oscar 19:55
Becker, Osker 15:287
Becker, Peter 21:134
Becker, Philip 1:114; 8:45; 21:134
Becker, William 6:8; 7:86; 9:235; 16:146
Becker, William S. 11:135
Beckerdite, Alson 9:235; 26:216
Beckerman, Hermann 24:64
Beckers, Joseph 12:47

Beckers, William 21:203
Beckerstaff, Tom 17:127; 24:188
Becket, Albert 25:140
Becket, Francis 11:135
Becket, George W. 19:4
Becket, Richard F. 18:229; 26:14
Becket, Solomon 17:234
Becket, Winters 18:270
Beckett, Alexander 21:96
Beckett, Archibald 17:258
Beckett, Charles 23:112
Beckett, Henry 24:165
Beckett, J. 22:330
Beckett, James 27:23
Beckett, James M. 10:171
Beckett, John 22:518
Beckett, Joseph 22:415
Beckett, T. W. 7:86
Beckett, William 12:47
Beckford, Daniel 21:300
Beckford, Dennis M. 21:300
Beckford, Edward 9:116
Beckford, J. 14:36
Beckford, Lyman 17:98
Beckford, W. H. 26:121
Beckham, D. 25:281
Beckham, F. B. 3:20
Beckhart, Jacob 18:121
Beckholdt, Frederick 23:132
Beckler, J. 25:140
Beckles, Henry 22:232
Beckley, G. 3:20
Beckley, S. 3:20
Beckley, W. 3:20
Becklin, O. 1:116
Beckman, Benjamin C. 13:128
Beckman, C. P. 16:172
Beckman, F. 15:29
Beckman, Fletcher 4:64
Beckman, George 6:28
Beckman, Henry 7:86; 9:235; 21:300; 22:117
Beckman, John 22:160
Beckman, Philip 19:4
Becknel, Isaac 10:40
Becknell, Thomas S. 20:103
Beckner, George 21:47
Beckner, Jacob W. 22:65
Beckner, Philip 16:89
Beckner, Washington 22:289
Beckols, W. 3:20
Becks, R. 17:271
Beckshire, J. 3:20

Beckstead, Frederick 25:141
Beckstein, Herman 12:12
Becktol, J. 27:142
Beckwelt, George 19:55
Beckwelt, Herbert D. 19:55
Beckwith, C. 3:20
Beckwith, C. C. 15:102
Beckwith, Charles 15:262
Beckwith, Charles B. 14:130
Beckwith, E. 3:20
Beckwith, F. 1:16
Beckwith, Francis 20:206
Beckwith, G. 12:94; 25:141
Beckwith, George 5:9; 15:357
Beckwith, George R. 23:304
Beckwith, George W. 12:12
Beckwith, Gilbert 10:40; 20:206
Beckwith, H. D. 13:61
Beckwith, H. G. 15:183
Beckwith, Herbert 7:55
Beckwith, J. 1:20
Beckwith, J. H. 18:63
Beckwith, J. P. 10:13
Beckwith, James 17:75
Beckwith, John 4:10
Beckwith, John P. 26:11
Beckwith, Joseph 4:10
Beckwith, L. 17:143
Beckwith, Lafayette 21:300
Beckwith, Martin 15:183; 22:65
Beckwith, Nicholas 20:206
Beckwith, Rufus J. 13:9
Beckwith, S. 1:18
Beckwith, Stewart W. 4:10
Beckwith, W. 16:172
Beckworth, Francis 10:102
Beckworth, G. 20:153
Beckworth, James 1:13
Beckwoth, Joel 7:7
Becky, Levi 23:290
Becroft, John T. 22:65
Bectold, Charles 21:47
Becuet, Baltic 8:45
Bedall, S. 14:36
Bedden, H. R. 26:15
Beddlecomb, George 23:105
Bede, Richard 24:47

Bedee, Charles 16:172
Bedee, Richard 11:410
Bedell, Alonzo A. 4:10
Bedell, J. L. 9:168; 19:247
Bedell, James 21:242
Bedell, James T. 16:138
Bedell, Jesse 19:4
Bedell, L. 9:168; 19:273
Bedell, Walter 21:64
Bedford, Alexander 10:157; 19:148
Bedford, Charles 22:447
Bedford, G. W. 1:116
Bedford, George W. 10:40; 20:206
Bedford, Henry 23:127
Bedford, J. 8:45
Bedford, John 21:134
Bedford, John R. 13:9
Bedient, James S. 21:134
Bedinger, R. 21:96
Bedker, Frederick 17:29
Bedllion, David 25:141
Bedman, C. 21:185
Bedon, Ashel 17:241
Bedork, David 18:121
Bedorke, David 8:8
Bedorthy, H. K. 12:7
Beds, Joe 11:223
Bedwell, James 9:235; 26:216
Bedwell, James M. 21:47
Bedwell, James R. 7:86
Bedwell, Robert M. 8:79
Bedwell, Tilghman H. 23:59
Bedz, Martin 25:141
Bee, Benjamin F. 7:64
Bee, C. O. 14:36, 132
Bee, Daniel 23:201
Bee, Francis 11:137
Bee, George 3:20
Bee, Hugh 25:141
Bee, J. 9:65
Bee, Thomas 3:20
Beeb, J. 11:257
Beebe, A. 21:119
Beebe, B. F. 26:152
Beebe, Charles A. 15:164; 27:142
Beebe, Charles E. 11:103
Beebe, Charles W. 23:85
Beebe, Clark 24:12
Beebe, David B. 23:19
Beebe, Edwin 16:138
Beebe, Franklin H. 11:285
Beebe, H. H. 22:177
Beebe, Hosmer P. 8:79
Beebe, J. E. 3:20
Beebe, John 3:20

Beebe, Joseph 11:123; 13:104
Beebe, L. M. 25:14
Beebe, Leroy 21:197
Beebe, M. L. 1:15
Beebe, N. A. 10:147
Beebe, Nathan L. 24:91
Beebe, Oliver 15:63
Beebe, P. J. 9:168
Beebe, R. 17:287
Beebe, W. H. 22:8
Beebe, Waldo 11:135
Beebe, William 19:148
Beebe, William W. 10:40
Beebe, Y. A. 18:45
Beebee, Charles 18:391
Beebee, David E. 11:399
Beebee, Gilbert 4:10
Beebee, H. S. 14:36
Beebee, Milton 22:65
Beebee, T. J. 19:247
Beebee, W. H. 20:206
Beeber, John 11:237
Beeby, Goblin 9:11
Beech, A. L. 11:428
Beech, E. L. 1:112
Beech, Edward 21:300
Beech, James M. 22:473
Beech, John E. 20:29
Beech, Lyman A. 10:157
Beech, Samuel R. 15:183
Beecham, Charles 8:8; 18:121
Beecham, Joseph A. 23:133
Beecher, C. H. W. 11:198
Beecher, Charles 8:8; 18:121
Beecher, Ephraim 26:150
Beecher, Franklin 10:157
Beecher, George 18:302
Beecher, Jessie 18:24
Beecher, Joseph A. 23:244
Beecher, L. 14:140, 253
Beecher, N. C. 22:19
Beecher, Philip 17:453; 24:185
Beecher, Robert T. 9:11
Beecher, S. N. 18:337
Beecher, Zebn 11:258
Beechman, John 19:55
Beechnor, Casper 17:63
Beed, Hiram 17:25
Beede, F. I. 9:139
Beede, T. J. 27:16
Beede, William S. 14:140
Beedle, F. W. 7:19
Beedleman, George W. 12:13
Beedlemann, A. H. 18:274

Beedy, Nathaniel 18:302; 26:92
Beegel, Henry W. 16:116
Beegle, C. W. 1:109
Beeham, P. 16:173
Beehan, John 18:187
Beehiel, Philip 15:29
Beehler, Daniel 3:223
Beek, Cornelius 11:52
Beek, J. 15:63, 183
Beek, J. G. 16:287
Beekel, William 9:32
Beekelshyrner, H. 23:19
Beeker, Christian 15:164
Beeker, Henry I. 10:40
Beeker, Jacob 22:65
Beekey, William 1:113
Beekman, C. P. 13:126
Beekman, Charles 18:391
Beekman, Frank 13:9
Beekman, Henry 4:10; 26:216
Beekman, Henry J. 23:284
Beekman, John 4:10
Beekman, Robert 7:117
Beekman, William H. 16:21
Beekner, George 19:243
Beel, Isaac 8:37
Beel, James 17:107
Beeler, C. 18:187
Beeler, Christine 23:133
Beeler, Daniel 17:504; 22:499
Beeler, G. 16:172
Beeler, George W. 18:213
Beeler, John 18:204; 26:120
Beeler, John W. 14:1
Beeler, Joseph 22:241
Beeler, Louis 23:19
Beeler, Nathan 17:294
Beeler, P. 17:127; 24:187
Beeler, William 22:241
Beelman, George M. 20:38
Beelor, Fred 20:206
Beelre, Frederick 10:40
Beels, John G. 1:18
Beelville, Archibald 8:8
Beem, Abraham 9:75
Beem, Beuben 9:218
Beem, P. P. 9:139
Beem, Reuben 18:362
Beem, William P. 23:59
Beeman, A. 27:23
Beeman, B. F. 17:29
Beeman, C. 14:36
Beeman, Charles F. 9:116; 27:18
Beeman, Francis 1:114

Beeman, J. M. 14:36
Beeman, James M. 25:141
Beeman, James W. 1:16
Beeman, Richard 3:20
Beeman, S. 25:141
Beeman, William 25:268
Beemer, A. 25:19
Beemer, Albert 2:8
Beemer, Michael 17:75
Beemis, G. 14:239
Been, Daniel 20:144
Been, J. 16:173
Been, W. E. 5:9
Beene, David 11:24
Beene, Jeremiah 14:140
Beener, S. 3:20; 20:38
Beenfry, Sank 26:150
Beenier, S. 5:9
Beeny, Samuel 20:144
Beer, A. J. 20:55
Beer, D. 11:103
Beer, J. 21:193
Beer, Joseph 13:9
Beer, Samuel 12:66;
    15:63
Beer, Shedrack 21:300
Beer, Solomon 21:9
Beerbower, John W.
    10:102; 20:206
Beerd, John 1:15
Beerly, M. 25:15
Beerman, Daniel 15:85
Beerry, Isaac 22:177
Beers, A. 3:20
Beers, C. T. 23:19
Beers, Caleb 11:23
Beers, D. S. 17:497
Beers, Giles E. 9:11
Beers, Hiram S. 25:141
Beers, J. 7:19
Beers, James 13:9
Beers, Lucas M. 11:115
Beers, Peter 16:89
Beers, T. S. 22:350
Beers, Thaddeus S.
    22:459
Beers, Uriah 10:40;
    20:206
Beers, Wesley 27:23
Beers, William 5:9;
    25:141
Beers, William R. 24:12
Beersick, Charles W. 8:8
Beery, Solomon 24:74
Bees, A. 14:140
Bees, Simon 18:77
Beesack, Nicholas 23:59
Beeshenie, T. 9:139
Beesicks, George H. 9:15
Beesing, Louis 24:12

Beesley, J. W. 18:229;
    26:15
Beesley, James 17:170
Beesley, William T.
    10:40; 20:206
Beesman, Martin 13:9
Beesman, T. C. 9:107
Beesmer, Milton 22:460
Beesom, Milto 21:193
Beesom, William H.
    21:193
Beeson, James H. 22:65
Beeson, Richard 24:58
Beeson, U. O. 11:299
Beeson, William 13:9
Beet, A. 14:140
Beetenschiag, Johann
    23:19
Beethely, --- 11:285
Beetley, Lewis 24:12
Beetman, Adam 4:10
Beets, Augustus H. 1:15
Beets, J. 14:318; 25:268
Beewer, A. F. 11:25
Beezley, C. C. 9:218;
    18:362
Beezley, H. 17:497
Beezley, Joseph M.
    22:241
Beff, N. 9:75; 26:12
Before, George 23:305
Befurt, John 15:329
Befust, John 19:55
Begelow, Henry 13:9
Beger, Michael 16:363
Beges, Enoch 18:117
Begg, A. 1:111
Begg, William 17:354
Begham, J. H. 25:141
Begle, John 14:264
Begley, J. A. 17:296
Beglin, John 22:417
Beguette, Julian 18:45
Begwell, Isom H. 10:102;
    20:206
Behaige, Cornelius 18:204
Behan, John 24:12
Behand, James A. 3:20
Behar, Hannon 10:40
Behays, Cornelius 8:79
Behen, George 12:13
Beherstine, David 18:290
Behka, C. 16:173
Behlen, George 21:220
Behlen, John 10:13
Behlike, Henry 21:250
Behm, J. 23:19
Behm, John 19:337
Behm, Otto 19:55
Behn, John 15:102
Behr, B. 24:12

Behr, John 4:10
Behre, William 17:351
Behreas, A. 3:20
Behrens, J. C. 19:247
Behrens, John 23:19
Behrens, John C. 9:168
Behrman, Michael 9:18
Behrns, Henry 24:12
Behuke, Henry 25:16
Beidelman, Alexander H.
    23:19
Beider, I. 16:116
Beidleman, Samuel
    23:105
Beif, Charles 11:118
Beigelow, T. H. 25:18
Beighle, C. 23:19
Beighler, Enoch 24:47
Beightel, J. F. 3:20
Beihl, Nicholas 4:10
Beiler, William B. 23:133
Beilly, John 10:206
Bein, Adam 1:13
Beindisch, Frank 26:216
Beiner, Henry F. 21:97
Beinhammer, Fred 20:206
Beinhammer, Frederick
    10:102
Beir, Reuben 7:117
Beiran, S. 21:185
Beirn, Stephen 19:289
Beirnes, James 8:103
Beirs, James C. 3:20
Beiry, Jacob 22:136
Beiry, William 13:61
Beisaker, Jacob 21:119
Beisel, Aaron 9:116;
    27:18
Beisel, G. M. 9:107
Beiser, Nicholas 23:112
Beisterfield, Henry 21:17
Beistle, J. 12:66
Beistle, Jacob 19:148
Beitel, Heman 11:138
Beiter, Benedict 23:19
Beitley, Charles 9:205
Beitzell, Benjamin F.
    18:213
Bekel, Joseph 18:24
Bekwith, J. E. 23:19
Belan, Hank 26:151
Belance, Oliver 9:168
Belander, James 15:297
Belby, John 19:4
Belch, Henry 21:250
Belch, Josiah 22:177
Belcher, Andrew 11:399
Belcher, B. F. 5:9; 25:141
Belcher, Charles G. 9:18
Belcher, E. W. 13:104
Belcher, Fred. E. 9:168

Belcher, Frederick E.
19:235
Belcher, G. 1:110
Belcher, Henry A. 25:141
Belcher, Ira B. 22:400
Belcher, James 11:24
Belcher, John 8:61
Belcher, L. T. 1:17
Belcher, Samuel 17:153
Belcher, Stephen 16:21
Belden, Charles E. 17:320
Belden, Charles F. 22:177
Belden, D. F. 21:300
Belden, Eugene C. 23:119
Belden, G. W. 14:140
Belden, Hamlet 17:404
Belden, Harman J. 17:417
Belden, Harry 11:135
Belden, Henry 13:9
Belden, Herman 24:155
Belden, W. 19:235
Belden, Walter 9:168
Belden, William 3:21
Beldin, W. D. 1:111
Belding, F. 3:21
Belding, William W.
20:180
Beldof, Jacob 19:337
Beldon, Orland 7:19
Beldron, S. 1:14
Bele, Nelson 14:36
Belen, Hank 8:37
Beler, George D. 20:121
Belew, Solomon 17:258
Belfard, John 26:91
Belfinger, A. 14:4
Belford, Charles C. 20:94
Belford, David 13:9
Belford, J. H. 11:22
Belford, John 3:21;
18:302
Belford, Joshua 22:177
Belfour, R. C. 13:104
Belge, R. 13:61
Belge, Rudolph 19:55
Belger, Henry 17:48
Belger, I. W. 15:339
Belger, J. W. 16:363
Belger, Patrick 8:8;
18:121
Belger, W. 1:110
Belhart, G. 14:4; 16:266
Belhimer, L. 1:109
Belia, Jacob 20:88
Belick, I. 24:12
Belihiemer, J. 1:112
Belisky, J. 3:21
Belk, Green 20:182
Belk, John 10:94
Belknap, Franklin 22:460
Belknapp, L. R. 20:191

Bell, --- 18:171; 24:100
Bell, --- (Mrs.) 18:187
Bell, A. 3:20
Bell, A. J. 26:93
Bell, A. P. 15:339; 16:363
Bell, Albert 17:170
Bell, Alexander 6:24;
9:116; 22:289; 27:11
Bell, Alfred 9:205; 11:133
Bell, Andrew 10:170
Bell, Andrew J. 18:290
Bell, Archi'l 26:210
Bell, Austin 10:102;
20:206
Bell, B. B. 3:20
Bell, Benjamin 17:127;
19:44; 24:188
Bell, Benjamin F. 22:65
Bell, C. 10:211
Bell, Calvin 8:99
Bell, Cave Johnson
23:270
Bell, Charles 8:117;
17:161; 19:44, 315;
21:300
Bell, Charles M. 15:288
Bell, Christian 1:18
Bell, D. 5:35; 21:108
Bell, D. C. 13:61; 19:55
Bell, D. M. 17:290
Bell, D. S. 3:20; 17:427
Bell, David 13:9; 20:95;
22:523
Bell, David R. 22:65
Bell, Doctor S. 24:182
Bell, E. 25:141; 26:210
Bell, E. S. 3:20
Bell, Edward 11:198
Bell, Edwin 4:10
Bell, Edwin A. 1:19
Bell, Eli 23:133
Bell, Elijah 5:9
Bell, Elisha 17:234
Bell, Enoch 22:400
Bell, Ephraim M. 22:460
Bell, Francis 18:24;
25:141
Bell, Frank 22:136
Bell, Fred. K. 7:117
Bell, G. 9:168; 19:247
Bell, G. A. 20:4
Bell, George 3:20; 9:168,
205; 14:140; 16:173;
17:409; 22:117;
27:20
Bell, George C. 13:9
Bell, George H. 19:148
Bell, George W. 23:187
Bell, Gleason C. 25:15
Bell, H. 3:20; 12:85;
16:287

Bell, H. C. 3:20; 22:177
Bell, Henry 7:77; 11:90;
17:170; 25:293
Bell, Henry C. 9:48
Bell, Hiram 7:86
Bell, Horace 17:170
Bell, I. 1:109; 18:171
Bell, Irpeth 8:8
Bell, Isaac 17:278; 26:151
Bell, Isman 17:170
Bell, J. 1:18, 112; 3:20;
9:139; 11:137; 18:63;
24:109; 27:15
Bell, J. C. 7:86
Bell, J. H. 22:496
Bell, J. R. 3:20
Bell, J. W. 18:45
Bell, Jackson 7:86
Bell, James 5:9; 7:19;
12:13; 15:183;
16:173; 17:396, 417,
446; 22:20, 177;
24:12, 155, 169;
25:141
Bell, James D. 22:117
Bell, James M. 9:116;
27:19
Bell, Japseth 18:121
Bell, Jefferson 22:499
Bell, Jesse 12:172
Bell, John 1:15; 11:90,
222, 325; 16:89;
18:107, 274; 22:289;
23:15, 308; 25:141
Bell, John C. 22:417
Bell, John R. 8:103
Bell, John T. 9:75
Bell, John W. 21:97
Bell, Jonathan F. 26:10
Bell, Jos. E. 16:173
Bell, Joseph 1:17, 113;
3:20; 6:27; 7:86;
21:300; 22:177;
23:283; 25:141
Bell, Joseph A. 10:13
Bell, Josiah 12:150
Bell, L. W. 11:189
Bell, Leander W. 21:64
Bell, Leonard 17:170
Bell, Lewis 1:13
Bell, M. 15:183
Bell, Moses 22:416;
25:141
Bell, N. N. 11:138
Bell, Nathan 21:300
Bell, Nelson 21:264
Bell, Newell W. 19:148
Bell, Orlando 16:287
Bell, P. 16:173
Bell, Peter 8:112
Bell, Peter S. 8:112

Bell, R. 15:85; 16:173
Bell, R. F. 17:316
Bell, R. W. 1:13
Bell, Richard 16:173;
    19:55; 26:210
Bell, Robert 9:169, 205;
    12:66; 18:24;
    19:247; 22:65;
    24:189; 25:141;
    26:216
Bell, Robert J. 22:241
Bell, Robert W. 16:116
Bell, Samuel 16:173;
    19:55
Bell, Samuel H. 8:103
Bell, Samuel J. 21:300
Bell, Samuel R. 11:14
Bell, Sandy 25:285
Bell, Shelby 9:70
Bell, Snyder 26:152
Bell, Stephen 25:141
Bell, Sydney 8:61
Bell, Sylvester 9:18
Bell, Taylor 21:264
Bell, Thomas 3:20; 11:23,
    102, 134
Bell, Thomas C. 22:415
Bell, Thomas E. 8:103
Bell, Thomas J. 24:35
Bell, Thompson M.
    11:321
Bell, V. N. 6:8
Bell, W. 11:298
Bell, W. A. 22:177
Bell, W. C. 11:380; 12:86;
    16:287
Bell, W. D. 19:299
Bell, W. H. 11:197;
    14:37; 25:141
Bell, W. I. 10:40
Bell, W. J. 20:206
Bell, W. M. 25:281
Bell, Washington 21:264
Bell, Washington L. 13:9
Bell, Watson 7:117
Bell, Will 7:86
Bell, William 3:20; 9:205,
    218; 10:40; 11:90;
    13:61; 16:173;
    17:278; 18:63, 102,
    362; 20:34, 206;
    21:300; 23:177, 240;
    24:47, 89; 25:18,
    278, 285, 310
Bell, William D. 8:79;
    18:213
Bell, William H. 5:35;
    16:89; 23:59
Bell, William J. 17:358
Bell, William P. 12:54
Bell, William S. 22:241

Bell, Zephaniah 21:64
Bellair, Anthony 9:205
Bellamy, E. A. 18:229;
    26:15
Bellamy, Harvey 16:21
Bellamy, Henry H. 20:29
Bellamy, James 20:177
Bellamy, Thomas J.
    17:234
Bellany, Harvey 13:56
Bellard, G. B. 23:133
Bellare, James 17:287
Bellars, G. 9:139
Belle, Ezra 20:188
Belle, Robert 3:21
Bellegard, G. 20:206
Beller, George W. 24:12
Beller, Henry 7:20
Belles, H. 7:55
Belles, Silas 2:8; 25:15
Bellesom, Charles 22:330
Belleville, Freeman
    11:133
Bellew, Colledge C.
    22:117
Bellfield, William H.
    23:10
Bellgard, Gregore 10:41
Bellgard, John F. 7:86
Bellimes, S. 12:66
Bellinger, A. 13:83
Bellinger, Christopher
    10:13
Bellinger, G. 3:21
Bellinger, William M.
    24:107
Bellings, Jose 24:151
Bellington, W. T. 19:4
Bellis, James 15:289
Bellis, John 25:13
Bellis, Joseph 16:173
Bellman, C. 1:16
Bellman, Franklin R.
    23:240
Bellman, Lewis 15:53
Bellman, William 17:127;
    24:188
Bellon, Theodore 24:91
Bellony, John 27:143
Bellow, Joseph 26:236
Bellow, Nathaniel 19:148
Bellows, Charles 20:110
Bellows, E. 12:86; 16:287
Bellows, Edwin 21:17
Bellows, George 5:9;
    25:141; 27:16
Bellows, Horace 12:54
Bellows, Nathaniel 10:157
Bellows, O. M. 22:177
Bells, J. H. 3:21
Bells, R. 13:77; 14:37

Bells, Thomas 9:75
Bellshaw, John 16:21
Bellville, Archibald
    18:121
Bellville, Thomas 19:4
Bellwa, John 14:140
Bellwood, Theodore
    10:157; 19:148
Belmar, Archer 23:197
Belner, Cornelius 11:24
Belo, Christian 1:114
Belogy, Israel 4:10
Belonia, Alpha 13:9
Belor, George 21:250
Belote, Darwin N. 23:276
Belote, James L. 22:460
Beloyer, George M.
    18:334
Belp, W. 14:37
Belson, Isaac 21:17
Belsor, Henry M. 22:65
Belt, Charles 10:41
Belt, G. A. 18:302; 26:93
Belt, H. 23:262
Belt, Henry E. 24:47
Belt, John W. 22:241
Belt, Josiah H. 23:19
Belt, Nathaniel D. 21:97
Belt, Thomas 22:448
Belt, William T. 20:95
Beltham, William 4:10
Beltner, John 18:213
Belton, Joseph 18:213
Belton, Robert A. 7:66
Belton, T. J. 16:116
Belton, Thomas H. 22:330
Belts, Adam 15:150
Belts, C. H. 21:17
Belts, J. K. 13:61; 16:173
Belts, James F. 20:206
Beltz, Abraham 14:334
Beltz, Charles 4:10
Beltz, Joseph 26:150
Beltz, N. W. 3:21
Beltz, William 4:10
Belve, John M. 24:189
Belville, Henry 11:279
Belvri, Louis 18:117
Belwood, Levi 20:4
Belz, John 18:187
Bema, E. 23:187
Beman, G. 27:22
Beman, Job 19:148
Beman, Stephen 21:203
Beman, William S. 8:103
Bemans, S. 18:411
Bembooter, George
    18:121
Beme, Alonzo 7:19
Bement, Clement C.
    11:102

Bement, M. L. 15:183
Bement, Sylvester 21:64
Bemer, John 10:26;
    19:299
Bemer, Solomon 27:19
Bemis, --- 22:8
Bemis, A. D. 14:140
Bemis, C. 22:472
Bemis, Charles 3:21
Bemis, Charles B. 1:20
Bemis, G. 16:89
Bemis, H. 3:21
Bemis, I. W. 9:139
Bemis, J. W. 15:90
Bemis, Joseph 12:61
Bemis, M. L. 7:47
Bemis, Morris C. 1:13
Bemis, P. 18:24
Bemiss, James W. 22:136
Bemmer, Joseph 11:117
Bemmis, William 17:265
Bemner, Joseph 10:102
Bemon, Andrew 8:8
Bemon, B. 16:277
Bemont, J. 1:110
Bems, Lewis 9:239
Ben, Frank W. 18:12
Bena, R. 12:61
Benadum, Nelson 24:176
Benar, Edward 9:205
Benaston, Albion 24:156
Benastow, Albion 17:442
Benaway, Peter 11:103
Benaway, T. 25:141
Benbann, I. 9:139
Benbee, G. 10:147
Benbow, Benjamin 11:51
Benbow, Edom 23:85
Benbow, John M. 21:220
Benbrook, G. E. 8:61
Benc, G. M. 7:73
Bence, James 26:16
Bencel, Augustus 20:206
Bench, Aaron 7:86
Bench, G. 15:183
Bench, Harvey S. 27:20
Bench, William 17:439;
    24:151
Bencifield, William
    17:439; 24:151
Benda, Frantz 16:143
Bendall, C. 1:18
Bendel, G. D. 14:268
Bendel, William 18:302;
    26:91
Bendell, A. 14:37
Benden, H. 1:93
Bender, Andreas 22:65
Bender, C. 3:21
Bender, Charles 21:17
Bender, Charles L. 22:177

Bender, Damon 12:171
Bender, Daniel 12:13
Bender, F. J. 14:37
Bender, Frederick 24:64
Bender, George 3:21
Bender, H. 20:144
Bender, Jacob 13:10
Bender, James 9:75; 26:10
Bender, John 12:13;
    13:104
Bender, L. 14:295;
    17:470; 27:20
Bender, Lewis 12:53
Bender, Peter 4:10;
    10:102; 20:207
Bender, S. 16:15
Bender, William 20:182
Bendere, E. C. 25:20
Bendikson, Benedick
    24:47
Bendill, William 8:70
Bending, Jeremiah 6:15;
    18:77
Bendle, H. 14:279
Bendler, Christopher 8:8
Bendon, H. B. 17:29
Bendure, John 22:417
Beneby, James A. 10:89
Benechilt, Charles 27:22
Benecken, D. 1:116
Benedick, Allen 11:24
Benedick, G. R. 2:8
Benedick, George 15:183
Benedick, H. 9:169
Benedick, J. M. 2:8
Benedict, A. 21:300
Benedict, Anson W.
    23:133
Benedict, C. 22:65
Benedict, Crance 22:460
Benedict, E. 12:145
Benedict, Flavel 21:119
Benedict, G. H. 10:153
Benedict, G. L. 25:14
Benedict, George 22:136
Benedict, H. 19:247
Benedict, H. S. 19:340
Benedict, Henry 23:85
Benedict, J. 1:116; 17:153
Benedict, J. M. 1:113;
    25:19
Benedict, Jacob 7:86
Benedict, John 4:10
Benedict, John E. 24:12
Benedict, John P. 22:416
Benedict, Joseph B.
    19:287
Benedict, L. H. 5:9;
    10:144
Benedict, Lorman 11:24
Benedict, Moses 14:321

Benedict, N. B. 23:133
Benedict, Norman 12:150
Benedict, P. S. 19:4
Benedict, Russell 22:136
Benedict, Theo. B. 9:11
Benedict, Thomas 22:460
Benedict, W. 1:20
Benedict, William 11:235;
    14:140
Benedine, A. A. 21:119
Benedund, Jesse 27:21
Benedus, George 1:17
Beneel, Augustus 10:102
Benefiel, John K. 17:233
Benefiel, Robert S. 21:220
Beneker, Henry 7:86;
    21:300
Bener, Joseph 7:47
Benerly, Napolean 24:155
Beneroft, John G. 15:183
Beners, John 7:55
Benet, J. 19:148
Benezia, Joseph 6:24
Benfield, J. D. 25:141
Benfield, John H. 22:417
Benfli, Sauk 8:37
Benford, Philip 22:289
Benfro, W. M. 21:185
Bengal, Charles 11:331
Benge, James 25:332
Benge, Joseph 8:8
Bengee, Benjamin 13:126
Bengel, Frederick 4:10
Bengman, J. 22:20
Bengman, W. H. 3:21
Bengston, Lewis 26:10
Bengston, Louis 9:75
Benhack, Henry 20:84
Benham, Dempster B.
    23:59
Benham, G. K. 25:293
Benham, Henry D. 27:12
Benham, J. 17:290
Benham, J. M. 17:63
Benham, Joel A. 11:285,
    291
Benham, M. C. 17:161
Benham, Preston 11:52
Benham, Robinson 12:150
Benham, Rowland 21:300
Benham, S. E. 17:63
Benhane, W. A. 21:300
Benhard, Alex 11:135
Benhart, John 13:128
Benhoff, L. 25:141
Beniah, J. 1:111
Benie, Benedict 19:44
Benika, Arnold 22:117
Benis, G. W. 27:16
Benitlif, Thomas 18:171
Benitz, Edmund 23:19

Benix, S. M. L. 8:45
Benjamin, A. C. 16:173
Benjamin, Alcart 21:300
Benjamin, Allen 22:8
Benjamin, Ambrose S.
21:250
Benjamin, C. 1:17
Benjamin, Chancelor
12:13
Benjamin, Charles 7:81;
19:148; 25:293
Benjamin, Charles F.
9:41; 26:121
Benjamin, Charles H.
10:157
Benjamin, D. 14:37
Benjamin, D. L. 11:236
Benjamin, E. B. 1:96
Benjamin, Edwin 23:10
Benjamin, F. O. R. 25:141
Benjamin, Frederick
18:229; 26:15
Benjamin, Grant B. 19:55
Benjamin, H. 13:103;
14:4; 16:266; 21:109
Benjamin, H. E. 27:13
Benjamin, Harris 23:197
Benjamin, Harvey N.
23:187
Benjamin, Henry 10:41
Benjamin, J. 1:17; 14:37
Benjamin, J. B. 16:21
Benjamin, J. W. 14:141
Benjamin, James 10:41
Benjamin, James F. 17:73
Benjamin, Jesse 11:102
Benjamin, John 4:10
Benjamin, John P. 13:10
Benjamin, Lathrop 13:10
Benjamin, Laythrop 16:21
Benjamin, M. 1:112
Benjamin, Marcellus
17:63
Benjamin, Oley 9:75;
26:10
Benjamin, P. 1:111
Benjamin, Park 9:169
Benjamin, S. F. 8:45
Benjamin, Samuel F.
21:17
Benjamin, T. O. B. 5:9
Benjamin, W. Y. 1:116
Benjamin, William
11:380; 14:37
Benjamin, William S.
18:391
Benjia, Joseph 5:9
Benjiman, Grant B.
15:283
Benjimin, W. G. 15:289
Benke, William 22:417

Benker, John 4:10
Benker, Thomas 7:19
Benkler, Nicholas 13:10
Benlis, J. M. 3:21
Benlit, F. 3:21
Benlon, E. 16:173
Benlow, William 11:51
Benly, Henry 8:112
Benn, Abraham 26:11
Benn, L. 12:81; 16:287
Benn, Peter 20:177
Benn, William 25:283
Bennd, C. 9:199; 19:289
Bennd, G. D. 14:279
Bennedict, L. H. 19:148
Bennefield, John 24:35
Bennell, Albert 9:169;
19:273
Bennell, Frank 10:7
Bennell, Martin B. 8:79
Bennell, William 26:153
Benner, A. E. 3:21
Benner, B. S. 22:496
Benner, C. 13:83
Benner, Castle 17:170
Benner, Christian 23:281
Benner, F. C. 9:75
Benner, F. M. 17:275
Benner, Fieden 23:278
Benner, Franklin 9:169;
19:269
Benner, H. 14:141
Benner, J. 1:110, 116
Benner, Joseph H. 23:59
Benner, L. 14:37; 23:85
Benner, P. 13:104
Benner, W. 1:19
Benner, W. A. 3:21
Benner, W. T. 21:203
Benner, William 3:21
Benner, William E. 12:13
Bennet, C. W. 15:183
Bennet, Charles 18:271
Bennet, D. A. 20:153
Bennet, F. 15:157
Bennet, Henry A. 26:92
Bennet, J. A. 8:119
Bennet, Jacob 11:138
Bennet, John J. T. 11:135
Bennet, John W. 22:177
Bennet, Pat 25:293
Bennet, Richard 15:171
Bennet, Samuel 18:274;
20:207
Bennet, Thomas 15:63
Bennet, William 5:49;
8:70
Bennether, --- 3:21
Bennett, --- 1:13; 3:21;
25:15

Bennett, A. 1:20; 3:21;
9:108, 226
Bennett, A. A. 7:19
Bennett, A. H. 11:234
Bennett, A. J. 12:98
Bennett, A. O. 13:83
Bennett, A. S. 1:111
Bennett, Abram 11:197;
22:417
Bennett, Albert 17:73
Bennett, Alderson 20:132
Bennett, Alfred C. 22:417
Bennett, Allen 11:420
Bennett, Andrew 18:213,
362
Bennett, Andrew J. 20:29
Bennett, Andrew T. 8:79
Bennett, Anthony 23:278
Bennett, Augustus 13:10
Bennett, Austin 25:18
Bennett, B. 18:213
Bennett, B. F. 25:17
Bennett, Ben 21:264
Bennett, Benjamin F.
11:23; 22:164
Bennett, C. 1:18; 3:21;
12:121; 15:118
Bennett, C. A. 22:473
Bennett, C. B. 3:21
Bennett, C. E. 1:13
Bennett, C. H. 22:473
Bennett, C. W. 1:13;
26:153
Bennett, Caleb N. 10:102
Bennett, Carlisle 16:138
Bennett, Charles 12:13;
13:10; 15:53
Bennett, Charles E. 9:32;
11:257
Bennett, Charles F. 10:41;
20:207
Bennett, Charles W. 23:59
Bennett, D. 9:139; 14:37;
27:16
Bennett, Daniel 23:133
Bennett, Daniel F. 9:48
Bennett, David J. 17:442;
24:156
Bennett, E. 1:13; 11:384;
23:133
Bennett, E. M. 11:236
Bennett, E. S. 9:169
Bennett, Eber 8:112
Bennett, Edgar 5:9;
17:231
Bennett, Edson C. 24:48
Bennett, Edward F.
21:300
Bennett, Eli 5:9; 17:75
Bennett, Elias 19:4
Bennett, Elie 25:141

Bennett, Elisha D. 15:118, 349
Bennett, Emery 22:417
Bennett, Ephraim 18:229; 22:177; 26:14
Bennett, Erastus 1:113
Bennett, Eugene H. 11:180
Bennett, F. 14:37
Bennett, F. J. 14:1; 18:45
Bennett, F. P. 19:235
Bennett, Ferdinand 23:187
Bennett, Fernando 23:284
Bennett, Francis 21:300
Bennett, Francis J. 7:55
Bennett, Francis M. 9:116
Bennett, Franklin 12:141; 20:207; 22:136
Bennett, Fred 9:205
Bennett, G. 23:133
Bennett, G. A. 12:66; 14:141; 15:21
Bennett, G. B. 14:279
Bennett, G. E. 7:86
Bennett, G. H. 15:315; 19:55
Bennett, G. W. 8:70
Bennett, Gay 7:117
Bennett, George 8:8; 9:169; 12:53; 14:141; 18:121, 290; 19:55; 23:133
Bennett, George H. 11:399; 13:10; 20:29
Bennett, George J. 23:133
Bennett, George N. 16:21
Bennett, George S. 17:262
Bennett, George W. 4:10; 12:58; 13:10
Bennett, Gilbert 21:264
Bennett, H. 8:45; 14:28; 16:287; 18:229; 22:518; 26:15
Bennett, H. H. 11:236; 24:35
Bennett, H. K. 11:297
Bennett, H. O. 23:19
Bennett, Hanford 9:169
Bennett, Harrison 13:10
Bennett, Henry 10:41; 14:141; 17:170; 18:323; 20:207; 21:134, 264; 22:20
Bennett, Henry A. 9:18; 18:302
Bennett, Henry C. 13:10
Bennett, Henry D. 12:66
Bennett, Hiram 9:108
Bennett, Hiram H. 22:20
Bennett, I. I. 10:152

Bennett, I. W. 15:339
Bennett, Ira 16:87; 17:358
Bennett, Irving T. 13:10
Bennett, Isaac 21:220
Bennett, J. 1:113; 3:21; 11:22; 14:277; 16:173; 21:17; 23:19; 24:35; 25:141; 27:12
Bennett, J. B. 10:41, 89
Bennett, J. F. 8:103; 14:37
Bennett, J. H. 3:21; 14:141
Bennett, J. J. 18:45
Bennett, J. K. 1:15
Bennett, J. L. 16:287
Bennett, J. R. 25:17
Bennett, J. T. 25:141
Bennett, J. W. 11:299; 16:363
Bennett, Jacob 5:9; 17:450; 20:105; 24:177
Bennett, James 1:192; 9:71; 10:41, 102; 11:135, 295; 15:63; 18:229; 20:207; 21:300; 23:19; 25:141; 26:13, 15
Bennett, James D. 21:300
Bennett, James H. 13:10
Bennett, James W. 22:164
Bennett, Jesse H. 21:114
Bennett, John 7:86; 8:112; 14:141; 17:13; 19:4; 20:207; 22:20, 65, 415, 460, 475; 23:60, 127; 25:316
Bennett, John A. 25:316
Bennett, John B. 18:204
Bennett, John C. 7:19
Bennett, John F. 21:300
Bennett, John G. 22:474
Bennett, John H. 5:9; 7:86; 19:4
Bennett, John L. 23:255
Bennett, John M. 10:102, 157; 19:148; 20:207
Bennett, John W. 10:157; 19:148
Bennett, Joseph 1:17; 20:47
Bennett, Joseph P. 22:65
Bennett, Joseph W. 17:448; 24:173
Bennett, Joshua 22:65
Bennett, K. 9:139; 21:64; 27:13
Bennett, L. 3:21; 11:236; 13:104
Bennett, L. A. 3:21
Bennett, L. J. 3:21

Bennett, L. L. 9:169
Bennett, Lawrence 16:116
Bennett, Lemuel 21:64; 22:496
Bennett, Lemuel W. 23:281
Bennett, Leonard 19:5
Bennett, Leonard S. 19:5
Bennett, Levi 10:102; 20:207
Bennett, Levi B. 22:177
Bennett, Louis 21:264
Bennett, M. 1:109
Bennett, M. T. 1:16
Bennett, Mason 23:19
Bennett, Milton 23:133
Bennett, Moses 9:48
Bennett, N. H. 19:285
Bennett, N. L. 3:21
Bennett, O. A. 14:4
Bennett, Orien 9:32; 18:290; 26:93
Bennett, Orlando 22:65
Bennett, P. 23:133
Bennett, P. A. 17:98
Bennett, Peter G. 7:55
Bennett, Philip 8:103
Bennett, Polite 25:316
Bennett, R. 1:17; 9:18; 13:83
Bennett, R. F. 11:299
Bennett, R. H. 15:21
Bennett, R. N. 3:21
Bennett, Reuben H. 12:66
Bennett, Richard 11:14; 13:9
Bennett, Robert 18:229; 24:12; 26:15
Bennett, Robert A. 10:41
Bennett, Robert L. 8:100
Bennett, Rufus 21:264
Bennett, S. 15:339; 16:363; 17:213
Bennett, Samuel 10:102; 17:209
Bennett, Samuel F. 23:60
Bennett, Samuel S. 20:27
Bennett, Sanford 26:12
Bennett, T. 22:350
Bennett, T. F. 19:55
Bennett, T. G. 14:37
Bennett, T. H. 1:115
Bennett, Theophilus 13:10; 16:21
Bennett, Thomas 4:10; 10:157; 12:63; 14:141; 18:45, 213; 19:55; 22:241
Bennett, Thomas A. 21:300
Bennett, Thomas J. 20:95

Bennett, Thoms 19:148
Bennett, Thurman C. 17:63
Bennett, V. 16:173
Bennett, Virgil 22:447
Bennett, W. 1:110; 16:363
Bennett, W. A. 4:10
Bennett, W. E. 12:150
Bennett, W. H. 22:136
Bennett, W. J. 1:112
Bennett, W. O. 1:116
Bennett, Warren 6:20
Bennett, Warren H. 9:244
Bennett, Washington 7:86
Bennett, Wesley 16:173
Bennett, William 9:32;
    10:41; 14:37;
    15:339; 17:199;
    18:229, 411; 19:148;
    20:143, 182, 207;
    22:65, 177; 25:141,
    317; 26:15, 150, 153
Bennett, William A. 18:391
Bennett, William B. 8:61; 21:17
Bennett, William H. 7:86; 9:32; 11:134
Bennett, William M. 24:12
Bennett, William S. 9:218; 18:362; 22:20
Bennett, William W. 11:14
Bennett, Willis A. 24:63
Bennett, Z. P. 19:55
Bennette, J. F. 15:164
Bennetts, Philip 16:143
Benney, A. F. 1:112
Benney, S. 21:119
Bennie, Ida 26:217
Bennie, John 18:270
Bennilta, John 6:24
Bennine, Charles 20:110
Benning, E. J. 15:118
Benning, J. 19:55
Benning, J. W. 16:277
Benning, John 3:21
Benning, William H. 10:41
Benningfield, John H. 17:234
Bennington, Alva 9:32
Bennington, George 9:41
Bennington, Samuel 10:41; 20:207
Bennington, T. 27:142
Bennington, V. 22:177
Bennington, William 22:117
Bennion, John 1:17

Bennior, William J. 20:207
Bennitt, A. B. 18:24
Bennitt, H. 19:55
Bennman, L. 3:21
Bennon, Henry B. 9:116
Bennoni, Gifford 20:188
Bennor, William 23:133
Bennott, Robert A. 20:207
Bennsey, Seth 18:440
Bennt, A. 27:15
Benny, I. 25:141
Benny, Thomas A. 9:71
Benny, W. 22:241
Benoit, Eugene 17:17
Benondia, Emmet 19:148
Benor, H. 3:21
Benord, William 21:300
Benosh, Wenzell 9:169
Benoy, Joseph 1:113
Benron, Francis 10:157
Bensanger, D. 25:141
Bense, B. 12:150
Benser, Jacob 6:29; 25:317
Benshooter, George 8:8
Bensingen, Adam 21:300
Bensinger, John 14:318; 25:287
Bensizer, Moses 17:231
Bensley, Charles 1:17
Bensmyer, J. 14:37
Bensoble, George 21:300
Benson, --- 11:89; 18:411; 25:17
Benson, A. 3:21; 9:139, 226; 16:138; 18:362; 25:141
Benson, A. L. 5:9
Benson, A. P. 1:19
Benson, Aaron 15:63
Benson, Abraham 5:35
Benson, Albert 7:77; 25:293; 27:14
Benson, Alexander 20:121
Benson, B. P. 20:207
Benson, Benjamin T. 10:41
Benson, Bradley 22:276
Benson, C. 9:169
Benson, Charles 13:104
Benson, Charles B. 7:19
Benson, Chester 21:127
Benson, D. A. 8:45
Benson, David 22:473
Benson, Edward 15:29; 25:141
Benson, Enoch 15:63
Benson, Francis 19:148
Benson, Francis A. 21:88

Benson, Frank J. 16:88
Benson, G. 27:13
Benson, G. W. 25:141
Benson, George 9:139; 11:335; 23:104
Benson, George W. 5:9; 13:10
Benson, H. 16:173
Benson, H. L. 19:247
Benson, H. S. 15:118
Benson, Henry 5:9; 11:23
Benson, Henry L. 7:19; 9:169
Benson, Isaac 5:9; 8:45
Benson, J. 25:141
Benson, J. A. 10:209
Benson, J. B. 27:19
Benson, J. C. 19:247
Benson, Jacob 1:13
Benson, James 5:35; 25:141
Benson, James B. 9:116
Benson, Jerome 4:10
Benson, Jesse W. 16:21
Benson, John 9:41; 21:301; 26:121
Benson, John C. 9:242
Benson, John H. 10:13
Benson, John M. 11:384
Benson, John W. 11:325
Benson, Jonah 5:9
Benson, Lucien N. 21:301
Benson, Michael 22:289
Benson, O. M. 11:236
Benson, Orin 19:5
Benson, P. F. 1:16
Benson, Perry 22:460
Benson, Peter 8:103
Benson, R. L. 25:141
Benson, Richard 11:285
Benson, Rodway L. 5:9
Benson, Samuel 1:15; 6:15; 18:77
Benson, Stephen 4:10
Benson, Sylvester C. 10:102; 20:207
Benson, Thomas 9:11
Benson, W. H. 1:14
Benson, W. M. 11:325
Benson, W. N. 19:244
Benson, W. R. 16:363
Benson, William 7:15; 16:173
Benson, William H. 9:157
Bent, Elijah 7:86
Bent, George Fletcher 1:14
Bent, George W. 15:289
Bent, Henry 15:15
Bent, Luther M. 1:15
Bent, W. A. 22:330

Bent---, A. J. 24:109
Benta, Ferdinand 20:47
Bentar, Frederick 10:41
Bente, Alexander 12:13
Bente, Fred 19:55
Bente, William 1:115
Bentear, Anthony 4:10
Benter, A. 17:29
Benter, Max 7:15
Bentford, Augustus 7:86
Bentle, A. 9:18
Bentler, George 23:283
Bentler, H. 18:45
Bentler, William A. 9:32
Bentley, --- 5:49
Bentley, ---- 18:344
Bentley, Albion G. 15:277
Bentley, Augustus 22:136
Bentley, Augustus C. 9:41
Bentley, C. 3:21
Bentley, Constantine
    20:207
Bentley, Constine 10:102
Bentley, Enok 19:279
Bentley, Francis M.
    18:121
Bentley, G. 15:289;
    16:173; 21:301
Bentley, George 17:158,
    358
Bentley, George A. 12:13
Bentley, H. 3:21
Bentley, J. 1:103; 17:29;
    25:141
Bentley, J. E. 11:299
Bentley, J. L. 26:12
Bentley, James 3:21;
    18:24; 22:136
Bentley, John 15:2
Bentley, Joseph 7:86
Bentley, M. L. 18:411
Bentley, M. W. 3:21
Bentley, Orrin S. 14:37
Bentley, P. T. 4:10
Bentley, T. 3:21
Bentley, Thomas 24:12
Bentley, W. 9:108; 11:138
Bentley, W. C. 15:339;
    16:363
Bentley, William 21:301
Bentley, Wilson A. 4:10
Bentlif, Thomas 10:179
Bentliff, John 13:61
Bently, A. G. 25:141
Bently, Albert 22:475
Bently, E. 15:157
Bently, Francis M. 8:8
Bently, G. 1:113
Bently, James S. 19:148
Bently, John C. 19:55
Bently, Levi 19:5

Bently, Smith 16:173
Bently, William 13:76;
    16:173
Bentner, James 3:21
Benton, --- 14:141;
    18:187
Benton, A. 14:264
Benton, A. E. 23:19
Benton, Barnes 8:103
Benton, C. 25:293
Benton, C. W. 3:21; 17:63
Benton, Charles 20:207
Benton, D. D. 14:37
Benton, E. H. 11:236
Benton, Elisha 10:102;
    20:207
Benton, Frank 6:27; 18:77
Benton, Fred 20:207
Benton, G. 16:173
Benton, G. C. 17:29
Benton, G. E. 17:158
Benton, G. W. 1:115;
    18:24
Benton, George 8:8;
    13:61; 15:297;
    16:173
Benton, H. W. 21:301
Benton, Hamilton 27:17
Benton, Harrison 8:37;
    26:151
Benton, Henry 4:10;
    19:55
Benton, Hiram 18:121
Benton, Horace 9:139;
    27:16
Benton, Isaac 21:165
Benton, Israel 23:270
Benton, J. 1:14; 9:48
Benton, James 14:286
Benton, John 6:15;
    10:102; 18:77;
    20:207
Benton, John M. 20:207
Benton, L. 3:21
Benton, Lucius 27:142
Benton, Miles P. 18:391
Benton, Nelson 25:142
Benton, O. 14:287;
    23:133
Benton, Philip 9:41
Benton, Samuel O. 12:98;
    15:366
Benton, T. J. 16:173
Benton, Thomas 18:424;
    21:264
Benton, W. 27:21
Benton, W. C. 14:37
Benton, W. P. 21:185
Benton, Wiley 7:117
Benton, William 8:8, 79
Benton, Y. N. 1:109

Bentony, Lawrence
    21:301
Bentrupp, Florence H.
    24:91
Bents, Christian 10:7
Bents, Joseph 10:89
Bentuny, Edward 13:104
Bentz, George 12:13
Bentz, Joseph 20:207
Bentzinger, George 12:13
Benum, Willis 11:197
Benver, Charles 25:19
Benway, C. 3:21
Benway, Henry 16:277
Benway, J. 19:247
Benway, Joseph 9:169
Benway, Thomas 5:9
Beny, James 7:47
Benz, Charles 21:250
Benz, Conrad 25:142
Benzam, John 20:207
Benze, Joseph 18:121
Benziger, August 18:302;
    26:93
Benzton, N. 3:21
Benzy, George 9:169
Beoeistine, David 9:32
Beolim, Henry 15:164
Beontin, Hiram A. 8:8
Beot, Isaac 3:21
Beovins, Daniel 19:5
Bepee, William 24:109
Bepelmim, Henry 18:121
Bequeath, Solomon
    15:183
Berager, Isaac 19:5
Berbaker, Charles 16:277
Berbee, L. 13:126
Berch, Andrew 1:19
Berchard, Frank 16:146
Berchfield, W. R. 3:21
Berchnal, Wiley 19:5
Bercon, Jacob 8:79
Bercy, John 17:160
Berd, James 13:10
Berdan, Eli 10:147
Berdan, Spencer 9:11
Berdan, W. 18:45
Berdan, Wellington
    10:147
Berden, Eli 18:45
Berdine, A. A. 3:21
Berdine, Abram 17:75
Berdine, Samuel 9:70
Berdine, V. 1:13
Berdinge, Telesianna
    12:172
Berdslee, John 15:29
Berdsley, E. T. 11:399
Berdson, George 8:9

Berean, William H. C. 22:472
Beren, Edward 16:89
Bereniger, Adam 10:102; 20:207
Berenley, W. 7:47
Beresford, Frank P. 21:220
Beresticks, Abram 9:116
Beretler, Frank 25:15
Berett, A. H. 23:201
Berett, James 17:253
Berfford, W. H. 9:41
Berfoot, R. 3:21
Berford, William 20:182
Berg, Adam 19:56
Berg, Edmund 23:119
Berg, G. W. 1:19
Berg, Hezekiah 9:65
Berg, James 8:79; 10:102; 20:207
Berg, Lars N. 21:250
Berga, John 20:29
Bergan, Thomas 1:16; 20:185
Berge, A. J. 20:135
Berge, Andrew C. 20:110
Berge, Henry 22:178
Berge, John 6:23; 15:339; 16:363
Berge, M. C. 25:18
Berge, Nelson W. 13:10
Berge, Valentine 22:117
Bergeman, August 10:102
Bergemann, August 20:207
Bergen, Daniel 27:15
Bergen, James 12:98
Bergen, John 9:101; 18:337; 26:121
Bergendine, J. B. 9:48
Berger, August 25:332
Berger, Benjamin F. 21:64
Berger, C. 14:37; 15:293; 16:173
Berger, Charles 7:14; 9:239
Berger, Daniel 15:183
Berger, George 16:131
Berger, Godlip 1:16
Berger, Hamilton 17:153
Berger, J. 3:22
Berger, Jacob 8:9; 18:122; 19:5
Berger, James 15:366
Berger, John 11:137; 18:411
Berger, John W. 1:18
Berger, Joseph 4:10; 22:20
Berger, Martin M. 14:141

Berger, Samuel 17:127; 24:189
Berger, William 15:317; 19:56
Berger, Willis 17:170
Bergert, John 23:133
Berget, John W. 22:416
Berggnist, G. 1:113
Berghanson, Augustus 12:66
Berghausen, August 15:80
Berghorn, Charles 21:97
Bergin, William 14:37
Bergins, C. 14:37
Bergit, E. 26:204
Bergle, H. 9:169
Bergman, Aug 22:507
Bergman, E. 1:19
Bergman, Lewis 17:470; 27:20
Bergman, Louis 14:295
Bergmann, August 17:98
Bergrath, Anthony 24:150
Berham, H. 3:21
Berhens, William 12:164
Berian, Patrick 10:13
Berien, B. 17:320
Berin, Frederick 14:141
Beringer, John 21:9
Beringer, Samuel 19:148
Beringer, Titus 8:112
Berington, James 12:150
Berk, Adam H. 18:121
Berk, J. 14:295; 17:469; 27:20
Berk, J. S. 2:7
Berke, William 18:122
Berkenhaden, Anton 12:13
Berker, Solomon 10:152
Berkey, Abiah 4:10
Berkey, John 7:86
Berkham, Easton 22:400
Berkhamer, Joseph 7:86
Berkhardt, Caspar 21:109
Berkhart, Andrew 7:81
Berkiger, B. 3:21
Berkingstock, William 23:133
Berkley, Charles P. 13:10; 16:21
Berkley, John 12:63
Berkley, John W. 22:474
Berkley, Levi L. 11:135
Berkley, M. 3:22
Berkley, Samuel 15:183
Berkpile, Jeremiah 22:330
Berks, G. 3:22
Berkshire, E. A. 11:435
Berkshire, Samuel C. 11:53

Berkshire, T. J. 23:133
Berky, E. H. 1:17
Berky, Solomon 18:45
Berler, J. 25:142
Berlew, Isaac T. 15:118
Berlick, Inlius 9:169
Berlick, Julius 19:247
Berlin, Charles A. 21:301
Berlin, Charles H. 7:86
Berlin, Cor. J. 21:17
Berlin, E. 16:116
Berlin, J. B. 23:19
Berlin, Jacob 20:182
Berlin, James 3:22
Berlin, John 21:17
Berliner, Lewis 15:183
Berling, Samuel 25:142
Berlingam, A. J. 3:22
Berlow, Isaac T. 12:121
Berman, Christian 10:102; 20:207
Berman, H. 16:89
Bermingham, Th. 21:17
Bernahard, Joseph 11:51
Bernal, Dolares 12:171
Bernant, G. A. 1:112
Bernard, Andrew 25:293
Bernard, Bassell 21:301
Bernard, C. 7:117
Bernard, C. C. 21:18
Bernard, Charles 8:45; 21:135
Bernard, Edward 18:63
Bernard, G. 21:301
Bernard, G. P. 25:277
Bernard, George 23:19
Bernard, J. 24:188
Bernard, James M. 12:13
Bernard, John 17:127; 21:97, 109
Bernard, S. D. 21:301
Bernard, S. G. 9:169; 19:279
Bernard, Samuel 9:239
Bernard, Shelby 22:117
Bernard, Sylvanus 21:301
Bernard, Tho. J. 20:207
Bernard, Thomas J. 10:41
Bernard, William 8:77
Bernardy, Nicholas 24:91
Berner, A. I. 27:24
Berner, A. J. 14:239
Berner, David 22:499
Berner, Gottleib 4:10
Berner, Jacob 23:133
Berners, H. 14:37
Bernes, C. 10:192; 18:171
Berness, Albert 3:22
Bernett, Benjamin 22:473
Bernett, Miss 17:108
Berney, Frederick 14:314

Bernham, Carlton 15:63
Bernham, Robert S.
    11:137
Bernham, Sylvanus B.
    12:53
Bernhamer, J. 15:309
Bernhardt, Archer 13:10
Bernhardt, W. F. 1:19
Bernhauer, Cajotan
    23:112
Bernian, Conrad 16:21
Bernine, J. B. 9:48
Bernis, G. E. 14:250
Berniss, --- 11:134
Bernnett, C. D. 10:204
Berns, Anthony 22:178
Bernsey, John 18:24
Berokwater, Columbus
    8:79
Beron, Frank 9:75
Beron, Stephen 18:187
Berrer, Peter 16:89
Berrian, Charles H.
    22:177
Berrian, Conrad 13:10
Berrian, George W. B.
    13:10
Berrian, R. H. 15:183
Berrias, Thomas S. 9:169
Berrich, Merrick C. 12:94
Berrick, Merrick C.
    15:357
Berridge, Claudius 19:5
Berridge, George W.
    22:136
Berrien, C. W. 9:48
Berrien, Charles H.
    22:460
Berrier, Martin 22:177
Berrill, Adolphus C.
    21:215
Berrill, Beverly 7:117
Berrill, Silas P. 13:10
Berritt, George 10:208
Berrold, William F. 8:103
Berry, --- 1:114; 11:236;
    23:303
Berry, A. L. 19:235
Berry, A. P. 14:333
Berry, Aaron P. 22:177
Berry, Albert L. 9:169
Berry, Alfred 17:165
Berry, Allen 9:156
Berry, Alonzo 18:24
Berry, Anderson 21:264
Berry, Andrew J. 23:307
Berry, Arthur A. 12:13
Berry, B. 12:150
Berry, Bazil 9:157
Berry, Benjamin 10:89;
    20:207

Berry, C. H. 3:21
Berry, Calvin J. 22:115
Berry, Charles 5:35;
    10:13; 11:52; 25:142
Berry, Charles E. 4:10
Berry, Charlotte 26:217
Berry, Conrad 15:277
Berry, Daniel 17:258
Berry, David 20:4
Berry, David H. 7:86;
    21:301
Berry, David I. 8:8
Berry, David J. 18:122
Berry, E. 17:170; 21:119
Berry, E. A. 17:153
Berry, Edgar 8:103
Berry, Edwin 7:79; 25:293
Berry, Elijah 10:13
Berry, Ellis 27:17
Berry, Etlis 9:128
Berry, F. M. 15:183;
    21:18
Berry, G. 3:21; 22:177
Berry, Garrett 21:87
Berry, George 9:203;
    18:77; 21:301
Berry, George E. 22:447
Berry, George H. 19:5
Berry, George W. 16:113
Berry, H. 18:229; 26:14
Berry, H. F. 11:299
Berry, H. H. 11:138
Berry, Hale P. 26:138
Berry, Harrison 18:213
Berry, Henry 3:21; 9:205;
    10:98; 12:47; 18:63;
    20:207; 21:18
Berry, I. 15:183
Berry, Isaiah 17:17
Berry, J. 1:20; 11:22;
    16:173
Berry, J. C. 3:21
Berry, J. E. 13:62
Berry, J. H. 14:37
Berry, J. M. 3:21
Berry, J. R. 8:45
Berry, J. W. 9:48; 17:254
Berry, Jacob 20:207
Berry, Jake 8:37; 26:150
Berry, James 10:147;
    11:407; 17:278;
    18:45; 20:207
Berry, James F. 8:103
Berry, James L. 12:164
Berry, James M. 8:8;
    17:389; 18:122
Berry, Jeremiah 1:17
Berry, Jessie E. 19:56
Berry, John 4:64; 11:298;
    17:170; 22:289;
    25:142

Berry, John A. 11:123;
    26:121
Berry, John B. 20:207
Berry, John L. 15:63
Berry, John S. 12:61
Berry, Jonathan 17:417;
    24:155
Berry, Jordan 21:18
Berry, Joseph 5:9; 9:169;
    11:230; 19:266;
    22:137, 511, 517
Berry, Lambert 17:246
Berry, Levi 9:75; 26:11
Berry, Lewis 6:15, 28;
    7:66; 16:173; 18:77
Berry, Martin 7:19;
    16:116; 21:48
Berry, Mathers 22:241
Berry, Merriman 18:229;
    26:14
Berry, Michael 19:287
Berry, N. 14:141
Berry, P. 14:37
Berry, P. S. 9:218; 18:362
Berry, Patrick 19:235;
    26:150
Berry, Richard 7:86
Berry, Samuel 22:20, 289;
    23:284
Berry, Samuel S. 13:60
Berry, Sergeant 17:63
Berry, Simon S. 21:215
Berry, Solomon 17:170
Berry, Stephen 18:290;
    26:93
Berry, T. 22:177
Berry, T. A. 7:86
Berry, Thom 21:163
Berry, Thomas 17:75;
    22:289; 25:293
Berry, Thomas M. 15:309
Berry, V. 25:142
Berry, Vincent 5:35
Berry, W. 9:139
Berry, Walter 7:8
Berry, Westley 22:177
Berry, William 11:51,
    198; 14:141; 20:207;
    21:220; 22:417;
    23:270; 27:14
Berry, William H. 7:8
Berry, William J. 23:201
Berry, Zip 8:37; 26:151
Berryan, James H. 12:13
Berryhill, Alex. A. 24:12
Berryhill, H. A. 25:293
Berryhill, M. 27:20
Berryhill, William B.
    8:100; 17:462;
    24:177
Berryman, Eli 11:51

Berryman, Green B. 21:64
Berryman, Ira K. 17:401
Berryman, James 25:142
Berryman, John 19:5
Berrywood, --- 17:363
Bersh, E. 3:22
Bersha, John 3:22
Bersheim, T. 27:16
Bershers, Alvers 11:420
Bersner, P. 25:142
Bertan, Henry 12:168
Bertan, I. 3:22
Bertell, Charles 9:169
Berten, Richard 9:11
Bertha, John 17:128;
    24:188
Berthold, Jacob 20:4
Bertholds, Gustavus
    22:178
Berthole, Horace 11:410
Berthoud, Stephen
    10:102; 20:207
Bertin, F. 3:22
Bertin, William 4:10
Bertle, J. B. 12:13
Bertler, James V. 9:169
Bertlesen, Frederick 17:98
Bertlins, W. 18:45
Bertner, John 9:176
Bertolet, A. 16:363
Bertolet, A. F. 15:339
Berton, Calvin 21:220
Berton, Joseph 1:114
Bertouns, Lewis 4:10
Bertram, --- 14:141
Bertram, Addison 4:10
Bertram, David 22:20
Bertrand, E. P. 18:102
Bertrand, Eli 22:160
Bertrand, M. 10:26
Bertro, August 23:133
Bertsch, William 1:16
Bertz, Philip 20:121
Berwell, Porter 17:158
Berwick, David H. 7:19
Berwick, G. 16:173
Berwick, James 23:19
Berwick, Thomas 23:292
Beryman, William 22:448
Besamore, Charles 10:9
Besand, Paul 9:75; 26:10
Besanon, Peter 3:22
Besant, Joseph 20:88
Besbegier, Julian 27:21
Bescenson, Frank 17:75
Besensaydeer, George
    11:83
Besey, W. S. 16:89
Besha, L. H. 26:153
Beshears, Thomas D.
    22:448

Besimer, William 16:89
Besler, Sebastian 10:41
Beson, Frank 26:16
Beson, Yenas 26:13
Beson, Zenas 18:229
Bess, Humphrey 9:48
Bess, J. F. 25:142
Bess, J. W. 26:16
Bess, John A. 9:75
Bess, R. 25:142
Bess, William 17:170
Bessa, Henry A. 7:86
Besse, C. C. 14:295;
    17:472; 27:20
Besse, C. W. 24:12
Besse, G. C. 13:124
Besse, G. W. 1:111
Besse, Joseph S. 8:117;
    19:315
Besse, L. E. 1:110
Bessee, Alphonse 7:86
Bessell, Edward H. 7:86
Bessell, Lewis 5:9
Besselmann, Henry 8:9
Besser, Alexander 4:10
Besseth, Jeremiah 5:9
Bessetie, Didasse 21:18
Bessett, Albert 12:7
Bessex, Isaac 21:301
Bessey, Albert 21:301
Bessey, Amos 20:188
Bessey, E. 1:111
Bessey, Isaac 7:117
Bessey, Peter 17:73
Bessey, R. 1:110
Bessey, Samuel D. 7:73;
    25:293
Bessey, William 21:301
Bessick, I. 23:276
Bessie, Eugene L. 22:400
Bessie, John 13:104
Bessing, Herman 10:41
Bessley, George 4:10
Besson, William 3:22
Bessy, James 9:108
Bessy, Miles K. 23:177
Best, A. E. 9:108
Best, Adam 24:12
Best, Alexander 1:113
Best, B. 1:116
Best, Harvey 10:41;
    20:207
Best, Henry 14:141; 24:64
Best, Hezekiah 7:86
Best, Horatio B. 22:417
Best, I. 10:26
Best, Jacob 10:171;
    19:148
Best, Jesse A. 20:38
Best, John 1:15; 14:37;
    19:56

Best, John T. 22:178
Best, John W. 8:9; 18:122
Best, Nathan 22:276
Best, Peter G. 7:86
Best, Tipt 19:299
Best, W. 27:15
Best, W. E. 1:14
Best, W. M. 9:139; 27:14
Best, William 3:22; 22:66;
    25:16
Bestell, Henry 9:18;
    18:320
Bester, D. H. 11:235
Beston, William 17:170
Bestor, Sebastian 20:207
Beswick, Charles E. 16:75
Beswick, John M. 22:473
Betcher, William 14:37
Beteman, Francis Joseph
    11:53
Betenburgh, --- 12:13
Beth, Joseph 15:102
Beth, Peter 15:53
Bethel, Bluford 7:19
Bethel, Charles 24:189
Bethel, Edwin R. 17:75
Bethel, Marion 18:391
Bethel, Thomas B. 23:133
Bethel, William 1:13
Bethel, William A. 20:38
Bethell, Norman 27:157
Bether, E. 15:337
Bethom, A. 21:301
Bethowner, Jimberent
    18:230
Bethwig, L. 25:142
Betinger, J. B. 19:56
Betley, Ephraim 21:301
Betney, John 12:13
Betosh, James L. 7:19
Betsinger, G. W. 7:86
Betson, Thomas 15:29
Better, Joseph 16:21
Better, Lewis 11:298
Better, William 16:173
Betterton, George 7:86
Betterton, William 11:380
Bettick, F. M. 10:103;
    20:207
Bettinger, Nicholas 7:19
Bettis, A. 27:142
Bettis, A. M. 17:294
Bettis, Edmond 22:20
Bettis, H. M. 17:294
Bettis, M. 23:19
Bettis, R. 1:20
Bettler, Henry 9:116;
    27:19
Betton, Alvis 23:96
Betton, Joseph N. 26:91
Bettork, James M. 21:238

Bettrice, John 22:241
Betts, A. 11:338
Betts, Alvin D. 22:178
Betts, B. H. 13:10
Betts, G. 1:110
Betts, George 4:10
Betts, Godfrey 7:86
Betts, John W. 21:264
Betts, Joseph F. 10:41
Betts, Oskar 9:101
Betts, P. 3:22
Betts, Samuel 22:178
Bettsel, George 8:80
Betty, Joseph 8:45
Bettyes, L. 15:118
Bettz, Even 22:178
Bety, John 27:22
Betz, Alexander 14:253
Betz, Henry 22:178
Betz, Ira C. 20:21
Betz, Reuben 4:11
Betz, Samuel 10:41;
   20:207
Betzer, J. N. 14:277
Betzer, Peter 20:95
Betzler, Matthew 9:203
Betzler, William 19:328
Beuford, William 22:66
Beugman, P. 19:247
Beule, A. R. 21:18
Beumet, Josiah 22:448
Beumret, C. 3:22
Beunett, John 22:418
Beur, Henry 7:20
Beurman, George 20:207
Beuscoter, A. 25:19
Beush, Wenzel 19:276
Beutch, Louis 18:204
Beutz, E. H. 7:13
Beuzy, G. 19:247
Bevaid, James M. 18:391
Bevan, Henry 22:330
Bevan, John M. 11:137
Bevan, William 9:235
Bevans, Adams 20:182
Bevans, C. 10:103;
   20:208
Bevans, George 25:142
Bevans, J. C. 18:107
Bevard, H. 14:37
Bevard, Jessew 18:204
Bevard, William H.
   24:151
Bevear, L. S. 14:37
Bevell, Drainville H.
   20:208
Bevell, Drarville H.
   10:103
Bevels, Jacob 4:11
Bevens, A. 1:111

Bevens, Henry 9:128;
   27:17
Bever, M. R. 9:48
Beverley, William 24:165
Beverlin, Madison 24:35
Beverly, A. W. 1:113
Beverly, Balts 16:131
Beverly, Charles 9:199;
   19:279
Beverly, H. 16:173
Beverly, John 6:15; 18:77
Beverly, John A. 21:9
Beverly, W. J. 1:112
Beverly, Wyeth 1:192
Beverson, Edward 12:54
Bevier, George 14:37
Beville, David R. 22:241
Bevin, Edward 9:169;
   22:66
Bevin, James E. 6:9
Bevin, Joseph 13:124
Bevin, Stacey 9:32
Bevin, Thomas R. 22:474
Bevine, Bartholomew
   7:92
Bevington, Aug 22:178
Bevington, John A.
   19:266
Bevins, A. 10:192
Bevins, E. 19:287
Bevins, George 13:104
Bevins, Reason 22:178
Bevins, T. A. 18:171
Bevis, A. J. 9:18
Bevis, Joseph 24:107
Bevnad, Loftus 12:66
Bevny, Joseph 1:17
Bevo, John 11:138
Bevy, James 23:133
Bevy, William 20:144
Bew, Thomas 7:86;
   21:301
Bewler, Jacob 16:287
Bewley, James A. 20:174
Bewmon, Thomas 9:226
Bewsticks, Plenty 9:128
Beydon, George M. 7:20
Beyea, J. 25:142
Beyed, James 7:8
Beyel, John M. 26:121
Beyer, Albert 4:11
Beyer, Augustus 18:187
Beyer, Charles 19:316;
   22:20, 330
Beyer, D. C. 1:110
Beyer, George 4:11
Beyer, Henry 19:5
Beyergant, Eli 12:151
Beyers, John 17:29
Beyler, --- 20:180
Beymer, Alonzo F. 23:20

Beytes, George D. 4:11
Bezeke, Joe 27:18
Bezel, Francis 4:11
Bezzen, Andrew 5:35
Bezzer, A. 25:142
Bhaine, Monroe 23:20
Bhomback, Frederick
   17:210
Bhueress, Jacob 8:103
Biahu, Jacob 19:337
Bial, John 15:80
Biark, Gustave 10:41
Bias, Henry G. 12:61
Bias, Presley 22:241
Bib, Albert 9:160
Bibb, Edward 22:290
Bibb, Frank 22:290
Bibb, James 22:241
Bibb, James R. 17:48
Bibb, John 22:290
Bibb, John A. 22:290
Bibb, Moses 22:289
Bibb, R. 1:20
Bibb, William 22:290
Bibber, Henry R. 21:301
Bibbions, A. F. 17:322
Bibbith, G. W. 7:47
Bibbith, William 18:434
Bibbles, G. F. 13:83
Bibbs, J. 22:290
Bibbs, John 19:322
Bibbs, Jonathan 14:318;
   25:282
Bibbs, Squire 22:290
Bibby, George W. 15:157
Bibby, J. W. 21:119
Bibee, J. 20:208
Bibee, --- 14:321; 23:183
Bible, G. W. 23:133
Bible, J. 1:111
Bible, Lewis 11:135
Bible, Noah L. 22:241
Bible, Richard Owen 4:64
Bible, W. 3:22
Bibler, Harrison 22:178
Bibles, Alexander 3:22
Bibley, George 3:22
Bibley, J. 3:22
Bice, Benjamin 16:89
Bice, H. 1:116
Bice, Hamilton 20:38
Bice, Hiram C. 11:275
Bice, Jacob 22:178
Bice, James 14:141
Bichel, Humphrey 26:16
Bichel, J. H. 11:258
Bichford, T. 16:363
Bichop, William 25:142
Bick, J. 9:18; 18:302;
   26:93

Bickel, George 10:41; 20:208
Bickel, Humphrey 18:229
Bickel, John 26:120
Bickel, S. R. 3:22
Bickelhaupt, W. 1:16
Bickell, Henry C. 24:48
Bickenhaltz, H. 12:121
Bicker, Henry 16:138
Bicker, John 9:75
Bicker, M. F. 18:45
Bicker, S. L. 25:317
Bickerstaff, John 2:8; 25:13
Bickerstith, J. 25:14
Bicket, E. H. 3:22
Bicket, Nathaniel 17:271
Bickett, Everman 22:117
Bickford, Andrew 21:301
Bickford, Asel 21:301
Bickford, Bennett 21:301
Bickford, Charles L. 11:284
Bickford, Edwin 1:16
Bickford, G. F. 19:235
Bickford, J. W. 7:20
Bickford, James H. 4:11
Bickford, Kendall 4:11
Bickford, Marshall 9:169; 19:247
Bickford, Oliver 1:112
Bickford, P. 21:18
Bickford, S. 1:19
Bickford, Stephen 22:115
Bickford, W. H. 1:112
Bickford, Washington 10:41
Bicking, Isaac D. 7:14
Bicking, K. 1:19
Bicking, P. D. 7:55
Bicking, Richard 14:141
Bickland, James E. 23:133
Bickle, D. G. 7:86
Bickle, Daniel 21:48
Bickle, George W. 22:330
Bickle, John 22:400
Bickle, Paul 12:13
Bickle, Samuel E. 17:75
Bickler, Frank 21:301
Bickley, G. 14:141
Bickley, G. W. 8:45
Bickley, Henry H. 12:13
Bickley, John 13:10
Bickman, I. 15:183
Bickmore, L. F. 14:141
Bicknell, Aaron 21:301
Bicknell, Anson 21:301
Bicknell, David 17:271
Bicknell, N. B. 16:83
Bicknell, Thomas 17:271
Bickner, J. 1:116

Bicknor, James 24:99
Bicks, Frederick 20:208
Bickson, Andrew E. 18:229
Bidd, William 9:169; 19:266
Biddell, Charles 9:108
Bidder, John 14:37
Biddett, Charles 1:13
Biddey, Daniel 8:9
Biddinger, M. 3:22
Biddinger, Nicholas 22:20
Biddison, Amon 21:135
Biddison, Josiah 12:151
Biddle, A. 11:257
Biddle, Andrew 17:48
Biddle, David 1:18
Biddle, E. 20:38
Biddle, G. 1:116
Biddle, Heland 13:105
Biddle, Isaac 17:246
Biddle, John W. 19:5
Biddle, Martin 21:48
Biddle, Mathias 20:121
Biddle, Miles H. 24:88
Biddle, Perry 8:9; 18:122
Biddleman, J. 25:142
Biddleman, William H. 22:137
Bidell, George 13:62
Bidell, R. A. 13:124
Bidenharn, Otto 25:142
Bider, Henry 15:297
Bidgeley, James 14:141
Bidgood, William 12:151
Bidleman, D. 23:20
Bidman, William 6:24
Bidmeed, James 3:22
Bidon, S. 3:22
Bidurel, Richard 15:297
Bidwell, A. L. 24:74
Bidwell, B. F. 1:18
Bidwell, C. 3:22
Bidwell, Cyrus 10:103; 20:208
Bidwell, D. D. 16:11
Bidwell, Elisha 9:32; 11:137
Bidwell, G. C. 14:37
Bidwell, George 22:20
Bidwell, Henry 12:67
Bidwell, Hiram 15:63
Bidwell, J. 3:22
Bidwell, Richard 16:173
Bidwell, Solomon 18:302; 26:91
Bidwell, William W. 11:399
Bie, --- 16:89
Bieber, H. 11:123

Biedlen-an, William H. 23:187
Biegler, John 15:53
Biehl, Frank 21:18
Biehl, George 23:133
Biehle, Anton 25:16
Biehler, James E. 22:401
Biel, S. 3:22
Bieland, Gottlieb 21:301
Bieller, F. 23:20
Bien, R. B. 6:29; 25:317
Bien, W. D. 20:38
Biener, John 23:20
Bieney, M. 2:8
Bier, S. 13:83
Bierce, James M. 22:460
Biere, Ira A. 10:41; 20:208
Biere, Samuel 20:208
Bieri, Samuel 10:103
Bierly, James 22:416
Bierman, Joseph 22:20
Biern, R. P. 27:13
Biers, S. 3:22
Bierson, W. J. 5:49
Biertselp, S. 9:139
Bierwith, Francis V. 15:93
Biery, W. 19:56
Biery, William 19:56
Bieter, R. 1:111
Bietz, George 11:135
Biewald, Paul 4:11
Biffen, N. 23:197
Biffinger, Henry 8:9; 18:121
Biffle, Benjamin 22:290
Biffley, William L. 26:10
Bifill, William 26:210
Big Aleck 25:332
Big Bill 25:332
Big Jim 25:332
Big Mush 25:332
Bigalow, John L. 13:10
Bigalow, Samuel L. 13:10
Bigards, Henry H. 14:141
Bigby, Aaron 8:103
Bigdon, James 16:173
Bigdy, G. C. 12:86; 16:287
Bigelow, --- 11:217
Bigelow, A. D. 15:29
Bigelow, Anson D. 12:63
Bigelow, C. 1:109; 3:22
Bigelow, G. 3:22
Bigelow, G. M. 20:55
Bigelow, Henry 16:21
Bigelow, Horace 22:415
Bigelow, James H. 23:60
Bigelow, Jeremiah 16:151
Bigelow, John 9:8
Bigelow, Joseph H. 4:11

Bigelow, S. J. 20:55
Bigelow, S. S. 17:151
Bigelow, Samuel L. 16:21
Bigelow, Thomas 9:11
Bigelow, W. H. 4:11
Bigford, Charles 5:49
Bigford, George 9:169
Bigg, Henry 25:142
Bigg, John G. 16:89
Bigg, Mathew 26:13
Biggard, F. 12:91; 16:287
Biggard, J. 14:37
Bigge, Frank 26:92
Bigger, Alex 13:10
Bigger, James A. 11:22
Biggerstaff, Anderson G.
    23:96
Biggerstaff, George L.
    26:13
Biggerstaff, Henry 18:229
Biggerstaff, Lafayette
    17:417
Biggerstaff, William J.
    17:48
Biggerstaff, William T.
    24:13
Biggins, Ezekiel 8:37;
    26:151
Biggins, Hugh 1:15
Biggins, J. H. 22:178
Biggle, J. S. 21:301
Biggle, William 17:29
Biggot, Gabriel 17:128
Biggott, Gabriel 24:188
Biggs, A. 14:318
Biggs, A. W. 1:192
Biggs, Benjamin 21:48
Biggs, Frank 18:302
Biggs, George W. 21:220
Biggs, H. 22:178
Biggs, H. L. 8:70
Biggs, Harrod 22:178
Biggs, J. H. 1:116
Biggs, John 6:29; 15:347;
    16:363; 25:317
Biggs, John W. 23:312
Biggs, Levi 5:49
Biggs, Marquis L. 17:389
Biggs, Mathew 18:229
Biggs, Noah 8:9; 18:122
Biggs, Paul 27:142
Biggs, Randall 17:128;
    24:188
Biggs, Richard 24:189
Biggs, William 8:116;
    13:10; 18:330; 22:66
Biggs, William M. 17:17
Biggs, Wilson 22:241
Biggs, York 10:170
Bigham, D. 9:139; 27:20
Bigham, George W. 21:18

Bigham, John 23:20
Bigham, Simon 26:15
Bigler, A. 3:22
Bigler, George 16:173;
    21:301
Bigler, H. 23:20
Bigler, John 10:41
Bigler, M. 3:22
Bigler, Michael 12:56
Bigler, T. 17:290
Bigley, A. J. 23:20
Bigley, Arthur 21:301
Bigley, H. 18:362
Bigley, Martin 7:86
Bigley, Thomas 1:113
Bigley, W. R. 25:17
Bigley, William 21:165
Biglow, B. H. 7:86
Biglow, Charles P. 16:363
Biglow, Henry 10:171;
    19:149
Biglow, J. G. 11:285
Biglow, John 3:22
Biglow, John C. 7:63
Biglow, L. 3:22
Biglow, M. P. 17:63
Biglow, Simon 14:141
Biglow, Solomon 17:439;
    24:151
Biglow, William 3:22;
    7:20
Biglow, Zedrick 11:24
Bigly, H. 9:218
Bigney, John 8:80
Bigney, Stephen 11:51
Bigney, Thomas 22:137
Bignoli, Frederick 12:13
Bigott, James 18:12
Bigs, Frederick 15:315
Bigsby, Andrew E. 7:20
Bigsby, Hiram 21:185,
    290
Bigstaff, Jack 24:189
Bigtree, Isaac 18:187
Bikholder, Christian
    23:177
Bikley, John 19:149
Bilby, Richard 11:22
Bildenbock, Charles 8:45
Bilderback, Charles H.
    21:250
Bilderback, Friend B.
    21:135
Bilderback, P. J. 20:188
Bildhasten, W. 16:173
Biles, Arnold 18:113
Biles, Henry 22:290
Biles, Thomas 22:330
Bileter, Hezekiah 11:90
Bilgen, William I. 11:51
Bilger, William 14:141

Bilkington, William 11:23
Bilks, John 18:229; 26:13
Bill, B. S. 3:22
Bill, Daniel H. 24:48
Bill, Indian 20:208
Bill, James 8:70
Bill, Mathew 27:22
Bill, Robert 25:142
Bill, Stephen 11:197
Billam, --- 10:153
Bille, R. 21:97
Billenten, Harrison 20:208
Biller, B. 18:246
Billett, E. 14:37
Billeve, T. R. 22:350
Billey, B. J. 11:418
Billey, George 7:77;
    25:293
Billhimer, James E.
    22:499
Billhover, L. 9:139
Billhurt, A. 24:64
Billian, Benjamin R.
    22:241
Billiar, J. 1:15
Billiard, Joseph 8:60;
    12:172
Billiard, William 23:60
Billiardes, W. G. 22:241
Billick, Alonzo 22:20
Billick, L. 11:237
Billig, J. S. 3:22
Billing, A. J. 23:133
Billing, A. T. 21:301
Billing, G. W. 23:133
Billing, George 13:10
Billinger, W. 1:110
Billingham, J. G. 1:93
Billings, A. 1:14
Billings, A. J. 9:213
Billings, Amos 20:110
Billings, C. 2:7
Billings, C. W. 12:151;
    21:301
Billings, Charles 4:11
Billings, Dennison 23:20
Billings, E. E. 23:85
Billings, E. W. 27:23
Billings, Elihu 13:83
Billings, George P. 21:301
Billings, Hiram 19:149
Billings, Hiram H. 10:157
Billings, Isaac 22:330
Billings, J. 3:22
Billings, J. D. 11:331
Billings, J. W. 15:183;
    21:301
Billings, John 5:49; 8:80;
    20:2; 25:142
Billings, Joseph 3:22;
    17:439

Billings, L. 20:29
Billings, Lucius 21:206
Billings, M. 25:142
Billings, Martin 5:9
Billings, Pliny 13:10
Billings, R. D. 23:133
Billings, R. M. 1:15
Billings, Rufus 20:110
Billings, W. 3:22
Billings, W. H. 23:20
Billings, W. W. 3:22
Billings, William R. 22:20
Billingsby, A. T. 21:301
Billingsby, Henry 19:44
Billingsby, J. 3:22
Billingsby, L. 22:330
Billingsfield, William G. 22:164
Billingsley, John W. 23:96
Billingsley, Joseph 10:103
Billingsly, Joseph 20:208
Billingsly, Samuel 22:473
Billington, Charles L. 15:183
Billington, George 4:11
Billington, J. D. 5:9; 25:142
Billington, Owen 9:108
Billington, Rufus 10:103; 20:208
Billington, Thomas W. 23:20
Billington, William 12:7
Billington, Z. J. 21:87
Billips, Lee 7:77; 25:293
Billis, W. N. 14:4
Billis, W. W. 13:83
Billiter, Harrison 10:89
Billman, Henry A. 24:48
Billman, Jacob 7:20
Billman, John 12:151
Billman, William L. 19:5
Billmeyer, W. H. 1:20
Billow, E. 1:112
Billow, John C. 22:276
Billows, E. F. 14:37
Billows, John 3:22
Bills, Charles 4:11
Bills, Delos 14:141
Bills, Elisha T. 7:86
Bills, George 17:17; 24:165
Bills, H. C. 20:144
Bills, Jabez P. 24:61
Bills, John G. 27:13
Bills, Reuben 26:151
Bills, S. 19:235
Bills, S. D. 1:113
Bills, Thompson 1:115
Bills, Walter 14:141

Bills, William H. 16:363
Billsbery, Stephen 22:290
Billson, Henry 25:18
Billy, Indian 16:21
Billy Bowlegs 25:332
Bilton, Thomas 18:302
Bimble, H. 11:294
Bimelein, Gottleib 10:41
Bimert, Isaac B. 13:10
Bimetin, G. 20:208
Bimnell, G. 27:23
Binard, Thomas 21:18
Binbarry, John 26:150
Binch, D. 17:158
Bincham, George 10:103
Binche, --- 18:406
Binchfield, Henry 17:170
Bind, William 14:37
Binder, A. 14:37
Binder, John 3:22
Binder, Joseph 11:384
Binder, Robert 24:169
Bine, J. 1:110
Bine, William R. 9:218
Binec, L. 12:86
Binee, L. 16:287
Bing, --- 20:87
Bing, A. J. 14:37
Bingal, John 12:13
Bingaman, --- 15:183
Binger, Ludwig 11:90
Bingham, Albert 21:146
Bingham, Alfred 17:358
Bingham, B. 15:150
Bingham, Burt 17:146
Bingham, C. D. 3:22
Bingham, C. K. 8:45
Bingham, Cavey 4:11
Bingham, Charles 18:229; 26:14
Bingham, Charles K. 21:250
Bingham, Charles L. 21:135
Bingham, Chester 21:238
Bingham, David 10:13
Bingham, Ebben 23:133
Bingham, Edward D. 22:66
Bingham, Eli 11:135
Bingham, Elias 22:66
Bingham, Ezra 15:53
Bingham, F. D. 11:394
Bingham, G. G. 18:63
Bingham, G. H. 8:45
Bingham, H. L. 11:22
Bingham, H. S. 19:328
Bingham, J. W. 13:10
Bingham, James 9:169; 11:256; 15:63
Bingham, James A. 7:20

Bingham, James B. 24:58
Bingham, James H. 8:103
Bingham, John 17:146
Bingham, K. 8:45
Bingham, L. H. 1:109
Bingham, L. M. 9:116
Bingham, Luther B. 10:204
Bingham, Oscar H. 20:105
Bingham, Porter 8:70
Bingham, Robert 11:24
Bingham, S. A. 15:329; 19:56
Bingham, Simon 18:229
Bingham, William 25:142
Binginim, William G. 16:173
Bingle, G. 24:13
Bingle, Washington 11:319
Binglersdorf, F. 25:317
Binglespaugh, Abram 11:298
Bingman, John 21:301
Bingoman, W. R. 23:20
Bings, G. 3:22
Bining, W. H. 20:208
Binington, George 26:121
Bink, S. 15:29
Binkard, John 19:5
Binker, J. W. 5:56
Binker, James 16:116
Binker, Samuel 11:299
Binker, W. 23:60
Binkhard, Levi 23:85
Binkhart, J. E. 12:151
Binkley, Amos 17:75
Binkley, Irom 10:41
Binkley, Jacob 22:290
Binkley, L. S. 21:119
Binkley, W. 14:279
Binley, Tobias 11:409
Binley, William 11:134
Binner, George 11:399
Binner, Granville L. M. 24:64
Binner, L. 18:12
Binnett, Caleb N. 20:208
Binney, J. L. 23:255
Binning, --- 14:37, 141
Binning, Henry 9:48
Binning, J. M. 20:208
Binning, John M. 10:41
Binns, James C. 22:330
Binson, Thomas 18:362
Bintle, A. 1:13
Binz, Jacob 20:4
Bio---, J. 24:13
Biorge, Nelson Ole 24:185
Biork, Gustar 20:208

Biotte, Peter 11:230
Bious, A. 1:116
Bipler, Madison 22:137
Bipple, A. 14:287; 23:20
Biraus, Joshua 11:299
Birch, --- 5:49; 25:142
Birch, A. Jackson 17:90
Birch, A. L. 1:114
Birch, B. H. 11:279
Birch, Elijah 10:103;
  20:208
Birch, George 17:215
Birch, James 18:434
Birch, James C. 5:35
Birch, James H. 11:103
Birch, James R. 13:60
Birch, John 13:10; 17:90
Birch, John H. 21:87
Birch, John M. 24:35
Birch, L. F. 3:22
Birch, Nathan 13:10
Birch, Richard 15:329;
  19:56
Birch, Samuel 18:284;
  26:134
Birch, Thomas 4:11
Birch, Thomas S. 20:21
Birch, W. H. 14:141, 253
Birch, Warren J. 15:183
Birch, William 18:171;
  26:144
Birch, William I. 11:51
Birchard, A. P. 15:283
Bircher, George 7:20
Birchfield, A. H. 10:41;
  20:208
Birchfield, Lewis 22:178
Birchfield, William H.
  21:48
Birchler, Martin 9:203
Birck, T. A. 3:22
Bird, --- 15:183
Bird, A. 23:312
Bird, Anson 17:442;
  24:156
Bird, Arthur C. 8:113
Bird, Benjamin 12:121;
  15:118
Bird, Benjamin W. 24:71
Bird, Black 25:332
Bird, C. 14:141
Bird, Charles 17:241
Bird, Daniel 7:77; 22:66;
  25:293
Bird, Edward 19:149
Bird, F. 14:37
Bird, F. G. 1:116
Bird, G. W. 19:5
Bird, George 9:18; 14:37;
  18:302; 26:93
Bird, H. 18:24

Bird, Harrison 7:117
Bird, Henry C. 25:142
Bird, Isaac 21:265
Bird, J. 3:22; 12:86;
  14:279; 16:287
Bird, J. A. 19:5
Bird, J. E. 27:15
Bird, J. H. 15:297
Bird, J. M. 14:38
Bird, J. P. 10:178
Bird, J. W. 1:116; 12:151
Bird, James 10:185;
  12:13; 14:38; 20:45;
  22:232, 241
Bird, Jesse S. 24:35
Bird, John 4:11; 9:32;
  14:38; 18:290;
  22:111; 26:93; 27:12
Bird, John H. 16:173
Bird, Joseph 27:21
Bird, Joseph W. 20:208
Bird, Joshua W. 10:41
Bird, Josiah 16:21
Bird, L. C. 18:122
Bird, Lee 17:234
Bird, Levi 14:38
Bird, M. 3:22
Bird, Monell 8:100
Bird, Monnel 17:459;
  24:156
Bird, Nancy E. 10:171;
  19:149
Bird, P. 3:22
Bird, Pat 25:317
Bird, Patrick 6:29
Bird, Pierson 22:20
Bird, Rabo 7:117; 21:301
Bird, S. H. 3:22
Bird, S. P. 10:151
Bird, Samuel 8:9; 10:41;
  15:53; 20:208
Bird, Simon D. 22:241
Bird, Thomas 11:435;
  18:63
Bird, Thompson 13:10
Bird, Virgil C. 21:97
Bird, W. D. 14:279
Bird, W. E. 22:523
Bird, W. L. 16:21
Bird, W. O. 14:279
Bird, W. T. 3:22
Bird, William 9:213;
  11:399, 421; 18:274;
  21:301; 22:241, 517
Bird, William E. 25:142
Bird, William G. 17:241
Bird, William H. 12:80;
  21:250; 25:142
Birden, --- 22:350
Birdenstein, F. F. 9:75
Birdner, Christian 21:301

Birds, William F. 4:11
Birdsall, Albert I. 15:29
Birdsall, Allen 7:87
Birdsall, C. M. 20:135
Birdsall, George 20:110
Birdsall, H. J. 25:142
Birdsall, Marion 20:4
Birdsall, W. 19:149
Birdsall, Watson 10:157
Birdsall, William 22:178
Birdsel, Calvin 12:151
Birdsel, Isaac F. 22:460
Birdsell, --- 14:141
Birdsell, D. 3:22
Birdsell, Edwin 14:141
Birdsell, Frank 14:141
Birdsell, William 23:276
Birdseye, J. 3:22
Birdson, George 18:122
Birdsong, George 10:26;
  19:299
Birdsong, J. W. 9:218
Birdsony, J. W. 18:362
Birdswell, F. 25:142
Birdswell, Francis 5:35
Birers, Jacob 25:142
Birge, Boswell 25:17
Birge, G. M. 23:20
Birge, Mancil 21:244
Birgis, E. 3:23
Birgle, Christian 10:146
Birkenhaltz, H. 15:118
Birkenmeyer, John 15:118
Birkett, David 10:171;
  19:149
Birkett, W. D. 3:22
Birkey, Christian 12:13
Birkheimer, I. 9:139
Birkman, N. 4:11
Birkmeyer, Isaac 27:13
Birlenbach, John 22:20
Birler, Peter 10:41;
  20:208
Birley, Peter 3:22
Birmen, John 9:18
Birmingham, J. 19:235
Birmingham, John 16:21;
  26:150
Birmingham, Patrick
  23:133
Birminster, Charles
  20:208
Birmis, G. 27:24
Birney, D. 9:139
Birney, David H. 27:14
Birney, Joseph 8:123
Birney, William 25:142
Birnham, H. 3:22
Birns, Reuben 6:12
Birrell, M. L. 3:22
Birriet, B. R. 20:91

Birsey, George 5:35
Birsey, Theo. E. 9:169
Birt, B. 22:290
Birt, James 23:251
Birtsch, Christian 1:116
Bisb, James 15:183
Bisbee, H. K. 7:87
Bisbee, James C. 27:14
Bisbee, Joseph C. 9:139
Bisbee, Luther J. 7:87
Bisbee, Mark 20:102
Bisbing, Charles 7:20
Bisbing, George M. D. 12:13
Bisbing, Jerbase 13:10
Bisby, Henry 22:511
Bisby, Hiram 13:10
Biscar, August 20:208
Bischoff, Casper 17:29
Biscoe, William W. 12:13
Biscott, A. 18:122
Bisdorph, John 20:208
Bise, Jacob 16:131
Bisel, B. 3:23
Bisel, James 3:23
Bisel, Joseph 22:66
Bisenger, Stephen 10:89
Biser, C. B. 19:56
Bisgrove, Isaac 3:23
Bish, J. 3:23
Bisher, Noah 11:410
Bishline, David 15:102
Bishman, J. P. 16:21
Bishop, A. 1:116; 3:23; 23:20, 133
Bishop, Acsolver 11:278
Bishop, Albrich 17:448; 24:173
Bishop, Artemus 7:87; 21:301
Bishop, Ash M. 14:141
Bishop, Austin 1:18
Bishop, B. 9:95; 14:38
Bishop, B. H. 3:23
Bishop, Bart 1:16
Bishop, Beal 22:401
Bishop, Benjamin 25:142
Bishop, C. 3:23; 15:184
Bishop, C. O. 25:317
Bishop, C. W. 18:24; 25:142
Bishop, Charles 19:349; 20:208
Bishop, Charles A. 10:13
Bishop, Charles O. 6:29
Bishop, Cyrus 7:87; 21:301
Bishop, D. 17:501
Bishop, D. A. 19:247
Bishop, D. S. 3:23
Bishop, Daniel 23:133

Bishop, David 11:420; 19:5
Bishop, David A. 9:169
Bishop, Dean 14:141
Bishop, Drury 22:20
Bishop, E. 3:23; 14:141; 16:77
Bishop, E. R. 16:363
Bishop, Edmond 4:11
Bishop, Elijah 1:13
Bishop, Ezra 9:108
Bishop, F. M. 23:20
Bishop, Frank 25:142
Bishop, Frederick 21:199
Bishop, G. 13:83; 14:38
Bishop, G. B. 7:66
Bishop, G. T. 16:116
Bishop, G. W. 9:100
Bishop, George 6:29; 8:9; 18:122; 25:317
Bishop, George H. 9:15; 22:401
Bishop, H. 11:135; 12:173
Bishop, H. A. 11:278
Bishop, H. C. 1:114
Bishop, Henry 22:8
Bishop, Henry R. 22:417
Bishop, Hicks 14:141
Bishop, Hiram 1:192
Bishop, Hollis 14:141
Bishop, I. S. 24:60
Bishop, Isaac M. 14:268
Bishop, Israel 15:150
Bishop, J. 1:17; 17:90; 23:20
Bishop, J. C. 3:23
Bishop, J. E. 1:20
Bishop, J. H. 11:298
Bishop, J. M. 21:302
Bishop, J. N. G. 14:132
Bishop, J. W. 18:45
Bishop, J. W. A. 14:38
Bishop, Jackson 10:103; 20:208
Bishop, James 9:18; 11:325; 13:105; 18:302; 22:241; 25:317; 26:92
Bishop, Joab 23:112
Bishop, John 4:11; 8:103; 18:171; 25:143
Bishop, John W. 22:241
Bishop, Jonathan 17:199
Bishop, Joseph 8:59; 11:410; 17:346; 19:276
Bishop, Josiah 7:87
Bishop, L. 14:279
Bishop, Lander 24:13
Bishop, Lemouel 10:103
Bishop, Lemuel 20:208

Bishop, Lewis 16:89; 21:302
Bishop, M. 14:295; 17:473; 25:143; 27:20
Bishop, Mack 16:173
Bishop, Miles 24:64
Bishop, Morris 5:9; 6:15; 18:77
Bishop, Myron G. 11:19
Bishop, N. 1:18; 13:103; 14:4; 16:266
Bishop, O. 15:184; 20:144
Bishop, Owen 21:97
Bishop, P. 3:23
Bishop, R. 11:285
Bishop, Richard 11:196
Bishop, Richard J. 22:137
Bishop, Robert 22:117
Bishop, Robert M. 13:10
Bishop, S. 3:23; 27:23
Bishop, S. S. 8:60; 12:168
Bishop, Samuel 21:193, 221
Bishop, Silas 24:13
Bishop, Simeon 10:94
Bishop, T. 3:23; 17:501; 25:143
Bishop, Thomas 11:23, 435
Bishop, W. 3:23
Bishop, W. B. 1:116
Bishop, W. D. 20:208
Bishop, W. M. 1:16
Bishop, W. R. 18:274
Bishop, Walter 14:141
Bishop, Walter R. 22:17
Bishop, William 9:75; 10:41; 11:135; 16:174; 21:302; 22:507; 23:133; 26:11
Bishop, William D. 10:41
Bishop, William H. 13:10
Bishop, William I. 8:9
Bishop, William J. 18:122
Bishop, William L. 16:363
Bishop, William P. 22:447
Bishop, Zachariah 11:90
Bisk, E. 23:201
Bisk, F. 23:201
Biskar, George F. 10:103; 20:208
Bisker, August 10:103
Bisley, R. 16:174
Bisley, Samuel C. 10:13
Bisnett, J. 16:174
Bisnett, James 13:105
Bisonette, S. 16:138
Bispham, John 14:141

Bispham, Thomas E. 13:10
Bissaw, Henry 4:11
Bissel, Ephraim C. 19:328
Bissel, Henry 15:29
Bissel, Lawson L. 22:137
Bissel, R. S. 12:148
Bissell, A. E. 1:114
Bissell, Albert 7:87; 17:272
Bissell, C. 15:184
Bissell, C. J. 9:31
Bissell, Edward 12:91; 16:287; 23:133
Bissell, H. 1:111
Bissell, J. 3:23
Bissell, J. S. 3:23
Bissell, John M. 11:136
Bissell, L. 1:18
Bissell, Marcellus J. 17:287
Bissell, Oscar 22:137
Bissell, R. N. 21:302
Bissenger, Stephen 20:208
Bisser, George J. 23:255
Bissey, J. 9:48
Bissey, Thomas E. 19:266
Bisshele, John 10:103; 20:209
Bissing, H. 20:209
Bissinger, Henry 17:75
Bissitt, J. 18:45
Bisson, Charles S. 20:209
Bist, Alfred 11:52
Bistole, Michael 23:240
Bisvey, Joseph H. 15:184
Biteman, I. H. 18:102
Biter, Albert 18:12
Bitgood, Joseph A. 1:17
Bither, J. 3:23
Bitler, Patrick 7:87
Bitley, J. S. 22:448
Bitner, A. 3:23
Bitner, John 17:233
Bitner, Samuel 23:20
Bitnor, John 15:184
Bitsor, John 3:23
Bittenzer, E. T. 27:22
Bitter, George J. 9:18
Bitter, H. 3:23
Bitter, Josiah M. 22:20
Bitters, W. H. 25:14
Bitting, Joseph 15:184
Bittinger, A. J. 16:116
Bittinger, H. P. 20:153
Bittings, Henry 22:417
Bittle, Mat 13:76
Bittman, J. 3:23
Bittner, S. I. 14:38
Bitts, James M. 24:35
Bitts, John 16:174

Bitz, Isaac H. 10:41
Bivans, Alonzo 1:115
Bivans, James 15:184
Bivens, Morris 21:302
Bivens, William 11:185, 407
Biver, N. 3:23
Bivins, George W. 11:118
Bivins, T. 25:143
Bivins, Thomas J. 20:177
Bix, Hosea 15:29
Bix, Moses 12:67
Bixby, A. 16:266
Bixby, A. R. 19:56
Bixby, Almon 7:20
Bixby, Ashley 22:178
Bixby, Benjamin 20:29; 23:85
Bixby, D. A. 14:38
Bixby, Henry C. 10:41; 20:209
Bixby, J. A. 13:83
Bixby, John T. 16:83
Bixby, Mansel 27:18
Bixler, --- 19:299
Bixler, D. 3:23
Bixler, George J. 26:92
Bixler, George W. 7:20
Bixler, J. G. 18:302
Bixler, Kim 19:299
Bixley, A. R. 15:334
Bixley, J. 14:4
Bixley, Mannel 9:116
Bixley, Russell 14:38
Bjorge, Old Nelson 17:453
Bl--e, A. 24:109
Bla---, Jacob 23:201
Blacher, C. 25:143
Blachly, N. 11:257
Black, --- 14:287
Black, A. 2:8; 10:26; 11:134; 19:299
Black, A. M. 21:18
Black, Adam 9:108; 15:184; 21:119
Black, Albert 1:113
Black, Alex 20:209
Black, Alexander 7:87; 10:41; 23:105
Black, Alfred H. 9:95
Black, Anderson 18:63
Black, Anson 15:85
Black, Benjamin 22:117; 27:142
Black, C. 16:21
Black, C. G. 1:16
Black, Charles 7:20; 11:117; 13:56
Black, Charles O. 17:309
Black, Cyrus A. 23:20

Black, D. 21:146, 302
Black, Dan 9:108
Black, Daniel 11:24; 25:268
Black, David 10:94; 21:210
Black, Derritt 12:97
Black, E. 16:174
Black, Eli 27:23
Black, Ezra 11:257
Black, Francis 11:384
Black, Francis M. 10:41; 20:209
Black, Franklin 19:44
Black, Fred J. 7:87
Black, G. W. 3:23
Black, Gabriel 23:133
Black, George 14:141; 17:128; 21:302; 24:189
Black, George F. 8:9
Black, George K. 11:218
Black, George M. 8:9; 18:122
Black, George W. 20:142; 22:178, 510; 25:15
Black, Gustavus H. 21:64
Black, H. 3:23
Black, H. C. 3:23
Black, Henry 4:11; 17:170; 23:60
Black, Henry C. 8:9
Black, Henry P. 19:149
Black, Hiram D. 11:298
Black, Hugh 9:239
Black, I. 12:98
Black, Isaac 17:29
Black, J. 3:23; 15:150; 16:174; 19:56
Black, J. C. 21:119
Black, J. F. 23:20
Black, J. H. 3:23
Black, J. L. 18:45; 21:18
Black, J. S. 16:115
Black, Jacob 17:170
Black, Jake 17:191
Black, James 3:23; 11:420; 14:142; 23:177
Black, James A. 3:23; 11:295
Black, James B. 5:9; 25:143
Black, James C. 21:18
Black, James F. 10:171; 19:149
Black, James H. 7:20
Black, James J. 23:60
Black, James P. 26:217
Black, James R. 9:235
Black, James S. 22:447

Black, John 1:15, 18;
  5:36; 8:117; 9:65;
  10:13; 11:23, 138;
  12:13; 14:142;
  17:146; 18:274;
  19:149, 315; 21:48,
  302; 22:330; 24:13;
  25:143
Black, John A. 22:20
Black, John C. 23:60
Black, John Q. 23:133
Black, John R. 11:23
Black, John T. 14:38
Black, Jonathan 21:203
Black, Joseph 7:20; 13:10;
  14:38; 22:241
Black, Joseph H. 22:20
Black, Joseph L. 8:113
Black, L. 1:111; 3:23
Black, M. 17:17; 25:143
Black, Martin V. 4:11
Black, Mathew 12:67;
  15:63
Black, Moses 17:399
Black, Moses H. 22:460
Black, N. 20:4
Black, N. H. 1:93
Black, Napoleon 16:174
Black, Norton W. 22:276
Black, O. 15:29; 22:178
Black, O. D. 12:67
Black, Oliver 9:213
Black, P. 10:147; 18:45
Black, P. J. 16:174
Black, P. P. 13:105
Black, Peter 18:24
Black, R. M. 23:20
Black, R. T. 19:266
Black, Richard 21:210
Black, Richard F. 9:169
Black, Robert 9:116;
  12:13; 16:363; 27:19
Black, Robert A. 20:209
Black, Robert C. 4:11
Black, Robert E. 23:96
Black, Robrt 15:339
Black, Rose 23:276
Black, Rufus 7:87
Black, S. 22:178
Black, Samuel 8:70;
  18:122; 26:153
Black, Samuel G. P. 24:74
Black, Simon 1:13
Black, T. C. 18:229; 26:15
Black, Thomas 22:20
Black, U. J. 1:17
Black, W. F. 1:115
Black, W. H. 1:20, 112
Black, W. O. 3:23
Black, W. R. 22:330
Black, W. W. 23:201

Black, Walter W. 23:133
Black, Washington 17:396
Black, William 7:14; 9:32,
  75; 10:41; 17:309;
  18:290; 19:5; 20:209;
  21:18, 302; 23:60;
  26:93; 27:21
Black, William H. 17:415
Black, William T. 9:169
Blackall, G. 16:89
Blackall, P. 13:105
Blackallen, --- 18:102
Blackbern, P. 19:56
Blackbon, George 21:302
Blackburn, B. 13:83
Blackburn, Francis 23:105
Blackburn, G. 17:170
Blackburn, George 3:23;
  27:21
Blackburn, George W.
  24:165
Blackburn, I. 11:138
Blackburn, J. 14:38
Blackburn, J. R. 14:142
Blackburn, James 3:23;
  7:87; 22:447
Blackburn, John 11:257;
  18:284; 21:302;
  24:165; 26:134
Blackburn, John R.
  10:146; 20:209
Blackburn, Joseph D.
  12:67
Blackburn, M. 27:23
Blackburn, Martin 22:330
Blackburn, Mathas F.
  22:178
Blackburn, Miles 17:201
Blackburn, R. 12:92;
  16:287
Blackburn, Rankin 9:164
Blackburn, Richard 8:80
Blackburn, Samuel
  17:396; 22:20
Blackburn, Samuel D.
  8:103
Blackburn, T. F. 27:16
Blackburn, Thomas 4:11;
  7:20
Blackburn, W. A. 11:258
Blackburn, William
  15:184; 20:144;
  22:66
Blackburn, William H.
  20:185
Blackburne, J. F. 9:139
Blackcock, John M.
  17:128; 24:188
Blacke, John 3:23
Blackeher, W. H. 3:23
Blackeley, R. T. 16:363

Blacken, John 21:302
Blacken, Thomas 21:302
Blacker, A. 23:20
Blacker, George 18:392
Blacker, Jacob 18:214
Blacketer, Norman 8:80
Blackford, Henry 1:115;
  26:138
Blackford, L. 1:112
Blackford, S. C. 22:473
Blackford, Samuel 16:11
Blackford, W. T. 10:41
Blackford, William P.
  20:209
Blackguard, Jasper 11:51
Blackhall, J. 18:24
Blackhead, A. 15:63
Blackinan, W. 3:23
Blackled, Gilbert 21:302
Blackledge, Clarkson
  20:110
Blackledge, L. P. 11:236
Blackley, S. 23:133
Blacklidge, Martin R.
  20:34
Blackly, George 3:23
Blackman, A. 3:23
Blackman, Anson 22:111
Blackman, Austin 19:331
Blackman, C. 1:14
Blackman, C. A. 1:111
Blackman, Charles 20:55
Blackman, Cicero 8:37;
  26:151
Blackman, Daniel 22:290
Blackman, Elisha M.
  18:302
Blackman, F. L. 23:20
Blackman, Fred. A. 4:11
Blackman, George 8:61
Blackman, George E. 1:14
Blackman, Harrison
  9:128; 27:17
Blackman, Henry 4:11;
  8:9
Blackman, J. 3:23
Blackman, J. C. 1:20
Blackman, James 18:440;
  25:17
Blackman, Lawrence
  11:189
Blackman, R. G. 18:302;
  26:92
Blackman, R. J. 9:18
Blackman, S. 3:23
Blackman, Theodore
  10:147; 18:45
Blackman, Thomas
  19:235
Blackman, W. 3:23

Blackman, William 9:169; 19:266
Blackman, Z. 12:98; 15:366
Blackmer, E. 14:4
Blackmer, H. 1:19
Blackmore, A. 1:18
Blackmore, John 21:97
Blackmore, Nelson 12:13
Blackmore, Philip 9:205
Blackmy, B. 3:23
Blackner, H. R. 25:143
Blackner, Thomas 3:23
Blackney, T. J. 21:165
Blackney, Thomas 21:215
Blacknor, A. 22:290
Blackrey, David 19:5
Blacksome, Jeremiah 17:442; 24:156
Blackson, Benjamin 12:47
Blackson, John J. 24:35
Blackson, John W. 21:302
Blackson, William 12:47
Blackstein, Frederick 16:90
Blackstein, M. 18:229; 26:14
Blackston, --- 22:523
Blackston, Keenard 22:448
Blackston, S. 11:22
Blackstone, C. 25:279
Blackstone, J. 14:38
Blackstone, Newton 18:392
Blackstone, Thomas 7:87
Blackwaddle, Fred 9:75
Blackweddle, Frederick 26:12
Blackwedle, Henry 20:209
Blackweedle, Henry 10:103
Blackwell, Allen 9:199; 19:289
Blackwell, B. D. 15:26
Blackwell, Benjamin D. 12:67
Blackwell, C. 11:22
Blackwell, Christopher C. 24:90
Blackwell, Daniel 11:338; 14:142
Blackwell, Douglass 22:290
Blackwell, E. 25:143
Blackwell, Edward 22:290
Blackwell, Emanuel 5:35
Blackwell, George 14:318
Blackwell, Hampton 10:41
Blackwell, Hiram 21:302

Blackwell, Isaac M. 10:13
Blackwell, J. V. 19:149
Blackwell, James 1:115
Blackwell, James S. 12:13
Blackwell, John 27:18
Blackwell, Judy 10:170; 19:149
Blackwell, Morgan 7:87
Blackwell, Philip 22:290
Blackwell, W. 25:143
Blackwell, W. E. 4:11
Blackwell, William 10:103
Blackwood, G. W. 3:23
Blackwood, George 9:41; 26:121
Blackwood, Ira 18:229; 26:16
Blackwood, J. 3:23
Blackwood, John 9:128
Blackwood, Robert C. 22:401
Blackwood, W. 3:23
Blacmier, Herman 22:164
Blacthley, D. 25:143
Blade, Harry 11:136
Blade, William 9:218; 18:362
Bladen, Frank 9:169; 19:266
Blades, Henry 22:330
Blades, J. 7:20
Blades, James 12:47
Blades, Major G. 15:4
Bladgett, D. T. 14:38
Bladt, Louis 7:87
Bladwell, George W. 12:58
Blaes, Bangame 18:229
Blagg, Peter H. 26:92
Blagg, Peter K. 9:18
Blagley, John 14:142
Blahang, W. 15:29
Blaick, Charles 18:107
Blaid, G. W. 21:185
Blaik, Henry E. 18:122
Blain, A. B. 22:242
Blain, Alexander 22:242
Blain, Alvin 22:117
Blain, Charles H. 17:13
Blain, Frank 22:511
Blain, George 21:64
Blain, Hugh 16:83
Blain, John 1:19
Blain, Metcalfe B. 23:60
Blain, Robert 22:418
Blain, W. D. 23:250
Blaine, William C. 22:418
Blair, Adam 13:124
Blair, Addison 23:270
Blair, Charles G. 24:173

Blair, Chrs. G. 17:448
Blair, D. 3:24
Blair, David F. 22:448
Blair, Emanuel 18:406
Blair, F. 13:62
Blair, Frank 23:307
Blair, George 3:24; 14:38; 18:229; 26:13
Blair, George F. 20:209
Blair, George W. 10:41; 20:209
Blair, H. 3:24
Blair, Henry 1:115; 22:178; 23:270
Blair, Henry N. 10:157; 19:149
Blair, J. 1:96; 7:20; 13:83; 14:142, 253; 15:332; 19:56
Blair, J. G. 1:20; 3:24
Blair, J. H. 9:65
Blair, J. W. 3:24; 25:143
Blair, James 3:24; 8:70; 10:41; 20:135, 209; 21:18; 23:85
Blair, James H. 18:274
Blair, James K. 22:416
Blair, Jeremiah 4:11
Blair, John 3:24; 7:20; 11:22; 13:105; 14:142; 15:171; 17:98; 23:20
Blair, Joseph 14:38
Blair, Joseph F. 18:77
Blair, Josiah 20:121
Blair, L. 25:143
Blair, L. D. 15:184
Blair, L. P. 23:20
Blair, Levi 11:189
Blair, Lewis 5:9
Blair, Manly 23:20
Blair, Moses 17:450; 24:176
Blair, Peter S. 22:178
Blair, R. 1:19
Blair, Robert 16:90; 22:164; 25:143
Blair, Robert S. 17:48
Blair, Samuel 4:11; 17:17
Blair, Silas J. 20:121
Blair, Stephen 12:13
Blair, T. 14:4
Blair, Thomas 19:56
Blair, V. 12:147
Blair, W. 1:109; 9:139
Blair, W. A. 25:143
Blair, W. H. 14:38
Blair, W. M. 16:174
Blair, W. P. 25:143
Blair, William 16:174; 19:299; 27:14

Blair, William A. 5:9
Blair, William C. 22:276
Blair, William P. 12:80
Blais, Bongame 26:14
Blais, Frank 20:135
Blaisbell, Sanford 15:102
Blaisdale, C. H. 25:19
Blaisdall, M. W. 9:75
Blaisdell, --- 15:118
Blaisdell, Charles F.
    10:157
Blaisdell, Enoch 20:182
Blaisdell, George C.
    19:225
Blaisdell, H. 10:157
Blaisdell, Henry 18:274;
    19:149
Blaisdell, J. 9:139; 27:13,
    16
Blaisdell, James C. 6:29
Blaisdell, L. G. 25:19
Blaizdall, C. 3:24
Blaize, H. 14:287; 23:60
Blake, A. H. 15:29
Blake, A. J. 25:143
Blake, A. P. 15:184
Blake, Adam 9:48
Blake, Albert 16:174
Blake, Alex 12:47
Blake, Allen 18:24
Blake, Arthur P. 19:5
Blake, Augustus 1:14
Blake, Benjamin F.
    20:121
Blake, C. H. 23:20
Blake, Charles 21:302
Blake, Charles A. 7:83;
    21:302
Blake, Charles N. 1:18
Blake, Charles S. 21:64;
    22:474
Blake, David 22:290
Blake, David L. 21:193
Blake, E. 3:23
Blake, E. P. 13:10
Blake, E. T. 17:439;
    24:151
Blake, Edward 19:56
Blake, Edwin 5:49;
    25:143
Blake, F. 25:19
Blake, Fred 27:13
Blake, G. 25:143
Blake, George 3:23; 9:235
Blake, George K. 23:281
Blake, George M. 14:142
Blake, George Mead
    19:56
Blake, Granville 5:9
Blake, H. 1:19; 4:11
Blake, Hanson 22:401

Blake, J. 27:142
Blake, J. F. 3:23
Blake, J. J. 14:38
Blake, J. M. 16:174
Blake, J. N. 13:62
Blake, J. R. 7:87
Blake, James 11:137;
    17:170; 20:135
Blake, James H. 1:16
Blake, James R. 16:132
Blake, James T. 20:209
Blake, Jedediah 1:115
Blake, John 7:117; 8:103;
    9:8, 139; 13:56;
    14:250; 17:452;
    20:38; 22:330;
    24:182; 25:14; 27:14
Blake, John D. 14:38
Blake, John H. 23:20
Blake, John L. 12:13
Blake, John T. 14:142
Blake, Joseph 17:442;
    24:156
Blake, Josiah 24:35
Blake, L. B. 19:224
Blake, L. R. 9:169
Blake, Lewis 9:169;
    19:231
Blake, N. K. 14:264
Blake, P. 2:8; 25:19
Blake, Pino 9:128; 27:17
Blake, R. 11:90
Blake, Richard 25:268
Blake, S. H. 23:20
Blake, S. T. 1:109
Blake, Samuel 9:128;
    27:17
Blake, Samuel A. 21:48
Blake, Seneca 21:245
Blake, T. 1:110; 2:8
Blake, T. B. 19:149
Blake, Theopholis 18:392
Blake, Thomas 13:10, 56;
    14:38; 16:21, 81
Blake, Thomas M. 10:41;
    20:209
Blake, W. D. 3:23
Blake, W. H. 11:443;
    14:26; 18:392;
    19:235
Blake, Ward 10:41;
    20:209
Blake, Warren H. 9:169
Blake, Wesley 22:66
Blake, William 3:23;
    10:103; 11:279;
    20:209; 21:97; 27:22
Blake, William L. 17:75
Blake, William P. 15:90
Blakeby, M. 14:250
Blakeley, Charles 14:142

Blakeley, George 20:209
Blakeley, Levi 20:209
Blakeley, Philip 18:24
Blakeley, Robert 24:91
Blakeley, S. 5:36
Blakely, Arthur 7:20
Blakely, F. H. 1:113
Blakely, George W. 13:10
Blakely, H. 25:143
Blakely, Hardin P. 22:66
Blakely, Harvey 23:177
Blakely, Hiram 18:171
Blakely, Isaac A. 24:35
Blakely, J. D. 25:277
Blakely, Jackson 11:186
Blakely, Jacob 7:47
Blakely, James L. 10:13
Blakely, James M. 22:164
Blakely, John I. 8:9
Blakely, John J. 18:122
Blakely, John N. 7:117
Blakely, Levi 10:41
Blakely, Levi S. 20:188
Blakely, Napoleon 17:170
Blakely, Newman P.
    23:20
Blakely, R. 3:23; 13:103
Blakely, R. J. 22:178
Blakely, S. 25:143
Blakely, Thomas 17:128;
    24:187
Blakely, Wesley C. 22:20
Blakely, William 13:105;
    21:302
Blakely, William G.
    23:134
Blakely, Z. 21:302
Blakeman, Elisha 9:19
Blakeman, Elisha M.
    26:92
Blakeman, Horace 7:55
Blakeman, John W.
    22:137
Blakeman, Philip 17:128;
    24:188
Blakeman, R. 25:143
Blakeman, Robert 5:36
Blakeman, Sidney 1:113
Blakeney, B. 9:48
Blakeney, Charles 19:5
Blakenship, Madison
    10:41
Blaker, George E. 22:66
Blaker, Jonathan 22:8
Blaker, Joseph 1:16
Blaker, Robert 22:330
Blakerly, M. 14:239
Blakesby, Ferdinand
    11:103
Blakeslee, James W.
    10:13

Blakeslee, N. N. 11:83
Blakesley, Joel 10:103;
  20:209
Blakesley, M. 27:24
Blakesley, Peter 26:15
Blakesley, R. 19:247
Blakesley, Robert 9:169
Blakesley, Seth 21:97
Blakesley, W. F. 9:19
Blakesly, Peter 18:229
Blakesly, S. S. 26:12
Blakestery, H. 3:24
Blaketler, E. C. 9:139
Blakey, R. 14:5
Blakie, George 15:184
Blakley, James W. 12:151
Blakley, S. S. 9:75
Blaknenhein, John 22:474
Blakney, Charles 12:58
Blakson, W. H. 18:24
Blal, John 12:67
Blaloch, William A.
  18:229
Blalock, Thomas J. 23:60
Blalock, William A. 26:15
Blamley, W. 21:146
Blan, Clifton 17:278
Blan, David 24:189
Blan, Tim 24:189
Blan---, J. W. 24:109
Blanahard, William W.
  25:143
Blanberg, Peter A. 9:116
Blanc, A. 19:279
Blanc, Branch 21:302
Blance, Albert 9:169
Blancet, James 11:420
Blanch, Elijah 8:45
Blanch, F. 19:279
Blanchan, Franklin 27:18
Blanchan, Franklin F.
  9:116
Blanchard, --- 13:126;
  25:17
Blanchard, A. 3:23
Blanchard, A. J. 14:142;
  16:174
Blanchard, Aaron 13:10
Blanchard, Allen 19:289
Blanchard, Alonzo C.
  23:85
Blanchard, Andrew 9:95;
  26:11
Blanchard, B. G. 10:157
Blanchard, D. 13:83
Blanchard, Daniel 14:38,
  142
Blanchard, E. 3:24; 8:45
Blanchard, Edmund L.
  10:103; 20:209

Blanchard, Edward 4:11;
  7:20; 14:142; 21:302
Blanchard, Elijah 21:135
Blanchard, Enoch 22:290
Blanchard, Erwin W. 4:11
Blanchard, F. 9:139;
  27:15
Blanchard, Fred 7:117
Blanchard, G. 3:24
Blanchard, G. P. 1:113
Blanchard, George 10:41;
  16:174; 17:241, 390;
  20:209
Blanchard, George S.
  12:13
Blanchard, George T.
  12:13
Blanchard, H. 25:17
Blanchard, J. 16:174
Blanchard, J. P. 16:174
Blanchard, James 3:24;
  25:143
Blanchard, James M.
  11:103
Blanchard, Jasper 11:115
Blanchard, John D.
  20:135
Blanchard, John H. 9:169
Blanchard, Jonathan D.
  22:20
Blanchard, Joseph 21:302
Blanchard, L. 3:23, 24
Blanchard, L. M. 1:110
Blanchard, Lyman 13:105
Blanchard, Martin 13:10
Blanchard, Merit A. 10:89
Blanchard, Moses 9:205
Blanchard, O. S. 3:23
Blanchard, Oliver 15:63
Blanchard, Oliver H.
  22:137
Blanchard, Oscar 3:23
Blanchard, S. 19:225
Blanchard, S. B. 16:146
Blanchard, S. F. 15:21
Blanchard, Sargent J.
  21:135
Blanchard, Spencer M.
  23:105
Blanchard, T. C. 15:339
Blanchard, Tyler 10:157;
  19:149
Blanchard, W. H. H.
  18:392
Blanchard, W. M. 15:102
Blanchard, W. W. 27:142
Blanchard, Wesley 13:10
Blanchard, William 8:9;
  18:122
Blanchard, William F.
  26:13

Blanchard, William T.
  18:229
Blanchard, William W.
  5:9
Blanchear, Peter 4:11
Blanchett, C. E. 1:114
Blanchford, W. S. 14:38
Blanckard, T. C. 16:363
Bland, A. C. 9:48
Bland, Charles 22:117
Bland, David 15:53
Bland, E. 11:123, 230
Bland, Ellis 17:170
Bland, Fletcher 17:278
Bland, G. W. 7:87
Bland, J. 20:209
Bland, J. H. 20:209
Bland, James 9:229
Bland, John 10:157;
  19:149
Bland, Joseph 21:64
Bland, M. 1:19
Bland, Taylor 13:10;
  16:21
Bland, W. J. 26:236
Bland, William 17:170;
  21:97; 23:307
Blanderig, William A.
  8:80
Blandfield, Edward
  11:256
Blandford, Stephen 5:36
Blandin, A. 1:112
Blanding, J. E. 25:143
Blanding, Osmond L.
  22:232
Blane, --- 18:171
Blane, D. A. 19:328
Blane, Lewis 21:210
Blane, Series 21:265
Blanehard, George 13:78
Blaner, David A. 22:178
Blaney, George 10:157
Blaney, J. S. 1:110
Blaney, James 18:230;
  26:14
Blaney, Samuel 16:174
Blaney, William H. 16:3
Blanford, Stephen 25:143
Blank, F. 9:169
Blank, George 12:13
Blank, George F. 18:122
Blank, H. 14:142, 253
Blank, J. 11:321
Blank, Jacob 10:89;
  20:209
Blank, Joel 22:401
Blank, John 11:383;
  21:193
Blank, Joseph H. 18:392
Blank, Nicholas 1:19

Blankanship, S. H. 11:325
Blankeman, August 23:178
Blanken, Claus 21:97
Blankenbaker, David L. 24:35
Blankenbecker, Thompson 22:415
Blankenshife, J. W. C. 8:45
Blankenship, A. 21:97
Blankenship, Caleb 17:452; 24:182
Blankenship, Hezekiah 21:97
Blankenship, Isam 24:165
Blankenship, J. D. 10:41; 20:209
Blankenship, John 10:41; 20:209; 22:20
Blankenship, Joshua 22:117
Blankenship, M. 8:9; 18:122; 20:209
Blankenship, Robert 8:80
Blankenship, Thomas 17:151
Blankenship, V. M. 9:65; 18:274
Blankenship, Vincent 17:146
Blankenship, William 11:88
Blankernst, J. W. 10:34
Blankey, F. 4:11
Blankingship, J. 19:149
Blankinship, Charles 17:165
Blankinship, Henry 17:128
Blankinship, Isaac 11:383
Blankinship, J. 10:171
Blankinship, John 16:21
Blankinship, Joseph C. 11:83
Blankinship, Nelson 17:128; 24:188
Blankley, Hiram 10:185
Blanks, William 15:357
Blanlett, Wesley 21:265
Blann, John 20:142
Blanningford, Alex. 8:113
Blanpied, T. 13:83
Blanse, E. 21:302
Blansfield, C. 25:143
Blant, Nelson 25:143
Blanten, Peter 20:209
Blanter, Peter 20:209
Blantford, Henry T. 22:117
Blanton, A. J. 11:23

Blanton, Peter 10:41, 103
Blanton, William 17:234
Blanvelt, Abm. 19:149
Blanvelt, Isaac I. 23:119
Blany, Patrick 12:13
Blarault, George B. C. 11:102
Blarfield, Charles 5:9
Blarkley, R. 16:266
Blasdel, James F. 15:6
Blasdell, C. E. 18:45
Blasdell, H. M. 24:35
Blasdell, J. C. 25:317
Blasdell, John F. 21:221
Blase, Samuel 17:450
Blaser, Conrad 11:420
Blaser, F. 22:178
Blaser, H. 14:264
Blaser, Samuel 24:176
Blash, George 8:80
Blasidal, William 9:71
Blasier, David 22:276
Blask, William 11:52
Blason, G. K. 22:473
Blass, J. 23:255
Blass, Obediah 22:137
Blass, Philip A. 4:11
Blasse, F. 21:302
Blasser, Noah 20:209
Blatchley, H. D. 13:83
Blatchley, Joseph 24:13
Blatchly, A. A. 19:149
Blathman, George 26:152
Blatsley, M. 12:7
Blatt, Horatio D. 4:11
Blatt, W. 1:109
Blattan, Jacob 22:178
Blattman, Benjamin 17:13
Blatz, H. 14:295; 17:482; 27:20
Blauvelt, William 3:24
Blauvelt, William J. 10:13
Blaxon, William D. 17:17
Blaxter, James 21:302
Blaxton, D. W. 14:38
Blaycer, Joseph 22:474
Blaye, Jos 16:364
Blaye, Joseph 15:339
Blaytick, John 26:152
Blazdell, J. P. 9:108
Blaze, Charles G. 10:103; 20:209
Blazen, William 10:89
Blazer, David 11:258
Blazier, Charles W. 17:29
Blazier, Phillip 27:12
Blazoor, C. F. 13:105
Bleack, Samuel 8:9
Bleak, Harrison 22:473
Bleams, Dillard 22:242
Blean, Joseph 26:210

Bleber, Thomas 23:20
Blechem, Charles E. 12:13
Bleck, Andrew 22:417
Blecker, William J. 24:91
Blecksley, J. J. 4:11
Bledsoe, David R. 13:10
Bledsoe, Green 21:265
Bledsoe, Solomon 11:335
Bledsoe, William 10:41
Bledson, Daniel 16:174
Bledson, Thomas 10:41
Bledson, William 20:209
Bleedney, Hugh 4:11
Bleekley, Francis D. 4:11
Bleeldat, Thomas 10:208
Bleiler, Christopher 26:121
Bleiler, E. 16:15
Blell, George 22:447
Blem, Jacob 17:429
Blemberg, Peter A. 27:11
Blemhoff, A. 11:117
Blemons, Alexander 23:251
Blen, Harvey 22:66
Blenard, Roger 8:37; 26:151
Blencoe, N. 27:13
Blenden, S. 25:143
Blengly, James G. 22:401
Blenker, Henry 1:14
Blenker, Paul 23:250
Bleock, D. 9:199
Blerins, R. 18:362
Blerius, Jacob 8:37
Blern, Jacob 24:186
Blesdale, J. H. D. 19:231
Blesi, Melchior 22:161
Bless, A. C. 15:150
Bless, W. H. 25:16
Blessdale, Stephen 21:302
Blesser, Charles 25:143
Blessing, C. 3:24
Blessing, Michael 10:103; 20:209
Blessing, Pius 3:24
Blessington, H. 19:235
Bleuler, J. J. 1:116
Bleven, Thomas 12:13
Blevens, G. M. 23:20
Blevies, Louis 21:265
Blevin, Timor 17:146
Blevin, Walter 22:242
Blevins, Benjamin 7:47
Blevins, J. 22:242
Blevins, Jacob 26:151
Blevins, Nathaniel 21:12
Blevins, R. 9:218
Blevins, Solomon 17:258
Blevins, T. H. 11:325
Blevins, Thomas 23:21

Blevins, William 22:66
Bleviz, Adam 18:102
Blew, Samuel 16:151
Blewer, W. W. 9:19;
    18:320
Bley, Henry 4:11
Bleyman, J. 1:19
Blickenstaff, Jacob 22:66
Blie, D. 14:142
Bliffington, H. 9:169
Blight, Joseph 11:121
Blimber, Turner 17:48
Blimmer, C. 13:83
Bline, David I. 8:9
Bline, P. H. 22:66
Blineboy, William 7:20
Blink, Godeby 9:75
Blinker, John 26:11
Blinkman, H. Y. 16:288
Blinn, Clinton A. 13:10
Blinn, E. A. 9:19
Blinn, Noble A. 22:276
Blint, Anthony 9:164
Bliss, A. N. 21:302
Bliss, Andrew 17:146
Bliss, Augustus E. 24:60
Bliss, B. 22:469
Bliss, C. B. 23:301
Bliss, Charles 9:139;
    11:14
Bliss, Charles W. 22:66
Bliss, D. 1:15
Bliss, D. A. 25:143
Bliss, D. L. 19:235
Bliss, David A. 5:9
Bliss, David L. 9:169
Bliss, Donald 17:262
Bliss, E. 27:23
Bliss, E. L. 11:134
Bliss, Edwin A. 10:41
Bliss, Edwin H. 16:7
Bliss, F. H. 3:24
Bliss, Franklin R. 23:187
Bliss, G. F. 1:112
Bliss, George C. 4:11
Bliss, Harrison 4:11
Bliss, Henry 4:11
Bliss, J. W. 11:53; 13:105
Bliss, Jacob 15:277
Bliss, James 1:19
Bliss, James H. 3:24
Bliss, John A. 23:60
Bliss, John F. 13:62;
    16:174
Bliss, John T. 16:174
Bliss, Julius C. 24:64
Bliss, M. D. 24:74
Bliss, Merit 7:47
Bliss, Nathaniel 22:276
Bliss, P. 1:112
Bliss, S. 19:327

Bliss, Samuel 9:116
Bliss, Seth 7:66
Bliss, Simon 1:15
Bliss, Thomas 11:237
Bliss, W. H. 10:26;
    19:299
Bliss, William 1:15; 20:95
Bliss, Willis D. 10:103;
    20:209
Blissitt, William 23:21
Blithman, F. 23:134
Bliton, Thomas 26:93
Blitter, James 10:41
Blitter, Jasper 20:209
Blitton, Thomas 9:19
Blitzner, Ferdinand 4:11
Bliven, Calvin P. 10:103;
    20:209
Blivins, E. 13:83
Blivon, P. C. 10:103;
    20:209
Blizard, Samuel 24:74
Blizard, W. H. 12:151
Blizzard, --- 19:149
Blizzard, F. 10:153
Blizzard, Henry G.
    10:153; 19:149
Blizzard, James 12:13
Blizzard, Oliver 22:461
Blizzard, William 11:399
Blizzard, William D.
    23:60
Blo---, E. D. 18:230;
    26:14
Blobus, Peter 9:199;
    19:289
Blocher, William 1:16
Blocher, William L.
    22:350
Block, D. 19:289
Block, Everett Van 20:209
Block, G. A. 14:38
Block, George 14:142
Block, J. P. 3:24
Block, John C. 23:187
Block, R. 11:186
Block, S. P. 21:165
Block, Samuel 17:29
Block, Valentine 13:10
Blockberger, John 22:330
Blocker, James 21:265
Blocker, Robert A. 11:24
Blockley, Matthias 21:64
Blockman, John 16:90
Blockmay, E. 13:83
Blockson, M. 25:293
Blockson, Minus 7:77
Blockwell, George 25:279
Blockwell, Hampton
    20:209
Blodget, Alonzo 11:102

Blodget, Hiram L. 11:180
Blodget, John 8:103
Blodget, Nelson 25:143
Blodgett, A. S. 25:143
Blodgett, A. Z. 3:24
Blodgett, Albert 13:10
Blodgett, Alex 26:151
Blodgett, Andrew 10:26
Blodgett, Andrew T.
    18:392
Blodgett, C. S. 11:399
Blodgett, Calvin A.
    22:517
Blodgett, E. J. 1:109
Blodgett, G. F. 21:302
Blodgett, George 14:142
Blodgett, Henry 9:7;
    12:13
Blodgett, Henry H. 22:66
Blodgett, J. 15:83
Blodgett, J. J. 25:16
Blodgett, J. S. 1:113
Blodgett, Jackson 12:67
Blodgett, James H. 15:184
Blodgett, James M.
    14:142
Blodgett, Jerome 22:137
Blodgett, John D. 10:157
Blodgett, Pearley J. 4:11
Blodgett, W. A. 19:5
Blodgett, W. M. 12:98
Blodgett, W. Walter
    26:216
Blodgett, William 9:235
Blodson, Thomas 20:210
Blodt, James 14:142
Bloedt, Joseph 14:142
Bloes, John 6:20
Blogg, Peter K. 18:302
Bloisdell, C. H. 2:7
Blomer, --- 15:164
Blonde, Joseph 22:164
Blonden, John 18:392
Bloner, A. C. 24:13
Blood, Alyah W. 19:5
Blood, Amas 9:156
Blood, B. C. 1:116
Blood, Charles 21:302
Blood, Ebert L. 26:10
Blood, Elert L. 9:75
Blood, Elias 22:66
Blood, G. P. 3:24
Blood, George D. 25:143
Blood, H. P. 12:7
Blood, Herson 16:138
Blood, J. W. 21:302
Blood, L. 3:24
Blood, L. W. 16:21
Blood, Lyman R. 19:56
Blood, R. R. 1:18
Blood, Senaca 11:410

Blood, T. B. 3:24
Blood, William F. 14:142
Bloodaugh, James W. 5:9
Bloodough, J. W. 25:143
Bloom, Adam 3:24
Bloom, Charles 21:198
Bloom, D. 1:20
Bloom, David 18:24
Bloom, F. 1:93
Bloom, Gabriel 8:9;
    18:122
Bloom, H. E. 15:29
Bloom, J. 3:24; 25:143
Bloom, John 5:9
Bloom, Robert 10:103;
    20:210
Bloom, S. 14:38
Bloom, William 8:9;
    13:79; 16:174;
    18:122
Bloomage, Henry 22:178
Bloomer, Ancil 11:257
Bloomer, Benjamin
    21:221
Bloomer, H. 3:24; 18:12
Bloomer, Hans 13:10
Bloomer, J. 3:24
Bloomer, James 11:297
Bloomer, John C. 17:205
Bloomer, Joseph 1:114
Bloomer, W. H. 1:111
Bloomfield, E. 11:295
Bloomfield, Henry 22:20
Bloomfield, S. P. 25:143
Bloomfield, William 4:11
Bloomingbury, M. 14:38
Bloomis, Louis 21:210
Bloomker, W. 3:24
Blosage, S. 16:266
Bloser, Jonah 3:24
Blosey, Newton 21:193
Bloss, Charles 27:13
Bloss, Frank 23:119
Bloss, H. 16:288
Bloss, J. 12:86
Bloss, J. P. 23:21
Bloss, Martin 17:108
Bloss, O. 23:117
Bloss, P. 3:24
Blosser, J. 23:134
Blosser, Noah 10:89
Blossom, Charles 3:24
Blossom, Fred. C. 7:87
Blotensberger, Abram
    17:427
Blotkamp, Henry 15:6
Blotman, George 8:61
Blottenberger, Abraham
    24:181
Blough, Francis H. 16:132
Blough, Isaac 11:52

Blough, R. 25:143
Blough, Rufus 5:9
Bloughard, Edw. 1:13
Blount, A. 21:302
Blount, Cornelius 22:276
Blount, John B. 4:11
Blount, Jonathan 11:235
Blount, Riley 4:11
Blour, John 9:48
Blouser, John 9:32
Blow, George 24:74
Blow, J. 14:38; 21:18
Blow, Lewis 21:242
Blowers, Andrew J.
    15:119
Blowers, B. 9:108
Blowers, Barton 9:156
Blowers, George 20:95
Blowers, Harrison 22:66
Blowers, Ira 22:137
Blowers, Peter 14:142
Blowers, Washington J.
    22:137
Blowers, William 22:330
Bloxham, Joseph 17:421;
    24:163
Bloyer, John 8:70
Bloyer, Thomas 22:276
Blublaw, John 1:19
Bluch, George 25:15
Blucher, John L. 12:58
Bluck, Fredrick 27:18
Bludgett, A. C. 16:21
Blue, Benjamin 22:290,
    417
Blue, David 4:64; 22:178
Blue, David J. 18:122
Blue, Edwin 18:230;
    26:16
Blue, Ennis 12:151
Blue, George 22:290
Blue, J. 21:18
Blue, Jackson 7:117
Blue, Jacob 27:23
Blue, James 24:155
Blue, John 17:246
Blue, Joseph 27:12
Blue, L. 7:87
Blue, Michael 21:221
Blue, Reubin 18:230;
    26:15
Blue, S. 24:74
Blue, W. R. 18:362
Blue Bat 25:332
Bluebucker, John 11:137
Bluemour, John H. 18:63
Bluett, John C. 8:9;
    18:122
Bluff, Henry 9:203
Bluff, John 16:174
Bluis, William S. 25:14

Blum, I. 14:142
Blum, John 12:170
Blume, Theodore 16:90
Blumener, C. 14:5
Blumenstein, N. 1:19
Blumey, H. 1:18
Blumhart, Jacob 15:164
Blumley, Guy W. 4:11
Blumly, E. 3:24
Blund, Peter 9:19
Blunket, Mathew 27:23
Blunt, A. 9:153
Blunt, Anthony 25:317
Blunt, B. C. 16:90
Blunt, B. M. 18:63
Blunt, G. W. 21:303
Blunt, Granville 9:164
Blunt, Henry 13:10
Blunt, J. 1:20
Blunt, J. F. 16:174
Blunt, J. H. 21:303
Blunt, James G. 22:20
Blunt, John 10:41; 20:210
Blunt, Perry 27:143
Blunt, Reuben 24:176
Blunt, T. H. 16:21
Blurkman, Henry 18:122
Blush, Curtis 18:448
Blush, Curtis A. 18:420
Blutzstein, C. 1:14
Bly, E. P. 13:10
Bly, Isaac 10:89; 20:210
Bly, Jackson 11:410
Bly, John 11:198
Bly, John M. 23:60
Bly, Lysander 10:204
Bly, Nicholas 24:107
Bly, Simon 11:198
Bly, Thomas 21:18
Blydenburgh, Charles
    1:19
Blye, Benjamin F. 22:523
Blye, Joseph H. 12:13
Blynn, Daniel 22:10
Blyohe, David 26:11
Blystone, William 13:105
Blyth, Henry C. 9:95
Blyth, O. 3:24
Blythe, C. B. 22:178
Blythe, Daniel 18:274
Blythe, David 9:75
Blythe, George F. 13:10
Blythe, George T. 16:22
Bnakman, A. 3:24
Boace, Joseph 11:380
Boadup, H. 14:5
Boadwee, John 4:11
Boaez, David 22:117
Boag, Sim 17:128; 24:187
Boak, J. J. B. 9:139
Boaks, Berry S. 18:399

Boal, William F. 13:10
Boaley, J. J. 7:47
Boaling, R. M. 17:48
Boals, Samuel T. 18:392
Board, Albert 9:206
Board, C. 17:48
Board, Charles 11:198
Board, Dennis 9:164
Board, L. 16:174
Board, W. 17:278
Board, William 17:275
Boarden, Levy 21:303
Boardman, Andrew J. 9:11
Boardman, F. 18:25
Boardman, Frederick A. 18:334
Boardman, George M. 10:41
Boardman, John 20:210
Boardman, L. O. 1:115
Boardman, Viras N. 12:7
Boardman, W. 1:13
Boares, A. 3:24
Boarman, Paul 17:128; 24:188
Boarn, M. 16:175
Boarnan, Augustine 10:94
Boarsem, Isea 19:279
Boarts, P. 1:20
Boas, A. 23:21
Boas, John 21:119
Boas, Michael 21:90
Boas, Washington 27:22
Boast, J. B. 14:38
Boatman, B. F. 22:473
Boatman, George 10:42; 20:34, 210; 27:143
Boatman, Jeremiah 24:35
Boatman, L. W. 15:287
Boatman, Lorenzo 26:151
Boatman, Perry 10:41
Boatman, S. D. 21:165
Boatman, William 21:48
Boatright, Hiram 22:20
Boatwright, Robert 22:117
Boatwright, T. J. 8:61
Boaz, Hudson 22:20
Boaz, William J. 22:242
Boban, Thomas 9:161
Bobb, A. 21:185
Bobb, Isaac 7:87
Bobb, Jacob 11:410
Bobb, John 22:242
Bobb, William 14:39
Bobbett, Harrison 17:348
Bobee, C. 1:19
Bobenmyer, David 23:134
Bobinder, A. 21:109
Boblett, L. E. 7:87

Bobp, William 20:210
Bobson, Allen 15:358
Bocet, C. H. 15:63
Boch, John 13:106
Bochard, Ferdinand 23:134
Bochbour, John 23:105
Bock, Adam 16:22
Bock, Adams 13:10
Bock, Charles 22:276
Bock, H. 18:25
Bock, Hembold 22:276
Bock, Henry 20:142
Bock, Jacob 4:11
Bock, John 11:297
Bock, Samuel 3:24
Bock, Thomas J. 7:87
Bock, William 22:401
Bockell, Henry 20:102
Bocker, C. 14:253
Bocket, C. 16:174
Bockett, J. 22:518
Bocklins, John A. 12:13
Bockman, William 22:66
Bockmei, O. 19:56
Bockmeyer, Emil 10:89
Bockmeyer, Emile 20:210
Bocock, Benjamin F. 8:9
Bod, R. 11:118
Boday, Adam 22:179
Boddorf, Israel 10:103; 20:210
Boddy, James 25:16
Bode, A. 3:24
Bode, Christian 9:71
Bode, Frederick 1:17
Bode, Henry 25:19
Bode, William 23:60
Bodecker, --- 15:29
Bodecker, August 8:9; 18:122
Bodel, Samuel 10:32
Bodeman, O. H. 21:303
Boden, J. 14:318; 25:279
Boden, Joseph 17:358; 18:45
Boden, S. D. 23:21
Boden, Thomas 9:163; 15:184
Bodenburg, Charles 22:232
Bodenhammer, S. 14:250
Bodenhort, W. 14:39
Bodet, Ely 10:13
Bodett, Peter 21:303
Bodette, Louis 22:20
Bodey, George 15:102
Bodfish, Benjamin 10:204
Bodge, Charles H. 25:18
Bodge, S. D. 3:24
Bodgen, W. A. 20:210

Bodgers, Thomas F. 26:210
Bodicher, D. 25:143
Bodier, David 23:308
Bodihay, J. 3:24
Bodin, T. S. 3:24
Bodine, Allen 22:66
Bodine, Antonio 5:9
Bodine, George W. 22:21
Bodine, Mortimer C. 17:287
Bodine, Napoleon 16:22
Bodish, Elisha 7:87
Bodius, A. 1:13
Bodkin, E. L. 3:24
Bodkin, J. 13:83
Bodkin, W. J. 3:24
Bodkin, William 3:24
Bodking, E. 17:335
Bodkins, George 18:284; 26:134
Bodkins, P. 3:24
Bodkins, R. 25:19
Bodkins, Robert 2:8
Bodla, J. 12:164
Bodlay, R. H. 19:44
Bodle, Alonzo K. 22:415
Bodle, F. 26:152
Bodle, Richard 17:144
Bodle, William 9:95
Bodles, Daniel 3:24
Bodley, Elisha 11:51
Bodley, Jesse 11:136
Bodley, Philo 20:95
Bodley, W. 14:39
Bodly, D. 1:14
Bodman, B. 18:302; 26:92
Bodman, Charles 16:146
Bodman, H. 11:395
Bodman, W. J. 10:204
Bodman, W. S. 18:406
Bodon, Napoleon 13:10
Bodsey, Joseph 23:308
Bodsford, Albert 7:117
Bodson, William 12:13
Bodtcher, Christopher 23:60
Bodwell, Charles A. 1:18
Bodwell, Isaac 10:157
Bodwell, John A. 25:143
Bodwell, William 4:11
Body, M. 12:85
Body, Samuel 1:13
Body, Sandy 17:171
Boe, John 11:52
Boedecker, Charles 22:330
Boegelt, Frederick 21:117
Boegler, John 19:279
Boehling, O. 15:317
Boehm, C. 1:112

Boehm, Charles H. 21:133
Boehman, John 12:94
Boehning, Henry 22:164
Boellenrucher, Jacob
  17:29
Boely, M. 16:288
Boeman, John 12:48
Boemaster, J. 3:24
Boen, Thomas 25:317
Boenton, W. E. 17:275
Boergley, William N.
  11:339
Boering, Thomas 22:242
Boerner, Julius 1:15
Boery, Henry 10:103;
  20:210
Boes, John 17:48
Boes, Peter 10:42; 20:210
Boessling, E. A. 24:63
Boethier, W. F. 8:9
Boeticher, Augustus H.
  23:112
Boettcher, A. 9:65
Boetyler, George 8:9
Boey, Francis 20:105
Bofeet, Francis 14:142
Boff, John 27:22
Boffman, Baker 22:418
Bofman, Daniel 11:198
Bofman, W. H. 17:290
Bog---, H. 24:189
Bogain, N. 14:39
Bogan, James B. 16:174
Bogan, James P. 6:11
Bogan, Palmer 10:171;
  19:149
Bogan, S. F. 23:60
Bogar, David 3:24
Bogar, James 15:319
Bogard, J. 1:14
Bogard, John R. 3:24
Bogard, W. D. 26:93
Bogard, William 17:108
Bogard, William D. 9:19
Bogardis, George D.
  20:105
Bogardus, G. E. 1:15
Bogardus, H. L. 9:169;
  19:224
Bogardus, S. P. 15:277
Bogart, A. 1:13
Bogart, Andrew J. 10:103
Bogart, Andrew M. 25:17
Bogart, George 15:293;
  16:174
Bogart, Henry 15:29
Bogart, John 3:24; 13:11;
  16:22
Bogart, Kersey 1:115
Bogart, Lafayette 20:135

Bogart, Nelson 6:7;
  18:107
Bogart, P. E. 8:9; 18:122
Bogart, Theodore 16:90
Bogart, Vincent 21:221
Bogart, Wallace 13:10;
  16:22
Bogarth, Reason 17:71
Bogarth, William M.
  17:48
Bogden, William A. 10:42
Bogel, Samuel 17:444
Boger, F. H. 1:96
Boger, Harvey 21:248
Boger, Joseph H. 10:42
Bogert, Charles 10:42;
  20:210
Bogert, Isaac 20:210
Bogert, Peter L. 8:80
Bogert, William H. 20:210
Bogg, G. 14:239
Bogg, James C. 11:237
Boggess, Jeremiah F.
  17:17
Boggs, --- 14:39, 142;
  18:426
Boggs, Albert 15:63
Boggs, Benham 23:21
Boggs, Edward 6:15;
  18:77
Boggs, Francis M. 22:66
Boggs, George 9:32
Boggs, H. C. 3:24
Boggs, Hazel 7:117
Boggs, Hugh 21:241
Boggs, J. 25:144
Boggs, J. C. 12:166
Boggs, J. L. 9:32
Boggs, John 5:36; 9:128;
  27:17
Boggs, John F. 10:103;
  20:210
Boggs, Joseph W. 11:236
Boggs, L. 9:48
Boggs, Lafayette 17:29
Boggs, M. 14:39
Boggs, Sandford 18:274
Boggs, W. S. 21:303
Boggs, William 7:117;
  23:134
Boggy, Charles 24:189
Boghee, W. B. 25:144
Bogine, Charles 17:73
Bogle, A. 25:144
Bogle, Harmon 11:407
Bogley, J. E. 3:24
Bogman, John 11:299
Bognard, Philip 4:64
Bogno, Walter 7:117
Bograth, A. 17:439
Bogue, C. L. 10:185

Bogue, Elias 22:179
Bogue, John 10:103;
  20:210
Bogue, Richard H. 7:20
Bogue, S. P. 18:274
Bogus, Benjamin 11:198
Bogwell, A. 11:24
Bohale, John 18:274
Boham, Daniel 20:210
Bohaman, J. 7:20
Bohan, George 21:303
Bohan, John 22:117
Bohannan, Asa 1:115
Bohannan, D. 16:288
Bohannan, Elijah 20:210
Bohannon, Elijah 10:103
Bohannon, J. G. 27:15
Bohannon, J. L. 17:278
Bohanon, J. 3:24
Bohanow, D. E. 14:39
Bohart, Samuel 11:53
Bohein, C. 3:24
Bohein, J. 3:24
Bohen, Philip 3:24
Boher, H. 20:210
Boherper, E. 10:26
Bohin, C. 14:142
Bohl, Frederick 25:17
Bohl, H. 3:24
Bohl, W. M. 17:73
Bohler, Leo 12:13
Bohler, Nelson 11:196
Bohler, Sullivan 12:48
Bohm, William H. 21:135
Bohman, S. 17:251
Bohme, Peter 22:179
Bohmer, William 11:137
Bohmer, Wilm 15:157
Bohn, Andrew 22:8
Bohn, Benjamin 5:36
Bohnat, I. 1:109
Bohne, Herman 15:317;
  19:56
Bohnger, John 23:183
Bohni, John 15:339;
  16:364
Bohnmiller, J. 3:24
Bohnson, --- 24:35
Bohnson, W. 3:24
Boholar, P. 23:21
Bohrer, Casper 16:132
Bohrman, William 13:11
Bohrmann, William 16:22
Bohrper, E. 19:299
Boice, A. 21:18; 25:144
Boice, Austin 25:144
Boice, Cornelius 7:20
Boice, G. A. 3:25
Boice, J. 3:25
Boice, John 22:460
Boice, W. A. 18:45

Boicourt, David 23:60
Boid, John R. 22:242
Boid, Joseph 11:24
Boid, Michael 19:280
Boigenson, J. 23:200
Boil, Charles 15:291
Boil, Patrick 11:53
Boil, Samuel 18:122
Boin, John 20:210
Bointon, Andrew A. 9:116
Boir, George W. 27:17
Boise, A. 1:17
Boise, J. 25:14
Boise, Marion 12:151
Boisne, S. 17:170
Boisonnault, F. N. 3:25
Boiss, J. 25:144
Boist, John 5:9
Boisvert, Adolphus 13:11
Boitram, John S. 3:25
Bokaske, Benjamin 9:228
Boker, J. A. 9:139
Boker, James 15:95
Boker, James B. 20:210
Boker, John M. 11:410
Boker, Stephen 11:198
Bokewood, D. 25:144
Bolan, Benjamin 10:94
Bolan, D. 15:184
Bolan, Daniel 1:17
Bolan, P. 22:164
Bolan, R. 8:9; 18:122
Boland, Daniel 3:25
Boland, Fred 19:149
Boland, Frederick 10:153
Boland, James 3:25
Boland, John 24:13
Boland, Margaret B. 26:217
Boland, Peter 15:184
Bolander, William J. 11:298
Bolby, D. 3:25
Bolby, H. 11:138
Bolcolm, Russell 1:112
Boldbrie, Samuel R. 17:409
Bolden, Anthony 23:290
Bolden, Elisha 10:94
Bolden, James M. 17:29
Bolden, John 7:77; 25:293
Bolden, Moses 7:117
Bolden, Robert 21:265
Boldin, S. 7:77; 25:293
Boldin, Samuel 7:77
Boldin, Sol 25:293
Boldman, James 7:117
Boldock, D. H. 8:45
Boldrey, Clark 11:384
Bole, John 11:23

Bole, Sampson 6:29; 25:317
Boleer, J. 18:430
Bolen, --- 22:350
Bolen, Alex H. 17:210
Bolen, Christopher 10:103; 20:210
Bolen, E. 3:25
Bolen, George W. 21:84
Bolen, J. B. 25:144
Bolen, James 17:93
Bolen, S. 11:420
Bolen, William J. 23:21
Bolenbaugh, John 24:91
Bolenburgh, George 11:137
Bolenger, Joseph 11:325
Boles, Alexander 18:188
Boles, F. 3:25
Boles, G. 3:25
Boles, H. 3:25
Boles, J. 3:25
Boles, James 24:74
Boles, M. B. 3:25
Boles, Robert 22:511
Boles, W. G. 3:25
Boles, William 3:25; 9:235; 15:81
Bolestell, David 13:11
Bolestelle, Daniel 16:22
Boleston, Frederick 12:141
Bolew, William 26:216
Boley, A. J. 3:25
Boley, John H. 17:29
Boley, Peter 3:25
Bolger, --- 27:15
Bolger, Michael 21:303
Bolhuger, William 18:171
Bolian, George 7:87
Bolibeaugh, Jacob 18:274
Bolin, --- 9:239
Bolin, Edward 13:134; 19:346
Bolin, Eli 17:335
Bolin, George 26:10
Bolin, James 23:60
Bolin, John 16:364; 17:170; 20:88
Bolin, John E. 22:21
Bolin, Nelson 15:184
Bolin, Noah M. 24:35
Bolin, O. 23:21
Bolin, P. M. 11:52
Bolin, Thomas 11:51
Bolin, Upton 17:191
Bolin, William 8:61; 18:77; 26:152
Bolin, Wright 17:235
Bolinder, Oliver 22:179

Boling, Alexander 10:103; 20:210
Boling, William 3:25
Boling, William H. 9:32
Boling, William H. H. 11:325
Bolinger, George 23:134
Bolinger, J. 1:13, 18
Bolinger, Jacob 14:142; 15:53
Bolinger, John 20:210
Bolinger, Robert 11:217
Bolinger, Samuel 21:18
Bolington, Alexander 21:64
Bolington, Moses 22:66
Bolio, Charles 23:260
Bolio, G. W. 24:74
Bolis, E. 1:110
Bolivar, J. 21:146
Bolivar, John 21:215
Bolkhan, Ferdinand 9:116
Bolkhart, John 12:13
Boll, W. D. 10:26
Bolla, Emanuel 8:9
Bollair, Alphonse 7:87
Bollan, D. G. 27:24
Bolland, Hovial 19:247
Bolland, W. H. 9:19
Bolland, William 20:210
Bollard, Robert 9:169
Bollardick, William 10:103; 20:210
Bollardson, F. 16:266
Bolleher, John 4:11
Bollen, Emanuel 18:122
Bollenger, David 9:75
Bolles, F. 20:176
Bolles, H. D. 1:115
Bolles, R. J. 10:210
Bolleston, Fred 20:210
Bollier, David 15:102
Bollin, James 11:383
Bolling, James P. W. 26:16
Bollinger, --- 16:90
Bollinger, Alexander 17:108
Bollinger, John 10:103
Bollinger, S. W. 20:210
Bollinger, W. H. 13:124
Bollman, S. 27:22
Bollnison, Christian 22:179
Bollow, D. G. 14:239
Bollunback, William 12:167
Bolman, Israel 25:268
Bolmar, Edward 17:163
Bolmer, B. 23:134
Bolmer, John 11:53

Boloer, Alexander 7:117
Bolona, P. 14:39
Bolp, William 10:42
Bolser, James S. 21:135
Bolser, Peter 13:11
Bolster, D. M. 19:56
Bolster, Francis J. 23:119
Bolster, James 27:19
Bolster, Joseph 12:13
Bolsward, Sebastian 8:9
Bolswon, Charles 26:149
Bolswow, Sibastur 18:122
Bolt, Benjamin 13:11
Bolt, Frederick 18:122
Bolt, J. H. 3:25
Bolt, S. 21:18
Bolt, William G. 17:29
Bolte, Frederick 8:9
Bolten, John 23:15
Bolten, William L. 17:351
Bolthroff, John W. 10:42
Bolthroff, R. W. 20:210
Boltinghouse, Joseph S. 20:27
Bolton, Abraham 15:10
Bolton, Calvin J. 22:242
Bolton, Charles 11:123
Bolton, E. W. 20:210
Bolton, Edward 17:63
Bolton, George 15:150
Bolton, J. 13:83
Bolton, J. R. 25:293
Bolton, Jacob 21:265
Bolton, James 9:101;
    10:42; 14:39;
    15:184; 18:337;
    20:211
Bolton, James K. 7:73
Bolton, James L. 22:448
Bolton, James M. 13:60
Bolton, John 10:103;
    20:211
Bolton, Joseph 9:32;
    18:290; 26:93
Bolton, L. W. 9:242
Bolton, Mylo S. 22:161
Bolton, N. P. 3:25
Bolton, Orsel 22:137
Bolton, P. 16:174
Bolton, R. 12:81; 16:288;
    20:132
Bolton, Richard R.
    12:167; 19:347
Bolton, S. M. 1:111
Bolton, Thomas B. 21:64
Bolton, W. 13:83
Bolton, William C. 7:47
Bolts, Daniel 19:5
Boltz, Adolph 11:23
Boltz, Frederick 4:11
Bolwin, Hiram C. 18:122

Bolyard, Joshua 15:85
Bolyn, Daniel 18:230;
    26:15
Bolza, C. 15:93
Bomah, John 25:15
Boman, Abner 14:142
Boman, Charles 26:13
Boman, Edmon 10:151
Boman, G. 3:25
Boman, J. 3:25
Boman, John 23:21
Boman, Samuel 3:25
Bomand, William 14:39
Bomarger, V. 14:39
Bomassa, Daniel 14:143
Bomback, Sylvester
    15:171
Bombard, A. 1:116
Bombard, J. E. 25:144
Bomberg, Frederick
    10:103
Bomeling, T. 15:29
Bomer, B. 27:20
Bomer, C. 14:39
Bomer, Frederick 9:116
Bomer, John 10:103;
    20:211
Bomer, William 17:29
Bomers, James 3:25
Bomgardner, Levey 23:21
Bommar, John 1:15
Bomoster, M. 19:56
Bomyea, R. 1:112
Bon, Henry 25:144
Bon, James W. 19:149
Bon, Nicholas 22:179
Bon---, E. L. 24:35
Bonaparte, Jerome 17:170
Bonaparte, Napoleon
    21:210
Bonar, David 26:151
Bonbrake, Isaac 11:319
Bond, --- 18:77
Bond, Allen 22:21
Bond, Amos H. 11:137
Bond, Bazil J. 22:448
Bond, Benjamiin 18:204
Bond, Benjamin F. 19:149
Bond, Charles 6:15;
    18:77; 22:290;
    25:144
Bond, Charles C. 3:25
Bond, Charles F. 10:13
Bond, Charles T. 7:64
Bond, Daniel 12:67; 15:2
Bond, David 9:19; 18:320
Bond, E. M. 10:42;
    20:211
Bond, Edwin 16:22
Bond, Elisha 16:116
Bond, F. M. 23:134

Bond, Frederick 22:179
Bond, G. 25:144
Bond, George 5:36;
    21:265
Bond, H. 7:20; 9:218;
    18:230, 362; 26:13
Bond, H. C. 25:144
Bond, Harrison 9:169
Bond, Henry 12:13
Bond, Henry D. 7:72
Bond, Henry G. 22:460
Bond, Herbert 9:116;
    27:19
Bond, Hezekiah 14:142
Bond, I. 7:10
Bond, J. 3:25; 14:39
Bond, J. D. 1:93; 25:144
Bond, James 22:473
Bond, James G. 7:87
Bond, Jerome 10:103;
    20:211
Bond, Joel D. 22:474
Bond, John 21:200
Bond, John D. 5:9
Bond, John H. 22:290
Bond, Joseph 16:80
Bond, Josiah G. 16:138
Bond, L. 20:153
Bond, Oliver 9:229;
    20:211
Bond, Osgood W. 17:17
Bond, Philip 25:14
Bond, R. J. 14:318
Bond, R. S. 23:134
Bond, Raphael 22:290
Bond, Robert 5:9
Bond, S. F. 3:25
Bond, Samuel 6:15;
    18:77; 21:303
Bond, Silas 11:198
Bond, Simeon 1:113
Bond, Stephen 19:5
Bond, Sylvester 13:11
Bond, T. Benjamin 10:157
Bond, Thomas F. 21:303
Bond, Thomas I. 10:42
Bond, Thomas J. 20:211
Bond, Thomas W. 16:175
Bond, Wesley 22:21
Bond, Wiley W. 11:237
Bond, William 4:11;
    10:42; 21:97, 129
Bond, William W. 22:242
Bondage, J. L. 21:303
Bondan, G. W. 21:18
Bonde, Samuel 26:15
Bondee, Joseph 27:20
Bonder, Joseph 9:116
Bonder, P. 3:25
Bondle, J. 7:47

Bondon, John 9:128; 27:17
Bondrant, E. 11:394
Bonds, Ellis 7:87
Bondurant, John 17:146
Bondurant, W. 17:147
Bondwell, E. 25:144
Bondy, Andrew 8:80; 17:257
Bondy, John J. 9:116; 27:19
Bondy, Joseph P. 12:13
Bone, A. 3:25
Bone, Almond W. 10:103; 20:211
Bone, Daniel 22:290
Bone, George W. 25:268
Bone, H. C. 26:151
Bone, Henry 11:297
Bone, James 17:209
Bone, John J. 11:118
Bone, Joseph 21:97
Bone, Michael 17:29
Bone, Samuel 7:87; 20:211
Bone, Samuel M. 10:42
Bone, William 22:499
Bone, William A. 22:164
Bone, William D. 15:85
Bonean, Pierre 22:66
Bonebrake, Augustus 8:80
Bonebrake, W. S. 8:45
Bonebrake, Wilson S. 21:64
Bonel, G. F. 16:364
Bonel, Richard 6:35
Boner, Adam 15:310; 19:56
Boner, Charles J. 21:215
Boner, F. 21:200
Boner, Henry 16:175
Boner, J. 1:111
Boner, John 7:62; 11:257; 17:75
Boner, John S. 11:235
Boner, N. B. 15:339
Boner, Samuel 21:242
Bones, J. 14:39
Bones, Jackson 14:143
Bones, John 11:236
Bones, Thomas 23:21
Bonested, George 14:143
Bonesteel, Albert 14:143
Bonestell, Albert 14:39
Bonestine, W. H. 3:25
Bonewell, W. W. 3:25
Boney, M. 25:144
Boney, Montague 5:36
Boney, Simon L. 22:179
Bongayon, Constant 6:29

Bonghner, Ebenezer 23:250
Bongie, John 3:25
Bongleton, J. 14:287
Bonham, A. 1:113
Bonham, Benjamin W. 24:48
Bonham, Johnson 22:474
Bonham, M. 14:250
Bonham, S. 25:144
Bonhame, Joseph 11:189
Bonhanberger, A. 3:25
Bonhorr, Charles 20:211
Bonhour, Charles 10:42
Boni, Louis 22:473
Bonie, Richard 16:22
Bonifant, Thomas G. 17:425
Boniger, Jacob 10:103; 20:211
Boninsk, Frederick 7:15
Bonis, Eli 7:77; 25:293
Bonk, Carston 11:123
Bonk, Henry 11:123
Bonk, S. 18:230
Bonker, G. B. 9:139
Bonker, John R. 5:49
Bonley, James 3:25
Bonman, Elisha 9:19
Bonman, M. 11:135
Bonn, Charles S. 17:75
Bonn, H. W. 14:39
Bonnamham, M. 18:45
Bonnel, G. F. 15:339
Bonnell, Aaron H. 23:187
Bonnell, Casper 16:90
Bonnell, James 22:496
Bonnell, Joseph 5:9; 25:144
Bonnell, R. W. 22:473
Bonnell, S. M. 20:188
Bonnell, Silas 7:87
Bonnell, William 24:74
Bonnenberg, J. 21:303
Bonner, --- 17:396; 23:270
Bonner, Alfred 11:420
Bonner, Benjamin F. 24:48
Bonner, David 22:447
Bonner, E. L. 15:119
Bonner, F. 14:39
Bonner, G. W. 15:6
Bonner, George W. 12:67
Bonner, John 11:103
Bonner, Joshua 17:278
Bonner, L. J. 25:14
Bonner, N. 25:144
Bonner, Noah 5:36
Bonner, R. 9:48

Bonner, Robert 15:293; 19:56
Bonner, Samuel E. 24:35
Bonner, Thomas 7:87
Bonner, William 18:25
Bonnet, J. 25:144
Bonnett, Emile 10:103
Bonnett, J. M. 23:85
Bonnett, Jacob 5:9
Bonnett, S. P. 1:17
Bonneville, J. 4:11
Bonney, Benjamin 22:416
Bonney, Edwin A. 21:135
Bonney, George W. 14:143
Bonney, Isaac 7:117
Bonney, J. 21:303
Bonney, Jack 7:117
Bonney, L. L. 18:45
Bonnie, Herman 12:13
Bonnott, Emile 20:211
Bonns, John 14:143
Bonny, L. L. 10:147
Bonny, Lyman 22:137
Bonsall, James 12:13
Bonsall, L. 20:211
Bonsall, Levi 10:42
Bonsall, William H. 12:13
Bonser, George 12:48
Bonser, Joseph H. 10:103
Bonsher, John 25:144
Bonsher, Joseph 11:410
Bonshir, John 5:49
Bonsie, Joseph 21:303
Bonson, J. B. 19:149
Bonsoon, John 11:189
Bontell, Victor 20:211
Bonti, Frederick 15:315
Bontom, J. H. 25:144
Bonton, Charles 7:79
Bonton, John 27:17
Bonton, John E. 9:169
Bontrell, C. 3:25
Bontrell, O. 3:25
Bonty, Robert 12:55
Bonum, Emos 8:37
Bonum, Enos 26:150
Bonurn, J. 25:144
Bony, J. W. 20:121
Bonyer, J. 17:503
Bonzes, Dilton 19:149
Boo, Greenby S. 8:80
Boo, J. 21:18
Boobe, John M. 11:185
Boober, J. 9:108
Boobur, William 3:25
Boocher, David 22:66
Bood, Adam 14:143
Booden, Edward 21:303
Boodry, John 7:87
Boody, Charles H. 17:403

Booe, M. 8:45
Boogs, Irving 17:215
Booher, Alfred 17:276
Booher, J. D. 21:84
Booher, Martin 22:164
Booher, Samuel 25:144
Book, --- 1:110
Book, C. 3:25
Book, Frank 10:153
Book, Henry 26:121
Book, J. E. 1:17
Book, John 17:392
Book, Willis 17:267
Book 25:332
Bookart, Abel 21:12
Booker, --- 18:284; 26:134
Booker, ---ennis 24:189
Booker, A. J. 13:83
Booker, Alvin 19:225
Booker, Asa 10:9
Booker, H. 18:12
Booker, Henry 11:198; 17:278
Booker, J. 17:153
Booker, Jacob 7:87; 17:170
Booker, James 8:9; 18:123
Booker, James T. 22:111
Booker, John H. 4:12
Booker, Joseph 10:157; 19:149
Booker, Moses 11:197
Booker, Peter 10:209
Booker, Ruell 20:16
Booker, Samuel 15:277; 22:66
Booker, Wilson 25:144
Bookey, Christian 23:259
Bookey, E. M. 14:39
Bookhart, M. D. 26:151
Booking, Isaac 20:103
Books, Albert 10:154
Booksland, A. 18:188
Booley, J. 16:174
Booley, W. 19:225
Booley, William 9:169
Bools, William 24:48
Boom, W. P. 3:25
Boomer, B. F. 3:25
Boomer, Charles D. 9:71
Boomer, George B. 16:8
Boomer, M. 11:236
Boomershine, Amos 22:179
Boomhover, David 21:90
Booms, Joseph 22:290
Boon, A. 9:139
Boon, Benjamin 1:192
Boon, Benjamin F. 24:48
Boon, Charles 21:115

Boon, Daniel S. 25:144
Boon, E. 15:329
Boon, Emanuel 19:56
Boon, Fielding W. 22:418
Boon, Francis 10:13
Boon, George W. 9:75; 21:48
Boon, I. K. 8:9; 18:123
Boon, J. T. 10:211; 18:464
Boon, James A. 9:169
Boon, Jefferson 18:214
Boon, John 17:128, 454; 23:112; 24:188, 189
Boon, John B. 24:35
Boon, John M. 20:185
Boon, Lewis 21:265
Boon, Major 21:303
Boon, Math 17:439; 24:151
Boon, Richmond 17:171
Boon, S. 16:174
Boon, Samuel 24:58
Boon, Stephen 12:48
Boon, Sylvester M. 9:229; 20:211
Boon, Valentine 8:9
Boon, Will 9:158
Boon, William 7:87; 27:23
Boon, William S. 9:139
Boone, A. 21:119; 26:16
Boone, B. 8:77
Boone, Burrill 18:25
Boone, George H. 26:12
Boone, J. 1:15
Boone, James 3:25; 12:13
Boone, James A. 19:247
Boone, Lewis 10:155
Boone, Major 7:117
Boone, Peter 16:174
Boone, Robert 25:15
Boone, Samuel 7:117
Boone, Sylvester 25:279
Boone, William 11:23, 89; 18:204
Boons, Alex. R. 19:149
Boons, Alexander 10:176
Boonson, A. B. 8:9
Boony, Jo 20:132
Boor, Benjamin F. 24:156
Boor, Leonard 22:115
Boor, M. 20:144
Boor, Stephen A. 8:9; 18:123
Booran, M. 27:24
Boord, George 9:41; 26:120
Booream, David 23:134
Booreen, O. 3:25
Boorhorst, Henry 9:95

Boorman, E. 25:144
Boorman, J. 3:25
Boorom, Isaac H. 20:144
Booron, Jacob N. 4:12
Booron, Peter 4:12
Boors, G. T. 18:45
Boos, J. 17:108
Boos, John 15:53
Boos, Philip 9:15
Boose, M. 14:27
Boose, Moses P. 22:475
Boot, William 25:16
Boote, Paul 7:118
Bootes, E. N. 3:25
Bootey, W. W. 1:110
Booth, C. 19:247
Booth, C. F. 19:149
Booth, E. 15:325
Booth, E. M. 17:276
Booth, Edward 17:108
Booth, Elijah D. 11:123
Booth, George 8:103; 20:153
Booth, George W. 4:11
Booth, H. 11:421
Booth, H. T. 1:17
Booth, Harrison 21:48; 22:66
Booth, Henry 19:44
Booth, Isaac 17:235
Booth, J. 3:25; 19:56; 25:144
Booth, J. A. 12:164
Booth, J. C. 9:48; 14:39
Booth, J. S. 25:144
Booth, J. W. 23:251; 27:13
Booth, James 10:103; 20:211; 27:12
Booth, James I. 24:90
Booth, James L. 8:70
Booth, John 7:17; 12:13; 13:11; 27:12
Booth, John A. 26:152
Booth, John B. 16:288
Booth, John H. 23:134
Booth, M. H. 22:179
Booth, Marquis L. 20:4
Booth, Mary M. 26:217
Booth, Otis 21:115, 265
Booth, Robert 4:11
Booth, Samuel 5:49
Booth, Seth 17:63
Booth, Silas S. 7:87
Booth, Stephen 17:387
Booth, Thomas 21:64
Booth, W. H. 1:114
Booth, Wilson L. 17:101
Boothby, H. 25:144
Boothe, Benjamin 12:151
Boothe, E. 19:56

Boothe, J. 21:18
Boothe, John H. 22:242
Boothe, R. 14:39
Boothe, Z. 3:25
Boothly, Henry 5:9
Boothwick, William 13:11
Bootle, William 5:9;
  25:144
Bootman, John 11:384
Bootman, William O.
  10:157; 19:149
Bootright, Richard
  17:128; 24:188
Boots, J. A. 1:18
Boots, Jacob W. 19:5
Boots, Martin 22:179
Bootz, Lewis 22:66
Boover, Joseph 24:8
Boovoski, William 9:116
Booz, Aaron 19:5
Booz, T. H. 1:114
Booze, M. 12:94
Boozer, Eli 23:284
Boozer, John 23:290
Boozer, Peter 22:415
Bopnd, William 20:211
Boquet, Joseph A. 24:35
Borah, George 26:10
Borah, George L. 9:75
Borah, H. C. 18:230
Borah, John C. 22:21
Borah, W. C. 26:14
Boran, Jacob 22:66
Borard, J. 7:20
Boray, George 12:67
Borban, S. 1:16
Borce, Horace 11:135
Borchers, H. 15:5
Borchers, Henry 20:21
Bord, John A. 18:188
Bord, Valentine 14:39
Bordabow, J. A. 1:109
Bordage, Henry 5:9
Bordan, G. W. 13:11
Bordare, H. 25:144
Borden, --- 10:151
Borden, Albert 15:184
Borden, Alfred 14:143
Borden, E. 3:25; 17:290
Borden, F. 9:139; 27:13
Borden, F. L. 14:235
Borden, Isaac 7:47
Borden, Isaac T. 20:211
Borden, J. 1:16
Borden, J. E. 19:247
Borden, J. L. 18:25
Borden, James E. 9:169
Borden, John 21:146
Borden, John Y. 17:205
Borden, Lorenzo 10:103;
  20:211

Borden, Thomas P.
  11:102
Borden, Valentine 11:399
Borden, W. 16:266
Borden, W. L. 9:213
Borden, William 7:87;
  9:41; 22:474
Bordenstedt, F. 16:116
Border, David 11:23
Border, John 23:21
Border, Nathaniel 11:90
Borders, Harvey 26:11
Borders, Jacob 11:53
Bordier, Frank 21:303
Bordier, Frank C. 20:182
Bordin, W. 15:29
Bordine, Daniel 23:134
Bordley, Alonzo 10:103;
  20:211
Bordley, John 17:171
Bordley, King 7:118
Bordman, Frank 14:235
Bordman, H. 21:303
Bordman, James 14:39
Bordner, H. 11:298
Bordon, Andrew 15:311;
  19:56
Bordow, Andrew 15:354
Bordu, James 23:178
Bordun, Frank 7:118
Bordus, Henry 9:75
Bordwell, D. 1:111
Bore, Austin D. 11:134
Bore, George W. 15:85
Boreff, W. 11:53
Boreland, S. R. 13:124
Borem, Israel 9:199
Borem, M. 3:25
Boreman, W. H. 1:17
Boren, Daniel 1:18
Boren, Harmon 22:416
Boren, Isaac 21:18
Boren, J. 21:18
Boren, John W. 23:60
Boren, William K. 17:348
Borer, James 11:52
Borer, John W. 10:211
Boreskey, J. 16:175
Borett, D. 13:83
Borg, Peter 15:53
Borga, S. 25:144
Borgair, Charles 19:5
Borge, Christopher 23:187
Borge, George C. 13:105
Borger, Gideon F. 16:116
Borger, Samuel H. 10:103
Borgois, Moses 17:17
Borgordous, J. P. 25:144
Boric, --- 11:420
Boright, Americus 21:90
Boring, George W. 22:66

Boringer, Philip 17:75
Bork, J. 13:83
Borken, Dwight 19:149
Borker, Theobald 21:240
Borlan, George 15:102
Borland, J. W. 25:17
Borland, James 12:13
Borland, James R. 22:232
Borland, Jerome L.
  18:274
Borland, John 4:12
Borland, R. D. 10:145;
  19:149
Borland, William A.
  21:117
Borlean, A. 27:24
Borley, Hiram 18:230
Borly, Hiram 26:13
Borm, W. 3:25
Borman, C. A. 9:75
Borman, Jacob 7:47
Borman, John 13:11
Bormand, C. A. 26:12
Borment, Joseph 11:338
Bormey, J. H. 8:80
Bormsey, J. K. 14:39
Born, Frederick 23:134
Born, Jacob 17:76
Born, John 26:121
Born, Lewis 26:217
Born, William 8:80
Born, William F. 18:107
Borne, Charles 8:9;
  18:123
Borne, Chester 21:303
Borneau, Paul 23:21
Borner, Fredric 27:19
Bornett, George 26:93
Borngesser, J. A. 26:217
Bornheimer, J. 20:211
Bornhill, George 24:189
Bornhimer, J. 9:229
Bornor, Ezra 14:143
Bornthom, James 18:440
Bornwell, L. C. 9:48
Boroff, W. C. 11:297
Borohan, Thomas 14:318
Boroker, Levi 18:123
Boroles, Almond E. 12:94
Borough, Curtis 8:45
Borough, Henry 4:12
Boroughs, James 24:74
Borouski, William 27:19
Borran, M. 14:239
Borrer, Harvey 13:11
Borrer, Henry 16:22
Borres, James 16:22
Borrie, Reason 20:211
Borrios, Darwin 19:56
Borrough, William 21:64

Borroughs, Clifford 16:175
Borroughs, M. H. 9:240
Borrows, John J. 22:401
Borst, J. 3:25
Borst, Lewis 18:63
Borst, William 21:303
Borst, Wilson 7:87
Bort, George D. 19:5
Bort, Henry C. 7:87
Bort, W. 26:152
Bort, W. L. 16:90
Borte, H. 1:111
Bortges, F. 14:39
Borth, Charles 9:169
Borthead, George 21:212
Borthy, R. A. 8:70
Bortle, G. W. 1:113
Bortle, H. 23:134
Bortless, Beldon 15:29
Bortner, Andrew K. 23:21
Borton, Peleg 5:9
Borts, William N. 15:150
Borum, Jerome 5:36
Borz, Ferdru 11:135
Bosa, Harmon 20:211
Bosard, M. S. 13:124
Bosart, H. G. 13:62
Bosart, Petro 19:149
Boscam, H. 20:211
Boscam, Hiram 10:42
Bosco, Robert 15:157
Boscrark, John M. 9:48
Bose, George 15:63
Bose, William 22:170
Boseker, John M. 20:182
Boseley, Martin V. 17:272
Bosely, Bob 7:118
Bosely, Solomon 7:118
Boseman, John 23:312
Bosert, Lodyk 1:15
Bosey, F. 18:64
Bosh, David 1:16
Bosh, H. 14:39
Bosher, A. 13:83
Bosher, George 17:108
Bosher, Miles 7:20
Boshet, J. 7:55
Boshler, Thomas 15:53
Boshner, Michael 18:274
Boskon, John W. 21:303
Bosler, M. 5:49; 25:144
Bosler, Samuel Aug 26:92
Bosley, Caesar 7:118
Bosley, Edward 15:184
Bosley, J. 18:362
Bosley, James 9:218; 22:331
Bosley, Lewis 9:100
Bosley, Milton 9:19
Bosley, Philip 8:9

Bosley, Phillip 18:123
Bosley, Thomas 15:53
Bosley, Zeno 7:118
Bosman, David 20:211
Bosman, Thomas 22:179
Bosom, Joseph 9:32
Bosquet, A. J. 1:112
Bosrett, James M. 8:103
Boss, Abraham 21:303
Boss, Daniel A. 19:149
Boss, F. 25:145
Boss, Herman 22:276
Boss, James T. 9:239
Boss, John H. 11:51
Boss, John R. 21:215
Boss, Sumner 27:12
Boss, T. W. 1:14
Boss, William 5:49
Boss, William G. 26:12
Bossa, Harmon 10:42
Bossard, Vance 22:290
Bossard, William 15:6
Bossard, William H. 12:67
Bossell, J. R. 14:143
Bossert, A. 22:472
Bosshammer, John 23:134
Bossick, Jacob 20:4
Bosslan, John 15:53
Bossman, David 10:103
Bost, Azariah 11:135
Bost, Levi 22:179
Boster, Peter 16:115
Bostick, Abraham 27:18
Bostick, Ebenezer 22:21
Bostick, Peter 22:179
Bostick, Spencer 27:17
Bostie, Robert 11:103
Bostman, L. W. 19:56
Boston, A. 25:145
Boston, A. J. 6:29; 25:317
Boston, Alonzo 17:171
Boston, C. 1:112
Boston, Enoch S. 22:66
Boston, F. M. 13:83
Boston, George 10:103; 20:211
Boston, J. 3:25; 25:145
Boston, Jacob 5:9
Boston, Jacob B. 17:76
Boston, James G. 13:128
Boston, Jeremiah 17:13
Boston, John T. 20:185
Boston, John W. 7:87; 22:330
Boston, N. 19:231
Boston, Nathan 9:169
Boston, Robert 25:14
Boston, S. 23:255
Boston, Stephen 13:56
Boston, Thomas F. 9:169; 19:225

Boston, W. T. 27:15
Boston, William K. 20:16
Bostrand, Oscar 23:85
Bostrick, F. A. 8:70
Bostrum, A. 1:20
Bostwick, A. 15:184
Bostwick, Dana 11:399
Bostwick, George H. 21:18
Bostwick, J. C. 20:179
Bostwick, John 25:18
Bostwick, Joseph 4:64
Bostwick, M. H. 11:298
Bostwick, N. 1:14
Bostwick, R. 15:339
Bostwick, R. S. 3:25
Bostwick, Romeo 24:91
Bostwick, Samuel 25:18
Bostwick, Samuel E. 22:21
Bostwick, Stephen A. 17:403
Boswell, Abraham 8:113
Boswell, C. H. 14:39
Boswell, Charles S. 9:169
Boswell, Chris 21:97
Boswell, Edson 22:137
Boswell, G. W. 23:21
Boswell, Garland 21:64
Boswell, Gasten 8:45
Boswell, H. A. 9:48
Boswell, I. W. 8:9
Boswell, J. W. 18:123
Boswell, James S. 24:60
Boswell, John 21:265
Boswell, Leonard 25:317
Boswell, Levi H. 11:51
Boswell, Riel 20:121
Boswell, S. 17:171
Boswell, Theo 9:75
Boswell, Thomas 12:48; 26:13
Boswell, W. E. 8:61; 26:152
Boswell, W. F. 25:293
Boswerth, H. 3:25
Boswick, George L. 9:218
Boswith, A. N. 3:25
Bosworth, D. 21:18
Bosworth, E. 19:273
Bosworth, Edward 9:169
Bosworth, Frank H. 7:55
Bosworth, H. 21:303
Bosworth, H. B. 7:20; 22:179
Bosworth, H. T. 11:25
Bosworth, H. W. 23:134
Bosworth, Hosea A. 13:11
Bosworth, J. H. 24:74
Bosworth, John E. 7:87

Bosworth, Joseph T. 15:80
Bosworth, Judson A. 13:11
Bosworth, Samuel P. 19:149
Bosworth, W. H. 3:25
Boszon, F. J. 11:257
Botarfe, William 15:184
Botcher, H. 25:145
Botell, John 1:14
Botes, Ashbury 13:105
Both, Henry 12:13
Botham, Sanford 15:292; 19:56
Bothby, W. 13:83
Bothereks, Julius 8:80
Botherton, Silas C. 11:23
Bothie, A. L. 14:277
Bothinger, Aaron 12:13
Bothwell, --- (Mrs.) 18:424
Bothwell, A. 12:98
Bothwell, L. 11:134
Botimer, Jacob 22:8
Botkin, C. 14:39
Botkin, Jesse C. 23:21
Botkin, T. H. 11:257
Botkins, William 10:89
Botler, D. 11:383
Botler, James R. 12:67
Botlolph, M. 25:145
Botman, C. 7:47
Botmer, John 19:5
Botner, James 10:42, 89; 20:211
Botsford, Henry S. 23:21
Botsford, Levi 11:399
Bott, Charles 15:325; 19:57
Bottenberg, William 7:20
Bottinger, Aaron 12:13
Bottle, Fitch 24:189
Bottle, H. 10:26
Bottle, Peter 22:290
Bottom, Dwight 10:157
Bottom, Iverson 17:402
Bottom, J. 13:83
Bottom, M. 26:11
Bottomley, J. F. 18:64
Bottoms, Edward 10:42; 20:211
Bottoms, J. M. 3:25
Bottoms, John 17:48
Bottoms, M. S. 11:394
Botton, F. M. 16:266
Botton, Joe N. 18:302
Botton, Philip 26:120
Bottorf, David 14:143
Bottorf, Francis M. 24:35
Botts, A. C. 14:143

Botts, Aaron 17:76
Botts, George 21:303
Botts, Harrison 17:171
Botts, John M. 23:134
Botts, Lysander 19:5
Botts, Peter 21:90
Botts, Robert 17:48
Botts, William 21:135
Botts, Wilson A. 11:135
Botzfield, William 11:23
Botzler, George 18:123
Bouch, Isaac 15:63
Bouch, John 1:13
Bouch, John G. 19:5
Bouch, Joseph 12:7
Bouchard, Enoch 7:118
Bouchen, James 5:49
Boucher, Peter 21:303
Boucher, W. 3:26
Bouckare, Frank 1:115
Boud, John 14:39
Bouden, James 14:143
Bouder, John 21:303
Bouderiot, E. L. 22:473
Boudin, Joseph 20:188
Boudish, Elisha 21:303
Boudish, Frank 19:5
Boudon, Ernest 21:303
Boue, Syms 7:20
Bough, Amos 17:48
Bough, Joseph G. 20:212
Bough, Marshall 20:212
Bougham, Henry L. 16:22
Bougham, James 8:121
Bougham, Samuel 10:42
Bougher, John W. 22:179
Bougher, W. 3:25
Bougher, W. M. 3:25
Bougher, William 15:184
Boughers, Joseph 21:18
Boughman, W. D. 17:90
Boughner, Marion 21:303
Boughner, William H. 11:103
Boughter, M. 3:25
Boughton, Abram C. 20:179
Boughton, Benjamin 13:11; 16:22
Boughton, Charles W. 15:53
Boughton, Clement A. 23:187
Boughton, Edgar 27:142
Boughton, G. W. 22:286
Boughton, H. 7:20
Boughton, Isaac 15:150
Boughton, J. 1:20, 114
Boughton, John 7:20
Boughton, Levi L. 22:137

Boughton, Lionel Judson 21:64
Boughton, Myron 17:358
Boughton, W. 18:274
Boughton, W. A. 19:149
Boughue, Oscar 21:303
Bouis, Nelson 7:118
Boulby, William 1:16
Bouldin, N. H. 16:22
Bouler, Joseph 7:66
Bouling, Stephen 26:120
Boullish, Joseph 19:57
Boulls, William C. 15:184
Bouls, Almond G. 15:358
Boulster, James 9:116
Boulter, Hiram 22:331
Boulton, George I. 12:13
Boulton, H. 25:15
Boulton, T. 3:26
Boultry, Welcome W. 4:12
Boulyou, A. 3:26
Bouman, J. 14:143
Bound, Phillip 16:22
Bounds, Ellis 21:303
Bounds, John 7:87
Bounds, Thomas M. 24:64
Bouner, Michael 11:135
Boura, Pierre 21:303
Bourd, J. D. 17:445; 24:165
Bourdalowe, Michael 17:348
Bourder, Thomas B. 12:58
Bourer, --- 20:5
Bourgoyne, Cornelius 14:143
Bourguin, Lewis 23:85
Bouri, Reason 10:42
Bourjoice, Charles 22:67
Bourke, P. 9:139
Bourke, Pat 27:14
Bourke, Thomas 8:60
Bourland, Andrew 24:13
Bourland, Otway D. 22:117
Bourland, T. 1:17
Bourland, W. W. 21:18
Bourman, --- 3:26
Bourman, A. 3:26
Bourn, Robert 11:135
Bourn, William 9:229
Bourne, Charles L. 23:187
Bourne, G. H. 27:13
Bourne, James 16:22; 17:246
Bourne, Paul 9:15
Bouse, Adolphus 21:303
Bouse, John G. 16:175
Bouser, A. D. 1:18
Bouser, G. 3:26

Bouser, James L. 17:494
Bouser, John W. 17:433;
  24:156
Bouser, Joseph H. 20:211
Boush, S. A. 13:83
Bousman, Freeman
  17:313
Bouth, James S. 15:85
Bouton, Charles 14:143
Bouton, George 14:143
Bouton, J. 1:17
Bouton, J. E. 19:244
Boutright, Thomas J.
  26:152
Bouts, Benjamin 10:47
Boutsman, Jacob 12:48
Boutwell, D. C. 10:152;
  18:45
Boutwell, W. C. 21:303
Boutwell, W. G. 1:114
Boutwright, A. 3:25
Bouty, Joseph 11:410
Bouyea, Singleton 5:36
Bovard, Abner 17:143
Bovard, G. M. 11:257
Bovard, George W.
  19:149
Bovart, J. 15:184
Bovee, James 2:7; 25:19
Bovee, James M. 23:105
Boven, W. H. 14:253
Boven, William H. 14:143
Bovie, Andrew D. 11:331
Bovier, Philip 7:118
Bovin, Joseph 11:134
Bovish, Perry 12:14
Bow, James 3:26
Bow, James W. 10:176
Bow, Joseph 14:39
Bow, Seth 23:21
Bowan, A. 15:184
Bowan, Dennis 26:16
Bowan, I. R. 26:150
Bowan, John S. 10:42
Bowan, S. 3:26
Bowan, S. S. 18:171
Bowan, Thomas 14:39
Bowars, E. B. 26:151
Bowby, N. B. 21:19
Bowcholz, Alex 24:109
Bowck, Benjamin F.
  18:123
Bowden, Albert 26:210
Bowden, Ernest 23:260
Bowden, Henry 25:317
Bowden, James M. 17:76
Bowden, L. 3:26
Bowden, P. 21:146
Bowden, S. B. 22:331
Bowden, W. 3:26
Bowden, William 20:111

Bowden, William H.
  22:472
Bowdick, J. 14:39
Bowdirn, H. 11:123
Bowdish, E. T. 21:303
Bowditch, William 7:66
Bowdle, C. W. 22:472
Bowdoin, Ernest 7:87
Bowe, Edward 10:157
Bowe, Walter 24:91
Bowe, William L. 24:61
Bowel, William 10:103;
  20:211
Bowels, Amos 12:67
Bowels, F. J. 1:111
Bowels, Henry C. 10:103
Bowels, J. W. 10:89
Bowelson, S. N. 10:103;
  20:211
Bowely, James 11:384
Bowen, --- 10:157
Bowen, A. C. 15:63
Bowen, Abner 9:19; 26:92
Bowen, Addison 9:75
Bowen, Andrew J. 4:12
Bowen, B. D. 9:41;
  26:120
Bowen, Benjamiin 17:171
Bowen, Benjamin 14:295;
  17:471
Bowen, C. 17:30
Bowen, C. H. 1:14
Bowen, Caleb 14:143
Bowen, Charles 7:47
Bowen, D. 21:19
Bowen, Daniel 8:45
Bowen, Eli D. 17:262
Bowen, Fayette 10:42
Bowen, Felix 21:250
Bowen, Francis 10:103;
  20:211
Bowen, G. W. 19:225;
  27:21
Bowen, George 19:5
Bowen, George W. 9:169;
  22:67
Bowen, Gilbert 22:276
Bowen, H. 14:39
Bowen, Henry 9:242
Bowen, Hezekiah 22:242
Bowen, Isaac 20:105
Bowen, Israel 21:109
Bowen, J. 3:26; 15:184
Bowen, J. A. 9:108
Bowen, J. B. 18:430
Bowen, J. Q. A. 7:73
Bowen, J. W. 9:234
Bowen, James 11:22;
  26:10
Bowen, James (Mrs.) 1:16
Bowen, James A. 18:64

Bowen, Joel 21:19
Bowen, John 10:42;
  18:452; 19:5, 57;
  20:211; 21:303;
  22:447; 23:85
Bowen, John A. 11:137
Bowen, John R. 13:11
Bowen, Joseph W. 10:42;
  20:211
Bowen, L. C. 14:143
Bowen, Leroy 10:42;
  20:211
Bowen, Lewis R. 21:64
Bowen, M. R. 1:93
Bowen, M. W. 9:169;
  19:247
Bowen, Nathan 15:354
Bowen, Nathaniel 19:57
Bowen, Oliver 7:20
Bowen, Peter 21:248
Bowen, Richard 15:102
Bowen, Rodeny S. 22:401
Bowen, Russel 22:67
Bowen, S. M. 22:242
Bowen, Smith 8:9
Bowen, T. H. 3:26
Bowen, Thomas 13:133;
  14:39; 20:211;
  21:135
Bowen, Thomas C. 8:9;
  18:123
Bowen, W. 25:19
Bowen, W. F. 17:13
Bowen, W. G. 8:9; 18:123
Bowen, W. H. H. 26:93
Bowen, Wenderline 17:48
Bowen, William 2:8;
  20:211; 22:137
Bowen, William H. 7:20
Bowen, William S. 21:303
Bowens, George 12:48
Bowens, John H. 11:410
Bower, --- 15:358; 19:57
Bower, A. 16:364
Bower, Abner 18:302
Bower, Adam 11:297;
  17:17
Bower, Anthony 15:339
Bower, Benjamin 3:26
Bower, Benjamin F.
  18:392
Bower, C. 3:26; 24:74
Bower, Cassius 22:473
Bower, E. 18:230; 26:14
Bower, Edmond 20:34
Bower, F. 3:26; 22:475
Bower, Frederick 23:105
Bower, G. W. 3:26
Bower, Godfrey 13:11
Bower, H. 3:26; 10:147

Bower, Henry 17:404; 24:74
Bower, Hiram A. 11:257
Bower, J. 3:26
Bower, John 3:26; 10:103; 12:14; 20:211; 23:288; 25:145
Bower, John H. 24:48
Bower, Joseph 6:29
Bower, L. E. 11:236
Bower, Lewis C. 22:179
Bower, M. 12:94; 15:358; 19:57
Bower, N. B. 16:364
Bower, Nicholas 1:114
Bower, P. 1:103
Bower, Paul 13:11
Bower, Peter W. 22:21
Bower, S. 23:21
Bower, Thomas 5:9
Bower, W. H. 9:139
Bower, William A. 22:415
Bowering, William A. 17:425
Bowerman, Addison 22:137
Bowerman, Daniel 9:235; 26:216
Bowerman, Deforrest A. 22:137
Bowerman, R. 3:26
Bowerman, Stephen 19:5
Bowermaster, S. K. 3:26
Bowers, A. 3:26
Bowers, A. J. 14:250; 22:473
Bowers, A. M. 22:179
Bowers, Adam 9:32; 13:11
Bowers, Alfred 23:60
Bowers, Andrew 11:230; 23:134
Bowers, B. F. 22:242
Bowers, Benjamin 27:20
Bowers, C. 21:119
Bowers, C. F. 19:57
Bowers, Charles 1:14; 15:352; 16:277
Bowers, Charles E. 9:95
Bowers, Christian 9:160
Bowers, E. 7:20
Bowers, E. B. 8:61
Bowers, Edmund T. 22:416
Bowers, F. 3:26
Bowers, Frank 10:103; 20:211
Bowers, Franklin 18:77
Bowers, G. F. 21:303
Bowers, G. R. 19:328

Bowers, George 1:113; 17:199
Bowers, George H. 17:390
Bowers, George W. 22:179
Bowers, H. 15:184
Bowers, H. U. 27:12
Bowers, Hemmans R. 10:7
Bowers, Henry 1:15; 14:143
Bowers, I. 15:184
Bowers, J. 3:26; 11:25; 13:83; 16:175; 21:185; 26:10
Bowers, J. C. 7:20
Bowers, J. H. 14:253
Bowers, Jacob 11:135; 17:287; 22:8
Bowers, Jacob C. 14:143
Bowers, James 11:118
Bowers, Jesse 20:29
Bowers, Jessee 10:157
Bowers, Jessie 19:150
Bowers, John 1:113; 9:65, 75, 139; 11:52; 13:83, 105; 14:5, 39; 18:274; 22:242
Bowers, Jordan 17:171
Bowers, Joseph 9:49; 25:317
Bowers, L. A. 22:242
Bowers, Madison 22:111
Bowers, Marion 11:52
Bowers, Marquis L. 21:97
Bowers, Martin F. 10:103; 20:211
Bowers, Michael 11:21; 22:331
Bowers, Moses 10:89
Bowers, O. F. 15:317
Bowers, Patrick 11:180; 25:19
Bowers, Robert 19:150; 21:265
Bowers, S. 11:50
Bowers, S. J. 1:110
Bowers, Samuel 9:71
Bowers, Samuel W. 1:15
Bowers, Solomon 9:95
Bowers, Stephen 20:211; 22:472; 23:278
Bowers, T. 3:26; 23:85
Bowers, T. H. 17:390
Bowers, Theodore 9:116; 27:19
Bowers, V. 11:21
Bowers, Valentine 17:165
Bowers, W. 15:16; 22:179
Bowers, W. H. 3:26; 23:134; 27:19

Bowers, W. P. 18:123
Bowers, William 12:14; 14:143; 21:303; 25:145
Bowers, William A. 10:171
Bowers, William H. 21:64; 22:242
Bowers, William S. 23:255
Bowersox, --- 20:153
Bowery, Peter 7:87
Bowess, James 13:11
Bowey, G. 16:175
Bowey, James 16:364
Bowgardner, George 22:137
Bowhan, H. A. 3:26
Bowhan, Thomas 25:271
Bowhard, William 11:89
Bowher, Luke 15:293
Bowick, John 11:236
Bowie, David 9:116; 27:19
Bowie, Ellsworth 7:8
Bowie, H. 1:109
Bowie, J. 16:90
Bowie, James W. 9:71
Bowie, Richard 13:56
Bowin, E. 19:57
Bowin, Gus 24:185
Bowin, James 18:25
Bowin, Natham 15:308
Bowker, G. B. 27:15
Bowker, H. 18:45
Bowker, J. 1:110
Bowker, J. R. 25:145
Bowker, J. W. 27:13
Bowker, Joseph A. 22:242
Bowker, Levi 8:9
Bowker, Louis F. 22:475
Bowker, Luke 16:175
Bowker, Richard 17:171
Bowkin, William 3:26
Bowl, L. 2:8
Bowlan, J. 3:26
Bowland, Thomas R. 25:281
Bowlby, George L. 20:121
Bowlby, George W. 22:179
Bowlby, Joseph 23:134
Bowlds, Frank 10:103; 20:212
Bowlds, James C. 17:48
Bowler, C. F. 3:26
Bowler, H. A. 3:26
Bowler, J. C. 8:9; 18:123
Bowler, J. R. 25:145
Bowler, J. W. 12:81; 16:288

Bowler, Michael 17:348
Bowler, S. W. 10:104
Bowler, Sylvender W. 20:212
Bowles, Amos 15:63
Bowles, C. L. 21:19
Bowles, D. M. 19:5
Bowles, Elijah 11:102
Bowles, George W. 22:67
Bowles, Henry C. 20:212
Bowles, J. A. 23:134
Bowles, Jacob 9:206
Bowles, James 16:175
Bowles, James A. 17:358
Bowles, Jerry 21:265
Bowles, Jesse 22:448
Bowles, John 7:8
Bowles, L. H. 3:26
Bowles, W. H. 11:89
Bowles, William 23:307
Bowles, William J. 21:19
Bowlett, Joseph 13:11; 16:22
Bowley, A. 15:312; 19:57
Bowley, Addison 1:18
Bowley, E. 1:109
Bowley, J. 3:26
Bowley, James M. 24:64
Bowley, Kingsbury H. 13:11
Bowley, R. H. 16:175
Bowley, T. J. 18:12
Bowley, William 3:26
Bowlighter, S. 3:26
Bowlin, Austin 10:42; 20:212
Bowlin, B. 25:145
Bowlin, E. B. 22:499
Bowlin, John M. 23:134
Bowlin, Louis 17:171
Bowling, C. M. 17:147
Bowling, D. E. 25:145
Bowling, Elias 17:442; 24:156
Bowling, Green 20:185
Bowling, J. 3:26
Bowling, J. V. 1:115
Bowling, James A. 20:16
Bowling, James P. W. 9:75
Bowling, Robert E. 11:90
Bowling, Stephen 9:41
Bowling, W. B. 11:438
Bowling, William 11:384; 22:399
Bowling, Woodson 17:48
Bowlington, John W. 22:117
Bowlis, John W. 15:63
Bowls, F. 1:14
Bowlsby, George 21:115

Bowman, --- 15:267
Bowman, A. 3:26
Bowman, Alfred 11:14
Bowman, Andrew 22:511
Bowman, B. 12:92; 16:288
Bowman, B. F. 25:15
Bowman, Benjamin 7:118; 24:48
Bowman, Benjamin W. 11:24
Bowman, Bobert 26:16
Bowman, C. 1:109; 25:145
Bowman, Ch. H. 21:19
Bowman, Charles 5:36; 14:143; 18:230, 271
Bowman, Charles A. 24:13
Bowman, Conrad 8:80
Bowman, D. H. 1:113
Bowman, David 6:11; 18:107; 22:397
Bowman, Dennis 18:230
Bowman, E. 1:114
Bowman, E. M. 17:509; 20:191
Bowman, Edmond 10:178
Bowman, Elias 26:120
Bowman, Elias T. 24:13
Bowman, Elisha 18:302; 26:93
Bowman, F. 9:139
Bowman, Frank 21:303
Bowman, Fred 21:265
Bowman, George 10:42; 11:21; 15:309; 19:57; 20:212; 23:60
Bowman, George H. 23:60
Bowman, George W. 16:156
Bowman, Gustus 27:143
Bowman, H. 3:26; 17:128; 24:187
Bowman, Henry 3:26; 24:35
Bowman, Henry C. 22:67; 23:134
Bowman, Howard H. 23:134
Bowman, I. 15:339
Bowman, I. G. 15:184
Bowman, Ira 10:13
Bowman, Isadore 18:426
Bowman, J. 1:109; 3:26; 11:53; 12:7; 16:364; 25:145
Bowman, J. F. 11:257
Bowman, J. H. 12:14
Bowman, J. R. 8:80

Bowman, J. S. 10:179; 18:171
Bowman, J. Z. 18:362
Bowman, Jack 17:128; 24:189
Bowman, Jacob 11:180; 19:150
Bowman, James 10:42, 185; 15:184; 17:278; 18:171; 20:212
Bowman, James M. 20:188
Bowman, Jerry 11:197
Bowman, Jesse 22:331
Bowman, John 3:26; 7:77; 8:9; 11:197; 12:14; 18:123; 21:19, 304; 22:242; 23:134; 24:64; 25:293; 26:120
Bowman, John A. 17:48
Bowman, John G. 21:304
Bowman, John H. 22:21
Bowman, John W. 12:67; 15:25
Bowman, Joseph 11:321; 22:518
Bowman, Joseph M. 13:11
Bowman, L. 3:26; 25:145
Bowman, L. W. 20:191
Bowman, Lewis 10:104
Bowman, Lott 27:22
Bowman, Louis 20:212
Bowman, M. 2:7; 25:14
Bowman, Martin 6:11; 9:15; 18:107; 22:242
Bowman, Nathaniel 17:147
Bowman, Newton 18:230; 26:14
Bowman, Oliver P. 20:212
Bowman, Oliver T. 10:104
Bowman, Peter 23:119
Bowman, R. 18:45
Bowman, R. D. 13:11
Bowman, R. J. 17:30
Bowman, Robert F. 24:64
Bowman, S. 11:384; 18:25
Bowman, S. B. 21:19
Bowman, S. G. 25:317
Bowman, Samuel 1:115; 7:64; 9:108; 19:57; 22:242; 23:255
Bowman, Silas 22:242
Bowman, Sylvanus 1:17
Bowman, T. 27:16
Bowman, Theo 9:139

Bowman, Thomas 26:10
Bowman, W. H. 11:22; 25:15
Bowman, W. J. 14:39
Bowman, W. P. 15:185
Bowman, W. W. 1:114
Bowman, Wellington N. 20:27
Bowman, Will 14:143
Bowman, William 1:116; 9:108, 206; 14:39; 23:60; 24:151; 25:16
Bowman, William H. 21:19
Bowmaster, John 11:409; 24:35
Bown, B. 24:100
Bown, J. 14:143
Bowne, Curtis 12:14
Bowns, W. P. 8:9
Bownson, A. B. 18:123
Bowreman, Jacob 8:80
Bowrod, Fletcher B. 26:134
Bowse, F. O. 21:19
Bowser, J. F. 1:116
Bowser, J. R. 1:109
Bowser, Jacob 19:57
Bowsit, Milner 7:66
Bowsman, J. 16:266
Bowsteak, T. D. 3:26
Bowsticks, Plenty 27:17
Bowswell, W. T. 7:73
Bowts, John 13:105
Bowyer, Felix J. 24:58
Bowyer, Francis C. 9:169
Bowyer, James M. 24:13
Bowyer, John 11:22
Bowyer, W. F. 17:246
Bowyer, W. R. 10:89
Bowzee, Dilton 10:157
Box, G. 3:26
Box, George 4:12
Box, Jack 9:206
Box, Josiah 10:94
Box, Michael 12:81; 16:288
Box, R. R. 26:13
Box, William 26:120
Boxbury, Frederick 13:105
Boxby, Charles 18:302; 26:92
Boxell, Henry J. 22:401
Boxendine, George 11:180
Boxenil, Samuel 22:472
Boxley, Anderson 22:290
Boxter, James 8:9
Boxter, John 4:12
Boy, Buswell 9:169

Boy, J. O. 20:212
Boyan, Joshua E. 19:150
Boyat, G. V. 16:175
Boyce, A. 3:27
Boyce, Alexander 23:201
Boyce, Anthony 23:119
Boyce, Arthur D. 8:80
Boyce, Austin L. 21:97
Boyce, B. 1:116
Boyce, B. G. 14:143
Boyce, Benjamin 20:16
Boyce, C. 26:121
Boyce, E. S. 25:145
Boyce, E. T. 5:9
Boyce, I. 15:339
Boyce, J. 12:94; 15:358; 16:364
Boyce, J. W. 1:110; 7:87
Boyce, James 8:45
Boyce, James H. 13:11
Boyce, James W. 14:143
Boyce, John 15:325; 19:57
Boyce, John G. 11:14
Boyce, John W. 22:401
Boyce, Joseph 17:417; 24:156
Boyce, M. 21:185, 247
Boyce, Matthew 14:39, 330
Boyce, Nelson 22:415
Boyce, R. 3:27; 14:40
Boyce, R. J. 25:17
Boyce, S. D. 27:21
Boyce, S. R. 10:42; 20:212
Boyce, Solomon E. 10:13
Boyce, Thomas 21:304
Boyce, Thomas D. 13:11
Boyce, W. H. 15:339; 16:364
Boyce, W. L. 18:25; 23:21
Boyce, William 19:57
Boyce, William W. 8:45
Boyd, --- 18:214
Boyd, A. 5:36; 11:383; 18:214
Boyd, A. D. 3:26
Boyd, A. M. 3:26
Boyd, Alex 19:57
Boyd, Alexander C. 17:233
Boyd, Alfred 25:145
Boyd, Allen 12:151; 27:143
Boyd, Andrew H. 14:143
Boyd, Andy 17:171
Boyd, Archibald 20:5
Boyd, B. F. 3:26
Boyd, Bird 19:44
Boyd, C. 14:39

Boyd, C. W. 25:16
Boyd, Calvin 24:173
Boyd, Charles 11:279; 17:17
Boyd, Charles P. 11:257
Boyd, D. E. 23:301
Boyd, David H. 19:320
Boyd, David W. 16:116
Boyd, Doydor 23:10
Boyd, E. 14:40
Boyd, E. H. 24:13
Boyd, Erastus 4:12
Boyd, F. 3:27; 22:291
Boyd, F. M. 9:49; 22:473; 26:152
Boyd, Franklin 21:19
Boyd, Frederick S. 22:475
Boyd, Furnace J. 17:423; 24:173
Boyd, George 27:17
Boyd, George W. 10:104; 20:212
Boyd, H. 16:175; 17:48
Boyd, H. J. 3:26
Boyd, H. P. 3:27
Boyd, Henry 11:23; 20:16; 23:312
Boyd, Henry H. 18:230; 26:14
Boyd, Howell 21:129
Boyd, I. 13:130
Boyd, J. 1:112; 14:143, 253; 16:175; 24:74; 25:145
Boyd, J. E. 3:26
Boyd, J. H. 19:269; 24:13; 25:145
Boyd, J. M. 3:35
Boyd, J. P. 17:30
Boyd, J. S. 6:11
Boyd, J. T. 1:13
Boyd, J. W. 15:53
Boyd, Jacob 16:115
Boyd, James 8:77; 9:170; 10:94, 179; 12:14; 15:13; 18:171; 21:265; 22:179; 25:271
Boyd, James F. 22:242
Boyd, James H. 5:9; 10:42; 20:212
Boyd, James J. T. 3:26
Boyd, James M. 14:143
Boyd, Jesse 9:170; 19:280
Boyd, John 4:12; 5:9; 9:128; 10:151, 178; 13:11; 19:57; 22:290; 23:60; 24:13; 27:18
Boyd, John H. 9:170
Boyd, John L. 18:107
Boyd, John M. 9:41

Boyd, John W. 21:19
Boyd, Joseph 5:36; 17:46
Boyd, Joseph L. 17:417
Boyd, Joshua J. 13:11
Boyd, King 9:164
Boyd, L. 3:26
Boyd, L. D. 19:150
Boyd, Lafayette 9:75; 26:11
Boyd, Lansus 23:301
Boyd, Lewis 1:192
Boyd, M. 1:110; 3:27
Boyd, M. C. 14:40
Boyd, Manuel 11:197
Boyd, Michael 9:170
Boyd, Milton F. 9:9
Boyd, N. 25:145
Boyd, Nathaniel T. 23:85
Boyd, Neil 14:295; 17:475; 27:21
Boyd, Norman 4:12
Boyd, O. 21:129
Boyd, R. 14:40
Boyd, R. I. 8:9
Boyd, R. J. 18:123
Boyd, Reuben 15:283; 19:57; 22:511
Boyd, Richard 22:291, 511
Boyd, Robert 12:55; 22:291
Boyd, S. 22:473
Boyd, S. A. 1:17
Boyd, S. I. 17:48
Boyd, Samuel 25:19
Boyd, Taylor 9:128; 27:17
Boyd, Thomas 1:15; 3:26; 8:80; 10:42; 13:11; 20:212; 22:291
Boyd, Thomas J. 16:90
Boyd, Thornton 22:290
Boyd, W. 17:30; 20:84
Boyd, W. C. 9:139; 27:15
Boyd, W. E. 25:16
Boyd, W. F. 3:26
Boyd, W. H. 3:26
Boyd, W. P. 18:188
Boyd, W. S. 19:150
Boyd, W. T. 9:65
Boyd, Walter 11:135
Boyd, William 4:12; 11:136; 15:351; 16:175, 364; 17:17, 422; 20:5, 103; 21:265; 22:331, 416; 24:48; 27:142
Boyd, William E. 27:142
Boyd, William F. 11:23
Boyd, William L. 11:24
Boyd, William R. 11:89; 24:13

Boyd, William T. 18:274
Boyd, Wilson 26:152
Boyd, Wilson J. 23:96
Boyde, George 9:128
Boyden, A. J. 25:145
Boyden, Alfred 16:116
Boyden, Andrew 9:159
Boyden, Henry 23:187
Boyden, Jack 9:159
Boyden, Justice L. 4:12
Boyder, A. L. 3:27
Boydjun, J. 25:145
Boye, John 25:18
Boyen, Thomas T. 22:21
Boyer, A. 14:143
Boyer, Albert 16:175
Boyer, Alfred S. 24:91
Boyer, C. 1:20
Boyer, C. P. 1:17
Boyer, Charles F. 22:415
Boyer, Christopher C. 10:104; 20:212
Boyer, D. 1:111; 3:27
Boyer, Daniel 1:18; 19:57; 27:16
Boyer, David 11:103; 22:470
Boyer, Ed 26:93
Boyer, Edward 18:302
Boyer, Eli 11:258
Boyer, Elias 12:14
Boyer, Elijah W. 22:21
Boyer, F. 3:27
Boyer, Frank 25:276
Boyer, Gilbert 7:82; 21:304
Boyer, H. 20:2; 25:145
Boyer, Henry 16:175; 19:57
Boyer, Henry C. 22:137
Boyer, I. 14:280
Boyer, Israel 27:14
Boyer, J. 1:15; 3:27; 9:139
Boyer, J. D. 7:77; 25:293
Boyer, J. F. 25:18
Boyer, J. M. 3:27
Boyer, Jacob 7:71; 14:143; 24:48
Boyer, James K. P. 1:13
Boyer, Jeremiah 1:15; 23:134
Boyer, Jerome H. 19:57
Boyer, Jesse 13:56
Boyer, John 1:18; 11:138, 230; 12:14; 16:116; 22:67, 111
Boyer, John B. 3:27
Boyer, Joseph 19:57
Boyer, Joseph H. 20:212
Boyer, L. 11:138; 25:145

Boyer, L. L. 1:18
Boyer, Levi 5:36
Boyer, Martin L. 17:90
Boyer, Michael 10:104; 20:212
Boyer, P. 3:27
Boyer, Richard 9:41; 14:143; 26:121
Boyer, S. 22:460
Boyer, S. D. 14:295; 17:478
Boyer, Samuel 8:80
Boyer, T. 3:27
Boyer, V. 1:20
Boyer, W. H. 18:188
Boyer, William 1:113; 14:143; 23:134
Boyer, William B. 22:179
Boyer, William H. 7:71
Boyers, David 23:292
Boyers, George 15:185
Boyers, J. 25:145
Boyers, John 5:9
Boyers, John W. 10:154; 19:150
Boyers, Martin K. 13:11
Boyes, G. M. 24:61
Boyes, H. 5:36
Boyes, J. M. 3:27
Boyes, S. 20:121
Boyes, W. 22:331
Boyes, William L. 14:235
Boyett, Bennett 19:280
Boyett, G. T. 19:5
Boyett, J. 23:201
Boyington, Everett 7:8
Boyington, Thomas 4:12
Boyken, --- 9:160
Boyl, Patrick 18:123
Boyl, Silas M. 18:123
Boyl, William 18:123
Boylan, A. 22:179
Boylan, Anthony 1:16
Boylan, C. 3:27
Boylan, Luke 10:157; 19:150
Boylan, P. R. 10:204
Boylan, Patrick 13:105
Boylan, Philos 21:265
Boylan, R. R. 18:406
Boylan, William 20:38
Boyle, Alexander 22:8
Boyle, Bryan 12:67; 15:29
Boyle, C. 14:253
Boyle, Charles 1:15; 14:40
Boyle, Charles A. 10:157
Boyle, Cornelius 16:288
Boyle, D. 13:83
Boyle, Daniel 5:9

Boyle, Edward 21:304;
    23:281
Boyle, Ephraim 9:19;
    18:302; 26:92
Boyle, Francis 11:299
Boyle, H. 3:27
Boyle, Henry F. 11:395
Boyle, Hinas A. 8:113
Boyle, I. 17:290
Boyle, J. 1:17; 13:83;
    14:295; 17:478;
    27:20
Boyle, J. C. 1:111
Boyle, J. R. 9:108
Boyle, James 8:61; 20:47;
    21:146; 26:152
Boyle, James R. 1:15
Boyle, Jeremiah 16:116
Boyle, John 5:49; 23:119;
    24:64; 25:145
Boyle, John A. 22:179
Boyle, M. 1:110; 19:150
Boyle, Nathaniel 9:206
Boyle, P. 1:113; 3:27;
    19:57
Boyle, Patrick 3:27; 8:9;
    11:24
Boyle, Peter 18:274;
    19:149; 20:21
Boyle, Peter F. 25:14
Boyle, Philip 20:212
Boyle, R. 27:21
Boyle, R. C. 3:27
Boyle, Reuben 15:262
Boyle, Richard 22:137
Boyle, Robert 4:12
Boyle, S. 18:107
Boyle, Silas W. 8:9
Boyle, Spencer 4:64
Boyle, Stephen 16:22
Boyle, T. 3:27
Boyle, Thomas 15:29
Boyle, Thomas J. 19:149
Boyle, Thomas R. 15:289;
    16:175
Boyle, Timothy 21:117
Boyle, Tolbert 11:53
Boyle, U. H. 27:12
Boyle, W. H. 3:27
Boyle, Wallace 17:278
Boyle, William 1:15; 8:9;
    10:157
Boyle, William F. 8:70
Boyle, William O. 17:318
Boylen, James 3:27
Boylen, Patrick 1:14
Boyler, Edward 9:19
Boyles, Artemus 20:95
Boyles, Curtis R. 18:392
Boyles, Cyrus 21:64
Boyles, Daniel J. 21:65

Boyles, David 18:411
Boyles, Edgar S. 5:9
Boyles, J. 23:21
Boyles, John M. 21:94
Boyles, Philip 10:42
Boyles, T. 1:14
Boyley, D. 9:48
Boyne, C. L. 18:171
Boyne, George 22:137
Boyne, Robert 14:143
Boynton, A. L. 16:364
Boynton, Andrew H.
    27:19
Boynton, G. W. 9:169
Boynton, George W.
    24:71
Boynton, H. E. 1:111
Boynton, Horace 7:8
Boynton, Ira 17:326
Boynton, James E. 19:5
Boynton, Lorenzo 12:67
Boynton, Otis B. 13:11
Boynton, R. 1:112
Boynton, S. C. 25:15
Boynton, Seth A. 10:42;
    20:212
Boynton, Timothy 10:157
Boynton, W. 15:10
Boyon, Christian 15:185
Boys, Perry 18:107
Boyse, J. 19:57
Boyt, L. B. 9:49
Boyte, Henry 10:170
Boyton, Edward 25:15
Boyts, Hiram 1:113
Bozard, Lewis 22:291
Bozard, William B. 23:21
Bozarth, Benjamin 10:94
Bozarth, Joseph 23:127
Bozarth, Josiah 10:42
Bozarth, Richard 1:15
Boze, James H. 10:104;
    20:212
Boze, M. 15:358
Bozell, J. F. 3:27
Bozeman, M. 16:22
Bozen, D. 14:40
Bozzell, H. C. 1:111
Bozzolos, H. 1:111
Br---, Edwin 16:175
Br---, Joseph 25:16
Braam, Laurence 7:87
Braan, John 22:173
Brabaker, Amos 11:51
Brabaugh, Matthew 12:14
Brabazon, Thomas E.
    22:137
Brabham, George 3:28
Brabham, Joseph 26:144
Brabham, William 17:258
Brabrook, W. W. 11:285

Brabson, Alexander 26:12
Brabson, W. F. 7:66
Brabster, Jeffrey 23:312
Brabston, James S. 22:243
Brace, Daniel 13:105
Brace, George W. 20:5
Brace, J. D. 10:42; 20:212
Brace, James 20:212
Brace, James H. 9:32
Brace, John 17:387
Brace, John B. 23:134
Brace, Joseph 10:42
Brace, Samuel 4:64
Brace, W. G. 20:212
Bracey, Aleck 7:118
Bracey, Charles 9:170
Bracey, George 7:55
Bracey, John W. 9:170
Bracey, Shavey 9:95
Bracher, Berry 17:49
Bracher, Enos W. 17:461
Bracher, Joseph A. 23:96
Brachtel, Nelson 9:229
Brack, John H. 18:392
Brack, Rans 17:171
Bracke, Henry 23:134
Bracken, Craig 23:134
Bracken, James 7:20;
    8:100; 12:14
Bracken, James A.
    17:459; 24:156
Bracken, John L. 22:179
Bracken, M. C. 26:153
Bracken, Thomas J.
    22:448
Bracken, Timothy 10:157
Bracken, William 12:14
Brackendor, J. H. 11:22
Bracker, Enos W. 24:165
Bracker, J. 14:237
Brackerty, John 14:40
Bracket, F. 13:105
Bracket, John 23:201
Bracket, N. W. 25:15
Bracket, W. T. 23:201
Brackett, A. M. 14:40
Brackett, B. S. 11:89
Brackett, Benjamin F.
    26:11
Brackett, C. H. 15:185,
    347
Brackett, Clarence 9:95
Brackett, Edward 15:93;
    21:304
Brackett, John 7:47
Brackett, Marshall M.
    17:235
Brackett, Michael 14:143
Brackett, S. 3:28
Brackett, Seth W. 21:48
Brackett, T. 14:143

Brackett, Timothy 6:7; 18:107
Brackett, Tucker 21:265
Brackett, W. F. 13:83; 14:5
Brackett, Walter S. 21:114
Brackin, S. Denis 3:28
Brackley, C. H. 7:87
Brackley, John 19:6
Brackman, Charles 7:47
Bracksmith, W. H. 26:92
Brackson, Samuel 10:104; 20:212
Bracy, Charles 19:225
Bracy, J. W. 19:225
Bracy, Marbin 9:116
Bracy, Marrion 27:19
Bracy, Wythe 4:64
Bradall, R. P. 1:18
Bradberry, B. 14:40
Bradberry, J. S. 11:24
Bradberry, James R. 21:129
Bradberry, William 21:19
Bradborn, J. 9:140
Bradburn, G. 11:21
Bradburn, James 17:94
Bradburn, P. H. 15:29
Bradburn, Peter H. 12:67
Bradbury, Andrew J. 22:21
Bradbury, B. M. 25:293
Bradbury, Benjamin M. 7:73
Bradbury, E. 1:14
Bradbury, Hugh M. 15:10
Bradbury, John 21:250
Bradbury, R. 25:145
Bradbury, Robert 5:10
Bradbury, S. B. 21:48
Bradbury, S. F. 14:143
Bradbury, Samuel 10:13
Bradbury, W. S. 9:213; 21:304
Bradbury, Wiley 16:22
Bradd, Ira 19:57
Bradden, A. J. 22:242
Braddesley, J. 19:57
Braddock, Francis 9:128; 27:11
Braddock, Frank 17:425
Braddock, S. J. 16:150
Braddock, W. H. 17:161
Braddock, William 3:27
Braddon, Ashby 9:206
Braden, A. 1:18
Braden, Alexander S. 18:123
Braden, Anderson 10:104; 20:212
Braden, Charles 18:392

Braden, J. 14:40
Braden, James 22:67
Braden, Uriah 8:103
Braden, W. C. 13:62
Bradenburgh, W. K. 21:19
Bradenbury, Henry 4:12
Brader, A. B. 15:157
Bradey, Charles 14:144
Bradey, Daniel W. 9:170
Bradey, J. 1:110
Bradey, Jackson 17:103
Bradfield, B. L. 3:28
Bradfield, Chandler 20:182
Bradfield, David 22:418
Bradfield, Francis A. 22:67
Bradfield, John 20:135
Bradfield, Peter 11:136
Bradfield, William J. 22:179
Bradford, Alexander 22:416
Bradford, Andrew 22:291
Bradford, Andrew S. 22:21
Bradford, Benjamin 17:128; 24:188
Bradford, C. G. 1:20
Bradford, Charles 7:20; 9:170; 19:235
Bradford, D. 3:28
Bradford, D. B. 3:28
Bradford, David 9:235; 26:216
Bradford, Edward D. 20:111
Bradford, Francis 7:15
Bradford, Franklin 9:116; 27:19
Bradford, George 9:213; 14:40; 21:304
Bradford, George W. 18:392
Bradford, H. A. 3:28
Bradford, H. B. 9:235; 26:216
Bradford, H. C. 1:20
Bradford, Henry 7:77; 25:293
Bradford, Hosea 9:235
Bradford, J. 3:28; 17:346
Bradford, J. D. 11:90
Bradford, J. E. 13:83; 14:5
Bradford, James 11:285; 12:67; 15:30
Bradford, John 25:17
Bradford, John L. 9:218; 18:362
Bradford, Joseph 9:128; 27:18

Bradford, King 22:291
Bradford, L. 3:28
Bradford, Larkin 22:291
Bradford, Lester 21:65
Bradford, Nathaniel F. 9:68
Bradford, P. H. 26:138
Bradford, Peter 9:75; 22:179; 26:11
Bradford, Robert 17:63
Bradford, Robert Y. 18:230; 26:16
Bradford, Samuel 7:79; 22:67; 25:293
Bradford, T. A. 8:80
Bradford, Thomas 22:242, 291
Bradford, Thomas B. 11:180
Bradford, William 5:36; 10:13; 12:7; 23:278
Bradford, William B. 22:137
Bradfute, J. R. M. 17:363
Bradieans, Charles 22:8
Bradin, N. S. 15:347
Bradish, Addison 12:67
Bradish, Cyrus 17:358
Bradish, Hugh 17:446; 24:169
Bradish, J. L. 9:140; 27:15
Bradisk, F. 3:28
Bradle, George 17:63
Bradler, Rachard 16:132
Bradley, --- 16:22; 18:45; 19:322
Bradley, A. 3:27; 16:175
Bradley, A. M. 20:144
Bradley, Abram 11:197
Bradley, Alanson P. 20:95
Bradley, Alex 11:136
Bradley, Alexander 3:27
Bradley, Alfred 8:103
Bradley, Augustus B. 12:14
Bradley, B. 3:27; 5:36; 8:77; 25:145
Bradley, Berry 21:304
Bradley, Bigelow 10:179
Bradley, Bradley 7:118
Bradley, C. 14:40
Bradley, Charles 9:75; 15:349; 16:364; 22:291; 26:10
Bradley, Clinton 10:42; 20:212
Bradley, Cupid 9:116; 27:18
Bradley, Dalton 11:258
Bradley, Daniel 1:14; 11:52, 53

Bradley, David 21:304
Bradley, E. 3:27; 16:175
Bradley, E. M. 9:75;
26:12
Bradley, Edmund 16:71
Bradley, Edward 13:105;
26:150
Bradley, Eli A. 22:242
Bradley, Elijah 12:151
Bradley, Ezra I. 5:36
Bradley, F. 14:40
Bradley, F. H. 10:42;
20:212
Bradley, Francis 23:85
Bradley, Francis M.
22:418
Bradley, G. 14:40; 27:14
Bradley, G. B. 24:13
Bradley, G. G. 18:12
Bradley, G. W. 1:113;
9:218; 18:362; 27:24
Bradley, George 1:191;
3:27; 14:144; 26:153
Bradley, George J. 22:67
Bradley, George W.
10:42; 17:278;
20:212
Bradley, H. 14:40;
16:175; 17:435
Bradley, Henry S. 9:235;
26:217
Bradley, J. 1:109, 111;
9:140; 10:157;
11:279; 12:151;
15:119; 16:22;
19:150; 25:145
Bradley, J. C. 10:42;
20:212
Bradley, J. H. 1:19; 26:16
Bradley, J. Miles 17:351
Bradley, Jacob 9:65
Bradley, James 7:20;
10:26, 94; 14:144;
22:331; 24:91;
25:145
Bradley, Jeremiah 13:11
Bradley, John 3:27; 5:36;
7:87; 13:105;
16:175; 18:45;
21:117; 25:145
Bradley, John J. 24:36
Bradley, John L. 24:90
Bradley, Joshua 17:30
Bradley, M. 3:27; 14:40
Bradley, Monroe 1:115
Bradley, N. C. 7:79
Bradley, N. J. 25:293
Bradley, N. W. 20:212
Bradley, Nicholas W.
10:42
Bradley, Noah P. 11:51

Bradley, Oliver 4:12
Bradley, Patrick 12:14;
13:105
Bradley, Peter 12:14;
17:49, 396
Bradley, Philip 22:243
Bradley, Robert 20:121;
26:16
Bradley, S. 8:45
Bradley, Samuel 18:25;
21:94
Bradley, Samuel B. 9:32
Bradley, Simon 26:10
Bradley, Stephen 7:87
Bradley, T. W. 15:30
Bradley, Theodore 9:11
Bradley, Thomas 4:12;
8:9; 11:197; 18:123;
26:120
Bradley, Thomas J. 7:20
Bradley, Thornton 10:94
Bradley, W. 14:40
Bradley, W. F. 1:115
Bradley, William 5:10, 36;
8:9; 17:98; 18:123,
230; 20:111, 177;
22:67; 25:145; 26:15
Bradley, William M.
12:14; 17:278
Bradley, William R.
20:135
Bradlif, Thomas 11:197
Bradly, James 17:49
Bradman, A. M. 3:28
Bradman, L. W. 8:70;
26:153
Bradman, W. H. 13:124
Bradock, Stephen S. 15:95
Bradon, James 23:119
Bradon, L. 14:295;
17:480; 27:20
Bradpite, I. R. J. 22:350
Brads, James 25:145
Bradshare, G. W. 20:213
Bradshaw, A. 9:170;
18:230; 19:266;
26:14
Bradshaw, A. G. 3:27
Bradshaw, A. W. 17:351
Bradshaw, C. W. 7:20
Bradshaw, D. J. 19:6
Bradshaw, Frank 22:291
Bradshaw, G. 22:179
Bradshaw, George 17:17
Bradshaw, George W.
23:134
Bradshaw, H. 3:27
Bradshaw, Harvey 22:242
Bradshaw, Henry 18:230;
26:15
Bradshaw, Hiram 11:257

Bradshaw, Isaac W. 22:21
Bradshaw, J. P. 16:22
Bradshaw, Jackson 19:44
Bradshaw, James 9:206;
23:240
Bradshaw, James R. 23:60
Bradshaw, Joel J. 8:113
Bradshaw, John D. 9:11
Bradshaw, John T. 22:415
Bradshaw, Joseph 11:380
Bradshaw, Joseph P.
21:65
Bradshaw, Mason 21:48
Bradshaw, O. 20:213
Bradshaw, Octave 10:42
Bradshaw, P. P. 13:11
Bradshaw, R. 3:27
Bradshaw, Richard
10:104; 20:213
Bradshaw, Sam. C. 24:14
Bradshaw, Seth J. 23:96
Bradshaw, Stephen
17:287
Bradshaw, Theophilus
17:235
Bradshaw, Thomas 24:13
Bradshaw, William
15:336; 19:57; 22:67
Bradshear, Joseph 17:294
Bradshoe, Frank 24:189
Bradt, Augustus 27:13
Bradt, George 12:14
Bradt, Oliver 11:295
Bradt, Samuel 10:13
Bradton, J. 27:14
Bradway, Edwin 9:218;
18:362
Bradway, Sylvanus
11:115
Bradway, T. B. 11:53
Bradwin, John W. 22:21
Brady, --- 16:364
Brady, Alex 12:47
Brady, Andrew J. 11:23
Brady, Barnard 1:114
Brady, Barney 4:12
Brady, Benjamin 7:15
Brady, C. 7:47
Brady, C. M. 1:114
Brady, Calvin L. 7:87
Brady, Charles 16:288;
19:322
Brady, Crawford 17:278
Brady, D. W. 19:280
Brady, Dennis 16:90
Brady, E. 1:116
Brady, Elias 11:51
Brady, Elizabeth 16:71
Brady, Ernest 23:135
Brady, Eugene 15:310;
19:57

Brady, F. 3:28; 15:185
Brady, Freeman 21:65
Brady, G. W. 17:49
Brady, George 21:304;
   27:142
Brady, Henry 4:12
Brady, Isaac 10:176;
   19:150
Brady, J. 3:28; 15:164;
   24:87; 25:145
Brady, J. A. 19:57
Brady, J. L. 26:152
Brady, James 1:16; 7:20;
   14:336; 16:22;
   17:233; 21:304;
   22:243
Brady, James A. 22:232
Brady, John 1:116;
   11:134; 14:144;
   18:102; 19:325;
   22:331, 417, 499;
   23:284; 25:18
Brady, John S. 12:161
Brady, John W. 4:12;
   22:243
Brady, Lewis 15:171
Brady, Mathew 21:304
Brady, Michael 1:113;
   4:12; 9:116; 15:335;
   19:57; 27:20
Brady, Mike 24:165
Brady, Nathaniel 10:14;
   13:11
Brady, Oscar 4:64
Brady, P. 6:11
Brady, Patrick 15:185
Brady, Patrick G. 13:11
Brady, Peter 14:144
Brady, Philip 23:21
Brady, R. 3:28; 14:295;
   17:480; 27:20
Brady, R. M. 16:175
Brady, R. R. 9:49
Brady, Richard 13:124
Brady, Robert 1:15
Brady, S. 17:128; 24:187
Brady, S. A. 2:7; 25:17
Brady, Samuel 7:118;
   17:354
Brady, Thomas 14:40;
   21:48
Brady, W. H. 17:351
Brady, Walter 7:20
Brady, William 20:144
Brady, William B. 22:117
Braeney, E. 12:161
Brafford, J. 18:64
Braford, --- 9:163
Brag, Orrin 21:304
Braga, Hiram 9:170;
   19:248

Bragant, H. M. 9:49
Bragden, S. A. 25:145
Bragdon, Aaron 7:88;
   21:304
Bragdon, Albert 5:10
Bragdon, H. H. 15:157
Bragdon, John J. 13:11
Bragdon, John W. 11:135
Bragdon, Ora 19:225
Bragg, A. J. 11:51
Bragg, Bartemus 20:185
Bragg, Elmer 7:20
Bragg, George 15:21
Bragg, George E. 12:63
Bragg, George M. 16:77
Bragg, George W. 23:119
Bragg, Henry 10:157
Bragg, J. C. 3:28
Bragg, James 18:25
Bragg, James W. 8:103
Bragg, Joel 21:242
Bragg, John 15:328; 19:57
Bragg, Joseph 8:61;
   11:14; 26:151
Bragg, L. 13:105
Bragg, Lewis 12:161
Bragg, Nelson C. 22:137
Bragg, S. 20:141
Bragg, S. F. 1:20
Bragg, Samuel 22:331
Bragg, Thomas 11:420
Bragg, Thomas J. 4:12
Bragg, Willard 1:113
Bragg, William 9:199;
   19:280
Braggum, Charles 4:12
Braginton, George F.
   22:179
Bragkett, A. M. 24:74
Bragton, Samuel A. 5:9
Braham, Catharine 26:217
Braham, Emma C. 26:217
Brahany, Charles 24:107
Brahler, Louis 15:317;
   19:57
Brahm, August 27:142
Brahmyer, H. 3:27
Braid, George W. 21:304
Brailer, Josiah 7:87
Brailey, J. 3:28
Braily, George W. 1:16
Braimels, C. 19:248
Braimon, Michael 26:11
Brain, William 3:28
Brain, William H. 18:123
Brainard, Amos T. 22:8
Brainard, Ansen 20:213
Brainard, Anson 10:42
Brainard, Benjamin 24:13
Brainard, Clark D. 17:241
Brainard, Edward 20:5

Brainard, F. E. 27:14
Brainard, Fred 11:24
Brainard, George 11:298
Brainard, George W.
   22:276
Brainard, J. 9:140
Brainard, J. B. 17:69
Brainard, J. P. 3:28; 12:94
Brainard, James 22:67
Brainard, James P. 15:358
Brainard, Joseph 22:276
Brainard, Lewis C. 20:135
Brainard, Samuel A. 19:6
Brainard, T. E. 9:139
Brainer, F. 25:145
Brainhart, Martin 11:319
Braiser, H. 19:57
Braisey, Hampton 20:213
Braisted, Austin A. 10:14
Braithwaite, Wilson 15:90
Brake, B. F. 10:104
Brake, Benjamin F.
   20:213
Brake, George 9:11
Brake, J. 3:27
Brake, James M. 20:213
Brakeman, Wilson S.
   17:404
Braken, Samuel 17:201
Braken, Timothy 19:150
Brakenridge, J. H. 19:6
Braker, C. 9:41
Braker, Isaac 7:118
Braker, Philip 21:215
Brakman, David 12:67
Braley, E. B. 19:150
Braley, George 8:70
Braley, James 27:17
Bralnistiem, A. 14:277
Bralt, Peter 22:137
Bram, Abner M. 9:170
Bram, Albert E. 15:277
Bram, Alfred 21:48
Bram, John 11:197
Bramald, James 9:140
Braman, B. 1:110
Braman, Charles 14:40
Braman, Henry 17:164
Braman, L. 5:9
Braman, W. H. 4:12
Brame, Orrington 7:87
Brame, William 13:124
Bramen, Irving 17:241
Bramer, David 26:15
Bramer, Henry 17:147
Bramer, William 20:213
Brames, William A. 8:10
Bramhall, George P. 11:99
Bramhart, Hiram 14:144
Bramiller, William 11:89
Bramin, L. 25:145

Bramlet, Alexander W. 22:242
Bramlet, Thomas 11:23
Bramlet, William H. 22:242
Bramlett, James M. 9:49
Bramlett, Joseph 24:13
Bramlette, Noah 21:265
Bramley, J. R. 15:171
Bramley, Thomas 21:185
Bramly, Fred 3:28
Brammell, James W. 22:67
Brammer, Columbus H. 17:71
Bramon, Henry 5:9
Bramon, Leroy 8:9
Bramon, Nathaniel 8:9
Bramstaedt, John 21:135
Bramwell, James 20:111
Bran, W. 16:266
Bran, W. T. 7:87
Bran, William 14:144
Branagan, J. 1:110
Branagan, James 22:137
Branagan, P. 1:15
Branan, John 17:94
Branan, L. 3:27
Branan, M. 15:119
Branar, Alexander 26:150
Branard, Leander 10:37
Branard, S. F. 14:144
Branard, William 14:40
Branberry, Francis 26:152
Brance, S. 17:13
Branch, B. 14:295; 15:185; 17:472
Branch, Barney 23:60
Branch, C. 11:285
Branch, Charles 1:115
Branch, Edward 22:21
Branch, Edwin 22:170
Branch, Frank W. 13:134; 19:346
Branch, G. W. 9:101
Branch, George L. F. 9:116; 27:19
Branch, George W. 18:337
Branch, Henden 27:143
Branch, Henry 11:134; 16:22
Branch, Hezekiah 20:177, 188
Branch, J. 3:28
Branch, J. J. 14:40
Branch, L. 27:14
Branch, Lewis 18:230; 26:15
Branch, P. 27:21

Branch, William 7:118; 16:175; 21:265; 25:20
Branchard, John 11:133
Branchet, J. H. 11:384
Brancisco, Moses 20:107
Branciva, Joseph 9:207
Brand, A. 18:77
Brand, Alfred 6:12
Brand, D. H. 22:21
Brand, David J. 15:30
Brand, Denis A. 23:119
Brand, H. 10:192; 18:172
Brand, Jeremiah 22:137
Brand, John V. 21:250
Brand, Joseph 7:47
Brand, L. C. 3:28
Brand, Lawrence 21:304
Brand, N. H. 1:20
Brand, Orington 21:304
Brand, P. 22:179
Brandan, John J. 12:173
Brandcherry, Levi 24:74
Branden, Franklin 22:242
Branden, J. F. 19:57
Branden, O. 3:28
Brandenburgh, E. 23:135
Brandenburgh, Henry 17:337
Brandent, Mathew 23:135
Branderberg, Jacob 15:6
Branderburg, James 16:22
Brandford, W. 25:145
Brandhorst, Arnold 21:250
Brandhurs, William 8:9
Brandiger, F. 3:27
Brandine, John 26:150
Brandis, John 21:304
Brando, Robert 9:161
Brandon, Adolphus 14:144
Brandon, Alex 9:218; 18:362
Brandon, B. F. 25:145
Brandon, Benjamin T. 5:10
Brandon, C. 3:223; 17:504
Brandon, D. A. 23:21
Brandon, Daniel 22:291
Brandon, J. 15:119; 17:191
Brandon, J. C. 23:117
Brandon, J. F. 15:318
Brandon, John 3:28; 9:32
Brandon, John F. 9:32
Brandon, John L. 18:290; 26:94
Brandon, John R. 9:9

Brandon, Parker 9:75; 26:12
Brandon, Richard B. 24:13
Brandon, Samuel T. 17:212
Brandon, T. 18:25
Brandon, Thomas J. 7:87
Brandon, W. 25:145
Brandon, William C. 20:213
Brandon, William V. 11:133
Brandow, W. 20:121
Brandstater, John B. 10:42
Brandstutter, J. B. 20:213
Brandt, Clark 16:145
Brandt, Ford 15:30
Brandt, George 12:48; 16:22; 18:275; 23:21
Brandt, Gilbert C. 20:5
Brandt, Henry S. 13:11
Brandt, Isaac 23:21
Brandt, J. 24:74
Brandt, John 11:51
Brandt, Lewis 13:105
Brandt, M. H. 22:67
Brandt, William 1:20; 13:84
Brandy, --- 15:171
Brandy, John 18:25
Branel, B. 21:185
Branen, James 11:237
Braner, George 8:10
Braner, Perry 8:37
Braney, Louis C. H. 18:25
Branfield, J. F. 19:6
Brangle, J. 13:84; 14:5
Branham, Charles 22:291
Branham, Edwards 24:165
Branham, Orille 17:351
Branham, William 16:22
Branigan, J. 11:185
Branigan, P. K. 10:157
Brank, Samuel 10:42; 20:213
Branlette, Wesley 21:265
Branly, Samuel 6:24
Branman, J. 15:185
Branman, Joseph 20:213
Brann, A. M. 19:285
Brann, Calvin N. 7:73
Brann, D. 13:84
Brann, John 25:293
Brann, L. G. 9:163
Branna, Elias 3:27
Brannagan, W. 27:15
Brannagin, C. 3:27
Brannagin, J. 3:27
Brannan, A. 25:146
Brannan, I. B. 14:330

Brannan, J. F. 18:303
Brannan, J. R. 14:40;
26:93
Brannan, J. T. 9:19
Brannan, James 3:27
Brannan, James H. 12:146
Brannan, John 26:93
Brannan, John D. 10:104;
20:213
Brannan, M. 12:121; 14:5
Brannan, P. A. 3:27
Brannan, P. J. 23:21
Brannan, Patrick 7:87;
26:94
Brannan, Peter 25:15
Brannan, Thomas 7:87
Brannan, William 1:19;
9:242; 22:232
Brannan, William M.
22:179
Brannen, J. 16:175
Brannen, Peter 1:18
Brannen, William 22:67
Branner, David 18:230
Branner, Fred. 8:103
Branner, William 23:306
Brannigan, John 3:27
Brannilly, John W. 16:22
Brannin, A. 8:45
Brannin, T. 1:14
Brannock, C. 3:27
Brannock, F. 3:27
Brannock, J. H. 15:185
Brannon, Alexander
23:135
Brannon, Chanton 8:9
Brannon, Chester 18:123
Brannon, Dennis 22:397
Brannon, H. 21:97
Brannon, J. 1:109; 3:27
Brannon, James 14:314
Brannon, John 18:290
Brannon, Joseph S. 22:21
Brannon, Leroy 18:123
Brannon, M. 13:84
Brannon, P. 3:27; 15:185
Brannon, Patrick 9:32;
18:290
Brannon, Philander
20:213
Brannon, Richard 22:117
Brannon, S. S. 17:439
Brannon, Samuel S.
24:151
Brannon, Thomas 8:45;
21:304; 22:164
Brannon, William 21:185
Branon, A. B. 15:30
Branon, William 3:27
Branon, Willis 17:128;
24:188

Brans, Seyborn N. 21:48
Bransburg, Taylor 17:335
Branscom, P. 22:291
Bransetter, Adam O.
23:112
Bransin, Levi T. 10:34
Bransom, E. 3:28
Branson, Anthony 9:116
Branson, Benjamin F.
18:214
Branson, F. 27:15
Branson, George 9:75
Branson, H. C. 18:45
Branson, James H. 22:447
Branson, Jeremiah 23:60
Branson, John J. 21:97
Branson, R. C. 12:94;
15:358; 19:57
Branson, Robert D. 9:75
Branson, Thomas 11:325
Bransteeter, S. 13:62
Branstell, L. 16:175
Branstetter, Charles
16:143
Branstiter, C. M. 1:115
Brant, A. 3:27; 18:337
Brant, B. B. 3:27
Brant, C. 18:45; 21:119
Brant, Charles 3:27
Brant, D. 23:312
Brant, Daniel 18:284;
26:134
Brant, David S. 11:23
Brant, G. 25:146
Brant, George 15:277
Brant, George W. 23:278
Brant, Ivor 10:104;
20:213
Brant, Jacob 7:87
Brant, John 9:11
Brant, Martin 17:76
Brant, Milton 1:13
Brant, William 8:70
Branthover, Daniel 17:90
Brantley, C. B. 24:11
Brantley, Daniel 6:29
Brantley, John N. 22:242
Brantley, Julius 21:221
Brantling, W. P. 18:420
Brantly, Daniel 25:317
Brantly, G. W. 21:304
Brantonyes, Frank 20:34
Brants, Martin 7:118;
21:304
Brantt, Joseph 12:151
Brantz, August 19:6
Brantz, W. B. 14:240
Branum, A. 21:19
Branum, W. H. 17:235
Branum, William H.
11:335

Brarerty, Edward 7:15
Brarksmith, William N.
18:302
Brary, Oscar 19:235
Brase, Augustus 7:87
Brasel, Joseph 11:420
Brasfield, Aaron 22:164
Brash, Frederick 12:151
Brash, Michael 18:123
Brash, Nicholas 8:9
Brashe, Jack 18:64
Brashear, John 8:61
Brashears, C. W. 10:185
Brashears, Mathew 18:123
Brashen, Oscar W.
18:230; 26:15
Brasher, Charles 7:118
Brasher, F. M. 20:121
Brasher, John 17:94
Brasher, Lafayette 10:42
Brasher, LaFayette 20:213
Brashers, C. W. 18:172
Brashford, Allen 10:94
Brashier, G. W. 18:417
Brashing, W. 15:171
Brasier, S. 3:27
Braskette, William 11:135
Brason, W. J. 5:36
Brass, Esau 9:128
Brass, Joseph 20:213
Brass, William 9:170;
19:294
Brasse, E. C. 11:189
Brassel, J. 1:13
Brassen, Andrew 21:304
Brasser, M. 18:230
Brasses, M. 26:14
Brassfield, William 7:88
Brassing, Henry 21:304
Brassington, J. 1:110
Brasteg, D. W. 7:87
Brastle, Christian 17:13
Braswell, Allen 17:30
Braswell, Jacob 10:104;
20:213
Bratcher, Enos 8:100
Bratcher, Merideth 17:252
Bratcher, Morgan 20:185
Bratcher, William P.
20:185
Brate, Peter 8:103
Brates, T. S. 25:146
Bratis, Thomas 4:12
Bratly, Jonathan W.
23:288
Bratman, Perry 20:213
Braton, C. H. 1:15
Braton, F. M. 3:28
Braton, George 10:171;
19:150
Bratshone, G. M. 26:91

Bratstrone, G. M. 18:303
Bratt, Abijah 11:285
Bratt, G. 3:28
Bratt, John 12:7
Bratt, Lewis 4:12
Bratt, M. S. 20:47
Bratt, W. H. 15:102
Brattam, Thomas 10:42;
    20:213
Brattan, William 22:179
Brattenstein, --- 13:132
Bratterbray, John 16:22
Brattlebough, H. 25:146
Bratton, G. W. 1:111
Bratton, H. C. 11:135
Bratton, Henry 7:47
Bratton, Horace 22:499
Bratton, J. 11:319
Bratton, Jerry 17:396
Bratton, Job 15:349
Bratton, John 9:160
Bratton, John R. 23:135
Bratton, W. R. 6:29;
    25:317
Brauchat, Nicholas 7:20
Brauell, John 8:70
Brauer, Gustav 21:97
Brauer, John 11:53
Braugh, David 18:25
Braugh, J. 27:15
Braughman, Reuben
    27:21
Brauham, William 17:201
Braukman, Augustus 7:20
Braumer, R. 15:339
Braun, Eberhard 23:60
Braun, Henry 25:317
Braun, J. 1:109
Braun, Nehemiah C.
    22:401
Braun, O. W. 1:109
Braun, Peter 10:146
Braun, Xavier 23:187
Braundy, John 13:11
Braunwalder, D. 14:40
Brauser, A. 15:185
Braw, Rukes 18:172
Braward, H. A. 18:64
Brawdy, William 1:19
Brawley, J. 1:109
Brawn, Allison 18:392
Brawn, Humphrey 18:392
Brawner, William 20:135
Brawning, Daniel 21:304
Brawson, H. C. 10:147
Braxton, C. S. 18:172
Braxton, George G.
    23:135
Braxton, Isaac 17:191
Braxton, Robert 16:288
Braxton, Samuel 21:304

Bray, A. 11:278; 13:84
Bray, Amos 15:185
Bray, Anthony 10:98
Bray, Asa W. 12:98
Bray, Calvin 10:104;
    20:213
Bray, E. 11:420
Bray, Ebenezer 12:14
Bray, Edward D. 24:8
Bray, Eli 20:95
Bray, F. E. 16:23
Bray, Francis 10:104;
    20:213
Bray, Francis E. 13:11
Bray, George 15:30
Bray, H. N. 3:28
Bray, J. 9:114; 14:40
Bray, James 7:20; 17:147
Bray, James N. 9:19;
    18:320
Bray, Joel E. 22:67
Bray, John 15:185; 25:146
Bray, John W. 23:85
Bray, Joseph 14:144
Bray, Lafayette 1:113
Bray, Luther C. 7:55
Bray, Martin R. 10:104;
    20:213
Bray, Milo 1:19
Bray, Orrin J. 10:104;
    20:213
Bray, R. 7:87
Bray, R. A. 9:199; 19:280
Bray, Richard 11:89
Bray, Samuel 18:25
Bray, T. 3:28
Bray, Thomas 22:401
Bray, W. 1:112
Bray, W. H. 9:140
Bray, W. R. 21:165
Bray, William 23:21
Bray, William H. 27:15
Bray, William N. 10:104;
    20:213
Bray, William P. 23:135
Brayden, A. 12:7
Brayden, Henry P. 8:80
Brayden, John J. 16:22
Braydon, John 22:232
Brayer, Willis M. 17:278
Brayford, W. H. 1:111
Brayier, John 9:19
Brayley, Watson 23:276
Braylie, James C. 25:19
Brayman, George 9:170
Brayman, J. T. H. 12:14
Brayman, John 19:6
Brayman, Samuel 15:30
Brayman, William 18:123
Braynard, Conant, Mrs.
    15:185

Braynard, Joseph 13:11
Brayton, A. 25:146
Brayton, Asa 9:32
Brayton, B. F. 9:140
Brayton, Benjamin F.
    27:14
Brayton, J. F. 1:14
Brayton, Job 15:119
Brayton, W. L. 14:250
Brayton, William 22:474
Braze, Lafaett 19:150
Braze, Lafayette 10:157
Brazeal, W. H. 26:92
Brazee, J. 9:170; 19:244
Brazee, Martin 14:144
Brazee, P. 13:105
Brazel, Zeke 9:164
Brazell, John 8:9; 18:123
Brazelle, Anthony 22:170
Brazelton, George 17:335
Brazelton, Joshua 18:214
Brazelton, Oliver C. 7:87
Brazen, Abraham 10:94
Brazenton, Eli 22:401
Brazer, W. P. 2:7
Brazie, David 12:14
Brazie, E. 1:14
Brazier, Nathan 21:304
Braznell, William 1:116
Brbo, Adam 18:123
Breading, Robert F. 22:21
Breadlover, R. 11:258
Breadshaw, Isaac I. 4:12
Breah, David 15:297
Breaix, Oscar 21:304
Break, David 16:175
Breaker, Isaac 21:304
Breakison, Daniel 20:95
Brealy, James 14:40
Breanam, B. F. 15:277
Breanny, J. 3:28
Breart, James M. 16:175
Brease, Oscar 7:88
Breast, Aaron 11:123
Breast, Henry L. 5:10
Brebinger, C. N. 26:94
Brebriston, Robert 15:308
Brecenridge, Milton 19:44
Brechdold, William 8:80
Brechenridge, William
    14:40
Brecht, F. 17:71
Brecht, Jacob O. 9:76
Brechtol, Christopher
    11:384
Breck, C. 7:47
Brecken, M. C. 8:70
Breckenbridge, --- 25:15
Breckenridge, --- 3:28
Breckenridge, A. 17:128,
    404; 24:188

Breckenridge, Andrew 22:291
Breckenridge, Charles H. 25:268
Breckenridge, David 22:291
Breckenridge, G. W. 1:18
Breckenridge, George A. 24:99
Breckenridge, Harvey 10:204
Breckenridge, Henry 17:171
Breckenridge, J. 7:47
Breckenridge, J. E. 26:153
Breckenridge, John 17:30; 18:77
Breckenridge, Linwood 11:180
Breckenridge, M. 18:230
Breckenridge, Thomas J. 22:243
Breckenridge, W. 26:14
Breckenridge, William K. M. 20:150
Breckerish, Nicholas 10:42
Breckles, F. 1:111
Breckman, Henry 21:304
Breckmeck, H. 3:28
Breckwood, C. W. 2:8
Brecount, John S. 18:214
Bred, W. H. 21:185
Breddell, Lewis 1:115
Brede, Daniel 13:11
Breden, Elias 25:146
Bredhemer, Hiram 22:179
Bredlon, William B. 9:75
Bredlow, William B. 26:12
Bredon, Reuben 19:6
Bredony, W. 18:12
Bredwell, John 23:301
Bree, Edward 13:105
Breece, Garrett 11:399
Breece, J. M. 20:38
Breece, John 21:19
Breech, Jacob 12:14
Breed, G. E. 25:13
Breed, J. 1:93
Breed, Nelson 21:146, 210
Breed, Reuben O. 22:137
Breed, William 14:40, 132
Breedan, James F. 10:89
Breeden, Henry W. 10:147; 18:45
Breeden, S. S. 11:257
Breeder, James P. 20:213
Breedin, Calvin 11:420

Breeding, Benjamin F. 25:317
Breedland, Jesse 22:447
Breedlon, Charles 20:144
Breedlorr, Charles 8:10
Breedlove, Allison 22:243
Breedlove, Charles 18:123
Breedlove, Henry J. 17:49
Breedlove, Thomas 8:10
Breedlove, William 11:23
Breek, George 21:304
Breel, Jacob 3:28
Breem, George H. 9:170
Breem, Hugh 26:94
Breen, A. 3:28
Breen, B. 6:7; 18:107
Breen, Charles H. 7:88
Breen, Dennis 25:146
Breen, Edmond 10:157
Breen, Henry H. 21:304
Breen, John 9:11; 20:213
Breen, John H. 22:507
Breen, Thomas 15:325
Breen, William 14:144
Breene, Hugh 9:32; 18:290
Breer, Oliver 4:12
Brees, E. 15:304
Brees, Ezra 16:175
Brees, John 17:30; 22:331
Brees, Noah 21:19
Breese, C. W. 1:19
Breese, D. 3:28
Breese, F. 19:248
Breese, George 23:119
Breese, Joseph 7:55
Breesley, William 27:24
Breeton, Samuel 13:11
Breeves, H. A. 8:45
Breeze, Franklin 9:170
Breeze, J. T. 23:21
Breezee, George H. 22:507
Brehen, Abraham 10:104
Brehl, Henry 12:58; 16:153
Brehm, Charles 22:173
Brehmer, Ferdinand 21:305
Brehn, Abraham 20:213
Brehn, H. G. 12:14
Brehorn, Willis 9:170; 19:280
Breicks, H. 9:170
Breidan, E. 3:28
Breidninger, Sidney R. 16:151
Breikwith, John M. 22:179
Breim, A. 3:28
Breindan, Johnson 10:42

Breing, John 19:6
Breinstedt, Louis 9:75
Breinthet, Aaron 5:49
Breirer, A. V. 9:49
Brekel, Augustus 25:18
Breker, John 22:21
Brell, Francis 19:6
Brelsch, J. 25:18
Brem, John 10:42; 17:417; 24:156
Brem, Wolfgang 10:157; 19:150
Breman, B. 25:279
Breman, J. 19:248
Breman, Noah 9:229
Breman, Patrick 22:401
Bremann, Gotlieb H. 26:150
Bremen, --- 21:165
Bremen, John 22:331
Bremer, Andrew 15:358
Bremer, George W. 20:213
Bremer, John 1:115; 17:128; 24:188
Bremer, Lewis 10:104; 20:213
Bremer, Louis 8:121
Bremer, Thomas 3:28
Bremman, John R. 20:103
Bremmer, Frederick 9:10
Bremon, Francis 24:13
Bremon, James 13:105
Bremon, Louis 26:10
Brenan, John 22:21
Brenan, O. 15:325
Brenard, J. N. 20:213
Brenard, Oliver 15:53
Brenbook, Henry 4:12
Brenchley, William 19:248
Brenden, W. T. 19:57
Brendle, J. E. 23:135
Brendon, Johnson 20:213
Brendren, William 10:104
Brene, Jeremiah 14:144
Brenegan, John 14:144
Brenell, John 26:153
Breneman, B. F. 25:146
Breneman, Harmon S. 23:135
Breneman, Miles 7:20
Brenenstal, Danne 20:213
Brenenstall, Duane 10:104
Brener, F. M. 24:13
Brener, J. 25:16
Brenerger, H. W. 20:213
Brenger, Henry 25:317
Brenio, August 9:105
Brenkman, Frederick 11:53

Brenlinger, W. R. 3:28
Brennan, A. 9:140
Brennan, Charles A. 7:83
Brennan, Chris 14:144
Brennan, Edward 4:12
Brennan, George 10:42
Brennan, Henry 8:113
Brennan, J. 12:81; 14:144;
    16:288
Brennan, James 1:15
Brennan, Jeremiah 25:332
Brennan, John 9:170;
    10:10; 21:305; 24:63
Brennan, M. 1:20
Brennan, Melcher 20:213
Brennan, Owen 23:112
Brennan, Pat 14:144
Brennan, Patrick 10:14;
    16:23; 20:121
Brennan, Peter 15:283;
    19:57
Brennan, Thomas 21:135
Brennan, Thomas S. 13:11
Brennan, William 7:83;
    16:138; 21:305
Brennen, James 15:185
Brennen, M. 1:18
Brennen, W. 7:47
Brenner, David 15:185
Brenner, F. C. 26:12
Brenner, Frederick 1:114
Brenner, J. 13:84; 14:5
Brenner, John 10:42;
    15:185; 20:213
Brenner, Melchior 10:89
Brenner, Michael 13:11
Brenner, N. 3:28
Brenner, Philip 21:48
Brenning, C. F. 7:88
Brenning, Joseph 7:88
Brennley, M. 12:151
Brennon, M. 3:28
Brennon, Peter 23:119
Brenson, --- 10:157;
    19:150
Brenson, William P. 12:67
Brent, Charles 22:21
Brent, Coleman 17:128;
    24:189
Brent, Fred 14:40
Brent, Henry 17:171
Brent, J. 16:175
Brent, John L. 19:57
Brent, L. 18:25
Brent, Stephen 10:211
Brent, William H. 14:40
Brent, William M. 22:21
Brentel, A. 25:146
Brentel, Aaron 25:146
Brentez, Aaron 5:49
Brenthan, C. 25:146

Brentley, N. 11:83
Brentley, S. 27:12
Brentley, William 9:170
Brentlinger, D. 1:16
Brenton, A. J. 20:121
Brenton, F. J. 9:140
Brenton, George D.
    21:215
Brenton, Henry K. 17:272
Brenton, James 20:88
Brenton, N. 25:146
Brenton, R. S. 17:272
Brenton, Thomas 14:263
Brenton, W. 11:53
Brenton, William C.
    21:221
Brentzel, Peter 16:90
Breny, James 3:28
Brereton, William 19:150
Brersford, M. 3:28
Bresang, C. 3:28
Brescott, A. 8:10
Bresden, John 8:103
Bresee, John 10:104;
    20:213
Bresh, Peter 6:10
Breshaben, Patrick 9:159
Bresihan, J. 25:13
Bresler, Linsday 4:12
Bresley, M. 14:5
Bresley, W. 14:5
Breslin, Dennis 15:30
Breslin, James 25:146
Breslin, John 14:144
Bresnehan, John 2:8
Bresse, Hinman 17:17
Bressell, Warren 16:175
Bressett, Isaac 22:397
Bressford, Augustus
    21:305
Bressu, H. 11:257
Brest, Ferdinand 11:103
Brest, George W. 21:305
Brest, Isaac 7:88
Breston, James M. 11:53
Brethouner, Jimberant
    26:14
Brethunker, George
    13:105
Bretly, William 14:144
Bretsnyder, J. 3:28
Brett, B. 14:5
Brett, D. N. 25:18
Brett, E. I. 15:339
Brett, E. J. 16:364
Brett, James 3:28
Brett, John 23:21
Bretts, John 15:185
Bretts, L. 22:21
Bretty, Joseph 9:19
Bretty, William 14:144

Bretz, A. 11:298
Bretz, Henry 1:114
Bretz, Jac 27:23
Bretz, John 17:504
Bretz, Martin 9:76
Bretz, William 14:144
Bretzki, C. 1:19
Breul, Erhardt 17:199
Breum, J. 3:28
Breverd, Julius A. 17:30
Breverton, Patrick 4:12
Brevett, John 9:203
Brewaster, John H. 18:77
Brewen, Luther 26:144
Brewer, --- 14:144;
    21:129
Brewer, A. J. 21:119
Brewer, A. W. 11:325
Brewer, Aaron 25:146
Brewer, Anderson 15:10
Brewer, C. 21:185
Brewer, C. A. 18:102
Brewer, C. P. 1:93
Brewer, Charles 18:290;
    26:93
Brewer, Charles W. 4:12
Brewer, Cyrus J. 22:21
Brewer, D. C. 3:28
Brewer, Darrell 17:287
Brewer, David 17:409;
    22:117
Brewer, E. 1:18
Brewer, Edward 9:32;
    18:290; 26:93
Brewer, Eli 16:175
Brewer, Ernest 13:11
Brewer, Fred 3:28
Brewer, G. E. 3:28
Brewer, G. P. 15:185
Brewer, G. W. 10:94
Brewer, George 8:80;
    14:40
Brewer, George W.
    10:104
Brewer, Green 4:12
Brewer, H. 3:28; 9:65;
    11:134
Brewer, H. O. 7:74;
    25:293
Brewer, H. Z. 3:28
Brewer, Henry 8:80;
    27:142
Brewer, Hiram M. 24:91
Brewer, I. 15:339
Brewer, I. A. 20:144
Brewer, J. 3:28; 13:84;
    14:5; 16:364
Brewer, J. E. 14:41
Brewer, J. S. 3:28
Brewer, J. W. 20:38
Brewer, Jacob 11:135

Brewer, James 9:49;
11:53; 17:108;
22:243; 23:21;
25:317
Brewer, James H. 23:60
Brewer, James R. 4:12
Brewer, John 17:76; 22:21
Brewer, John C. 13:11;
16:23
Brewer, John L. 15:311
Brewer, John W. 22:117
Brewer, Justus 19:337
Brewer, L. 1:17
Brewer, Lewis 18:188
Brewer, M. 3:28
Brewer, Martin 6:11
Brewer, Nicholas 7:20
Brewer, Oliver 23:85
Brewer, P. 22:179
Brewer, Paris A. 23:135
Brewer, Real 24:58
Brewer, Richard 9:95;
22:117
Brewer, Robert 4:12
Brewer, Robert M. 22:448
Brewer, Ryal 17:94
Brewer, S. 3:28
Brewer, Samuel R. 19:150
Brewer, Thomas 20:213;
21:19
Brewer, Thomas J. 22:243
Brewer, Thomas O. 8:80
Brewer, W. E. 10:204
Brewer, W. H. 3:28
Brewer, W. J. 27:22
Brewer, W. L. 8:10;
18:123
Brewer, W. N. 10:42
Brewer, W. T. 3:28
Brewer, William 7:88;
14:41; 21:221;
23:60; 24:91
Brewer, William N.
20:213
Brewer, William R.
20:213; 22:243
Brewer, Willis 21:221
Brewers, Charles 9:32
Brewington, Richard
19:44
Brewington, Shanly 19:44
Brewman, Thomas 19:6
Brewn, J. D. 25:278
Brewser, E. A. 11:410
Brewster, A. 26:12
Brewster, Amon 10:157
Brewster, C. 1:19; 25:146
Brewster, C. F. 21:305
Brewster, Charles 5:10;
25:146
Brewster, Clemuel 17:272

Brewster, David 9:76;
26:10
Brewster, E. H. 7:47
Brewster, Harvey 23:267
Brewster, Hiram 11:52
Brewster, Isaac 10:104;
20:213
Brewster, J. C. 1:14
Brewster, J. F. 21:305
Brewster, James 13:11;
19:334
Brewster, John 6:15
Brewster, John F. 27:17
Brewster, John P. 22:67
Brewster, John W. 25:278
Brewster, L. W. 19:150
Brewster, R. 25:317
Brewster, Robert 15:354;
19:57
Brewster, Robert J. 4:12
Brewster, Samuel 10:157;
19:150
Brewster, William 8:80
Brewton, Albert T. 25:146
Brham, Warner 17:262
Briace, J. R. 3:29
Brian, Charles 3:29
Brian, James 16:175
Brian, James O. 22:243
Brian, John M. 21:135
Brian, P. O. 16:175
Brian, Peter 25:16
Brian, R. 25:146
Brian, Robert 5:36
Brian, Thomas 16:71
Briant, H. 20:89
Briant, Harvey 10:204
Briant, John 10:27;
19:299
Briant, L. A. 3:29
Briant, William 9:49
Briar, Horace A. 4:12
Briarlin, Michael 4:12
Briarsly, W. S. 14:235
Briazeal, W. H. 18:303
Brice, Chancey E. 15:185
Brice, F. 13:124
Brice, Isaac 13:11
Brice, J. C. 3:29
Brice, John 22:21
Brice, P. 21:165
Brice, Robert 11:103
Brice, U. 25:146
Brice, William 19:44;
25:14
Brice, William A. 20:91
Bricholas, J. 14:41
Brick, --- 9:240
Brick, Barney 23:135
Brick, J. J. 1:111
Brick, Samuel 11:137

Brick, Thomas G. 21:48
Brickback, Casper 4:12
Brickell, John 7:20
Brickenstaff, --- 3:29
Bricker, Bery 14:144
Bricker, G. B. 1:17
Bricker, George W.
21:305; 23:135
Bricker, H. 1:20
Bricker, J. 1:116
Bricker, J. J. 3:29
Bricker, James M. 11:135
Bricker, John H. 23:135
Bricker, Joseph 12:14;
24:13
Bricker, Nicholas 9:19
Bricker, Samuel I. 12:56
Bricker, W. H. 11:134
Bricker, William 16:175;
17:509
Brickerly, Louis B. 18:12
Brickett, J. H. 15:289
Brickett, W. D. 11:53
Brickey, John M. 20:132
Brickey, Peter 11:420
Brickford, F. 13:84
Brickhilt, W. 1:13
Brickhouse, --- 2:8
Brickhouse, Raymond
10:171; 19:150
Brickinal, P. 1:13
Brickler, John 17:98
Brickman, George 8:80
Brickman, Henry 7:88
Brickman, Michael 14:144
Bricknel, George 9:170
Bricknell, Anderson 24:13
Bricknell, B. F. 15:185
Bricks, Frederick 10:104
Bridaham, H. W. 3:29
Briddle, George W. 17:94
Bride, B. M. 1:110
Bride, Emile 8:121
Bride, Robert 1:19
Bride, Samuel 9:235;
26:217
Bridegood, --- 18:411
Bridell, S. 3:29
Bridenbaugh, John 20:132
Bridenbourgh, William
18:406
Bridenbucher, John 24:36
Bridenstine, M. 22:21
Brider, H. 16:175
Bridewell, Carter 26:14
Bridewell, John E. 22:164
Bridewell, S. D. 1:13
Bridg---, Andrew 25:18
Bridge, Coolie 21:265
Bridge, Henry 12:14
Bridge, Simon 19:57

Bridge, Wellington 15:90
Bridgeford, T. 26:16
Bridgefort, Peter 11:335
Bridgehouse, Timothy
    9:32
Bridgeman, Abram N.
    17:205
Bridgeman, Ansil O.
    11:298
Bridgeman, Frances 20:55
Bridgeman, James 22:21
Bridgeman, William
    22:417
Bridgement, Chris. S.
    20:182
Bridgens, Robert 23:178
Bridges, A. B. 12:141;
    20:214
Bridges, Abraham 18:123
Bridges, Alcana 22:243
Bridges, Alfred 13:11
Bridges, B. 1:14; 9:170
Bridges, Beal 26:15
Bridges, Benjamin 22:67
Bridges, Bennell 19:280
Bridges, Berl 18:230
Bridges, D. 12:7; 14:287;
    23:201
Bridges, Elias 11:197
Bridges, G. W. 10:42;
    20:214
Bridges, George A. 8:80
Bridges, George W. 8:45
Bridges, H. J. 11:383
Bridges, J. 12:7
Bridges, J. E. 19:57
Bridges, J. N. 21:305
Bridges, J. O. 19:150
Bridges, Jackson 10:94
Bridges, James 9:76;
    10:104; 17:147;
    20:214; 21:265;
    26:11
Bridges, James M. 10:42;
    20:214
Bridges, Jesse 17:171
Bridges, John C. 15:10
Bridges, John F. 10:14;
    16:23
Bridges, Julian T. 9:76
Bridges, L. W. 21:129
Bridges, M. E. 3:29
Bridges, Richard A. 17:17
Bridges, T. J. 10:192;
    18:172
Bridges, W. J. 3:29
Bridges, Wesley T. 21:305
Bridges, William 26:12
Bridget, George 26:15
Bridget, H. J. 1:18
Bridgett, W. 9:140; 27:16

Bridgewater, Abraham
    10:98
Bridgewater, C. 9:19
Bridgewater, E. 11:24;
    26:92
Bridgewater, G. 25:146
Bridgewater, George
    10:89
Bridgewater, George N.
    5:36
Bridgewater, John 11:53
Bridgewater, Lewis B.
    21:221
Bridgewater, Martin V.
    20:16
Bridgford, H. 23:21
Bridgham, G. W. 9:140;
    27:16
Bridgham, J. S. 1:112
Bridgman, A. M. 17:216
Bridgman, Edwin S. 17:76
Bridgman, Patrick 12:14
Bridgwater, E. 18:303
Bridgway, J. 3:29
Bridle, Sebastian 11:99
Bridler, A. 16:175
Bridsing, Abraham 11:197
Bridsley, W. 22:350
Bridwell, Carter 18:230
Bridwell, Cuthburth 20:95
Bridwell, H. 17:496
Bridwell, H. C. 3:29
Bridwell, J. W. 20:135
Bridwell, John J. 22:243
Bridwell, Orlando 8:45;
    21:221
Brieden, F. T. 26:13
Briefierd, J. 13:105
Briel, John 12:169, 170
Brielman, William 17:76
Briely, P. G. 19:57
Brien, Daniel O. 7:55
Brien, David 4:12
Brien, E. 15:164
Brien, F. O. 5:10
Brien, Henry J. 20:105
Brien, J. O. 7:47; 16:175
Brien, James 3:29
Brien, John 15:30
Brien, Joseph O. 15:150
Brien, P. O. 7:20
Brien, Pat O. 7:20
Brien, Reuben 11:196
Brien, T. O. 15:312;
    16:175
Brien, Thomas O. 16:176
Brier, L. 11:257
Brierly, E. 16:176
Brierly, John 17:49
Brierton, James 22:21
Briesnhen, Daniel 1:115

Briest, Henry 11:197
Briett, Charles 20:5
Brieulaugh, Charles 6:11
Brigain, A. A. 11:293
Brigby, Alvin 10:104
Brigerstaff, Aaron 8:45
Briget, George 18:230
Brigg, George 14:133,
    264
Brigg, W. 14:295; 17:475;
    27:21
Brigger, William 11:180
Briggis, R. L. 14:5
Briggle, J. 26:121
Briggs, --- 3:29; 16:17
Briggs, A. 1:111
Briggs, A. L. 21:185
Briggs, A. W. 23:304
Briggs, Abner 11:331
Briggs, Alack A. 14:144
Briggs, Andrew 3:28
Briggs, Augustus D. 19:6
Briggs, C. W. 1:110
Briggs, Cassius 22:179
Briggs, Charles 13:11;
    21:305
Briggs, Charles N. 23:105
Briggs, D. 7:47; 16:176;
    24:13
Briggs, D. B. 9:140
Briggs, Daniel C. 17:90
Briggs, Daniel D. 27:14
Briggs, David 27:22
Briggs, E. 1:14; 3:29
Briggs, E. A. 7:20
Briggs, Edwin 25:16
Briggs, Emanuel 22:137
Briggs, Enoch 17:17;
    24:48
Briggs, Ethan C. 11:134
Briggs, F. 3:29
Briggs, F. S. 26:11
Briggs, Filmore 24:189
Briggs, Franklin S. 9:76
Briggs, Frederick 19:58;
    26:236
Briggs, G. 10:147, 192;
    14:41; 18:45, 172
Briggs, G. A. 18:204
Briggs, G. L. 25:293
Briggs, George 4:12;
    15:185; 20:214;
    21:48
Briggs, George L. 7:74
Briggs, George W. 22:164
Briggs, H. 3:29; 23:21
Briggs, H. J. 9:218;
    18:362; 24:74
Briggs, Henry 13:11
Briggs, J. 1:111; 3:29;
    7:47; 16:288

)

Briggs, J. C. 3:29; 10:204
Briggs, J. H. 20:91
Briggs, Jacob 17:128;
  24:188
Briggs, James 1:17; 13:11;
  15:90
Briggs, James S. 22:21
Briggs, Jasper 7:47;
  16:132
Briggs, John 10:27;
  11:136; 15:53;
  17:153; 19:299
Briggs, John C. 1:14
Briggs, John H. 13:11,
  134; 19:346
Briggs, John W. 22:416;
  23:312
Briggs, Justin 10:14
Briggs, L. 17:30
Briggs, L. B. 1:114
Briggs, L. H. 26:152
Briggs, Lewis 13:11
Briggs, Lewis O. 10:14
Briggs, Maring 19:58
Briggs, Martin 13:62
Briggs, Mayberry G.
  16:156
Briggs, Melvin J. 23:85
Briggs, Michael S. 13:11
Briggs, N. 1:111
Briggs, Nat 9:206
Briggs, P. R. 16:364
Briggs, R. 25:146
Briggs, R. S. 13:84
Briggs, Ransom 5:10
Briggs, Robert J. 13:11
Briggs, Roswell 1:16
Briggs, S. 14:41
Briggs, S. D. 7:20
Briggs, S. J. 25:146
Briggs, Samuel 20:111
Briggs, Sylvester F. 15:83
Briggs, Thomas 17:17;
  22:21
Briggs, W. 3:29
Briggs, W. H. 3:29;
  16:364
Briggs, W. H. M. 27:22
Briggs, W. J. 26:13
Briggs, W. W. 3:29
Briggs, Walter S. 16:116
Briggs, Weston 12:14
Briggs, William 8:80;
  9:128; 21:198;
  22:291; 26:12; 27:11
Briggs, William H. 22:137
Briggs, William J. 23:183
Briggs, Wilson 3:28;
  26:151
Brighall, Josiah 11:384
Brigham, C. L. 1:115

Brigham, David 3:29
Brigham, George W.
  17:262
Brigham, Ira L. 16:132
Brigham, J. W. 16:23
Brigham, L. C. 19:58
Brigham, L. M. 27:12
Brigham, T. C. 15:364;
  25:18
Bright, A. 8:103
Bright, Abram 21:221
Bright, Adam 3:29
Bright, Alexander 18:214
Bright, Andrew J. 11:135
Bright, Benjamin 18:214
Bright, Bennett 9:170
Bright, C. 22:180
Bright, Daniel W. 7:83
Bright, David 22:448
Bright, E. 3:29
Bright, E. R. 23:312
Bright, Emsley 22:416
Bright, George 19:58
Bright, George N. 11:23
Bright, J. 14:253
Bright, J. W. 16:176
Bright, James 14:144
Bright, John 3:29; 22:67,
  170
Bright, Joseph T. 21:247
Bright, M. 22:291
Bright, M. D. 17:327
Bright, Mason 17:171
Bright, N. 3:29
Bright, Nelson 17:171
Bright, Thomas 8:113;
  19:272
Bright, W. 25:310
Bright, W. C. 1:17
Bright, William 9:76;
  10:42; 19:6; 26:16
Brightbill, Samuel 1:115
Brightenhauger, Frederick
  22:67
Brightill, C. 17:90
Brightman, C. 3:29
Brightman, Ed 27:23
Brightman, Erastus 1:114
Brightman, Josiah 4:12
Brightman, Sylvester 19:6
Brighton, Aaron 21:48
Brighton, Bard 7:118
Brighton, Isaac N. 22:21
Brighton, John 15:185
Brightop, D. 17:294
Brightwell, John 10:90;
  20:214
Brigindine, W. L. 10:104;
  20:214
Brigman, John 22:243
Brigman, Reuben 10:14

Brigum, C. S. 15:185
Brihiner, John W. 8:119
Briker, J. 3:29
Briles, George 24:74
Briles, John W. 10:204
Briles, Samuel 11:258
Briley, Charles 19:58
Briley, E. 22:243
Briley, George W. 22:117
Briley, John 17:276
Briley, Silas W. 8:10;
  18:123
Brill, Benjamin F. 17:76
Brill, C. 3:29
Brill, Charles 24:8
Brill, D. N. 19:233
Brill, Daniel L. 9:170
Brill, H. N. 25:146
Brill, Henry 1:16
Brill, Horatio M. 5:10
Brill, J. 1:116; 21:305
Brill, James P. 22:179
Brill, John 17:76
Brill, Michael 22:117
Brill, Oliver 1:17
Brill, P. A. 1:112
Brill, S. A. 22:179
Brillhat, J. 12:81
Brilton, J. S. 1:112
Brim, J. 18:45
Brimberry, F. 8:61
Brimm, J. 10:147
Brimpton, I. 14:41
Brims, Foster M. 22:447
Brinan, Owen 19:58
Brinckerhoff, Herman C.
  24:36
Brinckman, John 20:16
Brinde, Christ 11:23
Brindle, A. W. 25:17
Brindle, C. 14:250
Brindle, David 25:16
Brindle, J. 24:74
Brindle, Jacob 13:11
Brindle, Joseph 1:114
Brindle, L. W. 15:185
Brindley, Henry 24:176
Brindley, John 8:100;
  24:212
Brindley, John W. 17:459;
  24:156
Brindsmaid, Old 4:64
Brine, Charles 12:63;
  15:63
Brine, Daniel O. 24:213
Brine, Thomas O. 8:103
Brine, William 15:10
Brinegan, H. W. 10:43
Brineley, A. 3:29
Brinell, N. 18:64
Briner, George 18:123

Briner, J. 23:255
Briner, J. W. 17:348
Briner, Jacob 21:221
Briner, James 4:12
Briner, Jesse 22:67
Briner, John 18:303;
　26:92
Briner, L. 13:84
Briney, J. 1:14
Briney, J. L. 12:161
Briney, Joseph 3:29
Bringat, John 27:142
Bringer, Harry 6:29
Bringer, John 22:21
Bringham, Henry D.
　21:305
Bringham, J. 1:109
Bringham, L. E. 14:41
Bringle, Francis M. 22:67
Bringle, George 12:14
Bringle, William N.
　18:214
Bringley, Henry 5:10
Bringley, L. 9:76
Brinhomer, J. 3:29
Brinin, Samuel 23:135
Brining, Jacob J. 24:176
Brink, C. 3:29
Brink, David 1:13
Brink, E. O. 13:77;
　16:176
Brink, Elias 1:18
Brink, F. 3:29; 17:63
Brink, Francis E. 20:111
Brink, George 7:20
Brink, H. 1:112
Brink, Harvey 22:21
Brink, J. L. 17:153
Brink, James 22:417
Brink, John 4:12
Brink, Joseph 16:138
Brink, Nathaniel 19:6
Brink, Norman 15:157
Brink, S. 20:144
Brink, S. H. 15:297;
　16:176
Brink, Samuel H. 16:176
Brink, Taylor 4:12
Brink, Thomas B. 22:179
Brink, Tyler 9:15
Brink, V. 20:5
Brink, W. 22:401
Brink, W. L. 18:464
Brinkenhoff, Martin 22:21
Brinker, Bernard 25:279
Brinker, Clark 10:104;
　20:214
Brinker, George 23:135
Brinker, H. A. 1:109
Brinker, Israel 22:474
Brinker, J. 3:29

Brinker, M. 27:22
Brinkerman, L. 3:29
Brinkey, Morris 3:29
Brinkey, W. L. 3:29
Brinkley, Alexander 7:118
Brinkley, Davis I. 17:49
Brinkley, G. T. 16:176
Brinkley, Isaac 25:146
Brinkley, J. 22:180
Brinkley, L. K. 21:129
Brinkley, Robert 21:146
Brinkman, Adolph 15:4
Brinkman, Augustus
　23:178
Brinkman, Henry 7:47
Brinkman, Jacob 11:285
Brinks, Henry 18:123
Brinland, T. 1:14
Brinn, W. H. 7:74; 25:293
Brinnell, J. 25:146
Brinsley, J. 9:49
Brinstadt, Lewis 26:13
Brinston, James R. 22:67
Brint, John 22:474
Brinth, Edward 18:123
Brinton, George D. 21:65
Brinton, George L. 19:58
Brinton, Isaac 21:193
Brinton, J. 3:29
Brinton, J. W. 3:29
Brinton, M. J. 3:29
Brinur, Andrew 12:94
Brion, Charles 1:16
Brion, J. 6:29
Briot, A. 24:48
Brisbane, William 22:401
Brisbin, Benjamin S.
　10:42
Brisbin, Perry S. 20:214
Brisbine, E. T. 20:214
Brisbine, Edward T. 10:90
Brisby, F. M. 23:303
Brisco, J. A. 1:110
Brisco, Jacob 19:296
Brisco, Levi 26:152
Brisco, Thomas 22:291
Briscoe, Constantine 6:24
Briscoe, John M. 17:278
Briscoe, Michael 19:150
Briscoe, Shad 17:171
Briscoe, William M.
　17:472
Briscol, Joseph 24:58
Briser, C. B. 15:309
Briseve, William M. 27:20
Brish, F. 15:102
Brishaham, J. 15:102
Brisham, William 21:19
Brisher, James I. 12:48
Briska, Nace 6:24
Briskley, H. 3:29

Briskman, P. 9:153
Brisland, Edward 16:364
Brisling, John 16:277
Brison, James 8:10;
　18:123
Brison, Valentine 22:179
Brissell, J. 25:146
Brissell, William 17:17
Brissie, L. 11:298
Brisslon, D. 19:58
Brist, Edward 15:119
Bristah, Thomas S. 21:97
Bristel, Richard B. 22:474
Bristleton, Robert 4:64
Bristley, Conrad 11:114
Bristline, A. M. 11:319
Bristo, H. 26:151
Bristo, Thomas 17:422
Bristol, A. 14:28
Bristol, Alex 18:45
Bristol, Alexander 10:147
Bristol, Benjamin W.
　18:214
Bristol, C. B. 11:25
Bristol, H. A. 17:63
Bristol, J. A. 14:253
Bristol, James 6:15; 18:77
Bristol, John 19:44
Bristol, John D. 11:295
Bristol, L. F. 13:12
Bristol, L. P. 16:23
Bristol, Lawrence F. 13:12
Bristol, N. P. 19:58
Bristol, R. T. 19:150
Bristol, Robert 10:157;
　19:150
Bristoll, George 21:305
Briston, John H. 22:473
Bristow, E. 20:214
Bristow, Ephraim 10:42
Bristow, F. G. 18:409
Bristow, George W.
　10:151, 178
Bristow, Thomas 24:165
Brit, R. R. 26:150
Britanskey, J. 3:29
Britchetts, J. B. 21:305
Britchol, M. 1:110
Brite, M. 26:12
Briten, Zachariah 13:11
Brithuret, William 20:214
Brithwest, William 9:229
Britman, Henry 9:128
Britman, Joseph 21:248
Britman, P. 27:15
Briton, D. H. 21:65
Britry, Alf 27:22
Britt, Albert 11:325
Britt, C. 1:111
Britt, David 10:170;
　19:150

Britt, Emanuel 9:49
Britt, Emray 11:420
Britt, J. 16:277
Britt, James 12:167
Britt, John C. 19:299
Britt, Joseph 21:305
Britt, Osborne 6:27
Britt, Riley 22:243
Britt, T. 17:216
Britt, Thomas 4:12; 24:8
Britt, Thomas H. 17:205
Britt, W. 18:362
Britt, William 9:226;
    20:5; 24:64
Brittain, Andrew 16:23
Brittain, G. A. 17:363
Brittall, John 1:14
Brittan, Whitney 12:14
Brittell, G. W. 23:112
Britten, Edward 27:18
Britten, I. 10:27
Britten, J. 19:299
Brittenham, J. 3:29
Brittian, Daniel 22:67
Brittin, Ryley 10:42
Brittingham, Isaac 20:214
Brittingham, T. B. 11:256
Brittman, Henry 27:17
Britton, --- 14:268;
    15:157; 18:12
Britton, A. R. 3:29
Britton, Adelbert A.
    20:214
Britton, Adlebert 10:104
Britton, Alexander 11:197
Britton, Alfred D. 7:88
Britton, Andrew 13:11
Britton, B. H. 3:29
Britton, C. L. 1:112;
    15:319
Britton, Charles 11:135;
    23:135
Britton, Cullen 22:117
Britton, Daniel A. 7:20
Britton, E. 8:45; 21:19
Britton, Edward 9:128;
    12:67
Britton, Francis M.
    22:180
Britton, G. W. 1:115
Britton, George 10:104;
    20:214
Britton, George F. 10:42
Britton, H. 3:29; 7:20
Britton, Harlan P. 11:399
Britton, Harrison 12:14
Britton, Henry 11:136
Britton, Henry C. 13:11
Britton, Henry T. 17:358
Britton, J. 3:29; 13:84;
    14:5, 144; 17:501

Britton, J. C. 12:147
Britton, J. M. 11:22
Britton, James 7:20;
    14:280, 334
Britton, James F. M.
    22:499
Britton, John 1:115; 22:9
Britton, Lewis 6:23
Britton, Linderman 12:14
Britton, Luther D. 17:76
Britton, M. 7:20
Britton, Robert 11:137
Britton, S. W. 21:19
Britton, Thomas 14:41
Britton, W. H. 4:12
Britton, William F. 25:146
Brittop, Edward 15:30
Britwell, J. W. 22:180
Britz, Joseph 18:303;
    26:93
Britzer, L. B. 3:29
Brizeal, N. H. 9:19
Bro---, H. 19:151
Broach, E. 15:185
Broad, Isaac N. 13:12
Broad, Isaac W. 16:23
Broad, O. 27:23
Broadback, Frederick
    13:12
Broadback, M. 25:146
Broadbeck, Adam 3:31
Broadberot, John 15:63
Broadbrook, George
    12:14
Broadbrook, Rufus 20:214
Broadby, James 3:31
Broades, John W. 10:104;
    20:214
Broadhead, Abel 7:66
Broadhead, David 18:25
Broadhead, J. B. 18:25
Broadhead, Simon D.
    9:116
Broadhead, Simon V.
    27:19
Broadley, John 4:13
Broadrie, M. 17:494
Broadrup, H. 13:84
Broadstone, E. 1:110
Broadstreet, C. B. 3:32
Broadway, --- 16:23
Broadway, A. 5:36;
    25:146
Broadway, Jackson
    22:511
Broadwell, Darwin 1:14
Broadwell, George 5:49
Broadwell, W. 13:12
Broadwright, H. 14:41
Broady, Andrew C.
    22:499

Broan, Frederick 14:144
Broannum, Joseph 21:48
Broat, A. 27:21
Brobeck, J. 23:135
Brober, M. D. 25:17
Brobet, Samuel 10:14
Brobson, Alexander 9:76
Brobst, J. 3:31
Brobst, Simon 12:14
Brocan, Michael 8:80
Brocan, Thomas 6:27
Broccett, William 9:226
Brocdon, S. 23:183
Broce, F. M. 21:65
Broce, William C. 17:49
Brocetard, James 18:77
Brochers, John 27:19
Brochet, W. 18:362
Brochman, D. 15:63
Brochsit, James 22:21
Brochtezend, J. 25:146
Brochus, G. W. 16:288
Brocius, G. W. 12:81
Brock, A. 22:511
Brock, Albert 14:145
Brock, B. 9:76
Brock, C. 3:31
Brock, Caleb A. 10:104;
    20:214
Brock, Calvin 23:135
Brock, Charles 18:25
Brock, Charles H. 4:13
Brock, Elias 21:185
Brock, Freeman 12:63;
    15:10
Brock, George H. 1:20
Brock, Henry 11:325;
    21:94
Brock, Hugh 22:243
Brock, J. 17:246
Brock, J. H. 12:161
Brock, Jesse 17:147
Brock, John 11:395;
    17:76; 22:447;
    24:163
Brock, John M. 16:83
Brock, Josephus 21:65
Brock, Leonard 19:6
Brock, Montery 7:118
Brock, Reese 22:350
Brock, Robert 21:119
Brock, Shirling 11:395
Brock, Strather 21:305
Brock, William 3:31
Brock, William R. 4:13
Brockelbank, L. 1:110
Brocker, J. K. 21:119
Brockers, William K.
    22:243
Brockett, Salem A. 22:115
Brockfhurst, I. 11:138

Brockham, J. W. 16:90
Brockhiler, J. 3:31
Brockleband, John A. 27:22
Brockler, H. 3:32
Brockleston, Hamilton 9:128
Brockleton, Hamilton 27:17
Brockley, Frederick 15:185
Brockman, B. F. 10:104
Brockman, Benjamin S. M. F. 20:214
Brockman, Ewitt 22:460
Brockman, George M. 21:305
Brockman, George W. 17:30
Brockman, H. 24:65
Brockman, Job 17:287
Brockman, William 10:43; 20:214
Brockrhoff, B. 21:119
Brocks, Warren 5:49
Brocksmith, Henry 11:299
Brocksteller, --- 19:287
Brockus, William 17:272
Brockway, A. 27:23
Brockway, C. 3:31
Brockway, Charles 10:43; 20:214
Brockway, E. 2:8
Brockway, Ephraim C. 20:105
Brockway, M. 3:31
Brockway, P. 1:20
Brockway, Samuel 20:91, 95
Brockway, Scott 7:88
Brockway, Simon 21:198
Brockway, Thomas C. 25:332
Brockwell, Thomas 19:58
Broctcher, A. 24:74
Brocton, J. W. 9:108
Brodan, M. 1:111
Broddie, J. 25:146
Brode, J. 14:295; 17:478; 27:20
Brodee, Jacob 9:105
Brodegan, Conrad 20:121
Broden, David C. 9:206
Broden, W. S. 16:364
Broderick, C. 25:17
Broderick, Edward 26:144
Broderick, H. 22:350
Broderick, J. S. 3:31
Broderick, James 22:499
Broderick, John 13:12
Broderick, Michael 12:14

Broderick, Virgil 15:119
Broderick, W. 3:31
Broderick, William 5:10; 25:17
Brodes, Emory 1:114
Brodess, Thomas M. 7:21
Brodie, John 16:83
Brodie, R. 11:237
Brodiers, William L. 13:56
Brodock, John 22:448
Brodrick, Daniel 24:8
Brodwater, Noble 19:6
Brody, Alvin 23:308
Broeman, F. 9:41
Broemmel, Fitz 19:58
Broffman, George 18:290; 26:94
Brofman, George 9:33
Brogan, C. H. 7:88
Brogan, J. M. 3:32
Brogan, John 3:32; 21:305
Brogan, Patrick 18:434
Brogan, William H. 21:305
Brogart, O. P. 21:119
Brogden, Stephen 9:128
Brogdens, Stephen 27:18
Brogg, G. 27:24
Broghill, George 7:88
Broghton, Jonas R. 23:178
Brogle, --- 14:144
Brogle, Lewis 7:55
Broglin, Thomas 19:328
Brogy, William 22:331
Brohan, W. H. 1:113
Brohead, J. Z. 12:161
Brohst, F. 14:41
Broiler, William 27:21
Broiles, Berry 23:135
Broils, Frederick 11:325
Broils, S. 3:223; 17:504
Broils, William 25:279
Brokan, J. M. 9:33
Brokan, Thomas S. 25:279
Brokaw, Abraham 21:221
Brokaw, George E. 25:18
Brokaw, John 23:85
Brokaw, Joshua 22:475
Broke, J. G. 25:146
Brokely, John 23:284
Broken, Henry A. 27:142
Broker, George 8:70
Broker, H. 27:142
Broker, Joseph 24:64
Broker, N. 14:144
Broket, Charles 16:143
Brokett, W. P. 27:142
Brokinizer, F. 3:32
Brollier, J. 27:15

Brollies, W. 19:58
Brollur, J. 9:140
Bromage, D. B. 19:6
Bromaghim, Alexander 15:119, 349
Bromald, J. 27:13
Broman, C. 3:31
Broman, H. 14:145
Bromberg, Exil 21:305
Bromberg, Frederick 20:214
Bromberger, John 2:8; 25:19
Bromeling, Thomas 12:67
Bromer, Adam 21:265
Bromery, John 5:36; 25:146
Bromfield, Edwin 21:250
Bromfield, F. 20:214
Bromfield, Floyd 10:43
Bromfield, John 1:191
Bromlet, William H. 22:21
Bromley, H. 3:32; 27:15
Bromley, Henry 23:60
Bromley, J. 3:32; 14:145
Bromley, John 8:80; 17:30, 94
Bromley, John R. 17:258
Bromley, Joseph 21:65
Bromley, Riley 18:214
Bromley, Thomas 21:221
Brommel, W. 1:116
Brommell, Fritz 12:94
Brommer, Andrew 15:30
Brommer, Harrison 22:447
Bromsteed, G. 3:31
Bromwell, C. 14:5
Bron, Timothy 9:76
Bronagan, M. 3:31
Bronck, Lewis 8:37
Broncon, Thomas 10:104
Brondfit, Andrew B. 22:475
Brondwell, Baldwin 21:305
Bronell, J. G. 7:21
Brong, E. 1:109
Bronhard, J. 20:214
Bronhard, Jonathan 10:43
Bronis, Nathan R. 17:231
Bronner, Martin 7:21
Bronson, Albert S. 11:52
Bronson, Amos J. 22:137
Bronson, Anthony 27:18
Bronson, Christian 4:13
Bronson, David 20:84
Bronson, Edwin O. 11:103

Bronson, Ellis 9:128;
 27:18
Bronson, F. 9:154
Bronson, Franklin 16:17
Bronson, G. M. 10:43;
 20:214
Bronson, George 27:17
Bronson, Henry 21:19
Bronson, Henry W.
 11:325
Bronson, J. 25:146
Bronson, James 5:36
Bronson, Jesse H. 4:13
Bronson, P. 21:19
Bronson, Thomas 20:214
Bronson, W. H. 20:84
Bronson, Will 27:12
Bronson, William W.
 9:170
Bronsonger, John 5:49
Bronswell, William
 11:383
Bront, S. 15:321
Bronton, James 18:303
Bronton, Joseph 9:19;
 26:92
Brontz, A. 1:116
Broo, F. 3:31
Broodrick, Thomas
 11:136
Brook, Burbig 1:14
Brook, Caleb T. 4:13
Brook, Henry V. 16:176
Brook, Louis M. 18:320
Brook, Thomas 11:133;
 13:130
Brook, William 25:147
Brooke, E. 14:41
Brooke, Robert 7:21
Brookelsby, John 22:180
Brooker, Antoine 11:52
Brooker, J. 1:19
Brooker, J. R. 25:147
Brooker, John R. 10:14
Brookerhoff, Washington
 17:448
Brookerhoof, Wash
 24:173
Brookers, J. M. 3:32
Brookers, R. H. 14:41
Brookes, Isaac 25:317
Brookfield, A. 25:147
Brookfield, Alexander
 5:36
Brookfield, B. 25:147
Brookfield, Benjamin
 5:36
Brookfield, J. 25:147
Brookfield, Joseph 5:36
Brookfield, M. 1:93
Brookhart, John 4:13

Brookhart, M. D. 8:61
Brookhart, William 3:31
Brookhill, Alfred 11:410
Brookie, William T. 23:21
Brookings, Crosby R.
 16:77
Brookings, Samuel C.
 16:77
Brookins, B. C. 8:10;
 18:123
Brookins, Thomas 23:135
Brookling, S. M. 26:120
Brookman, C. 23:187
Brookman, Charles C.
 22:67
Brookman, Charles V.
 15:53
Brookman, J. E. 3:31
Brookman, James 21:305
Brookman, Jerome
 18:230; 26:15
Brookman, John 23:240
Brookmeyer, G. W. 3:32
Brookmeyer, S. 16:116
Brooknall, James 16:288
Brookover, George 3:31
Brooks, --- 5:49; 12:169;
 24:109
Brooks, A. 25:147
Brooks, A. J. 14:5
Brooks, A. O. 9:170;
 19:244
Brooks, A. S. 15:185
Brooks, Albert 5:36
Brooks, Alden S. 22:276
Brooks, Alex 24:74
Brooks, Alfred 22:291
Brooks, Alli--- 19:150
Brooks, Allison 10:176
Brooks, Almon 22:21
Brooks, Amos 25:285
Brooks, Amos G. 7:21
Brooks, Andrew 1:17
Brooks, Andrew J. 15:85
Brooks, Ashley 22:331
Brooks, Astrabel 18:275
Brooks, Austin 7:118
Brooks, B. 18:25
Brooks, Benjamin 22:118
Brooks, Boss 16:176
Brooks, C. 25:147
Brooks, Cephas 25:147
Brooks, Chapman 22:448
Brooks, Charles 5:10;
 15:185
Brooks, Clark 9:116;
 27:19
Brooks, D. 13:84
Brooks, D. M. 27:15
Brooks, D. S. 3:31

Brooks, David 8:112;
 9:49; 11:14, 420
Brooks, E. 1:111; 3:31
Brooks, Eben 13:12;
 16:23
Brooks, Edward 9:206;
 10:157
Brooks, Edward N.
 19:150
Brooks, F. S. 14:239, 250
Brooks, Francis 17:313
Brooks, Francis E. 17:209
Brooks, Francis M.
 20:121
Brooks, G. 10:179; 15:85;
 18:172
Brooks, G. H. 7:88; 8:113
Brooks, George 7:88;
 11:115; 12:67;
 13:105; 18:77; 19:6,
 58; 21:210
Brooks, George L. 10:14
Brooks, George S. 18:25
Brooks, George W. 23:61
Brooks, Greenberry
 11:420
Brooks, H. 1:93; 18:25
Brooks, H. A. 25:147
Brooks, H. J. 13:84
Brooks, H. V. 15:289
Brooks, Hardy C. 22:448
Brooks, Henry 9:41, 116;
 19:244; 21:305;
 22:164; 24:36; 27:18
Brooks, Henry A. 5:10
Brooks, Hiram J. 22:21
Brooks, Hollis 19:6
Brooks, Homer 4:13
Brooks, I. 6:30; 14:41
Brooks, Ira H. 22:473
Brooks, Isaiah 8:80
Brooks, J. 1:112; 3:31;
 7:48; 11:409; 14:280;
 16:176; 25:317
Brooks, J. C. 10:179
Brooks, J. D. 1:17
Brooks, J. E. 14:41
Brooks, J. G. 25:147
Brooks, J. J. 21:19
Brooks, J. S. 1:116; 2:8
Brooks, J. T. 18:284;
 26:134
Brooks, J. W. 16:176;
 22:164
Brooks, Jackson 17:108
Brooks, Jacob 13:56;
 16:23
Brooks, James 1:14;
 15:185; 16:176;
 17:108, 128; 24:188

Brooks, James C. 10:104;
20:214
Brooks, James G. 5:10
Brooks, James H. 17:279
Brooks, James P. 4:13
Brooks, Jasper 9:116;
27:18
Brooks, Jasper N. 8:10;
18:123
Brooks, Jesse Y. 22:118
Brooks, Joel L. 22:22
Brooks, John 9:156, 213;
13:62; 19:6, 58;
21:305; 22:331;
23:255
Brooks, John A. 22:243
Brooks, John J. 17:241;
22:447
Brooks, John T. 1:14
Brooks, John W. 12:63;
18:392; 24:35
Brooks, Jonas 15:53
Brooks, Joseph 11:256;
17:434; 24:169
Brooks, Joseph S. 21:114
Brooks, Kelsey H. 15:349
Brooks, Levi 21:48
Brooks, Levi W. 21:305
Brooks, Lewis C. 17:351
Brooks, Lewis M. 16:8
Brooks, Louis M. 9:19
Brooks, Lucien 7:118
Brooks, M. 26:12
Brooks, Martin 14:268
Brooks, Matthew 9:76
Brooks, Morris 11:285
Brooks, Newton G.
22:118
Brooks, Oliver 11:52;
12:14
Brooks, P. 14:235; 19:248
Brooks, Paul 7:118
Brooks, Perry L. 24:91
Brooks, Peter 9:170;
21:305; 22:397, 472
Brooks, Preston 22:243;
26:16
Brooks, R. 13:84
Brooks, Robert H. 22:67
Brooks, Royal A. 10:104;
20:214
Brooks, S. 25:147; 26:13
Brooks, S. T. 3:31; 25:19
Brooks, Samuel 1:113;
7:118; 8:103;
14:145; 21:210, 265
Brooks, Sherod 17:17
Brooks, Silas 5:36
Brooks, Spencer 17:200
Brooks, Stephen 7:118
Brooks, Stephen P. 17:94

Brooks, T. S. 27:24
Brooks, Thomas 4:13;
9:128; 16:176;
17:279, 396; 18:78;
20:214; 21:305;
27:17
Brooks, Thomas J. 8:10;
18:123
Brooks, Thomas M. 4:13
Brooks, Virgil 15:53
Brooks, W. 15:185;
25:147
Brooks, W. B. 6:24
Brooks, W. D. 3:31
Brooks, W. E. 9:213;
21:305
Brooks, W. M. 10:192;
18:172
Brooks, W. R. 19:248
Brooks, William 5:36;
7:118; 15:185;
17:392; 21:265;
23:61; 25:277
Brooks, William A. 9:170;
14:145
Brooks, William H. 12:67;
15:10; 23:240
Brooks, William J. 9:95
Brooks, William L.
21:135
Brooks, Wilson 19:44
Brooks, Zach 23:201
Brookshere, Robert
18:214
Brookshire, James W.
17:49
Broom, D. 1:17
Broom, Samuel S. 22:67
Broom, Thomas J. 22:499
Broombaugh, James 22:67
Broomfield, Charles E.
21:221
Broomfield, E. 21:19
Broomfield, F. 25:147
Broomfield, G. 14:145,
253
Broomfield, M. 20:214
Broomhalt, Sidney 12:63;
15:85
Brooms, Henry 20:16
Broomsteel, S. A. 3:31
Broon, James 1:114
Brooner, George 20:95
Broooks, W. 3:31
Broots, W. 24:36
Brooze, M. 19:58
Broozen, Thomas 10:104
Broozom, Thomas 20:215
Brophay, J. 16:176
Brophey, John F. P.
16:364

Brophy, James 8:10;
18:124
Brophy, Lewis 13:105
Brophy, M. 3:31
Brophy, Mathew 24:48
Brophy, Thomas 24:8
Brophy, William 4:13
Brosan, Thomas 2:8
Brosby, J. 27:31
Brose, John 15:185
Brosey, Samuel 5:10
Brosh, Nicholas P. 11:136
Brosheans, Mathew 8:10
Brosius, John H. 18:188
Brosman, Michael 7:55
Brosom, W. C. 15:185
Bross, C. 18:230; 26:15
Bross, David 21:185
Bross, Edward 20:29
Bross, George 4:13
Bross, James 17:171
Brosser, Henry L. 20:12
Brossesault, M. 3:32
Brossman, T. I. 20:55
Brossney, William 11:180
Brot, D. 15:339; 16:364
Broth, John 24:35
Brothen, F. 20:215
Brother, A. F. 11:237
Brother, Benjamin 8:61;
26:152
Brother, Duffield 7:55
Brothers, A. 25:147
Brothers, Benjamin 25:13
Brothers, D. 3:32
Brothers, Francis 10:43
Brothers, J. 13:129; 21:87
Brothers, J. R. 9:49
Brothers, James M.
22:118
Brothers, John 9:116
Brothers, John W. 25:147
Brothers, Lewis 16:176
Brothers, M. 25:147
Brothers, Stephen 21:185
Brotherton, F. 1:15
Brotherton, Henry 25:278
Brotherton, Hugh 10:25
Brotherton, I. 17:49
Brotherton, John F. 10:94
Brotherton, W. H. 3:32
Brothes, Duffield 14:1
Brotochi, Ad 12:92
Brotschi, A. D. 16:288
Brott, Anthony 3:31
Brott, Freeman K. 17:346
Brott, William 22:137
Brotten, Enoch 18:25
Brotzman, Abner 7:55
Brouchton, William
14:235

Brouck, Lewis 26:151
Broudbeck, Gottleib 24:61
Brough, David 8:103
Brough, J. 9:140
Brough, Leon 6:24
Brougham, Nelson 5:10
Brougher, Manias 18:64
Brougher, Samuel H. 12:14
Broughman, Daniel 21:48
Broughman, N. 25:147
Broughman, W. 11:138
Brought, Charles 3:32
Brought, George 26:151
Brought, Richard W. 24:64
Brought, S. O. 11:14
Broughter, J. H. 18:25
Broughton, D. 3:31
Broughton, H. 3:31
Broughton, Henry 10:14
Broughton, J. H. 15:185
Broughton, James 22:21
Broughton, William 9:242; 13:12
Broullet, E. 25:288
Broun, A. L. 15:63
Broun, Balston 15:63
Broun, D. 1:116
Broun, Edward 15:63
Broun, John J. 19:150
Broun, T. R. 15:63
Brounell, Jasper 12:67
Brouner, J. H. 4:13
Brounland, James 15:64
Brouse, Francis C. 15:185
Brouse, Henry 11:123
Brouse, J. W. 14:145
Broussa, Peter 7:118
Brouyette, Adolph 20:111
Brova, John O. 25:317
Brow, C. W. 1:112
Brow, D. 16:176
Brow, E. J. 9:49
Brow, I. 17:482
Brow, J. 14:295; 21:146; 27:20
Brow, John 14:145
Brow, R. 10:185
Brow, R. L. 9:218; 18:363
Brow, Thomas A. 21:221
Broward, U. A. 27:15
Browd, Aaron 23:270
Browdens, P. 3:31
Browder, Gilbert 22:180
Browder, H. V. 3:31
Browder, Jeremiah L. 22:118
Browder, John 4:65
Browdie, John 19:6
Browdy, Freedom 18:327

Brower, A. J. 14:295; 17:475
Brower, A. L. 19:150
Brower, C. F. 15:103
Brower, Charles 1:16
Brower, E. 16:146
Brower, Ezekiel G. 17:403
Brower, Frederic 11:133
Brower, J. 3:31; 16:266
Brower, L. F. 3:31
Brower, Martin L. 10:104; 20:215
Brower, R. D. 9:244
Brower, Shadrack 1:113
Brower, Thomas 10:104
Brower, William R. 10:104
Browiller, G. 14:267
Browing, John W. 20:16
Browings, Almond L. 13:12
Browleith, Joseph 26:216
Browley, John 14:41
Browlittle, Jacob 9:235
Browman, G. 3:31
Browman, Henry 13:105
Browman, Lafayette 22:180
Browman, Tho. W. 20:215
Brown, --- 8:124; 11:50; 12:94; 15:13; 17:246; 19:300; 22:243; 24:8, 109; 25:147
Brown, A. 3:30, 31; 12:151; 15:30; 21:200; 22:416; 23:85; 24:74; 25:147; 27:16
Brown, A. A. 25:293
Brown, A. B. 12:67; 16:176
Brown, A. C. 1:110, 114; 13:62; 23:262
Brown, A. D. 14:145
Brown, A. E. 8:103
Brown, A. F. 20:215
Brown, A. G. 16:176
Brown, A. H. 9:170; 19:235, 244; 23:135
Brown, A. J. 1:16; 17:18; 27:21
Brown, A. L. 1:113; 25:147
Brown, A. L. M. 24:61
Brown, A. M. 16:176
Brown, A. O. 3:30
Brown, A. P. 25:293
Brown, A. R. 12:161
Brown, A. S. 20:176
Brown, A. S. A. 12:67

Brown, A. T. 3:30; 14:295; 17:475; 21:305; 27:20
Brown, A. W. 14:145; 21:305; 27:13
Brown, Aaron 21:305
Brown, Aaron B. 21:305
Brown, Aaron J. 19:6
Brown, Abiza 15:185
Brown, Abner 21:221
Brown, Abraham 18:230; 24:48; 26:14
Brown, Abraham D. 14:318; 25:279
Brown, Abram 9:128; 27:11
Brown, Adam 9:128; 15:64; 21:265; 27:17
Brown, Adams 14:145
Brown, Adna 20:86
Brown, Adrian V. 5:10
Brown, Albert 8:103; 9:76, 226; 11:51; 16:23; 17:153; 18:363; 21:305; 22:67
Brown, Alex 12:67; 17:70
Brown, Alex. B. 9:116; 27:18
Brown, Alex. C. 17:417
Brown, Alexander 6:15; 7:47; 10:157; 11:198, 256; 12:161; 18:78; 19:151; 21:305; 24:58
Brown, Alexander D. 22:446
Brown, Alfred 7:118; 9:206; 17:171; 21:305
Brown, Alfred E. 1:14
Brown, Allen 7:88; 21:305; 25:147
Brown, Almstead 21:305
Brown, Alonzo 12:14
Brown, Alphonzo 9:15
Brown, Amos 7:21; 11:189; 14:295; 17:482; 24:74; 27:20
Brown, Amos D. 24:36
Brown, Amos G. 22:67
Brown, Anderson 22:291
Brown, Andrew 4:65; 5:36; 9:49; 13:12; 14:145; 15:289; 16:176
Brown, Andrew F. 10:43
Brown, Andrew J. 1:191; 7:21
Brown, Andrew L. 10:43
Brown, Ansel 20:5

Brown, Anthony 9:128; 27:18
Brown, Antoine 15:297
Brown, Archibald D. 17:209
Brown, Archimedeus 11:237
Brown, Armstead 7:88
Brown, Arthur 11:103
Brown, Asa 21:305
Brown, Augustus 3:29; 23:10
Brown, Augustus A. 7:74
Brown, Austin 22:447
Brown, B. 1:113; 5:10; 16:138, 176; 22:291; 25:147
Brown, B. E. 20:144
Brown, B. F. 1:109; 7:66; 11:53; 20:215
Brown, B. M. 3:30
Brown, B. T. 10:43
Brown, B. W. 17:252
Brown, Barnabas 22:137
Brown, Bartlett 8:10; 16:80; 18:124
Brown, Benedict 22:118
Brown, Benjamin 7:77; 9:128; 12:48; 17:409; 21:265; 22:117, 350; 24:87; 25:293; 27:18
Brown, Benjamin A. 7:118
Brown, Benjamin C. 22:22
Brown, Benjamin F. 22:180
Brown, Bowman 22:291
Brown, Bradish B. 7:66
Brown, Brutus 17:171
Brown, Bunell 25:317
Brown, C. 1:20; 3:30, 31; 5:36; 10:154; 14:41; 15:150; 19:58, 151, 289
Brown, C. A. 13:84; 14:5; 18:124
Brown, C. B. 9:170
Brown, C. C. 14:42; 18:466
Brown, C. E. 25:147
Brown, C. F. 23:290
Brown, C. G. 21:19
Brown, C. H. 3:30; 9:76; 17:153; 26:11; 27:14
Brown, C. J. 21:19; 25:147
Brown, C. K. 19:248
Brown, C. L. 7:48; 9:49; 20:91

Brown, C. N. 9:49; 18:230; 25:293; 26:16
Brown, C. O. 8:10
Brown, C. P. 13:105
Brown, C. W. 11:384; 17:358; 20:144
Brown, Caleb S. 7:21
Brown, Calvin 7:88; 9:206
Brown, Calvin W. 11:23
Brown, Charles 1:14, 20; 3:30; 6:15, 23; 7:118; 9:15, 128, 140, 170; 10:157; 11:180; 12:48; 14:321; 15:30, 103; 17:128, 171; 18:78, 230, 270, 303; 19:58, 151, 289; 21:265, 306; 22:291; 23:10, 85, 135; 24:13, 188; 25:18, 147; 26:13, 121, 244; 27:12
Brown, Charles 27:17
Brown, Charles A. 23:61
Brown, Charles B. 2:8
Brown, Charles C. 17:76
Brown, Charles E. 5:10; 17:171
Brown, Charles F. 17:390; 21:65
Brown, Charles H. 9:11; 20:33; 23:61; 24:36
Brown, Charles J. 13:12
Brown, Charles L. 11:90
Brown, Charles M. 8:80; 25:147
Brown, Charles S. 17:151; 23:85
Brown, Charles W. 20:38; 25:147; 26:93
Brown, Charley 11:197
Brown, Chauncey L. 17:241
Brown, Christian A. 26:150
Brown, Christopher 11:380
Brown, Clabourne 7:118
Brown, Clarence 22:118
Brown, Clark H. 24:13
Brown, Clement 16:176; 17:272
Brown, Clifford T. 4:12
Brown, Clinton 17:215
Brown, Colburn 13:12
Brown, Cornelius 8:10; 9:128; 18:124; 27:18
Brown, Cortlan 23:85
Brown, Cullen D. 18:214

Brown, Curley 14:145
Brown, Curtis H. 10:171; 19:151
Brown, Cyrus 13:12; 16:23; 17:429
Brown, D. 1:20; 3:29, 30, 31; 5:49; 7:21; 9:140; 12:85; 14:5; 15:185; 16:176, 288; 18:45, 108; 25:19; 27:16, 142
Brown, D. C. 13:84
Brown, D. L. 15:64
Brown, D. M. 20:135
Brown, D. W. 1:116
Brown, Dallas 6:9
Brown, Danid 6:24
Brown, Daniel 1:191; 13:105; 18:270
Brown, Daniel C. 12:14
Brown, Daniel F. 20:215
Brown, Daniel H. 20:38
Brown, Daniel M. 18:458
Brown, David 2:7; 4:12; 7:55; 9:33; 17:403; 18:290; 21:306; 23:135; 25:147, 268; 26:93
Brown, David B. 16:83
Brown, David F. 8:10
Brown, David J. 8:80
Brown, David W. 9:19
Brown, Dawson M. 22:67
Brown, Delose 21:306
Brown, Dennis 17:171
Brown, Dr. 9:170
Brown, E. 3:30; 11:51, 298; 13:62; 14:41; 17:276; 22:473; 25:147
Brown, E. A. 16:364; 18:363
Brown, E. B. 1:111
Brown, E. C. 1:19
Brown, E. D. 16:23
Brown, E. G. 3:30
Brown, E. H. 1:14; 16:116
Brown, E. J. 16:176
Brown, E. L. 10:104; 20:215
Brown, E. M. 3:29; 18:411
Brown, E. R. 3:30
Brown, E. S. 14:145
Brown, E. S. H. 24:35
Brown, E. T. 13:62; 25:147
Brown, E. W. 3:31; 7:21
Brown, Ed 7:118
Brown, Edmund 24:36

Brown, Edward 1:115; 7:21; 10:43, 104; 20:215; 25:147; 27:142
Brown, Edward G. 8:120
Brown, Edward R. 10:14
Brown, Edwin 22:460
Brown, Edwin A. 9:218
Brown, Edwin N. 15:157
Brown, Elbert 9:129; 16:90; 27:17
Brown, Eli 19:6; 22:447
Brown, Elias A. 8:103
Brown, Elijah 5:36; 12:48; 17:30; 21:306; 22:243
Brown, Elijah B. 21:48
Brown, Elisha 16:176; 20:135; 27:15
Brown, Elisha K. 8:10; 18:124
Brown, Elkanah 9:68
Brown, Ellia A. 16:23
Brown, Ellid A. 13:12
Brown, Emanuel 26:151
Brown, Emmanuel 8:37
Brown, Emmerson 21:306
Brown, Enos 4:12
Brown, Eugene 10:171; 19:151
Brown, Ezekiel 17:49
Brown, F. 5:10; 7:10; 12:121; 14:41; 16:176; 20:215; 25:147
Brown, F. A. 10:14
Brown, F. H. 19:328
Brown, F. M. 7:66; 11:384; 23:21
Brown, F. N. 25:15
Brown, F. S. 9:240
Brown, Ferdinand 5:10
Brown, Forrester 1:114
Brown, Francis 7:118; 10:144; 11:137; 17:147; 19:6, 151; 27:22
Brown, Francis E. 17:346
Brown, Francis M. 20:102; 24:13
Brown, Frank 7:17; 9:129; 27:17
Brown, Franklin 1:115; 18:231; 26:14
Brown, Franklin L. 18:124
Brown, Franklin S. 8:10
Brown, Frantz 24:72
Brown, Fred 18:12, 78
Brown, Frederic 17:63

Brown, Frederick 6:10; 8:10, 113; 13:124; 18:124; 22:117; 24:13
Brown, G. 1:14; 3:30, 31; 9:49; 13:81; 14:41, 253; 16:176; 21:19, 109; 25:147; 27:23
Brown, G. A. 19:248; 25:14, 147
Brown, G. E. 1:112; 3:31
Brown, G. G. 24:75
Brown, G. H. 1:18; 3:30, 31
Brown, G. L. 3:30; 19:235
Brown, G. M. 3:31; 21:306
Brown, G. N. 23:135
Brown, G. R. 25:147
Brown, G. S. 14:41
Brown, G. T. 1:110
Brown, G. W. 7:21; 9:213; 16:266; 21:185, 306
Brown, George 1:19, 192; 3:30, 31; 5:36; 7:88; 8:46; 9:101, 238; 10:94, 157; 12:14, 48; 13:12, 56; 14:41, 145; 15:185, 297; 16:176, 177; 17:63, 415; 19:151, 319; 21:65, 97, 109, 265; 22:118, 291; 24:100, 151; 25:19; 26:217; 27:13
Brown, George A. 4:13; 5:10; 11:23
Brown, George B. 22:118, 137
Brown, George D. 20:111
Brown, George E. 9:33
Brown, George F. 10:43; 20:215
Brown, George H. 9:15; 11:51; 18:108; 20:47
Brown, George L. 1:18; 24:13
Brown, George M. 7:48; 13:12
Brown, George R. 17:30
Brown, George S. 22:67; 25:148
Brown, George W. 4:13; 7:21; 8:10; 10:151, 178; 12:48; 17:30, 391; 18:25, 124; 20:16; 22:180; 23:21, 276; 24:8
Brown, Gilbert 6:24
Brown, Gilman N. 7:88

Brown, Gotlieb 20:34
Brown, Gray D. 17:396
Brown, Green 17:215
Brown, H. 2:8; 3:30, 31; 7:65; 8:70; 9:154; 10:192; 11:137; 14:145; 16:177; 17:435; 18:172, 275; 20:38; 24:176; 25:19; 27:15
Brown, H. A. 24:75
Brown, H. B. 9:101
Brown, H. C. 2:7; 25:13
Brown, H. D. 13:12
Brown, H. E. 16:23; 18:12; 20:215
Brown, H. G. 1:113
Brown, H. H. 3:30; 8:113; 25:148
Brown, H. J. 9:49; 20:215
Brown, H. L. 9:49; 13:105; 16:177
Brown, H. M. 16:177
Brown, H. N. 9:76; 13:105; 26:12
Brown, H. S. 3:30
Brown, H. T. 19:296
Brown, H. V. 25:148
Brown, Harmon 17:205
Brown, Harriet 21:207
Brown, Harrison 1:191; 11:118
Brown, Harrison C. 11:136
Brown, Harry 22:511
Brown, Henry 1:13; 2:8; 3:29; 6:24; 7:88; 8:70; 9:157; 10:43; 12:48; 13:12; 14:314; 16:23; 17:392; 18:12, 25, 214; 19:6, 325; 20:215, 399; 22:180; 23:112; 25:310; 27:22, 143
Brown, Henry C. 18:327
Brown, Henry E. 10:43; 21:135
Brown, Henry F. 23:135
Brown, Henry H. 1:17; 5:10; 8:80
Brown, Henry J. 4:12
Brown, Henry K. 22:507
Brown, Henry L. 8:80
Brown, Henry M. 12:14; 13:12
Brown, Henry O. 22:22
Brown, Herman 4:13
Brown, Hiram P. 10:104; 20:215
Brown, Horace 9:65; 22:161

Brown, Horace R. 17:241
Brown, Horace W. 8:70
Brown, Hudson 23:278
Brown, Hugh 8:121; 22:118, 137
Brown, Hugh S. 22:473
Brown, Hustin 23:312
Brown, Huston 1:113
Brown, I. 14:41; 17:279; 25:148
Brown, I. L. 18:291
Brown, I. N. 21:13
Brown, I. R. 24:13
Brown, Ira 1:20
Brown, Isaac 5:36; 7:118; 8:10; 9:15; 14:41; 17:209; 18:25, 124; 22:291
Brown, Isaac V. G. W. 21:65
Brown, Isaiah 24:75
Brown, Ises 19:280
Brown, Isham T. 7:64
Brown, Isom 22:291
Brown, J. 1:109, 112; 3:29, 30, 31; 9:108, 154, 199; 10:43; 11:123, 298; 12:151; 13:84; 14:41, 145, 295; 15:185, 186, 339; 16:364; 17:90, 478; 18:25, 78, 188; 19:225, 235; 20:144, 215; 22:180, 517; 23:21, 201; 25:17, 148; 26:11; 27:16, 20
Brown, J. A. 14:145, 253; 15:64
Brown, J. B. 1:17; 3:30, 31; 17:298; 20:215
Brown, J. C. 3:30; 9:33, 140; 11:51; 14:41; 15:119; 25:18; 27:16
Brown, J. D. 3:31
Brown, J. E. 8:45; 14:145
Brown, J. F. 7:77; 13:84; 14:5; 25:148, 293
Brown, J. G. 19:235
Brown, J. H. 3:30; 10:43; 12:7; 13:105; 14:41, 314; 20:215; 23:21; 26:16
Brown, J. J. 16:23; 22:499
Brown, J. L. 1:112; 10:32; 14:41; 21:185; 26:93
Brown, J. M. 3:30; 14:41; 16:177; 20:215; 22:518
Brown, J. Q. 9:108
Brown, J. Q. A. 25:293

Brown, J. S. 8:80; 9:140; 10:94; 11:299; 14:145; 20:55; 27:15
Brown, J. T. 3:29; 6:12; 11:339
Brown, J. W. 10:211; 13:62; 14:145; 16:177; 17:30, 258; 20:5, 215; 24:109; 25:17
Brown, Jackson 9:116; 19:151; 23:308; 26:216; 27:19
Brown, Jackson A. 21:48
Brown, Jackson V. 20:5
Brown, Jacob 7:118; 9:41; 17:335; 18:25, 231; 26:14, 120
Brown, Jacob G. 22:22
Brown, Jacob L. 22:9
Brown, Jacob W. 9:76
Brown, James 3:30; 4:13, 64; 5:10, 36; 7:81, 118; 8:37, 45; 9:11, 76; 10:43, 104, 179; 11:14, 197, 222; 12:14, 164; 13:12, 62; 15:164, 186; 16:177, 364; 17:90, 108, 313, 392, 424, 450; 18:25, 303, 440; 19:58; 20:111, 215; 21:117, 210, 221, 306; 22:22
Brown, James 22:67, 173, 291, 499, 517; 24:175, 176; 25:148, 285, 293, 317; 26:92, 151, 210; 27:22
Brown, James A. 4:13; 9:11; 20:21; 21:48; 22:417
Brown, James B. 8:46; 21:135
Brown, James C. 17:460; 24:156
Brown, James D. 5:10
Brown, James E. 14:145; 21:135; 24:8
Brown, James F. 15:11; 17:442; 24:156; 26:152
Brown, James G. 9:170
Brown, James H. 7:62, 66; 21:19; 25:148
Brown, James K. 8:80; 25:17
Brown, James L. 2:7; 21:306

Brown, James M. 17:49, 453; 18:172; 19:6; 21:94; 22:169; 23:85
Brown, James N. 22:473
Brown, James P. 17:30
Brown, James R. 10:210
Brown, James S. 15:333
Brown, James T. 21:221
Brown, James W. 9:11; 17:71; 19:151; 24:182
Brown, Jared 20:21
Brown, Jasper H. 7:21; 21:214
Brown, Jasper M. 19:316
Brown, Jathro 9:76
Brown, Jefferson 1:114; 12:14
Brown, Jefferson H. 22:67
Brown, Jemmie 22:67
Brown, Jeremiah 7:88; 9:140, 170; 21:306; 27:14
Brown, Jerry 25:294
Brown, Jesse 15:103; 21:193; 24:91
Brown, Jessie 18:231; 26:15
Brown, Joab 20:5
Brown, Joel 26:153; 27:23
Brown, Joel Y. 21:65
Brown, John 1:13; 2:8; 3:30, 31; 4:12; 5:10; 6:15, 28; 7:74, 118; 9:41, 76, 108, 129, 140, 157, 170, 199, 206, 229; 10:43, 94, 98, 157; 11:52, 102, 123, 137, 196, 217, 256; 12:14, 56, 58, 86; 13:12, 62, 105; 14:145; 15:85, 103, 186; 16:23, 131, 177
Brown, John 16:288; 17:49, 202, 279; 18:12, 78, 204, 270, 303, 323; 19:151, 280; 20:215, 399; 21:221, 306; 22:22, 161, 165, 232, 417, 473; 23:22, 135; 24:75; 25:19, 148, 287; 26:12, 16, 92, 120; 27:13, 16, 17
Brown, John A. 3:31; 14:321; 20:136; 21:306; 27:12
Brown, John B. 7:88; 17:348
Brown, John C. 1:16; 12:48; 25:285

Brown, John D. 10:43;
20:215; 21:65; 22:22,
67
Brown, John E. 13:12;
19:6
Brown, John G. 8:121;
19:225
Brown, John H. 13:12;
16:23; 17:235, 395,
417; 22:243; 23:61;
25:332
Brown, John J. 19:6
Brown, John L. 13:62;
18:78
Brown, John M. 5:10;
7:88; 10:14; 16:138;
22:180
Brown, John M. M. 24:75
Brown, John N. 22:472
Brown, John P. 7:118
Brown, John S. 6:15;
17:316; 20:121, 215
Brown, John T. 5:36;
22:117
Brown, John V. 17:18;
22:416
Brown, John W. 10:43;
17:30, 76; 21:135;
22:180, 243; 26:120
Brown, John William
10:43
Brown, John Y. 17:18
Brown, Jonathan F. 10:14
Brown, Jordan 8:58;
21:146
Brown, Jos. M. 8:103
Brown, Joseph 7:21, 66,
118; 9:170; 10:154;
11:53; 12:80; 13:56;
19:151, 331; 21:306;
22:161, 416; 25:148
Brown, Joseph B. 20:215;
22:118
Brown, Joseph E. 10:104;
13:12
Brown, Joseph F. 21:19
Brown, Joseph G. 11:237
Brown, Joseph H. 6:7
Brown, Joseph M. 18:108;
19:151
Brown, Joseph R. 11:23
Brown, Joseph T. 12:63;
15:25
Brown, Joseph W. 22:22
Brown, Josephus 10:43
Brown, Joshua 10:14
Brown, Joshua P. 22:115
Brown, Josiah 13:56
Brown, Josiah R. 14:145
Brown, Judg 24:182
Brown, Judge 17:453

Brown, K. N. 14:41
Brown, Keely J. 21:221
Brown, L. 3:30; 13:105;
14:145, 254; 15:349;
16:177; 17:199;
25:148
Brown, L. A. 22:331
Brown, L. F. 1:18
Brown, L. J. 11:22
Brown, L. L. 9:49; 15:103
Brown, L. M. 15:171
Brown, L. P. 15:186;
18:64
Brown, L. T. 13:62;
16:177
Brown, Leland 20:111
Brown, Lemon 8:103
Brown, Leonard 8:10;
10:14; 19:58; 26:149
Brown, Leonard A. J.
23:135
Brown, Lewis 4:64; 5:36;
6:15; 7:118; 15:333;
16:288; 18:78; 21:9;
22:243; 26:152
Brown, Lewis H. 10:147;
18:45
Brown, Lewis P. 13:12
Brown, Loney 7:118
Brown, Louis 19:58
Brown, Luther S. 22:474
Brown, Lyman 11:24
Brown, Lyon S. 9:129;
27:16
Brown, M. 3:30; 10:192;
14:295; 17:469;
27:21
Brown, M. (Mrs.) 18:188
Brown, M. A. 10:94; 20:5
Brown, M. B. 26:216
Brown, M. M. 11:90;
14:41
Brown, Mack H. 11:407
Brown, Madison 22:499
Brown, Mahlon 22:418
Brown, Malcom 4:12
Brown, Marins L. 25:148
Brown, Marion 11:380;
18:456
Brown, Mark C. 22:232
Brown, Martin 7:88;
13:12; 20:185
Brown, Martin L. 22:417
Brown, Martin S. 11:285
Brown, Martin W. 17:49
Brown, Mason 8:37;
9:155; 26:151
Brown, Mather 24:187
Brown, Mathew 8:103;
17:128
Brown, Matthew 17:396

Brown, McKee 22:165
Brown, Merritt 9:33
Brown, Michael 10:157;
19:151; 22:460;
23:135
Brown, Miles S. 21:19
Brown, Miller Jeremiah
18:108
Brown, Milton 7:118
Brown, Milton J. 17:13
Brown, Morton W. 23:15
Brown, Moses 16:177;
17:205
Brown, Moses H. G.
18:214
Brown, Mott 24:61
Brown, N. 14:41; 25:148
Brown, N. D. 14:41
Brown, N. H. 9:235
Brown, N. L. 1:14, 16
Brown, N. S. 22:473
Brown, Napoleon B.
13:12
Brown, Nathan 21:265
Brown, Nelson 22:137
Brown, Nicholas 10:210;
19:151
Brown, Noah 22:180
Brown, O. 3:30; 5:36;
13:84; 25:148
Brown, O. D. 15:186
Brown, O. M. 23:135
Brown, O. P. 21:306
Brown, O. W. 8:70
Brown, Oliver 13:128;
17:267
Brown, Oliver F. 18:108
Brown, Oran B. 18:330
Brown, Orin B. 8:116
Brown, Oscar V. 22:276
Brown, Oscar W. 1:16
Brown, Otis P. 10:43
Brown, Owen 9:226;
18:363; 21:265;
22:401
Brown, P. 1:109; 3:30;
9:170
Brown, Pardon 7:88
Brown, Patrick 11:217;
22:417
Brown, Patrick H. 11:14
Brown, Patton 22:22
Brown, Perry 7:118; 8:70
Brown, Peter 6:10; 7:21,
118; 9:41, 161, 206;
10:104; 11:123;
12:48; 16:177;
17:171; 18:78;
20:215; 22:180;
23:135; 25:148;
26:120

Brown, Peter H. 22:243
Brown, Philip 19:7
Brown, Pierson 24:48
Brown, Primus 10:208
Brown, Quincey 8:46
Brown, R. 14:264, 287;
     18:172, 231; 23:135;
     25:148; 26:15, 16
Brown, R. B. 7:88; 22:22
Brown, R. E. 16:288
Brown, R. M. 18:78
Brown, R. P. C. 11:237
Brown, R. S. 10:185;
     18:172
Brown, Ralph 24:71
Brown, Ransond 25:148
Brown, Reuben 1:115;
     21:306; 23:96;
     25:148
Brown, Richard 4:13;
     22:9; 23:127; 25:148
Brown, Richard F.
     10:157; 19:151
Brown, Richard H.
     10:104; 20:215
Brown, Richard R. 21:97
Brown, Riley B. 12:14
Brown, Robert 1:113;
     8:37; 9:206; 11:123;
     17:30; 18:64;
     20:188; 26:151;
     27:13
Brown, Robert A. 17:30
Brown, Robert C. 18:108
Brown, Robert G. 25:271
Brown, Robert H. 1:15
Brown, Robert K. 22:415
Brown, Robert M. 6:9
Brown, Robert O. 24:13
Brown, Robert P. 22:473
Brown, Rodolphus 25:16
Brown, Ruf. C. 19:151
Brown, Rufus 9:71; 25:16
Brown, Rufus C. 10:171
Brown, Russell 11:325
Brown, S. 2:8; 10:104;
     13:84; 14:41;
     16:177; 20:215;
     21:19; 25:13, 148;
     27:13
Brown, S. E. 21:109
Brown, S. F. 21:306
Brown, S. G. 1:112; 26:93
Brown, S. H. 15:16
Brown, S. J. 25:294
Brown, S. S. 19:325
Brown, S. W. 18:323;
     22:180; 25:18
Brown, Samuel 1:16;
     3:30; 5:36; 7:21;
     9:161; 19:151;

21:265; 22:22, 180;
     23:135; 24:36, 100,
     169
Brown, Samuel G. 9:33;
     18:291; 22:180
Brown, Samuel N. 21:48;
     22:67
Brown, Samuel S. 10:104;
     17:422; 20:215
Brown, Seemon 27:23
Brown, Shadrack 11:22
Brown, Sheldon 4:12
Brown, Sidney 18:351
Brown, Sidney F. 8:80
Brown, Silas 6:23
Brown, Simeon F. 21:306
Brown, Smith 11:257;
     18:124
Brown, Smith P. 11:121
Brown, Solomon 7:21;
     11:394; 24:75
Brown, Soveryn 4:12
Brown, Spencer R. 20:2
Brown, Squire 7:118
Brown, Stephen 9:76,
     129; 14:145; 25:148;
     27:18
Brown, Stephen A. 8:10;
     18:124
Brown, Stephen B.
     10:104; 20:216
Brown, Stephen N. 26:10
Brown, Sylvester L.
     12:58; 16:153
Brown, T. 1:20; 3:29, 30;
     11:186, 297; 13:84;
     14:145; 16:23;
     19:248; 22:243
Brown, T. B. 9:108
Brown, T. E. 9:49; 24:35
Brown, T. I. 14:41
Brown, T. K. 21:306
Brown, T. N. 14:41
Brown, T. W. 14:41
Brown, Theodore 9:140;
     10:43; 13:12; 20:216;
     21:215
Brown, Thomas 1:114;
     4:13; 5:36; 7:118;
     8:103; 9:76, 95, 170,
     206; 10:104; 11:136;
     14:145, 235; 17:171;
     18:25, 78, 231, 303,
     406; 19:7; 20:216;
     22:118, 291, 499;
     23:135; 24:212;
     25:148; 26:14, 93
Brown, Thomas A. 24:75
Brown, Thomas B. 18:231
Brown, Thomas D. 25:16

Brown, Thomas E. 9:170;
     22:22
Brown, Thomas H. 8:45;
     21:97
Brown, Thomas J. 5:10;
     13:12; 15:186;
     20:103; 22:22
Brown, Thomas L. 7:88
Brown, Thomas P. 26:14
Brown, Thomas W. 8:103
Brown, Tilman 5:36
Brown, Timothy 26:11
Brown, V. 11:380
Brown, Volney N. 22:115
Brown, Voories M. 7:48
Brown, W. 1:19; 3:29, 30;
     10:147; 11:298; 12:7;
     14:41, 145; 15:26;
     16:90; 18:25, 45;
     19:58; 20:216;
     21:119, 185; 25:148
Brown, W. A. 4:12;
     21:306; 23:290
Brown, W. B. 14:42;
     18:25
Brown, W. E. 19:151;
     25:148
Brown, W. F. 1:18; 3:30;
     8:80
Brown, W. G. 23:117
Brown, W. H. 1:20; 3:31;
     9:140; 16:177;
     19:294; 20:216;
     21:129; 22:243;
     26:153
Brown, W. I. 23:22
Brown, W. J. 18:420;
     19:7; 20:89, 216
Brown, W. L. 16:364;
     25:148
Brown, W. M. 7:21;
     10:179
Brown, W. P. 4:13
Brown, W. R. 18:45
Brown, W. S. 13:105;
     15:339
Brown, W. T. 14:42
Brown, W. W. 7:118;
     25:19; 26:153
Brown, Walter 7:118;
     20:188
Brown, Walter G. 27:12
Brown, Warren 3:29
Brown, Welkard 8:80
Brown, Wesley A. 18:214
Brown, William 1:14,
     116; 3:30; 5:10; 6:7,
     12, 15; 7:21; 8:10,
     70, 80; 9:11, 49, 100,
     206; 10:14, 43, 104,
     208; 11:117, 133,

185, 198, 236, 299, 325;
12:58, 67; 13:12, 84, 105;
14:145, 280; 15:313, 325,
354; 16:23, 116, 132,
177; 17:18, 30, 76,
358
Brown, William 18:78,
108, 124, 204, 231;
19:7, 58; 20:111,
121, 216; 21:19, 97,
129, 185, 193, 265,
306; 22:137, 180,
291, 401, 473; 23:61,
178, 312; 24:13, 36;
25:148; 26:15, 16;
27:12
Brown, William A. 22:415
Brown, William B.
21:306; 23:292
Brown, William D. 26:11
Brown, William E.
19:151; 24:87
Brown, William F.
17:435; 22:243
Brown, William G. 15:164
Brown, William H. 4:13;
7:63, 88; 9:170;
10:43, 104; 11:24;
13:12; 14:145;
17:279; 20:188, 216;
22:22; 23:292;
24:91; 27:14
Brown, William H. H.
18:303
Brown, William Henry
15:186; 22:474
Brown, William J. 20:34;
22:401; 23:15
Brown, William K.
20:216
Brown, William L. 10:43
Brown, William M. 16:90;
22:243; 24:109
Brown, William R. 10:37;
22:243
Brown, William S. 7:66;
23:119
Brown, William T. 20:45;
24:177
Brown, William V.
22:180
Brown, William W.
21:306
Brown, Willis 5:36;
10:43; 20:216
Brown, Wilson 1:18
Brown, Wyabt 8:37
Brown, Wyatt 26:150
Brown, Young 8:103
Brown, Zachariah J.
21:193

Brownall, Jasper 15:53
Browne, Charles 19:151
Browne, James 22:417
Browne, John F. 11:90
Browne, Lewis 11:325
Browne, W. S. 1:112
Browne, William F. 8:113
Brownell, A. G. 3:31
Brownell, Augustus 13:12
Brownell, Cibel 9:159
Brownell, G. W. 14:145
Brownell, I. 1:18
Brownell, John C. 20:216
Brownell, John W. 16:288
Brownell, Richmond 1:15
Brownell, Robert 11:399
Brownels, B. 21:146
Browner, H. 16:177
Browner, John 3:31
Browner, John E. 16:23
Browner, Johnson 13:12;
16:23
Browner, Leonard 18:124
Browner, R. 25:149
Browner, W. H. 27:14
Browney, I. 5:36
Brownfield, Michael
10:43
Brownfield, R. J. 1:110
Brownfield, R. M. 11:52
Brownfield, Rayson
9:129; 27:17
Brownfield, Z. 14:42
Browning, --- 11:297;
26:244
Browning, A. G. 10:185;
18:172
Browning, Abel W. 11:90
Browning, Albert 10:98
Browning, C. W. 9:49
Browning, Daniel 7:118
Browning, E. 22:416
Browning, E. B. 16:138
Browning, E. C. 14:5
Browning, E. F. 14:42
Browning, E. G. 13:84
Browning, G. W. 17:396
Browning, George C.
10:104; 20:216
Browning, H. A. 1:110
Browning, Hawkins 10:43
Browning, J. 3:31; 9:108;
11:217
Browning, J. J. 11:438
Browning, Jacob 23:22
Browning, James 12:151;
22:9
Browning, John 22:22
Browning, Lewis 22:67
Browning, Marshal 24:13
Browning, O. H. 20:191

Browning, R. 5:36
Browning, Sanford 21:94
Browning, Thomas 3:31
Browning, Walter 17:147
Browning, Wiley 10:43;
20:216
Browning, William 17:76
Brownings, Almond L.
16:23
Brownlee, James 21:147;
22:67
Brownlee, Robert 22:180
Brownley, Edward 19:58
Brownley, John P. 9:76
Brownley, William 17:30
Brownlow, John H.
19:323
Brownlow, Obid J. 23:288
Browns, William 11:223
Brownsaugh, Isaac 13:105
Brownsick, C. 1:114
Brownson, --- 18:392
Brownson, Edgar W. 8:10
Brownson, Edwin 13:62
Brownson, H. O. 9:229;
20:216
Brownson, Henry 20:216
Brownswell, C. 13:84
Brownvill, F. 10:212
Brownwell, G. W. 20:87
Brownwell, Joseph S.
10:43
Brownyard, Edward
23:119
Browre, J. W. 3:32
Brows, L. F. 15:119
Browson, Edgar W.
18:124
Broxmire, Thomas 3:32
Broyce, John 21:306
Broyden, D. C. 3:32
Broyer, J. 3:31
Broyle, T. 21:109
Broyles, George F. 22:243
Broyles, Richard W.
17:442; 24:156
Broyles, Samuel 17:453;
24:182
Broyles, W. 26:92
Broyles, William 9:19;
18:303
Broyson, Frederick 9:76
Bruback, Alexander
21:221
Brubaker, B. P. 3:32
Brubaker, E. 1:112
Brubaker, Emanual
15:186
Brubaker, G. 14:287
Brubaker, J. 14:42
Brubaker, J. M. 11:133

Brubaker, Jacob 19:7
Brubaker, Jeremiah 27:21
Brubaker, John 17:346
Brubaker, Otis 23:135
Brubecker, G. 14:264
Bruce, --- 18:411
Bruce, A. 3:32
Bruce, Aaron 21:307
Bruce, Abraham 15:53
Bruce, Albert 5:10
Bruce, Alfred 17:171
Bruce, Charles 21:250;
    22:416
Bruce, Charles A. 18:392
Bruce, D. 1:93
Bruce, D. R. 16:177
Bruce, Daniel 17:235
Bruce, E. 25:149
Bruce, Elias 8:80
Bruce, G. 19:7; 25:149
Bruce, George 5:36; 9:33
Bruce, George F. 16:23;
    22:415
Bruce, George T. 13:12
Bruce, H. 3:32
Bruce, H. W. 20:144
Bruce, Hiram 17:171
Bruce, J. 6:15; 18:78
Bruce, J. B. 3:32
Bruce, J. E. 1:18
Bruce, J. F. 11:90
Bruce, J. W. 3:32; 9:49;
    13:84
Bruce, Jacob 23:22
Bruce, Jacob W. 17:128;
    24:188
Bruce, Jerry 17:171
Bruce, John 3:32; 8:46;
    22:180
Bruce, John C. 12:55
Bruce, John H. 18:420
Bruce, Jonas C. 7:88
Bruce, Joseph S. 1:19
Bruce, Michael 1:113
Bruce, Nelson D. 17:258
Bruce, Peter 17:455;
    21:307; 23:201
Bruce, Robert 14:42;
    18:303; 26:91
Bruce, S. M. 12:151
Bruce, Sanford 25:149
Bruce, Theodore L. 10:90
Bruce, V. 1:96
Bruce, W. H. 13:62; 19:58
Bruce, W. J. 14:5
Bruce, Wilford H. 22:415
Bruce, William 4:13;
    11:137
Bruce, William G. 10:43
Bruce, William H. 20:121
Bruce, William W. 22:67

Brucer, Job 13:105
Bruch, George 21:115
Bruchner, Gustave 9:116
Bruckett, Ben. F. 9:76
Brudenwold, Jacob
    11:135
Bruedley, William H.
    9:229
Bruen, E. 25:15
Bruen, John 13:105
Bruen, L. B. 1:111
Bruer, James 19:151
Bruett, Samuel 27:22
Brufel, Levi H. 11:135
Bruff, B. 26:151
Bruff, Carrington 9:129;
    27:17
Brug, --- 14:42
Bruga, Frank 17:73
Bruin, J. J. 14:42
Brukins, C. 25:149
Brum, Wilkard 18:204
Brum, William 20:216
Brumage, Allen E. 15:85
Brumaghin, F. 3:32
Bruman, H. 3:32
Bruman, William 14:42
Brumback, W. A. 26:121
Brumbarger, William
    23:61
Brumbey, George 3:32
Brumbough, J. 1:16
Brumby, Thomas 1:19
Brumel, Z. C. T. 21:207
Brumelle, Louis 24:63
Brumeman, Abner 7:55
Brumeyard, Charles
    17:502
Brumfield, Charles 21:19
Brumfield, I. F. 15:186
Brumfield, John W.
    11:137
Bruminger, Henry 8:10
Bruminster, Charles 10:43
Brumler, J. 25:14
Brumley, Charles W.
    22:416
Brumley, W. T. 12:151
Brummage, John 9:33
Brummagin, A. J. 25:149
Brummel, W. G. 10:179
Brummell, C. 14:42
Brummell, Fritz 15:358
Brummell, John 5:36
Brummell, William
    17:235
Brummer, John 18:204
Brummer, Uriah 11:23
Brummett, B. 3:32
Brumming, Rudolph 6:8;
    18:102

Brumwelt, A. D. 17:504
Brumwelt, H. D. 3:223
Brun, James 21:163
Brun, Richard 9:49
Brunage, James 12:14
Brunagin, Andrew J. 5:10
Brunaller, Charles 24:91
Brunamar, Joseph 5:10
Bruncage, Isaac 8:103
Brunce, J. H. 15:13
Brunck, Frank C. 25:268
Brund, W. 13:105
Brundace, Levi 15:16
Brundage, James 20:38
Brundage, L. B. 16:23
Brundage, Levi B. 13:12
Brundage, Wesley 13:12
Brundege, Levi E. 21:65
Brundehurt, William
    18:124
Brunderberg, James 13:12
Brundge, John 8:10
Brundy, Joseph P. 22:448
Brune, John 12:63
Brunell, E. J. 13:128
Bruner, Albert 16:90
Bruner, B. 14:295; 17:477
Bruner, Berry 26:151
Bruner, George 11:52
Bruner, George S. 9:95
Bruner, Henry 16:23;
    24:36
Bruner, Henry D. 23:61
Bruner, James 10:105;
    11:384; 20:216
Bruner, John 11:51; 13:12
Bruner, John D. 11:53
Bruner, John L. 23:135
Bruner, Samuel 17:171
Bruner, Samuel T. 21:19
Bruner, William 19:248
Brunes, C. 14:145
Brunes, James 14:280
Brunett, Henry 19:296
Brunette, Sanford 9:76
Brunfield, Thomas 22:291
Brungham, Truman 21:65
Brunig, B. 3:32
Bruning, C. 3:32
Bruning, J. 23:135
Brunk, C. F. 16:11
Brunk, Romulus 9:199;
    19:280
Brunkley, Charles 10:176
Brunkley, Peter 12:48
Brunkly, Charles 19:151
Brunn, John M. 20:121
Brunnamer, L. 19:58
Brunne, John B. 22:180
Brunnel, W. 18:172
Brunneman, L. 15:328

Brunner, Bruno 1:113
Brunner, Jacob 4:13;
19:300
Brunner, James 24:75
Brunner, John 21:265
Brunner, John H. 17:272
Brunner, Matthew 23:187
Brunner, R. M. 20:144
Brunnett, Francis M.
24:36
Brunnon, Louis 9:76
Brunnor, Nathaniel
18:124
Bruno, --- 15:30
Bruno, Edgar 17:262
Brunridge, A. 26:153
Bruns, Hamilton 18:275
Bruns, I. 17:49
Brunskill, J. 1:20
Brunson, A. 12:98;
15:347, 366
Brunson, Byron C. 17:287
Brunson, Eli 15:90
Brunson, Eugene H.
22:460
Brunson, G. W. 22:180
Brunson, Isaac 10:105
Brunson, James G. 24:61
Brunson, James H. 22:417
Brunson, Otis E. 21:185
Brunson, Robert D. 26:11
Brunson, Smith A. 22:170
Brunson, Stephen 17:453;
24:185
Brunson, W. A. 26:121
Brunson, W. F. 15:30
Brunson, William 4:13
Brunt, Frederick 1:115
Brunt, James 26:12
Brunt, Stephen 18:456
Brunt, William H. 22:417
Brunton, L. F. 10:105;
20:216
Brurn, John R. D. 8:46
Brusa, Hector 21:307
Bruse, David R. 10:153
Brush, C. W. 17:439;
24:151
Brush, Drury 17:323
Brush, Henry 26:217
Brush, James 9:108
Brush, John 9:235; 26:216
Brush, John S. 10:43;
20:216
Brush, Joseph 10:43
Brush, R. 7:48
Brush, S. F. 25:149
Brush, William 8:103
Brushell, George H. 9:203
Brusher, Theodore 17:13
Brusk, William 14:145

Brusle, J. 21:19
Bruson, Andrew 18:124
Bruss, Joseph 10:43
Brussa, Peter 21:307
Brussett, W. P. 21:307
Brust, A. 23:22
Brust, J. 3:32
Bruster, John F. 9:129
Bruster, William 23:276
Brutche, E. 3:32
Bruten, Calvin 23:305
Bruthers, F. 21:19
Bruton, H. M. 20:216
Bruton, Hamilton 9:129
Bruwell, Isaac 10:157
Bruza, Mataza 25:294
Bruzer, Martin 7:77
Bry, William H. 23:61
Bryan, --- 11:297
Bryan, A. 27:24
Bryan, A. A. 8:103
Bryan, A. E. 10:14
Bryan, Adolphus 12:98;
15:366
Bryan, Albert C. 12:14
Bryan, Benjamin 12:14
Bryan, D. 23:22
Bryan, D. L. 25:310
Bryan, E. 1:20
Bryan, E. E. 11:137
Bryan, G. H. 17:108
Bryan, G. W. 4:13
Bryan, George 9:140;
10:43; 17:231;
20:216
Bryan, George G. 7:88
Bryan, Gilbert 9:49
Bryan, Guy 21:9
Bryan, H. C. 11:138
Bryan, H. R. 14:277;
23:178
Bryan, Hallot 21:48
Bryan, Isaac 15:186
Bryan, J. 25:317
Bryan, J. W. 13:79
Bryan, James 20:216
Bryan, John 1:15; 6:30;
7:88; 23:105; 25:317
Bryan, John J. 13:12;
16:23
Bryan, John O. 7:21
Bryan, Joseph 10:43
Bryan, Joshua E. 10:158
Bryan, Josiah 18:231;
26:13
Bryan, L. 3:32
Bryan, Lewis 16:178
Bryan, Luke W. 7:55
Bryan, Mathew 16:90
Bryan, Moses M. 11:103
Bryan, Orville 8:113

Bryan, P. 3:32
Bryan, Peter O. 24:165
Bryan, Philip 6:24
Bryan, R. 3:32
Bryan, Richard 8:103
Bryan, Robert C. 27:17
Bryan, Spencer Y. 18:214
Bryan, Thomas 11:256;
26:216
Bryan, Thomas W. 18:468
Bryan, W. W. 26:134
Bryan, William 3:32;
9:19; 10:105; 16:90;
20:216
Bryan, William F. 11:137
Bryan, William W. 18:284
Bryand, J. J. 7:88
Bryans, Edward 10:105;
20:216
Bryant, A. 9:154
Bryant, A. E. 8:10; 18:124
Bryant, A. J. 5:10; 25:149
Bryant, A. S. 1:17
Bryant, Adolphus 15:347
Bryant, Albert S. 14:146
Bryant, Amos 11:257
Bryant, Archy L. 23:22
Bryant, B. 22:243
Bryant, Benjamin 7:118;
20:121
Bryant, Benjamin F. 23:61
Bryant, Bernhardt 26:217
Bryant, Buffalo 6:20
Bryant, C. 12:86; 14:280;
16:288
Bryant, C. A. 14:146
Bryant, C. C. 14:42
Bryant, C. F. 3:32
Bryant, Charles 9:129;
20:216; 27:17
Bryant, Charles H. 8:113
Bryant, D. 3:32
Bryant, D. H. 1:112
Bryant, D. Scott 13:12
Bryant, Daniel 21:307;
22:447
Bryant, Daniel B. 23:243
Bryant, Daniel W. 15:16
Bryant, E. 16:90
Bryant, Edward 8:10;
9:206; 15:186;
21:265; 26:149
Bryant, Ellenhaht 16:288
Bryant, G. A. 14:5
Bryant, G. P. 25:294
Bryant, G. W. 14:42;
18:426
Bryant, Gainton 10:43
Bryant, Ganton 20:216
Bryant, Gardner 1:114

Bryant, George 7:79;
　　14:146; 27:13
Bryant, George W. 17:76
Bryant, H. 3:32
Bryant, Henry 1:192
Bryant, Isaac 5:10
Bryant, J. 15:53; 16:177;
　　22:243, 331; 25:149
Bryant, J. A. 13:84
Bryant, J. C. 19:7
Bryant, J. F. 14:146
Bryant, J. S. 11:89
Bryant, J. W. 17:147;
　　27:12
Bryant, James 9:218;
　　10:105; 11:90;
　　15:171; 18:363
Bryant, James A. 3:32
Bryant, Jesse 17:90, 147
Bryant, Joel 15:329; 19:58
Bryant, John 17:453;
　　21:307; 22:243, 331;
　　24:182
Bryant, John H. 22:118
Bryant, John M. 18:188
Bryant, John P. 20:111
Bryant, John S. 11:103
Bryant, Joseph 18:231;
　　26:15
Bryant, Joshua 13:105
Bryant, L. 2:8; 25:20
Bryant, Leroy 18:12
Bryant, Lewis 18:64
Bryant, M. 16:177
Bryant, M. M. 19:285
Bryant, Moses 17:267
Bryant, Nelson W. 21:19
Bryant, P. 1:18; 11:257
Bryant, P. H. 17:504
Bryant, P. R. 9:140
Bryant, Pascal G. 21:199
Bryant, Peter 24:187
Bryant, R. 15:6, 339;
　　16:364; 22:331, 523
Bryant, R. M. 25:149
Bryant, R. R. 27:14
Bryant, Richmond 17:171
Bryant, Robert 17:49,
　　171; 22:243
Bryant, Robert S. 22:22
Bryant, Rosco L. 14:146
Bryant, S. J. 1:19
Bryant, Samuel 21:129;
　　22:331; 25:149
Bryant, Silas 20:106
Bryant, Simons 17:49
Bryant, Spencer A. 21:250
Bryant, Stephen 9:129;
　　27:18
Bryant, T. 14:42
Bryant, Thomas 9:238

Bryant, W. 25:149
Bryant, W. A. 3:32
Bryant, W. C. 3:32
Bryant, W. P. 17:307
Bryant, W. T. 9:170;
　　19:235
Bryant, Washington
　　17:267
Bryant, William 5:10;
　　9:95; 12:48; 18:231;
　　23:267; 26:15
Bryant, William E. 22:511
Bryant, William W. 22:22
Bryant, Winston 13:127
Bryar, Moses 11:198
Bryarts, J. 14:5
Bryber, Lewis 27:21
Bryburn, Caleb 18:204
Bryce, Andrew J. 7:55
Bryce, John 22:416
Bryden, W. 25:288
Bryden, William 18:108
Brydon, E. D. 1:116
Bryent, O. 22:350
Bryer, Henry 7:21; 19:7
Bryer, Joseph Q. 7:14
Bryer, L. 14:42
Bryer, Robert T. 21:221
Bryler, J. 7:21
Bryman, William 8:10
Bryne, R. 22:350
Bryner, T. J. 15:262
Bryngeldsen, Asbjorn
　　21:251
Bryning, George 17:49
Bryon, C. 12:164
Bryscon, Francis 9:108
Brysell, James 8:113
Bryslin, Josiah 17:246
Bryson, Andrew 10:105;
　　20:216
Bryson, David 10:105;
　　20:217
Bryson, Henry I. 9:9
Bryson, J. 3:32; 14:277;
　　15:64; 23:183
Bryson, John 13:105
Bryson, Samuel 20:185
Bryson, William 22:276
Bryson, William H. 4:13
Bryte, Cyrus C. 7:56
Buad, Lyman 19:58
Buayer, Samuel 22:417
Bub, George 15:63
Bubb, Isaac 23:10
Bubb, John W. 8:80
Bubb, R. 11:321
Bubbles, Joseph 20:84
Bubby, M. C. 21:307
Buber, J. 1:110
Bubier, Frank 5:10

Bubier, George 12:121;
　　15:119
Bubiling, J. 14:42
Buble, Charles E. 11:180
Buble, L. J. 15:186
Bubler, J. W. 3:32
Bubold, C. 18:78
Bubolty, F. 25:15
Bubolz, William 19:343
Bubs, H. 3:32
Bucanon, C. L. 15:186
Bucans, St. Alvin 18:78
Buccaud, St. Alvin 6:12
Buceley, George 20:144
Buch, Silas 19:59
Buch, William E. 12:14
Buchalter, O. W. 9:68
Buchan, Charles 1:15
Buchan, William 11:22
Buchanan, A. 1:109;
　　23:22
Buchanan, Aaron 17:128;
　　24:189
Buchanan, Albert L.
　　10:158
Buchanan, Bartholomew
　　8:80
Buchanan, C. A. 18:12
Buchanan, C. C. 14:146,
　　254
Buchanan, D. 24:13;
　　25:274
Buchanan, Daniel 13:105
Buchanan, Eli 17:165
Buchanan, G. A. 25:317
Buchanan, George 12:14;
　　18:392; 21:48;
　　22:291
Buchanan, George A.
　　23:135
Buchanan, H. 8:46
Buchanan, Harrison
　　18:214
Buchanan, Harry 18:303;
　　26:93
Buchanan, Henry 9:19;
　　19:328; 22:291
Buchanan, J. 12:80;
　　25:149
Buchanan, J. A. 20:144
Buchanan, Jackson 4:13
Buchanan, James 1:16;
　　12:63; 20:217
Buchanan, James T. 5:10
Buchanan, John 7:118;
　　10:43; 21:307; 24:48
Buchanan, John W.
　　16:116
Buchanan, Jonah M. 7:88
Buchanan, Joseph 11:420;
　　22:22, 416

Buchanan, L. D. 11:136
Buchanan, Leartus 22:291
Buchanan, Lewis 21:265
Buchanan, Lucius 23:135
Buchanan, Matthew
    17:502
Buchanan, Michael 8:126
Buchanan, Peter 21:210
Buchanan, Pl'n't 15:6
Buchanan, Pleasant 12:67
Buchanan, R. 14:42;
    19:59
Buchanan, Robert 20:103
Buchanan, S. 16:177;
    22:180
Buchanan, Sandy 18:231;
    26:14
Buchanan, T. S. 1:113
Buchanan, Thiopolis
    11:103
Buchanan, Thomas
    15:186
Buchanan, Thomas M.
    17:417
Buchanan, W. 11:297
Buchanan, W. B. 19:7
Buchanan, W. R. 18:231;
    26:14
Buchanan, W. W. 21:19
Buchanan, William 7:118;
    17:502; 21:265;
    22:180, 232, 518
Buchanan, William E.
    10:105; 20:217
Buchanan, William W.
    22:22
Buchannan, Henry 22:165
Buchannan, J. 10:43
Buchannan, John 19:59
Buchannon, S. 3:32
Buchanon, J. 3:32
Buchanon, John 20:217
Buchanon, W. 23:201
Buchart, George 7:88
Buched, Jacob 8:10
Bucher, George 17:76;
    26:91
Bucher, Henry 12:67
Bucher, J. 23:261
Bucher, J. A. 9:160;
    14:327
Bucher, Jacob 21:19
Buchin, Fridrig 23:22
Buchle, Martin 1:115
Buchlin, Charles A. 12:14
Buchlin, John 22:165
Buchman, Adam 11:137
Buchman, Ferdinand
    22:277
Buchman, John 19:151

Bucholley, William
    11:331
Buchson, Emery W. 23:22
Buck, --- 1:16; 3:32
Buck, Artemus 18:231;
    26:13
Buck, B. F. 3:32; 11:298;
    12:121; 15:119
Buck, B. T. 3:32
Buck, C. 15:186
Buck, C. C. 1:16
Buck, C. E. 1:114
Buck, Charles 14:146;
    21:65; 25:149
Buck, Charles E. 20:106
Buck, D. 12:151
Buck, D. C. 3:32
Buck, David A. 8:80
Buck, David H. 22:22
Buck, E. 1:110; 14:42
Buck, E. D. 18:460
Buck, Eben R. 10:158;
    19:151
Buck, F. M. 1:19
Buck, Francis M. 8:10;
    26:149
Buck, George 24:90
Buck, George W. 17:262
Buck, Gregerous 14:146
Buck, Gustave 9:101
Buck, H. 3:32; 18:45
Buck, H. A. 11:22
Buck, Henry 4:13
Buck, Hiram 1:114;
    22:180
Buck, J. 1:16
Buck, J. H. 15:325
Buck, J. W. 9:170; 15:186
Buck, James 11:14;
    17:171; 19:59; 22:68
Buck, John 1:115; 7:88,
    118; 9:19, 170;
    11:257; 17:445
Buck, John A. 8:61; 23:85
Buck, John B. 7:21
Buck, John C. 6:30;
    25:317
Buck, John L. 23:119
Buck, Joseph 11:23, 135;
    20:121
Buck, Joseph W. 7:88
Buck, L. 15:21
Buck, M. 13:84
Buck, M. H. 4:13
Buck, Marion 17:252
Buck, Martin 10:7; 22:291
Buck, Mathew 9:71
Buck, Michael 11:14
Buck, Miles 8:99
Buck, N. F. 25:19
Buck, Noah 20:5

Buck, O. H. 18:46
Buck, Osborne 7:67
Buck, Peter 20:217; 23:61
Buck, R. 25:294
Buck, S. A. 13:124
Buck, Samuel 8:103
Buck, Scott 9:206
Buck, Silas 12:94
Buck, Simeon 21:307
Buck, Thomas 16:23
Buck, W. H. 2:7; 15:354;
    25:14
Buck, Walter 17:98; 19:7
Buck, William 1:15;
    9:160; 14:327;
    16:177; 27:13, 23
Buck, Willis H. 22:68
Buckam, J. 3:33
Buckaman, J. 25:149
Buckanan, James 9:19
Buckanon, J. A. 11:257
Buckard, Macks 4:13
Buckas, James 11:198
Buckbee, B. F. 23:135
Buckbier, Joseph 3:33
Buckecker, Isaac 24:75
Buckeley, P. 25:149
Bucker, Alex 20:217
Bucker, Charles 7:118
Bucker, George W. 7:88
Bucker, John 1:13
Bucket, Charles 14:146
Bucket, Robert 21:19
Bucketmeyer, John 24:65
Buckew, J. 1:93
Buckey, Elijah 17:13
Buckey, J. E. 1:112
Buckfenk, Jacob 1:115
Buckford, C. 7:21
Buckford, E. 16:266
Buckford, William H.
    21:307
Buckhalter, James S.
    10:105; 20:217
Buckhanan, Reason 22:68
Buckhannah, W. 3:32
Buckhannon, G. 15:186
Buckhard, Charles 8:10
Buckhardt, --- 14:287
Buckhart, E. 3:32
Buckhart, Frederick A.
    10:43
Buckhart, H. 18:64
Buckhart, Henrich 26:150
Buckhart, J. 1:111
Buckhart, Jacob 7:56
Buckhart, Joseph 24:13
Buckhaus, J. 26:217
Buckhauser, August 16:23
Buckhoet, P. 12:164
Buckholey, Henry 17:257

Buckholly, --- 18:334
Buckholly, William 18:334
Buckholt, P. 26:152
Buckingham, C. 15:119
Buckingham, Charles 10:179; 18:172
Buckingham, Charles W. 11:135
Buckingham, G. 9:108
Buckingham, Hamilton 23:85
Buckingham, John E. 7:9
Buckingham, Lewis 22:416
Buckingham, M. 16:90
Buckingham, M. S. 13:105
Buckingham, R. K. 18:424
Buckingham, S. M. 25:149
Buckingham, Sed 5:10
Buckingham, William J. 22:415
Buckingham, Z. 15:186
Buckingham, Z. P. 22:243
Buckland, A. A. 11:257
Buckland, Chester 9:19
Buckland, James 20:217
Buckland, S. W. 14:146
Buckland, Thomas 6:27
Buckle, J. R. 13:84
Bucklebank, Joseph 1:18
Buckler, Conrad 11:136
Buckler, Nicholas 16:23
Buckler, Robert 11:90
Buckler, W. G. 23:22
Buckles, Elisha 11:23
Buckles, Francis 22:68
Buckles, John 20:217
Buckles, Joseph 9:19
Buckles, Lynus 11:420
Buckles, S. J. 27:21
Bucklew, --- 1:18
Bucklew, Wesley 16:23
Buckley, --- 17:247; 26:204
Buckley, A. M. 3:32
Buckley, Abner 26:120
Buckley, B. 14:295; 17:469; 27:21
Buckley, Charles 17:171; 22:9
Buckley, Charles H. 21:307
Buckley, D. 9:49
Buckley, David 24:107
Buckley, Dennis 23:119
Buckley, E. G. 4:13
Buckley, F. 14:42

Buckley, George 3:32; 9:170; 19:269
Buckley, George W. 21:307
Buckley, Hiram 9:164
Buckley, J. 1:109; 15:293; 16:177; 25:149
Buckley, J. B. 1:18
Buckley, J. G. 3:32
Buckley, J. W. 11:217
Buckley, James 8:70; 12:14; 26:152
Buckley, James W. 23:112
Buckley, Jeremiah 19:7
Buckley, Jesse 25:149
Buckley, Joe 5:49
Buckley, Joel 9:108
Buckley, John 3:32; 16:116; 23:10; 27:22
Buckley, John J. 3:32
Buckley, Lorenzo 12:151
Buckley, Michael 8:80; 18:204
Buckley, Miles 11:123
Buckley, Moses 7:48
Buckley, Patrick 15:277; 21:9; 25:149
Buckley, Philip 5:10
Buckley, Samuel L. 17:421
Buckley, T. 13:84
Buckley, W. 3:32
Buckley, William 11:90
Bucklin, G. A. 1:116
Bucklin, William 13:12
Buckloe, Alfred 18:271
Buckman, --- 3:33
Buckman, George 6:28
Buckman, H. 1:109
Buckman, Henry 9:229
Buckman, J. A. 22:180
Buckman, Jonathan 1:15
Buckman, Joseph M. 23:97
Buckman, Thomas 17:171
Buckmaster, David 23:135
Buckmaster, F. 3:33
Buckmaster, F. M. 18:392
Buckmaster, George W. 10:43; 20:217
Buckmaster, J. 3:33
Buckmaster, John 20:16
Buckmaster, Levi 10:94
Buckmaster, Nicholas 26:13
Buckmaster, Samuel 11:52
Buckmaster, Synire 8:80
Buckmaster, Thomas 11:410
Buckminister, H. A. 9:140

Buckminster, A. 25:17
Buckminster, H. A. 27:16
Bucknell, Ellis 21:203
Buckner, Adam 3:33
Buckner, Alfred 11:198
Buckner, Alfred M. 26:120
Buckner, C. 11:83
Buckner, C. J. 21:307
Buckner, Christian 9:95
Buckner, Ed 17:267
Buckner, Frank 18:406
Buckner, George 3:33; 9:164; 25:317
Buckner, Gustave 27:18
Buckner, Henry 18:231; 21:307; 26:16
Buckner, J. T. 23:270
Buckner, James 3:33
Buckner, Jeremiah 22:118
Buckner, N. 14:42
Buckner, R. G. 17:404
Buckner, Robert 21:307
Buckner, Samuel M. 13:12
Buckner, Thomas 11:197
Buckner, W. 14:42; 22:180
Buckner, Wesley 13:12
Buckner, William 11:198; 22:291
Buckner, William E. 17:18
Buckney, David C. 21:265
Bucknoy, William 18:204
Buckoly, Anthony 11:236
Bucks, John 11:257
Bucks, O. 15:364
Bucks, Samuel J. 22:401
Bucks, Willis 21:266
Buckshot, John 7:56
Buckson, Charles 5:36
Buckstave, Benjamin 9:199
Bucktooth, Ira 25:13
Buckwalter, R. 15:119
Buckway, Mason 21:307
Buckwith, John P. 9:76
Buckworth, A. 25:317
Buckworth, William 19:285
Bucy, Joseph 24:189
Bucy, N. 22:180
Bud, J. 19:59
Budd, --- 25:13
Budd, Benjamin 23:22
Budd, Caleb 22:181
Budd, Charles H. 10:210
Budd, D. 11:256
Budd, George W. 11:230
Budd, Harvey M. 4:13

Budd, Henry 10:9
Budd, Henry C. 20:182
Budd, Jackson 10:43;
 20:217
Budd, John 4:13
Budd, John T. 18:214
Budd, Martin G. 17:76
Budd, S. 12:94; 15:358
Budd, Samuel 10:43;
 20:217
Budde, John G. 21:251
Budden, John 21:307
Buddery, William 14:42
Buddy, John L. 9:170;
 19:277
Buddy, R. S. 13:62
Budenback, Max 21:9
Budew, William 14:146
Budge, James E. 19:7
Budgeman, Oscar 25:13
Budger, Nathan 9:108
Budges, Frank 19:7
Budges, Jackson 9:49
Budk, Charles 13:56
Budley, Hope 21:266
Budsall, S. 23:22
Budson, John 3:33
Bueche, Alfred 23:301
Buek, James 19:7
Buel, Austin G. 22:138
Buel, Edward E. 10:105
Buel, J. 3:33
Buel, John 15:103; 18:124
Bueler, Morgan H. 26:94
Bueler, Morgan Honer
 18:303
Buell, David 8:103
Buell, Edward E. 20:217
Buell, Frank M. 11:285;
 22:137
Buell, G. W. 3:33
Buell, Henry 8:10; 18:124
Buell, John 8:10
Buell, John H. 16:177
Buell, W. M. 7:88
Buer, Henry 24:36
Buerick, James 1:14
Buerkle, Joseph 21:97
Buerly, Francis 17:63
Buesick, Frederick 23:112
Bufert, S. 11:321
Buff, --- 11:50
Buff, Henry 24:13
Buff, John 14:42, 132;
 17:409; 22:118
Buffam, Benjamin 8:113
Buffam, L. 14:146
Buffett, T. A. 25:149
Buffin, Chesley 17:279
Buffin, John 14:42
Buffin, Matt 21:307

Buffington, David 10:43;
 20:217
Buffington, O. W. 16:364
Buffington, Thomas 9:96
Buffington, William 17:76
Buffinton, B. 3:33
Buffinton, Jacob 17:76
Buffman, C. 9:76; 26:12
Buffman, H. C. 3:33
Buffom, Alonzo M. 20:47
Buffon, E. W. 7:56
Bufford, Solomon 21:266
Buffum, George R. 15:94
Buffum, J. 18:64
Buffum, L. 3:33
Bufington, W. S. 11:24
Bufleb, Charles 1:18
Bufler, Edward 15:13
Buford, John 11:198
Buford, T. 17:128; 24:187
Bufort, Charles 21:266
Bufort, Henry 11:197
Bugance, James A. 21:129
Bugas, Thomas 17:18
Bugbee, C. 7:48
Bugbee, Henry F. 12:67;
 15:30
Bugbee, John C. 10:43;
 20:217
Bugbee, Leander 10:158
Bugbee, W. 1:110
Bugbee, W. H. 15:339
Bugbee, W. W. 1:112
Bugbee, William H.
 16:364
Bugbee, William L.
 19:328
Bugbee, William R.
 17:209
Bugbee, Wilson 14:42,
 146
Bugby, Alvin 20:217
Bugby, Lanson L. 24:91
Bugby, Nehemiah 11:23
Bugenberg, F. R. 20:5
Bugg, J. M. 26:152
Bugg, Noah H. 16:23
Bugg, Noah K. 13:12
Buggard, G. W. 11:237
Bugge, P. 17:109
Bugger, Ebenezer 7:88
Buggins, George 16:90
Buggle, John 9:41
Bugglen, John H. 19:151
Buggs, Fred 13:105
Buggs, J. M. 8:70
Buggy, Dennis 12:14
Bugh, Alfred 10:105;
 20:217
Bughanan, D. H. 11:236
Bughly, William 3:33

Bugion, Stephen 4:13
Bugle, H. 19:248
Bugler, Abel 19:7
Bugler, John 12:67; 18:25
Bugler, Peter 7:88
Bugley, Joseph 20:217
Bugmeyer, A. 10:27
Bugo, Robert 21:247
Bugul, Samuel 8:80
Buhard, J. 12:86
Buhler, H. 10:90
Buhner, John H. 11:53
Buhol, T. B. 11:230
Buhrer, Louis 25:17
Buiche, John 10:204
Buick, J. 1:116
Buil, James P. 11:134
Buirtch, E. 15:186
Buise, H. H. 16:177
Buitt, T. J. 21:20
Buk, --- 15:30
Buke, William 18:188
Buker, John 17:128
Bukonski, Emil 7:81
Bukowski, Em 25:294
Bulard, J. 18:231; 26:15
Buldac, L. 3:33
Bulden, L. 1:116
Bulen, A. N. 8:61
Bulen, J. W. 3:33
Bulen, Morgan L. 10:105;
 20:217
Buler, Fred 20:5
Buler, Henry 8:80
Buler, John 8:80; 11:321
Buler, John W. 7:48
Buley, John T. 8:80
Bulfin, John 14:42
Bulfinch, Byron 12:67
Bulger, James 10:144;
 19:151
Bulgers, James 13:12
Bulhman, William 19:300
Bulinger, J. F. 1:18
Bulingham, W. N. 21:109
Bulkely, E. A. 3:33
Bulkley, F. O. 9:140
Bulkman, William 10:27
Bulkun, James 9:158
Bull, A. A. 17:358
Bull, A. W. 26:152
Bull, Alonzo 27:18
Bull, Charles H. 24:91
Bull, E. L. 9:140; 27:14
Bull, E. W. 25:18
Bull, Eiosego 9:116
Bull, Elisha 7:88
Bull, Frank 3:33
Bull, Frank M. 16:143
Bull, J. C. 1:115
Bull, J. T. 24:91

Bull, Jarrard 24:13
Bull, Jesse J. 22:243
Bull, John H. 22:181
Bull, Morgan 21:210
Bull, N. 14:42
Bull, Randolph G. 2:7
Bull, Stephen C. 14:146
Bull, W. C. 20:55
Bull, W. T. 25:149
Bull, William 17:171
Bull, William J. 5:10
Bulla, Levi 16:135
Bulla, W. H. 11:51
Bullam, William 21:307
Bullard, Albert 15:293;
  18:125
Bullard, Arthur M. 19:151
Bullard, Asa 23:119
Bullard, J. A. 15:117
Bullard, J. S. 11:375
Bullard, James M. 17:18
Bullard, John 13:12
Bullard, Joseph 14:263
Bullard, Moses 22:291
Bullard, N. N. 18:303
Bullard, Reuben 18:392;
  22:277
Bullard, Thomas 7:118;
  22:118
Bullard, W. N. 26:91
Bullard, William T. 16:83
Bullen, Henry 15:16
Bullen, Samuel W. 14:42
Buller, W. J. 3:33
Bullerdick, Henry 23:112
Bullet, C. 9:199
Bullet, Sandy 17:171
Bullett, I. 10:204
Bullett, Mose 24:189
Bullett, William 17:455;
  24:189
Bulletts, J. 16:177
Bullfinch, Byron 15:53
Bullied, James 3:33
Bullier, William 3:33
Bullin, Charles B. 19:151
Bullin, G. 9:68
Bullin, S. W. 14:43
Bullinger, James 10:94
Bullinger, John 14:146
Bullington, J. W. 23:22
Bullion, James M. 11:420
Bullis, Amos 14:146
Bullis, Calvin 18:78
Bullis, Charles H. 20:217
Bullis, D. W. 16:23
Bullis, David 14:43
Bullis, Lewis 10:14
Bullis, Wilbur I. 15:186
Bullitt, Mose 17:455

Bullman, Frederick
  16:288
Bullman, H. S. 23:22
Bullman, John 20:111
Bullman, L. 1:19
Bullock, Amos 22:22
Bullock, C. 24:75
Bullock, Chancey 16:277
Bullock, D. W. 24:58
Bullock, David 22:68
Bullock, David S. 9:116;
  27:18
Bullock, E. 3:33
Bullock, F. 27:13
Bullock, George 9:41;
  26:120
Bullock, George W. 4:13
Bullock, H. 1:20
Bullock, H. B. 8:46
Bullock, Illman 26:13
Bullock, J. 25:149
Bullock, J. M. 1:20
Bullock, J. S. 27:14
Bullock, James W. 7:21
Bullock, John S. 9:140
Bullock, Joseph 17:454;
  24:185
Bullock, L. 16:177
Bullock, Ralph 12:14
Bullock, T. 25:149
Bullock, W. H. 3:33
Bullock, William A.
  10:105; 20:217
Bullock, William Z.
  19:151
Bullon, Dennis 22:68
Bullones, Jesus 6:20
Bullow, --- 21:307
Bulls, Charles H. 10:43
Bullsen, E. F. 3:33
Bullsgos, --- 8:125
Bulluck, A. 15:186
Bully, Charles 9:7
Bully, John 11:137
Bullymore, R. 16:11
Bulman, L. 1:16
Bulock, Tillman 18:231
Bulski, Carl 15:103
Bultham, Henry 10:14
Bulton, C. 18:46
Bulvert, Henry 26:11
Buly, John 17:205
Buly, Thomas 17:205
Buly, William 17:76
Buman, Noah 20:217
Bumbas, David C. 19:151
Bumberry, J. B. 21:307
Bumble, Henry 18:125
Bumcroft, J. S. 7:88
Bumer, Alex. 8:80
Bumer, Vinyard 22:243

Bumford, James 19:59
Bumganer, M. 1:110
Bumgard, John S. 12:14
Bumgarden, M. 1:116
Bumgardener, B. 14:5
Bumgarder, Ephraim
  22:68
Bumgarder, M. 19:235
Bumgardin, H. 14:43
Bumgardner, --- 3:33
Bumgardner, A. 20:144
Bumgardner, B. 13:84
Bumgardner, C. F. 15:186
Bumgardner, D. 16:116
Bumgardner, Joel 3:33
Bumgardner, John H.
  21:221
Bumgardner, W. 13:84
Buminger, Leonhardt
  21:97
Bumley, Christian 9:76
Bumm, Albert 13:12
Bummel, E. 16:266
Bummels, Charles 9:170
Bummer, Andrew 19:59
Bummer, Henry 13:12
Bummer, James 22:291
Bummerman, Herman
  5:10
Bummert, John 9:105
Bummet, David 8:80
Bumner, Joseph 20:217
Bump, Allen 1:14
Bump, Belois 21:307
Bump, George M. 23:85
Bump, Henry 13:12
Bump, Highland 12:14
Bump, J. 1:112; 11:292
Bump, James H. 16:151
Bump, L. 9:49
Bump, Samuel 20:191
Bumpers, David C.
  10:158
Bumps, John S. 25:16
Bumpton, George 25:310
Bumpus, B. F. 9:108
Bumpus, E. L. 11:99
Bumpus, J. W. 18:231;
  26:15
Bumpus, M. 1:109
Bums, George W. 7:56
Bums, Peter 9:170
Bumsley, James M. 22:22
Bumsted, Joseph 21:117
Bumsteller, Henry 9:19
Bumsworth, Christian
  11:53
Bumyan, Henry 15:335
Bun, David 14:5
Bunacker, Charles 14:146
Bunberry, John 11:102

Bunbey, M. J. 3:33
Bunce, Albert 7:88
Bunce, Clarence 13:56
Bunce, Francis M. 22:138
Bunce, Henry 21:307
Bunce, Hiram A. 21:65
Bunce, Orland 16:177
Bunce, Samuel 8:103
Bunce, Theodore L.
    20:217
Bunch, A. 14:133
Bunch, Anderson 17:94
Bunch, Andrew 10:147;
    18:46
Bunch, D. A. 19:7
Bunch, F. 14:280
Bunch, George 21:266
Bunch, Greenberry 22:243
Bunch, Harvey 21:147
Bunch, Henry 21:266
Bunch, J. 20:136
Bunch, J. F. 25:149
Bunch, James 11:186
Bunch, Jesse 10:105;
    20:217
Bunch, Samuel 14:43
Bunch, T. J. 18:363
Bunch, William 17:165
Bunderle, Robert 22:470
Bundick, C. A. 27:24
Bundiger, Jacob 17:76
Bunding, L. 16:177
Bundock, J. 14:25
Bundrek, J. 15:363
Bundren, William 20:217
Bundry, Henry 9:206
Bundstein, Augustus
    12:14
Bundy, Alex. 8:80
Bundy, C. 1:110
Bundy, C. T. 9:239
Bundy, Christian 26:10
Bundy, E. M. 20:89
Bundy, Edgar 22:474
Bundy, Freedom 8:80
Bundy, George W. 11:236
Bundy, H. 21:20
Bundy, Harden 20:217
Bundy, Hurden 10:105
Bundy, J. L. 17:70
Bundy, Jacob 11:137
Bundy, James 10:105;
    20:217
Bundy, John 18:125
Bundy, Joseph 3:33
Bundy, Joseph F. 22:329
Bundy, L. 15:297
Bundy, Nelson 17:424;
    24:175
Bundy, Orin 9:240
Bundy, Reuben 4:13

Bundy, William 1:112
Bundy, William F. 22:401
Bunell, James 14:146
Buner, Joseph 19:7
Buner, Thomas P. 24:48
Buner, William H. 21:65
Bunerantz, B. 13:124
Bunfill, Hamilton 10:43
Bunge, Isaac 11:51
Bungle, Fred 11:22
Bunham, D. 24:14
Bunham, L. D. 19:269
Bunham, Linsley 10:208
Bunie, C. W. 18:205
Bunion, J. O. 12:86;
    16:288
Bunis, Martin 17:202
Bunk, M. 19:248
Bunk, Matthias 9:170
Bunke, Samuel W. 20:177
Bunker, A. D. 16:177
Bunker, C. 3:33
Bunker, C. C. 9:41;
    26:121
Bunker, C. L. 1:111
Bunker, Charles H. 22:9
Bunker, Francis A. 4:13
Bunker, George H. 13:12
Bunker, J. 1:93
Bunker, J. F. 3:33
Bunker, J. U. 25:149
Bunker, James S. 18:46
Bunker, Jesse 11:299
Bunker, John 11:237
Bunker, Joseph 26:150
Bunker, L. 1:19
Bunker, M. 1:116
Bunker, Nathaniel 14:146
Bunker, R. 12:81; 16:288
Bunker, R. B. 3:33
Bunker, S. A. 3:33
Bunker, William 1:113
Bunker, William M.
    12:151
Bunkley, T. 21:147
Bunks, Henry 8:10
Bunks, Jackson 22:292
Bunley, W. 21:307
Bunmerman, C. 5:36
Bunn, B. W. 21:20
Bunn, Francis M. 24:91
Bunn, J. R. 1:111
Bunn, James 21:97
Bunn, John 16:117
Bunn, Louis 22:475
Bunn, Thomas 19:151
Bunn, William W. 22:474
Bunnara, A. 27:15
Bunnel, P. E. 15:186
Bunnell, C. D. 18:406
Bunnell, C. R. 19:151

Bunnell, Chelson 1:114
Bunnell, George 21:266
Bunnell, J. 21:307
Bunnell, James M. 10:14
Bunnell, John H. 22:401
Bunner, Lafayette 18:392
Bunner, Solomon 18:392
Bunner, Valman 18:392
Bunniss, Leroy 22:243
Bunnon, Christopher
    20:106
Bunsford, William J.
    11:122
Bunson, John J. 11:52
Bunt, Alexander 18:25
Bunt, H. William 22:475
Buntain, C. A. 10:43
Buntain, Henry C. 17:417
Buntain, Joseph 22:401
Buntan, N. G. 22:181
Bunter, William 8:70
Buntin, Alexander 22:511
Buntin, George A. 22:417
Buntin, Joseph W. 22:165
Buntin, Robert 21:20
Buntin, Sylvanus 21:307
Buntin, Thomas 11:197
Bunting, Henry 17:171
Bunting, J. 13:124
Bunting, James H. 21:65
Bunting, Joseph M.
    13:105
Bunting, William 17:161
Bunton, C. A. 20:217
Bunton, Henry 9:170;
    19:248
Bunus, H. L. 7:56
Bunyan, John W. 11:137
Bunzam, John 10:102
Buoy, John C. 19:151
Buoy, W. 1:112
Buoyson, James 22:292
Bupp, L. 3:33
Bups, D. 17:364
Bur, John 19:280
Bura, William 12:48
Burahan, E. F. 25:14
Burbage, Thomas 22:22
Burbaker, Henry H.
    21:215
Burbank, A. J. 21:251
Burbank, Andrew A. 7:21
Burbank, C. H. 25:20
Burbank, Charles H. 2:7;
    25:19
Burbank, DeWitt C. 15:90
Burbank, John 7:88; 21:48
Burbank, O. 10:153;
    19:151
Burbanks, J. 3:34
Burbanks, W. L. 19:7

Burbeck, William W. 22:22
Burbee, C. N. 9:140
Burber, George W. 4:13
Burbic, W. 1:116
Burbinger, C. W. 18:291
Burbride, Charles 18:124
Burbridge, --- 11:137
Burbridge, Charles 8:10
Burbridge, Franklin 11:24
Burbridge, H. W. 7:119
Burbridge, Henry 7:119
Burbridge, John 22:292
Burbridge, Robert 23:22
Burby, Robert M. 11:136
Burch, Alfred 17:390
Burch, Andrew 11:257
Burch, Benona 23:105
Burch, Charles 17:191; 21:307
Burch, Charles J. 22:68
Burch, Colburn 24:109
Burch, Crawford K. 17:49
Burch, D. 25:15
Burch, Dewitt C. 20:191
Burch, Ebenezer 22:181
Burch, H. 16:90; 21:307
Burch, Henry 11:23
Burch, J. 25:149
Burch, J. G. 14:146
Burch, James 10:94; 15:103
Burch, James A. 13:105
Burch, James L. 22:118
Burch, James M. 22:232
Burch, Jesse 10:105; 17:30; 20:217
Burch, John 11:275; 15:186; 19:287; 21:307
Burch, L. S. 11:257
Burch, Michael A. 24:36
Burch, Mitchell 21:193
Burch, Nathan 16:23
Burch, Nathaniel E. 17:287
Burch, S. 15:186
Burch, Thomas 13:13
Burch, Thomas W. 18:231; 26:15
Burch, W. 3:35
Burch, W. H. 21:307
Burch, William 8:61
Burch, William H. 10:105; 20:217
Burcham, George 20:217
Burcham, J. 3:34
Burcham, John 7:21
Burcham, Levi 8:81
Burcham, Smith G. 22:418

Burcham, W. J. 19:151
Burchans, Jesse 20:121
Burchard, A. P. 19:59
Burchard, Hiram A. 21:65
Burchardt, Zach 23:95
Burchel, John 25:15
Burchell, Theodore 4:13
Burcher, Green 9:206
Burcherd, C. 3:34
Burchett, Francis M. 17:258
Burchett, George 7:48
Burchetts, J. 7:48
Burchfield, Charles 11:298; 17:147
Burchfield, J. H. 7:48
Burchfield, James 9:229; 20:217
Burchfield, Jesse 1:15
Burchfield, M. 21:307
Burchfield, Michael 17:354
Burchfield, Samuel 6:24
Burchfield, William H. 21:221
Burchill, G. 12:151
Burck, George M. 20:217
Burcker, John 16:177
Burckinger, Lewis 4:13
Burcol, George 10:105; 20:217
Burd, Adam 5:10
Burd, George D. 5:10
Burd, Jacob H. 22:181
Burd, W. H. 3:34
Burdage, L. E. 8:46
Burdan, H. 1:20
Burdan, Samuel O. 21:127
Burddeck, L. 3:34
Burdeck, --- 3:34
Burdeck, C. 3:34
Burdell, John 17:49
Burdell, Lansey 8:81
Burdell, Lot 10:204
Burden, David 12:15
Burden, H. 24:14
Burden, Henry 4:65
Burden, Thomas 12:48
Burder, D. M. 14:43
Burdess, James 23:281
Burdeth, Lewis H. 17:425
Burdeti, W. C. 21:65
Burdett, Aaron 13:13
Burdett, Charles F. 12:15
Burdett, George 22:181
Burdett, H. F. 15:358; 19:59
Burdett, Henry C. 22:244
Burdett, I. 17:171
Burdett, James L. 22:416

Burdett, John 11:90; 17:291
Burdett, Lewis H. 24:176
Burdett, Noah R. 22:244
Burdette, G. W. 11:275
Burdge, L. 3:35
Burdhampt, A. 12:81
Burdhaupt, A. 16:288
Burdick, A. 3:34
Burdick, Albert 15:64
Burdick, Alfred A. 1:17
Burdick, Augustus A. 20:21
Burdick, Benjamin 4:13
Burdick, Benjamin F. 15:80
Burdick, Bruce R. 23:85
Burdick, C. A. 14:239, 251
Burdick, Charles 10:14
Burdick, Charles E. 22:461
Burdick, G. A. 13:13
Burdick, G. W. C. 16:23
Burdick, George D. 23:85
Burdick, George J. 10:94
Burdick, H. A. 20:217
Burdick, H. W. 22:277
Burdick, Harrison A. 10:44
Burdick, Horace 7:88
Burdick, James M. 22:22
Burdick, Joel G. 13:13
Burdick, Merritt 25:16
Burdick, R. 15:164
Burdick, Reuben 10:90; 20:217
Burdick, S. 14:251
Burdick, Stephen H. 15:80
Burdick, Theo 3:34
Burdick, W. 11:24
Burdick, W. C. 1:17
Burdick, W. H. 9:76
Burdick, Ward 1:115
Burdickson, Daniel 4:65
Burdict, Henry 1:114
Burdin, Calvin H. 16:77
Burdine, Doc 21:307
Burdine, Elijah 17:205
Burdine, M. V. 14:287; 23:22
Burdine, Robert 22:244
Burdine, Samuel P. 22:244
Burdis, G. 3:34
Burdis, George W. 21:307
Burditt, --- 12:94
Burditt, F. 24:187
Burditt, George W. 22:244
Burditt, James F. 27:22

Burdman, L. G. 22:331
Burdock, J. 12:121
Burdock, J. S. 27:12
Burdock, L. 3:34
Burdock, Nelson 24:61
Burdock, W. H. 26:11
Burdon, Jerry 22:292
Burdrick, Albert 12:67
Burdsell, Peter 1:13
Burdy, E. L. 4:13
Burdy, J. 16:266
Burean, Francis 14:43
Bureles, G. D. 1:109
Burer, Noah 8:103
Burfield, C. 3:35
Burfit, Norris 12:48
Burford, W. 25:149
Burfort, Jeremiah 10:25
Burg, Charles 9:234
Burg, Henry 21:20
Burg, Hiram 21:307
Burg, J. 21:109
Burg, John 21:20
Burg, Michael K. 21:90
Burg, Peter 11:21
Burgan, James A. 11:384
Burgan, L. 3:34
Burgan, Michael 18:124
Burgdoef, Christian
    22:170
Burgdorf, Frank 10:44
Burge, Adam 1:15
Burge, Joseph 17:30
Burge, Richard 17:326
Burge, Solon 17:348
Burge, Wilkinson 22:118
Burgees, David R. 17:276
Burgen, Charles 7:56
Burgen, J. 9:226
Burgen, Michael 8:10
Burgener, Frederick 15:30
Burgeon, J. 18:363
Burger, Amos 22:138
Burger, B. 22:9
Burger, Charles 15:30
Burger, Edward T. 12:67;
    15:30
Burger, F. 17:90
Burger, John 1:14
Burger, S. O. 13:105
Burger, William 1:113;
    23:260
Burger, William H. 12:15
Burges, Henry 19:59
Burges, Samuel 18:231
Burgeson, William 22:277
Burgess, --- 13:128;
    15:103
Burgess, A. 1:17; 14:43
Burgess, A. C. 21:307
Burgess, A. L. 19:225

Burgess, Alfred 17:30
Burgess, Andrew J. 5:10
Burgess, Archy 7:119
Burgess, Austin 20:217
Burgess, Auston 10:44
Burgess, B. B. 8:46; 21:48
Burgess, C. H. 15:336;
    16:177
Burgess, C. L. 18:64
Burgess, Charles B.
    16:138
Burgess, Charles H.
    19:151
Burgess, D. 1:20
Burgess, Daniel 9:96
Burgess, Daniel O. 22:418
Burgess, David 13:105
Burgess, E. D. 7:67
Burgess, E. S. 9:170
Burgess, F. M. 11:90
Burgess, George 14:43;
    22:460
Burgess, George W.
    19:340; 22:181
Burgess, H. 3:34; 21:185
Burgess, Henry 15:325
Burgess, Horace 16:90
Burgess, I. F. 14:43
Burgess, J. 14:146
Burgess, J. W. B. 1:115
Burgess, Jacob 10:44
Burgess, Jacob S. 20:217
Burgess, James K. 14:334
Burgess, Jeremiah 17:210
Burgess, John 11:407;
    12:67; 15:64; 20:95;
    22:68
Burgess, John A. 1:14
Burgess, Jordan 11:180
Burgess, Joseph 20:217;
    21:307
Burgess, Levi 11:103;
    13:106
Burgess, N. F. 2:7; 25:19
Burgess, Nelson 7:79;
    25:294
Burgess, S. 18:231; 26:13
Burgess, Samuel 26:13
Burgess, W. C. 19:59
Burgess, W. T. 3:34
Burgess, Weston 1:13
Burgess, William 11:51;
    13:13
Burgess, William A.
    23:103
Burgess, William H. 24:65
Burgess, William O. 12:15
Burget, H. 1:16
Burget, Isaac 7:119
Burget, J. 1:116
Burget, Samuel H. 21:221

Burgett, Alfred 22:118
Burgett, G. R. 26:121
Burgett, Lewis F. 13:56
Burgett, M. 21:119
Burgett, W. F. 11:135
Burghardt, Moritz 20:217
Burghardt, Morritz 10:44
Burghart, Charles L.
    10:105; 20:218
Burgher, Jacob 13:134;
    19:346
Burgher, William C.
    22:448
Burghouse, J. 13:105
Burgi, Joseph 22:165
Burgie, Gotleit 13:13
Burgie, Gotlieb 16:23
Burgin, A. 3:35
Burgin, Hugh 23:119
Burgla, B. 14:43
Burgman, Andrew 21:307
Burgmier, Antoine 7:56
Burgness, William 23:308
Burgoine, Thomas J.
    12:151
Burgon, James R. 10:204
Burgoyne, C. 14:146
Burgoyne, Thomas 9:105
Burgun, M. 20:34
Burgus, John R. 7:48
Burham, C. L. 20:218
Burham, D. 1:18
Burham, E. P. 22:401
Burham, John 18:124
Burham, W. 3:34
Burhanee, Henry C. 20:29
Burhardt, Andrew J. 11:53
Burhong, L. 17:265
Burhous, George 15:103
Burhull, George 21:307
Burier, F. 25:149
Burill, --- 25:19
Buris, Abram 6:12
Burk, A. 18:46; 19:248
Burk, Alexander 16:135
Burk, C. 3:34; 11:298
Burk, E. F. 13:84
Burk, Edward 26:16
Burk, Elias 14:5
Burk, Francis M. 18:124
Burk, G. W. 8:46; 13:106
Burk, George M. 10:105
Burk, George W. 17:30
Burk, Gilbert 10:105
Burk, Gilman 23:187
Burk, Henry 9:49; 11:394;
    16:90
Burk, Isaac 10:105;
    20:218; 21:221;
    22:118

Burk, J. 9:108; 14:146; 17:18
Burk, J. D. 3:34
Burk, James 3:34; 7:21; 12:81; 16:288, 365; 25:317
Burk, James H. 22:416
Burk, James W. 8:81
Burk, John 7:21; 9:76; 11:197; 17:18, 49, 73; 19:7; 21:307, 308; 25:274
Burk, John L. 26:120
Burk, John R. 10:43; 22:244
Burk, Jonas 22:499
Burk, Joseph 2:7; 15:53, 95; 21:308; 25:16
Burk, Louis H. 24:165
Burk, Lyman A. 20:188
Burk, Michael 10:14, 105; 12:15; 20:218
Burk, Nelson 23:308
Burk, O. 3:34
Burk, P. 10:105; 14:146
Burk, Perry 9:108
Burk, Peter 12:67; 17:76
Burk, Philip 15:187
Burk, R. C. 9:49
Burk, Richard 15:187
Burk, Robert 20:182
Burk, Sam 24:188
Burk, Samuel 17:129; 24:165
Burk, T. 1:109
Burk, Thomas 1:13, 14; 9:49, 108; 16:365
Burk, Thomas C. 14:146
Burk, Thomas J. 17:202
Burk, Thomas M. 19:7
Burk, Tobias 23:97
Burk, W. A. 8:46; 11:438; 21:20
Burk, Walter 12:63
Burk, Wesley 11:24
Burk, William 10:43
Burk, William A. 17:76
Burk, William B. 21:119
Burk, William G. 8:81
Burka, Thomas 16:364
Burkart, George 22:68
Burke, --- 2:8; 25:19
Burke, Alexander 9:170
Burke, C. D. 16:177
Burke, Coleman S. 11:51
Burke, D. S. 23:22
Burke, E. D. 19:7
Burke, E. F. 14:5
Burke, E. T. 25:149
Burke, Edmund 17:202; 22:499

Burke, Edward 18:78
Burke, F. M. 17:364
Burke, G. 27:12
Burke, G. F. 9:108
Burke, G. M. 14:146
Burke, George 12:7; 27:142
Burke, Gilbert 20:218
Burke, H. J. 22:292
Burke, Henry 11:197; 20:144
Burke, J. 1:109; 3:34; 15:309; 19:59; 25:19
Burke, J. C. 1:19
Burke, J. H. 3:34
Burke, J. T. 23:22
Burke, James 1:114; 6:30; 11:279; 15:334; 18:231; 25:268; 26:13
Burke, James H. 21:308
Burke, James N. 7:88
Burke, John 1:114, 115; 3:34, 223; 4:13; 7:21; 15:164; 16:83, 288; 17:504; 18:303; 21:135; 25:149; 26:91
Burke, John A. 18:392
Burke, John C. 8:10; 18:124
Burke, John F. 22:161
Burke, John G. 7:8
Burke, John J. 17:49; 22:447
Burke, John R. 20:218
Burke, John T. 11:374
Burke, Joseph 20:218
Burke, L. 3:34
Burke, Lawrence 23:22
Burke, Lewis F. 17:76
Burke, Louis F. 13:13
Burke, M. 1:96
Burke, Michael 9:108; 16:288; 17:49
Burke, Myron 24:91
Burke, P. 20:218; 24:14
Burke, P. M. 14:43
Burke, Patrick 4:13; 5:10; 25:149
Burke, Peter 15:64
Burke, Proome 21:185
Burke, R. 3:34
Burke, Richard 25:288
Burke, Robert 9:129; 27:16
Burke, Samuel 8:10; 14:146; 18:124
Burke, Stephen 8:10; 18:124

Burke, Thomas 8:120; 9:170; 12:161, 171; 13:13; 14:43; 16:9; 19:235, 328; 22:518
Burke, Tillman A. 22:244
Burke, V. R. 24:75
Burke, Victor 12:15
Burke, W. H. 3:34
Burke, W. T. 7:88
Burke, Walter 15:30
Burke, Wesley 17:171
Burke, Weston 10:94
Burke, William 9:71; 11:53, 383; 14:43; 18:440; 20:218; 23:85, 303; 24:48
Burke, William A. 22:22
Burke, William C. 7:12
Burke, William E. 18:12
Burke, William H. 17:30
Burkee, Joseph 10:43
Burkee, Nelson 21:308
Burkell, Moses 12:15
Burkeor, Henry 11:278
Burker, H. 15:297
Burker, J. K. 11:236
Burkes, Charles 1:191
Burkessel, H. 3:34
Burket, C. 13:62; 19:59
Burket, Daniel 20:218
Burket, Eli 22:68
Burket, J. 23:251
Burket, J. S. 5:10
Burket, John 7:21; 17:90
Burket, R. 23:251
Burket, S. 14:43
Burket, William 10:105; 20:218
Burkett, Daniel 10:44
Burkett, Edward 9:76
Burkett, Ephraim 21:308
Burkett, Lewis H. 4:13
Burkett, Philip 12:56
Burkett, Stephen 22:474
Burkewart, Peter 22:22
Burkey, G. W. 21:119
Burkey, M. 12:98
Burkhalter, William 22:181
Burkham, James 9:156
Burkhamer, Jesse 23:201
Burkhammer, George W. 15:85
Burkhams, W. H. 22:523
Burkhard, Charles 18:124
Burkhard, Gattlid 13:13
Burkhardt, Andrew 13:13
Burkhardt, Bester 22:22
Burkhardt, Charles 13:13
Burkhardt, Christopher 21:308

Burkhardt, E. 24:213
Burkhardt, George W. 11:102
Burkhardt, John M. 21:221
Burkhardt, W. 20:139
Burkhardt, William A. 21:215
Burkharmer, Isaac 15:187
Burkhart, C. 3:34
Burkhart, E. 23:135
Burkhart, Emanuel 21:221
Burkhart, George 14:146
Burkhart, Gotlieb 16:23
Burkhart, Isaac 8:46
Burkhart, Jacob 8:10
Burkhart, James 17:235
Burkhart, John 13:13
Burkhart, John R. 22:68
Burkhart, Paul 20:136
Burkhart, William 24:48
Burkhartz, Michael 10:105; 20:218
Burkhe, Thomas 19:59
Burkhead, Green B. 21:221
Burkhead, W. 3:35
Burkheart, David 13:106
Burkhey, Thomas 15:325
Burkholder, D. A. 1:110
Burkholder, F. 13:106
Burkholder, J. 23:105
Burkholder, L. V. 23:22
Burkholder, Thomas B. 15:187
Burkirk, William 15:53
Burkland, James 10:105
Burkley, A. W. 1:116
Burkley, J. M. 14:43
Burkley, John 15:53
Burkley, T. W. 11:237
Burkman, Peter 20:121
Burks, Hamilton 24:48
Burks, James 19:59
Burks, John S. 13:77
Burks, Richard 21:97
Burks, William N. 21:308
Burkshire, Aaron 22:292
Burkshire, Thomas 24:14
Burky, Oliver 22:416
Burkyard, Fred 9:116
Burkyard, Frederick 27:20
Burl, A. C. 22:331
Burland, John 18:417
Burlassow, E. K. 21:308
Burleigh, Benjamin F. 21:185
Burleigh, H. W. 1:112
Burleigh, L. 3:35
Burleigh, Robert F. 23:10
Burles, George 23:266

Burleson, James 22:244
Burleson, Rufus O. 13:13
Burlew, G. W. 1:114
Burlew, Lewis E. 23:127
Burley, C. 3:35; 14:146
Burley, Ebenezer 12:15
Burley, Francis M. 16:117
Burley, Francisco 10:105; 20:218
Burley, George W. 22:181
Burley, H. 1:110
Burley, H. S. 1:111
Burley, Harrison 22:181
Burley, Horace 11:394
Burley, J. 21:308
Burley, James 20:177
Burley, Joshua 18:392
Burley, Marshall P. 22:68
Burley, P. 11:298
Burley, William 1:16; 11:134
Burley, William L. 26:120
Burlin, J. A. 9:108
Burlin, Jesse 23:22
Burlin, William 25:310
Burling, Samuel 9:218; 18:363
Burlingame, Benjamin F. 7:67
Burlingame, C. 16:177
Burlingame, C. D. 13:106
Burlingame, Charles 26:150
Burlingame, Cyrus L. 19:7
Burlingame, E. 25:15
Burlingame, Freeman 8:46
Burlingame, J. M. 1:15
Burlingame, Jacob 7:88
Burlingame, N. H. 7:48
Burlingame, Spencer 7:83; 21:308
Burlingame, Sylvanus 23:136
Burlingame, W. D. 25:149
Burlingame, Z. 7:67
Burlingane, John F. 21:135
Burlingcaunt, L. 23:136
Burlingham, C. L. 25:16
Burlingham, Frank 15:187
Burlingham, George 14:147
Burlingham, T. A. 25:149
Burlington, Benjamin B. 21:221
Burlington, W. D. 5:10
Burlinson, J. B. 12:166
Burlison, Ambrose 23:105
Burlison, L. 9:171; 19:248
Burlison, S. 17:63
Burlow, M. 14:43

Burlson, Joseph 8:70
Burly, --- 14:147
Burly, George 16:289
Burly, James 12:48
Burman, Alexander 17:400
Burman, James 18:124
Burman, Nelson 18:275
Burman, W. A. 19:7
Burmeyer, H. 19:300
Burminger, Henry 18:124
Burmingham, Michael 25:15
Burmington, J. M. 12:53
Burminster, John 20:218
Burn, Hugh L. 17:94
Burn, John 3:34; 8:37
Burn, Patrick 19:59
Burn, Rufus H. 21:185
Burnam, A. O. 14:314
Burnap, G. W. 8:46
Burnap, W. R. 15:187
Burnard, C. C. 15:187
Burnbaum, George 4:13
Burnby, John 9:49
Burndege, O. 22:181
Burne, Mathew 17:30
Burne, William 8:10
Burnell, Alpheus 27:23
Burnell, Franklin M. 19:7
Burnell, Freeman 12:151
Burnell, John 5:49; 25:149
Burnell, Joseph 11:52
Burnell, Luther S. 11:123
Burnell, Samuel R. 24:36
Burnell, Thomas A. 7:88
Burner, Franklin 22:22
Burnes, A. S. 21:308
Burnes, Anthony 19:59
Burnes, B. B. 21:14
Burnes, Charles 9:229
Burnes, Charles W. 5:10
Burnes, D. B. 3:34
Burnes, Devande 9:129
Burnes, Eli 27:143
Burnes, George 16:177
Burnes, Henry 26:151
Burnes, J. 14:43; 25:149
Burnes, J. C. 14:43
Burnes, J. W. 14:43
Burnes, James 12:67; 25:332; 26:16
Burnes, John 3:34; 5:10; 9:129; 17:49; 24:107; 27:18
Burnes, M. 14:147
Burnes, Michael 9:116
Burnes, Miles O. 12:67
Burnes, P. 14:43
Burnes, Patrick 9:140

Burnes, Paul 16:289
Burnes, Richard 16:177
Burnes, Sober 9:116
Burnes, T. M. 21:20
Burnes, Thomas 11:189;
  12:67; 14:43; 15:4;
  16:117; 21:251
Burnes, W. C. B. 20:34
Burnes, William 5:10
Burnesley, Edwin 22:68
Burness, James 18:25
Burness, Peter 19:248
Burness, Thomas 14:147
Burnet, Doctor 6:27
Burnet, Henry S. 23:105
Burnet, Thomas J. 20:218
Burnett, --- 3:33
Burnett, A. A. 1:113
Burnett, Alfred J. 17:30
Burnett, Andrew 13:13
Burnett, Benjamin F.
  20:218
Burnett, C. G. 25:149
Burnett, C. H. 1:15
Burnett, C. R. 24:14
Burnett, Charles 9:76
Burnett, Charles F. 1:13
Burnett, Charlton 19:300
Burnett, D. W. 17:71
Burnett, E. C. 11:236
Burnett, E. S. 19:273
Burnett, Edwin 17:30
Burnett, Francis M. 27:19
Burnett, George 21:308
Burnett, Green 22:292
Burnett, H. 1:20
Burnett, Henry 17:241;
  21:266
Burnett, Henry C. 24:36
Burnett, Hezekiel 4:13
Burnett, Ira 21:203
Burnett, Isaac 4:65;
  11:296; 21:119
Burnett, J. 3:33; 14:43
Burnett, J. D. 27:15
Burnett, J. H. 25:149
Burnett, J. L. 14:43
Burnett, J. N. 8:61
Burnett, J. S. 11:24
Burnett, Jacob 17:76
Burnett, James 10:14;
  26:152
Burnett, James A. 21:251;
  24:65
Burnett, James E. 22:68
Burnett, John 18:108;
  21:247
Burnett, John J. 22:23
Burnett, John L. 23:22
Burnett, John W. 22:474

Burnett, Joseph 3:33;
  24:14
Burnett, Joseph N. 24:36
Burnett, L. 9:140
Burnett, Lennox 20:38
Burnett, Leonard 23:270
Burnett, Levi 27:15
Burnett, M. 3:33
Burnett, Marion 10:27;
  19:300
Burnett, Mason 8:10;
  18:124
Burnett, Nathan 7:119;
  21:308
Burnett, Nathaniel 20:218
Burnett, Oliver C. 25:149
Burnett, Peter 13:106
Burnett, R. 14:43
Burnett, R. P. 20:145
Burnett, Robert 23:97
Burnett, Robert P. 12:67;
  20:145
Burnett, S. 22:181
Burnett, S. H. 3:33
Burnett, Samuel 3:33;
  21:308
Burnett, Samuel N.
  17:442; 24:156
Burnett, Saraphan 20:218
Burnett, Seraphan 10:105
Burnett, Seth T. 22:181
Burnett, Silas 4:13
Burnett, Simon 6:12
Burnett, T. B. 21:165
Burnett, Thomas 17:247;
  23:119
Burnett, Thomas H.
  22:244
Burnett, W. 12:166
Burnett, W. H. 4:13;
  17:392
Burnett, William 9:238;
  16:23; 17:18, 272;
  19:44
Burnett, William G.
  11:275
Burnett, William L.
  22:499
Burnett, William T. 8:81
Burnetts, B. F. 10:105
Burney, G. 14:239; 27:24
Burney, John 4:13
Burney, Thomas 14:43
Burngardner, L. 11:138
Burnham, --- 1:109
Burnham, A. S. 4:13
Burnham, Alanson O.
  23:105
Burnham, Albert 21:308
Burnham, Alfred W.
  23:250

Burnham, Ansel 1:16
Burnham, B. C. 18:25
Burnham, David T. 23:61
Burnham, E. M. 1:19
Burnham, E. W. 9:170;
  19:235
Burnham, Elijah B. 22:23
Burnham, Enok 19:235
Burnham, Essex 17:144
Burnham, Ford 26:153
Burnham, G. W. 27:12
Burnham, George 15:187
Burnham, George P.
  22:170
Burnham, H. A. 9:108
Burnham, J. 3:34; 25:17
Burnham, J. C. 27:16
Burnham, J. D. 9:170
Burnham, J. E. 9:140
Burnham, James 17:147
Burnham, John 1:17
Burnham, Leander T.
  16:90
Burnham, Levi 15:187
Burnham, Lincoln 12:53
Burnham, M. 11:297
Burnham, Mark 10:105;
  20:218
Burnham, P. P. 4:13
Burnham, Robert 4:13
Burnham, Samuel M.
  22:23
Burnham, T. 23:22
Burnham, W. 1:93
Burnham, W. H. 21:200
Burnhard, John 17:18
Burnhardt, Samuel 17:231
Burnheart, John 14:147
Burnhill, Thomas 21:84
Burnian, Cornelius 21:221
Burninger, Henry 26:149
Burningham, A. H. 25:17
Burnitt, B. 3:33
Burnitt, J. K. 8:71
Burnley, James A. 20:218
Burnley, P. G. 20:218
Burnnett, Munroe 10:146
Burns, --- 9:217; 15:30,
  85; 19:287, 328
Burns, A. 8:46; 9:203;
  12:92; 13:62, 76, 84;
  14:43; 16:177, 289;
  18:78, 231; 19:59;
  26:15
Burns, A. P. 13:12; 16:23
Burns, Adam R. 8:119
Burns, Alexander 10:105;
  20:218; 21:97
Burns, Allen G. 11:134
Burns, Andrew J. 22:418
Burns, Aurel 9:11

Burns, B. 3:34; 21:12
Burns, Barney 21:20
Burns, Benjamin 15:85
Burns, C. 11:134; 18:46; 26:13
Burns, C. L. 24:14
Burns, Charles 14:147; 20:218; 21:308; 22:115
Burns, Christopher 19:316
Burns, Clement A. 21:266
Burns, Conrad 7:88
Burns, D. 18:231; 26:13
Burns, D. O. 15:187
Burns, Daniel 3:34
Burns, David 21:308
Burns, Dennis 17:387
Burns, Dervando 27:17
Burns, E. 1:16
Burns, E. J. 3:33
Burns, E. M. 21:49
Burns, E. P. 22:118
Burns, Edward 17:387
Burns, Elias E. 23:22
Burns, Eugene 25:149
Burns, Francis M. 17:76; 22:68
Burns, Frank 22:518
Burns, Frederick 13:106
Burns, George 14:314, 321; 17:30
Burns, George E. 16:83
Burns, George H. 25:268
Burns, George M. 23:61
Burns, George W. 14:147
Burns, Gleason 22:331
Burns, H. 1:112; 3:34; 18:102
Burns, H. F. 21:308
Burns, H. N. 24:14
Burns, Harrison H. 17:71
Burns, Henry 8:37; 17:13; 19:59
Burns, Henry C. 11:180
Burns, Henry N. 17:279
Burns, Hezekiah 21:193
Burns, Hiram 15:318
Burns, Hugh 9:65; 18:275; 25:18
Burns, I. 10:27
Burns, Irvin 18:363
Burns, Isaac 17:172; 22:292
Burns, Israel 14:147
Burns, J. 1:14, 20, 111; 3:34; 13:84, 131; 15:83; 16:277; 21:20
Burns, J. D. 1:115
Burns, J. H. 1:109; 9:49
Burns, J. M. 16:177
Burns, J. W. 3:34

Burns, James 1:115; 3:34; 9:41, 76, 171, 226; 11:118, 137, 278; 12:14, 15; 14:147; 18:214, 363; 19:7, 151; 20:37; 21:308; 23:85; 26:11, 120; 27:22
Burns, James A. 26:152
Burns, James D. 23:112
Burns, James K. 11:88
Burns, James T. 13:12
Burns, Jasper P. 22:474
Burns, John 1:114; 3:33, 34; 7:67, 88; 8:81; 9:10, 11; 10:14, 105; 11:257; 12:140; 13:12; 15:30, 315; 16:24, 90; 17:391, 442; 18:102; 19:59; 20:218; 21:95, 308; 23:85, 119, 136; 24:156; 25:17; 26:150; 27:12, 13
Burns, John E. 9:226; 22:68
Burns, John F. 18:363
Burns, John H. 4:13
Burns, John J. 17:147
Burns, John W. 22:499
Burns, Joseph 7:21
Burns, Lafayette 16:90; 22:118
Burns, M. 1:14, 19; 3:34
Burns, M. F. 22:331
Burns, M. G. 3:34
Burns, M. O. 15:30
Burns, Mathew 22:181; 23:22
Burns, Mathew B. 22:68
Burns, Michael 8:100; 9:68; 16:90; 17:462; 23:119, 187; 24:36, 177; 27:19
Burns, N. 25:271
Burns, N. H. 3:34
Burns, Owen 3:33
Burns, P. 1:19; 3:34; 19:248
Burns, Patrick 9:19; 16:24, 90; 22:138; 23:10; 27:16
Burns, Peter 1:113; 7:88; 22:23; 25:18
Burns, R. F. 2:8
Burns, R. S. 12:98
Burns, Richard V. 23:61
Burns, Robert 19:235; 20:38; 21:308; 22:331; 25:150
Burns, Robert C. 16:152

Burns, Robert L. 10:14
Burns, Robert S. 20:5
Burns, S. A. 1:20; 3:33
Burns, Samuel 3:33
Burns, Sielney 24:189
Burns, Sober 27:18
Burns, Stephen 9:199
Burns, T. 3:34; 25:285
Burns, T. R. 1:109
Burns, Thomas 1:15; 8:46; 10:43; 11:22; 13:12; 15:30, 187; 17:76; 18:12; 21:65; 22:23
Burns, Thomas E. 17:279
Burns, W. 1:116; 3:34; 25:150
Burns, W. D. 9:49
Burns, W. H. 11:51
Burns, W. M. 23:136
Burns, W. W. 20:141
Burns, William 8:113; 9:206; 11:23; 16:177; 18:64; 21:206; 25:150, 283
Burns, William A. 12:151
Burns, William D. 25:150
Burns, William H. 7:67
Burns, William W. 20:34
Burnsheller, Abram 9:162
Burnsheller, Adam 27:23
Burnshine, A. E. 23:136
Burnside, Charles 21:308
Burnside, Frank 7:67
Burnside, George 14:147
Burnside, J. 27:12
Burnside, J. M. 7:88
Burnside, R. 19:248
Burnside, Robert 9:170
Burnside, Taylor 24:189
Burnside, W. N. 22:331
Burnside, William H. 18:284; 26:134
Burnsides, William 14:147, 254
Burnson, William 22:232
Burnsworth, Levi 22:68
Burnsworth, Milton 13:84
Burnt, J. 15:352
Burnt, John 25:19
Buron, J. C. 8:100
Burr, A. 1:109; 15:64
Burr, C. 1:110
Burr, Charles 7:118; 10:105; 20:218
Burr, David 13:84
Burr, Davis 10:14
Burr, E. 3:35
Burr, Edwin 10:158; 19:151
Burr, Emen 12:151
Burr, Eugene 20:111

Burr, F. 1:112
Burr, F. W. 11:137
Burr, Francis M. 18:214
Burr, Francis W. 15:2
Burr, George 9:108;
 11:180; 12:14
Burr, Harvey 22:181
Burr, Henry C. 20:145
Burr, Hiram 22:181
Burr, J. C. 20:91
Burr, J. N. 16:117
Burr, James 12:14; 22:511
Burr, Jewell 19:59
Burr, Joel 12:94; 15:358
Burr, Lewis M. 13:13;
 16:24
Burr, N. E. 25:150
Burr, R. H. L. 21:308
Burr, Robert 22:292
Burr, Rufus H. 21:290
Burr, S. P. 15:339
Burr, T. 1:111
Burrage, D. C. 10:105;
 20:218
Burrall, S. H. 26:150
Burrel, W. H. 16:117
Burrell, A. S. 13:106
Burrell, Abner L. 8:10;
 18:125
Burrell, Ananias 17:76
Burrell, B. 25:294
Burrell, Charles 9:76;
 26:11
Burrell, Charles J. 15:103
Burrell, Decatur 13:13
Burrell, Eli W. 8:113
Burrell, George 18:231;
 26:15
Burrell, George W.
 19:328
Burrell, J. 18:12
Burrell, James 14:254
Burrell, James J. 27:21
Burrell, James W. 21:65
Burrell, John E. 25:17
Burrell, Simon P. 20:95
Burrell, T. 23:187
Burrell, W. L. 19:59
Burrell, Washington
 19:289
Burrell, William 22:472
Burrell, William A.
 17:390
Burren, George 3:34
Burress, Jacob 8:81
Burress, W. 20:27
Burress, Wesley 8:71
Burrett, Louis 21:266
Burrible, Daniel 7:119
Burrick, F. 18:25
Burrie, Strange 17:205

Burrier, Peter 11:298
Burries, Isaac W. 20:103
Burries, John 1:13
Burril, Joseph E. 15:186
Burrill, Daniel 21:308
Burrill, Henry C. 16:83
Burrill, O. M. 25:18
Burrill, William 3:35
Burrill, William L. 2:8
Burrington, W. W. 19:327
Burris, Abraham 10:98
Burris, Albert 21:308
Burris, Alonzo L. 9:218;
 18:363
Burris, Benjamine 19:300
Burris, Charles 20:103
Burris, Clark 21:9
Burris, Daniel 22:417
Burris, David 15:85
Burris, Eli 22:417
Burris, Francis 11:410
Burris, H. I. 10:44
Burris, H. J. 20:218
Burris, Henry H. 8:10;
 18:125; 24:36
Burris, Isaac 22:9
Burris, J. 19:300
Burris, J. C. 20:218
Burris, J. H. 10:44
Burris, James 22:243
Burris, Mathew E. 11:298
Burris, Moses 22:68
Burris, Owen 22:331
Burris, Samuel 22:118
Burris, Silas D. 24:48
Burris, Walter 10:105;
 20:218
Burris, Wesley A. 26:153
Burris, Wilburn 18:125
Burris, Wiley 9:218;
 18:363
Burris, William 11:135
Burriss, Leroy 22:243
Burritt, --- 1:19
Burritt, Benjamin S.
 22:138
Burritt, Daniel M. 22:507
Burrns, W. 14:268
Burros, Wilson 23:284
Burroughs, A. 19:248
Burroughs, A. M. 24:75
Burroughs, Abel 24:14
Burroughs, Alfred 18:275
Burroughs, Andrew
 9:170; 19:269
Burroughs, Austin 9:170
Burroughs, C. F. 27:15
Burroughs, David P.
 10:105; 20:218
Burroughs, E. A. 12:166
Burroughs, G. W. 25:14

Burroughs, H. 23:22
Burroughs, Henry 17:396
Burroughs, Horatio 9:96
Burroughs, J. 20:84
Burroughs, James 17:415
Burroughs, Jeremiah
 17:262
Burroughs, John K. 7:88
Burroughs, Joseph
 11:103; 16:113
Burroughs, R. 15:157
Burroughs, S. A. 25:317
Burroughs, Stephen
 22:292
Burroughs, William
 16:178
Burroughs, William H.
 21:308
Burrous, Dickerson 13:13
Burrow, Cornelius R.
 23:85
Burrow, J. 22:161
Burrow, William M.
 18:172
Burrowes, J. 1:20
Burrows, --- 25:15
Burrows, Albert 14:147
Burrows, D. 15:336
Burrows, Dickinson 16:24
Burrows, E. E. 11:399
Burrows, Earl 8:10;
 18:125
Burrows, Frank 10:151,
 178
Burrows, Franklin 13:13
Burrows, George 27:23
Burrows, H. 3:34; 26:151
Burrows, Henry 17:18;
 22:447
Burrows, Horace 17:425
Burrows, J. 3:34; 9:49;
 25:150
Burrows, James 5:10
Burrows, James H. 9:76
Burrows, James M.
 20:191
Burrows, Jesse R. 7:119;
 21:308
Burrows, John 22:68
Burrows, Joshua 11:275
Burrows, Josiah 22:460
Burrows, Nathaniel 3:34
Burrows, R. B. 14:43
Burrows, S. 9:235; 26:216
Burrows, T. 11:22
Burrows, W. 9:140; 27:20
Burrows, Warren 18:13
Burrows, William 12:15;
 27:14
Burrrows, G. R. 1:111
Burrs, Esau 27:18

Burrs, W. 3:35
Burrul, J. 11:134
Burrup, W. C. 14:43
Burruss, Alfred 17:109
Burry, John 24:63
Burry, Miles 7:88
Burry, W. 3:35
Burs, Zachery 14:147
Bursaym, Thomas 18:334
Bursha, Thomas 3:34
Burshen, F. 3:34
Bursick, Charles W. 18:125
Burslem, E. T. 15:172
Burson, H. 25:150
Burson, John M. 23:201
Burson, Robert 22:23
Burst, John 11:298
Bursteel, John 3:34
Burt, --- 25:14
Burt, Abraham 23:61
Burt, Albert B. 10:90
Burt, Alonzo 23:136
Burt, Alvin 25:150
Burt, Andrew 9:218; 18:363
Burt, Augustus C. 26:121
Burt, B. 19:334
Burt, Baannah 9:244
Burt, Barrett 22:138
Burt, C. E. 3:34
Burt, Calvin 9:76; 26:16
Burt, Charles 14:239, 251; 27:24
Burt, Charles H. 13:13
Burt, Elijah 7:88
Burt, Elmer P. 9:203
Burt, George 9:240
Burt, H. 23:201
Burt, Henry 22:292
Burt, J. 3:34
Burt, J. G. 14:147
Burt, J. L. 27:14
Burt, John 8:81; 9:171
Burt, John H. 16:178
Burt, Julius 21:308
Burt, L. 25:16
Burt, Nathaniel 22:138
Burt, R. J. 21:308
Burt, Ransom 10:43; 20:218
Burt, Robert 17:77
Burt, Silas 1:114
Burt, Silas W. 11:14
Burt, W. O. 9:171
Burt, William 9:171; 11:285; 18:214
Burt, William B. 22:138
Burt, William G. 22:23
Burt, William M. 12:151
Burt, William O. 19:273

Burt, Wilson 22:170
Burtch, F. W. 15:164
Burten, Daniel 4:13
Burthart, J. 3:35
Burtis, William 27:20
Burtle, Samuel 13:79
Burtlett, Charles 9:139
Burtlis, George 10:171
Burtnell, William 10:14
Burtney, James 25:288
Burton, --- 19:59; 25:17
Burton, A. 1:115
Burton, A. H. 13:84
Burton, Aaron 20:180, 191
Burton, Abraham 11:51
Burton, Abram 21:266
Burton, Albert D. 20:219
Burton, Alex M. 13:13
Burton, Alfred P. 10:210; 18:468
Burton, Almeson 1:114
Burton, Anthony 8:37; 26:150
Burton, B. 11:325
Burton, Benjamin 21:266
Burton, Burrell 20:142
Burton, C. 3:33
Burton, Caleb 26:13
Burton, Charles 7:77; 11:53; 15:352; 16:277; 23:187; 25:293
Burton, D. W. 20:219
Burton, Daniel 7:21
Burton, Daniel B. 9:213
Burton, Drury W. 10:44
Burton, E. 1:17
Burton, Edward 16:138
Burton, Eli 10:10
Burton, Elijah 7:48
Burton, Extra 6:15; 18:78
Burton, F. 14:43
Burton, G. 11:24
Burton, G. E. 3:33
Burton, G. W. 19:59
Burton, George 3:33; 6:12, 27; 11:198; 12:151; 18:78, 125
Burton, George W. 17:450; 23:10; 24:176
Burton, H. M. 10:44
Burton, H. W. 4:13
Burton, Harlow 10:209
Burton, Henry 3:33; 6:28; 13:62
Burton, Horace 13:13
Burton, Isaac 10:44; 20:219
Burton, J. 21:308

Burton, J. A. 26:236
Burton, J. H. 26:153
Burton, J. J. 16:178; 25:150
Burton, J. L. 17:107
Burton, J. M. 7:88
Burton, J. R. 20:55
Burton, Jacob 21:266
Burton, James 7:119; 13:13; 16:24
Burton, James F. 18:424
Burton, James H. 1:14
Burton, James M. 22:244
Burton, James R. 24:58
Burton, Jared M. 12:63
Burton, Jered M. 15:64
Burton, Jesse L. 21:97
Burton, John 3:33; 22:9, 474; 24:75
Burton, John J. 5:10
Burton, John L. 14:239; 27:24
Burton, John M. 21:193
Burton, Joseph 25:268
Burton, Joshua 8:61; 18:205
Burton, Josiah H. 22:68
Burton, L. G. 1:111
Burton, Lafayette 3:33
Burton, Lemuel 21:65
Burton, Lorenzo T. 17:241
Burton, Luther C. 22:23
Burton, M. 25:150
Burton, Marion 11:384
Burton, Mark 5:36
Burton, Matt 9:199
Burton, Meat 19:289
Burton, N. 3:33; 7:77; 14:147
Burton, N. B. 26:152
Burton, N. S. 27:20
Burton, Nelson 17:129; 24:189
Burton, O. S. 3:33
Burton, Richard 7:14; 17:18
Burton, Robert E. 18:108
Burton, Roswell 17:205; 22:232
Burton, S. J. 14:251
Burton, Samuel 11:23; 15:288; 17:49; 23:276
Burton, Sanford 11:134
Burton, Th. B. 21:20
Burton, Thomas 1:191; 17:258; 21:147
Burton, Tillman 3:33
Burton, Turner 21:308
Burton, W. 8:70; 14:43

Burton, W. B. 3:33; 8:61
Burton, W. G. 13:62
Burton, W. S. 13:84
Burton, W. W. 21:20
Burton, Washington
    21:266
Burton, William 3:33;
    7:88; 8:10; 17:147,
    202, 442; 18:125;
    20:399; 23:136;
    24:156
Burton, William M. 1:20
Burton, William N. 22:68
Burton, William S. 17:471
Burton, Winslow 13:13
Burtram, G. 1:14
Burtrand, M. 19:300
Burtrass, W. H. 8:46
Burtrey, James 14:318
Burts, William 17:63
Burtselt, Stephen 27:15
Burtwell, W. H. 23:22
Burum, John R. D. R.
    21:65
Burus, Thomas 19:324
Burwell, G. W. 1:13
Burwell, J. H. 19:151
Burwell, James 15:187
Burwell, James H. 17:392
Burwell, W. J. 27:142
Burwick, George 13:124
Burwick, S. 14:239; 27:24
Bury, Frederick 10:105;
    20:219
Busbee, C. C. 3:35
Busbee, C. M. 27:16
Busbie, E. 23:136
Busby, Henry 13:13
Busby, Jacob 17:442;
    24:156
Busby, R. A. 10:105;
    20:219
Busby, Washington
    17:129; 24:187
Busby, William 5:36; 7:89
Busby, William H. 22:401
Busby, William J. 12:67
Busch, Johanna 16:24
Buschart, W. 21:20
Buschaug, George 11:137
Busche, W. 21:20
Buscher, Lewis 18:303;
    26:93
Buscher, Louis 9:19
Buscow, A. J. 14:43
Buse, Joseph H. 9:19
Buse, William 1:20
Busenberg, Daniel 21:65
Bush, A. 1:17; 3:35; 19:59
Bush, A. B. 4:14
Bush, A. J. W. 18:430

Bush, A. P. 21:309
Bush, A. W. 11:123
Bush, Alex 23:283
Bush, Anna W. 1:96
Bush, Asa L. 21:242
Bush, Benjamin 11:197
Bush, C. 19:248
Bush, C. P. 14:295;
    17:471; 27:20
Bush, Caesar 12:48
Bush, Ch. A. 21:90
Bush, Charles 9:171;
    23:105
Bush, Charles H. 16:24
Bush, Chauncy 17:144
Bush, Christian 4:14
Bush, Clayton 27:15
Bush, Clinton 7:21
Bush, D. D. W. 13:84
Bush, Daniel 22:474
Bush, David 3:35
Bush, David F. 17:417
Bush, E. 14:43
Bush, Edward 15:187
Bush, F. 15:150; 17:172
Bush, F. C. 15:187
Bush, G. 23:136
Bush, George 1:18;
    11:197
Bush, George B. 17:31
Bush, George E. 21:49
Bush, George H. 15:288;
    19:59
Bush, George V. 17:63
Bush, George W. 23:255
Bush, H. 1:116
Bush, H. H. 3:35
Bush, Henry 9:206;
    24:189
Bush, Henry C. 11:53
Bush, Henry E. 17:98
Bush, Hiram 23:136
Bush, Hugh 17:326
Bush, Israel 4:13
Bush, J. M. 1:109
Bush, J. S. 21:20
Bush, Jacob 1:15; 14:43;
    17:49
Bush, James 8:10; 11:395;
    18:125
Bush, James F. 21:215
Bush, John 9:49; 11:134;
    14:147; 22:181;
    23:22; 26:13
Bush, Jordan 16:178
Bush, Joseph 1:115;
    9:171; 14:147;
    19:248
Bush, Josephus 19:7
Bush, Joshua 22:292
Bush, L. 25:150

Bush, Laurence 7:21
Bush, Leander 8:81
Bush, Levi 11:399
Bush, Levin 6:24
Bush, Lewis 4:14; 5:10
Bush, London 26:15
Bush, Londow 18:231
Bush, Luke 17:396
Bush, M. 17:153
Bush, Middleton 24:65
Bush, Milton H. 22:170
Bush, N. W. 16:178
Bush, Ned 25:150
Bush, Oscar N. 19:7
Bush, P. 15:297; 16:178
Bush, Peter 18:78; 21:238
Bush, R. 17:129; 24:189
Bush, Ransom 12:15
Bush, Rosina 1:96
Bush, S. A. 14:5
Bush, Samuel 9:41;
    12:145; 22:23;
    26:216
Bush, Sindey 4:14
Bush, T. J. 27:20
Bush, Thomas 3:35
Bush, Thomas B. 20:185
Bush, Uriah H. 8:81
Bush, W. 3:35; 14:147
Bush, W. H. 7:89
Bush, William 2:7;
    13:106; 14:43;
    20:219; 21:309;
    23:136; 25:19
Bush, William B. 23:262
Bush, William F. 17:316;
    27:142
Busham, Amos 1:13
Busham, P. 21:20
Bushaw, Charles L.
    22:181
Bushby, N. 3:35
Bushel, Edward 4:14
Bushel, H. A. 9:49
Bushel, Jacob 18:125
Bushelberry, F. 15:340
Bushell, Davrn D. 15:53
Bushell, William 3:35
Bushelloy, F. 16:365
Busher, A. 2:8
Busher, Narcissus 20:219
Busher, W. J. 26:151
Bushfield, Michael F.
    23:284
Bushfield, Thomas 13:13
Bushhammer, S. 13:84
Bushley, David 20:219
Bushley, William 3:35
Bushman, Andrew 26:12
Bushman, J. R. 3:35
Bushnel, David 15:30

Bushnel, John 4:14
Bushnell, A. 3:35
Bushnell, A. C. 23:251
Bushnell, A. W. 9:242
Bushnell, Charles 4:14;
 14:147
Bushnell, Clovius V.
 21:135
Bushnell, D. D. 12:63
Bushnell, E. 9:96
Bushnell, Edwin 10:170
Bushnell, Ewolis 18:25
Bushnell, Ezra 8:81
Bushnell, H. 1:116
Bushnell, Hiram 9:19
Bushnell, James H. 10:14
Bushnell, Joseph S.
 20:121
Bushnell, Orsamus 22:68
Bushnell, S. 9:171;
 19:244
Bushong, Jacob H. 9:19;
 18:303
Bushong, John 17:77
Bushor, Narcissus 10:105
Bushre, --- 20:84
Bushrod, M. 7:48
Bushshawn, Eli 22:181
Bushwell, Ovid 11:23
Bushy, Henry 16:24
Bushy, Oliver 1:112
Busick, Augustine 8:71
Busick, C. 22:244
Busick, J. S. 21:49
Busick, R. H. 14:287;
 23:22
Busick, Sample C. 10:44
Busick, Sample P. 20:219
Busick, W. A. 3:35
Busing, G. K. 23:22
Busk, --- 16:132
Buska, F. 26:236
Buska, Theopolis 19:59
Buskdall, L. 18:108
Buskey, F. 25:19
Buskey, Frank 2:7
Buskholder, H. 9:140
Buskholder, Henry 27:16
Buskirk, --- 17:482; 27:20
Buskirk, A. 3:35
Buskirk, G. V. 23:15
Buskirk, George W.
 26:150
Buskirk, James 17:395
Buskirk, O. 3:35
Busler, H. 14:251
Busley, William 14:239
Busman, G. 14:43
Busnige, John 19:152
Buss, Ferdinand 27:22
Buss, J. 25:150

Buss, James 24:91
Buss, Joseph 5:10
Buss, Thomas 5:10
Buss, William 8:81, 116
Bussard, Daniel B. 13:128
Bussard, Jefferson 22:292
Bussard, Nathaniel D.
 17:415
Bussard, P. A. 16:135
Busse, Daniel 17:18
Busse, James 24:100
Bussell, W. 19:225
Busser, William 22:161
Bussert, Martin 22:68
Busset, George 6:35
Bussill, H. 1:19
Bussing, W. 15:187
Bussing, W. J. 18:64
Bussinger, William
 11:384
Bussler, Abram 1:18
Busson, Augustus 4:14
Bussum, Alexander
 21:210
Bust, A. 25:150
Bust, Abner 5:10
Bust, J. C. 14:147
Bust, Thomas 1:16
Bustell, Nathaniel 20:103
Buster, John B. 9:11
Bustin, H. 13:84
Bustire, Charles 14:43
Bustner, Mack 11:51
Bustod, David 24:189
Buston, B. 3:35
Buston, Charles 22:292
Buston, D. O. 15:187
Buston, J. H. 15:336
Buston, John 21:309
Buston, Nicholas 21:309
Bustoo, David 17:455
Bustrong, Job H. 26:92
Buswell, C. S. 19:225
Buswell, N. C. 23:22
Buswell, Stephen 14:147
Buswick, Charles 11:51
Buswill, R. J. 21:309
Butchells, J. B. 7:89
Butcher, C. 9:49
Butcher, Charles C.
 10:171; 19:152
Butcher, David 17:18
Butcher, Elvin 24:88
Butcher, F. M. 10:44;
 20:219
Butcher, J. 1:111; 11:375
Butcher, J. A. 1:17; 27:23
Butcher, J. F. 18:231;
 26:13
Butcher, James 11:23
Butcher, James D. 16:117

Butcher, James S. 22:68
Butcher, John 12:67;
 13:13; 14:147; 15:30
Butcher, John C. 22:244
Butcher, John W. 22:23
Butcher, Joseph 1:113;
 10:105; 20:219;
 22:23
Butcher, L. 12:92; 14:43;
 16:289
Butcher, Marshal 7:21
Butcher, Michael 10:105;
 20:219
Butcher, Peter 3:35
Butcher, Robert 26:210
Butcher, Samuel 23:22
Butcher, William S. 22:68
Butchler, Peter 7:21
Butell, C. 19:235
Buthoff, --- 25:317
Butle, Solomon 15:30
Butler, --- 25:332
Butler, A. 3:35; 11:90;
 13:84
Butler, A. F. 3:35
Butler, A. H. 12:67; 15:16
Butler, Aaron 21:49
Butler, Abraham 21:309
Butler, Adam 7:119;
 22:292
Butler, Albert 4:14
Butler, Albert E. 23:119
Butler, Alex 14:147
Butler, Alfred 10:14
Butler, Allen 4:14;
 14:147; 21:221
Butler, Alonzo B. 17:265
Butler, Andrew 9:116;
 22:292; 27:19
Butler, Armstead 17:172
Butler, Augustus 23:105
Butler, B. 25:150
Butler, Ben. F. 24:175
Butler, Benjamin 17:449;
 20:145
Butler, C. 14:43; 19:59
Butler, C. P. 3:35
Butler, Caleb P. 10:105
Butler, Calip P. 20:219
Butler, Calvin B. 7:89
Butler, Champness D.
 23:97
Butler, Charles 12:15;
 16:24; 17:144;
 18:303; 22:138;
 26:92
Butler, Charles M.
 18:231; 26:16
Butler, Charles W. 9:49,
 76

Butler, Christopher 24:100
Butler, D. 3:35; 21:20; 25:150
Butler, D. S. 14:43
Butler, Daniel 5:11
Butler, Daniel B. 21:309
Butler, Daniel W. 10:145; 19:152
Butler, Dennis 25:16
Butler, E. 4:14; 25:150
Butler, E. A. 14:43
Butler, E. C. 11:24
Butler, E. H. 14:44
Butler, E. W. 1:115
Butler, Edmond A. 22:181
Butler, Edward 4:14; 5:11; 7:48; 17:265; 22:417
Butler, Elbert K. 15:187
Butler, Eldad 16:3
Butler, Eli 20:179
Butler, F. 1:112
Butler, Ferdinand 25:283
Butler, Francis M. 9:76; 26:12
Butler, Frank 10:208
Butler, Fruly 22:118
Butler, G. 17:153
Butler, G. A. 12:81
Butler, G. M. 25:294
Butler, G. W. 17:77
Butler, George 5:11; 7:21, 89; 10:176; 11:198; 12:15; 14:277; 15:187; 19:44, 152; 23:136; 25:150
Butler, George B. 22:23
Butler, George C. 3:35
Butler, George M. 7:74
Butler, George S. 22:244
Butler, George W. 24:88
Butler, Glasgow 17:191
Butler, H. 18:46
Butler, H. C. 24:75
Butler, H. J. 1:112
Butler, H. M. 7:56
Butler, Harris 7:15
Butler, Harry 25:16
Butler, Henry 6:24; 7:89, 119; 16:138; 21:309; 22:331; 23:202
Butler, Henry B. 19:7
Butler, Henry M. 22:68
Butler, Herbert 11:230
Butler, Hiram S. 9:116; 27:18
Butler, Horace 9:206
Butler, Ignatius 1:15
Butler, Isaac 9:206; 18:64

Butler, J. 1:20, 116; 3:35; 12:161; 21:165
Butler, J. D. 1:116
Butler, J. H. 9:140; 17:31; 27:15
Butler, J. J. 3:35
Butler, J. L. 1:113
Butler, J. N. 19:269
Butler, J. P. 14:44; 27:15
Butler, J. T. 23:23
Butler, J. W. 21:87; 23:23
Butler, Jacob 10:44; 20:219; 25:294
Butler, James 9:76, 242; 13:56; 14:147; 18:13; 21:65; 23:23; 27:21
Butler, James E. 16:83
Butler, James M. 10:94
Butler, James O. 18:231; 26:16
Butler, Jefferson 8:37; 26:151
Butler, Jeffrey 7:119
Butler, Jeremiah 15:277; 25:150
Butler, John 1:17, 114; 7:119; 8:10, 71, 113; 10:176; 11:135, 278; 12:15, 48; 14:147; 15:30, 172; 16:178; 17:31, 172; 18:125; 19:152; 24:65; 25:150
Butler, John F. 6:15; 18:78
Butler, John M. 7:21
Butler, John S. 22:138
Butler, John T. 20:191
Butler, John W. 21:309
Butler, Jones 4:14
Butler, Joseph 17:320; 27:17
Butler, Joseph H. 17:31
Butler, L. 7:89; 21:309
Butler, Leverett L. 10:158
Butler, Lorenzo D. 22:460
Butler, M. 3:35
Butler, M. R. 11:325; 12:166; 25:318
Butler, Mathias 22:181
Butler, Mitchell 27:23
Butler, Moses 11:53; 14:147
Butler, N. 1:111
Butler, N. H. 1:16
Butler, Nance 18:78
Butler, Nelson 10:105; 20:219
Butler, O. 12:85
Butler, Oliver 23:23
Butler, Oran A. 9:116

Butler, Orrin A. 27:19
Butler, Owen 18:275
Butler, P. 3:35; 7:21; 13:84; 14:5; 25:150, 294
Butler, Patrick 5:11
Butler, Peter 5:36; 17:172; 24:187
Butler, Phelim 7:77
Butler, R. 21:20
Butler, Randolph 22:118
Butler, Richard 10:176; 19:152
Butler, Riley 20:219
Butler, Rob 17:129
Butler, Robert 24:188
Butler, S. H. 1:16
Butler, Samuel 13:56; 22:417
Butler, Simon 10:98
Butler, Solomon 22:232
Butler, Stephen 10:14
Butler, Sylvester 22:23
Butler, Thomas 3:35; 7:81; 14:147; 25:294
Butler, Tobias 12:151
Butler, Trueman 8:117
Butler, W. 1:115; 3:35; 13:84; 14:280; 25:150
Butler, W. B. 1:112; 25:150
Butler, W. G. 15:297
Butler, W. H. 19:225
Butler, W. L. 19:59
Butler, W. W. 3:35
Butler, Walter 1:113
Butler, William 1:15; 3:35; 4:14; 5:36; 6:24; 9:49; 10:14, 44; 16:178; 20:219; 21:20; 309; 23:105; 25:18, 150
Butler, William C. 17:279
Butler, William D. 22:23, 460
Butler, William E. 5:11
Butler, William F. 15:315
Butler, William H. 5:10; 22:181; 23:183
Butler, William O. 22:181
Butler, Wilson S. 9:218; 18:363
Butlor, J. W. 20:219
Butman, A. D. 26:13
Butman, George 17:395
Butman, J. 21:147
Butman, N. D. 9:76
Butmubaugh, M. 21:20
Butner, John 25:150
Butner, L. B. 3:35

Butoff, R. 3:35
Butr---, W. 18:46
Butram, Granville 22:118
Butsch, Henry 11:52
Butsell, Mack 8:103
Butson, Thomas 23:136
Butt, B. 11:383
Butt, Cornelius 11:299
Butt, J. C. 14:147
Butt, Jacob W. 20:5
Butt, James 12:141
Butt, James F. 21:65
Butt, Joseph 7:119
Butt, N. 14:44
Butt, Thomas G. 11:23
Buttan, W. H. 14:26
Buttenmayer, F. 20:142
Butter, A. 3:35
Butter, Amos 10:90
Butter, C. M. 3:35
Butter, H. J. 3:35
Butter, J. D. 3:35
Butter, J. W. 8:46
Butter, James 3:35; 20:89
Butter, L. J. 3:35
Butter, Laura J. 26:217
Butterbaugh, A. L. 25:15
Butterbaugh, George 7:21
Butterfield, --- 25:15
Butterfield, Abram G.
    22:418
Butterfield, Albert 22:507
Butterfield, Albert F. 8:81
Butterfield, B. S. 21:135
Butterfield, C. W. 9:140;
    27:14
Butterfield, Charles E.
    9:101
Butterfield, D. 17:63
Butterfield, D. J. 21:90
Butterfield, Erastus 11:14
Butterfield, Ettis 17:316
Butterfield, F. 14:44
Butterfield, Henry F.
    21:114
Butterfield, J. 5:49
Butterfield, James 3:35
Butterfield, John 17:279
Butterfield, Joseph 1:115
Butterfield, Lewis 21:309
Butterfield, Lyman C.
    22:277
Butterfield, M. 14:147
Butterfield, Peter 21:309
Butterfield, S. 21:165
Butterfield, Samuel W.
    11:180
Butterfield, Smith 22:138
Butterfield, Stephen A.
    1:13
Butterfield, W. O. 20:219

Butterfield, W. W. 1:110
Butterfield, Willard O.
    10:44
Butterfield, Z. A. 1:115
Butterford, T. 9:49
Butterman, Henry 10:102
Butterman, M. A. 23:312
Butters, George 25:150
Butters, J. 3:35
Butters, James 10:105;
    20:219
Butters, Theodore S.
    16:83
Butters, William 9:239;
    18:275
Butterwick, Henry 27:12
Butterworth, Josiah
    16:117
Buttholph, R. 10:44
Buttiker, T. 20:34
Buttingham, Isaac 12:141
Buttler, G. A. 16:289
Buttler, O. 16:289
Buttler, William 20:219
Buttles, Lyman 20:111
Buttoff, John W. 22:496
Buttolph, David O. 23:23
Buttolph, R. 20:219
Buttolph, William H.
    23:262
Buttom, J. 16:266
Button, A. 14:44
Button, David 4:14
Button, Dorathal 22:170
Button, E. A. 21:203
Button, E. D. 3:35
Button, Edward 9:171;
    19:244
Button, F. 16:178
Button, Fred 7:21
Button, George 1:17
Button, Hosea 21:210
Button, J. 1:20
Button, J. W. 16:113
Button, John 24:156
Button, John T. 8:100;
    17:460
Button, Wilson 14:268
Buttons, L. D. 19:152
Buttram, --- 12:86
Buttram, John 7:21
Buttram, T. L. 16:289
Buttrick, Alanson E.
    19:152
Buttrick, Alden 15:103
Butts, A. 3:35
Butts, A. G. 24:14
Butts, Benjamin 10:94
Butts, C. 14:44
Butts, C. D. 1:96
Butts, C. W. 25:150

Butts, Charles M. 20:191
Butts, Charles W. 26:11
Butts, G. H. 9:218; 18:363
Butts, Henry 8:37; 26:150
Butts, Henry H. 15:340;
    16:365
Butts, James 9:164;
    25:318
Butts, John 3:35; 15:119
Butts, John R. 11:51
Butts, Joseph 1:114
Butts, O. P. 4:14
Butts, Philip 1:115
Butts, Philip W. 10:90;
    20:219
Butts, Richard 23:117
Butts, Robert 11:395
Butts, Thomas 17:31
Butts, William 25:150
Butts, William E. 23:105
Butwater, W. 25:150
Butwistle, George 14:147
Buty, Samuel 24:75
Butz, Augustus 12:147
Butz, W. 14:44
Buvy, John C. 10:171
Buxford, Daniel 25:150
Buxom, C. 25:150
Buxto, --- 12:63
Buxton, C. M. 24:61
Buxton, E. W. 4:14
Buxton, George 12:61;
    15:90
Buxton, George A. 23:202
Buxton, Greenberry S.
    9:33
Buxton, J. L. 25:277
Buxton, Thomas 3:35;
    11:102
Buyer, H. 3:35
Buyer, Oliver 27:12
Buys, James 17:262
Buys, Jeremiah 4:14
Buyton, Nicholas 7:119
Buzbee, C. W. 25:310
Buzbee, Elizabeth 25:310
Buzbee, F. W. 25:310
Buzbee, S. 25:310
Buzbee, T. J. 25:310
Buzby, Benjamin 22:415
Buzeel, James 18:323
Buzell, S. 16:178
Buzhard, John 15:119
Buzinait, George 7:48
Buzine, R. S. 25:318
Buzinham, Oliver 17:348
Buzyard, Perry W. 19:7
Buzzard, George 23:23
Buzzard, J. 7:48
Buzzard, Jacob 4:14
Buzzard, James 7:21

Buzzard, John 11:136
Buzzard, John J. 8:71
Buzzard, William 20:84
Buzzell, Charles V. 16:80
Buzzell, E. K. 1:109
Buzzell, Solon 21:309
Buzzell, Solon D. 9:213
Buzzell, Stephen S.
    21:309
Byam, G. 1:110
Byam, P. A. 19:59
Byam, S. A. 13:62
Byand, Paul 5:11
Byant, Ambrose 17:18
Byard, Abram J. 22:181
Byard, Andrew J. 8:103
Byard, Cornelius 12:67
Byard, Frank 6:8
Byard, George L. 12:15
Byas, Alexander 11:198
Byatt, James E. 21:9
Byatt, William 14:147
Bybee, Joseph J. 23:97
Bybell, --- 14:321; 23:183
Byck, Enis 18:26
Byden, Lucius 12:15
Bye, George J. 23:23
Byebee, J. F. 9:140
Byens, Andrew M. 5:11
Byer, Albert 4:14
Byer, G. B. 23:178
Byer, George B. 23:178
Byer, John 4:14
Byeril, C. 1:111
Byerly, Amos 23:23
Byerly, Cyrus P. 18:108
Byerly, Jacob 20:29
Byerly, James 3:35
Byerly, John 22:68
Byerly, Noah 21:20
Byerly, Smith 19:7
Byerly, W. N. 3:35
Byerly, William 3:35;
    17:147
Byerns, J. 3:36
Byers, A. 25:150
Byers, Adam 11:134
Byers, E. 22:292
Byers, Emanuel 5:11
Byers, George 11:137
Byers, J. 3:36; 11:236;
    13:84
Byers, J. G. 14:44
Byers, James 22:68
Byers, John 4:14; 15:64;
    22:416; 25:18
Byers, John W. 8:46;
    21:20
Byers, Joseph 22:181
Byers, Lawson 14:261
Byers, O. D. 23:136

Byers, Samuel F. 17:31
Byers, William 9:41;
    13:13; 22:68, 496;
    26:121
Byers, William P. 11:52
Byford, Q. I. 21:12
Byington, A. E. 11:285
Byington, C. E. 18:46
Byland, Franklin D. 21:65
Bylema, Oscar 22:138
Bymun, Thomas 13:84
Bymun, Townsend 26:151
Byndick, F. 12:98
Bynes, A. M. 25:150
Bynorn, J. W. 3:36
Bynos, John S. 11:22
Byns, Thomas 22:181
Bynum, Townsend 8:37
Byons, H. G. 15:6
Byons, Richard 6:24
Byram, C. K. 21:12
Byram, Hardy L. 19:152
Byram, Joseph N. 23:243
Byram, W. C. 18:64
Byram, William 20:219
Byraman, John 10:158
Byramen, John 19:152
Byran, William 10:105
Byrd, A. 14:330
Byrd, Anderson 8:37
Byrd, Benjamin 7:119
Byrd, Clay 20:153
Byrd, J. 9:140; 19:7;
    27:14
Byrd, James 20:153
Byrd, L. C. 8:10
Byrd, M. S. 22:473
Byrd, S. I. 8:10
Byrd, S. J. 18:125
Byrd, Tho. 20:219
Byrd, Thomas 10:44
Byrens, Allen T. 25:310
Byrens, R. 1:110
Byres, George 3:36
Byrett, L. 15:349
Byreum, Thomas 14:5
Byrington, H. 1:113
Byrke, Joe 9:129
Byrket, J. S. 25:151
Byrkett, Eli 18:214
Byrkett, Peter 18:214
Byrkit, Peter 24:36
Byrllen, E. 9:49
Byrn, Patrick 22:9
Byrne, J. 1:16; 9:49
Byrne, James 13:13
Byrne, James A. 10:105
Byrne, James O. 15:13
Byrne, John 7:8
Byrne, M. 25:16
Byrne, Peter 13:13

Byrne, Thomas 23:127
Byrne, W. C. 11:257
Byrne, William 16:147;
    21:251
Byrnes, --- 15:187
Byrnes, F. 6:30; 25:318
Byrnes, John 4:14
Byrnes, Peter 23:10
Byrnisser, John 11:180
Byroad, P. 23:136
Byrod, Anderson 26:151
Byrom, James 22:511
Byron, A. 14:251
Byron, Emanuel 25:285
Byron, Fred 11:398
Byron, H. M. 3:36
Byron, Harrison 11:399
Byron, Henry 25:151
Byron, J. 3:36
Byron, J. F. 7:74; 21:309;
    25:294
Byron, J. M. 23:136
Byron, Jacob 15:187;
    19:152
Byron, James 11:383
Byron, James C. L.
    18:231; 26:14
Byron, John 20:121
Byron, Leonard 25:288
Byron, Lewis 15:297
Byron, Patrick 22:331
Byron, Peter 9:171
Byron, William H. 22:68
Byron, Z. 1:109
Byrum, George 22:23
Byrum, Henry 7:89
Byrum, J. F. 11:90
Byrum, Joe 8:46
Bywater, J. 9:65
Bywater, James 18:275
Byxbee, John 27:19
Byxbee, John T. 27:14
Byxber, John 9:116

C

C---, --- 10:27, 186;
    20:55; 23:23; 25:151
C---, A. 11:237; 20:38;
    25:151
C---, A. H. 11:339
C---, A. J. 11:301
C---, A. W. 17:364;
    24:109
C---, Albert B. 19:296
C---, B. 9:51; 11:385;
    24:36
C---, B. B. 21:207
C---, B. F. 24:109
C---, Bellew W. 21:309

C---, C. 15:30; 21:165; 25:151
C---, C. O. 12:141
C---, C. W. 20:86
C---, Charles D. 25:23
C---, D--- 23:61
C---, D. 15:192; 16:91; 22:350; 23:202; 26:156
C---, D. W. 11:218
C---, Dennis 11:25
C---, E. 20:91; 22:350; 23:202; 26:210
C---, E. B. 8:71
C---, E. D. 11:299
C---, E. P. 15:192; 20:55
C---, F. 11:321; 17:346
C---, G. 17:509; 23:197; 24:109
C---, G. S. 15:103
C---, G. W. 17:216; 27:24
C---, George 15:192, 297
C---, H. 11:339; 17:109; 20:141, 153; 21:20; 23:262
C---, H. B. 19:64
C---, H. C. 2:9
C---, H. H. 11:27
C---, I. 17:296
C---, I. D. 11:421
C---, I. P. 17:296
C---, J. 18:26; 20:5, 55; 21:165, 309; 23:202, 251
C---, J. A. 20:34
C---, J. B. 14:268; 16:366; 20:154
C---, J. C. 21:207
C---, J. F. 23:267; 24:213; 26:156
C---, J. H. 11:259; 20:219; 24:109; 25:21; 26:156
C---, J. M. 26:156
C---, J. N. 20:55
C---, J. Q. 12:99
C---, J. R. 15:258; 20:219
C---, J. S. 24:213
C---, J. W. 11:299; 21:207
C---, John 20:219
C---, John M. 23:267
C---, L. 23:260
C---, L. J. 21:165
C---, M. 11:279; 24:109; 25:20; 26:156
C---, M. J. 12:86
C---, M. R. 25:310
C---, M. T. 20:136
C---, N. 20:180; 21:165
C---, N. W. 23:292
C---, O. H. P. 26:156

C---, O. P. 19:64
C---, Otis 20:136
C---, P. 26:156
C---, Peter M. 15:21
C---, R. 11:299; 15:95; 19:64
C---, S. 9:213; 17:216; 20:38
C---, S. H. 17:296
C---, S. L. 21:207
C---, T. 23:85; 24:213
C---, T. M. 24:109
C---, Thomas 11:325
C---, V. S. 10:32
C---, W. 2:9; 17:355; 20:55, 121, 219; 22:350; 24:109
C---, W. A. 19:300; 23:267
C---, W. B. 16:366
C---, W. C. 21:135
C---, W. E. 20:219
C---, W. F. 21:207
C---, W. H. 18:26; 20:34
C---, W. J. 25:24
C---, W. O. 11:339
C---, William 11:339; 12:141; 15:172
C---, William S. 25:21
C----, J---- 22:244
C----, R. 22:181
C---g, William 17:271
C---kers, John 25:26
Ca, James 13:13
Ca---, William 19:59
Caarl, --- 1:121
Caban, William 27:28
Cabanski, Michael 20:27
Cabassier, Frank 23:242
Cabb, C. W. 15:349
Cabbage, George A. 15:325
Cabbage, Henry S. 17:417; 24:157
Cabe, Job 22:69
Cabel, Henry 24:65
Cabell, David 8:71
Cabell, James 6:22
Cabell, M. J. 14:147
Cabella, F. 24:65
Cabellero, --- 19:322
Caberly, Levi D. 21:309
Cabey, F. 16:178
Cabin, William 9:140
Cable, Benjamin 8:81
Cable, Benjamin H. 9:11
Cable, C. 3:36
Cable, C. H. 24:14
Cable, J. S. 1:23
Cable, Jacob W. 17:161

Cable, James 6:15; 9:108; 18:78
Cable, James H. 22:420
Cable, William 7:119; 10:158; 16:178; 19:152; 22:23
Cabler, Daniel 10:44; 20:219
Cabler, Philip 8:81
Cables, Henderson 7:119
Cablisher, J. 11:141
Cabner, John 19:152
Cabun, R. H. 11:27
Caby, W. 11:141
Cace, M. A. 11:285
Cacrone, J. H. 9:49
Cada, William 11:421
Cadal, Andrew 22:449
Caddehay, Ed 25:151
Caddell, Andrew 10:44
Caddell, Martin V. 24:58
Caddell, Richard 25:283
Cadding, J. C. 3:36
Caddington, Elton 9:116
Caddle, William 14:314
Caddy, James 21:309
Cade, Elbert B. 8:10; 18:125
Cade, Enoch 22:23
Cade, Ezra 10:7
Cade, James 17:346
Cade, W. P. 21:309
Cadell, Amos 4:14
Cadell, Peter 11:88
Cader, Daniel 19:152
Cader, H. 14:44
Cadey, Henry 4:14
Cadey, John 22:244
Cadigan, Michael 1:120
Cadison, I. 10:27
Cadle, John 14:147
Cadle, Z. P. 26:217
Cadman, N. W. 1:119
Cadmes, William H. 11:124
Cadmus, Adam C. 16:91
Cadmus, C. 3:36
Cadmus, J. W. 17:387
Cadnell, C. B. 15:340
Cadogan, H. 12:98
Cador, Maximilian 25:318
Cadry, B. F. 15:340
Cadwalader, Silas 26:122
Cadwallader, Elisha 22:69
Cadwallader, J. B. 22:69
Cadwallader, Thomas B. 22:23
Cadwell, A. 21:309
Cadwell, A. G. 23:283
Cadwell, Alex 9:240

Cadwell, Alfred 14:147
Cadwell, B. W. 14:295;
    17:470; 27:31
Cadwell, C. B. 16:365
Cadwell, Charles D.
    13:127
Cadwell, E. D. 11:190
Cadwell, G. 16:178
Cadwell, J. 1:122
Cadwell, P. 1:120
Cadwell, Samuel 23:23
Cadwell, William 5:50
Cadwellader, Silas 9:41
Cadwick, William A.
    10:204
Cady, Addison 10:171;
    19:152
Cady, Andrew 1:21
Cady, Arod 20:5
Cady, Augustus 1:120
Cady, B. F. 16:365
Cady, C. 1:97; 22:331
Cady, C. F. 19:59
Cady, Charles 4:14;
    21:309
Cady, Charles M. 9:240
Cady, Demetrius 22:23
Cady, Dennis 13:13;
    16:24
Cady, Edward 1:120
Cady, F. 13:106
Cady, G. F. 15:314
Cady, George 3:36
Cady, George A. 22:461
Cady, George W. 22:461
Cady, H. W. 15:302
Cady, Harrison 22:138
Cady, Henry I. 24:91
Cady, Henry W. 16:178
Cady, J. 3:36; 12:63;
    13:106; 15:16
Cady, J. J. 3:36
Cady, James B. 24:72
Cady, James D. 23:85
Cady, James M. 10:105;
    20:219
Cady, John 10:44; 22:69
Cady, Joseph 17:18
Cady, Joseph B. 13:13
Cady, Lee D. 23:283
Cady, M. 17:153
Cady, Mike 16:91
Cady, P. W. 13:62;
    16:178
Cady, Patrick 22:23
Cady, R. B. 19:7
Cady, S. H. 1:119
Cady, Thomas P. T. 10:44
Cady, Thomas T. P.
    20:219
Cady, Vernon F. 1:22

Cady, William 9:101;
    18:337
Caefer, Conrad 22:331
Caesar, Daniel 25:151
Caetid, John 18:231
Caff, Charles 15:303
Caffee, J. 27:26
Caffelt, A. C. 22:23
Caffery, W. 1:120
Caffey, Joshua 27:29
Caffray, J. 9:140
Caffray, Thomas 24:14
Caffren, G. H. 1:25
Caffrey, J. 27:26
Caffrey, John 17:77
Cagal, C. 14:44
Cage, Henry 21:309
Cage, J. W. 14:147
Cage, John 11:198
Cage, John W. 23:97
Cage, Melebizibel C.
    22:401
Cage, S. C. 19:235
Cager, John 9:116; 27:30
Cagg, A. 14:147, 254
Cagher, Thomas 14:147
Cagle, Elijah 17:428;
    24:150
Cagle, Rufus 22:500
Cagle, W. 17:49
Cagur, Atonie 9:49
Cahartt, William 8:10
Cahaw, B. 8:71
Cahen, C. 13:106
Cahil, --- 19:59
Cahile, L. J. 27:27
Cahill, --- 15:286
Cahill, A. 19:152
Cahill, E. J. 17:404
Cahill, Francis 7:14;
    23:250
Cahill, J. 1:117, 118;
    11:300
Cahill, J. H. 3:36
Cahill, James 12:15;
    19:338; 27:25
Cahill, James A. 11:140
Cahill, John 9:19; 18:303;
    26:94
Cahill, L. 10:105; 20:219
Cahill, Lawrence 11:218
Cahill, Michael 10:105;
    20:219
Cahill, Nicholas 18:303;
    26:95
Cahill, Peter 9:11
Cahill, T. 19:152
Cahill, Thomas 9:33;
    18:291; 26:95
Cahill, Timothy 21:309

Cahill, William 3:36;
    14:147
Cahles, Thomas 5:11
Cahon, N. J. 3:36
Cahoon, Charles 12:15
Cahoon, Daniel W. 21:20
Cahoon, Joseph 21:163
Cahoun, B. B. B. 18:125
Cahow, William 9:15
Cahue, Henry 18:26
Caid, John 11:124
Caig, James 18:205
Caige, W. H. 8:46
Cail, Christopher 22:401
Cailas, F. 14:27
Caillot, John 4:14
Caily, Y. C. 22:23
Cain, --- 7:77; 10:158
Cain, A. N. 13:13
Cain, Alford 26:18
Cain, Alfred 10:90
Cain, Allen M. 18:125
Cain, Alpin 20:219
Cain, Andrew 20:55
Cain, Anthony 7:21
Cain, Augustus 17:144
Cain, Charles 17:442;
    21:20; 24:157
Cain, Charles C. 20:55
Cain, Christopher D.
    10:14
Cain, D. 24:75
Cain, F. 13:84; 14:5
Cain, Francis 23:10
Cain, G. 14:44
Cain, George 14:44
Cain, George W. 19:7
Cain, Harvey 7:21
Cain, Henri 26:22
Cain, Henry B. 22:476
Cain, Henry J. 13:79
Cain, Horace 4:14
Cain, J. F. 11:293
Cain, Jacob 17:316
Cain, Jacob L. 4:14
Cain, James 11:55; 21:12
Cain, James H. 19:7
Cain, Jesse 12:15; 21:97
Cain, John 1:21; 9:49, 76;
    11:258, 385; 16:91;
    17:205; 26:19
Cain, John C. 17:18
Cain, Joseph 11:55
Cain, M. 1:119, 122; 3:36
Cain, Nelson 15:352;
    16:277; 22:401
Cain, Owen 16:289
Cain, P. 1:118; 21:20
Cain, P. C. 1:23
Cain, Patrick 25:151
Cain, R. A. 8:116; 18:330

Cain, Richard 14:235
Cain, Russell A. 8:81
Cain, T. 5:11; 15:187; 25:151
Cain, Thomas 3:36; 10:44; 20:47, 219
Cain, W. 1:121
Cain, William 1:119
Cain, William F. 10:94; 15:289; 16:178
Cain, Wizery 9:206; 18:64
Cainco, Len 26:155
Caine, Alfred 9:76
Caine, George W. 22:446
Caine, J. 1:118
Cainer, George 21:49
Caines, Arthur 14:147
Cainlett, E. M. 9:108
Caio, Adolphus 23:10
Cair, Jesse 8:46
Cairnes, James 18:26
Cairnes, William 22:23; 27:25
Cairs, Alexander 15:187
Caited, John 26:19
Caiter, G. 14:319
Caithorn, Charles 17:94
Cake, George F. 16:83
Cakill, Patrick 17:253
Cakin, Reuben J. 19:269
Cakin, William 9:229
Cal, James R. 11:140
Cal, S. H. 11:104
Calabine, Peter A. 14:334
Calahan, Alexander 23:136
Calahan, B. F. 11:83
Calahan, C. A. 15:119
Calahan, George 7:119
Calahan, I. 15:187
Calahan, Patrick 15:30
Calahan, William 20:220
Calamazoo, Sargent 22:292
Calamine, Alexander 12:10
Calander, Jack 9:70
Calaway, Charles 10:44
Calaway, Monroe 10:44
Calb, R. C. 9:41
Calback, H. 11:299
Calbert, Joseph 22:292
Calbfalls, J. 1:23
Calborn, Joseph 8:81
Calcord, Lewis 13:13
Calcutt, Samuel W. 20:219
Calden, James 1:21
Calder, E. H. 21:20
Calder, J. D. 27:27
Calder, John A. 9:19

Calderhead, John 7:56
Calderwood, A. H. 10:153; 19:152
Calderwood, E. S. 9:171
Calderwood, Eben S. 19:225
Calderwood, H. A. 2:8; 25:23
Caldhan, L. C. 3:36
Caldnell, J. H. 25:151
Caldorell, Robert 13:60
Caldron, Rush B. 4:14
Caldway, Nathaniel 7:119
Caldwell, A. 3:36; 20:121
Caldwell, A. J. 3:36; 17:247
Caldwell, Alfred 17:460; 24:157
Caldwell, Andrew 20:5
Caldwell, Archie 11:26
Caldwell, Augustus 20:192
Caldwell, Benjamin 10:44; 20:219
Caldwell, Benoni 22:244
Caldwell, C. 1:117
Caldwell, C. A. 16:91
Caldwell, Cassius M. 21:251
Caldwell, Charles 12:169
Caldwell, David 17:262
Caldwell, David T. 20:145
Caldwell, David W. 20:16
Caldwell, F. 14:239
Caldwell, G. L. 17:151, 402
Caldwell, George 10:158; 11:25
Caldwell, Henry 22:418
Caldwell, Hiram P. 17:391
Caldwell, Isaac 18:108; 21:251
Caldwell, J. 3:36
Caldwell, J. D. 16:178
Caldwell, J. E. 13:79
Caldwell, J. G. 25:151
Caldwell, J. H. 23:136
Caldwell, James 13:13; 22:244
Caldwell, James A. 18:125
Caldwell, James H. 5:11
Caldwell, James M. 10:14
Caldwell, James N. 8:10
Caldwell, John B. 10:14
Caldwell, Jonathan F. 22:23
Caldwell, Joseph C. 19:59
Caldwell, Leonidas 8:81
Caldwell, Levi 11:104

Caldwell, M. 1:23; 2:9
Caldwell, M. D. 22:181
Caldwell, McS. 23:243
Caldwell, Moses 17:109
Caldwell, P. 3:36; 11:339
Caldwell, R. 1:118
Caldwell, Reuben 22:292
Caldwell, S. A. 3:36
Caldwell, Samuel 13:13; 18:231; 26:20
Caldwell, Samuel M. 16:117
Caldwell, T. 27:33
Caldwell, Thomas 11:421; 17:172; 23:61
Caldwell, W. A. 26:144
Caldwell, W. H. 17:272
Caldwell, W. P. 15:13
Caldwell, W. W. 19:7
Caldwell, Warton 16:160
Caldwell, William 3:36; 9:19; 22:244; 25:24; 26:155
Caldwell, William D. 21:97
Caldwell, William R. 13:13
Cale, H. H. 14:239
Cale, J. 3:36
Cale, J. H. 25:151
Cale, James M. 23:23
Cale, James W. 8:81
Cale, Jeremiah F. 8:81
Cale, S. J. 21:200
Cale, W. H. 3:36
Caleb, Emanuel 17:172
Caleen, Charles 14:148
Calef, Jonathan 1:20
Calehan, H. 12:151
Calehoof, Henry 12:15
Caleman, James H. 8:81
Caleman, Lind 3:36
Calender, Isaac 24:14
Calender, John 22:69
Calendine, Daniel 18:78
Calent, Kele 24:190
Caler, Jesse 8:81
Caler, William 22:9
Cales, Thomas J. 10:44
Calesley, J. 3:36
Caley, David 11:411
Caley, William 22:181
Calfa, A. W. 27:32
Calgin, --- (Mrs.) 26:218
Calgrove, Caleb E. 22:23
Calhan, J. C. 12:151
Calheart, Hugh 18:26
Calherand, Charles 18:64
Calhoin, Alva 17:296
Calhoon, E. A. 1:121
Calhoon, John C. 20:219

Calhorm, Ottaway 21:309
Calhoun, Albert 8:81;
    18:26
Calhoun, Andrew H.
    10:105; 20:219
Calhoun, Bailer B. B. 8:10
Calhoun, G. S. 12:95;
    15:358
Calhoun, Hamilton 11:385
Calhoun, J. 1:117
Calhoun, J. H. 9:49
Calhoun, James 10:44;
    20:220
Calhoun, James E. 24:36
Calhoun, James R. 17:313
Calhoun, John 7:67
Calhoun, John C. 9:199,
    229; 19:280
Calhoun, Joseph 17:425;
    24:177
Calhoun, Lafayette 22:292
Calhoun, Mack 22:292
Calhoun, S. 9:140; 27:27
Calhoun, Samuel 9:140;
    10:105; 20:220
Calhoun, W. 1:23
Calhoun, William 20:188;
    22:181
Calhuna, Daniel 22:518
Calib, Alfred 26:19
Calico, George 10:44;
    20:220
Calicott, Samuel W. 10:44
Calicut, John 18:231;
    26:21
Califf, Jewel 22:69
Calihan, David 8:103
Calihan, G. 16:365
Caliman, Benjamin F.
    13:56
Caling, Ed 3:36
Calk, George 10:176;
    19:152
Calkens, F. A. 1:119
Calkin, Arsten Y. 7:89
Calkin, George W. 7:89
Calkin, Jacob 23:23
Calkin, Marion 9:76
Calkin, Rueben J. 9:171
Calkins, A. 1:26; 11:339
Calkins, Alfred 26:217
Calkins, C. 5:50
Calkins, Calvin 1:22
Calkins, Cornelius 22:181
Calkins, E. 1:93
Calkins, George 14:44;
    20:151; 24:14
Calkins, J. 7:21
Calkins, James 13:13
Calkins, James E. 17:63;
    22:181

Calkins, Joseph 21:309
Calkins, Marion 26:18
Calkins, O. H. 27:27
Calkins, O. N. 9:140
Calkins, R. 1:118
Calkins, S. V. 3:36
Calkins, Stephen B. 20:21
Calkins, William 21:309
Calkins, William B.
    22:138
Calkins, Z. J. 12:15
Call, Charles 22:292, 449
Call, E. 15:187
Call, George 1:25; 14:239;
    15:351; 16:365, 373;
    23:136; 27:33
Call, George B. 23:23
Call, H. D. 1:25
Call, Henry 8:46
Call, Hugh 22:331
Call, Isaac 22:181
Call, Isaac M. 26:155
Call, J. 11:237; 23:136
Call, J. J. 1:121
Call, J. M. 25:21
Call, John 4:14; 22:476
Call, John M. 12:151
Call, Joseph H. 10:105;
    20:220
Call, Julius N. 9:11
Call, L. 14:44
Call, Luther 22:181
Call, M. 26:19
Call, Moses 1:21
Call, P. 25:151
Call, P. S. 22:292
Call, Patrick 5:11
Call, Robert F. 12:170
Call, Rufus H. 21:90
Call, Warner 9:76
Call, Washington 22:292
Call, William 7:21; 24:36
Call, William R. 16:132
Callagan, Martin 23:200
Callagan, R. 15:328
Callaghan, --- 16:289
Callaghan, C. 3:36
Callaghan, D. 1:24
Callaghan, D. M. 7:56
Callaghan, Davis 10:158
Callaghan, Jerry 13:13
Callaghan, Mathew
    16:178
Callaghan, Michael 1:120
Callaghan, Nathaniel
    13:13
Callaghan, T. O. 1:25
Callaghan, Thomas 20:47
Callagher, C. 3:36
Callagher, James 9:108
Callagher, John 11:55

Callahan, A. 25:151
Callahan, C. 1:117
Callahan, David 19:152
Callahan, David M.
    22:401
Callahan, Dennis 10:185
Callahan, George 21:309
Callahan, Henry 22:244
Callahan, J. 25:151
Callahan, James 3:36
Callahan, Jeremiah 11:139
Callahan, John 5:11;
    21:97
Callahan, Mathew 15:303
Callahan, O. M. 21:309
Callahan, Oth 17:335
Callahan, P. 3:36; 14:148
Callahan, Patrick 10:171;
    12:67; 13:13; 27:33
Callahan, Peter 15:64
Callahan, S. B. 9:240
Callahan, Solomon 21:309
Callahan, T. S. 22:23
Callahan, Thomas 14:44
Callahan, W. 3:36; 16:365
Callahan, W. P. 27:24
Callahan, William 10:105;
    11:400
Callaher, G. W. 26:17
Callam, M. 3:36
Callam, Michael 10:158
Callamore, S. E. 27:28
Callan, James 16:365
Callan, Samuel 14:147
Callargus, O. 25:151
Callaway, Charles 20:220
Callaway, Isaac 17:455;
    24:190
Callaway, John 24:109
Callaway, M. 20:220
Callbrock, J. 3:36
Calle, A. J. 11:325
Callea, Andrew 22:292
Callen, James 16:24
Callen, John 7:62
Callendar, Matthias 9:49
Callender, William H.
    11:83
Callery, John 25:268
Calleson, Alfred 17:428
Calley, Alexander 19:152
Calley, John S. 19:277
Callher, Roger 9:11
Calliat, Adrian 23:283
Callidge, Stephen 5:11
Calligan, James 3:36
Calligan, Peter 8:113
Calligon, M. 1:119
Callihan, D. H. 1:21
Callihan, Edw. 14:148
Callihan, G. 15:340

Callihan, H. 3:36
Callihan, J. 3:36
Callihan, John 3:36
Callihan, Patrick 3:36;
    12:15
Callihan, R. 3:36
Callihan, Samuel 3:36
Callihan, Thomas 3:36
Callin, Joseph 11:411
Callins, Charles R. 22:500
Callins, Norman 11:124
Callis, H. G. 18:205
Callison, Isaac 22:420
Callison, J. 19:300
Callison, J. T. 14:44
Callison, R. R. 15:187
Callison, Thomas 11:104
Callnis, S. S. 22:69
Calloden, Daniel 4:14
Callogg, H. 24:14
Callon, William A. 22:69
Calloner, John 17:247
Callord, George 13:13
Callory, Hugh 19:152
Callos, M. 19:153
Calloway, Albert 9:129;
    27:29
Calloway, J. W. 25:151
Calloway, John W. 5:37
Calloway, Leander 23:278
Calloway, William 3:36
Cally, Thomas 27:29
Cally, William 13:13
Calmeston, C. 9:49
Calnane, D. 25:151
Calnane, Daniel 5:11
Calohen, Dennis 18:172
Caloman, Thomas 7:119
Calony, E. 3:36
Calorie, D. 14:44
Calp, Samuel G. 22:72
Calpin, Andy 11:200
Calprence, M. S. 26:17
Calriock, John 14:44
Calsom, William 12:67
Calson, Charles 24:14
Calson, John C. 21:90
Caltinbaugh, William
    22:111
Calton, William 10:105
Calum, A. H. 11:83
Calvanoll, James 11:200
Calvay, G. 27:28
Calvell, William 19:59
Calver, A. 26:19
Calver, George W. 7:67
Calverly, Joseph M.
    23:178
Calvers, John A. 13:13
Calvert, Ardel 27:27
Calvert, Eli 22:475

Calvert, Francis 8:46
Calvert, Francis A. 21:65
Calvert, G. F. 3:36;
    14:148
Calvert, G. W. 23:136
Calvert, George N. 22:419
Calvert, Hutchinson 22:23
Calvert, J. J. 6:30
Calvert, J. R. 23:136
Calvert, John 14:44
Calvert, Martha Jane
    27:27
Calvert, Peyton L. 23:112
Calvert, R. 22:244
Calvert, R. R. 3:36
Calvert, Richard 4:14
Calvert, Sanford D.
    17:259
Calvert, Thomas 21:309;
    22:118
Calvert, William 19:44
Calvert, William I. 22:118
Calvert, William M.
    25:279
Calvey, Edward A. 24:14
Calvin, --- 19:59
Calvin, Alfred 7:119
Calvin, Charles G. 22:69
Calvin, D. C. 16:135
Calvin, Daniel 17:94
Calvin, Demetrius 18:102
Calvin, Edward 14:334
Calvin, G. W. 27:27
Calvin, George W. 23:284
Calvin, Hugh 22:418
Calvin, Ira 21:49
Calvin, Isaac 9:171
Calvin, J. 8:71
Calvin, J. B. 22:181
Calvin, J. J. 8:81
Calvin, James H. 20:121
Calvin, John 18:108;
    22:23
Calvin, John W. 1:191;
    24:36
Calvin, M. 15:187
Calvin, Martin 17:355
Calvin, Mathew D. 16:24
Calvin, Milan 8:113
Calvin, Morris 20:29
Calvin, Moses 24:65
Calvin, N. O. 14:44
Calvin, Robert 9:76
Calvin, Thomas H. 21:49
Calvin, W. 18:13
Calvin, W. C. 27:32
Calvin, William 7:89;
    27:31
Calvin, William H. 22:69
Calvin, William M.
    22:181

Calvington, R. 3:36;
    14:148
Calway, E. C. 14:277
Calwell, Henry 18:78
Calwell, James B. 12:151
Calwell, John 11:139;
    17:346
Calwell, M. B. 12:151
Calwell, Patten 21:309
Calwell, Warren 8:81
Calwin, Jesse P. 18:205
Calyer, Wesley 8:81
Camack, William 22:293
Camahan, H. 7:65
Caman, James 9:218
Caman, Jerome S. 9:171
Caman, Lawrence 9:171
Camance, F. W. 14:44
Camba, Henry 6:30
Cambel, W. 21:20
Cambell, D. 16:365
Cambell, Daniel 19:272
Cambell, David N. 13:133
Cambell, J. S. 25:151
Cambell, R. 14:277
Cambell, W. 11:186
Cambell, William 3:37
Camberford, Patrick J. K.
    20:142
Cambert, Charles 14:44
Camble, Henry 17:172
Camblin, Thaddeus D.
    24:36
Cambol, R. C. 17:446
Cambridge, J. 21:185
Cambridge, P. H. 12:151
Cambs, J. H. 14:44
Camden, George 18:323
Camden, J. S. 16:24
Camden, Shelby 9:171
Camden, Thomas R.
    14:148
Came, John M. 20:220
Cameil, J. L. 1:97
Camel, Abraham 23:312
Camel, C. 18:13
Camel, Frank 27:28
Camel, John D. 11:421
Camel, M. 9:129
Camelio, J. E. 12:151
Camell, J. 3:37
Cameron, A. 12:97
Cameron, Alexander
    15:187
Cameron, B. H. 19:153
Cameron, Benton 16:24
Cameron, Bernard 7:9;
    19:7
Cameron, Charles 14:148
Cameron, Clinton 22:244
Cameron, D. 3:37

Cameron, Daniel 26:17
Cameron, David D. 22:69, 420
Cameron, Duncan 17:161
Cameron, Ed. W. 21:20
Cameron, F. 3:37; 17:18
Cameron, F. M. 7:89
Cameron, Finley 9:213
Cameron, George N. 18:334
Cameron, Glea 15:187
Cameron, Green 21:309
Cameron, H. 3:37
Cameron, Hardin 8:11
Cameron, Henry 22:232; 26:122
Cameron, Hiram 18:125
Cameron, J. 1:118; 15:53
Cameron, J. F. 10:105; 20:220
Cameron, James 12:151; 14:44
Cameron, John 3:37; 7:21; 9:108, 229; 14:148; 20:220; 22:9; 25:151; 27:33
Cameron, Joseph 7:89; 21:309
Cameron, L. 21:309
Cameron, Larzinski 19:153
Cameron, Lewis B. 4:14
Cameron, Lorzinski 10:158
Cameron, Nelson 22:244
Cameron, Norid 15:258
Cameron, Oscar F. 24:75
Cameron, R. 1:25
Cameron, Richard 20:220
Cameron, Robert C. 21:309
Cameron, S. P. 17:291
Cameron, Silas 17:98
Cameron, Simeon 18:205
Cameron, Thomas 11:237
Cameron, William 3:37; 14:148; 21:309
Cameron, William H. 22:475
Camerson, George 22:507
Cames, W. H. 19:7
Cameters, William I. 8:11
Camfield, J. 14:5
Camfield, James 11:25
Camfield, Merritt 20:220
Camfield, Thomas 22:331
Camhill, Charles 16:24
Camie, Orin 9:49
Camile, George 1:192
Camins, J. R. 20:220
Camion, J. C. 14:44

Camis, L. 14:44
Camm, John 11:140
Camm, Stephen 23:136
Cammel, David 8:59
Cammel, Frank 9:129
Cammel, James 12:171
Cammel, James M. 19:7
Cammel, Joseph 13:13
Cammel, Mazarini 27:28
Cammel, Pierre 9:206
Cammell, J. 3:37
Cammell, Joseph 16:24
Cammell, S. 1:118
Cammell, Samuel 22:292
Cammer, W. 14:5
Cammerson, John 15:187
Cammick, Peter 11:200
Cammire, William 22:23
Cammock, William 14:44
Cammon, J. 14:44
Cammon, William 24:99
Cammons, Jacob 11:411
Camohan, Silas 10:44
Camon, Edward S. 5:11
Camon, George W. 22:244
Camon, James 18:363
Camp, Albert 9:116; 27:29
Camp, Alexander 1:25
Camp, C. 21:193; 25:22
Camp, Charles 23:23
Camp, Christopher 11:237
Camp, Cyrus M. 17:31
Camp, E. H. 1:121; 11:238
Camp, Elis Van 9:76
Camp, Ezra L. 23:23
Camp, F. M. 8:11; 18:125
Camp, Franklin 25:23
Camp, G. M. 20:151
Camp, G. W. 18:231; 26:21
Camp, George 15:187
Camp, George M. 20:192
Camp, H. 1:122
Camp, H. L. 22:181
Camp, Henry 1:25; 12:48; 22:293
Camp, Hezekiah 11:321
Camp, Hiram 19:59; 27:33
Camp, I. M. 15:187
Camp, Isaac 17:153
Camp, J. 1:119, 122; 14:277
Camp, J. M. 13:84; 14:5
Camp, J. W. 20:145
Camp, James 9:76; 10:105; 16:24; 17:241; 20:220; 26:18

Camp, James W. 20:106
Camp, John 25:151
Camp, Jonah 21:114
Camp, L. F. 24:75
Camp, Levi B. 7:21
Camp, Luther 9:10
Camp, Michael 4:14
Camp, N. 3:37
Camp, N. J. 23:112
Camp, Nathaniel 23:188
Camp, Nathaniel J. 24:61
Camp, Orion 16:178
Camp, Peter 1:25
Camp, Robert 11:55
Camp, Samuel 9:33; 18:291; 26:95
Camp, Sterling W. 10:44; 20:220
Camp, W. S. 17:494
Camp, W. W. 3:37
Camp, William 10:179; 18:172
Camp, William B. 22:499
Camp, William H. 13:13
Campans, John 13:84
Campbell, --- 2:9; 12:168; 19:317
Campbell, A. 1:23, 119, 123; 8:61; 9:19; 15:187; 25:151; 26:95, 154
Campbell, A. A. 16:178
Campbell, A. D. 20:136
Campbell, A. H. 12:67; 15:11
Campbell, A. J. 9:140
Campbell, A. M. 16:132
Campbell, A. V. 20:220
Campbell, Aaron V. 10:44
Campbell, Adam 9:206; 14:148; 18:64; 22:244
Campbell, Alexander 4:14; 21:90; 22:244
Campbell, Alexander D. 24:14
Campbell, Andrew 7:89; 16:289
Campbell, Andrew J. 27:28
Campbell, Angus 22:138
Campbell, Anthony 17:129; 24:192
Campbell, Archelist 23:119
Campbell, Archibald 24:61
Campbell, Augustine 27:28
Campbell, Austin 21:266
Campbell, B. 3:37

Campbell, B. A. 17:202
Campbell, B. M. 5:11;
25:151
Campbell, Benjamin
23:136
Campbell, C. 9:159;
12:149; 15:119;
25:151; 26:217
Campbell, C. A. 3:37
Campbell, C. H. 19:225
Campbell, C. I. 12:121
Campbell, C. J. 15:119
Campbell, C. M. 27:25
Campbell, Charles 10:105,
208; 12:98; 13:13;
15:347; 16:24;
20:220; 22:292
Campbell, Charles C.
24:91
Campbell, Charles H.
10:106; 20:220
Campbell, Charles P.
24:48
Campbell, Charles W.
21:309
Campbell, Clark 22:182
Campbell, Cornelius
22:292
Campbell, Cyrus M.
21:310
Campbell, D. 1:119; 3:36;
15:150
Campbell, D. A. 3:37
Campbell, D. K. 22:138
Campbell, D. W. 21:95
Campbell, Daniel 8:59;
9:19; 18:303;
19:153; 25:25; 26:94,
95
Campbell, Daniel M.
8:37; 18:323; 26:155
Campbell, David 9:33,
171; 17:63, 241;
18:291; 19:248;
23:61
Campbell, David B.
23:136
Campbell, David F.
22:138
Campbell, David H. 24:91
Campbell, David N.
20:220
Campbell, David W.
10:106; 20:220
Campbell, Dean 8:113
Campbell, Dexter 10:158;
19:153
Campbell, Donald 7:21
Campbell, E. 1:119, 121;
11:237; 16:24; 21:21

Campbell, Edward 11:25;
12:15; 15:187
Campbell, Edward O.
15:31
Campbell, Eli 25:24
Campbell, Elijah 22:69
Campbell, Enoch 21:310
Campbell, F. B. 26:153
Campbell, F. M. 23:136
Campbell, Foodman 9:129
Campbell, Footman 27:24
Campbell, Francis 21:310
Campbell, Francis M.
16:24
Campbell, Frederick
23:105
Campbell, G. 13:124;
16:178; 24:63
Campbell, G. A. 14:287
Campbell, George 9:70,
171; 10:44, 98;
11:19, 199; 14:264;
17:129, 358; 19:235;
20:111, 220; 22:292,
449; 24:191
Campbell, George D. 1:21
Campbell, George F.
14:319; 25:276
Campbell, George H.
9:49; 23:105
Campbell, George N.
23:61
Campbell, George T. 3:37
Campbell, George W.
7:67, 89; 10:44, 106;
17:355; 20:220;
21:310; 22:182
Campbell, H. 1:24;
18:303; 25:22
Campbell, H. G. 7:21
Campbell, Henry 7:21;
15:11, 188; 17:144
Campbell, Henry C.
13:13; 23:136
Campbell, Howard 15:188
Campbell, Hugh 13:13;
19:153
Campbell, Isaac 14:148;
21:210
Campbell, Isaac S. 5:11
Campbell, Isaiah 16:289
Campbell, Ison 22:244
Campbell, J. 1:22, 119;
2:8; 3:37; 10:192;
15:31, 188, 352;
17:153, 279; 18:78,
172, 231; 25:25;
26:20
Campbell, J. A. 11:259;
22:244

Campbell, J. B. 3:36;
14:44, 148; 23:136
Campbell, J. C. 1:25;
16:365
Campbell, J. D. 16:117
Campbell, J. E. 23:136
Campbell, J. H. 13:84;
14:5; 21:49; 23:301
Campbell, J. M. 3:37
Campbell, J. N. 10:106;
20:220; 25:151
Campbell, J. P. 10:179;
18:172
Campbell, J. R. 15:119
Campbell, J. S. 22:182
Campbell, J. W. 1:25;
9:226; 18:284, 363;
24:14; 26:134
Campbell, Jackson 25:285
Campbell, Jacob 7:21;
15:64
Campbell, James 3:36, 37;
8:11, 81, 103; 9:76,
226; 10:44, 106;
12:171; 13:13;
14:148; 15:188, 330;
16:24; 17:31; 18:46,
125, 363; 19:59;
20:220; 21:215;
22:165, 397; 23:281;
24:88
Campbell, James H.
10:106; 20:220
Campbell, James L. 20:39;
22:138
Campbell, James M. 8:103
Campbell, James O.
11:259; 18:46
Campbell, James S. 22:69,
181
Campbell, James V.
10:147
Campbell, James W.
22:244
Campbell, Jerry 21:14
Campbell, Joel N. 22:419
Campbell, John 4:14;
6:12; 7:89; 8:37, 61;
9:203; 10:44, 90,
106; 11:238, 279;
12:15, 67; 14:148;
15:64; 17:164, 279;
19:153; 20:220;
21:221; 22:9, 181,
244; 23:85; 25:22,
151, 287; 26:17, 95,
155; 27:157
Campbell, John A. 10:90
Campbell, John B. 7:21,
56; 25:22

Campbell, John F. 1:21;
9:33; 18:291
Campbell, John H. 4:65
Campbell, John J. 19:153;
22:23
Campbell, John R. 22:244
Campbell, John T. 20:220
Campbell, John W. 8:81;
13:13; 15:31
Campbell, John Y. 10:90
Campbell, Jordan 24:191
Campbell, Joseph 4:14;
11:141; 17:498;
22:244; 25:24, 268,
318
Campbell, Joseph A.
16:152
Campbell, Joshua 22:181
Campbell, Knox 14:148
Campbell, L. 18:363
Campbell, L. B. 3:36
Campbell, Lawson 22:499
Campbell, Levi 11:284;
15:150
Campbell, Lewis 23:303;
24:75
Campbell, Louis 23:136
Campbell, Lowery 22:69
Campbell, M. 3:37;
21:185
Campbell, M. V. 15:283;
19:59
Campbell, M. V. B.
25:151
Campbell, Marion 22:23
Campbell, Martin V. B.
5:11
Campbell, Mathew 22:181
Campbell, Milton 4:14;
16:117
Campbell, Morton 10:106;
20:220
Campbell, Moses 27:31
Campbell, Moses T.
22:244
Campbell, N. 14:45
Campbell, Napoleon
22:511
Campbell, Nathan S.
21:97
Campbell, Nelson 22:512
Campbell, Nemiah W.
11:115
Campbell, O. E. 16:178
Campbell, O. H. 3:37
Campbell, O. N. 14:45
Campbell, O. S. 16:117
Campbell, Oliver 22:69
Campbell, Oliver M.
23:61
Campbell, Orin E. 13:62

Campbell, P. S. 20:39
Campbell, Patrick 5:11
Campbell, Peter 8:100;
17:463; 24:185;
26:155
Campbell, Philip 22:292
Campbell, Preston 11:421
Campbell, R. 10:27;
15:263; 19:300;
24:75
Campbell, R. C. 14:45
Campbell, R. D. 3:37
Campbell, R. E. 11:83
Campbell, R. G. 3:37
Campbell, R. J. 16:24;
25:24
Campbell, Richard 13:13;
25:274
Campbell, Robert 3:37;
4:14; 7:89; 16:24;
17:13; 19:222;
22:449; 23:183
Campbell, Robert C.
21:129
Campbell, Robert K. 8:11;
18:125
Campbell, Robert M.
22:421
Campbell, Roswell 4:14
Campbell, S. 1:24, 118;
21:185
Campbell, S. B. 3:37
Campbell, S. D. 16:117
Campbell, S. L. 3:37
Campbell, S. P. 9:19
Campbell, S. S. 4:14
Campbell, Sampson
11:199
Campbell, Samuel 3:37;
6:30; 8:11; 18:125;
23:86; 25:21, 318
Campbell, Samuel D.
22:23
Campbell, Samuel P.
23:136
Campbell, Selon 22:277
Campbell, Silas M. 20:47
Campbell, Solomon
22:182
Campbell, Sylvester
10:158; 19:153
Campbell, T. 11:238
Campbell, T. J. 8:61;
15:352; 16:277
Campbell, Taylor 17:77
Campbell, Theodore
25:21
Campbell, Thomas 7:21;
9:171; 11:25, 138;
15:336; 16:178;
17:49; 19:248;

Campbell, Thomas
22:138, 500
Campbell, Thomas C.
9:76; 26:17
Campbell, Thomas E.
9:171; 19:277
Campbell, Tubal 8:11;
18:125
Campbell, W. 3:36, 37;
7:21; 15:277; 18:303;
25:25; 26:94
Campbell, W. A. 9:101
Campbell, W. C. 3:37;
27:27
Campbell, W. E. 24:157
Campbell, W. F. 23:23
Campbell, W. G. 23:283
Campbell, W. H. 22:499
Campbell, W. J. 23:136
Campbell, W. T. 18:13
Campbell, W. W. 12:15
Campbell, Ward 5:11
Campbell, Wesley 8:46;
21:65
Campbell, Wesley H. 4:14
Campbell, Whiting J.
22:182
Campbell, William 1:22,
120; 3:36, 37; 6:30;
9:19, 100; 10:106;
11:25, 55, 199;
16:178; 17:101, 400;
18:78, 108, 323;
20:84, 221; 21:185,
240, 310; 22:292;
23:112, 263; 24:100;
25:25, 151, 318;
27:32
Campbell, William A.
17:90
Campbell, William C.
8:11; 18:125
Campbell, William E.
17:442; 22:420
Campbell, William H.
12:15; 18:337
Campbell, William N.
22:23
Campbell, William R.
17:359; 21:21
Campbell, York 9:129;
27:28
Campell, Ira 11:199
Camper, F. E. 1:97
Camper, Henry 7:119
Camper, J. H. 18:79
Camper, John H. 6:12
Camper, Washington
19:44
Campf, Squire 11:140

Campfield, Benjamin 14:148
Campfield, Cyrus 9:154
Campfield, J. 13:84
Campfield, J. W. 8:46
Campfield, John 15:188
Campher, Levin 5:37
Campion, J. 1:24
Campion, John 10:106
Campiron, P. J. 7:89
Cample, Henry 21:266
Cample, W. D. 15:337
Campman, Sidney 7:89
Campman, Tim 14:148
Campsey, James 3:37
Campton, George 20:145
Campton, Robert 9:105
Campton, William C. 26:121
Campy, William J. 23:312
Camron, Harrison 17:272
Camron, Henry 9:41
Camron, James 21:49
Cams, W. W. 11:400
Cams, William 15:188
Camway, H. 3:37
Can, Edward 13:77
Can, George T. 16:178
Can, James 16:178
Canada, A. 17:346
Canada, Alex 11:54
Canada, Alfred 1:23
Canada, Ira 13:62
Canada, Isham 21:266
Canada, J. 25:151
Canada, James 13:13; 23:255
Canada, John H. 21:241
Canada, Thomas 7:89
Canada, W. H. 17:439
Canada, William H. 24:151
Canaday, Charles W. 24:36
Canadin, Shelby 19:277
Canado, O. F. C. 14:263
Canady, A. 25:151
Canady, Andrew J. 21:221
Canady, Bennett M. 22:9
Canady, Eli 11:295
Canady, Horace P. 20:5
Canady, Matthew 8:112
Canady, Samuel 7:21
Canady, William W. 23:263
Canaga, C. L. 13:13
Canaghan, P. 1:21
Canahan, Daniel 14:148
Canahy, James 16:178
Canak, James 4:14
Canalton, Richard 16:178

Canan, L. 19:269
Canan, W. 14:45
Canant, J. R. 25:22
Canard, George 18:46
Canard, J. Q. A. 3:37
Canary, Thomas 18:214
Canary, W. 1:123
Canatt, Peter 11:385
Canbee, Brazil 1:120
Canby, Dennis 7:81
Canby, G. C. 3:37
Canby, J. 8:69
Canby, John 13:56
Canby, T. A. 21:310
Cancher, A. H. 16:178
Cancre, Stephen 4:65
Cancright, W. 21:21
Canculd, George W. 2:9
Cand, Jerome G. 21:310
Candage, George B. 13:13; 16:24
Candall, Aaron 18:125
Candall, Thomas F. 12:15
Candamus, Richard 18:125
Candee, D. M. 3:37
Candeis, Morris 25:26
Candell, W. M. 9:242
Candenus, Richard 8:11
Cander, John 14:319; 25:282
Candett, Asko 4:14
Candie, W. B. 18:64
Candish, Samuel D. 17:450
Candle, John 11:91
Candle, John H. 24:166
Candlish, Alex M. 13:13
Candrith, C. F. 9:49
Candus, W. H. 11:190
Candy, John 8:103
Candy, Seth 23:301
Candy, W. 26:217
Cane, B. 13:79
Cane, Charles 9:129; 22:23
Cane, George 26:153
Cane, James 10:106; 20:221
Cane, James A. 12:63
Cane, John 3:37; 21:310
Cane, John G. 23:178
Cane, Joseph 24:191
Cane, M. 14:5
Cane, Michael 4:14
Cane, Richard 18:125
Cane, Warren 4:14
Cane, William H. 4:14
Cane, Willis 22:118
Canedy, Philo 16:24
Canefield, J. 4:14

Canefield, James 4:14
Canefield, William L. 19:153
Canence, John 14:148
Caneth, A. J. 9:49
Caney, C. C. 3:37
Caney, John A. 22:138
Canfield, --- 27:33
Canfield, A. 11:400
Canfield, A. E. 2:8; 25:20
Canfield, A. T. 1:26
Canfield, A. W. 21:21
Canfield, Aaron 22:286
Canfield, Amos 12:15
Canfield, C. 1:23
Canfield, D. A. 1:122
Canfield, D. W. 1:120
Canfield, Daniel 10:94
Canfield, David L. 9:100
Canfield, Don C. 21:97
Canfield, E. 25:151
Canfield, Edward 19:7
Canfield, Edwin M. 12:15
Canfield, F. 14:45
Canfield, Francis M. 13:13
Canfield, Frederick 15:64
Canfield, George 15:150
Canfield, Henry 13:134; 19:346
Canfield, Ira 17:63
Canfield, Ira L. 22:461
Canfield, J. 1:26
Canfield, James L. 22:401
Canfield, Johnson G. 11:83
Canfield, Merritt 10:44
Canfield, Nathaniel S. 20:47
Canfield, Orin S. 22:182
Canfield, P. 7:56
Canfield, R. S. 14:45
Canfield, Robert 19:153
Canfield, Thomas 11:141
Canfield, William 1:25
Canflew, S. 22:182
Canghorn, W. 21:95
Canham, Alfred 19:337
Canier, Joseph 1:26
Canifax, William T. 20:221
Canifer, William T. 10:106
Canile, J. S. 21:310
Canine, Jerome 19:153
Canks, George 11:385
Canlar, W. C. 20:221
Canler, James M. 18:125
Canley, John 9:108
Canley, T. A. 7:89
Canlin, Allen 12:15

Canlius, J. H. 5:11
Canlogue, P. 21:21
Canlon, John 15:188
Canman, Alexander
    10:158
Canman, John 11:139
Cann, A. 20:55
Cann, J. M. 15:172
Cann, John 19:327
Cann, Julius 11:421
Cann, Leonard 18:205
Cann, Robert 8:46
Cann, Seth 16:365
Cann, T. W. 5:11
Cann, William 19:153
Canna, John 21:21
Cannada, James 5:37
Cannada, Spicer 20:145
Cannahan, Amos 27:28
Cannals, John 22:182
Cannan, Henry 9:19
Cannan, Ralph 20:136
Canneda, William 27:28
Cannel, Robert N. 22:245
Cannell, Henry A. 22:111
Cannells, William 16:88
Cannelly, Patrick 12:172
Canner, John 16:130
Cannet, Benjamin 19:7
Canney, Benjamin 21:310
Cannihan, Richard 22:293
Canning, E. 27:27
Canning, F. 15:119
Canning, William 10:144
Cannington, Edward J.
    10:94
Cannion, D. 14:45
Cannion, Michael 10:7
Cannis, George F. 27:26
Canniston, Hans 17:231
Cannon, A. 3:37; 14:148
Cannon, Benjamin B.
    17:49
Cannon, C. 9:140; 27:26
Cannon, Charles W.
    22:182
Cannon, Daniel 1:120
Cannon, E. 25:294
Cannon, Edwin 21:266
Cannon, Elbert S. 21:97
Cannon, Elijah 7:77
Cannon, Francis 10:192
Cannon, Fred 19:153
Cannon, G. W. 15:267
Cannon, George 7:77;
    24:165; 25:294
Cannon, Isaac 9:116;
    27:31
Cannon, Isaac H. 8:61;
    26:153
Cannon, J. 1:97; 16:179

Cannon, J. W. 7:77
Cannon, James 25:151
Cannon, James E. 17:77
Cannon, James H. 17:49;
    22:118
Cannon, James M. 17:49
Cannon, James S. 10:158
Cannon, John 13:13;
    16:24; 22:293;
    24:166
Cannon, John C. 24:151
Cannon, John F. 19:153
Cannon, L. 16:179
Cannon, Lewis 18:188
Cannon, Marshall 9:203
Cannon, Ned 7:119
Cannon, Patrick 5:11;
    10:106; 20:221
Cannon, R. C. 15:318;
    19:60
Cannon, R. H. 22:350
Cannon, Reuben 13:13
Cannon, Robert 7:119;
    22:475
Cannon, Robert H. 22:449
Cannon, S. W. 25:294
Cannon, Samuel 9:19
Cannon, Sandy 22:138
Cannon, U. 1:117
Cannon, W. 21:207
Cannon, W. E. 1:97
Cannon, W. J. 10:185
Cannon, W. S. 18:172
Cannon, William 1:191;
    3:37; 22:69
Cannon, William H. 12:15
Cannon, William P.
    17:276
Connor, Oldrick 9:129
Connor, William 12:15
Cannot, William 4:14
Cannover, William H.
    5:37
Canns, Moses 21:266
Canny, Robert 22:245
Canody, J. 1:118
Canon, Charles 24:8
Canon, J. 14:45
Canon, J. D. 13:134
Canon, James 3:37
Canore, M. 14:45
Canott, J. J. 11:91
Canover, William B.
    16:179
Canoway, David R. 27:29
Canoy, J. 19:316
Canpano, John 14:5
Canpelt, John 17:259
Canrod, John 15:6
Cansady, Thomas 26:153
Cansata, Thomas 8:11

Cansdy, Philo 13:13
Cansey, I. 21:21
Cansey, James M. 20:5
Cansickle, J. W. 15:147
Canstan, James I. 20:221
Canstiner, Frank 11:25
Cansy, Michael 12:63
Cant, James 7:119
Cant, John 26:121
Cant, William 4:14
Cantabury, John W. 27:32
Cantell, Richard 11:421
Canter, Charles 11:27
Canter, John 26:21
Canterbury, Griffin 15:85
Canterrel, R. 19:263
Cantetion, John 22:9
Cantewell, John 21:119
Canthers, William J.
    18:125
Cantillion, James 19:346
Cantin, Aug 27:28
Cantleberry, John 23:136
Cantlin, Henry 25:294
Cantline, Henry 7:74
Cantnor, R. 23:61
Canton, A. 14:148
Canton, L. 25:310
Cantonwine, George
    10:44
Cantonwino, George
    20:221
Cantor, John 18:232
Cantrell, Edward 19:341
Cantrell, Elsperry 25:288
Cantrell, George W.
    21:129
Cantrell, Isaac 20:106
Cantrell, J. 21:90
Cantrell, John 21:248
Cantrell, M. 3:37
Cantrell, William 21:215
Cantwell, A. L. 15:6
Cantwell, David 11:199
Cantwell, J. W. 9:242
Cantwell, John 9:242
Cantwell, John A. 22:69
Cantwell, Joseph H.
    15:333
Cantwell, K. 1:25
Canup, Noah 19:8
Canute, James 22:476
Canwell, C. 1:23
Cape, Daniel 8:81
Cape, Joseph 21:135
Cape, W. 20:91
Cape, W. S. 18:232; 26:20
Capehart, H. 3:37
Capeland, James 21:245
Capelin, B. A. 22:500
Capeling, G. W. 4:14

Capell, A. E. 22:182
Capell, C. 3:37
Capelman, Oliver 11:411
Capen, E. S. 21:310
Capen, George A. 21:251
Capen, James M. 21:135
Capern, John E. 16:179
Capers, Thomas 21:310
Capery, Bartley 19:327
Capgar, Asa 25:21
Capin, C. H. C. 9:101
Capinio, Daniel 9:116
Capino, Daniel 27:30
Capino, F. 15:120
Caplain, --- 27:33
Capland, J. 1:21
Caple, Hamilton 13:14;
    16:24
Caples, T. 25:151
Caplinger, Levi 18:275
Capon, Stephen B. 16:179
Capp, Charles M. 9:171
Capp, George 11:139
Capp, Isaac M. 10:44
Capp, P. H. 11:200
Capp, W. 23:312
Capp, William G. 18:214
Cappell, Lewis 13:127
Cappell, William L. 12:15
Cappen, Alonzo H.
    23:104
Capper, D. 23:137
Capper, John 16:91
Cappers, Henry 14:148
Capple, David 8:81
Capple, Silas 17:423
Capples, John K. 7:89
Capps, Albert 11:91
Capps, Benjamin 22:245
Capps, Elisha 17:463;
    24:183
Capps, George 18:232;
    26:21
Capps, Isaac 20:221
Capps, James 22:245
Capps, John 27:143
Capps, M. H. 27:143
Capps, Robert 10:106;
    20:221
Capps, Robert R. 21:129
Capps, Siles 24:173
Capps, William 22:245
Cappy, H. H. 11:55
Capret, D. 22:165
Capron, C. 9:19
Capron, Charles 6:8;
    18:102
Capron, Ed. P. 26:94
Capron, Edward P. 18:303
Capron, H. E. 1:120
Capron, James 21:310

Capron, S. R. 21:49
Caps, J. 25:151
Caps, Jonas 5:37
Capsay, J. 3:37
Capsin, Charles H. 18:337
Capson, Arnold 15:258
Capson, Nathaniel 13:14
Capus, George G. 17:425
Capwell, J. O. 14:148
Car, --- 17:364
Car, Edward 19:8
Car, John 13:14
Car, Joseph 15:363
Car, Robert 18:117
Car---, John 24:190
Carabine, D. W. 22:350
Caragan, P. 19:285
Caraket, Daniel 1:21
Caraner, James M. 20:221
Caravan, A. 14:280
Caraway, J. B. 20:221
Caraway, Joseph B. 10:45
Caray, A. 14:254
Carbage, Alicle 22:331
Carbary, Zebulon 9:129;
    27:29
Carbaugh, Emanuel 7:89;
    21:310
Carbaugh, M. 1:23
Carbaugh, T. M. 9:33;
    18:291
Carben, John William
    10:44
Carber, Fred. K. 11:14
Carberry, Edward 11:385
Carberry, George W.
    25:279
Carberry, John 21:185
Carbeth, Anthony 4:15
Carbino, Joseph 4:15
Carborius, W. 3:39
Carbough, T. M. 26:95
Carbour, James 23:18
Carbrook, F. W. 11:55
Carcaran, Lawrence
    22:118
Carcevay, William 25:318
Carcey, John 12:15
Carch, S. 14:45
Carcy, John 11:14
Card, A. 3:39
Card, A. C. 16:277
Card, Cornelius C. 21:310
Card, G. 3:39
Card, Jacob 11:300
Card, John 16:179
Card, Oscar B. 19:8
Card, Roland 15:188
Card, T. P. 14:45
Card, Thomas 17:129;
    24:191

Card, W. H. 15:340;
    16:365
Card, William 17:446;
    24:169
Card, William C. 17:262
Cardelia, A. 16:179
Cardell, Isaac 12:151
Carden, A. K. 3:38
Carden, Monroe 11:199
Carden, Robert 3:38
Carder, Henry 10:44
Carder, James M. 18:406
Cardin, Robert 17:453;
    24:183
Cardinal, John 18:46;
    24:65
Cardinal, Joseph 22:170
Cardinell, John 15:103
Cardington, Jesse 9:76
Cardner, H. H. 9:50
Cardoba, Felipe 12:171
Cardon, Thomas A.
    18:188
Cardrick, Dusign 11:411
Cardwell, Elizabeth
    19:325
Cardwell, H. 10:154
Cardwell, M. 22:331
Cardwell, Thomas 22:119
Cardwell, W. C. 3:38
Cardwill, W. C. 3:38
Cardwin, Archy 22:512
Cardy, Francis 15:16
Care, D. 16:365
Care, George 9:71
Care, Glasco 25:151
Care, John 19:289
Care, William M. 19:8
Cared, George 12:160
Carefield, William 17:322
Carel, A. 25:151
Carel, To 21:207
Caren, Edward 22:293
Caren, W. B. 23:276
Cares, William 9:41
Caret, Robert 20:55
Careter, James M. 8:11
Caretthus, Joseph 24:100
Carey, --- 16:91
Carey, Adkins M. 27:143
Carey, Alex 7:22
Carey, Alfred 14:321;
    23:86
Carey, Alfred F. 23:86
Carey, Amorois 21:310
Carey, B. W. 19:60
Carey, Barney 23:137
Carey, Benjamin 8:61
Carey, Butler 8:77
Carey, C. E. 1:24
Carey, Calvin P. 22:69

Carey, Charles 5:37
Carey, Charles G. 25:151
Carey, Charles H. 26:95
Carey, Dennis 14:148
Carey, Dyer 24:170
Carey, E. W. 9:108
Carey, Edwin 21:221
Carey, Eri 13:124
Carey, Ernest D. 22:277
Carey, Frank 24:109
Carey, Franklin H. 11:103
Carey, G. 1:97
Carey, George 17:18
Carey, Harrison E. 20:192
Carey, Henry 27:25
Carey, J. 14:239; 23:23
Carey, James 9:11, 203;
    15:16; 19:44; 22:23
Carey, Jeremiah W. 21:65
Carey, John 7:89; 9:171;
    12:67; 13:14; 15:64;
    16:24, 91; 22:182;
    25:152, 318
Carey, John F. 16:77
Carey, Levi 10:44
Carey, Livi 20:221
Carey, Lucius J. 23:119
Carey, Luther 25:22
Carey, Mathias 4:15
Carey, Mesillan 9:199
Carey, N. G. 4:15
Carey, O. 1:117
Carey, O. E. 9:171
Carey, P. 1:93
Carey, S. 9:218; 18:363
Carey, Samuel 9:41
Carey, Sheldon 22:138
Carey, Smith 21:310
Carey, Stephen 16:115
Carey, T. 3:39; 13:81
Carey, T. P. 16:115
Carey, Thomas 8:121;
    21:310
Carey, W. B. 26:19
Carey, William 4:14
Carey, William F. 21:221
Carfield, D. T. 19:60
Carfield, Henry 15:358
Carg, A. 3:39
Cargil, Daniel C. 10:106;
    20:221
Cargile, J. H. 21:310
Cargill, B. D. 1:120
Cargill, C. 3:39
Cargill, G. C. 2:9
Cargill, Ralph C. 10:10
Cargille, Solomon H.
    15:120
Cargle, Abner S. 23:61
Carguille, B. 8:46

Carible, George W.
    21:193
Carico, James 10:44;
    20:221
Carie, Bush 12:160
Carier, J. H. 19:300
Caries, Henry 9:218
Cariher, F. 25:23
Carin, B. 11:141
Carine, Abraham 22:420
Cariner, John 14:148
Carion, F. 24:36
Carison, John 17:49
Carithers, John A. 9:160
Carithers, S. H. 11:56
Carkener, Joel 21:310
Carker, Abraham 11:118
Carl, Amos G. 4:15
Carl, Andrew 14:148
Carl, Andrew J. 13:14;
    16:24
Carl, C. 2:9; 25:20
Carl, Charles 13:14
Carl, Chauncey 13:14
Carl, D. 25:22
Carl, Daniel 19:60
Carl, Frederick 4:15
Carl, George 9:19;
    18:303; 26:95
Carl, H. C. 23:23
Carl, Henry 18:214
Carl, Hiram 1:120
Carl, J. M. 3:38
Carl, Jacob 8:11
Carl, James 11:90; 13:14
Carl, John 23:303
Carl, Joseph 3:38
Carl, L. 3:38
Carl, Lewis 13:106
Carl, Michael 12:15
Carl, Peter 1:23; 13:14;
    20:29
Carl, W. P. 22:475
Carlace, James 16:365
Carlaley, --- 11:339
Carlan, Napoleon 26:210
Carlan, William 9:218;
    18:363
Carland, Michael 9:244
Carldon, James W. W.
    4:15
Carle, Abram 21:251
Carle, E. 14:263
Carle, F. 3:39
Carle, G. W. 1:121
Carle, John 17:494
Carle, John H. 13:62
Carle, Joseph 18:46
Carle, Sylvester 23:263
Carle, W. 16:266
Carlen, F. 26:21

Carlen, Presley 23:10
Carlen, Robert 16:179
Carlentyere, G. 3:39
Carlepp, Andrew 16:24
Carleppo, Andrew 13:14
Carles, F. 15:358
Carleton, --- 14:148, 254
Carleton, Benjamin F.
    22:277
Carleton, H. 16:289
Carleton, H. D. 1:120
Carleton, Thomas H.
    18:117
Carlett, Martin 15:2
Carley, George R. 10:106;
    20:221
Carley, H. M. 19:8
Carley, John 7:48
Carley, Loren P. 10:14
Carley, W. C. 3:38
Carley, William 8:104
Carli, M. 15:150
Carligh, S. 24:110
Carlile, J. W. 19:8
Carlile, Peter 25:152
Carlin, Charles 7:14
Carlin, F. 18:232
Carlin, James A. 5:50
Carlin, John 11:181
Carlin, John C. 18:79
Carlin, Joseph 11:139
Carlin, Joseph L. 24:48
Carlin, M. 3:39; 15:164
Carlin, Mahlon 23:127
Carlin, P. 1:122
Carlin, Thomas 18:46
Carlin, William P. 21:65
Carlington, W. H. 14:45
Carlins, Owen 22:23
Carlis, F. 12:95; 19:60
Carlis, William 21:310
Carlish, --- 3:38
Carlisle, --- 15:188
Carlisle, Alva 25:294
Carlisle, Amazon 18:232;
    26:20
Carlisle, Don J. 25:152
Carlisle, Henry 21:310
Carlisle, Hiram 22:23
Carlisle, J. 1:25
Carlisle, James 8:81
Carlisle, James H. 7:89
Carlisle, John C. 21:310
Carlisle, John Don 12:80
Carlisle, Joseph 27:32
Carlisle, Newman O.
    25:283
Carlisle, R. 16:289
Carlisle, Royal M. 17:287
Carlisle, S. M. 10:106;
    20:221

Carlisle, Samuel 26:22
Carlisle, W. H. 14:133; 18:363
Carlisle, William 23:23
Carlisle, William H. 9:218
Carll, Lauriston B. 21:65
Carlo, Thomas 15:6
Carlock, John 10:44; 20:221
Carlock, William 10:44
Carlock, William N. 24:65
Carlon, Robert 13:76
Carlough, George 9:244
Carlson, Christian 24:14
Carlson, Jacob 26:244
Carlson, Peter J. 21:90
Carlson, William 7:22
Carlton, --- 21:49
Carlton, Andrew 1:22
Carlton, C. C. 1:117
Carlton, Edward 11:141
Carlton, G. 3:39
Carlton, J. 14:45
Carlton, J. L. 3:39
Carlton, James 16:24
Carlton, Louis 22:245
Carlton, Marcus A. 22:138
Carlton, Merriman 24:48
Carlton, S. G. 11:142
Carlyle, Abram 9:171
Carlyle, Armstead 10:106; 20:221
Carmac, T. 3:39
Carmack, E. 23:137
Carmahan, Lorenzo 16:25
Carmall, James 9:77
Carman, C. D. 23:137
Carman, Elijah 22:23
Carman, G. 1:97
Carman, George 10:158; 21:119; 23:23
Carman, George W. 19:153
Carman, H. 11:237
Carman, Henry 13:62
Carman, J. B. 11:419
Carman, James E. 19:153
Carman, Jeremiah 21:310
Carman, John 20:111; 21:9
Carman, Jonathan 11:140
Carman, Julius 19:8
Carman, O. 1:122
Carman, Samuel 9:226
Carman, Samuel D. 13:14
Carman, Thomas 6:30
Carman, Thomas J. 18:392
Carman, W. P. 3:39
Carman, Warren R. 6:8

Carman, Wilet 15:188
Carman, William 11:395; 13:56
Carman, William C. 18:232; 26:21
Carmangear, Henry 6:30
Carmanger, H. 25:318
Carme, Jerome 10:154
Carmel, Daniel 20:141
Carmel, James 26:18
Carmel, Jeremiah 23:278
Carmen, F. H. 3:38
Carmen, George 19:153
Carmen, John W. 22:448
Carmen, Michael 12:173
Carmer, A. A. 1:123
Carmer, Andrew 3:39
Carmer, Charles 16:117
Carmer, Henry 19:8
Carmeyer, William 21:90
Carmichael, Abraham 17:49
Carmichael, Alfred 15:31
Carmichael, Andrew 10:90; 20:221
Carmichael, Daniel 8:11; 18:125
Carmichael, David 22:401
Carmichael, E. T. 18:188
Carmichael, George 3:38
Carmichael, J. 22:245
Carmichael, J. A. 9:108
Carmichael, James 15:120
Carmichael, John 15:188
Carmichael, Joseph J. 21:49
Carmichael, L. 22:245
Carmichael, Lee 9:33; 18:291
Carmichael, Patrick 8:81
Carmichael, T. 22:245
Carmichael, William 12:172
Carmichael, William H. 11:190; 21:221
Carmichal, Lee 26:95
Carmichall, John B. 11:25
Carmickle, Eden 11:259
Carmickle, M. 17:31
Carmienky, William 22:470
Carmin, Asal. G. 23:61
Carmine, David C. 17:77
Carmine, S. 11:259
Carmine, Teman M. 17:77
Carmines, S. 25:152
Carmire, P. 3:39
Carmis, Alfred 15:31
Carmon, B. 14:45
Carmons, John 11:140
Carmouche, Furman 7:119

Carmouche, John 21:310
Carn, Amos 18:108
Carn, Calib 26:156
Carn, J. 13:84
Carn, Marion 8:46
Carn, William 3:38
Carnaham, G. M. 3:38
Carnahan, A. W. 3:39
Carnahan, Benjamin F. 13:14
Carnahan, J. C. 11:321
Carnahan, James 23:106
Carnahan, John 10:106; 17:348, 351; 20:221
Carnahan, John J. 17:320
Carnahan, Lorenzo 13:14
Carnahan, Peter H. 22:69
Carnahan, Silas 20:221
Carnal, A. F. 9:108
Carnal, John 12:15
Carncross, D. 13:84
Carned, R. 14:149
Carneham, Charles 3:39
Carnell, F. H. 14:45
Carnell, Israel 4:65
Carnell, J. H. 22:182
Carnell, John H. 9:96
Carnell, Samuel 26:218
Carner, Andrew 3:38
Carner, DeWitt 1:121
Carner, Edward 22:9
Carner, H. 7:48
Carner, Henry 18:363
Carner, Hugh C. 4:15
Carner, John 22:245
Carner, W. 1:97
Carner, Conner, Or Carver, Jo. 16:117
Carnes, Alfred 9:76
Carnes, G. H. 13:62
Carnes, George B. 19:60
Carnes, H. 3:38
Carnes, Isaac 22:182
Carnes, James C. 11:83
Carnes, John C. 18:214
Carnes, John E. 10:45; 20:221
Carnes, M. 18:26
Carnes, Patrick 22:245
Carnes, R. 18:172
Carnes, Richard 11:199; 22:69
Carnes, Robert 1:21
Carnes, T. 3:38
Carnes, T. M. 18:205
Carnes, W. 3:38
Carnes, William 11:139; 14:45; 26:144
Carnet, Christ 6:9
Carnett, William 11:238
Carney, A. 17:153

Carney, Absalom 22:69
Carney, Alonzo 20:39
Carney, Andrew 22:138
Carney, Benjamin W. 22:170
Carney, Bryan 19:153
Carney, D. 11:54
Carney, D. J. 3:38
Carney, David 1:120
Carney, Francis 3:39
Carney, G. 1:22
Carney, George 22:138
Carney, George W. 7:22
Carney, Henry 1:25
Carney, J. 1:118; 25:152
Carney, J. E. 17:158
Carney, James 11:295; 13:106; 15:172; 21:65; 22:69
Carney, James A. 17:71
Carney, John 20:185
Carney, John A. 15:53
Carney, Joseph 21:310
Carney, M. 3:39
Carney, Mark 25:152
Carney, Michael 15:21
Carney, Nicholas 11:421
Carney, P. 18:26
Carney, Patrick 11:14; 20:111
Carney, Peter 10:171; 15:188
Carney, Philip 25:152
Carney, Rupert 22:496
Carney, S. B. 7:22
Carney, Thomas 22:138
Carney, Tim 22:331
Carney, W. 7:22
Carney, William 16:179
Carney, William B. 22:182
Carney, William W. 22:245
Carnie, Silas D. 9:240
Carnifex, John 23:23
Carnifox, James 17:172
Carnine, John 16:91
Carniss, James D. 23:202
Carnochan, W. 1:24
Carnot, Henry 9:49
Carnough, Michael 1:22
Carnovan, Thomas 19:328
Carnrike, William C. 23:119
Carns, Calvin 9:218
Carns, James 22:182
Carns, Perry B. 11:326
Carns, R. 10:185
Carns, W. 24:75
Carnstien, Henry 8:62
Carnth, William 11:199

Carny, R. 3:38
Carol, James 27:143
Carolin, James 21:310
Carolin, Samuel I. 18:353
Carolin, Samuel J. 22:507
Carolus, J. 23:263
Caron, Patrick 25:23
Carons, Henry 14:149
Carorer, Jacob H. 18:125
Carothers, Albert 22:518
Carothers, George 22:138, 421
Carothers, Richard 21:311
Carover, Israel P. 22:245
Carow, Levi 19:248
Caroy, John 18:108
Carp, J. S. 3:39
Carp, Wesley 18:64
Carpenter, --- 8:71; 15:188; 26:18
Carpenter, A. 18:108; 25:24
Carpenter, A. A. 20:221
Carpenter, A. B. 9:157
Carpenter, A. J. 11:285
Carpenter, A. W. 7:22
Carpenter, Abraham 6:7
Carpenter, Albert 13:14; 24:65
Carpenter, Albert A. 10:90
Carpenter, Alexander 9:116; 11:200; 27:31
Carpenter, Alfred 17:172; 22:182
Carpenter, Allen 9:206; 10:158; 18:64; 19:153
Carpenter, Alonzo 20:95
Carpenter, Amasa B. 11:339
Carpenter, Andrew T. 11:428
Carpenter, Arnold 17:215
Carpenter, Austin 8:99
Carpenter, B. 13:106; 14:287; 23:184
Carpenter, Benjamin 8:81; 21:221
Carpenter, Benjamin F. 10:44; 20:221
Carpenter, C. 1:26; 13:84; 15:31; 16:179
Carpenter, C. G. 10:37; 20:221
Carpenter, C. H. 16:91
Carpenter, C. L. 21:21
Carpenter, Calvin 12:15
Carpenter, Charles C. 17:286
Carpenter, Charles M. 21:135

Carpenter, D. 1:97; 15:188
Carpenter, D. C. 18:26
Carpenter, D. J. 1:22
Carpenter, D. T. 1:22
Carpenter, D. V. 1:21
Carpenter, David 14:235
Carpenter, David B. 11:139
Carpenter, E. 1:120
Carpenter, E. C. 15:340; 16:365
Carpenter, E. D. 25:24
Carpenter, E. H. 4:15
Carpenter, Ed 23:137
Carpenter, Edward 5:11; 9:203; 18:64
Carpenter, Eleazer 19:8
Carpenter, Ephras 4:15
Carpenter, F. 9:213; 11:124; 21:310
Carpenter, F. E. 20:55
Carpenter, F. M. 1:121
Carpenter, F. S. 19:153
Carpenter, Fielding 17:455; 24:190
Carpenter, Frank 3:37; 10:158; 20:90
Carpenter, Frank L. 26:21
Carpenter, Franklin 9:76
Carpenter, G. 3:37; 14:5
Carpenter, G. A. 8:46
Carpenter, G. J. 11:237
Carpenter, G. M. 26:18
Carpenter, G. W. 13:106
Carpenter, George 4:15; 14:149; 15:53, 364
Carpenter, George H. 7:22
Carpenter, George M. 21:215
Carpenter, George W. 15:64; 18:411
Carpenter, Gilbert 22:69
Carpenter, Gillam 22:182
Carpenter, H. 1:123; 9:154; 15:31; 16:179; 25:152; 27:27
Carpenter, H. A. 3:37
Carpenter, H. B. 3:37
Carpenter, H. E. 26:154
Carpenter, Harding 13:14; 16:25
Carpenter, Haydock 12:67
Carpenter, Henry 7:64; 8:123; 16:278; 20:21
Carpenter, Henry W. 4:15
Carpenter, Horatio 19:8
Carpenter, Isaac 12:15; 17:31

Carpenter, J. 1:123; 11:141; 22:182; 25:152

Carpenter, J. A. 16:25

Carpenter, J. C. 19:325

Carpenter, J. H. 1:119

Carpenter, J. K. 1:119

Carpenter, J. M. 11:124

Carpenter, J. W. 9:140; 13:14; 16:278; 27:27

Carpenter, J. W. B. 2:8

Carpenter, James 4:15; 20:221; 21:119; 26:210

Carpenter, James M. 23:61

Carpenter, Jefferson 5:37

Carpenter, Jeremiah 24:58, 90

Carpenter, Jesse 11:55

Carpenter, John 8:11, 46, 71; 9:76; 12:98; 13:106; 18:125, 424; 19:325; 22:245; 25:26; 26:17

Carpenter, John A. 21:90

Carpenter, John B. 14:261

Carpenter, John D. 9:117

Carpenter, John F. 14:261; 20:221

Carpenter, John H. 21:310; 23:106

Carpenter, Joseph 18:291; 26:95

Carpenter, Joseph O. 22:277

Carpenter, Joshua C. 11:385

Carpenter, L. 1:117; 3:37; 7:22; 10:208

Carpenter, L. B. 15:188

Carpenter, Levi 5:50; 16:91; 22:69

Carpenter, Lewis H. 22:138

Carpenter, M. 11:124; 17:31

Carpenter, M. C. 14:5

Carpenter, M. E. 13:84

Carpenter, M. J. 9:33

Carpenter, Michael J. 17:259

Carpenter, Millard 26:95

Carpenter, Mose 17:455; 24:190

Carpenter, N. D. 23:137

Carpenter, Nelson 17:163

Carpenter, O. B. 3:37

Carpenter, O. F. 1:118

Carpenter, O. H. 11:115

Carpenter, O. P. 18:363

Carpenter, Octavius 15:54

Carpenter, Orlando T. 23:188

Carpenter, Orville P. 9:218

Carpenter, P. 1:118; 3:37; 25:152

Carpenter, P. P. 20:221

Carpenter, Pardon E. 21:206

Carpenter, Peter 5:37

Carpenter, Philip 23:290

Carpenter, Preston P. 10:44

Carpenter, R. C. 22:401

Carpenter, R. S. 11:258

Carpenter, Reuben 19:8; 22:182

Carpenter, Richard 9:96

Carpenter, Robert 10:44; 20:221

Carpenter, S. 3:37; 19:60

Carpenter, S. A. 1:121

Carpenter, S. J. 11:332

Carpenter, S. M. 4:15

Carpenter, S. N. 9:76

Carpenter, Samuel 11:25, 331; 17:322; 22:245

Carpenter, Solomon 7:89

Carpenter, T. J. 16:117

Carpenter, T. U. 25:152

Carpenter, Thomas 17:94; 21:185

Carpenter, Thomas W. 5:11

Carpenter, U. C. 3:37

Carpenter, V. R. 1:117

Carpenter, W. 14:149

Carpenter, W. E. 1:97

Carpenter, W. F. 11:258; 21:185

Carpenter, W. H. 14:149

Carpenter, W. M. 15:318; 23:23

Carpenter, W. R. 1:24

Carpenter, W. T. 14:149

Carpenter, White 3:37

Carpenter, Willard 18:291

Carpenter, William 3:37; 7:22; 21:88; 22:448

Carpenter, William G. 21:310

Carpenter, William H. 9:105; 22:401

Carpenter, William N. 19:60

Carpenter, William P. 9:76

Carpenter, Williard 9:33

Carpetner, Joseph 9:33

Carplenter, John J. 27:30

Carps, Edwin 9:41; 26:122

Carps, William H. 12:15

Carpt, Ezra 17:213

Carquill, L. 24:14

Carr, --- 10:25

Carr, A. 3:38

Carr, Aaron 21:311

Carr, Alden S. 25:288

Carr, Alex 14:45

Carr, Alexander 27:25

Carr, Alfred L. 22:182

Carr, Amos 1:121; 6:9

Carr, Anderson 22:245

Carr, Andrew 19:8

Carr, Andrew J. 11:140

Carr, Anthony 8:104

Carr, Archy 11:199

Carr, Asa 4:65

Carr, Ashel 17:63

Carr, B. 3:38; 15:64

Carr, B. F. 7:22

Carr, B. H. 14:45

Carr, B. L. 12:15

Carr, Barney 23:23

Carr, C. 13:106

Carr, C. D. 25:152

Carr, C. M. 19:248

Carr, C. W. 18:64

Carr, Caleb 8:38

Carr, Cassius M. 17:396

Carr, Charles 9:199; 14:235; 15:172

Carr, Clancy D. 5:11

Carr, Clemance 19:60

Carr, D. 3:38; 14:45; 15:351

Carr, Daniel 7:22

Carr, David 10:106; 20:221

Carr, Dempsey 21:311

Carr, Edmund S. 12:58

Carr, Edward 21:311

Carr, Edward B. 17:109

Carr, Edward E. 17:247

Carr, Erastus H. 9:96

Carr, F. 3:38

Carr, Fan 8:104

Carr, Frank 11:326

Carr, G. 1:122

Carr, G. B. 18:26

Carr, G. W. 1:119

Carr, George 4:15

Carr, George A. 3:38

Carr, George D. 14:239; 27:33

Carr, George F. 17:77

Carr, George W. 7:89; 16:25; 19:8; 23:61

Carr, Green 22:293

Carr, H. 8:46

Carr, H. C. 21:311
Carr, Henry 21:147; 27:32
Carr, Henry H. 23:284
Carr, Henry P. 19:153
Carr, Isaac 5:11; 21:311
Carr, J. 3:38; 9:140;
    13:84; 18:79;
    25:152; 27:26
Carr, J. B. 1:118; 14:277;
    23:188
Carr, J. H. 1:21
Carr, J. M. 16:179; 18:26
Carr, J. S. 1:120
Carr, J. W. 13:106;
    17:144; 22:182;
    23:23
Carr, Jacob 12:151; 13:84
Carr, James 1:25; 7:15;
    8:11; 10:9; 12:15;
    14:149; 18:125;
    20:2; 21:266; 22:23
Carr, James M. 10:106;
    20:221
Carr, Jason 9:203
Carr, Jehial 22:170
Carr, Joel 1:21
Carr, John 1:119; 7:89;
    9:96; 11:14; 15:31;
    16:179; 21:251;
    23:281; 25:25
Carr, John H. 14:149
Carr, John J. 22:245
Carr, John W. 8:46; 21:21
Carr, Joseph 4:65; 18:46
Carr, Josiah 17:446
Carr, Lafayette 24:91
Carr, Leander 22:138
Carr, Leo 25:21
Carr, M. 18:46; 21:119
Carr, M. M. 12:15
Carr, Michael 1:121;
    15:81
Carr, Moses 11:103
Carr, Mungo 1:192
Carr, Nathan S. 7:89
Carr, Nathaniel S. 9:11
Carr, Noah J. 24:36
Carr, Orson S. 16:81
Carr, P. 3:38
Carr, P. C. 25:25
Carr, Patrick 11:54;
    22:401
Carr, R. B. 27:27
Carr, Robert 7:89; 19:343;
    21:311; 22:165, 401
Carr, Roderick 22:69
Carr, Rufus 22:512
Carr, S. 15:293; 16:179
Carr, S. A. 1:25
Carr, Samuel 8:113;
    23:276

Carr, Sandford 22:421
Carr, Silas A. 18:205
Carr, Smith 7:89
Carr, T. 7:22
Carr, Thomas 1:192;
    10:106; 20:221;
    21:49
Carr, Thomas A. 13:14
Carr, Timothy 25:283
Carr, W. 11:411; 21:21;
    25:152
Carr, W. A. 25:152
Carr, W. E. 1:121
Carr, W. H. 19:153;
    25:152
Carr, W. R. 7:89
Carr, Wesley 23:283
Carr, William 3:38; 4:15;
    5:11; 7:22; 10:106,
    176; 15:120; 16:84;
    17:129; 19:153;
    20:221; 24:190
Carr, William H. 5:37
Carr, William I. 19:8
Carr, Wilson 24:190
Carragon, George W.
    10:14
Carraka, James M. 21:21
Carral, James H. 8:81
Carrall, Alex 16:25
Carrath, Enoch 9:33
Carraway, David 11:421
Carraway, J. 5:50; 25:152
Carraway, James 5:50
Carre, Peter 7:89
Carre, Thomas 10:45;
    20:221
Carrel, Joseph 22:69
Carrell, Francis 11:88
Carrell, H. 12:140; 20:221
Carrell, James 19:60
Carrell, James H. 23:23
Carrell, James M. 26:95
Carrell, John 22:331
Carrell, M. 26:19
Carrell, Martin 11:300
Carrell, Nelson 22:245
Carrell, S. E. 1:123
Carren, Lawrence 24:150
Carrens, James 21:266
Carret, J. 16:266
Carrett, Archie 17:450
Carrett, W. C. 25:21
Carrew, Lawrence 8:100
Carrey, Elijah 25:152
Carrey, William 17:172
Carrfield, J. L. 9:108
Carrick, J. B. 11:279
Carrick, Joseph H. 10:44;
    20:221
Carrico, Henry 23:251

Carrico, J. B. 11:279
Carrico, Levi 8:37; 11:421
Carrico, M. 17:31
Carrico, Richard 24:191
Carrie, Anderson 17:49
Carrie, Benjamin 14:45
Carrie, R. B. 23:184
Carrier, C. C. 3:39
Carrier, D. 11:411
Carrier, D. B. 3:39
Carrier, Daniel J. 7:89
Carrier, Ezra 11:398
Carrier, F. J. 1:26
Carrier, Henry H. 21:311
Carrier, John 10:44;
    20:221
Carrier, John D. 17:70
Carrier, M. H. 21:311
Carrigan, --- 19:317
Carrigan, Amos 22:182
Carrigan, Christopher C.
    22:245
Carrigan, F. 1:122
Carrigan, Henry 18:26
Carrigan, Hy 14:235
Carrigan, J. 16:179
Carrigan, James 22:9
Carrigan, John 12:67;
    16:91; 20:111;
    22:518
Carrigan, Thomas 12:169
Carriher, Carley C. 23:61
Carrill, James 4:15
Carrin, Lawrence 17:459
Carrington, --- 22:350
Carrington, Alfred 16:13
Carrington, Ed 9:156
Carrington, H. 26:154
Carrington, James 3:38
Carrington, John 24:36
Carrington, Lester 4:15
Carrington, Service 24:36
Carrington, Thomas 21:21
Carrington, William 14:45
Carrion, Hill 27:143
Carrion, Patrick 14:149
Carris, William 7:119
Carriss, S. J. 19:60
Carro, Jacob 21:311
Carro, James 15:172
Carrody, Lewis 18:26
Carroes, Arch 10:98
Carrol, Arthur 13:106
Carrol, George 18:188
Carrol, J. 11:25; 16:266
Carrol, John 8:81
Carrol, M. 1:118
Carrol, P. 1:118
Carrol, Samuel 15:26
Carroll, --- 1:21; 5:55;
    18:172

Carroll, A. 3:38; 27:24
Carroll, Albert 21:251
Carroll, Alexander 13:14
Carroll, Anthony 17:212
Carroll, Augustus G. 4:15
Carroll, Boon F. 23:86
Carroll, C. 1:22; 3:38
Carroll, C. A. 9:8
Carroll, Charles 20:192
Carroll, Charles E. 7:14
Carroll, Charles J. 16:77
Carroll, Dennis 9:117;
    21:311
Carroll, E. 16:179
Carroll, Edward 21:311
Carroll, F. 9:140
Carroll, Ferrell 24:91
Carroll, Francis 12:98
Carroll, Frank 27:26
Carroll, G. 22:293
Carroll, George 12:121;
    15:120
Carroll, H. 9:140
Carroll, H. W. 1:123
Carroll, Henry 27:26
Carroll, J. 1:119; 3:38;
    15:31
Carroll, J. C. 26:210
Carroll, J. H. 23:23
Carroll, J. J. 19:60
Carroll, J. K. 18:64
Carroll, J. M. 1:122
Carroll, J. R. 3:38
Carroll, J. S. 17:31
Carroll, J. W. 1:24
Carroll, Jacob 23:137;
    24:58
Carroll, James 1:24; 3:38;
    6:12; 8:113; 12:67;
    14:149; 15:188;
    18:79, 411; 20:111;
    21:311; 23:283;
    25:22, 152
Carroll, James M. 7:22
Carroll, Jasper N. 10:106;
    20:221
Carroll, John 4:15; 5:37;
    9:11; 18:430; 23:106
Carroll, John A. 8:11, 81;
    18:125
Carroll, John C. 20:95
Carroll, John G. 17:98
Carroll, John H. 25:152
Carroll, John W. 22:69
Carroll, Joseph 3:38; 4:15;
    16:25
Carroll, Josiah 19:153
Carroll, L. 3:38; 14:5
Carroll, M. 16:147;
    19:235
Carroll, Martin 9:171

Carroll, Michael 7:22;
    21:311; 23:119;
    25:23
Carroll, Michael L.
    23:119
Carroll, Moflet H. 22:69
Carroll, Morris 9:11
Carroll, Moses 9:206
Carroll, O. J. 3:38
Carroll, Owen 12:151
Carroll, P. 1:26; 3:38
Carroll, Page 9:108
Carroll, Patrick 1:120;
    7:22; 9:159; 12:170;
    20:110
Carroll, Peter 14:149;
    18:26; 19:60, 235
Carroll, Robert 7:119;
    16:25; 17:165
Carroll, Simpson 8:38;
    26:155
Carroll, T. 3:38; 14:45
Carroll, T. A. 15:31
Carroll, T. W. 1:117
Carroll, Tennis 27:30
Carroll, Thomas 1:20;
    13:14; 15:103;
    17:252; 22:518
Carroll, Thomas J. 27:143
Carroll, Thomas W.
    17:390
Carroll, W. 3:38; 13:85;
    14:45
Carroll, William 10:7,
    106; 16:179; 17:440;
    20:221; 21:115;
    24:151; 27:32
Carrollton, George C.
    21:311
Carrolton, George 12:151
Carrolton, Ira 22:24
Carron, A. 10:14
Carron, Joseph 13:106
Carron, O. 3:38
Carroth, Elijah 21:266
Carroth, Enoch 18:291;
    26:95
Carrothers, James 23:137
Carrouth, Albert 4:15
Carrow, Antoine 17:73
Carrow, Levi 9:171
Carrs, George H. 17:241
Carrs, H. 1:119
Carruthers, Abraham
    21:266
Carruthers, Calvin 21:266
Carry, J. J. 18:64
Carry, T. K. 2:9
Carry, Thomas 14:149
Carse, John 22:331
Carseray, William 6:30

Carsey, John P. 22:476
Carsie, Richard D. 19:153
Carsin, Ben 20:221
Carsinon, Philip 20:221
Carslisle, Charles 19:153
Carson, --- 18:275
Carson, A. C. 17:71
Carson, A. J. 8:61
Carson, Alexander 16:179
Carson, Andrew 17:404
Carson, Benjamin 11:199
Carson, Bosse 20:222
Carson, Bowse 10:44
Carson, C. B. 21:215
Carson, D. 21:9
Carson, Daniel 11:139
Carson, Daniel B. 13:106
Carson, David 16:156
Carson, E. 3:39
Carson, Eli 9:218
Carson, Emery 27:32
Carson, Ezra 13:14
Carson, George 21:311
Carson, George O. 12:15
Carson, George W. 14:149
Carson, Henry L. 10:90
Carson, J. 25:152
Carson, J. G. 3:39
Carson, J. H. 16:365
Carson, J. M. 12:98
Carson, J. W. 15:297;
    16:179
Carson, Jackson 17:172
Carson, Jacob 7:22
Carson, James 11:408;
    21:311; 23:308
Carson, James M. 22:419
Carson, James P. 17:94
Carson, Joel 22:69
Carson, John 5:11; 9:108;
    18:26; 21:21, 311
Carson, John A. 18:13;
    22:245
Carson, John C. 10:44;
    20:222
Carson, John F. 8:81
Carson, Levi C. 21:311
Carson, M. 15:31
Carson, Matt B. 19:153
Carson, Matthew B.
    10:158
Carson, McKinza 21:198
Carson, Orison 20:222
Carson, P. 25:152
Carson, Prime 5:11
Carson, R. 19:60
Carson, R. S. 11:300
Carson, Robert 9:228;
    18:363
Carson, Robert A. 4:15
Carson, S. 11:300; 18:79

Carson, Samuel 19:269
Carson, Stephen 11:199
Carson, Sylvester 6:12
Carson, T. 23:23
Carson, Thomas 9:71;
    11:180
Carson, W. 14:149;
    21:119
Carson, Wesley 14:45
Carson, William 8:11;
    9:19; 18:125
Carson, William A.
    23:188
Carson, William F. 23:137
Carson, William H. 5:37
Carss, Fred. A. 5:11
Carstine, Henry J. 26:154
Carswell, John 11:385
Carswell, N. 19:248
Cart, Md. 3:39
Cart, William 22:420
Cartel, N. 5:37
Cartell, G. 15:340; 16:365
Carter, --- 3:37; 15:188;
    18:64; 23:202
Carter, A. 5:11; 25:152
Carter, A. H. 2:8; 25:20
Carter, A. J. 3:37; 9:226;
    13:14; 18:363
Carter, Aaron 15:188
Carter, Abner 9:206
Carter, Albert 10:151
Carter, Alden G. 9:213
Carter, Alexander 9:76;
    26:17
Carter, Alfred 22:24
Carter, Allan G. 21:311
Carter, Allen 10:98;
    14:314, 321; 23:202;
    26:154
Carter, Alonzo 7:89
Carter, Andrew 22:118
Carter, Archibald 11:54;
    24:14
Carter, B. 1:25
Carter, B. F. 12:151
Carter, Barney 15:273
Carter, Benjamin 4:15;
    21:266; 24:191
Carter, Benjamin N.
    25:279
Carter, Bruce 16:179
Carter, C. A. 3:38; 15:188
Carter, C. F. 21:311
Carter, C. H. 5:11
Carter, C. N. 14:149
Carter, C. T. 1:117; 8:59;
    19:285
Carter, Cager 11:198
Carter, Calvin 13:14

Carter, Charles 11:259;
    14:149; 21:241;
    22:331
Carter, Charles A. 23:188
Carter, Charles L. 9:171;
    19:273
Carter, Charles M. 25:20
Carter, Charles W. 20:5
Carter, Charley 21:311
Carter, Clinton 17:129;
    24:191
Carter, Creed 21:311
Carter, Cyrus 21:266
Carter, D. 18:79
Carter, D. B. 25:294
Carter, Dallas 17:172
Carter, Daniel B. 7:74
Carter, David 8:11, 104;
    9:161; 17:77; 18:125;
    27:28
Carter, Davis 10:94
Carter, E. D. 23:23
Carter, E. J. 21:21
Carter, Ed 3:38
Carter, Edmund J. 13:14
Carter, Edward 4:15;
    13:56
Carter, Edward D. 14:332
Carter, Edwin 18:26
Carter, Edwin N. 7:7
Carter, Elmore 10:44;
    20:222
Carter, F. 7:89; 12:98
Carter, F. M. 11:141
Carter, F. W. 22:523
Carter, Frank 7:22; 11:200
Carter, G. D. 10:44;
    20:222
Carter, G. N. 10:27;
    19:300
Carter, G. W. 25:152
Carter, George 9:206;
    17:94; 19:325
Carter, George H. 26:122
Carter, George W. 11:421;
    13:14
Carter, Graves 14:319;
    25:282
Carter, H. B. 21:21
Carter, H. C. 3:38
Carter, H. J. 5:11
Carter, Henry 3:37; 7:119;
    9:129, 161; 24:58;
    25:318; 27:29
Carter, Herman 8:104
Carter, Hiram 16:166
Carter, Hiram L. 21:21
Carter, Horace 4:15
Carter, Hyatt 18:232
Carter, I. W. 17:291
Carter, Isaac 13:56

Carter, J. 1:117; 3:38;
    10:10; 11:141; 17:31;
    18:26; 19:244
Carter, J. B. 3:38
Carter, J. D. 17:94;
    18:232; 26:20
Carter, J. E. 18:26
Carter, J. F. 22:182
Carter, J. M. 11:258
Carter, J. R. 14:130;
    15:263
Carter, J. W. 11:259;
    27:143
Carter, Jackson 9:129;
    23:137; 27:29
Carter, Jacob 22:293
Carter, James 7:73, 119;
    8:11, 38; 9:49;
    11:200; 12:67; 15:54;
    16:179; 17:158, 172;
    18:125, 284; 21:49;
    22:69, 293; 24:75;
    25:152; 26:134, 155
Carter, James A. 21:311
Carter, James B. 15:54
Carter, James F. 22:476
Carter, James L. 6:14;
    18:79; 22:119
Carter, James M. 17:49
Carter, James T. 11:55
Carter, Jefferson 21:311
Carter, Jefferson K.
    22:245
Carter, Jesse A. 23:61
Carter, Jessie 18:26
Carter, John 3:38; 6:12;
    7:119; 8:11, 104;
    9:171, 206; 13:85;
    15:26, 318; 17:151,
    161, 402; 18:79, 125;
    19:60; 20:39; 21:65,
    311; 22:293; 23:188;
    25:152
Carter, John B. 23:137
Carter, John H. 7:48; 9:15
Carter, John J. 17:313
Carter, John M. 22:293
Carter, John T. 20:5, 154
Carter, Joseph 9:117, 206;
    10:106; 18:64;
    20:222; 21:311;
    22:245, 331; 27:30
Carter, Joseph B. 22:420
Carter, Josiah 12:15;
    17:31
Carter, Judson W. 22:461
Carter, Lavilla 18:64
Carter, Legran 20:222
Carter, Lem 7:74
Carter, Lemuel 25:294

Carter, Leonard 10:44; 20:222
Carter, Levi 17:77; 18:434; 19:8; 24:100
Carter, Lewis 24:48, 191
Carter, Loma T. 22:420
Carter, Lyman 23:284
Carter, Lyra 4:15
Carter, M. 18:26
Carter, M. H. 22:475
Carter, Marcus D. 19:8
Carter, Margaret 27:31
Carter, Marling 22:24
Carter, Maynard 22:138
Carter, Michael 13:14
Carter, Miles 7:119
Carter, N. 25:152
Carter, N. M. 1:26
Carter, N. W. 7:89
Carter, Nelson 5:37
Carter, Newman B. 14:149
Carter, Nicholas 21:266
Carter, Oliver 15:319
Carter, P. 1:21
Carter, P. S. 9:33
Carter, Perkins 22:293
Carter, Pleasant 21:266
Carter, Powell 22:245
Carter, R. J. 20:91
Carter, Richard 25:152
Carter, Richard D. 21:248
Carter, Richard P. 21:129
Carter, Robert 17:172; 19:153; 21:267, 311; 23:289
Carter, Robert H. 23:97
Carter, Robert J. 12:15
Carter, Robert T. 24:14
Carter, Robin W. 13:14
Carter, Rollin W. 16:25
Carter, Rubert 10:176
Carter, Russell 21:311
Carter, S. 13:85; 14:6; 16:88
Carter, S. H. 1:21
Carter, S. W. 9:101
Carter, Samuel 21:88
Carter, Sandy 22:293
Carter, Seth C. 22:69
Carter, Silas 18:79
Carter, Simon 22:293
Carter, Spencer 11:199
Carter, Stanley 21:210
Carter, T. F. 1:22
Carter, T. N. 12:151
Carter, Tazwell 24:48
Carter, Theodore 23:97
Carter, Thomas 3:38; 9:70; 11:55; 14:314; 17:253

Carter, Thomas J. 24:165
Carter, Timothy 10:44; 16:25; 20:222
Carter, W. 3:38; 17:129; 24:190, 191
Carter, W. A. 14:149; 22:161
Carter, W. B. 3:38
Carter, W. E. 19:273; 23:188
Carter, W. F. 9:49
Carter, W. H. 19:248
Carter, W. J. 3:38; 9:242
Carter, W. M. 25:23
Carter, Walter P. 1:23
Carter, Warren M. 12:15
Carter, Wash 17:129; 24:191
Carter, Washington 7:119
Carter, Wiley 8:69
Carter, William 3:37; 7:22, 48; 11:56, 218, 408, 422; 13:14, 85; 17:172; 21:186; 22:420; 23:86; 24:191; 25:332
Carter, William C. 17:31
Carter, William D. 1:192
Carter, William E. 9:171
Carter, William H. 18:411; 23:61
Carter, William I. 8:11
Carter, William J. 18:126; 20:95
Carter, William M. 15:94
Carter, William P. 22:182
Carter, William R. 11:139
Carter, Willis 19:8
Carter, Wilson 7:119
Carter, Wyatt 26:21
Carterthers, Nelson 22:518
Cartey, Barney 7:89
Carthcart, G. W. 15:150
Carthier, Thomas 10:27
Carthwell, --- 12:15
Carthy, David 19:300
Cartillian, James 13:134
Cartis, Benjamin 26:19
Cartiss, James H. 11:104
Cartlan, Patrick 16:179
Cartland, Francis 16:25
Cartle, James H. 20:222
Cartleman, Jacob 25:318
Cartman, Austin 18:337
Cartman, David 22:293
Cartman, James 21:267
Cartner, J. D. 3:38
Cartney, A. 3:38
Cartney, John 11:421
Cartney, P. 13:85

Cartney, Peter 19:153
Cartney, Thomas 9:19
Cartnill, William 22:69
Carton, George 15:64
Carton, P. 15:64
Cartridge, --- 25:24
Cartright, And--- 25:25
Cartright, John 15:188
Cartright, Leyrand 19:300
Cartright, Lorenzo D. 24:175
Cartrill, Elspeny 14:319
Cartry, C. O. 9:229
Carts, P. 16:365
Cartwell, George 11:338
Cartwell, James 11:55
Cartwright, --- 27:26
Cartwright, A. L. 27:32
Cartwright, Alvin S. 17:359
Cartwright, C. 27:33
Cartwright, C. E. 26:95
Cartwright, C. S. 2:9; 25:25
Cartwright, Charles 14:149
Cartwright, Charles E. 9:33; 18:291
Cartwright, E. 3:39; 14:149
Cartwright, G. S. 8:61; 26:154
Cartwright, H. T. 22:24
Cartwright, Henry 9:76; 26:17
Cartwright, Hill 22:293
Cartwright, J. D. 9:49
Cartwright, J. G. 22:418
Cartwright, James 21:222
Cartwright, James C. 22:69
Cartwright, James W. 23:61
Cartwright, Jesse L. 5:11
Cartwright, John 7:56; 8:11; 10:14; 13:14; 17:18; 18:126; 22:182
Cartwright, John T. 18:392
Cartwright, Joseph 13:14
Cartwright, Lorenzo 17:449
Cartwright, N. 25:152
Cartwright, Nicholas 8:117; 19:315
Cartwright, P. W. 9:140
Cartwright, Peter 21:311
Cartwright, Reuben 8:38; 26:155

Cartwright, Thomas 10:44; 20:222
Cartwright, W. F. 22:277
Cartwright, William 1:24; 13:81; 16:179; 24:14
Carty, C. A. 20:222
Carty, D. 1:123
Carty, Horatio 25:20
Carty, M. 15:31
Carty, Michael 8:11; 18:126
Carty, Newton 11:199
Cartz, Robert F. 13:14
Caruch, George B. 12:63
Caruford, P. 15:347
Carultiers, William E. 7:22
Carurike, George H. 11:124
Caruth, Adam 21:147
Caruthers, Holbert 10:204
Caruthers, Lemuel 11:300
Caruthers, M. C. 14:327
Carvan, James 12:169
Carver, A. N. 8:46
Carver, Andrew J. 10:44; 20:222
Carver, Augustus H. 22:401
Carver, Carthulo 17:454
Carver, Daniel 12:67; 15:26
Carver, Edward 4:15
Carver, Edwin 4:15
Carver, Frank 1:25
Carver, H. 14:295; 17:478; 27:31
Carver, J. 21:109
Carver, J. D. 25:152
Carver, J. W. 18:26
Carver, Jacob H. 8:11
Carver, James 11:199; 12:141; 14:262; 17:147; 20:222
Carver, James A. 17:235
Carver, James C. 23:137
Carver, James S. 22:182
Carver, John 11:237
Carver, John G. 3:39
Carver, John T. 26:210
Carver, Justus M. 13:14
Carver, Kathelo 24:170
Carver, L. 1:119
Carver, Lewis 16:25
Carver, Louis 17:161
Carver, Lucius 5:11
Carver, Mathias 18:334
Carver, P. 1:97; 19:236
Carver, Philip 9:171
Carver, Reuben H. 17:205
Carver, S. H. 11:325

Carver, Samuel 12:151; 21:251
Carver, T. S. 12:151
Carver, William 21:311
Carver, William A. 22:518
Carver, William B. 23:97
Carver, William H. 17:359
Carver, Conner, Or Carner, Jo. 16:117
Carvers, James 14:149
Carvey, John 10:210
Carvil, Jacob 9:50
Carvin, Lewis 15:188
Carvine, George 16:179
Carvine, R. W. 11:385
Carwall, H. D. 9:71
Carwell, Armstead 12:160
Carwell, Thomas 12:169
Carwin, T. W. 10:45
Carwine, John 12:151
Cary, Clay 19:44
Cary, Dyer 17:422
Cary, Edward 9:171; 19:248
Cary, Franklin John 15:165
Cary, George L. 14:149
Cary, H. 13:62; 19:60
Cary, J. 15:150
Cary, J. A. N. 21:21
Cary, James 12:61
Cary, Jeremiah 4:15
Cary, John 6:30; 19:8
Cary, Lawrence 13:106
Cary, Marvin 9:240
Cary, Masselan 19:280
Cary, Patrick 15:188
Cary, Samuel 13:106
Cary, Spencer 9:218
Cary, T. M. 5:11; 25:153
Cary, Thomas 3:39; 15:188
Cary, W. B. 9:76
Cary, William 23:188
Cary, William H. 4:15
Caryl, A. 19:233
Casad, A. D. 10:106; 20:222
Casad, J. A. 16:91
Casad, James 21:222
Casbury, John 25:23
Casco, James 18:126
Casdorph, W. H. 14:45
Case, A. F. 3:39
Case, A. P. 3:39
Case, Aaron 4:15
Case, Augustus 11:285
Case, Benjamin P. 20:21
Case, C. 12:67
Case, C. E. 8:46
Case, Charles 1:22

Case, Columbus 4:15
Case, Daniel 3:39
Case, Daniel W. 14:149
Case, David 9:19; 18:303; 26:95
Case, E. 3:39; 13:85
Case, E. J. 22:182
Case, Edwin A. 11:104
Case, F. 22:293
Case, Frank 23:61
Case, G. M. C. 9:226
Case, G. W. C. 18:363
Case, George 16:132; 18:232, 303; 26:19, 95
Case, George M. 23:61
Case, George W. 11:140; 20:21
Case, H. 1:120; 23:23
Case, H. J. 3:39
Case, Harrison W. 9:77
Case, Henry H. 18:232; 26:20
Case, Hiram A. 21:222
Case, Hiram H. 11:55
Case, Horace 12:15
Case, Hosey E. 25:153
Case, Isaac 9:77
Case, J. B. 11:83; 14:280; 17:494
Case, J. J. 18:323
Case, J. W. 11:300
Case, James 4:15; 8:11; 15:85; 16:179; 26:155
Case, James F. 8:11; 18:126
Case, James M. 23:61
Case, John 10:45; 15:304; 16:179; 20:222; 23:106
Case, John H. 17:279; 22:420
Case, John J. 22:182
Case, John M. 20:222
Case, Joseph 16:289; 17:63, 287
Case, L. 3:39
Case, Levi S. 22:139
Case, Lewis 9:206
Case, Luaso P. 19:60
Case, Madison 11:54
Case, Maxim 21:90
Case, N. D. 1:26
Case, N. M. 27:25
Case, Oliver C. 15:2
Case, Orville J. 15:2
Case, P. O. 11:395
Case, Perry L. 10:7
Case, Peter C. 9:106
Case, R. 22:331

Case, S. 14:45, 149
Case, S. G. 19:249
Case, Samuel 8:113
Case, Samuel D. 22:69
Case, Smith G. 9:171
Case, Theodore 22:138; 23:128
Case, Thom 11:140
Case, Thomas 12:85; 16:289
Case, Valentine 10:171
Case, Valt 19:153
Case, W. B. 19:8
Case, W. H. 1:117
Case, William 9:218; 10:106; 23:23; 26:18
Case, William C. 25:20
Case, William E. 2:9
Casebeer, Jacob D. 12:15
Casebeer, John B. 12:15
Casebeer, W. H. 20:132
Casebolt, Lloyd H. 22:24
Casens, William 20:222
Casewell, H. W. 26:22
Casey, A. E. 10:14
Casey, A. M. 16:25
Casey, Adolphus 10:106; 20:222
Casey, Asa 10:106; 20:222
Casey, Charles F. 22:401
Casey, Charles John 21:311
Casey, Cornelius 18:79
Casey, D. 16:91
Casey, D. W. 21:14
Casey, Daniel 16:91
Casey, Edward 23:252
Casey, Ellis 17:172
Casey, Frederick C. 16:65
Casey, G. 14:277; 23:104
Casey, George W. 23:270
Casey, Henry 22:69; 293
Casey, Hiram H. 7:89
Casey, Isaac J. 22:245
Casey, J. 3:39; 13:85; 20:39
Casey, J. E. 1:117
Casey, J. R. 7:74; 25:294
Casey, James 4:15; 15:64, 188
Casey, Jeremiah F. 4:15
Casey, John 1:24; 3:39; 10:14; 11:115, 139, 222; 12:151; 13:81; 14:45; 15:103, 188; 18:188; 20:121; 22:421
Casey, John C. 22:245
Casey, John S. 22:9
Casey, Joseph 15:188

Casey, L. B. 24:14
Casey, M. 3:39; 19:60; 23:137
Casey, Martin 22:182
Casey, Mathew 22:24
Casey, Michael 13:106; 14:149; 15:349; 16:365; 18:202; 26:210
Casey, Miles 15:31
Casey, Nelson 9:206
Casey, O. 14:6
Casey, P. 1:122; 3:39; 13:85
Casey, Patrick 12:151; 20:136; 23:106
Casey, Presley 7:89
Casey, R. 9:226
Casey, Richard 12:68; 15:81
Casey, S. 20:39
Casey, Samuel B. 7:89; 21:311
Casey, T. S. 11:443
Casey, Theodore 18:102
Casey, Thomas 1:21; 15:333; 19:60; 22:24
Casey, Thomas I. 10:106
Casey, Thomas J. 20:222
Casey, Timothy 11:25
Casey, William 3:39; 10:106; 15:340; 16:365; 20:222
Caseys, William 12:15
Casgriff, Arthur 22:69
Casgriff, William 17:449; 24:175
Casgrove, J. 11:141
Casgrove, William 16:179
Cash, --- 11:218
Cash, C. 14:45
Cash, Charles E. 27:33
Cash, F. 12:95; 15:358; 19:60
Cash, Felix 25:24
Cash, Frederick 11:90
Cash, George 21:222
Cash, Henry 13:106
Cash, Jacob 8:38; 26:155
Cash, James C. 17:49
Cash, John A. 19:60
Cash, John M. 8:81
Cash, Kendrick S. 22:449
Cash, Philip 3:39
Cash, Samuel 11:54
Cash, U. 1:23
Cash, W. 5:50; 20:222; 25:153
Cash, Wesley 18:232; 26:21
Cash, William L. 22:69

Cash, William Y. 10:45
Cash---, --- 24:190
Cashaw, John 12:95
Cashdollar, Levi 26:95
Cashell, W. 1:122
Cashenberry, John 5:37
Cashier, John 14:264
Cashier, William 14:149; 18:275
Cashin, Nicholas 9:33
Cashion, J. 1:26
Cashion, James 10:14; 12:140
Cashman, H. C. 15:347
Cashman, Jacob 12:15
Cashman, James 11:190
Cashmore, C. M. 17:500
Cashnard, J. E. 1:120
Cashra, Frederick 10:153
Cashron, Thomas 23:202
Cashway, Pascal 18:46
Casiday, Jameson 8:81
Casingham, Frederick 22:182
Casity, John F. 23:23
Caskadder, Charles 9:77
Casker, S. 11:139
Casket, S. 17:77
Caskey, E. 1:117
Caskey, J. 24:75
Caskey, Thomas 23:283
Caskill, Dav. W. 19:8
Caskill, W. B. 17:404
Caskins, S. 22:350
Casky, S. C. 14:280
Casler, A. J. 25:25
Casler, F. W. 17:63
Casler, Joseph 15:31
Casler, Oliver 19:60
Casler, Smith 11:115
Caslett, William C. 17:18
Caslin, Edward 18:411
Caslint, Charles 22:418
Caslit, John H. 22:24
Casmer, H. H. 11:139
Casmer, Joseph 16:179
Casner, Daniel 4:15
Casner, John 8:62
Casner, Nixon 21:311
Casner, Noah 4:15
Casner, P. 20:222
Casner, R. 22:183
Casner, Samuel 22:461
Casner, Samuel F. 22:24
Casner, Samuel L. 4:15
Casner, Thomas 1:120
Casner, W. 25:153
Casner, William 5:11
Caso, C. W. 8:11
Cason, J. B. 10:45; 20:222
Cason, W. H. 25:153

Caspares, Nathan S. 22:401
Casper, A. 14:45
Casper, Backman 17:318
Casper, John 20:95; 24:14
Casper, Joseph 16:289
Casper, Lewis 20:95
Casper, Peter 25:268
Casper, William 10:147; 18:46
Caspill, James 22:9
Caspino, Lewis 1:24
Caspley, A. 2:9
Casporas, William I. 15:90
Cass, Benjamin Q. 4:15
Cass, C. R. 11:189
Cass, C. W. 18:126
Cass, Edwin 16:278
Cass, George 18:337
Cass, J. W. 11:259
Cass, John 18:46
Cass, Leonard 8:81
Cass, Lewis P. 8:81
Cass, P. 1:118
Cass, Rufus 9:77; 26:18
Cass, W. 9:140; 27:26
Cass, W. W. 10:45; 20:222
Cass, William 6:20; 12:86; 13:106; 16:289
Cassad, John A. 22:419
Cassada, Andrew S. 21:65
Cassada, John 12:15
Cassada, William 22:139
Cassaday, J. R. 27:25
Cassady, Alexander 18:214
Cassady, Amaziah 11:139
Cassady, George W. 17:241
Cassady, H. 20:142
Cassady, Henry 22:69
Cassady, J. 3:39
Cassady, John 6:30
Cassady, Robert 18:215; 21:222
Cassady, William 7:81; 10:106; 20:222
Cassall, J. B. 17:63
Cassatt, Joseph 18:392
Cassau, John 18:284
Casse, William 20:132
Cassedy, Augustus S. 4:15
Cassedy, George 4:15
Cassedy, James 5:11
Cassedy, John H. 8:81
Cassedy, Mat 15:172
Cassedy, W. 17:191

Cassedy, William W. 17:49
Cassel, A. H. 25:24
Cassel, C. P. 1:120
Cassel, John E. 22:69
Casseldon, J. 14:280
Cassell, Adam L. 22:245
Cassell, C. D. 9:33
Cassell, Calvin 12:151
Cassell, D. 3:39
Cassell, George 23:137
Cassell, George E. 7:67
Cassell, Gustaff A. 21:65
Cassell, Horace 22:138
Cassell, James W. 11:139
Cassell, W. B. 17:469
Cassell, W. R. 14:295; 27:32
Cassell, Whitney 8:104
Cassell, William H. 22:69
Cassells, Samuel 3:39
Casselman, A. 15:31
Cassender, Warren 4:15
Casser, Stephen A. 10:106
Casser, Stephen Antone 20:222
Casserly, Thomas 7:22
Cassett, James W. 11:139
Cassey, --- 25:22
Cassey, George W. 22:119
Cassey, James 3:53
Cassey, M. 18:232
Cassey, Thomas L. 5:37; 25:153
Cassiart, John 22:402
Cassida, P. 26:155
Cassiday, John 23:97
Cassiday, William H. 8:81
Cassiday, William R. 24:48
Cassidey, Michael 9:171
Cassidey, Patrick 1:24
Cassido, William F. 7:67
Cassidy, Edward 10:158; 19:153
Cassidy, Frank 19:317
Cassidy, G. 9:140; 27:28
Cassidy, J. 9:140; 27:26
Cassidy, James 12:15; 14:45; 16:88; 22:332; 25:318
Cassidy, Jeremiah 14:149
Cassidy, John 13:14; 14:45, 149; 15:103; 16:91
Cassidy, John S. 22:69
Cassidy, Joseph 9:50
Cassidy, Lewis 14:235
Cassidy, M. 9:159; 19:249
Cassidy, Michael 21:84
Cassidy, P. 1:25; 14:149

Cassidy, Samuel 14:149
Cassidy, T. 12:81; 16:289
Cassidy, Thomas 9:171; 19:236
Cassidy, Thomas E. 24:8
Cassidy, William 14:45; 25:294
Cassie, George 9:19
Cassildine, John 17:501
Cassimere, John 9:15
Cassinder, B. 9:171
Cassing, Henry 12:151
Cassingham, Thomas A. 11:25
Cassity, James 25:153
Cassius, John S. 3:39
Cassler, Albert 12:68
Cassley, J. C. 18:232; 26:21
Cassman, A. 3:39
Cassman, Charles B. 8:11; 18:126
Cassman, E. 17:31
Casson, B. 16:289
Casson, John 26:134
Casson, Samuel 9:171; 19:269
Casson, Simon 7:82
Casswell, Alexander 22:293
Casswell, Harvey S. 22:183
Casswell, Thomas 12:169
Cast, H. 18:215
Castable, J. 3:39
Castano, J. 3:39
Caste, Amthee 9:157
Caste, David 15:188
Casteel, Benjamin 23:137
Casteel, Hiram 24:58
Casteel, J. A. 22:500
Casteel, Jeremiah 22:245
Casteel, Thomas 8:62
Castel, Jeremiah 4:15
Castel, William 22:449
Castelan, Adam 17:209
Castelio, M. H. 9:171
Castell, Archibald 20:145
Castell, William 22:449
Castella, M. H. 19:236
Castello, Antonio Jose 8:124
Castello, F. 14:45
Castello, John 17:144; 19:60
Castello, Michael 10:90
Castello, Patrick 10:14
Castello, Peter 19:331
Castello, Thomas 16:179; 22:182
Castello, W. F. 7:48
Castello, William 9:33

Casteo, C. B. 25:23
Caster, Albert 10:178
Caster, Edwin B. 11:139
Caster, George 17:31
Caster, J. L. 21:49
Caster, J. M. 21:65
Casterbough, D. 16:266
Casterger, Charles 12:98
Casterline, William 13:14
Casterlough, L. 14:6
Casterly, John 15:358
Casterman, T. 8:62
Castertine, William 26:144
Castham, Thomas 15:165
Castigan, Lawrence 12:15
Castile, George R. 10:45
Castile, J. R. 11:421
Castill, George R. 20:222
Castillo, George A. 19:153
Castillo, M. 20:222
Castillon, Robert 7:48
Castills, John 19:8
Castimore, Charles 11:301
Castin, Nichols 18:291
Castina, H. 21:311
Castine, J. S. 22:17
Casting, Richard 7:119; 21:311
Castle, Andrew 22:245; 27:143
Castle, C. 3:39; 22:182
Castle, C. H. 3:39
Castle, C. L. 25:153
Castle, Charles A. 5:11
Castle, Curran H. 18:303
Castle, Curren H. 26:94
Castle, Emery 4:15
Castle, F. 3:39
Castle, George 27:32
Castle, J. W. 3:39
Castle, John 5:11; 17:172; 24:165; 25:153
Castle, M. 19:153
Castle, Martin 15:2
Castle, Martin V. 22:139
Castle, Melborn 11:139
Castle, R. 11:339
Castle, Robert R. 10:94
Castle, S. B. 1:119
Castle, Thomas 6:30; 25:318
Castle, W. 27:27
Castle, William 3:39; 7:72; 12:7
Castle, William S. 16:25
Castleburg, Daniel 21:21
Castlebury, R. J. 11:19
Castleman, Hiram H. 9:96
Castleman, Jacob 6:30

Castleman, Joseph 1:21
Castleman, Moses 22:245
Castleman, W. 16:179
Castler, Emory W. 7:22
Castler, Theodore 4:15
Castles, Eli 22:245
Castline, George 22:165
Castly, John 15:64
Castner, John 11:139
Castner, John N. 22:245
Castner, Josiah 10:147; 18:46
Castner, William 9:65; 18:275
Casto, Jesse 3:39
Castoe, A. 13:85
Castolo, J. M. 5:11
Caston, Nathan 9:206
Caston, S. B. 4:15
Caston, Samuel 7:119; 21:311
Castor, --- 4:15; 8:46
Castor, A. 16:266
Castor, David 11:56
Castor, Edward 21:311
Castor, J. B. 9:68
Castor, James 19:294
Castor, Jesse 22:518
Castor, Miles 21:222; 22:119, 449
Castor, Perry C. 8:46
Castor, Philip 21:311
Castor, Silas 16:143
Castrupe, Henry 22:420
Caswall, Harvey 9:77
Caswell, Alfred 17:252
Caswell, E. C. 12:15
Caswell, F. 3:39
Caswell, Francis M. 22:119
Caswell, G. 3:39
Caswell, H. 1:26
Caswell, J. F. 1:122
Caswell, J. S. 3:39
Caswell, John 16:84
Caswell, John M. 9:7
Caswell, Landall 12:171
Caswell, Nelson 9:171
Caswell, Richard 10:158
Caswell, Robert 17:406
Caswell, S. 14:45
Caswell, Samuel H. 21:311
Caswell, Samuel S. 18:205
Caswell, Thomas 7:22
Caswell, W. 14:45
Caswell, W. H. 12:121
Caswell, W. W. 15:120
Cat---, F. A. 22:24
Cata, William D. 4:15

Catacurt, Robert 3:40
Catch, James 16:179
Catch, Killer 25:332
Catcham, John M. 11:27
Cate, A. 25:153
Cate, A. P. 11:400
Cate, Augustus 5:11
Cate, Charles 7:89; 21:312
Cate, Elijah 11:421
Cate, Eugene 7:89; 21:312
Cate, George 7:22
Cate, James M. 22:24
Cate, John 9:171; 10:34; 19:232
Cate, Joseph H. 24:14
Cate, Joshua 21:49
Cate, Noah 23:61
Cate, William S. 10:106; 20:222
Caten, M. 3:40
Cater, A. 15:150
Cater, George H. 15:64
Cater, Isaac 9:240
Cater, William H. 9:171
Catern, George O. 18:126
Cates, Charles 10:106; 20:223
Cates, E. 14:149
Cates, J. 3:39; 16:179
Cates, J. C. 1:121
Cates, J. J. T. 25:153
Cates, John 21:267; 23:251
Cates, John C. 17:49
Cates, John E. 10:106; 20:223
Cates, Lewis 26:161
Cates, M. W. 8:46
Catey, M. J. 21:119
Cathaather, Osborne 9:77
Cathan, John F. 11:399
Cathbath, W. H. 19:8
Cathburn, A. 21:109
Cathcart, Hugh 17:98
Cathcart, James 1:22
Cathcart, Samuel 21:135
Cathcart, Thomas K. 23:23
Cathcart, W. 14:295; 17:479; 27:31
Cathcart, William 12:16; 20:21
Cathcart, William H. 20:182
Catheon, J. 11:438
Cather, James 21:267
Catherall, Isaac 12:16
Catherman, Benjamin 17:90

Catherman, Lewis M. 23:178
Cathey, A. I. 8:11
Cathey, David E. 8:62
Cathey, Thomas 19:300
Cathin, Delon 13:106
Cathir, J. 22:461
Cathlin, John 14:45
Cathoon, Obad A. 9:116
Cathraine, S. 3:40
Catiller, William 22:350
Cating, Robert 11:421
Catipie, Paul 7:119
Catlen, George M. 15:21
Catlen, James S. 8:11
Catler, C. P. 27:27
Catler, George 22:475
Catlern, George W. 8:11
Catlet, James 21:267
Catlett, Samuel 17:172
Catlett, T. M. 11:56
Catlin, C. 1:97
Catlin, Clinton J. 20:121
Catlin, David M. 15:31
Catlin, Edward W. 23:106
Catlin, Harrison 18:215
Catlin, Israel 17:31
Catlin, James S. 18:126
Catlin, Joseph M. 14:149
Catlin, Simon 16:179
Catlon, Lewis 16:179
Caton, J. D. 1:21
Caton, James 14:149
Caton, John 17:13
Caton, R. 7:119
Caton, Thomas 10:106; 20:223
Caton, W. T. 3:40
Catrell, William G. 26:122
Catrell, Willis 11:198
Catrick, Lewis 14:149
Catrill, L. 3:40
Catrin, Eli 14:45
Catron, Andrew J. 17:498
Catron, Henderson 21:267
Catron, Hudson 21:211
Catron, William A. 11:181
Catshaw, S. 22:183
Catt, E. C. 19:249
Catt, Emile C. 9:171
Catt, Fielding 11:55
Catt, John 22:245
Catt, Morris 21:21
Catt, N. 11:259
Cattargus, Otto 5:50
Cattel, William 9:42
Cattell, G. W. 14:45
Cattelle, James 21:267
Cattern, William 17:210
Catterton, M. 5:50

Cattiss, Henry F. 11:141
Cattle, Samuel R. 27:30
Cattlekock, F. 3:40
Caty, J. H. 11:385
Catz, George W. 22:9
Cauble, William H. 23:61
Cauch, Charles E. 24:157
Caudill, Benjamin L. 17:235
Caughey, James 14:149
Caughlem, William 17:49
Caughlin, B. 3:40
Caughlin, John 13:14; 15:188
Caughlin, Michael 22:245
Caughman, Nelson B. 10:185; 18:172
Caughney, James 22:23
Caukey, Daniel C. 18:26
Caul, Charles 24:75
Caul, John 13:106
Cauldwell, Robert 8:81
Cauldwell, Samuel 16:25
Caulee, William C. 10:45
Cauley, Abner 21:206
Cauley, Henry W. 11:299
Cauley, Richard 12:48
Caulfie, D. T. 15:287
Caulk, R. B. 10:185; 18:172
Caulkin, Alfred 9:235
Cault, Albert 3:40
Caulthart, W. 16:25
Cauman, Alex 19:153
Cauncy, T. 14:239
Cauneign, John S. 8:100
Caunston, Caunt 18:363
Cauntson, Cannt. 9:218
Courtores, Julius 12:171
Causarr, Daniel 11:54
Causeris, Charles E. 9:117
Causey, John 15:172
Causey, Merrick 7:119
Causlin, Oliver 14:149
Causon, Lucius 9:117
Caustright, Chauncey 19:8
Cautin, L. 1:117
Cautney, Hugh 11:91
Cautry, Daniel 16:91
Cautts, Anderson 11:199
Cauty, Enoch 26:18
Cavalry, Isaac 16:150
Cavalry, Lorenzo Dow 11:141
Cavan, T. A. 15:340
Cavan, Thomas 25:318
Cavanagh, Charles 19:153
Cavanagh, J. F. 27:26
Cavanagh, Michael 16:115

Cavanagh, Patrick 19:324; 22:332
Cavanagh, Thomas 18:108
Cavanah, W. 5:50
Cavanaugh, Arthur 4:15
Cavanaugh, C. W. 8:62; 26:154
Cavanaugh, Charles 10:106; 20:223
Cavanaugh, Christopher C. 23:178
Cavanaugh, Dennis 21:312
Cavanaugh, E. F. 18:232; 26:20
Cavanaugh, J. 23:23
Cavanaugh, J. F. 9:140
Cavanaugh, James 14:148
Cavanaugh, John 3:40; 8:124; 9:19; 18:303; 23:178; 26:94
Cavanaugh, Michael 13:14; 14:314; 24:14
Cavanaugh, P. 3:40; 12:16
Cavanaugh, Peter 19:8; 23:23
Cavanaugh, Thomas D. 23:188
Cavanaugh, Thomas H. 20:223
Cavanaugh, W. W. 26:218
Cavanaugh, William D. 19:153
Cavaner, James M. 10:45
Cavangh, Dennis 7:89
Cavannaugh, George 4:15
Cavdish, James 16:365
Cave, Cyrus 4:15
Cave, Robert 1:25
Cavein, John 17:253
Cavel, Henry 18:26
Cavelin, James 13:128
Caven, William 24:165
Cavena, Daniel 9:171
Cavenaugh, John 3:40
Cavenaugh, Michael 11:83
Cavenaugh, William 9:218; 18:363
Cavender, George W. 18:232; 26:21
Cavender, J. L. 3:40
Cavender, John 12:16
Cavender, John B. 17:18
Cavender, John P. 17:18
Cavendish, J. 27:143
Cavendish, James 22:293
Cavendish, Thomas 11:299
Cavener, Thomas 5:11
Cavens, Thomas 25:153

Caver, H. C. 11:218
Caver, William 7:89
Caverley, John 25:294
Caverly, Cynes 14:149
Caverly, D. E. 9:140
Caverly, John 7:81
Caverly, Levi D. 7:89
Caverly, Nathaniel 25:153
Caverly, Philip D. 21:222
Cavern, Silas D. 19:316
Caverner, Bernard 12:16
Cavert, Nicholas 9:117;
    27:30
Cavesley, Nathaniel
    15:277
Cavet, Robert 3:40
Cavett, G. 25:278
Cavey, William 13:14
Cavil, Charles 16:179
Cavil, William 10:106;
    20:223
Caviler, R. B. 21:267
Cavileron, Frank 27:33
Cavilier, Peter B. 21:115
Cavin, J. 3:40
Cavin, James 3:40
Cavinder, B. 19:266
Caving, P. 11:115
Cavins, William W.
    23:301
Cavis, C. P. 18:46
Cavis, William 26:121
Cavit, J. 20:181
Cavitt, Francis M. 22:420
Cavitt, William T. 20:181
Cavnell, J. 1:117
Cavrian, H. 11:27
Cawan, A. 14:280
Cawather, O. 26:17
Cawfield, D. 13:106
Cawford, Charles G.
    18:126
Cawgill, E. D. 11:25
Cawish, George 15:188
Cawkins, L. 11:88
Cawley, John 26:210
Cawley, M. 14:45
Cawley, Thomas 1:23
Cawlin, Thomas 7:89
Cawling, George 27:32
Cawood, I. T. 25:271
Cawood, Jacob H. 17:31
Cawrol, L. 13:85
Cawton, F. M. 14:45
Caxton, John W. 16:179
Cay, John 11:299
Cay, William H. 4:65
Cayan, Nelson 21:251
Cayel, William 11:218
Cayey, Lewis M. 22:401
Cayfort, J. 13:85

Cayhardt, Samuel 15:189
Cayhee, Fuffield 15:157
Cayle, Edward 15:292
Cayle, Patrick 13:106
Cayler, Elijah 22:183
Cayler, Leonard 15:31
Caylor, Benjamin 26:144
Caylor, Benjamin F.
    22:475; 26:144
Caylor, D. 18:363
Caylor, David 9:218
Caylor, Isaac S. 21:222
Cayner, Edward 20:177
Cayson, Thomas 11:199
Cayton, John W. 15:302
Caywood, Adelbert 4:15
Caywood, Charles F.
    20:121
Cazart, Mukin H. 22:245
Cazenau, Pierre 10:45
Cazier, W. S. 19:8
Cea, Charles 21:312
Ceafas, E. W. 1:118
Ceahm, George 16:179
Cealrow, W. 16:278
Ceams, P. 8:71
Cearer, D. 3:40
Cearley, Edward 18:126
Cearls, Henry 14:149
Cearns, Robert 11:83
Ceasar, W. 1:97
Cease, Alexander 17:129;
    24:190
Ceaser, Henry 13:106
Ceavley, Edmond 8:11
Cebers, M. 15:31
Cechum, C. 14:295;
    17:470
Cecil, James 9:219
Cecil, Jerry 16:179
Cecil, M. B. 10:45;
    20:223
Cecil, R. N. 23:23
Cecil, Solomon 22:119
Cecil, William P. 8:124
Cecily, James 18:363
Ceder, Robert 20:223
Ceefer, J. H. 3:40
Ceeil, Stephen 19:8
Ceffers, Preston C. 12:16
Cefton, W. H. 21:312
Ceicy, Maley 16:289
Ceicy, Maly 12:86
Ceigler, Joseph 10:106;
    20:223
Celary, J. H. 3:40
Celbring, Albert 14:149
Celegg, Thomas 8:104
Celester, Louis 21:312
Celestin, Joseph 21:312

Celestine, Charles 7:119;
    21:312
Celestine, Ira 7:119
Celey, Shelden 15:31
Celieher, Jettefans 17:235
Cellar, Thomas 24:100
Celley, J. D. 16:179
Cellon, J. 17:497
Celwell, A. 19:60
Cemer, William H. 26:17
Cemline, David C.
    14:295; 17:477;
    27:32
Cence, N. 11:258
Cennandy, Cornelius
    9:171
Cennay, Joseph W. 12:68
Cennis, W. 21:49
Cenntly, C. C. 12:121
Cent, James J. 16:179
Center, E. R. 3:40
Center, George W.
    10:158; 19:153
Centers, W. 7:22
Centher, John 15:189
Centre, A. 3:40
Ceole, Philip 9:163
Ceperly, D. H. 21:165
Ceperly, Martin 24:14
Cephus, Richard 10:176;
    19:153
Cephy, Henry 25:25
Cepins, W. 25:153
Ceplias, L. 3:40
Cept, I. 3:40
Ceran, Edward 15:297
Cerbin, Alonzo 13:14
Cerer, William H. H.
    22:476
Cerets, William 23:188
Cereville, Samuel 16:289
Cerfoss, Daniel 13:14
Cering, John 10:45
Cerley, --- 23:312
Cermmon, B. 12:147
Cern, Jacob 10:45
Cerns, Jacob 20:223
Cerrighan, Thomas 4:15
Cerrney, John 9:108
Cersey, Martin 11:421
Cerstiruppleicutt, W.
    15:31
Certre, J. 13:62
Cerwekh, Jacob 11:26
Ceryer, W. 15:189
Cesar, J. L. 12:16
Cessions, H. 18:46
Cetchum, C. 27:31
Ceurtis, Theodore 25:23
Ceutis, George 19:44
Ceuyh, John F. 10:178

Ceville, Reiveson 19:322
Cew, C. 1:24
Cezen, J. 14:6
Ch---, Austin F. 19:154
Ch---, E. P. 15:172
Ch---, William 11:259, 339
Ch---n, Charles 23:106
Chaadt, V. 7:22
Chabel, George 4:16
Chabin, C. 4:16
Chace, J. F. 16:91
Chace, R. S. 19:273
Chace, William 1:121
Chacon, A. W. 3:41
Chadaley, S. 1:21
Chadbourn, Charles 12:16
Chadbourn, Edward C. 15:11
Chadbourne, Simon 9:117; 27:30
Chadburn, C. M. 7:22
Chadburn, John 18:291; 26:95
Chadderdon, George 22:161
Chadderdon, Phile D. 16:278
Chaddock, D. 17:70
Chaderick, George W. 12:68
Chadlayne, George 26:17
Chadman, Benjamin 7:74
Chadrick, Francis B. 24:151
Chadvin, Isaac P. 17:202
Chadwell, E. M. 22:476
Chadwell, Jesse R. 21:21
Chadwick, Amasa 11:104
Chadwick, C. E. 3:40
Chadwick, Charles 10:45; 20:223
Chadwick, D. 14:295; 17:472; 27:32
Chadwick, Daniel 10:106; 20:223
Chadwick, Eugene A. 22:24
Chadwick, F. W. 17:432
Chadwick, G. W. 15:16
Chadwick, J. H. 22:351
Chadwick, Jabez 11:104
Chadwick, James 22:332; 23:188
Chadwick, Jeremiah 16:150
Chadwick, John 21:203
Chadwick, John H. 15:189
Chadwick, M. 3:40
Chadwick, R. 12:16

Chadwick, Robert 9:117; 21:90
Chadwick, Samuel 23:61
Chadwick, William 8:11
Chadwick, William H. 9:11
Chael, Charles D. 21:312
Chafee, Edgar 15:103
Chafee, Jerome 10:171
Chaffee, A. J. 16:91
Chaffee, C. P. 15:120
Chaffee, Jerome 19:154; 21:312
Chaffee, R. A. 3:41
Chaffee, T. E. 20:145
Chaffee, W. R. 7:22
Chaffee, William E. 12:68
Chaffer, E. A. 19:8
Chaffer, George W. 17:320
Chaffer, W. E. 15:21
Chaffer, William 12:16
Chaffey, Royal 5:50
Chaffin, James 22:183
Chaffin, John C. 8:11
Chaffin, Louis 11:140
Chaffin, N. 1:23
Chaffin, Sam 9:203
Chaffin, W. F. 24:75
Chaffin, William 7:22
Chaffin, William M. 24:36
Chaffle, Tom 7:119
Chafin, A. 14:331
Chafin, J. T. 9:219; 18:363
Chaflin, Alden H. 21:90
Chafman, George 14:149
Chagnon, E. 3:41
Chailders, Joseph 10:45
Chailer, D. C. 14:45
Chaille, J. C. 7:56
Chain, Thomas 9:164
Chainbury, S. C. 14:6
Chalafauk, Nelson 16:289
Chalborn, John 9:33
Chaldbourn, W. R. 15:189
Chalenbenberg, C. 7:89
Chaley, J. H. 25:24
Chalfan, Joseph 11:300
Chalfant, Matthias 22:419
Chalfant, Ralph W. 17:31
Chalin, James 15:189
Chalis, James 3:40
Chalk, Michael 10:45; 20:223
Chalker, M. J. 15:120
Chalker, Oren S. 17:161
Challacomb, William 10:204
Chalmers, H. 14:46
Chalmers, Robert 21:267

Chalrant, Charles S. 9:50
Chalson, Peter 15:189
Chalton, William 20:223
Chaman, Decatur S. 9:171
Chamat, George 20:34
Chambelain, M. J. 12:68
Chamber, J. S. 3:41
Chamberlain, --- 13:14
Chamberlain, A. 14:150
Chamberlain, A. B. 23:137
Chamberlain, Allen 21:312
Chamberlain, Augustus 20:5
Chamberlain, B. F. 7:89
Chamberlain, C. 3:40; 12:7; 16:289
Chamberlain, C. P. 3:40; 7:22; 21:312
Chamberlain, Charles B. 4:15
Chamberlain, Charles L. 3:40
Chamberlain, Curtis J. 22:170
Chamberlain, D. 14:46
Chamberlain, D. F. 1:119
Chamberlain, E. 14:46; 17:63
Chamberlain, E. A. 4:15
Chamberlain, E. E. 11:124
Chamberlain, Edward 17:159
Chamberlain, F. O. 22:161
Chamberlain, Francis G. 13:14
Chamberlain, Francis W. 23:61
Chamberlain, Frank 1:119
Chamberlain, Franklin 7:79
Chamberlain, G. 12:86; 14:254
Chamberlain, George 4:15; 12:16
Chamberlain, George A. 4:15
Chamberlain, H. 3:40; 14:239; 25:25
Chamberlain, H. H. 16:179
Chamberlain, H. W. 20:223
Chamberlain, Henry 2:8; 14:150
Chamberlain, Henry C. 22:507
Chamberlain, Henry W. 10:45
Chamberlain, I. 3:40

Chamberlain, Ira 7:89
Chamberlain, Isaac
  14:150; 17:18
Chamberlain, J. 25:153
Chamberlain, J. B. 3:40;
  9:141
Chamberlain, Jacob
  23:137
Chamberlain, James C.
  20:47
Chamberlain, Jay B. E.
  4:15
Chamberlain, John 9:15;
  17:101; 22:461;
  23:106
Chamberlain, John B.
  27:27
Chamberlain, L. W. 8:46
Chamberlain, Levi
  15:329; 19:60
Chamberlain, Lorenzo S.
  11:398
Chamberlain, Lucas
  22:183
Chamberlain, M. 1:121
Chamberlain, N. 22:161
Chamberlain, P. 14:46
Chamberlain, S. 14:150,
  254
Chamberlain, Samuel B.
  22:420
Chamberlain, Simeon G.
  17:73
Chamberlain, W. C. 1:119
Chamberlain, W. H.
  14:150
Chamberlain, William
  6:20; 7:67; 9:140;
  14:46; 16:25, 147
Chamberlain, William H.
  15:189
Chamberlain, William S.
  14:261
Chamberlain, William W.
  18:79
Chamberlain, Willis D.
  23:119
Chamberlan, L. 25:26
Chamberlan, M. 15:31
Chamberlan, W. S. 27:27
Chamberland, Owen
  15:189
Chamberland, W. H.
  25:24
Chamberlin, --- 10:158;
  16:91
Chamberlin, B. 12:7; 15:6
Chamberlin, C. P. 7:83
Chamberlin, D. 14:46
Chamberlin, D. H. 1:21

Chamberlin, Ebenezer B.
  21:65
Chamberlin, Elihu M.
  7:89
Chamberlin, F. 25:294
Chamberlin, G. B. 9:50
Chamberlin, H. 27:33
Chamberlin, H. M. 9:101
Chamberlin, L. G. 15:11
Chamberlin, Samuel 9:19
Chambers, A. 9:77; 14:46
Chambers, Alexander
  11:186; 27:25
Chambers, C. 17:435
Chambers, C. C. 24:177
Chambers, Charles 9:77;
  20:223
Chambers, David 4:65
Chambers, David F.
  18:337
Chambers, David S. 9:101
Chambers, E. R. 8:11;
  18:126
Chambers, Eli 8:11;
  18:126
Chambers, Elijah 12:16
Chambers, Eugene H.
  22:475
Chambers, F. P. 10:204
Chambers, G. 1:24
Chambers, G. W. 22:476
Chambers, George 13:76;
  16:180; 17:396
Chambers, George C. 8:46
Chambers, George M.
  21:215
Chambers, George W.
  16:25; 19:8
Chambers, H. 22:245
Chambers, H. A. 22:245
Chambers, H. M. 21:21
Chambers, Hamilton 19:8
Chambers, Harvey 16:25
Chambers, Henry 15:64;
  22:512
Chambers, Hezekiah
  11:140
Chambers, Hiram 9:77;
  18:232; 26:19, 20
Chambers, Humphrey
  17:129; 24:192
Chambers, I. 3:41
Chambers, Isaac 13:14
Chambers, Isaiah B. 21:97
Chambers, J. 1:26; 3:41;
  15:335; 17:172;
  19:60
Chambers, J. B. 8:46
Chambers, J. M. 27:27
Chambers, J. W. 1:120

Chambers, James 9:140;
  14:150; 23:188
Chambers, James M. 7:89;
  17:449; 24:175
Chambers, John 10:45;
  20:223
Chambers, John W. 7:22
Chambers, Legrand 7:67
Chambers, Lemuel 11:421
Chambers, M. 16:180
Chambers, M. V. 23:137
Chambers, Martin L.
  18:215
Chambers, Moses 22:499
Chambers, Nathaniel
  15:315; 19:60
Chambers, R. 15:31
Chambers, R. B. 13:14;
  16:25
Chambers, R. S. 3:41
Chambers, Richard
  26:144
Chambers, Robert 19:60;
  23:23
Chambers, S. 1:24; 16:180
Chambers, S. C. 14:150
Chambers, Samuel
  24:177; 27:25
Chambers, Sheven 27:29
Chambers, Stephen 1:24;
  9:129
Chambers, Thomas 9:101;
  16:180; 18:337;
  21:186; 22:139, 183;
  24:8
Chambers, W. 3:41
Chambers, W. H. 1:117;
  26:217
Chambers, W. R. 23:61
Chambers, Wesley 24:14
Chambers, William
  23:137; 24:157
Chambers, William B.
  22:500
Chambers, William E.
  23:23
Chambers, William G.
  24:48
Chambers, William H.
  4:16; 9:235; 11:321
Chambers, Williams
  17:417
Chamblain, Lorenzo
  25:24
Chambleis, J. H. 18:232
Chambless, John 22:183
Chambliss, J. R. 3:40
Chamblus, J. H. 26:20
Chamburg, --- 16:91
Chamell, Leonard 21:312
Chammond, R. 16:289

Champ, A. V. 23:289
Champ, G. 25:153
Champ, George 5:37
Champ, Samuel 19:154
Champ, Thornton 21:66
Champ, William 8:46;
   17:71; 21:21
Champagne, Frank 22:461
Champe, Arnold 9:42;
   26:122
Champeny, F. E. 19:249
Champer, John 22:70
Champier, Joseph 22:245
Champion, Charles 7:89
Champion, E. 20:55
Champion, Ezra 13:14
Champion, John 20:223
Champion, Smith B.
   24:169
Champion, Thomas 12:16
Champion, William 16:25
Champion, William M.
   24:75
Champlain, George H.
   23:240
Champlain, George W.
   9:213; 21:312
Champlain, H. 3:41
Champlain, William H.
   12:16
Champlin, B. A. 23:23
Champlin, Davis B. 21:90
Champlin, E. 14:46
Champlin, E. E. 11:27
Champlin, George W.
   13:14
Champlin, Joel R. 11:237
Champlin, John R. 22:24
Champlin, Lewis 10:158;
   16:25; 19:154
Champlin, Smith B.
   17:434
Champlin, W. 3:41
Champlin, William P.
   17:31
Champlin, William R.
   13:14
Champney, Elliot J. 24:91
Champney, P. A. 3:41
Champny, W. 15:189
Champon, S. 26:19
Champoux, David 17:70
Champside, J. 16:289
Chamside, J. 12:81
Chana, J. 12:63
Chanabery, James M.
   23:289
Chanand, J. 16:289
Chance, A. 11:325
Chance, A. J. 3:41
Chance, Benjamin 18:102

Chance, Burnell 18:126
Chance, Cyrus 23:61
Chance, Henry C. 11:300
Chance, James 8:81;
   18:215
Chance, Purnell 8:11
Chance, Samuel 9:129
Chance, William 8:11;
   26:153
Chancey, Dennis 12:16
Chancey, James C. 23:106
Chancey, John 22:518
Chancy, Ezekiel 21:135
Chancy, John 14:261
Chancy, John C. 15:263
Chancy, John W. 22:419
Chancy, Michael 23:242
Chancy, O. 23:252
Chandaler, C. A. 13:106
Chander, Campbell 9:171
Chandle, O. P. 19:300
Chandler, --- 9:117; 27:24
Chandler, A. 1:25
Chandler, A. F. 7:22
Chandler, Adon M. 15:16
Chandler, Adoniram
   12:68
Chandler, Alfred 7:22
Chandler, B. F. 8:11;
   18:126
Chandler, Benjamin F.
   22:70
Chandler, Charles 7:119
Chandler, Charles D.
   24:36
Chandler, Charles F.
   18:232
Chandler, Charles G.
   18:108
Chandler, Charles S.
   26:20
Chandler, Clark 15:189
Chandler, D. H. 9:96;
   27:25
Chandler, D. W. 8:62;
   26:154
Chandler, E. D. 20:2
Chandler, E. O. 11:279
Chandler, Ed 27:31
Chandler, Edward 9:117
Chandler, Esquire 10:106;
   20:223
Chandler, George 17:129;
   24:191
Chandler, George B.
   17:318
Chandler, George D.
   21:312
Chandler, George W.
   10:106; 20:223

Chandler, H. 1:103;
   21:312
Chandler, H. A. 14:150
Chandler, H. G. 17:501
Chandler, H. J. 17:499
Chandler, Henry 12:53
Chandler, Henry D.
   22:402
Chandler, Isaac 18:303;
   26:94
Chandler, Isaiah 10:151,
   178
Chandler, J. 23:23
Chandler, J. D. 10:179;
   18:172
Chandler, J. E. 11:26
Chandler, J. H. 1:118
Chandler, J. L. 12:121
Chandler, J. M. 5:11;
   11:54; 15:120;
   19:225; 25:153
Chandler, J. T. 9:50
Chandler, James 10:45;
   20:223
Chandler, James W. 22:70
Chandler, Jason M. 9:171
Chandler, Jesse 9:19
Chandler, John 8:62;
   18:232; 21:312;
   26:19
Chandler, John L. 21:312
Chandler, Joseph 21:312
Chandler, L. 1:22
Chandler, L. A. 9:50
Chandler, L. E. 14:46
Chandler, M. 3:41
Chandler, Marshall M.
   12:16
Chandler, Morris I. 8:11
Chandler, Nero 9:129;
   27:29
Chandler, O. P. 10:27
Chandler, R. O. 23:23
Chandler, S. 25:153
Chandler, S. N. 14:295;
   17:474
Chandler, S. T. 25:153
Chandler, S. W. 27:32
Chandler, Smith 22:183
Chandler, Solomon F.
   8:104
Chandler, Solomon K.
   23:97
Chandler, T. 5:37
Chandler, W. F. 14:46
Chandler, W. H. 12:164;
   26:156
Chandler, William 1:22;
   22:24
Chandler, William H.
   21:312

Chandley, William 13:14
Chandoin, Henry W. 21:14
Chane, J. 15:81
Chaner, Alfred 20:5
Chanerey, D. 16:289
Chanery, D. 12:81
Chaney, Albert 7:77
Chaney, Ambrose 11:115
Chaney, Charles H. 17:46
Chaney, George A. 7:79
Chaney, I. 9:140
Chaney, J. 27:27
Chaney, J. A. 21:21
Chaney, J. J. 14:130
Chaney, James 11:140; 15:31
Chaney, James B. 11:140
Chaney, John 11:141
Chaney, Joshua Y. 23:61
Chaney, Josiah 7:22
Chaney, L. 11:138
Chaney, S. 1:122
Chaney, S. I. 22:461
Chaney, Samuel 27:29
Chaney, W. 17:309
Chaney, William 22:332; 25:153; 26:154
Chaney, William B. 22:402
Chaney, William J. 22:24
Chang, Devan 18:392
Change, William 8:62
Chanley, Isaac 18:188
Chanley, Wesley 7:119
Channan, Jasper 14:327
Channel, Aaron N. 23:305
Channell, William E. 17:295
Channer, Charles J. 20:21
Channy, Abraham 17:346
Chant, J. O. 17:153
Chany, G. H. 12:63
Chaoon, W. P. 9:68
Chapel, Alfred S. 12:16
Chapel, C. 3:41
Chapel, Charles F. 27:25
Chapel, Ezra H. 11:190
Chapel, Gustavus 24:61
Chapel, J. B. 18:64
Chapel, J. O. 18:65
Chapel, Jacobb 16:365
Chapel, James 25:153
Chapel, James L. 22:245
Chapel, Morace 19:244
Chapel, R. 3:41
Chapell, A. 3:41
Chapell, Andrew J. 20:223
Chapell, D. F. 13:106

Chapell, O. D. 9:219; 18:363
Chapen, Alex 9:77
Chapfield, William 3:41
Chapin, A. 26:19
Chapin, C. A. 10:14
Chapin, C. F. 25:153
Chapin, Caleb D. 5:11
Chapin, Captain 19:154
Chapin, Charles B. 7:48
Chapin, D. S. 11:400
Chapin, Elisha C. 22:418
Chapin, Emil 17:18
Chapin, F. B. 14:6
Chapin, F. W. 8:71; 26:154
Chapin, George F. 11:56
Chapin, H. 19:60
Chapin, Harry 16:289
Chapin, J. A. 3:41
Chapin, J. E. 21:49
Chapin, J. L. 3:41
Chapin, James 3:41; 23:86
Chapin, K. W. 19:222
Chapin, Kimball 18:232; 26:20
Chapin, L. C. 11:300
Chapin, Lucius D. 16:8
Chapin, Marvin M. 23:23
Chapin, Nelson 13:106
Chapin, Scott H. 13:14
Chapin, T. 3:40
Chapin, T. B. 13:85
Chapin, T. W. 11:301
Chapin, Theodore N. 22:139
Chapin, W. C. 15:103
Chapin, William H. 4:16
Chapine, E. A. 19:225
Chaplain, --- 15:263
Chaplain, E. B. 9:15
Chaplain, G. W. 25:22
Chaple, John 20:223
Chaplin, G. W. 2:9
Chaplin, Lorenzo 20:111
Chaplin, W. 13:85
Chapman, --- 1:22; 3:40; 14:46
Chapman, A. 11:199
Chapman, A. M. 21:312
Chapman, A. W. 25:318
Chapman, Albert 10:210
Chapman, Alfred A. 13:14
Chapman, Alvin 18:232; 26:21
Chapman, Ames 1:120
Chapman, Amos M. 23:119
Chapman, Anson 17:212
Chapman, B. 22:293; 24:191

Chapman, B. D. 22:475
Chapman, Benjamin 8:112
Chapman, Berry 17:129
Chapman, C. 3:40; 13:85
Chapman, C. C. 10:94
Chapman, C. T. 7:56
Chapman, Charles E. 9:15
Chapman, Charles W. 20:111
Chapman, D. 19:154
Chapman, D. W. 11:90
Chapman, David 5:50
Chapman, David L. 10:106; 20:223
Chapman, Decatur S. 19:225
Chapman, E. 25:153; 27:32
Chapman, E. E. 11:26
Chapman, E. H. 7:56; 14:150
Chapman, E. M. 1:21; 5:11
Chapman, Edward 11:26
Chapman, Edwin B. 16:180
Chapman, Eli 23:137
Chapman, Elisha B. 22:418
Chapman, Everett M. 9:117; 27:30
Chapman, Ezra L. 23:188
Chapman, F. 1:22
Chapman, F. L. 1:120
Chapman, Francis 12:151; 16:91
Chapman, Francis A. 16:91
Chapman, Frank 22:293
Chapman, G. 1:22, 121; 3:40; 14:295; 17:473; 27:31
Chapman, George 3:40; 6:12; 12:55; 15:302; 16:180; 17:129; 18:79; 24:191
Chapman, George W. 17:354; 18:392
Chapman, Grandison E. 27:143
Chapman, H. 3:40; 18:393
Chapman, H. A. 12:16
Chapman, H. C. 17:247
Chapman, H. J. 20:223
Chapman, H. P. 13:62
Chapman, H. Z. 19:8
Chapman, Henry 11:200; 21:66; 24:14
Chapman, Henry J. 21:66
Chapman, Hiram 20:5
Chapman, Hugh R. 23:61

Chapman, Ira H. 22:24
Chapman, J. 1:117; 3:40; 24:14; 25:318
Chapman, J. C. 1:119; 9:50; 26:18
Chapman, J. F. 1:119
Chapman, J. L. 13:106
Chapman, Jacob 20:223; 23:86
Chapman, James 9:15, 50; 11:83; 16:135; 21:21; 22:24, 139; 23:137
Chapman, James B. 9:171
Chapman, Jesse 22:70
Chapman, Joel 12:7
Chapman, John 8:104; 11:26; 14:150; 21:215; 22:476
Chapman, John H. 23:10
Chapman, John M. 22:350
Chapman, John S. 9:77
Chapman, K. 3:40
Chapman, L. A. 13:62; 16:180
Chapman, Lak. T. 16:365
Chapman, Luke T. 15:347
Chapman, Lyman W. 20:111
Chapman, Miles 23:24
Chapman, N. C. 27:31
Chapman, Nathan 14:150
Chapman, Nicholas S. 21:312
Chapman, O. C. 1:119
Chapman, O. G. 25:153
Chapman, Orin D. 16:143
Chapman, R. 15:189; 25:153
Chapman, R. E. 1:24
Chapman, R. H. 22:161
Chapman, R. L. 8:11; 18:126
Chapman, Reuben 9:50
Chapman, Richard 5:11
Chapman, Robert 10:106; 20:223; 22:24
Chapman, S. D. 18:172; 22:183
Chapman, S. H. 14:46
Chapman, S. J. 4:16
Chapman, Samuel 16:180; 18:232; 26:20
Chapman, Silas J. 4:16
Chapman, Stephen 21:242
Chapman, Stephen W. 11:139
Chapman, T. C. 12:151
Chapman, Thomas 14:150; 26:154

Chapman, Thomas I. 12:16
Chapman, Thomas J. 11:385
Chapman, Townsend 4:16
Chapman, Urban 22:111
Chapman, W. 1:121; 21:21
Chapman, W. A. 19:60
Chapman, W. C. 14:295; 17:475
Chapman, W. E. 19:244
Chapman, W. F. 19:60
Chapman, W. H. 7:48; 9:140; 27:28
Chapman, Washington 13:14; 16:25
Chapman, William 1:121; 8:113; 9:117; 11:140; 14:150; 27:31
Chapman, William A. 15:315
Chapman, William E. 8:11; 9:171
Chapman, William H. 21:66
Chapman, William S. 9:213; 21:312
Chapmane, William E. 18:126
Chapmen, William 1:21
Chappel, C. S. 8:11
Chappel, Carter 27:143
Chappel, Emory 18:126
Chappel, Giles R. 11:285
Chappel, J. C. 5:50; 25:153
Chappel, Jacob 15:349
Chappel, James 23:137
Chappel, Paddy 26:155
Chappell, Albert G. 20:21
Chappell, Andrew I. 10:45
Chappell, C. S. 18:126
Chappell, D. 13:85; 14:6
Chappell, E. 3:41
Chappell, E. S. 18:271
Chappell, Emory 8:11
Chappell, G. H. 9:171; 19:244
Chappell, Horace 9:171
Chappell, James 5:11
Chappell, Jesse J. 11:293
Chappell, M. F. 19:154
Chappell, Turner 9:171; 19:273
Chappell, W. D. 10:45; 20:223
Chappell, W. H. 22:183
Chappell, William C. 22:119
Chappell, William T. 20:5

Chappens, John 21:90
Chappin, J. M. 21:312
Chappis, L. 19:61
Chapple, Simeon 11:395
Chapplear, C. 17:291
Chaprer, John C. 18:126
Chapron, Seth L. 21:238
Chapter, Charles 21:267
Charaw, Solomon 16:289
Charbound, Paul 21:312
Chard, James 8:60; 12:170
Chard, William H. 8:116
Chards, William W. 8:81
Chare, William 13:62
Charge, George 22:24
Charge, Philip 18:79
Charity, Jake 11:300
Charles, --- 9:50; 13:85; 21:312; 26:22
Charles, A. 15:329; 19:61
Charles, A. F. 12:16
Charles, Ceaser 9:206
Charles, Crazar 18:65
Charles, D. S. 1:120
Charles, F. 3:41
Charles, F. C. 12:121; 15:120
Charles, G. 11:218
Charles, J. E. 8:62
Charles, J. G. 25:153
Charles, Jackson 23:24
Charles, James H. 7:67
Charles, John 7:119; 22:24
Charles, John H. 15:354
Charles, Joseph N. 4:16
Charles, Lorenn 17:73
Charles, R. J. 3:41
Charles, William 5:11; 22:232
Charleston, George 13:56
Charlett, E. A. 25:153
Charlton, Henry 22:24
Charlton, Henry C. 17:396
Charlton, Isaac 7:89
Charlton, James W. 22:245
Charlton, W. H. 9:50
Charman, George 18:232; 26:20
Charman, Henry 11:138
Charmelia, S. 1:22
Charmer, James H. 9:19
Charmer, Milroy 22:24
Charpman, Daniel S. 23:260
Charrian, F. 12:81
Charrion, T. 16:289
Charrity, M. 16:117
Chart, C. W. 3:41
Charter, Joseph 23:188

Charter, Nelson 17:247
Charter, Winfield S. 12:16
Charters, John 14:46
Charters, William 20:145
Chary, A. 25:294
Chase, A. 3:40; 15:318;
  18:79; 25:153
Chase, A. H. 19:296
Chase, A. L. 1:118
Chase, A. P. 21:312
Chase, A. T. 15:189
Chase, A. W. 17:31
Chase, Alfred 4:16; 19:61
Chase, Alonzo 5:11
Chase, Alpheus 11:285
Chase, August 13:14;
  16:25
Chase, Braddock R.
  9:213; 21:312
Chase, C. 1:118
Chase, C. D. 14:150
Chase, C. M. 25:294
Chase, C. W. 25:294
Chase, Caleb 8:62; 26:154
Chase, Charles 11:25;
  13:106
Chase, Charles D. 24:71
Chase, Charles G. 23:24
Chase, Charles R. 19:61
Chase, Charles V. 15:306,
  354
Chase, Charles W. 7:79;
  17:18; 21:135
Chase, Chassius M. 7:79
Chase, Cornelius 14:150
Chase, D. 9:171; 19:226
Chase, D. C. 13:85
Chase, Darion 19:346
Chase, Darwin 13:134
Chase, David 19:61
Chase, David O. 15:336
Chase, Dennis 13:14
Chase, Dennis E. 1:21
Chase, E. B. 15:189
Chase, E. F. 9:171
Chase, E. L. 1:119; 3:40
Chase, E. S. 3:40
Chase, Ebenezer 10:14;
  22:139
Chase, Edwin 22:183
Chase, Emerick 10:106;
  20:223
Chase, Eugene 23:106
Chase, F. W. 3:40; 9:171
Chase, Francis A. 10:158
Chase, Francis E. 19:154
Chase, Frank 10:14
Chase, Frank E. 19:277
Chase, Franklin 7:7
Chase, G. L. 1:118
Chase, G. M. 3:40

Chase, G. W. 1:26
Chase, George 23:137
Chase, George E. 19:61
Chase, George W. 7:22
Chase, Gideon R. 9:203
Chase, Gustavus 18:79
Chase, H. 1:21
Chase, H. H. 19:226
Chase, H. M. 1:25
Chase, H. R. 1:21
Chase, Heller 14:150
Chase, Henry A. 11:332
Chase, Henry C. 10:106;
  20:223
Chase, Henry E. 9:15;
  10:158; 19:154
Chase, Homer 26:19
Chase, Horner 9:77
Chase, Isaac C. 7:89
Chase, Isaac F. 16:162
Chase, Isaiah 4:16
Chase, J. B. 1:119; 13:85;
  14:254
Chase, J. F. 1:123; 13:14
Chase, J. H. 26:218
Chase, J. T. 12:16
Chase, James 10:45, 106;
  20:223
Chase, James A. 16:84
Chase, James B. 21:312
Chase, James H. 10:106;
  13:14; 20:223;
  21:312
Chase, James P. 17:404
Chase, John 3:40; 9:213;
  21:312
Chase, John B. 24:63
Chase, John H. 10:34
Chase, John S. 19:8
Chase, John W. 19:154
Chase, Joseph 13:62;
  16:180
Chase, Joseph W. 23:188
Chase, Kelly 25:153
Chase, L. 3:40
Chase, L. A. 1:22
Chase, Lester 23:305
Chase, Levi A. 24:75
Chase, Lewis 7:89; 13:56;
  16:25
Chase, Lucien H. 17:73
Chase, M. 3:40; 7:89
Chase, M. M. 3:40
Chase, M. O. 1:26
Chase, Marcellus 16:143;
  19:226
Chase, Marcus 25:153
Chase, Myron 15:189
Chase, N. D. 9:140; 27:26
Chase, N. F. 3:40
Chase, Newby 23:86

Chase, O. 1:26
Chase, O. H. 21:312
Chase, Otis 9:171; 19:232
Chase, R. S. 9:171
Chase, Randel S. 25:23
Chase, Richard M. 13:14
Chase, Richard W. 22:232
Chase, Royal 10:158;
  19:154
Chase, S. M. 3:40
Chase, Silas 11:139
Chase, Simeon 13:14
Chase, Stephen H. 4:16;
  12:16
Chase, T. B. 14:6
Chase, T. M. 3:40
Chase, Thomas 23:119
Chase, Thomas D. 17:404
Chase, Thomas G. 9:171;
  19:266
Chase, Thomas H. 10:45;
  20:223
Chase, Thomas S. 7:119
Chase, V. 3:40
Chase, Valentine M.
  10:14
Chase, Victory 1:21
Chase, W. 19:226
Chase, W. W. 1:22; 7:22
Chase, Wallace M. 7:8
Chase, Wellington 7:89
Chase, Wesley C. 4:15
Chase, William 7:79;
  9:171; 12:56; 17:98;
  19:61; 20:223;
  25:294
Chase, William E. 21:313
Chase, William H. 9:155
Chase, Wilson 21:87
Chasekill, H. 14:280
Chasen, C. 16:180
Chasm, Thomas 16:25
Chason, Thomas 13:14
Chassee, Dela 11:91
Chassin, Charles J. 20:180
Chastain, J. W. 10:106;
  20:223
Chasteen, Austin 17:205
Chasteen, John 8:11
Chasteen, William 22:397
Chasteen, William P.
  22:119
Chasten, David C. 7:89
Chasteno, M. P. 20:223
Chastern, William 11:55
Chastien, C. P. 17:364
Chastine, Joseph 18:205
Chastine, T. 18:232; 26:20
Chastun, John 18:126
Chatbourne, H. A. 7:89
Chatburn, H. 3:40

Chateman, S. M. 3:41
Chaterson, Caleb 24:14
Chates, Cyrus A. 12:16
Chates, W. 25:153
Chatfield, A. 1:26
Chatfield, Charles H. 23:24
Chatfield, David 9:235; 26:217
Chatfield, Henry 23:260
Chatfield, J. 1:25
Chatfield, James 22:461
Chatham, Clem 22:245
Chatham, J. 27:28
Chatman, A. W. 16:365
Chatman, C. H. 19:226
Chatman, Joseph 14:150
Chatman, Thomas 8:62
Chatman, W. 11:237
Chatsin, W. M. 3:41
Chattenay, J. 3:41
Chatterson, Jefferson 10:106; 20:223
Chatterson, Robert W. 22:419
Chatterton, A. J. 23:137
Chatterton, J. 3:41
Chatterton, John R. 22:475
Chatterton, M. 25:153
Chatterton, Siral 4:16
Chattle, Benjamin 8:113
Chattle, H. 19:232
Chattle, N. 18:65
Chattock, Alphonse 21:313
Chatwick, Henry E. 4:16
Chaudion, Jesse P. 21:66
Chaudler, Morris J. 18:126
Chaul, Alphonso A. 4:16
Chauncey, Michael 22:183
Chauncy, T. 27:33
Chaundy, Charles 10:14
Chaunley, C. 11:285
Chavers, Juan 8:123
Chavez, Juan 8:123
Chavez, Rafael 19:321
Chavis, A. 16:180
Chawgo, M. W. 1:117
Chawson, Peter 11:189
Chaychis, Richard 18:232
Chayo, Syvanius 11:19
Chays, John B. 19:61
Che, Thomas 13:62; 16:180
Cheadle, Daniel D. 10:106; 20:223
Chean, Augustus 21:313
Cheardon, Daniel 21:313

Cheat, E. 14:46
Cheatam, C. A. 20:142
Cheatam, Thomas 22:9
Cheaten, Samuel 18:13
Cheatham, Harrison 6:22
Cheatham, Jasper C. 24:15
Cheatham, Nelson 25:153
Cheatham, William A. 22:183
Cheatley, Samuel 10:45; 20:223
Cheaton, S. 5:37; 25:153
Cheatty, H. H. 8:11
Check, Elias 13:106
Check, Fenno 16:25
Check, W. F. 3:41
Chedester, John 15:85
Chedwick, Robert 27:30
Cheek, Benjamin 23:24
Cheek, E. J. 21:12
Cheek, Fenno 13:14
Cheek, Henry 11:200
Cheek, I. E. 18:172
Cheek, James M. R. 20:122
Cheek, John F. 22:183
Cheek, Maben 17:445
Cheek, Maber 24:166
Cheek, Nelson 24:65
Cheek, R. 3:41
Cheek, Robert 19:61
Cheek, William 10:27; 19:300; 21:129
Cheeman, J. 12:81
Cheenan, J. 16:289
Cheeney, Charles 23:137
Cheeney, Deran 9:101
Cheenshaw, Jones 22:511
Cheenworth, C. 14:46
Cheeny, Richard 7:90
Cheer, W. 18:188
Cheers, Frazier 21:267
Cheers, James 9:206
Cheesbro, H. 19:249
Cheesbro, Isaac 1:22
Cheesbrough, Spicer 16:25
Cheese, Thomas S. 21:313
Cheeseborough, Spicer 13:14
Cheeseman, C. F. C. S. 25:21
Cheeseman, J. 14:327
Cheeseman, J. W. 15:120
Cheeseman, Joseph H. 8:113
Cheeseman, O. G. 18:26
Cheeseman, William 12:56
Cheesman, C. 1:121
Cheesman, Jasper 9:160

Cheesney, Jesse 9:100
Cheetam, G. W. 26:156
Cheever, Barney 13:14
Cheever, Josiah 4:16
Cheever, W. 15:189
Cheffey, Daniel 10:45
Cheffy, Daniel 20:223
Chegston, Hugh 12:16
Cheif, Charles 9:108
Cheis, W. 25:153
Chellis, H. W. 25:23
Chellis, J. F. 1:118
Chelsea, John 11:199
Chelsey, Joseph M. 16:80
Chelson, John W. 15:285; 19:61
Cheltz, A. 14:6
Chemran, J. W. 15:363
Chen, John 16:180
Chenall, Philip 10:45; 20:224
Chenaworth, H. 25:153
Chency, C. 19:154
Chenette, F. 15:189
Cheneworth, William 3:41
Cheney, A. B. 15:340
Cheney, A. R. 16:365
Cheney, Albert 19:61; 25:294
Cheney, Alexander 20:136
Cheney, Charles L. 20:5
Cheney, Edward 17:98
Cheney, G. A. 25:294
Cheney, Hiram O. 9:33
Cheney, Julius C. 22:476
Cheney, Nathan C. 15:189
Cheney, Philips 25:283
Cheney, Rufus 21:242
Cheney, S. 3:41; 25:25
Cheney, Smith C. 4:16
Cheney, Stephen 22:139
Cheney, William R. 24:15
Cheney, Wilson 17:247
Chenic, Elijah 25:153
Chenkins, Andrew 10:98
Chennan, J. W. 12:121
Chenning, Isaac 14:327
Chenock, Frank 7:56
Chenoweth, Alfred D. 22:420
Chenoweth, Isaac 22:477
Chenoweth, Isaac N. 22:421
Chenowith, Jacob 11:254
Chenowith, Joseph 11:275
Chenown, William 20:224
Chenwick, C. 9:50
Chenworth, Alfred D. 11:55
Cheny, Frank 15:165
Cheny, John M. 18:205

Cheonut, S. 22:511
Chepwell, Thomas 11:25
Cherman, J. W. 14:25
Cherold, William 21:109
Cherrett, George B. 1:22
Cherrey, Dexter E. 16:8
Cherrington, Sp'r. 15:54
Cherrington, Spencer 12:63
Cherry, A. 25:20
Cherry, Alexander 17:50; 25:153
Cherry, Alfred 2:9
Cherry, Charles 14:150
Cherry, David 9:108
Cherry, F. R. H. 13:62
Cherry, Isaac 11:138
Cherry, James 3:41; 9:77, 96, 117; 27:30
Cherry, James J. 26:19
Cherry, John 14:46
Cherry, John D. 10:106; 20:224
Cherry, Noah 25:153
Cherry, R. 25:153
Cherry, Richard 5:37
Cherry, Savory 2:9
Cherry, Sidney 23:24
Cherry, Solomon H. 11:385
Cherry, Stephen J. 22:139
Cherry, W. H. D. 21:313
Cherry, William 11:55
Cherry, William W. 22:70
Chersmon, W. D. 23:266
Cherteley, E. A. 17:109
Chery, William 18:13
Chesbro, Almond M. 16:117
Chesbro, Dennis W. 23:178
Chesbro, J. A. 12:151
Chesbro, Sylvester 1:120
Chesebrow, Giles 4:16
Chesemore, Nathan R. 22:277
Chesessier, Rene 27:29
Chesettro, Ephraim 9:206
Chesheir, Samuel 21:119
Cheshier, A. 12:81
Cheshier, Wesley 10:45
Cheshier, William 24:15
Cheshire, Benjamin 21:267
Cheshire, W. 20:224
Chesihier, A. 16:289
Chesley, C. 14:6
Chesley, G. H. 1:119
Chesley, John 19:61
Chesley, Joseph 14:150
Chesley, P. S. 3:41

Chesley, Samuel C. 7:90
Chesley, Simon P. 13:106
Chesley, W. W. 1:122
Chesming, Isaac 9:160
Chesney, A. 14:46
Chesney, E. D. 17:214
Chesney, John 14:46
Chesnut, Andrew J. 16:69
Chesnut, Bruce 22:293
Chesnut, J. N. 15:90
Chesnut, Jasper N. 12:68
Chesnut, John 22:419
Chesnut, Samuel 22:418
Chesnuts, O. W. 18:46
Chess, Jonas 9:108
Chessbro, H. 9:172
Chesser, Martin 10:106; 20:224
Chesser, Samuel 12:152
Chesser, William H. 9:66
Chesshire, L. B. 23:137
Chessman, Edward B. 4:16
Chestain, John W. 10:106; 20:224
Chester, A. 3:41
Chester, Charles M. 11:139
Chester, Charles W. 10:106; 20:224
Chester, G. W. 12:148
Chester, George 22:293
Chester, George W. 11:186
Chester, James 8:46
Chester, John 19:61; 22:183
Chester, Nicholas 9:19; 18:303; 26:94
Chester, Samuel 15:64
Chester, William 10:158; 19:154; 22:512
Chestey, John 3:41
Chestin, William 11:91
Chestleson, Asiak 24:91
Chestner, Daniel 17:129; 24:190
Chestnut, A. 14:46
Chestnut, Frank 24:191
Chestnut, J. W. 21:313
Chestnut, Joseph W. 11:259
Chestnut, O. W. 10:152
Cheston, Charles 15:172
Chetneynd, Charles 18:108
Cheud, Richard 7:56
Chevalere, Edward 15:31
Chevessier, B. 9:117
Chevin, A. 15:340
Chevney, Watson 12:16

Chew, Henry 26:121
Chew, Henry H. 22:449
Chew, John 3:41
Chew, Robert 11:258
Chewits, Axel 19:154
Chezen, Samuel 25:274
Chibauhan, John 10:45
Chicester, David 25:22
Chichester, Cyrus 17:247
Chichester, J. A. 1:23
Chichester, V. R. 22:183
Chick, J. H. L. 14:150
Chick, John 12:86; 16:289
Chick, W. S. 9:50
Chickchester, C. H. 3:42
Chicken, William 23:137
Chickenaineu, Peter 18:303
Chickenaman, Peter 9:19
Chickenanun, Peter 26:95
Chickman, F. 9:50
Chicks, James 20:111
Chidders, W. A. 9:77
Chidls, Jarius 23:137
Chidsey, Daniel 21:21
Chiele, J. E. 27:24
Chifender, John 2:9
Chifeulor, J. 25:23
Chiffert, Charles 9:117
Chiknahan, John 20:224
Chilcoat, James L. 11:55
Chilcoat, Mordecai 24:157
Chilcoat, Mordecia 17:417
Chilcote, James A. 3:41
Chilcote, William 22:476
Chilcutt, H. A. 9:50
Child, A. F. 3:41
Child, Ashell E. 21:21
Child, H. 3:41
Child, Mark A. 7:22
Childern, Phelan 11:199
Childers, Alfred 10:45; 20:224
Childers, C. H. 3:41
Childers, E. 3:41
Childers, J. 3:41
Childers, J. F. 24:110
Childers, J. M. 3:41
Childers, James 14:319; 25:282
Childers, James M. 17:94
Childers, Jasper 20:224
Childers, John 22:70
Childers, Joseph 10:45; 11:411; 20:224
Childers, Joseph W. 22:119
Childers, Levi 13:14
Childers, Marvin R. 22:70

Childers, Robert 22:500
Childers, Samuel W. 11:25
Childers, Thomas L. 3:41
Childers, W. 3:41; 23:24
Childers, W. E. 3:41
Childers, William 10:106; 20:224; 22:449
Children, M. 9:172
Children, Madison 19:289
Childres, Charles W. 17:50
Childress, Berrill 22:293
Childress, W. 14:240
Childress, William 23:24
Childriss, William 21:313
Childromile, J. 22:351
Childs, A. 3:41
Childs, A. M. 18:26
Childs, Asa B. 27:25
Childs, Barton 9:160; 14:327
Childs, Darius 22:139
Childs, G. 3:41
Childs, G. A. 3:41
Childs, G. W. 20:224
Childs, H. W. 21:313
Childs, Henry 27:33
Childs, Henry W. 7:90
Childs, J. 16:180
Childs, Jacob L. 17:402
Childs, Jenkins 17:172
Childs, John 10:106; 22:111
Childs, Lewis 17:172
Childs, S. 25:154
Childs, S. C. 12:7
Childs, S. P. 3:41
Childs, Seldon 5:37
Childs, Sylvanus 4:16
Childs, T. G. 27:27
Childs, Theodore R. 21:251
Childs, Victor 9:206
Childs, Wilkin B. 22:277
Childs, William 3:41
Chiles, Amos 17:235
Chiles, John 20:224
Chiles, Jonathan 26:154
Chill, John 13:62
Chillcoat, Samuel G. 22:232
Chilles, B. 11:275
Chilles, C. 11:139
Chillick, Henry 15:103
Chillingeworth, William 13:106
Chillis, James 17:267
Chillson, King A. 13:15
Chilly, C. 13:85
Chilsey, C. A. 18:46

Chilson, A. W. 14:46
Chilson, Daniel 4:16
Chilson, John H. 11:26
Chilson, John W. 26:144
Chilson, Joseph 8:113
Chilt---, James K. 23:119
Chilton, Francis M. 23:112
Chimell, Elias B. 22:461
Chin, George 13:56
Chin, Henry J. 16:180
Chine, George L. 5:11
Chinerworth, Henry 17:272
Chingbury, A. 3:41
Chinn, Charles 9:129; 27:29
Chinn, James S. 7:90
Chinn, Oliver J. 22:461
Chipley, William 22:119
Chipman, Albert 11:140
Chipman, C. B. 11:237
Chipman, E. B. 15:302
Chipman, E. E. 1:96
Chipman, Henry G. 9:156
Chipman, J. F. 1:121
Chipman, James 9:157
Chipman, John 4:16; 19:44
Chipman, John T. 17:109
Chipman, Lane 14:150
Chipman, V. F. 20:224
Chipman, V. P. 10:45
Chippen, Nathan R. 19:154
Chippendle, C. 3:41
Chipper, Tiberius 17:247
Chipps, J. Martin 7:90
Chiquet, Joseph 23:86
Chirens, Hiram W. 12:68
Chirgwin, Edward 11:103
Chiridy, Leander 12:68
Chisaling, William 19:61
Chisam, T. 1:121
Chisan, John 11:181
Chisen, Henry 21:313
Chisholm, A. 7:79; 25:294; 27:25
Chisholm, J. H. 3:41
Chisholm, J. M. 3:41
Chisis, Jonathan 8:62
Chisler, R. 25:154
Chisley, C. A. 10:152
Chism, Henry 7:119
Chism, R. 1:117
Chism, Samuel R. 17:205
Chism, W. J. 11:279
Chisman, Harrison 6:20
Chisman, Noyes 21:66
Chisman, S. 14:150
Chissm, Aleck 20:224

Chister, J. 1:117
Chiston, Elijah 9:77
Chistwood, Richard 18:126
Chitester, Ephram 20:224
Chitister, Ephraim 10:45
Chittenden, A. W. 25:154
Chittenden, C. C. 18:26
Chittenden, J. F. 9:226; 18:363
Chittianson, Michael 18:126
Chitting, A. J. 11:398
Chittum, Thomas M. 11:223
Chitwood, D. 3:41
Chitwood, D. M. 14:46
Chitwood, H. H. 19:9
Chitwood, J. H. 3:41
Chitwood, Joel 18:126
Chitwood, Shadrack 23:259
Chivas, Robert John 18:334
Chivens, Hiram W. 15:54
Chizlett, William 1:24
Chloe, Celestin 18:65
Chneider, L. R. 21:109
Choat, Clinton 17:216
Choat, Jacob 14:150
Choat, John 12:152
Choat, Samuel H. 11:237
Choat, William 3:42
Choate, Erasmus M. 20:95
Choate, Jacob B. 18:355
Choate, John 27:33
Chodrow, R. 14:46
Choel, Charles D. 7:90
Cholgerra, Marcella 21:313
Chollar, Lucius A. 17:320
Choller, Sally 26:210
Chope, John 17:346
Chopin, J. S. 12:161
Chopman, J. 3:42
Choppe, A. S. 16:267
Choppel, Paddy 8:38
Choraly, Henry 15:358
Choraty, Henry 19:61
Chord, Samuel 21:186
Chorpenning, W. H. 1:117
Chorrely, Henry 12:95
Chouse, James 11:141
Chover, B. 1:119
Chovey, Frederick 2:9
Chovey, T. 25:25
Chovin, A. 16:365
Chown, William 24:48
Chram, Thomas 21:313
Chrehore, Charles 21:313
Chrieber, Charles 21:313

Chrinstwood, Richard 8:11
Chris, W. 5:50
Chrisatim, G. 15:329
Chriscamp, Henry 10:106
Chrise, J. T. 18:46
Chrisenson, P. 3:42
Chrish, Alexander 10:45
Chrish, Henry R. 10:45
Chrish, J. E. 20:224
Chrish, Jacob E. 10:45
Chrisholm, A. K. 22:183
Chrisinger, Michael L. 12:16
Chrisler, H. 1:25
Chrisler, Reuben 5:37
Chrisman, Charles 18:233
Chrisman, H. 1:118
Chrisman, J. M. 18:393
Chrisman, John W. 22:119
Chrisman, William 26:19
Chrismore, Joseph 20:136
Christ, A. E. 23:137
Christ, Fred 15:315; 19:61
Christ, G. S. 1:103
Christ, H. 13:85
Christ, H. R. 20:224
Christ, J. 9:42
Christ, Jacob 16:117
Christ, John 10:204
Christ, Joseph 14:150
Christ, Stephen 10:211; 18:456
Christ, William 19:9
Christ, Z. 26:122
Christafercer, James 11:400
Christanna, G. 16:91
Christansen, Ola 13:15
Christel, J. 21:21
Christenat, P. G. 13:78
Christenat, R. G. 16:180
Christenberg, James M. 22:245
Christenberry, R. J. 3:42
Christenburg, John B. 11:56
Christener, A. E. 5:37
Christensen, Caspar 4:16
Christenson, E. 9:172; 19:249
Christerzune, P. 14:6
Christey, John 18:406
Christfield, John G. 7:14
Christian, --- 18:411
Christian, A. F. 26:154
Christian, A. T. 8:62
Christian, E. 1:26
Christian, G. 8:11; 18:126
Christian, G. W. 1:120

Christian, George 18:126
Christian, H. I. 8:11
Christian, H. J. 18:126
Christian, Henry 8:11; 18:126
Christian, Henry C. 21:313
Christian, J. 3:42; 17:498; 21:163
Christian, J. W. 9:50
Christian, James 11:258; 13:79; 16:180
Christian, John 3:223
Christian, John H. 18:393
Christian, L. F. 18:232; 26:20
Christian, L. R. 26:95
Christian, Law. R. 18:291
Christian, Lawrence 9:33
Christian, Marshall 17:129; 24:191
Christian, Martin 23:61
Christian, P. G. 8:11; 18:126
Christian, R. H. 12:148
Christian, Robert L. 22:70
Christian, Robert W. 18:215
Christian, Samuel 22:139
Christian, William 10:158; 11:54
Christian, William E. 22:119
Christian, William L. 12:16
Christiansen, C. 11:238
Christiansen, Charles 10:14
Christiansen, Guttrand 23:188
Christiansen, J. 3:42
Christiansen, Mathias 21:251
Christiansen, Ole L. 21:251
Christianson, C. 1:21
Christianson, Francis 26:17
Christianson, Frank 9:77
Christianson, George 8:11
Christianson, James 9:9
Christianson, John 16:289
Christianson, Michael 8:11
Christianson, Ola 16:25
Christie, A. M. 3:42
Christie, Alex 22:332
Christie, Andrew 16:180
Christie, Garn M. 15:64
Christie, H. C. 9:141
Christie, John 16:65

Christie, John T. 16:143
Christie, Joseph 10:45; 20:224
Christie, Robert 11:410
Christie, Robert W. 22:418
Christie, W. A. 13:127
Christie, William 9:66; 18:275
Christie, William H. 16:180
Christin, J. 12:152
Christin, Robert C. 12:152
Christine, S. 24:75
Christine, William 22:24
Christinger, P. 13:85
Christinson, O. 18:108
Christison, George 10:107; 20:224
Christler, Johnson 4:16
Christman, C. 14:150
Christman, Charles 26:20
Christman, D. 9:141
Christman, D. C. 27:27
Christman, Daniel 11:104
Christman, I. 14:150
Christman, J. E. 3:42
Christman, Jacob 13:15
Christman, Jacob T. 21:98
Christman, John 24:48
Christman, Levi 20:16
Christman, Thomas 24:190
Christman, W. 1:117
Christmann, William 9:77
Christmas, C. H. 1:25
Christmas, J. 3:42
Christnat, Albert 14:150
Christnear, James 17:172
Christofosin, Peter 10:107; 20:224
Christon, Armstrong 10:107; 20:224
Christonson, A. 4:16
Christopersen, Abe 9:19
Christophason, Abe 18:303
Christopher, Abe 26:94
Christopher, Charles 9:172; 19:280
Christopher, F. 8:77
Christopher, George 21:215
Christopher, Hiram 17:144
Christopher, I. 9:129
Christopher, J. 27:28
Christopher, John 4:65
Christopher, Richard 16:25

Christopher, Samuel 13:15; 16:138
Christopher, Thomas 7:90; 19:154; 22:246
Christopherson, Franz 21:251
Christopherson, H. 23:188
Christopherson, Halver 22:277
Christopherson, Ola 18:337
Christune, M. 7:48
Christwell, Benmul 18:65
Christwood, Ezekiel 18:126
Christy, A. 15:31
Christy, Andrew P. 12:16
Christy, D. 7:48
Christy, E. 13:85; 18:232; 26:20
Christy, George W. 4:16
Christy, H. L. 1:118
Christy, J. 3:42
Christy, J. R. 1:22
Christy, John 5:50; 11:238; 23:137
Christy, John F. 20:16
Christy, L. M. 8:46
Christy, Leander 15:81
Christy, Leander H. 21:135
Christy, Levi W. 17:257
Christy, O. 11:141
Christy, S. H. 5:11
Christy, Samuel P. 4:16
Christy, Thomas 17:109; 22:24
Christy, W. 3:42
Christy, William 22:183
Christy, William I. 12:16
Chriswell, Mallard 17:494
Chritewood, Joel 8:11
Chrittenden, H. 25:154
Chritwood, Hezekiah 8:11
Chronister, --- 25:22
Chronister, J. 25:154
Chronister, John 5:11
Chronister, John D. 15:64
Chronister, Joseph A. 22:70
Chrotty, H. H. 18:126
Chruse, Francis H. 10:107; 20:224
Chrysler, D. E. 21:119
Chrysler, E. 13:106
Chrysty, Joseph 22:421
Chubaer, A. K. 15:352
Chubb, Charles 7:90
Chubb, Hector 17:63
Chubb, James 16:278
Chubb, Lucius 12:16

Chubuck, Job W. 12:16
Chuck, John 8:71
Chuck, John H. L. 14:150
Chuder, John 17:98
Chudwick, William 18:126
Chuff, James E. 15:352
Chughs, David 25:154
Chum, Jacob J. 8:104
Chummey, Jesse 3:42
Chunk, David 8:46
Chuny, A. 17:295
Chuoniger, E. A. 7:67
Church, --- 12:99
Church, A. 3:42
Church, A. B. 23:24
Church, Almon S. 21:114
Church, Alonzo B. 24:75
Church, Andrew A. 20:5
Church, Bishop 23:10
Church, C. H. 3:42
Church, C. K. 1:121
Church, C. L. 3:42
Church, D. H. 9:20; 18:303; 26:94
Church, E. 3:42
Church, F. M. 3:42
Church, Francis 4:16
Church, Frank 20:224
Church, Fred. J. 21:313
Church, Frederick A. 20:106
Church, G. 10:147; 17:77
Church, George E. 9:11
Church, George W. 21:66
Church, H. C. 24:75
Church, Harrison 17:447; 24:172
Church, Harry 15:64
Church, Horace L. 16:365
Church, Howard P. 11:103
Church, Isaac M. 9:117; 27:31
Church, J. 14:46, 150, 254; 26:156
Church, J. B. 16:91
Church, J. H. 19:9
Church, J. L. 17:158
Church, J. M. 20:145
Church, J. W. 27:31
Church, James T. 5:11
Church, John 1:22; 24:48
Church, John W. 9:117
Church, Jonathan 13:15
Church, Joseph 7:90
Church, Joseph P. 10:158
Church, L. 21:313
Church, L. C. 14:6
Church, L. L. 13:85
Church, M. 14:46

Church, Miles H. 8:11; 18:127
Church, Moses 9:213; 21:313
Church, N. F. 1:25
Church, Oliver P. 15:189
Church, Otho 9:77
Church, Reuben 22:24
Church, S. 13:106; 16:180
Church, Stephen 21:114
Church, Thomas 4:16; 15:340; 16:365; 19:9
Church, W. 11:325; 16:365
Church, W. G. 9:172
Church, W. H. 3:42; 18:446
Church, W. W. 5:50; 21:313; 25:154
Church, Wiley 11:141
Church, William 11:124, 332; 12:7, 16; 18:188
Church, William E. 20:224
Church, William O. 23:262
Church, William P. 22:277
Churchan, C. 22:523
Churches, O. 13:106
Churchfield, John 11:141
Churchfield, Patrick 18:420
Churchill, Asa B. 23:178
Churchill, B. L. 16:180
Churchill, C. H. 13:62; 19:61
Churchill, Calvin 13:15; 16:25
Churchill, Casmere 4:16
Churchill, Charles H. 12:16; 21:251
Churchill, Charles W. 10:145; 19:154
Churchill, D. 9:172; 11:331; 19:244
Churchill, E. R. 11:100
Churchill, Edmond P. 20:33
Churchill, Ezra 19:154
Churchill, Ezra S. 10:158
Churchill, F. 14:46; 20:55
Churchill, G. W. 3:42
Churchill, H. M. 10:14
Churchill, Henry 8:38; 26:155
Churchill, J. N. 7:22
Churchill, John 18:205; 21:66
Churchill, John H. 8:81

Churchill, Lyman S. 19:296
Churchill, N. 11:190
Churchill, N. M. 15:189
Churchill, O. H. 27:25
Churchill, Orson 22:402
Churchill, Samuel 12:91; 16:289
Churchill, T. J. 3:42
Churchill, Thomas 15:352; 16:278
Churchill, W. R. 1:118
Churchill, Wallas 7:90
Churchman, Joseph 8:71
Churchouse, John 8:71
Churchward, A. R. 3:42
Churchwell, E. 3:42
Churd, William H. 18:330
Churdee, --- 16:180
Churdel, M. 13:81
Churin, M. T. 9:50
Churkin, Samuel 19:249
Chusman, J. R. 25:154
Chusterson, F. 3:42
Chute, A. M. 3:42
Chute, Francis 21:91
Chyastes, T. C. 14:46
Cibben, Edward 21:313
Cibbrel, Frederick 12:16
Ciboromes, Albert 9:117
Ciborovius, Albert 27:30
Cicial, John 17:99
Cicotle, John B. 15:333
Ciercey, John L. 17:259
Ciggins, M. 11:200
Cigin, J. 13:85
Ciller, John W. 17:235
Cilley, Charles L. 25:154
Cilley, Charles S. 5:11
Cilley, E. 14:46
Cilley, Judia 1:120
Cimmerman, William 1:120
Cimper, Lewis 22:293
Cinclair, --- 8:11; 26:153
Cincque, F. 15:358
Cindair, --- 18:127
Cindall, Thomas 8:11; 18:127
Cinimon, W. H. 24:91
Cinn, William 24:191
Cinque, F. 12:95
Cinthroe, J. 14:240
Ciopp, T. H. 11:141
Ciperlie, Alexander 10:107
Ciperlie, Peter 20:111
Ciperline, Alexander 20:224
Cipfert, Charles 22:332
Ciphens, John S. 21:245

Ciphus, William 5:37
Cipperly, G. 25:154
Circle, Joseph 15:189
Circle, Madison 17:77
Cirfett, J. C. 17:495
Cirlarge, Jesse 9:95
Cirttenden, L. J. 11:199
Ciscle, H. 25:154
Cisco, Benjamin F. 11:104
Cisco, Harrison 13:15
Cisco, James A. 8:11; 18:127
Cisco, Milton 8:81
Cisco, William 21:21
Cisk, Esau 22:500
Cisk, William 17:151
Cisney, Stephen 17:77
Cisnia, James A. 22:232
Cison, J. A. 15:120
Cissel, Joseph 20:103
Cistle, John T. 8:104
Citron, Tony 16:289
Citz, Edward 27:33
Claary, R. 21:215
Clabaugh, J. 3:43
Clabaugh, Martin 22:246
Claburne, Thomas 23:312
Clack, Columbus 8:12
Clackey, E. J. 22:24
Clackman, James 2:7
Clackson, Charles 8:12
Clacue, John 12:16
Cladway, Nathaniel 21:313
Clady, Charles 7:120
Clady, William C. 9:219
Clady, William H. 18:363
Claffee, C. P. 15:349
Clafferty, P. M. 15:31
Claffey, Thomas 22:420
Claffin, D. 21:313
Claffin, George 21:313
Claffin, William J. 17:233
Clafflin, K. E. 16:91
Clafflin, M. 14:46
Claflin, F. G. 3:43
Claflin, Ira W. 25:318
Claflin, L. D. 1:120
Claflin, William 12:141; 20:224
Clage, Clarkston 11:408
Clage, S. 3:43
Clager, Joseph 11:141
Clagg, Hosfield 23:188
Claggart, L. 16:180
Claggett, James W. 22:183
Claghorn, H. D. 9:77
Claiborne, Marion 17:205
Claig, M. 14:151, 254

Clain, David B. 12:140
Clair, Charles 26:22
Clair, George 5:12, 37
Clair, Irwin 18:26
Clair, Levi 10:46; 20:224
Clair, S. S. 25:154
Clair, W. H. 20:224
Clair, William 20:37
Clair, William H. 10:46
Clam, C. 22:351
Clam, Chauncey 12:63
Clammand, George 22:246
Clammoon, Lewis 24:65
Clamon, Joseph M. 19:61
Clampart, William J. 22:402
Clan, Clemen 15:287
Clan, Samuel 18:393
Clancey, John 13:15
Clancey, Michael 8:12
Clancey, Robert 3:43
Clancey, William B. 12:16
Clancy, J. 13:124; 14:46
Clancy, J. W. 3:43
Clancy, Jacob 22:351
Clancy, James 10:107; 17:462; 20:224; 24:176
Clancy, Michael 4:16; 18:127
Clancy, Patrick 19:328; 20:225
Clandell, Nicholas 13:15
Clane, H. 3:43
Claney, F. 16:267
Claney, James 8:100
Claney, William 22:449
Clangy, Thomas 22:183
Clanin, Samuel H. 22:419
Clanin, Thomas J. 24:15
Clann, A. L. M. 14:295
Clanser, David 22:419
Clanson, Henry 3:43
Clanson, J. 11:438
Clanten, William 17:401
Clanton, Jesse 22:24
Clanton, Thomas 5:37
Clap, R. P. 22:246
Clapham, Henry I. 10:46
Clapham, Jacob 10:46
Clapp, A. 22:183
Clapp, A. D. 19:236
Clapp, Charles C. 19:245
Clapp, Charles E. 27:25
Clapp, E. A. 9:172
Clapp, E. S. P. 1:117
Clapp, Eli 21:251
Clapp, Elish 25:154
Clapp, Elisha 5:12
Clapp, George 18:275

Clapp, Henry E. 14:151
Clapp, J. C. 15:120
Clapp, J. H. 10:185;
  18:172
Clapp, Monroe 22:246
Clapp, P. 14:47
Clapp, Parrion 15:273
Clapp, Samuel 4:16
Clapp, Seamons 21:66
Clapp, W. 19:154
Clapp, William 9:172;
  19:236
Clapp, William R. 21:193
Clapper, Anson 9:42
Clapper, E. 25:154
Clapper, Eldridge 5:12
Clapper, George W. 13:15
Clapper, Jacob 8:12;
  18:127
Clapper, James 11:428
Clapper, Jeremiah 11:139
Clapper, John 7:90;
  22:419; 25:22
Clapper, John D. 12:16
Clapper, William D.
  11:138
Clappin, Ed 22:183
Clapsaddle, George W.
  22:70
Clapson, Charles 9:141;
  27:28
Clapton, Charles 21:267
Clara, Robartus 22:24
Claradon, E. H. 15:189
Clardy, William 9:96
Clare, John 18:420
Clare, S. S. 20:89
Clare, T. 17:355
Clare, William 14:151
Claremont, Joseph 19:61
Claren, J. P. 9:77
Claret, John 7:90
Clarey, B. 25:154
Clarey, James 25:25
Clarey, Paris 5:37
Clarida, John B. 22:449
Claridge, Ira 9:117; 27:29
Clarisey, D. 14:151
Claristine, A. 14:47
Clark, --- 1:121; 3:42, 43;
  15:6, 273; 18:102,
  411; 19:61, 154;
  23:62
Clark, A. 1:23; 3:42; 8:62;
  9:141; 12:92; 16:180,
  289; 19:154; 25:154;
  26:154; 27:28
Clark, A. B. 16:25
Clark, A. E. 3:42
Clark, A. G. 23:278
Clark, A. H. 3:42; 7:83

Clark, A. J. 8:62; 26:154
Clark, A. M. 22:183
Clark, A. S. 18:108
Clark, Aaron 20:122
Clark, Aaron A. 16:152
Clark, Able W. 4:16
Clark, Abraham C. 24:15
Clark, Abram 7:22
Clark, Adam 7:64; 27:32
Clark, Addison S. 23:137
Clark, Albert 3:42;
  23:301; 24:49
Clark, Albert H. 27:33
Clark, Alexander 5:37;
  13:15; 22:293
Clark, Alexander M.
  22:419
Clark, Alfred 4:16; 13:56;
  14:151
Clark, Alfred B. 13:15
Clark, Allen M. 22:70
Clark, Allen S. 9:117
Clark, Alonzo 7:8
Clark, Alphonso 10:45
Clark, Alphonzo 9:15;
  20:225
Clark, Alvin S. 27:30
Clark, Ambrose 7:64
Clark, Andrew 17:63;
  22:496
Clark, Ansel F. 7:90
Clark, Anson H. 15:103
Clark, Artemus 16:139
Clark, Arthur 4:16
Clark, Arthur F. 1:24
Clark, B. 27:27
Clark, B. C. 19:226
Clark, B. F. 7:22, 83;
  9:172; 25:21
Clark, B. O. 21:313
Clark, Barnabus F. 19:236
Clark, Barney 16:84
Clark, Benajah 17:291
Clark, Benjamin 13:106;
  16:91; 19:226
Clark, Benjamin F. 21:215
Clark, Benzine 9:141
Clark, Bernard 9:117;
  27:31
Clark, Bernhard 26:155
Clark, Burn 17:456;
  24:213
Clark, Bwoney 18:188
Clark, C. 1:22, 119; 3:42,
  43; 11:124; 14:47;
  17:191; 18:79;
  19:249; 21:21; 23:24;
  27:33
Clark, C. C. 23:24
Clark, C. E. 21:119

Clark, C. H. 3:42; 11:99;
  15:189; 19:61
Clark, C. M. 7:48
Clark, C. W. 26:154
Clark, Caleb B. 23:188
Clark, Calvin 11:332
Clark, Calvin C. 9:20
Clark, Calvin E. 18:303;
  26:94
Clark, Carey 11:421
Clark, Cassius 4:16
Clark, Cerlies 24:100
Clark, Charles 4:16; 6:12;
  7:22; 8:12; 9:129;
  10:158, 208; 13:15;
  14:151; 16:25, 91,
  365; 18:13, 440;
  19:61, 154; 21:135;
  27:33
Clark, Charles E. 12:53
Clark, Charles F. 9:77;
  10:147; 18:46
Clark, Charles H. 7:67;
  10:158; 13:15;
  19:154; 20:182
Clark, Charles John
  26:218
Clark, Charles N. 11:104
Clark, Charles P. 11:332;
  12:16
Clark, Charles W. 21:313
Clark, Chr. 3:42
Clark, Christopher 22:293
Clark, Clement 9:172
Clark, Columbus 18:127
Clark, Cornelius 11:398
Clark, Cyrus 22:293
Clark, D. 3:42; 14:6, 268,
  280; 18:79; 22:70
Clark, D. C. 15:297;
  16:180
Clark, D. F. 14:47
Clark, D. H. 26:19
Clark, D. N. 1:120
Clark, D. O. 14:47
Clark, Dallas 21:313
Clark, Dan'l D. 22:232
Clark, Dana B. 25:281
Clark, Daniel 8:71;
  10:158; 15:189;
  18:26, 215, 393;
  19:154; 21:49
Clark, Daniel B. 17:63
Clark, Daniel E. 10:45
Clark, Daniel G. 23:276
Clark, Daniel H. 9:77
Clark, Darius 1:120
Clark, David 6:12; 13:15,
  85; 17:99; 18:232;
  20:91, 111; 26:21

Clark, David A. 4:16; 17:233
Clark, David C. 22:476
Clark, David E. 20:225
Clark, Dennis 8:46
Clark, Denton 7:22
Clark, E. 3:42; 5:50; 14:47
Clark, E. B. 3:43
Clark, E. E. 20:225
Clark, E. G. 15:157
Clark, E. J. 1:118; 11:410; 19:154
Clark, E. P. 21:313
Clark, E. R. 8:12; 14:151; 18:127
Clark, Ed 17:172
Clark, Edgar 15:340; 16:365
Clark, Edward 1:24; 10:45; 11:26; 20:225; 21:313; 25:154
Clark, Edward B. 21:200
Clark, Edward F. 10:14
Clark, Edward K. 27:30
Clark, Edward R. 12:92; 22:24
Clark, Edwin 10:45; 20:225
Clark, Edwin A. 10:45; 20:225
Clark, Edwin D. 13:62; 19:61
Clark, Edwin L. 22:139
Clark, Elbridge 17:31
Clark, Elijah I. 10:107
Clark, Elijah J. 20:225
Clark, Elisha C. 11:254
Clark, Elizay C. 10:45
Clark, Elvin 15:64
Clark, Enoch 15:13
Clark, Enos B. 18:215
Clark, Erastus A. 22:461
Clark, Ethan A. 21:251
Clark, Ethan Allen 21:119
Clark, Ezekiel 9:50
Clark, Ezra B. 5:12; 25:154
Clark, Ezra E. 21:313
Clark, F. 3:42; 11:141
Clark, F. A. 20:225
Clark, F. B. 19:232
Clark, F. D. 3:43
Clark, F. H. 1:117
Clark, F. J. 3:42; 19:224
Clark, F. K. 24:191
Clark, F. M. 14:47; 20:225
Clark, F. W. 21:313
Clark, Felix 22:183

Clark, Francis 10:158; 19:154
Clark, Francis A. 10:45
Clark, Francis G. 21:251
Clark, Francis M. 9:172; 10:45; 11:55; 19:280
Clark, Frank 24:190
Clark, Frank B. 9:172; 12:167; 19:347
Clark, Frank M. 7:22
Clark, Fred 14:47
Clark, Frederick 12:169
Clark, Frederick D. 16:91
Clark, Frederick G. 22:518
Clark, G. 1:22; 3:43; 11:400; 23:86; 25:154
Clark, G. A. 22:511
Clark, G. B. 7:48
Clark, G. E. 8:46
Clark, G. F. 8:12; 17:439; 18:127
Clark, G. H. 1:121; 7:90
Clark, G. P. 19:325
Clark, G. W. 1:122; 3:42, 43; 11:55
Clark, George 3:42; 5:37; 7:22, 119; 8:62; 9:15; 11:26; 12:16, 99; 13:15; 14:151; 15:21; 16:91; 19:9; 20:145; 22:419; 23:24; 25:22, 24
Clark, George A. 9:77; 15:11
Clark, George B. 17:109
Clark, George E. 5:12
Clark, George H. 26:154
Clark, George K. 11:115
Clark, George M. 11:19
Clark, George W. 9:11; 10:14; 13:15; 21:49
Clark, Getson J. 20:106
Clark, Gideon F. 24:150
Clark, Grace J. 16:71
Clark, H. 1:119, 122; 3:42, 43; 16:278; 25:154; 26:22
Clark, H. C. 23:137
Clark, H. H. 3:42; 24:99
Clark, H. L. 17:287
Clark, H. M. 1:122; 3:43
Clark, H. R. 16:150; 19:236
Clark, H. S. 3:42; 13:62
Clark, H. W. 19:61; 21:21
Clark, Harrison 8:58; 9:114; 21:147
Clark, Harvey 11:199
Clark, Harvey W. 25:276

Clark, Henderson 8:12; 18:79, 127
Clark, Henry 5:37; 7:22, 47; 8:81; 9:77; 10:147; 11:25, 199; 14:151; 15:189; 21:313; 22:70; 26:18
Clark, Henry B. 9:172
Clark, Henry C. 13:62; 16:180
Clark, Henry E. 16:180; 22:402
Clark, Hiram 11:141, 237; 17:158; 21:66
Clark, Hiram H. 26:210
Clark, Horace 25:24
Clark, Horace J. 4:16
Clark, Horatio M. 17:262
Clark, Hugh 13:15
Clark, Hyman 8:104
Clark, I. 15:65; 19:61
Clark, Ira 23:62
Clark, Ira W. 10:45; 20:225
Clark, Isaac 1:24; 11:26; 12:16; 13:15; 17:316
Clark, Isaac P. 20:89
Clark, J. 1:118, 119, 122; 3:42, 43; 5:50; 13:85; 14:6, 47, 151; 16:180; 17:129; 18:46; 19:61; 21:21; 23:24, 240; 24:191; 25:23, 154; 27:27
Clark, J. A. 10:45; 20:225
Clark, J. B. 3:43; 14:151; 22:402
Clark, J. C. 3:42; 14:151
Clark, J. D. 3:42; 12:68; 15:65
Clark, J. F. 1:121; 14:319; 17:247; 21:313; 25:268
Clark, J. F. M. 19:327
Clark, J. G. 23:137
Clark, J. H. 21:313; 25:154
Clark, J. J. 12:152
Clark, J. M. 11:91
Clark, J. O. 14:47
Clark, J. P. 1:93
Clark, J. R. 3:42; 11:27
Clark, J. S. 11:54; 13:62; 21:49
Clark, J. W. 9:50; 10:24, 192; 11:56; 15:6; 18:173; 23:24; 25:154
Clark, Jack 7:119
Clark, Jackson 7:119

Clark, Jacob 7:22; 17:77; 18:284; 26:134
Clark, Jacob L. 10:45; 20:225
Clark, Jahue 9:77
Clark, James 1:121; 3:42; 5:12; 7:22, 90; 9:206; 10:14, 45, 95, 147; 11:55, 124, 259; 13:15; 16:25; 17:31, 272, 313; 18:440; 19:9; 20:225; 21:119, 193; 22:183, 418, 476; 25:22, 154, 268
Clark, James A. 15:90; 20:5; 21:313
Clark, James C. 10:45; 20:225
Clark, James E. 12:16; 17:359; 21:49
Clark, James F. 11:237
Clark, James H. 2:8; 4:16; 10:107; 20:225; 22:183; 23:62; 25:25
Clark, James L. 21:222
Clark, James M. 10:107; 16:278; 20:225; 24:37
Clark, James N. 18:363; 21:127
Clark, James R. 10:204
Clark, James S. 22:24
Clark, James W. 9:227
Clark, Jasper 22:507
Clark, Jeremiah W. 23:62
Clark, Jerome A. 12:16
Clark, Jerome J. 13:15
Clark, Jerry 8:46; 21:267
Clark, Jesse 11:25; 20:225
Clark, Joel 22:70
Clark, John 3:42; 4:16; 7:22, 90, 119; 8:38, 116; 10:45, 107, 176; 11:19, 384; 12:63; 14:47, 151, 254; 15:65, 189; 17:31, 153, 172, 247, 253, 316; 19:61, 154; 20:225; 21:119, 222, 313; 22:24, 246, 419; 23:62; 26:155
Clark, John A. 4:16; 25:22
Clark, John B. 22:332
Clark, John C. 18:393; 23:62
Clark, John D. 23:106
Clark, John E. 23:62
Clark, John F. 17:403
Clark, John G. 10:14; 27:25

Clark, John H. 7:90; 20:111; 22:419; 25:25
Clark, John J. 17:259; 18:232; 26:20
Clark, John M. 18:393; 21:193; 23:62
Clark, John P. 9:101; 20:47
Clark, John R. 11:141
Clark, John S. 8:62
Clark, John W. 5:12; 15:16; 22:165; 23:24, 178
Clark, Johnson 10:45; 20:225
Clark, Jonas 12:16
Clark, Jonathan 21:313
Clark, Jordan 17:172
Clark, Joseph 14:151; 17:50; 21:313; 27:32
Clark, Joseph C. 19:9
Clark, Joseph M. 13:15
Clark, Joseph R. W. 22:119
Clark, Joseph W. 16:25; 17:409; 22:24
Clark, Joseph Z. 15:65
Clark, Josiah F. 11:104; 22:139
Clark, L. 1:122; 3:43; 22:499
Clark, L. B. 13:77
Clark, L. F. 13:106
Clark, L. H. 25:271
Clark, L. J. 25:22
Clark, L. M. 5:12; 25:154
Clark, Lamon 22:139
Clark, Leander 17:442; 24:157
Clark, Lemuel B. 24:15
Clark, Leonard 17:263; 21:21
Clark, Leonard J. 2:9
Clark, Lewis 3:42; 5:50; 9:219; 11:295; 18:363; 19:249; 25:154
Clark, Lewis G. 13:15
Clark, Lewis H. 8:104
Clark, Lman 4:16
Clark, Lorenzo J. 21:9
Clark, Lorin E. 13:15
Clark, Louis 17:172
Clark, M. 3:43; 6:30; 12:61; 14:47; 25:318
Clark, M. A. 11:332
Clark, M. J. 8:62
Clark, M. V. B. 1:24
Clark, Manville 13:129

Clark, Marcellus A. 10:107; 20:225
Clark, Marshall 24:36
Clark, Martin 9:50
Clark, Martin D. 7:90; 21:313
Clark, Martin L. 13:15
Clark, McGune F. 25:154
Clark, Michael 12:53
Clark, Milton 18:215; 22:25
Clark, Mitchell 7:119
Clark, Morris C. 23:184
Clark, Moses 26:217
Clark, N. 9:213; 21:314
Clark, N. S. 14:295
Clark, Nathan 22:25
Clark, Nathan M. 22:70
Clark, Newel N. 1:22
Clark, Noah 9:50
Clark, O. 18:232; 25:23; 26:21
Clark, Octavius M. 14:151
Clark, Orlando B. 10:107; 20:225
Clark, Orni 2:8
Clark, Oron 8:38
Clark, Orrin L. 20:91
Clark, Orris 13:15
Clark, Oscar 11:300
Clark, Owen 26:156
Clark, P. 1:122; 3:43; 14:47
Clark, P. M. 3:42
Clark, Patrick 9:77, 172; 13:15; 16:25
Clark, Peter 12:48; 13:62; 14:151; 16:180; 22:183
Clark, Peter J. 12:16
Clark, Phililp A. 17:202
Clark, R. 3:43; 16:135; 24:75; 27:33
Clark, R. R. 17:107
Clark, R. W. 3:43; 16:25
Clark, Ransom 22:165
Clark, Riley 24:165; 25:285
Clark, Robert 8:46; 9:172; 20:5; 21:49; 22:293, 500; 23:270
Clark, Royal G. 22:119
Clark, Russell W. 13:15
Clark, S. 3:42, 43; 11:141; 27:24
Clark, S. E. 19:245
Clark, S. H. 25:23
Clark, S. M. 19:154
Clark, Samuel 10:46; 11:321; 20:225; 25:154

Clark, Samuel A. 17:287
Clark, Samuel E. 9:172
Clark, Samuel H. 2:8
Clark, Samuel I. 25:154
Clark, Samuel P. 22:402
Clark, Sandy 18:65
Clark, Silas B. 4:16
Clark, Silas S. 17:77
Clark, Solomon 11:199;
  23:86
Clark, Solomon I. 10:45
Clark, Solomon J. 20:225
Clark, Spencer 17:456;
  24:213
Clark, Stephen 9:157;
  21:314; 27:143
Clark, Stephen A. 19:61
Clark, Stephen E. 25:154
Clark, Steven 9:213
Clark, T. 1:121; 10:147;
  18:46
Clark, T. D. 1:97
Clark, T. K. 17:129
Clark, T. T. 7:90
Clark, Theodore 3:43
Clark, Thomas 1:21; 7:15;
  11:26; 16:365;
  17:355, 415; 18:232;
  19:61; 21:314;
  22:510; 23:24;
  24:213; 26:20, 236
Clark, Thomas A. 8:11;
  18:127
Clark, Thomas B. 22:183
Clark, Thomas H. 15:65;
  22:232
Clark, Thomas J. 14:151
Clark, Thomas L. 22:420
Clark, Thomas W. 21:215
Clark, Tillman 22:183
Clark, Timothy 17:241
Clark, Ulysses B. 17:31
Clark, Uriah 22:232;
  25:22
Clark, Vincent 12:16
Clark, W. 3:42, 43; 12:99;
  25:154
Clark, W. A. 13:15
Clark, W. B. 15:189
Clark, W. C. 3:43
Clark, W. E. 1:118
Clark, W. F. 25:155
Clark, W. H. 1:122; 7:90,
  119; 17:499; 18:26;
  19:294
Clark, W. J. 9:172; 23:24;
  26:154
Clark, W. J. H. 21:49
Clark, W. L. 3:42
Clark, W. P. 25:155
Clark, W. R. 22:477

Clark, W. T. 11:56;
  20:225
Clark, W. W. 16:91
Clark, Walter 22:139
Clark, Walter F. 5:12
Clark, Warren 22:332
Clark, Washington 17:396
Clark, Watson A. 10:171;
  19:154
Clark, Widdens M. 21:66
Clark, William 3:42; 6:15,
  20; 7:22, 48, 119;
  8:12; 9:50, 206, 227;
  10:27, 45; 11:55,
  122, 199, 300; 12:55;
  15:65; 16:365; 17:77;
  18:79, 127, 232, 275,
  363; 20:225; 21:314;
  22:25, 139, 246, 402;
  26:19
Clark, William A. 16:25;
  20:192; 22:139
Clark, William C. 21:49
Clark, William E. 19:61
Clark, William F. 16:25,
  26
Clark, William H. 10:45;
  20:225; 21:314;
  22:183
Clark, William L. 16:289
Clark, William M. 12:55;
  19:300; 20:151;
  22:70, 277
Clark, William P. 18:215
Clark, William P. H.
  16:180
Clark, William P. J. 13:62
Clark, William R. 22:476
Clark, William S. 13:15
Clark, William T. 10:45;
  13:15
Clark, William W. 16:117;
  21:98
Clark, Wills 7:90
Clark, Z. 3:43
Clark, Zachariah 4:16
Clarke, B. F. 8:81
Clarke, Benjamin 14:331
Clarke, C. 1:21
Clarke, C. M. 1:93
Clarke, Calvin 8:81
Clarke, Charles 8:81;
  26:155, 210
Clarke, Charles C. 27:24
Clarke, Charles M. 18:202
Clarke, D. 4:16
Clarke, E. 27:24
Clarke, E. D. 1:23
Clarke, Ed. R. 16:289
Clarke, George E. 15:31;
  17:322

Clarke, George H. 4:16
Clarke, George W. 8:81
Clarke, Gilbert 22:293
Clarke, H. H. 22:397
Clarke, Henry 4:16; 18:46
Clarke, J. 11:300; 12:7;
  14:47
Clarke, J. A. 14:321
Clarke, J. J. 11:259
Clarke, Jahue 26:18
Clarke, James 8:81;
  11:300; 13:15; 18:46
Clarke, James A. 8:81
Clarke, James H. 9:71
Clarke, Jesse 11:259
Clarke, Jewett 11:300
Clarke, John 4:16; 22:9
Clarke, John B. 4:16
Clarke, John C. 1:25
Clarke, John W. 18:108
Clarke, Joseph 4:16;
  24:100
Clarke, Leroy 20:5
Clarke, Lewis 4:16
Clarke, Lyman 8:81
Clarke, Milo 8:81
Clarke, N. S. 17:480;
  27:31
Clarke, P. 19:249
Clarke, Ralph P. 8:81
Clarke, Richard 4:16
Clarke, Robert 17:50
Clarke, S. B. 4:16
Clarke, Sacra 4:16
Clarke, Vincent 4:16
Clarke, Warren 22:183
Clarke, William 8:81
Clarke, William R. 21:314
Clarkin, John 14:151
Clarks, George 21:314
Clarkson, --- 3:43
Clarkson, Aaron 7:119;
  11:25
Clarkson, B. F. 14:151
Clarkson, Charles 18:127
Clarkson, E. 1:22
Clarkson, Eli 17:172
Clarkson, Frank B. 21:21
Clarkson, H. 17:94
Clarkson, J. M. 14:47
Clarkson, James 22:119
Clarkson, John 22:119,
  246
Clarkson, John H. 9:129;
  27:29
Clarkson, John W.
  17:417; 24:157
Clarkson, Julius 22:70
Clarkson, Q. C. 25:24
Clarkson, W. 19:285
Clarkson, W. H. 20:225

Clarkson, William 9:33;
18:291; 26:95
Clarkson, William H.
10:46
Clarkston, T. 16:180
Clarkstone, John H.
17:352
Clarmondy, Daniel 25:24
Clarmont, Joseph 15:358
Clarnage, J. 14:47
Clarno, Andrew 22:277
Clarson, John 13:106
Clary, B. 1:26
Clary, C. 20:225
Clary, Cyrus M. 17:31
Clary, Dennis 24:15
Clary, Edward 11:91
Clary, Edward D. 10:158
Clary, Edward R. 7:67
Clary, Eli 8:38; 26:155
Clary, Francis M. 23:301
Clary, Henry D. 23:120
Clary, James 16:117
Clary, Joseph J. 22:183
Clary, M. 21:163
Clary, Patrick 20:185
Clary, Phelix 23:15
Clary, T. 13:85
Clary, Watson 24:15
Clary, William 9:77
Clase, Adam 12:152
Clase, D. 11:218
Clase, J. 14:6
Clase, S. 22:183
Clasen, Andrew 23:24
Clason, William S. 10:204
Claspill, Aaron C. 22:70
Claspill, Z. T. 11:300
Claspy, Amstead 22:139
Class, George W. 23:128
Class, William L. 12:152
Classen, Joel 21:314
Classic, Bartholomew
11:230
Classin, Martin 6:9
Classon, Abraham 10:14
Classon, Amasa 21:91
Classon, Amos 8:46
Classon, Amos C. 22:139
Classon, P. S. 17:99
Clathery, T. H. 15:150
Claton, Thomas 15:324
Clatry, William 22:183
Clatter, F. 3:43
Clatter, Henry 16:166
Clatter, L. 13:85
Claud, A. L. M. 27:31
Claudener, J. E. 15:363
Clauders, S. 1:118
Claugh, Charles 18:127
Claugh, John 26:18

Claugh, John D. 3:43
Claugh, William 22:332
Claughlin, Walter 27:25
Claun, A. L. M. 17:479
Claunch, Lafayette 17:202
Claus, David 25:22
Claus, John C. 1:24
Clausby, J. 3:43
Clause, Charles 26:18
Clause, Joseph 25:268
Clause, Justice 25:155
Clausman, Jacob 9:96
Clauson, L. L. 23:252
Clauson, Seaman G.
21:251
Clausy, David 5:12
Clautman, C. C. 18:393
Clauton, Benjamin 8:77
Clavanaugh, Joseph M.
16:26
Clavell, A. F. 11:139
Claver, A. R. 1:119
Claver, G. 25:155
Clavill, Milton H. 17:205
Clavin, A. 22:293
Clavland, G. E. 25:155
Clawson, B. 20:225
Clawson, Barney 10:46
Clawson, D. 1:118
Clawson, Elijah 10:46;
20:225
Clawson, G. 11:259
Clawson, Granville
20:225
Clawson, H. 8:71; 26:154
Clawson, Hiram 11:410
Clawson, J. 25:155
Clawson, Joseph 10:107;
20:225
Clawson, Oliver 26:121
Clawson, Phineas 21:66
Clawson, Thomas 11:411;
22:402
Clawson, Vinte 22:70
Clawson, W. N. 1:26
Clax, George 16:91
Claxton, Arthur 11:279
Claxton, Floyd 17:396
Claxton, Richard 21:314
Claxton, Riley 17:94
Claxton, W. 14:327
Claxton, William 9:160
Claxton, William H.
17:494
Clay, --- 23:244
Clay, A. 21:109
Clay, Aaron 20:6
Clay, Cassius 17:396
Clay, Charles M. 19:9
Clay, Daniel 21:314
Clay, David 9:141

Clay, David T. 10:204
Clay, Francis 7:90
Clay, Francis M. 20:45
Clay, Frank 11:230
Clay, Franklin 17:429;
24:186
Clay, Fred 23:106
Clay, G. M. 1:25
Clay, G. W. 9:68
Clay, George W. 13:15
Clay, H. 1:117; 3:43
Clay, Henry 1:118; 3:43;
6:12, 15; 7:119;
9:161; 11:199;
16:181; 17:129, 172,
191; 18:79, 411;
19:289; 21:267;
22:293, 512; 24:191;
25:155; 27:143
Clay, Horculus 25:155
Clay, J. M. 1:21
Clay, J. P. 25:155
Clay, Jacob 22:70
Clay, James 17:173;
26:155
Clay, John 17:50, 173;
24:165; 26:19
Clay, John H. 2:9
Clay, John I. 5:12
Clay, John S. 9:68
Clay, Kais 24:107
Clay, Lilly 6:28
Clay, Louis 17:173
Clay, O. 3:43
Clay, Philip 22:293
Clay, Samuel 23:308
Clay, Shadrack 25:285
Clay, T. C. 18:65
Clay, Thomas 26:210
Clay, W. 17:173
Clay, W. H. 7:119; 16:181
Clay, Warren W. 21:314
Clay, William 7:119;
10:7; 22:293
Clay, Wilson 20:39
Claybaugh, Daniel 22:402
Claybaugh, G. W. 3:43
Claybaugh, John 12:58
Clayborn, Joel T. 24:166
Clayborn, Joseph H.
17:205
Clayborne, W. 21:147
Clayborne, William
17:190
Claybourne, Archy 27:28
Claybourne, Lewis 7:119
Clayburne, Archey 9:129
Claychie, Richard 26:22
Claycomb, David R.
22:449
Claycome, S. A. 3:43

Clayfoot, David B. 24:181
Clayford, W. F. 4:16
Clayhough, Samuel 22:246
Clayman, H. 23:137
Claymer, Charles 20:225
Claymt, A. 16:181
Clayner, Michael 26:154
Claypole, James 17:267
Claypole, S. R. 1:120
Claypole, Thomas C. 24:191
Claypole, Thomas J. 17:129
Claypool, William 18:26
Claypoole, Levi 15:120
Claypoole, S. 16:181
Claypoor, William 14:235
Clayson, E. 1:24
Clayson, H. 11:237
Claysy, W. 15:13
Clayton, --- 16:289
Clayton, C. P. 17:327
Clayton, Charles 22:183
Clayton, Christopher 22:477
Clayton, D. J. 3:43
Clayton, Daniel C. 23:128
Clayton, E. 13:85; 14:6
Clayton, E. B. 3:43
Clayton, George 17:129; 19:61; 24:191
Clayton, George C. 12:121
Clayton, George W. 18:215
Clayton, H. 10:46; 20:225
Clayton, Henry 20:16
Clayton, Isaac 12:68; 15:27
Clayton, J. 1:119; 3:43; 25:155
Clayton, J. R. 22:246
Clayton, James F. 8:81
Clayton, John 21:222
Clayton, John B. 5:12; 25:155
Clayton, John C. 9:33
Clayton, John F. 10:14
Clayton, John H. 9:33; 18:215
Clayton, Joseph 4:16; 24:190
Clayton, L. 3:43
Clayton, M. L. 19:327
Clayton, O. 17:153
Clayton, R. 13:85
Clayton, Robert 9:77; 17:129; 24:191; 26:19
Clayton, Thomas 23:24

Clayton, W. P. 1:122
Clayton, W. W. 19:9
Clayton, William 13:15; 14:327; 20:122; 25:268
Clayton, William T. 22:402
Claywell, Milton H. 22:448
Clazey, William 12:68
Cle---, Martin 15:189
Cleak, A. J. 11:326
Clean, John 23:252
Clear, Abraham 23:62
Clear, James 3:43
Clear, John 21:314
Clear, P. 2:9
Clear, William B. 20:188
Cleareland, H. C. 16:181
Clearer, Empson 22:477
Clearmond, J. 12:86
Clearmont, R. 12:86
Clearnes, Jeremiah 10:45
Clearwater, W. B. 1:117
Cleary, B. 20:174
Cleary, Cornelius 16:80
Cleary, James 21:86; 22:161
Cleary, John 7:90; 11:408
Cleary, Michael 21:109
Cleary, P. 3:43
Cleary, Patrick 25:268
Cleary, R. 21:200
Cleary, Sylvester 8:82
Cleary, Thomas 7:48
Cleason, S. 14:280
Cleaveland, A. 18:46
Cleaveland, C. F. 5:50; 25:155
Cleaveland, George E. 5:12
Cleaveland, George P. 10:95
Cleaveland, L. 10:14
Cleaver, Albert 7:48
Cleaver, G. J. 11:385
Cleaver, George R. 21:66
Cleaver, George W. 22:25
Cleaver, Joseph 22:419
Cleaver, Rufus 9:172
Cleaver, W. 3:43
Cleaver, William H. 22:232
Cleaves, Allison 27:30
Cleaves, Allison G. 9:117
Cleaves, John 21:314
Cleaves, R. 19:236
Cleaves, Samuel 18:26
Cleeche, Charles 18:127
Cleekley, Lewis 11:200
Cleeland, A. K. 16:278

Cleeland, S. H. 1:117
Cleen, William 14:151
Clees, Ellis 22:9
Cleeves, W. 3:43
Clefton, George H. 20:225
Cleg, M. 15:54
Clegett, Philip 21:186
Clegg, Francis 8:62
Clegg, J. 16:91
Clegg, James 7:22
Clegg, Jesse H. 13:15; 16:26
Clegg, John 14:47
Clegg, Joseph 21:314
Clegg, Joseph C. 24:15
Clegg, Moses 12:68
Clegg, W. P. 13:85
Cleggett, Charles H. 4:65
Cleggett, M. 3:43
Cleghorn, R. 25:310
Cleghorn, William L. 21:66
Cleimger, Thornton 8:82
Clein, A. J. H. 20:225
Clelan, William 13:15
Cleland, A. 1:21
Cleland, Jos 19:154
Cleland, Joseph 10:158
Clelland, George 10:46; 20:225
Clelland, J. 10:185; 18:173
Clellum, M. 16:181
Clem, Ellis 10:107; 20:225
Clem, George 8:82
Clem, H. A. 12:141
Clem, Henry 8:104
Clem, Isaac M. 14:47
Clem, Jackson 7:48
Clem, W. H. 3:43
Cleman, Pat 8:12
Clemane, Clinton 20:226
Clemans, J. H. 15:172
Clemans, Joseph H. 20:95
Clemans, Samuel 7:22
Clemans, William W. 11:279
Clemant, N. 1:97
Clemburg, J. 3:43
Clemene, William 19:337
Clemens, --- 14:151
Clemens, A. 3:43
Clemens, Andy 21:267
Clemens, Archibald 27:32
Clemens, C. 1:22
Clemens, Charles 22:119
Clemens, Charles W. 22:70
Clemens, Clinton 10:46
Clemens, D. 3:43

Clemens, E. 14:47; 15:189
Clemens, E. T. 17:18
Clemens, George 10:46;
  20:226
Clemens, Henry 12:61;
  14:280
Clemens, Hudson 13:15
Clemens, I. 14:47
Clemens, J. 3:43; 26:18
Clemens, J. C. 7:56
Clemens, J. D. 3:43
Clemens, James 9:66;
  17:318; 18:275;
  23:24
Clemens, James T. 18:205
Clemens, John 10:107;
  12:16; 19:9; 20:226;
  21:49, 314
Clemens, Joseph 24:37
Clemens, N. 16:181
Clemens, Nicholas 23:10
Clemens, O. H. 21:314
Clemens, Pat 20:226
Clemens, Patrick 10:46
Clemens, Philip 17:318
Clemens, R. 14:47
Clemens, William 14:151
Clemens, William H.
  27:32
Clement, --- 15:21
Clement, Alonzo 20:111
Clement, Charles 17:359
Clement, E. C. 15:150
Clement, Ezra 9:159
Clement, F. S. 9:141;
  27:26
Clement, G. W. 1:26
Clement, George 22:476;
  25:25
Clement, H. H. 1:117
Clement, Henry 11:55
Clement, I. C. 8:12
Clement, J. B. 12:16
Clement, J. C. 18:127
Clement, Jacob 23:10
Clement, James 10:95
Clement, Marcus 8:112
Clement, Martin 17:241
Clement, Mathias 22:277
Clement, Moses G. 16:88
Clement, O. F. 19:9
Clement, Richard 9:203
Clement, Theodore 16:26
Clement, W. B. 17:263
Clement, W. C. 9:71
Clements, A. 15:31
Clements, Aaron 1:22
Clements, Charles 26:218
Clements, Daniel 10:46;
  20:226
Clements, David J. 20:29

Clements, E. B. 7:48
Clements, Evatus 16:289
Clements, G. W. 24:99
Clements, George 18:233;
  26:21
Clements, H. 1:23
Clements, I. 9:141
Clements, J. H. 7:90;
  9:141
Clements, J. N. 21:314
Clements, James 3:43;
  14:151; 21:314
Clements, James O.
  16:181
Clements, James W.
  22:119
Clements, John 21:49, 98
Clements, John H. 11:54;
  27:27
Clements, John W. 9:33
Clements, Joseph 25:155
Clements, L. 3:43
Clements, L. D. 7:67
Clements, N. 15:297
Clements, Nathan 23:62
Clements, Nelson 16:181
Clements, Patrick H.
  21:49
Clements, Prince 18:233
Clements, Samuel 10:46;
  20:226
Clements, Thomas E.
  22:448
Clements, W. 3:43; 12:92;
  16:290
Clements, W. H. 9:15
Clements, William 10:46
Clements, William H.
  4:65; 12:16
Clements, William M.
  13:15
Clements, William R.
  10:107; 20:226
Clementson, William
  15:103
Clemets, Prince 26:22
Clemevis, James T. 8:82
Clemhern, M. 16:181
Clemie, William 18:127
Clemings, Thomas 3:43
Clemison, Thomas 22:25
Clemmans, Charles 10:14
Clemmens, George
  17:455; 24:190
Clemments, James
  15:189; 17:31
Clemments, R. 15:189
Clemmon, John 7:120;
  14:287; 23:112
Clemmons, A. 14:151

Clemmons, Charles C.
  22:476
Clemmons, Hiram R.
  21:135
Clemmons, James 19:61
Clemmons, S. L. 22:183
Clemmont, E. 4:16
Clemons, A. 13:15
Clemons, H. 10:107;
  20:226
Clemons, Henry 15:90
Clemons, James 22:523
Clemons, M. V. 1:22
Clemons, Matthew 20:103
Clemons, R. 13:124
Clemont, A. H. 5:12
Clemont, Theodore 13:15
Clempson, H. 22:183
Clen, Henry 22:25
Clenaly, James 14:47
Clenard, John 22:332
Clenard, M. 9:50
Clenbats, George 22:476
Clency, Mary Ellen 27:31
Clency, Richard 9:219;
  18:363
Clendeman, Thomas 7:56
Clendenan, Washington
  15:65
Clendenin, George W.
  20:95
Clendenin, Robert 22:332
Clendenin, Washington
  12:68
Clendening, A. P. 13:15
Clendening, C. W. 1:117
Clendening, Joseph 21:91
Clendening, R. M. 18:215
Clendening, W. 14:254
Clendennan, C. L. 3:43
Clendennin, Alfred 8:82
Clendenning, A. 20:192
Clendenning, R. C.
  17:355
Clendenning, Thomas
  22:70
Clendining, A. P. 16:26
Clenenger, Seth 18:215
Clengin, Nathan 9:96
Clenk, George W. 7:48
Clenk, R. R. 7:22
Clenk, W. H. 7:22
Clenn, I. M. 14:151
Clent, W. 23:312
Clent, W. B. 23:301
Clerest, H. 16:267
Clerk, John 1:121
Clerman, Pat 18:127
Clerman, Robert A.
  21:314
Clermento, H. 3:43

Clermont, Joseph 12:95
Clery, D. 27:26
Clesby, Thomas 19:155
Cleson, Peter 9:106
Cless, Jacob 25:155
Cleton, William 11:118
Cleveland, --- 11:141
Cleveland, A. 22:293
Cleveland, A. D. 9:33;
18:291
Cleveland, A. H. 2:9;
25:26
Cleveland, Aburt 10:147
Cleveland, Albert 20:192
Cleveland, Alexander
22:183
Cleveland, Andrew W.
22:277
Cleveland, Baf 20:29
Cleveland, Benjamin
25:155; 27:32
Cleveland, Charles H.
15:103; 21:165
Cleveland, Clark 20:47
Cleveland, David 21:314
Cleveland, E. 3:44;
25:155
Cleveland, Elisha E. 8:82
Cleveland, Elmadore
23:62
Cleveland, Erastus 19:9
Cleveland, Ezra 5:12
Cleveland, Ezra N. 20:106
Cleveland, F. 25:155
Cleveland, Francis 5:37
Cleveland, G. W. 15:189
Cleveland, Henry 17:241
Cleveland, Isaac 25:155
Cleveland, M. G. 18:65
Cleveland, N. 20:177
Cleveland, P. D. 22:402
Cleveland, Peter H. 15:31
Cleveland, S. J. 22:332
Cleveland, Thomas 5:12
Cleveland, William H.
1:22
Cleveland, William H. H.
22:139
Clevely, J. 11:238
Cleven, S. 14:268
Clevenger, Andrew C.
17:31
Clevenger, Charles C.
11:421
Clevenger, D. 7:72
Clevenger, John 21:49
Clevenger, Josh. B. 20:6
Clevenger, Seth 11:259
Clevenger, Thomas 4:17;
23:97

Clevenger, William
22:499
Clever, C. 1:117
Clever, Joel 12:16
Clever, John 15:120
Clevering, Peter A. 9:172
Cleverly, John M. 7:90
Cleverstine, David 4:17
Cleverstine, John 10:107;
20:226
Clevey, George H. 22:70
Clevine, P. A. 19:280
Clevinger, David 23:62
Clevinger, J. 24:37
Clew, Martin 10:154;
19:155
Clewell, Eugene T. 7:90
Clews, Charles 16:71
Cleyhorn, G. 14:254
Cleyn, A. 11:186
Cleyton, William 24:75
Clibaugh, J. 19:300
Cliborn, J. H. 17:216
Cliborn, W. B. 9:50
Cliburn, B. F. 10:46
Clich, James 14:47
Click, H. 22:476
Click, Henry 22:519
Click, Joseph 22:183
Click, Mathias M. 11:421
Click, Solomon 22:70
Click, Thomas 21:314
Click, Washington 11:421
Clickner, John F. 11:139
Cliff, T. J. 9:50
Cliff, W. 14:280
Cliff, William E. 12:16
Cliffin, William 11:186
Clifford, Alonzo 11:141;
20:192
Clifford, C. 14:151, 254
Clifford, C. Contrell 10:10
Clifford, Charles 3:44;
27:30
Clifford, Charles W. 16:71
Clifford, D. 7:22
Clifford, E. B. 17:355
Clifford, E. R. 17:153
Clifford, Ephraim 22:418
Clifford, G. 22:170
Clifford, G. R. 25:21
Clifford, George 3:44;
22:170, 332
Clifford, H. C. 3:44
Clifford, H. E. 18:233
Clifford, Henry 23:137
Clifford, I. 14:6
Clifford, J. 3:44; 13:85;
14:47
Clifford, J. G. 7:56
Clifford, James 17:173

Clifford, John 4:17; 7:74;
10:176; 19:155;
25:294
Clifford, John C. 24:91
Clifford, Lyonel 4:17
Clifford, Michael 25:155
Clifford, N. 12:7
Clifford, Nicholas 23:128
Clifford, R. 10:147; 18:47
Clifford, S. 16:365
Clifford, Samuel 23:305
Clifford, Thomas W.
15:120
Clifford, W. 19:61
Clifford, W. E. 26:20
Clift, W. 13:106
Clifton, C. H. 26:19
Clifton, Charles 9:156
Clifton, Daniel 9:33, 77;
18:291; 26:17, 95
Clifton, David 12:16
Clifton, DeWitt C. 23:188
Clifton, F. M. 20:226
Clifton, G. J. 23:263
Clifton, George 16:26
Clifton, George H. 10:46
Clifton, H. 9:77
Clifton, Harrison Y. 7:48
Clifton, Jackson 17:440;
24:151
Clifton, James 14:47, 151
Clifton, John 8:12; 18:127
Clifton, Josiah 8:12;
18:127
Clifton, Orton A. 17:18
Clifton, Sidney 20:34
Clifton, Sidney A. 20:34
Clifton, Wyete 17:307
Cligan, James K. P.
22:499
Cligse, John 8:46
Clileters, J. 9:108
Clille, John 22:277
Clim, William 14:47
Climan, Conrad 13:124
Climan, James O. 13:62
Climer, Isaac D. 11:325
Climer, John T. 21:129
Climer, Joseph 17:355
Climmer, Sherman 14:47
Clinard, B. 9:50
Clinch, George E. 3:44
Clinch, Joseph John
25:294
Cline, A. J. 1:121
Cline, Abraham 9:235
Cline, Abraham C. 26:217
Cline, Albert 1:21
Cline, Allen 22:277
Cline, Ambrose 23:86
Cline, B. 3:44

Cline, Benjamin 7:22
Cline, C. 7:22; 14:334
Cline, C. C. 11:237
Cline, C. K. 1:119
Cline, Charles 26:144
Cline, Christ 17:404
Cline, Christian 14:151
Cline, Daniel A. 22:246
Cline, Davis 4:17; 15:54;
   18:364
Cline, E. W. 9:117; 27:30
Cline, F. 3:44
Cline, Frederick 13:106;
   23:178
Cline, G. L. 25:155
Cline, George 8:82; 9:77;
   10:46; 20:226
Cline, George W. 22:475
Cline, Isaiah 21:119
Cline, J. 3:44; 10:27;
   12:81; 13:85;
   16:290; 19:300
Cline, J. C. 14:47
Cline, J. E. 14:47
Cline, J. N. 20:226
Cline, J. W. 3:44; 26:156
Cline, Jacob 5:12; 9:229;
   10:171; 19:155;
   20:226
Cline, John 3:44; 10:171;
   11:319; 17:31;
   19:155
Cline, John C. 10:46
Cline, John M. 7:90;
   8:104
Cline, John W. 22:119,
   277
Cline, Jonas 11:14
Cline, Jonathan 17:90
Cline, Joseph 8:82
Cline, K. 3:44
Cline, M. 3:44; 20:226;
   23:24
Cline, Martin 10:90; 19:9
Cline, Milton 13:15
Cline, P. M. 18:233;
   26:20
Cline, Richard 7:90
Cline, Robert 10:27;
   19:300
Cline, S. M. 3:44
Cline, Samuel 22:70
Cline, Thomas 15:165
Cline, Thomas L. C.
   14:334
Cline, Thomas L. W. 7:22
Cline, W. 3:44
Cline, W. C. 20:226
Cline, W. F. 14:295;
   17:479; 27:31
Cline, W. L. 8:71

Cline, William 1:24
Cline, William B. 11:400
Cline, William C. 10:46
Cline, William P. 21:251
Clinefogle, Charles 9:71
Cliner, A. 1:119
Clinesmith, Oliver 21:66
Cling, C. 3:44
Cling, Davis 9:219
Cling, Jacob 3:44
Clingan, John 25:20
Clinger, John 21:98
Clinger, John W. 23:255
Clinger, Samuel 21:98
Clinger, W. H. 3:44
Clingham, James 11:380
Clingman, Hiram 20:122
Clingman, I. 14:327
Clingman, J. 3:44
Clingman, Jefferson
   18:215
Clingman, Miles 11:25
Clink, F. 23:137
Clink, Homer H. 23:24
Clinkenbeard, William
   17:173
Clinkhammer, Peter 1:120
Clinkinbeard, J. 11:238
Clino, M. 14:151
Clinsing, Caspar J. 24:37
Clint, Peter 11:139
Clinton, Allen 17:272
Clinton, Auber 27:143
Clinton, Charles 21:109
Clinton, David 27:143
Clinton, Edward 26:218
Clinton, George 23:86
Clinton, Horace 13:15
Clinton, John 9:46;
   26:122
Clinton, Jones 18:65
Clinton, L. 21:147
Clinton, Lewis 21:211
Clinton, Luman W.
   17:359
Clinton, R. 3:44; 14:151
Clinton, Tines 9:206
Clinton, W. H. 20:226
Clinton, William 7:120;
   27:25
Clinton, William H. 10:46
Clintuck, Tom M. 19:155
Clintzman, George 25:155
Clipp, Benjamin F. 22:70
Clippand, John 17:109
Clippenger, Samuel D.
   23:137
Clipper, George 8:38;
   26:155
Clipper, Phil. O. 18:188

Clippinger, John H.
   23:202
Clirage, James 26:18
Clisbee, James 26:17
Clisbee, Louis 10:46
Clisbell, James 9:77
Clisby, Lewis 20:226
Clise, Elias 26:18
Clise, Martin F. 4:17
Clissold, S. 25:24
Cliston, Haywood 17:129;
   24:189
Clitcher, Elisha M. 6:7
Cliton, Mathew 21:267
Clive, John 19:9
Cliver, S. 21:49
Cliver, William H. 21:314
Clivinger, H. 20:226
Clivinger, Hamilton 10:46
Clizt, W. D. 14:321
Clock, Charles H. 12:7
Clock, D. W. 16:147
Clock, Emanuel 12:7
Clock, H. R. 25:155
Clock, Harvey 22:293
Clockey, John 17:247
Clockton, Willis 21:267
Clodell, Eugene 10:46;
   20:226
Clodfelte, John W. 21:66
Cloduis, Charles 25:23
Cloe, J. W. 26:138
Cloe, John W. 9:31
Cloeman, L. A. 27:31
Cloggett, C. H. 21:215
Cloine, J. 20:91
Cloister, B. F. 8:62
Clokie, J. W. 3:44
Clon, N. 24:15
Clonay, J. 3:44
Clongensmith, J. 9:50
Clongher, H. 18:47
Clonner, --- 19:249
Clookey, Louis 26:155
Clooman, P. 3:44
Cloon, George W. 18:127
Clooney, William 1:23
Clopp, Levi 24:37
Clorich, John 9:77
Clorke, Samuel 14:47
Cloro, B. F. 18:364
Clorson, C. 14:6
Clory, D. 14:47
Close, Abraham 4:17
Close, Christian 11:124
Close, David 11:124
Close, J. 13:85
Close, J. A. 1:123
Close, James A. 23:120
Close, John L. 22:420
Close, John W. 22:351

Close, Jonathan 20:111
Close, Levi 15:90; 19:61
Close, Levy 12:61
Close, Lewis M. 14:151
Close, Nathan 13:15
Close, R. 1:26
Close, R. H. 18:406
Close, Robert 21:120
Close, William 9:160;
    14:327
Closen, Eliza D. 18:215
Closky, Lewis 6:9
Closs, J. 1:97
Closs, William 25:155
Clossen, Daniel 1:23
Clossett, John P. 17:322
Clossin, C. 13:85
Closson, Amos P. 10:107;
    20:226
Closson, Joel 9:213
Clotfelter, Columbus
    21:215
Clottey, John 23:137, 173
Clotty, H. 24:75
Clouch, H. W. 27:25
Clouch, James 22:119
Cloucher, H. 10:147
Cloud, --- 11:218
Cloud, Andrew 17:276
Cloud, C. S. 15:336;
    16:181
Cloud, Charles H. 14:151
Cloud, Francis M. 23:137
Cloud, George 21:314
Cloud, Gilbert 18:233;
    26:20
Cloud, J. M. 8:71; 26:154
Cloud, James 18:420
Cloud, Nathan 20:177
Cloud, Samuel 22:419
Cloud, William 24:37
Cloud, William C. 24:88
Cloudfelter, John 10:46
Cloudfether, John 20:226
Cloudh, S. I. 25:155
Cloudy, Harrison 11:199
Cloudy, John M. 10:107;
    20:226
Clough, Albert 7:90
Clough, B. 3:44
Clough, Cary A. 14:151
Clough, Charles 8:12
Clough, Charles H.
    23:103
Clough, Daniel M. 21:314
Clough, Edward 16:181
Clough, F. 1:117
Clough, George 10:15;
    16:365; 18:47
Clough, George O. 1:22
Clough, Henry A. 16:5

Clough, Homer E. 22:420
Clough, J. B. 4:17
Clough, J. E. 1:122
Clough, J. H. 10:15; 16:26
Clough, J. W. 1:119
Clough, Joel 21:314
Clough, John H. 23:86
Clough, M. M. 15:189
Clough, Oliver 23:263
Clough, Richardson
    22:461
Clough, T. H. 25:21
Clougher, William 23:24
Cloupf, Andrew 4:17
Clouse, Charles 25:283
Clouse, James M. 24:75
Clouse, Luther 23:137
Clouse, William H. 15:65
Clouser, John 20:122
Clout, F. 3:44
Cloutman, Benjamin
    12:58
Clover, Bonypart 11:199
Clover, D. 11:300
Clover, Daniel 19:44
Clover, George W. 8:12
Clover, Richard 8:58;
    21:147
Clover, Thomas 14:295;
    17:475; 27:31
Cloves, M. 3:43
Cloves, Robert 13:106
Clovish, C. E. 16:278
Clow, Andrew J. 21:135
Clow, B. F. 9:219
Clow, Edward 24:191
Clow, Louis 7:56
Clow, William 17:73
Cloy, J. 25:155
Cloy, John 5:37; 22:139
Cloyd, Peter 17:355
Cluck, --- 18:173
Cluck, D. A. 9:50
Cluck, George 21:222
Cluck, J. W. 17:161
Cluckey, L. 18:108
Clue, Thomas 13:62
Cluff, James M. 11:324
Cluhan, C. 12:86; 16:290
Cluire, Joseph 7:90
Clum, Chauncey 15:31
Clum, Henry C. 21:222
Clum, Hiram 11:140
Clumusan, I. 14:47
Clune, Frank 17:73
Clune, J. C. 20:226
Clune, P. 1:122
Clunolan, --- 13:62
Clurburk, J. 15:165
Clure, C. M. 17:129;
    24:191

Clure, Dan D. 26:19
Clure, L. M. 17:129;
    24:191
Clure, M. 14:254
Clurkin, Samuel 9:172
Clusson, D. M. 9:50
Clusterman, J. 3:44
Clustin, B. 14:6
Cluta, J. 12:91
Clute, Charles W. 22:277
Clute, F. 1:26
Clute, George 21:117
Clute, George W. 14:151
Clute, H. V. 3:44
Clute, J. 15:54
Clute, John 9:172; 19:249
Cluter, James K. 12:152
Cluts, Jacob 16:290
Clutter, Andrew J. 23:137
Clutter, John 21:49
Clutter, L. 3:44; 14:6;
    16:267
Clutter, M. 1:97
Clutter, W. 11:238
Clutz, G. W. 1:117
Cluxton, Galen 25:155
Cluyton, --- 18:173
Clvi, --- 20:91
Cly, John 4:17
Clyburne, J. J. 17:422
Clyde, Charles 16:117
Clyde, W. J. 25:20
Clyens, J. P. 3:44
Clymar, James 16:26
Clymer, Charles 10:46
Clymer, D. H. 24:15
Clymer, Henry C. 22:70
Clymer, James 13:15
Clymer, John W. 9:77;
    26:22
Clymer, N. 15:189
Clymer, Solomon 22:402
Clyne, E. F. 3:44
Clyne, Nathaniel 22:25
Clyson, Peter 12:152
Cn., Reid 27:25
Co-mon-chee 25:332
Co-wet-a-hajo 25:332
Coab, George 17:446
Coach, Andrew 19:280
Coache, Andrew 9:172
Coachman, E. F. 25:155
Coady, James 4:17
Coak, George 1:24
Coakely, Jacob 22:184
Coakir, Fred 18:393
Coakley, Charles 6:24
Coakley, J. 16:84
Coakley, James 25:155
Coakley, Jeremiah 22:9
Coakley, Martin 19:9

Coakley, William 7:22
Coakley, William J.
  15:103
Coakson, Isaiah 27:26
Coal, Alva 13:15
Coal, Constant 22:477
Coales, S. H. 19:61
Coalman, Arthur 10:107;
  20:226
Coalman, C. S. 3:44
Coalman, H. 3:44
Coalman, John 9:129
Coals, John S. 19:61
Coan, George S. 18:323
Coan, Henry 21:314
Coan, S. 11:259
Coane, Charles 22:446
Coanes, William 3:44
Coaplined, Martin 18:188
Coar, William 20:226
Coard, William F. O.
  21:135
Coarhan, R. 14:47
Coate, John G. 11:55
Coates, Brazilla 12:16
Coates, D. 21:147
Coates, Francis 19:155
Coates, G. W. 14:151
Coates, George 15:31
Coates, George H. 3:44
Coates, J. G. 17:417
Coates, John 16:181;
  27:143
Coates, Lewis 18:79
Coates, Major 19:44
Coates, Miles 11:384
Coates, S. R. 3:44
Coates, Sewell 9:15
Coates, Thomas D. 7:56
Coates, Tom 21:314
Coats, --- 24:190
Coats, Anthony 6:12
Coats, Benjamin 20:226
Coats, Benjamin L. 10:46;
  20:226
Coats, C. 1:117
Coats, Elihu 23:62
Coats, Francis 10:158
Coats, Frederick P. 11:218
Coats, G. W. 9:50
Coats, George 11:19, 384;
  25:23
Coats, Heber D. 15:277;
  25:155
Coats, Herbert E. 10:46
Coats, J. H. 11:141
Coats, James 7:67
Coats, John 1:23
Coats, Lewis 19:9
Coats, Milan W. 21:242
Coats, N. 21:314

Coats, Oliver R. 17:265
Coats, R. 5:50; 25:155
Coats, Ralph 25:23
Coats, Rufus 3:44
Coats, S. 18:364
Coats, S. R. 3:44
Coats, Samuel 9:219
Coats, Tom 7:120
Coats, W. 21:314
Coats, W. A. 20:226
Coats, William 15:85;
  20:226
Coats, William H. 9:42
Coatt, E. J. 3:44
Coaty, Sypin 21:314
Cobahan, John 21:215
Cobang, J. E. 25:22
Cobb, --- 27:25
Cobb, A. 13:106
Cobb, A. J. 11:100
Cobb, Alex. 8:12
Cobb, Alexander 18:127
Cobb, Andrew 27:26
Cobb, Barzilla S. 12:58
Cobb, Bryant 17:259
Cobb, C. A. 9:172; 19:245
Cobb, C. B. 1:23; 13:62
Cobb, C. W. 16:365
Cobb, Charles B. 16:181
Cobb, Charles J. 4:17
Cobb, D. 17:289
Cobb, Daniel 1:24
Cobb, Derrick W. 10:15
Cobb, Drew 18:233;
  26:20
Cobb, E. 3:44
Cobb, E. L. 16:181
Cobb, Edwin 7:90
Cobb, Elisha 7:56
Cobb, F. M. 15:189
Cobb, Franklin B. 13:15
Cobb, G. 3:44
Cobb, G. S. 25:318
Cobb, George W. 9:117;
  27:30
Cobb, H. H. 17:387
Cobb, Henry 11:200
Cobb, Henry E. 25:24
Cobb, I. 24:110
Cobb, J. B. 25:155
Cobb, J. C. 15:85
Cobb, J. H. 1:24
Cobb, J. L. 1:120
Cobb, J. S. 19:61
Cobb, James 3:44; 22:294
Cobb, James A. 6:28;
  22:246
Cobb, James C. 12:68
Cobb, John 21:315
Cobb, John T. 18:393;
  22:461

Cobb, Joseph H. 23:86
Cobb, Lawrence W.
  17:259
Cobb, Levi 25:155
Cobb, M. C. 21:315
Cobb, Marion 17:94
Cobb, N. S. 9:141
Cobb, Newton 11:421
Cobb, Perry 14:6
Cobb, R. C. 26:122
Cobb, Samuel 23:308
Cobb, Sidney 1:23
Cobb, Silas 24:90
Cobb, Walter S. 21:315
Cobb, William 1:121;
  17:165
Cobb, William T. 12:16
Cobban, Frank 20:145
Cobbern, N. 3:44
Cobbett, Jamison 9:239
Cobbett, Sebastian 11:25
Cobbett, William R. 10:46
Cobble, J. C. 20:226
Cobble, John C. 10:46
Cobble, W. M. 18:47
Cobbs, William 12:16
Cobbs, William J. 22:119
Cobder, John 18:188
Cobeam, S. L. 15:120
Cobean, S. L. 12:121
Cobel, James L. 22:461
Cobel, Levi 22:184
Coben, Charles M. 10:46
Cobert, F. C. 3:44
Cobes, S. 11:300
Cobey, Delaney 10:204
Cobiant, --- 11:218
Cobin, J. M. 3:44
Cobin, John 4:17
Coblage, C. 14:47
Coble, Jacob 21:66
Cobleigh, H. E. 25:25
Cobleigh, S. W. 1:122
Coblentz, W. H. H.
  11:140
Coblin, H. C. 26:154
Coborn, Dallas 8:12
Coborn, Guy 9:129
Cobran, H. 16:290
Cobran, K. 12:86
Cobridge, James 17:429
Cobrock, Thomas 17:231
Cobtney, I. 8:62
Coburg, W. C. 3:44
Coburn, C. M. 1:23
Coburn, Charles H. 4:17
Coburn, D. F. 18:27
Coburn, F. J. 25:21
Coburn, George 22:507
Coburn, Guy 27:28
Coburn, H. 16:181

Coburn, Henry 23:120
Coburn, Isaiah 13:15
Coburn, J. C. 14:47
Coburn, James 22:294
Coburn, James A. 22:25
Coburn, Jesse 16:117
Coburn, John 16:26;
  21:21; 23:24
Coburn, Milton 11:55
Coburn, Moses 9:50
Coburn, S. 13:130
Coburn, S. C. 21:315
Coburn, S. M. 22:332
Coburn, Samuel 21:66
Coburn, Virgil 9:42;
  26:122
Coburn, W. T. 12:68;
  15:54
Coburn, William 7:90;
  22:70
Coche, B. 14:47
Cochems, John 9:77;
  26:18
Cochrael, Thomas 17:147
Cochraham, A. 13:85
Cochrahan, A. 14:6
Cochrain, James E.
  25:155
Cochran, --- 21:207
Cochran, Andrew J.
  22:475
Cochran, B. T. 14:151
Cochran, C. 3:44
Cochran, C. H. 24:15
Cochran, Cementous
  22:70
Cochran, Charles 23:138
Cochran, D. S. 25:294
Cochran, David 17:287
Cochran, Edward 11:54;
  20:6
Cochran, G. 21:120
Cochran, G. W. 14:295;
  17:477; 27:31
Cochran, H. 14:47; 26:19
Cochran, H. C. 14:151
Cochran, Henry 19:289;
  20:39
Cochran, Isam 23:290
Cochran, J. 16:181
Cochran, J. H. 2:8; 25:20
Cochran, J. S. 22:475
Cochran, Jacob 22:184
Cochran, James 3:44;
  13:15
Cochran, James F. 15:85
Cochran, James W.
  22:418
Cochran, John 3:44; 4:17;
  5:50; 6:20; 8:82;
  14:268; 16:181;

Cochran, John 17:31, 272;
  18:79; 23:10; 25:155
Cochran, Josiah 24:15
Cochran, L. A. 22:70
Cochran, M. 1:26; 3:44
Cochran, Madison 22:461
Cochran, Martin 22:446
Cochran, Oran 10:107;
  20:226
Cochran, Peter 21:222
Cochran, R. H. 4:17
Cochran, Robert 26:122
Cochran, Robert B.
  20:103
Cochran, Robet 9:42
Cochran, S. 9:20
Cochran, S. D. 24:110
Cochran, Samuel B. 11:25
Cochran, Simon 18:303;
  26:94
Cochran, T. 25:155
Cochran, Thomas 10:46;
  20:227
Cochran, W. 21:21
Cochran, W. G. 23:24
Cochran, W. L. 20:179
Cochran, W. T. 22:184
Cochran, W. W. 19:155
Cochran, William 13:15;
  15:189; 22:246
Cochran, William D.
  10:15
Cochran, William M. 19:9
Cochran, William R.
  22:449
Cochran, Wilson 11:199
Cochrane, Henry 21:267
Cochrane, John 8:82;
  15:293
Cochrane, Robert 11:115
Cochrane, Stephen 22:294
Cochrane, Thadeus 8:82
Cochrane, William H.
  23:128
Cochrane, William P.
  10:107; 20:227
Cochren, David 13:127
Cochren, J. E. 25:21
Cochrin, Dennis 11:200
Cock, Alfred 21:247
Cock, Lewis 8:38; 26:156
Cockayne, Henry C. 23:86
Cockburn, Joseph 10:107;
  20:227
Cocker, A. E. 1:119
Cocker, C. 25:155
Cockeran, J. 25:155
Cockerel, William 21:165
Cockerell, Abraham 9:20
Cockerell, J. F. 22:476
Cockerhan, D. M. 20:227

Cockerhan, William 17:31
Cockerhand, William
  13:85
Cockeril, M. 16:181
Cockerill, William 8:100
Cockerrum, James M.
  22:246
Cockerton, Benjamin F.
  10:90; 20:227
Cockesham, David M.
  10:46
Cockingham, S. 1:22
Cockoran, J. 14:47
Cockraft, A. 14:47
Cockran, E. G. 21:315
Cockran, J. S. 19:9
Cockran, James 11:83
Cockran, John 5:12;
  15:165
Cockran, M. P. 19:9
Cockran, William 12:152
Cockrane, William 15:347
Cockrell, George 8:104
Cockrell, Israel 21:267
Cockrell, N. 24:15
Cockrell, William A.
  15:54
Cockrell, William G.
  24:177
Cockrill, Israel 21:211
Cockrill, William W.
  17:462
Cockrow, B. 14:47
Cocks, William 13:124
Cockson, Isaiah 9:141
Cockson, J. 3:44
Cocktilo, L. C. G. 11:26
Cocoinne, John 18:79
Cocomne, John 6:15
Cod, William 16:181
Codall, C. A. 16:27
Codd, W. 20:227
Coddington, Alfred P.
  11:285
Coddington, Elting 27:30
Coddington, Samuel F.
  19:9
Coddington, W. J. 3:44
Coddington, William 3:44
Coddle, T. 22:165
Coddon, O. 1:121
Code, Christian 18:275
Code, Garrett 24:92
Code, John 9:141; 27:26
Coder, D. 1:118
Coder, E. 3:44
Coder, John D. 12:16
Coder, Robert 10:46
Codill, Peasny 16:181
Codinson, E. H. 14:153
Codle, Hamilton 22:246

Codman, Cornelius 9:117
Codray, F. 12:86
Codron, Anthony 17:18
Codwell, Lewis M. 20:34
Codwell, Warren 18:205
Cody, Jay 7:90
Cody, John 7:90; 20:227
Cody, Lyman H. 4:17
Cody, Stephen 16:84
Cody, William 19:155;
    21:251
Cody, William H. 22:246
Coe, Alsan 15:54
Coe, Caesar 22:294
Coe, E. J. 19:61
Coe, Elmer 10:107;
    20:227
Coe, George W. 3:44
Coe, H. M. J. 25:318
Coe, John H. 18:108
Coe, William 20:122
Coen, Michael 15:189
Coen, Nicholas 22:25
Coen, William 9:77
Coens, George 7:22
Coenzler, P. J. 11:14
Coer, James B. 25:25
Cofam, W. 3:45
Cofer, Henry C. 22:419
Coferth, J. C. 26:22
Cofey, Joseph M. 19:331
Coff, Adam 6:24
Coff, Charles 25:24
Coff, J. M. 14:48
Coff, James 3:45
Coffa, Joshua 18:108
Coffe, James 19:61
Coffe, Samuel 5:37
Coffee, C. C. 11:326
Coffee, Cornelius 11:321
Coffee, D. 19:236
Coffee, Daniel 9:172
Coffee, Frank 17:50
Coffee, I. 9:141
Coffee, J. 19:155
Coffee, J. G. 16:26
Coffee, J. K. 25:155
Coffee, James 21:66
Coffee, Jesse 7:67; 21:98
Coffee, John 18:27
Coffee, John W. 12:16
Coffee, Mayor 22:294
Coffee, Miles 17:173
Coffee, P. 19:249
Coffee, Pat 14:151
Coffee, Patrick 9:172
Coffee, S. 25:155
Coffee, Thomas 24:165
Coffee, William T. 24:165
Coffeen, A. H. 1:25
Coffeen, Moses J. 17:359

Coffein, Francis 23:24
Coffel, John 10:158
Coffelt, Daniel 10:151
Coffeman, T. 16:290
Coffen, J. 13:81
Coffer, Franklin 7:22;
    14:334
Coffer, Joshua B. 22:165
Coffery, M. 15:189
Coffery, Martin 7:90
Coffes, Charles M. 21:315
Coffett, Daniel 10:178
Coffett, George L. 20:227
Coffey, Bonapart 17:313
Coffey, Christopher C.
    20:16
Coffey, Cleveland 22:449,
    499
Coffey, Copernicus H.
    23:62
Coffey, Daniel 19:273
Coffey, Daniel F. 11:186
Coffey, Henry 17:13
Coffey, James 12:68
Coffey, James F. 17:318
Coffey, Jeremiah 24:75
Coffey, John 9:66
Coffey, Joseph 26:22
Coffey, Leander H.
    22:119
Coffey, Lewis 9:96
Coffey, Stephen R. 22:70
Coffey, Virgil 17:259
Coffield, William 19:155
Coffill, Andrew J. 13:60
Coffin, A. R. 3:45
Coffin, Abram 9:129;
    27:31
Coffin, Albert B. 4:17
Coffin, Albert G. 18:406
Coffin, Frank 16:77
Coffin, G. 24:213
Coffin, George H. 15:283;
    19:61
Coffin, Gorham 16:84
Coffin, H. F. 15:31
Coffin, J. 11:237; 16:181
Coffin, James 8:82
Coffin, L. F. 15:358;
    19:62
Coffin, L. M. 13:106
Coffin, M. O. 18:27
Coffin, Nelson H. 21:315
Coffin, R. 24:107
Coffin, Robert G. 10:204
Coffin, S. B. 25:155
Coffin, Simeon B. 5:12
Coffin, Stephen 7:90
Coffin, W. H. 18:233
Coffin, W. L. 25:155
Coffin, W. Y. 14:152

Coffin, Walter S. 5:12
Coffin, William H. 26:21
Coffin, William O. 10:158
Coffinger, Joseph 10:7
Coffit, George L. 10:107
Coffland, Jacob 10:46;
    20:227
Coffman, F. 3:44
Coffman, H. H. 21:21
Coffman, Isaac H. 21:98
Coffman, J. W. 12:121;
    15:121
Coffman, John 10:46;
    20:227; 23:24
Coffman, Joseph 7:120;
    17:417
Coffman, Joshua J. 22:421
Coffman, L. T. 11:118
Coffman, Lewis 21:267
Coffman, Maurice M.
    22:421
Coffman, Nicholas 22:449
Coffman, S. A. 19:266
Coffman, S. E. 9:172;
    19:280
Coffman, Solomon 9:172
Coffman, T. H. 23:301
Coffman, V. 23:306
Coffman, William 3:45;
    21:222; 22:184
Coffman, William B.
    21:222
Cofford, R. S. 15:150
Coffran, Augustine 27:32
Coffran, John 4:17
Coffrey, Edward 25:332
Coffrin, E. E. 1:26
Coffron, L. F. 12:95
Coffy, William H. 8:12;
    18:127
Cofield, P. 12:81; 16:290
Cofield, Peter 7:120
Cofman, Conrad 11:190
Cofman, J. H. 23:24
Cofman, Nathan 6:30
Cofman, Nathaniel 25:318
Cofren, Kendall H. 16:80
Coga, Nathaniel 23:86
Cogan, Benjamin 21:49
Cogan, J. B. 1:117
Cogan, Jacob 17:129;
    24:190
Cogan, John 13:15;
    18:108; 27:28
Cogan, Thomas 6:30
Cogan, W. H. 25:156
Cogan, William H. 5:12
Cogan, William J. 17:90
Cogel, Owen 18:205

Coger, Jackson 17:129; 24:191
Coger, James 17:129; 24:191
Cogeswell, Richard 17:73
Coggbin, H. J. 14:48
Cogger, W. 3:45
Coggin, Launcelot 24:92
Coggins, John F. 21:315
Coggins, John T. 7:120
Coggswel, John 4:17
Coggswell, Ebenezer R. 22:470
Coggswell, J. C. 22:402
Cogill, John M. 21:84
Cogins, Joshua 14:152
Cogle, J. H. 9:50
Cogn, E. 14:48
Cognie, Edward 25:318
Cogsell, Gideon 22:184
Cogsley, H. J. 1:25
Cogswell, Amos 16:91
Cogswell, E. 21:315
Cogswell, Frederick 12:167
Cogswell, George 16:117
Cogswell, Isaiah 10:46
Cogswell, John 11:285
Cogswell, Joshua 20:227
Cogswell, Marion 9:33
Cogswell, R. 1:22
Cogswell, S. 3:45
Cogswell, Thomas 1:120
Cogwell, Watson 15:189
Cohagen, J. H. 3:45
Cohall, N. 25:156
Cohan, D. 3:45
Cohan, J. 25:20
Cohart, David 22:332
Cohart, George 14:240
Cohash, John 3:45
Cohasky, Nelson A. 7:48
Cohee, Benjamin 23:62
Cohen, John W. 23:138
Cohen, W. 21:315
Cohen, William 7:90
Coher, David 24:177
Cohill, Daniel 13:79; 16:181
Cohill, J. 1:24
Cohle, F. 13:62
Cohlhepp, Kaspar 20:132
Cohn, B. 23:255
Cohn, E. 14:48
Cohn, J. W. 17:19
Cohniff, J. J. 16:91
Cohoe, David 17:450
Cohoon, A. 25:156
Cohoon, Samuel 22:70
Cohoon, Simon 1:119
Cohotze, John 4:17

Cohrit, S. 14:48
Cohron, James H. 22:119
Cohrs, Henry 21:315
Cohurst, John 20:227
Cohvell, Robert 9:71
Cohxy, Samuel 18:272
Coil, Barney 22:518
Coil, Isaac 1:23
Coil, Isaac C. 22:25
Coil, J. T. 1:121
Coil, N. N. 11:139
Coil, Oliver H. 22:119
Coil, P. 3:45; 13:85
Coil, Peter H. 23:138
Coil, Samuel W. 17:77
Coile, James 22:448
Coile, P. 14:6
Coilen, P. 14:314
Coilie, William 13:106
Coines, J. A. 9:50
Coistum, W. 3:45
Coit, Benjamin J. 20:179
Coit, David W. 10:158
Coit, William H. 13:15
Coke, Joseph 22:25
Coke, Sandy 21:267
Coke, Silas M. 23:97
Cokely, A. 25:21
Cokely, George 21:315
Cokely, John 21:315
Cokely, Nathan 24:75
Coker, Jonathan 10:107; 20:227
Coker, Smith 22:246
Col---l, H. William 25:22
Colam, F. 8:12
Colaman, John 26:21
Colan, Frederick 3:45
Colan, Joseph 5:12
Coland, Tom 26:21
Coland, Tony 18:233
Coland, William 18:139
Colany, Charles 21:98
Colart, Michael 18:127
Colb, L. 14:48
Colbath, Alfred 17:394
Colbath, G. W. 1:21
Colbath, Richard N. 13:16
Colbatt, James 10:158
Colbaugh, Charles W. 22:397
Colbeck, George 7:23
Colber, Ambrose 14:152
Colbern, D. C. 25:156
Colberson, J. J. 27:25
Colbert, Albert 11:338
Colbert, Alfred M. 17:453; 24:183
Colbert, Benjamin 9:219; 18:364
Colbert, Charles H. 24:91

Colbert, David 10:147; 18:47
Colbert, E. 1:118
Colbert, J. G. 9:219; 18:364
Colbert, James 22:246
Colbert, John 8:104
Colbert, John W. 4:17
Colbert, Joseph 17:309
Colbert, M. 21:315
Colbert, Nelson 18:79
Colbert, Thomas E. 8:12; 18:127
Colbert, W. 14:240
Colbfy, Will F. 25:156
Colborn, W. H. 1:21
Colbourn, C. 9:66
Colburn, --- 15:189; 23:245
Colburn, A. 3:44
Colburn, C. 3:44
Colburn, Chandler E. 16:366
Colburn, George 1:22; 16:139
Colburn, George W. 5:12
Colburn, J. 1:119
Colburn, J. S. 13:85; 14:6
Colburn, James 21:267
Colburn, John 17:215
Colburn, Lewis 20:177
Colburn, Norman 21:251
Colburn, Robert 23:24
Colburn, Thomas 3:46; 22:332
Colburn, Warren 3:46
Colburn, William E. 14:152
Colburne, Daniel M. 4:17
Colburns, Lorenzo O. 7:23
Colbut, James 19:155
Colbut, Nelson 6:15
Colby, --- 25:26
Colby, A. C. 14:319; 25:279
Colby, A. D. 17:153
Colby, A. J. 16:290; 19:232
Colby, Andrew J. 9:172
Colby, Benjamin A. 14:152
Colby, Charles 9:172; 19:232
Colby, Charles B. 21:315
Colby, Charles M. 17:403
Colby, Daniel F. 9:141
Colby, Daniel L. 27:28
Colby, E. 26:18
Colby, Ebenezer 9:77
Colby, Enos A. 22:161

Colby, Foster 24:61
Colby, G. A. 9:172; 19:236
Colby, G. F. 21:315
Colby, George 8:113; 21:315
Colby, George H. 17:403
Colby, H. A. 1:121
Colby, Henry 2:9; 7:67
Colby, Henry A. 1:24
Colby, Ira 17:31
Colby, Isaac 11:190
Colby, J. 15:95
Colby, J. C. 1:26, 118
Colby, J. G. 25:156
Colby, J. J. 15:189
Colby, J. T. 25:156
Colby, Jesse F. 5:12
Colby, John 22:139
Colby, John M. 3:46; 7:56
Colby, L. J. 13:85
Colby, Orlando 21:88
Colby, R. L. 25:24
Colby, Solomon D. 4:17
Colby, T. W. 7:23
Colby, Thomas H. 21:21
Colby, W. A. 26:18
Colby, William 16:26
Colby, William J. 17:263
Colby, Z. 1:122
Colcazier, Philip 23:278
Colchartbert, William 27:33
Colclaser, G. W. 16:290
Colclasure, Noah 18:364
Colclazer, Joseph 21:222
Colclazier, Philip 23:278
Colclusure, Noah 9:219
Colcord, Louis 16:26
Cold, William M. 15:351
Coldboth, Charles 21:215
Coldburn, Grey 9:129
Coldecote, C. W. 21:315
Colden, P. T. 10:204
Colden, William 17:173
Colder, Clarence H. 4:17
Colderon, William B. 17:445
Coldhan, John 7:23
Coldier, A. 8:12; 26:153
Colding, C. H. 22:277
Coldiron, Henry 22:119
Coldiron, Jesse 8:12; 18:127
Coldiron, William B. 24:166
Coldiron, William S. 17:202
Coldron, Adam 12:17
Coldron, J. 15:121
Coldron, Jacob 20:182

Coldstream, George 21:315
Coldwell, A. F. 17:337
Coldwell, H. 17:161
Coldwell, James W. 21:98
Coldwell, John 22:71
Coldwell, W. 17:173
Coldwell, William 3:46; 8:38
Coldwell, William S. 22:461
Cole, --- --- 15:258
Cole, A. 1:119; 15:190
Cole, A. B. 1:21
Cole, A. C. 15:157
Cole, A. H. 3:45; 9:172; 16:77; 19:280
Cole, A. J. 13:106; 21:21
Cole, A. M. 14:152
Cole, A. W. 10:46; 20:227
Cole, Abraham 17:50
Cole, Alexander 22:139
Cole, Alfred 11:385
Cole, Alvah 16:26
Cole, Ambrose 19:9
Cole, Ambrose B. 24:92
Cole, Ambu C. 20:227
Cole, Ambue C. 10:107
Cole, Amos E. 13:15
Cole, Andrew 11:54
Cole, Andrew A. 9:108
Cole, B. 3:45; 16:181
Cole, Benjamin 13:56; 20:29
Cole, Benjamin F. 23:103
Cole, Benjamin H. 9:71
Cole, Benjamin P. 10:46; 20:227
Cole, Benjamin S. 17:348
Cole, Benjamin W. 4:17
Cole, Burrows 22:170
Cole, Byron 4:17
Cole, C. 1:119
Cole, C. C. 9:77; 26:17
Cole, C. H. 27:25
Cole, C. S. 12:68; 15:31
Cole, Caleb 17:241
Cole, Campbell 15:65
Cole, Carole P. 25:23
Cole, Charles 10:46; 20:227; 21:66; 22:294; 27:25
Cole, Charles D. 9:101
Cole, Charles E. 23:15
Cole, Charles F. 11:122
Cole, Charles L. 10:15
Cole, Charles P. 22:461
Cole, Christopher 27:33
Cole, Consider 4:17
Cole, Corwin 10:171; 19:155

Cole, D. 13:76, 85; 14:48; 15:340; 16:366
Cole, D. A. 25:25
Cole, D. D. 16:278
Cole, D. E. 11:421
Cole, D. S. 11:140
Cole, D. T. 1:121
Cole, Daniel 1:24; 9:172; 19:233
Cole, Daniel M. 16:26
Cole, David 17:173
Cole, Dorran 16:181
Cole, E. 1:122
Cole, E. B. 3:45
Cole, E. J. 1:119
Cole, E. L. 21:66
Cole, Eben 1:23
Cole, Edward 21:251; 22:246
Cole, Edwin S. 8:117; 19:315
Cole, Emery 9:50
Cole, Emory 4:17
Cole, Ephraim T. 12:16
Cole, Ethan 23:62
Cole, Ezekiel 14:152
Cole, F. 25:24, 156
Cole, F. A. 26:19
Cole, F. B. 14:152
Cole, F. F. 16:181
Cole, F. H. 1:25
Cole, Ferguson 24:15
Cole, Francis A. 18:275
Cole, Frank 5:12
Cole, Franklin 16:91
Cole, Frederick 8:113
Cole, G. 1:122
Cole, G. B. 13:106
Cole, G. H. 20:227
Cole, G. T. 19:226
Cole, G. W. 1:21; 21:315
Cole, George 3:45; 11:385; 17:31; 18:27, 233; 26:21
Cole, George A. 16:181; 22:332
Cole, George B. 13:15; 16:26
Cole, George H. 18:334
Cole, George M. 3:45
Cole, George W. 4:17; 7:120; 17:212; 22:71
Cole, Giles E. 10:107; 20:227
Cole, H. 15:150; 25:156
Cole, H. H. 11:138
Cole, H. O. 3:45
Cole, Harvey L. 22:419
Cole, Henry 17:63; 18:233; 22:139, 294; 26:21

Cole, Henry A. 18:393
Cole, Henry O. 1:21
Cole, Hezekiah V. 24:165
Cole, Ira 5:12; 25:156
Cole, Isaac 11:139;
    23:103, 290
Cole, Isaac D. 11:259
Cole, Isaac H. 4:17
Cole, J. 16:181; 25:156
Cole, J. A. 7:8
Cole, J. B. 1:25
Cole, J. C. 3:45; 19:62
Cole, J. E. 18:364
Cole, J. H. 10:46; 11:139;
    15:297; 16:181
Cole, J. J. 27:25
Cole, J. L. 13:85; 14:6
Cole, J. N. 15:5
Cole, J. W. 26:19
Cole, Jacob H. 22:170
Cole, Jacob J. 7:90
Cole, James 11:395;
    15:318; 16:290;
    19:62; 21:115
Cole, James B. 1:22
Cole, James C. 11:25;
    22:246
Cole, James F. 17:404
Cole, James J. 27:25
Cole, James O. 19:155
Cole, James W. 18:205;
    23:62
Cole, Jason W. 21:315
Cole, Jeremiah 5:12;
    22:170
Cole, Jeremiah F. 18:205
Cole, John 1:26, 191;
    3:45; 4:17; 7:67;
    11:25, 55; 21:267;
    22:71; 23:138
Cole, John B. 23:62
Cole, John F. 12:17
Cole, John H. 7:56
Cole, John J. 3:45
Cole, John S. 9:172;
    21:21
Cole, John T. 21:315
Cole, John W. 7:90; 9:77;
    11:326; 21:222, 240;
    22:246
Cole, Johnston A. 22:184
Cole, Joseph A. 20:122
Cole, L. 1:121
Cole, L. B. 1:24
Cole, L. N. 1:26; 18:27
Cole, L. R. 18:27
Cole, Lewis H. 13:15
Cole, Lithan 21:315
Cole, M. 3:45; 15:104;
    17:153; 20:227
Cole, M. D. 25:21

Cole, Martin L. 4:17
Cole, Martin R. 23:62
Cole, Merriman 7:120
Cole, Michael 10:46
Cole, Milton 22:332
Cole, Miro 18:27
Cole, Moses 16:139
Cole, Myron 10:46;
    20:227
Cole, N. M. 21:315
Cole, Nathan 11:380
Cole, Nelson 1:23
Cole, Noah 9:163
Cole, Ollis I. 12:16
Cole, Ora 19:9
Cole, Orville B. 15:54
Cole, Owen 20:39
Cole, P. A. 13:62
Cole, P. B. 27:27
Cole, P. H. 27:25
Cole, Peter 22:294
Cole, Philip 25:318
Cole, R. J. 1:24
Cole, R. S. 3:45
Cole, Richard 21:315
Cole, Riley 13:15
Cole, Robert 17:267;
    22:476
Cole, Robert C. 11:140
Cole, Rufus 15:90
Cole, S. 1:21; 21:21
Cole, S. F. 18:364
Cole, S. L. 21:207
Cole, S. M. 9:77
Cole, Samuel 22:71
Cole, Sandy 21:211
Cole, Sidney 22:25
Cole, Simon P. 15:172
Cole, Stephen 7:56
Cole, Stephen R. 7:90
Cole, T. 3:45
Cole, T. A. 18:233
Cole, Theodore 12:7
Cole, Thomas 11:26;
    17:77
Cole, Thomas D. 14:48
Cole, Volney A. 15:90
Cole, W. 5:50; 15:31;
    16:181
Cole, W. A. 9:50; 19:249
Cole, W. C. 3:45; 15:157
Cole, W. H. 3:45; 15:85;
    21:315
Cole, W. J. 1:122
Cole, W. L. 25:25
Cole, W. M. 7:90
Cole, W. W. 15:172;
    16:366
Cole, Walker 21:315
Cole, Walter 7:120
Cole, Warren E. 23:284

Cole, Washington 17:191
Cole, Washington F.
    22:165
Cole, William 6:24; 8:12,
    104; 11:418; 15:304;
    18:47; 20:122;
    21:315; 22:246, 419;
    24:75; 25:156
Cole, William A. 9:172;
    16:139
Cole, William H. 1:22, 24;
    4:17; 12:68; 15:190;
    16:139; 20:106
Cole, William M. 24:49,
    157
Cole, William N. 20:95
Cole, William Q. 4:17
Cole, William R. 8:12;
    18:127
Cole, William T. 20:95
Cole, William W. 24:65
Colebaugh, N. 3:46
Colebuck, C. 22:119
Colecliff, Joseph 7:23
Colef, William 14:48
Colegrove, I. 23:138
Colegrove, W. 1:118
Colehouse, John 22:232
Colein, John 10:46
Colelaser, G. W. 12:92
Colelesh, Charles 19:62
Coleley, A. 3:46
Coleman, --- 15:277;
    21:315; 23:303
Coleman, A. 3:46; 14:48;
    19:62; 26:19, 122
Coleman, Absalom 9:77
Coleman, Adam 17:346
Coleman, Alex 26:155
Coleman, Alex. 8:38
Coleman, Alexander
    22:294
Coleman, Allen 7:120
Coleman, Amons 11:385
Coleman, Anthony 6:24
Coleman, Archie 18:233;
    26:21
Coleman, Azel 16:26
Coleman, B. 7:48; 9:114
Coleman, Benjamin A.
    20:122
Coleman, C. 3:46; 25:25
Coleman, C. H. 20:142
Coleman, Charles 12:63;
    15:6, 13; 16:181
Coleman, Clark 2:9
Coleman, D. 22:332
Coleman, Daniel 23:62;
    26:122
Coleman, Daniel C. 21:66
Coleman, Daniel T. 16:26

Coleman, David 17:173
Coleman, David C. 23:86
Coleman, Dennis 24:165
Coleman, E. 25:156
Coleman, E. J. 18:27
Coleman, Edward 22:294
Coleman, Elisha W.
  21:315
Coleman, Ezra 5:12
Coleman, Frank 26:22
Coleman, G. 3:45
Coleman, George 7:23;
  8:77; 9:199; 17:129,
  173; 21:22; 22:294,
  475; 24:190
Coleman, George W.
  22:419
Coleman, H. 16:181
Coleman, H. H. 8:62;
  26:153
Coleman, Henry 12:64;
  15:4; 17:129;
  18:173; 24:190;
  25:26
Coleman, I. 17:129
Coleman, Israel 27:143
Coleman, J. 3:45, 46;
  14:6, 152; 16:267;
  21:22; 24:190
Coleman, J. B. 11:331
Coleman, J. C. 13:85;
  21:315
Coleman, J. W. 14:296;
  17:471; 27:31
Coleman, Jackson 6:24;
  9:206; 18:65
Coleman, James 1:120;
  6:24; 14:152;
  18:108; 20:111
Coleman, James N. 22:25
Coleman, James R. 18:108
Coleman, Jeremiah 11:400
Coleman, Jerry M. 22:71
Coleman, Joel 20:6
Coleman, John 10:107;
  15:190; 17:173;
  18:233, 275; 20:227;
  21:84, 129; 22:184;
  26:20; 27:29
Coleman, John L. 9:71
Coleman, Jonas 22:518
Coleman, Jordan 18:434
Coleman, Joseph J. 8:82;
  18:215
Coleman, L. N. 22:184
Coleman, M. 10:154;
  21:315
Coleman, Mat 17:335
Coleman, Miles 22:294
Coleman, Ned 22:294
Coleman, Othe 6:28

Coleman, Patrick 17:109
Coleman, Perry 7:120
Coleman, Peter 19:62;
  20:227
Coleman, Peter A. 10:46
Coleman, R. 13:106
Coleman, Reuben 22:294
Coleman, Richard 7:15
Coleman, Robert 22:139,
  294
Coleman, Robert A.
  23:188
Coleman, S. 5:37; 25:156
Coleman, S. F. 1:25
Coleman, Samuel M.
  24:65
Coleman, Thomas 8:38;
  9:199; 10:176; 17:50;
  19:280; 25:156;
  26:155
Coleman, W. 16:181
Coleman, W. B. 18:233;
  26:19
Coleman, Washington
  4:65
Coleman, William 4:65;
  9:206; 10:107; 11:55,
  321, 374; 12:48;
  20:227; 21:315;
  22:71, 294; 23:62;
  24:61; 25:156
Coleman, William C.
  11:90
Coleman, William D.
  22:119
Coleman, William M.
  20:139
Coleman, William T.
  17:109
Coleman, Wilson 22:294
Coleman, Zedor 21:98
Colenck, N. 16:181
Colens, John 9:172
Coleon, J. 25:156
Coler, Jeff 9:206
Coler, P. W. 1:120
Colerick, N. 15:317
Coles, C. 1:118; 11:300
Coles, D. 22:294
Coles, David 18:275
Coles, J. W. 3:45
Coles, James A. 6:28
Coles, John W. 9:77
Coles, Ludwig 12:17
Coles, Philip 10:46;
  20:227
Coles, Samuel 5:50;
  25:156
Coles, W. J. 11:25
Coles, William 3:45;
  18:127

Coles, William J. 18:215
Coles, William M.
  15:351; 19:340
Colesberry, Ernest J. B.
  23:24
Colesman, Corn 6:12
Coleson, John 11:411
Colewell, B. 3:45
Colewell, T. J. 21:267
Colewell, William 18:109
Coley, I. P. 18:108
Coley, R. C. 12:86
Coley, W. 25:156
Coley, William 5:12
Colfin, John 14:152
Colflish, Charles 15:325
Colgan, B. 8:60
Colgan, Brannan 12:170
Colgan, James M. 21:135
Colgan, W. 15:16
Colgan, William 12:68
Colgden, Michael 25:25
Colghamon, Thomas 5:12
Colgin, M. 1:25
Colglazier, David B.
  17:313
Colgrove, Henry A.
  19:155
Colgrove, James 21:315
Colgrove, James A.
  22:119
Colgrove, John 21:186
Colgrove, John S. 21:315
Colgrove, S. H. 9:141;
  27:26
Colgrove, T. D. 1:23
Colgrove, William 14:152
Colhane, Patrick 4:17
Colider, E. 15:190
Colieas, Henry 22:246
Colier, A. 9:77
Colier, D. 15:16
Colier, Jacob H. 14:152
Colier, John J. 3:46
Colier, William H. 11:27
Colier, William T. 10:107;
  20:227
Coligan, W. 16:181
Colin, A. J. 17:165
Colin, George W. 9:141
Colin, M. 3:45
Colinder, William 5:37
Colings, S. 19:62
Colins, A. J. 3:45
Colins, Lawrence 9:77
Colitz, Charles 15:263
Colks, W. H. 13:88
Coll, H. H. 14:240
Coll, John 14:152
Coll, Robert 9:206

Coll, William 16:366; 17:107
Collagan, M. 3:46
Collage, George 7:48
Collamer, Solomon 1:22
Collamon, Foster H. 13:16
Collamore, Foster H. 16:26
Collamore, S. E. 9:141
Collamore, W. P. 9:141
Collamore, Warren P. 27:26
Colland, A. D. 1:24
Colland, James H. 1:24
Colland, James L. 12:121
Colland, John W. 20:227
Collander, Henry 17:352
Collar, Charles 24:15
Collar, David 15:172
Collar, E. 3:46
Collar, H. 3:46
Collar, John 10:107; 20:227
Collar, John G. 20:227
Collar, Thomas 15:31
Collard, Elijah 10:107; 20:227
Collard, F. N. 21:315
Collard, James L. 15:121
Collard, John 13:106
Collawin, J. 8:46
Collay, B. J. 5:12
Collection, --- 19:232
Colledge, S. 25:156
Colleig, W. 10:186
Collen, Lewis 13:15
Collen, Owen 19:249
Collen, S. 20:227
Collens, M. 19:236
Coller, Henry 22:71
Coller, Jacob 23:10
Coller, William 1:120
Collerin, Thomas 12:17
Collers, S. 24:75
Collesten, B. F. 26:156
Collet, J. C. 11:138
Collet, James D. 22:71
Colleth, William R. 20:227
Collett, George 14:48
Collett, J. A. 17:165
Collett, James 3:46
Collett, James W. 22:476
Collett, Jeremiah 11:421
Collett, Stephen W. 20:47
Colley, Charles H. 4:17
Colley, Isaac S. 17:77
Colley, J. R. 17:50
Colley, James P. 21:14
Colley, Robert H. 9:213
Colley, W. 14:254; 15:157

Colley, W. A. 9:77
Collhart, William 14:48
Collick, I. 19:44
Collidge, H. D. 14:26
Collier, A. B. 14:152
Collier, Alexander 10:46
Collier, Benjamin 22:294
Collier, C. P. 20:227
Collier, C. Q. B. 20:227
Collier, C. S. 7:90
Collier, Charles 18:215
Collier, Commodore P. 10:46
Collier, Elihu 8:82
Collier, Elisha 21:66
Collier, Elshuer 8:46
Collier, Frank 7:90; 8:38; 21:267; 26:155
Collier, Gaston 18:47
Collier, H. J. 11:259
Collier, Horace 15:121
Collier, J. M. 24:15
Collier, J. S. 22:402
Collier, James 1:22; 10:107; 20:227
Collier, John 8:38; 21:267; 26:155
Collier, Lewis 21:147
Collier, Milton 11:199
Collier, Thomas 22:165
Collier, Wesley 17:63
Collier, William 10:27; 19:300; 27:32
Colliers, Allen Ethan 18:303
Colliers, Ethan Allen 26:95
Collihan, Patrick 15:31
Collin, J. 2:9
Collin, James 17:173
Collin, John 3:45; 14:152
Collin, Levi 5:37
Collin, William 3:45
Collinbine, P. 14:48
Colling, N. 18:173
Collings, George 17:267
Collings, George W. 21:49
Collings, J. A. 14:48
Collings, J. S. 18:108
Collings, James L. 22:475
Collings, John 21:315
Collingwood, D. 15:190
Collingwood, George 23:138
Collingwood, William 26:155
Collins, --- 15:31, 190
Collins, A. 1:117; 3:45; 5:50; 14:48, 296; 15:297; 17:473;

Collins, A. 25:156; 27:31
Collins, A. C. 8:12; 18:127
Collins, A. E. 15:190
Collins, A. F. 6:30; 25:318
Collins, Aaron 16:366; 17:235
Collins, Achilles 22:119
Collins, Adam C. 23:138
Collins, Albert F. 25:318
Collins, Alfred 17:129, 313; 24:191
Collins, Allen 9:20
Collins, Alphens 10:171
Collins, Alpheus 19:155
Collins, Anderson 18:233; 26:20
Collins, Andrew 10:15
Collins, Andrew J. 23:10
Collins, Archiball 16:181
Collins, Asa L. 23:62
Collins, B. 14:48
Collins, B. F. 14:130; 20:55
Collins, Barney 21:9
Collins, Benjamin 7:120; 21:315; 22:9
Collins, C. 3:45; 9:159; 19:280; 23:24
Collins, C. C. 14:48
Collins, C. L. 18:65
Collins, C. R. 3:45
Collins, Carl 17:247
Collins, Charles 1:22; 9:172, 206; 17:173
Collins, Charles M. 22:277
Collins, Charles O. 10:46; 20:227; 25:332
Collins, Charles W. 11:237; 16:77
Collins, Cordillo 16:117
Collins, Cornelius 13:16; 16:26
Collins, Cyrus 18:79
Collins, D. 3:45; 22:246
Collins, D. P. 1:119
Collins, Dan 9:172
Collins, Daniel 4:17
Collins, David 10:46; 20:227
Collins, David W. 16:132
Collins, E. 1:25; 23:138
Collins, E. B. 9:108
Collins, E. F. 13:85
Collins, E. R. 25:295
Collins, Edward 8:12; 18:127
Collins, Edward F. 1:25
Collins, Elijah 8:82

Collins, F. 1:122; 14:6
Collins, F. M. 8:12, 104; 18:127
Collins, Francis 27:29
Collins, Francis M. 11:55; 20:136
Collins, Freeman 23:138
Collins, G. 3:45
Collins, G. B. 8:12, 13
Collins, G. H. 26:18
Collins, G. W. 1:120; 27:25
Collins, Gaston 10:147
Collins, George 14:152; 15:5; 16:131; 18:47; 21:222; 24:37
Collins, George B. 18:127
Collins, George E. 7:90
Collins, George M. 14:152
Collins, George W. 22:139
Collins, Gideon W. 9:15
Collins, H. 1:24; 11:339; 12:121; 14:152, 254
Collins, H. C. 8:62
Collins, H. F. 18:65
Collins, H. P. 13:85; 14:6
Collins, Harry 8:12
Collins, Harvey 24:190
Collins, Henry 3:45; 14:280; 18:127; 22:246, 294; 23:112; 24:92
Collins, Hubbard 21:186
Collins, I. 25:156
Collins, Ira 14:152
Collins, Isaac 5:37; 17:129; 24:189
Collins, J. 1:26; 3:45; 11:326; 12:95; 14:48; 15:190, 358; 19:62, 232, 236; 25:20, 24, 310; 26:19
Collins, J. C. 1:117; 14:48; 26:155
Collins, J. E. 1:25
Collins, J. H. 3:45; 11:118
Collins, J. M. 9:50
Collins, J. R. 21:315
Collins, J. S. 21:22
Collins, J. W. 14:48
Collins, Jacob 4:17
Collins, James 3:45; 4:65; 7:120; 8:121; 9:71, 129; 13:62; 16:26;
Collins, James 18:420; 19:62; 23:112, 178; 27:27
Collins, James H. 21:49
Collins, James M. 1:22

Collins, James W. A. 11:186
Collins, Jeremiah 10:158; 19:155
Collins, John 1:24; 3:45; 7:23, 81, 90; 9:20, 77, 159, 172, 219, 235; 11:400; 14:48; 15:94; 16:164; 17:279, 352; 18:303, 364; 21:9, 315; 22:9, 475; 24:15; 25:156; 26:94; 27:33
Collins, John C. 14:152; 17:241
Collins, John D. 8:104
Collins, John E. 8:104; 11:90
Collins, John H. 23:86
Collins, John J. 1:23
Collins, John P. 9:77; 26:19
Collins, John S. 15:190
Collins, John W. 13:127
Collins, Joseph 8:104; 13:106; 15:326; 19:62
Collins, Joseph P. 10:107; 20:227
Collins, Joshua 23:312
Collins, Josiah 23:240
Collins, L. 16:181; 25:156; 26:18
Collins, L. C. 8:12; 18:127
Collins, Leander 9:96; 25:156
Collins, Lenard 27:143
Collins, Levi 4:17; 7:120
Collins, Lewis 22:71
Collins, Lewis C. 13:129
Collins, Loren 9:77
Collins, Louis 7:90; 21:316
Collins, M. 3:45; 20:174; 21:127; 25:156
Collins, M. N. 25:22
Collins, Martial 9:172
Collins, Martin 5:37
Collins, Mayse S. 23:112
Collins, Melvin 8:12
Collins, Michael 4:17; 10:107; 12:58; 15:165; 20:227; 22:25
Collins, Myron 22:475
Collins, N. 14:319; 23:24; 25:276
Collins, Nicholas 22:332
Collins, O. C. 24:15
Collins, Onesimus 11:55

Collins, Orville 11:104
Collins, Owen 22:332
Collins, P. 27:24
Collins, P. H. 1:117
Collins, Paddy 7:120
Collins, Patrick 4:17; 14:152; 19:9; 20:111
Collins, Peter 9:129; 13:16; 18:424; 24:15; 27:29
Collins, Philip C. 10:144; 19:155
Collins, Poindexter 10:107; 20:227
Collins, R. 3:45; 13:16
Collins, R. F. 26:218
Collins, Richard 17:31; 18:13
Collins, Riley J. 21:316
Collins, Robert 16:26; 25:156
Collins, Rubins 19:44
Collins, Rufus E. 7:74
Collins, Rufus L. F. 17:202
Collins, S. 17:173; 22:246
Collins, S. B. 15:31
Collins, S. F. 9:219
Collins, Samuel 9:108; 11:199; 15:21; 19:290; 20:95
Collins, Solomon 22:500
Collins, Stephen 18:13; 21:316
Collins, Stephens 9:206
Collins, T. 1:119; 3:45
Collins, Thomas 3:45; 10:46, 107, 158; 20:228; 22:332
Collins, Thomas J. 21:49
Collins, Thomas R. 20:228
Collins, Timothy 12:173; 19:62
Collins, Troy 22:246
Collins, W. 3:45; 13:85; 14:6; 22:232
Collins, W. J. 1:120
Collins, W. M. 1:117
Collins, W. W. 15:157
Collins, Warren 7:48
Collins, Warrin J. 11:115
Collins, Washington 13:106
Collins, Whitefield 10:95
Collins, William 1:120, 121; 6:24; 7:120; 9:96, 129; 11:419; 13:124; 14:152; 17:173, 392; 18:109; 19:62, 344; 21:316;

Collins, William 22:246, 499; 23:138, 188; 27:29
Collins, William E. 14:152
Collins, William H. 7:90; 17:348, 498; 20:102; 24:49
Collins, William M. 8:82; 22:419
Collins, William P. 20:103
Collins, Zacharias 7:90
Collinson, Alfred 24:184
Collis, James 10:107; 20:228
Collis, Melloin 18:127
Collison, Arthur 15:273
Collison, George 11:54
Collister, John O. 22:25
Colliston, William 25:271
Collman, J. N. 25:156
Collo, G. T. 18:127
Collom, John A. W. 1:22
Collon, J. L. 15:31
Collon, Joshua 21:316
Collonoy, G. 9:141
Collor, Luther 22:419
Collott, Thomas B. 20:102
Collough, James R. 12:17
Colloway, John 22:402
Collry, Frank 14:240
Collulm, Benjamin 18:233
Collum, Benjamin 26:21
Collum, George 1:24
Collum, Isaiah 24:61
Collum, Peter 24:61
Collum, T. 21:22
Collum, W. M. 17:440
Collum, W. W. 27:25
Collum, William M. 24:151
Collur, John 15:190
Collville, William 8:113
Colly, John M. 19:328
Colly, Lorenzo 19:9
Collyer, A. 1:24
Collyer, David W. 10:107; 20:228
Collyer, J. 3:46
Collyer, James 1:23
Collyer, John 20:228
Colman, A. 9:42
Colman, Charles H. 18:393
Colman, F. 18:127
Colman, J. E. 25:156
Colman, James D. 17:425
Colman, John C. 25:310
Colman, L. A. 14:296; 17:473

Colman, M. 19:155
Colman, Samuel 16:181
Colman, Thomas 7:81; 19:155; 25:295
Colman, Thomas C. 16:181
Colmans, Preston 17:337
Colna, Cunningham 9:71
Colon, Francis M. 10:15
Colon, H. H. 26:18
Colony, Charles 12:17
Colony, J. M. 25:156
Colony, James E. 21:66
Color, Ansberry 4:65
Colors, Jacob 4:17
Colp, Albert 22:170
Colpetzer, George 22:232
Colran, James 10:95
Colrige, James 24:213
Colser, R. 1:123
Colsgrove, J. W. 1:120
Colshear, William 21:222
Colsheir, William 9:172
Colshier, William 19:277
Colson, A. G. 17:63
Colson, Aaron 9:213; 21:316
Colson, Eben 7:74; 25:295
Colson, Edward W. 14:152
Colson, Frederick 13:16
Colson, George F. 9:77; 26:17
Colson, Herman 11:25
Colson, Ira F. 23:62
Colson, John 21:66
Colson, John A. 7:67
Colson, Lafayette 10:107; 20:228
Colson, Thomas 16:290
Colson, William 2:9; 9:117; 22:419; 25:25; 27:31
Colspur, Joseph 11:411
Colstan, William 20:228
Colsten, Casper 21:316
Colstock, John 21:22
Colston, Peter 11:200
Colston, William 12:141
Colt, David W. 19:155
Colt, John 3:46
Colt, Larsi 17:77
Colt, Sidney W. 1:23
Colt, W. L. 1:119
Colter, A. W. 10:107; 20:228
Colter, Charles 18:27
Colter, H. 11:123
Colter, Henry B. 23:62
Colter, J. E. 19:9

Colter, J. W. 20:228
Colter, James 14:296; 17:469; 23:86; 27:31
Colter, John 15:322; 21:316
Colter, Mathew 7:23
Colter, Patrick 15:351
Colter, Samuel E. 21:316
Colter, William A. 25:25
Colteran, Ira A. 20:122
Colterer, Henry W. 10:46
Coltey, Henry 14:152
Colther, William 22:184
Coltier, W. 3:46
Coltoeton, --- 9:172
Colton, D. D. 20:174
Colton, Franklin 10:15
Colton, George C. 4:17
Colton, H. H. 19:62
Colton, Henry 8:46; 11:421; 25:26
Colton, J. 16:181
Colton, James 10:107; 20:228
Colton, James H. 9:172
Colton, James W. 22:184
Colton, Luther 15:190
Colton, Milton E. 21:91
Colton, Richard 21:22
Colton, S. A. 21:316
Colton, William 14:48
Colton, Z. F. 3:46
Coltour, Stephen R. 17:313
Coltrain, Charles H. 17:247
Coltraine, Linden 11:258
Coltrane, G. W. 14:48
Coltrar, Edwin 17:253
Coltrie, Andrew J. 22:277
Coltrie, Oliver L. 22:277
Colts, R. E. 3:46
Colty, Thomas 19:317
Colum, William 20:91
Columbia, J. 10:204
Colver, Horace 14:152
Colvert, John 16:26
Colville, G. H. 10:27; 19:300
Colville, John M. 23:24
Colville, R. W. 27:143
Colvin, A. B. 20:228
Colvin, Alanson 20:141
Colvin, Bryant 10:171; 19:155
Colvin, Daniel 7:90
Colvin, E. O. 3:45
Colvin, Frederick 15:16
Colvin, George 3:45; 22:184
Colvin, George W. 20:95

Colvin, Henry G. 10:107; 20:228
Colvin, John 20:228
Colvin, L. H. 24:75
Colvin, Maylon 18:323
Colvin, Nathan D. 13:16
Colvin, Nathaniel B. 10:46
Colvin, Nimrod S. 9:50
Colvin, Robert 26:17
Colvin, S. 15:190
Colvin, S. G. 25:21
Colvin, S. R. 1:93
Colvin, Thomas 21:215
Colvin, W. 20:39
Colvin, W. H. 11:331
Colvin, William 14:296; 17:202, 469
Colwell, Alfred 12:17; 26:217
Colwell, Andy 7:120
Colwell, Charles 22:71
Colwell, Charles M. 11:411
Colwell, D. C. 3:45
Colwell, Daniel 11:299
Colwell, Edward 22:184
Colwell, I. 25:156
Colwell, J. 3:45
Colwell, J. H. 3:45
Colwell, John 5:37; 8:12; 10:107; 17:267; 18:127
Colwell, John M. 20:29
Colwell, Nathan 5:37; 26:156
Colwell, Patten 7:120
Colwell, Samuel 13:107; 16:181
Colwell, T. 16:182
Colwell, W. W. 22:246
Colwell, William 9:20; 11:26
Colwin, Bennett 10:46; 20:228
Colwin, O. W. 25:24
Colyer, B. 3:46
Colyer, Edward 14:152
Colyer, John 10:107
Colyer, Joseph 24:100
Com---, Andrew 23:283
Coman, William 7:23
Comaree, Thomas J. 22:419
Comaster, Philip 3:46
Comb, Elijah 5:12
Comb, J. M. 9:50
Comban, T. 16:182
Combes, A. P. 25:21
Combs, B. 3:46
Combs, Byron 17:235

Combs, David 4:17
Combs, Dyer B. 22:184
Combs, Eberill 22:461
Combs, Ed. A. 3:46
Combs, Edward 9:164
Combs, Edwin R. 15:190
Combs, Farmer 18:393
Combs, George 3:46
Combs, George E. 13:16
Combs, George W. 23:138
Combs, H. M. 25:156
Combs, Henry Clay 10:27
Combs, J. 3:46; 14:153
Combs, J. H. 8:62
Combs, James 8:38; 9:77; 26:17, 155; 27:30
Combs, James L. 26:218
Combs, James N. 13:16
Combs, John 3:46; 18:393; 20:185
Combs, John B. 24:59
Combs, John H. 20:21; 23:138
Combs, Leonard 24:165
Combs, Milton 24:191
Combs, Robert 15:27
Combs, S. 3:46
Combs, Samuel 22:449
Combs, Thomas Clay 19:300
Combs, W. 14:48
Combs, William 13:85; 14:7
Combs, William C. 11:55
Combs, William H. 8:82
Combston, J. 3:46
Comby, Silas 24:37
Come, Samuel 25:157
Comedas, George 18:233
Comeggs, Benjamin 1:22
Comelford, James 14:153
Comell, Lamartine 11:124
Comer, A. P. 25:156
Comer, Archibald 13:128
Comer, J. T. 15:321
Comer, James F. 11:259
Comer, Richard 18:173
Comer, Samuel 5:12
Comer, William 8:104; 10:46, 179; 20:228
Comerford, John 24:49
Comerford, Patrick 19:155
Comerfort, John 8:124
Comers, Robert 16:182
Comes, E. 25:156
Comes, G. 23:25
Comes, S. B. 10:95, 107; 20:228
Comestock, C. 25:156
Comey, Manlius 5:12

Comford, David 12:64; 15:31
Comford, Michael 23:25
Comfort, E. M. 25:23
Comfort, G. 1:22
Comfort, J. 13:85; 14:7
Comforth, John 13:16
Comicle, F. 3:46
Coming, D. H. 25:157
Coming, Deer 10:204
Coming, John 20:228
Comingo, J. G. 15:172
Comins, S. 15:312
Cominsky, Philip 13:16
Comley, John 11:331
Comley, Nathan 19:155
Comly, B. 13:107
Comly, William 21:316
Commankie, Bolham 7:120
Commansone, Lewis 7:90
Commar, W. 27:27
Commeal, John 14:153
Commerath, C. 14:287
Commerce, A. 10:107; 20:228
Commerford, Hugh 21:115
Comming, Charles 7:90
Comming, John 14:314
Commings, Jeremiah 27:29
Commings, M. 1:121
Commings, W. J. 10:158
Commins, Alexander H. 1:24
Commins, James 19:331
Commins, Nathan B. 12:169
Commins, Thomas 13:107
Commins, W. D. 19:155
Commiskey, Francis 21:136
Common, H. W. 16:182
Common, Thomas 25:157
Commons, Calvin 4:17
Commons, Henry 10:107; 20:228
Commons, John M. 21:207
Commons, R. B. 11:56
Commons, R. R. 9:77
Commons, William 4:17
Comneily, Abner 26:21
Comneity, Abner 18:233
Comnons, Reason 26:21
Comon, William 9:101
Comp, J. J. 11:56
Comp, Jacob 15:190
Comphn, Peter C. 11:124
Compo, E. 1:119

Compston, John 12:68
Compston, Jonathan 23:25
Compston, S. L. 8:125
Compston, W. 23:245
Compt, Clairmont 25:24
Compton, A. 13:107
Compton, Andrew J. 8:82
Compton, D. P. 12:152
Compton, E. L. 8:12;
18:127
Compton, F. G. 3:46
Compton, F. W. 15:190
Compton, Francis 11:385
Compton, Frazee 13:60
Compton, G. 25:23
Compton, George 8:46
Compton, H. H. 3:46
Compton, H. S. 12:161
Compton, J. 15:27
Compton, J. B. 23:245
Compton, Jacob 27:143
Compton, John 9:244;
11:258; 17:19, 272;
22:71, 499
Compton, John D. 23:138
Compton, John H. 10:107;
20:192, 228
Compton, Jonas 19:272
Compton, L. 1:26
Compton, Lewis 9:117;
27:29
Compton, Nester 23:62
Compton, P. T. 4:17
Compton, S. 24:15
Compton, Samuel 11:25;
22:71
Compton, Samuel C.
10:90
Compton, Samuel E.
20:228
Compton, Simon 7:120
Compton, W. 14:277
Compton, William
23:104; 24:165;
25:157
Compton, William A.
22:119
Compton, William H.
1:21; 17:235
Comptson, S. S. 12:61
Comrose, G. 3:46
Comstag, E. 8:71
Comstock, A. 19:155, 236
Comstock, Albert 17:319
Comstock, Ambrose L.
20:111
Comstock, Artemus 9:172
Comstock, Benjamin B.
20:48
Comstock, C. 5:12
Comstock, C. H. 19:155

Comstock, Charles M.
11:332
Comstock, D. 1:21
Comstock, E. 13:124
Comstock, E. B. 19:155
Comstock, Ellis 16:139
Comstock, Eugene 7:90
Comstock, G. 19:155
Comstock, G. W. 1:120
Comstock, George F.
19:155
Comstock, George W.
11:26; 20:21
Comstock, Henry 16:152
Comstock, J. 9:50
Comstock, J. H. 17:446;
24:170
Comstock, James 5:12;
20:84; 21:316;
25:157
Comstock, Jem. R. 7:90
Comstock, Josephus 15:54
Comstock, Julius R.
22:461
Comstock, Lewis 18:27
Comstock, Mannus 9:101
Comstock, Marius 18:337
Comstock, Mark 10:107;
20:228
Comstock, Melvin 22:139
Comstock, O. 21:186
Comstock, O. A. 27:24
Comstock, Orlando
21:251
Comstock, S. 15:190
Comstock, Thomas
24:110
Comstock, W. 9:71
Comstock, William J.
24:49
Comvell, J. F. 3:46
Comway, C. C. 3:46
Comwell, Henry 16:117
Con, B. 23:202
Con, Moseby 6:27
Conaghen, A. F. 23:138
Conal, Robert H. 23:128
Conally, H. 14:48
Conally, Hugh 14:130
Conaly, J. 15:293; 16:182
Conaly, James 15:293
Conaly, Thomas 21:109
Conaman, J. 13:124
Conant, Abraham F.
22:139
Conant, Ahan F. 27:24
Conant, C. R. 14:130
Conant, Francis 8:104
Conant, George C. 9:20
Conant, George W.
11:291

Conant, H. S. 20:141
Conant, J. B. 13:124
Conant, James A. 12:17
Conant, John F. 21:135
Conant, L. 25:26
Conard, A. 3:47
Conard, George 22:184
Conarday, Thomas 17:77
Conart, C. R. 15:263
Conaught, C. S. 3:47
Conaut, John E. 10:210
Conaway, Benjamin
21:120
Conaway, D. 11:259
Conaway, David R. 9:129
Conaway, H. 20:145
Conaway, John W.
17:442; 24:157
Conaway, Moses 15:190
Conaway, Patrick 9:71
Conaway, Thomas 11:407
Conboy, Isaac 24:92
Conbs, Erwin 9:242
Conch, Sterling 16:182
Conch, William 8:12
Conch, William A. 8:12
Conch, William H. 8:12
Conche, John 10:90
Concher, A. H. 13:107
Concklin, Charles 19:155
Conclin, T. 13:85
Concord, Edward 4:18
Concright, Charles 11:400
Condant, Joseph 13:16
Conden, E. T. 9:172
Conden, G. D. 16:182
Conden, George W. 13:16
Conden, James 13:16;
16:26
Conden, W. H. 3:47
Conderman, W. 17:346
Condin, --- 19:62
Condis, John D. 8:71
Condit, A. L. B. 19:155
Condit, Amazia L. B.
10:158
Condit, Daniel M. 24:49
Condit, Philip H. 22:184
Condley, Edmund 17:235
Condo, B. B. 1:118
Condo, D. 18:27
Condo, Elias 13:76
Condo, Jose 12:172
Condon, --- 12:95; 15:358
Condon, A. B. 1:25
Condon, E. T. 19:226
Condon, Edward 19:317;
21:316
Condon, H. 3:47
Condon, J. 15:190
Condon, J. Larkin 23:138

Condon, James 7:23
Condon, John 2:9; 12:99; 25:25
Condon, Owen 14:153
Condon, R. 14:49, 296; 17:475; 27:31
Condon, Ransom C. 10:209
Condon, Richard 21:316
Condon, Seth 1:22
Condon, Thomas 3:47; 13:107
Condon, William 22:71
Condon, William M. 20:179
Condor, A. 18:27
Condor, Adam 18:27
Condor, Eleven N. 17:279
Condor, John 25:26
Condor, Stephen G. 17:279
Condray, William S. 22:165
Condren, Dennis 21:316
Condrey, John 24:176
Condron, Michael 14:153
Condry, Jefferson 16:26
Condry, John M. 24:183
Conds, E. 16:182
Condy, John 18:233; 26:22
Cone, A. 22:523
Cone, Austin 20:29
Cone, C. J. 27:26
Cone, C. W. 1:120
Cone, Cornelius 19:155
Cone, G. F. 9:141
Cone, H. C. 11:319
Cone, Hallette 17:19
Cone, J. 21:316
Cone, James 5:37
Cone, Patrick 16:182; 20:228
Cone, R. 3:47
Cone, S. 3:47
Cone, Thomas 17:31
Cone, W. M. H. 23:202
Cone, William 11:385
Coneet, Wesley 7:56
Conefield, J. 14:48
Conel, J. 3:47
Conelas, George 26:20
Conelius, J. 3:47
Conell, James M. 15:85
Conelly, Charles 14:48
Conelly, J. 15:358
Conelly, Patrick 3:46
Conelton, A. 18:79
Conely, Dan 1:24
Conent, Hamliton H. 7:90
Coner, Alex 18:291

Coner, Alexander 26:95
Coner, C. W. 3:47
Coner, P. C. 25:157
Coner, Samuel 20:179
Conerly, Dennis 9:20
Coneroy, Israel A. 22:111
Conery, J. 1:96; 25:157
Conery, John 8:12; 18:127
Cones, John 24:110
Conestock, William 7:23
Conevoy, Owen 17:235
Coney, James 13:107
Coney, T. 3:47
Coney, W. M. 15:121
Confare, William 20:136
Confer, Daniel L. 16:91
Confer, John 4:17
Confer, William 18:173
Confrey, Michael 16:88
Confru, W. H. 1:22
Congal, C. C. 14:48
Congden, E. 3:47
Congdon, A. G. 16:366
Congdon, Chancey 17:422
Congdon, Chauncy 24:169
Congdon, J. S. 27:25
Congeo, T. 1:119
Conger, Hiram 11:199
Conger, Jacob B. 14:153
Conger, James 3:47
Conger, Joseph 11:199
Conger, L. 14:49
Conger, Lewis B. 21:135
Conger, Nathaniel F. 11:296
Conger, W. H. H. 12:68; 15:31
Congler, Benjamin 4:65
Congleton, John F. 23:62
Congleton, William 23:284
Congo, William T. 16:366
Congreve, E. 3:47
Congue, Lewis B. 8:46
Congus, S. 7:91
Conhoff, David 22:246
Conica, James 8:82
Conice, J. D. 3:47
Conier, Wallace 25:157
Coniff, Austin 7:48
Conine, H. 23:138
Conine, Lewis 13:16
Conion, C. 12:164
Conis, David G. 11:400
Conivay, S. 16:182
Conk, Hiram 10:47
Conkelman, Ferdinand 1:121
Conkey, William 9:172; 19:249

Conkia, Michael 10:47
Conkin, Hagans 22:246
Conkley, Patrick 10:9
Conklin, A. 3:47
Conklin, Amzi 26:95
Conklin, Ansey 9:20
Conklin, Arnsey 18:304
Conklin, B. H. 14:264, 287
Conklin, Barnabas 16:65
Conklin, Benjamin H. 23:97
Conklin, C. 9:172; 19:249
Conklin, Charles 25:25
Conklin, E. 3:47
Conklin, E. O. 13:85
Conklin, Edward S. 13:16
Conklin, F. 14:153
Conklin, Francis 13:16
Conklin, Frederick 17:13
Conklin, G. 15:32
Conklin, G. W. 27:25
Conklin, George 9:77; 10:10; 14:49; 15:190; 26:18
Conklin, Harrison 11:124
Conklin, Hezekiah 22:71
Conklin, I. J. 1:25
Conklin, J. B. 8:71; 17:153
Conklin, J. H. H. 12:68; 15:32
Conklin, J. J. 1:120
Conklin, J. R. 3:47
Conklin, James 14:153
Conklin, James H. 17:359
Conklin, John 7:67; 12:68; 15:190; 21:206
Conklin, John H. 21:316
Conklin, John J. 22:277
Conklin, John L. 10:15
Conklin, Joseph 4:17; 23:62
Conklin, Josiah 1:24
Conklin, Lafayette 13:107
Conklin, Lewis 18:233; 26:21; 27:31
Conklin, N. 3:47
Conklin, Oliver 1:24
Conklin, Patrick 5:12
Conklin, Peter R. 9:172
Conklin, Philip 22:461
Conklin, S. 3:47; 26:18
Conklin, Seth 21:316
Conklin, Silas 9:77
Conklin, Stephen 4:17; 12:17
Conklin, T. 16:267
Conklin, T. R. 19:249
Conklin, U. 20:228

Conklin, U. S. 1:24
Conklin, W. H. 15:32
Conklin, Walter 21:115
Conklin, William 7:82
Conklin, William P. 22:71
Conklin, William W.
    13:107
Conkling, Albert G.
    10:107; 20:228
Conkling, G. E. 21:22
Conkling, H. 15:32
Conkright, Samuel 22:418
Conkright, William
    22:119
Conkrite, James 8:12
Conlan, J. 7:23
Conlan, John 2:8; 25:25
Conlan, Patrick 16:9
Conlan, Peter 16:84
Conlan, Thomas 19:249
Conlet, Henry 25:157
Conley, Andrew 22:25
Conley, C. M. 10:95
Conley, Charles 23:120
Conley, Dennis L. 9:77;
    26:17
Conley, E. G. 8:82
Conley, Elijah 10:95
Conley, Francis 20:6
Conley, Franklin M. 24:37
Conley, Garrett 14:153
Conley, George 7:120
Conley, J. 7:56
Conley, J. H. 3:47
Conley, James 7:83;
    12:152; 18:188;
    22:518
Conley, James D. 8:71
Conley, John 8:46;
    18:270; 20:6; 22:25
Conley, L. 14:49
Conley, Nathan 10:145
Conley, Owen 22:25
Conley, P. 14:49
Conley, Pat 22:332
Conley, Patrick 22:294
Conley, Samuel H. 9:71
Conley, T. 1:24; 15:32
Conley, Thomas 13:16;
    16:26; 21:165;
    22:397
Conley, W. 1:93; 3:47
Conley, William 18:215;
    21:251; 22:25;
    26:155
Conlin, Daniel 3:47
Conlin, David 12:17
Conlin, M. 11:331
Conlin, Owen 13:107
Conlin, Patrick 21:316
Conlin, Tim 3:47

Conliss, Augustus H. 7:8
Conlon, Peter 15:283;
    19:62
Conlong, T. L. 12:91;
    16:290
Conly, G. C. 17:440;
    24:151
Conly, John 17:235
Conly, Michael 21:251
Conly, Stephen 15:4
Conly, William 16:117
Conman, Bartha 8:71
Conn, Asa T. 13:16
Conn, David 21:316
Conn, E. 9:235; 12:121;
    26:217
Conn, Francis M. 21:222
Conn, George W. 7:23;
    13:16
Conn, J. 1:97; 15:65
Conn, Jerry 12:68
Conn, John 25:318
Conn, John P. 16:91
Conn, Jordon 21:203
Conn, Samuel M. 12:152
Conn, T. M. C. 21:22
Connahan, W. 3:47
Connally, Thomas I.
    18:102
Connan, James 21:316
Connan, John 14:153
Connant, Samuel 19:9
Connar, Amos Gregg
    18:215
Connar, Jerome S. 19:273
Connard, C. H. 25:24
Connard, Dennis 10:47;
    20:228
Connard, George 16:182
Connars, John 3:47
Connary, J. 1:23
Connatser, J. P. 11:326
Connaught, A. E. 9:108
Conne, John 6:30
Connegan, Joseph 13:16
Connel, --- 23:202
Connel, Charles M.
    16:117
Connel, H. 11:103
Connel, James 20:132
Connel, M. M. 11:299
Connel, Patrick 17:461;
    21:222
Connel, Thomas 16:26
Connel, Thomas O. 9:117
Conneley, John 8:121
Connell, Allen 22:71
Connell, Charles 9:10;
    21:9
Connell, D. 11:56
Connell, D. M. 12:99

Connell, Daniel O. 19:337
Connell, E. C. 9:50
Connell, G. W. 10:15
Connell, J. 3:46
Connell, J. L. 9:108
Connell, J. O. 3:46;
    16:182
Connell, James 23:62
Connell, James L. 17:352
Connell, James P. 27:25
Connell, John 14:49;
    15:121; 19:349
Connell, John W. 7:23
Connell, Joseph 9:172;
    22:184
Connell, Levi 17:456;
    24:213
Connell, Logan 22:294
Connell, Loven 18:323
Connell, M. 1:123
Connell, Michael 21:316;
    22:71
Connell, O. 13:76
Connell, P. 16:366
Connell, Patrick 8:100;
    22:332; 24:166
Connell, R. A. 21:316
Connell, Robert A. 21:316
Connell, T. 3:46
Connell, T. J. 18:215
Connell, Thomas 4:17;
    15:81; 22:9
Connell, William 21:316
Connell, William H.
    25:283
Connelley, Frank 11:279
Connelly, Anthony 9:172
Connelly, Bernard 7:90;
    23:120
Connelly, C. C. 15:363
Connelly, Daniel 25:295
Connelly, Dennis 15:150;
    21:9
Connelly, Edward 16:26
Connelly, F. 3:46; 18:275
Connelly, F. M. 24:37
Connelly, George 9:240
Connelly, Hiram 21:316
Connelly, Hugh 12:17
Connelly, J. 12:95; 15:157
Connelly, James 9:172
Connelly, John 20:174;
    21:98; 22:246
Connelly, Josiah W.
    18:452
Connelly, Levi I. 8:12
Connelly, Levi J. 18:128
Connelly, M. 1:26; 3:46
Connelly, Michael 4:17;
    21:316

Connelly, Middleton 24:49
Connelly, Patrick 9:77, 117; 27:30
Connelly, Peter 27:25
Connelly, W. H. 7:90
Connelly, William 3:46
Connelly, William H. 24:75
Connelton, A. 6:12
Connely, John 19:9
Connely, Patrick 8:60
Connely, W. 12:149
Conner, A. 9:114; 11:230
Conner, A. S. 26:156
Conner, Abner P. 14:153
Conner, Allen 21:267
Conner, Andrew 23:270
Conner, B. F. 12:152
Conner, B. O. 24:92
Conner, Benjamin 21:66
Conner, C. 14:49
Conner, Caleb W. 22:71
Conner, Charles 22:184; 23:120
Conner, D. 3:46; 24:37
Conner, D. O. 13:107
Conner, Daniel H. 22:419
Conner, David 22:111
Conner, David S. 22:25
Conner, Edward 21:316
Conner, Felix 20:228
Conner, Francis 9:172
Conner, George 11:139; 16:91
Conner, Harris 12:17
Conner, Henry 3:46; 23:178
Conner, Henry D. 17:313
Conner, J. 1:117; 11:238; 13:107; 14:49
Conner, J. A. 14:240
Conner, J. B. 3:46
Conner, J. C. 11:25
Conner, J. N. 3:46
Conner, J. O. 18:13
Conner, J. S. 17:144; 20:228
Conner, J. W. 17:31
Conner, James 14:7; 22:25
Conner, Jeremiah 22:173
Conner, Jessie G. 27:143
Conner, John 9:117; 11:181; 13:107; 14:49; 15:54; 21:109; 23:62, 97; 25:157; 27:30
Conner, John A. 9:106
Conner, John C. 23:306
Conner, John H. 22:25

Conner, John M. 21:86
Conner, John O. 7:83
Conner, Joseph 19:296
Conner, Joseph D. 21:316
Conner, L. F. 25:157
Conner, Lawrence 10:95
Conner, M. 19:249
Conner, Martin 18:215
Conner, Martin V. 22:419
Conner, Michael 9:172
Conner, Mosiah 21:267
Conner, Mosick 21:211
Conner, Nicholas 16:154
Conner, O. 16:182
Conner, P. 3:46; 14:49
Conner, P. O. 15:340
Conner, R. 14:7
Conner, Richard 6:8
Conner, Robert 22:402
Conner, Robert F. 22:119
Conner, Samuel 20:95
Conner, Samuel L. 16:132
Conner, Sovance M. 20:228
Conner, T. 1:122
Conner, T. O. 16:182
Conner, Thomas 13:107; 21:66
Conner, Thomas C. 9:172
Conner, Thomas N. 8:12; 18:128
Conner, Timothy 15:90
Conner, W. A. 3:46
Conner, W. D. 23:138
Conner, Wesley 22:173
Conner, William 14:153; 16:290
Conner, William B. 22:232
Conner, William E. 21:222
Conner, William F. 11:293
Conner, William H. H. 17:388
Conner, William J. 22:449
Conner, Z. 14:153
Conner, Carner, Or Carver, Jo. 16:117
Connerly, James 18:128
Connerly, James H. 8:82
Conners, Allen 11:428
Conners, E. 3:47
Conners, James 10:171
Conners, Michael 7:83
Conners, Nathan O. 12:61
Conners, P. 15:104
Conners, Patrick 18:304; 26:94
Conners, Seth 20:228
Conners, Thomas 16:278

Connerty, L. 25:157
Connerty, Luke 5:12
Connery, Andrew 22:449
Connery, J. 1:120
Connery, J. P. 1:121
Connery, Joseph 25:22
Connery, Michael 9:77
Conness, J. 25:157
Connett, Daniel 3:47
Connett, Edward 11:199
Connett, H. 19:155
Connett, Henry 10:158
Connett, Hiram M. 17:235
Connett, John F. 21:194
Connety, J. 19:62
Conneval, W. H. 25:157
Conney, Patrick 7:23
Conney, Valentine 13:16
Connic, W. 25:157
Connick, John 23:260
Connick, Levi F. 27:143
Connie, James H. 10:15
Connier, Titus A. 20:228
Conniff, John D. 10:158; 19:155
Connigan, John 16:26
Conningham, B. 27:33
Connis, M. C. 23:25
Connley, W. 1:93
Connoble, J. T. 20:122
Connoley, Andrew 22:184
Connolly, Anthony 19:280
Connolly, C. A. 1:25
Connolly, C. C. 15:121
Connolly, D. 3:46
Connolly, D. S. 14:49
Connolly, Ferdinand 21:316
Connolly, J. 1:123
Connolly, James 19:280; 21:316
Connolly, James B. 24:92
Connolly, Patrick 13:16
Connolly, Richard 7:120
Connolly, Thomas 14:49, 153
Connoly, James 8:113
Connor, A. 14:254
Connor, Aldrich 27:29
Connor, Alex 9:33
Connor, B. J. 5:12
Connor, C. 3:46
Connor, Charles 22:449, 518
Connor, D. 3:46; 17:173
Connor, Daniel 10:46; 17:173; 20:229
Connor, Date T. 17:279
Connor, Daviel 18:215

Connor, Davis L. 10:107; 20:229
Connor, E. 25:157
Connor, Elias 5:37
Connor, Eugene 22:332
Connor, F. 19:249
Connor, Felix 10:46
Connor, Francis 9:242
Connor, George 1:21
Connor, H. 3:46; 12:161
Connor, Hugh 12:85; 16:290
Connor, J. 1:121; 3:46; 12:166; 27:27
Connor, J. A. 27:33
Connor, J. J. 18:65
Connor, J. R. 19:155
Connor, J. W. 1:24
Connor, James 10:158; 13:85; 18:215; 19:155
Connor, James B. 11:139
Connor, John 1:25; 3:46; 8:77; 23:25
Connor, John S. 10:46
Connor, Joseph 9:77, 242; 26:17
Connor, Levi 1:21
Connor, Louis 22:294
Connor, M. 27:26
Connor, M. O. 1:26
Connor, Martin B. 21:316
Connor, Michael 1:24
Connor, O. 17:158
Connor, P. 3:46; 7:23
Connor, P. O. 19:62
Connor, Patrick 12:17; 19:324
Connor, Peter 20:29
Connor, Reuben 19:155
Connor, Richard 18:102
Connor, Richard O. 18:128
Connor, S. 3:46
Connor, S. A. 25:157
Connor, S. B. 8:46
Connor, Samuel 8:38; 26:155
Connor, Smith A. 5:12
Connor, T. 1:25, 121; 3:46
Connor, T. C. 1:25
Connor, Thomas 8:46; 19:155; 25:318
Connor, Thomas C. 19:249
Connor, Thomas W. 21:317
Connor, Titus A. 10:107
Connor, W. 19:9
Connor, William 22:475

Connors, C. 1:25
Connors, Edward 10:107; 20:229
Connors, George 15:190
Connors, Henry 8:12; 18:128
Connors, James 19:155
Connors, John 4:18; 19:324
Connors, Michael 21:317
Connors, Patrick 9:20
Connors, Thomas 15:352
Connortore, John 24:8
Connsilor, N. 25:157
Connway, A. 20:229
Conoary, P. 1:118
Conody, Stephen 25:157
Conol, O. B. 3:47
Conolly, Edward 11:14
Conolly, F. 21:317
Conoly, John 12:161
Cononan, Hugh 13:62
Conor, John 21:129
Conora, Edward 18:205
Conordy, Thomas 17:235
Conorr, James 5:12
Conorter, James 21:317
Conovell, Frank 9:33
Conover, C. 21:317
Conover, Combs 20:229
Conover, Coombs 10:47
Conover, Dominicus 20:185
Conover, Isaac 11:237
Conover, Jacob A. 11:300
Conover, James 24:190
Conover, John 15:190
Conover, John C. 11:26
Conover, John D. 12:151
Conover, Joseph 17:455
Conover, P. 7:90
Conover, R. 13:85
Conover, S. 3:47
Conover, W. A. 26:144
Conover, W. D. 15:298
Conover, William 21:215
Conoway, Enoch W. 17:355
Conoy, Patrick 22:9
Conquest, William 17:50
Conrad, --- 16:91
Conrad, Adam 1:25
Conrad, Albert 13:107
Conrad, Armstead 22:332
Conrad, Augustus 17:99
Conrad, B. 16:91
Conrad, Christian 20:185
Conrad, Daniel 23:138
Conrad, Edsen 3:46
Conrad, Eli 8:62; 26:154
Conrad, F. 14:49

Conrad, Fletcher B. 18:284
Conrad, Frederick 1:24
Conrad, George 8:12, 82; 18:128; 21:317
Conrad, George W. 10:107; 20:229
Conrad, H. 1:117, 122; 11:27
Conrad, H. S. 21:317
Conrad, Hendrich C. 7:90
Conrad, Henry 25:157
Conrad, Henry L. 6:20
Conrad, Humphrey 10:15
Conrad, J. 1:122
Conrad, Jacob 25:157
Conrad, James 16:182
Conrad, James H. 21:317
Conrad, John 7:23; 11:140; 12:17, 161; 14:153
Conrad, Joseph W. 12:17
Conrad, Josephus 22:71
Conrad, L. C. 14:314
Conrad, Mathias 26:22
Conrad, N. 12:152
Conrad, Neal 21:222
Conrad, Nelson 11:200
Conrad, P. 13:85
Conrad, R. P. 3:47
Conrad, W. 3:47
Conrad, W. H. 17:417
Conrad, W. W. 25:157
Conrad, William 24:156
Conrad, William C. 12:17
Conrad, William F. 24:61
Conrad, William H. 18:215; 22:71
Conrad, William W. 5:12
Conrade, Levi 20:106
Conradt, John 16:26
Conray, Elenor 8:104
Conray, H. 9:172
Conray, J. 16:290
Conray, Patrick 9:219
Conroe, Darling 12:68
Conroe, William 18:346
Conrow, Darling 15:27
Conroy, Charles 25:157
Conroy, D. 1:118
Conroy, H. 11:124
Conroy, Henry 27:27
Conroy, I. 19:347
Conroy, J. 7:23; 12:167
Conroy, James 16:366; 17:19
Conroy, John 17:94
Conroy, Joseph 21:109
Conroy, Michael 4:18
Conroy, Owen 17:50
Conroy, P. H. 12:161

Conroy, Pat 25:295
Conroy, Patrick 7:23
Conroy, Thomas 25:295
Conroy, Timothy 11:259
Conroy, William 13:16;
  16:26; 21:135
Conry, John 26:19
Conry, Thomas 22:518
Consana, Cornelius 9:219
Consby, John 3:47
Conse, Albert 17:475
Conseal, C. 26:19
Consee, --- 10:7
Consgry, Edward 15:313
Conshau, Thomas 8:12
Consla, John 19:62
Consle, Samuel M. 19:9
Conson, Joseph 9:50
Constable, Jacob 21:317
Constable, Noah 22:71
Constad, --- 8:104
Constad, F. 26:154
Constant, Andrew 8:47;
  21:98
Constant, John 3:47
Constant, Newton V.
  17:199
Constantine, George
  14:153
Constantine, J. 1:22; 7:81;
  25:295
Constantine, Samuel W.
  21:87
Constantine, William 7:15
Conston, James J. 9:229
Consuegra, J. 1:117
Contance, John 4:17
Contant, David 14:153
Contee, N. 25:157
Content, Peter 25:157
Conterman, Thomas 13:16
Conthe, Ferdinand C.
  10:47
Contoy, P. 3:47
Contras, Henry 16:182
Contrel, J. A. 8:62
Controy, William 2:8
Conur, J. I. 21:186
Convers, Charles 23:15
Convers, W. E. 21:317
Converse, C. W. 25:24
Converse, Clark 23:62
Converse, D. B. 11:26
Converse, E. W. 15:364;
  19:62
Converse, George W.
  10:107; 20:229
Converse, Henry 20:55
Converse, Josiah 17:422;
  24:169
Converse, Merrick B. 16:8

Converz, John 4:17
Convis, J. D. 26:156
Convoy, H. 9:141
Convoy, Patrick 18:364
Conway, --- 10:15
Conway, Alonzo 10:47
Conway, Bernard 12:17
Conway, C. 25:157
Conway, Dennis 11:321
Conway, F. 3:47
Conway, Francis 4:17
Conway, G. 9:141; 27:26
Conway, George 23:138
Conway, J. 3:47; 11:258;
  12:92; 15:190;
  16:147; 27:27
Conway, J. A. 14:49;
  17:192
Conway, J. C. 1:118
Conway, James 1:24;
  14:49; 15:32; 18:420;
  21:317
Conway, James F. 18:270
Conway, Jeremiah 9:129;
  27:29
Conway, John 7:23, 63;
  13:85; 14:7, 49;
  17:31; 26:155
Conway, John P. 27:25
Conway, Jones 25:332
Conway, Joseph 1:192;
  22:71
Conway, Joseph W. 15:85
Conway, M. 17:147
Conway, Michael 22:25
Conway, Neil 22:119
Conway, Orrin T. 19:9
Conway, Owen 5:12
Conway, P. 1:117; 18:79
Conway, Pat 8:12; 18:128
Conway, Patrick 4:17;
  14:153
Conway, Peter 10:15
Conway, Philip 17:447;
  24:172
Conway, Rinalds 17:216
Conway, Samuel 23:138
Conway, Silas 9:206
Conway, T. 1:23, 24
Conway, Thomas 1:25;
  3:47; 15:32; 22:448
Conway, Valentine 16:26
Conway, W. 12:92;
  16:182, 290; 27:27
Conway, W. E. 3:47
Conway, William 7:23;
  12:17; 16:9; 17:291;
  22:351
Conway, Willis 9:203
Conwell, George W.
  18:215; 21:222

Conwell, James 11:300
Conwell, Murray M.
  8:104
Conwell, P. 3:46
Conwell, Thomas S. 5:12
Conydon, Eugene D.
  20:95
Conyers, James M. 10:47
Conyers, John A. 24:15
Conyne, Isaiah D. 22:139
Conzett, David 23:86
Conzil, H. 14:49
Coo, Clark C. 13:16
Coob, Henry 9:206
Cooch, H. 11:427
Cood, J. 1:118
Cood, Orlando 20:179
Coodis, Z. 3:223; 17:496
Coody, C. 15:32
Cooer, William 15:81
Coogan, F. 14:153
Coogan, P. 1:24
Coogle, Joseph M. 17:109
Coogrove, F. 3:48
Cooin, Flore 21:317
Cook, --- 20:181; 26:210
Cook, A. 13:103; 16:182
Cook, A. I. 10:47
Cook, A. J. 20:229
Cook, A. L. 16:27
Cook, A. T. S. 20:21
Cook, Abner 22:421
Cook, Abraham 7:120
Cook, Adam 11:411;
  22:294
Cook, Albert 6:30;
  14:153; 19:9; 21:317;
  23:62; 25:318
Cook, Albert C. 9:117;
  27:30
Cook, Alexander 9:129;
  27:29
Cook, Alfred 6:27
Cook, Alfred E. 16:147
Cook, Allen 15:32;
  24:191
Cook, Alonzo H. 24:92
Cook, Alpheus M. 11:56
Cook, Alvah J. 10:158
Cook, Alvin 19:155
Cook, Alvin N. 25:157
Cook, Alvin V. 5:12
Cook, Amos 13:107
Cook, Amos G. 21:317
Cook, Archibald 13:85
Cook, Arthur 9:206
Cook, Asa 24:76
Cook, Asa L. 19:156
Cook, Augustus W.
  24:166
Cook, B. F. 1:119

Cook, B. P. 1:117
Cook, Benjamin 4:65; 7:10; 19:44; 21:222; 25:281
Cook, Bradford 23:106, 202
Cook, Bradley M. 22:165
Cook, Britton 21:133
Cook, Brune 8:47
Cook, C. 14:49
Cook, C. G. 13:85; 14:7
Cook, C. H. 3:47
Cook, Calvin 11:300
Cook, Cassius M. 22:71
Cook, Charles 10:176; 14:49; 19:156; 21:186; 24:75
Cook, Charles A. 2:8; 18:233; 25:25; 26:21
Cook, Charles C. 17:448; 24:172
Cook, Charles H. 9:117, 172; 13:16; 19:236
Cook, Charles R. 13:62; 16:182
Cook, Chester 19:249
Cook, Christian 8:12; 18:128
Cook, Clark C. 16:27
Cook, Conrad 17:355
Cook, Curtis 9:15
Cook, D. 11:56
Cook, D. C. 8:12; 18:128
Cook, D. D. 15:352
Cook, D. F. 9:50
Cook, Daniel 6:28; 16:92; 23:25
Cook, David 17:94, 295
Cook, E. 9:20; 20:229; 25:157
Cook, E. L. 19:156
Cook, Eben 8:117; 19:315
Cook, Ed 17:173
Cook, Edward 1:121; 5:37; 10:15; 11:55; 13:16; 21:317
Cook, Edward F. 10:144; 19:156
Cook, Edward H. 22:25
Cook, Edward J. 24:15
Cook, Edwin B. 21:251
Cook, Eli S. 22:25
Cook, Elias M. 19:156
Cook, Elihu 10:47
Cook, Elijah 9:78; 26:17
Cook, Elisha D. 23:120
Cook, Emanuel 17:455; 24:190
Cook, Enos 11:124
Cook, Ernest 10:47; 20:229

Cook, Ether A. 12:152
Cook, Ezekiel 9:20; 18:320
Cook, F. A. 9:172; 19:224
Cook, F. H. 18:13
Cook, F. M. 1:117
Cook, Fairfield 9:117; 27:29
Cook, Fesse C. 23:276
Cook, Francis M. 8:82
Cook, Frank 14:153; 19:156; 20:229
Cook, Franklin 13:16
Cook, Fred 15:158; 19:62
Cook, Frederick 23:62
Cook, Fredrick W. 6:7
Cook, Freeman 8:38; 26:156
Cook, G. C. 1:21; 5:50
Cook, G. M. 15:121
Cook, G. P. 3:47
Cook, G. W. 3:47; 19:245; 27:24
Cook, George 3:47; 9:46; 13:77; 17:409; 20:95; 22:25, 184, 419; 24:15; 25:23; 26:122
Cook, George H. 10:107; 20:229; 23:255
Cook, George W. 14:49; 16:182; 22:332
Cook, H. 2:9; 11:56; 12:152; 20:39; 25:20
Cook, H. J. 19:62
Cook, H. L. 10:204
Cook, H. W. 10:47; 20:229
Cook, Harry 22:294
Cook, Henry 11:118; 17:129; 22:247, 332; 24:191
Cook, Henry A. 9:117; 27:30
Cook, Henry C. 21:135
Cook, Henry S. 22:71
Cook, Hiram 11:141; 17:417; 20:6
Cook, Holden 16:182
Cook, I. F. 23:25
Cook, Ira 9:31
Cook, Isaac 5:37; 16:27; 17:31, 404
Cook, J. 1:119, 123; 3:47; 5:37; 7:23; 16:366; 17:153; 21:22, 147; 23:202; 25:157
Cook, J. A. 11:299
Cook, J. Addison 15:190
Cook, J. B. 1:117; 12:152
Cook, J. F. 13:124; 18:47
Cook, J. G. 1:23

Cook, J. H. 10:171; 19:156
Cook, J. J. 3:47
Cook, J. M. 11:218
Cook, J. P. 3:47; 9:50; 20:55
Cook, J. R. 12:152
Cook, J. T. 13:124
Cook, J. W. 9:172
Cook, Jacob 10:47; 13:16; 17:77; 20:229; 22:477; 23:305
Cook, James 6:27; 8:62; 9:42; 11:295, 400; 13:16; 14:153; 18:27; 20:48, 229; 21:267; 22:184; 25:310; 26:154; 27:27
Cook, James A. 10:47; 20:229; 25:279
Cook, James M. 8:12; 17:94; 18:128
Cook, James S. 17:77
Cook, Jared L. 23:25
Cook, Jerome 12:17
Cook, Jerry 22:512
Cook, Jesse S. 21:49
Cook, Joel B. 17:322
Cook, John 1:23; 3:47; 7:23; 8:82; 9:20, 66; 10:27, 108, 158; 11:56, 199; 13:107; 16:182; 18:205, 304; 19:300; 20:229; 23:97; 26:94
Cook, John C. 16:182
Cook, John E. 22:277
Cook, John G. 22:475
Cook, John H. 1:22; 7:65
Cook, John M. 26:121
Cook, John P. 12:171
Cook, John S. 22:184
Cook, John T. 22:71, 119
Cook, John W. 4:18; 23:86; 27:32
Cook, John Y. 18:411
Cook, Jonas 8:82
Cook, Jonathan 25:157
Cook, Joseph 9:50; 10:47; 14:153; 17:94; 21:317; 23:255; 24:92
Cook, L. 14:49
Cook, L. B. 3:47
Cook, L. J. 1:118
Cook, Laorenzo W. 11:104
Cook, Lebi 1:23
Cook, Lee 7:120
Cook, Lewis 3:47; 10:171; 18:79; 19:156

Cook, Lewis C. 7:64
Cook, Lewis H. 15:190
Cook, Leyo 20:29
Cook, Lloyd W. 4:18
Cook, Luther 22:294
Cook, Lyman 17:450
Cook, Lyman A. 24:177
Cook, M. 11:54; 18:13; 22:469
Cook, M. H. 17:435; 25:23
Cook, Marion 22:512
Cook, Mark 1:23
Cook, Marshall L. 9:240
Cook, Martin J. 16:81
Cook, Michael 1:22
Cook, Monroe J. 19:236
Cook, Mordecai H. 24:177
Cook, Morris C 20:151
Cook, Moses 7:71
Cook, Munroe J. 9:172
Cook, N. 3:47
Cook, N. B. 25:22
Cook, Nathan 8:113
Cook, Nelson O. 15:165
Cook, O. L. 13:16
Cook, Orin 20:229
Cook, Orrin 10:47
Cook, Orson J. 24:92
Cook, P. 1:118; 15:326
Cook, P. F. 11:27
Cook, Paul 7:48
Cook, Perry 25:157
Cook, Peter 1:120; 13:16
Cook, Philemon 7:91
Cook, Preston 19:62
Cook, R. 1:23
Cook, Richard 8:77; 17:294; 20:95, 120; 22:184; 25:157
Cook, Richard C. 24:49
Cook, Robert 1:23; 11:200; 21:194; 22:294, 332
Cook, Robert B. 23:288
Cook, Robert F. 8:12; 18:128
Cook, S. 23:138
Cook, S. B. 1:119
Cook, S. C. 25:157
Cook, S. F. 16:27; 25:157
Cook, S. H. 17:337
Cook, S. S. 24:110
Cook, S. W. 13:107
Cook, Samuel 9:206; 14:314, 321; 19:156; 22:139
Cook, Samuel B. 18:233; 21:317; 26:20
Cook, Samuel E. 22:294

Cook, Samuel H. 23:97
Cook, Sandy 21:66
Cook, Sanford 8:12; 18:128
Cook, Scott 18:233; 26:21
Cook, Smith G. 14:334
Cook, Solomon H. 22:139
Cook, T. 20:154
Cook, T. D. 25:157
Cook, T. M. 17:199
Cook, Tennessee 22:247
Cook, Theodore 3:47
Cook, Theodore S. 25:157
Cook, Thomas 10:144; 11:91; 17:205; 19:156; 20:6; 22:247
Cook, Thomas D. 5:12
Cook, Thomas W. 17:31
Cook, Valentine 9:117; 27:31
Cook, Vaness V. 20:106
Cook, W. 1:21, 117; 21:109; 22:351; 25:157
Cook, W. D. 18:27
Cook, W. G. 11:26
Cook, W. H. 3:47; 13:85, 107; 16:267; 17:144
Cook, W. M. 11:279
Cook, W. P. 3:47; 24:15
Cook, W. S. 12:17; 20:122
Cook, W. V. 11:218
Cook, W. W. 1:23
Cook, Walcott 13:107
Cook, Walter 15:32
Cook, Wellington 22:139
Cook, Welsey 7:120
Cook, Wesley 1:120; 26:20
Cook, Wiley 18:233
Cook, Willard S. 1:23
Cook, William 4:18; 5:12; 7:120; 8:62; 9:157; 10:15; 11:25, 55, 411; 14:153; 15:54; 16:182; 20:16; 22:119
Cook, William A. 8:82
Cook, William C. 23:138
Cook, William H. 25:288
Cook, William H. H. 21:242
Cook, William J. 26:17
Cook, William P. 11:100
Cook, William T. 9:78
Cook, William W. 19:9
Cook, Willoby 12:172
Cook, Wilmore 22:294
Cook, Winfield S. 11:140
Cooke, Adolph 7:16

Cooke, Albert E. 18:109
Cooke, Charles H. 16:27
Cooke, Chester 9:173
Cooke, F. 15:323
Cooke, Frederick W. 18:109
Cooke, J. L. 9:108
Cooke, J. W. 22:9
Cooke, John 13:16; 16:27
Cooke, S. W. 18:109
Cooker, J. W. 11:25
Cooker, John R. 12:17
Cooker, Robert N. 10:204
Cookley, John 15:150
Cookman, J. 16:366
Cookman, James 15:65
Cookran, James 12:68
Cooks, Albert 21:211
Cooks, John L. 11:55
Cooks, Joseph 14:49
Cooks, Nathaniel R. 14:153
Cooksey, Alexander F. 21:66
Cooksey, E. C. 20:2
Cooksey, James 24:177
Cooksey, James M. 11:26
Cooksey, James S. 8:82
Cooksey, John 17:173
Cooksey, Woolford 9:77
Cookson, John M. 21:317
Cookson, William O. 23:138
Cooksy, James 17:450
Cool, H. 5:12; 25:157
Cool, J. B. 3:48
Cool, J. H. 14:153
Cool, Jacob 18:128
Cool, John 13:16
Coolbaugh, A. K. 16:117
Coolbeth, W. D. 25:295
Coolbeth, Winthrop D. 7:79
Cooldridge, M. 3:48
Coole, John 21:203
Coole, Thomas J. 20:229
Cooledge, Asker E. 20:229
Cooleh, Homer H. 23:188
Coolendess, W. 25:157
Coolenger, J. 22:9
Coolery, J. J. 19:62
Cooley, --- 15:277
Cooley, Adamanter 10:47
Cooley, Adamantus 20:229
Cooley, Adonirom J. 20:16
Cooley, Archibald S. 20:136
Cooley, Benjamin 4:18

Cooley, Benjamin F. 21:67, 248
Cooley, Charles H. 1:23
Cooley, D. H. 8:71
Cooley, David 10:108; 17:425; 20:229; 24:177
Cooley, Dennis 18:320
Cooley, Dill 10:47; 20:229
Cooley, E. 5:37; 25:158
Cooley, F. K. 20:229
Cooley, Francis K. 10:47
Cooley, G. 3:48
Cooley, Gabriel N. 25:158
Cooley, George W. 15:90; 25:158
Cooley, Hiram R. 10:47
Cooley, Hossa 21:120
Cooley, Hy 3:48
Cooley, J. 3:48
Cooley, J. B. 1:26
Cooley, J. C. 11:238
Cooley, J. J. 13:62
Cooley, James 23:62
Cooley, Jesse 19:9
Cooley, John 4:65; 12:58; 16:154; 23:138
Cooley, L. 24:76
Cooley, Louis 11:299
Cooley, Myron R. 20:229
Cooley, Myron Reuben 26:218
Cooley, Nathan M. 25:21
Cooley, Oscar T. 24:15
Cooley, R. B. 23:178
Cooley, Robert M. 21:317
Cooley, S. 25:271
Cooley, Silas 11:25
Cooley, Thomas 9:78; 22:402; 26:17
Cooley, W. 1:122
Cooley, William 9:78; 14:49
Cooley, William A. 1:23
Cooley, William E. 26:17
Coolidge, David 22:161
Coolidge, Melville G. 21:67
Coolidge, Oscar E. 10:47
Coolidge, S. 1:119
Coolidge, Theophilus 15:190
Coolis, John W. 14:153
Coolley, John F. 12:152
Coolman, Cornelius 27:31
Cools, Charles W. 9:33
Cools, Joseph 11:399
Cooly, A. 3:48
Cooly, John 12:86; 16:290
Cooly, John S. 24:49

Cooman, George W. 11:139
Coombes, Isaac 14:153
Coombs, C. H. 14:49
Coombs, E. M. 15:352; 16:278
Coombs, George 3:48
Coombs, George E. 16:27
Coombs, J. G. 21:317
Coombs, John 3:48; 17:144; 23:250
Coombs, Joseph E. 14:153
Coombs, Samuel 14:153
Coombs, Solomon 17:401
Coombs, Wesley 7:120; 21:317
Coombs, William E. 22:420
Coomer, James 22:119
Coomer, William C. 17:235
Coomes, J. M. 3:48
Coomfar, H. 15:326
Cooms, H. 18:430
Cooms, Henry M. 5:12
Cooms, William 22:402
Coon, --- (Mrs.) 26:155
Coon, A. B. 14:321
Coon, A. D. 1:23
Coon, Alexander 9:240
Coon, Alphus 26:155
Coon, And. B. 14:314
Coon, Andrew B. 23:106
Coon, B. 14:49
Coon, Benjamin 15:6
Coon, Charles 13:16
Coon, Charles H. 10:95
Coon, D. 1:93
Coon, Enos 20:229
Coon, Evans 10:47
Coon, F. 17:432
Coon, Franklin 24:151
Coon, G. W. 25:21
Coon, George 3:48
Coon, George F. 3:48
Coon, George W. 16:27
Coon, H. S. 3:48
Coon, Henry 9:68; 11:123; 18:291; 23:63
Coon, I. 14:153
Coon, J. 1:122; 14:254
Coon, J. H. 3:48; 25:21
Coon, J. W. 7:120
Coon, James 12:17
Coon, Jesse H. 8:82
Coon, John 9:78; 21:194; 22:139; 23:97, 106; 26:17
Coon, John W. 23:120
Coon, K. N. 24:191

Coon, Leonard 18:79
Coon, Levi 9:160; 14:327
Coon, Michael 26:156
Coon, Milton D. 12:17
Coon, Nathan 3:48
Coon, Perry 22:184
Coon, R. 1:26
Coon, Ralph M. 20:91
Coon, Richard D. 22:139
Coon, S. 1:122
Coon, Samuel 11:103
Coon, Simpson 22:475
Coon, Stephen B. 17:247
Coon, T. C. 9:219; 18:364
Coon, Thornton 22:184
Coon, W. H. 1:122
Coon, William 11:138; 18:420; 20:132, 182; 22:184; 26:17
Coon, William I. 10:47
Coon, William J. 20:229
Coonan, J. 3:48
Coonce, J. 11:25
Cooncer, Harvey 1:21
Cooner, Henry 9:129; 27:28
Coones, George 25:158
Cooness, Joseph 5:37
Cooney, Charles 12:64
Cooney, F. 3:48
Cooney, I. 9:20
Cooney, J. 18:304; 26:94
Cooney, John 14:49; 17:13, 32
Cooney, S. 25:158
Cooney, Stephen 5:12
Cooney, W. H. 1:120
Coonfar, H. 19:62
Coonley, J. 19:236
Coonrad, Mathias 9:78
Coonrod, Columbus 17:272
Coonrod, Emanuel 20:16
Coonrod, H. L. 18:79
Coons, Andrew J. 10:90; 20:229
Coons, C. T. 11:26
Coons, Daniel 9:173; 19:270
Coons, David 1:24; 3:48
Coons, F. 3:48
Coons, George 9:20
Coons, George H. 11:104
Coons, George W. 22:71, 475
Coons, H. 25:158
Coons, Henry 5:12
Coons, Henry C. 18:393
Coons, J. M. 21:317
Coons, James 9:173; 19:226, 290; 25:158

Coons, John 2:9; 15:54
Coons, John W. 9:10
Coons, Levi 7:91; 21:317
Coons, Peter 22:25
Coons, R. 1:25
Coons, S. A. 17:77
Coons, Samuel C. 10:108; 20:229
Coons, T. 3:48
Coons, W. 18:65
Coons, W. B. 7:91
Coons, W. S. 21:317
Coons, William 22:421
Coonse, William 22:25
Coonts, Edwin 13:127
Coop, Francis 18:393
Coop, John 2:9; 19:156; 25:21
Coop, Merrick 21:22
Coop, W. A. 1:121
Coopage, William 24:190
Cooper, --- 10:158; 18:215
Cooper, A. 1:24, 122; 14:49
Cooper, A. H. 3:48
Cooper, A. P. 11:27
Cooper, Aaron 19:319
Cooper, Abner 12:17
Cooper, Abraham 4:18
Cooper, Albert 2:9
Cooper, Alcaney 20:229
Cooper, Alcany 10:47
Cooper, Alfred 10:98; 11:218
Cooper, Ambrose C. 8:82
Cooper, Amos 26:122
Cooper, Arthur L. 17:19
Cooper, B. F. 1:121; 10:108
Cooper, Benjamin F. 20:229
Cooper, C. 3:47; 18:47
Cooper, C. E. 18:393
Cooper, C. W. 1:21
Cooper, Charles 6:15; 13:134; 18:79; 19:346
Cooper, Charles H. 14:153
Cooper, Charles W. 9:173
Cooper, Chesley 8:82
Cooper, Christopher 1:121
Cooper, Colf 7:120
Cooper, Colonel 9:206
Cooper, D. 8:12; 14:49; 18:129
Cooper, D. C. 14:49
Cooper, Daniel 13:16; 18:411

Cooper, David 8:47; 9:235; 14:130; 15:258; 22:139
Cooper, David J. 13:16
Cooper, E. 3:48; 12:95; 15:358; 19:62
Cooper, E. F. 19:62
Cooper, E. H. 14:49; 25:158
Cooper, E. W. 10:147; 18:47
Cooper, Edwin 1:22
Cooper, Elisha M. 23:258
Cooper, Enoch R. 12:152
Cooper, Enos M. 11:319
Cooper, Ephraim 20:192
Cooper, Eugene H. 5:12
Cooper, Ezra 23:276
Cooper, F. 25:20
Cooper, Francis 15:54
Cooper, Francis M. 11:139
Cooper, Frederick 22:402
Cooper, G. W. 3:48
Cooper, George 6:15, 30; 8:58; 9:15; 18:79; 21:147; 22:294, 418; 24:49; 25:21
Cooper, George A. 22:184
Cooper, George J. 17:19
Cooper, George L. 13:16
Cooper, George M. 20:6
Cooper, George N. 11:181
Cooper, George W. 8:82; 11:238; 14:49
Cooper, H. 1:118; 22:294; 25:158
Cooper, H. A. 11:300
Cooper, H. D. 11:124; 15:340; 16:366
Cooper, H. O. 24:76
Cooper, H. P. 19:156
Cooper, H. T. 18:284; 26:134
Cooper, Henry 7:120; 8:12; 9:9, 199; 17:455; 18:128; 19:290; 24:190
Cooper, Heston P. 10:171
Cooper, Horace 19:45
Cooper, I. 9:141
Cooper, Ira B. 17:73
Cooper, Isaac 11:421; 17:19
Cooper, Isaac N. 22:9
Cooper, J. 3:48; 27:25, 26
Cooper, J. A. 15:6
Cooper, J. B. 17:210
Cooper, J. C. 13:62; 19:62
Cooper, J. D. 17:502
Cooper, J. E. 25:21

Cooper, J. H. 9:114; 17:19
Cooper, J. J. 17:417
Cooper, J. P. 7:23
Cooper, J. S. 14:49
Cooper, J. V. 9:227
Cooper, Jackson 22:71
Cooper, Jacob 11:54; 22:294
Cooper, Jacob S. 21:49
Cooper, James 3:48; 11:199; 14:153; 15:65; 18:79; 21:317; 25:158
Cooper, James F. 18:444
Cooper, James G. 10:47; 20:229
Cooper, James M. 17:50
Cooper, James S. 18:233; 26:20
Cooper, Jasper 22:71
Cooper, Jeremiah 12:68
Cooper, Jesse J. 12:152
Cooper, Joel 8:12; 18:128
Cooper, John 4:18; 7:23; 8:12, 82; 11:407; 16:182; 20:6, 229; 21:9; 22:71, 247; 26:153
Cooper, John C. 11:139
Cooper, John D. 15:305
Cooper, John F. 9:50
Cooper, John H. 22:449
Cooper, John J. 24:156
Cooper, John L. 10:108
Cooper, John R. 12:172
Cooper, John W. 9:219; 18:364
Cooper, Joseph 14:336
Cooper, Joseph H. 1:23
Cooper, Joseph M. 22:419
Cooper, Joshua B. 22:25
Cooper, Josiah F. 19:62
Cooper, Josiah G. 7:14; 10:15
Cooper, K. 15:190
Cooper, L. C. 9:50
Cooper, Leroy 22:25
Cooper, Levi G. 11:238
Cooper, Lewis 4:65; 7:23; 23:279
Cooper, M. 11:258; 18:364; 26:19
Cooper, M. L. 11:331
Cooper, Martin 9:77; 17:202
Cooper, Matthias 9:199; 19:290
Cooper, Milton H. 8:82
Cooper, N. 3:48; 10:192
Cooper, Nelson 10:171; 19:156

Cooper, Oliver 21:22
Cooper, Oliver B. 19:156
Cooper, Osborn 22:184
Cooper, Peter 18:79, 188
Cooper, Preston 21:317
Cooper, R. B. 26:20
Cooper, R. R. 18:233
Cooper, Radon 16:182
Cooper, Ralph 18:291; 26:95
Cooper, Richard 7:79; 17:129; 24:15, 110, 190; 25:295
Cooper, Robert F. 5:50
Cooper, Samuel 9:129; 13:16; 18:27; 27:29
Cooper, Shepherd 6:28
Cooper, Silas 3:48
Cooper, Simeon 12:58; 16:154
Cooper, Solomon A. 27:29
Cooper, Spencer 8:38; 26:155
Cooper, Spencer F. 23:63
Cooper, Stephen 2:8; 16:366
Cooper, T. 1:118; 3:47; 14:153
Cooper, T. H. 21:317
Cooper, Theodore 7:81
Cooper, Thomas 7:120; 10:34, 95; 12:48; 15:95; 21:49, 317; 23:138; 25:295; 26:218
Cooper, Thomas F. 9:129; 21:22; 27:28
Cooper, Thomas H. 21:67
Cooper, Thomas L. 11:238
Cooper, Timothy 27:32
Cooper, Tobias 20:39
Cooper, V. B. 11:140
Cooper, Vincent 13:16
Cooper, W. 17:279; 18:173; 25:23
Cooper, W. C. 15:190
Cooper, W. D. 1:118
Cooper, W. H. 12:147
Cooper, W. L. 7:56
Cooper, W. W. 10:108; 20:229
Cooper, William 2:9; 6:24; 7:77; 9:173; 13:107; 17:77, 215, 279; 19:266; 20:91; 25:20, 158, 295
Cooper, William C. 21:222

Cooper, William H. 5:37; 7:120; 21:129; 23:97; 25:158
Cooper, William H. H. 23:10
Cooper, William J. 21:251; 23:97
Cooper, William S. 20:132, 229; 21:251
Cooper, William T. 10:90
Coopermire, J. 19:266
Coopland, Richard 9:129
Cooplin, David 9:20
Coopride, Daniel 23:63
Coopridore, N. 19:266
Coopridore, Newton 9:173
Coot, Henry 17:322
Cooter, Barnard 11:421
Cooterlough, L. 13:85
Coots, A. 21:147
Coots, B. F. 25:25
Coover, George H. 22:496
Coover, Martin 21:49
Coovert, Archibald 10:108; 20:229
Coovert, D. 3:48
Copass, William R. 22:523
Copber, Elijah A. 22:71
Cope, Ambrose 18:205
Cope, George 25:318
Cope, George W. 17:268
Cope, Isaac 8:12
Cope, J. 13:85; 14:268; 26:18
Cope, J. B. 3:48
Cope, James E. 24:61
Cope, John 14:280; 25:24
Cope, John H. 21:222
Cope, Leroy 11:421
Cope, Martin 9:71
Cope, O. J. 23:138
Cope, Peter 18:393
Cope, Samuel 18:205
Cope, Sanford 8:104
Cope, Thomas 15:333
Cope, William 21:194
Copel, Elijah 10:47; 20:229
Copeland, A. 13:86
Copeland, B. 3:48
Copeland, Benjamin A. 22:247
Copeland, C. 3:48
Copeland, Charles 19:156
Copeland, Charles K. 19:156
Copeland, David 10:47; 20:229
Copeland, Edward 6:24

Copeland, G. W. 23:292
Copeland, George 16:27
Copeland, George W. 10:47; 20:229
Copeland, Henry 22:71
Copeland, Isaac H. 16:113
Copeland, J. 3:48
Copeland, J. E. 8:104
Copeland, J. H. 15:190
Copeland, Jackson 9:129; 27:29
Copeland, James 2:9
Copeland, John 9:42; 12:17; 22:184; 26:122
Copeland, Jordan 9:206
Copeland, Lewis 11:259
Copeland, Richard 20:229; 27:29
Copeland, Richard E. 10:47
Copeland, T. S. 11:138
Copeland, Taylor J. 22:500
Copeland, Thomas 11:55; 20:6
Copeland, W. B. 9:20
Copeland, Warren 14:49
Copeland, William 11:186
Copeley, John 19:156
Copelin, John W. 10:108; 20:230
Copell, James 25:158
Copely, A. C. 14:262
Copen, V. A. 3:48
Copenbeaver, William 3:48
Copenhaver, Adam A. 11:54
Copening, John W. 24:65
Copenire, Jacob 9:173
Coper, William 25:158
Coperland, Richard 24:15
Copers, P. 15:32
Copers, Thomas 7:120
Coph, James 15:32
Copies, H. 14:7
Copland, George 13:57
Copland, James 25:20
Cople, H. 3:48
Copley, Daniel 20:48
Copley, John 10:171
Copley, John B. 10:108
Copley, Selah 24:92
Coplin, Eli F. 9:78; 26:17
Coply, John B. 20:230
Copner, James E. 17:200
Copp, Alonzo 14:153
Copp, Dominick 10:47; 20:230
Copp, Edward 1:22

Copp, H. 9:7
Copp, James 12:68
Copp, Samuel 11:14
Copp, Samuel S. 1:22
Coppage, B. 17:191
Coppage, Dewitt C. 22:449
Coppage, William 17:455
Coppe, G. 14:287
Coppenhaven, Richard 17:77
Copper, Hiram 7:120
Copper, Ralph 9:33
Coppernal, Charles E. 4:18
Coppersmith, A. 1:25
Coppersmith, F. L. 13:16
Coppersmith, P. 25:158
Copperwaite, L. 1:23
Coppies, D. D. 11:339
Coppin, John 11:140
Coppin, Joseph 22:119
Copple, Eli 11:26
Copple, F. 3:48
Copple, Morgan 11:26
Copple, W. C. 21:22
Copple, William 22:25
Coppock, Derrick 11:54
Coppock, John 7:91
Coprs, Henry 7:91
Cops, Nicholas 17:32
Copsy, F. 1:122
Copter, Henry 17:19
Copus, Henry 13:86
Coquillette, Isaac 4:18
Cora, James L. 11:54
Corad, Barzil 23:25
Corady, J. 17:435
Corai, Christian 22:9
Coram, Elijah M. 23:184
Coram, Orizian 22:247
Corath, J. 14:49
Coray, William 6:30
Corb, William 3:49
Corba, John 10:204
Corban, George 17:316
Corban, James 17:205
Corban, William H. 24:76
Corbant, George 14:49
Corbat, Rees 9:78
Corbath, J. 14:49
Corbatt, R. 26:19
Corbean, William 24:90
Corben, John W. 20:230
Corben, Timothy 11:339
Corbert, M. 19:245
Corbet, J. L. 25:158
Corbet, John 11:124
Corbet, Napoleon 11:325
Corbet, W. M. 3:48
Corbett, Andrew J. 22:247

Corbett, B. R. 25:158
Corbett, Charles P. 15:11
Corbett, Daniel 16:92
Corbett, E. 3:48
Corbett, G. W. 27:27
Corbett, H. 14:49
Corbett, Isaac 25:158
Corbett, J. S. 15:277
Corbett, James 27:32, 33
Corbett, John 21:317
Corbett, L. B. 3:48
Corbett, M. 25:22
Corbett, Michael 9:173; 17:50
Corbett, Owen C. 23:106
Corbett, Patrick 18:420
Corbett, S. C. 21:317
Corbett, Thomas 3:48; 27:33
Corbett, William C. 9:155
Corbey, Joseph E. 18:271
Corbin, Alonzo 16:27
Corbin, Amasa M. 22:402
Corbin, B. F. 3:48
Corbin, Benjamin 26:156
Corbin, Benjamin J. 8:62
Corbin, C. H. 27:26
Corbin, D. W. 1:24
Corbin, George 14:50
Corbin, George W. 24:37
Corbin, Hiram D. 22:25
Corbin, Ira 16:117
Corbin, Isaac 5:37
Corbin, J. 25:158
Corbin, J. S. 14:254; 16:92
Corbin, Jerry 13:107
Corbin, Joshua M. V. 4:18
Corbin, L. B. 5:12
Corbin, L. W. 19:62
Corbin, M. 3:48; 23:138
Corbin, P. W. 18:79
Corbin, Parker 6:15
Corbin, Thomas 14:314
Corbin, W. 3:48
Corbin, William 6:27; 8:62; 26:156
Corbint, A. G. 20:177
Corbis, J. 3:49
Corbit, J. 23:106
Corbit, Martin 18:304; 26:94
Corbitt, George T. 12:17
Corbitt, J. 1:23
Corbitt, John 3:48
Corbitt, Martin 9:20
Corbitt, Michael 9:20
Corbitt, W. H. 9:242
Corbitt, William 5:12; 25:158
Corbon, John B. 8:104

Corboran, Dallas 18:128
Corbran, Alexander 17:503
Corby, John W. 10:158; 19:156
Corby, Thomas 19:62
Corcoran, Henry 17:63
Corcoran, J. C. 11:124
Corcoran, James 10:158; 19:156
Corcoran, John 1:24; 20:230
Corcoran, Joseph 13:16; 18:334
Corcoran, L. 19:249
Corcoran, Lawrence 9:173
Corcoran, M. 14:50; 16:290
Corcoran, Michael 1:120; 7:23; 19:9
Corcoran, P. 1:121
Corcoran, Richard 15:340; 16:92, 366
Corcoran, Stephen 4:18
Corcoran, Thomas 15:318; 19:62
Corcoran, W. J. 9:78
Corcoran, William 22:287
Corcoran, William I. 26:17
Cord, Charles M. 26:21
Cord, James M. 20:21
Cord, Lorenzo W. 24:15
Cord, W. N. 20:154
Cord, William N. 20:182
Cordell, C. 21:22
Cordell, Charles F. 16:27
Cordell, Charles T. 13:16
Cordeman, William 13:16
Corden, C. 18:47
Corden, J. W. 21:186
Corder, Benjamin 18:233; 26:21
Corder, J. 22:184
Corder, J. A. 14:50
Corder, Jackson 17:291
Corder, James 22:184
Corder, James M. 10:204
Corder, John 23:25
Corderry, William 17:235
Cordery, W. H. 22:185
Cordindorfee, D. 14:50
Cordiner, John 11:56
Cording, Jacob 11:199
Cording, W. A. 20:230
Cording, William A. 10:47
Cordman, Samuel 23:279
Cordnay, David 22:418
Cordon, C. 10:147
Cordova, Juan 12:169

Cordray, J. J. 3:48
Cordray, Josephus 22:9
Cordray, T. 16:290
Cordright, Levi 4:18
Corduan, William H. 23:128
Core, H. 10:27; 19:300
Core, J. 13:86; 14:7; 15:312; 19:63
Core, J. H. 24:76
Core, Joseph H. 16:117
Corea, Joseph 17:442
Coreson, Edward H. 11:285
Coresoy, H. 19:249
Corett, James M. 17:294
Corey, A. B. 17:290
Corey, B. W. 15:306
Corey, C. A. 3:48
Corey, Charles 25:158
Corey, Charles A. 4:18
Corey, Charles H. 18:291
Corey, Charles R. 22:139
Corey, E. 13:16; 16:27
Corey, George 1:120
Corey, J. A. 18:47
Corey, J. M. 20:39
Corey, James 1:21
Corey, John 9:117; 27:30
Corey, John W. 12:17
Corey, Joseph W. 9:96
Corey, Nelson H. 22:71
Corey, Oscar M. 19:9
Corey, Philip 24:185
Corey, Samuel 8:82, 113; 18:327
Corey, Spencer 18:364
Corey, William 15:190
Coreyel, A. 15:340
Corfail, Thomas 26:95
Corgalt, P. T. 20:230
Corgan, J. 21:165
Corgatt, Peter T. 10:47
Corhis, S. 21:67
Coriell, A. 23:138
Coriell, S. 16:147
Corigan, H. 25:158
Corin, Flore 7:91
Corion, O. P. 15:285
Corison, John 21:244
Corjial, Thomas 9:33; 18:291
Cork, Albert 7:91
Cork, John H. 16:182
Cork, William 5:50; 25:158
Corkell, F. M. 22:185
Corkell, John 1:25
Corken, Gideon 12:17
Corkill, B. 11:380
Corkins, Egbert C. 11:259

Corkins, Eugene 22:25
Corkins, Henry H. 24:37
Corkran, Daniel 11:279
Corkrite, James 18:128
Corkson, Patrick 11:395
Corkwell, George W. 15:191
Corl, C. C. 3:48
Corlen, John 21:165
Corlen, Warren 26:122
Corlens, Warren 9:42
Corler, Alfred 4:18
Corless, R. 3:49
Corlett, Daniel 17:231
Corlett, James 21:223
Corlett, Thomas 17:313
Corlette, Hilty 9:159
Corley, D. H. 26:154
Corley, John 18:284
Corley, Michael 3:48
Corley, Noah E. 7:23
Corlie, Presley 14:314
Corlin, L. P. 23:86
Corlis, Hayen J. 23:284
Corlis, J. 10:186; 18:173
Corliss, Amos 14:153
Corliss, Daniel 22:185
Corliss, G. A. 9:78
Corliss, J. C. 21:22
Corliss, Samuel 25:158
Corlock, William 20:230
Corlue, P. 14:321
Corly, John 26:134
Cormack, Jeremiah 24:99
Cormack, John 13:16; 23:25
Corman, Samuel 18:364
Cormed, J. J. 11:230
Cormell, J. 1:97
Cormick, J. 15:165
Cormick, J. M. 16:182
Cormick, John 12:68; 15:32
Cormick, Patrick 19:63
Cormick, William 5:37
Cormish, Isaac 16:182
Cormody, Simon 11:91
Cormore, John 13:107
Cormwright, S. 1:121
Corn, A. 9:78
Corn, George 7:67
Corn, Harrison 22:295
Corn, Ishman 9:20
Corn, J. C. 11:299
Corn, James 22:71
Corn, Jerry 17:173
Corn, Jesse 7:48
Corn, Peter 20:91
Corn, Samuel 22:71
Corn, Timothy 17:259
Corn, W. R. 17:505

Corndon, James 8:12
Corne, James 9:199
Corneal, Vincent 11:199
Cornegie, John L. 24:175
Cornelious, G. H. 9:96
Cornelisor, James 14:153
Cornelius, A. 1:25
Cornelius, Albert 22:332
Cornelius, Charles T. 25:25
Cornelius, David 8:100; 17:461; 24:169
Cornelius, E. 3:48
Cornelius, Edward 8:12; 18:128
Cornelius, Ephraim C. 22:71
Cornelius, George 22:295
Cornelius, J. B. 18:27
Cornelius, J. G. 25:23
Cornelius, J. J. 1:21
Cornelius, J. W. 15:347; 16:366
Cornelius, James 3:48
Cornelius, Jefferson 6:24
Cornelius, L. C. 3:48
Cornelius, Samuel 22:25
Cornelius, William 3:48; 10:47, 108; 20:230
Cornelius, Willis 17:400
Corneliusen, Charles 21:251
Cornell, Adrian 13:16
Cornell, Albert 20:39
Cornell, Alfred 11:200
Cornell, Ambrose G. 22:25
Cornell, Asa 22:139
Cornell, Cornelius 23:188
Cornell, Harrison 22:184
Cornell, Isaac 17:64
Cornell, J. 1:122
Cornell, James 22:295
Cornell, John 7:16
Cornell, Jonathan 24:76
Cornell, Lafayette 10:47
Cornell, Lewis 22:295
Cornell, M. 13:86; 14:7
Cornell, Peter 23:305
Cornell, R. B. 1:23
Cornell, Robert 24:37
Cornell, S. C. 19:156
Cornell, Samuel 17:415
Cornell, Solomon 7:91
Cornell, Tho. 21:67
Cornell, Thomas 13:16
Cornell, William 21:251
Cornell, William L. 17:233
Corner, Ephraim M. 21:67
Corner, George 18:393

Corner, L. 25:158
Corner, Martin 23:138
Corners, Robert 13:107
Cornes, James 9:117
Corness, George 14:50
Cornet, Romance 13:16
Cornett, Christ 18:79
Cornett, W. 17:147
Cornett, Wesley 17:109
Cornett, William H. 21:86
Cornette, Laurence 8:113
Corney, C. 16:183
Corney, Charles 9:206; 15:95
Corney, Ipock 19:156
Corney, John 19:156
Corney, Thomas 19:156
Cornfare, D. 15:158
Cornfield, John 26:155
Cornford, Sylvan 17:287
Cornham, H. 14:50
Cornhe, Pans 13:62
Cornhe, Parris 16:183
Cornhill, William 12:58
Cornick, Daniel 25:158
Cornick, G. 1:117
Cornin, J. 24:15
Cornine, William H. 21:67
Corning, Alfred 9:117
Corning, David 23:138
Cornish, A. 3:48
Cornish, Almon 10:47
Cornish, Almond A. 20:230
Cornish, Charles P. 1:192
Cornish, Edward 12:48
Cornish, Henry 18:79
Cornish, Jacob 14:153
Cornish, James 14:153
Cornish, M. 19:249
Cornish, Matthew 9:173
Cornish, Thomas 7:71
Cornish, W. E. 19:156
Cornish, William 14:154
Corniss, George 5:12
Cornly, B. 16:183
Cornman, F. J. 1:25
Cornman, Oscar 15:25
Cornmesser, J. L. 4:18
Cornock, T. 1:26
Cornog, William 16:27
Cornon, Frederick 10:171
Cornor, Samuel 19:45
Cornoy, William 13:16
Cornoy, William L. 19:329
Cornry, John 10:171
Cornstock, G. E. 3:49
Cornstuble, Green B. 22:25

Cornultia, N. 25:158
Cornurty, James 8:12
Cornville, Edward 22:232
Cornwall, Charles 22:277
Cornwall, Edgar 13:16; 16:27
Cornwall, George H. 25:25
Cornwall, Homer 19:156
Cornwall, Homes 10:171
Cornwall, John 22:402
Cornwall, Morgan 9:66
Cornwall, William 22:397
Cornwall, William J. 22:332
Cornway, Henry 24:107
Cornwell, A. S. 20:89; 21:98
Cornwell, B. F. 18:291; 26:95
Cornwell, Bennett H. 21:223
Cornwell, Elias 7:77
Cornwell, Enos 20:230
Cornwell, J. S. 8:82
Cornwell, J. W. 17:390
Cornwell, Jackson 17:50
Cornwell, Lewis 10:108; 20:230
Cornwell, Martin 7:23
Cornwell, Morgan 18:275
Cornwell, Thomas 8:82
Coroat, C. W. 14:154
Coroden, James M. 16:154
Coron, Charles 3:49
Coroner, C. 9:160
Corothers, William W. 18:426
Corpe, William J. 17:70
Corperts, A. H. 22:332
Corpinlis, John 25:287
Corpion, F. 1:122
Corps, Park 14:50
Corpstein, J. S. 24:76
Corpstine, J. 11:339
Corral, George 22:111
Corrall, A. 21:98
Corran, Edward 16:183
Corran, John 9:108
Correll, C. 24:76
Correll, J. Daniel 22:475
Correll, John 10:158
Correll, Lafayette 20:230
Correll, Levi 15:191
Correll, W. H. 11:54
Correy, Philip 17:429
Corridon, James 18:128
Corrien, Henry 9:33
Corrigan, Hugh 5:12
Corrigan, James 15:81

Corrigan, John 15:32; 17:50; 23:128
Corrin, Charles 3:49
Corring, W. S. 21:317
Corrington, J. B. 18:79
Corrish, Frank 14:334
Corrison, W. N. 25:158
Corrivan, Daniel 25:158
Corrmens, C. 18:117
Corroll, John N. 11:55
Corrow, Willy 24:65
Corry, C. W. 13:86; 14:7
Corse, Asa 19:9
Corse, Charles 24:92
Corse, H. B. 4:18
Corse, Silas 3:48
Corse, William H. 11:319
Corsen, Eli 18:364
Corsen, Thomas 23:63
Corsens, Lewis 11:199
Corser, Anthony B. 22:420
Corser, George A. 10:158; 19:156
Corser, True 22:71
Corsom, C. H. 15:191
Corson, Abijah 7:14
Corson, Alexander 13:107
Corson, B. S. 3:48
Corson, C. M. 13:107
Corson, G. A. 1:122
Corson, Isaac 14:7
Corson, J. 1:122
Corson, John 25:158
Corson, Lemuel 26:122
Corson, Levi C. 9:213
Corson, Tunis 27:30
Corson, W. 1:118
Corson, William S. 22:71
Corst, James 3:49
Cort, John 24:90
Corter, C. J. 25:158
Corter, H. A. 19:9
Corter, H. O. 19:63
Corter, J. 14:50
Corter, John W. 14:50
Cortes, D. 13:86
Cortin, E. H. 9:141
Cortis, D. 14:7
Cortis, Joel 13:107
Cortiss, Francis L. 4:18
Cortman, George 23:138
Cortner, Samuel E. 23:63
Cortney, George W. 20:21
Cortney, J. 26:153
Cortney, Thomas 18:304; 26:94
Cortney, William 25:20
Cortnight, Daniel 4:18
Corton, H. M. 25:23
Corton, Milo 11:124

Cortor, Henry 21:317
Cortrell, W. W. 5:12
Cortrocke, P. 8:104
Corts, Abraham 18:393
Cortter, H. O. 15:326
Cortwell, Joseph 19:63
Corurtney, Edward 21:223
Coruthers, Henry 8:82
Corvill, H. F. 16:183
Corvill, Joseph A. 20:230
Corville, Edward 13:16
Corville, Joseph Antoine 10:47
Corwall, William 26:156
Corway, George 7:83
Corwein, Stephen 23:120
Corwell, Adam 11:332
Corwell, Peter 11:411
Corwin, C. W. 21:120
Corwin, D. L. 13:77; 16:183
Corwin, Frederic 17:64
Corwin, H. C. 11:385
Corwin, Henry 17:19, 173
Corwin, J. 3:48
Corwin, J. F. 22:139
Corwin, J. V. 3:48
Corwin, James 14:50
Corwin, Jonas D. 20:94
Corwin, M. T. 22:139
Corwin, Nathan 10:47; 20:230
Corwin, Nelson W. 20:29
Corwin, P. M. 15:104
Corwin, T. W. 20:230
Corwin, Theodore 7:23
Corwin, William R. 19:300
Cory, Abraham 20:16
Cory, Albert 1:25
Cory, C. W. 16:267
Cory, Enos 19:63
Cory, Leander 18:215; 22:402
Cory, Leander C. 22:419
Cory, O. E. 19:249
Cory, Robert Z. 22:71
Cory, Thomas E. 24:15
Cory, William 25:318
Corya, Joseph W. 11:238
Coryeb, A. 16:366
Coryell, Daniel 23:86
Coryell, Edw. C. 9:102
Coryell, J. W. 21:165
Corzin, Thompson C. 24:15
Corzolt, M. H. 9:96
Cos, John F. 16:117
Cosad, J. P. 14:50
Cosart, Lewis 16:27
Cosart, Wilson 27:32

Cosbin, William H. 17:50
Cosby, Overton 9:203; 18:65
Cose, Isaac 26:17
Coselman, W. H. 14:268
Coseman, Foster 11:91
Cosevay, George 21:317
Cosey, Daniel 20:174
Cosflock, H. A. 3:49
Cosgrone, S. 16:183
Cosgrove, A. H. 11:299
Cosgrove, Arthur 1:22
Cosgrove, James 23:15
Cosgrove, John 11:15
Cosgrove, Michael 9:109
Cosgrove, S. 13:77
Cosgrove, Thomas C. 19:343
Cosgrove, William 15:298
Coshey, Lebons B. 15:65
Cosier, John 11:325
Cosland, G. 14:7
Coslet, M. 26:154
Coslete, Alexander 17:19
Coslin, Abraham 10:208
Cosmer, Joseph 13:63
Cosmer, Judson 10:204
Cosner, P. H. 22:473
Cosper, James S. 24:37
Coss, Edward 15:352
Coss, Levi 23:284
Cosse, Isaac 18:128
Cosselman, G. 3:49
Cossins, S. 11:27
Cosson, B. 12:85
Cossy, M. 26:20
Costagan, Wesley 5:12
Costalo, Michael 25:21
Costard, George 7:120
Costell, E. M. 11:190
Costelle, Peter 22:333
Costello, Charles 15:65
Costello, James 4:18
Costello, John 12:95
Costello, M. 12:164
Costello, Michael 6:20; 23:63
Costello, Patrick 9:11
Costello, Thomas 11:258; 12:17; 15:293
Costellow, Samuel W. 21:91
Costelly, John C. 22:448
Costelow, Daniel W. 22:185
Costerman, Jacob 8:12
Costigan, Daniel 8:113
Costigan, W. 25:158
Costillo, Joseph 8:12
Costills, Joseph 18:128
Costin, Henry W. 22:420

Costin, Richard 23:63
Costley, John 12:68
Costley, Nelson 21:136
Costo, Simon 15:85
Coston, Frederick 23:86
Coston, J. 3:49
Coston, W. L. 13:107
Costrel, S. 18:173
Coswell, Samuel 8:82
Cot, T. J. 20:154
Cotanch, Henry 19:156
Cotcomb, Fred 24:166
Cotean, William 10:47; 20:230
Cotee, Francis 14:154
Cotes, E. 22:25
Cotes, Edwin 14:154
Cotes, Mariner W. 21:91
Cotes, W. W. 11:286
Coteul, William S. 22:185
Cotey, J. S. 15:191
Cothall, William G. 9:42
Cotherman, Jacob 18:128
Cothingin, Henry 8:12
Cothour, John 22:295
Cothran, David S. 17:417
Cothy, David 12:147
Cotier, Elihu 16:11
Cotillo, Thomas 22:402
Cotlendafer, George 14:152
Cotlier, H. 25:26
Cotmody, Cornelius 19:233
Cotner, Frederick 22:71
Cotner, John 11:259
Cotner, Thomas 22:71
Coto, Joseph 21:317
Cotrall, John 22:477
Cotray, J. 11:339
Cotrell, J. 11:141
Cotrell, John 15:191
Cotrell, Joseph 16:92
Cotrell, Perry 8:104
Cott, G. T. 8:12
Cott, John S. 15:329; 19:63
Cottar, Samuel 14:154
Cottein, Elisha 9:173
Cottel, John 19:156
Cottell, Isaac 21:67
Cottengan, William 22:247
Cottepair, J. 15:340; 16:366
Cotter, Benjamin 11:104
Cotter, George W. 11:118
Cotter, J. 21:317
Cotter, J. A. 17:216
Cotter, Marion 11:421
Cotter, Patrick 16:366

Cotter, W. A. 2:9
Cotter, William 11:218
Cotteral, Perrey W. 20:189
Cotterell, Abram 26:144
Cotterell, Benjamin J. 22:185
Cotterman, A. 23:139
Cotterman, Isaac 19:9
Cottie, Henry 2:9
Cottil, Henry 2:9
Cotting, George P. 7:23
Cottinger, Frank 10:158
Cottinger, Frank H. 19:156
Cottinger, John 14:154
Cottingham, --- 11:199
Cottingham, G. W. 11:238
Cottingham, Isaac T. 23:279
Cottingham, James E. 21:84
Cottingham, John 10:108; 20:230
Cottingham, T. 1:26
Cottingin, Henry 18:128
Cottle, Ben. R. 23:188
Cottle, Enoch G. 22:185
Cottle, J. 25:318
Cottle, James H. 10:108
Cottle, Samuel R. 9:117
Cottner, H. W. 20:230
Cotton, --- 25:319
Cotton, Addison 24:213
Cotton, Addison R. 17:423
Cotton, Cyrus 24:100
Cotton, Elisha 15:54
Cotton, Eugene 17:417; 24:157
Cotton, George 10:170; 19:156
Cotton, George A. 21:49
Cotton, George T. 11:443
Cotton, George W. 22:402
Cotton, H. 9:141; 21:109; 27:28
Cotton, J. 3:49
Cotton, J. B. 20:132
Cotton, J. C. 10:95
Cotton, J. H. 19:226; 21:12
Cotton, James 12:17
Cotton, James H. 22:419
Cotton, John 6:24; 11:103; 15:191
Cotton, John O. 22:71
Cotton, N. F. 17:291
Cotton, Otis A. 20:192
Cotton, P. 25:158
Cotton, Robert 22:9

Cotton, Sampson 27:29
Cotton, Samuel 9:129
Cotton, Thomas 8:77
Cotton, W. C. 17:32
Cotton, William 17:77
Cottonwood, H. D. 14:50
Cottrel, J. W. 7:48
Cottrell, A. H. 23:117
Cottrell, Abraham 10:108; 20:230
Cottrell, P. 3:49
Cottrill, A. 1:122
Cottrill, M. 3:49
Cotts, Isaac 25:21
Cottsrell, G. W. 3:49
Coty, Henry 24:92
Cou, T. 14:50
Couburn, George 19:63
Couch, A. 21:147
Couch, Benjamin 1:24; 3:49
Couch, Charles 13:16
Couch, Charles M. 7:91
Couch, E. B. 16:183
Couch, Enoch Anderson 11:115
Couch, George H. 21:317
Couch, H. 18:128
Couch, Henry 22:25
Couch, J. H. 9:50
Couch, John 21:317; 25:23
Couch, John A. 12:145; 26:217
Couch, John G. 24:37
Couch, John W. 13:63
Couch, Jonathan 22:421
Couch, M. W. 16:183
Couch, R. C. 14:154
Couch, Thomas M. 10:27; 19:300
Couch, William 18:128; 22:333
Couch, William A. 18:128
Couch, William F. 22:420
Couche, J. 18:65
Couche, John 20:230
Couchlin, Lewis 9:117
Coudry, John M. 17:453
Couffman, L. 14:50
Cough, B. 7:67
Cough, Daniel 21:317
Cough, E. 13:86
Cough, Samuel 9:70
Cougher, J. M. 15:191
Coughill, Jackson 21:49
Coughlan, J. 1:117
Coughlin, Cornelius 19:327
Coughlin, James 18:430
Coughlin, Jeremiah 4:18

Coughlin, John 1:120; 16:27
Coughman, C. Y. 20:122
Coughman, G. H. 7:91
Coughman, Jacob 17:415
Coughran, D. 1:96
Coughran, Michael 21:317
Cougill, John 11:276
Couillard, James A. 24:92
Coulard, Charles 13:107
Coulbourn, G. W. 25:158
Couler, William 3:49
Couley, J. 19:63
Couley, John 14:50
Coullier, Alexander 20:230
Coulogn, Robert 21:317
Coulon, Lorence 11:140
Coulson, Chauncey R. 17:442
Coulson, Chauncy R. 24:157
Coulson, Cornelius B. 11:411
Coulson, George H. 23:139
Coulson, George W. 17:359
Coulson, Jesse 22:185
Coulson, Job V. 22:476
Coulson, John W. 24:157
Coulson, S. W. 22:185
Coulten, J. W. 19:63
Coulter, Edward 19:63; 21:318
Coulter, Fred C. 20:230
Coulter, H. 15:65
Coulter, Henry 12:68
Coulter, J. C. 22:476
Coulter, J. W. 10:47
Coulter, James 4:18; 23:178
Coulter, John 19:63
Coulter, Levi 1:120
Coulter, M. 3:49
Coulter, M. V. B. 24:76
Coulter, Michael 12:95
Coulter, S. 25:319
Coulter, Samuel L. 9:117
Coulter, Samuel R. 27:30
Coulter, W. James 21:251
Coulter, Warren W. 11:450
Coulter, William 15:150
Coulthard, Robert 9:10
Coulthart, W. 13:16
Coultner, Mike 19:63
Coultner, Nicholis 15:358
Coulton, Edward 15:354
Coulton, James R. 21:247

Coultrain, Jackson 16:27
Coun, John 17:173
Counahan, Andrew J. 7:23
Council, Matter S. 18:205
Council, S. 25:159
Councillor, Sol 23:252
Counnings, William 21:318
Counrod, Abson 7:23
Counselbraun, G. B. 4:18
Counsellor, Benjamin F. 22:420
Counselman, A. 14:50
Counsil, H. 10:47
Count, G. 14:7
Counter, Baptiste 12:48
Counter, James 19:280
Counter, M. 14:50
Counter, Nicholas 8:113
Counterlean, Erin 17:396
Countraman, James M. 5:13
Countryman, --- 3:49
Countryman, A. 8:47
Countryman, Alexander 21:67
Countryman, Alfred 25:159
Countryman, James 4:18
Countryman, Joseph 23:303
Countryman, Simon 4:18
Counts, Caesar 27:29
Countue, G. 11:83
County, James 4:18
County, Shelby 21:267
Countz, Aaron 20:34
Coup, J. R. 7:91
Coup, J. S. 24:76
Coup, Jacob 13:124
Coup, W. F. 1:121
Coupant, G. F. 10:144
Coupin, John 18:128
Couplantz, G. W. 20:39
Cour, William 10:108
Courad, Frank 11:91
Couradt, John 13:16
Courds, Caesar 9:129
Courier, George 5:12; 9:78; 26:18
Courier, John 20:230
Courier, Lucien A. 4:18
Courin, P. 25:276
Cournal, Frank 23:202
Course, Albert 14:296
Coursen, Abraim 23:120
Courser, Hiram J. 11:91
Coursey, G. D. 11:275
Coursey, Matt. B. 25:285
Coursey, Silas 22:333
Courson, B. W. 11:384

Courson, D. H. 3:49
Courtain, Felix 17:423; 24:172
Courtenay, George 18:79
Courtenay, J. H. 27:31
Courteny, J. C. 23:25
Courter, Robert W. 22:461
Courter, William P. 16:162
Courting, Joseph 11:141
Courtley, H. 25:159
Courtnay, W. 3:49
Courtney, C. J. 15:32
Courtney, F. 1:23
Courtney, G. 11:299
Courtney, George 6:15, 22
Courtney, H. 11:91
Courtney, Henry 11:200
Courtney, J. 26:18
Courtney, J. F. 3:49
Courtney, J. H. 10:108; 14:296; 17:470; 20:230
Courtney, Jacob M. 17:94
Courtney, James 8:47; 9:78; 23:139; 25:21; 26:18
Courtney, John 17:287
Courtney, Levi 15:191
Courtney, M. 18:27
Courtney, Pat 3:49
Courtney, Samuel 22:25
Courtney, Smith R. 17:109
Courtney, Thomas 17:50
Courtney, W. W. 14:50
Courtney, William 1:22; 13:16
Courtney, William H. 22:72
Courtny, John Thomas 23:25
Courtraman, J. M. 25:159
Courtright, A. 11:230
Courtright, Adam A. 17:320
Courtright, George 8:82; 17:355; 18:327
Courtright, R. 1:119
Courtright, S. E. 15:191
Courtright, Vance T. 17:71
Courtright, William 11:55
Courtwright, C. C. 19:236
Courtwright, Charles 9:173
Courtwright, J. L. 25:159
Courtwright, Jefferson 25:159

Courtwright, Manassas 19:156
Courtwright, S. 1:23
Courtwright, William 4:18
Cousans, C. 18:364
Couse, Albert 27:32
Couse, Charles W. 22:333
Cousicil, Walter S. 8:82
Cousin, William A. 23:86
Cousino, M. 19:325
Cousins, Alphonso C. 5:12
Cousins, Charles E. 27:29
Cousins, James A. 16:27
Cousins, Moses 19:325
Cousins, T. D. 1:121
Coustney, John M. 11:26
Coutant, William H. 21:67
Coutcher, David 20:189
Couter, James E. 23:25
Coutes, William 10:90
Coutr, David 21:211
Couts, Peter 23:139
Couts, William A. 10:47
Couturi, Israel 4:18
Couzers, N. H. 7:74
Couzins, N. H. 25:295
Cova, Charles 4:18
Covall, Charles H. 25:310
Cove, Samuel 21:242
Covekett, Thomas J. 10:108; 20:230
Covell, A. 7:48
Covell, Isaac 7:23
Covell, Lyman 19:157
Covell, Martin 15:315
Covell, Zenus 22:25
Covensfarrow, D. 19:249
Covenstance, Joseph 20:111
Cover, Ephaim 18:109
Cover, Ephraim 6:7
Cover, G. W. 1:121
Cover, John 3:49
Cover, Joseph 17:320
Cover, L. 3:49
Cover, Peter 9:20; 18:304; 26:95
Cover, S. 14:50
Cover, W. A. 21:318
Cover, William H. 14:154
Coveran, John 11:259
Coverbrink, H. 20:230
Coverbrink, Henry 10:47
Coverdell, J. J. 20:230
Coverdill, James 21:318
Coverdill, James J. 10:47
Coverston, L. J. 21:120
Covert, A. S. 22:418
Covert, Benjamin 1:21; 25:21

Covert, E. 3:49
Covert, Francis 4:18
Covert, J. H. 21:165
Covert, John 9:71
Covert, Nathan 12:121
Covert, Nathaniel 15:121
Covert, Samuel 22:72
Covert, William A. 23:284
Covett, Martin 19:63
Covey, Alfred C. 16:27
Covey, Alfred E. 13:16
Covey, Charles H. 9:33
Covey, D. 1:97
Covey, E. 1:117
Covey, Hiram 27:32
Covey, John B. 14:50
Covey, William 19:45
Covil, James L. 22:461
Covil, William 3:49
Covill, Andrew J. 20:111
Covill, Elisha 16:84
Covill, Hiram C. 10:210
Covington, A. 3:49
Covington, A. J. 21:318
Covington, Andrew 22:295
Covington, Charles 22:333
Covington, E. B. 11:254
Covington, Elijah 16:27
Covington, George B. 18:215
Covington, J. B. 3:49
Covington, VanBuren 10:179; 18:173
Covington, William 11:325
Covington, William H. 8:13; 18:128
Covly, R. B. 14:277
Cow, William 15:191
Cowall, William 10:108
Cowan, Alexander 21:67
Cowan, C. 21:318
Cowan, David F. 10:108; 20:230
Cowan, David H. 5:13
Cowan, Edward 23:260
Cowan, Ezra W. 22:402
Cowan, F. H. 9:50
Cowan, Francis 9:20; 18:304; 26:94
Cowan, G. A. 13:63; 19:63
Cowan, G. P. 17:99
Cowan, George 25:159
Cowan, George A. 18:338
Cowan, H. 13:86
Cowan, Henry 26:138
Cowan, Hugh M. 22:26
Cowan, Hugh Q. 25:274

Cowan, J. 14:50
Cowan, James 14:50
Cowan, James D. 19:157
Cowan, John 4:18; 15:32; 17:242; 24:8
Cowan, John A. 11:141
Cowan, John H. 22:185; 25:22
Cowan, Joseph 9:78; 26:19
Cowan, N. 23:306
Cowan, Robert H. 21:242
Cowan, Samuel 22:185
Cowan, W. 25:24
Cowan, William M. 21:67
Cowans, John M. 11:259
Coward, S. 17:129; 24:191
Coward, Thomas 22:247
Cowarn, William 15:2
Cowary, J. B. 16:366
Cowdel, W. 16:183
Cowden, B. W. 10:179; 18:173
Cowden, Charles L. 22:185
Cowden, Daniel 18:304
Cowden, Daniel A. 9:20; 26:94
Cowden, G. D. 13:107
Cowden, R. 24:212
Cowden, William 13:86; 14:7; 22:26
Cowder, Stephen A. 22:140
Cowdey, Russel 23:25
Cowdin, --- 23:289
Cowe, George E. 19:9
Coweas, A. 25:20
Cowell, Edward 16:27
Cowell, Emanuel 8:71
Cowell, G. 16:183; 21:67
Cowell, John 3:49; 12:68; 15:27
Cowell, Lewis 4:18
Cowell, Moses 21:251
Cowell, S. 11:326
Cowell, Samuel 24:151
Cowell, W. 14:7
Cowell, William 12:17
Cowels, Charles 22:139
Cowen, Abner 9:50
Cowen, Andrew 10:90
Cowen, Andrew J. 20:230
Cowen, Andy 6:27
Cowen, Calvin 16:183
Cowen, David 23:251
Cowen, Dennis 6:9
Cowen, E. 8:62; 18:188; 26:154
Cowen, Emory H. 20:122

Cowen, George 7:120
Cowen, H. 14:7
Cowen, J. 3:49
Cowen, Jeff 17:173
Cowen, John 1:21
Cowen, John F. 24:151
Cowen, Joseph 21:223
Cowen, Moses 15:7
Cowen, Robert 20:231
Cowens, A. 2:9
Cowens, York 9:129; 27:28
Cower, John 25:24
Cowerley, D. E. 27:27
Cowers, J. 27:31
Cowers, N. L. T. 22:461
Cowes, Frederick S. 21:251
Cowey, George 21:98
Cowger, J. E. 10:186; 18:173
Cowger, William 10:186; 18:173
Cowgill, Daniel 17:450; 24:177
Cowgill, M. H. 1:119
Cowgill, Robert H. 17:242
Cowham, John M. 21:251
Cowhen, David 27:33
Cowherd, Francis M. 21:50
Cowhorn, John 22:247
Cowill, J. B. 16:92
Cowin, E. 17:337
Cowin, J. 11:326
Cowin, James H. 12:17
Cowing, John T. 17:415
Cowings, Edward B. 10:108; 20:231
Cowish, John 11:385
Cowl, J. 25:159
Cowl, James 5:13
Cowler, James M. 17:425
Cowler, John 18:304; 26:94
Cowles, Asa S. 21:136
Cowles, B. H. 23:202
Cowles, D. 3:49
Cowles, E. 15:165
Cowles, E. V. 16:183
Cowles, George 9:163; 25:319
Cowles, Giles M. 13:63
Cowles, Giles N. 19:63
Cowles, Hale 17:359
Cowles, J. 14:296
Cowles, Leonard 14:296; 17:477; 27:31
Cowles, Lewis G. 12:17
Cowles, M. A. 19:157
Cowles, Manly T. 22:277

Cowles, Nathan 7:67
Cowles, R. 15:151
Cowles, R. W. 22:139
Cowles, Robert 15:335
Cowles, S. W. 19:236
Cowles, W. 18:173
Cowles, Z. H. 1:120
Cowley, E. 18:13
Cowley, Eason P. 8:13
Cowley, Edwin P. 18:128
Cowley, F. 14:50
Cowley, J. 14:50
Cowley, John 22:161;
    25:159
Cowley, Josiah 1:22
Cowley, R. 17:13
Cowling, David 7:91
Cowling, Thomas 10:171;
    19:157
Cowlis, John M. 10:171
Cowlis, Marshall 10:171
Cowls, J. 17:473
Cowman, Clark R. 22:111
Cowman, William M.
    20:21
Cowpe, John 23:139
Cowper, Henry 26:153
Cowperthwaite, D. R.
    5:13
Cowpland, R. H. 16:117
Cowrier, John 10:47
Cowrser, E. 16:183
Cowser, Abraham 11:335
Cowser, Samuel 11:300
Cowville, J. W. 10:47;
    20:231
Cox, --- 18:109; 22:523;
    23:267
Cox, A. B. 3:49; 14:240;
    27:33
Cox, A. C. 17:388
Cox, A. E. 3:49
Cox, Aaron 9:229;
    20:231; 22:419
Cox, Aaron O. 18:468
Cox, Abraham 21:223
Cox, Acton 18:393
Cox, Alex 21:318
Cox, Alfred 6:7
Cox, Andrew 22:165;
    23:270; 24:76
Cox, Atlas 8:13; 18:128
Cox, B. 17:129; 24:191
Cox, B. F. 11:83
Cox, Bartlee G. 22:165
Cox, Benjamin 11:275;
    22:185
Cox, Buck 26:22
Cox, Charles 8:13;
    10:108; 14:50, 334;

Cox, Charles 18:128;
    20:231; 27:33
Cox, Charles P. 17:205
Cox, D. 1:24; 3:49; 9:141;
    27:26
Cox, D. C. 3:49
Cox, D. M. 14:50
Cox, Daniel 7:91; 22:185
Cox, David 12:48
Cox, Edmond 20:231
Cox, Edmund 10:47
Cox, Elias 21:318
Cox, Elijah 21:223
Cox, Ezra 18:233; 26:19
Cox, F. 13:86; 25:319;
    27:26
Cox, Franklin 20:185
Cox, G. W. 16:17
Cox, George 11:421;
    17:247; 20:6; 23:112
Cox, George C. 19:346
Cox, George W. 9:96;
    10:108; 20:231;
    23:290
Cox, H. 3:49; 10:154;
    19:157
Cox, Hall 21:267
Cox, Henry 25:281
Cox, Horton 22:499
Cox, Howell L. 24:37
Cox, I. W. 25:310
Cox, Isaac 8:104; 17:32,
    247
Cox, Isaac D. 21:22
Cox, Israel B. 9:173;
    19:266
Cox, Iverson 6:27
Cox, J. 14:50; 16:267;
    18:233, 364; 20:122;
    21:203; 25:159;
    26:21
Cox, J. A. 3:49; 18:233;
    26:21
Cox, J. B. 22:185
Cox, J. D. 11:218
Cox, J. H. 11:91; 21:50
Cox, J. J. 8:113; 26:19
Cox, J. K. 21:318
Cox, J. M. 10:108; 20:231
Cox, J. S. 19:157
Cox, J. W. 11:54
Cox, Jackson 10:47;
    20:231
Cox, Jacob 21:50
Cox, Jacob L. 11:259
Cox, James 3:49; 9:33;
    10:47; 17:94; 18:291;
    20:231; 22:26;
    23:281; 24:37; 26:95
Cox, James A. 19:157
Cox, James E. 20:143

Cox, James H. 22:119
Cox, James M. 23:267
Cox, James R. 10:47;
    20:231
Cox, Jesse W. 17:235
Cox, Joel 7:120
Cox, John 5:37; 9:47, 219;
    10:108; 11:54, 380;
    15:273; 17:77, 307;
    18:215; 19:63;
    20:142, 174, 231;
    21:267; 23:202;
    24:59; 26:142
Cox, John H. 12:95;
    15:358; 19:63
Cox, John J. 9:78; 22:26
Cox, John S. 7:14
Cox, John W. 22:402
Cox, Joseph 3:49; 9:33;
    10:108; 14:235;
    18:27, 291; 20:231;
    21:241; 24:88; 26:95
Cox, Joseph F. 17:90
Cox, Joshua E. 16:183
Cox, Josiah 21:98; 24:173
Cox, Kate H. 26:218
Cox, L. 3:49; 23:202
Cox, L. N. 9:50
Cox, Lawrence 22:72
Cox, Linsey 17:205
Cox, Lorenzo H. 12:17
Cox, Loven 14:296;
    17:475; 27:31
Cox, Luman C. 11:410
Cox, M. 20:231
Cox, Madison 23:63
Cox, McLoro 18:411
Cox, Micajah 10:47;
    20:95
Cox, Miness 23:97
Cox, Morgan 17:19
Cox, N. 11:91
Cox, N. J. N. 22:499
Cox, Nelson 9:206; 23:97
Cox, Newell 27:29
Cox, Newton 21:109
Cox, Nicholas 22:72
Cox, O. 1:123
Cox, O. H. P. 8:71
Cox, Orlando A. 20:188
Cox, Orville N. 21:318
Cox, P. 3:49; 23:25
Cox, Patrick 11:19
Cox, Perry 18:233; 26:21
Cox, Peter 22:185
Cox, Peter A. 22:119
Cox, Richard 15:16;
    25:295
Cox, Robert 11:259;
    24:37
Cox, Robin 16:183

Cox, S. 11:90; 14:7
Cox, S. J. 22:185
Cox, S. M. 21:120
Cox, Samuel 11:103;
13:86; 21:267
Cox, Samuel C. 22:499
Cox, Sherrill B. 24:49
Cox, Silas F. 12:152
Cox, Squire M. 22:448
Cox, Stephen 21:98
Cox, T. 9:141
Cox, T. A. 3:49
Cox, Taylor 10:108;
20:231
Cox, Theodore 6:8;
18:102
Cox, Thomas 8:13, 104;
9:141; 10:95;
18:128; 19:9; 24:37
Cox, Thomas H. 10:159;
19:157
Cox, Thomas P. 11:54
Cox, Turner T. 17:32
Cox, Virgil S. 20:231
Cox, W. 25:159, 279
Cox, W. A. 3:49
Cox, W. C. 3:49; 23:63
Cox, W. F. Dolan 25:159
Cox, W. R. 7:23
Cox, Warner 21:223
Cox, William 1:121; 4:18;
5:13; 8:104; 9:106;
10:47; 11:411, 421;
12:170; 13:86; 14:7,
319; 15:86; 20:231;
22:420
Cox, William F. 22:420;
23:63
Cox, William G. 22:26
Cox, William H. 21:67;
22:419
Cox, William H. H. 17:32
Cox, William J. 23:184
Cox, William M. 10:90;
11:55; 20:231
Cox, William P. 11:325
Cox, William T. 7:91;
18:128
Cox, Z. A. 11:15
Coxall, Henry 21:318
Coxan, George 17:50
Coxe, Jesse E. 19:9
Coxe, Robert 9:68
Coxen, William 2:8; 25:23
Coxey, James 7:67
Coxley, Solon 25:23
Coy, Á. 11:138
Coy, Asa 7:23
Coy, B. 19:249
Coy, E. G. 1:121
Coy, Eliab W. 25:159

Coy, Francis 22:421
Coy, G. 16:267
Coy, G. C. 18:188
Coy, Henry 11:139
Coy, J. H. 20:231
Coy, J. M. 17:173; 19:249
Coy, John 22:72
Coy, John H. 3:49
Coy, Joseph H. 10:47
Coy, Kindall H. J. 20:231
Coy, N. A. 22:185
Coy, Sidney 17:64
Coy, Silas 22:476
Coy, William 9:50
Coyad, S. 22:518
Coydam, William B.
21:318
Coyer, --- 10:151, 178
Coyer, Joseph 17:359;
20:151, 192
Coyer, William 8:13
Coyers, C. W. 9:50
Coyfort, J. 16:267
Coygins, Thomas 12:48
Coyheadall, Wesley 9:33
Coykendall, Adolphus
21:247
Coykendall, D. 3:49
Coykindale, H. J. 9:229
Coylay, C. J. 2:8; 25:20
Coyle, A. B. 9:78; 26:17
Coyle, Beverly 9:206
Coyle, C. 3:49
Coyle, C. D. 16:117
Coyle, D. B. 11:279
Coyle, Daniel 19:10
Coyle, Edward 3:49;
16:183
Coyle, H. 3:49
Coyle, J. 1:121
Coyle, J. G. 16:117
Coyle, James 12:68;
13:16; 15:27; 16:117;
19:10, 63
Coyle, John 20:122
Coyle, M. 3:49
Coyle, M. B. 1:118
Coyle, Mark 4:18
Coyle, Michael 17:355
Coyle, N. 9:109
Coyle, Patrick 16:183
Coyle, Richard 22:119
Coyle, S. 14:50
Coyle, S. H. 22:185
Coyle, Thomas J. 23:63
Coyle, William 23:25
Coyna, Peter 24:15
Coyne, John 7:23; 21:318
Coyne, M. 3:49
Coyne, Simon 7:67
Coyne, Thomas 25:319

Coyner, George W. 3:49
Coynor, William C. 21:22
Cozard, Edward 13:16
Cozard, W. H. H. 15:86
Cozart, J. 1:122
Cozel, William 1:23
Cozens, A. 25:159
Cozgill, J. C. 25:26
Cozin, William 4:18
Cozine, William G.
17:202
Cozzen, Ezzra 16:183
Crab, Lewis 5:37
Crabaugh, Jeremiah N.
16:132
Crabb, A. J. 16:135
Crabb, F. M. 22:185
Crabb, Ira 17:32
Crabb, J. F. 20:87
Crabb, John H. 22:419
Crabb, Robert 16:290
Crabb, W. H. 15:121
Crabb, William H. 12:121
Crabb, William J. 22:140
Crabbett, Barney 22:247
Crabble, Levi M. 10:48
Crabbs, Charles 23:139
Crabe, A. B. 1:118
Craber, Jackson 20:181
Crabill, Martin 22:185
Crabill, William 22:185
Crable, L. M. 20:231
Crabs, Benedick 26:17
Crabs, Benedict 9:78
Crabs, H. K. 22:477
Crabton, Charles 8:104
Crabtree, --- 17:279
Crabtree, Abner 9:219;
18:364
Crabtree, Abraham 7:64
Crabtree, Amey 17:202
Crabtree, B. F. 21:318
Crabtree, C. 24:191
Crabtree, Daniel 6:35;
10:47; 17:173;
20:231
Crabtree, E. 21:186
Crabtree, G. W. 12:81;
16:290
Crabtree, George 27:33
Crabtree, Hiram 22:26
Crabtree, J. 1:121
Crabtree, J. P. 19:10
Crabtree, J. W. 7:23
Crabtree, Jackson 20:185;
21:186
Crabtree, James 22:448
Crabtree, John 21:98;
22:247
Crabtree, Joseph 26:210
Crabtree, M. L. 22:165

Crabtree, Noah 17:129; 24:191
Crabtree, Robert T. 17:94
Crabtree, Seth 9:117; 27:31
Crabtree, Solomon 24:165
Crabtree, William 10:108; 11:395; 17:202; 20:231; 22:399
Crabtree, William C. 22:247
Crackel, M. 23:25
Cracken, J. M. 1:117
Crackenberg, John 9:20
Cracraft, John 17:32
Craddick, Thomas 19:319
Craddock, --- 8:71; 26:154
Craddock, E. T. 10:192
Craddock, John 24:65
Craddock, Presley 9:78
Craddock, R. 26:18
Craddock, Thomas J. 10:159; 19:157
Cradel, Arnst 21:318
Crader, P. 15:191
Cradle, S. 23:112
Cradlebaugh, J. K. 21:120
Cradock, Pleas't. G. 22:499
Crady, Alex. M. 10:145; 19:157
Crady, Columbus 17:352
Crady, Felix 17:352
Crady, M. 11:100
Craegan, Michael 24:92
Craf, Newton 15:337
Craffen, O. 26:20
Crafford, Daniel 13:107
Craford, J. D. 21:109
Craft, A. 3:49
Craft, A. B. 13:107
Craft, Antoine 10:204
Craft, B. 3:49
Craft, C. H. 21:318
Craft, Charles 10:108; 20:231; 22:277
Craft, Courtland 10:15
Craft, D. P. 9:141; 27:26
Craft, Daniel 16:183
Craft, Fred 9:106
Craft, G. B. 11:395
Craft, G. C. 14:154
Craft, George 12:99; 15:347, 366
Craft, Henry 22:333; 24:169
Craft, Henry S. 17:32
Craft, I. S. 25:159
Craft, J. B. 14:240
Craft, J. L. 22:186

Craft, J. S. 21:95
Craft, James 9:117; 16:183; 27:30
Craft, James H. 8:82
Craft, James L. 22:185
Craft, Jesse 23:139
Craft, John 10:108; 20:231
Craft, Newton 19:63
Craft, Richard 19:10
Craft, S. B. 20:145
Craft, Samuel O. 27:30
Craft, Thomas 8:13; 11:410; 18:129
Craft, Thomas H. 22:26
Craft, W. S. 15:318
Craft, Walter 9:129; 27:29
Craft, William Z. 23:97
Crafton, John 22:26
Crafts, E. T. 3:49
Crafts, F. A. 25:159
Crafts, Samuel O. 9:117
Crafts, William C. 16:92
Crag, I. 18:188
Crag, N. C. 20:142
Cragan, G. 3:50
Cragen, Elisha 11:54
Crager, G. 14:50
Crager, J. 3:50
Crager, J. V. 21:22
Cragg, Thomas 17:32
Cragill, Alonzo M. 16:183
Cragle, Alexander 25:23
Cragle, J. T. 25:159
Cragle, John T. 5:13
Cragle, W. 16:117
Crago, I. 1:25
Crago, John 22:185
Crague, C. 21:98
Craick, Samuel 9:229; 20:231
Craid, Jacob 11:27
Craifton, Lawrence 7:91
Craig, --- 18:188
Craig, A. F. 11:400
Craig, Albert L. 18:80
Craig, Alexander 1:22; 22:469
Craig, Andrew 18:233; 25:295; 26:20
Craig, Augustus 21:318
Craig, D. 3:50
Craig, D. R. 7:48
Craig, Darius 10:47
Craig, David E. 20:96
Craig, Davis 20:231
Craig, E. 14:287; 22:185
Craig, Edward 9:229; 20:231
Craig, F. 3:50; 15:32, 54
Craig, Francis 11:411

Craig, Frank 12:68
Craig, G. W. 13:17
Craig, George 20:96
Craig, H. 25:159
Craig, Henry 10:108, 208; 20:231
Craig, Henry W. 6:20; 18:80
Craig, Hiram 5:13
Craig, Isaac A. 22:26
Craig, J. 3:50
Craig, J. G. 3:50
Craig, James 11:321; 17:247; 24:87
Craig, James G. D. 5:13
Craig, James L. 21:22
Craig, James M. 17:32
Craig, Jefferson 16:183
Craig, John 8:13; 12:86; 17:101; 18:129; 19:157; 24:59
Craig, John A. 24:37
Craig, John L. 21:215
Craig, John S. 18:215
Craig, John W. 11:319; 21:22, 318
Craig, Jonathan 11:410
Craig, Joseph 4:18; 11:300
Craig, Lafayette 11:395
Craig, M. E. 9:227; 18:364
Craig, Michael 12:167
Craig, Noah 7:23
Craig, O. P. 18:47
Craig, Orlando 9:109
Craig, Orrin 22:72
Craig, R. 1:122
Craig, R. B. 4:18
Craig, Reason 17:316
Craig, Renzel 10:204
Craig, Richard 1:23; 20:111
Craig, Robert 20:189
Craig, Robert E. 27:32
Craig, Robert H. 11:385
Craig, S. 3:50; 14:264; 25:159
Craig, S. G. 21:318
Craig, Samuel 15:191; 22:449; 23:25; 24:99
Craig, Smiley 17:144; 22:421
Craig, Stacey 13:17
Craig, Stacy 16:27
Craig, T. 1:123
Craig, Thomas 7:48; 15:258; 23:270
Craig, Thomas J. 23:63
Craig, W. 3:50; 25:22
Craig, W. A. 3:50

Craig, W. H. 1:117; 23:25
Craig, W. W. 12:141
Craig, Wesley 15:90
Craig, Wilford 24:15
Craig, William 3:50;
18:27; 23:63, 139
Craig, William H. 15:16;
22:9
Craig, Willis 11:91
Craig, Z. H. 8:71
Craige, Hugh 10:108;
20:231
Craige, James 12:17
Craige, Samuel 20:6
Craigen, G. F. 1:23
Craiger, --- 25:24
Craiger, A. 15:267
Craiger, John W. 10:108;
20:231
Craiger, Z. 15:323
Craiger, Zach 19:63
Craigg, Thomas 4:18
Craighead, Lerry 21:267
Craighton, J. W. 11:141
Craighton, Michael
14:154
Craighton, William 1:120
Craigle, William H. 22:72
Craigue, E. 13:107
Crail, D. O. 11:91
Crail, Hugh 21:251
Crail, James 10:47;
20:231
Crain, A. J. 26:144
Crain, Ausker J. 20:231
Crain, David S. 20:231
Crain, J. 3:50
Crain, John 9:20; 22:420
Crain, John M. 21:223
Crain, R. O. 3:50
Crain, William 21:22
Craine, C. 18:27
Craine, Francis 13:107
Craine, Peter 8:82
Crainer, E. 14:7
Craines, John 23:104
Craisel, Samuel C. 10:95
Craiton, John 14:51
Craivner, William 16:183
Crakl, J. E. 12:86; 16:290
Crale, Hue 8:47
Craley, Fred 25:21
Crall, D. 13:86
Crall, John H. 23:139
Crallen, Edward 26:218
Crallen, Thomas 26:217
Cralty, Edmund 17:313
Cram, A. 3:50
Cram, C. L. 20:151
Cram, Eliphalet C. 15:191
Cram, H. 12:121

Cram, H. C. 25:159
Cram, James 12:68; 15:32
Cram, Joseph 12:121;
15:121
Cram, L. 12:121
Cram, Landon 4:18
Cram, Oscar I. 10:47
Cram, R. 3:50
Cram, S. F. 1:25
Cram, William 18:291
Crambaugh, J. 7:48
Cramblet, William 19:349
Crame, A. 1:122
Crame, C. E. 15:151
Crame, Howell 23:188
Cramer, A. 3:50
Cramer, Alex 7:23
Cramer, B. M. 14:154,
254
Cramer, C. 9:141; 27:28
Cramer, Charles E. 19:63
Cramer, Conrad 19:10
Cramer, Cornelius 1:120
Cramer, David 19:63;
22:185
Cramer, Dota 1:22
Cramer, E. 3:50; 13:86
Cramer, E. A. 16:183
Cramer, Elias 17:320
Cramer, F. 9:141; 13:124;
25:159; 27:28
Cramer, F. T. 22:185
Cramer, Frederick 7:91;
9:33
Cramer, Henry 7:91
Cramer, J. 1:121; 5:50;
9:141; 22:295;
25:159; 27:28
Cramer, J. M. 3:50
Cramer, J. W. 15:191
Cramer, Jacob 7:23
Cramer, James 22:421
Cramer, James H. 23:188
Cramer, Jeremiah 1:121
Cramer, John 1:22;
22:232; 24:37
Cramer, John D. E. 17:13
Cramer, John G. 22:185;
23:188
Cramer, Joseph 1:25;
22:185, 295
Cramer, Lewis 21:242
Cramer, Louis 22:477
Cramer, M. 14:154, 254
Cramer, Marcus 24:92
Cramer, Nicholas 24:37
Cramer, Philip 18:215
Cramer, Samuel 19:10
Cramer, Solomon 24:37
Cramer, T. H. 11:83
Cramer, T. Y. 19:277

Cramer, W. 13:86
Cramer, Walter 9:96
Cramer, Warren A. 23:63
Cramer, William H. H.
17:355
Cramer, William S.
22:277
Crames, Dillard 22:499
Cramie, John 7:23
Cramlet, John C. 11:139
Cramley, George 3:50
Crammel, Valley 21:267
Crammer, John 19:63
Crammund, C. C. 18:27
Cramner, Ezra 19:157
Cramonan, Daniel 18:129
Cramp, C. E. 1:120
Cramp, George 6:24
Cramp, Thomas 11:91;
22:161
Cramp, William 17:287
Crampson, H. 26:156
Crampton, A. 3:50
Crampton, A. B. 3:50
Crampton, H. 8:62; 13:86
Crampton, James 16:84
Crampton, Michael 6:12
Crampton, Oscar 18:444
Cramshaw, J. W. 26:19
Cramt, J. P. 3:50
Cran, James W. 8:82
Cran, Joe W. 25:159
Cranahan, R. 24:107
Crance, John 12:17
Crance, Richard 7:91
Cranch, William 11:91
Cranchan, Ephraim
24:173
Cranchan, Ephriam
17:448
Crandal, A. 19:63
Crandall, A. W. 18:233;
26:21
Crandall, Charles 22:476
Crandall, Clara 26:218
Crandall, Cleon 8:13
Crandall, D. 1:24
Crandall, Dudley W.
19:157
Crandall, Ephraim 27:25
Crandall, G. F. 19:63
Crandall, George W.
19:157
Crandall, H. 1:117
Crandall, H. H. 18:65
Crandall, H. M. 21:22
Crandall, H. S. 18:393
Crandall, Harriet B.
26:218
Crandall, J. 3:50
Crandall, J. H. 8:47

Crandall, John A. 21:136
Crandall, Joseph C. 9:173
Crandall, Joshua 23:305
Crandall, L. 3:50
Crandall, Mary A. 26:218
Crandall, Nelson 11:115
Crandall, P. 9:141
Crandall, Paul 27:28
Crandall, R. 3:50
Crandall, W. 1:117
Crandall, William H.
  5:13; 23:10
Crandall, Zanoni G. 24:49
Crandalls, A. G. 19:157
Crandell, C. 13:86
Crandell, C. H. 25:159
Crandell, C. J. 16:92
Crandell, Charles M.
  17:242
Crandell, D. 3:50
Crandell, Daniel 12:17
Crandell, Dennison G.
  21:251
Crandell, Dudley 10:159
Crandell, Eli 14:154
Crandell, Frank 12:53
Crandell, G. 1:118
Crandell, J. L. 19:249
Crandell, P. 14:51
Crandell, Thomas 15:151
Crandell, W. M. 3:50
Crandell, William 21:252
Crandell, William H.
  17:263; 25:159
Crandle, A. 26:236
Crandle, B. F. 10:48;
  20:231
Crandle, Charles 15:191
Crandle, J. F. 3:50
Crandle, John D. 13:17
Crandle, Silas 7:23
Crandole, A. C. 10:153
Crane, A. A. 25:22
Crane, A. J. 20:231
Crane, A. M. 11:25
Crane, Allen W. 16:278
Crane, Amos 22:185
Crane, Asa F. 23:25
Crane, Benjamin F.
  11:122
Crane, Byron 4:18
Crane, Charles C. 11:115
Crane, Charles O. 21:318
Crane, Conleton D. 11:54
Crane, Cyrus 23:202
Crane, D. H. 8:13
Crane, D. W. 18:129
Crane, David 15:321
Crane, E. 18:65
Crane, E. A. 1:118
Crane, Earl 8:104

Crane, Edmund 24:107
Crane, Edward 1:22
Crane, Elisha 7:91
Crane, Francis 12:172
Crane, G. B. 8:12, 13
Crane, G. W. 26:217
Crane, George 18:129
Crane, George W. 9:236;
  22:165
Crane, H. 1:26; 3:49;
  15:121; 21:147
Crane, H. J. 16:290
Crane, Henry 10:159;
  16:183; 19:157
Crane, Ira J. 22:72
Crane, J. E. 25:159
Crane, James E. 20:29
Crane, James G. W. 21:67
Crane, James H. 8:13;
  18:129
Crane, James S. 21:22
Crane, James W. 20:21
Crane, Jefferson 20:89
Crane, John 1:21; 17:19;
  18:304; 21:200;
  22:476; 25:20; 26:94
Crane, John D. 10:152
Crane, John M. 23:86
Crane, Jonas K. 22:72
Crane, Jonathan M. 24:37
Crane, Joseph 22:403
Crane, Josiah W. 20:192
Crane, L. 21:165
Crane, L. W. 1:118
Crane, Lee 18:233; 26:22
Crane, Lewis A. 10:47;
  20:231
Crane, Lewis H. 13:17;
  16:27
Crane, Lewis T. 25:159
Crane, Lindsay 26:156
Crane, M. 3:49; 13:86;
  17:130; 24:190
Crane, Martin 19:63
Crane, Newman 12:68;
  15:21
Crane, Noah 27:32
Crane, Oscar I. 10:47
Crane, Samuel 7:91; 13:86
Crane, Silas B. 9:203
Crane, Stephen M. 18:47
Crane, Theo. F. 20:231
Crane, Theodore F. 10:90
Crane, Thomas 17:252;
  22:185, 247; 24:76
Crane, Thomas C. 22:140
Crane, Timothy 11:26
Crane, W. 22:185
Crane, W. E. 11:56
Crane, W. S. 11:56

Crane, William 11:395;
  17:147; 26:95
Craner, Charles 12:48
Craner, M. F. 11:259
Craner, Thomas J. 22:421
Cranes, James 19:280
Craneson, William P.
  11:291
Craney, Samuel 13:17
Craney, W. H. 14:237
Crangle, Elijah 25:282
Crank, --- 17:506
Crank, A. 14:7
Crank, F. 14:280
Crank, Hiram 20:231
Crank, Joseph 8:47; 21:98
Crank, Leonard 13:79
Crank, T. 24:15
Cranke, James 3:50
Crankite, C. M. 18:304;
  26:95
Cranley, George 21:318
Cranmer, Abram 21:136
Cranmer, C. H. 18:47
Cranmer, J. C. 10:108;
  20:231
Crann, Michael 18:129
Crannel, William 22:26
Crannell, C. 15:191
Crannell, Marvin 12:17
Crannell, Solon 1:121
Crannons, Charles 12:17
Crans, David 22:475
Crans, William 4:18
Cranshaw, James 22:185
Cranson, A. B. 5:13
Cranson, Andrew 8:82
Cransten, Michael 14:268
Cranston, Earl 21:136
Cranston, Henry 7:91
Cranston, James 10:15;
  15:191
Cranston, Michael 13:17
Cranston, William 16:92
Crant, J. 1:118
Cranter, M. 16:183
Crantz, W. B. 14:240
Cranwell, Thomas 19:10
Crap, Charles 11:26
Crape, Henry C. 12:7
Crapen, Arms 9:42
Crapen, J. 3:50
Crapes, Martin 11:285
Crapo, Eliakim 15:121
Crapo, John F. 19:10
Crapo, M. 10:47; 20:232
Crappel, J. P. 17:109
Crapps, Joseph 7:91
Craps, Job H. 7:14
Craps, M. D. L. 22:140
Craps, Samuel 11:25

Craptree, Joseph 4:18
Crareers, William 8:82
Crarey, B. F. 8:47
Crark, Jacob 15:277
Crarston, T. C. 1:118
Crary, Charles 4:18
Crary, F. 11:83
Crary, George 18:173
Crary, George M. 10:34
Crary, Newton 22:185
Crary, Osgood S. 11:140
Crasby, Benjamin 10:159
Crasby, Henry 24:190
Crasby, M. 3:50
Crasby, N. B. 22:476
Crasen, J. 3:50
Crasey, William R. 17:19
Crass, J. 23:139
Crass, John 22:449
Crass, William P. 24:15
Crassen, A. 15:54
Crassen, Edward 8:13
Crassman, Josiah 9:50
Crassman, W. F. 8:47
Crasson, D. P. 1:118
Crasson, John 16:84
Craswell, Samuel 3:50
Crasy, S. P. 3:50
Craten, Barney 4:18
Crater, Jacob H. 15:65
Crater, John 12:68
Crathers, J. 25:159
Crathers, James 5:37
Crathurd, George 8:82
Cratin, August 9:129;
  27:28
Crato, Charles 11:300
Craton, Andrew 25:319
Craton, L. M. 16:183
Cratt, A. W. W. L. 11:421
Cratting, Michael 7:23
Crattley, Henry 11:301
Cratz, Phillip 8:82
Craun, William J. 22:185
Crausver, Daniel 18:129
Craut, Charles F. 22:185
Cravat, John 17:212
Cravatt, William 10:108;
  20:232
Crave, George 18:275
Craven, A. J. 3:50
Craven, Allen 11:275
Craven, Austin 18:27
Craven, Charles P. 22:26
Craven, John 11:259;
  17:130; 21:50;
  24:189
Craven, P. 21:109
Craven, Peter 20:136
Craven, Reason 7:23
Craven, Samuel W. 21:50

Craven, Thomas 10:48;
  20:232
Craven, William 10:48
Craven, Zeno 19:327
Cravener, J. 19:63
Cravens, Horace P.
  24:186
Cravens, Howell P.
  17:429
Cravens, Patrick 9:159
Cravenstine, Charles
  19:10
Craver, Chester L. 13:17
Craver, George 13:17
Craver, M. T. 25:25
Craver, Thomas H. 21:67
Craver, William 11:104
Cravey, Jonas 25:295
Cravin, William 20:232
Cravity, Christian 10:108
Cravner, S. P. 3:50
Cravoly, Alex 16:27
Craw, Abraham 24:191
Craw, Adam 12:152
Craw, Henry 7:56
Craw, I. 11:410
Craw, J. S. 11:54
Craw, Jacob W. 12:17
Craw, Shellon 18:205
Craw, William 1:22
Craw, William T. 9:96
Crawback, George 14:51
Crawell, James 17:233
Crawer, T. Y. 8:59
Crawford, A. 3:50; 11:279
Crawford, A. G. 16:27
Crawford, Alfred 21:267,
  268
Crawford, Andrew
  21:147, 268; 22:295
Crawford, B. 21:318
Crawford, Barnell 21:268
Crawford, Boswell 21:147
Crawford, C. 9:50
Crawford, C. S. 27:26
Crawford, Carroll 21:268
Crawford, Cato 18:233;
  26:21
Crawford, Charles 9:141;
  12:17; 15:32; 22:147,
  185
Crawford, Charles G.
  8:13; 26:153
Crawford, Columbus
  26:210
Crawford, D. 1:117
Crawford, D. S. 17:19
Crawford, David 11:411
Crawford, Davis 22:500
Crawford, Duncan 11:380

Crawford, E. 1:122;
  25:159
Crawford, Ebenezer A.
  22:26
Crawford, Edward 22:247;
  23:25; 26:210
Crawford, Edward C.
  23:288
Crawford, Edward S
  22:476
Crawford, Edwin E.
  22:496
Crawford, Elisha 15:191
Crawford, F. 8:113
Crawford, F. J. 18:173
Crawford, G. 23:139
Crawford, George 3:50;
  15:121
Crawford, George W.
  9:78; 26:17
Crawford, H. 18:109;
  22:295
Crawford, H. C. 10:108;
  20:232
Crawford, H. E. 19:249
Crawford, Henry 21:136,
  268; 22:512
Crawford, Henry W.
  20:145
Crawford, Herman 11:104
Crawford, Hezekiah
  17:389
Crawford, Hillane 6:9
Crawford, Hiram B.
  17:109
Crawford, Horace 24:61
Crawford, Isaac 24:61
Crawford, J. 3:50; 7:56;
  25:310
Crawford, J. A. 19:277
Crawford, J. H. 15:191
Crawford, J. J. 10:27;
  19:300
Crawford, J. J. T. 1:122
Crawford, J. M. 9:102
Crawford, J. N. 18:338
Crawford, Jacob 24:76
Crawford, James 1:23;
  3:50; 12:17; 18:173;
  21:268; 27:30
Crawford, James A. 7:23;
  9:173
Crawford, James H. 22:26
Crawford, James M.
  23:284
Crawford, James R. 9:42;
  10:108; 20:232
Crawford, John 3:50;
  7:120; 9:199; 19:63,
  290; 22:402; 23:260
Crawford, John A. 12:7

Crawford, John I. 20:232
Crawford, John L. 10:108
Crawford, John W. 8:82
Crawford, Johnson A. 23:139
Crawford, Joseph 3:50
Crawford, Josiah 17:64
Crawford, K. 14:254
Crawford, L. 3:50
Crawford, L. O. 20:232
Crawford, Lemuel 22:72
Crawford, M. 3:50; 9:42
Crawford, M. H. 12:68; 15:32
Crawford, Marcus 22:295; 24:49
Crawford, Martin 17:94
Crawford, Moses L. 17:272
Crawford, N. M. 18:173
Crawford, P. 15:191; 22:523
Crawford, Peter 13:17; 19:63
Crawford, R. 11:299
Crawford, R. J. 19:10
Crawford, R. M. 11:321
Crawford, R. S. 1:121; 19:280
Crawford, Richard 22:295
Crawford, Robert 18:27; 24:76
Crawford, Robert S. 9:173
Crawford, S. 11:258; 23:139
Crawford, Sam W. 17:423
Crawford, Sam. W. 24:172
Crawford, Samuel 11:90; 14:314; 18:434; 21:318; 22:185, 507
Crawford, Samuel C. 22:287
Crawford, Silas 10:48; 21:318
Crawford, Smith 22:402
Crawford, T. J. 10:179
Crawford, T. T. 12:86; 16:290
Crawford, Taylor 21:223
Crawford, Thomas 13:17; 22:295
Crawford, Thomas F. 14:51
Crawford, Thomas P. 10:48
Crawford, W. 7:48
Crawford, W. H. 20:232
Crawford, W. M. 10:179
Crawford, W. S. 11:408

Crawford, W. W. 10:48; 20:232
Crawford, Walter 15:32
Crawford, Walter J. 22:140
Crawford, William 1:119; 7:23; 8:82; 9:157, 173; 11:258; 13:17; 16:27, 117; 17:440; 19:273; 20:39; 21:129, 318; 22:295, 448; 24:151; 26:156
Crawford, William C. 17:417; 24:157
Crawford, William E. 9:173
Crawford, William H. 10:108
Crawford, William J. 24:107
Crawford, William M. 9:33; 10:48
Crawford, William P. 6:10
Crawford, William S. 10:15; 22:185
Crawford, William W. 22:232
Crawghan, Michael 13:107
Crawk, Thomas 11:259
Crawley, Abraham 16:117
Crawley, Alex 13:17
Crawley, Charles 9:33; 26:95
Crawley, Cornelius 9:173
Crawley, David 20:143
Crawley, G. 9:141; 27:26
Crawley, J. 25:26
Crawley, Jeremiah 9:173
Crawley, John 15:298; 16:183
Crawley, Nathan 7:23
Crawley, Preston 17:348
Crawley, Stephen 11:294
Crawling, William W. 17:50
Crawn, William 23:139
Crawshaw, Job 22:185
Cray, --- 25:159
Cray, A. L. 1:118
Cray, Andrew 22:185
Cray, Charles 23:283
Cray, David B. 10:90
Cray, F. M. 13:127
Cray, M. 24:76
Cray, N. 13:107
Craycraft, Joseph 22:26
Craycraft, William B. 22:449
Craycroft, C. John 14:7
Craycroft, J. 13:86

Crayen, Laymen 9:33
Crayho, Joseph 21:67
Craymer, J. A. 14:254
Craymer, R. 13:107
Crayton, Lawrence 21:318
Crayton, Stephen 14:154
Craze, William 14:51
Crazier, William 14:51
Crazinn, J. 3:50
Cready, Richard 22:119
Creagar, Elmore W. 22:72
Creagar, Henry 7:67
Creager, Charles A. 23:178
Creal, J. M. 19:10
Crealmen, C. 1:121
Creamer, --- 16:113
Creamer, Andrew 17:77
Creamer, Arthur 22:403
Creamer, E. 3:50
Creamer, Elias 17:32
Creamer, George 13:17
Creamer, J. 11:299
Creamer, J. T. 1:26
Creamer, Jacob 16:15
Creamer, Jesse 23:25
Creamer, John 19:157
Creamer, John W. 10:90; 20:232
Creamer, Levi 9:173
Creamer, Marcus 11:103
Creamer, Michael 19:10
Creamer, Webster 9:173
Creammer, Webster 19:226
Crease, John 19:157
Crease, John B. 16:27
Creaser, W. 25:23
Creashbaum, G. 1:24
Creasin, Gilpen 26:17
Creasin, Gilpin 9:78
Creasy, Jesse 14:154
Creath, Owen M. 20:136
Crebo, George 18:233; 26:21
Crecelous, John H. 22:421
Credan, Timothy 20:106
Crede, Homer 10:108
Cree, Calvin 23:267
Cree, R. B. 21:120
Creeas, John R. 22:26
Creech, George T. 23:97
Creech, H. 14:51
Creech, Isaac 23:63
Creech, Valentine 21:98
Creech, William H. 22:26
Creed, G. B. 2:9
Creede, Homer 20:232
Creedy, J. M. 4:18
Creek, George 7:23; 13:86

Creek, John 10:108; 20:232
Creek, John W. 11:385
Creek, William W. 17:205
Creeke, George 14:7
Creekpan, H. J. 9:102
Creekpaun, Jasper 20:232
Creekpaun, Joseph 10:108
Creeks, Isaiah 19:301
Creeks, James 10:27
Creel, W. C. 21:318
Creelina, B. F. 11:395
Creemer, Anthony 10:48; 20:232
Creemer, John 22:419
Creeney, James H. 21:318
Creeper, J. 9:96
Creese, James H. 18:129
Creete, L. 25:159
Creever, Henry I. 7:91
Creff, J. 16:183
Cregan, John 19:10
Creger, James 20:21
Cregg, J. 3:50; 14:51
Cregg, Michael 17:454; 24:185
Cregger, J. F. 3:50
Cregger, W. H. 3:50
Creghton, --- 16:290
Crego, Albert 16:183
Cregswell, Harrison 11:411
Creig, Ezra W. 9:50
Creiger, Carl F. 25:283
Creight, A. O. M. 26:20
Creighton, --- 12:81
Creighton, Alexander 16:117
Creighton, Benjamin 4:18
Creighton, Henry 21:67
Creighton, M. 1:118
Creighton, Patrick 17:19
Creighton, William 17:231
Creisler, John 9:207
Creitser, Solomon 18:47
Crell, F. M. 14:7
Creller, L. 23:25
Cremble, James 7:138
Creme, N. B. 5:13
Cremean, Jesse J. 17:212
Cremer, George 3:50
Cremer, Hubert L. 22:277
Cremers, William 25:22
Cremmer, A. 26:154
Cremmer, Levi 19:226
Cremonds, Cornelius 16:290
Cremones, D. 3:50
Cremor, --- 12:172
Crenell, Henry 21:318

Crenger, Henry 24:15
Crenshall, Calvin 22:295
Crenshaw, J. W. 9:78
Crenshaw, Peter 21:268
Crenshaw, S. W. 9:78
Crent, Charles 11:124
Creppin, John A. 26:94
Crepps, J. C. 17:90
Crepps, Joseph 26:122
Crepwell, G. B. 18:359
Creridon, John 16:147
Cresal, John 15:104
Cresey, N. F. 3:50
Cresfield, Abraham 22:140
Cresishan, Boone 7:23
Cresivell, --- 11:54
Cresler, J. W. 16:92
Cresm, R. B. 15:191
Creso, James H. 8:13
Creson, George W. 21:223
Cress, H. 22:9
Cress, James 17:247
Cress, John 12:152
Cress, William 12:17
Cress, William T. 17:259
Cressey, D. 27:27
Cressey, Henry W. 23:188
Cressey, Marquis L. 21:136
Cressey, Osgood D. 22:475
Cressey, W. P. 26:17
Cressford, William Henry 19:157
Cressinger, Daniel J. 19:157
Cressinger, Samuel J. 10:171
Cresswell, William 7:120
Cressy, Albert B. 12:55
Cressy, Charles F. 10:15
Cressy, Ebenezer 19:157
Cressy, James C. 7:120
Cressy, N. P. 9:78
Crest, C. D. 19:63
Creswell, James M. 24:37
Cretcher, Charles 25:159
Cretons, H. F. 11:385
Crettenson, Almon 13:63
Cretzel, Englebert 22:333
Creuse, John B. 13:17
Creveling, J. B. 13:86
Creveslin, Levi 20:96
Creviston, Aaron 22:72
Crevity, Christian 20:232
Crew, J. L. 27:27
Crew, John L. 26:122
Crew, John W. 4:18
Crew, Thomas 9:42; 26:122

Crewe, Elam 22:72
Crewell, John H. 12:17
Crewet, William 14:333
Crewis, William E. 5:13
Crews, Andrew 18:129
Crews, E. M. 3:50
Crews, Francis A. 10:108; 20:232
Crews, G. 3:50
Crews, J. 9:50
Crews, Levi 11:56
Crews, Peter 11:198
Cria, Augustus 9:173
Cribben, John 20:232
Cribben, Sam 25:26
Cribbin, John 10:108
Cribbing, John 22:523
Cribble, Daniel 11:142
Cribbs, D. 14:51
Crible, George W. 21:50
Cribles, S. 25:159
Crichfield, R. 18:173
Crick, F. 14:27
Crick, J. W. 15:65
Crick, Uriah F. 15:191
Cricket, D. 25:159
Crickporm, Hugh 11:55
Criddlebaugh, B. 8:47
Cridell, W. 15:258
Crider, Charles D. 19:157
Crider, E. 11:259
Crider, Francis 8:82
Crider, Jacob M. 22:448
Crider, John B. 22:120
Crider, Joseph 18:233; 26:21
Crieler, Isaac 23:63
Crien, E. F. 10:108; 20:232
Crier, J. F. 9:50
Criff, Goowon 4:65
Criffy, James 23:304
Criger, Solomon 11:140
Crigg, John 17:212
Crigger, William 8:100; 17:460; 24:157
Cright, Charles M. 25:274
Crigsby, Burges 24:100
Crile, George 12:17
Crill, John 22:186
Crilley, C. W. 3:51
Crilly, Nicholas 12:17
Crim, C. 3:51
Crim, Henry G. 17:279
Crimer, Nelson R. 10:159
Crimes, George 9:71
Crimm, M. D. 14:154
Crimm, W. 11:27
Criner, J. C. 26:18
Cringer, Jacob 5:13
Crink, J. Mc. 27:33

Crinnian, R. 18:47
Crins, M. S. 11:421
Crip, J. K. 21:318
Cripe, David R. 8:82
Cripe, John 22:419
Cripe, Sylvester 23:63
Cripliver, James 22:186
Cripliver, James F. 17:32
Cripman, S. 3:51
Crippen, Aborn 20:232
Crippen, Abram 10:48
Crippen, G. F. 3:51
Crippen, John A. 9:20
Crippen, Nathan R.
    10:171
Cripple, Solomon 6:24
Cripps, John 16:92
Cris, William 11:55
Criscamp, Henry 20:232
Crise, Aaron K. M. 22:72
Crise, C. 23:25
Crise, Charles 13:107
Crish, M. 18:27
Crisinger, George W.
    10:25
Crisler, James M. 11:25
Crisler, T. 16:183
Crisler, William R. 18:47
Crisles, Albert 17:397
Crisley, J. 3:51
Crisman, Jacob 23:202
Crisman, Michael 22:232
Crisman, William 22:72
Crisner, C. 25:159
Crisner, Isaac 9:78
Crisp, Allen H. 23:25
Crisp, Ansil 8:13
Crisp, Charles 17:263
Crisp, G. 1:120
Crisp, Orrin 7:120
Crispel, John H. 22:140
Crispen, William 21:67
Crispin, Gilbert 10:108;
    20:232
Crispin, James 17:32
Crisple, D. 7:120
Criss, Andrew C. 4:18
Criss, James 21:50
Criss, James A. 15:191
Criss, W. C. 21:223
Crissinger, William
    11:301
Crissman, A. 17:173
Crissman, James 3:51
Crisson, Jacob 22:247
Crisswell, William 20:145
Crist, David 26:121
Crist, Henry T. 18:215
Crist, J. 22:186
Crist, J. D. 3:51
Crist, John I. 22:72

Crist, John M. 13:17
Crist, M. 14:51
Crist, Martin 11:118
Crist, Michael 9:109
Crist, Orrin 22:475
Crist, W. H. 21:223
Cristemon, M. 22:72
Cristfelter, Stephen 22:26
Cristie, William 20:21
Cristy, Albert 19:285
Cristy, Garvey M. 12:68
Cristy, Jonathan 8:13
Cristy, P. 7:67
Crisup, James 18:65
Criswell, George B. 10:7
Criswell, J. 3:51
Criswell, Jackson 1:21
Criswell, M. 1:26
Criswell, S. M. 14:254
Critchel, Legrand B.
    10:108
Critcherson, C. 19:280
Critchet, J. W. 1:121
Critchet, Legrand B.
    20:232
Critchett, W. H. 21:318
Critchfield, J. R. 10:179;
    26:204
Critchfield, John 10:108;
    20:232
Critchfield, L. 3:51
Critchfield, Moses 18:448
Critchfield, Zachariah
    10:108; 20:232
Critchison, Charles 9:199
Critchlow, Adam W.
    16:27
Critchlow, J. 1:122
Critchlow, Wellington
    22:120
Crites, A. G. 9:229;
    20:232
Crites, D. 14:154
Crites, Daniel 21:50
Crites, Frederick 23:63
Crites, Jacob 17:32
Crites, John 18:216
Crithfield, William 22:26
Critman, R. E. 15:191
Critser, George 22:72
Crittenden, Aretus 22:277
Crittenden, B. F. 13:124
Crittenden, Cash 6:28
Crittenden, Edmund W.
    11:237
Crittenden, George
    18:233; 26:21
Crittenden, Henry 20:6
Crittenden, J. K. 9:8
Crittenden, John J. 22:247
Crittenden, Thomas 22:26

Crittenden, W. A. 14:154
Crittendon, Harvey 5:37
Crittendon, Noah 17:64
Crittenton, Almon 16:183
Critz, Albert 8:59
Crizer, W. 3:51
Croace, L. 13:17
Croak, Almont 21:268
Croak, George 20:136
Croaker, Hugh 10:108;
    20:232
Croch, J. B. 1:119
Crochet, J. C. 17:432
Croching, J. B. 14:7
Crocke, H. 3:51
Crocke, S. W. 14:51
Crocker, B. 7:91
Crocker, C. F. 9:51
Crocker, Charles 3:51
Crocker, D. 3:51
Crocker, E. S. 17:90
Crocker, F. 19:63
Crocker, George 3:51;
    22:161
Crocker, George W.
    13:17; 23:25
Crocker, H. 14:1
Crocker, H. C. 13:107
Crocker, H. L. 4:18
Crocker, J. 3:51
Crocker, J. H. 4:18
Crocker, Joseph W.
    22:420
Crocker, M. 22:186
Crocker, M. M. 18:393
Crocker, Nelson 10:171;
    19:157
Crocker, S. H. 13:107
Crocker, Samuel 13:107;
    14:154
Crocker, W. H. 25:159
Crocker, William B. 21:50
Crocket, Leroy 1:21
Crockett, --- 9:107;
    22:351
Crockett, A. W. 3:51
Crockett, C. 9:173; 21:109
Crockett, C. P. 19:236
Crockett, Charles 17:173
Crockett, Daveny 10:108
Crockett, Davney 20:232
Crockett, Granville 23:290
Crockett, Isaac 9:207
Crockett, J. H. 20:232
Crockett, Thomas 22:475
Crockett, W. 1:118
Crockett, William 22:295
Crocraft, Samuel 17:397
Croe, John 17:402
Crofard, G. M. 16:183
Crofer, Stephen 11:410

Croffard, James 9:117
Crofford, James R. 26:122
Crofford, Nathan 9:71
Crofoot, A. 21:194
Crofoot, Isaiah 22:461
Crofoot, James H. 22:140
Crofoot, John C. 20:189
Crofoot, Philip 21:200
Croft, Abram 9:109
Croft, C. L. 8:104
Croft, C. W. 10:15
Croft, G. H. 1:122
Croft, George 11:200
Croft, Henry 20:96
Croft, Mannissah 17:199
Croft, Peter 18:275
Croft, R. 27:27
Croft, Samuel 9:163
Croft, Thomas 10:48; 20:232
Croft, W. F. 8:47
Crofton, --- 26:244
Crofton, James 24:65
Crofton, James H. 20:16
Crofts, E. B. 1:23
Crofut, Levi 13:17
Crogan, W. E. 8:71
Crogan, William H. 9:42
Croger, William 18:129
Croghan, Edward 1:120
Croghan, John 3:51
Crognon, Thomas 22:518
Crohan, Patrick 13:17
Croil, Thomas 11:54
Croin, S. 16:27
Croker, H. 14:51
Croker, Henry 9:33
Croker, William F. 1:191
Croker, William J. 21:50
Crolius, John D. 10:15
Croll, S. R. 15:340; 16:366
Crolley, Noah 10:108; 20:232
Crolton, M. A. 27:33
Crom, Philip 14:154
Crom, William H. 4:18
Croman, George H. 14:51
Croman, J. 7:67
Cromark, J. 3:51
Crombie, Charles H. 11:83
Cromblet, A. J. 3:51
Cromboa, Henry 18:234
Crombough, --- 20:233
Crome, Henry 21:319
Cromel, Joseph 7:48
Cromen, M. 14:154
Cromer, Daniel C. 9:33
Cromer, G. D. 1:26
Cromer, George 7:67

Cromer, Joseph A. 10:108; 20:233
Cromer, P. 14:296; 17:479; 27:31
Cromfoot, D. W. 11:399
Cromian, John 3:51
Cromie, Charles H. 25:159
Cromingburger, C. 3:52
Cromis, A. 13:63
Cromiter, Peter 7:120
Cromley, James 11:411
Cromley, Lewis 10:176; 19:157
Cromley, M. 1:120
Crommet, J. C. 25:159
Crommet, John W. 5:13
Crommett, S. A. 16:183
Crommey, Owen 4:18
Crommond, M. E. 20:233
Crommor, M. C. 25:24
Cromnia, Charles E. 15:315
Crompson, C. J. 21:319
Crompson, Felix 21:319
Crompter, James 3:51
Crompton, George W. 22:9
Crompton, John 1:21
Cromshaw, John 19:63
Cromwall, Charles R. 10:108; 20:233
Cromwell, Albert 19:45
Cromwell, C. 25:295
Cromwell, Charles 4:18
Cromwell, D. 3:51
Cromwell, Diner 9:109
Cromwell, E. 14:154, 254
Cromwell, Edwin 8:104
Cromwell, G. W. 3:51
Cromwell, James 13:107
Cromwell, M. 21:22
Cromwell, Morgan 8:104
Cromwell, O. B. 25:22
Cromwell, P. 1:122
Cromwell, Philamon 22:449
Cromwell, S. R. 3:51
Cromwell, T. 3:51
Cromwell, W. H. 3:51
Cromwell, William 12:55
Cron, John 19:10
Cron, Peter 8:104
Cronah, H. H. 9:78
Cronan, Cornelius 12:170; 23:188
Cronan, Daniel 4:18
Cronan, J. 15:318; 21:22
Cronan, James 9:173; 19:249
Cronan, Joseph 10:15

Cronan, Pat 5:50; 25:159, 295
Cronan, Patrick 7:79; 16:27
Cronce, Ephraim 25:21
Crone, Alexander A. 22:72
Crone, George F. 10:108; 20:233
Crone, Jared 21:252
Crone, John 22:277
Crone, Nelson 22:26
Cronebaugh, H. 23:86
Cronell, C. P. 14:7
Cronemeyer, F. 25:24
Cronen, Dennis 22:461
Croner, Linsey 5:37
Croner, Michael 11:15
Croney, D. 21:109
Croney, E. S. 22:477
Cronicker, Jacob 7:23
Croniett, Hiram 10:15
Cronin, Ambrose 7:67
Cronin, Andrew J. 10:108; 20:233
Cronin, D. 1:23
Cronin, Daniel 1:24
Cronin, Michael 12:17
Cronin, P. 25:25
Cronin, Parick 11:100
Cronin, Patrick 2:9
Cronin, Philip 13:107
Cronin, Thomas 8:124
Cronin, Timothy 7:91; 11:124
Cronin, W. 2:9
Croning, Alfred 27:30
Croninshields, C. 3:51
Cronise, H. G. 7:48
Cronister, S. 27:33
Cronk, A. 1:21
Cronk, Aaron 14:7
Cronk, Andrew 23:188
Cronk, Charles R. 18:275
Cronk, George 12:17
Cronk, Henry 15:32
Cronk, J. S. 1:25
Cronk, John 20:29, 91
Cronk, L. 25:159
Cronk, Luther 12:58
Cronk, Rensler 20:192
Cronk, Stephen 19:157
Cronk, T. 27:28
Cronk, W. G. 19:249
Cronk, William 10:108; 20:233; 21:67
Cronkin, Charles 2:9
Cronkirt, C. M. 9:20
Cronkite, Alfred B. 20:29
Cronkite, Byron 10:48; 20:233

Cronkite, Solomon 17:64
Cronkite, Wallace 10:48;
  20:233
Cronkright, A. 25:295
Cronkwright, Alex 7:74
Cronley, David E. 18:216
Cronley, Robert 9:117
Cronmet, S. A. 13:63
Cronover, Daniel 8:13
Cronville, Odell 24:190
Croo---, George W.
  22:247
Crook, E. H. 3:51
Crook, F. C. 1:23
Crook, Frederick 15:277;
  25:160
Crook, H. 14:51, 154
Crook, J. 9:141
Crook, James A. 23:25
Crook, James E. 21:91
Crook, Jonathan 10:171;
  19:157
Crook, Joseph 24:59
Crook, N. R. 14:154
Crook, Pleasant 13:127
Crook, Samuel 12:55
Crook, Samuel B. 23:106
Crook, Samuel F. 24:110
Crook, Simon 17:130;
  24:190
Crook, Thomas 7:120;
  21:319
Crook, W. D. 15:172
Crook, W. O. R. 16:366
Crook, William 10:108;
  20:233; 27:32
Crooke, John R. 20:96
Crooke, W. 1:93
Crooker, Almon L. 21:319
Crooker, Almond L. 9:212
Crooker, C. S. 27:33
Crooker, E. 11:398
Crooker, J. B. 7:83
Crooker, Z. B. 9:173;
  19:249
Crooks, A. J. 22:496
Crooks, Charles M.
  21:240
Crooks, George W. 15:65
Crooks, J. M. 3:51
Crooks, John 9:236; 11:14
Crooks, Joseph M. 17:90
Crooks, Mathew 20:132
Crooks, Thomas 14:51
Crooks, W. A. 21:87
Crooks, W. B. 3:51
Crooks, William 13:86;
  17:46; 22:72
Crooks, William H.
  10:108; 20:233

Crooks, William O. R.
  15:340
Crookshank, Alexander
  18:129
Crookshank, Simon K.
  17:389
Crookshanks, Alex. 8:13
Crookshanks, William
  9:15
Crookson, John N. 11:26
Crookston, J. C. 23:25
Croom, John 22:186
Croome, George 26:144
Crooms, Jesse 21:319
Croon, F. C. 9:242
Croon, John De 19:63
Croopts, T. 16:290
Croos, H. E. 23:25
Crootps, T. 12:86
Crop, Franklin S. 21:319
Crop, Henry 21:319
Cropin, Edward 18:129
Cropley, C. B. 1:21
Cropley, E. 1:119
Cropp, George 11:139
Cropper, George 12:48
Cropper, L. 16:183
Cropper, Lewis 17:77
Croppern, John E. 18:304
Cropsey, Thomas 1:21
Cropwhite, James M.
  22:247
Crory, Hugh 11:301
Crosan, James M. 19:157
Crosbey, E. 3:51
Crosbey, Eli 20:233
Crosbie, James 19:63
Crosby, Aaron F. 14:154
Crosby, Abijah 16:77
Crosby, Allanson 22:470
Crosby, B. 3:51
Crosby, Byron 9:141;
  27:26
Crosby, C. O. 7:91
Crosby, C. S. 21:22
Crosby, Charles 10:147;
  18:47
Crosby, Columbus 25:271
Crosby, D. 9:66; 25:160
Crosby, E. P. 13:107;
  16:183
Crosby, Edward 15:335;
  19:63
Crosby, Ely C. 24:99
Crosby, Franklyn 8:113
Crosby, G. E. 1:23
Crosby, G. H. 20:102
Crosby, George 10:90;
  20:233
Crosby, George W. 12:68
Crosby, H. 1:118

Crosby, H. N. 14:154
Crosby, Henry 15:121;
  17:130
Crosby, Horace F. 20:29
Crosby, I. 14:154
Crosby, J. 3:51; 14:296;
  17:473
Crosby, J. A. 23:25
Crosby, J. H. 19:63
Crosby, James 15:335
Crosby, James F. 23:63
Crosby, Jesse A. 10:48;
  20:233
Crosby, John 1:22; 17:77;
  21:319; 22:186;
  24:92
Crosby, John T. 10:15
Crosby, L. E. 9:109
Crosby, L. G. 9:117;
  27:30
Crosby, L. H. 27:27
Crosby, M. 3:51
Crosby, Norton 18:393
Crosby, O. 27:24
Crosby, O. C. 21:319
Crosby, P. L. 1:119
Crosby, Patrick 9:173;
  19:249
Crosby, R. 8:47; 14:296;
  17:477; 25:20; 27:32
Crosby, Reuben 7:23
Crosby, Richmond 14:154
Crosby, Robert 2:9
Crosby, Sherman O.
  21:242
Crosby, Steven 18:80
Crosby, T. F. 11:238
Crosby, Thomas 7:91
Crosby, Thomas H. 8:121
Crosby, W. 3:51
Crosby, William 4:18;
  22:475
Crosby, Williard 19:157
Crose, E. F. 3:52
Croseby, Jonathan 18:129
Crosell, William 26:21
Croshyer, A. B. 15:191
Crosier, Daniel 21:319
Crosier, J. 19:249
Crosier, Robert P. 24:37
Croskey, Edward 22:26
Crosle, G. 25:25
Crosley, Isaac F. 21:223
Crosley, W. 1:26
Crosque, John 20:96
Cross, A. 1:122; 13:86
Cross, A. J. 19:232; 25:26
Cross, A. L. 22:140
Cross, Acel 9:50
Cross, Albion P. 9:213
Cross, Alfred T. 21:136

Cross, Amos 25:160
Cross, Anderson 9:173
Cross, August 8:13;
    18:129
Cross, B. W. 14:51
Cross, C. 1:121; 2:9;
    25:20
Cross, Calvin W. 10:90;
    20:233
Cross, Cassius 25:21
Cross, Charles 15:32
Cross, Charles H. 20:89
Cross, Charles J. 12:68
Cross, E. 3:51; 17:77
Cross, Ebenezer 22:72
Cross, Ed 22:469
Cross, Eli 12:152
Cross, Elias V. 20:39
Cross, Elijah T. 10:95
Cross, F. 3:51
Cross, Fitshue 13:107
Cross, Fred 14:154
Cross, G. 13:86
Cross, G. C. 1:23
Cross, George 1:24
Cross, George W. 3:51;
    16:84; 21:120
Cross, Green 9:117; 27:29
Cross, H. 11:141
Cross, Ira W. 3:51
Cross, Isaac 8:82
Cross, J. 5:37; 9:236;
    14:255; 17:436
Cross, J. D. 3:51
Cross, J. G. 1:22; 19:222
Cross, J. H. 18:338
Cross, J. R. 20:145
Cross, J. S. 3:51
Cross, J. W. 5:50; 25:160
Cross, James 11:141, 385;
    22:26; 25:25; 26:217
Cross, James B. 21:120
Cross, James M. 24:183
Cross, John 9:219;
    22:186; 24:191
Cross, John C. 22:475
Cross, John H. 8:13;
    18:129
Cross, John M. 16:366
Cross, John W. 13:17;
    22:475
Cross, Joseph 10:108;
    20:233; 26:18
Cross, Joseph A. 23:63
Cross, Joseph D. 24:157
Cross, Josiah B. 17:247
Cross, L. C. 17:326
Cross, Lewis 13:17
Cross, M. 12:85; 14:51;
    16:290
Cross, M. C. 3:51

Cross, McHenry 22:403
Cross, Nelson 13:17;
    15:83; 16:27
Cross, Nicholas 7:23
Cross, Noah 3:51
Cross, Othello B. 23:263
Cross, R. H. 18:13
Cross, Reuben 11:303
Cross, Robert 4:65
Cross, S. 15:104
Cross, Samuel 14:235;
    18:27
Cross, Samuel H. 22:140
Cross, T. C. 2:9; 25:20
Cross, Thomas 21:252
Cross, Thomas L. 7:91
Cross, Tilman F. 23:63
Cross, Timothy S. 10:109;
    20:233
Cross, W. 23:139
Cross, W. H. 18:27
Cross, W. R. 16:183
Cross, William 16:183;
    17:337; 22:186, 476
Cross, William A. 10:48;
    20:233
Cross, William B. 15:191
Cross, William H. 16:92
Cross, William R. 17:215
Cross, Willis 19:10
Crossan, James M. 10:171
Crossan, William 15:191
Crossart, H. H. 26:19
Crossell, William 18:234
Crossen, Alexander 12:68
Crossen, G. M. 17:291
Crossen, John 11:142
Crossen, Solomon 20:122
Crosser, James F. 23:301
Crosser, Joseph M. 20:16
Crosser, Michael 22:72
Crosser, W. 3:51
Crossey, James 4:18
Crossgrow, Joseph S. 20:6
Crossland, Samuel 11:56
Crossley, J. L. 21:319
Crossley, James M. 7:14
Crossley, John A. 15:293
Crossley, Luke 1:120
Crossley, Mathias 13:17
Crossley, Thomas 12:53
Crossling, John 10:48
Crossman, Charles 11:115
Crossman, Dexter 15:191
Crossman, H. J. 3:51
Crossman, Mathew T.
    20:233
Crossman, Matthew T.
    10:109
Crossman, Orrin 4:18
Crossman, R. F. 1:26

Crossman, Robert 22:295
Crossman, W. H. 25:160
Crossman, W. T. 21:22
Crossman, William H.
    5:13
Crosson, J. 23:139
Crosswait, G. 16:183
Crosswait, Stanf 6:12
Crosswart, H. W. 18:393
Crossy, A. 14:51
Crostey, T. D. 11:142
Croswell, Frederick 6:15;
    18:80
Crotby, Daniel 8:62
Crotchet, John C. 24:151
Crotchett, William 11:100
Crothers, Christopher
    13:17
Crothers, Cornelius
    18:393
Crothers, David 9:238;
    26:217
Crothers, Samuel G.
    22:477
Crothin, Henry 16:27
Crothin, Henry G. 13:17
Crotley, Daniel 26:154
Crotter, M. A. 14:240
Crottondollar, C. 24:49
Crotts, George W. 23:25
Crotts, James 22:247
Crotts, James H. 20:16
Crotts, William H. 22:403
Croty, D. 1:119
Crouch, A. 8:58
Crouch, Bailey 14:130
Crouch, Daniel W. 17:316
Crouch, Edwin L. 15:16
Crouch, Flavel 22:111
Crouch, George 9:173;
    19:273; 23:279
Crouch, George B. 15:54
Crouch, H. C. 14:130;
    15:263
Crouch, Henry 8:38;
    21:194; 26:155
Crouch, Henry D. 11:237
Crouch, Hezekiah 10:109;
    20:233
Crouch, Hiram 18:338
Crouch, Hiram J. 9:102
Crouch, J. 14:51
Crouch, J. A. 11:258
Crouch, J. C. 5:13
Crouch, J. M. 4:18
Crouch, J. W. 1:191
Crouch, James 17:99
Crouch, Jefferson 27:32
Crouch, John 7:91
Crouch, Joseph 22:111
Crouch, Joseph D. 11:186

Crouch, King 22:295
Crouch, L. D. 13:107
Crouch, Levi 3:51
Crouch, Samuel 22:277
Crouch, Thomas F. 1:24
Crouch, W. 1:117
Crough, John J. 11:237
Crougher, Jefferson 21:319
Crouk, Aaron 13:86
Crouk, James 13:107
Crouk, Leonard 16:183
Crouk, N. 21:319
Crouk, Stephen 10:159
Crouncun, Miles 7:48
Croup, John 17:242
Croup, W. S. 3:51
Crouse, Charles 16:139
Crouse, Edward 23:139
Crouse, Emanuel 19:10
Crouse, F. 3:51
Crouse, G. W. 7:23
Crouse, George 3:51
Crouse, H. 3:51
Crouse, Henry 14:51
Crouse, J. 3:51; 23:139
Crouse, J. A. 3:51
Crouse, James A. 25:160
Crouse, John 11:141
Crouse, John D. 20:233
Crouse, L. 14:155
Crouse, Levi 14:51
Crouse, W. 1:22
Crouse, W. A. 3:51
Crouse, William H. 26:155
Crouser, John 9:20
Crout, Elihu F. 17:77
Croutt, W. H. 19:226
Crow, A. 1:25; 22:461
Crow, Abraham 15:191
Crow, Alpheus C. 11:285
Crow, B. 3:51
Crow, Benjamin 20:179
Crow, C. C. 17:165
Crow, Calvin P. 21:319
Crow, Chancey 17:77
Crow, Daniel B. 21:50
Crow, E. 9:50; 16:366
Crow, E. P. 22:476
Crow, F. 3:52
Crow, Frank S. 10:211; 18:456
Crow, George 10:109; 20:233
Crow, H. 1:117, 118; 12:92; 14:51; 16:290
Crow, Harvey 4:65
Crow, Haywood 17:337
Crow, Henry C. 11:325
Crow, I. 17:130

Crow, J. 3:51; 24:190
Crow, J. H. 11:139
Crow, James L. 21:319
Crow, John 10:109; 11:411; 17:130; 19:63; 20:233; 24:191
Crow, John S. 22:111
Crow, M. 13:86; 14:7
Crow, Pat 14:155
Crow, Stephen 9:10
Crow, T. 13:86
Crow, Thomas 11:54
Crow, Thornton 15:191
Crow, W. H. 24:65
Crow, William 10:109; 20:233
Crow, William G. 13:17
Crow, William P. 26:17
Crowall, William 20:233
Crowan, David 9:244
Crowdel, Riley 21:147
Crowder, Daniel J. 22:523
Crowder, Francis 19:281
Crowder, J. 21:22
Crowder, James K. 23:63
Crowder, Ryland 21:268
Crowder, William 16:27
Crowe, Barton 8:82
Crowe, Shelton 8:82
Crowell, C. H. 1:23, 97
Crowell, C. P. 13:86
Crowell, Calvin E. 21:319
Crowell, Charles 21:319
Crowell, Daniel 6:30; 17:32; 25:319
Crowell, David 25:268
Crowell, Edward 22:403
Crowell, G. W. 16:184
Crowell, J. 25:160
Crowell, J. B. 15:287
Crowell, J. W. N. 20:233
Crowell, James M. 22:418
Crowell, James W. 24:99
Crowell, John W. M. 10:48
Crowell, Jonathan 19:10
Crowell, S. F. 21:319
Crowell, S. T. 9:213
Crowell, S. W. 1:119
Crowell, Sandford 21:319
Crowell, Sanford 9:213
Crowell, T. B. 19:63
Crowell, W. 24:110
Crowell, W. A. 16:139
Crowell, W. B. 11:139
Crowell, William E. 20:16
Crowfoot, J. 22:517
Crowfoot, Jesse 22:507
Crowford, G. 16:184
Crowford, Henry 15:104

Crowford, Thomas P. 20:233
Crowhile, John 3:51
Crowl, F. 14:51
Crowl, J. 11:56
Crowl, J. H. 18:47
Crowl, M. F. 27:26
Crowl, Mich. 9:42
Crowl, Michael 26:121
Crowl, N. T. 9:141
Crowl, T. 14:7; 16:267
Crowl, William 16:117
Crowley, C. 19:232
Crowley, Charles 18:291
Crowley, Cornelius 10:48; 20:233
Crowley, D. 3:52
Crowley, Daniel 10:159; 19:157
Crowley, F. 1:25
Crowley, J. 1:122, 123; 19:236; 21:319
Crowley, James 9:203
Crowley, Jeremiah 18:426
Crowley, John 20:233; 22:72, 333
Crowley, Joseph 16:27
Crowley, Levi 22:26
Crowley, Lewis 6:27
Crowley, M. C. 11:385
Crowley, Michael 27:33
Crowley, P. J. 20:132
Crowley, Philip 21:319
Crowley, R. W. 27:30
Crowley, S. 3:52
Crowley, Timothy 16:145
Crowley, William 14:155; 22:419
Crowly, Pat 3:51
Crown, Henry 11:124
Crown, Joseph 12:152; 22:419
Crownen, Daniel 8:13
Crowner, Benjamin 7:120
Crowner, Irvin 7:10
Crowner, J. 10:186; 18:173
Crowner, James V. 10:109; 20:233
Crowner, Samuel C. 17:46
Crownhart, W. C. 20:192
Crowning, H. 3:51
Crowningshield, Arnold 12:17
Crowningshield, J. 14:155
Crowningshield, L. 16:184
Crownosse, Patterson 11:259
Crowrer, William 11:400
Crows, William 21:50

Crowta, J. D. 1:122
Crowther, --- 25:20
Crowthers, J. 14:28
Crowthers, J. H. 3:52
Crox, N. 14:277
Croxdale, Avin 11:395
Croxdale, Edward 17:165
Croxton, E. M. 23:202
Croxton, J. 1:123
Croy, A. 23:120
Croy, David P. 20:233
Croy, Eliah 18:188
Croy, J. 3:51
Croy, James 10:109;
    20:233
Croyier, John 25:23
Croyle, G. 27:27
Croyle, George 9:141
Croyle, John 19:10
Croyle, William H. 13:17
Croze, William 21:215
Crozer, Robert 17:173
Crozier, George 21:319
Crozier, Isaac 9:117;
    27:30
Crozier, J. 24:76
Crozier, James 9:173
Crozier, John 9:78; 26:18
Crozier, Robert 7:91
Crozier, Samuel 7:91
Crritzn, Solomon 10:147
Crubb, P. 11:190
Crubbs, E. 15:104
Cruben, Nox 18:47
Crubun, Nox 10:147
Cruce, D. 14:7
Cruch, Enoch P. 11:91
Crucher, I. 9:207
Cruddis, William 21:133
Cruder, R. 21:147
Crudney, Pierre 21:319
Cruess, Alfred 10:48;
    20:233
Cruffy, Albert 19:272
Cruger, Julius 11:190
Crugin, Ridgeway P.
    23:188
Cruikshank, William
    17:392
Cruis, Marcus 8:123
Cruiser, Curtis 4:19
Cruit, William 23:305
Cruk, William B. 11:54
Crulip, W. B. 1:119
Crum, Alexander 22:120
Crum, Alfred 21:98
Crum, Daniel 11:259;
    12:17
Crum, E. 11:326
Crum, F. A. 23:139
Crum, George 4:19

Crum, Henry J. 4:19
Crum, Ira 4:19
Crum, Isaac 8:47; 21:120;
    23:25
Crum, J. W. 11:259
Crum, James W. 20:145
Crum, John D. 18:47
Crum, Michael 8:13
Crum, Moses 24:165
Crum, N. B. 25:160
Crum, N. M. 18:173
Crum, Peter 11:56
Crum, R. 14:287; 23:139
Crum, William 20:6;
    22:165
Crum, William B. 24:49
Crumb, A. 1:96
Crumb, Chandler 13:107
Crumb, G. H. 2:8; 25:20
Crumb, M. 17:210
Crumb, O. 3:52
Crumb, Peter H. 9:78;
    26:17
Crumb, S. S. 1:23
Crumb, Simon 12:17
Crumb, Thomas T. 12:17
Crumbaker, Manley H.
    23:139
Crumbey, Hiram 21:319
Crumbly, C. C. 14:25
Crumbly, Thomas M.
    22:16
Crumboa, Henry 26:21
Crumett, Carl 8:62
Crumford, C. 14:296;
    17:482; 27:31
Crumitisky, M. 22:518
Crumley, H. W. 1:120
Crummel, L. 25:160
Crummel, L. A. 9:173
Crummell, L. A. 19:226
Crummell, Nelson 5:37
Crummet, Joseph H. 7:8
Crummett, L. M. 19:226
Crummit, Orchard N. 7:91
Crummy, William H.
    10:159
Crumnell, John 11:300
Crumney, A. E. 19:63
Crump, Benjamin 11:199
Crump, Elmore B. 10:109;
    20:233
Crump, John 8:38; 26:155
Crump, Lewis 15:191
Crumt, William P. 12:17
Crumune, Isaac 11:141
Crune, A. J. 9:51
Crune, George B. 18:127
Crune, Levi 21:268
Crunger, J. M. 21:319
Crunlich, Herman 4:19

Cruns, Andrew 8:13
Crup, Hasel 18:129
Crur, Leoosier 11:140
Crusa, Henry 22:72
Crusader, Thomas 18:129
Crusan, John W. 16:118
Cruse, D. 1:21
Cruse, E. 3:52
Cruse, T. J. 4:19
Cruselery, Edward 26:21
Cruser, Christian 22:72
Crushaw, Thomas 18:129
Crusher, F. 22:295
Cruson, John 7:91
Crusselery, Edward
    18:234
Crussell, Walter 27:25
Crust, A. 10:204
Crust, William 3:52
Crustree, J. 27:33
Crutch, John 14:240
Crutchburg, Christian
    10:109
Crutcher, R. M. 22:510
Crutcher, Reuben 22:449
Crutcher, Samuel 17:130;
    24:190
Crutcher, Thomas J.
    17:279
Crutcher, William 17:130;
    24:191
Crutchfield, Albertina
    8:123
Crutchfield, H. H. 17:94
Crutchfield, Jackson
    17:50
Crutchfield, James 21:268
Crutchfield, John 10:98
Crutchfield, M. 11:53
Crutchfield, Michael N.
    12:139
Crutchfield, R. 20:84
Crutchfield, Stephen
    22:295
Crutchfield, Zopher
    26:155
Cruthers, James 22:511
Crutree, J. 14:240
Crutsberg, Christian
    20:233
Cruver, Orton 7:91
Cruz, William 1:21
Cruzan, Amos 22:72
Cruzan, John 22:72
Cruzan, Oliver 22:26
Cruzan, Oliver H. 22:420
Cruzen, Leaman 26:95
Cruzen, Leander 18:291
Crwys, W. E. 25:160
Cryder, Caldof 15:121
Cryling, George 17:336

Crysler, J. S. 19:157
Crysler, James H. 23:188
Cryster, J. F. 25:23
Crytseer, J. 14:255
Crytzer, Amos 12:58
Cu---, P. 20:154
Cubbage, C. H. 3:52
Cubbage, G. A. 19:63
Cubbage, George W. D. 23:139
Cubbage, John 16:27
Cubber, William 15:315
Cubberly, Thomas 11:258
Cubbins, J. M. 16:184
Cubbison, James C. 22:186
Cubbitt, John 18:27
Cube, Nicholas 12:81; 16:290
Cuberly, Dennis 22:140, 421
Cuberson, Henry 19:63
Cubine, A. P. 17:165
Cubner, John 10:172
Cubrine, Michael 10:147
Cuch, John 10:48; 20:233
Cuckendoff, Orsimous 4:19
Cuddlebuck, John 12:17
Cuddy, Charles 19:329
Cuddy, Edward 11:339
Cuddy, John 7:91
Cuddy, N. B. 14:155
Cuddy, P. 1:23
Cuddyback, P. G. 17:287
Cuder, Daniel 10:159
Cudiff, Solomon S. 22:26
Cudjoc, Moses 7:77
Cudjoe, Moses 25:295
Cudley, Ezkiel 20:233
Cudney, Ezekiel 10:48
Cudworth, Edwin 13:63; 19:64
Cudworth, O. 13:86
Cuff, Michael 22:9
Cuff, Parker 16:184
Cuff, S. 3:52
Cuff, William H. 18:80
Cuffee, J. 25:160
Cuffey, Alexander 18:27
Cuffey, Jack 5:37
Cuffey, Joshua 9:129
Cuffle, Henry 21:194
Cuffle, Jonathan 7:91
Cuffman, Best 22:295
Cuffy, M. 5:56; 25:160
Cuggerty, W. A. 21:319
Cugh, John F. 10:151
Cughten, John 14:155
Cuigley, P. 7:23
Cuin, J. 18:234; 26:22

Cuine, Florian 22:140
Cuis, A. M. 11:375
Cul---, William 20:55
Culber, Martin J. 21:319
Culberson, Henry 15:364
Culberson, J. 1:122
Culberson, R. F. 20:122
Culberson, Samuel J. 17:77
Culberson, Z. B. 20:132
Culbert, J. 3:52
Culbert, W. 3:52
Culberton, J. 19:64
Culberton, John 3:52
Culberton, S. 3:52
Culbertore, Walter 10:15
Culberts, R. 10:27
Culbertson, A. J. 11:385
Culbertson, D. J. 11:139
Culbertson, Franklin 23:139
Culbertson, George 23:25
Culbertson, J. 15:305
Culbertson, J. D. 11:385
Culbertson, John 12:17
Culbertson, John F. 17:13
Culbertson, Lewis 3:52
Culbertson, Martin 22:186
Culbertson, Uriah 18:216
Culbertson, William 23:139
Culbertson, William H. 17:205
Culbertson, William W. 17:259
Culbertzen, Frank 9:49
Culd, A. D. 23:25
Culfen, Lewis 20:233
Culgee, Adam 3:52
Cull, Abram 4:19
Cull, Michael 16:164
Cull, Peter 22:397
Cullan, John 5:55
Cullan, Michael 19:157
Cullans, H. C. 11:400
Cullard, Francis 10:109; 20:233
Cullen, A. 21:319
Cullen, Christopher 24:92
Cullen, Felix 21:9, 268
Cullen, Frank 12:64; 15:32
Cullen, Frederick A. 20:192
Cullen, G. 25:160
Cullen, Garett 5:13
Cullen, Henry D. 21:194
Cullen, J. 7:23; 11:141
Cullen, James 7:91; 8:82; 13:17; 16:92

Cullen, John 10:159; 19:157; 24:92
Cullen, M. 3:52; 14:155
Cullen, M. F. 15:318
Cullen, Mathew 22:120
Cullen, P. 1:121
Cullen, Patrick 14:155
Cullen, Simon 21:136
Cullen, Sodden 10:48
Cullen, T. P. 3:52
Cullen, Thomas 12:58
Cullen, Thomas M. 13:128
Cullen, William 13:17; 16:27
Cullens, Benjamin 21:268
Culler, David 11:410
Culler, John J. 10:90; 20:233
Culler, John W. 19:10
Culler, Michael 22:26
Cullerts, R. 19:301
Cullery, Hugh 10:159
Culley, A. 11:438
Culley, C. 12:80
Culley, E. M. 14:280
Culley, J. 25:160
Cullicutt, Henry 19:157
Cullie, R. 19:249
Cullier, V. V. 15:172
Culligan, Charles 19:45
Culligen, Arthur L. 12:17
Cullin, M. 14:51
Cullin, Martin 17:266
Cullinane, Timothy 19:329
Culling, William 3:52
Cullingford, P. 3:52
Cullins, Amos D. 21:67
Cullip, John C. 15:191
Culliron, B. 6:9
Cullison, Fred 23:139
Cullison, J. H. 11:141
Cullison, Kinsey 23:139
Cullison, Noah D. 10:48
Cullison, W. D. 20:233
Culliston, Thompson 20:235
Culliver, John B. 22:247
Cullney, James 9:129; 27:29
Cullock, J. M. 21:319
Culloe, Oli 22:333
Cullon, Daniel 22:9
Cullors, George 22:419
Cullpper, Milichi 20:6
Culls, Henry 7:120; 21:319
Cully, Henry 17:109
Cully, Rusko 19:290
Cully, Thomas 9:129

Culman, M. 1:21
Culmer, R. N. 15:165
Culnine, M. 18:47
Culp, A. B. 1:25
Culp, Amos 7:48
Culp, Cornelius 25:160
Culp, G. K. 26:218
Culp, George 23:86, 139
Culp, J. 22:186
Culp, John 17:64
Culp, Mark 9:207
Culp, P. K. 3:52
Culp, Polk 22:295
Culp, S. 1:97; 14:321
Culp, Samuel 14:314;
    23:139
Culp, Samuel G. 18:216
Culp, Simon P. 17:265
Culp, William E. 24:15
Culpeper, John 21:319
Culpepper, John 7:120
Culps, Simon 22:295
Culton, Augustus B.
    17:202
Cults, E. 13:86
Culum, James 1:25
Culver, A. A. 14:280
Culver, A. L. 3:52
Culver, Alvin B. 13:17;
    16:27
Culver, C. O. 11:258
Culver, Farris 17:259
Culver, Frederick D. 15:2
Culver, G. E. 10:109;
    20:234
Culver, George M. 12:121
Culver, George W. 15:121
Culver, Harrison 21:223
Culver, Henry 10:159;
    19:157
Culver, Horatio 9:78;
    26:17
Culver, J. 3:52
Culver, J. H. 15:263
Culver, J. W. 3:52
Culver, James 9:173;
    19:249
Culver, John A. 22:72
Culver, John C. 15:277;
    25:160
Culver, John D. 11:91
Culver, John T. 10:7
Culver, Levi 17:64
Culver, M. A. 16:92
Culver, Oliver N. 16:139
Culver, Parmenus 13:17
Culver, S. 1:25, 120
Culver, Samuel G. 22:111
Culver, T. M. 5:13
Culver, W. 1:119; 23:245

Culver, William 4:19;
    14:268; 17:498
Culver, William H. 1:25
Culverson, Benjamin
    18:80
Culverton, Benjamin 6:15
Culvimet, C. 15:151
Cum, J. 16:267
Cumaham, Amos 9:129
Cumbaa, John 17:109
Cumbaugh, David M.
    22:403
Cumber, Lyman M. 13:17
Cumberland, Albert
    19:157
Cumberland, L. 11:26
Cumberland, Thomas 3:52
Cuming, Isaac 20:234
Cumings, Moses 15:298
Cummer, J. 16:184
Cummer, John H. 4:19
Cummerman, George
    13:17
Cummeth, Conrad 23:25
Cumming, A. 8:71
Cumming, A. G. 1:23
Cumming, Francis 8:13
Cumming, Isaac 10:48
Cumming, J. W. 7:23
Cumming, John 14:155
Cumming, John F. 7:23
Cumming, William 1:21
Cummings, --- 3:52;
    18:173; 25:268
Cummings, A. 3:52
Cummings, A. B. 3:52
Cummings, A. W. 1:21
Cummings, Albert 8:47;
    14:155
Cummings, Alonzo 16:7
Cummings, Ambrose
    10:15
Cummings, Andrew 20:6
Cummings, Asa W. 7:91
Cummings, B. 19:301;
    25:160
Cummings, Benjamin
    5:37; 8:104; 13:17;
    16:27
Cummings, Benjamin F.
    22:120
Cummings, C. 14:51;
    25:160
Cummings, Cyrus 11:141
Cummings, D. 3:52;
    25:23, 160
Cummings, D. M. 20:132
Cummings, Daniel 15:90
Cummings, David 13:17
Cummings, E. C. 19:249

Cummings, Ebenezer
    21:67
Cummings, Edward
    9:173; 23:11
Cummings, Edward R.
    22:333
Cummings, Eleck 9:129
Cummings, Elleck 27:29
Cummings, F. 21:22
Cummings, Francis
    18:129
Cummings, G. 7:91
Cummings, G. W. 1:24,
    117; 17:191; 21:23
Cummings, George
    18:304; 26:94;
    27:143
Cummings, George A.
    21:319
Cummings, George W.
    10:109; 11:140;
    20:234; 23:281
Cummings, Harvey 21:22
Cummings, Henry 11:141;
    13:17; 23:178
Cummings, Hiram H.
    23:120
Cummings, Isaac 21:319
Cummings, J. 3:52;
    11:398; 21:165;
    25:160
Cummings, J. B. 21:319
Cummings, J. D. 8:82
Cummings, J. N. 3:52
Cummings, J. R. 17:494
Cummings, J. T. 1:118
Cummings, J. W. 11:331
Cummings, James 9:68;
    18:364; 20:234
Cummings, James B.
    22:140
Cummings, James E.
    22:140
Cummings, James L.
    23:120
Cummings, John 5:13;
    7:56; 8:125; 9:78;
    12:61; 13:17; 20:136
Cummings, John B. 23:25
Cummings, John E.
    18:275
Cummings, Johnson 17:50
Cummings, Jos. 8:125
Cummings, Michael
    18:13; 22:333
Cummings, Mortimer
    13:17
Cummings, Moses 16:184
Cummings, N. 13:63;
    19:64; 23:202
Cummings, N. D. 26:18

Cummings, N. H. 20:91
Cummings, Nathan H. 20:111
Cummings, Noah J. 12:152
Cummings, Norman D. 9:78
Cummings, O. H. 1:97
Cummings, O. W. 1:97
Cummings, Oliver 24:76
Cummings, Oscar 23:106
Cummings, Otis 25:21
Cummings, Patrick 17:14
Cummings, Perry C. 11:384
Cummings, Peter 11:199
Cummings, R. 3:52
Cummings, R. B. 11:421
Cummings, Reuben 21:319
Cummings, Robert 13:63; 19:64
Cummings, Robert L. 22:186
Cummings, S. 3:52; 10:186; 26:17
Cummings, Samuel 24:92
Cummings, Seymour M. 20:111
Cummings, Stephen 9:78
Cummings, T. F. 20:6
Cummings, Thomas 10:48; 20:234
Cummings, Timothy 10:9
Cummings, W. 3:52; 13:86
Cummings, W. H. 14:51; 15:191
Cummings, W. S. 3:52
Cummings, William 7:91; 8:38; 13:107; 22:295; 26:155
Cummings, William A. 20:234
Cummings, William H. 11:103
Cummings, William M. 4:19
Cummins, A. F. 23:139
Cummins, Charles W. 7:91
Cummins, Franklin J. 16:3
Cummins, George 9:20
Cummins, George B. 23:86
Cummins, George W. 15:121
Cummins, H. 1:117
Cummins, Hugh 22:186
Cummins, J. 1:122
Cummins, J. R. 9:230

Cummins, James 9:219; 10:48
Cummins, John G. 22:475
Cummins, Joseph G. 23:139
Cummins, Milton 22:120
Cummins, Thomas 10:204; 17:50
Cummins, W. 14:7
Cummins, W. A. 9:173
Cummins, William 17:19; 23:120
Cummins, William A. 17:235; 19:250
Cummins, William E. 20:34
Cummiskey, John A. 12:17
Cummons, William 15:4
Cummus, T. 16:184
Cumner, V. S. 19:64
Cumon, W. C. 16:184
Cump, Andrew 25:160
Cumpson, Thomas 15:85
Cumpton, Scott 15:263
Cumstock, Hiram 11:104
Cumton, R. 3:52
Cunan, Alfred 8:71
Cunch, J. 3:52
Cunder, Lyman M. 16:27
Cundiff, Elias 22:448
Cundiff, James L. 23:276
Cundiff, John C. 23:97
Cunent, Abraham 10:48
Cuney, John 10:48; 20:234
Cunger, Henry N. 8:100; 17:462
Cunier, --- 9:117
Cunier, Alexander 10:48
Cuning, Thomas 23:252
Cunk, J. 14:240
Cunncen, Michael 17:359
Cunnigham, Moses 18:364
Cunnignham, John L. 20:234
Cunnignham, Patrick 17:320
Cunning, A. A. 22:186
Cunning, G. N. 15:32
Cunning, Ira S. 23:139
Cunning, William 19:157
Cunningham, --- 14:155; 20:234
Cunningham, A. 1:25
Cunningham, A. D. 22:247
Cunningham, Albert 14:155
Cunningham, Alex 9:11

Cunningham, Andrew 22:72
Cunningham, B. 1:22, 118
Cunningham, B. H. 18:393
Cunningham, Charles 8:112; 23:15; 25:23
Cunningham, Chauncy 20:45
Cunningham, Cyon 18:393
Cunningham, Cyre 22:295
Cunningham, D. 26:134
Cunningham, D. H. 25:23
Cunningham, Dacon 11:141
Cunningham, Daniel E. 15:104
Cunningham, David 18:284
Cunningham, E. 14:51; 25:278
Cunningham, E. S. 1:119
Cunningham, Edward 16:77
Cunningham, Elias 22:247
Cunningham, Eugene 9:78
Cunningham, Francis 10:172; 19:157; 25:21
Cunningham, G. V. 12:161
Cunningham, G. W. 26:19
Cunningham, George W. 7:120; 23:63
Cunningham, H. 12:48, 161; 20:234
Cunningham, H. L. 11:190
Cunningham, Harry 21:319
Cunningham, I. 1:25
Cunningham, J. 1:26; 3:52; 13:86; 15:191; 18:47; 22:295
Cunningham, J. Franklin 15:85
Cunningham, J. L. 13:86
Cunningham, J. T. 14:51
Cunningham, Jacob 13:17
Cunningham, James 8:82; 10:48; 12:141; 17:263, 422; 20:234; 22:397; 24:157
Cunningham, James L. 21:223
Cunningham, James S. 10:109; 20:234
Cunningham, James V. 22:120

Cunningham, Jesse 7:91; 11:26

Cunningham, Jim 10:204

Cunningham, John 7:23, 91; 11:122, 142, 339; 12:68; 15:2; 18:323; 21:23, 319; 22:351, 403; 25:160

Cunningham, John F. 20:106

Cunningham, John L. 10:109

Cunningham, John P. 10:15

Cunningham, John T. 17:50

Cunningham, John W. 12:171

Cunningham, Johnson J. 22:420

Cunningham, Joseph 4:19; 10:109; 20:234

Cunningham, Joseph W. 16:132

Cunningham, L. 7:24

Cunningham, Lowell 13:17

Cunningham, M. 9:114, 219; 19:301

Cunningham, M. C. 20:234

Cunningham, M. P. 10:48

Cunningham, Mark 23:25

Cunningham, Martin 12:17

Cunningham, Mat'w. M. 8:82

Cunningham, Michael 14:155

Cunningham, N. 20:234

Cunningham, Nicholas 12:141; 17:422

Cunningham, O. H. 1:117

Cunningham, Orasius A. 21:67

Cunningham, P. 7:24; 16:290; 19:287; 25:160

Cunningham, R. 3:52

Cunningham, R. B. 13:86; 14:7

Cunningham, R. G. 12:68

Cunningham, R. T. 15:83

Cunningham, Richard 17:130; 24:189

Cunningham, Robert 10:25; 14:155

Cunningham, Robert P. 20:17

Cunningham, S. 1:22

Cunningham, Samuel 11:26, 259; 14:155; 23:178

Cunningham, Silas 8:104

Cunningham, T. 3:52; 21:166

Cunningham, Thomas 10:48; 14:155; 17:90; 22:111; 26:19

Cunningham, Timothy 17:19

Cunningham, W. 1:119, 123; 14:296; 17:481; 18:47, 25:160; 27:32

Cunningham, W. H. 25:160

Cunningham, Washington F. 11:421

Cunningham, Wesley 22:419

Cunningham, William 3:52; 11:384; 14:51; 17:19, 427; 22:518; 24:183

Cunningham, William A. 15:95

Cunningham, William H. 10:90; 14:155

Cunol, Pat 20:234

Cunol, Patrick 10:90

Cuntzman, Samuel 23:139

Cuny, Henry 16:184

Cuny, J. 16:184

Cuny, John 15:191

Cunzick, Stephen 20:86

Cuper, John 22:233

Cupick, B. 3:52

Cupid, John 26:22

Cupp, George 10:48; 20:234

Cupp, J. 15:158

Cupp, Michael 9:20

Cupp, W. 17:77

Cupper, C. 10:147

Cuppert, J. 3:52

Cupples, John K. 21:319

Cupps, Elias 17:272

Cupps, Elisha 8:100

Cupps, George 14:155

Cuppy, Moses 17:272

Cups, Joseph L. 9:42

Curby, --- 7:18

Curby, B. 16:184

Curby, F. 14:155

Curch, Francis 10:48

Curch, Nathan 20:234

Curchil, C. F. 13:106

Curchill, C. 3:53

Curchman, Jacob 4:19

Curd, James 17:130; 24:190

Curd, John H. 23:97

Curd, Washington 17:267

Curden, Patrick 12:17

Curdley, James 12:56

Curdy, A. 14:287; 23:202

Cure, J. 24:76

Cure, William M. 20:154

Cureck, Michael 5:13

Curett, Mathew 10:48

Curey, D. 3:52

Curgadd, Joseph 22:247

Curicre, Levi S. 9:109

Curie, Charles 23:139

Curier, B. Frank 4:19

Curier, Henry H. 7:91

Curkindale, Jacob 26:154

Curl, D. 14:7

Curl, J. 25:20

Curl, J. H. 23:139

Curl, William 13:86; 22:120

Curlaugh, William 14:155

Curler, Henry 22:186

Curler, J. 13:17

Curley, A. M. 1:122

Curley, A. W. 14:7

Curley, Charles 16:81

Curley, Daniel 18:65

Curley, Edward 22:277

Curley, Francis 1:21

Curley, James 15:277; 25:160

Curley, James N. 20:185

Curley, John 12:68

Curley, P. 3:53

Curley, Patrick 1:23

Curley, R. 25:160

Curley, Thomas 25:22

Curley, W. 21:14

Curlin, J. 16:27

Curlis, Lovell 18:129

Curlis, R. A. 18:129

Curly, John 15:32

Curly, King 10:109; 20:234

Curm, Nathan 8:104

Curmons, Alonzo 12:17

Curn, J. 14:7

Curnan, Henry H. 22:111

Curne, --- 19:301

Curne, D. M. 25:160

Curnell, J. D. 19:64

Curnell, John H. 9:96

Curnett, Noah 10:95

Curney, John 21:320

Curnian, Victor 8:13

Curnings, Benjamin 3:53

Curnutt, John 22:73

Curnutt, William 23:63

Curr, Daniel 11:138

Curran, J. G. 11:299

Curran, James 22:9
Curran, Jeremiah 10:159
Curran, John B. 9:78;
 26:17
Curran, Michael 17:107;
 19:287
Curran, P. 12:92; 16:291
Curran, Patrick 1:24
Curran, Thomas 7:56;
 12:18
Curran, William 19:338;
 21:320
Curran, William B.
 21:223
Curray, John 5:13
Currell, H. G. 3:53
Currell, W. H. 23:25
Curren, Alfred 26:154
Curren, Andrew 24:107
Curren, F. 3:53
Curren, Felix 4:19
Curren, Giles 4:19
Curren, J. M. 14:51
Curren, Jeremiah 19:157
Curren, John C. 16:92
Current, Abraham 20:234
Currey, John A. 10:90
Currey, Stephen 5:38
Currey, W. F. 3:52
Currian, Victor 18:129
Currie, Arthur L. 22:115
Currie, John 21:320
Currie, M. 21:320
Currie, Robert 26:17
Currie, Robertson 9:78
Currie, S. M. 9:20
Currie, T. 1:119
Currie, Thaddeus 13:17
Currie, Thaddeus F. 16:28
Currie, W. 18:420
Currie, W. H. 25:160
Currie, William 19:157;
 25:160
Currier, C. C. 25:160
Currier, Edward 21:67
Currier, G. 25:160
Currier, George W.
 12:161; 22:277
Currier, Harry 19:157
Currier, J. H. 10:27
Currier, William 3:53
Currin, Aleck 20:234
Currin, Isaac 19:45
Currin, S. M. 26:94
Curringer, J. M. 21:320
Curry, A. 14:296; 17:479;
 27:31
Curry, Alonzo 25:271
Curry, Archibald 3:52
Curry, Bernard 1:121
Curry, Christopher 22:73

Curry, David M. 23:97
Curry, David P. 22:120
Curry, E. 13:86; 14:51
Curry, E. G. 17:307
Curry, Edward 8:83
Curry, Elijah 17:496
Curry, G. W. 11:331
Curry, George 22:295
Curry, Green 9:117; 27:29
Curry, H. 8:47
Curry, Henry 24:16
Curry, Hiram M. 24:15
Curry, Isaac 22:295
Curry, Isham H. 22:120
Curry, J. D. 19:10; 27:26
Curry, J. H. 21:120
Curry, J. L. 9:141
Curry, J. T. 11:91
Curry, J. W. 3:52
Curry, James 11:140, 200;
 17:77; 22:140
Curry, James W. 24:15
Curry, Jason 13:17
Curry, John 3:52; 12:68;
 15:32, 191; 19:236;
 22:397; 25:160
Curry, John A. 20:235
Curry, Joseph 7:91; 15:32;
 22:72
Curry, Lewis 6:35
Curry, Marion 4:19
Curry, Nathan 9:117;
 27:30
Curry, Nathan H. 17:32
Curry, Neal 4:19
Curry, R. M. 18:409
Curry, Richard 16:291
Curry, Robert 14:155
Curry, Robert A. 3:52
Curry, S. 3:52; 9:51;
 13:86
Curry, Samuel 19:329
Curry, Thomas 9:236;
 26:217
Curry, Thomas M. 17:50
Curry, Tisdale E. 22:421
Curry, W. H. 3:52
Curry, W. P. 10:147;
 18:47
Curry, William 21:214;
 22:72, 419
Curry, William H. 23:285
Curtain, Michael 10:7
Curtain, Patrick 13:81
Curter, J. H. 23:63
Curterue, Napoleon 7:24
Curtes, --- 16:291
Curtes, George 19:64
Curtes, William 19:64
Curtess, John 23:25
Curtilla, William 22:449

Curtin, B. 3:53
Curtin, D. 27:26
Curtin, Elkarch 17:272
Curtin, Francis 4:19
Curtin, Henry S. 10:159
Curtin, Patrick 16:184
Curtin, Thomas 10:152
Curtins, T. 18:234
Curtis, --- 25:23
Curtis, A. 3:52; 7:24
Curtis, Abe. T. 21:247
Curtis, Andrew J. 17:242;
 22:140
Curtis, Augustus 21:320
Curtis, Barton J. 22:140
Curtis, Benjamin 9:78;
 22:295
Curtis, Benjamin F. 22:73
Curtis, Benjamin L.
 21:320
Curtis, Benjamin M.
 17:242
Curtis, C. 17:309
Curtis, C. R. 20:111
Curtis, C. S. 16:184
Curtis, Charles 7:91;
 10:109; 11:181;
 16:184; 20:234;
 25:20
Curtis, Charles F. 10:159;
 16:8
Curtis, Charles H. 18:420;
 19:10; 22:507
Curtis, Charles L. 17:495;
 26:155
Curtis, D. 21:186
Curtis, Daniel R. 22:403
Curtis, David 26:144
Curtis, David C. 7:24
Curtis, E. 13:127
Curtis, E. W. 25:295
Curtis, Edmond 10:159
Curtis, Edward 26:22
Curtis, Edward J. 22:351
Curtis, Elias 26:19
Curtis, Elias E. 22:140
Curtis, Elijah 17:313
Curtis, Erwin W. 7:74
Curtis, F. 1:118
Curtis, F. B. 17:64
Curtis, Frank B. 16:77
Curtis, Franklin 9:129;
 27:28
Curtis, Franklin W. 17:77
Curtis, Fred 20:234
Curtis, G. F. 1:117
Curtis, George 10:159;
 13:17; 17:19; 19:157;
 21:206; 25:160
Curtis, George H. 23:285
Curtis, Gustave 15:121

Curtis, H. 15:191; 27:26
Curtis, H. W. 18:460
Curtis, Hanford 12:68; 15:2
Curtis, Henry 10:48; 20:234; 22:449
Curtis, Henry L. 19:158
Curtis, Hiram C. 13:17
Curtis, Hiram H. 11:104
Curtis, Horace 24:92
Curtis, Howard 7:91
Curtis, J. 1:97, 117, 118; 18:109
Curtis, J. A. 11:279
Curtis, J. G. 7:24; 20:234; 21:320
Curtis, J. J. 25:161
Curtis, J. M. 8:47
Curtis, James 4:19; 7:67; 9:78; 22:295, 333; 27:143
Curtis, James A. 21:50
Curtis, James E. 21:252
Curtis, James H. 10:48
Curtis, Jerome H. 20:234
Curtis, Jesse 7:120; 23:139
Curtis, Job C. 10:48
Curtis, John 3:52; 7:91; 9:130; 15:191; 17:191, 259; 18:80; 20:122
Curtis, John G. 11:258
Curtis, John J. 5:13
Curtis, John M. 22:120
Curtis, John V. 20:183
Curtis, John W. 21:98; 22:26
Curtis, Jordan 17:235
Curtis, Joseph 7:67; 10:48; 20:234
Curtis, L. 1:122; 25:161
Curtis, Lewis 5:38
Curtis, M. D. 3:52
Curtis, M. J. 25:25
Curtis, Major 13:57
Curtis, Marion J. 2:9
Curtis, Myron S. 10:109; 20:234
Curtis, N. 3:52
Curtis, N. B. 11:237
Curtis, Nathan 16:366
Curtis, O. F. 1:118
Curtis, Orin G. 17:46
Curtis, Oscar 22:420
Curtis, P. 15:340
Curtis, R. B. 1:23
Curtis, R. J. 25:161
Curtis, R. N. 26:153
Curtis, R. V. 8:13
Curtis, Ransom 7:64

Curtis, Richard 7:67; 15:21
Curtis, Robert 10:48; 20:234; 22:295
Curtis, Sandy 6:24
Curtis, Silas 1:119
Curtis, T. J. 8:71; 26:154
Curtis, Theodore E. 13:17
Curtis, Thomas 12:68; 15:7
Curtis, Thomas J. 16:92
Curtis, Thompson 4:19
Curtis, W. 20:91
Curtis, W. A. 3:52
Curtis, Wallace 18:430
Curtis, Washington J. 18:468
Curtis, William 1:121; 9:78, 130; 11:25; 13:17; 15:315; 16:147; 17:147; 18:234; 23:285; 26:18, 21; 27:25, 29
Curtis, William G. 18:109
Curtis, William L. 4:19
Curtis, William M. 20:234
Curtis, William S. 10:15
Curtiss, Bela 14:155
Curtiss, Charles E. 14:155
Curtiss, D. 17:154
Curtiss, F. J. 14:51
Curtiss, George R. 10:15
Curtiss, H. 9:141
Curtiss, Henry L. 11:115
Curtiss, J. 14:51; 27:27
Curtiss, J. A. 22:186
Curtiss, James 22:186
Curtiss, John 27:28
Curtiss, John W. 14:155
Curtiss, R. J. 5:50
Curtiss, S. C. 14:51
Curtiss, T. 27:27
Curtiss, Wade H. 22:247
Curtius, T. 26:22
Curtler, F. H. 16:184
Curtley, Milton 5:38
Curtney, P. 16:267
Curts, Calvin 22:73
Curts, Thomas 8:104
Curts, Walter 4:19
Curtwright, L. 3:53
Curtz, Frederick 10:48
Curver, J. H. 3:53
Curvin, S. M. 18:304
Curvy, Robert 14:264
Curyell, Abraham D. 23:63
Cusack, Benjamin 9:130
Cusack, Pen 27:29
Cusens, Neal 16:184
Cush, James P. 16:92

Cush, M. 11:385
Cush, T. M. 19:64
Cushin, Nicols 26:95
Cushinberry, George 17:267
Cushing, Augustus C. 21:320
Cushing, C. H. 14:51
Cushing, Charles 21:320
Cushing, Charles E. 3:53
Cushing, Dennis 17:50
Cushing, G. W. 1:122
Cushing, H. B. 14:155
Cushing, Ira W. 9:213; 21:320
Cushing, J. B. 14:155
Cushing, James 15:192
Cushing, John Z. 9:42
Cushing, Miles S. 19:158
Cushingbery, E. 25:161
Cushionbery, J. 25:161
Cushman, Charles T. 27:33
Cushman, Corydon S. 7:91
Cushman, E. J. 9:173
Cushman, E. L. 19:226
Cushman, Edward 13:107
Cushman, F. 15:11
Cushman, Fairfield 12:61
Cushman, George W. 22:186
Cushman, H. C. 15:192
Cushman, Horace 27:33
Cushman, J. C. 9:141
Cushman, J. E. 27:26
Cushman, O. J. 12:68
Cushman, W. 15:192
Cushmer, Charles 7:91
Cusic, W. C. 23:189
Cusick, H. 17:64
Cusick, Hiram 22:140
Cusick, J. 1:25
Cusick, Jerry 7:48
Cusick, Leander 11:141
Cusick, M. 25:161
Cusick, M. H. 23:139
Cusick, Patrick 22:333
Cusick, Peter 8:71
Cusick, Richard A. 22:140
Cusick, William 7:91
Cusley, Wadson B. 21:23
Cuss, J. 11:139
Cuss, P. 25:161
Cussans, --- 8:47
Cusser, R. 17:64
Cussick, J. M. 17:164
Cussick, Mathew J. 11:181
Custar, Charles 11:55
Custard, A. 13:81; 16:184

Custard, George M. 7:91
Custard, J. N. 13:107
Custard, John 21:223
Custard, Martin 11:300
Custer, Henry C. 21:67
Custer, J. B. 9:68
Custer, James C. 22:73
Custer, Joseph 11:140
Custer, Samuel L. 4:19
Custer, Washington 20:96
Custerman, F. 3:53
Custin, Agustus 9:141
Custin, D. 9:141
Custner, James 14:155
Custra, B. 14:51
Custy, Joseph 7:120
Cutchlon, Adam W.
    10:15; 13:17
Cutcomb, Morris 24:151
Cutcomb, Willis 17:440
Cute, A. 3:53
Cuter, C. H. 18:420
Cuter, Henry 12:16
Cuthbert, Ralph W.
    23:284
Cuthbert, W. H. 1:122
Cuthbertson, Edw. A.
    13:17
Cuthel, C. 3:53
Cuthnock, William 11:27
Cutland, Milton 16:28
Cutle, George 15:192
Cutlep, William 7:24
Cutler, --- 11:301
Cutler, A. 3:53
Cutler, Aaron M. 12:56
Cutler, Allen J. 21:223
Cutler, B. F. F. 20:39
Cutler, C. F. 3:53
Cutler, Charles 8:113;
    10:15; 19:10
Cutler, F. H. 1:26
Cutler, Forrest 25:161
Cutler, G. 25:25
Cutler, G. O. 27:24
Cutler, George 20:235
Cutler, Henry 22:26
Cutler, Henry A. 9:173
Cutler, James 11:411
Cutler, Jason 7:91
Cutler, John 11:55
Cutler, Joseph B. 21:320
Cutler, S. W. 11:285
Cutler, William 26:121
Cutler, Yerson 21:320
Cutlin, M. 19:64
Cutling, Charles H.
    18:304
Cutlip, Enos 11:300
Cutrell, James 22:26
Cutry, L. 3:53

Cutsdaphner, D. J. 3:53
Cuttell, H. 14:51
Cutter, C. E. 27:27
Cutter, C. H. 1:117
Cutter, Carrie E. 19:158
Cutter, Charles F. 21:320
Cutter, Edward 11:400
Cutter, Fred. B. 8:83
Cutter, G. 2:9; 16:113
Cutter, George 10:109
Cutter, George F. 19:158
Cutter, H. A. 19:236
Cutter, Henry J. 18:393
Cutter, J. P. 3:53; 14:155
Cutter, Jibena 21:320
Cutter, John 11:385
Cutter, Nicholas 18:323
Cutter, R. P. 15:165
Cutter, William 3:53
Cutting, C. H. 26:94
Cutting, Chapin 21:252
Cutting, Charles H. 16:8
Cutting, Horatio A. 13:17;
    16:28
Cutting, John 27:33
Cutting, William 8:119
Cuttiston, Thompson
    10:109
Cuttle, John A. 26:217
Cuttle, Paul 7:10
Cuttler, A. 14:155
Cuttler, A. H. 14:51
Cuttler, L. 14:51
Cuttler, Orrin C. 21:50
Cuttrell, Isaac 22:73
Cutts, E. 14:7
Cutts, Loren 7:24
Cutts, O. W. 3:53
Cutts, William 6:11;
    14:155; 18:109
Cuttshall, Henry F. 17:32
Cutwright, N. 14:51
Cuvalier, Cornelius
    15:192
Cuver, James H. 24:107
Cuvere, J. W. 3:53
Cuvvie, P. 14:52
Cuykendall, Newell
    22:140
Cuyler, H. 3:53
Cuyler, Joseph 9:130;
    27:29
Cuzzell, Davis P. 17:358
Cuzzin, William 4:19
Cwins, Charles 13:79
Cyford, J. 14:7
Cyloss, James 17:397
Cynus, Kincaid 22:295
Cypher, Eugene 27:25
Cypher, J. 17:154

Cypher, William 10:109;
    20:235
Cypher, William J.
    10:159; 19:158
Cyphers, A. 24:16
Cyphers, Coe 19:158
Cypper, James 19:10
Cyrus, John 9:207
Cysk, James 18:173
Cysser, C. 25:161
Cysser, Charles 5:38
Czar, George 20:235
Czariskie, Charles 22:277
Cziar, J. 27:25

D

D'Orsay, Patrick 14:160
D---, --- 10:27
D---, B. J. 11:239
D---, B. T. 23:25
D---, D. J. 11:260
D---, David 11:326
D---, E. 8:63; 11:105;
    15:151; 20:235;
    26:158; 27:143
D---, E. E. 22:351
D---, E. M. 25:27
D---, F. P. 17:216
D---, G. 18:65; 25:295
D---, G. W. 20:235
D---, George 15:32;
    19:161
D---, H. 23:267; 24:110
D---, H. C. 20:154
D---, H. W. 16:92
D---, I. 24:110
D---, J--- 10:27
D---, J. 11:301; 17:19,
    216; 18:27; 19:301;
    20:235; 21:208;
    24:110, 213
D---, J. C. 20:55; 26:158
D---, J. E. 11:339
D---, J. F. 11:259
D---, J. H. 15:54
D---, J. Q. 26:158
D---, J. T. 11:239
D---, James 17:236
D---, John 25:161
D---, K. 23:267
D---, L. 15:195
D---, M. 24:92
D---, M. C. 8:47
D---, M. D. 11:286
D---, M. J. 11:239
D---, M. L. 11:279
D---, Matt. L. 20:50
D---, N. 11:301
D---, P. 24:213

D---, R. 19:161
D---, R. B. 11:83
D---, R. H. 25:310
D---, S. 10:192; 17:217
D---, S. D. 11:339
D---, T. 11:239
D---, V. 11:301
D---, W. 11:238, 339; 17:364; 20:235
D---, W. F. 25:319
D---, W. H. 11:238; 20:235
D---, W. M. 19:67; 22:351
D---, W. T. 24:37
D---, William 11:239, 339; 15:165
D---, William S. 27:34
D----, B. W. 22:111
D---ge, Ephraim D. 25:29
D---it, C. 15:195
D---wn, --- 17:200
Da---, David 11:218
Daa, William 11:143
Daas, I. T. 24:65
Dabb, George 18:129
Daber, G. 3:53
Dabney, B. 3:53
Dabney, James D. 17:165
Dabney, John 22:449
Dabney, William 21:268
Daboo, Celestine 7:120
Dabough, John 23:95
Daby, John 15:192
Dabylon, Jeremiah 13:17; 16:28
Dace, C. 25:279
Dachety, Johann 9:106
Dachtler, H. 13:107
Dachtter, H. 16:184
Dack, John 19:250
Dacken, William 9:42
Dacker, Eli 11:395
Dacker, J. 7:24
Dacker, Jacob 11:144
Dackworth, J. A. 8:13; 18:129
Dacon, John 15:358; 19:64
Dacoster, Charles W. 22:403
Dacous, Edward 7:24
Dacy, G. 3:53
Dacy, John 9:160
Dade, Daniel M. 18:65
Dade, Gibson 11:201
Dade, James M. 24:16
Dade, John 6:35
Dade, Thomas 11:201
Daden, James C. 17:109
Dadley, John W. 25:161
Daergard, James 15:192

Daey, Timothy C. 25:278
Dafer, Joseph 23:285
Daffan, John H. 24:37
Dafferty, J. 16:184
Daffin, Sam 11:57
Daffney, I. 3:53
Daffondall, P. H. 3:53
Dafford, John 21:320
Dafford, Rice 22:247
Daffron, M. F. 19:10
Dafty, Martin 4:19
Dager, William 15:121
Dagerson, Charles 13:57
Daget, A. J. 1:93
Dagett, Richard 7:91
Daggart, R. 16:184
Daggatt, Horace W. 4:19
Dagger, Franklin 8:83
Dagger, Madison 22:403
Dagger, Wortley 11:201
Daggert, W. W. 11:239
Daggert, William G. 10:48
Dagget, A. G. 1:28
Daggett, Alvah E. 19:10
Daggett, Charles R. 11:27
Daggett, Darius 25:319
Daggett, George 22:478
Daggett, Jacob 17:19
Daggett, James G. 1:26
Daggett, John 22:140
Daggett, L. 14:155
Daggett, Lyman 14:268
Daggett, Nelson 1:28
Daggett, O. 21:320
Daggett, Orin H. 23:26
Daggett, W. G. 20:235
Daggitt, C. R. 16:366
Daggott, Darius 6:30
Daggy, Silas J. 17:271
Dagle, Alexander 23:290
Dagle, George V. 15:2
Dagnau, Charles 3:53
Dagne, John 14:155
Dagner, William T. 17:50
Dagnett, Joseph 17:160
Dagonia, Joseph 21:23
Dague, Aaron 12:18
Dague, Cyrus C. 24:76
Dague, Jonathan 25:29
Dague, Robert H. 23:285
Dahal, J. 14:52
Dahl, Ole E. 21:252
Dahlberg, M. 1:29
Dahle, Sylvester 7:24
Dahlem, John 22:186
Dahler, Jacob 22:186
Dahomey, Andrew 18:234; 26:23
Dahsteol, Andrew 21:244
Dahurty, Richard 5:13
Daicy, Thomas 22:165

Daigh, Thomas F. 25:332
Daiily, H. 15:192
Dailey, A. 3:53; 21:23
Dailey, Albert D. 7:63
Dailey, Andrew J. 20:29
Dailey, Asa 10:7; 18:359
Dailey, Benjamin T. 20:17
Dailey, Charles 17:160; 24:212
Dailey, D. 15:104; 25:161
Dailey, D. E. 20:55
Dailey, Daniel 18:27; 20:122
Dailey, E. 14:52
Dailey, Edwin R. 7:91
Dailey, Flemings 22:295
Dailey, Francis 17:469
Dailey, Harry 23:308
Dailey, Henry 11:400
Dailey, J. F. 18:27
Dailey, James 9:20, 199; 17:279, 348; 21:86
Dailey, James H. 17:14
Dailey, James M. 11:57
Dailey, Jeremiah 13:17; 21:98
Dailey, John 4:19; 5:13; 10:204; 12:99; 21:320; 22:519
Dailey, John B. 12:56
Dailey, John C. 23:178
Dailey, John W. 19:45
Dailey, Lewis N. 24:49
Dailey, M. 3:53; 15:65
Dailey, P. 1:127; 7:24
Dailey, Patrick 9:20
Dailey, Richard 22:295
Dailey, Robert G. 9:96
Dailey, Sylvanus 17:279
Dailey, Thimothy 15:32
Dailey, Thomas 4:19; 8:13; 18:129
Dailey, W. 18:27
Dailey, W. G. 12:81; 16:291
Dailey, William 1:28; 3:53; 7:91; 10:48; 14:314; 20:235
Dailey, William B. 22:111
Dailing, E. 14:7
Daily, A. M. 24:16
Daily, Aaron 25:27
Daily, B. H. 22:186
Daily, Charles 19:158
Daily, D. A. 22:186
Daily, F. 18:65
Daily, Francis 14:296; 27:38
Daily, Henry C. 11:144
Daily, I. 14:155
Daily, J. 1:125; 3:53

Daily, J. F. 12:161
Daily, J. J. 1:29
Daily, James 19:290
Daily, James A. 9:236
Daily, John 9:71; 11:57;
  13:79; 14:155;
  16:184; 17:50
Daily, Michael 27:35
Daily, Patrick 11:143;
  18:304; 26:96
Daily, Peter 13:17
Daily, Timothy 12:64;
  20:122
Daily, Warren B. 11:125
Dain, James M. 22:507
Daine, J. F. 15:158
Daine, W. W. 5:50;
  25:161
Daines, Daniel 8:83
Dains, Clark L. 19:273
Dair, Beriga 8:47
Dair, Eber H. 18:338
Daire, Thomas J. 21:320
Dairger, Madison 8:83
Daist, Andrew S. 11:143
Daisy, Robert 23:63
Dake, E. L. 10:48; 20:235
Dake, G. 3:53
Dake, Henry 22:247
Dakenfelt, J. 3:53
Dakens, Zephaniah 10:25
Dakin, J. A. 22:477
Dakin, Jeremiah 27:39
Dakin, L. T. 15:192
Dakin, Paul 21:252
Dakin, Robert 9:173
Dakin, W. V. 9:173
Dakin, Watson W. 22:449
Dakin, William G. 15:86
Dalahunty, James 22:333
Dalany, R. 14:52
Dalber, W. A. 18:393
Dalbey, J. M. 24:110
Dalbow, Henry 20:235
Dalburg, John P. 18:393
Dalby, Abner 24:16
Dalby, James 3:53
Dalden, G. H. 14:52
Dalden, J. 21:147
Dale, A. 21:166
Dale, A. G. 9:173
Dale, Alfred 20:235
Dale, C. 13:86; 14:7
Dale, Charles 15:340;
  16:366
Dale, Clarinda 26:219
Dale, Columbus 18:393
Dale, D. 11:239
Dale, David N. 21:320
Dale, Decatur 9:236;
  26:218

Dale, E. V. H. 15:192
Dale, Edward 8:104
Dale, Enoch 17:442;
  24:157
Dale, Evans 25:161
Dale, H. 16:92
Dale, Harry 18:80
Dale, Henry 6:15; 23:86
Dale, J. B. 21:320
Dale, James 8:62, 83
Dale, James A. 17:62, 276
Dale, James R. 20:55
Dale, John 12:152; 22:512
Dale, John P. 21:98
Dale, John R. 23:120
Dale, Landis 9:78
Dale, Martin 8:104
Dale, Myley 20:235
Dale, N. 21:186
Dale, Simeon C. 17:99
Dale, William 22:26
Dale, Wyley 10:48
Dalen, Simon 16:184
Dales, Albert 9:96
Dales, James 15:267
Daley, Alexander 8:83
Daley, Amor 9:95
Daley, Amos 26:25
Daley, Andrew 22:333
Daley, Andrew J. 15:54
Daley, Daniel 13:17
Daley, Daniel E. 17:247
Daley, E. C. 11:28
Daley, Erving 19:233
Daley, H. P. 25:161
Daley, Irving 9:173
Daley, J. 1:123; 27:35
Daley, James 3:53; 7:48;
  14:264; 18:109;
  22:295; 23:26
Daley, John 1:28; 3:53;
  18:109; 19:158;
  24:110
Daley, M. 27:35
Daley, Michael 19:10;
  23:202
Daley, N. C. 13:17
Daley, Nesley 25:30
Daley, Patrick 21:320
Daley, Peter 13:17; 16:28
Daley, Robert 21:320
Daley, S. 3:53
Daley, Thomas 19:321
Daley, Tim F. 9:173
Daley, V. D. 27:37
Daley, William 16:9
Dalgam, John 23:63
Dalgleish, George 16:92
Dalhe, C. O. 11:332
Dalhueyer, John 9:96
Dalibone, Daniel 21:23

Daliel, Patrick 17:14
Dalien, P. 1:126
Dalin, Solomon 17:173
Dalkin, William A. 22:26
Dall, E. 14:52
Dall, John 17:130; 24:192
Dall, Landis 26:22
Dall, Martin 26:219
Dall, R. C. 15:33
Dallar, George 25:277
Dallas, Harrison 22:26
Dallas, John 14:155
Dallas, Samuel H. 21:23
Dallbeck, G. A. 12:86
Dallem, Lewis 9:199;
  19:281
Dalley, Henry P. 5:13
Dalley, James 18:13;
  21:320
Dalley, James A. 26:218
Dalley, W. J. 1:124
Dalliard, D. 11:143
Dalliere, John B. 10:153
Dallinger, W. C. 3:53
Dallis, George M. 12:48
Dallon, Thomas 25:161
Dallrumple, Robert 4:19
Dally, C. F. 27:157
Dally, John H. 22:186
Dally, Noah J. 22:186
Dalmelder, A. 12:121;
  15:121
Dalmin, K. 19:250
Dalon, C. 3:53
Dalover, John 11:57
Dalrimple, Samuel H.
  22:422
Dalrimple, T. 11:100
Dalrimple, Thomas
  18:129
Dalrumple, Thomas 8:13
Dalryample, R. C. 7:64
Dalrymple, Jesse 15:352;
  16:278
Dalrymple, R. 9:141
Dalrymple, W. 13:86;
  14:7
Dalten, James 3:53
Dalten, John A. 8:62
Daltman, Jonathan 18:205
Daltmer, George 11:28
Dalton, A. 11:83
Dalton, A. J. 9:51
Dalton, Bernard 8:100;
  17:459; 24:150
Dalton, D. B. 18:234;
  26:23
Dalton, E. M. 19:64
Dalton, E. W. 9:11
Dalton, F. 2:10; 25:27
Dalton, G. 14:52

Dalton, George 13:17; 16:28
Dalton, Hugh 11:260
Dalton, Isaac 17:235
Dalton, J. 11:186; 21:320
Dalton, James 13:79; 16:184; 20:145; 21:320
Dalton, Jasper 11:144
Dalton, John 12:18; 18:47; 22:111, 186
Dalton, John A. 26:158
Dalton, Michael 9:78; 14:155; 20:6; 26:22
Dalton, N. W. 26:158
Dalton, P. 16:184
Dalton, Patrick 9:173; 19:250
Dalton, Peter 8:13; 18:129
Dalton, R. K. 22:186
Dalton, Robert C. 20:111
Dalton, T. 16:184
Dalton, W. H. H. 23:26
Dalton, William 8:83; 19:64
Dalton, William E. 22:120
Daly, Charles 26:135
Daly, E. 17:109
Daly, J. 1:123; 15:7
Daly, James 18:304; 26:95
Daly, Joe 15:158
Daly, John 3:53; 10:15; 25:281
Daly, M. 16:28; 17:337
Daly, Matthew 14:155
Daly, Michael 3:53; 13:17
Daly, Patrick 19:158
Daly, T. 1:28; 3:53
Daly, V. D. 14:296; 17:479
Daly, W. 1:124
Daly, William 15:121
Dalye, Michael 12:7
Dalzell, Floren 22:186
Dalzell, J. G. 3:53
Dalzell, Martin 17:253
Dalzelle, William 27:34
Dalziel, Robert 21:136
Dalziel, W. 3:53
Dam, Charles E. 16:5
Dama, Daniel 22:165
Damain, Isaac 11:238
Damann, August 23:63
Damant, G. W. 14:52
Damar, Andrew 8:83
Damback, John 22:165
Dambadier, Christopher 21:242
Dambo, John 21:320
Dambusky, Henry 19:10
Damby, John 25:295

Dame, George 20:111; 25:161
Dame, J. L. 14:52
Dame, John 10:48
Damel, Levi 11:91
Damell, I. F. 10:48
Damen, Jarrel 8:13
Dameny, William 25:161
Damer, Stephen D. 22:161
Damerigo, Louis 21:320
Dameron, Yancey 10:109; 20:235
Damerst, --- 15:192
Damersy, A. P. 17:451
Damerwood, E. H. 1:126
Damery, John 3:53
Damhockle, E. 3:53
Damhum, Daniel J. 16:28
Damiens, Joseph 24:8
Daming, C. W. 14:52
Damkeith, Samuel 25:283
Damlos, James 17:247
Dammert, Charles F. 23:112
Dammig, Henry 16:113
Damn, Henry 25:28
Damon, A. 1:27
Damon, Albert H. 16:28
Damon, Albert K. 13:17
Damon, Alfred A. 22:508
Damon, D. N. 4:19
Damon, David 19:158
Damon, Fred 7:91
Damon, G. 9:173; 19:250
Damon, Irin 24:16
Damon, J. D. 3:53
Damon, Joshua L. 10:159
Damon, L. F. 14:155
Damon, M. 8:121
Damon, Milo N. 23:26
Damon, R. 3:53
Damon, Samuel 17:322
Damon, Thomas 14:155
Damon, Thomas H. 26:23
Damon, William 21:91
Damond, John 9:130
Dampey, John 3:53
Dampire, --- 2:10
Dampman, Richard 14:155
Dampsey, Jeremiah 18:291
Damrin, Charles M. 12:68
Damson, Alexander 7:120
Damuth, William 10:109; 20:235
Dan, C. 1:126
Dan, Christian 10:48
Dan, Darius 21:252
Dan, George 15:304; 16:184

Dan, Thomas A. 9:157
Dan, William 12:87; 16:291
Dan, William H. 27:37
Dana, Josiah H. 17:359
Dana, Michael 9:173
Dana, R. F. 22:333
Danabaugh, Christopher 20:235
Danah, John 11:104
Danah, W. W. 14:7
Danaho, Peter 10:109; 20:235
Danark, Thomas R. S. 16:28
Danas, J. H. 1:97
Danasa, Augustus 11:235
Danbar, D. A. 16:184
Danber, Peter 17:464; 24:213
Danburg, Aaron 26:96
Danbury, Aaron 9:20
Danbury, Anson 18:304
Danby, C. 25:27
Dance, Jacob 20:122
Dance, Patrick 13:107
Dancer, Henry C. 17:64
Dancer, John 19:10
Dancer, Samuel 17:173
Dancey, Allen 7:120
Danchy, William 16:118
Dancil, --- 25:27
Dancley, H. M. 25:161
Dancy, Joseph 20:183
Dand, George W. 22:333
Dand, J. 12:161
Dandel, Joseph 1:27
Dandelion, F. 3:54
Dandenmarkle, D. 14:8
Dandrich, Rolla 21:268
Dandridge, Alexander 21:211
Dandridge, Alfred 6:15; 18:80
Dandridge, Richard 18:434
Dandroff, W. 1:93
Dandy, Daniel 19:10
Dane, Albert G. 14:156
Dane, Andrew 3:54
Dane, C. Y. 26:23
Dane, Francis 23:63
Dane, H. L. 15:192
Dane, Henry 19:64
Dane, Joe 4:19
Dane, John 12:18; 18:27
Dane, M. G. 2:10
Dane, Marshall 22:73
Danegh, James 25:161
Danell, J. E. 10:95

Danenhower, I. I. 16:291
Danenhower, J. J. 12:85
Daner, I. 3:54
Danerigo, Louis 7:91
Daneton, John 19:158
Daney, Philip 16:92
Danfelt, John 14:156
Danfirth, George A. 3:54
Danford, James 14:156
Danford, Johnson N. 4:19
Danford, Malon F. 15:192
Danford, R. 1:125
Danford, William 2:10; 25:26
Danforth, Charles 9:102
Danforth, D. 16:366
Danforth, E. N. 1:29
Danforth, Edwin S. 12:18
Danforth, Henry 23:120
Danforth, J. R. 20:48
Danforth, Jeremiah 16:84
Danforth, Joseph 21:320
Danforth, S. E. 25:161
Danforth, Samuel 24:61
Danforth, Stephen E. 5:50
Dangan, --- 12:169
Danger, Lewis 9:230; 20:235
Dangerfield, Alfred 7:120
Dangerfield, B. F. 23:255
Dangerfield, John 1:191
Dangerfield, William H. 20:96
Danghenbach, W. H. 20:174
Dangiles, Milton 9:78
Danglass, William J. 12:173
Danglemyre, Jacob 24:76
Dangler, Elias 12:18
Dangler, W. G. 3:53
Dangon, W. 25:161
Danice, George 21:320
Danice, William 16:92
Daniel, --- 3:53; 26:24
Daniel, A. J. 24:110
Daniel, E. J. 14:8
Daniel, George 15:258
Daniel, H. 21:109
Daniel, J. 14:52
Daniel, J. E. 13:86; 14:8
Daniel, J. O. 17:455; 24:192
Daniel, James 10:176; 22:333
Daniel, James W. 11:91
Daniel, John 10:32
Daniel, John L. 21:223
Daniel, John P. 16:184
Daniel, Joseph 11:57
Daniel, Levi B. 18:275

Daniel, Lewis 22:333
Daniel, P. 23:139
Daniel, R. 3:53
Daniel, R. M. 19:10
Daniel, Robert 19:10, 329
Daniel, Robert B. 13:18; 16:28
Daniel, S. 1:127
Daniel, Samuel 7:91; 9:51
Daniel, T. 15:293
Daniel, W. 13:86; 18:234; 26:25
Daniel, William C. 22:73
Danield, George 14:52
Danields, J. A. 22:500
Daniells, M. D. 4:19
Daniels, --- 14:287
Daniels, A. 20:235
Daniels, A. G. 9:109
Daniels, A. H. 9:20
Daniels, Abraham 10:48
Daniels, Alfred 10:109; 20:235
Daniels, Allen 8:83
Daniels, Alvin 8:104
Daniels, And. J. 27:37
Daniels, Andrew J. 9:117; 11:27
Daniels, Archibald 21:211
Daniels, Arthur M. 21:91
Daniels, Asa R. 8:13; 18:129
Daniels, August 4:19
Daniels, B. 8:104
Daniels, B. S. 25:161
Daniels, Calvin 18:216
Daniels, Charles 10:176; 12:18; 15:310; 19:64, 158
Daniels, Charles H. 21:320
Daniels, Chester W. 8:113
Daniels, D. W. 11:15
Daniels, David 10:144; 17:235; 21:91
Daniels, David C. 19:158
Daniels, E. 25:161
Daniels, E. A. 15:340
Daniels, E. L. 14:264
Daniels, Edward 4:19
Daniels, Eugene L. 23:26
Daniels, Ezra 5:13
Daniels, F. W. 15:277; 25:161
Daniels, Fred. W. 9:173; 19:270
Daniels, G. F. 15:172
Daniels, George 8:104
Daniels, George E. 20:136
Daniels, George W. 22:351

Daniels, H. 1:125
Daniels, Harman 21:215
Daniels, Harrison 17:130; 22:277; 24:192
Daniels, Henry 1:27; 16:184; 21:248, 321
Daniels, Henry W. 16:7
Daniels, Hiram 24:92
Daniels, Isaac 24:110
Daniels, Isaac H. 4:19
Daniels, Isaiah 10:48
Daniels, J. 1:123; 7:77; 19:250; 25:295; 26:22
Daniels, J. C. 16:267
Daniels, J. F. 9:20
Daniels, J. S. 20:39
Daniels, James 9:173; 14:52; 19:158
Daniels, James M. 22:247
Daniels, James W. 22:403
Daniels, John 9:102; 20:235; 22:277, 477
Daniels, Jonah 9:78
Daniels, Jonathan 17:235
Daniels, Joseph 23:313
Daniels, Joseph B. 11:186
Daniels, L. M. 27:35
Daniels, Levi B. 9:66
Daniels, Lewis 6:22; 7:77
Daniels, Liner M. 25:29
Daniels, Louis 16:366; 25:295
Daniels, Luke H. 17:109
Daniels, M. 1:125
Daniels, M. V. 25:28
Daniels, Merritt 22:461
Daniels, Myron M. 16:7
Daniels, N. H. 18:304; 19:334; 26:96
Daniels, Nelson 10:109; 20:235
Daniels, Oscar G. 9:11
Daniels, Patrick 21:268
Daniels, Peter 17:445; 24:166
Daniels, R. 7:79; 25:295
Daniels, Reuben 23:63
Daniels, Richard 17:130; 18:65; 24:192
Daniels, Samuel 18:65
Daniels, T. 1:126; 16:366
Daniels, Thomas 10:90; 20:235
Daniels, Thomas W. 21:67
Daniels, W. 1:27
Daniels, W. D. 26:158
Daniels, William 8:38; 10:48; 12:148; 17:99; 20:235; 26:157, 218

Daniels, William B. 10:109; 20:235
Daniels, William F. 15:151
Daniels, William H. 17:436; 24:185
Daniels, William W. 21:186
Daniels, Zach 9:51
Danier, Nelson 11:124
Danim, William 3:53
Danior, W. H. 3:54
Danish, John 14:8
Danish, L. 27:157
Danison, George W. 7:48
Danity, Timothy 11:105
Danke, William 26:97
Dankel, Mathias 25:28
Danken, J. 14:287
Danker, Daniel 20:235
Danker, J. 23:97
Dankers, Daniel 7:24
Dankhour, George 10:48
Dankid, J. 14:264
Dankie, William 11:143
Danks, C. O. 11:58
Danks, Henry C. 10:109; 20:235
Danles, William W. 21:166
Danley, A. J. 9:219; 18:364
Danley, C. 13:86
Danley, C. L. 25:27
Danley, Elisha 11:105
Danley, George W. 4:19
Danley, Joel M. 22:186
Danley, Levi 14:334
Danley, William 8:13
Danley, Z. 13:17
Danly, William 9:157
Dann, A. 14:52
Dann, Alfred 23:106
Dann, Henry 23:26
Dann, J. 14:52
Dann, J. A. 18:188
Dann, John 20:235
Dann, L. 18:131
Danna, H. 3:54
Dannan, Andrew 12:152
Dannehover, J. 14:156
Dannell, James 7:120
Danner, Adam 15:165
Danner, Anton 21:98
Danner, James H. 22:186
Danner, John 11:143; 22:477
Danner, Joseph 22:27
Danner, Lewis 11:235
Danner, S. 11:28
Danner, VanBuren 12:18

Danney, C. 14:52
Dannier, P. 9:141
Danning, Samuel A. 19:158
Danning, W. 3:54
Danns, Mathew 15:192
Dannser, J. 26:156
Dannser, S. 18:129
Danny, Frederick 12:18
Danolo, John 5:13
Danolt, Remming 21:321
Danon, John H. 9:173
Danour, George 20:235
Danouth, Charles 10:48; 20:235
Danovins, Patrick 22:449
Dans, Simon 10:95
Dans, W. H. 2:10
Dansbaugh, Christopher 10:109
Dansforth, H. 25:161
Dansing, A. 3:54
Danson, J. 3:54
Danson, Josiah 18:173
Danson, Matthew 12:64
Danson, Oliver 8:83
Danster, David 11:238
Dant, I. M. 3:54
Dant, Samuel 5:38
Dant, T. B. 25:26
Danthan, James M. 17:392
Danton, Alfred 23:63
Danton, Henry C. 14:52
Danton, Thomas 15:347
Dantry, B. 21:23
Danuho, A. 15:192
Danuser, I. 8:13
Danvoack, Harry 11:143
Danwalder, Charles 11:27
Danway, Benjamin 10:98
Danwin, C. W. 15:11
Dany, Daniel 13:107
Danylois, J. T. 14:255
Danzeglock, Gustav 27:34
Danzigar, Moses 26:25
Danziger, N. 1:28
Dapall, J. 16:367
Dapee, Fortunatus 17:130; 24:192
Dapol, Charles 7:92
Dapp, Alonzo T. 23:26
Daprembple, W. 16:267
Dapron, C. 13:18
Dar, D. 21:23
Dar---, J. 26:24
Daran, Wilson 13:57
Darande, Julius 12:18
Daratt, Louis 3:54
Darby, Archibald 10:109; 20:235

Darby, Christopher 22:247
Darby, G. S. 15:27
Darby, Greenleaf S. 12:68
Darby, Henry 17:130; 24:192
Darby, Hugh 7:83
Darby, J. J. 10:109; 20:235
Darby, James 17:71; 22:120
Darby, James H. 17:32
Darby, L. L. 14:52
Darby, Leander 18:109
Darby, Newton 9:70
Darby, Royal 7:81; 25:295
Darby, S. E. 14:240
Darcey, Edward 5:13
Darcey, J. C. 14:280
Darcy, E. 25:161
Darden, B. 9:242
Darden, J. 9:68
Dardenne, Edward 20:89
Dardingkiller, Fred 10:15
Dardis, E. 25:26
Dardis, Edward 2:10
Dare, Henry A. 21:23
Dare, Hugh 25:161
Dare, J. W. O. 1:126
Dare, John 14:52
Dare, Moses 25:28
Dare, Wesley 10:48
Dareen, Patrick 26:210
Darenuss, David A. 15:172
Darer, Daniel 17:454; 24:186
Darew, T. 3:54
Darey, John 1:29
Darfee, Courtland E. 5:13
Dargan, P. 14:156
Darge, John 24:58
Dargen, Jeremiah 9:173
Darhelf, James 9:117
Darimples, George 11:295
Daring, Emil 22:186
Daring, F. 16:184
Daring, J. 16:185
Daringer, Madison 18:205
Darity, W. J. 14:8
Dark, G. 7:67
Dark, J. A. 11:239
Darker, William 3:54
Darkin, Michael 14:156
Darkin, William 26:122
Darkins, Richard 18:80
Darkiss, J. V. 20:132
Darkitalder, Leonard 18:129
Darkman, John 27:37
Darl, Thomas 11:28

Darland, Ally 19:11
Darland, Cornelius
    10:109; 20:235
Darley, D. 5:50
Darley, Henry 15:158
Darley, I. 3:54
Darley, James 26:157
Darley, Levi 7:24
Darley, William 11:190
Darling, A. B. 1:28
Darling, A. L. 15:21
Darling, Alexander
    11:190
Darling, Arthur 4:19
Darling, Benjamin H.
    19:226
Darling, Charles 22:287
Darling, D. K. 7:48
Darling, D. O. 1:26
Darling, D. W. 3:54
Darling, Daniel 1:27
Darling, E. 13:86; 19:64
Darling, E. S. 26:25
Darling, Ephraim 25:27
Darling, Francis 18:327
Darling, Frank 16:291
Darling, Franklin 4:19
Darling, G. 17:296
Darling, G. H. 3:54
Darling, H. 1:124
Darling, H. M. 12:80;
    25:161
Darling, Herman G. 13:18
Darling, I. 3:54
Darling, Irenus 22:278
Darling, J. A. 25:27
Darling, J. P. 11:144
Darling, Joseph 7:92
Darling, Killus 18:462
Darling, L. 13:107
Darling, R. 23:139
Darling, S. G. 1:123
Darling, Samuel I. 10:48
Darling, Samuel J. 20:235
Darling, Seth 23:26
Darling, Simeon 21:206
Darling, T. 25:26
Darling, Thomas J. 23:106
Darling, Truman 7:67
Darling, William 14:156
Darlint, Francis 8:83
Darlon, T. 2:10
Darman, A. 25:161
Darmbaash, Harm 17:94
Darn, Cornelius 10:159
Darn, Nicholas 22:333
Darnaby, Ephraim 15:192
Darnell, Elias 20:111
Darnell, G. W. 18:47
Darnell, George W.
    10:152

Darnell, J. F. 20:235
Darnell, John R. 21:115
Darnell, Thomas 24:16
Darnell, W. J. A. 19:64
Darnell, William 22:247
Darnes, Joseph W. 9:11
Darning, Edward 14:156
Darnold, James L. 16:28
Darnold, R. 1:29
Darr, John 20:96
Darr, John F. 21:321
Darr, Milton 22:73
Darr, P. 2:10; 25:29
Darr, Philip S. 12:56
Darr, Singleton 25:161
Darr, William H. 18:129
Darragh, W. E. 21:120
Darrah, Charles 8:62
Darrah, John 15:33
Darrah, Joseph 21:136
Darrah, William A.
    18:109
Darrel, Andrew 27:39
Darrell, William 22:470
Darres, A. J. 9:219
Darrey, Patrick 15:33
Darrigan, Richard 16:13
Darrigh, John 13:86
Darrin, Israel 18:338
Darriston, --- 18:27
Darrixon, G. 14:8
Darrone, C. A. 17:211
Darrone, Charles 15:332
Darrow, Clark 9:141
Darrow, Ezra 10:48;
    20:235
Darrow, J. H. 19:245
Darrow, James M. 26:144
Darrow, L. F. 1:28
Darrow, N. 13:86
Darrow, Seymour F. 9:102
Darsey, M. 3:54
Darsham, Christian
    21:223
Darst, B. 15:273
Darst, Samuel T. 22:27
Darsy, J. 27:38
Dart, Alford 15:121
Dart, Charles W. 3:54
Dart, Harry 22:140
Dart, John K. 22:477
Dart, Joshua F. 12:18
Dart, W. R. 19:158
Dart, William H. 13:18
Dartch, E. 21:321
Darter, Nicholas 24:16
Darthe, Allen 14:52
Dartword, John 9:78
Darun, J. S. 3:54
Darvin, M. W. 3:54
Darvoe, --- 16:92

Darwark, David 9:78
Darwen, William 23:15
Darwin, Charles 11:201
Darwin, Israel P. 9:102
Darwin, John 9:20
Darwood, Henry 11:15
Darymple, J. 1:28
Dascher, Henry 19:250
Dascomb, E. 16:80
Dasen, N. 3:54
Dasey, A. W. 23:26
Dash, Jacob 20:176
Dash, Stephen 9:42;
    26:122
Dash, William 16:28
Dasha, John 13:63;
    16:185
Dasher, Henry 11:57
Dasher, Levi 9:141; 27:36
Dasin, Charles 9:11
Daskey, James 27:37
Dasson, James 23:112
Dasson, Jeremiah 11:201
Daster, H. D. 20:39
Dasting, Henry B. 26:158
Dasting, Henry P. 18:130
Data, Noah 17:199
Date, James 27:36
Date, P. M. 2:9
Date, S. 21:321
Daten, Edwin 9:219
Dater, F. M. 8:83
Dater, George A. 18:80
Dater, Jacob 14:52
Dates, Jacob 17:19
Dates, William J. 17:287
Dathman, --- 11:339
Datin, James 27:144
Datrol, J. 15:325
Datson, B. B. 12:152
Datson, William 11:105
Datton, H. 25:161
Datzuis, Philip W. 7:67
Daub, J. 18:47
Daubenspeck, D. 16:185
Daubert, Frederick 1:27
Daubing, --- 11:181
Dauble, John 23:97
Daucer, Frank 20:122
Dauchtr---, A. 23:202
Dauge, A. 21:203
Daugh--caugh, Jacob
    17:294
Daughenbaugh, J. 1:124
Daugherty, A. M. 20:46
Daugherty, B. 25:161
Daugherty, D. 17:199
Daugherty, F. 1:125
Daugherty, George 25:161
Daugherty, George P.
    22:120

Daugherty, Henry L. 21:50
Daugherty, Hezekiah W. 23:63
Daugherty, J. 24:76
Daugherty, Jacob 11:57
Daugherty, James R. 21:50
Daugherty, Jesse 22:186
Daugherty, John 11:143; 22:449
Daugherty, L. 16:267
Daugherty, Samuel 23:86
Daugherty, Thomas H. 15:158
Daugherty, W. T. 21:120
Daugherty, William 15:172
Daughter, R. J. 16:278
Daughterty, Harvey 17:397
Daughtery, Joseph 25:161
Daughtery, Samuel 22:73
Daughty, Benjamin B. 15:151
Daughty, G. W. 16:267
Daughty, Lyman 22:421
Daughty, Robert H. 13:18
Daughurburg, Charles 14:156
Dauks, William 18:304
Dauliffe, Henry 21:321
Daulton, --- 11:142
Daulton, John 10:159
Daumueller, John 10:109; 20:236
Daun, R. 3:54
Daunanay, Charles H. 24:16
Daunard, N. 3:54
Daunt, William 15:65
Daurwolf, Auguste 21:321
Dauson, August 11:190
Dav---, J. 18:234
Davaes, Andrew 7:120
Davalt, J. A. 21:23
Dave, --- 10:204
Dave, John 24:92
Davee, Richard H. 20:6
Davees, L. 9:51
DaVelle, T. 1:125
Davenbrook, I. 3:55
Davene, J. 3:55
Davenport, A. 1:124
Davenport, Albert W. 25:29
Davenport, Benjamin 25:29
Davenport, Charles 7:24
Davenport, Charles W. 22:333

Davenport, Cornelius 23:139
Davenport, Daniel 12:18
Davenport, E. M. 15:7
Davenport, Erasmus M. 12:61
Davenport, F. 16:185
Davenport, George 23:313
Davenport, George W. 7:13; 10:159; 19:158
Davenport, H. S. 18:27
Davenport, H. W. 1:29
Davenport, Henry 5:13; 25:27
Davenport, Henry D. 11:144
Davenport, Hy 2:9
Davenport, I. 15:192
Davenport, J. 3:55
Davenport, James 3:55
Davenport, James E. 26:25
Davenport, Jesse 23:202
Davenport, John 23:86
Davenport, John J. 1:27; 17:242
Davenport, L. 8:62; 26:158
Davenport, Leonard 10:204
Davenport, M. C. 16:28
Davenport, N. 9:141; 27:36
Davenport, P. 8:62
Davenport, R. G. 19:226
Davenport, R. J. 14:52
Davenport, Samuel 18:440
Davenport, Valentine 10:15
Davenport, Vincent 15:192
Davenport, W. 14:296; 17:481; 20:239; 27:39
Davenport, Warren 1:27
Davenport, William 8:38; 10:49; 21:238; 26:157
Davenport, William B. 17:242
Davenport, William J. 18:65
Davenson, I. 3:55
Daveport, Robert S. 23:120
Daver, Patrick 7:67
Daverin, W. 1:126
Davey, A. J. 14:156
Davey, C. B. 16:185
Davey, David C. 23:189

Davice, George W. 21:321
David, A. 14:52
David, Alexander 23:106
David, Archy 6:35
David, Barton 22:296
David, Charles 7:63
David, D. 9:154; 15:32
David, D. P. 3:55
David, D. T. 16:135
David, Daniel 22:296
David, E. M. 22:140
David, G. N. 11:27
David, Isaac 11:143
David, J. B. 13:86
David, J. W. 23:259
David, James 14:52
David, James M. 17:71
David, John 11:142; 15:192
David, John W. 22:508
David, Joseph 22:403
David, Knar 22:233
David, Lomig 8:13
David, Loring 18:129
David, Thomas E. F. 22:478
David, W. 22:477; 23:245
David, William 9:130, 207; 27:37
Davids, A. 9:173
Davids, Chester W. 8:83
Davids, William J. 13:107
Davidsaw, Ed. A. 19:11
Davidsizer, H. 22:233
Davidson, --- 14:156
Davidson, A. 20:84
Davidson, A. H. 22:187
Davidson, Adam 17:267; 21:321
Davidson, Alexander 21:136; 23:305
Davidson, Amos 22:27
Davidson, Andrew J. 24:16
Davidson, Benjamin G. 17:209
Davidson, C. 3:55
Davidson, C. H. 14:280
Davidson, Ch. 21:23
Davidson, Charles 3:55; 11:201; 22:449
Davidson, Charles E. 16:28
Davidson, Charles M. 22:333
Davidson, Cyrus 22:187
Davidson, D. 14:240
Davidson, Daniel 11:181; 23:139
Davidson, Daniel B. 24:49

Davidson, David 10:49; 18:364; 20:236
Davidson, David H. 20:96
Davidson, E. K. 17:77
Davidson, Edw. H. 13:18
Davidson, Elias B. 17:71
Davidson, Francis 16:185
Davidson, Frank 21:268
Davidson, Franklin M. 10:109; 20:236
Davidson, G. 3:55; 14:52; 15:192; 17:173
Davidson, George 3:55; 14:52
Davidson, George F. 8:13; 18:129
Davidson, George W. 8:13; 14:156; 18:129; 22:477
Davidson, Gideon 19:11
Davidson, Giles 22:421
Davidson, Granbury 23:285
Davidson, Gustav 15:315
Davidson, Gustave 19:64
Davidson, H. 1:124; 9:66; 14:28; 17:173
Davidson, H. C. 14:333; 23:305
Davidson, Henry 4:19; 18:275; 21:321; 22:73; 24:177
Davidson, Hugh 23:120
Davidson, I. 23:140
Davidson, I. H. 3:55
Davidson, I. W. 19:11
Davidson, Isaac E. 24:49
Davidson, J. 1:29, 103, 126; 11:301; 13:107; 27:34
Davidson, J. A. 7:24; 14:313
Davidson, J. C. 9:51
Davidson, J. E. 20:236
Davidson, J. G. 21:23
Davidson, J. H. 1:123; 10:49; 20:236
Davidson, Jackson 20:103
Davidson, James 9:117; 11:57, 201; 15:54; 25:29
Davidson, James E. 22:170
Davidson, James F. 22:120
Davidson, James L. 8:83
Davidson, James M. 22:73
Davidson, Jeremiah 14:156

Davidson, John 9:173; 10:109; 14:52; 20:236
Davidson, John F. 8:83
Davidson, John I. 18:205
Davidson, John L. 20:185
Davidson, John S. 22:27
Davidson, Jonathan K. 17:19
Davidson, Joseph 7:92
Davidson, Louis 16:28
Davidson, M. 1:126
Davidson, Marcus 20:6
Davidson, Martin 14:52
Davidson, Martin A. 17:50
Davidson, Nathan 23:15
Davidson, O. S. 14:53
Davidson, Ole 21:67
Davidson, P. 22:296
Davidson, P. S. 3:55
Davidson, R. 11:142
Davidson, R. W. 16:185
Davidson, Radford 22:248
Davidson, Richard 22:422
Davidson, Robert C. 4:19
Davidson, S. 15:33; 23:276
Davidson, S. A. 18:189
Davidson, S. B. 27:143
Davidson, Samuel 3:55; 10:109
Davidson, Samuel M. 23:279
Davidson, Silas F. 11:386
Davidson, Solomon 22:296
Davidson, T. J. 17:322
Davidson, T. K. 23:26
Davidson, Theodore 19:64
Davidson, Thomas 19:158; 24:110
Davidson, Thomas D. 21:129
Davidson, W. 3:55; 14:156; 27:35
Davidson, W. L. 11:124
Davidson, W. P. 7:92
Davidson, William 9:219; 15:65; 17:442; 22:187; 24:37, 157
Davidson, William H. 10:15
Davidson, William J. 25:29
Davidson, William T. 16:28
Davidson, Wilson 8:47
Davien, John 21:268
Davies, E. 27:35
Davies, Elijah C. 9:78
Davies, James 26:96

Davies, Joseph 26:122
Davies, Milton J. 21:247
Davies, Seth 18:393
Daville, Oliver S. 20:236
Davin, M. 19:250
Davine, Dennis 24:16
Davis, --- 9:109; 15:104, 340; 16:367; 17:228; 18:65, 444; 26:236
Davis, A. 7:24; 9:78, 173; 10:90; 11:57; 12:87; 14:53; 15:192; 16:291; 17:173; 19:250; 20:236; 21:23, 163; 24:76; 26:25
Davis, A. C. 1:125; 18:129; 20:174
Davis, A. Drake 27:39
Davis, A. E. 5:13; 10:48
Davis, A. G. 19:222; 20:236; 22:500
Davis, A. H. 15:104
Davis, A. J. 15:340; 16:367; 23:263, 267
Davis, A. M. 9:51
Davis, A. S. 16:118
Davis, A. W. 5:13; 25:161
Davis, Aaron 17:448; 20:236; 22:295; 24:172
Davis, Abner B. 17:294
Davis, Aldin B. 15:122
Davis, Alex 7:24
Davis, Alexander 4:19; 5:38; 16:185
Davis, Alexander H. 15:192
Davis, Alfred 4:19; 7:48; 21:136; 22:73
Davis, Alfred G. 10:109; 20:236
Davis, Alfred M. 22:140
Davis, Alfred W. 15:16
Davis, Alice 25:285
Davis, Allen 16:28; 22:140, 295; 23:279; 27:37
Davis, Allin 21:321
Davis, Almond 13:18
Davis, Alson W. 7:48
Davis, Alvan 11:115
Davis, Alvin 21:321
Davis, Alwood L. 11:190
Davis, Ambrose 7:121
Davis, Anderson 8:38; 26:157
Davis, Andrew 3:54; 8:13; 18:129; 21:321; 22:187
Davis, Andrew J. 22:27

Davis, Ansel 19:236
Davis, Anthony 8:38;
  9:130; 26:157; 27:36
Davis, Arch 22:247
Davis, Archibald 17:78
Davis, Archy 22:296
Davis, Arnold 23:140
Davis, Asa 7:24; 9:173
Davis, Asa E. 25:161
Davis, Asa O. 16:132
Davis, Augustus 9:130
Davis, Azro W. 15:104
Davis, B. 3:54; 8:47;
  9:141; 11:27; 27:35
Davis, B. B. 14:53
Davis, B. F. 10:109;
  23:140
Davis, Beales 24:166
Davis, Benjamin 2:10;
  7:121; 12:18; 14:53;
  21:98
Davis, Benjamin A. 11:57
Davis, Benjamin C. 23:63
Davis, Benjamin F.
  20:236; 21:321
Davis, Benson 1:27
Davis, Boston 7:120
Davis, Burke 22:296
Davis, C. 1:29; 3:54, 55;
  9:154; 14:235;
  23:140; 26:158
Davis, C. A. 3:55
Davis, C. B. 7:24
Davis, C. C. 7:56; 14:27;
  19:64
Davis, C. H. 1:124; 11:83;
  25:161
Davis, C. L. 17:144
Davis, C. M. 1:97
Davis, C. S. 10:49; 20:236
Davis, C. W. 27:34
Davis, Ca's. 23:97
Davis, Carl 15:340
Davis, Celestine 21:321
Davis, Charles 1:27; 7:92;
  9:20; 12:18; 13:18;
  17:19, 336; 18:27,
  304, 327; 19:11;
  21:321; 26:95
Davis, Charles B. 10:109;
  20:236
Davis, Charles C. 12:95;
  14:156; 15:358
Davis, Charles D. 17:460;
  24:157
Davis, Charles E. 19:64;
  21:223; 23:140
Davis, Charles H. 5:13;
  13:18; 22:27
Davis, Charles L. 9:78;
  26:22

Davis, Charles M. 15:172
Davis, Charles S. 22:187
Davis, Charles W. 8:83;
  14:156; 18:327;
  20:106; 21:252;
  22:461
Davis, Chris. C. 19:11
Davis, Christopher 11:27;
  21:321
Davis, Clark 3:55; 12:18;
  13:107; 24:92
Davis, Clark L. 9:173
Davis, Clearbourne 12:48
Davis, Cornelius J. 22:421
Davis, Cornelius P.
  19:158
Davis, Creighton 21:186
Davis, D. 3:55; 15:267;
  20:132; 27:35
Davis, D. C. 25:27
Davis, D. M. 12:161
Davis, D. T. 1:124
Davis, D. W. 1:125
Davis, Daniel 8:13, 83;
  10:109; 14:53, 156;
  17:202; 18:129;
  20:236
Davis, Daniel W. 20:122
Davis, Darius 4:19
Davis, David 7:24; 8:83;
  10:15; 11:143, 230;
  12:81; 14:156;
  15:267; 16:291;
  17:440; 22:233;
  23:26; 24:151
Davis, David D. 17:259
Davis, David J. 13:18
Davis, David M. 23:63
Davis, Dexter P. 15:158
Davis, Dock 11:326
Davis, Drewry 22:73
Davis, DuPuy 24:61

Davis, E. 9:154; 11:91;
  15:192, 290; 16:185;
  20:236; 21:23;
  25:161; 26:158;
  27:34, 35
Davis, E. A. 20:236
Davis, E. B. 9:51
Davis, E. Cozer 10:49
Davis, E. G. 1:29
Davis, E. H. 11:301
Davis, E. J. 3:55; 18:80;
  23:26
Davis, E. P. 11:57;
  14:156, 255
Davis, E. S. 18:27
Davis, E. W. 1:28; 25:162
Davis, Ebb 27:36
Davis, Ebenezer 10:49

Davis, Edmond 6:22;
  22:296
Davis, Edmond P. 16:81
Davis, Edmund 10:186;
  17:397; 21:268
Davis, Edward 6:15; 8:71;
  9:130; 13:57; 18:80;
  23:26
Davis, Edward E. 16:28
Davis, Edward L. 23:189
Davis, Edward W. 5:13;
  10:7
Davis, Edwin 13:18;
  18:109
Davis, Edwin F. 17:99
Davis, Elbridge 7:92
Davis, Eli 10:49; 20:236
Davis, Elias C. 22:403
Davis, Elias P. 24:16
Davis, Elijah 10:109;
  20:236; 22:247
Davis, Elisha A. 10:49
Davis, Elvert S. 12:53
Davis, Enoch 11:260
Davis, Enos 22:27
Davis, Eph. B. 25:26
Davis, Ephraim 13:18;
  21:240
Davis, Ephraim B. 2:10
Davis, Esquire 24:76
Davis, Eugene 8:13;
  18:129
Davis, Evan 15:54;
  22:187
Davis, Ezekiel 7:24
Davis, Ezra 10:15
Davis, F. 9:51; 21:321
Davis, F. A. 9:51
Davis, F. B. 13:107;
  20:174
Davis, F. K. 17:217
Davis, F. L. 19:158
Davis, F. M. 22:295
Davis, F. W. 20:236;
  22:187
Davis, Francis 23:140
Davis, Francis I. 20:6
Davis, Francis K. 17:205
Davis, Frank 7:121
Davis, Frank N. 20:181
Davis, Franklin 10:48;
  20:236
Davis, Franklin W. 10:48;
  20:122
Davis, Fred. E. 24:110
Davis, Frederick 7:24;
  10:15; 22:403;
  26:157
Davis, G. 1:123, 125;
  3:54, 55; 10:147;
  14:53; 15:192;

Davis, G. 16:185; 18:47;
20:39; 25:162;
26:157
Davis, G. A. 1:127
Davis, G. C. 3:54
Davis, G. D. 21:321
Davis, G. E. 4:19
Davis, G. F. 7:49
Davis, G. H. 7:24
Davis, G. L. 17:440
Davis, G. S. 19:236
Davis, G. W. 3:54, 55;
10:179; 12:152
Davis, Gabriel 10:208
Davis, Garson M. 22:450
Davis, Gen 18:80
Davis, General 6:12
Davis, George 1:27; 7:77,
92; 10:159, 208;
11:218; 12:64;
15:16; 17:173;
18:234; 19:158, 329;
20:96; 21:186, 198,
268, 290; 23:63, 270;
25:295; 26:24;
27:144
Davis, George B. 11:286
Davis, George D. 22:403
Davis, George E. 22:248
Davis, George F. 19:64
Davis, George H. 15:54,
192
Davis, George L. 13:18;
24:152
Davis, George M. 7:67;
11:422
Davis, George R. 23:26
Davis, George S. 9:173
Davis, George W. 7:92;
9:96; 15:16; 17:144;
18:173; 19:64; 22:73,
170; 23:26
Davis, Gilmore 5:13;
9:165
Davis, Guthery 22:295
Davis, H. 1:126; 3:54, 55;
7:121; 10:27;
16:185; 19:301;
23:26
Davis, H. A. 16:185;
19:226
Davis, H. B. 15:311;
19:64
Davis, H. C. 1:125
Davis, H. D. 1:123
Davis, H. E. 7:24
Davis, H. F. 25:319
Davis, H. G. 5:13; 21:23;
25:162
Davis, H. H. 9:96; 17:254

Davis, H. J. 19:11;
21:120; 25:162
Davis, H. L. 9:51
Davis, H. O. 19:158
Davis, H. P. 11:57
Davis, H. R. 3:54
Davis, H. S. 17:146
Davis, H. T. 3:55
Davis, H. W. 1:29
Davis, Hall W. 9:78;
26:23
Davis, Haly D. 23:63
Davis, Hamilton 7:121
Davis, Hamilton F. 6:30
Davis, Harden 22:27
Davis, Harman 25:295
Davis, Harmon 7:74
Davis, Harry 15:349;
16:367; 23:178
Davis, Harvey 17:307
Davis, Henry 7:92; 8:47;
9:109; 10:10, 49;
11:190, 201, 260;
13:18; 17:147, 163,
415; 18:234, 344;
20:236; 21:109;
24:152; 26:23
Davis, Henry A. 9:71;
17:390
Davis, Henry C. 1:26;
19:11; 22:27, 422
Davis, Henry E. 3:54
Davis, Henry G. 26:218
Davis, Henry H. 9:11;
22:140, 278
Davis, Henry J. 16:92
Davis, Henry M. 22:140;
25:27
Davis, Henry W. 17:439;
24:150
Davis, Herbert B. 23:260
Davis, Hezekiah 17:276
Davis, Hiram 11:239
Davis, Horatio L. 13:18;
16:28
Davis, I. 1:29; 17:469;
22:187
Davis, I. B. 11:395
Davis, I. F. 3:55
Davis, I. I. 3:55
Davis, I. W. 3:55
Davis, Ira 3:55; 18:205;
23:140
Davis, Ira A. 21:321
Davis, Isaac 3:54; 7:121;
8:77, 83; 11:380;
17:349; 22:278;
26:24
Davis, Isaac M. 24:183
Davis, Isaac O. 18:234
Davis, Israel 27:144

Davis, J. 1:27, 123, 124,
125; 3:54; 9:51;
11:239, 301; 13:86;
14:8, 255, 296;
15:172; 18:189;
19:64, 325; 20:145;
21:321; 23:189;
25:162, 319; 26:210;
27:37
Davis, J. A. 7:56, 92;
10:27; 19:301; 20:6;
21:23
Davis, J. B. 9:51; 13:86;
14:8; 22:333; 23:112
Davis, J. C. 14:53; 15:65,
192
Davis, J. D. 21:129
Davis, J. H. 9:227; 13:18;
18:109, 234, 364;
21:23; 24:16; 26:24
Davis, J. J. 8:13; 18:130
Davis, J. K. 16:28
Davis, J. K. P. 1:125
Davis, J. M. 1:27; 3:54;
13:108; 17:411;
22:500
Davis, J. N. 1:93, 127;
26:158
Davis, J. O. 21:321
Davis, J. P. 3:54; 9:109;
21:321
Davis, J. R. 1:126; 9:213;
17:147; 21:321
Davis, J. S. 1:30; 10:109;
14:156; 18:173;
20:236
Davis, J. T. 1:124; 9:20;
10:109; 14:280;
15:321; 19:64;
20:236; 21:23
Davis, J. W. 1:27; 3:54;
20:154; 21:23
Davis, Jackson 21:186;
23:26
Davis, Jackson C. 21:186
Davis, Jacob 1:28; 4:19;
10:109; 18:234;
20:236; 24:49; 26:23
Davis, Jacob A. 27:36
Davis, Jacobs 11:385
Davis, James 1:28; 3:55;
4:65; 7:92, 121; 9:20,
78, 164, 219; 10:109;
11:20, 28, 260;
12:18; 13:18, 86,
108; 14:8, 53, 235;
16:28; 18:109, 234,
304, 364, 393; 19:64;
20:33, 236; 21:50,
127, 321; 22:73, 187,
296; 23:106;

Davis, James 24:192, 193; 25:162, 319; 26:23
Davis, James 26:24
Davis, James A. 8:83; 10:109; 20:236
Davis, James B. 13:60; 14:53; 21:321
Davis, James D. 10:109; 20:236
Davis, James E. 19:158
Davis, James G. 15:33
Davis, James H. 21:321; 22:73
Davis, James I. 10:49
Davis, James J. 20:236; 22:187
Davis, James M. 4:19; 10:109; 12:169; 20:237
Davis, James R. 16:28; 18:80
Davis, James S. 23:26
Davis, James W. 15:192; 17:427; 21:129; 24:183
Davis, Jason J. 24:150
Davis, Jeff 25:295
Davis, Jefferson 7:77
Davis, Jennie 26:219
Davis, Jeremiah 16:135; 17:32
Davis, Jerome 17:451; 22:73; 23:87
Davis, Jerry 10:109; 20:237
Davis, Jesse 11:201, 321; 17:453; 22:247
Davis, Jesse O. 18:216
Davis, Jesse P. 26:24
Davis, Jesse W. 24:16
Davis, Jessie P. 18:234
Davis, Jethro O. 4:19
Davis, Jirome 24:177
Davis, Jo. L. 8:13; 18:130
Davis, Joel 26:156
Davis, John 1:29; 2:10; 3:55; 5:13; 7:24, 92, 121; 8:100; 10:7, 26, 49, 109, 159, 172, 204; 11:259, 380; 12:169; 13:18, 86, 130; 14:8, 156; 15:33, 65; 16:28, 132; 17:130, 241, 349, 460, 501; 18:216, 393; 19:11, 64, 158; 20:237; 21:268; 22:27, 140; 22:187, 248, 278; 23:26, 304;

Davis, John 24:49, 157, 192; 25:29; 26:25; 27:34, 144
Davis, John A. 5:38; 8:104; 11:260; 20:94
Davis, John B. 9:109
Davis, John C. 7:92
Davis, John E. 7:24; 9:78; 17:32; 22:140, 422; 26:23
Davis, John G. 22:247
Davis, John H. 7:16, 121; 8:83; 10:90; 11:27; 18:393; 19:158; 22:403; 24:37
Davis, John J. 7:49, 92; 25:162
Davis, John L. 17:235; 24:49
Davis, John M. 11:100; 21:200
Davis, John R. 21:321; 23:178; 24:76; 25:27
Davis, John S. 9:96; 10:159, 179; 19:158; 20:39; 22:73
Davis, John T. 22:27; 23:97
Davis, John W. 9:102; 18:338; 21:268; 22:73, 247, 351
Davis, Jonathan 10:109; 20:237
Davis, Joseph 7:121; 9:42; 10:208; 16:185; 21:321; 22:9, 461; 25:280; 27:39
Davis, Joseph B. 17:99
Davis, Joseph H. 22:248
Davis, Joseph L. 15:165
Davis, Joseph P. 22:27
Davis, Joseph R. 22:422
Davis, Joshua 21:252; 22:73; 23:63; 25:162
Davis, Josiah 18:216
Davis, K. 3:54; 9:173
Davis, L. 1:124; 3:54; 5:38; 9:141; 14:156; 21:321; 25:162
Davis, L. C. 12:121; 15:122
Davis, L. D. 25:162
Davis, L. E. 10:147; 13:77; 18:47
Davis, L. H. 20:21
Davis, L. M. 2:9; 25:30
Davis, L. R. 17:247
Davis, Lanson 21:50
Davis, Larkin 10:109; 20:237
Davis, Lawley 21:321

Davis, Leander D. 21:136
Davis, Leonard 7:24
Davis, Leonard A. 22:248
Davis, Lerain 24:92
Davis, Leroy 3:54
Davis, Levi 1:26; 3:55; 10:172; 21:50; 23:178
Davis, Levi H. 7:24
Davis, Levy 19:159
Davis, Lewis 11:143; 14:156; 16:132; 19:65
Davis, Lewis B. 4:19
Davis, Lorenzo D. 11:386
Davis, Loring 22:27
Davis, Lorz. D. 1:28
Davis, Louis 9:20; 18:304; 26:96
Davis, Lowell 21:321
Davis, Lucius 7:121
Davis, Luther 27:35
Davis, M. 5:13; 17:432; 18:80; 25:162
Davis, M. C. 25:27
Davis, M. H. 7:92
Davis, M. L. 5:38; 25:162
Davis, M. W. 11:144, 239
Davis, Madison 10:49; 17:233; 20:237; 24:37
Davis, Malachi 18:102
Davis, Mansion 22:73
Davis, Mariner O. 10:159
Davis, Marion 10:49; 20:237; 27:39
Davis, Marshall 10:204
Davis, Martin 6:20; 24:151
Davis, Mathew 17:252
Davis, Mathew M. 17:78
Davis, Mathias 15:7
Davis, Melvin F. 7:92
Davis, Michael 8:13; 10:170; 18:130; 22:233
Davis, Mila. L. 17:359
Davis, Miles 12:68; 15:33
Davis, Miles H. 15:54
Davis, Milton 11:239; 22:247
Davis, Morgan 11:201
Davis, Morris 7:121
Davis, Morris C. 1:27
Davis, Moses 10:95; 13:18; 16:77
Davis, Myron 4:19
Davis, N. 7:121; 24:37
Davis, N. A. 1:26
Davis, N. I. 3:55
Davis, N. J. 4:19

Davis, N. L. 4:19
Davis, Nathan 19:65
Davis, Nehemiah 14:156
Davis, Nelson 3:54; 17:64
Davis, Noah 17:130;
  18:80; 24:192
Davis, Norris S. 17:417
Davis, O. 1:124
Davis, O. C. 8:13; 24:76
Davis, O. D. 9:173
Davis, O. E. 14:53
Davis, O. F. 3:55
Davis, O. L. 22:248
Davis, O. O. 25:162
Davis, O. P. T. N. 18:65
Davis, Obediah P. 9:20
Davis, Octavius 14:156
Davis, Oliver C. 23:26
Davis, Oliver O. 5:13
Davis, Orrin S. 8:83
Davis, Orson 18:27
Davis, Owen 17:173
Davis, P. 3:55; 25:162;
  27:35
Davis, P. A. 14:53;
  16:185
Davis, Pascall 26:157
Davis, Pascuel 8:38
Davis, Patrick 23:63
Davis, Patten 10:95
Davis, Peter 5:13; 8:77,
  112; 9:51, 141;
  12:18; 14:156; 18:13
Davis, Peter M. 20:21
Davis, Peter W. 20:237
Davis, Philander 21:321
Davis, Philip 7:120;
  10:15; 19:11;
  21:321; 24:100
Davis, Phineas 22:73
Davis, Pleasant 21:23
Davis, Princeton 10:208
Davis, Prosser 22:296
Davis, R. 9:141; 15:2;
  17:173; 19:266;
  21:147; 23:140;
  25:162, 295
Davis, R. A. 1:28
Davis, R. F. 1:123; 7:67
Davis, R. McKee 24:16
Davis, R. T. 9:109
Davis, R. W. 23:97;
  25:162
Davis, Randolph 12:68
Davis, Reading 13:18
Davis, Redin 17:389
Davis, Reese T. 24:92
Davis, Reuben 8:13;
  18:130; 23:304

Davis, Richard 3:54; 8:38,
  99; 11:28; 17:316;
  21:186; 26:157
Davis, Richard M. 24:37
Davis, Richard O. 22:248
Davis, Robert 5:13, 38;
  9:207; 11:143; 13:18;
  17:173; 18:393;
  20:139; 22:120, 247;
  27:35
Davis, Robert F. 20:48
Davis, Robert P. 11:201
Davis, Rolla 9:165;
  25:319
Davis, Romeo 9:207
Davis, S. 3:54; 6:30;
  14:53; 15:192;
  17:295; 19:65;
  22:333, 351; 25:319
Davis, S. B. 1:123
Davis, S. F. 1:26; 8:47;
  21:91
Davis, S. H. 9:96
Davis, S. O. 1:28
Davis, S. S. 23:26
Davis, S. W. 22:187
Davis, Sam 21:23
Davis, Sampson 16:28
Davis, Samuel 8:13, 47,
  83; 10:109; 18:130;
  20:237; 25:162;
  26:25, 158
Davis, Samuel C. 16:77
Davis, Samuel J. 22:477
Davis, Samuel R. 10:109;
  20:237; 22:247
Davis, Samuel T. 23:11
Davis, Samuel T. S.
  22:477
Davis, Sandford 21:321
Davis, Sanford 13:63
Davis, Scipio 27:36
Davis, Shepard 21:67
Davis, Sidney 27:144
Davis, Silas 21:321
Davis, Silas E. 25:29
Davis, Silas N. 23:87
Davis, Simon 8:38;
  26:157
Davis, Simon E. 13:18
Davis, Stephen 14:156
Davis, Stillman P. 7:8
Davis, Stuart 20:17
Davis, Sumner A. 16:84
Davis, T. 1:126; 15:329;
  21:147; 25:162
Davis, T. J. 21:120
Davis, T. M. 1:125;
  11:408
Davis, Theodore 9:117;
  11:15; 27:37

Davis, Theron 21:136
Davis, Thomas 1:28; 3:54;
  6:28; 9:203; 11:28;
  12:18; 14:262;
  16:291; 17:267;
  18:234; 19:65; 20:29;
  21:211, 321; 22:333;
  23:140, 308; 24:49;
  26:24
Davis, Thomas A. 23:106
Davis, Thomas B. 22:247
Davis, Thomas E. 9:106
Davis, Thomas H. 22:27
Davis, Thomas J. 5:50;
  17:19; 24:16; 25:162
Davis, Thomas P. 21:136
Davis, Thomas W. 10:49;
  18:284; 20:237;
  26:134
Davis, Thompson 5:13
Davis, Timothy C. 10:15
Davis, V. W. 14:157
Davis, Victor 21:321
Davis, W. 1:27, 125; 3:54,
  55; 7:24; 11:301;
  13:86; 14:53; 18:47;
  21:50; 26:157
Davis, W. A. 18:47
Davis, W. G. 7:24; 19:226
Davis, W. H. 1:125; 3:54;
  7:92; 14:53, 264,
  287; 17:451; 23:26,
  140; 24:177; 25:29;
  26:25
Davis, W. H. H. 27:38
Davis, W. I. 15:340
Davis, W. J. 17:64
Davis, W. L. 3:54
Davis, W. R. 16:147;
  19:236
Davis, W. T. 11:260
Davis, W. W. 1:97; 14:53;
  18:27
Davis, Walter R. 4:19
Davis, Warren 1:27
Davis, Washington
  19:321; 20:96
Davis, Waterman 9:173;
  19:250
Davis, Watson 22:296
Davis, Watson W. 10:109;
  20:237
Davis, Wesley 22:187
Davis, Wesley C. 9:51
Davis, Wilbur F. 22:165
Davis, Wiley 11:186
Davis, William 1:26, 28,
  29; 3:54, 55; 4:19;
  7:92, 121; 8:47, 83;
  9:42; 10:49, 90, 109;
  11:15, 91, 411;

Davis, William 13:18, 134; 14:53, 157; 15:33, 193, 277; 16:185; 17:109; 18:47, 364; 19:65, 222, 346; 20:34, 237; 21:109, 321, 322; 22:27, 187, 421; 23:120, 303
Davis, William 25:162
Davis, William A. 22:421
Davis, William B. 20:6
Davis, William C. 10:176; 19:159
Davis, William D. 18:102; 22:233
Davis, William E. 10:49; 11:260; 20:237
Davis, William F. 21:322; 24:170
Davis, William G. 9:173; 16:28; 22:187
Davis, William H. 10:15; 12:141; 15:328; 19:65; 20:237; 21:50, 223; 22:477
Davis, William I. 14:334
Davis, William J. 7:24, 92; 16:367
Davis, William M. 7:56; 11:395; 14:157; 15:193
Davis, William R. 9:173; 17:355
Davis, William S. 23:26
Davis, William T. 17:78, 423; 21:194
Davis, William V. 22:140
Davis, William W. 11:83; 18:27; 21:98
Davis, William Y. 9:141; 27:36
Davis, Wilson S. 11:15
Davis, Z. C. 22:187
Davis, Z. P. 11:190
Davis, Zachariah 17:235
Davise, J. 10:147; 18:47
Davison, C. 19:236
Davison, Charles 11:142
Davison, Charles E. 13:18
Davison, David P. 15:83
Davison, Francis 15:302
Davison, G. 14:8
Davison, George 14:157
Davison, H. 3:55
Davison, James 1:26
Davison, John 4:19; 12:152; 19:281
Davison, John E. 10:49
Davison, M. 3:55

Davison, Martin V. 17:287
Davison, Samuel 20:237
Davison, W. 14:53
Davison, Walter 6:9
Davison, William 19:301
Davison, William H. 18:109
Davisson, Daniel 22:73
Davisson, Jesse E. 22:73
Davley, William 18:130
Davlin, Michael 15:352
Davns, John W. 19:159
Davrah, John 12:68
Davy, C. 1:29
Davy, Edward 21:9
Davy, Elias C. 11:28
Davy, F. 3:55
Davy, H. 3:55
Davy, Isaac 15:193
Davy, J. J. 3:55
Davy, Jacob 9:102; 18:338
Davy, James 9:117
Davy, Peter 9:102
Davy, R. 3:55
Davy, William 22:187
Davyson, W. 3:55
Daw, J. 15:65
Daw, Patrick 19:266
Dawalt, Jackson 23:63
Dawd, George 18:271
Dawd, P. 14:53
Dawe, Christian 20:237
Dawes, Edmund 18:173
Dawes, F. L. 19:65
Dawes, Jacob 9:78
Dawes, Jacob R. 7:16
Dawes, James 14:157
Dawes, M. M. 3:55
Dawes, W. P. 25:26
Dawes, William 21:120
Daweshower, J. 14:53
Dawkins, Austin 21:268
Dawkins, H. W. 10:147; 18:47
Dawkins, Lewis 21:268
Dawkins, Thomas C. 11:83
Dawley, Philander 11:295
Dawlie, John 14:53
Dawling, J. K. 12:172
Dawling, James 9:78
Dawn, C. D. 25:27
Dawner, Thomas B. 9:33
Dawney, Albert 18:393
Dawney, George 3:55
Dawns, Owen 5:38
Dawolon, John 25:162
Dawrin, L. 3:55
Dawry, --- 18:13

Daws, George 7:24
Daws, H. 3:55
Daws, W. P. 2:10
Dawsay, S. B. 17:218
Dawsey, Daniel 5:38
Dawsey, Peter 5:38
Dawsey, Samuel 16:185
Dawson, --- 10:186; 18:173; 26:22
Dawson, A. 16:185; 18:234; 26:23
Dawson, Abijah 17:144
Dawson, Abraham 12:18
Dawson, Alexander 22:27
Dawson, Alphonzo 7:24
Dawson, Andrew 21:186
Dawson, Benjamin F. 25:28
Dawson, Bloomington 18:173
Dawson, C. E. 15:340
Dawson, C. H. 11:15
Dawson, Charles D. 16:367
Dawson, Crawford 21:322
Dawson, D. 3:55
Dawson, D. L. 20:84
Dawson, Enos 22:73
Dawson, F. 15:193
Dawson, Frederick 19:65
Dawson, G. B. 11:260
Dawson, George 8:38; 18:411; 26:157
Dawson, Harrison 17:190
Dawson, Henry R. 19:11
Dawson, Hiram 21:268
Dawson, Ignatius 23:97
Dawson, Isaac L. 22:422
Dawson, J. 23:26
Dawson, J. A. 20:17
Dawson, J. C. 18:393
Dawson, J. E. 17:364
Dawson, J. M. 14:53
Dawson, J. W. 1:125
Dawson, James 6:12; 9:109; 11:83; 13:18; 22:187, 296; 26:218
Dawson, James P. 18:393
Dawson, Jeremiah 10:110; 20:237
Dawson, John 1:191; 7:121; 8:62; 14:53; 17:173; 21:322; 22:333, 403; 25:30; 26:157
Dawson, John F. 11:58
Dawson, John M. 16:92
Dawson, Joseph 21:23
Dawson, L. 16:185
Dawson, L. B. 25:162
Dawson, Levi 21:67

Dawson, Lewis 8:77
Dawson, Lewis B. 5:13
Dawson, M. 19:317
Dawson, M. M. 1:124
Dawson, Manassah 17:349
Dawson, Mathew 15:33
Dawson, Milton 17:130; 24:192
Dawson, N. C. 9:20; 18:304; 26:96
Dawson, N. D. 15:258
Dawson, Naamen 22:187
Dawson, Noah 8:83
Dawson, Poten 21:23
Dawson, R. T. 23:140
Dawson, Robert 13:18
Dawson, S. 14:296; 17:471; 27:38
Dawson, S. J. 19:159
Dawson, Smiley C. 14:314, 321
Dawson, Smiley J. 23:26
Dawson, Stephen 10:172
Dawson, Thomas 16:92
Dawson, W. 25:162
Dawson, William 5:13; 10:27; 11:143; 16:185; 17:161; 21:186
Dawson, William H. 10:49; 20:237
Dawson, William L. 21:252
Dawson, William S. 12:18
Dawson, Wylie G. 24:37
Dawson, Zadock 10:49
Day, A. 11:58; 12:81; 14:53; 16:291; 21:198
Day, A. J. 13:86
Day, A. M. 12:81; 16:291
Day, Abner M. 22:10
Day, Albert F. 7:92; 21:322
Day, Alexander H. 4:20
Day, Alson L. 4:20
Day, Amos 14:296; 17:474; 27:38
Day, Andrew Henry 3:55
Day, Andrew I. 10:49
Day, Andrew J. 11:142
Day, B. D. 11:301
Day, Brice 26:23
Day, C. 21:147
Day, C. A. 10:49; 20:237
Day, C. C. 25:162
Day, C. E. 16:92
Day, C. N. 9:174; 19:250
Day, Caleb 17:233
Day, Charles 14:157

Day, Charles C. 5:13
Day, Charles F. 10:159
Day, Charles W. 21:67
Day, D. B. 3:55
Day, D. C. 25:162
Day, Daniel 16:92; 18:234; 22:187; 26:24
Day, David 18:234; 26:24
Day, Dennis 14:53, 157
Day, E. 1:125
Day, Edgar G. 18:271
Day, Edward 17:400
Day, Edwin 1:27
Day, Eli F. 8:83
Day, Elijah H. 27:38
Day, Elisha R. 17:64
Day, Ellis 20:48
Day, Ephraim 11:143
Day, Evan 20:17
Day, Francis 12:152
Day, Freedman H. 11:104
Day, G. 15:329
Day, G. W. 20:39; 26:157
Day, Gabriel 19:65
Day, George 3:56; 4:20; 22:73, 187
Day, George E. 15:11
Day, George W. 16:28
Day, George William 13:18
Day, H. 1:97
Day, H. C. 22:187
Day, H. K. 1:93
Day, Harry 17:130; 24:192
Day, Henry 10:159; 11:260; 19:159
Day, Hubert J. 21:252
Day, I. 3:55; 17:473
Day, I. D. 3:56
Day, I. W. 3:55
Day, Ira W. 13:18
Day, Isaac 21:322
Day, J. 1:126; 7:74; 14:157, 296; 17:469; 25:295; 27:38
Day, J. H. 19:301
Day, J. M. 11:104
Day, J. N. 4:20; 9:174
Day, J. W. 14:53
Day, Jackson 10:110; 20:237
Day, Jacob L. 16:291
Day, James 9:174; 19:236; 27:37, 39
Day, James F. 23:11, 140
Day, James W. 15:193
Day, Jesse 20:39; 22:500; 25:319; 27:39
Day, Jim 6:30; 12:166

Day, John 4:19; 7:56; 13:18; 14:53; 21:50, 98
Day, John D. 12:18
Day, John F. 11:143; 14:296; 17:473; 22:403; 27:37
Day, John M. 22:187
Day, John P. 22:140
Day, John W. 9:117; 27:37
Day, Joseph W. 10:49; 20:237
Day, Josephus B. 8:62; 26:158
Day, Julian 15:104
Day, Justis C. 10:15
Day, Levi 11:144
Day, Lewis A. 22:73
Day, Lewis P. 22:351
Day, M. 14:157; 18:430
Day, M. A. 18:394
Day, M. H. 13:108
Day, Martin 13:63; 19:65
Day, Melville C. 16:77
Day, Miller C. 17:64
Day, Morgan 7:121
Day, Nicholas 4:65
Day, Norton 17:173
Day, Orlander F. 4:20
Day, P. C. 12:8
Day, Pratt 13:18; 16:28
Day, Putnam 12:61; 15:94
Day, R. A. 7:74; 25:295
Day, Richard 22:296
Day, Richard W. 22:248
Day, Rufus 7:92; 9:109
Day, S. Edward 22:470
Day, S. H. 9:117; 27:37
Day, Samuel M. 19:11
Day, Simon O. 15:158
Day, T. W. 13:86
Day, Thomas 7:92; 12:141; 21:252; 22:333; 27:157
Day, Thomas G. 23:87
Day, Thomas J. 1:27
Day, Thomas R. 18:216
Day, Virgil 9:96
Day, W. 9:51; 25:162
Day, W. B. 14:53
Day, W. E. 19:65
Day, W. F. 3:55
Day, W. S. 16:278
Day, Wesley 11:57
Day, William 3:55; 5:38; 7:83; 9:130; 11:408; 14:53; 18:275; 21:198, 322; 22:141; 27:36
Day, William A. 22:248
Day, William H. 16:77

Day, William W. 15:83
Day, Winfield 17:287
Dayale, Frank 9:207
Dayer, James 20:237
Dayford, R. 5:13
Daygo, John 3:56
Dayhoff, Theopolis 8:104
Dayle, William 3:56
Dayley, William 14:157
Daylie, J. 14:287
Dayman, O. F. 17:247
Daymond, Ebenezer 13:18
Dayne, Mortimer 12:8
Dayo, William A. 10:10
Days, Andrew 7:121
Days, James 7:121
Daysark, R. 27:34
Dayson, John 10:90;
    20:237
Dayton, C. 3:56
Dayton, C. W. 21:322
Dayton, Charles K.
    18:275
Dayton, Charles R. 9:66
Dayton, Elmer 22:187
Dayton, F. 27:34
Dayton, Frederick F.
    20:183
Dayton, George 11:286
Dayton, H. C. 13:18;
    16:28
Dayton, Hamilton 7:92
Dayton, James 9:51
Dayton, John 8:13; 18:130
Dayton, John S. 23:189
Dayton, Neal 15:122
Dayton, Simon 18:406
Dayton, W. 1:124
Dayton, Winthrop 18:234;
    26:25
Daywalt, David 17:19
Daywalt, S. 1:126
Dazer, J. 14:157
De, --- 18:130
De---, Milor 12:99
Deabolt, G. R. 13:86
Deaborne, C. H. 9:141
Deabyshire, George
    14:157
Deacon, C. A. 27:34
Deacon, E. A. 1:29
Deacon, G. W. 25:26
Deacon, Garrett F. 2:10
Deacon, J. 3:56; 20:34
Deacon, Richard 18:47
Deacon, Solomon 11:56
Deacon, William 9:236
Deaconheart, Frederick
    18:338
Dead, Lemel P. 18:291
Dead, S. G. 26:96

Deadler, J. F. 14:8
Deadmore, J. 18:234;
    26:23
Deadstein, Abraham 9:174
Deafenbaugh, Theodore
    17:32
Deagan, Peter 4:20
Deagene, James 14:53
Deake, William 8:47
Deakin, Ivie 22:500
Deal, Alonzo 9:20; 26:96
Deal, C. S. 14:157
Deal, Daniel 5:13; 25:162
Deal, Eli 4:20
Deal, F. 3:56
Deal, Frederick 22:141
Deal, G. 1:123
Deal, Henry W. 21:50
Deal, J. 1:123; 22:477
Deal, James 6:9; 9:130;
    18:109
Deal, John 9:96
Deal, Martin 10:211;
    18:456
Deal, S. 13:127; 14:53
Deal, Strattern 17:313
Deal, W. 22:477
Deal, William 22:403
Dealey, John 25:162
Dealey, Oliver 9:79
Dealney, L. D. 3:56
DeAlton, Thomas H.
    22:519
Dealy, John 15:193
Deam, Thomas F. 22:422
Deamon, Henry 14:157
Dean, A. 3:59; 16:185
Dean, A. J. 25:162
Dean, A. R. 19:236
Dean, Aaron 18:65
Dean, Abner 23:255
Dean, Abraham 9:78
Dean, Alex 26:123
Dean, Alfred J. 5:13
Dean, Alvin R. 9:174
Dean, Anthony 22:27
Dean, B. F. 1:97
Dean, B. L. 14:280
Dean, B. P. 20:237
Dean, Benjamin 11:319;
    17:506
Dean, Byron W. 20:145
Dean, C. 3:56; 14:157;
    16:28
Dean, C. J. 1:125
Dean, C. N. 25:26
Dean, Calvin C. 13:18
Dean, Charles 11:332;
    17:154; 20:237;
    22:461
Dean, Charles A. 14:157

Dean, Charles N. 2:10
Dean, Columbus 9:33
Dean, D. 1:123
Dean, Daniel 13:18; 16:28
Dean, Daniel J. 20:96
Dean, Daniel M. 21:67
Dean, Darius 24:37
Dean, David W. 21:223
Dean, E. 21:23
Dean, E. B. 21:322
Dean, E. H. 9:174; 19:250
Dean, E. J. 22:333
Dean, E. W. 20:237
Dean, Edward 6:22; 18:80
Dean, Elber 25:162
Dean, Elhanon W. 10:90
Dean, Elisha 24:37
Dean, Francis 17:316
Dean, Frederick 9:96
Dean, George 12:18
Dean, George B. 19:159
Dean, George S. 9:96
Dean, George W. 14:157
Dean, H. 13:86; 22:296
Dean, H. A. 7:67
Dean, H. Elune 11:326
Dean, Henry 9:130;
    14:157
Dean, Henry C. 9:117;
    27:37
Dean, Henry W. 15:65
Dean, Hiram 18:411
Dean, Isaac 1:27
Dean, Isaac C. 23:140
Dean, Isaac V. 18:394
Dean, J. 3:56; 20:39
Dean, J. B. 23:263
Dean, J. F. 7:92
Dean, J. N. 21:322
Dean, J. W. 10:49;
    14:280; 20:237
Dean, Jacob B. 21:67
Dean, James 5:38, 50;
    21:322; 25:162
Dean, James M. 9:33, 141
Dean, James S. 9:78
Dean, James T. 12:18;
    21:136
Dean, Jasper 6:24
Dean, Jesse D. 6:30;
    25:319
Dean, Jesse P. 12:68
Dean, Jessee P. 15:90
Dean, John 3:56; 7:24;
    9:11, 118; 27:37
Dean, John A. 12:18
Dean, John D. 14:157
Dean, Jonathan 4:20
Dean, Joseph 22:73
Dean, Joseph F. 21:241
Dean, Joseph S. 7:24

Dean, Joseph T. 21:50
Dean, Josiah 11:104
Dean, Josiah R. 18:394
Dean, M. C. 15:277;
  25:162
Dean, M. W. 9:51
Dean, Marcellus 10:110
Dean, Marcillus 20:237
Dean, Marcus 21:322
Dean, Michael 27:34
Dean, N. P. 15:83
Dean, Oliver 22:397
Dean, Oscar 11:124
Dean, P. 13:86
Dean, Patrick 10:179;
  18:173
Dean, R. 3:56
Dean, Robert 22:111
Dean, Rowe 14:157
Dean, S. D. 15:305
Dean, S. G. 23:26
Dean, Samon 7:121
Dean, Samuel 3:56; 6:27;
  12:99; 15:347;
  18:275
Dean, Silas 11:105
Dean, Stephen H. 14:157
Dean, Stonewall G. 9:33
Dean, T. Z. 26:23
Dean, Thomas 16:185;
  18:216, 323
Dean, W. 7:24; 25:162
Dean, W. H. 23:26
Dean, W. S. 12:8
Dean, Westbrook 7:24
Dean, William 1:28; 5:38;
  6:30; 14:53, 157;
  18:216; 25:319;
  26:158
Dean, William F. 14:53
Dean, William H. 9:242;
  14:157; 22:187;
  23:87
Dean, William J. 19:326
Dean, William P. 22:73
Dean, Z. 1:126
Deane, Dneuman C.
  17:235
Deane, George 19:159
Deane, George C. 13:63
Deane, Henry 27:34
Deane, Jesse W. 14:268
Deane, John 22:403
Deane, John H. 10:15
Deane, Thomas 13:108
Deane, Zeadrick 25:271
Deang, J. 21:322
Deanis, John C. 21:211
Deans, --- 14:157
Deans, Cyrus F. 22:27
Deans, Jonathan 17:242

Deanslow, David 4:20
Dear, Jeremiah G. 8:83
Dear, Lyman 22:421
Dear, R. 3:56
Dearbean, Augustus
  13:124
Dearbirn, F. C. 14:53
Dearborn, C. E. 13:124
Dearborn, C. H. 27:35
Dearborn, G. 3:56
Dearborn, G. M. 17:158
Dearborn, H. W. 19:236
Dearborn, Henry C. 15:25
Dearborn, W. H. 19:226
Dearborn, William H.
  9:174
Dearbro, R. 14:296;
  17:479
Dearburn, F. A. 13:108
Dearburn, George 14:157
Dearburn, George W. F.
  22:10
DeArcy, W. E. 18:13
Deardorf, John 23:255
Dearham, Henry 9:199
Dearholt, H. 18:420
Dearing, Abner H. 21:14
Dearing, Charles 13:63;
  19:65
Dearing, Elisha R. 11:57
Dearing, S. 27:34
Dearing, William 15:352;
  16:278
Dearinger, H. 27:34
Dearinger, Henry C. 20:21
Dearman, Elliot 15:86
Dearman, M. L. 9:244
Dearmith, J. 1:97
Dearmond, Mathew J.
  22:73
Dearmond, W. C. 17:64
Dearmont, J. K. 3:56
Dearmord, John M. 26:22
Dearmott, Samuel 16:118
Dearson, John 7:92
Dearth, Edward D. 20:6
Dearth, Hugh 20:112
Dearth, John A. 22:27
Dearth, Noah 22:187
Deartoo, R. 27:37
Dearwood, Sylvester
  13:108
Deary, James 21:322
Deary, P. 14:53
Deas, Abraham 3:56
Dease, Dennis 22:296
Deason, James P. 22:27
Deason, Samuel 8:47;
  21:23
Deastein, A. 19:250
Death, Michael J. 21:252

DeAtley, Alfred H. 22:27
Deaton, G. W. 23:26
Deaton, J. M. 23:26
Deaton, J. W. 25:295
Deaton, James 21:223
Deaton, Joseph 23:26
Deaton, Levi 20:86
Deaton, S. 9:51
Deaton, S. G. 9:51
Deaton, Spencer 12:85
Deaton, William L. 20:6
Deats, --- 11:83
Deats, J. 7:56
Deaver, David H. 22:187
Deaver, Ezekiel 11:57
Deaver, J. 24:65
Deaver, J. H. 20:237
Deaver, J. W. 10:110
Deaver, Levi H. 22:73
Deaver, Thomas R. 11:57
Deaver, William H. 23:63
Deball, George 4:20
Deban, T. W. 27:37
DeBar, George 5:13
Debar, George 25:162
Debar, Hiram 17:99
Debar, Leander 17:359
Debar, Lewis W. 16:29
Debare, David 8:47
DeBarnes, P. M. 3:56
Debarry, Moses D. 4:20
Debass, Horatio 4:20
Debat, Lewis 9:203
Debaugh, George 14:53,
  155
Debaughan, Isaac 10:170
Debaune, Jeremiah 7:67
Debbins, --- 19:265
Debble, J. 1:126
Debble, Spencer 14:327
DeBell, George W. 22:477
DeBell, William 19:65
DeBelle, William 13:63
Debenport, M. 1:28
Debitt, Isaac 9:109
Deblady, Edward 12:18
Debling, G. 27:39
Deboard, George J. 23:87
Deboard, H. A. 3:56
Deboard, Logans 17:445
Deboard, Soyars 24:166
DeBock, Paul 19:11
Deboffom, Frederick
  20:132
DeBogata, Lewis 7:77
DeBogota, Louis 25:295
Deboice, J. 16:185
Deboid, Littleton 22:73
Debois, Levi 21:322
Debold, John 10:90;
  20:237

Debold, Lewis 19:341
Debolt, Henry W. 23:140
Debolt, J. F. 22:27
Debolt, J. W. 11:28
Debolt, John 16:132
DeBond, Collin 8:83
DeBonds, G. F. 16:367
DeBoosh, James 26:157
Debord, Andrew J. 22:73
Debord, G. 11:28
Deborde, Nelson 22:403
Debose, Allen 7:92
DeBosh, James 8:38
Debouch, Felecine 22:278
Deboys, George 23:26
Debra, David A. 17:276
DeBrady, DeYoung 16:29
Debras, J. 3:56
Debree, Joseph 11:201
Debretz, Michael 15:54
Debrick, T. J. 13:86
Debrigne, F. 25:163
Debrigue, Francis 5:13
DeBrock, John 7:92
Debroett, Charles 13:18
Debrow, George 11:201
Debrude, David 11:28
Debruler, J. I. 24:76
Debut, John 23:313
DeCam, Joel 26:25
Decamp, Fred 17:263
Decamp, H. 15:193
DeCamp, Joel 9:78
DeCamp, Leander 13:18
Decard, Daniel 12:18
DeCarr, Lionell T. 23:120
DeCasta, Charles W. 18:275
Decat, B. 18:234
Decat, Bousdley 26:24
Decater, John 25:332
Decater, Philip 22:296
Decatur, Webster C. 12:18
Decatur, William 10:15
DeCay, George S. 18:338
Decay, Stephen 12:53
Decener, M. W. 23:26
Dech, Alfred 7:92
Dechard, Campbell 22:187
Dechert, Gustavus 21:98
Deck, Charles 20:237
Deck, Edward 13:18
Deck, Martin 13:18
Deckars, John 21:252
Decker, A. 3:56; 15:193, 363
Decker, Armon 12:18
Decker, B. F. 3:56
Decker, Benjamin 15:293; 16:185; 19:11

Decker, Benjamin J. 20:189
Decker, C. 1:124; 3:56
Decker, C. L. 1:93
Decker, Charles E. 1:28
Decker, Clarkson H. 15:172
Decker, Daniel 24:65
Decker, Daniel D. 15:193
Decker, David 16:367
Decker, E. C. 9:141; 27:36
Decker, Elisha 8:13; 18:130; 23:140
Decker, Ethel 8:83
Decker, G. 1:125; 3:56; 15:33; 16:185
Decker, G. S. 3:56
Decker, George 7:9; 12:68; 14:157; 19:11, 159; 20:189
Decker, George H. 17:424
Decker, George L. 24:175
Decker, George S. 9:102
Decker, Gideo 19:11
Decker, H. 19:250
Decker, Henry 1:27; 9:174
Decker, I. 3:56
Decker, I. L. 16:92
Decker, Ira 22:141
Decker, Isaac 13:18; 17:316; 22:422
Decker, J. 9:240; 11:91; 12:166; 14:53, 336
Decker, J. H. 1:93
Decker, J. P. 3:56
Decker, J. T. 13:108
Decker, J. W. 13:108
Decker, Jacob 11:400
Decker, Jacob B. 19:159
Decker, Jacob R. 10:159
Decker, James 3:56; 13:63; 16:185, 291
Decker, John 1:28; 8:13, 100; 13:18; 14:53; 15:324; 17:271; 18:130; 19:65
Decker, John B. 9:174; 19:250
Decker, John C. 1:26
Decker, John H. 1:26
Decker, John I. 5:13
Decker, Joseph E. 10:7
Decker, L. 1:29, 125; 3:56
Decker, Leonard 18:28
Decker, Levi 8:113; 27:34
Decker, Ly 13:87
Decker, M. 1:126
Decker, Moses 18:364
Decker, Nathan 4:20

Decker, Nicholas 11:118; 12:68
Decker, P. 3:56; 25:163
Decker, P. C. 19:159
Decker, Philip 13:124
Decker, R. 1:123
Decker, R. W. 22:170
Decker, S. G. 22:73
Decker, Sidney A. 4:20
Decker, Squire I. 17:50
Decker, Stephen 14:157
Decker, T. 19:250
Decker, Thomas 14:157
Decker, Townsley 9:174; 19:250
Decker, W. 26:25
Decker, W. E. 8:62; 26:158
Decker, W. H. 8:71; 26:158
Decker, Walter 25:29
Decker, William 11:124
Decker, William H. 23:120
Decker, William R. 5:13
Deckers, Mathias 11:28
Deckman, Frederick 15:193
Deckman, J. G. 3:56
Deckman, John 3:56
Decknan, Charles 14:157
Decks, John 21:322
Deckson, William 19:45
DeClayton, Thomas H. 10:110; 20:237
Declercy, W. E. 3:56
Decom, William 26:218
DeCorsey, George O. 5:38
DeCorsie, Richard 10:172
DeCosta, Frank 21:322
Decosta, Peter 19:11
Decostan, John 25:163
Decoster, John 5:50
Decourcey, Richard 10:110
Decourcy, Richard 20:237
DeCoursey, James E. 22:422
DeCoy, Garritt 6:12
DeCroon, John 15:315
Dede, K. 11:125
DeDeglorff, Platt 19:250
Dedemar, Edward 11:286
Dedemond, H. H. 9:42; 26:123
Dederick, L. M. 25:163
Dedney, J. 21:99
Dedon, George W. 18:189
Dedrell, Andrew 21:120
Dedrich, George 21:268

Dedrick, H. A. 8:100; 17:462
Dedrick, Henry 11:279
Dedrick, Henry H. 24:175
Dedrick, P. 3:56
Dedrick, P. J. 14:8
Dedrick, William 10:204; 17:272
Dee, --- 12:167
Dee, James 11:385
Dee, John 4:20
Dee, Moses 10:208
Dee, Nicholas 12:121; 15:122
Dee, Orson 11:411
Dee, Patrick 16:29
Dee, W. J. 18:364
Dee, William J. 9:219
Deecher, John 11:286
Deeds, Charles 16:367
Deeds, J. 3:56
Deeds, John 9:71
Deegan, Dennis 9:12
Deegan, John 1:28
Deegan, Patrick 10:15
Deek, Charles 10:110
Deeker, John 17:460
Deeker, Moses 9:219
Deeker, S. 3:56
Deel, W. H. 24:16
Deeler, William 22:73
Deelman, Adam 23:64
Deelon, Francis 8:13
Deem, Hiram P. 18:216
Deem, Thomas 21:203
Deem, Thomas H. 22:523
Deems, P. 3:56
Deen, Abraham 26:22
Deen, D. 14:53
Deen, J. H. 8:47
Deen, James H. 21:67
Deen, W. M. 26:158
Deener, John 1:27
Deeney, Daniel 12:18
Deens, H. 16:185
Deens, William 22:141
Deeny, Charles 18:28
Deep, Geo 3:56
Deer, H. 3:56
Deer, J. 18:234; 26:25
Deer, Jefferson 18:234
Deer, John 16:84; 27:34
Deer, Marion I. 10:49
Deer, Marion J. 20:237
Deer, Michael 25:163
Deer, Thomas H. 23:64
Deer, W. J. 15:165
Deerdaff, Thomas 21:215
Deeren, William 17:471; 27:38

Deerhammer, John H. 22:278
Deering, Addison G. 21:322
Deering, J. 21:322
Deering, John S. 5:13; 25:163
Deering, Peter 4:20
Deering, R. N. 21:322
Deerrnier, P. 27:35
Deers, G. 26:158
Deervester, J. 27:143
Dees, G. 8:62
Dees, Griffin 21:14
Dees, William 10:172; 19:159
Deeten, D. 11:301
Deeter, Andrew F. 23:87
Deeter, Jacob 24:37
Deeter, Thomas 19:159
Deets, B. H. 11:142
Deets, Charles 15:341
Deets, H. 1:93
Deets, R. 3:56
Deetsh, Jacob 17:359
Deety, D. R. 24:16
Deetz, James 8:83
Deever, William 24:110
Deevit, J. A. 16:185
Deevus, John H. 8:13
Deezur, Zeno 9:174
DeFay, Thomas 10:110; 20:237
Defenbaugh, Francis N. 21:120
Defenbaugh, L. 11:27
Defenbaugh, Wesley 21:223
Defentry, W. 15:7
Deffamore, William F. 15:193
Deffel, Joel 17:32
Deffenbacher, Frederick 21:99
Deffenbacker, Jacob 14:157
Deffenderfer, Emanuel 22:422
Deffer, G. 11:238
Deffer, Louis 3:56
Deffey, Charles 10:172
Deffy, Charles 19:159
Defintey, Henry 12:68
Deflibaugh, W. K. 3:56
Defoe, Edmond 15:358
Defoe, Louis 11:105
DeFor, Edry 19:65
Defor, Edward 12:95
Deford, Jonas 22:73
Deford, Shaford R. 27:39
Deford, Stephen 25:332

Deford, William 22:403
Defore, Robert 27:39
DeForest, Amade 19:159
Deforest, Hiram 13:18
DeForest, Samuel 11:143
DeForest, William 19:159
DeForrest, E. H. 1:29
DeForrest, Francis 21:252
DeForrest, W. M. 1:126
Defree, James 3:56
Defries, A. 10:27; 19:301
DeFrise, Thomas 13:57
Degains, J. 1:28
Degains, Thomas 14:251
Degammo, J. 3:56
Degan, A. 1:123
Degan, John 7:24
Degan, Patrick 16:185
Degard, H. 3:56
DeGarmo, W. R. 25:163
Degbee, William 18:304; 26:96
Degin, P. 1:123
Degnan, Thomas 10:15
Dego, Aaron 24:65
Dego, William 18:80
Degonelier, J. S. 9:109
Degonier, Thomas 26:23
Degonies, Thomas 9:78
Degraff, M. 1:103
DeGraff, William 11:27
Degrant, --- 10:147; 18:47
DeGroat, Charles 22:278
DeGroat, E. 14:53
DeGroat, N. H. 14:157
Degroff, E. 22:477
Degroff, G. 3:56
DeGroff, Watson 21:252
Degroodt, Lofe 24:110
Degroot, H. 3:56
Degroot, Obadiah 27:36
DeGroot, Peter 23:260
DeGroot, Simon 24:61
Degroot, W. 3:56
DeGrot, George 9:141
Degrote, John N. 10:147; 18:47
Degrounor, B. 14:54
Degrout, A. 14:54
DeGrout, George 8:62
Degue, Antoine 19:281
Degue, Ben 7:121
DeGuer, E. 19:250
Deguire, Richard 7:121; 21:323
Deham, John 21:322
Dehan, Joshua 21:322
Deharer, Reuben 24:87
Dehart, D. 7:56
Dehart, G. 11:144
DeHart, Hiram 21:67

Dehart, Ira B. 9:78; 26:22
Dehart, J. W. 21:322
DeHart, John 6:15; 18:80
DeHart, Lorenzo D. 23:255
DeHart, Richard 8:83
Dehaven, Daniel 21:186
DeHays, W. H. 18:103
Dehl, John 9:33; 18:291; 26:96
Dehne, Henry 1:27
Dehoff, Joseph 10:49
Dehome, J. 13:108
Dehoof, Joseph 20:237
DeHovey, David 21:242
Dehoy, Garrett 18:80
Dehrell, Paul 8:13; 18:130
Dehtold, Eman 24:74
Dehuff, C. H. 1:125
DeHuxley, William 23:87
Deide, Lewis 12:18
Deidrich, Julius 23:104
Deids, Eli 8:83
Deifenbock, P. 25:29
Deig, Andrew 1:28
Deihl, C. 14:54
Deihl, J. 22:477
Deii, J. R. 25:30
Deike, W. 11:292
Deikhart, Fred 18:304
Deikmeyer, Charles 11:301
Deiks, C. 3:57
Deilen, C. C. 21:14
Deily, William 3:56
Deimer, Frederick 8:83
Deinastas, I. 3:56
Deingue, Thomas 6:15
Deinlein, Dankutz 26:96
Deinlein, Daukaty 18:304
Deinlim, Denkraty 9:20
Deinsett, Constant 18:411
Deipert, A. 22:187
Deir, J. R. 2:9
Deisroth, G. 16:118
Deitch, --- 27:39
Deiteman, H. 1:124
Deiter, Sarah 22:351
Deiterlen, Fred 26:96
Deiterlin, Frederick 9:20
Deith, Gustav 19:159
Deitling, Augustus 16:84
Deitrich, A. 10:147; 18:47
Deitrich, Adam 7:92
Deitrichoodien, George 18:130
Deitrick, J. W. 14:157
Deitrick, John 1:26
Deitrick, William H. 11:57
Deits, Andrew 17:64

Deits, C. 19:65
Deits, G. 13:103
Deits, George F. 22:403
Deitsback, John 11:143
Deitsh, Carl 24:92
Deitton, W. M. 23:313
Deity, Henry 11:143
Deity, William 21:322
Deitz, A. 1:124
Deitz, G. 14:8
Deitz, Henry 22:333
Deitzel, Frederick 9:174
Deitzer, Mathias 20:238
Deitzer, Nicholas 11:276
Deitzinger, John 12:18
Deitzler, Henry 13:60
Deivire, Dennis 3:56
Deixheimer, J. 15:326
Dejarnes, Henry 19:45
DeJarnett, Thomas 13:18
Dejean, George 7:121
DeJean, V. 1:28
Deke, Louis 21:215
Dekenson, J. C. 18:234
DeKittridge, Carlisle 4:20
DeKnight, Christopher 10:110; 20:238
DeKruif, John P. 4:20
Delabar, Joseph 17:90
Delacosta, J. 1:124
Delaine, John A. 14:157
Delaire, Oliver 21:322
Delamater, Martin 13:18
DeLaMater, W. 25:27
Delameter, Martin 16:29
Delan, Leon 12:95
Delana, Mary Jane 26:218
Delanah, E. B. 3:56
Delancey, Anthony 13:18
Delancey, Benjamin 20:39
Delancey, John 20:122
Delancey, L. 9:142
Delancy, J. 3:57
Delancy, James 11:27, 142
Delancy, William 22:161
Deland, Alvin S. 7:67
Deland, Charles D. 18:275
Deland, R. A. 1:124
Deland, T. 18:65
Delane, Ed 14:157
DeLane, Oscar 8:83
Delaney, --- 1:27
Delaney, Alexander 25:283
Delaney, B. 1:124
Delaney, C. 3:57; 16:185
Delaney, C. W. 14:281
Delaney, Charles 14:281
Delaney, Charles M. 12:18

Delaney, Daniel 14:157; 15:13
Delaney, Dennis 1:28
Delaney, E. 3:56, 57
Delaney, E. M. 13:129
Delaney, Edward 15:298
Delaney, F. 19:159
Delaney, George 17:503
Delaney, H. 3:56
Delaney, H. E. 25:319
Delaney, Harry 17:397
Delaney, J. 1:124; 8:47; 25:163; 27:36
Delaney, J. C. 1:29
Delaney, J. P. 19:281
Delaney, Jacob 3:56
Delaney, James 9:174; 19:281
Delaney, James M. 16:92
Delaney, John 3:56; 6:28; 7:83; 8:113; 11:15; 12:69; 15:33; 22:333
Delaney, John R. 8:83
Delaney, John W. 10:49
Delaney, Louis I. 17:19
Delaney, M. 1:126; 3:56
Delaney, Mather 9:8
Delaney, Michael 11:28; 17:355
Delaney, P. 25:27
Delaney, Patrick 7:16; 12:69; 22:248
Delaney, Samuel 9:78; 26:25
Delaney, Squire 22:422
Delaney, Thomas 9:78
Delaney, W. 11:260
Delaney, W. H. 8:62; 26:157
Delaney, William 1:28; 5:50; 10:159; 12:8; 19:159; 20:6
Delano, Asa C. 10:110; 20:238
Delano, David 19:325
Delano, E. 3:57
Delano, Eben R. 22:141
Delano, Edgar C. 25:283
Delano, Harvey 22:141
Delano, Hatzil 20:112
Delano, John 18:364
Delano, Leon 15:359
Delano, Macey 15:33
Delano, S. 14:54
Delano, Smith 22:111
Delano, Stephen B. 20:106
Delano, Walter 22:111
Delansy, James 6:11
Delantise, Francis 18:28
Delany, Charles 21:322

Delany, D. 15:158
Delany, Edward 19:11
Delany, J. 1:124
Delany, John 5:13; 21:322
DeLany, Josephus 26:122
Delany, N. 16:185
Delany, Nicholas 13:63
Delany, Patrick 15:193
Delany, T. 26:22
Delany, William C. 17:205
Delap, Albert G. 23:64
Delap, Anderson 26:218
Delap, Edward 21:252
Delap, Harrison 13:18
Delap, W. A. 7:83
Delap, William A. 21:322
Delaplain, S. J. 23:26
Delapp, Anderson 9:236
Delapp, William 24:92
DeLaReve, Anthony 16:29
Delarue, Benjamin W. 11:57
Delashwent, F. 3:57
DelaTreaux, M. 7:24
Delaughter, Absalom 8:83
Delaum, --- 15:94
Delaus, John 9:219
Delaware, Joseph F. 13:18
Delax, Robert 9:102
Delay, Dennis 18:234; 26:25
Delay, J. 26:25
Delay, J. S. 21:120
Delay, Jeremiah 9:78
Delay, P. 11:28
Delberk, C. A. 16:291
Delbert, O. A. 14:54
Delbragher, H. 18:48
Delbridge, William 17:154
Deleal, Charles 14:54
Delemater, D. 1:27
Deleno, Leon 19:65
Delergue, --- 15:33
Delevan, G. 23:27
Delewood, D. 8:77
Delezar, Joseph 19:11
Delf, E. 14:157
Delf, F. 3:57
Delfs, Charles 22:165
Delhanta, William 3:57
Delhanty, P. 15:83
Delhanty, Patrick 12:69
Delimore, E. 16:185
Delind, Curtis 7:49
Deling, Richard 5:13
Delinger, A. 16:118
Delinger, Jacob 11:260
Delisle, Moses 19:250

Deliver, John 21:322
Delivery, A. J. 20:238
Delk, E. 14:54
Delkerson, J. 16:291
Delkey, George 2:10; 25:29
Delks, William J. 1:28
Delkson, J. 12:87
Dell, Edward 17:454; 24:185
Dell, J. M. O. 18:130
Dell, James H. O. 25:271
Dell, John H. 11:57
Dell, Peter 21:322
Dellard, Moses 8:38
Dellart, Henry 9:12
Dellen, T. 14:54
Deller, Valentine 9:174
Delleson, James B. 8:104
Dellett, Moses 14:157
Dellew, J. D. 7:92
Dellig, J. 21:88
Delliner, LeRoy 19:324
Delling, R. 25:163
Dellinger, Christian 17:32
Dellinger, David 15:193
Dellinger, Henry P. 11:143
Dellinger, Oscar 8:13
Dellinger, William H. 23:64
Dellingham, A. 5:13
Dellion, J. 17:279
Dellno, Christian 8:23
Dellon, James 21:322
Dellu, Charles 20:238
Dellup, Z. S. 3:57
Dellworth, Franklin 17:235
Dellzeit, Anthony 22:187
Delmart, C. A. 21:136
Delmer, Wilson 12:56
Delmont, P. 8:13; 18:130
Delmore, E. 15:298
Delmore, George 14:157
Delmore, W. 3:57
Delmot, --- 16:92
Delodge, Joseph 17:456; 24:213
Deloice, J. J. 25:30
Delome, N. 25:163
DeLong, Albert 7:92
Delong, C. R. 5:13
Delong, Charles O. 4:20
DeLong, George E. 1:28
Delong, H. 1:126
Delong, J. 1:124
DeLong, James 7:56
Delong, James E. 23:87
Delong, John H. 20:39
Delong, John J. 10:204

Delong, John W. 23:87
Delong, Merritt C. 20:112
Delong, N. 4:20
Delong, Nicholas 22:187
Delong, Oscar 11:400
DeLong, Peter 13:18
Delong, Peter 15:311, 354
DeLong, Peter 16:29
DeLong, Silas 13:57
DeLong, Silas H. 16:29
Delono, M. 3:57
Delony, Peter 19:65
Delord, G. 21:23
DeLosh, John 4:20
Delosier, A. B. 23:184
Delph, J. T. 13:79
Delrue, John 2:10
Delty, Enoch M. 16:132
DeLuce, Reuben 10:159
DeLury, Dennis 22:508
Delvey, Allen I. 10:49
Delvin, James 21:322
Delworth, Thomas 7:24
Dely, Peter R. 20:189
Delyle, Moses 9:174
Delzell, Robert 22:422
Delzell, S. P. 18:364
Demagan, J. 18:234
Demahrl, I. 19:343
Deman, C. 10:147; 18:48
Demar, J. E. 25:281
Demaranville, Elisha P. 22:27
DeMaranville, Nehemiah 22:27
DeMaranville, Samuel 22:27
Demard, W. J. 9:42
Demarer, Baptiste 16:29
Demarest, D. 3:57
Demarest, Martin V. B. 15:27
Demarias, J. 16:367
Demaris, D. 1:27
Demarra, Xavier 17:70
Demars, J. 1:125
Demars, Peter 19:65
DeMartigna, L. 1:28
Demary, Myson 19:11
Demas, Isaac 14:8
Demas, Nicholas 8:38; 26:157
Demasils, J. 18:364
DeMaw, J. 1:30
Demay, John 3:57
Dement, Andrew 7:92; 21:323
Dement, Benjamin 22:73
Demere, Franklin 10:49
Demeree, D. 3:57
Demeresh, William 7:24

Demerest, G. W. 13:87; 14:8
Demerest, George 14:157
Demerest, H. V. 3:57
Demerest, Horace E. 21:99
Demerest, Philip 8:13
Demerest, Phillip 18:130
Demerin, Jefferson 22:296
DeMerritt, John Y. 9:7
Demers, C. L. A. 24:63
Demerst, John W. 22:73
Demet, I. D. 15:193
Demett, G. O. 24:16
Demevert, Samuel 16:185
Demevitt, C. J. 25:319
Demgan, J. 26:24
Demgon, Peter 8:13
Demias, Clement 16:29
Demick, Franklin 15:54
Demick, Oscar 14:157
Demil, Daniel 11:143
Deming, Benjamin O. 21:50
Deming, George A. 9:130; 27:36
Deming, George M. 4:20
Deming, Harvey L. 19:329
Deming, J. 23:106
Deming, J. Martin 14:319; 25:268
Deming, John H. 4:20
Deming, W. 16:185
Demington, John 11:385
Demint, Lewis 19:159
Demis, S. 27:36
Demiter, Thomas 22:296
Demkin, John H. 22:248
Demly, William 19:45
Demman, Francis 22:403
Demmice, C. S. 18:48
Demmick, James 11:200
Demming, Augustus E. 10:210
Demming, B. O. 3:57
Demming, F. M. 3:57
Demming, George 11:201
Demming, H. 1:126
Demming, L. 3:57
Demming, Robert 6:20
Demming, W. H. 17:168
Demmler, John 21:252
Demmons, Fernando E. 13:18
Demo, George W. 22:187
Demobille, James A. 10:49; 20:238
Demon, B. V. 16:29
Demon, C. 9:174; 19:250
Demon, J. 23:27

Demona, Stephen 22:187
Demond, John B. 22:421
Demond, Joseph 8:83
Demoney, D. H. 18:48
DeMont, George 8:83
Demont, L. 22:141
Demony, D. H. 10:147
Demorar, Baptiste 13:18
Demorest, William 13:108
Demory, Jacob 11:143
Demoss, Andrew 11:58
Demoss, Benjamin L. 11:260
Demoss, D. 18:65
DeMoss, F. 22:333
Demot, John A. 13:129
Demott, Benjamin 10:159; 19:159
DeMott, George 5:13
DeMott, James 25:29
Demouth, --- 16:367
Demouth, F. 15:151
Demouth, T. 1:28
Demp, George W. 17:101
Dempey, W. T. 23:306
Demprey, J. M. 26:23
Demprey, Robert 26:23
Dempry, John 24:16
Dempsey, Daniel 23:140
Dempsey, David L. 17:449; 24:175
Dempsey, Ely 6:23
Dempsey, Farley 23:97
Dempsey, H. S. 1:126
Dempsey, James 6:30; 9:174; 12:167; 19:273; 20:48; 24:92; 25:28, 163, 319
Dempsey, Jeremiah 9:33
Dempsey, John 25:163
Dempsey, M. 1:124
Dempsey, Mark 19:65
Dempson, T. 9:51
Dempster, G. F. 7:24
Dempsy, August 22:187
Dempsy, James 5:14
Dempsy, Jeremiah 26:96
Dempuy, John 10:15
Demroke, Edward 9:174
Demsby, John 7:74
Demsey, Jacob 21:323
Demsey, James 25:163
Demshea, Edwill 19:289
Demsing, A. 14:158
Demsnap, John 12:18
Demston, Thomas A. 7:49
Demuens, Francis 9:12
Demund, Henry 22:141
Demuth, H. W. 19:11
Demuth, Jacob 13:108
Demuth, John 23:64

Den, Jefferson 26:24
Den, S. 17:337
Den, William 16:185
Denald, Charles 7:67
Denard, M. D. 14:277; 23:120
Denatt, Paul 7:121
Denbo, Joseph 18:216
Denbo, William R. 11:143
Denbone, James 18:394
Denby, Isaac 25:163
Denby, Leander S. 24:16
Denby, W. 25:163
Dencaster, Henry 11:27
Denchar, E. M. 23:140
Denchuis, Davis 26:25
Denck, Daniel 26:156
Denck, David 18:130
Deneare, Franklin 20:238
Deneen, Henry S. 15:122
Deneen, R. 25:29
Deneen, Solan 13:18
Deneen, Solon 16:29
Denek, Daniel 8:13
Denel, Asa 13:18
Denel, James 22:27
Dener, Carll 25:163
Denerenger, George 11:27
Denery, John 11:190
Denesore, J. M. 27:38
Denett, William H. 13:18
Deney, E. A. 9:42
Deney, Edward M. 13:18
Deney, Henry A. 10:159
Denfair, Seth B. 4:20
Denfetney, James 15:33
Dengel, G. M. 18:130
Dengerpool, B. 9:51
Dengher, D. F. 25:163
Dengle, G. 15:65
Dengon, N. H. 7:56
Denham, B. 9:142; 23:27
Denham, Eli 25:295
Denham, J. W. 10:90
Denham, James W. 20:238
Denham, Joseph 15:7
Denham, R. 3:57
Denham, Thomas 11:407
Denham, W. S. 19:159
Denhart, W. 3:57
Denhor, A. 14:54
Denhurst, James 8:83
Denich, William 19:159
Denick, V. 1:124
Denick, William 10:159
Denigon, Peter 18:130
Denika, Henry 17:355
Deniker, David H. 15:13
Denim, James 18:48
Denin, Cail 27:38

Denin, Carl 14:296; 17:474
Denin, Patrick 8:121
Denis, James 20:238
Denis, Richard 15:22
Denise, William T. 22:187
Denison, --- 16:185
Denison, Cornelius 12:18
Denison, D. A. 17:154
Denison, F. N. 20:238
Denison, H. M. 15:193
Denison, Joseph S. 25:163
Denison, W. H. 10:110; 20:238
Denison, William 20:238
Deniston, Andrew 11:142
Deniston, George M. 10:110
Deniston, J. 1:124
Denivan, J. 21:323
Denize, William 24:76
Denker, Frederick 12:58
Denkey, J. M. 9:78
Denley, Washington 5:38
Denlinger, David 23:140
Denly, William 25:163
Denman, Albert 21:269
Denman, Benajah 17:78
Denman, John H. 22:74
Denmark, --- 27:36
Denmark, A. 2:9; 25:28
Denmark, Hamilton 18:420
Denmark, J. 9:142
Denmark, J. J. 20:192
Denmore, C. L. 2:10
Denmore, Thomas 16:367
Denn, J. H. 20:238
Denn, L. H. 3:57
Denn, S. 14:54
Dennan, Martin 11:144
Dennan, Richard 11:190
Dennan, S. 3:57
Dennan, W. 3:57
Dennean, James 10:159; 19:159
Dennen, George 16:93
Dennett, Charles 9:163
Dennett, J. C. 27:35
Dennett, R. M. 1:126
Dennette, J. C. 9:142
Denney, --- 20:91
Denney, Alfred 6:24
Denney, David 9:42
Denney, George W. 1:29
Denney, H. L. 18:48
Denney, L. 1:124
Denney, Robert M. 23:27
Denney, W. 15:65
Denney, W. H. 1:125

Denney, William 1:27; 20:238
Dennick, E. W. 21:186
Dennick, John A. 22:421
Dennin, Anderson 11:201
Dennin, David Wallace 21:67
Denning, Aseph C. 11:239
Denning, Benjamin F. 23:64
Denning, Franklin 10:15
Denning, General 22:248
Denning, J. 1:126
Denning, James 3:57; 23:120
Denning, L. 14:158
Denning, Mathias 26:158
Denning, Nathan 18:130
Denning, V. T. 25:26
Denning, W. 3:57
Denning, William M. 17:440; 24:151
Denninger, William 17:313
Dennings, G. A. 3:57
Dennings, Jackson 21:269
Dennington, South 19:65
Dennip, Benjamin 3:57
Dennis, A. 1:124; 19:296; 25:163; 27:39
Dennis, A. A. 3:57
Dennis, Aaron 19:45
Dennis, Abraham 21:323; 23:140
Dennis, Alexander 23:27
Dennis, Allen 24:88
Dennis, Andrew 9:42
Dennis, Arnold 25:163
Dennis, Benjamin 12:18
Dennis, C. 3:57
Dennis, Caleb F. 22:27
Dennis, Charles 6:24; 8:14; 18:130; 22:27
Dennis, Charles J. 19:65
Dennis, Courtland 1:27
Dennis, D. 21:120
Dennis, D. S. 22:477
Dennis, Daniel 18:394
Dennis, David 22:187
Dennis, E. 16:147
Dennis, Edward 9:207
Dennis, Elihu 13:18
Dennis, Francis M. 21:23
Dennis, G. W. 9:71
Dennis, Gabriel 9:219; 18:365
Dennis, George 9:213; 21:323
Dennis, George W. 7:92
Dennis, H. 26:122
Dennis, Henry 15:172

Dennis, Hugh 10:110; 20:238
Dennis, Isaac 11:105; 13:87; 16:185
Dennis, J. 12:98; 13:87; 14:8; 21:323
Dennis, J. C. 21:147
Dennis, J. J. 7:24
Dennis, Jac 11:27
Dennis, James 10:49, 159; 19:159
Dennis, James L. 11:27
Dennis, Jessie 18:109
Dennis, John 9:174; 15:357; 16:278; 18:13; 19:65; 22:333; 25:163
Dennis, John C. 22:74
Dennis, John L. 25:27
Dennis, John T. 18:80
Dennis, John W. 24:65
Dennis, Lee 20:238
Dennis, Leo 10:110
Dennis, Levi 6:28
Dennis, M. 11:144; 19:301
Dennis, M. E. 23:202
Dennis, Ned 6:24
Dennis, Noah 9:79; 26:23
Dennis, Oscarr B. 19:11
Dennis, Peter 9:142
Dennis, Richard 24:100
Dennis, Robert 21:211
Dennis, S. 9:130
Dennis, S. A. 13:18
Dennis, Samuel 6:15; 17:279; 18:80; 19:11
Dennis, T. H. 18:365
Dennis, Thomas 3:57; 21:323
Dennis, Thomas H. 9:219
Dennis, Thomas J. 17:235
Dennis, Thomas P. 24:37
Dennis, William 4:20; 19:250; 23:106
Dennis, William H. 20:6; 23:140
Dennis, York 11:201
Dennison, A. 11:143
Dennison, A. D. 13:108
Dennison, Arthur 8:62
Dennison, Charles 10:49; 20:238; 23:120
Dennison, Charles E. 11:230
Dennison, Charles H. 24:49
Dennison, Chauncey 22:461
Dennison, Clement 13:18
Dennison, Daniel 9:33

Dennison, E. D. 10:146
Dennison, E. G. 1:29
Dennison, Eben 12:18
Dennison, Emery W. 20:112
Dennison, F. N. 10:90
Dennison, G. 22:187
Dennison, G. A. 1:123
Dennison, H. 3:57
Dennison, Henry J. 17:397
Dennison, J. 3:57; 18:109
Dennison, J. C. 1:29
Dennison, J. M. 14:296; 17:475
Dennison, James 10:49; 22:477
Dennison, James W. 8:113
Dennison, John 6:9; 23:27
Dennison, Joseph 22:165
Dennison, Joseph T. 5:14
Dennison, L A. 12:18
Dennison, Robert 20:238
Dennison, Sylvester 13:129
Dennison, W. 3:57; 13:60; 20:145
Dennison, William 10:49; 22:461
Dennison, William H. 8:83
Denniss, E. 3:57
Dennissen, T. 3:57
Denniston, E. 19:296
Denniston, George M. 20:238
Dennoits, J. 3:57
Dennon, Isaac J. 9:66
Denns, W. A. 24:17
Dennse, John 27:34
Denny, --- 11:144; 21:323
Denny, Andrew 7:92
Denny, C. H. 19:11
Denny, Charles 14:314; 19:341
Denny, Charles C. 22:73
Denny, David 19:290; 22:469; 26:122
Denny, George 7:92
Denny, Henry 17:247
Denny, Jacob 11:57
Denny, Jeremiah 14:158
Denny, Jesse A. 22:422; 23:64
Denny, John 3:57; 7:121
Denny, Lernings 21:323
Denny, O. 21:323
Denny, Patrick 10:110; 20:238
Denny, Ralph 22:296

Denny, S. L. 19:65
Denny, Selah 10:110; 20:238
Denny, Walter H. 22:73
Denny, William 9:230
Denoe, Oliver 24:92
Denon, B. V. 13:18
Denorf, F. 3:57
Denorrville, John 24:8
Denoya, W. H. 3:57
Denrerst, S. 13:77
Densan, Albert 13:108
Dense, E. W. 19:159
Denshell, John 22:187
Densinger, John 11:279
Denslor, --- 27:39
Densman, H. 3:57
Densmond, --- 1:29
Densmore, C. L. 25:26
Densmore, Charles 17:247
Densmore, Coleman 11:143
Densmore, E. 3:57
Densmore, J. S. 13:87
Densmore, L. 17:154
Densmore, Oliver J. 8:83
Densmore, W. H. 23:312
Densmore, William 3:57
Denson, A. 16:185
Denson, Benjamin 13:124
Denson, E. 13:87
Denson, Edward 9:79; 26:22
Denson, Edward S. 17:205
Denson, James B. 22:248
Denson, John R. 21:136
Denson, Leonard 22:27
Denson, Merel 16:278
Dent, Alexander 9:165
Dent, Andrew B. 17:359
Dent, F. 16:185
Dent, James H. 7:24
Dent, John F. 23:189
Dent, S. 25:163
Dent, W. A. 3:57
Dent, W. M. 17:272
Dent, William R. 18:234; 26:23
Dentberg, Benjamin 25:278
Denten, Hazeltine 20:112
Dentermont, V. 12:61
Dentler, George L. 22:233
Dentler, Henry 3:57
Denton, E. 3:57
Denton, Frederick 21:323
Denton, G. 3:57
Denton, George M. 22:333
Denton, Huston 11:422

Denton, Iron 8:83
Denton, J. 17:95
Denton, J. C. 18:406
Denton, J. W. 8:62; 26:158
Denton, James 21:23
Denton, James W. 17:144
Denton, John 3:57; 9:219; 18:365; 23:27
Denton, John W. 22:450
Denton, Jonas 23:27
Denton, M. B. 20:238
Denton, Marion 17:50
Denton, Martin B. 10:49
Denton, N. B. 11:380
Denton, Nathaniel 22:248
Denton, Oziah 21:323
Denton, Phillip 3:57
Denton, S. H. 17:242
Denton, S. W. 17:263
Denton, Samuel R. 26:157
Denton, Thomas 22:74; 23:27
Denton, W. 19:250
Denton, Walter 9:174
Denton, William 8:104; 22:74
Denton, William S. 11:143
Dentrement, V. 8:125
Denure, Albert 22:27
Denver, Abraham 27:36
Denver, Henry 23:27
Denver, J. L. 3:57
Denver, Peter 1:28
Deny, Ford 3:57
Deny, Michael 19:159
Denyoe, John B. 9:109
Denzar, Charles 18:65
Denzberger, John 21:23
Denzer, Dennis 9:219
Deol, Alonzo 18:304
Deon, R. E. 20:48
Deorrings, C. A. 14:54
Deoss, Job T. 20:238
Depance, Wallace L. 24:37
Departy, W. 3:57
Depas, A. 3:57
Depaugh, --- 18:28
DePay, John 18:304
Depeer, B. F. 8:83
Depen, Isaac L. 7:92
Depenport, --- 18:65
Deper, Reuben 8:104
Deperoin, --- 11:118
Depert, Jacob 17:32
Deperty, Z. 13:19
Depew, E. H. W. 9:79
DePew, Hugh 13:57
Depew, James W. 21:223

Depew, Levi 19:159
Depew, Lyman 22:477
Depew, S. 17:147
Depew, Thomas 17:109
Depey, John 9:20
Dephard, T. 3:57
Depmecole, A. 15:341
Depne, C. 25:29
Depne, William 14:251
Depoaly, William 1:29
Depolston, Hiram 9:96
Deport, Henry 12:171
Depositer, John 23:252
Depp, Henry H. 9:12
Deppert, John A. 8:14
Deppy, George H. 11:104
Deprew, Benjamin 18:205
Depriest, Asa 22:27
Deprow, C. 16:29
DePue, J. A. 3:57
Depue, John I. 10:49
Depue, Moses 10:49
Depue, Philip 7:121
Depue, Ralph 10:110;
    20:238
Depugh, C. 1:27
Depugh, Evan 13:19
Depung, C. L. 1:29
Deputy, Henry 15:7
Deputy, Jesse 9:79
Depwood, Samuel 11:201
Dequeir, P. 18:48
Dequin, Englebert 20:112
Der---, Henry 15:193
DeRalt, F. 3:57
Deraney, Patrick 7:24;
    14:335
Derbin, A. J. 14:158
Derbin, Adolph 7:121
Derbin, Charles E. 7:121
Derbin, Frederick 16:93
Derbin, Mathew 9:219;
    18:365
DerBott, George H. 27:38
Derbro, Sydney 14:158
Derby, E. M. 25:30
Derby, Edwin A. 16:278
Derby, F. H. 1:28
Derby, G. W. 1:27
Derby, John 20:106
Derby, John L. 22:141
Derby, S. E. 14:240;
    27:39
Derby, William 11:27
Derdine, M. V. 14:264
DeReading, John 19:11
Deremer, Mahlon 23:178
Deremer, Morris 25:29
Derese, Thomas 7:56
Derewish, Edward 20:238
Derewith, Edward 10:49

Dergan, James 12:18
Dergram, James 6:27
Dergue, Antonie 9:199
Dergun, M. 10:27; 19:301
Derh, Joseph 19:65
Derhan, Patrick 13:108
Derherd, Jeff 11:142
Derick, David 22:74
Derick, George 22:74
Derick, Thomas 11:58
Derickson, W. W. 3:58
Derigan, Thomas 19:322
Derimare, John 7:64
Deringer, Edward 4:20
Deringer, J. 1:29
Derkin, S. 11:293
Derlin, J. Y. 19:65
Derlin, James R. 22:233
Derling, Aaron 6:15;
    18:80
Dermady, W. C. 25:26
Derman, A. 3:58
Dermandy, Jeremiah
    16:118
Dermett, S. 3:58
Dermint, J. 1:125
Dermis, George 7:24
Dermitt, William 25:28
Dermody, Philip 20:238
Dermody, Thomas 3:57
Dermond, G. M. 17:387
Dermond, L. F. 9:174
Dermot, --- 27:38
Dermot, James 18:275
Dermott, John 14:158
Dermott, L. 3:58
Dermott, Levi B. 25:163
Dermott, Patrick M. 8:14
Dermott, Samuel 25:163
Dermwith, John P. 22:74
Dern, Silas 20:96
Dernkee, David 9:102
Dernont, --- 14:297;
    17:474
Dernton, Thomas B. 9:174
Dero, Francis J. 22:27
Deroff, Thomas 12:18
Derolt, Joseph E. 2:10;
    25:26
Derome, Michael 18:65
DeRosh, Hector 8:38
Derosia, Joseph 25:163
Derosia, Lewis 12:18
Derosier, Morris 19:349
DeRost, Hector 26:157
Deroucher, Stephen 19:65
Derr, Aaron 12:18; 23:255
Derr, Adam 19:334
Derr, B. 11:301
Derr, Charles 14:158
Derr, George R. 25:28

Derr, Henry 14:54
Derr, J. 1:123
Derr, J. H. 1:28
Derr, J. W. 1:127
Derr, James 12:18
Derr, John 5:14
Derr, John S. 21:323
Derr, Richard M. 12:18
Derr, Samuel 12:95;
    15:359
Derr, William R. 4:20
Derrald, Cornelius 8:104
Derrick, Hadley 22:512
Derrick, J. W. 16:185
Derrick, William 22:278
Derrickon, John W. 23:64
Derrickson, G. 13:87
Derrickson, J. D. 15:104
Derrine, John 19:349
Derring, August 17:74
Derringer, H. 3:57
Derringer, J. 3:57
Derrint, Lewis 10:172
Derrit, J. 25:163
Derrit, Joseph 22:296
Derritt, George 18:406
Derrnody, Philip 10:110
Derroin, N. 16:185
Derroshet, O. 1:123
Derry, E. N. 26:122
Derry, Edward M. 16:29
Derry, James 25:319
Derry, Joseph 6:30
Derry, Moses 5:38
Derry, W. 25:163
Derryman, Joseph 8:83
Derson, William 6:24
Dertrichvodien, George
    8:14
Derum, Edward 13:19
DeRush, Samuel 3:58
Dervay, Moses 9:79
Derverest, William F.
    16:185
Dervey, Hugh 8:104
Dervey, James H. 18:48
Dervier, E. F. 22:403
Dervis, J. R. 14:240
Dervit, B. 18:205
Dervitt, Henry S. 18:412
Derwent, Samuel 22:27
Derwey, John S. 23:189
Derwichter, John 14:158
Derwin, N. 15:293
Derwin, P. 1:125
Derwince, George 9:51
Dery, Edwin E. 10:15
Derzback, George 7:92
Desamur, Ned 7:77
Desann, Ned 25:295
Desart, John 21:67

DeSawyer, C. 25:163
Descem, W. H. 14:8
Descol, S. 3:58
Desek, John 19:250
Desellen, J. 16:186
Desendener, Clement 21:323
Desern, W. H. 13:87
Desertar, I. R. 25:283
Deseter, J. R. 14:319
Deshago, Paul H. 21:323
Deshay, Charles 8:38; 26:157
Deshea, W. 22:296
DeSheild, Benjamin 27:37
Deshelter, D. L. 15:21
Deshield, Benjamin 9:130
Deshields, William 15:13
Deshler, Joseph E. 11:239
Deshuser, C. 9:236
Deshuzer, C. 26:218
Desilitus, Carlos 18:275
Desin, L. 1:126
Desinger, John 11:91
Deslock, Jacob 18:130
Desman, T. 14:158
Desment, Michael 14:158
Desmier, Daniel 8:71
Desmold, D. 13:87
Desmond, D. 3:58
Desmond, Daniel 7:56; 10:10
Desmond, F. 13:108
Desmond, John 11:301
Desmond, T. 14:54
Desmond, W. 1:125
Desmond, William F. 23:27
Deson, Henry 22:296
Deson, T. H. 21:215
Desore, Noah 21:238
Desow, J. W. 14:54
Despain, William 23:27
Despart, F. A. 25:310
Despenet, John G. 17:259
Despers, Joseph 9:79
Despond, James H. 21:323
Desrehan, Elijah 14:158
Dessa, Jo. 8:38
Dessa, Joe 26:157
Dessart, Gustaf 13:19
Dessellun, M. 3:58
Dessing, J. T. 22:165
Dessinger, John 12:18
Desslock, Jacob 8:14
Dessotell, J. 3:58
Destler, Fred 3:58
Desvae, Joseph H. 19:159
Desysler, L. Y. 21:323
Detchon, Francis 11:301

Detchon, W. F. 1:125
Detchon, William 22:187
Detel, C. A. 18:28
Deter, Jacob 14:158
Determan, Harman 9:20
Detheridge, James 11:200
DeThiell, H. 11:239
Dethro, R. F. 11:438
Detling, G. 14:297; 17:471
Detlmher, Romaine 15:352
Detman, James 7:24
Detmering, H. 1:126
Detrad, Dudley 17:174
Detrech, Gustavus 9:230
Detrich, C. 3:58
Detrich, J. B. 9:227
Detrich, Jeremiah 22:27
Detrick, August 10:49
Detrick, Eli 13:19
Detrick, George 15:54
Detrick, Gustavus 20:238
Detrick, J. B. 18:365
Detrick, John 10:153; 19:159
Detriler, G. 1:125
Detrow, Wilh. 16:291
Detrow, Will 12:92
Detsler, Henry 19:11
Detterick, August 20:238
Detterman, Herman 18:304
Detterson, J. 17:64
Dettinger, Romanis 16:278
Dettner, H. 3:58
Detus, Henry 1:27
Detwiler, Charles 12:18
Detwiler, Christian J. 24:49
Detzell, F. 19:250
Detzon, Mathew 27:39
Deuble, Sebastian 12:18
Deubner, John P. 22:278
Deubois, Isaac 1:27
Deuce, Wesley 22:27
Deuel, Daniel 20:106
Deulke, S. 23:285
Deun, J. H. 10:49
Deury, H. 27:37
Deuschle, George 23:64
Deuse, T. 1:124
Deusinbar, John 8:47
Deutsh, George 9:155
Deval, Olney 8:83
Devall, Elias 9:118; 27:37
Devalt, Henry 20:238
Devalt, M. 14:54
Devan, Charles A. 23:285
Devan, George W. 3:58

Devan, James 12:18
DeVan, Joseph 18:80
Devan, Robert W. 25:163
Devan, William 6:15
DeVan, William 18:80
Devance, B. 13:130; 20:238
Devaney, Owen 4:20
Devans, Henry 15:2
Devans, W. E. 13:79
Devans, William E. 16:186
Devare, Solomon 10:49
Devatt, Henry 10:49
Devaugn, Samuel 21:50
Devaul, Moses H. 23:202
DeVault, Andrew 24:49
DeVault, Frank 22:248
Devault, J. 11:142
Devault, Simon H. 20:21
Devausa, William 23:64
Deveaux, Joseph 6:27
Develin, A. 3:58
Develin, E. 16:93
Develin, Michael 10:110; 20:239
Develin, Patrick 19:237
Develin, William 22:141
Deven, George 16:186
Devendorf, A. 11:301
Devendorf, J. 7:49
Deveney, John 15:352; 16:278
Devenport, John W. 27:143
Devens, John 17:109
Devens, Theodore 23:120
Devenshier, John 9:130
Dever, Alney 18:205
Dever, Benjamin 11:56
Dever, Columbus 23:259
Dever, E. 19:237
Dever, Edward 24:16
Dever, George P. 9:242
Dever, J. M. 18:48
Dever, J. W. 10:179; 18:173
Dever, M. 16:186
Dever, R. 13:81; 16:186
Dever, William N. 7:24
Deveraeux, Albert E. 22:27
Deveraux, --- 12:18
Deveraux, Henry 22:141
Deveraux, W. 1:29
Deverax, Joseph 26:157
Devere, Solomon 20:239
Devereaux, --- 2:10
Devereaux, Dwight M. 23:189
Devereaux, George 4:20

Devereaux, Joseph 8:38
Devereaux, Ralph 20:39
Devereux, Frank 16:77
Devereux, J. 1:126
Deverey, Pat 20:239
Deverick, Philip 23:15
Devericks, John H. 23:64
Deverney, H. 3:58
Devers, H. T. 20:239
Devery, Patrick 10:49
Devery, S. 17:290
Devese, Joseph 22:74
Devet, Christ 11:201
Devez, A. 1:29
Devil, Charles 3:58
Devilbirs, George 26:96
Devilbiss, George 18:304
Devilin, William 22:233
Deville, Francis 9:174
Devin, Charles 13:19
Devin, J. 3:58
Devin, M. 10:27
Devine, --- 12:172
Devine, A. 1:124
Devine, A. B. 21:323
Devine, Abraham 26:23
Devine, Ami 5:14
Devine, Barnard 19:11
Devine, Clark 10:49;
    20:239
Devine, D. S. 5:14
Devine, George 3:223;
    17:78, 499
Devine, J. 5:50; 16:291;
    19:250; 25:163
Devine, John 7:16; 9:174;
    12:91; 21:269
Devine, M. 16:186;
    19:301
Devine, Martin 4:20
Devine, Michael 22:27
Devine, Patrick 10:159
Devine, Peter 22:519
Devine, Robert 4:20
Devine, Thomas 9:240;
    16:93
Devine, William 9:130;
    21:201; 27:36
Deving, Thomas 21:223
DeVinney, J. W. 21:23
Devinney, Philip S. 19:65
Devinny, Aaron B. 22:74
Devins, George 25:163
Devins, Henry A. 18:271
Devins, Michael 9:174
Devins, Silas D. 9:20
Devire, A. 16:278
Devit, T. C. 14:297;
    17:469; 27:38
Devits, G. 3:58
Devitt, A. 25:28

Devley, J. 3:58
Devlin, Alex 12:18
Devlin, E. 3:58
Devlin, Edward 4:20
Devlin, F. 11:91
Devlin, George 10:159;
    19:159
Devlin, Henry 12:18
Devlin, I. 3:58
Devlin, Isaac 9:159
Devlin, J. 17:14
Devlin, J. A. 19:250
Devlin, John 9:9; 17:212;
    21:323; 23:64
Devlin, John J. 24:8
Devlin, Joseph 1:27;
    12:18
Devlin, Michael 16:278
Devlin, Patrick 9:174;
    12:18
Devlin, Patrick S. 25:27
Devlin, S. 13:63
Devo, Henry 14:54
Devoe, Daniel S. 15:193
Devoe, Isaac J. 16:29
Devoe, John 1:28
DeVoe, John 22:278
Devoe, Joseph 8:104
Devoe, William 8:104
Devoir, Edward 21:120
Devol, Edw. P. 18:291
Devolie, Lewis 18:305
Devolle, Lewis 26:96
Devolt, Joseph H. 9:219;
    18:365
Devon, John 16:118
Devon, Joseph 6:27
Devon, T. John 22:333
Devond, Henry 22:296
Devons, J. B. 11:125
Devonshire, Joseph 27:36
Devor, Robert 17:78
Devor, Thompson J. W.
    23:11
Devora, C. W. 26:157
Devore, Cornelius 21:115
Devore, Henry 17:78
Devore, Isaac 23:11
Devore, Isaac J. 13:19
Devore, N. 21:23
Devore, William 22:112
Devort, Cyrus C. 12:18
Devort, John 8:59
Devos, Job T. 10:90
DeVos, P. 16:93
Devour, William K.
    14:158
Devoy, Calvin 16:29
Devoyes, Henry 12:99
Devren, William 14:297
Devul, J. H. 20:55

Devurd, J. 1:123
Dew, Andrew J. 10:110;
    20:239
Dew, Gershom 17:46
Dewal, E. P. 26:96
Dewalt, D. S. 14:158
Dewalt, Henry 23:27
Dewalt, John 19:11
Dewalt, Robert 22:188
Dewar, A. 25:163
Dewar, Joseph 13:19
DeWaters, Joseph 11:104
Dewberry, Charles 17:352
Dewberry, J. 13:87; 14:8
Dewear, Andrew C.
    11:144
Dewease, Irwin 17:51
Dewees, Benjamin F.
    23:64
Dewees, Caleb 16:132
Dewees, John W. 18:130
Deweese, C. S. 18:48
Deweese, John 20:185
Deweese, W. L. 20:239
Deweese, William L.
    10:49
Dewel, David 10:110
Dewel, Henry 20:239
Dewel, J. W. 10:49
Dewell, Alfred 22:462
Dewell, David 20:239
Dewell, George A. 12:18
Dewell, Henry 10:49
Dewell, J. E. 17:442;
    24:157
Dewell, J. W. 20:239
Dewell, Peter 9:118
Dewell, Samuel 15:193
Dewella, Charles 11:57
Dewes, C. 14:8
Dewese, P. 21:120
DeWest, Thomas 23:140
Dewett, Cornelius 9:130
Dewey, C. 15:122
Dewey, Calvin 13:19
Dewey, Clinton 22:141
Dewey, Curtis E. 25:163
Dewey, Daniel D. 15:55
Dewey, Edwin 13:108
Dewey, Erastus 17:200
Dewey, F. 25:319
Dewey, Francis 21:252
Dewey, Frank 8:14;
    10:204
Dewey, G. W. 7:24
Dewey, H. A. 19:159
Dewey, J. 7:81; 25:295
Dewey, J. J. 1:123
Dewey, James H. 10:110;
    20:239
Dewey, John W. 23:87

Dewey, M. 1:125
Dewey, Moses 26:25
Dewey, Orville S. 16:11
Dewey, Otis C. 13:19
Dewey, R. C. 1:126
Dewey, Reuben S. 12:18
Dewey, S. H. 25:163
Dewey, Thomas 12:18;
    19:65
Dewey, W. F. 8:47
Dewey, William 10:26;
    18:394
Dewhurst, Horsfall 10:159
Dewight, Mygatt 14:158
DeWilt, Reuben 8:83
DeWire, W. 19:11
Dewison, John 22:296
DeWit, Andrew 16:93
Dewits, John 10:49
Dewitt, A. 22:187
Dewitt, Abner 21:67
Dewitt, Alfred O. 21:223
Dewitt, C. 16:29
DeWitt, C. 23:27
Dewitt, C. S. 15:341;
    16:367
Dewitt, Columbus 13:19
Dewitt, Cornelius 27:36
DeWitt, D. 19:65
Dewitt, Daniel 5:14
Dewitt, David 14:331
Dewitt, Elepparz 27:39
Dewitt, Elijah R. 21:99
Dewitt, Ezery 20:239
Dewitt, Ezra 10:110
Dewitt, F. M. 18:394
Dewitt, George E. 4:20
Dewitt, J. E. 1:124
Dewitt, J. M. 13:87
Dewitt, Jacob 9:118
DeWitt, Jacob 27:37
DeWitt, James M. 17:51
Dewitt, John 8:47
DeWitt, John 10:49
Dewitt, John 10:110;
    20:239
Dewitt, John C. 11:279
Dewitt, Johnson C. 26:122
Dewitt, Johnson O. 9:42
Dewitt, Joseph 3:58
DeWitt, L. B. 5:14
Dewitt, Logan 11:276
Dewitt, M. 3:58
Dewitt, Oscar 22:187
Dewitt, Owen 17:316
DeWitt, S. C. 3:58
Dewitt, Simeons 7:24
Dewitt, Simon J. 21:67
DeWitt, Stephen 20:136
Dewitt, Thomas J. 23:27
Dewitt, W. H. 16:29

Dewitt, W. T. 20:239
DeWitt, William 13:57
Dewitt, William 13:108;
    22:74
Dewitt, William T. 10:49
Dewitts, Yancey 24:192
DeWitts, Yancy 17:130
DeWolf, A. 10:90; 20:239
DeWolf, Andrew 10:110
Dewolf, Andrew 20:239
Dewolf, C. 25:163
DeWolf, Charles 4:20;
    5:14
DeWolf, David 20:7
Dewolf, Delos 18:394
DeWolf, M. 1:27
DeWolff, Leon 25:288
Dewoss, N. 19:159
Dewrey, James 18:13
Dewrey, L. A. 3:58
Dews, C. 13:87
Dewsey, G. C. 25:163
Dewton, H. H. 11:57
Dewtraw, P. 25:163
Dewy, G. P. 25:29
Dewy, G. W. 14:335
DeWyne, William 4:20
Dexhamer, Jacob 19:65
Dexter, Albert 20:106
Dexter, Amos 23:106
Dexter, Charles 10:159;
    19:159
Dexter, Darius T. 12:18
Dexter, David 12:18
Dexter, F. E. 18:234;
    26:24
Dexter, George R. 10:15
Dexter, Ira 6:9; 18:109
Dexter, J. 3:58
Dexter, James K. P. 22:74
Dexter, Jeremiah 21:23
Dexter, Jesse 27:34
Dexter, Joseph 22:10
Dexter, Levi 13:19
Dexter, Norvon 4:20
Dexter, Samuel 15:94
Dexter, Thomas 10:159
Dexter, William E. 21:323
Dey, Amos 19:11
Dey, Austin 12:69
Dey, Austin H. 15:27
Dey, D. W. 5:50; 25:163
Dey, Frank 8:38; 26:157
Dey, James 18:189
Dey, Jerard 25:164
Dey, Reuben B. 24:177
Deyarman, John 15:86
Deyarmon, C. 1:126
Deyer, William 7:121
Deyman, J. 16:267
Deyo, David 7:16

Deyo, James A. 4:20
Deyo, Reuben 17:451
Deyo, William 6:15
DeYoung, J. W. 14:54
Deys, Robert 15:323;
    19:65
Dezaly, Charles 11:400
Dezarn, Jasper 17:202
Dezotell, William 18:365
Dhoetty, R. 25:164
Diabal, D. A. 25:28
Diaboct, G. R. 14:8
Dial, A. 24:76
Dial, E. 24:76
Dial, J. 16:186
Dial, John 22:27
Dial, L. D. 11:301
Dial, Phil 23:27
Dial, R. 3:58
Diamond, --- 15:122
Diamond, George 9:96
Diamond, James 17:78
Diamond, R. 1:27
Diamond, William 19:11
Diamond, William H.
    22:141
Dian, F. 14:8
Dias, George 14:158
Diaueaut, William 5:14
Dibben, Henry 23:202
Dibble, Alfred H. 16:88
Dibble, C. 25:30
Dibble, Charles J. 8:14;
    18:130
Dibble, David N. 23:120
Dibble, E. B. 14:54
Dibble, F. 3:58
Dibble, H. 14:277;
    21:323; 23:120
Dibble, J. 25:164
Dibble, John 23:189
Dibble, Joseph 5:14
Dibble, Julius 20:239
Dibble, Randall 10:49;
    20:239
Dibble, S. 11:332
Dibble, Spencer 9:160;
    27:38
Dibble, Wallace 20:189
Dibbs, Julius 10:110
Dibell, Moro W. 11:332
Dibert, C. H. 11:27
Dible, D. J. 16:367
Dible, M. 15:104
Dible, Sylvanus H 22:449
Dibley, William 14:158
Dibner, Lewis 14:158
Dibztil, L. 3:58
Dice, --- 10:159
Dice, Emory 14:158
Dice, Ezekiel J. 22:170

Dice, Francis 10:110; 20:239
Dice, George W. 11:143
Dice, Henry 10:110; 20:239
Dice, John 12:48
Diche, J. 15:165
Dichel, Espy 3:58
Dichmeyer, Christian 27:37
Dichouse, James W. 24:157
Dick, --- 9:174
Dick, Benjamin 3:58
Dick, C. L. 21:23
Dick, Charles 3:58
Dick, D. 1:126
Dick, David 22:74
Dick, Franklin M. 24:92
Dick, Henry 14:158; 23:308
Dick, Henry T. 11:142
Dick, James 24:49
Dick, John 9:174; 13:19
Dick, Leander 11:27
Dick, P. 13:108
Dick, Philip 10:49; 20:239
Dick, Richard 6:35
Dick, Robert 25:164
Dick, Samuel 22:74
Dick, Thomas 4:20
Dick, Thomas A. 21:136
Dick, W. M. 17:213
Dick, William 4:20; 11:321
Dickant, Frederick 9:20
Dickason, J. M. 20:239
Dickason, R. 20:145
Dickason, Samuel S. 16:29
Dicken, George W. 11:395
Dicken, Isaac 23:140
Dicken, John F. 7:24
Dicken, William J. 20:7
Dickens, A. 11:58
Dickens, Charles 3:58
Dickens, David 10:179
Dickens, Eli 25:164
Dickens, Ely 5:14
Dickens, Henry 22:477
Dickens, Jackson 22:523
Dickens, James 14:158
Dickens, Jefferson 21:147
Dickens, John 5:14
Dickens, Jonah 11:201
Dickens, Mathew 21:194
Dickens, Nelson 8:77
Dickens, S. F. 25:295
Dickens, Sherman 17:78

Dickens, William T. 26:157
Dickenson, A. H. 23:27
Dickenson, C. B. 18:235
Dickenson, G. W. 24:16
Dickenson, George V. 11:190
Dickenson, J. 1:29
Dickenson, J. C. 26:25
Dickenson, John 21:323; 24:76
Dickenson, Lafayette 22:188
Dickenson, Milton S. 9:33
Dickenson, Stephen 9:165
Dickenson, Thomas D. 4:20
Dicker, Fowler 4:20
Dicker, J. B. 18:305
Dicker, J. J. 17:144
Dicker, James W. 22:27
Dicker, L. H. 16:93
Dicker, L. T. 14:8
Dicker, M. 16:93
Dicker, Peter 5:14
Dicker, W. R. 25:164
Dicker, William 20:239
Dicker, William H. 23:106
Dickerhoff, C. 1:125
Dickerhoff, Daniel 22:188
Dickerhoff, John 22:74
Dickerman, C. H. 26:158
Dickerman, C. M. 8:62
Dickerman, I. 25:164
Dickerman, Joel C. 16:88
Dickerman, John P. 9:142
Dickerman, W. B. 3:58
Dickerson, Andrew 22:296
Dickerson, Daniel 12:152
Dickerson, David 17:276
Dickerson, Dick 22:512
Dickerson, E. A. 12:18
Dickerson, E. A. Q. 14:158
Dickerson, E. F. 10:15
Dickerson, Eli 22:477
Dickerson, Francis M. 22:27
Dickerson, G. 16:186
Dickerson, G. M. 5:38; 25:164
Dickerson, George 10:110; 20:239; 22:233
Dickerson, H. H. 8:83
Dickerson, Henry 7:92; 21:323
Dickerson, Henry C. 21:99
Dickerson, Isaac 12:18

Dickerson, Isom 21:215
Dickerson, J'h. 17:462
Dickerson, J. H. 7:92
Dickerson, J. W. 9:51; 10:49; 14:158; 20:239
Dickerson, Jackson 27:39
Dickerson, James 10:49; 11:200; 20:239
Dickerson, James D. 22:188
Dickerson, Jesse N. 22:74
Dickerson, John 8:100; 14:54; 22:188
Dickerson, John W. 23:87
Dickerson, Josephus 23:197
Dickerson, Joshua 24:177
Dickerson, Lee 22:296
Dickerson, M. 13:87; 16:267; 20:132
Dickerson, Martin L. 10:15
Dickerson, P. E. 1:27
Dickerson, Reuben 22:188
Dickerson, S. 25:164
Dickerson, Samuel C. 18:173
Dickerson, Silas M. 22:188
Dickerson, T. 16:186
Dickerson, Thomas 9:79; 12:69
Dickerson, W. 1:27; 17:174
Dickerson, W. R. 22:333
Dickerson, William 14:158
Dickerson, Wilson 17:130; 24:192
Dickerson, Zeddick 22:74
Dickert, Philip 10:49; 20:239
Dickey, B. 21:120
Dickey, Charles H. 16:29
Dickey, D. A. 23:27
Dickey, E. C. 25:319
Dickey, Edmon A. 20:239
Dickey, Edmund A. 10:110
Dickey, G. A. 16:139
Dickey, George 14:158; 23:308
Dickey, George S. 8:124
Dickey, J. C. 11:260; 14:158
Dickey, James 9:33; 18:394; 20:179; 21:269
Dickey, John 22:188
Dickey, Joseph M. 22:248

Dickey, Joseph P. 11:143
Dickey, Josiah 22:296
Dickey, L. W. 1:124
Dickey, M. 1:97
Dickey, Madison 7:67
Dickey, Orvin 12:69
Dickey, P. 21:129
Dickey, Philip 21:269
Dickey, R. J. 9:20
Dickey, Robert 17:95
Dickey, Robert D. 22:112
Dickey, Samuel 23:64
Dickey, W. A. 26:25
Dickey, William 9:79;
    17:32
Dickey, William H.
    10:110; 20:239
Dickhart, Fred 26:96
Dickhorner, William
    17:313
Dickins, David 18:173
Dickins, Jackson 16:367
Dickinson, C. 18:80
Dickinson, C. B. 26:24
Dickinson, Cornelius 6:15
Dickinson, D. 25:164
Dickinson, D. L. 7:24
Dickinson, E. 1:29;
    25:164
Dickinson, Edward
    22:171
Dickinson, F. 18:48;
    25:164
Dickinson, Franklin
    9:130; 27:36
Dickinson, George L.
    18:235; 26:23
Dickinson, Green 21:269
Dickinson, H. A. 19:237
Dickinson, J. H. 23:202
Dickinson, Jacob 3:58
Dickinson, James A.
    20:86
Dickinson, John H.
    21:323
Dickinson, L. A. 12:145
Dickinson, N. J. 1:125
Dickinson, Nathaniel
    11:385
Dickinson, Philander
    21:323
Dickinson, Robert 6:15;
    18:80
Dickinson, Thomas 15:22;
    23:120; 26:23
Dickinson, W. 3:58; 9:51;
    18:28
Dickinson, William 18:28;
    21:323
Dickinson, William T.
    22:141

Dickison, H. N. 17:217
Dickison, Samuel 7:49
Dickison, William 22:27
Dickman, A. 11:301
Dickman, B. 13:130;
    20:239
Dickman, Charles 17:422;
    24:166
Dickman, Charles C.
    14:158
Dickman, Francis 21:215
Dickman, J. 1:123
Dickman, John 11:286
Dickman, Val 11:143
Dickman, William 17:78
Dickon, Albert 9:20
Dicks, Andrew G. 24:38
Dicks, John B. 22:120
Dicks, Valentine 9:15
Dickson, A. 17:64
Dickson, Albert J. 21:99
Dickson, Alonzo 20:27
Dickson, Andrew 17:211
Dickson, Andy 20:145
Dickson, Archibald 7:56
Dickson, Booker 22:351
Dickson, D. 3:58
Dickson, Edward 4:20;
    25:29
Dickson, F. 12:87;
    16:291; 17:217
Dickson, George B. 12:19
Dickson, H. 16:291
Dickson, J. 1:125; 25:164
Dickson, J. M. 27:35
Dickson, Jackson 11:422
Dickson, James 17:144;
    21:323; 26:157
Dickson, James H. 18:305
Dickson, James W. 8:62;
    24:90
Dickson, Jerry 10:176;
    19:159
Dickson, John 7:121;
    14:158; 21:203;
    25:164
Dickson, John E. 15:16
Dickson, John W. 22:421
Dickson, Joseph H. 26:96
Dickson, M. 14:158
Dickson, Madison 22:477
Dickson, N. B. 10:49;
    20:239
Dickson, Nathaniel
    15:104
Dickson, Nathaniel S.
    17:411; 22:523
Dickson, Richard 19:159
Dickson, Rosell 4:20
Dickson, Samuel S. 13:19
Dickson, Sheldon 20:29

Dickson, Silas 17:418;
    24:157
Dickson, Simon A. 22:28
Dickson, Thomas 18:424
Dickson, Thomas E.
    23:279
Dickson, W. 11:28;
    22:333
Dickson, William 14:159;
    22:165
Dickson, William H.
    19:159
Dickson, William S.
    12:69; 15:65
Dickson, Willis 9:174;
    19:281
Dickwall, William 3:58
Dicky, Owen 15:11
Diclute, John 20:132
Dicy, Dana H. 19:65
Didamus, Thomas 17:235
Diddleton, Robert 18:202
Diddy, William 10:110;
    20:239
Diderick, L. M. 5:50
Didier, Jefferson F.
    25:332
Didlake, R. F. 15:338
Didlake, R. S. 15:354
Didler, J. F. 13:87
Didler, John S. 23:27
Didleton, Robert 26:210
Diebald, Stephen 19:159
Diebler, --- 16:367
Diebler, Henry 11:419
Diebold, Stephen 10:159
Diecenroth, Frank 16:93
Diecey, C. 3:58
Diedrick, Jacob 6:24
Diefe, August 22:296
Diefenbach, Paul 16:158
Dieffenbaugh, David
    16:137
Dieffendeffer, C. 14:159
Dieffendorf, E. 14:159
Diegal, John 26:25
Diegle, D. 9:142; 27:35
Diehl, Francis 15:309
Diehl, H. 27:34
Diehl, Henry 7:24
Diehl, Solomon 9:156
Diehouse, James W.
    17:442
Diehr, Frederick 16:145
Diel, Daniel 17:32;
    22:422
Diel, S. F. 3:58
Diell, English 14:130
Diemer, Henry 16:93
Diemon, James 21:323

Diendonnie, M. 12:69; 15:33
Diengan, James 21:323
Dierdorff, E. 1:29
Diereks, Henry 3:58
Dierfield, James H. 15:65
Dierkies, Charles 15:55
Dierling, Jacob 23:140
Dies, James 21:23
Diesch, John 22:28
Diet, F. 3:58
Dieter, John R. 24:88
Dieter, Lester 22:148
Dieterlen, Fred 18:305
Dietrich, C. 25:164
Dietrich, Joseph 22:10
Dietrick, C. 5:14
Dietrick, L. 16:93
Dietsick, J. 17:432
Diety, F. 25:28
Diety, L. S. 25:28
Diety, Moses 22:28
Dietz, Augustus 24:150
Dietz, Casper 13:108
Dietz, Henry 25:268
Dietz, James 18:205
Dietz, John Y. B. 26:219
Dietz, William 27:35
Diew, Dennis 9:207
Diezal, John 9:79
Dife, John 23:308
Difendof, R. 3:58
Diffenbaugh, John K. 11:143
Diffield, Thomas 18:48
Diffin, Richard 23:308
Digan, T. N. 1:124
Digby, Hamilton 14:54
Digby, J. M. 11:239
Diggins, Alonzo 24:49
Diggs, Albert 11:83
Diggs, David M. 10:95
Diggs, Edward 6:15; 18:80
Diggs, Frank 12:48
Diggs, George C. W. 22:422
Diggs, Giles 27:144
Diggs, J. 8:83; 25:164
Diggs, J. G. 3:58
Diggs, James A. 8:14; 18:130
Diggs, John 9:9
Diggs, John G. 3:58
Diggs, Johnson 13:57
Diggs, L. 14:54
Diggs, William 9:34; 18:291; 26:96
Diggs, William H. 17:32
Dighton, Sevestus 7:92
Digman, H. 14:54

Digman, John 13:87; 14:8
Dignam, M. 14:159
Dignan, Andrew 17:459; 24:151
Dignan, Thomas 9:244
Dignew, Andrew 8:100
Dignon, S. 3:58
Digroot, Obediah 9:130
Digs, George 11:201
Dihery, T. 16:291
Dihring, Maximillian 19:329
Dike, Edgar 19:11
Dike, Henry 22:248
Dike, William H. 22:188
Dikeman, A. S. 18:272
Dikeman, Samuel P. 10:159; 19:159
Dikeman, T. 1:126
Dikes, James 18:80
Dikes, T. 14:240
Dikey, T. 12:92
Dikon, George 9:65
Dilan, Edward 3:58
Dilard, Taylor 11:386
Dilback, --- 18:412
Dilber, Jacob 16:93
Dilberd, Frank 23:308
Dilcan, W. H. 2:9
Dilcher, H. 12:95; 15:359
Dilchner, H. 19:65
Dildey, James 18:189
Dildine, Andrew J. 16:132
Dildine, J. 3:58
Dildine, John H. 7:67
Dildley, W. R. 11:125
Dile, --- 22:351
Dile, George W. 7:74
Dilenger, John 23:15
Diley, Clinton 9:34
Diley, Levi 9:96
Dilg, Jacob 11:301
Dilger, John 22:333
Dilk, --- 20:92
Dill, A. J. 1:125
Dill, Albert 22:188
Dill, Ambrose 7:92
Dill, C. H. 14:130; 15:273
Dill, C. P. 3:58
Dill, Calvin H. 19:11
Dill, Daniel W. 25:28
Dill, G. W. 25:295
Dill, J. 11:301
Dill, J. F. 11:255
Dill, John C. 21:67
Dill, John W. 8:83; 11:105
Dill, Knowles 18:412
Dill, Oveston 11:422
Dill, P. 11:28
Dill, S. 19:250

Dill, Samuel 11:200
Dill, Stephen 9:174
Dill, Thomas I. 10:49
Dill, Thomas J. 20:239
Dill, Thomas M. 10:49; 20:239
Dill, William B. 9:66; 18:275
Dill, William H. 7:24
Dill, Z. 3:58
Dillabaugh, Reuben 22:278
Dillaha, T. R. 9:51
Dillam, F. 15:341; 16:367
Dillan, Henry 12:152
Dillan, James A. 17:501
Dillara, Starling 18:205
Dillard, Burch 24:100
Dillard, Eli 24:16
Dillard, Elias 22:296
Dillard, John R. 11:186
Dillard, Joseph 6:22
Dillard, Martin 21:269
Dillard, P. M. 21:23
Dillard, R. H. 21:99
Dillard, Robert 7:92
Dillard, S. P. 21:147
Dillard, W. 21:23
Dillard, William 10:110; 20:239
Dillard, Zack 22:296
Dillarvay, Jeff 17:174
Dillason, Samuel 17:231
Dillaway, Granville 17:174
Dille, Charles 3:58
Dille, Louis 16:118
Dille, M. 12:98
Dille, W. H. 11:144
Dillemot, John 4:20
Dillen, Andrew 5:38
Dillen, Chamberlain 6:24
Dillen, Colion 24:16
Dillen, Isaac H. 21:23
Dillen, M. B. 24:16
Dillen, Matthew 17:440; 24:151
Dillen, Michael 9:12
Dillens, Jackson 15:341
Diller, A. 25:164
Diller, F. 3:58
Diller, O. M. 3:58
Diller, V. 19:265
Dilley, A. 14:159
Dilley, A. J. 18:235; 26:24
Dilley, Alson C. 23:140
Dilley, Avery 1:29
Dilley, Cyntan 26:97
Dilley, F. 1:27
Dilley, George W. 10:37

Dilley, H. 3:58; 22:188; 26:158
Dilley, I. 5:14
Dilley, J. 25:164
Dilley, Jonathan 9:34; 23:285
Dilley, Thomas B. 18:394
Dilley, W. H. 23:27
Dilley, Z. 8:62
Dillian, P. E. 11:28
Dilliard, Francis M. 21:216
Dilliard, Moses 26:157
Dilliard, R. H. 8:47
Dillick, August 15:193
Dillie, M. 15:357; 16:278
Dillihunt, William 12:69
Dillinder, John N. 10:110
Dillinder, John W. 20:239
Dilling, Henry 7:92
Dilling, James D. 14:159
Dilling, Meredith 20:239
Dillinger, Daniel 15:193
Dillinger, John G. 11:56
Dillinger, John S. 23:140
Dillinger, Oscar 18:130
Dillingham, --- 19:270
Dillingham, Albert 25:271
Dillingham, Albert M. 14:319
Dillingham, Benjamin 9:174; 19:226
Dillingham, Derrane 8:83
Dillingham, E. H. 13:63; 16:186
Dillingham, Edwin 7:8
Dillingham, J. M. 3:58
Dillingham, James 9:174
Dillingham, Jerome B. 21:223
Dillingham, John G. 12:19
Dillingham, L. 15:122
Dillingham, Richard 18:216
Dillingham, Samuel 4:20
Dillingham, Samuel J. 27:37
Dillingham, Sidney 9:230; 20:239
Dillingham, W. O. 3:58
Dillings, Aaron R. 11:238
Dillion, D. H. 25:276
Dillion, J. 25:276
Dillizlyham, J. E. 23:303
Dillman, Adams 19:159
Dillman, Charles 10:9
Dillman, H. 14:54
Dillman, William O. 17:19
Dillmann, John 4:20
Dillmore, Jacob 25:28

Dillon, A. A. 1:125
Dillon, A. I. 15:193
Dillon, Alfred 10:95
Dillon, B. E. 7:49
Dillon, D. 18:48
Dillon, D. H. 14:319
Dillon, E. T. 11:91
Dillon, E. W. 11:56
Dillon, Eli H. 23:285
Dillon, Elijah 23:87
Dillon, Francis 18:130
Dillon, Frank 7:92
Dillon, G. W. 25:274
Dillon, George W. 1:28
Dillon, H. 21:186
Dillon, Isaiah N. 23:140
Dillon, J. 1:28, 125; 14:255
Dillon, J. D. 11:239
Dillon, James 23:140; 25:268
Dillon, James P. 22:188
Dillon, John 7:49; 21:109, 323
Dillon, Joseph 6:15; 7:49; 18:80; 21:23
Dillon, Levi 10:49
Dillon, M. 1:125
Dillon, M. T. 4:20
Dillon, Michael 25:295
Dillon, Newton 22:403
Dillon, P. 1:125
Dillon, Patrick 10:15
Dillon, Richard 25:164
Dillon, Thomas 17:51
Dillon, Timothy 16:186
Dillon, W. 1:123; 22:188
Dillon, W. B. 14:54
Dillon, W. H. 14:159, 255
Dillon, William 4:65; 10:146
Dillone, J. 14:281
Dillow, A. 21:23
Dillwood, Alonzo 17:51
Dillworth, J. J. 14:54
Dilly, Cyrinton 18:291
Dilly, J. 1:126
Dilly, Jonathan 18:291; 26:97
Dilly, W. 15:158
Dillyon, James 13:19
Dilman, James T. 17:276
Dilman, Oliver 11:386
Dilmoith, J. Q. A. 9:242
Dilridge, Adam 17:190
Dilthey, F. 26:25
Dilthy, Ferdinand 9:79
Dilthy, John M. 24:65
Dilton, George 18:13
Dilton, Michael 7:81
Dilts, Charles J. 24:16

Dilts, Herman H. 24:16
Dilts, Nathan 23:140
Dilts, Peter D. 20:7
Dilwood, Daniel 9:161
Dilworth, George M. 24:58
Dilworth, John R. 11:56
Dilworth, R. S. 23:140
Dim, W. F. 12:87
Dim, William F. 16:291
Diman, Robert 22:296
Dimes, Martin 20:240
Dimes, R. 11:239
Dimham, L. 3:58
Dimick, Edward 18:334
Dimick, Edward A. 19:273
Diming, Michael 21:240
Diminick, M. 1:123
Dimit, Elias 23:140
Dimit, W. C. 25:319
Dimitton, W. J. 11:57
Dimm, F. A. 23:27
Dimm, J. 3:58
Dimmica, C. S. 10:147
Dimmick, Edw. A. 9:174
Dimmick, G. H. 3:58
Dimmick, H. 15:304
Dimmick, Harvey M. 20:7
Dimmitt, William H. 20:96
Dimmons, John 14:54
Dimon, A. 19:266
Dimon, Arthur 9:174
Dimon, F. B. 26:156
Dimond, --- 25:27; 27:157
Dimond, F. 3:58
Dimond, J. P. 25:27
Dimond, James 25:287
Dimond, Sidney B. 15:193
Dimond, Vincent 20:240
Dimum, Stephen P. 18:130
Dinan, Patrick 26:244
Dinckhardt, George 13:19
Dinden, William 22:296
Dinder, Hiram 4:20
Dindon, Edwin 17:352
Dine, John 12:19
Dinelli, Angelo 21:9
Dines, James A. 23:140
Dinfel, John 13:19
Ding, Lewis 5:14
Dingal, Benjamin 16:186
Dingby, C. 3:59
Dinge, Charles 19:250
Dingee, C. H. 21:114
Dingee, James 18:13
Dinger, Reuben 23:87
Dingfelter, Conrad 18:235

Dingle, Joseph 12:167
Dingle, O. 3:59
Dingle, Samuel 19:11
Dingler, Daniel 5:14
Dingler, Selena 26:244
Dingley, --- 23:27
Dingman, A. W. 1:126
Dingman, Alonzo 25:164
Dingman, D. 1:124
Dingman, Edward 10:7
Dingman, Elijah 15:193
Dingman, H. H. 8:113
Dingman, J. 1:124
Dingman, John 22:233, 421
Dingman, Levi 20:7
Dingman, Peter 17:319
Dingman, W. D. 14:159
Dingman, William 3:59; 7:92
Dingmon, Lorenzo 11:105
Dingo, Smith 16:186
Dingre, Franklin 14:159
Dings, L. 25:164
Dings, M. 11:142
Dings, W. 21:323
Dingus, David C. 17:259
Dingus, Thomas 18:81
Dinkele, John 16:367
Dinkins, J. W. 11:142
Dinkins, James 20:96
Dinkle, L. 1:126
Dinley, John 11:142
Dinn, John 3:59
Dinn, Patrick 3:59
Dinneson, M. 1:123
Dinnick, Wallace A. 24:49
Dinning, Henry 22:120
Dinnis, Josiah 11:428
Dinock, Ira 20:112
Dinsamore, S. F. 3:59
Dinser, Charles 18:13
Dinsimore, Daniel 26:158
Dinslow, B. F. 3:59
Dinsmore, E. H. 18:271
Dinsmore, F. H. 22:188
Dinsmore, Francis M. 23:64
Dinsmore, G. W. 14:54
Dinsmore, George 21:323
Dinsmore, J. S. 14:8
Dinsmore, James F. 17:418; 24:157
Dinsmore, John 14:54
Dinsmore, Oliver J. 18:205
Dinsmore, Peter O. 22:28
Dinsmore, Samuel J. 22:188
Dinsmore, W. H. 12:58
Dinsmore, W. T. 11:260

Dinsmore, William 13:19, 87
Dinsmore, William H. 16:154
Dinst, John 13:19
Dinston, Peter 9:157
Dintinger, Charles 14:159
Dinton, M. 3:59
Dinum, M. 11:326
Dinwiddie, J. 21:24
Dinwiddie, R. 9:51
Dinwiddle, Benjamin 6:20
Dinwiddle, Simon E. 20:22
Dinwidle, A. 11:260
Dinzman, Alonza 15:151
Diogfelter, Conrad 26:24
Diona, Romeo 19:319
Diper, O. 3:59
Dipon, Thomas 26:24
Dippart, John H. 18:130
Dipper, J. 12:92; 16:291
Dipper, James 14:54
Dipple, S. 3:59
Dippler, Joseph 11:427
Dippolt, John 16:84
Dipson, Thomas 18:235
Dirby, Henry 21:323
Dire, Charles 11:201
Dirett, Peter 14:159
Diribachter, John 23:120
Diring, Thomas 8:83
Dirkens, --- 24:16
Dirkman, Henry 11:125
Dirnick, H. 16:186
Diro, O. 18:235; 26:23
Dirr, H. H. 20:154
Dirrim, James G. 20:96
Dirst, Herman 22:421
Dirst, Sylvester 11:142
Dirt, Isom 22:296
Dirt, James 12:48
Dirt Seller 25:332
Dirt Thrower 25:332
Dirth, C. 3:59
Dirts, James 12:152
Disart, John B. 11:301
Disborm, A. 20:240
Disbro, --- 15:193
Disbroe, J. P. 3:59
Disbron, William 12:19
Disbrow, Abraham 10:110; 20:240
Disbrow, Albert 15:165
Disbrow, Charles 14:159
Disbrow, Frederick 19:159
Disbrow, G. W. 14:159
Disbrow, George 14:159
Disbrow, H. 15:332; 19:65

Disbrow, Lemeul S. 23:64
Disbrow, Peter W. 23:140
Disbrow, W. 25:164
Disbrow, William 5:14
Disby, William 9:20
Disch, John 9:174
Discoll, H. C. 3:59
Dise, Daniel 12:69
Diseal, Alexander 7:24
Diselms, R. 11:142
Disemling, J. W. 18:235; 26:24
Disgue, John 11:57
Dish, Andrew 23:27
Disharoon, James 7:49
Disher, Thomas 11:411
Dishinger, Christian 9:118
Dishler, Edward 8:14; 18:130
Dishman, --- 16:186
Dishman, Andrew 16:29
Dishman, J. C. 17:147
Dishman, Lewis 17:252
Dishner, Francis 11:143
Dishon, Jacob 17:316
Dishong, George W. 10:159; 19:160
Dishong, Israel D. 14:159
Dishrow, A. 10:50
Dishrow, Theodore 9:9
Disinger, Frank 18:48
Disinger, Henry 21:323
Dismald, D. 14:8
Dismany, William 17:51
Dismond, John 11:125
Dismore, Nathaniel 27:37
Dismow, Nathaniel 9:118
Disney, Charles 23:64
Disney, E. W. 3:59
Disney, Judson 7:92
Disney, L. L. 17:318
Disney, Patrick 17:389
Disort, Richard 25:164
Dispenett, Newton 16:29
Dissenger, Sol 15:193
Dissmore, T. 27:34
Disterheff, John C. 22:478
Distill, Nacious 24:100
Ditch, Henry 22:333
Ditch, John 13:87
Diterly, W. 15:165
Ditman, H. 1:123
Ditner, John 14:159
Dito, G. 16:267
Ditrick, Charles 14:159
Dits, John 3:59
Ditson, B. 11:339
Ditter, B. T. 11:142
Ditter, C. 8:47
Ditter, Colander 21:91
Ditterline, C. 1:29

Ditterly, Martin 17:279
Dittesline, John F. 25:271
Dittey, John P. 12:152
Dittherb, Frederick 4:20
Dittman, Emiel 25:27
Dittman, H. 1:29
Dittman, Henry 12:19
Dittman, N. 1:125
Dittmore, Francis M. 23:97
Dittmyre, George 17:494
Ditto, Davis D. 22:188
Ditto, James W. 24:16
Ditto, Jefferson 20:240
Ditto, John 3:59
Ditto, Michael 23:87
Ditto, Miles 8:38; 26:157
Ditweller, Samuel 9:20
Ditzel, Christ'r 22:233
Ditzer, Robert 17:32
Ditzler, J. 22:188
Ditzlor, George W. 24:38
Divan, Walter 23:189
Divan, William A. 17:323
Divel, John 25:27
Divelbliss, Caleb 20:7
Dively, George 22:422
Dively, Lorenzo 17:316
Divenny, Add. G. 7:92
Diver, C. 3:59
Diver, Edward 9:174; 21:323
Diver, Isaac 7:92
Diver, J. 3:59
Diver, Thomse C. 16:152
Dividina, Charles 18:235; 26:23
Divier, J. 1:29
Divilbiss, John 20:240
Divine, Charles 19:321
Divine, David 8:83; 13:19; 25:276
Divine, G. 21:120
Divine, James 10:50, 147; 20:240
Divine, McKey 12:19
Divine, Michael 13:108; 18:365
Divine, Patrick 19:160
Divine, Patrick C. 21:9
Divine, Samuel D. 13:130
Divine, Silas D. 18:305; 26:96
Diving, George 11:419
Divit, Thomas 16:139
Divoll, Charles P. 4:20
Divoll, George W. 21:323
Divon, Francis 14:159
Dix, --- 9:230; 16:71; 20:240

Dix, Daniel 15:278; 25:164
Dix, George 3:59; 7:71
Dix, George F. 22:112
Dix, John P. 17:323
Dix, Miles A. 17:78
Dix, Philip 8:119
Dix, Willis 17:174
Dixen, William 20:240
Dixey, Moses 10:176
Dixie, Christopher 21:323
Dixie, Moses 19:160
Dixon, --- 8:38; 26:157
Dixon, A. 15:172; 27:38
Dixon, Abraham 16:186
Dixon, Albert E. 16:152
Dixon, Alex 15:165
Dixon, Allen S. 9:236; 26:218
Dixon, Alonzo 17:287
Dixon, Andrew 21:67
Dixon, Azariah 27:38
Dixon, B. 3:59
Dixon, C. 1:126
Dixon, Caesar 11:200
Dixon, Charles 8:47; 21:323
Dixon, Clay 6:15, 22; 18:80
Dixon, E. 1:125; 11:260
Dixon, Elisha H. 20:122
Dixon, F. M. 20:154
Dixon, Felton 17:205
Dixon, Frank 5:38
Dixon, G. J. 7:24
Dixon, George 16:186; 24:92
Dixon, George L. 17:235
Dixon, George W. 8:83; 10:110; 20:240
Dixon, H. 5:14
Dixon, Harper 11:201
Dixon, Henry A. 8:83
Dixon, Horace 21:324
Dixon, Ira G. 17:279
Dixon, J. 1:124; 3:59; 17:231; 23:11; 27:35
Dixon, J. N. 14:55
Dixon, James 1:29; 11:411; 17:359; 19:65; 20:55
Dixon, James M. C. 22:74
Dixon, John 3:59; 9:142; 22:477
Dixon, John J. 16:29
Dixon, John Q. 11:57
Dixon, Joseph K. 23:87
Dixon, Lewis 27:38
Dixon, M. 26:23
Dixon, Martin 9:79
Dixon, Michael F. 20:240

Dixon, Moses 19:321; 21:324
Dixon, Oliver B. 21:324
Dixon, Peter 12:19
Dixon, Pleasant 21:269
Dixon, Polk 23:184
Dixon, Prince 21:147
Dixon, Robert 9:34; 18:291
Dixon, Robert A. 15:55
Dixon, Roland 10:159
Dixon, S. 14:55
Dixon, S. S. 23:140
Dixon, Sam 17:279
Dixon, Samuel Y. 5:14
Dixon, Stephen 16:186
Dixon, Theodore 7:92
Dixon, Thomas 14:55; 22:297; 24:193
Dixon, Thomas E. 9:227; 18:365
Dixon, Thomas J. 10:110; 20:240
Dixon, W. C. 1:29
Dixon, William 1:27; 8:100; 9:199; 10:50; 11:91; 13:19; 17:461; 18:81; 19:290; 22:297, 421; 24:164
Dixon, William C. 11:28
Dixon, William R. 11:57
Dixson, Robert 26:96
Dixson, S. Y. 25:164
Dixson, William 22:188
Djurken, Nittert 20:122
Dlawso, G. 1:125
Dlener, Jacob 13:79
Dnip, Ditrich 4:20
Doahue, A. 25:164
Doak, J. V. 3:59
Doaland, James 9:236
Doan, Christian A. 21:238
Doan, Franklin 16:186
Doan, J. 27:36
Doan, James 11:386
Doan, Joseph 24:16
Doan, Wilson 17:390
Doane, E. E. 16:186
Doane, Ed. I. 18:338
Doane, J. S. 19:160
Doane, Robert 10:50; 20:240
Doane, Van 24:100
Doane, William 7:92
Doap, M. 3:59
Doar, Phineas 3:59
Doban, Bemhard 9:20
Dobbin, John W. 12:19
Dobbin, Samuel 7:92
Dobbin, William H. 22:171

Dobbins, A. C. 22:512
Dobbins, Andrew 22:333
Dobbins, David 9:20;
18:320
Dobbins, Franklin 20:7
Dobbins, Fred 25:29
Dobbins, G. W. 27:35
Dobbins, George W.
9:142
Dobbins, Horace 25:29
Dobbins, J. 1:125
Dobbins, James 22:403
Dobbins, James T. 8:14;
18:131
Dobbins, John 10:50;
20:240
Dobbins, Lorenzo 21:324
Dobbins, Patrick 7:92
Dobbins, Thomas 15:33
Dobbins, William 21:324
Dobbins, William H.
21:136
Dobbins, William T.
23:306
Dobbs, G. B. 25:164
Dobbs, George W. 22:28
Dobbs, Jesse W. 10:110;
20:240
Dobbs, John 8:14; 18:131
Dobbs, Michael 25:164;
26:156
Dobbs, Paris 11:422
Dobby, Joseph 11:385
Dobel, E. 26:25
Dobel, Ernest 9:79
Dober, Joseph 22:28
Dobert, Frederick 14:159
Dobie, James C. 9:34;
26:97
Dobin, Peter 11:292
Dobins, J. M. 18:235;
26:24
Dobkins, H. S. 7:72
Doblan, William 22:248
Dobner, L. 7:24
Dobody, James 17:64
Dobratz, Charles 10:50;
20:240
Dobson, Andrew B. 17:51
Dobson, Calvin 11:57
Dobson, Daniel M.
18:216
Dobson, Elijah 12:160
Dobson, Frederick 25:28
Dobson, Henry 9:207;
26:25
Dobson, J. 19:65, 251
Dobson, J. M. 3:59
Dobson, J. R. 3:59
Dobson, Jacob 24:16

Dobson, James 11:122;
17:51
Dobson, James H. 18:81
Dobson, James M. 22:28
Dobson, John 14:55
Dobson, Joseph W.
22:248
Dobson, King 22:297
Dobson, Peter 17:51
Dobson, Taylor 22:248
Dobson, W. H. 20:240
Dobson, W. J. 9:96
Dobson, William H.
10:50; 23:97
Doby, Jessie 18:235
Docathy, Anthony 13:19
Docherty, Christopher
11:190
Docherty, David 25:164
Docherty, J. J. 24:65
Dock, Abram 18:205
Dock, C. 3:59
Dock, H. 22:297
Dock, Philip 9:42; 26:123
Dock, W. 13:63
Docken, Robert 19:45
Docker, John 25:164
Docker, Perry 18:28
Dockery, J. D. 7:24
Dockey, Doctor C. 21:24
Dockey, W. H. 18:131
Dockhall, J. H. 1:28
Dockham, George 19:65
Dockham, R. R. 1:124
Dockhem, George 15:359
Dockhen, George 12:95
Dockins, R. B. 17:307
Dockke, Frantz 7:92
Docksey, Joseph 21:324
Doctdorf, J. 14:55
Doctonbeer, Joseph 11:91
Doctsch, P. J. 2:9; 25:26
Dodd, A. 9:79
Dodd, A. G. 13:108
Dodd, Alfred 8:38; 26:157
Dodd, Benjamin 3:59
Dodd, Caleb 22:333
Dodd, Charles 3:59; 20:55
Dodd, Darius H. 21:50
Dodd, F. 21:12
Dodd, Francis S. 4:20
Dodd, G. W. 3:59
Dodd, George E. 21:223
Dodd, George W. 22:421
Dodd, H. H. 14:55
Dodd, H. M. 9:51
Dodd, Henderson 9:165;
25:319
Dodd, Henry 24:17
Dodd, J. 3:59
Dodd, J. A. 3:59

Dodd, James 10:192;
18:173
Dodd, John 10:50; 13:19;
14:55; 20:240
Dodd, John H. 8:105
Dodd, John L. 22:449
Dodd, John M. 4:20
Dodd, John T. 17:95
Dodd, Joseph 5:14
Dodd, Lewis 22:74
Dodd, M. 25:164
Dodd, N. A. 1:29
Dodd, Patterson P. 22:74
Dodd, R. 9:142; 27:35
Dodd, Robert 22:120
Dodd, S. 3:59; 8:14;
26:158
Dodd, Samuel 18:275
Dodd, Thomas 22:74
Dodd, Tilman 22:74
Dodd, W. 22:248
Dodd, W. C. 14:55
Dodd, W. H. 1:27;
17:346; 20:132, 240
Dodd, Wesley 11:105
Dodd, William 12:98
Dodd, William H. 10:50
Dodd, William H. H.
17:276
Dodd, William P. 20:22
Dodd, Zach 18:235; 26:24
Doddis, James L. 4:20
Doddridge, Benjamin F.
8:60
Doddridge, Julian B.
17:78
Dodds, C. 22:28
Dodds, F. 8:83
Dodds, Henry W. 7:25
Dodds, I. L. 15:193
Dodds, John 11:57
Dodds, John C. 15:122
Dodds, Joseph 10:110;
20:240
Dodds, Joseph H. 23:11
Dodds, T. H. 12:141;
20:240
Dodds, W. M. 21:166
Dodds, William 12:61;
15:22; 23:141
Dodds, William H. 24:38
Doddson, William 11:91
Dodean, Albert 9:79
Dodge, --- 3:59
Dodge, A. 14:159
Dodge, A. H. 1:28
Dodge, A. O. 7:8
Dodge, A. W. 14:321;
23:202
Dodge, Abram M. 17:359
Dodge, Addison 27:34

Dodge, Albert F. 20:189
Dodge, Albin 9:102
Dodge, Allen 11:142
Dodge, Benjamin H. 25:281
Dodge, C. F. 3:59
Dodge, C. L. 1:124
Dodge, C. R. 16:367
Dodge, Cassius C. 7:92
Dodge, Columbus 9:34
Dodge, David 25:164
Dodge, Davis 5:14
Dodge, Devill A. 11:125
Dodge, E. D. 17:152
Dodge, Edwin 6:15, 22; 18:81
Dodge, Eldridge 18:235; 26:25
Dodge, Elias 1:28
Dodge, F. C. 21:324
Dodge, Francis R. 13:19
Dodge, G. H. 15:172
Dodge, G. W. 21:324
Dodge, George W. 7:25
Dodge, H. H. 20:240
Dodge, Harmon 17:64
Dodge, Henry C. 15:2
Dodge, Henry H. 10:50
Dodge, Homer F. 22:141
Dodge, J. 11:57, 400; 20:55; 27:35
Dodge, J. P. 14:159
Dodge, J. R. 22:188
Dodge, Jacob 9:142
Dodge, James 1:26; 15:193
Dodge, James M. 9:20
Dodge, John A. 21:324
Dodge, John C. 21:120
Dodge, John M. 10:50; 20:240
Dodge, L. 25:164
Dodge, Leroy 19:11
Dodge, Lewis 25:164
Dodge, Luwellyne 5:14
Dodge, Lyman W. 19:160
Dodge, Lyrus 11:296
Dodge, Mathew 5:14
Dodge, Mordecia 26:24
Dodge, Mordica 18:235
Dodge, Norman 20:240
Dodge, Norman E. 10:110
Dodge, P. F. 21:324
Dodge, Peter 14:159
Dodge, Philip 18:338
Dodge, Ranson 12:19
Dodge, Silas 11:28
Dodge, Thomas A. 3:59
Dodge, William 17:276; 22:74
Dodge, William H. 10:15

Dodge, William R. 21:87
Dodge, Z. 14:55
Dodrick, Louis 3:59
Dodrick, William 17:401
Dodson, --- 10:186
Dodson, A. 21:147
Dodson, A. F. 17:364
Dodson, Albert 26:23
Dodson, C. 15:86
Dodson, Charles 12:69
Dodson, Daniel 22:28
Dodson, E. 3:59
Dodson, G. 22:297
Dodson, Geary 20:240
Dodson, George 11:422
Dodson, Henry 17:355
Dodson, J. T. 14:55
Dodson, James 18:468; 21:269
Dodson, James G. 21:216
Dodson, John S. 23:64
Dodson, Joseph 23:64
Dodson, R. 16:186
Dodson, R. B. 3:59
Dodson, Robert 21:269
Dodson, S. J. 19:65
Dodson, Samuel 22:297
Dodson, Samuel H. 9:219; 18:365
Dody, Alonzo A. 4:20
Doe, Andrew W. 9:7
Doe, C. A. 25:28
Doe, H. 17:158
Doe, L. B. 25:30
Doebling, Herman 26:123
Doebold, Francz 18:406
Doeld, Denis 17:469
Doeld, Dennis 14:297
Doer, S. 3:59
Doerathy, G. W. 13:87
Doerfler, G. C. 23:27
Doering, Charles 20:7
Doering, Julius 18:48
Doerlinger, --- 12:19
Doey, A. H. 22:161
Doffler, G. P. 14:55
Doffnlough, J. 14:55
Dogan, E. 1:124
Dogan, J. 1:127
Doge, John C. 8:47
Dogget, Philetus M. 19:160
Doggett, Benjamin W. 17:259
Doggett, George 14:55
Doggett, L. 3:59
Doggett, Philehis M. 10:159
Doggett, William 17:95
Dogherty, John 19:270
Dogherty, John H. 21:24

Dogherty, Patrick 19:265
Doging, F. N. 3:59
Doh, Christian 7:25
Dohany, James 24:72
Dohart, Seigel 18:235; 26:23
Doherty, Daniel 10:172; 11:28; 19:160
Doherty, J. 27:36
Doherty, John 5:55; 10:15
Doherty, Michael 16:84
Doherty, Niel 16:278
Doherty, Patrick B. 7:92
Doherty, W. 14:55
Dohl, J. 13:87
Dohn, P. 25:164
Dohu, Peter 5:14
Doig, David 21:50
Doig, John C. 11:15
Doile, Benjamin 14:159
Doile, John 13:108
Doilhasey, A. 9:96
Doine, J. 1:125
Doizier, George 6:15
Doizier, Joseph 6:15
Doke, Benjamin C. 22:141
Dokken, Knud O. 21:252
Dokken, Lars O. 22:278
Dolaher, James 16:9
Dolan, Arthur 24:17
Dolan, Barney 14:159
Dolan, Bernard 18:305; 26:96
Dolan, Charles 22:120
Dolan, David 21:324
Dolan, E. 15:172
Dolan, Edward 12:19
Dolan, Felix 27:34
Dolan, Hugh 7:25
Dolan, J. 1:103; 3:59; 11:28
Dolan, James 3:59; 4:20; 11:143; 12:19; 15:2; 26:211
Dolan, Jerry 23:120
Dolan, John 21:67, 201
Dolan, John J. 18:103
Dolan, M. 3:59
Dolan, Michael 5:14; 10:15; 25:165
Dolan, N. 25:165
Dolan, P. 3:59; 14:297; 17:475; 19:65; 25:165
Dolan, Pat 7:92; 15:172
Dolan, Perry F. 19:329
Dolan, Peter 5:14, 14:159; 18:81
Dolan, Robert A. 9:118

Dolan, Thomas 7:14; 11:332; 15:278; 21:324; 22:233; 25:165
Dolan, W. 19:251
Dolan, William 1:28; 9:174; 23:189
Doland, C. H. 25:165
Doland, Charles H. 5:38
Doland, Eugene 10:159
Doland, J. L. 21:120
Doland, John 14:159
Doland, L. 19:160; 25:165
Doland, Lewis 5:38
Doland, P. 21:109
Doland, R. W. 5:14
Doland, S. A. 25:165
Dolans, John 17:247
Dolas, Thomas 15:193
Dolbeck, Adolph 27:38
Dolbold, Franz 10:204
Dolde, Phil 15:193
Dole, Amos G. 19:237
Dole, Charles B. 3:59
Dole, E. H. 15:193
Dole, M. M. 9:230; 20:240
Doleck, --- 19:286
Dolelly, John 7:81
Dolen, J. 1:124
Dolen, N. F. 10:15
Dolen, William 26:123
Dolend, Peter A. 27:37
Doley, James 21:324
Doley, Thomas 13:108
Dolf, Sylvanus 3:59
Dolinger, Edward 9:66
Dolinger, William 5:55
Doliol, W. O. 22:351
Dolison, A. 9:219; 18:365
Dolittle, Norman 26:96
Dolittle, W. M. 20:240
Dolivan, John 9:174; 19:251
Doll, Edward 23:305
Doll, George 4:20
Doll, J. 14:8
Doll, Jacob 8:59; 19:273
Doll, Jacob H. 11:181
Doll, Joseph 21:99
Doll, L. 11:118
Doll, Peter 21:324
Doll, R. 3:59
Dollands, N. 9:154
Dollans, N. 27:35
Dollar, Levi Cash 9:34; 18:291
Dollar, Peter 22:278
Dollard, John 18:109
Dollenger, W. M. 24:99
Doller, Edward 17:109

Dolles, James 22:10
Dolley, Derby T. 7:92
Dolley, T. H. 9:174
Dolley, William A. 7:25
Dollibar, F. 1:125
Dolling, J. M. 27:143
Dolloway, Theodore 25:27
Dolman, Cyrus J. 23:141
Dolman, Lewis 27:144
Dolph, Davis 11:260
Dolph, F. G. 1:29
Dolph, John 15:193
Dolph, Joseph O. 20:183
Dolph, N. 21:324
Dolph, S. 3:59
Dolph, Simon 11:286
Dolph, W. H. 15:278
Dolph, William H. 25:165
Dolpheider, George 9:219
Dolphelder, George 18:365
Dolphin, Louis F. 17:434; 24:170
Dolphit, Henry 25:285
Dolsen, James M. 23:87
Dolson, Frank 15:33
Dolson, Fred 9:42
Dolson, Frederick 26:122
Dolson, John 9:174
Dolson, Samuel 19:45
Dolt, George 13:108
Dolt, John 12:69
Dolt, Martin 14:159
Dolt, P. M. 24:110
Dolterman, Henry 9:51
Dolthrop, George E. 10:110
Dolton, James 1:29
Dolton, John 10:147
Doluff, Lyman 9:109
Doly, J. 14:159
Doly, Jesse 26:24
Dolz, J. 3:59
Doman, Albert N. 22:165
Doman, C. 14:55
Doman, J. 14:55
Domanget, Perry H. 11:58
Dome, Elijah 23:64
Domeny, William 5:50
Domer, Joseph 12:92
Domers, Joseph 16:291
Domeust, G. W. 16:267
Domick, E. 3:59
Domina, Perry 24:107
Domine, Priest 13:19
Domine, William 19:329
Dominick, Leopold 22:188
Dominie, Priest 16:29
Dommas, F. 1:124

Dommey, David 11:385
Domolas, --- 19:66
Don, F. 14:55
Don, Hiram J. 11:28
Don, J. C. 25:27
Don, Joseph 20:29
Don, R. S. 6:30
Don, W. L. 1:29
Donaby, Dennis 12:19
Donagan, J. 1:126
Donagan, J. R. 14:55
Donagan, John 13:19
Donagan, M. 27:37
Donagan, Michael 14:159
Donagan, Patrick 10:147; 18:48
Donagha, J. 1:126
Donaghue, E. H. 19:11
Donaghy, W. 1:126
Donahoe, James 21:324
Donahoe, Preston 22:351
Donahoe, William 21:99
Donahue, --- 24:76
Donahue, Alexander 20:27
Donahue, Andrew 24:38
Donahue, Augustus 5:14
Donahue, Bartley 22:120
Donahue, Charles 9:79
Donahue, Daniel 4:21; 17:279; 20:102
Donahue, Francis 20:122
Donahue, Frank 25:30
Donahue, H. 3:60; 25:280
Donahue, Henry 18:81
Donahue, J. 12:19; 27:35
Donahue, James 23:87
Donahue, John 8:83; 22:28
Donahue, Martin 8:105
Donahue, P. 3:60; 25:271
Donahue, Patrick 19:316; 25:165
Donahue, Peter 4:21; 12:95
Donahue, S. 3:60
Donahue, T. 11:230
Donahue, Thomas 5:14; 12:19
Donahue, William 17:154
Donahue, Wilson Z. 22:28
Donahugh, John 7:93; 21:324
Donaigan, Thomas W. 15:193
Donaker, Charles 22:188
Donald, A. D. 11:181
Donald, Charles 4:21
Donald, Edward M. 12:19
Donald, J. 7:49
Donald, J. O. 15:559

Donald, J. P. 12:95
Donald, James M. 18:394
Donald, John 22:512
Donald, John M. 11:142
Donald, Kennis 7:121
Donald, Lewis 21:269
Donald, Martin 7:92
Donald, Moses 16:186
Donald, S. M. 1:97
Donald, Sangas 17:477
Donald, Sangus 27:38
Donald, Saugus 14:297
Donald, Seth A. 5:14
Donalds, E. 7:92
Donaldson, --- 25:26
Donaldson, A. M. 9:142
Donaldson, Amb. A.
   27:36
Donaldson, E. M. 26:158
Donaldson, Edward
   24:107
Donaldson, F. W. 7:72
Donaldson, George L.
   10:110; 20:240
Donaldson, J. 12:8;
   18:235; 23:27; 26:25
Donaldson, Jackson
   11:238
Donaldson, James 7:56;
   17:19; 23:141
Donaldson, James W.
   11:143
Donaldson, John 9:174;
   11:125; 14:159
Donaldson, Joseph 22:233
Donaldson, Michael 17:51
Donaldson, S. 1:28;
   14:281
Donaldson, S. P. 11:238
Donaldson, Samuel 21:84
Donaldson, Thomas
   22:297
Donaldson, W. 1:29
Donaldson, William 1:29;
   7:16, 121; 11:422
Donally, J. 14:8
Donally, John 19:160
Donally, Pat 24:166
Donalon, M. 3:60
Donalson, Charles G. 5:14
Donalson, James 18:394
Donalson, John 18:394
Donalson, Joshua 8:105
Donant, C. 2:10
Donarth, Herman 16:152
Donat, Thomas R. S.
   13:18
Donathan, Benjamin
   18:305; 26:96
Donaughen, J. 3:60
Donaval, Jerry B. 9:174

Donavan, Charles M. 4:21
Donavan, D. 22:74
Donavan, Daniel 5:14
Donavan, George 14:159
Donavan, J. 19:237
Donavan, J. V. 19:11
Donavan, John 9:174;
   27:143
Donavan, Mich 13:19
Donavan, Michael 12:58;
   22:233
Donavan, T. 12:81
Donavan, Tim 27:34
Donaway, J. 3:60
Donaway, John 18:235
Donaway, William 24:151
Doncaster, J. T. 23:281
Doncey, J. S. 11:57
Doncisen, William 4:21
Doncklefson, Christian
   4:21
Doncy, Richard 17:448
Dond, James 14:159
Dond, S. L. 1:125
Dond, T. 15:65
Dond, Wilbur 22:74
Dondall, B. 3:60
Dondel, Owen 23:27
Dondes, A. 9:242
Dondle, Robert 3:60
Dondna, B. S. 10:186
Done, Edw. J. 9:102
Done, Enos 7:74
Done, H. H. 1:123
Doneahoe, James 16:291
Doneal, Michael 4:21
Donegan, F. 1:27
Donegan, John 4:21
Donegan, Patrick 19:160
Donegan, Perry 17:174
Donegan, W. M. 1:29
Donegan, William 5:14;
   17:160
Donehoe, Peter 15:359
Donehoe, Thomas 18:291
Donehogh, Thomas 26:97
Donehon, F. 1:29
Donehue, James 5:50
Donehue, Michael 4:21
Donel, George W. 26:23
Donel, John H. 25:28
Donell, Austin 17:326
Donell, P. O. 15:193
Donelly, Arthur 13:81;
   16:186
Donelly, C. H. 13:19
Donelly, Edward 10:110;
   20:240
Donelly, George G. 7:83
Donelly, Owen 20:240
Donelly, Richard 7:83

Donelly, William 13:63
Donelson, D. C. 19:66
Donelson, James 24:157
Donelson, Lavan 18:412
Donelson, Lemuel 17:503
Donelson, P. 22:351
Donelson, W. C. 17:454
Donelson, Walter 15:33
Donelson, William
   11:301; 14:159
Donely, Phillip 16:278
Doner, T. 23:27
Dones, S. M. 3:60
Donetic, P. 12:81
Donetie, P. 16:291
Donetoff, Andio 25:165
Donevan, Michael 26:157
Donevan, Peter 23:279
Doney, J. W. 3:60
Doney, Paul 10:110;
   20:240
Doney, Wellington 22:278
Dongeison, John 22:188
Dongham, J. 1:126
Donham, Isaac 13:108
Donham, J. M. 20:132
Donham, J. P. 16:186
Donham, Reece 22:421
Donhouson, George 1:28
Donhue, T. 1:29
Donica, James 9:96
Donilly, B. 14:159
Donins, George 8:14
Donivan, D. 23:141
Donivan, George 9:239
Donivan, Richard 11:428
Donkan, S. O. 20:241
Donkle, Charles 23:141
Donklin, M. A. 12:141
Donlap, John 5:14
Donlean, James 12:152
Donless, B. F. 8:105
Donley, Alexander O.
   22:297
Donley, Benjamin 25:165
Donley, E. J. 3:60
Donley, Edward 15:33
Donley, George 22:233
Donley, James 3:60; 8:62;
   26:157
Donley, John 14:159;
   19:11
Donley, M. 3:60
Donley, Nelson 7:93
Donley, P. 1:124; 14:159
Donley, Stephen 22:74
Donley, Thomas 19:334
Donley, Walter 25:332
Donlin, J. 3:60
Donlon, James 13:124
Donly, Calvin 23:64

Donly, John 7:9
Donly, Samuel 11:200
Donn, Romaser 27:34
Donn, Valentine 14:159
Donn, Wallis 27:34
Donnahue, John 4:21
Donnahue, Jonathan 4:21
Donnahue, William 4:21
Donnal, J. 9:51
Donnally, Dudley 16:67
Donnally, J. 13:87
Donnally, James 18:103
Donnan, Andrew 5:50
Donnathy, J. A. 23:27
Donnavan, Jeremiah 4:21
Donnegan, James 16:29
Donnegan, Patrick 10:159
Donnel, James 8:62
Donnel, James L. 7:93
Donnell, --- 21:324
Donnell, F. 3:60
Donnell, F. W. 21:324
Donnell, George O.
    26:158
Donnell, Henry 9:42
Donnell, Hugh B. 9:118
Donnell, John 14:297;
    17:469; 27:38
Donnell, Joseph 22:74
Donnell, Joseph C. 20:189
Donnell, Michael M.
    25:165
Donnell, Michael O. 4:20
Donnell, Orin 14:159
Donnell, Patrick O.
    15:193
Donnell, Thomas O.
    15:283
Donnell, W. 3:60
Donnellan, Thomas 7:25
Donnelley, John 7:49
Donnelley, William
    20:241
Donnelly, C. 22:351
Donnelly, Charles 24:17
Donnelly, David 25:29
Donnelly, E. 11:385
Donnelly, Edward 4:20;
    12:69; 17:73, 130;
    24:192
Donnelly, George 25:285
Donnelly, George H.
    25:29
Donnelly, H. 1:28
Donnelly, Hugh 6:30;
    12:19; 19:11; 25:319
Donnelly, J. 1:126; 3:59;
    12:8
Donnelly, James 3:59;
    12:19; 13:19; 18:323

Donnelly, John 1:27;
    10:110, 159; 20:241;
    21:95; 22:519
Donnelly, Josiah 18:452
Donnelly, Owen 10:110
Donnelly, P. 1:29; 3:59
Donnelly, Patrick 17:266;
    19:160
Donnelly, Patrick H.
    20:39
Donnelly, Peter A. 18:275
Donnelly, Reuben 4:20
Donnelly, Samuel 25:295
Donnelly, T. D. 7:49
Donnelly, Thomas 20:174
Donnelly, William 10:50;
    22:333
Donnelon, James 22:10
Donnels, James 7:93
Donnelson, John 9:159
Donnelson, W. C. 24:186
Donnely, George 23:120
Donnely, James 4:21
Donnely, John 8:121
Donner, A. 17:64
Donner, D. 14:268
Donner, Job 13:19
Donner, M. 3:60
Donner, William 24:17
Donnety, C. A. 16:29
Donney, H. 3:60
Donney, Patrick 9:79
Donneyhas, T. 14:8
Donneyhue, T. 13:87
Donnie, D. 14:281
Donnitt, John 16:186
Donno, C. D. 14:55
Donnolly, Thomas J.
    23:97
Donns, M. 11:142
Donns, Nath 27:36
Donnwan, Patrick 12:168
Donoghey, John 14:55
Donoghue, William
    26:210
Donohae, J. D. 15:193
Donoho, John 27:39
Donoho, William 18:235
Donohoe, --- 15:33
Donohoe, Hugh 21:324
Donohoe, James 15:33
Donohoe, Jeremiah
    21:117
Donohoe, Thomas 21:324
Donohoe, William 26:24
Donohue, Barnard 17:470
Donohue, Bernard 14:297
Donohue, Edward 14:159
Donohue, H. 1:27;
    15:293; 16:186
Donohue, J. 7:25; 14:255

Donohue, James 7:25;
    17:51
Donohue, John 14:159;
    18:430; 22:10
Donohue, Michael
    14:160; 19:66
Donohue, P. 3:60
Donohue, Patrick 13:19;
    15:193
Donohue, Peter 19:66
Donohue, R. S. 13:108
Donohue, T. 25:165
Donohue, Thomas 1:28;
    13:19
Donoley, Michael 15:33
Donor, Frank 16:29
Donoran, M. 14:255
Donott, Ernest 14:160
Donough, Charles 11:125
Donovan, Alfred 18:284;
    26:134
Donovan, C. 1:127
Donovan, C. J. 7:49
Donovan, D. 3:60
Donovan, D. W. 12:122;
    15:105
Donovan, Daniel 15:105;
    25:165
Donovan, Francis 13:19
Donovan, G. H. 19:222
Donovan, J. 1:29; 3:60
Donovan, J. B. 19:278
Donovan, James 9:242
Donovan, John 16:291;
    18:48
Donovan, John A. 18:275
Donovan, M. 21:324
Donovan, Mich'l 22:248
Donovan, Michael 16:154
Donovan, Patrick 13:108
Donovan, Richard 21:324
Donovan, T. 16:291
Donovan, William 1:27;
    15:55
Donovan, William C.
    10:110; 20:241
Donoven, J. 23:178
Donoway, John 26:24
Donoway, William 17:440
Donriell, Moses 7:56
Donson, --- 11:230
Donst, S. M. 1:126
Dontaz, Alfred 14:321
Donth, Edward E. 8:14
Dontin, Patrick 15:359
Dontman, James 13:124
Donty, L. 16:186
Donyes, John 4:21
Doodenhafer, George
    14:160

Doodle, Henry 8:38; 26:157

Doodridge, Benjamin 12:170

Doody, John 7:49

Dooey, John 18:81

Doolan, --- 15:33

Doolan, John 17:279

Doolan, Patrick 13:19; 16:291

Dooland, James 26:218

Doolen, Patrick 10:15

Dooley, Attellus 19:266

Dooley, Charles Louis 20:136

Dooley, Henry G. 21:68

Dooley, I. 11:190

Dooley, Isaac 17:202

Dooley, James 1:28; 21:324; 22:248; 23:27

Dooley, John 7:49; 9:219; 17:389; 18:365

Dooley, Jonathan 12:152

Dooley, Leonard J. 7:56

Dooley, Oliver 26:23

Dooley, Philip 11:260

Dooley, Thomas W. 8:47

Dooley, William 14:55; 22:334

Dooley, William J. 21:68

Doolin, David 24:166

Doolin, William 17:435; 24:181

Dooling, Patrick 12:64; 15:33

Dooling, Richard 9:118; 27:37

Doolittle, A. W. 1:124

Doolittle, Alvin D. 22:422

Doolittle, C. 11:125

Doolittle, Charles 9:102

Doolittle, Charles F. 23:141

Doolittle, Egbert D. 10:110; 20:241

Doolittle, G. S. 3:60

Doolittle, G. W. 11:124

Doolittle, Henry 18:346

Doolittle, Ira 24:38

Doolittle, J. H. 11:286

Doolittle, Joel 8:83

Doolittle, Lorenzo S. 9:118; 27:37

Doolittle, M. B. 20:241

Doolittle, Marcus B. 10:50

Doolittle, N. J. 19:160

Doolittle, Norman 9:34; 18:291

Doolittle, Samuel H. 23:189

Doolittle, W. 3:60

Doolittle, William M. 10:50

Doolittle, Willis 22:233

Dooly, Benjamin F. 12:141

Dooly, James 3:60; 22:287

Doomas, M. 11:286

Doonane, Henry 19:45

Doop, H. 11:238

Door, Charles B. 12:19

Door, Frank 17:502

Door, Jackson C. 12:19

Door, John 13:108; 25:165

Door, P. 11:301

Door, W. W. 2:10

Doores, C. W. 18:365

Doorhamp, C. 9:96

Dootater, Levi 25:27

Dootey, A. 9:174

Dopke, F. 9:228; 18:365

Dopp, J. 11:286

Dopp, Lewis G. 11:125

Dora, John G. 13:19

Dorall, P. O. 16:267

Doram, James 3:60

Doram, McKum 3:60

Doramus, P. J. 12:19

Doran, Andrew 11:28

Doran, E. L. 9:109

Doran, George 9:219; 27:39

Doran, H. H. 3:60

Doran, Henry 1:27

Doran, Hugh 18:189

Doran, Isaac 1:28; 11:57

Doran, J. 1:126

Doran, J. M. 3:60

Doran, James 7:67; 16:93; 21:324

Doran, John 14:160; 19:12, 322

Doran, M. 10:95

Doran, Nelson 14:160

Doran, P. 3:60; 18:48

Doran, Silas 26:25

Doran, T. 16:186

Doran, Thomas 26:158

Doran, U. B. 19:329

Doran, Valentine 20:37

Doran, W. 9:142; 27:35

Dorbins, Robert 22:297

Dorbon, James 10:10

Dorcey, Curtis 22:74

Dorcey, John 17:357

Dorcey, John H. 21:324

Dorchester, H. S. 3:60

Dore, Clifford M. 10:176

Dore, H. L. 9:174; 19:232

Dore, J. 16:93

Dore, James N. 21:324

Dore, John 25:268

Dore, Patrick 23:120

Dored, Theodore 19:66

Doremire, George W. 4:21

Doremus, C. 1:29; 3:60

Doremus, Jacob 12:19

Doremus, W. 1:125

Doren, George 18:365

Dorenick, H. 20:241

Dorety, Michael 16:186

Dorety, Phil 26:157

Dorety, Phil. 8:38

Dorey, George 9:156

Dorey, William 22:334

Dorf, Ferdinand 14:55

Dorfe, E. 14:55

Dorfe, F. 14:55

Dorflin, John 14:55

Dorgan, James 9:214; 21:324

Dorgan, Jeremiah 19:281

Dorger, John 9:174

Dorherty, L. 14:262

Dorhman, Daniel 17:109

Dorie, Peter H. 11:28

Doris, J. 14:55

Dorithy, Anthony 16:29

Dority, C. E. 13:63; 19:66

Dority, J. 25:28

Dorkin, Thomas C. 11:279

Dorking, George 26:218

Dorland, A. N. 3:60

Dorley, Patrick 12:19

Dorliffe, J. T. 21:324

Dormady, Chr. 10:16

Dorman, Isaac E. 16:118

Dorman, J. M. 11:301

Dorman, Jesse A. 16:77

Dorman, John B. 19:12

Dorman, M. C. 9:20

Dorman, Nathaniel 21:199

Dorman, P. J. 15:122

Dorman, Patrick 15:193

Dorman, Philip 9:71

Dorman, William H. 21:194

Dorman, William M. 11:57

Dormity, M. 3:60

Dormity, P. 3:60

Dormody, William 16:367

Dormoy, G. 23:27

Dorms, William 17:279

Dorn, A. E. 11:239

Dorn, C. H. 18:330

Dorn, Charles H. 8:83, 116
Dorn, Emma M. 18:189
Dorn, John 11:144; 17:442; 24:157
Dorn, John J. 16:29
Dorn, L. P. C. 20:34
Dorn, Wendell 16:118
Dornholper, C. 14:160
Dornmoyer, L. 1:124
Dornon, Joseph 26:122
Dorohn, J. H. 15:193
Doron, Robert P. 3:57
Doroy, William 14:160
Dorr, Daniel G. 19:160
Dorr, E. B. 21:324
Dorr, H. A. 7:25
Dorr, H. C. 10:148; 18:48
Dorr, J. H. 7:49
Dorr, J. N. 21:324
Dorr, John D. 4:21; 20:106
Dorr, Joseph 19:160
Dorr, Luke 15:193
Dorr, Peter 20:106
Dorrah, W. W. 13:87
Dorrance, Alexander P. 24:49
Dorrance, William B. 13:19; 16:29
Dorrel, Arunt 27:37
Dorrel, Henry 20:7
Dorrel, J. M. 20:55
Dorrel, James M. 10:110; 20:241
Dorrell, Henry 7:25
Dorrell, J. 21:24
Dorrell, Sanders 7:121
Dorrigan, Patrick 9:66
Dorring, M. 1:123
Dorris, J. 18:235; 26:25
Dorrough, Joseph 21:223
Dorrow, B. 18:189
Dorrow, N. 14:8
Dorry, Samuel 7:121
Dorsan, G. F. 16:186
Dorsby, R. H. 9:240
Dorse, --- 16:186
Dorse, John 22:188
Dorset, Hanibal 16:93
Dorsett, Calvin H. 22:120
Dorsett, Clement 17:418; 24:157
Dorsey, A. L. 3:60
Dorsey, A. T. 23:141
Dorsey, Charles 10:90; 20:241
Dorsey, Charles W. 12:48
Dorsey, D. 15:13; 25:165; 27:34

Dorsey, Edward 1:28; 4:21; 9:207
Dorsey, Emanuel 12:48
Dorsey, Fred 16:187
Dorsey, G. 25:165
Dorsey, George 5:38
Dorsey, H. F. 22:403
Dorsey, Hamilton 11:218
Dorsey, Henry 1:191
Dorsey, Isaac 7:93
Dorsey, J. 1:27
Dorsey, J. C. 14:281
Dorsey, Jacob 7:121
Dorsey, James 12:122; 15:122; 23:141
Dorsey, James H. 17:205
Dorsey, Jeremiah 12:48
Dorsey, John H. 7:121
Dorsey, L. C. 25:165
Dorsey, Michael M. 18:205
Dorsey, N. 16:187
Dorsey, P. 25:165
Dorsey, Parker M. 17:205
Dorsey, Philip H. 6:23
Dorsey, R. J. 9:20
Dorsey, Samuel 15:194
Dorsey, Sullivan 4:65
Dorsey, Thomas 13:108
Dorsey, Thomas J. 8:83
Dorsey, Timothy 22:188
Dorsey, William 12:19; 16:115, 187
Dorsims, Jean B. 22:278
Dorsitt, W. D. 7:25
Dorson, B. 26:210
Dorson, George 14:160
Dorson, H. 4:21
Dorson, Henry 25:311
Dorson, J. 19:66
Dorson, L. 3:60
Dorson, Mitchell 8:14; 18:131
Dorson, Sam 7:121
Dorster, Frederick 27:39
Dorsy, Edward 4:21
Dorsy, John C. 23:27
Dort, C. R. 3:60
Dort, H. S. 14:160
Dort, Ira L. 20:7
Dort, R. 3:60
Dorther, William 11:201
Dorthup, George E. 20:241
Dortis, John 10:172; 19:160
Dortley, George 21:24
Dorus, Peter 18:13
Dorvet, Joseph W. 9:79
Dorwark, D. H. 26:23
Dorwin, C. 3:60

Dose, --- 15:33
Dosher, Henry 9:174
Dosier, Major 7:71
Dosier, Thomas 19:160
Dosile, Daniel 11:201
Dosk, J. 21:194
Doss, F. F. 18:48
Doss, G. W. 20:241
Doss, J. S. 3:60
Doss, Nicholas 22:477
Doss, Thomas S. 25:274
Dossett, Henry 11:385
Dossett, Robert 11:186
Dostee, John W. 8:84
Dosten, John 16:166
Dot, Levi 18:365
Doten, Edwin 18:365
Doten, J. W. 1:126
Dotherty, Michael 13:77
Dothiratie, C. 22:188
Dotler, Theodore 17:242
Dotn, P. E. 25:29
Dotre, Charles 1:29
Dotsey, J. 3:60
Dotson, A. 7:25
Dotson, C. Y. 10:110; 20:241
Dotson, David 20:103; 22:297
Dotson, Z. M. 20:241
Dotson, Zachariah M. 10:50
Dott, Abraham 5:38; 25:165
Dotter, M. 1:123
Dotter, Morris 17:247
Dotts, Eli 22:188
Dottson, John W. 17:349
Dotty, John 3:60
Doty, Benjamin 23:64
Doty, Daniel F. 22:477
Doty, E. E. 3:60
Doty, Edward 17:32
Doty, Elihu V. 22:10
Doty, Frank 16:187
Doty, G. W. 20:136
Doty, George 18:81
Doty, George F. 9:102
Doty, George W. 17:90
Doty, H. 17:174
Doty, Horace B. 24:61
Doty, J. H. 1:29
Doty, John 13:63; 16:187; 17:130; 24:192
Doty, John B. 24:65
Doty, Joshua M. 22:74
Doty, Julius 11:286
Doty, K. 16:118
Doty, Leonard 13:134; 19:346
Doty, Levi 9:219

Doty, Martin 22:477
Doty, Martin C. 17:242
Doty, N. 15:65
Doty, N. W. 10:26
Doty, Nathan W. 18:394
Doty, Nathaniel 12:69
Doty, S. 1:93
Doty, Samuel 9:21
Doty, Sidney 24:17
Doty, T. 1:125
Doty, Timothy F. 19:237
Doty, Willard A. 24:93
Doty, William 13:19;
  19:12; 24:38
Douavan, J. 27:34
Doub, George 8:14
Double Jack 25:332
Doubleday, Francis M.
  10:16
Doubleday, J. 25:165
Doubleday, J. H. 25:165
Doubleday, John H. 5:14
Doubleday, William O.
  16:81
Doubleset, I. 24:65
Doubty, Benjamin 23:309
Doucher, James 20:241
Doud, Alexander 18:394
Doud, Cordon P. 17:323
Doud, Daniel 3:61
Doud, Hiram S. 17:242
Doud, Lorenzo 25:165
Doud, Milo P. 17:323
Doud, Samuel 17:90
Doud, Theodore 13:63
Doude, Samuel 11:201
Doudes, Michael 8:14
Doudlan, Jesse 15:105
Doudy, Levin 15:288
Douer, Joseph F. 15:352
Dougal, James M. 27:157
Dougal, R. C. 1:28
Dougall, John E. 16:152
Dougan, James 4:21
Dougan, Turner 16:278
Dougerty, G. A. 18:235
Dougherty, --- 3:60; 8:71;
  16:135
Dougherty, A. 13:87;
  15:263
Dougherty, B. 25:165
Dougherty, Benjamin 5:14
Dougherty, Bernard
  10:159; 19:160
Dougherty, C. 1:124;
  25:29
Dougherty, Charles 10:50;
  20:241
Dougherty, Charles M.
  21:325

Dougherty, Cornelius
  12:19
Dougherty, D. 3:60
Dougherty, D. B. 3:60;
  8:14; 18:131
Dougherty, D. L. 5:14
Dougherty, Daniel 13:87;
  14:8
Dougherty, E. 14:160
Dougherty, E. L. 3:61
Dougherty, E. T. 3:61
Dougherty, Edward 9:71
Dougherty, Edward M.
  21:68
Dougherty, F. 3:61;
  14:160
Dougherty, F. V. 19:66
Dougherty, Felter 19:160
Dougherty, Ferrer 10:172
Dougherty, Francis
  11:118
Dougherty, Francis M.
  11:380
Dougherty, Frank 12:19
Dougherty, G. A. 26:25
Dougherty, G. W. 14:9
Dougherty, George 10:16;
  11:57; 14:160;
  21:147
Dougherty, H. 14:55
Dougherty, Henry 6:8;
  18:103; 19:66;
  21:223; 24:193
Dougherty, Hugh 15:65
Dougherty, J. 1:124, 126;
  3:60
Dougherty, J. B. 8:14;
  18:131
Dougherty, J. H. 1:124
Dougherty, J. J. 1:123
Dougherty, J. W. 13:87;
  14:9
Dougherty, James 8:71;
  10:110; 14:133;
  15:194; 16:115, 367;
  21:325; 23:11;
  25:165
Dougherty, James R.
  20:96
Dougherty, Jessey 22:403
Dougherty, John 9:9, 142,
  174; 10:110; 15:298;
  16:187; 18:109;
  20:241; 23:120
Dougherty, John F. 10:50;
  20:241
Dougherty, John H. 4:21;
  21:136
Dougherty, John M. 20:96
Dougherty, John W. 12:19
Dougherty, Joseph 4:21

Dougherty, L. B. 8:59;
  19:278
Dougherty, L. F. 23:141
Dougherty, Levi D. 9:109
Dougherty, M. 1:26; 3:61;
  10:16; 13:87; 14:9,
  160, 255; 17:494
Dougherty, Michael
  10:110; 14:160;
  15:122; 19:12;
  20:241
Dougherty, Milton T.
  10:205
Dougherty, O. 3:60
Dougherty, Oliver M.
  11:57
Dougherty, Owen 12:19
Dougherty, P. 1:93; 27:39
Dougherty, Pat 9:174
Dougherty, Patrick 9:15
Dougherty, Philip 26:25
Dougherty, R. I. 15:352
Dougherty, Robert 19:160
Dougherty, Sybel 10:172;
  19:160
Dougherty, T. V. 15:335
Dougherty, Thomas 3:60;
  9:102; 18:13
Dougherty, Timothy
  10:209
Dougherty, W. G. 14:314
Dougherty, W. H. 3:60
Dougherty, W. H. H.
  11:57
Dougherty, W. J. 13:87
Dougherty, W. John
  25:311
Dougherty, W. L. 14:55,
  160
Dougherty, William
  8:123; 11:181; 14:55;
  21:325; 22:329
Doughlass, Robert 24:93
Doughman, A. G. 24:17
Doughman, Henry 17:265
Doughman, James F. 20:7
Doughman, Samuel 17:51
Dought, John 11:301
Doughtery, James 20:241
Doughtery, John 4:21
Doughtery, John Thomas
  17:51
Doughtery, Levi 22:188
Doughtery, M. 1:29
Doughtey, George 6:15
Doughtry, Charles M.
  20:241
Doughty, George 21:211
Doughty, George E. 7:49
Doughty, J. B. 15:321
Doughty, J. N. 25:29

Doughty, John 7:121
Doughty, John B. 19:66
Doughty, Joseph B. 23:279
Doughty, L. G. 2:9; 25:29
Doughty, R. W. 24:76
Doughty, W. H. 11:419
Doughty, William 1:27
Douglas, A. C. 5:14
Douglas, Alfred 14:314
Douglas, Archibald 12:58
Douglas, Asa P. 11:181
Douglas, Ashahel 18:271
Douglas, B. F. 25:27
Douglas, C. A. 1:126
Douglas, Charles H. 14:160
Douglas, D. 3:60
Douglas, David M. 23:303
Douglas, Dudley M. 24:93
Douglas, Edward 15:65
Douglas, Edward M. 24:88
Douglas, George 3:60; 23:267
Douglas, Henry 9:96
Douglas, Henry C. 11:27
Douglas, J. A. 1:29; 9:228; 18:365
Douglas, J. C. 1:27; 27:39
Douglas, J. H. 14:160
Douglas, J. P. 1:123
Douglas, J. T. 13:87
Douglas, J. W. 1:27
Douglas, James 18:440
Douglas, James A. 21:136
Douglas, James H. 17:130; 24:192
Douglas, John 9:106; 11:200; 12:58; 18:216, 334
Douglas, M. 3:60
Douglas, Marion 9:219; 18:365
Douglas, Orman L. 9:241
Douglas, P. 3:60
Douglas, Richard 21:24
Douglas, S. E. 19:301
Douglas, Samuel 1:28; 17:209
Douglas, Stephen 8:116
Douglas, Thomas 23:240
Douglas, W. 3:60; 8:113
Douglas, Wallace 18:271
Douglas, William 1:29; 8:100; 14:160; 18:327; 24:157
Douglas, --- 16:291; 20:55
Douglass, A. 23:117
Douglass, A. J. 1:123

Douglass, A. P. 25:165
Douglass, Allen 12:19
Douglass, Anderson 22:512
Douglass, Anthony 21:269
Douglass, Arch 9:203
Douglass, B. 21:325
Douglass, Banth 18:305
Douglass, C. M. 21:325
Douglass, David 13:19
Douglass, David H. 21:50
Douglass, David M. 23:141
Douglass, E. H. 26:157
Douglass, E. R. 15:194
Douglass, Enos 22:508
Douglass, Frank 27:37
Douglass, George 15:90; 17:346; 27:35
Douglass, George A. 16:93
Douglass, George T. 22:449
Douglass, George W. 16:93
Douglass, Gibson 21:211
Douglass, H. J. 26:157
Douglass, Henry 19:290
Douglass, Henry A. 12:19
Douglass, Henry C. 10:110; 20:241
Douglass, Henry L. 22:422
Douglass, I. J. 17:109
Douglass, Isaac 10:110; 20:241
Douglass, J. 12:19; 16:187; 25:165
Douglass, J. H. 21:325
Douglass, J. T. 14:9
Douglass, J. W. 15:194
Douglass, James C. 22:248
Douglass, James L. 7:93
Douglass, James W. 22:161
Douglass, Jilson 22:120
Douglass, John 17:78; 22:28; 23:285
Douglass, John L. 17:295
Douglass, John M. 21:68
Douglass, John S. 11:56
Douglass, John W. 13:57
Douglass, Joseph 5:38
Douglass, L. S. 14:55
Douglass, Laney 24:17
Douglass, Leroy 11:143
Douglass, Miles 21:24
Douglass, Nathan 9:21; 26:97

Douglass, Ned 22:297
Douglass, Neely 21:269
Douglass, Nelson 11:422
Douglass, Ora B. 10:110; 20:241
Douglass, Prentice A. 9:34
Douglass, R. B. 14:277; 23:106
Douglass, Reuben H. 21:325
Douglass, Richard W. 22:74
Douglass, Robert 19:66
Douglass, Robert A. 10:110; 20:241
Douglass, Roberts 8:62
Douglass, S. E. 10:27
Douglass, Samuel 17:287
Douglass, Samuel B. 22:141
Douglass, T. 19:251
Douglass, Thomas 9:174
Douglass, Thomas J. 17:279
Douglass, Thomas M. 19:12
Douglass, William 8:84; 16:118; 17:460; 22:297, 334
Douglass, William B. 10:110; 20:241
Douglass, William L. 12:19
Douglass, William W. 19:12
Dougle, Patrick 27:39
Douins, George 18:131
Douk, N. 19:66
Doule, J. 3:61
Doule, J. H. 16:367
Douley, John 14:55
Douley, M. 3:60
Douley, Nelson 21:325
Douls, Michael 18:131
Douly, William 16:187
Doun, P. C. 1:27
Douney, J. L. 19:160
Douning, F. 14:55
Dounold, J. O. 19:66
Douphman, Thomas 20:84
Douse, A. 11:439
Douse, Lewis 21:325
Douth, Edward E. 18:131
Douthelt, William S. 22:496
Douthy, F. 14:55
Doutt, R. 1:125
Douty, Joseph 10:110; 20:241
Dovall, Malcomb 21:325

Dove, Charles 12:69
Dove, Clif. M. 19:160
Dove, D. 24:17
Dove, G. S. 25:165
Dove, George W. 18:205
Dove, Henry 15:13
Dove, John F. 22:248
Dovee, Gil. Van 27:39
Dovennis, C. W. 17:33
Dover, John 16:139;
    22:523
Dover, Joseph 16:278
Dover, Park 17:33
Dovers, Lewis 15:65
Doverspike, H. 1:123
Doville, Oliver S. 10:111
Dow, Albert 27:37
Dow, Albert S. 9:118
Dow, Albion 14:160
Dow, Amos 4:21
Dow, Andrew 23:87
Dow, B. 1:125
Dow, B. J. R. 24:17
Dow, Carlos C. 17:403
Dow, Charles H. 4:21
Dow, Charles M. 19:160
Dow, Cornelius 27:37
Dow, Daniel G. 10:172
Dow, Daniel H. 24:58
Dow, Enoch C. 16:77
Dow, Enoch S. 4:21
Dow, Enos 25:296
Dow, G. F. 14:160
Dow, G. K. 9:174
Dow, G. R. 19:232
Dow, George 11:115
Dow, H. A. 3:61
Dow, Henry S. 22:422
Dow, Horace L. 21:91
Dow, J. E. 1:97
Dow, J. M. 1:124
Dow, James 10:205
Dow, James G. 21:68
Dow, Joseph 10:172
Dow, Lewis 14:160
Dow, Lewis R. 18:216
Dow, Lorenzo 9:46, 158;
    26:122
Dow, Lynas W. 22:403
Dow, M. 3:61
Dow, Ocar H. 4:21
Dow, Reno 24:101
Dow, Robin 7:121
Dow, S. E. 1:124
Dow, W. K. 1:124
Dow, William A. 15:194
Dow, William H. 9:118
Dowal, Moses 9:79
Dowall, W. V. 26:158
Dowd, Alfred 4:21
Dowd, F. 3:61

Dowd, F. A. 11:260
Dowd, Ira C. 27:39
Dowd, J. 19:348; 20:174
Dowd, J. W. 3:61
Dowd, Jerome 1:27
Dowd, John 7:25
Dowd, N. 18:28
Dowd, Thomas 16:187;
    25:165
Dowdell, Eli 24:177
Dowden, Andrew 23:189
Dowden, Daniel 22:297
Dowden, T. N. 20:145
Dowder, Joseph 3:61
Dowderop, Horace 22:470
Dowdey, Green 18:235
Dowdle, Isaac 23:141
Dowdle, William 14:160
Dowdra, B. S. 18:173
Dowds, John 14:160
Dowds, R. 15:65
Dowdy, George 7:64
Dowdy, Green 26:24
Dowdy, Martin V. 24:17
Dowdy, Wesley 26:25
Dowdy, William J. 23:251
Dowe, S. D. 1:27
Dowed, L. A. 17:247
Dowel, Moses 26:22
Dowell, A. S. 22:188
Dowell, Alex B. 11:385
Dowell, Bird 17:279
Dowell, G. 24:17
Dowell, George W. 22:28
Dowell, J. 22:74
Dowell, John 12:19; 23:87
Dowell, Reuben 22:165
Dowell, W. F. 11:408
Dowell, W. L. 3:61
Dowell, William 11:408
Dowels, John A. 1:27
Dowen, A. J. 1:103
Dowen, Henderson
    11:374
Dowen, John 18:28
Dower, C. 16:367
Dower, James 8:84
Dower, Patrick 9:174;
    19:266
Dowerbry, F. 21:325
Dowers, George 21:325
Dowers, Jacob 26:23
Dowers, Samuel 21:325
Dowers, Washington
    11:28
Dowey, John 15:364
Dowin, Andrew 15:326
Dowin, Harrison 23:267
Dowing, Stewart 18:81
Dowland, Bernard 27:38
Dowle, Daniel 14:161

Dowle, Dennis 14:161
Dowler, Edward 24:65
Dowler, Irwin 17:335
Dowley, George 19:160
Dowling, Andrew 9:207;
    18:65
Dowling, Edward 12:122;
    15:122
Dowling, G. 27:35
Dowling, J. 26:23
Dowling, James 15:65,
    105
Dowling, James A. 1:27
Dowling, John 12:99
Dowling, John P. 23:128
Dowling, Joseph 11:407
Dowling, M. 20:241
Dowling, Mathew 20:241
Dowling, Michael 4:21
Dowling, Mitchell 10:50
Dowling, Nathan 10:50
Dowling, P. 1:126
Dowling, Patrick 12:95;
    19:66
Dowling, W. H. 15:341;
    16:367
Dowling, William 13:19
Dowly, Thomas 21:99
Dowman, James H.
    22:399
Down, Cornelius 9:118
Down, E. 14:160
Down, George P. 4:21
Down, Giles 11:27
Down, Henry 7:121
Down, James 18:205
Down, John 17:174;
    22:334
Down, William 4:21
Downard, George 17:389
Downard, James S.
    10:111; 20:241
Downard, W. G. 26:123
Downen, William 10:111;
    20:241
Downer, A. 3:61
Downer, A. P. 3:61
Downer, Anthony 21:136
Downer, Charles 4:21
Downer, E. P. 21:115
Downer, Frederick 1:28
Downer, Henry 13:19
Downer, Job 16:29
Downer, Nelson 25:165
Downer, R. 17:130;
    24:192
Downer, S. 3:61
Downer, Simon A. 22:461
Downer, Thomas B.
    18:292; 26:96
Downer, Thomas W. 9:34

Downer, W. H. 16:367
Downes, Henry 22:334
Downes, James 22:278
Downes, John W. 22:278
Downes, Martin H. 17:259
Downes, Michael 7:25
Downes, Samuel P. 22:422
Downes, Stephen 13:19
Downes, T. 1:97
Downess, Henry C. 25:29
Downey, --- 10:186; 16:115
Downey, Albert 1:28
Downey, Andrew 19:12
Downey, B. 9:174; 19:237
Downey, Benjamin 10:50; 20:241
Downey, Byron 9:174
Downey, Elder St. John 22:141
Downey, George W. 9:130
Downey, H. 15:55
Downey, Henry 12:69
Downey, I. A. 3:61
Downey, J. 1:126
Downey, James 9:102; 25:165
Downey, James L. 10:159
Downey, Joel 3:61
Downey, John 13:19
Downey, Joseph 18:338
Downey, M. H. 9:219
Downey, Martin B. 18:365
Downey, Michael 4:21
Downey, P. 12:161
Downey, Patrick 10:159; 20:39; 26:22
Downey, Peter 12:19; 14:160
Downey, Philip 22:115
Downey, R. 18:235; 26:24
Downey, Richard 24:172
Downey, S. M. 3:61
Downey, Samuel 4:21
Downey, Simon 8:14
Downey, Sinson 18:131
Downey, Tarlton 22:450
Downey, Thomas 16:84; 23:11
Downey, W. 20:145
Downey, William H. 8:14; 18:131
Downham, John 21:223
Downham, Wesley 21:50
Downie, John 5:50
Downie, Nelson 18:438
Downie, Philip 11:143

Downie, S. 9:142; 27:35
Downie, William 10:90; 20:241
Downin, J. L. 25:165
Downing, Albert 21:325
Downing, Allen C. 23:27
Downing, Asell 1:27
Downing, B. 25:165
Downing, Benjamin G. 15:194
Downing, Brant 11:91
Downing, Butler 5:14
Downing, C. 21:186
Downing, C. R. 18:235; 26:25
Downing, D. 7:25
Downing, Daniel 19:12
Downing, Edmond 9:12
Downing, G. 3:61
Downing, George 3:61; 18:235; 21:325; 26:25
Downing, George H. 4:21
Downing, George W. 27:36
Downing, H. 1:124
Downing, H. C. 22:188
Downing, Henry 11:201
Downing, Henry F. 10:111; 20:241
Downing, Henry R. 24:93
Downing, J. 1:125; 9:236; 26:218
Downing, J. D. 26:96
Downing, J. N. C. 19:320
Downing, Jacob 12:48
Downing, James A. 22:421
Downing, John C. 16:118
Downing, John W. 12:122; 15:122
Downing, Joseph D. 18:292
Downing, Joshua D. 9:34
Downing, M. 3:61
Downing, P. 19:237
Downing, P. S. 10:186
Downing, Patrick 9:174; 19:160
Downing, R. S. 18:173
Downing, Riley 18:173
Downing, S. 14:268, 281
Downing, Samuel 7:93
Downing, Simon B. 21:24
Downing, Solomon 9:207
Downing, Thomas H. 14:160
Downing, Thomas J. 7:49
Downing, W. 9:109
Downing, W. N. 8:62

Downing, William 14:160, 281; 21:325; 25:26
Downing, William E. 13:19
Downing, William H. 9:130; 22:403; 27:36
Downley, Samuel 9:109
Downord, David W. 17:200
Downs, A. 7:25
Downs, Albert 11:20
Downs, Alfred 23:128
Downs, Alonzo 14:160
Downs, B. J. 19:12
Downs, Benjamin 22:74
Downs, Bradford S. 10:16
Downs, Burton J. 23:261
Downs, C. 7:25
Downs, C. T. 26:144
Downs, Charles 10:50; 14:55; 20:241
Downs, E. 3:61
Downs, Edward 14:55
Downs, Edwin W. 17:391
Downs, Floyd 10:50; 20:241
Downs, Francis E. 22:278
Downs, G. W. 17:482; 27:38
Downs, I. R. 3:61
Downs, Isaac S. 17:279
Downs, J. 1:27; 3:61; 13:87; 14:9
Downs, J. S. 26:144
Downs, James 23:97
Downs, James B. 10:16
Downs, James D. 22:421
Downs, James M. 2:10
Downs, John 25:274
Downs, John W. 10:176
Downs, Joseph 7:93
Downs, Julius P. 24:170
Downs, Junius 17:446
Downs, L. 21:325
Downs, Levi 17:159
Downs, M. 25:26
Downs, Nathaniel 9:142
Downs, O. 25:165
Downs, Patrick 12:69; 13:124; 15:33
Downs, R. A. 14:161
Downs, Samuel 1:26
Downs, Stephen 16:29
Downs, T. 1:126
Downs, Thomas 13:19
Downs, Thomas J. 11:260
Downs, Timothy 14:161
Downs, W. 11:292
Downs, Walter A. 9:15
Downs, William 11:27

Downs, William L. 22:74
Downs, William S. 22:477
Downson, John 4:21
Dowrey, James 14:161, 255
Dowse, Charles 22:141
Dowse, James 21:252
Dowse, James G. 12:69
Dowtard, Cam 18:202; 26:210
Dowtich, E. T. 21:325
Dox, Newell 9:129
Dox, T. 1:124
Doxie, John R. 15:283; 19:66
Doxison, John C. 25:28
Doxtaber, Daniel 9:118
Doxtader, Daniel 22:74
Doxtater, Dan B. 27:37
Doxtater, H. 1:29
Doxtater, John 7:93
Doxtater, Paul 9:79; 26:25
Doxtoter, B. 1:28
Doyd, Richard 11:57
Doyel, James 10:111; 20:241
Doyen, H. L. 16:187
Doyier, William 16:187
Doyl, John 18:131
Doyl, Michael 21:325
Doyle, Andrew 10:50; 20:241
Doyle, Carlisle H. 17:279
Doyle, D. 1:125; 13:87
Doyle, E. 1:123
Doyle, Edward 22:519
Doyle, Garrett 17:33; 20:34
Doyle, Green 17:174
Doyle, H. 3:61; 17:147
Doyle, H. H. 14:161
Doyle, J. 1:125, 126; 3:61; 9:142; 11:301; 14:55; 20:241; 23:141; 27:35
Doyle, J. B. 14:55
Doyle, J. W. 20:39
Doyle, James 3:61; 4:21; 13:19; 15:122, 298; 16:29, 187; 17:235; 27:37
Doyle, James K. 10:50; 20:241
Doyle, John 3:61; 8:14; 11:142; 15:194; 21:325; 25:165
Doyle, John A. 17:51
Doyle, Lawrence 10:159; 19:160
Doyle, Leander 9:109
Doyle, Leyman 27:38

Doyle, M. 9:142; 27:35
Doyle, M. O. 13:63; 19:66
Doyle, Mathew 15:313
Doyle, Matthew 19:66
Doyle, P. 3:61; 9:142; 11:238; 14:55, 161
Doyle, Pat 14:161
Doyle, Patrick 9:10, 230; 12:19; 20:132, 241; 22:334
Doyle, Paul 11:181
Doyle, Peter 7:121; 21:325
Doyle, R. 14:55
Doyle, Richard 22:449; 23:64
Doyle, Robert 5:50
Doyle, S. A. 10:27; 19:301
Doyle, Sanford 17:33
Doyle, Taylor 25:319
Doyle, Thomas 11:239; 14:55; 15:194; 26:97
Doyle, W. 3:61; 27:36
Doyle, W. P. 8:14
Doyle, W. S. 1:29
Doyle, William 1:27; 2:9; 8:84; 25:29
Doyle, William P. 18:131
Doyne, William C. 16:187
Dozen, Hiram L. 17:404
Dozenbaker, Lewis H. 4:21
Dozer, B. 14:161
Dozier, George 18:81
Dozier, Joseph 18:81
Dozier, Valen 25:165
Draan, R. H. 3:61
Draber, William 15:65
Drackarm, L. 3:61
Draf, August 12:19
Drafton, Hanson 21:325
Dragan, D. 17:191
Drager, Fred 14:161
Draghess, H. 15:194
Dragit, William 1:27
Dragon, John 8:84
Dragoo, B. 25:28
Dragoo, Daniel 11:260
Dragoon, H. 3:61
Dragoon, N. 14:161
Dragstren, Samuel 10:111; 20:241
Draher, A. 11:259
Draher, W. 1:124
Drain, Jasper N. 20:39
Drain, John 7:16
Drain, R. 15:194
Drain, William 15:194
Draine, Benjamin 11:201
Draine, Lewis 11:201

Draine, William 11:201
Draing, John 21:325
Drake, A. 1:125
Drake, A. J. 26:23
Drake, Abra 18:365
Drake, Abraham 9:227; 27:39
Drake, Alexander 22:233
Drake, Alfred 17:154
Drake, Aliez 15:194
Drake, Andrew 8:14; 18:131
Drake, Andrew S. 20:22
Drake, Asbury 23:260
Drake, Augustus 12:19
Drake, B. C. 16:291
Drake, Benjamin F. 17:191
Drake, Bob 7:121
Drake, Brittan 22:173
Drake, C. 3:61; 25:165
Drake, C. M. 20:242
Drake, Charles 6:15; 10:50; 12:19; 18:81; 20:242; 21:325; 22:297
Drake, Charles C. 3:61
Drake, Charles H. 21:252
Drake, Curtis M. 10:50
Drake, D. 1:126; 10:210
Drake, D. B. 3:61
Drake, D. W. 3:61
Drake, David 15:194; 23:27
Drake, E. C. 3:61
Drake, E. S. 9:109
Drake, Edward P. 20:7
Drake, Edwin L. 13:19
Drake, Eli 17:46
Drake, F. 5:14; 25:165
Drake, Francis 18:109
Drake, Francis E. 12:69; 15:11
Drake, Friend 27:38
Drake, G. 18:424
Drake, G. W. 7:25
Drake, George 9:199; 15:90; 18:65; 19:290; 22:188; 23:141
Drake, George B. 11:104
Drake, George L. 23:189
Drake, George W. 17:144
Drake, Guy F. 12:69; 15:86
Drake, H. 1:123; 11:142
Drake, H. D. 17:402
Drake, Henry 21:24
Drake, Hyram 12:19
Drake, Isaac C. 10:159; 19:160
Drake, J. 11:301; 24:17

Drake, J. A. 25:28
Drake, J. E. 25:296
Drake, J. H. 3:61
Drake, J. M. 11:100
Drake, J. T. 17:327
Drake, Jacob 11:385;
22:188
Drake, James E. 21:216
Drake, James F. 1:28
Drake, James P. 24:17
Drake, Jeremiah 13:77
Drake, John 4:21; 21:136
Drake, John A. 11:144
Drake, John B. 13:19
Drake, John E. 26:25
Drake, John F. 3:61
Drake, John J. 19:66
Drake, John M. 10:159;
19:160
Drake, John R. 7:25
Drake, John T. 17:78
Drake, John V. 23:141
Drake, John W. 22:75
Drake, Jonathan 10:159;
19:160
Drake, Joseph 8:84
Drake, Joseph H. 10:7
Drake, Julius A. 9:174
Drake, K. 11:201
Drake, L. 12:161
Drake, L. A. 27:34
Drake, Lemuel 21:50
Drake, M. 20:399
Drake, M. A. 1:126
Drake, Malville 18:13
Drake, Martin 20:48
Drake, Michael 14:161
Drake, Milan M. 11:104
Drake, Moses A. 10:159
Drake, Moses R. 19:160
Drake, Nathaniel 7:56
Drake, Nelson 9:207;
18:65
Drake, Norman 18:235;
26:24
Drake, O. F. 16:147
Drake, O. P. 15:165
Drake, P. 22:248
Drake, R. R. 3:61
Drake, Renselar 4:21
Drake, Richard J. 23:279
Drake, S. 1:27; 21:325;
23:27
Drake, S. L. 10:205
Drake, S. M. 11:105
Drake, Salmon 16:187
Drake, Samuel 3:61
Drake, Silas 7:83
Drake, Silas A. 23:141
Drake, Silas C. 22:75
Drake, Stephen H. 23:189

Drake, T. 1:125; 3:61
Drake, T. B. 21:24
Drake, Thomas 17:174;
25:319
Drake, Thomas W. 17:64
Drake, W. 13:87; 14:9;
17:101
Drake, W. A. 1:29; 22:189
Drake, William 3:61;
11:201; 17:446;
24:170
Drake, William B. 23:304
Drake, William M. 12:58
Drake, William W. 20:242
Draker, William W.
10:111
Drakes, J. B. 9:42
Drams, Charles 25:274
Drane, W. 20:242
Drang, Samuel 18:81
Dransfield, John 3:61
Dransfield, Samuel B.
7:25
Drany, Stonewall 9:34
Draper, --- 26:219
Draper, Alex 11:200
Draper, Allenson 21:325
Draper, B. Y. 15:151
Draper, E. 1:126
Draper, G. A. 25:165
Draper, George A. 5:14
Draper, George W. 13:19;
16:29
Draper, H. 22:189
Draper, Isaac F. 7:67
Draper, J. P. 19:232
Draper, James 9:174;
11:301
Draper, John 10:90;
12:141
Draper, John A. 21:136
Draper, John C. 22:28
Draper, John W. 1:26
Draper, L. 3:61
Draper, Lorenzo 11:380
Draper, M. V. 12:152
Draper, Margaret 26:219
Draper, Merritt 23:267
Draper, Milton W. 23:260
Draper, Ondi 26:96
Draper, Oned 9:21
Draper, Oudi 18:305
Draper, Samuel P. 24:17
Draper, Stephen 10:111;
20:242
Draper, William 22:461
Drapler, Moses 18:131
Drapo, M. 1:124
Drasson, B. 9:203
Draton, Spencer 16:291
Draux, Jacob 16:29

Draw, J. W. 18:189
Drawn, George 3:61
Drayer, --- 15:194
Drayer, John 12:170
Drayer, William 13:63;
19:66
Drayers, Gerret H. 21:136
Drayton, M. 27:39
Drayton, March 9:154
Drear, R. B. 1:123
Dreatz, Benjamin 11:142
Dreck, John 8:47
Drecold, D. 3:61
Dreem, Graham 9:79
Dreggs, John 16:367
Dreher, August 10:160;
19:160
Dreher, Peter 22:477
Dreibelbis, John A. 21:68
Dreillis, John A. 8:47
Dreis, John 21:91
Dreld, Denis 27:38
Dreman, Jordan 27:44
Dremer, Frederick 18:205
Drendies, David 9:79
Drenery, Calvin 11:142
Drenkle, J. A. 3:61
Drennan, John 20:123
Drennen, James H. 24:17
Drennen, William J.
10:111; 20:242
Drennon, John W. 22:75
Drennon, Rasebery
22:422
Drensdorf, Henry 7:25
Drescall, Michael 11:144
Dreschal, Charles 9:244
Dresher, Louis 13:19
Dresher, W. 1:125
Dreskill, Philip T. 20:185
Dreslines, Henry 17:78
Dresman, James 21:325
Dress, Henry 22:75
Dress, Jonathan 12:19
Dressel, George 4:21
Dresser, A. 1:125; 25:26
Dresser, A. A. 10:144;
19:161
Dresser, A. S. 25:165
Dresser, Albert 2:10
Dresser, C. 3:61
Dresser, C. C. 9:174
Dresser, Charles 19:237;
25:165
Dresser, Ezra 12:161
Dresser, N. 9:174; 19:251
Dresser, Robert 9:175;
19:251
Dressler, Moses 8:14;
26:156
Dressler, S. 25:166

Dressler, Samuel 5:14
Dressor, Charles F. 13:108
Dressus, O. 26:158
Drestler, John 4:21
Dreu, Sol 15:194
Dreutler, L. 16:291
Drew, --- 25:166
Drew, A. 19:12
Drew, Asa 12:55
Drew, C. 1:93
Drew, Charles 16:367; 21:325
Drew, E. 3:61
Drew, F. 3:61
Drew, Francis M. 9:15
Drew, George 7:121; 14:161; 21:99
Drew, George W. 21:99
Drew, H. 3:61
Drew, H. C. 1:125
Drew, H. F. 27:37
Drew, H. T. 9:118
Drew, Henry 23:128
Drew, J. F. 1:124
Drew, J. S. 25:29
Drew, Jacob S. 1:29
Drew, James 22:141
Drew, John 12:55; 13:19; 20:242
Drew, Lycurgus D. 17:64
Drew, Michael 25:29
Drew, Pliney F. 1:28
Drew, Robert 26:157
Drew, S. 1:123
Drew, Samuel 9:12
Drew, Stephen H. 12:58
Drew, Theo. H. 25:166
Drew, Walter 21:242
Drewing, Samuel 11:381
Drewlock, Andrew 7:56
Drewry, Frank 18:131
Drexel, Jacob 12:19
Drey, Minor 4:65
Dreyer, Peter 15:194
Dreyer, Sylvester 12:139
Dribblebiss, Jacob 10:111
Dricker, B. J. 26:96
Dricoll, Dennis 10:160
Drier, Thomas D. 9:21
Driery, Levi 18:216
Driesbillis, C. W. 7:25
Driesbillis, G. W. 7:25
Driesler, M. 7:25
Driess, Henry 17:359
Driezke, Andrew 17:210
Drigg, A. 14:55
Driggs, C. M. 14:240
Driggs, Henry 7:93
Drigshouse, T. 18:292

Drigshouse, Timothy 26:96
Drilling, H. 1:126
Dringle, Robert 5:50
Drink, D. N. 4:21
Drinker, Joe 10:205
Drinkwater, George 12:69; 15:81
Drinkwater, H. 15:313; 19:66
Drinn, --- 12:173
Drinth, Hugh 18:434
Drisbord, Doc 14:314
Driscall, D. 15:357
Driscall, Daniel 8:84
Driscol, Alexander 20:102
Driscol, Cornelius 19:251
Driscol, Henry 23:251
Driscol, John 23:27
Driscol, S. W. 12:152
Driscoll, C. 1:29
Driscoll, Charles 7:93
Driscoll, D. 1:126
Driscoll, Daniel 16:279
Driscoll, Dennis 13:19; 19:161
Driscoll, Doctor 22:297
Driscoll, F. 1:124
Driscoll, Florence 9:199
Driscoll, J. 7:83; 22:28
Driscoll, James 13:19; 21:325
Driscoll, Jeremiah 13:19
Driscoll, John 21:325
Driscoll, John S. 10:50
Driscoll, M. 3:61
Driscoll, Silas 26:157
Driscoll, Simon 22:421
Driscoll, Timothy 21:325
Driscoll, William 25:28
Driscult, Silas 8:38
Drisdell, William 17:252
Drisgue, F. 3:61
Drishel, Peter 23:313
Driskel, Daniel 25:332
Driskell, G. V. 23:27
Driskels, F. 19:281
Driskoll, Cornelius 26:123
Driskoll, John 7:63
Drisland, Richard 17:349
Driss, Michael 18:65
Driswold, Elldridge 21:325
Drite, S. 8:105
Dritman, William 3:61
Driver, David 17:202; 22:446
Driver, George 22:297
Driver, George R. 22:75
Driver, L. 27:35
Driver, M. 9:51

Driver, Robert C. 17:19
Drivre, --- 3:61
Drizsdale, F. 3:61
Drobisch, P. 25:166
Droeber, Heinrick 16:93
Droff, J. I. 11:279
Droham, Edward F. 1:28
Dromanett, W. 3:62
Drommond, Lott D. 20:242
Dronaniller, Philip 12:64
Dronmiller, Ph. 15:33
Drosselmeyer, H. 11:88
Drot, Cyrus A. 16:150
Drouis, Henry 19:161
Droumiller, Mathias 22:450
Droun, Albert 10:153; 19:161
Droun, Thomas 10:16
Drous, Henry 10:154
Drowley, George 17:33
Drown, Benjamin 19:161
Drown, H. 1:125
Drown, O. 25:29
Drown, Osborn 2:10
Drown, Thomas E. 22:75
Drown, W. B. 15:194
Drown, William O. 11:286
Drown, Zdotes 13:19
Droxler, --- 5:50
Droydlin, Philip 10:111; 20:242
Drozier, J. W. 27:35
Drubaker, G. E. 9:109
Druckenmiller, John 13:19
Drue, James A. 8:62; 22:28
Druery, H. 14:297; 17:473
Drueschler, Julius 18:81
Drueson, Benjamin 22:297
Druetler, L. 12:91
Druggan, James 23:285
Druinin, Levi 12:48
Druining, D. 14:255
Drul, A. B. 27:38
Drul, S. B. 14:297; 17:475
Drulin, J. A. 9:175
Drullinger, Thomas 23:279
Drum, A. 3:62
Drum, G. 3:62
Drum, Graham 26:22
Drum, James N. 21:325
Drum, John 14:240
Drum, M. 27:38
Drum, Martin V. B. 20:22
Drum, N. 15:165

Drum, Patrick 24:93
Drum, Peter 10:50;
 20:242
Drum, Samuel 27:38
Drumagin, D. 15:194
Druman, S. R. 22:189
Drumbel, J. 21:120
Drumbower, J. 14:281
Drumhaller, E. 22:189
Drumheller, Daniel 24:76
Drumm, P. H. 11:125
Drummer, A. 15:158
Drummindo, Milton
 11:104
Drummon, James 22:120
Drummond, Alexander
 13:19
Drummond, David
 10:160; 19:161
Drummond, Henry 4:21
Drummond, J. 3:62
Drummond, J. F. 25:166
Drummond, James 16:29;
 24:17
Drummond, Lot D. 10:50
Drummond, Nile 7:25
Drummond, S. A. 14:328
Drummond, William 6:15;
 18:81
Drumner, Frost 20:242
Drumny, John 17:107
Drumpford, William
 9:207
Drunks, Henry 9:79
Drurior, Joseph 23:141
Drury, Colbert J. 22:75
Drury, G. W. 3:62
Drury, James A. 22:75
Drury, James E. 18:48
Drury, James H. 22:120
Drury, James T. 17:109
Drury, John S. 17:51
Drury, Silas O. 21:325
Drury, T. 21:24
Drury, W. C. 16:29
Drury, W. H. 13:19; 14:56
Druse, C. T. 23:27
Drusenbrock, Frederick
 4:21
Drushell, Benjamin
 21:325
Druson, Charles 9:207
Drusten, Peter 9:130
Drusvin, Michael 22:248
Druyre, William 13:108
Dry, Robert 19:45
Dry, Samuel B. 4:21
Dry, Wesley 26:23
Dryan, J. 27:35
Dryant, Silas 11:144
Dryden, C. D. 9:51

Dryden, Charles 9:34
Dryden, Joseph 26:144
Dryden, William 11:201
Dryer, Frederick 7:93
Dryer, H. 1:123; 3:62
Dryer, Hun 11:143
Dryer, Jeremiah 9:12
Dryer, John 8:60
Dryer, Z. 21:325
Dryfoos, Marcus 1:27
Drykeman, John 19:12
Drynan, John 12:171
Drysdale, James B. 22:421
Drysdale, John 10:111;
 20:242
Duacke, Francisco 12:171
Duain, Thomas 25:319
Duaine, Thomas 6:30
Duan, James H. 22:500
Duan, Martin 27:39
Duan, Solomon 27:39
Duane, Burnard 11:27
Duane, F. 3:62
Duane, Henry 21:325
Dubach, W. 22:189
Dubber, Lawrence 11:143
Dubber, S. A. 3:62
Dubblebiss, Jacob 20:242
Dubbs, John O. 11:142
Dube, James 10:111;
 20:242
Dube, John 22:397
Dubendorff, Herman
 10:111
Dubendorff, Hermen
 20:242
Dubenthal, H. 3:62
Duber, Valentine 12:8
Duberry, William 17:51
Dubert, Fred 18:131
Dubert, Fred. 8:14
Duble, Henry 3:62
Dubley, James 14:56
Dubley, W. J. 10:111
Dubley, Wilson 22:297
Dublin, A. 1:125
Dubois, Ablenis 10:172
Dubois, C. 25:166
Dubois, Charles 5:14;
 9:214; 13:57; 18:81;
 21:325
DuBois, Charles 22:461
Dubois, E. A. 9:21;
 18:305; 26:96
Dubois, E. B. 8:84
Dubois, E. F. 8:71; 26:158
Dubois, Emile 22:334
Dubois, George W.
 22:421
Dubois, H. 25:166
Dubois, Henry 9:175

Dubois, Isaiah 16:29
Dubois, Isiah 13:57
Dubois, Jacob 14:161
Dubois, Jeheil 7:25
Dubois, John 7:13; 19:161
Dubois, Joseph 13:81;
 16:187
Dubois, Levi 7:121
Dubois, Oblenis 19:161
Dubois, Peaser 21:325
Dubois, Treat S. 23:64
Dubois, W. H. 25:166
Dubois, William 9:203
Dubois, William H. 5:38
Duboise, Charles 18:109
Duboys, Henry 19:251
Dubple, S. 1:125
Dubray, Frank 7:79
Dubre, John 17:235
Dubre, Jonathan 20:183
Dubrysafle, J. E. 3:62
Dubuny, J. 16:267
Ducan, John 25:166
Ducat, Dornat 11:57
Ducat, Isaac 22:75
Duchane, Joseph 13:19;
 16:29
Duchemin, Eli 11:143
Duchene, Benjamin
 22:141
Ducher, Fayett 25:28
Ducherme, John 22:449
Duchine, Alexander 21:51
Duchmin, William O.
 22:75
Duck, Jesse 22:165
Duck, Robert A. 23:27
Duckensheet, David
 17:247
Ducker, G. 25:166
Ducker, J. L. 10:111;
 20:242
Ducker, John B. 22:75
Ducket, Isaac 11:27
Ducket, John 2:10; 25:27
Ducket, R. 1:126
Duckett, David 24:49
Duckett, Edward G.
 23:279
Duckett, H. 7:49
Duckett, Isaiah 24:49
Ducklin, W. 1:124
Duckreth, Ansey 18:109
Ducks, J. 25:274
Duckworth, J. 3:62;
 14:161
Duckworth, John 21:9
Duckworth, L. 14:56
Duckworth, Leander
 21:68
Duckworth, W. B. 3:62

Duckworthy, G. S. 14:336
Duclo, A. 26:23
Dudden, E. W. 13:87
Duddleston, Hamilton 21:252
Duddy, R. 1:29
Dudeck, Alexander 12:69; 15:33
Dudenhoefer, F. 11:57
Dudgeon, Thomas J. 23:97
Dudley, Aaron 19:12
Dudley, Adolphus 18:235; 26:24
Dudley, Alfred 18:13
Dudley, Anson 9:130
Dudley, Asa 10:50
Dudley, Aug. F. 21:325
Dudley, Augustus 7:93
Dudley, C. J. 14:264, 287; 23:141
Dudley, Charles 15:55; 18:216
Dudley, Daniel 21:326
Dudley, David F. 22:334
Dudley, E. 1:126; 23:117
Dudley, Edward W. 10:160
Dudley, Elias 10:176; 19:161
Dudley, Elijah 24:38
Dudley, Freeman 12:19
Dudley, G. D. 9:109
Dudley, G. N. 16:29
Dudley, George 9:102; 11:201
Dudley, George A. 9:130; 27:36
Dudley, George W. 13:19; 21:24
Dudley, H. C. 11:125
Dudley, H. M. 1:125
Dudley, Henry 17:174
Dudley, Henry A. 21:87
Dudley, Ira 13:108
Dudley, J. 14:56; 16:29; 25:166
Dudley, J. C. 3:62
Dudley, J. W. 3:62
Dudley, Jerry 24:192
Dudley, Jesse 21:326
Dudley, John 5:38; 8:99; 9:31; 18:305; 26:97
Dudley, John G. 18:394
Dudley, John W. 5:14
Dudley, Joseph 16:187; 17:78; 23:97
Dudley, Joseph A. 21:326
Dudley, L. 25:166
Dudley, L. B. 25:29
Dudley, Lewis 5:14

Dudley, Loren 17:359
Dudley, M. A. 20:242
Dudley, M. N. 13:130
Dudley, Moses 13:108
Dudley, Mott N. 25:27
Dudley, Paul 13:108
Dudley, Reuben 21:194
Dudley, Samuel 3:62; 23:270; 27:36
Dudley, Seppy 22:75
Dudley, Stephen B. 17:33
Dudley, T. 1:127
Dudley, W. 13:87
Dudley, W. J. 20:242
Dudley, W. R. 18:189
Dudley, Wentworth E. 16:152
Dudley, Wiley J. 18:216
Dudley, William J. 19:161
Dudley, William L. 11:386
Dudly, I. 15:194
Dudly, John F. 23:189
Dudman, Charles 15:33
Duds, Joseph B. 11:143
Dudtrick, H. 11:239
Dueen, Pinkney H. 11:408
Duel, Alonzo F. 21:252
Duel, G. E. 18:65
Duel, J. M. 25:166
Duel, Jacob N. 5:14
Duel, James H. 18:394
Duel, John 18:131
Duel, Peter 27:37
Duell, Tobias 22:10
Duenner, August 17:33
Duer, Bernard 9:34; 18:292; 26:97
Duer, Edward M. 12:152
Duer, Thomas D. 18:305; 26:95
Duerney, Isaac 14:161
Duerr, Jacob 18:334
Duesimo, L. L. 16:267
Duett, John 9:109
Dufeer, William R. 21:240
Dufer, R. 14:297; 17:479
Duff, --- 17:279
Duff, A. 16:187
Duff, A. B. 26:157
Duff, A. J. 11:181
Duff, Abraham 9:96
Duff, Alvan 1:29
Duff, Ansel D. 22:449
Duff, Benjamin R. 16:29
Duff, Caleb W. 22:233
Duff, Charles 3:62
Duff, Daniel 17:130; 24:192
Duff, E. 14:56
Duff, Everett 9:156

Duff, George 16:187
Duff, I. 3:62
Duff, J. 1:125
Duff, J. C. 14:255
Duff, J. M. 11:239
Duff, J. W. 3:62
Duff, James 8:62, 84
Duff, James A. 16:30
Duff, James S. 22:248
Duff, John G. 22:161
Duff, John W. 11:239
Duff, Morris 17:174
Duff, N. 20:242
Duff, Nathaniel 10:50
Duff, Robert 13:63; 16:187
Duff, William 4:21; 17:130; 24:192
Duffe, James 20:242
Duffee, D. 12:64; 15:4
Duffee, Frank 15:363
Duffee, John 9:142
Duffee, Patrick 7:93
Duffee, Richard B. 2:9
Duffee, T. 1:124
Duffees, George E. 16:30
Duffel, Stacey K. 13:20
Duffer, James 10:50
Duffert, Thomas 27:37
Duffert, William 9:118
Duffey, A. 3:62
Duffey, E. 3:62
Duffey, Francis N. 8:84
Duffey, George 10:146
Duffey, Hugh 11:301
Duffey, J. 15:65
Duffey, James 3:62; 7:49; 11:385; 12:69
Duffey, James K. 14:161
Duffey, John 9:51; 12:69; 22:334, 351
Duffey, Michael J. 23:64
Duffey, Patrick 13:108; 24:71
Duffey, Thomas 17:78
Duffey, William 9:21; 18:305; 26:96
Duffie, Frank 19:66
Duffie, J. 3:62
Duffie, James 26:158
Duffie, James Y. 19:161
Duffie, Thomas 14:161
Duffield, A. 15:194
Duffield, B. 8:71
Duffield, L. C. 8:71
Duffield, W. H. H. 8:119
Duffield, W. S. 14:161
Duffield, William 22:28
Duffield, William J. 19:224
Duffin, A. 14:56

Duffin, Samuel 23:87
Dufford, Chrouce 15:65
Duffrey, J. R. 14:56
Duffries, John 15:194
Duffy, C. J. 25:29
Duffy, C. R. 1:29
Duffy, D. 25:166
Duffy, Eugene H. 23:16
Duffy, Francis 9:109; 21:9
Duffy, Frank 21:326
Duffy, G. 3:62; 11:279
Duffy, George J. 2:9
Duffy, Henry 23:121
Duffy, J. 3:62; 21:326
Duffy, James 14:329;
   15:7; 17:73
Duffy, John 9:34; 15:33;
   22:189, 461, 519;
   27:36
Duffy, Joseph 1:27; 13:79;
   16:187
Duffy, Michael 10:16;
   26:210
Duffy, P. 14:56
Duffy, Patrick 21:326;
   25:166
Duffy, Peter 10:160;
   17:51; 19:161;
   23:121
Duffy, Philip 21:326
Duffy, Samuel 21:91
Duffy, Simon 1:27
Duffy, Stephen A. 19:321
Duffy, T. 1:29; 27:34
Duffy, Thomas 25:166
Duffy, Thomas C. 21:51
Duffy, W. 3:62
Duffy, William 13:76;
   16:147, 187
Duflow, John 11:105
Dufrane, O. 17:70
Dugal, --- 25:28
Dugal, Edward 16:187
Dugal, G. H. 26:156
Dugan, Albert 17:427
Dugan, D. 3:62; 12:8
Dugan, Dennis 22:233
Dugan, E. F. 10:50;
   20:242
Dugan, Francis 23:305
Dugan, Frank 11:27
Dugan, Hamilton 22:248
Dugan, Isaac F. 23:27
Dugan, J. C. 21:109
Dugan, John 9:118, 142;
   10:160; 12:19;
   16:30; 19:161;
   21:68; 23:27
Dugan, Joseph 8:62;
   17:130; 24:192

Dugan, L. T. 18:235;
   26:24
Dugan, Martin 8:14;
   18:131
Dugan, Michael 23:141
Dugan, R. 11:143
Dugan, T. 14:255
Dugan, Thomas 3:62;
   10:172; 19:161
Dugan, W. 26:218
Dugan, William 9:236
Dugan, William H. 21:238
Dugcan, J. R. 3:62
Dugel, G. M. 8:14
Dugen, James 25:166
Dugeon, J. D. 19:66
Dugeon, J. H. 15:326
Dugeon, James 1:28
Duger, Hardin 22:28
Dugg, William A. 10:111
Duggan, Albert 24:183
Duggan, Daniel 18:440
Duggan, James 16:187
Duggan, John 17:320
Duggan, William 19:66;
   23:184
Dugger, George M.
   11:422
Dugger, H. 11:28
Dugger, Henry C. 22:248
Dugger, James A. 24:17
Dugger, James E. 7:73
Dugger, James W. 11:422
Dugger, T. 17:279
Dugger, William 19:301
Duggett, Samuel W. 10:16
Duggin, J. R. 16:30
Duggin, William A.
   20:242
Duggins, James 22:120
Duggon, Robert 16:30
Duglas, C. 16:187
Duglass, Andrew J. 15:86
Duglass, J. A. 8:47
Duglass, James B. 23:289
Duglass, John 8:121
Duglass, William F. 17:64
Dugley, C. E. 27:38
Dugley, William 8:47
Duguett, John 19:66
Duhamel, John 22:278
Duheime, Lizeder 27:143
Duhurst, Albert 4:21
Duican, James D. 7:49
Duih, Emil 15:33
Duin, W. 15:16
Duiney, John 24:192
Duinont, P. 23:267
Dukale, John 3:62
Dukate, James 22:75
Duke, A. B. 22:189

Duke, A. J. 9:79
Duke, Aaron B. 21:326
Duke, Benjamin 7:56
Duke, D. F. 25:166
Duke, E. 15:158
Duke, Ferd 26:157
Duke, Fred. 8:38
Duke, George 7:25
Duke, George H. 22:75
Duke, Henry 22:297, 421
Duke, Jehu 22:248
Duke, John 9:175
Duke, R. F. 22:189
Duke, Thomas 11:143
Duke, William 3:62;
   14:56
Duke, William R. 18:365
Duker, John 24:157
Dukes, A. 7:49; 8:71
Dukes, Crawford 18:216
Dukes, Isaac 9:175
Dukes, Isaac A. 19:266
Dukes, J. D. 23:292
Dukes, John L. 22:165
Dukes, Peter 24:72
Dukes, Robert B. 21:51
Dukes, William C. 22:421
Dukes, William R. 9:219
Dukeworth, James 23:202
Dulac, Stephen 20:189
Duland, G. W. 3:62
Dulay, G. 1:29
Dule, Levi 3:62
Dulen, James 8:71
Dulesmond, Nicholas 7:93
Duley, John 9:175; 19:251
Duley, William 10:111;
   20:242
Dulgenbonto, Jacob 18:48
Dulhaut, John 16:291
Dulian, Gilbert 9:51
Duliere, John P. 19:161
Dulin, Atwell 7:49
Dulin, John F. 20:185
Dulin, P. 27:37
Dulinan, Henry 27:36
Duling, John 19:12
Dulivan, Samuel 27:36
Dull, --- 19:322
Dull, Andrew 10:111;
   20:242
Dull, E. Wesley 22:189
Dull, George 15:285;
   19:66
Dull, George W. 4:21
Dull, Jeremiah 27:38
Dull, John 8:14
Dull, W. 3:62
Dull, W. C. 14:56
Dullard, William 21:326
Dullen, John Van 19:66

Dulliord, Samuel 9:130
Dullivan, Henry 9:130
Dully, J. R. 17:453;
    24:183
Dulsey, Frank 25:296
Dulu, John 20:29
Duly, Edward 20:46
Duly, J. 1:97
Duly, Martin 15:194
Dulyeburk, H. 3:62
Dulzo, Nicholas 10:160;
    19:161
Dum, J. 3:62
Duman, Joel 21:223
Dumand, John 11:105
Dumaran, John 3:62
Dumas, B. F. 23:184
Dumas, J. P. 3:62
Dumas, John 1:26
Dumas, Paul 15:194
Dumbar, Alexander
    22:397
Dumbaugh, James M.
    22:189
Dumbauld, John A. 25:28
Dume, Maranco 19:317
Dumend, George W.
    19:266
Dumers, Gotzian 23:117
Dumersy, A. P. 24:177
Dumfee, I. 1:27
Dumford, Daniel 22:189
Dumford, T. 1:126
Dumfry, Denis 3:62
Dumfry, Henry 15:194
Duming, Mathias 8:14
Dumire, Andrew 23:281
Dumm, Vincent 22:422
Dummer, R. O. 9:109
Dummerigh, J. A. 1:125
Dummerressy, J. 14:56
Dummers, Frost 9:230
Dummet, --- 22:351
Dummill, William H.
    18:440
Dummond, Franklin
    11:400
Dumnell, Peter 13:63
Dumon, Joseph 9:42
Dumond, A. 3:62
Dumond, C. 3:62
Dumond, Cornelius W.
    21:9
Dumond, J. H. 3:62
Dumond, John 3:62
Dumond, Paul 10:111;
    20:242
Dumont, John F. 19:334
Dumont, W. 3:62
Dumoss, J. 20:56
Dumpey, M. 13:63; 19:66

Dumpford, J. 24:77
Dumphany, Edward
    15:194
Dumphrey, Daniel 17:390
Dumphy, Ansel W.
    22:278
Dumphy, Patrick 22:334
Dumpprope, Henry
    20:112
Dumpson, Henry 27:34
Dumton, Peter 27:36
Dun, David 13:135
Dun, F. 18:81
Dun, H. W. 1:123
Dun, J. H. 18:28
Dun, R. B. 3:63
Dun, S. 15:290
Dun, Samuel 19:66
Dunagan, William 11:385
Dunagin, J. 14:56
Dunahoe, George 22:422
Dunan, --- 15:194
Dunardy, R. C. 13:108
Dunarun, U. 15:194
Dunavan, James W. 20:7
Dunavan, Thomas 7:56
Dunaway, Jacob E. 22:189
Dunaway, M. 11:279
Dunbab, William 5:38
Dunbar, A. B. 11:100
Dunbar, Adelbert 17:242
Dunbar, Alexander 3:62
Dunbar, Anthony 17:109
Dunbar, Caleb 17:174
Dunbar, D. 1:27
Dunbar, D. F. 9:175
Dunbar, E. 1:124
Dunbar, George 11:422
Dunbar, George H. 21:51
Dunbar, George W.
    21:186
Dunbar, Green 18:235;
    26:25
Dunbar, H. E. 19:66
Dunbar, Henderson 21:24
Dunbar, Hugh M. 17:205
Dunbar, J. 3:62; 11:56
Dunbar, James 8:14;
    18:131
Dunbar, James M. 11:422
Dunbar, John 15:194
Dunbar, Joseph 23:97
Dunbar, Levi 9:79
Dunbar, Oliver 19:66
Dunbar, Theo 26:236
Dunbar, Thomas 3:62
Dunbar, W. 9:109
Dunbar, William 4:22;
    14:161
Dunbar, Willis 17:206
Dunbar, Zeras 11:230

Dunbell, S. F. 18:28
Dunberger, George 3:63
Dunblare, George E.
    14:161
Duncan, --- 11:339;
    15:258; 26:218
Duncan, A. 3:62
Duncan, A. H. 15:278
Duncan, A. J. 25:166
Duncan, Aaron 12:152
Duncan, Alexander
    17:397
Duncan, Americus B.
    22:28
Duncan, Andrew 21:51
Duncan, Benjamin 21:24
Duncan, C. 1:123
Duncan, Chapen 10:50
Duncan, Charles 27:34
Duncan, Charles H.
    17:211
Duncan, Cridenden
    11:200
Duncan, Dwight 23:106
Duncan, E. 3:223; 17:130;
    24:192
Duncan, E. H. 14:268
Duncan, Edgar 12:19
Duncan, Elbridge 17:499
Duncan, Erasmus D.
    20:136
Duncan, Evan 22:297
Duncan, F. 27:35
Duncan, Francis 8:14;
    18:131
Duncan, Fred 27:36
Duncan, Frederick 9:130
Duncan, G. 1:123; 21:186;
    25:166; 26:23
Duncan, G. W. 3:62
Duncan, Gabriel 26:123
Duncan, Gam 27:34
Duncan, George 5:38;
    9:79; 10:111; 20:242;
    22:351; 23:104
Duncan, George H.
    18:344
Duncan, George Thomas
    17:501
Duncan, H. 15:258
Duncan, H. P. 3:62
Duncan, Harrison 17:294
Duncan, Henry 10:111;
    11:201; 20:242;
    21:326; 22:297
Duncan, Hiram 26:23
Duncan, Ichabod 21:99
Duncan, J. B. 5:14;
    25:166
Duncan, J. C. 14:56
Duncan, J. M. 3:62; 22:75

Duncan, J. W. 14:240;
27:39
Duncan, James 12:171
Duncan, James E. 17:19
Duncan, James M. 18:48
Duncan, Jason 7:83
Duncan, Jesse 10:50;
20:242
Duncan, Jm. 8:100
Duncan, John 13:124;
15:278; 17:78, 95,
165, 459; 22:249;
24:151, 192
Duncan, John D. 10:111
Duncan, John H. 7:25;
22:189
Duncan, John L. 17:272
Duncan, John M. 22:422
Duncan, Joseph 11:422
Duncan, Joshua 23:178
Duncan, Josiah S. 11:411
Duncan, Leroy 11:395
Duncan, Marion 22:500
Duncan, Mitchell 17:235
Duncan, Nathan 17:130;
24:192
Duncan, Oran J. 10:95
Duncan, Orin 24:193
Duncan, R. 12:171;
15:172
Duncan, Richard 22:249
Duncan, Robert B. 22:141
Duncan, S. 17:131;
24:192
Duncan, Sanford 21:269
Duncan, Seth 23:98
Duncan, Stephen P. 8:14;
26:156
Duncan, T. S. 10:50;
20:242
Duncan, Theodore 27:39
Duncan, Thomas 21:51
Duncan, W. H. 9:142;
19:233; 25:27; 27:35
Duncan, W. H. H. 27:34
Duncan, W. M. 3:62
Duncan, W. W. 8:71
Duncan, Washington
22:297
Duncan, William 1:26;
8:14; 9:235; 11:200;
18:131, 235, 420;
22:28, 249; 24:101;
26:24
Duncan, William A.
17:144
Duncan, William H. 9:175
Duncan, William M.
24:17
Duncan, William S. 23:64

Duncan, William T.
17:236
Duncaster, Thomas
22:334
Dunco, George 4:21
Duncommon, John 20:242
Dundardy, R. C. 16:187
Dunderdale, W. 20:242
Dunderdale, William
10:50
Dundore, W. E. 23:27
Dunell, Milton N. 9:156
Duneman, John 10:50
Duner, John G. 17:456;
24:213
Dunevan, John D. 20:243
Dunfer, --- 8:84
Dunforth, J. 18:189
Dunfy, John 21:252
Dungan, A. H. 25:166
Dungan, D. 16:160
Dungan, J. C. 16:187
Dungan, Simon 15:352
Dungans, Newell 25:166
Dungberry, W. H. 14:161
Dungeon, William 13:108
Dungy, A. J. 9:79
Dunham, --- 21:206
Dunham, Alburtus 22:28
Dunham, Amos J. 7:25
Dunham, B. D. 24:88
Dunham, Benjamin 4:21
Dunham, Daniel B. 24:99
Dunham, Daniel J. 13:20
Dunham, David F.
10:111; 20:243;
23:64
Dunham, E. 23:245
Dunham, Edward A.
22:422
Dunham, Enoch W. 11:15
Dunham, Ephraim 12:19
Dunham, George 11:104;
15:331; 19:67; 22:28
Dunham, George H. 15:5
Dunham, George L.
24:110
Dunham, George W. 4:21
Dunham, H. 9:142;
16:187; 21:326;
27:35
Dunham, Harvey 13:76;
16:187
Dunham, Ira 17:33
Dunham, J. 19:233
Dunham, J. B. 23:28
Dunham, J. H. 8:71;
25:166
Dunham, J. P. 15:293
Dunham, J. S. 3:63
Dunham, James 19:67

Dunham, John 11:105,
321
Dunham, John B. 10:16
Dunham, John H. 5:14
Dunham, John M. 22:278
Dunham, John R. 15:33
Dunham, Jonathan 22:28
Dunham, Joseph 9:175
Dunham, Josiah 11:218
Dunham, Marion 22:189
Dunham, Nathan 24:38
Dunham, Nathan L.
10:111; 20:243
Dunham, O. 20:243
Dunham, Orson 11:57
Dunham, Ozro 10:50
Dunham, Peter 7:93
Dunham, Robert F. 24:49
Dunham, Samuel W. 4:21
Dunham, T. J. 16:187
Dunham, Thomas L.
16:145
Dunham, W. 12:80;
25:166
Dunham, W. E. 15:165
Dunham, W. H. 15:194
Dunham, William 14:297;
17:472; 27:38
Dunhart, W. 3:63
Dunigan, Percy G. 16:30
Dunihue, Gardner 24:38
Dunihue, Isaac D. 24:38
Duning, E. 14:268
Dunivan, Henry 22:297
Dunivan, J. 13:87
Dunk, S. 20:151
Dunkal, Jacob 13:20
Dunkan, Ludwell 24:38
Dunkan, W. H. 25:296
Dunkard, Achilles 9:219;
18:365
Dunkel, Abraham 21:120
Dunkel, John 15:347
Dunkelberger, Joel 22:75
Dunkell, John 11:28
Dunken, A. 16:187
Dunken, T. 3:63
Dunken, W. H. 18:338
Dunkenbring, Henry
10:50
Dunker, Jasper 17:242
Dunkert, Daniel 10:50
Dunkin, C. 18:365
Dunkinfield, George
16:118
Dunkinson, Thomas 10:25
Dunkirk, John 21:136
Dunkle, Benjamin F.
13:20
Dunkle, John 25:166
Dunkle, Reuben 7:64

Dunkle, Watson 13:20
Dunkleberry, E. A. 14:56
Dunklee, Peter S. 19:161
Dunkley, J. H. 12:152
Dunkow, J. 14:56
Dunkweits, William 14:56
Dunlap, A. 23:313
Dunlap, Alex 12:19
Dunlap, C. 3:63
Dunlap, David 21:326
Dunlap, Edward 13:20
Dunlap, Erasmus 17:404
Dunlap, F. 21:147
Dunlap, Galvin C. 21:326
Dunlap, George H. 21:68
Dunlap, George W. 23:288
Dunlap, Hugh 10:16
Dunlap, J. 25:166
Dunlap, J. J. 11:301
Dunlap, J. S. 16:30
Dunlap, James 1:28; 15:323; 21:24; 22:189; 23:87
Dunlap, James T. 10:95
Dunlap, Jeremiah 4:22
Dunlap, John 10:160; 19:161
Dunlap, John A. 21:68
Dunlap, John M. 11:301
Dunlap, John W. 21:252
Dunlap, Josiah 10:172; 19:161
Dunlap, M. B. 9:51
Dunlap, Martin 12:19
Dunlap, P. 8:62
Dunlap, Patton 26:158
Dunlap, Philip 25:287
Dunlap, S. 14:56
Dunlap, S. C. 9:79
Dunlap, S. M. 22:519
Dunlap, S. O. 26:25
Dunlap, Samuel 22:496
Dunlap, Taylor 21:269
Dunlap, Thomas 11:239
Dunlap, Thomas J. 11:301
Dunlap, W. 3:63; 15:55; 25:166
Dunlap, W. F. 9:162
Dunlap, W. J. 14:161
Dunlap, Warren 17:392
Dunlap, William 12:19; 22:28, 189
Dunlap, William F. 27:38
Dunlass, William 12:69
Dunlavey, George 8:125
Dunlavy, George 19:320
Dunlavy, J. 11:301
Dunlavy, James 1:28
Dunlavy, Patrick 27:39
Dunlear, D. F. 19:226

Dunleary, Francis 10:160; 19:161
Dunlep, John 14:161
Dunlevy, Thomas 23:189
Dunlop, Hugh 10:10
Dunlop, John S. 14:161
Dunlop, S. R. 16:30
Dunman, Robert S. 16:279
Dunmar, Edward 4:21
Dunmer, Levi 11:238
Dunmoore, A. 14:56
Dunmore, John R. 11:27
Dunmore, Thomas 12:48
Dunmore, W. 1:125
Dunmore, William 15:122
Dunn, --- 14:161
Dunn, A. 12:152
Dunn, Adam 19:327
Dunn, Adolphus E. 7:16
Dunn, Alexander 3:63
Dunn, Alfred O. 22:249
Dunn, Alvin 17:99
Dunn, Ammon 9:21; 18:305; 26:95
Dunn, Ananias 22:477
Dunn, Andrew 7:16
Dunn, Andrew J. 22:28
Dunn, Anthony 25:288
Dunn, Archibald 10:111
Dunn, B. J. 8:47
Dunn, B. W. 10:144; 19:161
Dunn, Berry 17:131; 24:192
Dunn, Boston 9:207
Dunn, C. 3:63; 17:291
Dunn, C. A. 11:395
Dunn, C. C. 18:216
Dunn, C. E. 1:123
Dunn, C. W. 14:277; 23:28
Dunn, Cain 7:77; 25:296
Dunn, Calvin 15:55
Dunn, Catharine 12:170
Dunn, Chancey 25:27
Dunn, Charity L. 10:160; 19:161
Dunn, Daniel 7:93; 10:50; 20:243; 21:326; 22:297
Dunn, David 7:56; 19:346; 23:141
Dunn, E. 13:87; 24:17; 27:35
Dunn, Edward 5:14; 9:12; 15:195; 25:166
Dunn, Edward H. 15:105
Dunn, Emanuel M. 22:249
Dunn, Enos 22:189
Dunn, Ezra E. 22:141

Dunn, F. H. C. 25:280
Dunn, F. M. 9:68
Dunn, G. 3:63
Dunn, G. E. 3:62
Dunn, George 20:7
Dunn, George W. 20:29
Dunn, H. 14:297; 17:475; 27:37
Dunn, Harvey 6:24
Dunn, Helam H. 11:57
Dunn, Henry 11:57
Dunn, Hiram 8:14; 18:131
Dunn, J. 3:63; 14:56; 24:177
Dunn, J. A. 21:109
Dunn, J. M. 27:35
Dunn, J. M. C. 22:115
Dunn, J. T. 21:24
Dunn, J. V. 3:62
Dunn, J. W. 20:177
Dunn, James 3:62; 8:47; 10:10, 160; 11:181; 12:19, 122; 18:131; 19:161; 21:166; 22:161; 25:166; 26:157
Dunn, James A. 19:161
Dunn, James F. 23:276
Dunn, James H. 10:95
Dunn, James M. 25:29
Dunn, John 3:62, 63; 7:15; 9:118; 10:152; 11:422; 14:161; 15:55; 16:291; 17:14, 359; 18:13, 48, 235; 19:12, 161; 20:96, 243; 21:326; 22:249; 23:11, 28, 64; 24:65; 26:23; 27:37
Dunn, John A. 22:397
Dunn, John C. 17:425
Dunn, John M. 15:165; 25:166
Dunn, John R. 12:19
Dunn, John T. 11:239
Dunn, Joseph 11:28; 14:56; 17:355
Dunn, Joseph N. 25:166
Dunn, L. 1:124
Dunn, L. H. 17:158
Dunn, Lafayette 21:109
Dunn, Lawrence 25:166
Dunn, Lemuel 10:50; 20:243
Dunn, Levi 20:189
Dunn, Lewis 20:243
Dunn, M. 3:62; 14:297; 17:477
Dunn, M. S. 25:319
Dunn, Martin 14:297; 17:474

Dunn, McKee 22:422
Dunn, Michael 11:104; 21:9
Dunn, Milton 7:64
Dunn, N. 1:126; 25:166
Dunn, N. R. 17:95
Dunn, Nicholas 22:334
Dunn, Owen 3:62
Dunn, P. 3:62; 19:226
Dunn, P. T. 11:428
Dunn, Patrick 9:175; 11:15; 15:195; 16:88
Dunn, Peter 13:20; 16:367; 22:334; 23:28
Dunn, Pt. James 15:122
Dunn, R. 3:63
Dunn, R. G. 4:21
Dunn, R. H. 12:69; 15:33
Dunn, Rease 16:187
Dunn, Robert 18:81; 19:161
Dunn, Rufus R. 14:56
Dunn, Samuel 7:56
Dunn, Samuel B. 19:12
Dunn, Samuel H. 23:141
Dunn, Solomon 12:48; 14:297; 17:481
Dunn, Stephen 22:297
Dunn, Thomas 13:20; 14:56; 18:109; 22:120; 23:141; 24:17
Dunn, Thomas B. 11:286
Dunn, W. 25:167
Dunn, W. H. 17:495
Dunn, W. W. 3:63; 25:311
Dunn, Wesley 5:14
Dunn, William 5:38; 8:63; 9:157; 10:16; 13:63; 15:105; 19:12, 66; 22:297
Dunn, William A. 7:25
Dunn, William G. 12:19
Dunn, William H. 13:20; 16:118
Dunn, William J. 17:206
Dunn, William M. 22:249
Dunn, Wilson 4:21
Dunnan, Joseph 4:21
Dunnan, L. 21:147
Dunnan, Lewis 10:172
Dunnan, Robert S. 15:352
Dunnan, Smith 4:21
Dunnaway, Isaac J. 11:91
Dunnaway, William 22:403
Dunnborough, S. 14:56
Dunne, E. 9:142
Dunne, G. 23:112

Dunnegan, James 13:20
Dunneheigh, Thomas 9:34
Dunnell, Henry C. 16:93
Dunnell, William A. 8:84
Dunnels, Albert 25:167
Dunner, Albert 9:207
Dunner, George 18:394
Dunnigan, H. 25:167
Dunnigan, John 18:65
Dunnigan, Perey E. 13:20
Dunnigan, Peter 24:77
Dunning, Amos 20:29
Dunning, Charles 9:156
Dunning, D. 14:161
Dunning, E. 14:281
Dunning, Francis M. 8:84
Dunning, J. W. 17:279
Dunning, James 22:297
Dunning, John 10:16
Dunning, John J. 16:93
Dunning, S. P. 3:63
Dunning, William A. 25:167
Dunningan, Joseph 11:259
Dunninger, Thomas 9:109
Dunnings, John 13:124
Dunnivan, John 22:449
Dunnoran, John 9:79
Dunnrise, --- 12:19
Dunoff, N. P. 14:56
Dunos, B. F. 3:63
Dunrand, P. 3:63
Dunridie, John 7:121
Dunroe, P. F. 3:63
Duns, Timothy W. 11:301
Dunscob, William G. 8:105
Dunscomb, Horace 9:70
Dunsmoore, John 19:337
Dunsmore, Carmi S. 22:477
Dunsmore, D. 25:167
Dunson, D. 14:56
Dunson, E. 14:56
Dunson, F. 9:142
Dunson, Howard 23:285
Dunson, Joseph 13:20
Dunson, L. F. 3:63
Dunston, Andrew 26:138
Duntley, Sylvanius 11:286
Dunton, David A. 16:30
Dunton, Duran A. 13:20
Dunton, F. B. 19:251
Dunton, John 25:274
Dunton, Nathaniel 4:21
Dunton, O. E. 14:161
Dunton, O. F. 25:28
Dunton, Prince A. 16:84
Dunton, Thomas 6:27
Dunton, W. H. 13:63
Dunton, William A. 23:87

Dunton, William H. 19:67
Dunton, Wilmot W. 14:161
Dunway, J. 18:13
Dunwell, Henry 26:122
Dunwell, Samuel 3:63
Dunwiddie, John 21:326
Dunwoodie, James 25:319
Dunwoodie, L. 21:99
Dunwoody, Ebenezer 9:51
Dunwoody, James 18:420
Dunwoody, L. D. 7:93
Dunz, David 20:35
Duor, Joseph H. 20:243
Dupee, Francis 27:37
Dupee, Henry 23:189
Dupee, Samuel 17:64
Dupel, L. 1:126
Dupenette, Newlin 13:20
Duper, R. 27:38
Duphrey, Henry 21:326
Dupis, George 21:326
Duplesse, Julius 7:25
Dupney, S. W. 7:56
Dupon, Francis 3:63
Dupont, C. 14:56
Dupont, Duam 11:278
Dupont, Ira 13:108
Dupont, Mady D. 10:50
Dupont, Meady D. 20:243
Dupont, Severe 21:326
Dupose, Silas 26:24
Dupp, Edwin C. 7:49
Duppe, Francis 9:118
Dupre, Isaac 22:249
Dupree, E. 18:235; 26:23
Dupree, Harman 10:111
Dupree, Harmon 20:243
Dupree, James K. 18:235; 26:24
Duprene, John 9:207
Duprey, Harrison L. 17:64
Dupries, Charles 14:161
Dupse, Silas 18:235
Dupue, Abraham 10:50; 20:243
Dupue, John J. 20:243
Dupue, Moses 20:243
Dupull, I. 15:341
Dupuy, J. 21:68
Dupuy, John 21:223
Dupyee, Charles 16:291
Duquane, William 25:285
Duquitte, John 13:63
Dural, Isaac 18:131
Dural, Norman 19:324
Durall, Frank 13:108
Durall, Henry 19:322
Duralle, Lewis W. 12:99
Duram, James 25:319
Duran, Antonio 8:123

Duran, George 7:8
Duran, Joseph 25:26
Duran, Thomas 22:10
Durance, James 9:230;
    20:243
Durand, Charles 11:27
Durand, Farand A. 10:95
Durand, George 9:175
Durand, H. 3:63
Durand, James C. 3:63
Durand, Juba 13:20; 16:30
Durand, Robert B. 23:87
Durand, Walter H. 20:22
Durant, F. 20:56
Durant, George 19:232
Durant, John 25:319
Durant, Samuel 12:19
Durant, Thomas 21:326
Durant, W. H. 23:141
Durant, William P. 21:326
Durban, M. 3:63
Durbin, C. 21:326
Durbin, D. H. 15:86
Durbin, E. 11:279
Durbin, Eli S. 15:195
Durbin, J. W. 12:95;
    15:359
Durbin, John W. 14:27;
    17:445; 24:166
Durbin, Joseph 11:143
Durbin, Lewis 17:131;
    24:192
Durbin, P. 20:243
Durbin, Philip 10:50
Durbron, Walter L.
    15:123
Durby, Edward 24:192
Durchmiller, P. 13:108
Durchonp, Peter 27:39
Durden, Robert 3:63
Durdon, Adam 24:101
Durdon, David 21:326
Durell, H. E. 9:214;
    21:326
Duren, Thomas 8:100;
    17:461; 24:169
Durer, John T. 7:121
Dures, S. H. 20:243
Durfee, Andrew 25:167
Durfee, C. A. 25:167
Durfee, Edwin 20:154
Durfee, James 3:63; 8:63
Durfee, R. J. 17:242
Durfee, William J. 7:16
Durflinger, Philip 17:418;
    24:157
Durfrance, --- 1:27
Durgan, Charles P. 21:326
Durgan, Daniel 9:175
Durgan, R. 24:65
Durge, Edmund 24:107

Durgin, D. F. 19:237
Durgin, D. V. 19:232
Durgin, E. R. 25:29
Durgin, Henry S. 9:79
Durgin, John 14:161;
    25:27
Durgin, Leavitt B. 16:84
Durgin, W. 1:126
Durgin, Z. 3:63
Durham, A. 14:56
Durham, A. B. 1:126
Durham, Ab 3:63
Durham, Abraham 13:20
Durham, Allen G. 18:292;
    26:97
Durham, B. F. 10:50;
    18:65; 20:243
Durham, Charles 13:63
Durham, David 17:403
Durham, E. A. 8:63;
    26:158
Durham, George H. 22:75
Durham, H. C. 9:175;
    19:251
Durham, H. J. 1:125
Durham, Henry 19:290
Durham, Henry C. 12:48
Durham, Isham 9:70
Durham, J. 22:28
Durham, John 1:28; 4:22
Durham, John H. 18:28
Durham, Nathan 7:121
Durham, Polk 11:186
Durham, R. H. 3:63
Durham, Wesley 17:397
Durham, William 17:147
Durheim, Bernard 27:35
Durhous, B. 3:63
Duric, James 13:108
Durin, William S. 22:249
During, Christian 24:71
During, F. 14:57
During, Paul 13:20
Duringer, J. 7:93
Durisco, C. L. 16:30
Durk, Henry 15:195
Durkee, A. 23:141
Durkee, Alvah B. 10:160
Durkee, Charles 17:359
Durkee, R. 1:28
Durkee, Sidney 10:153
Durkee, Walter F. 21:252
Durkey, C. F. 1:93
Durkey, J. C. 17:109
Durkin, J. W. 1:126
Durkin, P. 1:124; 24:17
Durks, Henry 26:22
Durland, John 4:22
Durland, John M. 4:22
Durlbiss, John 10:111
Durlein, Lymme 1:27

Durley, Robert 22:28
Durlin, J. C. 18:235;
    26:24
Durller, William 23:11
Durm, Thomas 16:132
Durman, George 18:131
Durman, Lewis 19:161
Durmann, George 8:14
Durn, Berry 16:30
Durnan, James 15:291
Durnel, A. 23:28
Durner, G. H. 25:167
Durnill, H. B. 7:93
Durning, M. 1:29
Durning, T. 1:124
Durnshee, William N.
    18:305
Durnshes, W. N. 26:96
Durobis, William 3:63
Duross, Henry 1:28
Durphy, Edmund 22:334
Durphy, Henry 19:12
Durr, Israel 16:145
Durr, John 3:63
Durr, William H. 8:14
Durrall, John H. 23:28
Durran, Joseph 6:30
Durrant, B. 3:63
Durrant, John 6:30
Durre, John 16:139
Durree, John F. 21:326
Durrell, William H. 9:34
Durrenburg, D. 14:9
Durrham, James 4:22
Durrice, James H. 6:23
Durryberry, W. H. 14:255
Durst, Dennis 1:28
Durst, Herbert 21:10
Durst, Jacob 23:98
Durst, John 10:111;
    20:243
Durstin, George M. D.
    12:19
Durstine, Jacob 11:238
Durvan, John 26:23
Dury, Green 11:201
Duryea, G. W. 7:72;
    26:158
Duryea, W. 1:125
Duryee, George 22:141
Dusaing, Scott 27:39
Dusalt, A. 3:63
Dusan, J. 3:63
Dusang, Samuel E. W.
    15:7
Duscin, J. B. 21:24
Dusenberry, Charles
    20:243
Dusenberry, D. 13:87
Dusenberry, George 14:57

Dusenberry, Henry 4:22; 16:30
Dusenberry, J. H. 20:243
Dusenberry, John M. 23:87
Dusenberry, Martin 18:292
Dusenberry, S. B. 8:125
Dusenbery, --- 16:367
Dusenburg, Charles 10:50
Dusenburg, James H. 10:50
Dusenbury, L. 15:341
Dusenbury, Martin 26:97
Dusey, E. 14:161
Dush, John 9:21; 18:305; 26:96
Dusham, Joseph 15:332
Dushane, Joseph 19:67
Dushey, Anthoney 15:55
Dushid, Lewis W. 4:65
Dushuttle, H. L. 19:161
Dushuttle, Henry L. 10:160
Dusick, William 15:165
Dusinberry, Isaac 15:195
Dusinbury, Henry 13:20
Duskett, Pius 25:167
Dusler, Frederick 10:50
Duslor, Fred 20:243
Dusman, George D. 22:75
Dusney, Josiah 7:121
Duso, Stephen 20:189
Dusold, J. G. 15:5
Dusseldorf, Peter 13:20
Dustan, Daniel 25:27
Duster, Holmes 17:78
Dustin, Albert 16:118
Dustin, B. F. 21:326
Dustin, Benjamin H. 12:19
Dustin, Charles J. 21:24
Dustin, D. D. 15:195
Dustin, Timothy 21:326
Dustin, W. 19:232
Dustin, Walter 13:108
Dustin, William 9:79
Dusting, Henry B. 8:14
Duston, J. S. 23:141
Dutch, Benjamin T. 26:23
Dutch, J. P. 9:142; 27:35
Dutch, James 7:25
Dutch, Joseph 18:81
Dutch, Michael 11:190
Dutcher, A. 20:243
Dutcher, Albro 10:50
Dutcher, Andress 23:106
Dutcher, E. B. 14:57
Dutcher, Fred. A. 18:394
Dutcher, G. 7:25
Dutcher, G. W. 16:187

Dutcher, Harry 22:334
Dutcher, J. 1:127
Dutcher, J. H. 1:123
Dutcher, Newton 11:122
Dutcher, Platt 4:22
Dutcher, W. 27:143
Dutcher, William 22:141
Dutches, William R. 11:276
Dute, William 19:329
Duter, David 10:16
Dutlee, C. 17:64
Dutreman, W. 3:63
Dutro, John 18:48
Dutro, S. H. 20:145
Dutrom, Irdell 3:63
Dutrombley, F. 8:14
Dutrombly, F. 18:131
Dutsick, John 24:151
Dutten, E. 24:59
Dutten, G. F. 9:51
Dutterer, Levi 17:78
Dutterman, Herman 26:97
Duttin, S. 3:63
Dutto, John 27:39
Dutton, --- 15:123
Dutton, A. 25:167
Dutton, Andrew J. 22:278
Dutton, David D. 27:38
Dutton, Frank A. 22:10
Dutton, G. L. 18:66
Dutton, George H. 22:10
Dutton, H. 16:187
Dutton, J. 21:194
Dutton, J. P. 26:122
Dutton, J. R. 15:33
Dutton, James 7:15; 10:50; 20:243; 23:276
Dutton, John 13:108
Dutton, John H. 19:270
Dutton, John W. 9:175
Dutton, Joseph 23:313
Dutton, Myranda 23:104
Dutton, Theodore 10:160; 19:161
Dutton, Victor F. 11:105
Dutton, William 1:29; 10:50; 20:243
Dutton, William F. 13:20
Dutton, William H. 3:63
Duttry, Andrew 11:15
Dutwiler, J. W. 21:198
Duty, William 24:38
Duval, E. 1:28; 14:240; 27:39
Duval, Francis 19:273
Duval, Isaac 8:14
Duval, W. 1:124
Duval, William R. 22:120
Duvale, Benjamin 18:420

Duvall, Benjamin 22:120
Duvall, Charles P. 22:10
Duvall, D. W. 19:245
Duvall, E. O. P. 9:34
Duvall, G. W. 9:175
Duvall, George W. 7:93
Duvall, Hilary H. 17:101
Duvall, I. H. 1:28
Duvall, Jacob 7:121
Duvall, John T. 23:64
Duvall, John W. 23:28
Duvall, John W. D. 20:243
Duvall, Nelson 7:121
Duvall, Peter 17:131; 24:192
Duvall, T. 1:124
Duvall, Thomas 22:233
Duvall, W. A. 22:477
Duvall, Wallace 7:121
Duvall, William 23:189
Duvall, William L. 22:120
Duvan, Jacob 17:161
Duvarris, Lucien 7:121
Duvier, Louis 21:24
Duvigneand, Joseph 24:93
Duvine, G. 3:63
Duvitt, J. S. 3:63
Duxans, H. 25:167
Duyer, James 10:50
Duyer, John 16:187
Duyer, Michael 16:187
Duyer, P. 3:63
Duysing, O. 25:319
Duzan, William W. 19:266
Duzen, D. T. 9:175
Duzenberry, Martin 9:34
Dvis, Caleb 19:11
Dweer, John 11:422
Dwelley, Samuel L. 16:77
Dwelling, Archer 22:75
Dwer, Mark 20:89
Dwick, J. S. 21:24
Dwiggans, James 22:478
Dwight, E. 15:286; 19:67
Dwight, G. S. 17:78
Dwilbiss, George 9:21
Dwinell, James 17:495
Dwinell, R. E. 16:187
Dwiner, James 18:109
Dwinnels, Joseph 7:93
Dwire, Michael 9:219; 13:63; 18:394
Dwold, Louis 9:21
Dwyel, Philip 11:238
Dwyer, Clifton 17:389
Dwyer, Dennis 18:365
Dwyer, Edward 7:25
Dwyer, J. 19:251
Dwyer, James 22:334

Dwyer, John 20:145
Dwyer, Michael 9:21; 21:326
Dwyer, Patrick 25:167
Dwyer, Richard 21:202
Dwyer, T. 1:126
Dwyer, William 19:161; 21:326
Dwyer, William H. 20:35
Dwyre, Hezekiah G. 20:22
Dwyse, --- 19:67
Dyal, Amos A. 11:15
Dyar, Israel D. 4:22
Dyar, John 17:233
Dyar, Thomas J. 20:17
Dyar, William M. 20:17
Dyas, G. W. 21:326
Dyas, Henry 13:20
Dyas, Moses 22:28
Dyas, Thomas 26:218
Dyball, J. 14:161
Dybell, Allen N. 10:111; 20:243
Dychman, D. 14:57
Dyctill, William 9:219
Dye, Abel 13:20
Dye, Abram 8:84
Dye, Adams 15:195
Dye, Alfred 22:75
Dye, Asa 20:142
Dye, B. T. 20:139
Dye, Curtis S. 5:14
Dye, D. F. 18:305; 26:96
Dye, D. T. 9:21
Dye, David G. 17:19
Dye, E. 9:96
Dye, Elam 4:22
Dye, George W. 1:26
Dye, Henry 9:21; 18:276, 305; 26:96
Dye, I. C. 3:63
Dye, J. 1:126
Dye, James 3:63; 12:69; 15:55
Dye, John 11:260; 22:10
Dye, John A. 9:227; 18:365
Dye, John E. 20:17
Dye, John H. 22:120
Dye, John S. 19:161
Dye, Joseph 22:500
Dye, Lewis 13:20; 16:30
Dye, Oliver 8:77
Dye, Robert T. 17:279
Dye, Samuel 14:161
Dye, Silas H. 17:206
Dye, V. 16:367
Dyer, Albert H. 17:51
Dyer, Alfred 18:216
Dyer, Andrew H. 10:111; 20:243

Dyer, Benjamin 7:93; 21:327
Dyer, Benson B. 10:16
Dyer, Charles 17:276
Dyer, Charles R. 19:67
Dyer, Edmund 14:161
Dyer, Edward M. 19:334
Dyer, Ephraim F. 11:422
Dyer, Fordyce A. 10:160
Dyer, G. M. 21:327
Dyer, G. W. 3:63
Dyer, H. 3:63; 9:51
Dyer, H. C. 12:122; 15:123
Dyer, H. P. 16:30
Dyer, Hadley 9:79
Dyer, Hadley P. 26:22
Dyer, Henry C. 17:259
Dyer, Henry J. 13:20
Dyer, Hudson K. 18:13
Dyer, I. 3:63
Dyer, Isaac B. 22:249
Dyer, J. A. 10:27; 19:301
Dyer, J. C. 2:9; 3:63; 25:27
Dyer, James 8:14; 18:131; 20:7; 23:197
Dyer, John 9:100; 14:161, 314, 321; 15:86; 16:81; 22:28, 421; 23:98
Dyer, John W. 3:63
Dyer, Joseph 23:189
Dyer, Knowles H. 7:93
Dyer, Lawson 10:50; 20:243
Dyer, N. H. 15:95
Dyer, Owen 8:14; 18:131
Dyer, Peter 4:65
Dyer, Rev. C. 19:161
Dyer, S. 3:63; 23:141
Dyer, S. C. 18:434
Dyer, Stephen H. 10:160
Dyer, Stephen K. 19:161
Dyer, T. J. 16:187
Dyer, Thomas 15:273
Dyer, W. 3:63
Dyer, W. W. 1:123
Dyer, William 9:233; 10:210; 23:28
Dyer, William H. 20:243
Dyer, William N. 25:271
Dyer, William R. 10:50
Dyermond, John 9:203
Dyers, Jerome W. 22:75
Dygert, George H. 24:185
Dygert, James F. 22:421
Dygut, George H. 17:429
Dying, William 8:113
Dyke, A. 1:97; 14:161, 255

Dyke, C. 13:108
Dyke, F. 3:63
Dyke, Frederick A. 24:93
Dyke, H. J. 15:315; 19:67
Dyke, Henry 25:30
Dyke, James H. 21:99
Dyke, John W. 22:189
Dyke, Joseph M. 21:253
Dyke, Manlis E. 22:75
Dyke, Noah 4:22
Dyke, W. B. 25:296
Dyke, William 1:28; 8:63
Dykeman, D. 3:63
Dykeman, F. 3:63
Dykeman, John J. 11:27
Dykeman, Martin 13:20
Dykeman, Michael 13:20
Dykeman, Simon 10:111; 20:243
Dykeman, W. 1:124
Dyker, Henry 9:159
Dykes, J. F. 12:166
Dykes, James 6:12
Dykes, John F. 25:319
Dykes, L. 3:63; 14:161
Dykes, Pleasant 3:223; 17:504
Dykes, S. 25:29
Dykes, Stephen 2:9
Dykes, William 17:202
Dykman, J. 27:34
Dykman, Martin 16:30
Dyks, Basil 25:28
Dyman, George B. 20:243
Dymond, George 13:20; 16:30
Dymond, Jacob F. 25:27
Dymond, Vincent 10:50
Dyne, James W. 4:22
Dyne, W. E. O. 16:291
Dynman, George B. 10:111
Dyon, Russell 18:235; 26:24
Dyon, William 5:38
Dyons, John H. 8:84
Dyr, R. V. 1:97
Dyre, Lyman S. 11:319
Dyre, W. 3:63
Dyre, William 3:63
Dyringer, Henry 23:263
Dyringer, Isaac 23:263
Dysart, S. 9:227; 18:365
Dysart, Stephen 22:10
Dysen, W. 25:167
Dysert, Samuel 23:276
Dysert, T. K. 12:152
Dysing, Henry 9:130; 27:36
Dyson, J. 13:87; 14:9
Dyson, J. C. 18:81

Dyson, Joseph 18:394
Dyson, Mathias 10:111;
  20:243
Dyson, Reuben 21:327
Dyson, Robert 19:45
Dysort, Silas 11:144
Dyton, Sevestus 21:327

E

E---, --- 12:99; 17:506;
  23:28, 64
E---, A. J. 11:326
E---, A. P. 19:286
E---, C. 15:196
E---, C. D. 19:301
E---, Charles 11:326;
  12:99
E---, D. B. 9:51; 24:110
E---, D. E. 27:42
E---, David 11:302
E---, F. M. 20:243
E---, G. 16:291
E---, G. B. 23:313
E---, George 9:51
E---, H--- 26:236
E---, H. 20:56; 24:110;
  26:159
E---, J. 10:32; 12:141;
  18:28; 24:110, 213;
  26:159
E---, J. A. 17:509
E---, J. B. 14:268
E---, J. G. 17:355
E---, J. J. 20:243
E---, J. M. 11:339
E---, J. W. 15:267
E---, Joseph B. 22:351
E---, L. A. H. 11:339
E---, L. W. 16:291
E---, M. L. 24:110
E---, S. J. 23:203
E---, S. M. 21:208
E---, T. 10:34; 19:301;
  25:31
E---, T. H. 10:186
E---, T. P. 18:366
E---, W. 17:296; 20:84,
  181; 24:110; 25:311
E---, W. A. 16:113
E---, W. F. 11:29
E---, W. H. 18:28
E---, W. L. 23:313
E---, W. M. 11:239
E---, Z. M. 26:159
E----, David 22:141
E---a, John 15:165
E---th, J. 15:151
Eachnes, J. L. 23:203
Eachody, W. H. 22:189

Eades, J. M. 7:25
Eades, James 3:64
Eades, L. J. 1:30
Eadie, J. 1:127
Eadley, Levi 3:64
Eadons, H. H. 9:51
Eads, Asa 17:206
Eads, David 15:195
Eads, Henry 22:450
Eads, Jackson 17:267
Eads, John B. 17:453;
  24:183
Eads, Samuel 11:59
Eads, Zachariah 22:121
Eady, D. 14:57
Eady, H. 9:207; 18:66
Eady, J. W. 14:57
Eaens, David 15:195
Eagan, Charles 3:64
Eagan, F. C. 20:243
Eagan, James 16:65
Eagan, John 3:65; 10:111;
  20:185; 23:121
Eagan, M. 25:274
Eagan, Martin 8:14
Eagan, Patrick 25:287
Eagan, Philip 13:108
Eagan, R. 17:501
Eagan, T. C. 12:142
Eagans, J. 14:57
Eagear, H. E. 12:87;
  16:291
Eagen, Eugene 23:64
Eager, Daniel E. 12:19
Eager, H. 7:56
Eager, Nathaniel 21:136
Eager, Stephen 10:160;
  19:161
Eaggleston, William 3:65
Eagin, J. 20:39
Eagin, Martin 18:426
Eagland, William 17:352
Eagle, Edward 22:189
Eagle, G. W. 7:72
Eagle, George 16:279
Eagle, George B. 12:98;
  15:357
Eagle, Henry M. 20:132
Eagle, John 9:21; 15:123;
  18:305; 26:97
Eagle, John H. 22:189
Eagle, Nelson 13:87
Eagle, William S. 17:161
Eaglebrath, H. 14:235
Eagler, John 25:319
Eagles, Charles L. 1:30
Eagles, Nelson 14:9
Eagles, Wilson 14:9
Eagleson, Mathew 15:315
Eagleston, C. 25:167
Eagleston, D. 1:128

Eagleston, Daniel 11:145
Eaglison, Mathew 19:67
Eagon, James 15:33
Eairly, James 22:120
Eaken, Samuel 10:111;
  20:243
Eakes, Andrew J. 22:75
Eakin, Franklin A. 8:14;
  18:131
Eakin, Joseph B. 18:365
Eakin, William 20:243
Eakins, J. 14:281
Eakins, Joseph 20:243
Eakman, Aaron 22:233
Eakman, George 2:10;
  25:31
Eaks, Hillman 20:35
Eal, Andrew 22:450
Ealen, James W. 22:189
Eales, Lucius S. 15:195
Ealey, William 20:243
Ealy, Daniel 17:236
Eames, Charles 4:22
Eames, George T. 9:142
Eames, Jacob 16:187
Eames, John E. 13:20
Eames, L. C. 15:298
Eames, Martin 9:118;
  27:41
Eames, Samuel 4:22
Eames, Walter J. 4:22
Eamick, J. 25:167
Eamsbry, Anson E. 4:22
Eanes, Charles 10:27
Eanos, Charles 19:301
Ear, John W. 18:189
Eardman, Henry 13:108
Earehart, Samuel 26:97
Eareheart, Samuel 18:305
Eares, Jacob 8:38
Earhart, E. 25:30
Earhart, George C. 10:50
Earhart, James 22:423
Earhart, Nicholas 12:61
Earhart, William F. 8:14;
  18:131
Earheart, George 14:240
Earheart, George C.
  20:244
Earickson, J. P. 9:244
Earl, Alfred 11:145
Earl, Arthur 4:22
Earl, C. 3:64
Earl, Charles 9:175;
  22:423
Earl, D. 3:64
Earl, Daniel 13:20
Earl, G. W. 3:64
Earl, George 22:297
Earl, George B. 6:14;
  18:81; 20:123

Earl, George W. 5:14
Earl, H. 3:64
Earl, Isaac 21:253; 23:28
Earl, J. 8:47
Earl, James H. 3:64;
    11:260
Earl, Joseph W. 21:327
Earl, Nathan 25:31
Earl, Nelson 22:423
Earl, Royal F. 15:349
Earl, S. C. 7:73
Earl, Seth C. 24:17
Earl, Spencer V. 10:16
Earl, William 3:64;
    18:131; 22:297
Earld, Robert 15:151
Earle, Abraham 4:22
Earle, G. H. 16:187
Earle, George W. 16:5
Earle, James 1:31
Earle, James M. 12:19
Earle, John 9:12
Earle, John W. 7:25
Earle, Joseph W. 9:214
Earle, Nelson 17:109
Earle, R. E. 1:30
Earle, Robert 8:84
Earle, Royal F. 16:367
Earle, Thomas 1:31
Earlenbough, George 7:63
Earles, Charles W. 22:512
Earles, James W. 17:73
Earles, Ran 1:31
Earles, William H. 8:100;
    24:157
Earley, Andrew 24:88
Earley, Barney 9:219;
    18:365
Earley, Charles 27:40
Earley, George 22:297
Earley, James 11:302;
    20:244
Earley, N. C. 27:40
Earley, Solomon 16:187
Earley, Thomas 19:67
Earley, William 10:50;
    26:26
Earlinley, E. D. 4:22
Earlis, Henderson 25:319
Earlman, J. 3:64
Earls, Hozy H. 22:249
Earls, Robert 22:297
Earls, William 8:47; 21:51
Earls, William H. 17:460
Earlston, D. 22:478
Early, Charles 9:130
Early, Christopher 22:278
Early, Daniel 9:175
Early, Daniel W. 19:273
Early, Edward 13:20
Early, Elias 23:178

Early, George 20:39
Early, H. T. 16:30
Early, J. Q. 17:217
Early, John 4:22; 9:203;
    17:346; 24:107
Early, John H. 22:334
Early, John N. 21:199
Early, Joshua 15:195
Early, Leland 21:194
Early, M. 9:142
Early, Mich. 9:42
Early, Samuel 11:145
Early, Silas D. 16:30
Early, T. 4:22
Early, William 11:381;
    12:19
Earmisse, J. 8:47
Earms, Henry 4:22
Earnest, A. 20:179
Earnest, Charles 19:12
Earnest, David 21:68
Earnest, H. C. 3:64
Earnest, Henry D. 22:75
Earnest, Oliver P. 11:422
Earnest, Samuel 18:292
Earnest, Thomas P.
    23:112
Earnest, W. 20:244
Earney, Cassianus 10:111;
    20:244
Earns, Mathew 19:12
Earns, W. T. 9:219
Earnst, William 10:51
Earp, William H. 8:14;
    18:131
Ears, Thomas 6:30;
    25:319
Earse, Andrew 12:145
Earson, A. J. 26:159
Earwood, F. M. 10:186;
    18:173
Easby, Clairborne 10:111
Easeley, A. 20:244
Easeley, Claibore 20:244
Easenbeck, M. 3:64
Easer, Oliver 14:161
Easler, William 9:21
Easley, Ambrose 10:51
Easley, Ed 17:174
Easley, John A. 19:161
Easley, Miller 10:51
Easley, Thomas 25:271
Easley, Thomas H. 10:51
Easley, William A. 3:64
Easly, Hamilton 17:352
Easly, James H. 17:202
Easly, Wesley 21:269
Easly, William H. 17:352
Eason, Charles 11:286
Eason, Edward 7:25
Eason, Edwin E. 21:253

Eason, Enos B. 15:172
Eason, Jack 25:167
Eason, Joel B. 19:251
Eason, Moses 22:28
Eason, R. 21:163
Eason, William 21:269;
    22:249
Eason, William M. 22:28
Eassey, William 18:235;
    26:26
East, Alra 19:12
East, Bailey 21:51
East, E. 26:26
East, Edward 9:79
East, I. R. 3:64
East, J. 14:57
East, James D. 22:189
East, John 4:22
East, Jonathan 17:33
East, William 20:136
Eastbowne, D. 12:19
Eastbrook, Charles 10:51;
    20:244
Eastburn, Thomas F.
    21:24
Eastell, Henrich 23:262
Easten, Milton E. 20:244
Easter, --- 16:93
Easter, G. 14:162, 255
Easter, Jacob 10:51; 11:58
Easter, James 15:319
Easter, Robert 1:30
Easter, William 17:131;
    22:297
Easter, William E. 10:51
Easterbrook, S. 5:14;
    25:167
Easterbrook, Sanford T.
    10:16
Easterbrooks, G. F. 1:128
Easterday, Peter 12:56
Easterling, Thomas
    11:395
Easterly, H. E. 1:128
Easterly, Harmon 24:63
Easterly, J. 15:195
Easterly, Thomas 3:64
Easterly, William A.
    10:160
Eastern, Thomas 3:64
Eastern, William A.
    19:161
Eastern, William P. 22:75
Eastey, David 8:84
Eastham, J. H. 11:144
Eastham, John W. 17:279
Easthom, John J. 15:273
Eastlack, J. G. 12:69
Eastland, Allen J. 24:17
Eastlow, J. 1:128

Eastman, --- 11:319;
 15:165
Eastman, A. D. 15:16
Eastman, Albert A. 20:22
Eastman, Ambrose 22:278
Eastman, Benjamin
 23:106
Eastman, C. 1:127;
 15:195; 25:167
Eastman, C. H. 6:30
Eastman, Charles A. 16:30
Eastman, Charles H.
 13:20
Eastman, Charles R. 21:51
Eastman, Chauncey H.
 10:111; 20:244
Eastman, Clark 5:14
Eastman, D. 3:64
Eastman, Daniel 9:214;
 21:327
Eastman, Dunbar 12:62
Eastman, Dwight 13:20;
 16:30
Eastman, Dyer B. 23:285
Eastman, E. H. 25:319
Eastman, F. C. 19:161
Eastman, George S.
 21:114
Eastman, George W. D.
 21:68
Eastman, H. W. 21:327
Eastman, I. 11:105
Eastman, Israel C. 12:69;
 15:65
Eastman, J. 3:64; 9:142;
 27:40
Eastman, James 12:172
Eastman, James R. 12:19
Eastman, John L. 1:30
Eastman, Lorenzo D.
 13:20
Eastman, Lyman C.
 22:141
Eastman, Malvin 4:22
Eastman, Mathew H.
 23:64
Eastman, O. E. 13:63
Eastman, O. R. 16:187
Eastman, S. C. 16:279
Eastman, S. S. 15:352
Eastman, Salathial 22:28
Eastman, Simon 11:400
Eastman, Thomas 7:93
Eastman, W. 3:64
Eastman, W. D. 21:248
Eastman, W. H. 1:30
Eastman, Wallace 7:93
Eastman, William 3:64;
 11:286
Eastmorgan, Lewis 9:79
Easton, D. H. 9:66

Easton, Dan 16:291
Easton, Daniel 18:109
Easton, E. E. 3:64
Easton, E. M. 14:162, 255
Easton, Isaac 21:327
Easton, J. 3:64
Easton, J. C. 27:41
Easton, J. H. 9:15; 14:162
Easton, John 9:118;
 13:20; 20:183; 27:41
Easton, Johnson 8:84
Easton, Joseph 22:29
Easton, Mark L. 21:24
Easton, Morgan 9:109
Easton, Phillip 17:313
Easton, Reddick 21:327
Easton, S. L. 23:28
Easton, W. 14:162
Easton, William 24:193;
 25:167
Eastor, Daniel 12:92
Eastwood, Constantine
 13:130; 20:244
Eastwood, Cyrus B. 9:12
Eastwood, E. 3:64
Eastwood, Ithamar G.
 20:112
Eastwood, J. 14:57;
 25:167
Eastwood, J. H. 1:128
Eastwood, James H. 21:51
Eastwood, John 20:151
Eastwood, John K. 22:278
Eastwood, Oscar 10:145
Eastwood, Wilber 15:105
Eastwood, William 9:51
Easty, Solomon W. 12:55
Eat---, Joseph E. 25:31
Eaten, James 8:63
Eates, William 14:235
Eatis, James 22:297
Eatle, Joseph 22:165
Eatno, Charles O. 24:93
Eaton, A. 3:64
Eaton, A. H. 8:14
Eaton, Alehaner 19:67
Eaton, Alexander 26:219
Eaton, C. 12:152; 19:243
Eaton, Carrol J. 7:93
Eaton, Charles 9:102, 175;
 13:81; 16:188
Eaton, Cyrus 26:144
Eaton, D. 9:142; 11:144;
 27:40
Eaton, Daniel 15:27
Eaton, David H. 16:84
Eaton, Ebenezer 18:66
Eaton, Ed 21:88
Eaton, F. 7:67
Eaton, F. W. 3:64
Eaton, Francis S. 23:240

Eaton, Frank S. 11:322
Eaton, Franklin A.
 10:111; 20:244
Eaton, G. 1:127
Eaton, G. W. 27:41
Eaton, George 24:17
Eaton, George I. 18:276
Eaton, George O. 18:353
Eaton, George W. 10:160;
 19:161
Eaton, Granville 10:111;
 20:244
Eaton, H. 11:58; 25:311
Eaton, H. J. 27:41
Eaton, Henry 12:20
Eaton, Henry C. 13:20;
 16:30
Eaton, Henry J. 10:111;
 20:244
Eaton, Herman A. 12:62;
 15:16
Eaton, Ira F. 7:56
Eaton, Isaac 16:118
Eaton, Isaiah V. 16:77
Eaton, J. 1:127
Eaton, J. A. 25:167
Eaton, J. H. 1:127
Eaton, J. L. 25:167
Eaton, J. M. 23:106
Eaton, Jackson R. 23:64
Eaton, James 20:244;
 26:159
Eaton, James D. 15:11
Eaton, Joel 17:495
Eaton, John 10:111;
 20:244
Eaton, John S. 9:175
Eaton, John W. 1:30;
 22:75
Eaton, Joseph 17:131;
 24:193
Eaton, L. C. 21:12
Eaton, Levi 22:165
Eaton, Lewis 8:63; 22:423
Eaton, Loren 16:93
Eaton, Marshal S. 24:59
Eaton, N. 25:30
Eaton, N. J. 1:127
Eaton, Nat 3:64
Eaton, Nelson 25:274
Eaton, Orrin D. 20:189
Eaton, Owen D. 8:105
Eaton, R. 3:64
Eaton, R. B. 7:93
Eaton, Robert 9:230;
 11:105; 20:244
Eaton, S. 17:154
Eaton, Samuel A. 9:71
Eaton, Sidney W. 10:111;
 20:244
Eaton, Solon S. 19:226

Eaton, Stephen 7:8
Eaton, T. 1:127
Eaton, Thomas 1:31
Eaton, Thomas D. 8:14
Eaton, W. 3:64; 14:288; 19:67; 23:28
Eaton, W. A. 19:12
Eaton, W. H. 3:64; 12:99; 16:130
Eaton, W. M. 14:264
Eaton, W. S. 9:219
Eaton, W. W. 16:188
Eaton, William 4:22; 19:226
Eaton, William S. 18:365
Eatonhall, N. E. 24:65
Eaun, Martin 14:162
Eavans, --- 25:31
Eavans, Alfred 12:152
Eavans, John 25:31
Eavans, T. 25:31
Eave, James 11:381
Eave, Moses 6:15; 18:81
Eaveheart, Samuel 9:21
Eavens, G. W. 15:341
Eavens, Henry 9:118
Eavens, James 10:179
Eavens, Julius B. 9:118
Eavers, E. 25:31
Eavers, John 20:183
Eavery, John F. 9:118
Eaves, George 6:16; 18:81
Eaves, Jacob 26:159
Eaves, Jeny 16:188
Eaves, Stephen 6:16; 18:81
Eayers, William A. 17:359
Eba, Wesley 24:38
Ebarhart, George A. 9:79
Ebaugh, William D. 22:75
Ebbert, A. 15:33
Ebberts, John E. 15:328; 19:67
Ebbin, Joseph W. 18:216
Ebe---by, Christian 15:195
Ebel, Christopher 25:296
Ebel, E. 12:8
Ebelhardt, A. 12:20
Ebell, Christian 7:81
Eben, Hardy 12:48
Ebenhart, C. K. 8:63
Ebensberger, John 8:14
Ebenst, Henry 26:219
Eber, Henry 21:327
Eber, James 3:64
Eber, Samuel 18:236; 26:26
Eberand, G. 14:57
Eberbein, Ferdinand 24:63

Eberhard, Jonathan 7:56
Eberhardt, Jacob 22:278
Eberhardt, John 23:141
Eberhardt, W. 22:189
Eberhart, Andrew 16:30
Eberhart, Edward 23:28
Eberhart, F. 26:159
Eberhart, Samuel 10:111; 20:244
Eberle, Henry 22:29
Eberle, Jacob 1:30
Eberle, John 15:22; 17:14
Eberle, Judson 22:403
Eberle, Ludwig 19:67
Eberling, William 9:219
Eberly, E. O. 15:195
Eberly, Godfrey 22:233
Eberly, Isaac 16:30
Eberly, Joshua 11:59
Eberly, William 21:327
Eberman, H. W. 16:367
Ebersal, S. 27:40
Ebersol, S. 9:142
Ebersole, John C. 23:179
Eberson, George M. 8:84
Ebert, C. 1:31
Ebert, Charles 2:10; 4:22
Ebert, D. S. 7:25
Ebert, George 6:7; 12:20; 18:109
Ebert, Isaac 11:59
Ebert, John 21:51
Ebert, Lenions 1:30
Ebert, R. 25:31
Ebert, Reuben 2:10
Eberts, John 12:69
Eberwine, Frederick J. 22:423
Ebey, Byron 25:167
Ebhart, J. 3:64
Ebhime, Jo 20:132
Ebinger, John 10:111; 20:244
Ebington, H. S. 10:111
Ebinier, H. 16:188
Eblers, J. E. 11:301
Eblp, W. M. 1:31
Ebner, Charles 3:64
Ebner, E. 1:30
Ebnon, Charles S. 24:193
Eby, Abraham 23:65
Eby, John 25:167
Eby, Monroe 26:144
Eby, Peter 8:14; 18:131
Eby, VanBuren 3:64
Eby, William 24:38
Eccart, P. 14:57
Eccles, David 9:51
Eccles, M. 11:302
Eccles, Roger 14:162
Eccles, S. F. 17:497

Eccles, William 23:121
Eccleston, O. A. 7:25
Ecert, Joseph 27:40
Echarat, Ida 21:327
Echard, Henry 14:162
Echart, Samuel 14:162
Echart, Thomas 15:151
Echart, W. 11:261
Echartt, William 14:57
Echelbarger, A. F. 20:123
Echelberry, Davis 23:141
Echembett, Oliver T. 21:327
Echerson, William 14:57
Echert, David S. 21:242
Echert, E. 22:351
Echman, J. 1:128
Echner, Philemon 24:93
Echols, George 21:187
Echols, Joseph 8:105
Echols, Wilford C. 8:14
Echols, Wilford E. 18:131
Echtranch, John 18:66
Echtrauch, John 9:203
Eck, Benjamin 14:162
Eckard, G. W. 15:195
Eckard, William 1:31
Eckart, J. 15:315
Eckelberry, E. 4:22
Eckels, Benjamin 17:78
Eckels, F. 14:57
Eckels, James 25:30
Eckeman, D. 1:127
Eckenbach, C. 14:57
Eckendorff, George R. 14:162
Eckenrodes, I. 1:128
Eckenrodes, T. 1:128
Ecker, Charles 13:108
Ecker, D. N. 22:478
Ecker, J. 3:64
Ecker, Tilden 17:70
Ecker, W. 23:28
Eckerman, David F. 23:87
Eckerman, Frank W. 11:145
Eckers, John F. 19:12
Eckerson, Simoen 21:327
Eckerson, W. 16:292
Eckert, Adam 9:118
Eckert, Eckert K. 19:161
Eckert, H. 13:20
Eckert, John 4:22
Eckert, Jonathan 19:67
Eckert, Lucas 20:88
Eckert, Pete 9:109
Eckert, V. 25:31
Eckert, William 19:251
Eckert, William R. 1:30
Eckes, J. 11:125
Eckhard, Henrick 10:51

Eckhart, David 25:167
Eckhart, Francis W. 23:141
Eckhart, H. 16:30
Eckhart, Henry 20:244
Eckhart, J. 3:64
Eckhart, L. 14:162
Eckhart, Levi 14:57
Eckhart, Martin 11:286
Eckle, John 22:75
Eckler, Adam 16:154
Eckler, Edmund 21:269
Eckler, J. J. 1:31
Eckler, Peter 13:20
Eckles, A. 17:154
Eckles, E. 3:64; 21:147
Eckles, James 23:28
Eckles, Orlando 12:20
Eckles, P. 14:9
Eckles, Rufus 11:202
Eckles, Valentine 14:162
Eckley, Charles 13:108
Eckley, Jonathan 17:440; 24:152
Eckley, Levi 5:14; 25:167
Eckliff, O. 7:25
Eckly, W. J. 23:28
Eckman, Eli 17:14
Eckman, Peter 1:31
Eckols, Edward 21:269
Eckorp, William 9:175
Ecksteen, S. 13:108
Eckstein, Any 11:58
Eckstein, Emanuel 26:159
Eckstein, John 7:25
Eckstine, A. 1:31
Eckternan, William 11:105
Eclan, John 11:386
Ecorn, L. 25:288
Ecroyd, Hargraves 4:22
Ecut, Joseph 9:130
Edaline, F. 11:125
Edam, John C. 20:35
Eddem, Ephraim 18:323
Eddeman, A. J. 11:59
Eddens, Judd 19:290
Edder, James A. 20:151
Eddes, James E. 17:504
Edding, Joseph 21:269
Eddinger, A. 18:235; 26:26
Eddings, William I. 22:249
Eddington, Austin 20:39
Eddington, David 9:79
Eddington, G. B. 3:64
Eddington, James 9:21
Eddington, Jesse 26:26
Eddington, John 8:47; 21:137; 22:249

Eddins, C. 14:162
Eddins, Milton B. 18:216
Eddins, Thomas 19:290
Eddlebleete, E. W. 24:77
Eddleman, George C. 10:16
Eddleman, Jacob 22:75
Eddles, James E. 3:223
Eddy, --- 21:187
Eddy, A. 22:523
Eddy, A. H. 24:17
Eddy, Alfred 11:145
Eddy, C. 21:24
Eddy, C. A. 12:20
Eddy, Charles B. 15:105
Eddy, Charles E. 17:247
Eddy, Constrank 8:113
Eddy, Daniel E. 9:79
Eddy, E. W. 16:367
Eddy, Eben 8:84
Eddy, Edwin 16:367
Eddy, Emaziah 11:115
Eddy, F. M. 22:141
Eddy, Francis 18:276
Eddy, G. 1:30
Eddy, G. W. 14:315
Eddy, George 27:41
Eddy, George E. 14:297; 17:473
Eddy, J. E. 17:33
Eddy, J. S. 1:127
Eddy, James 18:235; 20:106; 26:26
Eddy, Jasper 27:41
Eddy, Martin 15:158
Eddy, Nathan 1:30
Eddy, Orrin 22:462
Eddy, Robert 1:30
Eddy, Sam 17:425
Eddy, Samuel 24:177
Eddy, Thomas 9:79; 26:26
Eddy, W. E. 1:97
Eddy, W. H. 25:31
Eddy, W. M. 19:162
Eddy, William 14:162, 240; 27:42
Eddy, William B. 10:172
Eddy, William N. H. 22:141
Eddybum, Calvin 9:16
Ede, B. T. 1:30
Edeburn, H. P. 20:33
Edeley, L. S. 15:195
Edelman, M. 25:167
Edelman, Michael 5:14
Eden, Stephen 14:162
Edens, Jesse 11:422
Edens, John 15:86
Eder, L. C. 16:188
Edes, Edward 11:100
Edes, Thomas G. 22:189

Edes, W. 3:64
Edey, William B. 19:162
Edgar, Addison 16:132
Edgar, G. W. 18:66
Edgar, J. 11:239; 17:433
Edgar, J. C. 7:93
Edgar, Jacob 18:468
Edgar, James 15:328; 22:423
Edgar, James C. 21:187
Edgar, John 18:456; 24:163
Edgar, Joseph 23:305; 24:49
Edgar, Samuel 25:30
Edgar, William H. 3:64
Edgard, E. 13:87
Edgarly, Henry T. 5:15
Edgarton, C. M. 12:48
Edge, R. D. 12:55
Edgecomb, L. A. 23:141
Edgeley, M. 4:22
Edger, Charles 25:167
Edger, William 20:92
Edgerly, Amos 15:55
Edgerton, A. A. 1:31
Edgerton, Charles 8:47; 15:173
Edgerton, Charles L. 21:137
Edgerton, F. 25:31
Edgerton, Frank 2:10
Edgerton, G. 25:167
Edgerton, G. C. 25:167
Edgerton, George C. 5:15
Edgerton, H. A. 18:48
Edgerton, Herbert J. 21:327
Edgerton, Jerome C. 21:68
Edgerton, S. R. 20:192
Edgerton, William J. 20:112
Edgeston, H. J. 7:93
Edgeworth, John 19:162
Edgington, Jacob 22:29
Edgington, James 9:79
Edgington, Thomas E. 20:96
Edgly, J. 15:195
Edgo, Charles 5:38
Edick, Joseph 14:162
Edimmiller, W. 9:21
Edinburgh, John 19:296
Edinger, E. 13:108
Edings, Charles 8:14; 18:131
Edington, D. S. 26:26
Edington, Francis A. 21:51
Edington, Frank 21:51

Edington, H. S. 20:244
Edington, J. 22:29
Edington, John 17:131;
    24:193
Edison, William 1:31
Edkins, John 21:223
Edleman, George 9:21
Edleman, Thomas 9:21;
    18:305
Edler, Henry 9:219;
    18:365
Edlewan, Thomas 26:97
Edlin, John F. 18:81
Edman, Tobias 11:202
Edmands, James T. 16:84
Edmister, C. W. 14:9
Edmister, G. W. 13:87
Edmister, Reuben 8:105
Edmiston, J. W. 3:64
Edmond, Cornelius
    19:287
Edmond, Ellis 10:111
Edmond, Isaac 13:127
Edmond, Lester 8:14
Edmonde, E. 7:93
Edmonds, B. 3:64
Edmonds, E. 25:167
Edmonds, Ellis 20:244
Edmonds, Ethelbert 10:51
Edmonds, F. 15:195
Edmonds, George 11:218;
    12:20
Edmonds, Henry 21:147;
    22:297
Edmonds, Hugh 15:278
Edmonds, Isaac 22:75
Edmonds, J. A. 9:51
Edmonds, J. C. 27:144
Edmonds, J. M. 25:278
Edmonds, Jacob R. J.
    25:271
Edmonds, James H. 13:20
Edmonds, John 22:249
Edmonds, L. 3:64
Edmonds, Moses 15:293
Edmonds, Peter 10:153;
    19:162
Edmonds, Richard 10:95
Edmonds, S. 13:128
Edmonds, William 12:20;
    18:420
Edmondson, --- 23:203
Edmondson, Andrew J.
    7:49
Edmondson, Charles S.
    24:49
Edmondson, Frank 22:297
Edmondson, H. 21:327
Edmondson, Jesse F.
    17:147

Edmondson, William W.
    23:87
Edmons, P. 7:77
Edmonson, Mathew
    18:216
Edmonson, P. 25:296
Edmonson, Samuel 7:121;
    14:329
Edmonson, T. F. 12:81;
    16:292
Edmonson, W. F. 23:141
Edmonson, William 22:75
Edmonston, William H.
    21:109
Edmund, Austin 14:162
Edmund, William 10:111;
    20:244
Edmunds, E. 20:244
Edmunds, Edward E. 1:30
Edmunds, H. S. 21:327
Edmunds, Hugh 25:167
Edmunds, Joel S. 21:68
Edmunds, Morgan 15:195
Edmunds, W. B. F.
    18:394
Edmunds, William H.
    21:290
Edmundson, Francis
    22:423
Edmundson, James 24:17
Edmundson, Theodore
    15:55
Edmundson, William
    17:394
Edney, Andrew 11:144
Edney, George 26:123
Edons, C. 14:57
Edridge, Joseph W. 13:20
Edsall, Barton 11:400
Edsall, William 11:144
Edset, --- 18:271
Edson, Albert H. 16:93
Edson, Alfred 20:180
Edson, Alonzo 13:20
Edson, Dewitt C. 24:152
Edson, Edwin 11:190
Edson, George G. 15:195
Edson, H. 1:127
Edson, Herbert 25:31
Edson, J. M. 25:167
Edson, James I. 22:121
Edson, John 3:64
Edson, L. M. 9:175;
    19:237
Edson, Leander 8:113;
    18:323
Edson, Lorenzo D. 13:20
Edson, Rennselaer L.
    20:91
Edson, Robert 9:230
Edson, T. 1:127

Edson, Timothy N.
    10:111; 20:244
Edson, W. 3:64
Edson, William 8:59;
    19:272; 22:478
Edson, William B. 4:22
Edson, William M.
    10:111; 20:244
Edunds, John 16:132
Edwads, Thompson 21:99
Edward, B. 1:127
Edward, C. S. 3:64
Edward, Hogan 11:202
Edward, J. 1:128; 14:57
Edward, N. W. 1:127
Edward, Thomas 14:57
Edward, William 10:98
Edwards, --- 18:28;
    20:244; 21:166;
    25:31; 27:42
Edwards, A. F. 26:26
Edwards, A. J. 9:21;
    18:305; 26:97
Edwards, A. R. 19:12
Edwards, A. T. 18:235
Edwards, Aaron 23:65
Edwards, Abraham
    10:111; 20:244
Edwards, Abram 7:121
Edwards, Absalom 8:84
Edwards, Albert M. 10:16
Edwards, Allen 22:508
Edwards, Altaire H.
    21:253
Edwards, Amos 9:242
Edwards, Archibald 19:12
Edwards, B. 7:25; 22:298;
    27:42
Edwards, Benjamin 7:121
Edwards, Brewey 10:205
Edwards, C. 3:64; 13:87
Edwards, C. C. 11:279
Edwards, C. D. 3:64
Edwards, C. F. 3:64
Edwards, C. W. 9:79
Edwards, Callahan 17:95
Edwards, Charles 7:121;
    11:125; 24:193
Edwards, Charles V.
    17:19
Edwards, Clayborn 9:51
Edwards, Crittenden 4:22
Edwards, Cyrenus 10:111;
    20:244
Edwards, D. 1:31; 25:167
Edwards, D. L. 25:167
Edwards, Danford 21:51
Edwards, David 10:205;
    11:190; 22:298
Edwards, Davis 7:121
Edwards, Douglass 23:11

Edwards, E. 1:127; 8:47; 27:144
Edwards, E. B. 21:208
Edwards, E. H. 22:519
Edwards, Edward 11:422; 22:298
Edwards, Edwin H. 13:20
Edwards, Elias 4:22
Edwards, Elijah 24:61; 27:144
Edwards, Ensley 22:297
Edwards, Evan 16:152
Edwards, Francis M. 20:123
Edwards, Frank 21:269
Edwards, Frederick 20:29
Edwards, G. 16:188
Edwards, G. W. 1:128; 9:16; 21:327; 27:40
Edwards, George 5:15; 7:121; 9:118; 10:16; 11:261; 14:162; 21:68; 22:141; 25:167
Edwards, George S. 7:93; 13:20; 16:30
Edwards, Gilbert 17:147
Edwards, Gustavus H. 23:65
Edwards, H. 1:30; 3:64; 14:57; 22:297
Edwards, H. C. 1:30; 11:302
Edwards, H. N. 18:66
Edwards, H. R. 11:58
Edwards, H. S. 3:64
Edwards, Hamilton 15:86
Edwards, Hamilton C. 17:78
Edwards, Hartman 13:20
Edwards, Hasket 27:42
Edwards, Henry 9:207; 14:321; 16:367; 18:28, 66; 23:203
Edwards, Henry J. 19:324
Edwards, Hiram B. 7:25
Edwards, Horace 9:118; 23:121; 27:41
Edwards, Isaac J. 11:239; 13:20
Edwards, Ison M. 10:51
Edwards, J. 1:30, 127; 3:64; 11:230; 15:66; 27:40
Edwards, J. A. 1:31
Edwards, J. C. 9:71; 20:244; 22:249
Edwards, J. G. 1:128
Edwards, J. H. 10:51; 11:255
Edwards, J. J. 12:152

Edwards, J. K. P. 9:175; 19:251
Edwards, J. L. 25:30
Edwards, J. M. 20:245; 25:167
Edwards, J. N. 11:422; 20:244
Edwards, J. P. 23:28
Edwards, J. W. 3:64; 10:51, 154; 14:57; 19:162; 21:187; 25:167
Edwards, Jackson D. 22:450
Edwards, Jacob 1:191
Edwards, James 8:14, 84, 112; 9:118, 130; 10:111; 11:201; 12:147; 17:33; 18:81, 132; 19:301; 20:245; 22:298; 25:31, 319; 27:41
Edwards, James A. 22:29
Edwards, James B. 21:99
Edwards, James H. 16:30; 17:51
Edwards, James N. 5:15; 22:249
Edwards, James W. 7:93
Edwards, Jeremiah 7:93; 11:338
Edwards, Jerry 22:298
Edwards, Jesse 17:280
Edwards, Jirm 16:188
Edwards, Joel S. 8:47
Edwards, John 1:30; 3:64; 7:121; 8:63; 9:230; 10:170; 11:144, 279, 302; 13:20; 15:195; 16:188; 17:159; 19:162; 20:245; 21:327; 23:28; 24:212
Edwards, John C. 19:162
Edwards, John H. 7:25; 16:30
Edwards, John J. 12:20
Edwards, John S. 1:30; 12:55
Edwards, Jos. R. 15:158
Edwards, Joseph 17:307
Edwards, Joseph B. 22:75
Edwards, Joshua 9:219; 18:365
Edwards, L. 3:64; 13:87; 15:195; 26:159
Edwards, L. B. 11:400
Edwards, Lee T. 22:450
Edwards, Levi 11:58; 22:29
Edwards, Lewis 23:87

Edwards, Louis 21:269
Edwards, Manuel 21:327
Edwards, Milton 11:395; 22:450
Edwards, Morton J. 22:500
Edwards, Moses 16:188; 22:298
Edwards, N. H. 14:315
Edwards, N. S. 3:64
Edwards, O. J. 3:64
Edwards, Olin 27:42
Edwards, P. 12:64; 25:167
Edwards, Patrick 13:79; 16:188; 21:327
Edwards, Pierce 18:66
Edwards, Pierre 9:207
Edwards, Pleasant 8:38; 26:159
Edwards, R. 1:31
Edwards, Richard 12:58
Edwards, Riley 11:239
Edwards, Robert 14:57
Edwards, S. 3:64; 13:76; 16:188; 19:67
Edwards, S. F. 15:123
Edwards, Samuel 11:118; 12:48; 22:29; 26:26
Edwards, Simon 7:56
Edwards, Simon J. 10:160
Edwards, Squire C. 23:141
Edwards, Stephen 27:41
Edwards, T. 1:128
Edwards, T. B. 11:302
Edwards, T. H. 11:59
Edwards, Thomas 7:138; 11:145; 14:57; 17:387; 22:297
Edwards, Thomas B. 18:13
Edwards, Thomas D. 16:30
Edwards, Thomas J. 9:230; 11:58; 20:245
Edwards, Thomas P. 1:31
Edwards, Thompson 8:47
Edwards, Tobias 15:195
Edwards, U. 21:24
Edwards, Vincent 7:121
Edwards, W. 18:420; 21:121; 22:297
Edwards, W. B. 25:31
Edwards, W. H. 6:23
Edwards, W. M. 7:25
Edwards, W. N. 18:406
Edwards, W. P. 10:27
Edwards, W. W. 10:205
Edwards, Wesley 9:51
Edwards, Wiley H. 22:249
Edwards, Will 21:269

Edwards, Willett 18:412
Edwards, William 3:64;
  9:130; 10:111;
  11:125, 218, 286;
  15:55, 267, 341;
  16:367; 18:81;
  20:245; 21:211, 223;
  22:422; 23:65, 141;
  24:17; 25:274; 27:40
Edwards, William B. 7:25
Edwards, William E.
  22:141
Edwards, William F. 9:79;
  26:25
Edwards, William H.
  20:136; 21:194;
  24:38
Edwards, William L. 20:7
Edwards, William M.
  21:68
Edwards, William T.
  21:327
Edwards, Willis 22:297
Edwards, Wilson 17:95
Edwer, Rodney 17:165
Edwin, Peter 6:16
Edwinson, I. 1:31
Edy, J. 27:40
Eeaster, Jacob 20:123
Eeaton, Thomas L. 18:131
Eek, Joseph 7:25
Eelle, Tiffany 20:22
Eels, E. 19:251
Eels, Edward 9:175
Eernisse, Jacob 21:137
Eeterman, Gustar 15:90
Eferhart, Thomas 18:48
Eff, P. 23:28
Effen, --- 19:322
Effing, John 18:235;
  26:26
Effinger, J. 1:128
Effingham, --- 18:284;
  26:134
Egan, --- 21:327
Egan, H. H. 14:57
Egan, James 14:162;
  21:327; 23:121
Egan, John 20:245
Egan, Joseph 21:327
Egan, Martin 18:132
Egan, Patrick 18:109, 205
Egan, Thomas 21:327
Egan, W. 25:167
Egan, William 5:15;
  21:327
Egar, Henry 11:322
Egar, J. 25:167
Egar, Martin 17:78
Egart, Charles 7:57
Egben, John H. 9:79

Egbert, Charles 10:16
Egbert, Frank 13:63
Egbert, John H. 26:26
Egbert, John L. 21:327
Egbert, Obadiah 24:193
Egbert, Obediah 17:131
Egbert, W. H. 17:64
Egbert, William 22:403
Ege, A. 25:31
Ege, H. J. 2:10
Ege, Jacob 25:168
Egel, Charles 4:22
Egeland, Osmund 21:68
Egellmer, William 11:29
Egenes, Thomas L. 20:123
Eger, Paul 27:40
Egerton, George 21:241
Egerton, W. Irving 22:403
Egester, Joseph 24:77
Egg, Christian 21:51
Eggan, Nelson S. 24:49
Eggart, August 10:51
Eggbert, H. 26:26
Egge, Thomas 18:109
Eggelton, H. 3:65
Eggemeier, --- 16:292
Eggens, J. 7:25
Egger, Joel 22:249
Egger, John 1:30
Egger, Michael 10:111;
  20:245
Eggerman, C. 7:49
Eggert, August 20:245
Eggert, Charles A. 17:454;
  24:185
Eggert, Joseph 17:352
Eggert, William A. 20:7
Eggerton, J. R. 12:152
Eggles, Robert 17:174
Eggleson, Edward 7:93
Eggleson, George 18:305;
  26:97
Eggleston, A. J. 1:127
Eggleston, Abraham 13:20
Eggleston, C. 25:168
Eggleston, Cornelius 5:15
Eggleston, Ellery S.
  17:263
Eggleston, F. 1:128
Eggleston, George 9:21
Eggleston, H. C. 7:25
Eggleston, Henry 18:351
Eggleston, Hiram 10:111;
  20:245
Eggleston, L. H. 21:327
Eggleston, Lewis H.
  9:214; 16:143
Eggleston, Lucius 21:15
Eggleston, Peter 22:75
Eggleston, Reuben R.
  23:121

Eggleston, Samuel 8:38;
  26:159
Eggleston, William
  17:287
Eggleton, A. 14:57
Eghart, Henry 9:79
Eginston, J. 21:68
Eglan, Charles 24:193
Eglan, Henry 20:245
Egland, Peter 24:49
Eglaw, Henry 10:111
Egler, J. 1:127
Egleston, Harrison 11:302
Egleston, N. 16:367
Egli, Edward 18:103
Eglin, Charles 1:192
Eglin, R. B. 16:188
Eglison, H. S. 1:127
Egman, Nathan 22:403
Egner, W. 9:142; 27:40,
  41
Egnew, Jeff L. 8:14;
  18:132
Egnew, John 22:423
Egnor, C. 18:235; 26:26
Egnow, Alvin 11:58
Egoll, John 15:195
Egra, Hiram 12:20
Egsillim, P. H. 3:65
Ehaler, Anthony 10:111;
  20:245
Ehenger, C. 13:87
Ehirt, W. H. 27:42
Ehle, Chauncey 12:20
Ehle, John H. 4:22
Ehle, N. G. 25:30
Ehler, Israel 16:30
Ehler, Julius 13:20
Ehlers, T. H. 11:218
Ehlert, Ferdinand 23:117
Ehlscheid, Ch. 11:92
Ehman, A. 3:65
Ehman, Frederick 20:123
Ehman, John 9:109
Ehnurghans, Earnest
  9:118
Ehochobic, --- 18:417
Ehrgood, John H. 12:20
Ehrhard, D. 1:128
Ehrhardt, Benjamin 22:29
Ehrhardt, Theodore
  18:305; 26:97
Ehrhart, J. 1:127
Ehrhart, Samuel H. 22:75
Ehrie, Michael 9:175
Ehrit, W. H. 14:297;
  17:479
Ehrke, Joachim 23:189
Ehrle, George 16:267
Ehrlic, M. 19:251
Ehrman, F. 7:49

Ehrman, John 11:59
Ehrmin, Davis 1:30
Ehrnest, Samuel 9:34
Ehtinger, John A. 20:112
Ehunghaus, Ernst 27:41
Ehvensberger, John 18:132
Eibers, Henry 3:65
Eiberson, J. 3:65
Eich, Fred 20:245
Eichalz, John 27:144
Eichel, Casper 10:90; 20:245
Eichelberger, George W. 23:28
Eichelberger, Peter 24:172
Eichelburger, William 5:15
Eichellinger, Peter 17:448
Eichendure, A. 15:33
Eichenor, J. 13:108
Eicher, A. R. 18:292; 26:97
Eicher, John 25:168
Eichert, Frederick 23:128
Eichert, John 26:144
Eichhorn, L. 11:118
Eichhorst, Frederick 22:278
Eichlin, John 13:20
Eichman, A. 14:57
Eichman, John 9:96
Eichnor, C. 3:65
Eichoff, John 22:10
Eichoff, Peter 23:98
Eickhoffs, Frank 11:15
Eicklin, John 16:30
Eicleberger, M. 14:162
Eides, Thomas 19:226
Eiding, J. 1:31
Eidle, F. 1:30
Eidom, John 9:79
Eidson, Dewitt C. 17:415
Eiershan, --- 16:93
Eifler, Charles 26:123
Eifler, W. 26:219
Eigart, E. L. 26:159
Eigenschen, Joseph 24:152
Eighelbrecht, August 9:21
Eignor, J. 19:67
Eignson, Joseph 17:440
Eike, William 11:260
Eikelberg, H. 1:31
Eikens, E. M. 1:128
Eikler, George 11:144
Eilcoman, G. 17:19
Eilenburger, D. B. 22:29
Eiler, Israel 10:16
Eilse, R. 5:50
Einbers, Lingo 19:290

Einbrest, L. 9:199
Einbury, Charles 10:51
Eing, John 10:51; 20:245
Einseidel, H. 22:10
Einwechter, H. 1:128
Eipick, Isaac 14:162
Eiro, F. 26:26
Eis, Peter 18:305; 26:97
Eischen, Adam 17:429; 24:185
Eisele, Charles 23:141
Eisele, Frank 1:30
Eisell, Jacob 15:151
Eiseman, Ferdinand 19:12
Eiseman, Gattfr 9:219
Eiseman, Gotler 18:365
Eisenberg, Justice 16:93
Eisenberger, B. F. 23:179
Eisenbower, George W. 9:96
Eisenbrise, John B. 5:50
Eisendick, Casper 22:165
Eisenhart, M. 14:162
Eisenhath, G. T. 1:128
Eisenhour, Philip 11:118
Eisenhower, W. L. 23:288
Eiser, Jacob 16:93
Eisile, Joseph 26:123
Eisle, R. 25:168
Eisley, John 3:65
Eisner, August 21:253
Eisten, John 26:26
Eister, A. 11:145
Eister, Louis 15:33
Eistis, W. 14:27
Eitel, John 22:171
Eiteman, M. 10:51
Eiten, Peter 4:22
Eivens, B. F. 14:240
Eiver, T. 8:47
Ekarett, Christ 24:77
Ekart, Cornelius 17:418; 24:157
Ekart, Jonas 22:423
Ekel, J. H. 11:145
Ekel, John 19:162
Ekey, Levi M. 7:93
Ekhard, William Henry 22:423
Ekis, Larkin D. 19:12
Ekis, Levi 7:64
Ekis, Michael 22:29
Ekleberry, Marshall 17:161
Eklir, John 11:118
Eksen, Allen 21:269
Ela, William H. 16:84
Elam, Lemuel A. 7:93
Elany, Patrick 21:327
Elason, R. 15:341; 16:367
Elau, A. 25:31

Elbars, Peter 9:79
Elberhart, J. 4:22
Elberson, Benjamin 21:115
Elberson, Henry 16:113
Elberson, William 4:22
Elbert, C. 14:162
Elbert, Frederick 10:112; 20:245
Elbert, G. W. 21:327
Elbert, H. 14:162
Elbert, Horace 7:122
Elbert, Levi 11:411
Elbert, Nicholas 8:84
Elbord, John 9:118
Elbrnom, Thomas 11:260
Elbum, William 21:223
Elchert, B. 9:109
Elcook, William 14:162
Eldege, C. 14:162
Elden, F. 14:9
Elden, Sam 17:174
Elden, William 12:20
Elder, A. S. 1:31
Elder, Adam 15:123
Elder, B. F. 7:25
Elder, Charles 8:38; 26:159
Elder, Clark 15:195
Elder, Edwin P. 22:121
Elder, Ephraim 11:408
Elder, F. 13:87
Elder, Francis E. 22:75
Elder, George 14:162; 22:141
Elder, J. 11:239; 21:14
Elder, J. D. 27:40
Elder, Jacob 23:141
Elder, James 9:199; 19:290
Elder, John 23:65
Elder, John D. 9:142
Elder, Leonard 21:24
Elder, M. E. 11:145
Elder, Martin 23:141
Elder, P. 3:65
Elder, R. B. 9:118; 27:39
Elder, Robertson 25:168
Elder, Robinson 5:50
Elder, Samuel 7:25
Elder, Samuel D. 8:14; 18:132
Elder, Theo R. 9:68
Elder, Thomas 12:20; 15:313; 19:67
Elder, W. 1:127
Elder, William R. 22:249
Elderfield, Thomas 8:84
Elderidge, Ashley D. 13:108
Elderken, J. 15:86

Elderkien, Samuel 18:305
Elderkin, D. M. 13:77; 16:188
Elderkin, E. 7:65
Elderkin, J. B. 13:108
Elderkin, Jackson 12:69
Elderkin, Nicholas S. 21:137
Elderkin, Samuel 9:21; 26:97
Elderman, Andrew 21:24
Elders, Isaiah 22:189
Eldery, B. 3:65
Eldide, H. C. 1:127
Eldon, T. S. 1:127
Eldred, C. C. 1:128
Eldred, C. W. 16:188
Eldred, Egbert 20:106
Eldred, G. U. 13:63
Eldred, Gilbert 8:14
Eldred, H. 3:65
Eldred, H. W. 14:163
Eldred, J. 3:65
Eldred, P. E. 15:195
Eldred, W. H. 18:28
Eldred, William H. 22:462
Eldredge, D. D. 2:10
Eldredge, Franklin 20:96
Eldredge, Rufus H. 20:22
Eldrid, Gilbert 18:132
Eldrid, Hiram W. 9:16
Eldridge, --- 25:30
Eldridge, A. C. 16:188
Eldridge, Adam 11:400
Eldridge, Albert 7:25
Eldridge, Alfred 22:141
Eldridge, B. 22:512
Eldridge, C. 1:128
Eldridge, Charles F. 14:163
Eldridge, D. D. 25:168
Eldridge, D. K. 1:128
Eldridge, Daniel 8:14; 18:132
Eldridge, David 16:31
Eldridge, E. 3:65; 21:327
Eldridge, E. W. 13:108
Eldridge, Eli 10:112; 20:245
Eldridge, Hyde 14:163
Eldridge, J. 16:188
Eldridge, J. B. 23:28
Eldridge, J. D. 20:39
Eldridge, James 17:95
Eldridge, James V. 15:55
Eldridge, Jason F. 12:20
Eldridge, John 7:93
Eldridge, John R. 10:144; 19:162
Eldridge, John W. 16:31
Eldridge, Joseph 19:162

Eldridge, Louis 13:20
Eldridge, Nathan R. 24:17
Eldridge, Neal D. 15:33
Eldridge, Oscar 18:66
Eldridge, Rodney 20:106
Eldridge, Solomon 13:20; 16:31
Eldridge, Thomas 21:24
Eldridge, William 9:175; 11:411
Eldridge, William G. 10:16
Eldrige, D. D. 25:31
Eldrige, Mathew 25:31
Elee, William 14:57
Elefritz, James 11:144
Elege, John 24:88
Eleleres, Thomas 19:12
Eleman, Enos W. 10:112
Elenberger, P. 3:65
Elerson, Elias B. 27:41
Eleton, N. 3:65
Eleven, Henry 13:20
Elexson, A. 13:87
Eley, Erastus 24:77
Eley, Jesse 17:14
Eley, Joseph 5:15; 25:168
Elfield, Albert 7:122
Elfrey, Peter 11:125
Elfring, Ernest 11:91
Elfry, B. S. 3:65
Elgen, William 24:38
Elgin, --- 18:426
Elgin, Faank 9:175
Elgin, Frank 19:289
Elgin, Thomas 1:30
Elha, D. 3:65
Elheny, E. L. 15:293
Elheny, E. Mq. 16:188
Elhy, Michael 13:20
Eli, Rachelle 7:122
Eli, Thomas 8:14; 18:132
Eli, W. 3:65
Elias, George 17:147
Elias, Henry 11:201
Elias, Samuel 25:332
Elibear, --- 12:145
Elican, J. 25:280
Elifler, --- 9:236
Elifritz, Martin 22:189
Eligah, John 27:39
Eligan, --- 16:367
Elighury, Porter L. 17:78
Elijah, Absent 21:327
Elin, Charles 12:20
Eline, John A. 16:31
Eline, John H. 13:20
Elineer, T. B. 11:153
Elingsworth, Joseph 14:163
Elington, John W. 22:249

Elingwood, R. 19:67
Eliot, E. 3:65
Eliott, A. A. 25:30
Eliott, John 3:65
Eliott, W. H. 11:181
Elisha, Perry 21:269
Elison, James 15:66
Elive, E. 11:339
Elixon, A. 14:9
Elkar, C. 1:30
Elker, Jacob 4:22
Elkert, J. 19:251
Elkey, Henry 13:20
Elkey, Lewis 11:118
Elkin, --- 16:292
Elkin, David W. 24:65
Elkin, Henry 12:20
Elkin, John V. 23:98
Elkington, J. W. 18:81
Elkins, A. 7:93
Elkins, Albert 14:163
Elkins, Aloz F. 27:40
Elkins, Daniel K. 21:51
Elkins, E. 17:147
Elkins, Freeman 13:20
Elkins, G. S. 1:31
Elkins, Henry 8:84
Elkins, J. 17:33
Elkins, James 14:57
Elkins, Jesse 14:297; 17:470
Elkins, John 8:84
Elkins, Louis J. 22:249
Elkins, M. M. 14:163, 255
Elkins, Marwell 23:98
Elkins, R. D. 11:302
Elkins, S. 14:163, 255
Elkins, Stephen 17:346
Elkins, W. 9:109
Elkins, W. A. 14:57
Elkins, William H. 16:188
Elkir, Jacob 4:22
Ellan, John 10:98
Ellard, Andrew J. 11:59
Ellard, George 13:21
Ellard, John 8:121
Ellbut, --- 20:181
Ellcott, L. 15:195
Elldridge, Edward T. 21:327
Ellebrant, Robert 12:58
Elledge, Joel H. 24:17
Elledge, William 13:20
Elledge, William J. 22:500
Elleman, Enos W. 20:245
Ellen, H. H. 14:57
Ellen, J. 1:128
Ellenbecker, Nicholas 22:29
Ellenberger, August 16:93
Ellenwood, A. W. 1:127

Ellenwood, Horace 24:71
Ellenwood, L. 3:65
Ellenwood, William 1:30
Eller, David 11:386
Eller, George 24:65
Eller, James M. 17:418
Eller, S. 11:261
Ellerson, A. G. 8:14; 18:132
Ellery, A. J. 11:261
Ellery, T. 7:49
Elles, Joseph H. 11:59
Elleson, Benjamin F. 19:12
Ellester, Samuel H. 25:30
Elleston, James P. 20:245
Ellet, Isaac 22:512
Ellet, J. W. 11:59
Elleth, Joseph 20:245
Ellett, Johnson M. 7:93
Ellett, Joseph 10:51
Elleveson, Elleve 13:21
Elley, Henry H. 16:188
Ellickson, John 7:93
Ellicott, George N. 5:15
Ellie, John 21:327
Ellimoore, Eli 10:16
Ellinfritz, George 9:34
Ellinger, Jacob 14:163
Ellinger, Jacob S. 21:51
Ellinger, John 14:163
Ellinger, P. 3:65
Ellingood, Miles H. 19:222
Ellingson, Johann 10:112; 20:245
Ellingto, George 11:202
Ellington, Abraham 17:51
Ellington, Albert 17:272
Ellington, Dabney 7:122
Ellington, David C. 17:280
Ellington, George 17:397
Ellington, J. 3:65
Ellington, John A. 22:298
Ellington, William 17:267
Ellingwood, Charles O. 17:211
Ellingwood, H. O. 21:327
Ellingwood, Hiram 11:59
Ellins, Johnson 21:327
Ellinwood, H. 22:189
Ellinwood, Lyman 13:63
Elliot, --- 14:163; 26:26
Elliot, C. G. 16:292
Elliot, Eli 20:136
Elliot, F. P. 3:65
Elliot, G. A. 10:172
Elliot, George 14:163
Elliot, Hacon 19:12
Elliot, Henry 5:15; 18:236

Elliot, J. 19:67
Elliot, Jason 6:8
Elliot, John 11:302; 15:305
Elliot, John R. 10:90
Elliot, Park B. 17:359
Elliot, William 17:33
Elliote, Absalom 10:95
Elliott, --- 2:10; 25:31
Elliott, A. 3:65; 14:57
Elliott, A. J. 11:365
Elliott, Aaron 24:17
Elliott, Andrew S. 24:77
Elliott, B. 22:189
Elliott, Bacon 26:123
Elliott, Baker 15:7
Elliott, Bartholomew 22:121
Elliott, Bason 9:42
Elliott, Benjamin F. 16:93
Elliott, Benson 11:105
Elliott, Brown 17:236
Elliott, C. 1:30, 127; 3:65
Elliott, C. C. 12:152
Elliott, C. G. 12:85; 14:57
Elliott, C. H. 12:80; 25:168
Elliott, Charles 11:145; 21:253, 327; 23:28
Elliott, D. M. 9:34; 18:292; 26:97
Elliott, David 14:297; 17:477; 27:41
Elliott, Dawson 24:38
Elliott, E. 14:57
Elliott, E. J. 23:28
Elliott, Edward J. 22:189
Elliott, Embray 22:478
Elliott, Ezekiel 13:21
Elliott, F. 14:57
Elliott, Frank 23:141
Elliott, Franklin 17:404
Elliott, G. R. 19:12
Elliott, George 7:93; 14:57; 18:28, 394; 24:193
Elliott, George C. 13:127
Elliott, Griffith 10:112; 20:245
Elliott, H. 10:27; 25:168
Elliott, H. H. 12:152
Elliott, H. R. 17:131; 24:193
Elliott, Hamton 5:38
Elliott, Henry 1:31; 16:188
Elliott, Henry E. 11:84
Elliott, Henry P. 21:114
Elliott, Hiram 8:15; 18:132
Elliott, I. S. 18:216

Elliott, Isaac 20:174; 24:175
Elliott, Isaac I. 22:75
Elliott, Isaac M. 11:58
Elliott, Israel 17:449
Elliott, J. 1:127; 3:65; 7:25; 11:29; 25:168
Elliott, J. D. 26:219
Elliott, J. H. 3:65
Elliott, J. P. 3:65; 17:404
Elliott, J. R. 20:245
Elliott, J. W. 7:25; 25:319
Elliott, J. Y. 16:31
Elliott, Jacob 13:135; 19:346
Elliott, Jacob W. 23:189
Elliott, James 7:25; 11:201; 17:247; 22:189; 24:157
Elliott, James A. 22:450
Elliott, James E. 9:236; 26:219
Elliott, James L. 4:22
Elliott, Jason 18:103
Elliott, Jason M. 21:129
Elliott, Jefferson 17:257
Elliott, Joah 9:21
Elliott, John 1:31; 5:38; 9:219; 11:365; 14:321; 15:34; 18:365; 20:123; 22:17, 403; 23:28
Elliott, John C. 22:75; 23:141
Elliott, John H. 17:51; 21:51
Elliott, John J. 20:7
Elliott, John W. 22:249
Elliott, Jonas D. 23:285
Elliott, Jordan 22:298
Elliott, Joseph 7:57; 14:57
Elliott, L. 3:65
Elliott, Lander 24:49
Elliott, Levi 22:189
Elliott, Lewis 12:56; 22:10, 512
Elliott, Lewis B. 13:21
Elliott, Lewis C. 22:279
Elliott, Malachi 11:59
Elliott, Mark 17:131; 24:193
Elliott, Monroe 27:41
Elliott, O. P. 13:21
Elliott, O. W. 1:31
Elliott, Perkins 23:28
Elliott, Peter B. 22:500
Elliott, R. W. 21:327
Elliott, Reuben 17:259
Elliott, S. 14:57, 281
Elliott, S. T. 15:293; 16:188

Elliott, Samuel W. 4:22
Elliott, Silas 11:59
Elliott, Simon 17:415
Elliott, Solomon 22:298
Elliott, T. 1:127
Elliott, Thomas 3:65; 13:21; 21:187; 22:278, 403
Elliott, Thomas W. 21:223
Elliott, Uriah 22:189
Elliott, V. H. 9:51
Elliott, W. 3:65; 25:320
Elliott, W. H. 17:71
Elliott, William 1:31; 8:113; 9:51, 68; 22:423; 23:65; 25:31
Elliott, William B. 21:24
Elliott, William M. P. 22:121
Elliott, William P. 14:268
Elliott, William S. 10:112; 20:245
Elliott, Winslow 22:298
Ellis, --- 25:332
Ellis, A. 1:127; 3:65; 5:15; 25:168
Ellis, A. B. 19:222; 20:245
Ellis, A. E. 17:154
Ellis, A. G. 17:295
Ellis, A. H. 22:462
Ellis, A. J. 8:47
Ellis, Albert 10:16
Ellis, Alonzo B. 10:51
Ellis, Amon 24:49
Ellis, Andrew 7:122
Ellis, Benjamin 9:203
Ellis, C. 3:65; 14:57
Ellis, C. C. 23:28
Ellis, C. F. 1:31
Ellis, C. G. 22:278
Ellis, C. O. 3:65
Ellis, Cabdial 16:292
Ellis, Calvin G. 22:278
Ellis, Carl 22:141
Ellis, Charles 3:65; 22:10
Ellis, Chester A. 19:162
Ellis, Curtis 22:278
Ellis, D. 3:65; 14:57, 281
Ellis, Daniel 13:20; 20:141
Ellis, Darius S. 7:25
Ellis, David 11:279
Ellis, David A. 10:7
Ellis, E. 3:65; 17:174; 23:65
Ellis, E. S. 15:158
Ellis, Edward 19:251
Ellis, Edward H. 21:327
Ellis, Edward J. 9:175
Ellis, Elijah 9:200

Ellis, Ellis Ellis 21:68
Ellis, F. 3:65
Ellis, Frank 10:25
Ellis, G. 1:127; 19:67
Ellis, G. W. 27:40
Ellis, George 1:30; 10:112; 11:29; 15:195; 16:188; 19:12; 20:245; 22:141; 25:31
Ellis, Gilbert W. 14:163
Ellis, H. 7:67; 14:58, 163
Ellis, H. C. 3:65
Ellis, H. H. 3:65
Ellis, H. T. 21:327
Ellis, Hector 23:270
Ellis, Henry 7:57; 9:21; 13:20; 17:99; 19:45
Ellis, Henry C. 12:69
Ellis, Henry E. 10:172; 19:162
Ellis, Hiram 13:20
Ellis, Hiram H. 1:30
Ellis, I. H. 3:65
Ellis, Isaac 17:349
Ellis, Isaac B. 11:145
Ellis, J. 1:103; 3:65
Ellis, J. H. 15:90
Ellis, J. J. 17:429
Ellis, J. L. 9:219; 18:365
Ellis, J. W. 1:30; 18:236; 20:245; 26:26
Ellis, Jacob 11:422; 19:290
Ellis, Jacob B. 22:478
Ellis, James 8:63; 9:230; 17:174; 20:245; 22:478; 23:263; 25:333
Ellis, James A. 20:7
Ellis, James E. 21:238
Ellis, James F. 14:163
Ellis, James H. 12:69
Ellis, James Mason 22:519
Ellis, James S. 18:271
Ellis, James W. 21:24
Ellis, John 7:57; 11:58, 381; 16:31, 137; 17:359; 19:13; 22:189; 24:65
Ellis, John I. 20:245
Ellis, John J. 10:112; 22:462; 23:87
Ellis, John M. 12:152
Ellis, John O. 23:28
Ellis, John Q. 9:34; 18:292; 26:97
Ellis, John W. 15:313; 19:67; 23:65
Ellis, Johnson 7:93

Ellis, Joseph 8:38; 14:58; 19:290; 22:403; 26:159
Ellis, Joseph A. 22:278
Ellis, Joseph S. 7:93
Ellis, Joseph W. 5:15
Ellis, L. 27:40
Ellis, L. E. 1:127
Ellis, Leo 27:41
Ellis, Levi 23:255
Ellis, M. 9:142; 27:41
Ellis, Martin 22:29
Ellis, Nathan 11:401; 17:425; 24:177
Ellis, Nathan S. 12:20
Ellis, Nelson 22:298
Ellis, Noah 22:478
Ellis, Nolty D. 21:244
Ellis, O. W. 1:128
Ellis, Orland D. 22:403
Ellis, Orrin 4:22
Ellis, P. M. 3:65
Ellis, Phineas 24:49
Ellis, R. 26:26
Ellis, R. H. 3:65
Ellis, Reuben 9:79; 26:26
Ellis, Richard 11:191; 24:110
Ellis, Robert J. 10:112; 20:245
Ellis, Rodman 9:79
Ellis, S. 9:142; 27:40
Ellis, Samuel 13:87; 16:31
Ellis, Samuel R. 24:59
Ellis, Solomon 5:15
Ellis, Sorel 11:125
Ellis, Stephen 7:57; 22:112
Ellis, T. G. 19:67
Ellis, Theodore 22:75
Ellis, Thomas 16:188; 17:174; 25:30
Ellis, Thomas G. 10:112; 20:245
Ellis, W. 3:65
Ellis, W. A. 8:47; 10:90
Ellis, W. H. 19:162
Ellis, W. M. 11:260
Ellis, W. R. 5:51
Ellis, W. T. 14:241
Ellis, Wash 24:193
Ellis, Washington 22:165
Ellis, Wesley 22:298
Ellis, William 3:65; 4:22; 7:122; 8:71; 9:118, 130; 16:11; 18:236; 20:136; 23:292; 26:26, 159; 27:40
Ellis, William A. 20:245; 21:68
Ellis, William D. 11:411

Ellis, William H. 7:122
Ellis, Wyatt 16:188
Ellise, J. 14:240; 27:42
Ellison, --- 15:94; 17:503
Ellison, A. J. 21:328
Ellison, Benjamin 17:174
Ellison, E. B. 9:118
Ellison, Gabriel 22:121
Ellison, George W. 7:93
Ellison, Hebris 24:63
Ellison, I. 14:58
Ellison, Isaac 3:65; 15:105
Ellison, J. 14:9
Ellison, J. B. 9:142; 27:40
Ellison, J. K. 14:58
Ellison, James 9:79; 14:163; 26:25
Ellison, Jesse 24:193
Ellison, Jesse S. 18:216
Ellison, John 14:241
Ellison, L. 25:168
Ellison, Lawson 5:38
Ellison, M. H. 20:245
Ellison, Morgan 11:202
Ellison, Oliver 24:17
Ellison, Pleasant 7:93
Ellison, R. 13:108
Ellison, Slaughter 22:423
Ellison, W. 3:65
Ellison, W. A. 11:145
Ellison, W. C. 11:191
Ellison, William 14:58
Ellison, William H. 13:108
Ellison, William J. 23:251
Elliston, G. 1:31
Elliston, J. 15:173
Ellithrop, Charles 21:68
Ellitt, Harris S. 4:22
Ellmare, Henry 12:152
Ellmer, Solomon 21:328
Ellmore, Jonas 16:31
Ellot, R. 16:93
Ellrye, --- 9:71
Ells, Charles 1:31
Ells, G. 1:128
Ells, Perry 3:65; 16:17
Ellsaesser, Joseph 23:141
Ellsbarry, F. H. 20:245
Ellsberg, Joseph 10:27
Ellsberry, Frederick H. 10:51
Ellsburg, Joseph 19:301
Ellsing, Benjamin 24:38
Ellson, Christian 21:328
Ellson, Isaiah 11:239
Ellston, M. W. 1:127
Ellsworlt, A. 19:67
Ellsworth, A. 12:95; 15:359

Ellsworth, A. E. 22:519
Ellsworth, Atwater 6:8
Ellsworth, H. J. 15:341; 16:367
Ellsworth, I. 14:58
Ellsworth, J. 14:58
Ellsworth, James 24:93
Ellsworth, Jason C. 4:22
Ellsworth, Job 21:68
Ellsworth, John 16:145
Ellsworth, L. 20:145
Ellsworth, Nelson H. 17:359
Ellsworth, Newman 24:17
Ellsworth, Oliver C. 22:141
Ellsworth, Orison 15:34
Ellsworth, R. 1:30
Ellsworth, Sylvester 13:21
Ellsworth, W. 18:28
Ellsworth, Wesley W. 21:51
Ellwell, B. A. 21:328
Ellwell, G. W. 16:367
Ellwell, Henry 22:403
Ellwood, Frank 16:31
Ellwood, W. V. 27:40
Ellwood, William 21:328; 23:121
Ellworth, John 7:25
Elma, David 19:67
Elman, Frederick 7:93
Elman, N. 3:65
Elmer, C. 1:128
Elmer, C. B. 19:13
Elmer, Caleb W. 17:65
Elmer, Ebein 4:22
Elmer, H. 1:31
Elmer, Henry 16:31
Elmer, John 13:108; 14:58
Elmer, John E. 20:96
Elmer, Noah 11:338
Elmer, Parley 11:105
Elmer, Robert 7:49
Elmer, Washington 21:147
Elmer, William 16:188
Elmere, Curtis H. 9:175
Elmerpot, Holden 11:400
Elmor, R. G. 25:168
Elmore, A. 9:175; 19:273
Elmore, Archer 18:81
Elmore, Archey 6:16
Elmore, B. A. 1:127
Elmore, Curtis H. 19:251
Elmore, George 21:187
Elmore, James 1:31
Elmore, Jesse 17:442; 24:157
Elmore, P. J. 17:233
Elmore, Sylvanus 24:93

Elmore, Wesley C. 20:86
Elmore, William M. 23:65
Elmoth, Atwater 18:103
Elmrick, David 20:245
Elms, James 25:168
Elms, W. 15:341
Elms, W. F. 16:368
Elmuck, David 10:51
Elonding, William 18:132
Elording, William 8:15
Elph, John T. 13:21
Elrah, John 13:87
Elrick, Ruggles 23:11
Elrick, Thomas J. 23:87
Elridge, Charles 14:58
Elridge, J. B. 14:281
Elright, Benjamin 3:65
Elright, S. C. 15:195
Elrod, Alexander 23:98
Elrod, Dennis 15:195
Elrod, George 21:203
Elrod, John 22:249
Elrod, Leonard G. 22:75
Elrod, Samuel L. 11:58
Elrod, Stephen L. 21:25
Elrod, Thomas 21:203
Elroth, C. H. 26:211
Els, Emil 13:81; 16:188
Els, Enril 16:188
Elsa, William 18:305; 26:97
Elsboy, T. 11:401
Elsbree, Joshua 15:273
Else, Dennis 18:81
Elsea, Rudolph H. 22:422
Elsen, J. D. 9:68
Elsenninger, T. 11:125
Elsert, Charles 25:31
Elsessor, P. 1:31
Elsey, Daniel 6:16; 18:81
Elsey, E. 1:31
Elsey, James 22:450
Elsey, John 7:122
Elsey, Joshua 12:69; 15:86
Elshack, Joseph 11:230
Elsie, Arthur 4:65
Elsie, James 11:386
Elsington, D. R. 16:188
Elsnor, F. 21:137
Elson, James 5:15; 25:168
Elson, John 10:112; 20:245
Elson, Tunis 22:189
Elson, W. M. 11:144
Elst---, B. 25:31
Elster, William 23:141
Elston, David R. 8:84
Elston, F. 3:66
Elston, F. N. 26:159
Elston, James 3:66

Elston, James P. 10:112
Elston, James V. 3:66
Elston, John 18:365
Elston, John H. 22:189
Elston, Marion 11:59
Elston, William G. 1:30
Elstow, John 9:219
Elsum, Thomas 1:30
Elswert, J. 1:128
Elswick, Isaac 24:166
Elsworth, A. G. 17:291
Elsworth, Daniel 8:84
Elsworth, Daniel H.
    22:141
Elsworth, David 12:8
Elsworth, John 17:51
Elsworth, Orl. I. 15:195
Elter, Valentine 3:66
Elters, Henry 3:66
Eltzroth, J. A. 11:239
Elvdid, C. D. 13:108
Elvin, Albert 22:75
Elvord, John 27:41
Elwel, L. 7:74
Elwel, W. S. 7:74
Elwell, A. 20:245
Elwell, Abraham 10:51
Elwell, C. C. 16:93
Elwell, Charles E. 1:30
Elwell, E. D. 15:173
Elwell, F. 15:326
Elwell, Freeman 19:67
Elwell, John 25:168
Elwell, Joseph 14:163
Elwell, L. 25:296
Elwell, M. G. 7:25
Elwell, Nelson E. 17:65
Elwell, Newell 27:40
Elwell, Thomas 21:51
Elwell, Timothy 4:22
Elwell, W. 3:66
Elwell, W. S. 25:296
Elwell, William 4:22
Elwell, William H. 23:107
Elwood, Franklin 13:21
Elwood, George 15:27
Elwood, J. M. 22:334
Elwood, James 25:271
Elwood, John 26:138
Elwood, W. F. 9:142
Elwood, W. M. 1:31
Ely, --- 19:349
Ely, A. R. 19:67
Ely, Amos 24:77
Ely, Daniel 25:31
Ely, David 17:265
Ely, E. R. 20:245
Ely, F. 15:195
Ely, Frederick 12:167;
    19:347
Ely, G. 14:262

Ely, George 14:163
Ely, George W. 23:141
Ely, J. 1:128
Ely, J. C. 21:25
Ely, Jacob 23:263
Ely, John 5:15; 10:98
Ely, John B. 19:45
Ely, John W. 8:84
Ely, M. 9:21; 18:305;
    26:97
Ely, William M. 23:141
Elyea, James E. 11:296
Elyea, James S. 11:239
Elyer, Hugo 18:48
Elza, James M. 20:96
Elzey, J. 14:58
Emanard, Philip 12:95
Emanert, Philip 19:67
Emans, Andrew 22:189
Emanuel, A. 22:75
Emanuel, Victor 13:63;
    16:188
Emanuel, William 9:130;
    27:40
Emart, Jacob 10:51;
    20:245
Ematinger, C. 1:128
Emay, E. H. 19:233
Ember, W. 27:40
Emberry, William 8:99
Emberson, Lors 11:190
Emberton, George T.
    17:236
Emberton, Nathan H.
    22:121
Emberton, Silas 11:284
Emberton, W. H. 8:15;
    18:132
Emberton, William B.
    17:206
Embery, Charles 20:245
Embody, J. 17:435
Embody, Jona M. 24:177
Embree, Cyrenus 21:238
Embree, J. F. 12:161
Embree, M. 1:128
Embree, Watson C.
    10:112; 20:245
Embree, William 20:22
Embree, William B. 20:22
Embry, Ossas 15:288
Emburg, Edward 10:148
Emburger, Henry 23:179
Embury, Edward 18:48
Emch, John 20:245
Emchy, Thomas 21:269
Emdee, --- 14:163
Emeby, William 20:39
Emeh, John 10:112
Emel, Henry 21:269

Emely, Alonzo 12:69;
    15:27
Emerick, G. 7:25
Emerick, Jeremiah
    11:234; 22:397
Emerick, John 9:230;
    20:246; 23:65
Emerick, P. F. 10:186;
    18:174
Emerine, Joseph 21:223
Emerith, Peter 13:21
Emerson, A. P. 19:251
Emerson, Amos 7:93
Emerson, Andrew P.
    9:175
Emerson, B. 23:267
Emerson, C. A. 17:154
Emerson, Calvin 1:30
Emerson, Charles 14:163
Emerson, Daniel W. 8:47;
    21:68
Emerson, F. F. 14:262
Emerson, Frank 11:84
Emerson, Franklin 21:87
Emerson, G. 15:195
Emerson, G. W. 3:66
Emerson, Gentry 19:290
Emerson, H. B. 5:51
Emerson, Henry 14:163;
    22:404
Emerson, J. 3:66
Emerson, J. L. 1:127
Emerson, J. R. 16:31
Emerson, J. S. 1:127
Emerson, Jacob 9:219;
    18:365
Emerson, James 9:200;
    19:290
Emerson, James E. 8:47
Emerson, John 7:67;
    9:230; 13:21; 20:246
Emerson, John C. 22:189
Emerson, John S. 18:276
Emerson, John T. 9:175
Emerson, Joseph S. 8:47
Emerson, L. 16:188
Emerson, Logan 23:65
Emerson, M. D. 1:127
Emerson, Martin E.
    21:238
Emerson, Muity 11:319
Emerson, Ole 10:112
Emerson, P. 9:175
Emerson, Reuben 11:58
Emerson, S. T. 19:226
Emerson, Samuel 16:31;
    23:290
Emerson, T. 1:31; 21:25
Emerson, W. 25:168
Emerson, Washington
    27:41

Emerson, William 17:163; 19:162
Emertson, Timothy O. 22:134
Emery, A. P. 16:292
Emery, A. T. 1:127
Emery, Aaron 19:13
Emery, Adam 15:66
Emery, Alfred 9:21; 18:305; 26:97
Emery, Alvin 14:321; 23:28
Emery, C. 23:28
Emery, C. T. 3:66
Emery, E. D. 18:48
Emery, E. R. 13:63
Emery, Edward 16:189
Emery, Ennis 17:174
Emery, F. 15:311; 19:67
Emery, Frederick V. 15:34
Emery, George 11:191; 17:211
Emery, H. S. 25:168
Emery, Ira 16:81
Emery, Isaac 7:25; 8:105
Emery, J. 3:66
Emery, James 11:29, 319; 19:13
Emery, John S. 12:20
Emery, Jonas 15:7
Emery, Louis 17:174
Emery, M. A. 7:67
Emery, Mark 9:159
Emery, N. 25:168
Emery, N. M. 20:89
Emery, Richard 4:22; 25:30
Emery, S. R. 9:142; 27:40
Emery, Samuel 19:270
Emery, Stephen 10:51; 20:246
Emery, Thomas 16:368
Emery, Thomas B. 24:38
Emery, William 10:51; 11:58; 20:246
Emery, William H. 17:73
Emes, J. 1:127
Emet, Jacob 20:27
Emge, Jacob 10:51
Emhuff, Andrew 8:63
Emick, Benedict 8:84
Emig, Jesse 23:142
Emig, Martin 12:58
Emigh, Charles 25:168
Emigle, A. 1:127
Emil, Adolph 11:276
Emin, Peter 18:81
Eming, G. A. 24:16
Eminger, H. 18:48
Eminger, Hiram 10:152
Eminhizer, A. 1:127

Eminker, H. 27:41
Emis, Alfred 18:81
Emison, G. 3:66
Emitt, Peter 10:176
Emler, Lee 22:249
Emley, Thomas 15:34
Emly, Charles 21:328
Emmans, Levi 13:124
Emmedy, Alexander R. 7:122
Emmel, P. 1:31
Emmell, Henry 7:49
Emmenert, Philip 15:359
Emmerson, F. F. 3:66
Emmerson, George 14:163, 255
Emmerson, H. B. 25:168
Emmerson, H. H. 3:66
Emmerson, Jeremiah 13:130; 20:246
Emmerson, John 7:122
Emmerson, L. P. 22:189
Emmerson, Ole 20:246
Emmerson, R. K. 15:173
Emmerson, S. 13:108; 23:189
Emmerson, W. 3:66
Emmerson, Washington 9:118
Emmerson, William 5:38
Emmerson, William H. 25:31
Emmert, I. C. 3:66
Emmert, Jacob 23:65
Emmert, W. 14:58
Emmery, Alvin 14:315
Emmery, J. 14:163, 255
Emmes, Henry 1:30
Emmet, --- 26:236
Emmet, E. R. 10:112
Emmet, Reuben 11:202
Emmett, John S. 22:249
Emmett, Robert 7:122
Emmett, W. 3:66
Emmette, Andrew 21:328
Emmick, L. S. 3:66
Emming, David 9:79
Emmings, J. J. 11:145
Emmit, E. R. 20:246
Emmond, J. P. 14:241
Emmonds, A. 3:66
Emmonds, Cassius 5:15
Emmonds, W. 3:66
Emmons, A. 1:30
Emmons, Asher 14:163
Emmons, Benjamin 10:112
Emmons, C. 20:133
Emmons, C. H. 21:25
Emmons, Daniel 9:130; 27:40

Emmons, Ephraim 21:328
Emmons, Everett 19:227
Emmons, George M. 16:189
Emmons, George W. 20:96
Emmons, H. B. 25:31
Emmons, Harly 11:302
Emmons, Harrison W. 7:57
Emmons, Henry C. 1:30
Emmons, Hiram 10:16
Emmons, Jacob 6:24
Emmons, James W. 22:141
Emmons, John 12:20
Emmons, Jonathan 8:15; 18:132
Emmons, Joshua 9:130; 27:41
Emmons, Smedley 27:144
Emmons, William 8:15; 18:132
Emmons, William H. 21:206
Emo, Joseph 7:138
Emory, Adam 12:69
Emory, Frederick 9:175
Emory, Frederick V. 12:69
Emory, G. 1:128
Emory, H. 1:94
Emory, Harrison E. 5:15
Emory, I. 9:109
Emory, J. W. 9:109
Emory, James 7:93; 27:40
Emory, Joseph G. 1:31
Emory, Moses D. 16:77
Emory, Nathaniel 5:15
Emory, Robert 24:193
Emory, Samuel 9:175
Emory, Silas 18:420
Emory, T. 25:168
Emory, Thomas 5:38
Emory, William 13:21
Emory, William W. 15:123
Empoy, Robert 3:66
Empy, Samuel 13:108
Empy, Frederick 9:96
Emrer, Frederick 9:96
Emrich, Henry 15:34
Emrich, Valentine 4:22
Emrick, Henry I. 12:69
Emrick, John 11:145
Emrison, D. G. 3:66
Emry, E. M. 9:175
Emry, John C. 11:29
Emstreet, A. P. 15:289; 16:189
Emtree, P. J. 18:409
Emviet, John 9:79

Enacks, William 9:42
Enary, Wash 17:131;
  24:193
Enbanks, J. 3:66
Enburg, Alfred 19:340
Encel, Charles 14:163
Encell, Joseph 12:56
Ench, Michael 24:17
Encher, Abraham A. 9:34
Encillis, Fred 13:109
Encram, R. C. 9:51
Encron, Magonis 10:172
Ency, Abram 23:98
Enda, Christ 14:163
Ende, Henry 12:58
Endecott, Melvin C. 20:96
Enderly, Joel 20:246
Endermill, John 3:66
Endersbee, J. 25:168
Endicott, David 23:240
Endicott, Joseph 10:51;
  20:246
Endicott, Newland G.
  21:187
Endicott, Thomas H.
  23:65
Endicott, William 13:63
Endicott, Williard 19:67
Endricks, F. 24:17
Ends, William 11:58
Endsley, J. C. 25:271
Endsley, Jacob W. 22:76
Eneking, John B. 20:246
Enens, Simon 21:269
Enepey, Nelson 13:109
Enes, Lewis 16:189
Enfield, Charles 20:145
Enfield, John 18:236;
  26:26
Enfield, William J. 17:313
Eng, Christian 11:190
Engalergy, Charles 20:246
Engall, W. 3:66
Engals, Nicholas 21:328
Engard, J. E. 4:22
Engart, Hugh D. 10:112
Engebretson, Ole 24:63
Enged, George 25:168
Engel, Jacob 18:132
Engel, Samuel 11:419
Engelberg, Charles 10:51
Engelob, William 1:30
Engels, Augustus 4:22
Enger, August 19:251
Enger, J. 3:66
Engerman, A. 14:297;
  17:472
Engermann, A. 27:41
Engers, Christian 16:147
Engesser, August 22:29
Engey, F. 19:251

Engfer, John 20:246
Enghert, John 25:168
Engla, --- 17:151
Englan, Thomas W. 21:51
England, --- 10:27; 19:301
England, Andy 17:103
England, E. 8:48
England, Ezekiel 3:66
England, G. 3:66
England, George 7:122;
  9:96
England, Harrison 18:276
England, I. 14:58
England, J. 19:251
England, J. H. 10:27;
  19:301
England, James 17:425
England, Jefferson 24:17
England, John 9:175;
  19:251; 22:29
England, Thomas J. 24:65
England, W. C. 27:41
England, William 23:184
Engle, Alex 26:97
Engle, Alexander 9:21;
  18:305
Engle, B. 1:127
Engle, Charles 9:118;
  27:41
Engle, D. 1:128
Engle, D. H. 22:478
Engle, Fred 18:28
Engle, G. W. 21:99
Engle, Hamilton E.
  14:163
Engle, Henry 10:51;
  14:163; 20:246
Engle, Hiram 18:132
Engle, Hiram J. 8:15
Engle, J. 20:39
Engle, J. B. 23:142
Engle, Jacob 8:15;
  14:163; 20:246
Engle, John 9:42; 14:58;
  20:133; 22:190;
  24:38
Engle, John C. 26:144
Engle, John T. 26:144
Engle, Joseph 21:253
Engle, Levi 8:100;
  17:462; 24:177
Engle, Otho 22:189
Engle, Peter 3:66
Engle, Thomas 4:22
Engle, Vincenns 24:77
Engle, William 21:51
Engle, William B. 22:189
Engle, William T. 17:51
Englebrecht, August
  18:305; 26:97
Englebroth, H. 18:28

Engledon, J. M. 20:246
Engledore, J. M. 10:90
Englee, Gasper 7:16
Englehart, C. 17:154
Englehart, G. 25:168
Englehart, Jacob 17:247;
  23:252
Englehart, John M. 21:51
Englehrat, J. 25:168
Engleman, C. 1:128
Engleman, Henry M.
  22:423
Engleman, William 8:15;
  10:51; 18:132;
  20:246
Engler, Frank 16:189
Engler, J. 8:15; 18:132
Engler, John 3:66; 6:30
Engler, M. 24:77
Engler, Silas H. 11:278
Englert, Marx 16:93
Engles, Charles W. 13:21
Engleson, N. 10:205
Engleston, F. 21:121
Engleton, S. S. 21:121
Engley, Isaac 19:227
Englis, C. F. 14:9
English, Albon H. 17:143
English, Allen 22:249
English, C. F. 13:87
English, C. H. 7:26
English, Darius 21:211
English, David 22:512
English, Dennis 21:269
English, E. W. 22:190
English, Edward 12:20
English, G. 3:66
English, George 15:66;
  20:399
English, Granville 11:201
English, Grean 26:159
English, Green 8:38
English, Henry 19:13
English, J. 7:26; 9:51;
  19:237
English, J. C. 3:66
English, James 3:66;
  9:175; 14:58
English, James A. 1:30
English, John 14:163;
  24:17
English, Joseph 19:287
English, M. 15:341;
  16:368
English, N. 19:67
English, Nelson 11:201
English, Oliver 16:93
English, P. 17:174
English, Pat 14:163
English, R. 14:241; 27:42
English, Richard 23:309

English, S. 21:328
English, Samuel J. 10:160; 19:162
English, Samuel N. 24:49
English, Sarvair 8:38
English, Seth 15:289; 16:189
English, Solomon 23:28
English, Survain 26:159
English, T. M. 17:95
English, Thomas 4:22; 22:141
English, W. P. 11:302
English, William 9:70; 11:422; 20:106
English, William C. 10:112; 20:246
Englut, J. 25:168
Engraff, John 21:121
Engrewark, J. 1:128
Engste, --- Charles 16:189
Engster, Charles 13:79
Enhart, H. 3:66
Enhoff, Jacob 4:22
Enichs, Isaac 22:190
Eninger, R. 13:21; 16:31
Enis, Alfred 6:12
Enis, J. W. 27:40
Enke, Frederick 22:334
Enloe, Anderson 7:122
Enloe, F. 20:246
Enloe, Felix 10:51
Enlons, John 18:236; 26:26
Enlow, Homer 10:51; 20:246
Enlow, Jonathan 17:257
Enlow, Thomas B. 22:121
Ennerer, William 10:160
Enney, John E. 9:175
Ennis, Andrew 3:66
Ennis, Daniel 9:21
Ennis, Dayton 10:16
Ennis, E. T. 27:41
Ennis, H. 15:151; 25:168
Ennis, J. 1:127
Ennis, J. F. 25:168
Ennis, J. W. 9:142
Ennis, Jeremiah 26:144
Ennis, John 4:22; 9:130; 12:56; 19:45; 21:51; 25:168; 27:40
Ennis, John F. 5:15
Ennis, L. B. 10:51
Ennis, Lawrence 11:59
Ennis, Mat 21:328
Ennis, Robert D. 23:107
Ennis, Thomas 20:112
Ennis, William 3:66
Ennos, J. E. 20:246
Eno, Clephus 15:55

Eno, Franklin 10:51; 20:246
Eno, Stephen H. 22:298
Enoch, Hyatt 18:236; 26:26
Enoch, James 22:76
Enochs, James 22:190
Enocks, William 26:123
Enoff, N. 3:66
Enos, E. 1:127
Enos, G. W. 25:168
Enos, George 11:91
Enos, Isaac A. 5:15
Enos, Jesse 25:168
Enos, Michael 17:446; 24:170
Enos, Thomas 24:17
Enos, W. R. 7:26
Enos, William H. 9:175; 19:251
Enos, William I. 8:15
Enos, William J. 18:132
Enosense, John 16:93
Enoveys, John M. 21:328
Enox, Horace 15:283; 19:67
Enrhard, John 1:30
Enri, J. M. 23:301
Enright, David 13:21; 16:31
Enright, Michael 1:31
Enscore, R. S. 27:41
Enser, Conrad 16:279
Ensighu, N. 25:168
Ensign, --- 19:162
Ensign, Benjamin 18:28
Ensign, E. 14:163
Ensign, J. 3:66
Ensign, Joseph A. 23:11
Ensign, Salmon 8:84
Ensigner, H. A. 25:31
Ensing, R. B. 19:67
Ensinger, Hy. A. 2:10
Ensler, John 9:109
Ensler, Samuel 16:31
Ensley, C. 3:66
Ensley, John 20:145
Ensley, W. H. 3:66
Ensley, William 3:66
Enslow, D. Y. 10:51
Enslow, Lyman 8:84
Enslow, Perry A. 20:22
Ensminger, B. 14:163
Ensom, H. 22:298
Enstrom, C. 14:255
Enswer, --- 19:162
Ensworth, John 3:66
Entenmann, Jacob 4:23
Entepil, G. 23:65
Enthill, Thomas B. 2:10
Entler, Philip 22:190

Entrekin, J. W. 20:2
Entrophistle, John 21:10
Entry, Isaac 16:31
Entsinenger, G. A. 7:26
Entulen, B. C. 3:66
Entwistle, R. 13:81
Entwistle, Ralph 13:81; 16:189
Enty, Isaac 13:57
Entzminger, John 21:51
Enwright, Thomas 13:21
Enyart, Hugh D. 20:246
Enyart, James M. 22:76
Enyart, John 17:442; 24:157
Enyart, Oliver B. 22:76
Enyart, Saben 11:58
Eoff, Joseph L. 23:112
Eoff, Leander 15:55
Eoff, William 21:25
Eomes, H. C. 15:263
Epler, Samuel 14:163
Epler, William 9:71
Epley, George 4:23
Epley, J. 1:31
Epley, Thomas 22:190
Eppard, Allen 22:76
Eppauline, Henry 13:109
Eppel, William 10:51
Eppercan, Joseph 14:321
Epperly, W. S. 20:246
Epperly, William S. 13:130
Eppers, J. D. 1:93
Epperson, B. 14:58
Epperson, J. W. 17:165
Epperson, James C. 7:49
Epperson, Jasper 23:184
Epperson, P. B. 23:28
Epperson, Perry J. 23:113
Epperson, Samuel A. 10:112; 20:246
Epperson, William 20:96
Epperson, William P. 11:422
Epperstone, J. H. 9:51
Eppert, S. C. 3:66
Epping, Frederick 14:163
Eppinger, M. 1:30
Eppinson, Samuel 24:193
Epple, William 20:246
Epple, William H. 19:320
Eppler, J. B. 1:31
Eppler, M. G. 1:93
Eppley, Josh A. 20:246
Eppmier, John 23:28
Epps, Anthony 13:109
Epps, Edward 17:174
Epps, Henry 21:269
Epps, James 17:46
Epps, N. O. 11:422

Epps, Squire 8:38; 26:159
Eppusm, Jasper 14:315
Epron, Louis 19:287
Epsey, Alloway 7:122
Epsom, W. J. 21:214
Epson, O. 1:30
Epson, William 19:13
Eranea, J. 1:128
Erans, S. J. 15:165
Erans, W. 3:66
Erason, Alex 18:132
Erault, E. E. 18:330
Eraw, Sidney 17:395
Erb, Henry 18:28
Erb, J. 3:66
Erb, John 11:58
Erb, William 17:470;
    27:41
Erbe, Charles 14:58
Erbedience, J. 3:66
Erbert, Frank 19:13
Erde, F. 14:58
Erdebauch, C. 3:66
Ereland, A. 26:97
Ereles, Thomas 9:175
Erener, William 26:211
Erginger, G. 13:109
Erhart, Daniel 22:497
Erhart, F. 15:165
Erhart, Fred 19:346
Erhart, G. 19:251
Erhart, George 9:175
Erhart, J. 16:189
Erhart, Jacob 22:29
Erhart, Nicholas 15:66
Erichlson, Augustus
    11:386
Erichson, Almer 4:23
Erick, Henry 20:33
Erick, J. 3:66
Erick, John 11:58
Ericksen, Erick 22:279
Erickson, C. 3:66; 12:152;
    14:288
Erickson, Chr. 16:3
Erickson, Christian
    23:189
Erickson, Heige 20:112
Erickson, J. P. 19:334
Erickson, John 1:30;
    9:207
Erickson, Ole 8:63;
    22:279
Erickson, Oliver 23:28
Erickson, Paul 20:48
Erickson, Peter 9:244;
    12:69; 15:81; 19:331
Erickson, Simon 21:137
Erickson, Theodore
    21:328

Erickson, Thorbjorn
    22:508
Erickson, Toby 7:122
Erickson, Truils 23:244
Ericson, --- 14:58
Ericson, J. 17:70
Ericson, Just 11:386
Ericson, Magonis 19:162
Ericson, O. L. 8:15
Erin, F. 18:236
Eringer, Casper 8:63
Eris, Stephen 21:25
Erisman, Abraham 17:291
Erisman, John 23:65
Erisson, T. H. 22:469
Eritts, Joseph 27:41
Erkem, Haywood 21:269
Erkinbes, F. R. 21:25
Erkne, E. 9:200
Erl, J. 14:58
Erle, John 18:66
Erles, H. 14:58
Erlich, William 19:270
Erline, T. 13:109
Erlins, A. 16:189
Erman, Joseph 13:87
Erment, Edward 8:15;
    18:132
Ermine, Henry 17:33
Ermitanger, Isaac 17:99
Ermman, Nathaniel
    22:141
Ermmick, Robert B. 4:23
Ermy, John C. 19:266
Erne, Joseph 10:112;
    20:246
Ernerheisen, Samuel
    12:20
Ernest, Amos 13:60
Ernest, Anthony W. 16:31
Ernest, Charles 25:31
Ernest, G. W. 9:71
Ernest, Igraice 19:286
Ernest, J. 1:128
Ernest, John 20:246
Ernest, Julius 6:8
Ernest, Moses 9:71
Ernest, Nathan 21:328
Ernest, Philip 22:249
Ernest, Samuel 13:21
Ernest, William 10:112;
    20:2, 246
Ernestine, Frederick
    22:190
Ernests, F. 7:26
Ernet, Henry 16:189
Ernin, John 24:17
Ernmie, Gabmaria 11:411
Ernset, Jacob 23:128
Ernst, A. 18:236; 26:26
Ernst, A. V. 23:29

Ernst, Anthony 13:21
Ernst, Christian 26:144
Ernst, Daniel G. 11:319
Ernst, Edwin 18:132
Ernst, F. 22:478
Ernst, John 23:179; 24:49
Ernst, Julius 18:103
Ernst, Phillip 14:163
Ernst, Samuel 26:97
Ernstain, Ernest 16:31
Erp, William S. 22:76
Errer, James T. 10:160
Errets, James 3:66
Errichson, P. 14:58
Errick, William 3:66
Errickson, Nelse A.
    22:423
Erricson, S. 3:66
Erriman, J. B. 19:67
Erring, D. 14:58
Errinman, J. B. 15:305
Errisman, S. D. 23:142
Erritt, M. 1:30
Errixon, John 17:443
Errixson, John 24:157
Erron, John 8:15; 18:132
Errukoo, Jonathan 16:368
Erseht, Theo. T. 12:152
Erskin, Andrew 22:478
Erskin, I. 14:58
Erskin, J. 1:127
Erskin, Jacob 10:51;
    20:246
Erskin, Samuel B. 22:190
Erskin, Wesley 11:91
Erskine, A. 19:281
Erskine, Andrew H. 13:21
Erskine, E. 1:128
Erskine, Freeman 18:346
Erskine, George B. 2:10;
    25:31
Erskine, James A. 14:163
Erskine, L. R. 25:296
Erskine, Mayo 7:74;
    25:296
Erskine, Theodor 15:34
Erskine, Thomas 13:109
Erskins, L. R. 7:79
Erskins, Lewis 15:55
Erst, James 3:66
Erster, J. C. 8:84
Erty, Michael 26:123
Ertz, John 6:7; 18:109
Ertzman, F. 1:128
Erva, Eugene 4:23
Ervey Or Ewey, G. W.
    16:139
Ervin, John 11:395;
    19:227
Ervin, Leroy 22:298
Ervin, Thomas J. 14:321

Ervin, Timothy 8:38; 26:159
Ervin, William E. 17:318
Ervin, William H. 18:236
Ervin, William R. 23:184
Ervine, John 9:175
Ervine, Norman M. 12:20
Erving, Arthur H. 8:15; 26:158
Erving, Franklin 8:15
Erving, J. F. 1:93
Erving, J. G. 9:51
Erving, James 12:152
Erving, John 11:411
Erving, Samuel D. 11:118
Erving, T. J. 13:87
Erving, W. F. 21:117
Ervons, John 18:28
Erwin, A. 18:13
Erwin, C. 3:66
Erwin, D. 25:169
Erwin, George 1:30
Erwin, H. 16:189
Erwin, Henry 15:330; 19:67
Erwin, I. 25:271
Erwin, John 14:58, 163; 27:41
Erwin, Jonas 23:29
Erwin, Joseph A. 21:51
Erwin, Joseph W. 16:147
Erwin, L. C. 14:58
Erwin, Robert E. 22:76
Erwin, W. 25:280
Erwin, W. J. 11:29
Erwin, W. W. 9:51
Erwing, Robert 1:30
Es-fan-na-hop-pa-yah 25:333
Esback, J. W. 13:21
Esbern, John 19:67
Esberne, John 15:324
Escher, Christian 9:220
Esco, Breno 9:207
Escue, H. 3:66
Esdees, J. M. 11:91
Eselbeth, H. A. 19:162
Esell, Gillone 8:105
Esenberg, William 23:107
Esenbraun, A. 1:30
Esenhardt, J. 14:255
Esenthal, F. 3:66
Esep, Corhelius 12:20
Esgat, William 7:26
Esgate, C. W. 8:48
Esgate, Charles W. 21:68
Esgett, Harry J. 23:283
Eshalman, Martin 14:163
Esham, John 6:24
Eshellnear, J. 12:161

Eshelman, Benjamin 17:313
Eshelman, F. 1:31
Eshleman, Abraham 11:411
Eshleman, William 13:109
Esiegh, Jacob 3:67
Eske, T. 1:128
Eskels, Joel 23:142
Eskew, E. H. 9:51
Eskew, Henry 16:31
Eskew, James W. 1:30
Eskew, John M. 23:240
Eskidge, James 14:9
Eskin, Joseph B. 9:227
Eskine, Henry 13:21
Eskins, S. 27:42
Eskridge, Oakley 3:67
Eslay, George W. 12:69
Esler, David 18:205
Esley, John 11:239
Eslick, A. 15:151
Eslics, James 4:23
Eslinger, Adam 24:38
Eslinger, J. 14:58
Eslinger, Robert 14:58
Eslinger, William 22:500
Eslow, D. Y. 20:246
Esmarch, N. 25:30
Esmay, Rufus 16:368
Esmer, George 25:169
Esmey, Jerome 10:16
Esmon, William 22:29
Esmond, William 20:106
Esolink, J. 25:169
Espie, James 19:162
Espleman, Francis 19:162
Espring, A. J. 24:17
Espy, James 3:67
Espy, James R. 22:249
Esra, J. W. 14:58
Esray, Theodore 12:20
Essaman, James 9:230; 20:247
Esselon, Michael 18:284; 26:134
Esselston, C. 1:97
Esseltine, John 7:26
Essenger, M. 11:144
Essex, A. 1:127
Essex, James 23:29
Essex, Richard 17:164
Essex, William 9:51
Esshorn, E. F. 7:93
Essick, J. 1:31
Essig, Frederick 13:21
Essig, William 26:97
Essing, John 21:328
Essing, William 18:305
Essings, Oliver 17:471; 27:41

Essington, Hiram F. 20:247
Essington, Hiram T. 10:112
Essler, Hardy 27:41
Essler, I. C. 18:205
Essling, John 5:15
Esslinger, C. 17:101
Essom, John 22:233
Esster, Handy 9:118
Essworthy, J. A. 14:58
Est, J. 11:202
Estabrontes, George A. 9:12
Estabrook, David 12:152
Estabrook, James E. 16:8
Estabrook, Warren D. 23:11
Estal, Abram 21:328
Estas, John 9:79
Estay, George W. 15:11
Estbrook, Andrew J. 21:68
Estbrook, C. H. 18:28
Este, John 20:123
Esteff, J. 3:67
Estel, W. H. 2:10; 25:31
Estell, --- 21:216
Estell, Albert 22:298
Estell, Andrew J. 12:69
Estell, B. 1:30
Estell, D. F. 24:17
Estell, H. 21:137
Estell, Isaac F. C. 21:216
Estell, Jeremiah 17:276
Estell, William J. 1:30
Estella, John 7:122
Estep, David 14:162
Estep, Joel 17:236
Estep, Martin 14:163
Esteph, B. E. 25:169
Ester, F. M. 8:15; 18:132
Ester, James 19:67
Ester, John W. 12:20
Ester, W. A. 3:67
Esterbrook, Chauncey 20:112
Esterbrook, Frederick K. 21:328
Esterbrooks, Elisha 24:93
Estergreen, Frank 11:29
Estes, A. W. 16:93
Estes, George 17:131; 24:193
Estes, George W. 22:298
Estes, George Y. 23:29
Estes, Isaac 8:84
Estes, J. 7:26
Estes, J. B. 15:351; 16:368
Estes, James B. 20:27

Roll of Honor Index

Estes, James H. 17:109
Estes, John 11:91
Estes, John A. 24:65
Estes, Peter 10:112;
    20:247
Estes, R. 21:166
Estes, Samuel 15:16
Estes, Thomas 8:15;
    18:132
Estes, Wiley 20:96
Estes, William L. 21:328
Estes, William W. 9:21;
    18:320
Estey, E. E. 3:67
Estey, H. P. 16:189
Estey, James R. 16:8
Esthel, J. 15:158
Estile, Daniel 14:163;
    15:123
Estill, E. W. 3:67
Estill, Hawkins 21:25
Estis, C. J. 9:175
Estis, J. 1:127
Estis, James H. 22:190
Estis, John M. 16:31
Estis, Joseph M. 9:96
Estiss, Joseph 7:93
Estius, Andrew 11:386
Estman, Adam 4:65
Eston, A. H. 18:131
Estookin, William 22:249
Estrich, J. 23:142
Estrick, Joseph 11:302
Estridge, John 9:242
Estridge, William 17:392
Estrike, Christian 4:23
Estuff, John 3:67
Estus, A. 27:40
Estus, Alvin 9:142
Estus, W. H. 13:109
Estus, William 18:28
Esty, John M. 11:100
Esworthy, W. 1:128
Etal, Benjamin 24:50
Etchison, Isaac 10:95
Etchison, William 27:41
Etdress, N. D. 21:91
Eteal, L. 10:179; 18:174
Eten, Francis 16:189
Eters, --- 10:186
Eters, James 10:179
Ethaman, Isaac 26:159
Ethams, Isaac 8:38
Ethell, W. A. 26:159
Etherge, Jerome 16:189
Etheridge, J. 20:56;
    25:169
Etheridge, J. N. 9:79;
    26:26
Etheridge, Joshua 5:38
Etherige, J. 16:189

Etherington, Phillip
    18:132
Etherten, Thomas D. H.
    22:249
Etherton, A. 21:25
Etherton, C. S. 11:422
Etherton, L. 21:328
Etherton, Moses 21:68
Etherton, Thomas 18:206
Ethiar, J. 3:67
Ethington, Philip 8:15
Ethridge, Jerome 15:293
Ethridge, William 3:67
Etler, Paris 23:29
Etlers, James 18:174
Etnyer, George 22:76
Etoches, E. I. 11:386
Eton, J. 27:40
Etrod, James B. 11:58
Ettens, Asa 10:51
Etter, Jacob Y. 11:302
Etter, James 10:90; 20:247
Etter, William T. 10:34;
    19:301
Etterman, Henry 9:118
Etters, Asa 20:247
Etters, B. J. 1:127
Etters, D. 3:67
Ettian, William 27:40
Ettien, Philip 23:288
Ettiman, M. 20:247
Ettinger, Francis 1:30
Ettis, Alonzo 25:30
Ettle, J. 20:40
Etton, C. C. 18:189
Etzel, William 1:30
Eubank, H. V. 11:302
Eubanks, Isaac 17:397
Euberger, Goddard 11:59
Euchenbroth, Fred 21:25
Euck, E. 11:144
Euddard, Edward 24:10
Eudoly, E. J. 18:66
Euford, Ernest 25:169
Eugard, William 18:206
Eugelberger, Dom 23:121
Eugene, Egbert 22:471
Eugene, Patrick 4:23
Eugfer, John 10:112
Eugh, John 3:67
Eugliter, C. 1:30
Eukmirger, L. 26:26
Eulans, J. P. 14:163
Euler, Mathias 20:142
Eulick, Charles 14:164
Euling, James C. 19:274
Eunas, J. W. 15:195
Euneking, J. B. 10:90
Eunice, F. V. 26:97
Eunice, Frank V. 18:292
Eunice, Franklin V. 9:34

Eunis, E. T. 11:92
Eunis, James 8:15
Euniss, Bernard 10:16
Eures, A. O. 12:98
Eurich, John 26:25
Euright, Thomas 4:23
Euse, Conrad 15:352
Eustace, G. C. 3:67
Eustace, James 23:113
Eustace, W. 19:67
Eustice, William 12:95;
    15:359
Eustin, James H. 14:164
Eustin, Thomas 14:164
Eustis, --- 20:87
Eustis, W. W. H. 17:19
Eustus, Irez 27:39
Euterman, Augustus 22:10
Eutsey, David 19:67
Eutwythe, H. 9:79
Euzart, Levi 11:58
Eva---son, --- 25:30
Evald, Hy 14:164
Evan, David 26:219
Evan, James 15:34
Evann, Jay 16:31
Evans, --- 21:117
Evans, A. E. 20:92, 112
Evans, A. R. 16:139
Evans, Abner 7:93
Evans, Acquilla 21:25
Evans, Albert E. 21:25
Evans, Alex 17:174
Evans, Alexander 9:207
Evans, Alfred 14:164
Evans, Alson 7:74; 25:296
Evans, Anderson T. 7:93
Evans, Andrew 4:65;
    16:189
Evans, Andrew J. 22:422
Evans, Andrew M. 11:58
Evans, Andrew R. 16:139
Evans, Ashbury 17:355
Evans, B. 1:94, 128
Evans, B. G. 21:328
Evans, Balis 22:249
Evans, Benjamin 7:122;
    22:76
Evans, Benjamin F. 7:49;
    11:58; 26:26
Evans, Benjamin T.
    18:236
Evans, Bernard 10:205
Evans, C. 14:297; 17:469;
    24:77; 27:42
Evans, C. H. 15:298
Evans, Calvin C. 19:162
Evans, Charles 5:38; 8:84,
    105; 20:96; 21:223;
    22:298; 25:169
Evans, Charles H. 16:189

Evans, Cossett 22:422
Evans, Cyrus 18:216;
    21:269
Evans, D. B. 24:38
Evans, D. S. 24:77
Evans, Daniel 10:172;
    19:162; 22:298;
    24:193; 27:41
Evans, David 5:38; 9:236;
    21:269; 23:29;
    25:169
Evans, David A. 9:79
Evans, David E. 22:478
Evans, David T. 8:15;
    18:132
Evans, Dolphus 12:62
Evans, Don G. 27:144
Evans, E. 1:31; 12:92;
    14:59; 16:292
Evans, E. M. 3:67
Evans, E. T. 11:58
Evans, Edward 9:142;
    10:98; 27:40
Evans, Ellery 21:328
Evans, Eugene F. 22:190
Evans, Evan 4:23; 20:142;
    21:253
Evans, Evan D. 20:145
Evans, Evandor 4:23
Evans, F. 20:2
Evans, F. G. 21:14
Evans, F. W. 13:63
Evans, Ferdinand E. 17:51
Evans, Frank 3:67
Evans, Franklin 21:328
Evans, G. 1:127
Evans, G. M. 24:185
Evans, G. S. 15:105
Evans, G. W. 3:67;
    10:205; 11:260;
    16:368
Evans, George 4:23;
    10:205; 22:423
Evans, George A. 13:21;
    21:328
Evans, George E. 19:162
Evans, George W. 17:429;
    18:217; 22:76
Evans, George W. L. 4:23
Evans, Gideon 25:30
Evans, Gustavus 4:23
Evans, H. 3:67; 8:71;
    9:66; 14:59
Evans, H. A. 27:41
Evans, H. L. 16:292
Evans, Harrison 21:269
Evans, Harry 16:118
Evans, Hawking 21:269
Evans, Hawley 21:269
Evans, Henderson 17:280

Evans, Henry 16:84;
    18:189, 217; 21:147,
    269; 27:41
Evans, Henry A. 15:364
Evans, Isaac 23:65; 27:40
Evans, J. 1:31, 127; 3:67;
    14:164; 19:301;
    21:25; 23:142;
    25:169; 26:25
Evans, J. D. 11:145;
    17:163
Evans, J. F. 1:31; 13:87
Evans, J. G. 14:59
Evans, J. H. 1:128; 13:87;
    14:9; 20:247
Evans, J. M. 14:9; 26:159
Evans, J. W. 8:63
Evans, Jack 24:193
Evans, Jackson 10:51;
    20:247
Evans, Jacob 5:38
Evans, James 1:31; 3:67;
    5:38; 9:79; 10:51;
    13:21; 17:247, 363;
    18:174; 20:247;
    21:208; 22:190, 478;
    23:29, 142
Evans, James A. 18:206
Evans, James C. 8:15
Evans, James E. 18:132
Evans, James H. 24:193
Evans, James M. 17:259,
    318
Evans, James P. 7:26
Evans, James T. 21:224
Evans, Jerry 22:298
Evans, Jesse F. 10:51;
    20:247
Evans, John 4:23; 7:93;
    11:28, 411, 422;
    12:48; 14:9; 16:368;
    17:99, 107, 165;
    18:189; 20:247;
    21:25, 245, 328;
    22:121
Evans, John A. 7:57
Evans, John B. 14:263;
    19:162
Evans, John E. 16:31;
    17:355
Evans, John F. 1:31
Evans, John H. 10:51;
    13:21; 16:31; 17:440
Evans, John M. 13:87;
    20:112
Evans, John P. 1:31
Evans, John S. 6:23
Evans, John W. 24:152
Evans, Jonathan 9:34,
    236; 26:219

Evans, Joseph 9:96;
    12:20; 15:7; 16:189
Evans, Joseph E. 22:423
Evans, Josiah 22:190
Evans, Judson A. 1:30
Evans, Julius B. 27:41
Evans, Killis J. 17:206
Evans, L. 1:127; 3:67;
    25:169
Evans, L. B. 19:233
Evans, Lafayette 5:38
Evans, Lemuel 22:423
Evans, Levcott 12:69
Evans, Levert 15:2
Evans, Levi 27:40
Evans, Lewis 15:195;
    20:247
Evans, Lewis B. 12:20;
    20:183
Evans, Louis 10:112
Evans, Lyman 17:446;
    24:170
Evans, Lyman B. 9:175
Evans, M. 3:67; 9:154;
    27:40
Evans, M. B. 20:247
Evans, M. O. 18:236;
    26:26
Evans, M. P. 8:84
Evans, Marcus L. 17:33
Evans, Mathew D. 10:51
Evans, Meredith F. 23:285
Evans, Michael 24:77
Evans, Moses 8:48
Evans, N. L. 3:67
Evans, Norfolk 21:269
Evans, O. 15:105
Evans, O. L. 26:159
Evans, Oliver 22:190
Evans, Oliver M. 22:76
Evans, Oliver P. 17:259
Evans, Orlando D. 9:12
Evans, Owen 10:51;
    20:247
Evans, Peter H. 23:87
Evans, Philip 2:10
Evans, R. 1:127
Evans, Richard 15:195
Evans, Richard A. 22:76
Evans, Robert 7:122;
    8:84; 18:189; 21:147;
    24:170, 193
Evans, Robert T. 22:29
Evans, Rufus 10:112;
    20:247
Evans, Ryan 26:159
Evans, S. 14:59, 164
Evans, S. D. 3:67
Evans, S. M. 21:25
Evans, S. S. 21:328
Evans, S. W. 11:58; 23:29

Evans, Sam 11:15
Evans, Samuel 3:67; 4:23; 9:130; 14:59, 164; 20:29; 22:249
Evans, Samuel A. 8:15; 18:132
Evans, Samuel K. 10:112; 20:247
Evans, Shadrick 15:195
Evans, Sidney 18:189
Evans, Simon 21:211
Evans, Stephen 1:31
Evans, T. 20:145
Evans, Thomas 9:68; 17:392; 18:81; 19:13; 22:29, 423, 512; 23:16
Evans, Thomas C. 10:112; 20:247
Evans, Thomas H. 20:145
Evans, Thomas R. 12:170
Evans, Virgil M. 17:202
Evans, W. 1:127; 7:62; 13:21; 16:31, 267; 24:77; 25:169
Evans, W. E. 27:157
Evans, W. H. 14:59; 15:341; 16:368; 20:247
Evans, Walker 18:28
Evans, Walter 1:31; 21:328
Evans, Wesley 13:21; 16:31
Evans, William 3:67; 5:15, 38; 7:67; 8:15, 105; 9:42; 10:51; 11:144; 13:87; 14:9, 59, 164; 15:34; 16:118; 17:131, 154; 18:132, 276, 292; 20:112, 247; 24:193; 26:97, 123
Evans, William B. 21:224
Evans, William D. 22:450
Evans, William E. 10:112; 16:143; 20:247
Evans, William F. 20:123
Evans, William H. 13:21; 18:276
Evans, William J. 4:23
Evans, Willis 20:247
Evans, Zachariah 22:249
Evanson, Evans S. 20:247
Evanson, Hountz 7:26
Evard, C. H. 26:159
Evard, Leopold 22:76
Evarton, Henry 22:423
Evarts, D. 1:31
Evarts, E. 1:128
Evarts, Elijah S. 10:160

Evarts, Eugene 17:415; 24:152
Evarts, Iris 24:170
Evarts, J. V. 9:175
Evarts, John V. 19:245
Evarts, Oliver 22:462
Evatt, William 11:428
Eve, Benjamin 11:381
Eveland, Amos 23:29
Eveland, E. 25:30
Eveland, James S. 23:240
Eveland, L. G. 8:15; 18:132
Eveland, P. 15:329; 19:67
Evelin, Albert 11:201
Evelin, Robert 23:121
Evell, William 7:93
Evenly, William 13:87
Evens, C. W. 3:67
Evens, Charles 3:67
Evens, G. S. 3:67
Evens, George 13:21
Evens, Harry 11:260
Evens, J. 10:27
Evens, J. M. 3:67
Evens, John 3:67
Evens, Sanford 10:112; 20:247
Evens, Selah 1:30
Evens, T. 3:67
Evens, W. O. 15:357
Evens, William 17:51, 267
Evens, William H. 10:51
Evens, Willis 10:51
Evenson, Abraham 10:51
Evenson, Evan S. 10:51
Evenson, Haloor 17:448
Evenson, Holver 24:172
Evenson, James 17:99
Everage, John 16:189
Everden, Edwin J. 23:121
Everding, Henry C. 10:51; 20:247
Everels, George W. 12:152
Everest, Charles J. 22:142
Everest, J. W. 1:30
Everest, John D. 22:462
Everet, E. 23:65
Everet, J. B. 16:189
Everett, --- 17:346
Everett, A. T. 3:67
Everett, Ambrose M. 11:145
Everett, C. M. 18:276
Everett, Charles 9:175; 19:266
Everett, D. 14:297; 17:477; 27:41
Everett, Dr. 20:154

Everett, E. 14:164; 18:365; 27:41
Everett, Edward 4:23
Everett, Francis 20:112, 151
Everett, Frank 18:28
Everett, G. 18:48
Everett, George 10:152
Everett, George W. 15:83
Everett, H. 25:169
Everett, Hamilton 22:142
Everett, Harvey 13:21
Everett, Henry C. 9:8
Everett, Hugh 19:287
Everett, J. 3:67; 19:232
Everett, James 9:175; 21:211
Everett, Jeremiah 17:291
Everett, John 3:67; 10:176; 19:162
Everett, John L. 12:20
Everett, Joseph 6:16; 18:81
Everett, Joseph F. 22:29
Everett, Joseph J. 22:76
Everett, Kelly 9:51
Everett, Lewis 23:142
Everett, Marsenia S. 21:68
Everett, Moses 25:169
Everett, R. 15:105
Everett, R. J. 11:321
Everett, S. 11:144
Everett, Thomas M. 4:23
Everett, W. 1:128
Everett, W. J. 18:66
Everett, William 14:164
Everett, William H. 12:20; 17:323
Everett, William L. 10:112; 20:247
Everetts, S. 1:31
Everhard, Andrew B. 21:253
Everhart, A. B. 18:351
Everhart, Andrew 13:21
Everhart, George A. 26:26
Everhart, J. B. 7:26
Everhart, Jacob 9:242
Everhart, James H. 23:250
Everhart, Jeremiah 13:81; 16:189
Everhart, Lewis H. 23:65
Everhart, N. A. 23:267
Everhart, Simeon 10:112; 20:247
Everhart, W. 11:302
Everhart, William 22:141
Everheart, Adam 17:272
Everingham, S. 11:302
Everison, A. 20:247
Everitt, B. F. 25:169

Everitt, David 15:55
Everitt, Edwin 9:220
Everland, G. 21:25
Everley, F. N. 18:305
Everling, W. 18:365
Everly, Evan 9:16
Everly, F. M. 26:97
Everly, Francis M. 20:185
Everly, G. 3:67
Everly, Henry B. 10:112;
    20:247
Everly, Isaac 13:21
Everly, T. M. 9:21
Everly, William 12:153;
    14:9
Everman, Allen H. 17:280
Everman, Evan H. 12:20
Evern, John 16:189
Evernham, Joseph 4:23
Evernhart, Clayton B.
    15:173
Evers, B. 3:67
Evers, B. F. 14:241
Evers, Benard 18:406
Evers, E. H. 11:302
Evers, L. 11:301
Evers, William E. 21:328
Eversole, G. W. 23:29
Eversole, S. 1:128
Eversole, Wolery 22:121
Eversoll, William 23:313
Everson, David H. 12:20
Everson, J. H. S. 1:127
Everson, Ole 17:99;
    21:137; 22:508
Everson, S. 17:99
Everson, Thomas 10:51;
    20:247
Evert, Iris 17:423
Evert, John A. 10:112;
    20:247
Evert, Thomas 14:315
Everton, G. R. 25:169
Everton, William F. 7:57
Everts, Eli B. 20:247
Everts, Eli R. 20:247
Everts, Henry 16:31
Everts, John C. 22:142
Everts, Levi B. 10:112
Everts, Levi R. 10:112
Everts, Myron 11:105
Everts, T. P. 3:67
Evertts, I. R. 19:13
Every, James 22:404
Eves, I. 12:166
Eves, Wilson 16:189
Evett, David 8:112
Evett, William 21:328
Evetts, John S. 10:112;
    20:247
Evilsizer, Minor 21:224

Evilsizer, Spencer 22:76
Evingfelt, Jacob 3:67
Evingham, Warren 14:164
Evington, Thomas J.
    17:51
Evins, B. F. 8:84
Evins, G. H. 19:13
Evins, James 18:132
Evins, John 11:145
Evins, Ryan 8:38
Evins, W. T. 18:365
Evirst, Richard 19:68
Evitt, E. 14:297; 17:475
Evley, Isaac 9:175
Evolt, Joseph 22:298
Evy, R. 1:127
Ewale, William 11:190
Ewall, Horace 9:79
Ewalt, Edward E. 8:84
Ewards, George 14:164
Ewart, T. C. 1:128
Ewarts, Daniel A. 17:19
Ewatt, Ed. E. 8:117
Ewbank, Christopher
    24:38
Ewell, Al 17:174
Ewell, Eden 17:174
Ewell, H. 1:128
Ewell, J. H. 23:313
Ewell, Job 4:23
Ewell, R. N. 16:189
Ewell, Samuel 1:30
Ewell, William F. 15:195
Ewen, J. S. 1:128
Ewen, T. J. 14:9
Eweng, D. 3:67
Ewening, Arthur 18:133
Ewens, Edward J. 15:55
Ewer, James T. 19:162
Ewer, Reuel 21:137
Ewer, Ruel 8:48
Ewers, E. 2:10
Ewers, J. E. 16:189
Ewers, John G. 11:145
Ewers, W. O. 16:279
Ewerton, J. T. 22:165
Ewey, George E. 22:279
Ewey Or Ervey, G. W.
    16:139
Ewin, James 18:394
Ewine, J. W. 15:196
Ewing, Abraham 17:131;
    24:193
Ewing, Amos 19:45
Ewing, Barbon 21:270
Ewing, Corwin 11:145
Ewing, Daniel L. 11:58
Ewing, Edmund 7:122
Ewing, Franklin 18:133
Ewing, George 11:400
Ewing, George B. 22:190

Ewing, H. P. 20:247
Ewing, Henry 21:270;
    22:512
Ewing, Homer 22:478
Ewing, Hugh P. 10:51
Ewing, Jackson 18:236;
    26:26
Ewing, James 27:41
Ewing, James C. 9:175
Ewing, James E. 25:30
Ewing, James H. 20:136
Ewing, James M. 9:118
Ewing, John 10:112;
    14:59; 20:247
Ewing, John M. 23:142
Ewing, John W. 21:328;
    22:142
Ewing, R. 17:131; 24:193
Ewing, Robert 4:23; 7:26;
    21:270
Ewing, Robert E. 9:34
Ewing, Robert J. 22:190
Ewing, S. A. 1:127
Ewing, S. J. 11:100
Ewing, Samuel G. 22:29
Ewing, Samuel M. 22:29
Ewing, Samuel P. 1:30
Ewing, Stephen W.
    22:142
Ewing, T. 21:147
Ewing, T. J. 14:9
Ewing, Thomas 21:270;
    22:76
Ewing, Thomas E. 22:29
Ewing, William 17:276;
    18:217
Ewing, William B. 21:224
Ewing, William H. 26:26
Ewinger, Gabriel 22:298
Exell, William 22:478
Exgenmon, --- 14:59
Exison, P. 25:283
Exlene, Jacob 3:67
Exlie, James D. 23:142
Extell, William B. 11:190
Exum, Henry G. 21:129
Exum, Joseph J. 21:129
Exum, William 21:270
Eyball, Isaac 11:408
Eybett, James 3:67
Eychoymer, H. 3:67
Eydroner, R. 3:67
Eye, Andy 13:21
Eyebonds, William 22:29
Eyed, Alfred 12:62
Eyer, Alfred 15:34
Eyer, D. 1:97
Eyer, George 11:332
Eyer, Jacob 13:109
Eyer, John 22:233
Eyer, John D. 11:411

Eyer, Philip 20:7
Eyerly, J. 22:190
Eyler, A. 1:31
Eylor, Christian 16:158
Eyman, George 23:276
Eyman, L. J. 12:164;
  26:159
Eymann, E. C. 24:18
Eyre, Joseph 27:39
Eyrick, Isaac 14:164
Eysenhour, John 14:164
Eyster, Solomon 12:20
Eyton, Henry 15:55
Ezel, Clyburn 8:71
Ezell, J. 21:25
Ezell, Joseph B. 25:287
Ezell, Thomas 20:110
Ezell, Thomas L. 21:12
Ezelle, Andrew J. 22:29

F

F---, --- 25:169; 26:248
F---, A--- 26:236
F---, A. 11:30; 25:320
F---, A. M. 20:151
F---, B. 20:56
F---, B. P. 23:283
F---, B. T. 15:258
F---, C. 23:98; 26:160
F---, C. S. 26:160
F---, D. 20:56; 23:179
F---, Daniel 15:198
F---, E. W. W. 25:320
F---, F. 16:93
F---, F. B. 21:187
F---, F. E. 20:7
F---, G. H. 11:239
F---, G. S. 23:303
F---, George C. 9:52
F---, H. 11:219; 20:247;
  23:270
F---, H. D. 11:428
F---, H. G. 12:148
F---, Henry 15:198
F---, J. 11:302, 339;
  16:113, 292; 18:28;
  21:25; 25:320;
  26:160
F---, J. A. 17:19
F---, J. C. 8:63
F---, J. F. 17:19
F---, J. L. 14:269
F---, J. M. 11:219
F---, J. O. 25:169
F---, James H. 21:137
F---, John 20:85
F---, L. 16:118; 20:56
F---, L. W. 24:111
F---, Ly 23:203

F---, M. 21:166
F---, M. M. 17:91
F---, N. 19:165; 23:203
F---, P. 9:227
F---, P. H. 20:40
F---, P. L. 11:339
F---, P. M. 23:29
F---, Peter J. 17:296
F---, R. 9:52; 11:302;
  21:328
F---, S. 11:340; 14:269;
  15:198, 326; 23:65;
  24:110
F---, S. J. 14:269
F---, S. M. 24:110
F---, S. W. 20:92
F---, T. 14:269; 23:203;
  27:42
F---, V. 17:213
F---, W. 11:261; 15:198;
  23:113; 24:166, 213
F---, W. E. 19:70
F---, W. H. 20:247
F---, X. F. 17:355
F---, L. 22:190
F---ann, W. F. 23:189
F---ier, William 15:198
F---lk, J. 16:189
F---wk, William 27:157
F--er, Robert 23:203
Fa, B. F. 3:67
Faads, Joseph 24:77
Fabbinger, H. 14:59
Fabens, W. P. 1:130
Faber, A. 1:131
Faber, Benjamin 17:247
Faber, D. J. 23:87
Faber, J. C. 1:131
Faber, Silas D. 23:87
Faber, W. 21:25, 121
Fabers, Charles 10:112;
  20:247
Fabery, Joseph 23:179
Fabian, M. 14:59
Fable, John 11:146
Fably, Denis 15:34
Face, C. 3:67
Face, J. 3:67
Face, W. H. 3:67
Facer, William 3:67
Fachback, John 11:92
Fachler, George 9:34
Facker, J. W. 12:166
Facker, L. 3:67
Fackler, George 4:23;
  18:292; 26:98
Facon, H. W. 1:130
Facott, John 12:153
Facy, E. 26:27
Fadden, Charles 15:66
Fadden, George E. 9:203

Fadder, J. W. 14:265
Fadderky, Henry 23:29
Faddin, Isaac 13:21
Fadeley, John 15:86
Fadell, William H. 13:127
Faden, C. 25:279
Fader, William 13:63;
  19:13
Fadley, John 18:236;
  26:28
Faes, Jacob 13:21
Fagain, J. D. 13:87
Fagam, M. 3:67
Fagan, Alexander 4:23
Fagan, Alfred 12:48
Fagan, Andrew 27:42
Fagan, B. H. 18:133
Fagan, Charles 15:196
Fagan, James 17:65;
  22:334
Fagan, Joseph 12:48
Fagan, Leonard 9:165
Fagan, M. F. 2:11
Fagan, Marcus D. 9:34
Fagan, Michael 9:79, 109,
  214; 13:21; 26:27
Fagan, O. 3:67
Fagan, Patrick 10:160;
  19:162
Fagan, R. 3:67
Fagan, W. H. 19:162
Fagan, William 14:59,
  164
Fagan, William E. 10:7
Fage, Allen 9:165
Fagen, Aseph 22:112
Fagen, Cornelius 13:127
Fagen, T. D. 3:67
Fager, F. 18:236; 26:28
Fager, J. 1:131
Fagerty, William 21:270
Fagg, Alexander 9:51
Fagg, Henry C. 17:206
Fagg, William 22:351
Faggott, Daniel 14:164
Fagian, J. D. 14:9
Fagin, D. 1:131
Fagin, W. H. 10:160
Fagle, --- 19:68
Fagley, John 20:40
Fagley, Reuben 10:112;
  20:247
Fago, Fostine 7:122
Fago, James F. 21:328
Fagontus, T. 3:67
Fagrety, F. 3:67
Fague, David R. 22:76
Fague, Henry 11:59
Fague, Larkin 7:93
Fah, Sebastian 22:121
Fahey, T. 18:49

Fahl, Calvin 24:77
Fahliman, Frederick 18:66
Fahnestock, John 7:57
Fahr, William 22:479
Fahrer, John D. 13:21
Fahy, John 3:67
Faidley, William 22:190
Faigue, Andrew 15:196
Failer, Charles 11:279
Failes, A. J. 17:446
Failey, Frank H. 10:160;
19:162
Failey, George 8:15
Failey, John A. 26:160
Failing, Robert 21:137
Failor, J. 7:26
Fails, John 18:28
Fails, M. L. 1:131
Fain, Elisha 11:303
Fain, John J. 20:103
Faine, W. A. 9:242
Fainegan, James 8:15
Fainter, J. A. 11:232
Fair, Alexander M. 26:145
Fair, Allen 14:164
Fair, Amos 22:190
Fair, Andrew 15:196
Fair, David 8:84
Fair, E. P. 14:59
Fair, James 21:329
Fair, James W. 20:35
Fair, John 21:91
Fair, Joseph 19:13
Fair, Joseph J. 20:40
Fair, Leonard 17:78
Fair, N. 14:164
Fair, Oliver 14:164
Fair, Richard S. 19:13
Fair, Samuel B. 17:33
Fair, Thomas I. 11:146
Fair, Wesley 22:501;
26:145
Fair, William H. 13:21
Fairbach, Jacob 9:21
Fairbank, Cyrus 13:21
Fairbank, F. G. 15:359
Fairbank, John 25:288
Fairbanks, Alex 3:67
Fairbanks, Almon 22:29
Fairbanks, B. F. 9:42
Fairbanks, Charles H.
13:21
Fairbanks, D. 14:164
Fairbanks, D. F. 26:123
Fairbanks, E. 3:68
Fairbanks, F. C. 21:329
Fairbanks, F. G. 12:95;
19:68
Fairbanks, F. M. 14:164
Fairbanks, G. 15:318;
19:13, 68

Fairbanks, H. 14:59
Fairbanks, J. 3:68
Fairbanks, J. H. 16:279
Fairbanks, John 3:68
Fairbanks, Lafayette
13:21; 16:31
Fairbanks, Lewis 24:50
Fairbanks, Maryland E.
7:26
Fairbanks, N. 1:33
Fairbanks, Oscar 18:109
Fairbanks, R. 1:129
Fairbanks, Richard 15:196
Fairbanks, S. S. 25:169
Fairbanks, Sanford S. 5:15
Fairbrother, Frank 16:77
Fairbrother, H. 3:68
Fairbrother, Irwin 13:21
Fairbrother, O. C. 1:32
Fairbrother, Thomas 8:48
Fairchields, Henry 14:315
Fairchild, Addison 13:21
Fairchild, Benjamin 10:16
Fairchild, Ephraim G.
10:112; 20:247
Fairchild, George 10:90;
20:247
Fairchild, George L. 20:29
Fairchild, H. C. 17:242
Fairchild, Henry 11:303
Fairchild, J. F. 15:341
Fairchild, John 8:121
Fairchild, Levi 23:107
Fairchild, Robert 10:160
Fairchild, Samuel 4:23
Fairchild, Squire A. 10:90
Fairchild, W. 1:33
Fairchild, William 4:23;
25:296
Fairchild, William H.
17:263
Fairchild, William J.
20:247
Fairchild, William L.
10:51
Fairchilds, Charles 22:142
Fairchilds, Daniel C.
11:29
Fairchilds, G. L. 3:68
Fairchilds, H. 1:32
Fairchilds, Henry 23:200
Fairchilds, J. H. 19:13
Fairchilds, J. V. 16:368
Fairchilds, Jesse 3:68
Fairchilds, Robert 19:162
Fairchiles, Henry 14:321
Fairclough, Nat 19:163
Fairclough, Nathan
10:176
Fairfax, Charles 3:68
Fairfax, George 17:174

Fairfax, Henry 6:16; 18:81
Fairfield, B. 5:51; 25:169
Fairfield, Edwin 22:161
Fairfield, H. J. 17:242
Fairfield, J. M. 1:129
Fairfield, W. S. 1:34
Fairland, William 12:122
Fairley, James H. 21:240
Fairley, Kries 11:147
Fairley, Samuel 15:66
Fairley, Thomas 7:64
Fairman, E. 1:97
Fairman, George 24:50
Fairman, H. B. 3:68
Fairman, James B. 13:21
Fairman, R. J. 11:322
Fairo, A. 3:68
Fairrall, John 24:58
Fairs, Chambers 15:66
Fairweather, H. 16:189
Fairweather, John 6:16;
18:81
Fairwell, C. S. 19:163
Fairwell, Colman S.
10:160
Fait, A. 25:169
Faite, W. D. 3:68
Faith, Alex 3:68
Faith, George W. 10:51;
20:248
Faith, John 13:79
Fakey, Thomas 10:152
Fakin, N. 1:130
Falby, Dennis 12:69
Falch, Jacob 19:163
Falcht, John 24:65
Falcier, Walter H. 6:30
Falck, Jacob 10:160
Falcomby, James 8:84
Falconburg, J. R. 3:68
Falconer, Robert 16:31
Faldar, Michael 7:93
Faldman, John 7:26
Fale, Isaac E. 21:329
Fale, Isaac R. 9:214
Fales, Albert 15:83
Fales, C. Y. 7:26
Fales, George F. 16:84
Fales, J. A. 1:129
Fales, N. 14:59
Fales, Orick J. 24:170
Fales, P. 1:131
Fales, R. O. 14:59
Faley, Patrick 11:279
Faley, Thomas 22:424
Faling, Pat 15:196
Falix, W. 15:86
Falk, Gustus 13:109
Falk, J. 1:33
Falk, Jacob 10:90; 20:248
Falk, John 25:32

Falk, N. A. 9:66
Falk, S. 5:51
Falk, W. 3:68
Falke, F. 24:77
Falke, R. 1:131
Falkenberry, Jefferson 10:112; 20:248
Falkenburg, Willis M. 21:224
Falkerson, J. 3:68
Falkerson, William M. 22:121
Falketts, J. 16:139
Falkinborough, Samuel 17:418
Falkiner, Hiram 11:412
Falkinstein, F. 3:68
Falkner, A. L. 10:179
Falkner, Albert 23:142
Falkner, George 22:249
Falkner, Henry 17:280
Falkner, James 4:23
Falkner, John 7:57
Falkner, P. 21:121
Falkner, Riley 11:147
Falkner, W. 1:129
Falkner, W. H. 20:248
Falkswick, Jasper 7:93
Fall, Edward 4:23
Fall, F. R. 4:23
Fall, H. 14:9
Fall, Hen. 25:32
Fall, Henry 2:11
Fall, J. B. W. 19:266
Fall, J. S. 26:236
Fall, J. W. 14:164
Fall, Josiah 20:179
Fall, O. 13:87
Fall, O. W. 1:129
Fall, Samuel 12:81; 16:292
Fall, Samuel H. 22:423
Fall, T. N. 22:190
Fallagber, A. 24:77
Fallamsbe, W. 16:189
Fallansbe, W. 13:63
Fallansbee, C. N. 9:142
Fallbright, John 16:147
Fallege, Michael 26:123
Fallen, Benjamin 9:130
Fallen, Greenville 23:87
Fallen, James 5:51
Fallen, Jeremiah 6:14
Fallen, O. 20:248
Fallen, P. 8:71
Fallen, Patrick 3:68
Fallen, T. 1:129
Fallenger, Peter 8:15
Faller, Nicholas 19:163
Faller, P. 26:160
Falles, T. J. 23:142

Falley, Bernard 5:15
Fallick, C. W. 1:129
Fallin, Barton S. 11:240
Fallman, Phineas 13:21
Fallon, B. 21:329
Fallon, George 11:240
Fallon, James 25:169
Fallon, Patrick 12:20; 23:29
Falloon, D. 18:66
Falloon, Jeremiah 18:81
Falls, A. C. 1:130
Falls, Aaron 12:48
Falls, Elias 21:270
Falls, G. 23:142
Falls, J. K. 14:59
Falls, J. T. 16:139
Falls, James 11:122
Falls, James A. 8:63
Falls, Norman S. 13:109
Falls, Robert 8:105
Falls, Stephen 10:16
Falls, Thomas K. 14:281
Fallz, Adam 25:169
Falmatier, John 23:189
Falmy, Garrett 13:109
Falner, J. 12:95
Falon, James 15:196
Falon, John 15:298
Faloy, John 25:33
Falsker, Frederick W. 12:145
Faltax, Frederick 10:16
Faltman, C. 12:166
Faltner, William S. 11:59
Faltock, Robert M. 15:7
Falton, Thomas 9:220; 18:366
Faltz, J. 12:153
Faltz, William 11:29
Falue, George 9:175; 19:251
Falvy, James 25:169
Famble, Andrew 21:329
Famburg, M. W. 9:79
Fameef, Eli 7:26
Famile, E. 3:68
Faminan, Richard 9:130
Fammings, T. 16:189
Fan, G. 11:326
Fanar, C. E. 13:87
Fanar, John 10:51
Fanbook, H. 15:196
Fancher, A. 25:169
Fancher, David 10:51; 20:248
Fancher, Jay H. 20:112
Fancher, John H. 20:189
Fancher, R. 14:288; 23:29
Fancher, R. H. 23:29

Fanchey, M. 17:291
Fanchier, Jacob F. 10:112
Fanchier, Jacob T. 20:248
Fandisle, S. 3:68
Fane, James 23:270
Fane, L. 25:169
Fanel, L. A. 10:51
Fanell, John 19:163
Fanell, Patrick 11:332
Faner, Sandy 21:329
Faner, Wilson W. 4:23
Fanfield, J. E. 13:63
Fanghey, E. 22:479
Fank, F. 7:26
Fankel, William H. 10:112
Fankell, W. H. 20:248
Fankhouser, John 20:248
Fanks, Benjamin W. 21:25
Fanle, John 1:32
Fanlett, L. D. L. 20:248
Fann, Garrett 14:59
Fann, Martin L. 22:249
Fannagan, Thomas 17:415
Fannandes, J. 18:81
Fanneas, Peter J. 8:105
Fannel, J. C. 14:281
Fannell, Jacob C. 17:500
Fanner, David 10:51
Fanner, Nathan 9:21
Fanner, Samuel 20:248
Fanney, John 17:33
Fannin, James 24:59
Fanning, Edward 9:230; 20:248
Fanning, H. L. 9:79; 26:27
Fanning, Henry C. 15:2
Fanning, John 25:287
Fanning, Lafayette 9:79
Fanning, Malacky 15:196
Fanning, Michael 24:93
Fanning, P. 1:131; 16:93
Fanning, S. C. 24:18
Fanning, William 12:58; 21:238; 22:519
Fanning, William D. 12:173
Fannings, Joe 26:160
Fannis, Anthony 12:69
Fannon, A. 3:68
Fannon, G. K. 3:68
Fannton, H. 3:68
Fanow, John 10:51
Fanow, John W. 7:49
Fanraw, William H. 16:31
Fansett, William 22:519
Fansey, William 7:26
Fanshaw, A. 27:42
Fanshaw, S. A. 16:279
Fanshier, William H. 21:224
Fansler, George H. 17:209

Fansnaugh, William H. 12:69
Fanssen, John F. 16:93
Fanstermaker, J. 18:49
Fanthrop, George W. 19:13
Fantlinger, F. 3:68
Fanton, H. 1:128
Fants, A. J. 9:118
Fantz, A. 12:20
Fanver, H. F. 25:33
Fanver, L. 13:87; 14:9
Fanver, William 10:112; 20:248
Fapless, --- 12:20
Faradice, Jacob B. 10:52
Farbaugh, Barnard 4:23
Farber, Daniel 9:118; 27:44
Farber, Joseph 20:248
Farble, Charles 21:329
Farbuck, Philip 8:84
Farce, Albert 18:271
Farce, F. 3:68
Farchild, William A. 18:394
Fard, Haunewell 6:24
Fard, Isaac 9:130
Fard, James 13:57
Farde, S. J. 9:220
Fardley, Samuel 22:76
Farelwell, William 14:59
Faret, Henry 17:78
Farewell, Cromwell 22:29
Farewell, David M. 24:61
Farewell, E. 3:68
Farewell, J. 7:74
Farfield, George W. 12:20
Fargett, James 17:500
Fargo, Franklin A. 22:161
Fargo, Henry 17:65; 22:462
Fargo, Thomas 15:341; 16:368
Fargo, W. R. 9:175
Fargo, Waldo R. 19:237
Fargrave, M. B. 3:68
Fargueson, Robert F. 22:450
Farhine, C. 3:68
Farhon, E. 24:18
Farier, G. W. 18:366
Faril, Dennis 20:143
Faris, Clayborn 17:33
Faris, J. 9:21; 26:219
Faris, Joshua 18:305; 26:97
Faris, Rees M. 10:90
Faris, Thornton 17:424; 24:173
Farisder, H. 3:68

Farl, John 18:276; 22:279
Farl, William 26:160
Farlan, L. 22:478
Farland, T. 3:68
Farleigh, Andrew 19:321
Farles, Robert 12:153
Farley, A. 17:147
Farley, Amabel 4:23
Farley, Archibald 21:194
Farley, B. F. 18:109
Farley, E. M. 18:330
Farley, F. H. 17:456
Farley, G. W. 9:227
Farley, George 18:133
Farley, H. 1:130
Farley, H. H. 18:284
Farley, Harry H. 26:134
Farley, Hugh 16:118
Farley, J. 1:131; 11:60; 13:87; 14:9; 18:81
Farley, James 10:16; 13:63; 14:241; 16:189; 17:33; 27:47
Farley, Jesse 23:261
Farley, John 11:29
Farley, John A. 8:63
Farley, Joseph 3:68
Farley, Michael 14:164
Farley, P. 20:141
Farley, Peter 15:105; 21:329
Farley, R. 25:169
Farley, Samuel 9:96; 12:69; 16:189
Farley, Sylvanius 22:190
Farley, T. H. 24:213
Farley, Thomas 17:147
Farley, Tom 24:193
Farley, W. 3:68; 25:169
Farley, W. F. 10:27; 19:301
Farley, William 4:23; 23:142
Farley, William C. 18:292
Farlin, Charles P. 23:258
Farlin, Lucien 10:52
Farling, Burt 15:86
Farling, Joseph 11:105
Farling, Michael 7:49
Farling, P. F. 7:57
Farlon, Perry C. 21:253
Farlon, Robert 15:359
Farlow, F. A. 24:38
Farlow, J. F. 20:40
Farlow, Robert 12:95; 19:68
Farlow, Tilgham A. 21:224
Farly, John 10:176; 19:163
Farman, David A. 22:142

Farman, John 12:153
Farman, Joseph 11:412
Farman, T. 1:130
Farmandy, Lewis 9:200
Farme, Isaac 9:242
Farmer, A. F. 8:71
Farmer, B. 23:29
Farmer, Benjamin 24:18
Farmer, Benjamin F. 21:248
Farmer, David 11:29, 147; 20:248
Farmer, E. E. 19:237
Farmer, E. L. 3:68
Farmer, E. W. 9:175
Farmer, Eli 9:34
Farmer, F. 1:34; 3:68
Farmer, F. G. 12:153
Farmer, Finkley S. 18:133
Farmer, G. S. 3:68
Farmer, George 21:329
Farmer, Grain 22:29
Farmer, H. 1:33; 8:84; 25:320
Farmer, Harrison 11:261
Farmer, Harvey H. 22:121
Farmer, Henry 9:200; 19:281
Farmer, J. H. 22:249
Farmer, J. L. 17:337
Farmer, Jacob 22:423
Farmer, James 12:57
Farmer, Jefferson 8:63
Farmer, John 10:51; 19:68; 20:248; 22:121
Farmer, John A. 24:93
Farmer, John L. 16:31
Farmer, John R. 7:49
Farmer, Mortimer 9:175; 19:251
Farmer, N. 6:30
Farmer, O. W. 9:175
Farmer, Owen 19:237
Farmer, P. 12:8
Farmer, Samuel 9:230
Farmer, Samuel H. 21:68
Farmer, T. B. 9:52
Farmer, Thomas 24:193
Farmer, W. 3:68; 15:2
Farmer, William 17:499; 18:338; 20:103, 104
Farmer, William B. 11:423
Farmer, William L. 24:18
Farmer, William M. 16:31
Farming, Samuel M. 13:21
Farmingham, W. 3:68
Farmington, J. W. 22:161
Farmington, Miles 20:248

Farn, C. 3:68
Farna, W. B. 17:252
Farnagan, Thomas 24:152
Farnam, J. D. 25:169
Farnam, Paul 12:58
Farne, Patrick 26:211
Farnel, A. 17:51
Farnell, H. 11:146
Farnell, Parrett 24:89
Farnell, Reuben 12:64;
15:66
Farnell, W. E. 27:43
Farnem, Thomas 13:21
Farner, Charles 9:165
Farnes, A. 12:161
Farnes, E. J. 17:499
Farness, James 12:161
Farnesworth, G. W.
11:105
Farnesworth, J. 13:88
Farnett, M. 14:59
Farney, F. 8:84
Farngot, M. 9:80
Farnham, --- 16:11
Farnham, A. 3:68
Farnham, A. A. 14:59
Farnham, C. 3:68
Farnham, Charles R.
15:105
Farnham, Earl 22:29
Farnham, F. E. 25:169
Farnham, H. 7:57
Farnham, J. A. 9:142;
27:43
Farnham, J. C. 12:98
Farnham, John C. 15:357;
16:279
Farnham, John M. 10:16
Farnham, L. B. 3:68
Farnham, L. D. 3:68
Farnham, M. B. 3:68
Farnham, Orchelaus
17:359
Farnham, R. S. 9:142;
27:43
Farnham, Sydney B. 12:20
Farnham, W. 9:175;
19:232
Farnham, W. H. 1:34
Farnham, William 14:59
Farnhill, J. S. 7:26
Farnhire, Peter 20:123
Farnlay, C. F. 9:80
Farnnant, E. 14:265
Farnold, William 18:28
Farnon, James 25:169
Farns, Charles H. 11:374
Farnsbroth, C. 16:93
Farnsworth, A. F. 7:79;
25:296
Farnsworth, Allen 22:279

Farnsworth, C. H. 11:302;
19:227; 21:25
Farnsworth, Charles 11:29
Farnsworth, Charles H.
9:175
Farnsworth, D. W. 21:329
Farnsworth, David
15:352; 16:279
Farnsworth, E. T. 10:186;
18:174
Farnsworth, Edwin W.
10:16
Farnsworth, Gilbert 9:175
Farnsworth, H. 25:169
Farnsworth, J. 1:130; 14:9
Farnsworth, James C.
10:16
Farnsworth, Josephus 8:84
Farnsworth, Marvin O.
21:91
Farnsworth, Michael
25:33
Farnsworth, S. 3:68
Farnsworth, S. F. 18:13
Farnsworth, T. 22:10
Farnsworth, W. 3:68
Farnsworth, W. C. 21:121;
23:117
Farnsworth, W. L. 11:146
Farnum, C. W. 12:8
Farnum, Charles H.
21:329
Farnum, Cyrus H. 17:391
Farnum, E. 3:68
Farnum, Luther 15:278;
25:169
Farnum, Phidussa 14:164
Farnun, Lemuel 4:23
Farnworth, G. 19:245
Faro, Abraham 12:69
Faroclough, R. 3:68
Farole, G. 3:68
Farquare, J. 15:196
Farqueson, Robert 22:190
Farquier, L. S. 11:438
Farquire, E. 26:160
Farr, A. 14:59; 20:123
Farr, Abram 15:86
Farr, Charles 1:33; 23:276
Farr, D. J. 1:130
Farr, E. D. 18:236; 26:28
Farr, E. M. 15:151
Farr, Edward 25:320
Farr, Edward B. 16:88
Farr, George C. 13:21
Farr, Haskell 16:132
Farr, M. 10:16
Farr, Robert 9:130; 27:45
Farr, S. M. 12:153
Farr, William 12:164
Farra, N. L. 1:32

Farra, W. J. 25:169
Farrab, J. H. 21:25
Farrabee, F. W. 21:329
Farrall, C. 1:129
Farrall, Charles 11:122
Farrall, Francis 26:159
Farrall, P. 16:189
Farran, Abraham 11:386
Farran, Joliah 26:27
Farrand, F. S. 1:129
Farrand, Henry 17:65;
22:462
Farrand, Hezekiah 21:121
Farrand, Magordus 22:142
Farrand, Richard 8:15
Farrand, Rubard 18:133
Farrand, Thomas 11:401
Farrap, Edward 1:33
Farrar, C. E. 14:9
Farrar, C. S. 25:169
Farrar, Caswell 21:270
Farrar, D. 1:33; 7:57
Farrar, Eben 5:15
Farrar, G. W. 1:103
Farrar, H. 15:196; 19:232
Farrar, Jehit 9:80
Farrar, W. J. 5:15
Farrar, Ward 21:329
Farrar, Wesley 21:329
Farrar, William 14:164;
27:42
Farras, James 3:68
Farraud, J. B. 14:59
Farray, Frederick 21:329
Farree, J. 19:68
Farrel, Aaron 26:159
Farrel, Adam 24:38
Farrel, B. 19:287
Farrel, J. 19:251
Farrel, John 21:25
Farrel, John C. 12:153
Farrel, L. 27:43
Farrel, Michael 15:347
Farrel, P. 16:93
Farrell, Aaron 8:38
Farrell, Andrew 22:121
Farrell, C. 3:68
Farrell, Dominick 10:153
Farrell, Edward 4:23;
15:105; 22:76
Farrell, Edward J. 15:318;
19:68
Farrell, Francis 21:329
Farrell, George 9:114
Farrell, George C. 23:179
Farrell, Harmon 18:323
Farrell, Henderson 21:329
Farrell, Isaac 15:86
Farrell, J. 1:128, 129; 7:49
Farrell, J. B. 1:131
Farrell, J. E. 26:97

Farrell, J. H. 3:68
Farrell, James 3:68; 9:68; 16:189
Farrell, James F. 3:68
Farrell, John 8:48; 9:175; 10:112, 160; 15:311, 354; 19:68; 20:248
Farrell, John E. 18:305
Farrell, John J. 23:142
Farrell, L. A. 20:248
Farrell, Lawrence 9:142; 25:32
Farrell, M. 1:34; 3:68
Farrell, Martin 23:107
Farrell, Michael 16:368
Farrell, Michael J. 10:16
Farrell, P. 25:169
Farrell, P. O. 22:190
Farrell, Pat 15:173
Farrell, Patrick 13:21; 15:298; 16:31; 20:104
Farrell, Richard 4:23
Farrell, Robert P. 21:329
Farrell, Seth 21:329
Farrell, Stephen 22:190
Farrell, T. 1:34
Farrell, Thomas 19:163
Farrell, William 9:80; 10:7; 23:113; 26:27
Farrelly, Matthew 22:17
Farrelly, Thomas 25:296
Farren, Charles 12:20
Farren, F. 16:189
Farren, James F. 3:68
Farren, Patrick 18:109
Farren, Warren 17:159
Farrer, George F. 19:163
Farrer, George P. 10:160
Farrer, J. G. 19:163
Farrer, James 3:68
Farrer, James W. 11:100
Farrer, Jeremiah 18:206
Farrer, Walde 16:145
Farrew, George M. 10:172
Farrier, Andrew 11:240
Farrier, Andrew J. 21:99
Farrier, Robert 20:97
Farrill, George C. 9:106
Farrill, Peter 9:160
Farrin, Abner S. 1:33
Farrin, Adam 11:423
Farrin, F. 3:68
Farrington, B. H. 1:32
Farrington, C. A. 1:129
Farrington, Daniel 19:163
Farrington, Eben 16:77
Farrington, George 2:10; 14:165
Farrington, George T. 10:160

Farrington, Gustavus 7:93; 21:329
Farrington, Henry 13:21; 16:31
Farrington, John 16:31
Farrington, John E. 16:84
Farrington, Josiah 15:105
Farrington, Miles 10:51
Farrington, Patrick 16:93
Farrington, William 17:147
Farrington, William A. 20:112
Farris, A. M. 12:153
Farris, A. V. 12:20
Farris, Albert 15:123
Farris, Alexander L. 22:121
Farris, Alfred L. 20:248
Farris, C. 3:68
Farris, Charles 15:105
Farris, Hardy H. 8:100
Farris, Harvey H. 17:460
Farris, J. 10:27; 19:301
Farris, J. F. 21:329
Farris, John 8:84; 9:118
Farris, R. E. 15:123
Farris, R. R. 11:395
Farris, William 17:272
Farris, William C. 21:51
Farris, William H. 24:88
Farris, William S. 13:124
Farrns, William 9:52
Farroll, W. 1:33
Farron, D. W. H. 10:148
Farron, W. 1:34
Farror, D. W. H. 18:49
Farror, Minot J. 12:20
Farrow, Francis M. 11:59
Farrow, J. B. 14:59
Farrow, J. P. 11:59
Farrow, Samuel R. 22:450
Farrow, W. 3:68
Farrow, William 17:144
Farrowen, Henry 21:91
Farry, Samuel 14:165
Farryco, Lewis 24:193
Farsie, Charles 7:74
Farson, J. B. 17:307
Farst, Henry 11:181
Farthengell, H. 14:9
Farthing, George 20:7
Farthing, O. 16:189
Farthing, William 1:34; 20:104
Farton, John 12:20
Farwater, William R. 24:66
Farwell, E. G. 25:169
Farwell, Edwin P. 21:137
Farwell, Eugene E. 5:15

Farwell, Francis M. 13:21; 16:31
Farwell, J. 25:296
Farwell, James F. 22:479
Farwell, W. E. 9:142
Farwig, Henry 17:502
Fary, John 5:15; 25:169
Farz, Epoch R. 18:394
Fasburg, A. 1:131
Fasburg, Robert 12:20
Fase, Augustus A. 9:12
Fasel, Antoine 8:15; 18:133
Fashbaker, William 15:13
Fashbaugh, Lewis 23:142
Fashler, Fritz 4:23
Fasker, J. 1:32
Faskil, Orlo 1:33
Fasmyer, Joseph 12:69
Fasnahat, Charles 3:68
Fasnaught, Edward 9:80
Fasno, Jacob 18:81
Fasnot, Jacob 6:9
Fass, L. M. 20:248
Fasse, A. S. 11:332
Fassenacht, Samuel B. 13:21
Fassett, F. 9:109
Fassett, G. P. 13:88
Fassett, J. 19:68
Fassett, James F. 20:106
Fassette, Amest 16:147
Fassitt, E. C. 9:176
Fassitt, Elbridge C. 19:227
Fassitt, William J. 9:176
Fast, Daniel 10:52; 20:248
Fast, Henry 23:285
Fastad, John H. 22:279
Fastenson, Frederick 22:171
Faster, Alexander 19:163
Faster, G. R. 24:107
Faster, Isaac 4:23
Faster, Robert 11:59
Fasters, Daniel 7:26
Fastin, J. 14:59
Fatbrook, William 16:31
Fatcher, Sandy 7:122
Fate, George 17:280; 18:189
Fate, Ira 11:29
Fate, Valentine 20:123
Fatem, Robert 17:51
Fates, Anthony 12:69
Fath, George 23:113
Fathergill, H. 13:88
Fatherstone, Joseph 17:78
Fatland, Thomas 10:112; 20:248
Fatman, Ezra 23:276

Fatman, Pemberton 6:24
Fatmer, N. B. 20:123
Fatro, George 11:303
Fatte, Joseph 4:23
Fattig, Joseph 18:206
Fattman, B. 3:68
Fatty, E. F. 16:11
Fatzpatrick, C. 13:109
Faubert, E. 1:131
Faubion, Noah 21:51
Fauble, J. 1:130
Faucault, Michael 22:29
Fauce, Thomas 14:315
Faucett, Benjamin F.
    22:76
Faucett, I. 3:68
Faucett, J. T. 22:190
Faucett, John A. 12:153
Faucett, Joseph 18:133
Faucette, George 18:217
Faucler, Andrew 18:394
Faught, O. F. 7:13
Faul, Martin 8:121
Faulconer, Robert 13:21
Faulk, Andrew Thomas
    27:144
Faulk, George 24:66
Faulk, J. C. 21:329
Faulk, Jacob W. 22:478
Faulk, John 11:146
Faulkner, A. 24:77
Faulkner, A. L. 26:204
Faulkner, Charles 22:298
Faulkner, Charles E.
    13:21
Faulkner, D. 20:29
Faulkner, Francis 13:109
Faulkner, Franklin 11:20
Faulkner, George N.
    20:185
Faulkner, J. 25:296
Faulkner, J. L. 18:174
Faulkner, John H. 19:13
Faulkner, John W. 21:329
Faulkner, L. C. 1:129
Faulkner, Levi 11:239
Faulkner, Peter 9:207
Faulkner, Riley 8:63;
    26:160
Faulkner, Robert D. O.
    17:19
Faulkner, Samuel 11:302
Faulkner, Thomas 21:224;
    22:190
Faulkner, W. H. 10:52
Faulkner, William 17:174
Faulkner, William J.
    22:29
Fault, Peter R. 11:411
Faunce, A. 1:130
Faunce, Lemuel B. 18:49

Faunrer, A. 21:329
Faunsaught, W. H. 15:66
Fauntleroy, A. L. (Miss)
    25:311
Fauntleroy, D. 25:311
Fauntleroy, V. D. (Miss)
    25:311
Fauntroy, Moses 17:397
Faurk, --- 14:9
Faurke, --- 13:88
Faurnis, Thomas 22:497
Faush, H. 15:196
Faushier, J. D. 14:165
Faushire, --- 3:69
Fausler, Moses W. 22:142
Fausnaught, Bernard
    22:233
Fausse, Pierre 18:66
Faust, A. 25:34
Faust, Daniel 17:276
Faust, David 12:20
Faust, G. W. 23:29
Faust, H. 12:20
Faust, Henry 25:32
Faust, Jacob 16:31
Faust, John 22:500
Faust, Peter L. 11:181;
    16:135
Faustormaker, James
    10:152
Favis, Ruse M. 20:248
Favneer, Pinkney G. 8:15
Favon, William 12:153
Favor, John W. 11:19
Favors, Andrew 19:290
Fawbush, Docton W.
    25:275
Fawcett, J. 1:128
Fawcett, James 23:16
Fawcett, Joseph 20:97
Fawcett, Joseph A. 24:50
Fawcett, R. D. 27:42
Faweebt, Joseph 8:15
Fawgett, Ph. A. 24:77
Fawkes, Issac 16:189
Fawks, William 3:69
Fawn, Samuel 14:165
Fawyer, Joseph C. 25:32
Faxler, Hugh 11:412
Faxon, Henry M. 9:142
Faxton, Elihu J. 16:11
Faxton, H. M. 27:43
Fay, A. 15:151
Fay, A. J. 14:332
Fay, Adam 10:16
Fay, C. E. 13:109
Fay, Carlos B. 20:112
Fay, Charles 24:8
Fay, Daniel 10:52; 20:248
Fay, Emmerson C. 15:83
Fay, Eugene 22:161

Fay, G. W. 15:123
Fay, Harris 8:15
Fay, Henry 22:29
Fay, Hous 18:133
Fay, Isaac 12:57
Fay, J. 1:131
Fay, J. W. 3:69; 22:190
Fay, James 7:26; 14:336
Fay, John 1:33; 3:69;
    17:33; 27:44, 46
Fay, Mark G. 21:206
Fay, Michael 15:80
Fay, Milton C. 11:292
Fay, Myron H. 21:87
Fay, Newton R. 21:253
Fay, Patrick 22:10
Fay, R. 22:190
Fay, S. W. 12:122; 14:25
Fay, Stephen 11:146
Fay, Sylvester 7:62
Fay, T. 3:69
Fay, W. M. 7:67
Fay, William 4:23
Fay, William A. 17:33;
    23:29
Fay, William N. 24:93
Faybury, William 11:435
Fayette, James R. 13:57
Fays, Frank 5:15
Fayshan, John 4:23
Fazzier, John 2:10; 25:32
Feackle, J. F. 9:142
Fead, G. 3:69
Feaer, W. 26:160
Feagler, Ernest 7:57
Feagles, G. A. 15:293;
    16:189
Feagley, William M.
    23:113
Feagne, Nathaniel 8:15
Feague, Larkin 21:329
Feahy, P. 19:251
Feak, N. 16:267
Feakins, Thomas 7:93
Feal, Samuel 17:174
Fealey, John 18:133
Fealix, R. 19:281
Fealt, William 18:366
Fealy, Patrick 9:176;
    19:251
Fear, A. B. 15:258
Fear, George 26:145
Fear, William A. 23:279
Fearather, John F. 23:65
Fearing, Dudley 19:316
Fearing, J. 1:130
Fearing, J. J. 3:69
Fearman, Samuel 7:122
Fearnley, J. 18:49
Fearnley, Joseph W. 17:65
Fearnley, W. 3:69

Fears, J. 23:29
Feas, Samuel 17:423
Feasel, H. 3:69
Feasley, James H. 17:218
Feasley, Levi 3:69
Feast, George 3:69
Feaster, James 21:68
Feaster, Silas 22:10
Feath, William 9:220
Feather, J. B. 3:69
Feather, Jefferson 7:26
Feather, Joseph 4:23
Feather, Lucius S. 11:181
Featherby, George 25:296
Feathers, Daniel 22:29
Featherstone, J. 3:69
Feats, S. M. 7:26
Feauge, James 16:279
Feb, Frank 8:48
Febay, John W. 13:21
Febis, Autwine 16:189
Febols, Charles B. 13:63
Febra, Hock 6:35
Feddon, Elisha 20:248
Feder, W. 8:63
Federly, Daniel 18:338
Federman, Christian
    23:128
Fedinberg, --- 3:74
Fedison, Chris 18:305;
    26:98
Fee, Daniel 7:94
Fee, George W. 3:69
Fee, Hiram 17:147
Fee, James 9:71; 12:139
Fee, John 23:65
Fee, L. 15:263
Fee, Michael 1:34
Fee, Samuel 12:69; 15:66
Fee, William 11:261;
    15:151
Feeback, I. S. 11:92
Feeck, E. 14:9
Feed, Dan 9:176
Feed, Daniel 19:274
Feedly, Daniel 14:327
Feel, Noah 9:70
Feeler, Antonie 8:48
Feeler, G. 27:43
Feeley, Edward 7:26
Feeley, J. 19:251
Feeley, James 16:189
Feeley, John A. 22:423
Feeley, Thomas 22:519
Feely, Martin 9:118;
    27:45
Feenay, John 15:278
Feeney, Ignatius 18:109
Feeney, James 7:26;
    19:251
Feeney, John 25:169

Feeney, P. 1:34
Feeney, Patrick 18:292;
    26:98
Feeney, Thomas 22:334
Feenig, H. 14:297; 17:469
Feeny, Charles 15:341;
    16:368
Feeny, Michael 19:68
Feer, Harvey J. 23:29
Fees, Charles 12:20
Feet, Marvin 19:13
Feet, Solomon 7:26
Feeter, Stephen 13:21
Feetgan, Joseph 8:121
Fegan, John 3:69; 17:259
Fegan, William 14:59,
    165
Fegely, Augustus 9:118;
    27:44
Fegg, Richard V. 21:51
Fegi, Michael 24:18
Fegles, Silas 7:26
Fehland, August 21:99,
    253
Fehliman, L. 11:146
Fehr, H. 24:18
Fehr, Joseph 19:317
Fehrenkamp, Mehut
    11:191
Fehtil, Peter 10:16
Feifer, A. 14:255
Feiffer, Albert P. 24:72
Feighner, Alfred 8:15;
    18:133
Feighner, W. A. 7:94
Feight, Frederick 16:93
Feilder, George 10:112;
    20:248
Feilds, James 12:69
Feiley, M. 3:69
Feiney, James 9:176
Feinstinaker, William G.
    17:392
Feinthal, J. 17:309
Feirbach, Jacob 18:305;
    26:98
Feisel, C. 11:295
Feiser, --- 18:49
Feiten, John 24:93
Feitzell, Frederick 5:51;
    25:169
Felbrick, E. L. 3:69
Felch, David F. M. 21:91
Felch, F. H. 11:145
Felch, J. 1:130
Felch, J. P. 14:165
Felcorn, Nelson 8:15
Felder, Spencer 8:112
Feleson, John 13:21
Felger, T. 15:105
Felicier, W. H. 25:320

Felick, Christopher
    10:112; 20:248
Felie, Enos 20:248
Felinger, Andrew J.
    11:145
Felio, A. 15:293
Felio, Enos 10:112
Felix, C. H. 13:109
Felix, George 21:329
Felix, Robert 9:200
Felix, Tumor 4:23
Felix, Warren 12:69
Felker, George 15:304
Felker, John 23:11
Felker, Lomis J. 19:68
Felkner, Andrew 15:196
Fell, Aaron 25:169
Fell, Adam 7:26
Fell, George 16:118
Fell, Henry 15:105
Fell, J. 14:165
Fell, James G. 16:118
Fell, John 14:165
Fell, S. 11:147
Fell, William 17:449;
    24:175
Felland, Samuel 11:202
Fellbaum, August 22:279
Fellenger, Joseph D.
    25:33
Feller, Jesse 10:112;
    20:248
Feller, John 10:112;
    20:248
Feller, Nicholas 14:165
Feller, Robert 10:112
Feller, Robert W. 8:84
Fellers, E. 24:77
Fellers, J. 23:142
Fellers, W. 23:142
Fellett, Eugene 20:249
Felley, James 14:165
Felliber, Jacob A. 22:508
Fellingast, Charles 14:165
Fellinger, George 11:105
Fellinger, N. 14:241
Fellingham, George
    10:112; 20:249
Fellingham, John D.
    22:334
Fellou, George O. 22:190
Fellows, A. M. 9:96
Fellows, Eratus G. 11:105
Fellows, H. 15:173
Fellows, Henry A. 12:20
Fellows, Hubert 21:216
Fellows, J. C. 3:69
Fellows, Jacob 17:19
Fellows, John 19:13
Fellows, Lewis 17:295
Fellows, Milton D. 24:77

Fellows, Stork 9:157
Fells, Elias 9:95
Fells, Rudolph 7:81
Fells, S. W. 19:13
Fellton, John H. 9:80
Felmott, Henry D. 24:89
Felpecker, Jacob 9:21
Felps, --- 18:174
Felps, Daniel 3:69
Fels, Rudolph 25:296
Felsinger, Christian
    22:233
Felson, John M. 14:165
Felt, A. C. 25:170
Felt, A. W. 1:34
Felt, Alden L. 17:33
Felt, John W. 10:52;
    20:249
Felt, P. L. 11:60
Feltenverger, William
    4:23
Felter, F. 3:69
Felter, H. M. 3:69
Felter, J. J. 9:142
Feltham, H. W. 9:109
Felthouse, H. H. 3:69
Feltman, John 13:109
Feltner, Edw. 27:45
Feltner, Edward J. 9:118
Feltner, John 17:147
Felton, A. 25:170
Felton, Abram 22:501
Felton, Ambros 9:34
Felton, Ambrose 18:292
Felton, Burklay 22:142
Felton, C. S. 1:129
Felton, Chawney 11:411
Felton, E. H. 1:130
Felton, Francis 11:146
Felton, Frederick 13:21
Felton, George 3:69
Felton, George W. 20:249
Felton, H. 23:179
Felton, J. 14:255
Felton, J. C. 15:173
Felton, James 9:42;
    26:123
Felton, L. 15:123
Felton, R. R. 13:63
Felton, W. 14:281
Felts, Amos 22:29
Felts, James W. 22:249
Felts, William S. 21:69
Felwick, H. 3:69
Femoil, William 14:165
Femworth, Hennan
    17:461
Fenall, J. 3:69
Fenant, Arthur 8:105
Fenant, John C. 14:165
Fench, Miles 6:12

Fenchell, J. F. 27:43
Fenchter, Fred 16:368
Fenchter, Frederick
    15:341
Fenda, Martin 19:13
Fendel, Samuel H. 4:23
Fenden, Joseph P. 18:133
Fender, J. 26:160
Fender, Joseph P. 8:15
Fender, Samuel 25:275
Fenderson, T. D. 1:34
Fendly, Daniel 9:102
Fenegan, Stephen 15:354
Fenelon, T. H. 16:84
Fenenson, John 7:9
Fenerbroch, J. 14:59
Fenerison, John 19:13
Feners, Aaron 11:261
Feney, Patrick 9:34
Fenian, John J. 22:462
Fenical, J. 12:87
Fenicle, C. 14:59
Fenig, H. 27:46
Fenis, Augustus 14:165
Fenix, John 10:52; 20:249
Fenk, H. K. 8:15
Fenkner, John P. 13:21
Fenleson, John 4:23
Fenley, A. 23:113
Fenley, J. 9:142
Fenley, R. 3:69
Fenley, Westley 19:163
Fenly, John 8:15
Fenly, Westly 10:154
Fenn, J. 1:129
Fenn, John 17:65
Fenn, William P. 25:271
Fennell, Enoch 22:76
Fenner, Byron A. 4:23
Fenner, G. W. 15:196
Fenner, John A. 23:128
Fenner, Joseph E. 14:265
Fenner, Lynford 12:20
Fenner, T. G. 11:239
Fennerham, William
    20:249
Fennerhan, William 10:52
Fennery, John 21:329
Fenney, Peter 25:170
Fenni, John 17:352
Fennick, Salem 27:46
Fennimore, Charles
    21:224
Fennimore, Henry 11:60
Fennimore, Richard E.
    24:18
Fennis, William H. 9:80
Fenno, I. H. 8:84
Fenno, William W. 12:20
Fenny, Michael 23:128
Fenny, William 22:462

Fensall, Wilson 6:20
Fensger, Philip 12:20
Fenson, L. 1:97
Fentinean, Francis 24:18
Fenton, Abraham 7:122
Fenton, Albert 25:280
Fenton, Arthur 9:176;
    19:251
Fenton, C. 1:128
Fenton, Charles 12:20
Fenton, D. C. 1:129
Fenton, Edward 14:165
Fenton, F. H. 1:97
Fenton, Henry 15:66
Fenton, Isaac 27:42
Fenton, J. 2:11; 3:69;
    25:31
Fenton, J. W. 3:69
Fenton, John 10:95
Fenton, John L. A. 22:190
Fenton, Michael 5:15
Fenton, Samuel J. 20:136
Fenton, T. 14:59
Fenton, Thomas 23:65
Fenton, W. 1:130
Fenton, William 13:21
Fenton, William D. 20:7
Fenton, William H.
    25:170
Fentress, G. W. 25:170
Fentress, George W. 5:38
Fentress, William 18:217
Fentriss, William 21:211
Fentz, John C. 9:176
Fenwick, Abraham 27:44
Fenwick, Abram 9:130
Fenworth, Hennan 8:100;
    24:166
Feogo, H. 3:69
Feon---, Ed 23:203
Feozee, Thomas 22:29
Ferailleger, W. 3:69
Ferand, A. 3:69
Ferber, Michael 24:77
Ferbert, Stephen 17:280
Ferbich, H. S. 27:43
Ferbush, George 8:84
Ferbuson, Thomas H.
    22:249
Ferce, R. S. 3:69
Ferch, Earnest 6:23
Ferchens, Fred 20:249
Ferchinger, Joseph 22:279
Ferd, Robert E. 24:93
Ferder, Zachariah L. 7:94
Ferdinand, George 22:29
Ferdinand, Leonard 10:52;
    20:249
Ferdon, George 12:95;
    15:359; 19:68
Fereheus, Frederick 10:52

Fergason, D. 20:249
Fergason, H. 11:326
Fergen, Peter 7:122
Fergen, William 8:48
Fergerson, J. 1:33; 8:71
Fergerson, Uriah 18:29
Fergerson, William 1:33
Fergeson, George 17:463; 24:183
Fergeson, Julius 16:147
Fergesson, Forger 11:332
Ferguerer, Martin 8:105
Fergueson, Nathaniel 11:59
Fergurson, A. D. 1:34
Fergurson, Dryden 23:142
Fergurson, George 9:7
Fergurson, John 17:349
Ferguson, --- 2:10; 12:61; 16:31, 135; 17:435; 18:189
Ferguson, Abraham 9:142; 19:320
Ferguson, Alexander 1:32
Ferguson, Anderson 20:50
Ferguson, Andrew J. 17:51
Ferguson, Arch 17:175
Ferguson, B. S. 27:42
Ferguson, C. 21:329
Ferguson, Casper 10:90
Ferguson, D. 22:142; 24:77
Ferguson, David 10:52
Ferguson, David B. 10:52; 20:249
Ferguson, E. M. 15:105
Ferguson, Elijah 10:52; 20:249; 22:500
Ferguson, F. 14:9
Ferguson, Fenus 17:131
Ferguson, Fergus 22:279
Ferguson, Frank 22:479
Ferguson, Frank M. 11:412
Ferguson, G. 9:52
Ferguson, G. W. 1:129; 23:142
Ferguson, George 9:161
Ferguson, George B. 10:52
Ferguson, George H. 14:165; 22:76
Ferguson, George N. 1:34
Ferguson, George W. 11:146
Ferguson, H. C. 3:69
Ferguson, H. W. 3:69
Ferguson, Henry 4:23; 5:38

Ferguson, Henry M. 22:397
Ferguson, J. 1:31, 94; 13:135; 14:297; 17:481; 19:346
Ferguson, J. B. 21:329
Ferguson, J. E. 1:130
Ferguson, J. H. 8:59
Ferguson, Jackson 20:249
Ferguson, James 4:23; 15:55; 17:202; 19:13
Ferguson, James R. 5:15
Ferguson, James T. 8:48; 21:69
Ferguson, Jason D. 20:136
Ferguson, John 12:95; 14:9; 17:236; 21:329; 22:29, 298; 25:333
Ferguson, John P. 10:112; 20:249
Ferguson, Joseph 3:69; 9:176, 207
Ferguson, Josephus 21:253
Ferguson, L. 25:33
Ferguson, Lafayette 23:113
Ferguson, Lewis 3:69
Ferguson, Luke 22:298
Ferguson, M. 11:428; 26:160
Ferguson, M. L. 8:63
Ferguson, M. W. 1:129
Ferguson, Nathaniel 25:170
Ferguson, P. 14:297; 17:481; 27:46
Ferguson, Peter 21:224
Ferguson, Prince 27:45
Ferguson, R. 11:326
Ferguson, Reuben 7:122
Ferguson, Robert 12:60; 17:175
Ferguson, Robert F. 10:52
Ferguson, Robert M. 21:253
Ferguson, S. 14:59, 165, 255
Ferguson, Samuel 10:160; 11:261; 19:163; 23:87
Ferguson, Samuel T. 11:146
Ferguson, Scott M. 15:66
Ferguson, Stephen 21:270
Ferguson, T. H. 14:281
Ferguson, Thomas 17:502; 24:18, 93
Ferguson, Thornton 19:45
Ferguson, Vanest 25:33
Ferguson, W. 8:63; 26:97

Ferguson, W. B. 18:133
Ferguson, W. W. 14:281; 17:497
Ferguson, William 5:15; 7:94; 8:48; 9:12, 31; 18:305; 22:249; 26:160
Ferguson, William H. 21:51
Ferguston, F. 14:59
Feril, Charles 19:68
Feril, J. B. 10:112; 20:249
Ferley, Thomas 11:146
Ferman, --- 9:106
Ferman, Edward 26:159
Ferman, H. 25:34
Ferman, Marcellus 7:94
Fern, A. P. 27:42
Fern, Hugh 10:146
Fern, Owen 25:34
Fern, Robert 10:112; 20:249
Fern, William 9:80; 26:28
Fernald, Benjamin W. 23:65
Fernald, G. W. 9:163; 25:320
Fernald, Joseph 21:329
Fernam, Marcellas 21:329
Fernando, James 21:270
Fernardey, Peter 21:329
Fernarld, Joseph 9:214
Fernell, Delos 17:446
Ferney, Ambrose 9:204
Ferngruber, M. 15:326
Fernitt, J. 3:69
Fernold, C. G. 3:69
Fernon, J. 3:69
Fernum, C. 27:42
Fernz, John 11:118
Ferole, Chancey 18:133
Ferole, Cheney 8:15
Feron, Louis O. 7:122
Ferrarow, Andrew 21:329
Ferrce, William 26:123
Ferree, C. 3:69
Ferree, James M. 2:10
Ferrel, Christopher 3:69
Ferrel, Frederick 14:241
Ferrel, James 10:52
Ferrel, William C. 15:196
Ferrele, A. 14:59
Ferrell, --- 11:60
Ferrell, Alvah 10:95
Ferrell, Bernard 9:176
Ferrell, C. C. 15:196
Ferrell, Chester 13:22
Ferrell, Fred 27:46
Ferrell, George C. 19:163
Ferrell, J. 3:69; 18:366
Ferrell, J. M. 25:34

Ferrell, James 20:249
Ferrell, James O. 22:450
Ferrell, M. C. 3:69
Ferrell, Walter 23:142
Ferrell, William 9:220
Ferren, William E. 15:333
Ferrenex, Pierre 9:165
Ferrer, Amos 9:80
Ferrett, Philip H. 10:153
Ferretzy, Julius 16:94
Ferrey, Aaron G. 20:48
Ferrics, Charles 4:23
Ferrieco, John 11:240
Ferriel, Burt 18:394
Ferriel, Lemuel 18:395
Ferrier, John F. 10:112;
  20:249
Ferrigor, Michael 18:395
Ferrill, Harvey 17:165
Ferrill, Isaiah 21:137
Ferrill, J. 18:366; 20:249
Ferrill, James 8:71
Ferrill, John N. 8:71
Ferrill, Thomas 11:395
Ferrill, Warren 11:202
Ferrill, William 23:98
Ferrin, Jesse M. 21:51
Ferrin, John M. 22:500
Ferrin, Leroy 17:259, 318
Ferrin, Robert 9:157
Ferrin, William 7:94
Ferrin, William E. 19:68
Ferrio, Benjamin 9:200;
  19:281
Ferris, --- 11:218; 15:297;
  16:189
Ferris, A. 1:130
Ferris, Alfred L. 10:52
Ferris, Amos 17:175
Ferris, Charles D. 4:23
Ferris, David M. 11:335
Ferris, E. B. 15:293;
  16:190
Ferris, Ebenezer 22:462
Ferris, Edward 24:18
Ferris, F. B. 14:165
Ferris, G. W. 1:129
Ferris, George 5:38;
  25:170
Ferris, Gilmore 9:130;
  27:44
Ferris, Harvey H. 24:157
Ferris, Henry 22:142
Ferris, Henry I. 23:11
Ferris, Hiram G. 7:26
Ferris, J. 14:255
Ferris, J. W. 3:69
Ferris, Jacob B. 21:51
Ferris, Joel 24:38
Ferris, John 3:69; 21:329;
  27:44

Ferris, John J. 2:10; 25:34
Ferris, Joseph 3:69
Ferris, Loretso 11:60
Ferris, Phillip H. 15:196
Ferris, R. 25:170
Ferris, R. H. 15:341;
  16:368
Ferris, Richard 5:15
Ferris, Robert 3:69
Ferris, Theodore H. 21:69
Ferris, William H. 26:28
Ferris, William J. 21:329
Ferris, William R. 11:59
Ferritt, P. H. 19:163
Ferrol, --- 9:71
Ferrus, E. 14:59
Ferry, Alfred 18:29
Ferry, Amos 15:55
Ferry, B. 11:145
Ferry, Benjamin 11:181
Ferry, Freeman 11:303
Ferry, George 21:238
Ferry, George B. 1:32
Ferry, Hugh 17:51;
  20:185
Ferry, James 8:84
Ferry, John 16:94; 21:137;
  24:18
Ferry, Marion 27:46
Ferry, Noah H. 16:139
Ferry, Orien E. 16:31
Ferry, R. 18:366
Ferry, Richard 9:220
Ferry, W. 3:69
Ferryman, Robert 11:146
Ferson, Howard 10:52
Ferstner, J. 1:130
Fert, George W. 21:95
Ferterd, Lawson 11:202
Fertile, Charles L. 9:244
Ferwilleger, E. 3:69
Feschuer, L. 10:153
Fesetto, Lewis 9:12
Fesgo, Edgar P. 11:89
Fesler, A. 23:29
Fesler, H. 16:190
Fess, Lewis 23:87
Fessell, George M. 18:366
Fessell, John 8:105
Fessenden, Eben 21:91
Fessenden, F. A. 22:161
Fessenden, James O.
  19:163
Fessenden, N. E. 3:69
Fessenden, Ransom M.
  17:90
Fessenden, S. R. 1:131
Fessendon, H. 1:34
Fesser, Benjamin 4:23
Fessington, Clinton 15:2
Fessler, Martin 21:91

Fessmeyer, Joseph 15:13
Fest, Jacob 25:170
Fester, Francis E. 4:23
Fester, John M. B. 22:450
Fester, Samuel 15:66
Festi, August 15:311
Festie, August 19:68
Festler, Nathaniel 6:23
Festman, John H. 21:201
Fetcer, Fred 20:249
Fetcher, Samuel 16:279
Feteer, F. 24:77
Fetein, G. L. 11:239
Feterly, Benjamin 23:107
Fetherling, W. 27:43
Fetherman, Henry 27:44
Fetherston, James 10:16
Fethton, A. 3:69
Fethy, George 20:249
Fetrick, John 7:26
Fetroe, Jeremiah 13:22
Fetten, James 11:145
Fetter, George W. 10:52
Fetter, James J. 27:42
Fetter, John A. 24:50
Fettering, W. 9:142
Fetterley, Jesse W. 24:170
Fetterley, William 1:33
Fetterly, Jesse W. 17:446
Fetterly, W. I. 15:196
Fetterman, Daniel 17:70
Fetterman, J. 3:69
Fetterman, William F.
  19:329
Fetters, A. E. 11:145
Fetters, C. 11:302
Fetters, Henry 17:452;
  24:181
Fetters, L. 18:49
Fetters, Samuel 22:190
Fetterson, Henry 9:118;
  27:45
Fetton, Ambrose 26:98
Fetts, Horatio 22:334
Fettut, Frederick 1:33
Fetty, A. J. 9:21
Fetty, Andrew 22:190
Fetty, George 10:52
Fetty, Isaac 26:219
Fetty, John H. 15:158
Fetzer, Frederic 10:90
Feuder, J. 8:71
Feulner, Frank 22:249
Feutford, Marion F.
  22:500
Feutherstone, Thomas
  21:10
Fevatt, John 26:27
Feveason, Andrew 15:105
Feverbaugh, James 11:59
Fevris, Thadeus 15:196

Few, Walter Payne 26:219
Few, William 10:16
Fewell, W. A. 25:170
Fewitt, J. W. 11:29
Fey, Frederick 13:22
Feyhe, Charles 1:33
Feyler, W. H. 25:296
Fiarvin, Jacob 11:186
Fibbett, William H. 16:190
Fibert, B. 20:89
Fiblet, James 27:47
Fich, John 3:69
Fichel, F. 17:436; 24:187
Fichler, August 18:133
Fichter, C. 9:70
Fick, C. 1:130
Fick, George 21:253; 23:259
Ficke, W. P. 3:69
Ficken, Christopher 15:196
Fickens, A. 17:33
Ficker, J. 19:290
Fickett, John 4:23
Fickle, W. H. 21:25
Fickles, I. 11:332
Fickles, Isaac 11:291
Ficklin, M. T. 23:279
Fiddle, Willis 25:170
Fiddler, George A. 10:52; 20:249
Fiddler, Louis 17:99
Fiddler, William F. 18:133
Fidelis, F. 19:281
Fidgett, Oswell 7:71
Fidler, Conroy 20:123
Fidler, James 9:118; 27:45
Fidler, W. 15:7
Fidler, William C. 8:15
Fiecharch, --- 19:274
Fiedero, Theodore 16:31
Fiedler, L. E. H. 22:76
Fiedler, Valentine 10:112; 20:249
Fiedman, J. 7:26
Fiedner, Theodore 13:22
Fieerne, James 18:426
Fiefer, J. D. 11:29
Fieg, Henry 16:31
Fiegely, Samuel 12:55
Fiel, Geen 19:278
Fiel, Michael 7:94
Field, Albin 21:329
Field, Barrett 6:12
Field, Benjamin F. 15:86
Field, Calvin S. 16:84
Field, Charles A. 17:359
Field, Charles C. 21:329
Field, Charles H. 21:329

Field, Christopher 25:33
Field, Daniel H. 17:20
Field, Dennis 1:191
Field, E. O. 18:29
Field, E. W. 19:13
Field, Ed. C. 18:276
Field, Edwin 16:84
Field, Francis M. 21:99
Field, G. W. 25:33
Field, George A. 17:266
Field, George W. 22:191; 23:65
Field, Green 9:176
Field, H. A. 12:122; 15:123; 27:42
Field, Henry 19:13
Field, J. 1:129; 21:121, 201
Field, J. F. 25:296
Field, J. P. 1:131
Field, Jacob 3:69
Field, James 25:296
Field, John 7:122
Field, John A. 20:151
Field, John E. 20:192
Field, Joseph 8:15; 26:27
Field, Julius 12:20
Field, Mark L. 9:71
Field, Morris 13:109
Field, Patrick 25:33
Field, Richard 23:29
Field, Richard W. 19:163
Field, S. 3:69
Field, S. L. 18:395
Field, Taimor 18:236
Field, Thomas 11:386
Field, Thomas J. 22:191
Field, W. 14:59
Field, Walter O. 22:279
Field, William 7:94; 22:512
Field, William F. 11:146
Fielder, Benjamin 7:122
Fielder, James 8:15; 18:133
Fielder, William R. 22:29
Fieldhouse, H. 1:34
Fielding, --- 3:70
Fielding, Andrew 7:94
Fielding, Edward 23:29
Fielding, John 11:202
Fielding, Philip 10:160
Fieldman, W. 25:276
Fields, A. E. 1:34
Fields, Alexander 17:409
Fields, Alexander A. 22:121
Fields, Andrew 7:122
Fields, Augustus C. 11:84
Fields, B. 18:82
Fields, C. 1:129; 16:190

Fields, Charles 11:122; 13:63; 19:68
Fields, Charles B. 13:22; 16:32
Fields, Charles W. 7:94
Fields, D. 1:129
Fields, D. B. 15:196
Fields, D. C. 23:142
Fields, Daniel C. 11:181
Fields, E. 3:69
Fields, Edgar 11:261
Fields, Esquire 22:501
Fields, F. 3:69; 13:109; 20:154
Fields, F. M. 12:153
Fields, Francis M. 17:210
Fields, G. 1:130
Fields, George 21:127
Fields, George W. 22:76
Fields, Harvey 23:142
Fields, Haywood G. 17:352
Fields, Henry 13:22; 16:190; 22:76
Fields, Isaac 11:202
Fields, J. 16:190
Fields, J. F. 7:74
Fields, J. H. 18:29; 25:32
Fields, J. M. 11:29
Fields, J. W. 20:145
Fields, James 4:65; 7:77; 9:200; 12:48; 15:66; 19:290; 22:121
Fields, James H. 23:142
Fields, Jeremiah 24:59
Fields, John 9:80; 10:208; 14:165; 22:512
Fields, John S. 15:55
Fields, Joseph 7:94; 9:80; 18:133
Fields, Joseph S. 9:241
Fields, Lancaster 20:35
Fields, Leander J. 22:462
Fields, Leonard 22:142
Fields, Leroy 9:42; 26:123
Fields, Lindsey 17:175
Fields, Lott 17:247
Fields, Lyman 12:99
Fields, Mathew 22:479
Fields, Miles 9:80
Fields, Myron H. 15:34
Fields, N. 3:70
Fields, Nelson 17:400
Fields, Orin 11:398
Fields, P. 9:154
Fields, Palmer 26:28
Fields, Patrick 22:191
Fields, Robert 10:112; 16:190; 20:249
Fields, Samuel 27:42
Fields, W. 17:432

Fields, Washington
25:170
Fields, Westley 26:160
Fields, Wiley 24:152
Fields, William 8:69;
17:236; 26:160
Fields, William H. 21:224
Fieldstad, Martin 22:279
Fieldstadt, Andrew 22:279
Fiender, Isaac 11:419
Fieres, H. 15:105
Fiero, S. A. 1:131
Fiers, James 1:33
Fiery, J. 14:9; 16:267
Fiesmier, John 7:26
Fiess, B. 8:63; 26:160
Fiess, Stephen 23:189
Fiest, Harrison 16:32
Fiester, Gabriel H. 20:145
Fife, Amos 21:330
Fife, J. 3:70
Fife, J. M. 11:240
Fife, James 9:230; 20:249
Fife, John 22:334
Fife, Newton 22:404
Fifeld, John H. 10:113
Fifer, A. 14:165
Fifer, Alex 1:34
Fifer, Charles 3:70
Fifer, Clayborne 11:202
Fifer, David 22:424
Fifer, M. 25:320
Fifer, Valentine 10:148;
18:49
Fiffe, Benjamin 26:211
Fiffey, H. 3:70
Fifield, George E. 10:16
Fifield, Joseph 20:29
Fifield, T. 25:33
Fifield, William E. 21:25
Figaet, John 9:21
Figert, Henry 1:33
Figg, Anthony 6:28
Figg, Daniel 11:105
Figger, S. 1:129
Figgins, Daniel 22:76
Figgins, W. 21:121
Figgord, William H. 5:51
Fight, William A. 22:29
Figley, A. M. 22:191
Figley, T. W. 1:32
Figlos, Salem 7:26
Figne, James 13:22
Fignet, John 18:320
Fike, Chauncey 22:191
Fike, S. 1:130; 19:13
Fike, Tobias 3:70
Fike, W. P. 14:165
Fike, Wesley 23:142
Filben, T. 14:297; 17:470
Filbert, T. J. 11:147

Filbert, Wilson 7:26
Filbrick, --- 19:68
Filbrick, J. A. 14:165
Filbrin, Martin 17:14
Filbur, T. 27:46
Filby, A. 3:70
Filby, W. 22:191
Filby, William 22:478
Filch, G. P. 3:70
Filch, Michael 18:206
Filcom, Nelson 18:133
Filds, R. G. 3:70
Filds, Thomas J. 17:202
File, Amos 7:94
File, C. 3:70
File, C. E. 9:31
File, Napoleon B. 27:45
File, R. 3:70
File, Samuel 26:27
File, W. M. 23:29
Fileds, W. H. 18:66
Filer, J. H. 3:70
Filer, John 7:49
Files, John G. 23:29
Fileston, Ebenezer B. 7:26
Filey, F. 12:8
Filfield, John H. 20:249
Filharty, T. 1:34
Filiob, Harvey 22:191
Filker, Charles 20:17
Filkins, Anthony 15:81
Filkins, Cornelius R.
21:238
Filkins, Nolan 10:52;
20:249
Filkins, Stephen 19:13
Filkner, Tipton 11:261
Fillbrick, --- 12:168
Fillbrook, John H. 9:118
Fille, Frank 20:181
Fillebrown, H. G. 15:318
Filler, H. C. 21:99
Filler, Joseph 21:330
Filler, N. 13:63
Fillers, L. 14:59
Fillers, T. V. 17:252
Filletsor, Orlando M.
12:20
Filley, Hiram 20:106
Filley, J. M. 14:59
Filley, Jeremiah 23:142
Filley, Jesse 20:249
Filley, Sol 18:236; 26:28
Filley, William 10:113;
20:249
Fillhauer, William 16:292
Fillinger, F. M. 22:191
Fillinger, Samuel A.
23:279
Fillis, George 15:196
Fillman, J. 13:77

Fillman, Judah 16:190
Fillman, Lewis 8:38;
26:159
Fillmore, Albert N.
21:117
Fillmore, Lemuel 22:142
Fillmore, O. W. 10:160
Fillmore, Seymore L.
21:91
Filloon, Abington J. 24:50
Fillowe, H. 25:32
Fillport, Isaac 7:122
Fillson, Robert F. 23:87
Filly, Jesse 10:52
Filly, John 10:34
Filmore, Augustus P.
22:29
Filmore, C. H. 22:479
Filmore, L. 8:48
Filmore, Milton 18:434
Films, William 4:23
Filoszimmans, William F.
18:395
Filpot, M. 17:272
Filsan, George M. 22:450
Filson, Charley 18:217
Filson, H. H. 26:160
Filson, J. W. 10:95
Filson, James 18:217;
22:76
Filson, Newton B. 22:29
Filson, Thomas 21:25
Filtner, George B. 22:424
Filton, Edmund 24:193
Filton, Frederick 16:32
Filton, H. 16:190
Filtz, Edward 14:165
Filun, John G. 12:20
Filyer, William 3:70
Fimple, P. C. 19:317
Fin, J. H. 19:68
Finah, Eugene 13:22
Finbeq, J. 19:68
Fince, Henry 1:32
Fincer, John 22:191
Finch, A. 3:70
Finch, A. L. 25:32
Finch, Allen 23:309
Finch, Aurelius 10:113;
20:249
Finch, C. 3:70; 7:26
Finch, Charles 22:298
Finch, Daniel 16:32
Finch, Dennis 22:351
Finch, Dorsan 4:24
Finch, E. 7:49
Finch, F. A. 15:355; 19:68
Finch, F. W. 3:70
Finch, Francis 21:117
Finch, Frederick 24:93
Finch, G. H. 16:118

Finch, George 17:404
Finch, H. 3:70
Finch, H. O. 22:233
Finch, Hiliard 22:298
Finch, Hy 3:70
Finch, I. M. 25:32
Finch, Irvin M. 2:11
Finch, J. 22:250
Finch, J. B. 3:70
Finch, J. K. P. 9:52
Finch, James 3:70; 14:59,
    281; 15:7
Finch, John 7:94; 8:84;
    10:16
Finch, John H. 20:249
Finch, Joseph T. 21:25
Finch, Laban 18:174
Finch, Leander C. 7:26
Finch, Louis 9:80; 26:27
Finch, Miles 18:82; 20:29
Finch, Nathan 12:20
Finch, Newton 18:236;
    26:28
Finch, Parks 22:298
Finch, R. 15:22; 16:77
Finch, Reuben 11:202
Finch, Richard D. 12:62
Finch, S. B. 4:24
Finch, S. M. 9:66
Finch, Samuel A. 16:190
Finch, Samuel M. 9:80
Finch, Samuel N. 26:26
Finch, Stephen M. 18:276
Finch, Thomas 13:22
Finch, W. 14:59; 19:13;
    25:170
Finch, William 4:24
Finch, William H. 25:170
Finch, Willington 11:29
Finchbaugh, William
    14:165
Fincher, Henry 17:397
Fincher, J. 11:386
Fincher, John B. 22:250
Finchey, Isaac 9:70
Finchum, William 13:88
Finck, Jasper 8:15
Finck, W. H. 19:13
Fincks, William 21:330
Fincucan, John 3:70
Findale, George W. 2:11
Findell, G. W. 25:34
Findlater, H. 3:70
Findle, Frederic 18:189
Findler, Gideon 9:176
Findley, Andrew 3:70
Findley, Charles W.
    23:260
Findley, Christopher C.
    10:113; 20:249
Findley, I. 14:59

Findley, James A. 21:10
Findley, John 14:315
Findley, L. C. 1:32
Findley, Logan 11:203
Findley, Russel H. 8:117
Findley, Thomas 23:11
Findley, William 17:395
Findley, William A. 22:29
Findling, Phillip 23:142
Findly, William 20:46
Fine, Owen W. 24:61
Finegal, John C. 22:142
Finegan, B. 13:81
Finegan, C. 14:60
Finegan, Daniel 16:190
Finegin, P. 3:70
Finehout, Daniel C. 10:52;
    20:249
Finele, Daniel 13:22
Finer, Peter 21:270
Fineral, Patrick 21:330
Finerty, John 13:22
Finerty, Owen 7:49
Fines, L. D. 22:191
Finet, Francis 13:22
Finey, --- 19:68
Finey, John W. 9:80
Finfrock, A. 1:131
Finger, J. 14:165
Finger, James 11:423
Finger, W. 14:255
Fingley, John 3:70
Fingley, Richard 19:163
Fingley, S. 3:70
Fingusson, J. H. 19:277
Finical, J. 16:292
Finigan, John 7:16
Finigan, P. 25:170
Finigan, Stephen 15:311
Finisty, Thomas 22:250
Fink, Alonzo 7:94
Fink, Amelia F. 27:43
Fink, Eli 4:23
Fink, Emanuel 12:122;
    15:123
Fink, F. 18:13
Fink, G. 1:130
Fink, George 17:423;
    24:170
Fink, H. B. 4:23
Fink, H. K. 18:133
Fink, Henry 14:165;
    17:78; 23:189
Fink, J. 7:49
Fink, J. G. 20:249
Fink, J. P. 3:70
Fink, John 9:80; 11:261;
    18:49
Fink, L. 3:70
Fink, M. A. 7:94
Fink, Martin 7:94

Fink, Michael 20:154
Fink, P. 14:297; 17:479
Fink, Peter 3:70
Fink, R. 27:46
Fink, Seth 7:94
Fink, Thomas W. 27:45
Fink, W. H. 19:251
Fink, William 7:26; 9:16;
    14:60; 17:79
Finke, T. 16:190
Finkenwinter, Jacob 4:24
Finker, Benjamin F.
    10:151
Finker, Joseph 6:16; 18:82
Finkin, Henry 15:2
Finkle, Barton 24:18
Finkle, C. 19:251
Finkler, Louis 13:22
Finkmer, Benjamin F.
    10:178
Finkpener, Charles 12:92;
    16:292
Finks, John 20:249
Finkstine, W. 3:70
Finkum, William H. 8:15;
    18:133
Finlan, James 3:70
Finland, Robert 11:125
Finlay, George 25:320
Finlay, Samuel 22:10
Finlay, Webster 22:191
Finlayson, Henry 13:22
Finler, Thomas 15:359
Finley, A. 3:70
Finley, Angus 6:24
Finley, Anthony 16:32
Finley, Daniel 18:29
Finley, E. 14:60
Finley, F. 17:51
Finley, G. W. 7:94
Finley, George 6:30
Finley, H. 14:60
Finley, J. W. 18:395
Finley, James 6:24;
    13:109
Finley, James A. 22:298
Finley, James W. 9:42
Finley, John 1:33; 13:88;
    21:121; 22:501
Finley, John H. 1:33
Finley, Newton 6:16;
    18:82
Finley, Robert 10:172;
    19:163
Finley, Robert E. 8:105
Finley, Thomas 10:52;
    20:249
Finley, W. 15:196
Finley, William 8:63
Finlin, J. 16:94
Finlow, John 2:10

Finly, William 15:81
Finman, Azro 17:265
Finn, Florentine 23:142
Finn, Franklin 10:52;
20:249
Finn, John 20:249; 22:450
Finn, L. 1:131
Finn, M. 15:34
Finn, Marcus R. 21:187
Finn, Michael 12:64;
15:34
Finn, P. 24:63
Finn, Patrick 20:189;
23:121
Finn, Stephen 11:29
Finnasson, William
21:330
Finnefrock, J. J. 16:118
Finnefrock, Samuel
16:118
Finnegan, --- 15:173
Finnegan, J. B. 21:330
Finnegan, James 18:133
Finnegan, Peter 10:113;
20:249
Finnegan, Stephen 19:68
Finnegan, William 13:109
Finnel, --- 16:190
Finnel, Fontain 9:34
Finnel, J. 11:29
Finnel, James 21:242
Finnel, Robert M. 17:147
Finnell, G. W. 1:129
Finner, David A. 11:381
Finner, Files 21:330
Finnerly, P. 3:70
Finnerty, John 16:32
Finnerty, P. 14:165
Finnerty, Patrick 12:20
Finnesy, R. 1:129
Finney, --- 15:364
Finney, A. T. 10:209
Finney, Clayborn 11:202
Finney, E. D. 16:368
Finney, H. 1:129
Finney, Herbert 6:16;
18:82
Finney, Ira J. 15:11
Finney, James B. 9:80
Finney, James N. 23:142
Finney, James W. 22:423
Finney, John 14:333
Finney, John W. 26:27
Finney, Michael 19:13
Finney, Owen 21:248
Finney, R. L. 25:170
Finney, William J. 7:94
Finnick, Charles 22:298
Finnick, Joseph 12:49
Finnigan, G. 12:166
Finnigan, J. 25:320

Finnman, B. 16:190
Finns, --- 15:34
Finny, Robert L. 5:15
Finska, August 9:52
Finsley, J. 21:25
Finson, Leu 8:105
Finstine, Emanuel 8:100
Fint, George 11:261
Finton, John 2:11; 25:34
Finton, Josiah 22:76
Finton, M. 25:170
Finton, Thomas 3:70
Finton, W. 1:130
Fiper, Pleasant 21:194
Fipett, C. C. 12:140
Fippen, Lot 11:147
Fipscomb, G. 9:52
Firbish, H. S. 9:142
Firecoat, Henry 8:84
Fireman, George 12:49
Fireman, Jeremiah 24:18
Fires, General Jackson
17:51
Firestine, Emanuel
17:460; 24:158
Firestone, --- 3:70
Firestone, C. 8:63
Firestone, John A. 9:118
Firestone, Joseph 13:109
Firil, Daniel 18:420
Firing, Samuel 25:32
Firk, I. 3:70
Firk, J. 14:165
Firkland, Robert F. 18:133
Firman, E. C. 1:131
Firman, H. 2:11
Firman, J. 27:43
Firman, Jacob 5:38
Firman, V. 3:70
Firmeny, John 7:49
Firre, William 11:181
Firrimerman, C. 25:170
Firsetine, John R. 20:249
First, Henry 10:52
Firth, Edward A. 24:99
Firth, George 13:109
Firth, John 22:191
Firth, R. E. 9:142; 27:43
Firth, Thomas 13:22
Firth, Thomas J. 16:32
Firtmer, Peter 27:46
Firtz, Jo 13:109
Firy, William 22:30
Fiscell, Albert 4:24
Fisch, Frederick 17:79
Fischer, D. 3:70
Fischer, Daniel 19:163
Fischer, John C. 24:77
Fischner, D. 3:70
Fiscus, Aaron 17:79
Fiscus, Jacob 21:224

Fiser, G. W. 11:29
Fish, --- 3:70
Fish, A. G. 20:174
Fish, A. H. 16:118
Fish, A. W. 9:176; 19:237
Fish, Alonzo L. 21:330
Fish, Austin O. 15:196
Fish, Charles 15:278;
25:170
Fish, Charles E. 14:165
Fish, Charles S. 5:15
Fish, Charles W. 3:70
Fish, Christian 9:16
Fish, Cornelius 7:94
Fish, D. L. 1:32
Fish, David K. 21:330
Fish, E. 9:109
Fish, E. C. 1:130
Fish, E. R. 9:142; 27:43
Fish, Ephraim 22:30, 423
Fish, Evan 17:415
Fish, Francis 4:24
Fish, G. W. 19:237
Fish, George 8:84; 18:29
Fish, George M. 24:158
Fish, George W. 22:478
Fish, H. 21:25
Fish, Harry 15:34
Fish, Henry 11:303;
12:64; 15:80, 289,
352; 16:11, 190
Fish, Henry C. 11:59
Fish, Henry D. 14:165
Fish, Henry S. 17:109
Fish, Henry T. 22:142
Fish, Hiram 15:123
Fish, Horace 7:26
Fish, Horatio N. 5:15
Fish, Isaac 11:386;
18:236; 26:28
Fish, J. 3:70
Fish, J. B. 14:60
Fish, J. H. 9:176
Fish, J. L. 10:144
Fish, J. M. 23:29
Fish, James 27:46
Fish, John 9:16; 10:9;
17:164
Fish, John J. 19:163
Fish, John M. 21:99
Fish, John W. 15:196
Fish, Joseph 11:145
Fish, Joseph H. 9:118;
27:44
Fish, L. D. 9:220; 18:366
Fish, L. V. 3:70
Fish, Leonard 8:120
Fish, Lorenzo D. 17:443;
24:158
Fish, M. 15:196
Fish, Nathaniel 25:170

Fish, Oscar P. 16:190
Fish, R. W. 7:74; 25:296
Fish, Robert 21:330
Fish, S. V. 4:24
Fish, Samuel 15:313;
 19:68
Fish, Sylvester 23:29
Fish, W. 3:70
Fish, William 3:70; 4:24;
 21:330; 22:191
Fish, William E. 10:160
Fish, William M. 17:359
Fishback, Benjamin
 11:202
Fishback, H. 17:175
Fishback, John W.
 10:113; 20:249
Fishback, Wash 17:131;
 24:193
Fishburn, Jacob 20:185;
 22:191
Fishel, Eben B. 17:79
Fisher, --- 11:261; 19:329;
 23:292
Fisher, A. 1:130; 7:26;
 14:60; 15:22;
 16:190; 17:254;
 21:25
Fisher, A. C. 12:20
Fisher, A. E. 27:45
Fisher, A. W. 16:32
Fisher, Adam 7:94;
 10:155; 11:146;
 19:163
Fisher, Adolphus 12:64;
 15:34
Fisher, Albert 12:69
Fisher, Albert W. 26:27
Fisher, Alex 19:290
Fisher, Alexander 9:200
Fisher, Amos 22:161
Fisher, Andrew 8:100;
 10:52; 17:462;
 20:249; 26:145
Fisher, Andrew J. 22:424;
 24:177
Fisher, Anthony 21:330
Fisher, August 7:94; 9:42
Fisher, Augustus 14:165;
 26:123
Fisher, B. A. 24:18
Fisher, B. M. 3:70
Fisher, Barnard 4:24
Fisher, C. 3:70
Fisher, C. B. 3:70
Fisher, C. M. 16:11
Fisher, C. P. 3:71
Fisher, C. U. 3:70
Fisher, Charles 3:70;
 21:199
Fisher, Conrad 3:71

Fisher, D. 3:70
Fisher, D. F. 19:163
Fisher, D. W. 21:25
Fisher, Daniel 3:70;
 11:125; 22:77
Fisher, Daniel E. 11:186
Fisher, David 17:317;
 25:275
Fisher, David T. 10:176
Fisher, Deidrich 17:20
Fisher, Dort George
 18:133
Fisher, E. 19:68
Fisher, E. B. 23:142
Fisher, E. D. 5:15; 25:170
Fisher, E. I. 9:234
Fisher, E. S. 1:128
Fisher, Elijah 22:77
Fisher, Ezra R. 12:69;
 15:11
Fisher, F. 11:401; 13:109
Fisher, Felix 10:113;
 20:250
Fisher, Francis H. 20:7
Fisher, Francis W. 9:34
Fisher, Franklin 10:95
Fisher, Fred 24:93
Fisher, Frederick 1:31;
 4:24
Fisher, G. 1:129
Fisher, G. A. 1:129
Fisher, G. W. 1:33
Fisher, George 7:122;
 8:15; 13:22; 14:165;
 16:32; 21:330;
 25:170
Fisher, George D. 11:146
Fisher, George H. 23:29
Fisher, George W. 14:165;
 21:224; 23:184
Fisher, H. 3:70, 71;
 14:165; 16:368;
 21:25; 22:191;
 25:170
Fisher, H. D. 25:269
Fisher, Hamilton 7:122
Fisher, Harris D. 16:368
Fisher, Harry 5:15
Fisher, Henry 16:279;
 22:298
Fisher, Henry F. 25:33
Fisher, Hiram 7:74; 21:99;
 25:296
Fisher, Hushel 22:112
Fisher, Isaac 25:170
Fisher, J. 1:34; 8:101;
 9:109; 11:231, 261;
 13:88; 14:9, 60, 241;
 15:173; 16:368;
 25:31, 170
Fisher, J. B. 12:8

Fisher, J. C. 15:165
Fisher, J. D. 13:109
Fisher, J. E. 12:153
Fisher, J. F. 3:70
Fisher, J. H. 14:60
Fisher, J. M. 1:129
Fisher, J. W. 15:332;
 19:68
Fisher, Jackson 7:122
Fisher, Jacob 1:33; 10:52;
 20:250; 21:187;
 22:191
Fisher, James 9:161;
 11:261; 17:79;
 18:426
Fisher, James H. 17:20
Fisher, James S. 13:109
Fisher, Jason C. 19:227
Fisher, Jeremiah 11:59
Fisher, Jesse 22:191
Fisher, Joel R. 5:15
Fisher, John 1:34; 3:70;
 4:24; 5:15; 8:15;
 9:34, 106, 176;
 10:113; 14:130;
 16:292; 17:502;
 18:133, 292; 19:251;
 20:250; 22:76;
 23:121; 24:8, 50;
 26:98
Fisher, John C. 11:145
Fisher, John H. 6:16;
 17:236; 18:82
Fisher, John R. 23:98
Fisher, John S. 11:303
Fisher, Joseph 8:15;
 10:91, 113; 18:133;
 20:250
Fisher, Joseph C. 24:50
Fisher, Joshua 17:460;
 24:157
Fisher, Julius 11:146
Fisher, L. 3:71
Fisher, L. J. 1:34
Fisher, Lawrence 10:113;
 20:250
Fisher, Leander 18:29
Fisher, Leonard 14:235
Fisher, Lewis 12:49;
 13:22; 24:38
Fisher, Louis 9:220;
 17:175; 18:366;
 19:68
Fisher, M. 14:237; 16:190
Fisher, M. P. 3:70
Fisher, Marion 20:250
Fisher, Martin 12:148
Fisher, Michael 22:76
Fisher, N. G. 11:100
Fisher, Nathan 5:39

Fisher, Nicholas 8:15; 18:133
Fisher, Nick 27:46
Fisher, Noah 8:15; 18:133
Fisher, O. 25:170
Fisher, Omil L. 11:302
Fisher, Otis 5:15
Fisher, Otto 16:11
Fisher, Owen 14:60
Fisher, P. O. 17:33
Fisher, Paul 4:24
Fisher, Pela 4:24
Fisher, Peter 12:55; 22:191
Fisher, Philip 11:240; 22:423
Fisher, Phillip A. 7:26
Fisher, R. F. 9:220; 11:100
Fisher, R. R. 21:290
Fisher, Randolph 10:16
Fisher, Reuben 13:22; 17:175
Fisher, Robert 9:21; 18:206; 23:107
Fisher, Robert H. 21:25
Fisher, Rufus 25:296
Fisher, S. 1:32; 19:251; 21:187, 247
Fisher, Samford 7:62
Fisher, Samuel 10:176; 14:165; 19:163
Fisher, Simon 9:21; 18:305; 26:97
Fisher, Sol 25:296
Fisher, Solomon 25:320
Fisher, Solomon J. 9:165
Fisher, Sylvester 11:59
Fisher, T. 1:130; 13:88
Fisher, Theodore 21:330
Fisher, Thomas 11:60; 19:13; 20:399
Fisher, Thomas C. 21:194
Fisher, Thomas H. 1:33
Fisher, Uriah 22:76
Fisher, W. 1:31, 130; 3:70, 71; 18:82; 23:142
Fisher, W. F. 15:196
Fisher, W. H. 11:145
Fisher, W. M. 18:217
Fisher, William 6:10, 16; 11:60; 12:49, 56; 13:22, 109; 15:335; 16:32; 18:82, 236; 19:68; 22:30; 26:28
Fisher, William A. 22:76; 23:142
Fisher, William G. 1:31
Fisher, William H. 20:112; 24:50

Fisher, William M. 10:91; 13:22; 20:250
Fisher, William O. 18:292; 26:98
Fisher, Wilson A. 9:34
Fisherdeck, J. S. 21:330
Fisherman, G. 27:45
Fisherman, Garrett 9:130; 27:44
Fisherman, N. 5:38
Fisherman, N. J. 25:170
Fishless, John W. 10:113
Fishman, Charles 12:95
Fishwater, George 15:196
Fisk, Alexander 20:183
Fisk, Ansel A. 25:33
Fisk, Charles 9:176
Fisk, Charles S. 25:170
Fisk, Clifton E. 11:401
Fisk, E. P. 18:82
Fisk, Eldridge 6:14
Fisk, Erastus 13:22
Fisk, G. 14:277
Fisk, G. W. 12:99
Fisk, George A. 17:33
Fisk, George N. 22:142
Fisk, George W. 9:176
Fisk, Gilbert E. 23:186
Fisk, H. 3:71
Fisk, I. B. 3:71
Fisk, J. 3:71
Fisk, J. H. 19:237
Fisk, James 22:404
Fisk, John 16:94; 25:33
Fisk, John D. 21:330
Fisk, John W. 10:52; 20:250
Fisk, M. W. 15:341; 16:368
Fisk, O. F. 13:63
Fisk, Richard 11:398
Fisk, Rossalas 7:94
Fisk, S. H. 10:16
Fisk, Samuel 7:94; 8:105
Fisk, Samuel B. 20:192
Fisk, W. B. 25:170
Fisk, Washington B. 5:15
Fisk, Wilbur H. 21:69
Fisk, William 11:261
Fisk, William E. 19:163
Fiske, Charles 19:251
Fiske, Edgar A. 16:84
Fiske, M. 12:8
Fiske, Nathan 15:278
Fisklin, Robert F. 8:15
Fismire, William 16:190
Fiss, E. G. 19:68
Fissel, Elias 11:15
Fissell, Randolph 11:386
Fissler, N. 16:190
Fist, C. 3:71

Fist, W. P. 3:71
Fiste, H. 11:240
Fister, E. A. 9:176
Fister, F. 3:71
Fister, Franklin 15:123
Fister, John 7:94
Fister, Joseph 26:159
Fister, Otis S. 9:176
Fisti, August 15:355
Fit, A. 15:151
Fitch, A. 3:71
Fitch, Adrian 23:143
Fitch, C. 3:71; 19:251
Fitch, C. P. 3:71
Fitch, Charles E. 26:138, 145
Fitch, Charles P. 4:24
Fitch, Christian 9:176
Fitch, Daniel 9:130; 27:44
Fitch, E. M. 18:338
Fitch, E. W. 9:102
Fitch, Edward 13:109
Fitch, Edwin 22:191
Fitch, F. 3:71
Fitch, George 9:176; 19:286
Fitch, Henry 17:33
Fitch, Henry M. 20:102
Fitch, Irvin L. 15:196
Fitch, J. C. 11:125
Fitch, James 9:118; 27:45
Fitch, Jasper 18:133
Fitch, John 7:57; 20:22, 123
Fitch, John F. 22:279
Fitch, Joseph 17:352; 23:143
Fitch, Luther W. 4:24
Fitch, M. J. 21:109
Fitch, Marcus E. 20:112
Fitch, Morris E. 23:283
Fitch, N. 17:175
Fitch, P. 14:60
Fitch, Patrick 7:26
Fitch, Robert 8:84; 20:85
Fitch, S. H. 1:94
Fitch, Samuel 19:68; 22:462
Fitch, Samuel A. 15:291
Fitch, W. 1:130
Fitch, W. A. 10:95
Fitch, W. F. 3:71
Fitch, William 1:32; 17:14
Fitchell, David 6:12
Fitchett, Andrew 16:190
Fitchett, D. 18:82
Fitchett, E. 25:170
Fitchett, Edward 5:39
Fitchett, O. 19:68
Fitchler, August 8:15
Fitchman, Abraham 12:49

Fitchor, Samuel 15:352
Fite, Andrew 10:113; 20:250
Fite, J. 11:339
Fite, John R. 21:137
Fite, Leoman L. 18:133
Fite, Leonard L. 8:15
Fite, Nicholas 8:105
Fite, Samuel 9:80
Fitemaster, James W. 17:259
Fitey, Samuel 22:191
Fither, C. 3:71
Fithian, David C. 22:77
Fithian, H. C. 11:181
Fitlebrown, H. C. 19:69
Fitse, --- 3:71
Fitsh, C. D. 4:24
Fitsick, O. S. 15:309
Fitspatrick, Pat 20:250
Fitsymonds, Patrick 9:34
Fitterly, John W. 22:404
Fitters, Isaac 11:29
Fitting, S. 11:60
Fittle, Clint 21:12
Fitts, Charles A. 16:8
Fitts, James F. 21:206
Fitugen, William 11:303
Fity, J. L. 21:330
Fitz, --- 3:71
Fitz, Isaac 9:159
Fitz, J. D. 1:131
Fitz, James 15:16
Fitz, Richard R. 13:22
Fitz Gerald, --- 8:116
Fitz-Patrick, Michael 13:109
Fitzborn, --- 1:34
Fitzenny, Ernel 14:165
Fitzer, Jeremiah 21:25
Fitzer, S. H. 25:296
Fitzer, S. T. 7:81
Fitzgerald, --- 3:71; 13:109
Fitzgerald, A. 14:165
Fitzgerald, Andrew M. 19:329
Fitzgerald, B. 22:191
Fitzgerald, Charles E. 4:24
FitzGerald, Christopher 9:156
Fitzgerald, D. H. 14:165, 255
Fitzgerald, E. 22:299
Fitzgerald, Edward 8:15; 18:133; 21:270; 22:10
Fitzgerald, Frederick 14:165

Fitzgerald, George W. 5:15; 25:170
Fitzgerald, H. 3:71
Fitzgerald, Henry 21:330
Fitzgerald, I. 3:71
Fitzgerald, Irene 24:107
Fitzgerald, J. 7:26; 9:176; 13:79; 16:190; 18:236; 19:237; 20:85; 25:170; 26:28
Fitzgerald, James 1:32; 3:71; 23:11
Fitzgerald, James C. 24:18
Fitzgerald, John 5:15; 8:48; 9:16; 11:181; 12:20; 15:27; 17:363; 20:180; 21:99; 22:77; 23:121; 25:33
Fitzgerald, Jonathan 17:79
Fitzgerald, Joseph 17:20
Fitzgerald, Leonard O. 22:462
Fitzgerald, M. 1:130; 3:71; 14:165; 21:109
Fitzgerald, Maurice 22:397
Fitzgerald, Michael 5:15; 7:94; 18:13; 23:65, 128; 25:170
Fitzgerald, N. 3:71
Fitzgerald, N. H. 25:170
Fitzgerald, Owen 13:22; 16:32
Fitzgerald, P. 1:34, 131; 7:26; 14:60
Fitzgerald, Patrick 22:191
Fitzgerald, R. 15:196
Fitzgerald, R. D. 11:332
Fitzgerald, Richard 22:279
Fitzgerald, S. 1:129
Fitzgerald, Squire 23:184
Fitzgerald, T. 1:129
Fitzgerald, Thomas 3:71
Fitzgerald, W. 1:128, 131; 27:46
Fitzgerald, William 8:48, 117; 14:297; 17:474; 19:315; 20:183; 21:51; 24:18
Fitzgerald, William H. H. 25:33
Fitzgibbon, Thomas 3:71
Fitzgibbons, James 26:211
Fitzgibbons, John 1:32
Fitzgibbons, Patrick 15:55
Fitzgrober, William 7:26
Fitzhenry, Robert 12:20
Fitzherbert, Samuel 7:94
Fitzhorn, James 14:166
Fitzhue, W. M. 27:42

Fitzhugh, --- 11:15
Fitzhugh, F. 8:15
Fitzinger, Gideon 25:170
Fitzinger, L. B. 8:63
Fitzinger, Samuel 16:118
Fitzmaurice, Thomas 21:330
Fitzner, John 7:26; 16:94
Fitzpatrick, --- 14:166; 19:69
Fitzpatrick, B. 16:190
Fitzpatrick, Cornelious 15:197
Fitzpatrick, Dennis 20:123
Fitzpatrick, Edward 22:142
Fitzpatrick, G. W. 26:160
Fitzpatrick, George W. 22:77
Fitzpatrick, H. A. 9:220
Fitzpatrick, Hugh 13:22
Fitzpatrick, J. 1:129; 5:15; 7:49; 11:240; 22:191
Fitzpatrick, James 3:71; 10:160; 18:272; 24:58
Fitzpatrick, James H. 10:113; 20:250
Fitzpatrick, John 4:24; 8:15; 14:166; 15:55, 263; 18:133, 284; 21:109; 22:404; 24:77; 26:134
FitzPatrick, John B. 15:347
Fitzpatrick, Joseph 19:13
Fitzpatrick, K. D. 1:128
Fitzpatrick, Luke 20:123
Fitzpatrick, M. 3:71
Fitzpatrick, Marion 24:166
Fitzpatrick, Mathias 22:450
Fitzpatrick, Michael 15:66
Fitzpatrick, N. 25:32
Fitzpatrick, Nicholas 2:11
Fitzpatrick, O. 3:71; 10:179; 26:204
Fitzpatrick, P. 1:130; 15:291
Fitzpatrick, Patrick 10:52
Fitzpatrick, Pleasant C. 17:317
Fitzpatrick, S. 22:287
Fitzpatrick, Samuel 16:190
Fitzpatrick, T. 1:129; 21:330
Fitzpatrick, Thomas 11:146
Fitzpatrick, W. 14:166

Fitzpatrick, William 1:32;
18:109; 24:66
Fitzrof, R. 15:34
Fitzroy, Reginald 12:69
Fitzsimmons, --- 15:329;
19:69
Fitzsimmons, Henry 12:20
Fitzsimmons, J. M. 1:130
Fitzsimmons, J. P. 23:29
Fitzsimmons, James
21:330
Fitzsimmons, John 9:16;
13:109; 17:90
Fitzsimmons, Matthew
9:107
Fitzsimmons, P. 1:33
Fitzsimmons, R. 5:15
Fitzsimmons, Thomas
10:160; 19:163
Fitzsimmons, Thomas A.
23:29
Fitzsimmons, William
22:334
Fitzsimmons, William A.
7:64
Fitzsimonds, Joseph
15:302
Fitzsimons, P. 1:34;
15:291; 16:190
Fitzwater, --- 18:406
Fiun, Albert 19:13
Fix, Andrew 14:166
Fix, George 26:160
Fix, John 17:73
Fizer, D. G. 23:29
Fizone, Isaac 15:158
Fl---, George 18:49
Fla, Frederick 15:197
Flachman, Henry 24:66
Flack, F. Marion 20:123
Flack, Harvey 11:303
Flack, Isaac A. 4:24
Flack, James M. 23:87
Flack, John H. 20:123
Flack, P. E. 11:332
Flag, C. 3:71
Flag, I. P. 3:71
Flag, John W. 22:479
Flag, L. 3:71
Flag, Samuel 13:22
Flag, Thomas 15:335
Flagell, F. H. 23:143
Flager, John 1:34
Flagerty, J. 16:267
Flagg, C. 27:43
Flagg, Charles S. 4:24
Flagg, E. H. 1:131
Flagg, Frederick 14:166
Flagg, George 14:166
Flagg, J. A. 9:242
Flagg, Job B. 16:154

Flagg, Silas 14:60
Flagg, Thomas 10:98
Flagger, James 14:166
Flagle, M. M. 27:46
Flagler, William 3:71
Flaglor, Myron 11:286
Flaharty, John 24:18
Flaherty, D. O. 9:142;
27:43
Flaherty, J. 25:171
Flaherty, John 4:24; 7:94
Flaherty, Martin 13:22;
19:69
Flaherty, Patrick 10:16;
13:22
Flaherty, Timothy 22:334
Flaherty, William 8:15;
18:133; 21:10
Flaherty, William O. 8:15;
18:133
Flahty, David 7:9
Flaig, Thomas 19:69
Flaig---, J. 23:203
Flake, Albert 9:95; 26:27
Flake, George W. 21:129;
22:77
Flake, Matt 21:270
Flake, R. S. 23:306
Flake, S. E. 16:160
Flakefield, C. 19:163
Flamboy, C. L. 19:252
Flamburg, Martin 13:109
Flamer, Joseph 25:171
Flamlee, Jacob 25:171
Flammer, F. 15:66
Flammer, Thomas 12:69
Flamming, John 4:24
Flamming, Robert 4:24
Flamyan, William 18:133
Flanagan, Edward 26:27
Flanagan, Floyd 10:113
Flanagan, George 25:320
Flanagan, J. 3:71; 19:252;
25:171, 311
Flanagan, John 14:166;
19:252; 21:69
Flanagan, John D. 10:113
Flanagan, M. 27:45
Flanagan, Michael 17:109
Flanagan, Patrick 22:121
Flanagan, Thomas 10:113;
16:113; 20:250
Flanagan, William 1:32
Flanaghan, John 25:32
Flanagin, Michael 7:83
Flanchea, A. 14:281
Flander, Charles 26:27
Flander, Titus H. 20:250
Flandereau, J. S. 1:130
Flanders, Alex 12:8
Flanders, B. 19:227

Flanders, Charles H.
26:28
Flanders, Charles L. 3:71
Flanders, Charles W. 9:80
Flanders, E. C. 1:32
Flanders, George C.
22:404
Flanders, I. G. 3:71
Flanders, J. 25:171
Flanders, J. H. 14:166
Flanders, J. M. 1:34
Flanders, James F. 23:189
Flanders, Jefferson 8:39;
26:159
Flanders, John H. 21:88
Flanders, L. 25:34
Flanders, M. 15:318;
19:69
Flanders, Martin V. 1:34
Flanders, N. N. 9:80;
26:27
Flanders, O. 3:71; 14:255
Flanders, Oscar B.
10:113; 20:250
Flanders, R. F. 25:33
Flanders, S. 16:190
Flanders, Titus H. 10:113
Flanders, Volney R. 10:16
Flanders, W. E. 15:258
Flanders, W. W. 1:94
Flanders, Wesley 21:330
Flandrau, David 12:21
Flanegan, Charles 18:133
Flanegan, George 14:166
Flanegan, James R. 8:15
Flanegan, Lloyd 20:250
Flanegan, Michael 16:94
Flanery, John 16:190
Flanigan, Archibald
11:146
Flanigan, Charles 8:15
Flanigan, Edward 3:71
Flanigan, F. 10:113
Flanigan, Henry O. 7:49
Flanigan, John 9:176
Flanigan, John B. 9:80;
26:28
Flanigan, L. F. 11:59
Flanigan, M. 3:71; 16:190
Flanigan, Miles 11:92
Flanigan, P. 3:71
Flanigan, William 14:60
Flaning, W. 3:71
Flankers, Robert 11:146
Flannagan, James 4:24
Flannagan, John 15:173;
20:250
Flannagan, Timothy 4:24
Flannagan, Vincent 15:91
Flannaghan, P. 3:71

Flannegan, James R. 18:133
Flanner, Thomas 13:109
Flannery, E. 26:219
Flannery, F. F. 1:32
Flannery, John 15:305
Flannery, Pat 7:94
Flannery, Philip 9:42; 26:123
Flannery, William 18:206
Flanney, Michael 8:16
Flanney, P. 14:60
Flanney, William 8:84
Flannigan, Albert 17:397
Flannigan, B. 25:171
Flannigan, Bryant 20:178
Flannigan, Edward 9:80
Flannigan, F. 20:250
Flannigan, George 9:165
Flannigan, James 26:211
Flannigan, John 3:71; 5:15
Flannigan, Michael 21:330
Flannigan, P. 1:32; 22:334
Flannigan, Patrick 12:57; 17:276
Flannigan, R. 13:22
Flannigan, Richard 26:219
Flannigan, T. 1:131
Flannigan, William 8:16
Flanning, I. 3:71
Flanny, I. 14:60
Flansburg, Spencer 10:160; 19:163
Flanshburg, Henry C. 10:52
Flanshin, O. 14:281
Flarchmann, John 8:15
Flarer, David 10:52
Flarerty, O. 3:71
Flaris, Michael 11:29
Flarney, Michael 26:159
Flarun, J. 15:197
Flary, B. 22:479
Flasbury, N. 16:279
Flashburgh, M. 15:352
Flasher, James 25:271
Flashman, John T. 12:21
Flashouse, B. 3:71
Flat, Lewis 8:126
Flatch, A. 1:33
Flatcher, George E. 9:80
Flather, Henry 10:113
Flather, Henry G. 20:250
Flatoff, T. 3:71
Flatt, Lewis 11:286
Flatt, Robert S. 22:30
Flatter, Jesse 21:224
Flatter, Richard 21:51
Flatter, Robert 21:330

Flattich, George 1:32
Flaugherty, Anthony 12:20
Flaurance, J. A. 13:63
Flaut, G. 1:94
Flax, Samuel 11:146
Flaxmore, Charles 25:320
Fleage, Henry 12:69
Fleager, Henry A. 24:50
Fleaker, Charles H. 9:118
Fleck, Christopher 27:46
Fleck, David 10:9
Fleck, Frederick 14:166
Fleck, J. 1:34
Fleck, James 2:10; 25:33
Fleck, L. E. 25:171
Fleck, Luther E. 5:15
Fleckinger, J. 3:71
Fleckison, J. 3:71
Fleckner, John 13:22
Flee, W. 21:25
Fleece, Joseph B. 22:423
Fleech, Jacob B. 27:43
Fleeck, Mallon 14:166
Fleed, W. E. 14:60
Fleegell, Jacob B. 12:21
Fleegle, J. B. 9:142
Fleehr, --- 3:71
Fleek, Charles 10:113; 20:250
Fleek, R. 13:88
Fleek, William 15:55
Fleeman, William 22:501
Fleenboy, Charles L. 9:176
Fleener, William 8:48
Fleener, William F. 22:77
Fleeson, R. C. 14:166, 255
Fleet, Charles 15:318; 19:69
Fleet, Michael 19:252
Fleetwood, Ansel 21:242
Fleetwood, Charles 18:406
Fleetwood, William 22:77
Flegal, Z. P. 25:171
Fleigle, John 22:10
Fleivelling, N. 1:129
Flement, Arthur F. 22:462
Flement, Richard 21:330
Flemery, M. 3:71
Fleming, A. J. 7:74
Fleming, Alexander 8:105; 21:51
Fleming, Alfred 10:52; 20:250
Fleming, Alonzo 21:270
Fleming, Charles H. 10:172
Fleming, D. Boyd 11:59

Fleming, David 27:44
Fleming, E. 20:40
Fleming, E. B. 22:478
Fleming, Edmund 8:105; 26:27
Fleming, Edward 10:113; 20:250
Fleming, Elias 22:404
Fleming, F. 22:30
Fleming, Frederick 9:102
Fleming, G. W. 20:123
Fleming, Gabriel 21:270
Fleming, George 22:299
Fleming, Gottleib 18:133
Fleming, Gottlert 8:16
Fleming, H. P. 22:479
Fleming, Henry E. 22:30
Fleming, Isaac 10:52; 20:250
Fleming, J. 1:130; 9:52; 19:232; 23:29
Fleming, J. C. 20:56
Fleming, J. E. 14:166
Fleming, J. H. 14:265
Fleming, J. M. 11:381
Fleming, J. V. 20:179
Fleming, J. W. 14:288; 23:29; 25:296
Fleming, James 14:60
Fleming, James G. 22:30
Fleming, James W. 10:52; 20:250
Fleming, Jerry 24:18
Fleming, John 9:176; 13:22, 77, 129; 16:190; 18:440; 21:84; 22:30
Fleming, John C. 17:247
Fleming, John T. 26:27
Fleming, Joseph 11:147; 22:191
Fleming, Lewis G. 15:86
Fleming, M. 25:171
Fleming, Major 5:39
Fleming, Michael 22:519; 27:45
Fleming, Moses 17:397
Fleming, P. 3:71
Fleming, Patrick 22:30
Fleming, R. 20:250
Fleming, Reuben 9:230
Fleming, Robert Van 18:13
Fleming, S. B. 22:479
Fleming, Samuel 11:240; 22:299
Fleming, T. 19:163
Fleming, Thomas 15:16; 18:426
Fleming, W. W. 3:72

Fleming, Washington 9:207
Fleming, William 12:49; 27:44
Fleming, William A. 23:98
Fleming, William J. 13:57
Flemming, Charles H. 19:163
Flemming, David J. 7:26
Flemming, Davis 7:122; 9:130
Flemming, Frank 23:121
Flemming, Harris 17:131; 24:193
Flemming, J. E. 16:32
Flemming, J. R. 1:130
Flemming, J. W. 1:33
Flemming, James 4:24; 7:26; 18:236; 20:123; 23:290; 26:28
Flemming, John 1:31; 16:32
Flemming, Michael 9:118
Flemming, Muntry 3:71
Flemming, Parker 26:219
Flemming, Parker (Mrs.) 26:219
Flemming, R. 3:71
Flemming, Samuel 4:65
Flemming, Spencer 7:122
Flemming, William 7:122; 9:130
Flemming, William H. 20:40
Flemmings, Henry 7:26
Flemons, James P. 22:121
Flener, Samuel A. 11:386
Flenn, C. 1:129
Flenner, John 13:22
Fleppin, Isham 20:250
Flesher, B. 15:197
Flesher, H. G. 23:143
Fleshman, Eusebius 20:97
Flesuer, William 21:99
Fletch, John 18:426
Fletcher, A. 1:128; 20:250
Fletcher, A. J. 21:25
Fletcher, Abraham 16:143
Fletcher, Adelbert 13:22; 16:32
Fletcher, Andrew 21:253
Fletcher, Austin 10:52
Fletcher, Bailey M. 22:30
Fletcher, C. 12:167; 19:348
Fletcher, Charles 16:32; 27:44
Fletcher, Charles M. 9:130

Fletcher, D. A. 18:14
Fletcher, D. M. 21:330
Fletcher, Daniel 13:22; 21:270
Fletcher, Dennis 17:415; 24:152
Fletcher, Duncan 15:341; 16:368
Fletcher, Edmond 6:29
Fletcher, Ezra F. 4:24
Fletcher, Franklin 20:7
Fletcher, Frederick 12:21
Fletcher, G. E. 1:129
Fletcher, George 18:29; 23:143
Fletcher, George F. 12:140
Fletcher, George H. 22:462
Fletcher, H. C. 7:94
Fletcher, H. M. 8:48
Fletcher, Hall 22:299
Fletcher, Henry 22:299
Fletcher, Hiram M. 21:69
Fletcher, J. 3:71
Fletcher, J. B. 15:341; 16:368
Fletcher, J. K. 16:135
Fletcher, J. M. 10:151, 178; 12:21
Fletcher, Jackson 22:299
Fletcher, James 13:109; 16:113
Fletcher, James B. 9:96
Fletcher, John 9:34; 17:79; 18:292; 22:299; 26:98
Fletcher, John C. 11:92
Fletcher, John M. 18:206
Fletcher, John W. 22:30
Fletcher, Johnel 7:26
Fletcher, Jordan 21:270
Fletcher, Joseph E. 17:313
Fletcher, Josiah 11:395
Fletcher, L. D. 26:27
Fletcher, Lawson W. 11:422
Fletcher, Lewis D. 9:80
Fletcher, Martin 9:130; 27:44
Fletcher, Michael 7:26
Fletcher, Mingo 22:299
Fletcher, N. 22:334
Fletcher, Noah R. 4:24
Fletcher, Oliver 15:11
Fletcher, Oran 20:250
Fletcher, Orrin 12:142
Fletcher, Peter 9:142
Fletcher, Peyton 22:334
Fletcher, Rufus 11:59
Fletcher, Rufus R. 20:7

Fletcher, Sampson 21:270
Fletcher, Samuel J. 8:48
Fletcher, Simeon 22:299
Fletcher, Theodore 15:91
Fletcher, Thomas 9:207; 23:65
Fletcher, Thomas J. 20:250
Fletcher, W. 13:88; 14:9; 16:81
Fletcher, W. I. 10:52
Fletcher, W. J. 20:251
Fletcher, William 3:71; 10:16; 12:98; 13:22; 17:65
Fletcher, William F. 23:87
Fletcher, Willis 18:236; 26:28
Flether, Robert 14:166
Fletter, Samuel 11:59
Flevra, Francis 18:29
Flewellen, Robert 20:17
Flexer, Elias B. 16:279
Flexir, Elias B. 15:357
Flexor, William 27:44
Flich, David 17:102
Flich, Joseph 14:166
Flick, D. 4:24
Flick, Daniel 18:29
Flick, James 18:49
Flick, John 10:113; 20:251
Flick, Joseph 14:166
Flick, L. 3:71
Flick, W. L. 16:292
Flick, William 21:51
Flickenger, E. 1:97
Flickenger, John 22:191
Flickenger, M. 11:145
Flicker, John 14:166
Flickinger, Charles 12:21
Flickinger, F. M. 11:261
Flickinger, Samuel 16:368
Flickwinger, Thomas 12:21
Fliege, Henry 15:22
Fliel, Aquilla 12:49
Fliestine, L. 3:71
Flifin, H. 3:72
Fliger, James 18:305
Flight, Edward 10:172; 19:163
Flight, H. 14:60
Fligle, Daniel 25:34
Fligor, James 9:21; 26:98
Flimey, Michael 18:133
Fliming, J. 3:72
Fling, T. J. 3:72
Flinn, --- 21:330
Flinn, Charles B. 22:478; 26:145

Flinn, David 22:10
Flinn, Dennis 13:109
Flinn, Dominick 27:45
Flinn, Edgar 23:143
Flinn, F. A. 23:143
Flinn, F. T. 8:105
Flinn, George C. 19:69
Flinn, Henry 11:408
Flinn, I. 14:60
Flinn, Isaac 10:113;
    20:251
Flinn, J. 3:72; 14:60;
    20:251
Flinn, J. F. 20:133
Flinn, James 21:137
Flinn, James B. 9:52
Flinn, Jerome 10:52
Flinn, John 16:292
Flinn, Joseph 22:250
Flinn, M. 14:166
Flinn, Michael 8:113;
    16:85
Flinn, Richard 17:20
Flinn, Silas W. 14:166
Flinn, Thomas 23:121
Flinn, Timothy 11:29
Flinn, William 5:15;
    9:176; 10:160;
    14:166; 19:163;
    22:250; 27:45
Flinn, William J. 23:65
Flinner, E. 22:233
Flint, A. S. 24:66
Flint, Albert S. 9:118;
    27:44
Flint, C. B. 3:72
Flint, C. R. 1:131
Flint, C. W. 3:72; 18:103
Flint, Charles 19:252
Flint, D. B. 23:267
Flint, David 11:191; 17:79
Flint, Edson 17:154
Flint, Elijah 19:13
Flint, Francis T. 16:85
Flint, G. N. 18:103
Flint, G. W. 9:176; 19:274
Flint, George B. 17:263
Flint, George H. 21:330
Flint, George W. 10:151,
    178
Flint, Henry 1:33
Flint, J. A. 27:144
Flint, James 8:16; 18:134
Flint, James P. 22:30
Flint, John S. 22:10
Flint, Joseph 21:253
Flint, Loren R. 22:462
Flint, Marcus 8:84
Flint, Morey J. 17:246
Flint, R. 15:341; 16:368
Flint, Seneca 18:346

Flint, T. 21:163
Flint, Thomas 21:290
Flint, Warren A. 22:112
Flint, William 9:176;
    11:125; 19:237
Flinthan, G. L. 12:69
Flintoff, F. 14:166
Flinton, George L. 15:13
Flipp, F. 11:118
Flippen, Albert R. 21:130
Flippin, Isham 10:113
Flishmar, W. 11:412
Flitcher, August 1:32
Flixor, William M. 9:118
Flo, --- 21:330
Flock, J. H. 21:330
Flock, W. 18:109
Flock, W. V. 17:231
Flocker, John 7:26
Flockmere, William
    11:395
Flodland, Ole 27:45
Flogans, William 25:32
Flohr, D. 11:181
Floid, George 19:290
Floid, James H. 21:224
Flommoy, Joseph 18:236;
    26:28
Flond, John D. 13:22
Flood, Arthur 13:22
Flood, E. 15:66; 25:33
Flood, Eli 24:111
Flood, F. 25:283
Flood, George 9:200
Flood, J. 25:171
Flood, James 9:130;
    12:171; 27:44
Flood, James M. 15:285;
    19:69
Flood, John 13:22;
    14:166; 16:32;
    17:359; 25:278
Flood, John E. 21:270
Flood, Michael 9:176;
    15:197
Flood, N. 9:220; 18:366
Flood, P. 27:43
Flood, Patrick 22:279
Flood, Robert 13:22
Flood, T. 14:297; 17:475;
    27:46
Flood, Thomas 7:49;
    10:172; 19:163
Flood, W. C. 21:331
Flood, William 9:130;
    27:44
Floon, R. 21:331
Flora, A. 14:166, 255
Flora, Felix 11:125
Flora, J. M. 11:303
Flora, Jacob B. 23:143

Flora, James 22:77
Flora, Jesse R. 14:297;
    17:479; 27:46
Flora, John 20:56
Flora, Jonas 11:386
Florance, James A. 19:69
Flord, J. N. 15:34
Florence, B. 3:72
Florence, C. 1:130
Florence, J. J. 3:72
Florence, Peter 13:109
Florer, David 20:251
Flores, --- 19:322
Florey, David 22:77
Florian, Anfance 11:291
Flories, W. H. 7:94
Flork, A. D. 21:331
Floro, Daniel 4:24
Flory, Francis M. 23:87
Flory, G. A. 9:66
Flory, George 4:24
Flory, George A. 18:276
Flos, George 19:163
Flosum, George W.
    10:160
Flottman, Fred 20:251
Flottman, Frederick 10:52
Flout, Henry 8:105
Flout, John 5:15
Flow, Cadmus 23:29
Flowar, G. W. 11:240
Flower, Charles 19:13
Flower, Franklin 16:32
Flower, Lewis 7:26
Flower, Rudolf 9:176
Flower, W. 1:33
Flowers, Artemus D.
    25:32
Flowers, Arthur 24:90
Flowers, H. B. 26:98
Flowers, Harrison B.
    18:292
Flowers, Henry 13:22
Flowers, Isaac L. 22:142
Flowers, James 17:427;
    18:305; 23:65;
    24:183
Flowers, James H. 1:32
Flowers, John 27:46
Flowers, John N. 22:191
Flowers, N. L. 11:291
Flowers, W. F. 3:72
Flowers, William 9:21;
    11:147; 26:98
Flowers, William P. 3:72
Flowers, William W.
    10:113; 20:251
Floyd, A. 3:72
Floyd, Albert J. 21:137
Floyd, B. 3:72; 16:292
Floyd, Benjamin 15:34

Floyd, Conrad 14:166
Floyd, Daniel M. 21:51
Floyd, Dolly 27:45
Floyd, Eli B. 17:346
Floyd, F. M. 25:171
Floyd, G. E. 3:72
Floyd, H. 1:129
Floyd, Henry 14:319;
    16:190; 25:288
Floyd, J. 17:145
Floyd, J. A. 23:29
Floyd, J. M. 21:208
Floyd, Jacob 8:84
Floyd, James 17:51, 175
Floyd, John 17:247
Floyd, L. F. 25:171
Floyd, Lyman 9:176;
    19:237
Floyd, M. 14:60
Floyd, Osgood 7:26
Floyd, Philip 6:16; 18:82
Floyd, R. A. 25:171
Floyd, Robert C. 11:255
Floyd, Thomas 16:191;
    17:202; 23:260
Floyd, W. G. 18:236;
    26:27
Floyd, William 11:60
Floyd, William M. 22:424
Fluck, P. L. 15:66
Fluck, Peter L. 12:69
Fluckey, William C. 22:77
Fludder, Henry 17:443;
    24:158
Fludland, Ole 9:118
Flueker, William 9:207
Flugels, Charles 25:171
Flugge, Christian 13:22
Fluhart, William V. 13:22
Fluke, J. 3:72
Fluke, Lyman 8:48; 21:69
Flume, Hugh 11:125
Flungiers, Hiram J. 19:69
Fluno, Henry A. 23:189
Fluno, Oscar 3:72
Fluor, R. 19:252
Flurchman, John 18:134
Flurdy, Stephen 7:122
Flusser, --- 10:160
Fluter, Patrick 10:10
Fly, Alfred W. 9:214;
    21:331
Fly, D. 18:49
Fly, Daniel 10:152
Fly, James 21:25
Flye, H. H. 5:51
Flye, John 16:85
Flyn, I. 14:297
Flyn, James 10:10
Flynn, Arthur 21:331
Flynn, C. M. 27:45

Flynn, D. 16:191; 19:69
Flynn, D. M. 15:197
Flynn, Daniel 21:201, 291
Flynn, E. 9:142; 27:43
Flynn, Edward 16:32
Flynn, F. 27:43
Flynn, Florence 7:94
Flynn, George W. 17:95
Flynn, Henry 7:94
Flynn, I. 3:72; 17:479
Flynn, J. 1:129, 131; 3:72;
    27:46
Flynn, J. F. 1:131
Flynn, James 8:16; 13:22;
    14:60, 166; 16:88;
    18:134; 26:159
Flynn, John 9:71; 18:110;
    19:69; 20:251
Flynn, John C. 27:46
Flynn, John H. 20:89;
    21:331
Flynn, M. 1:129; 3:72
Flynn, Martin 17:352
Flynn, Michael 9:80;
    12:69; 17:143;
    23:283
Flynn, Michael J. 26:28
Flynn, Patrick 9:176;
    22:500
Flynn, Peter 12:21;
    21:331; 25:269
Flynn, Richard 8:16;
    18:134
Flynn, S. 3:72
Flynn, Thomas 4:24; 9:21;
    18:306; 26:98
Flynn, Thomas J. 11:147
Flynn, W. 3:72; 25:171
Flynn, William 9:118;
    19:237
Flynton, George 12:8
Fo---, Andrew 25:33
Fo---, Jacob 11:261
Foahn, George 10:113
Foaja, F. 1:131
Foaley, William 24:18
Fobas, William 14:60
Fober, S. H. 16:267
Fobes, B. 1:129
Fobes, Benjamin F. 24:50
Fobes, Caleb W. 24:50
Fobes, Ferdinand F.
    11:319
Fobes, Joseph 9:34
Fobet, John 12:81; 16:292
Fobin, Michael 3:72
Fobs, Hiram 10:52
Fock, James 7:122
Focks, Christian 21:331
Focord, E. 14:60

Fodge, David 10:52;
    20:251
Foe, James 1:34
Fog, C. 9:142
Fogaly, John 21:331
Fogan, B. H. 8:16
Fogarty, Bartley 16:32
Fogarty, Patrick 9:176
Fogarty, William 18:110
Fogel, G. H. 3:72
Fogel, John 4:24
Fogeman, M. 16:191
Fogerty, Daniel 19:69
Fogerty, John 21:51
Fogerty, N. 1:34
Fogerty, Patrick 19:281
Fogerty, Richard 13:132
Fogg, Almon 21:331
Fogg, B. F. 3:72
Fogg, C. G. 19:163
Fogg, C. M. 20:151
Fogg, Charles M. 20:192
Fogg, E. G. 10:160
Fogg, Esa 21:331
Fogg, G. M. 19:163
Fogg, George H. 10:16
Fogg, George L. 13:22
Fogg, H. 12:70; 15:66
Fogg, J. 19:227
Fogg, James 9:176
Fogg, John 22:299
Fogg, Lucien 25:32
Fogg, Oris 12:21
Fogg, Robert 21:270
Fogg, S. 13:109
Fogg, S. J. 12:10
Fogg, S. W. 25:171
Fogg, Sylvanus N. 5:15
Fogg, Thomas W. 17:359
Fogg, William 21:331
Fogg, William H. 19:163
Foggan, Michael 21:331
Foggen, John 9:118;
    27:45
Fogle, A. 20:145
Fogle, Andrew 19:13
Fogle, J. 14:166
Fogle, John F. 17:452;
    24:181
Fogle, P. 1:130
Fogle, Philip 23:143
Fogle, R. M. 23:143
Fogle, Royal 23:143
Fogle, William 16:32;
    17:51; 22:423
Fogleman, Z. T. 23:98
Fogler, William 12:21
Fogley, C. 3:72
Fogus, Jasper 22:77
Fogwill, Jacob 17:418
Fohl, Jacob 25:269

Fohnsbelly, C. 3:72
Foin, D. B. 11:279
Foins, Fains Levi 26:219
Foisher, Taylor S. 21:238
Foit, August 5:15
Foitle, Thomas 26:28
Folan, John 25:34
Foland, Felix L. 21:10
Folard, James 3:72
Folay, Michael 22:77
Folay, Patrick 22:77
Folbrook, William 13:22
Fold, Paul 9:242
Folder, Robert 13:22
Foldin, H. 3:72
Fole, J. 1:131
Folensbee, C. M. 27:43
Foler, Austin 18:351
Folerson, R. D. 18:134
Folet, D. 3:72
Foley, C. 13:88; 14:9
Foley, Cornelius 15:34
Foley, Daniel 3:72; 24:66
Foley, E. 14:334
Foley, Edward 23:179;
    24:18
Foley, F. 3:72
Foley, Francis 22:191
Foley, George 12:21
Foley, H. J. 11:303
Foley, J. 9:143; 14:297;
    16:32; 17:473; 27:43,
    46
Foley, James 13:22, 109;
    23:121, 189
Foley, James G. 20:17
Foley, John 9:102; 11:29;
    18:49, 338
Foley, M. 7:26, 49; 15:27;
    25:32
Foley, Michael 22:334;
    24:18
Foley, Morgan 12:70;
    15:81
Foley, Owen 13:22
Foley, P. J. 13:109
Foley, Patrick 7:8;
    21:331; 22:334
Foley, Russell 7:122
Foley, Stephen 9:118;
    27:44
Foley, Thomas 10:113;
    11:125; 13:124;
    16:191; 19:69;
    20:251
Foley, William 10:113;
    19:163; 20:251; 24:8
Folgee, Edward P. 25:269
Folger, Augustus 15:66
Folger, Charles G. 25:171
Folger, Henry 13:22

Folger, William 17:242
Foliand, W. 3:72
Foliard, Edwin A. 10:160
Folick, H. 14:315
Folin, William H. H.
    25:171
Folitt, William 23:268
Folk, A. P. 3:72
Folk, C. 3:72
Folk, Charles 22:423
Folk, J. 11:218
Folk, James W. 14:166
Folk, L. 3:72
Folk, Marcellus 14:167
Folk, Paul 19:326
Folk, S. 14:60; 25:171
Folk, William 16:132
Folke, W. 1:97
Folkerson, C. 18:464
Folkerts, John G. 16:139
Folks, Jordon 19:290
Folks, Salmon 16:191
Folks, W. H. 14:9
Follansbee, G. R. 9:214
Follansby, A. 14:167
Follard, Edwin A. 19:163
Follausber, G. R. 21:331
Follen, Andrew J. 22:423
Follen, George 22:299
Follet, T. 15:341; 16:368
Follet, Weber 10:91
Follett, A. H. 16:292
Follett, Charles 21:331
Follett, Edward 13:22
Follett, Egbert W. G.
    10:113; 20:251
Follett, Eugene 10:52
Follett, George 4:24
Follett, Gerome V.
    10:144; 19:163
Follett, Jerome 4:24
Follett, L. D. 1:129
Follett, Luther D. L. 10:52
Follett, Sal. O. 4:24
Follett, Webber 20:251
Follett, William 11:30
Follett, Zander 8:16
Follett, Zauder 26:160
Folley, L. A. 22:191
Folley, William 13:63;
    16:191
Follin, David F. 22:191
Follinger, J. 1:130
Follis, Alexander 10:113;
    20:251
Folliver, Archibald 4:24
Follman, Warren L. 10:16
Follner, Charles 21:331
Follow, M. 1:34
Follows, John 20:251
Folly, Thomas 17:202

Folman, French 24:193
Folsom, Alfred E. 20:183
Folsom, E. A. 27:43
Folsom, E. T. 19:237
Folsom, Ephraim P. 16:32
Folsom, George W. 8:16
Folsom, Henry C. 1:32
Folsom, Henry W. 4:24
Folsom, Nelson H. 24:50
Folsom, W. B. 20:7
Folsome, George W.
    18:134
Folson, Benjamin F. 12:58
Folson, Ezra T. 9:176
Folson, I. 9:143
Folsten, Frederick W.
    26:219
Folston, A. 20:251
Folston, Absalom 12:142
Folt, Richard D. 12:62
Foltd, Daniel 1:31
Folten, J. 18:29
Folton, Samuel 5:15
Folts, Richard D. 15:91
Foltz, Eli J. 22:191
Foltz, Erwin 22:191
Foltz, J. 12:85; 16:292
Foltz, James K. 4:24
Folwell, J. D. 20:251
Folwell, James D. 10:52;
    12:21
Foly, J. 21:25
Foman, Joseph 4:24
Fomlius, Michael 26:28
Fomskill, Henry C. 11:147
Fon, Miner 5:39
Foncannon, Harrison
    22:423
Foncannon, John 22:77
Foncas, G. H. 12:85
Foncks, H. P. 3:72
Fonda, Conrelius J.
    22:142
Fondren, E. 21:147
Fondren, J. W. 9:21
Fondy, George W. 22:30
Foneas, G. H. 16:292
Foney, Dudley 26:28
Fonier, William 19:69
Fonitellott, Lewis J.
    20:252
Fonlan, Patrick 21:241
Fonnder, James 7:122
Fonnell, James 14:167
Fonner, Thomas 15:86
Fonse, Benjamin 17:90
Fonse, William L. 19:69
Font, A. 18:49
Font, Alex 13:109
Fontaine, Amy 19:13
Fontaine, Garland 7:122

Fontaine, Henry 10:172; 19:164
Fontes, Augustus M. 22:142
Fonts, A. J. 27:42
Fonts, John C. 19:270
Fonts, Osborn 25:171
Fonts, Samuel 25:171
Fonts, William 26:27
Fontz, Andrew J. 22:423
Foodle, William 17:397
Foody, W. 7:94
Fook, Truman 16:191
Fooks, Albert C. 25:33
Foomard, A. 13:103
Foor, Daniel 12:153
Foor, M. 13:88
Foorman, David N. 17:233
Foose, Ben. F. 17:418
Foose, Benjamin 24:213
Foot, --- 1:32
Foot, Abraham 27:42
Foot, Andrew T. 22:142
Foot, Asa A. 17:65
Foot, Austin 20:189
Foot, Charles 5:15; 25:171
Foot, Cornelius C. 22:142
Foot, Curtis 22:479
Foot, David 22:142
Foot, Gainset J. 27:45
Foot, George 1:32; 17:99
Foot, Herman 15:302
Foot, Hiram R. 22:142
Foot, Isaac 6:16; 18:82
Foot, J. A. 11:29
Foot, James 19:45; 21:270; 27:42
Foot, James A. 4:24
Foot, Jasper 21:270
Foot, M. M. 15:123
Foot, Richmond 5:39
Foot, Seneca H. 10:16
Foot, Simeon S. 16:191
Foot, Simon P. 13:63
Foot, Truman 15:302
Foot, W. S. 25:171
Foot, William 21:194
Foot, William A. 20:106
Foot, Z. 25:32
Foote, Alanson C. 22:142
Foote, Charles S. 8:121
Foote, Dennis 21:331
Foote, Herman 16:191
Foote, James 9:21; 20:87
Foote, James H. 22:142
Foote, Oscar E. 21:253
Foote, Richmond 25:171
Foote, Roswell J. 22:191
Foote, W. R. 7:122

For, W. 3:73
Fora, Josephus 23:301
Foracre, David 17:33
Foraker, David L. 20:123
Foraker, William 8:48
Foral, G. W. 27:144
Foram, William 2:11
Foran, Patrick 15:105
Foran, William 25:31
Foraster, Thomas 7:94; 21:331
Forban, Gabriel 4:24
Forbash, G. H. 14:60
Forbens, E. P. 21:99
Forber, Joseph 10:52
Forbert, Isaac L. 10:16
Forbes, --- 7:74; 10:160; 12:85; 16:292
Forbes, A. S. 20:251
Forbes, Albert 22:479
Forbes, Andrew J. 11:239
Forbes, Arthur S. 10:52
Forbes, Benjamin 9:12
Forbes, Boyd 23:143
Forbes, Charles 1:32; 14:235; 17:73; 18:29; 25:33
Forbes, D. A. 15:359
Forbes, D. M. 1:129
Forbes, Duncan 14:167
Forbes, J. 18:49; 21:187
Forbes, J. B. 21:331
Forbes, James 25:32
Forbes, Jeremiah 21:331
Forbes, John 14:167; 17:502
Forbes, John H. 23:143
Forbes, John W. 7:94
Forbes, Moses D. 17:79
Forbes, Nathan 17:51
Forbes, R. A. 7:26
Forbes, S. F. 11:261
Forbes, Samuel 9:34; 17:33
Forbes, Thomas 17:452; 24:181
Forbes, W. H. 15:151
Forbes, Watson 10:52
Forbes, William 10:52, 113; 20:251; 21:14; 24:61
Forbes, Willie 26:219
Forbridge, B. H. 1:31
Forbs, B. 19:69
Forbs, B. S. 3:72
Forbs, C. 3:72
Forbs, Hiram 20:251
Forbs, John 22:191
Forbs, Robert C. 22:250
Forbs, William 20:251
Forby, D. 12:95

Forby, William 23:29
Forby, William C. 9:34; 26:98
Force, Albert 9:80
Force, C. 1:128
Force, Cummings 24:18
Force, D. 12:8
Force, David 23:143
Force, G. W. 14:167
Force, George B. 16:75
Force, J. 1:33; 24:77
Force, J. H. 23:29
Force, M. H. 1:34
Force, Richard 17:131; 24:193
Forchner, John 26:138
Ford, --- 5:51; 15:94; 17:242
Ford, A. 3:72; 15:158
Ford, A. J. 24:38
Ford, Abner 22:191
Ford, Abraham 7:122
Ford, Abram B. 20:251
Ford, Absalom 21:114
Ford, Alex 9:165; 13:109; 25:320
Ford, Alexander B. 11:186
Ford, Alfred 12:21
Ford, Allan C. 21:331
Ford, Allen 22:142
Ford, Allen M. 23:107
Ford, Alonzo A. 18:330
Ford, Ambrose B. 10:52
Ford, B. I. 21:99
Ford, B. K. 1:32
Ford, B. W. 23:143
Ford, C. A. 9:52
Ford, Chancey 23:87
Ford, Charles 15:83; 23:260
Ford, Charles H. 10:170
Ford, Choice 18:406
Ford, Christopher M. 21:240
Ford, D. 25:278
Ford, D. B. 1:129
Ford, D. C. 22:469
Ford, D. W. 12:70; 15:95
Ford, Daniel 25:34
Ford, David 11:146
Ford, Dennis 11:202
Ford, Dominick 22:77
Ford, Dwight 13:57; 16:32
Ford, E. 21:88
Ford, E. T. M. 11:401
Ford, E. V. 3:72
Ford, Edmund 11:88
Ford, Edw. 27:44

Ford, Edward 1:32; 4:24; 9:130; 19:337
Ford, Elie 24:101
Ford, F. M. 14:60
Ford, Francis M. 10:113; 20:251
Ford, Frank 27:43
Ford, G. H. 21:331
Ford, George 14:167; 23:113, 189
Ford, George W. 7:26
Ford, H. 15:293; 16:191
Ford, H. W. 14:167
Ford, Henry 7:57; 13:109
Ford, Hiram 22:250
Ford, I. 19:164
Ford, Isaac 22:450
Ford, J. 9:109; 13:88; 14:10
Ford, J. C. 17:20
Ford, J. L. 7:94
Ford, J. W. 9:176
Ford, Jacob C. 22:497
Ford, James 11:29; 12:70; 13:109; 15:81; 16:32; 20:133
Ford, James B. 8:113
Ford, James E. 9:80
Ford, James H. 19:13
Ford, Jefferson 7:122
Ford, Jeremiah 20:22
Ford, John 7:26; 8:63; 9:102; 10:160; 15:2; 17:165; 19:13, 69; 20:56, 251; 21:331; 27:144
Ford, John A. 7:26; 26:211
Ford, John C. 22:423
Ford, John H. 5:39; 10:176; 25:171
Ford, John K. 19:164
Ford, John L. 19:164
Ford, John W. 15:197; 22:450
Ford, Jonathan H. 22:250
Ford, Joseph 16:85
Ford, Joseph E. 13:22
Ford, Josiah 1:32
Ford, Julius 12:81; 16:292
Ford, Kinney S. 17:51
Ford, L. D. 17:33
Ford, L. G. 9:230; 20:251
Ford, L. N. 7:67
Ford, Lanson A. 8:84
Ford, Lanson H. 8:117
Ford, Leander C. 23:301
Ford, Lewis 12:21; 21:270
Ford, Lyman A. 17:313
Ford, Lyman F. 11:125
Ford, Mary Jane 26:219

Ford, Michael 4:24
Ford, Michael F. 21:10
Ford, Miles H. 11:29
Ford, Milton 17:317; 22:142
Ford, N. 3:72; 20:85
Ford, O. E. 20:133
Ford, Ozias C. 16:132
Ford, P. 3:72
Ford, P. H. 14:60
Ford, Perry 19:69
Ford, Perry F. 22:77
Ford, R. 14:61
Ford, Robert 13:63; 19:69
Ford, S. 1:33
Ford, S. D. 8:71; 26:160
Ford, Samuel P. 7:122; 21:331
Ford, Samuel R. 11:239
Ford, Samuel W. 22:497
Ford, Slater 7:14
Ford, Stephen 16:130
Ford, Thomas 3:72; 8:63; 12:153; 13:22; 17:33, 51; 21:331; 26:160
Ford, Thomas C. 20:251
Ford, Tobias 9:130; 27:44
Ford, W. 11:60; 18:103
Ford, W. R. 13:88
Ford, W. S. 20:251
Ford, Walter 7:10; 19:45
Ford, Washington 17:175
Ford, William 3:72; 7:49, 94; 9:80, 230; 20:251; 22:191, 250; 23:65; 24:38; 26:211
Ford, William C. 20:133
Ford, William H. 5:15; 12:153; 25:171
Ford, William N. 17:387; 22:250
Ford, William S. 10:52; 23:65
Ford, Z. 19:164
Fordan, G. D. 17:470
Forde, Azriah 17:51
Forde, J. H. 19:252
Forde, John 17:20; 19:164
Forde, S. J. 18:366
Forden, Robert H. 21:224
Forderhacken, Frank 20:251
Forderhackin, Frank 10:113
Fordham, Albert 21:331
Fordham, Cephas 22:77
Fordice, Amos B. 21:69
Fording, William 10:113; 20:251
Fordner, Frank 22:299

Fordney, Benjamin C. 22:165
Fordney, G. W. 3:72
Fordy, John 22:334
Fordyce, J. B. 20:251
Fordyce, William 24:38
Fordyce, William A. 10:52; 20:251
Fore, M. 25:171
Foreacre, Jasper 11:240
Foreacre, W. 3:72
Foreaker, A. 1:129
Foreaker, William H. 21:137
Forebaugh, Solomon 12:99
Foreber, A. 3:73
Foreel, Reuben 24:193
Forehand, David 8:16
Foreier, Francis 25:171
Forel, Daniel W. 12:70
Foreland, David 18:134
Foremall, Joshua 11:202
Foreman, A. 3:72; 21:201
Foreman, A. H. 23:279
Foreman, Augt 9:80
Foreman, Augustus 26:27
Foreman, Basil 22:121
Foreman, E. 6:35
Foreman, F. 11:191; 21:148
Foreman, Francis M. 11:59
Foreman, Frederic 17:109
Foreman, G. S. 3:72
Foreman, G. W. 10:52
Foreman, George 18:66
Foreman, H. B. 9:176
Foreman, H. R. 19:252
Foreman, I. M. 1:32
Foreman, J. F. 26:27
Foreman, J. M. 1:34
Foreman, James 9:80
Foreman, John 1:192; 8:39; 11:145; 26:159
Foreman, John D. 17:265
Foreman, Joseph 1:192
Foreman, Michael K. 17:90
Foreman, Nathan 19:329
Foreman, Philip 11:284
Foreman, Robert 4:24
Foreman, Samuel 17:272
Foreman, Thomas 10:91; 18:82; 23:143
Foreman, W. R. 3:72
Foreman, William 5:16; 20:7; 24:88; 25:171
Forenbeck, W. 19:69
Foresman, F. 16:191
Foreson, William 19:301

Forest, W. 14:297; 17:471
Forest, W. C. 8:71
Foreston, John A. 27:45
Forey, --- 15:34
Forey, Jack 21:331
Forey, Michael 21:331
Forfe, Jacob 15:302; 16:191
Forge, Robert 10:113; 20:251
Forgenin, Peter 14:167
Forgus, William 19:164
Forinash, George 18:206
Fork, John A. 11:19
Fork, Matthew 8:105
Forkenstan, J. 1:131
Forkes, George W. 13:22
Forkner, John 20:46
Forkner, Joseph 22:250
Forkner, Judson 27:45
Forkner, W. 18:395
Forks, Richard 4:24
Forley, John 19:13
Forlin, L. 20:251
Forlinberg, D. K. 14:167
Forman, E. 14:167
Forman, F. 11:29
Forman, James A. 7:64
Forman, John 12:49
Forman, John W. 17:33
Forman, Thomas 6:12
Forman, W. 1:130
Formels, James 8:48
Former, Harry 22:335
Former, Moses 19:164
Forn, E. 1:32
Fornar, Daniel 17:46
Fornard, August 8:16; 18:134
Fornash, George 22:191
Fornay, D. 3:72
Forncrook, A. 19:69
Forne, H. 21:331
Fornea, Augustus 9:176; 19:270
Forner, Edward 4:24
Forner, H. 11:239
Forney, Alexander 23:143
Forney, George 3:72
Forney, John 13:63; 17:33
Forney, Samuel 12:57
Forney, Solomon 23:143
Forneyburg, John 18:29
Fornholty, Louis 14:167
Forp, Charles 7:27
Forr, J. C. 3:73
Forrenback, W. 15:309
Forrer, Howard 26:145
Forrest, Alexander D. 25:34
Forrest, Charles 21:270

Forrest, George 23:65
Forrest, H. 25:32
Forrest, Henry 10:113
Forrest, Ira W. 7:94
Forrest, Isaiah 22:171
Forrest, James 23:29
Forrest, James C. 21:240
Forrest, James H. 17:321
Forrest, John S. 23:29
Forrest, John W. 22:508
Forrest, Joseph A. 22:191
Forrest, Joseph B. 9:10
Forrest, Moses 19:334
Forrest, Perry 15:326
Forrest, R. 14:61
Forrest, S. 3:73
Forrest, Samuel 13:22
Forrest, Thomas 3:73
Forrest, W. 3:73; 27:46
Forrest, W. C. 26:160
Forrest, William 22:423
Forrest, William E. 10:52; 15:66; 20:251
Forrester, A. W. 21:331
Forrester, Archable B. 15:66
Forrester, Daniel 11:186
Forrester, F. M. 22:17
Forrester, G. W. 1:129
Forrester, George 17:165
Forrester, George W. 16:94
Forrester, Isadore 27:42
Forrester, James 22:250
Forrester, John W. 17:499
Forrester, R. L. 25:296
Forrester, S. W. 9:143
Forrester, Samuel C. 13:22; 16:32
Forrester, St. Clair 22:335
Forrester, William 17:147
Forresters, S. 15:197
Forrey, W. 3:73
Forrier, William 15:309
Forrow, John 20:251
Forsha, James 10:113; 20:251
Forshall, Henry 24:93
Forshay, A. 3:72
Forshee, Caleb 23:98
Forsher, Monroe 9:70
Forshey, Elijah 17:79
Forshey, T. T. 18:29
Forshma, W. 3:72
Forsie, Charles 25:296
Forslay, William K. 3:72
Forsman, John 17:257
Forson, Anthony 21:331
Forsst, William D. 10:160
Forst, John 15:55
Forst, P. 14:61

Forstell, Charles 16:32
Forster, Fred. 8:121
Forster, Robert 1:32
Forstniggar, Joseph 22:171
Forsyth, Abraham 21:137
Forsyth, Charles 17:359
Forsyth, Charles W. 20:22
Forsyth, Eli 11:84
Forsyth, Elijah 12:153
Forsyth, H. 3:72
Forsyth, I. 11:30
Forsyth, J. 3:72; 18:110
Forsyth, J. R. 11:88; 25:171
Forsyth, James 14:167; 27:45
Forsyth, John 6:9
Forsyth, John A. 5:16
Forsyth, Lee 1:33
Forsyth, Robert M. 12:70
Forsyth, Stillman 4:24
Forsythe, A. 8:48
Forsythe, George 15:197
Forsythe, T. 11:29
Forsythe, Thomas C. 17:51
Fort, C. W. 15:105
Fort, George 24:101
Fort, Harley 21:331
Fort, Hugh 21:331
Fort, J. L. 14:167
Fort, James L. 12:21
Fort, Moses F. 21:331
Fort, Oscar 4:24
Fort, S. 20:40
Fort, Tait 7:122
Fort, U. S. 15:278
Fort, William 1:32
Forte, James 18:306; 26:97
Forten, Joseph 7:94
Fortenberry, D. K. 14:61
Fortescue, William 21:331
Forth, Franklin 4:24
Forth, J. M. 14:61
Forth, John 16:191
Forth, R. 3:72
Forth, R. L. 23:143
Forthham, --- 3:72
Forthy, Thomas 9:80
Fortman, Lewis 22:30
Fortna, Henry 10:172; 19:164
Fortner, Benjamin F. 8:16; 18:134
Fortner, Eldridge 9:80
Fortner, Elijah 26:27
Fortner, Isaac 7:94; 21:331
Fortner, J. P. 23:65

Fortner, Job 23:313
Fortner, John 3:72; 9:68; 19:281
Fortner, Marion D. 23:243
Fortner, Robert 9:68
Fortner, T. F. 19:301
Fortner, T. S. 10:27
Fortney, B. J. 23:179
Fortneys, H. 15:258
Fortriey, Henry 19:13
Forttilson, Neil 3:73
Fortune, F. A. 7:57
Fortune, James 23:128
Fortune, John 9:236; 26:219
Fortune, Lewis 1:192
Fortune, Richard 12:49
Fortune, Robert 16:191
Fortune, W. N. 24:18
Forward, Marshall 24:93
Forward, S. 3:73
Fosen, David 9:106
Fosgate, Henry 3:73
Fosket, R. M. 1:131
Foskett, B. O. 11:29
Foskett, Elizur H. 23:189
Foskins, G. L. 18:276
Fosmer, Abraham 16:368
Fosnight, John H. 22:192
Foss, A. J. 9:143; 15:278; 25:171; 27:43
Foss, Amos 20:7
Foss, Austin 11:15
Foss, C. A. 16:94
Foss, Charles 13:22
Foss, Charles H. 21:331
Foss, Charles W. 16:368
Foss, Daniel 13:22
Foss, Elfin J. 16:77
Foss, Eugene 4:25
Foss, G. E. 1:128
Foss, H. C. 8:101; 17:459; 24:152
Foss, H. I. 14:61
Foss, J. W. 20:56
Foss, James G. 11:60
Foss, James M. 10:16
Foss, John 9:109; 22:450
Foss, John W. 10:16
Foss, L. H. 21:331
Foss, Lewis 5:15
Foss, Lorenzo W. 10:52
Foss, Nathan A. 15:11
Foss, Nathaniel A. 12:70
Foss, Nathaniel H. 24:38
Foss, O. 27:43
Foss, Richard F. 9:159
Foss, S. F. 9:214
Foss, T. 1:130
Foss, Uriah H. 9:7
Foss, William L. 23:29

Fossee, W. H. 18:29
Fosselman, Jacob 21:51
Fosselman, William 19:14
Fossett, M. 14:61
Fossett, Robert M. 15:11
Fost, Philip 11:386
Fost, William 9:207
Fostelle, Charles 13:23
Foster, --- 15:363; 16:191; 17:296; 19:69; 25:34
Foster, A. 1:129, 131; 3:73; 8:63; 9:52; 12:81; 14:61; 16:191, 292; 20:145, 251; 21:25; 26:160
Foster, A. B. 19:14
Foster, A. E. 19:237
Foster, A. G. 2:11; 25:34
Foster, A. H. 25:171
Foster, A. J. 3:73; 21:130
Foster, Albert G. 16:368
Foster. Albert J. 24:38
Foster, Alexander 10:160
Foster, Andrew 1:33
Foster, Andrew J. 17:276
Foster, Ansen G. 20:251
Foster, Anson H. 10:113
Foster, Anthony 9:165
Foster, Arthur 1:32
Foster, Azariah 10:52
Foster, B. 17:175
Foster, B. B. 3:73
Foster, Benjamin F. 23:189
Foster, C. 1:131; 25:171
Foster, C. A. 11:419
Foster, C. J. 25:33
Foster, C. T. 12:99
Foster, C. W. 3:73
Foster, Calvin R. 22:30
Foster, Canoles 13:23
Foster, Carlos B. 9:12
Foster, Carroles 16:32
Foster, Cassius 5:16
Foster, Charles 13:22; 14:167; 18:395; 21:270
Foster, Charles B. 2:10
Foster, Charles G. 4:24
Foster, Charles R. 3:73
Foster, Crawford 22:450
Foster, D. G. 1:129
Foster, Dallas 10:52; 20:251
Foster, Daniel 14:167; 16:191; 22:335
Foster, Daniel S. 22:142
Foster, Dr. 18:82
Foster, E. 14:167; 21:331
Foster, E. B. 8:16; 18:134
Foster, E. C. 21:332

Foster, E. D. 16:191
Foster, E. J. 18:29
Foster, E. R. 3:73
Foster, E. S. 1:129; 3:73
Foster, Edward S. 25:171
Foster, Edwin B. 13:22
Foster, Edwin O. 13:22
Foster, Elroy 27:42
Foster, Enos 27:42
Foster, F. 25:171
Foster, F. A. 25:33
Foster, F. D. 13:63
Foster, F. F. 8:71
Foster, F. H. 14:167
Foster, F. J. 26:160
Foster, F. M. 23:29
Foster, Franklin F. 22:279
Foster, Fred B. 9:176
Foster, Frederick 12:169; 19:317
Foster, G. 1:34
Foster, G. F. 10:205
Foster, G. H. 26:27
Foster, G. L. 19:252
Foster, G. W. 1:130, 131
Foster, Galvin O. 10:16
Foster, George 1:34; 4:24
Foster, George H. 9:80
Foster, George K. 19:69
Foster, George L. 9:176
Foster, George W. 13:23; 16:32
Foster, H. 1:131; 3:73
Foster, H. B. 3:73; 20:154
Foster, H. C. 3:73
Foster, H. F. 15:293
Foster, H. M. 1:33
Foster, H. P. 2:10; 25:34
Foster, Hacus 18:206
Foster, Henry 9:159; 15:105; 22:191
Foster, Henry A. 24:50
Foster, Henry C. 22:250
Foster, Henry S. 15:197
Foster, I. 11:146; 14:61
Foster, Ira O. 18:344
Foster, Isaac 1:32
Foster, Isum 17:397
Foster, J. 3:73; 9:52; 13:63, 88, 109; 14:10, 61, 167; 19:252
Foster, J. C. 1:130; 14:61
Foster, J. D. 25:171
Foster, J. E. 10:113; 20:251
Foster, J. J. 22:250
Foster, J. N. 9:12; 21:25
Foster, J. R. 16:191
Foster, J. S. 11:240

Foster, Jacob 7:49; 22:191, 233
Foster, Jacob C. 15:34
Foster, James 1:31; 3:73; 4:24; 9:31; 10:113; 12:140; 13:23; 15:197; 17:175, 318; 20:40, 252; 23:65
Foster, James F. 23:65
Foster, James G. 21:91
Foster, James H. 9:240
Foster, James S. 10:160
Foster, James T. 22:121
Foster, Jeremiah 10:113; 20:252
Foster, Jesse 14:236
Foster, Jesse K. 22:479
Foster, Jessel 9:176
Foster, Joe 17:418
Foster, John 1:33; 3:73; 4:24; 7:57, 122; 8:84; 9:52; 11:202; 13:22; 17:65, 79; 22:191; 23:143, 263; 25:33
Foster, John B. 12:21; 22:233; 23:143
Foster, John C. 22:501
Foster, John E. 7:27
Foster, John H. 22:478
Foster, John L. 23:87
Foster, John O. 8:16
Foster, John P. 18:134
Foster, John W. 14:167; 24:50
Foster, Jonathan 22:30
Foster, Joseph 8:39; 13:109
Foster, L. 9:143; 11:261; 27:43
Foster, M. 8:63; 14:61
Foster, M. W. 12:80; 25:171
Foster, Mario 22:77
Foster, Marmaduke 7:63
Foster, Martin 10:52; 20:252
Foster, N. J. 20:84
Foster, N. O. 15:34
Foster, N. W. 7:49
Foster, Nathan 7:94
Foster, Nicholas 4:65
Foster, O. 15:298; 16:191
Foster, Orange 22:30
Foster, Otis 19:274
Foster, Otis A. 27:42
Foster, P. H. 2:10
Foster, P. S. 12:21
Foster, Paul 25:171
Foster, Peter 23:203
Foster, Philip H. 15:2

Foster, Prea. B. 19:237
Foster, R. 10:27; 19:301
Foster, R. T. 1:32
Foster, Ralph S. 13:23; 16:32
Foster, Richard 22:299
Foster, Richard T. 23:143
Foster, Robert 18:14, 29; 20:252
Foster, Robert C. 18:217
Foster, Robert J. 17:280
Foster, Robert M. 3:73
Foster, Rufus 13:23
Foster, Russell 22:501
Foster, S. 3:73; 4:24; 7:65; 18:29
Foster, S. E. 25:171
Foster, S. W. 12:161
Foster, Samuel 15:197; 17:247; 24:50
Foster, Samuel C. 3:73
Foster, Seth 10:113; 20:252
Foster, Solomon W. 21:137
Foster, T. B. 7:94
Foster, T. M. 16:191
Foster, Thatcher B. 7:27
Foster, Theodore 23:189
Foster, Thomas 4:24; 9:200; 10:27; 11:423; 15:197; 19:281, 301; 22:501; 24:93
Foster, Thomas L. 10:113; 20:252
Foster, W. 2:10; 3:73; 16:94; 25:34
Foster, W. A. 13:88; 14:10
Foster, W. C. 8:71
Foster, W. E. 18:174
Foster, W. George 13:23
Foster, W. H. 1:130; 13:63; 22:191
Foster, W. Henry 22:478
Foster, W. J. 14:315
Foster, W. R. 21:332
Foster, Wilfred 12:21
Foster, William 1:32; 4:24; 11:59, 261; 12:21; 14:61, 321; 21:25, 332; 23:65; 25:171
Foster, William B. 19:337
Foster, William E. 26:160
Foster, William F. 15:197
Foster, William J. 1:34
Foster, William L. 21:137
Foster, William M. 17:359
Foster, William P. 22:30
Foster, William R. 17:109

Foster, Zachariah 10:113; 20:252
Foswell, Littleton 8:39; 26:159
Foten, M. 4:24
Fother, Elijah 9:80
Fotheringham, Hamilton 10:113; 20:252
Fothner, E. A. 20:252
Fothner, E. Allen 10:52
Fotson, Isaac 21:91
Fotte, Adelbert 4:24
Fouaker, Francis 11:145
Fouch, B. 23:143
Fouch, J. 1:129
Fouch, James 11:147
Fouch, Obanion 11:276
Fouch, Simpson R. 23:30
Fouch, W. 23:30
Fouch, William F. 11:60
Foucher, G. D. 11:284
Foucher, John C. 11:231
Foucht, Jonas 27:45
Foucht, Jones 9:118
Fouck, John E. 12:153
Fouck, Philip 11:146
Foucker, William H. 8:48
Fought, M. J. 4:25
Fought, Simon 7:67
Fougue, John 8:48
Foul, J. H. 20:87
Fould, John J. 22:462
Foulds, John E. 23:104
Foulett, C. A. 15:359
Foulk, Benjamin 16:191
Foulk, John 1:32
Foulk, Levi 23:143
Foulk, Peter L. 11:411
Foulk, Samuel 20:252
Foulke, C. 14:61
Foulke, Peter 3:73
Foulke, S. 1:130
Foulkrod, Samuel L. 4:25
Foulks, Harrison 22:399
Foulks, John W. 22:77
Fouls, Z. N. 10:211
Foults, M. 3:73
Fountain, Charles 18:14
Fountain, David W. 7:49
Fountain, Edwin M. 22:423
Fountain, H. B. 16:139
Fountain, Herdon 18:189
Fountain, J. H. 1:32
Fountain, Joseph 12:21; 22:299
Fountain, Oliver 11:20
Fountain, Pleasant 10:205
Fountain, R. S. 14:241; 27:47
Fountain, Robert 12:49

Fountain, S. H. 19:164
Fountain, W. A. 19:69
Fountain, W. H. 3:73
Fountaine, Solomon
10:172
Founts, John 20:252
Fouracre, William H.
22:192
Fourlinson, John M.
18:134
Fourlough, A. 3:73
Fournier, Bragzede
19:164
Fourtelbette, C. A. 12:95
Fourth, Jacob 22:479
Fourtney, P. 3:73
Fousber, John B. 17:20
Fousch, Christopher 20:17
Fouse, G. W. 4:25
Fouse, John 25:296
Foust, Henry 20:252
Foust, J. P. 22:192
Foust, J. W. 11:381
Foust, Josiah 24:77
Foust, L. B. 22:478
Foust, Leroy 23:65
Foust, P. W. 16:368
Foust, S. L. 3:73
Foust, Sylvester 17:165
Foust, Wiley G. 11:422
Foustalot, C. A. 19:69
Fouster, J. O. 14:61
Fout, George 15:197
Fout, Henry F. 22:450
Fout, Henry T. 22:121
Fout, Thomas J. 11:145
Fouta, Soloman 21:121
Foutenbaiher, Fried'k.
4:25
Fouts, John 10:91
Fouts, Joseph 8:84
Fouts, Lemon 22:30
Fouts, Samuel 22:424
Fouts, Zimri N. 18:468
Foutz, J. A. 1:34
Fowel, R. F. 14:10
Fowell, R. F. 13:88
Fowh, E. 21:26
Fowl, D. W. 1:131
Fowl, George W. 23:143
Fowle, James 4:25
Fowle, Stephen M. 17:391
Fowler, A. 16:143; 19:164
Fowler, Anderson 27:45
Fowler, Andrew L. 22:479
Fowler, Anivick 9:109
Fowler, Ben 9:207
Fowler, C. B. 5:16;
25:171
Fowler, Caleb 27:45
Fowler, Charles 9:52

Fowler, Charles B. 1:33
Fowler, Charles E. 23:65
Fowler, Charles H.
17:259; 24:38
Fowler, D. W. 27:43
Fowler, Daniel 22:404
Fowler, Daniel H. 11:59
Fowler, David 20:189
Fowler, E. 17:175
Fowler, Eli 12:49
Fowler, Francis 19:317
Fowler, Frank A. 10:16
Fowler, G. L. 19:252
Fowler, George 10:53;
20:252; 22:142;
24:50
Fowler, Gideon 19:252
Fowler, H. 10:186;
11:202; 18:174
Fowler, H. C. 1:130
Fowler, H. H. 1:128
Fowler, Henry 8:16;
18:134
Fowler, Henry B. 9:34
Fowler, Hiram 20:252
Fowler, I. 10:53
Fowler, Israel 20:3
Fowler, J. 3:73; 14:241;
17:495; 20:252;
27:47
Fowler, J. E. 14:277
Fowler, J. F. 14:61, 167
Fowler, J. W. 9:244;
14:61; 23:143
Fowler, Jacob 22:479
Fowler, James 10:53;
14:61; 20:252;
22:351
Fowler, James B. 11:20
Fowler, James H. 9:12;
10:53
Fowler, James M. 25:32
Fowler, James N. 20:252
Fowler, John 3:73; 7:122;
8:16; 18:134; 20:7;
23:143
Fowler, John T. 23:143
Fowler, Joseph G. 22:30
Fowler, Joseph J. 18:292;
26:98
Fowler, Justin 17:79
Fowler, L. N. 16:32
Fowler, L. W. 13:23
Fowler, Lewis 11:202
Fowler, Lucius 21:332
Fowler, M. E. 10:186;
18:174
Fowler, Manuel 15:55
Fowler, Moses C. 17:236
Fowler, N. C. 14:61

Fowler, Orin 9:214;
21:332
Fowler, Osbrey 21:271
Fowler, Peter 18:306;
26:98
Fowler, Robert 10:53;
20:22, 252
Fowler, Robert A. 12:21
Fowler, Rowland 20:17
Fowler, Rufus 21:332
Fowler, Rufus H. 22:500
Fowler, S. 9:143; 27:45
Fowler, S. B. 16:32
Fowler, S. G. 14:281
Fowler, Samuel 1:33;
3:73; 21:332
Fowler, Samuel A. 11:59
Fowler, Sandy 11:202
Fowler, Stephen 22:250
Fowler, T. 5:16; 25:172
Fowler, Theodore E.
21:117
Fowler, Thomas 9:80;
10:53; 12:95; 19:69;
20:252; 26:27
Fowler, W. 10:144, 186;
18:174; 19:164
Fowler, W. G. 25:172
Fowler, W. H. 5:16; 26:98
Fowler, W. P. 16:191
Fowler, W. R. 15:197
Fowler, W. W. 18:306
Fowler, Washington 4:25
Fowler, Washington F.
22:77
Fowler, Wesley 6:20;
18:82
Fowler, William 7:27, 94;
8:85; 9:118; 14:167;
17:20; 19:14; 22:250;
27:44
Fowler, William C.
22:250
Fowler, William H. 9:21
Fowles, A. 1:129
Fowles, Thomas 11:29
Fowta, J. A. 11:302
Fox, --- 8:72
Fox, A. 3:73; 9:102
Fox, A. I. 26:27
Fox, A. J. 9:80
Fox, Aaron 15:34
Fox, Abram 22:142
Fox, Adam 22:77, 250
Fox, Alex 12:8
Fox, Alfred M. 9:42;
26:123
Fox, Alvin 11:286
Fox, Andrew 7:94
Fox, Andrew J. 22:77
Fox, B. 3:73

Fox, B. F. 23:143
Fox, Barney 24:18
Fox, Barton 1:33
Fox, Benjamin 21:84; 22:299
Fox, Black 25:333
Fox, C. 3:73
Fox, C. A. 14:61
Fox, C. D. 11:105
Fox, C. H. 22:497
Fox, Caesar 22:512
Fox, Charles 1:34; 10:113; 12:21; 18:29; 20:252; 25:33
Fox, Charles E. 13:23; 23:143
Fox, Charles F. 16:94
Fox, Christian 23:243
Fox, D. 11:261; 14:61
Fox, Daniel 7:122
Fox, David 10:208
Fox, Dennis 24:59
Fox, Dewitt C. 7:27
Fox, Dexter 27:46
Fox, Dixon 10:53
Fox, E. 2:10; 3:73; 25:34
Fox, Edward 17:175
Fox, Edward T. 13:23
Fox, Elijah 23:184
Fox, Emmanuel 4:25
Fox, Ezekiel 21:224
Fox, Ezra A. 8:105
Fox, Francis M. 4:25
Fox, Frank 15:197
Fox, Frederick 1:33
Fox, G. 1:129
Fox, G. H. 19:14
Fox, G. W. 21:332
Fox, George 3:73; 4:25; 8:63, 113; 9:102; 14:129; 18:338; 19:69; 20:252; 22:299; 24:8; 25:172
Fox, George C. 1:34; 13:135
Fox, George H. 27:46
Fox, George W. 10:53; 12:142; 20:252
Fox, H. 3:73
Fox, H. A. 13:109
Fox, H. C. 3:73
Fox, Henry 27:45
Fox, Herman 13:23
Fox, Isaac 7:122; 26:236
Fox, J. 1:130; 13:88; 14:10; 17:436
Fox, J. B. 13:124
Fox, J. F. 21:187
Fox, J. H. 15:197; 21:26
Fox, J. W. 16:368

Fox, Jacob 10:113; 12:21; 20:252; 24:183
Fox, James 3:73; 7:94; 11:386; 19:69; 27:45
Fox, James F. 16:33
Fox, James G. 24:89
Fox, James O. 14:28
Fox, James W. 12:21
Fox, Jerry 8:16; 18:134
Fox, John 4:25; 8:16; 9:109; 11:145, 276, 302; 14:61; 15:197, 335; 16:191; 18:134; 20:252; 22:478, 519; 23:143
Fox, John A. 22:462
Fox, John C. 4:25
Fox, John F. 17:95
Fox, John I. 23:30
Fox, John N. 23:104
Fox, John W. 4:25; 23:121
Fox, Jordan 9:130; 27:44
Fox, Joseph 22:121
Fox, Joseph W. 4:25; 20:123
Fox, Josiah 14:61
Fox, Josiah B. 22:424
Fox, K. 15:165
Fox, L. 16:191
Fox, Lar 27:46
Fox, Levi 10:16; 27:46
Fox, Lorenzo 13:57
Fox, Luther T. 22:77
Fox, Lyman 27:42
Fox, M. 3:73
Fox, Michael 14:61
Fox, Miram 4:25
Fox, Nathaniel 14:167
Fox, Nicholas 12:53
Fox, Norman 15:197
Fox, Oscar 11:386
Fox, Owen 8:85
Fox, Owin 18:327
Fox, P. 1:33; 18:49
Fox, P. F. 15:298
Fox, Pat 17:470; 27:46
Fox, Patrick 14:297; 16:292
Fox, Peter 9:16; 13:64; 17:154; 19:69; 25:172
Fox, R. 3:73
Fox, R. J. 1:33
Fox, Ransom 7:57
Fox, Robert 12:21; 21:115; 22:250; 23:143
Fox, Robert Nelson 11:423
Fox, Rudolph 14:167

Fox, S. W. 15:197
Fox, Sidney 25:172
Fox, Simon 9:130; 27:44
Fox, Sol 14:61
Fox, Solomon 5:51; 25:172
Fox, Sylvester 17:70
Fox, Thomas 1:34; 14:61; 18:14; 22:233; 26:159
Fox, Thomas E. 19:334
Fox, W. 3:73; 7:27; 15:86; 25:172
Fox, W. A. 1:130
Fox, W. H. 8:85
Fox, Whitcomb 7:57
Fox, William 1:31; 5:16; 7:94; 12:62, 64; 14:61; 15:34, 66, 91; 17:147; 22:250; 23:240
Fox, William F. 8:16; 9:34; 18:292; 26:98
Fox, William George 20:106
Foxel, William 13:64
Foxworth, John 6:22
Foy, Albert M. 15:291
Foy, Dennis 25:172
Foy, E. 25:172
Foy, G. C. 14:61
Foy, John 25:285
Foy, John C. 21:332
Foy, Mart 26:28
Foy, Patrick 10:145; 19:164
Foy, Reuben 22:77
Foy, Thomas 1:34
Foy, William 10:113; 20:252
Foyd, John 14:167
Foye, G. F. 1:130
Foye, John 9:119
Foyle, Ephraim 21:332
Foyle, J. W. 7:68
Foyles, N. 7:68
Foyster, S. P. 21:332
Fozzard, James 11:29
Fr---, G. 23:203
Fr---, Martin 25:32
Frace, William A. 20:29
Frack, George 17:404
Fradcis, Isaac 19:164
Fradd, Jacob 18:334
Fradenburgh, George L. 5:16
Fragar, Milo 20:17
Frager, M. S. 15:331
Fraggart, James 13:109
Fragleigh, A. 19:69
Frahar, P. 3:73

Frahes, George 11:145
Frahm, John 20:112
Frahn, George 26:160
Frahworth, F. 3:73
Fraiar, S. C. 21:332
Fraige, John 9:68
Fraigien, S. 9:52
Frail, George 10:148;
    18:49
Frail, Martin 10:37
Frailer, VanBuren 3:73
Frailey, I. 8:63
Frain, Hugh 21:332
Frain, Miller 12:21
Frainer, Patrick 12:70
Frair, J. 14:10
Frair, John W. 11:186
Fraisier, W. 18:236
Fraisure, Henry 22:250
Frake, --- 3:73
Fraker, D. 21:121
Fraker, Edmond 10:152
Fraker, John W. 17:91
Fraker, Joseph 23:65
Fraker, Levi H. 17:165
Fraker, Robert 18:49
Fraker, Samuel 22:192
Fraker, Wiley M. 21:51
Frakes, Frederick 8:85;
    18:217
Frakes, J. 22:404
Frakes, John 22:77
Frakes, Joseph 8:16
Frakes, Leonard 9:34;
    18:292; 26:98
Frakes, Sebron 11:59
Frakin, Charles 18:236;
    26:28
Fraland, C. 25:172
Fralech, --- 14:167
Fraley, Ansel 11:146
Fraley, F. 23:143
Fraley, M. 1:34
Fraley, Peter 4:25; 23:179
Fralick, Abraham 7:27
Frall, Patrick 21:332
Fram, Isaac I. 8:16
Fram, John 15:197
Framblay, James 21:332
Frame, Charles W. 18:134
Frame, Hiram 17:443;
    24:177
Frame, Isaac J. 18:134
Frame, John 10:179;
    18:174
Frame, W. 3:74; 8:48
Frame, Watson 21:69
Frame, William 9:21;
    18:306; 26:98
Frames, T. H. 18:29
Framton, T. H. 1:129

Frana, Charles W. 8:16
Frananburg, Jacob 15:34
France, --- 2:10; 25:33
France, Arnold 14:167
France, George 21:332
France, H. A. 14:61
France, Isaac 17:33
France, Jeremiah 8:85
France, John W. 23:143
France, Peter 9:42; 26:123
France, Robert 17:165
France, S. 22:501
France, Thomas 17:296
France, Thomas C. 4:25
France, Thomas J. 17:276
France, William A. 8:113
Francell, Oto 3:73
Frances, A. 20:145
Frances, Benjamin 9:130
Frances, George A.
    14:167
Frances, John 16:191
Frances, M. 25:172
Franch, Joseph S. 15:80
Francher, Andrew J. 22:30
Francher, David B. 20:107
Francher, William 11:202
Franchion, F. 1:34
Francil, P. L. 3:73
Francis, --- 18:327
Francis, A. J. 11:145
Francis, Alexander 19:287
Francis, Ashland 10:113;
    20:252
Francis, Benjamin 27:44
Francis, Benjamin D. 9:9
Francis, Charles 1:32;
    16:191; 19:14;
    21:332
Francis, Charles H. 4:25
Francis, Cyrus S. 12:21
Francis, D. 21:26
Francis, E. S. 17:192
Francis, Edward 6:16;
    9:244; 18:82
Francis, F. 3:73
Francis, Frederick 18:82
Francis, George 6:16;
    18:82
Francis, George W.
    22:462
Francis, H. 3:73
Francis, Henry 12:21;
    25:281
Francis, I. J. 20:252
Francis, Isaac 1:32
Francis, J. 1:33; 3:73;
    21:332
Francis, J. F. 3:73
Francis, J. J. 10:113

Francis, James 10:53;
    13:64; 15:34; 17:355;
    26:27
Francis, John 10:53;
    20:252; 22:299
Francis, John A. 7:71
Francis, John M. 9:176
Francis, John W. 19:245
Francis, Joseph 12:21;
    17:95
Francis, Kermis 17:175
Francis, L. 10:27; 25:172
Francis, Leonard A. 12:21
Francis, Lewis 5:16
Francis, Lorenzo 7:81
Francis, M. 14:281
Francis, M. H. 18:29
Francis, M. J. 21:332
Francis, Marion 17:165
Francis, Milton 5:39
Francis, P. 27:43
Francis, S. 16:191
Francis, S. G. 20:179
Francis, Samuel 7:94;
    10:113; 20:253
Francis, Samuel L. 22:250
Francis, Solomon 7:63
Francis, T. 19:266
Francis, Theodore 9:176
Francis, Thomas 18:189;
    22:77; 23:179
Francis, W. 21:26
Francis, W. L. 19:301
Francis, William 11:276
Francisco, A. 14:61
Francisco, Abraham 10:53
Francisco, Abram 20:253
Francisco, C. 21:26
Francisco, C. H. 20:192
Francisco, James 20:253
Francisco, James R.
    15:197
Francisco, K. 3:74
Francisco, Samuel C.
    10:16
Francisco, William 4:25;
    8:85
Francisco, William A.
    22:143
Franciva, Joseph 18:66
Francois, N. 9:207
Francose, Max 4:25
Franders, Charles 9:80
Frandler, Joseph 20:112
Franger, Philip A. 25:288
Franigan, W. J. 1:34
Frank, --- 12:21
Frank, A. B. 11:146
Frank, Alexander B.
    23:179
Frank, Almond B. 4:25

Frank, Anton 16:118
Frank, Augustus 1:34
Frank, B. F. 20:17
Frank, C. N. 25:33
Frank, Charles 22:351
Frank, Charles A. 10:25
Frank, Christian 1:34;
9:176; 19:252
Frank, Constantine 11:302
Frank, Daniel 21:332
Frank, Daniel L. 17:425
Frank, Elijah H. 23:88
Frank, F. W. 3:74
Frank, Frederick 7:7;
24:77
Frank, Fritz 13:109
Frank, G. 11:191
Frank, G. H. 1:129
Frank, George 15:197;
19:69; 20:253
Frank, Gustavus 12:21
Frank, H. 12:85; 16:191,
292; 25:34
Frank, H. P. 20:253
Frank, Henry 2:10; 14:61
Frank, J. 1:33, 34, 131
Frank, J. W. 11:181
Frank, Jackson 7:57
Frank, James B. 12:153
Frank, Joel 9:34; 23:143
Frank, John 1:33; 11:15;
13:23; 14:61;
18:323; 21:253;
24:150
Frank, John W. 12:57
Frank, Joseph 10:113;
20:253
Frank, Konrad 15:197
Frank, L. G. 23:30
Frank, Lewis 14:167
Frank, Louis 23:107
Frank, N. P. 10:113
Frank, P. 13:88; 14:10
Frank, R. 5:51; 25:172
Frank, R. L. 3:74
Frank, Rolan C. 13:23;
16:33
Frank, S. G. 10:113;
20:253
Frank, W. W. 3:74
Frank, William 20:253
Frankberger, Vincent
17:443
Frankberger, Vinct 24:158
Franke, Charles 23:121
Franke, John 11:60
Franke, John T. 20:7
Franke, R. H. 21:99
Frankenberger, J. K.
22:335

Frankenberry, Benjamin
10:113; 20:253
Frankenthen, Augustus
25:172
Franker, Edmond 18:49
Frankey, William 21:271
Frankfather, George
11:145
Frankford, Henry 23:143
Frankford, Washington
15:351; 16:368
Frankhouser, C. 17:294
Frankhouser, Frederick
22:77
Frankhouser, John 10:53
Frankil, W. N. 19:237
Frankisch, J. K. 2:11;
25:34
Frankle, John L. 9:176
Franklin, --- 14:319;
15:197, 273; 25:276
Franklin, A. 21:121
Franklin, A. C. 21:332
Franklin, Albert 21:332
Franklin, Alex 9:130
Franklin, Alexander 27:44
Franklin, Allen 11:202
Franklin, Andrew 8:105
Franklin, Arch 6:16;
18:82
Franklin, B. 9:52, 65;
17:175; 22:299;
26:160
Franklin, Benjamin 1:192;
9:176; 17:131, 400;
18:206; 19:222, 281;
21:271; 24:193;
25:320
Franklin, Benjamin K.
20:40
Franklin, Brice 8:77
Franklin, Buck 9:165
Franklin, C. 14:61
Franklin, Charles 6:12
Franklin, Charles F.
21:203
Franklin, D. 11:125;
24:18
Franklin, Daniel 17:131;
24:193
Franklin, David 7:122;
11:203; 21:51
Franklin, E. 17:175
Franklin, E. J. 9:71
Franklin, Easom 22:250
Franklin, Edgar F. 23:107
Franklin, Edward 13:57;
16:33
Franklin, Elford 21:332
Franklin, Eli 27:43
Franklin, Elia 9:131

Franklin, Elijah 22:30
Franklin, Elliott 14:167
Franklin, Erastus 21:239
Franklin, F. 1:130
Franklin, G. 20:151
Franklin, G. W. 23:143
Franklin, Gabriel 1:191
Franklin, George 9:200;
10:53; 20:253
Franklin, H. 5:16; 25:172;
27:46
Franklin, Harrison 12:153
Franklin, Henry H. 11:59
Franklin, Hiram 20:87
Franklin, Isaac 8:126
Franklin, J. 1:34, 130;
3:74
Franklin, J. G. 11:125
Franklin, J. W. 11:411
Franklin, James 1:32;
10:95; 11:20, 202
Franklin, James S. 23:65
Franklin, James W. 7:57
Franklin, Jeremiah 21:224
Franklin, Joab 12:21
Franklin, Joel 18:409
Franklin, John 3:74;
7:122; 17:175;
22:404; 23:143, 173
Franklin, John B. 14:167
Franklin, Jonathan 13:23
Franklin, Jordon 21:271
Franklin, Joseph 10:53;
20:253
Franklin, K. 3:74
Franklin, L. 22:192
Franklin, Lewis C. 22:423
Franklin, Loudon H. 4:25
Franklin, Luther 16:139;
21:26
Franklin, M. 14:10
Franklin, Martin 8:69
Franklin, Massals 8:105
Franklin, N. G. 9:21
Franklin, O. H. 9:176
Franklin, Ollen 19:245
Franklin, Olmstead 9:165
Franklin, P. 16:191
Franklin, Pleasant 21:52
Franklin, R. 12:87; 16:292
Franklin, Robert 13:23;
22:250
Franklin, Rolly 20:183
Franklin, Roswell 4:25
Franklin, S. 8:113
Franklin, S. B. 17:247
Franklin, Samuel D. 20:40
Franklin, Samuel M.
10:53; 20:253
Franklin, T. 21:148

Franklin, Thomas 20:133, 253; 21:211; 22:250, 299
Franklin, Thomas J. 21:26
Franklin, Vandy 23:11
Franklin, W. 11:240; 16:369
Franklin, W. E. 1:33
Franklin, W. G. 23:252
Franklin, Wesley 9:131; 27:44
Franklin, Wilburn 18:134
Franklin, William 6:24; 8:16, 48, 77; 9:220; 10:53; 15:341; 16:94; 18:366; 20:253; 22:192, 250; 23:30, 143; 25:172
Franklin, William G. 7:94
Franklin, Willis 9:200; 19:290
Franklinburg, C. 3:74
Franklow, R. L. 16:33
Frankohl, Fred 7:94
Franks, C. R. 18:236; 26:28
Franks, Charles 17:79; 26:160
Franks, E. 14:167
Franks, F. 15:106
Franks, J. 24:18
Franks, J. D. 26:219
Franks, James H. 21:332
Franks, John 1:32
Franks, Louis 7:94
Franks, M. P. 1:130
Franks, Mary Ann 26:219
Franks, O. 9:131; 27:44
Franks, W. H. 15:197
Franks, W. I. 26:28
Franks, W. L. 18:236; 26:28
Franks, William 15:197; 22:423
Franks, William H. 17:51
Franner, Marcus 25:320
Fransburg, Henry C. 20:253
Franscois, N. 18:66
Fransh, John H. 18:323
Fransk, A. 25:32
Fransworth, P. 1:130
Franton, J. D. 16:369
Frantz, F. J. 3:74
Frantz, Henry M. 10:113; 20:253
Frantz, Jac 3:74
Frantz, Louis 20:253
Frantz, Marion 22:30
Frantz, Peter 12:21
Franueprets, C. 18:29

Frany, T. 19:164
Franzen, A. A. 21:332
Frarrow, Robert 18:49
Frary, J. 13:88; 14:10
Frary, Jerome A. 16:33
Frary, T. 10:153
Fraser, Alfred 18:49
Fraser, J. H. 3:74
Fraser, Louis 21:332
Fraser, Ransom 9:102
Fraser, Thomas 8:16
Frasey, J. B. 11:261
Frash, J. 27:144
Frasher, J. 19:296
Frasher, Joseph 4:25
Frasier, C. 16:191
Frasier, H. C. 16:369
Frasier, Jacob 22:423
Frasier, James 3:74
Frasier, Joseph 10:114; 20:253
Frasier, Perry 8:77
Frasier, Simon 26:160
Frasier, W. 26:28
Frask, Stephen 9:80
Frask, W. P. 16:191
Frask, Warren 24:170
Fraskey, John 22:335
Frass, Lewis 3:74
Frassary, Casper 16:33
Frasure, Andrew 5:39
Frauer, W. 23:88
Fraunch, Frank 11:118
Fravel, Jesse 23:128
Fraver, L. 3:74
Fraville, J. 16:191
Fravis, Jacob S. 18:395
Fravo, John 25:172
Fravosse, A. F. 15:197
Fraw, Orin R. 10:16
Frawley, J. 26:160
Frawley, Patrick 13:135; 19:346; 22:335
Fray, --- 14:167
Fray, Henry 21:332
Fray, Isaac B. 11:29
Fray, Jasper 2:10
Fray, Jerome A. 13:23
Fray, John 14:167; 25:33
Fray, John F. 9:80
Fray, William H. 22:143
Frayden, W. J. 12:153
Frayer, A. 15:322
Frayer, Daniel 3:74
Frayer, Fred. H. 21:332
Frayer, J. C. 9:52
Frayley, James 14:269
Frayor, John 16:191
Fraypat, --- 3:74
Frayser, Philip 25:296

Frayshure, Joshua R. 18:366
Frazbugh, A. 19:69
Fraze, Jonathan 15:13
Frazee, Alva H. 23:88
Frazee, George 21:52
Frazee, Isaac 20:253
Frazee, Oliver 21:224
Frazell, Azarias 17:20
Frazell, J. 23:143
Frazell, M. M. 21:26
Frazer, Albert B. 4:25
Frazer, David 17:175; 24:39
Frazer, Edwin 11:115; 13:23
Frazer, George 17:51
Frazer, Henry 17:161
Frazer, J. H. 1:97
Frazer, James 9:131; 24:18
Frazer, Jarrett 10:155
Frazer, John 9:119
Frazer, John W. 14:167
Frazer, L. L. 11:145
Frazer, Martin 9:42
Frazer, O. E. 11:84
Frazer, P. 7:27
Frazer, S. 1:97
Frazer, Squire 17:175
Frazer, Walter 14:167
Frazey, John 20:40
Frazier, --- 1:131; 15:197; 19:164
Frazier, A. 19:69; 22:479; 25:172
Frazier, A. L. 14:61
Frazier, Adam W. 7:122
Frazier, Albert 17:95; 19:45
Frazier, Alex 22:478
Frazier, Alexander 5:39
Frazier, Andrew 1:32
Frazier, Asa 17:175
Frazier, C. C. 27:43
Frazier, C. O. 9:42; 26:160
Frazier, Catharine 27:45
Frazier, D. W. 1:33
Frazier, David M. 4:25
Frazier, Ed 17:175
Frazier, Edmond 22:299
Frazier, Edward A. 22:479
Frazier, Edwin 16:33
Frazier, F. 25:172
Frazier, Frank J. 5:16
Frazier, Frederick 24:193
Frazier, Freeman 24:170
Frazier, G. G. 9:143
Frazier, G. W. 1:32
Frazier, George 21:332

Frazier, George W. 23:30
Frazier, Hardrick 11:302
Frazier, Henry L. 19:69
Frazier, I. 1:32
Frazier, Ira M. 21:26
Frazier, Isaac 10:114
Frazier, Isaac D. 20:141
Frazier, Israel 21:332
Frazier, J. 1:32; 13:88
Frazier, J. F. 9:143
Frazier, J. H. 9:143; 27:43
Frazier, J. L. 17:147
Frazier, James 1:33;
    18:82; 24:18, 111;
    27:44
Frazier, Jesse 10:53;
    20:253
Frazier, John 1:33; 3:74;
    7:49; 18:206; 19:14;
    22:192; 27:45
Frazier, Joseph 22:30
Frazier, M. 21:333
Frazier, Milton S. 19:69
Frazier, Nicholas 4:25
Frazier, Oliver K. 11:302
Frazier, Robert 19:164;
    21:26
Frazier, S. 14:61
Frazier, Thomas 9:21;
    18:134, 320
Frazier, Thomas G. 17:95
Frazier, W. 9:109
Frazier, William 8:101;
    9:200; 12:55;
    17:460; 21:130;
    22:77; 24:157
Frazier, William H. 4:25
Frazier, William J. 22:171
Frazler, J. 14:10
Frazuer, Freeman 17:423
Frazur, C. R. 3:74
Fre, Samuel 24:50
Freals, James 16:369
Frears, Daniel 9:109
Freary, John 3:74
Freas, George 18:49
Freas, J. 27:43
Freas, John E. 9:72
Frease, G. 23:30
Freazer, Rufus 14:167
Freck, S. 3:74
Fred, Charles 21:52
Fred, George 21:333
Fred, James 15:341
Fredail, M. 14:10
Fredd, John W. 22:192
Freddle, Dallas 17:397
Frede, Charles 18:134
Fredembirg, Delos W.
    15:22
Fredenberger, --- 23:203

Fredenburg, Delos W.
    15:22
Fredenburg, E. R. 1:34
Fredenburg, F. 3:74
Fredenburg, Frank B. 8:16
Fredenburg, George
    11:261
Fredenburg, Henry 21:203
Fredenburgh, Harvey
    21:291
Frederic, Jacob 18:284;
    26:134
Frederich, John 14:61
Frederich, Q. 14:61
Frederick, --- 3:74; 18:29
Frederick, A. J. 17:323
Frederick, Adrian 21:247
Frederick, B. 25:172
Frederick, Benjamin 20:17
Frederick, C. 3:74
Frederick, Corvin B.
    24:50
Frederick, D. 1:130
Frederick, David 8:85
Frederick, Edward 9:159;
    20:154
Frederick, Fritz 10:53
Frederick, G. 3:74
Frederick, George 4:25;
    14:277; 17:276;
    23:184
Frederick, H. K. 9:80;
    26:27
Frederick, Henry 10:152
Frederick, J. 1:94
Frederick, Jacob 9:80;
    10:53; 20:253; 26:27
Frederick, James M.
    22:192
Frederick, John 3:74;
    11:386; 12:70;
    14:236; 15:66;
    22:192
Frederick, Julius 12:70
Frederick, Kundt 11:29
Frederick, L. 3:74; 18:14
Frederick, Lewis 10:53;
    20:253
Frederick, M. 17:337
Frederick, Nelson A.
    17:73
Frederick, Omeman
    16:369
Frederick, Philip 8:16
Frederick, Phillip 18:134
Frederick, Reuben 17:352
Frederick, Samuel 10:53;
    20:253
Frederick, W. R. 17:443;
    24:158
Frederick, William 22:424

Fredericks, Augustus 4:25
Fredericks, D. 25:172
Fredericks, David 5:16
Fredericks, Edward 1:33
Fredericks, George 1:32
Fredericks, John 18:110
Fredericks, Q. A. 3:74
Frederickson, Hans C.
    4:25
Frederidge, A. 3:74
Fredgil, M. 13:88
Fredick, J. H. 25:172
Fredie, Charles 8:16
Fredingil, T. 9:143
Fredingill, L. 27:43
Fredline, Isaac 26:159
Fredly, David 5:16
Fredmore, F. N. 19:69
Fredough, George 3:74
Fredrew, Charles R. 26:27
Fredwood, George 18:29
Free, C. 3:74
Free, C. H. 16:292
Free, Charles 15:197
Free, Chauncey 11:286
Free, Christ 24:111
Free, George 18:236;
    26:27
Free, Henry 8:16; 18:134
Free, J. 1:32; 3:74; 25:34
Free, James 10:186;
    18:174
Free, John 4:25; 11:401
Free, M. 3:74
Free, R. C. 11:219
Free, W. S. 12:166
Free, William 10:53;
    18:49; 20:253
Freeborn, James S. 22:479
Freeborn, Philip P. 20:137
Freeborn, S. 25:172
Freece, William 23:143
Freed, A. 25:34
Freed, J. B. 24:77
Freed, Jacob 7:27
Freed, John 24:39
Freed, Richard 1:33
Freed, Solomon 26:159
Freed, William H. 1:33
Freedenberg, Fred 20:253
Freedlander, C. 3:74
Freedline, John 11:145
Freeham, Jesse D. 25:32
Freehouse, Samuel 4:25
Freel, A. F. 20:253
Freel, Austin F. 10:53
Freel, G. W. 14:288;
    23:98
Freel, George 14:265
Freelan, Lucius 9:204
Freelan, William 9:157

Freeland, B. F. 15:197
Freeland, C. 12:21
Freeland, Charles 5:16; 11:105
Freeland, Clark 13:23
Freeland, Henry 27:43
Freeland, J. H. 25:172
Freeland, T. J. 9:52
Freeland, W. 14:61
Freeland, W. J. 25:172
Freeland, William 1:34
Freeley, Daniel 9:160
Freeleyhouse, Edward 21:333
Freelind, --- 1:131
Freelock, William 14:167
Freelove, H. 3:74
Freelove, James 18:353
Freelove, W. 26:27
Freelow, L. 21:333
Freeman, --- 25:320
Freeman, A. 1:130; 12:8
Freeman, A. J. 21:333
Freeman, A. M. 22:30
Freeman, A. S. 21:333
Freeman, A. W. 4:25
Freeman, Aaron 8:16; 18:134
Freeman, Adam 4:25
Freeman, Alexander 6:24
Freeman, Alonzo 12:70; 15:34
Freeman, B. 3:74
Freeman, B. C. 16:369
Freeman, Benjamin 25:320
Freeman, C. 14:61
Freeman, C. D. 9:176; 19:237
Freeman, C. O. 19:164
Freeman, C. R. 3:74
Freeman, Charles 5:16; 7:122; 9:131; 22:279
Freeman, Charles W. 7:27
Freeman, D. 3:74; 9:143
Freeman, Daniel 1:33; 7:94
Freeman, Daniel L. 11:92
Freeman, David 9:21; 18:306
Freeman, Dean 11:202
Freeman, Dennis 4:25
Freeman, E. 11:29
Freeman, E. E. 5:39
Freeman, Ed 17:159
Freeman, Edward 6:16; 7:122; 12:21; 24:39
Freeman, Edwin R. 24:93
Freeman, Enes 25:172
Freeman, Francis 15:197

Freeman, Franklin 10:160
Freeman, G. 1:130; 17:291
Freeman, G. E. 2:11; 25:32
Freeman, G. F. 25:271
Freeman, G. L. 1:32
Freeman, G. P. 1:129
Freeman, G. T. 7:57
Freeman, G. W. 22:192
Freeman, Gardner C. 20:107
Freeman, George 1:32; 8:48; 10:53; 12:49
Freeman, George M. 4:25
Freeman, George W. 15:66; 21:253, 333
Freeman, Gerard 19:287
Freeman, H. 25:173
Freeman, H. H. 13:88
Freeman, Harrison 8:105
Freeman, Henry 5:39; 6:16; 11:125; 15:197; 21:271
Freeman, Henry B. 24:18
Freeman, Henry W. 7:122
Freeman, Hiram 19:164
Freeman, Horace 22:143
Freeman, Hosea H. 24:59
Freeman, Howard W. 22:30
Freeman, J. 25:172
Freeman, J. A. 9:52
Freeman, J. C. 1:129; 23:144; 25:172
Freeman, J. W. 7:79; 21:333; 23:144; 25:296
Freeman, Jackson 4:65
Freeman, Jacob 7:27; 11:202
Freeman, James 8:16; 10:160; 19:164; 21:84; 22:450
Freeman, James E. 22:121
Freeman, James H. 25:288
Freeman, James M. 17:160
Freeman, James N. 9:21; 18:306; 26:97
Freeman, Jerkin 22:462
Freeman, Jesse N. 23:98
Freeman, Jesse S. 21:86

Freeman, John 3:74; 10:53; 11:105, 255; 16:33, 191; 20:253; 21:253; 22:250; 23:65
Freeman, John E. 22:121
Freeman, John F. 13:109

Freeman, John H. 9:12, 131
Freeman, John L. 17:70
Freeman, John W. 8:85; 11:261; 27:43
Freeman, Jordan 9:131
Freeman, Joseph 5:39; 10:172; 19:164; 24:183
Freeman, Julius 16:191
Freeman, L. 9:114; 14:62
Freeman, L. E. 25:172
Freeman, Levi 23:270
Freeman, Lewis 15:341; 16:369
Freeman, M. L. 6:30; 25:320
Freeman, Mary Jane 26:219
Freeman, N. 17:265
Freeman, N. N. 1:33
Freeman, Nathan 18:217
Freeman, Orin 21:137
Freeman, Orlan 11:276
Freeman, Peter 8:16
Freeman, Porter 24:101
Freeman, R. E. 12:140
Freeman, R. M. 3:74
Freeman, S. 1:130; 5:51; 10:205; 14:133; 25:172; 27:144
Freeman, Samuel D. 21:91
Freeman, Sandy 22:299
Freeman, Tarquin 7:122
Freeman, Thomas 6:23; 9:52
Freeman, Thomas J. 22:77
Freeman, Titus 21:333
Freeman, Victor 8:16; 18:134
Freeman, W. 3:74; 5:51; 25:172
Freeman, W. L. 22:351
Freeman, W. M. 3:74
Freeman, W. R. 25:172
Freeman, Washington L. 11:59
Freeman, Watson E. 11:92
Freeman, William 10:114; 20:253; 22:519; 23:30
Freeman, William F. 12:21
Freeman, William L. 22:450
Freeman, William M. 18:346
Freeman, William W. 21:253
Freemann, Josiah 4:25
Freemont, J. 3:74

Freemont, O. 1:33
Freer, Moses 13:23
Freer, Samuel 7:94;
   15:364; 19:69
Freer, Simon 16:94
Freer, Solomon 8:39
Frees, G. W. 14:265
Frees, George A. 9:42
Frees, J. H. 20:253
Frees, Joseph 17:321
Frees, W. 14:288
Freese, G. W. 23:144
Freese, H. 1:130
Freese, Isaac P. 12:21
Freese, William 20:17
Freeser, Terance 15:197
Freet, J. 3:74
Freezar, James 9:96
Freeze, Anniel 25:32
Freeze, H. 9:143
Freeze, John 17:313
Frefry, Charles F. 4:25
Frego, Amos 5:16; 25:172
Frei, F. 20:154
Freiburgh, Henry 10:53
Freidenburg, William
   15:66
Freiderberg, Fred 10:53
Freidly, Samuel 21:333
Freiholtz, Ferdinand
   23:88
Freil, George 14:265
Freise, John 1:33; 3:74
Freitzland, Frank 7:122
Freiud, Andy 8:72
Frek, Philip 27:45
Freks, F. 3:74
Freleigh, C. 25:172
Frelestree, George 11:191
Freligh, Charles 5:16
Frelinger, William 11:92
Frells, William H. 22:30
Frelst, --- 21:201
Freltz, Jasper 19:69
Fremain, Don 8:16;
   18:134
Freman, C. O. 10:172
Freman, Charles 27:44
Freman, D. 27:45
Freman, David 27:43
Freman, Ed 27:44
Fremas, William 15:55
Fremier, Enoch 21:333
Frenald, B. W. 1:129
French, --- 25:33
French, A. 3:74; 14:286
French, A. B. 14:62
French, A. E. 1:129
French, Albert 9:143;
   27:45
French, Alexander 4:25

French, Alfred E. 12:21
French, Alice 27:45
French, Alonzo 9:80
French, Annus 10:53
French, Anthony M. 22:30
French, Armus 20:253
French, C. D. 13:109;
   14:241
French, C. R. 12:70;
   15:81
French, C. S. 27:47
French, Chancey 24:93
French, Charles 12:21;
   14:167, 281; 17:392
French, Charles E. 8:117;
   19:315
French, Clayton H. 22:77
French, D. 1:131
French, D. B. 1:130;
   26:160
French, D. C. 14:331
French, D. L. 14:62
French, David 17:175
French, David J. 15:7
French, Davis 19:164
French, Durbin 11:60
French, Edward R. 4:25
French, Eli 8:85
French, Ephraim 12:21
French, Ephriam 17:276
French, Erastus 10:160
French, Erastus D. 19:164
French, F. 16:369
French, Francis 23:283
French, Francis M. 11:386
French, Franklin 11:423
French, G. 1:129
French, G. C. 21:333
French, G. H. 1:131
French, George 3:74;
   15:197
French, George L. 4:25
French, George S. 7:94
French, George W. 7:27;
   11:84; 20:189;
   22:166
French, H. F. 15:197
French, Hallis 9:42
French, Hayden F. 18:217
French, Henry 14:334;
   16:369; 25:173
French, Henry C. 11:423
French, Hollis 26:123
French, Ira J. 13:23; 16:33
French, J. 3:74
French, J. E. 21:333
French, J. H. 14:62;
   20:137
French, J. M. 21:333
French, J. O. 17:310

French, James 1:34; 3:74;
   7:68; 8:113; 12:172;
   19:14
French, James M. 9:161;
   14:327
French, John 8:16;
   10:114; 14:62;
   16:191; 17:242;
   18:134; 20:253;
   23:179; 25:173
French, John C. 3:74
French, John H. 8:113;
   15:34
French, Jonas 14:167
French, Joseph 10:17;
   23:144
French, Josiah 22:423
French, Lewis J. 20:123
French, M. 11:105
French, M. F. 9:42
French, Marion S. 20:22
French, Martin A. 22:279
French, Milton 17:397
French, N. W. 19:224
French, Noah 12:99;
   15:347, 366
French, O. 13:109
French, Orion 14:167
French, Peter 16:131
French, Philip 10:53;
   20:253
French, Quincy 17:14
French, R. 15:341
French, Robert 8:39, 48
French, Robert G. 22:121
French, Robert H. 21:114
French, S. 9:109
French, S. B. 13:88
French, S. W. 1:34
French, Samuel 9:200
French, Shadrick 11:326
French, Theodore S. 10:91
French, Thomas J. 17:276
French, William 24:61
French, William B. 8:85
French, William G. 12:21
Frenchman, John 9:207
Frenck, James W. 11:59
Frenck, Joseph 3:74
Frenden, Simon H. 19:69
Frendes, Jacob 14:168
Frenon, C. C. 18:66
Frensh, M. A. 11:29
Frentleman, Charles 8:85
Frento, Lewis 16:94
Frenwith, Robert 16:191
Freny, George 16:191
Fresboure, H. 13:88
Freschuer, L. 19:164
Fresel, G. 27:43
Fresel, H. A. 14:62

Fresgate, James 15:16
Fresh, Conrad 18:306; 26:98
Fresh, Henry W. 11:15
Freshbergar, Henry 20:253
Freshberger, Henry 10:53
Freshman, Charles 15:359; 19:70
Freshour, J. 23:144
Freshour, James 17:79, 355
Freshour, John 21:52
Freshour, U. F. 22:479
Freshour, William 22:250
Freshours, Charles 15:158
Freshwater, W. 1:32
Fresil, Frederick 9:52
Frestone, Franklin 17:273
Fretcher, M. 3:74
Fretnall, T. E. 14:281
Frets, Henry B. 22:233
Fretty, L. D. 15:298
Fretwell, F. E. 14:281
Fretze, Isaac 16:33
Freulick, J. 1:34
Frevart, Charles 8:72
Frew, John 2:11
Frew, Joseph 1:32
Frew, R. 11:386
Frey, A. J. 15:197
Frey, Albert 13:127
Frey, Christian 23:121
Frey, George 17:73
Frey, H. 15:258
Frey, Henry 23:144
Frey, I. F. 26:28
Frey, Jacob 16:94, 118
Frey, James 15:165
Frey, Jasper 25:34
Frey, John 14:168
Frey, John M. 4:25; 12:70
Frey, Mathias 16:152
Frey, Nidas 9:220; 18:366
Frey, Sandford 27:42
Frey, Urias 9:52
Freymayer, Jacob 12:21
Freymoyer, F. 1:34
Freytag, Henry 25:173
Frezlich, Abraham 11:412
Friar, E. 18:366
Friar, F. 9:220
Friar, John 23:30
Friar, Joseph 12:95
Fribble, Benjamin F. 20:253
Frible, William 7:27
Frick, Benjamin 11:29
Frick, C. 1:129
Frick, Franklin S. 23:11

Frick, George 15:318; 19:70
Frick, J. 1:130
Frick, John D. 19:14
Frickel, Conrad 22:479
Fricker, G. 1:131
Fricker, Henry 23:179
Frickey, Christopher 22:192
Fricking, F. 21:333
Frickle, John 10:53; 20:253
Frickle, Lucian 21:333
Fricks, A. 3:74
Fricks, Aaron 9:143
Fricks, Daniel D. 22:250
Fricks, Walter 13:23
Frida, E. H. 25:173
Fridager, John 22:192
Friday, Adam 22:519
Friday, E. A. 5:16
Friday, H. 14:62
Friday, Henry 12:87; 16:292
Friday, John 10:114; 20:253
Friday, Peter 20:107
Friday, S. T. 3:74
Fridenburgh, Albert 26:27
Frider, Valentine 15:197
Fridge, A. C. 18:236; 26:28
Fridland, George 11:302
Fridley, D. 25:173
Fridley, Henry 16:369
Fridley, J. 24:77
Fridley, Russel H. 19:315
Frie, R. C. 22:192
Frieand, T. A. 15:13
Frieburg, Henry 20:253
Fried, George D. 23:144
Fried, Jacob D. 22:10
Fried, John 7:27; 10:9
Fried, S. 3:74
Friedle, Samuel 23:113
Friedline, A. 1:32
Friedly, Dan 27:46
Friedman, Adam 26:236
Friedmann, N. 23:30
Friedriskie, Frederick 24:58
Friedt, Hardin 21:26
Friel, D. 3:74
Friel, George 9:200
Friel, J. 1:130
Friel, William H. 7:14
Frieland, Henry 9:143
Friell, W. J. 23:98
Friem, Elisha 14:168
Friend, A. J. 14:168
Friend, Alfred 27:42

Friend, Anton Will 22:30
Friend, Bacharies 21:333
Friend, Charles 17:169; 22:77
Friend, Daniel 11:146
Friend, Elijah 15:13
Friend, Francis A. 12:70
Friend, J. 9:228; 18:366
Friend, Jacob 23:144
Friend, Joseph 14:168; 18:110
Friend, Levi M. 22:192
Friend, Nelson 22:77
Friend, Peter 24:39
Friend, S. 8:48
Friend, William 11:29
Friend, William D. 26:27
Friendly, Samuel 21:333
Friends, D. P. 18:174
Frier, Henry M. 12:161
Frier, J. 12:81; 16:292
Frier, James 9:34; 18:292; 26:98
Frier, John 3:223
Frier, Joseph 15:359; 19:70
Frierstine, Jacob 18:292
Frierwood, George 23:65
Friery, J. 13:88
Fries, Daniel L. 15:66
Fries, F. 10:146
Fries, George L. 26:123
Fries, Gilbert 15:197
Fries, J. B. A. 25:173
Fries, James E. 5:16
Friesback, Charles 19:164
Friesch, C. H. 9:109
Friesistoni, Jacob 9:34
Friesner, Joseph 17:321
Friest, W. 25:32
Friestine, Jacob 26:98
Friezel, G. 9:143
Friffin, W. B. 19:232
Frigate, David 11:59
Frigate, Preston 9:72
Frigle, Edward 7:27
Frigle, Esard 14:335
Frigold, C. 22:30
Frigts, Lewis 16:293
Friks, Thomas 21:333
Frill, G. 19:281
Frill, G. E. 15:341; 16:369
Frill, Joseph 27:46
Frilledge, Charles 20:253
Frimood, Adam 21:69
Fringle, Jacob 10:17
Frinier, Austin 18:29
Frink, Alonzo 21:333
Frink, B. 17:79
Frink, C. 20:137; 25:173
Frink, Charles 12:21

Frink, Christopher 5:16
Frink, D. 1:129
Frink, G. W. 25:33
Frink, Horace K. 20:7
Frink, John 4:25
Frink, Thomas W. 9:119
Frink, W. 14:62
Frinkham, J. 13:88
Frinkle, Peter 21:333
Frior, James K. 24:66
Fripp, A. J. 12:142
Fripp, E. G. 12:95
Frisbee, H. 3:75
Frisbee, J. 25:173
Frisbee, James 21:333
Frisbee, John H. 26:27
Frisbee, M. B. 9:143;
　　27:43
Frisbee, T. H. C. 14:168
Frisbee, William A.
　　17:212
Frisbey, Christopher
　　9:176
Frisbey, Vincent 17:65
Frisbie, Caleb 21:253
Frisbie, James 15:278
Frisbie, William A.
　　15:106
Frisbie, Z. 3:75
Frisborne, H. 14:10
Frisby, A. 3:75
Frisby, Charles 13:57;
　　24:177
Frisby, Charles G. 17:425
Frisby, Enos 24:18
Frisby, G. C. 21:137
Frisby, John 5:39
Frisby, Levi 3:75
Frisby, N. 15:263
Frisby, R. W. 17:79
Frisby, Ran'd. 1:32
Frisby, William L. 3:75
Frisch, J. G. 15:263
Frische, John F. 1:34
Frischknect, J. 1:128
Frischmann, George
　　22:192
Frisener, Eli 27:45
Frish, A. 1:32
Friske, M. N. 25:33
Frisler, Jeremiah 1:33
Frisley, William B. 22:112
Frissle, H. A. 14:62
Frissler, H. 18:49
Frist, Henry 20:253
Fristermacher, Abraham
　　25:269
Fritch, Alise 13:109
Fritcher, Edward L.
　　20:137
Fritchler, A. 1:34

Fritchler, D. 7:27
Frith, George 4:25
Fritig, John 23:179
Fritig, John P. 23:179
Frits, Andrew 25:173
Frits, E. 26:27
Fritsch, R. 20:253
Fritsche, H. 19:301
Fritsha, August 4:25
Fritts, Alvin W. 10:114;
　　20:253
Fritts, David C. 21:69
Fritts, Samuel 20:137
Frity, A. 25:173
Fritz, --- 22:77
Fritz, A. 3:75
Fritz, Charles 7:27; 14:62
Fritz, D. 3:75
Fritz, Dexter 23:144
Fritz, E. 9:80
Fritz, Franklin 10:53
Fritz, G. 14:297; 17:470;
　　27:46
Fritz, G. W. 23:144
Fritz, Henry 9:21; 18:306;
　　22:30; 26:97
Fritz, Henry A. 9:119;
　　27:45
Fritz, I. 26:27
Fritz, Isaac 13:23
Fritz, J. 3:75; 9:220;
　　18:366
Fritz, Jack 22:143
Fritz, Jacob 11:146
Fritz, Jer 1:33
Fritz, John 11:146; 22:233
Fritz, John K. 2:10; 25:32
Fritz, Joseph 15:267
Fritz, Josiah 9:80
Fritz, L. 1:33
Fritz, Lawrence 21:253
Fritz, Levi 9:109
Fritz, Lewis W. 24:89
Fritz, Louis 17:503
Fritz, Michael 22:192;
　　25:173
Fritz, Peter A. 1:32
Fritz, Thomas 17:95
Fritz, Walter 14:168
Fritz, William H. 10:114;
　　20:254
Fritzenshal, Conrad
　　21:333
Fritzhue, F. 18:134
Fritzman, J. W. 3:75
Fritzs, F. 20:254
Fritzs, Fred 20:254
Fritzshe, H. 12:146
Frizell, J. W. 27:46
Frizell, James H. 22:30
Frizen, John W. 22:351

Frizzee, John 23:30
Frizzell, Alonzo 17:212
Frizzell, Henry 17:212
Frizzell, Hugh 17:389
Frizzell, Winston 17:51
Frizzett, C. C. 18:409
Frizzle, John 7:57
Frizzle, Riley 9:220
Frock, B. T. 12:21
Frock, J. W. 15:197
Frock, Michael 22:424
Froebe, Nicholas 18:306;
　　26:98
Froechlick, W. 15:106
Froelich, Antonie 9:176
Froelin, J. W. 12:70
Froeline, J. W. 15:91
Froeman, J. 9:154
Frogg, Francis J. 17:52
Frohan, George 20:254
Frohbart, Ferdinand 13:23
Frohen, George 8:16
Froisdorff, Ferdinand
　　24:70
Froleck, A. 19:281
Froley, John 3:75
Frolich, William 11:401
Frolier, Jacobs 18:440
Froman, J. 16:267
Froman, Wilson 17:131
Fromard, A. 14:10
Fromer, William A. 9:34
Frompton, Caleb M. 19:14
Fromy, David 9:176
Frondin, Brownlow
　　17:165
Froney, Robert 22:335
Front, Andrew 14:168
Front, John O. 13:23
Front, Tobias 4:65
Fronta, Charles 9:165
Frontione, John 25:173
Froome, Franklin 21:26
Frosh, C. 15:267
Froshet, John 26:211
Fross, J. 3:75
Frossary, Casper 13:23
Frost, A. 3:75; 14:62
Frost, Aaron H. 21:253
Frost, Allen 9:131; 27:44
Frost, Andrew J. 4:25
Frost, B. 3:75; 14:168,
　　255
Frost, C. 14:130
Frost, C. B. 13:64
Frost, C. C. 9:109
Frost, Charles 15:123
Frost, Christopher 9:230;
　　20:254
Frost, Constant 22:501

Frost, Curtis 12:122; 15:123
Frost, D. 3:75
Frost, E. 14:168, 255; 18:237; 26:28
Frost, E. G. 10:114; 20:254
Frost, E. M. 9:227
Frost, E. R. 1:130
Frost, Edwin B. 21:203
Frost, Eli 22:299
Frost, Emory 9:109
Frost, Feilder 9:119
Frost, Filiber 27:45
Frost, Francis 23:144
Frost, Francis M. 22:508
Frost, Frederick 21:99
Frost, G. 22:192
Frost, G. W. 8:105; 13:109
Frost, G. W. H. 16:192
Frost, George 15:34
Frost, George C. 21:333
Frost, George W. 19:286
Frost, H. 26:236
Frost, H. E. 20:151
Frost, Henry 17:346
Frost, I. C. 19:270
Frost, J. A. 20:254
Frost, J. W. 18:82
Frost, James 9:176; 15:318; 19:227
Frost, James A. 10:53
Frost, James R. 8:16; 18:134
Frost, John 4:25; 17:20, 415; 21:333
Frost, John A. 10:160; 19:164
Frost, John H. 9:34; 18:292; 26:98
Frost, John J. 24:152
Frost, John W. 21:253
Frost, Merritt C. 12:21
Frost, Nathaniel S. 21:253
Frost, P. 1:131
Frost, Robert B. 22:192
Frost, S. 11:303, 395
Frost, S. W. 1:128
Frost, Samuel 22:250
Frost, Sardine 21:203
Frost, Solomon 22:450
Frost, Sumner 7:57
Frost, T. 19:227
Frost, Thomas 9:176
Frost, W. H. 9:119; 27:45
Frost, W. T. 18:174
Frost, Wallace 7:94
Frost, Westley 22:31
Frost, William 10:53; 14:168; 15:106;

Frost, William 16:192; 17:496; 20:254
Frost, William H. 9:119
Frost, William T. 10:186
Frost, Wilson C. 11:296
Froster, William 21:333
Frothengham, Charles 18:276
Frother, Jerome 22:192
Frothingham, Charles 9:66
Frothingham, Edw. 16:85
Frothingham, G. 13:109; 16:192
Froule, F. 3:75
Frout, John W. 15:283
Frouville, Lewis 17:20
Frowler, Joseph D. 9:34
Froy, Frank 14:168
Frozer, J. 1:97
Fruby, John 9:176
Frudbury, Frank B. 18:134
Frudenburgh, Albert 9:80
Fruitt, Jeff 15:165
Frukerson, H. R. 7:57
Fruly, P. 3:75
Fruman, D. S. 20:254
Fruman, Edward 18:82
Frun, P. 14:10
Frund, William 9:80
Fruny, Isaac 8:112
Frur, Thomas 7:57
Fruschley, F. 3:75
Frusdale, John 22:192
Frusell, G. W. 3:75
Frusher, Daniel 17:242
Fruss, George 10:148
Frutinger, Peter 4:25
Frutz, S. J. 17:79
Fry, --- 21:69
Fry, A. 1:130; 3:75; 9:143
Fry, Abram 22:233
Fry, Alexander 3:75
Fry, Alfred 14:168
Fry, Allen 11:319; 27:43
Fry, Andrew J. 9:220; 18:366
Fry, C. 13:64
Fry, Calvin 17:148
Fry, Charles 4:25; 10:53; 20:254; 22:143
Fry, Christopher 16:192
Fry, D. 8:48
Fry, David 10:114; 20:254
Fry, David C. 21:69
Fry, E. 1:131
Fry, E. C. 21:333
Fry, Enoch 10:114; 20:254
Fry, F. 14:62; 16:267

Fry, Flavins 17:280
Fry, Frank 13:88
Fry, Franklin 16:192
Fry, G. R. 22:250
Fry, George 17:79; 21:88; 22:192
Fry, George W. 22:233
Fry, H. 16:192
Fry, Henry 3:75; 9:21; 22:299
Fry, Isaac 12:70; 15:66; 23:30
Fry, J. 1:130
Fry, J. C. 16:192
Fry, J. R. 14:168
Fry, Jacob 3:75; 20:255; 22:31, 479
Fry, James 8:16; 18:134; 19:290
Fry, James L. 21:69
Fry, James S. 13:23
Fry, Joel 17:199
Fry, John 3:75; 4:25; 7:57; 14:62; 21:333; 25:173; 26:159
Fry, John D. 22:478
Fry, John P. 23:66
Fry, Jonathan 18:237; 26:28
Fry, L. F. 17:20
Fry, Levi 22:31
Fry, Lewis 7:94; 23:144
Fry, M. 1:131; 3:75
Fry, Marion 22:279
Fry, N. 1:131
Fry, Peter 9:34; 14:62, 168
Fry, Peter S. 7:27
Fry, Ransford H. 22:143
Fry, Reuben 10:53; 20:254
Fry, S. 3:75
Fry, Samuel 22:479
Fry, Simeon 23:30
Fry, Thomas 15:198; 17:91; 19:164; 24:101
Fry, W. 1:32
Fry, W. P. 19:227
Fry, William 23:301
Fry, William L. 3:75
Fryant, John 13:109
Fryar, John T. 17:504
Fryar, P. 16:279
Fryberger, Philip 12:21
Frydebolt, F. 1:32
Frye, Augustus 19:164
Frye, Charles 16:164
Frye, David 23:30
Frye, Ira 11:218
Frye, J. C. 1:128

Frye, John 4:25; 16:164
Frye, William 9:96
Fryer, Charles 13:23;
    27:46
Fryer, Edward 16:33
Fryer, Francis N. 11:29
Fryer, George 15:198
Fryer, Henry 12:21
Fryer, I. 15:341
Fryer, J. 13:88; 16:369
Fryer, J. F. 1:129
Fryer, James J. 17:52
Fryer, John H. 4:25
Fryer, P. H. 20:254
Fryer, P. N. 10:114
Fryer, W. L. 3:75
Fryling, W. 12:99
Fryman, Jacob 24:77
Fryman, Matthew 23:98
Fryman, P. 18:49
Frymon, James 11:303
Frymyer, William 22:233
Fryor, James R. 1:32
Frys, W. F. 25:173
Frysher, Joshua B. 9:220
Frysinger, S. R. 1:131
Frysler, H. 10:148
Fub, George 15:198
Fuch, Charles 27:46
Fuchs, George 10:114;
    20:254
Fuchs, John 25:173
Fuchs, Seigel 18:110
Fuchtman, F. 9:109
Fucks, H. 3:75
Fucks, John 21:333
Fudge, Henry 22:77
Fudge, William 10:95
Fuedell, John 7:27
Fuel, Ephraim 17:33
Fuel, John 10:208
Fuelder, Aaron 11:422
Fuell, Silas 24:213
Fuft, E. 3:75
Fugate, Marion 17:161
Fugate, William W.
    22:192
Fugett, Henry A. 17:453
Fugett, W. 3:75
Fugg, William 11:231
Fugie, Paul 10:10
Fugit, G. 7:27
Fugitt, Henry A. 24:183
Fugitt, James B. 17:501
Fugleberg, John 17:359
Fugna, George 5:39
Fugua, G. 25:173
Fuguson, Joseph 18:426
Fuke, George 7:27
Fuks, George 7:27
Fulbert, Sam 22:512

Fulcher, Joseph 18:395
Fulcher, William 19:164
Fulconier, J. 1:131
Fulda, Hugo 19:14
Fulden, D. 14:168
Fulevider, Andrew 24:158
Fulford, Edward 25:173
Fulford, R. J. 25:173
Fulgan, Joseph 19:317
Fulgham, E. 25:173
Fulghum, J. W. 23:292
Fulhamer, W. 12:92
Fulheart, Samuel 19:267
Fulk, Charles 22:404
Fulk, Francis M. 23:66
Fulk, Jacob 9:52
Fulk, James 12:53
Fulk, John A. 22:77
Fulk, Joseph 14:62
Fulk, Samuel 10:91
Fulk, Thomas J. 22:424;
    23:66
Fulk, W. 22:192
Fulk, William 22:77
Fulkenson, Charles D.
    4:25
Fulkerson, C. F. 14:62
Fulkerson, Henry F.
    22:497
Fulkerson, J. J. 1:130
Fulkerson, Loriston A.
    17:287
Fulkerson, W. 3:75
Fulkes, N. 14:315
Fulkinson, James 1:31
Fulkison, --- 3:75
Fulkison, Thomas R.
    17:33
Fulks, Charles 20:97
Fulks, Coleman 11:408
Fulks, Drew 22:299
Fulks, John 9:236; 26:219
Fulks, Joseph W. 16:33
Fulks, Samuel 9:131;
    27:44
Fulks, William T. 23:98
Full, A. 9:52
Full, George 18:189
Full, Peter 22:192
Full, William 20:254
Full, William A. 25:33
Fullager, William H. 4:25
Fullam, Lawrence 7:49
Fullbo, Nels 17:449
Fullbright, James B.
    20:183
Fullenwider, James D.
    23:88
Fuller, --- 18:346
Fuller, --- (Mrs.) 18:430

Fuller, A. 1:130; 3:75;
    7:72
Fuller, A. B. 17:435
Fuller, A. F. 26:160
Fuller, A. H. 20:33
Fuller, Abram 15:106
Fuller, Alb 19:14
Fuller, Albert 7:27
Fuller, Albert B. 24:177
Fuller, Albert T. 21:99
Fuller, Alexander 25:285
Fuller, Alfred 22:512
Fuller, Alvin 11:401
Fuller, Amos L. 7:68
Fuller, Anson 20:17
Fuller, B. 12:49
Fuller, B. F. 14:62, 168
Fuller, Benjamin 11:105;
    12:21
Fuller, Bennet 20:254
Fuller, Bennett C. 22:423
Fuller, Bermott 10:53
Fuller, Bethael 25:173
Fuller, C. 3:75; 11:125
Fuller, C. H. 19:237
Fuller, C. W. 3:75
Fuller, Calvin 19:70
Fuller, Charles 20:107
Fuller, Charles C. 24:93
Fuller, Charles D. 1:33
Fuller, Charles H. 9:176;
    22:279
Fuller, Coleby E. 4:25
Fuller, Daniel 17:446;
    24:170
Fuller, Daniel C. 20:22
Fuller, David 8:16; 18:135
Fuller, E. 9:143; 21:333
Fuller, E. B. 22:335
Fuller, Edward C. 23:189
Fuller, Edwin G. 25:33
Fuller, Elijah 8:16; 18:135
Fuller, Ellick 1:32
Fuller, F. 11:145; 25:271
Fuller, Ferry C. 18:66
Fuller, Fred. R. 17:65
Fuller, G. 3:75; 13:88;
    14:10
Fuller, G. A. 3:75; 26:27
Fuller, G. H. 7:74; 25:296
Fuller, George 3:75; 13:57
Fuller, George A. 9:80
Fuller, George J. 15:11
Fuller, George W. 24:93;
    25:173
Fuller, Gilbert F. 15:165
Fuller, Gordon 10:17
Fuller, H. 3:75; 22:192
Fuller, H. A. 15:151
Fuller, H. C. 3:75; 8:48
Fuller, Henry 6:24; 7:27

Fuller, Henry A. 14:168; 15:341
Fuller, Henry G. 5:16
Fuller, Henry H. 16:369
Fuller, Henry W. 13:23
Fuller, Ihrimintus 7:94
Fuller, Ira B. 3:75
Fuller, Irvin 3:75
Fuller, Isaac H. 8:16; 18:135
Fuller, J. 11:302; 25:33
Fuller, J. B. 3:75
Fuller, J. D. 1:129
Fuller, J. F. 15:198
Fuller, J. H. 14:168; 17:291
Fuller, J. H. H. 1:32
Fuller, J. M. 14:168
Fuller, J. P. 1:129; 13:23; 16:33
Fuller, Jacob D. 17:313
Fuller, James 1:192; 9:21; 18:306, 430; 19:164; 26:98
Fuller, James G. 21:333
Fuller, Jasper M. 22:423
Fuller, Jeremiah 7:94
Fuller, John 12:21; 23:144
Fuller, John A. 14:168
Fuller, John H. 22:31
Fuller, John K. 22:450
Fuller, John M. 9:12
Fuller, John R. 23:30
Fuller, Joseph 15:7; 21:26
Fuller, Levi 5:16; 25:173
Fuller, Lewis 21:333
Fuller, Lorenzo 10:114; 20:254
Fuller, Lyman 20:112
Fuller, M. 25:173
Fuller, M. J. 1:32
Fuller, M. J. L. 27:43
Fuller, M. S. 8:16; 18:135
Fuller, Marcellus R. 22:121
Fuller, Martin V. R. 10:17
Fuller, Morgan 10:114; 20:254
Fuller, Moses 5:39
Fuller, N. 3:75
Fuller, N. T. 14:168
Fuller, Nathan 22:77
Fuller, Nelson 19:14
Fuller, Nichols 10:172
Fuller, O. A. 13:23
Fuller, O. B. 11:60
Fuller, O. M. 9:80
Fuller, O. N. 26:27
Fuller, Orlando V. 23:88
Fuller, Oscar E. 11:105
Fuller, Philip 11:146

Fuller, Robert 20:254
Fuller, Romandel 25:32
Fuller, Russell 8:72
Fuller, S. 1:34; 3:75
Fuller, S. W. 5:16; 25:173
Fuller, Salon 8:113
Fuller, Samuel 16:94; 22:143
Fuller, Samuel A. 25:33
Fuller, Sidney 21:253
Fuller, Spencer J. 20:22
Fuller, Squire 1:33
Fuller, Stephen 4:25; 24:39
Fuller, Stephen G. 22:143, 462
Fuller, Stillman 27:45
Fuller, W. 3:75; 14:168, 255; 15:34; 17:33
Fuller, W. C. 15:329; 19:70
Fuller, W. H. 1:129
Fuller, William 1:33; 12:21; 20:254
Fuller, William A. 15:198; 24:93
Fuller, William B. 20:29
Fuller, William D. 25:173
Fuller, William H. 11:118; 21:117
Fuller, William L. 20:107
Fuller, William O. 1:31
Fuller, William S. 9:80
Fuller, Y. 16:192
Fullerton, A. B. 1:131
Fullerton, Benjamin 22:351
Fullerton, C. W. 16:369
Fullerton, Corwin 10:98
Fullerton, David 10:114
Fullerton, E. 3:75
Fullerton, George W. 8:85
Fullerton, J. 3:75; 24:77
Fullerton, J. E. 22:192
Fullerton, James B. 22:10
Fullerton, John 15:25
Fullerton, Joseph 12:21
Fullerton, Thomas 18:395
Fullerton, W. H. 17:352
Fullerton, W. M. 25:33
Fullerton, William 10:114; 20:254
Fullerton, William M. 11:145
Fullhart, Samuel 9:176
Fullhill, George W. 8:85
Fullingston, G. E. 19:301
Fullington, L. B. 20:254
Fullington, Lucien B. 10:53
Fullman, August 23:128

Fullman, Frederick 22:404
Fullman, Michael 22:31
Fullman, Phineas 16:33
Fullmer, Abr 20:40
Fulls, John 22:299
Fullum, M. 27:43
Fullum, Samuel 12:49
Fully, Joshua 8:85
Fully, Samuel 11:60
Fulman, George C. 19:14
Fulmber, David 4:25
Fulmer, David 11:261
Fulmer, Edward C. 17:79
Fulmer, J. 19:70
Fulmer, Jacob 9:72
Fulmer, James S. 22:479
Fulmer, John 22:192
Fulmer, M. 14:168
Fulmer, William M. 11:261
Fulner, J. 15:359
Fulp, Emanuel 12:70
Fulper, Theodore 14:336
Fulsk, Thomas J. 22:192
Fulsome, H. O. 25:173
Fulter, Smith D. 27:46
Fulterman, Henry 24:39
Fultersmith, D. 14:297; 17:477
Fultig, Joseph 8:85
Fultingson, G. E. 10:27
Fultner, Andrew M. 8:105
Fulton, A. K. 17:322
Fulton, Anthony 5:39
Fulton, Charles 15:198
Fulton, Charles C. 18:29
Fulton, Chester G. 13:23; 16:33
Fulton, D. C. 17:143
Fulton, David 20:254
Fulton, David R. 14:168
Fulton, E. 11:412
Fulton, G. H. 1:33
Fulton, George E. 13:23
Fulton, Harry 7:27
Fulton, Horatio P. 18:276
Fulton, J. 1:130; 25:297
Fulton, J. C. 13:109
Fulton, J. S. 15:151
Fulton, James 15:315; 17:148
Fulton, James F. 16:293
Fulton, John 10:17
Fulton, Joseph 7:77; 19:70
Fulton, Nelson G. 23:66
Fulton, Philip 8:69
Fulton, R. 1:130
Fulton, R. D. 1:34
Fulton, Robert 25:173
Fulton, Robert A. 7:27
Fulton, Robert K. 19:70

Fulton, S. 25:173
Fulton, Thomas A. 3:75
Fulton, W. 2:11; 25:31
Fulton, W. T. 7:49
Fulton, William 11:59;
  14:168; 19:287;
  23:240
Fulton, William J. 11:303
Fulton, Winfrey 8:16;
  18:135
Fultonling, --- 16:293
Fults, --- 9:236
Fulty, Christian 22:450
Fulty, George 26:159
Fulty, Jasper 13:64
Fulty, Nathaniel 13:88
Fultz, Cyrus 21:271
Fultz, D. 26:219
Fultz, George 20:40
Fultz, George W. 1:33
Fultz, J. B. 20:56
Fultz, John 13:109;
  24:111
Fultz, R. A. 14:62
Fulwider, Andrew 17:418
Fulwider, J. W. 17:145
Fuly, Thomas 15:198
Fuman, F. E. 21:137
Fumerich, Julius 15:35
Fumwalt, Isaac 14:168
Funck, J. B. 1:128
Funck, John 23:30
Fund, David 7:27
Funderback, George
  21:271
Funderburg, Jacob W.
  20:7
Funderburk, Abel E.
  10:91
Funderburk, C. C. 14:62
Funderbusk, William
  21:187
Funderlover, John 14:168
Fundern, Adam 21:52
Fundiberg, William
  22:192
Funds, F. 27:42
Fundy, F. 3:75
Funer, John 18:440
Funiack, J. 1:34
Funk, Abraham 19:14
Funk, Boone 23:144
Funk, Charles 19:325
Funk, Frederick 20:104;
  24:77
Funk, George 25:320
Funk, H. P. 11:419
Funk, Henry 10:114;
  11:59; 14:168;
  20:254
Funk, Jacob 18:217

Funk, Jacob R. 22:479
Funk, James 17:79
Funk, James G. 4:25
Funk, Jethro 23:144
Funk, John 17:248; 26:27
Funk, John M. 11:145
Funk, Joseph 19:70
Funk, L. 3:75
Funk, Miles 6:11
Funk, Milton P. 15:198
Funk, S. 1:131
Funk, W. 21:52
Funk, William 12:21;
  14:169; 15:81
Funk, William D. 8:85
Funk, Wrenklin 1:33
Funke, Charles 8:85
Funke, John 13:109
Funkes, E. E. 23:30
Funkhoun, John 14:62
Funkhouser, John 3:75
Funks, William 3:75
Funky, John 25:33
Funn, A. P. 9:119
Funnell, Edward 21:245
Funnell, James 22:299
Funnell, W. H. 17:152
Funston, James 23:113
Fuping, F. 23:113
Furay, Arthur 12:21
Furback, C. 15:198
Furbeck, Seymour H.
  19:14
Furber, Marsh 21:333
Furbinger, M. 20:254
Furbish, Charles 7:8
Furborn, J. W. 14:62
Furbringer, Matthias
  10:53
Furbrow, William 12:168
Furbur, Joseph 16:85
Furbush, John 25:320
Furbush, William 1:33
Furby, G. M. 11:29
Furby, Isaac 11:146
Furch, John H. 10:114
Furcham, W. 14:10
Furderburgh, Hiram 8:105
Furey, Franklin 14:169
Furey, Joseph 23:189
Furg, William J. 19:165
Furgarson, John 20:254
Furgason, Benjamin 12:21
Furgason, G. B. 20:254
Furgason, H. 25:173
Furgason, J. 27:46
Furgason, J. R. 25:173
Furgason, James 21:130
Furgason, Robert F.
  20:254
Furge, Isaac 7:79; 25:297

Furgeon, William 13:110
Furgerson, A. 25:33
Furgerson, Charles 11:303
Furgerson, Daniel 19:70
Furgerson, J. 19:70
Furgerson, J. R. 18:440
Furgerson, James K. 19:70
Furgerson, John 16:192
Furgerson, Jones G.
  12:161
Furgerson, Samuel 14:169
Furgerson, William
  21:333
Furgeson, David 15:320
Furgeson, DeWitt 10:17
Furgeson, George W.
  23:301
Furgeson, Jacob 17:273
Furgeson, John 13:88;
  16:94
Furgeson, Joseph A.
  16:119
Furgeson, S. 13:88
Furgeson, W. 3:75
Furgson, W. T. 11:84
Furgueson, Henry 11:202
Furgurson, J. H. 16:192
Furgurson, W. B. 8:16
Furguson, Daniel 22:250
Furguson, Daniel W.
  23:144
Furguson, E. H. 18:174
Furguson, Fenus 24:193
Furguson, G. M. 10:95
Furguson, H. 3:75
Furguson, Ham 17:280
Furguson, J. 1:129;
  17:148; 24:111
Furguson, J. K. 3:76
Furguson, J. M. 3:76
Furguson, Jackson 10:53
Furguson, John 3:76;
  15:359
Furguson, John W. 8:85;
  23:240
Furguson, O. P. 22:335
Furguson, Oscar F. 22:423
Furguson, Owen W. 9:156
Furguson, Samuel 11:202;
  24:177
Furguson, T. 3:76
Furguson, W. R. 3:76
Furguson, William 17:14;
  22:121
Furguson, William A.
  21:224
Furguss, --- 15:165
Furgusson, Joseph 19:270
Furgusson, Zachariah 8:85
Furleson, A. 13:64
Furling, Patrick 12:64

Furlong, J. 12:81; 16:293
Furlong, Patrick 15:35
Furlong, Robert 16:147
Furlong, S. P. 21:121
Furlough, Benjamin F. 20:139
Furlough, S. 3:76
Furman, D. 3:75
Furman, E. 25:173
Furman, George 14:169
Furman, J. 23:179; 25:173
Furman, James 15:283; 19:70
Furman, W. M. 13:110
Furnace, J. 25:32
Furnace, Joseph 21:333
Furnald, Charles 17:46
Furndes, Furdes 7:27
Furneld, Samuel F. 12:153
Furner, A. A. 12:153
Furner, W. E. 1:129
Furness, Benjamin 12:153
Furney, James 25:173
Furney, N. 1:130
Furnham, Thomas S. 16:33
Furnice, E. 7:27
Furnice, J. 2:11
Furnish, Charles S. 21:52
Furniss, Henry 21:333
Furnister, George 1:33
Furnum, Thomas 16:33
Furock, Gustave 11:125
Furr, E. 3:76
Furr, George 22:251
Furr, William W. 23:98
Furrel, Henry 17:452
Furrey, N. 20:40
Furry, D. C. 11:60
Furry, E. 11:261
Furry, James 19:14
Furry, John 8:72
Furry, Patrick 16:119
Furry, William M. 22:77
Furse, Robert 11:145
Fursin, George 15:198
Furst, Charles 22:479
Furstine, John R. 10:53
Furth, F. 3:76
Furton, William 7:27
Fury, James 10:114; 20:254
Fus, John 8:72
Fusby, S. 19:165
Fusche, William 24:170
Fusheller, Max 7:94
Fusho, John 15:335
Fushya, Solomon 1:32
Fusick, J. 13:81
Fusiher, Camille 21:333
Fusing, Henry 18:66

Fusner, J. E. 3:76
Fuson, A. J. H. 24:77
Fuson, Amos H. 10:95
Fuss, Mathias 25:173
Fusselman, Michael 22:77
Fussleman, J. 3:76
Futcher, Sandy 21:333
Fute, James 7:95
Futherstoen, Chris 11:202
Futrell, William 10:114
Futrell, William H. 20:255
Futtman, Frederick 25:281
Futts, Patrick 22:10
Fuver, E. 3:76
Fuze, James 16:192
Fye, David 11:191
Fye, Jacob 10:114
Fyer, Wesley 13:110
Fyn, M. 12:21
Fytt, B. 17:95

G

G---, A. 27:47
G---, A. J. 23:203
G---, A. W. 11:428
G---, Alonzo 20:92
G---, B. 17:192
G---, C. 26:162
G---, C. J. S. 17:217
G---, D. 11:262; 16:119
G---, D. C. 25:35
G---, D. N. 11:303
G---, Daniel 15:201
G---, David 15:298
G---, E. 20:154; 21:166
G---, E. D. 17:357
G---, E. M. 11:240
G---, E. N. 11:303
G---, E. W. M. 26:162
G---, F. 14:269; 20:92
G---, F. C. 15:201
G---, F. J. 9:119
G---, G. 15:326; 22:351; 23:268
G---, H. 11:261; 26:162
G---, H. C. 18:103
G---, H. D. 15:151
G---, H. R. 20:56
G---, Henry 11:119
G---, I. 10:27
G---, I. B. 15:201
G---, Isaac 11:241
G---, J. 14:269; 15:201; 17:364; 20:255; 23:263; 24:214
G---, J. C. 16:192
G---, J. E. 19:167
G---, J. G. 26:220
G---, J. H. 23:259; 24:66

G---, J. J. 18:66
G---, J. M. 11:340
G---, J. P. 17:337
G---, J. P. C. 11:303
G---, J. S. 17:217
G---, J. W. 18:83
G---, Jacob 11:303
G---, James 18:285; 26:134
G---, John 24:214; 27:47
G---, L. 17:364; 18:238
G---, L. B. 11:241
G---, L. E. 16:192
G---, M. 24:111
G---, M. B. 26:162
G---, M. V. 27:48
G---, Marshall H. 9:214
G---, N. 23:276
G---, O. 25:37
G---, P. 9:227
G---, R. 12:166; 18:29; 19:167; 22:351
G---, R. F. 15:263
G---, S. D. 23:292
G---, S. F. W. 11:240
G---, S. M. 11:286
G---, T. 23:85, 268
G---, T. E. 22:351
G---, T. J. 27:47
G---, T. M. 24:109
G---, W. 17:192
G---, W. A. 10:192; 16:94; 26:204
G---, W. H. 12:142; 20:255
G---, W. L. 17:364
G---, W. M. 19:73
G---, W. P. 17:364
G---, W. R. 25:297
G---, W. S. 9:52
G---, W. W. 17:248; 20:255
G---, William 16:119
G---, William E. 15:298
G-----, ----- 22:31
G---r, George 23:30
G---r, H. 25:36
G., L. 26:31
Ga---, --- 17:502
Gabbart, S. B. 11:395
Gabbert, Henry M. 18:395
Gabbett, G. 12:92; 16:293
Gabble, Henry 11:262
Gabble, J. 11:203
Gabbott, J. F. 14:62
Gabbott, William 20:255
Gabel, Charles 11:115
Gabel, William 17:33
Gabert, Herbert 16:192
Gabert, Isaac 14:169
Gable, G. W. 10:53

Gable, Jacob 12:8
Gable, Joel C. 10:17
Gable, Philip 18:217
Gabler, George 4:26
Gabler, Henry 21:224
Gabott, William 10:53
Gabran, P. 14:62
Gabrial, Jacob 19:70
Gabriel, Charles 8:16; 18:135
Gabriel, Dennis 22:335
Gabriel, F. 27:49
Gabriel, I. N. 22:192
Gabriel, Isaac 9:207
Gabriel, Jacob 26:162
Gabriel, James 13:57; 16:192
Gabriel, Joseph 7:123
Gabriel, Reuben 7:122; 21:333
Gabriel, Richard 22:192
Gabrielson, Gabriel 8:117; 19:315
Gabulison, J. 3:76
Gaby, John 15:198
Gachdon, Benjamin F. 14:169
Gachet, Sherman L. 14:336
Gachwind, Charles 9:22
Gacon, Alexander 16:94
Gadd, Frank 22:31
Gaddie, Alfred W. 20:185
Gaddie, George 11:92
Gaddies, Norman W. 20:7
Gaddin, Daniel 14:169
Gaddis, --- 15:123
Gaddis, Daniel 17:52
Gaddis, Henry H. 23:98
Gaddis, Hiram 18:412
Gaddis, James W. 17:280
Gaddis, Jesse 9:131; 27:50
Gaddis, Nathan 17:427
Gaden, John 21:333
Gades, Thomas 26:29
Gadiact, William 27:144
Gadis, Thomas 9:95
Gadkin, G. H. 3:76
Gadner, B. 12:161
Gae, Sabina 27:51
Gaertner, H. 16:147
Gaeser, Peter 10:114; 20:255
Gaff, Henry 8:105
Gaff, Lindsay O. 16:33
Gaff, R. 3:76
Gaffeny, Patrick 26:162
Gaffeny, Richard 23:121
Gaffering, John 3:76
Gaffield, Thomas 2:11

Gaffing, Thomas 18:338
Gaffney, John 10:10
Gaffney, Michael 25:37
Gaffney, P. 7:72
Gaffney, T. H. 1:132
Gaffney, Timothy 9:80; 26:29
Gafford, James 21:203
Gafforey, Peter 21:334
Gaffy, William 18:217
Gagahan, John 25:173
Gagan, James 22:335
Gagan, Thomas 3:76
Gage, --- 27:53
Gage, A. 1:133
Gage, A. P. 16:293
Gage, Albert 4:26
Gage, Amos 9:52
Gage, B. 24:111
Gage, Benjamin 19:165
Gage, Charles E. 11:105
Gage, Daniel B. 21:114
Gage, E. 25:38
Gage, Edmund C. 2:11
Gage, Elias 16:94
Gage, Franklin 13:23
Gage, Godfrey 17:33
Gage, H. 9:66
Gage, H. C. 13:64; 16:192
Gage, Henry 19:165
Gage, Isaac 25:297
Gage, J. 1:37
Gage, Josiah H. 13:23; 16:33
Gage, L. D. 25:173
Gage, M. I. 10:160
Gage, M. J. 19:165
Gage, Michael 22:519
Gage, Nelson 27:47
Gage, Peter 22:299
Gage, Samuel C. 9:176
Gage, Samuel H. 7:8
Gage, W. H. 19:14
Gage, W. L. 1:133
Gage, William 6:14; 18:82
Gage, William C. 12:21
Gager, George 11:203
Gager, J. 14:169, 255
Gaggerty, W. A. 7:83
Gaghan, William 3:76
Gaghigan, J. 14:297; 17:473
Gagin, John 8:85
Gahaer, J. 14:269
Gahagan, John 13:64
Gahide, Henry 1:36
Gahle, Franklin 7:95
Gahlier, --- 9:176
Gaibel, H. 7:49
Gaicia, --- 19:322
Gaier, G. 3:76

Gaige, William H. 21:69
Gail, --- 7:27
Gail, Lewis 9:207
Gailag--er, Michael 15:198
Gailamore, Elisha 9:34
Gaile, Jack 6:16
Gaile, John 18:82
Gailes, John G. 9:21; 18:306; 26:98
Gailey, J. 13:88
Gailord, --- 15:198
Gaily, John R. 22:425
Gaily, Simon 13:79
Gaily, Solomon 13:127
Gaim, James 22:251
Gaimes, Augustus W. 18:189
Gaimes, Mary C. 18:189
Gaimo, F. 25:173
Gain, J. 21:334
Gaines, --- 26:211
Gaines, A. 3:76
Gaines, Alfred 25:173
Gaines, C. 3:76
Gaines, C. W. 16:192
Gaines, Charles 9:207
Gaines, F. 19:281
Gaines, Ferdinand 9:176
Gaines, G. 25:173
Gaines, George 24:39
Gaines, Green 24:194
Gaines, Harriet 16:71
Gaines, Henry 18:237; 26:30
Gaines, James 7:71; 22:299
Gaines, John 22:251
Gaines, John M. 11:412
Gaines, John P. 22:121
Gaines, Joseph H. 18:135
Gaines, L. 18:434
Gaines, Lewis 7:123
Gaines, Louis 21:334
Gaines, Maria 16:71
Gaines, Mary Thomas 26:211
Gaines, Ore B. 19:165
Gaines, Parker 16:71
Gaines, Pleasant 7:123
Gaines, Robert 7:123
Gaines, Samuel 18:49
Gaines, T. B. 21:334
Gaines, William 26:29
Gainor, F. 27:49
Gains, David 17:131; 24:194
Gains, Eli 21:26
Gains, George B. 20:97
Gains, J. H. 19:70
Gains, Sullivan 11:401

Gainsey, Theodore 15:173
Gainy, Thomas 12:22
Gairam, Taylor 26:161
Gairety, P. 22:251
Gairo, James 9:207
Gaiser, Ernest J. 20:7
Gaith, Edward 11:203
Gaither, James 20:56
Gaither, M. G. S. 17:14
Gaithwaite, Henry 24:158
Gaiton, Hugh 12:22
Gakston, Marion 21:239
Gal---ender, J. 25:37
Galaeway, Francis 19:70
Galager, P. 25:173
Galagher, E. 3:76
Galagher, J. 1:37
Galahe, J. M. 18:237;
    26:31
Galaher, L. M. 24:18
Galamo, J. W. 23:240
Galasha, J. E. 7:27
Galaway, Calvin C.
    20:255
Galb, J. A. 9:96
Galberson, Samuel B.
    18:189
Galbradson, A. 9:242
Galbraith, C. 3:76
Galbraith, E. 22:299
Galbraith, G. W. 3:76
Galbraith, H. 27:48
Galbraith, Johnson 22:404
Galbraith, L. S. 3:76
Galbraith, M. 9:143
Galbraith, Robert A.
    22:31
Galbraith, Samuel J.
    22:404
Galbrath, William 17:387
Galbreath, John W. 8:85
Galbreth, George W.
    18:306; 26:99
Galbreth, Robert 12:153
Galcher, John 8:85
Galday, Peter 27:47
Galder, William 8:105
Gale, --- 21:334
Gale, A. 21:334
Gale, Alfred 12:49
Gale, Andrew H. 23:121
Gale, B. 3:76
Gale, George 3:76
Gale, George W. 10:25;
    23:66
Gale, H. Wallace 22:31
Gale, Hollister E. 21:334
Gale, James 6:16; 18:82
Gale, James S. 27:48
Gale, John 17:391
Gale, Justus F. 21:133

Gale, Lewis 14:319;
    16:192
Gale, Louis 25:272
Gale, Orlando 9:176;
    19:237
Gale, Robert 18:82
Gale, S. G. 1:133
Gale, Spencer H. 10:114;
    20:255
Gale, T. 23:117
Gale, Walter 3:76
Galegher, Robert 26:123
Galena, P. H. 14:333
Galenar, H. C. 22:193
Galentine, William A.
    12:22
Gales, Alexander 24:18
Gales, Frank 17:175
Gales, Isaiah 12:49
Gales, S. W. 16:369
Gales, W. H. 26:99
Gales, William H. 9:21
Galey, Fisher 18:217
Galey, James 7:27
Galey, Simon 16:192
Galey, William 18:217
Galfilland, R. 13:88
Galgan, James 22:251
Galgean, G. 22:251
Galghan, Pat 14:169
Galhoun, H. 12:164
Galiger, Anthony 16:192
Galiger, P. 14:62
Galigher, Patrick 17:202
Galigher, Robert 9:42
Galihan, William Henry
    27:51
Galiher, Daniel 10:114;
    20:255
Galihorn, G. 17:252
Galimus, Michael 5:51
Galispie, Pat 22:251
Gall, Anton 23:113
Gall, George W. 10:17;
    13:23
Gall, J. F. 22:11
Gall, Jacob A. 22:193
Gall, Jeff 9:200; 19:290
Gall, John Z. 17:415
Gall, R. H. 14:62
Gall, Robert 16:33
Gallacan, Martin 23:200
Gallachal, Peter 27:48
Galladay, Major 22:299
Gallagar, Richard 19:70
Gallager, J. 15:173
Gallager, James 19:14
Gallager, John 17:33
Gallager, William 4:26
Gallagher, --- 8:125;
    19:320, 322

Gallagher, A. 14:62
Gallagher, Abraham
    23:179
Gallagher, Charles H.
    14:169
Gallagher, E. 1:132
Gallagher, Edmond
    23:144
Gallagher, Edward 4:26;
    14:169
Gallagher, Elza 11:303
Gallagher, F. 3:76; 13:23;
    16:33, 119; 27:49
Gallagher, Francis 22:335
Gallagher, G. 3:76
Gallagher, H. 14:169
Gallagher, H. O. 7:27
Gallagher, Hugh 14:241;
    18:276; 27:53
Gallagher, I. 3:76
Gallagher, J. 1:37; 16:119
Gallagher, J. D. 12:53
Gallagher, James 10:27;
    16:94, 119; 19:165,
    301; 22:335; 25:37
Gallagher, James S.
    18:395
Gallagher, Jeremiah
    16:152
Gallagher, Jerry 16:33
Gallagher, John 8:85;
    16:293, 369; 21:334
Gallagher, John M.
    10:160; 19:165
Gallagher, L. 14:169
Gallagher, L. G. 1:132
Gallagher, Luke 11:92
Gallagher, M. 21:26
Gallagher, Michael 20:37,
    255; 23:242
Gallagher, P. 3:76; 25:297
Gallagher, Patrick 19:329;
    22:11
Gallagher, Preston 22:501
Gallagher, Robert 10:160;
    19:165
Gallagher, Samuel 8:16;
    18:135
Gallagher, T. 16:369
Gallagher, Thomas 14:62;
    19:317
Gallagher, William 1:36;
    3:76; 12:53
Gallagher, William J. 7:14
Gallahan, J. 3:76
Gallaher, C. 15:86
Gallaher, C. B. 18:135
Gallaher, Crawford 12:70
Gallaher, George H. 9:80
Gallaher, George W.
    17:109

Gallaher, Hugh 15:35
Gallaher, James 3:76
Gallaher, John 21:115, 271
Gallaher, M. B. 20:151
Gallaher, Michael 10:114
Gallaher, P. 3:76
Gallaher, William 18:237; 25:35; 26:31
Gallahur, Harrison 10:95
Gallam, Nathan C. 26:29
Gallan, William 16:117
Gallar, James 9:177
Gallard, Thomas H. 11:279
Gallaspie, John 21:271
Gallaspie, William 21:271
Gallaspy, Henry 27:52
Gallat, James 18:135
Gallatin, Antony 7:123
Gallatin, Joseph 22:166
Gallavin, J. 3:76
Gallavin, Michael 4:26
Gallaway, Benjamin 20:255
Gallaway, Calvin C. 10:53
Gallaway, D. W. 11:303
Gallaway, Elias A. 13:76
Gallaway, Elisha 16:192
Gallaway, Francis 15:329
Gallaway, G. 14:277
Gallaway, George 12:49
Gallaway, J. T. 19:14
Gallaway, Samuel 17:20
Gallaway, W. 27:53
Galleanor, David I. 23:144
Gallecheimer, George 10:114
Gallego, Prudencio 8:123
Gallegos, Felip 19:319
Galleher, John 8:101
Galleher, S. K. 23:144
Galleher, William 18:135
Gallemore, Elisha 26:99
Gallen, Thomas F. 17:79
Galler, James 19:252
Galler, L. 22:31
Galles, Orristus 4:26
Gallet, James 8:16
Gallett, L. 3:76
Galletts, W. 25:277
Galley, Alexander 10:155
Galley, N. 19:227
Galley, Nathaniel 9:177
Galley, Samuel 11:303
Galley, Samuel F. 7:27
Gallie, Joseph 25:36
Gallier, F. H. 15:66
Galligan, Peter 10:9
Galligan, Philip 21:334

Galligar, George 19:70
Galliger, A. 13:64
Galliger, Charles 23:113
Galliger, Dennis 9:236; 26:219
Galliger, Eugene 22:351
Galliger, F. 3:76
Galliger, George 13:64
Galliger, J. 16:94; 27:48
Galliger, W. 3:76
Galliger, William 12:22; 13:110
Galligers, John 12:22
Gallighan, Henry 9:119
Gallighan, Mathew 7:95
Gallighar, Frank 20:255
Galligher, F. 3:76
Galligher, J. 9:143
Galligher, James 14:169
Galligher, Michael 10:53
Galligher, P. 3:76
Galligher, Patrick 5:16; 15:305; 19:70
Galligier, Thomas 19:14
Galliher, C. B. 8:16
Galliher, C. W. 24:77
Galliher, Frederick R. 20:17
Galliher, Gaines M. 22:251
Galliher, James 12:142
Galliher, John 17:460; 24:158
Galliher, William 8:16
Gallimicks, T. H. 27:53
Gallimore, W. A. 24:19
Gallin, J. 1:131
Gallin, Scioto 18:189
Gallion, David 9:21; 18:306; 26:99
Gallis, Joseph 2:11
Gallis, Nathan 24:183
Gallison, J. M. 17:165
Gallison, William 19:70
Gallivan, Patrick 15:364; 19:70
Gallivan, T. R. 16:85
Gallman, William 16:33
Gallmicks, T. H. 14:241
Gallocks, W. C. 11:423
Galloman, Patrick 13:23; 16:33
Gallop, Henry 12:62
Gallop, Leroy 11:398
Gallop, Lewis C. 26:99
Gallop, Louis 18:306
Gallop, W. 25:174
Gallops, Louis C. 9:21
Gallough, Joseph 2:11
Galloway, A. A. 20:183
Galloway, C. 18:110

Galloway, Charles 6:9
Galloway, Clinton 10:98
Galloway, Cyrus M. 11:241
Galloway, Elijah 21:52
Galloway, F. C. 3:76
Galloway, George 8:85; 22:233
Galloway, Isaac 10:98; 11:204
Galloway, J. 16:369
Galloway, James 22:251
Galloway, Joseph W. 23:16
Galloway, Martin 22:251
Galloway, Peter 10:17
Galloway, T. J. 17:165
Galloway, W. B. 26:145
Gallows, Peter 13:79
Gallup, Charles A. 12:22
Gallup, George 7:123
Gallup, George H. 13:23
Gallup, Giles A. 23:98
Gallup, Hiram 25:37
Gallup, Levi P. 21:26
Gallup, Samuel 1:192
Gallup, W. T. 1:37
Gallup, William 16:143
Galm, John 17:423
Galnil, Jacob E. 11:30
Galoman, Jacob 8:105
Galop, Henry 15:91
Galpin, Charles 11:401
Galpin, Charles E. 21:91
Galt, Joseph 8:16; 18:135
Galt, William J. 8:85
Galtey, Paul F. 21:253
Galtimer, Andrew 19:70
Galtin, J. 19:70
Galugan, G. 27:53
Galuscha, F. 15:66
Galush, W. 3:76
Galusha, A. 1:35
Galusha, Giles 11:291
Galusha, J. 1:134
Galushe, U. S. 1:36
Galven, J. H. 18:237; 26:30
Galvin, And 17:475
Galvin, And. 27:52
Galvin, Andrew 14:297
Galvin, I. 10:53
Galvin, J. 20:255
Galvin, John 9:109; 18:271
Galvin, Lewis 23:30
Galvin, M. 1:35, 94
Galvin, Thomas 16:293
Galvin, W. 3:76
Galvin, William 16:293
Galwatty, E. H. 12:22

Galway, David H. 22:31
Galway, James 9:177
Galway, Thomas 10:17; 13:23; 16:33
Galway, William 9:177; 19:281
Galwich, J. H. 14:241
Galy, Charles 26:29
Galyon, Samuel B. 22:251
Gamball, George 15:283; 19:70
Gamball, Nathan 21:271
Gambel, Robert 4:26; 10:114; 20:255
Gambel, W. 19:267
Gambell, Robert 22:299
Gambell, W. T. 14:10
Gambell, William D. 18:135
Gamble, A. 21:26
Gamble, A. J. 3:76
Gamble, Alex 7:27
Gamble, Alfred 17:202
Gamble, Benjamin 20:255
Gamble, Corydon C. 20:17
Gamble, Frederick 10:114
Gamble, G. B. 14:169
Gamble, George 13:64; 14:62; 19:70
Gamble, I. M. 14:169
Gamble, Jacob E. 10:17
Gamble, James O. 7:95
Gamble, John 7:95; 23:203
Gamble, Pomeroy 22:31
Gamble, Robert 24:170
Gamble, S. S. 16:192
Gamble, Samuel F. 22:121
Gamble, Seth 14:169
Gamble, Sylvanus C. 24:50
Gamble, W. H. 17:34; 21:334
Gamble, W. T. 13:88
Gamble, Wesley 24:158
Gamble, Wiley 9:177
Gamble, William 6:20; 23:179
Gamble, William A. 18:82
Gambler, Fred 17:482
Gambler, George 15:198
Gambler, James M. 14:169
Gambois, William 27:51
Gambol, James 25:37
Gambol, Wesley 17:418
Gambol, William 13:88
Gambold, J. 1:134
Gamboll, W. 14:10
Gambrel, Gordon 23:98

Gambrel, Henry 11:326
Gambrel, James 9:34
Game, Henry 23:203
Gamel, Robert 12:70
Gamer, Davis 7:64
Gamer, E. 14:281
Gamer, George S. 10:172
Gamer, J. A. 3:76
Gamer, Riley 22:251
Gamer, Stephen 16:192
Games, Samuel 10:150
Gamet, Peter 7:77
Gamett, James 8:16
Gamiel, William 21:52
Gamill, A. B. 13:88
Gaming, Alexander 15:198
Gammell, A. B. 14:10
Gammell, Matthias 4:26
Gammell, William 22:512
Gammon, A. C. 19:70
Gammon, Andrew 7:27
Gammon, Henry 16:33
Gammon, I. C. H. 11:279
Gammon, J. 3:76; 20:255; 25:297
Gammon, J. G. 7:79
Gammon, John A. 22:279
Gammon, R. T. 14:169
Gammon, T. H. 18:189
Gammon, W. 22:121
Gammons, George N. 19:165
Gamner, Anthony 11:147
Gamon, James 9:177
Gamos, A. R. 12:22
Gamsby, John 5:39
Gamto, Owen 10:53
Ganard, Richard 18:14
Ganathy, Richard 14:169
Ganatt, I. 10:53
Ganaway, Louis 7:57
Ganby, George E. 14:298; 17:472
Ganby, Lewis 7:123
Gance, Isaac 7:77
Ganda, Otho 11:241
Gandee, George 10:91
Gandell, Marcus 8:16
Gandisse, Charles 10:114
Gandley, R. 16:94
Gandrow, Levi 5:16
Gandy, David 22:233
Gandy, F. E. 25:36
Gandy, Samuel 10:114; 20:255
Gandy, Thurman 17:71
Ganebe, T. 27:53
Ganepp, Theodore 13:23; 16:33
Ganes, Allen 9:207

Ganes, Austin 18:189
Ganes, John M. C. 20:123
Ganes, Ora B. 19:165
Ganett, E. H. 23:144
Ganett, John T. 10:91
Ganey, C. 3:76
Ganey, John M. 17:502
Ganey, Patrick 21:334
Ganford, Bradford 18:237; 26:30
Gangan, John 18:135
Gangen, Herman 11:126
Ganger, George 17:394
Ganger, William 18:292; 26:99
Gangerty, James 24:61
Ganges, Peter 27:50
Ganghim, Ovid 22:299
Gangle, Anthony 26:29
Gangle, H. 18:237; 26:30
Gangloff, G. 22:193
Gangtoff, Charles 16:192
Gangumus, Louis 20:255
Ganibler, Frederick 27:53
Ganibull, Thomas 21:271
Ganison, S. 1:37
Ganiss, S. J. 15:285
Ganitt, Samuel 21:224
Ganly, George E. 27:52
Gann, J. W. 3:76
Gann, N. E. 21:12
Gann, N. G. 10:205
Gann, Smith 14:62
Gannan, N. J. 19:14
Gannaum, Henry 7:27
Ganner, Allen 18:66
Ganner, K. 9:110
Gannett, F. 3:76
Gannett, J. W. 22:77
Ganning, T. 1:132
Gannis, David 17:65
Ganno, Thomas 14:169
Gannon, Austin 16:369
Gannon, George N. 22:501
Gannon, J. L. 9:109
Gannon, J. W. 3:76
Gannon, James 19:252
Gannon, James J. 25:320
Gannon, John 21:253
Gannon, N. H. 23:313
Gannon, P. D. L. 1:37
Gannon, Patrick 21:334
Gannon, Peter 23:30
Gannon, S. 3:76
Gannon, Thomas 16:94
Gannon, William 18:412
Gannott, Lewis 20:255
Gannte, P. 14:62
Gannue, Thomas 16:75
Gannuel, Robert 15:27

Gano, Henry 11:386
Ganon, William 12:70
Ganow, F. 22:299
Gans, Lewis 22:171
Ganse, R. 3:76
Ganseig, Francis 12:172
Gansen, John 18:306;
  22:479; 26:99
Gansey, S. 6:20
Ganstine, Christian
  22:425
Gansto, R. R. 25:272
Gant, Charles 27:50
Gant, David A. 24:183
Gant, George W. 10:148
Gant, Henry 26:30
Gant, J. A. 24:214
Gant, J. R. 3:76
Gant, Job 18:217
Gant, Patrick M. 22:121
Gant, Thomas 7:123
Ganther, Lewis 11:149
Gantholz, Gathiel 15:4
Gantley, Timothy 22:251
Gantly, Hugh 17:425
Gantner, Matthias 21:137
Gants, James L. 15:198
Ganty, Enoch 9:80
Gantz, H. 7:49
Gantz, John 11:261
Gantz, L. 14:62
Gantz, Peter 19:70
Gantz, Samuel 22:78
Ganwich, Samuel 12:22
Gapham, John M. 11:88
Gapin, Alfred 18:217
Gaptill, William 27:51
Garabout, James J. 10:17
Garagan, James H. 1:35
Garbary, J. 1:133
Garbeck, Isaac D. 8:114
Garbee, L. H. 7:49
Garbelt, William 25:277
Garben, John 10:114
Garber, Christopher
  22:279
Garber, John 20:255
Garber, Silas C. 17:452;
  24:181
Garber, William 12:55
Garberick, John H. 21:121
Garbes, Richard 10:53
Garbey, John 17:265
Garbine, George 15:298
Garbinson, Joseph 21:194
Garboden, W. H. 11:61
Garbreth, Isaac 22:299
Garcell, Henry 17:415;
  24:152
Garcelon, A. H. S. 25:174

Garcia, Jesus 8:124;
  12:171
Gard, B. H. 14:281
Gard, Burtis M. 14:269
Gard, C. 18:395
Gard, Daniel H. 22:424
Gard, David 18:395
Gard, James 13:23
Gard, John 22:193
Gard, Joseph M. 20:56
Gard, M. 21:26
Gard, Mahlon B. 23:66
Gard, Samuel G. 23:279
Gard, W. 15:198
Gard, W. P. 24:107
Gard, William M. 6:11;
  18:110
Gardain, Edward A. 27:52
Garde, John 17:79
Garden, G. W. 15:173
Gardener, C. W. 18:320
Gardener, L. 25:174
Gardener, R. 1:37
Gardener, S. P. 23:30
Garder, John 19:14
Gardin, J. W. 12:22
Gardiner, A. S. 10:53
Gardiner, Charles H. 4:26
Gardiner, Edward F.
  12:22
Gardiner, G. 12:81
Gardiner, I. 15:341
Gardiner, Jacob 10:53
Gardiner, Peter 21:334
Gardiner, Samuel H. 7:77
Gardiner, Solomon C.
  1:36
Gardiner, T. D. M. 17:257
Gardiner, W. C. 25:297
Gardiner, William 20:189
Gardiner, William C. 7:74
Gardiner, William H.
  19:45
Gardiner, William P.
  22:193
Gardiner, Z. R. 26:211
Gardipur, Joseph 4:26
Gardley, William 10:172
Gardman, P. 25:174
Gardman, Peter 5:39
Gardner, --- 3:77; 12:99;
  15:258, 366; 19:291;
  23:203
Gardner, A. 1:135; 3:77
Gardner, A. G. 17:346
Gardner, A. P. 7:57
Gardner, A. S. 20:255
Gardner, Abner L. 13:23
Gardner, Abraham 3:76
Gardner, Adam M. 23:66
Gardner, Agustus 11:147

Gardner, Albert L. 16:33
Gardner, Alexander
  22:233, 512
Gardner, Amos 25:174
Gardner, Anthony 17:34;
  25:37
Gardner, Arthur 6:24
Gardner, B. 14:298;
  17:479; 25:174;
  27:52
Gardner, B. F. 8:48
Gardner, Benjamin 5:39
Gardner, Bradford 11:191
Gardner, C. 3:77; 14:63
Gardner, C. G. 15:198
Gardner, C. L. 8:63;
  26:161
Gardner, C. R. 1:35
Gardner, C. W. 15:106
Gardner, Caleb M. 13:23
Gardner, Charles 11:61;
  25:37
Gardner, Charles F.
  11:106
Gardner, Charles L. 4:26
Gardner, Charles T.
  16:119
Gardner, Chauncey 9:156
Gardner, D. 3:77; 14:63
Gardner, Daniel 22:233
Gardner, Dick 24:101
Gardner, Dunvin 18:366
Gardner, Durwin 9:220
Gardner, F. 1:134; 25:38
Gardner, F. M. 16:33
Gardner, F. W. 17:164
Gardner, Francis 13:23
Gardner, Frank 1:36; 2:11;
  18:189
Gardner, Franklin E.
  12:22
Gardner, G. 1:35; 3:77;
  12:99; 15:366;
  26:162
Gardner, G. D. 13:110
Gardner, Gabe 18:237
Gardner, Gabi 26:31
Gardner, George 4:26;
  8:119; 21:115, 271
Gardner, George F. 20:86
Gardner, George G. 7:95
Gardner, George W.
  10:114; 11:319;
  20:255; 22:31
Gardner, H. 3:76, 77;
  25:174
Gardner, H. W. 19:14;
  20:255
Gardner, Harrison 14:169

Gardner, Henry 5:39; 20:123; 22:335; 27:144
Gardner, Henry F. 9:157
Gardner, Henry M. 22:251
Gardner, Henry W. 10:53
Gardner, Herman C. 11:125
Gardner, Hiram H. 21:26
Gardner, Hugh 21:187
Gardner, I. 9:143; 14:63
Gardner, I. W. 8:63
Gardner, Isaac 20:40
Gardner, Isaac M. 17:387
Gardner, J. 4:26; 9:177; 16:136, 192, 293, 369; 18:110, 366; 19:252, 281; 27:49
Gardner, J. A. 21:334
Gardner, J. B. 11:60; 15:198
Gardner, J. G. 7:95
Gardner, J. H. 12:99, 153
Gardner, Jackson 21:216
Gardner, Jacob 9:220; 11:148; 20:255
Gardner, Jacob M. 21:240
Gardner, James 8:48; 9:131, 177; 11:423; 12:153; 16:192; 17:418; 20:255; 24:158
Gardner, James C. 12:49
Gardner, James F. 23:263
Gardner, James G. 10:160
Gardner, James S. 7:27
Gardner, Jefferson 7:123
Gardner, Jeremiah 27:50
Gardner, Jermiah 12:22
Gardner, Joel 17:319
Gardner, Joel W. 19:71
Gardner, John 1:37; 8:117; 9:220; 11:147, 148; 15:7; 19:315; 24:39
Gardner, John C. 15:151
Gardner, John L. 22:424
Gardner, John S. 22:31
Gardner, John W. 22:451
Gardner, Joseph 10:53; 23:203
Gardner, L. 24:19
Gardner, L. L. 13:110
Gardner, Lambert B. 24:50
Gardner, Leander 22:193
Gardner, Lewis 22:143
Gardner, Logan E. 17:65
Gardner, M. 25:174; 27:47
Gardner, Miner 5:39
Gardner, Moses 20:399

Gardner, N. 11:61
Gardner, Newton 22:299
Gardner, O. 1:132; 3:77
Gardner, O. C. 21:52
Gardner, Obediah 21:52
Gardner, P. 1:133
Gardner, Pennington 17:423; 24:170
Gardner, R. 3:77; 13:64; 19:71
Gardner, Richard 7:95
Gardner, S. 1:132, 134
Gardner, S. O. 14:169
Gardner, Samuel 10:95; 21:52, 216; 22:78; 25:297
Gardner, Sidney 5:16
Gardner, Stephen N. 10:160
Gardner, Tee 15:198
Gardner, Thaddeus 10:160
Gardner, Theodeaus 19:165
Gardner, Thomas 1:37; 20:112; 21:10
Gardner, Thomas H. 7:95; 21:334
Gardner, Thomas N. 22:193
Gardner, V. M. 22:335
Gardner, W. A. 20:255
Gardner, W. C. 24:77
Gardner, W. F. 18:49; 19:237
Gardner, W. H. 3:77; 19:71
Gardner, W. R. 11:61
Gardner, Wallace P. 21:69
Gardner, Walter F. 9:177
Gardner, Warren H. 13:23
Gardner, William 3:77; 18:237; 20:179; 22:121; 24:177; 26:30
Gardner, William A. 10:53
Gardner, William H. 10:205; 21:26
Gardner, William P. 13:23
Gardner, William W. 19:14
Gardner, Winfield L. 9:177
Gardues, Joseph 9:200
Gare, Owen P. 10:37
Gare, William 19:71
Garell, Jacob P. 8:85
Garely, T. 14:169
Garen, Dodson 17:95
Gares, Thomas 7:49
Garette, C. 3:77

Garey, Leonard 22:121
Garey, Perry 9:42; 26:123
Garey, Simpson 22:121
Garfelt, William 20:255
Garfield, D. 1:35
Garfield, Henry 12:95; 19:71
Garfield, John W. 8:63; 26:161
Gargan, P. 1:134
Gargenfeld, F. 21:99
Gargins, Patrick 10:146
Garh, M. 12:70
Garham, J. 8:48
Garheart, W. D. 24:77
Garigan, John 8:16
Garing, John 16:33
Garis, Fletcher 22:78
Garison, H. T. 14:169
Garitt, Samuel 7:82
Garkue, John 8:48
Garl, Charles 19:270
Garland, A. 1:37; 25:174
Garland, Alva 12:80
Garland, Bayram 11:262
Garland, David 17:165; 22:251
Garland, Eli M. 7:74; 25:297
Garland, F. 14:169
Garland, F. A. 27:53
Garland, Francis 18:206
Garland, Frank K. 16:94
Garland, G. M. 7:74; 25:297
Garland, G. W. 1:94
Garland, George H. 18:135
Garland, Isaiah 12:22
Garland, J. 14:255
Garland, J. L. 7:57
Garland, James 21:137
Garland, James K. 19:14
Garland, John 17:166
Garland, John M. 22:351
Garland, John W. 15:25
Garland, Joseph 11:280
Garland, Joseph W. 21:224
Garland, Lewis 12:22
Garland, Richard 10:53; 20:255
Garland, Samuel 17:95
Garland, W. 3:77
Garland, William 18:217
Garlap, Joseph H. 20:192
Garlaugh, Frank 15:91
Garley, I. D. 8:16
Garlick, E. 27:53
Garling, Melch 16:192
Garlinger, A. 17:109

Garlisk, E. A. 4:26
Garlock, Charles 14:298;
   17:475
Garlock, John 3:77
Garlock, John Wesley
   20:30
Garlon, William 3:77
Garluck, Charles 27:52
Garly, H. 3:77
Garmage, Osborne 22:279
Garman, Charles 22:451
Garman, E. 3:77
Garman, Henry 16:192
Garman, J. A. 7:27
Garman, Jacob 10:17
Garman, Leander 22:279
Garman, M. 25:174
Garman, Timothy 10:114;
   20:255
Garmen, John B. 22:31
Garmiage, O. D. 8:72
Garmm, N. G. 18:406
Garmon, B. 3:77
Garmon, John 17:445
Garmoro, E. D. 21:26
Garn, L. 3:77
Garnall, Jesse 8:16
Garnard, Thomas 9:200;
   19:281
Garnder, Henry 19:331
Garnell, Jesse 26:161
Garner, Albert 21:148
Garner, Bu 9:242
Garner, C. 3:77
Garner, E. 9:220; 14:281;
   18:366; 21:26
Garner, George 15:315;
   19:71
Garner, George S. 19:165
Garner, H. 16:192
Garner, Henry 19:45, 71
Garner, Henry G. 21:334
Garner, J. K. P. 8:72;
   26:162
Garner, J. M. 20:85
Garner, James 9:177
Garner, John V. 17:206
Garner, Joseph A. 8:123
Garner, Lorenzo 6:7
Garner, P. 9:177
Garner, S. 13:88
Garner, Sampson 23:289
Garner, Washington
   22:251
Garner, William 14:169
Garner, William P. 24:66
Garner, Winfield L.
   19:274
Garnes, J. 13:88; 14:10
Garnet, D. 25:174
Garnet, Peter 25:297

Garnett, --- 16:192
Garnett, A. 15:55
Garnett, Adam 19:71
Garnett, Alex 11:203
Garnett, Archie 24:177
Garnett, C. D. 15:198
Garnett, Daniel 25:174
Garnett, Daniel S. 15:198
Garnett, George 17:397
Garnett, James 18:135
Garnett, Robert 21:69
Garnett, Robert H. 11:61
Garnett, William 2:11;
   18:285; 25:34;
   26:134
Garnett, William G. 8:85
Garney, John 22:193
Garney, Joshua A. 12:139
Garney, W. H. 27:47
Garney, William 3:77
Garnham, Robert 1:38
Garnick, George 11:31
Garnish, William 9:52
Garno, David 15:258
Garnsey, Arthur 8:120
Garom, T. 14:169
Garoner, B. 15:341;
   16:369
Garoon, J. 13:88
Garoutte, William 19:349
Garoy, A. 14:63
Garr, James M. 22:424
Garrabraut, Charles S.
   7:16
Garrad, Daniel 17:307
Garrad, Henry 17:175
Garrad, Tyre 17:203
Garrad, William 17:203
Garrall, L. 3:77
Garrard, Alfred 21:52
Garrard, Henry 5:39
Garrard, Maneil 22:121
Garrat, William 17:175
Garratt, John 21:334
Garraty, Edward 27:47
Garraty, Patrick 7:27
Garraud, William 7:16
Garraugh, J. 1:37
Garrelly, Michael 4:26
Garreson, George 19:45
Garret, George H. 23:144
Garret, George L. 17:145
Garret, J. R. 20:181
Garret, James H. 20:255
Garret, John 24:19
Garret, Joseph 23:144
Garret, Judge 23:197
Garret, Levi 23:144
Garret, Philip 11:203
Garret, W. J. 25:297

Garretson, Benjamin H.
   12:22
Garretson, E. G. 14:63
Garretson, J. R. W. 11:419
Garretson, William 24:50
Garrett, --- 15:198; 20:56;
   21:166
Garrett, Amos 20:255
Garrett, Andrew 11:203
Garrett, B. 14:63
Garrett, Benjamin O.
   11:30
Garrett, C. 17:34
Garrett, Cyrus J. 22:31
Garrett, D. 14:63
Garrett, F. 14:169
Garrett, Fielding 17:215
Garrett, Frank 17:148
Garrett, Franklin 8:16;
   18:135
Garrett, George 11:335
Garrett, George W. 11:84
Garrett, H. 22:299;
   25:174; 27:49
Garrett, H. F. 27:47
Garrett, Harry 24:194
Garrett, Henry 11:148
Garrett, J. 13:88; 20:255;
   25:174; 27:50
Garrett, J. M. 14:63; 23:30
Garrett, J. W. 14:169
Garrett, Jacob 11:92;
   18:82
Garrett, James 3:77; 8:16;
   16:33; 18:135
Garrett, James A. 9:110
Garrett, James F. 8:105
Garrett, James H. 10:114
Garrett, James P. 17:280
Garrett, James R. 13:60
Garrett, James W. 4:26
Garrett, January 9:131
Garrett, Jeremiah 22:512
Garrett, John 1:35;
   11:241; 16:192;
   18:206
Garrett, John T. 20:255
Garrett, John W. 20:146
Garrett, Joseph 5:16
Garrett, Joseph H. 22:251
Garrett, Joshua 17:52
Garrett, Levi 12:153
Garrett, Louis J. 7:27
Garrett, M. J. 3:77
Garrett, Mathias V. 7:95
Garrett, Meredy 18:82
Garrett, Mondy 6:16
Garrett, Moses 26:162
Garrett, Noah 10:114;
   20:255; 24:93
Garrett, Omas 10:53

Garrett, Patrick A. 9:52
Garrett, Richard 7:123
Garrett, S. H. 3:77
Garrett, S. N. 25:174
Garrett, Sampson 22:299
Garrett, Samuel 13:23
Garrett, T. 3:77
Garrett, Thomas 9:96; 20:255; 22:299
Garrett, Thomas J. 11:147
Garrett, W. B. 19:14
Garrett, William 17:175; 22:251, 299
Garrett, Willis 11:203
Garrett, Zack 20:133
Garrette, Samuel H. 21:334
Garretts, J. L. 20:255
Garretts, Lewis 12:142
Garrety, Thomas 18:110
Garrey, E. T. 14:169
Garrey, James 22:501
Garrey, Patrick 25:333
Garricks, John 18:338
Garries, J. K. 22:31
Garrig, J. 3:77
Garrigan, J. 3:77
Garrigan, T. 1:132
Garrigus, F. J. 1:134
Garrin, Milton 15:67
Garringer, Isaac 10:152
Garringer, J. 18:49
Garringer, Samuel 22:78
Garris, Amos 4:26
Garris, John 11:322
Garris, Peter 23:263
Garrison, A. 3:77; 9:177, 236; 19:252; 20:137
Garrison, A. C. 9:52
Garrison, A. F. 26:219
Garrison, Asahel 24:77
Garrison, Benjamin C. 18:49
Garrison, Benjamin R. 10:152
Garrison, C. 25:174
Garrison, Charles 5:39; 9:16; 19:291; 21:198, 216
Garrison, Charles H. 13:57
Garrison, D. 10:179; 15:341; 16:369; 18:174
Garrison, Daniel 6:16; 17:131; 18:82; 24:194
Garrison, David 8:125
Garrison, Edward 4:65; 17:131; 24:194

Garrison, F. 16:193; 25:320
Garrison, Florence A. 22:404
Garrison, Fran. H. 19:165
Garrison, Franklin H. 10:172
Garrison, G. B. 14:265
Garrison, G. M. 12:153
Garrison, G. W. 15:198
Garrison, H. 14:169
Garrison, Henry 13:23
Garrison, Henry W. W. 24:19
Garrison, Isaac 25:37
Garrison, J. 3:77
Garrison, J. B. 24:19
Garrison, J. D. 24:111
Garrison, J. F. 22:31
Garrison, J. N. 9:143; 27:48
Garrison, J. O. 21:334
Garrison, J. W. 19:71
Garrison, John 9:242; 10:53; 11:401; 16:293; 17:509; 20:255
Garrison, John H. 27:49
Garrison, John J. 12:22
Garrison, Joseph 12:62; 15:7; 17:95
Garrison, Lewis 11:61
Garrison, Mason 22:31
Garrison, McKinzie 21:69
Garrison, Monroe 21:130
Garrison, Mortimor 16:94
Garrison, Oliver 10:53; 20:255
Garrison, P. 1:36
Garrison, R. A. 16:369
Garrison, Robert 6:16; 9:177; 18:82
Garrison, Robert M. 24:50
Garrison, Rosseter 19:165
Garrison, Samuel 8:16; 18:135; 27:53
Garrison, Thomas 7:123; 21:334; 23:290
Garrison, Value 7:123
Garrison, W. 3:77
Garrison, W. H. 13:23
Garrison, William 21:99, 334
Garrison, William H. 16:33
Garrison, William T. 23:66
Garrisond, David 7:49
Garriss, J. T. 26:236
Garrith, B. 12:85; 16:293
Garrith, J. M. 14:63

Garritt, Daniel 5:39
Garritt, J. S. 8:105
Garritt, James 5:16
Garrity, E. 25:174
Garrity, Patrick 20:255
Garrity, William 15:35
Garro, Adolphus 11:15
Garron, G. N. 21:194
Garron, I. 3:77
Garrott, James 22:193
Garrott, W. 16:193
Garrow, George 16:193
Garrow, John 13:110
Garrow, Joseph 24:93
Garrow, Peter 21:137
Garrsy, Patrick 20:255
Garry, Michael 22:501
Garry, Thomas M. 10:17
Garry, Thomas O. 7:27
Garse, A. C. 15:106
Garser, Jacob C. 19:71
Garsham, C. A. 26:30
Garst, Christian 20:40
Garst, Davy 23:270
Garth, James 9:207
Garth, John 22:299
Garth, L. 1:132
Garth, William 21:334
Gartham, John M. 16:33
Garthland, Thomas 13:23
Garthoffer, John 11:147
Garthwait, D. B. 1:36
Garthwait, H. 5:51
Garting, M. 13:81
Gartland, --- 3:77
Gartling, Patrick 12:22
Gartman, Antonie 9:102
Gartman, Daniel J. 17:143
Gartner, John 18:366
Gartner, W. 9:52
Garto, Lewis 15:106
Garton, H. B. 1:132
Garty, M. 15:35
Garty, William 18:293
Garve, I. 14:63
Garver, C. M. 10:114; 20:256
Garver, George W. 12:22
Garver, John 3:77
Garver, Martin C. 21:242
Garver, Samuel 8:117; 22:425
Garverich, Joseph 26:99
Garvey, James 3:77; 7:95
Garvey, Joseph 18:292
Garvey, Luke 12:22
Garvey, Patrick 22:451
Garvin, Charles 17:313
Garvin, Cornelius 10:17

Garvin, E. 1:103
Garvin, Henderson 1:35
Garvin, John 3:77
Garvin, Levi 24:77
Garvin, Samuel R. 16:119
Garvin, T. 1:133
Garvin, W. W. 7:57
Garvin, William 22:335
Garvine, John 24:212
Garvis, Peter 23:270
Garwin, Mitchell 11:408
Garwood, Charles J. 17:257
Garwood, George W. 19:324
Garwood, L. 25:174
Garwood, M. L. 20:256
Garwood, Marcus L. 10:53
Garwood, Marion 11:147
Garwood, S. 11:149
Garwood, Samuel 5:16
Garwood, William 12:142
Gary, Alfred 10:91; 20:256
Gary, Asa H. 23:144
Gary, Charles 13:23
Gary, John A. 23:107
Gary, Lovet 20:256
Gary, M. 25:174
Gasaway, George 18:83
Gasaway, George W. 23:66
Gasaway, William 24:39
Gasber, W. W. 27:47
Gaschtetter, Joseph 22:166
Gascon, George 9:204
Gashbank, Philip 11:148
Gashearer, J. 14:63
Gasher, Abraham 20:97
Gashriz, J. 27:49
Gask, I. 3:77
Gaskell, Abram 22:193
Gaskell, Caesar 9:131
Gaskell, John 21:253
Gaskell, S. 7:77
Gasker, John 10:54; 20:256
Gaskey, John 23:144
Gaskey, William 17:46
Gaskil, Caesar 27:51
Gaskill, Abram 23:250
Gaskill, Amos 21:224
Gaskill, Charles 13:23
Gaskill, Charles F. 22:31
Gaskill, G. W. 1:134
Gaskill, J. W. 11:262
Gaskill, Jacob 11:412
Gaskill, R. 10:152; 18:49
Gaskill, S. H. 18:189

Gaskill, William H. 8:85
Gaskin, G. K. 8:48
Gaskin, J. M. 7:74; 25:297
Gaskin, John 25:297
Gaskins, Elijah 9:114
Gaskins, George K. 21:137
Gaskins, H. J. 1:134
Gaskins, I. H. 18:206
Gaskins, James F. 8:85
Gaskins, John S. 8:105
Gaskins, W. G. 7:27
Gaskins, W. I. 14:336
Gaskins, William B. 12:99
Gaslene, A. 18:292
Gasler, Joseph 16:132
Gasler, Powell 13:23
Gaslin, Charles 14:169
Gaslin, Edgar G. 19:317
Gaslin, G. 22:161
Gasline, Aurelius 26:99
Gasmal, Charles 21:137
Gasner, Edgar 4:26
Gasner, J. 15:106
Gason, Samuel N. 7:95
Gaspar, James M. 19:14
Gaspar, John 9:177
Gasper, John 19:281
Gasper, Nathaniel C. 18:14
Gasper, William 13:79
Gass, Ellis 19:165
Gass, James 14:169, 255
Gass, John 9:207; 18:66; 22:31
Gass, Newman 22:143
Gass, Thomas 12:22
Gass, William C. 22:451
Gassal, C. A. 8:48
Gassard, S. C. 25:37
Gassaway, George 6:16
Gassett, George 10:54; 20:256
Gassett, James 22:251
Gassey, John 21:224
Gassham, C. A. 18:237
Gassler, P. 3:77
Gasson, Pierre 19:329
Gassoway, Henry 17:145
Gast, John W. 22:171
Gast, W. H. 3:77
Gastell, G. W. 18:29
Gaster, Stephen 11:381
Gastillo, F. 14:169
Gastin, Stephen 8:39; 26:161
Gaston, Alexandria 19:71
Gaston, C. 14:169
Gaston, David 17:20
Gaston, J. B. 17:231
Gaston, J. K. 20:256

Gaston, J. R. 10:114
Gaston, J. W. 23:30
Gaston, James A. 21:69
Gaston, John 12:62; 15:91; 26:219
Gaston, John C. 11:30
Gaston, John R. 25:35
Gaston, R. M. 27:47
Gaston, Theodore 7:68; 23:30
Gaston, Thomas 11:303
Gaston, W. H. 24:19
Gaston, William 19:165
Gaston, William H. 23:66
Gasway, James 19:267
Gaswell, Benjamin 9:177; 19:281
Gaswell, C. 8:48
Gatchel, Uriah D. 12:153
Gatchell, --- 26:161
Gatchett, Sylvester 24:78
Gate, William J. 18:206
Gateford, James 4:65
Gateh, J. 9:52
Gately, Isaac 18:237; 26:30
Gately, J. G. 20:177
Gately, Patrick 18:338; 19:222
Gates, A. E. 9:80; 14:130
Gates, Abraham 11:61
Gates, Albert 20:48
Gates, Barnett 10:114; 20:256
Gates, Burtis 10:8
Gates, Clark 21:243
Gates, D. 18:49
Gates, E. E. 15:258
Gates, Edwin O. 12:22
Gates, F. S. 1:36
Gates, Fordy A. 22:404
Gates, G. W. 11:84; 23:30
Gates, George 13:23; 25:333
Gates, George R. 18:353; 22:11
Gates, George W. 18:395; 21:91
Gates, H. 1:133; 3:77; 17:175; 20:27
Gates, H. A. 26:29
Gates, Harvey A. 8:85
Gates, Henry 4:26; 18:271
Gates, Henry A. 21:334
Gates, Horatio 12:22
Gates, I. 3:77; 14:169
Gates, J. O. 24:166
Gates, J. S. 11:381
Gates, Jacob 11:92
Gates, James 8:16; 15:67; 18:135; 22:78

Gates, James M. 11:387
Gates, Jefferson 19:14
Gates, John 15:91
Gates, John L. 18:14
Gates, Jonathan 7:68
Gates, L. 1:134
Gates, Lewis 26:161
Gates, Loring 9:72
Gates, Louis A. 10:91;
    20:256
Gates, Marion 18:29
Gates, Marion M. 26:161
Gates, Orrin F. 23:285
Gates, Peter 21:271
Gates, Polandy 11:203
Gates, Ross 21:271
Gates, S. 9:177; 13:88
Gates, S. W. 15:341
Gates, Samuel 8:16;
    11:241; 18:135
Gates, Silas H. 9:96
Gates, Stephen 11:30
Gates, Stephen H. 9:163
Gates, T. J. 20:123
Gates, W. G. 27:47
Gates, W. H. 11:386
Gates, Walter 25:37
Gates, William H. 18:306;
    22:193, 451
Gatewell, Joseph 1:192
Gatewood, Charles 1:36;
    17:131; 24:194
Gatewood, James 27:51
Gatewood, Jefferson
    22:299
Gatewood, John M. 22:78
Gatewood, Joseph 21:271
Gatewood, Robert 22:78
Gatewood, Theph 6:12
Gatewood, William B.
    8:117; 19:315
Gathain, B. 16:193
Gather, James 24:19
Gather, M. 3:77
Gathericole, Francis V.
    20:137
Gathermann, Andreas
    23:189
Gathers, H. 1:134
Gathman, Henry 12:153
Gatho, Simeon 24:66
Gathwaite, Henry 17:418
Gatilff, H. 3:77
Gatlen, Dempsey 26:161
Gatliff, B. 13:130
Gatliff, M. 17:433
Gatliff, Moses 24:166
Gatlin, Dempsey 8:39
Gatlin, Isaac 22:31
Gatling, Joseph 25:174
Gatson, N. D. 8:105

Gatt, William P. 23:66
Gatten, George W. 15:359
Gatten, J. 15:359
Gattenberry, V. N. 12:81;
    16:293
Gattings, Michael 7:95
Gattis, Samuel 17:161
Gattis, William H. 22:193
Gatton, George W. 12:95
Gatton, J. 12:95
Gatwood, James 9:119
Gatwood, Robert B.
    11:262
Gaty, Charles 9:80
Gatz, Jacob 20:256
Gatz, John B. 12:22
Gaube, Henry 16:166
Gaude, Bev'y. 8:39
Gaude, Beverly 26:161
Gaudy, Joseph 17:276
Gaues, Isaiah 15:198
Gauff, H. 21:26
Gaugen, Godfrey M.
    8:105
Gauger, William 9:34
Gaugh, Jeff 18:83
Gaul, George 11:147
Gaul, John F. 13:23;
    16:33
Gaul, William 10:114;
    20:256; 27:50
Gaul, William H. 9:131
Gauld, A. P. 12:153
Gauley, J. J. 15:198
Gaulk, --- 16:94
Gault, Frank M. 22:425
Gault, George C. 9:177
Gault, John 8:85; 25:174
Gault, L. 19:252
Gault, L. J. 1:36
Gault, Leonard 9:177
Gault, Robert 11:15
Gault, William 17:443;
    24:158
Gault, William W. 21:253
Gaulth, W. A. 7:49
Gaumer, William 22:78
Gaunt, David 17:427
Gaunt, G. 13:88
Gaunt, Joseph H. 9:16
Gaunt, Redden M. 11:276
Gaunt, Richard 18:276;
    25:174
Gaunt, William 3:77
Gaus, Ernest 10:17
Gaus, Peter 23:270
Gausey, B. 3:77
Gausker, G. W. 15:165
Gauss, Denny 16:193
Gausy, B. 14:169
Gaut, George W. 18:49

Gauther, F. 15:106
Gauther, Lewis 21:334
Gautier, Joseph 9:177
Gauz, Arnold 10:205
Gavabront, A. 14:63
Gavanagh, W. 25:174
Gaven, C. 18:237; 26:31
Gaven, J. M. 16:267
Gaven, Michael 22:335
Gaves, John 9:21
Gavet, A. D. 21:334
Gavett, Samuel 21:334
Gavey, Anson 15:35
Gavin, T. 1:37
Gavitt, D. H. 9:143
Gavitt, P. 1:35
Gavitt, William 1:37
Gavon, Michael 21:163
Gavy, Anson 12:64
Gaw, J. 21:166
Gaw, John G. 12:153
Gaw, R. P. 1:132
Gawdy, Thomas 3:77
Gawer, Israel 1:35
Gawey, John 3:77
Gawley, A. 9:227
Gawlt, G. C. 19:252
Gawn, Wesley 22:351
Gawthrop, James 22:31
Gay, --- 18:206
Gay, Abner 13:23
Gay, Alvaro 22:31
Gay, Andrew 26:162
Gay, C. R. 3:77
Gay, Carl 27:48
Gay, David 10:54; 20:256
Gay, Earl 10:172; 19:165
Gay, Edward 21:10
Gay, Fred 16:193
Gay, George C. 24:172
Gay, George H. 23:104
Gay, Hiram 12:22
Gay, Ira E. 22:143
Gay, J. 3:77
Gay, John 21:224; 22:404;
    23:30; 27:50
Gay, John G. 20:256
Gay, John L. 25:174
Gay, Levi 17:455; 24:194
Gay, Milo S. 4:26
Gay, N. 16:33
Gay, Robert 8:16; 18:135
Gay, Rufus 21:271
Gay, S. H. 21:334
Gay, S. W. 21:26
Gay, Samuel 10:114;
    20:256
Gay, Semour C. 24:66
Gay, T. K. 11:428
Gay, W. E. 8:72
Gay, William B. 17:34

Gay, William H. 22:451
Gayer, R. 21:334
Gayetty, Levi 27:50
Gayety, Levi 9:119
Gayhurt, Hiram 11:30
Gayland, March 27:53
Gaylard, Oliver C. 20:256
Gayle, Purnell B. 21:334
Gaylom, Henry 9:34
Gaylor, John 19:45
Gaylord, A. 7:50
Gaylord, A. H. 23:30
Gaylord, Abel 13:23
Gaylord, Albert 15:16
Gaylord, Alexander 21:69
Gaylord, Charles 16:94
Gaylord, James G. 14:169
Gaylord, Lewis 26:31
Gaylord, Oliver C. 10:54
Gaylord, Ransom A.
    21:253
Gaylord, S. B. 11:261
Gaylord, Wilber 11:255
Gaylord, William B.
    22:193
Gaylord, William F.
    8:105; 21:69
Gayman, E. 9:220; 18:366
Gaymor, Phillip 14:169
Gayner, Godfrey 17:175
Gayner, Thomas 10:114;
    20:256
Gaynes, Sarah C. 18:189
Gaynon, Joseph 11:15
Gaynor, James 1:35
Gaynor, Marcus 25:35
Gayot, Marion J. 22:462
Gayport, George 17:109
Gays, David C. 22:251
Gayway, George 9:207
Gayzle, Jason 10:178
Gaza, Peto 7:95
Gaze, S. 15:199
Gazely, Delos M. 21:117
Gazett, Edward K. 25:174
Gazzenway, Joshua 6:27
Gcohman, Henry 19:165
Ge--ul, --- 25:36
Geadell, Daniel 17:323
Geager, Alex. 8:39
Geager, George 8:17
Geahart, Levi 14:298;
    17:470
Gealing, Thomas 11:60
Gealnor, Charles 7:27
Gealock, J. 19:270
Gealy, Cyrus 13:23
Gealy, John W. 4:26
Geaorge, M. 19:281
Gear, Charles M. 7:14
Gear, James 15:199

Gear, John 13:23
Gear, Richard 23:88
Gear, W. R. 7:27
Gear, W. W. 11:148
Gearer, George 22:508
Gearhan, S. 3:77
Gearhardt, J. W. 7:50
Gearhart, Gabriel 9:42
Gearhart, J. 1:132
Gearhart, Lafayette
    10:114; 20:256
Gearhead, Alfred 21:334
Gearheart, Levi 27:53
Gearing, Earnest 9:119
Gearing, Ernest 27:51
Gearls, John 11:219
Gearman, William 22:143
Gearon, Albert 20:256
Gearry, Thomas 1:35
Gears, James A. 22:31
Gearson, Albert 10:114
Geary, C. 14:10
Geary, D. 3:77
Geary, Francis 15:91
Geary, G. 13:88
Geary, George 23:263;
    27:53
Geary, Horatio 18:66
Geary, J. S. 1:36
Geary, James 3:77
Geary, John 1:35; 21:334
Geary, L. M. 17:265
Geary, Lovett 10:54
Geary, Peter V. 21:115
Geary, Stephen 18:110
Geary, T. 1:134
Gease, O. 9:177; 19:281
Geasland, Jackson L.
    22:251
Geast, Francis 22:11
Geates, S. 19:274
Geaugue, Lewis 11:148
Geave, P. H. 25:320
Geawith, Anthony 27:52
Gebber, J. 11:240
Gebbhardt, John 22:166
Gebert, E. L. 1:134
Gebhart, M. G. 9:12
Gebmann, Louis 21:253
Gechurn, J. 3:77
Gecke, William 6:16
Geddes, J. 1:37
Geddi, H. 14:277
Geddis, James 27:51
Geddis, Perry 22:352
Geddis, Samuel 11:203
Gedlin, James 7:27
Gedney, Seth M. 21:137
Gedra, Lemon 21:335
Gedrich, B. 13:110
Gee, A. C. 25:297

Gee, Abriski G. 7:79
Gee, Am's 22:352
Gee, Benjamin H. 10:54
Gee, Bond H. 20:256
Gee, Charles H. 7:50
Gee, Eastman 4:26
Gee, Edmond 18:338
Gee, George 8:17; 18:135;
    21:271
Gee, J. M. 7:74; 25:297
Gee, John 8:48
Gee, John W. 12:70
Gee, Josephus 16:94
Gee, Robert 17:52
Gee, Sol. L. 18:395
Gee, Solomon 11:401
Gee, Thomas M. 8:39;
    26:161
Gee, Volney B. 1:37
Gee, W. 8:48
Gee, W. H. L. 13:88
Gee, William H. 19:301
Gee, Wilson 21:69
Geeger, John 8:17
Geehavey, Michael 4:26
Geek, G. W. 1:35
Geeke, William 18:83
Geen, G. G. 25:174
Geer, Atley W. 18:189
Geer, Carlton 7:27
Geer, Eli 24:19
Geer, Ellmore 11:148
Geer, Francis 1:35
Geer, George W. 20:123
Geer, H. 23:144
Geer, Harlow 4:26
Geer, Israel S. 11:147
Geer, J. 16:279
Geer, J. F. 1:133
Geer, James M. 12:122
Geer, Joel 18:338
Geer, John W. 17:257
Geer, Joseph 11:61
Geer, Leroy 11:106
Geer, Marshall 9:42
Geer, Mascal 26:124
Geer, Philip 9:80; 26:31
Geer, S. W. 1:132
Geer, Thomas 12:58
Geer, W. C. 16:267
Geer, William 17:271;
    20:7
Geer, William H. 10:17;
    13:23; 16:33
Geere, F. 16:369
Geerhard, John 23:30
Geerhart, L. S. 1:132
Geering, John 13:24
Geers, Thomas 8:17;
    18:135
Geertry, James H. 8:17

Geese, John H. 14:169
Geesebreth, W. 15:199
Geffney, T. 1:133
Gefford, Daniel D. 10:114
Gefford, Daniel G. 20:256
Gegan, C. 1:133
Gegenict, J. 14:63
Geger, George W. 17:418
Gegge, Ely 24:19
Gegor, D. R. 25:174
Geguanta, George 7:12
Gehenge, Alvid 13:24
Geheugen, Bartholomew 4:26
Gehinger, Aloid 16:33
Geho--, Addeson 15:199
Gehoe, Benn 25:174
Gehr, C. 2:11; 25:35
Gehr, D. 19:71
Gehr, L. D. 15:67
Gehr, Louis D. 12:64
Gehr, Martin 8:17; 18:135
Gehre, Benjamin 5:16
Gehreb, J. R. 16:369
Gehret, I. R. 15:341
Gehrett, Adam 4:26
Gehrett, Amos 11:147
Gehrig, Anthony 21:69
Gehring, Jacob 19:315
Gehringer, Xavier 17:71
Geiberlick, J. 19:252
Geidner, Timothy 22:31
Geier, Albert 23:144
Geier, Henry 1:36
Geiffith, George H. 9:119
Geiger, B. 2:11; 25:37
Geiger, Daniel 12:22
Geiger, Fred 11:240
Geiger, George 16:33
Geiger, George W. 24:158
Geiger, Jacob 23:179
Geiger, Joseph 22:193
Geiger, Mathias 11:181
Geiger, W. 1:133
Geigher, William H. 11:322
Geil, Solomon 10:172
Geilet, Isabel 14:170
Geiner, J. 16:139
Geirger, John 21:69
Geisel, F. 14:63
Geisentanner, Charles 11:326
Geiser, Charles 3:77
Geiser, Jacob 4:26
Geisler, Frank 1:36
Geisler, James W. 16:33
Geisler, Lewis 11:31
Geiss, John 20:30
Geist, Charles 10:114; 20:256; 25:36

Geist, James 4:26
Geist, William 11:15
Geisz, D. 11:303
Geitlomason, Tellof 18:135
Geizer, John 18:135
Gelalt, C. W. 19:14
Gelaspy, George 23:252
Gelberts, --- 18:66
Gell, A. 18:135
Gellaspie, J. J. 21:26
Gellecheimer, George 20:256
Geller, M. 9:110
Gellerne, George 26:161
Gellert, A. 11:125
Gellespie, John L. 17:453
Gellespie, Leander 4:26
Gelo, A. 3:77
Gelse, John 21:26
Gelter, Jacob 19:71
Geltner, Andrew J. 17:349
Gelven, Lamb 14:170
Gelwick, Daniel 22:193
Gemcy, James C. 17:440
Gemderson, M. 27:51
Geminder, W. 1:132
Gemmes, W. E. 18:237
Gemminger, J. 1:37
Gemmings, Thomas 7:15
Gemmons, Joseph 15:2
Gemons, John P. 12:153
Gemperling, William 3:77
Gemsy, James C. 24:152
Gender, Jacob 3:77
Generous, Peter 16:139
Genesh, G. M. 7:57
Gengan, James 15:2
Gengingle, Jacob 1:35
Gengle, John 24:19
Genicke, P. 25:174
Genis, P. 21:335
Genkinger, M. 14:63
Gennerville, F. 16:369
Genness, John W. 14:170
Gennings, I. 3:78
Gennings, R. 15:357
Gennony, A. 14:63
Genoer, Isaac 2:11
Gensardi, Thomas 3:77
Gensen, P. 1:133
Gensill, J. F. 11:147
Gensle, John 3:77
Gensler, Michael 24:61
Genter, Martin 17:175
Genter, Peter 12:70
Genter, S. 19:281
Genter, Seville 9:177
Genters, Martin 24:173
Gentey, A. 16:369
Genther, Newell W. 9:177

Genther, Thomas S. 10:17
Gentis, W. 11:262
Gentle, George M. 12:70
Gentle, George W. 15:55
Gentle, Shipley 14:63
Gentleman, Newell H. 19:227
Gentner, G. 14:255
Gentnum, David 14:332
Gentry, E. 13:88
Gentry, Edward 27:52
Gentry, Henry 9:34; 18:292; 26:99
Gentry, Isaac 9:100
Gentry, J. R. 21:26
Gentry, James 17:236
Gentry, James A. 17:259
Gentry, James M. 25:174
Gentry, John 17:131; 22:251; 24:194
Gentry, O. 18:83
Gentry, Orange 6:12
Gentry, P. 14:63
Gentry, P. N. 9:97
Gentry, R. F. 25:174
Gentry, Samuel S. 22:501
Gentry, Siilas 18:237
Gentry, Silas 26:30
Gentry, Thomas 17:335
Gentry, W. H. 22:251
Gentry, William 7:123
Gentry, Zimry 23:113
Gents, Christian 15:35
Genung, Palmer 21:253
Geoghengan, M. 1:37
Geohegan, John 7:68
Geohegan, Thomas 13:24
Geolzer, L. 1:36
Geom, Albert 11:148
Geopling, Augustus 11:30
George, --- 12:99; 18:174; 26:31
George, A. 3:78; 21:26
George, A. J. 1:134
George, Aaron 23:30
George, Adam 9:34; 18:292; 26:99
George, Allen 21:211
George, Alonzo W. 14:170
George, Augustus 9:131; 26:145
George, C. C. 17:159
George, C. S. 1:132
George, Cap 9:102
George, Charles 13:24
George, Charles E. 21:69
George, D. 1:131
George, David 11:149; 19:165; 20:123
George, David C. 17:34

George, Deane 10:161
George, E. 1:135; 19:252
George, E. L. 9:143
George, Edgar 9:177
George, F. 3:78; 22:300
George, Flavius J. 23:66
George, Gulliver 9:131
George, H. 1:35, 132;
    13:88
George, H. A. 23:268
George, Henry 11:181;
    15:283; 19:71;
    21:271
George, Henry H. 14:170
George, Isaac 22:335
George, J. 1:132, 134
George, J. E. 24:78
George, Jacob 8:17;
    18:135; 22:31
George, James C. 27:52
George, James H. 8:105;
    23:98
George, John 9:200;
    19:291; 21:271;
    22:424; 23:98; 27:48
George, John R. 21:99
George, John W. 11:387
George, Joseph 7:95;
    16:369
George, Juey 11:106
George, Lawrence 18:83
George, Levi 23:88
George, M. 12:8; 16:369
George, Marion L. 21:10
George, Nathan 9:143
George, Nelson 22:279
George, O. A. 17:495
George, Osman G. B. 1:37
George, P. H. 17:424
George, Pleasant H.
    24:173
George, R. M. 22:193
George, R. O. 22:479
George, Rains 20:256
George, Reuben B. 13:24
George, Robert 17:248
George, Sandy 21:335
George, Sylvester 9:119;
    27:51
George, Thomas 1:35;
    22:78
George, Timothy M. 1:36
George, Victor 7:123
George, Vroom 20:30
George, W. 9:177;
    16:267; 21:99
George, W. A. 18:366
George, W. George
    11:428
George, William 8:117;
    11:148; 12:70;

George, William 13:88;
    15:67; 17:79; 18:237;
    19:277; 22:300;
    26:30, 219
George, William A. 7:95
George, William T.
    21:130
George, William W. 7:27
George 25:335
Georgen, Joseph 23:144
Georges, W. 1:36
Georgeson, George
    11:191
Georgeson, Henry 7:95
Georgia, John 9:80; 26:29
Georgia, William V. 21:99
Georing, John 9:143
Geourd, C. 3:78
Gepein, G. F. 9:177
Gepford, A. 24:78
Gephardt, Ambrose
    11:106
Gephart, John 1:36
Gephart, S. L. 10:114;
    20:256
Gepring, Jacob 8:117
Gerald, George W. 7:68
Gerald, James S. 9:12
Gerald, R. D. 19:227
Gerard, A. H. 15:165
Gerard, Frederick 3:78
Gerard, H. 3:78
Gerard, John 24:19
Gerard, John H. 9:80
Gerard, Joseph 20:123
Gerard, Joshua 22:78
Gerard, M. V. 19:165
Gerard, P. 14:63
Gerard, Perry 22:193
Gerard, S. 17:14
Gerbending, Charles
    12:22
Gerber, Alfred 22:193
Gerber, Charles 25:174
Gerber, J. J. 3:78
Gerbert, Adam 17:20
Gerbert, Jacob 19:165
Gerbrich, Thomas 9:159
Gerbrick, J. 1:134
Gerchwind, Charles
    18:315
Gerdan, Green B. 12:22
Gerdeman, Theodore
    20:256
Gerden, Anderson 19:45
Gere, Eli 27:51
Gere, L. 20:174
Gere, O. B. 4:26
Gere, W. 1:132
Gerenger, William 1:35

Gerent, William 18:237;
    26:31
Gerfoss, Daniel 16:33
Gergee, J. 21:198
Gergen, N. 11:125
Gerhard, Gustavus
    10:145; 19:165
Gerhardt, H. 11:61
Gerhart, J. 3:78
Gerhart, John 13:24
Gerin, George 11:92
Gerin, P. 1:97
Gerk, G. 18:174
Gerke, E. 10:192
Gerkhere, David 10:54
Gerkin, F. 14:63
Gerkins, L. J. 14:277
Gerlach, Michael 13:24
Gerlack, J. 3:78
Gerlinde, H. 26:31
Gerllman, Thomas 23:309
Gerlock, D. 3:78
Gerlock, F. 22:171
Gerloff, F. 1:132
Germain, Henry 16:293
Germain, Hermain 21:335
Germain, James 21:117
Germaine, Frederick
    24:93
Germaine, Loyies 19:281
German, Charles E.
    17:273
German, E. 3:78
German, G. 25:174
German, George 5:39;
    13:135; 19:346
German, Henry H. 22:479
German, J. 13:88
German, J. H. 1:135
German, James 25:174
German, John S. 22:78
German, Lewis 20:256
German, M. 22:300
German, P. 3:78
German, Silas 4:26
German, Thomas 11:122;
    21:335; 27:48
German, Thomas C.
    11:412
German, W. H. 9:143
German, William 7:123;
    15:199
Germann, Bernard 16:94
Germer, Henry 25:174
Germine, Louis 19:281
Gerner, Martin 12:22
Gerney, Frederick 10:114;
    20:256
Gernon, Henry W. 23:121
Gernon, Patrick 20:142
Gerns, Samuel A. 15:106

Gernsey, Charles 1:35
Gerod, Lewis A. 22:193
Gerold, A. 20:256
Gerold, William 9:230; 20:256
Gerome, J. B. 7:27
Geron, A. 7:74; 25:297
Gerondal, Philip 20:256
Geront, Samuel 3:223
Gerould, James L. 11:106
Gerper, A. 1:94
Gerr, Mathias 25:37
Gerrald, A. P. M. 11:60
Gerrald, J. 1:133
Gerrald, R. 27:49
Gerrans, Thomas J. 19:165
Gerreit, Jacob 1:36
Gerrett, John 7:95
Gerrick, G. 11:231
Gerriets, John F. 8:17; 18:135
Gerrish, Frederick 10:17
Gerrish, Henry S. 9:119
Gerrish, Isaac 20:48
Gerrish, John 20:48
Gerritt, George 9:34
Gerrmell, A. 12:161
Gerrold, William 9:230
Gerry, E. 12:81; 16:293
Gerry, E. P. 3:78
Gerry, Edmund 14:170
Gerry, H. 1:36
Gerry, John L. 14:63
Gerry, William T. 13:24
Gersbaker, Richard 4:26
Gersh, Frederick 26:211
Gershan, David 19:14
Gershbacker, Amandus 10:114; 20:256
Gersiembane, John 11:219
Gersier, W. 25:175
Gerskemper, L. C. 20:35
Gerson, Otto 14:269, 281
Gerson, R. 1:37
Gerstenberger, John 21:121
Gersting, Frank 13:88
Gerswinger, --- 25:35
Gert, E. 23:189
Gerthe, John L. 9:102
Gerthoffer, J. 7:50
Gerths, A. 1:36
Gerting, Mack 21:335
Gertney, Christopher 22:78
Gerttomason, Tellof 8:17
Gervig, H. 1:134
Gervont, Samuel 17:504
Gervur, James 9:143
Gery, Robert 26:161

Gesalter, T. 16:193
Geschwind, Charles 26:99
Gesell, J. 1:37
Geser, John 11:30
Geshwender, Joseph 20:7
Gesler, Anna 25:175
Gesler, H. 17:191
Gesler, Henry 9:21; 18:320
Gesler, James 3:78
Gess, Joseph 19:14
Gessler, J. 14:170
Gesslerr, Jerome 14:63
Gessner, Henry N. 9:97
Gestbent, Nicholas 15:35
Gester, Conrad 25:37
Geston, F. J. 23:289
Getchel, L. G. 12:99
Getchell, C. L. 19:165
Getchell, Fred. C. 19:45
Getchell, J. Frank 25:37
Getchell, J. R. 13:124
Getchell, Jeremiah 4:26
Getchell, Prescott 19:327
Getchell, S. J. 13:110
Getler, Jacob 13:64
Getson, James 4:65
Gett, John 3:78
Gett, Theodore 11:61
Gett, Thomas E. 17:273
Getteam, Poney 22:300
Gettenher, D. M. 3:78
Gettes, James 15:199
Gettings, J. 20:257
Gettings, J. H. 3:78
Gettings, James 4:26
Gettings, Jeremiah 10:54
Gettis, David 9:159
Gettis, Delancois 14:170
Gettis, J. 25:175
Gettis, Jefferson 5:16
Gettis, John 21:335
Gettis, William 14:63; 24:78
Gettle, George 9:177; 19:274
Getton, George 19:71
Getts, B. 3:78
Getts, F. 3:78
Getty, Andrew 18:206
Getty, Charles H. 18:292
Getty, Daniel 22:463
Getty, David 7:95
Getty, Henry 18:420
Getty, J. 12:8
Getty, John W. 21:253
Getty, Lewis 21:335
Getty, R. 9:143
Gettys, F. 14:63
Getz, Fidel 4:26
Getz, George 4:26

Getz, Gustavo 23:98
Getz, Jacob 10:54
Getz, John 10:54
Getz, Louis 21:88
Getz, Martin 5:16; 25:175
Getz, Robert 27:48
Geuartz, P. 1:132
Geulford, J. 3:78
Geunnar, Moses 21:253
Geverance, Thomas J. 12:22
Gevondal, Philip 10:91
Gewe, Elia 9:119
Gewecke, F. 1:131
Geyer, Amaziah 21:216
Geyer, August 1:35
Geyer, Christian G. 11:30
Geyer, J. 21:121
Geyer, J. H. 24:78
Geyer, John 9:22; 18:306; 26:99
Gezain, Zella 9:80
Gezime, Vella 26:29
Gh--lie--ton, --- 25:38
Ghea, Dennis 17:52
Ghee, Thrd. 18:14
Ghent, Alvin 17:52
Gher, Henry 23:189
Gherfelt, William H. 14:298; 17:470
Ghir---, Joseph 25:35
Ghistwhite, John 17:91
Gholson, William 17:99
Ghonnater, A. 21:121
Ghorpelt, W. H. 27:52
Ghost, John 12:99
Giahl, Julius 18:135
Gian, Benjamin 3:78
Giarrapo, Charles 13:64
Giasco, Augustus 21:335
Gib, William 19:71
Gibany, A. N. 15:329
Gibb, M. 1:134
Gibb, Samuel 18:306
Gibb, W. G. 24:66
Gibben, L. 18:49
Gibbens, H. 25:175
Gibbens, John 20:257
Gibbens, William 4:26
Gibber, Frederick 8:72
Gibberd, John 15:67
Gibbin, P. T. 11:62
Gibbins, E. 25:175
Gibbins, Edward 5:16
Gibbins, James 15:309
Gibbins, W. I. 3:78
Gibble, John L. 11:92
Gibbon, James F. 10:114
Gibbon, James T. 20:257
Gibbon, W. 20:40

Gibbon, W. F. 14:170
Gibboney, Silas A. 23:144
Gibbons, Abraham 21:335
Gibbons, Austin 11:412
Gibbons, Barney 10:114;
20:257
Gibbons, C. A. 26:162
Gibbons, Daniel 11:261
Gibbons, Eugene F. 8:121
Gibbons, George James
20:22
Gibbons, Harry 5:39
Gibbons, J. B. 12:91;
16:293
Gibbons, James 18:189;
19:340
Gibbons, John 8:17;
10:54, 114; 18:135;
20:257
Gibbons, John H. 8:105
Gibbons, John W. 22:425
Gibbons, M. 3:78
Gibbons, M. J. 20:146
Gibbons, Marion 24:19
Gibbons, P. 1:134
Gibbons, Peter 22:78
Gibbons, Philip 23:144
Gibbons, Robert 20:139
Gibbons, S. 23:144
Gibbons, T. A. 20:133
Gibbons, Theo 1:35
Gibbons, Thomas 10:54,
161; 19:165
Gibbons, Thomas A.
20:183
Gibbons, Tobias 19:15
Gibbons, W. 1:131
Gibbons, W. F. 14:256
Gibbons, William 1:37;
3:78
Gibbons, Willis S. 23:144
Gibbow, James H. 15:67
Gibbow, Joseph 19:165
Gibbs, --- 15:67; 20:181
Gibbs, A. 5:39; 25:175
Gibbs, A. D. 21:335
Gibbs, A. J. 9:220; 18:366
Gibbs, Albert 17:359;
22:143
Gibbs, Albert S. 20:257
Gibbs, Amos 7:64
Gibbs, Benjamin 19:15
Gibbs, Benjamin F. 9:42;
26:124
Gibbs, C. 7:50; 13:103;
14:10; 16:267
Gibbs, Cassius R. 22:166
Gibbs, Charles 3:78;
16:152
Gibbs, David G. 23:66

Gibbs, Elisha 9:131;
22:31; 27:50
Gibbs, Francis 25:175
Gibbs, Frank L. 5:16
Gibbs, G. 21:335
Gibbs, G. W. 8:17; 18:135
Gibbs, George 9:131;
27:50
Gibbs, George T. 16:33
Gibbs, George W. 17:427;
24:183
Gibbs, George
Washington 22:31
Gibbs, Gershon A. 23:30
Gibbs, H. C. 8:59
Gibbs, H. H. 8:63
Gibbs, Hamilton 22:424
Gibbs, Hiram F. 9:236;
26:220
Gibbs, Hiram M. 17:359
Gibbs, I. A. 3:78
Gibbs, Isom 22:300
Gibbs, Israel 7:27
Gibbs, J. W. 13:88; 14:10
Gibbs, James 1:191; 9:72
Gibbs, James R. 22:501
Gibbs, John 9:207;
14:170; 25:175
Gibbs, Joseph 3:78; 7:77;
25:297
Gibbs, L. 16:139
Gibbs, Larkins 9:52
Gibbs, Levi B. 22:404
Gibbs, Louis 18:29
Gibbs, M. 14:63
Gibbs, M. F. 11:240
Gibbs, M. H. 3:78
Gibbs, Madison 27:53
Gibbs, Mason 17:175
Gibbs, Milton 8:72; 10:9
Gibbs, N. 1:134
Gibbs, Nathaniel 8:99
Gibbs, O. 14:255
Gibbs, P. 21:335
Gibbs, P. W. 11:438
Gibbs, R. 3:78; 14:170
Gibbs, Robert J. 20:107
Gibbs, S. 9:22; 14:63
Gibbs, S. G. 25:175
Gibbs, Samuel 26:99
Gibbs, Simon P. 8:85
Gibbs, Thomas 12:95;
15:359; 19:71
Gibbs, Timothy 6:24
Gibbs, W. A. 7:27
Gibbs, William 12:70;
15:35
Gibbs, William A. 21:26
Gibbs, William F. 21:216
Gibbs, William H. 11:60;
22:143

Gibbs, Zeno 1:35
Gibbson, Charles 5:39
Gibbson, F. 18:237; 26:30
Gibbson, Jerry 27:47
Gibby, David C. 21:224
Gibby, John J. 21:187
Giberlick, John 9:177
Gibernaster, John 24:19
Giberny, A. M. 19:71
Giberson, Harmon 21:240
Giberson, Henry H. 24:19
Giberson, O. D. 16:293
Giberson, Oliver C. 4:26
Gibes, T. 16:193
Gibeson, J. 3:78
Gible, C. 21:26
Gibley, Charles 22:31
Gibley, Rodolph 12:70
Giblin, Michael 27:53
Giblin, Peter 19:165
Giblong, Abraham 22:234
Gibner, Benjamin 17:34
Gibney, J. 1:133
Gibney, Peter 21:91
Gibney, T. 1:37
Gibney, Thomas 9:119;
12:70
Giboni, Henrich 20:123
Giboon, Joseph 20:146
Gibson, --- 9:157; 14:321;
19:165; 23:203;
26:162
Gibson, --- (Mrs.) 18:189
Gibson, A. 3:78
Gibson, A. C. 21:335
Gibson, Adam 22:300
Gibson, Adriel 23:107
Gibson, Alex 20:257
Gibson, Alexander 10:54;
16:279
Gibson, Benjamin 9:80;
26:29
Gibson, C. 25:175
Gibson, C. G. 3:78
Gibson, C. O. 19:15
Gibson, Calvin W. 21:247
Gibson, Charles 9:97;
13:24; 16:34, 193;
19:15
Gibson, Charles H.
10:161; 19:165
Gibson, Clark 16:193
Gibson, Collin 3:78
Gibson, D. 3:78; 11:15
Gibson, D. E. 3:78
Gibson, D. G. 3:78
Gibson, David 9:81;
22:193
Gibson, David S. 15:151
Gibson, E. 5:39; 21:148
Gibson, E. H. 15:27

Gibson, E. M. 9:214;
21:335
Gibson, Ed 19:45
Gibson, Edward 12:70
Gibson, Edward J. 1:36
Gibson, Elias 20:7
Gibson, Elisha 23:66
Gibson, Ephraim 21:211
Gibson, F. E. 11:240
Gibson, Francis M.
22:251
Gibson, Frederick 18:110
Gibson, G. 10:148; 18:49
Gibson, Garrett 21:224
Gibson, George 7:62;
11:293; 14:63;
22:161
Gibson, George C. 24:78
Gibson, H. D. 3:78
Gibson, H. H. 3:78
Gibson, H. T. 19:15
Gibson, Henderson 9:220
Gibson, Henry 8:105;
20:257; 26:219
Gibson, Henry C. 22:424
Gibson, Henry H. 7:80
Gibson, Henry M. 9:239;
19:337
Gibson, Howard 25:175
Gibson, I. 3:78
Gibson, Isaac 21:137
Gibson, Israel 12:62;
15:67
Gibson, J. 1:132; 3:78;
11:31; 22:479;
23:30; 25:35
Gibson, J. A. S. 23:30
Gibson, J. M. 23:258
Gibson, J. W. 14:63;
21:335
Gibson, Jacob 22:300
Gibson, James 3:78;
14:256; 20:17;
21:148, 211; 22:501
Gibson, James A. 17:95
Gibson, James B. 18:237;
26:31
Gibson, James D. 14:170
Gibson, James E. 8:48
Gibson, James M. 13:24
Gibson, James T. 20:7
Gibson, James W. 11:386;
12:153; 22:451
Gibson, Jefferson 17:131;
19:45; 24:194
Gibson, Jerry 16:369;
21:211
Gibson, Jesse A. 12:22
Gibson, Jesse R. 17:280

Gibson, John 3:78; 7:80;
11:88; 12:22, 58;
14:170; 21:187;
25:175, 297
Gibson, John A. 22:508
Gibson, John C. 19:45
Gibson, John F. 11:92
Gibson, John L. 23:66
Gibson, John U. 21:335
Gibson, Jonathan 10:114;
20:257
Gibson, Joseph 18:189;
26:220
Gibson, L. 22:300
Gibson, L. M. 1:34
Gibson, Lawson 22:78
Gibson, Lewis 8:112;
21:211
Gibson, M. 25:297
Gibson, Maftily 14:315
Gibson, Martin 7:74
Gibson, N. 25:320
Gibson, Norman 23:144
Gibson, O. P. 21:335
Gibson, Obed. J. 21:225
Gibson, Oliver F. 23:66
Gibson, Owen 17:389
Gibson, Peter 11:203
Gibson, Peter R. 11:30
Gibson, R. 3:78; 13:103;
14:10; 16:267
Gibson, R. A. 19:331
Gibson, R. W. 19:15
Gibson, Rial 17:389
Gibson, Robert 9:9
Gibson, Robert A. 9:12
Gibson, Robert M. 19:165
Gibson, Robert W. 10:91;
20:257
Gibson, S. 15:199
Gibson, S. F. 3:78
Gibson, S. G. 20:257
Gibson, S. J. 13:64
Gibson, S. T. 9:240
Gibson, Shepherd 17:166
Gibson, Simon 10:54;
20:257
Gibson, Solomon 24:89
Gibson, T. 25:35
Gibson, T. C. 27:49
Gibson, Thomas 8:63;
9:97; 12:70; 15:95,
199; 21:130
Gibson, Thomas B. 26:29
Gibson, W. 14:63
Gibson, W. A. 13:88;
14:10
Gibson, W. F. 19:71
Gibson, W. H. 16:73;
21:335
Gibson, Warren 19:252

Gibson, William 5:16;
6:12; 10:54; 12:153;
13:24, 64; 18:83,
237; 22:112; 23:30;
25:175; 26:30
Gibson, William C. 22:31
Gibson, William E. 17:95
Gibson, William M.
12:153
Gibson, William R.
20:151
Gibson, Wilson 24:39
Gibum, J. 21:148
Gice, C. M. 16:34
Gick, Fred 23:288
Gidder, James 17:65
Giddings, --- 23:292
Giddings, F. M. 11:303
Giddings, George 22:143
Giddings, I. 3:78
Giddings, J. A. 1:37
Giddings, W. R. 23:31
Gide, Harrison H. 9:72
Gideon, --- 19:71
Gideon, G. L. 23:260
Gideon, Greenville 11:61
Gideon, Isom 17:352
Gideon, T. 18:366
Gideon, Theodore 9:220
Gidney, S. M. 8:48
Giebel, John 25:283
Giebig, Godfried 4:26
Giee, Edward 9:81
Gieger, Joseph 11:181
Gier, O. 3:78
Gierhart, Joseph 9:68
Gies, A. 3:78
Giese, Christ 20:257
Giese, Christian 3:78
Giesenking, Frederick
23:113
Gieshafer, Ant 14:170
Giesler, Julius 8:17
Giesman, M. 15:35
Giess, Nicolaus 22:31
Gieswell, Edwin 15:91
Giether, I. 3:78
Giff, William 25:175
Giffard, M. 14:170
Giffard, W. H. 25:175
Giffeth, Jacob 17:161
Giffin, Abner D. 22:31
Giffin, G. W. 3:84
Giffin, Isaac 5:39
Gifford, --- 15:199
Gifford, A. 13:24
Gifford, B. 26:30
Gifford, B. F. 23:145
Gifford, C. 1:35
Gifford, C. H. 11:125
Gifford, Charles 11:387

Gifford, Charles E. 11:147
Gifford, Charles M. 21:69
Gifford, D. 16:193
Gifford, D. A. 1:133
Gifford, E. A. 1:37
Gifford, Eben 14:170
Gifford, Frank 25:175
Gifford, G. R. 1:38
Gifford, George 1:35
Gifford, German 11:381
Gifford, H. 1:37
Gifford, H. N. 3:78
Gifford, Henry C. 21:137
Gifford, I. 3:78
Gifford, J. 1:37
Gifford, James 19:252
Gifford, John M. 22:193
Gifford, Lewis P. 4:26
Gifford, Russell 4:26
Gifford, Samuel H. 9:16
Gifford, Simon 19:340
Gifford, W. 13:88
Gifford, William H. H. 8:17
Giffore, William 11:31
Giffroy, F. 14:28
Gift, John A. 22:78
Gift, Jonathan 17:394
Gift, Martin V. 15:13
Giger, Charles 4:26
Giger, George 13:24
Giger, John 4:26
Giger, John S. 9:81; 26:29
Giggen, Joseph 11:118
Gigley, George 7:50
Gigly, Rudolph 15:35
Gigsby, Reuben 20:123
Giher, P. 3:78
Gijr, August 24:39
Gilaisier, J. 25:175
Gilando, Lewis 6:23
Gilbeck, James 27:51
Gilber, Charles 14:241
Gilberson, James 7:27
Gilbert, A. 3:79; 15:165
Gilbert, A. D. 7:27
Gilbert, A. F. 3:79
Gilbert, A. H. 8:85
Gilbert, A. J. 18:237; 26:30
Gilbert, A. T. 15:307; 19:71
Gilbert, Albert 18:83; 22:470
Gilbert, Alexander 17:52
Gilbert, Alson I. 7:95
Gilbert, Alson J. 21:335
Gilbert, Asa B. 12:22
Gilbert, Benjamin 23:31
Gilbert, Benjamin F. 22:463

Gilbert, C. 1:133; 3:79; 14:63
Gilbert, C. P. 25:36
Gilbert, C. S. 15:5
Gilbert, Charles 14:170; 22:193; 26:220; 27:53
Gilbert, Charles H. 24:61
Gilbert, Charles M. 4:26
Gilbert, Charles P. 22:519
Gilbert, Charles S. 12:70
Gilbert, Cicero 20:7
Gilbert, Cornelius 22:78, 480
Gilbert, Cyrus J. 21:52
Gilbert, D. 3:79; 10:192
Gilbert, D. W. 7:27
Gilbert, David 12:70; 15:67
Gilbert, David W. 4:26
Gilbert, Dudley 18:174
Gilbert, E. 3:79; 16:150
Gilbert, E. D. 14:170, 256
Gilbert, Ewin F. 15:22
Gilbert, Ezekiel 6:29
Gilbert, F. 3:79
Gilbert, Frank 12:8
Gilbert, G. 9:110
Gilbert, G. W. 14:63
Gilbert, George 9:220; 11:20; 12:64; 13:57; 15:91; 17:404; 18:366; 21:27
Gilbert, George H. 5:16; 25:36
Gilbert, George L. 27:51
Gilbert, George P. 18:271
Gilbert, Gibson 8:17; 18:135
Gilbert, Grafton 19:348
Gilbert, Granville 19:71
Gilbert, H. 3:79; 13:88; 14:10; 17:148; 23:145
Gilbert, H. A. 3:79
Gilbert, H. E. 25:175
Gilbert, Harry 15:267
Gilbert, Henry 16:193; 22:300
Gilbert, Henry R. 12:22; 26:220
Gilbert, Herbert 13:79
Gilbert, Hiram 25:175
Gilbert, Hugh 1:35
Gilbert, Isaac 7:123; 14:329
Gilbert, J. 3:79; 21:335; 25:175
Gilbert, J. D. 15:306; 19:71
Gilbert, J. F. 22:479

Gilbert, James 8:85; 9:119, 143; 11:332; 27:48
Gilbert, James A. 18:217
Gilbert, James B. 8:63
Gilbert, James H. 11:319; 21:335
Gilbert, James R. 22:78
Gilbert, Job 1:37
Gilbert, John 3:79; 8:17, 85; 11:203; 18:135; 20:46; 23:66
Gilbert, John B. 19:71
Gilbert, John H. 19:165
Gilbert, John R. 11:147
Gilbert, John W. 10:172
Gilbert, Joseph F. 22:193
Gilbert, Lafayette H. 22:143
Gilbert, Lewis 12:153
Gilbert, Liman 4:26
Gilbert, Lyman B. 21:253
Gilbert, M. 14:298; 17:470; 27:52
Gilbert, Martin 21:244
Gilbert, Michael 7:95
Gilbert, Miles 8:85
Gilbert, Miles H. 10:8
Gilbert, N. 1:132
Gilbert, Nathan 21:271
Gilbert, P. 13:110
Gilbert, Philip 18:29
Gilbert, Pleasant 26:29
Gilbert, R. 14:63
Gilbert, Richard 19:15
Gilbert, Rufus 20:7
Gilbert, S. 3:79
Gilbert, S. M. 18:189
Gilbert, Samuel 9:131; 17:236; 27:50
Gilbert, Samuel M. 14:170
Gilbert, Simon 23:66
Gilbert, Squire 21:271
Gilbert, Stephen 8:48
Gilbert, Stephen E. 17:287
Gilbert, Sudam 7:123
Gilbert, Thomas 10:161; 17:91; 19:165; 22:300
Gilbert, Thomas C. 22:193
Gilbert, Thomas N. 22:479
Gilbert, U. 23:145
Gilbert, W. 7:57; 25:175
Gilbert, Walter 22:404
Gilbert, William 3:79; 5:16; 9:214; 10:54; 13:24; 14:170; 15:315; 17:326; 20:257

Gilbert, William A. 11:31
Gilbert, William E. 12:70
Gilbert, William F. 15:199
Gilbert, William R. 17:79
Gilberth, George W. 9:22
Gilberton, William 13:110
Gilbertor, Gilchrist
    Charles 18:320
Gilbertson, Thomas
    10:54; 20:257
Gilbertson, Thomas F.
    11:115
Gilbough, N. 16:193
Gilbraith, D. W. 10:54
Gilbraith, Green 11:203
Gilbraith, J. 14:63
Gilbraith, Robert S.
    22:193
Gilbrath, John T. 12:53
Gilbreath, Benjamin M.
    23:98
Gilbreath, Grey 21:271
Gilbreth, Edwin 20:8
Gilbreth, Henry 22:300
Gilbreth, J. H. 17:16
Gilbreth, John 23:309
Gilbreth, Thomas 11:203
Gilbreth, William 22:300
Gilbrith, R. 11:186
Gilbroth, Ira 19:165
Gilbs, D. 3:79
Gilchrist, Charles 9:22
Gilchrist, Edwin R. 22:31
Gilchrist, G. 3:78
Gilchrist, H. G. 14:63
Gilchrist, Hampton
    21:271
Gilchrist, Henderson 8:48
Gilchrist, Henry 22:31
Gilchrist, I. R. 3:78
Gilchrist, James 10:114;
    20:257
Gilchrist, James M. 17:34
Gilchrist, Sidney 17:175
Gilday, --- 12:168
Gilday, Edward 24:111
Gilde, J. 14:63
Gilden, D. 3:79
Gilden, Oliver 20:137
Gilder, J. A. 16:34
Gilder, P. 12:161
Gildersleve, Seymour
    10:17
Gildersleve, Stephen
    25:269
Gilding, H. 16:193
Gildman, John A. 22:335
Gilds, John 8:48
Gildwer, Francis 4:26
Gile, C. M. 1:134
Gile, Elias B. 22:404

Gileo, A. H. 19:71
Gilereas, John M. 16:3
Gileroy, Samuel J. 21:187
Giles, A. 23:145
Giles, C. 3:79; 23:252
Giles, Charles 16:147
Giles, Cicero 26:124
Giles, Cuffee 9:207; 18:66
Giles, Cyrenus 10:17
Giles, G. 18:306
Giles, H. 18:66
Giles, I. 25:34
Giles, Isaac W. 11:287
Giles, J. 9:22; 13:88;
    26:98
Giles, J. C. 11:303
Giles, J. M. 9:177; 19:227
Giles, J. V. 3:79
Giles, Jacob 1:37
Giles, James 7:123; 16:94
Giles, John 21:271;
    25:175
Giles, John W. 5:16
Giles, L. 25:175
Giles, M. C. 3:79
Giles, Martin 21:271
Giles, R. B. 23:31
Giles, Ransler 24:19
Giles, Richard 16:34
Giles, S. 2:11
Giles, S. P. 3:79
Giles, Samuel 9:207;
    10:170; 19:165
Giles, Stearns A. 18:276
Giles, T. 16:193
Giles, W. Irwin 11:148
Giles, William B. 17:346
Gilet, William 22:143
Gilf, A. C. 13:64
Gilfan, Joseph 11:340
Gilffer, M. 14:63
Gilfillan, James H. 23:31
Gilfilland, R. 14:10
Gilford, B. 18:237
Gilford, D. 20:133
Gilford, Hiram 13:110
Gilford, Myron S. 24:63
Gilford, William H. H.
    18:135
Gilg, Conrad 4:26
Gilgan, W. 3:79
Gilger, Charles W. B.
    22:78
Gilger, Samuel P. 13:24
Gilghrist, John E. 23:179
Gilham, Albert 18:135
Gilham, Dennis 22:335
Gilham, William C.
    21:194
Gilhard, H. 7:27
Gilhart, George 25:35

Gilhe, F. 16:193
Gilhouly, Peter 21:335
Gilhum, A. W. 8:85
Giliam, L. 11:438
Gilkep, A. K. 19:71
Gilkey, David J. 22:451
Gilkey, E. 1:133
Gilkey, Savilian W. 19:15
Gilkey, Thomas 11:262
Gilkison, John 22:193
Gilkry, A. J. 15:335
Gill, --- 25:333
Gill, A. 8:17; 18:237;
    26:31
Gill, A. C. 16:193
Gill, Abraham 22:300
Gill, Alex 20:257
Gill, Alexander 10:54
Gill, Augustine 14:321
Gill, Benjamin F. 4:26
Gill, Boyle 18:83
Gill, C. F. 12:153
Gill, C. H. 25:35
Gill, D. 1:133
Gill, Daniel 27:53
Gill, Edward 26:31
Gill, Edward R. 22:121
Gill, G. W. 3:79
Gill, George 1:36
Gill, Harrison 18:237;
    26:31
Gill, Henry 22:300
Gill, J. 20:40
Gill, J. A. 25:175
Gill, J. F. 3:79
Gill, J. H. 9:22; 18:306;
    26:99
Gill, James 10:172;
    15:165; 17:352, 418;
    19:165; 24:158
Gill, James D. 26:29
Gill, John 10:114; 20:257
Gill, Josiah 20:123;
    27:144
Gill, Marion 8:17
Gill, Michael 17:14;
    22:300
Gill, Mirion 18:135
Gill, N. 3:79
Gill, Peter 7:50; 21:271
Gill, Robert 7:123;
    14:329; 17:422;
    24:164
Gill, Scott 17:267
Gill, Solomon 19:165
Gill, W. F. 9:177
Gill, W. I. 3:79
Gill, William 7:27; 8:105
Gill, William A. 11:412
Gill, William C. 10:114;
    20:257

Gillam, Dallas 20:257
Gillam, Dennis 22:519
Gillam, William 4:27
Gillam, Zachariah 11:84
Gillamin, J. 3:79
Gillan, Dallas 10:54
Gillan, G. 12:153
Gillan, I. 3:79
Gillan, James 12:153;
    15:313
Gillan, O. 1:135
Gilland, Henry 8:48
Gilland, John 25:175
Gilland, P. 3:79
Gilland, William 16:193
Gillany, T. 14:63
Gillaran, J. H. 1:36
Gillard, James 27:50
Gillard, W. 3:79
Gillaspay, Aaron 7:27
Gillaspie, Harvey 17:259
Gilleard, George B.
    12:171
Gillelan, J. W. 11:147
Gilleland, William 25:175
Gillem, Jeffrey 21:271
Gillen, Arther 25:278
Gillen, Charles 11:286
Gillen, F. 12:22
Gillen, H. 19:252; 25:175
Gillen, Henry 9:177
Gillen, J. 11:240
Gillen, James 4:27; 19:71
Gillen, James S. 15:35
Gillen, John 5:16
Gillen, L. D. 1:134
Gillen, M'l. 16:193
Gillen, M. 3:79
Gillen, William H. 12:53
Gillenback, J. 3:79
Gillengham, R. 16:293
Gillens, A. 25:175
Gillenwother, Thomas
    17:110
Gilleo, H. 1:134
Giller, Christopher 13:24
Giller, Edgar 13:24
Gilleran, Thomas 16:132
Gillerd, James 9:131
Gillerm, George 18:135
Gillery, --- 15:35
Gilles, William 8:48
Gillesper, D. 16:34
Gillespie, --- 12:99
Gillespie, Andrew 22:335
Gillespie, Andrew H.
    23:31
Gillespie, B. F. 23:145
Gillespie, Charles 17:34
Gillespie, Cornelius
    22:193

Gillespie, D. 20:146
Gillespie, David 13:24
Gillespie, Edward 7:95
Gillespie, Franklin 22:300
Gillespie, George Y.
    23:88
Gillespie, H. 14:10
Gillespie, J. 1:133; 3:79
Gillespie, J. C. 11:147
Gillespie, J. D. 1:134
Gillespie, J. R. 1:36
Gillespie, J. S. 22:193
Gillespie, J. W. 1:134;
    3:79
Gillespie, Jacob 6:16
Gillespie, James 1:36;
    7:57; 17:321
Gillespie, Jesse 24:89
Gillespie, John 17:191;
    22:193
Gillespie, John L. 24:183
Gillespie, John W. 7:27
Gillespie, Josiah 22:31
Gillespie, Peter 12:53;
    25:175
Gillespie, S. 1:133
Gillespie, Samuel 12:153;
    13:64
Gillespie, Theophilus
    15:86
Gillespie, Thomas 21:271
Gillespie, Thomas H.
    10:114; 20:257
Gillespie, Wallace 27:50
Gillespie, Wallis 9:131
Gillespie, William 7:8;
    22:193
Gillespy, Thomas J.
    22:425
Gillestruss, W. H. 19:15
Gillet, C. R. 11:262
Gillet, Charles S. 23:31
Gillet, Curtis C. 10:161
Gillet, F. 19:165
Gillet, Nelson 19:15
Gillet, Silas W. 9:177
Gillett, --- 11:105
Gillett, A. L. 1:35
Gillett, Charles 24:50
Gillett, Chauncey F.
    20:137
Gillett, Curtis C. 19:165
Gillett, Edgar D. 10:161
Gillett, Eli S. 13:127
Gillett, Elihue 4:26
Gillett, G. W. 3:79
Gillett, George 15:22
Gillett, H. M. 15:199
Gillett, James 13:24;
    16:34
Gillett, James A. 22:501

Gillett, John B. 11:126
Gillett, John S. 10:114;
    20:257
Gillett, L. L. 20:257
Gillett, Leander M.
    21:253
Gillett, M. 1:133
Gillett, Nathan 10:17
Gillett, Olare 11:255
Gillett, Oliver 1:35
Gillett, Orson 15:199
Gillett, R. M. 4:26
Gillett, S. W. 19:252
Gillett, W. H. 25:36
Gillett, William 3:79;
    11:423
Gillette, Cyrus 18:338
Gillette, H. 1:103
Gillette, Jonah 17:65
Gillette, N. 8:114
Gillette, Samuel 14:170
Gilley, C. H. 26:99
Gilley, George C. 22:251
Gilley, Joseph 4:27;
    11:387
Gilley, M. 1:132
Gilley, Warren M. 26:161
Gilley, Warren W. 8:17
Gilley, William 10:114
Gillham, George 11:387
Gillham, L. 26:31
Gillhouse, Frederick
    16:119
Gillian, Albert 26:161
Gillian, J. 23:31
Gilliar, H. P. 15:199
Gillie, William T. 1:37
Gillied, Joseph 11:15
Gillifillan, Daniel L.
    16:293
Gilligan, Matthew 3:78
Gilligan, Thomas 15:35
Gilliham, R. 14:63
Gillihue, James W. 21:241
Gilliland, C. 16:34
Gilliland, Fielding L.
    23:66
Gilliland, I. 3:79
Gilliland, James 17:452
Gilliland, John 12:70;
    15:67
Gilliland, William 3:79
Gillilard, J. 9:52
Gillimann, John 3:79
Gillin, Eugene 11:401
Gillinan, Elias B. 27:52
Gillinea, D. 21:27
Gillinger, John 4:26
Gillingham, B. 3:78
Gillingham, Ira 21:335

Gillingham, R. 12:92; 16:293
Gillings, John 7:81; 25:297
Gillinwater, H. 22:193
Gillion, Abraham 5:39
Gillion, J. 1:134
Gillion, Joseph 18:135
Gillis, G. 3:79
Gillis, J. 15:199
Gillis, John 9:220; 18:366
Gillis, M. D. L. 20:257
Gillis, Patrick 21:127
Gillis, R. 1:133
Gillis, William 26:211
Gillis, William H. 8:17
Gillison, Henry 22:300
Gillison, John R. 12:22
Gillison, Joseph 8:17
Gillison, T. 2:11
Gillispie, Adam 18:83
Gillispie, Ebenezer 11:148
Gillispie, George 8:17; 18:135
Gillispie, H. 11:119; 13:88
Gillispie, Henry C. 22:193
Gillispie, Jacob 18:83
Gillispie, Samuel 19:71
Gillispie, William 16:193
Gillispie, William C. 22:193
Gilliss, John 3:79
Gillith, Cyrus 9:102
Gillitt, T. B. 1:132
Gillman, Albert 8:17
Gillman, C. C. 25:35
Gillman, Charles B. 22:143
Gillman, Ezra 10:8
Gillman, Frank W. 7:27
Gillman, G. N. 25:175
Gillman, George 8:105
Gillman, Henry 5:39
Gillman, J. 27:47
Gillman, John G. 11:401
Gillman, John H. 10:153
Gillman, Joseph 19:296
Gillman, L. 1:134
Gillman, Matthew 21:27
Gillman, S. A. 3:79
Gillman, William L. 16:85
Gillmann, Newill G. 4:26
Gillmor, Joseph M. 7:50
Gillmore, F. 14:63
Gillmore, G. A. 19:320
Gillmore, Henry T. 4:26
Gillmore, John 13:24
Gillmore, John S. 17:95
Gillmore, Joseph 10:98
Gillmore, Levi 4:26

Gillmore, M. 3:79
Gillmore, P. W. 14:63
Gillmore, Samuel 9:81
Gillmore, Willoughby A. 21:99
Gillo, Edgar 16:34
Gillock, A. 14:170
Gilloman, Joseph N. 11:331
Gillon, Hugh 5:51
Gillon, J. M. 26:98
Gillon, Joseph L. 18:306
Gillon, Solomon 10:114
Gillot, R. 14:170
Gillott, R. 14:256
Gillott, Reuben 24:62
Gillpatrick, Jesse 14:170
Gills, Charles 18:270
Gills, J. M. 25:175
Gills, James 3:79
Gills, James O. 9:81
Gills, S. 25:175
Gills, William H. 18:135
Gillsa, Samuel 8:63
Gillson, Alpheus 9:97
Gillson, Joseph 25:175
Gillson, R. M. 1:134
Gillson, Thomas 10:17; 21:253
Gillson, William 20:257; 25:37
Gillum, William C. 21:69
Gilly, William 20:257
Gilman, A. 19:232
Gilman, Albert 18:29
Gilman, Allen 18:306
Gilman, Alvah 9:177
Gilman, Benjamin 18:272
Gilman, C. C. 2:11
Gilman, C. M. 8:48
Gilman, C. W. 13:64
Gilman, Charles 12:8
Gilman, Chester M. 21:253
Gilman, Daniel 17:439; 24:150
Gilman, E. 9:52
Gilman, Frank 9:207
Gilman, G. N. 25:175
Gilman, G. W. 12:80
Gilman, George D. 12:22
Gilman, George W. 5:16
Gilman, H. S. 25:37
Gilman, Henry 15:35
Gilman, J. B. 9:110
Gilman, Jacob 19:15
Gilman, Jasper 8:85
Gilman, John 15:199
Gilman, Joshua C. 21:335
Gilman, Josiah 21:148
Gilman, Josiah C. 7:95

Gilman, M. B. 19:15
Gilman, N. 18:29
Gilman, William P. 24:158
Gilmark, Harod 2:11
Gilmartin, D. 25:175
Gilmartin, M. 10:17
Gilmartin, Michael 16:193, 293
Gilmartin, Thomas 12:22
Gilmer, Allen 9:22; 26:98
Gilmer, D. 13:89
Gilmer, J. B. 14:241
Gilmer, James C. 17:79
Gilmer, William 22:166
Gilmere, A. L. 17:242
Gilmoor, A. 19:274
Gilmord, A. K. 15:267
Gilmore, Archibald 14:170
Gilmore, Bradford 21:335
Gilmore, G. 9:220; 18:366
Gilmore, George 20:8
Gilmore, George A. 8:125
Gilmore, George M. 27:52
Gilmore, H. 18:420
Gilmore, H. R. 9:52
Gilmore, Henry J. 13:24
Gilmore, J. 3:79; 11:241; 16:136; 20:40
Gilmore, James 3:79; 10:95; 14:170; 18:14
Gilmore, John 10:54; 11:30; 20:257
Gilmore, Joseph 18:29; 27:51
Gilmore, Joseph B. 9:119
Gilmore, Martin 9:131; 27:49
Gilmore, Martin V. 18:103
Gilmore, Milford 17:206
Gilmore, R. 1:94, 134
Gilmore, R. P. 17:346
Gilmore, Samuel 22:251
Gilmore, William 11:241; 21:335
Gilmore, William S. 15:308
Gilmour, Alex 9:177
Gilmour, J. P. 11:428
Gilnott, Frederick 17:392
Gilny, James 7:28
Gilom, Solomon 20:257
Gilooly, Peter 22:11
Gilpatrick, E. 10:34
Gilpatrick, John M. 11:61
Gilpatrick, Nathaniel 12:22
Gilpatrick, Thomas 27:47

Gilpatrick, William H. 26:219
Gilpen, E. C. 18:49
Gilpen, Wesley 17:146
Gilphin, Henry 20:257
Gilpin, A. B. 22:143
Gilpin, Alexander 7:77; 25:297
Gilpin, Andrew J. 21:52
Gilpin, David P. 20:97
Gilpin, Enoch 21:27
Gilpin, J. 21:203
Gilpin, J. W. 20:257
Gilpin, John 11:92; 19:15; 22:451
Gilpin, Jonas 21:121
Gilpin, William 22:251
Gilroy, Barney 3:79
Gilroy, John 13:127
Gilroy, M. 16:279
Gilsby, P. 3:79
Gilso, Charles 14:170
Gilson, C. A. 9:143
Gilson, E. H. 27:49
Gilson, Eda 25:311
Gilson, Francis A. 23:11
Gilson, H. H. 25:297
Gilson, John E. 3:79
Gilson, John J. 17:34
Gilson, Justus M. 4:26
Gilson, L. C. 11:106
Gilson, S. G. 10:54
Gilson, Samuel 21:137
Gilson, William 7:28; 14:63
Gilspy, Samuel 18:14
Gilstrap, T. I. 18:174
Gilstrap, Thomas 10:179
Gilt, John 21:335
Giltgrease, J. 3:79
Gilthreath, D. W. 20:257
Giltner, F. 15:199
Giltner, George 24:50
Giltner, Henry P. 17:70
Gilton, Jasper N. 9:22
Gilverson, George N. 10:115; 20:257
Gilvery, Lafflin M. 11:30
Gilyon, Wiley 22:501
Giman, J. 3:79
Gimberline, J. 3:79
Gimble, Jacob 7:95
Gimmes, W. E. 26:31
Gimmill, John H. 12:171
Gimpel, Frederick 20:40
Gimpson, Alexander 7:95
Ginder, H. B. 21:335
Ginder, James 9:236
Gindray, Joseph 7:123
Ginern, John 7:28
Gingell, H. 1:132

Ginger, E. 10:205
Ginger, John C. 22:78
Gingerick, Jesse 20:133
Gingerick, John 11:31
Gingery, Daniel 11:148
Gingery, J. W. 11:287
Gingery, Joseph 23:285
Gingery, P. L. 3:79
Gingher, Benjamin F. 23:66
Gingrey, Henry 11:148
Gingrich, Allen 22:31
Gingry, Samuel 15:199
Ginhicks, G. P. 25:37
Ginie, Clarence W. 9:102
Ginings, P. 20:123
Ginley, Jeremiah 23:145
Ginley, W. H. 9:177
Ginlin, John 13:24
Ginn, --- 23:198
Ginn, J. B. 17:175
Ginn, Jerry 19:45
Ginn, Joshua M. 19:15
Ginnalls, George 12:99
Ginnas, A. 14:10
Ginnels, A. 14:10
Ginnels, Daniel 21:148
Ginnes, Samuel 16:193
Ginney, B. 25:175
Ginnick, Peter 3:79
Ginnold, George 10:210
Ginnoy, A. 14:64
Ginter, P. 15:67
Ginter, Samuel 26:31
Gintes, Samuel 9:200
Ginther, Joseph G. 4:27
Ginty, T. 11:191
Giphart, Thomas R. 11:147
Gipple, Henry 16:34
Gipple, Joseph 23:145
Gipprer, Jacob 9:35
Gipps, Frederick 8:48
Gipsey, J. 25:175
Gipsey, Jacob 5:39
Gipsom, George B. 22:78
Gipson, George 5:16
Gipson, John C. 22:251
Gipson, Johnson 22:300
Girard, Alexander 22:31
Girard, E. 14:64
Girard, Frank 4:26
Girard, Hezekiah 8:85
Girard, James 1:37
Girard, John 22:31; 26:29
Girard, Joseph 4:26
Girckero, Henry 18:395
Girdes, Rank 8:48
Girdner, J. J. 17:148
Girkin, H. 19:252
Girkin, Henry 9:177

Girkin, William 11:262
Girkon, David 20:257
Girle, H. 17:294
Girney, Thomas 27:51
Girrard, Jacob 11:30
Girrardean, V. D. G. 27:49
Girstung, Frank 14:11
Girt, E. S. 13:124
Girtler, H. 1:132
Girtley, Thomas 18:206
Girton, William 22:193
Girton, William H. 22:425
Girtone, Alfred 7:68
Girts, James R. 22:234
Gisbee, --- 15:35
Gisen, Frank 15:314
Gish, A. S. 23:117
Gish, H. A. 22:193
Gish, William 17:393
Gison, E. 25:175
Gison, Harvey 21:99
Gison, Henderson 18:366
Gison, Thomas 9:81
Gison, Wilson 9:207
Gispelker, L. 14:64
Gissmon, Jacob 11:119
Gist, S. 16:369
Gist, T. 7:57
Gister, James 9:207
Gists, H. 3:79
Gitchel, J. H. 9:220; 18:367
Gitchel, W. D. 15:17
Gitchell, James 27:52
Gitchell, O. 1:133
Gitchell, Roswell E. 9:214
Gitchouse, W. 27:52
Gitchouse, William 14:298; 17:470
Githens, J. W. 11:92
Githens, Jacob R. P. 9:35
Githens, James 22:251
Githens, Thomas J. 23:145
Githins, J. R. P. 26:99
Gitney, Thomas 15:35
Gitson, William 24:111
Gitt, John 7:95
Gittens, John 25:175
Gitter, John 19:329
Gitthens, Jacob R. 18:293
Gittings, --- 8:72; 26:162
Gittings, M. 22:193
Gittle, J. B. 16:193
Gittoly, John 12:22
Gitty, Joseph K. 11:181
Giull, Julius 8:17
Giungoclott, H. 3:79
Givans, Isaac 17:460
Givans, Thomas 20:257
Given, Alex 19:15

Given, Charles 3:79
Given, F. 14:11
Given, George 22:193;
   23:11
Given, Isaiah 6:16; 18:83
Given, John 6:20; 17:175
Given, N. 9:200
Given, Nat. H. 19:291
Given, Unman 9:177
Givens, Charles 24:194
Givens, E. 1:37
Givens, Edward 7:123
Givens, Frank 18:237
Givens, George 14:170;
   17:400
Givens, Green 17:131;
   24:194
Givens, Isaac 24:158
Givens, J. A. 3:79
Givens, John 10:54;
   20:257
Givens, Joshua 19:296
Givens, Major 7:123
Givens, Milton 20:257
Givens, P. H. 22:251
Givens, Perry 18:412
Givens, S. C. 24:193
Givens, S. R. 23:95
Givens, Samuel 5:39
Givens, William 22:251
Giver, John L. 23:288
Gives, Peter 9:22
Givinett, Charles 20:257
Givins, Frank 26:30
Givins, Isaac 8:101
Givins, James 19:71
Givins, Milton 10:115
Givisiez, Joseph 19:71
Gizzle, P. 16:193
Glabbort, H. 1:36
Glacebrooks, James
   17:131; 24:194
Gladd, A. H. 27:49
Gladden, John B. 9:177
Gladdin, Thomas 1:192
Gladding, Edward S.
   16:34
Gladding, J. 1:133
Gladding, James 10:8
Gladding, O. 1:37
Gladding, Timothy 15:3
Gladen, A. 3:79
Gladen, H. 25:175
Gladen, Peter 9:81
Gladen, William 22:251
Gladenon, W. 13:110
Gladfelder, David 23:258
Gladfeldter, --- 9:220
Gladfelter, --- 18:367
Gladfelter, David 22:31
Glading, Edw. S. 13:24

Glading, T. A. 13:110
Gladish, Leander J.
   10:115; 20:257
Gladman, Mathew 11:147
Gladman, T. 1:38
Gladmon, H. 3:79
Gladson, Andrew 21:137
Gladson, J. 27:53
Gladson, Joshua L. 24:19
Gladson, L. A. 8:85
Gladstone, William 3:80
Glaeser, C. 18:189
Glaeton, L. R. 14:64
Glage, Jacob 13:110
Glahn, John 9:177
Glahn, P. 19:252
Glair, J. 16:94
Glair, John 16:95
Glaise, Robert 22:300
Glaize, H. 14:288
Glake, N. 1:121
Glance, Archibald 8:105
Glancer, Solomon C.
   8:105
Glancey, J. 1:94
Glancey, J. J. 15:329
Glancey, P. 1:134; 3:80
Glancy, J. 16:193
Glancy, James 19:71
Glancy, Owen 27:53
Glancy, Patrick 7:80;
   25:297
Glanden, Sterling 9:52
Glander, A. 1:37
Glaney, John C. 18:189
Glannon, William 15:4
Glantor, T. 25:176
Glanville, Thomas 14:64
Glanwood, S. C. 7:50
Glanzer, Philip 20:35
Glara, F. 21:335
Glardon, Peter 26:29
Glardsly, Charles 15:199
Glare, A. J. 22:335
Glarescy, E. 19:331
Glarow, --- 25:35
Glasby, Andrew J. 22:121
Glasby, M. L. 19:321
Glasby, Scott 20:399
Glasby, William 19:15
Glascere, Robert 19:15
Glasco, Hiram 8:17;
   18:136
Glasco, W. 13:89
Glascock, Samuel P.
   11:326
Glascow, George 15:199
Glascow, William 18:14
Glascoy, William 7:50
Glase, --- 15:35
Glaser, David 4:27

Glasgom, John 18:237
Glasgon, John 26:29
Glasgow, E. 18:66
Glasgow, J. 12:99
Glasgow, James D. 20:22
Glasgow, James N. 16:34
Glasgow, Matthew 12:22
Glasgow, Robert M. 24:50
Glasgow, William 18:426
Glasha, George 7:62
Glasier, J. 5:51
Glason, Andrew 26:162
Glaspy, J. S. 11:92
Glass, --- 1:134; 11:219
Glass, A. 18:237; 26:30
Glass, A. B. 21:335
Glass, David 15:199, 347
Glass, E. J. 11:401
Glass, G. W. 1:134
Glass, Henry 14:64;
   21:198
Glass, Henry H. 19:227
Glass, Isaac 22:32
Glass, J. J. 26:161
Glass, James 15:86;
   17:406; 22:251
Glass, John 1:37; 7:63;
   8:17; 9:177; 12:70,
   81; 15:35; 16:293;
   17:34, 52; 18:136;
   19:252
Glass, John K. 23:189
Glass, John W. 20:139
Glass, Joseph 17:203;
   22:513
Glass, Joseph A. 21:187
Glass, Levi 13:64
Glass, Lowry M. 17:34
Glass, M. C. 19:15
Glass, R. 13:110
Glass, S. 22:397
Glass, S. H. 15:285
Glass, Samuel 16:160
Glass, Samuel S. 21:335
Glass, Solomon 21:254
Glass, William 3:80; 4:27;
   8:69; 11:386; 17:148,
   389
Glass, William H. 12:62;
   15:13; 22:519
Glassans, John W. 17:79
Glassbrener, George 20:17
Glassbrook, G. W. 11:286
Glassburner, J. 1:37
Glasscock, Elijah 17:280
Glasscock, J. H. 11:31
Glasscock, James H.
   22:31
Glasscott, J. 13:89
Glassford, Samuel S.
   23:31

Glassford, W. H. 25:176
Glassford, William H.
  15:278
Glassman, P. 3:80
Glassner, Frederick 12:22
Glasson, Amos A. 22:463
Glasspy, Silas 20:257
Glasur, Frederick 15:91
Glaton, J. A. 20:123
Glatts, William H. 4:27
Glaughlin, G. 13:110
Glave, Freder. 16:145
Glavish, Cornelius E. 9:35
Glay, Jacob 14:171
Glay, William 8:39;
  26:161
Glays, H. 14:265
Glaze, Andrew 13:124
Glaze, Henry 23:95
Glaze, John 23:66
Glaze, Nathan 22:78
Glaze, Samuel 23:31
Glaze, Stephen S. 12:22
Glazer, Adolph 13:110
Glazer, Asa 17:34
Glazer, Christopher 23:31
Glazer, H. M. 18:29
Glazier, Edward 22:11
Glazier, G. 7:50
Glazier, Harry 9:131
Glazier, Henry 27:50
Glazier, Jabez 4:27
Glazier, Jacob 9:110
Glazier, Thomas J. 12:55
Glaziner, Levi 15:165
Glazy, Marcus D. 10:115;
  20:257
Gle---, J. L. 15:263
Glead, William 19:237
Glean, J. H. 15:67
Gleancy, Francis 17:502
Gleaser, Louis 21:335
Gleaser, M. 25:34
Gleasman, George 25:176
Gleason, --- 25:285
Gleason, A. 8:63; 9:177;
  19:253
Gleason, C. W. 3:80
Gleason, Charles 5:16;
  15:199
Gleason, Charles A.
  15:199
Gleason, Charles F. 12:22
Gleason, Charles H. 4:27
Gleason, Cornelius 7:28
Gleason, Daniel 22:335
Gleason, E. 19:253
Gleason, E. M. 9:177
Gleason, Edward 9:177
Gleason, Emanuel 7:95
Gleason, Francis 23:145

Gleason, G. 23:31
Gleason, G. A. 1:132
Gleason, G. M. 3:80
Gleason, George 21:254
Gleason, George W.
  23:190
Gleason, Henry O. 9:177
Gleason, Hiram 22:193
Gleason, Howell 21:271
Gleason, J. 1:132
Gleason, J. D. 13:64
Gleason, J. P. 15:357
Gleason, J. T. 25:35
Gleason, James 8:48;
  19:222
Gleason, Jesse D. 16:193
Gleason, Joel 9:177;
  19:253
Gleason, John 15:278;
  17:79; 19:318; 21:27
Gleason, Joseph 27:52
Gleason, L. 1:135
Gleason, L. A. 1:135
Gleason, Michael B.
  13:24; 16:34
Gleason, Patrick 14:171;
  17:34; 21:335; 22:11
Gleason, Sumner A. 7:8
Gleason, Thomas 3:80;
  7:68; 22:335
Gleason, Thomas E. 11:31
Gleason, Timothy 21:335
Gleason, Volney R.
  23:179
Gleason, W. 19:15
Gleason, W. J. 1:132
Gleaton, W. N. 19:327
Glebe, Valentine 11:106
Gleek, George A. 12:22
Gleen, Francis 21:27
Gleen, James B. 16:34
Gleeson, Elisha 11:401
Gleeson, Frank 12:22
Gleeson, John 14:64
Gleeston, Manuel 7:123
Gleiser, --- 11:61
Gleitch, William 3:80
Glellan, William M. 7:95;
  21:335
Glem, G. A. 13:89
Glem, M. S. 25:35
Gleman, C. O. 13:82
Glen, James 18:83
Glen, P. B. 20:146
Glenard, William E.
  16:193
Glencross, John 19:165
Glendemer, G. W. 14:319;
  25:275
Glendenning, Henry
  10:115; 20:257

Glendenning, James J.
  10:54; 20:258
Glendenning, John G.
  7:95
Glendenning, William
  21:52
Glendon, John 11:30
Glendon, Richard 22:32
Glenes, C. 14:64
Gleney, J. 11:105
Glenfield, Adam 10:115;
  20:258
Glengross, W. M. 15:106
Glenmier, Charles 22:470
Glenn, --- 21:69
Glenn, Archibald 25:176
Glenn, C. H. 3:80; 10:54
Glenn, Christopher 17:397
Glenn, Daniel 13:24
Glenn, Francis 8:48
Glenn, G. A. 14:11
Glenn, H. C. 20:258
Glenn, Henry 21:271
Glenn, J. 9:52; 14:64;
  22:300
Glenn, James 6:12;
  17:175, 321
Glenn, James B. 13:24
Glenn, James L. 22:251
Glenn, John 7:64; 8:85;
  17:397
Glenn, John A. 9:35
Glenn, John B. 20:192
Glenn, John W. F. 10:115;
  20:258
Glenn, Jordan 17:175
Glenn, Josiah D. 20:40
Glenn, Ludwig 8:48
Glenn, M. S. 2:11
Glenn, Mathew 18:83
Glenn, Oliver 12:22
Glenn, R. 11:303
Glenn, Robert 21:27, 208;
  22:300
Glenn, Samuel T. 18:136
Glenn, Thomas 23:309
Glenn, William 3:80;
  11:30; 12:22; 20:258
Glenn, William M. 22:519
Glenn, William T. 4:27
Glenons, Patrick 1:35
Glense, Josiah 25:35
Glenson, T. S. 12:99
Glent, Jesse 9:35
Glenwood, Harry C.
  21:335
Glesbby, M. E. P. (Mrs.)
  27:49
Glesmon, William 18:83
Gleson, Chancy 19:71
Gleson, Dennis 14:171

Gleson, E. W. 19:237
Gleson, M. 18:83
Glessner, Edward C. 23:145
Glessner, Phillip 15:81
Glestine, James 12:22
Gleves, Thomas 22:335
Glewell, J. L. 15:199
Glick, Erasmus B. 17:349
Glidden, --- 10:161
Glidden, A. N. 7:8
Glidden, Benjamin F. 13:24
Glidden, G. 25:176
Glidden, J. C. 17:159
Glidden, Lysander 10:91
Gliddon, --- 19:166
Gliddon, Lysander 20:258
Gliddon, Wesley 12:22
Gliden, J. A. 19:227
Glidewell, James 11:30
Glidewell, Robert 8:17; 18:136
Glidwell, F. 3:80
Glifford, W. 15:322
Gliford, J. 1:135
Glifton, Walter 8:121
Glilton, George 5:16
Glim, J. 25:176
Glimanbaga, Michael 11:262
Glime, C. R. 24:78
Glimes, Jeremiah 19:325
Glimker, B. 18:49
Glimps, J. 1:132
Glin, Addison 20:258
Gliner, Charles 11:303
Glines, Albert 21:69
Glines, Clarence 18:338
Glines, Daniel L. 22:279
Glines, Frederick A. 14:171
Glines, George W. 17:248
Glines, J. 1:133
Glinfish, J. 14:64
Glinger, H. 21:91
Glinis, H. 17:159
Glinn, Addison 10:54
Glinn, James G. 1:36
Glinn, John 4:27; 5:16
Glinn, William 14:171
Glishman, William 6:20
Glispie, Jacob 7:50
Glisson, Elisha E. 23:66
Glisson, George W. 21:130
Glitch, J. 1:37
Glitz, Cesar 19:287
Gload, Joseph 4:27
Glocher, Jeremiah 7:57

Glodsberry, Stephen 10:54
Glodwell, Peter 22:352
Glofelt, Robert C. 15:199
Gloge, --- 18:412
Glogg, I. 8:48
Gloire, Brunoe 17:429
Glomas, J. 7:50
Glombey, Patrick 26:161
Glonghlin, --- 26:29
Gloobson, Walter 16:95
Gloon, J. G. 15:357
Gloor, Jacob 8:17; 18:136
Glore, Richard 17:308
Glorie, Brunoe 24:185
Gloss, Elijah 1:35
Gloss, Frederick 14:171
Gloss, Joseph 11:387
Glossan, Frederick 26:29
Glossen, Fred 9:81
Glosser, J. 11:84
Glossin, A. 3:80
Glossner, John 13:89
Glossup, C. F. 15:199
Glouchlen, John 16:132
Gloud, D. 1:132
Glove, Frederick 9:207
Glove, W. S. 8:63; 26:162
Glover, --- 19:329
Glover, Adam 9:200; 19:291
Glover, Alex 20:258
Glover, Alexander 10:54; 22:300; 25:35
Glover, B. W. 21:335
Glover, Cassius Q. 22:78
Glover, Christopher 4:65
Glover, Daniel T. 22:166
Glover, Edward D. 17:206
Glover, Francis 7:123
Glover, Fred 25:320
Glover, Frederick 6:30
Glover, G. 17:364
Glover, G. F. 9:52
Glover, G. W. 1:37
Glover, George 8:17; 18:136; 26:31
Glover, George A. 22:193
Glover, Gleam 21:335
Glover, Harrison 13:24
Glover, Harvey B. 16:369
Glover, Henry 9:22; 18:306; 26:99
Glover, James N. 17:236
Glover, Joel 4:27
Glover, Joel C. 16:279
Glover, John 7:123; 10:54; 20:258; 21:335
Glover, John F. 12:95; 15:359; 19:71

Glover, John H. 11:92
Glover, John R. 16:34
Glover, Joseph 11:262
Glover, L. 9:154; 27:49
Glover, Lemuel H. 17:46
Glover, M. S. 15:199
Glover, Philip L. 17:359
Glover, Reuben 10:161; 19:166
Glover, Robert M. 17:318
Glover, Samuel 9:119; 27:50
Glover, Thomas L. 1:35
Glover, W. R. 20:258
Glover, William 16:193
Glover, William R. 10:54
Gloyd, Ashael 4:27
Gloyd, William 1:37
Gluck, A. E. 3:80
Gluck, Lewis 10:172
Gluder, D. 14:64
Gluflegel, George 10:54; 20:258
Glum, H. C. 15:165
Glum, P. 18:237
Glum, Samuel T. 8:17
Glunkier, B. 10:148
Glunt, John 9:22
Glunt, Josiah 22:234
Glunt, S. 21:121
Glur, Fred 7:28
Glurm, P. 26:30
Glusky, John 19:287
Gluslir, J. 1:134
Gluth, Frederick 15:91
Gluthart, Leon 11:147
Glynn, Augustus 23:145
Glynn, G. F. 21:336
Glynn, James 6:30; 25:320
Glynn, Michael 15:199
Glynn, Patrick 20:33
Glyof, Augustus 24:66
Gm---mon, A. C. 15:323
Gnash, S. 14:171
Gnitt, George 11:398
Goad, Henry C. 11:280
Goalsby, Benjamin 22:300
Goamy, G. 3:80
Goans, Robert 10:27; 19:301
Goare, William 23:88
Goarley, W. M. 23:307
Goarty, John 21:225
Goatamont, P. 1:131
Goaume, J. 3:80
Gob---, C. B. 25:36
Gobal, Henry 7:95
Gobat, Frederick 22:78
Gobbert, Adam 17:34
Gobbie, William H. 1:34

Gobble, Hiram 17:236
Gobbles, William 5:16
Gobe, George 18:454
Gobeen, Milton C. 19:71
Gobel, John 12:53
Gobelet, Frederick 4:27
Goben, Charles M. 10:54
Goben, Thomas 24:213
Gober, Charles 21:271
Gobert, Celestius 7:28
Gobert, Nicholi 22:78
Gobin, Thomas 17:456
Goble, Daniel 22:404
Goble, Darwin L. 23:285
Goble, E. R. 12:22
Goble, H. 1:131
Goble, J. L. 22:480
Goble, Peter 19:15
Goble, T. O. 1:135
Goble, W. 1:131
Goble, W. H. H. 15:199
Gobles, W. 25:176
Goblon, A. T. 21:336
Gobsuch, Joshua 20:258
Gochenour, James M.
  23:145
Gochenour, John 23:145
Gochey, James 21:336
Gochlin, Benjamin 14:171
Gocia, Frank 21:336
Godale, George A. 9:119
Godard, William 17:446;
  24:170
Godbold, David 23:190
Godbold, F. A. 3:80
Godbold, William 3:80
Godbrey, Eugene 23:107
Goddard, --- 23:292
Goddard, A. 5:16
Goddard, George 10:95;
  15:199
Goddard, H. 3:80; 22:479
Goddard, J. 12:98
Goddard, James 8:72
Goddard, John 3:80;
  15:357; 16:279
Goddard, Moses 12:55
Goddard, Prentiss H.
  21:336
Goddard, Samuel 17:166
Goddard, William 17:79
Goddard, William A.
  25:176
Goddard, William H.
  17:62
Goddell, Ezekiel 22:480
Godder, Samuel 8:17
Goddings, J. W. 16:369
Godditt, Joseph 5:16
Godell, F. 3:80; 14:171
Goder, I. 25:35

Goders, J. D. 16:193
Godfrey, A. 1:133
Godfrey, Alfred 6:23
Godfrey, Alvin A. 20:189
Godfrey, Amos 3:80
Godfrey, Andrew S.
  11:295
Godfrey, Benjamin 12:22
Godfrey, Charles G.
  11:219
Godfrey, Charles N. 13:24
Godfrey, Edward 22:143
Godfrey, Elbridge 17:154
Godfrey, Eleazer 16:34
Godfrey, Francis 23:145
Godfrey, G. 14:64, 171
Godfrey, G. W. 11:381
Godfrey, George 11:92;
  21:69
Godfrey, George W. 17:99
Godfrey, Giles 11:387
Godfrey, Godfrey 21:247
Godfrey, Isaac 14:171
Godfrey, James 21:336;
  22:425
Godfrey, Jesse G. 11:61
Godfrey, John 21:187
Godfrey, John W. 9:97
Godfrey, L. 14:171
Godfrey, L. A. 16:95
Godfrey, L. H. 21:110
Godfrey, M. M. 25:297
Godfrey, Michael S.
  17:349
Godfrey, Morey 22:462
Godfrey, Robert 6:12
Godfrey, S. 16:193
Godfrey, S. R. 15:298
Godfrey, Solomon W.
  20:123
Godfrey, W. C. 15:341;
  16:369
Godfrey, W. W. 16:369
Godfrey, William 22:78
Godfrey, William C.
  15:67
Godfried, Adolph 10:205
Godfry, Mathew 6:20
Goding, G. P. 13:24
Goding, G. T. 16:34
Goding, Richard 10:170
Goditt, J. 25:176
Godkin, Benjamin W.
  12:22
Godkin, Thomas 19:253
Godley, D. 5:39
Godley, George W.
  11:395
Godlief, John 20:46
Godlin, Benjamin 14:171
Godlove, S. 15:199

Godly, D. 25:176
Godnan, John 18:29
Godpy, Andrew 11:255
Godrey, R. B. 16:139
Godrick, Charles 24:50
Godron, D. 22:300
Godsey, John A. 7:50
Godshath, Jacob 12:53
Godstran, J. 17:175
Godwin, George 22:78
Godwin, George W. 1:35
Godwin, J. 25:297
Godwin, Phineas W. 7:95
Godwin, Thomas M.
  18:237
Godwith, George 15:199
Goe, W. E. 10:115;
  20:258
Goebel, C. 1:132
Goebel, Jacob 21:69
Goebler, Frederick 22:424
Goeke, Lewis 24:214
Goen, Reuben 10:54
Goender, George 4:27
Goens, George W. 15:7
Goens, Jasper 22:251
Goer, James W. 10:115;
  20:258
Goertz, Daniel 18:110
Goes, E. G. 9:220; 18:367
Goesel, W. 1:133
Goetz, F. 16:85
Goetz, Hewie 17:52
Goff, A. C. 14:64
Goff, Amos 12:82; 20:107
Goff, Augustus 4:27
Goff, B. F. 14:171
Goff, Benjamin C. 24:39
Goff, C. 1:134
Goff, Charles 4:27
Goff, Christey 25:176
Goff, D. 1:134
Goff, Daniel S. 7:95
Goff, Dorr 22:279
Goff, Elias 14:298;
  17:480; 27:53
Goff, Gustavus 20:30
Goff, J. 14:64; 25:176
Goff, J. H. 25:176
Goff, James 5:16; 14:171;
  21:52; 23:203
Goff, John 3:80; 5:16;
  22:279
Goff, John G. 15:199
Goff, John R. 23:66
Goff, Joshua 12:22
Goff, Julius S. 10:54;
  20:258
Goff, Levi J. 18:237;
  26:30
Goff, Louis 11:92

Goff, Marchall C. 14:171
Goff, Martin W. 15:199
Goff, Michael 16:113
Goff, P. E. 3:80
Goff, S. B. 10:148
Goff, S. S. 14:64, 171
Goff, Simon M. 11:126
Goff, T. B. 18:49
Goff, T. M. 18:237; 26:31
Goff, Thomas 23:263
Goff, W. H. 17:475; 27:53
Goff, William 14:171, 332
Goff, William H. 14:298
Goffield, T. 25:35
Goffney, J. 3:80
Goffney, Michael 12:22
Goffney, Owen 19:70
Gofford, L. M. 15:199
Gofforth, Benjamin F. 20:258
Goffrey, Martin 8:105
Goffunt, P. 3:80
Goffy, John 19:70
Goffy, P. 3:80
Goforth, Benjamin F. 10:54
Goforth, James C. 9:81
Goforth, James M. 22:501
Goforth, L. T. 26:29
Goforth, St. T. 9:81
Goforth, William 13:24
Gogancamp, W. 1:35
Gogen, --- 15:35
Goggin, P. 1:133
Goggin, Richard 12:22
Goggin, William 20:192
Goggins, Alfred 11:203
Goggins, Pesh 17:175
Gogley, James H. 12:22
Gohagan, John 19:70
Gohagne, N. 14:64
Goheen, Charles E. 13:24
Goheen, John C. 22:424
Goheins, Samuel 18:430
Gohike, William 10:115
Gohlke, William 20:258
Gohn, John 25:176
Gohn, P. 14:171
Gohon, Joseph 8:17
Gohu, John 5:16
Goiles, John 5:16
Goilonis, R. 18:237; 26:31
Goin, Uriah 22:501
Goine, Louis 20:258
Goiner, G. 14:11
Going, C. E. 11:105
Going, Reuben 20:258
Goings, David 11:262
Goings, G. W. 12:62
Goings, John 24:111

Goins, Daniel P. S. 22:251
Goins, Galloway 22:121
Goins, William 22:352
Goit, J. A. 1:134
Goit, W. S. 18:395
Goky, Eugene 9:81
Goland, John W. 16:7
Golard, Joseph 9:207
Golby, Amos H. 18:66
Golcher, John 18:206
Gold, A. C. 13:110
Gold, A. W. 13:110
Gold, Bev'y. 8:39
Gold, Beverly 26:161
Gold, J. 25:176
Gold, John 24:39; 25:176
Gold, John M. 10:172; 19:166
Gold, Joseph A. 17:200
Gold, N. W. 15:106
Gold, R. 14:64
Gold, W. 1:134
Gold, William H. 15:318
Gold, William P. 20:30
Goldberg, Jacob 25:34
Goldberry, George 10:54
Golden, B. B. 14:241
Golden, C. 9:143; 27:48
Golden, Charles 9:81; 18:14; 26:28
Golden, D. 27:53
Golden, Dennis 21:336
Golden, E. 23:31
Golden, Eugene 21:203
Golden, George 8:17; 16:85; 18:136
Golden, George W. 14:171
Golden, H. C. 19:253
Golden, Hamilton 22:404
Golden, Henry 10:172; 19:166
Golden, Henry C. 9:177
Golden, J. 1:37; 3:80
Golden, J. H. 3:80
Golden, James 4:27; 9:177; 19:237; 22:251
Golden, John 14:171
Golden, John S. P. 22:166
Golden, Joseph 4:27
Golden, M. 14:64, 171
Golden, Marcus 22:251
Golden, Patrick 11:61
Golden, Peter 1:36
Golden, Thomas 23:242
Golden, W. H. 1:134
Golden, William 17:79
Golden, William G. 22:166

Golder, Archibald L. 22:78
Golder, Joseph 15:35
Goldestine, C. 13:110
Goldey, John 19:71
Golding, Alexander 7:123
Golding, C. 15:298
Golding, Charles 16:193
Golding, Charles H. 21:110
Golding, George 9:35
Golding, I. H. 14:171
Golding, John 10:172; 19:166
Golding, John H. 22:424
Golding, S. 23:145
Golding, Thomas M. 19:166
Golding, William B. 22:424
Goldman, David 18:217; 22:78
Goldner, Henry 23:190
Goldsberry, George 20:258
Goldsberry, Henry 9:81
Goldsberry, Stephen 20:258
Goldsbore, Charles 16:193
Goldsburg, James 11:61
Goldsbury, Charles 20:104
Goldsbury, P. 26:29
Goldschalk, William 15:341
Goldschmidt, Leopold 12:22
Goldsley, W. 18:276
Goldsmith, Charles W. 21:115
Goldsmith, G. 12:153
Goldsmith, Gustavus 18:334
Goldsmith, Jeremiah 12:53
Goldsmith, Julius 4:27
Goldsmith, Peter 18:14
Goldsmith, R. 25:176
Goldsmith, Richard 5:16
Goldsmith, S. 14:64
Goldsmith, W. H. 21:110
Goldsmith, W. H. H. 22:479
Goldsmith, W. R. 15:86
Goldsmith, William 3:80
Goldsmith, William R. 12:70
Goldstock, John 21:216
Goldstone, Joseph 7:123
Goldswood, C. 25:272

Goldwaith, Frank 7:28
Goldwin, Isaac 18:29
Goleanor, P. A. F. 23:305
Goles, Richard 17:448; 24:172
Golhher, W. A. 17:79
Golias, J. 1:132
Goliner, Charles 9:177
Goll, Jacob 23:190
Golladay, Russell 22:300
Golladay, Thomas T. 22:424
Gollady, C. 17:495
Gollaher, J. W. 23:259
Gollard, William 4:27
Golleda, M. P. 8:48
Gollerno, George 8:17
Golley, Louis 7:14
Gollier, Frank H. 12:70
Gollier, Philip 11:30
Gollong, Philip 10:34
Golt, Charles 20:258
Golterman, L. 3:80
Goltschalk, William 16:369
Gomer, Henry 12:153
Gomeray, George Y. 16:193
Gomery, A. 25:176
Gomery, Aaron 5:16
Gomes, F. 9:66
Gomez, Manuel 4:27; 27:51
Gomley, James 4:27
Gonan, Martin G. 16:34
Gonard, --- 15:199
Gonchriour, Daniel 22:193
Gond, G. B. 13:89
Gond, Johnson 11:423
Gonder, Michael R. 17:79
Gondon, T. 25:176
Gondoux, William J. 10:8
Gondy, James H. 22:193
Goned, I. 14:171
Goned, J. 14:256
Gonell, Solan 16:34
Gonger, James H. 11:303
Gongin, A. A. 12:95
Gonie, Louis 10:54
Gonier, D. 3:80
Gonir, Henry 13:64
Gonnigal, John 13:110
Gonnon, George W. 11:276
Gons, A. 16:193
Gonsalis, David 10:54; 20:258
Gonsery, Calvin 9:131
Gontly, Henry 26:30
Gonzales, Abner 21:336

Gonzalez, A. 25:176
Gonzaliby, William 1:35
Gonzel, M. 8:72
Gonzelez, Antonio 5:16
Gonzer, William H. 17:34
Goo---, H. 15:258
Gooch, A. 25:176
Gooch, A. B. 9:177; 19:227
Gooch, James 8:85; 13:89
Gooch, Peter 22:512
Gooch, Singleton 21:86
Goochman, Austin 9:12
Good, --- 20:146
Good, A. H. 16:34
Good, A. L. 10:54
Good, C. 15:67
Good, C. Y. 11:331
Good, Daniel K. 22:194
Good, David P. 25:36
Good, Edward 17:34
Good, F. 1:132
Good, Francis M. 4:27
Good, G. W. 23:145
Good, George 21:225
Good, Hartsell 22:251
Good, Havamiah 7:71
Good, Henry 9:200; 24:39
Good, Henry J. 22:78
Good, Isaac 27:50
Good, J. A. 22:251
Good, J. Milton 23:259
Good, Jacob 11:406
Good, James 22:194
Good, John 13:110
Good, L. J. 18:189
Good, Martin 18:103
Good, Robert 15:7
Good, Ross 27:50
Good, Samuel 22:78
Good, Samuel S. 22:424
Good, Shadrach 12:49
Good, Simon 21:336
Good, Washington 21:148
Good, William E. 22:425
Good, William R. 12:153
Good Dollar Young Bird 25:333
Goodacre, Robert 10:54
Goodaen, Robert 20:258
Goodale, George A. 27:47
Goodale, H. H. 23:31
Goodale, J. 27:48
Goodale, James 23:16
Goodale, L. P. 11:84
Goodale, Wesley C. 19:166
Goodale, Whittle 18:276
Goodall, Amos 21:336
Goodall, Asoph 15:35
Goodall, C. A. 13:24

Goodall, Charles H. 17:287
Goodall, David J. 17:393
Goodall, Davis 20:258
Goodall, Dexter S. 22:32
Goodall, E. 8:48
Goodall, Edward 21:137
Goodall, George 12:23
Goodall, George E. R. 19:329
Goodall, Isaac 25:35
Goodall, J. 13:89
Goodall, John 17:65
Goodard, James A. 5:16
Goodbarn, A. 15:55
Goodbarn, John H. 23:145
Goodbehere, J. S. 7:28
Goodbo, Jacko 17:34
Goodbraid, J. F. 3:80
Goodbrake, Isaac 20:142
Goodbrath, C. 3:81
Goodby, Oscar 12:70
Goodchild, H. 9:12
Goode, A. J. 20:258
Goode, J. 22:251
Goode, John E. 17:52
Goode, Thomas M. 22:32
Goodel, M. 3:81
Goodell, Andrew J. 22:425
Goodell, Austin 15:199
Goodell, Calvin 24:19
Goodell, D. E. 27:52
Goodell, Davis 10:115
Goodell, Francis 9:204
Goodell, J. 9:143
Goodell, John C. 19:15
Goodell, L. 1:132
Goodell, Lyman 21:88
Goodell, Omar R. 27:52
Goodell, P. A. 5:17; 25:176
Gooden, J. C. B. 14:64
Gooden, N. 17:95
Gooden, W. H. 11:412
Goodenburger, J. 1:131
Goodeno, Martin 18:293; 26:99
Goodenough, Abraham 9:81
Goodenough, D. 20:56
Goodenough, E. 1:37; 20:189
Goodenough, G. M. 3:80
Goodenough, J. 10:192
Goodenough, James 3:80
Goodenough, T. W. 1:36
Goodenough, William 14:171
Goodenow, Corinthius 23:31

Goodern, John W. 18:136
Goodfame, Alfred 12:70
Goodfellow, C. 13:89
Goodfellow, E. C. 3:81
Goodfellow, H. 14:171
Goodfellow, J. 1:35
Goodfellow, Robert
  23:121
Goodfellow, Wallace 4:27
Goodfrey, M. M. 7:74
Goodfrey, P. E. 8:72
Goodhardt, Samuel 26:31
Goodhastier, Richard
  11:381
Goodheart, B. 14:171
Goodheart, John 20:94
Goodheart, John F. 12:23
Goodheart, Philip 19:15
Goodhen, D. H. 14:171
Goodhen, W. H. 14:64
Goodhour, Joseph 8:17;
  18:136
Goodhue, --- 12:85;
  16:293
Goodhue, A. 1:133
Goodhue, E. P. 25:38
Goodhue, J. 21:336
Goodhue, Volony 17:236
Goodier, Lyman J. 19:245
Goodier, W. 25:176
Goodin, Frank 4:27
Goodin, Jeremiah 22:122
Goodin, Merida 23:266
Goodin, N. 3:80
Goodin, Olly 11:149
Goodin, William W.
  23:88
Goodine, Alexander 14:64
Gooding, A. D. 25:176
Gooding, G. D. 23:145
Gooding, Hale P. 11:401
Gooding, James 3:80
Gooding, Joshua 20:56
Gooding, P. 25:176
Gooding, Thomas 16:34
Gooding, William 17:248
Goodinow, Charles E.
  7:28
Goodison, E. H. 14:171
Goodle, John 22:143
Goodloe, Vivian 15:55
Goodlow, Edwin 22:300
Goodlow, G. 16:267
Goodman, --- 16:95
Goodman, A. 15:199
Goodman, A. H. 18:217
Goodman, Adam 22:234
Goodman, Albert 1:35;
  10:115
Goodman, Anderson
  22:501

Goodman, Andrew 12:22,
  57
Goodman, Anselm 17:259
Goodman, D. 16:193
Goodman, E. 11:303
Goodman, F. 3:80
Goodman, Francis 22:300
Goodman, Francis M.
  17:318
Goodman, George R.
  22:78
Goodman, H. Z. 3:80
Goodman, Henry 27:47
Goodman, Horace 22:335
Goodman, Isaac 23:285
Goodman, J. A. 3:80
Goodman, J. H. 10:54
Goodman, J. W. 9:177;
  19:253
Goodman, Jacob 11:395
Goodman, James 8:121;
  11:319; 25:285
Goodman, Jefferson 10:95
Goodman, John 3:80;
  9:162; 10:115; 17:79;
  18:49; 20:258; 27:53
Goodman, John D. 8:105;
  20:186
Goodman, K. 25:176
Goodman, Kaler 5:39
Goodman, L. H. 13:135;
  19:346
Goodman, M. O. 8:101
Goodman, Mabery 15:55
Goodman, Mathew 22:252
Goodman, Mayes O.
  17:460; 24:158
Goodman, Ole 10:115;
  20:258
Goodman, Otis S. 22:480
Goodman, Peter 16:34
Goodman, R. W. 19:15
Goodman, Richard 22:451
Goodman, Robert 3:80;
  10:205
Goodman, Robert D.
  11:240
Goodman, S. 3:80
Goodman, Sanford 18:330
Goodman, Sylvester
  15:199
Goodman, T. 1:132
Goodman, Thomas 10:37;
  20:258
Goodman, Virgil 21:271
Goodman, W. 3:80; 15:7
Goodman, William
  11:255; 17:52
Goodmate, Sanford 8:117
Goodnal, G. C. 14:64
Goodnell, George 11:181

Goodnell, Jeremiah
  11:147
Goodner, John 20:8
Goodner, Reuben 22:300
Goodner, Thomas 20:153
Goodnight, J. 11:62
Goodno, F. 1:98
Goodnon, J. 3:80
Goodnough, A. B. 26:29
Goodnough, Harwood
  19:15
Goodnough, I. 18:174
Goodnough, J. 15:35
Goodnough, William
  7:28; 10:161
Goodnow, Austin 13:24
Goodnow, Elisha P. 2:11
Goodnow, Irad H. 25:176
Goodnow, Martin 9:35
Goodnow, Oliver S.
  14:336
Goodnow, R. H. 5:16
Goodnow, T. H. 1:133
Goodon, William S. 7:28
Goodpastur, Noah 22:451
Goodpasture, Emanuel
  22:513
Goodpasture, W. C.
  11:303
Goodpasture, William H.
  23:88
Goodpick, G. I. 3:80
Goodplaster, Col. 11:203
Goodreath, Joseph 26:211
Goodrel, George C.
  23:145
Goodremont, Sanford
  8:85
Goodrich, --- 9:177
Goodrich, A. 1:37;
  19:166; 21:336
Goodrich, A. V. 11:92
Goodrich, Alex. B. 8:105
Goodrich, Alfred 23:16
Goodrich, Allen 12:70;
  15:35
Goodrich, Allen N.
  11:148
Goodrich, Allen W. 19:15
Goodrich, Arthur K.
  11:303
Goodrich, Asa L. 26:236
Goodrich, B. 14:313
Goodrich, Ben 17:110
Goodrich, C. O. 16:193
Goodrich, Ceaser 21:336
Goodrich, Charles 11:261
Goodrich, Charles H.
  13:24
Goodrich, Charles O.
  13:110

Goodrich, David 1:35
Goodrich, David A. 1:35
Goodrich, E. 7:57
Goodrich, Eleazer 22:194
Goodrich, F. 3:80
Goodrich, F. F. 20:123
Goodrich, Frank T. 17:154
Goodrich, Frederick M. 16:369
Goodrich, George 3:80; 15:199
Goodrich, Gustavus 18:346
Goodrich, H. 1:35; 12:87; 16:293
Goodrich, H. C. 11:401
Goodrich, Harvey 22:194
Goodrich, Henry S. 10:115; 20:258
Goodrich, Henry W. 21:137
Goodrich, Ira 27:53
Goodrich, Isaac A. 22:143
Goodrich, J. 1:37, 132
Goodrich, J. F. 24:111
Goodrich, J. S. 3:80
Goodrich, J. W. 3:80
Goodrich, James 5:17; 14:298; 17:481; 25:176; 27:52
Goodrich, Jarred 17:154
Goodrich, Joseph W. 16:369
Goodrich, L. H. 25:297
Goodrich, L. L. 15:199
Goodrich, Louis 23:66
Goodrich, Minister 21:336
Goodrich, R. 20:133
Goodrich, Richard 17:146
Goodrich, Robin 17:451
Goodrich, Rollin 24:177
Goodrich, S. 9:143; 27:48
Goodrich, S. E. 20:259
Goodrich, T. 7:50
Goodrich, Thomas 12:122; 15:123
Goodrich, W. 14:64
Goodrich, William 16:279
Goodrich, William C. 22:32
Goodrick, Albert B. 4:27
Goodrick, Christopher 10:54
Goodrick, Henry J. 11:30
Goodrick, James J. 20:112
Goodrick, S. E. 10:54
Goodrick, T. A. 4:27
Goodricks, Christopher 20:259
Goodridge, E. 1:36; 3:80

Goodridge, Henry E. 19:265
Goodridge, Heny E. 9:177
Goodridge, J. 11:381
Goodroad, A. 3:80
Goodroe, Francis 21:99
Goods, Peter 4:27
Goodsbery, Henry 22:300
Goodsell, Andrew G. 19:15
Goodsell, Daniel 21:91
Goodsell, Edward W. 15:55
Goodsell, Olive 19:325
Goodsey, William 20:88
Goodshall, William 10:161
Goodshaw, Joseph 17:454; 24:185
Goodsill, Francis W. 10:115; 20:259
Goodson, J. 9:52
Goodson, Joseph 10:54; 20:259
Goodson, O. D. 10:54; 20:259
Goodson, William N. 21:99
Goodson, William W. 22:112
Goodspeed, Benjamin 15:151
Goodspeed, Dyer H. 18:110
Goodspeed, Forest 1:35
Goodspeed, George W. 11:106
Goodspeed, J. 1:37
Goodspeed, James 10:172; 19:166
Goodspeed, James H. 16:133
Goodstall, William 19:166
Goodue, J. 9:214
Goodur, Lyman J. 9:177
Goodwill, Aaron B. 17:91
Goodwill, Ephraim 22:78
Goodwill, William 1:36
Goodwin, A. 3:80
Goodwin, Albert 13:110; 20:259
Goodwin, Alex 9:131
Goodwin, Almond 22:194
Goodwin, Alonzo 1:36
Goodwin, Amos 11:105
Goodwin, Arthur 15:11
Goodwin, B. 22:335
Goodwin, Benjamin F. 12:23
Goodwin, C. 1:135
Goodwin, C. D. 9:22

Goodwin, C. H. 9:143; 27:49
Goodwin, C. R. 11:303
Goodwin, Charles 1:35
Goodwin, D. 14:64; 15:293, 298; 16:193
Goodwin, David 22:501
Goodwin, Dexter 12:8
Goodwin, E. 1:36, 134
Goodwin, E. J. 14:315
Goodwin, Elijah 9:72; 22:122
Goodwin, Elisha 22:404
Goodwin, Flander 27:51
Goodwin, Foss G. 13:24
Goodwin, Frank 10:17
Goodwin, G. H. 7:95
Goodwin, G. S. 1:36
Goodwin, G. W. 8:48; 13:24
Goodwin, George 3:80; 9:143, 177; 19:227; 27:48
Goodwin, H. 21:13
Goodwin, H. E. 23:104
Goodwin, H. H. 1:37
Goodwin, Henry 4:27
Goodwin, Horace J. 21:69
Goodwin, Isaac 1:35; 16:293
Goodwin, J. 3:80; 5:51; 7:74; 15:335; 19:71; 25:176; 27:53
Goodwin, J. D. 18:306; 26:98
Goodwin, J. G. 25:176
Goodwin, J. R. 1:134
Goodwin, J. W. 17:70; 27:49
Goodwin, James 23:190
Goodwin, Jesse 8:48
Goodwin, John 14:64; 20:89; 22:194
Goodwin, John J. 21:27
Goodwin, John L. 27:52
Goodwin, John R. 25:176
Goodwin, John W. 8:17; 9:143
Goodwin, Joseph D. 10:161
Goodwin, Joseph L. 5:16
Goodwin, Josiah M. 10:153; 19:166
Goodwin, Levi 19:15
Goodwin, M. 25:272
Goodwin, M. T. 3:80
Goodwin, Noah 17:71
Goodwin, O. G. 23:203
Goodwin, Robert 26:162
Goodwin, S. 1:132; 12:80; 25:176, 272

Goodwin, Samuel 13:24
Goodwin, Samuel G.
  16:34
Goodwin, Silas 9:177;
  19:270; 22:32
Goodwin, Solomon 9:35
Goodwin, Thomas 9:177;
  11:191; 21:336;
  22:194
Goodwin, Thomas M.
  26:30
Goodwin, W. 5:17;
  14:171; 25:176
Goodwin, W. J. 20:27
Goodwin, W. P. 21:187
Goodwin, W. W. 11:61
Goodwin, Willard F.
  23:285
Goodwin, William 3:80;
  12:70; 18:29; 22:32
Goodwin, William W.
  17:273
Goodwine, Thomas J.
  23:66
Goodwith, A. B. 8:48
Goodwll, John H. 25:176
Goodwoods, G. 16:193
Goody, Charles 15:67
Goody, George A. 16:193
Goodyear, F. 3:81
Goodyear, Horace 13:110
Goodyear, Joseph 13:24
Goodyear, Joseph T.
  22:32
Goodyear, L. L. 21:336
Goodyear, Thomas 10:54;
  20:259
Goodyear, W. H. 12:22
Googe, George 22:300
Google, M. G. 15:341;
  16:369
Goohts, Austin 20:259
Gookins, James 22:404
Gool, A. 11:191
Goolah, Charles 4:27
Goold, Emerson 9:177
Goold, Henry 18:293;
  26:99
Goold, Wilson 1:35
Goolden, Thomas 19:71
Gooles, H. F. 3:80
Gooley, J. 3:80
Goolman, Jacob H.
  25:275
Goolsby, Henry 18:276
Goolsby, Thomas 22:252
Goon, John E. 3:81
Goon, Noah 15:199
Goon, Thomas 14:171
Goon, William 17:411
Goor, Frank 18:136

Gooram, Sam 6:28
Goosberry, William 18:83
Goosby, Charles 21:271
Goosey, Charles 11:203
Gooshar, W. T. 9:110
Goosuch, M. A. 3:80
Goot, J. P. 10:91
Gootman, Amos 7:122
Goots, James 22:335
Goots, William 25:37
Goove, Cyrus G. 9:119
Goove, Erasmus 9:119
Goovenst, John 9:81
Gooze, Hugh 19:71
Gopp, Herman 8:105
Gor, Jake A. 10:176
Gora, J. 14:64
Gora, Samuel 25:36
Goram, Henry 25:176
Goran, Manuel 8:39
Goratze, P. 16:293
Gorb, Henry 17:20
Gorb, S. 3:81
Gorbey, F. L. 3:81
Gorbey, S. 1:132
Gorbit, Francis A. 22:32
Gorby, H. 23:145
Gorby, Pierce 22:194
Gorcke, Henry 3:81
Gordan, Daniel 20:259
Gordan, G. 14:64
Gordan, I. W. 21:121
Gordan, J. A. 16:267
Gordan, J. Q. 1:37
Gordan, Jonathan H.
  16:34
Gorden, C. 11:105
Gorden, Eli 17:175
Gorden, Haffe 27:53
Gorden, John M. 17:20
Gorden, P. 17:176
Gorden, Robert 17:34
Gorden, W. A. 9:240
Gorden, W. W. 16:369
Gorden, William 17:273
Gorden, Zacheus 22:425
Gorder, Julius 21:254
Gordes, William 5:17
Gordey, Henry 4:66
Gordfield, J. 27:51
Gordflhy, Eleazer 13:24
Gordin, James B. 11:30
Gordiner, J. 14:64
Gordinier, Asa 22:143
Gordlon, G. 14:11
Gordon, --- 9:200; 10:161;
  12:170; 15:200;
  25:35, 38
Gordon, A. B. 3:81
Gordon, A. F. 7:28

Gordon, A. L. 9:220;
  18:367
Gordon, Aaron 11:203
Gordon, Alexander 12:70
Gordon, Anderson 7:10
Gordon, Andrew 22:194
Gordon, Anthony 22:32
Gordon, Augustus 18:30
Gordon, Benjamin 7:123;
  17:14
Gordon, Blueford 18:136
Gordon, Bluford 8:17
Gordon, C. H. 7:95
Gordon, C. M. 18:29
Gordon, C. W. 9:22
Gordon, Charles 3:81;
  21:211, 336; 25:177
Gordon, Charles M. 20:56
Gordon, D. B. 18:367
Gordon, Daniel 1:192;
  10:54; 13:24
Gordon, David 17:313
Gordon, E. 18:237; 26:30
Gordon, E. W. 21:336;
  23:145
Gordon, Edward 18:450
Gordon, Edward S. 17:20
Gordon, Edwin 8:101;
  17:463; 24:185
Gordon, Elijah 23:31
Gordon, Erastus 17:248
Gordon, Ezra 6:11
Gordon, F. D. 23:290
Gordon, Felix 22:300
Gordon, Francis S. 19:329
Gordon, Frederick 22:11
Gordon, G. 13:110
Gordon, G. S. 1:103
Gordon, G. W. 16:193
Gordon, George 17:34
Gordon, George L. 18:306
Gordon, George R. 19:287
Gordon, George S. 9:22;
  26:99
Gordon, George W. 2:11
Gordon, Henry 8:39;
  18:306; 22:122;
  26:99, 161
Gordon, Henry T. 23:113
Gordon, Heustis A. 23:88
Gordon, J. 3:81; 14:11, 65
Gordon, J. B. 1:134
Gordon, J. C. 22:194
Gordon, J. D. 16:119;
  25:177
Gordon, J. H. 7:95
Gordon, J. M. 13:77, 89;
  21:336
Gordon, J. W. 3:81; 19:71
Gordon, Jackson 11:387
Gordon, Jacob C. 21:199

Gordon, James 2:11; 3:81; 4:66; 7:95; 17:440; 18:237; 24:19, 158; 26:31
Gordon, James B. 13:24
Gordon, Jasper 1:36
Gordon, Jerry 24:194
Gordon, John 3:81; 8:85; 10:115; 20:123, 259; 22:79, 143
Gordon, John A. 27:53
Gordon, John C. 12:23
Gordon, John S. 13:24
Gordon, Jonathan 11:61
Gordon, Joseph 7:95; 13:110; 22:32
Gordon, Mark 7:123; 9:114; 14:329
Gordon, Martin 21:336; 22:335
Gordon, Munday 13:57
Gordon, N. 18:29; 23:31
Gordon, Nathaniel 11:204
Gordon, P. L. 21:336
Gordon, Patrick 18:217
Gordon, R. 3:81; 25:35
Gordon, R. A. 11:62
Gordon, R. W. 18:426
Gordon, Reynolds 22:194
Gordon, Richard 2:11
Gordon, Robert F. 22:143
Gordon, S. 3:81; 9:200
Gordon, S. L. 14:256
Gordon, Samuel 15:35
Gordon, Samuel G. 9:119
Gordon, Samuel I. 27:51
Gordon, Scott 13:24
Gordon, Silas H. 15:304
Gordon, Simon 21:336
Gordon, T. 1:133
Gordon, T. H. 11:62
Gordon, Thomas 21:225
Gordon, Toliff O. 21:254
Gordon, W. 3:81; 16:119
Gordon, W. C. 3:81
Gordon, W. D. 25:177
Gordon, W. H. 7:50; 9:52
Gordon, W. L. 3:81
Gordon, W. N. 3:81
Gordon, Walter D. 21:69
Gordon, Wanton H. 11:126
Gordon, William 3:81; 9:42; 14:65; 16:34; 22:166, 300, 425
Gordon, William A. 23:190
Gordon, William H. 13:24
Gordon, William S. 14:336; 24:19
Gordon, Young 21:271

Gordow, G. 13:103
Gordwine, D. 14:65
Gordy, George W. 20:97
Gore, Benjamin S. 26:28
Gore, Christopher W. 23:88
Gore, Cyrus 27:51
Gore, F. 3:81
Gore, Frank 10:176; 19:166
Gore, J. 27:48
Gore, James 9:177; 18:420
Gore, John 9:143; 14:65
Gore, Joshua R. 9:12
Gore, Melville H. 25:177
Gore, N. 3:81
Gore, Owen P. 20:259
Gore, Robert 10:205
Gore, William H. 22:122
Goreen, J. H. 3:81
Gorelon, William 26:123
Gorem, David 14:171
Gorer, Thomas 10:176
Goreton, --- 2:11
Gorett, J. 3:81
Gorey, John 22:451
Gorfrey, T. M. 14:65
Gorgan, Thomas 21:27
Gorgen, Louis 9:12
Gorgis, H. 14:171
Gorgo, Charles A. 4:66
Gorgus, Harrison 27:144
Gorham, Alonzo 21:27
Gorham, C. 23:31
Gorham, Danford 22:32
Gorham, Emanuel 11:186
Gorham, H. C. 22:279
Gorham, Harris 23:107
Gorham, Leveret 10:115; 20:259
Gorham, W. 15:298
Gorham, Wallace 16:193
Gorham, Willard 14:171
Gorhamer, Ole H. 10:115; 20:259
Gorin, Daniel 23:31
Gorinan, H. 27:53
Gorkey, Eugene 26:29
Gorkey, Nelson 26:28
Gorlin, Henry H. 25:36
Gorman, A. 25:320
Gorman, Aaron H. 22:508
Gorman, Andrew J. 21:86
Gorman, Charles 16:95
Gorman, Conrad 11:119
Gorman, D. 1:133, 134; 14:321
Gorman, Daniel 14:315
Gorman, Daniel F. 23:66
Gorman, E. 17:34

Gorman, Edward 11:231
Gorman, F. 3:81
Gorman, G. 1:37; 3:81
Gorman, George 11:147
Gorman, J. 1:133; 25:37
Gorman, J. A. 1:134
Gorman, James 3:81; 7:28; 11:181; 13:24; 15:307; 19:71
Gorman, John 1:35; 22:32
Gorman, John F. 20:22
Gorman, Joseph 2:11; 9:131; 27:51
Gorman, Lewis 9:200
Gorman, M. 1:133
Gorman, Maurice 19:338
Gorman, Patrick 13:24; 16:369; 19:166; 22:335
Gorman, Peter 18:14
Gorman, S. 5:39
Gorman, Thomas 17:34; 21:336; 25:36
Gorman, W. H. 22:479; 27:49
Gorman, William 3:81
Gormby, Patrick 8:17
Gormer, George 11:240
Gormilas, James 21:27
Gormley, --- 18:237; 26:31
Gormley, James 14:171
Gormley, Robert 12:23
Gormley, Thomas 7:28
Gormly, C. 22:519
Gorn, Huston 8:85
Gornell, Israel G. 8:17
Gornell, John G. 18:136
Gornto, Owen 20:259
Goro, William 18:367
Gorr, Frank 8:17
Gorrall, John W. 21:69
Gorrell, H. T. 10:115; 20:259
Gorrick, T. 1:36
Gorriman, J. 21:336
Gorrin, Kinney 9:70
Gorringer, Isaac 18:276
Gorse, Henry 12:23
Gorsie, David 25:177
Gorslin, J. J. 14:65
Gorsman, G. 24:19
Gorstine, James M. 25:37
Gorsuch, Mordecai M. 23:145
Gorsup, M. M. 14:277
Gorthans, W. W. 18:426
Gortley, Thomas 8:85
Gorton, Aaron 25:37
Gorton, B. E. 1:133
Gorton, C. S. 14:171

Gorton, Charles 15:200
Gorton, J. P. 17:154
Gorton, John 25:177
Gorton, W. I. 25:311
Gorty, William 26:99
Gorum, John 24:194
Gorvand, Florand 24:50
Gorvearet, I. 26:29
Gosage, Joel 22:79
Gosart, Henry 9:81
Gosby, J. 22:301
Gosch, Ezra 11:61
Goscie, Michael 7:50
Goselhurt, Henry 18:30
Gosey, Logan 22:301
Gosha, Nicholas 16:139
Gosham, Lewis 22:194
Goshan, J. 14:171
Goshart, W. R. 1:134
Goshen, Henry 23:31
Goshrow, C. 1:134
Gosley, Elbert 18:83
Gosley, Elbut 6:16
Gosley, William 9:35
Goslin, A. 12:80; 25:177
Goslin, Aurelius 9:35
Goslin, E. H. 3:81
Goslin, John L. 21:69
Goslin, R. M. 1:35
Gosmer, --- 16:267
Gosmore, John 14:11
Gosnef, Jesse 9:81
Gosnel, James 8:48
Gosnell, A. 19:301
Gosnell, Augustus 18:217
Gosnell, D. 24:19
Gosnell, Jessee 26:29
Gosnell, Joshua 13:24
Gosnell, Moses A. 12:70; 15:13
Gosnell, Price 12:23
Gosnell, Samuel D. 21:69
Gosnell, Wilson L. 23:31
Goss, Andrew 9:66
Goss, Bernard 14:171
Goss, Charles 13:64; 16:194
Goss, Daniel 22:166
Goss, David L. 20:259
Goss, Ellis 10:172
Goss, Frederick 10:115; 20:259
Goss, G. 19:227
Goss, G. W. 21:336
Goss, George 9:177; 17:91
Goss, George G. 20:123
Goss, George W. 22:194
Goss, Henry 12:161
Goss, J. 26:219
Goss, James 3:81; 4:66

Goss, John 22:397
Goss, Prince A. 21:271
Goss, William 25:177
Gossage, William 22:79
Gosset, John 23:145, 184
Gossett, James 22:252
Gossett, Joseph B. 24:39
Gossett, Stephen 1:37
Gossit, J. 14:256
Gossit, Peter 17:110
Gossman, William 13:24
Gossner, Benjamin F. 21:115
Gossom, Isaac 10:95
Gosson, M. 1:133
Goswick, Bird 23:243
Got, C. 1:131
Gotchell, B. E. 21:336
Goth, John 23:31
Goth, William 7:28; 21:211, 271
Gotham, F. H. 19:71
Gothan, W. 13:89; 14:11
Gothard, J. 3:81
Gothard, T. 1:134
Gothe, F. 21:27
Gothen, Charles 11:387
Gothenburg, George 15:106
Gothridge, David 23:107
Gotischal, Charles 9:236
Gotschel, --- 18:412
Gotsh, Green 11:61
Gotshalf, John 26:99
Gotshel, Wilson S. 22:32
Gotswald, Jacob H. 27:48
Gott, Albert H. 21:69
Gott, C. 3:81
Gott, C. H. 18:217
Gott, G. 3:81
Gott, H. 3:81; 14:171
Gott, John W. 11:92
Gott, William 10:115; 20:259
Gotta, Solomon D. 22:497
Gottbright, August 23:88
Gottchall, William 11:322
Gotte, Alexander 7:123
Gotte, Jacob 16:34
Gottinger, George 23:11
Gotton, R. 3:81
Gottry, Aaron A. 18:276
Gottschalk, John 18:306
Gottshall, J. G. 14:171
Gotty, A. S. 16:268
Gotwalt, H. 3:81
Gotz, John 20:259
Goubert, Zeb 18:67
Gouch, A. 8:48
Gouch, Edward 7:123
Gouchy, M. 3:81

Goud, G. B. 14:11
Gouderman, John H. 22:79
Goudy, --- 21:336
Goudy, C. W. C. 1:131
Goudy, Elijah 18:217
Goudy, George 23:66
Goudy, J. W. 20:146
Goudy, John 3:81
Gouge, George 1:36
Gouge, James K. 10:95
Gough, --- 27:157
Gough, H. 3:81
Gough, Hiram 11:303
Gough, J. 12:8
Gough, Jacob 21:52
Gough, James 18:110; 25:177
Gough, Jefferson 6:12
Gough, John 11:286; 16:194; 22:523
Gough, Lemuel 22:424
Gough, Peter 9:110
Gough, S. B. 13:24
Gough, Thomas 16:194
Goughery, John 12:23
Goughnour, D. N. 14:65
Goughtry, W. 20:123
Gougins, A. A. 15:359; 19:72
Goul, M. E. 3:81
Gould, A. C. 19:166
Gould, A. S. 27:47
Gould, Adam 15:307
Gould, Andrew 15:124
Gould, Anthony 21:336
Gould, Austin W. 17:319
Gould, Benjamin A. 11:84
Gould, C. 12:8
Gould, C. E. 14:65
Gould, C. L. 13:64; 19:72
Gould, Charles 11:30; 18:237; 26:30
Gould, Charles H. 4:27
Gould, Christop'r. 22:425
Gould, Cornelius 21:336
Gould, D. C. 25:36
Gould, D. H. 14:171
Gould, Daniel E. 10:115; 20:259
Gould, Densiel M. 23:121
Gould, Doctor 14:171
Gould, E. 3:81
Gould, E. A. 7:28
Gould, E. B. 1:132
Gould, Emerson 19:237
Gould, Ephraim 7:50
Gould, Frank A. 16:85
Gould, Frederick 13:24
Gould, G. H. 19:227
Gould, G. W. 14:65

Gould, George 11:30; 13:124
Gould, George H. 22:32
Gould, H. A. 12:122
Gould, Harrison A. 15:124
Gould, Henry 15:86; 16:194
Gould, Hiram S. 17:263
Gould, Isaac B. 21:336
Gould, Isaac H. 19:166
Gould, J. 1:35; 14:65
Gould, J. M. 3:81
Gould, J. O. 19:237
Gould, J. R. 15:200
Gould, J. W. 25:177
Gould, Jacob 9:212
Gould, Jacob O. 9:178
Gould, James 1:191
Gould, James H. 1:35
Gould, Jeremiah 25:177
Gould, John 4:27, 66; 5:17; 27:47
Gould, John H. 17:263; 19:227
Gould, John M. 5:17
Gould, Joseph 9:17; 11:286
Gould, Joshua 13:24; 16:34
Gould, L. 7:28
Gould, L. W. 25:297
Gould, Leander M. 10:161
Gould, Lemuel 14:315
Gould, Lorrentio E. 7:80
Gould, Luther H. 13:24
Gould, M. P. 17:65
Gould, Madison W. 22:32
Gould, Manson 19:166
Gould, Monson 10:161
Gould, Myron 9:178
Gould, N. 1:135
Gould, Nathan C. 23:190
Gould, Natt 21:336
Gould, O. A. 7:28
Gould, Oliver 21:239
Gould, Oliver A. 22:143
Gould, Oscar 19:72
Gould, P. H. 20:91
Gould, Peter 23:198
Gould, R. D. 1:135
Gould, Richard 3:81; 24:78
Gould, Samuel 11:115
Gould, Schyler D. 8:85
Gould, Smith 22:462
Gould, Stephen B. 21:52
Gould, Sylvanus 17:287
Gould, Sylvester J. 21:254
Gould, T. C. 25:297
Gould, T. W. 25:35

Gould, Theodore 8:126
Gould, Thomas B. 22:279
Gould, W. 1:98; 11:240; 24:78
Gould, W. C. 19:253
Gould, W. H. 19:72; 25:177
Gould, Wentworth H. 21:337
Gould, Wheeler 21:52
Gould, William 3:81; 7:95, 123; 15:305; 16:293; 19:72; 20:40; 21:225
Gould, William C. 9:177
Gould, William H. 12:23
Goulden, James 4:27
Goulden, Owen 19:15
Goulden, Patrick 15:200
Gouldie, Harrie 14:172
Gouldin, Charles 12:23
Gouldin, Seneca 23:98
Goulding, John 4:27
Goulding, W. R. 1:134
Goull, G. 16:194
Goulson, John W. 17:443
Goulty, Henry 18:237
Gound, Henry 9:35
Goundy, Thomas 3:81
Gouns, George 7:57
Gount, J. M. 3:81
Goupp, Augustus 13:24
Gourd, Samuel 23:179
Gourley, J. B. 9:143
Gourley, Samuel 1:36
Gousey, Charles 15:326
Gousley, J. B. 27:49
Gouton, William 13:24
Gov, Jake A. 19:166
Gova, Augustus 19:281
Govan, Emanuel 26:161
Govan, N. P. 16:119
Govatzs, P. 12:82
Gove, Augustus 9:200
Gove, Benjamin S. 9:81
Gove, Charles 19:166
Gove, Charles H. 16:145
Gove, Gardiner 21:114
Gove, George 7:68
Gove, H. H. 19:72
Gove, H. N. 8:17; 18:136
Gove, H. S. 11:106
Gove, Ira S. 12:58
Gove, J. 3:81
Govellena, John 4:27
Gover, Thomas 19:166
Goves, Addison 11:115
Govsuch, Joshua 10:115
Govurn, Squires 15:5
Gow, James 16:143
Gow, John 27:51

Gow, Nelson 8:17
Gow, R. 13:89
Gow, Thomas H. 21:194
Gow, William 4:27; 17:190
Gowan, Alex 16:293
Gowan, Charles M. 9:178
Gowan, David 22:279
Gowan, James 10:17
Gowan, Martin G. 13:24
Gowar, David C. 21:69
Gowdey, Daniel 12:161
Gowdy, Fleming 22:404
Gowdy, H. M. 21:27
Gowell, F. E. 7:74
Gowell, Leroy A. 16:293
Gowell, N. 3:81; 14:172
Gowell, Solon 13:24
Gowely, Thomas 17:176
Gowen, J. 3:81
Gowens, John A. 22:79
Gower, Charles 7:95
Gower, Duncan 11:30
Gower, Erwan 9:204
Gower, J. 3:81
Gower, J. C. 3:81
Gower, Lyman 14:172
Gower, T. F. 9:72
Gowers, J. A. 1:133
Gowey, Andrew 14:172
Gowin, C. M. 19:227
Gowin, John 11:148
Gowin, Solomon J. 20:112
Gowing, Benjamin F. 21:69
Gowins, William 22:252
Gowland, J. 23:31
Gowles, Robert 19:72
Gowling, L. 18:189
Gowney, J. 25:177
Gowrin, Patrick A. 10:9
Goyer, J. B. 26:211
Goyle, Nathan 7:28
Goza, N. B. 24:107
Goze, H. 15:359
Gozier, Andrew 14:172
Gozney, Edward 16:194
Gr---, J. A. 19:72
Gra---, Patrick 23:252
Graback, H. 1:132
Grabaugh, J. 3:82
Grabb, George 7:28
Grabb, Samuel 9:35
Grabb, Thomas 12:153
Grabb, Ulrich 9:22
Grabber, Henry 1:35
Grabe, A. 24:107
Grabe, Randolph 10:7
Grabe, Theo 22:335
Graber, I. 3:82

Graber, J. J. 1:133
Graber, J. T. 3:82
Grabett, Carl 26:161
Grabiel, Augustus 16:34
Grabill, Daniel 7:95
Grable, Asbury 22:79
Grable, Daniel 11:115
Grable, Josiah 17:79
Grable, Riley M. 22:122
Grabon, George 25:177
Grabool, B. 3:82
Graboski, Charles 22:11
Grabot, Julian 7:95
Grace, Albert 17:52
Grace, B. 25:177
Grace, Benjamin 5:17
Grace, Charles 4:27
Grace, Daniel T. 17:280
Grace, Evan T. 21:254
Grace, Francis 23:145
Grace, Herman 9:110
Grace, J. R. 8:49
Grace, James 25:38
Grace, John 25:177; 26:31
Grace, John P. 18:49
Grace, John R. 21:69
Grace, Joseph 7:28
Grace, Joseph M. 22:352
Grace, Martin 14:172
Grace, Patrick K. 19:72
Grace, Samuel E. 13:25
Grace, Samuel S. 16:34
Grace, Thomas 3:82
Grace, W. 3:82
Gracey, David 12:23
Gracey, W. D. 8:17
Gracia, W. W. 16:293
Gracie, W. W. 12:92
Gracier, Godfrey 17:79
Gracy, Daniel 14:172
Graddess, Josiah 22:425
Graddy, John 14:172
Grade, G. 17:280
Graden, J. W. A. 14:263
Graden, James M. 22:234
Graden, John 14:263
Graden, T. 1:133
Gradner, George 22:287
Gradon, Wallace 23:31
Gradwain, Davis C. 15:173

Grady, Armstrong 11:203
Grady, B. 11:219
Grady, Ernest 22:301
Grady, George W. 17:206
Grady, J. W. 23:31
Grady, James 15:309; 21:27
Grady, John 16:85
Grady, John E. 10:54
Grady, Joseph 19:166

Grady, L. 15:158
Grady, M. 3:83; 15:341; 16:370
Grady, Martin 20:8
Grady, Thaddeus 22:301
Grady, W. S. 16:34
Grady, W. W. 25:177
Grady, William 2:11; 25:34
Graef, Charles 11:412
Graem, J. B. 25:177
Graf, George 21:337
Graf, John 15:35
Graf, Joseph 25:177
Graff, A. 1:36; 14:28
Graff, A. I. 3:82
Graff, Albert 4:27
Graff, Charles W. 20:35
Graff, Clement 12:23
Graff, F. 3:82; 23:145
Graff, Frederick 8:17; 18:136
Graff, G. 11:240
Graff, George 11:61; 14:172; 22:425
Graff, Henry 9:143; 13:124; 27:49
Graff, Herman S. 27:47
Graff, John 10:153; 27:51
Graff, John A. 9:119
Graff, Michael 22:194
Graff, P. 3:82
Graff, S. 11:119
Graff, Samuel 16:194; 22:234
Graff, William 10:115
Graffice, I. 14:172
Grafh, Frederick 18:334
Graft, William F. 21:121
Graftner, H. D. 22:301
Grafton, Allen 19:45
Grafton, D. 3:82
Grafton, Jacob 1:36
Grafton, James 26:29
Grafton, James W. 23:145
Grafton, Luke 17:248
Grafton, Samuel 21:337
Grager, H. 3:82
Gragg, E. 17:291
Gragg, William K. 22:479
Graglee, W. 19:72
Gragon, James M. 26:160
Gragor, John 15:323
Gragory, William 18:174
Graham, --- 20:259; 21:254
Graham, A. T. 13:124
Graham, Abram S. 22:32
Graham, Adam 4:27
Graham, Allen 19:72
Graham, Allison 20:97

Graham, Andrew 11:61; 22:301
Graham, Arthur 25:37
Graham, Ashfield 11:401
Graham, Bendi M. 18:338
Graham, Benedict 9:102
Graham, Benjamin F. 19:15
Graham, C. 24:39
Graham, C. S. 21:95
Graham, Calvin 11:203
Graham, Charles 8:49; 9:81; 13:25; 17:176
Graham, Christian 11:126
Graham, D. 3:81; 18:30
Graham, D. S. 18:30
Graham, David 11:262; 18:338
Graham, E. 3:81
Graham, E. H. 12:99; 15:366
Graham, E. L. 8:59; 19:279
Graham, E. W. 11:262
Graham, Edmond 22:194
Graham, Edward 10:17; 25:275
Graham, Elijah 17:349
Graham, Ezekiel 20:185
Graham, F. 1:98; 12:82; 16:293
Graham, F. L. 17:291
Graham, G. 1:135; 10:186; 18:174
Graham, George 10:54; 11:241, 423; 20:259
Graham, George H. 8:17
Graham, George J. 22:252
Graham, George W. 3:81
Graham, Gilbert 13:110
Graham, Gorton 20:107
Graham, H. 1:37; 9:110; 26:220
Graham, Harrison 19:72
Graham, Henry 10:161; 17:176; 18:412; 23:107
Graham, Horace 24:93
Graham, Hugh F. 10:115; 20:259
Graham, I. L. 18:174
Graham, Isaac 17:65, 163
Graham, J. 1:94, 132, 133; 3:82; 7:50; 13:89; 21:27; 22:194
Graham, J. B. 11:148
Graham, J. G. 22:279
Graham, J. H. 26:31
Graham, J. L. 10:186
Graham, J. P. 21:198
Graham, J. W. 3:81

Graham, Jackson 17:131; 24:194
Graham, Jacob 6:16; 18:83
Graham, James 5:17; 7:95; 11:106; 17:308; 21:148; 22:11, 32, 252; 25:177
Graham, James W. 22:194
Graham, Jesse 9:131; 24:194; 27:50
Graham, Jesse H. 20:102
Graham, Job. H. 19:15
Graham, John 4:27; 6:7; 10:115; 11:92, 262; 14:172; 15:67; 18:110; 20:113, 259; 21:137, 337; 23:31, 190; 27:47
Graham, John A. 27:52
Graham, John H. 9:81, 178; 19:277
Graham, John L. 11:88
Graham, Joseph 9:66; 12:92; 16:293; 18:276
Graham, Joseph H. 24:39
Graham, L. 1:36; 9:143; 21:163
Graham, L. P. 26:162
Graham, L. R. 8:72
Graham, M. 14:65
Graham, M. H. 20:259
Graham, M. J. 3:82
Graham, Marion B. 11:381
Graham, Martin V. 22:194
Graham, Melvin 9:159
Graham, Michael 20:174
Graham, Milford 8:85; 22:462
Graham, Morgan H. 10:54
Graham, Moses 9:72; 27:53
Graham, Nelson 7:95
Graham, Oliver 18:206
Graham, P. 11:147; 25:177
Graham, Patrick 24:19; 27:48
Graham, Peter 5:17
Graham, R. 25:37
Graham, R. B. 13:89
Graham, R. P. 14:11
Graham, Randolph 21:130
Graham, Robert 2:11; 7:95; 8:49; 18:237; 26:30
Graham, Robert J. 10:17
Graham, Robert M. 15:67

Graham, Robert S. 22:122
Graham, S. 1:36; 14:11
Graham, Samuel 18:237; 26:30
Graham, Samuel L. 21:337
Graham, Seven 17:52
Graham, Seymour 15:7
Graham, Siblock 18:276
Graham, Silas 26:219
Graham, Simmons 12:70
Graham, Simon L. 7:123
Graham, Stephen 23:301
Graham, T. L. 1:37
Graham, Thomas 19:15; 22:404
Graham, W. 1:133; 3:82; 12:92; 14:65; 16:293
Graham, W. B. 11:147
Graham, W. F. 1:133
Graham, W. H. 10:152; 18:49; 27:47
Graham, W. I. 3:81
Graham, W. P. 22:11
Graham, Willard 26:211
Graham, William 3:81; 8:49, 69; 9:119, 236; 10:115; 11:423; 14:172; 16:293; 20:259; 22:425; 24:19, 107; 26:219; 27:51
Graham, William B. 12:23
Graham, William C. 23:98
Graham, William D. 22:122
Graham, William F. 17:151
Graham, William G. 8:17; 18:136
Graham, William H. 8:17, 105; 13:25; 18:136
Graham, Witham 7:28
Graham, Zachariah 21:245
Grahan, William 3:82
Graig, G. W. 18:412
Graig, John 22:301
Graigg, W. 3:82
Grainer, A. 8:72
Grairs, James 8:105
Graishaw, Joseph 9:119
Graken, Samuel 20:259
Gralock, James 9:178
Graly, David 26:29
Gram, July 27:47
Grambaugh, --- 3:82
Grambling, Levi C. 22:463
Gramblings, Solomon 15:67
Grame, George 24:78

Gramel, Peter 8:85
Gramer, J. 27:48
Grames, Charles B. 23:107
Gramford, Charles 19:329
Gramis, D. H. 9:143
Gramley, Frank 17:80
Gramling, F. C. 26:161
Grammar, John I. 26:31
Grammer, George W. 10:95
Grammer, William 10:115; 20:259
Grammett, H. 3:82
Grammons, James 3:82
Grampker, Frederick 22:122
Grampson, James 21:337
Grampy, N. I. 3:83
Gran, Daniel 26:99
Gran, John 14:172
Gran, Loues 19:326
Gran, William 22:301
Granard, Daniel 21:337
Granberg, F. 7:74; 25:297
Granburg, Evick V. 24:170
Granby, --- 27:53
Granby, B. 12:87; 16:293
Granby, John 10:161
Grancel, Joseph A. 22:234
Grancoe, Henry C. 16:370
Grand, George 22:301
Grand, S. H. 27:49
Granda, George W. 16:145
Grandall, George 12:70; 15:35
Grandee, George W. 23:186
Grandell, John J. 22:424
Grandell, W. M. 19:326
Grander, G. 25:177
Granderson, Alfred 7:123
Granderson, John 6:16; 18:83
Granderson, Norman 26:123
Grandeson, L. B. 1:36
Grandeville, Edmond 7:123
Grandfield, John 23:121
Grandidle, William 11:203
Grandine, D. S. 3:82
Grandipie, Charles 20:259
Grandley, W. D. 11:303
Grandlock, William 7:28
Grandson, Norman 9:43
Grandstaf, J. 15:200
Grandstaff, J. 9:220

Grandstaff, J. J. 17:79
Grandstaff, James A. 18:136
Grandstaff, James O. 8:17
Grandstaff, L. 23:145
Grandstaff, Riley 18:367
Grandvil, Jacob 26:161
Grandville, Jacob 8:39
Grandy, Charles 5:39
Grandy, John M. 5:17
Grandy, L. 1:134
Grandy, Stephen K. 7:68
Granell, J. S. 9:52
Granely, B. 14:65
Graner, Gottleib 25:333
Graner, Peter 18:136
Granes, John 17:357
Granfield, J. 14:277
Grang, Wolf 24:59
Grange, F. 24:78
Grange, R. 18:30
Granger, A. 3:82
Granger, A. E. 21:166
Granger, C. H. 13:110
Granger, C. P. 25:177
Granger, E. Buell 22:194
Granger, E. F. 23:145
Granger, E. H. 3:82
Granger, Francis W. 9:42; 26:123
Granger, Frederick 4:27
Granger, George 22:446
Granger, Gordon 20:30
Granger, Henry 22:79
Granger, Ira 21:225
Granger, Isaac 22:32
Granger, James 22:11
Granger, John 3:82
Granger, L. T. 1:35
Granger, Leman B. 14:172
Granger, Leonard 13:25
Granger, Manson 4:27
Granger, Samuel M. 22:424
Granger, T. 18:367
Granger, Thomas 9:220
Granger, W. 14:65
Granger, W. S. 23:31
Granger, William 1:36; 17:314
Granger, William G. 17:390
Grangers, H. 14:172
Grangier, G. 20:259
Graninger, F. 13:110
Graninger, Gottleib 10:54
Granis, William 6:23
Granley, Moses 15:326; 19:72
Granlish, G. 9:143
Granly, A. 27:52

Granman, G. 11:240
Granmiss, D. H. 27:49
Grannin, M. 14:172
Grannis, Henry S. 11:115
Grannon, Ward 23:283
Grannous, G. W. 14:65
Grannt, David 18:174
Grans, A. 24:39
Grans, Burk 17:176
Gransinger, Nicholas 21:225
Granson, Mathias 8:17; 18:136
Granson, Wesley 25:177
Grant, --- 9:143; 21:187; 27:48
Grant, A. 1:37
Grant, A. C. 1:134
Grant, A. H. 3:82
Grant, A. I. 22:519
Grant, A. J. 2:11; 25:37
Grant, Aaron 8:105
Grant, Alexander 22:122
Grant, Andrew T. 23:121
Grant, Asa 15:296; 16:194
Grant, B. F. 8:85
Grant, Benjamin 8:85
Grant, Benjamin W. 16:78
Grant, C. 3:82; 14:65; 23:203
Grant, C. M. 14:172, 256
Grant, Charles 5:39; 7:28; 9:131; 10:27; 15:17; 19:301; 25:177
Grant, Charles C. 11:287; 25:35
Grant, Charles G. 12:153
Grant, Charles H. 14:172
Grant, Cyrus 11:88
Grant, D. F. 23:31
Grant, D. W. 9:143; 27:49
Grant, Daniel 25:177
Grant, Daniel A. 22:424
Grant, David 9:119; 13:25; 27:51
Grant, Dennis 17:397
Grant, Edward 4:27
Grant, Edward F. 8:85
Grant, F. 13:110
Grant, F. M. 7:95
Grant, Ferdinand 18:338
Grant, Frank 3:82
Grant, Franklin C. 11:126
Grant, G. 1:132, 133; 3:82
Grant, G. A. 9:214; 21:337
Grant, G. W. 13:110
Grant, George M. D. 25:177
Grant, George S. 10:17

Grant, George W. 3:82; 11:261; 18:237; 26:30
Grant, H. 1:134; 23:303; 25:177
Grant, H. G. 3:82
Grant, Harrison B. 9:12
Grant, Hector 9:81; 26:28
Grant, Henry 5:39; 7:123; 17:190; 18:237; 24:39
Grant, Henry M. 17:286
Grant, Henry W. 23:98
Grant, I. R. 25:297
Grant, J. 3:82; 14:65; 25:177
Grant, J. A. 3:82
Grant, J. W. 1:134; 18:238; 26:30
Grant, James 8:105; 10:54; 13:25; 14:172; 20:259
Grant, James A. 7:8
Grant, Jeremiah 27:47
Grant, John 9:131; 16:370; 25:320; 27:50, 51
Grant, John E. 12:62; 15:13
Grant, Joseph P. 4:27
Grant, L. 6:31; 25:320
Grant, L. B. 9:52
Grant, L. E. 21:337
Grant, Lewis P. 18:395
Grant, M. 3:82
Grant, Marion 8:105
Grant, Miles 21:203
Grant, Moses 9:143; 27:48
Grant, Norman 23:31
Grant, Orin L. 15:166
Grant, Patrick 9:110
Grant, Pliney 18:276
Grant, R. 17:131; 24:194; 25:177
Grant, Richard 5:39
Grant, S. 18:14; 27:49
Grant, Samuel 10:8; 13:127
Grant, T. 15:200
Grant, Thomas 21:337
Grant, W. 1:134
Grant, W. F. B. 9:214
Grant, William 3:82; 4:27; 10:115; 18:276; 20:259; 21:337
Grant, William F. 19:72
Grant, William F. B. 21:337
Grant, William H. 9:217; 21:337

Grant, William K. 15:309
Grant, William R. 7:95
Grantham, Henry 21:337
Grantham, I. L. 17:291
Grantham, William 8:59
Granthan, Richard D. 22:252
Granton, G. G. 11:303
Grantt, Alexander J. 1:35
Grantz, F. 1:132
Grantzmiller, Louis 17:203
Granves, L. 25:37
Granville, E. 24:99
Granwell, William 22:122
Grany, N. W. 16:194
Granyville, Daniel 21:337
Graper, William 21:254
Graper, William F. 11:61
Grapp, William 17:506
Grapps, H. 3:82
Grarisloff, F. 3:83
Grary, Richard 24:93
Gras, G. W. 3:82
Grash, Fred 3:82
Grash, Frederick A. 7:50
Grashley, G. 17:20
Graskinsky, --- 1:132
Grasman, E. 3:82
Grass, A. 14:65
Grass, Augustus 8:123
Grass, C. 3:82
Grass, Edward 9:214
Grass, George E. 9:214
Grass, Henry 8:17; 18:136
Grass, J. 3:82; 15:106
Grass, William 26:99
Grasshopper, James G. 22:424
Grassmier, Adam 14:172
Grassmire, James R. 23:31
Grasstare, C. 16:194
Grast, J. W. 14:65
Grasvenor, D. 11:147
Gratam, John 3:82
Grate, Deidrich 20:8
Grate, George 4:27
Grated, George M. 19:72
Gratehouse, H. C. 8:63
Gratemuse, Irwin 22:32
Grath, W. H. 13:89
Grath, W. M. 14:11
Grath, Wilhelm F. 18:338
Gratham, John 23:66
Gratham, John S. 20:40
Graton, E. R. 19:166
Gratten, J. 14:27
Gratten, James 9:81
Gratton, A. A. 13:64; 19:72

Gratton, John 1:36
Gratton, John L. 26:220
Gratz, O. 2:11; 25:35
Gratz, William 12:55
Gratznousky, William 7:28
Grau, Charles 19:15
Graudy, Ezra 11:147
Grauer, C. 14:65
Grauff, Frederick 13:25
Grauit, David 10:179
Grauner, Joseph J. 9:81
Grause, J. B. 16:194
Grautz, Frederick 10:17
Gravatt, E. P. 1:36
Gravatt, R. 1:35
Grave, Benjamin 6:16; 18:83
Grave, John 8:72
Gravel, George W. 5:39
Gravel, Henry 24:78
Gravel, J. 3:82
Gravel, Peter 18:206
Gravell, William 3:82
Graven, Henry 11:262
Gravenberg, Antoine 21:337
Gravenburg, Antonie 7:123
Gravens, Thomas J. 24:39
Graver, C. L. 16:34
Graver, J. J. 13:25
Graver, John H. 11:412
Graveraet, G. A. 1:133
Graves, Abraham 11:203
Graves, Albert 22:425
Graves, Alexander 21:337
Graves, Allen 11:255
Graves, Alvin C. 20:97
Graves, B. 22:301
Graves, Benton 9:43
Graves, Berton 26:123
Graves, C. 1:133
Graves, C. B 13:64
Graves, C. S. 17:231
Graves, Chandler 7:95
Graves, Charles 16:34; 23:190
Graves, Charles E. 23:31
Graves, Charles H. 16:194
Graves, Charles P. 22:450
Graves, D. B. 5:17; 25:177
Graves, Dock 23:307
Graves, E. 18:14
Graves, Edward C. 8:72
Graves, Elijah 21:225
Graves, Ezekiel E. 7:95
Graves, F. 13:110; 15:35
Graves, F. M. 10:115; 20:259

Graves, Franklin 13:25
Graves, Frederick 4:27
Graves, G. 3:82; 20:22
Graves, G. B. 18:238; 26:30
Graves, G. W. 14:65; 25:177
Graves, George 20:259; 21:337
Graves, George M. 18:217
Graves, George W. 9:119
Graves, Henry 3:223; 9:66; 10:115; 17:504; 18:276; 20:259
Graves, Henry H. 7:7
Graves, Hiram S. 15:200
Graves, I. 23:31
Graves, Ira V. 22:451
Graves, Isaac 11:31
Graves, J. 3:82; 13:89; 16:119
Graves, J. C. 3:82
Graves, J. H. 26:162
Graves, J. S. 14:319; 25:282
Graves, Jacob 17:163; 23:66
Graves, James 3:82; 21:187
Graves, James L. 13:25; 16:35
Graves, John 8:17, 85; 11:61; 18:136; 23:31
Graves, Joseph 11:31
Graves, Joseph D. 10:212
Graves, Kneeland 20:107
Graves, L. 5:51; 22:301; 25:177
Graves, Leander W. 19:15
Graves, Leonard 8:17; 18:136; 21:337
Graves, Lysander 7:95
Graves, Mariom 22:79
Graves, Martin A. 22:501
Graves, Monroe 4:27
Graves, N. 25:320
Graves, Nat 11:203
Graves, Nathan 14:172
Graves, Peter 7:123
Graves, S. 18:367
Graves, S. S. 7:74; 19:166; 25:297
Graves, Samuel 7:123; 9:220
Graves, Simeon H. 4:27
Graves, Soweny 8:58
Graves, Squire 17:418
Graves, Stephen S. 10:172
Graves, T. 16:194
Graves, T. W. 21:27
Graves, Thomas G. 10:17

Graves, Thomas T. 16:35
Graves, W. 11:261
Graves, W. E. 3:82
Graves, W. F. 3:82
Graves, W. H. 18:306;
  22:32; 26:98
Graves, W. P. 25:177
Graves, W. S. 15:342;
  16:370
Graves, Walter M. 23:107
Graves, Warren 19:72
Graves, William 11:381
Graves, William J. 23:121
Graves, William N. 9:178
Graves, Willis 18:395
Gravet, George 8:39
Gravet, Paul 12:23
Gravett, John 22:335
Gravette, Simeon 22:279
Gravilins, H. 1:132
Gravis, G. 22:463
Gravitt, James 11:241
Gravlick, Martin 15:35
Gravly, James M. 18:206
Graw, A. 16:152
Graw, Benjamin S. 11:106
Graw, Charles 15:363
Graw, Daniel 18:293
Graw, E. 7:57
Graw, L. 14:298; 17:479;
  27:52
Graw, Owen M. 10:54;
  20:259
Graw, William 9:81
Graw, William A. 27:48
Grawforo, William 23:261
Grawlish, G. 27:49
Gray, --- 12:140
Gray, A. 11:293; 26:219
Gray, A. O. 17:291
Gray, A. S. 1:94; 22:479
Gray, A. W. 11:326
Gray, Aaron I. 4:27
Gray, Adam 15:352
Gray, Albert J. 13:24
Gray, Alexander 17:391
Gray, Alfred 22:301
Gray, Alva M. 12:70;
  15:83
Gray, Andrew 8:72
Gray, Andy 9:47; 26:123
Gray, Anthony 17:34
Gray, Augustus 10:115;
  20:259
Gray, Augustus N. 21:99
Gray, Austin L. 11:240
Gray, Benjamin 23:190
Gray, C. 3:82; 16:95
Gray, C. A. 18:190
Gray, C. D. 3:82
Gray, C. E. 18:306; 26:98

Gray, C. F. 14:172
Gray, C. H. 9:138
Gray, C. J. 9:22
Gray, Calvin 19:72
Gray, Charles 2:11; 14:65;
  16:35; 19:72; 25:177
Gray, Charles H. 23:66
Gray, Chris. A. 7:64
Gray, Clark 15:151
Gray, Cyrus 7:123
Gray, D. 13:89; 26:29
Gray, D. H. 9:220; 10:27;
  18:367; 19:302
Gray, D. L. 3:82
Gray, Daniel 10:151, 178;
  22:301
Gray, Daniel W. 20:30
Gray, Darrel 18:136
Gray, David 8:17; 10:24,
  54; 20:259; 23:31;
  26:161
Gray, Dennis 8:99
Gray, E. 13:77; 22:194
Gray, E. P. 15:200
Gray, E. S. 21:166
Gray, Edward 17:148
Gray, Edward C. 20:97
Gray, Edwin 7:16
Gray, Elijah 26:211
Gray, Ellery 14:172
Gray, Francis 13:57;
  20:259
Gray, G. S. 3:82
Gray, George 3:82; 7:95;
  10:176; 13:110;
  17:176; 19:166;
  20:259
Gray, H. 14:277; 18:238;
  23:145; 26:30
Gray, H. F. 3:82
Gray, H. H. 23:263
Gray, H. J. 17:440; 24:152
Gray, H. M. 26:204
Gray, H. V. 10:54
Gray, Harvey 10:95
Gray, Henry 15:86;
  18:276; 22:301;
  24:78; 27:50
Gray, Hiram 7:16; 14:172
Gray, Hor. M. 18:174
Gray, Hugh 9:22
Gray, I. W. 17:295
Gray, Ira 9:178; 19:270
Gray, Isaac 11:147
Gray, Isham 26:161
Gray, J. 1:133; 3:82;
  9:143; 13:103; 14:11;
  16:147, 268; 21:110;
  25:37
Gray, J. A. 11:322
Gray, J. C. 1:37

Gray, J. H. 13:110
Gray, J. M. 27:52
Gray, J. S. 1:132; 14:281
Gray, J. W. S. 18:395
Gray, Jackson 21:271
Gray, Jacob 26:161
Gray, James 3:82; 5:39;
  8:17, 101; 9:81, 97;
  16:95, 194; 17:20,
  463; 18:136, 238;
  22:143; 23:179;
  25:177; 26:29, 31
Gray, James A. 22:424
Gray, James H. 17:440;
  24:152
Gray, James M. 7:123;
  20:183; 22:112;
  23:98
Gray, James W. 8:85;
  11:261
Gray, Jeremiah 22:425
Gray, Jerry 2:11
Gray, John 3:82; 8:85;
  9:131; 10:115; 11:88,
  148; 13:25, 89; 15:7,
  124; 16:35, 293;
  18:110; 20:259, 260;
  21:254; 22:166, 335;
  23:66, 285; 25:177
Gray, John C. 17:429
Gray, John F. 8:77
Gray, John M. 9:119;
  17:110
Gray, John N. 15:55
Gray, John O. 18:30
Gray, John R. 18:395
Gray, John S. 16:78;
  17:506
Gray, John W. 3:223;
  7:95; 17:504
Gray, Joseph 24:177
Gray, Joshua B. 13:64;
  16:194
Gray, L. S. 23:145
Gray, Leonard S. 12:23
Gray, Lewis A. 17:71
Gray, Louis 27:51
Gray, M. 1:134; 3:82;
  10:179
Gray, M. B. 7:72
Gray, M. M. 13:77
Gray, Marshal 2:11
Gray, Marshall 21:337
Gray, Martin L. 8:116
Gray, N. 26:31
Gray, Nelson 27:50
Gray, Newton 13:25
Gray, Newton B. 21:52
Gray, O. I. 24:78
Gray, Oliver 7:123;
  21:121

Gray, Oscar 20:22
Gray, P. 1:133
Gray, Patrick 14:172;
  22:451
Gray, Philetus M. 22:424
Gray, R. 1:131
Gray, R. G. 15:35
Gray, R. H. 21:10
Gray, Richard 17:131;
  24:194
Gray, Robert 7:123;
  14:172
Gray, S. 25:177
Gray, S. H. 22:194
Gray, S. W. 15:200
Gray, Samuel 22:32
Gray, Samuel G. 9:97
Gray, Samuel N. 21:337
Gray, Samuel S. 22:32
Gray, Scipio 11:203
Gray, Seymour 22:279
Gray, Silas 13:25; 16:35
Gray, Solomon J. 7:95
Gray, Stephen 9:43
Gray, Sylveseter 17:259
Gray, T. 11:191
Gray, T. P. 10:192;
  18:174
Gray, T. W. 21:337
Gray, Thomas 7:95;
  10:54, 170; 20:260
Gray, Thomas J. 10:115;
  20:260
Gray, Tobias 15:151
Gray, W. 1:103; 15:151
Gray, W. D. 18:136
Gray, W. G. 12:161
Gray, W. H. 15:200;
  23:31
Gray, W. N. 20:260
Gray, Warner N. 10:54
Gray, Warren 12:23
Gray, Wash 17:131;
  24:194
Gray, Washburn 13:24
Gray, West 16:370
Gray, William 3:82; 8:17;
  13:64; 18:136;
  19:72; 20:124;
  21:337; 22:194, 301,
  397, 501; 23:121
Gray, William A. 11:428
Gray, William E. 12:70
Gray, William F. 11:61
Gray, William H. 4:27;
  11:106; 22:501
Gray, William I. 26:29
Gray, William J. 9:81
Gray, William P. 22:79
Gray, William R. 21:337
Gray, Willis 13:110

Gray, Wilson S. 17:495
Graybeel, Reuben 22:501
Graybill, E. 18:110
Graybill, Samuel 22:194
Graydon, James 8:125;
  12:61
Graydon, Peter 1:36
Grayham, James 26:31
Grayham, W. A. 15:106
Grayhle, Emanuel 6:9
Graylar, Henry 9:220
Graylor, Henry 18:367
Graylord, Charles H.
  11:387
Grayner, Charles 14:172
Grayson, Amos 27:50
Grayson, Amos H. 9:131
Grayson, Caesar 27:47
Grayson, Charles 9:131;
  27:50
Grayson, H. 17:34
Grayson, James M. 8:17
Grayson, John 27:50
Grayson, W. 22:301
Graystone, G. 19:253
Graystone, George 9:178
Grazie, Charles 21:27
Grazier, Andrew J. 20:185
Grazier, H. 14:65
Greadley, H. 3:83
Grealsh, Patrick 13:64
Greamer, I. 9:143
Greamsh, Patrick 16:194
Greany, W. 9:66
Grear, Alexander 21:130
Grear, R. 3:83
Grease, --- 25:333
Grease, William 20:174
Greaser, William D.
  17:425
Greason, Nelson 10:55;
  20:260
Great, Ander A. 21:337
Greatbead, John 22:234
Greathouse, Daniel
  20:124
Greathouse, David 9:81;
  26:31
Greathouse, H. 20:154
Greathouse, H. C. 26:161
Greathouse, J. 25:177
Greathouse, Richard
  15:86
Greathouse, T. 3:83
Greatrake, Henry 21:337
Greaves, George 3:83
Greaves, Lorry 21:148
Greaves, R. 23:179
Greaves, Wilson B. 9:34
Grebe, James 4:27
Grech, G. 17:473

Greck, G. 27:52
Greealy, A. 14:298;
  17:469
Greeby, David 9:81
Greech, G. 14:298
Greedee, Littleton 8:39
Greedley, Allen 4:28
Greedy, Thomas 22:301
Greeenlun, W. 22:194
Greegs, Lawson P. 9:81
Greek, C. H. 3:83
Greek, G. W. 11:219
Greek, Joseph H. 22:471
Greek, Nathan 7:77
Greek, Samuel 3:83
Greek, William 12:58
Greeley, --- 14:172
Greeley, B. B. 7:74;
  25:297
Greeley, Benjamin 18:49
Greeley, D. 15:293;
  16:194
Greeley, Horace 13:57
Greeley, Patrick 20:260
Greeley, Rufus 21:337
Greeley, Sheldon H.
  19:227
Greeley, William 18:50
Greely, Horace 27:144
Greely, Julius 23:285
Greely, Patrick 10:115
Greely, R. 21:121
Greeman, Lyman 17:110
Green, --- 5:17, 55;
  10:161; 19:166
Green, A. 7:95; 9:143;
  14:65; 15:35, 158,
  293; 17:496; 19:72;
  21:187; 27:48
Green, A. D. 10:55;
  20:260
Green, A. E. 19:166
Green, A. F. 11:125
Green, A. P. 1:133
Green, Abe S. 21:121
Green, Abial 13:79
Green, Abraham 11:147
Green, Adam 5:17; 9:131;
  27:50
Green, Addison 12:23
Green, Albert 11:61;
  13:81; 16:194;
  17:131; 18:238, 307;
  21:187; 22:194, 463;
  24:194; 26:31
Green, Albert C. 19:15
Green, Albert E. 10:161
Green, Albert G. 21:70
Green, Albert S. 7:8
Green, Albion 27:52

Green, Alex. F. 9:131; 27:49
Green, Alexander 10:55; 18:83; 19:45
Green, Alfred 17:176
Green, Algert 26:98
Green, Allen 10:91; 20:260; 22:301
Green, Alonzo 7:28, 123
Green, Amos 27:47
Green, Anderson 7:28; 21:272
Green, Andrew 4:28; 22:252, 301
Green, Anthony 9:119
Green, Armstrong 6:31
Green, Arthur 21:27
Green, B. 9:200
Green, B. C. 14:65
Green, B. T. 1:133
Green, Bayfield 21:272
Green, Benjamin 8:39; 10:98; 13:57; 26:161
Green, Benjamin F. 20:8
Green, Benjamin L. 10:91; 20:260
Green, Benjamin T. 4:28
Green, Bill 16:194
Green, Bowling 23:31
Green, Bradford 8:17
Green, Bury 27:53
Green, C. 3:83; 9:143; 20:260; 25:178; 27:48
Green, C. B. 11:106
Green, C. E. 24:99
Green, C. H. 25:178
Green, Calvin C. 10:55; 20:260
Green, Charles 1:34; 7:123; 11:105, 203; 14:173, 315; 21:110; 27:50
Green, Charles A. 9:12
Green, Charles B. 12:64; 21:337
Green, Charles C. 7:95
Green, Charles E. 9:131
Green, Charles F. 13:127
Green, Charles H. 5:39
Green, Charles M. 14:173
Green, Charles V. 7:95
Green, Charles W. 18:217
Green, Clark L. 21:91
Green, Claypool 6:35
Green, Cyrus 10:55
Green, Cyrus A. 5:17
Green, D. J. 7:96
Green, D. W. 21:187
Green, Daniel 19:329; 25:178

Green, David 18:238; 21:194, 337
Green, David L. 22:194
Green, David R. 11:61
Green, Decatur 1:36
Green, Dennis 1:192
Green, E. 1:132, 134; 3:83; 11:262; 14:65, 326
Green, E. B. 26:162
Green, E. K. 8:72
Green, E. P. 19:237
Green, E. T. 16:119
Green, Edgar 6:20
Green, Edgar P. 9:178
Green, Edmund 19:166
Green, Edward 13:110
Green, Edwin 1:35
Green, Eleon D. 19:72
Green, Elijah 19:15
Green, Elisha 7:28
Green, Elithan J. 21:243
Green, Espa 17:52
Green, Ezra 27:47
Green, F. 12:99; 27:49
Green, F. R. 14:130
Green, F. W. 24:93
Green, Francis S. 11:261
Green, Franklin 9:22
Green, Frederick 9:22
Green, G. 1:132, 134; 9:52; 15:67; 16:194; 27:48
Green, G. D. 25:178
Green, G. M. 14:173
Green, George 6:16, 25; 7:123; 10:55; 12:49; 15:106; 16:194; 17:79, 176; 18:83, 434; 20:260; 21:52, 337; 22:79
Green, George B. 8:49; 21:254
Green, George D. 19:72
Green, George F. 18:238; 20:183; 26:30
Green, George H. 1:36; 6:16; 17:52; 18:83
Green, George M. 22:451
Green, George W. 13:25; 17:71; 21:115
Green, Goling 19:291
Green, H. 12:82; 13:89; 16:293; 20:260
Green, H. A. 7:28
Green, H. H. 14:65
Green, H. P. 1:37
Green, H. W. 3:83; 12:82; 14:173; 16:293
Green, Harrison 7:123

Green, Harry 11:203; 21:337
Green, Harry C. 8:105
Green, Harvey 9:158; 22:335
Green, Harvey H. 22:425
Green, Henry 7:123; 8:39; 9:119; 11:148; 13:25; 17:176; 22:301; 26:161; 27:51
Green, Henry A. 20:260
Green, Henry E. 9:102
Green, Henry H. 22:79
Green, Henry J. 1:97
Green, Herbert 22:143
Green, Herny 23:305
Green, Hiram 7:95; 10:115; 20:260
Green, Horace 10:55; 21:272
Green, Isaac 9:43; 17:131; 21:337; 23:145; 24:194; 26:123
Green, J. 1:36, 134; 3:83; 9:52, 220; 12:85; 14:65; 16:293; 18:367; 22:79, 352; 23:31; 25:178; 26:162
Green, J. A. 1:36
Green, J. B. 3:83
Green, J. C. 3:83; 22:79
Green, J. D. 5:39
Green, J. F. 16:194
Green, J. G. 3:83
Green, J. H. 11:322; 20:260
Green, J. K. 16:194
Green, J. M. 11:332; 15:324; 17:280; 19:72; 24:19
Green, J. P. 1:132; 21:100; 25:34
Green, J. R. 9:227; 18:367; 25:320
Green, J. S. 18:50
Green, J. V. 21:337
Green, J. W. 9:81; 21:338; 23:145; 27:47
Green, Jack 17:176; 18:67
Green, Jacob 8:72; 26:162; 27:51
Green, Jacob H. 8:17
Green, Jake 10:98
Green, James 1:37; 6:25; 10:115, 170, 172; 11:148, 203; 13:25, 57, 127; 14:65; 16:35; 17:253, 443; 19:166; 20:260; 22:234, 252, 301;

Green, James 24:158;
 25:178, 272, 297
Green, James A. 22:451
Green, James B. 18:206
Green, James C. 24:39
Green, James H. 8:85;
 10:55, 115; 20:260
Green, James M. 11:147;
 19:45
Green, James P. 14:269,
 281
Green, James R. 22:79
Green, James T. 22:252
Green, Jasper N. 22:194
Green, Jeptha F. 9:72
Green, Jerry 17:131, 176;
 21:272; 24:194
Green, Jesse 21:272
Green, Joel 10:55; 20:260
Green, John 3:83; 4:28;
 7:28, 123; 9:9, 72,
 157, 207; 10:55, 161;
 11:423; 12:70, 139;
 13:110; 14:173;
 15:86, 106; 16:35,
 194; 17:20, 248;
 18:206; 19:15;
 20:107, 260; 21:337;
 22:17, 194, 301;
 23:31; 24:78; 26:29
Green, John A. 11:106
Green, John B. 11:181
Green, John J. 20:3
Green, John L. 10:91;
 20:260; 23:200;
 25:36
Green, John M. 10:115;
 20:260
Green, John O. 17:65
Green, John R. 1:35;
 18:444
Green, John S. 7:28
Green, John W. 14:173;
 17:355; 23:179
Green, Johnson 9:131;
 27:50
Green, Jonathan 17:418;
 25:35
Green, Joseph 4:66; 5:39;
 7:28; 9:9, 165;
 10:54; 11:423;
 16:194; 20:260;
 24:152
Green, Joseph A. 23:145
Green, Joseph H. 7:28;
 9:131; 10:8; 27:50
Green, Joseph W. 19:15
Green, Jupiter 9:131;
 27:50
Green, Kebula 12:49

Green, L. 13:124; 19:325;
 27:49
Green, L. D. 14:298;
 17:469; 27:53
Green, Len 18:67
Green, Leonard A. 25:36
Green, Levi 10:55;
 20:260; 27:52
Green, Levi M. 10:27
Green, Lewis 14:173;
 23:145
Green, Lindley 20:8
Green, London 18:83
Green, Loudon 6:16
Green, Louis 9:81, 207;
 25:178
Green, Luss 18:103
Green, Lyman 8:119
Green, M. 1:133; 3:83;
 11:262; 13:89;
 16:194
Green, M. P. 2:11; 25:34
Green, Madison 21:338
Green, Mainwaring 9:12
Green, Manning 9:131
Green, Marg. K. 24:111
Green, Marion 13:60
Green, Marmduke 25:36
Green, Martin 9:207;
 17:242; 21:91, 338;
 23:203
Green, Martin D. 17:317
Green, Mastin 16:35
Green, May 9:131; 27:50
Green, Merrihue 4:28
Green, Michael 9:35;
 20:192; 22:335;
 26:124
Green, Milo 17:154
Green, Monroe 8:39;
 26:161
Green, Morgan 17:233
Green, Morris 17:95
Green, Mortimer L.
 22:143
Green, Moses 10:205;
 21:338
Green, Moses H. 19:72
Green, Murry 21:272
Green, N. S. 1:132; 10:55;
 20:260
Green, Nat 25:297
Green, Nemon 20:17
Green, Newton 8:85;
 21:211, 272
Green, Noah 17:95;
 22:252
Green, Norman 15:292;
 19:72
Green, O. 3:83
Green, Obial 16:194

Green, Orrin L. 14:65
Green, Oscar C. 19:15
Green, P. 9:214; 27:51
Green, Paul 21:10
Green, Peris 11:92
Green, Peter 7:77; 11:401;
 25:297
Green, Philip 11:203
Green, Pleasant 11:203
Green, R. 11:241; 13:103;
 14:11; 16:268
Green, R. A. 25:37
Green, R. B. 1:36; 5:17
Green, R. M. 25:311
Green, R. W. 20:89
Green, Randolph 19:325
Green, Reuben 22:252
Green, Robert 11:203;
 22:252
Green, Robert H. 19:296
Green, Robert L. 22:32
Green, Robert W. 15:200
Green, S. 3:83; 15:106;
 25:178
Green, S. P. 12:23
Green, S. R. 1:134; 16:80
Green, S. T. 21:27
Green, S. W. 25:178
Green, Samuel 6:28;
 11:395, 408; 13:110;
 14:65; 17:352, 400;
 20:3; 21:272
Green, Samuel F. 21:203
Green, Samuel S. 22:425
Green, Samuel W. 5:39
Green, Scott 15:67
Green, Shelly 25:36
Green, Simon 21:338
Green, Solomon 16:194
Green, Stephen 4:28;
 13:25; 15:200
Green, Sterling 22:252
Green, Sylvanus 4:27
Green, Sylvester 4:28
Green, T. 27:49
Green, T. N. 11:223
Green, T. R. 15:263
Green, T. S. 8:106
Green, T. W. 15:35
Green, Thomas 4:28, 66;
 7:57, 77; 8:85; 17:95,
 176; 19:15, 166;
 22:79, 462; 25:35,
 297
Green, Thomas W. 12:70
Green, Timothy 9:16
Green, Tina 18:30
Green, Turner J. 15:124
Green, W. 1:132; 7:65;
 9:52; 13:89; 14:11;

Green, W. 15:200; 18:50; 21:121; 25:36
Green, W. A. 25:311
Green, W. D. 22:194
Green, W. H. 1:37, 133; 11:60, 322; 12:95; 19:72
Green, W. R. 1:134; 9:72
Green, W. S. 3:83
Green, W. W. 15:200
Green, Warner 22:143
Green, Whitman 17:263
Green, Willett S. 24:62
Green, William 4:28; 6:7, 31; 8:17; 9:31, 165; 10:152; 11:423; 12:82; 13:78; 14:173; 15:200; 16:194, 293; 17:20; 18:110, 136, 468; 21:13, 272, 338; 22:252, 301; 25:178, 320; 26:138
Green, William A. 12:70
Green, William C. 7:28; 9:81; 23:179
Green, William E. 16:81; 21:184, 214
Green, William G. 21:225
Green, William H. 7:95; 9:35; 15:359; 17:34; 22:425
Green, William L. 20:8; 22:32
Green, William M. 17:209, 355
Green, William Q. 20:17
Green, William S. 19:72
Green, Willis 9:7; 22:425
Green, Wilson 21:272; 25:320
Green, Winfield S. 17:154
Greenaway, A. 9:143
Greenaway, H. C. 11:186
Greenback, William 14:173
Greenbury, Dan 10:98
Greencan, James D. 23:145
Greene, --- 23:184
Greene, A. 19:274
Greene, Addison 9:178
Greene, Benjamin M. 16:35
Greene, Christian 9:16
Greene, David 13:25; 26:31
Greene, Edwin R. M. 17:79
Greene, George 9:143
Greene, Howard 18:334

Greene, I. W. 26:31
Greene, Jacob 18:136
Greene, James 18:30
Greene, James P. 14:281
Greene, John 13:25; 17:79
Greene, L. 9:143
Greene, Lewis 17:34; 26:31
Greene, Rudolph 18:136
Greene, Samuel 7:68
Greene, Thomas 3:83
Greenfather, J. 10:205
Greene, William 12:55; 18:426
Greene, William B. 22:143
Greener, Charles 1:36
Greener, E. 1:133
Greenfather, J. 10:205
Greenfield, D. 11:61; 25:178
Greenfield, E. 13:110
Greenfield, James 23:66
Greenfield, M. 9:143; 27:48
Greenfield, Robert 12:49; 22:301
Greenfield, W. S. 24:78
Greenham, N. 22:479
Greenhart, H. 15:200
Greenhoe, Henry 11:286
Greenhorn, Thomas 9:72
Greenhouse, John 13:64
Greening, Henry 21:338
Greening, J. 9:143; 27:49
Greening, Jacob 4:28
Greening, R. 23:31
Greening, W. 18:103
Greenland, Frank 22:479
Greenlaw, A. H. 15:351
Greenleaf, C. W. 7:81; 25:297
Greenleaf, Charles D. 21:338
Greenleaf, E. Q. 15:107
Greenleaf, F. 18:67
Greenleaf, G. 9:110
Greenleaf, George W. 16:194
Greenleaf, Isaac P. 19:286
Greenleaf, Robert E. 10:115; 20:260
Greenleaf, S. 1:135
Greenlee, Alex 3:83
Greenlee, George 14:173
Greenlee, Joseph 22:32
Greenlee, L. S. 16:152
Greenlee, Peter P. 18:395
Greenlee, R. 15:200
Greenlee, William H. 20:146
Greenley, J. 23:309

Greenlie, James M. 21:95
Greenlief, A. P. 15:200
Greenlin, R. 14:65
Greenlow, Christopher 11:286
Greenlow, J. M. 15:17
Greenly, Willett 22:508
Greenman, Charles 22:143
Greenman, D. 3:83
Greenman, Henry C. 18:174
Greenman, J. S. 3:83
Greenman, M. 17:65
Greenman, Matthew 12:23
Greenman, W. P. 19:243
Greenman, Walter P. 9:178
Greenough, A. 14:65
Greenow, Lewis 8:106
Greens, A. R. 14:65
Greens, Volney A. 10:161
Greenshaw, H. W. 22:32
Greenslit, Neal A. 23:31
Greensteitle, C. 1:36
Greenstreet, James 12:142; 20:260
Greenstreet, John 23:113
Greensvieg, Levi 9:119
Greenswall, G. 18:83
Greensway, A. 27:49
Greenswicke, William 9:16
Greenswright, R. H. 17:65; 22:463
Greenville, C. 15:5
Greenville, Charles 12:70
Greenwald, G. 19:15
Greenwald, I. 17:294
Greenwall, B. 3:83
Greenwalt, G. 3:83
Greenwalt, Henry 8:63
Greenwalt, M. 3:83
Greenwelt, Edward 14:173
Greenwith, A. C. 15:200
Greenwolt, John 14:173
Greenwood, Alfred C. 22:32
Greenwood, C. 10:148; 18:50
Greenwood, Dennis 19:45
Greenwood, Edward N. 9:178
Greenwood, Edwin N. 19:237
Greenwood, Enos L. 22:279
Greenwood, Frank A. 11:60
Greenwood, Franklin L. 17:20

Greenwood, Frederick 21:338
Greenwood, George T. 22:32
Greenwood, Hugh 23:190
Greenwood, I. 19:227
Greenwood, Israel 9:178
Greenwood, Jack 9:165
Greenwood, James H. 23:88
Greenwood, John 9:52; 16:119
Greenwood, Joseph 13:89
Greenwood, Lewis 17:429; 24:185
Greenwood, Martin 22:335
Greenwood, Nelson 7:28
Greenwood, Richard H. 22:32
Greenwood, S. 20:260
Greenwood, Samuel 9:178; 19:245
Greenwood, Thomas 22:32
Greenwood, Victor 24:107
Greenwood, W. 1:133; 3:83
Greenwood, W. A. 19:302
Greenwood, W. C. 27:52
Greenwood, W. F. 25:37
Greenwood, William 20:260
Greer, Alex 20:260
Greer, Asher M. 17:276
Greer, Benjamin 17:403
Greer, Calvin L. 22:501
Greer, David 19:331
Greer, Elias D. 9:178
Greer, F. L. 15:200
Greer, Franklin 18:307; 26:99
Greer, Frederick 22:252
Greer, G. G. 3:83
Greer, George 3:83; 17:65; 22:301
Greer, George W. 11:241
Greer, H. 17:166
Greer, J. A. 3:83
Greer, J. L. 10:55; 20:260
Greer, J. M. 12:23
Greer, J. O. 3:83
Greer, J. W. 20:40
Greer, James 11:240; 20:35
Greer, James V. 23:88
Greer, James W. 15:124
Greer, John 3:83; 10:115; 20:261
Greer, John A. 22:32

Greer, Lewis 11:203
Greer, Madison A. 17:276
Greer, Mark M. 8:117
Greer, Martin 12:23
Greer, Nathan 18:395
Greer, R. 20:40
Greer, R. J. 3:83
Greer, R. M. 8:63
Greer, Samuel 12:23
Greer, Thomas 7:14; 22:301
Greer, Thomas J. 22:194
Greer, W. 1:97
Greer, W. E. 13:89; 14:11
Greer, W. H. 23:66
Greer, Weasner 11:61
Greer, William H. 16:35
Greerman, Henry G. 10:186
Greeser, Andrew 10:115; 20:261
Greesey, J. 17:79
Greeson, A. B. 11:60
Greeson, Jacob 21:52
Greever, George 23:31
Greffith, John 15:364
Greger, W. 1:132
Greger, William H. 25:36
Gregg, Alexander 22:279
Gregg, Azariah 21:70
Gregg, Ezra 10:115; 20:261
Gregg, F. 1:133; 3:83
Gregg, G. 21:110
Gregg, Henry 22:479; 24:50
Gregg, Isaac 4:28; 22:194
Gregg, Israel 8:85
Gregg, J. 3:83
Gregg, Jacob 7:57
Gregg, James 11:61
Gregg, Jesse 18:412
Gregg, John 14:11; 15:306; 19:72
Gregg, John C. 1:36
Gregg, Joseph 15:200
Gregg, Joseph P. 19:72
Gregg, Lewis 10:172; 19:166
Gregg, R. 14:65
Gregg, R. W. 25:177
Gregg, Richard 24:194
Gregg, Rodney A. 26:29
Gregg, Samuel 22:335
Gregg, Stephen 8:39; 26:161
Gregg, W. 1:37; 14:173
Gregg, W. W. 15:258
Gregg, William 16:35
Gregg, William F. 18:190

Gregg, William H. 18:206; 23:145
Greggor, M. 12:166
Greggory, John C. 20:261
Greggs, D. 3:83
Greggs, J. 25:178
Greggson, Jesse 22:301
Gregison, L. 17:20
Gregley, Frank 20:261
Gregney, Edward 11:203
Gregoir, Major 27:50
Gregon, J. P. 26:31
Gregon, W. H. 26:123
Gregor, August 9:81; 26:28
Gregor, F. 25:178
Gregor, John 4:28; 19:72
Gregor, Samuel 10:115; 20:261
Gregore, H. 21:203
Gregorie, Robert 10:115; 20:261
Gregorry, F. 16:293
Gregory, A. 16:195; 25:178
Gregory, Alvin 4:28
Gregory, Augustus 27:50
Gregory, B. 1:36
Gregory, B. M. 7:96
Gregory, C. A. 18:238; 26:31
Gregory, C. B. 19:245
Gregory, C. H. 18:420
Gregory, Charles 11:423; 17:273
Gregory, Charles B. 9:178
Gregory, Charles W. 16:139
Gregory, Clinton 7:123
Gregory, Corwin 9:102; 18:338
Gregory, Curtis D. 10:115; 20:261
Gregory, Cyrus 26:145
Gregory, D. D. L. 3:83
Gregory, David 24:19
Gregory, E. 13:89; 14:173
Gregory, Erastus 18:67
Gregory, Eric 20:261
Gregory, Erie 10:55
Gregory, F. 12:92; 14:65
Gregory, Francis 22:11
Gregory, G. 1:36; 21:208
Gregory, G. W. 21:95
Gregory, George 8:49, 106; 15:107; 17:314
Gregory, George D. 21:254
Gregory, George M. 4:28
Gregory, George W. 17:423

Gregory, H. 3:83; 22:33
Gregory, Hardy 10:170
Gregory, Harrison 17:190
Gregory, Henry 11:241
Gregory, Hiram 22:122
Gregory, J. 24:107; 25:35
Gregory, J. G. 15:107
Gregory, J. W. 20:261;
    25:321
Gregory, James 17:34
Gregory, James C. 26:161
Gregory, James W.
    10:115; 15:87;
    20:261
Gregory, John 3:83;
    11:419; 14:319;
    25:277
Gregory, John C. 10:115
Gregory, John F. 20:261
Gregory, John G. 8:85
Gregory, John H. 24:93
Gregory, John M. 11:106
Gregory, John P. 9:81
Gregory, John T. 21:225
Gregory, John W. 10:55
Gregory, L. 3:83
Gregory, Landon 27:50
Gregory, Leroy 10:95
Gregory, London 9:131
Gregory, Major 9:131
Gregory, Norman 23:145
Gregory, Odgrs 27:47
Gregory, Oscar 4:66
Gregory, Owen 15:200
Gregory, Peter 17:176
Gregory, Ph. 15:4
Gregory, Philip 12:70
Gregory, R. 14:65
Gregory, R. P. 17:148
Gregory, Robert 9:100;
    22:335
Gregory, S. 11:280
Gregory, Stephen 17:148
Gregory, T. 11:60
Gregory, T. M. 9:81
Gregory, W. 8:63; 12:161
Gregory, W. E. 23:145
Gregory, W. M. 27:53
Gregory, Walter 17:337
Gregory, William 9:235;
    10:186; 18:421;
    26:162
Gregory, Willis 9:131;
    27:51
Gregory, Z. 1:131
Gregory, Z. H. 8:17;
    18:136
Grehoe, M. 3:83
Grei, John 11:126
Greiber, Henry J. 23:190
Greider, Joseph 4:28

Greig, Martin 18:306
Greig, Thomas 9:204
Greig, William 17:391
Greiggs, A. M. 4:27
Greightley, R. 19:227
Greightley, Robert 9:178
Greiner, Cyrus 11:303
Greiner, Edward 21:117
Greiner, G. O. 15:263
Greiner, George B. 16:133
Greiner, John 23:121
Greiner, N. 1:134
Greinzroerg, W. H. 4:28
Greira, Harman 26:145
Grell, John 19:166;
    21:254
Grellar, A. R. 12:85
Greller, A. R. 16:294
Grelon, Frederick 11:30
Greman, Fred 26:99
Gremm, Fred 18:307
Gremon, Joseph 10:55
Gren, Henry 17:248
Gren, W. M. 23:31
Grenable, Henry 23:32
Grenade, Charles 21:272
Grenchlune, George
    11:276
Grendrew, L. 25:178
Greneer, J. G. 11:280
Grenell, William H. 26:29
Grenenscheider, Henry
    23:32
Grenier, Michael 1:35
Greno, Miles 21:247
Grenon, Joseph 20:261
Grenough, Daniel S.
    11:100
Grenter, Thomas 22:512
Grenthouse, J. 3:83
Grere, G. 27:47
Grerling, Daniel 3:83
Grerson, A. R. 11:60
Grese, Christian 10:55
Greser, John 10:115;
    20:261
Gresham, F. C. 20:186
Gresham, James E. 23:67
Gresler, Julius 18:136
Gresman, Joseph W.
    22:79
Gresrate, C. P. 9:52
Gress, Jacob 25:178
Gress, Michael 1:37
Gress, Reuben 23:145
Gressell, T. J. 27:51
Gresser, M. 1:133
Gresseth, A. A. 23:107
Gresson, George W.
    24:101
Grestle, John 25:36

Greswell, Charles W. 7:50
Gretanda, A. 7:96
Gretner, C. 19:281
Gretner, Caspar 9:178
Gretsell, Andrew 11:148
Greutzmacher, Carl
    21:254
Grevet, George 26:161
Grew, Elias 10:115;
    20:261
Grew, I. 11:148
Grewell, Timothy A.
    23:88
Grewett, S. P. 3:83
Grey, A. H. 11:261
Grey, Alex 12:8
Grey, Alexander 4:27
Grey, Andy 26:124
Grey, August L. 15:200
Grey, Charles 11:31
Grey, Charles E. 22:33
Grey, David 9:81; 19:73
Grey, E. B. 4:27
Grey, Francis 7:68
Grey, G. H. 3:83
Grey, George C. 17:448
Grey, H. 7:13
Grey, Hasler S. 9:81
Grey, Henry 9:131; 12:23;
    17:280
Grey, J. 13:89; 27:49
Grey, J. C. 19:73
Grey, J. M. 11:240
Grey, James 17:154
Grey, Joel 21:338
Grey, John 1:36, 37;
    19:73; 22:301;
    23:145
Grey, John C. 24:185
Grey, John E. 18:238;
    26:31
Grey, Joseph 1:36
Grey, Joseph S. 19:73
Grey, L. 3:83
Grey, Louis 9:119
Grey, M. 25:37
Grey, Marshall 17:248
Grey, Moses 17:176
Grey, Moses F. 7:50
Grey, Nathan 22:194
Grey, Nelson 9:131
Grey, P. 3:83
Grey, Pat 3:83
Grey, Preston 11:203
Grey, R. L. 21:338
Grey, Richard 11:295
Grey, Silas 4:27
Grey, Thomas 3:83; 7:28,
    123
Grey, W. E. 15:55
Grey, W. H. 1:35

Grey, William 19:287; 24:78
Greyham, J. 11:322
Greys, L. 3:83
Greyson, Caesar 9:131
Greyson, D. 16:195
Greyson, John W. 9:131
Griago, Louis 18:426
Gribbons, Henry J. 15:55
Grice, David 23:67
Grice, Isaiah 20:261
Grice, N. M. 23:145
Grice, Samuel 15:151
Grichard, A. 21:338
Gridenwise, Peter 11:332
Grider, Frederick G. 17:52
Gridley, Alfred E. 18:346
Gridley, Benjamin F. 22:33
Gridley, Joseph 9:178
Gridley, L. B. 2:11; 25:34
Gridley, William 11:401; 16:152
Grieg, Martin 26:99
Grien, Armstrong 25:321
Griepger, J. 25:178
Grier, A. 6:31; 20:261; 25:321
Grier, A. L. 23:32
Grier, Absalom 10:55
Grier, Anthony 21:272
Grier, Francis 10:55
Grier, George 20:22
Grier, J. 3:84; 18:50
Grier, James A. 23:289
Grier, John W. 26:162
Grier, R. 1:133
Grier, R. M. 26:162
Grier, Samuel C. 11:319
Grier, Talmadge 5:51
Grier, Thomas G. 10:153; 19:166
Grier, W. 26:29
Grier, W. H. 9:81; 27:49
Griesel, John 22:115
Griesel, John D. 13:25
Grieser, William 24:177
Griesham, Wenderlin 9:97
Griff, John 14:173
Grifface, J. 14:173
Griffee, J. S. 22:252
Griffee, Sol. 23:313
Griffee, William W. 22:195
Griffen, Charles 22:523
Griffen, John 16:195
Griffen, Thomas 22:79
Griffeth, J. 25:178
Griffeth, Phelin 17:357
Griffeth, S. 3:84
Griffey, Calvin M. 14:173

Griffey, Cyrus M. 21:137
Griffey, George 22:79
Griffey, Richard 22:301
Griffey, Robert 22:252
Griffey, T. 22:513
Griffey, Thomas 22:301
Griffey, William T. 19:15
Griffic, William 17:427
Griffin, A. 1:37; 10:144
Griffin, Adna H. 20:48
Griffin, Alexander 11:408
Griffin, Alvin P. 12:23
Griffin, Asa H. 19:329
Griffin, B. 3:84
Griffin, Benjamin 17:496; 24:66
Griffin, Byron 10:145; 19:167
Griffin, C. 20:124
Griffin, C. L. 11:60
Griffin, Charles 6:29; 8:39; 18:238; 26:30, 161
Griffin, Charles D. 22:143
Griffin, Charles F. 25:37
Griffin, Charles M. 23:146
Griffin, Charles T. 22:143
Griffin, Charles W. 20:124
Griffin, Clarendon 9:7
Griffin, Columbus 23:146
Griffin, Cornelius 18:238; 26:30
Griffin, D. 3:84
Griffin, D. M. 17:176
Griffin, D. O. 11:30
Griffin, D. S. 14:65
Griffin, Daniel 12:167; 19:348; 27:53
Griffin, David 7:123; 21:338; 22:79
Griffin, David T. 16:35
Griffin, Denis 1:35
Griffin, E. 15:151
Griffin, Erastus C. 10:161; 19:167
Griffin, Fernando D. 21:137
Griffin, Frank 21:272; 22:352, 425
Griffin, Frank C. 15:200
Griffin, Frederick 9:178
Griffin, G. 3:84; 18:14
Griffin, G. M. 8:49
Griffin, G. W. 18:110
Griffin, George 6:7; 22:143
Griffin, George H. 16:35
Griffin, George W. 13:25
Griffin, H. 21:100

Griffin, H. C. 14:65; 24:89
Griffin, Henry 10:55; 12:23; 18:83
Griffin, Howard 8:63
Griffin, I. D. 21:163
Griffin, Isaac 22:252
Griffin, J. 1:38; 3:84; 13:89; 14:65; 16:195; 25:178; 27:49
Griffin, J. B. 3:84
Griffin, J. C. 3:84
Griffin, J. H. 9:52
Griffin, J. S. 16:35
Griffin, Jacob 22:252
Griffin, James 6:27; 9:154; 11:191; 20:261; 23:32, 179
Griffin, James A. 22:252
Griffin, James S. 21:70
Griffin, Jarvis M. 11:106
Griffin, John 3:84; 10:55; 17:415; 20:261; 22:335; 23:190, 270; 24:8, 152
Griffin, John A. 11:148
Griffin, John B. 11:332
Griffin, John J. 13:25
Griffin, John W. 14:66; 21:338
Griffin, Joseph 9:154; 10:55
Griffin, Julen 15:302
Griffin, Julien 16:195
Griffin, L. 22:161
Griffin, Lewis 7:77; 20:113
Griffin, Lewis B. 23:67
Griffin, Louis 25:297
Griffin, M. 7:96; 25:178
Griffin, M. H. 17:280
Griffin, M. W. 21:338
Griffin, Martin 24:194
Griffin, Michael 5:17; 11:181; 15:267
Griffin, Murray 18:83
Griffin, Murry 6:12
Griffin, N. 13:89; 14:11; 26:162
Griffin, N. B. 8:63; 26:161
Griffin, N. G. 1:97
Griffin, N. O. 21:338
Griffin, Nelson T. 21:137
Griffin, Noah 7:123
Griffin, O. 25:311
Griffin, P. 1:38; 17:191
Griffin, Patrick 7:96; 10:9; 11:295
Griffin, Polk 17:131; 24:194

Griffin, R. 3:84
Griffin, R. C. 9:143; 27:48
Griffin, R. H. 11:30
Griffin, Richard 22:252
Griffin, Robert 16:119;
　25:272
Griffin, S. 14:65
Griffin, Samuel 8:101;
　18:14
Griffin, Samuel L. 17:463;
　24:185
Griffin, Seth E. 18:103
Griffin, Silas 16:35
Griffin, Stephen 21:338
Griffin, T. 11:31
Griffin, T. S. 1:134
Griffin, Thomas 4:28;
　7:68; 14:173;
　18:190; 21:100
Griffin, Timothy 15:81
Griffin, W. 3:84; 9:242;
　23:283
Griffin, W. A. 3:84;
　17:148
Griffin, W. B. 9:178
Griffin, W. H. 1:132;
　11:125, 186
Griffin, Wedem 8:63
Griffin, William 3:84;
　12:49; 16:195;
　17:95; 25:178
Griffin, William W.
　21:137
Griffing, Allen 21:338
Griffing, J. C. 7:28
Griffing, James 18:14
Griffis, Henry O. 12:70
Griffit, John 21:338
Griffit, Joseph 23:67
Griffit, T. 9:52
Griffith, --- 9:81, 156
Griffith, A. 3:84; 14:66
Griffith, A. H. 14:173
Griffith, Albert A. 21:27
Griffith, Avery 15:319;
　19:73
Griffith, B. F. 8:49
Griffith, Barna 26:220
Griffith, Barney 9:236
Griffith, Belford 11:303
Griffith, Benjamin 10:55;
　20:261
Griffith, Benjamin F.
　18:421; 21:52
Griffith, C. 14:173
Griffith, Charles C. 20:35
Griffith, D. 8:49
Griffith, D. E. 14:173
Griffith, David 14:236;
　18:30; 21:138;
　22:252

Griffith, E. 12:70
Griffith, E. P. 3:84
Griffith, Edward 22:143
Griffith, F. 27:53
Griffith, Franklin 27:53
Griffith, George H. 27:51
Griffith, H. 14:66; 21:187
Griffith, H. P. 14:173
Griffith, Henry 15:17
Griffith, Hugh 8:106;
　13:25
Griffith, I. 18:67
Griffith, I. H. 19:253
Griffith, Isaac 9:178
Griffith, Isaac F. 18:395
Griffith, Isaac N. 20:261
Griffith, Isaac W. 10:55
Griffith, J. 1:133; 9:22;
　13:89; 15:67; 18:320;
　21:121; 25:178
Griffith, J. H. 3:84
Griffith, J. M. 10:148
Griffith, James 5:17
Griffith, James A. 4:28;
　23:98
Griffith, Jerry 22:301
Griffith, John 12:70;
　14:28; 19:73; 22:79;
　24:39, 194
Griffith, John D. 22:425
Griffith, John J. 11:125
Griffith, John R. 10:115;
　20:261
Griffith, John W. 9:214
Griffith, L. 1:132
Griffith, Lucas 22:79
Griffith, Michael 21:244
Griffith, Peter 22:33;
　26:211
Griffith, Philip L. 11:322
Griffith, R. 22:301
Griffith, R. P. 23:146
Griffith, Riely 22:33
Griffith, S. 2:11; 3:84;
　25:34
Griffith, S. F. 26:162
Griffith, Samuel 12:99;
　22:33
Griffith, Spencer 21:27
Griffith, Syrus 7:28
Griffith, T. G. 26:29
Griffith, T. M. 18:50
Griffith, Thomas 10:115;
　11:148; 20:261;
　21:338; 22:195
Griffith, W. 9:110; 13:89;
　14:11; 17:34
Griffith, W. H. 14:265
Griffith, Wallace 11:125
Griffith, Wesley 15:67

Griffith, William 12:153;
　21:27; 22:33, 234
Griffith, William H.
　14:173; 18:395
Griffith, Willis 25:36
Griffiths, F. O. 16:35
Griffiths, John C. 21:254
Griffiths, S. T. 7:72
Griffiths, William 18:344
Griffler, Daniel N. 11:240
Grifford, L. 3:84
Griffs, Henry O. 15:35
Griffy, Willis 17:433;
　24:158
Grifill, John 7:123
Grifin, James H. 17:287
Grifit, William 24:19
Griflow, Aaron 24:19
Grigg, Alexander 9:52
Grigg, Cassius 4:28
Grigg, John 25:178
Grigger, Nathaniel 9:119
Griggley, A. F. 19:270
Griggs, C. M. 17:433
Griggs, J. C. P. 12:153
Griggs, J. R. 9:52
Griggs, Jacob 5:39
Griggs, James S. 23:67
Griggs, John D. 17:79
Griggs, Luther 10:55;
　20:261
Griggs, Oscar 9:81
Griggs, Ransom C. 9:35
Griggs, Reuben 11:105
Griggs, Samuel M. 24:163
Griggs, T. 14:66
Griggs, V. 13:89
Griggs, W. P. 19:73
Griggs, William 11:30
Griggs, William H. 22:425
Griggsby, Jesse 22:513
Griggsley, A. F. 9:178
Griggsley, W. M. 10:179
Griggy, Nathaniel 27:51
Grignon, Charles 17:429;
　24:185
Grignon, Robert B.
　21:254
Grigs, W. P. 15:329
Grigsby, Alfred 17:131;
　24:194
Grigsby, Andrew 26:124
Grigsby, Charles 6:20;
　22:33
Grigsby, Enoch 21:272
Grigsby, Fedman 26:29
Grigsby, Jefferson 22:301
Grigsby, Joseph 22:166
Grigsby, L. 14:66
Grigsby, Oscar 11:203
Grigsby, Readman 9:81

Grigsby, William J.
    18:217
Grills, William 17:336
Grilly, Eldridge 12:55
Grilmartin, A. 3:84
Grim, A. 13:89
Grim, A. S. 1:132
Grim, Aaron 11:181
Grim, Adam W. 15:67
Grim, Albert 17:355
Grim, Charles 21:121
Grim, David H. 22:112
Grim, F. 25:276
Grim, George W. 22:79
Grim, Harrison 8:77
Grim, Henry 17:451;
    24:177
Grim, J. S. 9:143; 15:200;
    27:48
Grim, John H. 20:261
Grim, Joseph S. 21:70
Grim, Nicholas 23:179
Grim, Randall 11:203
Grim, Reuben 20:261
Grim, William 3:84
Grimand, Virgil 13:25
Grime, A. 12:166
Grimer, William 8:72
Grimes, --- 19:167; 20:56
Grimes, A. 15:351
Grimes, A. J. 26:162
Grimes, Absolm 21:201
Grimes, Adam 25:36
Grimes, Albert 19:73
Grimes, Charles S. 8:86
Grimes, D. 23:11
Grimes, Daniel 25:36
Grimes, David 17:317
Grimes, Ellis 6:28
Grimes, F. 1:37; 25:178
Grimes, G. W. 21:187
Grimes, J. 1:135
Grimes, J. A. 23:203
Grimes, J. H. 19:73
Grimes, James 6:28; 9:43;
    11:181; 17:148;
    18:50; 21:194;
    24:19; 26:123; 27:48,
    52
Grimes, James S. 26:145
Grimes, James W. 14:173
Grimes, John 9:43, 119;
    11:148; 13:25;
    21:272; 26:123;
    27:51
Grimes, John R. 7:123
Grimes, L. 25:34
Grimes, Levi 2:11
Grimes, Lewis 20:17
Grimes, M. M. 15:22
Grimes, Oliver 14:66

Grimes, P. 12:99
Grimes, R. H. B. 24:78
Grimes, Rufus 21:338
Grimes, Samuel 23:107
Grimes, T. O. 3:83
Grimes, Thomas 22:252
Grimes, W. 11:60; 25:272
Grimes, W. H. 11:262
Grimes, W. R. 18:238
Grimes, William 7:28;
    9:12, 22; 11:261;
    20:189
Grimes, William R. 26:31
Grimley, C. 25:178
Grimly, Patrick 18:136
Grimm, A. 14:11; 25:178
Grimm, Adam 5:17
Grimm, Charles 21:100
Grimm, Daniel 3:84
Grimm, John L. 15:151
Grimm, Ludwig 17:99
Grimm, Thomas 8:17
Grimm, William 21:100
Grimmage, B. 27:47
Grims, Demester 12:23
Grims, J. 21:121
Grims, William 3:84
Grimsby, Charles 5:39
Grimshaw, J. N. 1:37
Grimshaw, Joseph 27:51
Grimshaw, S. 15:200
Grimshaw, Thomas
    13:135; 19:346
Grimsley, Abraham
    18:444
Grimsley, Harrison 27:53
Grimstaff, George 9:52
Grimstaff, Greene 7:68
Grimstone, Arthur 14:173
Grimwood, Samuel H.
    19:167
Grinan, F. 27:49
Grinder, E. F. 21:338
Grinder, Jeremiah 4:28
Grinder, W. H. 14:298;
    17:479; 27:52
Grinder, William 15:283
Grinderod, James 25:178
Grindle, Daniel H. 7:96
Grindle, Harvey 7:96;
    21:338
Grindle, Otis 25:178
Grindley, Joseph 19:227
Grindling, A. 1:131
Grindstaff, J. 18:367
Grindstaff, William N.
    22:252
Grindstaff, Wilson 22:252
Grine, Reuben 10:115
Grinem, Thomas 18:137
Griner, C. 1:134

Griner, G. 13:89
Griner, G. A. 14:26
Griner, George E. 17:79
Griner, George W. 21:52
Griner, J. 1:37, 134
Griner, J. N. 25:178
Griner, James 11:84
Griner, Jonathan 27:51
Griner, Peter 8:18; 22:79;
    26:160
Griner, Samuel F. 17:34
Gringer, J. 25:178
Gringer, Leonard C.
    11:332
Grinley, Henry 23:146
Grinn, T. 1:132
Grinn, William 26:162
Grinnell, Edward 16:152
Grinnell, John 3:84; 27:53
Grinnell, John G. 15:200
Grinnell, W. H. 9:81
Grinnells, O. 11:147
Grinnels, A. 13:89
Grinner, Joseph 7:28
Grinnett, Peter 11:203
Grinnul, N. 1:134
Grinstead, F. R. 3:84
Grinstead, Francis M.
    21:225
Grinstead, J. P. 17:280
Grinstead, James 23:98
Grintiney, J. 14:66
Grinum, Frederick 22:195
Gripey, S. 7:50
Gripon, M. 26:30
Grippen, A. Judson
    22:279
Gripple, Henry 13:25
Grippman, J. 3:83
Gripps, Frederick 21:254
Grisaman, James M. 17:34
Grisby, W. M. 18:175
Griscom, W. B. 22:195
Grise, H. 13:89
Griselle, Moses K. 22:425
Grisen, A. 11:326
Grisham, Richard 22:252
Grisham, S. 25:178
Grisham, William H.
    22:33
Grisieham, John 21:338
Grisler, William 15:200
Grison, C. 3:84
Grisot, Thomas 11:60
Grispom, M. 18:238
Griss, John 14:173
Grissam, William 22:335
Grissel, Henry 23:309
Grissell, John 17:176
Grissible, Balthesar 22:33
Grissins, C. 1:134

Grissitt, J. G. 21:338
Grisso, J. 15:258
Grister, Philip 24:19
Gristian, Silas 11:203
Gristie, Andrew 13:77
Gristold, A. M. 11:149
Griswald, F. 16:95
Griswald, James H. 16:95
Griswell, John 14:173
Griswell, Thomas J. 3:84
Griswell, W. H. 3:84
Griswold, A. 15:200;
    25:34
Griswold, B. F. 3:84
Griswold, Cyrus 25:178
Griswold, E. 2:11; 22:510
Griswold, E. A. 15:319
Griswold, Elliott 10:161
Griswold, Ephraim 18:323
Griswold, Erastus A.
    19:73
Griswold, Francis 21:27
Griswold, Fred 23:283
Griswold, Gabe 9:207
Griswold, George W.
    12:153
Griswold, Guy E. 22:143
Griswold, Henry 9:220
Griswold, Henry A. 12:23
Griswold, Henry E.
    18:367
Griswold, Irwin 8:114
Griswold, J. 17:154;
    25:178
Griswold, Jacob 22:301
Griswold, John 5:17
Griswold, John C. 13:25
Griswold, Joseph 25:36
Griswold, L. 16:147
Griswold, Luther H.
    22:462
Griswold, M. H. 14:66
Griswold, Merrit D. 4:28
Griswold, Moses N.
    21:100
Griswold, Noah 18:334;
    22:508
Griswold, Preston 15:302;
    16:195
Griswold, Rufus 11:105
Griswold, S. 1:132; 14:66
Griswold, S. A. 25:297
Griswold, S. Y. 7:28
Griswold, Stephen A. 7:80
Griswold, Thomas 3:84
Griswold, W. M. 14:173
Griswold, Walter B. S.
    18:444
Griswold, William H.
    22:404
Griswold, Z. P. 3:84

Grites, H. 11:340
Gritton, G. 3:84
Gritton, M. 3:84
Gritzer, A. 24:111
Griven, J. P. 21:194
Grizzle, Azariah 22:252
Grizzle, John H. 27:48
Grizzle, William A. 24:39
Gro---, G. 20:56
Groadway, Martin 12:23
Groash, C. 10:211
Groat, A. 14:11
Groat, A. J. 19:253
Groat, Andrew J. 9:178
Groat, Ferdinand 9:102
Groat, John William 16:8
Groat, Peter 10:115;
    20:261
Groat, William H. 24:93
Grobb, Ulrich 18:307
Grobb, Ulrick 26:98
Grobe, Jacob 7:96
Groben, Newman 9:178
Grober, Herman 22:11
Grober, L. 19:253
Grobet, Augustus 13:25
Grobis, Chris 13:110
Groblh, W. H. 23:32
Groce, G. W. 9:52
Groce, George 10:172
Groce, J. 25:178
Grochel, Henry 1:35
Grocher, G. 25:36
Groda, Conrad 10:115;
    20:261
Grodge, James L. 8:106
Groemet, --- 2:11
Groenendyke, Amos
    22:425
Groenendyke, Henry
    21:225
Groeper, John 21:117
Groesbeck, George W.
    21:70
Groesbuck, C. A. 26:99
Groesier, G. 9:110
Groesot, Charles 16:154
Groesser, Thomas 23:190
Groff, Charles 5:51
Groff, G. 14:66
Groff, J. F. 23:146
Groff, Leo 13:25
Groff, Samuel 25:321
Groff, William 20:261
Groff'h, A. 13:89
Groffen, O. 18:233
Groft, Isaac 7:96
Grogan, D. 3:84
Grogan, Frank 20:151
Grogan, J. 13:110
Grogan, James 18:272

Grogan, John 21:10
Grogan, Robert 24:19
Grogan, Thomas 10:55;
    20:261
Grogan, William E.
    26:162
Groge, George 19:167
Grogg, Joseph 15:87
Grogg, Nathaniel 23:146
Grogg, Patterson G.
    22:252
Groggins, Pesh 17:176
Groht, Henry 7:68
Groins, S. 25:179
Groissant, G. 25:35
Grokin, Samuel 10:55
Grolevant, C. J. 27:48
Grolon, Peter 9:204
Grolter, C. S. 19:281
Gromer, Isaac G. 23:67
Gromer, Peter W. 21:338
Gromes, John 17:203
Gron, Philander 25:36
Gronbuck, C. A. 18:307
Grone, George W. 10:55
Gronefield, Seward
    21:254
Gronekle, Lewis 26:123
Groner, Charles F. 25:179
Groner, H. 3:84
Gronna, Leopold 21:338
Gronnie, Charles 26:29
Gronshaw, C. 3:84
Groo, John 17:143
Groom, Joseph 11:30
Groom, Michael 7:123
Groom, S. C. 20:261
Groom, Shadrach C.
    10:55
Groom, W. H. 25:179
Groom, William H. 5:17
Grooman, Charles 20:174
Grooman, W. 21:201
Groome, Ferdinand
    11:223
Groomer, Solomon 13:57
Grooms, Benjamin F. 7:13
Grooms, H. 26:29
Grooms, James 11:203;
    23:146
Grooms, John 14:315;
    22:301
Grooms, Judah L. 19:277
Grooms, Michael 21:338
Grooms, Richard 21:338
Grooms, Samuel 22:301
Grooms, William 17:393
Grooms, William R.
    22:301
Groosman, L. 1:133
Groosner, Charles 4:28

Groot, J. P. 20:261
Groots, Edward 25:37
Groover, Charles 11:148; 12:23
Groovis, Benjamin F. 20:48
Groovus, Judah L. 9:178
Grophard, Peter 19:73
Grorger, J. 14:173
Grosbeck, G. W. 8:49
Grosbernar, Silas N. 19:73
Groscaust, S. 3:84
Grose, Henry L. 4:28
Grose, William D. 17:65
Groser, --- 15:35
Groser, Augustus 13:127
Grosfent, F. 1:35
Groshneld, Jacob 18:50
Groshueld, Jacob 10:148
Groskeits, Frederick 22:166
Grosmeyer, John 18:338
Grosner, John 13:25
Gross, A 25:179
Gross, Abraham 20:97
Gross, Adam 14:66
Gross, Benjamin 19:45
Gross, C. 1:132, 133; 3:84; 26:161
Gross, Charles 13:25; 16:370
Gross, Charles H. 20:124
Gross, D. 17:273
Gross, Daniel W. 21:70
Gross, David L. 19:73
Gross, E. 2:11; 25:37
Gross, Ed 26:161
Gross, Edward 17:110
Gross, Edward G. 11:148
Gross, Fred 25:321
Gross, Frederick 9:165; 18:206; 19:73
Gross, George 9:102
Gross, George E. 21:338
Gross, Green 16:195
Gross, H. 14:298; 17:479; 27:52
Gross, Henry A. 4:28
Gross, Henry R. 9:12
Gross, Isaac 4:28; 15:200; 18:206
Gross, J. 3:84; 14:298; 15:200; 17:480; 27:52
Gross, J. J. 14:66
Gross, Jacob 12:49
Gross, James 9:81; 17:271; 26:29
Gross, James A. 23:67
Gross, James W. 17:248

Gross, John 3:84; 13:25; 21:338; 25:179
Gross, John T. 8:72
Gross, Joseph 1:35; 3:84
Gross, Julius 20:113
Gross, L. 1:37, 133
Gross, Lewis 9:35
Gross, M. 20:146
Gross, Michael 8:18; 18:137
Gross, N. 16:195
Gross, Nathaniel 9:9
Gross, Philip 14:173
Gross, R. 25:179
Gross, Richard 9:52
Gross, Robert 5:39
Gross, S. 3:84; 8:63
Gross, Samuel 3:84
Gross, Stephen 25:179
Gross, Thomas 18:83
Gross, W. D. D. 8:106
Gross, W. M. 2:11; 10:205
Gross, William 9:35; 17:440; 18:293; 24:152
Gross, William M. 25:37
Grossbeck, Charles 4:28
Grosse, W. O. 1:135
Grosser, C. 23:117
Grosser, Charles 23:289
Grossett, Charles 12:58
Grossfriend, William H. 19:253
Grossinan, John 10:115
Grossmaier, W. D. 14:173
Grossman, F. 9:178; 19:253
Grossman, John 20:261
Grossman, Nicholas 14:66
Grossmeyer, John 9:102
Grossner, Samuel H. 25:36
Grosvenor, Joseph A. 15:3
Grosvenor, S. N. 13:64
Groth, A. 14:11
Groth, Frederick 15:201
Grothcopp, John 23:32
Grother, H. 10:28; 19:302
Grotoms, Ky 27:48
Grotomsky, --- 9:143
Grotstaff, Riley 9:220
Grotte, Carl 14:173
Grotten, A. 15:326
Grotten, H. 19:73
Grotter, Hiram 20:3
Grotter, Thomas S. 9:178
Grotuant, G. N. 1:36
Grotz, A. 20:261
Grotz, Antonie 10:55

Grotzer, Charles 8:18; 18:137
Groubeck, C. A. 9:22
Groucher, J. 3:84
Grougan, T. 25:179
Groupe, D. 3:84
Grouse, C. 1:36
Grouse, G. 3:84
Grouse, John 14:66
Grout, M. S. 1:36
Grout, O. 13:89
Grouter, M. 15:289
Groutz, John 18:334
Grouz, Jacob 11:322
Grov, Michael 18:293
Grove, Abselon 13:25
Grove, Elias 11:412
Grove, F. 14:66
Grove, George 22:480
Grove, George J. 23:146
Grove, George W. 15:87; 20:261
Grove, H. H. 15:318
Grove, J. W. 18:293; 26:99
Grove, John 5:17, 39; 25:179
Grove, John B. 20:261
Grove, John S. 21:339
Grove, Levi 23:146
Grove, Michael 26:99
Grove, Perry 22:404
Grove, S. W. 12:92; 14:66; 16:294
Grove, W. C. 1:133
Grove, William P. 12:64; 15:67
Grovemet, --- 25:35
Groven, Bryan 25:179
Groven, James 3:84
Grovenburg, Adolphus 24:62
Grovendyke, G. E. 7:96
Grovendyke, G. G. 21:338
Grover, C. 9:143; 27:49
Grover, Dennis 16:35
Grover, Dilbert 9:214
Grover, Fayette 27:144
Grover, Filmore 7:123
Grover, Francis 7:28
Grover, George 12:153
Grover, George F. 14:66
Grover, George H. 12:23
Grover, Gilbert 21:339
Grover, Harras 23:32
Grover, I. 21:121
Grover, J. 15:201
Grover, J. A. 15:298
Grover, J. C. 21:339
Grover, Jacob 25:179

Grover, James 3:84; 14:173
Grover, James H. 15:331; 19:73
Grover, Jeremiah 27:52
Grover, John 17:20; 18:136; 21:339
Grover, John B. 22:33
Grover, John C. 13:25
Grover, L. G. 11:240
Grover, L. M. 26:31
Grover, Lewis 22:424
Grover, Lyman 14:173
Grover, N. 1:94
Grover, Oscar 19:73
Grover, P. 15:201
Grover, Peter 17:91
Grover, R. L. 25:298
Grover, Riley L. 7:80
Grover, S. M. 18:238
Grover, Sam C. 17:80
Grover, Samuel 12:70; 15:27
Grover, Stephen A. 25:269
Grover, T. F. 13:60
Grover, W. 1:132
Grover, William W. 1:37
Groves, --- 21:216
Groves, A. T. 3:84
Groves, Alexander 25:269
Groves, Archibald 22:79
Groves, Benjamin 11:203
Groves, Charles 22:79
Groves, Charles A. 5:17
Groves, Daniel 21:194
Groves, George 22:497
Groves, George M. V. 22:195
Groves, George W. 23:67
Groves, Isaac 11:61
Groves, J. 16:195
Groves, J. F. 1:36
Groves, J. H. 1:134
Groves, J. L. 19:167
Groves, Jacob W. 20:124
Groves, James 24:19
Groves, Joel W. 1:34
Groves, John 8:17
Groves, John B. 10:55
Groves, L. 3:84
Groves, M. H. 9:22
Groves, Nathan 23:146
Groves, P. F. 12:153
Groves, Thomas J. 19:167
Groves, William A. 23:146
Groves, William C. 21:254
Groves, William H. 22:143

Grow, Charles H. 21:339
Grow, David 9:35
Grow, Henry A. 10:55
Grow, J. B. 15:318; 19:73
Grow, John 14:66
Grow, John H. 23:146
Grow, Lewis F. 23:190
Grow, Matthew 25:243
Grow, Samuel 4:28; 17:321
Growas, Peter 25:35
Growell, Joseph J. 24:50
Grower, Benjamin H. 22:33
Grower, Emanuel 27:51
Growes, Edwin 1:35
Growhurst, Henry H. 21:70
Grown, Martin 17:242
Growr, Daniel 27:53
Grows, G. E. 1:133
Groyer, Charles B. 17:432; 24:152
Groynn, Thomas 22:462
Grub, G. R. 23:146
Grub, Jacob 23:121
Grubb, Abram 22:195
Grubb, Alfred 19:302
Grubb, B. 24:78
Grubb, David 11:423
Grubb, DeWitt C. 17:52
Grubb, Ephraim 22:301
Grubb, G. W. 14:281
Grubb, George W. 14:269
Grubb, J. 7:57
Grubb, J. L. 16:294
Grubb, Jacob 1:35
Grubb, Jedediah 23:99
Grubb, Joe 18:175
Grubb, John 11:148; 17:404; 21:195
Grubb, Joseph 15:201
Grubb, M. 19:302
Grubb, M. P. 3:85
Grubb, Myron 11:30
Grubb, Nelson 25:333
Grubbs, Abram 22:195
Grubbs, Duren 22:122
Grubbs, G. W. 9:144; 27:47
Grubbs, J. 3:85
Grubbs, Joe 10:186
Grubbs, John 23:313
Grubbs, John S. 22:234
Grubbs, Joseph T. 9:22; 18:307
Grubbs, M. 10:28
Grubbs, S. 14:173, 256
Grube, Barney 17:259
Gruber, Charles 22:279
Gruber, Henry 9:161

Gruber, John 4:28
Grubera, Henry 27:53
Gruberry, Pier 7:124
Grubs, George W. 11:148
Grubs, Joseph 11:408
Grubs, Joseph T. 26:99
Gruby, Stephen 11:148
Gruder, F. 3:84
Grudgings, William 22:33
Grudman, W. 25:179
Gruell, Thomas C. 20:40
Gruesbeck, Omer 11:61
Gruesbeck, Walter 11:61
Grueter, J. 18:307; 26:99
Grugan, Henry 5:17
Gruglan, Silas 11:387
Gruin, S. 13:89
Gruitt, J. 14:11
Gruler, Ernest 11:148
Grum, Columbus 10:55
Grum, H. H. 9:97
Grum, J. F. 9:52
Grum, James 21:272
Grum, Lewis 18:238; 26:30
Grum, William 3:84
Grumaker, Joseph 10:115; 20:261
Grumburg, Eze 17:446
Grumman, Frederick A. 22:399
Grummer, Francis 9:119
Grummitt, Stanford 22:301
Grummon, William 24:50
Grummond, George W. 19:329
Grummond, Reuben B. 22:143
Grummonds, Andrew 7:96
Grumon, Francis 27:51
Grumons, Philander 19:16
Grumsey, J. 22:352
Grumshey, C. P. 27:49
Grumus, Lewis 22:301
Grun, Madison 24:101
Grun, R. 3:84
Grun, Robert 11:326
Grunard, Daniel 7:124
Grunbles, P. B. 16:35
Grund, C. 27:144
Grundier, J. 9:110
Grunds, L. 3:84
Grundy, Alexander M. 22:33
Grundy, Henry S. 18:276
Grundy, Jacob 6:22; 18:83
Grundy, John 19:16
Grundy, L. W. 10:115; 20:261
Grundy, R. G. 3:85

Grundy, Samuel 11:203
Gruner, Matthias 9:178;
  19:270
Gruner, Peter W. 7:124
Grunion, Moses 22:79
Grunl, A. 25:179
Grunley, James 3:84
Grunnell, Charles 9:81
Grunnell, John 3:84
Grunon, John N. 5:17
Grunston, David 12:23
Grunsving, Love 27:51
Grur, Riley 4:28
Grusel, Gabriel 10:55
Grushost, E. 14:66
Grussell, G. 20:261
Gruster, Peter 17:80
Grutham, James 21:339
Gruthier, Peter 24:63
Grutte, G. 3:84
Grutz, James 20:8
Grutzell, Durutz N. 18:67
Gruur, J. 10:148
Gruver, G. W. 27:47
Gruver, Joseph 10:55
Gryon, Henry 8:114
Gschwend, Francis 4:28
Gteinet, G. W. 18:50
Guain, Michael 22:335
Guain, William 19:16
Gualb, J. H. 19:302
Gualy, A. 18:367
Guant, A. 3:85
Guard, Hiram T. 11:387
Guard, Samuel 13:25
Guard, Weston 21:138
Guarly, John 15:201
Gubb, E. H. 13:89
Gubbins, Patrick 26:30
Gubbons, Patrick 18:238
Gubby, G. W. 21:52
Gubener, George 9:52
Gubera, Jose H. 8:121
Gubtail, Ephraim 21:339
Gucinzins, G. 11:293
Gude, Henry 9:52
Gudemann, K. 7:74
Guder, Littleton 26:161
Guderman, R. 25:298
Gudgeon, Samuel 7:50
Gudny, W. 18:293
Gudon, Joel 17:165
Gudy, David 9:165
Gue, Isaac 8:18; 26:161
Gue, W. L. 1:132
Gue---, Isaac 18:137
Guegue, Napoleon 1:36
Guehring, John 12:23
Gueiler, F. 14:66
Guelck, Conrad 14:130
Guender, John 25:36

Guep, David 17:294
Guerin, Robert M. 10:116;
  20:261
Guerin, William 18:137
Guernsey, Birney 11:126
Guernsey, George H.
  12:23
Guerting, James H. 26:161
Gueserwich, John 17:20
Guesford, Davis 4:28
Guess, A. 16:370
Guess, Jacob R. 20:40
Guest, A. 8:69
Guest, Alonzo 22:404
Guest, Frank B. 8:106
Guest, G. 14:66
Guest, Henry C. 20:189
Guest, James 22:79
Guest, John R. 17:418;
  24:158
Guest, Joseph 11:262
Guest, Martin V. 11:326
Guestry, James H. 18:137
Guff, Erastus S. 4:28
Guff, William M. 25:179
Guffe, Peter 20:107
Guffey, Fidela C. 20:88
Guffey, H. 17:148
Guffey, J. 11:293
Guffey, J. L. 17:203
Guffey, James C. 20:261
Guffey, R. 3:85
Guffey, W. C. 11:326
Guffey, William 8:106
Guffin, George 20:262
Guffin, George E. 10:116
Guffy, Charles 20:262
Guffy, Eli 22:195
Guffy, James C. 10:116
Guffy, William R. 10:55;
  20:262
Gufton, Frederick 19:253
Gug, John 14:11
Gugett, A. 1:132
Gugette, L. 1:37
Guggenheim, E. 27:47
Gugle, John W. 11:31
Gugremus, Louis 10:55
Guhe, William 19:45
Guhlie, E. 24:39
Guiatt, J. 14:321
Guiatt, Joseph 23:113
Guiaw, S. 14:11
Guibert, George 22:79
Guidley, J. H. 18:50
Guidry, Joseph 21:339
Guiher, I. 25:179
Guild, C. 3:85
Guild, C. L. 20:133
Guild, Ferdinand E. 17:70
Guild, G. 1:134

Guild, James 3:223;
  17:504
Guild, Robert 7:96
Guild, William 12:161
Guilds, H. 1:37
Guile, A. L. 3:85
Guile, John 15:201; 21:52
Guile, Martin 21:272
Guiles, A. 1:133
Guiles, A. A. 22:463
Guiles, James E. 10:116;
  20:262
Guilett, Samuel 9:95
Guilford, G. 19:227
Guilford, H. W. 9:22
Guilfoyle, Daniel 14:173
Guillermo, Pedro 25:37
Guillott, Peter 17:65
Guim, Jonathan 9:119
Guin, Levi 21:13
Guin, M. 21:13
Guinau, John 7:28
Guinby, L. C. 3:85
Guiner, John 13:25
Guiniss, David 1:35
Guinn, Caleb F. 7:96
Guinn, F. 26:29
Guinn, Henry 7:124
Guinn, Jacob 11:412
Guinn, John 8:49; 10:28;
  18:137, 276; 19:302
Guinn, John W. 21:100
Guinn, M. 17:291
Guinn, W. C. 8:18
Guinn, William 8:18;
  24:19
Guinness, W. W. 25:179
Guinnip, William 22:79
Guinor, John 16:35
Guinor, S. H. 27:49
Guion, Edward 10:170
Guion, Joseph 15:289
Guiott, Joseph 14:315
Guire, Burse 22:33
Guire, F. 20:262
Guire, T. 15:342; 16:370
Guire, Thomas M. 8:18
Guirm, James P. 9:220
Guisart, W. 11:241
Guisbeck, A. 1:36
Guise, H. 14:173
Guise, William H. 23:67
Guist, J. W. 3:85
Gulbertson, J. H. 18:67
Gulbranson, Peter 19:340
Gulclave, A. D. 23:268
Gulclave, John 23:268
Guler, Andrew 23:88
Gulick, Edward D. 21:254
Gulick, Robert 19:253
Gulick, S. 15:201

Gulick, W. O. 26:162
Gulick, William 10:9;
20:23
Gulifogle, Patrick 7:57
Gulk, P. 3:85
Gull, Henry 14:66
Gull, John Z. 24:152
Gull, Thomas 7:96
Gulla, James 10:116;
20:262
Gulle--, D. D. 20:56
Gullett, A. 3:85
Gullett, Daniel 24:166
Gulley, Moses 21:195
Gulleyhone, Rowsey 4:28
Gulliger, Frank 10:53
Gulliland, James 24:181
Gullington, Lewis B.
20:95
Gullip, Washington 5:39
Gulliver, George 27:50
Gullory, Arusmo 9:178
Gullson, William 3:85
Gullum, Henry 18:293
Gully, Josiah 17:409;
22:451
Gully, W. R. 11:280
Gulore, Henry 26:99
Guls, Robert 9:178
Gulse, T. E. 3:85
Gulvere, David 3:85
Guly, David 10:209
Gulz, --- 3:85
Gulzer, Moses 9:43
Gum, Burrell G. 12:8
Gum, Cyrus 5:17
Gum, Harrison N. 22:425
Gum, Harvey 15:201
Gum, J. 20:146
Gum, L. 19:253
Gumbert, A. 3:85
Gumbo, William 18:238;
26:30
Gumekle, Lewis 9:43
Gumion, James 8:18
Gumly, Wiley 9:35
Gump, H. 1:132
Gumple, Earnest 4:28
Gumps, George W. 19:16
Gums, John A. 26:162
Gums, William 15:201
Gun, Abraham 24:194
Gun, Alexander M. 4:28
Gun, Perry 23:309
Gunahan, --- 3:85
Gunbell, William D. 8:18
Guncannon, Thomas
25:36
Gundalock, F. 3:85
Gunder, James 18:412
Gunder, Mathew 22:234

Gunder, William 19:73
Gunderman, William
14:315
Gunderson, Andrew
10:116; 20:262
Gunderson, H. 3:85
Gunderson, Knud 21:254
Gunderson, M. 9:144
Gunderson, Miles 19:331
Gundert, W. 12:80;
25:179
Gundlach, Frederick
23:190
Gundly, J. 3:85
Gundolah, Philip 10:116
Gundolph, Philip 20:262
Gundry, Henry 9:66
Gundry, John E. 15:25
Gundry, Randolph 24:111
Gundunn, Joshua 19:16
Gundy, J. 23:146
Gundy, J. H. 9:22; 18:307;
26:98
Gundy, Wiley 26:99
Gunehode, James 15:278
Gunens, Neil 15:289
Guner, L. 19:253
Gunery, C. 3:85
Gunion, James 18:137
Gunkel, George 13:25
Gunn, A. 22:301
Gunn, A. O. 17:265
Gunn, Aaron C. 21:27
Gunn, Abraham 17:131
Gunn, Alexander 3:85;
21:203
Gunn, Almon 22:479
Gunn, Calvin 3:85
Gunn, Charles 17:308
Gunn, Coleman 17:176
Gunn, Columbus 20:262
Gunn, Daniel 17:95
Gunn, George 9:144;
27:48
Gunn, Harrison 11:387
Gunn, John 20:262;
23:190
Gunn, Leonard 17:265
Gunn, M. 14:11
Gunn, Morrison 22:79
Gunn, Nela K. 25:37
Gunn, Ouveris 22:519
Gunn, Pleasant 10:176
Gunn, Pleasent 19:167
Gunn, Simpson 17:433;
24:158
Gunn, T. 1:35
Gunnels, Daniel 4:28
Gunner, James 7:28
Gunner, John 16:195
Gunnerman, M. 27:49

Gunnery, Calvin 27:50
Gunnett, Michael 24:39
Gunnier, Elias 13:110
Gunnigle, James 14:174
Gunning, Charles 20:124
Gunning, Hiram 19:16
Gunning, Leonard 12:23
Gunnings, John 14:174
Gunnison, Francis 16:294
Gunnison, G. A. 1:36
Gunsaeel, Charles 11:147
Gunsatius, S. 25:37
Gunsatius, Samuel 2:11
Gunsaulis, John 21:206
Gunsaulus, Samuel 27:51
Gunsenhouser, John 11:61
Gunsolus, Abner 9:214
Gunson, Samuel 2:11
Gunsteall, Thomas 21:339
Guntel, Martin 21:254
Guntelfinger, Daniel 7:96
Gunter, D. 27:49
Gunter, George N. 22:79
Gunter, Henry 19:73
Gunter, James B. 9:220;
18:367
Gunter, Jesse 22:33
Gunter, John 3:85
Gunter, R. C. 3:85
Gunter, William 4:28
Gunter, William S. 11:219
Gunther, --- 15:35
Gunther, Daniel 9:144
Gunther, David 10:17
Gunther, Henry 7:28
Gunther, I. G. 9:144
Gunther, J. G. 27:48
Gunther, Martin 17:448
Gunther, Peter 17:61
Gunther, Samuel 10:55;
20:262
Gunther, William 15:201
Guntner, John 25:36
Gunton, James 7:50
Guntt, F. H. 11:106
Guolt, J. A. 10:28
Guppe, William 10:55;
20:262
Guptell, Irons 7:96
Guptell, L. P. 21:339
Guptill, John P. 24:63
Guptill, William S. 9:119
Gur---, H---n 15:201
Gurde, John 23:190
Gurdy, William H. 26:123
Gure, James 19:270
Gurerson, G. W. 3:85
Gurgent, G. 1:132
Gurick, Jacob 23:240
Gurl, William 4:28
Gurley, --- 5:51

Gurley, A. 26:161
Gurley, Addison 17:80
Gurley, Charles 25:321
Gurley, J. D. 18:137
Gurley, James 25:179
Gurley, John 27:52
Gurley, Saban 10:55; 20:262
Gurley, W. H. 19:237
Gurley, William H. 9:43; 18:190
Gurlin, Benjamin 11:61
Gurname, B. S. 3:85
Gurnee, Marcenus 20:192
Gurner, John 7:28
Gurner, Marion 13:110
Gurnesey, Seth W. 22:143
Gurney, A. J. 21:339
Gurney, Charles 16:85
Gurney, D. 1:133
Gurney, George W. 10:116; 20:262
Gurney, H. C. 23:146
Gurney, J. F. 3:85
Gurney, Jacob 7:96
Gurney, John 9:234; 21:203
Gurney, Richard 13:64; 19:73
Gurney, S. S. 1:37
Gurnish, J. 1:133
Gurnsey, C. 13:110
Gurnsey, Charles 24:101
Gurnsey, James O. 25:179
Gurnsey, Samuel 22:33
Gurr, Henry 11:401
Gurree, Feliciana 9:207; 18:67
Gurrin, Frederick 13:25
Gurrode, James 18:421
Gurry, J. 25:37
Gursler, I. 14:174
Gurss, James 8:106
Gurtes, Samuel 19:281
Gurther, Abner 19:16
Gurtler, George 14:174
Gury, A. 14:66
Gushom, Jos. 22:501
Guslenburg, August 8:18; 18:137
Gusler, William 23:32
Gusotte, Benjamin 27:52
Gusset, S. 25:179
Gussey, Edward 12:23
Gussman, William 13:25
Gusston, Simon 22:302
Gust, Adam 14:174
Gustafin, Charles 8:72
Gustell, Aaron 10:8
Gusten, C. R. 9:144

Gusten, H. C. 12:64; 15:67
Gustiff, J. 25:179
Gustin, Amos W. 10:116; 20:262
Gustin, C. R. 27:48
Gustin, Charles S. 17:354
Gustin, F. 14:11; 16:268
Gustin, George 13:110
Gustin, I. S. 15:342
Gustin, J. S. 16:370
Gustin, Jehiel 8:86
Gustin, John M. 11:61
Gustin, Samuel 21:339
Gustin, V. 14:66
Gustliff, John 5:39
Guston, William 10:172
Gustus, Charles A. 23:260
Gustus, John H. 19:73
Gutel, Samuel M. 8:86
Gutelins, J. S. 16:119
Gutemuth, Frederick 15:17
Guter, Joseph 19:289
Guth, H. 3:85
Guthard, Julius 21:339
Guthbrod, Lorenz 23:113
Guthens, L. 15:201
Gutherry, Shader K. 22:252
Guthorel, John J. 23:146
Guthpeck, M. 26:31
Guthpeet, M. 9:81
Guthray, Benjamin 19:73
Guthree, E. 26:211
Guthrey, M. H. 19:16
Guthrie, Amos 11:223
Guthrie, Anderson 9:220; 18:367
Guthrie, Calvin 22:16
Guthrie, Daniel B. 22:79
Guthrie, E. W. 9:144
Guthrie, G. S. 23:263
Guthrie, H. 24:19
Guthrie, Henry 18:238; 26:31
Guthrie, J. 3:85
Guthrie, J. A. 11:322
Guthrie, J. T. 14:174
Guthrie, J. W. 16:119
Guthrie, James H. 11:147
Guthrie, John B. 22:173
Guthrie, Joseph K. 23:146
Guthrie, Joseph P. 21:52
Guthrie, Joshua 18:217
Guthrie, Martin 17:410; 22:122
Guthrie, Robert 13:64; 19:73
Guthrie, S. 19:167

Guthrie, S. W. 1:132
Guthrie, Samuel M. 7:28
Guthrie, Seymour 22:302
Guthrie, W. B. 3:85
Guthrie, W. H. 1:35
Guthrie, W. L. 5:17; 25:179
Guthrie, William 9:207; 12:163; 17:34
Guthrill, J. W. 12:153
Gutieres, Azaphite 6:20
Gutlebb, Michael 8:106
Gutman, N. 14:174
Gutridge, Alvin 11:147
Gutry, Henry 27:53
Gutscher, Jacob 10:161; 19:167
Gutsel, John 16:370
Gutterman, J. 3:85
Gutterson, G. 3:85
Guttry, B. 21:52
Gutzer, Moses 26:123
Gutzler, Jacob 15:55
Guva, John 18:30
Guy, A. 25:179
Guy, Alex 25:298
Guy, Alexander 7:77
Guy, Andrew 11:340
Guy, Elijah 7:124; 17:400
Guy, G. W. 20:124
Guy, J. 16:268
Guy, Jackson 22:425
Guy, John 6:27; 18:83
Guy, John J. 22:195
Guy, Joseph 6:25
Guy, M. S. 19:270
Guy, Morgan S. 9:178
Guy, William F. 12:153
Guyer, Ephraim 16:154
Guyer, F. 3:85
Guyer, John M. 2:11; 25:37
Guyer, S. 7:50
Guyer, Timothy 13:125
Guyer, William 3:85
Guyger, N. 13:110
Guyiniss, Franklin 8:86
Guyld, A. 16:195
Guyman, John 22:33
Guyman, William P. 11:60
Guynn, John 8:18
Guyton, B. 9:144; 27:49
Guyton, John 10:55; 20:262
Guyton, William 10:116; 20:262
Guzze, Hugh 12:95
Guzzle, Jason 10:151
Gwaye, M. S. 18:175
Gwess, John H. 20:40

Gwin, Alphus 17:453
Gwin, J. R. 20:262
Gwin, James 10:98
Gwin, James P. 18:367
Gwin, John H. 10:55
Gwin, John R. 10:55
Gwin, Michael 12:145
Gwin, Samuel 8:86
Gwin, T. 13:89
Gwiney, Samuel R. 8:86
Gwining, P. E. 12:23
Gwinn, Elias P. 22:252
Gwinn, Elisha 22:252
Gwinn, John 4:28; 9:66
Gwinn, Newton 22:253
Gwinn, W. C. 18:137
Gwinnett, Charles 10:55
Gwyn, William T. 22:33
Gwynn, Edward A. 12:23
Gwynne, J. M. 14:66
Gye, William 20:146
Gyer, C. 15:173
Gyer, George 22:451
Gyer, J. 1:35
Gyer, Otto 17:148
Gyger, Samuel 11:324
Gygoria, Fores 12:172

H

H---, --- 11:340; 17:192;
    19:302; 24:19
H---, A. 15:263, 267;
    18:30; 20:23, 35;
    23:203; 27:55
H---, A. J. 21:208
H---, A. P. 11:340
H---, A. T. 20:262
H---, B. 17:296; 23:190
H---, C. 11:64; 20:146;
    24:78
H---, C. B. 23:289
H---, C. H. 12:140
H---, C. S. 24:111
H---, C. T. 23:259
H---, C. W. 10:192;
    25:298
H---, D. 16:370; 19:16;
    25:40
H---, D. F. 24:111
H---, D. G. 11:340; 19:16
H---, D. J. 23:268
H---, D. W. 15:273
H---, Dudley 25:42
H---, E. 23:203
H---, E. H. 9:214
H---, E. M. 17:217;
    23:203
H---, Ed. R. 20:56
H---, Edward 18:30

H---, Ever B. 19:78
H---, F. R. 17:364
H---, G. 11:340; 27:54
H---, G. H. 12:99
H---, G. S. 11:242
H---, G. W. 25:43
H---, H. 20:8; 24:93
H---, H. G. 20:262
H---, H. J. C. 10:192
H---, H. R. 15:205
H---, H. W. 17:297
H---, I. 12:122
H---, I. D. 16:151
H---, I. N. 23:203
H---, J--- 21:148
H---, J. 2:12; 11:64, 304,
    340; 15:205; 16:113,
    151; 17:110, 364,
    411, 509; 18:30, 466;
    19:171; 20:154;
    21:166, 339; 23:270;
    25:40, 43, 298; 27:54
H---, J. A. 17:217; 18:103;
    27:54
H---, J. B. 15:205; 22:352
H---, J. C. 15:205
H---, J. F. 17:364
H---, J. L. 11:231; 20:262;
    24:111
H---, J. M. 15:173
H---, J. R. 21:166, 208
H---, J. S. 23:301
H---, J. V. 20:85
H---, J. W. 17:236; 27:144
H---, James 15:67;
    19:171; 20:85
H---, John 15:205;
    23:121; 25:42
H---, John T. 21:166
H---, L. 11:152
H---, L. C. 10:28
H---, L. L. 10:186
H---, M. 15:166; 17:355;
    19:171; 24:111
H---, M. B. 26:166
H---, M. M. 15:205
H---, M. W. 25:311
H---, N. 14:269
H---, N. R. 20:92
H---, Nathan 16:119
H---, O. K. 17:364
H---, O. S. 15:267
H---, Ossley John 19:78
H---, P. 18:30; 27:63
H---, P. A. 15:349
H---, Peter 15:22
H---, Ph--- 11:293
H---, R. 19:302; 20:56;
    23:313
H---, R. B. D. 23:313
H---, R. C. 11:64

H---, R. T. 24:214
H---, R. W. 25:311
H---, Ralph 19:171
H---, Richard 19:78
H---, S. 9:228; 11:340;
    15:205; 18:369;
    23:67; 26:204
H---, S. A. 14:269
H---, S. C. 15:298; 19:302
H---, S. H. 25:40
H---, S. S. 27:54
H---, Solomon 11:304
H---, T. 11:340; 14:269;
    18:421; 23:292
H---, T. B. 26:211
H---, T. J. 21:166
H---, T. L. 23:146
H---, T. N. 11:84
H---, T. R. H. 26:221
H---, V. B. 26:166
H---, W. 19:302; 20:262;
    24:214
H---, W. E. 18:30
H---, W. G. 24:111
H---, W. H. 25:44
H---, W. H. Q. W. H.
    24:39
H---, W. S. 20:179;
    21:339
H---, William 11:287;
    15:151; 20:41;
    21:339
H---, William H. 13:64,
    132
H----, --- 22:352
H----, J. 22:352
H---met, Jacob 15:151
H---nm, R. 25:189
H---sch, Nathan H. 23:203
H--d, Sterling 8:39
H--ng---, --- 25:42
H--ry, --- 25:42
H--ton, William 8:39
Ha---, Thomas 12:99
Ha---ll, J. 11:340
Ha-i-ton, H. 21:342
Haack, Charles F. 12:58
Haag, Jacob 18:412
Haag, P. 1:138
Haake, Thomas 3:85
Haaker, Henry 23:32
Haare, Charles 19:289
Haas, Adolf 7:96
Haas, Francis 24:8
Haas, J. 1:139
Haas, M. 1:138
Haas, Peter 22:195
Haas, Vetus 23:285
Haas, William 10:116;
    20:262
Haase, D. 13:64

Haase, Henry 20:35
Haass, Christoper 1:42
Haat, German 14:335
Habbard, A. 3:85
Habbard, B. 3:85
Habbill, Cyrus 18:137
Habble, Don. O. 17:155
Habbner, F. 3:85
Habecker, J. W. H. 1:138
Habel, Charles 13:25
Haber, Charles 27:63
Haber, John 14:66
Haberdank, Frederic
    11:62
Haberer, George 10:17
Haberland, Benjamin
    18:307; 26:101
Habermaker, F. M. 15:201
Haberman, John 4:28
Haberman, L. 1:139
Habernah, Lewis 16:35
Haberom, Bernard 24:63
Haberstrump, H. 20:262
Haberstrump, Henry 10:55
Habes, Anthony 23:32
Habin, George 14:174
Habinson, E. 25:179
Hablizel, Philip 4:28
Habor, Charles 14:298;
    17:475
Habs, D. 3:85
Habue, Westley 17:267
Hachler, David 22:173
Hack, Benjamin 7:124;
    21:339
Hack, C. 10:148
Hack, Charles 9:102;
    18:339
Hack, H. 12:87
Hack, J. 3:85
Hack, John 15:291
Hack, Joseph 16:195
Hack, Martin 11:63
Hackat, E. 24:78
Hackathon, Benjamin
    24:78
Hackathorn, J. 1:136
Hackaway, George 20:262
Hackenberry, Michael
    18:293
Hackenburg, Hiram 8:18;
    18:137
Hackenburg, J. W. 15:67
Hackenburg, Michael
    26:102
Hackenburg, Samuel 5:17
Hackenburg, William E.
    23:67
Hacker, Charles E. 15:35
Hacker, David 10:116;
    20:262

Hacker, David M. 24:8
Hacker, Ed. W. 23:32
Hacker, George H. 21:27
Hacker, H. 11:191; 21:100
Hacker, Harvey G. 22:33
Hacker, Joseph 22:253
Hacker, Joseph F. 11:31
Hacker, Philip 4:28
Hacker, Thomas A. 21:52
Hacker, W. 19:253
Hacker, William 9:178
Hacker, William A. 23:67
Hacker, William B. S.
    20:262
Hacker, William S. 10:116
Hackersmith, George
    13:25
Hacket, E. 7:74
Hacket, J. 3:85
Hackett, A. S. 21:339
Hackett, Aaron 17:455;
    24:196
Hackett, C. 3:85
Hackett, Charles 22:79
Hackett, E. 9:144; 25:298
Hackett, Emery E. 24:170
Hackett, George H. 10:17;
    16:35
Hackett, Henry 4:66
Hackett, J. 1:43; 3:85
Hackett, J. E. 1:44
Hackett, J. P. 7:28
Hackett, James 22:253
Hackett, John 14:174
Hackett, Moses 18:83
Hackett, Nathan T. 4:28
Hackett, P. 16:195
Hackett, Patrick 24:150
Hackett, S. 1:42
Hackett, T. 7:28
Hackett, Thomas 19:16
Hackett, W. G. 1:136
Hackett, William M.
    21:216
Hackhart, Peter 23:279
Hackkess, E. C. 8:18
Hackleman, Hezekiah
    22:79
Hackley, C. 25:179
Hackley, James W. 23:99
Hackley, S. 18:395
Hackman, A. 2:12; 25:39
Hackman, Abraham
    15:166
Hackman, H. 13:110
Hackman, Hendrick
    22:143
Hackman, J. J. 25:179
Hackney, Benjamin
    22:234
Hackney, Daniel 8:63

Hackney, Isaac 9:220;
    18:367
Hackney, Thomas H. 8:63
Hackney, W. R. 14:265
Hacks, G. 15:173
Hacks, R. 27:61
Hackson, John 23:301
Hackstoff, H. 1:137
Hackuty, J. 3:85
Hackwelder, G. W. 11:149
Hackwell, S. A. 17:506
Hackwitt, Charles 14:174
Hackworth, George
    22:508
Hackworth, S. E. 8:101;
    17:463; 24:187
Hacting, Daniel 19:331
Hacxley, J. J. 19:73
Hacy, G. 13:89
Hadden, C. 3:85
Hadden, Charles 18:238;
    26:37
Hadden, Christopher
    19:73
Hadden, J. M. 14:174
Hadden, John H. 10:116;
    20:262
Hadden, John S. 14:174
Hadden, Robert 15:309;
    19:73
Hadden, Robert D. 20:262
Hadden, Robert D. C.
    10:55
Hadden, S. F. 13:77
Hadden, S. T. 16:195
Hadden, Tim 16:370
Haddesoll, C. 3:85
Haddin, J. H. 22:480
Hadding, Henry 19:270
Haddington, Noah 10:91
Haddish, J. 3:85
Haddix, James M. 10:55;
    20:262
Haddock, --- 11:241
Haddock, H. 26:125
Haddock, Harvey 10:95
Haddocks, V. B. 10:95
Haddon, C. C. 25:179
Haddon, W. 25:179
Haddox, C. M. 13:25
Haddox, George 17:259
Haddox, Silas 22:513
Haddox, Thomas I. 7:96
Hadduan, William 19:167
Hade, D. W. 22:480
Hade, J. 14:174
Hade, John 8:114
Hade, R. 14:174
Hade, William 1:38
Haded, Geen 19:291
Haden, Andrew 11:93

Haden, Franklin 17:267
Haden, John 11:263
Haden, William 17:267
Hadfield, J. 23:32
Hadgeman, Amos 20:27
Hadie, J. 24:111
Hading, George 18:238
Hading, John 11:107
Hadley, A. 1:41; 9:66
Hadley, Alras 14:174
Hadley, Amos 18:276
Hadley, Bennett H.
   21:339
Hadley, C. C. 7:28
Hadley, Cassius M. 27:62
Hadley, Charles 12:70
Hadley, D. W. 15:201
Hadley, Daniel 1:42
Hadley, David 21:225
Hadley, E. B. 15:315;
   19:73
Hadley, Edward A. 21:216
Hadley, Edwin 11:106
Hadley, G. 1:139; 25:179
Hadley, H. C. 15:318
Hadley, H. H. 18:277
Hadley, I. 26:35
Hadley, Isaac N. 15:7
Hadley, Isiah 22:519
Hadley, J. 18:238; 22:302
Hadley, J. H. 23:32
Hadley, J. L. 25:179
Hadley, James 11:63
Hadley, John 8:86; 18:323
Hadley, Langdon S.
   21:254
Hadley, Levi 8:86
Hadley, Noah 14:66
Hadley, S. J. 1:135
Hadley, Simon 24:172
Hadley, T. W. 15:201
Hadley, Uriah 20:183
Hadley, W. J. 14:66
Hadley, Walter F. 21:84
Hadley, Warren 9:81
Hadley, William A. 21:70
Hadlock, A. 1:139
Hadlock, Samuel 18:277
Hadly, Simon 17:448
Hadon, Charles E. 16:195
Hadrian, G. 25:41
Hadrick, John 18:395
Hadsall, John L. 19:73
Hadsell, J. C. 15:293;
   19:73
Hadseth, William 15:173
Hadxstud, P. 11:191
Haederty, Urias 6:31
Haefenner, D. 1:141
Haeffer, Andrew 18:110
Haeget, Peter 6:31

Haehl, M. 11:62
Haelton, H. 25:179
Haenser, Carl 18:110
Haenssler, J. C. 1:136
Haerger, G. 5:17
Haes, Hiram M. 25:179
Haes, J. 22:352
Haest, George 1:40
Hafer, James J. 21:70
Haff, John 27:59
Haff, M. 3:85
Haffarer, Thomas 15:201
Haffarmin, Pat 14:11
Haffeny, S. 14:66
Hafferty, John 23:281
Haffey, B. 25:44
Haffey, Edward 17:80
Haffey, James M. 4:28
Haffey, Jerome 18:238;
   26:35
Haffey, John 5:17; 25:179
Haffham, C. 14:174
Haffingle, J. 3:85
Haffit, Lewis 4:28
Haffkill, A. 9:178
Haffman, --- 16:35
Haffman, T. J. 20:189
Haffner, George 25:43
Haffner, James 24:78
Haffron, Thomas 23:121
Hafkille, A. 19:224
Hafley, Henry 8:86
Hafman, R. M. 19:16
Hafner, --- 25:39
Hafner, G. 1:141
Hafner, Michael 13:25
Hafner, Nicholas 25:333
Haft, Paul 13:110
Haft---, W. 25:43
Hafterling, A. B. 13:25;
   16:35
Haga, Andrew 17:453;
   24:183
Haga, Thomas 11:222
Hagaar, Ernst 18:339
Hagaboom, S. 1:43
Hagadome, B. A. 9:68
Hagadorn, Cyr 1:40
Hagadorn, Horace 19:73
Hagadorn, Horas 15:291
Hagadorn, Samuel 13:110
Hagale, Jacob 3:85
Hagaman, Everet H.
   23:190
Hagaman, Henry 6:16;
   18:83
Hagaman, J. 3:85
Hagaman, J. D. 27:144
Hagaman, W. E. 12:140;
   20:262
Hagan, A. 9:52

Hagan, C. 21:163
Hagan, C. A. 21:339
Hagan, Charles 13:64;
   20:263
Hagan, David 22:336
Hagan, F. 20:263
Hagan, Francis 15:363
Hagan, J. 9:110; 15:201
Hagan, James 16:195
Hagan, John 14:174;
   25:272
Hagan, John T. 11:93
Hagan, Joseph 9:159
Hagan, L. 16:294
Hagan, Owen 11:15
Hagan, R. 9:52
Hagan, Richard J. 12:23
Hagan, Robert 23:99
Hagan, Stephen 17:131;
   24:195
Hagan, Thomas 15:201
Haganbuoh, William
   23:179
Hagans, John 15:158
Hagar, John 25:298
Hagar, Thomas 14:67
Hagard, Phillip 18:137
Hagarman, D. 19:281;
   25:41
Hagart, S. 1:38
Hagathorn, J. 27:56
Hagden, Michael 16:154
Hage, A. 19:167
Hageleton, Charles 13:110
Hageley, T. 9:54
Hageman, E. 20:263
Hageman, Isaac 22:480
Hageman, Joseph 11:126
Hageman, R. 14:174
Hageman, R. C. 9:35
Hageman, Samuel P.
   25:39
Hagen, A. 3:85
Hagen, Aloes 22:195
Hagen, Charles 10:116
Hagen, D. 1:43
Hagen, James T. 9:119
Hagen, Jeremiah 22:336
Hagen, Patrick 3:85
Hagen, William 24:66
Hagenbuck, William
   22:79
Hagenstein, Carl 10:116
Hagenstein, Carol 20:263
Hagenwood, C. 19:75
Hager, --- 3:85
Hager, Asa 22:195
Hager, Caleb 24:196
Hager, Charles 19:319
Hager, Ernest 9:102
Hager, Henry 22:171

Hager, Isaac 17:132
Hager, J. D. 18:339
Hager, Jacob 22:122
Hager, John 2:12; 7:78
Hager, Jonah 25:41
Hager, Julius 22:33
Hager, Phineas A. 23:107
Hager, S. 24:78
Hager, T. 1:136
Hager, William 9:178
Hagerman, Charles 4:28
Hagerman, D. 9:178
Hagerman, Edward 22:144
Hagerman, Ellsey 10:55
Hagerman, Franklin 22:79
Hagerman, G. W. 22:195
Hagerman, Isaac A. 23:88
Hagerman, J. 12:161
Hagerman, James 3:85
Hagerman, John B. 22:195
Hagerman, N. 17:295
Hagerman, R. 3:86
Hagerman, Samuel 6:16; 18:83; 20:183
Hagerman, Theodore D. 23:121
Hagerson, William 2:12; 25:42
Hagertone, Elizur 4:28
Hagerty, Conrad 9:207
Hagerty, D. G. 3:86
Hagerty, James 25:42
Hagerty, John 1:42; 9:159
Hagerty, Mathew 15:201
Hagerty, Michael 21:245; 22:144
Hagerty, Patrach 20:263
Hagerty, Patrick 10:116
Hagerty, Peter 22:33
Hagerty, W. R. 3:86
Hagerty, William 3:86; 4:28
Hageton, Daniel 11:115
Hageyar, P. 15:331
Hagg, Henry 23:146
Hagg, Thomas E. 27:61
Hagg, William T. H. 20:263
Haggard, E. 3:86
Haggard, G. W. 7:96; 21:339
Haggard, Jack 17:132; 24:195
Haggard, James 21:27
Haggard, James E. 7:124
Haggard, L. B. 18:137
Haggard, Thomas 6:16; 18:83
Haggard, W. F. 27:144

Haggardone, H. 1:136
Haggart, Davis 7:96
Haggart, James 22:519
Haggart, Richard 17:176
Haggarty, Benjamin 17:132
Haggarty, James 22:463
Haggarty, Michael 1:38; 21:15
Haggendorn, Stephen 22:397
Haggerte, J. J. 1:43
Haggerty, Barney 11:231
Haggerty, Benjamin 24:195
Haggerty, Cornelius 20:8
Haggerty, D. 14:67
Haggerty, James 2:12; 22:352
Haggerty, Jeremiah 9:72
Haggerty, John 8:114; 10:17; 14:174; 19:340
Haggerty, Jona 24:50
Haggerty, Joseph D. 15:292
Haggerty, M. 1:42; 21:27
Haggerty, Nelson 17:160
Haggerty, Thomas 7:28
Haggett, F. H. 12:23
Haggett, P. 3:86
Haggett, Reuben 23:190
Haggett, William 9:35
Haggett, William G. 22:33
Haggin, O. 17:176
Haggisht, Jacob 19:73
Hagin, Thomas 18:137
Haginey, F. 3:86
Haginnis, W. 3:86
Hagins, J. C. 9:53
Hagins, S. 25:179
Hagland, F. 14:67
Hagle, Blan 17:35
Hagle, I. 9:144
Hagle, Isadore 27:57
Hagle, Patrick 7:96
Haglebarger, G. 22:195
Haglef, Dempsey 10:116; 20:263
Hagler, George 21:187
Hagman, H. 18:83
Hagmon, George 19:270
Hagner, Henry 14:174
Hagner, John 15:201
Hagoen, Robert 10:17
Hagorth, H. 14:11
Hagsith, H. 16:268
Hagsworth, Sylvanus 17:146
Hagt, Asa 11:149
Hague, E. 1:135

Hague, Lewis S. 12:62
Hague, Marion 4:28
Hague, Peter 17:461; 24:167
Hague, Samuel 16:95
Hague, William 14:67
Haha, Joseph 14:319; 25:272
Hahantal, G. 14:67
Haheimer, George W. 17:52
Hahn, C. 3:86
Hahn, Charles 14:174; 27:63
Hahn, Conrad 10:55; 20:263
Hahn, D. 13:89
Hahn, Daniel 14:11
Hahn, G. 1:137
Hahn, George 7:57
Hahn, Henry 10:95
Hahn, John 7:124; 10:116; 20:263
Hahn, Paul 22:33
Hahn, Peter 23:179
Hahn, S. 15:67
Hahn, Sidney 12:70
Hahn, William 25:179
Hahn, Winchester 10:116; 20:263
Hahoris, C. S. 22:451
Haig, D. C. 15:158
Haig, Samuel 15:298
Haigh, M. 7:50
Haight, A. W. 17:242
Haight, Abraham L. 9:106
Haight, Abram 18:334
Haight, Alonzo 11:401
Haight, Benjamin 12:23
Haight, Christian 18:137
Haight, Edgar 13:110
Haight, Ellsworth 15:107
Haight, Eugene W. 22:33
Haight, George E. 11:319
Haight, George W. 4:28
Haight, H. 13:125
Haight, H. H. 17:65
Haight, J. E. 3:86
Haight, Morris P. 21:254
Haight, Peter A. 22:144
Haight, Thomas B. 16:35
Haight, Tobias B. 13:25
Haight, William 17:110
Haigler, William M. 22:482
Haignett, John 12:170
Haihne, George S. 18:50
Haihrilo, S. 1:44
Hail, E. E. 5:17
Hail, H. C. 6:31; 25:321
Hail, John 17:349

Hailare, R. 3:86
Haild, Jesse 11:394
Haile, James R. 17:154
Hailen, Gotfried 3:86
Hailes, John 22:481
Hailey, Charles 22:405
Hailey, David 7:62
Hailey, John 24:19
Hailey, Thomas 1:43
Hailey, William 18:30
Hailgardner, David 23:146
Hailman, Benjamin 7:28
Hain, Arthur 14:174
Hain, E. A. 16:133
Hain, John 9:178
Hain, Joseph 22:502
Hain, Samuel 16:195
Haine, Adam 10:205
Haine, D. 11:33
Haine, George 25:179
Haine, I. H. 9:144
Haineg, John H. 17:52
Hainer, Jacob 18:367
Haines, --- 15:201
Haines, Andrew 18:206
Haines, Benjamin F. 9:72
Haines, Bentley E. 21:53
Haines, C. C. 25:179
Haines, Charles E. 7:96
Haines, Charles L. 11:150
Haines, Clayton 10:116; 20:263
Haines, D. 22:405
Haines, D. C. 4:28
Haines, David 12:8
Haines, David G. 20:113
Haines, Davis 20:41
Haines, Dewitte 16:162
Haines, E. 11:187
Haines, E. M. 25:179
Haines, E. S. 7:124
Haines, F. 20:146
Haines, G. 3:86
Haines, G. A. 10:55; 20:263
Haines, G. H. 23:32
Haines, G. W. 14:67
Haines, George 8:39; 26:165
Haines, H. 3:86; 14:174
Haines, Harlow 13:64; 19:73
Haines, Harrison 11:63
Haines, Henry 16:195; 26:145
Haines, Howard 25:40; 26:165
Haines, J. 1:137, 141; 3:86; 11:387; 19:73
Haines, J. A. 3:86

Haines, James 10:55; 11:151
Haines, John 4:28; 13:25; 22:11
Haines, John B. 23:146
Haines, John C. 22:144
Haines, John H. 15:201
Haines, John W. 15:201
Haines, Jordan 11:205
Haines, Lewis 19:73
Haines, M. 22:481
Haines, M. S. 9:22
Haines, Moses 25:285
Haines, N. 16:268
Haines, N. S. 3:86; 14:174
Haines, Philip 20:183
Haines, R. 3:86
Haines, Richmond 9:230
Haines, S. D. 1:139
Haines, S. W. 18:367
Haines, Samuel 14:174
Haines, Sanford S. 22:195
Haines, Simon S. 8:86
Haines, Smith 21:339
Haines, Sylvester L. 15:35
Haines, T. H. 25:179
Haines, Theo 3:86
Haines, Thomas 25:179, 180
Haines, W. 13:79
Haines, W. H. 21:339
Haines, William 10:55; 11:107; 20:263; 21:339; 22:195, 302
Haines, William H. 23:146
Haines, Winfield W. 18:110
Hainey, O. 22:253
Hainford, Thomas 12:82; 16:294
Haingan, Pat 8:101
Hainist, E. 13:89
Hainlind, Elias 23:32
Hainmond, Barlett 16:195
Hains, Andrew 17:415
Hains, Charles D. 23:103
Hains, Ed. H. 19:73
Hains, H. J. 20:263
Hains, J. B. 27:55
Hains, John 10:55
Hains, Wail 8:18
Hainson, Charles 26:165
Hainson, Sylvester 26:165
Hainston, G. 23:32
Hainsworth, J. W. 1:41
Hainsworth, John 27:59
Hainsworth, W. 16:268
Hainz, Franz 11:119
Hair, C. C. 23:289
Hair, Daniel B. 15:35

Hair, Daniel W. 11:150
Hair, F. 3:86
Hair, G. 3:86
Hair, Gilbert 11:63
Hair, Henry 8:58
Hair, I. W. 14:67
Hair, Jacob 1:41
Hair, John 21:216
Hair, John B. 16:35
Hair, P. M. 20:85
Hair, Robert L. 22:253
Hair, Silas 4:28
Hair, W. J. 16:35
Hair, William 11:182
Hairis, Isem 23:198
Hairsine, Anthony 18:137
Haisch, John 19:274
Haiseh, John 9:178
Haiser, J. 23:67
Haist, Seth H. 9:178
Hait, A. B. 19:281
Hait, Charles 14:174, 256
Hait, Joseph 1:43; 14:174
Hait, William 14:174
Haiter, Nathaniel 26:102
Haitley, T. H. 23:313
Haitman, Harrison 10:55
Haitnell, I. 17:287
Haiton, Alex 20:263
Haiton, Alexander 10:55
Haitranft, Flighman 11:32
Haives, A. M. 1:39
Hakaion, F. 3:86
Hake, H. 14:67
Hake, William 3:86
Hakeman, R. 16:370
Haker, Frank 27:64
Haker, Frederick 14:298; 17:473
Haker, Henry H. 8:106
Haker, W. 19:281
Haker, William 9:178
Hakes, B. 1:140
Hakes, George 22:195
Hakes, George W. 10:116; 20:263
Hakes, J. 1:94
Hakes, L. 1:42
Hakey, Hugh L. 7:28
Hakill, Francis M. 8:18; 26:165
Hakin, Vincent H. 23:146
Hakons, James 26:212
Hal-lis-fix-fek 25:333
Hal-lok-to-mie-marrah 25:333
Haladay, W. W. 12:153
Halar, Lyman 22:115
Halberkan, William 10:116

Halberkann, William 20:263
Halbert, A. H. 3:86
Halbert, Chester A. 16:35
Halbert, Earl 15:283; 19:73
Halbert, F. 3:86
Halbert, George 21:91
Halbert, George F. 15:91
Halbert, James W. 27:61
Halbert, L. 3:86
Halbert, William K. 22:80
Halbfas, --- 15:95
Halbung, George 16:95
Halburger, T. 22:195
Halchew, I. 9:144
Halcomb, A. N. 9:35; 26:103
Halcomb, A. W. 18:293
Halcomb, Benjamin 15:201
Halcomb, Franklin M. 17:453; 24:183
Halcomb, H. C. 8:63
Halcomb, Margnes D. 11:150
Halcomb, R. 5:17
Halcomb, Samuel 17:154
Halcombe, Francis M. 8:18
Halcott, Nathan 4:29
Halcott, R. B. 14:336
Halcroft, Edward 16:294
Haldaman, Henry 23:107
Haldeman, N. A. 20:263
Haldeman, Newton A. 10:56
Haldeman, Reuben 2:13; 25:38
Halden, Charles W. 18:334
Halder, William 11:31
Halderman, Aaron 18:444
Halderman, Joseph 18:217
Halderman, Peter H. 19:16
Haldridge, Dudley 19:267
Haldridge, W. H. 25:180
Haldridge, William 1:44
Haldron, Dudley 12:153
Haldwell, S. 21:148
Hale, A. J. 21:339
Hale, A. V. 20:92
Hale, A. W. 3:86
Hale, Alexander 21:244, 339
Hale, C. 11:149, 335
Hale, C. N. 26:32
Hale, Charles 12:139; 14:174
Hale, Charles H. 9:178

Hale, Charles K. 18:395
Hale, Daniel 22:279
Hale, Davis 18:395
Hale, E. E. 25:180
Hale, Eber 26:33
Hale, Edmond P. 19:167
Hale, Edra 10:55
Hale, Edward P. 16:145
Hale, F. 12:142; 13:89; 14:11
Hale, F. S. 12:153
Hale, Francis B. 21:70
Hale, Frank 20:263
Hale, Frank A. 18:334
Hale, G. A. 14:67
Hale, G. S. 20:263
Hale, G. W. 1:40
Hale, George 12:92; 22:195
Hale, George C. 15:35
Hale, H. C. 3:86
Hale, Henry 8:106
Hale, Hiram 22:234
Hale, Horatio S. 22:519
Hale, Ira 3:86
Hale, J. 13:89; 26:34
Hale, J. B. 19:237
Hale, J. C. 20:263
Hale, J. K. P. 26:100
Hale, J. M. 26:211
Hale, J. P. 12:64; 15:25
Hale, J. R. P. 9:22
Hale, Jacob 10:98
Hale, James 11:93
Hale, James O. 16:195
Hale, James P. 22:482
Hale, James S. 22:501
Hale, James W. 14:175
Hale, Jeremiah 21:10
Hale, Jesse F. 20:8
Hale, John 10:55; 11:64; 20:263; 21:14; 22:253
Hale, John H. 2:12; 20:154; 25:43
Hale, John L. 11:84
Hale, John M. 11:423
Hale, John N. 18:395
Hale, John S. 21:166
Hale, John T. 17:287
Hale, John W. 22:33
Hale, Joseph 10:55; 20:263
Hale, Joseph B. 9:178
Hale, Joseph W. 11:100
Hale, Justice 22:482
Hale, L. 26:33
Hale, Levi 20:146
Hale, M. 26:33
Hale, M. F. 22:253
Hale, Madison 21:225

Hale, Mathew 9:81
Hale, Morgan 22:253
Hale, P. J. 7:57
Hale, P. R. 16:35
Hale, Peter 22:513
Hale, Philip 23:32
Hale, Powel 27:63
Hale, R. 14:67
Hale, Richard 17:191
Hale, S. 20:89
Hale, S. B. 3:86; 25:44
Hale, S. G. 10:55
Hale, S. H. 20:90
Hale, S. V. 2:12
Hale, Sewell 19:227
Hale, Stephen B. 19:270
Hale, T. 20:263
Hale, T. M. 13:89; 14:11
Hale, Talburt G. 17:233
Hale, Thomas 17:233
Hale, Thomas J. 24:59
Hale, Volney F. 12:70; 15:67
Hale, Walter H. 13:25
Hale, William 1:38; 9:220; 10:116; 17:443; 18:367; 20:263; 24:159
Hale, William C. 7:74; 23:107
Hale, Z. L. 22:195
Halebury, Isaac 22:480
Halem, Charles 11:152
Haleman, M. 3:86
Halenbeck, S. 3:86
Haler, F. 21:121
Hales, William H. 21:27
Haley, --- 25:180
Haley, A. 10:28; 19:302
Haley, Adam W. 22:302
Haley, Albert 12:49
Haley, Andrew J. 21:100
Haley, B. 9:53
Haley, Benjamin 7:124; 21:339
Haley, C. 23:67
Haley, C. H. 3:86; 9:53
Haley, Edward 14:67
Haley, F. 14:175
Haley, George 15:201
Haley, J. 27:57
Haley, J. M. 9:43
Haley, James 19:287
Haley, James A. 7:96
Haley, Joel 9:220
Haley, John 8:18; 12:49; 14:236; 18:30, 137
Haley, Joseph 7:8
Haley, L. 14:67
Haley, M. 14:67; 15:107
Haley, Martin 15:124

Haley, Michael 19:73
Haley, P. 14:175; 24:78
Haley, Patrick 12:122;
13:64; 14:67;
15:124; 19:74
Haley, Thomas 13:25;
16:95; 19:167;
21:339
Haley, Timothy 22:80
Haley, W. 12:8
Haley, Wiley 9:208; 18:67
Haley, William 10:116;
20:263; 22:302, 336
Haley, William H. 8:86;
22:426
Haley, William O. 23:308
Half, C. C. 15:158
Halferty, John W. 21:138
Halferty, W. 21:27
Halferty, William 21:254
Halfhill, Hiram E. 10:56
Halfhill, William S.
21:225
Halfield, Andrew 11:408
Halfill, J. 17:14
Halfin, Lawr 1:40
Halfinger, Bergen 9:81
Halford, G. W. 15:173
Halford, George 23:240
Halford, I. 21:130
Halford, J. R. 21:27
Halfpenny, John 22:234
Halfrer, J. A. 3:86
Halgner, John 17:425
Haliards, Daniel 10:161
Haliburton, J. H. 21:339
Haliday, George E. 16:195
Halienieb, James M. 9:81
Haligan, J. F. 13:89
Haligan, J. T. 14:11
Halin, George 21:239
Haline, D. T. 26:32
Halke, Thomas 25:288
Halkeld, J. 18:83
Halker, Moses 19:270
Halkner, J. T. 21:53
Halkner, T. J. 21:53
Hall, --- 2:12; 16:195;
21:339; 25:38
Hall, A. 1:140, 141; 3:86;
5:40; 16:195;
21:208; 23:245;
25:180
Hall, A. B. 1:41; 16:370
Hall, A. D. 13:110
Hall, A. G. 15:347;
16:370
Hall, A. H. 13:64
Hall, A. I. 9:144
Hall, A. J. 21:339
Hall, A. P. 15:17

Hall, A. R. 25:298
Hall, Aaron 10:56; 20:263
Hall, Abner 22:144
Hall, Abraham 4:29
Hall, Adam 11:151
Hall, Albert 11:149;
15:35; 21:88
Hall, Albert R. 7:74
Hall, Albus 5:17
Hall, Alexander 3:86;
11:327; 12:23, 153;
17:337; 21:211
Hall, Alfred 21:225; 22:33
Hall, Allen 21:272
Hall, Almond 11:413
Hall, Amos 27:58
Hall, Andrew 22:302
Hall, Andrew J. 9:220;
17:80; 18:367
Hall, Anna 27:61
Hall, Anson 25:39
Hall, Aquilla 17:317
Hall, Augustus 5:17;
11:115
Hall, Austin 7:124; 10:56;
20:263; 21:339
Hall, Avery 22:33
Hall, B. 3:86; 23:309;
25:180
Hall, B. C. 9:230; 20:263
Hall, B. F. 21:339
Hall, Benjamin 3:86; 4:29;
5:40; 11:150; 16:195
Hall, Benjamin F. 25:42
Hall, Benjamin J. 14:175
Hall, Benjamin W. 22:287
Hall, Benjamin Ward
18:217
Hall, Berdman 11:32
Hall, Brown 22:302
Hall, Byron B. 25:282
Hall, C. 1:140; 3:86;
11:106; 14:67, 277;
23:121
Hall, C. A. 2:12; 3:86;
25:39
Hall, C. B. 26:163
Hall, C. C. 25:321
Hall, C. E. 2:12; 25:44
Hall, C. H. J. 17:35
Hall, C. M. 16:151
Hall, C. N. 9:81
Hall, C. T. 23:107
Hall, C. W. 14:175
Hall, Calvin E. 9:35;
18:293; 26:102
Hall, Charles 1:44; 3:86;
7:96; 8:63; 9:208;
11:15, 402; 14:67;
16:195; 22:195

Hall, Charles A. 10:116;
20:263
Hall, Charles G. 27:54
Hall, Charles M. 17:248
Hall, Charles T. 22:79
Hall, Christopher C. 11:93
Hall, Clark W. 5:17
Hall, Clarke 4:28
Hall, Clay 11:204
Hall, Clemont F. 4:29
Hall, Cornelius 18:217;
27:145
Hall, Cornelius C. 10:116;
20:263
Hall, Cyrus 1:41
Hall, D. 1:141; 3:86
Hall, D. E. 14:175
Hall, D. F. 25:321
Hall, D. K. 25:180
Hall, D. L. 1:38; 7:96
Hall, D. O. 11:263
Hall, D. W. 15:330; 19:74
Hall, Daniel 18:190;
25:180; 26:211
Hall, David 17:336;
18:421; 22:253
Hall, David D. 22:144
Hall, David J. 10:161;
19:167
Hall, E. 1:135, 136;
9:131; 14:265, 288;
18:190
Hall, E. G. 25:180
Hall, E. H. 27:59
Hall, E. P. 7:28
Hall, E. S. 14:67
Hall, E. Z. 1:136; 7:64
Hall, Edward 3:86;
11:412; 13:25;
21:187; 22:405
Hall, Edwin 3:86
Hall, Eley 19:16
Hall, Eli 9:131; 10:95;
21:211
Hall, Eli W. 16:195
Hall, Elias 15:201
Hall, Elijah 13:25; 19:16
Hall, Elisha 10:56, 91;
20:263
Hall, Emanuel 9:178
Hall, Erastus P. 22:79
Hall, Ezekiel H. 22:122
Hall, Ezra 14:265; 27:62
Hall, F. 3:86; 27:56
Hall, F. M. 11:191
Hall, Fleming 12:95
Hall, Flemming 15:359;
19:74
Hall, Francis 13:110
Hall, Francis A. 22:144

Hall, Frank 6:16; 10:55; 18:83; 22:144, 508
Hall, Frederick 15:351
Hall, G. H. 3:86
Hall, G. S. 1:136
Hall, G. W. 3:86; 9:144; 14:175; 17:433; 27:57
Hall, George 4:29; 12:49; 14:67; 16:294; 17:349; 18:83; 20:8; 21:339; 24:39; 25:180
Hall, George A. 7:96; 16:35
Hall, George H. 11:115
Hall, George W. 4:29; 5:17; 10:116; 12:71; 20:263; 24:159
Hall, Green B. 22:122
Hall, H. 3:86; 9:217; 10:148; 14:133; 16:268; 18:50; 21:339
Hall, H. C. 3:86; 23:146; 25:321
Hall, H. D. 16:195
Hall, H. E. 17:14
Hall, H. F. 19:167
Hall, H. H. 3:86; 14:175
Hall, H. I. 18:175
Hall, H. J. 1:137
Hall, H. M. 12:23
Hall, H. O. 19:74
Hall, H. P. 20:146
Hall, H. W. 17:424; 23:32; 24:173; 26:34
Hall, Haley H. 1:42
Hall, Harris 9:161
Hall, Henry 1:43; 3:86; 9:102; 10:116, 161; 13:25; 18:67, 339; 19:167; 20:56, 97, 263; 21:272; 22:195, 405; 23:267, 268; 24:152
Hall, Henry C. 11:31; 18:217; 22:426
Hall, Henry L. 14:175
Hall, Hiram 13:25; 25:43
Hall, Hiram A. 21:339
Hall, Hiram H. 23:88
Hall, Hit 22:302
Hall, Horace R. 11:106
Hall, Howard 10:179
Hall, Hugh 7:78; 25:298
Hall, Irvin 3:86
Hall, Irving 25:40
Hall, Isaac A. 8:18; 18:137
Hall, Isaac W. 19:167

Hall, Ishmael 1:191
Hall, J. 1:135, 137, 140, 141; 3:86; 9:53, 81; 13:89; 14:11, 67; 15:81, 332; 19:74; 25:40, 44; 26:33
Hall, J. A. 10:116; 20:263
Hall, J. C. 10:116; 19:74
Hall, J. D. 1:142
Hall, J. E. 9:144
Hall, J. F. 3:87
Hall, J. G. 27:56
Hall, J. J. 3:87
Hall, J. L. 3:87
Hall, J. M. 3:87; 15:352; 16:279; 18:190
Hall, J. N. 9:53
Hall, J. R. 7:96; 16:139
Hall, J. R. P. 18:308
Hall, J. S. 19:287
Hall, J. W. 1:137; 3:87; 9:81; 23:32
Hall, Jacob 7:68; 10:17; 14:175
Hall, James 3:86; 4:29; 9:35; 12:70; 13:25; 15:201; 16:195; 17:176; 18:293; 19:45, 74; 20:192, 263; 21:14, 27; 22:480, 502; 23:285; 26:102
Hall, James C. 8:18
Hall, James F. 22:452
Hall, James G. 25:278
Hall, James H. 15:283; 19:74
Hall, James L. 22:426
Hall, James M. 7:96; 11:381; 20:263
Hall, James R. 17:65
Hall, James S. 9:178
Hall, James W. 8:18; 10:56; 15:310; 17:52; 18:137; 19:74
Hall, Jasper 8:18; 18:137; 27:58
Hall, Jeremiah 22:427
Hall, Jesse 14:175; 21:339
Hall, Joel A. 11:32
Hall, Joel C. 10:116; 20:263
Hall, John 3:86; 4:29, 66; 5:17; 7:68, 96; 8:18, 77; 9:22; 11:16, 63; 12:23; 13:25; 14:67, 175, 256; 18:137, 190, 277, 307; 21:53, 211, 339; 22:11, 234; 23:146; 24:19; 25:180; 26:33, 100;

Hall, John 27:62
Hall, John A. 1:38, 41
Hall, John B. 12:49; 17:280, 291
Hall, John C. 12:49; 25:39
Hall, John D. 4:29; 13:25
Hall, John F. 22:166
Hall, John G. 4:28; 13:25
Hall, John H. 10:116; 16:195; 20:264; 25:180
Hall, John L. 14:175
Hall, John P. 9:81; 26:32
Hall, John R. 14:67
Hall, John S. 8:49; 21:70
Hall, John T. 21:27
Hall, John W. 13:25; 22:79
Hall, Jones 10:56
Hall, Joseph 8:86; 9:110, 178; 15:355; 17:20, 148, 236; 19:245; 21:339; 22:253; 23:32
Hall, Joseph L. 18:206
Hall, Joseph S. 22:79
Hall, Joseph T. 16:35
Hall, Josiah 17:418
Hall, L. 1:136, 140; 3:87; 21:148; 27:55
Hall, L. A. 1:141
Hall, L. B. 10:186; 18:175; 25:180
Hall, L. D. 15:201
Hall, L. E. C. 13:89
Hall, L. F. 16:268
Hall, Leander 20:133
Hall, Lemuel 15:336; 19:74
Hall, Leonard 25:180
Hall, Levi 17:248
Hall, Lorenzo I. 7:96
Hall, Louis 17:176
Hall, Lucius 21:195
Hall, Ludius 21:225
Hall, Luther 10:56; 20:264
Hall, M. 1:41; 3:87
Hall, M. J. 1:40
Hall, M. M. 6:31; 25:321
Hall, M. V. B. 20:41
Hall, Major 17:423; 24:170
Hall, Marcius 10:56; 20:264
Hall, Martin 11:408; 18:285; 26:135
Hall, Mary 27:56
Hall, Mathew 8:86
Hall, Miles 10:56; 20:264
Hall, Milford D. 7:16

Hall, Milton 17:259; 21:27; 22:427
Hall, Milton P. 20:189
Hall, Monroe 1:41
Hall, Myron M. 22:144
Hall, Nathan 22:195
Hall, Ned 7:124
Hall, Newman 1:41
Hall, Newton 8:18; 18:137
Hall, O. 3:87
Hall, O. R. 8:49
Hall, Oliver 22:302
Hall, Omer C. 11:107
Hall, Orlando R. 21:254
Hall, Orson 12:23
Hall, Orwin S. 12:8
Hall, Oscar 22:482
Hall, Owen 17:236
Hall, P. 20:146
Hall, P. F. 1:42
Hall, Peter 3:87; 7:78; 12:82; 13:110; 16:294; 25:298
Hall, Philip 21:339; 22:144
Hall, Pleasant M. 22:112
Hall, R. 19:281
Hall, R. A. 3:86
Hall, R. B. 25:43
Hall, R. E. 10:116; 20:264
Hall, R. F. 9:178
Hall, R. H. 3:87
Hall, R. P. 1:141
Hall, Richard 13:25; 24:66
Hall, Riley 9:35; 18:293; 26:102
Hall, Robert 7:96; 9:178; 11:32, 33; 17:176; 20:264; 21:272; 22:144; 26:32
Hall, Robert M. 11:88; 19:167
Hall, Robinson 9:178; 19:281
Hall, Rollo 21:53
Hall, S. 3:87; 14:67; 18:30
Hall, S. E. 8:49
Hall, S. H. 3:87
Hall, S. L. 3:87
Hall, S. M. 1:138; 14:175
Hall, S. V. 25:38
Hall, Sam. J. 19:167
Hall, Samuel 4:28; 7:124; 11:186; 14:236
Hall, Samuel G. 7:96
Hall, Samuel M. 18:307
Hall, Samuel Miller 26:101

Hall, Samuel W. 10:116; 20:264
Hall, Seth J. 23:179
Hall, Sewell 9:178
Hall, Sherdon 6:23
Hall, Silas 11:262
Hall, Silas E. 21:70
Hall, Stephen B. 9:178
Hall, Sylvanus 22:144
Hall, Sylvanus A. 19:167
Hall, T. 3:87; 14:67; 16:195
Hall, T. A. G. 13:125
Hall, T. B. S. 22:195
Hall, T. H. 15:83
Hall, Thear J. 10:161; 19:167
Hall, Theodore 7:28; 26:124
Hall, Theodore H. 12:71
Hall, Thomas 8:119; 9:178; 11:387; 17:267; 19:253; 20:186, 264; 23:184, 307; 24:66, 194
Hall, Thomas B. 14:67, 281
Hall, Thomas D. 1:191
Hall, Thomas G. 23:67
Hall, Thomas J. 7:28; 18:217
Hall, Timothy 14:175
Hall, Tyra R. 10:56; 20:264
Hall, W. 3:87; 13:89; 14:11
Hall, W. D. 17:233
Hall, W. F. 27:61
Hall, W. G. 3:87
Hall, W. H. 1:139; 18:238; 20:264; 25:38; 26:36
Hall, W. N. 20:264
Hall, W. P. 8:49
Hall, W. R. 3:87; 9:227; 18:367
Hall, W. S. 13:89; 21:340
Hall, Warren 21:138, 340
Hall, Watson 7:28
Hall, Wesley 19:167
Hall, Wilburn 10:116; 20:264
Hall, William 1:38; 3:87; 7:96; 8:114; 11:64, 204, 263; 14:67, 175; 15:201; 16:35; 17:259, 418; 18:323; 20:264; 21:117, 187; 22:425; 24:51, 159; 25:269; 27:61

Hall, William C. 3:87; 17:71; 22:471; 25:298
Hall, William E. 9:236; 26:220
Hall, William H. 10:56; 11:412; 18:190; 22:144
Hall, William H. H. 8:49; 21:225
Hall, William N. 1:42; 10:56
Hall, William P. 8:18; 18:137
Hall, William S. 24:19
Hall, William T. 1:40
Hall, William W. 10:56; 20:264; 22:80
Hall, Wilson 22:302
Hall, Z. 16:195
Hall, Zach 7:96
Hall, Zera W. 22:33
Hallabaugh, L. 14:67
Hallabaugh, S. 16:294
Hallack, Charles H. 10:17
Hallack, J. M. 9:110
Halladay, F. 9:144
Hallahan, John 25:298
Hallam, F. 11:31
Hallam, George 19:327
Hallam, William C. 19:167
Hallan, George 18:353
Hallar, John 3:87
Hallar, William 3:87
Hallard, W. 18:238; 26:36
Hallaway, G. W. 16:268
Hallaway, William 23:252
Halleck, Aaron 8:101
Halleck, Arny 19:277
Halleck, Daniel 14:175
Halleck, Flavel B. 21:70
Halleck, Hiram 10:56
Halleck, J. L. 16:95
Halleck, John 7:96
Halleck, William 24:8
Halleck, William M. 9:81; 26:32
Hallen, John 21:272
Hallen, W. 18:238; 26:35
Hallenback, N. 19:237
Hallenback, William 16:35
Hallenbar, A. 9:81
Hallenbeck, Henry 13:25
Hallenbeck, W. 26:32
Hallenbeck, William 11:219
Hallenberg, Hal 9:35
Haller, --- 24:111
Haller, Baldwin 11:126

Haller, Christian 23:146
Haller, D. 3:87
Haller, Ebenezer 14:175
Haller, F. 25:44
Haller, H. 3:87
Haller, Israel 19:267
Haller, Jacob 22:481
Haller, James 9:236
Haller, John 22:481
Haller, Joseph P. 22:166
Haller, Martin 10:17
Haller, Peter 3:87
Haller, R. 1:139
Halleran, Michael 12:23
Hallerman, Adam 17:393
Hallerman, Marius C.
    21:216
Hallet, B. 16:195
Hallet, Bradford 14:175
Hallett, Charles 24:39
Hallett, D. 25:321
Hallett, N. 1:39
Hallett, Oliver S. 11:305
Halley, A. J. 8:49
Halley, Davis 26:37
Halley, Elisha 22:425
Halley, J. 3:87
Halley, John 6:23; 7:28
Halley, L. 25:180
Halley, M. B. 7:50
Halley, P. 21:148
Halley, T. 3:87
Halley, W. 3:87
Halley, William H. 20:113
Halley, Zachariah 22:302
Hallfield, D. W. 21:340
Hallfish, C. 15:294
Hallford, J. A. 3:87
Halliard, Daniel 19:167
Halliday, F. 27:56
Halliday, G. 25:180
Halliday, Harvey 12:99;
    15:366
Halliday, Robert 25:180
Hallie, E. 19:274
Halligan, J. 3:87
Halligan, Thomas 5:17
Halliger, C. 3:87
Hallihan, James 7:81
Halliker, Jerome 14:175
Halliman, Patrick 4:29
Hallinger, Edward 23:146
Hallinger, George 17:71
Hallins, L. 18:14
Halliville, James 22:195
Halliwell, D. 1:136
Hallman, B. 1:98
Hallman, Samuel 19:16
Hallman, William C.
    10:161
Hallmark, --- 3:87

Hallock, Aaron 17:459;
    24:152
Hallock, H. H. 23:32
Hallock, Hiram 20:264
Hallock, Martin 24:51
Halloran, Daniel 14:175
Halloran, Herman 11:293
Halloran, Thomas 25:180
Halloran, William 24:66
Hallorn, Michael 15:319;
    19:74
Hallow, Thomas O.
    17:429
Halloway, Edwin 9:131
Halloway, George W.
    15:91
Halloway, J. 3:87
Halloway, James 18:307;
    26:100
Halloway, John 6:25
Halloway, Levi 21:272
Halloway, Lovell S.
    22:253
Halloway, Peter 6:22
Halloway, Thomas 11:63;
    27:145
Halloway, Watson 23:240
Halloway, William 11:107
Halloway, William H.
    22:33
Hallowell, Charles
    13:135; 19:346
Hallowell, G. 1:138
Hallowell, H. 1:39; 17:35
Hallowell, James 24:39
Hallows, J. 25:180
Hallows, James 5:17
Halls, E. 5:40; 25:180
Halls, Fred. R. 11:241
Hallsa, Frances Ann
    26:221
Hallsa, George W. 26:221
Hallsa, Rebecca Ann
    26:221
Hallstead, Samuel 5:17
Hallsted, Peter L. 23:146
Hallus, William F. 13:110
Hallwell, Stephen 21:272
Hally, Charles 26:102
Hally, L. 25:180
Hally, W. W. 9:242
Hally, William 20:8
Hallyard, William N.
    21:340
Halm, John 11:62
Halm, T. 1:137
Halman, A. 16:195
Halman, Hugh 12:23
Halman, J. H. 16:195
Halmark, John 17:95

Halmer, Charles W.
    21:340
Halmsby, John 6:22
Halnagle, J. C. 9:22
Haloran, D. 14:175
Haloran, Pat 18:175
Haloway, John 26:35
Haloway, W. 26:34
Halowell, Edward 25:288
Halp, J. 14:67
Halphons, John 9:178
Halpin, --- 19:74
Halpin, James 23:128
Halpin, John 3:87
Halpin, P. 3:87
Halpin, Thomas 1:42
Halpin, William 19:16
Halpin, William P. 15:55
Halsberg, Charles 27:63
Halsby, N. 19:281
Halsch, G. 1:139
Halse, P. 16:195
Halsee, J. 19:74
Halseg, W. 1:39
Halseh, J. 15:359
Halsel, William 22:336
Halsenberger, John 13:25;
    16:35
Halser, J. 14:27
Halsey, Anson 10:24
Halsey, Henry W. 16:35
Halsey, Ira 15:201
Halsey, J. 12:95
Halsey, James 16:35
Halsey, Jasper 21:121
Halsey, Joseph 25:39
Halsey, Nicholas 9:200
Halsey, Silas 20:48
Halsey, William 1:40
Halsford, Thomas 15:201
Halshutt, A. 3:87
Halsinger, W. H. 21:27
Halsinger, William 16:195
Halsner, John 16:195
Halso, George 16:195
Halsom, John 21:272
Halsom, William 15:35
Halson, D. 17:500
Halson, David 3:223
Halson, George 15:317
Halstead, C. 1:137
Halstead, Elliott 23:32
Halstead, H. A. 22:481
Halstead, Hiram 10:161;
    19:167
Halstead, J. W. 3:87
Halstead, Jesse 1:192
Halstead, John 15:258
Halstead, R. 11:64
Halstead, William C.
    19:167

Halsted, Albert 11:126
Halsted, James 9:16
Halsted, P. A. 9:12
Halsted, William H.
  20:264
Halstine, William 8:86
Halt, Chesley 22:253
Halt, Gideon 26:33
Halt, John 14:67
Halt, William P. 26:204
Halt Hill, H. E. 20:263
Halter, J. E. 26:33
Halter, John 12:23
Halter, Mitchell 26:32
Halter, Stephen 11:304
Halter, W. 3:87
Halterman, Aaron 26:145
Halterman, Christian J.
  23:67
Halterman, J. 20:35
Haltin, Philip 12:53
Haltmeed, E. L. 8:72
Halton, A. J. 15:201
Halton, E. 18:50
Halton, F. M. 3:87
Halton, James 18:412
Halton, Philip 4:29
Halts, G. F. 17:148
Halts, William 3:87
Haltshourke, Henry 9:81
Haltuck, James M. 9:66
Halty, George 24:66
Haltzel, D. 14:11
Haltzell, William B. 9:218
Halum, E. 10:56
Halvarson, Lars 20:113
Halverand, Barnard 20:85
Halverson, Halver 10:91;
  17:323; 20:264;
  26:101
Halverson, Ole 10:91;
  20:264; 22:508
Halverson, Peter S.
  14:298; 17:474;
  27:64
Halverton, William 26:37
Halvorsen, Oliver 20:48
Halvorson, Halvor 18:307
Halvorson, John 20:151
Halvorson, Lars 21:254
Haly, Alexander T. 23:32
Haly, John 12:23; 22:33
Haly, Oscar P. 20:48
Haly, Thomas 12:23
Haly, W. 3:87
Haly, William 3:87
Ham, --- 8:106
Ham, A. H. 15:326
Ham, Alexander 17:236
Ham, B. A. 25:180
Ham, B. F. 8:18

Ham, Beuben 27:62
Ham, Charles 14:175
Ham, Daniel 2:13; 25:38
Ham, E. 7:28; 10:192;
  18:175
Ham, E. E. 18:137
Ham, Edward 25:43
Ham, Edward B. 22:280
Ham, Edward R. 10:116;
  20:264
Ham, Ephraim T. 22:80
Ham, F. 13:89
Ham, George P. 13:26
Ham, J. H. 3:87
Ham, J. W. 9:144; 27:57
Ham, James 11:65
Ham, James A. 22:80
Ham, James H. 20:46;
  22:253
Ham, John 12:147; 19:274
Ham, Lawson 22:427
Ham, O. F. 25:298
Ham, O. T. 7:74
Ham, Philo 17:35
Ham, Sidney 22:451
Ham, W. F. 26:163
Ham, W. H. 19:74
Ham, Wash 24:196
Ham, Washington 17:455
Ham, Wellington 6:7
Ham, William 14:67;
  26:125
Hamacher, --- 16:294
Hamaford, William 12:23
Hamamun, H. 25:180
Haman, --- 15:67
Haman, Arthur 4:66
Haman, David 11:413
Haman, J. 3:87
Haman, L. 19:253
Hamans, James 16:35
Hamar, N. 11:62
Hamar, Robert 24:78
Hamasay, P. 16:268
Hambaugh, A. 8:77
Hambelain, --- 25:44
Hamber, John 10:172;
  19:167; 26:211
Hamberger, William
  11:15
Hambert, Simon 9:81
Hambleton, G. 25:180
Hamblett, Atwell J.
  11:333
Hamblett, Horace 13:26
Hamblett, L. 1:137
Hamblin, Caleb 21:211
Hamblin, D. 17:248
Hamblin, D. J. 1:142
Hamblin, Eli 1:40
Hamblin, Frank 21:340

Hamblin, Frederick S.
  5:17
Hamblin, George 20:124
Hamblin, George C.
  18:395
Hamblin, Jesse B. 13:26
Hamblin, Joel 20:113
Hamblin, John 14:67
Hamblin, Reuben 11:401
Hamblin, William 10:116;
  20:264; 21:340
Hambold, William 4:29
Hambric, Jilson 17:236
Hambrick, Alexander
  22:302
Hambrick, Archibald
  22:302
Hambrick, Y. 22:302
Hambridge, James 11:326
Hambright, Hardin 22:253
Hambrough, H. 9:178;
  19:270
Hamburg, F. 19:74
Hamburg, William 1:43
Hamburger, Andrew
  15:27
Hamby, Isaac N. 20:104
Hamby, J. T. M. 20:140
Hamcotter, John 18:190;
  26:211
Hame, Joseph 19:243
Hame, William 13:128
Hamel, C. N. 17:291
Hamel, Jonathan W. 4:29
Hamel, T. C. 9:97
Hamel, Wesley B. 10:56
Hameley, George 4:29
Hamell, A. 11:303
Hamelton, Elander 19:74
Hamelton, John 16:196
Hamelton, T. 25:180
Hamely, Pat 12:23
Hamens, James 18:367
Hamer, Adrian C. 22:497
Hamer, C. 14:67
Hamer, James 24:19
Hamer, P. 25:40
Hamer, R. 14:67
Hamer, Series 10:17
Hamer, Thomas 10:161;
  19:167
Hamer, William A. 18:395
Hamer, William H. 25:44
Hamerden, F. 7:96
Hamerly, William C. 8:18;
  18:137
Hamern, Calvin H. 18:206
Hamers, Nathaniel 24:196
Hames, D. H. 12:161
Hames, F. 7:50
Hames, Hiram 16:35

Hames, Zelis 19:16
Hamesson, J. S. 25:40
Hamey, George 4:66
Hamick, James M. 21:53
Hamilin, W. 21:27
Hamilin, Zenon 9:208
Hamiling, A. C. 11:263
Hamill, A. 16:35
Hamill, D. 27:58
Hamill, David 25:180
Hamill, M. E. (Mrs.)
    20:92
Hamill, Thomas 15:353
Hamilton, --- 1:39; 11:127
Hamilton, A. 7:124; 9:82;
    11:262; 18:83; 26:33
Hamilton, A. F. 19:222
Hamilton, A. G. 11:31
Hamilton, A. J. 21:340
Hamilton, A. T. 10:56;
    20:264
Hamilton, Alexander
    21:130; 22:33; 23:88
Hamilton, Alfred 10:116;
    20:264
Hamilton, Almon E.
    21:340
Hamilton, Alva P. 23:190
Hamilton, Alvin W.
    21:254
Hamilton, Anderson 12:49
Hamilton, Andrew S.
    8:18; 18:137
Hamilton, Arthur T. 15:91
Hamilton, Avery G.
    21:254
Hamilton, B. 1:44; 8:49
Hamilton, Bedwell 20:264
Hamilton, Benjamin
    15:87; 21:53
Hamilton, Benjamin F.
    17:35
Hamilton, Bidwell 10:116
Hamilton, Brentor 8:86
Hamilton, C. W. 15:258
Hamilton, Cassius M.
    21:70
Hamilton, Charles 7:124
Hamilton, Charles C. 7:96
Hamilton, Charles T. 1:41
Hamilton, Charles W.
    12:99
Hamilton, D. 1:135; 3:87;
    13:130; 25:43
Hamilton, David 9:22, 82;
    18:320; 22:195
Hamilton, E. 20:178
Hamilton, Edwin 8:72
Hamilton, Edwin M.
    24:51
Hamilton, Eli 7:14

Hamilton, Elias 15:36
Hamilton, Elisha B.
    10:116; 20:264
Hamilton, Elliott 25:180
Hamilton, Ennis 5:40
Hamilton, Erastus H.
    21:340
Hamilton, Evander 12:95;
    15:359
Hamilton, F. 6:31; 25:321
Hamilton, Fandy 27:63
Hamilton, Frank 18:238;
    26:36
Hamilton, G. H. 1:44
Hamilton, G. W. 11:263;
    17:154
Hamilton, George 10:56;
    11:338; 17:176;
    19:16; 20:264;
    23:244
Hamilton, George F.
    18:238; 26:36
Hamilton, George N.
    18:339
Hamilton, George S.
    22:481
Hamilton, George W. 4:29
Hamilton, Gustavus 5:40
Hamilton, H. 3:87; 8:72;
    25:180
Hamilton, H. B. 20:264
Hamilton, H. C. 1:138;
    9:144
Hamilton, H. F. 13:110
Hamilton, H. J. 27:55
Hamilton, H. M. 11:327
Hamilton, H. P. 13:111
Hamilton, Hancey 15:3
Hamilton, Helen 9:110
Hamilton, Henry 5:40;
    11:31; 21:272
Hamilton, Henry B. 10:56
Hamilton, Henry N.
    22:253
Hamilton, Hugh B. 7:28
Hamilton, Hunter 20:264
Hamilton, I. 3:87; 24:66
Hamilton, I. R. 21:27
Hamilton, J. 1:43; 3:87;
    16:196; 17:176;
    21:208
Hamilton, J. A. 17:273;
    25:180
Hamilton, J. B. 14:175;
    27:145
Hamilton, J. F. 1:94;
    19:267
Hamilton, J. G. 3:87
Hamilton, J. H. 22:253
Hamilton, J. S. 11:149;
    23:146

Hamilton, J. W. 25:38
Hamilton, Jackson
    17:132; 24:195
Hamilton, Jacob 21:27
Hamilton, James 11:263,
    413; 12:23; 13:26;
    15:201; 21:255;
    22:253; 25:180;
    27:144
Hamilton, James C.
    11:276
Hamilton, James D.
    17:317
Hamilton, James M. 8:49;
    21:70
Hamilton, James W. 22:33
Hamilton, Jefferson 7:124
Hamilton, Jer 26:100
Hamilton, Jeremiah 9:22;
    18:307
Hamilton, John 3:87;
    4:29; 7:29, 124;
    11:305; 14:67;
    15:298; 16:3; 17:151;
    18:67; 22:451;
    25:298
Hamilton, John A. 5:17
Hamilton, John F. 9:178
Hamilton, John H. 4:29
Hamilton, John J. 22:122
Hamilton, John L. 22:508
Hamilton, John S. 1:38
Hamilton, Joseph 20:146
Hamilton, Joseph V.
    19:331
Hamilton, Julius P. 11:107
Hamilton, July 9:131;
    27:59
Hamilton, L. 10:28;
    19:302
Hamilton, L. R. 1:136
Hamilton, L. W. 16:196
Hamilton, M. 18:30
Hamilton, M. S. 17:291
Hamilton, Marcus 10:95
Hamilton, Marion T.
    21:195
Hamilton, Mark 22:80
Hamilton, Michael B.
    22:11
Hamilton, Myron 23:32
Hamilton, N. J. 14:175
Hamilton, Norris 22:33
Hamilton, P. 5:40; 9:178;
    19:294; 25:180
Hamilton, P. S. 3:87
Hamilton, Permission
    22:405
Hamilton, Peter 7:57
Hamilton, R. A. 26:37
Hamilton, R. F. 25:321

Hamilton, R. T. 9:82
Hamilton, Reuben 21:340
Hamilton, Richard 24:101
Hamilton, Richard S.
  17:233
Hamilton, Richard W.
  1:191
Hamilton, Robert 7:96;
  10:116; 11:31;
  13:111; 14:67;
  20:264; 22:33, 171
Hamilton, S. 3:87;
  11:181; 20:124
Hamilton, S. C. 1:42
Hamilton, S. S. 1:39
Hamilton, Samuel 7:57;
  21:340; 22:80; 23:67
Hamilton, Stephen 7:124;
  17:397
Hamilton, Stewart 18:238;
  26:36
Hamilton, T. H. 6:31
Hamilton, Thomas 3:87;
  4:66; 5:40; 7:29, 80;
  17:176; 23:67;
  25:298
Hamilton, Thomas B.
  22:405
Hamilton, Tillman 23:146
Hamilton, Verdamon
  10:116
Hamilton, Verdeman
  20:264
Hamilton, W. 11:292;
  18:238; 22:302;
  24:78; 26:37
Hamilton, W. A. 8:49
Hamilton, W. C. 15:201
Hamilton, W. D. 21:100
Hamilton, W. L. 23:190
Hamilton, W. L. S. 22:161
Hamilton, Wade 7:124
Hamilton, Warren 7:124;
  21:340
Hamilton, Wesley 11:413
Hamilton, Wesley B.
  20:264
Hamilton, William 3:87;
  4:29; 9:97; 12:153;
  13:26, 111; 15:56;
  17:145; 18:30;
  21:138, 225; 22:336;
  25:180; 26:125;
  27:59
Hamilton, William A.
  11:287; 21:70
Hamilton, William C.
  18:239; 26:36
Hamilton, William Foster
  22:33

Hamilton, William H.
  9:131; 16:82
Hamilton, William M.
  8:106
Hamilton, William S.
  11:191; 23:281
Hamilton, Wilson 12:99
Hamin, Elijah 22:33
Hamitt, J. 14:67
Hamler, Henry 8:72
Hamler, Isaac 11:304
Hamlet, Benjamin 16:147
Hamlet, Franklin C.
  22:425
Hamlet, J. 1:139
Hamlet, William 22:302
Hamley, Joseph 21:340
Hamlier, John 3:87
Hamlin, A. 1:98; 16:196
Hamlin, Abra J. 24:78
Hamlin, Andrew 24:93
Hamlin, B. 1:42
Hamlin, B. F. 9:178;
  19:253
Hamlin, Bolin 19:291
Hamlin, Caleb 21:247
Hamlin, Calvin R. 8:86
Hamlin, Charles 24:72
Hamlin, Christopher
  Columbus 21:70
Hamlin, Ferdinand 21:272
Hamlin, George 21:53
Hamlin, H. P. 3:87
Hamlin, Henry 18:239;
  26:35
Hamlin, Isaac 22:144
Hamlin, J. 15:202
Hamlin, J. H. 3:87
Hamlin, Jacob L. 22:161
Hamlin, James 7:96;
  15:67
Hamlin, Jesse S. 21:91
Hamlin, John 8:18;
  18:137; 22:195;
  25:321
Hamlin, Leroy 17:110
Hamlin, P. A. 27:55
Hamlin, Philip 16:145
Hamlin, Stephen 22:427
Hamlin, William 9:35,
  102; 18:293; 26:102
Hamm, Eugene 26:124
Hamm, J. 3:88
Hamm, John 16:196
Hamm, William 10:116
Hammack, J. W. 3:88
Hamman, Gotfried 16:119
Hamman, Lucas C. 11:413
Hamman, Samuel J. 13:26
Hamman, W. H. 3:88

Hamman, Walker G.
  25:180
Hamman, William 11:401
Hammard, H. C. 1:40
Hammel, A. 11:149
Hammel, Bernard 15:36
Hammel, John 12:153
Hammel, Thomas H.
  17:20
Hammell, H. 1:42
Hammell, Isaiah 17:20
Hammell, John 4:29
Hammelt, William 13:26
Hammer, A. 3:88; 14:67
Hammer, A. C. 25:321
Hammer, A. G. 9:163
Hammer, Christian 16:166
Hammer, D. B. 13:110
Hammer, David V. 23:88
Hammer, Dennis S. 24:51
Hammer, Edward 10:210
Hammer, F. 26:164
Hammer, George 17:209
Hammer, J. 14:175;
  16:196; 19:253
Hammer, James D. 19:16
Hammer, John 3:88;
  9:178; 24:66
Hammer, L. B. 14:175,
  256
Hammer, N. 12:99
Hammer, Nelson 7:124
Hammer, P. W. 14:67
Hammer, Richard 21:70
Hammer, S. 3:88
Hammer, William 20:33
Hammercher, Gottfried
  10:56
Hammers, H. 17:359
Hammerslee, William M.
  1:42
Hammersmith, F. 20:265
Hammersmith, Frank
  10:56
Hammerston, George
  22:33
Hammes, J. 3:88
Hammett, Harrison 7:124
Hammett, W. B. 1:141
Hammide, A. 3:88
Hammill, D. 9:144
Hammill, George 23:88
Hammill, James 19:167
Hammilt, William 16:35
Hammilton, George 1:39
Hamming, Amos 9:214
Hamming, Pleasant
  16:196
Hammis, J. M. 9:43
Hammmond, William D.
  16:147

Hammock, George 17:52
Hammock, J. H. 16:35
Hammock, James L. 23:32
Hammock, John C.
　21:133
Hammock, Malon 17:295
Hammock, Martin V. B.
　15:87
Hammock, Philip 24:51
Hammocks, W. 21:203
Hammon, Charles 17:110
Hammon, Charles E. 7:96
Hammon, Eugene 9:43
Hammon, Henry 6:31;
　25:321
Hammon, Ira 11:93
Hammon, Jonas 22:427
Hammon, Paul 25:41
Hammon, Samuel 22:352
Hammon, William R.
　22:452
Hammond, --- 8:49
Hammond, A. 1:141;
　20:264; 21:340
Hammond, A. C. 1:39
Hammond, A. H. 25:181
Hammond, A. P. 11:327
Hammond, Alex 19:167
Hammond, Alexander
　9:230; 10:176
Hammond, Alfred 22:501
Hammond, Andrew
　22:482
Hammond, Anson 27:61
Hammond, Apollos 7:96
Hammond, B. 22:302
Hammond, Barthel 13:64
Hammond, C. 1:138;
　13:89; 14:11;
　15:201; 16:196
Hammond, Calvin A.
　22:80
Hammond, Carey 22:302
Hammond, Charles 19:16
Hammond, Cornelius
　23:121
Hammond, D. 16:95
Hammond, D. F. 11:152
Hammond, David 9:82
Hammond, Dugal 9:242
Hammond, E. 9:144;
　22:523; 27:58
Hammond, E. A. 27:61
Hammond, Edwin 24:19
Hammond, Elias 24:39
Hammond, F. 12:164;
　26:164
Hammond, F. D. 13:110
Hammond, Frank 16:294;
　22:302
Hammond, G. 9:163

Hammond, G. A. 1:141
Hammond, G. E. 7:29
Hammond, G. M. 1:137
Hammond, G. W. 3:88
Hammond, George 3:88;
　9:144; 22:195; 27:56
Hammond, Greenville G.
　21:70
Hammond, H. 14:11, 67
Hammond, Henry C.
　23:301
Hammond, J. 3:88; 19:16;
　24:78
Hammond, J. B. 1:139
Hammond, J. K. 13:89;
　14:11, 67
Hammond, J. S. 21:340
Hammond, James 20:97;
　22:195
Hammond, James E.
　27:63
Hammond, Joab M. 7:96
Hammond, John 8:18;
　17:259; 18:137;
　22:33
Hammond, John A. 23:88
Hammond, John H. 9:72
Hammond, Joseph
　10:161; 19:167
Hammond, Joshua 23:67
Hammond, L. 12:95;
　15:359; 25:181
Hammond, L. D. 17:445
Hammond, Lemuel F.
　24:39
Hammond, Levi 21:121
Hammond, Loren M.
　17:263
Hammond, Louis 21:86;
　22:336
Hammond, Louis P.
　18:307; 26:102
Hammond, Luther 27:60
Hammond, Lyman D.
　24:164
Hammond, M. 16:196
Hammond, N. 9:53
Hammond, N. F. 25:181
Hammond, Nathan 18:277
Hammond, Oliver 13:26
Hammond, Perry H. 22:33
Hammond, R. T. 9:119
Hammond, Randolph 7:96
Hammond, Rubin 23:244
Hammond, S. 3:88; 13:89;
　25:285
Hammond, S. C. 9:82
Hammond, S. D. 20:265
Hammond, S. E. 10:205
Hammond, Samuel 22:302

Hammond, Samuel D.
　10:56
Hammond, Samuel W.
　13:26
Hammond, Sanford 11:32
Hammond, Solomon 7:29
Hammond, T. J. 25:181
Hammond, W. 3:88;
　14:67
Hammond, W. A. 20:265
Hammond, W. E. 19:16
Hammond, W. H. 1:98
Hammond, W. P. 20:265
Hammond, Westle 23:285
Hammond, William
　14:175; 17:35, 176;
　24:19
Hammond, William A.
　10:56
Hammond, William H.
　11:150; 12:172;
　17:273
Hammond, William M.
　17:65
Hammond, William W.
　23:107
Hammonds, G. G. 8:49
Hammonds, Henry W.
　22:502
Hammonds, Jefferson
　24:59
Hammonds, John 17:52
Hammonia, F. 7:29;
　14:334
Hammons, George 11:387
Hammons, Isaac 19:319
Hammons, Thomas 17:52
Hammons, Wiley 22:253
Hammonstrees, Thomas
　11:327
Hammontree, Joseph L.
　19:16
Hammontrer, P. 3:88
Hammor, L. 5:40
Hammuston, Jos. W.
　8:114
Hamnausten, N. P. 15:359
Hamner, H. 13:89
Hamner, Jacob 13:64
Hamon, Jacob 21:211
Hamon, K. 14:68
Hamon, R. 16:196
Hamon, William A.
　18:217
Hamond, Daniel 21:27
Hamons, Ezekiel 26:163
Hamor, Frederick 25:181
Hamp, George H. 11:402
Hamp, K. 9:178
Hamp, Rafer 19:274
Hampe, Charles 10:56

Hampe, F. 1:98
Hampel, Joseph 7:96
Hamper, Adolphus 11:381
Hampfling, H. 17:347
Hamphill, J. 14:288; 23:67
Hampkins, James A. 9:228
Hample, Joseph 21:340
Hampo, Charles 20:265
Hampson, C. P. 19:270
Hampson, James B. 23:146
Hampson, Solomon C. 17:91
Hampton, --- 4:66
Hampton, Amos M. 11:305
Hampton, B. F. 8:63
Hampton, Benjamin F. 7:96
Hampton, Charles B. 10:116; 20:265
Hampton, David 8:106
Hampton, E. J. 10:209
Hampton, E. W. 25:276
Hampton, Edward 8:106
Hampton, Ephraim T. 10:116; 20:265
Hampton, G. S. 11:63
Hampton, Henry 24:71
Hampton, Horace H. 10:116; 20:265
Hampton, J. A. 3:88
Hampton, J. H. 17:280
Hampton, J. R. 24:78
Hampton, J. S. 17:166
Hampton, J. W. 11:93
Hampton, J. W. N. 18:239; 26:34
Hampton, James 8:106; 22:405
Hampton, James M. 20:104
Hampton, Joel 8:119
Hampton, Joel A. 22:451
Hampton, John 9:161; 10:116; 14:327; 17:132; 20:265; 23:242; 24:195
Hampton, John C. 1:41
Hampton, John W. 21:27
Hampton, Jonathan 20:113
Hampton, Joseph 17:347
Hampton, Lewis L. 22:452
Hampton, N. 9:53
Hampton, Nicholas 22:302
Hampton, Peter 21:272

Hampton, Philip 22:405
Hampton, R. 25:281
Hampton, R. M. 23:146
Hampton, R. W. 11:65
Hampton, Robert 11:387; 12:87; 14:68; 16:294
Hampton, Samuel 10:172; 19:167
Hampton, Seras 21:340
Hampton, Thomas 7:96; 14:68
Hampton, W. 21:27
Hampton, Wade 23:290
Hampton, William 9:230; 20:265
Hampy, W. H. 23:148
Hamrick, S. S. 25:42
Hamrick, Samuel J. 24:39
Hamrick, W. H. 27:63
Hamrick, William 22:352
Hams, Lewis 8:106
Hams, Peter 20:265
Hamsley, James W. 9:208
Hamson, B. 19:274
Hamson, G. M. 25:181
Hamson, John 14:68
Hamson, Joseph 18:293
Hamson, Thomas 8:18
Hamstead, J. 3:88
Hamstead, James 27:59
Hamston, Andy 22:302
Hamstred, Holzy 26:103
Hamton, John 14:327
Hamur, Levi J. 12:71
Han, A. 1:139
Han, F. 14:11
Hana, H. 14:175
Hanaburg, Michael 17:107
Hanach, L. 3:88
Hanafer, J. 14:298; 17:470
Hanaford, Benjamin 9:119; 27:60
Hanagan, I. 17:475; 27:63
Hanagan, J. 14:298
Hanagan, Patrick 17:460; 24:159
Hanaghan, D. 25:40
Hanah, D. S. 11:413
Hanahan, Michael 22:336
Hanak, C. L. 3:88
Hanakota, Fred 18:320
Hanaley, Tyler 23:279
Hanaman, Hugh 12:154
Hanan, John 26:100
Hanan, P. 27:61
Hanan, W. 23:147
Hanar, A. 1:38
Hanard, A. C. 14:175
Hanard, J. B. 3:88
Hanasan, Thomas 20:265

Hanasen, Thomas 9:230
Hanass, C. H. 9:53
Hanatan, Samuel 15:353
Hanault, Samuel 21:203
Hanawait, --- 11:150
Hanaway, E. 1:142
Hanaway, Stephen 11:387
Hanber, Charles P. 9:220
Hanber, J. F. 13:64
Hanber, John 9:220; 18:190
Hanberry, John 23:32
Hanbert, Handsman 8:106
Hanbey, P. 14:298
Hanbit, J. F. 16:196
Hanby, Abram 16:35
Hanby, Adam 13:26
Hanby, P. 17:477
Hance, A. 11:126
Hance, J. D. 13:125
Hance, J. M. 18:239
Hance, James 8:39; 26:165
Hance, James H. 19:16
Hance, Joseph R. 11:327
Hance, Samuel 17:154
Hance, Willis 11:126
Hancey, James 13:26
Hanch, August 7:57
Hanch, H. L. 21:27
Hanchell, Arnst 11:413
Hanchett, Henry J. 20:48
Hanck, G. M. 21:121
Hanco, I. W. 26:35
Hancock, Balise 18:137
Hancock, Barless 8:18
Hancock, Benjamin 21:148
Hancock, C. P. 12:71
Hancock, Charles G. 18:421
Hancock, Claiborne 6:22
Hancock, Edwin R. 15:91
Hancock, F. E. 7:57
Hancock, Francis M. 22:80
Hancock, G. 9:144; 27:57
Hancock, G. E. 1:135
Hancock, George G. 24:20
Hancock, George L. 21:340
Hancock, George W. 8:124
Hancock, Gilbert F. 21:91
Hancock, H. D. 19:16
Hancock, Ham 22:302
Hancock, I. I. 8:18
Hancock, J. 14:68, 298; 17:480; 27:64
Hancock, J. J. 18:137
Hancock, J. O. 15:25

Hancock, James 14:286
Hancock, James L. 24:66
Hancock, Joel 22:452
Hancock, John 8:77;
    14:263; 20:17;
    21:70; 22:195
Hancock, John W. 22:352
Hancock, L. 1:137
Hancock, Lewis 22:253
Hancock, M. 24:39
Hancock, N. W. 14:68
Hancock, Oscar S. 21:195
Hancock, R. 3:88
Hancock, Robert 24:107
Hancock, Samuel 24:194
Hancock, W. 3:88
Hancock, W. H. 25:283
Hancock, William 9:208;
    14:175; 26:166
Hancomb, James E.
    10:148
Hancson, N. 1:137
Hancy, James 16:36
Hancy, Levi 17:460
Hand, --- 15:347; 16:370
Hand, Barney 10:116;
    20:265
Hand, Clement E. 9:179;
    19:277
Hand, Daniel H. 4:29
Hand, Davis 10:17
Hand, E. E. 8:18
Hand, Edward 25:40
Hand, Elias 19:16
Hand, Francis F. 25:39
Hand, G. 3:88; 14:175
Hand, George E. 9:208
Hand, H. 3:88
Hand, H. S. 3:88
Hand, Henry 16:196
Hand, Isaac 12:23
Hand, J. 13:89; 14:11;
    16:196
Hand, J. C. 14:175
Hand, J. E. 9:53
Hand, James 12:99;
    14:175
Hand, Joel R. 21:70
Hand, John 1:38, 39;
    15:67; 24:107
Hand, Joseph 9:179
Hand, Josiah 7:14
Hand, L. 3:88
Hand, Lewis 14:175
Hand, M. C. 21:110
Hand, Martin 10:151, 178
Hand, Nathan 12:23
Hand, P. 23:263
Hand, Patrick 17:14
Hand, Silas 10:116;
    20:265

Hand, Thomas 1:42;
    16:119, 166
Hand, Thomas H. 22:405
Hand, William 13:26
Handcock, Robert 14:175
Handel, Valentine 13:26
Handemer, George 22:302
Hander, Daniel 23:32
Handerson, James 17:287
Handey, James B. 19:227
Handford, Horace S.
    9:119
Handgerton, H. 24:78
Handin, G. W. 3:88
Handland, H. 3:88
Handle, William B. 20:17
Handler, John 13:26
Handless, John 22:336
Handley, A. G. 5:17
Handley, Aaron 10:56;
    20:265
Handley, Albert 4:29
Handley, Daniel 10:210
Handley, F. J. 14:68
Handley, Frank 19:296
Handley, J. D. 11:152
Handley, James 15:124
Handley, John 6:31;
    22:336
Handley, Mathew 9:22
Handley, Matthew 18:307
Handley, N. S. 10:56;
    20:265
Handley, R. P. 9:53
Handley, Samuel B.
    22:481
Handley, Thomas 10:153
Handlin, Samuel 16:279
Handlin, Thomas 27:56
Handlin, Walter 13:26
Handlon, Rufus R. 6:31
Handly, John 8:106
Handly, Mathew 26:99
Handorf, Henry 18:395
Hands, Clark 26:35
Hands, George 21:340
Hands, J. 3:88
Handshaw, Joshua 10:56
Handsler, George 15:298
Handy, Alfred 19:46
Handy, Andrew J. 14:175
Handy, C. 15:158
Handy, C. H. 1:141
Handy, Charles W. 8:114
Handy, Clark 18:239
Handy, Daniel 19:267
Handy, George 3:88
Handy, George W. 25:181
Handy, H. 9:208
Handy, Henry 6:16; 18:83
Handy, Jacob 6:12

Handy, Joel 3:88
Handy, John 9:131; 19:74;
    27:59, 62
Handy, M. 1:38
Handy, Moses 3:88
Handy, S. H. 15:298
Handy, Thomas 6:31;
    7:29; 9:131; 27:59
Handy, Thomas B. 20:133
Handy, W. 1:136
Handy, William 6:12;
    18:84
Hane, Amos C. 9:82
Hane, Henry A. 22:481
Hane, John R. 9:236
Haneberger, D. 25:181
Haned, Alvin 11:287
Haned, Charles 12:49
Haneford, Joseph 13:26
Hanel, Nelson 19:167
Hanelton, T. W. 8:49
Haneman, Emanuel 9:220
Hanenstein, J. 12:82
Haner, Alexander 17:242
Haner, Charles 16:370
Haner, Ellis W. 17:35
Haner, Hiram 13:26
Haner, Jacob 1:44
Haner, Oscar 20:107
Haner, W. P. 1:137
Haners, Philip 9:22
Hanes, Andrew 22:195;
    25:42
Hanes, Charles 9:22;
    18:307; 26:100
Hanes, David 9:53;
    20:177
Hanes, F. G. 25:181
Hanes, I. 15:342
Hanes, James 24:20
Hanes, John 22:195
Hanes, John H. 22:336
Hanes, R. M. 25:42
Hanesly, Abraham 18:285
Haney, A. 14:68
Haney, A. E. 11:242
Haney, Alva 23:190
Haney, Ashel N. 22:253
Haney, B. 1:45
Haney, C. 14:68
Haney, Charles W. 19:348
Haney, Daniel 24:93
Haney, Elijah 25:41
Haney, G. M. 9:66
Haney, H. 3:88
Haney, Henry 25:298
Haney, J. 3:88; 24:111
Haney, Jacob 11:107
Haney, James 7:96
Haney, John 13:26; 16:36;
    23:147

Haney, Levi 8:101; 24:159
Haney, Lewis 23:147
Haney, Martin 22:11
Haney, Patrick 22:451
Haney, Robert 23:147
Haney, S. J. 23:32
Haney, Stockton D. 24:159
Haney, T. 23:32
Haney, Theron 22:336
Haney, Thomas 3:88
Haney, W. 15:201; 22:352
Haney, William 10:116; 20:265
Haney, William H. 12:23
Hanff, Paul 15:304
Hanford, C. J. 1:45
Hanford, Charles H. 9:156
Hanford, Chauncey 13:26
Hanford, George E. 10:56; 20:265
Hanford, H. 15:173
Hanford, Hiram 12:23
Hanford, Horace 27:60
Hanford, J. 16:196
Hanford, Joseph 16:36
Hanford, Mathew 22:451
Hang, E. 14:241
Hang, G. 1:137
Hang, Lewis 15:151
Hang, M. 25:181
Hangas, George 18:84
Hange, E. 18:430
Hanger, Solomon 23:279
Hanger, Thomas 19:16
Hanghers, R. 11:304
Hanghey, C. W. 26:163
Hanghman, A. 3:88
Hangliter, C. M. 15:67
Hango, Shango 26:220
Hangor, L. S. 3:88
Hangue, Lewis S. 15:91
Hangus, George 6:16
Hanh, Frederick 17:394
Hanibal, James 17:391
Hanick, Charles 14:175
Hanico, J. 18:239
Hanie, J. P. 8:49
Hanier, Daniel 9:179
Hanighugh, Charles W. 9:22
Haning, E. A. 14:175
Haning, M. W. 22:195
Hanion, John 10:9
Hanison, John 19:253
Hank, B. 21:203
Hank, George D. 3:88
Hank, J. 25:41
Hank, J. M. 21:340
Hank, J. W. 11:150

Hank, James T. 15:36
Hank, John 10:172; 19:167
Hank, John H. 7:50
Hank, N. H. 20:92
Hank, Peter 11:93
Hank, R. 27:63
Hank, Richard 14:327
Hankell, J. 3:88
Hanken, J. H. 1:138
Hanker, B. 25:181
Hanker, John C. 13:26
Hanker, R. 3:88
Hankerson, Robert 11:305
Hankery, Chancelor 12:71
Hankey, C. 15:87
Hankhurst, W. J. 15:201
Hankins, Alex 20:265
Hankins, C. R. 20:265
Hankins, George 3:88; 15:67
Hankins, H. T. 9:179
Hankins, Henry 21:340
Hankins, James 15:202
Hankins, John 17:276
Hankins, Joseph 15:7
Hankins, L. 20:174
Hankins, Richard 10:56; 20:265
Hankins, William 9:208, 220; 18:367
Hankley, Abraham 21:28
Hankley, J. B. 14:175
Hankly, Jordan 16:196
Hanks, --- 21:340
Hanks, A. 3:88
Hanks, Cyrus W. 15:315
Hanks, David 17:176
Hanks, G. 11:305
Hanks, George 11:151
Hanks, J. 3:88
Hanks, James B. 22:480
Hanks, James W. 19:74
Hanks, Jeremiah H. 20:23
Hanks, M. 14:175
Hanks, Moses 17:177
Hanks, Nelson 3:88
Hanks, T. W. 11:33
Hanks, Wallace B. 22:427
Hanks, William 22:501
Hankston, Elmon 11:149
Hanky, John 20:183
Hanlenbeck, W. H. 19:253
Hanlette, Everette 17:259
Hanlewbeck, W. H. 9:179
Hanley, --- 11:231
Hanley, Charles J. 22:144
Hanley, D. 3:88
Hanley, F. 3:88
Hanley, F. M. 11:413
Hanley, Franklin 21:225

Hanley, George M. 22:427
Hanley, J. 2:12; 25:38
Hanley, John 9:179; 14:298; 17:470; 19:74, 238; 27:64
Hanley, Lemuel 8:39
Hanley, M. 9:53
Hanley, Martin 20:56
Hanley, T. 3:88
Hanley, Thomas 11:231
Hanley, W. 3:88
Hanley, William 3:88; 14:176
Hanley, Z. 21:121
Hanlin, Joseph 23:147
Hanline, I. W. 25:181
Hanlon, James 12:82; 15:36; 16:294
Hanlon, John 7:15; 9:82; 21:53; 25:181
Hanlon, Samuel M. 23:147
Hanlon, Thomas 3:88
Hanlon, W. 26:33
Hanly, Daniel 1:40
Hanly, R. 27:64
Hanly, Reuben 21:273
Hanly, Thomas 19:167
Hanmacher, G. 20:265
Hanman, George 17:248
Hanman, J. M. 20:124
Hanmer, John C. 15:342
Hanmer, William 20:189
Hanmore, W. 18:50
Hann, --- 16:370
Hann, Adam 24:89
Hann, George 12:71
Hann, Hermann 22:508
Hann, J. B. 18:339
Hann, James 9:165
Hann, James T. 22:253
Hann, John N. 12:64; 15:7
Hann, John W. 15:7
Hann, Joseph C. 19:16
Hann, Peter 10:56
Hann, S. 10:155
Hann, W. 8:18; 18:137
Hanna, Abraham 1:42
Hanna, Adam 15:158
Hanna, Charles 23:147
Hanna, D. 16:119
Hanna, G. W. 25:298
Hanna, Henry 16:36
Hanna, J. A. 14:68
Hanna, J. B. 23:292
Hanna, J. R. 21:340
Hanna, James 18:217
Hanna, John 3:88; 5:17; 16:370; 17:248, 253
Hanna, John J. 11:63
Hanna, Joseph 19:287

Hanna, Julian J. 23:147
Hanna, Lewis 10:56
Hanna, N. N. 22:481
Hanna, P. 3:88
Hanna, R. 14:176
Hanna, Robert 18:217;
25:321
Hanna, Robert P. 23:67
Hanna, W. F. 3:88
Hanna, William A. 12:64;
15:7
Hanna, William T. 23:305
Hannaford, John 9:239;
19:337
Hannagan, Leverett
21:216
Hannagan, Patrick 4:29
Hannah, Aaron 21:28
Hannah, Benjamin 22:336
Hannah, D. 15:294;
16:196
Hannah, E. B. 16:36
Hannah, George W. 7:74
Hannah, H. 3:88
Hannah, Henry 13:26
Hannah, James 7:80;
25:298
Hannah, John 22:80
Hannah, Joseph 21:138
Hannah, L. T. 24:20
Hannah, Robert 9:165
Hannah, Thomas 3:88;
7:68
Hannah, William 11:63
Hannahan, A. 3:88
Hannahen, Thomas
16:370
Hannahs, Delivan 18:367
Hannam, F. 17:154
Hannam, John F. 6:11
Hannam, John T. 18:110
Hannaman, Francis 24:93
Hannan, --- 15:36
Hannan, D. 19:253
Hannan, Geron 12:71
Hannan, James H. 10:56
Hannan, John 4:29
Hannan, Patrick 13:26;
27:54
Hannanas, James 13:26
Hannar, Jeremiah 11:205
Hannard, G. 1:136
Hannas, William H. 1:40
Hannassey, J. 7:57
Hannay, Michael 23:67
Hannegan, John 10:34
Hannegan, John L. 20:151
Hannel, D. 12:154
Hanneman, E. 1:44
Hannen, John 9:22
Hannen, Lawrence 9:82

Hanner, Charles 15:347
Hanner, Decater 11:412
Hanner, Edward 22:195
Hanner, John 1:38; 11:305
Hanner, L. G. 15:56
Hanner, Nelson 22:513
Hanner, Ole 14:288
Hanner, William 11:423;
19:270
Hannerott, John 23:147
Hannes, J. B. 9:82
Hanney, J. 1:41
Hanney, M. N. 25:42
Hannhas, J. 19:74
Hannibal, E. 18:137
Hannibal, Watson 4:29
Hannibal, William 9:12
Hannible, Franklin 21:340
Hannicoolt, Thomas
20:265
Hannicott, Thomas 10:116
Hannig, Mark 3:89
Hannigan, M. 1:42
Hanniker, Charles 4:29
Hanning, Amos 21:340
Hanning, F. 11:287
Hanning, H. 3:89; 7:50
Hannington, Jeremiah
27:62
Hannis, Elias 16:95
Hannison, J. T. 15:14
Hannison, W. H. 9:144
Hanniton, Joseph H.
18:323
Hanno, George 15:299;
16:196
Hannolds, L. 14:68
Hannon, C. H. 23:32
Hannon, Charles 11:150
Hannon, Henry 18:207
Hannon, J. 14:68
Hannon, James 25:321
Hannon, John 18:103
Hannon, Josiah 9:82
Hannon, Lawrence 26:33
Hannon, Peter 21:340
Hannon, Peter E. 10:56
Hannon, W. F. 20:265
Hannons, William M.
20:113
Hannor, Robert 11:205
Hannosay, A. 3:89
Hanns, Charles 20:265
Hanns, Elijah 5:17
Hannschild, David 20:137
Hannsen, Peter 9:236
Hannuell, George 11:262
Hannum, A. S. 21:121
Hannum, James 22:195
Hannum, John A. 23:88
Hannum, R. B. 23:147

Hannum, Silas 21:340
Hannuon, Louis P. 9:22
Hannvet, C. 14:68
Hanny, Christian 10:116;
20:265
Hanny, D. 3:89
Hanny, Lord B. 22:280
Hano, William 14:332
Hanobin, John 19:222
Hanoler, George 19:291
Hanolin, John 19:222
Hanon, John B. 10:56
Hanon, Peter E. 20:265
Hanoper, J. 27:64
Hanor, Frank 3:89
Hanor, Mathias 8:114
Hanover, Allen 17:291
Hanover, Henry 7:96
Hanover, James 16:294
Hanover, John T. 14:176
Hanover, W. R. 17:110
Hanowdel, W. H. 4:29
Hanrahan, Patrick 23:32
Hanray, Prince A. 7:124
Hans, A. H. 1:44
Hans, August 24:93
Hans, Carl 26:165
Hans, Charles 18:421
Hans, G. W. 19:16
Hans, George T. 22:33
Hans, John 3:89; 24:195
Hans, Lewis 26:166
Hans, Samuel 9:22
Hansacker, G. 15:359
Hansard, W. 22:482
Hansart, Peter 19:343
Hansberry, E. A. 3:89
Hansbro, Henry 4:66
Hansburg, Frederick
26:32
Hansbury, Frederick 9:82
Hansbury, M. 17:177
Hanscom, J. P. 7:68
Hanscom, John O. 25:181
Hanscom, Newell 20:48
Hanscomb, Cyrus 4:29
Hanscomb, James E.
18:50
Hanscomb, Lewis 12:23
Hanscomb, Nathaniel 4:29
Hanscon, George 7:29
Hanse, Benjamin 7:29
Hansel, Conrad 19:167
Hansel, David 21:28
Hansel, Francis Merrian
16:119
Hansel, Llewellyn 19:270
Hansell, Isaac 10:56;
20:265
Hansell, Josiah 23:285
Hansell, L. 9:179

Hansell, William A. 10:116; 20:265
Hanselman, W. 24:79
Hansen, A. 9:220
Hansen, Andrew 24:51
Hansen, Hans 21:91; 23:190
Hanser, James H. 8:18
Hanser, Mathias 21:340
Hansey, G. 3:89
Hansfield, William 19:167
Hansfire, Alfred 22:80
Hansford, Benjamin 11:423
Hansford, F. 27:56
Hanshan, Thomas 18:239
Hanshaw, James 17:143
Hanshaw, Thomas 26:35
Hanshear, Josiah 20:265
Hansien, Oscar A. 21:340
Hansinger, Charles N. 27:60
Hansley, Pleasant 17:52
Hansley, Robert 10:176; 19:168
Hanslog, Arnold 14:176
Hansman, John 9:144
Hansman, Louis 11:33
Hansman, Michael 9:35
Hansmid, Anthony 8:18
Hansom, H. 14:265
Hansom, Ransom 24:20
Hanson, A. G. 7:96
Hanson, A. H. 27:55
Hanson, Almond 19:168
Hanson, Amond 10:161
Hanson, Anderson 22:34
Hanson, Andrew 22:34
Hanson, Anton 22:166
Hanson, Augustine 24:66
Hanson, Austin 16:78
Hanson, B. 9:214
Hanson, Benjamin 7:29; 11:191
Hanson, Brown 9:179
Hanson, C. 3:89; 18:239; 22:352; 26:35
Hanson, Charles 13:26; 16:36
Hanson, Charles B. 10:116; 20:265
Hanson, Charles D. 14:176
Hanson, Christian 17:80; 22:508; 26:164
Hanson, Cornelius 8:18; 18:137; 27:55
Hanson, D. 3:89
Hanson, Daniel 22:80
Hanson, E. 16:196
Hanson, E. H. 9:110

Hanson, Edward 15:13
Hanson, F. A. 3:89
Hanson, Frank 3:89
Hanson, Frank B. 10:161
Hanson, Frederick 17:446
Hanson, Frederick H. 24:170
Hanson, Gilbert 21:70
Hanson, Gontleet 8:18
Hanson, Gottlieb 18:137
Hanson, H. 9:119; 14:68, 288; 18:110; 27:60
Hanson, H. B. 13:26; 21:340
Hanson, H. H. 11:149; 16:294
Hanson, Halvor 6:9
Hanson, Hans 10:161; 11:33; 19:168; 22:280
Hanson, Hans Carl 17:359
Hanson, Harris 11:191
Hanson, Henry 17:21
Hanson, Hilliard 17:397
Hanson, J. 1:44; 3:89; 14:68, 269; 26:32
Hanson, J. A. 26:32
Hanson, J. W. 10:116; 20:265
Hanson, Jacob 16:196; 22:336; 24:94
Hanson, James 9:22; 18:84, 307; 26:100
Hanson, Jesse 9:82
Hanson, John 5:51; 10:116; 11:191; 12:23; 17:16; 19:16, 344; 20:265; 25:181
Hanson, John A. 9:82
Hanson, John C. 22:195
Hanson, Joseph 26:102
Hanson, L. 3:89
Hanson, Lewis 18:239; 26:35
Hanson, Lewis A. 22:195
Hanson, M. 22:280
Hanson, N. A. 27:57
Hanson, Noble 18:14
Hanson, O. 26:34
Hanson, O. C. 21:341
Hanson, Ole 23:88
Hanson, Oran 9:82
Hanson, P. 9:144; 17:432; 27:55
Hanson, Patrick 14:335
Hanson, Peter 12:49; 24:150
Hanson, R. 3:89
Hanson, Rasmus 10:116; 20:265
Hanson, S. G. 25:181

Hanson, Samuel 7:74; 10:116; 20:265; 22:80; 25:298
Hanson, Samuel K. 22:451
Hanson, Sears 22:280
Hanson, Siren 21:341
Hanson, Theodore 17:449; 24:185
Hanson, Thomas 1:40; 6:31; 25:321
Hanson, Vandy 24:195
Hanson, W. 1:137; 3:89
Hansoom, P. A. 25:42
Hansor, Vandy 17:132
Hansow, L. 14:176
Hansru, Henry 18:395
Hanstan, B. 3:89
Hanston, John 22:34
Hant, --- 26:100
Hant, Jacob 9:22
Hant, John 14:68
Hant, Richard 27:64
Hanter, Allen D. 22:513
Hantilius, H. 17:236
Hantly, John W. 17:393
Hantor, John 15:36
Hantrel, Chris 19:316
Hanttier, Brinkley 5:17
Hanum, Robert N. 11:305
Hanun, S. 19:168
Hanway, John 12:71
Hanwing, Eli 14:176
Hanwood, Herman A. 7:96
Hanxwell, William 4:29
Hapage, Lewis 13:111
Hape, R. 14:68
Hapeman, John W. 23:262
Hapeny, Nicholas 22:336
Hapes, H. 3:89
Hapgood, Cornelius 20:56
Hapgood, John 12:23
Hapkish, W. 26:33
Hapleton, Granville 20:265
Hapner, Jesse 9:22; 26:101
Hapner, Nathan 9:22
Hapner, Nelson 8:86
Happ, Christian 13:80
Happ, John 26:124
Happ, Moses 19:267
Happer, Anson 26:124
Happer, R. 14:68
Happer, Wash 21:341
Happy, Jacob 10:172; 19:168
Happy, William 9:131; 27:58
Haps, Michael 9:82

Hapsar, Jacob 24:173
Hapsess, J. 9:82
Hapson, Francis 26:35
Hapstontal, C. W. 9:97
Hapton, James 22:34
Hapwood, G. 13:89
Har---, Flanigan 24:196
Har---c, Charles 9:236
Hara, D. O. 1:44
Hara, Michael C. 16:36
Haraden, Albert 22:34
Haradon, Charles W. 20:97
Haradon, Henry 20:265
Harager, William 12:24
Harald, J. 16:196
Haraldson, Seibert 22:280
Haran, P. 13:26
Harare, John 9:53
Harb, F. 1:140
Harbach, Wilson 27:60
Harback, Cassius 20:189
Harback, D. 1:39
Harback, John 9:119; 27:60
Harbarger, J. 20:265
Harbaugh, Bishop R. 11:63
Harbaugh, C. H. 21:203
Harbaugh, E. A. 14:176
Harbaugh, George 5:18
Harbaugh, H. 1:39
Harbaugh, Jonathan 27:64
Harbaugh, Peter 23:305
Harbaugh, Thomas 25:275
Harbaugh, Wesley 21:138
Harbaugh, Wilson 9:119
Harben, Perry 22:81
Harber, I. 21:148
Harberger, Jacob 10:57
Harbermehl, Michael 23:147
Harbert, J. 1:138
Harbert, J. H. 10:179
Harbert, Joseph F. 22:81
Harbert, T. J. 11:293
Harbin, H. G. 23:147
Harbin, Joseph E. 20:124
Harbin, William 21:341; 22:336
Harbin, William C. 17:273
Harbine, John W. 15:56
Harbison, James 10:116; 20:265
Harbison, James H. 22:196
Harbison, James W. 22:426
Harbison, John S. 21:100
Harbit, James 23:147

Harbold, Henry 20:2
Harbolt, Jonathan B. 1:40
Harbon, F. 27:58
Harbon, Frederick 9:144
Harbon, John 13:26
Harbor, Isaac 21:273
Harbor, John D. 22:81
Harborough, J. H. 3:89
Harbough, G. 25:181
Harboure, L. 1:44
Harbrecket, J. 9:110
Harbridge, George H. 22:166
Harburger, I. 14:68
Harchbuyer, Peter 14:176
Harcourt, Joseph 17:387
Harcross, George I. 27:63
Hard, Duane 27:61
Hard, J. H. 17:52
Hard, John 22:463
Hard, John L. 11:107
Hard, Peterson 21:273
Hard, Thomas 12:142
Hard, William 3:89
Harda, L. C. 3:89
Hardacre, Milton 11:149
Hardaway, B. M. 19:17
Hardaway, J. H. 19:17
Hardaway, Peter 21:273
Hardcastle, William 22:452
Hardee, Dallas 11:263
Hardee, F. 12:166
Hardee, James 25:298
Hardee, Louis L. 27:62
Hardee, Milton R. 21:100
Hardee, N. 12:82
Hardee, R. 1:135
Hardee, Richard 11:280
Hardee, T. 1:43
Hardee, Thomas 25:321
Hardee, W. 16:294
Hardeen, C. 12:87; 16:294
Hardeman, Martin 20:266
Hardeman, Stephen 20:265
Harden, --- 3:89
Harden, Albert 12:171
Harden, Albert G. 22:34
Harden, Andrew J. 23:301
Harden, Benjamin F. 4:29
Harden, Charles 16:279; 18:412
Harden, Cyrus 17:455; 24:196
Harden, David 23:95
Harden, E. 7:57
Harden, E. A. 1:140
Harden, E. K. 14:68
Harden, Eli 11:187

Harden, Even 10:117; 20:265
Harden, George W. 21:341
Harden, H. D. 9:53
Harden, John M. 23:147
Harden, John P. 22:502
Harden, Joseph W. 23:147
Harden, M. 3:89
Harden, Mack 21:273
Harden, Oliver P. 23:32
Harden, S. H. 9:82
Harden, Thomas 11:149; 15:315
Harden, W. S. 7:97
Harden, Whatt 16:196
Harden, William 10:117; 20:266
Harden, William P. 17:280
Hardenberg, H. M. 19:74
Hardenburg, J. 25:181
Hardenburg, J. A. 1:38
Hardenburg, J. W. 5:18
Hardenburgh, Henry 12:154
Hardendorff, C. W. 15:124
Hardendorph, R. 1:139
Harder, C. 14:68
Harder, J. S. 7:97
Harder, Jerome 19:17
Harder, Lewis 15:330; 19:74
Harder, Peter 22:34
Harderliuty, --- 18:30
Harderly, E. 25:321
Harderman, Stephen 10:117
Harderty, Nelson 11:305
Hardester, Henry 10:57; 22:122
Hardestry, S. 20:266
Hardesty, Charles 22:451
Hardesty, George 11:149
Hardesty, Henry 22:482
Hardesty, James 17:132; 22:196; 24:195
Hardesty, James W. 17:321
Hardesty, Joseph 12:161
Hardesty, S. 24:78
Hardey, James 14:176
Hardfellow, Gootlieb 27:60
Hardfetter, Gotlieb 9:119
Hardia, M. M. 14:321; 23:32
Hardick, S. 1:43
Hardick, W. 11:149
Hardie, Martin U. 14:315

Hardigan, Daniel 19:340
Hardiman, A. C. 19:232
Hardiman, Martin 10:57
Hardin, --- 17:310; 26:166
Hardin, B. 17:99
Hardin, C. C. 11:423
Hardin, Calvin 7:29
Hardin, E. 17:177
Hardin, F. M. 17:191
Hardin, Frank 17:132;
  24:195
Hardin, G. 11:327
Hardin, G. W. 3:89
Hardin, George 18:346
Hardin, H. 18:239; 26:36
Hardin, Henry 24:196
Hardin, Henry C. 17:308
Hardin, Ira 22:80
Hardin, Isaac 17:35
Hardin, Jesse N. 8:86
Hardin, John 8:106;
  9:200; 11:419;
  14:68; 19:291
Hardin, John C. 11:84
Hardin, John W. 8:18
Hardin, Joseph 22:451
Hardin, Joseph G. 9:22
Hardin, Leonard 17:242
Hardin, Levi 22:253
Hardin, Marion S. 22:80
Hardin, Moses 17:177
Hardin, Nicholas 26:166
Hardin, R. 24:111
Hardin, Robert 8:49;
  18:239; 26:34
Hardin, Robert M. 21:70
Hardin, Rowen 17:148
Hardin, S. 10:150; 18:50
Hardin, S. B. 11:151
Hardin, S. H. 26:34
Hardin, Samuel H. 26:34
Hardin, W. 11:280
Hardin, W. E. 23:33
Hardin, W. P. 8:72
Hardinbrook, Charles
  14:176
Hardinburgh, Solomon
  11:107
Harding, --- 11:63; 26:164
Harding, A. M. 1:44
Harding, A. S. 20:266
Harding, Augustus 21:255
Harding, Aurelius 10:57
Harding, B. F. 1:141
Harding, Ben. E. 24:214
Harding, C. 3:89
Harding, Charles 22:80
Harding, Cyrus 7:74;
  25:298
Harding, D. 14:288;
  16:196; 19:238

Harding, Darius 9:179
Harding, G. W. 17:110;
  25:181
Harding, George W. 5:40
Harding, H. 8:49
Harding, H. A. 12:24
Harding, H. D. 15:202
Harding, H. P. 9:240
Harding, Henry 9:179;
  13:111; 21:341
Harding, Henry C. 17:259
Harding, J. 25:181
Harding, J. D. 17:265
Harding, James H. 7:8
Harding, John 13:26;
  15:91
Harding, John C. 16:36
Harding, John W. 15:202;
  18:137
Harding, Joseph 17:177
Harding, L. 1:43
Harding, Lewis 22:196
Harding, Mathew 18:277
Harding, N. 11:263
Harding, P. 22:196
Harding, Peter R. 23:88
Harding, Robert 22:336
Harding, Samuel C.
  21:187
Harding, Stephen 10:161;
  19:168
Harding, T. 17:217
Harding, Theodore 13:26
Harding, Thomas 17:212;
  19:74
Harding, Thomas J.
  22:426
Harding, W. 9:144;
  25:181; 27:58
Harding, W. D. 1:41
Harding, W. H. 1:141;
  3:89; 26:124
Harding, Warren 5:18
Harding, William H.
  22:144, 196
Harding, William P. 18:50
Harding, Ziba 13:26
Hardinger, Daniel 23:147
Hardinger, W. 3:89
Hardinorick, J. 3:89
Hardinson, Hiram 15:359
Hardison, B. B. 25:181
Hardison, G. 3:89
Hardison, Hiram 19:74
Hardison, M. H. 21:198
Hardison, William H. 5:18
Hardison, Wilson 22:303
Hardisty, Archibald
  22:196
Hardly, Henry 9:22
Hardman, D. M. 22:480

Hardman, E. M. 22:523
Hardman, George W. 8:86
Hardman, H. 19:17
Hardman, Thomas 19:46
Hardner, W. 10:34
Hardpence, James 11:65
Hardsan, D. 14:331
Hardsan, Daniel 24:51
Hardsaw, D. 7:73
Hardsock, T. W. 25:181
Hardtman, George 20:8
Hardway, D. B. 3:89
Hardway, George 11:205
Hardway, N. 8:69
Hardwell, D. 18:190;
  26:211
Hardwell, Norton 25:39
Hardwich, Energy P.
  20:46
Hardwick, H. 13:26
Hardwick, J. W. 21:341
Hardwick, James W.
  17:52
Hardwick, John 5:18
Hardwick, John W.
  18:217
Hardwick, Noah 10:117
Hardwick, Richard 11:396
Hardwick, Thomas 23:147
Hardy, A. 14:298; 17:470;
  27:63
Hardy, A. E. 12:62
Hardy, A. W. 10:56;
  20:266
Hardy, Abraham 12:24
Hardy, Albert 11:304
Hardy, Allen 22:303
Hardy, Andrew 21:28
Hardy, B. 26:34
Hardy, Benjamin 13:26
Hardy, Blanchard 9:82
Hardy, Chauncey 4:29
Hardy, D. S. 14:241
Hardy, D. W. 21:341
Hardy, E. 1:140
Hardy, E. R. 8:64
Hardy, E. S. 3:89
Hardy, Eli 22:280
Hardy, F. 25:181
Hardy, G. E. 25:181
Hardy, George 5:51;
  25:181
Hardy, George H. 27:63
Hardy, Gustavus 5:18
Hardy, H. 11:242; 14:68
Hardy, Har. N. 1:38
Hardy, Henry 1:40; 26:99
Hardy, I. M. 14:332
Hardy, J. 1:45, 135, 139;
  3:89; 9:144; 25:181;
  27:58

Hardy, J. C. 13:89
Hardy, J. H. 1:136; 17:35
Hardy, J. T. S. 17:308
Hardy, James 22:80
Hardy, James D. 21:53
Hardy, James H. 13:26
Hardy, James M. 16:36
Hardy, John 3:89; 10:17;
  15:80; 18:239;
  24:78; 26:35
Hardy, John H. 9:179;
  19:238
Hardy, Joseph 5:40; 25:39
Hardy, Joshua 24:39
Hardy, Josiah W. 10:117;
  20:266
Hardy, Lewis S. 21:70
Hardy, M. C. 21:201
Hardy, Moses D. 22:80
Hardy, N. G. 25:43
Hardy, O. D. 9:227;
  18:367
Hardy, Orean H. 27:60
Hardy, Orod H. 9:119
Hardy, Patrick 10:161
Hardy, R. 19:238
Hardy, Richard 6:21
Hardy, Robert 9:179;
  19:238
Hardy, Samuel 27:59
Hardy, T. 25:181
Hardy, Thomas 5:18;
  10:145; 15:202;
  17:443; 19:168;
  22:34; 24:159
Hardy, Thompson 20:124
Hardy, W. 3:89
Hardy, W. S. 7:74; 25:298
Hardy, Warren C. 10:161
Hardy, William 7:124;
  9:131; 17:451;
  24:178; 27:59
Hardzog, C. 11:63
Hare, A. 14:176
Hare, Daniel 22:482
Hare, E. J. 1:138
Hare, E. O. 15:258
Hare, G. 21:28
Hare, George A. 22:34
Hare, Henry 21:148
Hare, J. J. 9:82; 26:34
Hare, Jacob 9:82; 18:339;
  27:54
Hare, Jacob S. 22:427
Hare, James 25:333
Hare, Jesse 21:255
Hare, John 16:147; 21:273
Hare, John D. 20:177
Hare, John O. 21:341
Hare, John R. 21:341
Hare, Joseph 21:341

Hare, Josiah 12:24
Hare, M. Henry 10:145
Hare, M. S. 27:55
Hare, M. W. 17:65
Hare, Mik 25:333
Hare, Nelson 9:200
Hare, Peter 14:176
Hare, Porter 7:97
Hare, Robert 17:355
Hare, Thomas O. 19:296
Hare, W. 9:53
Hare, W. B. 25:181
Hare, William 14:68;
  19:245
Hare, William Henry
  19:168
Haredinger, Ellis 7:29
Hareling, Charles 14:176
Harelt, Joshua 24:79
Haren, Joseph G. 10:172
Harener, Chapman 22:480
Harer, H. W. 1:142
Harewood, E. 15:17
Harewood, Martin J. 8:86
Harey, Robinson 22:303
Harfert, J. 11:263
Harford, B. 10:26
Harford, John W. 13:26
Harga, Jason 16:196
Hargan, James D. 22:34
Hargas, Adam 18:84
Harge, Levi T. 23:132
Harger, Jason 15:336
Harger, John 8:18; 22:197
Harger, N. B. 26:163
Harger, Nelson 11:263
Harger, William 20:266
Harges, J. C. 9:220
Harges, Thomas J. 18:367
Hargess, John 7:97
Harget, Frederick 9:82
Hargett, Daniel H. 22:451
Hargett, F. 26:32
Hargett, H. 21:28
Hargett, John 14:176
Hargett, N. 5:40; 25:181
Hargham, James G.
  21:225
Hargis, J. C. 18:367
Hargis, Samuel V. 21:100
Hargis, William 11:327
Hargood, George 16:196
Hargraives, J. 19:253
Hargrates, Edward 9:221
Hargrave, E. 18:367
Hargrave, Edward 18:367
Hargrave, Joseph 7:17
Hargrave, Samuel Q.
  19:17
Hargrave, Thomas J.
  22:80

Hargraves, Edward 16:36
Hargraves, G. W. 21:28
Hargraves, James 9:179
Hargraves, John 9:230;
  17:21; 20:266
Hargraves, Nathan 17:52
Hargreaves, Edwards
  13:26
Hargress, Henry 10:57
Hargress, John 9:220;
  18:367
Hargries, H. 20:266
Hargroove, James 10:150
Hargrove, James 18:50
Hargrove, Pleasant 8:39;
  26:165
Hargroves, William 18:67
Hargt, Peter 25:321
Hargus, H. 9:154; 27:57
Hargus, J. M. 21:100
Hargus, Thomas J. 9:220
Harguss, Adam 6:16
Harhainter, James 13:27
Harhianter, James 16:36
Hari, George S. 17:166
Harian, H. 16:196
Haridan, George 18:175
Hariff, W. D. 11:149
Hariget, J. H. 23:203
Harigg, Lewis 4:30
Harilson, J. H. 23:198
Haring, C. P. 18:307;
  26:101
Harington, G. 1:44
Harington, Melville E.
  20:23
Harison, Paris H. 20:266
Hark, Jacob 13:26
Hark, William 11:119
Harkee, John W. 23:156
Harkee, Richard 24:66
Harkenessell, F. 21:341
Harkensmith, Thomas
  27:64
Harker, --- 11:149
Harker, Elisha B. 23:147
Harker, George 17:246
Harker, John 11:335;
  23:107
Harker, John M. 17:209
Harkerly, Philip 11:262
Harkerson, Harrison
  19:267
Harkey, Eli 8:18; 18:137
Harkey, J. J. 26:164
Harkey, Levi 8:18; 18:137
Harkey, Nat 19:282
Harkey, Thomas H.
  26:164
Harkins, D. S. 3:89
Harkins, Edward 14:176

Harkins, Eli 18:368
Harkins, H. 3:89; 17:191
Harkins, James 7:81;
    25:298
Harkins, M. 3:89
Harkins, Michael 23:128
Harkins, R. W. 20:85
Harkins, William 17:148
Harkison, H. 9:179
Harkles, John P. 19:168
Harkless, George W.
    25:39
Harkless, John P. 10:172
Harkless, Philip 22:197
Harkless, Travis 22:303
Harkner, Frank 10:34
Harkness, Alexander
    23:147
Harkness, Darwin 13:26
Harkness, Francis 24:94
Harkness, Howard H.
    24:94
Harkness, John E. 23:147
Harkness, Lysander G.
    19:340
Harkness, M. V. B.
    23:289
Harkness, T. 14:68
Harkness, W. 7:29
Harkness, William 20:23;
    23:33
Harkwart, John 18:367
Harl, James W. 16:133
Harlan, Aloa 18:137
Harlan, George 17:248
Harlan, George W. 14:176
Harlan, H. 14:176
Harlan, Henry 13:125
Harlan, J. 25:41
Harlan, J. C. 3:89
Harlan, James 9:82
Harlan, John 11:205
Harlan, John Y. 23:179
Harlan, Louis 14:176
Harlan, Thomas 6:29
Harlan, William 15:36
Harlan, William C. 16:139
Harland, C. D. 21:341
Harland, J. M. 11:33
Harland, Jefferson 13:64;
    16:196
Harland, John 15:67
Harland, Robert 27:57
Harland, William 22:81
Harlane, James 25:181
Harlbush, William 15:202
Harle, B. B. 5:18; 25:181
Harle, Harry 17:355
Harle, William H. 11:401
Harleman, William 21:341
Harler, J. C. 24:66

Harler, John 3:89
Harless, Francis M. 21:28
Harless, Johnston 13:89
Harless, Joseph 19:17
Harless, Samuel 12:71
Harlet, M. 3:89
Harleton, William H.
    18:207
Harley, Alfred 3:89
Harley, Anice 27:56
Harley, Charles 9:200;
    19:282
Harley, George 10:176;
    19:168
Harley, George W. 17:439
Harley, Isaac 9:68
Harley, J. M. 1:140
Harley, J. S. 3:89
Harley, James 13:27; 20:8
Harley, John 22:405
Harley, Luke 12:71
Harley, Michael 11:16
Harley, Nat 9:200
Harley, Robert 17:177
Harley, W. 15:56
Harley, William 12:71
Harligood, John 4:66
Harlin, Enoch 22:426
Harlin, Joshua 20:23
Harlin, M. 11:31
Harlin, T. 17:177
Harlin, Tilghman S. 23:67
Harling, A. 3:89
Harling, August 23:190
Harling, Channon 11:205
Harling, George 25:181
Harlison, David 21:214
Harlon, Alon 8:18
Harlon, Edward H. 21:53
Harlow, B. 14:12
Harlow, C. F. 19:74
Harlow, D. 13:90
Harlow, F. E. 9:110
Harlow, H. 21:70
Harlow, H. G. 13:90
Harlow, Harvey 3:89
Harlow, Henry 11:287
Harlow, Henry C. 5:18
Harlow, Hosea 7:74;
    25:298
Harlow, J. 25:181
Harlow, Jacob 13:111
Harlow, James H. 20:142
Harlow, John 16:36
Harlow, O. 17:495
Harlow, Thomas 20:104
Harlow, W. 19:267
Harlow, W. H. 17:297
Harlow, W. S. 13:90;
    14:12

Harlow, William 9:179;
    17:443; 19:238;
    24:159
Harlow, William F. 10:56;
    20:266
Harlow, William P. 1:41
Harlowe, Daniel 23:67
Harlsman, Christopher
    11:93
Harlyfield, Joseph 10:117;
    20:266
Harm, Myson 10:8
Harm, Samuel 8:86
Harm, W. P. 7:72
Harma, H. 1:137
Harman, A. P. 3:89
Harman, Albert J. 20:113
Harman, Andrew H.
    21:100
Harman, Archer S.
    10:117; 20:266
Harman, Charles 27:55
Harman, David 8:86
Harman, Eli 22:196
Harman, F. 8:72
Harman, Francis M.
    20:137
Harman, George 17:35;
    22:80
Harman, Henry 15:87
Harman, J. 3:89; 12:87;
    14:12; 16:294
Harman, J. T. 16:196
Harman, Jacob 24:39
Harman, James 16:36;
    20:266
Harman, James W. 17:453
Harman, John 3:89; 17:35
Harman, John A. 7:97
Harman, Johnson 16:36
Harman, Joseph 17:393
Harman, Josiah 26:33
Harman, L. 3:89; 8:72
Harman, Lazarus 12:49
Harman, Louis 21:341
Harman, Luther C. 22:427
Harman, M. 25:181
Harman, Martin 10:161;
    19:168
Harman, Michael 5:17;
    12:60
Harman, O. J. 1:42
Harman, Patrick 9:119
Harman, R. R. 16:139
Harman, S. 14:176
Harman, Sylvanus S.
    22:144
Harman, Theron 15:36
Harman, Thomas 24:20
Harman, William H.
    16:119

Harmanda, D. 14:27
Harmany, George 12:24
Harmasay, Pat 14:12
Harmell, H. C. 13:90;
    14:12
Harmer, George 1:41
Harmer, John 15:124, 349
Harmer, Samuel 12:24
Harmes, C. 9:66
Harmidown, M. 14:241
Harmin, John 25:44
Harming, H. F. 24:79
Harmish, Samuel 18:217
Harmley, John 21:138
Harmon, A. 21:341
Harmon, A. J. 14:68
Harmon, Albert 9:66;
    18:277
Harmon, Alonzo 22:80
Harmon, Alvin 4:29
Harmon, B. 7:50
Harmon, C. R. 11:304
Harmon, C. W. 26:163
Harmon, Clarence C.
    18:110
Harmon, Daniel 16:36;
    17:276
Harmon, Darius C. 24:39
Harmon, David 8:63;
    26:33, 164
Harmon, E. P. 19:227
Harmon, Edwin J. 11:241
Harmon, Elijah 23:67
Harmon, Francis M. 8:18
Harmon, Frederick 1:38
Harmon, Frunis M.
    18:138
Harmon, G. 16:197
Harmon, George W.
    23:279
Harmon, H. 11:31; 13:90
Harmon, H. T. 8:18;
    18:138
Harmon, Harrison 1:192
Harmon, Henry I. 8:18
Harmon, J. 1:43; 13:90;
    21:148
Harmon, J. G. 10:95
Harmon, J. J. 11:100
Harmon, J. P. 24:20
Harmon, James 11:182;
    13:26
Harmon, James H. 5:17;
    20:266
Harmon, James W. 24:183
Harmon, Jasper 20:97
Harmon, John 3:89;
    13:111
Harmon, John A. 21:255
Harmon, John H. 11:305
Harmon, Johnson 13:26

Harmon, L. 21:341; 27:55
Harmon, M. 13:90
Harmon, Moses 11:423
Harmon, O. 22:352
Harmon, R. B. 1:94
Harmon, Richard C. 9:179
Harmon, Robert 17:318
Harmon, Rolla A. D.
    13:26
Harmon, Smith 21:341
Harmon, T. 5:40; 25:181
Harmon, W. F. 12:142
Harmon, W. L. 9:179;
    19:253
Harmon, William 5:17;
    7:97; 17:360; 25:181
Harmon, William M.
    27:61
Harmond, G. W. 19:302
Harmond, Lucius 9:179
Harmond, W. 10:28
Harmony, Hiram 20:41
Harmony, J. 3:89
Harmony, Jeremiah
    20:266
Harmott, George 12:24
Harms, C. 18:277
Harmstad, Charles S.
    14:176
Harn, George A. 22:482
Harnady, E. B. 15:202
Harnaker, Morgan 21:28
Harnard, George 25:181
Harnard, Nathan 20:141
Harnasay, Pat 13:90
Harnback, S. B. 11:93
Harnbeck, William 11:93
Harnbenst, John 2:12
Harnden, Henry 10:56
Harned, John 20:88
Harner, A. 1:44
Harner, Charles M. 12:71
Harner, G. D. 14:68
Harner, Isaac 9:179
Harner, J. 15:263
Harner, Michael 22:196
Harner, W. P. 2:12
Harner, William H. 4:29
Harness, A. 9:100
Harness, Adam 22:481
Harness, Philip 18:320
Harness, William 22:196;
    23:99
Harnett, John 10:56
Harney, Chris 20:266
Harney, Christian 10:56
Harney, D. R. 18:67
Harney, G. W. 2:12
Harney, J. 14:12
Harney, James 4:29
Harney, James P. 13:27

Harney, James T. 18:207
Harney, John 4:29
Harney, John M. 21:225
Harney, Mathew 22:80
Harney, Patrick 16:370
Harney, R. 1:137
Harney, Robert 24:79
Harnick, George 11:107
Harnicker, John 19:302
Harnies, B. C. 18:30
Harning, E. A. 14:176
Harning, G. 16:197
Harnish, E. 14:12; 16:268
Harnish, Joseph 14:332
Harnish, W. 16:197
Harnot, Julius 15:36
Harnret, W. O. 16:197
Harnsberger, George M.
    11:276
Harnsman, Henry 9:43
Harnson, J. 15:67
Harnson, John 12:71
Harntenst, J. H. 25:44
Harnurg, George 13:64
Harny, John 23:67
Harok, Richard 9:161
Haroke, Henry C. 18:320
Harold, Aug 1:41
Harold, James 20:266
Harold, P. G. 21:14
Harols, Charles F. 14:298
Haron, G. W. 22:196
Harouff, J. 1:141
Harp, Benajer 17:148
Harp, Benjamin A. 23:121
Harp, David 5:51; 25:181
Harp, George F. 23:190
Harp, Henry 12:122;
    15:124
Harp, Isaac 17:35
Harp, J. H. S. 9:53
Harp, Jacob 7:29
Harp, James 21:187
Harp, John 20:30
Harp, L. W. 23:203
Harp, N. 16:197
Harp, Thomas 22:196
Harp, W. F. 15:202
Harp, William 22:34
Harp, William M. 17:388
Harpe, Joseph D. 8:18
Harpe, W. 14:176
Harpel, J. A. 20:41
Harpell, Seth 16:95
Harpending, John 9:53
Harpending, M. 14:176
Harper, --- 23:313
Harper, A. 13:90; 14:12;
    25:181
Harper, A. H. 23:88
Harper, A. J. 20:266

Harper, Alexander 5:40
Harper, Andrew J. 7:29; 10:57
Harper, Andrew W. 15:278
Harper, Benjamin 22:303
Harper, Benjamin F. 22:34
Harper, C. D. 15:316
Harper, Charles D. 19:74
Harper, D. 3:89
Harper, David 17:177; 23:148
Harper, E. 15:202
Harper, Edward 19:74
Harper, Elisha 22:397
Harper, G. W. 17:406
Harper, George 19:302; 21:88; 22:81
Harper, George E. A. 24:20
Harper, George F. 8:86
Harper, George W. 22:34
Harper, Green 22:513
Harper, Henry 17:177; 22:196
Harper, Hetter 19:296
Harper, Isaac 17:35; 20:183
Harper, J. 1:141; 3:89; 7:50
Harper, J. A. 15:202
Harper, J. B. 1:44
Harper, J. H. 3:89
Harper, J. J. 1:41
Harper, J. W. 22:196
Harper, James 1:40; 18:30
Harper, Jeremiah 17:199
Harper, John 14:68
Harper, John J. 23:113
Harper, John M. 8:18; 18:138
Harper, John S. 26:220
Harper, John W. 17:21
Harper, Joseph 15:3
Harper, Joseph D. 18:138
Harper, L. D. 15:107
Harper, Lee 11:205
Harper, Lewis 9:82; 17:35
Harper, Lorenge 9:72
Harper, Mathew 22:303
Harper, Moses 11:204
Harper, Nelson 7:124
Harper, Peter W. 15:87
Harper, R. 3:89
Harper, R. A. 17:21
Harper, R. B. 11:327
Harper, Robert 20:113
Harper, Robert W. 22:508
Harper, S. 1:44
Harper, S. H. 1:135

Harper, S. M. 22:196
Harper, Samuel 13:64; 19:74
Harper, T. P. 22:253
Harper, Thaddeus 24:178
Harper, Thomas 20:266; 27:55
Harper, Tobias E. 9:179; 19:267
Harper, W. 3:89; 14:28
Harper, W. E. 1:39
Harper, W. T. 23:279
Harper, William 7:29; 14:176; 21:225
Harper, William C. 23:242
Harper, William H. 23:88
Harper, Wilson B. 15:56
Harper, Z. 25:43
Harpin, E. H. 21:13
Harpister, D. N. 14:176
Harply, Abraham 23:147
Harpole, Henry 10:95
Harpool, M. V. 21:100
Harppart, L. 25:182
Harps, B. 15:359
Harps, David 19:74
Harpsler, Thomas 19:74
Harpst, Jacob 12:24
Harpst, T. 1:140
Harpster, H. H. 13:111
Harpster, Thomas 15:324
Harpstruth, John 7:57
Harr, J. 1:140
Harr, Jacob 9:102
Harrah, J. C. 18:395
Harrah, J. H. 12:161
Harrall, Elias 18:138
Harrall, P. 14:69
Harrall, Philip 22:303
Harramann, John G. 16:11
Harrat, Charles 23:33
Harre, George 24:166
Harrel, A. 26:33
Harrel, Nelson 10:155
Harrell, Benjamin F. 22:80
Harrell, G. 3:89
Harrell, John 10:117; 20:266
Harrell, John C. 22:80
Harrell, Philip 7:97
Harrell, Richard 26:124
Harrell, Samuel 7:29
Harren, F. J. 3:90
Harrep, John C. 11:151
Harrett, Robert 9:208
Harrew, Hamser 21:88
Harriam, John F. 22:34
Harrick, Alanson 26:34
Harrick, Benjamin 17:65
Harrick, P. 4:29

Harridan, Walter 17:177
Harridon, George 7:97
Harridon, Horace 21:341
Harridon, J. T. 23:104
Harries, Phil 3:90
Harriet, Robert 10:161; 19:168
Harrigan, Harden 8:58; 21:148
Harrigan, Jacob 22:11
Harrigan, James 16:95
Harrigan, John 1:38
Harrigan, M. 25:38
Harrigan, T. 16:95
Harrigan, T. J. 1:43
Harrigan, Timothy 7:57
Harrigan, W. 1:137; 13:26
Harriger, Reuben 12:24
Harrill, James B. 18:138
Harrill, S. 14:277
Harriman, A. 1:135
Harriman, G. L. 25:42
Harriman, H. 19:74
Harriman, H. G. 10:161
Harriman, Horatio 7:8
Harriman, J. 15:56
Harriman, John 21:225
Harriman, Lorenzo 9:10
Harriman, Walker G. 5:18
Harriman, William B. 17:146
Harrimus, S. F. 12:122
Harrinan, James 4:29
Harringson, David 22:502
Harrington, --- 23:281
Harrington, A. 1:138; 13:90; 15:294; 16:197; 20:192
Harrington, A. H. 9:22; 18:307; 26:102
Harrington, Aaron 13:111
Harrington, Abram S. 21:255
Harrington, Albert 9:102; 14:298; 17:472; 18:339; 27:63
Harrington, Anderson 19:296
Harrington, Ben 26:102
Harrington, Benjamin 9:35; 18:293
Harrington, C. 3:90
Harrington, C. L. 18:277
Harrington, Charles S. 8:86
Harrington, Cornelius 22:336
Harrington, Cyrus 5:18
Harrington, D. 11:305; 25:182
Harrington, D. L. 4:29

Harrington, Daniel 11:33; 16:119; 21:216
Harrington, Dennis 19:168
Harrington, E. 2:12; 25:38
Harrington, E. D. 8:86
Harrington, E. F. 21:110
Harrington, Ed. R. 10:17
Harrington, Edward C. 18:323
Harrington, Emory R. 23:99
Harrington, Erwin 17:161
Harrington, Francis 12:154
Harrington, Frank 12:24; 17:423
Harrington, Frank M. 24:173
Harrington, Frederick 15:202
Harrington, G. 3:90
Harrington, G. M. 1:140
Harrington, George 10:57; 11:287; 18:395; 20:266; 21:10; 22:34; 25:44
Harrington, George G. 16:8
Harrington, H. 10:28; 19:302; 25:41, 182
Harrington, H. C. 20:193
Harrington, Henry 5:40; 22:144
Harrington, I. G. 14:176
Harrington, I. M. 12:154
Harrington, J. 15:202; 21:138, 341
Harrington, J. G. 3:90; 27:157
Harrington, J. H. 19:168
Harrington, J. T. 20:266
Harrington, J. W. 3:90
Harrington, James 9:119; 18:110; 19:324; 22:336; 26:166; 27:61, 63
Harrington, James S. 21:341
Harrington, Jeremiah 4:29; 13:26
Harrington, John 1:40; 3:90; 16:119; 21:100, 341; 25:182
Harrington, Jordan 7:97
Harrington, Joseph 15:95; 21:341
Harrington, L. 19:75; 22:480
Harrington, L. C. 15:124

Harrington, Lowall W. 22:144
Harrington, M. 9:144; 15:22, 202; 19:168, 253
Harrington, Michael 8:72; 9:179; 21:341
Harrington, Morey 10:117; 20:266
Harrington, Nelson 13:26
Harrington, Pat 3:90
Harrington, Patrick 12:173
Harrington, S. 1:141
Harrington, S. B. 21:198
Harrington, S. J. 3:90
Harrington, S. M. 3:90
Harrington, T. 3:90
Harrington, Timothy 25:43
Harrington, W. 1:139
Harrington, William 10:17; 17:165; 21:341; 23:277; 27:62
Harrington, William J. 23:190
Harrington, William M. 23:121
Harriott, E. 7:50
Harriott, O. B. 12:154
Harris, --- 8:63; 11:149; 18:30, 190; 25:39; 26:211; 27:55
Harris, A. 3:90; 11:263; 12:85; 14:69; 16:294; 21:163; 25:182
Harris, A. A. 20:266
Harris, A. F. 7:29
Harris, A. G. 3:90
Harris, A. H. 21:28
Harris, A. I. 8:18
Harris, A. J. 18:138
Harris, A. L. 9:227; 18:367
Harris, A. S. 8:49; 9:110
Harris, A. T. 14:336
Harris, Aaron 25:182
Harris, Aaron M. 22:428
Harris, Abraham 22:144
Harris, Abram 22:302
Harris, Adam 10:98
Harris, Albert 7:68; 9:208; 22:195
Harris, Albert S. 10:161; 19:168
Harris, Alexander 21:273; 22:302
Harris, Alfred 5:40; 10:10; 17:80; 25:182
Harris, Anderson 17:177

Harris, Andrew 17:397; 19:75
Harris, Andrew J. 24:152
Harris, Anson 11:333
Harris, Ashley C. 22:80
Harris, Augustus A. 10:56
Harris, B. 21:163
Harris, B. F. 9:35
Harris, B. J. 18:239; 26:34
Harris, B. R. 7:29
Harris, B. S. 3:90
Harris, Banks 10:91; 20:266
Harris, Benjamin 9:131; 13:26; 21:341; 27:59
Harris, Benjamin F. 23:67
Harris, Benjamin J. 21:273
Harris, Berry 21:273
Harris, Bradford D. 19:17
Harris, C. 1:138; 3:90; 12:122; 15:124; 22:302; 26:165
Harris, C. M. 13:125
Harris, C. S. 19:296
Harris, Cato 27:54
Harris, Charles 1:40; 4:29; 6:16; 7:124; 8:72; 18:84; 21:273, 341
Harris, Charles E. 13:26
Harris, Charles M. 18:218; 22:425
Harris, Charles T. 16:95
Harris, Christopher 11:335
Harris, Columbus 6:25; 8:72
Harris, Cornelius 10:56; 20:266
Harris, D. 9:154; 27:57
Harris, Daniel 14:176; 23:33
Harris, David 10:95; 11:304; 17:418; 21:273
Harris, David D. 9:82; 26:32
Harris, David W. 23:88
Harris, Delos 16:139
Harris, E. 1:141; 16:279; 25:182
Harris, E. A. 24:111
Harris, E. B. 21:28
Harris, E. D. 3:90
Harris, E. J. 16:36
Harris, E. K. 3:90
Harris, E. P. 11:241
Harris, Edson J. 24:94
Harris, Edward 8:106; 11:93; 12:24; 21:28
Harris, Eli J. 23:67

Harris, Eli T. 11:64
Harris, Elijah 11:107; 18:67; 21:341
Harris, Elijah M. 17:314
Harris, Elisha 22:195
Harris, Elwood 11:63
Harris, Even 8:63
Harris, F. 1:40; 25:182
Harris, F. J. 7:29
Harris, Fielding 22:122
Harris, Foster 12:161
Harris, Frank 7:124; 11:205
Harris, Fred 19:75
Harris, Frederick 5:18; 26:211
Harris, G. 9:53; 14:69; 23:33
Harris, G. E. 17:495
Harris, G. W. 3:90
Harris, Genis 9:208; 18:67
Harris, George 4:29; 5:18; 9:131, 220; 12:49; 15:36, 318; 16:197; 17:177; 18:367; 21:273; 24:8; 25:182; 27:58
Harris, George F. 25:44
Harris, George H. 10:56; 20:266
Harris, George M. 22:196
Harris, George S. 17:263
Harris, George W. 9:68; 11:427
Harris, Gilbert T. 24:94
Harris, Gilmore 18:190
Harris, Granville 22:303
Harris, H. 1:38; 6:25; 15:158; 21:148
Harris, Harrison 9:165; 25:321
Harris, Henderson 10:56; 20:266
Harris, Henry 10:161; 11:204, 287; 12:49; 14:176; 18:84; 19:168; 20:50
Harris, Henry S. 4:29
Harris, Hiram J. 10:56
Harris, Horatio 22:497
Harris, Hosea B. 23:179
Harris, Howard 8:39
Harris, I. I. 15:342
Harris, Ira A. 22:280
Harris, Irving 19:46
Harris, Isaac 8:72; 10:117; 20:46, 266; 27:62
Harris, Israel B. 9:144
Harris, J. 1:140; 3:90; 14:69; 15:36; 16:370; 17:177;

Harris, J. 22:352; 25:285; 27:64
Harris, J. A. 7:96; 9:43
Harris, J. B. 14:69
Harris, J. C. 1:136
Harris, J. D. 25:182
Harris, J. E. 3:90; 7:96; 14:177
Harris, J. F. 14:69
Harris, J. H. 17:145; 26:124
Harris, J. Henry 9:7
Harris, J. S. 3:90
Harris, Jacin 27:62
Harris, Jacob 9:220; 20:154; 21:341; 25:182
Harris, Jacob F. 11:150
Harris, James 8:18; 9:82, 242; 10:176; 11:149; 12:71; 14:286; 15:81; 18:67, 138, 421; 19:46, 168; 20:8; 22:195, 302; 25:182, 321
Harris, James B. 10:117; 20:267
Harris, James C. 21:248
Harris, James H. 11:242
Harris, James L. 22:80
Harris, Jared 11:402
Harris, Jesse 9:53; 16:197
Harris, Jesse M. 17:209
Harris, Job 19:238
Harris, Joe 27:145
Harris, John 9:12; 10:56; 11:231; 12:49; 13:26; 14:177, 256; 17:203, 322; 20:267; 22:166, 253, 501; 24:66; 25:182; 27:54, 61
Harris, John B. 18:277
Harris, John D. 22:134; 24:39
Harris, John F. 18:84; 20:124
Harris, John G. 24:107
Harris, John L. 22:80
Harris, John M. 10:211; 18:464; 21:13, 70
Harris, John N. 20:30
Harris, Jordan 22:80
Harris, Joseph 7:96; 8:72; 9:119; 14:177; 17:35, 80; 19:17; 21:273; 22:196; 26:166; 27:60
Harris, Josh 9:179
Harris, Joshua 9:240
Harris, Justin 9:156

Harris, L. 1:135; 9:53; 22:513
Harris, L. E. 15:202
Harris, L. J. 8:117; 18:330
Harris, L. R. 1:43
Harris, Lawrence J. 8:86
Harris, Levi 7:124
Harris, Lewis 15:202, 326
Harris, M. 14:177; 24:20
Harris, M. C. 3:90
Harris, M. O. 21:201
Harris, M. T. 26:220
Harris, Marcellus 10:117; 20:267
Harris, Martin V. 23:240
Harris, Matha 18:30
Harris, Mathew 22:302
Harris, Michael 20:8; 25:40
Harris, Miles W. 10:117; 20:267
Harris, Montgomery 7:64
Harris, Morgan 11:387
Harris, Moses 7:50; 21:273
Harris, Myron 22:34
Harris, N. 13:103
Harris, N. B. 13:26
Harris, N. D. 11:387
Harris, N. J. 14:69
Harris, Nash 18:138
Harris, Nathan 17:102
Harris, Nelson 12:24
Harris, Noah 17:132; 24:195
Harris, Oliver 9:97
Harris, P. 13:90; 14:12; 27:55
Harris, P. S. 21:341
Harris, Perry 21:148
Harris, Peter 8:58; 17:355; 21:148; 22:34
Harris, Peter G. 24:63
Harris, R. 16:197; 25:182
Harris, R. E. 19:75
Harris, R. J. 23:147
Harris, R. P. 23:308
Harris, Richard 18:84; 20:267; 22:470
Harris, Robert 11:276; 15:67; 18:190
Harris, Rodolphus 11:423
Harris, Rollin T. 21:225
Harris, Roswell 22:144
Harris, S. 16:197; 22:196; 26:164
Harris, S. B. 16:197
Harris, S. G. 16:139
Harris, S. W. 9:220
Harris, Sampson 11:204

Harris, Samuel 9:179;
    19:282; 21:341;
    22:80
Harris, Samuel B. 21:133
Harris, Samuel R. 7:96
Harris, Smith 9:204
Harris, Stephen 11:413
Harris, Stephen N. 22:34
Harris, Susan 19:168
Harris, T. 25:182
Harris, T. J. 26:212
Harris, Taylor 27:59
Harris, Thomas 3:90;
    5:40; 7:78; 20:89;
    22:253; 25:298;
    26:163
Harris, Thomas J. 17:453;
    24:183
Harris, U. 3:90
Harris, Vincent 22:122
Harris, W. 1:140; 9:110;
    13:90; 14:12, 69;
    16:279; 18:14
Harris, W. F. 2:12; 25:38,
    182
Harris, W. H. 16:197;
    18:175; 21:341
Harris, W. K. 21:341
Harris, W. P. 11:280
Harris, Walter 13:57
Harris, Washington 7:124;
    8:49
Harris, Westley 9:240
Harris, Willard N. 11:287
Harris, Willard P. 23:262
Harris, William 1:40, 41;
    3:90; 4:29; 5:40;
    9:179; 10:56, 117,
    148; 11:287; 17:327,
    397; 18:50; 19:267;
    20:267; 22:166, 302,
    480; 23:113; 25:182;
    27:145
Harris, William C.
    11:151; 19:17
Harris, William F. 5:40
Harris, William G. 11:62;
    22:427
Harris, William H. 11:241
Harris, William H. H.
    11:93
Harris, William J. 16:197
Harris, William L. 21:28
Harris, William N. 13:26;
    16:131
Harris, William S. 22:196
Harris, William W. 17:280
Harris, Willis 10:117
Harris, Wilson 6:16;
    18:84

Harrison, --- 9:200;
    19:329
Harrison, A. 16:197;
    19:274
Harrison, A. H. 8:18;
    15:289; 16:197
Harrison, A. M. 18:138
Harrison, Aaron 8:18;
    18:138
Harrison, Alex 11:205;
    20:267
Harrison, Alex. Y. 20:124
Harrison, Alexander
    10:117
Harrison, Alphens 9:179
Harrison, Americus 21:70
Harrison, B. 21:341
Harrison, B. G. 22:196
Harrison, B. R. 18:138
Harrison, Benjamin 9:53
Harrison, Bennett G.
    23:279
Harrison, C. L. 11:191
Harrison, C. N. 11:241
Harrison, Carter 23:67
Harrison, Charles 8:39;
    10:117; 20:267;
    22:196
Harrison, Charles D.
    21:341
Harrison, Cheatam 18:84
Harrison, Cheatham 6:16
Harrison, Cornelius F.
    18:218
Harrison, D. 3:90; 14:177
Harrison, D. M. 22:481
Harrison, Daniel C.
    21:341
Harrison, Daniel H. 7:97
Harrison, David 9:82;
    22:303
Harrison, David A. 22:81
Harrison, David W. 26:32
Harrison, E. 12:142
Harrison, E. H. 11:304
Harrison, Edward 12:24
Harrison, Edward B.
    16:139
Harrison, Edwin 10:56;
    20:267
Harrison, Elihu 17:53
Harrison, Emelius 21:341
Harrison, Frederick
    15:124
Harrison, G. 1:140, 142;
    22:196; 23:309
Harrison, G. W. 8:72;
    9:22; 18:307; 26:100,
    163
Harrison, General 9:208

Harrison, George 4:29;
    9:200; 17:148, 177,
    397; 19:17, 291;
    22:303
Harrison, George C.
    11:126
Harrison, George W.
    8:106
Harrison, Green 23:99
Harrison, H. H. 9:53
Harrison, H. M. 1:141
Harrison, Harvey 6:35
Harrison, Henry 3:90;
    6:16; 7:124; 17:35,
    215, 400; 18:84;
    19:46; 20:267;
    21:239; 26:165
Harrison, Henry J. 18:138
Harrison, Hower 9:22
Harrison, Hudson 20:23
Harrison, Isaac 10:208
Harrison, J. 3:90; 10:205;
    12:154; 14:277;
    16:197; 23:147
Harrison, J. C. 18:110
Harrison, J. F. 9:53
Harrison, J. H. 7:50
Harrison, J. R. 21:341
Harrison, J. W. 3:90;
    16:197
Harrison, Jacob 21:138
Harrison, James 4:29;
    9:22, 240; 12:49;
    14:177; 15:353;
    18:307; 19:17;
    26:101
Harrison, James H. 17:352
Harrison, James M. 20:41
Harrison, Jesse 17:21;
    21:53
Harrison, Joel 22:122
Harrison, John 7:124;
    9:110; 17:80; 18:239;
    23:11, 67; 26:35;
    27:60, 62
Harrison, John B. 17:206
Harrison, John F. 12:71
Harrison, John H. 9:179
Harrison, John J. 23:147
Harrison, John M. 9:119;
    19:331
Harrison, John Q. 23:285
Harrison, John R. 22:253
Harrison, John W. 9:35;
    17:53
Harrison, Joseph 10:56;
    11:205; 19:17;
    20:267; 22:451
Harrison, Joseph N.
    22:144
Harrison, L. 21:341

Harrison, Levi T. 10:117; 20:267
Harrison, Lewis F. 22:397, 523
Harrison, M. 14:12; 23:33
Harrison, M. H. 8:63
Harrison, M. W. 9:163; 25:321
Harrison, Mahlon 25:321
Harrison, Marion 20:97
Harrison, Martin 21:244
Harrison, Mathew 19:318
Harrison, McCarty 10:117
Harrison, Morgan 10:117; 20:267
Harrison, Nathan 19:17
Harrison, Nelson 9:208; 24:196
Harrison, Norman 8:114
Harrison, O. 3:90
Harrison, Ogden 11:16
Harrison, Peter 4:66
Harrison, Philip 22:34
Harrison, Presley 27:157
Harrison, Purris H. 10:117
Harrison, R. 22:463
Harrison, R. L. 1:94
Harrison, Reuben 23:285
Harrison, Robert 5:40; 8:39; 11:327; 19:265; 23:250; 26:165
Harrison, Robert M. 16:65
Harrison, S. H. 11:305
Harrison, S. W. 12:24
Harrison, Sample 18:277
Harrison, Samuel 6:16; 8:49; 9:131; 10:98; 12:154; 18:84; 27:58
Harrison, Solomon 23:289
Harrison, Sylvester 8:39
Harrison, T. 4:29
Harrison, Thomas 8:39; 11:65; 18:138; 22:336; 26:163
Harrison, Thomas C. 17:46
Harrison, Thomas J. 24:51
Harrison, W. 1:138; 26:166
Harrison, W. H. 1:38, 135; 18:239; 25:182; 26:35, 124, 164; 27:56, 59, 63
Harrison, W. J. 25:42
Harrison, Wesley 11:204
Harrison, William 7:29, 78, 124; 8:63; 9:16; 10:117; 11:65, 204; 17:161; 20:267; 22:336; 25:182, 298

Harrison, William H. 8:39; 9:43, 72, 132; 14:298; 17:479; 24:39; 26:165
Harrison, William M. 22:405
Harrison, William P. 15:91
Harrison, Willis R. 17:46
Harrison, Winfield Scott 23:11
Harriss, Lapells 10:17
Harriss, Robert 10:17
Harrit, J. 12:161
Harritt, J. W. 1:39
Harritt, Richard E. 22:196
Harrod, Edward J. 11:255
Harrod, Enos 23:147
Harrod, James A. 11:322
Harrold, H. 18:424; 21:110
Harrold, Henry 21:273
Harrold, Thornton F. 23:67
Harrold, William H. 11:319
Harroldton, D. J. 14:69
Harroll, James 10:57
Harron, Charles 11:107
Harron, Elias E. 11:276
Harron, M. 21:121
Harrop, T. 1:136
Harrover, Isaac 5:18
Harrover, William J. 5:18
Harrow, Peter 23:270
Harrower, I. 25:182
Harrowood, Perry 8:86
Harrows, W. J. 25:182
Harrt, H. C. 18:190
Harry, A. 3:90
Harry, B. F. 3:90
Harry, D. 3:90
Harry, D. S. 27:65
Harry, E. A. 14:241
Harry, Henry 7:124
Harry, James B. 14:299
Harry, John 17:451
Harry, Joshua 7:124; 21:341
Harry, L. 27:63
Harry, M. 1:140
Harry, Oliver 10:57
Harry, P. D. 3:90
Harry, R. 23:288
Harryman, --- 10:186; 18:175
Harryman, E. T. 18:175
Harryman, J. P. 18:190
Harryman, John 17:71
Harryman, Walter 7:97
Harsch, William 5:18

Harsh, A. 15:7
Harsh, Alexander 9:82; 26:33
Harsh, C. P. 11:242
Harsh, C. W. 14:69
Harsh, Daniel 22:166
Harsh, David 11:388
Harsh, Hiram 19:340
Harsh, Jonas 17:21
Harsh, Nathan 11:413
Harsh, Sylvester D. 22:196
Harsh, William 25:182
Harsha, John H. 22:196
Harshaw, Albert 8:49
Harshaw, Albert K. 21:138
Harshbarger, Jacob 19:75
Harshberger, A. J. J. 11:305
Harshberger, Christian 22:196
Harshberger, Jacob 12:82; 16:294
Harshberger, William 22:196
Harsher, Andrew 23:33
Harshley, Joseph 17:154
Harshman, J. K. 3:90
Harshman, Peter 3:90
Harshman, William 9:102
Harsin, William M. 10:117; 20:267
Harsley, Evans 10:57
Harson, Gideon 10:57
Harst, A. 14:299; 17:475; 27:64
Harst, J. M. 8:72
Harswell, John 8:49; 21:138
Hart, --- 17:110; 18:190
Hart, A. 1:44; 3:90; 12:87; 14:288; 16:294; 23:33
Hart, A. B. 1:98; 9:179
Hart, Albert S. 22:144
Hart, Alexander 14:177
Hart, Alonzo A. 17:35
Hart, Andrew D. 13:57
Hart, Andrew R. 15:158
Hart, Archer 23:291
Hart, B. 25:43
Hart, Balaam S. 24:66
Hart, Benjamin H. 10:56; 20:267; 21:255
Hart, C. 7:50; 22:197; 25:182
Hart, C. B. 25:182
Hart, C. C. 22:480
Hart, Calvin 11:443; 22:253

Hart, Case 11:205
Hart, Charles 1:43; 4:29; 7:50; 18:110; 22:303
Hart, Cornelius 13:80
Hart, Cyrus 21:225
Hart, D. 11:20; 12:24; 17:21
Hart, D. R. 3:90
Hart, David 16:197; 21:187, 291
Hart, David B. 22:80
Hart, David E. 13:26
Hart, David J. 23:179
Hart, E. 1:140; 3:90
Hart, Ephraim H. 24:94
Hart, Febus 11:322
Hart, Francis 8:86
Hart, Francis J. 13:26
Hart, Francis M. 11:280
Hart, Fred. P. 26:164
Hart, G. 1:141; 14:299; 17:480; 25:182
Hart, G. E. 14:69
Hart, G. W. 9:53, 221; 18:367
Hart, George 3:90; 5:40; 9:82; 11:374; 17:276; 19:75
Hart, George F. 10:117; 20:267
Hart, H. 16:139; 23:313
Hart, H. C. 3:90; 8:49; 26:211
Hart, H. H. 25:182
Hart, H. M. D. 14:69
Hart, H. W. 25:182
Hart, Hard 8:18
Hart, Harrison E. 13:60
Hart, Henry 8:86; 10:56; 18:30; 20:267; 24:20
Hart, Herman 21:198
Hart, Hiram C. 10:173; 19:168
Hart, Hugh 20:267
Hart, Hurd 18:138
Hart, I. 14:69
Hart, J. 1:137, 138; 3:90; 11:322; 16:139; 20:133; 22:303; 23:122; 25:182
Hart, J. A. 1:135
Hart, J. B. 1:139
Hart, J. D. 26:220
Hart, J. J. 5:18
Hart, J. P. 11:262
Hart, J. R. 3:90
Hart, J. S. 7:96
Hart, Jacob 18:138
Hart, James 6:25; 9:82; 10:98; 12:24; 14:69;

Hart, James 19:17; 22:336; 23:67; 26:37
Hart, James L. 10:91; 20:267
Hart, Jeffrey 12:24
Hart, John 1:42; 3:90; 4:29; 7:124; 13:26; 14:69, 177; 16:294; 22:427; 23:121; 24:101
Hart, John F. 21:28
Hart, John M. 11:413
Hart, John N. 10:17
Hart, Joseph 11:63
Hart, Joseph P. 22:501
Hart, Joshua 11:395
Hart, Joshua P. 22:144
Hart, Josiah 17:80
Hart, L. 1:44
Hart, Levi 8:49; 21:255
Hart, Lewis 7:96
Hart, Loyd 17:161
Hart, M. 3:90
Hart, Martin S. 22:405
Hart, Michael 12:82; 16:294; 19:168
Hart, Miles 22:336
Hart, Nathan 12:146; 19:302
Hart, Nathaniel 9:221; 18:367; 23:285
Hart, P. 14:281
Hart, Peter 4:29; 8:72; 13:64; 19:75
Hart, Peter M. 20:137
Hart, Philip 14:269
Hart, Robert 23:33
Hart, S. 3:90; 11:84
Hart, S. L. 3:90
Hart, Samuel 13:26; 24:62
Hart, Sherwood 22:144
Hart, Simon 9:82; 26:34
Hart, T. 25:182
Hart, Thomas 5:40; 9:144; 15:67; 21:342; 27:57
Hart, Thomas J. 22:253
Hart, W. 3:90; 15:258; 18:239; 25:182; 26:35
Hart, W. B. 20:267
Hart, W. E. 26:164
Hart, W. H. 1:137; 27:63
Hart, William 1:44; 3:90; 8:86; 9:70; 11:387; 19:75; 22:426
Hart, William A. 23:88
Hart, William B. 10:56
Hart, William F. 4:29
Hart, William H. 9:161; 14:177
Hart, William T. 22:463

Hart, Willis 27:60
Hart, Wilson C. 11:319
Hartcler, J. 11:62
Harte, James 16:294
Harte, John C. 4:29
Hartel, George 22:171
Harten, Husten A. 11:408
Harten, James 11:126
Harten, Michael 19:329
Harten, Thomas 21:273
Harter, F. 3:90
Harter, Francis M. 23:147
Harter, George W. 10:117; 20:267; 21:225
Harter, Henry 27:61
Harter, Henry R. 9:119
Harter, J. A. 1:135
Harter, J. M. 15:166
Harter, Jacob M. 19:17
Harter, James 6:22; 14:69
Harter, John A. 23:147
Harter, Jonathan 11:63
Harter, Joshua 22:144
Harter, Madison W. 12:58
Harter, Nathaniel 18:293
Harter, Sol. I. 25:275
Harter, T. S. 11:263
Harteston, William 8:86
Hartesty, W. J. 22:196
Hartey, Henry 21:225
Hartfield, G. 25:182
Hartfield, John 16:36
Hartfield, William P. 10:56
Hartford, A. 12:122; 15:107
Hartford, Abraham G. 23:147
Hartford, Charles H. 10:8
Hartford, G. E. 9:144; 27:56
Hartford, George D. 22:34
Hartford, George T. 22:34
Hartford, H. 3:90
Hartford, J. L. 1:139
Hartford, John 4:29
Hartford, Leslie 7:97
Hartford, Luther 4:29
Hartford, N. C. 23:285
Hartgrave, David L. 20:267
Hartgraves, David L. 10:117
Harth, John E. 11:93
Harther, H. 15:202
Harthorns, J. G. 25:298
Harthougt, William B. 7:50
Harties, Richard 12:71
Hartig, William 11:149
Hartigan, James 22:122

Hartigan, John 12:24
Hartinar, August 19:75
Harting, Daniel 13:111
Harting, Frederick 22:196
Harting, N. 15:333
Hartings, A. 21:28
Hartle, John 12:24
Hartle, Simon 23:147
Hartleib, Chris 18:307; 26:101
Hartleman, William 7:124
Hartley, Benjamin F. 16:133
Hartley, F. 27:61
Hartley, Francis M. 11:388
Hartley, G. H. 1:40
Hartley, Green 7:96
Hartley, Henry 16:85
Hartley, Hiram 14:177
Hartley, Isaac 3:90
Hartley, Isaiah D. 21:84
Hartley, J. 1:44
Hartley, J. B. 13:125
Hartley, James 15:158
Hartley, James A. 1:41
Hartley, Jesse H. 8:18
Hartley, Joseph 13:26
Hartley, Stephen Z. 7:7
Hartley, T. 1:136; 25:321
Hartley, Thomas M. 23:285
Hartley, William 13:26
Hartley, William H. 12:24
Hartlick, C. 3:90
Hartliffe, John F. 17:21
Hartlin, Elias 8:72
Hartline, S. 1:43
Hartline, William G. 19:168
Hartly, B. F. 18:421
Hartly, Benjamin 17:110
Hartly, Jesse H. 18:138
Hartly, John 24:20
Hartman, A. 11:423; 14:69; 25:182
Hartman, A. S. 5:17
Hartman, Abraham 5:17
Hartman, August 9:179; 12:95; 19:253
Hartman, Augustus 5:17
Hartman, B. 1:139
Hartman, Bernhard 12:53
Hartman, Charles 11:64
Hartman, Charles F. 21:342
Hartman, Daniel 17:463; 24:181
Hartman, Daniel H. 8:101
Hartman, David 13:26
Hartman, Diebrich 22:523

Hartman, Dudley 7:124
Hartman, E. 1:38
Hartman, E. B. 7:50
Hartman, E. N. 11:119
Hartman, Eather 11:412
Hartman, Francis 13:127
Hartman, G. P. 13:111
Hartman, George 11:33
Hartman, H. 3:91
Hartman, H. H. 1:135
Hartman, Harrison 20:267
Hartman, Henry 8:64; 10:205; 23:147; 25:40; 26:163
Hartman, Henry A. 21:255
Hartman, Hiram H. 16:152
Hartman, I. 3:91
Hartman, J. 1:140; 13:90; 18:30; 25:182
Hartman, J. M. 11:242
Hartman, Jacob 1:39; 5:17; 18:293; 22:427, 482; 26:102
Hartman, John 9:102; 11:126, 319; 16:294; 17:161
Hartman, John C. 21:70
Hartman, John D. 9:102
Hartman, John F. 22:112, 497
Hartman, John T. 23:147
Hartman, Joseph 17:80; 22:81
Hartman, L. S. 9:144
Hartman, Lewis 1:40; 20:267; 22:122
Hartman, Louis 10:56; 13:26; 22:508
Hartman, M. 3:91
Hartman, Mathew 9:47
Hartman, N. S. 27:57
Hartman, Philip 22:196
Hartman, Robert 22:497
Hartman, Samuel B. 25:41
Hartman, T. R. 1:141
Hartman, V. 1:137; 3:91
Hartman, W. 1:139; 20:267
Hartman, W. O. 9:144; 27:57
Hartman, William 10:56; 12:24; 25:41, 283
Hartman, William H. 15:5
Hartmand, A. J. 25:183
Hartmann, Louis 16:36
Hartmon, John 12:82
Hartneddy, P. 14:69
Hartnell, John 20:267
Hartness, M. M. 9:242
Hartnette, J. H. 1:43

Hartney, E. 3:91
Harton, D. 12:99
Harton, Horace 21:255
Harton, Isaiah 22:81
Harton, L. 1:135
Hartong, Boswell 11:31
Hartress, Hezekiah 7:124
Hartromft, Ezra 24:20
Harts, Fred 11:106
Harts, J. 16:370
Harts, Jacob 20:17
Harts, John 3:91
Harts, Samuel 21:273
Hartsaet, Nelson 18:110
Hartsborn, C. 16:294
Hartsburger, A. 14:177
Hartsell, G. 15:67
Hartsell, G. L. 14:177
Hartsell, George 3:91; 12:71
Hartshonies, A. 1:137
Hartshorn, C. 12:85
Hartshorn, Elmer 23:147
Hartshorn, J. C. 10:117; 20:267
Hartshorn, Jesse 21:91
Hartshorn, Joseph 6:25
Hartshorn, L. E. 3:91
Hartshorn, Martin 21:206
Hartshorn, Thomas B. 24:79
Hartshow, J. F. 21:342
Hartsman, John C. 17:402
Hartsock, --- 3:91
Hartsock, L. D. 19:75
Hartson, A. C. 22:482
Hartson, J. H. 1:43
Hartson, J. A. 1:135
Hartson, Palmer 22:171
Hartsook, Henry E. 23:288
Hartsough, David 21:70
Hartsough, E. 1:141
Hartstein, J. 27:54
Hartstein, Jacob 9:119
Hartung, William 13:111; 25:41
Hartup, Lewis 22:80
Hartus, Richard 15:4
Hartwell, A. J. 13:111; 17:152
Hartwell, Albert 27:60
Hartwell, Alfred 24:62
Hartwell, C. W. 5:51; 15:338; 19:75; 25:183
Hartwell, George 8:49
Hartwell, George W. 21:255
Hartwell, Henderson 21:342

Hartwell, John D. 23:277
Hartwell, Nathan H. 20:30
Hartwell, Obed 13:26
Hartwell, S. 14:281
Hartwell, William H. 23:67
Hartwell, Willis 19:17
Hartwick, William H. 4:29
Hartwigson, Thor 20:48
Harty, George 21:14
Harty, H. 26:163
Harty, J. 14:265
Harty, John B. 18:207
Harty, T. 25:44
Harty, Thomas 11:84
Hartye, H. 8:72
Hartz, J. 23:179
Hartz, J. J. 7:29
Hartz, J. T. 1:41
Hartz, Jacob 23:179
Hartz, James 3:91
Hartz, John 17:243
Hartz, Michael 1:39
Hartz, Mike 12:23
Hartz, Peter 23:11
Hartzburger, Amos 14:69
Hartzel, W. 18:190
Hartzel, W. H. 7:29
Hartzell, D. 15:202
Hartzell, E. 22:234
Hartzell, George H. 22:34
Hartzell, James H. 15:202
Hartzell, James O. 9:35
Hartzell, John 22:197
Hartzell, John J. 18:139
Hartzell, S. 3:91
Hartzell, S. C. 1:137
Hartzer, F. 3:91
Harvell, Harry 17:456
Harvell, W. F. 17:71
Harvers, W. H. 14:69
Harves, Questly 1:191
Harveston, Andrew 10:117; 20:267
Harveston, James 9:179
Harveston, Jonas 19:282
Harvey, --- 9:230; 17:297; 25:39
Harvey, A. 14:69
Harvey, A. S. 21:342
Harvey, Abraham 24:8
Harvey, Albert 7:96; 10:117; 20:267; 22:303
Harvey, Albert B. 9:82
Harvey, Albert J. 16:36
Harvey, Albert M. 17:403
Harvey, Anderson 11:205
Harvey, Andrew J. 23:184
Harvey, B. R. 25:42
Harvey, B. W. 11:93

Harvey, Byron 22:196
Harvey, C. L. 13:111
Harvey, Charles 3:91; 23:67
Harvey, Charles D. 24:20
Harvey, Charles H. 11:401
Harvey, Chester F. 15:304; 16:197
Harvey, D. 13:90; 14:12
Harvey, D. B. 12:154
Harvey, D. M. 3:91
Harvey, Daniel 10:56; 20:267; 24:79
Harvey, David 15:259
Harvey, David A. 22:427
Harvey, David P. 23:67
Harvey, E. 27:65
Harvey, E. P. 9:110
Harvey, Edward H. 9:43
Harvey, Elias 4:29
Harvey, F. 12:82; 16:294
Harvey, Frederick 19:17; 22:303
Harvey, G. B. 22:501
Harvey, G. C. 5:17
Harvey, George 4:29; 22:171
Harvey, George W. 10:117; 12:161; 20:267; 22:253
Harvey, Godfrey W. 7:96
Harvey, H. 18:84
Harvey, H. E. 1:135
Harvey, H. H. 14:69
Harvey, H. R. 25:43
Harvey, Head 7:82
Harvey, Henry 10:117; 17:155; 20:267
Harvey, Hiram 7:97
Harvey, Isaac 26:164
Harvey, J. 1:140; 12:85; 15:17, 299; 16:294; 20:177; 26:165
Harvey, Jacob 11:387; 16:119
Harvey, James 9:82; 10:17; 11:150; 12:71
Harvey, James A. 11:84; 12:24
Harvey, James B. 27:64
Harvey, James E. 21:70
Harvey, James H. 21:71
Harvey, James R. 7:68
Harvey, James S. 10:37; 20:267
Harvey, Jesse 16:197
Harvey, John 1:39; 5:17; 7:29; 12:55; 16:119; 17:409; 22:34; 23:122, 240; 24:178
Harvey, John A. 5:17

Harvey, John D. 25:40
Harvey, John G. 8:86
Harvey, John Smith 17:280
Harvey, John T. 22:196
Harvey, John W. 11:150
Harvey, Jonathan C. 10:117; 20:267
Harvey, Jones 26:164
Harvey, Joseph 21:28
Harvey, L. 18:30
Harvey, Leonard 4:29
Harvey, Lewis 7:97; 13:111
Harvey, Liman 4:29
Harvey, M. 14:69
Harvey, M. C. 10:28; 19:302
Harvey, M. H. 12:87; 16:294
Harvey, Marcus L. 23:67
Harvey, Martin 11:322
Harvey, Martin H. 23:67
Harvey, Michael 16:370
Harvey, Morgan 3:91
Harvey, Nathan 22:280
Harvey, Oscar 10:56
Harvey, P. 15:202
Harvey, Patrick 9:22; 18:307; 26:101
Harvey, Perry 17:53
Harvey, Pierce 16:85
Harvey, R. J. 25:183
Harvey, Robert 20:176
Harvey, Robert M. 8:18; 10:56; 18:138; 20:267
Harvey, Rufus L. 5:17
Harvey, S. 14:69
Harvey, S. J. 3:91
Harvey, Sampson 22:253
Harvey, Samuel 12:71; 15:80
Harvey, Samuel A. 22:501
Harvey, T. 2:12; 25:43
Harvey, Thomas 9:179; 19:253
Harvey, V. H. 7:57
Harvey, Walter 4:29
Harvey, William 9:35; 11:412; 18:30; 20:146
Harvey, William F. L. 15:87
Harvey, William H. 8:18
Harvie, --- 17:177
Harville, A. 9:82
Harville, James 11:106
Harville, William 16:36
Harvoeth, W. 1:138
Harvy, Henry 16:197

Harvy, Jacob R. 26:145
Harvy, James 26:32
Harvy, James B. 17:475
Harvy, S. 23:33
Harvy, Sylvester 23:33
Harvy, William 11:242
Harvy, William H. 18:138
Harwell, Harry 24:213
Harwell, Nat 14:329
Harwich, William 26:100
Harwick, A. 14:177;
    15:359
Harwick, Jacob 22:34
Harwick, William 18:307
Harwington, O. 3:91
Harwood, E. 25:183
Harwood, E. W. 15:166
Harwood, Ebenezer
    11:387; 22:80
Harwood, Edgar 11:401
Harwood, G. 3:91
Harwood, George 17:323
Harwood, J. 21:28
Harwood, John W. 20:113
Harwood, Samuel J.
    22:144
Harwood, W. N. 17:440
Harwood, William H.
    24:153
Hary, John 16:370
Hary, N. C. 22:253
Has, Adam 21:110
Hasack, John M. 15:353
Hasard, C. W. 5:40
Hasbouck, Cyrus 15:107
Hasbrook, Alexander
    7:124
Hasbrook, George S. 7:97
Hascall, Arthur F. 15:36
Hascomb, O. P. 27:54
Hase, Adam 22:197
Hase, John 9:208
Hase, L. 14:69
Hase, William 18:307;
    26:100
Hasell, Oscar 9:110
Haseltine, Moses 15:17
Haselton, A. 7:9
Haselton, C. 16:197
Haselton, Charles 6:25
Hasemeir, Henry 10:57
Hasenback, W. 1:136
Hasenfling, S. D. 16:370
Hasenplug, D. S. 15:349
Hasens, Andrea N. 11:387
Hasenwinkle, F. 9:221
Hasenwinkle, Frederick
    18:368
Hasey, William H. H.
    10:17

Hasfet, J. 25:39
Hasfle, J. 3:91
Hasford, Wiley 11:412
Hash, Andrew 20:186
Hashar, N. A. 16:36
Hashberger, Noah 22:81
Hashett, W. L. 5:18
Hashide, Norman 15:159
Hasid, A. 1:135
Hasier, Edward M. 22:197
Hasin, Henry 18:175
Hask, H. 18:30
Haskall, B. F. 1:38
Haskall, M. 25:44
Haskel, Clarence 19:168
Haskel, Theo 9:53
Haskell, A. S. 10:153;
    19:168
Haskell, Abner 10:161;
    12:24
Haskell, Abraham 16:36
Haskell, Albert 14:177
Haskell, Charles 7:74;
    14:177; 25:298
Haskell, Chauncey 16:133
Haskell, Clarence 10:173
Haskell, D. B. 8:121
Haskell, Daniel F. 10:153
Haskell, G. 14:256
Haskell, George A. 21:342
Haskell, I. C. 8:18
Haskell, J. 15:202; 17:168
Haskell, J. C. 18:138
Haskell, J. L. 1:43
Haskell, James E. 25:41
Haskell, James F. 10:57;
    20:267
Haskell, James M. 16:85
Haskell, John A. 24:39
Haskell, John H. 7:97
Haskell, Joseph 13:111
Haskell, L. J. 17:273
Haskell, Leander 10:17
Haskell, M. H. 9:179
Haskell, Moody 2:12
Haskell, N. B. 9:179;
    19:227
Haskell, Parsons F. 24:51
Haskell, S. 25:298
Haskell, W. 1:44
Haskell, Warner 12:8
Haskell, William L.
    22:427
Haskell, Willis F. 22:34
Hasket, Daniel 21:195
Hasket, J. B. 8:72
Hasket, John 21:195
Haskett, Roger 25:183
Haskett, Thomas 22:81
Haskett, William 25:183

Haskett, William A.
    21:225
Haskil, W. H. 19:286
Haskill, A. M. 19:17
Haskill, Abraham 13:27
Haskill, B. 25:298
Haskill, C. 1:39
Haskill, C. W. 1:94
Haskill, D. W. 1:139
Haskill, Daniel 19:168
Haskill, G. 1:138
Haskill, J. W. 1:137
Haskill, Leonard 20:23
Haskill, Mariot 19:17
Haskin, F. M. 14:69
Haskines, Walter 23:184
Haskins, --- 26:236
Haskins, A. C. 21:342
Haskins, Abram 22:144
Haskins, C. 27:144
Haskins, Charles 13:27
Haskins, Eli 9:221
Haskins, Elma 4:30
Haskins, Enoch 7:97
Haskins, Franklin 22:81
Haskins, George 9:72;
    21:110
Haskins, George H.
    20:193
Haskins, George P.
    22:197
Haskins, George W. 18:50
Haskins, H. 3:91; 18:30
Haskins, Harvey 22:303
Haskins, Harvey B.
    20:268
Haskins, J. 3:91; 25:183
Haskins, J. A. 1:140
Haskins, J. J. 20:267
Haskins, J. M. 24:111
Haskins, James 3:91;
    7:97; 9:16; 22:81
Haskins, James D. 7:68
Haskins, James E. 24:8
Haskins, Jason 11:205
Haskins, John 3:91; 5:40;
    17:148
Haskins, John D. 12:170
Haskins, John G. 20:113
Haskins, Leonard 21:342
Haskins, Luther 17:21
Haskins, Miles A. 10:57
Haskins, Miles J. 20:267
Haskins, R. 20:267
Haskins, Ransom 20:8
Haskins, Romanter 10:57
Haskins, Rufus 1:39
Haskins, Thomas B. 24:39
Haskins, W. 4:30; 25:41
Haskins, William 18:67;
    24:196

Haskins, William F.
11:327
Haskins, William W. 8:18
Haskions, Lyman G.
22:197
Haskitt, A. 3:91
Haslam, Charles 9:144;
27:55
Hasleff, J. 10:57
Hasler, C. 3:91
Hasler, J. W. 10:57
Hasler, Louis 20:23
Hasler, M. 3:91
Hasler, Thomas 23:147
Haslet, Samuel 8:18;
18:138
Haslett, W. 1:39
Hasley, John 27:62
Hasley, R. G. 25:183
Hasley, William C. 22:253
Hasliss, --- 11:150
Haslitte, Richard 18:412
Hasner, Henry 19:168
Haso, James 11:151
Hasper, Nelson 11:107
Hasper, Samuel 16:279
Hass, E. 15:36
Hass, Franklin 10:117;
20:268
Hass, Frederick 14:177
Hass, Gidson 16:197
Hass, H. B. 11:106
Hass, Henry 8:49
Hass, J. F. 3:91
Hass, R. 13:111
Hass, Richard 14:69
Hass, Stephen 12:8
Hassa, Frederick 4:30
Hassa, Joseph 7:97
Hassacher, G. 19:75
Hassan, George 4:30
Hasse, Charles 16:143
Hasse, Detlef 19:73
Hasse, John 3:91
Hasse, Wilhelm 7:29
Hasseiman, G. 1:40
Hassel, C. 1:137
Hasselbring, Fred 4:30
Hassell, Green 11:204
Hassell, Jacob 19:75
Hassell, John W. 16:36
Hassell, Joseph 23:309
Hassell, Joshua 10:173;
19:168
Hassell, Richard 27:59
Hassell, Robert 22:303
Hassellmid, George
18:395
Hasselman, Charles 10:57;
20:268
Hasselmann, Fred 20:124

Hassemier, Henry 20:268
Hassen, H. 3:91
Hassen, H. C. 23:33
Hassen, Jacob 20:8
Hassen, John C. 20:107
Hassen, John W. 22:197
Hassenplug, J. H. 12:24
Hasserberk, Frank 4:30
Hassett, Eugene E.
10:117; 20:268
Hassett, J. B. 27:57
Hassett, John 17:400
Hassett, M. 19:238
Hassett, Martin 9:179
Hassett, P. 15:202
Hassey, Charles 25:183
Hassey, D. H. 25:44
Hassie, John 11:107
Hassiler, Benjamin 16:119
Hassitt, David 12:24
Hassle, Thomas 22:253
Hassleff, J. 20:268
Hassler, A. 14:177
Hassler, John 11:387
Hassler, Joseph 4:30
Hasslett, George 11:33
Hassman, G. 1:44
Hassman, P. 20:268
Hassman, Philip 10:57
Hassner, Jesse 18:307
Hassock, Thomas 22:34
Hassom, Andrew M.
11:150
Hasson, Alexander 16:294
Hasson, B. F. 20:146
Hasson, Thomas 7:14
Hasson, W. 1:138
Hast, Joseph B. 13:27
Hast, Valentine 10:146
Hast, William 6:27
Haste, Aaron 23:190
Haste, William 3:91
Hasteller, Adam 4:30
Haster, Frank 11:413
Hastey, Willis 23:33
Hastie, James R. 20:124
Hastill, William 11:63
Hastin, G. 3:91
Hastin, Jacob 12:24
Hasting, George 14:177
Hastings, A. 3:91; 14:177
Hastings, Albert 17:152
Hastings, Andrew 25:42
Hastings, C. 13:90; 19:75
Hastings, D. C. 17:231
Hastings, D. L. 15:124
Hastings, Daniel 17:72
Hastings, Daniel W. 22:34
Hastings, Edward 20:113
Hastings, Edwin O.
22:197

Hastings, G. F. 19:168
Hastings, George 7:64;
23:277
Hastings, George H.
10:173
Hastings, H. C. 20:193
Hastings, Hugh 18:307;
26:100
Hastings, J. 1:140; 3:91;
13:90
Hastings, J. C. 13:64;
16:197
Hastings, J. P. 1:42
Hastings, J. W. 17:440
Hastings, James W.
24:153
Hastings, Leonard 21:53
Hastings, Nicholas 19:75
Hastings, R. 1:138
Hastings, Robert M.
9:230; 20:268
Hastings, S. 19:238
Hastings, S. R. 20:268
Hastings, Samuel 9:179
Hastings, T. 1:141
Hastings, Thomas 12:24;
13:128
Hastings, Thomas M. 1:39
Hastings, W. O. 1:138
Hastings, William 8:106;
20:151
Hastler, George 23:33
Hastlieb, Christ 9:22
Hastlings, Calvin T. 24:20
Haston, --- 11:280
Hasty, Benjamin F.
21:130
Hasty, Robert 16:139
Hasty, Simon 27:59
Hasty, William 11:64
Hasty, William C. 20:142
Haswell, Eugene 10:17
Haswell, Godfrey 7:13
Haswell, John C. 23:190
Haswell, William 12:154
Hataway, Edward 7:17
Hatch, --- 26:236
Hatch, A. 1:137; 25:298
Hatch, A. S. 1:137
Hatch, A. W. 7:97
Hatch, Alansen 9:106
Hatch, Albert 16:95
Hatch, Alfred 5:18
Hatch, Alonzo 7:75
Hatch, C. 15:202
Hatch, Charles 22:405;
23:122
Hatch, Charles M. 9:82
Hatch, Collyn C. 21:342
Hatch, Colon C. 9:214
Hatch, D. G. 1:43

Hatch, E. P. 10:17
Hatch, Eli A. 10:17
Hatch, Eugene 7:80; 25:298
Hatch, F. B. 14:281
Hatch, G. 7:75
Hatch, G. H. 14:177
Hatch, George 9:156; 13:27; 22:161
Hatch, George B. 18:277
Hatch, George W. 14:69
Hatch, H. 14:69, 177, 256; 16:295
Hatch, Harvey W. 22:197
Hatch, Henderson 21:273
Hatch, Henry 23:33
Hatch, Hiram 24:79
Hatch, Horace J. 7:29
Hatch, Horatio C. 8:18; 18:138
Hatch, J. C. 3:91
Hatch, J. E. 21:342
Hatch, J. F. 3:91
Hatch, James 21:273
Hatch, James F. 1:42
Hatch, James J. 27:54
Hatch, James N. 16:370
Hatch, James S. 22:197
Hatch, Jason C. 15:202
Hatch, Jesse P. 18:395
Hatch, John 1:41
Hatch, John B. 4:30
Hatch, M. 1:136
Hatch, Miles 7:97
Hatch, Miles P. 21:342
Hatch, Millard F. 13:27
Hatch, Nathan H. 22:508
Hatch, O. M. 22:197
Hatch, Oliver 7:14
Hatch, P. 7:81; 25:298
Hatch, Robert 25:183
Hatch, Roswell 12:24
Hatch, S. 3:91; 14:69
Hatch, S. W. 7:9
Hatch, Samuel 11:204
Hatch, Samuel O. 16:78
Hatch, T. 1:138
Hatch, W. 9:144; 27:55
Hatch, W. N. 27:60
Hatch, W. S. M. 14:69
Hatch, William 12:154; 23:11; 26:163
Hatch, William H. 8:64
Hatch, William N. 9:119
Hatch, Wilson 21:273
Hatchaway, John 19:17
Hatchcock, J. T. 9:53
Hatchell, R. W. 21:342
Hatcher, And. 22:513
Hatcher, C. 18:239; 26:34

Hatcher, George 18:239; 26:37
Hatcher, Henry 11:205
Hatcher, I. 9:234
Hatcher, Mayland N. 9:12
Hatcher, Moses 11:204
Hatcher, Reuben 20:268
Hatcher, Thomas 23:147
Hatchet, John C. 20:35
Hatchett, C. 1:140
Hatchett, Harvey 13:27
Hatchett, James H. 18:424
Hatchett, Peter 17:132; 24:195
Hatchkiss, E. C. 18:138
Hatcock, T. 1:138
Hater, J. J. 8:49
Hates, Charles 3:91
Hates, Orin 17:169
Hatfield, --- 15:56
Hatfield, A. 16:370
Hatfield, A. G. 3:91
Hatfield, Amos 15:342
Hatfield, Andrew 10:205
Hatfield, Anthony 11:33
Hatfield, Archibald 7:63
Hatfield, C. 27:64
Hatfield, Calvin H. 11:106
Hatfield, David 8:86; 17:236; 22:81
Hatfield, Elias 11:149
Hatfield, George 13:27; 16:36
Hatfield, George W. 3:91
Hatfield, Henley 8:86
Hatfield, Henry 22:481
Hatfield, Herman H. 22:11
Hatfield, J. 1:137, 140; 3:91
Hatfield, Jasper 6:9
Hatfield, Jeremiah 24:166
Hatfield, John N. 11:93
Hatfield, John R. 21:225
Hatfield, John T. 14:177
Hatfield, John W. 10:57; 20:268; 22:480
Hatfield, Joseph 17:477; 27:63
Hatfield, L. 3:91
Hatfield, Ober 26:145
Hatfield, S. E. 12:53
Hatfield, Samuel 7:124; 11:149
Hatfield, W. 11:263
Hatfield, W. J. 7:97
Hatfield, William M. 22:34
Hatfield, William P. 20:268
Hatgell, I. 17:291
Hath, Andrew J. 12:24

Hathans, G. W. 13:111
Hathaway, --- 25:44
Hathaway, A. 1:138; 16:197
Hathaway, A. J. 1:138
Hathaway, A. P. 1:137
Hathaway, Adolphus 16:197
Hathaway, Alpheus 7:97
Hathaway, Andrew 22:144
Hathaway, Avery N. 12:24
Hathaway, Ben 6:22
Hathaway, Benjamin 6:16; 18:84
Hathaway, C. 14:177, 256
Hathaway, Calvin 15:83
Hathaway, Charles 3:91; 15:36
Hathaway, Charles W. 25:183
Hathaway, D. F. 9:221
Hathaway, D. H. 14:69
Hathaway, D. L. 18:368
Hathaway, D. S. 17:155
Hathaway, E. 22:481
Hathaway, E. B. 7:29
Hathaway, Eleazer S. 20:107
Hathaway, Franklin 13:111
Hathaway, George 10:57; 11:402
Hathaway, George N. 17:243
Hathaway, George R. 22:34
Hathaway, H. E. 1:142
Hathaway, Henry 14:177
Hathaway, Henry C. 10:161
Hathaway, Henry H. 22:463
Hathaway, Isaac 7:29; 23:113
Hathaway, J. 17:435; 24:182
Hathaway, J. A. 1:139
Hathaway, J. F. 19:302
Hathaway, J. S. 20:85
Hathaway, James 10:57; 20:268
Hathaway, Jesse 10:173; 15:67
Hathaway, Jessie 19:168
Hathaway, John 8:86; 22:81
Hathaway, Joseph 17:243
Hathaway, Joseph W. 4:30
Hathaway, L. 10:210
Hathaway, L. A. 18:468

Hathaway, Lawson 7:50
Hathaway, Leonard W. 22:253
Hathaway, Levi 8:86
Hathaway, Lewis 7:97
Hathaway, Louis H. 22:112
Hathaway, N. 19:272
Hathaway, Nelson 9:179
Hathaway, R. A. 11:65
Hathaway, Richard 19:168
Hathaway, Robert J. 7:57
Hathaway, Royal 4:30
Hathaway, S. 3:91
Hathaway, Taylor 11:205
Hathaway, W. 2:12; 25:44
Hathaway, William R. 23:95
Hathaway, York C. 11:106
Hathelly, Alexander 11:187
Hatherway, E. 25:183
Hathett, Moses 6:16
Hatheway, E. 5:51
Hatheway, M. J. 24:20
Hathfen, W. S. 15:67
Hathfield, C. 14:299; 17:472
Hathfield, F. W. 1:141
Hathfield, Joseph 14:299
Hathorn, A. 15:318
Hathron, A. 19:75
Hathway, Isaac M. 23:147
Hathway, W. 23:147
Hation, Enoch 21:342
Hatkins, Daniel 18:239; 26:35
Hatler, T. 11:242
Hatley, C. 20:57
Hatmaker, Aaron 22:405
Hatmaker, John 7:29
Haton, John 21:53
Hatson, J. 14:69
Hatsough, Th. H. 11:126
Hatt, R. C. 7:29
Hattan, James 4:30
Hattell, Philip 7:50
Hatten, E. P. 11:304
Hatten, James 9:157
Hatter, Christopher 11:149
Hatter, Daniel 23:67
Hatter, Francis M. 11:93
Hatter, J. F. 14:12
Hatter, J. S. 13:90
Hatter, James 9:82
Hatter, Mitchell 9:82
Hatter, Robert S. 22:426
Hatterman, W. 17:440

Hatterman, William H. H. 24:152
Hatters, Henry 10:152
Hattery, Andrew 11:151
Hattery, Jesse 9:22; 18:307; 26:101
Hattery, Jonas 22:197
Hattey, Aaron 22:253
Hattimer, B. 23:33
Hattin, John 13:27; 16:36
Hattles, J. 19:253
Hatto, Charles 8:119
Hattock, William 15:291
Hatton, E. 9:8; 11:395
Hatton, Edward 10:57; 20:268
Hatton, Ezekiel 22:481
Hatton, Morris 10:117
Hatton, Robert 11:62
Hattorn, Michael 19:75
Hatts, Thomas 7:124
Hatz, Henry 9:119; 27:59
Hauan, John 18:307
Haub, J. P. 24:195
Haub, J. T. 17:132
Hauber, Charles P. 18:368
Hauber, John 18:368
Haubert, L. 14:69
Haubpard, H. 24:20
Haubranck, Prestler 17:415
Hauce, C. 3:91
Hauenstein, J. 16:295
Hauer, G. 15:107
Hauer, John H. 26:220
Hauer, W. 22:197
Hauff, Jacob C. 8:19; 18:138
Hauff, Paul C. 16:197
Hauff, William 19:168
Hauffman, George 13:27
Hauft, Christian 8:19
Haugenbarry, John 21:71
Haugh, A. W. 4:30
Haugh, Benjamin F. 21:225
Haugh, Hewry 18:14
Haugh, J. W. 12:24
Haugh, John 11:62
Haugh, M. 3:91
Haugh, P. W. 7:29
Haugh, Robert W. 12:24
Haugh, William 15:107
Haugh, William A. 14:177
Haugh, William H. 11:151
Haughan, S. 14:69
Haughaorth, Lefferd 19:17
Haughay, J. H. 24:79
Haughenberg, John 8:49

Haughenberry, Joseph 10:57; 20:268
Haughey, Charles F. 17:280
Haughey, John 3:91
Haughey, R. 23:33
Haughland, C. A. 8:72
Haughlin, Jerry 10:161
Haughtaling, Samuel 14:69
Haughteling, Fenimore 9:119
Haughton, H. 27:65
Haughton, M. 15:151
Haughton, N. 14:241
Haughton, William 1:39
Haugk, ---astus 25:40
Haugo, Shango 9:236
Hauker, Christian 9:204
Haukins, Alexander 10:117
Hauks, George 20:8
Haul, C. 21:342
Haulbert, William H. 4:30
Haum, Valentine 17:314
Haumer, J. C. 16:370
Haumm, William 20:268
Haumpreys, Benjamin I. 23:191
Haun, Levi 7:29
Haunesay, J. 15:17
Haunson, A. 13:90
Haunson, Peter 26:220
Haunstad, Charles S. 10:146
Haunward, Greenville 8:49
Haupst, Christ 11:63
Haupt, Justus 17:80
Haupt, Peter 9:144
Hauptman, Charles 19:17
Hauptman, J. 25:41
Haurmy, L. 22:303
Haus, John 17:132
Hausborough, Isaac 7:124
Hausby, James 7:13
Hause, Adam 9:119
Hause, Alonzo 9:119
Hause, Amos P. 23:190
Hause, Edwin R. 7:97
Hause, John 1:39; 3:91
Hause, L. D. 23:147
Hause, L. M. 18:307; 26:100
Hause, Reuben 17:288
Hausen, A. 18:368
Hauser, David 13:111
Hauser, Frederick 1:41
Hauser, G. 25:183
Hauser, J. 1:44
Hauser, John 23:113

Hausler, J. 1:43
Hausman, Emanuel 18:368
Hausman, G. 3:91
Hausman, John 27:58
Hauson, E. 21:121
Hauson, Peter 22:34, 161
Hausted, George 21:243
Haut, Henry 18:307
Haut, Jacob 18:307
Hautsaut, Chris 9:240
Havah, Henry 18:50
Havan, John 20:268
Havard, J. W. 25:183
Havard, Sterling 27:145
Haveland, Charles H. 12:71
Haveland, George 14:177; 23:147
Haveland, George W. 21:53
Haveley, Warner 22:34
Haven, Allen 22:336
Haven, B. F. 13:90; 14:12
Haven, Brook 9:179
Haven, C. H. W. 24:51
Haven, C. M. 25:39
Haven, Charles 1:41; 16:36
Haven, Charles W. 16:7
Haven, Clayton D. 4:30
Haven, Daniel D. 21:216
Haven, Edward 12:71
Haven, Eli 18:110
Haven, J. C. 19:224
Haven, J. D. 26:34
Haven, J. S. 19:286
Haven, J. T. 9:82; 26:33
Haven, Loren 16:36
Haven, Louis 13:27
Haven, O. 7:29
Haven, Theodore 20:268
Haven, Thomas 10:91
Haven, Thomas D. 7:29
Haven, William 18:84
Havendish, John 4:30
Havenfield, James 23:147
Havenmaster, John 16:15
Havens, Aaron 21:225
Havens, Charles 19:17
Havens, Charles F. 10:17
Havens, D. 9:82; 13:90
Havens, E. N. 3:91
Havens, Edward 15:27
Havens, Egbert L. 13:27
Havens, H. 3:91
Havens, Hamser 21:88
Havens, J. B. 3:91
Havens, J. D. 27:55
Havens, J. R. 25:41
Havens, J. S. 1:44

Havens, Richard 1:39
Havens, S. 3:91; 25:183
Havens, Samuel D. 17:211
Havens, Shaldon 8:117
Havens, Sheldon 8:86; 18:330
Havens, Thomas W. 22:81
Havens, W. 1:138
Havens, W. C. 23:252
Havens, William 18:110
Haver, A. 1:139
Haver, John 11:152
Haverill, Lucian 11:191
Haverslight, H. 3:91
Haverstick, Amos 13:27
Haverstick, James 16:9
Haverstick, John 20:268
Haverstick, Michael 11:15
Haverstock, John 10:91
Haverstraw, Augustus 7:62
Haverstraw, William 1:38
Haverstrumdpf, Martin 18:103
Haverty, D. 15:3
Haverty, Daniel 12:62
Haverty, Timothy 17:236
Havett, Bully 26:165
Havier, P. 14:12
Haviland, A. A. 1:136
Haviland, Alfred 13:27
Haviland, C. H. 15:27
Haviland, Daniel 22:144
Haviland, G. 18:31
Haviland, H. 3:91
Haviland, Joseph J. 21:115
Haviland, Nathan 24:94
Haviland, Robert 17:397
Havington, E. 16:370
Havins, Samuel 22:34
Havious, Benjamin 23:67
Havis, J. McD. 13:90
Havlin, William S. 22:34
Havous, William 20:27
Havrell, Elias 8:19
Havrill, James B. 8:19
Haw, Joshua D. 7:124
Haw, Thomas 22:280
Hawaley, Edward J. 16:36
Haward, George W. 12:154
Haward, Joseph 12:154
Haway, P. A. 21:342
Hawbrick, Joseph 23:33
Hawell, Henry 11:64
Hawell, Nat 7:124
Hawell, Nath 21:342
Hawenstein, J. 25:183
Hawes, Columbus 6:22
Hawes, F. 1:41

Hawes, George 7:97
Hawes, George H. 16:143
Hawes, J. 16:197
Hawes, Jefferson 22:399
Hawes, John F. 17:95
Hawes, LeRoy 16:197
Hawes, Lester L. 10:95
Hawes, M. B. 24:111
Hawes, Robert M. 21:216
Hawes, Samuel 22:122
Hawes, W. C. 22:253
Hawh, William 25:183
Hawhe, Isaiah 18:218
Hawhee, William S. 22:426
Hawk, A. 14:69
Hawk, A. C. 14:69
Hawk, Asa 4:30
Hawk, Benjamin 11:62
Hawk, C. 1:141
Hawk, Charles 4:30
Hawk, David C. 7:97
Hawk, E. 1:136
Hawk, Francis P. 19:327
Hawk, H. 9:227; 11:31
Hawk, Henry 22:197
Hawk, J. 23:147
Hawk, Jacob 23:147
Hawk, John 10:57; 20:268
Hawk, Joseph 9:179
Hawk, L. 14:177, 256
Hawk, Lafayette 11:149
Hawk, Lewis A. 22:112
Hawk, Peter 18:412
Hawk, V. 1:141
Hawk, William 9:82; 25:183; 26:32
Hawke, H. J. 7:57
Hawkenberry, S. 16:197
Hawkensmith, Thomas 17:469
Hawker, A. 16:197
Hawker, C. 26:34
Hawker, Charles 26:34
Hawker, David 24:20
Hawkes, Alton 4:30
Hawkes, B. F. 27:57
Hawkes, Dwight 24:20
Hawkes, George W. 9:179
Hawkes, J. F. 7:57
Hawkes, Robert 19:75
Hawkes, Willard W. 19:75
Hawkes, William S. 18
Hawkey, Thomas 21:342
Hawkhurst, W. H. 1:43
Hawkin, T. D. 16:95
Hawkins, A. S. 11:64
Hawkins, Albert 22:197
Hawkins, Alex 19:291
Hawkins, Alexander 9:200

Hawkins, Alfred 12:53; 22:463
Hawkins, Allen 9:12
Hawkins, Alphonse 7:50
Hawkins, Andrew 22:303
Hawkins, Arvine 12:53
Hawkins, Asel 17:314
Hawkins, B. 17:177
Hawkins, Ben 21:273
Hawkins, Benjamin 23:33
Hawkins, C. C. 8:19; 18:138
Hawkins, Calvin R. 10:57
Hawkins, Charles 13:57
Hawkins, Charles A. 10:117; 20:268; 25:183
Hawkins, D. 14:177
Hawkins, D. F. 3:91
Hawkins, Daniel G. 17:21
Hawkins, David 9:82; 21:273; 26:32
Hawkins, E. 1:142; 3:91; 21:110; 22:336
Hawkins, Edw. 11:205
Hawkins, Elijah 11:62
Hawkins, Francis 13:27
Hawkins, Frank 24:212
Hawkins, Freeman 20:146
Hawkins, G. 10:148
Hawkins, G. W. 5:40; 25:183
Hawkins, George 7:124; 18:84, 239; 21:342; 26:36; 27:61
Hawkins, George W. 9:120; 20:268; 25:183
Hawkins, H. 16:95; 17:166; 18:50; 22:303
Hawkins, H. W. 21:121
Hawkins, Henry 6:16; 7:124; 12:49; 17:166; 18:84
Hawkins, Hiram 27:145
Hawkins, I. H. 23:33
Hawkins, I. S. W. 18:218
Hawkins, J. 1:43; 10:155; 16:197; 18:31; 19:169; 21:342; 22:197, 253
Hawkins, J. M. 12:71; 18:368
Hawkins, J. N. 15:22
Hawkins, J. T. 16:197
Hawkins, J. W. 3:92
Hawkins, James 7:29; 9:72; 17:443; 20:107; 24:159
Hawkins, James A. 17:72

Hawkins, James O. 24:62
Hawkins, James R. 20:104
Hawkins, James S. 16:80
Hawkins, John 4:30; 9:97; 11:204; 22:81; 23:270
Hawkins, John L. 18:138
Hawkins, John O. 22:197
Hawkins, John S. 8:19
Hawkins, John W. 20:140
Hawkins, Joseph 12:49, 71; 22:197
Hawkins, Joshua 10:57; 20:268
Hawkins, Jourdan 24:195
Hawkins, Jourdon 17:132
Hawkins, Leroy J. 22:34
Hawkins, Moses 17:393
Hawkins, N. W. 3:92
Hawkins, Nelson 22:35
Hawkins, O. 9:200
Hawkins, O. J. 19:169
Hawkins, Oliver 1:191
Hawkins, Ores 19:291
Hawkins, Patrick 1:192
Hawkins, Paul 7:124
Hawkins, Perry 7:124
Hawkins, Preston 21:130
Hawkins, R. S. 9:22; 22:481
Hawkins, Reuben 22:336
Hawkins, Richard 7:124
Hawkins, Robert 18:239; 21:342; 23:148; 26:35
Hawkins, Rollin 9:200
Hawkins, Rowland 11:205
Hawkins, S. 25:183
Hawkins, S. D. 3:92
Hawkins, Samuel 5:40
Hawkins, Samuel W. 21:255
Hawkins, Solomon 23:270
Hawkins, T. 11:304
Hawkins, T. L. 1:135
Hawkins, Taylor 11:205
Hawkins, Thomas 9:22; 11:63; 15:202; 17:132, 433; 18:320; 24:159, 195, 196; 25:333
Hawkins, Thomas J. 22:253
Hawkins, Thomas W. 22:426
Hawkins, Tilghman H. 8:86
Hawkins, Valent B. 22:502
Hawkins, VanBuren 22:81

Hawkins, W. 14:69, 241; 16:197; 27:65
Hawkins, W. H. 4:30
Hawkins, W. T. 16:113; 21:225
Hawkins, Walker 16:36
Hawkins, Warren 18:458
Hawkins, William 7:124; 9:179, 208; 10:176; 13:27; 15:202; 16:67; 17:177, 273; 19:169; 21:342; 22:122; 26:212
Hawkins, William C. 13:27; 16:36
Hawkins, William H. 13:111
Hawkins, William O. 12:24
Hawkins, William R. 13:127
Hawkins, Zuriah F. 19:17
Hawkinson, Charles 20:124
Hawks, B. F. 9:144
Hawks, Edwin R. 7:57
Hawks, John F. 21:342
Hawks, S. B. 18:50
Hawks, William 5:51; 25:183
Hawks, William U. 13:64
Hawler, George 21:342
Hawley, A. B. 26:163
Hawley, C. 3:92
Hawley, Charles H. 17:243
Hawley, Daniel 10:57
Hawley, David 20:268
Hawley, Edward 10:161; 19:169; 21:342
Hawley, Edward A. 17:65
Hawley, Everett 4:30
Hawley, George 22:144
Hawley, George W. 22:144
Hawley, H. 25:40
Hawley, Henry 9:179; 14:177
Hawley, Henry M. 16:36
Hawley, Hiram R. 23:122
Hawley, Horace A. 4:30
Hawley, I. 14:177
Hawley, J. 14:256
Hawley, James 9:82; 26:32
Hawley, James S. 9:12
Hawley, Jeremiah 10:117; 20:268
Hawley, John 4:30
Hawley, John L. 10:57
Hawley, John W. 8:106

Hawley, Lemuel 26:165
Hawley, M. J. 27:63
Hawley, Phil. C. 27:145
Hawley, R. 8:106
Hawley, R. A. 3:92
Hawley, Thomas 10:161;
   15:202
Hawley, W. H. 2:12;
   25:43
Hawley, William 13:27;
   14:69; 16:295
Hawley, William A. 23:89
Hawley, William F. 7:124;
   21:342
Hawley, William W.
   20:113
Hawlins, W. H. 21:28
Hawmacher, --- 12:92
Hawn, E. A. 3:92
Hawn, George E. 1:42
Haworth, --- 21:195
Haworth, J. R. 8:64;
   26:164
Haworth, William 11:187
Hawre, John 12:122
Haws, A. 15:342; 16:370
Haws, J. 11:280
Haws, John 11:387
Haws, Samuel A. 16:371
Haws, W. 14:265
Haws, William 9:163
Hawsen, William 3:92
Hawser, J. 14:69
Hawsey, J. 12:92; 16:295
Hawsey, Joseph 7:124
Hawson, H. C. 17:95
Hawthorn, G. A. 25:298
Hawthorn, Ira 18:31
Hawthorn, J. B. 1:138
Hawthorn, Noah 18:138
Hawthorne, Alexander
   9:35
Hawthorne, George 14:70
Hawyer, Henry 12:154
Haxton, Benjamin 15:332;
   19:75
Haxton, Timothy 1:40
Hay, A. C. 25:183
Hay, Addison C. 5:18
Hay, Charles 26:37
Hay, David 21:100
Hay, G. F. 11:242
Hay, George 10:57
Hay, H. 14:70
Hay, H. H. 16:119
Hay, Henry C. 15:17
Hay, J. W. 1:138
Hay, James 18:218
Hay, James R. 17:206
Hay, John 22:513
Hay, John C. 22:11

Hay, John D. 7:57
Hay, Joshua 20:146
Hay, Lewis 7:81
Hay, Peter 23:113
Hay, Richard 11:205
Hay, Robert M. 21:342
Hay, Rufus T. 9:82
Hay, V. S. 14:288; 23:122
Hay, Vincent S. 14:265
Hay, W. 1:139
Hay, W. J. 11:242
Hay, W. T. 9:47
Hay, William 3:92;
   18:293; 26:102
Hayan, John B. 22:35
Hayatt, L. P. 3:92
Haybea, Elisha 20:268
Hayberger, David 4:30
Hayburn, Samuel 16:119
Hayck, C. W. 14:70
Haycock, E. G. 15:342
Haycock, H. 1:98
Haycox, William 14:70
Hayde, A. 23:148
Hayde, Mathews 15:14
Hayden, --- 9:22, 230;
   18:67; 20:268
Hayden, Alex 17:191
Hayden, Allen 7:78;
   25:298
Hayden, Alonzo C.
   16:145
Hayden, Anderson 7:124
Hayden, Benjamin F.
   10:57
Hayden, Charles 11:32;
   12:167; 19:348
Hayden, Daniel 7:97
Hayden, Frank 19:17
Hayden, Franklin 12:64;
   15:17
Hayden, G. L. 15:342;
   16:371
Hayden, H. 1:138; 16:197;
   21:342
Hayden, Henry J. 21:255
Hayden, J. 1:140
Hayden, J. B. 7:29;
   22:481
Hayden, James 8:86
Hayden, John 4:30;
   20:268
Hayden, Joseph B. 22:81
Hayden, L. L. 25:41
Hayden, Luther 21:28
Hayden, Lyman H. 24:94
Hayden, Michael 12:58
Hayden, P. 14:70, 282
Hayden, Pinkney 11:333
Hayden, Presley 6:12

Hayden, R. B. 18:307;
   26:101
Hayden, Samuel E.
   18:239; 26:35
Hayden, Stevens W.
   22:451
Hayden, Thornton 9:9
Hayden, W. 18:14
Hayden, W. H. 9:144;
   27:55
Hayden, William 7:124
Hayden, William H.
   14:335
Haydenberk, Daniel
   22:145
Haydon, Benjamin F.
   20:268
Haydon, Clemond 18:84
Haydon, G. 1:39
Haydon, John 10:57
Haydon, W. P. 11:33
Haye, Andrew J. 11:32
Hayen, S. C. 9:179
Hayer, D. A. 9:144; 27:57
Hayer, G. 1:137
Hayer, John 18:138
Hayeres, Benjamin H.
   21:342
Hayerstrom, John C.
   11:33
Hayes, --- 17:495
Hayes, A. 14:12; 16:268
Hayes, A. B. M. 21:342
Hayes, Alexander 9:102;
   16:197
Hayes, Alfred 7:29
Hayes, Antony 7:124
Hayes, Benjamin 8:77; 9:9
Hayes, C. B. 1:135
Hayes, Carl 20:268
Hayes, Charles 17:132;
   24:195
Hayes, Charles B. 15:124
Hayes, Charles N. 18:207
Hayes, D. 19:253
Hayes, Daniel 17:21;
   22:336
Hayes, Dennis 9:179
Hayes, E. P. 7:29
Hayes, Edson 17:449
Hayes, G. H. 19:253
Hayes, G. W. 1:137;
   25:183
Hayes, George 9:208;
   10:176; 13:27, 111;
   14:70; 19:169
Hayes, H. L. 16:295
Hayes, Hannibal 16:37
Hayes, Harry 9:120
Hayes, Henry 9:120;
   18:84; 21:342

Hayes, Horatio 9:179
Hayes, Isaac N. 23:113
Hayes, J. 1:140; 3:92;
 14:12; 19:282
Hayes, J. A. 17:327
Hayes, J. C. 3:92; 21:343
Hayes, J. D. 9:102
Hayes, J. H. 10:17
Hayes, J. J. 21:343
Hayes, J. M. 1:138
Hayes, James 1:39; 3:92;
 9:120, 132, 179;
 18:239; 19:282;
 21:255; 22:303;
 25:40; 26:36; 27:54
Hayes, James B. 22:35
Hayes, James P. 22:35
Hayes, James W. 22:35
Hayes, Jem 26:34
Hayes, Jerry 17:35
Hayes, John 1:38; 4:30;
 9:97; 11:241, 413;
 12:82; 13:27;
 14:262; 16:295;
 21:343; 22:336
Hayes, John F. 21:343
Hayes, John G. 21:343
Hayes, John H. 10:170
Hayes, John T. 27:61
Hayes, John W. 4:30
Hayes, Joseph G. 15:166
Hayes, Lawrence 23:11
Hayes, Lester L. 20:268
Hayes, Lloyd T. 18:138
Hayes, Loyd T. 8:19
Hayes, Michael 1:44;
 12:24; 16:37; 22:35;
 26:32
Hayes, Morris 10:170
Hayes, N. 22:303
Hayes, Nat. 15:289;
 16:197
Hayes, Nel'm. 1:39
Hayes, Nicholas 8:121
Hayes, Oliver 27:62
Hayes, P. 3:92
Hayes, Patrick 16:119;
 21:343
Hayes, Peter 1:41
Hayes, R. 21:166
Hayes, R. W. 1:98
Hayes, Richard 17:80
Hayes, Robert 20:27
Hayes, S. 1:43, 141; 12:8;
 14:70
Hayes, Samuel 20:113
Hayes, Samuel E. 21:216
Hayes, Seth 8:19
Hayes, T. 12:82; 19:169
Hayes, Thomas 15:202,
 347

Hayes, W. 17:236
Hayes, W. H. 12:99
Hayes, W. J. 21:28
Hayes, W. L. 12:85
Hayes, W. T. 26:142
Hayes, William 16:37,
 197; 21:240; 27:63
Hayes, William B. 15:68
Hayes, William M. 15:11
Hayes, William P. 10:205
Hayes, Wright 9:157
Hayford, A. E. 3:92
Hayford, J. 1:43
Hayford, Joel 1:40
Hayhow, Samuel 22:145
Hayhugh, J. W. 12:82
Hayhurst, Elias 23:89
Hayhurst, Thomas M.
 22:81
Hayless, Henry 22:303
Haylett, J. 3:92
Haymaker, G. E. 11:292
Hayman, Hendrick 16:95
Hayman, Henry T. 18:218
Hayman, J. 16:119
Hayman, William 21:216
Haymer, R. H. 8:49
Haymile, Frank 23:277
Haymond, George 9:179
Haymons, H. 12:161
Haymouth, W. 3:92
Haynard, Franklin 16:37
Hayne, Andrew 25:41
Hayne, C. 1:141
Hayne, George W. 8:86
Hayne, J. 16:371
Hayne, John 22:336
Hayne, Peter 8:101
Hayner, B. 3:92
Hayner, George 9:11
Haynes, A. D. 19:169
Haynes, Abraham 19:278
Haynes, Abram 9:179
Haynes, Alonzo 22:336
Haynes, Alvin 23:122
Haynes, Andrew B. 8:86
Haynes, Benjamin H. 7:97
Haynes, Bethuel M. 4:30
Haynes, C. E. 3:92
Haynes, C. G. 8:72
Haynes, C. J. 22:336
Haynes, D. 11:287;
 22:480
Haynes, D. M. 17:95
Haynes, D. P. 17:35
Haynes, Davis 17:35
Haynes, E. 3:92
Haynes, Eli 17:355
Haynes, F. G. 5:18
Haynes, G. 1:137
Haynes, George G. 21:343

Haynes, George H. 21:343
Haynes, H. 1:139
Haynes, H. B. 1:41
Haynes, Harrison 10:208
Haynes, Henry 18:138
Haynes, Isaac 18:31
Haynes, J. 11:263; 15:326
Haynes, J. B. 12:154
Haynes, J. C. 17:152
Haynes, J. F. 13:111
Haynes, J. M. 9:53
Haynes, J. W. 18:239;
 27:56
Haynes, Jacob 14:319;
 25:281
Haynes, James 5:40;
 20:269; 21:343
Haynes, James L. 18:111
Haynes, James P. 23:240
Haynes, James T. 10:91
Haynes, Jeremiah C.
 22:145
Haynes, John 3:92;
 22:197
Haynes, John B. 18:218
Haynes, John L. 18:368
Haynes, Jonathan 10:57;
 20:269
Haynes, Joseph W. 17:259
Haynes, Lester L. 10:117
Haynes, M. 27:56
Haynes, Martin 21:225
Haynes, Michael 27:56
Haynes, Napoleon B.
 22:502
Haynes, P. 3:92
Haynes, Parco 10:161
Haynes, Rawlings 18:207
Haynes, Reuben 8:39;
 26:165
Haynes, Robert 21:273
Haynes, Samuel 11:280
Haynes, Samuel A. 22:452
Haynes, Samuel M. 20:46
Haynes, Samuel T. 7:97
Haynes, Seymour P.
 10:117; 20:269
Haynes, Solomon 21:343
Haynes, T. 16:295
Haynes, Theron 21:245
Haynes, Thomas 5:51;
 9:97
Haynes, Thomas H. 5:18
Haynes, W. 1:141; 3:92;
 14:265; 18:84; 19:17
Haynes, W. C. 3:92
Haynes, W. F. 14:332
Haynes, W. I. 4:30
Haynes, William 21:343;
 22:197

Haynes, William E. 16:133
Haynes, Wilson 12:24
Haynesworth, W. 13:90
Haynew, H. 11:231
Hayney, Fannel 26:165
Hayney, Fanuel 8:39
Haynie, James P. 21:71
Haynor, L. 3:92
Hayns, A. 11:304
Hayns, Charles 11:219
Haypitch, John 8:86
Hayres, Henry 8:19
Hays, --- 14:177, 262; 19:75
Hays, A. 13:103
Hays, A. J. 25:183
Hays, Abraham J. 5:18
Hays, Abraham L. 15:87
Hays, Albert C. 10:57
Hays, Albert R. 8:86
Hays, Alex 18:339
Hays, Alexander 21:53
Hays, Alfred 11:93
Hays, Bardin 18:239; 26:37
Hays, Benjamin 26:166
Hays, Bernard 11:93
Hays, Boswell F. 15:36
Hays, C. 3:92
Hays, Charles A. 23:99
Hays, Charles W. 11:32
Hays, D. C. 27:56
Hays, D. G. 9:144
Hays, D. S. 12:154
Hays, D. W. 19:17
Hays, David 7:29; 22:253
Hays, DeLoss 11:401
Hays, E. 27:54
Hays, E. R. 15:159
Hays, Ed 19:17
Hays, Edson 24:175
Hays, Edward 3:92; 18:239; 26:36
Hays, Elisha A. 10:57; 20:269
Hays, Engle D. 20:17
Hays, Ezekiel 18:395
Hays, F. 2:12; 25:43
Hays, Felix 22:254
Hays, George W. 22:81
Hays, H. 17:132; 22:254; 24:196
Hays, Hannibal 13:27
Hays, Harrison 22:122
Hays, Harry 27:59
Hays, Horatio 19:267
Hays, Ira T. 15:202
Hays, Isaac R. 20:97
Hays, J. 13:90; 14:70; 18:368

Hays, J. F. 3:92
Hays, J. K. 1:139
Hays, J. L. 25:40
Hays, J. W. 7:29
Hays, Jackson 10:57; 20:269
Hays, Jacob 10:117, 146; 20:269
Hays, James 23:148; 27:58
Hays, James H. 22:197
Hays, Jerry 18:239
Hays, Jesse 21:71
Hays, John 5:18; 9:22; 10:8; 14:70, 177; 16:295; 17:243, 421; 18:434; 22:254, 336, 427; 23:67; 25:183, 272
Hays, John B. 17:393
Hays, John F. 8:86
Hays, John M. 24:164
Hays, Mahlon 18:218
Hays, Mathew 22:253
Hays, Michael 11:31; 13:27
Hays, Moses H. 10:17
Hays, P. 3:92
Hays, P. H. 16:371
Hays, Peter 17:177
Hays, Philander 24:94
Hays, Pompey 27:62
Hays, R. S. L. 14:331
Hays, Reuben G. L. 20:186
Hays, Richard 22:253
Hays, Robert 9:22
Hays, S. H. 14:177
Hays, Samuel J. 20:8
Hays, Seth 18:138
Hays, Shannon 22:197
Hays, Thomas 7:124
Hays, Thomas U. 18:307
Hays, Thomas W. 9:22; 26:101
Hays, W. 9:144; 27:57
Hays, W. L. 14:70
Hays, W. M. 3:92
Hays, Wilbern 26:32
Hays, Wilburn 9:82
Hays, William 7:97; 12:71; 13:27; 22:81
Hays, William A. 8:86
Hays, William B. 26:33
Hays, William F. 27:64
Hays, William H. 8:64; 26:163
Hays, Wilson T. 20:17
Hays, Worcester 23:67
Haysborn, Charles P. 9:82
Hayse, Francis N. 4:30

Hayse, John 27:63
Hayse, P. 15:124
Hayse, W. W. 25:311
Hayse, William 22:197
Hayse, William M. 12:71
Haysell, Joseph 14:177
Haysellton, Alexander 14:177
Hayser, A. S. 21:343
Hayser, John 21:100
Hayship, J. L. 22:405
Hayship, Samuel 17:404
Hayslip, --- 25:269
Hayslip, Henry 23:148
Hayslip, R. C. 23:148
Hayslip, Wesley 22:303
Haysworth, Francis M. 8:86
Hayt, Wil 25:183
Hayth, J. 17:191
Hayvert, B. 3:92
Hayward, A. J. 11:182
Hayward, Austin 23:107
Hayward, C. 25:183
Hayward, C. E. 19:227
Hayward, C. O. 9:179
Hayward, C. S. 8:86
Hayward, Elihu 8:86
Hayward, Franklin 13:27
Hayward, George 16:133
Hayward, Henry 22:405
Hayward, J. W. 12:24; 25:183
Hayward, John 9:68
Hayward, Oliver R. 21:10
Hayward, Thomas 7:97
Hayward, W. G. 3:92
Hayward, William H. 1:41
Haywood, --- 3:92
Haywood, A. J. 3:92
Haywood, Abner 4:30
Haywood, Caleb 5:18
Haywood, E. A. 9:179; 19:238
Haywood, E. M. 21:184, 214
Haywood, George 9:208
Haywood, Harry 15:151
Haywood, Henry 21:343
Haywood, J. 21:163
Haywood, J. B. 3:92
Haywood, J. F. 21:343
Haywood, J. L. 15:202
Haywood, Jacob 10:57
Haywood, James 4:30; 22:145
Haywood, James S. 11:32
Haywood, Joel 17:360
Haywood, John W. 5:40
Haywood, Judd 22:303
Haywood, Michael 12:168

Haywood, O. 5:18
Haywood, P. A. 13:90
Haywood, Robert 8:39;
  26:165
Haywood, Rotheans 9:72
Haywood, S. G. 3:92;
  14:177
Haywood, Sandy 27:58
Haywood, Sundy 9:132
Haywood, W. 27:56
Haywood, William 18:84
Hayword, O. 25:183
Hayworth, Charles K.
  22:11
Hayworth, F. 3:92
Hayworth, L. 23:33
Hayzlett, Edward 23:89
Hazard, Hubbard 4:30
Hazard, J. A. 25:44
Hazard, Jacob 19:46
Hazard, L. B. 8:19
Hazard, Phillistus 8:19
Hazben, Elisha 10:57
Haze, John J. 7:29
Haze, L. 18:67
Haze, Warty 11:84
Hazebrigg, James 10:57
Hazel, George 3:92
Hazel, Henry 13:27;
  24:107
Hazel, J. 3:92
Hazel, Jacob 24:19
Hazel, James W. 17:360
Hazel, Joseph 10:95
Hazel, Luther 19:322
Hazel, Richard 9:132
Hazelbaker, Andrew J.
  22:426
Hazelett, W. 17:479;
  27:64
Hazelett, William 14:299
Hazelger, Richard S.
  10:91
Hazelgrove, Andrew S.
  16:37
Hazelhurt, P. 19:321
Hazeligg, H. L. 18:218
Hazelins, Erick 21:138
Hazell, A. E. 19:17
Hazell, F. 13:81
Hazell, Henry 16:37
Hazell, J. 1:139
Hazell, William 15:202
Hazelmeyer, William
  12:24
Hazelmyer, William
  18:307; 26:99
Hazelrig, Mareum 22:303
Hazeltine, Jonas E. 24:94
Hazeltine, Moses 12:71

Hazeltine, Nathaniel S.
  21:138
Hazelton, David 21:225
Hazelton, Enoch E. 15:25
Hazelton, Henry 23:89
Hazelton, Herman 21:255
Hazelton, M. 25:299
Hazelwood, George L.
  6:21
Hazelwood, James 22:254
Hazelwood, W. S. 6:21
Hazen, A. 3:92
Hazen, Charles 9:156
Hazen, Charles B. 12:122
Hazen, Francis 25:41
Hazen, George W. 4:30
Hazen, Hazeriah 17:387
Hazen, Henry 10:179
Hazen, Isaac B. 10:117;
  20:269
Hazen, J. M. 5:51
Hazen, Jacob 15:17;
  17:323
Hazen, James A. 22:481
Hazen, M. 23:148
Hazen, M. J. 3:92
Hazen, William B. 11:443
Hazenbaugh, Caleb 19:75
Hazenflincy, I. 3:92
Hazens, Daniel 12:24
Hazens, James F. 27:59
Hazer, C. 14:70
Hazer, Frederick 13:27
Hazer, John 3:92
Hazey, William 5:18
Hazin, P. 14:70
Hazle, Henry 22:11
Hazle, J. 24:195
Hazle, Jo 17:132
Hazleger, R. S. 20:269
Hazlet, William 20:269
Hazleton, Augustus 11:32
Hazleton, B. 21:343
Hazleton, Bernard 21:343
Hazleton, George B. 22:35
Hazleton, Henry G. 4:30
Hazleton, Herbert 10:17
Hazleton, John W.
  10:117; 20:269
Hazleton, Lyman W.
  9:102
Hazleton, P. 25:183
Hazlett, Alexander 18:353
Hazlett, Henry 11:149
Hazlett, John 10:57;
  20:269
Hazlett, William 3:92;
  10:57
Hazlewood, J. H. 3:92
Hazlewood, J. S. 11:280

Hazlewood, Samuel
  17:132; 24:194
Hazlip, Mastron C. 22:451
Hazlitt, M. O. 26:221
Hazrick, John 21:343
Hazurigg, James 20:269
Hazzard, A. 9:132; 27:59
Hazzard, James 16:139;
  22:497
Hazzard, John T. 7:29
Hazzard, Lavinia 27:61
Hazzard, W. S. 15:159
Hazzer, W. 3:92
Hazzleton, Philip 5:40
Hea, D. O. 12:166
Heaber, Austin 21:216
Heaberling, John G.
  20:269
Heac, R. 3:92
Heacock, J. N. 1:141
Heacock, James O. 22:280
Heacock, Joel 11:32
Heacock, William H.
  18:396
Head, --- 19:291
Head, A. J. 9:53
Head, Daniel 3:92
Head, Elijah 25:183
Head, George W. 12:58
Head, Henry H. 8:86
Head, Isaac H. 7:97
Head, J. Henry 25:39
Head, James M. 22:197
Head, John C. 24:39
Head, Marius 11:219
Head, N. 18:239; 26:34
Head, P. 9:179; 19:232;
  21:28
Head, Parker 17:177
Head, R. F. 13:77
Head, R. J. 3:92
Head, Thomas 3:92
Head, Thomas C. 21:100
Head, W. C. 18:339
Headding, John W. 24:51
Headen, R. 22:513
Headen, Thomas 17:80
Heading, J. 1:139
Heading, Nelson W. 21:71
Heading, Zachariah 19:46
Headlee, Henry M. 22:11
Headlee, Jacob 20:23
Headley, Andrew 22:303
Headley, C. 20:133
Headley, Charles W.
  11:122
Headley, Cyrus 11:107
Headley, Daniel 10:179
Headley, Daniel E. 22:81
Headley, Harvey F. 1:39

Headley, J. 13:132; 20:269
Headley, J. D. 3:223; 17:504
Headley, J. W. 7:29
Headley, James 15:349
Headley, Jeptha 23:33
Headley, Oscar 4:30
Headley, William 21:225
Headly, John W. 15:203
Headly, Richard G. 24:71
Headly, Uriah 27:61
Headreck, George 8:86
Headrick, John 11:326
Heads, Nelson 26:165
Heady, Nathan S. 11:93
Heady, Uriah 9:120
Heaffy, Michael 19:75
Heagan, J. 3:92
Heagan, J. T. 11:187
Heagg, James T. 9:179
Heagles, Joseph 1:40
Heaglin, John 12:24
Heaglitt, J. W. 23:148
Heagney, James R. 21:71
Heagy, B. 1:42
Heakin, J. 1:136
Heal, Alton P. 24:62
Heal, C. H. 19:227
Heal, Isaac T. 7:97
Heal, L. J. 21:343
Heal, M. C. 19:227
Heal, Pressley M. 23:99
Heal, S. W. 25:42
Heal, T. A. 19:238
Heal, W. E. 16:197
Heald, A. 1:138; 25:41
Heald, Alfred 1:43
Heald, C. 1:44
Heald, H. H. 3:92
Heald, J. S. 15:166
Heald, James H. 7:29
Heald, John 26:145
Heald, John A. 19:75
Heald, M. 12:154
Heald, Nathan 16:133
Heald, Payson T. 12:24
Heald, Samuel W. 18:239; 26:35
Heald, W. S. 27:63
Heald, William 3:92
Heald, William S. 13:27
Heale, A. 19:227
Heales, William 10:117; 20:269
Healey, Daniel 16:198
Healey, Davis B. 5:18
Healey, H. 25:183
Healey, J. 15:203
Healey, Jer--- 25:39

Healey, John 18:138; 19:17; 20:23
Healey, Owen 19:319
Healey, Stephen E. 22:81
Healey, T. J. 16:85
Healey, Thomas 23:276
Healey, William 23:148
Healin, V. 14:70
Healley, H. 3:92
Heals, Joshua 9:35
Healstead, J. 14:282
Health, Tony 18:239
Healy, --- 18:412
Healy, C. E. 21:91
Healy, C. M. 14:282
Healy, George 27:54
Healy, Henry 18:103
Healy, J. 13:90; 14:12
Healy, J. B. 3:92
Healy, Jacob 3:92
Healy, James 24:40
Healy, John 10:17; 16:279
Healy, L. 9:114
Healy, S. 11:305
Healy, Samuel 12:53
Healy, Thaddeus 25:183
Healy, Thomas 12:71
Healy, W. 1:138
Heam, Frederick 10:95
Heam, Horace H. 6:23
Heaman, J. 1:45
Heamburger, Charles 10:117; 20:269
Heanestrand, James 9:132
Heany, J. M. 11:387
Heany, J. T. 11:149
Heap, Andrew 25:299
Heap, Andrew L. 7:80
Heap, B. O. 22:481
Heap, Frederick 9:179
Heape, Samuel 23:33
Heaper, Nathan H. 10:57; 20:269
Hear, John 11:126
Hearand, Robert 12:71
Heard, Alexander 23:313
Heard, W. 13:90
Heards, Nelson 8:39
Heardt, Frederick 23:68
Heardy, A. E. 15:14
Heardy, Samuel 9:132
Hearing, Daniel 12:95
Hearld, Jesse 21:273
Hearld, Joseph 21:273
Hearlsey, W. 12:82; 16:295
Hearn, Benjamin 20:23
Hearn, Dennis A. 13:111
Hearn, Jacob M. 17:46
Hearn, Jesse 11:62
Hearn, M. C. 1:40

Hearn, Peter 24:72
Hearn, Samuel 17:80
Hearne, Biough 19:253
Hearne, John 3:92; 14:177
Hearner, John W. 4:30
Hearop, Jacob 16:37
Heart, Charles 11:150
Heart, Columbus W. 21:100
Heart, Fielden 15:203
Heart, G. O. 11:181
Heart, George 13:125; 17:132; 24:195
Heart, Henry 14:262
Heart, James 21:100
Heart, John 3:93
Heart, John M. 21:216
Heart, John W. 22:35
Heart, Philip 14:282
Heart, Simon 23:148
Heart, Willis A. 9:120
Hearth, Robert 11:387
Heartless, S. 3:93
Heartley, Franklin 10:117; 20:269
Heartly, Simon 9:132
Heartly, William 22:197
Heartman, --- 18:31
Heartwell, Albert 9:120
Hearty, George 25:183
Heartzel, George T. 14:178
Heartzog, William C. 21:53
Hearvey, J. E. 3:93
Heary, C. 1:137
Heas, I. 18:277
Heas, Luther 20:124
Hease, Edwin 11:151
Heasley, A. 1:136
Heasley, George W. 22:280
Heasley, John 19:17
Heastly, G. 13:111
Heaston, J. N. 15:203
Heasy, William 25:183
Heat, A. O. 21:187, 291
Heat, John 13:80
Heath, --- 18:272, 277
Heath, A. 25:183
Heath, A. M. 10:28; 19:302
Heath, Albert 4:30
Heath, Asa 10:57; 20:269
Heath, Avery H. 12:24
Heath, B. 3:93
Heath, Calvin 7:97
Heath, Charles 7:68
Heath, Charles A. 22:197
Heath, Charles C. 21:255
Heath, Charles H. 4:30

Heath, Charles R. 1:45
Heath, Clark 21:343
Heath, Collin 7:58
Heath, Daniel 18:67
Heath, Daniel S. 21:343
Heath, E. A. 21:71
Heath, E. M. 14:178
Heath, E. R. 1:38
Heath, Edward H. 16:143
Heath, Edwin 10:57; 20:269
Heath, F. E. 16:295
Heath, George 27:60
Heath, George F. 9:120
Heath, Griffin 11:187
Heath, H. 7:29
Heath, H. B. 25:183
Heath, H. G. 18:396
Heath, H. H. 1:135
Heath, H. L. 25:299
Heath, Henry 22:197
Heath, Henry L. 7:80
Heath, Hial 4:30
Heath, Homer B. 11:387
Heath, Hosie 27:62
Heath, Isaac 4:30
Heath, Israel 22:197
Heath, J. 3:93
Heath, J. C. 1:138
Heath, J. M. 14:70; 23:148
Heath, J. W. 9:110
Heath, James 13:77; 16:198
Heath, James A. 25:183
Heath, John 15:309; 16:198; 19:75
Heath, Justice 21:343
Heath, L. 1:138
Heath, Lorenzo 1:41
Heath, Magis E. 12:24
Heath, Martin 22:452
Heath, Matthew H. 10:57
Heath, Michael 21:138
Heath, N. C. 21:343
Heath, Oliver 1:40
Heath, Perry 27:54
Heath, Reuben P. 10:161; 19:169
Heath, Richard 25:41
Heath, S. S. 1:136
Heath, Samuel 4:30; 22:35
Heath, Samuel H. 21:100
Heath, Schuyler 17:65
Heath, Sidney 12:58
Heath, Sidney B. 7:29
Heath, Sylvanus 4:30
Heath, T. 21:121
Heath, T. P. 22:197
Heath, Thomas 21:255

Heath, Toney 26:36
Heath, Uriah 6:16; 18:84
Heath, W. 3:93; 25:183
Heath, W. H. 20:269
Heath, William 10:34, 161; 12:24; 19:75, 169; 27:62
Heath, William C. 21:71
Heath, William G. 22:254
Heath, William O. 5:18; 25:184
Heathbrook, H. 14:241; 27:65
Heathcate, Giles 20:48
Heathcoat, R. 26:32
Heathcock, Benjamin H. 22:513
Heathcock, William 12:49
Heather, A. 11:33
Heather, Noah 22:35
Heatherby, John 3:93
Heatherstreet, James C. 8:86
Heatherton, --- 15:36
Heathierlp, John 11:187
Heathman, Grundy 21:273
Heathon, Joseph 14:178
Heating, William E. 26:165
Heatley, Isaac 4:30
Heatly, James B. 20:23
Heatman, J. 14:12
Heaton, A. 25:184
Heaton, Alfred 5:18
Heaton, Amos 3:223; 17:502
Heaton, Bivan 11:264
Heaton, Ebenezer 22:427
Heaton, Eithel 23:148
Heaton, Franklin G. 4:30
Heaton, Henry 23:16
Heaton, Hill 9:100
Heaton, Hylon E. 21:10
Heaton, Jesse 26:164
Heaton, Joseph 26:164
Heaton, Peter 9:208
Heaton, S. 17:509
Heaton, S. G. 15:151
Heaton, Samuel 10:57; 20:269
Heaton, W. 17:248
Heatt, J. M. 7:29
Heatterly, Garret 17:440; 24:153
Heavawa, R. 15:14
Heave, Paul 9:22
Heavener, G. W. 1:141; 21:28
Heavener, Josiah 21:71
Heavener, Theodore 23:148

Heavenridge, John 10:57; 20:269
Heavens, J. 16:268
Heaver, Daniel 12:154
Heaver, John 12:154
Heavering, George 20:269
Heavey, Thomas 16:37
Heavs, J. 16:371
Heavy, Christopher 7:97
Heavy, Thomas 13:27
Heaydy, James 14:177
Heazlitt, James B. 23:179
Hebard, Albert L. 25:40
Hebber, Paul 12:71
Hebbert, Albert 24:62
Hebden, S. 12:122; 15:125
Hebener, J. 21:28
Hebenstrite, Frederick 22:35
Heberlig, W. 23:148
Heberly, Albert 17:80
Heberly, G. W. 20:89
Hebler, J. 22:234
Hebner, Augustus 17:99
Hebner, Carl 14:178
Heburger, Henry 25:184
Heburn, C. 16:198
Hecathorm, Henry 9:144
Hecathorn, Henry 17:409; 22:81
Hecathorn, Robert H. 22:427
Heck, C. 1:44
Heck, G. 3:93
Heck, George W. 17:91
Heck, J. 1:140
Heck, John B. 20:8
Heck, Joseph 14:178
Heck, M. H. 23:148
Heck, William 6:9; 18:84
Heckart, J. 1:138
Heckatham, H. 27:58
Heckathan, A. 13:111
Heckathorne, H. 9:144
Hecke, James 3:93
Heckel, Depr 12:24
Heckelmire, Thomas 22:197
Hecker, Frederick 11:304
Hecker, G. 3:93
Hecker, L. E. 21:343
Hecker, R. W. 11:428
Heckerhon, A. 23:122
Heckerman, John 10:25
Heckey, C. C. 26:33
Heckey, M. 3:93
Heckey, William 17:95
Heckinbridge, --- 3:93
Heckinstatter, John 19:318

Heckler, Frank R. 26:145
Heckler, John 3:93
Heckman, Benjamin 14:178
Heckman, Henry 24:94
Heckman, J. W. 23:148
Heckman, John 18:207
Heckman, Nathan B. 8:86
Heckman, Peter P. 17:80
Heckman, S. 1:136
Heckman, W. 11:34
Heckner, Conrad 10:57
Hecknor, Conrad 20:269
Heckthom, Christian 10:91
Heckthoon, Christian 20:269
Heckton, J. S. 12:161
Heckworth, J. 3:93
Hecolett, George 26:236
Hecter, Albert 11:296
Hector, George H. 5:40
Hectrick, J. 15:68
Hedd, William 8:19
Hedden, James O. 17:206
Hedden, Jonathan 17:425; 24:178
Hedden, R. E. 17:291
Hedden, William 1:43
Heddensheimer, David 21:100
Hedding, F. G. 26:220
Hedding, Walter 12:80
Heddings, E. 1:135
Heddington, W. 3:93
Heddle, William 3:93
Heddon, Nathan C. 22:171
Heddricks, William A. 22:197
Heddy, Martin V. 21:100
Hede, Carl 22:81
Hedfield, Richard 4:30
Hedge, --- 8:49
Hedge, Frank 18:239; 26:36
Hedge, Samuel 21:343; 22:145
Hedge, Stillman 7:29
Hedge, Thomas 23:33
Hedgecock, Thomas 19:320
Hedgeman, H. 13:27
Hedgepeth, C. P. 17:297
Hedger, Moses J. 17:35
Hedgers, John W. F. 22:81
Hedges, George 18:239; 26:37
Hedges, Gideon 10:91; 20:269

Hedges, H. M. 1:43
Hedges, J. 21:343
Hedges, J. H. 22:480
Hedges, Josephus 17:352
Hedges, Justus 22:145
Hedges, Samuel 22:145
Hedges, Silia 11:263
Hedges, T. W. 9:35
Hedges, W. W. 16:37
Hedgs, Henry A. 6:7
Hedl, William 18:139
Hedleen, John 14:299; 17:476
Hedless, John 27:64
Hedley, Joseph 23:122
Hedlie, M. 14:178
Hedric, William 17:35
Hedrick, Charles E. 17:502
Hedrick, Daniel W. 8:125
Hedrick, G. W. 7:58
Hedrick, H. 1:43
Hedrick, H. D. 22:197
Hedrick, James M. 17:259
Hedrick, William 13:111; 17:418; 24:158
Heedge, William 17:271
Heeds, C. 3:93
Heeds, Edward 12:71
Heefaker, John W. 11:327
Heefall, A. 9:179
Heeffins, Green 24:196
Heehun, Martin 10:8
Heek, G. Jacob 10:34
Heekand, John 17:95
Heeke, Henry 11:263
Heekman, Jesse 11:388
Heeles, William 19:274
Heeley, T. 15:36
Heeling, Celsus 10:161
Heelkins, Burlington 22:81
Heelman, George H. 9:161
Heelman, John 14:178
Heeman, John 3:93
Heen, August 13:27; 16:37
Heen, J. W. 2:12; 25:39
Heenan, J. 1:140
Heenan, Michael 15:203
Heener, James 18:239
Heeney, John 7:29
Heer, Frederick 22:280
Heerd, A. 18:31
Heerlein, John 23:128
Heershu, Samuel M. 22:145
Hees, Henry 8:114
Heeson, Jacob U. 24:182
Heet, J. M. 7:29

Heeten, Oliver 14:178
Heeters, J. H. 3:93
Heetfall, Amos 19:253
Heether, James 15:68
Heetly, O. 25:184
Heetor, G. W. 25:184
Hefenstein, Adolph 11:182
Heff, J. 11:310
Heff, John 8:86
Heffelfinger, Henry 7:97
Heffenfinger, Enos 12:24
Hefferan, James 20:124
Hefferer, Michael 5:18
Hefferman, Patrick 12:59
Heffernan, James 22:463
Hefflefinger, V. 3:93
Heffley, W. A. 11:276
Hefflin, H. 14:321
Hefflin, Henry 23:68
Heffner, Andrew 9:35
Heffner, C. R. 19:17
Heffner, Conrad 21:100
Heffner, George 17:80
Heffner, J. 1:94; 9:82
Heffner, Jacob 15:125
Heffner, Joel 22:35
Heffner, William 17:80; 24:20
Heffren, John 11:263
Heffron, Walter 24:79
Hefften, Edward 18:84
Hefland, Henry 14:315
Hefley, Edward 21:71
Hefley, James 18:239; 26:36
Hefner, D. 14:70
Hefner, Francis M. 24:51
Hefner, Jacob 13:111
Hefner, W. H. 11:327
Hefron, John 25:43
Heft, Ezra 21:71
Heft, Joseph 22:197
Heft, S. 23:148; 27:64
Hefty, Nicholas 22:35
Hegan, Thomas 23:11
Hegans, Charles A. 4:30
Hegans, Nelson 20:124
Hegar, H. 22:451
Hegard, Frank W. 19:324
Hegbman, Charles 13:79
Hege, James 21:343
Hegenburg, William 3:93
Heger, Joseph 22:81
Heggekjar, P. 19:75
Heggele, T. 25:184
Heggin, C. 3:93
Heghton, M. 22:254
Heglin, I. 4:30
Hegrick, F. 1:41
Hegwo---, A. 24:51

Hegwood, George W. 21:71
Hehn, Harry 25:184
Hei, Charles 27:62
Hei---, Fred 16:95
Heib, Charles 9:120
Heicker, J. D. 14:70
Heicker, Sebastian 14:178
Heicks, J. W. 11:149
Heidel, Bruno 11:151
Heider, Henry 17:443
Heider, John P. 8:49; 21:138
Heiderbreder, H. 22:115
Heidler, John 26:145
Heidleson, J. 23:148
Heidman, Detrick 22:427
Heidman, Henry 6:25
Heidy, Adam 19:75
Heier, George 23:113
Heifenbock, Philip 2:12
Heifey, Michael 15:323
Heighboom, James 21:343
Heigholtzer, Gottleib 18:307; 26:100
Height, Jacob 9:43
Height, James M. 18:277
Height, Jesse 21:225
Height, W. H. 9:53
Heighton, Joseph 8:114
Heihl, J. 9:179
Heiker, Simon 8:106
Heiks, David 7:29
Heil, Charles 27:59
Heil, John 27:56
Heil, Peter 10:117; 20:269
Heil, Stephen 15:203
Heil, William 20:269
Heilberd, E. 12:24
Heilbroun, George 25:184
Heild, George 25:184
Heileg, H. H. 14:241
Heilenor, F. 21:195
Heiler, Gotleib 11:241
Heilers, Berherd 21:203
Heilman, Martin 12:167; 19:348
Heilstein, Saffrera 21:243
Heily, Leonard 22:35
Heim, C. 21:343
Heiman, J. 18:84
Heimback, G. H. 1:138
Heime, Robert 17:418; 24:158
Heimstone, J. M. 21:343
Hein, F. 20:179
Hein, John 22:171; 23:148
Hein, Peter 17:360
Hein, Xavier 4:30
Heinbach, Philip 18:307

Heinback, --- 18:84
Heinback, S. 3:93
Heinbacker, I. 16:95
Heinbluth, William 24:72
Heine, Charles W. 13:27
Heine, Ernest 18:111
Heine, Frederick 9:43
Heine, Henry 11:106
Heine, J. 16:198
Heineman, Henry 1:40
Heinemann, F. 23:148
Heiner, Jacob 20:17
Heiner, John 22:197
Heines, A. C. 18:175
Heines, Simon 24:40
Heineseman, C. 18:67
Heing, Charles 9:200
Heinick, --- 3:93
Heinig, Herrman 18:103
Heinley, George W. 21:71
Heinline, John W. 22:197
Heinrich, Henry J. 19:169
Heins, F. 12:24
Heins, Foster 18:430
Heins, John 20:269
Heinseler, B. 15:68
Heinshott, W. 3:93
Heinsler, Jacob 22:166
Heinstreet, Alonzo 9:23
Heintrye, T. 13:80
Heintz, J. 1:135
Heintz, John G. 27:59
Heintze, Charles T. 16:198
Heintze, Frederick 16:198
Heintzelman, D. 9:144
Heintzelman, Joseph 4:30
Heir, J. 3:93
Heirg, John 11:152
Heirly, John E. 12:24
Heirnisch, Charles R. 11:32
Heirs, Holster 14:236
Heis, Ferdinand 21:343
Heise, C. 16:198
Heise, Frederick 15:91
Heise, George 23:242
Heise, J. 23:33
Heise, William 13:127
Heise, William H. 16:154
Heisel, Abraham 17:80
Heisel, James B. 21:204
Heiser, A. 21:28
Heiser, Hiram 17:80
Heiser, J. 1:137, 139
Heiser, J. P. 22:480
Heishman, Levi 24:40
Heiskopps, Jacob 9:179
Heisleman, Jacob 9:120; 27:60
Heisler, --- 14:70

Heisler, C. 1:139
Heisler, Christian 4:30
Heisler, Conrad 21:343
Heisler, Frederick 21:28
Heisman, George 14:178
Heiss, Elam W. 20:17
Heiss, George 13:64
Heiss, R. 25:184
Heist, D. 20:146
Heist, William 15:309
Heistand, B. F. 3:93
Heistand, J. 1:44
Heister, Cyrus 26:164
Heister, David 18:139
Heister, Franklin 12:122
Heister, John 15:203
Heisterberg, Henry 17:21
Heitman, Adrian C. 9:12
Heitman, Lewis 7:97
Heitzel, J. 18:84
Heitzeman, Joseph 24:107
Heivea, Fred 26:124
Heizel, John 8:86
Hekley, James 11:126
Helaiggle, J. 15:318
Helan, William 7:97
Helav, James 18:190
Helba, John 25:184
Helbe, John 15:347; 16:371
Helbelk, Charles 12:24
Helbert, F. J. 1:43
Helbert, William 18:50
Helbey, George W. 21:343
Helbling, Celens 19:169
Helburt, William 10:148
Held, Adam 23:107
Held, G. 7:68
Held, G. Washington 22:446
Held, Harvey 23:179
Held, Henry 15:203
Held, John 23:191
Held, P. 23:148
Helde, Valentine 18:307; 26:100
Helderman, Jacob 21:100
Heleck, E. 1:42
Helen, Thomas J. 7:97
Helen, Walter M. 21:138
Helen, William 14:178
Helener, Francis 14:178
Helens, John 12:24
Heler, Henry 17:35
Heley, Joel 18:367
Heley, Thomas 10:161
Helfeo, L. 10:57
Helfer, Samuel 11:305
Helffine, Elias 21:53

Helficher, Jacob 18:308; 26:99
Helfinger, John 1:40
Helfrey, S. W. 21:343
Helfric, John C. 7:97
Helgerson, Henry 18:139
Helgerson, K. 12:24
Helgeson, Gulbrand 21:255
Helgeson, Gustav 22:112
Helgeson, Hans I. 22:280
Helin, K. W. 14:70
Helin, W. H. 14:70
Heline, Thomas 15:278
Helk, Lewis C. 8:86
Hell, T. H. A. 15:259
Hella, Charles 7:29
Hellam, Henry 26:163
Hellan, Henry 24:101
Hellas, Peter 7:97
Helleker, Martin J. 4:30
Hellems, S. 1:41
Hellenbeck, I. F. 14:332
Heller, --- 19:75
Heller, A. 3:93
Heller, Andrew 23:148
Heller, Benjamin F. 22:198
Heller, Charles 11:305
Heller, D. 1:141
Heller, Elias 13:27
Heller, F. 1:139
Heller, H. 14:70
Heller, Henry 17:387
Heller, J. 21:28; 25:184
Heller, J. B. 20:146
Heller, James M. 27:59
Heller, John 10:91; 117; 13:90; 20:269
Heller, Jonathan 7:97
Heller, Lewis 23:128
Heller, Rahney 21:122
Heller, W. H. 1:140
Heller, W. M. 1:142
Heller, William 3:93; 17:404
Hellesther, --- 13:64
Helleys, J. H. 16:371
Helliker, Elias P. 13:27
Helliker, Elias R. 16:37
Helline, Thomas 25:184
Helling, Henry 10:173; 19:169
Hellinger, W. 11:322
Hellinngh, W. 14:70
Hellishhom, Peter 16:198
Hellison, Julius 13:27
Hellman, A. 14:256
Hellner, Francis 14:178
Hellner, Michael 22:281
Hellock, C. H. 16:371

Hellock, Ole 15:342
Hellreigel, George 23:179
Hellrigel, Joseph 9:16
Helly, Lawrence 27:61
Hellyer, George 21:343
Helm, A. J. 16:37
Helm, B. 15:203
Helm, David 15:203
Helm, Edward 22:197
Helm, G. W. 10:57; 20:269
Helm, George 11:241
Helm, George W. 22:197
Helm, Harry 5:51
Helm, Henry 18:285; 26:135
Helm, J. M. 17:291
Helm, Jacob R. 22:81
Helm, John 6:16; 18:84; 22:197
Helm, Philip 11:322
Helm, Stephen 24:195
Helm, Tobias 24:20
Helm, William 12:139; 24:20
Helm, Willis 15:5
Helman, Daniel 12:59
Helman, Martin 10:117; 20:269
Helmbold, Alexander 23:11
Helmboldt, Charles 21:117
Helmer, Charles 15:166
Helmes, E. 21:343
Helmes, Jacob 9:16
Helmes, William 21:343; 22:303
Helmich, Frederick 21:138
Helmich, Gustavus 19:17
Helmick, B. R. 23:33
Helmick, Darwing 25:184
Helmick, Eli D. 10:91; 20:269
Helmick, Isaiah 7:97
Helmick, Jackson 17:212
Helmick, James M. 26:32
Helmick, John M. 10:57; 20:269
Helmick, John R. 8:86; 18:218
Helmick, Uriah 10:205
Helminger, Christian 13:27
Helmohl, Frederick 23:68
Helmrick, E. 11:119
Helms, Abe J. 11:63
Helms, Albert 19:169
Helms, Daniel 15:278; 25:184

Helms, George W. 11:319
Helms, Jacob 9:35; 18:293; 26:102
Helms, James 22:511
Helms, Joseph 25:272
Helms, Loten 11:107
Helms, Michael 23:68
Helms, Philander 20:30
Helms, Robert 20:269
Helms, Thomas 9:82; 26:33
Helms, W. H. 8:106
Helms, Warren 17:447
Helms, William 10:117; 20:269
Helms, William F. 22:145
Helmus, Warner 24:170
Helns, Albert 10:161
Help, Carl 3:93
Helpel, William 8:106
Helper, Jacob 10:117; 20:269
Helper, L. 20:269
Helpin, Patrick 10:161; 19:169
Helriggle, J. 19:75
Helrus, Henry 10:17
Helsal, Homer 11:106
Helsby, H. 20:124
Helser, A. 1:141
Helsey, J. 21:91
Helsey, M. M. 20:140
Helsin, Charles 17:35
Helsis, Ira 11:287
Helson, George 3:93
Helson, M. 1:42
Helsper, T. 11:264
Helstab, John 17:429; 24:185
Helstand, H. J. 12:154
Helston, Charles 4:30; 6:16; 18:84
Helston, Jonas N. 18:111
Heltgell, D. 13:90
Heltinberger, Jacob 9:23
Heltmayer, Jacob 16:37
Helton, Alfred 16:37
Helton, Andrew 17:430
Helton, Basel 21:100
Helton, Canada 22:254
Helton, Eli 11:84
Helton, Elisha 22:81
Helton, Peter 9:110
Helton, Robert 17:53
Helton, Samuel H. 21:84
Helton, Stokeley 17:280
Helton, William 24:71
Heltz, G. 19:17
Heltz, Nelson W. 8:114
Heltzler, John 20:270
Heltzter, John 10:117

Heluck, J. 15:324
Helverson, Byron 11:191
Helverson, James 11:413
Helverton, William
  18:239
Helvie, N. C. 3:93
Helvin, Charles 9:23
Helwick, Amos 18:84
Helwick, George 27:61
Hely, Allen 11:262
Hely, John 20:270
Helyerson, Henry 8:19
Hem---, --- 12:99
Heman, H. 1:137
Heman, O. 14:265
Heman, Old 14:265
Heman, R. 11:280
Heman, William 7:97
Hemance, J. 3:93
Hemance, James H. 7:29
Hemassee, John 22:35
Hemback, Philip 26:101
Hembill, Alfred 11:402
Hembray, J. 17:177
Hemchauser, Michael
  7:97
Hemden, --- 9:208
Hemdimon, L. 21:100
Hemdricks, David P.
  18:293
Hemdricks, Joseph 18:293
Hemel, William 11:305
Hemenger, Harris 11:287
Hemer, John 15:302;
  16:198
Hemerly, John 22:234
Hemerly, Wilbert W.
  17:35
Hemicks, B. 17:320
Hemierdinger, G. 7:50
Hemimwell, Richard 9:82
Heminger, George F.
  21:71
Heminger, Jacob P. 24:40
Heminger, John 9:82
Heminger, Marcus 22:145
Hemings, Otto 24:66
Hemingway, Charles
  11:151
Hemingway, Samuel
  16:37
Hemley, Frederick 16:119
Hemm, Francis 16:371
Hemman, John 19:169
Hemmann, John 10:161
Hemmel, J. 20:57
Hemmelreich, George
  27:62
Hemmer, C. 14:178
Hemmerdon, F. 21:343
Hemmes, E. M. 3:93

Hemmett, John 23:107
Hemming, F. M. 11:151
Hemming, J. C. 14:299;
  17:482
Hemming, William
  22:502
Hemminger, Frederick
  22:81
Hemminger, L. 19:75
Hemminghuus, William
  8:19
Hemmings, A. 1:44
Hemmings, John H. 12:64
Hemmingway, Francis J.
  11:107
Hemmingway, Samuel
  13:27
Hemn, Adam 1:39
Hemny, Andy 18:84
Hemonway, William A.
  23:117
Hemp, David H. 4:30
Hemp, George A. 4:30
Hempe, Frederick 23:148
Hempell, John 7:58
Hempemker, Charles 8:19
Hempfield, E. 15:203
Hempfield, Edward
  15:203
Hempfling, Frederick
  17:314
Hemphase, Louisa 25:299
Hemphill, D. 16:119
Hemphill, Francis M.
  17:80
Hemphill, Harry 11:150
Hemphill, James 14:265
Hemphill, Richard 13:27
Hemphill, Samuel 13:111
Hemphill, Stephen 23:113
Hempinker, Charles
  18:139
Hemple, Gustavus 11:396
Hempleman, E. 10:211;
  18:460
Hempleman, Moses
  11:305
Hempleman, Nelson
  23:148
Hempshill, Louis L.
  22:405
Hempstead, George W.
  23:33
Hempstead, Nelson 10:57
Hempsteak, D. 1:42
Hempstod, John E. 12:24
Hempton, Charles G.
  21:343
Hemrick, L. 14:12
Hemsley, Edward 18:84
Hemsley, H. W. 13:129

Hemstock, Adolph 25:43
Hemstred, Holzy 18:308
Hemstreet, Fayette 14:70
Hemstreet, William 4:30
Hemt, L. 3:93
Hemting, John 27:54
Hen---, John C. 15:203
Hen-mueh 25:333
Henacholes, H. 14:70
Henager, William 12:154
Henal, A. 14:178
Henan, R. 23:33
Henbdier, Gustave 18:139
Henby, H. H. 21:187
Hencame, Edward 21:343
Hence, F. 14:70
Hence, John 15:125
Hencethy, Timothy 14:70
Hench, F. 9:144; 27:58
Henchauser, Michael
  21:344
Henchell, Harris 16:95
Henck, C. W. 9:120
Henckle, Adolph 13:27
Henckle, Henry 10:205
Hencliff, Frederick 11:322
Hendecker, William
  27:145
Hendee, Solomon 24:51
Henden, --- 18:67
Henden, William 14:70
Hendenboot, J. 14:70
Henderlein, Frederick
  19:270
Henderlider, George
  22:463
Henderline, Fred 9:180
Henderset, J. 23:148
Hendershatt, V. T. 12:154
Hendershont, David 24:88
Hendershot, A. 13:90;
  14:12
Hendershot, Albert W.
  15:159
Hendershot, F. 25:184
Hendershot, I. 14:70
Hendershot, John 3:93
Hendershot, John W.
  22:35
Hendershot, L. H. 7:29
Hendershot, William A.
  22:35
Hendershott, F. F. 3:93
Hendershott, Francis 5:18
Hendershott, Jeremiah
  13:27
Henderson, --- 11:33;
  14:288; 16:279;
  26:221
Henderson, A. 3:93;
  21:110

Henderson, A. G. 3:93
Henderson, A. J. 15:203
Henderson, A. M. 9:221;
    18:368
Henderson, Aaron 11:31
Henderson, Alex 20:270
Henderson, Alexander
    10:117; 21:344
Henderson, Alexander F.
    22:35
Henderson, Alvy W.
    21:225
Henderson, B. 21:100;
    22:35
Henderson, B. F. 21:101
Henderson, Beecher B.
    20:8
Henderson, Benjamin H.
    22:427
Henderson, Beverly 8:64
Henderson, C. 25:184
Henderson, C. C. 11:408
Henderson, Charles 5:18;
    23:148
Henderson, Christopher
    7:58
Henderson, Clinton D.
    11:423
Henderson, D. 3:93; 9:82;
    18:103
Henderson, D. C. 23:33
Henderson, D. M. 12:161
Henderson, D. W. 25:184
Henderson, Daniel 11:92;
    22:337
Henderson, Darius 26:32
Henderson, E. 25:184
Henderson, Ed 24:79
Henderson, Edwin 21:28
Henderson, Elias 22:254
Henderson, Elion 11:263
Henderson, F. 5:18;
    15:107; 25:184;
    26:33
Henderson, Francis M.
    21:71
Henderson, G. 9:234;
    10:211; 18:430
Henderson, G. L. 10:179;
    18:175
Henderson, G. W. 11:264;
    14:263
Henderson, George
    10:173; 12:71;
    15:14; 17:132;
    19:169; 21:202, 291;
    22:303; 24:195
Henderson, George W.
    12:168
Henderson, Gilbert 7:124
Henderson, H. J. 11:64

Henderson, H. N. 21:344
Henderson, H. T. 23:276
Henderson, Henry W.
    12:59
Henderson, Irwin 24:196
Henderson, Isaac 9:144;
    27:58
Henderson, J. 3:93;
    10:161; 15:353;
    16:279; 18:239;
    19:169; 21:344;
    26:35
Henderson, J. A. 10:186
Henderson, J. D. 21:28
Henderson, J. H. 14:178;
    24:79
Henderson, J. K. 3:93;
    9:23
Henderson, J. M. 7:58
Henderson, J. P. 13:90
Henderson, J. Q. 1:39
Henderson, J. W. 21:344
Henderson, Jack 17:177
Henderson, Jackson 18:85
Henderson, Jacob 9:208
Henderson, James 7:12;
    8:86; 9:100; 11:150;
    18:50; 21:344; 24:66
Henderson, James B.
    11:32
Henderson, James M.
    22:254
Henderson, James S.
    21:130
Henderson, Joel 9:132;
    27:58
Henderson, John 1:38;
    6:16; 7:29, 124; 9:82;
    13:27; 16:37, 80;
    18:85, 396; 23:279
Henderson, John A.
    22:254
Henderson, John C.
    22:122
Henderson, John H. 1:39;
    11:205
Henderson, John M.
    11:126
Henderson, John N.
    18:218
Henderson, John W.
    22:451
Henderson, Joseph 21:344
Henderson, Joshua 8:39;
    26:165
Henderson, Kelly 20:270
Henderson, L. 22:303
Henderson, Levi 24:79
Henderson, Lyman 15:22

Henderson, M. 1:44;
    14:277; 23:203; 25:41
Henderson, Mathew H.
    9:120
Henderson, Monroe 22:82
Henderson, N. W. 15:203
Henderson, Nathan 27:61
Henderson, P. 3:93
Henderson, Peter 25:272
Henderson, R. 11:64
Henderson, Robert 3:93;
    11:396; 12:169;
    22:35, 463; 23:89
Henderson, Robert J.
    20:35
Henderson, Robert L.
    17:254, 259
Henderson, S. 5:40; 9:53;
    16:198; 18:175;
    25:184
Henderson, S. S. 1:137
Henderson, S. W. 1:38;
    3:93
Henderson, Samuel 5:40;
    6:16; 18:85
Henderson, Stephen 21:28
Henderson, Stilm 6:12
Henderson, Sylvester
    24:94
Henderson, Thomas
    11:295; 15:68; 19:17;
    24:40
Henderson, Thomas F.
    22:198
Henderson, Thomas M.
    11:151
Henderson, W. 14:178;
    20:46
Henderson, W. A. 17:177
Henderson, W. G. 20:17
Henderson, W. H. 21:344
Henderson, W. J. 3:93;
    18:239; 26:36
Henderson, W. R. 20:23
Henderson, Warren 5:18
Henderson, Wesley 25:39
Henderson, William 5:51;
    8:49; 14:70, 256,
    299; 15:166; 17:280,
    473; 18:85; 21:138,
    273; 22:254, 513;
    25:184; 26:163, 220;
    27:59, 63
Henderson, William C.
    24:111
Henderson, William H.
    12:24
Henderson, William R.
    17:231
Hendfist, J. B. 3:93
Hendirchson, W. 9:53

Hendix, John H. 6:31
Hendley, H. 14:282
Hendley, J. 3:93; 14:178
Hendley, R. 14:71
Hendly, David 18:175
Hendman, John 17:440;
24:153
Hendon, Aaron 6:12
Hendon, Henry H. 17:439
Hendren, A. 3:93
Hendren, J. 14:71
Hendren, William 3:93;
17:236; 20:177
Hendri, W. F. 12:92;
16:295
Hendri, W. H. H. 8:49
Hendric, Russell 20:270
Hendric, W. 20:270
Hendrich, James B. 12:24
Hendrichs, Augustus
12:24
Hendrichson, C. 8:49
Hendrichson, P. 14:71
Hendrick, --- 11:93;
17:499
Hendrick, A. C. 21:117
Hendrick, Allen 11:423
Hendrick, B. 21:110
Hendrick, B. F. 18:67
Hendrick, Bird 21:28
Hendrick, Chauncey E.
15:173
Hendrick, D. 16:198
Hendrick, Daniel 22:463
Hendrick, David A.
11:387
Hendrick, E. L. 14:178
Hendrick, E. P. 18:339
Hendrick, Francis 4:31
Hendrick, George O. 7:68
Hendrick, H. 13:90
Hendrick, H. L. 7:29
Hendrick, Henry 8:106
Hendrick, J. 1:41; 9:144;
14:321; 23:128
Hendrick, James 19:17
Hendrick, John 11:408;
17:506
Hendrick, John T. 11:62
Hendrick, L. 16:268
Hendrick, M. 14:12
Hendrick, Mordecai 7:68
Hendrick, Moses B. 13:27
Hendrick, Patrick 12:24
Hendrick, Peter 16:37
Hendrick, R. 21:138
Hendrick, Russell 10:57
Hendrick, Samuel A.
21:29
Hendrick, Wesley 17:132
Hendricks, Abram 25:41

Hendricks, Charles
10:117; 20:270;
22:198
Hendricks, David P. 9:35;
26:102
Hendricks, E. N. 23:99
Hendricks, Edgar J.
21:216
Hendricks, Franklin B.
22:427
Hendricks, Frederic
11:413
Hendricks, George 27:61
Hendricks, George B.
9:120
Hendricks, George C.
23:68
Hendricks, George W.
22:35
Hendricks, H. 14:288;
21:101; 23:180
Hendricks, J. 3:93; 9:40
Hendricks, J. H. 7:29;
10:57; 20:270;
25:321
Hendricks, J. J. 17:148
Hendricks, J. N. 10:205
Hendricks, J. P. 21:225
Hendricks, J. W. 23:33
Hendricks, Jacob 21:273
Hendricks, James 9:208;
11:263; 13:27
Hendricks, James J. 16:37
Hendricks, James W.
22:122
Hendricks, John 17:132;
24:66, 195
Hendricks, Joseph 20:57;
26:102
Hendricks, Louis 23:301
Hendricks, Mahlon 23:68
Hendricks, N. 3:93
Hendricks, N. P. 10:57;
20:270
Hendricks, Nathan 24:51
Hendricks, Peter 13:27
Hendricks, Philomel
23:148
Hendricks, Robert 21:239
Hendricks, Rufus 9:23;
18:308; 26:100
Hendricks, Thomas J.
22:81
Hendricks, W. P. 9:221;
18:368
Hendricks, Wesley 24:195
Hendricks, William 10:57
Hendricksen, H. 14:178
Hendricksen, William
14:178

Hendrickson, Augustus
6:8
Hendrickson, E. 12:99;
21:29
Hendrickson, Elias 22:171
Hendrickson, George
19:17
Hendrickson, George W.
20:124
Hendrickson, H. 16:371
Hendrickson, John
14:315; 21:344
Hendrickson, Jonah
18:396
Hendrickson, Mathias M.
20:124
Hendrickson, Milo F.
24:153
Hendrickson, Morton H.
23:33
Hendrickson, N. 12:24
Hendrickson, Oscar 11:33
Hendrickson, R. 7:29;
11:64; 12:142;
20:270
Hendrickson, S. H. 21:53
Hendrickson, Stephen
19:169
Hendrickson, Swan
11:115
Hendrickson, Thomas
17:280
Hendrickson, W. 1:141
Hendrickson, W. H. 17:95
Hendrickson, Wellington
19:75
Hendrickson, William
25:40
Hendrickson, William J.
22:11
Hendricus, J. 13:130
Hendrin, W. M. H. H.
21:14
Hendrix, A. 20:270
Hendrix, James 19:75
Hendrix, John 7:97
Hendrix, M. K. 1:141
Hendrix, Marcus 17:281
Hendrix, P. O. 11:65
Hendrix, William H.
22:427
Hendrixon, A. 12:154
Hendrixson, Miles F.
17:440
Hendry, A. 1:141
Hendry, Abram 17:166
Hendry, Amagum 15:203
Hendry, James H. 5:51;
25:184
Hendry, John 21:344
Hendry, William 23:33

Hendsey, James 22:303
Hendsley, Thomas 6:17; 18:85
Hendushot, R. 8:72
Hendy, Charles 16:198
Henehaw, Evans 27:61
Heneison, John 16:119
Henenhow, Evans 9:132
Hener, I. 9:53
Henerson, John 25:321
Henery, Israel 18:368
Henery, James W. 23:148
Henery, John 7:97; 18:207
Henery, Mathew 13:27
Henery, S. K. 16:295
Henesey, P. 3:93
Henesley, H. 16:295
Henessey, Richard 21:344
Henessy, M. 15:359
Henesy, T. 20:154
Heney, C. E. 14:178
Heney, C. L. 25:184
Heney, John 24:79
Henford, William 9:120
Hengelin, Gustave 8:19
Hengg, Joseph 26:163
Hengle, Lewis 5:18
Hengrece, William 11:322
Hengsteller, George 20:97
Henhoefer, John 22:81
Henico, J. 26:34
Heniey, William 23:11
Henigan, John 17:65
Heniger, J. W. 11:33
Henimghans, William 18:139
Hening, Thomas A. 19:17
Henion, S. W. 22:405
Henisey, M. 19:75
Henisler, Peter 12:71
Henison, H. 18:31
Heniztine, W. 9:144
Henke, William 24:94
Henkel, Adam 4:31
Henkel, E. G. 14:178
Henkel, F. 1:43
Henkell, Martin 21:71
Henken, John 12:170
Henkins, J. S. 9:53
Henkins, Joseph H. 22:502
Henkle, E. G. 14:256
Henkle, Francis 27:63
Henkle, Nathaniel 25:184
Henkle, S. W. 9:23
Henksby, G. 15:36
Henkston, P. 17:177
Henlard, Davis F. 17:281
Henlen, Elias P. 11:63
Henley, C. 3:93
Henley, Charles 9:179

Henley, Cyrus 21:344
Henley, E. M. 9:53
Henley, J. 1:136; 11:327; 23:148
Henley, James 25:39
Henley, Jesse 26:212
Henley, John 10:58; 23:252
Henley, R. 1:44
Henley, Thomas C. 17:80
Henley, Thomas I. 20:97
Henlin, D. H. 20:270
Henlin, Franklin 9:163
Henlink, Henry 14:321; 23:89
Henly, A. J. 24:20
Henly, C. C. 16:37
Henly, David 22:82
Henly, Elijah 22:81
Henly, Miles M. 9:221; 18:368
Henman, Aaron 25:184
Henman, Charles D. 24:20
Henman, E. H. 17:456
Henman, W. L. 7:29
Henmon, H. 16:198
Henn, Charles 21:202
Henn, Christ 24:20
Henn, Jacob 1:38; 9:23
Henn, P. 7:58
Henn, P. A. 18:14
Henn, Thomas 21:245
Hennan, John M. 12:71; 15:87
Hennan, Joseph W. 15:68
Hennan, Robert 20:270
Hennant, J. 2:13
Henndun, James H. 17:65
Hennelly, Michael 22:519
Hennemeyer, George G. 22:81
Hennen, William 21:344
Hennenold, Antone 9:97
Henner, Charles H. 13:27
Hennershote, John 25:39
Hennesberry, W. H. 19:75
Hennesey, J. 3:93; 12:71
Hennesey, John 20:193; 22:337
Hennesey, M. 3:93
Hennesey, Michael 10:117
Hennesey, W. D. 14:178
Hennessey, J. 1:40
Hennessey, John 8:86
Hennessey, Michael 8:64; 20:270
Hennessey, Nich's. 22:336
Hennessey, Patrick 19:17
Hennessey, W. D. 14:71
Hennessy, Lawrence 16:95

Hennessy, M. 12:95
Hennesy, John 23:148
Hennesy, William 4:30
Henni, I. 15:342
Henni, J. 16:371
Henni, J. J. 26:164
Hennig, Frederick 18:468
Henniger, Peter 3:93
Henniker, John 23:33
Henning, A. 26:33
Henning, C. 3:94
Henning, E. 23:33
Henning, Ezekiel 17:53
Henning, H. 1:44; 27:64
Henning, Henry 15:68
Henning, Philip 4:30
Henning, Thomas A. 12:71
Henning, W. 17:404
Henninger, F. 1:135
Henninger, N. 23:148
Hennings, William H. 9:208
Henningway, P. 8:49
Hennion, W. D. 1:138
Hennis, Daniel 3:94
Hennis, Hezekiah 17:14
Hennis, J. J. 1:137
Hennis, James 9:23
Hennis, Levi 23:148
Hennisen, Frederick 17:91
Hennison, --- 16:37
Hennison, Daniel 21:273
Henniss, W. H. 10:117; 20:270
Hennmill, Able 9:82
Hennoger, Joseph 18:239; 26:34
Henny, R. 19:302
Henny, Thomas 1:40
Henon, John 10:96
Henorthy, T. 14:71
Henrahan, John 22:122
Henreich, --- 1:138
Henrich, Paul 22:122
Henrich, Peter 21:53
Henrick, A. 5:18
Henrick, A. P. 14:71
Henrick, Henry 17:393
Henrick, I. S. 14:71
Henrick, John 9:82; 10:58; 12:55; 20:270
Henrick, Patrick 27:55
Henricks, E. 3:94
Henricks, John W. 24:51
Henrickson, George W. 4:31
Henrickson, O. 3:94
Henrickson, T. 9:241
Henrie, E. W. 3:94
Henrie, James 23:271

Henrie, John L. 18:50
Henries, A. J. M. 8:72
Henrietta, J. B. 23:33
Henrietta, Yean 21:344
Henriha, William 25:184
Henrotin, H. F. 18:277
Henry, --- 8:39; 15:307;
    18:111, 430; 19:75;
    25:44
Henry, A. 3:94; 5:40;
    11:327; 25:184
Henry, A. B. 3:94; 16:295
Henry, A. C. 21:273
Henry, A. L. 11:263
Henry, Aaron 9:68
Henry, Adolph C. 25:269
Henry, Albert 8:72;
    13:128
Henry, Albert D. 10:17
Henry, Albert H. 11:204
Henry, Alexander 4:31
Henry, Alfred 4:31
Henry, Allen 23:309
Henry, Amos 17:177
Henry, Andrew 19:17
Henry, Andrew J. 20:23
Henry, B. M. 4:31
Henry, Bailey 6:28
Henry, Burt 18:308;
    26:101
Henry, C. 19:274
Henry, Charles 1:42; 4:31;
    8:99; 9:179; 17:177;
    21:273; 26:124
Henry, Charles G. 21:344
Henry, Chubb 10:8
Henry, Cyrus 18:285;
    26:135
Henry, Daniel 11:204;
    21:273; 22:81
Henry, David 11:93;
    16:371; 22:198
Henry, E. 3:94; 18:31
Henry, E. P. 16:295
Henry, Ebenezer 17:91
Henry, Eleazer 17:314
Henry, Elijah 11:263
Henry, Ephraim 10:96;
    22:254
Henry, F. P. 12:85
Henry, Francis 17:161
Henry, Frank W. 23:191
Henry, Frederick 14:178
Henry, G. W. 3:94;
    20:270
Henry, George 9:66;
    17:132, 177, 349;
    24:195
Henry, George K. 22:81
Henry, George M. 22:427

Henry, George W. 10:58;
    22:81
Henry, H. 9:240; 24:20
Henry, H. A. 9:53
Henry, Harrison 10:57
Henry, Henry 15:319
Henry, Hole 12:24
Henry, Hudson 20:189
Henry, Hugh 18:239;
    26:35
Henry, I. A. 9:144
Henry, I. R. 22:480
Henry, Isaac 7:125;
    22:303
Henry, Israel 9:221
Henry, J. 1:135; 3:94;
    16:198; 19:169;
    21:344; 25:184
Henry, J. A. 27:56
Henry, J. C. 24:79; 27:145
Henry, J. D. 21:29; 25:184
Henry, J. F. 1:45
Henry, J. H. 1:135; 11:219
Henry, J. T. 13:129
Henry, Jacob 11:152
Henry, James 1:45; 3:94;
    5:18; 11:116, 127,
    322; 13:129; 14:315;
    19:287; 21:273, 344;
    23:268, 309
Henry, James F. 7:125
Henry, James W. 21:344
Henry, John 5:18; 9:12,
    132, 179, 208; 10:57,
    117, 161; 11:32, 63,
    107, 151; 12:171;
    13:64, 111; 14:178;
    16:198; 17:259, 335;
    18:239; 19:18, 169,
    282; 20:137, 270;
    21:225, 273, 291;
    22:513; 26:36; 27:59,
    157
Henry, John A. 4:31;
    12:53
Henry, John C. 11:152
Henry, John F. 22:35
Henry, John H. 17:394
Henry, John J. 8:64
Henry, John R. 22:254,
    427
Henry, John S. 19:169;
    22:81, 122
Henry, John W. 21:195
Henry, Joseph 3:94; 4:31;
    9:165; 15:203;
    22:280; 23:149;
    27:63
Henry, Joseph B. 21:198
Henry, L. 1:44
Henry, L. P. 22:234

Henry, Levi 16:37
Henry, Levy 13:27
Henry, Lewis 10:161;
    12:71
Henry, Luther D. 22:198
Henry, M. 14:71
Henry, M. R. 11:412;
    24:79
Henry, Matthew 16:37
Henry, Michael 21:10,
    344
Henry, Miles 7:97
Henry, N. B. 20:270
Henry, Napoleon B. 10:57
Henry, Norman 9:72
Henry, Norman F. 11:107
Henry, Owen W. 17:53
Henry, P. 3:94; 14:71
Henry, P. H. 3:94
Henry, Patrick 11:182;
    23:263
Henry, Peter 12:171;
    18:240; 23:68; 26:35
Henry, Philip 6:25
Henry, R. 9:200; 10:28;
    19:291
Henry, R. T. 11:33
Henry, R. W. 3:94
Henry, Ransom W. 4:31
Henry, Richard 21:273
Henry, Robert 9:23;
    15:36, 294; 16:198
Henry, S. 9:82
Henry, S. D. 5:51
Henry, S. P. 14:178
Henry, Samuel 10:99;
    11:150, 428; 12:49,
    71
Henry, Sherred 8:39
Henry, Sherrod 26:163
Henry, Simeon 22:425
Henry, Stanford 9:179
Henry, Stephen 9:132;
    18:31; 22:198; 27:59
Henry, T. 9:144; 26:33;
    27:57
Henry, T. H. 13:90
Henry, Tazewell 7:125
Henry, Thomas 9:132;
    10:186; 12:172;
    16:198; 18:175;
    26:204; 27:58
Henry, Thomas F. 9:100
Henry, W. 1:137, 141;
    9:53, 114; 17:190
Henry, W. A. 10:151, 178
Henry, W. F. 9:221
Henry, W. L. 1:136
Henry, W. P. 3:94
Henry, Walp 24:51
Henry, Webb 11:204

Henry, William 1:192; 3:94; 4:31; 5:18; 6:35; 7:29, 124; 8:19; 9:200; 11:63, 241; 12:24; 13:111; 14:71; 15:203; 16:198; 17:177; 18:103, 139; 19:18; 21:273, 344; 25:184, 299; 27:54, 145
Henry, William E. 22:35
Henry, William F. 18:368
Henry, William H. 22:198
Henry, William J. 6:16; 18:85; 22:161
Henry, William L. B. 22:81
Henry, William O. 1:44
Henrys, Charles G. 13:27
Henschen, A. 23:122
Henschen, Francis 23:122
Hensdon, J. H. 8:72
Hense, Peter 16:198
Hensel, Conrad 10:161
Henseley, J. M. 3:94
Hensell, Conrad 11:263
Hensell, John W. 17:80
Henser, Homer 9:43
Henser, N. 1:137
Hensey, John 11:32; 23:33
Henshaw, Alonzo 17:506
Henshaw, Charles 4:31
Henshaw, Daniel 20:17; 22:303
Henshaw, Eli H. 22:234
Henshaw, George W. 22:198
Henshaw, Henry C. 9:120; 27:59
Henshaw, Hoyt 17:263
Henshaw, James 11:327
Henshaw, Martin 8:86
Henshaw, Milton 21:344
Henshey, S. A. 15:203
Henshow, A. J. 14:282
Hensil, John 23:113
Hensinger, --- 3:94
Henskill, Edward 9:180
Hensler, J. 21:148; 26:164
Hensler, Jacob 22:234
Hensler, W. C. 25:185
Hensley, Abraham 26:134
Hensley, Adolph H. 24:40
Hensley, Amos 10:91; 20:270
Hensley, D. 14:71
Hensley, Frank 22:35
Hensley, H. 12:85
Hensley, Isaac 22:112
Hensley, J. A. 22:122

Hensley, J. C. 17:281
Hensley, J. H. 23:33
Hensley, Jacob 23:99
Hensley, James 11:31, 93
Hensley, James W. 22:254
Hensley, John 11:31, 63; 23:33
Hensley, John B. 10:58; 20:270
Hensley, N. 20:270
Hensley, Nicholas 10:58
Hensley, Robert P. 22:254
Hensley, S. 23:307
Hensley, Samuel 11:187
Hensley, W. 15:87
Hensley, W. J. 15:7
Hensley, W. T. 22:82
Hensley, Wakefield 10:117; 20:270
Hensley, William 17:281
Hensley, William J. 22:405
Hensley, Z. 14:71
Hensman, Henry 25:185
Hensome, Adam 22:82
Henson, Alfred 17:203
Henson, Andrew J. 20:27
Henson, Charles 1:192; 13:90
Henson, G. W. 3:94
Henson, H. 6:16
Henson, Henry 13:64; 16:295
Henson, Henry E. 22:35
Henson, Isaac 17:21
Henson, J. 1:44
Henson, James 22:254
Henson, James R. 24:152
Henson, Jesse F. 22:35
Henson, John 25:185
Henson, John E. 22:35
Henson, Joseph 8:49
Henson, M. 3:94
Henson, Nat. 16:198
Henson, Robert 12:24
Henson, Samuel 6:16; 8:106; 18:85
Henson, W. 21:53
Henson, W. B. 11:33
Henson, W. J. 21:14
Henson, William 21:29; 22:254
Henson, William H. 21:101; 22:254
Henster, William 9:102
Henstis, Aristides 12:25
Henstis, Benjamin 8:19
Henstis, Joel D. 8:87
Henston, Joseph 21:273
Henston, Thomas 9:154
Henston, William D. 8:87

Henstregt, Alonzo 16:95
Hensy, Charles D. 15:17
Hentelm, Joseph 15:353
Hentgal, Peter 6:31
Henthcult, Richard 9:82
Henthom, Jackson 20:270
Henthorn, A. 1:140; 22:81
Henthorn, Amos M. 22:81
Henthorn, Jacob 10:58
Henthorn, John 23:191
Henthorn, Noah 8:19
Henthorn, R. W. 23:149
Henthorn, William 23:33
Henton, C. P. 23:290
Henton, L. 1:137
Henton, Peter 22:337
Henton, W. 1:41
Hentsley, A. 3:94
Hentz, Henry 20:270
Hentz, John G. 9:120
Hentz, William 17:502
Hentzel, Peter 6:31
Hentzer, Henry 10:58
Hentzer, J. B. 16:37
Hentzline, W. 27:58
Henvey, J. 7:58
Henwick, L. 16:268
Henwood, Charles 15:203
Henyen, W. 3:94
Henyler, Lorenzo 13:27
Henyon, Earl H. 22:35
Henz, --- 18:359
Henzie, John 10:7
Henzoo, Eli 19:349
Heoffer, Jacob 22:198
Heogler, Joseph 18:323
Heoklen, Alexander 9:180
Heopock, Henry 11:119
Heorge, Patrick 12:71
Hep, M. 14:71
Hepborn, W. M. 13:27
Hepburn, Magnus 10:161
Hephry, Edward 13:111
Hepinger, L. 15:284
Hepington, W. A. 27:64
Hepker, H. 18:368
Hepker, Herman 9:221
Hepkirk, William 9:82
Hepler, John 15:203
Hepp, Augustine 19:18
Hepp, John M. 11:388
Heppel, John 12:25
Hepper, D. 1:41
Hepper, Rodolph 22:198
Hepron, Samuel 12:56
Hepsey, A. 3:94
Hepshire, Henry 8:19; 18:139
Heptars, I. F. 14:130
Heralb, Alfred 22:123
Herald, Daniel 11:62

Herald, J. 11:438
Herald, John L. 15:22
Herald, Joseph A. 9:43
Herald, Louis 21:344
Herald, Theophilus 7:125
Herald, William 15:36
Heraldson, William 5:18
Heramer, Jacob 11:231
Heratage, Thomas 3:94
Herb, Daniel S. 19:18
Herbaman, S. 9:110
Herbard, P. 15:166
Herbbell, Reuben 18:139
Herbeck, Lewis 4:31
Herber, George 22:337
Herbert, A. 7:50
Herbert, A. H. 25:41
Herbert, A. P. 7:58
Herbert, E. J. 22:82
Herbert, Eells 24:79
Herbert, J. 1:140
Herbert, J. S. 3:94
Herbert, James 4:66;
    12:82
Herbert, John W. 11:182
Herbert, Joseph 16:295
Herbert, Michael 13:27
Herbert, Otto 3:94
Herbert, R. 25:185
Herbert, S. 1:138; 12:82;
    16:295
Herbert, S. L. 20:89
Herbert, Vilat 7:62
Herbert, William 3:94;
    23:33
Herbester, C. 16:119
Herbison, William 14:178
Herbit, D. 1:42
Herbott, Daniel 3:94
Herbousen, B. 20:270
Herbrant, Joseph 1:38
Herbst, Albert H. 22:426
Herbst, Henry 22:35
Herbstreet, G. 11:280
Herbstritt, Charles 12:59;
    16:154
Herbut, Eli 16:198
Herch, Charles F. 20:270
Herchilrode, John 21:53
Hercht, George 14:179
Hercules, Louis 27:54
Hercy, V. 14:71
Herd, W. 16:268
Herd, William 8:19;
    18:139; 26:165
Herdendorf, Elisha 11:126
Herder, Hiram 15:288
Herder, Lewis 18:111
Herdester, H. 20:270
Herdindorf, Germ 1:40
Herdman, B. 1:44

Herdman, J. H. 1:139
Herdson, J. C. 9:144
Heredith, W. 21:29
Hereford, George W.
    18:218
Hereford, Isaac V. 21:240
Herell, W. 3:94
Herendon, Samuel 22:426
Herendon, W. 1:135
Hereshberger, Martin 4:31
Hereson, Gideon 20:270
Herford, William 14:71
Herfrich, George 16:119
Herger, Michael 12:71;
    15:68
Hergeshemer, J. L. 9:221
Hergeshermer, J. L.
    18:368
Hergitt, John 3:94
Herholtzer, J. C. 23:149
Herick, --- 16:119
Herick, A. C. 27:56
Herilage, J. 3:94
Herim, Nelson 9:208
Herin, O. 18:31
Hering, N. 3:94
Hering, P. 3:94
Hering, S. 11:303
Herizinger, Frederick
    23:113
Herken, Peter 21:344
Herkins, James 22:35
Herkness, T. 16:295
Herley, George W. 24:150
Herlinger, William H.
    17:449; 24:173
Herlong, Jesse 9:165
Herlsow, Albert 22:303
Herman, Alexander 12:25
Herman, C. F. 18:67
Herman, Charles 22:134
Herman, Charles F. 1:40
Herman, Christian 9:204
Herman, Cornelius 4:31
Herman, David 10:117;
    20:270
Herman, Elisha 24:111
Herman, F. 14:68, 179;
    26:163
Herman, F. G. 14:179
Herman, Frank 20:271
Herman, George 15:203
Herman, Godf'd. 1:39
Herman, H. 1:43; 3:94
Herman, Henry 5:51;
    12:64; 15:68; 20:41;
    25:185
Herman, J. 1:139
Herman, J. C. 9:180
Herman, John 12:173;
    14:179; 20:271

Herman, John G. 10:18
Herman, Joseph 20:113;
    27:62
Herman, Joseph A. 25:269
Herman, Karl 4:31
Herman, Louis 10:54
Herman, P. 3:94
Herman, Peter 22:145
Herman, Richard B. 22:82
Herman, S. C. 9:110
Herman, Sylvester 21:344
Herman, W. N. 11:119
Herman, Winser 22:82
Hermance, E. 14:71
Hermance, F. C. 3:94
Hermance, Isaac H. 10:18
Hermandet, Margill 7:97
Hermann, Augustus
    17:110; 23:122
Hermann, Conrad 22:166
Hermann, John 14:179
Hermann, John L. 17:74
Hermans, Evert 23:122
Hermans, John 3:94
Hermin, --- 16:371
Hermis, Barney 23:149
Hermitage, Thomas
    25:185
Hermon, R. 3:94
Hermond, G. N. 10:28
Hermore, D. 27:62
Hermy, Louis 16:37
Hern, George 2:12
Hern, J. O. 15:342;
    16:371
Hern, John 23:107
Hern, Joseph 9:156
Hern, M. 27:63
Hern, Michael 10:117;
    20:271
Hernadas, Nugent 15:359
Hernandes, J. 12:95
Hernandez, Antonio
    19:319
Hernando, James 21:211
Hernands, J. 19:75
Hernden, E. M. 10:58
Herndon, A. 18:85
Herndon, Allen A. 22:35
Herndon, E. M. 20:271
Herndon, John B. 22:123
Herndon, S. 8:101
Herndon, Solomon P.
    17:460; 24:159
Herndon, Thomas C.
    22:123
Herne, B. 20:271
Herne, E. 14:12
Hernel, John 9:221
Herner, Charles 19:169
Herner, James 26:37

Hernes, John 10:18
Herney, L. P. 14:241
Hernick, S. P. 14:71
Herning, Lawrence 11:381
Hernkey, E. 1:39
Hernley, D. U. 1:43
Hernman, Joseph H. 23:190
Hernoler, George 9:200
Herod, Loomis 17:35
Heroir, D. 13:64
Herold, Joseph A. 26:124
Herold, Kilean 22:198
Heron, G. W. 20:271
Heron, John 3:94; 11:32; 14:179
Heron, Moses 22:82
Heron, N. D. 11:263
Heron, T. O. 25:185
Heron, William 22:502
Heron, William H. 22:35
Herpen, F. 24:20
Herr, Benjamin 22:198
Herr, Conrad 9:230; 20:271
Herr, Daniel 22:427
Herr, Gabriel 22:198
Herr, H. 1:138
Herr, Henry 25:185
Herr, Jacob 4:31
Herr, James D. 24:20
Herr, John 6:27; 12:25; 22:482
Herr, Joseph 6:9
Herr, William 10:118; 20:271
Herrald, James A. 22:502
Herrell, Edward 23:68
Herrell, John 21:195
Herrell, William 8:87
Herret, W. 27:56
Herrich, William 13:111
Herrick, A. A. 25:38
Herrick, A. C. 9:144
Herrick, A. M. 19:238
Herrick, Amos 21:344
Herrick, Austin A. 2:12
Herrick, C. 3:94
Herrick, C. W. 27:61
Herrick, Edwin M. 10:9
Herrick, G. H. 13:90
Herrick, George 11:332
Herrick, George H. 7:30
Herrick, Henry 22:145
Herrick, Ira 11:151
Herrick, Ira I. 4:31
Herrick, James 14:179
Herrick, James W. 13:27
Herrick, John 26:32
Herrick, John E. 21:243
Herrick, Joseph 9:204

Herrick, M. 1:135
Herrick, Milton 17:80
Herrick, Mormon 27:61
Herrick, Nelson 10:118; 20:271
Herrick, Orville 20:151
Herrick, P. 8:49
Herrick, Thomas 12:25
Herrick, Thomas W. 17:360
Herrick, W. H. 15:107
Herrick, William 3:94; 20:107
Herrick, William L. 9:180
Herricks, John G. 19:75
Herridan, George 10:186
Herridan, W. F. 21:344
Herriff, H. 1:140
Herrigan, Michael 8:19
Herrign, J. 1:141
Herriman, Charles E. 16:78
Herriman, J. 1:136
Herriman, Sylvester 9:214
Herriman, William 11:219
Herrin, Richard 22:173
Herrin, Thomas 9:180
Herrin, Tobias 19:277
Herring, C. 1:40; 25:185
Herring, Charles 9:120
Herring, Daniel 15:359; 19:75
Herring, Delavan S. 10:58
Herring, Elisha 23:33
Herring, George 10:58
Herring, Henry 22:35
Herring, J. A. 1:42
Herring, J. H. 1:136
Herring, John 21:138; 24:20
Herring, John R. 25:311
Herring, Josiah 4:31
Herring, L. 9:68
Herring, L. G. 20:177
Herring, Levi 13:27
Herring, Lewis 13:27
Herring, Michael 22:82
Herring, S. S. 22:11
Herring, T. 22:497
Herring, W. B. 8:49
Herring, W. W. 1:43
Herring, William B. 21:71
Herring, Woodry 17:132; 24:196
Herrington, A. G. 19:76
Herrington, Andrew J. 11:64
Herrington, Hiram 14:288
Herrington, Isaac 14:179
Herrington, J. 23:149
Herrington, J. A. 20:124

Herrington, J. M. 13:111
Herrington, Levi 11:151
Herrington, M. 14:179
Herrington, Thomas 18:218
Herrington, Timothy 11:151
Herrington, Uroy 12:71
Herrington, William 8:87, 117
Herrington, William A. 17:21
Herrinion, William 18:330
Herrison, S. M. 22:405
Herritt, S. 15:342
Herrix, Martin 22:11
Herrod, James K. 17:80
Herrold, G. 25:185
Herrold, Richard D. 22:82
Herron, Alexander 23:68
Herron, Carter 8:19
Herron, Daniel 11:151; 18:111
Herron, E. 13:90
Herron, F. M. 26:33
Herron, G. W. 10:58
Herron, I. 26:36
Herron, J. 18:240
Herron, James 17:418; 24:159
Herron, James D. 22:480
Herron, Jasper 24:196
Herron, John 9:180; 19:286; 25:269
Herron, John E. 4:31
Herron, M. 14:71
Herron, Pat 3:94
Herron, Robert 9:230
Herron, Samuel 20:23
Herron, Shadrick 19:278
Herron, Sherdock 9:180
Herron, Thomas 18:67
Herron, Thomas O. 5:18
Herron, W. 1:141; 11:93
Herron, William 2:12; 23:68, 149; 25:38
Herron, William H. 20:86
Herrondon, George W. 23:68
Herrvel, John 18:368
Herry, John 25:41
Herry, Lewis 15:36
Hersch, A. 23:149
Hersch, Charles F. 10:58
Herschner, Lewis 19:75
Herse, Herman 13:27
Hersel, Conrad 19:75
Herselman, Herman 9:242
Hersentine, Follen 16:37
Hersentine, Tollen 13:27
Herser, Christian 16:371

Herser, John 18:139
Herset, --- 26:236
Hersey, Charles E. 1:41
Hersey, J. 9:144; 27:55
Hersey, J. Q. 1:41
Hersey, John B. 12:59
Hersey, John R. 11:182
Hersey, Joseph N. 25:43
Hersh, J. 16:198
Hersha, A. 1:139
Hersha, Charles 12:59
Hersha, Christian 10:173
Hershal, Christian 19:169
Hershey, Tobias M. 19:169
Hershian, A. 3:94
Hershman, Henry 22:82
Hershow, J. 11:242
Hersky, A. 21:344
Hersman, F. 21:138
Hersog, A. 14:299; 17:474; 27:64
Hersom, A. 1:44
Herson, B. F. 14:282
Herssler, Henry 8:116
Herter, Francis M. 22:482
Herter, J. 20:271
Hertgog, W. E. 16:198
Hertlin, Joseph 16:279
Hertue, John 21:273
Hertz, John 25:43
Hertzein, Herman 12:25
Hertzog, Godfred 13:27
Hertzoy, Charles 10:162
Hervey, G. W. 3:94
Hervey, Lewis 22:145
Hervey, William S. 19:346
Hervey, William T. 22:451
Hervit, Dan 19:169
Herzag, F. 1:135
Herzer, E. B. 8:72
Herzog, Alvis 22:11
Hesard, C. 25:185
Hesco, Reuben 12:154
Hesel, Henn H. 22:427
Hesford, D. 26:33
Hesh, Robert 8:87
Heshilman, A. 1:39
Heskell, B. 7:75
Heskes, Henry 1:40
Hesketh, T. 1:44
Hesler, Elisha 11:305
Hesler, Martin 1:43
Hesler, Morris 23:301
Hesley, --- 18:190
Hesley, Yost 9:102
Hesling, W. 1:136
Heslink, Henry 14:315
Heslop, E. 1:98

Hess, --- 5:51; 25:185
Hess, A. 1:136
Hess, A. W. 7:97
Hess, Adam 23:34
Hess, Albert 12:25
Hess, Anthony 9:23; 18:308; 26:101
Hess, C. 13:90; 14:12
Hess, Charles 5:18; 21:204
Hess, D. 13:90; 14:12
Hess, Daniel 4:31
Hess, Daniel A. 5:18
Hess, David 17:80
Hess, Edward 19:76
Hess, Edwin A. 16:95
Hess, Eli 9:23; 12:59; 18:308; 26:101
Hess, Florin 19:76
Hess, G. 3:94
Hess, George W. 22:82
Hess, H. 3:94; 13:90; 15:359; 19:76
Hess, Harvey 8:87
Hess, Henry 10:58; 20:271
Hess, Henry F. 22:35
Hess, I. 15:366
Hess, J. 1:135; 3:94; 12:99; 13:90; 14:12; 16:268; 17:364
Hess, J. W. 17:448; 24:172
Hess, John 1:40; 10:8; 17:14; 22:145, 198
Hess, Joseph 25:38
Hess, Lafayette 23:149
Hess, Lewis 15:203
Hess, M. 11:151; 14:71
Hess, Matthias 8:49; 21:101
Hess, N. 12:95
Hess, Nicholas 19:76
Hess, Nicholas M. 22:35
Hess, Philip 18:308; 26:102
Hess, Randolph 5:18
Hess, S. G. 14:179
Hess, Samuel 14:315; 15:68
Hess, Samuel W. 22:82
Hess, Saulte 9:66
Hess, Saultee 18:277
Hess, Stephen 21:71
Hess, T. 19:76
Hess, W. F. 3:94
Hess, William 1:40; 12:64; 15:56, 203
Hessbinon, --- 12:25
Hessdorfer, Andrew 23:128

Hesse, Conrad 27:61
Hesse, F. 11:33
Hesse, Herman 16:37
Hessec, Isaac 18:207
Hesseldon, J. W. 13:111
Hesselpot, J. F. 3:94
Hesseltine, Myron 7:80
Hesselton, H. D. 1:42
Hesselton, J. K. 14:179
Hesselton, R. R. 17:159
Hesselton, W. O. 10:118; 20:271
Hessen, Michael 7:97
Hessenflow, John S. 21:71
Hessenger, William F. 11:304
Hesser, Thomas 2:12
Hessilton, Alva 9:159
Hessimer, Lewis 23:89
Hessimer, Philip 3:94
Hessinger, H. 1:42
Hessinger, Joseph 12:25
Hessinger, L. 19:76
Hessington, W. A. 17:476
Hessington, William A. 14:299
Hessitten, S. A. 7:50
Hessler, Christian 9:35
Hessler, Jacob 22:123; 23:89
Hessleward, Frederick 21:344
Hesson, J. 19:302
Hesson, Jacob 17:427
Hesson, James 21:344
Hesspard, James 18:67
Hestand, Turner 23:99
Hester, Bassett 22:254
Hester, David 8:19; 21:274
Hester, E. 24:111
Hester, F. M. 12:154
Hester, George 11:204
Hester, J. 13:90; 14:12
Hester, J. P. 3:94
Hester, Jefferson 21:345
Hester, Jeremiah 10:58
Hester, John 3:94
Hester, John W. 22:519
Hester, Patrick 17:53
Hester, R. 25:299
Hester, Robert 21:114
Hester, William 12:154
Hestolate, John 3:94
Heston, Daniel 11:387; 27:144
Heston, P. D. 9:144; 27:57
Heston, Samuel 19:18
Heston, William C. 12:154

Hestover, Charles 16:37
Hetch, H. W. 17:35
Heth, R. 3:94
Heth, W. C. 8:49
Hetha, Philip 17:425
Hethel, James 10:58;
  20:271
Hether, Augustus 4:31
Hetherby, J. 13:129
Hetherington, J. O. 23:34
Hetherington, Joseph
  14:179
Hetherton, Edw. H. 13:27
Hetherton, Thomas
  18:396
Hethington, R. M. 10:58
Hetinger, Jacob H. 13:27
Hetinger, William 13:111
Hetrick, B. J. 17:231
Hetrick, J. M. 17:314
Hetrick, Jacob C. 21:138
Hetrick, Marer 17:110
Hetson, Charles 13:111
Hettick, Henry 11:62
Hettiker, John 24:51
Hettinger, George W.
  17:80
Hettinger, J. 1:41
Hettlen, Charles 11:151
Hettler, Adam 7:58
Hetton, Samuel 9:242
Hettzel, John J. 8:19
Hetuck, Jeremiah 19:76
Hetwich, Joseph B.
  21:195
Hetye, August 8:19
Hetz, Samuel 9:110
Hetzel, Gottlieb 24:40
Hetzell, J. 13:90
Heubelin, --- 26:165
Heuch, James A. 19:291
Heudon, Henry H. 24:150
Heun, Jacob 18:308;
  26:101
Heurtes, B. 3:94
Heuse, Conrad 9:120
Heuser, John 8:20
Heustis, Benjamin 18:139
Heuston, D. 25:185
Heustus, C. 14:12
Heuttander, George 27:58
Hevely, J. B. 17:248
Hevener, Charles E.
  16:198
Heverly, Owen 15:203
Hevron, P. 1:135
Hew, W. P. 14:71
Heweban, G. 14:179
Hewenleban, Conrad
  20:271
Hewer, Henry 10:162

Hewes, David 20:113
Hewes, E. B. 16:198
Hewes, George C. 12:25
Hewes, George W. 17:263
Hewes, J. 3:94
Hewes, M. 19:76
Hewes, Orlan 15:125
Hewes, R. 3:94
Hewes, William 19:253
Hewet, Elijah S. 20:271
Hewets, King 8:39
Hewett, Alonzo 4:31
Hewett, Bully 8:39
Hewett, Elijah S. 9:12
Hewett, George 23:107
Hewett, H. H. 14:71
Hewett, Hiram 15:314
Hewett, Ira J. 19:222
Hewett, J. 14:71
Hewett, J. C. 17:445
Hewett, James 26:165
Hewett, Joseph 24:94
Hewett, Joseph C. 24:164
Hewett, Joseph M. 8:106
Hewett, Philander 18:308;
  26:101
Hewett, Stephen 17:166
Hewett, W. 1:98; 18:240
Hewett, Winfield 19:18
Hewey, William S. 13:135
Hewick, Nelson 3:94
Hewing, D. S. 20:271
Hewings, William 15:17
Hewis, John 10:58
Hewitt, Aaron 21:10
Hewitt, Adam H. 12:25
Hewitt, Andrew 11:255
Hewitt, Andrew J. 21:101
Hewitt, Charles W. 22:145
Hewitt, Daniel 10:173
Hewitt, Edwin P. 17:253
Hewitt, George 7:97
Hewitt, George W. 22:145
Hewitt, H. 20:154
Hewitt, Henry 1:39
Hewitt, Henry H. 20:107
Hewitt, Henry S. 4:31;
  22:145
Hewitt, Hiram 19:76
Hewitt, Horace 21:345
Hewitt, J. C. 1:38
Hewitt, Jacob 10:58;
  20:271
Hewitt, Jeptha 7:97
Hewitt, John A. 4:31
Hewitt, John F. 19:337
Hewitt, John M. 22:82
Hewitt, John T. 21:255
Hewitt, Joseph 23:68
Hewitt, Joseph C. 21:71
Hewitt, Joseph M. 18:218

Hewitt, L. 16:371
Hewitt, Moses 21:225;
  24:20
Hewitt, Philander 9:23
Hewitt, Preston 6:25
Hewitt, S. 22:11
Hewitt, Simeon V. 22:11
Hewitt, Thomas 2:12;
  25:44
Hewitt, W. 26:34
Hewitt, W. H. 1:141
Hewitt, W. J. 23:34
Hewitt, Wesley 18:85
Hewitt, William 22:234
Hewlett, Ephraim 4:31
Hewlett, H. 1:137
Hewlett, Samuel 18:31
Hewley, Charles H. 24:20
Hewlick, Amos 6:21
Hewlit, Louis 22:303
Hewlitt, J. 20:271
Hewman, Richard 9:23
Hews, D. S. 26:34
Hews, F. H. 19:245
Hews, Henry A. 19:169
Hews, William 19:18
Hewthorn, Alexander
  26:102
Hewton, Hiram 21:345
Hewzman, S. 16:198
Hexford, William 27:60
Hexhor, J. E. 10:186
Hey, Anderson 9:35
Hey, Augustus 10:118;
  20:271
Hey, Lewis 25:299
Hey, William 9:35
Heyden, --- 16:95
Heyden, B. D. 17:281
Heyden, Henry M. 11:15
Heydenreich, A. 25:299
Heydt, Jessais M. 15:203
Heyekiob, Patrick 22:303
Heyl, J. 23:191
Heyland, J. 16:268
Heyman, Joseph 7:58
Heyman, Thomas 4:31
Heynard, Calvin M. 20:30
Heynard, Charles T. 20:30
Heyner, Charles G. 4:31
Heynolds, Marcellus
  21:233
Heysell, H. 8:64
Heythorn, Merris 15:36
Heywood, Frank 7:125
Heywood, John 12:25
Heywood, W. 18:240;
  26:36
Heywood, Willis 10:176;
  19:169
Hezeltine, John F. 21:255

Hezikieh, Comter 7:30
Hezlip, George P. 21:29
Hi---, --- 15:166
Hialinger, Jacob 10:58
Hiatt, Eli 20:183
Hiatt, G. B. 8:19
Hiatt, J. W. 1:140
Hiatt, John H. 11:262
Hiatt, Lewis 10:58;
    17:418; 20:271
Hiatt, S. 9:227; 18:368
Hiatt, William 22:82
Hibbard, --- 25:38
Hibbard, D. M. 9:144
Hibbard, D. W. 5:18
Hibbard, H. 15:330; 19:76
Hibbard, James B. 9:82
Hibbard, O. V. 1:39
Hibbard, William 9:180;
    19:253
Hibber, J. 14:71
Hibbet, William 3:95
Hibbets, James 1:40
Hibbetts, W. 11:305
Hibbitz, B. 3:95
Hibbons, J. 3:95
Hibborn, Thomas 3:95
Hibbrath, M. H. 3:95
Hibbs, E. 14:71
Hibbs, Joseph 18:240;
    26:36
Hibbs, Robert L. 4:31
Hibbs, S. B. 14:237
Hibdon, James M. 11:327
Hiblack, John 23:244
Hiblar, Samuel 17:177
Hibler, A. 3:95
Hibler, Alfred 21:148
Hibler, J. 21:148
Hibler, P. 15:36
Hibler, Sidney 11:33
Hibler, Snider I. 21:53
Hibley, Miles B. 9:102
Hibner, H. 24:79
Hice, Christian 27:62
Hice, George 9:214;
    21:345
Hice, Isaac 3:95
Hice, J. S. 9:145; 27:55
Hice, Jesse 22:82
Hicenaugle, John B. 10:58
Hichborn, Isaac 23:258
Hichcock, R. M. 25:185
Hichens, Jacob 20:271
Hichock, M. 7:125
Hichox, J. W. 1:41
Hick, George 18:139
Hick, Joseph 14:179
Hickcox, M. R. 3:95
Hickcox, Marcus 7:16

Hickenbotom, James
    24:167
Hicker, C. 3:95
Hickernell, J. D. 23:149
Hickerson, Joseph 22:481
Hickerson, Tallman
    22:174
Hicket, E. 27:55
Hickey, Andrew 21:345
Hickey, Cornelius 21:345
Hickey, D. C. 3:95
Hickey, Daniel 14:179
Hickey, George H. 4:31
Hickey, H. 20:124
Hickey, Henry C. 23:289
Hickey, James 4:31;
    19:169; 22:519
Hickey, John 16:85;
    19:18; 25:299
Hickey, John S. 20:124
Hickey, Lucius 15:107
Hickey, Michael 17:53
Hickey, Patrick 21:345
Hickey, Peter 15:81;
    17:80
Hickey, T. 1:137; 14:71
Hickey, Thomas 3:95;
    21:88; 27:54
Hickey, W. W. H. 12:142;
    20:271
Hickey, William D. 13:28
Hickhart, S. 14:71
Hicklen, John 10:58;
    20:271
Hickler, C. 26:164
Hickler, John C. 21:345
Hickler, Joseph 10:118;
    20:271
Hickley, Charles 5:40
Hickley, Charles W. 5:18
Hickley, J. S. 3:95
Hickley, John 3:95; 19:18
Hicklin, C. 8:64
Hickman, A. 8:72; 17:177
Hickman, A. C. 13:90;
    14:12
Hickman, Alfred 11:401;
    26:166
Hickman, C. 14:71
Hickman, Charles 11:115
Hickman, Columbus
    17:81
Hickman, D. 3:95
Hickman, Daniel 18:218
Hickman, E. 3:95; 11:33
Hickman, Elijah 23:34
Hickman, F. 14:71
Hickman, F. M. 12:154
Hickman, George 6:25
Hickman, George W.
    15:36

Hickman, H. 18:424
Hickman, Harvey C.
    11:327
Hickman, Henry 1:39;
    11:304
Hickman, Ira W. 24:51
Hickman, Isaac 8:106
Hickman, J. 21:71; 25:185
Hickman, J. C. 18:85
Hickman, J. H. 21:345
Hickman, J. M. 11:305
Hickman, James W. 7:68
Hickman, Joseph 5:40
Hickman, Lemuel 17:95
Hickman, Nathan 22:82
Hickman, Pleasant 7:30
Hickman, Richard 7:30
Hickman, Riley 11:263
Hickman, Robert 1:39;
    10:58; 20:271
Hickman, Robert B.
    17:260
Hickman, T. 1:141; 3:95
Hickman, Thomas 9:132;
    21:29; 345; 22:254,
    480; 27:58
Hickman, W. H. 10:28;
    19:302
Hickman, W. M. 11:327
Hickman, Wesley 17:81
Hickman, William 3:95;
    22:254
Hickmont, William
    14:179
Hickmoot, C. 12:82
Hickmot, C. 16:295
Hicknaugh, John B.
    20:271
Hickock, --- 11:322
Hickok, H. C. 20:133
Hickok, Lewis 17:21
Hickor, Edson 9:23
Hickor, James H. 10:118;
    20:271
Hickory, Daniel 24:111
Hickox, Emilius A. 17:81
Hickox, James 14:179
Hickox, John E. 21:130
Hicks, A. 14:265; 16:198
Hicks, A. G. 8:49
Hicks, A. R. 7:50
Hicks, Abraham 11:150
Hicks, Andrew 14:265
Hicks, Andrew D. 23:107
Hicks, Asa 9:106
Hicks, Benjamin 24:196
Hicks, Benjamin F. 19:18
Hicks, Byron 14:179
Hicks, Byron D. 7:97
Hicks, C. 3:95
Hicks, C. F. 9:66; 18:277

Hicks, C. Wesley 20:41
Hicks, Christopher C. 11:119
Hicks, Cornelius 11:33
Hicks, D. 7:50; 8:112
Hicks, Daniel 17:14
Hicks, Darius 8:49
Hicks, E. 3:95
Hicks, E. J. 13:28
Hicks, E. M. 1:140
Hicks, Elizabeth 17:65, 107
Hicks, Ephraim 24:152
Hicks, Ephriam 17:440
Hicks, F. 3:95
Hicks, Francis 9:180; 19:253; 20:107, 141
Hicks, Francis E. 11:295
Hicks, G. W. 3:95
Hicks, Garrett S. 1:40
Hicks, George 8:19; 9:144; 11:241; 18:139; 20:193; 22:35, 198, 303; 27:56, 57
Hicks, George F. 11:62
Hicks, George W. 2:11; 15:203; 25:38
Hicks, Gilbert 17:177
Hicks, H. 3:95; 15:203; 25:185
Hicks, H. J. 14:71
Hicks, H. W. 25:185
Hicks, Harrigan 10:118; 20:271
Hicks, Henry 5:40; 8:87; 21:255
Hicks, Henry E. 21:29
Hicks, Hermon 22:171
Hicks, Hiram 21:187
Hicks, I. 25:185
Hicks, Isaac 5:40; 9:221; 23:99, 291
Hicks, J. 3:95; 14:71; 25:185
Hicks, J. B. 21:166, 187
Hicks, J. C. 20:271
Hicks, J. E. 27:63
Hicks, J. F. 1:136; 3:95; 9:53
Hicks, J. H. 1:139
Hicks, J. M. 3:95
Hicks, J. S. 1:141
Hicks, J. W. 18:368
Hicks, Jacob 7:125
Hicks, James 9:221; 10:58, 173; 18:368; 19:46; 20:271
Hicks, James H. 21:187; 25:333

Hicks, James W. 10:18; 11:63
Hicks, Jeff 17:190
Hicks, Joel M. 17:243
Hicks, John 1:39; 9:236; 12:173; 14:71; 17:166; 18:240; 19:18, 76; 26:36, 164
Hicks, John C. 24:51
Hicks, John D. 22:35
Hicks, John F. 21:122
Hicks, John K. 14:179
Hicks, Joseph C. 21:187
Hicks, L. 9:154; 27:57
Hicks, Lester 21:345
Hicks, Lewis 4:31
Hicks, M. O. 2:12
Hicks, Maddison L. 8:87
Hicks, Madison L. 18:218
Hicks, Marion 22:463
Hicks, Milton 11:92
Hicks. Moses 22:166
Hicks, P. 3:95
Hicks, Patrick 8:106
Hicks, Peter 7:125
Hicks, Richard 22:519
Hicks, Robert 8:19; 12:161; 13:64; 18:139
Hicks, Robert C. 21:71
Hicks, S. 9:200
Hicks, Sally 19:169
Hicks, Samuel G. 21:53
Hicks, Selester 19:282
Hicks, Silas 26:34
Hicks, Smith 21:274
Hicks, Solomon 9:221; 18:368
Hicks, Stephen 19:18
Hicks, Sylvester 9:72
Hicks, T. 1:137
Hicks, Thomas 4:31
Hicks, Thomas A. 24:166
Hicks, V. A. 22:198
Hicks, W. 3:95; 25:185
Hicks, W. B. 11:280
Hicks, W. H. 1:137; 3:95
Hicks, William 8:77; 12:161; 17:248, 440; 21:255; 22:405; 24:153
Hicks, William A. 20:186
Hicks, William F. 10:58; 20:271
Hicks, William H. 8:19; 18:139; 23:243
Hicks, William J. 10:58; 20:271
Hicks, Y. 16:198
Hickson, Charles 12:25
Hickson, Daniel 3:95

Hickson, David 21:226
Hickson, George 3:95; 10:186; 15:299
Hickson, H. 26:163
Hickson, Henry 3:95
Hickson, Hiram 25:185
Hickson, J. P. 9:53
Hickson, Moses 22:303
Hickson, Robert 9:69
Hickson, Thomas 13:28
Hickson, Thomas J. 17:35
Hickson, W. T. 10:179
Hickson, William H. 4:31; 20:97
Hickston, Dick 17:397
Hicktenback, M. 13:28
Hicky, John 25:41
Hicock, George P. 14:331
Hiddrick, H. 3:95
Hide, Charles 9:12
Hide, James 17:281
Hide, John 11:327
Hide, M. L. 11:31
Hide, Niles H. 10:18
Hide, Samuel 8:49
Hideham, Reuben 17:243
Hidenburgh, Daniel 9:120
Hider, Henry 24:159
Hider, Joshua M. 16:119
Hidey, William 2:12
Hidge, Henry A. 18:111
Hidgeman, H. 16:37
Hidicer, J. W. 18:368
Hidy, George 21:53
Hiece, Elijah 24:58
Hieght, Jacob 26:124
Hiel, J. 9:145
Hieliman, Godfred 22:480
Hieman, J. 14:71
Hierman, Daniel 16:113
Hierman, J. H. 3:95
Hiers, J. 9:82; 26:33
Hiers, J. M. 20:92
Hiers, James 22:35
Hiesfand, Bentley 22:166
Hiestand, Martin 11:304
Hiestand, Samuel 21:226
Hiet, Joseph 22:198
Hiett, Jesse 10:58; 20:271
Hietziel, C. 3:95
Hiffner, Jacob 12:122
Hifford, A. 3:95
Hiffron, Michael 19:274
Hifner, G. 3:95
Higainyear, Henry 10:118
Higanyear, Henry 20:271
Higbee, Edwin G. 22:35
Higbee, Henry W. 20:271
Higbee, J. 21:122
Higbee, Martin 23:180

Higbee, S. M. 18:240; 26:36
Higbee, William H. 1:40
Higby, C. 14:71
Higby, E. I. 15:203
Higby, H. F. 1:135
Higby, M. P. 25:299
Higby, Merritt P. 7:75
Higdom, B. 15:321
Higdon, Alexander B. 23:99
Higdon, B. 19:76
Higdon, Francis 11:93
Higdon, Jesse 11:335
Higdon, Jesse M. 17:53
Higdon, John T. 20:186
Higerson, M. 14:71
Higgans, J. W. 27:144
Higgarty, F. 1:42
Higgeler, Frederick 5:18
Higgenbottom, James 17:445
Higgens, H. 11:241
Higgens, Hiram 12:154
Higgens, Joseph H. 18:368
Higgens, L. N. 18:368
Higgin, Caleb B. 12:25
Higginbotham, Joseph R. 20:97
Higginbottom, J. 17:177
Higgins, --- 15:36
Higgins, A. 3:95
Higgins, A. W. 1:137
Higgins, Albert 22:508
Higgins, Alfred 17:267
Higgins, Almerian 4:31
Higgins, Amos 22:82
Higgins, B. 25:185
Higgins, C. 15:107
Higgins, Charles 14:179; 15:203
Higgins, Charles C. 10:118; 20:271
Higgins, Christopher 22:166
Higgins, D. E. 25:299
Higgins, Daniel 13:129
Higgins, David 7:30
Higgins, David E. 7:80
Higgins, David M. 22:166
Higgins, Dewitt C. 23:240
Higgins, F. 1:42, 140
Higgins, G. D. 25:299
Higgins, G. H. 22:166
Higgins, G. R. 13:90
Higgins, George 25:321
Higgins, George D. 7:75
Higgins, George F. 19:316
Higgins, George W. 22:254

Higgins, Harvy 11:241
Higgins, Henry 7:15; 12:71; 15:22; 16:198
Higgins, Hubert R. 18:396
Higgins, Hugh 24:20
Higgins, Ira E. 11:381
Higgins, J. 3:95; 9:145; 14:179; 21:29; 27:55
Higgins, J. E. 10:211
Higgins, J. L. 20:271
Higgins, J. M. 10:91; 16:295; 25:42
Higgins, J. W. 3:95
Higgins, Jackson 22:303
Higgins, James 7:30, 125; 11:304, 305; 16:95; 17:35; 27:56
Higgins, James M. 12:82
Higgins, John 4:31; 6:11; 8:87; 16:87; 25:43; 26:145, 220
Higgins, John C. 10:58; 20:271
Higgins, John R. 21:71
Higgins, John W. 21:53
Higgins, Joseph 9:221; 14:179
Higgins, L. 25:185
Higgins, L. N. 9:221
Higgins, M. 15:299
Higgins, M. G. 20:8
Higgins, M. P. 3:95
Higgins, Matt 22:287
Higgins, Melvin W. 20:113
Higgins, Michael 24:58; 26:138
Higgins, Michael W. 20:113
Higgins, Miles 23:34
Higgins, Milo 21:71
Higgins, N. 1:139
Higgins, Nelson 11:107
Higgins, O. 17:177
Higgins, Oringdon 4:31
Higgins, Orland H. 18:277
Higgins, P. 21:163
Higgins, P. D. 1:141
Higgins, Patrick 10:118; 20:271; 21:10, 345
Higgins, Paul 9:208
Higgins, R. B. 16:295
Higgins, Robert 7:125
Higgins, S. A. 21:345
Higgins, S. C. 11:231
Higgins, S. H. 11:292
Higgins, Samuel 9:145; 19:169; 22:35
Higgins, Solomon 5:40
Higgins, T. 1:42, 139; 13:90

Higgins, T. W. 17:70
Higgins, Thomas 4:31; 8:106; 11:64; 17:203; 21:345; 22:82, 198
Higgins, Tim 22:337
Higgins, W. 1:42; 3:95; 11:31; 13:90
Higgins, W. E. 3:95
Higgins, W. R. 21:29
Higgins, William 10:18, 58; 11:205; 14:71; 20:271
Higgins, William B. 22:166
Higgins, William H. 23:34
Higgins, Wilson 17:81
Higgisn, Lucius 11:408
Higgison, Charles 22:35
Higgleman, James 11:149
Higgs, Andrew J. 21:130
Higgs, George W. 11:64
Higgs, H. W. 20:271
Higgs, Hiram W. 10:58
Higgs, James 22:254
Higgs, John 1:41
Higgs, L. 3:95
Higgs, Stephen 17:21
Higgs, Wesley 22:427
Higgs, William H. 22:36
Higgts, A. 14:256
High, A. 23:313
High, Alexander 4:31
High, Anson 14:71
High, Benjamin F. 22:337
High, H. 21:204
High, Henry 21:29
High, J. 15:203
High, J. W. 7:97
High, M. 3:95
High, Richard S. 8:87
High, Robert 24:158
High, Thomas 11:204
High, William 23:34
Higham, Richard 23:242
Highbanks, Henry 11:205
Highberger, A. L. 1:39
Highbie, James 11:64
Highfil, John 20:272
Highfill, Fielding S. 21:53
Highill, John 10:58
Highland, C. 3:95
Highland, Daniel 4:31
Highland, Edward 11:151; 22:337
Highland, J. W. 21:187
Highland, Jacob 21:345
Highland, James 7:97; 18:139
Highland, John A. 21:345
Highland, Washington 22:166

Highland, William 11:150
Highly, Albert 21:345
Highman, George M. 17:393
Highree, John 18:396
Highsmith, I. O. 26:36
Highsmith, J. O. 18:240
Hight, Alexander M. 20:97
Hight, J. M. 9:66
Hight, James 4:31
Hight, James G. 7:30
Hight, Jordan 23:276
Hight, Riely 18:85
Hight, Riley 6:17
Hight, S. C. 3:95
Hight, William 24:20
Hightman, Charles H. 22:112
Hightoner, P. H. 27:56
Hightower, Campbell 22:254
Hightower, Charles B. 20:272
Hightower, Daniel 11:31
Hightower, James R. 17:319
Hightower, Lewis 8:39; 26:163
Hightower, W. 21:13
Hightower, W. J. 11:263; 23:203
Hightown, Charles B. 10:118
Higler, Aaron 8:77
Higler, Austin 23:149
Higley, --- 19:169
Higley, A. J. 18:31
Higley, Albert 7:97
Higley, B. H. 8:49
Higley, C. W. 25:185
Higley, Edward 11:15
Higley, G. G. 18:31
Higley, G. K. 24:99
Higley, Harton 22:36
Higley, Herman 11:107
Higley, Joel P. 11:412
Higley, John H. 9:110
Higley, Levi H. 12:25
Higley, M. F. 3:95
Hignard, Frank 12:173
Hignett, Nathan 13:111
Hignett, W. H. H. 15:333
Hignight, William 22:36
Hignutt, W. H. H. 19:76
Higuerra, Francisco 12:171
Hihold, George H. 8:106
Hilam, William 21:345
Hiland, Bonaparte 18:139
Hiland, James 17:201

Hiland, Patrick 9:83
Hilant, James 8:19
Hilber, G. 12:92; 16:295
Hilber, Henry 8:106
Hilber, James 21:274
Hilbert, G. 3:95
Hilbert, Henry 15:107
Hilbert, James 24:101
Hilbert, John B. 17:241
Hilbert, Joseph I. 10:58
Hilbert, Joseph J. 20:272
Hilbert, Thomas J. 22:82
Hilbold, Alfred 15:125
Hilbon, T. W. 16:371
Hilborn, William H. 4:31
Hilborne, L. G. 13:111
Hilbourn, William R. 10:118; 20:272
Hilbrand, E. J. 9:236
Hilburd, D. M. 27:57
Hilburn, James 9:72
Hilburn, Levi G. 21:53
Hilburn, William 22:254
Hilbuth, A. 21:208
Hildan, George N. 18:339
Hildborn, James M. 17:319
Hildbrandt, H. 12:164
Hildebran, S. 11:64
Hildebrand, --- 11:219
Hildebrand, Franklin 17:91
Hildebrand, Frederick 17:53
Hildebrand, H. 11:122
Hildebrand, Henry 22:82
Hildebrand, J. 1:38, 135; 11:241
Hildebrand, N. 3:95
Hildebrand, W. 23:149
Hildebrand, William 10:118; 20:272
Hildebrandt, Augustus 5:18
Hildebrandt, George 10:58
Hildebrant, Francis R. 17:349
Hildebrant, George 20:272
Hilderbank, Edward 22:36
Hilderbaugh, Leo 14:179
Hilderbran, E. 11:62
Hilderbran, W. M. 21:166
Hilderbrand, A. 25:185
Hilderbrand, Charles 9:200
Hilderbrand, Hartman 11:413
Hilderbrandt, August 9:97
Hilderbranel, C. 19:282

Hildrath, Alex 17:443
Hildredth, Francis F. 17:319
Hildreth, A. 21:211
Hildreth, Alexander 24:159
Hildreth, Alfred 8:87
Hildreth, Allen B. 20:272
Hildreth, Allen E. 10:118
Hildreth, E. 1:94
Hildreth, Ephraim 8:87
Hildreth, H. 3:95
Hildreth, J. A. 3:95
Hildreth, J. P. 11:263
Hildreth, James 12:99
Hildreth, John W. 9:102
Hildreth, Newton M. 19:18
Hildreth, R. J. 8:50
Hildreth, S. C. 3:95
Hildreth, William 1:42
Hildreth, William H. 17:209
Hildridge, Moses 5:40
Hildrum, George M. 9:102
Hile, M. 22:337
Hile, O. 4:31
Hile, Samuel 14:179
Hileg, Michael 23:122
Hiler, William 14:179; 18:207
Hiler, William I. 20:272
Hiles, Ama 10:118
Hiles, Amos 20:272
Hiles, George 16:120; 24:79
Hiles, Jonathan 13:28
Hiles, Thomas 8:106
Hiley, H. R. 14:292
Hiley, J. 9:66
Hiley, James 17:260
Hilgate, Andrew 23:34
Hilger, Peter 1:41
Hilgers, Peter 16:120
Hilgert, J. 1:139
Hilgert, U. S. 9:145
Hilgert, W. S. 27:58
Hilgher, F. 16:295
Hilgus, Joseph 10:58; 20:272
Hiliman, John 22:198
Hilkenbaugh, William S. 12:25
Hilkey, John 22:82
Hilkie, John 8:106
Hilkins, George 25:185
Hill, --- 15:151; 16:199; 17:326; 25:42
Hill, A. 1:42, 45; 9:53; 20:272; 22:198; 23:191

Hill, A. A. 3:95
Hill, A. G. 1:135
Hill, A. I. 20:272
Hill, A. J. 1:39; 3:95;
    19:169
Hill, A. L. 14:329
Hill, A. M. 1:136; 10:18
Hill, A. P. 11:151
Hill, A. T. 10:118; 15:107
Hill, Aaron 3:95; 18:240;
    26:36
Hill, Abraham 17:53
Hill, Adam 9:145; 27:58
Hill, Alexander 7:125;
    9:72; 21:345
Hill, Allen 21:345
Hill, Amos 25:185
Hill, Anderson 10:58
Hill, Andrew 21:345;
    22:123
Hill, Andrew J. 7:30;
    10:118; 20:8, 272
Hill, Archy 22:513
Hill, Augustus 20:91
Hill, B. W. 4:31
Hill, Bartley E. 11:401
Hill, Benjamin 8:19;
    13:28; 18:139;
    23:301
Hill, Benjamin C. 18:50
Hill, Benjamin F. 13:28
Hill, C. 14:71
Hill, C. C. 13:28
Hill, C. J. 3:95
Hill, C. T. 20:154
Hill, C. W. 25:44
Hill, Caleb 7:50; 18:207;
    21:274
Hill, Charles 9:23; 12:25;
    15:22; 16:199;
    18:308; 19:46;
    22:508; 26:100
Hill, Charles E. 23:128,
    149
Hill, Charles J. 7:30
Hill, Charles W. 19:18
Hill, Church 12:64; 15:95
Hill, Clark 11:387
Hill, Cornelius 16:199
Hill, D. C. 17:65; 25:43
Hill, D. L. 3:95
Hill, D. T. 13:90
Hill, Daniel 17:360; 25:43
Hill, David 3:95; 8:49;
    10:58; 20:124, 272;
    25:42
Hill, E. 3:96; 17:273
Hill, E. A. 15:309; 19:76
Hill, E. B. 22:480
Hill, E. C. 19:76
Hill, E. J. 15:56

Hill, E. M. 20:272
Hill, E. P. 3:96; 14:179
Hill, E. S. 27:57
Hill, Ebenezer 13:28
Hill, Eber 9:102
Hill, Edward 18:190
Hill, Edward J. 12:71
Hill, Edwin E. 23:107
Hill, Elias 22:508
Hill, Elijah 14:179
Hill, Elisha M. 12:64;
    15:25
Hill, Emanuel 1:41; 5:40
Hill, Erastus 10:58;
    20:272
Hill, Ezra 10:58
Hill, F. 3:96; 11:126;
    20:57
Hill, F. J. 14:71
Hill, F. W. 9:145; 27:57
Hill, Ferdinand 11:15
Hill, Francis D. 10:118;
    20:272
Hill, Frank 3:96; 13:28
Hill, Franklin 9:180;
    19:265
Hill, Frederick 1:39;
    19:18
Hill, G. B. 27:62
Hill, G. D. 14:71, 179
Hill, G. H. 1:136
Hill, G. I. 27:63
Hill, G. W. 12:82; 14:179;
    16:199, 295; 23:34
Hill, Gaspar 14:179
Hill, George 3:96; 7:16;
    10:118, 148; 12:25;
    17:21, 352; 18:14,
    50; 20:272; 22:82
Hill, George E. 21:345
Hill, George H. 4:31; 7:98
Hill, George S. 9:82;
    26:32
Hill, George W. 1:40;
    6:17; 14:72; 18:85;
    22:82; 23:99, 122
Hill, Gilbert R. 20:272
Hill, Gust. B. 23:309
Hill, H. 1:39; 5:18; 13:90;
    16:371; 25:185, 283
Hill, H. C. 3:96
Hill, H. D. 18:240; 26:35
Hill, H. F. 25:38
Hill, H. J. 15:203
Hill, H. S. 24:20
Hill, Harvey 9:242
Hill, Henry 3:96; 4:66;
    9:23, 200; 10:91;
    11:412; 13:57; 15:87;
    16:37; 17:21; 18:308;
    19:291; 20:272, 399;

Hill, Henry 21:226, 274,
    345; 22:198, 254;
    23:305; 26:100;
    27:64
Hill, Henry F. 2:12
Hill, Henry J. 23:68, 149
Hill, Hilan 21:345
Hill, Hiram 19:267
Hill, Horace 11:33
Hill, Howard 25:185
Hill, I. 19:348
Hill, I. C. 11:388
Hill, Ira A. 10:118;
    20:272
Hill, Isaac 22:198
Hill, Isaac B. 14:179
Hill, Isaiah 12:49; 18:218
Hill, J. 3:96; 8:49; 11:241;
    16:199; 17:110, 177;
    19:238; 21:345;
    23:34; 25:185
Hill, J. B. 13:90
Hill, J. E. 3:96
Hill, J. H. 3:96; 16:37
Hill, J. K. P. 26:100
Hill, J. L. 7:30
Hill, J. P. 13:127
Hill, J. R. P. 18:308
Hill, J. S. 8:114
Hill, Jacob 11:219;
    14:179; 21:84, 345
Hill, Jacob V. 18:240;
    26:35
Hill, James 7:30; 9:53;
    10:148; 13:28, 90,
    125; 16:37, 120;
    18:50, 111, 285;
    21:101; 22:36;
    25:185; 26:135
Hill, James A. 17:35, 319;
    22:198
Hill, Jerome 25:41
Hill, Jes 18:85
Hill, Jesse 12:92; 16:37,
    295
Hill, John 1:40; 8:87;
    9:82, 132; 11:181,
    235; 12:161; 13:28;
    15:342; 16:199, 371;
    17:53, 281; 19:169;
    22:36, 425, 501;
    23:68, 128; 26:32;
    27:59, 62
Hill, John D. 22:11;
    23:122
Hill, John F. 20:272
Hill, John H. 14:72
Hill, John O. 15:17
Hill, John S. 9:12; 10:58
Hill, John W. 11:396

Hill, Joseph 7:30; 8:106; 18:240; 21:243; 26:36
Hill, Joseph C. 22:426
Hill, Joseph H. 12:71
Hill, Joshua 5:18
Hill, Josiah 9:180
Hill, Jothan M. 21:29
Hill, L. 1:140; 3:96; 18:139
Hill, L. D. 8:19
Hill, L. F. 24:88
Hill, L. H. 12:8
Hill, L. M. 11:305
Hill, Leroy 22:254
Hill, Levi F. 24:21
Hill, Levi P. 21:345
Hill, Lewis 22:11
Hill, Lewis G. 21:226
Hill, Lorenzo D. 23:279
Hill, Lucius 25:44
Hill, Lucius A. 2:12
Hill, M. 7:50; 25:185
Hill, M. A. 3:96; 14:179
Hill, M. E. 21:345
Hill, Martin 9:236; 23:68; 26:220
Hill, Mathew 9:43
Hill, Matthew 17:392; 26:124
Hill, Melvin J. 22:198
Hill, Michael 22:337
Hill, Moses 22:36
Hill, O. P. 20:155
Hill, Orzora 10:118; 20:272
Hill, Oscar 10:58; 20:272; 24:94
Hill, P. 3:96; 18:240; 26:35
Hill, P. A. 9:180
Hill, P. J. 1:139
Hill, Percival 12:64
Hill, Perry Harvey 20:272
Hill, Peter 7:125; 16:95
Hill, Phelps E. 20:113
Hill, Philander 9:35; 18:293; 26:103
Hill, Philip 9:53; 16:139
Hill, Pleasant 6:25
Hill, Plimpton 11:107
Hill, R. 3:96
Hill, R. F. 19:253
Hill, Randall 21:274
Hill, Reuben 17:132; 24:195
Hill, Richard 25:185
Hill, Richard G. W. 11:19
Hill, Richmond 11:423

Hill, Robert 9:159, 238; 10:18; 18:240; 24:150; 26:35
Hill, Robert E. 10:58; 20:272
Hill, Robert M. 10:118; 20:272
Hill, Rufus 9:236; 26:220
Hill, S. 14:72
Hill, S. A. 12:99
Hill, S. B. 10:145; 19:169
Hill, S. H. 21:110
Hill, S. N. 3:96
Hill, S. S. 22:198
Hill, S. W. 1:136
Hill, Samuel 1:41; 9:132; 18:14; 21:202; 22:82; 27:58
Hill, Samuel H. 26:32
Hill, Samuel N. 9:82
Hill, Shoemaker 23:122
Hill, Simeon 11:205
Hill, Solomon 11:63
Hill, Soponas 15:203
Hill, T. 16:268
Hill, T. A. 19:253
Hill, T. C. 11:304
Hill, Thomas 3:96; 4:31; 8:64; 12:25; 15:68; 17:253; 20:8; 25:42; 26:163
Hill, Thomas E. 11:63
Hill, Thomas H. 8:49
Hill, Thomas J. 10:58
Hill, Titus 21:345
Hill, Truman 20:8
Hill, W. 1:136; 3:96; 16:199; 25:38
Hill, W. D. 1:43
Hill, W. H. 11:62; 17:155
Hill, W. L. 3:96; 14:179
Hill, Warren 10:58; 20:272
Hill, Weldon 9:157
Hill, Wesley 25:185
Hill, Wilkison C. 22:82
Hill, William 1:44; 9:72, 162; 10:118, 173; 11:63, 401; 13:28, 111; 17:236, 276; 18:440; 19:169; 20:107, 272; 21:274, 345; 22:11, 198, 254; 27:59, 63
Hill, William A. 11:340; 17:281; 24:40
Hill, William B. 10:91
Hill, William E. 14:179
Hill, William F. 10:18
Hill, William H. 7:83; 17:70

Hill, William H. H. 10:58; 20:272
Hill, William I. 12:98
Hill, William J. 21:345; 23:34
Hill, William McD. 1:45
Hill, William R. 20:273
Hill, William W. 13:28; 15:353; 16:279
Hill, Wilson 17:499, 501
Hilland, Buonaparte 8:19
Hilland, H. 14:299
Hillard, Enas 18:31
Hillard, G. G. 19:233
Hillard, H. 17:476; 27:64
Hillard, John 9:110
Hillard, John F. 9:242
Hillard, S. 3:96
Hillary, George 22:280
Hillbaugh, N. 19:18
Hillberry, William H. 21:345
Hillbrand, H. L. 26:220
Hillbrant, A. 25:185
Hillburt, J. 18:240; 26:35
Hilldredge, M. 25:185
Hilldreth, Morris E. 8:114
Hille, I. 17:472
Hillebrand, Helwig 4:31
Hillebrand, Theodore 23:34
Hilled, F. S. 4:31
Hillen, A. 25:185
Hillen, E. 18:240
Hillen, John 4:31
Hillen, N. 25:185
Hillenthal, James 3:96
Hiller, D. 3:96
Hiller, E. 26:35
Hiller, F. 22:36
Hiller, H. 11:304
Hiller, J. 9:53; 23:34
Hiller, J. C. 9:23
Hiller, John 15:203
Hiller, John E. 8:64
Hiller, John L. 10:118; 20:273
Hiller, Nelson 5:40
Hiller, S. 3:96
Hiller, Stephen 25:43
Hiller, T. C. 18:308; 26:100
Hiller, William T. 10:118
Hillery, E. 13:90
Hilles, D. E. 11:263
Hilles, Robert R. 17:53
Hillet, --- 5:55
Hilley, Tradean 21:188
Hillgart, Jacob 17:14
Hillhause, W. H. 18:396
Hilliar, W. S. W. 12:154

Hilliard, Eli 14:72
Hilliard, Fletcher 14:179
Hilliard, Francis H. 12:25
Hilliard, George 3:96
Hilliard, George H. 13:28
Hilliard, Gilbert S. 9:180
Hilliard, J. 1:140; 3:96
Hilligar, --- 3:96
Hilligrass, F. L. 15:151
Hilliker, John F. 1:38
Hilliker, M. 1:140
Hilliland, J. A. 21:71
Hilliman, Edward 9:120
Hilliman, J. 21:345
Hillings, Laurence M.
    7:98
Hillingsworth, James
    19:278
Hillis, Alexander 21:29
Hillis, David D. 10:162
Hillis, G. A. 11:263
Hillis, Milton 18:396
Hillis, Tho. P. 18:396
Hillis, W. 1:138; 3:96
Hillman, August 18:139
Hillman, Daniel 13:28;
    16:37
Hillman, George 1:40
Hillman, George F. 23:68
Hillman, George W.
    20:193
Hillman, Henry 7:125
Hillman, J. 13:90
Hillman, John S. 19:76
Hillman, Jonathan 9:83
Hillock, B. 13:28; 16:37
Hillon, A. C. 19:227
Hillon, James B. 20:273
Hillon, John B. 10:118
Hillon, John W. 8:87
Hillory, E. 14:13
Hillow, Washington
    12:145
Hillowan, Ed 27:60
Hills, A. E. 1:138
Hills, Albert 11:107
Hills, E. 13:90
Hills, Eber H. 18:339
Hills, Elisha H. 9:53
Hills, G. S. 21:138
Hills, George 16:85
Hills, Giles 6:9
Hills, H. C. 11:387
Hills, J. 14:299; 27:54, 63
Hills, J. B. 3:96
Hills, Jacob 10:91; 20:273
Hills, James 9:35; 18:293;
    26:102
Hills, Jessey 25:283
Hills, Jessy 14:319

Hills, John 7:97; 11:107;
    14:72
Hills, Percival S. 15:3
Hills, S. 14:282
Hills, Thomas 17:502
Hills, W. 25:185
Hills, William 22:145
Hills, William H. 23:149
Hills, William O. 11:84
Hills, Willis 5:40
Hills, Wilson 16:199
Hillsgrove, John P. 9:180
Hillsinger, Martin 12:82;
    16:295
Hillsman, J. 17:102
Hillsman, Michael 23:122
Hillson, A. J. 5:40
Hillyer, J. 25:186
Hilm, H. 3:96
Hilman, August 8:19
Hilman, G. 3:96
Hilman, H. 3:96
Hilman, John 19:18
Hilman, Joseph 20:9
Hilman, Louis 10:91;
    20:273
Hilmer, C. 3:96
Hilms, Samuel 25:186
Hilping, P. 14:72
Hilsenberg, M. 1:40
Hilsendegen, J. H. 1:140
Hilstead, E. A. 13:64
Hilt, Caleb 8:87
Hilt, J. 12:167
Hilt, John 3:96; 27:65
Hilt, Peter 16:120
Hilt, Simon 7:97
Hiltebrand, S. M. 8:50
Hiltebrant, James 14:179
Hilterbridle, W. 15:152
Hilton, A. 14:72
Hilton, A. B. 25:186
Hilton, A. F. 3:96
Hilton, Alfred 8:58
Hilton, Alonzo C. 17:347
Hilton, Alvin 16:87
Hilton, Andrew 11:395;
    24:150
Hilton, B. 8:49
Hilton, D. B. 21:130
Hilton, Franklin 24:9
Hilton, George 7:78;
    10:58; 20:273;
    25:299
Hilton, George W. 9:214;
    21:53, 345
Hilton, Granville 17:233
Hilton, H. 1:141
Hilton, H. F. 17:102
Hilton, Henderson 24:21

Hilton, Henry 17:243;
    23:180
Hilton, I. 16:151
Hilton, J. 1:138
Hilton, J. E. 16:199
Hilton, John 3:96; 12:59;
    17:387; 22:82
Hilton, Joseph 26:142
Hilton, Joseph J. 9:47
Hilton, L. D. 17:102
Hilton, Levi P. 24:40
Hilton, Lewis 21:290
Hilton, Madison 9:132;
    27:59
Hilton, Mathew 12:49
Hilton, Nicholas 13:28;
    16:37
Hilton, Oliver 1:41
Hilton, P. 22:337
Hilton, Peter 21:114
Hilton, Rufus A. 17:288
Hilton, W. 6:31
Hilton, William 25:321
Hilton, Willis 22:425
Hilts, Byron 21:91
Hilts, Charles L. 15:203
Hilts, George A. 17:360
Hilts, Hiram G. 16:95
Hilvine, C. F. 26:100
Hilvine, Charles F. 18:308
Hilyanor, Enoch 11:151
Hilyard, P. F. 3:96
Hilyer, William 8:87
Himale, Christopher
    11:150
Himalo, Fred 11:32
Himball, N. 14:72
Himebaugh, William W.
    21:255
Himes, George 7:58; 8:50
Himes, George W. 17:248
Himes, Israel 23:180
Himes, James 15:3
Himes, John 21:345
Himes, Stephen 15:3
Himes, W. B. 14:256
Himestead, A. 15:299
Himling, Walter 27:60
Himmel, --- 15:203
Himmel, C. M. 7:98
Himmer, H. 2:11; 25:38
Himmer, Nelson 21:345
Himmill, J. 3:96
Himrick, Charles 11:119
Hin, J. W. 25:299
Hinchcliff, J. 3:96
Hincher, George 13:28
Hinchie, Andrew J.
    22:123
Hinchley, Daniel 13:111
Hinchley, J. H. 13:111

Hinchman, John 18:412
Hinchy, John E. 17:148
Hinck, Edward P. 20:273
Hinck, Thomas 14:72
Hinckle, Benjamin 20:273
Hinckle, John 20:273
Hinckle, Thomas 20:273
Hinckley, B. F. 1:137
Hinckley, Greshom
    22:463
Hinckley, Jesse 10:186
Hinckley, P. 1:39
Hinckley, P. F. 22:405
Hinckley, T. 1:138
Hincle, Harrison 8:87
Hincs, Philetus 12:25
Hind, George R. 17:317
Hind, John 14:72; 25:41
Hind, Patrick 8:87
Hind, W. J. 7:58
Hindback, August 6:9
Hindelang, Albert 13:28
Hindemah, Peter 15:166
Hindeman, S. 16:85
Hindes, John C. 22:145
Hindes, K. 19:238
Hindes, Peter 9:132
Hindle, Daniel 12:25
Hindley, Jordan 9:70
Hindley, Thomas 22:519
Hindman, David 23:244
Hindman, Eich'berger H.
    15:203
Hindman, J. 1:44
Hindman, Jackson 22:123
Hindman, James S.
    21:216
Hindman, Lewis 21:95
Hindman, McClellan
    22:234
Hindman, Samuel 21:71
Hindman, W. 1:139;
    15:355; 19:76
Hindmand, George 23:149
Hindmarch, George
    22:463
Hinds, C. H. 1:38
Hinds, David 24:21
Hinds, Enoch H. 12:71
Hinds, George 3:96
Hinds, George W. 17:428;
    24:183
Hinds, James J. 18:346
Hinds, John 9:53; 13:64;
    19:76
Hinds, L. C. 1:140
Hinds, O. 11:291
Hinds, Thomas 9:69;
    18:240; 26:36
Hinds, W. E. 17:217
Hinds, William W. 25:43

Hinds, Wilson 17:288
Hindshaw, John M.
    11:264
Hine, A. 23:149
Hine, Alva 20:273
Hine, Charles H. 9:12
Hine, Charles W. 16:37
Hine, F. E. 3:96
Hine, Frank 9:120
Hine, Fred 23:149
Hine, H. M. 8:106
Hine, John 8:19; 18:139
Hine, Lewis 21:345
Hine, S. 3:96
Hine, William 3:96
Hinebar, David 17:132;
    24:195
Hineber, C. 10:205
Hineberg, C. 18:406
Hineline, I. 1:44
Hineline, J. 25:40
Hineline, John 2:13;
    22:427
Hineman, E. L. 3:96
Hineman, Henry 5:18
Hineman, R. 1:138
Hiner, George 19:76
Hiner, J. E. 1:141
Hiner, John 17:464;
    24:214
Hines, A. 13:90; 14:13
Hines, A. B. 14:72
Hines, Adams 22:451
Hines, Andrew 5:18
Hines, Asa 16:133
Hines, B. H. 10:118;
    20:273
Hines, Ballard 19:18
Hines, Ben 24:195
Hines, C. 14:72
Hines, Charles 23:149
Hines, D. 3:96
Hines, D. F. 23:113
Hines, D. H. 25:186
Hines, Daniel 11:205
Hines, David 14:179;
    23:149; 26:33
Hines, E. 10:28; 19:302
Hines, Edward P. 9:10
Hines, Elias 24:178
Hines, Enoch 22:82
Hines, Francis 22:337
Hines, Frederick 22:337;
    24:79
Hines, George 15:324;
    20:146; 22:303;
    25:186
Hines, George W. 10:118;
    20:273
Hines, H. 18:240; 26:37
Hines, H. B. 14:179

Hines, H. H. 13:90; 14:13
Hines, Henry 1:42
Hines, Isaac M. 7:30
Hines, Isaiah B. J. 21:138
Hines, J. 1:40; 3:96;
    14:72; 20:41; 22:303
Hines, J. F. 14:180
Hines, J. H. 18:368
Hines, J. P. 19:18
Hines, J. W. 17:496
Hines, Jacob 22:198;
    23:149, 180
Hines, James 8:101;
    10:58; 12:82; 14:180;
    16:295; 17:459;
    20:273; 21:345;
    24:152
Hines, John 7:98; 9:83;
    10:9; 12:87; 16:9,
    295; 17:500; 18:207,
    396
Hines, John H. 9:221
Hines, John M. 22:280
Hines, John W. 9:180;
    19:267
Hines, Joseph 11:15, 33
Hines, Josiah 12:71
Hines, L. 3:96
Hines, M. 12:85
Hines, Mathew 14:299;
    17:471; 27:64
Hines, Michael 12:25;
    20:97
Hines, Mitchell 25:285
Hines, P. 1:192
Hines, Peter 11:204;
    21:274; 27:58
Hines, R. W. 7:58
Hines, Randolph L. 8:87
Hines, Robert 21:274
Hines, S. 3:96; 14:72,
    277; 23:186; 25:186
Hines, Samuel 5:18
Hines, Sanford 11:106
Hines, Seth 8:114
Hines, Silas 10:170;
    19:169
Hines, Squire F. 22:451
Hines, T. 15:263, 267
Hines, Thomas 22:198
Hines, W. 25:275
Hines, William 11:151;
    24:173
Hines, William H. 12:25
Hinestine, Thomas 10:162
Hineston, Thomas 19:169
Hiney, John 1:43
Hingery, A. 19:76
Hinging, B. 11:127
Hingleman, D. 27:57
Hingston, --- 10:152

Hingston, R. 18:50
Hink, C. E. 19:76
Hink, John 11:241
Hinkey, Benjamin 22:198
Hinkle, Benjamin 10:58
Hinkle, Henry 13:111;
 23:128
Hinkle, J. H. 11:64
Hinkle, Jacob 22:82
Hinkle, John 10:58;
 22:145; 23:191
Hinkle, Morris 19:76
Hinkle, Moses 17:443;
 22:427; 24:159
Hinkle, Paul 19:277
Hinkle, Philip 26:35
Hinkle, Philips 18:240
Hinkle, Sanford 17:132
Hinkle, Sanlord 24:195
Hinkle, Thomas 10:58;
 17:177
Hinkle, V. 9:180; 21:29
Hinkle, Wesley 12:25
Hinkle, William 22:198
Hinkle, William T.
 10:118; 20:273
Hinkley, A. 12:25
Hinkley, A. P. 1:138
Hinkley, B. 3:96
Hinkley, C. C. 18:31
Hinkley, D. 3:96
Hinkley, E. 9:180; 19:227
Hinkley, G. C. 3:96
Hinkley, Jesser 18:175
Hinkley, John 9:120;
 27:60
Hinkley, Leander P. 4:31
Hinkley, Leonard B.
 16:199
Hinkley, R. 25:186
Hinkley, Robert 7:98
Hinkley, S. 14:72
Hinkley, Timothy 21:346
Hinkly, Elijah 25:186
Hinkston, Harlow 10:118;
 20:273
Hinman, Charles 19:238
Hinman, Charles H.
 24:185
Hinman, E. S. 19:238
Hinman, Franklin 10:205
Hinman, George L.
 21:138
Hinman, H. M. 12:154
Hinman, Henry 20:273;
 22:427
Hinman, Henry M. 17:360
Hinman, J. C. 25:186
Hinman, James R. 5:18
Hinman, Jos. 15:125
Hinman, Joseph 12:122

Hinman, M. 19:253
Hinman, Myrtle 9:180
Hinman, Nathan 22:303
Hinman, O. K. 25:186
Hinman, O. R. 15:278
Hinman, Wait 15:36
Hinman, William 16:371;
 22:123
Hinn---, E. C. 23:122
Hinnigan, H. 21:71
Hinor, John 8:101
Hinricks, J. 3:96
Hinsdale, N. B. 20:102
Hinsel, Joseph 11:181
Hinshaw, A. 20:273
Hinshaw, Abner 10:58
Hinshaw, Charles 21:188
Hinshey, John 8:101
Hinsinger, A. 13:90;
 14:13
Hinskee, John 24:178
Hinsky, E. B. 3:96
Hinsky, John 17:463
Hinson, Daniel 5:40
Hinson, H. 18:85
Hinson, J. W. 3:96
Hinson, John 3:96
Hinson, John H. 18:85
Hinson, Robert 21:211
Hinston, Taylor 11:388
Hinsworth, George 24:182
Hint, Thomas 27:62
Hinten, Charles 8:64
Hinton, --- 9:23
Hinton, Alexander 23:149
Hinton, C. 18:190
Hinton, Charles 26:162
Hinton, E. 16:199
Hinton, E. C. 26:164
Hinton, Edward 27:62
Hinton, Elias 23:149
Hinton, F. G. 8:64
Hinton, Francis 18:308;
 26:101
Hinton, G. 25:186
Hinton, George 5:40
Hinton, Henry 19:267
Hinton, J. 3:96
Hinton, James F. 23:149
Hinton, James V. 20:27
Hinton, O. B. 12:87;
 16:295
Hinton, R. 12:25
Hinton, S. J. 13:64; 19:76
Hinton, Samuel 17:321
Hinton, T. 1:139
Hinton, Thomas 3:97;
 9:16
Hinton, Tobias 21:274
Hinton, Uriah P. 22:123
Hinton, V. 26:162

Hinton, W. 23:313
Hinton, William 3:97;
 12:25; 16:199
Hinton, William T. 21:226
Hintz, C. 1:138
Hintz, H. 14:180, 256
Hintz, John 4:31; 13:28
Hintze, John 16:37
Hintzel, Isaac 14:180
Hinze, Charles 11:33
Hinzle, Charles E. 23:34
Hiorchy, Thomas 14:179
Hipes, Joel 10:58; 20:273
Hipfinger, F. 9:53
Hipley, George 17:389
Hipman, Conrad 22:234
Hipp, Jacob 18:308;
 26:101
Hippard, John 15:14
Hipper, J. W. 14:269
Hipple, Marion 4:31
Hipple, Theo 1:40
Hipps, George 11:63
Hiprell, C. E. 24:21
Hipsels, Edward 9:69
Hipshire, Martin 21:204
Hiptemberger, Joseph
 20:107
Hirams, Joshua 18:85
Hirch, John 25:39
Hirch, P. 15:203
Hird, D. 3:97
Hire, Amzi 11:305
Hireld, Towson 20:146
Hirer, A. 25:42
Hires, William 16:199
Hirkson, George 18:175
Hirl, James 19:294
Hirley, C. P. 21:71
Hirrigan, Michael 18:139
Hirris, Henry 6:17
Hirris, John 8:87
Hirscfield, S. 3:97
Hirsch, Peter 9:97
Hirschi, Christian 21:255
Hirsh, E. 1:136
Hirshman, Fotlieb 9:23
Hirshman, Gottleib
 18:308; 26:101
Hirsley, Evans 20:273
Hirst, Alfred 25:40
Hirst, David 4:31
Hirst, L. D. 25:38
Hirst, Robert H. 9:110
Hirst, S. D. 2:12
Hirst, William J. 15:68
Hirt, Holsted 18:31
Hirt, John 10:118; 20:273
Hirth, Antonio 5:51;
 25:186
Hirth, William 14:72

His-cox, Mar. E. 16:95
Hischlay, Soph 20:133
Hiscitt, Benjamin F. 13:28
Hiscock, George 7:98;
  11:107
Hiscock, S. G. 1:137
Hiscons, R. H. 17:335
Hiscott, B. F. 13:90
Hiscott, D. 11:106
Hise, J. 18:240; 26:36
Hise, John 22:280
Hise, P. 3:97
Hisenbourg, John 10:58
Hiser, Aaron 8:19; 18:139
Hiser, Alfred 23:68
Hiser, H. 1:98
Hiser, Henry 9:110
Hiser, J. H. 12:161
Hiser, John 4:31
Hish, Henry 25:325
Hishboy, W. H. 9:120
Hisk, Chester C. 13:43
Hisk, Joseph 27:55
Hiskey, W. H. 26:165
Hiskey, William 27:59
Hisky, Harrison W.
  24:178
Hisky, W. H. 17:435
Hislip, James 17:281
Hisoer, Joel 11:127
Hisrembough, John
  20:273
Hisrodt, James E. 20:124
Hiss, John 25:186
Hiss, Ray 21:346
Hiss, T. 25:186
Hissay, Absalom 23:149
Hissel, J. 21:71
Hissington, H. 14:265
Hisson, William 19:316
Hissox, W. G. 1:140
Hister, Felix 17:421;
  24:164
Histerer, Joseph F. 16:279
Hitch, Benjamin 9:132;
  27:59
Hitch, E. 13:90; 14:13
Hitch, S. 3:97
Hitch, Thomas G. 18:218
Hitch, W. H. 14:180
Hitch, William 14:282
Hitch, William B. 22:254
Hitchcock, A. 15:17
Hitchcock, Asel 24:21
Hitchcock, Augustus 9:12
Hitchcock, C. B. 23:34
Hitchcock, C. W. 25:186
Hitchcock, Charles A.
  11:150; 15:203
Hitchcock, Charles W.
  5:18

Hitchcock, D. D. 25:333
Hitchcock, Dwight P.
  20:113
Hitchcock, E. 9:145;
  27:56
Hitchcock, F. 25:43
Hitchcock, G. 3:97
Hitchcock, Henry 16:95
Hitchcock, Henry C.
  9:208
Hitchcock, Hiram 20:41;
  22:280
Hitchcock, Israel 12:8
Hitchcock, J. C. 3:97;
  14:256
Hitchcock, J. F. 11:231
Hitchcock, J. R. 5:18;
  25:186
Hitchcock, James 22:280
Hitchcock, Jasper W.
  23:68
Hitchcock, John C. 17:295
Hitchcock, Joseph 10:155;
  19:169
Hitchcock, Lester B.
  17:317
Hitchcock, M. R. 16:199
Hitchcock, P. 14:72
Hitchcock, S. 2:12
Hitchcock, W. 18:50
Hitchcock, W. A. 3:97
Hitchcock, W. H. 4:31
Hitchcock, William 10:58;
  20:273
Hitchen, Daniel 16:37
Hitchen, Jacob 10:58
Hitchen, T. H. 16:199
Hitchengs, Charles 15:14
Hitchens, Frank S. 17:243
Hitchens, William 7:98
Hitchings, James 10:118;
  20:273
Hitchins, David 6:25
Hitchman, A. 1:136
Hitchock, Alfred 12:71
Hite, Fred 18:240; 26:37
Hite, George 22:198
Hite, J. E. 3:97
Hite, J. F. 15:204
Hite, John 13:64
Hite, Perry 1:41
Hite, R. D. 7:58
Hite, Scott 16:199
Hite, William 9:43
Hitekel, J. 20:133
Hiter, J. E. 26:163
Hiter, W. 17:297
Hites, John 10:58; 20:273
Hites, Lot D. 5:51
Hites, Tobias 27:62
Hithington, R. M. 20:273

Hitner, C. 11:439
Hitner, William 13:111
Hitsham, William 4:31
Hitsmiller, Samuel 21:195
Hitter, C. W. 11:304
Hitth, Jacob 26:124
Hittinger, William 23:191
Hittle, B. 3:97
Hittle, George 23:252
Hittle, J. 11:304
Hittle, Jacob 9:43
Hittle, William C. 25:39
Hittleson, Edward 11:32
Hitzelberger, Jacob 12:25
Hitzing, William 18:308;
  26:101
Hively, A. 22:352
Hively, J. 25:186
Hively, Jefferson 5:18
Hively, Jonathan 22:482
Hively, Josiah 17:155
Hively, Miles B. 18:339
Hively, Peter 11:305
Hively, Samuel 22:482
Hives, Isaac 9:157
Hix, Asa 17:206
Hix, James C. 21:216
Hix, John 11:413
Hix, William 5:18
Hixenback, John W. 6:23
Hixenbaugh, John B.
  21:71
Hixinbaugh, J. W. 18:85
Hixon, A. J. 19:76
Hixon, H. 15:152
Hixon, John 23:149
Hixon, John B. 22:254
Hixon, T. H. 13:90
Hixon, T. R. 14:13
Hixon, W. F. 26:204
Hixton, John 3:97
Hixwell, J. H. R. 15:204
Hizer, Christian 22:145
Hizer, Eugene 9:66
Hlle, B. F. 11:242
Hlll, Dallas A. 23:191
Hnderson, William S.
  9:132
Ho---, M. 17:509
Hoabley, Charles A. 1:42
Hoadley, C. 25:43
Hoadley, G. 14:72
Hoadley, Sylvester S.
  23:149
Hoadley, W. S. 7:98
Hoadly, Orlando 10:58
Hoaeiker, J. 3:97
Hoaey, James 5:19
Hoag, A. 14:241
Hoag, Cardinal 11:182
Hoag, D. C. 14:72

Hoag, George 26:138
Hoag, George W. 20:137
Hoag, Hamilton 11:398
Hoag, Herman 20:113
Hoag, J. 3:97
Hoag, J. M. 3:97
Hoag, John 20:97
Hoag, Judson 7:68;
  22:405
Hoag, Milo 21:53
Hoag, W. 15:308
Hoag, Walter 15:355
Hoag, William H. 17:447
Hoag, William L. 24:170
Hoagdom, William L.
  16:199
Hoage, Abraham 20:85
Hoages, Thomas 17:352
Hoaghen, John 16:199
Hoagland, C. A. 20:189
Hoagland, James B.
  18:271
Hoagland, John J. B.
  22:280
Hoagland, Lyman E.
  20:30
Hoagland, Theodore N.
  18:271
Hoah, John 14:72
Hoak, N. 11:64
Hoal, George W. 11:33
Hoaly, A. 3:97
Hoan, Timothy 14:180
Hoar, H. J. 3:97
Hoar, Wesley 22:198
Hoard, E. 13:90
Hoard, G. D. 21:110
Hoard, James 22:82
Hoard, Lorenzo 7:68
Hoard, W. 25:186
Hoard, William A. 11:241
Hoard, Z. 14:269, 282
Hoare, Charles 9:180
Hoare, U. 1:140
Hoarmon, J. 1:138
Hoarn, Thomas 23:11
Hoary, Patrick 25:186
Hoasch, George 12:71
Hoating, Jesse 13:57
Hoatland, John 1:41
Hoav, Martin 9:23
Hoback, H. 8:106
Hoback, Henry 25:186
Hoback, John W. 23:281
Hoback, Martin L. 22:123
Hoban, J. 25:186
Hobart, A. W. 14:180
Hobart, Anderson 21:138
Hobart, Charles 20:125
Hobart, Charles P. 9:97
Hobart, D. R. 14:237

Hobart, Isaac N. 22:426
Hobart, J. 21:188
Hobart, J. A. 19:169
Hobart, Lyman 17:418;
  24:158
Hobart, O. B. 2:12; 25:40
Hobart, Stanley 25:44
Hobart, W. M. 25:186
Hobart, Willie L. 16:152
Hobb, A. W. 20:273
Hobb, Waldron 7:98
Hobbard, --- 2:12
Hobbard, Russell 4:31
Hobbe, Thomas 16:295
Hobbell, Ray 12:25
Hobben, James 10:58;
  20:273
Hobbs, A. 3:97
Hobbs, A. E. 11:191
Hobbs, A. W. 10:118
Hobbs, Albert 20:137
Hobbs, Anthony 11:338
Hobbs, C. P. 25:186
Hobbs, Carl 19:169
Hobbs, Carlton 10:173
Hobbs, Charles B. 5:19
Hobbs, Charles C. 22:82
Hobbs, D. 14:72
Hobbs, George 25:186
Hobbs, Gustavus 23:68
Hobbs, H. N. 14:236
Hobbs, Harrison 22:425
Hobbs, Ira F. 25:186
Hobbs, J. 3:97
Hobbs, J. L. 19:267
Hobbs, J. M. 24:21
Hobbs, J. S. 9:180
Hobbs, James 1:38
Hobbs, James H. 10:118;
  20:273
Hobbs, John 6:7
Hobbs, John E. H. 20:155
Hobbs, John F. 4:31
Hobbs, John V. 21:53
Hobbs, Joseph J. 11:387
Hobbs, Joseph N. 9:83
Hobbs, L. 1:136
Hobbs, N. P. 10:18
Hobbs, Nelson 18:31
Hobbs, O. P. 17:21
Hobbs, R. S. 20:273
Hobbs, Richard 10:58
Hobbs, Sheldon 9:70
Hobbs, Thomas 11:31;
  12:85
Hobbs, Valentine E.
  17:276
Hobbs, W. M. 20:155
Hobbs, William 11:62
Hobbs, William C. 21:346
Hobbs, William H. 8:50

Hobby, I. W. D. 15:342
Hobby, J. W. D. 16:371
Hobby, John 22:254
Hobdier, Peter 8:19;
  18:139
Hobeirnick, William
  20:273
Hoberg, Henry 24:94
Hobert, A. 26:220
Hobert, Charles B. 4:31
Hobert, E. 14:72
Hobert, F. 14:72
Hobert, W. 12:149
Hobirnick, William
  10:118
Hobland, A. 24:66
Hoble, Theodore 18:308
Hobles, John 25:186
Hobley, D. J. 25:186
Hobley, George 17:177
Hoblit, G. 22:255
Hoblitzel, Jacob 10:118;
  20:273
Hobner, Michael 17:260
Hobs, Green 11:205
Hobs, Jacob I. 23:34
Hobson, A. J. 8:50
Hobson, Allen 17:132;
  24:195
Hobson, Archibald 22:36
Hobson, B. F. 3:97
Hobson, David 18:240;
  26:36
Hobson, Elijah 21:95
Hobson, Francis 17:110
Hobson, Jacob 17:449
Hobson, John 13:90;
  14:13
Hobson, Nicholas J. 21:71
Hobson, Peter 20:399
Hobson, Thomas 13:91;
  14:13
Hobson, W. 3:97
Hobson, William 3:97;
  21:346
Hobug, A. J. 3:97
Hobwick, Edwin 20:92
Hoby, Charles 13:111
Hobzworth, C. 1:43
Hoch, Benjamin F. 14:315
Hoch, Jacob 22:82
Hochenbaugher, William
  17:81
Hochkiss, N. 25:321
Hock, A. 26:163
Hock, C. 18:50
Hock, Charles 2:12; 25:43
Hock, Emma 26:221
Hock, Fred 15:166
Hock, George 8:19
Hock, T. 15:125

Hockaday, J. 1:44
Hockaday, Samuel E. 20:9
Hockebury, N. 3:97
Hockenbery, Jonathan 19:76
Hockenbrock, J. 3:97
Hockenburg, B. 1:139
Hockenburg, J. 25:41
Hockenburg, S. 25:186
Hockenjos, Charles 22:171
Hockensmith, Amos 10:145; 19:170
Hocker, D. 21:29
Hocker, Daniel 21:195
Hocker, H. C. 20:273
Hocker, Henry C. 10:58
Hocker, Nicholas 11:63
Hockert, J. P. 11:263
Hocket, John 15:204
Hockett, Patrick 17:439
Hockey, George 15:36
Hockhorn, J. 22:199
Hockinberger, Michael 11:305
Hocking, John 7:30
Hockins, Henry 22:83
Hockleberry, A. W. 4:32
Hockman, Andrew 8:106
Hockman, David 22:481
Hockman, Michael 17:265
Hockmuth, Sebastian 9:103; 18:339
Hocknall, Joseph 10:118; 20:273
Hocom, M. 15:294; 16:199
Hoctaw, E. 3:97
Hocum, Irving 25:42
Hocum, N. 12:25
Hocz, Hermon 18:51
Hodapp, Joseph 9:110
Hodchkiss, L. C. 1:42
Hoddie, John 15:17
Hodds, Benjamin 15:36
Hoddson, D. 1:140
Hode, Adam 22:304
Hode, Andrew 6:12
Hode, David 23:289
Hode, Philo 8:72
Hoden, Carl 9:83
Hodes, Louis 7:30
Hodgdon, A. B. 23:117
Hodgdon, E. F. 16:199
Hodgdon, George A. 13:28
Hodgdon, George E. 16:78
Hodgdon, R. 15:125
Hodgdon, William S. 16:78

Hodge, A. 21:29
Hodge, A. A. 22:199
Hodge, Amos 8:19
Hodge, Arnos 18:139
Hodge, B. F. 14:180
Hodge, C. 17:177
Hodge, Charles 20:193
Hodge, Charles M. 9:12
Hodge, E. F. 3:97
Hodge, E. S. 23:307
Hodge, G. H. 1:136
Hodge, G. W. 1:39
Hodge, Gaine 18:240
Hodge, Gains 26:36
Hodge, George 22:36
Hodge, George W. 10:179; 18:175
Hodge, Gerrard 11:93
Hodge, H. B. 22:337
Hodge, H. C. 17:319
Hodge, H. W. 1:136
Hodge, Harry W. 26:145
Hodge, Henry 21:226
Hodge, Horace 27:55
Hodge, J. H. 25:39
Hodge, James 18:85; 24:59
Hodge, James H. 2:12
Hodge, John 3:97; 11:423; 20:50; 25:299
Hodge, John C. 17:206
Hodge, Joseph 14:180
Hodge, Joshua 10:59
Hodge, Josiah 20:273; 25:42
Hodge, Lewis 9:200
Hodge, Martin 11:151
Hodge, Nelson 16:88
Hodge, Orell 22:463
Hodge, Philip S. 17:212
Hodge, Samuel 9:110; 17:397
Hodge, Samuel J. 21:255
Hodgeman, D. P. 22:481
Hodgeman, George 15:107
Hodgeman, Giles 11:402
Hodgeman, James 2:12
Hodgen, --- 3:97
Hodgen, Curtis Z. 10:118; 20:273
Hodgen, J. W. 3:97
Hodgers, I. 14:13
Hodges, --- 1:38; 12:87; 16:295
Hodges, A. 15:107; 23:34; 25:186
Hodges, Abraham 6:25
Hodges, Alex 16:37
Hodges, Andrew 11:205
Hodges, C. A. 9:53

Hodges, Capt. 19:170
Hodges, Daniel 9:180
Hodges, David 22:255
Hodges, E. R. 11:327
Hodges, Francis 9:120; 17:95, 110; 27:60
Hodges, Frank 9:66
Hodges, Gelon J. 21:71
Hodges, George 3:97; 9:132; 27:58
Hodges, H. G. 16:199
Hodges, Harry 21:130
Hodges, Heiman N. 20:9
Hodges, Henry 17:163; 19:46
Hodges, Horace 9:144
Hodges, Howell H. 22:255
Hodges, I. I. 17:271
Hodges, Isaac C. 24:20
Hodges, Isaiah W. 10:59
Hodges, J. 3:97; 13:91; 16:371; 25:186
Hodges, J. M. 3:97
Hodges, J. W. 9:180; 19:227
Hodges, James 6:12; 12:154; 19:76
Hodges, James B. 19:302
Hodges, John 3:97; 10:91; 19:170; 20:273
Hodges, L. 3:97
Hodges, Lorenzo 16:120
Hodges, M. 3:97
Hodges, M. J. 3:97
Hodges, Mathews G. 16:37
Hodges, Milton 11:119
Hodges, Moses 25:186
Hodges, Oscar E. 20:107
Hodges, S. 3:97
Hodges, S. J. 14:332
Hodges, Sidney 1:41
Hodges, T. 17:166
Hodges, Theodore 21:138
Hodges, Theodore C. 12:25
Hodges, Thomas 22:255; 26:33, 220
Hodges, Thomas E. 19:18
Hodges, W. F. 26:164
Hodges, William 9:221; 16:199; 17:389; 18:368; 27:145
Hodges, William C. 22:426
Hodges, William W. 13:28
Hodgin, G. S. 9:97
Hodgins, Charles H. 21:346

Hodgins, Josiah 22:513
Hodgins, Nicholas 21:255
Hodgkins, C. E. 1:137
Hodgkins, F. 1:140
Hodgkinson, W. 1:42
Hodgkiss, A. 19:170
Hodgman, E. W. 1:139
Hodgman, F. E. 1:40
Hodgman, J. A. 25:44
Hodgman, J. P. 19:296
Hodgman, Nathan 21:114
Hodgson, Benjamin 7:50
Hodgson, C. H. 17:506
Hodgson, E. 1:39
Hodgson, Ira 10:210
Hodgson, J. 9:110
Hodgson, Moses 15:204
Hodgson, Samuel 10:118;
    20:273
Hodgson, Thomas 25:41
Hodgson, Thomas R.
    24:94
Hodgson, W. L. 15:289
Hodgton, Henry C. 16:37
Hodgton, Henry O. 13:28
Hodil, F. 11:412
Hoding, George 26:35
Hoding, Thomas 17:418;
    24:158
Hodjkiss, Judson 7:64
Hodkinson, James 18:293;
    26:103
Hodman, Charles 19:316
Hodman, Lewis 9:230;
    20:273
Hodrick, Valentin 15:204
Hodsden, DeWitt C.
    22:426
Hodsden, F. 1:42
Hodsdon, Oliver P. 7:30
Hodsdon, T. S. 1:138
Hodskins, J. 27:55
Hodskins, W. S. 1:139
Hodskiss, --- 9:145
Hodson, Allen N. 22:83
Hodson, J. 13:91; 14:13
Hodson, John 17:309;
    25:186
Hodson, John M. 22:83
Hodson, L. B. 9:180;
    19:227
Hodson, N. R. 20:273
Hodson, Noah R. 10:58
Hodson, William 10:58;
    20:273
Hodstale, Virgil 11:401
Hodsten, Hamilton 13:28
Hodwell, John 9:236
Hoe, A. M. 11:32
Hoefer, Franz 10:9
Hoefer, Frederick 21:101

Hoeflen, Philip 11:126
Hoel, Jacob J. 24:94
Hoem, Max 13:65
Hoen, Halvor 20:113
Hoen, Oscar 22:123
Hoener, William 27:55
Hoere, James 4:32
Hoerigheit, George 20:274
Hoery, F. 3:97
Hoesell, Henry 21:346
Hoevell, Morris 9:230
Hoey, Arthur 12:25
Hoey, G. 14:13
Hoey, James 1:42
Hoey, John 7:50; 18:308;
    26:101
Hoey, Patrick 16:85
Hoey, Thomas 1:41
Hofadin, Joseph 1:42
Hofele, Nicholas 26:99
Hofer, Adam 12:25
Hofer, C. 1:139
Hofer, Fred 21:346
Hofer, John 16:95
Hoff, A. H. 21:346
Hoff, Abraham J. 23:128
Hoff, Albert 22:36
Hoff, Asa 19:76
Hoff, Charles 18:240;
    26:37
Hoff, E. C. 1:41
Hoff, G. 4:32
Hoff, Harlan 4:32
Hoff, Henry 1:43; 9:35;
    18:293; 26:102
Hoff, Isaac 11:423
Hoff, J. E. 4:32
Hoff, Jacob 16:133
Hoff, Leonard 4:32
Hoff, Louis 15:152
Hoff, Luther 10:118;
    20:274
Hoff, P. 22:304
Hoff, Robert W. 10:18
Hoff, Thomas W. 9:83
Hoff, William 14:180
Hoff, William D. 23:305
Hoffalt, H. 14:331
Hoffar, J. F. 1:43
Hoffard, John 3:97
Hoffeman, Pat 13:91
Hoffer, Herman 10:18
Hoffer, J. V. 1:44
Hoffer, Jack 22:497
Hoffer, S. 1:139
Hofferand, M. 19:76
Hofferband, N. 14:72
Hofferman, M. O. 9:23
Hoffey, B. 2:12
Hoffinee, B. 14:72
Hoffland, H. H. 3:97

Hoffler, William 19:76
Hofflin, Frederick 23:263
Hoffman, --- 9:180;
    12:168; 16:38;
    19:254
Hoffman, A. 1:142
Hoffman, A. L. 18:31
Hoffman, Aaron 17:418
Hoffman, Aaron B.
    11:295
Hoffman, Adam F. 23:68
Hoffman, Alex 11:151
Hoffman, Alfred 9:110
Hoffman, Andrew 10:25
Hoffman, Augustus 4:32;
    10:118; 20:274
Hoffman, B. 16:199
Hoffman, B. F. 19:170
Hoffman, Benjamin 1:40;
    21:274
Hoffman, Benjamin F.
    19:18
Hoffman, Brainard 10:173
Hoffman, C. 1:43; 3:97;
    12:82; 15:125;
    16:295
Hoffman, Charles 3:97;
    4:32; 7:98
Hoffman, Christian 1:39
Hoffman, Clement 18:111
Hoffman, Conrad 8:19;
    18:139
Hoffman, D. 3:97; 12:57;
    13:91; 14:13
Hoffman, Daniel 9:180;
    17:35; 19:270
Hoffman, David 14:180;
    15:36
Hoffman, David M. 24:40
Hoffman, Edward T.
    10:118; 20:274
Hoffman, Edwin 9:43
Hoffman, F. 1:39, 141
Hoffman, F. E. 9:103
Hoffman, Franklin 11:182
Hoffman, Fred 3:97
Hoffman, Frederick
    11:182; 25:269
Hoffman, G. A. 15:68
Hoffman, G. W. 3:97;
    7:30
Hoffman, George 1:38;
    6:27; 9:23; 10:59;
    14:180; 16:199, 279;
    18:85; 19:18; 20:274;
    21:346
Hoffman, H. 3:97; 16:199
Hoffman, H. R. 25:44
Hoffman, Hans 25:186
Hoffman, Harrison 9:69

Hoffman, Hiram 10:28; 19:302
Hoffman, Hy 5:51
Hoffman, I. 12:164
Hoffman, J. 1:43; 3:97; 9:145; 11:33, 93; 25:38, 186; 27:54, 56
Hoffman, J. H. 12:53
Hoffman, J. W. 25:40
Hoffman, Jacob 9:83
Hoffman, James 8:19; 18:139; 25:279
Hoffman, James C. 9:242
Hoffman, James H. 7:98; 21:346
Hoffman, John 2:12; 4:32; 10:91, 96; 12:25; 13:111; 18:111; 20:274
Hoffman, John D. 23:305
Hoffman, John E. 24:21
Hoffman, John H. 15:204
Hoffman, John W. 21:53; 22:199
Hoffman, Joseph 12:25; 20:35; 21:101; 23:149
Hoffman, Josiah 7:30
Hoffman, L. 5:40; 24:79
Hoffman, Leonard 11:115
Hoffman, Lewis 13:28; 16:38
Hoffman, M. 1:39; 24:94
Hoffman, Martin 23:99
Hoffman, Mitchell 13:28
Hoffman, Morgan I. 17:35
Hoffman, Nathan 21:346
Hoffman, O. A. 21:346
Hoffman, Oliver B. 18:396
Hoffman, Paul 6:8; 18:103
Hoffman, Peramas 7:30
Hoffman, Peter 17:387
Hoffman, R. 1:43; 3:97; 19:77
Hoffman, Reuben 7:62; 22:199
Hoffman, Rudolph 23:34
Hoffman, S. 3:97; 11:304; 12:122; 14:25; 15:363
Hoffman, Samuel 11:151
Hoffman, Samuel B. 24:173
Hoffman, Samuel P. 17:424
Hoffman, Spencer 13:111
Hoffman, T. K. 2:12
Hoffman, Thomas 17:501

Hoffman, Timothy 6:25; 7:125
Hoffman, Urias 9:43; 26:124
Hoffman, W. 12:92; 14:72; 15:316; 16:295
Hoffman, W. H. 1:41
Hoffman, W. M. 1:138
Hoffman, W. W. 25:187
Hoffman, Washington 15:204
Hoffman, William 4:32; 6:7; 10:118; 18:111; 19:18; 20:274; 23:34; 24:72
Hoffman, William H. 4:32; 17:99
Hoffman, William L. 14:180
Hoffman, William O. 18:320
Hoffmare, Charles C. 25:44
Hoffmaster, G. 3:97
Hoffmaster, L. 3:97; 16:158
Hoffmaster, Reuben 8:87
Hoffmire, Thomas E. 23:149
Hoffnay, W. 19:76
Hoffner, Jackson 22:482
Hoffner, James C. 8:19; 18:139
Hoffner, John 10:91
Hofford, D. 21:101
Hofford, Edward 11:16
Hoffron, Michael 8:59
Hoffs, M. 22:304
Hoffsletter, David 20:274
Hoffsmith, H. 14:180, 256
Hoffstater, J. 7:30
Hoffstetter, David 10:59
Hoffstetter, John 21:138
Hofgermerek, F. 3:97
Hofhints, F. 12:82; 16:295
Hofmaster, L. 3:97
Hofner, George 9:110
Hofner, Henry 13:28
Hofstatter, David 11:150
Hoftinger, Bergin 26:32
Hog, Augustus C. 17:307
Hogal, Jacob W. 8:106
Hogan, A. 1:136
Hogan, Andrew 22:337
Hogan, B. H. 25:187
Hogan, Bernard 16:78
Hogan, Charles 16:95
Hogan, D. 1:137
Hogan, David 4:32; 14:180

Hogan, Dennis 1:38
Hogan, Edward 23:250; 25:187
Hogan, Francis 12:122; 15:125
Hogan, G. W. 7:98
Hogan, George 15:125
Hogan, Guy 15:125, 349
Hogan, Henry 7:125; 26:33
Hogan, Horace 18:14
Hogan, Hugh 4:32
Hogan, J. 3:97; 27:56
Hogan, J. A. 19:18
Hogan, J. H. 21:166
Hogan, J. S. 8:50
Hogan, James 9:221; 18:67, 368, 462
Hogan, James M. 17:53
Hogan, John 7:98; 22:11; 25:287, 321
Hogan, John F. 11:100
Hogan, John J. 3:98
Hogan, Joseph 21:346; 25:321
Hogan, Lafayette 11:119
Hogan, Martin 18:240; 26:34
Hogan, Michael 23:99
Hogan, Nat 17:177
Hogan, Oscar 7:125
Hogan, Patrick 12:25; 21:29, 346
Hogan, R. D. 20:274
Hogan, Robert D. 10:59
Hogan, Robert R. 17:53
Hogan, Rody 9:244
Hogan, S. 1:42; 3:98
Hogan, Samuel C. 21:29
Hogan, Thomas 3:98; 7:98; 8:19; 18:85, 240; 26:36
Hogan, Thomas P. 6:9
Hogan, W. 21:110
Hogan, Walker P. 16:38
Hogan, William 8:87; 10:118; 20:274; 21:122
Hogancamp, W. 1:45
Hogans, David 15:278
Hogans, Jonathan 7:125
Hogans, Nelson 24:101
Hogard, Pat 15:204
Hogarth, James 18:277
Hogbin, C. 1:136
Hogden, R. 12:122
Hogdin, Miles Clay 22:83
Hogdon, M. L. 1:139
Hoge, E. 14:72
Hoge, G. 16:199
Hoge, Henry H. 16:38

Hogeboon, D. L. 1:103
Hogeboon, J. A. 1:139
Hogeboon, Stephen 1:38
Hogeman, --- (Mrs.) 1:138
Hogeman, Charles 16:199
Hogeman, Mathias 20:274
Hogen, U. 3:98
Hogenson, M. 12:85
Hogermann, Matthias 10:59
Hogers, Henry 20:274
Hogers, Rowland 11:187
Hogerson, M. 16:295
Hoges, Daniel 19:267
Hogg, --- 18:426
Hogg, C. 14:72
Hogg, Elbert A. 24:21
Hogg, Harvey 20:94
Hogg, John 15:17
Hogg, R. S. 14:72
Hogg, S. W. 25:283
Hogg, Seaton 21:274
Hogg, William 11:293; 14:180
Hoggard, James E. 21:346
Hoggard, Joseph 27:144
Hoggart, Alexander 27:145
Hogges, James 13:65
Hogget, Christopher 18:426
Hoggins, Frederick 7:125; 21:346
Hoggitt, R. 1:140
Hoggs, George W. 4:32
Hogham, John 15:294
Hogham, Wesley 11:119
Hoghton, A. 14:321
Hogincaus, John 8:106
Hogins, David 25:187
Hogintogle, S. 14:73
Hogland, Arthur 22:428
Hogland, F. 15:204
Hogland, Joseph 8:106
Hogland, Thomas 17:201
Hogle, Charles F. 20:107
Hogle, Dallas 20:30
Hogle, Franklin 8:106
Hogle, Gandon 21:29
Hogle, Henry P. 20:23
Hogle, James 8:87; 22:36
Hogle, M. 11:149
Hogle, R. 22:519
Hogle, Samuel 10:118; 20:274
Hogles, Charles 17:263
Hoglin, Harvey 20:146
Hoglin, William 21:346
Hogman, S. L. 25:187
Hogne, Esthas 26:211
Hogne, J. W. 25:39

Hogoith, H. 13:91
Hograss, Mathius 13:28
Hogrie, George W. 18:207
Hogron, Daniel 10:176; 19:170
Hogsington, A. 8:106
Hogstead, F. 9:110
Hogue, George R. 11:119
Hogue, J. A. 3:98
Hogue, James M. 20:113
Hogue, Lewis G. 1:40
Hogue, Samuel 12:25
Hogue, Solomon 20:17
Hogue, William H. 23:180
Hogus, William 26:145
Hogwood, F. 14:180
Hogwood, Frazier 14:73
Hoham, John 20:97
Hohan, Christian 22:337
Hohan, G. 13:28; 16:38
Hohan, John 5:19
Hohan, Michael 15:68
Hohe, J. 25:187
Hoheinstein, H. 1:141
Hohenberger, John 10:118; 20:274
Hohl, Jacob 19:254; 26:32
Hohle, Theo 26:101
Hohle, Theodore 9:23
Hohmeir, Thomas 10:59
Hohmen, J. 3:98
Hohn, Charles 11:387
Hohnorth, Henry 26:102
Hohrmior, Thomas 20:274
Hohuroth, Henry 18:308
Hoil, James 9:180
Hoile, George 20:37
Hoin, P. 3:98
Hoin, Peter 11:93
Hoisencon, E. L. 3:98
Hoisington, A. 16:139
Hoisington, Hiram 23:89
Hoisington, L. P. 14:269
Hoisington, William F. 20:48
Hoist, Michael 11:401
Hoit, D. 3:98
Hoit, E. 3:98
Hoit, George W. 20:274
Hoit, Philo 22:145
Hoit, William J. 18:14
Hoitt, G. F. 3:98
Hokd, John 18:67
Hoke, Andrew J. 21:130
Hoke, Anthony 11:151
Hoke, David J. 11:262
Hoke, Edwin 1:38
Hoke, F. M. 14:180
Hoke, George 9:35; 18:293; 26:102
Hoke, George N. 11:324

Hoke, John 14:180; 17:35
Hoke, L. M. 16:199
Hoke, Nathan 12:64
Hoke, Thomas M. 27:62
Hoke, William H. 24:40
Holabough, Samuel 19:170
Holaday, Robert R. 8:106
Holahan, M. 1:138
Holalr, David 11:319
Holan, G. M. 14:180
Holan, Thomas 3:98
Holandbeck, L. 1:140
Holaway, John 14:332
Holback, Charles F. 23:113
Holberg, Barney 23:149
Holbert, A. 18:51
Holbert, Irvin 22:255
Holbert, James 15:87
Holbert, Joel C. 8:19
Holbert, Joseph 15:342; 16:371
Holbert, Morris 9:12
Holbet, Joel C. 18:139
Holbon, Ezra 10:173; 19:170
Holbough, S. 1:139
Holbrew, James 9:208
Holbridge, Dudley 9:180
Holbrook, A. 14:180, 256
Holbrook, Charles 3:98
Holbrook, Daniel D. 22:83
Holbrook, Edw. 1:43
Holbrook, G. 3:98
Holbrook, George 19:170
Holbrook, George A. 24:51
Holbrook, Henry 27:54
Holbrook, J. 11:219
Holbrook, J. C. 19:77
Holbrook, J. E. 3:98
Holbrook, J. H. 19:296
Holbrook, James M. 19:170
Holbrook, John W. 20:113
Holbrook, Lera 20:113
Holbrook, Maurice 21:101
Holbrook, P. 9:180; 19:227
Holbrook, V. 12:80; 25:187
Holbrook, William 20:107
Holbrook, William A. 13:28; 16:38
Holbrook, William P. 17:387
Holburtt, Andrew J. 24:158
Holcamp, Henry 17:393

Holcham, Fred 26:124
Holcher, John G. 23:113
Holcher, Mathew 11:205
Holchew, J. 27:55
Holchien, A. 25:187
Holcomb, A. 3:98
Holcomb, A. B. 19:254
Holcomb, Aaron 22:280
Holcomb, Arden 10:91;
    20:274
Holcomb, C. 14:73
Holcomb, D. 3:98
Holcomb, David 9:23;
    18:308; 26:101
Holcomb, E. 14:73;
    21:201
Holcomb, Edward F.
    21:71
Holcomb, Francis M.
    18:139
Holcomb, G. 1:139
Holcomb, George H.
    23:89
Holcomb, H. C. 26:163
Holcomb, Hilas W.
    18:277
Holcomb, Isaac 20:102
Holcomb, J. 9:23; 18:308;
    26:101
Holcomb, J. B. 22:481
Holcomb, J. L. 22:352
Holcomb, James 7:58;
    14:180
Holcomb, John B. 4:32
Holcomb, John O. 9:97
Holcomb, Jonathan B.
    22:171
Holcomb, Jordan 10:118;
    20:274
Holcomb, Joseph L.
    20:151
Holcomb, L. 3:98; 18:51
Holcomb, L. B. 5:19
Holcomb, M. D. 3:98
Holcomb, Miles J. 9:12
Holcomb, N. 14:180
Holcomb, Newton 21:14
Holcomb, Orin 14:180
Holcomb, R. 25:187
Holcomb, R. T. 7:58
Holcomb, S. 14:13
Holcomb, Samuel 21:346
Holcomb, Seymour L.
    13:28
Holcomb, Simon 11:64
Holcomb, T. B. 1:43
Holcomb, Theo 3:98
Holcomb, W. 14:13
Holcomb, W. D. 20:274
Holcomb, William D.
    10:59

Holcombe, C. 1:139
Holcombe, S. 13:91
Holcombe, W. 13:91
Holcombs, J. 3:98
Holcome, Amos 1:38
Holcome, John S. 10:59
Holcome, Lewis 4:32
Hold, Conrad 1:43
Hold, Edward 23:309
Hold, Jacob 9:83
Hold, Nicholas 12:64;
    15:68
Hold, W. W. 11:423
Holdbrook, Warren
    14:180
Holdbrooks, James 23:34
Holdeman, J. 1:139
Holden, --- 23:282
Holden, Albert 5:51;
    22:199
Holden, Amos S. 7:58
Holden, B. 13:103; 14:13;
    16:268
Holden, Benjamin S.
    20:23
Holden, Dennis 22:36
Holden, Duane A. 18:111
Holden, E. 9:53
Holden, E. E. 7:50
Holden, Ezra 23:122
Holden, Ferdinand 14:180
Holden, Fred. H. 15:204
Holden, George 9:23
Holden, George N. 8:19
Holden, George R. 20:23
Holden, George W. 1:40
Holden, Green 21:188
Holden, H. B. 21:346
Holden, Henry 9:83
Holden, Isaac 3:98
Holden, J. 11:305;
    18:466; 21:110
Holden, J. R. 3:98;
    10:118; 20:274
Holden, James 16:9;
    17:14; 22:304
Holden, John 7:58; 14:73
Holden, John L. 21:249
Holden, Monroe 22:304
Holden, P. 3:98; 12:122;
    15:125
Holden, W. C. 21:188
Holden, W. E. 24:21
Holden, W. P. 7:30
Holden, Wesley 15:351;
    16:371
Holden, William 9:180;
    24:21
Holdenman, Henry 4:32
Holdenrider, F. 14:180
Holder, Anderson 11:205

Holder, George N. 18:139
Holder, George W. 22:426
Holder, Henry 26:32
Holder, John 11:33
Holder, Thomas S. 19:18
Holder, W. 19:238
Holder, William 1:39
Holderman, Jonas 11:64
Holderman, Lycurgus
    22:426
Holders, Hollis 15:17
Holders, Jesse 21:101
Holders, John 16:199
Holderson, Orin 11:205
Holdhaus, C. 3:98
Holdier, J. 14:256
Holdindick, Christian
    20:274
Holding, W. H. 14:73
Holdiway, William 22:255
Holdman, Jackson 21:29
Holdman, John 11:419
Holdman, Mathew 22:304
Holdman, Peter 17:177
Holdren, Benjamin F.
    23:68
Holdrew, W. 11:241
Holdrich, Charles H.
    22:405
Holdrich, W. H. 25:187
Holdridge, G. W. 25:187
Holdridge, George W.
    26:37
Holdridge, Hira 18:396
Holdridge, Martin 22:145
Holdridge, P. B. 9:214;
    21:346
Holdridge, W. H. 21:29
Holdsen, D. 23:252
Hole, Martin 10:118;
    20:274
Hole, O. W. 19:271
Holebrian, Anthony
    15:278
Holecome, John S. 20:274
Holeman, Edwin 10:148;
    18:51
Holeman, George 21:71
Holeman, Henry 7:125
Holeman, Miram 4:32
Holeman, William H.
    11:33
Holen, Enoch 11:151
Holen, G. W. 23:68
Holenback, D. C. 13:111
Holenbanger, Joseph
    17:265
Holenbeck, C. 3:98
Holenbeck, Nelson 19:18
Holenbrock, E. M. 1:39
Holenstine, John 17:260

Holenworth, James 23:307
Holers, William B. 10:96
Holesbrook, James 21:29
Holesome, Henry 23:313
Holeson, W. 10:192
Holeston, Walter 26:164
Holey, B. 25:321
Holey, E. 14:73
Holey, Edward 25:321
Holey, Philip 14:180
Holfer, J. 3:98
Holford, Daniel 9:180; 19:267
Holford, F. E. 4:32
Holford, John 21:249
Holfrich, Frederick 10:9
Holgate, F. 27:157
Holhass, Henry 16:38
Holher, W. H. 14:73
Holibaugh, A. J. 3:98
Holiday, G. E. 13:65
Holiday, G. H. 22:480
Holiday, James 11:396
Holiday, John B. 23:34
Holiday, Peter 17:35
Holiday, S. 3:98
Holiday, Thomas D. 18:308; 26:102
Holiday, W. 11:33; 12:142
Holiday, W. H. 25:276
Holier, William 26:37
Holinback, A. A. 1:38
Holinbrick, James 27:61
Holisch, Joseph 7:98
Holister, G. D. 1:141
Holister, Henry H. 22:405
Holister, J. 25:187
Holiven, G. E. 23:305
Holk, Oscar P. 20:48
Holkinger, Henry 17:35
Holl---, A. 25:41
Hollad, John B. 25:44
Holladay, F. M. 23:34
Holladay, Lindsey V. 11:263
Hollahan, Patrick 23:263
Hollan, Homer 18:396
Holland, --- 15:36
Holland, A. 16:199
Holland, A. A. 21:198
Holland, A. C. 23:268
Holland, A. S. 1:141
Holland, Albert 19:77
Holland, Alex 22:426
Holland, Andrew 4:32
Holland, B. 9:53
Holland, D. 1:41
Holland, Daniel 16:85
Holland, David 16:95

Holland, E. 3:98; 25:187
Holland, Ebenezer 5:19
Holland, F. J. 21:29
Holland, Frederick 9:23; 18:308; 26:100
Holland, George W. 7:125
Holland, H. 18:31
Holland, Henry 22:304
Holland, Herman 8:87
Holland, Isaac 9:132; 17:281; 27:59
Holland, J. 3:98; 11:31; 14:73; 19:46
Holland, J. B. 1:44; 22:480
Holland, J. L. 14:73
Holland, J. T. 1:137
Holland, J. W. 23:149
Holland, James 7:98; 18:67
Holland, John 6:9, 31; 9:23; 10:59; 16:199; 18:308; 20:274; 21:211; 25:321; 26:100
Holland, John C. 13:79
Holland, John P. 11:204
Holland, Joseph 4:32; 11:204
Holland, L. M. 9:221; 18:368
Holland, M. 14:73
Holland, Madison 22:304
Holland, Mark 22:304
Holland, Michael 10:162; 23:149
Holland, N. 18:368; 23:89
Holland, N. J. 23:149
Holland, Nathan 7:125
Holland, Pat 3:98
Holland, Patrick 21:346; 22:337
Holland, Philip 25:187
Holland, S. T. 11:387
Holland, T. 26:37
Holland, William 8:19; 9:221; 10:59; 16:199; 18:277; 20:274; 22:255; 23:99; 26:165
Holland, William B. 22:199
Hollander, L. P. 19:334
Hollands, H. 3:98
Hollands, Joshua 26:221
Hollands, Louisa 26:221
Hollandsworth, John 11:241
Hollanes, O. 17:434; 24:170
Hollar, Israel 9:180

Hollar, James 7:66
Hollard, --- 18:111
Hollarin, John 1:43
Hollaway, C. 16:199
Hollaway, Noah 22:255
Hollaway, William 22:255
Hollay, B. 14:73
Holle, G. 18:175
Holleman, W. A. 17:212
Hollen, George 3:98
Hollen, Johnson 11:205
Hollen, W. 3:98
Hollenbach, James 9:120
Hollenback, A. 3:98
Hollenback, Aaron 20:23
Hollenback, D. 3:98
Hollenback, Daniel H. 24:178
Hollenback, H. J. 3:98
Hollenback, Or. 19:77
Hollenbaugh, I. 1:38
Hollenbeck, S. 7:30
Hollenbeck, W. 15:159
Hollenbeck, W. H. 3:98
Hollenbeck, William 13:28
Hollenburg, William H. 23:149
Hollenger, Jacob O. 17:445; 24:166
Hollensback, Isaac 11:305
Hollensworth, J. 13:91
Holleque, Tostin 20:125
Holler, Hiram 8:19; 18:139
Holler, James 15:289; 16:199
Holler, James M. 9:120
Holler, M. 3:98
Holleran, John 9:106
Hollerfield, Joseph 13:28
Hollermire, W. 17:14
Hollet, Mark 11:263
Hollett, John A. 23:68
Holley, Albert 10:151, 178
Holley, Chancey 10:59; 20:274
Holley, Dallas 7:125
Holley, Dennis 12:49
Holley, Edward 9:163
Holley, Edward Burke 15:36
Holley, F. L. 20:274
Holley, Franklin L. 10:91
Holley, J. L. 1:44
Holley, Jacob 9:208
Holley, James 10:59; 11:150; 20:274; 22:83

Holley, John 10:91; 20:274
Holley, Joseph 6:21
Holley, N. 25:299
Holley, Norman 22:145
Holley, Robert 17:166; 22:481
Holley, Thomas R. 21:130
Holley, W. S. 7:30
Hollguith, Joseph 10:148
Hollgwith, Joseph 18:51
Holliard, C. 7:78; 25:299
Hollibaugh, W. 3:98
Hollibinton, A. J. 16:38
Hollida, M. C. 15:68
Holliday, Abraham 18:218
Holliday, Abram 8:87
Holliday, Alex 20:275
Holliday, Bassil G. 24:21
Holliday, Green 9:35; 18:293; 26:102
Holliday, H. 14:282
Holliday, Harvey 15:347
Holliday, J. 1:141
Holliday, J. B. 11:322
Holliday, John 5:40; 11:15; 16:199
Holliday, Marshall 19:46
Holliday, Martin 22:513
Holliday, Nathan 21:148, 274
Holliday, Peter 19:170
Holliday, Robert 21:346
Holliday, S. 3:98
Holliday, Thomas B. 24:51
Holliday, William 17:294
Holliman, Barzial 7:98
Holliman, James 7:98
Holliman, Thomas 7:98
Hollin, John 16:199
Hollinback, C. 11:31
Hollinback, David 17:425
Hollinback, J. A. 3:98
Hollinbeck, Norman 9:180
Hollinder, Mathias 19:170
Hollinder, Matthias 10:173
Hollinfield, Jacob 16:38
Hollinger, E. W. 13:28
Hollinger, Henry J. 11:412
Hollinger, J. 1:140
Hollinger, J. A. 15:289; 16:199
Hollinger, Jacob 20:275
Hollinger, John 8:19; 18:139
Hollinger, Thomas 13:111
Hollinger, William 12:25

Hollings, O. D. 13:65
Hollingshead, Henry 19:340
Hollingshead, John 24:51
Hollingshead, Levi 20:275
Hollingshead, S. 3:98
Hollingshed, John 17:263
Hollingsworth, Avanant 10:118; 20:275
Hollingsworth, B. F. 22:234
Hollingsworth, Bernard 22:426
Hollingsworth, Cyrus 22:36
Hollingsworth, E. 14:335
Hollingsworth, Enos 22:36
Hollingsworth, F. D. 27:56
Hollingsworth, G. 20:275
Hollingsworth, George 15:68
Hollingsworth, Horace C. 20:23
Hollingsworth, J. 11:205
Hollingsworth, J. A. 24:111
Hollingsworth, Jacob 12:71
Hollingsworth, James 9:180
Hollingsworth, Jesse 21:255
Hollingsworth, John 8:87; 9:35, 110; 11:423; 15:68; 18:293; 22:255
Hollingsworth, Joseph 8:19; 21:53
Hollingsworth, Joseph B. 22:427
Hollingsworth, M. 7:98
Hollingsworth, Noah 17:421
Hollingsworth, P. 22:352
Hollingsworth, Perry 22:83
Hollingsworth, Thomas 9:35; 18:293; 26:103
Hollingsworth, Wilburn 22:83
Hollingsworth, William J. 16:38
Hollington, Thomas C. 20:30
Hollingworth, E. 7:30
Hollingworth, J. 3:98
Hollingworth, Joseph 18:139

Hollingworth, Sylvester 12:25
Hollins, Harvey 17:132
Hollins, John 1:44
Hollinshead, Alfred 23:99
Hollinshead, Levi 10:91
Hollinsworth, --- 14:13
Hollinsworth, John 26:103
Holliper, Levi 22:199
Hollis, D. H. 11:31
Hollis, George 9:103; 18:339; 19:46; 21:138
Hollis, H. S. 17:62
Hollis, Henry 8:87
Hollis, Isaac 9:103; 18:339
Hollis, James 14:332
Hollis, Jesse 21:53
Hollis, Lewis 17:65
Hollis, Philip A. 22:123
Hollis, R. F. 15:342; 16:371
Hollis, William 11:150
Hollist, Francis 21:346
Hollister, A. 3:98
Hollister, Arthur A. 13:28
Hollister, Bridgeman J. 15:3
Hollister, D. 1:138
Hollister, F. G. 11:263
Hollister, Firman 10:18
Hollister, Joseph 5:19
Hollister, Oliver C. 12:25
Hollister, Samuel 21:346
Hollister, W. W. 17:231
Holliway, Charles 23:149
Holliway, Cleyborne 21:274
Holliworth, Henry 15:125
Hollman, George M. 20:275
Hollman, Joshua 9:35
Hollman, W. G. 26:102
Hollman, William G. 18:293
Hollmark, Daniel 21:346
Hollmart, George N. 22:255
Hollmen, James 11:32
Holloman, William 3:98
Hollopeter, A. 11:264
Hollorand, M. 15:326
Hollow, James 26:211
Holloway, Edwin 27:61
Holloway, G. W. 3:98; 13:91
Holloway, George 8:39; 26:165
Holloway, Giles 22:36
Holloway, H. B. 3:98

Holloway, Hamilton 22:145
Holloway, J. 3:98
Holloway, Jack 8:39
Holloway, Jacob 26:164
Holloway, James 9:23
Holloway, Jeremiah 20:275
Holloway, John 18:240; 24:21
Holloway, Lester W. 22:508
Holloway, Milo 22:304
Holloway, Peter 6:17; 18:85
Holloway, R. 3:98
Holloway, S. 15:27; 21:148
Holloway, Samuel 12:71
Holloway, Simon 21:211
Holloway, Watson 9:83
Holloway, William 22:337; 24:101
Holloway, William L. 20:97
Hollowell, L. 15:68
Hollowell, Stephen 21:274
Hollowell, William 23:68
Hollshoulel, Henry 26:32
Hollworth, William 19:18
Holly, Barton 22:427
Holly, Benjamin 6:17; 18:85
Holly, Charles 14:180
Holly, D. 14:299; 17:470; 27:64
Holly, Daniel 25:187
Holly, E. F. 3:98
Holly, J. D. 21:346
Holly, James 8:87
Holly, John 21:202, 291
Holly, Michael 14:181; 24:21
Holly, Nichols 7:80
Holly, Orlando 17:321
Holly, Stephen C. 17:81
Holly, V. H. 3:98
Hollycross, Perry A. 11:151
Hollyer, Julius 9:180
Holm, John 11:149
Holm, Oscar 22:11
Holman, --- 9:230
Holman, A. A. 9:53
Holman, A. L. 7:75; 25:299
Holman, A. O. 15:204
Holman, Albert H. 19:170
Holman, Allen 9:72
Holman, Asa 7:98

Holman, F. 3:98; 21:110
Holman, George 8:50; 17:91
Holman, H. A. 25:299
Holman, Henry 27:60
Holman, Henry A. 7:75
Holman, Henry H. 9:120
Holman, J. 18:368
Holman, J. T. 21:53
Holman, James 9:132; 19:18; 27:58
Holman, James A. 12:25
Holman, James H. 23:191
Holman, James J. 21:101
Holman, Jesse 9:180; 19:271
Holman, John 7:98; 22:166; 23:34
Holman, Joseph 10:118; 20:275
Holman, Lewis 18:240; 26:35
Holman, Luther 4:32
Holman, N. 20:275
Holman, Nicholas 10:59
Holman, P. 1:44
Holman, Peter 15:56
Holman, Philip F. 17:243
Holman, Solomon 22:304
Holman, Vinson 21:71
Holman, W. B. 11:242
Holman, William 22:502
Holmar, Daniel 9:180
Holmark, William 20:9
Holmer, Silas 27:54
Holmes, --- 26:220
Holmes, A. 19:228
Holmes, A. B. 14:181
Holmes, A. M. 20:46
Holmes, Aaron H. 4:32
Holmes, Alfred 8:39; 26:165
Holmes, Alfred C. 22:481
Holmes, Allyn 19:238
Holmes, Alonzo 10:118; 20:275
Holmes, Amos 25:42
Holmes, Andrew 20:23
Holmes, Ansell 25:187
Holmes, Anthony 11:204
Holmes, Arthur 9:180; 24:9
Holmes, Bennett 4:66
Holmes, C. 1:136; 3:98
Holmes, C. D. 13:111
Holmes, Charles 7:30, 125; 9:132; 18:426; 27:58, 145
Holmes, Charles C. 12:59; 16:154

Holmes, Charles E. 22:280; 25:42
Holmes, Christian 9:35
Holmes, Clarence 13:28; 16:38
Holmes, D. 15:166, 333; 19:77, 245; 21:346
Holmes, Daniel 9:214; 26:220
Holmes, Daniel H. 4:32
Holmes, David O. 21:139
Holmes, Davis 8:116
Holmes, Delawgen 21:29
Holmes, E. 1:40; 3:98; 10:118; 14:257; 22:304; 26:124
Holmes, E. P. 20:275
Holmes, E. W. 8:87
Holmes, Ed 26:102
Holmes, Edmund 16:95
Holmes, Edw. 8:87
Holmes, Edward 9:23; 12:170; 18:308
Holmes, Egbert S. 16:38
Holmes, Elias M. 20:125
Holmes, Emanuel 9:83
Holmes, Ephraim 12:49
Holmes, F. J. 3:98; 19:170
Holmes, Francis 4:66
Holmes, Frank 11:205; 13:91
Holmes, Frederick J. 10:162
Holmes, G. 1:94; 25:41
Holmes, G. W. 11:31
Holmes, George 5:19; 9:132; 11:287; 13:28; 22:304; 25:187; 27:58
Holmes, George E. 7:58
Holmes, George W. 14:181; 22:36
Holmes, Gilbert 18:240; 26:35
Holmes, Griffin 21:92
Holmes, H. 3:98; 19:238; 25:40
Holmes, H. P. 7:68
Holmes, Henry 7:125; 9:180; 13:28; 16:38
Holmes, I. 1:43
Holmes, Isaac 9:180; 17:53; 18:31; 19:267
Holmes, J. 1:39, 138; 3:98, 99; 11:31; 14:299; 17:479; 21:148; 27:58, 64
Holmes, J. B. 1:136; 18:31
Holmes, J. H. 14:130; 15:263

Holmes, J. M. 23:34
Holmes, J. R. 22:36
Holmes, J. W. 7:30
Holmes, James 3:99; 8:64;
9:180; 19:18, 238;
20:85; 22:83
Holmes, James H. 6:25
Holmes, James M. 11:84
Holmes, Jasper 8:19
Holmes, Jefferson 8:39;
26:163
Holmes, Jerry 21:211
Holmes, Jesse 17:81
Holmes, John 8:116, 117;
9:132; 11:151;
12:25; 17:91;
18:139; 19:77, 315;
20:9; 21:346; 27:59
Holmes, John D. 20:137
Holmes, John F. 14:181;
27:65
Holmes, John G. 21:346
Holmes, John K. 20:137
Holmes, John M. 27:62
Holmes, John T. 14:241
Holmes, John W. 8:19;
18:139
Holmes, Joseph 1:38;
9:132; 27:59
Holmes, L. 3:99
Holmes, L. D. 2:12
Holmes, L. T. 25:44
Holmes, Liman 12:71
Holmes, Lucian 14:181
Holmes, Lyman B. 15:83
Holmes, M. 1:43, 44;
20:85
Holmes, M. F. 27:65
Holmes, M. H. 19:18
Holmes, M. R. 15:125
Holmes, Martin 26:165
Holmes, Martin L. 7:71
Holmes, Michael 18:240;
26:34
Holmes, Orrin D. 19:77
Holmes, Paris 18:218
Holmes, Preston 17:349
Holmes, R. 1:138; 3:99
Holmes, R. P. 16:96
Holmes, R. R. 9:110
Holmes, Robert 9:242;
17:133; 24:195;
25:187
Holmes, S. 3:99
Holmes, S. D. 25:43
Holmes, Samuel 11:305
Holmes, Samuel B.
19:331
Holmes, Sidney 16:5
Holmes, Silas S. 9:120
Holmes, T. 1:141

Holmes, T. H. 25:43
Holmes, Thomas 1:39;
7:125; 8:60; 12:170;
13:28; 15:125;
25:321; 26:165
Holmes, Thomas B.
10:152; 18:51
Holmes, Timothy C. 23:89
Holmes, Uriah 8:87
Holmes, W. F. 14:241
Holmes, W. H. 20:155
Holmes, Wesley 3:99
Holmes, William 1:38;
7:98; 8:50, 87; 9:221;
10:118; 12:59;
14:181; 16:120;
20:275; 21:71; 22:83
Holmes, William H. 7:30
Holmes, William W.
23:281
Holmes, Williams 18:368
Holms, George S. 25:285
Holobaugh, Samuel
10:145
Holobaugh, T. 1:44
Holoway, Bank 18:241
Holoway, Frank 26:37
Holoway, J. H. 26:33
Holoway, Jeremiah 10:59
Holoway, William 21:226
Holpeter, Isaac 17:248
Holr, Michael 10:186
Holr, W. 10:179
Holroyd, Joseph 21:226
Holscher, G. 10:148
Holsclaw, Benjamin G.
22:83
Holsclaw, Charles V.
10:59; 20:275
Holsclaw, Jacob 11:263
Holsey, J. 21:204
Holsheiser, Lawrence
21:346
Holsinger, Elias 17:418
Holsinger, George 20:183
Holsinger, Isaiah 17:81
Holsinger, William H.
20:125
Holson, J. D. 11:305
Holson, William A.
22:480
Holst, Jacob 8:19; 18:139
Holstander, Jacob 4:32
Holstead, Calley 22:255
Holstead, Joshua R. 21:29
Holstead, William R.
21:239
Holsted, M. N. 12:99
Holstedd, William 18:207
Holster, Frederick 17:347
Holster, G. 18:51

Holston, Philip 19:46
Holston, Walter 8:64
Holston, William 22:36
Holt, A. 22:255
Holt, A. D. 15:25
Holt, Andrew 21:226
Holt, B. 14:73
Holt, Benjamin F. 4:32
Holt, Bobert R. 23:292
Holt, C. 1:44
Holt, C. H. 25:187
Holt, C. W. 9:180; 25:41
Holt, Caleb H. 5:19
Holt, Caswell 11:63
Holt, Charles 21:139;
22:519
Holt, Conway 16:199
Holt, Daniel S. 24:51
Holt, DeWitt C. 22:36
Holt, E. 16:136
Holt, E. K. 3:99
Holt, E. W. 1:136
Holt, Elias L. 17:360
Holt, Emery 22:199
Holt, F. E. 3:99
Holt, Frank 23:149
Holt, Frank M. 1:38
Holt, Franklin A. 17:443;
24:159
Holt, George 22:304
Holt, George D. 17:364
Holt, George W. 22:145,
199
Holt, Granvill 15:204
Holt, H. 4:32
Holt, Harper 18:277
Holt, Henry 9:70, 208;
18:67
Holt, Henry H. 13:28
Holt, Hines 11:187
Holt, Isaac 9:35
Holt, J. A. 25:44
Holt, J. N. 15:37
Holt, J. P. 25:38
Holt, J. S. 1:43
Holt, J. T. 1:40
Holt, James 12:25; 13:28;
22:304
Holt, James A. 9:244
Holt, James N. 19:334
Holt, Jeremiah 11:93
Holt, Joel 22:199
Holt, John 16:199
Holt, John H. 10:91;
20:275; 24:66
Holt, John M. 23:191
Holt, John S. 19:228
Holt, Joseph P. 21:71
Holt, Largan 10:59
Holt, Light 20:275
Holt, Longan 20:275

Holt, Louis 20:50
Holt, Lyman W. 21:346
Holt, M. 15:204
Holt, M. G. 9:180; 19:238
Holt, Nathan 22:482
Holt, Norman F. 13:28
Holt, O. W. 19:271
Holt, P. 17:35
Holt, Reuben 22:304
Holt, S. G. 7:80; 25:299
Holt, S. H. 1:136
Holt, Samuel 9:120; 27:60
Holt, Samuel B. 16:166;
   22:497
Holt, Samuel P. 15:204
Holt, Samuel S. 8:87
Holt, Sight 10:118
Holt, T. K. 25:187
Holt, Thomas 3:99
Holt, Thomas C. 10:59
Holt, Thomas G. 20:275
Holt, Thomas K. 5:19
Holt, W. P. 26:204
Holt, William 3:99; 7:30;
   18:175
Holt, William P. 18:175
Holtcamp, B. 3:99
Holter, Josephus W.
   22:481
Holter, Rufus G. 23:149
Holtgen, J. 3:99
Holthouse, H. 17:478;
   27:64
Holthouse, John 13:77
Holtman, Alfred 8:72
Holton, A. E. 10:118;
   20:275
Holton, C. A. 14:73
Holton, E. D. 17:152
Holton, Edward 15:107
Holton, G. E. 25:187
Holton, Granville E. 5:19
Holton, Henry 20:193
Holton, Hugh 22:123
Holton, J. C. 18:339
Holton, James 18:308;
   26:101
Holton, John 21:122
Holton, John C. 9:103
Holton, Lewis 7:66
Holton, M. 22:36
Holton, Nelson 17:400
Holton, P. 7:30; 14:335
Holton, Patrick 21:347
Holton, R. 21:347
Holton, Reuben B. 22:145
Holton, S. W. 3:99
Holton, W. H. 10:28
Holton, W. N. 19:302
Holton, William 11:327
Holton, William F. 23:68

Holtsberry, Isaac 24:79
Holtshour, John 23:180
Holtslander, John 22:463
Holtz, A. 3:99; 15:37
Holtz, David 18:421
Holtz, F. 21:53
Holtz, John W. 22:199
Holtz, W. 3:99
Holtzapple, John 23:149
Holtzell, J. 23:149
Holtzen, S. 14:265
Holtzer, S. 14:265
Holtzheimer, Hancy 11:31
Holtzlaw, John N. 22:337
Holtzman, John R. 17:81
Holtzman, S. 1:103
Holuns, J. 3:99
Holvenstot, H. 1:44
Holverson, Allen 18:51
Holvis, Kent 16:295
Holway, J. H. 9:83
Holwell, Samuel M.
   11:242
Holwill, W. 21:188
Holxam, George 21:166
Holy, Eliphalett 18:207
Holy, Joseph 25:275
Holycrogs, Volney 11:152
Holycross, George 23:149
Holycross, Joshua 23:149
Holycross, Lester M.
   23:149
Holyday, Alexander 10:91
Holyer, Julius 19:274
Holyfield, Warren A.
   18:241; 26:36
Holzham, Conrad 7:30
Holzmann, Charles H.
   7:63
Hom, John 16:371
Homan, Charles O.
   19:170
Homan, James E. 16:96
Homan, Theo 22:337
Homard, I. 24:79
Homberger, Joseph
   23:150
Hombuckle, J. C. W.
   11:84
Homby, Robert 9:83
Home, Isaac M. 23:34
Home, Luther 4:32
Homer, A. F. 13:91
Homer, A. J. 15:83
Homer, C. M. 15:37
Homer, Charles 17:451
Homer, E. 1:140
Homer, E. A. 19:228
Homer, G. M. 1:42
Homer, George W. 24:51
Homer, Henry 8:19

Homer, J. 25:44
Homer, J. A. 16:268
Homer, J. H. 1:44
Homer, J. P. 1:136
Homer, James A. 22:255
Homer, John 13:65;
   15:14; 17:35
Homer, Nathaniel 17:455
Homer, William 10:173;
   19:170
Homes, D. L. 11:262
Homes, Daniel 18:468
Homes, H. 25:187
Homes, I. C. 15:204
Homes, J. 25:187
Homesoth, F. 3:99
Homestreet, John 8:87
Homing, Henry 11:219
Homlebeck, Peter 22:280
Homlis, L. 1:43
Homman, John L. 23:68
Hommer, W. T. 15:311
Hommock, A. 11:84
Homoighausen, F. 3:99
Homoyear, Frederick
   10:118; 20:275
Hompfer, George 17:81
Homphry, James 20:275
Homprew, William
   21:347
Hompson, John 19:46
Homsley, Robert 19:46
Homstead, --- 3:99
Homteo, Elias 10:99
Honacker, John G. 25:311
Honacker, Mary C. 25:311
Honagg, Charles 9:180
Honaker, B. 25:187
Honaker, I. 11:152
Honaker, Isaiah 24:166
Honaker, Thomas 24:166
Honald, A. 9:110
Honales, C. 14:181
Honan, John 10:118
Honan, Martin 4:32
Honchins, Andrew J.
   11:413
Honchins, M. S. 7:58
Honck, John F. 25:41
Hondley, Orlando 20:275
Honds, F. 1:142
Hondshell, J. 14:319;
   25:272
Hone, G. 15:125
Hone, J. 12:80
Hone, John 15:125
Hone, O. S. 11:241
Hone, Reuben 16:140
Hone, William 9:180
Honegar, C. 3:99
Honegor, Lawrence 25:42

Honely, Ephraim R. 4:32
Honer Or Hoover, W. 16:136
Hones, B. E. 11:32
Hones, Samuel 15:304
Honesborough, Jacob 23:107
Honesty, Levi 13:28
Honesty, Lewis 6:12; 18:85
Honey, George W. 23:68
Honey, W. E. 22:145
Honey, William H. 18:277
Honeycut, Robert 22:83
Honeycutt, Green G. 7:125
Honeycutt, Jacob 10:148; 18:51
Honeycutt, William 11:423
Honeywell, Benjamin 15:204
Honeywell, Esra 22:199
Honeywell, T. 14:73
Honge, John C. 11:151
Honhan, Henry 22:304
Honiberger, Jacob 6:11
Honiford, M. 19:278
Honigman, Henry 24:67
Honin, Thomas 23:122
Honipson, --- T. 9:214
Honk, C. 18:51
Honk, J. 14:73
Honk, Johnson 17:35
Honk, Michael 15:302; 16:199
Honk, Nathan 15:37
Honk, William 11:32
Honley, Daniel 13:28
Honnell, F. R. 3:99
Honney, D. 14:282
Honniger, Frederic 9:204
Honnor, Dennis 16:38
Honnula, A. M. 21:29
Honoc, Zebulon 25:43
Honolt, George 11:149
Honregin, Patrick 10:118
Hons, John 9:235
Honsel, G. H. 10:118; 20:275
Honshaw, Henry 22:304
Honsigner, W. L. 3:99
Honsley, J. H. 13:111
Honsley, James W. 18:67
Honsley, Joseph 23:184
Honson, E. 16:200
Honsor, J. B. 18:31
Honssy, J. M. 11:287
Honton, John B. 18:51
Honts, John H. 9:23
Hontsch, C. R. 1:41

Hontz, John H. 18:308
Honvy, John 9:23
Hony, A. H. 16:200
Honyard, Charles H. 22:463
Hoobler, Daniel 17:355
Hoocher, D. R. 10:119
Hoock, Isaac 12:25
Hood, A. 13:91; 14:13
Hood, A. V. 11:241
Hood, Alexander 11:15
Hood, Allen H. 10:119; 20:275
Hood, Alonzo 10:59
Hood, Amos 22:199
Hood, Bradley 19:170
Hood, Charles 20:186; 21:347
Hood, David B. 10:59; 20:275
Hood, E. D. 21:347
Hood, Edward 1:38
Hood, Erasmus 24:21
Hood, F. 3:99; 12:167; 19:348
Hood, Fenson 8:99
Hood, Francis A. 19:18
Hood, Franklin 26:124
Hood, G. 3:99
Hood, George 17:177
Hood, George F. 12:53
Hood, H. 26:211
Hood, J. D. 3:99
Hood, J. H. 7:50
Hood, J. M. 17:291
Hood, James 15:289; 16:200; 23:68
Hood, Jesse 17:53
Hood, John 3:99; 10:119; 20:275; 22:83
Hood, Joseph H. 17:447
Hood, Joseph N. 24:170
Hood, Lookis 22:255
Hood, Lorenzo 11:32
Hood, Richard 10:205
Hood, Robert 22:337
Hood, S. A. 19:77
Hood, S. R. 16:200
Hood, Samuel 10:179; 18:175
Hood, Sterling 26:163
Hood, Thomas 1:39
Hood, W. 19:267
Hood, Washington 9:180
Hood, William 14:28; 22:36, 405
Hood, William A. 13:111
Hood, William B. 10:91; 20:275
Hood, William H. 22:83
Hooder, C. 16:200

Hoodlass, S. 11:305
Hoodlin, Joseph 13:57
Hoods, P. F. 9:43
Hoods, Peter F. 26:124
Hoofer, S. 23:150
Hoofman, E. 13:81
Hoofnagle, J. C. 18:308
Hoofstilter, Henry 10:18
Hoogan, Isaac 21:29
Hooge, James B. 10:28
Hoogland, E. 1:137
Hoogland, Isaac 21:53
Hook, Alexander 22:482
Hook, Barnard M. 21:71
Hook, Benjamin B. 21:347
Hook, Bernhard 11:119
Hook, Charles 17:161; 27:61
Hook, Cornelius 9:156
Hook, David 10:59; 20:275
Hook, Francis 12:57
Hook, Herman 17:143
Hook, J. 23:34
Hook, J. M. 3:99
Hook, Jacob 23:285
Hook, James J. 3:99
Hook, John 9:103; 11:62; 17:433; 18:339; 19:19; 24:159; 27:62
Hook, Joseph 11:16
Hook, M. S. 22:304
Hook, N. 3:99
Hook, Sylvania 12:25
Hook, W. H. 11:280
Hook, W. M. 25:187
Hook, Walter 21:10
Hook, William 25:42
Hooker, --- 15:125; 16:151; 24:94
Hooker, A. 3:99
Hooker, Alexander 19:265
Hooker, Casper H. 10:9
Hooker, Charles 22:145
Hooker, David 22:83
Hooker, Edwin H. 22:36
Hooker, F. 15:3
Hooker, F. L. 15:173
Hooker, Henry G. 21:195
Hooker, J. 21:188
Hooker, John B. 22:83
Hooker, N. C. 10:59; 20:275
Hooker, Robert 23:68
Hooker, T. 3:99; 12:71
Hooker, Virgil 20:140
Hooker, W. 23:150
Hooker, W. H. 1:41
Hooker, William 3:99; 9:53; 22:255

Hooker, William H. 9:103
Hooks, J. L. 3:99
Hooks, John 22:304
Hooks, T. 3:99
Hooks, W. 25:187
Hooks, William 10:59;
20:275
Hoole, F. J. 27:63
Hoole, William 20:35
Hoolehan, James 12:169
Hooley, J. 14:299; 17:481
Hoolihan, M. 11:33
Hooly, J. 27:64
Hoom, Philip 9:35
Hoomb, Daniel H. 4:32
Hoon, George 23:107
Hoon, M. 1:137
Hoonan, Patrick 9:23
Hoonty, J. 15:159
Hoop, A. T. 2:12; 25:40
Hoop, Brison 15:95
Hoop, H. 3:99
Hooper, --- 2:12; 12:87;
16:295; 25:39
Hooper, C. C. 9:221;
18:369
Hooper, C. S. 9:214;
21:347
Hooper, D. M. 8:19;
18:140
Hooper, David 11:423
Hooper, Elisha 22:199
Hooper, Ezekiel 12:49
Hooper, George W.
10:151, 178
Hooper, H. 19:228
Hooper, Harrison 9:180
Hooper, Isaac 17:419
Hooper, J. 3:99
Hooper, J. E. 9:145; 27:57
Hooper, James 8:87, 117
Hooper, James H. 22:280
Hooper, James W. 21:139
Hooper, John 9:103;
15:204
Hooper, Joseph E. 21:243
Hooper, Moses 21:274
Hooper, Orlando 9:214;
21:347
Hooper, R. 1:141; 13:91
Hooper, S. 17:291
Hooper, Samuel 3:223;
17:499
Hooper, W. H. 25:40
Hooper, W. M. 5:19
Hooper, William 13:57
Hooper, William H. 16:38
Hoopes, Frederick 11:423
Hoopes, Joseph 22:199
Hoops, Stamen 6:7
Hoops, Steyman 18:111

Hooritz, J. 14:73
Hoos, Alfred 8:87
Hoos, Christopher 7:98
Hoos, Conrad 21:101
Hoos, James 22:145
Hoosch, G. 15:56
Hoose, A. J. 1:139
Hoose, Reuben W. 7:50
Hoose, Sylvester J. 15:83
Hooser, Benjamin 24:194
Hooser, William 8:87
Hooshour, Sylvester
14:269
Hoosier, Benjamin 23:68
Hoosley, Fred 11:63
Hoot, C. R. 16:200
Hooten, Samuel 24:40
Hooter, Charles 4:32
Hooton, William F.
18:218
Hootus, Robert K. 11:62
Hoover, --- 12:169
Hoover, A. 3:99; 14:181
Hoover, A. M. 8:19;
18:140
Hoover, Abraham 11:413
Hoover, Benedict 19:19
Hoover, Benjamin 14:181,
332
Hoover, Benjamin B.
22:199
Hoover, Benjamin F.
23:68
Hoover, Benton 23:89
Hoover, Binton 11:62
Hoover, Charles 7:58;
9:180
Hoover, D. D. 20:275
Hoover, Daniel 3:99;
11:408
Hoover, David D. 10:59
Hoover, David D. 10:59
Hoover, E. 10:211;
18:460
Hoover, Eli 21:139
Hoover, Elias 21:53
Hoover, Elijah 1:40
Hoover, Emanuel 21:226
Hoover, Felix 17:35
Hoover, Fred 18:308
Hoover, Frederick 26:101
Hoover, George 14:181
Hoover, George H. 21:29
Hoover, George S. 9:145;
27:58
Hoover, George W. 7:58;
12:25
Hoover, H. C. 26:125
Hoover, Henry 17:148;
24:166
Hoover, Isaac 17:443;
24:159

Hoover, J. 3:99
Hoover, J. A. 21:53
Hoover, Jacob 10:59;
20:275
Hoover, James 8:87
Hoover, John 7:98;
11:413; 12:64; 15:56;
18:452
Hoover, John H. 21:53;
22:426
Hoover, Joseph 23:150
Hoover, Joseph T. 17:231
Hoover, Josiah 22:36
Hoover, Julius A. 23:150
Hoover, Lemanuel 21:29
Hoover, Levi 21:53
Hoover, Mark R. 22:83
Hoover, Martin B. 10:145
Hoover, Martin P. 19:170
Hoover, Morgan 9:23
Hoover, Nathaniel 9:120;
27:60
Hoover, Peter 17:91
Hoover, R. 3:99
Hoover, S. 3:99; 17:133;
24:195
Hoover, S. P. 3:99
Hoover, W. H. 3:99;
18:175
Hoover, William 11:150;
16:96; 18:207
Hoover, William N. 23:68
Hoover Or Honer, W.
16:136
Hooverstock, --- 11:303
Hoovler, F. 1:135
Hopburn, C. S. 18:396
Hope, --- 12:168
Hope, D. 14:278
Hope, David 23:184
Hope, David C. 17:440;
24:153
Hope, Eli 17:309
Hope, George W. 21:139
Hope, Hiram 14:288;
23:150
Hope, John 9:161; 16:120,
200; 17:21
Hope, Luke 13:28; 16:38
Hope, M. C. 14:73
Hope, R. 12:87; 16:295
Hope, Thomas B. 10:119;
20:275
Hope, William 17:254;
18:85
Hope, William T. 15:173
Hopeger, N. 7:30
Hopel, A. 16:196
Hopes, W. 3:99
Hopfner, Kasper 21:195
Hopgood, Reuben 7:98

Hoph, Ferdinand 17:14
Hophill, George 4:32
Hopily, Andrew 21:347
Hoping, John 8:50
Hopkins, A. 1:43; 3:99; 11:107
Hopkins, A. J. 2:12; 25:38
Hopkins, A. T. 12:82; 16:295
Hopkins, Alonzo 25:187; 27:60
Hopkins, Alonzo H. 9:120
Hopkins, Arden 21:274
Hopkins, C. S. 25:187
Hopkins, Caleb C. 23:68
Hopkins, Charles 13:28; 17:360; 22:36
Hopkins, Charles P. 22:463
Hopkins, Christian 11:62
Hopkins, D. 1:98
Hopkins, Daniel 7:58; 23:150
Hopkins, David 7:50
Hopkins, Dennison 10:18
Hopkins, E. 15:349; 16:371
Hopkins, Ebenezer 23:150
Hopkins, Elijah O. 17:53
Hopkins, Elt 20:57
Hopkins, F. A. 14:315
Hopkins, Franklin 9:23; 18:308; 26:101
Hopkins, Franklin B. 20:107
Hopkins, Freeman E. 13:28
Hopkins, G. 1:137
Hopkins, G. A. 9:110
Hopkins, G. H. 25:272
Hopkins, G. R. 3:99
Hopkins, George 5:19; 11:64; 12:25; 15:37; 17:295; 25:187
Hopkins, George P. 12:25
Hopkins, George R. 22:36
Hopkins, George W. 8:87; 20:275; 22:145, 427
Hopkins, H. 21:122
Hopkins, H. A. 12:25
Hopkins, H. C. 9:180; 19:228
Hopkins, Henry 14:263; 25:281
Hopkins, Henry W. 21:71
Hopkins, Hiram 16:140
Hopkins, Hiram C. 11:320
Hopkins, Ira E. 7:8
Hopkins, Isaac 9:132, 180; 18:241; 19:282; 26:37; 27:59

Hopkins, J. 11:241
Hopkins, J. C. 9:83
Hopkins, J. E. 21:29
Hopkins, J. G. 26:33
Hopkins, J. H. 14:181
Hopkins, J. L. D. 14:181
Hopkins, J. P. 11:305
Hopkins, Jackson W. 8:19; 18:140
Hopkins, Jacob W. 26:165
Hopkins, James 16:200; 22:337; 27:55
Hopkins, James A. 21:54
Hopkins, James C. 10:176; 19:170
Hopkins, James H. 22:199
Hopkins, Jeremiah 22:405
Hopkins, Jerome 7:78; 25:299
Hopkins, Jesse 15:326
Hopkins, Jessie 19:77
Hopkins, Joel 22:83
Hopkins, John 3:99; 4:32; 9:23; 17:243; 18:309; 26:101
Hopkins, Johnson B 22:470
Hopkins, Joseph 20:89; 22:145
Hopkins, Joshua 9:53
Hopkins, Lewis 7:30
Hopkins, Luther 18:271
Hopkins, Lyman F. 20:189
Hopkins, M. 14:181
Hopkins, Major 21:347
Hopkins, Martin 22:36
Hopkins, Matten 21:347
Hopkins, Milo 1:42
Hopkins, N. 1:39; 3:99
Hopkins, Nehemiah 17:81
Hopkins, Noah 22:83
Hopkins, Oliver 22:337
Hopkins, P. 15:83
Hopkins, P. H. 21:347
Hopkins, P. J. 16:96
Hopkins, Patrick 12:71
Hopkins, Philip 21:347
Hopkins, Primus 6:17; 18:85
Hopkins, R. B. 15:278; 25:187
Hopkins, Reuben 22:255
Hopkins, Richard M. 17:53
Hopkins, S. 11:293
Hopkins, S. D. 7:98
Hopkins, Samuel 21:226
Hopkins, Samuel C. 21:188
Hopkins, Sherman 19:19

Hopkins, Squire 22:304
Hopkins, T. 1:139; 15:68
Hopkins, Taylor A. 23:122
Hopkins, Thomas 10:119; 16:200; 20:275; 22:405
Hopkins, W. 3:99; 10:28; 17:308; 19:302
Hopkins, W. A. 10:119; 20:275
Hopkins, W. B. 17:21
Hopkins, W. G. 9:145; 12:154; 27:55
Hopkins, W. S. 24:79
Hopkins, William 12:62; 15:68, 329; 25:299; 27:62
Hopkins, William A. 26:164
Hopkins, William G. 16:38
Hopkins, William J. 22:145
Hopkins, William M. 19:77
Hopkins, William S. 19:170
Hopkinson, G. 19:228
Hopkinson, William R. 12:49
Hopkirk, Robert 21:71
Hopler, Daniel 10:59; 20:275
Hopling, J. B. 16:196
Hoplinger, Andrew 22:199
Hopner, Nelson 18:207
Hopp, Christian 16:200
Hoppe, H. 1:135
Hoppe, Walt 17:354
Hoppell, J. 12:80
Hoppenhoff, --- 13:28
Hoppens, Isaac 8:87
Hopper, Abraham W. 22:83
Hopper, Albert 4:32
Hopper, B. 1:136
Hopper, Charles 7:125
Hopper, D. W. 9:23
Hopper, Edward 16:295
Hopper, Edward M. 7:68
Hopper, Edwin 7:16
Hopper, Henry 9:114
Hopper, Henry A. 12:122
Hopper, J. 17:231
Hopper, J. W. 9:145
Hopper, Jackson C. 27:62
Hopper, James 18:330
Hopper, James B. 22:501
Hopper, Jesse N. 22:502

Hopper, John 17:260
Hopper, John D. 10:96
Hopper, Joseph 12:62
Hopper, M. 17:102
Hopper, Moses 25:187
Hopper, Solomon 22:501
Hopper, Thomas 10:28;
    19:302
Hopper, Thomas W. 27:61
Hopper, W. 25:40
Hopper, William H. 17:95
Hoppey, G. 3:99
Hoppin, James 8:114
Hopping, J. S. 16:152
Hopping, John A. 21:72
Hopping, Robert W.
    15:166
Hoppingartner, C. 1:41
Hoppins, D. M. 17:155
Hoppins, S. C. 17:155
Hopple, F. 9:145
Hopple, J. 27:57
Hoppock, A. 3:99
Hoppock, G. 3:99
Hopps, David 12:95
Hopps, George 10:155;
    19:170
Hopps, James 17:35
Hopps, Levi 7:63
Hopron, Franis 18:241
Hops, Isaac H. 1:40
Hopson, Addison E. 24:51
Hopson, Allen 1:41
Hopson, Robert 22:304
Hopson, Thomas 3:99
Hopson, William 22:255
Hopwood, G. 14:13;
    16:268
Hopwood, John 17:107;
    22:481
Hopwood, Thomas J. 20:9
Hopwood, William C.
    22:112
Horahan, Charles 4:32
Horan, Francis 14:26
Horan, H. 22:304
Horan, James 15:314;
    19:77
Horan, John 7:58, 98
Horan, L. 19:254
Horan, Lawrence 9:180
Horan, Michael 22:255
Horan, Michael B. 12:71
Horan, P. 16:38
Horan, Peter 11:33
Horan, T. 1:141; 19:254
Horan, Thomas 17:392
Horan, Timothy 9:180
Horan, William 22:234
Horant, E. A. 3:99
Horber, R. F. 24:51

Horborn, Thomas 11:408
Horbus, Adam 17:177
Horcher, D. R. 20:275
Hord, J. G. 9:23
Hord, Jarmon 22:304
Hord, William 8:106
Hord, William S. 23:150
Hord, Willis 20:183
Hordam, Charles 9:240
Horder, David 14:265
Horder, Fred 18:241
Hordey, Henry 21:347
Hordidge, George W. 9:83
Hordin, William 7:125
Hording, John 5:40
Hordling, B. T. 16:38
Hordson, F. B. 17:281
Hore, J. 25:187
Hore, R. 3:99
Hore, William 20:9
Horen, H. 9:53
Horex, William 1:43
Horfard, James 1:38
Horff, William 14:181
Horgan, Michael W.
    18:421
Horger, G. 25:187
Horgerab, --- 22:161
Horgin, --- 11:93
Horgue, S. B. 17:281
Horick, Joseph 17:430;
    24:214
Horidor, Frederick 26:35
Horisbergen, Peter 22:161
Horland, John 20:275
Horle, Augustus 13:28
Horman, Alfred 7:125
Horman, Gilbert 1:39
Horman, Maurice 7:98
Hormell, H. C. 16:268
Hormer, Charles 24:178
Hormich, John 14:73
Hormick, C. 3:99
Hormick, Thomas U.
    24:21
Horn, Alexander S.
    11:241
Horn, Anderson 20:3
Horn, Augustus 4:32
Horn, B. E. 10:186;
    18:175
Horn, B. F. 18:140
Horn, Caleb 13:28; 16:38
Horn, Charles 20:107;
    24:196
Horn, Charles L. 13:28
Horn, Conrad 20:125
Horn, D. A. 22:481
Horn, Daniel 23:150
Horn, E. H. 22:199
Horn, Eli 22:36

Horn, F. 3:99
Horn, G. 12:122; 14:26;
    15:363
Horn, George 13:111
Horn, H. C. 23:34
Horn, Harmon 18:175
Horn, Harris 20:186
Horn, Harrison 10:179
Horn, Henry 8:20
Horn, Ira B. 27:55
Horn, J. A. 16:38
Horn, J. T. 16:268
Horn, J. W. 21:54, 188
Horn, Jacob 17:419;
    24:158
Horn, James M. 14:181
Horn, James W. 8:20;
    26:165
Horn, Jefferson 10:59;
    20:275
Horn, John 9:53; 10:59;
    14:333; 15:342;
    20:275; 23:305
Horn, John L. 1:40
Horn, Joseph 23:150
Horn, Joseph B. 17:53
Horn, L. B. 22:199
Horn, Lewis 19:338
Horn, Louis 8:120
Horn, M. 14:299; 17:479
Horn, Martin 16:200;
    20:275
Horn, Michael 9:16
Horn, Samuel 27:145
Horn, Sterling R. 22:255
Horn, Thomas 18:31;
    23:313
Horn, William 14:181,
    257; 20:46
Horn, William H. 23:96
Horn, William W. 11:204
Hornaday, Clark 12:25
Hornback, J. 3:99
Hornback, John 22:405
Hornback, S. 27:55
Hornbaker, J. W. 19:77
Hornbard, John 17:496
Hornbeck, James 8:87
Hornbeck, James N.
    20:189
Hornbeck, John O. 22:481
Hornbeck, Noah 11:242
Hornbeck, S. 9:145
Hornberge, W. 9:53
Hornberger, Charles 2:12
Hornburren, James 14:73
Hornby, R. 26:33
Horne, A. 9:66
Horne, Gustavus 16:296
Horne, Henry 11:335
Horne, Jesse B. 10:119

Horne, John E. 10:119; 20:276
Horne, Joseph 21:347
Horne, Samuel W. 18:140
Horne, W. 1:141
Horne, William 21:347
Horner, Benjamin 10:119; 20:276
Horner, C. 12:82; 16:296
Horner, C. H. 7:30
Horner, Charles 23:69
Horner, D. 1:136; 3:99
Horner, F. 1:137; 18:51; 24:79
Horner, G. 1:137
Horner, George 20:97
Horner, George W. 6:10
Horner, H. 15:204
Horner, Henry 18:140; 22:482
Horner, J. 1:43, 136; 3:100; 19:254
Horner, J. A. 13:91
Horner, J. K. 13:125
Horner, J. Ross 16:96
Horner, Jacob 3:100
Horner, James 13:28
Horner, John 12:62
Horner, M. 25:187
Horner, Martin 5:40
Horner, Orange 22:83
Horner, P. W. 1:43
Horner, Robert M. 11:15
Horner, Robert S. 9:12
Horner, Samuel 21:347
Horner, Thomas A. 22:502
Horner, Thomas G. 17:166
Horner, Walter W. 12:53
Horner, William 13:111; 16:200; 25:187
Horner, William H. 23:180
Horner, William P. 21:226
Hornett, William 8:50
Horney, Francis M. 21:347
Horney, James 13:91; 18:218
Horney, L. P. 27:65
Horney, William A. 1:39
Horngan, --- 2:12
Hornipson, S. 21:347
Hornish, Jacob 14:181
Horns, Daniel 4:32
Hornset, W. 26:164
Hornton, J. J. 24:111
Horny, Julius 10:148
Horoser, Charles 7:58
Horr, Marcella 10:91

Horrace, C. H. 14:73
Horral, George W. 22:83
Horran, M. 21:29
Horrell, John H. 7:30
Horrer, J. 3:100
Horriford, M. 9:180
Horrigan, M. 27:57
Horrigan, Timothy 21:347
Horrigon, Thomas 19:329
Horris, Charles 21:274
Horry, G. W. 18:111
Horry, Oscar 20:276
Horryhill, Perry 10:59
Horsefall, G. 15:37
Horsefield, Charles 7:58
Horseley, Pollard 10:119
Horsely, Samuel W. 26:166
Horseman, Frank 9:23
Horseman, Goldson 26:124
Horseman, Henry 26:124
Horseman, William 3:100
Horsen, John 7:16
Horseright, George 10:59
Horsey, Henry 21:347
Horsey, Moses 19:46
Horsey, S. B. 23:34
Horsfall, Con 12:71
Horsfield, William 7:98
Horsford, James H. 19:170
Horsh, M. 15:285
Horsh, Michael 19:77
Horsha, E. 21:188
Horshaw, Charles 22:304
Horshaw, David 22:304
Horsheimer, John 19:271
Horsington, E. 12:161
Horsington, F. 1:39
Horsley, George H. 23:34
Horsley, Henry J. 22:280
Horsley, James A. 23:34
Horsley, Rolland 20:276
Horsman, Frank 18:309; 26:100
Horsman, James 7:68
Horst, Arland 7:125
Horst, Charles 21:101
Horst, Martin 14:257
Horstrope, S. H. 9:23
Hort, A. M. 14:336
Horten, John 21:274
Horter, Sandy 6:12
Horthan, John 11:32
Hortil, Frederick 1:40
Hortin, Sylvester 17:21
Hortin, W. C. 3:100
Hortin, William P. 9:23
Horting, P. 23:69
Hortman, I. 26:34

Hortman, Isaac 9:35
Horton, --- 21:347
Horton, A. 1:43, 136; 21:148
Horton, Adrian 21:206
Horton, Augustus 24:21
Horton, Barney R. 24:51
Horton, Bras 17:177
Horton, C. D. 10:119; 20:276
Horton, Charles 11:126; 16:147, 200; 19:19
Horton, David 10:59; 20:276; 22:199
Horton, E. 21:347
Horton, E. S. 7:30
Horton, Elisha 22:255
Horton, Evert 24:175
Horton, F. A. 26:163
Horton, F. H. 3:100
Horton, Frederick A. 4:66
Horton, Garland 11:204
Horton, George W. 9:83; 21:347; 24:40; 26:33
Horton, H. B. 25:187
Horton, Henderson 8:39; 26:165
Horton, Henry 5:19
Horton, Hiram 19:77
Horton, Ira C. 9:180; 19:254
Horton, Isaac J. 22:502
Horton, Isaiah 23:128
Horton, J. 1:135; 14:73; 21:149; 25:187
Horton, J. L. 21:29
Horton, J. T. 13:128
Horton, J. W. 8:50
Horton, Jacob W. 21:72
Horton, James 23:69
Horton, James A. 8:19; 26:165
Horton, James C. 11:150
Horton, James H. 12:25; 15:87; 21:85
Horton, John 9:240; 21:347; 24:101
Horton, John E. 14:181
Horton, John S. 2:12
Horton, Joseph C. 11:107
Horton, Joseph W. 10:119; 20:276
Horton, L. 19:254
Horton, Leonard 9:180
Horton, Lewis 1:38
Horton, Michael 9:180
Horton, P. 19:228
Horton, R. T. 8:50
Horton, Reuben 22:497
Horton, Reuben F. 24:40
Horton, Robert 12:25

Horton, S. 3:100; 12:8
Horton, Samuel 9:208;
    22:481
Horton, Silas 12:55
Horton, Simon 27:145
Horton, T. 19:238
Horton, T. D. 25:40
Horton, T. N. 8:72
Horton, Thaddeus 20:113
Horton, Thomas 9:180;
    22:11; 26:166
Horton, V. T. 18:51
Horton, W. 14:288
Horton, W. C. 9:83
Horton, W. P. 19:228
Horton, William 8:19;
    9:180; 18:140;
    19:278; 26:165
Horton, William D.
    14:181
Horton, William H. 8:87
Horton, William J. 17:91
Horton, William P.
    18:309; 22:145;
    26:100
Horton, William S. 7:30
Hortong, Christian 26:125
Hortsfield, James 14:73
Hortsman, H. 1:137
Hortstot, J. 23:263
Hortvet, Martin 10:119
Hortvet, Morton 20:276
Horvall, Paul 18:31
Hory, Cardina 21:347
Hory, Hartwell 4:32
Hory, J. 27:57
Hosack, Harrison 11:149
Hosack, John M. 16:279
Hosclaw, William 11:262
Hose, Caper 17:178
Hosenberger, William
    8:50
Hosentercer, John P.
    15:107
Hosford, David 9:83
Hosford, E. 18:51
Hosford, Eli R. 15:173
Hosford, Nathan F. 1:38
Hosford, W. F. 3:100
Hosier, A. W. 11:63
Hosier, Francis 7:98
Hosier, W. 15:204
Hosington, A. 14:13
Hosington, Wallace W.
    22:145
Hoskin, Charles 10:162
Hoskin, Monroe 21:139
Hoskins, Charles 19:170
Hoskins, Enos 22:427
Hoskins, Frank A. 4:32
Hoskins, H. 9:221; 18:369

Hoskins, John 23:150
Hoskins, John D. 12:170
Hoskins, John S. 4:32
Hoskins, Joseph 18:277
Hoskins, Miles 23:191
Hoskins, Thomas 15:4
Hoskins, W. 20:276
Hoskinson, A. 11:241
Hosley, F. C. 26:33
Hosley, T. C. 9:83
Hoslings, W. W. 17:65
Hosma, H. H. 12:25
Hosma, Lumas 15:323;
    19:77
Hosman, Peter 21:347
Hosmer, --- 11:241, 280
Hosmer, Daniel 11:107
Hosmer, Edward Jarvis
    19:238
Hosmer, Henry 21:347
Hosmer, N. D. 19:238
Hosmer, Newell A. 13:28
Hosmer, W. D. 9:180
Hosmick, E. 26:33
Hosned, Charles 14:73
Hosplehann, Henry
    23:150
Hoss, John M. 23:99
Hoss, Marcus 18:207
Hoss, William H. 22:501
Hossack, D. 12:25
Hossbaugh, J. A. 1:141
Hossett, J. B. 9:145
Hossheimer, John 9:181
Hossington, Benjamin F.
    22:36
Hossler, C. H. 21:195,
    211
Hossler, Charles H.
    21:226
Hosson, John 12:154
Hossor, W. C. W. 26:211
Hosstuttler, Jacob 23:150
Hosteller, John J. 12:71
Hosteter, Benjamin E.
    22:36
Hostetler, Emanuel 21:72
Hostetter, Alvin O. 21:54
Hostetter, Ben. F. 24:178
Hostetter, Benjamin F.
    17:435
Hostetter, D. 12:172
Hostetter, Jacob 8:87
Hostetter, John J. 15:68
Hostetter, Peter 22:112
Hostetter, Samuel 21:29
Hostettler, E. 24:79
Hostilter, John E. 8:106
Hostler, Samuel 13:28
Hoston, Elvert 17:449
Hostover, Charles 13:28

Hostutter, --- 15:87
Hotaling, Guy T. 13:28
Hotaling, Jacob H.
    10:119; 20:276
Hotchkins, Julius 9:23
Hotchkiss, A. 3:100
Hotchkiss, A. S. 15:107
Hotchkiss, C. E. 12:154
Hotchkiss, Charles 21:347
Hotchkiss, D. 1:41
Hotchkiss, E. A. 14:73
Hotchkiss, F. R. 14:181
Hotchkiss, George 21:117;
    24:51
Hotchkiss, H. 1:135;
    15:342; 16:371
Hotchkiss, H. W. 25:187
Hotchkiss, Henry C. 19:19
Hotchkiss, J. M. 15:68
Hotchkiss, Jesse 18:218
Hotchkiss, Normal 6:31
Hotchkiss, O. 1:42
Hotchkiss, O. W. 16:96
Hotchkiss, Rollin 20:57
Hotchkiss, Seth W. 5:19
Hotehode, A. 12:164
Hotell, John 17:91
Hotellin, Henry 9:242
Hotelling, Tobias 23:107
Hoten, George W. 13:135;
    19:346
Hothman, Augustus 4:32
Hotin, Austin 11:32
Hoting, George 21:166
Hotland, John I. 24:99
Hotnerr, Joseph 18:339
Hotock, William 16:200
Hottel, Enos 21:72
Hottel, James E. 10:119;
    20:276
Hotten, Thomas 15:204
Hottenrott, Edward
    11:126
Hottenstein, G. H. 3:100
Hottenstein, H. 3:100
Hottes, D. 14:73
Hottle, James D. 17:81
Hottmoyer, J. 19:77
Hotts, Fred 11:401
Hotts, Hiram 22:36
Hotzel, J. 14:288
Houbough, J. 3:100
Houch, Emanuel 26:35
Houchin, Anderson
    23:243
Houchin, William 22:405
Houck, --- 18:369
Houck, A. 16:133
Houck, Adam L. 10:119
Houck, B. W. 20:133
Houck, Emanuel 18:241

Houck, Francis M. 21:226
Houck, James E. 7:98
Houck, Joseph 3:100
Houck, W. 17:310
Houck, Warren 21:72
Houck, William 1:44;
    24:159
Houd, J. 15:107
Houder, Henry K. 23:34
Houder, Martin 14:332
Houdly, J. 14:257
Houer, Benedict 7:9
Houff, P. 14:73
Houg, John 4:32
Houga, Charles 23:263
Hough, A. 27:61
Hough, A. R. 25:187
Hough, Alex 11:204
Hough, Alfred 11:63
Hough, Allen R. 5:19
Hough, Broughton 16:96
Hough, Charles 10:59;
    20:276
Hough, D. F. 3:100
Hough, H. B. 17:404
Hough, James 11:107
Hough, John G. 20:181
Hough, John N. 16:38
Hough, John T. 8:50
Hough, John W. 13:29
Hough, Joseph 19:267
Hough, Joseph M. 17:53
Hough, Levi 16:371
Hough, M. T. 22:337
Hough, Nathaniel 22:280
Hough, Nehemiah 24:51
Hough, Oliver 22:234
Hough, Silas 9:208
Hough, Thomas 11:327
Hough, W. B. 25:187
Hough, William 21:139
Houghdaling, A. 12:71;
    15:37
Houghes, J. 1:42
Houghland, Charles
    26:166
Houghland, J. 24:40
Houghland, Samuel
    16:279
Houghlar, A. C. 3:100
Houghlin, John 14:315
Houghs, Luke 8:87
Hought, F. S. 18:51
Houghtailing, J. W. 4:32
Houghtailing, M. S. 1:41
Houghtailing, P. 1:140
Houghtalinger, M. 3:100
Houghtayler, H. 21:29
Houghtelin, James 22:234
Houghteling, C. 3:100
Houghting, E. 9:145

Houghting, Fenimore
    27:60
Houghtling, J. 16:200
Houghtling, John 13:111
Houghton, A. 23:34
Houghton, Alonzo 14:315
Houghton, Asa W. 22:145
Houghton, Danforth 9:103
Houghton, George 19:19
Houghton, George W.
    23:34
Houghton, H. W. 22:481
Houghton, J. 13:91
Houghton, J. G. 11:332
Houghton, James 11:443;
    20:176; 22:304
Houghton, Jerome M.
    22:145
Houghton, John 5:19
Houghton, Joseph 27:62
Houghton, Josiah 25:39
Houghton, Nelson 12:25
Houghton, S. 16:200;
    25:188
Houghton, Sandy 5:40
Houghton, W. B. 9:145;
    27:57
Hougland, C. C. 2:12;
    25:38
Hougland, J. N. 23:35
Houk, Daniel M. 9:83
Houk, David 22:405
Houk, John 11:64, 381
Houk, W. 20:155
Houk, William D. 17:443
Houlihan, James 9:16
Houlihan, John 7:50;
    11:149; 15:5
Houlihan, M. 1:38
Houlihan, William 11:242
Houltshouser, W. H.
    20:140
Houmchens, John 14:73
Houpt, Henry 18:218
Hour, James 3:100
Houragan, J. 1:44
Hourath, H. 8:87
Hourd, William A. J.
    22:255
Houregin, Patrick 20:276
Houri, J. 1:140
House, --- 15:152
House, Abraham 21:347
House, Adam 27:61
House, Alonzo 12:25;
    27:60
House, August 9:221
House, Clark 9:132; 27:59
House, Daniel 8:87
House, E. 25:188
House, E. D. 1:140

House, G. B. 11:304
House, George 26:35
House, I. 9:145
House, Israel W. 13:28
House, J. 27:55
House, J. E. 12:71
House, J. G. 10:59;
    20:276
House, J. H. 12:162
House, Jacob 24:40
House, John 17:36;
    22:304
House, John L. 22:463
House, John W. 22:123;
    23:89
House, Lewis 8:72;
    22:337
House, M. 8:114
House, Marcus 8:87
House, Mead 9:43
House, N. S. 14:181
House, Nathan 20:137
House, P. H. 11:33
House, Philemon 23:191
House, Robert 21:274
House, Samuel 14:315;
    20:125
House, Thomas L. 10:119;
    20:276
House, Wesley M. 22:463
House, William 14:181,
    282; 15:68, 204
House, William H. 8:87
House, William I. 14:269
House, William W. 9:181
Housedraper, James
    18:140
Housefield, Henry 17:419
Householder, B. W. 4:32
Householder, F. W. 14:73
Houseknecht, Christ
    15:107
Housel, Joseph 2:12;
    25:38
Housel, S. 1:138
Housel, W. 1:139
Housell, W. H. 19:170
Housell, Warner 21:347
Housely, Milton 9:208
Housem, Peter B. 10:25
Houseman, David 22:199
Houseman, George 14:73
Houseman, James 10:119
Houseman, W. G. 20:102
Housen, Samuel 24:40
Houser, Adam 4:32
Houser, Addison 22:199
Houser, Alexander 22:255
Houser, Alfred 12:25
Houser, Benjamin 4:32
Houser, Charles 1:40

Houser, D. 1:140
Houser, Daniel A. 10:25
Houser, David 11:64
Houser, Ferdinand 19:329
Houser, Frederick 14:181
Houser, George 11:327;
23:285
Houser, George W.
24:178
Houser, Homer 26:124
Houser, J. 1:142
Houser, Jacob 17:297;
21:72; 22:234
Houser, James H. 18:140
Houser, Jeremiah 22:199
Houser, John 18:139;
20:113
Houser, John B. 5:19
Houser, Jonathan 22:255
Houser, Maplon 8:64
Houser, O. 17:336
Houser, Simon 17:91
Houser, Thomas 17:166
Houser, W. R. 3:100
Houser, Walter M. 11:115
Houser, William 25:188
Housewick, Jacob 17:81
Houseworth, Doren C.
22:482
Houseworth, Euclia M.
17:271
Houseworth, Scott 15:204
Housewright, W. 8:72
Housewright, Wesley
26:166
Housh, Albert 14:181
Houshion, Seward 13:65
Housier, Adam 7:30
Housman, Jacob 1:38
Housman, James 20:276
Housman, N. 24:21
Houst, August 18:369
Houstin, H. 25:188
Housting, J. Chr. 24:111
Houston, A. M. 1:43
Houston, A. W. 27:59
Houston, Aaron W. 9:120
Houston, Alexander 4:66
Houston, Benjamin C.
10:119; 20:276
Houston, C. F. 7:75;
25:299
Houston, Charles 21:274
Houston, D. 3:100
Houston, D. S. 15:353
Houston, Daniel C.
22:427
Houston, Dock 7:125
Houston, E. 1:39; 3:100;
19:254; 22:502
Houston, Edward 9:181

Houston, G. W. 11:152
Houston, H. 3:100
Houston, Henry 5:19
Houston, Henry F. 22:405
Houston, J. 15:294;
16:200
Houston, J. A. 18:241;
26:34
Houston, J. C. 21:347
Houston, J. W. 20:276
Houston, Jacob 10:59;
20:276
Houston, James 21:274;
22:255; 24:89
Houston, James H. 22:37
Houston, Joel J. 21:347
Houston, John 11:93;
17:191; 22:452;
23:150
Houston, John S. 22:145
Houston, John W. 22:37
Houston, Lafayette 12:154
Houston, R. R. 24:21
Houston, Richard 23:150
Houston, Robert N. 8:20;
18:140
Houston, Samuel 8:39;
26:164
Houston, Samuel W.
22:405
Houston, W. E. 3:100
Houston, W. H. 19:286
Houston, W. S. 20:276
Houston, Wesley J. 4:32
Houston, William H.
17:133; 24:195
Houston, William S.
10:59
Hout, Adam L. 20:276
Houtailing, E. 27:57
Houts, Edward 19:77
Houts, Philip 23:150
Houts, William H. 10:59;
20:276
Houtz, J. 15:347
Houtz, John H. 26:101
Houver, George 17:35
Houze, James 21:226
Houzell, Cyrus 8:20
Houzer, James L. 26:145
Hovan, Michael B. 15:37
Hoveland, John 10:59
Hovender, William 9:83
Hover, George 5:51
Hover, George M. 22:481
Hover, Henry 18:140
Hover, J. 11:31
Hover, S. 17:291
Hover, William 24:89
Hoverle, B. 1:103
Hoverlin, B. 3:100

Hoverman, A. 9:181;
19:282
Hoverty, H. I. 1:39
Hovey, C. 25:41
Hovey, E. F. 20:174
Hovey, Edwin 23:35
Hovey, G. 16:268
Hovey, G. C. 13:111
Hovey, H. 1:136
Hovey, Josiah 1:42
Hovey, Pascal M. 23:191
Hovey, S. H. 15:22
Hovlerson, O. K. 18:51
Hovring, Charles 27:59
Hovy, Stephen 25:41
How, Daniel 12:154
How, Daniel B. 20:9
How, E. W. 23:313
How, Eli 22:405
How, Hiram T. 24:51
How, J. G. 18:309; 26:100
How, Joseph 18:111
How, Julius 5:40
How, M. 17:133; 24:196
How, Marcella 20:276
How, W. A. 15:326
How, Winfield 1:41
Howaly, J. 14:73
Howan, Nathan 18:369
Howard, --- 3:100; 7:65;
8:125; 10:186;
18:175; 19:170;
20:276; 27:145
Howard, A. 3:100; 8:50;
11:152; 15:342;
17:178
Howard, A. C. 7:30;
14:278; 23:122
Howard, A. E. 14:181
Howard, A. H. 16:371
Howard, A. J. 21:347
Howard, Abbot 18:85
Howard, Abbott 6:17
Howard, Albert 12:8;
21:139
Howard, Almond 16:371
Howard, Alonzo 17:440;
24:152
Howard, Alvin 22:426
Howard, Andrew 10:91;
20:276; 21:29
Howard, Andrew W.
22:123
Howard, Arthur 8:77
Howard, Asa F. 19:346
Howard, Asa W. 13:135
Howard, B. 17:178; 19:19
Howard, Ben 19:46
Howard, C. 3:100; 9:145;
27:57
Howard, C. B. 19:77

Howard, C. H. 15:324; 17:447; 24:170
Howard, C. M. 18:85
Howard, C. P. 13:125
Howard, Charles 9:132; 10:18; 16:200; 19:233; 21:347; 22:305; 27:54
Howard, Charles A. 22:145
Howard, Charles C. 21:226
Howard, Charles P. 12:49
Howard, Charles W. 27:55
Howard, Chester 21:347
Howard, Clay 22:304
Howard, Clayton 10:146
Howard, Cyrus A. 22:452
Howard, D. 11:33; 14:73
Howard, D. C. 9:53
Howard, D. H. 3:100
Howard, D. M. 3:100
Howard, Daniel S. 25:188
Howard, David 16:279; 21:54; 22:37
Howard, David H. 10:119; 15:37; 20:276
Howard, David P. 8:106
Howard, Dennis 22:513
Howard, E. F. 21:347
Howard, E. N. 1:135
Howard, E. V. 12:154
Howard, Edmund W. 16:147
Howard, Egbert B. 21:139
Howard, Elias 17:95
Howard, Elijah 17:21, 65
Howard, Emanna 18:31
Howard, Enos J. 23:122
Howard, Erastus 21:347
Howard, Ezekiel 22:255
Howard, Ezra 22:405
Howard, F. 17:432; 18:190; 27:54
Howard, F. A. 12:162
Howard, F. B. 3:100
Howard, F. D. 1:136
Howard, F. H. 1:139
Howard, F. M. 26:211
Howard, F. S. 3:100; 19:296
Howard, F. W. 16:96
Howard, Francis 24:152
Howard, Francis R. 24:51
Howard, G. 19:321
Howard, G. S. 3:100
Howard, G. W. 1:43
Howard, George 10:59; 11:126; 14:241; 15:56; 16:120;

Howard, George 18:111, 190; 20:276; 23:309; 26:211; 27:65
Howard, George A. 9:181
Howard, George C. 12:26
Howard, George D. 17:357
Howard, George H. 12:171
Howard, George P. 10:192
Howard, George W. 13:29; 21:139
Howard, Giles 11:335
Howard, Gregory 14:181
Howard, H. 14:181; 21:347
Howard, H. F. 1:138
Howard, H. H. 11:219
Howard, H. L. 22:145
Howard, H. M. 8:50
Howard, Harman B. 11:149
Howard, Harry 24:196
Howard, Henry 8:117; 11:62; 13:29; 14:299; 17:476; 21:211; 22:304; 27:64
Howard, Henry M. 21:72
Howard, Hiram B. 16:85
Howard, Homer D. 11:332
Howard, Hugh 21:72
Howard, I. 9:154
Howard, Iceum 21:347
Howard, Isaac 16:200; 19:46
Howard, J. 1:98, 139, 140; 3:100; 11:304; 16:200; 27:57
Howard, J. A. 13:91; 21:348
Howard, J. C. 16:38
Howard, J. E. 16:268
Howard, J. F. 1:41; 14:133; 21:348
Howard, J. H. 9:181; 19:233; 23:35
Howard, J. J. 21:348
Howard, J. W. 10:96; 11:33
Howard, Jackson P. 10:18
Howard, James 3:100; 11:126; 12:8; 17:95; 18:103, 396
Howard, James E. 21:348
Howard, James H. 10:8; 11:327
Howard, James W. 22:83
Howard, Jeff 22:304

Howard, John 7:125; 9:23; 10:162; 12:26; 14:73; 15:107, 326; 18:67, 309; 19:77, 170; 20:102; 21:130; 22:427; 26:101
Howard, John B. 9:103; 11:242; 24:51
Howard, John H. 9:23; 18:309; 26:101
Howard, John L. 11:151
Howard, John M. 16:200
Howard, John S. 10:28; 19:302
Howard, John W. 5:40
Howard, Joseph 18:67; 25:188
Howard, K. 1:42
Howard, L. 7:30
Howard, Laurin 13:111
Howard, Levi 12:26
Howard, Lewis 17:133, 403; 24:194
Howard, Lorenzo 7:98
Howard, Luven A. 18:140
Howard, M. F. 11:93
Howard, Mathew 19:170
Howard, Matthew 10:162
Howard, Melville 27:54
Howard, Meron 16:38
Howard, Mic 9:97
Howard, Michael M. 17:248
Howard, Miram 21:348
Howard, Morehead 23:180
Howard, Myron 13:29
Howard, N. C. 10:119; 20:276
Howard, Nathan 10:59; 20:276
Howard, Newton 22:405
Howard, Newton P. 23:307
Howard, Nicholas 14:181; 25:269
Howard, Noah S. 9:53
Howard, O. 12:122; 15:125
Howard, Olean 9:23; 26:101
Howard, Oramel 9:8
Howard, Orange F. 11:106
Howard, Orlean 18:309
Howard, P. 16:200
Howard, P. J. 10:119; 20:276
Howard, Patrick 13:111
Howard, Patrick J. 14:315
Howard, Perry 18:207

Howard, Philip 16:82
Howard, Purdy 8:114
Howard, R. 11:327;
    17:434
Howard, R. W. 11:423
Howard, Robert 24:170
Howard, S. 25:188
Howard, S. R. 13:91;
    14:13
Howard, Samuel 5:19;
    7:125; 8:39; 21:348;
    22:451; 26:163
Howard, Scott 12:166
Howard, Simeon 25:188
Howard, Simpson 8:87
Howard, Squire 22:426
Howard, Stephen 9:208;
    21:274
Howard, T. 1:136; 20:277
Howard, T. S. 1:140
Howard, Thomas 21:274;
    24:111
Howard, Thomas S.
    24:166
Howard, V. J. 22:199
Howard, W. 13:91; 18:51
Howard, W. F. 13:91;
    14:13
Howard, W. H. 18:293;
    19:46; 26:102
Howard, W. J. 1:139
Howard, W. M. 11:34;
    15:268
Howard, W. O. 7:98
Howard, Watson 23:69
Howard, Wells A. 19:19
Howard, William 3:100;
    5:40; 6:35; 7:30;
    8:77; 10:150;
    11:151; 12:49;
    13:29; 17:495;
    21:226, 274; 22:304;
    23:69
Howard, William G.
    22:451
Howard, William H. 9:35
Howard, William H. H.
    22:83
Howard, William J.
    21:201
Howard, William L. 10:18
Howard, William M.
    11:15
Howard, Wilson 7:71
Howarth, A. 15:204
Howarth, A. H. 25:43
Howarth, F. 12:82
Howarth, George 11:407
Howarth, George W.
    18:309; 26:102
Howarth, J. H. 25:321

Howath, F. 16:296
Howden, Joe 24:196
Howe, --- 15:204; 16:200
Howe, A. E. 17:155
Howe, A. R. 3:100
Howe, Alonzo F. 9:35
Howe, Asa 8:20; 18:140
Howe, B. B. 21:92
Howe, C. H. 3:100
Howe, C. K. 1:39
Howe, C. W. 1:42
Howe, Calvin 16:85
Howe, Chauncey P.
    10:119; 20:277
Howe, Cyrus B. 20:193
Howe, D. 1:135; 9:154;
    27:57
Howe, D. G. 13:65
Howe, Daniel 16:279
Howe, Dorcas 10:119;
    20:277
Howe, E. 16:85
Howe, E. H. 3:100
Howe, E. T. 11:65
Howe, Edmund 20:113
Howe, Edward 20:277
Howe, F. W. 22:145
Howe, Francis 1:43
Howe, Frank 16:38
Howe, G. 3:100; 27:144
Howe, G. E. 11:33
Howe, G. F. 1:139
Howe, G. G. 1:140
Howe, George A. 22:463
Howe, George H. 10:162;
    19:170
Howe, George W. 22:199;
    23:191
Howe, H. 14:73; 15:342;
    16:371
Howe, H. A. 1:138
Howe, H. M. 10:59;
    20:277
Howe, Henry 4:66; 12:25
Howe, Henry H. 13:29
Howe, Horace 17:397
Howe, Ira B. 9:145
Howe, J. 3:100; 25:188
Howe, J. B. 12:82; 16:296
Howe, J. F. 17:152
Howe, J. J. 26:163
Howe, J. W. 3:100
Howe, Jacob 11:242
Howe, James C. 24:111
Howe, John 10:119;
    15:25, 259; 22:199
Howe, John S. 12:26
Howe, Joseph B. 25:42
Howe, Joseph M. 2:12;
    25:39
Howe, L. A. 14:181

Howe, Leroy F. 17:429
Howe, Leroy T. 24:185
Howe, Lester B. 5:19
Howe, Lewis 22:234
Howe, Madison 11:205
Howe, Martin 10:91
Howe, N. 19:77
Howe, Nathan L. 18:51
Howe, Nicolas 15:37
Howe, Ora 15:173
Howe, Orrin W. 13:29
Howe, Ozra B. 16:200
Howe, P. 9:53
Howe, Patrick 12:26
Howe, Philip 11:205
Howe, R. 16:140
Howe, Richard T. 23:69
Howe, S. 3:100
Howe, S. W. 3:100;
    14:73; 15:342;
    16:371
Howe, T. B. 25:39
Howe, Thomas 22:337
Howe, Thomas R. 9:120
Howe, Titus F. 22:337
Howe, W. A. 19:77
Howe, W. B. 19:77
Howe, W. E. 15:292
Howe, W. H. 10:145;
    19:170
Howe, William 9:103
Howe, William F. 18:339
Howe, William G. 22:37
Howe, William H. 7:50
Howe, William Nelson
    12:25
Howe, Zachari 11:31
Howeker, Thomas 10:152
Howel, E. J. 14:73
Howel, G. H. 12:163
Howel, John 12:147;
    18:396
Howel, N. W. 14:73
Howel, Richard 26:165
Howeler, Daniel 8:50
Howell, --- 15:37
Howell, A. 3:100
Howell, A. J. 18:85
Howell, Adolphus 17:36
Howell, Albert J. 6:10
Howell, Alex 27:54
Howell, Alexander 9:120
Howell, Alfred E. 22:146
Howell, Allen 9:70
Howell, B. 15:342
Howell, C. R. 3:100
Howell, Charles G. 7:98
Howell, David 8:20;
    18:140
Howell, David M. 14:334
Howell, E. 20:178

Howell, E. P. 8:106
Howell, Edgar 22:481
Howell, Evans P. 17:236
Howell, F. 15:204; 27:57
Howell, Freeman 17:81
Howell, George 10:59;
    17:308; 19:170;
    20:277; 22:37
Howell, George M.
    17:263
Howell, Gilmore 17:321
Howell, H. 14:73
Howell, H. G. 1:43
Howell, Harloter 21:255
Howell, Harvey B. 16:38
Howell, Hedar 16:38
Howell, Henry 8:39;
    17:21; 20:9; 26:163,
    164
Howell, Isaac 9:97
Howell, Isaac M. 11:107
Howell, Isael H. 18:140
Howell, J. 1:44; 3:100
Howell, J. A. 1:94
Howell, J. B. 20:88
Howell, J. J. 8:64
Howell, J. W. 3:100;
    11:149, 152
Howell, James 11:84;
    12:71; 15:159;
    18:396; 26:163
Howell, James C. 25:272
Howell, James M. 8:20;
    18:140
Howell, Jesse H. 8:20
Howell, John 1:39; 8:114;
    17:21; 19:303
Howell, John E. 4:32
Howell, John J. 8:64
Howell, John T. 12:26
Howell, John W. 22:405,
    425
Howell, Joshua 25:44
Howell, L. H. 3:100
Howell, Lafayette 23:122
Howell, Lemuel 11:276
Howell, M. 22:199;
    23:150
Howell, M. C. 25:188
Howell, Milton 7:98
Howell, Morris 20:277
Howell, Moses 24:79
Howell, Richard 8:39
Howell, Robert 22:398
Howell, Samuel 16:200;
    22:482
Howell, Samuel K. 8:72
Howell, Stephen H. 20:17
Howell, T. 9:145
Howell, Thomas 22:37
Howell, V. 16:371

Howell, Virgil 25:39
Howell, W. 9:145; 14:73;
    27:57
Howell, W. H. 11:149;
    23:35
Howell, Wilburn 26:163
Howell, William 8:39;
    10:119; 11:187;
    13:29; 14:269;
    19:343; 20:277;
    25:188
Howell, William A.
    21:226
Howell, William B. 17:21
Howell, William C. 11:93
Howell, William W. 1:42
Howells, Rosser 25:41
Howeltt, J. 13:91
Hower, David 26:165
Hower, George 10:59;
    20:277
Hower, H. W. 10:186
Hower, John W. 22:83
Hower, Philip 21:348
Hower, Silas 17:273
Hower, William 7:98
Howerton, Braxton
    20:277
Howerton, Bruxton 10:59
Howerton, James 11:242
Howerton, John B. 22:452
Howery, A. 1:98
Howery, Jacob 10:59;
    20:277
Howes, Elisha 12:26
Howes, Henry 6:10
Howes, John 7:58; 8:20
Howes, Mead 26:124
Howes, S. 3:100
Howes, S. R. 1:137
Howes, Samuel 16:200
Howes, Wilson 17:178
Howett, James 14:181
Howewll, James 8:39
Howey, Lewis 21:348
Howher, Henry 11:205
Howie, John R. 21:139
Howington, John T. 10:59
Howington, Polk 24:159
Howith, Abednoza 12:26
Howith, Richard 9:43
Howitt, J. 15:56
Howitt, James 14:73
Howitt, William H.
    11:287
Howk, Benjamin R. 22:83
Howker, T. 18:51
Howkey, Thomas W. 7:98
Howland, A. 19:19
Howland, Benjamin
    22:337

Howland, Charles 22:337;
    27:62
Howland, E. 13:111
Howland, George 11:88;
    13:125
Howland, Henry C.
    23:122
Howland, Horace 1:38
Howland, I. 11:191
Howland, J. M. 23:150
Howland, L. R. 11:100
Howland, Marion 22:11
Howland, Nathan S. 9:35
Howland, O. M. 7:98;
    21:348
Howland, R. 9:154
Howland, Robert 9:154
Howland, William O.
    23:285
Howles, Hamel 9:23
Howlett, A. 13:91
Howlett, David 17:148
Howlett, James B. 9:83;
    26:32
Howlett, William 18:396
Howlett, William M.
    22:255
Howley, Daniel 16:38
Howley, Franklin L.
    15:204
Howley, Henry 19:238
Howley, Henry M. 13:29
Howley, John A. 11:305
Howley, John D. 9:181;
    19:274
Howley, M. 8:20; 18:140
Howley, Michael 19:19
Howley, Peter 18:309;
    26:102
Howley, Philp 24:111
Howley, W. 12:87
Howly, Peter 9:23
Howman, Daniel 17:395
Howmersley, I. 10:152
Howmessley, J. 18:51
Howorth, Joseph S. 1:41
Howrd, L. P. 1:44
Howrington, A. Polk
    17:443
Howry, John 18:309;
    26:101
Howse, John 20:277
Howser, Charles 19:19
Howser, Daniel 24:51
Howser, E. 23:150
Howser, George W.
    22:199
Howser, Gideon 21:195
Howser, Isaiah 25:275
Howser, Jacob 17:277
Howser, John 22:123

Howser, Melton 22:502
Howser, W. 13:91; 14:13
Howson, A. F. 3:100
Howstord, S. R. 24:101
Howth, Peter 9:236
Howzell, Cyrus 18:140
Howzen, William A.
  18:218
Hoxey, Garrett 10:18
Hoxice, Clarke 8:114
Hoxie, D. 27:54
Hoxie, H. 14:267
Hoxie, J. F. 1:44
Hoy, Edward 16:71
Hoy, Ephraim 9:120
Hoy, G. H. 14:181
Hoy, J. 3:100
Hoy, J. R. 17:218
Hoy, James 20:87
Hoy, John H. M. 10:28
Hoy, M. 18:67
Hoy, Ruphus 26:32
Hoye, D. 1:139
Hoye, I. 3:100
Hoye, J. 3:100
Hoye, Jacob 25:188
Hoye, Patrick 15:37
Hoyer, C. 16:200
Hoyer, George 13:112
Hoyer, William 1:40;
  17:21
Hoyes, Robert 18:309;
  26:101
Hoyle, Ben 18:175
Hoyle, James 4:32
Hoyle, Vincent 4:32
Hoys, J. 23:35
Hoysington, A. 1:138
Hoystrom, Charles P.
  26:32
Hoyt, A. D. 3:101
Hoyt, A. H. 8:50; 21:29
Hoyt, Albert J. 25:188
Hoyt, Albert T. 5:51
Hoyt, Alonzo 22:146
Hoyt, C. H. 19:77
Hoyt, Charles 9:110;
  21:243
Hoyt, Charles H. 7:30
Hoyt, Clinton 1:38
Hoyt, Dixie C. 10:162
Hoyt, E. S. 3:101
Hoyt, Eben S. 4:32
Hoyt, F. 14:262
Hoyt, F. M. 10:59; 20:277
Hoyt, F. S. 18:51
Hoyt, G. F. 25:188
Hoyt, G. P. 14:299;
  17:476
Hoyt, G. R. 27:64

Hoyt, George 7:98; 8:20;
  9:23; 16:200; 18:140,
  309; 26:100
Hoyt, George A. 19:19
Hoyt, George E. 11:33
Hoyt, George T. L. 23:191
Hoyt, George W. 9:103;
  18:339
Hoyt, H. 9:110; 16:200
Hoyt, H. H. 9:145; 27:56
Hoyt, H. J. 20:277
Hoyt, Henry 22:146
Hoyt, J. 1:136
Hoyt, J. L. 1:138
Hoyt, J. V. 23:122
Hoyt, James M. 10:96
Hoyt, Jesse 15:37
Hoyt, John 9:120; 27:61
Hoyt, John E. 7:80
Hoyt, Joseph 19:228
Hoyt, Levi M. 9:83; 26:32
Hoyt, Minor S. 20:107
Hoyt, Nathan R. 20:113
Hoyt, Nehemiah 27:60
Hoyt, Nicholas H. 25:43
Hoyt, O. B. 27:62
Hoyt, Oliver J. 24:21
Hoyt, R. 3:101
Hoyt, S. 19:245
Hoyt, S. P. 13:112
Hoyt, Samuel E. 12:122;
  15:125
Hoyt, Sperman 25:43
Hoyt, T. J. 25:188
Hoyt, T. S. 14:133
Hoyt, Thomas J. 5:19
Hoyt, Uphemiah 9:120
Hoyt, W. 1:140
Hoyt, W. D. 3:101
Hoyt, W. F. 25:43
Hoyt, William 17:65
Hoyt, William H. 24:71
Hoyt, Willser M. 19:171
Hoyup, Philip 9:181;
  19:282
Hozhstler, J. A. 25:188
Hozier, Andrew 7:68
Hozier, J. C. 26:211
Huat, T. 23:263
Hubacher, Jacob 13:29
Hubacher, Nicholas 21:54
Huband, A. 25:188
Hubanks, C. 3:101
Hubard, H. 26:35
Hubard, J. C. 21:29
Hubbanks, James 20:277
Hubbard, --- 19:77
Hubbard, A. 7:58
Hubbard, A. B. 9:83
Hubbard, A. M. 19:77
Hubbard, A. N. 17:436

Hubbard, Albert 20:102
Hubbard, Amos 9:36;
  18:293; 26:102
Hubbard, Andrew H.
  24:187
Hubbard, Austin 18:369
Hubbard, B. 14:236;
  25:285; 27:54
Hubbard, Ben 24:195
Hubbard, Benjamin
  17:133
Hubbard, C. 14:74, 236
Hubbard, C. P. 13:125
Hubbard, C. S. 13:65
Hubbard, Charles 7:125
Hubbard, Charles B.
  27:57
Hubbard, D. 7:98
Hubbard, David 4:66;
  17:281
Hubbard, Davis 7:125
Hubbard, Drake 20:30
Hubbard, E. 3:101
Hubbard, E. L. 21:29
Hubbard, E. P. 7:98;
  21:348
Hubbard, Edmund 8:20;
  18:140
Hubbard, F. 16:120; 20:57
Hubbard, Francis 24:62
Hubbard, G. F. 19:77
Hubbard, G. H. 27:55
Hubbard, G. W. 25:188
Hubbard, George 5:19;
  9:35; 16:200; 18:293;
  25:188; 26:37, 102
Hubbard, George B.
  26:212
Hubbard, George F.
  15:285
Hubbard, George M. C.
  13:29
Hubbard, H. 1:38; 7:125;
  18:241; 21:29, 348
Hubbard, H. D. 3:101
Hubbard, Henry 22:426
Hubbard, Howard 12:71
Hubbard, Howard A.
  15:91
Hubbard, Hugh 15:159
Hubbard, J. D. 23:35
Hubbard, J. H. 19:19
Hubbard, J. M. 9:236;
  26:220
Hubbard, J. W. 11:92
Hubbard, Jacob 18:396
Hubbard, James 10:59;
  12:49; 20:277
Hubbard, James M.
  23:259
Hubbard, James U. 15:289

Hubbard, James W. 22:199
Hubbard, John 14:181
Hubbard, John M. 8:87
Hubbard, Joseph 18:241; 26:34
Hubbard, Joseph A. 9:7
Hubbard, Joseph B. 18:218
Hubbard, L. 14:74
Hubbard, M. 10:162; 19:171
Hubbard, M. N. 25:299
Hubbard, Mathey 23:99
Hubbard, Molder 19:274
Hubbard, Monroe 21:255
Hubbard, Myron N. 7:75
Hubbard, Orange 21:348
Hubbard, P. A. 22:352
Hubbard, R. W. 16:200
Hubbard, S. 9:145; 27:56
Hubbard, Sala B. 18:31
Hubbard, T. I. 19:19
Hubbard, Terrance 13:29
Hubbard, Thomas 13:29
Hubbard, Vernon E. 17:81
Hubbard, W. 21:149
Hubbard, W. B. 9:23; 26:100
Hubbard, Washington 21:212
Hubbard, William 1:39; 13:125; 17:308, 347; 25:272
Hubbard, William A. 17:281
Hubbard, William B. 18:309
Hubbard, William G. 21:54
Hubbard, William H. 5:19
Hubbart, R. 1:43
Hubbel, --- 14:181
Hubbel, George 8:50
Hubbel, William J. 11:107
Hubbell, A. C. 1:43
Hubbell, Cyrus 8:20
Hubbell, Edward S. 7:50
Hubbell, Frank 21:188
Hubbell, G. 25:44
Hubbell, George 2:12; 21:101
Hubbell, Henry W. 17:360
Hubbell, Jacob O. 15:351; 16:371
Hubbell, John 5:19
Hubbell, Ralph 18:241; 26:37
Hubbell, Reuben 8:20; 22:83
Hubbell, W. N. 3:101

Hubber, D. 3:101
Hubbert, A. J. 1:43
Hubbert, A. M. 15:306
Hubbert, G. W. 3:101
Hubbert, J. 27:65
Hubble, B. D. 4:32
Hubble, Samuel 22:337
Hubble, W. H. 12:154
Hubboard, James 12:160
Hubbs, Curly 21:290
Hubbs, James G. 1:42
Hubbs, Milo A. 10:59; 20:277
Hubel, Francis 18:111
Hubel, John 23:117
Huber, Benjamin 22:482
Huber, Bernhard 4:32
Huber, C. 3:101
Huber, David 22:199
Huber, Edward 15:68; 18:111
Huber, F. 12:82; 16:296
Huber, Francis 9:23
Huber, Frederick William 20:146
Huber, George J. 8:87
Huber, Gottleib 21:117
Huber, H. 1:141
Huber, Henrich 22:280
Huber, J. 14:74
Huber, John 24:59
Huber, John A. 18:103
Huber, K. 27:63
Huber, Lawrence 4:32
Huber, Lewis 27:59
Huber, Louis F. 9:120
Huber, Martin 7:16; 10:25
Huber, Max 8:20; 18:140
Huber, Philip 10:59; 20:277
Hubert, Alonzo 12:26
Hubert, George 17:36
Hubert, Lysander 4:32
Hubert, M. 19:77
Hubert, M. F. 21:348
Hubler, Frederick W. 14:181
Hubley, D. W. 14:288
Hubrecht, John 23:35
Hubs, H. J. 23:150
Hubson, David 8:64; 26:164
Huch, Michael 5:19
Huchcraft, William 27:64
Huchens, Benjamin 18:207
Huchens, J. Q. 16:296
Huchins, William 16:201
Huchinson, J. 10:28
Huchison, S. R. 18:309
Huck, Charles 14:181

Huck, Francis 1:42
Huck, James 22:123
Huck, Joseph 12:99
Huck, Peter P. 10:59
Huck, W. 15:68
Huck, W. H. 19:254
Huckaba, Riley L. 22:37
Huckabee, A. J. 9:53
Huckaby, Joshua 20:35
Huckbone, William A. 10:9
Hucke, W. 20:277
Hucke, William 10:59
Huckelberry, James 23:35
Huckely, Robert A. 19:19
Huckenbock, James W. 12:71
Huckins, --- 11:219
Huckins, David M. 10:119; 20:277
Huckins, John A. 23:122
Huckinson, M. 3:101
Huckleby, J. C. 9:53
Huckleby, T. 3:101
Huckler, John 10:119; 20:277
Huckley, John 21:348
Huckley, John H. 20:9
Huckstep, J. D. 9:23
Huckstep, J. N. 18:309
Huckstip, J. H. 26:103
Hucktberry, Jacob 18:85
Hucktons, W. 17:254
Hud, E. L. 11:304
Hud, Eaten 11:205
Huddelson, James P. 20:277
Huddington, Noah 20:277
Huddlemeyer, F. 24:79
Huddleson, David 7:58
Huddleston, David 18:140
Huddleston, E. E. 17:203
Huddleston, J. J. 14:74
Huddleston, James H. 22:255
Huddleston, James P. 10:59
Huddleston, John W. 22:451
Huddleston, Rich 19:46
Huddlestone, David 8:20
Huddlestone, John 7:98
Huddock, L. 14:74
Hudgans, Cunningham 19:19
Hudgen, Richard W. 22:123
Hudgens, J. S. 20:277
Hudgins, J. 3:101
Hudgins, J. S. 10:59
Hudgnes, William 11:204

Hudiborg, William 22:83
Hudley, Abner 11:205
Hudman, J. L. T. 17:265
Hudson, --- 20:87
Hudson, A. B. 1:140
Hudson, Albert 8:39; 26:164
Hudson, Alebert 21:274
Hudson, Alexander 22:255
Hudson, Amos W. 19:303
Hudson, Andrew J. 23:89
Hudson, Augustus B. 4:32
Hudson, Austin 13:65; 19:77
Hudson, B. T. 3:101
Hudson, Benjamin 21:348
Hudson, Benjamin J. 21:54
Hudson, Berry D. 17:206
Hudson, C. 1:140; 14:74
Hudson, C. D. 9:36; 18:293; 26:102
Hudson, Charles 3:101; 18:396; 22:37; 23:283
Hudson, Charles H. 21:348
Hudson, D. M. 17:419
Hudson, Daniel M. 11:63; 24:159
Hudson, David 22:112
Hudson, E. 11:387
Hudson, Edwin S. 4:32
Hudson, Elijah 19:171
Hudson, Elisha 20:277
Hudson, F. 13:65; 19:77
Hudson, Foster 10:173; 19:171
Hudson, Frank 8:20; 18:140
Hudson, Frank P. 25:272
Hudson, G. H. 26:124
Hudson, G. W. 3:101
Hudson, George 11:32; 12:49; 14:74
Hudson, George W. 22:37
Hudson, H. 1:135, 136; 18:67
Hudson, H. C. 27:60
Hudson, H. R. 4:32
Hudson, Henry 11:151, 293; 21:348; 22:305
Hudson, Henry G. 22:123
Hudson, Iven D. 22:37
Hudson, J. 3:101; 8:121; 14:265
Hudson, J. A. 3:101
Hudson, J. B. 3:101; 21:88
Hudson, J. H. 14:181

Hudson, J. M. 3:101
Hudson, J. S. 3:101
Hudson, J. W. 14:288
Hudson, Jacob 6:17; 7:125; 18:85
Hudson, James 9:181; 11:263, 401; 19:77, 267; 23:69
Hudson, James N. 20:277
Hudson, Jarrett 23:69
Hudson, Jerry 6:17; 18:85
Hudson, Jesse 10:119; 20:277
Hudson, John 3:101; 17:178; 24:159; 25:275
Hudson, John J. 10:119; 20:277
Hudson, John L. 22:37
Hudson, John W. 22:83
Hudson, Johnson 22:427
Hudson, Joshua W. 23:150
Hudson, L. 1:44, 139; 12:145
Hudson, Manson 15:268
Hudson, Martin 17:163
Hudson, Milton C. 9:23; 18:309; 26:100
Hudson, Moses 9:208
Hudson, N. B. 15:204
Hudson, Nathan 21:348
Hudson, Reley 10:119
Hudson, S. R. 3:101
Hudson, Siegel 4:32
Hudson, Thomas 23:150; 24:79
Hudson, Thomas J. 7:75, 98; 25:299
Hudson, W. 3:101
Hudson, W. H. 3:101
Hudson, Washington 11:205
Hudson, William 8:20; 10:119; 18:140; 20:277; 21:204; 22:123; 24:166
Hudson, William D. 16:85
Hudson, William H. 17:422
Hudson, William R. 23:69
Hudson, Zac 18:85
Hudson, Zachariah 6:10
Hudsonpillar, R. L. 3:101
Hudspath, Thomas 16:162
Hudspith, J. J. 16:38
Huelsmann, Frank 21:139
Huendeen, James 12:26
Huerbert, M. 9:154
Hues, H. T. 11:439
Hues, P. H. 24:111

Hueslander, G. P. 1:139
Huestin, George 22:199
Huestis, John D. 18:207
Hueston, J. 9:145
Huet, John 20:125
Huett, J. M. 23:303
Huett, L. A. 11:263
Huetta, J. 19:327
Huey, John B. 26:221
Huey, Nefi 22:83
Huey, Robert 10:18
Huey, Samuel 14:181
Huey, Thomas 22:16
Huey, William H. 22:426
Huff, A. 17:143
Huff, Abraham 20:277
Huff, Abraham F. 24:51
Huff, Alexander 11:204
Huff, Arthur 3:101
Huff, August 24:214
Huff, B. L. 23:150
Huff, B. W. 10:179
Huff, Benjamin 3:101; 22:83
Huff, C. H. 13:112
Huff, Charles M. 7:98
Huff, Daniel 27:60
Huff, Daniel B. 9:120
Huff, David 23:89
Huff, E. 3:101
Huff, G. 1:140
Huff, Garrett 8:101
Huff, Hanson 22:428
Huff, Henry 8:64; 26:163
Huff, Hiram H. 12:55
Huff, J. 14:74
Huff, J. C. 3:101
Huff, J. T. 14:74
Huff, Jacob 22:481
Huff, James 9:120; 15:204; 27:61
Huff, James R. 7:98
Huff, John 12:54; 18:241; 26:36
Huff, Joseph 22:502
Huff, Joseph G. 17:464; 24:214
Huff, L. B. 14:282
Huff, Laman P. 14:269
Huff, Leonard F. 12:26
Huff, Lewis 7:125
Huff, Major 7:125
Huff, Morris 21:348
Huff, Nathaniel 9:181
Huff, P. 14:282
Huff, Richard 18:218
Huff, Robert 22:146, 427
Huff, Samuel 17:133, 178; 24:195
Huff, Samuel T. 14:181
Huff, Solomon W. 23:277

Huff, Theodore 25:39
Huff, Thomas 17:206, 281
Huff, Thomas A. 26:33
Huff, Thomas G. 10:59;
    20:277
Huff, Thomas H. 19:19
Huff, W. B. 18:175
Huff, W. L. 1:40
Huff, William 23:99
Huff, William D. 14:74
Huff, William H. 17:53
Huff, William J. 24:21
Huffaker, Andrew S.
    11:327
Huffaker, J. 3:101
Huffaker, J. B. 17:96
Huffer, John H. 20:125
Huffham, Calvin 14:181
Huffleton, J. 1:39
Huffman, --- 19:77
Huffman, Aaron 24:158
Huffman, Absalom 22:83
Huffman, Allen 11:93
Huffman, Benjamin 20:9
Huffman, Charles 3:101
Huffman, David 18:51
Huffman, Emanuel 20:133
Huffman, G. 13:91
Huffman, G. W. 11:287
Huffman, George 18:309;
    20:146; 22:37, 199;
    26:102
Huffman, H. C. 20:277
Huffman, Henry C. 10:59
Huffman, J. 1:139; 26:33
Huffman, Jacob 21:226
Huffman, James 21:217
Huffman, James M.
    11:242
Huffman, John 17:21
Huffman, John F. 17:452;
    24:182
Huffman, John H. 22:481
Huffman, Jonathan J.
    11:150
Huffman, Joseph 5:19
Huffman, L. 12:82;
    16:296; 25:188
Huffman, L. G. 23:150
Huffman, Lewis F. 17:206
Huffman, M. 16:38
Huffman, Moses 19:19
Huffman, Peter 13:128;
    22:199
Huffman, R. J. 3:101
Huffman, Sampson
    17:397
Huffman, Samuel 18:396
Huffman, Walter 4:33
Huffman, William 15:326;
    22:425

Huffman, William E.
    16:38
Huffnon, Ewell 26:124
Huffstetter, Samuel G.
    11:187
Huffurd, A. 23:35
Huffwagel, John 11:33
Hufhan, John A. 22:234
Hufleter, E. S. 1:103
Hufman, Fred 18:14
Hufnagel, James 4:33
Hufnagle, J. C. 26:100
Hufnagle, Lawrence
    11:387
Hufner, P. 1:138
Huft, William D. 11:191
Huftelen, David 7:30
Hufton, William 11:305
Hug, Charles 24:51
Hug, G. L. 22:199
Hug, Gustave 21:101
Hugaboom, William
    11:333
Hugamer, David J. 16:39
Hugan, James 15:299
Huganer, A. 3:101
Huganer, David J. 13:29
Hugck, W. O. 20:277
Hugel, H. 14:241
Hugel, John 3:101
Hugener, D. M. 3:101
Huges, Benjamin 22:305
Huges, J. S. 11:280
Huges, John 4:33
Huges, Thomas 8:121
Hugg, --- 12:122; 14:26;
    15:125, 363
Hugg, Casper 10:25
Hugg, Charles E. 12:26
Hugg, G. W. 7:98
Hugg, Johnson J. 11:33
Huggar, J. 1:138
Huggard, A. W. 12:49
Huggett, William 18:293;
    26:102
Huggins, Alexander
    18:396
Huggins, E. 21:348
Huggins, E. A. 11:32
Huggins, Henry 22:305
Huggins, I. G. 9:145
Huggins, J. G. 27:55
Huggins, J. P. 1:142
Huggins, Joel 5:19
Huggins, John 11:204;
    13:29; 25:188
Huggins, R. E. 9:145;
    27:58
Huggins, S. 27:56
Huggins, T. 18:175
Huggins, T. P. 10:179

Huggins, Thomas R.
    10:179; 18:175
Huggins, William 13:29
Huggins, William H.
    23:35
Hugh, Antone 23:263
Hugh, E. 1:137
Hugh, Henry T. 10:173
Hugh, John M. 12:26;
    13:29; 16:39
Hugh, R. 22:37
Hugh, Thomas 12:64
Hughart, John B. 17:46
Hughbanks, Nelson H.
    7:98
Hughboom, James 7:98
Hughes, --- 13:65; 15:204;
    19:77
Hughes, A. 14:241; 27:65
Hughes, A. D. 9:54
Hughes, A. J. 1:136
Hughes, A. M. 17:166
Hughes, Albert 18:309;
    26:100
Hughes, Amos 25:188
Hughes, Andrew 21:72
Hughes, Andy 18:241;
    26:36
Hughes, Anthony 10:18;
    13:29
Hughes, Arthur 11:401
Hughes, B. 1:44, 140
Hughes, Benjamin 3:101
Hughes, Bloomfield
    18:241; 26:36
Hughes, C. 14:241; 26:34
Hughes, C. W. 25:42
Hughes, Charles 12:169;
    18:309; 26:101
Hughes, Charles B. 1:42
Hughes, Cornelius 11:151
Hughes, D. L. 3:101
Hughes, Daniel 7:125;
    19:19
Hughes, David I. 22:37
Hughes, E. 3:101; 16:201
Hughes, E. G. 17:281
Hughes, Edgar 25:42
Hughes, Edy 27:55
Hughes, Eli 22:37
Hughes, F. J. 22:123
Hughes, Felix M. 7:98
Hughes, Frank 21:348;
    22:426
Hughes, Franklin 21:226
Hughes, G. R. 15:173
Hughes, G. W. 7:98;
    11:305
Hughes, George 15:204
Hughes, George W. 22:37
Hughes, Grefinin 16:201

Hughes, H. 8:64
Hughes, H. L. 18:31
Hughes, Harvey 22:123
Hughes, Harvey H. 17:206
Hughes, Henry 3:101;
    4:33; 11:33
Hughes, Henry C. 21:255
Hughes, Hezekiah 26:164
Hughes, Hiram 16:133
Hughes, Hugh 24:94
Hughes, Hugh W. 21:139
Hughes, Isaac 16:201;
    17:443; 23:69;
    24:159
Hughes, Isaac B. 21:348
Hughes, J. 1:138; 3:101;
    12:122, 154; 15:37;
    16:296; 21:122;
    27:55
Hughes, J. H. 14:74, 236;
    18:31
Hughes, J. M. 1:40;
    20:277; 25:39
Hughes, J. N. 1:141
Hughes, J. O. 1:135
Hughes, J. P. 1:140
Hughes, Jackson 22:199
Hughes, James 1:42; 4:33;
    5:40; 11:151; 13:29;
    14:181, 257; 21:201;
    22:305; 23:104, 268;
    24:21
Hughes, James B. 13:29;
    16:39
Hughes, James G. 22:37
Hughes, James M. 10:59;
    17:110; 20:277
Hughes, James O. 22:37
Hughes, Jesse 12:26, 160
Hughes, John 3:101; 5:19;
    7:50; 9:110, 120;
    12:72; 16:39; 19:77;
    22:37; 24:21;
    25:188; 27:60
Hughes, John G. 23:11
Hughes, John H. 14:181
Hughes, John W. 8:50;
    11:333; 17:81;
    21:226; 22:482
Hughes, Jonathan 14:335;
    21:226
Hughes, Joseph 7:125;
    11:33; 26:221
Hughes, Joseph M.
    15:204; 22:199
Hughes, L. 1:41
Hughes, L. M. 8:50
Hughes, Lewis 9:200;
    19:291
Hughes, M. 3:101
Hughes, Marcus 12:142

Hughes, Martin 7:68
Hughes, Michael 8:64;
    26:162
Hughes, Milton 4:33
Hughes, Mohard 23:200
Hughes, N. 21:166
Hughes, Nicholas 21:226
Hughes, O. H. 16:201
Hughes, Oliver 18:309;
    26:101
Hughes, Owen 21:255;
    23:128
Hughes, P. 3:101; 9:145
Hughes, P. H. 1:41
Hughes, Patrick 10:18;
    15:283; 19:77;
    21:117
Hughes, R. H. 25:40
Hughes, R. J. 15:126
Hughes, Reaso 12:147
Hughes, Reason 19:303
Hughes, Reece 20:146
Hughes, Richard 9:181;
    19:291
Hughes, Richard H. 21:72
Hughes, Robert 2:12;
    7:98; 9:208; 10:119;
    20:277; 25:39
Hughes, Robert H. 8:20
Hughes, Robert M. 18:140
Hughes, S. 13:91; 21:110
Hughes, S. A. 1:141
Hughes, S. H. 21:122
Hughes, S. L. 1:141
Hughes, Samuel 7:125
Hughes, Solomon 12:122
Hughes, T. 1:39; 21:29
Hughes, Thomas 1:44;
    3:101; 5:19; 11:263;
    12:26; 14:282; 15:37;
    16:371; 17:498;
    22:37; 26:212
Hughes, Thomas G.
    9:145; 27:56
Hughes, W. H. 3:101
Hughes, Wesley 13:57
Hughes, Westley 22:513
Hughes, William 3:101;
    7:98, 125; 8:77;
    9:242; 10:59; 14:236;
    18:31; 20:30, 277;
    22:83, 255, 481;
    27:58, 63
Hughes, William F. 7:51
Hughes, William G.
    21:130
Hughes, William H. 1:42
Hughes, William L. 22:37
Hughes, William M. 23:89
Hughes, Wilson 22:123
Hughevorline, H. H. 14:13

Hughey, J. B. 11:304
Hughey, James 3:101
Hughey, Victor 10:59;
    20:277
Hughlett, Charles 9:47
Hughnholtz, Christopher
    17:21
Hughnorline, H. H. 13:91
Hughs, --- 11:63
Hughs, A. 3:101
Hughs, Albert 9:23
Hughs, Alfred 22:513
Hughs, Armstead 17:178
Hughs, Charles 9:23
Hughs, David 9:83;
    24:196
Hughs, Elijah 20:186
Hughs, G. 15:68
Hughs, Gilford 11:423
Hughs, Gomer R. 11:413
Hughs, J. 12:82; 27:54, 56
Hughs, Jack 17:133;
    24:195
Hughs, James 11:413
Hughs, James M. 10:119
Hughs, James S. 18:51
Hughs, John 11:412;
    15:289
Hughs, John C. 10:119;
    20:277
Hughs, John D. 11:107,
    219
Hughs, M. H. 20:277
Hughs, N. J. 11:280
Hughs, Oliver 9:23
Hughs, P. 8:121
Hughs, Peter 13:112;
    22:305
Hughs, S. 14:13
Hughs, Silas 18:67
Hughs, W. E. 27:64
Hughs, William 10:119;
    17:409; 20:186, 277;
    22:37
Hughson, Charles A.
    19:19
Hughson, F. 1:136
Hughsten, John C. 22:235
Hughtalaing, C. 25:188
Hughton, J. 3:102
Hugin, John 21:240
Hugins, --- 15:14
Hugle, A. 20:278
Hugle, Albert 10:60
Hugle, C. H. 19:19
Hugle, Joseph 6:21
Hugle, Thomas L. 22:329
Huglet, Charles 26:142
Hugleton, F. M. 11:64
Hugley, C. W. 3:102
Hugo, Ed 18:241; 26:34

Hugo, John S. 23:242
Hugo, W. 21:29
Hugo, William 23:35
Hugoboom, Orin 23:191
Hugs, Isaac 11:204
Hugs, William G. 21:249
Hugtree, Austin 9:120
Huguet, John 8:118
Hugulet, Henry 24:51
Hugwood, L. 19:77
Huhn, A. 16:115
Huhn, E. 9:145; 27:55
Huhn, John 5:19
Huichniffe, Abraham
    21:348
Huick, A. 25:188
Huiton, Jacob 21:348
Huitt, John 11:241
Hukell, S. 11:149
Hukes, A. 26:163
Hukness, T. 12:92
Hulan, Osborn 22:502
Hulbard, A. B. 26:33
Hulbert, Chester A. 13:29
Hulbert, Dwight 7:98
Hulbert, George 9:120;
    27:60
Hulbert, Henry 4:33
Hulbert, J. H. S. 3:102
Hulbert, James W. 9:120
Hulbert, John 16:201
Hulbert, L. 23:35
Hulbert, Milo 13:29
Hulbert, Seymour 9:103
Hulburd, Benjamin
    15:205
Hulburt, Wallace 10:119
Hulbut, Jasper 19:19
Hulcapple, A. 15:166
Hulce, George 11:263
Hulce, Lester 23:150
Hulderman, G. W. 14:182
Hules, William 9:181
Hulet, Benjamin A.
    15:205
Hulet, Hiram 17:360
Hulet, J. 14:13
Hulet, James A. 22:83
Hulet, W. 3:102
Hulet, William 3:102
Hulett, Asa 8:20; 18:140
Hulett, George 16:39;
    22:463
Hulett, Miles 24:21
Hulett, S. 14:74
Hulette, George 13:57
Hulford, George 9:181
Hulfpen, John 3:102
Hulfrick, Christian 10:25
Huli, Hiram 11:401
Hulick, David S. 11:63

Hulin, Carroll H. 21:130
Huling, Edward T. 23:89
Hulit, R. N. 22:199
Hull, --- 8:124; 19:171
Hull, A. 11:62; 25:188
Hull, A. B. 1:135
Hull, A. E. 20:278
Hull, Aaron G. 22:199
Hull, Amos 11:219
Hull, Austin A. 23:89
Hull, Ben 8:69
Hull, C. T. 14:278
Hull, Chancey A. 19:77
Hull, Clark H. 27:61
Hull, D. 19:303
Hull, D. J. 20:278
Hull, Daniel V. 16:96
Hull, David 22:508
Hull, Edward E. 23:35
Hull, F. M. 26:166
Hull, George 18:14;
    20:137; 21:274
Hull, George H. 11:388
Hull, George W. 13:29
Hull, H. 12:82; 16:296
Hull, H. Ellsworth 10:162
Hull, H. H. 11:381
Hull, Harris 27:63
Hull, Harrison 10:60;
    20:278
Hull, Herman D. 15:37
Hull, Hiram G. 12:26
Hull, I. H. 11:219
Hull, J. 21:122
Hull, J. C. 11:119
Hull, J. E. 3:102
Hull, J. F. 23:277
Hull, Jacob 12:26
Hull, James C. 18:140
Hull, Jasper 9:145
Hull, Jesse 23:69
Hull, John 14:182; 21:30;
    22:83; 25:39; 26:211
Hull, Joseph 27:59
Hull, Joseph H. 9:120
Hull, L. F. 13:91
Hull, L. R. 9:221; 18:369
Hull, M. 3:102
Hull, Marion E. 20:125
Hull, N. 21:110
Hull, P. 21:30
Hull, R. W. 13:65; 19:77
Hull, Richard L. 15:3
Hull, S. 3:102; 22:480
Hull, Samuel 14:182
Hull, Samuel H. 15:56
Hull, Solomon 22:37
Hull, Sylvanus A. 10:173
Hull, Thomas T. 21:130
Hull, Thomas W. 10:119;
    20:278

Hull, Varnum D. 10:18
Hull, W. H. 25:188
Hull, Wesley 10:162
Hull, William 1:39;
    20:278; 22:123
Hull, William C. 13:29
Hull, Zury J. 25:188
Hullen, Mathias 8:87
Huller, John 21:226
Hullet, Charles W. 17:91
Hullett, J. 16:268
Hullett, John 18:207
Hullett, Robert 9:23;
    18:309; 26:100
Hulley, William 18:277
Hullibarger, Robert 17:36
Hullinger, J. 16:160
Hullock, A. 9:178
Hulls, William 10:60
Hulman, Eli 10:119;
    20:278
Hulme, James 22:337
Hulme, James M. 25:42
Hulme, Joseph 19:19
Hulmer, C. H. 16:140
Huls, Marion 21:54
Huls, Richard 22:83
Hulsars, Robert K. 17:243
Hulsay, G. 3:102
Hulse, A. B. 3:102
Hulse, George W. 23:267
Hulse, J. 9:54
Hulse, James A. 22:83
Hulse, Jermiah 20:97
Hulse, John 1:38
Hulse, L. 11:241
Hulse, M. F. 1:139
Hulse, Mary V. 25:311
Hulse, Nelson J. 23:35
Hulse, W. S. 3:102
Hulse, William 9:83
Hulse, William E. 13:65
Hulse, William R. 21:54
Hulsey, John 9:8
Hulshiser, C. 13:112
Hulsinger, Jacob 13:29
Hulsizer, Ellis W. 22:37
Hulsopple, Andrew J.
    22:83
Hulsopple, Philip 23:279
Hulsopple, William
    11:263
Hulstead, William F. 8:87
Hulston, C. H. 22:255
Hulston, J. A. 18:417
Hult, A. S. 21:101
Hult, George A. 3:102
Hulton, John 11:388
Hulton, Samuel 19:171
Hults, Henry 20:278
Hults, James 9:54

Hultz, J. 14:74
Hultz, William J. 26:33
Hulwick, Peter 11:32
Hum, Albert 4:33
Human, James 5:40
Human, Lewis 12:26
Humassey, David 7:30
Humbarger, John 17:419; 22:83; 24:159
Humbbard, G. H. 9:145
Humbell, John B. 19:282
Humber, --- 18:190
Humber, Charles H. 26:211
Humber, Mary 18:190
Humbert, F. R. 15:159
Humbert, Lewis 23:69
Humbert, M. 27:57
Humbert, Simon 26:33
Humbert, William 8:64
Humbill, Frank 9:132; 27:59
Humble, Cosly 18:396
Humble, David 17:145
Humble, Frederick 14:182
Humble, Jacob 14:182
Humble, John 23:150
Humble, John P. 9:181
Humble, Josiah 17:277
Humbore, John 11:84
Hume, Charles M. 10:119; 20:278
Hume, J. A. 3:102
Hume, James 9:236
Hume, John 17:36
Hume, Joseph D. 22:199
Hume, M. 11:305
Hume, W. B. 9:66
Hume, W. H. 21:122
Hume, Walter 21:255
Hume, William 17:295
Humel, H. J. 1:136
Humelbaugh, William 17:419
Humelkly, Frank A. 11:31
Humell, J. 14:299; 17:478; 27:64
Humer, Jacob 21:348
Humerick, F. W. 18:396
Humes, A. C. 10:192
Humes, Alexander 17:387
Humes, Benjamin G. 22:405
Humes, Ezra 5:19
Humes, George 7:75; 25:299
Humes, James 23:35; 26:220
Humes, James I. 21:92
Humes, Thomas 9:165
Humes, W. W. 21:166

Humeston, H. 1:42
Humeston, S. 26:163
Huminger, James K. 11:150
Huminslon, A. 15:205
Humma, Lewis 4:33
Hummel, Benjamin 4:33
Hummel, C. 25:322
Hummel, Calvin 25:43
Hummel, Peter M. 19:171
Hummel, S. C. 26:33
Hummel, T. 15:342; 16:371
Hummel, W. 16:371
Hummel, William 15:342
Hummell, Albert B. 22:37
Hummell, H. 1:42
Hummell, R. A. 19:77
Hummell, V. 11:303
Hummelsein, David W. 10:25
Hummer, B. 13:65
Hummer, Joseph D. 20:23
Hummer, P. C. 3:102
Humnison, Brunette 19:77
Humpayl, --- 7:63
Humpel, Nelson 20:278
Humphill, James 22:37
Humphrey, --- 3:102; 18:277
Humphrey, A. M. 13:29
Humphrey, Albert 21:217
Humphrey, Alex 19:291
Humphrey, Alexander 9:200
Humphrey, Benjamin 21:274
Humphrey, C. J. 1:139
Humphrey, David 22:199
Humphrey, E. 19:228
Humphrey, Eli 24:21
Humphrey, Eli D. 22:255
Humphrey, F. 15:299; 16:201
Humphrey, Francis 22:352
Humphrey, Fred 21:348
Humphrey, G. 12:95
Humphrey, G. W. 9:214; 21:348
Humphrey, George 17:178
Humphrey, George B. 9:23; 26:101
Humphrey, H. 23:150
Humphrey, Horace 8:50; 21:139
Humphrey, I. 27:63
Humphrey, J. 25:188
Humphrey, J. A. 10:18
Humphrey, J. P. 7:58; 18:190

Humphrey, James 5:19; 10:60; 14:182; 17:499
Humphrey, James M. 22:83
Humphrey, John 9:230; 18:434; 22:280; 23:150
Humphrey, Joseph 20:278
Humphrey, Lee 22:305
Humphrey, M. 23:35
Humphrey, M. W. 15:166
Humphrey, Marcus 20:137
Humphrey, Marion 8:101; 17:459; 24:152
Humphrey, Marquis E. 10:18
Humphrey, Moses 25:40
Humphrey, Peter 22:146
Humphrey, R. 24:88
Humphrey, S. 14:74
Humphrey, Samuel J. 21:72
Humphrey, Stephen D. 20:9
Humphrey, T. 16:201
Humphrey, W. 25:188
Humphrey, W. C. 16:201
Humphrey, W. G. 21:348
Humphrey, W. H. 15:173
Humphrey, William 5:40; 12:154; 18:396; 23:122
Humphrey, William N. 23:113
Humphrey, Wilson 21:275; 24:196
Humphrey, Young 11:423
Humphreys, A. 1:137
Humphreys, C. P. 1:40
Humphreys, Charles 21:275
Humphreys, Elias 11:84
Humphreys, Frank 15:205
Humphreys, G. 15:360; 19:77
Humphreys, George 4:33; 18:320
Humphreys, H. 3:102
Humphreys, H. B. 24:21
Humphreys, J. 1:136; 3:102; 14:299; 17:479
Humphreys, J. H. 26:211
Humphreys, Lewis 11:284
Humphreys, Robert W. 24:21
Humphreys, Sylvanus 5:51

Humphreys, Sylvester 25:188
Humphreys, T. 23:35
Humphreys, William 1:38; 3:102; 23:252
Humphries, A. 27:61
Humphries, Abijah 20:17
Humphries, Coray 10:173
Humphries, Corey 19:171
Humphries, F. E. 22:480
Humphries, George 9:23
Humphries, J. A. 27:57
Humphries, James A. 18:369
Humphries, John 22:37
Humphry, George B. 18:309
Humphry, J. J. 16:39
Humsteert, Charles H. 12:26
Hun, E. 18:67
Hun, Luther 14:182
Hunback, J. 3:102
Huncey, J. 14:257
Hunch, J. H. 1:136
Hund, Auton 11:443
Hund, I. F. 25:272
Hunderland, James 11:149
Hundley, A. B. 17:337
Hundley, G. A. 3:102
Hundley, Samuel 20:104
Hundley, Thomas 19:171
Hundmand, E. 17:178
Hundrell, James 21:348
Hundrick, Esline P. 9:102
Hune, Elias 9:145
Hune, George A. 22:37
Huneborger, W. 7:51
Huneningway, Levi 7:30
Huney, John 9:223
Huneyburn, Thomas 16:7
Hung, Daniel 11:332
Hungate, John 17:281
Hungen, John 9:83
Hunger, William F. 24:94
Hungerfard, C. 19:303
Hungerford, Abner 14:299; 17:476; 27:64
Hungerford, Alfred G. 22:200
Hungerford, C. 3:102
Hungerford, D. 1:137
Hungerford, Edwin R. 20:48
Hungerford, G. 25:188
Hungerford, J. C. 11:319
Hungerford, L. E. 1:38
Hungerford, M. 1:44; 3:102

Hungerford, Robert B. 13:29
Hungerford, T. B. 1:44
Hungerpard, C. 10:28
Hungton, Lester 7:30
Hunka, Ambrose 18:67
Hunker, Ambrose 9:208
Hunker, John C. 16:39
Hunker, William 26:220
Hunkers, William 19:238
Hunkins, H. B. 19:238
Hunley, Josiah T. 10:60
Hunley, M. 14:241
Hunn, Henry 19:19
Hunn, Horace 15:3
Hunn, Levi 13:112
Hunn, Samuel M. 12:26
Hunna, David 11:205
Hunnel, J. B. 1:41
Hunnell, Francis B. 24:51
Hunnell, J. 3:102
Hunnell, Thomas 15:205
Hunnerwell, J. 1:138
Hunneston, N. P. 12:95
Hunnewell, Colvin M. 15:107
Hunnington, --- 15:37
Hunningway, B. 21:30
Hunniston, Amos 16:96
Hunniston, Russell 22:146
Hunnycut, George 11:423
Hunold, William 22:167
Hunsaker, Solomon 22:200
Hunsberger, Henry 19:77
Hunsberger, M. J. 11:152
Hunsberger, Obadiah 20:17
Hunsdorfer, James 8:20
Hunsinger, A. 16:268
Hunsinger, Charles N. 9:120
Hunsinger, S. 1:42
Hunson, A. 14:13
Hunson, Christian 8:64
Hunson, William Henry 16:3
Hunster, Thomas 14:13
Hunston, Thomas 13:91
Hunsucker, W. 23:150
Hunt, A. 9:161; 18:85; 20:147; 27:63
Hunt, A. E. 1:135
Hunt, A. W. 14:74
Hunt, Abraham 22:255
Hunt, Albert 18:111
Hunt, Alexander 25:188
Hunt, Alfred 22:305
Hunt, Alfred F. 22:146
Hunt, Andrew 19:78
Hunt, B. 23:35

Hunt, B. D. 20:155
Hunt, Baisel 18:293; 26:103
Hunt, Baizel 9:36
Hunt, Basil 9:23
Hunt, Byron 20:30
Hunt, C. G. 23:35
Hunt, C. M. 21:348
Hunt, C. W. 3:102
Hunt, Caleb 7:30
Hunt, Calvin 22:84
Hunt, Charles 5:19; 19:19; 21:241; 22:123; 24:51
Hunt, Charles E. 7:98; 16:296
Hunt, Clayburn 10:119; 20:278
Hunt, D. C. 14:182
Hunt, David 21:275
Hunt, Decos 19:265
Hunt, Delas 11:191
Hunt, Delos 9:181
Hunt, E. 1:98; 26:34
Hunt, E. W. 7:51; 19:78
Hunt, Edwin 9:83
Hunt, Eli B. 22:425
Hunt, F. 14:74
Hunt, F. H. 26:164
Hunt, Foster M. 10:119; 20:278
Hunt, Francis 17:319
Hunt, Frank 25:40
Hunt, Frederick A. 23:150
Hunt, G. 7:30; 27:64
Hunt, G. A. 8:64
Hunt, Garret A. 11:287
Hunt, George 15:68; 18:31; 25:188
Hunt, George A. 1:40
Hunt, George W. 17:360; 23:69
Hunt, H. 1:38; 10:96
Hunt, H. A. 13:91
Hunt, Henry 8:20; 18:140; 23:122, 128; 26:100
Hunt, Henry C. 23:69
Hunt, Henry M. 1:45
Hunt, Herman 22:146
Hunt, Hiram R. 11:287
Hunt, Hiram S. 11:107
Hunt, Hugh 15:278; 25:189
Hunt, Ira 12:59; 16:154
Hunt, Isaac 21:30; 22:37
Hunt, Isaac T. 10:119; 20:278
Hunt, J. 1:44; 3:102; 16:201; 23:35
Hunt, J. A. 14:74; 16:296
Hunt, J. B. 10:28; 19:303

Hunt, J. C. 15:159
Hunt, J. F. 8:64; 26:163
Hunt, J. M. 17:360;
 26:163
Hunt, J. N. 20:41
Hunt, J. O. 19:78
Hunt, J. W. 18:31;
 19:267; 20:147
Hunt, Jackson 17:36, 393
Hunt, Jacob 18:207
Hunt, James 16:296
Hunt, James G. 18:396
Hunt, Jasper 23:307
Hunt, Jeff. G. 20:9
Hunt, Jeremiah W. 21:54
Hunt, Jesse 21:54
Hunt, John 1:42; 12:154;
 16:296; 17:273, 291;
 19:296; 20:278;
 21:204; 27:54
Hunt, John C. 8:87
Hunt, John D. 11:287
Hunt, John W. 9:181
Hunt, Jonathan 13:29;
 22:146
Hunt, Joseph 21:88; 27:60
Hunt, Joseph A. 11:242
Hunt, Joseph B. 23:69
Hunt, Joseph D. 4:33
Hunt, Josephus 9:120
Hunt, Julius 17:133;
 24:195
Hunt, L. H. 9:54
Hunt, L. T. 13:125
Hunt, Layborne 20:9
Hunt, Lerton D. 21:54
Hunt, Levi W. 22:427
Hunt, Lewis 13:112;
 15:205
Hunt, Louis 18:421
Hunt, M. 11:92, 152;
 22:305
Hunt, Martin D. 20:9
Hunt, Merril 7:30
Hunt, Michael 8:64
Hunt, N. 14:13
Hunt, Newton 11:126
Hunt, O. S. 1:137
Hunt, Oliver 20:41
Hunt, Owen 14:182
Hunt, P. 13:91
Hunt, Palmer C. 17:81
Hunt, Pat 14:74
Hunt, Patrick 16:120;
 22:337
Hunt, Paul S. 23:69
Hunt, Peter 22:305
Hunt, Phillip 16:201
Hunt, R. 22:200
Hunt, Ralph 23:150

Hunt, Richard H. 8:20;
 18:140
Hunt, S. 19:171; 21:348
Hunt, Samuel B. 24:51
Hunt, Samuel E. 23:69
Hunt, Stephen 12:154
Hunt, T. 16:136; 20:174
Hunt, T. H. 7:30
Hunt, T. J. 3:102
Hunt, Thomas 1:38; 16:96
Hunt, Thomas L. 10:119;
 20:278
Hunt, U. 13:91
Hunt, Urias 9:54
Hunt, W. 22:146
Hunt, W. B. 7:30; 16:140
Hunt, W. E. 15:308, 355
Hunt, W. H. 3:102;
 17:178
Hunt, W. L. 12:164
Hunt, Wiley 22:513
Hunt, William 10:10, 119;
 11:15, 381; 14:28;
 15:205; 17:110;
 19:19; 20:278;
 21:348; 22:523
Hunt, William A. 21:54
Hunt, William B. 13:29;
 16:39
Hunt, William Deel J.
 15:7
Hunt, William G. 8:20;
 18:140
Hunt, William H. 12:26;
 17:21, 178; 25:43
Hunt, William J. 17:253
Hunt, William P. 21:195
Hunt, William S. 13:129
Hunten, E. 20:278
Huntencoffer, George
 10:60
Hunter, --- 14:182;
 21:208; 23:203
Hunter, A. 21:198
Hunter, A. D. 24:21
Hunter, Alfred 17:133;
 24:195
Hunter, Benjamin 9:181;
 19:271
Hunter, C. 3:102
Hunter, Charles 11:423;
 25:333
Hunter, Charles E.
 18:355; 26:163
Hunter, Cornelius 18:85
Hunter, Creed 17:397
Hunter, D. 15:342; 16:371
Hunter, D. W. 12:26
Hunter, E. 1:137; 3:102;
 9:230
Hunter, Edward 11:204

Hunter, F. 17:133; 24:195
Hunter, F. D. 13:112
Hunter, F. F. 14:74
Hunter, Fidel 22:162
Hunter, Franklin 10:60;
 20:278
Hunter, Frederick A.
 21:72
Hunter, G. D. 25:189
Hunter, G. W. 3:102
Hunter, George 9:208
Hunter, George A. 25:189
Hunter, George D. 5:19
Hunter, George W. 12:139
Hunter, H. 1:98; 3:102;
 7:30; 17:307
Hunter, Hamilton 10:60
Hunter, Harry 21:275
Hunter, Henry 20:278;
 22:200
Hunter, Hingo 8:39
Hunter, Hings 26:165
Hunter, I. J. 24:21
Hunter, J. 1:43, 141;
 3:102; 12:85; 16:120,
 296; 25:189; 27:62
Hunter, J. A. 14:327
Hunter, J. B. 11:304
Hunter, J. C. 14:315
Hunter, J. F. 27:63
Hunter, J. H. 21:122
Hunter, J. L. 14:182
Hunter, J. M. 3:102
Hunter, J. T. 9:161;
 10:146; 12:154;
 17:281
Hunter, Jackson 15:205
Hunter, Jacob 18:241;
 26:36
Hunter, James 7:125;
 9:23, 54; 13:91;
 18:85, 309, 421;
 22:405; 23:180;
 24:79; 26:100
Hunter, James F. 23:151
Hunter, James M. 11:413
Hunter, James R. 9:100;
 21:54
Hunter, Jesse W. 21:72
Hunter, John 5:19;
 11:255; 13:65, 91;
 14:74; 16:201;
 17:133; 23:35;
 24:195; 25:285
Hunter, John F. 20:30
Hunter, John S. 18:241;
 26:35
Hunter, John W. 20:33;
 22:83
Hunter, Josiah 21:214
Hunter, L. 3:102

Hunter, Louis 19:321
Hunter, M. 9:24; 18:309; 26:100
Hunter, M. W. 3:102
Hunter, Mautton 9:145
Hunter, Memoral 6:27
Hunter, Monroe 6:27
Hunter, Moses 22:305
Hunter, N. 14:282
Hunter, N. B. 15:205
Hunter, O. 16:201
Hunter, O. K. 21:349
Hunter, P. S. 19:254
Hunter, Peter 21:226; 24:67
Hunter, Richard 17:429
Hunter, Robert 6:12; 8:20; 9:132; 18:85, 140, 293; 22:305; 27:58
Hunter, Robert B. 22:501
Hunter, Robert P. 9:36; 26:102
Hunter, Robert W. P. 11:150
Hunter, S. 24:79; 27:54
Hunter, S. B. 9:54
Hunter, Sam 25:280
Hunter, Samuel 21:226
Hunter, Sarah Jane 18:67
Hunter, Simeon 14:182
Hunter, T. 3:102
Hunter, T. A. 3:102
Hunter, T. T. 20:3
Hunter, Thomas 22:11, 200; 23:35
Hunter, Thomas H. 21:85
Hunter, Vitalis 24:79
Hunter, W. 1:141; 2:12; 3:102; 8:64; 9:54, 83, 145, 181; 14:282; 19:232; 25:43
Hunter, W. B. H. 18:241; 26:35
Hunter, W. C. 13:112
Hunter, W. H. 21:349
Hunter, Walter T. 17:248
Hunter, William 2:12; 6:27; 9:230, 236; 11:63; 14:182; 15:68; 20:278; 22:305, 513; 25:38; 26:162; 27:56
Hunter, William B. 23:35
Hunter, William C. 22:426
Hunter, William O. 15:205
Hunters, Joseph L. 5:19
Hunterstein, P. 1:140
Huntgee, Jacob 14:182

Hunting, A. R. 7:80; 25:299
Hunting, C. H. 14:74
Hunting, E. D. 23:268
Hunting, J. C. 16:201
Hunting, J. D. 21:349
Hunting, J. N. 3:102
Hunting, Jabez 23:191
Hunting, Miller 14:182
Hunting, Walter 9:120
Huntingdon, E. 14:321
Huntingdon, Edwin 14:315; 23:89
Huntingdon, John G. 20:23
Huntingdon, L. D. 21:349
Huntingdon, W. H. 16:78
Huntingee, J. 8:50
Huntington, A. S. 8:101
Huntington, Albert 10:162; 19:171
Huntington, Almon S. 17:463; 24:185
Huntington, C. 25:189
Huntington, Charles 5:19
Huntington, E. W. 20:278
Huntington, Ed. L. 18:355
Huntington, Edward 21:255
Huntington, George W. 21:226
Huntington, H. 13:91; 14:13
Huntington, Henry 9:120; 27:61
Huntington, J. 11:340
Huntington, J. D. 25:299
Huntington, James 8:72
Huntington, John 24:72
Huntington, Joseph C. 22:37
Huntington, L. 16:201
Huntington, Marion 11:387
Huntington, Matthew 18:323
Huntington, Samuel 7:30
Huntington, T. M. 1:140
Huntington, Thomas 23:285
Huntington, U. 1:42
Huntington, W. P. 16:96
Huntington, William T. 21:72
Huntley, --- 8:87
Huntley, A. H. 22:481
Huntley, Albert 10:162; 19:171
Huntley, Cyrus 26:164
Huntley, D. W. 7:98

Huntley, F. 15:302; 23:151
Huntley, F. Henry 10:60
Huntley, F. M. 19:254
Huntley, F. W. 20:278
Huntley, Francis M. 9:181
Huntley, H. 7:98
Huntley, Harvey 1:38
Huntley, Henry B. 9:103
Huntley, J. 22:523
Huntley, James F. 16:201
Huntley, James T. 20:278
Huntley, John 10:60
Huntley, Julian W. 22:37
Huntley, Justin R. 12:8
Huntley, Lewis 11:126
Huntley, Loring 11:100
Huntley, M. 27:65
Huntley, O. 12:82; 16:296
Huntley, Oscar F. 4:33
Huntley, R. 3:102
Huntley, Raynor K. 20:125
Huntley, S. 14:278; 22:200
Huntley, S. D. 16:160
Huntley, T. 23:151
Huntley, Whiteley 21:227
Huntley, William 3:102; 9:120; 22:200; 27:61
Huntley, William A. 4:33
Huntley, William C. 8:87
Huntley, William T. 8:87
Huntly, H. S. 25:189
Huntly, Ira 17:401
Huntman, H. 21:166
Hunton, D. M. 5:19; 25:189
Huntoon, F. B. 7:75; 25:299
Huntoon, William P. 23:35
Huntorn, John 11:401
Huntress, E. S. 9:145; 27:58
Huntress, George H. 15:107
Huntress, H. 19:78
Huntress, J. K. W. 7:98
Huntress, James 21:349
Huntsberger, Amos 22:200
Huntsier, W. H. 3:102
Huntsinger, Josiah B. 21:72
Huntsman, Thomas O. 13:29
Huntsmore, G. 3:102
Huntsniser, P. 18:175
Huntsucker, George 10:119; 20:278

Huntwork, G. 1:141
Hunty, W. H. 15:166
Huntzinger, C. F. 25:44
Huntzinger, John T. 2:12
Huonker, J. J. 1:45
Huoy, George 20:278
Huperty, Louis 22:11
Hupp, George 22:481
Hupp, H. 18:241; 26:34
Hupp, John A. 23:191
Hupp, William W. 23:151
Hupple, Jasper 11:64
Hupsteller, David 9:83
Hur---, W. J. 25:40
Hurber, James 15:205
Hurbert, Benjamin 7:125
Hurbert, D. 3:102
Hurbert, J. H. 18:175
Hurbert, Richard 17:248
Hurbert, W. C. 3:102
Hurbiron, James 16:279
Hurch, James 17:171
Hurd, --- 14:182
Hurd, A. H. 23:151
Hurd, Bradford 27:55
Hurd, Byron 11:126
Hurd, Charles R. 11:115
Hurd, Francis 12:26
Hurd, Francis G. 21:349
Hurd, George 9:230;
  20:278
Hurd, Henry A. 14:182
Hurd, Hiram 15:17
Hurd, Isam 8:39; 26:165
Hurd, J. 11:304; 15:333;
  16:201; 19:78
Hurd, J. H. 21:349
Hurd, Jacob 10:119;
  20:278
Hurd, James 12:162;
  15:68
Hurd, James H. 15:342;
  16:371
Hurd, John 13:112
Hurd, Norman L. 17:155
Hurd, Paul 12:26
Hurd, Philander 7:98
Hurd, Robert F. 21:255
Hurd, Simeon 14:182
Hurd, Stephen 17:160;
  21:188
Hurd, Thomas 12:72;
  15:68
Hurd, W. C. 13:91
Hurd, William 13:29;
  21:349; 23:35
Hurdeman, Rudolph 9:138
Hurden, Harrison 24:196
Hurdle, R. 27:54
Hurdle, W. 1:141
Hurdnell, --- 3:102

Hurdo, Samuel 4:33
Hurdy, L. 20:57
Hure, Daniel 17:288
Huret, Ed 21:212
Hurey, Charles 22:200
Hurford, D. 11:340
Hurgly, P. 17:291
Hurgy, Joseph 8:64
Hurick, Albert 11:107
Hurin, R. E. C. 22:405
Huring, Columbus 5:40
Hurison, Charles 23:122
Hurkill, Henry H. 6:12
Hurkleberry, Jacob 6:10
Hurl, William 3:102;
  11:127
Hurlain, Thomas 20:27
Hurlbart, H. E. 1:42
Hurlbert, Griffin 20:278
Hurlbert, S. B. 3:102
Hurlbird, L. W. 15:330
Hurlburt, E. 15:205
Hurlburt, Edgar 16:39
Hurlburt, G. Q. 1:136
Hurlburt, Griffin 10:119
Hurlburt, J. G. 18:330
Hurlburt, John 10:99
Hurlburt, S. H. 22:37
Hurlburt, S. P. 15:173
Hurlburt, Wallace 20:278
Hurlbut, Edgar 13:29
Hurlbut, Francis 19:19
Hurlbut, Th. J. 14:182
Hurlbut, W. P. 1:41
Hurlen, T. 1:140
Hurless, Samuel S. 17:503
Hurless, William 11:412
Hurley, Addison 17:36
Hurley, Bartholomew
  22:37
Hurley, C. 21:349
Hurley, Charles 22:37
Hurley, D. 3:102
Hurley, Daniel 16:9;
  24:158
Hurley, Elizabeth E.
  26:220
Hurley, George 4:33
Hurley, George W. 22:84
Hurley, Harrison D.
  17:443; 24:159
Hurley, J. 3:102, 103;
  25:43
Hurley, J. C. 3:103
Hurley, J. J. 1:136
Hurley, James 1:42;
  15:126
Hurley, James J. 10:162
Hurley, James P. 22:405

Hurley, John 5:51;
  16:120, 201; 22:11;
  25:189
Hurley, John W. 16:5
Hurley, Joseph 10:162
Hurley, L. 15:17
Hurley, M. 11:340
Hurley, Maurice 11:222
Hurley, N. 14:241
Hurley, Patrick 14:182
Hurley, Peter 11:152
Hurley, Samuel 17:260
Hurley, Silas 21:227
Hurley, Thomas 1:40;
  16:96
Hurley, William H.
  21:349
Hurley, William K.
  17:291
Hurley, William M. 7:98
Hurling, J. 25:299
Hurlings, J. 7:78
Hurlis, J. 3:103
Hurly, I. 15:342
Hurly, J. 16:371
Hurly, John 8:19
Hurmack, D. 11:304
Hurman, John 10:162
Hurman, Samuel B. 5:19
Hurmington, David 19:78
Hurn, R. 3:103
Hurns, Peter 8:64
Hurols, Charles F. 17:479;
  27:64
Huron, Emanuel 17:425
Huron, Nelson 21:275
Hurr, John 15:348
Hurrey, --- 25:44
Hurron, Alfred 15:126
Hurron, Caxter 18:140
Hurry, John 21:208
Hurry, T. J. 20:278
Hurse, Levy W. 13:29
Hurse, Samuel 4:66
Hurseman, Galdman 9:43
Hurset, --- 15:159
Hursey, George 22:200
Hursh, Jeremiah 23:279
Hursh, John 13:112;
  21:227
Hursley, John 8:87
Hursly, August 20:279
Hurst, A. 1:140; 24:21
Hurst, Albert 21:149
Hurst, Allen 21:30
Hurst, Amer 15:7
Hurst, Charles 13:29
Hurst, Edward 10:60;
  20:279
Hurst, Elias C. 20:279
Hurst, George P. 22:84

Hurst, Horace 22:305
Hurst, James 9:97; 24:152
Hurst, John 12:82
Hurst, Lemuel 21:72
Hurst, M. 9:110; 18:241; 26:36
Hurst, Major 21:275
Hurst, Martin 4:33; 8:87
Hurst, Pleasant 22:255
Hurst, R. V. 3:103
Hurst, Robert 20:279
Hurst, S. A. 14:282
Hurst, Thomas A. 22:482
Hurst, Thomas C. 10:119; 20:279
Hurst, Tillman 21:130
Hurst, William 10:28; 13:112; 19:303
Hurst, William E. 17:53
Hurt, A. 17:155
Hurt, A. W. 18:241
Hurt, Anthony 6:12
Hurt, Bowen P. 23:89
Hurt, Charles 9:157
Hurt, Henry 22:305
Hurt, Jacob 8:20
Hurt, Jesse 17:133; 24:195
Hurt, Jonathan 16:39
Hurt, Joshua 24:59
Hurt, L. W. 26:37
Hurt, Michael 10:162
Hurt, R. F. 8:50
Hurt, W. 3:103
Hurt, William 22:451
Hurtbut, M. R. 24:94
Hurter, A. B. 16:279
Hurth, Joseph 18:141
Hurtle, Joseph 8:20
Hurton, V. 8:64
Hurtz, Charles 19:243
Hurtzell, Peter 25:322
Hurtzet, G. 14:269
Hurz, August 18:141
Hus, Adam 11:119
Hus, John 19:78
Hus, Ole O. 21:92
Husa, Ferdinand 19:46
Husband, Sandy 7:78; 25:299
Huse, George 18:241
Huse, John 1:41
Huse, Spencer I. 25:283
Huse, Wade H. 8:87
Husenetler, Charles 20:279
Husenetter, Charles 10:119
Husenul, Henry 23:279
Huser, C. W. 5:19
Huser, Isaac 8:88

Huser, John 19:19
Huseton, J. 27:57
Husey, John 12:26
Husez, H. B. 25:272
Hush, John 21:227
Hushman, A. 3:103
Hushman, F. S. 15:205
Husk, G. 12:8
Huskey, G. 16:96
Huskey, William 22:255
Husking, William H. 18:141
Huskins, Joseph 10:119; 20:279
Husley, D. W. 14:288
Husman, John 19:171
Husman, Joseph 9:36
Huson, A. 14:13
Huson, George B. 14:182
Huson, Peter E. 21:255
Huss, James W. 22:84
Huss, John 14:182
Huss, W. 3:103
Hussey, Byron 9:155
Hussey, C. B. 14:74
Hussey, D. W. 4:33
Hussey, Elijah 7:51
Hussey, Fred 7:75; 25:299
Hussey, J. R. 3:103
Hussey, John 7:99
Hussey, Kendrick 22:255
Hussey, Orrin C. 9:9
Hussey, R. B. C. 1:138
Hussey, Walter 21:349
Hussey, Walter H. 21:349
Hussong, T. M. 8:106
Husstudler, James H. 9:242
Hust, George 23:151
Hustave, Joseph 9:181
Husted, B. M. 18:68
Husted, David 12:26
Husted, E. 10:18
Husted, F. 1:41
Husted, Francis 7:51
Husted, Freeman 26:124
Husted, J. 3:103
Husted, Jacob M. 21:72
Husted, W. 25:189
Husted, William H. 9:204
Hustedt, W. 5:19
Huster, Albert J. 4:33
Hustin, Augustus 1:39
Hustin, Sylvanius 22:200
Hustin, W. H. 22:425
Hustings, J. 14:13
Hustler, John 19:254
Huston, --- 20:279; 23:203
Huston, A. 13:91; 14:13
Huston, Abel C. 21:349

Huston, Alexander 17:265
Huston, Burrell 11:205
Huston, Charles 7:99
Huston, D. R. 26:220
Huston, Edward 24:79
Huston, Elijah 8:88
Huston, F. 14:74
Huston, Felix 7:125
Huston, G. C. 11:304
Huston, G. I. 24:79
Huston, George 9:36
Huston, H. 20:279
Huston, H. S. 12:80; 25:189
Huston, Henry 17:133; 24:195
Huston, Henry C. 11:381
Huston, Hezekiah 10:91
Huston, Ira T. 13:29
Huston, J. 1:94; 7:30
Huston, J. M. 10:60; 23:151
Huston, J. T. 25:41
Huston, James 3:103; 12:26; 23:69
Huston, Jeremiah 17:81
Huston, John 3:103; 13:65
Huston, Joseph 11:150; 21:212; 22:426
Huston, Joshua E. 26:34
Huston, P. M. 9:54
Huston, S. H. 21:30
Huston, Samuel J. 22:37
Huston, Seth 18:272
Huston, Thomas S. 20:97
Huston, W. D. 18:207
Huston, William 22:84
Huston, William H. 7:30
Hustons, Robert 15:205
Hustson, John 17:317
Hustson, Rufus 17:317
Hutbard, T. 14:74
Hutch, James 11:115
Hutchens, J. 24:40
Hutchens, W. 1:136
Hutchenson, --- 15:363
Hutchenson, Edward 9:72
Hutchenson, J. E. 1:137
Hutcher, Reuben 10:119
Hutcherson, E. R. 22:481
Hutcheson, John 18:218
Hutchin, Randal 23:271
Hutching, G. H. 15:294
Hutching, Thomas J. 9:83; 26:33
Hutchings, A. E. 19:78
Hutchings, A. S. 21:349
Hutchings, Charles F. 21:349
Hutchings, Dayton P. 17:81

Hutchings, G. H. 16:201
Hutchings, G. W. 7:30
Hutchings, George 10:18;
    13:29
Hutchings, H. W. 3:103
Hutchings, Henry H. 4:33
Hutchings, J. B. 1:136
Hutchings, John 10:119;
    20:279
Hutchings, John C. 9:181
Hutchings, L. D. 9:181
Hutchings, M. 18:85
Hutchings, O. 14:74
Hutchings, S. A. 3:103
Hutchings, W. 25:189
Hutchings, W. W. 1:44
Hutchings, William A.
    10:60
Hutchingson, Alexander
    21:349
Hutchingson, Andrew
    21:349
Hutchingson, G. 21:349
Hutchingson, Johnson
    5:19
Hutchingson, William
    21:349
Hutchins, --- 16:151
Hutchins, B. F. 11:319
Hutchins, Benjamin 8:88
Hutchins, Bryant 10:162;
    19:171
Hutchins, Charles F.
    9:214
Hutchins, Charles W.
    10:173; 19:171
Hutchins, D. F. 22:200
Hutchins, E. 11:100
Hutchins, F. M. 15:81
Hutchins, G. W. 3:103;
    14:74
Hutchins, George 9:24;
    15:37, 205; 18:309;
    26:101
Hutchins, George W.
    22:337
Hutchins, Hiram 9:120;
    27:60
Hutchins, Hollis 27:61
Hutchins, Ira B. 23:258
Hutchins, J. C. 18:175
Hutchins, J. E. X. 10:186
Hutchins, J. F. 1:137
Hutchins, J. Q. 12:82
Hutchins, J. W. 3:103
Hutchins, James 13:112
Hutchins, John 14:74;
    22:84
Hutchins, John A. 22:427
Hutchins, L. D. 19:228
Hutchins, Lewis 20:57

Hutchins, Martin 6:10
Hutchins, Meredy 20:147
Hutchins, Moses 12:170
Hutchins, Noah 14:182
Hutchins, R. N. 1:138
Hutchins, Robert 18:430
Hutchins, S. 3:103
Hutchins, Samuel 22:84
Hutchins, T. 22:200
Hutchins, T. C. 22:200
Hutchins, Theodore 22:84
Hutchins, Thomas 13:57
Hutchins, W. 9:221;
    18:369
Hutchins, W. H. 7:99
Hutchins, Warren 8:72
Hutchins, William 3:103
Hutchins, Zachariah
    21:130
Hutchinson, A. 13:65;
    16:201, 372
Hutchinson, A. P. 8:39;
    26:163
Hutchinson, Aaron B.
    18:353
Hutchinson, Albert 21:275
Hutchinson, Albert B.
    9:36
Hutchinson, Alex 10:91
Hutchinson, Alexander
    20:279
Hutchinson, Alfred 26:37
Hutchinson, Amos 9:24
Hutchinson, Amos J.
    18:309
Hutchinson, Andrew
    11:219
Hutchinson, Andrew J.
    11:32
Hutchinson, Benjamin F.
    25:189
Hutchinson, Bruce 22:451
Hutchinson, C. 1:42
Hutchinson, C. D. 17:409
Hutchinson, Charles 11:64
Hutchinson, Charles H.
    27:63
Hutchinson, Charles P.
    11:32
Hutchinson, Clayborn D.
    22:37
Hutchinson, Cyrus 9:16
Hutchinson, D. W. 7:99
Hutchinson, David 8:50;
    9:54
Hutchinson, E. 2:12;
    14:182; 25:38
Hutchinson, Enoch H.
    22:37
Hutchinson, Eugene W.
    23:260

Hutchinson, Evan 10:60
Hutchinson, F. 1:140;
    3:103
Hutchinson, G. A. 17:159
Hutchinson, G. L. 2:12;
    25:38
Hutchinson, George 17:91
Hutchinson, George P.
    22:11
Hutchinson, H. C. 1:135
Hutchinson, H. H. 17:158
Hutchinson, H. P. 1:135
Hutchinson, H. S. 25:276
Hutchinson, I. 24:21
Hutchinson, Isaac N. 7:58
Hutchinson, J. 3:103;
    9:145; 11:280;
    19:303; 21:349;
    25:189
Hutchinson, J. M. 8:64;
    26:164
Hutchinson, J. R. 22:12
Hutchinson, J. W. 11:322
Hutchinson, Jacob 10:60
Hutchinson, Jam. C.
    20:279
Hutchinson, James 9:24,
    83, 97; 11:187;
    18:320; 26:32; 27:57
Hutchinson, James C.
    10:119
Hutchinson, James N.
    22:84
Hutchinson, James O.
    11:413
Hutchinson, James W.
    9:12
Hutchinson, Jesse 22:305
Hutchinson, Jessie
    18:241; 26:36
Hutchinson, John 9:120;
    18:218; 22:255, 426;
    26:124
Hutchinson, John H.
    12:26
Hutchinson, John I. 22:84
Hutchinson, Joseph 22:84
Hutchinson, Josiah N.
    11:115
Hutchinson, L. 11:151
Hutchinson, M. C. 25:276
Hutchinson, Mathews
    20:142
Hutchinson, N. H. 7:30
Hutchinson, O. 14:74
Hutchinson, Orville W.
    13:29; 16:39
Hutchinson, R. 7:30;
    21:54; 25:189
Hutchinson, Reuben
    13:112

Hutchinson, Richard D. 7:99
Hutchinson, Robert 11:151; 19:19; 22:84
Hutchinson, S. K. 9:24
Hutchinson, S. R. 26:101
Hutchinson, Samuel 10:8, 119; 19:19; 26:165
Hutchinson, Saul 8:39
Hutchinson, Simson 22:406
Hutchinson, Smith 11:387
Hutchinson, Solon L. 11:62
Hutchinson, Sylvester 4:33
Hutchinson, Thomas 22:37
Hutchinson, W. 17:36
Hutchinson, W. B. 19:78
Hutchinson, W. F. 9:83
Hutchinson, W. H. 1:139
Hutchinson, William 1:41; 10:205; 12:26; 26:211
Hutchinson, William B. 4:33
Hutchinson, William C. 1:45
Hutchinson, William H. 18:111
Hutchinson, William W. 22:12
Hutchison, B. 11:263
Hutchison, Evan 20:279
Hutchison, J. 11:242; 17:203
Hutchison, J. A. 11:263
Hutchison, Richard 24:79
Hutchison, Samuel 20:279
Hutchison, William 15:299; 18:202; 22:200
Hutchman, Robert 5:19
Hutchson, John 27:60
Hutell, John 8:88
Huteson, W. E. 3:103
Huth, Andrew 23:285
Huthinson, Amos J. 26:100
Hutington, J. 1:138
Hutley, C. 12:80
Hutner, Henry 10:60
Huto, Charles 16:39
Huton, D. R. 9:236
Huton, Francis 21:30
Hutsell, Edward 11:63
Hutsell, Jacob 22:427
Hutsell, John 17:96
Hutson, E. J. 20:57
Hutson, Elisha 10:60

Hutson, J. 10:28; 14:74; 19:303
Hutson, J. E. 27:57
Hutson, Joel 19:171
Hutson, Joshua E. 18:241
Hutson, Peter 23:243
Hutson, R. 23:151
Hutson, Solomon 22:427
Hutson, William 11:63; 25:189
Hutt, A. J. 16:201
Hutt, Ed 11:333
Hutt, Henry 18:253
Huttenhouse, J. 13:81; 16:201
Hutter, C. G. 18:85
Hutter, John 10:119; 20:279
Huttie, John 16:39
Hutto, J. W. 18:68
Hutto, John 26:124
Hutton, Aaron 20:17
Hutton, Clement C. 20:107
Hutton, Elijah 23:250
Hutton, G. 1:135
Hutton, J. 11:119
Hutton, James 10:60; 20:279; 21:204
Hutton, James R. 7:71; 26:165
Hutton, Melville 14:269
Hutton, Morris 20:279
Hutton, S. 3:103
Hutton, S. D. 9:24
Hutton, Samuel 10:162
Hutton, William 23:122
Hutton, William R. 11:62
Huttoncoffer, George 20:279
Hutts, G. H. 9:145
Hutts, Henry 10:60
Hutts, James 17:36
Hutts, John 9:43
Huty, T. I. 26:35
Huty, T. J. 18:241
Hutzel, George I. 4:33
Hutzel, J. 14:13
Hutzell, John 23:35
Hutzell, Peter 25:322
Huub, William F. 11:63
Huves, D. 19:78
Huvet, Elijah S. 10:119
Hux, Thomas 7:125; 21:349
Huxley, Charles 15:304; 16:201
Huxley, D. E. 23:151
Huxley, D. W. 23:151
Huxley, Harvey 21:10
Huyck, Charles A. 22:146

Huyck, Hiram 23:151
Huyck, William O. 10:60
Huylehand, M. 1:43
Huyler, Lorenzo 16:39
Huzark, J. 14:182
Hyall, Charles G. 15:126
Hyam, D. 1:141
Hyan, Thomas 13:112
Hyand, Lawrence 11:387
Hyatt, --- 20:17
Hyatt, A. B. 18:141
Hyatt, Alfred 22:481
Hyatt, B. A. 22:255
Hyatt, Charles 23:279
Hyatt, Fudy 24:195
Hyatt, G. 9:234
Hyatt, G. B. 18:141
Hyatt, Henry C. 23:69
Hyatt, J. 3:103
Hyatt, J. W. 25:43
Hyatt, Jack 22:305
Hyatt, James 20:279
Hyatt, James G. 18:111
Hyatt, James H. 22:84
Hyatt, Jerome 21:54
Hyatt, John 22:200
Hyatt, Joseph 10:18, 60; 11:63
Hyatt, Ludy 17:133
Hyatt, M. 1:138
Hyatt, M. H. 22:200
Hyatt, Milton 7:99
Hyatt, O. B. 8:20
Hyatt, Samuel 21:198
Hyatt, Washington 16:201
Hyatt, William 15:205; 16:201; 18:31; 21:54
Hyatt, Wilson 11:64
Hyber, John 3:103
Hyde, --- 27:157
Hyde, A. D. 20:133
Hyde, A. L. 3:103
Hyde, Abel 7:99
Hyde, Alfred 17:96; 21:255
Hyde, C. 3:103
Hyde, C. V. 12:148
Hyde, Charles A. 16:96
Hyde, Charles F. 1:41; 24:79
Hyde, Charles H. 18:85
Hyde, Chauncey 5:51
Hyde, Chauncy 25:189
Hyde, Chester 14:182
Hyde, Croyden L. 7:99
Hyde, E. 3:103
Hyde, Edward 26:220
Hyde, Esek A. 20:279
Hyde, Esick A. 10:119
Hyde, Ethan M. 9:24
Hyde, Ezra 16:96

Hyde, Freeman 16:39
Hyde, G. 3:103
Hyde, George 13:112
Hyde, George B. 1:40
Hyde, German 14:335
Hyde, H. P. 25:38
Hyde, Henry 17:404;
     20:147
Hyde, Henry P. 2:12
Hyde, Isaac V. 13:29
Hyde, J. 16:140
Hyde, J. E. 15:205
Hyde, J. F. 3:103; 14:75
Hyde, J. G. 22:280
Hyde, J. P. 9:221; 18:369
Hyde, J. W. 20:279
Hyde, Jacob 7:30
Hyde, James S. 22:471
Hyde, Joel 21:139
Hyde, John D. 11:388
Hyde, John Henry 20:147
Hyde, John M. 13:29
Hyde, John W. 10:60
Hyde, Leonard M. 17:65
Hyde, Lycurgus 21:30
Hyde, M. A. 13:112
Hyde, Pelatiah 17:288
Hyde, Philip 22:305
Hyde, R. 12:80; 25:189
Hyde, Richard 3:103
Hyde, Robert J. 24:79
Hyde, S. H. 9:221
Hyde, Samuel 14:182
Hyde, W. 14:182
Hyde, W. G. 23:151
Hyde, W. H. 19:245
Hyde, William 16:201
Hyde, William H. 9:181
Hyde, Wilson 14:75
Hydenberg, Daniel 27:61
Hyder, Comfort 1:40
Hyder, James P. 21:101
Hyder, S. H. 18:369
Hyder, Theodore 4:33
Hydom, D. 1:44
Hydon, Nath 7:64
Hydran, Joseph 13:57
Hydrick, L. 1:139
Hydrom, H. 1:137
Hyer, A. 14:75
Hyer, James 14:183
Hyer, Mathew 13:135;
     19:346
Hyer, Thomas 12:26
Hyer, W. 14:183
Hyers, E. 3:103
Hyers, Jacob W. 10:60;
     20:279
Hyers, Josiah 15:27
Hyes, J. C. 3:103
Hyett, T. 15:205

Hyett, William 26:34
Hyette, S. N. 6:31
Hyffin, William 11:222
Hygate, Frank 7:64
Hyger, Thomas H. 4:33
Hyke, F. 19:254
Hyke, Frederick 9:181
Hyke, George A. 1:40
Hykes, J. 1:141
Hykes, John 11:64
Hyland, Charles 13:29
Hyland, G. G. 1:139
Hyland, John 12:26; 13:91
Hyland, Martin 7:30
Hyland, O. 3:103
Hyle, Thomas 22:502
Hyler, Daniel 17:395
Hyler, F. H. 22:481
Hyler, G. H. 11:438
Hyler, H. 21:30
Hyler, J. H. 13:112
Hyliard, A. J. 25:41
Hylton, James W. 11:93
Hyman, Anthony 11:401
Hyman, B. F. 16:201
Hyman, Frank 18:31
Hyman, Henry 18:309;
     26:101
Hyman, J. 3:103
Hymers, B. 3:103
Hymes, Frank 21:349
Hymes, William 15:69
Hymeyer, Simon 12:26
Hyndes, --- 15:205
Hyne, William W. 24:40
Hynemon, A. 11:219
Hyner, Joseph 9:181;
     19:267
Hynes, Bernis W. 4:33
Hynes, J. W. 26:35
Hynes, Jesse 22:513
Hynes, John 16:9
Hynes, M. 16:296
Hynes, Milton 22:84
Hynes, Terence 14:183
Hynes, Thomas W. 24:21
Hyney, John H. 25:189
Hynicka, C. C. 14:75
Hynly, John C. 5:19
Hynson, Charles 14:13
Hyrer, Charles 18:31
Hyrne, R. T. 7:99
Hyron, Thomas C. 27:55
Hyronemus, James 3:103
Hys, David 11:151
Hysel, Ogmia 9:24
Hysell, Addison 24:79
Hysell, Gabriel 14:183
Hysell, H. 26:163
Hysell, Richard 4:33
Hysen, B. 11:149

Hysenberger, Lewis 4:33
Hyslip, George 6:35
Hyslop, David 19:319
Hyson, Freeling 7:125
Hyson, Thomas G. 11:127
Hysong, S. C. 11:263

I

I---, B. F. 24:21
I---, D. 14:269
I---, E. B. 11:280
I---, H. M. 11:152
I---, I. 21:204
I---, I. W. 11:428; 17:281
I---, J. O. 11:242
I---, John H. 16:372
I---, Leopold 11:242
I---, N. B. B. 11:231
I---, P. R. 24:21
I---, T. B. 24:21
Ibbey, David 5:19
Ibeck, Carl 8:20
Ibelbeck, W. 3:103
Iber, J. 9:103
Ibes, Jacob 23:151
Ibes, John 10:91; 20:279
Ibrith, Carl 18:141
Ice, Andrew J. 21:122
Ice, Frederick 10:119;
     20:279
Ice, J. G. 14:75
Ice, James 22:428
Ice, Jesse A. 23:69
Ice, Thomas 17:422
Ich-har-se-yar-holer
     25:333
Ickes, D. 22:200
Icough, John 9:83
Ida, Eckhardt 7:99
Idall, C. 9:145
Idall, Comely 27:65
Iddings, Jacob O. 22:84
Iddings, James N. 24:40
Ide, Bernard 1:45
Ide, Darius 11:242
Ide, Edward D. 7:30
Ide, George W. 23:191
Ide, S. R. 3:103
Idel, Jacob 9:83
Idel, James 15:335
Idell, Edward 9:208
Idleman, Sylvester 9:54
Idlet, Robert 7:125
Idlett, William 9:239
Idner, Thomas 22:428
Idoax, John J. 22:123
Idol, Adam 14:75
Idol, Henry 23:198
Idol, James 15:335; 19:78

Idold, A. 3:103
Ifoes, William C. 15:56
Iglehart, John D. 22:452
Igo, J. 1:142
Igo, T. 3:103
Igon, James W. 20:41
Ihiecutt, F. J. 9:54
Ihle, S. 2:13; 25:45
Ihle, William 10:60; 20:279
Ihose, Eli 6:23
Ijams, Joseph H. 26:166
Ijanes, Joseph H. 8:20
Iker---, S. 24:51
Ilen, J. 18:339
Iler, Wilson S. 11:152
Iliff, John 18:207
Iliff, John G. 8:101; 17:459; 24:153
Iliff, T. F. 11:65
Iliff, Thomas H. 10:119; 20:279
Illenberger, John 19:19
Illinger, Jacob 11:242
Illingsworth, John P. 20:113
Illingsworth, Joseph 13:129
Illingsworth, W. P. 20:113
Illson, Silas F. 10:178
Illson, Silas T. 10:151
Illy, Tobias 3:103
Ilpenco, M. 23:180
Ilriger, E. 17:436
Ilsley, James 9:181
Ilsley, S. 19:228
Ilson, J. M. 15:353
Ilsted, William S. 4:33
Ilur, C. 3:103
Imber, Amos 13:29
Imbler, I. 24:99
Imboden, Eli 7:68
Imboden, J. 1:142; 3:103
Imbody, D. 1:142
Imbody, J. W. 1:94
Imbush, John 6:31
Imegan, --- 18:207
Imer, Frederick 15:87
Imer, J. 3:103
Imes, Giles 10:60; 20:279
Imes, J. H. 8:50
Imhoff, --- 3:103
Imhoff, J. 3:103
Imhoff, R. 3:103
Imhoff, Samuel G. 11:152
Imhope, Z. B. 1:45
Imil, John M. 22:428
Imlay, C. S. 19:228
Imlay, E. 3:103
Imlay, Robert 22:84
Imler, D. 1:142

Imman, Nath 18:190
Immel, --- 1:142
Immel, William 1:45
Immell, John R. 10:120; 20:279
Impson, Joseph 4:33
Impson, Samuel C. 12:26
Imus, Elon I. 18:396
Inbert, Cassius 9:181
Inch, J. L. 8:50
Inch, William 16:85
Inches, David D. 18:141
Inderin, Charles L. 9:110
Inders, Palentine 19:171
Indfield, Jacob 17:337
Indian, William 16:39
Indlecome, Adam 23:263
Inery, John K. 16:120
Infant, J. 1:142
Infer, John 9:66; 18:277
Ing, Edward 11:187
Ingalbe, Hamilton 4:33
Ingall, Robert L. 7:68
Ingalls, Andrew E. 22:406
Ingalls, Hiram 15:348
Ingalls, John P. 22:146
Ingalls, L. 1:142
Ingalls, M. 7:51
Ingalls, M. N. 15:17
Ingalls, Melvine 12:26
Ingalls, Perry 10:60; 20:279
Ingalls, W. 21:188
Ingalls, Walter 16:201
Ingalls, William B. 12:72
Ingalls, William H. 21:240
Ingalsve, Levi 13:112
Ingamells, Charles 21:139
Ingamells, I. R. 25:283
Ingel, Dexter W. 9:12
Ingersal, W. H. 18:369
Ingersol, Albert 13:29
Ingersol, S. G. 11:402
Ingersol, Samuel 11:413
Ingersoll, --- 14:299; 17:473
Ingersoll, Albert 16:39
Ingersoll, Benjamin 27:65
Ingersoll, C. 15:316
Ingersoll, Calvin 19:78
Ingersoll, Edward 6:21
Ingersoll, F. D. 25:189
Ingersoll, J. H. 20:41
Ingersoll, J. S. 10:60; 20:279
Ingersoll, James H. 22:37
Ingersoll, James N. 23:191
Ingersoll, John 17:440; 24:153
Ingersoll, R. 9:66

Ingersoll, Samuel 3:103
Ingersoll, Seth C. 8:88
Ingersoll, T. J. 1:45
Ingersoll, W. H. 9:221
Ingersoll, Willard 22:84
Ingersoll, William 13:91; 14:13
Ingerson, Frederick 13:29
Ingerson, S. 3:103
Ingham, C. 9:181; 19:228
Ingham, Charles 9:43
Ingham, Frank 21:275
Ingham, Hamilton 22:280
Ingham, Henry 21:275
Ingham, J. 3:103
Ingham, Jonathan 10:18
Ingham, William 22:337
Ingland, Anderson 10:60; 20:279
Ingland, Moses 7:51
Ingle, Almon 13:29
Ingle, Charles 14:75
Ingle, Charles H. 9:83; 26:37
Ingle, Elijah S. 21:54
Ingle, Francis M. 22:428
Ingle, J. R. 25:275
Ingle, James H. 20:89
Ingle, James S. 21:349
Ingle, Jesse 22:37
Ingle, John J. 8:106
Ingle, Murray 23:15
Ingle, Perley 26:138
Ingle, Reece B. 23:184
Ingle, William 9:24; 13:29; 18:309; 22:200; 26:103
Inglehardt, David 20:174
Inglehart, William 22:305
Ingleman, Robert 17:133
Ingleman, Samuel 17:178
Ingler, George 14:75
Ingler, William 3:103
Ingles, James 11:381
Inglesby, A. 23:35
Ingless, Samuel 7:99
Ingless, William 22:37
Ingleton, E. 14:75
Inglis, Archibald 21:227
Inglo, Albert 13:112
Ingman, Thomas 13:29
Ingmandson, Hiram 10:120
Ingmanson, Hiram 20:279
Ingmun, W. 11:152
Ingolls, David 16:39
Ingolls, L. 3:103
Ingols, David 13:29
Ingomar, Thomas 16:39
Ingosbie, R. 15:286
Ingraham, A. 7:68

Ingraham, A. W. 27:65
Ingraham, Agreen 22:428
Ingraham, Alexander
27:65
Ingraham, B. F. 23:113
Ingraham, C. B. 3:103
Ingraham, C. H. 21:349
Ingraham, D. 22:463
Ingraham, Douglass
11:287
Ingraham, George M. 4:33
Ingraham, George N.
19:171
Ingraham, George W.
16:120
Ingraham, Hardin 18:434
Ingraham, I. D. 17:291
Ingraham, J. 1:45; 22:38
Ingraham, Jacob 22:38
Ingraham, James K. 9:97
Ingraham, John 11:34;
17:91; 22:123
Ingraham, Joseph 12:140
Ingraham, L. J. 21:349
Ingraham, Lewis 21:275
Ingraham, Samuel 11:396
Ingraham, Smith 10:120;
20:279
Ingraham, T. 15:263
Ingraham, Thomas 23:122
Ingraham, W. L. 3:104
Ingraham, William
14:183; 18:31
Ingrahm, William 14:236
Ingram, A. F. 21:30
Ingram, C. 25:45
Ingram, Charles 17:166
Ingram, George N. 10:162
Ingram, George W. 8:106;
20:125
Ingram, Isaac P. 22:167
Ingram, J. 21:188
Ingram, James 8:112;
9:43; 26:125
Ingram, James A. 16:39
Ingram, John 11:396;
17:166
Ingram, John F. 20:23
Ingram, Kennedy 22:84
Ingram, L. 14:183, 257
Ingram, M. H. 18:51
Ingram, M. V. 18:51
Ingram, Meradath 24:153
Ingram, Meredith 17:440
Ingram, Nicholas 13:29
Ingram, T. 16:201
Ingram, Thomas 17:281
Ingram, Wesley 26:37
Ingram, William 10:120;
20:279

Ingram, William A.
17:447; 24:171
Ingrams, James 22:123
Ingrams, John W. 17:281
Inguson, P. 3:104
Inhoff, J. 12:87; 14:75;
16:296
Inhoff, John 22:482
Inhuff, F. P. 18:31
Inject, J. W. 7:99
Inker, Stephen 17:425
Inkess, G. 19:303
Inkis, I. 21:30
Inks, Hiram 10:120;
20:279
Inks, I. 15:342
Inks, J. 16:372
Inks, J. H. 1:142
Inland, James 9:83
Inlock, John 18:450
Inloes, L. 14:183
Inloff, Joseph 7:99
Inloff, S. 14:75
Inlok, John 10:211
Inlow, Hapsin 19:291
Inlow, Hopson 9:200
Inlow, John 17:443;
24:159
Inman, --- 19:171
Inman, A. H. 15:205
Inman, Abraham 21:241
Inman, Chandler 14:75
Inman, Darius H. 22:146
Inman, Ebenezer 17:321
Inman, Frank 21:217
Inman, G. 13:91; 14:13
Inman, George J. 16:7
Inman, Isaiah 17:66
Inman, J. L. 14:75
Inman, J. P. 3:104
Inman, J. R. 12:62; 15:56
Inman, J. T. 23:151
Inman, John 3:104; 10:60;
18:207
Inman, Joseph 10:120;
20:279
Inman, Leroy T. 23:301
Inman, Moses 27:65
Inman, Nathan 13:29
Inman, Philip 22:428
Inman, Timothy 21:198
Inman, W. 21:201
Inman, Welcome L. 20:30
Inman, Wesley 11:327
Inmann, --- 10:162
Inmann, J. P. 14:75
Inmans, Willis 22:502
Innerson, Lafayette 11:93
Innes, Benjamin 9:83
Innes, J. E. 1:45
Innes, P. 1:142

Innes, William 20:279
Inness, A. J. 11:34
Innis, Beverly 7:125
Innis, Chancey 19:19
Innis, Isaac 1:45
Innis, Michael 21:349
Innis, S. M. 21:30
Innis, William 10:60
Innison, E. 13:112
Innman, H. 22:399
Innman, W. 3:104
Innon, A. B. 21:86
Innuis, J. P. 13:130
Inom, M. 9:154
Insche, J. F. 12:26
Inscho, David D. 8:20
Inscho, David F. 22:428
Inscol, D. M. 19:171
Insign, Nelson 5:19
Inskeep, L. D. 1:142
Inskeep, Phineas S. 24:94
Inskess, G. 10:28
Inskip, Job 22:200
Inslee, H. 19:171
Insley, Henry 25:322
Insley, Joseph 22:112
Inwon, A. B. 21:208
Inwood, Arthur 23:69
Ioekel, George 16:85
Ioidiker, Charles 8:20
Ipe, J. 1:142
Ira, Pugsley 9:214
Irabinet, Archibald 16:39
Iraney, Lawrence 19:278
Irbing, John 7:125
Ireckson, George 14:75
Iredon, James C. 10:173
Iredon, John C. 19:171
Irelan, J. B. 10:28; 19:303
Irelan, John G. 21:227
Irelan, Robert 5:19
Ireland, Alex 13:112
Ireland, Alexander 17:36
Ireland, Bowens 12:26
Ireland, D. 1:45
Ireland, E. D. 26:221
Ireland, George 3:104;
12:148
Ireland, Goodwin S. 16:78
Ireland, H. C. 21:30
Ireland, Henry 10:60;
20:279
Ireland, J. S. 3:104
Ireland, James 18:51;
26:37
Ireland, James T. 10:148
Ireland, John D. 22:84
Ireland, John J. 11:242;
20:147
Ireland, Jonathan C.
23:151

Ireland, Jonathan R. 22:428
Ireland, L. 9:97
Ireland, N. B. 1:98
Ireland, Nathan 22:200
Ireland, Oscar 27:65
Ireland, R. 13:91; 14:13
Ireland, Reuben 11:182
Ireland, Rinaldo 15:11
Irens, Charles W. 22:146
Irescott, Solon M. 8:117
Ireson, J. 3:104
Ireton, T. R. 3:104
Irion, R. 25:189
Irion, Robert 5:19
Iris, G. 12:85; 16:296
Irish, A. J. 25:189
Irish, Albert J. 5:19
Irish, Alonzo 13:29
Irish, Andrew J. 22:463
Irish, Charles S. 19:78
Irish, Eli 26:166
Irish, G. 3:104; 14:75
Irish, George 18:346
Irish, Harvey 7:80; 25:299
Irish, Joseph 12:59
Irish, Noble 6:7
Irish, Pat 14:75
Irish, Robert 19:317
Irish, Sidney P. 17:243
Irish, Stephen 6:21
Iriss, William 18:369
Irlam, J. 1:142
Irlay, H. 3:104
Irmland, P. 14:75
Iroin, George 9:200
Iroin, James D. 8:20
Iroin, Robert 8:20
Iron, H. 3:104
Iron, John 8:20; 18:141
Irons, Birdsall C. 10:18
Irons, John M. 16:96
Irons, Loften 10:176;
    19:171
Irons, Phelon 7:125
Irons, Stephen 19:19
Irskip, Augustus 9:24
Irvan, Samuel 4:33
Irves, Levi 7:125
Irves, William 9:221
Irvin, A. 11:34
Irvin, Elijah 23:180
Irvin, Francis 11:305
Irvin, George 22:305
Irvin, Henry 16:96
Irvin, J. A. 11:152
Irvin, J. C. 14:299;
    17:479; 27:65
Irvin, J. T. 20:137
Irvin, James 8:106
Irvin, James C. 17:91

Irvin, James D. 18:141
Irvin, Jesse S. 22:452
Irvin, John 5:51; 25:189
Irvin, John D. 10:120;
    20:279
Irvin, John V. 4:33
Irvin, Joseph 12:26
Irvin, Martin 27:65
Irvin, Nicholas 22:235
Irvin, P. P. 3:104
Irvin, Robert 18:141;
    22:305
Irvin, T. H. 1:142
Irvin, T. W. 1:142
Irvin, Thomas 22:428
Irvin, W. 23:151
Irvin, William 23:69
Irvin, William J. 16:296
Irvin, William K. 22:123
Irvin, William R. 22:255
Irvin, Wyatt 7:125
Irvine, Anthony 17:397
Irvine, James 15:336;
    19:78
Irvine, John 24:79
Irvine, Thomas 12:8
Irvine, W. 17:191; 21:349
Irving, B. 19:291; 27:65
Irving, C. 14:75
Irving, Calhoun 21:275
Irving, Charles 27:65
Irving, David 17:36
Irving, Ester 3:104
Irving, G. C. 14:75
Irving, Henry 17:397
Irving, I. 15:342
Irving, James 16:120
Irving, John 4:33
Irving, Madison 10:173;
    19:171
Irving, Nelson N. 4:33
Irving, Oliver 7:125
Irving, W. 3:104
Irving, W. J. 22:519
Irvingpower, D. 14:299;
    17:479; 27:65
Irvins, Beverly 21:349
Irwen, David 5:19
Irwin, --- 23:277; 25:44
Irwin, A. 3:104
Irwin, Albert 1:45; 23:271
Irwin, Andrew J. 16:372
Irwin, Archibald S. 21:72
Irwin, C. 1:94; 14:183
Irwin, Charles 26:37
Irwin, Charles M. 23:180
Irwin, D. 20:41
Irwin, D. E. 1:142
Irwin, David 10:60;
    15:56; 20:279
Irwin, Edwin S. 18:15

Irwin, Eli 21:212
Irwin, Eli S. 24:52
Irwin, Elijah 9:165
Irwin, G. 1:142
Irwin, George 12:26;
    25:281
Irwin, George P. 8:50
Irwin, George R. 9:36
Irwin, H. 16:151
Irwin, Harrison 13:112
Irwin, Henry 9:208;
    17:443; 24:159, 182
Irwin, J. 1:142; 8:50;
    14:183, 257; 16:372
Irwin, James 8:99; 14:183
Irwin, Jerome B. 21:30
Irwin, Jesse 23:35
Irwin, John 9:110; 10:96;
    11:182
Irwin, John H. 23:151
Irwin, John M. 22:428
Irwin, L. 21:122
Irwin, L. H. 1:45
Irwin, Lafayette 22:406
Irwin, Lawson 11:205
Irwin, Marion 10:205
Irwin, Oliver 10:60;
    20:279
Irwin, Orin 18:68
Irwin, P. 11:219
Irwin, Patrick 17:419
Irwin, Robert 1:45;
    11:191; 15:22;
    20:280; 21:188
Irwin, S. P. 17:387
Irwin, Samuel 8:88
Irwin, Samuel G. 21:72
Irwin, Stewart 1:45
Irwin, T. 1:142
Irwin, Thomas 4:33;
    11:388; 22:398
Irwin, W. N. 1:142
Irwin, W. P. 11:34
Irwin, Wesley 22:84
Irwin, William 18:396;
    22:200
Irwine, A. B. 17:295
Irwing, George 19:291
Irwing, Robert 10:60
Irwins, Patrick 24:159
Isaac, Benjamin 17:36
Isaac, Harvey 26:37
Isaac, J. J. 23:117
Isaac, Pierre 21:349
Isaac, Thomas 19:78
Isaach, Thomas 13:65
Isaachson, I. 17:102
Isaackson, L. 25:189
Isaacs, Benjamin 22:428
Isaacs, Francis 17:260
Isaacs, Francis M. 22:428

Isaacs, G. W. 17:191
Isaacs, Harvey 18:241
Isaacs, Henry 3:104
Isaacs, James 21:275
Isaacs, P. 21:349
Isaacs, Preston 21:86
Isaacs, Spencer 22:305
Isaacs, W. 24:196
Isaacson, Ole 21:92
Isabel, Lewis 9:145
Isabel, Thomas 9:230
Isabell, A. 3:104
Isabell, Benjamin H.
    20:46
Isabell, G. 14:75
Isabett, J. M. 3:104
Isabit, John 22:305
Isacks, John 18:31
Isam, Henry H. 20:97
Isam, Richard 10:60
Isaman, Henry 12:26
Isans, Frederick 1:45
Isbel, E. 18:31
Isbell, Alfred 8:64
Isbell, John W. 20:46
Isch, Frederick 23:263
Ische, John 15:335
Ischi, John 19:78
Ischike, Thomas 9:181
Isdell, --- 15:95
Iseminger, Hiram 21:227
Isen, John H. 8:99
Isenberg, J. 23:35
Isenberger, Miles H.
    17:443; 24:159
Isenhart, Jacob B. 23:151
Isenhart, John 22:84
Isenhauer, J. J. 14:75
Isenhower, J. 3:104
Isensmith, Charles 9:110
Iserman, --- 12:168
Isert, Peter 12:96; 15:360;
    19:78
Isett, Fulton 24:52
Isett, John H. 18:396
Isett, M. G. 16:120
Isgreeg, Michael F.
    22:428
Isham, Andrew 17:178
Isham, D. 3:104
Isham, J. 22:38
Isham, Lewis J. 22:255
Isham, Nelson 22:352
Isham, W. B. 23:313
Ishart, N. 3:104
Ishler, Jacob 20:125
Ishmael, James 11:65
Ishmael, Levi 7:31
Ishmael, Louis 7:31
Ishmael, Thomas R. 22:84
Ishmael, William 22:200

Ishmail, George W.
    21:188
Ishmale, James 11:65
Ishman, Nelson 11:234
Isingoff, Henry 22:428
Isinhard, Nathaniel 17:81
Isinhart, S. 21:54
Isla, --- 7:65
Islan, R. 25:189
Island, George 26:221
Island, Patrick 1:45
Isle, James 25:189
Islep, George 15:91
Isley, A. M. 25:189
Isley, Charles 17:36
Isley, M. R. 17:96
Islicke, T. 19:274
Islingbrice, B. 17:53
Islinger, F. E. 15:205
Ismael, William 24:21
Isman, Henry 18:207
Ismer, J. 25:189
Ismon, Albert L. 10:120;
    20:280
Ismond, A. F. 23:260
Isnar, Adolphus 23:122
Isom, Andrew 22:305
Isom, Isaac 20:280
Isom, J. 17:178
Isom, Richard 20:280
Isom, Robert 7:99; 21:349
Isom, William 21:275
Ison, Isaac 10:60
Ispharding, Henry 12:26
Israel, Elisha 18:396
Israel, John 9:230; 20:280
Israel, S. 3:104
Israelson, Andrew 20:33
Israelson, J. G. 9:242
Isrig, M. S. 22:398
Issaman, Michael 19:19
Issup, I. 14:13
Ister, John 19:325
Istu, --- 8:106
Iswell, E. M. 14:75
Ite, John 11:340
Item, Jacob 21:92
Itle, John 15:69
Ittel, Lawrence 4:33
Itzenhauzer, John 22:38
Iv---, K. 11:305
Ivans, John 18:85
Ivans, William D. 13:29
Ivars, Daniel 19:171
Ivens, James 11:34
Ivers, Andrew H. 22:482
Ivers, Daniel 10:162
Ivers, James 16:96
Ivers, N. 1:142
Iverson, Elling 22:280
Iverson, J. B. 18:68

Iverson, J. S. 3:104
Iverson, Ole 17:70
Iverson, William 22:305
Iverton, Christian 4:33
Ivery, Norman 10:60
Ives, Albert 15:289;
    16:201
Ives, Anderson 22:305
Ives, C. H. 1:45
Ives, C. N. 11:287
Ives, George 9:240
Ives, Harrison P. 10:173;
    19:171
Ives, Hobert H. 19:254
Ives, Homer Levi 17:500
Ives, John 6:25
Ives, Joseph 10:162;
    19:171
Ives, R. J. 1:142
Ives, R. S. 1:94
Ives, Richard 22:305
Ivey, Edly 22:452
Ivey, Jackson 21:149
Ivey, S. 13:129
Ivin, J. 21:163
Iviner, Reuben 9:120
Ivline, Andrew J. 15:205
Ivory, H. D. 15:285; 19:78
Ivory, Jacob 21:149
Ivory, Jesse 21:275
Ivory, Norman 20:280
Ivory, Thomas 14:183
Ivy, Claiborne 21:349
Izer, Jeremiah 12:55
Izzard, A. J. 11:340

J

J---, --- 11:264, 340;
    16:372; 19:303
J---, A. 11:340; 20:280
J---, A. C. 24:21
J---, B. 15:336; 20:155;
    23:292
J---, B. A. 23:313
J---, C. 10:192; 24:214
J---, C. M. 16:296
J---, D. 9:54
J---, D. H. 23:313
J---, E. S. 23:292
J---, E. W. 16:372
J---, Ernst H. 16:201
J---, F. 10:192; 26:204
J---, G. S. 9:54
J---, G. W. 11:340
J---, George A. 15:285
J---, H. 9:54; 15:173;
    17:506; 21:349
J---, H. C. 23:313
J---, H. D. 23:313

J---, H. L. 9:54
J---, J. 19:303; 20:57; 23:313; 26:168
J---, L. 8:50; 11:153, 219
J---, L. H. 23:282
J---, M. 9:54; 15:207; 18:412
J---, M. B. D. 23:313
J---, N. R. 23:279
J---, O. 11:65
J---, O. Mc. 23:313
J---, P. 11:264; 16:296; 20:155
J---, P. S. 23:313
J---, Porter 11:264
J---, R. 17:217
J---, R. A. 20:57
J---, R. J. 25:46
J---, S. 22:352; 23:271, 313
J---, T. 10:28; 20:155; 21:166; 23:245
J---, W. 11:264; 15:37; 17:217, 364; 23:307
J---, W. A. 9:54
J---, W. H. 23:250
J---, W. J. 23:313
J---, W. M. 20:57
J---, W. R. 11:280; 21:208
J---, W. W. 20:57
J----, T. 22:169
J---leby, R. 11:322
J---lton, --- 11:439
J---s, Robert 25:193
J---y, A. 17:509
Jabbott, J. 1:143
Jabitt, J. 1:46
Jabo, Joseph 26:212
Jabocson, Jacob 10:60
Jaccards, S. A. 3:104
Jacent, P. 1:143
Jack, --- 22:337
Jack, A. 9:200
Jack, Benjamin S. 3:104
Jack, D. 22:482
Jack, David 22:256
Jack, Francis 21:349
Jack, G. T. 1:143
Jack, George E. 14:75
Jack, Harrison A. 9:7
Jack, J. D. 23:289
Jack, J. E. 12:142; 20:280
Jack, J. H. 1:143
Jack, J. P. 3:104
Jack, J. W. 3:104
Jack, James 18:175
Jack, Jesse J. 22:256
Jack, John 7:126
Jack, John P. 23:69
Jack, Michael 17:425; 24:178

Jack 25:333
Jack Walking Stick 25:333
Jackel, John Jacob 15:259
Jackett, Alonzo 10:162
Jackett, Ashley R. 4:33
Jackett, E. V. 22:463
Jackland, C. 3:104
Jacklin, Phillip 19:171
Jackman, A. J. 18:241; 26:39
Jackman, G. B. 1:144
Jackman, H. 25:322
Jackman, Henry 18:320
Jackman, M. 11:191
Jackman, Nathan 17:496
Jackman, R. A. 22:337
Jackman, Samuel 9:70; 18:241
Jackman, W. H. 9:181
Jackman, William 11:119
Jackmaw, W. H. 19:238
Jackner, Thomas 14:75
Jacko, Thomas 20:280
Jackobie, S. A. 1:46
Jackquens, C. 3:104
Jacks, Henry 25:285
Jacks, James M. 11:65
Jacks, John 13:135; 19:346
Jacks, John F. 21:227
Jacks, Laport 10:162
Jacks, Layport 20:280
Jacks, S. S. 20:280
Jacks, Thomas 10:60
Jackson, --- 11:153, 206; 18:68; 23:35, 268
Jackson, A. 3:104; 9:200; 16:201; 17:133; 18:31; 20:174; 21:122; 24:196; 27:66
Jackson, A. C. 9:24
Jackson, A. D. 27:69
Jackson, A. F. 1:46
Jackson, A. H. (Mrs.) 18:68
Jackson, A. J. 3:104; 18:309; 26:103
Jackson, A. W. 20:85
Jackson, Abraham 21:72
Jackson, Abram 7:71; 21:275
Jackson, Addison 7:99; 12:49
Jackson, Albert 9:208
Jackson, Alex 9:132; 10:120; 20:280
Jackson, Alexander 9:54; 17:453; 24:183; 25:189; 27:67

Jackson, Alf 25:299
Jackson, Alfred 4:33; 7:78; 15:291; 16:201; 19:46; 22:429
Jackson, Alonzo 4:33; 22:337
Jackson, Amos J. 21:212
Jackson, Anderson 24:52
Jackson, Andrew 6:12, 17, 25, 27; 7:126; 8:20, 40; 9:54, 132; 10:60, 208; 12:49; 17:102, 133, 161; 18:85, 141; 19:78; 20:280; 21:54, 139, 275, 349; 22:146, 305, 406, 513; 24:101, 197; 26:166, 167; 27:68
Jackson, Andrew P. 24:167
Jackson, Anthony 9:132; 12:26; 27:68
Jackson, Armistead 19:291
Jackson, Athol 22:429
Jackson, August M. 7:99
Jackson, Augustus 4:66
Jackson, Avery P. 22:255
Jackson, B 9:239
Jackson, B. 7:99; 21:349
Jackson, B. C. 16:113
Jackson, Benjamin 12:49
Jackson, Benjamin F. 25:46
Jackson, Burrel 19:46
Jackson, Byron S. 24:52
Jackson, C. 19:78; 25:189
Jackson, C. F. 1:143
Jackson, C. J. 7:126
Jackson, C. R. 14:75
Jackson, C. W. 8:50; 13:29
Jackson, Caesar 27:69
Jackson, Charles 9:132, 204; 12:49; 13:57; 17:62; 18:241; 23:191; 25:45; 26:38; 27:68
Jackson, Charles A. 7:31
Jackson, Charles H. 21:349
Jackson, Charles M. 22:305
Jackson, Charles S. 12:26
Jackson, Clark 14:183
Jackson, Cornelius 21:72
Jackson, D. J. 17:456; 24:214
Jackson, Daniel 15:299; 16:201; 19:46; 21:349; 23:277

Jackson, David 9:43;
    22:406; 26:125
Jackson, E. 11:243;
    13:103; 14:13, 75;
    16:269; 17:273;
    23:99
Jackson, E. D. 9:181;
    19:254
Jackson, E. J. 18:51
Jackson, Ed 17:265
Jackson, Edward 9:162;
    11:34; 13:57;
    15:348; 16:372;
    27:69
Jackson, Edward A.
    19:171
Jackson, Elbridge 22:429
Jackson, Elijah 8:88
Jackson, Ephraim 7:126;
    9:132; 27:65
Jackson, Everett W.
    23:151
Jackson, Eylbert D. 16:39
Jackson, Eylut D. 13:29
Jackson, F. 10:192;
    21:110; 24:101
Jackson, Foster 24:79
Jackson, Francis M.
    17:347
Jackson, Frank 7:126;
    10:176; 12:26;
    19:171; 24:21
Jackson, Franklin 9:132;
    18:397; 27:67
Jackson, Fred 15:205;
    16:201
Jackson, G. 13:91;
    16:269; 25:189
Jackson, G. A. 27:66
Jackson, G. H. 25:189
Jackson, G. J. 14:183
Jackson, G. M. 7:31
Jackson, G. W. 8:20;
    14:183; 16:201;
    18:141
Jackson, Gale 17:178
Jackson, General 24:101
Jackson, George 5:41;
    8:88; 9:181; 11:85;
    13:57; 14:319;
    16:201; 17:133, 203;
    18:207; 19:274;
    21:349; 23:309;
    24:79, 197; 25:281;
    27:65
Jackson, George G. 3:104
Jackson, George H.
    14:257
Jackson, George M. 8:88
Jackson, George T. 9:83

Jackson, George W.
    15:205; 20:113;
    21:349
Jackson, Gilbert 11:116
Jackson, Gilford 21:350
Jackson, Gobt 18:111
Jackson, Green 21:350
Jackson, Greenberry 8:88
Jackson, Greenville
    11:152
Jackson, H. 1:45; 3:104;
    15:37; 16:201;
    17:178; 21:122;
    25:189; 27:65
Jackson, H. A. 25:189
Jackson, H. C. 2:13
Jackson, H. S. 12:154
Jackson, H. W. 14:282;
    17:432; 24:153
Jackson, Hanibal 24:101
Jackson, Hanson 8:40;
    26:167
Jackson, Harris 21:275
Jackson, Henry 5:41;
    6:31; 7:126; 8:40, 50;
    9:24, 208, 213;
    12:72; 15:205;
    17:133, 390; 18:68;
    19:291; 20:9; 21:227,
    350; 22:428; 23:271;
    24:197; 26:37, 167
Jackson, Henry C. 24:159
Jackson, Henry G. 10:162;
    19:171
Jackson, Henry T. 9:83
Jackson, Herman 19:19
Jackson, Hiram 12:154;
    17:133; 18:31;
    24:197
Jackson, Hugh 25:189
Jackson, I. 8:40
Jackson, Isaac 11:108;
    15:205; 18:111;
    22:235
Jackson, J. 1:47, 144;
    3:104; 5:56; 9:54;
    12:82; 13:103;
    16:201, 269, 296;
    22:305; 23:35;
    25:189, 285; 26:167
Jackson, J. A. 9:72; 20:57
Jackson, J. D. 20:92
Jackson, J. F. 25:189
Jackson, J. H. 1:143;
    14:183; 16:201
Jackson, J. J. 11:335;
    13:112; 22:200
Jackson, J. L. 11:192
Jackson, J. M. 7:126;
    10:60; 20:280
Jackson, J. P. 25:277

Jackson, J. R. 17:91
Jackson, J. S. 3:104
Jackson, Jack 18:190
Jackson, Jacob 13:29;
    16:39; 17:53
Jackson, Jacob C. 20:27
Jackson, Jacob W. 12:26
Jackson, James 3:104;
    6:35; 7:31, 68, 126;
    8:20, 40; 9:54; 10:60;
    11:206; 13:57; 16:39,
    202; 17:36, 178;
    18:141; 20:280;
    21:350; 22:84;
    24:197; 26:167
Jackson, James A. 11:340
Jackson, James C. 22:167
Jackson, James H. 4:33;
    8:20; 18:141
Jackson, James M. 20:97
Jackson, James R. 21:54;
    22:256
Jackson, James V. 17:281
Jackson, James W. 17:243
Jackson, Jarvis W. 6:23
Jackson, Jeff 17:178
Jackson, Jeremiah 6:17;
    7:126; 18:86; 21:133
Jackson, Jerry 21:275;
    22:513
Jackson, Jesse 8:114;
    22:84
Jackson, Jesse D. 22:281
Jackson, Joel P. 13:29
Jackson, John 3:104; 4:33;
    5:19; 6:25; 7:78, 126;
    8:88, 106; 9:12;
    10:60, 120; 11:65;
    12:49; 13:57; 15:69,
    205; 16:39, 372;
    17:66, 178, 291, 406;
    18:218, 241; 20:280;
    21:54; 22:305, 502;
    23:69; 24:40; 25:189,
    299; 26:39
Jackson, John A. 1:45;
    17:206
Jackson, John B. 8:88
Jackson, John E. 4:33
Jackson, John F. 21:54
Jackson, John J. C. 22:281
Jackson, John L. 7:71
Jackson, John M. 19:46
Jackson, John W. 19:46;
    22:305; 23:305
Jackson, Jorden 9:54
Jackson, Joseph 1:45;
    5:41; 7:99; 10:60;
    11:243, 413; 17:260;
    21:350; 22:38;
    25:189; 26:168

Jackson, Joseph H. 17:236
Jackson, Joseph R. 11:388
Jackson, Josiah 19:46
Jackson, Julius A. 23:89
Jackson, L. 20:142
Jackson, L. C. 25:45
Jackson, L. M. 21:350
Jackson, L. T. 9:83; 26:38
Jackson, L. W. 14:282
Jackson, Lafayette 21:95;
24:67
Jackson, Lawson 7:126
Jackson, Lemon W.
22:428
Jackson, Leonard 7:126;
21:350
Jackson, Lewis 6:17;
18:86
Jackson, Lucas 17:415;
24:153
Jackson, Luther William
14:269
Jackson, Lysander 19:78
Jackson, Major 11:338
Jackson, Marshall 7:99
Jackson, Martin W.
10:120; 20:280
Jackson, Michael 22:38
Jackson, Milton M. 23:69
Jackson, Morris 18:31
Jackson, Moses B. 20:107
Jackson, Moses W.
22:406
Jackson, N. 3:104; 25:190
Jackson, Nathaniel 23:69
Jackson, Nelson 5:41
Jackson, O. P. 27:69
Jackson, O. W. 22:200
Jackson, Oliver 13:29
Jackson, Orlando 21:249
Jackson, Oscar C. 23:151
Jackson, Owen 16:39
Jackson, P. 7:31
Jackson, P. A. 16:202
Jackson, Patrick 12:26
Jackson, Paul 9:208
Jackson, Perry 8:20;
12:163; 14:183;
18:141
Jackson, Peter 17:178;
19:46
Jackson, Peter B. 22:305
Jackson, Peyton 6:28
Jackson, Prescott 22:171
Jackson, Preston 9:24
Jackson, R. 3:104; 8:50;
14:183; 16:202;
17:133; 24:196;
27:69
Jackson, R. C. 15:205
Jackson, R. John 10:60

Jackson, R. W. 3:104;
9:227; 16:372;
18:369
Jackson, Richard 8:40;
17:215; 26:167
Jackson, Robert 9:165;
17:133; 19:78;
24:197
Jackson, S. 1:143; 3:104;
11:306; 13:103;
14:183; 16:269
Jackson, S. E. 3:104
Jackson, Samuel 1:191;
9:208; 11:333;
21:350; 22:305;
26:38
Jackson, Sandford 27:67
Jackson, Sanford 9:132
Jackson, Scott 24:197
Jackson, Simeon 17:133;
24:196
Jackson, Spencer 17:178
Jackson, Spofford 14:334
Jackson, Stephen 15:348
Jackson, Stine 16:372
Jackson, T. 3:104
Jackson, T. A. 3:104
Jackson, T. B. 23:117
Jackson, T. C. 11:153
Jackson, T. J. 25:190
Jackson, T. M. 15:316
Jackson, Thatcher 21:275
Jackson, Theodore 7:126
Jackson, Thomas 4:66;
6:12; 11:20; 13:29;
15:69; 16:39, 202;
18:86; 19:19; 21:122,
227; 25:190; 27:66
Jackson, Thomas B. 22:84
Jackson, Thomas J.
22:167
Jackson, Thomas M.
19:78
Jackson, U. S. 3:104
Jackson, Ulrick B. 10:120;
20:280
Jackson, Valentine 7:126
Jackson, Vincent 23:282
Jackson, W. 1:46, 94, 144;
14:288; 15:126, 205;
21:30, 86; 23:69,
151; 25:190
Jackson, W. B. 21:30
Jackson, W. C. 20:280
Jackson, W. F. 11:388
Jackson, W. G. 13:91
Jackson, W. H. 14:13;
16:140; 24:21
Jackson, W. J. 9:157;
11:264

Jackson, W. P. 8:64;
26:167
Jackson, W. R. 3:104
Jackson, Wade 18:241;
26:39
Jackson, Warren N. 4:33
Jackson, Wellington
9:132, 181; 27:67
Jackson, William 3:104;
4:33; 5:41; 7:126;
8:50, 64, 88; 11:93,
127, 206; 12:122;
13:57; 14:183, 265;
16:202; 17:14, 133;
21:350; 22:305, 429;
23:151, 271; 24:52,
197; 25:285
Jackson, William A. 4:66
Jackson, William B. O.
17:206
Jackson, William C. 10:60
Jackson, William E.
17:347
Jackson, William H.
10:18; 22:38; 24:52;
25:45
Jackson, William J.
14:183
Jackson, William M.
21:166
Jackson, William N.
15:305; 19:78
Jackson, Wilson 5:41
Jackson, Y. 18:176
Jackson, Yaney 19:322
Jackwith, J. H. 12:26
Jaco, J. 1:142
Jacob, J. P. 17:36
Jacob, L. L. 17:101
Jacob, Martin 16:133
Jacob, S. 1:143
Jacob, Tipton 24:167
Jacobee, Benjamin F.
22:483
Jacobia, Webster 10:162;
19:171
Jacobin, P. 18:241
Jacobin, R. 26:39
Jacobison, Andrew 11:191
Jacobs, --- 2:13; 14:183;
15:205; 25:46
Jacobs, A. 13:91; 14:13
Jacobs, Adolphus 4:66
Jacobs, Alonzo 4:33
Jacobs, B. 16:202
Jacobs, B. G. 3:104
Jacobs, Boz 11:243
Jacobs, C. 17:209
Jacobs, C. C. 9:66; 18:277
Jacobs, C. O. 11:428
Jacobs, C. W. 11:264

Jacobs, Casper 1:46
Jacobs, Charles 9:181;
    10:120; 19:233;
    20:280
Jacobs, Christopher
    23:151
Jacobs, D. C. 11:243
Jacobs, Daniel 17:36;
    22:429
Jacobs, Daniel G. 21:30
Jacobs, E. 1:46
Jacobs, Ed. L. 17:248
Jacobs, Elias 10:120;
    11:85; 20:280
Jacobs, Eugene 9:181
Jacobs, G. 11:153
Jacobs, G. W. 11:306;
    19:78
Jacobs, George 4:66;
    17:81; 24:21
Jacobs, George A. 13:112
Jacobs, George C. 22:146
Jacobs, George D. 17:260
Jacobs, H. 3:104
Jacobs, Henry 8:124;
    17:152
Jacobs, Isaac 22:513
Jacobs, J. 14:183, 257,
    263
Jacobs, J. A. 16:202
Jacobs, J. B. 23:151
Jacobs, J. L. 3:104
Jacobs, Jacob 3:104;
    7:125; 21:350
Jacobs, James 9:208;
    18:86, 277; 22:38
Jacobs, James F. A. 7:31
Jacobs, Joel 23:11
Jacobs, John 9:24, 181;
    14:183; 15:273;
    18:218, 309; 19:254;
    26:38, 103; 27:65
Jacobs, John W. 3:104;
    10:120
Jacobs, John William
    20:280
Jacobs, Joseph 4:33;
    11:65
Jacobs, M. 16:202
Jacobs, N. S. 1:142
Jacobs, Ned 26:38
Jacobs, P. A. 15:205
Jacobs, P. O. 3:105
Jacobs, Peter 7:125
Jacobs, Philip 7:125;
    21:350
Jacobs, R. 1:143
Jacobs, S. K. 13:112
Jacobs, Samuel 10:60;
    20:280
Jacobs, T. 1:143

Jacobs, Thomas 17:397
Jacobs, U. D. 1:143
Jacobs, W. 9:145; 10:186;
    13:91; 27:66
Jacobs, W. B. 20:85
Jacobs, W. C. 3:105
Jacobs, W. D. 9:181
Jacobs, Washington 8:40;
    26:166
Jacobs, Willard 18:176
Jacobs, William 6:23;
    8:50; 11:65; 12:154;
    14:13; 18:86; 20:147;
    26:166
Jacobs, William H. 12:26
Jacobs, William I. 23:113
Jacobs, William J. 10:120;
    20:280
Jacobs, Willis 20:280
Jacobsky, Adolph 23:123
Jacobson, C. 13:91
Jacobson, Carl 22:281
Jacobson, E. 13:91; 14:14
Jacobson, Francis 9:12
Jacobson, J. 16:268
Jacobson, Jacob 20:280
Jacobson, John 23:191
Jacobson, Julius 4:33
Jacobson, O. 3:105
Jacobson, Otto F. 4:33
Jacobus, John 9:181;
    17:21
Jacobus, Levi K. 22:406
Jacobus, Thomas 22:519
Jacoby, Charles 12:169
Jacoby, David 12:26
Jacoby, Henry 17:81
Jacoby, James 4:33
Jacoby, John 7:125
Jacoby, John E. 23:191
Jacoby, John R. 17:355
Jacoby, Peter J. 11:153
Jacoby, T. 25:46
Jacolus, J. 14:75
Jacox, M. 23:35
Jacox, Nathaniel D.
    15:107
Jacoy, Edwin 10:120;
    20:280
Jacquemain, James A.
    10:192
Jacquet, J. 1:46
Jacquette, Antoine 13:29
Jacquith, Ambrose 9:103
Jacquith, Charles 14:28
Jacqumin, I. A. 18:176
Jacquott, Antoine 16:39
Jacrman, J. 9:163
Jadwin, Isaac 15:56
Jaeger, Herman 17:81
Jaeger, Peter 13:57

Jaepler, George M. 19:278
Jaffrey, John J. 21:255
Jafres, Jacob 7:51
Jagel, Lewis 4:33
Jagels, Peter 18:241;
    26:39
Jager, Aug 21:101
Jager, Charles 7:31
Jager, Douglas 12:154
Jager, Peter 4:34
Jager, T. 23:69
Jaggart, John 23:151
Jaggens, Benjamin F.
    22:256
Jagger, D. K. 22:482
Jagger, Daniel 16:39
Jagger, Daniel E. 13:29
Jaggers, Charles W.
    22:123
Jaggers, George 9:110
Jaggers, Jeptha 17:281
Jaggre, Lucius 9:120
Jaggus, Joseph 27:69
Jagler, Matteson 24:197
Jahn, Maximilian 10:120
Jahn, Maximillian 20:280
Jaideka, Charles 18:141
Jaine, W. A. 19:326
Jaines, T. A. 21:101
Jains, J. 1:45
Jairl, William H. 23:89
Jaistic, John 1:45
Jake, A. R. 3:105
Jake, William 7:126
Jakel, Charles 8:20;
    18:141
Jalber, J. W. 17:455
Jaleert, Cassins 19:254
Jaler, Amos 23:290
Jaleson, Edwin 11:191
Jam, A. 15:94
Jamar, Isaac 2:13
Jambeel, James 26:103
Jambrel, James 18:294
Jamerson, K. H. 13:112
Jamerson, S. 18:369
James, --- 8:20; 9:97, 181;
    12:87; 13:65; 26:167
James, A. 16:202; 19:46;
    25:190
James, A. A. 23:35
James, A. L. 13:112
James, Albert 22:84
James, Alfred 21:350
James, Allen 9:132
James, Alonzo 21:350;
    25:299
James, Andy 5:41
James, Arthur 22:256
James, B. 1:94
James, B. C. 19:326

James, B. W. 23:35
James, Boston 9:200
James, C. 24:99
James, Carey 9:221
James, Cary 18:369
James, Charles 12:64;
15:4; 18:32; 22:200
James, Charles E. 1:46;
18:15
James, Charles H. 18:32
James, Christian A. 8:106
James, Christopher 17:110
James, Clark 27:145
James, Colonel 27:69
James, Cornelius J. 20:48
James, Courtney M. 12:26
James, D. B. 23:151
James, D. L. 25:190
James, Daniel H. 10:120;
20:280
James, Daniel W. 18:241;
26:38
James, David 16:202
James, E. P. 12:142;
20:281
James, Ebenezer H.
16:153
James, Edward 11:34
James, Edward S. 4:34
James, Elijah 10:60;
20:281
James, Emanuel 22:200
James, Evan D. 12:26
James, Frank 14:183
James, Frederick A. 3:105
James, Freeman 17:314
James, G. 13:103; 17:273;
19:254
James, G. H. 1:143
James, Garrett 15:259
James, Geo O. 22:337
James, George 11:153;
15:69, 159; 17:96;
18:346; 20:183;
23:69
James, George L. 18:15
James, H. 1:143; 25:45,
275
James, Harrison 9:230;
20:281
James, Harvey 12:122;
15:126
James, Henry 6:17, 25;
9:100; 17:53; 18:86;
22:84; 23:69;
25:322; 27:67
James, Henry C. 9:69
James, Henry T. 22:200
James, Horace 9:242
James, Hubert D. 17:70
James, Hugh 22:84

James, Irven D. 7:99
James, Irvin D. 21:350
James, Isaac 6:13
James, Isaac M. 22:38
James, J. 23:304
James, J. A. 25:190
James, J. E. 23:35
James, J. F. 25:190
James, J. J. 26:167
James, J. R. 26:167
James, J. T. 26:38
James, Jacob 15:323;
19:78
James, James 18:32
James, James D. 11:306
James, James H. 8:20
James, Jesse 11:65
James, Jessie 26:212
James, John 1:46, 191;
4:66; 5:19; 8:40;
9:43; 11:153; 18:207;
19:19; 20:155;
21:275; 22:123, 503;
26:167
James, John C. 11:153
James, John H. 18:294;
26:167
James, John M. 16:5
James, John P. 18:103
James, John S. 22:123
James, John T. 21:204
James, John W. 10:120;
17:393; 20:281;
23:35, 252
James, Jonathan 10:120;
20:281
James, Joseph 10:205;
19:171
James, Joseph H. 18:141
James, Joseph O. 18:344
James, Joshua 10:173
James, L. 17:178; 21:188
James, L. Cass 22:509
James, Lorenzo 21:350
James, M. 16:202; 25:190
James, M. S. 10:60
James, Marc L. 21:350
James, Marion 11:153
James, Martin V. 1:46
James, Merril 24:101
James, Michael 7:126
James, Milo 22:200
James, Milton 17:53
James, N. 25:190
James, Nates A. 18:309
James, Nathan 17:110
James, Nelson 5:19
James, P. 16:202
James, P. G. 9:243
James, Perry 22:406

James, Philip 10:60;
20:281
James, Pierre 7:126
James, Prince 27:68
James, R. D. 1:46
James, Richard A. 5:52
James, Richard J. 25:46
James, Robert G. 1:45
James, Robert H. 6:25
James, S. L. F. 27:69
James, Samuel 16:120
James, Seth 11:153
James, Squire 21:275
James, T. 16:202
James, T. B. 9:54
James, Theodore 19:46
James, Thomas 11:34,
206; 12:26; 15:69;
16:96; 18:32, 421;
19:78
James, Vincent 9:208
James, W. 1:143; 3:105
James, W. A. 1:143
James, W. C. 23:282
James, W. D. 7:99
James, W. H. 26:167
James, W. J. 7:75; 25:299
James, W. S. 20:281
James, W. W. 14:75
James, Watt A. 26:103
James, William 1:46;
7:31; 8:121; 9:83;
14:321; 17:401;
18:86; 21:350;
23:243; 26:38
James, William A. 6:12;
9:24; 17:387
James, William D. 7:31
James, William H. 13:30;
22:16
James, William W. 10:25
Jameson, Abram 27:69
Jameson, Benjamin
22:513
Jameson, Charles 3:105
Jameson, Edward 9:103;
18:339
Jameson, Horace 19:326
Jameson, Isaac 8:20;
17:133; 18:141;
24:197
Jameson, J. F. 18:241
Jameson, J. R. 14:75
Jameson, James E. 15:37
Jameson, John 7:99; 9:208
Jameson, John R. 13:30
Jameson, Orin M. 23:191
Jameson, P. M. 10:60
Jameson, S. 1:46
Jameson, Siver 8:20;
18:141

Jameson, T. 16:202
Jameson, W. B. 14:75
Jameson, W. S. 26:125
Jameson, William 3:105
Jameson, William R. 22:146
Jamett, Thomas D. 16:39
Jamieson, J. 25:46
Jamieson, J. H. 14:14
Jamieson, J. S. 3:105
Jamieson, James 2:13
Jamieson, Stephen 19:239, 282
Jamine, James 3:105
Jaminman, M. N. 15:343
Jamison, A. 3:105
Jamison, Charles 18:421
Jamison, D. 12:166
Jamison, Daniel 22:84
Jamison, David A. 19:19
Jamison, E. 21:54
Jamison, Francis W. 13:30; 16:39
Jamison, H. 3:105
Jamison, Hugh 2:13; 18:219
Jamison, J. H. 13:91
Jamison, J. T. 26:38
Jamison, Jacob 22:84
Jamison, James E. 12:64
Jamison, James F. 22:38
Jamison, Jesse M. 20:17
Jamison, John 1:46; 9:181; 12:26; 23:151
Jamison, John A. 22:84
Jamison, John F. 20:104
Jamison, Joshua 22:305
Jamison, Merritt 23:89
Jamison, P. M. 20:281
Jamison, Q. 1:45
Jamison, Samuel 9:83
Jamison, Stephen 9:200
Jamison, W. E. 9:54
Jamison, William 9:43; 18:219
Jamison, William H. 12:49; 16:39
Jamison, William I. 11:65
Jamison, William W. 13:30
Jammison, John 10:153
Jamsey, Frederick 7:31
Jamson, Mills 16:147
Jamy, --- 26:212
Jandough, T. J. 23:151
Jane, D. 14:75
Janes, D. T. 1:46
Janes, F. 19:286
Janes, Isaac 9:97
Janes, J. A. 9:221
Janeson, G. 17:178

Janett, Allen 18:309; 26:103
Janett, Levi 17:36
Janier, George 9:181
Janier, W. A. 19:19
Janiper, J. 9:157
Janis, J. B. 12:154
Janks, J. P. 3:105
Jannes, Perry 12:154
Jannon, G. 27:65
Janny, --- 11:305
Jannygan, Alexander 21:275
Janorin, H. S. 13:125
Janot, Joseph 9:12
Jansel, Christian 12:154
Jansen, Claus 24:94
Jansen, Herman 15:27
Jansen, L. 9:200
Janson, Niel S. 22:509
Janson, Peter 19:171
Janson, S. 7:99
Janssen, Johann 15:173
January, John 22:256
Janvier, J. 25:45
Janviur, William F. 27:69
Jaquay, W. E. 23:35
Jaquayes, Oliver 22:463
Jaquays, B. C. 12:26
Jaquays, R. 3:105
Jaque, Joseph 10:152
Jaque, M. S. 10:186
Jaques, H. 3:105
Jaques, John L. 10:60
Jaques, Wilber 11:264
Jaquest, Christopher 21:227
Jaquets, E. H. 15:159
Jaquette, John 15:205
Jaquies, John 27:66
Jaquish, Emmet 9:66; 18:277
Jaquith, A. 10:18
Jaquith, George W. 13:30
Jaquith, H. 1:143
Jaquith, James 12:72; 15:11
Jaramille, --- 19:322
Jarbet, Morton 19:47
Jarboe, W. 7:31
Jared, Joel 23:35
Jarger, August 11:191
Jarinard, --- 19:78
Jarman, Arthur 20:9
Jarman, Gabe 17:178
Jarman, W. 8:50; 21:166
Jarman, William 9:204; 18:68
Jarmier, C. 3:105
Jarmin, Early I. 8:20
Jarmin, Early J. 18:141

Jarnegan, John 8:88
Jaro, W. 1:143
Jarosh, I. H. 13:112
Jarred, Johnson 17:178
Jarrell, William 17:349
Jarrett, A. 17:178
Jarrett, Allen 9:24
Jarrett, C. 9:181
Jarrett, Godfrey 9:200
Jarrett, James 27:68
Jarrett, Joseph 22:84
Jarrett, Lafayette 22:38
Jarrett, Owen 22:352
Jarrett, R. 14:75
Jarrett, Robert 17:360
Jarrin, Joseph 9:181
Jars, John 11:88
Jarvett, W. 3:105
Jarvis, --- 2:13; 25:46
Jarvis, A. R. 17:236
Jarvis, Adam 6:17; 18:86
Jarvis, Albert 17:81
Jarvis, Alexander 11:388
Jarvis, Burrel 27:66
Jarvis, C. E. 25:46
Jarvis, Charles 21:227
Jarvis, E. 3:105
Jarvis, F. 3:105
Jarvis, Francis 20:174
Jarvis, G. G. 18:277
Jarvis, Harrison 22:38
Jarvis, Isaac 20:41
Jarvis, J. 13:91; 21:350
Jarvis, James 18:219
Jarvis, John 10:120; 20:57, 281; 22:352
Jarvis, John M. 20:137
Jarvis, Jonas 11:127
Jarvis, Julius 13:30
Jarvis, Lawson 22:38
Jarvis, Lyman 17:243
Jarvis, Mead 22:200
Jarvis, Samuel A. 7:126
Jarvis, Thomas 15:309; 19:79; 21:227
Jarvis, W. D. 3:105
Jarvis, Wade 21:101
Jarvis, William 14:183; 17:402
Jarvis, William H. 10:18
Jasbol, John 8:107
Jasby, J. 25:190
Jasey, Isaac 18:327
Jasks, Silas 10:60
Jaslyn, J. 15:152
Jason, William 7:84
Jasper, A. 21:163
Jasper, Edward 22:305
Jasper, Franklin 17:133; 24:197
Jasper, George M. 9:181

Jasper, James 18:32
Jasper, Joseph 1:45
Jasper, Moses 18:241;
  26:39
Jasper, Robert 14:183
Jasper, Samuel 8:72
Jasper, W. 16:202
Jasper, William 3:105
Jassehlen, Abraham 6:21
Jasselyn, A. 14:14
Jasslyn, A. 13:91
Jastatt, Albert 23:151
Jaster, Aaron 19:171
Jastin, E. 27:66
Jaswait, Hector 7:126
Jate, Henry 18:202
Jate, William 18:202
Javer, E. M. 13:65
Javill, Russell 22:305
Jay, Alex 12:8
Jay, B. F. 7:99
Jay, F. 27:157
Jay, G. F. 3:105
Jay, George 23:107
Jay, H. 3:105
Jay, J. M. 18:241
Jay, John 3:105
Jay, John T. 20:281
Jay, Mills 6:21
Jay, Nathaniel P. 14:183
Jay, Price H. 11:153
Jaycox, Moses 9:132;
  27:67
Jaycox, Stephen 11:388
Jayne, Stephen 22:85
Jayner, J. E. 16:96
Jaynes, --- 18:111
Jaynes, A. J. 20:41
Jaynes, John L. 20:281
Jaynes, Pascal 19:79
Jaynes, Thornton 26:167
Jaynes, W. 23:151
Je---, P. D. 15:206
Jean, Barker D. 11:413
Jean, E. A. 20:281
Jean, W. S. 25:190
Jeane, Alex 11:280
Jeanes, J. R. 8:73
Jeanes, William 20:97
Jeanks, F. 14:183
Jeanpriter, Charles 26:103
Jeanputter, Charles 9:36
Jeans, E. A. 10:60
Jeaupreter, Charles 18:294
Jebb, P. J. W. 2:13; 25:46
Jebring, Nathan 1:45
Jecko, Peter 27:160
Jeddings, Julian A. 20:102
Jedenris, N. 25:190
Jedison, Christopher 9:24
Jedman, Christ 24:52

Jedwith, Sewell 5:19
Jeems, Jackson 10:99
Jeff, M. 3:105
Jeffen, David 17:428
Jefferies, H. 1:142
Jeffers, A. 15:166
Jeffers, David 24:184
Jeffers, Elias 21:30
Jeffers, Elijah 11:84
Jeffers, George K. 22:256
Jeffers, Henry E. 15:69
Jeffers, J. 3:105
Jeffers, James 17:236
Jeffers, John 10:120;
  20:281
Jeffers, Nicholas 20:186
Jeffers, Orville 13:30
Jeffers, Philip 13:30
Jeffers, Phillip 16:39
Jeffers, Thomas 24:52
Jeffers, William 1:45;
  3:105
Jefferson, --- 22:200;
  24:111
Jefferson, Austin 9:9
Jefferson, Charles 8:40;
  26:167
Jefferson, Ed 17:178
Jefferson, Edward 24:101
Jefferson, Francis D.
  15:206
Jefferson, Frank 27:69
Jefferson, George 22:305
Jefferson, George C.
  13:30
Jefferson, Henry 6:17;
  18:86
Jefferson, Isam 7:126;
  21:350
Jefferson, James 7:126;
  21:275
Jefferson, John 22:305;
  24:21
Jefferson, Milton 7:126
Jefferson, Nelson 22:85
Jefferson, Robert 27:67
Jefferson, Robert T. 9:132
Jefferson, Thomas 7:126;
  8:40; 9:208; 10:99;
  18:68; 19:79; 21:149,
  212; 26:167
Jefferson, Thomas J.
  17:260
Jefferson, William 6:17;
  18:86; 23:35
Jefferux, John 21:130
Jeffery, Leander 23:89
Jeffery, Richard E. 9:240
Jeffey, John 14:183
Jeffnass, J. J. 11:107
Jeffords, E. R. 22:201

Jeffrey, A. 3:105
Jeffrey, Abram 17:309
Jeffrey, B. 3:105
Jeffrey, Benjamin 22:483
Jeffrey, C. C. 8:50
Jeffrey, Charles 9:54
Jeffrey, F. 26:167
Jeffrey, George C. 21:255
Jeffrey, Gilbert L. 17:321
Jeffrey, H. E. 17:448
Jeffrey, Horace E. 24:173
Jeffrey, Robert 16:8
Jeffrey, W. 16:202
Jeffrey, William G. 16:82
Jeffreys, Barry 12:8
Jeffreys, Ellison 23:151
Jeffreys, I. 9:145
Jeffreys, J. 27:66
Jeffreys, R. B. 9:145;
  27:66
Jeffries, --- 17:297
Jeffries, C. 3:105
Jeffries, Charles 21:275
Jeffries, D. O. 20:281
Jeffries, D. P. 10:60
Jeffries, E. A. 18:397
Jeffries, H. 3:105
Jeffries, Henry E. 12:72
Jeffries, Inman H. 23:69
Jeffries, James 21:208;
  22:483; 23:69
Jeffries, James W. 22:85
Jeffries, John 17:397;
  22:200
Jeffries, John W. 10:96;
  22:452
Jeffries, M. 1:143; 22:38;
  25:190
Jeffries, Marvin 5:41
Jeffries, Milton 22:429
Jeffries, Peter 9:70
Jeffries, R. D. 10:146
Jeffries, Samuel B. 24:21
Jeffries, W. C. 21:227
Jeffries, W. H. H. 22:483
Jeffris, A. 25:190
Jeffry, David 17:81
Jeffry, Reading 4:34
Jeffs, David E. 20:9
Jeffs, William 24:67
Jefway, Adolphus 23:123
Jegbert, --- 11:264
Jehue, --- 9:54
Jekley, John S. 8:88
Jeks, George 21:243
Jelf, Lewis 8:88
Jelhi, Nathan 23:302
Jelioke, Charles 16:140
Jell, F. 16:96
Jellen, George H. 9:83
Jellett, G. E. 25:190

Jelley, James 23:113
Jellings, James 19:321
Jellison, Daniel 13:30
Jellison, Jeremiah F.
    21:92
Jellison, William 1:46
Jellot, George E. 5:20
Jelly, John 3:105
Jeman, Henry 8:88
Jemerson, R. G. 13:112
Jemerson, Samuel 9:221
Jemeson, W. 24:40
Jemieson, E. 11:335
Jemison, E. 25:46
Jemison, H. 14:75
Jemison, John K. 7:64
Jemison, S. R. 18:241;
    26:38
Jemmerson, J. D. 25:190
Jemmerson, R. B. 14:75
Jemmeson, Thomas 22:38
Jences, M. 16:296
Jencis, Nic 12:92
Jenckes, John 20:183
Jenem, Fred. G. 15:206
Jenett, N. F. 9:181;
    19:239
Jenfins, Lorenzo 17:288
Jenicar, W. A. 11:327
Jeninson, C. W. 3:105
Jenison, Enos 25:46
Jenison, S. A. 25:46
Jenkens, J. 1:94
Jenkens, W. 16:296
Jenkin, Adam 5:41
Jenkin, David 27:145
Jenkings, A. 25:190
Jenkins, --- 10:162;
    11:264; 13:30;
    15:95; 25:190
Jenkins, A. C. 22:502
Jenkins, A. J. 14:241
Jenkins, A. M. 23:35
Jenkins, Abraham 8:40;
    26:166
Jenkins, Alexander 22:306
Jenkins, Ames 21:275
Jenkins, Amos F. 10:120;
    20:281
Jenkins, Arthur 6:28
Jenkins, Austin 1:192
Jenkins, B. F. 19:19
Jenkins, B. W. 14:75
Jenkins, Benjamin 8:88;
    10:120; 18:207;
    20:281
Jenkins, Benjamin F.
    8:20; 18:141
Jenkins, Bristol 27:69
Jenkins, C. 18:32

Jenkins, Charles 8:112;
    16:39
Jenkins, Charles W.
    10:120; 20:281
Jenkins, Clestus 12:26
Jenkins, D. 13:91; 25:45
Jenkins, Daniel 24:22
Jenkins, David 8:107;
    11:306; 15:14
Jenkins, David M. 22:201
Jenkins, Dennis 27:145
Jenkins, E. 1:46
Jenkins, Edward 11:280
Jenkins, Erastus 10:120;
    20:281
Jenkins, Ezekiel 21:195
Jenkins, F. C. 4:34
Jenkins, Ferguson 7:51
Jenkins, Francis 10:120;
    20:281; 21:350
Jenkins, George 6:25;
    11:107; 15:299;
    16:202; 20:125;
    21:198
Jenkins, George S. 10:162
Jenkins, George W.
    21:127
Jenkins, H. 12:154;
    16:202
Jenkins, Henry 1:45; 6:17;
    8:73; 11:94; 18:86;
    21:149; 23:35
Jenkins, Henry C. 11:34
Jenkins, Hiram 13:30
Jenkins, Hopkin T. 18:103
Jenkins, Horatio 21:350
Jenkins, I. 11:396
Jenkins, Isaac 16:120
Jenkins, J. 17:499;
    21:149; 25:190
Jenkins, J. F. 14:75
Jenkins, J. M. 1:94
Jenkins, Jackson 22:305;
    23:36; 25:322
Jenkins, James 7:99;
    9:132; 10:155;
    11:243; 12:154;
    19:171; 20:48;
    21:275; 22:123;
    27:68
Jenkins, James H. 27:69
Jenkins, James L. 20:88
Jenkins, James S. 23:69
Jenkins, Jarrard W.
    17:352
Jenkins, Jeff 7:126
Jenkins, Jefferson 22:123
Jenkins, Jeremiah 22:503
Jenkins, John 5:41; 8:64;
    88; 9:83; 18:207;
    22:428, 452; 23:313;

Jenkins, John 24:89;
    25:190; 26:38
Jenkins, John A. 15:206
Jenkins, John C. 12:59
Jenkins, John H. 24:101
Jenkins, John W. 17:314
Jenkins, Jonas 23:99
Jenkins, Joseph 9:181;
    23:151
Jenkins, London 9:132;
    27:67
Jenkins, M. 3:105; 21:198
Jenkins, M. J. 13:112;
    14:75
Jenkins, N. F. 14:75
Jenkins, Nelson 15:353;
    16:280
Jenkins, Noah 19:47
Jenkins, P. 9:83
Jenkins, Pasley 16:39
Jenkins, Perry 17:133;
    24:196
Jenkins, Peter 9:132;
    27:68
Jenkins, R. 27:68
Jenkins, Ransom 22:38
Jenkins, Richard 10:96;
    21:350
Jenkins, Richard W.
    18:412
Jenkins, Rilman 26:221
Jenkins, Robert 22:483
Jenkins, S. 3:105
Jenkins, S. J. 13:125
Jenkins, Salathiel 12:26
Jenkins, Silas D. 22:256
Jenkins, Squire M. 17:237
Jenkins, T. 9:181; 19:239
Jenkins, Thomas 9:132;
    14:183; 21:350;
    27:68
Jenkins, Thomas N. 23:69
Jenkins, Tony 27:157
Jenkins, Virgil 9:132;
    27:68
Jenkins, W. 1:46, 47;
    3:105; 12:82; 14:75
Jenkins, W. A. 1:143;
    15:305; 19:79
Jenkins, W. H. 25:276
Jenkins, Walter 17:21
Jenkins, Washington
    22:306
Jenkins, Wes 24:197
Jenkins, Wesley 17:455
Jenkins, William 3:105;
    4:34; 8:20; 9:221;
    10:60; 11:424; 17:81,
    166, 178; 18:111,
    141, 369; 19:19, 47,
    171; 20:281

Jenkins, Willis 21:350
Jenkins, Z. 24:79
Jenkinson, --- 26:38
Jenko, Carl 24:112
Jenks, A. 16:140
Jenks, Benjamin 9:181
Jenks, Benjamin F. 14:336
Jenks, C. C. 1:47
Jenks, Charles 13:112;
14:183
Jenks, George 3:105
Jenks, Henry J. 15:206
Jenks, J. 18:51
Jenks, J. C. 3:105
Jenks, James 18:412
Jenks, James B. 15:206
Jenks, John 7:99
Jenks, John B. 12:64
Jenks, Julius C. 20:113
Jenks, Merrell 21:275
Jenks, Nelson 11:388
Jenks, Volney 14:183
Jenks, W. H. 13:125
Jenkson, Henry 25:322
Jenman, George 16:39
Jenmot, A. 19:286
Jenne, Franklin E. 11:402
Jenne, Lott 13:30
Jennedy, William 9:209
Jenner, Edward B. 13:30
Jenner, Henry 3:224;
17:502
Jenner, Jesse H. 25:190
Jenner, John 23:36
Jenner, Ludwig W. 24:94
Jenner, William 1:45
Jennerich, Christian
12:72; 15:37
Jenneryjohn, Christian
20:281
Jenness, Richard 20:281
Jennett, James M. 9:120
Jennett, Jonathan R.
22:429
Jenney, Horace 18:339
Jenney, J. 25:190
Jenney, James 19:172
Jenney, S. 1:142
Jenney, Sanford 10:162
Jenneyohn, Christian
10:120
Jennie, Wriah 11:107
Jennigan, G. B. 3:105
Jenning, Albert 14:332
Jenning, Hudson 22:171
Jenning, S. William 16:39
Jennings, --- 21:122
Jennings, A. A. 7:58
Jennings, Azar N. 21:139
Jennings, B. 17:168
Jennings, C. 3:105

Jennings, C. W. 1:45
Jennings, Charles 21:15
Jennings, Charles E. 16:75
Jennings, David 21:72
Jennings, Edward 8:20
Jennings, Elijah 24:52
Jennings, Elisha 17:133;
24:197
Jennings, Elwood 18:141
Jennings, Ezra 17:96
Jennings, F. G. 14:14
Jennings, Frank 11:107
Jennings, G. 7:51
Jennings, G. H. 3:105
Jennings, G. T. 13:91
Jennings, George 22:123,
429
Jennings, George W.
13:57
Jennings, H. 3:105;
25:190
Jennings, Harrison 22:429
Jennings, Henry H. 17:66
Jennings, I. 18:176
Jennings, Isaiah 23:36
Jennings, Israel F. 22:201
Jennings, J. 1:144; 7:51;
10:186; 11:305;
26:204
Jennings, J. A. 25:190
Jennings, J. P. 1:45
Jennings, J. R. 3:105
Jennings, Jackson 9:165
Jennings, James 8:20;
18:141
Jennings, James C.
10:120; 20:281
Jennings, James D. 7:16
Jennings, James J. 24:22
Jennings, James T. 19:20
Jennings, James W.
22:406
Jennings, John 3:105;
18:468
Jennings, Joseph 18:468
Jennings, Joseph A.
10:60; 20:281
Jennings, Levi 10:120;
20:281
Jennings, M. 25:190
Jennings, Nathan 8:88;
18:207
Jennings, R. 12:98;
16:280
Jennings, Reuben 11:408
Jennings, Royal H.
10:120; 20:281
Jennings, Samuel 23:151
Jennings, Thomas 19:20;
22:329; 24:40
Jennings, W. 1:98; 11:191

Jennings, W. H. 14:1, 332
Jennings, W. J. 17:237
Jennings, W. P. 18:309;
26:103
Jennings, William 10:60;
17:21, 66; 20:9
Jennings, William A.
18:219
Jennings, William H. 7:58
Jenninngs, Samuel 17:178
Jennipper, William 1:192
Jennis, William 5:41
Jennison, H. F. 19:172
Jennison, J. 19:239
Jennngs, Alexander
17:260
Jenny, --- 5:52; 25:190
Jenny, Charles N. 25:190
Jensen, Andrew 24:52
Jensen, Charles H. 17:360
Jensen, Christian 9:230
Jensen, J. 25:190
Jensen, John 26:38
Jensen, Louis 9:230
Jensen, Rasmus 23:191
Jensley, Levi 11:93
Jenson, A. 1:47
Jenson, Adolph 9:83;
26:37
Jenson, Carl 10:120;
20:281
Jenson, Christopher
20:281
Jenson, Halnor 22:201
Jenson, Hans 18:430
Jenson, James 5:20
Jenson, John 18:241
Jenson, Jonathan 22:201
Jenson, R. 14:288
Jentry, James 11:424
Jentry, Samuel 22:256
Jenway, Benjamin 11:327
Jeping, Christian 19:254
Jepperson, H. 13:91
Jepson, Joseph 10:120;
20:281
Jepson, William 12:26
Jer, C. K. 10:186
Jerald, Hezekiah N.
18:207
Jerald, W. H. 3:105
Jeraus, John 9:103
Jerdan, D. W. 3:105
Jerdan, I. 3:105
Jerdan, James 9:221;
18:369
Jerdo, Henry 18:32
Jerdon, Moses 20:113
Jeremiah, A. 20:147
Jergens, John 10:60;
20:281

Jericho, Lewis 10:120; 20:281
Jerigo, Mowrie 18:141
Jerky, Henry 15:206
Jermain, S. K. 11:65
Jerman, George 13:30
Jerman, John 20:125
Jerman, W. M. 27:65
Jermies, W. F. 14:183
Jerness, Richard 10:60
Jero, John 18:440
Jero, S. 1:143
Jerocher, M. A. 9:54
Jerolaman, William 22:497
Jerolds, Samuel W. 1:45
Jerome, --- 26:39
Jerome, Edward 5:20; 27:69
Jerome, James 21:350
Jerome, James E. 18:86
Jerome, Milton M. 20:107
Jerome, N. P. 26:125
Jerome, Oscar L. 1:46
Jerrald, Thomas A. 8:20; 18:141
Jerrard, Martin Van B. 10:162
Jerrards, John 1:46
Jerrell, Franklin 22:85
Jerrell, T. H. 19:20
Jerrett, Addison 22:306
Jerrett, W. 9:54
Jerrey, Monter 19:271
Jerrold, Ishmael 27:69
Jerry, Cornelius 19:172
Jersey, H. 15:206
Jersey, Isaac 8:88
Jersey, Phineas 18:15
Jerton, Wesley 21:212
Jervis, William 23:107
Jervy, Thomas 14:183
Jesal, F. 19:254
Jesoph, Simon 4:34
Jespersen, Christian 22:38
Jesrop, Winslow E. 21:227
Jess, B. 1:45
Jess, George 10:61; 20:281
Jess, W. 27:69
Jess, William 22:38
Jesse, Henry 5:41
Jesse, Joseph 9:238
Jesse, Thomas J. 20:97
Jessep, Joshua 20:281
Jessey, H. 25:190
Jessie, Joseph 26:221
Jessing, Christian 9:181
Jesson, A. 25:190
Jesson, C. 25:46

Jessup, Edward 16:71
Jessup, H. 11:287
Jessup, J. 13:91
Jessup, Joshua 10:61
Jessup, Samuel M. 21:101
Jessup, Sylvester M. 23:69
Jessup, Thomas 17:248
Jester, Ebenezer 11:65
Jester, Eleanor 9:24
Jester, Elkanah 18:309; 26:103
Jester, H. S. 11:243
Jester, J. A. 1:142
Jester, Madison 10:120; 20:281
Jester, Thomas B. 24:52
Jester, William H. 11:65
Jestive, L. 16:202
Jesup, William P. 11:65
Jeter, Theodore 10:120; 20:281
Jetlon, James 18:176
Jett, J. D. 10:205
Jett, James W. 22:256
Jett, John 10:120; 20:281
Jetterson, J. 3:105
Jetton, James 10:179
Jetzer, George 22:162
Jewall, W. 20:281
Jewart, R. 1:142
Jewel, H. 18:309
Jewel, Tim 24:197
Jewell, --- 10:205
Jewell, A. A. 13:77; 16:202
Jewell, Allen 22:306
Jewell, Andrew 17:317
Jewell, B. 14:76
Jewell, Benjamin B. 21:255
Jewell, Calvin B. 4:34
Jewell, Charles 9:208; 18:68
Jewell, Charles A. 11:191
Jewell, E. 14:76
Jewell, H. 26:103
Jewell, Henry 9:24; 24:196
Jewell, Horace 17:410; 22:146; 26:39
Jewell, Ira B. 8:20
Jewell, Isaac 21:122, 350
Jewell, J. 3:105
Jewell, J. G. 9:24; 18:309; 21:30; 26:103
Jewell, J. R. 3:105
Jewell, Jackson 10:61; 20:281
Jewell, James 11:264; 21:350
Jewell, James E. 7:99

Jewell, James L. 9:221; 18:369
Jewell, John 18:15, 334
Jewell, Joseph T. 18:219
Jewell, L. K. 23:36
Jewell, S. 25:190
Jewell, Seth 10:61; 20:281
Jewell, Simon 5:20
Jewell, Thomas 23:271
Jewell, W. 15:206
Jewell, W. A. 3:105
Jewell, William 10:61; 23:36
Jewell, Willis 19:47
Jewell, Zenas 15:69
Jewett, Benjamin F. 21:117
Jewett, Charles C. 8:88
Jewett, Charles G. 18:207
Jewett, Charles H. 19:20
Jewett, David N. 21:72
Jewett, Delos 7:99
Jewett, E. 3:105; 16:202
Jewett, E. M. 18:68
Jewett, Edward 1:46
Jewett, F. 3:105
Jewett, G. 3:105
Jewett, J. E. 14:299; 17:478
Jewett, Jasper 22:483
Jewett, John 22:509
Jewett, John H. 25:190
Jewett, John Q. 18:397
Jewett, Joshua 10:120; 20:281
Jewett, L. F. 1:142
Jewett, M. F. 19:239
Jewett, R. E. 19:20
Jewett, Stephen 11:93
Jewett, W. 16:140
Jewett, Warren 4:34
Jewett, William 17:133; 24:197
Jewey, Cornelius 10:176
Jewill, John 9:106
Jewire, T. 3:105
Jewis, J. 14:14
Jewitt, Elijah B. 8:88
Jewitt, J. E. 27:68
Jewitt, James 24:40
Jewitt, Jay 7:99
Jewitt, William T. 22:146
Jibson, William 15:206
Jickling, R. 1:142
Jiddleson, Lorenzo 22:481
Jidert, D. 10:28
Jiff, George B. 11:65
Jiff, J. 16:202
Jiffman, C. S. 16:280
Jifford, William 1:45
Jilert, D. 19:303

Jiles, --- 20:57
Jiles, William H. 22:256
Jillason, George 17:231
Jillett, J. 3:105
Jillings, James 8:125
Jillson, H. T. 1:46
Jimiller, Joseph 19:79
Jimison, John 19:79
Jimmeran, G. 14:76
Jimmerson, Archy 22:306
Jimmerson, Henry 7:126
Jimmy, E. H. 3:105
Jinehelt, George 14:183
Jines, John W. 22:85
Jinkins, David 9:239
Jinkins, Joseph 22:146
Jinkins, N. J. 17:217
Jinks, B. 19:239
Jinks, Calvin 27:145
Jinks, Richard 22:428
Jinn, Theo 5:20
Jinnings, L. 11:34
Jinnis, Robert 9:120
Jinny, --- 18:190
Jipp, Henry 8:20; 18:141
Jipson, G. F. 19:244
Jirango, Mecavio 8:20
Jirkins, Stephen 11:99
Jirman, Oliver 17:178
Jizen, Frank 19:79
Jleff, James R. 17:389
Jo., W. J. 26:167
Joasen, Iver 20:113
Job, James 22:167
Jobb, John 15:353
Jobbs, Josiah 25:46
Jobe, James C. 17:166
Jobe, William B. 18:241;
    26:39
Jobenour, L. 15:56
Jober, John D. 17:110
Joberts, Desire 18:277
Jobes, Allen L. 23:151
Jobes, George 22:201
Jobes, J. 3:106
Jobes, James S. 25:45
Jobes, John 16:202
Jobes, Robert 3:106
Jobes, Samuel 23:151
Jobinson, David R. 12:26
Jobler, J. W. 24:197
Jobling, F. W. 21:350
Jobling, John 21:350
Jobson, John 8:50
Jobson, L. 3:106
Jocelyn, Ely 13:112
Jocelyn, William 18:219
Jock, Alexander 2:13;
    25:46
Jock, James 10:179

Jock, William 17:434;
    24:171
Jockett, Alonzo 19:172
Joddy, Joseph 9:103
Joe, Daniel 15:159
Joe, M. P. 27:68
Joe, Willis 25:190
Joerg, Herman 1:46
Joerger, Christ 19:315
Joerger, Christ. 8:117
Joerson, J. B. 18:68
Joes, Amos 13:112
Joh, John W. 26:125
Joh---, Louis W. 19:79
Johanas, Martin 17:143
Johannis, C. 1:142
Johans, J. P. 11:34
Johers, William 14:183
Johes, Frank 19:329
John, --- 3:106
John, Abraham 6:25
John, Austin 9:36
John, Bane 11:152
John, Damon 27:67
John, Ernest 11:153
John, Frank 21:101
John, H. C. 15:11
John, Henry 4:34
John, John 23:151
John, Joseph 18:141
John, L. T. 23:184
John, Lewis 10:61; 20:281
John, P. 23:282
John, Pleasant 11:206
John, Richard 22:520
John, S. 15:95
John, Samuel J. 12:72
John, Stephen A. 10:99
John, Thomas 3:106
John, William 26:37
John, William L. 26:38
John 25:336
Johnas, William 18:86
Johne, John W. 19:20
Johnem, P. 15:206
Johnes, George 13:76
Johnkins, John 17:96
Johnrid, Charles 16:96
Johns, --- 15:310; 19:79
Johns, Allen E. 10:120
Johns, Alton E. 20:282
Johns, Andrew 23:191
Johns, Charles 11:187
Johns, D. 14:76
Johns, E. 23:69
Johns, E. K. 3:106
Johns, Elex 16:202
Johns, G. 17:190
Johns, H. M. 21:122
Johns, Henry 17:430
Johns, Isaac 11:206

Johns, J. 13:91
Johns, J. A. 11:153
Johns, John 9:24; 25:190
Johns, Joshua P. 15:91
Johns, Leroy 22:338
Johns, Levi 19:47
Johns, M. 11:243
Johns, Margaret 16:71
Johns, Morris 23:191
Johns, Patrick 9:200;
    19:291
Johns, Ralph 27:66
Johns, Robert 3:106
Johns, Samuel 21:351
Johns, Stephen S. 12:72
Johns, Thomas 8:88
Johns, Washington 7:126
Johns, William 9:83, 236;
    10:61; 11:153;
    20:113
Johns, William D. 12:72
Johns, Williamson 26:221
Johns, Willis 7:126
Johnsen, Charles 14:76
Johnson, --- 8:21; 9:106,
    182; 10:179; 11:322,
    340; 14:241; 15:268;
    16:71; 17:319, 482;
    18:32, 141, 176, 191,
    285; 19:172, 303;
    21:188; 22:256, 352;
    26:135; 27:65, 69
Johnson, A. 1:143, 144;
    3:106; 7:31; 9:83;
    14:76, 183, 299;
    17:476; 18:86; 19:79;
    21:110, 149; 25:191;
    26:38; 27:69
Johnson, A. B. 21:110;
    23:36
Johnson, A. F. 3:106
Johnson, A. G. C. 3:106
Johnson, A. H. 11:100;
    21:351
Johnson, A. L. 9:83; 26:37
Johnson, A. M. 20:33
Johnson, A. O. 3:106
Johnson, A. S. 3:106;
    15:56; 22:483
Johnson, A. W. 9:181;
    11:242; 19:239;
    21:351; 25:45
Johnson, Aaron 4:34
Johnson, Abraham 13:57;
    22:12
Johnson, Abram 7:126
Johnson, Aderson 9:120
Johnson, Adison 18:241;
    26:39
Johnson, Agustus 7:71

Johnson, Albert 11:127, 287; 21:149, 227; 24:52; 25:285
Johnson, Albert W. 2:13
Johnson, Alex 9:132; 18:86
Johnson, Alexander 6:10; 9:24, 103; 11:206; 14:183; 15:278; 18:309; 22:38; 26:103; 27:67
Johnson, Alexander A. 24:197
Johnson, Alfred 9:154, 165, 209; 13:57; 17:397; 21:351
Johnson, Allen 18:353; 22:85
Johnson, Allen B. 10:162
Johnson, Alonzo 1:46
Johnson, Alonzo P. 11:243
Johnson, Ambrose 15:206; 18:86
Johnson, Amego 20:113
Johnson, Amos 7:126; 18:450
Johnson, Ande 17:509
Johnson, Anderson 27:68
Johnson, Andison 9:208
Johnson, Andrew 7:99, 126; 8:88; 9:83, 201; 15:159; 17:166, 237, 423, 429; 19:282; 21:351; 22:306, 513; 23:69, 191, 271; 24:67, 171; 26:38
Johnson, Andrew B. 9:97, 103
Johnson, Andrew E. 21:255
Johnson, Andrew J. 8:21; 18:141
Johnson, Andrew N. 8:21; 18:141
Johnson, Andrew S. 9:214; 21:351
Johnson, Anson 8:107
Johnson, Ansteen 20:113
Johnson, Anthony 7:126
Johnson, Archie 18:68
Johnson, Arthur 11:320; 22:85
Johnson, Arthur L. 21:351
Johnson, Arthur O. 22:256
Johnson, Augustus 22:406
Johnson, Austin 22:201
Johnson, B. 3:106; 22:306; 23:263; 25:191; 27:69

Johnson, B. F. 3:106; 14:183; 18:277; 20:282; 25:46
Johnson, B. H. 18:191
Johnson, Barney D. 20:9
Johnson, Bartley 21:275
Johnson, Bayley 11:381
Johnson, Benj 9:154
Johnson, Benjamin 5:41; 6:21; 9:24, 100, 208; 14:76; 16:202; 18:309; 21:351; 22:306; 26:103
Johnson, Benjamin F. 10:61
Johnson, Benjamin I. 20:113
Johnson, Blackburn 22:256
Johnson, Bryant 7:75; 25:299
Johnson, Butler 22:519
Johnson, Byron W. 10:162; 19:172
Johnson, C. 1:143, 144; 3:106; 12:85; 14:184, 241; 16:202; 25:191; 27:69
Johnson, C. A. 9:154; 15:206; 18:430; 27:66
Johnson, C. C. 2:13; 3:106; 21:188; 25:46
Johnson, C. E. 15:37
Johnson, C. H. 1:143; 19:239
Johnson, C. J. 3:106; 16:296
Johnson, C. L. 23:184
Johnson, C. M. 3:106; 14:184
Johnson, C. R. 1:46
Johnson, C. S. 3:106
Johnson, C. T. 1:143
Johnson, C. W. 3:106
Johnson, Caleb 4:34
Johnson, Calvin 10:25; 20:282; 22:429; 23:291; 24:52
Johnson, Charles 5:41; 6:17; 7:58; 9:83, 132; 10:61, 120; 12:27; 13:112; 14:184, 331; 17:14, 133, 397; 18:68, 86, 440; 21:30, 275; 23:268; 24:196; 26:38; 27:67
Johnson, Charles A. 12:27; 23:191
Johnson, Charles B. 14:269

Johnson, Charles C. 26:39
Johnson, Charles E. 23:191
Johnson, Charles F. 9:7; 10:18; 20:125
Johnson, Charles H. 9:132, 182; 27:67
Johnson, Charles J. 10:120; 20:282
Johnson, Charles L. 7:31; 12:27; 13:57; 18:241; 20:282
Johnson, Charles M. 7:99; 8:107
Johnson, Charles O. 24:52
Johnson, Charles R. 7:99
Johnson, Charles S. 11:413; 12:142
Johnson, Charles W. 10:120; 12:50; 20:282; 22:146
Johnson, Chester I. 12:27
Johnson, Christ. C. 20:186
Johnson, Christian 14:184; 22:281
Johnson, Christopher 11:119
Johnson, Claborn 11:65
Johnson, Colman A. 22:167
Johnson, Cornelius 15:206; 17:133; 24:197
Johnson, Cornelius A. 11:191
Johnson, Cornelius N. 10:120; 20:282
Johnson, Courtland 10:25
Johnson, Cred 8:40; 26:166
Johnson, Curtis 23:271
Johnson, D. 1:46, 143; 3:106; 11:153; 16:202; 19:239, 254; 21:30, 163; 22:338; 24:80; 25:191; 27:65
Johnson, D. A. 14:242
Johnson, D. F. 19:79
Johnson, D. H. 7:51; 9:243
Johnson, D. H. C. 16:202
Johnson, D. Josiah 16:133
Johnson, D. R. 24:59
Johnson, D. T. 14:76
Johnson, D. W. 3:106
Johnson, Dan Noble 10:120; 20:282
Johnson, Daniel 9:132; 17:190; 18:32, 309; 21:275; 22:452; 26:103; 27:67

Johnson, Daniel E. 9:120
Johnson, Daniel M.
21:101
Johnson, David 5:20;
9:132, 181; 11:413;
13:30; 16:39;
17:133; 22:12, 38,
428; 24:80, 197;
27:67, 68
Johnson, David A. 9:13
Johnson, David L. 9:103
Johnson, David M. 7:14
Johnson, David R. 12:27;
16:96
Johnson, Davis 9:208
Johnson, Dean 9:201
Johnson, Dedrich 9:181
Johnson, Dennis 5:41;
19:291; 23:271
Johnson, Dexter 6:25
Johnson, Diana 19:291
Johnson, Diday 9:208
Johnson, Doc 11:206
Johnson, Dock 21:351
Johnson, Doctor F. 24:167
Johnson, Dr. F. 17:445
Johnson, E. 3:106;
10:148; 11:65;
17:179; 18:242, 369;
25:191; 26:39; 27:65
Johnson, E. A. 1:143;
3:106; 9:8; 20:282
Johnson, E. G. 16:162
Johnson, E. M. 9:230
Johnson, E. N. 3:106
Johnson, E. R. 15:302;
17:503
Johnson, E. S. 12:154
Johnson, E. T. 13:112
Johnson, E. W. 12:72;
14:76; 15:37
Johnson, Ed 17:179;
19:47
Johnson, Edw. S. 13:30
Johnson, Edward 6:27;
8:114; 9:208, 221;
10:162; 12:27;
18:434; 19:172;
22:338, 509
Johnson, Edward A. 9:9
Johnson, Edward F.
21:101
Johnson, Edward L.
21:244
Johnson, Edwin 13:30;
16:39; 20:48
Johnson, Edwin R. 16:202
Johnson, Eleazor 26:221
Johnson, Eleazur 23:151
Johnson, Eleim 17:103
Johnson, Eli 5:41; 20:35

Johnson, Elias 23:302
Johnson, Elijah 22:201
Johnson, Elikam 17:81
Johnson, Elmore S. 24:94
Johnson, Emerson 14:184
Johnson, Emery 24:167
Johnson, Emmet J. 15:91
Johnson, Enoch 23:267
Johnson, Enos 25:46
Johnson, Erastus 22:428;
24:9
Johnson, Eugene 9:103;
18:339
Johnson, Ezekiel 11:153
Johnson, F. 2:13; 3:106;
7:51; 14:76; 19:79;
20:282; 25:191
Johnson, F. A. 16:39
Johnson, F. M. 5:20
Johnson, F. M. J. 21:198
Johnson, Felix 23:113
Johnson, Felix M. 17:53
Johnson, Fink 24:80
Johnson, Fleet 16:39
Johnson, France 12:140
Johnson, Francis 7:31;
9:12
Johnson, Francis E. 9:12
Johnson, Francis M.
21:54, 72; 22:38
Johnson, Frank 4:66;
5:41; 12:27, 50, 154;
22:513
Johnson, Franklin 22:85
Johnson, Fred 17:179;
21:188
Johnson, Frederick 7:126;
9:156; 12:8; 18:277;
24:112
Johnson, Frisby 4:66
Johnson, G. 1:94, 143;
9:145; 10:186;
11:191; 16:203;
18:176; 25:191;
26:204; 27:66
Johnson, G. A. 16:372;
23:151
Johnson, G. B. 14:278;
23:191
Johnson, G. E. 2:13
Johnson, G. F. 1:46
Johnson, G. H. 14:321;
23:36
Johnson, G. M. 1:46
Johnson, G. P. 3:106
Johnson, G. W. 1:144;
3:106; 8:73; 11:264;
13:91; 14:14; 18:15
Johnson, Gabe 9:208
Johnson, Gabriel 17:133;
24:197

Johnson, George 4:66;
7:51; 8:50, 119; 9:9,
158, 204; 10:120;
11:264, 320; 12:145;
13:57; 14:130;
15:263; 16:203;
18:86, 242; 20:97,
177, 282; 21:101,
275; 22:38, 306;
23:11; 26:38; 27:69
Johnson, George A. 6:17;
9:132; 17:99; 27:67
Johnson, George B. 7:31
Johnson, George F. 12:27;
16:78
Johnson, George H.
10:120; 14:315;
20:282
Johnson, George M.
12:27; 15:360
Johnson, George W. 4:34;
11:116; 13:30; 18:86;
19:20; 20:282;
21:130; 22:85, 428;
25:45
Johnson, Gilbert L. 24:94
Johnson, Gordon C. 8:88
Johnson, Greenup 10:61
Johnson, Greenux 20:282
Johnson, Grey 11:107
Johnson, Gustus 10:120;
20:282
Johnson, H. 1:46, 142,
143; 3:106; 9:145,
154; 11:287; 12:154;
14:76; 17:99; 19:172;
21:149; 22:483;
23:36; 25:191; 27:66
Johnson, H. C. 1:142;
17:360
Johnson, H. F. 24:22
Johnson, H. H. 12:72;
15:37; 19:79; 22:256
Johnson, H. L. 1:144
Johnson, H. M. 18:285
Johnson, H. P. 20:125
Johnson, H. R. 23:151
Johnson, H. S. 11:152;
19:20
Johnson, H. W. 26:212
Johnson, Hampton D.
20:18
Johnson, Harrison 7:126;
17:91
Johnson, Harrison R.
22:85
Johnson, Harry 21:275
Johnson, Harvey 11:396
Johnson, Henry 1:46;
4:34, 66; 5:20; 6:17,
25; 7:99; 8:40, 88;

Johnson, Henry 9:132, 157, 165, 235; 13:57; 16:40, 96; 17:179; 18:86, 421; 22:509; 23:36; 24:22, 101, 153; 25:191; 26:167; 27:67

Johnson, Henry C. 8:114; 11:119; 17:360; 21:101; 22:497

Johnson, Henry E. 9:221; 22:12

Johnson, Henry H. 12:72; 15:7

Johnson, Henry L. 20:177

Johnson, Henry M. 5:20; 10:18; 17:319; 26:135

Johnson, Henry O. 17:360

Johnson, Henry S. 8:88; 18:327

Johnson, Hezekiah 21:227

Johnson, Hiram 17:281, 319

Johnson, Hollis 22:429; 25:191

Johnson, Horace 17:155; 19:47

Johnson, Howard 22:85

Johnson, Hugh 17:53; 22:201; 27:69

Johnson, I. 1:46; 21:30; 25:191

Johnson, I. F. 24:59

Johnson, Ingebret 22:508, 509

Johnson, Ira 22:85

Johnson, Ira A. 17:36

Johnson, Irah 15:56

Johnson, Isaac 3:106; 5:41; 10:120; 11:276; 16:133; 17:231; 20:282; 21:275; 22:428; 23:279; 26:167

Johnson, Isaac N. 22:482

Johnson, Isam 26:167

Johnson, Isum 8:40

Johnson, Iver 24:67

Johnson, J. 1:46, 143; 3:106; 4:34; 7:51, 58; 9:154, 221; 10:28, 155; 11:287; 12:72, 82; 13:91; 14:14, 76, 257, 299; 15:37, 108, 173; 16:203, 296; 17:215, 308, 470, 481; 18:51, 242, 369; 19:79, 172, 282, 303; 21:110;

Johnson, J. 22:201, 256; 23:263; 25:191, 283; 26:39; 27:66, 68, 69

Johnson, J. A. 1:98; 15:331

Johnson, J. B. 3:106; 13:65, 125; 23:262

Johnson, J. C. 10:32; 14:76; 18:242; 19:172; 20:282; 26:38

Johnson, J. D. 16:296

Johnson, J. E. 9:36

Johnson, J. G. 8:50; 11:243; 14:184; 15:152; 20:282

Johnson, J. H. 3:106; 11:327; 25:191

Johnson, J. J. 1:143; 3:106; 9:24; 18:68

Johnson, J. K. 9:24

Johnson, J. L. 14:242; 16:85

Johnson, J. M. 1:94; 7:75; 11:287; 17:145; 19:20, 334; 20:282; 25:299

Johnson, J. O. 26:39

Johnson, J. P. 18:242; 26:38

Johnson, J. R. 9:163; 14:315, 321

Johnson, J. S. 3:106; 5:20; 9:54; 25:191

Johnson, J. T. 1:142; 19:79; 23:36

Johnson, J. V. 16:203

Johnson, J. W. 1:143; 3:106; 4:34; 10:61; 11:306; 12:122; 15:126; 21:13, 101; 23:36; 25:46, 191, 275

Johnson, J. Y. 20:97

Johnson, Jack 8:77

Johnson, Jackson 11:388; 22:306

Johnson, Jacob 9:201; 13:112; 21:351; 26:212

Johnson, Jacob B. 25:46

Johnson, Jacob P. 22:201

Johnson, Jake 17:133

Johnson, James 4:34, 66; 5:20; 6:17; 7:58, 78, 126; 8:50; 9:16, 24, 36, 70, 133; 11:388, 407; 12:50, 154; 14:76, 265; 15:11, 206;

Johnson, James 17:133, 159, 166, 179, 360, 494; 18:86, 141, 294, 309, 424; 19:79; 20:9; 21:72, 351; 22:38, 85, 256, 306, 428; 24:197; 25:45, 191, 269; 26:103; 27:67

Johnson, James A. 17:53, 281; 22:452

Johnson, James A. C. 22:256

Johnson, James B. 21:249

Johnson, James D. 22:85

Johnson, James E. 18:294; 26:103

Johnson, James F. 21:54; 22:112

Johnson, James G. 9:110

Johnson, James H. 7:126; 11:153; 22:201

Johnson, James J. 17:151

Johnson, James K. 7:99

Johnson, James L. 10:120; 20:282

Johnson, James M. 10:61; 14:27; 17:260; 19:79

Johnson, James N. 12:96

Johnson, James P. 17:260

Johnson, James R. 15:206; 23:184

Johnson, James S. 10:162; 17:53; 19:172; 24:67

Johnson, James T. 10:120; 20:282

Johnson, James W. 10:61, 120; 20:282; 21:195

Johnson, James W. C. 10:120; 20:282

Johnson, James Y. 22:85

Johnson, Japtha A. 9:72

Johnson, Jared 11:65

Johnson, Jeans 26:167

Johnson, Jens 8:21

Johnson, Jeremiah W. 21:72

Johnson, Jerome 13:30; 16:40

Johnson, Jerry 16:96

Johnson, Jesse 5:20; 9:208; 11:306; 18:68; 21:188, 291; 23:151

Johnson, Joe 24:101; 25:299

Johnson, Joel 9:110

Johnson, John 1:45, 46; 4:34; 5:20, 41; 6:22; 7:58, 71, 99, 126; 8:21, 59;

Johnson, John 9:97, 133, 181, 182; 10:34, 61, 120, 151; 11:206, 264, 320; 12:26, 72, 85, 154; 13:30, 91, 112; 14:76, 184, 265, 335; 15:37, 206, 321, 338; 16:40, 162, 203, 296; 17:179, 260, 360, 429; 18:32, 141, 191, 242, 309, 334; 19:79, 274, 277; 20:41, 282; 21:54, 92, 117, 212, 255, 275; 22:38, 85, 123, 171, 306, 337, 520; 23:15, 36, 89, 191, 250; 25:46, 191; 26:38, 103, 125, 167, 221; 27:67, 69

Johnson, John A. 1:45; 8:64; 13:65; 16:203; 21:92

Johnson, John B. 16:40; 22:256; 25:276

Johnson, John C. 10:176; 12:62

Johnson, John Chris 15:91

Johnson, John E. 18:242; 26:38

Johnson, John F. 8:21; 18:141; 22:256

Johnson, John H. 7:126; 14:288; 16:203; 20:140; 21:255

Johnson, John I. 23:69

Johnson, John J. 7:99; 18:320; 22:502

Johnson, John Lucas 24:67

Johnson, John M. 12:26; 19:20

Johnson, John O. 9:83

Johnson, John R. 10:120; 20:283; 21:351; 22:85, 306

Johnson, John T. 18:369

Johnson, John W. 5:41; 7:99; 11:219; 13:30; 14:184; 17:397; 20:283; 21:72, 227; 22:123

Johnson, John Y. 11:243

Johnson, Jonathan 5:20

Johnson, Jordan 21:351

Johnson, Joseph 5:41; 9:54, 133; 11:320; 12:27, 50; 13:30; 16:40, 360a; 19:20; 20:30; 21:351; 22:256, 483;

Johnson, Joseph 27:65, 67

Johnson, Joseph A. 19:79

Johnson, Joseph E. 10:121; 20:283

Johnson, Joseph F. 9:214; 21:351

Johnson, Joseph L. 11:34

Johnson, Joseph M. 24:67

Johnson, Joseph R. 8:21; 18:141

Johnson, Joshua 9:36

Johnson, Joshua C. 10:61; 20:283

Johnson, Joshua H. 22:123

Johnson, Josiah L. 20:9

Johnson, Josiah W. 22:398

Johnson, Joyoforth 19:47

Johnson, Juba 20:50

Johnson, Kirk 21:275

Johnson, L. 1:142; 8:69; 16:203; 25:191

Johnson, L. A. 1:143

Johnson, L. D. 10:121; 20:283

Johnson, L. J. 27:69

Johnson, L. W. 3:107

Johnson, Lars 8:64; 20:33

Johnson, Lawson 21:227

Johnson, Leived 19:282

Johnson, Lemuel 13:30; 17:281

Johnson, Lemuel C. 7:99

Johnson, Leon 18:141

Johnson, Leonard 22:123

Johnson, Leven 8:21

Johnson, Levi 17:443; 21:149; 24:159; 26:167

Johnson, Lewis 8:40, 50; 11:34, 206; 14:184; 15:334; 16:203; 17:133, 267; 21:167; 24:197; 26:167

Johnson, Lewis D. 20:103

Johnson, Logan 22:306

Johnson, Louis C. 20:46

Johnson, Louisa 26:236

Johnson, Lucius 6:25

Johnson, Luther A. 13:30

Johnson, Luther M. 17:155

Johnson, Lyman J. 24:80

Johnson, M. 1:143; 3:107; 14:76; 16:203

Johnson, M. A. E. 27:68

Johnson, M. C. 13:112

Johnson, M. E. 21:351

Johnson, M. L. 8:50; 21:30, 206

Johnson, M. P. 27:69

Johnson, M. T. 7:31; 23:15

Johnson, M. W. 11:413

Johnson, Mack 22:306

Johnson, Major 22:513

Johnson, Marcus 20:114; 22:429

Johnson, Marion 10:61; 20:283

Johnson, Mark 9:133; 11:206; 13:30; 16:40; 21:243; 27:67

Johnson, Martin 7:126; 8:73; 9:36; 17:179, 317; 18:294; 22:429; 26:103

Johnson, Martin A. 19:20

Johnson, Mathew 16:120

Johnson, Mathias 25:45

Johnson, Matison N. 22:256

Johnson, Matthew S. 24:22

Johnson, Michael 12:27; 22:428; 27:145

Johnson, Milton 7:64; 26:38

Johnson, Minas 11:402

Johnson, Minerva 22:519

Johnson, Montgomery 9:156

Johnson, Morgan 22:201

Johnson, Morris 7:126

Johnson, Morrison 18:219

Johnson, Moses 6:35; 18:285; 19:296; 26:135

Johnson, Murdock D. 16:40

Johnson, N. 3:107; 9:201; 19:291

Johnson, N. H. C. 15:304

Johnson, N. P. 9:54

Johnson, N. W. 10:61; 20:283

Johnson, Nat 17:179

Johnson, Nathan 8:20

Johnson, Nathan L. 10:121; 20:283

Johnson, Nathaniel 22:85; 24:80

Johnson, Nathem 18:141

Johnson, Ned 9:120; 27:67

Johnson, Neils 25:191

Johnson, Nells 18:141

Johnson, Nels 8:21

Johnson, Nelson 8:40; 18:412; 26:167

Johnson, Newton 7:126

Johnson, Newton R. 12:27
Johnson, Nicholas 9:209;
    13:30; 23:151
Johnson, Nick 9:208
Johnson, Noah 6:17;
    18:86
Johnson, Noah B. 18:219
Johnson, Norman 9:10
Johnson, Norris 11:340
Johnson, O. 20:174;
    25:191; 26:39
Johnson, O. B. 3:107
Johnson, O. C. 14:184
Johnson, O. C. M. 25:191
Johnson, Ole 10:121;
    18:242; 20:48, 283;
    22:281, 509
Johnson, Oliver 5:41;
    9:230; 20:283;
    21:256
Johnson, Orsemus 11:116
Johnson, Oscar 23:36
Johnson, P. 1:46; 3:107;
    9:181; 17:281;
    18:242; 19:254;
    27:66
Johnson, P. B. 3:107;
    8:21; 18:142
Johnson, P. C. 16:203;
    23:152
Johnson, P. J. 1:144
Johnson, Pasco 21:351
Johnson, Patrick 19:320
Johnson, Perry W. 20:23
Johnson, Peter 8:20; 9:83,
    133, 181, 240; 12:27;
    16:203; 18:142;
    20:114; 21:351;
    22:281; 26:37; 27:67
Johnson, Peter M. 18:397
Johnson, Peter N. 11:116
Johnson, Philomon 8:107
Johnson, Phineas E. 15:37
Johnson, Presley 11:388
Johnson, Providence
    9:208
Johnson, R. 1:142, 143;
    3:107; 12:162;
    15:126; 16:203;
    17:179; 19:47;
    26:167
Johnson, R. A. 20:57
Johnson, R. G. 11:187
Johnson, R. J. 21:92
Johnson, R. P. 8:73; 25:45
Johnson, R. S. 8:124
Johnson, Ramon 21:351
Johnson, Randal 7:126
Johnson, Ransom 9:200
Johnson, Raswell W.
    22:38

Johnson, Reason 21:227
Johnson, Reed 22:306
Johnson, Reuben E. 22:85
Johnson, Rhinehal E.
    12:72
Johnson, Richard 6:17;
    9:182, 214; 18:86;
    19:20, 254; 21:351
Johnson, Richard F.
    20:283
Johnson, Richard M.
    23:240; 25:191
Johnson, Richard T.
    10:121
Johnson, Robert 1:45;
    4:34, 66; 7:16; 8:73;
    9:54, 133, 157, 181;
    10:121, 186; 16:120;
    17:455; 18:430;
    19:254, 267; 20:283;
    21:139, 351; 22:306;
    24:22, 72, 197;
    25:191; 27:67
Johnson, Robert B.
    10:121; 20:97, 283;
    21:351
Johnson, Robert E. 12:27
Johnson, Robert H. 20:9
Johnson, Robert P. 11:93
Johnson, Robert V.
    18:176
Johnson, Rufus 9:83;
    26:38
Johnson, Rutlif 13:30
Johnson, S. 1:142, 143;
    3:107; 5:52; 7:31;
    11:192, 264; 12:122;
    13:77; 14:321;
    15:126, 326; 22:482;
    23:152; 25:45, 191;
    26:38
Johnson, S. A. 9:181;
    19:254
Johnson, S. D. 8:60
Johnson, S. G. 10:96
Johnson, S. H. 22:38
Johnson, S. K. 1:143
Johnson, S. L. 3:107
Johnson, S. O. H. 25:191
Johnson, S. P. 18:51
Johnson, S. T. 26:38
Johnson, Sam 21:290
Johnson, Samuel 5:41;
    6:17; 8:40, 50; 10:61,
    121; 11:127, 264,
    333; 12:27, 55;
    14:315; 17:393;
    18:86; 19:79, 172;
    20:97, 283; 21:167,
    212, 275; 22:38;
    24:59, 197; 25:191;

Johnson, Samuel 26:166
Johnson, Samuel B. 8:88
Johnson, Samuel G. 7:51
Johnson, Samuel J. 10:205
Johnson, Sandy 9:133;
    27:67
Johnson, Schuyler W.
    22:146
Johnson, Sewell C. 12:27
Johnson, Sherman 19:20
Johnson, Silas 8:20;
    18:142
Johnson, Silas D. 24:52
Johnson, Simon 7:126
Johnson, Simon M.
    11:413
Johnson, Sion 22:452
Johnson, Solomon 8:21;
    11:243; 18:142;
    20:114
Johnson, Solomon J.
    22:256
Johnson, Spencer 10:61;
    20:283
Johnson, Spice 22:306
Johnson, Squire 17:260
Johnson, Stacy D. 12:172
Johnson, Stephen 9:121;
    13:80; 15:152; 16:40,
    203; 20:176; 27:68
Johnson, Stephen B. 9:83
Johnson, Stephen D.
    21:256
Johnson, Stiles J. 9:120;
    27:68
Johnson, Swain 22:85
Johnson, Sylvanus B.
    21:30
Johnson, Sylvester 13:57;
    16:40
Johnson, T. 1:143; 9:54;
    16:203; 22:502;
    25:45, 192
Johnson, T. A. 19:267
Johnson, T. K. 11:34
Johnson, T. N. 9:54
Johnson, T. P. 14:76
Johnson, T. R. 25:192
Johnson, T. S. J. 14:242
Johnson, Theo 13:112;
    16:372
Johnson, Theo. 8:21
Johnson, Theodore 5:41
Johnson, Thomas 1:46;
    5:52; 7:51; 9:12, 200;
    11:152, 153, 424;
    12:50; 13:30, 57, 65;
    15:56, 285; 17:265;
    18:142; 19:20, 47,
    79, 282; 20:283;
    21:115, 351;

Johnson, Thomas 22:201, 306, 337, 428, 519; 24:197; 25:45; 26:167; 27:68

Johnson, Thomas A. 9:182

Johnson, Thomas G. 17:260

Johnson, Thomas H. 9:121

Johnson, Thomas J. 21:256; 22:38; 23:69

Johnson, Thomas N. 16:40

Johnson, Thomas R. 22:201

Johnson, Thomas S. 20:9

Johnson, Thomas W. 13:30

Johnson, Uriah 10:61; 20:283

Johnson, V. 25:192

Johnson, Victor 9:208

Johnson, Virgil 19:47

Johnson, Volney 5:20

Johnson, W. 1:47, 143, 144; 2:13; 3:107; 11:306; 13:91, 92; 14:282; 16:96, 203; 21:163; 22:256; 23:117, 191

Johnson, W. A. 11:93

Johnson, W. B. 11:153

Johnson, W. C. 18:51

Johnson, W. D. 9:54

Johnson, W. F. 8:73

Johnson, W. H. 1:46; 2:13; 3:107; 4:34; 8:50; 9:110; 10:61; 13:65; 18:86; 19:172; 21:110, 351; 22:201; 25:192; 26:236

Johnson, W. J. 1:142; 14:133; 17:314

Johnson, W. L. 1:143

Johnson, W. M. 18:176

Johnson, W. N. 18:191

Johnson, W. P. 22:146

Johnson, W. S. 8:20; 18:142; 20:41; 27:65

Johnson, W. T. 8:50

Johnson, W. W. 1:143; 9:83; 13:112; 17:297

Johnson, Walter 21:351

Johnson, Warren 9:158, 165

Johnson, Wesley 8:40; 17:133; 22:85; 24:197; 26:166

Johnson, Wheeler P. 12:27

Johnson, Wiley 17:191

Johnson, William 1:46; 3:107; 4:34, 66; 5:20; 6:17; 7:99; 8:40, 64, 88; 9:83; 10:61; 11:16, 182, 327, 424; 12:26, 162; 13:30; 14:184; 15:56, 69, 166, 173; 16:203; 17:201, 445, 456; 18:86, 111, 191, 242, 406; 20:283; 21:227, 275, 351; 22:12, 38, 256; 22:281, 306, 337, 452, 502; 23:36, 99; 24:167, 171; 25:45, 192, 322; 26:37, 39, 167; 27:67

Johnson, William A. 11:153; 17:46; 22:85

Johnson, William C. 12:27; 21:128

Johnson, William E. 17:392

Johnson, William H. 5:20; 6:17; 9:161; 13:30; 16:40; 17:277; 19:79, 172; 20:283; 21:227; 22:513; 23:69; 25:46; 26:167

Johnson, William J. 10:91, 148; 15:108; 18:51, 86; 20:283; 21:227; 23:89

Johnson, William K. 18:219

Johnson, William L. 26:125

Johnson, William M. 10:186; 17:404; 20:97

Johnson, William P. 23:107

Johnson, William R. 10:208; 22:38

Johnson, William S. 22:201; 23:69

Johnson, William T. 21:72; 22:85

Johnson, William W. 17:360

Johnson, William Y. 17:206

Johnson, Willis 17:179; 21:275; 22:256

Johnson, Wilson 27:145

Johnson, Z. B. 16:203

Johnson, Z. C. 11:152

Johnson, Z. M. 9:43

Johnson, Zach'h. 22:306

Johnson, Zachariah 11:34

Johnson, Zebulon 20:49

Johnsteen, A. J. 12:154

Johnston, --- 13:30; 15:37, 206

Johnston, A. 1:46

Johnston, A. G. 3:107

Johnston, A. S. 12:72

Johnston, C. 1:45

Johnston, Christopher 24:40

Johnston, Clark 9:66; 18:277

Johnston, Cyrus 23:305

Johnston, Daniel 17:393

Johnston, David L. 18:339

Johnston, David W. 23:70

Johnston, Eli 11:153

Johnston, Enos 20:114

Johnston, George 9:66; 18:277

Johnston, H. 1:45

Johnston, H. E. 18:369

Johnston, Hamilton P. 24:89

Johnston, Harrison 22:201

Johnston, Hugh 1:45

Johnston, I. R. 17:291

Johnston, J. 3:107; 11:94; 17:291

Johnston, J. A. 3:107; 9:54; 17:441; 24:153

Johnston, J. B. 1:45; 15:206

Johnston, J. D. 12:92

Johnston, J. E. 1:46

Johnston, J. R. 15:206

Johnston, J. W. 3:107

Johnston, James 10:9; 12:27; 20:35; 21:54

Johnston, John 1:45; 9:24; 11:191; 18:117; 22:201

Johnston, John T. 9:221

Johnston, John W. 23:89

Johnston, Layman 9:221

Johnston, Lewis 23:152

Johnston, M. 3:107; 27:66

Johnston, Michael 24:40

Johnston, Peter 25:333

Johnston, R. A. 3:107; 9:54

Johnston, Rice 10:61

Johnston, Richard 11:206; 17:53; 24:167

Johnston, Richard M. 13:132

Johnston, Robert 24:67

Johnston, Samuel 24:178

Johnston, Stephen 16:40; 22:452; 25:322
Johnston, T. 9:54
Johnston, T. S. J. 14:242
Johnston, W. P. 17:96
Johnston, Wallace 18:103
Johnston, Wiley 25:333
Johnston, William 3:107; 13:30; 18:277; 24:52; 25:333
Johnston, William F. 21:227
Johnston, William W. 15:206
Johnston, Willis 1:192
Joho---, James 11:264
Johose, Franklin 18:142
Johsee, Franklin 26:167
Johsse, Franklin 8:21
Johynson, Abel 18:219
Joice, David R. 12:173
Joice, James 14:76
Joice, John 21:72
Joice, John F. 9:230
Joice, Michael 21:122
Joice, Oliver 17:360
Joice, Patsey 8:50
Joice, Richard 11:333
Joice, Thomas 3:107
Join, Harvey C. 11:219
Joiner, Alamo 12:50
Joiner, Amayah 26:166
Joiner, Amaziah 8:40
Joiner, C. C. 10:205
Joiner, Caesar 9:121; 27:68
Joiner, E. 9:145
Joiner, Elias 27:66
Joiner, Elisha 11:153
Joiner, Fred 26:125
Joiner, George 9:121; 27:68
Joiner, Gilbert 25:192
Joiner, H. B. 9:145
Joiner, H. P. 27:66
Joiner, Henry 18:32
Joiner, J. E. 16:203
Joiner, J. F. 25:192
Joiner, J. M. 3:107
Joiner, J. W. 16:296
Joiner, James T. 22:123
Joiner, Kinchen 10:155
Joiner, Kinchew 19:172
Joiner, Lafayette 22:201
Joiner, O. 21:30
Joiner, R. S. 14:299; 17:473; 27:68
Joiner, William 17:203
Joines, L. 25:192
Joinin, William 26:37
Joist, John N. 15:87

Jokler, Adam 12:59
Joles, Joseph F. 10:121; 20:283
Joliff, Richard A. 22:39
Joliffe, R. H. 14:184
Jolley, A. S. 14:14
Jolley, B. F. 10:121
Jolley, Benjamin 18:142
Jolley, Benjamin F. 20:283
Jolley, F. 3:107
Jolley, G. 3:107
Jolley, George W. 9:83; 21:351
Jolley, J. 3:107
Jolley, Reuben R. 22:428
Jolliff, E. 8:64
Jolliff, Richard 8:64; 26:167
Jollio, W. H. 27:66
Jolloff, John 16:96
Jolly, A. S. 13:92
Jolly, Benjamin 8:21
Jolly, J. 15:152
Jolly, John 10:61; 18:207; 20:283; 23:113
Jolly, Joseph 4:34
Jolly, Peter 15:37
Jolly, Robert 20:57
Jolly, Samuel 11:65
Jolly, Samuel C. 21:351
Jolly, William A. 11:34; 18:219
Jolly, William H. 21:227
Jollymore, B. C. 1:46
Jollymore, William 25:45
Joloph, James F. 16:96
Jonas, A. 3:107
Jonas, J. 3:107
Jonas, J. A. 11:152
Jonas, John 21:351
Jonas, Miles 22:406
Jonce, George W. 11:424
Joncoine, Lewis V. 15:285
Jondron, Eli 22:39
Jonegan, James 26:221
Joneles, --- 12:85; 16:296
Joneon, Isaac 15:206
Jones, --- 9:133; 11:65, 94; 13:65; 14:184; 17:364; 18:207; 19:79, 318, 327; 21:30; 25:45, 46
Jones, A. 1:45, 46, 142, 143, 144; 9:24; 11:65, 153; 13:129; 14:76, 278; 17:179; 18:51; 19:254; 22:306; 23:127; 25:192

Jones, A. B. 1:142; 7:51
Jones, A. H. 11:413; 14:76; 21:188; 25:192
Jones, A. J. 6:31; 20:150; 25:322
Jones, A. J. W. 11:127
Jones, A. S. 11:280
Jones, A. Y. 14:242; 27:69
Jones, Aaron 7:127; 13:30; 21:351
Jones, Abial H. 12:80
Jones, Abraham 14:184
Jones, Abram 21:275
Jones, Adam 13:57
Jones, Adomrome 27:65
Jones, Albert 8:40; 9:182; 19:286; 24:89; 26:166
Jones, Albert A. 15:159
Jones, Albert S. 17:405
Jones, Alex 9:133; 17:179
Jones, Alexander 5:41; 12:50; 20:97; 27:67
Jones, Alfred 9:103, 209; 18:68, 339; 21:351; 22:513, 523
Jones, Allen 19:47
Jones, Allin 20:9
Jones, Alonzo 7:78; 8:21; 18:142
Jones, Alphonzo 17:360
Jones, Altemus 19:172
Jones, Amos 22:257, 352
Jones, Amos D. 22:85
Jones, Anderson 9:221; 18:369
Jones, Andrew 9:209; 17:398
Jones, Andrew J. 19:254
Jones, Andrew T. 17:260
Jones, Andy 9:209; 18:68
Jones, Armstead 21:212
Jones, Asa W. 25:192
Jones, Atlas 25:192
Jones, Augustus 9:209; 19:303
Jones, B. 16:203
Jones, B. C. 19:326
Jones, B. F. 10:121; 25:192
Jones, B. H. 9:84; 26:38
Jones, B. R. 9:235; 18:421
Jones, Bartlett 19:172
Jones, Benjamin 11:107; 12:50; 17:260; 18:32; 19:47; 22:463; 23:152; 26:168
Jones, Benjamin C. 24:40

Jones, Benjamin D. 7:99; 10:121; 20:283
Jones, Benjamin F. 5:20; 20:283; 22:257, 483
Jones, Benjamin P. 16:203
Jones, Beverly 17:206
Jones, Bradford 17:423
Jones, Bradford B. 24:171
Jones, Buck 11:206
Jones, Buckara A. 25:192
Jones, Burel 18:369
Jones, Burel T. 9:221
Jones, Burl 7:127
Jones, Byron C. 21:54
Jones, C. 3:107; 7:58; 11:119; 13:92; 14:262; 25:299
Jones, C. B. 3:107
Jones, C. C. 18:15
Jones, C. E. 9:36, 54; 10:18; 21:351
Jones, C. H. 15:343; 16:372; 25:46
Jones, C. J. 13:30
Jones, C. R. 25:192
Jones, C. S. 16:372
Jones, C. W. 3:107
Jones, Caleb 4:134; 10:99
Jones, Calvin 7:8; 15:81
Jones, Charles 3:107; 11:94, 107, 413; 13:81; 14:184, 336; 15:289; 16:96, 203; 17:133, 148, 395; 18:32, 271; 19:326; 21:275; 22:257, 281; 24:197; 25:333
Jones, Charles B. 12:27
Jones, Charles D. 19:79
Jones, Charles E. 18:346
Jones, Charles P. 16:40
Jones, Charles R. 5:20; 10:121; 20:283
Jones, Charles T. 13:30
Jones, Charles W. 1:46; 4:34; 7:126
Jones, Clarkson 7:75; 21:227
Jones, Collins 7:127
Jones, Cornelius 20:89
Jones, Cyrus 7:126; 8:88
Jones, D. 3:107; 14:76; 19:327; 21:351; 23:152; 25:46, 192; 27:65
Jones, D. A. 17:145
Jones, D. C. 10:96; 14:76
Jones, D. H. 9:110, 145; 27:66
Jones, D. J. 2:13; 27:68
Jones, D. N. 20:92

Jones, D. W. 9:84; 14:76; 26:37
Jones, Daniel 5:41; 6:35; 10:121; 11:34; 20:283; 22:235; 23:99
Jones, Daniel R. 24:59
Jones, Daniel S. 17:422; 24:167
Jones, David 1:45; 4:66; 6:27; 7:99; 9:84, 121; 11:65, 413; 12:50; 17:133; 19:79, 172; 20:9; 21:227; 22:306, 307, 513; 23:11; 24:197; 27:66, 68
Jones, David B. 4:34
Jones, David E. 22:201
Jones, David T. 22:201
Jones, David W. 8:21; 18:142
Jones, Dennis 17:179
Jones, Dudley H. 22:452
Jones, E. 1:45; 3:107; 13:76, 112; 14:184; 16:203; 25:46, 192
Jones, E. B. 21:30; 25:192
Jones, E. C. 1:143; 3:107
Jones, E. D. 12:142
Jones, E. E. 9:230; 20:283; 23:307
Jones, E. S. 24:22
Jones, E. T. 23:152
Jones, E. W. 1:143; 9:54
Jones, Eaton 27:68
Jones, Ed 17:163
Jones, Ed. F. 16:280
Jones, Edmund 11:206; 13:30
Jones, Edward 5:41; 9:36; 15:17; 17:422; 21:276; 22:306; 24:167; 26:166
Jones, Edward O. 23:123
Jones, Edwin W. 9:13
Jones, Elias 17:504
Jones, Elijah 10:121; 16:203; 20:283
Jones, Elijah G. 8:88
Jones, Elisha 1:46; 17:36
Jones, Elizabeth Ann 22:353
Jones, Elmira 25:300
Jones, Elwood 14:184
Jones, Emerson 7:127
Jones, Emery 18:397
Jones, Emuel 16:40
Jones, Enfield 7:126
Jones, Enman W. 21:55
Jones, Enoch 22:124
Jones, Enoch A. 22:85

Jones, Enoch F. 17:81
Jones, Enos E. 17:425
Jones, Ephraim 7:126
Jones, Ephriam 18:242
Jones, Erasmus J. 24:40
Jones, Erastus W. 18:277
Jones, Eugene R. 23:89
Jones, Evan 7:99; 21:351; 25:45
Jones, Evan E. 22:483
Jones, Evans 18:86
Jones, Even G. 7:31
Jones, Ezra 8:21; 18:142
Jones, Ezra B. 17:281
Jones, F. 1:144; 25:192
Jones, F. B. 21:351
Jones, F. D. 10:145; 19:172
Jones, F. J. 25:300
Jones, F. M. 16:40
Jones, F. R. W. 21:30
Jones, File W. 4:34
Jones, Finnis 8:40
Jones, Francis 26:166
Jones, Francis B. 17:443; 19:172; 22:463; 24:159
Jones, Francis L. 22:85
Jones, Francis M. 17:314; 23:113
Jones, Francis W. 23:70
Jones, Frank 8:21; 11:206; 17:179; 18:142
Jones, Franklin 13:30
Jones, Franklin M. 22:428
Jones, Fred. C. 18:310
Jones, Fred. O. 16:40
Jones, Frederick C. 26:103
Jones, Frederick E. 7:99
Jones, Frederick O. 13:30
Jones, Frisbey 9:182
Jones, Frisby 19:282
Jones, G. 1:47, 142; 3:107; 14:76; 15:69; 24:112
Jones, G. A. 16:80
Jones, G. C. 3:107
Jones, G. J. 7:83; 21:351
Jones, G. L. 3:107
Jones, G. M. 27:66
Jones, G. O. 21:110
Jones, G. T. 25:46
Jones, G. W. 3:107; 9:145; 13:112; 16:40, 203; 25:192; 27:66
Jones, George 1:46; 4:66; 7:31; 8:40; 9:133, 157; 10:61; 12:72; 13:30, 58; 14:333; 15:206; 16:40, 203;

Jones, George 18:32;
20:283; 21:276;
22:85; 23:36;
26:167; 27:67, 69
Jones, George A. 9:221;
15:307
Jones, George F. 13:30;
14:184
Jones, George H. 7:51
Jones, George L. 24:52
Jones, George M. 22:429
Jones, George R. 23:70
Jones, George S. 23:268
Jones, George W. 5:20;
9:121, 236; 11:287;
16:78; 19:20, 319;
20:57; 26:221; 27:68
Jones, Green 18:242;
26:39
Jones, Green A. 23:89
Jones, Griffin 14:315
Jones, Gustus 8:40;
26:166
Jones, H. 3:107; 9:204;
10:176; 17:179;
18:68; 19:172; 20:85
Jones, H. B. 3:108; 7:99
Jones, H. C. 1:46; 3:108;
18:426
Jones, H. H. 1:143
Jones, H. H. H. 12:27
Jones, H. J. 18:15
Jones, H. L. 21:30
Jones, H. O. 15:278;
25:192
Jones, H. S. 3:108
Jones, H. T. 12:82; 16:296
Jones, H. W. 14:330
Jones, Harman 21:351
Jones, Harrison 17:81
Jones, Harrison P. 11:34
Jones, Hector 9:133;
27:67
Jones, Henderson 10:121;
20:283
Jones, Henry 1:45; 6:17;
7:83, 126; 8:40; 9:84,
133, 165; 10:61;
11:16; 12:50;
15:206; 18:68, 87,
426; 20:114, 283;
21:276, 351; 22:85,
256, 406, 429, 452;
24:40; 26:38, 166,
167, 236; 27:67
Jones, Henry C. 8:107;
9:69
Jones, Henry F. 12:27
Jones, Henry H. 7:14
Jones, Henry L. 13:30;
16:40

Jones, Henry P. 23:36
Jones, Henry W. 17:159
Jones, Herbert 14:184
Jones, Herman B. 10:61
Jones, Hiram 24:197;
26:125
Jones, Hiram P. 12:27
Jones, Hobart H. 9:182
Jones, Horace 22:429
Jones, Howard 4:34
Jones, Hugh 21:188
Jones, Hugh C. 15:159
Jones, I. 8:21; 14:184;
26:145
Jones, I. C. 18:68
Jones, Ira D. 9:121
Jones, Ira E. 17:21
Jones, Irwin 7:31; 21:352
Jones, Isaac 15:126;
17:273; 21:276;
22:85, 483
Jones, Isaac E. 20:18
Jones, Isaac M. 10:61;
20:283; 22:257
Jones, Isaac T. 10:61;
20:283
Jones, J. 1:46, 142, 143;
3:108; 7:51; 8:50;
9:69, 145, 154;
10:186; 11:280;
12:96; 13:103; 14:14,
77, 278, 299; 15:206,
259, 360; 16:120,
203, 269; 17:110,
179, 471, 480;
18:142, 176; 19:79;
21:352; 25:45, 192;
27:66, 69
Jones, J. A. 7:75; 15:206;
17:145; 25:300
Jones, J. B. 3:108; 14:184
Jones, J. B. W. 17:145
Jones, J. C. 1:142; 8:21;
18:142
Jones, J. E. 3:108
Jones, J. F. 3:108; 11:119
Jones, J. G. 19:79
Jones, J. H. 1:142;
16:203; 17:497
Jones, J. J. 19:255; 20:33
Jones, J. M. 3:108; 14:77,
242; 21:352
Jones, J. R. 3:108
Jones, J. T. 3:108; 11:242
Jones, J. W. 4:34; 5:41;
8:64; 14:77; 15:206;
16:40; 19:79; 20:283;
25:192, 322; 26:39,
167; 27:69
Jones, J. Willard 14:184
Jones, Jabez 8:64; 26:167

Jones, Jack 8:40; 26:166
Jones, Jackson 8:50;
19:296; 21:101
Jones, Jacob 8:21; 16:96;
18:142; 24:52
Jones, Jacob R. 17:206
Jones, James 1:46; 4:34;
7:99, 126; 8:64, 88;
9:54, 236; 10:121,
211; 11:34, 388;
12:50; 14:286;
16:203; 17:206, 428;
18:191, 450; 19:20,
303; 20:283; 21:95,
212, 240, 276, 352;
22:85; 23:70; 24:67,
183; 25:285; 26:221;
27:69
Jones, James A. 10:176;
19:172
Jones, James B. 11:127;
22:257
Jones, James C. 11:65
Jones, James D. 2:13
Jones, James E. 26:145
Jones, James F. 10:121;
20:283
Jones, James H. 9:182;
19:267
Jones, James M. 17:288
Jones, James P. 11:295;
19:79
Jones, James T. 20:125
Jones, Jardine 27:145
Jones, Jasper 18:32
Jones, Jeff 21:130
Jones, Jefferson 16:203
Jones, Jeremiah 21:149
Jones, Jeremiah A. 17:260
Jones, Jeremiah B. 11:388
Jones, Jeremiah C. 11:153
Jones, Jerry 1:191
Jones, Jesse 9:227;
10:121; 20:283;
21:212
Jones, Jesse E. 18:369
Jones, Jesse H. 22:502
Jones, Joel 11:127; 14:76
Jones, John 1:45; 4:34;
5:20; 6:17, 28; 7:83,
127; 8:40, 88, 114;
9:24, 163; 10:121,
180; 11:293; 12:8,
27, 72, 162; 13:128;
14:77; 15:56, 87,
108; 17:36, 179;
18:68, 87, 176, 242,
310; 19:20, 47, 278,
343; 20:35, 283;
21:55, 85, 240, 276;

Jones, John 22:39, 85, 201, 306, 307, 338, 429; 23:288; 25:192; 26:38, 39, 103, 125, 167
Jones, John A. 9:43; 18:87; 22:201; 26:125
Jones, John B. 11:231, 243; 22:257, 452
Jones, John D. 5:20; 7:31; 13:30
Jones, John E. 9:24; 21:352
Jones, John F. 9:182; 11:34; 25:45
Jones, John H. 8:21, 88; 18:142, 327, 412; 21:55, 276
Jones, John K. 4:34
Jones, John L. 23:36
Jones, John M. 8:107
Jones, John O. 13:30
Jones, John P. 12:50; 22:429; 23:89
Jones, John R. 6:17; 18:87
Jones, John S. 17:405
Jones, John T. 13:57; 22:39, 353, 452
Jones, John W. 8:21; 9:209; 10:61; 11:65; 16:78; 18:142; 20:9, 97; 22:39, 201, 256, 483
Jones, John Y. 17:314; 22:353
Jones, Jonathan 9:84; 23:107; 26:37
Jones, Jonthan 21:249
Jones, Joseph 8:40; 9:47, 235; 15:7, 206; 16:203; 18:242, 421; 19:20; 22:429; 26:39, 125, 167
Jones, Joseph C. 10:61; 20:283; 21:30
Jones, Joseph J. 9:182
Jones, Joseph L. 22:307
Jones, Joseph M. 7:31
Jones, Joshua A. 20:3
Jones, Josiah 8:88; 9:133; 21:131; 22:257; 27:67
Jones, Josiah A. 18:369
Jones, Jus. 1:46
Jones, L. 1:142, 143; 14:77; 17:179; 21:188
Jones, L. A. F. 12:142
Jones, L. A. J. 20:284
Jones, L. E. 15:268

Jones, L. P. 23:152
Jones, L. T. 13:30
Jones, Laburn 11:107
Jones, Lafayette 17:443; 21:55; 24:159
Jones, Lansing 12:160
Jones, Larkie 21:276
Jones, Laton 22:201
Jones, Leander M. 27:69
Jones, Lee H. 24:59
Jones, Leonard 9:182
Jones, Levi 21:31
Jones, Lewis 9:100; 19:20; 20:86; 21:276; 22:429; 25:333
Jones, Lewis L. 22:171
Jones, Licherton 9:209
Jones, Logan 19:291
Jones, Loofter 22:513
Jones, Lorenzo 17:66
Jones, Lorz 1:46
Jones, Louis 19:291; 23:268
Jones, Louis W. 22:85
Jones, Lucy 16:297
Jones, Luonas 5:20
Jones, M. 1:46; 5:41; 9:154; 13:92; 27:66
Jones, M. A. 21:188
Jones, M. B. 20:284
Jones, M. D. 22:338
Jones, M. K. 18:417
Jones, M. M. 19:20, 239
Jones, Marion 17:398
Jones, Martin 12:142
Jones, Martin M. 17:66
Jones, Martin V. 13:30
Jones, Marvin 7:126
Jones, Matthew 21:13
Jones, McDonald 22:399
Jones, McDuffie 22:85
Jones, Michael 7:71; 9:24; 17:21; 18:310; 26:103
Jones, Miles 8:40
Jones, Milford D. 21:55
Jones, Milton 8:40; 21:352; 23:191; 26:167
Jones, Milton R. 21:31
Jones, Morgan 22:497
Jones, Morris 10:208
Jones, Moses 12:27; 21:149, 276; 22:338; 24:197
Jones, Moses W. 15:91
Jones, Murdock 16:40
Jones, N. 1:143; 11:34; 16:203
Jones, N. C. 21:31
Jones, Nancy 21:352

Jones, Nat 22:338
Jones, Nathan 11:187
Jones, Nathaniel 9:43; 22:483; 26:125
Jones, Ned 9:204
Jones, Nelson 12:50; 22:307
Jones, Nelson W. 16:78
Jones, Newton 22:85
Jones, Noah T. 21:204
Jones, O. 3:108; 11:100; 14:77; 16:204
Jones, O. R. 15:360
Jones, Oliver 18:242; 26:39
Jones, Oliver A. 9:182
Jones, Oliver M. 4:34
Jones, Omstead 21:276
Jones, Orange S. 11:264
Jones, Orlando 19:20
Jones, Oscar D. 19:20
Jones, Oscar R. 19:79
Jones, Owen A. 22:39
Jones, Owen R. 12:96
Jones, P. 3:108; 12:8; 14:77; 25:192
Jones, P. D. 21:31
Jones, P. G. 14:184
Jones, Parker 1:192
Jones, Patrick 8:126; 13:112; 21:352
Jones, Paul 7:127
Jones, Perry 25:192
Jones, Peter 4:34; 5:41; 17:179; 18:15; 21:276; 22:256, 306, 513
Jones, Peter E. 22:338
Jones, Philip F. 4:34
Jones, Phineas 10:121; 20:284
Jones, Phineas P. 4:34
Jones, Pleasant 22:306
Jones, R. 3:108; 8:50; 11:264; 16:136, 204; 23:36; 25:45, 192, 272
Jones, R. E. 2:13; 25:45
Jones, R. H. 23:36
Jones, R. M. 16:204
Jones, R. P. 1:143
Jones, R. W. 3:108
Jones, Reason 17:179
Jones, Reuben 10:155; 12:8; 26:166
Jones, Reuchem 19:172
Jones, Rice 26:39
Jones, Richard 7:99; 10:121; 11:206; 12:50; 16:204; 17:398; 20:104, 284

Jones, Richard H. 22:406
Jones, Richard I. 11:231
Jones, Riley 8:88
Jones, Robert 4:34; 5:41;
    6:25; 7:126; 8:50;
    9:103, 133, 236;
    10:121; 11:206;
    12:50; 13:30; 16:40;
    17:36, 428; 18:68;
    19:79, 172; 20:284;
    21:122; 22:306, 452;
    24:183; 25:192;
    26:221; 27:67, 68
Jones, Robert A. 8:107;
    9:133; 11:93; 22:452
Jones, Robert H. 22:452
Jones, Robert N. 22:39,
    406
Jones, Robert R. 9:103
Jones, Robert W. 23:191
Jones, Rube 8:40
Jones, Rufus 10:121;
    20:284; 24:63
Jones, S. 1:47; 3:108;
    10:148; 13:92; 14:14,
    77; 15:351; 17:179;
    18:51; 25:192; 27:65,
    69
Jones, S. A. 21:122
Jones, S. D. 3:108; 17:53
Jones, S. F. 1:143
Jones, S. J. 22:338
Jones, S. M. 23:36
Jones, S. S. 15:4
Jones, S. W. 1:142;
    17:441; 24:153
Jones, Safford 21:31
Jones, Samuel 9:133, 154;
    10:61, 162; 11:206;
    12:50; 15:87; 17:323,
    390; 20:27; 21:128,
    276; 22:39, 306;
    24:80; 27:68, 69
Jones, Samuel S. 21:352
Jones, Samuel W. 9:24;
    18:310; 26:103
Jones, Seaban 17:273
Jones, Seth 9:182; 19:239
Jones, Shakespeare
    21:276
Jones, Sidney 7:127
Jones, Silas 10:61;
    16:204; 20:125, 284
Jones, Silas A. 19:79
Jones, Simon 10:121;
    20:284; 25:192
Jones, Sino 20:284
Jones, Solomon 7:127
Jones, Squire 17:179, 281

Jones, Stephen 6:17; 9:84;
    18:87; 21:241, 276;
    26:37
Jones, Stephen C. 22:307
Jones, Stewart 20:284
Jones, T. 1:143; 3:108;
    15:343; 16:269;
    23:36; 25:46, 192
Jones, T. C. 1:143; 11:153
Jones, T. F. 17:509
Jones, T. L. 12:87
Jones, T. M. 23:200
Jones, T. T. 25:193
Jones, T. W. 1:143
Jones, Thadeus 26:212
Jones, Theodore 11:388;
    21:245
Jones, Tho. C. 20:284
Jones, Thomas 1:46;
    3:108; 5:41; 8:118;
    9:36, 235; 10:99;
    11:153, 191, 264;
    12:27, 87, 170;
    13:65; 14:77; 16:297;
    17:74, 81; 18:242,
    421, 434; 19:20;
    20:23; 21:352; 22:12,
    201, 429; 25:300;
    26:38
Jones, Thomas B. 10:61;
    20:284
Jones, Thomas C. 10:61
Jones, Thomas D. 13:30;
    22:483
Jones, Thomas E. 26:212
Jones, Thomas G. 11:306
Jones, Thomas H. 7:14;
    24:22
Jones, Thomas P. 12:27
Jones, Thomas T. 5:20
Jones, Thornton 19:20
Jones, Tighlman N.
    22:406
Jones, Timothy 11:65
Jones, Tino 10:61
Jones, Tobias 16:120
Jones, V. 16:372
Jones, W. 1:46, 143;
    3:108; 18:310; 19:79;
    21:163, 245; 22:256,
    352; 23:289; 24:80;
    25:300; 26:103
Jones, W. A. 14:14;
    15:207
Jones, W. B. 10:61; 14:77;
    19:20; 20:284; 26:38
Jones, W. C. 7:31; 8:60;
    12:154, 172
Jones, W. E. 3:108
Jones, W. F. 3:108; 14:77

Jones, W. H. 1:142, 143;
    3:108; 11:152;
    14:269, 282; 15:360;
    19:79; 21:139;
    25:193; 27:67
Jones, W. J. 7:31; 12:163;
    22:235; 23:36;
    25:322; 26:38; 27:66
Jones, W. K. 7:58; 14:14
Jones, W. L. 11:423;
    21:95, 188
Jones, W. M. 3:108
Jones, W. P. 3:108; 9:24;
    13:92; 17:309; 23:36;
    26:103
Jones, W. R. 13:92; 21:31
Jones, W. S. 11:264
Jones, W. T. 3:108;
    17:297; 18:32
Jones, W. U. 9:145
Jones, W. W. 11:340
Jones, Wade 17:179
Jones, Waldo B. 15:11
Jones, Wallace 11:424
Jones, Waloo 7:126
Jones, Wat 17:421;
    24:164
Jones, Webster 17:336;
    21:204, 239
Jones, William 1:46;
    3:108; 4:34, 66; 6:23;
    7:99, 126, 127; 8:21,
    64, 88; 9:240; 10:18,
    99, 121; 11:219, 419;
    12:50, 64, 142;
    13:30; 14:77, 184,
    262, 332; 15:17, 37;
    16:204; 17:36, 133,
    134, 179, 203, 441;
    18:142, 219; 19:47,
    287; 20:177, 284;
    21:73, 188, 227, 352;
    22:12, 85, 124, 146,
    201, 235, 257; 23:70,
    113, 203; 24:196,
    197; 25:45, 193, 300
Jones, William A. 11:85;
    20:23
Jones, William B. 22:124,
    452
Jones, William C. 10:61;
    20:284
Jones, William D. 15:69;
    21:73; 23:191
Jones, William G. 13:30
Jones, William H. 4:34;
    7:31; 12:59, 96;
    17:243; 21:227;
    22:39; 23:180;
    24:153

Jones, William H. H. 23:152
Jones, William J. 5:41; 10:121; 11:187; 12:27; 20:284; 25:193
Jones, William M. 17:319
Jones, William P. 16:131; 18:310
Jones, William R. 10:61; 11:327; 12:162; 17:53; 23:70
Jones, William T. 11:243; 17:281
Jones, William W. 13:30; 16:40
Jones, Willis 7:68, 127
Jones, Wilson 16:40
Jones, Zachariah 17:91
Jonier, Frederick 9:43
Jonney, L. 3:108
Jonny, Horace 9:103
Jons, David L. 26:37
Jons, Ephraim 26:39
Jons, Miles 26:166
Jonslin, P. 9:145
Jonson, John A. 11:305
Jonson, John W. 15:316; 19:79
Jonson, William 27:145
Jonston, L. 18:369
Jonter, R. 18:51
Jonunk, A. O. 24:72
Joover, John 14:269
Joplin, Frederick 21:276
Joplin, J. H. 19:239, 274
Joraleman, David 12:55
Joray, Charles A. 11:65
Jorce, George 11:206
Jorce, Hillman 11:206
Jordan, --- 17:273
Jordan, A. 3:108
Jordan, A. E. 3:108
Jordan, A. T. 1:46
Jordan, Abram E. 11:34
Jordan, Amos 26:38
Jordan, Anderson 17:237
Jordan, Andrew 4:34; 12:155; 22:429
Jordan, B. 1:143
Jordan, B. W. 3:108
Jordan, C. H. 9:66
Jordan, Carry 25:193
Jordan, Charles M. 7:99
Jordan, David 8:64
Jordan, E. B. 19:20
Jordan, E. H. 25:193
Jordan, E. K. 7:99
Jordan, E. M. 11:34
Jordan, E. W. 9:214
Jordan, Edmond 7:127

Jordan, Edmund 26:236
Jordan, Edward 22:338
Jordan, Eli 17:314
Jordan, Elisha 21:352
Jordan, Emil 24:9
Jordan, Francis 9:84; 26:38
Jordan, Franklin 22:12
Jordan, G. D. 14:299
Jordan, George 8:40; 9:133; 23:36
Jordan, George F. 8:88
Jordan, George W. 18:111
Jordan, Gustin 10:121; 20:284
Jordan, H. 21:31
Jordan, Henry B. 22:39
Jordan, Hiram 25:46
Jordan, Isaac B. 10:121; 20:284
Jordan, J. 3:109; 10:152; 18:51
Jordan, J. A. 13:92; 14:14; 20:175
Jordan, J. M. 3:109
Jordan, J. P. 27:68
Jordan, James 9:182; 19:239; 21:55
Jordan, James D. 21:352
Jordan, James E. 15:11
Jordan, James H. 22:513
Jordan, James T. 11:65
Jordan, Jeremiah 21:352
Jordan, John 4:34; 13:112; 16:204; 18:207; 19:20; 20:23, 284; 21:276; 23:70; 24:9
Jordan, John J 21:31
Jordan, John R. 22:85
Jordan, L. S. 19:79; 27:68
Jordan, Lach 19:291
Jordan, Martin 15:69
Jordan, Mathew 22:257
Jordan, Moses 24:22
Jordan, N. 24:22
Jordan, N. H. 15:166
Jordan, Nathan 8:88
Jordan, Nehemiah 17:281
Jordan, Peter 9:84; 22:513; 26:37
Jordan, R. T. 9:214
Jordan, S. S. 15:343; 16:372
Jordan, Sahwell 20:186
Jordan, T. H. 21:31
Jordan, Thomas 3:109; 10:61; 17:415; 20:114, 284
Jordan, Thompson 24:153
Jordan, W. 19:20

Jordan, W. H. 12:82; 14:77; 16:297; 22:39
Jordan, W. L. 23:36
Jordan, William 7:75; 8:88; 9:84; 11:34; 17:200; 24:80
Jordan, William A. 10:121; 20:284
Jordan, William P. 21:73
Jordan, Willis 7:127; 24:196
Jordan, Wilson 8:21
Jorde, Kittle A. 21:256
Jorden, George 26:167
Jorden, R. 25:193
Jorden, William E. 10:99
Jordi, John 22:281
Jordon, Benjamin F. 21:85
Jordon, C. 27:69
Jordon, Charles H. 18:277
Jordon, Clinton G. 17:21
Jordon, Daniel 19:47
Jordon, E. 1:143
Jordon, Edward C. 15:207
Jordon, George 27:67
Jordon, George C. 18:397
Jordon, H. 23:114; 27:65
Jordon, J. 1:143
Jordon, J. H. 27:65
Jordon, John 10:121; 13:31; 16:40
Jordon, John J. 16:40
Jordon, Josiah 22:502
Jordon, L. C. 27:66
Jordon, Lawrence 17:190
Jordon, Louis S. 27:69
Jordon, M. M. 11:438
Jordon, Thomas 11:187; 18:219
Jordon, W. S. 16:78
Jordon, William 18:397; 25:300
Jordon, Willis 17:134
Jordon, Wilson 18:142
Joredan, Alex 9:204
Jorgenson, Gunder 21:256
Jorgeson, Nills P. 18:277
Jorgusson, Owen B. 18:334
Jornigan, James 9:236
Jortimer, John 18:279
Jose, Albert 14:184
Joselyn, G. R. 19:239
Joseph, --- 26:39
Joseph, A. S. 7:99
Joseph, Anthony 25:193
Joseph, F. 3:109
Joseph, Francis 13:31
Joseph, Isaac 7:14
Joseph, James 12:155
Joseph, John A. 23:152

Joseph, John P. 20:49
Joseph, Joseph 21:352
Joseph, L. 18:191
Joseph, L. D. 25:193
Joseph, L. R. 18:32
Joseph, N. 12:99
Joseph, Robert 26:212
Joseph, W. C. 3:109
Joseph, William 1:45
Joshua, William 22:338
Joskin, B. 19:79
Joslen, Albert W. 21:73
Joslin, David 9:84
Joslin, David D. 21:227
Joslin, Edward 9:145
Joslin, George M. 18:142
Joslin, J. 3:109
Joslin, James D. 23:70
Joslin, John A. 1:46
Joslin, John B. 18:219
Joslin, P. 27:66
Joslin, Rodney 18:219
Joslin, W. 18:32
Joslin, William 13:65
Joslyn, Americ 17:66
Joslyn, Daniel G. 10:121;
    20:284
Joslyn, E. A. 27:69
Joslyn, Edward J. 10:121;
    20:284
Joslyn, Edwin 25:45
Joslyn, F. 3:109
Joslyn, Frank B. 21:31
Joslyn, George 1:46
Joslyn, George M. 8:21
Joslyn, Herbert 25:46
Joslyn, Thomas G. 18:219
Joslyn, William 19:79
Joss, Samuel E. 14:185
Josselyn, A. J. 16:269
Josselyn, James H. 9:182
Josselyn, Luther 7:31
Joubert, Desire 22:406
Jouch, J. G. 12:96
Joughin, John 21:200
Jouls, Walter 4:34
Jount, John 12:99
Jourdan, Alex 18:68
Jourdan, B. 3:109
Jourdan, J. 20:133
Jourdan, Lewis 25:46
Jourdan, M. 3:109
Jourdon, John 14:185
Jourdon, William 23:276
Jourdron, M. 3:109
Jourman, Richard H.
    27:68
Journey, John 3:109
Journey, William 11:65
Journey, William L.
    23:242

Joute, J. G. 15:360
Jouter, R. 10:152
Jouton, M. 14:185
Jovees, F. 11:152
Jow, B. Goortrude 27:68
Jowe, John W. 16:209
Jowel, Joseph 11:100
Jowell, F. 15:207
Jowers, George 18:242;
    26:39
Jowers, J. W. 16:40
Jowgs, W. H. 11:243
Joy, A. E. 1:143
Joy, Albert S. 13:31
Joy, B. F. 21:352
Joy, Benjamin 13:112
Joy, Claybourn 7:127
Joy, D. V. 3:109
Joy, Dudley M. 13:31
Joy, Eli 8:21; 18:142
Joy, Granville W. 7:68
Joy, J. M. 26:39
Joy, John 16:85; 22:257
Joy, John T. 10:61
Joy, Joseph 21:55
Joy, Lewis 21:276
Joy, W. 24:22
Joy, W. H. 9:145
Joy, W. J. 16:40
Joyal, J. H. 25:193
Joyal, Joseph 21:352
Joyall, George 16:166
Joyboss, Arad 19:20
Joyce, A. 3:109
Joyce, Amos 18:242;
    26:39
Joyce, David K. 8:60
Joyce, George 10:8
Joyce, Henry 26:244
Joyce, James O. 11:187
Joyce, John 14:77
Joyce, John F. 20:284
Joyce, Matthew 4:34
Joyce, Michael 17:352
Joyce, Patrick 22:502;
    25:269
Joyce, Sullivan 16:40
Joyce, Thomas S. 22:429
Joyce, Walter 12:99
Joye, Cornelius 13:31
Joye, Lewis 17:398
Joyer, J. B. 18:191
Joylee, A. 18:191
Joyner, A. 25:193
Joyner, Amos 5:41
Joyner, D. M. 9:182;
    19:239
Joyner, John 22:39
Jrannep, J. 11:243
Juabett, S. 22:452
Jual, J. 11:280

Juan, Antonio 7:68
Juarado, Inocente 8:124
Jubb, John 16:280
Jubb, William 10:121;
    20:284
Jubenville, Francis 22:146
Juberg, Daniel 22:201
Jubilee, William 7:127
Juchem, Joseph 16:133
Juckey, H. S. 11:305
Juda, Andrew 17:66
Juda, G. 1:143
Judah, G. H. 11:88
Judas, M. 19:79
Judd, A. 18:242; 26:39
Judd, A. V. 12:171
Judd, Arya 21:256
Judd, Benjamin 15:294;
    16:204
Judd, C. A. 21:139
Judd, D. 10:18
Judd, D. H. 1:45
Judd, Daniel 23:200
Judd, E. 1:143
Judd, E. W. 1:46
Judd, Eli 11:34
Judd, F. 11:396
Judd, George 8:107
Judd, Henry 3:109
Judd, Henry M. 4:34
Judd, J. B. 9:182
Judd, J. E. 19:224
Judd, J. L. 1:142
Judd, John D. 19:172
Judd, John M. 22:502
Judd, Levi 12:82; 16:297
Judd, M. 24:214
Judd, Nathan 8:107
Judd, Volney 11:287
Judd, Warren L. 11:306
Judd, Watson W. 10:61;
    20:284
Judd, William 17:163, 503
Judd, Wilson F. 12:155
Juddy, G. W. 25:45
Juddy, George H. 2:13
Jude, H. 3:109
Jude, Henry 3:109
Jude, Hiram 24:167
Judge, James 15:95
Judge, John 10:162;
    19:172; 25:45
Judge, M. 24:112
Judge, Michael 15:37
Judge, Reemus 17:179
Judges, Josiah 9:133;
    27:68
Judgson, O. W. 10:61
Judkins, Franklin D.
    22:483
Judkins, H. T. 14:185

Judkins, Moses H. 13:31
Judkins, P. C. 25:45
Judkins, Thomas B. 7:99
Judkins, William H. 22:85
Judson, Charles 8:50
Judson, Chester 15:283;
  19:79
Judson, David 10:18
Judson, Edward L. 15:108
Judson, Edwin W. 10:18
Judson, Jerome D. 11:34
Judson, John 10:61;
  20:284
Judson, L. L. 20:284
Judson, Lucas F. 10:61
Judson, O. W. 20:284
Judson, S. C. 10:153
Judson, S. E. 19:172
Judson, Silas 9:16
Judus, John D. 8:114
Judy, George 17:179
Judy, George H. 12:27
Jugnet, A. B. 3:109
Juh, John W. 9:43
Juice, Horace 10:18
Juks, Simon 9:110
Jula, J. C. 11:280
Julerso, H. 3:109
Juley, Thomas J. 17:36
Julian, George 10:18;
  21:352
Julian, J. H. 8:50
Julian, James H. 21:55
Julian, John 27:66
Julian, Joseph 15:207
Julian, L. 20:284
Julian, Robert 11:413
Julian, Robert B. 20:9
Julian, Stephen 7:127
Julian, T. A. 11:264
Julian, Thomas 11:153
Julian, William 7:99
Julian, William C. 22:167
Julien, John 11:153
Julien, Joseph 18:242;
  26:39
Julien, Leonard 10:61
Julien, N. J. 11:264
Julien, Nathan 7:63
Julien, Thomas F. 22:85
Julier, Don A. 22:201
Julius, Charles 24:94
Jull, Charles M. 26:212
Jullman, George 22:452
Julson, John 17:99
July, F. 20:141
Juman, Israel 7:31
Juman, J. 7:31
Juman, Moses 9:121
Jump, Charles B. 11:127
Jump, D. P. 3:109

Jump, George 20:35
Jump, O. 3:109
Jump, Philo 15:304;
  16:204
Jump, Samuel L. 21:227
Jump, William 10:121;
  20:285
Jumper, Charles 18:310;
  26:103
Jumper, Jeremiah 11:152
Jumps, John W. 17:441;
  24:153
Junck, Ernest 26:166
Junck, J. 12:8
June, Hiram G. 22:146
June, James 13:31
June, John C. 17:419
June, Joseph 10:162;
  19:172
June, R. W. 1:46
June, Robert A. 10:162;
  19:172
June, Theron B. 19:20
Junel, J. 18:32
Jung, J. 20:155
Jung, Peter 19:303
Jung, Thomas 21:276
Jungham, Charles 11:119
Junian, Paul 11:428
Junice, Richard 17:53
Junior, Frank 9:165
Junios, Frank 25:322
Juniper, Abraham 22:201
Junis, Victor 24:107
Junk, Peter 16:97
Junk, William 19:327
Junker, E. 23:36
Junker, George 9:145
Junker, H. 11:242
Junket, Christian 18:32
Junkin, James A. 11:276
Junkins, James M. 10:146
Junot, Paul 4:34
Junstall, J. A. 9:54
Juntplate, F. 3:109
Juper, C. 3:109
Juprement, James 18:32
Jurder, James 14:185
Jurgens, Martin 24:67
Jurkins, J. 23:180
Jurles, M. 22:201
Jurwingo, J. 8:50
Jury, Adam 14:185
Jury, John M. 9:43
Jusel, Fred 9:182
Jusey, M. 9:182
Juskee, John N. 21:352
Juskins, George 18:68
Justice, Alexander L.
  23:70
Justice, Andrew 22:39

Justice, Cambridge 11:396
Justice, David E. 13:128
Justice, Edward 12:8;
  13:112
Justice, Francis M. 22:85
Justice, G. 10:148; 18:51
Justice, G. W. 8:101;
  21:122
Justice, George 9:84
Justice, George C. 2:13
Justice, George W. 3:109;
  17:463; 24:178
Justice, H. 3:109
Justice, Hiram 7:58
Justice, J. 3:109
Justice, J. W. 20:178
Justice, James B. 22:483
Justice, John 8:50; 13:31;
  21:139
Justice, John W. 22:201
Justice, Joseph 7:99
Justice, L. C. 14:77
Justice, L. G. C. 25:45
Justice, N. W. 9:145
Justice, Stephen 11:153
Justice, Thomas B. 19:172
Justice, W. N. 27:67
Justice, William 12:27
Justin, A. 17:354
Justin, C. 10:150
Justin, Conrad 17:36
Justin, George D. 10:18
Justin, John H. 20:9
Justis, D. S. 22:162
Justis, Elias 11:153
Justrice, N. 22:39
Justriel, Joseph M. 7:31
Justus, Daniel 21:195
Justus, George 26:38
Justus, J. M. 22:483
Justus, J. W. 22:201
Justus, William 20:103
Justus, William E. 23:152
Juttaaill, John 26:37
Juves, John J. 3:109
Juzi, Gustavus 17:388
Jyroe, J. W. 25:193
Jyther, Henry 19:80

K

K---, A. 15:173
K---, A. H. 11:341
K---, B. 21:101
K---, C--- 15:366
K---, C. 12:100
K---, C. E. 25:47
K---, C. J. 25:49
K---, C. M. C. 11:402
K---, C. W. 15:166

K---, D. 20:155; 24:214
K---, E. 25:49
K---, E. S. 21:352
K---, E. V. 21:208
K---, F. H. 16:136; 26:168
K---, F. R. 17:364
K---, G. 21:167
K---, G. W. 21:167; 23:263
K---, Gustavus 15:291
K---, H. 18:15; 27:70
K---, H. C. 15:208
K---, H. O. 20:155
K---, I. 11:243
K---, J. 12:147; 15:95; 19:303; 21:208; 25:47
K---, J. C. 16:97
K---, J. F. 9:121; 27:70
K---, J. M. 10:192
K---, J. R. 17:217
K---, J. W. 10:34
K---, Jacob 16:204
K---, Jacob N. 25:193
K---, James 20:175
K---, John 15:166
K---, L. M. 12:100; 15:208
K---, M. W. 16:297
K---, Morris 25:47
K---, N. 20:57; 24:214
K---, P. 11:155; 19:286
K---, R. 19:224
K---, R. E. 21:208
K---, S. 15:166
K---, S. B. 25:311
K---, S. M. 16:372
K---, T--- 26:236
K---, T. 18:87; 19:174; 25:49
K---, T. H. 8:64
K---, W. 11:94; 16:78; 23:259; 25:48
K---, W. A. 20:57
K---, W. E. 10:186
K---, William 8:51
K---, William E. 11:243
K----, E. W. 22:85
K---dre, Albert 11:322
Ka-metsh-hajo 25:333
Kabb, John 15:14
Kabe, William 12:92
Kable, Michael 17:81
Kach, A. C. 18:32
Kachell, E. H. 1:47
Kachholdt, Henry B. 24:80
Kachner, John 22:12
Kachner, Levi 19:172
Kadel, B. 13:31
Kadel, Nicholas 22:167

Kadell, Alfred 8:101
Kadle, B. 16:40
Kadle, W. 25:49
Kaeeghn, W. J. 24:22
Kaefer, George W. 17:81
Kaemerlyn, Frederick 14:77
Kaes, Jacob 22:281
Kaetwasser, L. 11:119
Kaffer, Joseph 4:34
Kafka, Martin 4:34
Kaford, John 26:40
Kage, Thomas 14:185
Kagle, John 23:70
Kagrice, J. 1:147
Kagy, J. A. 20:147
Kah-yer-skon-he 25:333
Kahalar, James 23:99
Kahl, Theodore 10:121; 20:285
Kahlah, G. 14:77
Kahle, Alex 9:182
Kahle, Frederick 11:243
Kahle, William F. 12:122; 15:126
Kahler, Charles 14:185
Kahler, Daniel 23:36
Kahler, Jacob 7:58
Kahn, Conrad 10:61; 20:285
Kahn, Emile M. 8:121
Kahns, Fred 20:285
Kahoon, Allen 5:20
Kahus, Frederick 10:61
Kahus, Reuben 4:34
Kaib, William 21:352
Kaichner, Levi 10:162
Kaifer, Fred K. 21:352
Kaifer, George 22:287
Kaigley, John F. 27:72
Kail, William 3:109
Kain, Elias P. 11:16
Kain, G. H. 11:154
Kain, George N. 25:47
Kain, J. F. 15:207
Kain, Pat 3:109
Kain, William A. 11:35
Kain, William H. 12:8
Kaine, A. 27:71
Kaine, John 12:27; 22:429
Kaine, John L. 17:419
Kaine, Joseph M. 7:31
Kaine, Rodgers 17:70
Kaine, William F. 15:289
Kains, Jacob 12:27
Kairman, Edward 4:34
Kaiser, Augustus 22:463
Kaiser, F. 23:152
Kaiser, Frederick 21:87
Kaiser, George 25:193

Kaiser, Gottleib 18:310; 26:104
Kaiser, Henry 23:123
Kaiser, John 4:34; 8:50
Kaiser, Matthias 7:31
Kaiser, Samuel 9:24
Kaison, Jacob 15:37
Kaiter, Robert 10:8
Kakle, Charles 14:77
Kalahar, John 12:72
Kalaran, Pat 18:142
Kalb, William 8:64
Kalcak, Alfred 21:31
Kale, Aaron 22:483
Kale, James 21:227
Kale, John B. 11:207
Kale, William J. 23:89
Kalehar, C. 1:49
Kaleir, R. 3:109
Kalemain, David 26:168
Kaleman, David 8:40
Kalenski, Charles 7:99
Kaler, George 20:285
Kaler, George W. 16:297
Kaler, J. 3:109
Kaler, J. D. 25:193
Kaler, John 5:20
Kaler, Walter 23:70
Kales, David 12:155
Kaley, Emanuel 22:201
Kaley, G. 3:109
Kaley, J. M. 26:125
Kaley, Michael 5:20
Kalford, John 18:242
Kaling, Leonard 16:204
Kalkrath, C. 3:109
Kall, P. 16:204
Kall, W. 21:352
Kalla, Christian 17:201
Kallenbrook, C. 19:80
Kaller, George 11:127
Kalley, Andrew 22:338
Kallhoff, Henry 23:99
Kallina, Martin 22:12
Kallman, N. 1:146
Kalls, John 11:108
Kallumry, Peter 15:207
Kalmback, Peter 19:80
Kalna, --- 21:352
Kalor, George 10:61
Kaloran, Pat 8:21
Kalps, J. 14:77
Kalriter, H. 1:144
Kalsan, Herman 19:173
Kalty, J. 3:109
Kam, James 22:124
Kamball, Edward P. 21:114
Kamboe, Barton 7:99
Kamerer, Adam 18:103
Kamerer, H. W. 19:173

Kamerer, P. L. 7:58
Kamerer, Sebastian 9:244
Kamerline, C. 1:49
Kames, Anthony 7:51
Kamley, John 12:27
Kammerer, Louis P. 23:152
Kammery, Daniel 22:201
Kammetz, Morris 4:34
Kammiake, Ernist 27:145
Kamp, Fred 17:314
Kampe, C. 23:152
Kamper, Samuel 10:173
Kampers, Henry 11:207
Kampf, M. R. 23:36
Kamron, Nicholas 11:155
Kan, A. 14:77
Kanada, C. 11:335
Kanaga, J. 3:109
Kanagan, Peter 9:182
Kanan, Jacob 14:336
Kanas, James P. 15:56
Kanbert, J. 11:127
Kanble, Eli 23:70
Kandle, John 25:322
Kandson, Andrew 18:142
Kane, Alexander 17:248
Kane, Andrew 15:37; 19:173
Kane, Antonia 18:397
Kane, C. 1:145; 18:111
Kane, Chales 27:71
Kane, Charles 4:34
Kane, Daniel 4:35
Kane, Dennis 22:338
Kane, Dennis H. 15:207
Kane, Eli 4:35
Kane, F. 3:109
Kane, G. N. 5:41
Kane, George 8:21; 12:62; 15:7
Kane, George M. 25:193
Kane, Gwin H. 4:34
Kane, H. 3:109
Kane, J. 1:145, 146, 147
Kane, J. S. 23:180
Kane, James A. 25:193
Kane, Jeremiah 23:36
Kane, John 8:21; 14:278; 18:142; 23:107
Kane, Joseph 3:109
Kane, Lucas 9:24; 18:310; 26:103
Kane, M. 21:55
Kane, Michael O. 17:21
Kane, Patrick 4:34; 7:16; 12:27; 14:185; 18:412; 21:122; 22:520; 27:71
Kane, Patrick F. 14:14
Kane, Peter 3:109

Kane, R. 13:76; 16:204
Kane, Richard 8:21; -18:32; 26:168
Kane, T. 1:48
Kane, Thomas 1:47; 8:88; 9:54
Kane, W. A. 15:322; 19:80
Kane, William 3:109; 11:154; 15:37; 25:282
Kanes, J. 25:193
Kanesmar, F. 1:144
Kaney, Martin 23:279
Kanio, August 9:204
Kanison, J. 11:66
Kank, J. S. S. 22:39
Kann, Henry 13:31
Kannar, O. 1:48
Kannarl, William 18:142
Kannion, David 21:352
Kano, Henry 16:40
Kanoble, John 22:12
Kanof, A. 25:193
Kanope, C. 3:109
Kanor, John B. 5:20
Kanpp, George 17:66
Kans, John 5:41
Kantanel, R. 14:299; 17:469
Kanter, Henry 18:32
Kanuss, David 20:137
Kanust, H. 3:109
Kapff, Paul 23:152
Kapilman, William 11:119
Kapital, S. 24:67
Kapler, Franklin 22:201
Kapone, --- 25:333
Kapp, D. 3:109
Kapp, John 16:97
Kappel, Christian 17:260
Kappel, H. 3:109
Kappelhof, F. 10:121
Kappelhof, T. 20:285
Kappell, Marcus 22:509
Kapper, Dick 9:103
Kappilman, Henry 24:67
Kappler, George 15:207
Kappler, Jacob F. 24:62
Karamer, Samuel 10:121
Karass, Abbott 1:47
Karch, J. 3:109
Karcher, Henry B. 22:146
Karcher, James 12:72
Karcher, Madkeas 19:21
Karck, Henry 23:36
Kardorff, August 8:21; 18:142
Karg, --- 26:236
Karge, Adam 23:129
Karger, Anton 6:10

Karger, H. 2:13
Kargner, George 17:460; 24:159
Kargo, William 17:449
Karier, Zack 22:483
Kariford, John C. 3:109
Kariger, Frederick 22:39
Karke, F. 1:49
Karker, J. 18:176
Karl, Charles 10:61
Karlan, P. 1:145
Karman, I. K. 20:285
Karman, W. K. 18:103
Karmels, Jacob A. 9:24
Karmin, F. 9:111
Karn, Charles 20:285
Karn, John 11:306
Karnaman, Henry 23:36
Karnasch, J. E. 23:36
Karne, P. 1:146
Karnes, Alexander 10:121; 20:285
Karnes, H. 11:340
Karnes, J. 3:109
Karnes, John 22:86; 25:49
Karnes, Joseph 11:306
Karnes, Owens W. 19:21
Karnes, William 18:242; 26:40
Karney, George 25:49
Karney, Henderson 21:276
Karney, Thomas J. 10:121; 20:285
Karnon, Edward 12:99; 15:366
Karns, F. 18:51
Karns, J. J. 3:109
Karns, John 2:13
Karns, Richard E. 7:31
Karps, M. 3:109
Karr, H. M. 16:160
Karr, Joseph 21:122, 256
Karr, Leander 22:464
Karr, M. H. 20:125
Karr, Robert 22:39
Karr, Samuel 18:421
Karr, Simeon 17:281
Karr, T. H. B. 11:155
Karr, Thomas H. 22:201
Karr, William 3:109
Karre, Andrew 10:153
Karrington, --- 23:281
Karrott, Klansons 13:31
Karsar, C. 25:48
Karsar, Charles 2:13
Karse, J. 18:242; 26:40
Karsh, Andrew 20:285
Karshubuter, Frederick 16:41
Karson, G. 15:207

Karson, H. B. 3:109
Karst, Andrew 10:61
Karston, Frank 19:329
Kart, Chauncey 21:352
Karthman, Dutrick 18:142
Karthmann, Detrick 8:21
Kartsinie, Charles 26:168
Karty, John 23:11
Kas, James A. 19:80
Kasa, --- 16:372
Kasabainn, Charles
    18:142
Kasay, C. 15:348
Kasburg, T. J. 21:14
Kase, F. 1:145
Kase, L. 11:182
Kase, R. J. 12:155
Kaseddin, J. 27:73
Kaser, Jacob 23:152
Kash, Elois 15:207
Kashadden, Charles 26:41
Kashew, W. 25:193
Kasinger, John A. 17:206
Kaske, William 13:65
Kasketter, L. 1:146
Kaskie, I. 14:185
Kaskie, J. 14:257
Kaskins, C. 25:193
Kasler, Abraham M.
    18:219
Kasman, William J.
    21:249
Kasper, J. 21:201
Kassabaum, Charles 8:21
Kassan, Alexander 15:207
Kassermaur, Christian
    11:116
Kassig, J. Handy 22:201
Kaste, Daniel A. 15:292
Kastel, Orton 24:80
Kasten, John 1:48
Kaster, Fitz 18:142
Kastner, Charles 11:119
Kastner, J. F. 1:49
Kastor, Fitz 8:21
Kat-coffa-la-sah 25:333
Katci, Joseph 20:285
Kate, William 16:297
Katen, H. 1:146
Katen, Wesley 1:47
Katens, Mary 20:57
Kater, N. 5:20
Katerman, T. H. 12:27
Kates, Wiley 10:61;
    20:285
Kath, W. D. 14:77
Kathalin, Frederick 13:31
Kathan, Charles W. 7:99
Kathan, J. 13:92
Kathburn, Henry 9:84
Katheiser, Nicholas 24:22

Katherson, John 21:31
Katill, A. 19:255
Katispalett, Casper 8:21
Katon, William 7:99
Katte, R. 20:285
Katte, Randolph 10:61
Katternia, --- 15:291
Katteshenny, J. W. 19:21
Kattle, Hubbard 18:142
Kattner, J. 1:146
Katto---, Be--- 16:204
Katts, Charles 13:60
Katz, Henry W. 7:31
Katza, Henry 21:31
Katzebue, Charles 11:154
Kauberg, Harry 11:16
Kauble, George W. 17:81
Kauer, John D. 19:320
Kauf, J. 3:109
Kauffin, John 11:66
Kauffman, B. F. 3:109
Kauffman, Gabriel 9:24
Kauffman, J. 15:318;
    19:80
Kauffman, J. R. 11:153
Kauffman, John 9:13;
    10:61; 13:112;
    20:285
Kauffmann, G. 14:185
Kaufman, --- 15:37;
    18:430
Kaufman, Andrew 17:321
Kaufman, Charistian 4:35
Kaufman, Christ L.
    22:430
Kaufman, Daniel F.
    14:315
Kaufman, Gabriel 26:104
Kaufman, George 10:61
Kaufman, J. 3:109
Kaufman, John 10:18;
    11:35; 15:207
Kaufman, William 24:52
Kaufmann, C. 1:145
Kauftman, J. T. 18:144
Kaughlin, Hugh 18:15
Kauhbaum, E. 3:109
Kaulback, Antonie 10:61
Kaull, David O. 23:152
Kaump, George C.
    17:454; 24:185
Kaump, Henry A. 15:91
Kaump, John F. 24:94
Kauphd, J. Charles 10:61
Kauron, William 11:154
Kause, J. 25:193
Kauses, S. 6:21
Kauskopf, George 1:47
Kauthold, Charles 20:285
Kautner, John 11:154
Kautney, W. 27:71

Kautz, Henry 22:497
Kautz, Loran 11:192
Kautzman, D. 24:80
Kauzman, John 22:483
Kavanagh, James 3:109
Kavanagh, John 7:99
Kavanaugh, B. H. 23:37
Kavanaugh, C. 17:179
Kavanaugh, L. 9:146;
    27:71
Kavanaugh, Michael
    27:73
Kavanaugh, Murty W.
    16:41
Kavanaugh, Patrick
    10:211
Kavanaugh, W. Minty
    13:31
Kavena, John 12:8
Kavnagh, Michael 14:299;
    17:473
Kawcliffe, --- 16:269
Kawell, James H. 3:109
Kay, Adam W. 21:352
Kay, Charles 18:242
Kay, George 23:37
Kay, Isaac 21:55
Kay, J. 1:146
Kay, J. C. 8:50
Kay, J. J. 10:61
Kay, James 10:96; 12:155;
    16:120; 23:70
Kay, John 11:306; 22:338
Kay, John L. 22:86
Kay, Nicholas 8:21;
    18:143
Kay, Robert 3:109
Kay, William 9:146;
    27:71
Kayler, Michael 22:202
Kaylor, Ed. B. 17:265
Kaylor, Henry 17:360
Kays, William 8:88
Kayser, George 8:101
Kayser, William 10:121;
    20:285
Kayson, John 22:353
Kayton, H. T. 20:133
Kaywood, James 17:237
Kazee, John L. 17:260
Kazue, John 17:248
Kea, J. S. A. 10:34
Keach, Harry 19:173
Keach, Henry 14:77
Keach, Stephen 19:21
Keader, R. J. 25:47
Keady, John 22:503
Keafer, Adam 11:320
Keafer, M. L. 1:145
Keagg, Michael 25:193
Keagle, William H. 22:39

Keal, Thomas E. 21:31
Kealey, John 26:168
Kealley, James 11:35
Keally, John 4:35
Keames, G. W. 20:285
Keames, Garrett 12:155
Keames, William 7:58
Kean, Dennis 17:391
Kean, James 19:329
Kean, John 17:203
Kean, Lester 10:61;
 20:285
Kean, Michael 22:146
Kean, P. W. 21:352
Kean, Thomas 13:31
Kean, William 11:155
Kean, Z. W. 9:182
Kean, Zadock W. 19:271
Keane, Michael 1:49
Keane, P. S. 25:193
Keans, Elijah 8:50
Keans, William R. 17:441
Keanskoff, L. 3:110
Keanting, Paul 11:94
Kearbey, Edmund 8:88
Kearicher, Jacob 23:37
Kearl, G. H. 13:112
Kearman, Thomas 22:338
Kearn, Charles S. 15:326
Kearn, James B. 24:40
Kearn, John D. 17:443;
 24:159
Kearn, T. 3:110
Kearne, A. 21:149
Kearnes, C. 14:185
Kearnes, Enoch B. 13:31;
 16:41
Kearnes, James 1:48;
 4:35; 7:31; 13:112
Kearnes, Michael 22:453
Kearnes, Nicholas 12:59
Kearnes, Perry J. 25:272
Kearney, --- 26:221
Kearney, Charles 19:296
Kearney, Edwin 14:185
Kearney, F. O. 19:80
Kearney, F. R. 15:326
Kearney, George W.
 24:63
Kearney, J. 16:71
Kearney, J. C. 7:100
Kearney, James 7:8
Kearney, John 5:20
Kearney, L. 3:110
Kearney, Stephen 8:126
Kearney, T. 1:146
Kearney, William 1:47;
 21:276
Kearns, Amos 15:319;
 19:80
Kearns, David 23:250

Kearns, James 22:429
Kearns, Jeremiah 19:21
Kearns, John 10:205
Kearns, Joseph 15:207
Kearns, Patrick 7:100
Kearns, Peter 23:104
Kearns, R. 10:61; 20:285
Kearns, Thomas 21:352
Kearns, Timothy 16:97
Kearns, W. 1:147
Kearns, William R.
 24:153
Kearny, Augustus 19:80
Kearny, John 19:21
Kearny, W. 3:110
Kears, J. 15:343
Kearshanbuter, Frederick
 13:31
Keartz, J. 14:14
Keasey, Mathias W. 13:31
Keasy, William B. 20:285
Keat, L. J. 11:243
Keatch, Stranther 10:96
Keath, Daniel 14:185
Keath, G. 14:77
Keath, H. C. 20:285
Keath, James 17:201
Keaths, Stephen 8:77
Keating, August 21:352
Keating, Charles 3:110
Keating, J. 1:47
Keating, Jeremiah 15:207
Keating, M. 3:110
Keating, Pat 7:99
Keating, Thomas 13:31
Keating, William 25:193
Keating, William E. 8:21;
 18:143
Keatings, James 16:120
Keaton, G. 11:281
Keaton, O. Y. 24:40
Keaton, William 17:203
Keaver, F. 10:28
Keavon, Leonard B. 4:35
Keay, James 11:265
Keay, William 24:9
Kebbee, George 19:81
Kebbery, Perry E. 13:31
Kebbs, V. S. 7:58
Keble, John 11:281
Kebler, P. 1:48
Kebley, Francis E. 15:318
Kebson, J. A. 21:73
Kech, H. 1:146
Kechle, Frederick 22:483
Keck, Daniel 10:121;
 20:285
Keck, David 7:100
Keck, E. W. 1:48
Keck, George 1:48
Keck, George W. 17:102

Keck, Halmon 7:100
Keck, John 20:285
Keck, Joseph L. 17:237
Keck, M. (Mrs.) 1:145
Keck, Mosheim G. 14:185
Keck, N. 22:202
Keckissor, John 21:353
Keckley, Joseph 23:152
Keckman, John 8:88
Keckner, A. 25:322
Keddall, Isaac G. 18:339
Kedder, Charles 15:207
Keder, Andrew 19:173
Kedgan, M. 3:110
Keding, Bernard 1:48
Kedler, George 11:94
Kedney, Augustus 15:316
Kedont, John 16:204
Kee, Bingham 10:62;
 20:285
Kee, Dwight L. 17:355
Kee, George 23:70
Kee, James 16:204
Kee, John 9:221; 18:369
Kee, Lindsay 21:256
Kee, Lorenzo M. 22:257
Kee--, R. 17:294
Keean, A. 3:110
Keebauch, Isaac 17:81
Keebaugh, William
 18:285; 26:135
Keeber, M. 11:127
Keebles, H. R. 11:243
Keece, William 21:239
Keech, E. 14:299; 17:476;
 27:73
Keech, M. 1:145
Keecher, Thomas 13:112
Keedy, Joseph 10:121;
 20:285
Keef, Charles 25:300
Keef, T. 3:110
Keef, Timothy W. 7:31
Keef, William 7:80;
 25:300
Keefanoer, Lebright 17:91
Keefe, --- 15:17
Keefe, D. 1:49
Keefe, J. 1:144
Keefe, James A. 3:110
Keefe, James O. 12:27
Keefe, John 3:110
Keefe, John O. 15:37
Keefe, M. 15:37
Keefe, Michael 7:58;
 20:125
Keefe, P. 27:70
Keefe, Patrick 9:146;
 23:37
Keefe, William 10:18
Keefer, B. 23:180

Keefer, J. 16:204; 25:48
Keefer, J. J. 25:193
Keefer, Jacob 2:13
Keefer, John 14:185;
  22:146
Keefer, John H. 21:353
Keefer, John O. 16:147
Keefer, Louis 3:110
Keefer, Michael 10:62
Keefer, Samuel 14:242;
  23:305
Keefer, William 12:55
Keeffe, John 17:355
Keefover, Jacob 16:280
Keegan, Frank 27:72
Keegan, George 23:129
Keegan, J. 16:204
Keegan, John 10:18
Keegan, John D. 11:287
Keegan, M. 1:94
Keegan, Thomas F. 19:21
Keegman, J. F. 3:110
Keeher, George 18:406
Keehler, James H. 18:219
Keehn, Charles F. 19:80
Keehn, Conrad 8:21;
  18:143
Keehn, Jacob 3:110
Keek, Henry 17:281
Keek, John 10:121
Keekley, Harvey 23:268
Keel, A. J. 20:92
Keel, Joel 22:202
Keel, M. L. 17:364
Keel, Phoenix 11:187
Keeland, Frank 9:157
Keeland, P. O. 19:80
Keele, Charles 20:49
Keele, J. C. 27:73
Keelen, James M. 17:206
Keeler, --- 9:182; 16:297
Keeler, A. D. 5:20
Keeler, Amos D. 15:91
Keeler, Andrew 10:176
Keeler, B. A. 12:27
Keeler, Benjamin 11:108
Keeler, C. L. 15:207
Keeler, Calvin 20:9
Keeler, Charles B. 4:35
Keeler, Frederick 11:108
Keeler, George W. 9:209
Keeler, Henry A. 18:357;
  23:191
Keeler, Jacob H. 5:20
Keeler, John 9:182; 19:21;
  20:9
Keeler, John L. 22:257
Keeler, Joseph 16:204
Keeler, Josiah 5:20
Keeler, Lewis E. 21:245
Keeler, Marion 23:70

Keeler, Martin 5:41
Keeler, Orvila 19:173
Keeler, Priela 10:162
Keeler, Robert 8:88;
  18:327
Keeler, Thomas 19:80
Keeler, William 11:108
Keeler, William H. 23:70
Keeley, G. W. 23:268
Keeley, Harvey 14:288
Keeley, Henry 14:265
Keeley, J. 12:8
Keeley, Michael 12:72
Keeley, W. 3:110
Keeling, Lawson T. 23:99
Keeling, M. 3:110
Keeling, Thomas I. 8:21
Keeling, Thomas J.
  18:143
Keeling, William 17:260
Keeller, Samuel B. 11:35
Keels, John 17:179
Keeltt, George 11:108
Keely, Eschol 22:398
Keely, J. 15:159
Keely, James 9:43
Keely, John 8:21
Keely, M. 16:269
Keely, Michael 8:21;
  15:81
Keely, Philip 14:185
Keely, William 3:110
Keeman, R. 14:77
Keen, A. I. 14:185
Keen, A. T. 14:77
Keen, Charles H. 19:222
Keen, Edwin 10:62;
  20:285
Keen, Ezekiel S. 9:36
Keen, Frank 5:20
Keen, Frederick 22:86
Keen, Hoza 3:110
Keen, J. 14:77; 23:152
Keen, J. S. 1:145; 3:110
Keen, James N. 17:36
Keen, John 6:27
Keen, John C. 16:78
Keen, Jordan 11:66
Keen, Joseph 22:338
Keen, Peter 11:85
Keen, R. F. 1:48
Keen, T. P. 1:145
Keen, W. E. 14:77
Keen, W. H. 27:71
Keen, William 7:100
Keen, William S. 21:31
Keenan, Bernard 12:27
Keenan, E. 1:144
Keenan, Henry 14:185
Keenan, Hugh 13:31;
  16:41

Keenan, J. 1:49
Keenan, James 9:146
Keenan, John 1:48; 7:31;
  13:31; 15:173; 16:41,
  147
Keenan, Patrick 15:37
Keene, Addison C. 14:77
Keene, Alfred B. 22:398
Keene, Charles 10:10;
  14:77
Keene, Cyrus H. 22:12
Keene, George 1:48
Keene, George W. 10:162;
  19:173
Keene, James B. 7:100
Keene, Joseph 9:244
Keene, S. H. 1:98
Keene, Thomas I. 5:20
Keene, William A. 15:207
Keener, Charles S. 23:123
Keener, E. B. 3:110
Keener, John 13:31
Keener, Joseph 7:51
Keener, R. L. 7:51
Keener, William W.
  22:257
Keenes, John 11:187
Keeney, A. W. 3:111
Keeney, Charles 9:182;
  19:278
Keeney, Curtis L. 10:62;
  20:285
Keeney, Daniel L. 12:27
Keeney, Daniel T. 23:89
Keeney, Henry 8:120
Keeney, J. C. 15:353;
  16:280
Keeney, James 5:20
Keeney, John 3:111
Keeney, Sampson 16:41
Keenholdt, C. 5:20
Keenholts, C. 25:193
Keenon, John G. 17:310
Keenright, J. 18:87
Keens, Joseph 17:309
Keeny, H. 27:70
Keeny, James H. 20:125
Keep, Aginnis 15:69
Keep, George 17:36
Keep, Horatio N. 11:34
Keep, Irwin H. 16:41
Keep, Marcus 4:35
Keep, W. H. 1:147
Keep, William 14:185
Keeper, F. 17:291
Keeper, Frederick 9:84
Keeper, Samuel 27:73
Keepers, Lewis M. 23:191
Keephart, H. 3:110
Keepinger, James 18:207
Keeply, Jacob 15:69

Keeps, John 8:21
Keer, Charles 18:15
Keer, Chrles A. 17:281
Keer, David 24:80
Keer, Erasmus 25:193
Keer, F. 25:48
Keer, J. 27:70
Keer, John 9:163
Keer, Joshua 24:112
Keer, P. A. 12:122; 15:126
Keer, Thomas 24:22
Keeran, John 15:56
Kees, James 22:406
Kees, Joseph 22:86
Keese, Edmond 6:25
Keese, H. 21:55
Keese, John 27:145
Keesfor, Elias 9:84
Keeshr, D. 15:319
Keeslar, D. 19:80
Keesler, Aaron 8:64
Keet, Robert 9:154
Keeter, William 9:133
Keeth, George 9:54
Keeth, John 10:155
Keetin, Alfred 18:430
Keeton, D. 21:122
Keeton, J. P. 23:152
Keever, David 4:35
Keever, Ignatius 21:92
Keever, John M. 9:84
Keever, Lucas 13:112
Keezer, George 23:152
Kefanber, George 21:227
Kefanber, Jacob 22:86
Kefer, J. 1:146
Kefer, W. 25:48
Keffeberg, Peter E. 9:182
Keffer, E. D. 23:252
Keffer, J. 14:77
Keffer, John 10:121; 20:285
Keffer, William 10:91
Kegan, James 23:37
Kegan, Patrick 17:352
Kegar, Hiram 27:72
Kegee, J. 14:77
Keger, John 3:110
Keggs, James S. 22:124
Keggs, W. 13:92
Keghen, John 15:278; 25:193
Kegley, Adam 11:66
Kegley, N. A. 19:267
Kegley, W. 16:41
Kehal, Michael 11:154
Keher, Thomas 25:193
Kehl, Louis 10:18
Kehl, William 21:115
Kehler, Joseph 17:81

Kehler, Lewis 21:256
Kehlin, Casper 22:124
Kehn, Lewis 25:193
Keho, John 10:62; 20:285
Kehoe, John 12:59; 21:353
Kehoe, Martin C. 25:47
Kehoe, Moses 3:110
Kehoe, T. 3:110
Kehoe, Thomas 15:69
Kehoe, William 5:20; 25:193
Kehol, Edward 10:18
Kehr, J. W. 15:17
Kehr, Samuel 17:231
Kehrl, --- 2:13
Kehten, J. B. 25:193
Kehune, Adam 22:338
Keiber, Francis E. 21:256
Keichman, Rolley A. 16:204
Keick, Christian 17:252
Keickler, John 11:192
Keif, E. 14:77
Keif, Jacob 26:125
Keif, James 11:206
Keifa, J. J. 5:52
Keifer, Adam 22:202
Keifer, Charles 16:41
Keifer, John 5:20
Keifer, Michael 23:129; 25:193
Keiffer, Eli 22:483
Keiffer, F. V. 9:111
Keiffer, P. 7:31
Keiffer, Valentine 4:35
Keiffin, Vincent A. 16:154
Keigan, Charles 17:91
Keigan, William 14:185
Keiger, Henry 8:88
Keiger, James 17:237
Keiger, William 8:88
Keighley, William 19:21
Keihl, George O. 9:221
Keihl, Ignatius 8:50
Keihl, Theodore 15:207
Keil, Herman 17:21; 19:329
Keil, Jacob 21:227
Keil, John 7:100
Keil, Lewis 17:74
Keil, Michael 22:39
Keiler, John 4:35
Keily, M. 13:92
Keim, Jacob 22:497
Keimer, Joseph 1:47
Keimpel, F. 16:120
Keims, W. P. 18:369
Kein, Mathias 8:21; 18:143

Kein, Michael J. 13:112
Keineath, Aden J. 22:39
Keiner, John 13:77
Keiney, Charles 19:291
Keininger, John 26:40
Keins, F. M. 8:88
Keins, Samuel 27:72
Keintzler, R. 3:110
Keipe, J. 15:207
Keipe, Jacob 9:24
Keippart, Isaac 21:353
Keirans, Michael 16:280
Keirman, Charles 16:85
Keirman, F. M. 11:192
Keirn, Nathan 11:322
Keirnan, J. 1:146
Keirnan, Mathew 11:66
Keirsey, John H. 22:257
Keirsh, Jacob 16:120
Keis, John 15:22
Keiselback, G. 8:64
Keiser, Albert A. 11:127
Keiser, Fred. W. 9:182
Keiser, J. F. 14:185
Keiser, Joseph 7:100
Keiser, Philip 17:461; 24:167
Keiser, Samuel 18:310; 26:104
Keiser, Ulric 10:121; 20:285
Keiser, William 7:100
Keisle, Hi 17:504
Keisler, G. H. 16:41
Keisse, James B. 22:483
Keister, A. L. 15:69
Keister, D. 1:144
Keister, J. M. 11:65
Keister, John H. 3:110
Keister, L. 11:306
Keit, George 18:111
Keith, --- 11:322
Keith, Benjamin 22:523
Keith, C. H. 19:173
Keith, Caleb H. 23:152
Keith, Daniel 21:201; 22:124
Keith, E. 21:31
Keith, Eben 7:100
Keith, F. 1:147
Keith, Fay 10:121; 20:285
Keith, Frank 22:257
Keith, H. R. 10:34; 19:303
Keith, Henderson 11:206
Keith, Henry C. 10:62
Keith, James 10:28; 19:21, 303; 21:31
Keith, James H. 10:121; 20:285
Keith, James W. 22:503

Keith, John 4:35; 17:206
Keith, John S. 11:243
Keith, Lewis 23:70
Keith, M. 25:193
Keith, Martin 5:41
Keith, Morris 7:100
Keith, N. 14:77
Keith, P. B. 1:48
Keith, Passe 18:32
Keith, Richard 22:503
Keith, Richard H. 19:21
Keith, S. B. 1:147
Keith, S. M. 10:152;
    18:51
Keith, Samuel J. 17:36
Keith, Simon 9:54
Keith, Thomas N. 22:430
Keith, Thomas T. 23:191
Keith, Walter 10:62;
    20:285
Keith, William 22:39
Keith, William A. 11:154
Keith, William G. 22:429
Keith, William H. 10:121;
    20:285
Keith, William S. 17:424;
    24:173
Keith, Y. S. 1:48
Keithley, Enoch M.
    20:193
Keitt, John 15:37
Keive, D. 21:353
Keizler, Frank 9:121;
    27:72
Kek, John 7:31
Kekeir, A. 12:166
Kelankle, H. 15:207
Kelber, J. H. 25:193
Kelble, Endroe 23:129
Kelbnon, John 8:21
Kelch, Abram 17:243
Kelch, L. 15:207
Kelcher, Jeremiah 25:322
Kelchner, Isaac N. 17:405
Keldon, R. W. 14:265
Kelehar, James 12:27
Kelely, J. 3:110
Kelemes, Samuel 10:62
Keler, John 19:278
Keles, Charles 12:72
Keley, --- 12:168
Kelffner, Anton 24:63
Kelgore, F. 1:144
Kelholty, Charles 11:154
Kelipfer, Elias 26:40
Kell, Charles 1:47
Kell, M. R. 3:110
Kella, Lewis 17:400
Kellar, A. 13:112
Kellar, J. 3:110
Kellar, Jacob S. 18:219

Kellar, James W. 10:148
Kellar, O. F. Isaac 10:148
Kellcher, Michael 10:162
Kellday, James 14:185
Kelle, George 16:204
Kelleb, John 11:67
Kelleher, Cornelius
    23:152
Kelleher, Michael 19:173
Kellelhere, Stephen
    14:185
Kellem, Warsom 10:62
Kelleman, Aug 17:21
Kellems, Daniel H. 22:86
Kellems, John 22:86
Kellenbeck, F. 23:11
Kellenbeck, M. 26:41
Keller, A. 1:49; 3:110;
    7:75; 25:300
Keller, Andrew 11:35;
    21:31; 23:283
Keller, Antoine 10:121
Keller, Anton 20:285
Keller, Benjamin 7:51;
    9:111
Keller, C. M. 15:207
Keller, Charles 7:100;
    8:73; 19:331
Keller, Daniel 7:100;
    17:81
Keller, David 20:133
Keller, Elias 11:35
Keller, Ernst 14:185
Keller, F. 15:69
Keller, F. M. 15:360
Keller, Fiedel 12:72
Keller, Frederick 12:27
Keller, Frederick L. 7:100
Keller, G. 1:146
Keller, George B. 12:168
Keller, George J. 4:35
Keller, George S. 9:24
Keller, George W. 17:355
Keller, H. H. 1:145
Keller, Henderson 21:353
Keller, Henry 4:35; 17:91
Keller, Isaac 9:103; 18:51
Keller, J. 3:110; 21:31,
    122
Keller, J. M. 12:96
Keller, J. W. 11:66
Keller, Jacob 21:131, 167;
    22:483
Keller, James 18:52
Keller, John 3:110; 4:35;
    11:35, 66
Keller, John F. 8:112
Keller, Joseph 9:36;
    18:294; 26:104
Keller, Joseph B. 1:48

Keller, Joshua 14:299;
    17:479
Keller, Levi 20:41
Keller, M. 3:110; 14:299;
    17:478; 25:193;
    27:73
Keller, Matthias 9:97
Keller, Nicholas 11:408
Keller, O. 1:49
Keller, Pleasant M. 8:21;
    18:143
Keller, R. W. 12:145;
    26:221
Keller, S. J. 20:133
Keller, Samuel 9:72
Keller, Samuel A. 10:62
Keller, Samuel S. 17:460;
    24:159
Keller, Simon 20:35
Keller, Thomas 19:80;
    25:193
Keller, W. 1:146
Keller, W. H. 1:146
Keller, Wesley 24:197
Keller, William 10:121;
    20:285; 22:202
Kelleran, James 22:39
Kellerhan, J. R. 22:257
Kellers, John 14:242;
    27:73
Kelles, Thomas 19:21
Kellett, John B. 3:110
Kelley, --- 11:153; 18:52,
    191; 22:503
Kelley, A. 26:40
Kelley, Alex 17:179;
    22:338
Kelley, Alexander 19:21;
    22:124
Kelley, Alonzo 9:182;
    19:271
Kelley, Amer 15:69
Kelley, Anderson 22:307
Kelley, Anthony 6:25
Kelley, B. F. 15:314;
    19:80
Kelley, Barnet 11:153
Kelley, Benjamin 9:182;
    17:134; 24:197
Kelley, Benjamin W.
    17:36
Kelley, C. 21:31
Kelley, Charles 15:207;
    16:120; 17:179;
    18:294; 21:227
Kelley, Charles T. 16:80
Kelley, D. 15:294;
    16:204; 19:80
Kelley, D. O. 17:110
Kelley, Daniel 1:48; 9:43;
    11:295

Kelley, E. 1:146; 3:110; 6:27; 7:51; 20:87
Kelley, E. D. 23:37
Kelley, E. M. 7:73; 24:80
Kelley, Edward 10:8
Kelley, Elias 23:152
Kelley, F. 1:47
Kelley, F. W. 7:31
Kelley, Francis 9:13; 17:81
Kelley, G. 25:48
Kelley, George 16:152, 204; 17:217; 22:338
Kelley, George O. 22:514
Kelley, George W. 11:66; 17:207; 22:235
Kelley, H. 12:82
Kelley, Henry 3:110; 22:307
Kelley, Hiram W. 20:285
Kelley, Horace 11:122
Kelley, J. 1:48, 145, 146; 14:278; 15:207; 16:204, 280; 18:52; 19:80, 239; 22:257; 23:37, 123
Kelley, J. A. 1:146
Kelley, J. C. 9:54
Kelley, J. H. 1:146
Kelley, J. M. 18:294; 25:194; 26:104
Kelley, J. Ross 18:369
Kelley, J. S. 1:147; 7:31
Kelley, J. T. 9:54
Kelley, J. V. 9:36
Kelley, Jacob 9:54; 22:86
Kelley, Jacob N. 21:131
Kelley, James 3:110; 9:84, 221; 11:35; 15:302, 319; 16:120, 204; 17:81; 20:285; 25:48; 26:125
Kelley, James B. 18:310
Kelley, James C. 18:369
Kelley, Jeremiah 15:38; 22:307
Kelley, John 3:110; 4:35; 6:35; 7:31, 75; 9:146, 182; 11:66; 12:96; 13:65; 14:185; 15:207; 19:80; 20:285; 21:55, 227; 22:338, 520; 24:159
Kelley, John B. 19:21
Kelley, John O. 11:287
Kelley, John W. 21:31, 55
Kelley, Joseph 7:31; 17:36
Kelley, Joshua 7:15
Kelley, Josiah 3:110; 22:39

Kelley, L. H. 14:77
Kelley, Lafayette 11:66
Kelley, Laurence 27:70
Kelley, Lawson 7:31
Kelley, Levi 9:54; 12:72; 17:53
Kelley, Lewis 17:36
Kelley, Lorenzo 17:37
Kelley, Louira A. 16:78
Kelley, M. 15:299, 329; 16:120, 204; 20:285; 22:257; 23:152; 25:194
Kelley, Martin 4:35; 11:16; 25:48
Kelley, Maurice B. 8:21
Kelley, Mich'l. 22:338
Kelley, Michael 19:21; 21:243; 25:48
Kelley, Michael H. 8:73
Kelley, Moses R. 27:72
Kelley, Nathaniel 20:107
Kelley, Nelson 15:159
Kelley, Newell H. 22:497
Kelley, Nicholas 9:182
Kelley, O. F. 3:110
Kelley, P. 1:146
Kelley, P. O. 10:186
Kelley, Patrick 1:48; 12:72; 19:21; 22:39; 23:152
Kelley, Peter 1:48; 3:110; 6:23; 12:72
Kelley, Philip 10:62; 20:286
Kelley, R. 21:188
Kelley, Richard 20:286
Kelley, Robert 9:54; 11:419; 17:179; 20:286; 22:39, 86
Kelley, Romelia 17:145
Kelley, S. 23:123
Kelley, S. A. 23:152
Kelley, S. B. 14:77
Kelley, Samuel 17:179
Kelley, Sidney 17:179
Kelley, Silas 20:181, 189
Kelley, Stephen 16:120
Kelley, T. 1:144; 3:110; 16:204; 22:307
Kelley, T. A. 8:64
Kelley, T. G. 25:194
Kelley, T. M. 19:80
Kelley, Theodore 19:80
Kelley, Thomas 1:47, 48; 14:185; 15:207
Kelley, Thomas G. 5:20
Kelley, Thompson 17:91
Kelley, Tyner 22:307
Kelley, W. 1:144; 18:242; 26:40

Kelley, W. H. 15:294
Kelley, Washington 19:47
Kelley, Wells C. 23:240
Kelley, William 3:110; 11:287; 13:76; 16:120; 18:310; 22:86, 307, 513; 24:197
Kelley, William A. 22:202
Kelley, William H. 16:204
Kelley, Willis H. 22:86
Kelley, Z. T. 23:37
Kellian, George W. 21:10
Kellich, George 26:39
Kelliher, D. 19:228
Kelliher, Daniel 9:182
Kelliher, M. 14:77
Kellinow, F. 26:41
Kellion, Peter 12:72
Kellips, Robert 8:51
Kellman, Albert 4:35
Kellmer, Isaac 5:41
Kellmer, Lawrence 14:77
Kellmer, Milton 21:353
Kellner, Charles W. 18:310; 26:104
Kellner, J. 1:48
Kelloch, George 9:84
Kellog, Alfred D. 16:204
Kellog, Beldig 12:146
Kellog, Belding 19:303
Kellog, Edward 7:9
Kellog, Henry 11:35; 16:97
Kellog, J. 18:242; 26:41
Kellog, Lewis 7:100
Kellog, M. 1:145
Kellog, R. 27:73
Kellog, R. B. 9:121
Kellog, Samuel C. 24:22
Kellogg, Albert 17:81
Kellogg, Bradford 22:483
Kellogg, C. 25:194
Kellogg, Charles 5:20; 20:125
Kellogg, Charles D. 17:319
Kellogg, Charles H. 4:35
Kellogg, Charles P. 22:281
Kellogg, D. M. 10:62; 20:286
Kellogg, David H. 1:47
Kellogg, E. D. 11:127
Kellogg, E. L. 3:110
Kellogg, E. V. 20:125
Kellogg, Edwin A. 9:24
Kellogg, G. T. 18:68
Kellogg, George L. 12:54
Kellogg, Hollis W. 22:281

Kellogg, Horace R. 16:205
Kellogg, James 1:47; 7:58
Kellogg, Jason 17:155
Kellogg, John W. 4:35; 20:107
Kellogg, L. 14:77
Kellogg, N. 23:37
Kellogg, P. M. 11:35
Kellogg, Peter 8:114
Kellogg, Ralph 20:9
Kellogg, Samuel S. 26:168
Kellogg, T. P. 21:353
Kellogg, Thomas O. 22:430
Kellogg, Wilson 27:145
Kellon, F. 21:189
Kellor, Wasson 20:286
Kellough, Orlando T. 17:266
Kelloy, Edward 19:303
Kells, Hylas 9:24; 18:310; 26:103
Kells, James 15:37
Kells, John 21:353
Kells, Samuel 12:72
Kellson, P. 12:162
Kellum, J. C. 17:53
Kellum, Orville 17:66
Kellum, Tillman H. 24:40
Kellum, William 16:205
Kelly, --- 17:425
Kelly, A. 18:242; 24:22
Kelly, A. J. 19:21; 25:194
Kelly, Abb 11:335
Kelly, Alazer 1:47
Kelly, Albert 21:31
Kelly, Albert G. 22:12
Kelly, Alexander 12:100
Kelly, Alfred 7:127
Kelly, Alva C. 27:72
Kelly, Andrew 16:297
Kelly, Asa 23:152
Kelly, Ashbury 25:194
Kelly, Aza 25:194
Kelly, B. M. 19:228
Kelly, Bartly 23:99
Kelly, Benjamin 9:182; 19:255
Kelly, Blackham 22:124
Kelly, Byron 9:182
Kelly, C. 8:51
Kelly, C. A. 23:37
Kelly, Charles 3:110; 22:12
Kelly, Charles D. 8:21; 18:143
Kelly, Charles G. 20:18
Kelly, Charles H. 3:110

Kelly, Clarence 10:162; 19:173
Kelly, Cornelius 26:244
Kelly, D. 1:145, 147; 3:110; 9:146; 27:71
Kelly, D. L. 14:78
Kelly, Daniel 21:73; 26:125
Kelly, David M. 21:353; 23:70
Kelly, Dennis O. 24:94
Kelly, E. 3:110; 21:353
Kelly, E. A. 13:112
Kelly, E. C. 25:194
Kelly, E. H. 18:68
Kelly, E. Meziah 12:27
Kelly, Edward 12:146; 16:372; 19:173; 21:353; 24:22; 25:194
Kelly, Edwin 9:106
Kelly, Elisha 18:87
Kelly, Enoch 1:48
Kelly, F. 3:110; 14:257; 15:108; 21:353
Kelly, Francis 10:18
Kelly, Frank 7:100
Kelly, Frank W. 12:27
Kelly, G. S. 1:146
Kelly, George E. 17:308
Kelly, H. 3:110; 9:154; 14:185; 16:297
Kelly, H. O. 16:372
Kelly, H. S. 3:110
Kelly, Henry 1:47; 7:127; 23:37, 70
Kelly, Henry C. 17:260
Kelly, Henry J. 23:37
Kelly, Henry O. 15:351; 21:276
Kelly, Henry P. 19:21
Kelly, Hiram W. 10:62
Kelly, Hugh R. 23:152
Kelly, Isaac 1:47; 15:56
Kelly, Isaiah 12:27
Kelly, J. 1:49, 144, 145, 146, 147; 3:110; 9:111; 13:92; 14:251; 27:70, 71
Kelly, J. A. 27:70
Kelly, J. B. 25:194
Kelly, J. J. 20:155
Kelly, J. S. 3:111
Kelly, J. T. 12:27
Kelly, J. W. 3:111
Kelly, James 3:110, 111; 9:24; 10:62, 153; 13:31; 14:185; 15:38, 81, 207; 16:143; 18:32, 310;

Kelly, James 19:80, 329; 21:353; 26:40, 103
Kelly, James A. 9:146
Kelly, James B. 26:104
Kelly, James N. 4:35
Kelly, James W. 1:47
Kelly, Jeremiah 12:50, 169
Kelly, John 1:48; 3:111; 7:127; 8:21, 125; 9:217; 10:62; 11:35; 13:31, 58; 14:27, 185; 15:38, 108, 360; 17:415; 18:103, 143; 19:80, 321; 20:9; 21:31, 101, 243, 353; 22:453; 24:60; 25:269; 27:70, 72
Kelly, John C. 11:108
Kelly, John F. 12:27
Kelly, John J. 16:41
Kelly, John S. 21:353
Kelly, John W. 1:47
Kelly, Joseph 22:430
Kelly, L. 3:111
Kelly, Lawrence 9:121; 23:152; 24:9
Kelly, Levi 15:81
Kelly, Lewis 6:17; 12:27; 18:87
Kelly, Louis 19:80
Kelly, Luke 16:97
Kelly, Lycurgus H. 21:31
Kelly, M. 1:145; 3:111; 14:318; 19:80, 255
Kelly, Martin 18:310; 19:329; 26:104
Kelly, Marurt B. 18:143
Kelly, Michael 7:64; 8:21; 9:24, 182; 10:62; 11:192; 14:185; 18:143, 310; 19:80; 24:107; 25:194; 26:104
Kelly, Milton 12:50
Kelly, Moses B. 9:121
Kelly, N. 16:372
Kelly, Newton 10:121; 20:286
Kelly, Nicholas 19:255
Kelly, O. W. 14:185
Kelly, Owen 14:185; 17:281
Kelly, P. 1:144, 145; 3:111; 15:69
Kelly, P. O. 18:176
Kelly, Pat 12:27
Kelly, Patrick 6:31; 7:100; 14:185; 15:27; 22:86; 23:129; 25:322; 27:145

Kelly, Peter 10:18; 18:32; 23:129
Kelly, Peter M. 24:22
Kelly, R. 1:49
Kelly, Richard 10:18, 62; 14:185; 19:173; 25:194
Kelly, Robert 9:243; 10:62; 15:126; 21:276; 22:307; 24:107
Kelly, S. L. 10:96
Kelly, Samuel 7:100; 12:27; 21:353
Kelly, Sheldon B. 12:100; 15:366
Kelly, T. 3:111
Kelly, T. A. 21:122
Kelly, Theodore 22:146
Kelly, Thomas 4:35; 8:21, 121; 9:244; 10:162; 12:27; 16:85; 18:143; 19:173; 22:167, 464
Kelly, Thomas A. 24:52
Kelly, Thomas E. 19:334
Kelly, Thomas M. 22:202
Kelly, Timothy 16:97
Kelly, Truman B. 9:24
Kelly, V. 14:78
Kelly, W. 1:146
Kelly, W. F. 13:31
Kelly, W. S. 11:306
Kelly, William 3:111; 7:100; 9:121; 10:18; 14:185; 15:14; 16:204; 24:22; 27:72
Kelly, William B. 12:55
Kelly, William D. 12:171
Kelly, William H. 20:27
Kelly, William Henry 26:244
Kelly, William M. 10:121; 20:286
Kelly, William R. 4:35
Kelly, Z. F. 4:35
Kelm, Frederick 22:86
Kelm, S. S. 20:140
Kelman, William 11:94
Kelmatine, Thomas 22:523
Kelmer, B. S. 18:242; 26:40
Kelmer, E. R. 9:182
Kelmer, Isaac 11:389
Kelms, Samuel 20:286
Kelnan, Thomas 25:333
Kelo, Bernard 15:108
Kelog, H. R. 15:302
Kelogg, C. H. 25:47
Kelogg, R. B. 27:70

Kelomer, Joseph 11:66
Kelon, John 22:202
Kelper, Henry 27:70
Kelper, P. 1:144
Kelperger, Joseph 8:88
Kelpert, William H. 1:47
Kelren, William 16:85
Kelsea, J. H. 1:98
Kelser, William 26:41
Kelsey, --- 8:88
Kelsey, Abram 13:31
Kelsey, Charles 13:112
Kelsey, Charles M. 4:35
Kelsey, E. 3:111; 13:112
Kelsey, E. A. 1:145
Kelsey, E. M. 14:185
Kelsey, F. 21:353
Kelsey, George 13:31
Kelsey, Harper 10:121
Kelsey, Irwin H. 17:419
Kelsey, J. H. 9:146; 27:71
Kelsey, John 3:111; 10:91; 18:111; 20:286; 21:244, 276
Kelsey, John W. 23:89
Kelsey, L. C. 3:111
Kelsey, Peter B. 4:35
Kelsey, Philip 11:127
Kelsey, R. D. 26:39
Kelsey, Ransom 21:243
Kelsey, Russell L. 9:84
Kelsey, S. A. 21:31
Kelsey, Thomas 21:101
Kelsey, William 18:242
Kelsheimer, William J. 17:37
Kelsing, Jacob 23:285
Kelso, Albert 19:327
Kelso, E. S. 3:111
Kelso, James T. 10:91; 20:286
Kelso, John 11:306; 15:207
Kelso, M. C. 1:48
Kelso, R. N. 15:7
Kelso, S. N. 18:369
Kelso, Samuel 12:92
Kelso, Stephen 18:219
Kelso, Sylvester N. 9:221
Kelso, W. 21:122
Kelsoe, William N. 17:273
Kelsow, Herman 10:162
Kelsy, Florilla M. 24:52
Kelt, John 12:72
Keltel, Warren 21:239
Kelthly, N. 8:73
Kelthur, Daniel 17:429
Keltner, M. V. 23:37
Kelton, J. E. 13:65
Kelty, Abraham 11:402

Kelty, J. T. 12:8
Kelty, John 12:171
Kelty, Silas N. 13:31
Kelty, Thomas 7:14; 13:65; 19:80
Kelun, Oliver F. 12:27
Kelvoy, Michael 14:186
Kely, Harper 20:286
Kemball, A. 19:21
Kemball, James 3:111
Kemball, S. 3:111
Kembell, George 7:58
Kemble, Alexander M. 20:18
Kemble, David 22:514
Kemble, Fletcher 1:47
Kemble, H. W. 21:31
Kemble, J. 25:311
Kemble, John 11:306
Kemble, Nathaniel 13:31
Kemble, William 8:107
Kembler, Ferdinand 19:303
Kemer, Thomas 9:13
Kemerle, Jacob 25:48
Kemery, Peter L. 23:70
Kemick, Samuel S. 9:182
Kemicuke, Henry 17:53
Kemir, Daniel 22:202
Kemkler, Christian 11:119
Kemly, D. 3:111
Kemmel, Cooper 8:21
Kemmery, John 25:194
Kemmfake, James 8:21
Kemniel, Carper 18:143
Kemp, Alva 9:72
Kemp, Amos 17:321
Kemp, Andrew J. 22:86
Kemp, Arthur 27:145
Kemp, C. H. 3:111
Kemp, Charles 2:13; 12:72; 15:56; 25:48
Kemp, Charles J. 11:35
Kemp, E. 3:111
Kemp, Edwin S. 10:121; 20:286
Kemp, Elihu 19:286
Kemp, F. 14:299; 17:473; 25:48; 27:73
Kemp, Francis 2:13
Kemp, George 12:72
Kemp, I. W. 14:186
Kemp, J. 27:70
Kemp, J. A. 14:78
Kemp, J. H. 1:146
Kemp, J. W. 1:145; 3:111
Kemp, James G. 10:121; 20:286
Kemp, John 14:186; 22:470
Kemp, L. 19:233

Kemp, Langdon 9:182
Kemp, Lewis 13:65
Kemp, Mapford 26:39
Kemp, Oscar 12:27
Kemp, Robert 11:66;
    25:333
Kemp, S. L. 1:144
Kemp, Samuel 15:108;
    19:21
Kemp, Silas 9:24; 18:320
Kemp, Solomon 22:146
Kemp, Thomas G. 9:235;
    18:421
Kemp, W. A. 17:159
Kemp, W. B. 15:338
Kemp, W. J. 20:41
Kemp, Wilkinson 22:86
Kemp, William 12:59;
    25:194
Kemp, William B. 16:205
Kemper, Bernard 18:207
Kemper, C. W. 24:80
Kemper, Elijah 7:127
Kemper, H. 27:73
Kemper, J. 3:111; 23:152
Kemper, John 14:242;
    17:81; 27:73
Kemper, Nelson 17:179
Kemper, R. 11:306
Kemper, Samuel 16:297
Kemper, William 9:54
Kempeter, H. 24:80
Kempf, Francis 23:11
Kemph, John 24:40
Kemph, Philip 21:353
Kemple, J. K. 14:78
Kemple, J. R. 12:92;
    16:297
Kemple, Jacob 13:31
Kemple, James 18:310;
    26:104
Kemple, John 23:108
Kemple, Jonas 9:24
Kemple, Patrick 22:338
Kemplon, William D.
    21:353
Kempp, O. 1:47
Kemps, Lewis 19:80
Kempster, Francis 16:41
Kempston, B. F. 3:111
Kempt, J. G. 22:338
Kempt, W. H. 14:78
Kempton, Benjamin
    11:306
Kempton, E. 3:111
Kempton, J. 1:145
Kempton, James 20:189
Kempton, L. B. 13:31
Kems, Samuel 9:121
Kenady, John A. 8:107
Kenard, Perry 11:94

Kenard, Richard 17:405
Kenarn, A. 3:111
Kenaston, Edgar D. 9:7
Kenaull, Freeling M.
    24:80
Kenball, A. H. 14:78
Kenbeagle, --- 17:254
Kenbridge, L. 17:471;
    27:73
Kenchler, James 7:75
Kendal, J. 23:152
Kendal, Thomas 22:86
Kendall, A. P. 21:353
Kendall, B. J. 1:144
Kendall, C. 14:257
Kendall, G. 1:48
Kendall, George D.
    17:273
Kendall, H. G. 1:144
Kendall, Horatio 27:73
Kendall, Isaac 17:37
Kendall, J. 1:47
Kendall, J. A. 22:257
Kendall, J. H. 21:353
Kendall, James 10:121;
    22:86, 257
Kendall, L. S. 21:353
Kendall, Lorenzo 15:56
Kendall, Lucas 21:139
Kendall, O. 12:82; 16:297
Kendall, Oscar 4:35
Kendall, R. 1:48
Kendall, R. A. 22:124
Kendall, S. 15:207
Kendall, Samuel 10:62;
    20:286
Kendall, T. D. 21:353
Kendall, T. J. 14:78
Kendall, Thomas 17:260
Kendall, Thomas A.
    10:62; 20:286
Kendall, W. 3:111
Kendall, W. L. 16:78
Kendall, Wesley C. 9:36
Kendall, William 9:10
Kendall, William W.
    12:155
Kendan, Jesse 12:155
Kendell, H. N. 7:31
Kendell, James 20:286
Kendell, John 14:185
Kendell, S. 16:205
Kendey, A. 25:194
Kendig, E. B. 13:125
Kendig, George 14:236
Kendig, Jacob 13:112
Kendig, M. L. 9:24
Kendig, Samuel H. 4:35
Kendig, William 13:112
Kending, Abram 5:20
Kending, E. B. 16:205

Kendle, George 1:48
Kendle, S. 11:88
Kendle, William H.
    11:154
Kendle, William P. 9:121
Kendler, Christopher
    18:143
Kendleter, John 11:219
Kendrich, H. 14:265
Kendrick, Alfred C.
    21:247
Kendrick, C. 1:147
Kendrick, David M.
    17:314
Kendrick, E. J. 21:31
Kendrick, George 12:82;
    16:297
Kendrick, M. C. 18:68
Kendrick, R. 16:205
Kendrick, Ralph 13:125
Kendrick, Robert 27:73
Kendrick, W. 26:212
Kendricks, Daniel 25:47
Kendricks, Thomas F.
    22:406
Kendrickson, Wellington
    13:65
Kendwecker, F. 22:202
Keneard, L. 25:194
Kenedey, John 14:299
Kenedy, --- 27:73
Kenedy, D. 15:173
Kenedy, Daniel 16:280
Kenedy, David 17:273
Kenedy, Felix 13:31
Kenedy, J. 18:52
Kenedy, Jackson 10:121
Kenedy, Jacob 11:206;
    13:112
Kenedy, James 11:35;
    19:21
Kenedy, James C. 22:147
Kenedy, John 21:31
Kenedy, Liberty H. 11:85
Kenedy, Michael 10:62
Kenedy, Nathaniel 22:86
Kenedy, Noah 10:62
Kenedy, Orion 10:62
Kenedy, Patrick 12:155
Kenedy, Price 17:53
Kenedy, William 10:62
Kenelster, Samuel 11:306
Kenerley, George 13:58
Kenerly, Napoleon B.
    17:419
Kenerson, B. 27:71
Keney, E. 15:207
Keney, L. 16:280
Keney, Levi 8:107
Keney, W. 24:112
Kengan, Sumner 17:447

Kengle, L. 25:194
Kengon, T. C. 16:269
Kenidy, I. 25:283
Kenigston, Michael 21:31
Kenihan, Martin 23:152
Kenion, F. 3:111
Keniston, S. E. 1:145
Kenkade, J. 25:194
Kenkapot, Levi 16:205
Kenkled, John 16:205
Kenle, John 9:182
Kenly, John 21:353
Kenman, George 15:207
Kenna, K. 1:47
Kenna, Michael 14:300;
  17:474; 27:73
Kennady, Daniel 23:198
Kennady, J. J. 1:145
Kennapake, James 18:143
Kennar, L. J. 1:145
Kennard, Charles 18:87
Kennard, Elbridge 9:36
Kennard, F. 9:65
Kennard, Francis 12:50
Kennard, Philip J. 23:152
Kennard, R. W. 17:388
Kennason, J. S. 21:353
Kennay, John 10:162;
  19:173
Kenne, Gustav 11:192
Kenneck, David 7:31
Kenneda, Champ F.
  22:124
Kenneda, G. W. 25:194
Kenneday, Owen 19:255
Kennedey, John M. 9:103
Kennedy, A. 1:49; 3:111;
  27:71
Kennedy, Abraham H.
  4:35
Kennedy, Abram 9:146
Kennedy, Albert 22:429
Kennedy, Alexander
  10:96
Kennedy, Allan 18:191
Kennedy, Amos 3:111
Kennedy, Andrew 14:78
Kennedy, Artemus E.
  11:327
Kennedy, B. 3:111
Kennedy, B. F. 8:88
Kennedy, Barnard 4:35
Kennedy, Benjamin F.
  22:39
Kennedy, C. 21:110;
  26:221
Kennedy, C. Y. 23:37
Kennedy, Charles 21:353
Kennedy, D. 1:144; 14:78
Kennedy, Dana 4:35

Kennedy, Daniel 9:182;
  21:353
Kennedy, David 1:47;
  9:204
Kennedy, David P. 23:153
Kennedy, Dennis 18:15
Kennedy, Earl P. 11:155
Kennedy, Edward 22:124
Kennedy, Edward M.
  22:520
Kennedy, Eugene 17:143;
  19:21
Kennedy, F. 14:78
Kennedy, Felix 16:41
Kennedy, Francis M.
  18:219
Kennedy, George 13:31
Kennedy, George D.
  21:131
Kennedy, George F.
  23:288
Kennedy, George W. 5:20
Kennedy, H. 1:146; 3:111
Kennedy, H. C. 27:71
Kennedy, H. I. 27:73
Kennedy, H. J. 14:300;
  17:479
Kennedy, Henry 15:351;
  16:372; 24:41
Kennedy, Hugh C. 8:88
Kennedy, I. 15:343
Kennedy, Ira 15:56
Kennedy, Irwin 23:89
Kennedy, J. 1:49, 144,
  145, 146; 3:111;
  16:372; 19:267;
  21:163
Kennedy, J. A. 1:146
Kennedy, J. D. 21:353
Kennedy, J. F. 1:144
Kennedy, J. J. 17:308
Kennedy, J. P. 3:111
Kennedy, J. W. 3:111
Kennedy, Jackson 20:286
Kennedy, James 3:111;
  8:21; 10:92; 12:91;
  15:14; 16:297;
  18:143; 24:52
Kennedy, James A.
  22:406
Kennedy, James G.
  22:429
Kennedy, James S.
  20:286; 24:22
Kennedy, John 1:49; 7:31;
  9:182; 10:91, 162,
  170; 11:276; 13:65;
  17:476; 18:397;
  19:21, 80, 173;
  20:140, 286; 22:338;

Kennedy, John 23:37;
  24:9; 25:47, 194;
  26:125; 27:73
Kennedy, John R. 22:429
Kennedy, John T. 17:237
Kennedy, John W. 11:375
Kennedy, Joseph 10:152;
  19:80, 287; 21:353
Kennedy, Joseph J. 22:86
Kennedy, Joseph R.
  27:145
Kennedy, Joseph W.
  22:429
Kennedy, Joshua 22:39
Kennedy, L. B. 3:111
Kennedy, Lawrence
  24:171
Kennedy, Louis H. 23:153
Kennedy, M. 3:111;
  11:388; 12:82;
  14:242; 16:147, 297;
  27:73
Kennedy, M. E. 3:111
Kennedy, M. H. 20:147
Kennedy, M. R. 9:146;
  27:70
Kennedy, Mathew 14:186;
  22:39
Kennedy, Matthew 12:27
Kennedy, Michael 12:28;
  17:201; 20:286
Kennedy, Morris 7:100
Kennedy, N. 11:155
Kennedy, Nathaniel S.
  4:35
Kennedy, Noah 20:286
Kennedy, Orion 20:286
Kennedy, Owen 9:182
Kennedy, Patrick 1:48;
  10:121; 13:31; 16:41;
  20:286
Kennedy, Patrick H.
  20:137
Kennedy, R. B. 20:178
Kennedy, R. E. 1:98
Kennedy, R. T. 17:308
Kennedy, Richard 9:121;
  22:430; 27:72
Kennedy, Robert 17:134;
  18:421; 24:197
Kennedy, Roger 4:35
Kennedy, S. 1:145
Kennedy, S. J. B. 3:111
Kennedy, Samuel 12:28
Kennedy, Silas H. 21:227
Kennedy, T. 1:47, 48,
  145; 21:110; 23:289
Kennedy, T. J. 24:112
Kennedy, Thomas 7:31;
  9:13; 14:186; 18:15;
  22:162, 307

Kennedy, Timothy 23:192
Kennedy, Timothy H.
　22:281
Kennedy, W. 3:111;
　26:104
Kennedy, W. A. 21:167
Kennedy, W. C. 12:72
Kennedy, W. H. H.
　10:162
Kennedy, W. O. 15:7
Kennedy, Walter O. 23:89
Kennedy, William 1:48;
　3:111; 4:35; 9:24,
　133; 11:424; 12:28;
　18:310; 20:89, 286;
　22:86; 23:108, 123,
　263; 25:47
Kennedy, William J. 4:35
Kennef, Cyrus 18:32
Kennefrick, Michael
　19:21
Kennel, Samuel 18:310;
　26:104
Kennell, Chanery 11:108
Kennell, Jesse 9:156
Kennell, Samuel 9:24
Kennelley, M. 1:145
Kennelly, Maurice
　17:415; 24:153
Kennelt, Charles 26:221
Kennemer, Prestley
　24:183
Kennemer, Prestly 17:453
Kenner, C. L. 18:32
Kenner, J. 11:327
Kenner, John 10:148;
　18:52
Kenner, R. 1:145
Kenner, Stephen 22:406
Kenner, Thomas 11:207;
　21:353
Kenner, William 21:353
Kennerday, A. 14:186
Kennerger, Charles 8:73
Kennerson, G. B. 1:98
Kennerson, W. R. 1:146
Kennesy, Edward 12:168
Kennett, J. 21:189
Kennett, Jacob 17:352
Kennett, James P. 24:52
Kennett, N. S. 19:239
Kennett, Stephen 17:207
Kennett, William M.
　22:430
Kennewanche, John 19:80
Kenneweg, F. 20:57
Kenney, --- 22:17
Kenney, A. J. 19:233
Kenney, A. M. 1:47
Kenney, Aaron 7:100

Kenney, Alonzo D.
　25:194
Kenney, Andrew J. 10:62
Kenney, C. W. 10:210
Kenney, Charles 21:353
Kenney, D. P. 9:84
Kenney, David 11:154
Kenney, Erastus 23:240
Kenney, George W.
　9:146; 16:205
Kenney, Isaac 17:320
Kenney, J. C. 14:78
Kenney, James 1:48;
　11:182; 25:194
Kenney, Joel 13:113
Kenney, John 11:154;
　13:31; 14:300; 15:38;
　17:476
Kenney, Joseph E. 20:33
Kenney, Michael 1:47;
　12:27
Kenney, O. 17:110
Kenney, P. 13:92; 14:14
Kenney, Patrick 16:97
Kenney, Peter B. 12:72;
　15:38
Kenney, Purchell 12:72
Kenney, S. 13:113, 129
Kenney, Thomas 12:27,
　169; 25:47
Kenney, Timothy 7:31
Kenney, W. 3:111; 16:205
Kenney, W. B. 18:32
Kenney, Washington C.
　11:413
Kenney, William 14:236;
　18:33; 22:39
Kennick, Harris 24:197
Kennicutt, Edgar S.
　22:112
Kennie, Edward 9:84
Kennigott, Edwin 10:173;
　19:173
Kennil, John 18:111
Kennin, Patrick 18:272
Kenning, Henry 10:121
Kennison, C. H. 1:145
Kennison, Callihill 7:58
Kennison, D. 22:338
Kennison, David 9:214
Kennison, Job 17:37
Kennison, L. E. B. 26:168
Kennison, Roswell 9:146
Kennison, S. J. 7:51
Kennison, William 9:72
Kenniston, Harry H. 9:159
Kenniston, James 25:194
Kenniston, W. 25:47
Kenniston, W. W. 25:194
Kenno, M. M. 24:112
Kennoerr, B. 20:90

Kennon, John 22:167
Kennon, W. A. C. 18:369
Kenny, Alonzo D. 5:52
Kenny, D. P. 15:126
Kenny, David 16:41;
　23:292
Kenny, G. A. 27:70
Kenny, Hiram 9:146
Kenny, J. J. 1:145
Kenny, John 27:73
Kenny, John F. 15:126
Kenny, Michael 14:186;
　23:99; 25:322
Kenny, Nelson 4:35
Kenny, Patrick 8:21
Kenny, William 3:111;
　19:81
Kenoff, Aram 5:20
Kenon, A. 9:230
Kenon, P. 27:73
Kenon, T. 14:300; 17:476
Kenou, C. A. 20:286
Kenouse, --- 15:81
Kenoyer, D. 27:70
Kenrick, A. F. 11:94
Kenrick, F. J. 25:194
Kenrick, S. N. 1:144
Kensan, N. A. 3:111
Kensel, Christian 14:186
Kensel, Miles G. 19:81
Kensell, E. M. 12:142;
　20:286
Kensella, John 8:125;
　14:236
Kenser, James 3:111
Kenser, U. 21:353
Kensey, George 11:88;
　14:186
Kensey, Jacob 13:113
Kenshrew, George W.
　13:31
Kensick, Frederick 14:186
Kensing, --- 15:38
Kensinger, David 7:31
Kensington, Edward
　21:353
Kensington, George
　21:353
Kensler, Joseph 18:243
Kensley, Fen 25:48
Kent, --- 16:297; 19:173
Kent, A. 21:123
Kent, A. W. 12:27
Kent, Abraham 22:307
Kent, C. 19:286
Kent, C. B. 12:72; 15:80
Kent, C. H. 22:146
Kent, C. J. 25:48
Kent, Charles 27:72
Kent, Charles F. 13:31;
　16:41

Kent, Cornelius 9:182
Kent, Daniel 6:31; 25:322
Kent, David 8:107; 9:24;
  18:310; 26:104
Kent, Douglas 10:162
Kent, E. 22:202; 24:80
Kent, E. L. 3:111
Kent, E. R. 19:173
Kent, Edward 7:100
Kent, Enoch 10:62;
  20:286
Kent, Francis R. 16:140
Kent, Frank 17:248
Kent, G. A. 1:145
Kent, George W. 15:87
Kent, H. 21:122
Kent, H. O. 1:48
Kent, J. 3:111
Kent, J. C. 16:97
Kent, J. L. 27:70
Kent, James 17:155;
  26:40
Kent, James H. 4:35
Kent, John 13:113; 19:21
Kent, John R. 12:27
Kent, John S. 15:3
Kent, M. C. 18:208
Kent, Oliver M. 7:31
Kent, P. 10:28; 19:303
Kent, Richard C. 22:147
Kent, Riley J. 22:39
Kent, S. 3:111
Kent, Segamund 25:194
Kent, William 21:139
Kent, William W. 8:64
Kentch, William 1:47
Kenter, A. W. 3:111
Kenter, Andrew F. 10:8
Kenter, Montgomery
  12:62
Kentigh, A. R. 22:497
Kentleberger, I. 14:78
Kentner, C. 23:153
Kenton, C. P. 23:290
Kenton, John 16:97
Kenton, Montgomery
  15:69
Kenton, William 22:514
Kenton, William C. 8:88
Kentzler, Henry 3:111
Kenvin, John 15:307
Kenwell, R. 3:111
Kenwood, Dennis 18:243;
  26:41
Kenyan, Benjamin 1:47
Kenyan, William L. 9:84
Kenyon, B. 25:194
Kenyon, George 25:194
Kenyon, Horace A. 16:41
Kenyon, J. L. 14:186
Kenyon, J. R. 1:47

Kenyon, James 21:353
Kenyon, James C. 19:81
Kenyon, John 16:205
Kenyon, John E. 8:88
Kenyon, Johnson R. 4:35
Kenyon, Orson 11:182
Kenyon, Orson T. 25:194
Kenyon, Ren 17:74
Kenyon, S. 17:179
Kenyon, Samuel 24:9
Kenyon, Sidney D. 17:314
Kenyon, Thomas 12:27
Kenyon, W. W. 19:21
Kenyon, William 26:39
Kenzel, Edward 23:70
Kenzie, E. 11:414
Kenzie, F. 25:47
Kenzier, A. R. M. 27:70
Kenzig, Doras 8:118
Kenzler, Philip 23:153
Kenzy, Nathan 13:31;
  16:41
Keo, A. 11:65
Keogh, Patrick 19:173
Keone, Louis 9:24
Keoring, --- 12:85
Keoring, F. 14:78; 16:297
Keorner, J. 1:146
Keough, Peter 3:111;
  13:31; 16:41
Keown, Alfred 21:256
Keown, Robert 10:122
Keown, V. 1:48
Kepcha, Henry H. 12:28
Keper, John 11:67
Kepford, Phillip 16:205
Kephart, A. 14:186
Kephart, C. B. 14:300;
  17:481; 27:73
Kephart, Conrad 24:52
Kephart, Levi 10:62;
  20:286
Keplar, Sam 20:147
Keplaton, J. P. 8:51
Kepler, Abraham H.
  23:153
Kepler, Charles 18:278
Kepler, I. 24:159
Kepler, J. 17:419
Kepler, Jacob 21:227
Kepler, James K. P.
  20:133
Kepler, John 21:55;
  22:202
Kepler, Josiah M. 23:153
Kepler, Peter 11:154
Kepler, S. 24:112
Kepley, Isaac 22:429
Kepley, Newell 25:275
Keplinger, Isaac M.
  23:285

Keplinger, J. 3:111
Kepner, A. 6:31
Kepner, D. 15:7
Kepner, G. W. 13:92
Kepp, August 17:91
Kepp, William H. 23:153
Keppart, Calvin 12:64
Keppart, Cyrus 7:31
Kepper, William 20:286
Keppering, D. 18:15
Keppers, D. 18:339
Keppers, F. 26:39
Kepple, Isaac 7:72
Kepple, Joseph S. 12:28
Kepple, M. G. 1:49
Kepple, William 11:231;
  15:108
Keppler, John 26:125
Keppner, Frank 18:278
Kepsha, Jacob 22:406
Kepshart, Caleb S. 7:100
Kept, George 21:353
Ker, Samuel 27:72
Ker---, Richard 25:48
Keran, Carlisle 10:62
Keran, Carlyle 20:286
Kerb, B. S. 21:128
Kerbey, J. M. 9:54
Kerbey, Job 14:186
Kerbey, Wesley 17:260
Kerbox, James 20:98
Kerby, E. B. 1:48
Kerby, George M. 22:453
Kerby, John 3:112;
  10:122
Kerby, King 22:307
Kerby, T. W. 19:303
Kerby, Thomas 11:306
Kerby, W. H. 14:78
Kerch, Victor 12:72
Kerchan, R. A. 15:294
Kerchen, Julius 16:41
Kercher, J. 13:31
Kercher, James 15:69
Kercher, Julius 13:31
Kerchey, James E. 18:143
Kerchmis, Jacob 9:97
Kerchner, George 15:299;
  16:205
Kerchner, L. 20:286
Kerchner, W. 25:272
Kereib, Jacob 3:112
Kerelfield, J. H. 11:402
Kerfman, Malachi 18:143
Kergan, John 15:207
Kerger, James 10:162;
  19:173
Kerice, Augustus 22:39
Kerigan, T. 27:71
Keriker, Jacob 21:189
Kerin, D. 1:146

Kering, Thomas 11:192
Kerkan, William 24:173
Kerkendall, Samuel 22:202, 257
Kerkham, --- 14:78
Kerknecker, J. 24:80
Kerlemin, Frederic 11:413
Kerlew, Rosewall 18:33
Kerley, Alonzo 9:36
Kerley, Daniel 21:110
Kerlin, James 7:58
Kerlin, William H. 23:180
Kerlinger, Samuel 8:107
Kerlock, Richard 9:201; 19:291
Kerlocks, L. 21:149
Kerman, Ebe 11:16
Kerman, O. F. W. E. 13:65
Kermene, John 10:62
Kermichael, John 8:88
Kern, Benjamin 21:243
Kern, C. L. 3:112
Kern, Erasmus 5:52
Kern, F. 14:78
Kern, Frank 25:300
Kern, Frederick 25:47
Kern, George 26:236
Kern, H. 24:22
Kern, H. J. 1:146
Kern, Henry B. 12:28
Kern, J. 1:147; 14:14; 25:194
Kern, James 15:38
Kern, Lewis 22:235
Kern, M. 21:123
Kern, Patrick 11:94
Kern, T. E. 1:147
Kern, W. 3:112
Kern, William 13:125
Kernall, Nathan 8:40
Kernan, James 18:33
Kerne, John 9:100
Kernedy, J. C. 20:287
Kernel, Moser 9:54
Kernell, Nathan 26:168
Kerner, Charles 10:173
Kerner, Fred C. 12:155
Kerner, Henry C. 11:187
Kerner, John 11:206
Kernes, Henry 8:118
Kernes, Henry T. 8:21
Kernes, John R. 21:227
Kernes, John W. 11:66
Kernes, L. D. 20:137
Kerney, James 19:81; 20:287
Kerney, John 12:8
Kerney, William 11:206
Kernick, G. H. 14:14
Kernon, Thomas 19:173

Kerns, Adam 21:353
Kerns, Franklin 22:39
Kerns, Henry 18:208; 19:315; 22:124
Kerns, John J. 15:14
Kerns, N. 22:307
Kerns, Owen 20:125
Kerns, P. 25:194
Kerns, Peter 22:202
Kerns, William 10:62; 20:287
Kerns, William R. 9:221
Kerns, Winburn 21:227
Kerny, Patrick 18:143
Kerr, A. 3:112
Kerr, Aaron 25:47
Kerr, Alexander 6:25
Kerr, B. 3:112
Kerr, Charles 8:59; 19:277; 22:406
Kerr, E. 3:112
Kerr, Edward C. 22:235
Kerr, Elliott W. 11:85
Kerr, Ferdinand 21:92
Kerr, H. 1:146; 3:112
Kerr, I. 14:186
Kerr, Isaac 22:202
Kerr, J. 1:94, 146
Kerr, J. H. 3:112
Kerr, J. L. 23:37
Kerr, Jacob 1:47
Kerr, James 6:21; 8:118; 20:141
Kerr, James M. 11:388
Kerr, Jessie T. 24:80
Kerr, John 5:20; 12:155; 22:124; 25:322
Kerr, John D. 9:227; 18:369
Kerr, John O. 14:78
Kerr, Joseph 14:78
Kerr, Nicholas F. 20:287
Kerr, P. A. 14:26
Kerr, R. H. 12:155
Kerr, Robert 15:69; 21:248
Kerr, Samuel M. 22:257
Kerr, Silas W. 9:54
Kerr, T. 1:144
Kerr, Thomas 10:62; 92; 20:287
Kerr, Thomas C. 23:180
Kerr, W. W. 10:205
Kerr, William 14:186; 26:40
Kerre, Henry T. 18:143
Kerrick, Samuel 3:112
Kerrick, Thacker 17:281
Kerrick, W. 1:94
Kerrigan, John 1:48
Kerrigan, Luke 16:280

Kerrigan, Thomas 7:78
Kerriger, William 3:112
Kerron, Richard 10:153; 19:173
Kersch, Henry 23:70
Kerschener, Jacob 13:31
Kerschner, William 11:413
Kersey, Ezra 24:41
Kersey, George 11:94
Kersey, Jasper 18:191
Kersey, Samuel 6:21
Kershaw, H. 1:144
Kershaw, M. E. 7:100
Kershaw, Thomas 7:31
Kersher, David 8:21
Kershner, Marcelius 21:55
Kershnick, F. G. 25:194
Kershoff, B. 3:112
Kershuskey, Alex 13:31
Kersler, F. 3:112
Kerson, Simeon E. 21:354
Kerstrine, Henry 11:231
Kerter, William 27:71
Kertz, Frank A. 12:28
Kertz, Samuel 12:100; 15:366
Kerve, Frank 7:80
Kerver, Mathew 9:106
Kerwan, Andrew 21:55
Kerwin, P. 14:14
Kerwin, Robert 7:58
Kerwish, John 22:39
Kerzy, John 18:208
Kescoddin, J. 14:242
Kesher, L. 8:51
Keshner, David 18:143
Kesinger, --- 15:152
Kesland, Jacob 16:85
Kesler, Albert D. 12:155
Kesler, Conrad 11:127
Kesler, F. 3:112
Kesler, Frederick 7:58
Kesler, George 22:483
Kesler, Henry 22:429
Kesler, J. 3:112
Kesler, Jacob 12:162
Kesler, James E. 26:125
Kesler, Jeremiah 20:147
Kesler, Joseph 22:39
Kesler, Josiah 22:483
Kesler, Lawson 8:64
Kesler, Richard H. 23:282
Kesner, W. 25:194
Kesner, William 5:20
Keson, David O. 21:128
Kesor, John 11:153
Kessel, C. 9:111
Kessell, W. 11:243
Kessimer, John 3:112
Kessinger, Andrew 11:428

Kessinger, Charles 25:194
Kessinger, J. M. 11:243
Kessington, O. 20:88
Kessler, --- 15:38
Kessler, Daniel 21:354
Kessler, Garrett B. 22:235
Kessler, Henry 11:443
Kessler, Herman 14:186
Kessler, J. 3:112
Kessler, J. E. 23:153
Kessler, John S. 7:58
Kessler, M. 19:255
Kessler, Martin 22:483
Kessler, Nicholas 23:114
Kessler, Samuel 23:286
Kessock, William 27:71
Kester, Asa 22:39
Kester, Charles 3:112
Kester, Israel 12:28
Kester, John 20:137
Kester, John L. 21:195
Kester, L. 3:112
Kester, Samuel 25:48;
    26:135
Kester, William 22:39;
    23:70
Kesting, John A. 21:101
Kestle, Piper 27:72
Kestler, C. 15:320
Kestler, Christian 19:81
Kestler, John 18:430
Kestler, John H. 10:173;
    19:173
Kestler, Joseph E. 22:202
Kestner, George 3:112
Keston, G. 1:48
Kestry, John 15:294;
    19:81
Ket, Robert 27:71
Ketch, George 6:10;
    18:111
Ketch, Lewis 23:153
Ketcham, C. A. 12:122
Ketcham, Daniel 19:173
Ketcham, F. 24:80
Ketcham, Jacob 18:397
Ketcham, William 18:397
Ketcham, Z. 1:146
Ketchem, William 9:84
Ketcher, Charles 14:78
Ketchner, D. 7:51
Ketchum, A. E. 11:264
Ketchum, Aaron 17:288
Ketchum, Alfred S. 27:70
Ketchum, Alonzo 15:320;
    19:81
Ketchum, Austin 10:205
Ketchum, Calvin R. 8:21;
    18:143
Ketchum, Charles 25:194
Ketchum, Daniel 10:162

Ketchum, G. 25:195
Ketchum, G. W. 3:112
Ketchum, Henry C.
    21:139
Ketchum, Isaiah 7:100
Ketchum, J. T. 14:78
Ketchum, Jerry 22:202
Ketchum, John 24:22
Ketchum, John R. 22:257
Ketchum, Leonidas
    17:102
Ketchum, Medade 4:35
Ketchum, P. G. 21:354
Ketchum, Rolla A. 16:205
Ketchum, S. 9:146; 27:70
Ketchum, Silas 21:149
Ketchum, Victor 22:429
Ketchum, W. 26:40
Ketering, William 12:155
Kethenen, Fred 16:205
Keting, J. 25:47
Ketnard, Jacob 22:523
Ketner, Andrew 21:195
Ketner, Charles P. 22:86
Ketrer, Sefra T. 23:180
Ketridge, Samuel M.
    10:62
Ketring, Abraham 22:86
Kettcher, T. S. 25:49
Kette, J. J. 4:35
Kette, L. 3:112
Kettell, Frederick S. 16:85
Kettell, James 3:112
Ketterer, George 14:78
Ketteres, Amdreas 20:9
Ketterman, John C.
    23:153
Kettle, C. B. 19:21
Kettle, E. H. 3:112
Kettle, Frederick S.
    15:207
Kettle, John 25:195
Kettle, P. 1:144
Kettle, Patrick 14:186
Kettle, William 1:47;
    20:193
Kettles, John 12:96;
    15:360; 19:81
Kettleson, Kneid 8:88
Kettlewell, Peter 15:126
Kettner, Silas 14:186
Ketty, Otis 15:207
Ketzer, Joseph H. 13:31
Keunard, Charles 6:17
Keuocke, William 10:18
Keurens, T. 1:145
Keuster, H. 8:51
Keustis, H. E. 23:277
Kever, H. H. 3:112
Kevi, Nathaniel 9:97
Kevinan, Michael 10:8

Kevis, W. 3:112
Kevon, Robert 20:287
Kew, John 14:78
Kew---, D. 15:207
Kewer, Matt 18:334
Kewin, James 20:114
Kewly, W. C. 21:123
Key, Alexander 1:48
Key, Andrew 22:429
Key, Arthur C. 4:35
Key, Charles 22:281
Key, Christopher 19:21
Key, George M. 22:453
Key, H. 25:278
Key, Harvey 8:69
Key, James E. 22:338
Key, Jasper 23:99
Key, Jesse 21:276
Key, Nathan 20:133
Key, Samuel 4:35
Key, Washington 23:271
Key, William D. 22:257
Key, Wyatt 21:276
Keyes, A. 18:87
Keyes, Alexander 25:195
Keyes, David H. 21:139
Keyes, E. R. 19:245
Keyes, Edward 9:138
Keyes, J. 1:145
Keyes, Jacob 15:127
Keyes, John 9:16, 133
Keyes, John L. 12:72
Keyes, M. 25:47
Keyes, Marcus 20:114
Keyes, Michael 23:114
Keyes, Miles 18:87
Keyes, O. S. 3:112
Keyes, Ovan B. 26:39
Keyes, Robert 19:294
Keyes, Samuel S. 5:52
Keyes, W. H. 16:97
Keyes, William 10:146
Keyes, William Worth
    22:453
Keyhill, S. 13:92
Keyling, William 7:100;
    21:354
Keymon, Abbey 9:54
Keyo, Alexander 3:112
Keys, A. F. 25:48
Keys, Albert 21:354
Keys, C. 3:112
Keys, C. D. 19:232
Keys, Cincinnati 4:35
Keys, David 14:185
Keys, E. 16:372
Keys, Edmond 15:360
Keys, Edward 12:96
Keys, Edwin 19:81
Keys, F. C. 14:186
Keys, Greenberry 9:36

Keys, Hugh Y. 22:39
Keys, J. C. F. 1:49
Keys, Jacob 12:122
Keys, John 15:289;
 16:205; 18:278;
 27:71
Keys, John W. 6:25
Keys, Levi P. 18:278
Keys, Manson H. 19:21
Keys, Mark 22:257
Keys, Matthew 12:28
Keys, Owen B. 9:84
Keys, Perry 7:127
Keys, R. 3:112
Keys, Richard 8:88
Keys, Robert 9:182
Keys, S. 1:144
Keys, Samuel 4:35
Keys, Southey 19:173
Keys, Thomas 22:39
Keys, Warren 10:62;
 20:287
Keys, William 3:112;
 6:28; 11:154
Keys, William R. 24:22
Keys, William Worth
 17:410
Keyser, Aaron 24:22
Keyser, G. W. 1:146
Keyser, George E. 15:207
Keyser, H. D. 21:354
Keyser, Henry 20:18
Keyser, Jeremiah 11:66
Keyser, John 15:207
Keyser, Joseph 15:207
Keyser, William 9:43;
 13:31; 26:125
Keyser, William L. 16:41
Keysler, George 14:186
Keystone, C. 3:112
Keyte, J. 26:168
Keyton, Isaac L. 9:36
Keyton, John 21:101
Khlomire, T. 12:82
Kholmine, T. 16:297
Khurst, --- 22:86
Kiale, George 8:51
Kibbe, D. 1:47
Kibber, George 11:396
Kibble, Amos 5:20
Kibbler, John 23:37
Kibburn, John 18:143
Kibby, Edward 13:135
Kibby, George 9:84;
 15:326
Kibby, James M. 23:37
Kibby, Lewis 8:77
Kibby, William 17:66
Kibby, William H. 18:412
Kiber, A. B. 7:100
Kibler, Isaac 23:286

Kibler, James N. 22:86
Kibley, Joseph 12:28
Kiblinger, John 22:430
Kibly, L. J. 17:145
Kibons, Thomas 15:38
Kick, Halmon 21:354
Kickapoo, Aaron 21:354
Kickling, Chester 22:202
Kicland, G. 18:219
Kidd, Ezra 17:421
Kidd, George 17:389;
 22:202
Kidd, H. 22:503
Kidd, J. L. 23:37
Kidd, James M. 22:39
Kidd, John 20:287
Kidd, John W. 11:154
Kidd, M. 16:297
Kidd, N. 12:92
Kidd, Owen 3:112
Kidd, Reuben 17:203
Kidd, W. H. 21:189
Kidd, W. R. 14:315
Kidd, W. W. 11:187
Kidd, Walter 7:31
Kidd, William 16:75
Kidden, John F. 4:35
Kidder, Charles A. 21:87
Kidder, E. 15:38
Kidder, Edward 2:13
Kidder, George M. 16:7
Kidder, Gustavis 16:205
Kidder, Horace E. 17:21
Kidder, J. D. 22:147
Kidder, Luther T. 24:9
Kidder, Reuben A. 21:139
Kidder, W. 18:68
Kidduff, Dennis 11:20
Kiddy, John 18:369
Kidito, Franklin 23:117
Kidney, H. J. 22:202
Kidney, Isaac 19:81
Kidney, James 23:70
Kidney, John 25:47
Kidney, Oliver 11:381
Kidney, P. 25:195
Kidney, Peter J. 20:189
Kidwell, G. W. 8:21;
 18:143
Kidwell, J. 3:112
Kidwell, John H. 17:201
Kidwell, Richard 12:147;
 19:303
Kidwell, S. 11:439
Kiedens, Jacob 16:297
Kief, Daniel 11:402
Kiefer, Frederick 11:94
Kieffer, Charles 13:31
Kieffer, John 25:195
Kieger, James 17:206
Kiehn, A. 1:145

Kiein, A. 19:81
Kieler, A. 3:112
Kielnecker, Jacob 11:323
Kiely, M. 14:14
Kieman, J. 27:70
Kien, Michael 16:205
Kiene, W. 17:335
Kiener, John 16:205
Kiepsicker, William 27:72
Kier, Joseph 23:291
Kier, William 17:291
Kieran, Patrick 19:173
Kierman, Patrick 13:113
Kiern, William 22:39
Kiernan, Thomas J. 22:12
Kierney, Michael 25:195
Kierney, S. H. 1:145
Kiernon, Thomas 10:162
Kiersey, Walter S. 17:243
Kierstead, Joseph 2:13;
 25:48
Kies, Alber 19:173
Kies, Albert 10:173
Kies, John 19:81
Kies, Lafayette 9:24
Kieskey, Emanuel 12:28
Kiester, Joseph W. 13:31
Kieth, O. S. 27:70
Kiffer, J. H. 21:31
Kigee, Alonzo 9:43
Kigel, Conrad 12:28
Kiger, Alonzo L. 26:125
Kiger, Elias D. 12:72;
 15:7
Kiger, George 22:39
Kiger, J. H. 3:224
Kiger, John 15:87
Kiger, M. 13:125
Kiger, William 3:112
Kigg, Stephen 1:47
Kight, West H. 10:205
Kightlinger, A. 14:78
Kightlinger, George
 11:182; 13:113
Kigles, William 14:78
Kihr, August 11:306
Kiker, William 16:121
Kil---, John 25:48
Kilbahre, F. 23:192
Kilbord, L. 11:35
Kilborn, Ancil D. 22:40
Kilborn, Frank 7:100
Kilborn, John 9:13
Kilborn, L. 16:205
Kilborn, Walter 10:9
Kilbourn, E. A. 1:144
Kilbourn, George W.
 20:30
Kilbourne, Charles 20:49
Kilbourne, D. W. 1:144
Kilbourne, Henry 18:219

Kilbraith, --- 26:221
Kilbrets, John 12:155
Kilbride, J. 3:112
Kilburn, Charles D. 4:35
Kilburn, Edward 11:243;
    18:271
Kilburn, G. A. 11:333
Kilburn, J. 1:145
Kilburn, J. A. 16:205
Kilburn, James R. 15:127
Kilburn, Lewis 25:48
Kilburn, Mervin A. 4:35
Kilburn, Thomas 15:207
Kilburne, G. 1:145
Kilby, A. L. 9:230; 20:287
Kilby, Ebenezer 16:372
Kilby, Edward 19:346
Kilby, Lloyd C. 21:31
Kilby, Mathew 18:434
Kilcea, F. W. 19:255
Kilch, R. 1:48
Kilcher, John 9:111
Kilcullen, J. 14:332
Kilcullin, Thomas 14:78
Kilday, Mathew 10:122;
    20:287
Kilderborn, William 9:13
Kildoyle, J. 1:145
Kilduff, O. 1:48
Kile, F. 13:92
Kile, George 21:139
Kile, Harman 21:227
Kile, Henry 21:239
Kile, James S. 4:35
Kile, John H. 22:86
Kile, Joseph 16:121
Kile, Lewis 18:208
Kile, Nathaniel 25:195
Kile, Nelson 21:139
Kilear, J. 12:87
Kileon, R. 15:208
Kiler, William D. 26:145
Kiles, Charles 15:69
Kiles, Timothy 10:122;
    20:287
Kiley, Eugene 12:72
Kiley, T. 15:38
Kilforle, Thomas 12:28
Kilgerif, Martin 21:354
Kilgore, Albert 22:40
Kilgore, B. F. 23:153
Kilgore, Ezekiel J. 22:406
Kilgore, F. A. 27:70
Kilgore, Isaac 22:147
Kilgore, J. 13:92; 14:14
Kilgore, James 11:66;
    17:179
Kilgore, James A. 15:8
Kilgore, Leroy P. 21:31
Kilgore, Stephen 24:59
Kilgore, T. J. 21:123

Kilgore, Thomas R. 20:3
Kilgore, William S.
    25:195
Kilgrow, William 22:257
Kiliplat, Caspar 18:142
Kiliran, Henry 4:35
Kill, A. 12:166
Kill, Frank 18:412
Killam, H. A. 7:58
Killan, Michael 14:186
Killan, Thomas 15:127
Killaught, William 8:107
Killborn, Beverly 7:127
Killbreth, J. 3:112
Killbride, Mark 25:195
Killday, James 14:186
Killduff, James 14:186
Killear, J. 16:297
Killem, J. 11:66
Killen, Asa 11:265
Killen, H. 6:31; 25:322
Killen, J. 14:242
Killen, Thomas P. 21:85
Killenger, John S. 7:31
Killer, C. G. 18:397
Killer, Francis 11:66
Killer, George 3:112
Killer, H. D. 15:343;
    16:372
Killer, R. J. 22:202
Killering, Samuel 19:81
Killgan, Wiseman 9:209
Killgore, John W. 12:155
Killinger, A. 1:48
Killinger, E. S. 17:37
Killinger, George S. 9:31
Killinger, Henry 17:81
Killingham, Joseph 8:21;
    18:143
Killingsworth, Charles
    8:21
Killingsworth, David 7:58
Killingworth, Charles
    18:143
Killion, George W. 11:65
Killion, M. 1:145
Killion, William A.
    17:349
Killip, Robert 21:256
Killips, Richmond C.
    22:281
Killis, John 21:354
Killison, John 22:281
Killman, --- 16:41
Killman, Patrick 19:173
Killmer, J. S. 1:146
Killner, Sanford 3:112
Killon, James R. 17:201
Killoran, Patrick 10:162
Killride, John 14:257
Killy, John 13:31

Kilm, Joseph 22:147
Kilman, O. P. 18:310;
    26:104
Kilmartin, Martin 23:12
Kilmer, Alonzo 9:24
Kilmer, J. 3:112
Kilmer, Joseph 17:288
Kilmore, John W. 27:70
Kilopsey, J. 14:78
Kilorne, M. 3:112
Kilpatrick, C. 3:112
Kilpatrick, George 10:173
Kilpatrick, J. 23:282
Kilpatrick, John 10:162;
    19:173; 21:354
Kilpatrick, Newton 7:68
Kilpatrick, R. 27:72
Kilpatrick, W. 25:195
Kilpatrick, W. B. 25:195
Kilpatrick, William
    15:152
Kilroy, Barney 21:87
Kilroy, J. M. 27:70
Kilroy, John 9:146; 13:65;
    16:205
Kilson, J. 3:112
Kilstrap, Peter 9:84
Kilstrup, Peter C. 26:40
Kilt, Edw. 8:88
Kilte, C. 18:460
Kiltner, D. 15:127
Kilts, W. L. 5:20
Kilty, William S. 15:273
Kilvey, John H. 24:22
Kim, George H. 12:155
Kimage, T. 1:146
Kimback, A. 1:48
Kimbair, Joseph 22:307
Kimbal, C. D. 16:140
Kimbal, C. W. 7:75
Kimbal, Granville 9:84
Kimbal, James 24:72
Kimbal, P. 13:92
Kimball, A. 1:145; 3:112
Kimball, Amos 11:66
Kimball, Andrew 15:3
Kimball, B. 1:49
Kimball, B. F. E. 23:37
Kimball, Benjamin 11:207
Kimball, Bradford B.
    12:28
Kimball, C. 19:239
Kimball, C. H. 11:388
Kimball, C. W. 25:300
Kimball, Catherine 1:146
Kimball, Charles 9:103,
    182; 18:111; 27:71
Kimball, Charles B. 9:146
Kimball, Charles E.
    10:162; 19:173

Kimball, Charles F. 19:228; 23:103
Kimball, Chauncey C. 21:256
Kimball, D. L. 18:351
Kimball, Daniel 25:195
Kimball, Deland 21:354
Kimball, E. 1:144, 146; 27:70
Kimball, Eliphat 27:72
Kimball, Elisha 17:349; 18:33
Kimball, Emanuel 7:100
Kimball, F. 9:209
Kimball, F. M. 18:243; 26:41
Kimball, Franklin 15:273; 20:133
Kimball, G. 12:122; 26:41
Kimball, G. F. 7:31
Kimball, George 22:86
Kimball, George A. 27:72
Kimball, George C. 21:73, 114
Kimball, George H. 10:92; 20:287
Kimball, H. H. 3:112
Kimball, Henry 18:334
Kimball, Henry G. 19:173
Kimball, Hiram 5:20
Kimball, J. 12:28; 15:311; 19:81
Kimball, J. E. 1:145
Kimball, J. F. 25:322
Kimball, J. N. 7:100
Kimball, J. T. 25:322
Kimball, J. W. 21:354
Kimball, Jacob 11:388; 22:307
Kimball, James 3:112; 10:205; 11:127
Kimball, Jeremiah B. 7:68
Kimball, Jerry 22:307
Kimball, John 3:112; 11:381
Kimball, John C. 11:155
Kimball, John W. 19:21
Kimball, Joseph 23:37
Kimball, Joshua 17:400
Kimball, Leander 21:139
Kimball, Louis 17:53
Kimball, Luther M. 7:16
Kimball, Mas 23:291
Kimball, Moses F. 13:31
Kimball, Nathan 8:51
Kimball, Newell 22:406
Kimball, O. S. 1:145
Kimball, R. 13:92
Kimball, R. H. 25:195
Kimball, R. S. 27:70

Kimball, Richard 15:303; 16:205
Kimball, Robert 21:276
Kimball, S. C. 20:147
Kimball, Solomon 7:58
Kimball, Timothy 27:72
Kimball, W. C. 12:57
Kimball, W. F. 27:71
Kimball, W. S. 14:78
Kimball, W. T. 17:495
Kimball, Wellman 12:72
Kimball, William 15:25; 22:40
Kimball, William F. 9:146
Kimbark, I. 19:255
Kimbark, Isaiah 9:182
Kimbel, Henry 23:304
Kimbell, H. 25:195
Kimbell, L. 27:70
Kimber, S. A. 16:205
Kimber, S. O. 15:304
Kimber, Simon 9:36; 26:104
Kimber, W. H. 22:497
Kimber, W. W. 9:54
Kimberlain, H. 13:92
Kimberley, F. 1:48
Kimberlin, John G. 15:69
Kimberling, Benjamin 11:413
Kimberling, M. 11:94
Kimberly, D. 25:195
Kimberly, David 23:153
Kimberly, George 11:108
Kimberly, Joseph 9:72
Kimberly, O. 3:112
Kimberly, S. 7:51
Kimble, Charles F. 9:182
Kimble, Charles W. 18:87, 117
Kimble, D. 15:95
Kimble, Degros A. 8:118
Kimble, E. 25:311
Kimble, George A. 9:121
Kimble, Hanibal 22:430
Kimble, Henry 12:72; 15:69; 17:82
Kimble, J. S. 6:31
Kimble, Jacob 25:195
Kimble, James 22:307
Kimble, John E. 27:70
Kimble, Joseph 10:122; 20:287
Kimble, Nathan H. 21:55
Kimble, Peter 6:17; 18:87
Kimble, R. A. 22:483
Kimble, S. 3:112
Kimble, S. D. 16:269
Kimble, Seymour W. 17:243
Kimble, Solomon 26:168

Kimble, William 23:153
Kimbler, Hiram 11:94
Kimbley, George W. 22:40
Kimbo, D. 25:195
Kimbo, David 5:41
Kimbo, P. 14:14
Kimbol, George 15:83
Kimborough, John 22:257
Kimbrell, William H. 21:73
Kimbro, George W. 22:503
Kimbro, Isaac 11:206
Kimbro, John J. 11:243
Kimbro, Moses 11:206
Kimbrough, George 17:398
Kimburley, Daniel 5:20
Kime, David I. 17:496
Kime, Jonas 19:81
Kime, Samuel A. 24:41
Kimel, John 26:41
Kimeling, John 17:179
Kimer, Alex 14:187
Kimer, Henry 23:153
Kimery, John J. 23:37
Kimes, Edward 22:86
Kimes, Francis W. 11:66
Kimes, James 22:407
Kimes, Richard 22:307
Kimes, Robert 9:221; 18:369
Kimes, William 23:263
Kimesford, Richard 19:255
Kimler, John 15:309
Kimler, Peter 25:47
Kimler, William 17:441; 24:153
Kimman, Richard 11:388
Kimmball, Theodore 24:107
Kimmbelher, Victor 14:332
Kimmel, A. 20:41
Kimmel, George W. 21:73
Kimmel, J. 11:154
Kimmel, Jacob 20:186
Kimmel, John C. 21:101
Kimmel, John D. 22:202
Kimmel, Zaccheus F. 21:73
Kimmell, David 23:286
Kimmell, George W. 15:316
Kimmell, William 23:286
Kimmell, William C. 22:202
Kimmerling, Josiah 9:221

Kimmerting, Josiah 18:369
Kimmey, D. 25:333
Kimmey, Jacob 1:47
Kimmons, Eli 11:388
Kimp, George 26:168
Kimper, M. H. 12:155
Kimpland, C. B. 15:38
Kimple, Adam 23:89
Kimple, E. 11:264
Kimple, J. D. 14:242
Kimple, John 14:186
Kimpley, Jacob 27:71
Kimrey, Asa P. 9:97
Kimsig, John 10:152
Kin, Herman 8:51
Kinaman, J. 13:92
Kinarch, M. 16:85
Kinard, Abraham 12:28
Kinard, John 5:41
Kinary, P. 14:186
Kinber, Simon 18:294
Kinble, Solomon 8:40
Kincade, --- 20:9
Kincade, A. 20:147
Kincade, B. D. 9:54
Kincade, Edwin 7:8
Kincade, J. 1:146
Kincade, J. A. 14:186
Kincade, P. 22:307
Kincade, Pete 17:134
Kincade, Peter 24:197
Kincaid, Alexander 23:12
Kincaid, E. 17:263
Kincaid, John R. 17:281
Kincaid, L. 5:41
Kincaid, S. 23:153
Kincaid, Thomas 22:257; 25:195
Kincaid, William 24:22
Kincair, William 23:279
Kincannon, S. P. 27:71
Kincheboe, W. B. 21:354
Kinchen, Taylor 21:212
Kinchler, James 25:300
Kincily, Aaron 13:125
Kind, Morit Z. 11:127
Kindall, James 14:78; 24:94
Kindall, Robert 11:154
Kindell, John S. 21:228
Kinder, Alexander 24:22
Kinder, F. 9:69
Kinder, George 7:31
Kinder, Henry 17:179
Kinder, Jeremiah M. 23:70
Kinder, John 10:148
Kinder, Lyman 17:248
Kinder, M. 26:40
Kinder, Miles W. 7:127

Kinderman, G. 3:112
Kindig, Jessie 22:86
Kindley, Jacob 9:121
Kindley, S. 21:31
Kindred, Andrew 7:100
Kindred, Carick 10:122; 20:287
Kindred, J. 26:40
Kindred, James 25:333
Kindred, John 9:84
Kindred, M. H. 19:21
Kine, Benjamin F. 12:54
Kine, Henry 12:28
Kine, Honet 19:239
Kine, Howard 9:182
Kine, Jonas 15:318
Kine, K. 9:182
Kinehart, Henry 17:37
Kineline, Abel P. 11:154
Kiner, William 11:108
Kinerly, F. 1:98
Kines, M. O. 3:112
Kinesley, J. 1:144
Kinfield, S. S. 11:108
Kinfolk, W. 19:47
King, --- 3:112; 15:208; 25:195; 27:73
King, A. 1:49; 5:41; 14:78, 186; 15:343; 16:372; 25:195
King, A. A. 11:243
King, A. J. 11:219; 18:33
King, Abel 17:405
King, Abraham 5:41
King, Adney 6:25
King, Albert 12:142; 14:186; 17:74
King, Alex 17:497
King, Alexander 3:224; 16:41; 23:37
King, Alfred A. 4:35
King, Allen 21:277
King, Almir 19:21
King, Almond 13:31
King, Almstead 7:127
King, Alom G. 4:35
King, Alvan J. 11:67
King, Alvestin 22:483
King, Alvin 13:113
King, Amasa 17:243
King, Ambrose 17:148
King, Anais 21:354
King, Andrew 22:483
King, Anthony H. 13:31
King, Arbney I. 8:22
King, Aubery J. 18:143
King, Aug 17:423
King, Augustus 24:171
King, B. R. 17:297
King, Benjamin 7:127
King, Benjamin F. 5:20

King, Benjamin M. 17:355
King, C. 3:112; 17:180
King, C. B. 15:299
King, C. L. 14:269
King, C. P. 7:100
King, C. S. 13:125; 25:48
King, C. W. 9:146; 27:71
King, Casser 17:179
King, Ceperate 21:354
King, Charles 7:31, 127; 17:53; 18:243; 21:354; 22:202; 23:153; 26:40
King, Charles D. 2:13
King, Charles S. 13:31
King, Chester B. 16:205
King, Christian 18:278
King, Conrad 17:82
King, Cornelius 25:195
King, Cyrel 15:38
King, D. 3:112; 9:154; 27:71, 145
King, Daniel 1:47; 9:36; 14:187; 21:195; 22:235
King, Daniel B. 23:277
King, David 22:430
King, David B. 16:87
King, David S. 17:501
King, David W. 8:89
King, Dudley 17:180, 400; 23:153
King, E. 3:112; 17:166; 20:92; 21:149; 27:72
King, E. A. 26:145
King, E. B. 21:354
King, E. D. 9:36
King, E. H. 8:51
King, Ed 21:277
King, Edgar 13:31
King, Edward 9:36; 18:294; 22:147; 26:104
King, Edwin H. 21:139
King, Elevin 1:48
King, Elias 17:14
King, Elijah 22:40
King, Emanuel 11:389
King, Enquire 17:152
King, F. 11:153; 18:176
King, F. F. 21:189
King, Felix 17:148
King, Francis E. 21:31
King, Francis L. 18:351
King, Frank 16:143
King, Franklin 22:281
King, G. 25:195
King, G. B. 9:146; 17:281; 27:71
King, G. W. 7:100

King, George 2:13; 5:41;
    7:127; 10:62, 122;
    11:306; 12:28;
    14:282; 17:82; 19:21,
    81; 20:287; 21:139,
    354; 22:235; 25:48,
    195; 27:72
King, George A. 16:372
King, George C. 17:37
King, George H. 13:31
King, George L. 22:453
King, George W. 5:21;
    14:187; 17:360;
    23:70
King, Gideon 9:209
King, Green 7:127;
    22:338
King, Greenberry 17:281
King, H. 11:85; 14:187,
    257
King, H. J. 1:146
King, H. M. 1:144, 145;
    25:311
King, H. O. 25:46
King, H. P. 1:49
King, Harmon 22:40
King, Harrison 8:58, 89;
    21:149
King, Henry 7:31; 8:22;
    18:143; 23:16
King, Henry B. 11:281
King, Henry N. 22:86
King, Henry P. 21:101
King, Henry W. 13:31;
    16:41
King, Hiram 12:28
King, Hiram R. 19:21
King, Horace W. 20:98
King, I. H. 17:503
King, I. M. 18:219
King, Isham 12:155
King, J. 1:144, 145, 146,
    147; 13:92; 14:79,
    265, 288, 300;
    16:297; 17:476, 502;
    19:81; 25:195; 27:73
King, J. B. 12:85; 14:79;
    16:297
King, J. C. 11:427; 16:41
King, J. E. 9:230; 20:287
King, J. G. 1:146
King, J. H. 13:65
King, J. K. 3:112; 17:217
King, J. M. 9:54
King, J. P. 9:161
King, J. R. 27:73
King, Jacob 10:62;
    17:237; 20:287;
    21:277; 22:202
King, James 1:48; 4:35;
    12:50; 16:7, 372;

King, James 17:180;
    20:23; 22:257, 513
King, James A. 9:182;
    12:28; 13:31; 19:267
King, James F. 3:224;
    17:504
King, James G. 17:321
King, James H. 9:201
King, James J. 14:187
King, James N. 21:189
King, James P. 9:84;
    26:39
King, James S. 21:131
King, James W. 19:291
King, Jeff 9:209
King, Jerome 17:14;
    20:287
King, Jerry 5:41
King, John 7:127; 9:66,
    111, 115, 236; 10:62,
    122; 11:16; 12:28;
    15:57, 208; 16:97;
    18:68, 278, 310, 369;
    20:287; 22:257;
    25:195; 26:104, 168,
    221; 27:72
King, John D. 10:122;
    20:287
King, John H. 8:89;
    16:205; 17:134;
    24:197
King, John M. 23:184
King, John W. 5:21;
    9:182; 11:265;
    15:152; 18:243;
    22:40; 25:195; 26:40
King, Jonathan 12:64
King, Joseph 10:62;
    14:187; 17:281, 309;
    18:33; 20:193, 287;
    21:101, 277; 23:70,
    282, 313; 25:195
King, Josiah 23:153
King, Josiah R. 17:207
King, Kelly 20:287
King, L. 1:146; 7:83;
    9:133
King, L. J. 25:195
King, Lafayette 9:55
King, Lavinus 21:55
King, Leander 3:112
King, Levi 21:277; 27:71
King, Levi P. 18:111
King, Levi R. 20:23
King, Lewis 15:299;
    16:205
King, Lysander 13:31;
    16:41
King, M. 3:113; 16:41;
    22:503
King, M. H. 1:146; 27:71

King, Madison 22:338
King, Marion 22:257
King, Marshall 22:147
King, Marshall H. 22:257
King, Martin 8:89
King, Martin B. 22:40
King, Marvin 15:108
King, Michael 17:21
King, Michael D. 23:70
King, Miles G. 15:292
King, Milton 9:209
King, Morgan 7:127
King, Moses P. 13:31
King, N. 3:113
King, N. J. 22:483
King, N. M. 17:110
King, N. S. 17:107
King, Nathan P. 23:153
King, Norman 16:140
King, O. 17:364
King, O. P. 21:354
King, Othy 7:64
King, Otis 19:21
King, Otis A. 10:163;
    19:173
King, Owen 15:127
King, P. 25:48, 195
King, Patrick 5:21; 14:79;
    21:240; 22:453
King, Paul 8:89
King, Paul F. 23:70
King, Peter 22:202
King, Peter B. 22:429
King, Philip 22:483
King, Pleasant 12:50
King, R. 3:113; 13:65;
    16:205
King, R. E. 1:48
King, R. M. 12:155
King, Reuben 15:328;
    19:81
King, Reuben D. 20:137
King, Richard 3:113;
    10:62; 20:287
King, Robert 7:127;
    10:62; 11:206, 320;
    20:287
King, Robert A. 23:70
King, Robert O. 21:86
King, Roland 11:207
King, Rufus James 24:80
King, Rufus W. 14:315
King, S. 1:144; 3:113;
    16:205
King, S. J. 20:141
King, S. M. 14:263;
    20:287
King, S. R. 11:192; 24:22
King, Samuel 9:209;
    11:154; 17:72;
    26:145

King, Samuel D. 20:3
King, Samuel I. 7:64
King, Silas 11:333
King, Silas G. 21:73
King, Simon 23:192
King, Stephen 12:72;
  15:69; 22:124
King, Stephen A. 22:429
King, Stephen M. 10:92
King, Sylvester 8:22;
  18:143
King, T. 1:144, 146;
  18:369; 21:31; 23:37
King, T. H. 23:302
King, T. P. 1:145
King, Thomas 9:221;
  11:424; 14:79, 187;
  15:87; 16:97;
  17:448; 18:370;
  20:88, 125; 21:10,
  354
King, Thomas D. 25:195
King, Thomas Green
  20:85
King, Thomas J. 16:41
King, Thomas S. 21:239
King, U. D. 19:272
King, Ulysses P. 21:228
King, Uriah S. 14:300;
  17:473; 27:73
King, Vincent 8:89
King, W. 14:187; 17:433;
  20:41; 21:206;
  25:195
King, W. A. 9:66
King, W. B. 10:148;
  18:52
King, W. C. 12:96;
  15:360; 19:81
King, W. E. 9:55; 17:151
King, W. H. 18:52;
  25:300
King, W. J. 27:70
King, W. V. 17:96
King, Walace 11:108
King, Warren 15:17
King, Webster M. 21:73
King, Wesley 9:70;
  17:180
King, Willard 16:17
King, Willard H. 21:73
King, William 7:78;
  10:62, 145; 12:28;
  16:205; 18:278;
  19:81, 173; 20:287;
  22:338; 23:153, 291;
  24:164; 26:125
King, William A. 15:208
King, William B. 8:51
King, William D. 8:89

King, William F. 21:228;
  23:153
King, William H. 10:162;
  19:173; 25:311
King, William H. H. 17:61
King, William R. 11:35
King, William W. 24:67
King, Willis 22:307
King, Wilson 7:127
King, Woolf 13:113
King, Wyatt C. 23:153
King, Y. L. 11:35
Kingcade, Thomas 15:208
Kingen, J. 26:40
Kingen, Joseph 23:37
Kingerry, Thomas 10:92
Kingery, J. 3:113
Kingery, John R. 23:153
Kingery, Thomas 20:287
Kingfisher, Jim 25:333
Kingham, --- 3:113; 19:81
Kinghayden, W. 25:195
Kinghorn, William A.
  21:244
Kingie, Fred 2:13
Kingkade, S. 3:113
Kingland, Elijah 8:51
Kingland, Robert 9:24
Kingle, A. 25:195
Kingler, Albert 20:287
Kingley, Isaac 8:84
Kingley, Jacob 9:72
Kingley, Loren 8:22
Kingman, Ed. S. 18:339
Kingman, Edward S.
  9:103
Kingman, Hector O.
  14:187
Kingman, L. 1:146
Kingon, Horace A. 13:32
Kingrey, Fulton 21:354
Kingrey, G. E. 23:153
Kingsbury, C. 3:113
Kingsbury, H. P. 3:113
Kingsbury, Harley 23:37
Kingsbury, Hiram O.
  11:35
Kingsbury, J. H. 3:113;
  7:75; 25:300
Kingsbury, J. J. 1:49
Kingsbury, J. M. 13:78
Kingsbury, J. W. 15:325
Kingsbury, James M.
  16:205; 21:247
Kingsbury, Levi P. 11:108
Kingsbury, Moses W.
  19:81
Kingsbury, O. P. 22:147
Kingsbury, R. C. 12:80
Kingsbury, S. C. 25:300
Kingsbury, Sidney C. 7:75

Kingseley, S. 3:113
Kingsey, James 24:41
Kingsford, R. 9:182
Kingshausen, Andrew
  6:23
Kingsland, Alfred 11:333
Kingsland, Charles B.
  9:84
Kingsland, Charles C.
  26:40
Kingsland, Elijah 21:167
Kingsland, Isaac 13:32
Kingsland, J. W. 12:64;
  15:38
Kingsland, Oscar 14:236
Kingsland, Oscar B. 18:33
Kingsland, W. H. 3:113
Kingsley, --- 9:182
Kingsley, A. 13:132
Kingsley, Adison 13:113
Kingsley, C. E. 14:187
Kingsley, Charles 18:426
Kingsley, D. C. 11:192
Kingsley, Elijah 5:52
Kingsley, G. A. 18:278
Kingsley, George W.
  24:94
Kingsley, H. 1:145
Kingsley, J. 3:113
Kingsley, John 19:173
Kingsley, John F. 9:121
Kingsley, Lovern 18:143
Kingsley, R. C. 25:195
Kingsley, Silas 9:36
Kingsley, Stephen 17:66;
  20:125
Kingsmill, H. J. 18:243;
  26:40
Kingsmith, D. 23:282
Kingston, Charles 20:287
Kingston, D. 1:49
Kingston, George 7:100;
  22:147
Kingston, John 22:147
Kingston, Judkins 15:38
Kingston, W. 14:242
Kingstrom, Charles 10:62
Kington, W. 27:73
Kinholtz, G. 1:146
Kiniler, John 19:81
Kininicier, L. 1:144
Kinivear, Carlton 27:70
Kink, John 19:303
Kinkade, A. L. 8:51
Kinkade, L. 14:187
Kinkade, L. C. 17:15
Kinkade, Munroe 23:271
Kinkade, Nathan 26:41
Kinkaid, James W. 9:84
Kinkaid, Robert G. 24:52
Kinkate, F. 25:49

Kinkead, Robert 21:133
Kinkelson, K. 11:333
Kinken, C. A. 16:202
Kinker, C. W. 18:191
Kinkle, John 3:113
Kinkley, Jacob 21:111
Kinklin, Henry 4:35
Kinle, John 10:28
Kinler, Henry 11:66
Kinley, A. J. 20:287
Kinley, A. L. 10:62
Kinley, John 17:180
Kinlock, D. 1:49
Kinman, A. 3:113
Kinman, T. J. 24:22
Kinman, William A.
     23:114
Kinn, John 11:16
Kinnafred, John 9:43
Kinnaman, J. 14:14
Kinnaman, John 23:263
Kinnamon, John 22:257
Kinnamon, Levi M. 17:37
Kinnan, David 4:35
Kinnan, James R. 11:182
Kinnan, Patrick 14:187
Kinnard, W. R. 9:236;
     26:221
Kinnberger, A. 8:121
Kinne, Cyrus A. 22:147
Kinne, George 26:39
Kinne, Warren O. 18:370
Kinneck, Ferdinand
     18:208
Kinnee, J. 3:113
Kinnel, Ralph 6:31
Kinnell, Adam 24:197
Kinnely, T. 3:113
Kinner, Adelbert 13:32
Kinner, J. 25:195
Kinner, James 13:32
Kinner, John 18:52
Kinner, Leonard T. 17:66
Kinnerd, J. 25:195
Kinnerman, John 20:85
Kinnescott, Walter J. 15:5
Kinnet, J. 24:80
Kinneth, Charles 17:203
Kinney, A. J. 9:182
Kinney, Aaron 21:354
Kinney, Alvin 10:163;
     19:173
Kinney, Andrew J.
     20:287; 22:406
Kinney, B. F. 17:203
Kinney, Barney 19:21
Kinney, C. 3:113; 14:187
Kinney, C. A. 22:463
Kinney, Charles 7:100
Kinney, Charles A.
     10:163; 19:173

Kinney, Charles M.
     18:143
Kinney, Chester D. 8:89,
     114
Kinney, Daniel 16:147;
     22:12
Kinney, David 1:47; 13:32
Kinney, Dennis 21:354
Kinney, G. F. 1:49
Kinney, George 1:192
Kinney, George H. 17:243
Kinney, George R. 11:243
Kinney, George W. 12:8;
     15:69
Kinney, H. 14:79
Kinney, Harrison 9:24;
     11:16
Kinney, J. 3:113
Kinney, J. B. 18:33
Kinney, J. W. 3:113
Kinney, James 9:201;
     19:286; 22:147;
     26:40
Kinney, James F. 21:245
Kinney, James M. 11:243
Kinney, Jeffrey 25:47
Kinney, John 11:293;
     22:202
Kinney, John C. 11:116;
     22:40
Kinney, John J. 17:54
Kinney, John W. 5:21;
     25:195
Kinney, Josiah 17:249
Kinney, Lamson 8:89
Kinney, Leander 11:154
Kinney, Lucas 3:113
Kinney, M. 3:113; 14:79
Kinney, Michael 19:329;
     20:107
Kinney, Morris 25:47
Kinney, Neil 22:257
Kinney, O. P. 26:39
Kinney, P. 22:353
Kinney, Percival 15:69
Kinney, Perry C. 12:155
Kinney, R. S. 19:173
Kinney, R. W. 25:322
Kinney, Rasford 17:496
Kinney, S. E. 16:297
Kinney, Samuel 23:123
Kinney, W. H. 11:291
Kinney, W. H. H. 19:173
Kinney, William 8:22;
     17:290; 23:153
Kinni, E. B. 26:39
Kinnie, Daniel 18:52
Kinnie, George 9:84
Kinnilley, Michael 22:453
Kinning, Henry 20:287

Kinning, John 10:122;
     20:287
Kinning, R. W. 12:166
Kinnis, J. M. 18:143
Kinnison, I. 23:153
Kinnison, Isaac 17:134;
     24:197
Kinnison, J. 14:289
Kinnison, W. W. 15:57
Kinniston, David 17:91
Kinny, --- 19:81
Kinny, William 18:143
Kinrade, Thomas 22:40
Kins, W. H. 3:113
Kinsable, Lenord 21:354
Kinsel, Adam 23:153
Kinsel, Fred. 15:108
Kinsel, H. M. 16:121
Kinsel, John 25:322
Kinsell, George 3:113
Kinsell, J. B. 4:35
Kinsell, William 10:18
Kinsella, John 19:321
Kinser, James C. 22:124
Kinser, Peter 10:122;
     20:287
Kinsey, B. B. 3:113
Kinsey, Benjamin 22:202
Kinsey, David 17:54
Kinsey, Harrison 18:310;
     26:104
Kinsey, J. W. 22:202
Kinsey, Joseph 11:389;
     17:82
Kinsham, M. 1:144
Kinshaw, Jacob 7:68
Kinside, John Francis
     11:264
Kinsig, John 18:52
Kinsler, Peter 26:168
Kinsley, --- 22:520
Kinsley, Alexander 8:89
Kinsley, Benjamin 13:32
Kinsley, Christian 24:9
Kinsley, G. Washington
     26:103
Kinsley, George B. 26:221
Kinsley, George W. 24:22
Kinsley, George
     Washington 18:310
Kinsley, Henry 11:66
Kinsley, John 5:21; 9:163;
     10:163; 11:35
Kinsley, S. 3:113
Kinsley, Samuel 12:155
Kinslow, Michael 4:35
Kinsman, B. W. 25:333
Kinsman, Charles 18:278
Kinsman, F. P. 3:113
Kinsman, J. E. 3:113
Kinsman, J. N. 19:174

Kinsman, Jerome 17:395
Kinsman, Joseph M. 10:163
Kinsman, Philonas 16:143
Kinsman, W. S. 3:113
Kinsman, William J. 17:502
Kinsol, John 22:430
Kinson, John 11:100
Kinson, Lewis 17:22
Kinson, Spencer 10:122; 20:287
Kinsor, John 15:208
Kinston, Thomas 8:22; 18:143
Kinter, H. 1:98
Kinter, John 7:64
Kinter, Robert 16:205
Kintigh, John E. 23:153
Kintner, Frank 24:80
Kinton, William H. 16:205
Kints, John 20:287
Kintyle, J. 20:287
Kintz, D. 14:79
Kintz, Edwin D. 17:82
Kintz, William 20:189
Kintzer, Charles 12:28
Kinutson, Kinute 10:122
Kinvery, William A. 18:143
Kinyon, Benjamin 21:31
Kinyon, Benjamin W. 5:20
Kinyon, D. P. 27:72
Kinyon, J. A. 1:48
Kinyon, Job W. 12:57
Kinyon, Lorenzo 25:195
Kinyon, P. T. 23:37
Kinyon, Sumner D. 24:171
Kinyon, V. L. 25:47
Kinzey, R. D. 19:278
Kinzie, G. 21:354
Kinzie, Isaac 17:37
Kinzler, Charles 23:153
Kions, Adam 23:70
Kions, Jacob 14:269
Kip, Charles S. 7:32
Kiper, L. J. 1:48
Kiper, Samuel 20:186
Kipler, Riperwick 18:426
Kipp, A. 18:52
Kipp, Andrew 10:152
Kipp, Benjamin 22:40
Kipp, C. 1:145
Kipp, Charles 11:127
Kipp, G. J. 1:145
Kipp, Henry 17:319
Kipp, J. B. 5:21; 25:195
Kipp, John W. 20:107

Kipp, Peter H. 21:256
Kipp, W. 3:113
Kipp, Walter B. 26:168
Kippetoe, J. M. 11:329
Kipping, Hans 14:130
Kipps, C. 25:300
Kipps, Corneling 7:80
Kiprio, J. 1:144
Kirby, --- 20:176
Kirby, A. 3:113
Kirby, A. J. 11:35
Kirby, A. W. 13:92
Kirby, Andrew 22:257
Kirby, Charles 3:113
Kirby, Christ'r. C. 8:89
Kirby, David W. 22:257
Kirby, Drissy 23:243
Kirby, Edward B. 17:393
Kirby, Ezra 14:187
Kirby, Garrison 21:228
Kirby, George E. 26:39
Kirby, Henry 23:89
Kirby, J. 3:113
Kirby, J. A. 3:113
Kirby, James 9:84; 26:40
Kirby, John 20:288; 24:59; 27:145
Kirby, John R. 11:154
Kirby, L. D. 11:94
Kirby, Lath 8:64
Kirby, Leonard 10:62
Kirby, Lewis 22:339
Kirby, Lowt 26:168
Kirby, Morgan 17:453; 24:183
Kirby, P. H. 10:176; 19:174
Kirby, Patrick 12:72; 15:69
Kirby, Peter 4:35
Kirby, Richard 20:50
Kirby, Ruston 6:31
Kirby, Smith V. 22:202
Kirby, Stephen 25:47
Kirby, T. W. 12:146
Kirby, W. 11:402
Kirby, Walter C. 15:208
Kirby, William 17:22, 37
Kirby, William E. 10:96
Kirby, William H. 9:236; 18:103; 26:221
Kirch, H. 3:113
Kirch, W. 2:13; 25:47
Kircher, John M. 11:388
Kirchhuebal, William 20:104
Kirchner, Henry 22:281
Kirchner, Lenast 10:62
Kirchner, Walter 5:41
Kirchoff, Henry 20:288
Kirchoff, John 11:35

Kirckberg, Ehrhardt 21:101
Kirfman, Malachi 8:22
Kirgan, Jonathan 9:84
Kirhn, Isaac 19:174
Kirhn, Thomas 8:107
Kirk, --- 8:22; 11:153; 18:143
Kirk, A. 1:144
Kirk, Abijah M. 22:257
Kirk, Alfred 14:282
Kirk, B. J. 3:113
Kirk, D. Vanbers 15:330
Kirk, Daniel E. 19:81
Kirk, David 7:127
Kirk, David E. 15:336
Kirk, E. 12:82; 16:297
Kirk, Elias W. 9:111
Kirk, Elmer 11:154
Kirk, G. W. 25:196
Kirk, George 12:64; 15:22
Kirk, Granville 10:62; 20:288
Kirk, Harris 9:133
Kirk, Hiram W. 21:131
Kirk, Horace 13:113
Kirk, Hugh A. 18:370
Kirk, Irwin 23:271
Kirk, Isaac 8:22; 18:143
Kirk, J. 22:202
Kirk, J. B. 14:79
Kirk, J. D. 9:121; 27:69
Kirk, Jacob 10:62; 11:34; 20:288
Kirk, James 12:160
Kirk, James W. 10:92; 20:288
Kirk, John 22:40
Kirk, Joseph 23:108
Kirk, Joshua 7:100
Kirk, L. S. 8:22; 18:143
Kirk, Lewis 12:155
Kirk, M. E. 21:101
Kirk, Martin 22:520
Kirk, Michael 7:14
Kirk, Mines 9:133
Kirk, Minos 27:71
Kirk, Nathan 11:16
Kirk, O. 14:79
Kirk, P. 3:113
Kirk, Paris 27:71
Kirk, R. 11:306
Kirk, Robert 12:100; 16:11; 22:86
Kirk, Samuel 20:125
Kirk, Samuel H. 12:59
Kirk, Thomas 1:47
Kirk, W. B. 23:153
Kirk, W. H. 12:87; 16:297

Kirk, William 10:18;
11:396; 13:113; 17:496
Kirk, William H. 24:41
Kirk, William J. 14:269
Kirk, William R. 22:40
Kirkbride, Asher 11:153
Kirkbride, H. K. 9:72
Kirkbride, William H.
21:115
Kirkendall, Ira 8:64
Kirkendall, Joseph W.
24:52
Kirker, C. 13:92
Kirker, M. 15:108
Kirkham, H. C. 3:113
Kirkham, James H. 10:62;
20:288
Kirkham, James R. 23:89
Kirkham, R. 11:413
Kirkham, T. 1:144
Kirkham, W. G. 25:322
Kirkhart, Michael 11:35
Kirkhead, Silas 8:51
Kirkier, C. 16:269
Kirkland, A. 1:49
Kirkland, Charles 11:127
Kirkland, Edward T.
17:360
Kirkland, J. 27:71
Kirkland, James 3:113;
17:54
Kirkland, Samuel 12:155
Kirkland, Taylor 22:430
Kirkland, Willard 15:127
Kirkland, William 7:127
Kirkland, William A.
22:503
Kirkland, William H. 7:63
Kirkland, William T.
19:21
Kirkland, Z. J. 17:54
Kirkle, Henry 14:187
Kirkley, A. W. 23:153
Kirkley, J. 25:285
Kirkley, Jack 8:40; 26:168
Kirkley, John 1:49
Kirklin, William M.
11:187
Kirkly, William 17:237
Kirkman, James 22:307
Kirkman, John 18:191
Kirkman, L. S. 1:145
Kirkman, Madison 15:8
Kirkman, S. 1:147
Kirkney, F. 3:113
Kirkoff, J. 1:146
Kirkpatrick, --- 22:124
Kirkpatrick, A. 20:288
Kirkpatrick, Albert 10:62
Kirkpatrick, Baltimore
4:35

Kirkpatrick, C. W. 10:62;
20:288
Kirkpatrick, Daniel M.
11:243
Kirkpatrick, David 22:86
Kirkpatrick, David E.
23:263
Kirkpatrick, Edward 1:47
Kirkpatrick, Ephraim
22:483
Kirkpatrick, Gus 18:243;
26:41
Kirkpatrick, Henry 13:32;
23:70
Kirkpatrick, J. 16:205
Kirkpatrick, J. F. 23:37
Kirkpatrick, J. M. 20:288
Kirkpatrick, James 15:69;
22:40, 257
Kirkpatrick, John 15:69;
17:281; 22:339
Kirkpatrick, John D.
11:35
Kirkpatrick, John G.
22:203
Kirkpatrick, John W.
22:86
Kirkpatrick, Joseph 10:62;
20:288
Kirkpatrick, Joseph M.
10:62
Kirkpatrick, King 22:307
Kirkpatrick, Mark 21:73
Kirkpatrick, R. 3:113
Kirkpatrick, R. B. 20:125
Kirkpatrick, Ralph 9:43;
26:125
Kirkpatrick, S. 3:113;
13:92; 14:14
Kirkpatrick, S. G. 20:288
Kirkpatrick, S. H. 8:107
Kirkpatrick, Selden G.
10:62
Kirkpatrick, Thomas
13:129
Kirkpatrick, W. A. 17:110
Kirkpatrick, W. W.
21:239
Kirkpatrick, William B.
5:21
Kirkpatrick, William C.
20:98
Kirkwick, Frederick G.
5:21
Kirkwood, Edmund
24:197
Kirkwood, H. 3:113
Kirkwood, Hugh 11:265
Kirkwood, John 1:47;
10:153; 17:308;
19:174

Kirkwood, John S.
10:122; 20:288
Kirkwood, William 19:81,
174
Kirlan, Hiram P. 22:235
Kirpsey, George 22:307
Kirrick, G. H. 16:269
Kirrler, T. 18:176
Kirsch, F. 27:71
Kirsch, M. B. 7:32
Kirsh, F. 9:146
Kirth, Augustus 22:12
Kirth, Henry 27:73
Kirthland, C. 22:174
Kirtland, James N. 9:66
Kirtz, George 18:294
Kirwen, M. 1:47
Kirwin, P. 13:92
Kirwin, Thomas 26:40
Kisby, Edward 8:73
Kiscie, Joseph A. 18:52
Kiscil, Joseph A. 10:148
Kise, Richard 18:208
Kisenger, Phillip 7:32
Kiser, B. M. 21:31
Kiser, Benjamin B. 22:87
Kiser, Frederick 27:72
Kiser, George 22:503
Kiser, Harrison 25:196
Kiser, Hiram 17:425
Kiser, J. S. 22:203
Kiser, John 21:204; 23:71
Kiser, John R. 22:12
Kiser, Lafayette 18:310;
26:103
Kiser, P. 14:14
Kiser, Philip 8:101
Kiser, Preston 22:87
Kiser, Reynolds 12:82;
16:297
Kish, Stephen 20:183
Kisham, Mitchell 17:110
Kishing, J. C. 8:51
Kishpaugh, George
23:263
Kishpaugh, William R.
13:32
Kisick, S. M. 9:221
Kisits, John 10:122
Kiskendall, Daniel 11:154
Kiskle, George W. 9:182
Kisley, G. 25:196
Kisling, Joseph C. 21:73
Kismiller, Frederick
11:276
Kisner, John 10:62
Kisner, John W. 21:101
Kisner, Samuel 1:48
Kisner, W. 23:308
Kisnor, John 20:288
Kisob, J. H. 8:51

Kissam, Oswald 22:509
Kissel, Austin 18:219
Kissel, J. H. 11:306
Kissell, Frederick 21:73
Kissell, Henry 12:28
Kissell, Michael 18:412
Kissenger, Ward W. 22:483
Kissing, E. 9:84
Kissinger, E. 3:113
Kissinger, Martin F. 9:24
Kissinger, R. 1:48
Kissinger, T. 23:276
Kissinger, W. 25:47
Kisska, John C. 16:133
Kissler, J. 1:48
Kissling, Joseph 22:203
Kissock, William 9:121
Kistar, Jeremiah 12:54
Kiste, A. 14:79
Kister, C. 14:79
Kister, Charles F. 14:187
Kister, O. P. 15:208
Kistler, John 21:228
Kistler, Levi D. 12:54
Kitch, Daniel R. 20:41
Kitcham, Jefferson 17:91
Kitchell, James 20:125
Kitchell, N. 19:291
Kitchell, S. 3:113
Kitchell, S. F. 2:13; 25:48
Kitchen, A. 1:146; 22:40
Kitchen, A. M. 22:203
Kitchen, Elisha 11:108
Kitchen, Eliza 26:221
Kitchen, George 17:54; 22:147
Kitchen, Henry 20:288; 23:37
Kitchen, J. F. 16:297
Kitchen, J. M. 10:192
Kitchen, J. N. 18:176
Kitchen, J. T. 12:85
Kitchen, John 9:209; 11:35; 23:99
Kitchen, Joseph 11:154
Kitchen, R. J. 7:75; 25:300
Kitchen, S. 14:79; 15:38
Kitchen, Stephen 12:72
Kitchen, Thomas A. 13:65
Kitchen, W. R. 20:288
Kitchen, W. W. 11:306
Kitchen, William 8:89
Kitchen, William E. 10:163; 19:174
Kitchen, William R. 10:62
Kitchenbarger, John 23:153
Kitchin, A. B. 13:32
Kite, A. J. 22:257

Kite, Adam 17:249
Kite, Alfred 22:257
Kite, Calvin 10:122; 20:288
Kite, E. 9:146; 27:72
Kite, Elijah 9:146
Kite, H. 14:79
Kite, Hiram 19:174
Kite, James F. 9:36; 18:294; 26:104
Kite, John 1:48
Kite, Richard 18:15
Kitenback, M. 16:41
Kiter, Daniel 15:208
Kithen, Henry 10:122
Kitles, George 23:180
Kitner, D. 12:122; 14:26; 15:363
Kitout, John 15:299
Kitsel, Michael 20:125
Kitt, J. W. 21:354
Kittelson, Ole 21:139
Kitterback, Joseph 9:182
Kitteridge, A. 1:49
Kitteridge, Samuel 9:97
Kittering, --- 12:96
Kittering, Samuel 15:360
Kitterman, F. M. 6:31
Kitterman, J. N. 15:208
Kitterman, Louis J. 9:84
Kitterman, T. M. 25:322
Kitters, John 7:100
Kittinger, Franklin B. 11:333
Kittinger, John 22:453
Kittle, Charles 7:58
Kittle, Solomon 23:123
Kittle, Valentine 20:30
Kittlefield, Charles H. 9:121
Kittman, L. I. 26:40
Kittredge, H. A. 21:354
Kittredge, James 21:354
Kittrell, Ned 22:307
Kittridge, G. P. 8:121
Kittridge, Samuel 20:288
Kittridge, William H. 4:35
Kitts, Allen H. 23:184
Kitts, Alonzo 18:33
Kitts, Mark 17:166
Kitung, Reuben 20:18
Kitzenberger, Frank 7:58
Kitzer, John 9:36
Kitzing, A. 1:48
Kive---, R. 16:205
Kivens, J. 17:495
Kivette, John L. 19:21
Kizer, Ben. F. 23:37
Kizer, Benjamin 17:387
Kizer, Charles 15:38
Kizer, D. 1:146

Kizer, Daniel 17:22
Kizer, G. W. 3:113
Kizer, John 22:483
Kizer, Nicholas P. 22:203
Kizer, P. 16:269
Kizer, Peter 22:87
Kizzer, Frank 11:207
Klabbats, Ed 7:100
Klade, F. 1:48
Klaffey, William 23:277
Klage, E. 3:113
Klages, Diedrich 25:196
Klahare, Herman F. 4:36
Klaman, H. 14:269
Klander, William 13:127
Klank, John 23:153
Klann, George G. 14:79
Klanrod, John 1:47
Klapp, William 11:66
Klapper, E. R. 11:153
Klara, Henry 18:191
Klass, Nicholas 24:95
Klauman, N. 25:49
Klauss, George 22:87
Klauss, Henry 17:91
Klebrenspies, --- 16:97
Klebuber, Joachim 12:28
Kleckner, George W. 23:12
Kleckner, John 12:28
Kleckner, Tilton 11:153
Kledhers, Jacob 12:82
Klee, Andrew 23:123
Kleep, Julius 15:208
Kleeschult, F. 22:115
Klegg, Joseph 7:100
Kleiber, Charles F. 11:127
Klein, A. L. 27:71
Klein, August 7:58
Klein, Conrad 26:168
Klein, Constance 15:38
Klein, Ernst Gustave 21:73
Klein, Frederick 14:187; 21:354
Klein, H. 1:47
Klein, Henry 9:121; 27:71
Klein, J. 19:282
Klein, John 9:182; 14:187
Klein, Martin W. 10:62
Klein, William 14:187; 19:174
Kleinbeigh, Julius 21:31
Kleine, C. 23:263
Kleine, William 19:174
Kleinert, Gol 1:47
Kleinhaus, Frank 7:100
Kleinhessling, Gerhard 19:331
Kleinhof, A. 1:145
Kleipping, H. 1:146

Kleisbee, C. 9:111
Kleist, John 11:231
Kleman, --- 12:100
Klenhuer, George W.
    23:37
Klent, William 21:354
Klenworth, --- 12:28
Klepfer, Amon 21:228
Kleppinger, J. 16:121
Klepser, F. B. 9:182
Klepson, Frederick B.
    19:255
Klernan, --- 15:366
Kley, A. E. A. 21:354
Kliber, Charles 14:79
Klice, Fred 16:205
Klien, Cleveland A.
    21:195
Kliezer, Henry 11:35
Kliff, Mehant 18:143
Kliff, Wehant 8:22
Kligle, Charles 8:107
Klim, Ross 3:113
Klimer, David 8:89
Klimpe, George 8:107
Klin, John D. 17:37
Klin, W. 1:146
Klindirt, A. 17:37
Kline, Aaron 10:18
Kline, Adam 15:38
Kline, Albert 11:413
Kline, Alexander 25:196
Kline, Andrew J. 7:32
Kline, Augustus 17:314
Kline, Barney 23:153
Kline, Benjamin 1:48
Kline, C. 22:203
Kline, C. T. 3:113
Kline, Cyrus 12:28
Kline, D. 15:127; 22:483
Kline, David 10:205
Kline, David C. 16:121
Kline, Edward 12:122;
    15:127
Kline, Eli P. 22:87
Kline, Elias 22:429
Kline, Enoch 14:79
Kline, F. 17:436
Kline, F. C. 22:235
Kline, Francis 24:178
Kline, G. 11:66
Kline, G. F. 1:144
Kline, G. H. 4:36
Kline, George 4:36;
    11:402; 13:32;
    16:140
Kline, Gottleib L. 22:203
Kline, Gustave 16:372
Kline, Gustune 15:343
Kline, Guy 19:81
Kline, H. 1:145

Kline, Henry 10:18;
    11:388
Kline, J. 1:145; 11:155;
    19:81
Kline, J. W. 1:48
Kline, Jacob 7:32; 26:145
Kline, James M. 10:122;
    20:288
Kline, John 11:234
Kline, John B. 13:32
Kline, John W. 22:87
Kline, Josiah 8:107
Kline, Lewis 15:127;
    22:87
Kline, Louis 16:15
Kline, P. K. 23:279
Kline, Peter 8:22, 114;
    18:143
Kline, Q. U. W. 20:288
Kline, Richard 11:182
Kline, Thomas 16:41
Kline, Thomas O. 13:32
Kline, W. H. 1:47
Kline, William 15:38, 91;
    17:54
Kline, Zephonia 22:406
Klinedinst, W. H. 1:49
Klinefelter, J. A. 18:15
Klinefelter, Joseph 16:133
Klinehaus, David 3:113
Klineland, L. 3:113
Klineman, Peter 11:119
Kliner, Henry 19:174
Klinesmith, Conrad
    11:154
Klinetoss, G. 7:58
Kling, Frederick 21:55
Kling, Gothard 23:99
Kling, M. 24:80
Klinger, David 17:251
Klinger, H. 21:101
Klinger, Joseph 13:32
Klingh, Jacob 4:36
Klinglar, Vortus 14:130
Klingler, Voisett 14:130
Klingman, John D. 25:269
Klingsmith, Alfred 21:31
Klingsmith, L. 13:113
Klingsmith, William
    13:113
Klingston, Michael 9:97
Klink, A. 3:114
Klink, F. 13:113
Klink, Nicholas 25:48
Klinker, John 18:191
Klinker, Valentine 15:268
Klinker, William 19:81
Klinn, Cornelius 18:144
Klinsmith, J. 3:114
Klintz, H. 3:114
Kliphan, --- 13:65

Klipp, H. 3:114
Klipp, Melcher 19:21
Klipstine, John W. 21:102
Klitz, George 11:154
Klock, DeWatt 15:357
Klock, Dewitt 16:280
Klock, G. W. 17:435;
    24:182
Klock, H. 24:159
Klock, Hunrich 17:415
Klock, Manning H. 4:36
Klock, Michael 22:162
Klock, Nathan 4:36
Klodt, Joseph 22:167
Kloen, W. 19:21
Klogs, Dietrich 15:278
Klohe, Anthony 27:70
Klokenhemper, F. 12:82;
    16:297
Klomer, John 17:37
Klope, John 24:108
Klopham, J. 19:81
Klopp, Peter 17:352
Klorppman, Henry 10:122
Klos, Clemens 22:124
Klosppman, Henry 20:288
Kloss, L. 3:114
Klotz, Christian 20:147
Klotz, F. A. 1:145
Klotz, Moses 15:208
Kloup, J. 14:79
Klouzer, S. 9:183
Klown, Hamilton 17:356
Kluckman, August 17:99
Klug, J. 12:82
Kluiklet, William 13:65
Klumb, August 23:192
Klump, G. 1:146
Klump, B. 1:47
Klumpp, W. 27:70
Klumpter, Henry 4:36
Klunder, Charles 3:114
Klushum, N. 14:79
Klusner, F. 3:114
Klute, Henry 22:203
Klutts, David 21:189
Klutz, Francis 11:66
Klynn, Cornelius 8:22
Knabaugh, Godlet 7:100
Knabe, Richard 22:257
Knaggs, Charles 22:281
Knap, D. O. 13:65
Knap, Daniel O. 16:205
Knap, Lyman T. 7:32
Knap, Michael J. 25:48
Knaper, J. H. 17:148
Knapher, Charles 10:122
Knapker, Charles 20:288
Knapp, --- 20:288
Knapp, A. 14:300;
    17:292, 481

Knapp, A. J. 14:79
Knapp, Albert D. 22:162
Knapp, Alonzo 20:183
Knapp, Alonzo B. 7:100
Knapp, Alonzo C. 22:463
Knapp, Andrew 7:100
Knapp, Azariah 10:62;
  20:288
Knapp, Benjamin P. 15:38
Knapp, Bernard 12:64;
  15:57
Knapp, C. 3:114
Knapp, C. A. 1:144
Knapp, Charles 22:509;
  25:48
Knapp, Charles C. 14:187
Knapp, Charles E. 13:32;
  20:142
Knapp, D. 5:21; 23:37;
  25:196
Knapp, D. N. 1:48
Knapp, Daniel A. 11:287
Knapp, David 3:114;
  16:97; 17:243
Knapp, E. P. 1:144
Knapp, Edward M. 20:94
Knapp, Edwin 11:414;
  23:12
Knapp, Elihu 4:36
Knapp, Elijah 9:121;
  21:73; 27:72
Knapp, Erastus 9:36;
  18:294; 26:104
Knapp, Ezekiel D. 4:36
Knapp, F. 11:100
Knapp, Francis W. 22:167
Knapp, Franklin 22:147
Knapp, G. W. 23:37
Knapp, George 19:21;
  25:282
Knapp, George W.
  21:204; 22:483
Knapp, H. 13:92
Knapp, H. P. 7:83
Knapp, H. T. 21:355
Knapp, Harris 25:196
Knapp, Henry 3:114
Knapp, Ira 13:80; 16:205
Knapp, Ira C. 19:22
Knapp, J. 3:114; 12:8;
  18:52
Knapp, J. V. 15:208
Knapp, James L. 12:59
Knapp, James P. 10:122;
  20:288
Knapp, John 5:41; 21:117
Knapp, John D. 22:463
Knapp, Justus W. 22:287
Knapp, Louis 17:424
Knapp, Ludwick 17:155
Knapp, M. C. 15:208

Knapp, Morris 17:273
Knapp, N. 27:73
Knapp, Nathaniel 10:62
Knapp, O. L. 9:47
Knapp, O. S. 26:142
Knapp, Oscar 10:62;
  20:288
Knapp, Osson 11:154
Knapp, Philip 3:114;
  12:62; 15:69
Knapp, Robert 14:187
Knapp, S. 11:127
Knapp, Thomas 3:114
Knapp, V. 14:79
Knapp, W. H. 9:84
Knapp, W. W. 27:72
Knapp, William 15:208
Knapp, William H. 8:107;
  26:40
Knapp, William O. 24:95
Knapp, William P. 19:174
Knapp, Xavier 5:52
Knappen, Benjamin F.
  22:406
Knappin, Malvin 11:108
Knapps, Joseph 21:355
Knarber, Adam 26:221
Knarenabalt, Joseph 12:28
Knarr, George 4:36
Knaub, Adam 21:102
Knauer, J. P. 25:196
Knauf, Philip 23:89
Knauff, Frederick 23:37
Knaufft, Theodore 24:183
Knaus, M. 22:203
Knause, John 21:256
Knause, L. 1:98
Knauss, William 11:35
Knauver, Anthony 14:187
Knavel, Thomas 11:155
Kneafsey, Michael 7:63
Kneal, James 25:47
Knealy, John 15:159
Kneas, Elvin 21:355
Knebler, Leonhart 7:59
Knebler, Clement 22:523
Knecht, Clemons 22:430
Knecht, Michael 11:306
Kneckerson, E. C. 25:196
Kneederbrooker, J. F.
  14:265
Kneedson, Ever 13:32
Kneeland, D. 5:21
Kneeland, R. 1:49
Kneeland, William 17:260
Kneele, David 14:187
Kneely, Benjamin 10:99
Kneerison, E. C. 12:80
Kneeshaw, George 27:72
Kneff, B. F. 24:22
Kneff, Harrison 9:97

Kneff, Joseph 24:90
Kneibeller, Victor 14:79
Kneibler, V. 14:79
Kneiderbrooker, T. 14:289
Kneiram, Ernst 12:59
Kneiskern, W. E. 1:146
Kneisley, Jacob M.
  26:145
Kneland, Benjamin
  21:355
Kneply, John 1:48
Knepp, William C. 21:228
Kneppel, W. 1:48
Knepper, Barnard 8:89
Knepper, N. 23:153
Kner, Edward 14:187
Knerrin, Emet 16:154
Kness, Albert 7:32
Kness, W. W. 7:32
Kness, William D. 17:453
Knettles, William H.
  15:127
Kneus, Elvin 7:100
Kneuton, T. 26:40
Knewson, Luther 15:69
Knibbs, Frederick 25:47
Knich, W. 14:79
Knicht, Frederick 13:113
Knickenbecker, William
  H. 16:121
Knickenbocker, L. 25:48
Knickerbocker, --- 14:28
Knickerbocker, Benjamin
  25:279
Knickerbocker, Charles
  13:32
Knickerbocker, George
  23:192
Knickerbocker, Hezekiah
  7:32
Knickerbocker, James
  4:36
Knickerbocker, Wilson
  17:22
Knide, Thomas 11:35
Knider, J. W. 3:114
Knidson, Peter 20:288
Knife, Albert 9:183;
  19:255
Knife, Charles 26:40
Knifer, Patrick 25:196
Kniffen, George 26:40
Kniffen, George C. 18:310
Kniffin, Anige 11:154
Kniffin, B. F. 23:37
Kniffin, George C. 26:104
Kniffin, Gilbert 21:355
Kniffin, J. W. 25:47
Kniffin, James H. 22:171
Kniffin, William H. 4:36
Kniffus, George 9:84

Knifin, Moses R. 10:62
Kniggs, A. 3:114
Kniggs, Charles 15:208
Knight, --- 3:114
Knight, A. B. 1:144
Knight, A. H. 8:22
Knight, A. W. 18:144
Knight, Albert F. 21:355
Knight, Alexander
   14:319; 23:99;
   25:288
Knight, Alford F. 24:22
Knight, Andrew 22:307
Knight, Benjamin 25:47
Knight, C. 1:146; 14:79
Knight, C. A. 9:97
Knight, C. L. 15:38
Knight, Calvin 17:37
Knight, Charles 3:114;
   5:21; 25:196
Knight, Charles H. 8:22
Knight, D. 1:147
Knight, D. H. 25:196
Knight, David H. 5:21
Knight, E. 1:144; 21:31
Knight, E. B. 9:84; 26:41
Knight, E. P. 22:40
Knight, Ebenezer C.
   22:453
Knight, Ed 26:104
Knight, Edward 18:310;
   23:241
Knight, Edwin 9:25
Knight, Elmer 17:91
Knight, Eoreth 11:424
Knight, F. 11:402
Knight, F. J. 1:144
Knight, F. S. 21:355
Knight, Fanary 11:265
Knight, G. 1:147; 16:205
Knight, G. E. 17:152
Knight, G. W. 21:355
Knight, Gad. 8:51
Knight, George 10:62;
   20:288
Knight, H. C. 14:187
Knight, H. E. 25:47
Knight, Haven 22:147
Knight, Henry 7:100;
   24:101
Knight, Henry R. 22:87
Knight, Hiram 24:22
Knight, Hiram T. 11:153
Knight, Isaac 22:87
Knight, J. 3:114; 13:92;
   14:14
Knight, J. B. 3:114
Knight, J. D. 1:145
Knight, J. F. 3:114
Knight, J. M. 9:121; 27:72
Knight, James H. 22:429

Knight, Jefferson 9:55
Knight, John 3:114; 8:51;
   9:36; 11:85; 12:28;
   18:294; 22:40;
   26:104
Knight, John B. 11:243;
   12:28
Knight, John H. 1:48
Knight, Jonathan M.
   13:32
Knight, Joseph 7:100
Knight, Joseph G. 20:125
Knight, Joshua 13:32;
   16:41
Knight, Judson 22:235
Knight, Levi 20:114
Knight, Levi E. 20:151
Knight, Martin 8:89
Knight, Miles J. 11:396
Knight, Morgan 26:221
Knight, Moses M. 10:63;
   20:288
Knight, Nathan 25:269
Knight, Nelson 10:145;
   19:174
Knight, Noah 9:72
Knight, Orland 24:112
Knight, Orrin H. 10:18
Knight, P. P. 9:146; 27:70
Knight, Paul 17:323
Knight, Primas 22:307
Knight, R. 18:33
Knight, R. A. 11:323
Knight, Ralph F. 16:69
Knight, Robert 10:122;
   20:288
Knight, Rodney 11:402
Knight, Russell T. 20:23
Knight, S. B. S. 6:31;
   25:322
Knight, Samuel 24:101
Knight, Scott 8:40; 26:168
Knight, Sebastian S. 9:214
Knight, T. 25:196
Knight, Thomas 5:41;
   21:277
Knight, Thomas H. 16:41
Knight, W. 1:147
Knight, W. D. 16:205
Knight, W. E. 9:55
Knight, W. F. 20:289
Knight, W. J. 1:146
Knight, W. S. 15:26
Knight, Washington 16:97
Knight, West. M. 18:406
Knight, William 1:47;
   3:114; 4:36; 7:100;
   8:58; 10:63; 17:445;
   20:288; 23:286;
   24:167

Knight, William A.
   21:102
Knight, William F. 10:63
Knight, William H.
   17:263; 27:72
Knight, William W.
   11:154
Knight, Z. 22:406
Knightlinger, J. 1:146
Knighton, Franklin 11:154
Knighton, William 25:195
Knile, Sidney 25:196
Knipe, Charles 18:243
Knipe, Henry 10:63
Knipe, Henry C. 7:32
Knipe, John 27:71
Knipe, Thomas 10:63;
   20:289
Knipp, T. 3:114
Knipple, C. 11:119
Knipple, L. 1:145
Knippy, H. 3:114
Knisley, Wilson 20:41
Kniss, Andrew 23:37
Knist, J. 16:206
Knit, William H. 18:144
Knitch, J. C. 1:145
Knite, William H. 8:22
Knittle, A. 1:145
Knittle, Archill 27:145
Knixer, Henry 20:289
Knobbe, Charles 8:89
Knobe, Charles 8:114
Knobeladorf, Charles 7:32
Knoblanch, Gustav
   11:119
Knoble, Casper 13:32
Knoble, Henry 13:113
Knoble, Kasper 16:41
Knoble, P. 3:114
Knoble, William 17:356
Knobles, J. 16:206
Knoblock, Christopher
   24:9
Knoblock, Frederick 7:64
Knoblock, George 17:430
Knobs, John 18:144
Knoch, H. 14:79
Knochen, Albert 21:228
Knock, Adam 17:82
Knock, Amos 22:407
Knock, Andrias 20:125
Knocke, John 23:89
Knocker, Henry 9:103
Knod, Armstead 11:206
Knodder, C. 14:79
Knodle, Sebastian 22:429
Knoell, Felix 21:228
Knoer, Joseph 11:155
Knoer, Theodore 1:47
Knoerer, John F. 19:22

Knoff, Jacob 8:22; 18:144
Knoff, William 24:67
Knofferi, John 10:92
Knoffert, John 20:289
Knoft, Thomas 17:453
Knoftman, I. T. 8:22
Knogg, Reuben 19:274
Knoid, John 16:206
Knoie, J. 14:14
Knoland, J. 23:37
Knoll, George 22:87
Knoll, Mois 18:68
Knollman, G. K. 26:212
Knoloff, Louis 7:59
Knols, J. C. 18:33
Knolte, Fred 3:114
Knoltman, Jacob 21:355
Knolton, David 10:18
Knolton, J. P. 10:18
Knolts, Joseph 16:297
Knop, William 20:186
Knopberger, C'k's 15:69
Knopberger, Charles
  12:72
Knopf, Sylvester 17:277
Knopp, Cornelius 10:96
Knopp, Holmes 22:167
Knopp, Lewis 24:176
Knorad, Jeremiah 12:28
Knorr, Charles 23:123
Knorr, Ruben 18:208
Knossker, Reuben M.
  17:99
Knote, O. S. 23:153
Knott, Eli 14:265
Knott, G. L. 14:331
Knott, George 15:108
Knott, J. B. 20:18
Knott, James 15:152;
  17:265
Knott, James H. 17:54
Knott, John 17:163
Knott, M. F. 16:131
Knott, Richard W. 17:282
Knott, William 17:22
Knotts, Isaac 22:430
Knotts, John 1:47
Knoulton, W. 27:73
Knouse, A. 14:300; 27:73
Knouse, B. M. 14:79
Knouse, C. 14:187
Knouse, Syl. V. 18:397
Knowd, J. 13:113
Knowe, William 8:22
Knowing, Edward 1:47
Knowl, F. W. 12:28
Knowl, H. 3:114
Knowland, W. 19:22
Knowlen, Albert 22:307
Knowlen, John 22:430
Knowles, C. W. 3:114

Knowles, Daniel 20:193
Knowles, David H.
  18:397
Knowles, E. 7:83
Knowles, Edgar 22:464
Knowles, Ephriam 19:228
Knowles, Ferdinand J.
  9:121
Knowles, George 25:48
Knowles, George M.
  17:288
Knowles, H. 3:114; 5:21
Knowles, H. T. 7:51
Knowles, H. W. 23:153
Knowles, Henry 21:149
Knowles, Hiram 11:291
Knowles, Horatio 18:458
Knowles, J. 14:187
Knowles, John 13:127
Knowles, Jonathan 27:72
Knowles, Lewis 21:149
Knowles, M. M. 1:49
Knowles, Marcus 23:71
Knowles, Peter 24:95
Knowles, Richard 14:187
Knowles, Russell 22:339
Knowles, Seth 13:81;
  16:206
Knowles, Stephen 18:243;
  26:41
Knowles, W. C. 1:146
Knowles, W. T. 1:145
Knowles, W. W. 21:355
Knowles, Wesley 8:40
Knowles, William E.
  19:174
Knowles, William H.
  9:236; 26:221
Knowlin, Nims 11:207
Knowls, Fd. E. 27:72
Knowls, H. 25:196
Knowls, Wesley 26:168
Knowlton, A. 14:79;
  18:243; 26:41
Knowlton, August 7:100
Knowlton, Austin C. 7:16
Knowlton, C. C. 15:17
Knowlton, C. R. T. 16:85
Knowlton, E. 3:114
Knowlton, F. 1:144
Knowlton, G. 19:239;
  21:355
Knowlton, G. G. 21:355
Knowlton, G. W. 27:71
Knowlton, Llewelyn
  12:28
Knowlton, M. 11:155
Knowlton, N. 12:28
Known, Reuben 8:89
Known, William 4:36
Knowse, A. 17:479

Knowse, E. 14:300;
  17:479
Knox, A. B. 4:36
Knox, B. 1:146; 23:153
Knox, C. 9:183
Knox, Charles 10:63;
  20:289
Knox, Dennis 7:127
Knox, Dexter 17:82
Knox, Edward 27:145
Knox, Erastus 9:146;
  10:63; 20:289
Knox, George 11:206;
  17:180; 22:406
Knox, George W. 20:289
Knox, H. 27:71
Knox, Henry 10:63
Knox, I. F. 25:196
Knox, J. 3:114; 14:79;
  16:269
Knox, J. L. 11:35
Knox, Jacob 15:208
Knox, James 17:445;
  20:289; 24:167
Knox, James M. 20:289
Knox, Jeremiah 23:313
Knox, John 10:122;
  11:243; 15:208;
  16:97; 17:74, 217,
  349; 20:289; 23:108
Knox, John J. 19:318
Knox, John M. 23:114
Knox, Jol 23:271
Knox, Levi 17:321
Knox, M. L. 11:292
Knox, N. 14:328
Knox, Reuben 9:183
Knox, Robert 9:209
Knox, Robert S. 22:40
Knox, S. 21:163
Knox, Samuel 5:21;
  11:182; 13:65;
  16:206
Knox, Solomon 22:514
Knox, T. T. 15:208
Knox, T. W. 14:79
Knox, W. E. 11:155
Knox, William 9:146;
  11:293; 13:32; 27:71
Knuckles, George 17:148
Knudsen, Knud 17:99
Knudson, Andrew 21:256
Knudson, Erick 21:256
Knudson, Halvor 21:139
Knudson, Ingebret 21:256
Knudson, Knud 21:256
Knudson, Nels 22:40
Knudson, Peter 10:63
Knudson, S. 26:40
Knuston, E. 12:155
Knutson, Ever 23:117

Knutson, Isaac 15:91
Knutson, Knud 20:288
Knutson, Thomas 15:91
Knuttle, F. 25:47
Knuttle, Frederick 2:13
Koan, R. F. 11:306
Kobaldt, Frederick 14:187
Kobb, W. 21:111
Kobe, Frederick 12:28
Koblan, G. 1:145
Koch, C. 19:255
Koch, Charles 22:171
Koch, Christian 10:63;
  20:289
Koch, Conrad 9:183
Koch, D. 7:68
Koch, Edwin 25:196
Koch, Francis C. 22:463
Koch, H. 3:114
Koch, H. F. 11:116
Koch, Jacob 24:67
Koch, John 22:429
Koch, Lewis 15:38
Koch, Ludwig 21:139
Koch, M. 23:180
Koch, Nathan 23:288
Koch, Peter 23:288
Koch, Philip 17:290
Koch, Robert 20:289
Koch, S. 1:48
Koch, Stephen 22:124
Kochansky, --- 5:52
Kochell, --- 22:235
Kochell, J. 3:114
Kochen, F. 1:48
Kochendorfer, C. 1:48
Kocher, Albert 17:22
Kocher, David 21:256
Kocher, F. 3:114
Kochler, F. 1:146
Kochler, John N. 19:278
Kochler, M. 11:340
Kochler, Thomas 14:327
Kock, A. 21:123
Kock, Burnett 8:51
Kock, Carl 26:41
Kock, Charles 4:36
Kock, Christian 27:72
Kock, Robert 10:63
Kockler, F. 27:73
Kockly, J. 1:145
Kocthe, Fred 19:81
Koefer, Carl 26:41
Koefouver, W. 19:81
Koehler, Adolf 4:36
Koehler, Adolph 16:373
Koehler, G. 25:46
Koehler, J. L. 15:108
Koehler, Wilhelm 22:87
Koeing, Fred 21:355
Koenig, Christian 19:22

Koenig, Henry 20:18
Koenig, John 4:36
Koenig, Joseph 23:71
Koenig, Theodor 22:509
Koenig, William 24:67
Koeniger, Louis 17:82
Koenigsmark, Joseph 20:9
Koepfyen, John A. 22:463
Koerner, Henry 9:230
Koesing, Throdore 17:99
Koethe, F. 19:81
Koethe, Fred 13:65
Koethe, William 23:117
Koffel, Rudolph 23:114
Koffer, John 19:22
Koffield, Elijah 7:127
Koffler, Joseph 15:91
Koffman, George 14:79
Koffman, M. 14:300;
  17:476; 27:73
Koffmann, Gabriel 18:310
Kogh, Fred. H. 11:119
Koghill, Josiah 20:18
Kogler, David 1:47
Kohan, Daniel 14:187
Kohen, Robert 18:243;
  26:41
Kohl, C. 3:114
Kohl, Christian 9:183
Kohl, Jacob 19:81
Kohl, Nicholas 17:22
Kohl, Peter 17:91
Kohlehan, Jacob 24:52
Kohlenburg, C. 3:114
Kohler, August 4:36;
  17:82
Kohler, Carl 18:111
Kohler, Charles 18:278
Kohler, Christian 12:8
Kohler, Earnest 23:252
Kohler, Fred 13:65
Kohler, Frederick 19:81
Kohler, Henry 22:167
Kohler, Herman 11:35
Kohler, Jacob 21:256
Kohler, John 9:25
Kohler, John G. 10:63
Kohler, John J. 15:57
Kohler, Josiah 4:36
Kohlhauf, Christian
  10:122; 20:289
Kohlmann, Henry W. F.
  20:98
Kohman, A. 20:289
Kohman, Andrews 10:63
Kohn, Charles 11:182
Kohn, Julius 9:221;
  18:370
Kohnke, John 22:281
Kohntopp, Henry 22:40
Kohrnel, George 15:22

Koil, J. 13:92
Koine, J. 25:196
Koka, John 9:209
Kokemore, Henry 22:87
Kolbe, Adolph 23:153
Kolby, George 19:239
Koleburg, William 4:36
Kolen, R. D. 15:166
Kolenbrander, H. 3:114
Koley, H. S. G. 18:15
Kolfeur, Carl 25:46
Kolford, Jacob 15:127
Kolgore, John V. B. 11:66
Kolhap, Henry 13:32
Koll, Moss 9:204
Kollaporth, Victor 11:119
Koller, John 17:99
Kolling, John M. 23:114
Kollman, G. H. 18:191
Kolme, John 25:287
Kolp, A. 14:79
Kolp, Jacob 10:122;
  20:289
Kolp, John 19:22
Komer, Charles F. 10:92;
  20:289
Komer, Henry 20:289
Komzig, John 19:22
Konader, C. 14:79
Kone, Alonzo 18:413
Kone, James 21:111
Kongune, A. 14:79
Konible, William H. 9:36
Konig, Max 25:196
Konig, William 9:66
Konkle, A. 14:14
Konklin, Philip W. 23:90
Konn, Lewis 23:305
Konold, Christian 14:187
Konrad, --- 20:89
Konstane, Andrew 21:167
Kontz, Moses 22:258
Konuck, Friday 9:13
Koof, George 24:171
Kooger, Daniel 18:52
Koogle, H. C. 10:146
Koohns, John 14:187
Kook, Lassa 17:74
Kook, William 17:292
Kooke, August 10:63;
  20:289
Kooken, John 25:47
Kooker, William 13:65
Kooker, William W. 19:81
Kooler, Abram 11:182
Koom, John 7:127
Koon, Calvin 17:66
Koon, David 14:187
Koon, Hiram 17:277
Koon, Jacob 17:425;
  24:178

Koon, James 11:219;
  17:314
Koon, Mark 22:87
Koon, Matthias 4:36
Koonce, F. 9:55
Kooner, Irwin 18:87
Koons, Jacob 23:123
Koons, John A. 22:112
Koons, Michael 4:36
Koons, Thomas 20:18
Koons, William 17:294
Koons, William W.
  23:123
Koontz, George L. 22:87
Koontz, George W. 8:22;
  18:144
Koontz, H. 21:102
Koontz, Isaac 4:36
Koontz, J. 1:146
Koontz, William 22:203
Koopp, William 11:276
Koops, Charles 21:102
Koot, Chancey D. 7:100
Koothman, U. W. 14:14
Koozer, Thomas 11:243
Kope, H. 1:146
Koperhefer, Daniel
  11:182
Koping, Ludwig 8:51
Kopiske, A. 23:153
Kopp, Carl 22:40
Kopp, Christopher
  10:122; 20:289
Kopp, Frederick 22:430;
  24:9
Kopp, G. 23:153
Kopp, George 14:265
Kopp, Jacob 9:84
Kopp, L. W. 1:146
Kopp, Moses 9:183
Kopp, Theodore 23:90
Koppa, Francis 19:22
Koptz, Philip 15:208
Korb, Nicholas 22:429
Korbick, Peter 10:63
Korby, Leonard 20:289
Korchoffer, Charles 19:22
Korder, J. 10:192
Kordle, W. 2:13
Kore, C. R. 18:191
Korfage, Frederick 11:278
Korff, Charles 22:87
Korger, H. 25:49
Koring, Henry 22:40
Korman, John B. 22:453
Korn, J. W. 13:92; 14:15
Korn, Jacob 22:203
Korne, William 14:79
Kornegay, George F. C.
  22:258
Korner, --- 11:35

Korps, William 9:183
Korrell, Gollford 11:182
Korschot, Dirk J. 20:49
Korsla, F. 21:102
Korsp, William 19:255
Korster, D. 11:243
Korte, Gotlieb 18:144
Korthman, Dietrick
  17:503
Korz, Martin 18:327
Kosa, S. K. 12:28
Kosier, Alex 13:32
Kosier, Alexander 16:41
Kosier, Jesse 15:69
Koslosker, A. 15:208
Kosmer, G. W. 16:269
Koss, George 4:36
Kosselitz, Philipp 22:171
Kossouth, W. 3:114
Koster, William 22:147
Kotcepel, Joseph 7:32
Kotch, John L. 7:16
Koter, Joseph 10:63
Kothe, Emil 24:23
Kotka, Augustus 23:71
Kotsmire, Christopher
  11:119
Kotterman, H. 19:282
Kotterman, Levi 4:36
Kottle, Hubbard 8:22
Kottnoff, Casper 9:244
Kouf, Frederick 19:255
Kough, J. 16:97
Kought, Margaret 22:353
Kouhl, John 3:114
Kouk, John 12:122;
  15:127
Koulchan, William H.
  2:13
Kounce, James C. 23:114
Kountz, Alfred 14:187
Kountz, John A. 4:36
Kourth, Jacob 10:122;
  20:289
Kouster, McChan 22:258
Koutchan, William H.
  25:48
Kouzen, George 22:203
Kowell, John 18:111
Koy, Henry 20:155
Koyn, William 23:37
Koyte, J. 8:64
Kraai, Thomas 12:28
Krabb, A. 25:196
Krabb, Andrew 5:21
Krabb, John 12:72
Kraeger, W. O. 3:114
Kraeselare, Peter 16:143
Kraff, August 25:269
Kraft, Alios 16:85
Kraft, Edward 22:112

Kraft, Emil 13:113
Kraft, Frederick 10:122;
  20:289
Kraft, H. 1:144
Kraft, Henry 12:96
Kraft, W. S. 19:81
Krafts, George 17:107
Kragenbrenk, William
  13:32
Krager, H. 1:145
Krah, George W. 10:122
Krahn, Fred 19:174
Krahn, Frederick 10:173
Kraig, Cornelius 12:28
Kraill, J. 3:114
Krais, Frederick 23:129
Krake, A. 1:144
Krake, J. H. 25:48
Krake, James O. 22:171
Krall, Zephaiah 11:388
Kram, --- 11:439
Kram, William 9:36
Krame, F. 16:206
Kramer, Albert 15:208
Kramer, Alvis 11:265
Kramer, Benjamin 12:9
Kramer, David 13:32
Kramer, Ernest 10:63;
  20:289
Kramer, Frederick 18:294;
  26:104
Kramer, George 3:114;
  22:40
Kramer, H. 15:318
Kramer, Henry 12:28;
  21:102
Kramer, J. 13:113
Kramer, Jacob 10:63
Kramer, Jacob I. 10:63
Kramer, John 10:122;
  17:82; 20:289
Kramer, Josiah 17:251
Kramer, P. 20:49
Kramer, P. P. 21:123
Kramer, Samuel 16:121;
  20:289
Kramer, Thomas 7:32
Kramer, Wintling 8:107
Krammelstacher, S. 12:28
Krammer, F. K. 8:64
Kran, T. C. 18:87
Kranier, R. 1:47
Kranklin, G. 19:282
Krant, Abraham 19:174
Krantz, H. 3:114
Krantz, J. 13:92
Krantz, John 12:28
Kranworth, C. 11:402
Kranz, George H. 20:125
Krapff, John G. 23:180
Krapple, John 14:187

Krappman, A. 16:97
Kraris, John 24:178
Krass, J. D. A. 15:330
Krassipass, K. 3:114
Krate, George W. 20:289
Kraton, J. M. 1:144
Kratz, A. 11:182
Kratz, A. P. 13:92
Kratz, John 17:393
Kratzer, A. 27:71
Kratzer, Henry 14:187
Krau, Thomas C. 6:14
Kraus, Frederick 8:22
Kraus, George 7:7
Krause, Charles 18:278
Krause, Ed. T. 16:97
Krause, Frederick 21:117
Krause, George 22:281
Krause, Magnus 23:192
Krause, Reinhold 23:192
Krausemick, F. 1:49
Krauser, Henry 8:51
Krauss, Edward 20:289
Krauss, Edward M. 10:92
Krauss, Gustave 24:80
Krauss, H. 15:208
Krauss, John 16:143
Krauth, Herman 19:81
Krauzer, S. 19:255
Kray, Charles 9:183
Kreager, F. 15:57
Kreager, William 14:187
Kreamer, E. 1:145
Kreamer, Jacob 20:289
Kreamer, John 16:373
Kreaner, M. 3:114
Kreas, John 17:425
Kreasy, William B.
    10:122
Krebs, Carl 4:36
Krebs, Chr. 24:80
Krebs, David 16:131
Krebs, John 3:114;
    23:180, 200
Krebs, K. 11:439
Kreckle, William 14:187
Krectzer, William 18:243
Kree, Louis 9:121; 27:72
Kreemer, Julius 10:63
Krees, --- 9:121
Kreffin, M. R. 20:289
Kregan, Henry S. 15:304
Kregar, Charles 17:37
Kregel, John 9:243
Kreger, Daniel B. C.
    16:41
Kregor, --- 25:48
Kreider, Godfried 12:55
Kreiger, J. 3:114
Kreiger, Peter 17:91
Kreiger, Purio 7:100

Kreighbaum, Cyrus 17:37
Kreighbaum, Peter 17:37
Kreigle, H. 3:114
Kreiner, P. 13:125
Kreis, William 16:97
Kreisel, L. 16:113
Kreiser, A. 24:23
Kreiss, Frank 10:122;
    20:289
Kreister, John E. 9:121
Kreitzer, A. H. 22:203
Krelan, A. 3:114
Krell, William 13:32;
    16:41
Kreller, George S. 10:173;
    19:174
Kremear, Julius 20:289
Kremer, F. 13:92
Kremer, J. 7:51
Kremer, Jacob 23:37
Kremer, R. 11:35
Kreney, James 10:122
Krennel, F. 14:15
Krentler, William 10:122;
    20:289
Krentz, Otto 8:89
Krentz, William 20:179
Krepp, E. 5:52; 25:196
Kreps, Jacob 13:32
Kreps, William 12:59
Krepsicker, William 9:121
Kresge, C. 19:81
Kresge, J. 1:144
Kresge, Josiah 12:28
Kresge, Paulin 23:180
Kreslin, F. 22:339
Kress, --- 27:71
Kress, G. G. 2:13
Kress, George W. 16:373
Kress, James J. 15:208
Kress, John 18:144
Kress, L. B. 20:133
Kress, William D. 24:183
Kressin, Charles 10:122;
    20:289
Kressin, F. 19:282
Kressle, P. 3:114
Kressler, William 24:9
Krest, H. 1:49
Kretzel, Nicholas 17:451;
    24:178
Kretzer, James 13:32
Kretzer, John 25:322
Kretzer, William 26:40
Kreutzer, John 24:23
Krewson, Simon 22:430
Krewzbeinter, --- 16:15
Krey, John 22:147
Kriaba, E. 3:114
Kribs, John 8:22
Krichoff, Henry 10:122

Krick, T. 3:114
Kridder, A. W. 16:297
Kridler, A. J. 22:203
Kridler, Joseph 11:419
Kridney, H. 13:80
Krieger, Conrad 23:154
Kries, --- 13:65
Krieser, Christian 18:440
Kriester, John E. 27:72
Kriez, --- 19:81
Krift, Frederick 20:35
Krige, Fred 9:25
Kriger, Frank 12:72
Kriger, Fred 9:25; 18:310;
    26:104
Krigg, Jacob 17:22
Krignow, F. 1:48
Krill, F. M. 13:92
Krim, John B. D. 23:286
Krinck, James 4:36
Krinebrook, William
    10:122
Kriner, Henry J. 4:36;
    23:37
Kring, D. 11:16
Kring, George W. 11:66
Kring, Isaac 24:80
Kring, James M. 11:276
Kring, Jansen 4:36
Kring, Joshua 17:54
Kring, Milton 17:319
Krinman, J. 26:40
Krins, Phillip 16:206
Krinsing, Alexander 7:32
Krisan, F. 20:289
Krise, Daniel 22:87
Krise, Daniel D. 4:36
Krise, Jacob 17:22
Krise, John 17:37; 22:430
Krise, Levi 18:219
Krise, William 24:23
Krisher, Jacob 22:203
Krisher, P. 23:305
Krisi, William 10:122;
    20:289
Krissiper, C. 3:114
Kriston, P. 27:71
Kritezer, --- 9:146
Kritzachmer, August
    7:100
Kritzer, Dala 22:87
Kritzer, John 6:31
Krizer, P. 13:92
Krober, Herman 20:289
Krober, Lewis 9:111
Kroche, Henry 18:339
Krocker, Herman 10:122
Krockman, John 18:191
Kroebe, Nicholas 9:25
Kroemmelbein, John
    23:90

Kroes, Peter 16:206
Kroger, Henry S. 16:206
Kroger, John 21:73
Kroger, Martin 26:125
Krogman, H. 9:111
Kroh, David 17:460; 24:159
Kroll, Frederick 4:36
Kroll, Simon 25:300
Krolow, H. 1:147
Krom, D. 16:297
Krom, J. B. 1:49
Krom, Martin 22:174
Kromert, Martiz 20:289
Kromiller, George 12:28
Kron, Samuel 23:71
Kronan, David 19:317
Krone, D. 12:91
Krone, Lewis 26:104
Krone, Louis 18:310
Kroon, C. E. 3:114
Kroon, Peter 8:22; 18:144
Krossin, Frederick 9:201
Krossler, J. 19:239
Krote, Gooliet 8:22
Krote, Henry 3:114
Kroth, David 8:101
Krott, Joseph 27:72
Krotusky, Ernot 22:124
Krotzer, Amos 24:80
Krouer, Morritz 10:63
Krouk, Peter 3:114
Kroupe, William H. 20:289
Krous, G. 7:59
Krouse, Frederick 18:144
Krouse, G. F. 14:187
Krouse, George 11:66
Krouse, H. 17:161
Krouse, H. W. 11:66
Krouse, John 11:66
Krouse, John D. 10:63
Krouse, M. 17:54
Krousse, William H. 10:122
Krout, John 17:54
Kroutwood, Conrad 22:203
Krow, Charles 11:265
Krowe, William 18:144
Krowley, Patrick G. 20:183
Krowser, G. R. 3:114
Krozier, John W. 8:89
Krueger, Gottleib 23:192
Kruer, Jacob 26:145
Krug, William 23:192
Kruger, F. 27:71
Kruger, Fred 26:104
Kruger, Harmon G. 21:256

Kruger, Henry 9:25; 26:104
Kruger, John Frederick 22:167
Kruise, Henry 8:22; 18:144
Krum, William F. 15:69
Krumeile, Henry 10:63
Krumelbein, William 11:119
Krumereide, Fred 20:289
Krummeil, Henry 20:289
Krummel, Christian 10:63; 20:289
Krumnide, H. 12:164
Krumpegle, Herman 22:12
Krumpeter, P. 25:300
Krumsoiden, H. 26:168
Krumwiede, F. 21:31
Krupp, J. 1:147
Krusa, J. 1:145
Kruse, Christian 24:41
Kruse, Christopher 17:54
Kruse, Harmon 22:430
Kruse, Herman 21:355
Kruse, J. 11:85
Kruse, W. 19:244
Kruse, William 22:483
Kruser, W. 9:183
Krushner, Nicholas 7:100
Krute, J. K. 3:115
Krutz, Carl 9:138
Kruzer, Charles 19:22
Kryder, S. 1:48
Krymer, J. 1:49
Krytzer, James 26:41
Kuazo, Samuel 9:13
Kuback, Charles 20:10
Kuben, A. 11:192
Kuber, Jacob 21:32
Kuble, Charles 10:63
Kubler, Henry 15:14; 22:281
Kubler, William 19:82
Kuch, Edward 10:122
Kuchenbrand, Charles 21:10
Kuchne, Levi 4:36
Kuck, Edward 20:290
Kuder, Charles 17:360
Kudwick, Peter 15:292
Kueer, S. 3:115
Kuehn, Frederick 18:346
Kuehn, Ludwig 23:192
Kuemmerly, Wilhelm 22:87
Kuenz, Jacob J. 19:174
Kuepper, Emanuel 21:55
Kuerr, Joseph 18:323
Kufferman, G. C. 9:25

Kufferschmidt, Simeon 22:398
Kuffman, S. D. 3:115
Kuffman, Thomas 22:453
Kufstetter, D. 26:40
Kuglegan, Jacob 21:355
Kugler, Albert 10:122
Kugler, J. 1:146
Kuglow, Adam 11:19; 23:259
Kuhl, Paul 25:47
Kuhle, Charles 20:290
Kuhle, F. 27:70
Kuhler, John 13:32
Kuhlman, Charles 22:281
Kuhlman, Richard 11:94
Kuhlum, John 23:37
Kuhlum, Joseph C. 23:38
Kuhms, James F. 19:82
Kuhn, Albert A. 4:36
Kuhn, Andrew 16:206
Kuhn, Charles E. 1:48
Kuhn, Daniel 4:36
Kuhn, Frank 23:38
Kuhn, Frederick 14:187
Kuhn, George 10:205; 23:192
Kuhn, Jacob 4:36; 13:113
Kuhn, Jesse M. 2:13
Kuhn, John 25:196
Kuhn, John George 12:28
Kuhn, Luding 8:114
Kuhn, Lyric 11:35
Kuhn, Marks 17:294
Kuhn, Peter 16:143
Kuhn, R. 3:115; 14:79
Kuhn, Richard 22:339
Kuhn, S. 21:32
Kuhn, William 22:235
Kuhnan, John P. 21:32
Kuhns, J. B. 20:290
Kuhns, John 12:28
Kuhns, John B. 10:63
Kuider, Mike 9:84
Kuitch, Christopher 11:119
Kukle, Josiah 1:47
Kukuk, G. F. 17:15
Kulbe, August 22:87
Kuler, George W. 12:82
Kules, George 18:243; 26:41
Kulke, A. 25:47
Kull, Christopher 18:311; 26:104
Kull, L. 3:115
Kullmer, George 16:41
Kullum, J. 25:196
Kulm, J. N. 25:47
Kulmen, Christopher 13:113

Kulmer, George 13:32
Kulp, H. 1:145
Kultz, A. 3:115
Kulu, N. B. 25:196
Kumanns, J. 1:146
Kumback, Anton 20:290
Kumfets, M. 7:75
Kumis, I. W. 8:22
Kumley, W. 1:47
Kummell, Ed. W. 19:82
Kummett, J. 3:115
Kump, W. E. 15:208
Kumpf, Ludwig 22:167
Kumple, Charles 27:73
Kumsereide, Frederick
    10:63
Kun, W. 1:147
Kunarl, William 8:22
Kunber, F. 26:168
Kunce, Noah 21:195
Kunder, Jacob 11:119
Kundson, A. 12:162
Kundson, Andrew 8:22
Kundson, George 21:139
Kundson, J. 3:115
Kune, David F. 17:510
Kune, Joseph 8:114
Kune, Patrick 22:339
Kunebrook, William
    20:290
Kunerd, Ferdinand 7:100
Kuney, George W. 3:115
Kung, John 20:290
Kungan, Harrison A. 9:84
Kunger, Charles 14:336
Kunkel, B. E. 23:154
Kunkel, George H. 15:8
Kunkel, P. 19:271
Kunkell, Peter 16:280
Kunkle, A. 13:92
Kunkle, B. 25:47
Kunkle, J. 13:92
Kunkle, J. C. 14:188
Kunkle, J. S. 14:15;
    15:208
Kunkle, John 16:121
Kunkle, S. D. 13:92
Kunks, James 11:306
Kunline, August 13:113
Kunman, J. 18:243
Kunmick, T. 3:115
Kunn, Ralph 25:322
Kunner, Andrew J. 7:51
Kunse, Solomon 13:32
Kunsey, Charles J. 27:73
Kunsman, Henry 23:114
Kunston, Ole 25:283
Kunston, Samuel 9:84
Kunston, Tuliff 9:84
Kunswruebe, J. 13:65
Kunth, Charles 9:106

Kunti, Harvey 19:291
Kuntz, Fred 4:36
Kuntz, George 9:36
Kuntz, H. 23:261; 25:47
Kuntz, Henry 2:13
Kuntz, John 23:90
Kuntz, Lewis 15:91
Kuntz, M. 1:147
Kuntzleman, John 3:115
Kunz, Jacob 10:205
Kunzel, F. 11:16
Kunzil, John 1:47
Kunzman, John 18:311;
    26:104
Kuper, Joel R. 22:147
Kupferly, Caspar 16:147
Kupmaul, M. 17:22
Kuppel, George 17:237
Kuppenheoffer, John
    22:497
Kupperschmidt, E. 15:283
Kupperschmidt, Ed 19:82
Kur, P. A. 15:363
Kurchen, P. 27:73
Kurchner, P. 14:300;
    17:476
Kurft, J. 14:282
Kurg, Charles 25:196
Kurger, Henry 18:311
Kurk, John 16:97
Kurker, C. 14:15
Kurn, D. O. 16:206
Kurna, Thomas 19:255
Kurnay, Andy 21:277
Kurney, Anderson 21:277
Kurr, John A. 11:306
Kurts, John 20:10
Kurty, P. 15:38
Kurtz, B. 24:80
Kurtz, Dan'l M. 22:203
Kurtz, Daniel M. 9:111
Kurtz, George 26:104
Kurtz, H. 1:146
Kurtz, Henry 1:48; 19:22
Kurtz, J. 3:115
Kurtz, Jacob 23:71
Kurtz, John 22:203
Kurtz, M. 1:144
Kurtz, W. 15:38
Kurtz, William 10:63;
    20:290
Kurtzart, John 27:70
Kurz, Ernst J. M. 18:311;
    26:104
Kurz, John 23:90
Kusda, John 8:118
Kuser, M. H. 1:47
Kush, William 13:113
Kushing, John G. 26:125
Kushing, M. G. 9:84
Kushner, Jacob 1:48

Kuslung, C. 14:79
Kusmitz, Ludwig 13:32
Kussick, T. B. 15:152
Kussing, J. 11:119
Kussman, Peter 17:37
Kussnau, --- 17:249
Kusteler, Joseph 14:188
Kuster, Martin 13:32
Kuston, E. 3:115
Kutch, John 11:243
Kuthesons, Sydney 9:103
Kutlebe, Frederick 20:23
Kuton, J. N. 19:22
Kutter, W. 18:444
Kutzachmer, August
    21:355
Kutzner, Julius 10:122;
    20:290
Kuver, J. M. 26:41
Kuyhendal, J. M. 11:327
Kuykendale, W. S. 21:355
Kuykendall, John 10:122;
    20:290
Ky, Moses 18:243; 26:40
Kyers, S. 22:353
Kyes, E. 20:41
Kyess, George L. 2:13
Kyger, W. 10:28; 19:303
Kylander, John 21:32
Kyle, A. 3:115
Kyle, A. D. 20:57
Kyle, Adam 7:32
Kyle, Benjamin 17:163
Kyle, Edward 22:40
Kyle, F. 18:103
Kyle, George A. 20:107
Kyle, H. 11:243
Kyle, I. 19:82
Kyle, Ira B. 11:154
Kyle, J. 12:96; 15:360
Kyle, Jacob 10:28; 19:303
Kyle, James 9:236
Kyle, James M. 20:104
Kyle, John 12:149; 26:221
Kyle, Levi 17:443; 24:159
Kyle, Richard 23:263
Kyle, Robert 11:94; 24:41
Kyle, Rouse 9:111
Kyle, S. H. 22:406
Kyle, T. M. 9:25
Kyle, Thomas 10:122;
    20:290
Kyle, W. B. 20:290
Kyle, William 3:115
Kyle, William A. 17:82
Kyle, William B. 10:63
Kyle, William H. 20:137
Kyler, Arnold 15:208
Kyler, Charles 20:290
Kyler, Darwin 23:71
Kyler, J. 25:47

Kyler, Stephen 21:277
Kyre, Joseph N. 22:203
Kyrk, John A. 18:397
Kyser, Asa W. 4:36
Kyser, George 23:283
Kyser, Jacob 14:79
Kyser, John 3:115
Kyser, Lewis 24:80
Kyser, Peter 10:122; 20:290
Kyser, Stephen 23:309
Kyson, Mathias 10:63
Kyson, Matthias 20:290
Kysonski, --- 4:36
Kyte, Thomas B. 23:90

L

L---, --- 15:17; 23:271
L---, A. 11:341; 20:290; 21:355
L---, A. F. 11:85
L---, A. M. 19:326
L---, A. W. 25:51
L---, B. 15:211; 19:177; 20:46; 26:170
L---, B. C. 15:211
L---, C. 19:177
L---, C. W. 18:33
L---, D. 23:203
L---, D. A. 14:269
L---, D. U. 23:279
L---, E. 21:355; 26:170
L---, E. C. 8:65; 26:170
L---, F. M. 11:307
L---, G. 11:244; 18:68
L---, G. A. 19:296; 20:41
L---, H. 24:112
L---, H. C. 8:73
L---, H. D. 11:265
L---, I. 14:269
L---, J. 23:117, 266; 24:214; 25:51
L---, J. H. 20:57, 290; 21:208; 25:51
L---, J. M. 23:114, 203
L---, J. S. 11:327
L---, J. T. 15:211
L---, J. W. 15:211; 20:290
L---, John 9:55
L---, Joseph 21:355
L---, K. 22:353
L---, L. 20:155, 175
L---, L. F. 19:177
L---, M. 16:373; 23:264; 25:50
L---, M. E. 12:91
L---, N. E. 23:268
L---, P. 18:69
L---, Patrick 16:297

L---, R. 14:269; 20:57
L---, S. N. 21:208
L---, S. W. 17:254
L---, T. H. 17:297
L---, Thomas 23:129
L---, W. 10:32, 192; 11:244; 19:303; 20:57; 21:355
L---, W. E. 20:57
L---, W. J. 24:112
L---, W. P. 11:402
L---, W. S. 20:290
L---, William 11:341; 15:211
L----, Y---- 22:40
L---a, --- H. 25:51
L---ellns, Mark 15:211
L---plant, M. 15:327
La'Bell, Edward 1:50
La---, J. 20:57
La---, John 23:16
Laabs, William 23:117
Laban, George F. 7:59
Laban, Jacob 9:165
Labanhard, Edward 22:40
Labanway, Charles 18:272
Labar, Calvin 14:188
Labarge, --- 10:28
Labarn, Ed 17:152
LaBaron, E. 1:150
Labarr, C. G. 18:397
Labarre, R. 3:115
LaBarron, A. W. 18:278
Labase, Pryor 17:337
Labau, Benjamin F. 22:87
Labaw, David L. 11:276
Labay, R. R. 16:297
Labbannon, J. T. 1:52
Labdell, Asbury 27:77
Labean, Lewis 9:201; 19:282
Labell, Louis 22:523
Labell, Thomas 14:188
Laber, M. 18:69
Labern, F. 11:335
Labey, R. R. 12:87
Labfleirk, George 18:144
Labius, D. P. 19:233
LaBlanc, W. C. 7:100
Lablance, A. 14:79
Lablede, James 21:355
Laboe, Anton 21:355
Labogteaux, Thomas 18:219
LaBolt, J. 3:115
LaBonney, H. 3:115
Labor, David T. 5:21
Labor, S. D. 15:309; 19:82
LaBounty, L. 14:79
LaBree, H. 24:23

Labree, J. 21:355
Labrie, O. 15:57
Labriel, W. H. 21:355
Labriel, William H. 7:127
Labrinch, George 3:115
Labrown, --- 14:80
Labuff, John 19:255
LaBuffer, John 9:183
Labur, Peter 26:126
Labutte, Eli 17:390
Laby, Edward 23:180
Laby, I. 11:157
Lacash, Francis 15:291
Lace, Joseph 4:36
Lace, Marcus 8:64
Lace, William 11:116
Lacelles, Mos 1:51
Lacer, Solomon 20:133
Lacerto, Joseph 23:38
Lacewell, Jasper 10:122; 20:290
Lacey, Charles 16:131
Lacey, Christian C. 20:290
Lacey, F. 9:55
Lacey, Henry 21:291
Lacey, J. 9:183
Lacey, Jacob 18:311; 26:105
Lacey, James F. 20:290
Lacey, James R. 24:80
Lacey, John 10:63
Lacey, John F. 10:63; 20:290
Lacey, John L. 20:290
Lacey, Leroy B. 10:63
Lacey, Nelson 9:209; 18:69
Lacey, S. G. 1:51
Lacey, S. S. 1:52
Lacey, Thomas 26:42
Lacey, William 22:124
Lachan, J. 1:148
Lachan, James 2:13
Lachan, Joseph 25:51
Lachard, L. 13:92
Lachay, James 21:355
Lachemyer, Charles 12:155
Lachetye, John 18:334
Lachey, J. 3:115
Lack, John 18:294
Lack, Peter 3:115
Lack, William H. 9:84
Lacker, Charles 5:42
Lacker, H. 3:115
Lackett, Samuel A. 21:239
Lackey, C. 1:147
Lackey, Elijah 14:188
Lackey, J. 1:147
Lackey, James 3:115

Lackey, John 22:124
Lackey, Marvin 15:83
Lackey, P. T. 3:115
Lackey, William 12:72
Lackey, William A. 24:167
Lackin, Daniel 8:114
Lackleid, J. 14:15
Lacklen, George 13:80
Lackman, Thomas 17:134; 24:198
Lacks, Lee 3:115
Lacky, Oliver 15:38
Laclaid, J. 13:92
Laclair, Alexander 15:208
Lacle, George W. 26:41
Laclese, Samuel 27:78
Lacock, Hugh 3:115
Lacock, John A. 22:235
Lacock, Thompson 22:407
Lacoler, James 18:144
Lacom, George 12:96
Lacombe, Louis 7:127
Lacompt, William 21:355
Lacon, Edward 22:339
Lacon, Perry 7:100
Lacons, John 11:36
Lacord, Gilbert 4:36
Lacost, J. M. 3:115
Lacost, Peter 21:355
Lacoste, H. 3:115
LaCount, Alexis 23:192
LaCount, Edward 9:243
Lacount, I. 21:32
LaCount, Zachariah 15:95
Lacoy, P. 3:115
LaCroix, Franklin 9:212
Lacroix, Franklin L. 21:355
Lacroix, R. 20:10
Lacross, John 10:92; 20:290
Lacruce, William 17:159
Lacy, A. 8:89
Lacy, Andrew B. 17:22
Lacy, Christian C. 10:92
Lacy, Conner 24:23
Lacy, Daniel 21:277
Lacy, E. 25:322
Lacy, H. 11:67
Lacy, H. H. 18:294; 26:105
Lacy, Henry 21:201
Lacy, J. 1:150; 21:163
Lacy, Jacob 9:25
Lacy, James A. 11:281
Lacy, James C. 18:208
Lacy, John C. 8:89
Lacy, Joseph 17:396
Lacy, Joseph C. 10:19

Lacy, Joseph R. 12:122; 15:127
Lacy, Keanas F. 24:167
Lacy, Levi 22:258
Lacy, Luc 26:169
Lacy, Thomas 17:252; 24:67
Lacy, Thomas W. 22:470
Lacy, W. 3:115
Lacy, W. C. 27:74
Lacy, W. S. 9:121
Lacy, Washington 22:203
Lacy, William 11:281; 16:97
Lacy, William B. 12:54
Lacy, William T. 8:64
Ladam, Peter 15:83
Ladbeater, James 3:115
Ladd, A. 3:115; 9:146; 27:74
Ladd, Albert 15:38
Ladd, Andrew J. 22:453
Ladd, C. 3:115
Ladd, Charles 16:133, 140
Ladd, Dustin 4:36
Ladd, George W. 1:50
Ladd, Henry 24:160
Ladd, J. 22:353
Ladd, J. A. 9:146; 11:155
Ladd, J. W. 23:38
Ladd, James 19:228
Ladd, Joseph 8:89
Ladd, Josiah 27:75
Ladd, Lathrop W. 21:73
Ladd, M. E. 17:99
Ladd, Michael 9:25
Ladd, Orange 17:22
Ladd, R. F. 19:224
Ladd, R. V. 7:100
Ladd, Reab 12:92
Ladd, Reuben 16:297
Ladd, Richard 18:311; 26:105
Ladd, Robert A. 22:124
Ladd, S. 25:196
Ladd, Samuel B. 7:100
Ladd, T. S. 27:78
Ladd, W. 13:92; 14:15
Ladd, W. S. 15:343; 16:373
Ladd, Warren 1:49
Ladd, William 14:80
Ladd, Wilson W. 20:186
Laddenbush, J. 3:115
Ladds, --- 18:191
Ladds, J. E. 23:252
Lade, Daniel 14:188
Laden, James 24:67
Laden, John 15:108
Laden, W. 12:92; 14:80
Lader, A. 3:115

Ladere, W. H. 16:280
Ladico, Charles 18:278
Ladiew, J. 3:115
Ladley, James 14:188
Ladon, Stephen 22:147
Ladon, W. 16:297
LaDow, Byron H. 10:122; 20:290
Ladow, William 11:127
Ladro, Peter 16:206
LaDuc, J. 3:115
Laduc, John 5:52
Ladue, A. 19:255
Ladue, Allen 9:183
Ladue, Daniel 12:28
Ladue, Edward H. 20:290
Ladue, Joseph 1:51
LaDuke, Frank 13:125
Laduke, John 11:116
Laduke, Peter 20:107
Lady, A. 3:115
Lady, Anny 26:212
Lady, C. P. 17:282
Lady, Thomas 9:84; 26:42
Laecry, John 19:82
Laer, H. 2:14
Laever, John 14:15
Lafan, W. D. 26:135
Lafang, George 11:155
Lafang, William 22:431
Lafaniel, Mat 24:198
Lafavre, David V. 23:192
Lafayette, J. 25:196
Lafayette, James 5:21
Lafayette, John 13:32; 22:307
Lafeaver, Joseph 7:32
Lafer, John 23:286
Laferman, J. 16:206
Laferry, John W. 9:221
Laferty, G. W. 1:147
Laferty, Michael 11:265
Laferty, Robert 23:312
Laferty, S. W. 11:341
Lafery, J. W. 18:370
Lafette, Henry 19:303
LaFever, D. W. 25:51
LaFever, Jesse H. 11:67
Lafevre, Eli 23:154
Laff, Charles 11:16
Laff, D. J. 20:147
Laffer, John 12:146
Lafferty, J. 1:149
Lafferty, J. B. 1:50
Lafferty, James 26:222
Lafferty, John 12:28
Lafferty, Leonard 14:188
Lafferty, Robert 17:180
Lafferty, William 3:115; 22:87
Laffin, J. 19:228

Laffin, John 1:51
Laffin, L. D. 10:63
Lafflin, Thomas O. 21:355
Lafflur, --- 13:65
Laffoon, W. H. 21:32
Laffy, William D. 22:124
Lafield, J. 19:82
Lafis, L. 1:149
Lafkins, C. P. 9:146; 27:75
Laflen, Augustus 9:209
Laflese, Joseph 7:32
Laflin, Isaac 22:87
Laflin, L. D. 20:290
Laflner, David 23:154
Lafollett, Joseph W. 21:55
Lafont, James W. 14:336
LaFope, Alfred 14:188
Laforce, D. 11:67
LaForce, G. 1:51
Laforce, Isaac M. 21:228
Laforce, Jacob 22:471
Laforce, John B. 18:144
Laforce, Joseph L. 24:41
Laford, Charles 22:147
Laford, Peter 7:100
Laforge, Eli 5:21
Laforge, Elie 25:196
Lafoth, Henry 10:28
Lafountain, John 12:28
Lafountain, Marshall 22:203
Lafountain, O. 22:203
LaFountain, P. 1:49
Laing, D. 1:150
LaFountain, R. 14:242
Lafuer, James 7:32
Lagaker, C. 25:196
Lagan, Thomas 10:63
Lagary, Edwin 22:464
Lagbun, Joseph 9:84
Lager, F. 19:255
Lager, Orten 7:51
Lagertrand, G. 27:74
Lagger, J. 3:115
Lagher, P. 16:297
Laghley, John 18:111
Lagier, David 6:7; 18:111
Lagley, T. 25:196
Lagne, Charles 7:75
Lago, A. 22:520
Lagore, John 18:111
Lagoy, Frank 3:115
LaGrand, G. 9:146
Lagrange, C. 14:80
Lagrange, H. 19:82
LaGrange, O. De. 15:87
LaGrangis, --- 12:64
Lagre---, H. 16:206
Lagru, James 22:339
Lague, Charles 7:80
Lah-te-ya-hola, 25:333

Laham, William H. H. 15:159
Lahan, Edward N 15:316
Lahay, James 7:100
Lahey, John 26:222
Lahey, P. 3:115
Lahflink, George 8:22
Lahguss, John M. 8:89
Lahiff, D. 3:115
Lahiff, Michael 15:353; 16:280
Lahley, --- 3:115
Lahman, Josiah 4:36
Lahn, Henry 20:290
Lahny, John 12:28
Lahser, A. 1:148
Lahue, George 22:431
Lahy, Kam 18:334
Laich, F. 3:115
Laidlaw, W. 14:80
Laighton, Stephen K. 12:169
Lailagaka, W. 16:269
Lain, David 4:66
Lain, F. M. 25:276
Lain, S. 3:115
Lain, S. H. 1:150
Lain, Thomas 4:36
Lain, W. H. 8:51
Lain, William 9:55
Laine, James 22:147
Laine, M. 7:32
Laing, Augs. C. 7:32
Laing, William M. 4:36
Lainkart, Jonathan 14:188
Lainsan, Alvin 18:278
Laint, John 15:299
Lair, G. 25:196
Lair, George 5:21
Lair, H. 25:51
Lairan, James 4:36
Lairch, John 12:72
Laird, Albert 1:50
Laird, C. 3:115
Laird, C. H. 21:102; 23:154
Laird, D. C. 16:140
Laird, Francis 13:113
Laird, George A. 15:305
Laird, J. 20:23
Laird, James 22:40
Laird, Jerome 11:335
Laird, John H. 10:19
Laird, Josiah 10:163
Laird, Reece D. 21:195
Laird, Richard P. 22:147
Laird, Robert 17:37
Laird, Samuel 15:25
Laird, T. S. 19:82
Laird, William 15:208

Laired, Alfred H. 23:114
Lairnine, C. 3:115
Lairson, Thomas 17:295
Laisen, Anders 18:278
Laitch, John 15:69
Laiton, H. B. 10:63
Laivson, D. 19:82
Laizure, J. 22:203
Lake, A. C. 25:50
Lake, A. P. 26:169
Lake, A. S. 7:32
Lake, Aaron 8:22; 18:144
Lake, Alfred 17:447
Lake, Benjamin 10:63; 20:290
Lake, Charles H. 22:203
Lake, Charles W. 17:388
Lake, Cyrel 22:203
Lake, Daniel 11:244
Lake, David 10:205
Lake, David D. 24:23
Lake, Edward 20:290
Lake, Elzy 10:36
Lake, G. W. 13:113
Lake, George 12:28
Lake, George H. 21:355
Lake, George W. 7:68; 12:28
Lake, Henry 11:36
Lake, Horace 3:115
Lake, Hurlburt F. 22:40
Lake, J. 1:148
Lake, James 14:319; 25:272
Lake, James C. 25:277
Lake, Jesse S. 22:203
Lake, John 21:88
Lake, John W. 9:183; 19:239
Lake, Joseph 4:36
Lake, Joseph M. 8:126
Lake, Lewis 11:207
Lake, Peter 21:277
Lake, Robert A. 12:50
Lake, Thomas 11:67
Lake, Vincent 9:36
Lake, W. H. 13:135
Lake, W. L. 19:346
Lake, William 3:115; 11:88; 21:212; 23:154
Lake---, William 25:50
Lakeman, C. 3:115
Lakeman, Charles E. 16:206
Laken, H. 9:146
Laker, E. 1:52
Laker, Oliver T. 10:163
Lakey, Daniel 3:115
Lakey, John W. 14:331
Lakin, A. 3:115

Lakin, H. H. 27:75
Lakin, John 18:144
Lakin, Joseph 8:107
Lakin, Newell J. 9:214
Lakin, S. P. 20:57
Lakins, John 17:22
Lakof, George 21:200
Laland, William 17:143
Laleing, J. O. 1:52
Lall, George 16:373
Lally, John 21:355
Lally, Michael 22:407
Lally, Peter 16:297
Lally, T. 16:97
Lalon, William J. 22:407
Lalor, --- 20:10
Lalor, J. 25:50
Lalson, Lulio 21:239
Lam, Donsy 18:144
Lam, Michael 24:23
Lama, J. 25:196
Lama, Joseph 5:21
Lamal, Andre 21:256
Laman, Adolf 19:244
Laman, C. 3:115
Laman, H. 23:154
Laman, Isaac 13:92
Laman, Jacob 20:107
Laman, John G. 17:260
Laman, Thomas 20:291
Laman, Truman 12:155
Lamar, --- 11:424
Lamar, Elijah 10:122;
   20:290
Lamar, James 23:38
LaMar, John 13:113
Lamar, William 20:291
Lamareau, A. 16:297
Lamareaux, A. 1:150
Lamaree, George 19:174
LaMark, Fred 17:360
Lamarsh, J. 1:148
Lamason, William B.
   21:217
Lamaster, D. D. 23:154
Lamasters, Joseph 22:203
Lamastus, E. 22:203
Lamay, G. B. 25:196
LaMay, Stephen 12:82
Lamay, Stephen 16:297
Lamb, --- 24:112
Lamb, A. 14:80
Lamb, A. C. 15:209;
   16:136
Lamb, Alexander 1:52
Lamb, Alfred B. 18:144
Lamb, Alfred K. 8:22
Lamb, Alvin W. 16:85
Lamb, Amos 13:113
Lamb, Anderson 21:195
Lamb, C. 3:115; 18:33

Lamb, Charles 7:32
Lamb, David 9:183
Lamb, David J. 21:228
Lamb, Dowry 26:168
Lamb, Drury 8:22
Lamb, Dustin 16:206
Lamb, Edward 8:40;
   26:169
Lamb, Edwin V. 21:73
Lamb, G. 9:103
Lamb, G. L. 18:191
Lamb, G. S. 9:214
Lamb, G. W. 3:115
Lamb, George 22:87
Lamb, George R. 7:101
Lamb, George W. 22:203
Lamb, H. 10:163
Lamb, H. C. 18:33
Lamb, Harvey 23:90
Lamb, Henry 19:174
Lamb, Hiram 4:66
Lamb, Isaac E. 10:122;
   20:291
Lamb, J. 9:146; 14:80;
   24:23
Lamb, J. H. 15:294;
   16:206; 19:239
Lamb, J. P. 9:222; 10:63;
   18:370; 20:291
Lamb, Jack 23:271
Lamb, Jacob 8:51; 10:173;
   19:174
Lamb, James 9:72
Lamb, John 27:75
Lamb, John F. 15:336;
   16:206
Lamb, John M. 20:176
Lamb, Joseph F. 11:16
Lamb, Joshua H. 9:183
Lamb, L. 16:206
Lamb, L. C. 7:51
Lamb, Larance 13:77
Lamb, Louis 17:180
Lamb, Lucien G. 16:206
Lamb, Mathew W. 16:41
Lamb, Middleton 8:22
Lamb, Milddleton 18:144
Lamb, Nathaniel 12:28
Lamb, Noah 22:258
Lamb, P. 14:80
Lamb, Robert 17:96
Lamb, S. 1:148
Lamb, S. C. 9:84; 26:42
Lamb, Samuel 12:59;
   16:154
Lamb, Sherborn 4:36
Lamb, T. W. 18:278
Lamb, Thomas 18:413;
   21:32; 22:40; 24:184
Lamb, W. 1:94
Lamb, W. A. 1:94

Lamb, W. P. 4:36
Lamb, William 9:84;
   10:63; 11:265; 19:82;
   20:291; 24:23; 26:41
Lamb, William C. 16:206
Lamb, Zenal C. 16:82
Lambach, Michael 18:144
Lamback, Samuel H.
   11:67
Lamback, William S. 7:68
Lambden, --- 12:147;
   19:303
Lambden, T. F. 9:16
Lambeck, Henry 10:122
Lamben, John 12:96;
   15:360
Lamberson, --- 1:150
Lamberson, Charles
   14:188
Lambert, --- 14:130;
   16:373
Lambert, A. 1:149; 3:116;
   21:189
Lambert, A. W. 18:397
Lambert, Aaron B. 18:370
Lambert, Aaron P. 9:222
Lambert, Alonzo A. 12:28
Lambert, Ambrose 8:89
Lambert, Amos S. 22:203
Lambert, B. 3:116; 9:240
Lambert, B. S. 7:101
Lambert, C. 3:116
Lambert, Charles 3:116;
   27:77
Lambert, Daniel 21:355
Lambert, David 12:28;
   19:267
Lambert, Edward 10:19
Lambert, Ephraim 22:40
Lambert, Erastus 24:167
Lambert, G. 14:80; 16:85
Lambert, Harrison 17:265
Lambert, Henry 19:22
Lambert, Hiram 22:281
Lambert, J. 1:148; 3:116;
   13:32; 21:189
Lambert, J. H. 17:149
Lambert, J. J. 14:289;
   23:204
Lambert, James 14:188;
   18:397; 20:98
Lambert, Jefferson 17:252
Lambert, Jeremiah 17:317
Lambert, Jerome 19:267
Lambert, Jesse 20:291
Lambert, Joel 19:174
Lambert, John 8:22;
   11:67; 15:87; 18:144
Lambert, John A. 22:258
Lambert, John W. 9:239

Lambert, Joseph 3:116; 15:57; 22:258
Lambert, Joseph S. 18:339
Lambert, Josiah 9:183; 19:267
Lambert, Luther R. 7:101
Lambert, Oscar 9:25
Lambert, R. F. 10:122; 20:291
Lambert, S. I. 26:125
Lambert, S. S. 22:203
Lambert, Samuel 16:97
Lambert, Sterling 7:127
Lambert, T. 1:52; 7:32; 23:243
Lambert, Thomas 22:87
Lambert, W. 3:116; 13:92; 14:15; 19:255; 21:163
Lambert, W. H. 25:276
Lambert, Wesley 23:154
Lambert, Wesley B. 21:228
Lambert, William 9:183; 11:156
Lambert, William F. 16:298
Lamberth, Jesse 10:122
Lamberton, George W. 22:40
Lamberton, J. C. 1:51
Lamberton, J. H. 1:52
Lamberton, Lawrence 8:89
Lamberton, William L. 22:87
Lambertson, William M. 17:22
Lambet, W. S. 9:121
Lambeth, Henry T. 9:222
Lambkin, Reuben A. 22:147
Lambkins, Dennis 21:277
Lambley, J. 3:116
Lamboly, Victor 23:286
Lambra, John 16:41
Lambrecht, John 15:302; 16:206
Lambright, A. 3:116
Lambright, J. 12:64; 15:57; 23:154
Lambsher, Jacob 23:277
Lambur, John 22:484
Lamburst, James O. 17:428
Lamburth, James O. 24:183
Lamby, John J. 11:16
Lame, Charles 3:116
Lame, Martin 23:71
Lame, Samuel 19:22

Lamen, F. 14:28
Lamer, George 16:298
Lamer, William 10:63
Lameran, John 22:147
Lamere, Frank A. 13:32; 16:41
Lamere, George 10:163
Lamet, J. J. 17:54
Lamey, Joseph 21:92
Lamey, W. H. 11:16
Lamfert, Otto 21:245
Lami, Peter 5:21
Lamie, George 20:291
Lamier, John 9:36
Lamigan, M. 3:116
Lamika, Edward 16:41
Lamison, George 19:22
Lamitte, Frank 7:127
Lamkin, Frank H. 20:107
Lamkins, J. M. 9:222
Lamkins, James 9:97
Lamley, George 21:355
Lamlilt, T. V. 3:116
Lammel, George 10:63
Lammie, Thomas 22:281
Lamming, John 10:145; 19:174
Lammis, W. B. 22:407
Lammon, L. 14:80
Lammoth, John A. 22:41
Lamney, John 13:113
Lamnon, George 26:125
Lamoine, Henry 16:42
Lamon, A. 11:155
Lamon, James 7:100
Lamon, James H. 10:63
Lamond, L. 14:80
Lamond, Louis 21:355
Lamons, Malcolm 10:122; 20:291
Lamont, Edward 17:74
Lamont, Joseph 25:323
Lamont, M. 1:148
Lamont, Thomas 14:300; 16:42; 17:476; 27:79
Lamont, W. B. 10:122; 20:291
Lamorean, A. 12:92
Lamoreaux, F. 1:149
Lamoreaux, J. R. 13:92
Lamorent, J. R. 16:269
Lamory, J. 25:196
Lamory, Julius 5:21
Lamot, A. 11:85
LaMotte, L. 13:92
Lamoy, W. H. 1:150
Lamp, Augustus 15:38
Lamparker, John 9:111
Lamparter, John G. 23:123
Lampe, August 21:139

Lampe, Christian 8:22
Lampell, Thomas 9:84
Lampert, R. 3:116
Lampford, Z. 16:206
Lamphair, H. D. 9:103
Lamphear, D. E. 1:148
Lamphear, E. 15:38
Lamphear, Thomas 15:152
Lampheart, George W. 16:97
Lampheir, L. O. 9:111
Lampher, D. 25:196
Lampher, David 5:21
Lampher, J. Y. 1:148
Lampher, Rufus G. 7:80
Lampher, T. W. 1:51
Lamphere, Alphonso S. 21:32
Lamphere, J. D. 1:52
Lamphere, Joel E. 22:41
Lamphier, Allstin 22:87
Lamphier, Charles 25:311
Lamphier, James 5:21
Lamphier, John 25:50
Lamphier, N. 1:149
Lamphier, R. G. 25:300
Lamphier, S. 27:75
Lamphier, W. N. 27:74
Lamphire, Byron W. 23:108
Lamphire, V. H. 1:52
Lamphire, William 4:36
Lamphur, E. 25:197
Lampier, Victor 7:127
Lampiman, Thomas 10:19
Lamping, John F. 1:51
Lampkens, J. B. 22:453
Lampkin, A. 23:304
Lampkins, Sidney G. 17:22
Lampley, J. 3:116
Lamply, E. 21:32
Lamply, G. A. 1:147
Lampman, Andrew 7:101
Lampman, J. 1:148
Lampman, John 18:397
Lampman, L. W. 16:140
Lampman, Luman 27:77
Lampman, Peter 13:32
Lampman, W. S. 3:116
Lampman, William N. 10:96
Lampmann, Peter 16:42
Lamport, B. 11:155
Lamprecht, William 13:32
Lamprell, Thomas 26:44
Lamprey, C. 1:51
Lampron, B. P. 27:78
Lampshire, S. 9:146
Lampson, A. S. 14:80

Lampson, Benjamin 7:63
Lampson, H. 9:146
Lampson, Romens 22:147
Lampson, Thomas 14:80
Lampson, William 16:206
Lampton, R. 25:51
Lams, John 9:121
Lamsford, Andrew 17:237
Lamson, A. 9:66
Lamson, A. H. 21:32
Lamson, Charles 22:339
Lamson, D. B. 21:355
Lamson, James M. 8:89
Lamson, Lorenzo D.
  23:71
Lamson, Patrick 9:106
Lamson, Thomas F. 7:101
Lamudge, Alexander
  27:74
Lan, Frederick 18:33
Lana, Alexander 22:407
Lanabel, Samuel B.
  21:355
Lanagan, John 2:14;
  19:267; 27:78
Lanaham, R. B. M. 22:484
Lanahan, James 19:22
Lanahan, Michael 12:59
Lanargan, Thomas 24:9
Lanback, Edwin H.
  20:107
Lanbeck, Henry 20:291
Lancaster, Abijah E.
  21:73
Lancaster, B. F. 9:84;
  26:41
Lancaster, C. 3:116
Lancaster, Charles 4:36
Lancaster, E. 3:116;
  22:497
Lancaster, Edward 6:25
Lancaster, Ezra C. 16:42
Lancaster, G. 17:134;
  24:198
Lancaster, G. H. 1:149
Lancaster, George 24:198
Lancaster, Henry 22:87;
  25:50
Lancaster, J. 1:148
Lancaster, J. C. 27:75
Lancaster, J. H. 9:146
Lancaster, J. W. 15:209
Lancaster, James 22:464
Lancaster, James H.
  20:103
Lancaster, John 25:334;
  27:76
Lancaster, L. L. 16:42
Lancaster, L. N. 18:370
Lancaster, L. O. 14:188
Lancaster, Lewis N. 9:222

Lancaster, M. 25:197
Lancaster, Madison 5:42
Lancaster, Mason S.
  18:243; 26:42
Lancaster, Moses 19:174
Lancaster, Rafe 9:70
Lancaster, T. M. 27:74
Lancaster, Thomas 13:32
Lancaster, W. 9:55; 18:87
Lancaster, W. K. 12:72
Lancaster, W. R. 15:27
Lancaster, W. T. 19:22
Lancaster, William J.
  22:258
Lancaster, Willis 6:13
Lancaster, Z. F. 24:198
Lancaster, Z. T. 17:134
Lance, Charles 21:32
Lance, Frederick 25:51
Lance, George W. 9:55
Lance, Isaac 22:203
Lance, Jacob A. 27:77
Lance, Jacob J. 9:121
Lance, John 11:187
Lance, Pomfrey 27:76
Lance, Pompey 9:133
Lance, R. 14:188
Lance, S. 18:243; 26:43
Lanceford, John D.
  22:503
Lanceford, William F.
  12:169
Lancer, John W. 26:244
Lancer, Louis 13:79
Lanch, E. 22:235
Lanchlin, S. 21:32
Lancre, William 4:36
Lancy, Augustus L. 9:84
Lancy, Byran 25:311
Lancy, Eugene 26:212
Lancy, George F. 27:74
Land, Adam 7:127
Land, Alphonso 9:103
Land, Anthony 7:127
Land, Bill 21:355
Land, C. M. 17:203
Land, Charles 26:42
Land, George 14:188
Land, George B. 1:50
Land, James M. 10:208
Land, John 18:33
Land, Laensa S. 15:166
Land, Mathew D. 13:32
Land, Merton J. 14:188
Land, Thomas 18:33
Land, Wesley A. 17:207
Land, Willis 17:54
Landaner, Moses 23:123
Landback, David 15:209
Landboys, William 18:339
Landcraft, S. W. 11:120

Landen, Cyre 20:291
Landen, George 8:89
Landen, John 19:82
Landen, Joseph 22:353
Landen, Richard 20:291
Landen, William 19:318
Landenbach, Bernard
  25:197
Landenberger, M. 11:265
Landenen, J. 27:75
Lander, --- 3:116; 9:183
Lander, Alden 25:197
Lander, Charles 20:291
Lander, Frank 4:36
Lander, James 27:77
Lander, Jesse 9:201
Lander, John 5:21; 25:197
Lander, Marion 6:11
Landerbaugh, D. 12:155
Landerdale, R. F. 18:397
Landergrab, John 7:101
Landerman, George
  11:156
Landerman, James 11:414
Landers, A. 9:146; 13:113
Landers, Alexander
  21:356
Landers, C. 3:116
Landers, Charles 14:80
Landers, Jacob 10:122;
  20:291
Landers, James 24:198
Landers, Joseph N. 19:239
Landers, Julius B. 9:25;
  18:311; 26:105
Landers, Michael 22:12;
  27:75
Landers, N. 9:146
Landers, Nathaniel B.
  22:430
Landers, Nicholas 23:154
Landers, P. 10:63; 20:291
Landers, S. 14:80
Landers, W. 16:206
Landers, W. H. 20:291
Landers, William H. 10:63
Landes, Abraham 27:75
Landes, Noah 22:431
Landess, Robert C. 21:123
Landetzer, Henry 21:217
Landfriel, George 24:67
Landguest, Charles 9:16
Landham, G. 3:116
Landiers, W. 11:428
Landies, T. J. 20:291
Landills, J. P. 13:32
Landis, Albert 17:180
Landis, Allen 12:28
Landis, Daniel 4:37
Landis, Jacob 22:203
Landis, John 5:21

Landis, John B. 13:32
Landis, William B. 23:90
Landley, J. W. 17:405
Landlin, William 24:59
Landman, Jourdan 22:307
Landman, William 5:42;
  22:514; 25:197
Landon, Almond 20:189
Landon, Andrew 1:49
Landon, Charles 10:122
Landon, Christopher C.
  22:112
Landon, Cyre 10:122
Landon, E. C. 1:148
Landon, Frederick 22:147
Landon, George W.
  18:208
Landon, Henry 17:435
Landon, J. 16:269
Landon, J. W. 11:265
Landon, James C. 23:108
Landon, John 17:37
Landon, L. 17:212
Landon, L. I. 25:197
Landon, Orin 21:256
Landon, W. O. 9:55
Landon, William 20:183
Landorney, Leonard
  24:101
Landower, Morris 23:38
Landpher, J. 25:197
Landre, Martin 9:209
Landreth, F. 26:169
Landreth, J. 23:252
Landreth, John 17:415
Landria, John 9:209
Landrills, J. P. 16:42
Landrith, John J. 24:153
Landroche, G. 1:149
Landron, Abram 7:127
Landrose, Samuel 18:191;
  26:212
Landrum, H. 5:42; 25:197
Landrum, James W.
  17:207
Landrum, John 7:101
Landry, C. 23:154
Landry, Wyatt 9:209
Landsburg, William
  25:197
Landsey, Benjamin
  21:356
Landt, William M. 12:55
Landthaler, George 19:82
Landue, Henry 24:175
Landus, Henry 19:174
Landwehr, Andrew
  22:124
Landwehr, Vicktor 24:52
Landy, A. B. 27:74
Landy, A. W. 22:203

Landy, Raymond 8:124
Landzebt, Phillip 19:22
Lane, --- 15:311; 19:82
Lane, A. 1:52, 94
Lane, A. B. 1:150
Lane, A. H. 1:51; 18:191
Lane, A. J. W. 22:258
Lane, Abraham 8:40;
  14:188; 26:169
Lane, Alex H. 11:36
Lane, Alfred E. 9:156
Lane, Allen 8:89; 17:419
Lane, Alonzo 17:102
Lane, Alonzo P. 23:277
Lane, Anderson 10:96
Lane, Andrew 17:180;
  21:14
Lane, Ann E. 27:75
Lane, Arnos 3:116
Lane, B. 11:243
Lane, Benjamin M. 13:32
Lane, C. 3:116; 10:28
Lane, C. W. 16:373
Lane, Charles 3:116; 9:84;
  26:42
Lane, Charles W. 11:35
Lane, D. 3:116; 22:307
Lane, D. E. 9:55
Lane, Daniel 21:139
Lane, Doctrine C. 17:273
Lane, Dustin 13:65
Lane, E. 11:327; 14:269,
  282; 16:206
Lane, E. P. 21:355
Lane, Edward 4:66; 7:101;
  14:188
Lane, Elias E. 24:9
Lane, G. H. 16:206
Lane, George 17:37;
  22:307
Lane, George W. 18:311;
  22:307; 26:105
Lane, Giles 22:430
Lane, H. B. 23:154
Lane, H. M. 25:197
Lane, Henderson 22:307
Lane, Henry 18:33
Lane, Horace 15:3
Lane, Hugh B. 22:41
Lane, J. 1:52, 148; 3:116;
  7:32
Lane, J. Congrave 10:123;
  20:291
Lane, J. D. 1:147
Lane, J. H. 3:116; 23:38;
  27:77
Lane, J. K. 25:49
Lane, J. M. 11:265
Lane, J. W. 3:116
Lane, Jacob H. 8:89;
  18:208

Lane, James 16:85; 19:82;
  21:277
Lane, James K. 2:14
Lane, James M. 22:503
Lane, James R. 9:84;
  26:41
Lane, Jerome H. 18:406
Lane, Job 11:333
Lane, John 11:182, 219;
  17:337; 19:174;
  22:258
Lane, John L. 1:52
Lane, John M. 9:201;
  19:291; 23:154
Lane, John W. 26:41
Lane, Joseph 9:43;
  22:399; 26:126
Lane, Joseph B. 10:92;
  20:291
Lane, Joseph L. 11:276
Lane, Joseph L. W.
  22:258
Lane, Joshua A. 9:84
Lane, Joshua D. 9:16
Lane, L. 11:265; 15:209
Lane, L. D. 9:146; 27:75
Lane, L. E. 3:116
Lane, Lemon 19:174
Lane, Lewis 18:406;
  24:198
Lane, M. 13:92; 19:82
Lane, M. C. 18:243; 26:44
Lane, Mack 9:160
Lane, Mark 7:71
Lane, Milrady 27:78
Lane, Morace 13:125
Lane, Moses H. 17:37
Lane, Nelson M. 24:52
Lane, Noah B. 24:174
Lane, P. A. 11:94
Lane, Patrick 21:355
Lane, Renson 25:197
Lane, Richard 6:17;
  18:87; 22:307
Lane, Richard A. 22:41
Lane, S. H. 1:51
Lane, S. M. 13:125
Lane, Sampson 17:149
Lane, Samuel 27:77
Lane, Sanders C. 24:89
Lane, Silas 10:63; 20:291
Lane, Stanton 15:38
Lane, Stuart L. 1:52
Lane, T. 16:206; 21:123
Lane, Thaddeus W.
  19:174
Lane, Thomas 9:159
Lane, Timothy 12:60
Lane, Trueman 2:14
Lane, Truman 25:51
Lane, V. 3:116

Lane, W. 1:149; 7:32
Lane, W. P. 7:101
Lane, West 21:277
Lane, William 7:127;
    10:63; 13:81, 113;
    16:206; 17:166;
    20:291; 21:356;
    22:258; 24:153
Lane, William A. 25:197
Lane, William B. 1:49
Lane, William D. F.
    21:228
Lanear, Henry 22:514
Laneb, Edward 13:113
Lanee, George W. 10:19
Laneer, Lewis 16:206
Laneer, M. 14:80
Lanegan, Andrew 18:339
Lanegan, John 26:221
Lanegar, John 16:97
Lanegon, J. F. 22:203
Lanels, John 8:22
Laner, John 4:36
Laner, John H. 17:110
Laner, William 27:77
Lanes, Wesley 7:101
Laneson, Regnald 11:333
Lanetirey, James 9:43
Laney, Andrew J. 23:71
Laney, C. 9:111
Laney, James 21:163
Laney, John 21:277
Laney, John J. 11:94
Laney, W. H. 14:80
Lanfell, Hans Oleson
    21:256
Lanfer, Rodolph 14:188
Lanfield, William 12:29
Lanfrear, A. 1:98
Lanfreet, Otto 21:102
Lang, --- 12:168
Lang, A. 3:116
Lang, Andrew 12:59
Lang, Augustus 18:117;
    19:329
Lang, Benjamin 7:127
Lang, C. 3:116
Lang, C. H. 1:50
Lang, Charles 18:243
Lang, F. 1:148
Lang, G. H. 14:80
Lang, George 1:50
Lang, H. R. 21:123
Lang, Harrison 7:127
Lang, Isaac 14:242
Lang, J. 3:116; 14:130
Lang, Jacob F. 8:51;
    21:139
Lang, James 7:101
Lang, James B. 21:55
Lang, James D. 15:353

Lang, James M. 22:484
Lang, John 7:101; 21:256;
    22:484; 27:146
Lang, Joseph 12:72; 15:38
Lang, L. 27:74
Lang, Lawrence 4:37
Lang, Levi 24:173
Lang, Lewis 17:423
Lang, Lorenz 22:281
Lang, M. 12:72
Lang, Peter 7:127
Lang, R. N. 4:37
Lang, Robert 7:127
Lang, T. L. 25:197
Lang, Thomas 19:318
Lang, W. W. 14:80
Lang, William 1:52;
    7:127; 22:520
Lang, William W. 3:116
Langan, J. 1:52
Langan, James 18:323
Langan, Patrick 10:63;
    20:291
Langanheim, L. 26:43
Langankeim, L. 18:243
Langbough, Samuel 13:65
Langdell, Miles 12:28
Langdell, William 3:116
Langden, George 6:17
Langden, Peter 12:54
Langdon, A. M. 3:116
Langdon, B. 1:147
Langdon, C. A. 1:148
Langdon, Daniel 22:87
Langdon, Frank 22:307
Langdon, George 22:235
Langdon, J. J. 25:197
Langdon, James 9:16
Langdon, L. M. 25:50
Langdon, Oliver 9:103;
    18:339
Langdon, Seth 22:115
Lange, Anias L. 16:42
Lange, Charles 13:32
Lange, H. 24:80
Lange, Henry 17:212
Lange, Leonard 21:356
Lange, Onias L. 13:32
Langenbury, A. 18:219
Langenckhousen, H.
    19:331
Langendefer, Michael
    19:22
Langenfelt, Fred 21:245
Langer, Edward 23:192
Langer, J. B. 2:14
Langerhand, Charles 9:66
Langey, Dennis 9:183
Langford, B. 14:242;
    27:79
Langford, G. M. 25:197

Langford, Harvey 10:63;
    20:291
Langford, Henry 8:40;
    26:169
Langford, James 17:91
Langford, James H.
    22:258
Langford, John 9:204
Langford, Lazarus 22:307
Langford, Peter 6:25
Langford, Robert 19:47
Langford, William 23:71
Langford, Zephaniah
    22:453
Langha, W. 3:116
Langham, George W.
    22:87
Langham, John W. 24:89
Langhemis, H. 14:188
Langhinais, J. L. 3:116
Langhlin, D. 3:117
Langhorst, Andreas
    21:117
Langhrey, L. C. 18:144
Langin, A. 3:116
Langinhouse, N. 22:307
Langkrick, Bruno 20:291
Langley, A. 1:147
Langley, Andrew A. 10:19
Langley, C. A. 21:356
Langley, Charles 10:63
Langley, E. 13:135;
    19:347
Langley, E. G. 3:116
Langley, G. 3:116
Langley, George 6:22;
    7:101; 12:28
Langley, George A. 21:73
Langley, George W.
    19:228
Langley, Henry 14:80
Langley, J. F. 17:102
Langley, John 11:396
Langley, Joseph K. 21:356
Langley, L. 9:183
Langley, L. F. 3:116;
    14:188
Langley, L. W. 9:146;
    27:75
Langley, Laurence 7:101
Langley, M. 9:161; 27:78
Langley, Samuel 5:42
Langley, Thomas 5:42;
    7:101; 21:356
Langly, J. G. 1:50
Langman, J. 14:315
Langood, George 13:32
Langribe, Augustus
    11:323
Langruff, William 25:197
Langry, S. 25:197

Langsaff, R. 3:116
Langsden, David 8:89
Langsden, John 16:42
Langsdon, Abner G. 11:94
Langston, --- 13:130
Langston, Isaiah 7:127
Langston, Jesse 26:169
Langston, R. 25:197
Langstone, Jesse 8:40
Langstrath, George 12:155
Langton, W. P. 10:123; 20:291
Languish, P. 21:111
Langulback, E. 15:209
Langwell, Thomas 23:114
Langworthy, L. C. 24:23
Lanham, Henry 3:116
Lanham, James A. 22:431
Lanham, James P. 22:453
Lanham, Samuel 21:55
Lanhan, William L. 23:99
Lanhardie, C. W. 18:33
Lanhill, --- 17:271
Lanhorn, Burton 24:41
Lanick, B. 15:57
Lanigan, Jacob 18:112
Lanigan, James 18:87
Lanigan, James F. 9:183
Lanigan, John 9:183; 23:12
Lanigan, O. 18:33
Lanigor, John 20:10
Laniker, Edward 13:32
Lanimger, Adam 12:54
Lanimore, William J. 21:14
Laning, R. E. 15:209
Laning, Robert 16:97; 18:243
Laning, Rufus 8:89
Lanis, --- 26:222
Lanis, B. C. 12:147
Lanis, James C. 11:36
Lanisch, W. P. 21:356
Lanisher, W. 15:343
Lanison, Wallace 3:116
Lank, --- 19:82
Lank, W. 15:4
Lanke, August 8:22
Lankerman, John L. 11:244
Lankester, Banjamin 8:51
Lankford, Daniel E. 19:22
Lankford, John J. 22:453
Lanklever, J. 16:206
Lankoff, Henry 13:65; 16:207
Lankoh, --- 21:167
Lankow, Frederick 11:192
Lanler, J. 14:257
Lanless, J. J. 16:42

Lanman, George 9:43
Lann, A. 24:88
Lann, Thomas 8:22
Lannaghan, E. 1:98
Lannan, Dennis 19:82
Lanner, William 1:50
Lannering, Thomas 8:73
Lanneringer, Theo 12:146
Lannigan, J. 25:49
Lannigan, M. 13:32
Lannigon, Henry W. 23:204
Lanning, A. 3:116
Lanning, F. 27:74
Lanning, G. 26:44
Lanning, George 9:84
Lanning, H. B. 3:116
Lanning, Henry 21:228
Lanning, Isaac 11:307
Lanning, James W. 24:80
Lanning, John 17:451
Lanning, Joseph 11:243
Lanning, L. M. 10:63
Lanning, Robert 26:43
Lanning, Thomas 21:356
Lanning, W. 1:147
Lanning, Z. M. 20:291
Lannis, Jacob 23:71
Lannis, T. 27:74
Lannon, A. W. 16:207
Lannon, Dennis 15:360
Lannox, William 27:74
Lannphare, G. W. 3:116
Lanoir, Julian 23:154
Lanon, J. L. 3:116
Lanovier, H. N. 21:356
Lanow, --- 14:269
Lanping, --- 15:57
Lanry, James 25:49
Lans, Henry 17:149
Lans, Peter 13:32
Lansbury, C. 27:78
Lansbury, William 3:116
Lansdale, Lewis 12:173
Lansdale, T. C. 15:8
Lansdale, Thomas C. 12:72
Lansdon, Richard 10:123
Lansdon, W. H. 3:116
Lansdown, Amos J. 22:41
Lansdown, Kizer A. 22:41
Lanse, L. M. 16:269
Lansell, R. P. 25:197
Lansey, W. 13:92
Lansford, James 26:42
Lansford, Marshall 22:307
Lansinberger, D. 9:111
Lansing, G. 3:116
Lansing, Isaac 14:282
Lansing, John 24:178
Lansing, Levi 24:101

Lansing, Osro 24:160
Lansing, Ozro 17:443
Lansing, Rufus 8:114
Lansing, William 3:116
Lanskin, W. C. 11:293
Lansley, Lorenzo 20:291
Lanson, Charles 10:123
Lanson, G. 1:147
Lanson, George 22:308
Lanson, J. 3:116
Lanson, P. J. 27:74
Lanson, Richard 16:67
Lanson, William 21:356
Lansop, J. 3:116
Lansphort, Zebina 9:240
Lanspon, Benjamin 11:424
Lansrear, Richard 22:41
Lansshear, G. F. 11:116
Lanster, Henry 1:49
Lansy, A. B. 19:174
Lant, Charles H. 12:169
Lant, F. 14:80
Lant, John W. 8:65
Lantenslayer, J. 9:183
Lantenslayer, Leonard 22:203
Lanterman, J. V. 2:14; 25:51
Lanthroop, William 16:42
Lanthrop, W. H. 19:22
Lantis, T. J. 10:63
Lanton, Rusha 9:133
Lanton, William 5:21
Lantrip, Miles G. 10:96
Lantrup, John 11:108
Lantry, John 15:94
Lantz, Albert 4:37
Lantz, Franklin 22:484
Lantz, Jacob 23:286
Lantz, William 3:117; 22:87
Lantzenheiser, D. 14:188
Lanx, J. 27:79
LaPage, A. 16:207
Lapaint, Charles 23:154
Lapairre, Joseph 21:356
Lapan, A. 25:197
Lapcam, A. 3:116
Lape, Andrew 7:101
Lape, C. 1:148
Lape, Edward 10:63
Lape, J. 3:116
Lape, John E. 7:101
Lape, Peter 4:37
Lape, W. 14:257
Lapede, Jacob 11:207
Lapel, Edward 23:108
Laper, William 9:43
Lapham, A. 1:147
Lapham, Amasa 15:57

Lapham, Amos 16:42
Lapham, D. 13:81; 16:207
Lapham, E. 11:320
Lapham, Ira B. 4:37
Lapham, J. 21:139
Lapham, Jonathan A.
16:42
Lapham, Jonathan H.
13:32
Lapham, R. 14:80
Lapham, W. W. 12:122
Laphand, John 9:16
Laphire, A. 17:249
Lapier, John 12:96;
14:188; 15:360;
19:82
LaPiere, N. 25:197
Lapin, Abraham 5:21
Lapine, Mathew 15:39
Laping, J. 16:207
Lapka, August 18:278
Lapland, John 12:50
Laplant, A. 1:51
Lapman, Daniel 25:197
Lapman, Simon 13:32
LaPoint, Alexander
22:203
LaPoint, Edward 17:360
LaPoint, Edwin 13:113
LaPoint, J. 8:114
LaPoint, Lewis 12:100
Lapoint, Otis C. 11:287
Lapoint, Peter 13:32
LaPointe, J. 8:117
Lapointe, J. 18:330
Lapointe, John 8:89
Lapold, John 12:29
Lapold, Martin 8:51
Laport, B. 15:127
LaPort, D. 9:146; 27:75
Laport, Oliver 9:163
Laport, Thomas C. 13:32
LaPorte, Isaac 23:71
Laporte, John 21:356
Laporte, L. 9:111
Lapp, Aaron 20:125
Lapp, B. J. 27:77
Lapp, E. 17:54
Lapp, Ed 24:198
Lapp, Edward 17:455
Lapp, John 22:147;
26:105
Lapp, Samuel 22:41
Lapp, Silas 10:163;
19:174
Lappam, W. W. 15:127
Lappan, L. H. 3:116
Lappen, P. 16:97
Lappine, Arthur 11:155
Lappins, W. H. 19:255
Lappue, H. J. 15:108

Laprirret, J. 3:116
Laps, S. J. 11:414
Lapse, Lewis 17:455;
24:198
Lapsley, Albert 7:127
Lapson, Mat 18:52
Lapter, J. P. 9:227
Laque, Charles 25:300
Larabe, Charles 27:77
Larabee, B. B. 16:298
Larabee, Charles E. 9:121
Larabee, G. 1:148
Larabee, Hiram 21:256
Larabee, J. B. H. 1:148
Larabee, L. M. 20:291
Larabee, N. H. 1:51
Larabee, T. E. 18:112
Larabee, Theo 20:291
Larach, W. H. 9:146
LaRache, Frank 9:13
Laracy, John M. 15:152
Larally, Joseph 10:163
Laramere, John C. 9:231
Larbay, John 20:41
Larbays, William 20:291
Larcan, Bowlan 17:395
Larcer, George E. 24:52
Larces, Benjamin 12:64
Larcks, G. 3:116
Larcom, William 15:209
Larcombe, John 9:111
Larcorn, Charles B. 17:37
Larcum, Austin 11:207
Lard, C. W. 19:282
Lard, F. 9:183
Lard, George B. 10:163;
19:175
Lard, H. O. 3:117
Lard, Jonas 21:206
Lard, Josiah 19:175
Lard, K. T. 11:333
Larder, G. W. 19:228
Larder, Z. 21:356
Lards, John 18:144
Lardwig, Lewis 9:111
Lare, C. E. 25:50
Lare, Richard M. 17:232
Lareen, Knoth 24:173
Lareia, Edwards 9:183
Laremore, John C. 20:291
Laren, George 4:66
Laren, William 20:291
Larenberg, Lewis 20:291
Larene, J. 21:204
Laretts, W. 15:209
LaReve, Anthony D.
13:32
Larew, I. 21:102
Larew, J. W. 17:166
Larew, Thomas J. 17:504
Larey, Armstrong 18:87

Larey, John O. 22:520
Larey, Joseph 20:291
Large, Allison H. 27:79
Large, Ambrose 17:15
Large, Andrew L. 22:258
Large, B. F. 12:72
Large, Christopher 21:139
Large, George 22:258
Large, Michael 3:117
Large, R. F. 15:57
Large, Robert 10:123;
20:291
Large, W. 11:265
Large, William 3:117;
17:37
Largeat, Nelson 20:98
Largem, Turner 19:175
Largent, J. W. 10:123;
20:291
Largent, James W. 21:228
Largent, Jonathan L.
24:52
Largerson, James 10:63
Larham, G. W. 14:80
Laribbe, L. 3:117
Laribee, John 23:154
Larid, John 22:339
Larid, L. 13:113
Larimer, J. 3:117
Larimer, John 17:321
Larimore, D. M. 21:240
Larimore, J. E. 1:148
Larimore, William B.
17:201
Laringer, Joseph 17:111
Larison, A. 3:117
Larison, A. J. 17:326
Larison, Gustavus 10:123;
20:291
Larke, J. A. 3:117
Larken, Miller 4:66
Larkey, Uriah F. 4:37
Larkie, Jesse 21:212
Larkin, A. M. 16:373
Larkin, Albious 20:291
Larkin, Charles 15:209
Larkin, George 10:63;
20:291
Larkin, George E. 7:101
Larkin, Henry S. 21:356
Larkin, Hugh 22:124
Larkin, J. C. 4:37
Larkin, J. J. 21:356
Larkin, J. J. 21:356
Larkin, James 3:117;
10:19, 96
Larkin, James H. 21:356
Larkin, John 8:22; 11:67
Larkin, L. C. 21:356
Larkin, Martin 19:175;
27:78
Larkin, Oliver E. 19:175

Larkin, P. 1:149, 150; 14:188
Larkin, Patrick 11:127; 21:217, 356
Larkin, Robert 9:25
Larkin, Thomas 17:155
Larkin, Timothy 19:82
Larking, James 13:32
Larking, Michael 23:12
Larkings, Anderson 17:134; 24:198
Larkins, Albions 10:123
Larkins, Daniel 12:29
Larkins, Edw. 1:52
Larkins, George 11:207
Larkins, J. 21:149, 201
Larkins, John 16:97
Larkins, John A. 19:175
Larkins, John P. 10:163
Larkins, Marshall 22:308
Larkins, N. W. 20:177
Larkins, R. 26:42
Larkins, Samuel 22:41
Larkum, L. H. 22:203
Larley, Leander C. 10:173
Larly, William E. 18:243; 26:43
Larmar, George 13:113
Larmarmore, H. F. 9:55
Larme, J. W. 27:78
Larmer, John H. 21:140
Larmer, W. A. 3:117
Larmon, Robert 19:324
Larnard, Edward A. 21:356
Larne, E. 25:197
Larne, Eli 5:42
Larne, John 24:23
Larne, William H. 21:228
Larned, Cryus 1:50
Larned, D. 20:92
Larned, James 13:32
Larner, G. B. 18:191
Larner, Theo 9:66; 18:278
Larnesen, Charles 11:116
Larnhum, John 9:36
Larnsdon, C. E. 3:117
LaRock, Thad 21:356
Larogue, Alphonso M. 10:163
Laromore, O. P. 17:273
Laron, John 22:167
Larose, A. 1:52
Larose, C. 1:147
Larose, Vincent 14:80
Larouche, W. H. 27:74
Larouge, Lewis 7:127
Larow, Thomas 3:224
Larpvin, M. 17:217
Larr, Jacob M. 22:87
Larr, John W. 20:125

Larr, Thomas J. 18:219
Larrabe, G. W. 19:228
Larrabee, E. 3:117
Larrabee, George N. 9:183
Larrabee, L. W. 10:63
Larrabee, O. S. 21:356
Larrabee, Seth 7:32
Larrabee, Theodore 10:63
Larray, H. 3:117
Larreby, G. 3:117
Larrence, G. H. 27:74
Larrevierre, Joseph 20:114
Larribee, Theodore 6:7
Larris, P. 25:197
Larrison, Robert 11:156
Larrison, William T. 22:124
Larry, Lewis 7:101; 8:69
Lars, Edward 22:41
Lars, Ejemess 22:41
Larsen, Lavritz 18:339
Larsen, Nels. H. 21:256
Larsen, Ole 22:281
Larson, C. J. 17:99
Larson, Christopher 17:99
Larson, Grinder 21:257
Larson, H. 18:33
Larson, Jens 22:509
Larson, Knud 22:281
Larson, Laos 8:22
Larson, Lars 18:144
Larson, Lavity 9:103
Larson, Lewis 9:103; 18:339; 23:114
Larson, N. H. 8:51
Larson, O. 22:353
Larson, Ole 20:114
Larson, Peter 9:103
Larson, R. 22:339
Larsten, Lars 18:339
Larston, Lars 9:103
Larue, D. O. 27:145
Larue, James L. 20:104
LaRue, Joseph 7:68
Larue, Leonard 20:291
Larue, Thomas L. 11:67
Larver, Jacob 18:413
Larver, William 12:142
Larvis, William 9:84
Larvost, Joseph 16:97
Larway, J. M. 4:37
Lary, D. O. 1:51
Larzalere, J. W. 14:188
Larzell, E. P. 25:50
Lasader, Lafayette 10:123; 20:292
Lasage, S. 16:97
Lasaman, Frederick 16:207
Lasame, John H. 9:222
LaSarr, Jesse B. 20:125

Lasater, C. C. 21:32
Lasater, John L. 8:73
Lasch, Henry 21:356
Lasco, J. 7:101
Lase---, L. 24:214
Lasell, Charles 4:37
Lasell, John A. 13:32
Laselle, C. 21:356
Laselle, Cephas 7:101
Lasenberg, William C. 9:84
Lasey, Henry 14:80
Lash, --- 11:341
Lash, Abraham 25:272
Lash, C. J. 15:159
Lash, D. L. 22:464
Lash, G. 25:197
Lash, George B. 18:208
Lash, Gotlieb 5:21
Lash, Henry 24:9
Lash, J. 3:117
Lash, John S. 21:55
Lash, Joseph K. 8:22
Lash, Joseph R. 18:144
Lash, Joshua 15:127
Lash, Philip 22:431
Lash, Stephen 10:123; 20:292
Lash, Wesley 7:51
Lash, William 18:294
Lash, William I. 9:36
Lash, William J. 26:105
Lashbrook, Jeremiah 22:87
Lashbrook, John W. 10:123; 20:292
Lashbrooks, George W. 12:29
Lasher, C. F. 20:147
Lasher, Charles 19:82
Lasher, Charles C. 21:356
Lasher, J. A. 25:197
Lasher, P. 13:113
Lashker, James A. 5:21
Lashley, James 11:67
Lasilla, Joseph 21:356
Lasinger, George 7:101
Lasker, J. 15:209
Laskey, Thomas 20:193
Laskins, M. C. 3:117
Lasler, C. M. 22:41
Lasley, David M. 24:41
Lasley, Harry 27:78
Lasley, J. 18:87
Lasley, James 9:165
Lasley, L. C. 19:175
Lasley, Lorenzo D. 10:63
Lasley, William H. 20:98
Laslie, Charles 16:5
Laslir, John 9:165
Lasnett, J. 1:147

Lason, Benjamin 3:117
Lason, James 15:159
Lasowger, John S. 9:103
Laspe, Otto 3:117
Lass, George 14:188
Lass, Henry 24:112
Lass, J. 1:149
Lassean, Y. O. 17:448;
   24:173
Lassell, George 7:101
Lassell, Silas 20:98
Lasselle, George 14:188
Lassen, Joseph 21:189
Lasser, Joseph 19:296
Lasser, Ope 11:333
Lasshana, Amerza 12:64
Lassing, James W. 6:31;
   25:323
Lassiter, Jesse 10:63;
   20:292
Lassius, Moritz 25:269
Lassly, R. 14:80
Lasson, L. 14:80
Lasson, Mat 10:150
Last, Ferdinand 15:91
Last, John 14:80
Lasted, John 7:83
Laster, Allen 22:308
Laster, J. 22:258
Laster, Robert 10:123;
   20:292
Laster, Thomas 21:356
Laster, Thomas G. 21:356
Lasterman, F. 9:146
Lastin, William 4:37
Lastley, W. B. 14:80
Lastman, F. 27:74
Lasty, J. 3:117
Lasur, John 8:73
Lasure, W. 3:117
Laswell, Joseph 22:407
Laswell, W. P. 1:52
Latch, J. 18:33
Latchaw, David 3:117
Latchs, Daniel 8:22
Late, D. 15:83
Late, David 12:72
Late, L. S. 14:81
Latem, L. F. 9:183
Laten, Daniel 17:180
Laten, William 12:29
Later, Charles 13:113
Latern, L. F. 19:228
Lath, Rowen G. 19:233
Lath, W. M. 1:50
Latham, Alexander 22:398
Latham, Bela E. 10:123
Latham, Bella E. 20:292
Latham, C. F. 14:188
Latham, F. 20:179

Latham, Franklin B.
   19:175
Latham, H. 16:373
Latham, H. V. 15:351;
   16:373
Latham, Henry 15:343
Latham, J. 20:41; 25:311
Latham, James H. 22:124
Latham, M. A. 19:224
Latham, M. C. 11:155
Latham, Peter 27:76
Latham, Russell 22:517
Latham, W. 3:117
Latham, William 1:51
Latham, William H. 21:73
Lathamer, S. C. 14:278;
   23:204
Lathan, Peter 9:133
Lathe, Owen G. 9:183
Lathenhouse, A. 16:207
Lathin, Ethan S. 25:197
Lathrop, A. 21:88
Lathrop, A. D. 1:51
Lathrop, Albert N. 16:373
Lathrop, C. B. 19:228
Lathrop, D. C. 7:59
Lathrop, E. H. 15:304
Lathrop, Edgar H. 16:207
Lathrop, Edward 10:145;
   19:175
Lathrop, Elijah 1:51
Lathrop, George 10:64;
   20:292
Lathrop, H. A. 5:21
Lathrop, H. B. 25:50
Lathrop, Horace 21:73
Lathrop, Isaac N. 16:78
Lathrop, J. K. 19:274
Lathrop, J. P. 16:207
Lathrop, Jay R. 22:147
Lathrop, John W. 22:41
Lathrop, Julius M. 9:8
Lathrop, Marion 17:498
Lathrop, Robert R. 20:183
Lathrop, S. H. 16:11
Lathrop, Simon D. 20:114
Lathrop, W. 3:117
Lathrop, W. B. 19:255
Lathrop, W. C. 23:154
Lathrop, W. F. 17:498
Lathrop, W. P. 14:270
Lathrop, W. W. 18:339
Lathrop, Whitney E. 9:13
Lathrop, William B. 9:183
Lathrop, William M.
   25:197
Lathrop, William R.
   18:346
Lathrope, A. U. 25:49
Lathrope, C. 25:51
Lathrope, H. G. 14:331

Lathrope, John 10:64
Lathrope, L. A. 20:155
Lathrope, M. 14:282
Lathrope, S. 13:92
Latimer, E. H. 19:22
Latimer, George B.
   22:399
Latimer, J. G. 5:21
Latimore, Samuel 24:160
Latin, C. 22:203
Latin, H. B. 18:243; 26:43
Latin, James S. 21:73
Laton, James H. 21:356
Laton, John R. 18:397
Laton, Peter 18:144
Laton, Reuben 6:17;
   18:87
Latonette, William 7:16
Latosganski, Simon
   26:169
Latoure, J. 12:82; 16:298
Latourette, David 23:123
Latourette, J. 3:117
Latrue, Lewis S. 17:361
Latshaw, James 7:64
Latshaw, Reuben 11:323
Latson, Andrew 23:309
Latson, Hiram 10:123;
   20:292
Latson, Samuel 22:87
Latta, I. W. 8:22
Latta, J. W. 1:50
Latta, T. B. 18:294;
   26:105
Latta, W. H. 3:117
Latta, W. M. 8:22; 18:144
Latta, William A. 21:228
Lattcher, D. 1:52
Latte, J. W. 18:144
Latten, J. M. 10:19
Latter, J. S. 14:81
Latterby, James M. 26:44
Latterly, James M. 18:243
Latterman, Adam 18:33
Latterno, W. 14:188
Lattey, John 16:298
Lattick, G. 17:294
Lattimar, Thomas 20:292
Lattimer, F. 8:73
Lattimer, J. C. 25:197
Lattimer, James H.
   10:123; 20:292
Lattimer, Myron 18:323
Lattimer, Thomas 10:63
Lattimore, W. H. 3:117
Lattin, C. 26:126
Lattin, Charles 9:103
Lattin, E. 3:117
Lattin, George M. 13:92
Lattin, George W. 14:15
Lattni, E. 9:43

Lattsill, William E. 26:42
Latty, Samuel 15:209
Lature, Alexander 12:170
Laty, John 12:82
Latz, Augustus 24:23
Laub, Jacob 1:50
Lauber, John W. 17:22
Lauberti, Charles 9:121
Lauchbaugh, Lewis
  20:292
Laucos, Haura 7:127
Laud, J. E. 27:74
Laud, Thomas 9:25
Laudenlazer, Frederick
  10:8
Lauderdeal, James A.
  23:184
Laudredge, Joseph 26:125
Lauer, William 1:52
Lauger, Owen 11:67
Laugh, Samuel 10:64
Laughan, Peter 12:29
Laughbough, Samuel
  16:207
Laugherty, William
  21:228
Laughery, J. 1:147
Laughery, James 13:32
Laughlan, J. 9:146
Laughlen, Edward W.
  10:92
Laughlin, --- 14:282
Laughlin, A. M. 10:28
Laughlin, Andrew 21:277
Laughlin, B. M. 10:123;
  20:292
Laughlin, Edward W.
  20:292
Laughlin, George 13:65
Laughlin, J. 3:117; 23:38;
  27:75
Laughlin, James 12:170;
  24:23
Laughlin, John 9:183;
  12:29; 22:431
Laughlin, John P. 17:15
Laughlin, Joseph L. 9:25
Laughlin, Judson J. 21:73
Laughlin, M. W. 3:117
Laughlin, Michael 11:108;
  16:86
Laughlin, Peter 11:231
Laughlin, R. M. 3:117
Laughlin, Robert 7:101
Laughlin, S. 11:307
Laughlin, T. A. 20:41
Laughlin, W. B. 1:103
Laughlin, William M.
  9:183
Laughlinback, William F.
  1:50

Laughman, J. 19:255
Laughner, James 7:32
Laughner, John H. 7:59
Laughray, James 23:38
Laughrey, J. 25:49
Laughrey, T. 15:8
Laughron, Barney 23:154
Laughter, Robert 22:258
Laughtery, James H.
  23:184
Lauhan, D. 1:148
Lauk, C. A. 25:51
Lauler, John 10:163
Lauman, Augustus 12:29
Launners, Frank 20:133
Launon, Thomas 12:59
Launsbury, C. 17:476
Launtenslayer, J. 19:271
Launterback, Gottleb 8:22
Launterlock, Gottlieb
  18:144
Lauper, David R. 12:29
Laupman, Luman 9:133
Laur, Ephraim 17:500
Laur, Noah 17:449
Laure, W. J. 4:37
Laured, John D. 7:32
Laurence, C. E. 27:74
Laurence, C. W. 27:74
Laurence, Dan 17:292
Laurence, H. 19:274
Laurence, J. T. 7:101
Laurence, Jabez F. 27:76
Laurence, John W. 19:175
Laurence, Joseph 27:76
Laurence, S. 27:79
Laurence, S. W. 12:155
Laurence, Sidney R.
  17:273
Laurence, Washington
  17:425
Laurens, Frank 19:232
Laurie, James 4:37
Laurne, N. 26:44
Laurson, A. 14:331
Laury, C. 14:245; 27:79
Laury, J. W. 27:75
Lausfallon, Sewell 9:183
Lauson, Charles 20:292
Lauson, J. M. 14:15
Lautenslaser, Philip 4:37
Lauter, Abram 7:101
Lauterman, John L.
  21:257
Lauton, W. D. 18:370
Lautz, Asable E. 23:305
Lautz, Jacob 12:29
Lautzenheimer, Samuel
  11:155
Laux, Jacob 25:51
Lauze, J. 21:164

Lavaby, John 16:140
Lavalley, A. B. 12:155
LaValley, Peter 16:140
Lavally, Joseph 19:175
Lavan, Ezekiel 22:41
Lavan, Willis 17:54
Lavanghee, W. O. 3:119
Lavassuer, Alex 1:50
Lavean, James E. 17:454
Laveden, J. 16:133
Lavee, Charles 9:201;
  19:282
Lavely, Franklin 22:87
Lavely, John 17:277
Laven, Edward 9:236;
  26:221, 222
Lavenberg, Louis 10:92
Lavender, Andrew J.
  17:358
Lavender, L. 18:243;
  26:44
Lavender, Willis 10:64;
  20:292
Laver, J. H. 14:81
Laver, William 19:322
Lavers, John 11:192
Lavers, R. 15:39
Laverty, David W. 23:71
Laverty, E. 1:52
Laverty, John 22:167
Lavery, D. 1:148
Lavery, H. 9:111
Lavey, Michael 22:41
Lavikleres, J. 15:299
Lavin, James 18:145
Lavin, Thomas 18:145
Lavis, G. 1:147
Lavonture, D. 1:51
Lavoodes, Harry 27:74
Lavore, L. A. 1:50
Lavy, C. 6:31
Law, A. 12:155
Law, Addison 10:19
Law, Benjamin E. 27:78
Law, C. 11:320
Law, D. 17:217
Law, David S. 17:207
Law, Ezra S. 22:12
Law, Francis 9:133; 27:76
Law, George 9:85; 26:41
Law, Henry 3:117
Law, J. 7:32
Law, James 12:72;
  18:311; 26:105
Law, James C. 7:101
Law, Joel 22:87
Law, John 15:209
Law, M. 14:81
Law, Noah L. 15:83
Law, S. S. 3:117
Law, Thomas 21:32, 356

Law, Thomas H. 10:19
Law, W. 25:197
Law, W. I. 11:67
Law, William 5:42
Lawaber, George 14:81
Lawbender, Joseph
    18:103
Lawber, Louis 10:19
Lawber, William P.
    16:207
Lawbroo, A. 1:52
Lawdon, J. 14:321;
    23:123
Lawdon, John 14:316
Lawdy, Andrew J. 19:255
Lawe, George 22:147
Lawe, J. 25:197
Lawellen, John 8:73
Lawer, Riley 11:36
Lawer, Thomas 25:197
Lawes, Lewis 17:134
Lawes, M. 21:102
Lawfer, M. 12:9
Lawhead, Reuben 22:147
Lawhead, W. J. 7:101
Lawhead, William 7:101
Lawhead, William J.
    21:356
Lawhom, M. 18:243
Lawhorn, Benjamin F.
    23:71
Lawhorn, M. 26:43
Lawinger, Oswold 13:33
Lawler, Denis 20:292
Lawler, Dennis 10:123
Lawler, Ezra C. 11:67
Lawler, Frederick T.
    15:11
Lawler, James 8:22;
    15:326; 19:82;
    26:168
Lawler, John 19:175;
    22:87; 25:49, 50
Lawler, M. 1:149
Lawler, O. D. 23:154
Lawler, P. 1:50; 23:38
Lawler, Richard 19:47
Lawler, Robert 10:123;
    20:292
Lawler, William P. 6:13
Lawler, William S. 18:87
Lawless, A. H. 13:92;
    14:15
Lawless, G. 1:52
Lawless, J. 1:147
Lawless, James 13:113
Lawless, M. 7:51; 15:127;
    25:197
Lawless, Mason 21:55
Lawless, Patrick 13:33
Lawless, S. H. 15:173

Lawless, Thomas 22:509
Lawley, Lucas 4:66
Lawlis, George W. 11:265
Lawliss, William 21:356
Lawlt, Lambert 25:197
Lawn, Adam 15:209
Lawn, David 9:227
Lawn, J. 21:55
Lawn, James 7:78; 25:300
Lawner, John 9:209
Lawney, Franklin 12:29
Lawrence, A. 1:149;
    3:117; 25:197
Lawrence, A. J. 21:357
Lawrence, A. M. 19:275
Lawrence, Abram 11:156
Lawrence, Albert 7:59
Lawrence, Albert M.
    9:183
Lawrence, Alfred 5:21
Lawrence, Almon 10:163;
    19:175
Lawrence, Austin 9:85
Lawrence, B. F. 3:117
Lawrence, B. L. 14:15
Lawrence, C. 3:117
Lawrence, C. W. 9:146
Lawrence, Charles 9:43;
    11:67; 20:133; 21:95;
    25:197; 26:126
Lawrence, Charles E.
    12:82; 16:298
Lawrence, Collier 24:101
Lawrence, D. 3:117;
    11:265
Lawrence, D. L. 13:92
Lawrence, E. 21:357
Lawrence, E. C. 1:148
Lawrence, Edward 13:32
Lawrence, Ervine 16:145
Lawrence, F. 13:92
Lawrence, Ferins 13:32
Lawrence, Frank 9:183;
    19:255
Lawrence, Frank H. G.
    22:464
Lawrence, Franklin
    25:197
Lawrence, G. 1:149
Lawrence, G. W. 11:307
Lawrence, George 6:14;
    16:140
Lawrence, George A.
    14:189
Lawrence, George W.
    19:22
Lawrence, Gilbert B.
    23:123
Lawrence, Gloho 21:357
Lawrence, H. 12:122;
    15:127, 209

Lawrence, H. B. 1:149
Lawrence, H. C. 17:155,
    263
Lawrence, Harrison 9:97
Lawrence, Harry 17:282
Lawrence, Henry 15:326;
    18:397; 19:82
Lawrence, Henry E. 10:19
Lawrence, Henry F. 21:32
Lawrence, Herman 14:189
Lawrence, Hiram 15:127
Lawrence, Horace 9:183
Lawrence, I. B. 7:32
Lawrence, Ira 10:64;
    20:292
Lawrence, Isaac N. 20:23
Lawrence, J. 1:148; 3:117;
    13:92, 113; 14:15;
    16:42; 19:255;
    22:171
Lawrence, J. B. 1:147;
    22:353
Lawrence, J. C. 3:117
Lawrence, J. H. 14:278;
    23:105
Lawrence, J. J. 11:101
Lawrence, J. L. 16:42
Lawrence, J. N. 18:243;
    26:43
Lawrence, Jabez S. 9:121
Lawrence, Jacob 9:43;
    11:307
Lawrence, Jacob S. 17:54
Lawrence, James 1:49;
    8:89; 9:183
Lawrence, James H. 20:30
Lawrence, James I. 26:105
Lawrence, James O.
    18:294
Lawrence, James P. 9:36
Lawrence, James W.
    11:187; 18:243;
    26:43
Lawrence, John 3:117;
    11:244; 12:155;
    14:81; 22:339
Lawrence, John B. 17:347
Lawrence, John W. 8:107;
    10:163
Lawrence, Joseph 4:37;
    9:133; 11:335;
    22:308, 407; 26:126
Lawrence, Joseph P.
    11:307
Lawrence, L. 25:197
Lawrence, L. G. 3:117
Lawrence, Lamson J.
    19:22
Lawrence, Lee 22:308
Lawrence, Leo 17:314

Lawrence, Lewis 18:87; 21:357
Lawrence, Lorenzo 22:147
Lawrence, Louis 6:17
Lawrence, Lyman 5:21
Lawrence, M. 13:65; 19:82
Lawrence, Nathaniel S. 24:95
Lawrence, Newman 6:25
Lawrence, O. 13:113
Lawrence, Oliver 8:22
Lawrence, Oliver V. 18:145
Lawrence, P. 13:92
Lawrence, Peter 7:101
Lawrence, Pr--- 15:209
Lawrence, R. 25:323
Lawrence, R. J. 3:117
Lawrence, R. P. 12:162
Lawrence, Richard 4:37; 9:165
Lawrence, Robert 1:50; 9:214; 18:243; 21:357; 22:87; 26:43
Lawrence, Russel B. 22:41
Lawrence, Russell F. 4:37
Lawrence, S. A. 18:69
Lawrence, S. D. 25:197
Lawrence, Salon 24:160
Lawrence, Samuel 21:277; 24:95
Lawrence, Simon 11:335
Lawrence, Solon 17:443
Lawrence, Spaulding 22:87
Lawrence, Stephen D. 5:21
Lawrence, Stephen L. 23:129
Lawrence, T. 18:243; 26:44
Lawrence, T. J. 25:300
Lawrence, Thomas 6:17; 18:87; 21:257
Lawrence, Thomas G. 17:54
Lawrence, Victor 21:357
Lawrence, W. 9:43; 22:308
Lawrence, W. A. 9:146; 27:76
Lawrence, W. S. 17:169
Lawrence, W. T. A. 22:258
Lawrence, Washington 24:178
Lawrence, Willard 15:209

Lawrence, William 14:81; 22:41, 308
Lawrence, William H. 15:353; 16:280
Lawrence, William L. 17:54
Lawrence, Zach 11:85
Lawrence, Zephraim 4:37
Lawrens, Martin 13:32
Lawrie, G. 1:147
Lawron, Calvin 26:44
Lawrson, John B. 18:145
Lawry, Ambrose 12:155
Lawry, Edward 15:108
Lawry, George 7:127
Lawry, John H. 7:101
Lawry, R. W. 14:81
Lawry, W. 14:15
Laws, Edward 12:50
Laws, Franklin 8:107
Laws, J. 16:207; 26:170
Laws, J. W. 17:450; 24:176
Laws, James 9:25
Laws, Jeremiah 17:273
Laws, John 5:42
Laws, Lewis 18:243; 26:44
Laws, Lindley D. 22:407
Laws, Sax. 16:207
Laws, Thomas 24:112
Laws, W. L. 14:81
Laws, William 24:198
Lawsa, V. 14:81
Lawsen, James 7:59
Lawson, --- 20:292
Lawson, A. 17:37; 27:157
Lawson, Abram 11:108
Lawson, Andrew 22:281
Lawson, Benjamin 11:295; 22:87
Lawson, Bryson 11:207
Lawson, C. M. 19:22
Lawson, Chancel 19:22
Lawson, D. 26:169
Lawson, D. G. 19:232
Lawson, David 21:149
Lawson, David G. 9:183
Lawson, David H. 22:41
Lawson, Delzell 18:219
Lawson, Dyer 17:166
Lawson, E. 25:197
Lawson, Edward 5:42
Lawson, Enoch 24:67
Lawson, Erick 11:192
Lawson, George 1:51; 9:236; 11:155, 187; 14:81; 21:195; 22:431
Lawson, George A. 23:71
Lawson, Gilbert 7:32

Lawson, H. G. 3:117
Lawson, H. T. 10:163
Lawson, Haman 20:104
Lawson, Henry 14:261; 27:78
Lawson, J. 1:148, 149; 3:117; 9:72; 20:292
Lawson, J. B. 22:258
Lawson, J. H. 19:255
Lawson, J. M. 13:92
Lawson, J. M. T. 11:187
Lawson, James 22:258; 24:23
Lawson, James D. 24:67
Lawson, Jesse R. 22:503
Lawson, John 11:414; 13:33; 15:278; 16:42; 17:96, 180; 25:198
Lawson, John T. 22:124
Lawson, John W. 11:281; 22:258
Lawson, L. B. 15:209
Lawson, M. 3:117
Lawson, Mat 1:51
Lawson, Oliver 10:123; 20:292
Lawson, R. C. 17:203
Lawson, Rufus D. 22:503
Lawson, S. 19:22; 21:149
Lawson, Spencer D. 7:51
Lawson, Thomas 16:3
Lawson, Thomas A. 17:37
Lawson, W. 22:308
Lawson, W. D. 9:228
Lawson, W. H. 9:111
Lawson, Wesley D. 22:484
Lawson, William 3:117; 15:209; 25:323
Lawson, William D. 18:370
Lawson, William H. 21:102; 22:41
Lawson, William W. 17:243
Lawson, Willis 9:25; 18:311; 26:105
Lawtan, George 12:172
Lawter, Abraham 21:357
Lawther, Alfred M. 21:102
Lawton, A. W. 21:357
Lawton, Albert H. 22:147
Lawton, Bartholomew 23:192
Lawton, C. M. 1:148
Lawton, Charles A. 10:163
Lawton, David 10:163; 19:175
Lawton, Door 18:103

Lawton, Edward O. 12:29
Lawton, George 8:60;
  16:86
Lawton, J. 1:150; 3:117
Lawton, James 3:117
Lawton, L. D. 19:175
Lawton, Peter 24:81
Lawton, Russia 27:76
Lawton, Sewell D. 10:163
Lawton, Thomas 12:168
Lawton, Thomas J. 19:175
Lawton, W. J. 11:219
Lawton, W. W. 23:38
Lawton, Wesley D. 9:222
Lawton, William 25:198
Lawwinger, Oswald 16:42
Lawyer, A. 11:287
Lawyer, Ezra 22:41
Lawyer, George 26:126
Lawyer, J. B. 3:117
Lawyer, James 3:117
Lawyer, John 10:26
Lawyer, Joseph 21:228
Lawyer, Stephen 8:22;
  18:145
Lawyer, William 25:198
Lay, Barrell 10:123
Lay, F. M. 27:78
Lay, Frank 15:159
Lay, G. W. 10:64; 20:292
Lay, Henry L. 25:272
Lay, Horace 15:3
Lay, J. 25:198
Lay, J. P. 10:28; 19:303
Lay, Jacob 5:21
Lay, Jesse 17:166
Lay, John 3:117; 10:64,
  173; 19:175; 20:292;
  22:431
Lay, Josiah 22:41
Lay, Louis 15:8
Lay, Passell 20:292
Lay, T. C. 15:17
Lay, Talton 17:353
Lay, Thomas S. 22:87
Lay, William 3:117
Lay, William S. 22:87
Layborn, Henry 17:82
Laycock, Allen B. 12:29
Laycock, John 10:123;
  20:292
Laycox, Richard 17:361
Layden, Michael 12:72
Layden, V. 14:81
Layder, James 21:357
Layeker, C. 12:80
Layer, Moses 7:127
Layer, Thomas 24:198
Layer, V. J. 16:373
Layfield, H. J. 14:15
Layfield, H. T. 13:92

Layford, Charles A.
  15:127
Layhan, J. 14:81
Layhee, John 18:112
Layhen, William 16:373
Layland, H. 19:82
Layman, A. H. 20:292
Layman, Abraham 22:147
Layman, Albert 9:222
Layman, Alfred 22:147
Layman, Augustus 21:357
Layman, C. 3:117; 17:347
Layman, David 8:107
Layman, Ephraim 15:69
Layman, F. 3:117
Layman, J. 14:15
Layman, J. H. 11:265
Layman, John 15:87
Layman, N. V. 15:8
Layman, Robert 22:258
Layman, William 15:8
Layman, William H.
  17:347
Laymar, Albert 18:370
Laymon, John E. 10:173
Laymon, John F. 19:175
Laymon, W. F. 3:117
Laymond, Lander M.
  17:326
Laynatt, William 25:272
Layne, --- 18:191
Layne, M. 14:15
Layne, William R. 24:67
Laypole, Nathan 11:156
Layport, John 1:50
Laysaya, S. B. 14:15
Layster, W. W. 27:76
Layton, Arelius 22:41
Layton, C. 1:49; 26:41
Layton, Charles H. 22:88
Layton, David 10:163;
  19:175
Layton, Fred P. 9:183
Layton, George C. 15:127
Layton, J. M. 1:50
Layton, James 16:207
Layton, John 15:209
Layton, Louis B. 11:35
Layton, M. C. 11:183
Layton, P. 3:117
Layton, Peter 10:19
Layton, Richard M.
  22:431
Layton, S. M. 16:207
Layton, Samuel 3:117
Layton, Stephen 3:117
Layton, Sylvester 7:59
Layton, T. H. 12:140
Layton, William 18:397
Laywell, W. D. A. 26:126
Lazar, Charles 22:88

Lazarman, Fred 16:207
Lazelle, Marshall 10:64;
  20:292
Lazier, W. D. 23:184
Lea, John 27:75
Lea, William W. 10:180;
  26:204
Leabman, E. R. 16:207
Leach, --- 19:82
Leach, A. 19:255
Leach, A. B. 27:77
Leach, A. J. 20:147
Leach, A. S. 1:149
Leach, Alex 9:183
Leach, Alfred J. 21:140
Leach, Allen S. 7:16
Leach, Almond 21:228
Leach, Austin 11:36
Leach, B. 12:147
Leach, B. F. 15:209
Leach, Bazil R. 17:82
Leach, Bernick 19:303
Leach, Byron 9:183;
  19:267
Leach, C. 15:324; 20:147
Leach, C. H. 3:117
Leach, Chauncy B. 8:60
Leach, Cyrus 11:156
Leach, D. 25:272
Leach, Daniel 22:12
Leach, Daniel B. (Mrs.)
  4:37
Leach, David 17:428;
  24:183
Leach, E. 1:149
Leach, E. B. 15:209
Leach, Ephraim B. 21:245
Leach, F. M. 17:273
Leach, G. 25:198
Leach, G. W. 14:81; 20:41
Leach, George 11:116
Leach, Granbury 5:21
Leach, Hiram 10:123;
  20:292
Leach, Hollis M. 21:87
Leach, Ira B. 22:464
Leach, J. 3:118; 15:209;
  25:198
Leach, J. P. 24:23
Leach, James 3:118; 9:55;
  23:184
Leach, John 8:107; 12:72
Leach, John W. 10:64;
  20:292
Leach, Joshua 12:122
Leach, Judge 24:101
Leach, L. D. 3:118
Leach, Lark 7:51
Leach, Lewis 18:243;
  26:44
Leach, P. F. 27:75

Leach, Philip 12:29
Leach, S. 3:118
Leach, S. H. 25:300
Leach, Stephen H. 7:80
Leach, T. H. 14:189
Leach, W. B. 1:148
Leach, W. P. 20:292
Leach, Warren B. 27:74
Leach, William 12:96;
　13:125; 15:360;
　19:82
Leach, William P. 10:64
Leachey, E. 22:235
Leachman, L. 8:51
Leacock, William 3:118
Lead, John 8:77
Leadbetter, Goliah 11:380
Leadbetter, J. 11:67
Leader, Charles H. 22:511
Leader, D. 11:265
Leadman, Arche 26:105
Leadman, Archy 9:25
Leadwell, Thomas 14:81
Leady, D. 23:38
Leady, John J. 16:373
Leady, William H. 27:145
Leadyard, Oliver 15:209
Leaf, John 20:10
Leafer, Joseph 9:55
Leafled, F. 16:97
Leaford, Thomas 22:258
Leagen, Louis 21:277
League, Samuel 21:131
League, William 14:236;
　18:33
Leahey, Daniel 1:51
Leahey, Michael 22:162
Leahey, William 15:327
Leahman, J. B. 15:294
Leahman, Solomon 13:65
Leahmberg, Charles
　10:123; 20:293
Leahy, Daniel 1:52
Leair, George W. 10:123;
　20:293
Leak, Chesley 18:219
Leak, Edward 1:50
Leak, Silas A. 24:41
Leake, Alexander F.
　23:154
Leake, C. F. 8:89
Leake, Elisha L. 16:133
Leake, John M. 8:89
Leake, Josiah 11:341
Leal, Junius E. 17:314
Lealy, E. A. 22:484
Leaman, Edward 16:143
Leamick, H. A. 7:32
Leaming, Sylvester 22:88
Leamon, G. 3:118
Lean, Dennis 11:36

Lean, J. 12:9
Lean, James M. 11:108
Leanard, Henry W. 23:192
Leanard, M. R. 25:198
Leaning, Joseph 19:175
Leany, Arthur 11:100
Leaony, W. H. 3:118
Leaper, Daniel E. 17:427
Leaper, James L. 17:356
Leaper, S. 11:243; 23:108
Lear, A. 13:92
Lear, Alexander 17:134;
　24:198
Lear, Frederick 23:108
Lear, George R. 26:44
Lear, H. C. 23:38
Lear, H. D. 9:85; 26:42
Lear, Jesse E. 22:124
Lear, John 11:307
Lear, S. W. 11:265
Lear, Thomas W. 7:63
Lear, William 10:96;
　23:180
Learch, F. G. 9:183
Learch, John 9:25
Learcke, F. G. 19:275
Leard, Homar 20:293
Leard, Homer 10:64
Learer, James H. 19:22
Learett, Nathan 27:78
Learett, W. R. 27:76
Learitt, Joseph 4:37
Learn, J. J. 21:357
Learn, Joseph 19:82
Learnard, C. 19:175
Learnard, W. A. 25:198
Learned, H. 19:82
Learned, J. L. F. 18:191
Lears, Thomas 3:118
Lears, William 21:357
Learsey, Michael 24:67
Leary, Andrew 22:503
Leary, Arthur 21:357
Leary, C. 3:118
Leary, C. O. 19:255
Leary, Charles 1:49
Leary, Cornelius 10:123;
　20:293
Leary, D. 3:118; 14:189,
　257; 25:49
Leary, Daniel 10:123;
　13:33; 18:243; 19:22;
　20:293; 26:43
Leary, E. 2:14
Leary, George 4:37
Leary, I. 17:297
Leary, J. 21:357; 25:51
Leary, J. O. 16:373
Leary, James 11:109;
　12:29; 21:32
Leary, James O. 4:37

Leary, John 9:111; 16:9;
　19:175
Leary, John O. 15:209
Leary, John S. 19:22
Leary, Michael 13:33;
　23:282
Leary, P. 19:245
Leary, Pat. O. 8:22
Leary, Patrick 9:183;
　22:124
Leary, Thomas R. 13:77;
　16:207
Leary, W. 1:149
Leary, William 19:83
Leary, William O. 1:51;
　17:327
Leas, James C. 11:156
Leasch, M. 1:52
Lease, George H. 9:36
Lease, Ira 11:265
Lease, J. 17:155
Lease, James 15:69
Lease, John W. 9:55
Lease, Rufus 4:37
Lease, Thomas 18:191
Leasell, A. 16:207
Leasiere, Isaac 3:118
Leasman, F. 11:244
Leasome, J. H. 18:370
Leason, Thomas 15:209
Leasun, Solomon 4:37
Leasur, Isaac 24:67
Leasure, Chesner 22:407
Leasure, F. 3:118
Leater, James S. 22:235
Leathe, Abner T. 7:101
Leather, Ezra 10:173;
　19:175
Leatherman, John 22:88
Leatherman, M. 3:118
Leatherman, William
　9:85; 26:44
Leatherman, Willis 23:292
Leathermore, Daniel W.
　21:32
Leathermore, George
　21:55
Leathers, C. 26:41
Leathers, Christian 9:85
Leathers, George W.
　10:123; 20:293
Leathers, H. 21:123
Leathers, J. B. 14:81
Leathers, James M.
　17:319
Leathers, John 16:207
Leathers, Larkin 22:453
Leathers, William 1:51
Leathers, William W.
　20:10

Leatherwood, Nath. M. 20:293
Leatler, W. H. 4:37
Leaton, R. 24:67
Leausure, Edward 22:88
Leaval, D. J. 18:397
Leavean, James E. 24:185
Leavell, Albert P. 23:71
Leavell, William L. 22:88
Leavelle, Benjamin F. 20:183
Leavens, James H. 16:86
Leaver, H. 19:255
Leavernway, Francis 22:41
Leavet, J. M. 25:300
Leavete, Daniel W. 11:67
Leavett, A. 8:51
Leavett, J. 1:149
Leavett, J. M. 7:75
Leavett, Nathaniel 21:102
Leavitt, A. D. 1:148
Leavitt, C. 11:67
Leavitt, C. N. 1:148
Leavitt, J. W. 21:357
Leavitt, Joseph 10:163
Leavitt, M. 1:150
Leavitt, Sylvester 13:33
Leavitt, W. B. 9:146
Leavy, D. 2:13
Leavy, Joseph 19:22
Leavy, T. 1:52
Leavy, William 6:31; 25:323
Leays, Daniel 14:189
Leazenby, G. W. 9:55
Lebanon, Otis D. 12:29
LeBaroa, --- 14:189
Lebatt, C. D. 25:198
Lebell, Peter 17:22
Leber, Frederick 4:37
Leberick, S. 25:198
Lebiz, William C. 23:180
Lebkurhner, Ferdinand 12:72
Lebkurthner, F. 15:39
LeBlanc, Leon 6:25
Leble, --- 15:94
Lebman, Thomas 8:65
Lebo, John J. 19:83
Lebo, W. W. 11:327
Lebolt, --- 11:16
Lebolt, Charles B. 16:207
Leboundy, William B. 4:37
Lebrant, Charles 10:64
Lebrick, J. 12:87
Lebroke, H. F. 1:51
Lebrook, John 3:118
Lebrune, Charles 7:59
Lebth, Linnt 26:41

Lebudd, J. 3:118
Leburn, E. 25:278
Lec---, J. H. 23:204
LeCarmegie, John 17:462
Lech, John 5:21; 25:198
Lech, Michael 22:203
Lechard, L. 14:15
Lechler, A. 18:52
Lechletner, Anthony 22:431
Lechterberg, Henry 15:209
Leciest, George 17:323
Lecke, J. C. 10:25
Lecker, L. 11:156
Leckie, William F. 1:52
Leckington, W. B. 12:85; 16:298
LeClair, C. 1:52
LeClear, C. P. 16:152
LeClere, Augustus L. 20:98
Lecomb, M. S. 17:91
Lecompt, A. 13:92
Lecompt, David 15:319
Lecompte, David 19:83
Lecompte, John 22:453
LeContre, Henry 4:37
Lecraw, W. P. 3:118
Lecron, John 14:319; 25:282
Leda, J. M. 11:307
Ledan, Joseph 15:127
Ledbeter, Jesse 10:92
Ledbetter, C. S. 8:22; 18:145
Ledbetter, Edwin M. 17:203
Ledderer, William 3:118
Leddey, Patrick 14:189
Leddis, James 15:294; 16:207
Leddy, J. 1:147, 149
Leddy, Thomas 9:43; 26:125
Ledebaer, William 22:464
Lederee, Leopold 26:169
Lederman, Jacob 10:9
Ledevick, Peter 23:12
Ledford, Enoch 10:123; 20:293
Ledford, J. A. 3:118
Ledford, John 8:22; 18:145
Ledford, Nancy Melvina 18:191
Ledford, Philip 18:243
Ledford, Robert G. 17:282
Ledford, William 16:42
Ledfowd, Philip 26:43
Ledger, James 10:152

Ledger, Joseph 18:243
Ledget, James 18:52
Ledi, Anthony 11:155
Ledirer, Joseph 26:44
Ledker, W. A. 11:307
Ledman, B. 23:154
Ledmans, Soloman 18:112
Ledsinger, James H. 21:55
Leduck, Christian 12:9
Ledwick, C. 3:118
Ledwick, T. M. 3:118
Ledwidge, Frank 1:51
Ledwig, Michael 9:111
Ledyard, H. D. 21:357
Ledyard, N. D. 7:83
Lee, --- 2:14; 3:118
Lee, A. 3:118; 20:293; 21:140
Lee, A. A. 11:381
Lee, A. J. 15:39
Lee, Absalom 10:64
Lee, Albert 22:41
Lee, Alex 9:159
Lee, Alexander 9:25
Lee, Alfred 9:9
Lee, Alfred S. 11:265
Lee, Andrew 7:128; 21:32
Lee, Andrew J. 10:123; 20:293
Lee, Arthur 6:17; 18:87
Lee, B. 23:154
Lee, B. A. 12:73; 15:22
Lee, B. E. 25:300
Lee, B. F. 9:222; 11:389; 18:243, 370; 26:43
Lee, Benjamin 10:28; 17:263; 18:87; 24:101
Lee, Benjamin F. 25:198
Lee, Benjamine 19:303
Lee, Bernhard 18:324
Lee, Brenhard B:114
Lee, C. C. 8:59
Lee, C. G. 18:33
Lee, C. H. 18:191
Lee, Charles 6:35; 8:59, 77; 13:33; 16:42; 19:272; 26:168
Lee, Charles W. 21:208
Lee, Chester 8:59; 19:272
Lee, Clark 20:86
Lee, Cornelius 3:118
Lee, D. 1:149; 11:341
Lee, Daniel 8:60; 12:171
Lee, Daniel H. 19:344
Lee, David 6:23; 9:25; 17:180; 19:343
Lee, Doctor 21:149
Lee, E. 15:173
Lee, E. C. 17:347
Lee, Ebenezer 7:59

Lee, Edward 22:520
Lee, Elijah 7:127
Lee, Elisha A. 22:88
Lee, Elwood H. 7:32
Lee, Emerson E. 19:175
Lee, Enoch 13:113;
    16:207
Lee, Eugene 7:128
Lee, F. 3:118; 25:198
Lee, F. M. 11:244
Lee, Ferdinand 5:42
Lee, Francis G. 10:173;
    19:175
Lee, Frank 7:128
Lee, Fred 7:128
Lee, Frederick G. 10:123;
    20:293
Lee, G. 14:189; 16:207;
    26:236
Lee, G. P. 18:191
Lee, G. W. 9:55
Lee, Gabriel 8:89
Lee, George 10:64;
    13:113; 14:81, 257;
    19:83, 175; 20:293;
    22:203
Lee, George W. 6:21;
    17:201
Lee, Gilbert 9:201;
    19:282; 21:277
Lee, Green D. 11:327
Lee, Gresham 22:430
Lee, Griffin 10:176;
    19:175
Lee, Guy 9:165
Lee, H. 14:81; 25:198
Lee, H. F. 1:98
Lee, H. H. 13:92
Lee, Hamilton 17:15
Lee, Harrison 22:308
Lee, Harry 22:308
Lee, Henry 3:118; 5:42;
    7:101; 9:201;
    11:156; 13:33;
    19:282; 21:357;
    23:282; 25:288;
    27:78
Lee, Herbert 25:198
Lee, Hilroy 7:101
Lee, Ira S. 22:407
Lee, J. 1:148; 16:207;
    18:15; 21:208
Lee, J. B. 1:148
Lee, J. H. 20:293
Lee, J. I. 18:176
Lee, J. M. 8:107
Lee, J. T. 12:155
Lee, J. W. 21:195; 23:38
Lee, Jabez C. 18:15
Lee, Jackson 17:400
Lee, Jacob 7:128; 15:94

Lee, Jacob J. 10:123;
    20:293
Lee, James 3:118; 6:17;
    9:222; 11:207; 12:29,
    83; 13:33; 16:298;
    18:87, 370; 20:30;
    24:101; 26:168, 222;
    27:76
Lee, James C. 10:19
Lee, James H. 10:64, 145;
    12:155; 16:133;
    19:175
Lee, James S. 23:99
Lee, James W. 7:101
Lee, Jerome 13:58
Lee, Jesse 9:227; 11:156
Lee, Jesse M. 9:36
Lee, John 1:50; 3:118;
    5:42; 7:32; 9:9, 154;
    10:64; 12:29; 13:113;
    15:327; 17:54;
    18:243, 421; 20:293;
    21:357; 22:308;
    25:198, 285; 26:43
Lee, John A. 22:124
Lee, John E. 22:407
Lee, John F. 11:67
Lee, John G. 11:328
Lee, John H. 10:212;
    21:73
Lee, John J. 7:101; 11:389
Lee, John M. 20:186
Lee, John S. 10:64; 14:81;
    20:293
Lee, John T. 11:307
Lee, John W. 11:276, 402
Lee, Jonathan 9:133
Lee, Joseph 1:51; 10:180;
    18:176; 20:186;
    22:204
Lee, Joseph A. 20:293
Lee, Joseph H. 20:10
Lee, Joseph S. 22:204
Lee, Joshua 7:128
Lee, Josiah A. 10:64
Lee, L. 5:42; 25:198
Lee, L. H. 16:97
Lee, L. W. 10:192
Lee, Lake 4:37
Lee, Lemuel 25:49
Lee, Levi 12:83; 16:298;
    17:111
Lee, Lewis 5:42; 9:133;
    14:189; 27:76
Lee, Louis 14:189
Lee, Lovett 26:212
Lee, Luther 23:267
Lee, M. 14:189
Lee, M. C. 26:41
Lee, M. J. S. 11:396
Lee, Madison 21:277

Lee, Manuel 7:128
Lee, Marshall G. 23:38
Lee, Martin 10:64;
    20:293; 27:146
Lee, Merrill C. 9:85
Lee, Michael 13:113;
    22:204
Lee, Mills J. 20:293
Lee, Milo Jackson 10:64
Lee, Morris 14:257
Lee, Moses 18:406;
    21:228
Lee, Nancy Caroline
    23:276
Lee, Nathan 21:357
Lee, Nathaniel 8:89
Lee, Oliver 14:189
Lee, Oscar B. 19:23
Lee, P. 1:147; 3:118;
    19:334
Lee, Patrick 10:176;
    11:94; 19:175
Lee, Perry N. 10:64
Lee, Peter 9:244
Lee, Peter H. 21:239
Lee, Pleasant A. 21:131
Lee, R. 21:167; 22:258,
    308
Lee, R. H. 20:147
Lee, Reason 11:207
Lee, Reuben 9:201;
    19:282
Lee, Richard 17:134;
    21:357; 24:198
Lee, Robert 8:40; 14:189;
    18:243; 24:23; 26:43,
    169
Lee, S. 3:118; 17:217
Lee, S. E. 21:111
Lee, Sampson 17:207
Lee, Samuel 7:128; 8:89;
    9:9
Lee, Silas H. 24:23
Lee, Silas M. 1:51
Lee, Simon 22:308; 25:52
Lee, Smith 25:198
Lee, Spencer 9:209
Lee, Stephen P. 11:244
Lee, Stephen R. 8:107
Lee, T. 1:148, 149
Lee, Theodore 23:38
Lee, Thomas 3:118; 4:37;
    9:85, 111, 163;
    11:127; 13:79;
    16:207; 18:191;
    24:67; 25:323; 26:41
Lee, Thomas A. 9:31
Lee, Thomas B. 20:125
Lee, Thomas E. 10:19
Lee, Thomas W. 7:75;
    25:300

Lee, Vincent 18:52
Lee, W. 1:94, 149; 15:39;
  21:167
Lee, W. A. 11:127
Lee, W. Charles 9:156
Lee, W. E. 3:118
Lee, W. H. 20:142, 293
Lee, W. S. 9:183; 19:233
Lee, W. W. 25:283
Lee, Warren 15:343;
  16:373
Lee, William 3:118; 8:22,
  73; 9:97; 11:381;
  16:207; 18:112, 145;
  22:12, 308; 26:170
Lee, William A. 7:101;
  11:155
Lee, William B. 10:123;
  20:293
Lee, William D. 19:23;
  22:453
Lee, William G. 20:140
Lee, William H. 10:64;
  13:58; 14:189; 16:42
Lee, William J. 17:82;
  21:189
Lee, William P. 20:186
Lee, William T. 22:430
Lee, William W. 13:33
Leebig, F. B. 14:15
Leeboss, C. 3:118
Leech, --- 15:39
Leech, David 17:249
Leech, F. A. 13:113
Leech, George 1:50
Leech, J. R. 15:39
Leech, J. W. 21:189
Leech, Jacob 11:155
Leech, James 5:21
Leech, John B. 22:464
Leech, Monroe 7:128
Leech, P. 15:39
Leech, P. S. W. S. 21:357
Leechman, Frederick
  17:361
Leechord, John 14:81
Leed, C. L. 16:373
Leed, Corman 15:209
Leed, W. J. 1:150
Leeder, Jacob B. 5:21
Leeders, Charles 22:204
Leeds, Andrew P. 22:431
Leeds, Arthur 18:33
Leeds, David 10:19
Leeds, G. W. 22:484
Leeds, H. C. 25:198
Leeds, Henry C. 5:21
Leeds, J. 3:118
Leedsinger, M. 14:81
Leedy, Augustus E. 22:88
Leedy, C. 20:147

Leedy, J. B. 25:198
Leef, Henry C. 23:154
Leeflar, F. 20:293
Leege, S. M. 12:155
Leegere, Jackson 8:22
Leegins, James 22:308
Leek, Charles 1:51
Leek, David H. 19:23
Leek, John 19:23
Leek, John S. 23:277
Leek, John W. 17:451;
  24:178
Leek, Thomas 12:29
Leek, William W. 25:49
Leekin, Newell G. 21:357
Leeky, Mark 22:339
Leel, Charles 22:88
Leelear, Charles 11:108
Leely, Alexander L.
  21:357
Leely, George H. 21:357
Leely, S. C. 21:357
Leely, W. 21:357
Leeman, James E. 4:37
Leeman, John 25:49
Leeman, S. B. 4:37
Leemon, John 23:264
Leemuster, John 18:176
Leenhaver, William H.
  11:428
Leent, John 17:273
Leep, Jacob 24:81
Leep, William 15:81
Leeper, Alex. O. 17:66
Leeper, Daniel E. 24:182
Leeper, George W. 24:23
Leeper, James 23:38
Leeper, Jesse 22:88
Leeper, John 20:178
Leeper, P. 24:81
Leeper, S. D. 27:77
Leer, F. 16:369
Leer, Stephen 12:140;
  20:293
Lees, A. 16:121
Lees, E. 14:270
Lees, Henry 25:49
Lees, Joseph P. 13:33
Lees, Samuel 18:145
Lees, W. H. 3:118
Leese, Benjamin 4:37
Leese, John 25:51
Leese, Oscar 17:353
Leese, William 12:29
Leeshiere, Eli 9:85
Leet, Franklin 20:189
Leetch, Frederick 8:22
Leeth, Robert L. 24:67
Leetle, Thomas 22:12
Leets, Albert H. 22:464
Leever, Felix E. 22:430

Leevonbroser, John 8:22
Lefaniel, Mat 17:134
Lefantz, John 8:119
Lefarge, E. R. 25:198
Lefebre, Odeline 22:162
Lefer, P. 13:93
Lefervre, Daniel 10:96
Lefest, R. A. 9:146
Lefever, D. W. 2:14
LeFever, J. C. 1:147
Lefever, M. V. 17:149
Lefever, T. 16:207
Lefevers, John 11:67
Lefevre, Daniel 10:123;
  20:293
Lefevre, George W. 12:29
Leffell, D. C. 1:51
Leffer, S. 14:81
Leffer, William 23:108
Leffers, Daniel 15:299
Leffingnell, L. B. 15:278
Leffingwell, Elyphus
  21:55
Leffingwell, Milon 10:64
Leffingwell, R. B. 15:294
Leffingwell, W. H. 1:149
Leffler, G. 25:50
Leffler, Jacob 22:204
Leffler, Peter 22:112
Leffler, Samuel L. 22:204
Leffords, Rufus 16:373
Lefhan, John 16:207
Lefingwell, R. B. 16:207
Lefland, Frank 17:428;
  24:183
Lefler, Franklin 10:64
Lefler, George 8:22;
  18:145
Lefler, John 10:64; 20:293
Lefon, W. D. 18:285
Leforrest, Lewis 22:147
Left, A. 14:81
Lefter, Stephen 21:102
Lefurre, W. E. 3:118
Legacy, James 12:83
Legacy, Joseph 16:298
LeGarde, Eustice 24:63
Leger, William 27:74
Leget, W. F. 25:300
Legg, A. 11:244, 365
Legg, A. E. 11:255
Legg, August A. 18:278
Legg, Charles H. 22:147
Legg, Constantine 11:244
Legg, G. H. 1:149
Legg, James 22:147
Legg, John 1:50
Legg, N. 8:51
Legg, Noah 21:123
Legg, Peter 20:98
Legg, W. M. 1:150

Legg, Washington 20:50
Legg, William 11:255
Legg, William H. 16:7
Leggatt, J. 21:357
Legget, John 15:209
Leggett, C. 27:74
Leggett, Charles 24:52
Leggett, Daniel 27:76
Leggett, Elijah 15:3
Leggett, George W.
    17:424; 24:174
Leggett, I. 7:32
Leggett, Joshua 13:135;
    19:347
Leggett, W. F. 19:83
Leggett, Washington
    11:155
Leggit, Daniel C. 9:121
Leggith, Robert 18:434
Leggitt, Archibald 8:22;
    18:145
Leggitt, M. K. 9:244;
    19:334
Leghner, Joseph 26:41
Legion, B. 18:52
Legion, Ransom 17:37
Legler, F. 19:327
Lego, George 3:118
Legran, Daniel S. 27:77
Legrand, Emile 20:293
LeGrand, George 14:261
Legrand, William 20:293
Legrande, Emile 10:123
Legrange, W. W. 18:351
Legrave, Cyrus 7:101
Legron, D. 3:118
Legrow, Daniel S. 9:121
Legue, James B. 13:65
Leguim, Urosin 21:357
Lehan, John 13:77
Lehansaler, R. A. 14:189
Lehau, Samuel 8:51
Leheon, William M. 7:68
Lehey, P. 1:49
Lehi, Joseph 17:66
Lehiffe, Timothy 9:183;
    19:239
Lehigh, W. 3:118
Lehing, Charles C. 25:198
Lehman, A. 15:209
Lehman, Abraham B.
    8:114
Lehman, B. F. 23:154
Lehman, Cyrus A. 12:29
Lehman, D. J. 1:150
Lehman, F. 1:52
Lehman, Fred 11:182
Lehman, G. 8:65
Lehman, H. 19:175
Lehman, Isaac 9:236;
    26:222

Lehman, John 22:41
Lehman, R. W. 14:300;
    17:479; 27:78
Lehman, S. 16:207
Lehman, Warner 17:82
Lehmerer, John 1:50
Lehn, Simon 17:356
Lehne, George 25:51
Lehner, John 23:192
Leho, W. H. 25:323
Lehone, Isaac 9:183
Lehrer, William 10:123;
    20:293
Lehrman, William 9:121;
    27:77
Lehur, Henry 8:73
Leib, J. 1:148
Leibald, John 11:155
Leibe, Joseph 15:57
Leibee, J. 20:10
Leiben, H. 25:323
Leiber, J. 11:155
Leibert, Gotlieb 20:35
Leibeusperger, Solomon
    9:121
Leibker, John 25:198
Leibmann, F. 1:50
Leibrand, John 10:64
Leiby, William 23:12
Leich, J. 15:57
Leichinger, J. 3:118
Leicht, Adam 4:37
Leidcick, Frank 19:83
Leideker, Peter 18:311;
    26:104
Leider, A. 23:117
Leiderburg, W. 18:176
Leidheiser, D. G. 1:147
Leidig, Philip 10:92;
    20:293
Leidle, E. 21:189
Leidner, Jacob 5:21
Leidsinger, W. S. 16:298
Leifels, Frank 19:83
Leifert, Jacob 22:339
Leiggett, J. 3:118
Leigh, Ichobod 22:41
Leigh, J. W. 27:77
Leigh, James 20:125
Leigh, John C. 21:357
Leigh, Joseph 7:128
Leigh, Marcus D. 22:407
Leigh, Richard 9:25
Leigh, William D. 21:131
Leighdon, W. 25:50
Leighland, Daniel 21:123
Leighman, John M. 13:33
Leight, E. P. 1:149
Leight, J. S. 9:43
Leighten, C. L. 26:169
Leightly, Allen 8:89

Leightly, John 24:167
Leightner, Jacob 5:21
Leighton, --- 9:183
Leighton, B. W. 12:29
Leighton, Frank 16:3
Leighton, H. 27:74
Leighton, H. G. 19:228
Leighton, Harvey E.
    22:147
Leighton, Henry 22:497
Leighton, Jefferson
    19:228
Leighton, John 7:101;
    9:231; 20:293
Leighton, John N. 5:21
Leighton, Peltere 1:50
Leighton, R. B. 8:51
Leighton, Samuel A. 1:51
Leighton, W. 7:32; 15:108
Leighton, W. A. 19:228
Leighton, W. G. 19:228
Leighton, William 3:118;
    15:343; 16:373
Leighton, William H. 1:49
Leighty, Daniel 24:23
Leighty, I. S. 26:126
Leigny, Louis 25:49
Leihimer, Matthew 21:140
Leik, Peter 22:204
Leiley, J. L. 24:52
Lein, August 20:23
Lein, C. H. 17:288
Lein, Jacob 21:244
Lein, Julius 9:201
Leindsey, Ephraim 19:175
Leine, --- 16:373
Leiney, J. 18:15
Leinhard, Conrad 9:106
Leinhart, James 10:123;
    20:293
Leinsey, W. H. 25:198
Leip, William 12:73
Leipird, Simon 11:414
Leippe, John 13:127
Leise, Jacob 22:88
Leiser, Boniface 24:95
Leiser, Jacob 1:49
Leish, Nicholas 8:51
Leisher, E. 26:42
Leisher, William B. 10:25
Leishess, Charles 13:65
Leishess, James 13:65
Leisme, W. 21:189
Leist, Amos S. 23:154
Leist, Harrison 13:33
Leist, William C. 23:277
Leiste, Julius 5:21
Leister, Anderson 8:22;
    18:145
Leister, H. 16:298

Leister, John 10:123; 14:15; 20:293
Leistes, Joseph 4:37
Leisure, John 13:33
Leisure, Jonathan 15:209
Leitch, N. 27:145
Leitchelfelden, Louis 10:64
Leitchwarth, John 10:64
Leiter, John H. 21:357
Leiter, Marcus 23:154
Leith, F. 13:93
Leith, Isaac L. 23:154
Leith, John W. 8:89
Leithon, S. 13:93; 14:15
Leitk, A. 3:118
Leituger, John 16:298
Leitus, Christian 18:145
Leitz, A. 14:15
Leitz, Michael 17:22
Leitz, William 3:118
Leitzberg, James 12:29
Leitzel, E. 1:51
Leize, John 12:29
Lekfield, John 7:64
Leknerder, A. 18:15
Leland, B. F. 12:100
Leland, Edson T. 10:19
Leland, G. H. 19:239
Leland, L. A. 21:357
Leland, Royal A. 10:163; 19:175
Leland, Thomas 11:36
Leland, William 26:145
Lelland, Gilbert H. 9:183
Leller, Benjamin F. 23:70
Lellers, S. F. 9:55
Lellgett, Richard 9:25
Lelye, Frederick 12:29
Lem, E. G. 19:83
Lemaczon, Aristede 19:23
Lemaire, Nicholas 17:260
Leman, Charles 22:430
Leman, Marshall 7:101
Leman, Willis 4:37
Lemans, William 17:96
Lemar, John 1:50
Lemarux, Joseph 3:118
Lemaster, George 15:209
Lemaster, Richard 17:237
Lemasters, Isaac 22:204
Lemasters, Jacob 11:67
Lemasters, John D. L. 22:88
Lembeck, Simon 22:88
Lemen, Alexander C. 22:464
Lemeraux, Squire H. 7:68
Lemermon, Jonas 12:29
Lemersville, C. 14:257
Lemey, Stephen 7:101

Lemhan, Jeremiah 10:19
Lemhew, Bartno 9:55
Lemier, John L. 20:293
Lemin, C. 25:198
Lemin, J. 17:434; 24:171
Leming, Charles 24:41
Lemins, Zerah 9:231
Lemins, Zuah 20:293
Lemke, Herman 23:252
Lemke, William 21:140
Lemler, John 22:281
Lemley, Truman 7:101
Lemm, John R. 21:10
Lemm, William B. 9:43
Lemman, A. H. 18:397
Lemmer, Jacob 25:198
Lemmitt, Horace 21:357
Lemmix, Isaac 11:402
Lemmon, James 18:208
Lemmon, Levi 8:89
Lemmon, N. 22:204
Lemmon, N. W. 15:319; 19:83
Lemmon, R. F. 24:23
Lemmons, Harrison 17:353
Lemmons, John 20:293
Lemmons, Samuel 20:293
Lemmons, William 9:66; 18:278
Lemmustine, Alexander 7:101
Lemmy, Alex 17:180
Lemner, Peter 7:101
Lemoin, L. K. 1:149
Lemon, A. 21:32
Lemon, Addison 9:103; 18:339
Lemon, C. W. 4:37
Lemon, Daniel 22:520
Lemon, Ezekiel 23:108
Lemon, Francis 25:334
Lemon, G. 21:85
Lemon, Henry 21:217
Lemon, J. 9:146; 27:75
Lemon, J. A. 25:51
Lemon, J. B. 17:145
Lemon, James H. 22:12
Lemon, John E. 3:118
Lemon, John F. 23:108
Lemon, L. 9:183; 19:267
Lemon, Levi 15:95
Lemon, P. H. 2:14
Lemon, Richard M. 22:88
Lemon, Simon 8:73
Lemon, W. 3:118
Lemon, William 17:409; 22:41
Lemon, William S. 22:41, 112
Lemons, Anthony 7:128

Lemons, David 23:192
Lemons, F. L. 25:49
Lemons, George P. 22:258
Lemons, John 10:123; 11:381
Lemons, Joseph 9:165
Lemons, M. 3:118
Lemont, A. 19:229
Lemont, O. H. 19:222
LeMoore, Augustus 11:183
Lemoreaux, J. R. 14:15
Lemory, Frderick 17:263
Lemping, Dominic 10:64
Lemson, Arthur F. 21:228
Lemvig, Ole 23:192
Len, Charles H. 16:42
Lenahan, Richard 22:41
Lenam, George W. 14:267
Lenard, --- 21:32
Lenard, A. A. 15:353
Lenard, George 10:180
Lenard, John 24:41; 25:287
Lenard, Patrick 19:175
Lenart, Paul 13:33
Lenaster, John 10:192
Lenbert, Joseph 25:300
Lench, Levi 11:16
Lenchlin, J. 3:118
Lenck, Daniel 9:236
Lender, D. 26:169
Lenderle, Israel 10:64
Lenderley, J. 20:293
Lenderson, Elisha W. 20:142
Lendner, John D. 14:189
Lendrum, Upton 19:23
Lenehan, Thomas 23:90
Lener, C. R. 11:265
Lener, William 18:33
Lenervor, Frederick 22:41
Lenet, V. 3:118
Lenex, D. 3:118
Leney, Henry 17:237
Lenfair, A. J. 12:9
Lenfist, R. A. 27:75
Leng, Fulton 12:87
Leng, William 20:293
Lenge, O. 1:150
Lengenholder, --- 19:275
Lenhart, C. H. 12:163
Lenhart, Elias 22:431
Lenhart, G. 1:150
Lenhart, Henry 24:23
Lenhart, J. 11:439
Lenhart, James 19:23
Lenhart, Samuel B. 21:217
Lenhurt, Charles 18:176
Lenier, John L. 10:92

Lenier, Robert A. 21:73
Lenig, Josiah 12:29
Leniger, Isaac 11:67
Lenim, Charles 5:21
Lening, G. J. 2:14
Leningham, James 13:130
Lenix, J. E. 20:293
Lenix, Samuel 22:235
Lenk, Charles J. 20:293
Lenkons, J. A. 27:77
Lenlie, H. 25:198
Lenliff, Edward F. 9:183
Lennen, M. 20:293
Lennen, Michael 10:64
Lennen, Peter B. 20:98
Lennew, C. 18:52
Lennex, G. M. 21:32
Lenney, John R. 12:29
Lennich, Barnet 17:454
Lennix, S. M. 8:51
Lennon, P. H. 25:51
Lennon, T. H. 23:104
Lennon, W. B. 26:125
Lennon, William G. 22:88
Lennon, William H. 20:189
Lennore, Dennis 12:96
Lennox, Abraham 10:64; 20:294
Lennox, G. 14:257
Lennox, G. M. 8:51
Lennox, S. 12:96
Lenny, D. 16:207
Leno, Henry 18:52
Leno, Jacob 7:75, 80; 25:300
Lenoir, Joseph 11:207
Lenon, Eli 24:81
Lenon, James 18:191
Lenord, E. 16:373
Lenoron, Robert 19:329
Lenoth, Joseph 16:207
Lenox, David 18:219
Lenox, E. A. 22:204
Lenox, G. 14:189
Lenox, George W. 12:29
Lenox, Henry 10:123; 20:294
Lenox, Henry C. 10:123; 20:294
Lenox, J. E. 10:64
Lenox, Jesse W. 23:154
Lenox, John 11:414
Lenox, Joseph 9:43; 26:126
Lenox, Robert 16:373
Lenox, S. 12:100; 15:360; 19:83
Lenox, William 4:37; 11:155
Lenseg, G. 20:294

Lensey, Thomas 10:123; 20:294
Lensky, Dennis 14:189
Lenssen, R. 1:150
Lent, A. 3:118
Lent, Albert 15:209
Lent, Charles I. 10:64
Lent, Charles W. 19:83
Lent, D. 18:243; 26:43
Lent, D. A. J. 18:243; 26:43
Lent, Francis 8:73
Lent, H. 3:118
Lent, Henry 15:209
Lent, Henry I. 15:343
Lent, Henry J. 16:373
Lent, John W. 26:169
Lent, W. F. 16:207
Lent, W. H. 13:79
Lent, William N. 16:207; 21:92
Lentell, James B. 21:357
Lenten, John 7:101
Lenter, James 18:243
Lents, Henry 17:46
Lents, Thomas W. 18:219
Lenty, Marshall 7:101; 21:357
Lentz, Eli A. 21:32
Lentz, Elias 25:51
Lentz, Franklin A. 12:83
Lentz, J. T. 20:155
Lentz, John H. 15:57
Lentz, Michael 24:63
Lentz, Nicholas 18:52
Lenville, James 9:161
Lenyer, M. 3:118
Lenzig, Gottleib 10:64
Leo, John 15:283, 343; 16:373; 19:83
Leo, L. W. 18:176
Leo, M. 19:83
Leod, John 11:16
Leolenwasser, William 1:50
Leolock, S. F. 18:311
Leomans, Benjamin F. 4:37
Leomun, J. 25:198
Leon, D. Juan 9:183
Leon, J. 25:323
Leon, Patrick 12:29
Leon, T. 21:357
Leonard, --- 21:291; 24:198
Leonard, A. 3:118
Leonard, A. A. 16:280
Leonard, A. C. 23:38
Leonard, Albert 18:219
Leonard, Alex. C. 19:175

Leonard, Alexander 10:173
Leonard, Alfred 17:419; 22:147
Leonard, Arthur C. 18:244; 26:43
Leonard, Bartlett 19:175
Leonard, C. H. 3:118; 7:128
Leonard, C. O. 25:198
Leonard, Cassius M. 11:67
Leonard, Charles 10:19; 12:73; 15:17; 21:357; 22:281
Leonard, Charles E. 13:33
Leonard, Charles O. 5:21
Leonard, D. 13:93; 14:15
Leonard, D. H. 18:244; 26:43
Leonard, Daniel 11:183
Leonard, E. 1:150
Leonard, E. D. 1:149
Leonard, Eli 22:520
Leonard, Elijah M. 22:88
Leonard, F. 12:96; 15:360; 16:280
Leonard, F. H. 20:294
Leonard, F. M. 3:118
Leonard, Franklin 22:407
Leonard, Frederick 11:108; 22:484
Leonard, Frederick A. 16:71
Leonard, G. 1:150
Leonard, George 3:118; 7:101, 128; 18:176
Leonard, George E. 13:33
Leonard, George F. 16:86
Leonard, H. 27:75
Leonard, H. C. 10:148; 18:52
Leonard, H. H. 12:162
Leonard, H. M. 11:265
Leonard, Henry 1:49; 21:247
Leonard, J. 1:149; 3:119; 9:146; 13:113; 14:81; 21:111, 189; 25:198; 27:75
Leonard, J. A. 24:88
Leonard, J. D. 16:42
Leonard, J. E. 15:83
Leonard, J. G. 3:119
Leonard, J. L. 12:29
Leonard, J. W. 3:119; 14:331
Leonard, Jacob 8:23; 18:145
Leonard, James 6:31; 7:32, 128; 8:23, 126;

Leonard, James 14:189;
    16:42; 18:145;
    24:198; 25:323;
    27:78
Leonard, James A. 22:115
Leonard, James G. 20:23
Leonard, James M.
    15:337; 26:237
Leonard, James R. 18:219
Leonard, Jerome 5:21
Leonard, John 2:14;
    3:119; 16:207;
    20:107, 108; 21:228;
    23:241; 25:49, 50,
    198
Leonard, John D. 23:108
Leonard, John J. 21:357
Leonard, John N. 5:21
Leonard, John W. 22:258
Leonard, Joseph 11:402;
    13:33
Leonard, Joshua 17:111
Leonard, Julius J. 21:140
Leonard, L. J. 2:14
Leonard, Lawrence 9:85;
    26:42
Leonard, Lemuel J.
    22:125
Leonard, Levi 16:42
Leonard, Mathew 20:294
Leonard, Matthew 10:64
Leonard, Melvin 21:357
Leonard, Orville 13:33
Leonard, Owen 1:50
Leonard, P. 1:49
Leonard, Pat 20:294
Leonard, Patrick 9:231
Leonard, Peter 13:33;
    16:42; 17:393
Leonard, Robert B.
    17:419
Leonard, Robert H.
    17:273
Leonard, S. 1:148; 15:351
Leonard, S. O. 10:64;
    20:294
Leonard, Silas 23:260;
    25:50
Leonard, Thomas C.
    23:154
Leonard, Thomas E. 12:29
Leonard, Thomas W.
    21:357
Leonard, W. 3:119
Leonard, W. E. 3:119
Leonard, W. P. 1:150
Leonard, W. S. 8:119
Leonard, William 7:128;
    10:64; 13:33; 20:10,
    294; 22:147

Leonard, William H.
    10:163; 26:169
Leonard, William N.
    15:39
Leonard, William S.
    22:235
Leonata, T. 9:183
Leonberger, William
    25:50
Leonderman, C. 1:150
Leonell, Omscn 26:42
Leonhard, P. 1:51
Leonhart, David 13:65;
    19:83
Leonord, Jacob 24:23
Leony, Peter 21:212
Leopard, John 20:18
Leopold, --- 21:189
Leopold, Gardner 1:50
Leopold, George 22:171
Leopold, Henry 14:189
Leopold, Lewis 11:120
Leopont, C. 3:119
Leor, William 11:122
Leord, Caleb B. 11:100
Leoroy, Elliott 22:147
Lepack, Henry 19:23
Lepard, Charles 24:23
Lepe, A. 3:119
Leper, Echer 15:57
LePert, James 9:183
Lepland, Charles 24:23
Lepley, Charles 3:119
Lepley, Samuel 10:123;
    20:294
Lepohart, Emanuel 25:198
Lepoldi, Henry 14:189
LePont, J. 3:119
Lepoon, W. P. 21:357
Lepp, Charles 13:128
Leppard, E. J. 14:81
Leppard, Thomas 22:41
Lepper, Alfred A. 22:112
Lepper, Jacob H. 21:358
Lepper, John S. 22:167
Lepper, S. 1:147
Leppert, O. 22:204
Lequi, Bonay 16:207
Ler, L. K. 18:176
Lerange, Joseph 4:37
Lerbingwood, W. H.
    25:198
Lerd, John 7:32
Lerelle, Thomas 3:119
Leringood, William H.
    5:21
Lerker, George A. 15:209
Lerkey, John W. 22:235
Lerman, George A.
    22:204
Lermgruber, --- 19:83

Lermond, A. S. 13:113
Lernart, C. Q. 7:32
Leroach, William T. 16:42
Leroy, A. 9:146; 14:81;
    27:75
Leroy, B. 10:64; 20:294
Leroy, F. 1:148
Leroy, Francis 23:12;
    26:222
Leroy, J. 1:98
Leroy, John 13:113;
    21:277
Leroy, R. 14:81
Leroy, Robert 11:381
Leroy, William 12:29
Lerrick, Benjamin 12:73
Lerroy, Francis 9:236
Lerrupkins, J. 14:81
Lerry, George 16:97
Lerry, George W. 15:209
Lerry, J. W. 15:209
Lerry, John 11:155
Lertey, A. 13:93
LeRump, Augustus
    23:204
Lervis, Isaac M. 18:397
Lervis, Richard 6:17
Leryelere, Henry 25:49
LeSage, Lewis 27:77
Lesage, Louis 9:121
Lesan, Solomon B.
    10:123; 20:294
Lesbley, D. P. 20:294
Lesch, Nicholas 21:257
Leseberg, Frederick
    22:407
Leser, Frederick 24:67
Lesh, David 17:265
Lesh, Lewis 6:10
Leshall, William 7:51
Lesher, Robert 16:121
Lesher, William 15:27
Leshorn, George 4:37
Leshot, Joseph 11:155
Lesk, Omar 17:232
Lesler, Thomas 9:36
Lesley, Allen 23:286
Lesley, Amos 9:36;
    18:294
Lesley, G. W. 16:207
Lesley, J. J. 21:102
Lesley, Jacob 21:245
Lesley, Morris 11:67
Leslie, --- 11:265
Leslie, Albert G. 20:125
Leslie, Andre 19:175
Leslie, Andrew 10:173
Leslie, Benjamin F.
    22:148
Leslie, Charles 10:163;
    18:330; 19:175

Leslie, Clarkson 22:41
Leslie, Frederick W. 25:275
Leslie, G. 14:283
Leslie, H. 11:265
Leslie, Humphrey 22:41
Leslie, J. 9:111
Leslie, James 9:183; 19:283; 22:204
Leslie, James P. 6:10
Leslie, John 12:166; 18:244; 25:323; 26:43
Leslie, Mark 7:64
Leslie, N. D. 1:49
Leslie, Robert 14:81
Leslie, W. H. 14:278; 23:185
Leslie, William 17:243; 21:32
Leslie, William J. 22:12
Lesly, Amos 26:105
Lesnet, Francis 23:154
Lesneur, M. C. 11:341
Lespe, Charles 23:154
Lesperance, Enos 22:464
Lespute, Edward 19:23
Lessabell, J. 1:150
Lessenger, George W. 8:89
Lesser, F. 9:183
Lesser, Solomon 16:97
Lessinger, J. C. 17:162, 405
Lesslie, John 23:38
Lesson, Alfred 5:42
Lestar, W. H. 3:119
Lestarky, C. 12:83
Lesten, John F. 12:62
Lester, E. 15:349; 16:373
Lester, E. W. 21:32
Lester, George 13:33
Lester, George F. 21:117
Lester, George W. 25:272
Lester, H. 12:92; 14:189
Lester, J. H. 21:358
Lester, J. S. 27:75
Lester, James 3:119
Lester, James D. 17:347
Lester, John 10:123; 13:93; 20:294
Lester, John F. 15:8
Lester, L. 1:51
Lester, N. C. 16:269
Lester, R. 1:98
Lester, Refer 17:155
Lester, Robert 17:82
Lester, S. A. 11:67
Lester, T. 1:149
Lester, T. L. 11:36
Lester, Thomas 11:265

Lester, W. 1:148
Lester, W. H. 1:150
Lester, Willard 12:73
Lester, William 10:123; 20:178, 294; 22:88
Lesters, James 11:207
Lestley, David P. 10:64
Leston, R. 25:199
Lestrange, M. 25:199
Lestruer, Lewis 14:81
Lestruff, C. 3:119
Lesure, Perry 23:38
Letarky, C. 16:298
Letcher, Ed 17:180
Letcher, Luke 19:175
Letcher, Nelson M. 10:64; 20:294
Letchworth, John 20:294
Lete, John W. 22:41
Lete, Jonathan 27:77
Letes, A. 16:207
Letever, Isaac 25:50
Letgen, E. 3:119
Leth, William 20:294
Lethe, Jacob 22:204
Letherwood, Nathan M. 10:123
Lethrop, C. D. 4:37
Letmolien, Lavel 20:49
Letner, Samuel 26:44
Letsinger, Alexander 23:71
Letsinger, James B. 23:71
Letsinger, Samuel W. 17:96
Letsinger, William 8:89
Letson, Jonathan 25:199
Letson, R. 5:52
Letson, Timothy 17:66
Lett, Lumbrius 18:33
Lett, Thomas J. 16:136
Lett, Willis 27:76
Lettage, J. 16:207
Letter, Edmond 18:145
Letter, James R. 11:67
Letteral, Jacob 21:277
Letti, Amos 1:50
Letting, F. S. 9:85
Lettner, David 21:73
Letts, James 1:50
Letts, Lemuel 23:129
Lettues, Samuel 9:85
Letty, Jacob 21:358
Letty, John 16:208
Letz, A. M. 14:81
Letz, John 14:189
Letzler, Thomas 12:73
Letzniger, David 17:353
Leubbett, M. S. 3:119
Leuderking, Rudolph 11:402

Leudon, H. 3:119
Leuloff, E. T. 19:275
Leuman, Andrew 22:484
Leuson, M. 18:69
Leutz, Franklin A. 16:298
Leutze, Charles 26:41
Levacy, Allen 15:209
LeValley, C. 3:119
Levaney, George H. 17:54
Level, Albert 17:180
Level, George 22:308
Level, Jonas 21:140
Level, Reuben 11:207
Level, Samuel 14:189
Level, Wilson 11:207
Leveler, E. 17:277
Levember, Nicholas 18:69
Lever, F. 14:81
Lever, George 12:29
Lever, H. B. 3:119
Lever, H. H. 3:119
Lever, John 13:93; 14:81
Levercomb, J. 1:149
Levere, M. 8:51
Leverens, Samuel 26:104
Leverett, N. 15:209
Leverich, William 20:137
Leveringhouse, John C. 14:189
Leverins, Samuel 18:311
Leverlon, P. 27:75
Leverri, A. 12:162
Levers, Jeremiah 13:33
Leverson, Anthony 17:288
Levert, M. 24:167
Leverton, R. 1:149
Levery, Tilman 12:50
Leves, Moses 21:277
Levett, James T. 11:108
Levey, William 14:81
Levi, C. 25:323
Levi, Chapel 6:31
Levi, Frank 22:514
Levi, Isaac 24:213
Levi, J. N. 17:504
Levi, M. 1:52
Levi, W. R. 22:258
Levick, Caspar 15:39
Levicount, Spencer E. 23:117
Levily, Jesse 9:236
Levin, C. 25:199
Levine, A. 25:199
Levine, William 11:36
Leving, Nelson 1:50
Levinger, Henry 18:87
Levinghouse, Benjamin 14:189
Levingood, G. 14:81
Levings, George 8:101; 17:464; 24:212

Levings, Orlando 10:123; 20:294
Levinns, Samuel 9:25
Levins, Leopold 9:97
Levis, D. D. 16:373
Levis, Isaiah 21:245
Levis, J. 22:148
Levison, Christian 21:358
Levison, L. 21:358
Levissee, Isaac 8:107
Levix, Joseph 22:407
Levly, Frank 7:32
Levy, --- 25:50
Levy, B. F. 16:42
Levy, Barney 13:33
Levy, Frank 3:119
Levy, H. J. 18:112
Levy, J. 8:121
Levy, William 12:166
Lew, John 7:33
Lewallen, Hall 25:199
Lewallen, J. 25:199
Lewallen, Joseph C. 16:280
Lewaller, James G. 15:353
Lewark, Elijah 23:71
Lewark, Francis M. 23:71
Lewellan, John 9:25
Lewellen, Abraham 22:204
Lewellen, J. 20:294; 26:170
Lewellen, J. T. 1:150
Lewellen, James M. 22:88
Lewellen, Josephus 10:64
Lewellen, Wilson 23:71
Lewelling, Thomas 8:51
Lewellyn, Samuel 4:37
Lewellyn, Thomas 21:102
Lewely, Jessee 26:222
Lewelyn, John 17:406
Lewelyn, M. 17:37
Lewelyn, R. 9:111
Lewens, Foster 11:155
Lewers, Jacob 22:125
Lewie, Dales 15:263
Lewilly, William 3:119
Lewin, J. 1:148
Lewin, Richard 23:180
Lewis, --- 9:25; 15:17; 26:170
Lewis, A. 1:147, 148, 149, 150; 3:119; 14:81; 15:209; 17:292; 21:201; 22:308; 25:199
Lewis, A. B. 12:155
Lewis, A. D. 17:402
Lewis, A. F. 11:187
Lewis, A. J. 10:96; 25:50
Lewis, A. K. 25:51

Lewis, Abner 21:73
Lewis, Abraham 5:42; 13:33; 25:199
Lewis, Albert J. 7:63
Lewis, Albert R. 9:227; 18:370
Lewis, Alexander 23:71
Lewis, Allen 9:121
Lewis, Allen H. 10:123; 20:294
Lewis, Almond D. 17:403
Lewis, Alvin T. 21:32
Lewis, Anderson 12:50
Lewis, Andrew 9:70; 22:509
Lewis, Andrew J. 22:88
Lewis, Andrew T. 10:123; 20:294
Lewis, Anthony 22:308
Lewis, Antonio 18:87
Lewis, Archie 25:199
Lewis, B. C. 17:37
Lewis, B. H. 8:51
Lewis, Baliff 11:207
Lewis, Benjamin 21:358
Lewis, Benjamin B. 11:307
Lewis, Benjamin F. 22:453
Lewis, Benjamin N. 22:235
Lewis, Benjamin R. 23:256
Lewis, Besha 12:147
Lewis, Bluford H. 21:102
Lewis, Bradford 9:13
Lewis, Burt W. 4:37
Lewis, C. 3:119; 6:31; 25:199, 323
Lewis, C. F. 3:119
Lewis, C. R. 13:113; 14:189
Lewis, C. V. 18:87
Lewis, C. W. 9:201; 19:291; 21:32; 25:199
Lewis, Calvin 12:160
Lewis, Charles 3:119; 5:42; 8:89; 9:133, 162, 209; 13:33; 16:208; 17:180; 20:125; 23:12; 24:72; 25:323; 27:76, 79
Lewis, Charles H. 12:29; 22:112, 430
Lewis, Charles V. 6:10
Lewis, Columbus E. 7:101
Lewis, D. 3:119; 14:283; 18:52; 23:154
Lewis, D. D. 8:51; 15:343
Lewis, D. H. 15:159

Lewis, D. S. 3:119
Lewis, Danforth A. 4:37
Lewis, Daniel 11:156; 17:398; 21:89; 25:49
Lewis, Daniel H. 23:250
Lewis, Daniel P. 20:177
Lewis, Daniel S. 12:64; 15:22
Lewis, Darius 15:39
Lewis, David 9:121; 10:123; 20:294; 22:308; 27:77
Lewis, David M. 18:327
Lewis, Decatur 10:176; 19:175
Lewis, E. 3:119; 9:133; 12:122; 14:81; 18:244; 21:111; 25:199; 26:43
Lewis, E. B. 24:23
Lewis, E. C. 9:85; 26:44
Lewis, E. G. 11:192
Lewis, E. W. 9:183; 19:267
Lewis, Eben 15:128
Lewis, Edgar S. 22:464
Lewis, Edmund 9:156
Lewis, Edmund E. 17:288
Lewis, Edw. 8:89
Lewis, Edward 15:69; 24:95
Lewis, Edward A. 15:343; 16:373
Lewis, Elijah 9:85; 25:287; 26:41
Lewis, Elisha 11:287; 12:73
Lewis, Emor 27:76
Lewis, Eugene 19:23
Lewis, Everett 10:176; 19:175
Lewis, F. 1:150; 3:119; 13:66; 14:189
Lewis, F. A. 3:119
Lewis, F. C. 17:159
Lewis, F. J. 25:199
Lewis, F. L. 3:119
Lewis, F. N. 25:199
Lewis, Fayette 8:51; 21:140
Lewis, Ferdinand 20:35
Lewis, Finle 17:134
Lewis, Finley 24:198
Lewis, Francis 23:155; 27:77
Lewis, Francis A. 16:86
Lewis, Francis P. 9:121; 15:152
Lewis, Frank 16:42; 25:199
Lewis, Frank P. 13:33

Lewis, Franklin 3:119
Lewis, Franklin H. 20:30
Lewis, Frederick 21:358
Lewis, G. 1:149; 15:314;
  25:199
Lewis, G. A. 26:170
Lewis, G. G. 3:119
Lewis, G. H. 3:119
Lewis, G. S. 19:23
Lewis, G. T. 10:64;
  20:294
Lewis, G. W. 3:119
Lewis, Garrison 4:37
Lewis, George 1:191;
  9:36; 11:307; 12:50;
  19:83; 21:85; 22:308,
  431
Lewis, George A. 9:121;
  27:77
Lewis, George F. 16:86
Lewis, George H. 7:101
Lewis, George M. 1:49
Lewis, George W. 7:32;
  11:36, 307; 22:112
Lewis, Gerdon 9:201
Lewis, Gideon 17:389
Lewis, Giles B. 13:33
Lewis, Gowan 9:13
Lewis, Granverville 5:42
Lewis, H. 12:92; 13:93;
  14:81; 16:298
Lewis, H. E. 17:232
Lewis, H. R. 14:242
Lewis, H. S. 19:255
Lewis, H. T. 20:294
Lewis, H. W. 8:73; 12:29
Lewis, Harrison 25:51
Lewis, Harvey 23:314
Lewis, Henry 6:17, 28;
  9:13, 85; 10:64;
  14:15; 17:134;
  18:87; 19:23, 47;
  20:294; 22:308, 453;
  24:198
Lewis, Henry D. 4:37
Lewis, Henry S. 9:183
Lewis, Horatio 8:23;
  18:145
Lewis, I. H. 23:38
Lewis, I. O. 14:82
Lewis, Ira 24:212
Lewis, Ira H. 21:358
Lewis, Isaac 10:64;
  11:265
Lewis, Isaac E. 4:37
Lewis, Isaac L. 7:32
Lewis, J. 1:50, 98; 3:119;
  9:146, 240; 14:300;
  16:208, 269; 17:473;
  18:311; 19:283;
  21:102; 25:199;

Lewis, J. 26:105; 27:77,
  78
Lewis, J. A. 14:81
Lewis, J. B. 1:148, 149;
  26:169
Lewis, J. C. 22:148
Lewis, J. D. 10:64; 15:209
Lewis, J. G. 14:82
Lewis, J. H. 9:240; 10:19;
  17:436; 24:187
Lewis, J. J. 25:280
Lewis, J. L. 14:82
Lewis, J. M. 17:292
Lewis, J. T. 5:42; 25:199;
  26:169
Lewis, J. W. 1:148;
  26:170
Lewis, Jacob 4:37; 22:258
Lewis, James 3:119; 6:17;
  8:73, 89; 9:31, 47,
  133, 183; 10:64;
  11:265; 12:50;
  14:189, 270, 283;
  15:17, 278; 17:237;
  18:87; 20:294; 22:41,
  308; 25:199, 311
Lewis, James A. 4:37;
  22:258
Lewis, James C. 6:21;
  17:237
Lewis, James F. 7:32
Lewis, James H. 22:259
Lewis, James J. 21:277
Lewis, James L. 20:31
Lewis, James M. 17:260
Lewis, James W. 11:155
Lewis, Jeremiah 19:348;
  22:258
Lewis, Jeremiah D. 8:101;
  17:460; 24:160
Lewis, Jerry 7:128
Lewis, Jesse 7:59; 22:308
Lewis, John 6:25; 7:63,
  101, 128; 9:209, 222;
  10:64, 146; 11:127,
  207, 307; 12:29, 50,
  92; 14:15, 81, 189;
  15:330; 16:298;
  17:134; 18:69, 370;
  19:83; 20:46, 114,
  294; 21:358; 22:148,
  258, 308, 353, 514;
  24:198
Lewis, John A. 16:8
Lewis, John B. 9:159;
  21:358
Lewis, John C. 17:91
Lewis, John D. 20:294
Lewis, John E. 13:33;
  22:88

Lewis, John F. 9:121;
  27:77
Lewis, John H. 9:146;
  11:424; 27:75
Lewis, John P. 21:167
Lewis, John R. 8:51
Lewis, Jonathan P. 9:97
Lewis, Jordan 9:183;
  19:291
Lewis, Jos. 22:514
Lewis, Joseph 5:42;
  7:101, 128; 15:8;
  20:103; 27:75
Lewis, Joseph H. 11:94
Lewis, Josiah 22:235
Lewis, L. 3:119; 18:244;
  26:43, 169
Lewis, L. A. 26:42
Lewis, L. J. 1:148
Lewis, Lee 21:358
Lewis, Lemuel 20:294
Lewis, Leonard 18:87
Lewis, Leonh 6:13
Lewis, Leroy 10:64;
  20:295
Lewis, Levi 9:209; 19:83
Lewis, Lewis 5:21; 26:126
Lewis, Lyman A. 9:85
Lewis, M. H. 7:32
Lewis, Major 12:173
Lewis, Mason 17:180
Lewis, Mather 14:189
Lewis, Merrett 19:303
Lewis, Merril 12:147
Lewis, Milton 11:36;
  17:180
Lewis, Milton G. 17:282
Lewis, N. 12:166; 14:82,
  257; 22:308; 25:323
Lewis, Nelson P. 10:64;
  20:295
Lewis, Newton 25:199
Lewis, O. P. 18:244;
  26:42
Lewis, Orson 22:483
Lewis, P. 3:119
Lewis, P. A. 3:119
Lewis, Peter 3:119
Lewis, Peter T. 18:69
Lewis, Philip 9:201
Lewis, Preston 17:180
Lewis, Q. C. 24:23
Lewis, R. 3:119; 11:323
Lewis, Ransker 22:353
Lewis, Richard 12:29;
  17:92, 180; 18:87
Lewis, Robert 6:31;
  14:189; 22:88;
  25:323; 26:43; 27:146
Lewis, Robert C. 13:125

Lewis, Robert L. 18:244
Lewis, Robert M. 8:51;
21:32
Lewis, Rockwell 9:121;
27:77
Lewis, Runyen C. 20:23
Lewis, S. 3:119; 20:57,
147; 21:358
Lewis, S. B. 8:65
Lewis, S. W. 11:244
Lewis, Samuel 6:25; 7:78;
10:64; 15:128;
16:208; 19:23;
21:358; 22:259;
25:300
Lewis, Samuel R. 16:136
Lewis, Sandy 21:358
Lewis, Scipio 17:134;
24:198
Lewis, Seymour R. 23:123
Lewis, Simeon 12:73
Lewis, Simon 23:117
Lewis, Smart 9:133; 27:77
Lewis, Solomon 22:259
Lewis, Stewart 9:209
Lewis, T. 20:295
Lewis, T. J. 5:52
Lewis, Thomas 6:17;
8:23; 12:29; 14:82;
18:87, 145; 21:32;
22:204, 258
Lewis, Thomas S. 22:88
Lewis, Timothy 7:16
Lewis, Ton 24:112
Lewis, V. G. 11:333
Lewis, Victor 7:128;
21:358
Lewis, Vinson 21:228
Lewis, W. 21:55
Lewis, W. A. 10:28;
15:294; 19:303
Lewis, W. F. 21:358
Lewis, W. G. 7:101
Lewis, W. H. 2:14; 15:39,
209; 23:38; 25:50, 51
Lewis, W. M. 18:244;
26:42
Lewis, W. O. 27:74
Lewis, W. P. 3:119
Lewis, W. S. 25:199
Lewis, W. V. 11:265
Lewis, Warren 9:157
Lewis, Wesley 22:204
Lewis, Wesley B. 17:445;
24:167
Lewis, Weston 6:25
Lewis, Will 16:208
Lewis, William 1:50;
5:42; 9:85, 222;
11:389, 424; 12:73;
13:66; 14:189;

Lewis, William 17:436;
18:33, 87, 370;
19:83; 20:31; 21:358;
22:88, 308; 23:38;
24:185; 25:199;
26:41
Lewis, William A. 8:89;
23:71
Lewis, William B. 8:23;
18:145
Lewis, William C. 5:42;
15:57
Lewis, William F. 22:204
Lewis, William H. 8:114;
9:36
Lewis, William W. 22:308
Lewis, Willis 22:308
Lewis, Wilson O. 11:402
Lewis, Zach. T. 20:295
Lewis, Zackariah T.
10:123
Lewis, Zebulon 10:64
Lewison, Alexander
21:257
Lewllyn, John 15:210
Lewman, David 21:73
Lews, Levi 13:66
Lewton, Sam 22:309
Lewtz, H. 14:333
Lex, Harson 9:183
Lexfield, Jacob 8:101;
17:462; 24:173
Ley, John W. 22:41
Ley, L. 11:231
Ley, Michael 16:156
Leybarckey, J. 23:71
Leybeyer, Isaac 21:245
Leydbickle, Jacob 27:78
Leyden, Martin 23:123
Leyer, Daniel 24:178
Leykin, Isaac P. 11:16
Leyman, John 12:54;
18:112
Leyman, Ment 27:78
Leyton, Jerry C. 9:85
Leyton, L. M. 13:77
Leyton, Surgen 16:373
Leyton, T 17:151
Lezarre, Primis 21:358
Lezier, James H. 23:71
Lhafttey, Peter 12:155
Libbart, George 8:89
Libbaugh, Philip 13:33
Libbe, William H. 16:373
Libbey, A. D. 7:75;
25:300
Libbey, A. G. 3:119
Libbey, Dallas H. 19:229
Libbey, John T. 6:7
Libbey, Joseph 18:340
Libbey, Thomas 20:295

Libbey, Thomas H.
10:123
Libbey, Virgil 12:29
Libby, --- 25:49
Libby, A. J. 10:19
Libby, Abrarads L. 9:214
Libby, Albans 14:189
Libby, Albert 9:184
Libby, Charles A. 7:8
Libby, D. 25:287
Libby, E. 27:145
Libby, E. O. 21:358
Libby, Edward 22:134
Libby, G. W. 1:52
Libby, H. C. 1:50; 15:319
Libby, H. H. 26:170
Libby, J. C. 1:51
Libby, J. F. 1:51; 6:31;
25:323
Libby, J. W. 9:111
Libby, James M. 21:358
Libby, John 15:39
Libby, L. H. 19:83
Libby, Richard 19:83
Libby, Robert 8:77
Libby, Sumner 14:189
Libby, W. 1:149
Libe, S. A. 16:42
Liberty, John 22:309
Libesey, William W.
26:168
Libold, Charles 22:125
Libolt, Albert 16:208
Librook, Henry 23:305
Libth, Lernit 9:95
Lice, J. C. 15:22
Licenby, Benjamin 20:295
Licet, D. 14:82
Lichefare, John H. 22:167
Lichenburg, Christ 26:169
Lichlenheld, --- 15:39
Lichlighter, John 22:88
Lichtenwater, David
23:242
Lichtess, Peter 10:64
Lichtman, George 23:155
Lichtner, Benjamin 4:37
Lichtner, J. F. 4:37
Lichty, Elias S. 18:397
Lichty, H. 1:51
Lichty, Joel M. 22:88
Lichty, Samuel 7:101
Lick, Alexander T. 22:430
Lick, Parmenias H. 24:41
Licken, Uriah 22:339
Lickenberger, John
24:214
Lickey, George 20:137
Lickfaer, Joseph 10:96
Lickings, Isaac 20:295
Lickley, James 20:108

Lickliter, Henry 3:119
Lickly, J. B. 3:119
Lickly, P. 3:120
Licombrose, John 18:145
Licon, Peter 9:184
Liconby, Benjamin 10:123
Lidale, Joseph 15:210
Lidd, James M. 22:484
Lidday, John 9:85
Liddel, L. 19:83
Lidden, William 8:73
Liddick, H. C. 27:79
Liddicke, H. L. 14:242
Liddle, Byron J. 23:108
Liddle, C. E. 7:101
Liddle, Henry 22:464
Liddle, John 5:21
Liddle, Thomas 21:140
Liddon, D. M. 9:43
Liddy, Hugh 23:155
Liddy, Levi 22:41
Liddy, P. 1:148
Lidenstick, J. A. 11:157
Lidey, Anthony 15:159
Lidey, J. 3:120
Lidford, George 17:398
Lidlinger, S. G. 14:82
Lidner, Jack 16:208
Lidrage, Adam 15:173
Lieb, C. C. T. 1:147
Lieb, Louis 13:33
Lieba, J. J. 8:121
Liebencuth, Goodhart 15:39
Liebensperger, Solomon 27:76
Liebrand, Godfrey 13:33; 16:42
Liebrand, John 20:295
Liebreck, G. S. 16:208
Liebrich, John 8:121
Lieby, B. F. 13:93
Lieby, Whitman 15:22
Liedinger, Charles 10:186
Liedsinger, M. S. 12:92
Liedy, Samuel 26:221
Liefferp, Frank 11:94
Liegler, August 11:155
Lieman, Peter 13:33
Lienage, M. 14:82
Lienhart, John 11:414
Lienlarker, W. 12:92
Lier, John 15:69
Lieser, Lewis 3:120
Liesley, J. 11:35
Liesner, A. 13:66
Liesner, A. H. 16:208
Liesner, William 3:120
Liessie, Emile 9:231
Lieter, Lester 22:148

Lieutz, Nichols 10:152
Liezman, Casper 22:235
Life, J. 14:82
Liff, Charles 8:51; 21:123
Liffie, Fred 20:126
Liffin, J. 1:148
Lifton, David 8:77
Liger, D. 22:309
Ligget, David C. 18:370
Liggett, David C. 9:222
Liggette, Samuel 22:431
Liggins, George 11:182
Liggins, John S. 9:222
Liggins, King 8:99
Lighall, Edward 13:113
Lighes, Henry 11:333
Lighfoot, G. 1:150
Lighshall, H. D. 5:21
Light, C. M. 16:42
Light, David 9:36
Light, Freeman 14:189
Light, Henry C. 15:57
Light, Jasper 8:89
Light, Mathias 15:57
Light, Michael 12:29
Light, Polk 18:219
Light, S. 3:120
Light, Simon 8:23
Light, Simpson 18:145
Light, Solomon 21:277
Light, Timothy 6:21
Lightbody, John 7:32
Lightbody, Pearce 26:44
Lightbody, Pierce 9:85
Lightcap, Jacob 7:101
Lightfoot, Edward 11:265
Lightfoot, J. 8:51
Lightfoot, James W. 21:73
Lightfoot, Jeptha 21:55
Lightfoot, Joseph 12:29; 24:23
Lightfoot, Leander 17:409; 22:88
Lightfoot, Walker F. 21:32
Lightfoot, William 3:120
Lightford, James 22:514
Lighthall, H. D. 25:199
Lightheart, Michael 15:210
Lighthizen, James J. 11:155
Lightholder, Patrick 23:129
Lighthouse, Jesse 23:264
Lightle, Peter 17:356
Lightman, John 12:29
Lightmire, J. 14:242
Lightner, Adam 17:249
Lightner, David 15:70
Lightner, J. 25:199

Lightner, J. M. 1:51
Lightner, John 14:82
Lightner, Richard 18:311; 26:104
Lightner, Samuel H. 22:204
Lightner, Thomas 25:51
Lighton, B. F. 26:42
Lighton, C. 8:65
Lighton, J. N. 25:199
Lighton, Richard 9:25
Lighton, Robert B. 21:87
Lightsinger, David 12:57
Lightwire, J. 27:79
Lighty, Solomon 11:389
Ligible, Lewis 18:88
Ligins, John S. 18:370
Lignion, Joseph 9:146
Ligrist, W. 3:120
Ligsby, A. 14:131
Lihtnen, Silas 14:189
Like, B. 14:82
Like, Francis 14:189
Like, Hiram 23:71
Like, John 17:449; 24:174
Like, Lemuel 13:66; 19:83
Liken, --- 15:210
Likeness, Stephen 9:133; 27:76
Likens, Edwin 10:152
Likens, George W. 22:281
Likens, T. W. 24:214
Likens, Williams 22:125
Likers, John 3:120
Likes, Martin 8:23; 18:145
Likes, S. M. 24:23
Likes, W. D. 15:109
Likes, William 18:219
Likins, Isaac 10:64
Likliter, Isaac P. A. 22:453
Liland, H. L. 10:64
Lilas, Columbus 22:453
Lile, Harrison 15:210
Lile, John M. 22:125
Lile, Joseph 17:22
Lile, W. L. 9:231
Liles, G. 27:77
Liley, G. R. 16:373
Lilie, Sherbert 17:15
Lilison, Daniel 16:42
Lill, J. F. 23:302
Lillard, Moses 11:207
Lillebridge, W. H. 3:120
Lillen, John 10:205
Liller, J. 12:92; 16:298
Liller, John 14:82
Lilley, Abram R. 22:88
Lilley, Alfred 9:103; 18:340

Lilley, Charles 25:199
Lilley, Charles H. 9:36
Lilley, Jacob 17:267
Lilley, James 10:64;
  20:295
Lilley, Joseph 12:29;
  18:397
Lilley, Richard 15:322
Lillia, John 24:67
Lillia, Levy N. 13:33
Lillibridge, W. R. 1:94
Lillich, Charles 23:155
Lillie, C. L. 11:439
Lillie, Dudley 22:281
Lillie, Elias 17:288
Lillie, George 8:65;
  26:169
Lillie, George C. 10:163;
  19:176
Lillie, Lyman P. 4:37
Lillienstein, E. 13:113
Lillienthal, Hans 21:73
Lillis, David G. 9:121;
  27:76
Lillis, Patrick 17:356
Lills, Samuel 14:82
Lilly, Albert 19:239
Lilly, Charles 21:358
Lilly, Clay 6:28
Lilly, David 8:73
Lilly, G. R. 15:343
Lilly, H. H. 8:73
Lilly, James A. 4:37
Lilly, John M. 10:123;
  20:295
Lilly, Lewis 10:177;
  19:176
Lilly, M. 24:81
Lilly, Mandus 5:52
Lilly, Nelson 17:37
Lilly, Samuel 17:92
Lilly, T. 14:15; 16:269
Lilly, Thomas 12:146;
  19:303
Lillygreen, O. 8:65
Lilridge, J. Q. A. 8:73
Lilton, George 16:43
Lily, Amandus 27:74
Lima, Peter 15:263
Limbarker, W. 16:298
Limbaugh, Albert T.
  10:123
Limbaugh, Allen T.
  20:295
Limbeck, Joseph 17:249
Limberger, Charles 1:50
Limbocker, A. S. 20:137
Limbocker, John W.
  21:257
Limbric, William F.
  17:260

Limbrick, Jacob 12:73
Limburger, W. 21:123
Limburgher, Lewis 16:208
Limburk, Jacob 15:39
Limeburg, W. 8:121
Limeiwise, W. 15:210
Limelle, Lewis 11:396
Limerick, Henry 16:97
Limet, Noah 19:232
Liminck, T. J. 18:421
Liming, Samuel 15:8
Limkins, George 4:37
Limmerman, Smith 7:128
Limmers, Frederick
  17:403
Limo, Hugh 10:64
Limorice, E. 18:52
Limp, P. 3:120
Limper, W. 2:14; 25:51
Limplin, William 9:66
Limpner, H. 16:208
Linard, John W. 23:38
Linaus, Benjamin 27:76
Linaweaver, Charles
  23:38
Linbernyer, John 9:67
Linburger, J. 3:120
Linburgher, Lewis 15:294
Linch, A. 25:323
Linch, B. 23:99
Linch, F. J. 26:41
Linch, G. 18:370
Linch, Henry 19:23
Linch, J. 14:289
Linch, James 7:128
Linch, John 13:113;
  26:142
Linch, M. 15:210
Linch, Patrick 21:358
Linch, Richard 8:59
Linchart, William 15:325
Linchien, F. 3:120
Linciedt, G. 14:283
Linck, Peter 16:97
Linckee, Bartholomew
  10:8
Linckle, C. 14:189
Lincoln, A. 3:120
Lincoln, Albert 23:277
Lincoln, Austin 22:464
Lincoln, B. C. 9:157
Lincoln, Caleb H. 22:464
Lincoln, Charles 8:118
Lincoln, Charles B.
  16:208
Lincoln, Charles D. 1:51
Lincoln, Clarence B.
  10:163
Lincoln, Dwight A.
  22:407

Lincoln, E. 16:208
Lincoln, Edward 21:358
Lincoln, F. 14:82; 25:199
Lincoln, Francis 9:85;
  26:41
Lincoln, G. H. 25:300
Lincoln, Garrad 17:180
Lincoln, George 1:49;
  20:193
Lincoln, George W.
  17:447; 24:171
Lincoln, J. S. 15:210
Lincoln, Jacob 17:151
Lincoln, James H. 24:95
Lincoln, James W. 1:50
Lincoln, Jefferson 13:135;
  19:347
Lincoln, John C. 1:50
Lincoln, John F. 8:59
Lincoln, Joseph 17:335
Lincoln, L. 1:51
Lincoln, Myers 9:209
Lincoln, Napoleon 9:133;
  27:76
Lincoln, Patrick 21:208
Lincoln, Perry 4:66
Lincoln, Russell 7:32
Lincoln, S. B. 14:82
Lincoln, Thomas 9:238;
  26:222
Lincolns, Seirett 8:73
Lind, F. S. 21:189
Lind, George 20:31
Lind, J. 9:146
Lind, John 27:75
Lind, Noah 9:184
Lind, Peter 1:50
Lind, Samuel 9:244
Lindal, P. A. 8:51
Lindall, Peter A. 21:257
Lindam, James K. 17:419
Lindamin, Frederick
  22:339
Linday, V. 3:120
Linday, Wallace 7:138
Linde, David 13:113
Lindeist, J. 13:113
Lindell, Byron N. 21:32
Lindell, Nelson 8:23;
  18:145
Lindeman, G. 9:69
Lindeman, James 11:414
Lindeman, John 18:430
Linden, A. P. 18:33
Linden, Calvin 4:37
Linden, F. 26:237
Linden, J. G. 26:169
Linden, James P. 15:27
Lindensmith, E. 3:120
Lindenster, J. 16:208

Lindenweber, Joseph 21:228
Linder, A. H. 8:65
Linder, C. 16:208
Linder, Charles 21:358; 22:204
Linder, Henry 24:23
Linder, J. F. 18:278
Linder, J. S. 8:65
Linder, J. T. 9:67
Linder, John 15:210
Linder, Martin 21:55
Linder, William A. 22:503
Linderman, A. 1:50
Linderman, Alonzo S. 22:41
Linderman, Cornelius 24:53
Linderman, H. A. 3:120
Linderman, J. H. 18:69
Lindermond, John 19:23
Lindermore, J. 9:146
Lindersmith, D. 20:179
Lindeur, Gotleib 17:54
Lindey, Charles 21:358
Lindey, Daniel 17:400
Lindgren, A. 23:38
Lindlay, Anton 25:285
Lindlay, D. 3:120
Lindle, William W. 21:228
Lindley, A. 1:150
Lindley, Aaron 11:67
Lindley, Andrew 22:235
Lindley, C. 3:120
Lindley, C. C. 21:33
Lindley, E. A. 17:66
Lindley, Henry 9:25; 18:311; 26:105
Lindley, James G. 8:89
Lindley, John H. 15:57
Lindley, Reuben 18:353
Lindley, Samuel C. 8:89
Lindley, Walter 20:18
Lindley, William 8:23; 17:243; 18:145; 23:71
Lindloe, Ole 22:281
Lindman, Aaron 4:37
Lindner, A. 1:51; 21:123
Lindo, Frederick 7:101
Lindon, Caleb 20:295
Lindon, John 17:82
Lindra, M. 7:78
Linds, Charles S. 17:263
Lindsat, Robert 18:69
Lindsay, --- 19:83
Lindsay, Allen 1:50
Lindsay, Caleb 22:431; 24:99

Lindsay, Charles 4:37; 15:210
Lindsay, Ephraim 12:54
Lindsay, Fleming S. 21:33
Lindsay, Francis 23:155
Lindsay, Frank 23:38
Lindsay, Henry S. 10:64
Lindsay, Hiram 10:64; 20:295
Lindsay, J. 1:52; 3:120
Lindsay, James 9:184; 10:64; 19:255; 22:259
Lindsay, John 1:50; 12:29
Lindsay, Joseph B. 21:33
Lindsay, M. 25:300
Lindsay, Merritt 22:41
Lindsay, Oliver 20:126
Lindsay, Powell J. 22:259
Lindsay, R. 14:283
Lindsay, R. G. 7:75; 25:301
Lindsay, S. 3:120
Lindsay, Solomon 10:173
Lindsay, Thomas 11:36
Lindsay, W. D. 24:23
Lindsay, Walter B. 10:123; 20:295
Lindsay, William 15:210
Lindsburger, Frank 19:329
Lindsey, A. 3:120
Lindsey, A. R. 3:120
Lindsey, Abner 9:165; 25:323
Lindsey, Alexander 11:333
Lindsey, Charles 9:85; 26:42
Lindsey, E. W. 14:82
Lindsey, Edwin 13:33
Lindsey, Elsey 21:85
Lindsey, Ephraim 10:145
Lindsey, George W. 7:32
Lindsey, Henry S. 20:295
Lindsey, J. 1:147; 23:155
Lindsey, J. H. 14:82; 18:278
Lindsey, James 13:33
Lindsey, James E. 11:307
Lindsey, James H. 10:123; 20:295
Lindsey, M. 18:15
Lindsey, N. C. 1:148
Lindsey, Nelson H. 18:219
Lindsey, R. 14:82
Lindsey, Samuel 19:176
Lindsey, Seaton 9:133; 27:76
Lindsey, Solomon 19:176

Lindsey, T. 1:51
Lindsey, T. J. 22:204
Lindsey, W. 1:148
Lindsey, William 11:36; 14:190; 24:67
Lindsey, Wilson 27:78
Lindslay, G. 1:149
Lindsley, A. 14:82
Lindsley, Abram S. 15:39
Lindsley, Erastus R. 17:66
Lindsley, Fran 1:51
Lindsley, H. H. 17:164
Lindsley, James G. 17:66
Lindsley, L. D. 11:419
Lindsley, M. 14:82
Lindsley, Robert 17:497
Lindsley, Silas S. 1:49
Lindsley, W. 1:50; 16:208
Lindsley, Walter P. 23:16
Lindsley, Watson 11:109
Lindsley, William 17:155
Lindsly, William 13:66
Lindsmill, Michael 11:183
Lindson, David C. 23:71
Lindusky, G. 3:120
Lindwall, August 10:65
Lindy, George W. 16:140
Lindy, Thomas 7:32
Line, H. 23:38
Line, James 27:74
Line, John 8:107
Line, Nathan S. 17:37
Lineback, John 22:259
Linebaugh, David 4:37
Linebaugh, J. 11:341
Lineburg, George 14:190
Lineger, Frederick 21:73
Linehan, Thomas 3:120
Linehart, Henry 22:520
Linenbitz, Charles 1:50
Linenbrinke, J. 1:149
Liner, A. 3:120
Liner, Lyman 18:145
Lines, A. 14:190
Lines, Aaron 23:71
Lines, D. 16:97
Lines, Elijah 18:219
Lines, Jacob 5:52; 22:204
Lines, James B. 10:163; 19:176
Lines, Jesse 19:23
Lines, L. 20:295
Lines, M. 11:265
Lines, M. A. 14:283
Lines, Marshall 14:190
Lines, S. E. 13:77; 16:208
Lines, William M. 22:88
Linesbury, Jacob 24:184
Linet, Charles 12:85; 16:298
Lineton, George 17:54

Linette, John H. 13:58
Linevall, August 20:295
Liney, --- 15:348
Linfisher, A. L. 21:73
Ling, C. B. 16:121
Ling, Charles 22:204
Ling, E. W. 27:145
Ling, John 3:120; 9:184
Ling, John V. 7:101
Ling, Mark 10:123; 20:295
Lingal, D. P. 25:199
Lingal, Daniel P. 5:21
Lingberg, S. A. 17:37
Lingear, John 22:514
Lingenfeller, John 22:431
Lingenhober, Joseph 9:184
Linger, F. J. 13:113
Linger, James 4:66
Linger, Lambert 19:255
Lingfellow, Charles 16:43
Lingfetter, --- 13:33
Lingham, Charles 7:128
Lingo, Cyrus B. 17:415; 24:153
Lingo, Henry 23:260
Lingo, James 17:505
Lingo, John 9:36; 12:50; 18:294; 26:105
Lingo, L. 14:82
Lingo, W. H. 14:82
Lings, Thomas 7:32
Lingston, John 18:88
Linhart, John H. 17:347
Linhart, W. 19:83
Lining, R. B. 11:67
Lininger, Josiah 15:319
Lininger, W. 14:82
Linis, Francis 22:484
Linis, J. 21:149
Link, Absalom 16:121
Link, Andrew 6:31
Link, Charles 12:29; 17:478
Link, Conrad 8:101; 17:462; 24:175
Link, David H. 15:91
Link, Edwin 14:190
Link, Ferdinand G. 23:265
Link, George 11:67
Link, George W. 9:103; 20:295
Link, Gotlieb 3:120
Link, Hartman 21:102
Link, Isaiah 22:113
Link, J. H. 25:323
Link, Jacob 27:77
Link, Jefferson 7:32
Link, John F. 22:281
Link, Joseph 11:156

Link, Solomon 16:43
Link, W. H. 11:281
Link, Washington D. 23:286
Link, William 4:37
Link, William Hardy 18:220
Linkel, F. 23:38
Linkelman, Lewis 7:32
Linker, C. 3:120
Linker, Henry 22:204
Linkhorn, Andy 17:180
Linkinbill, K. 21:189
Linkleter, Eugene 9:55
Links, Thomas 22:339
Linkun, Addison 9:85
Linley, William 11:244
Linly, James P. 8:89
Linn, Andrew J. 22:88
Linn, August 7:102
Linn, Buck 18:244; 26:43
Linn, David 21:358
Linn, Eli 22:453
Linn, Elias 17:162
Linn, H. 20:295
Linn, Henry 12:73; 15:70
Linn, Isaac 23:12
Linn, J. 12:142; 21:33
Linn, James 11:156
Linn, Joseph 22:204
Linn, Thomas 16:208; 18:244; 26:44
Linn, W. 22:204
Linnaberg, George 17:212
Linnegar, Edward 21:10
Linnekin, Gidson 26:44
Linnel, Giles 7:8
Linnell, Stuble 14:190
Linnelly, J. 27:74
Linneman, H. 23:155
Linnert, L. 3:120
Linnert, Lyman 8:23
Linniger, Washington 16:121
Linniken, J. F. 4:38
Linninger, W. 20:147
Linnius, Thomas 9:222
Linnscott, George 23:256
Lins, John 19:239
Linsay, D. 3:120
Linsay, J. 3:120
Linsay, James H. 18:244
Linsay, John 15:5
Linscott, Hiram 11:108
Linscott, J. 11:307
Linscott, James E. 7:101
Linscott, R. B. 23:155
Linscott, S. 14:82
Linscott, Thomas 9:184; 19:229
Linser, Matthias 9:13

Linsey, --- 12:87; 16:298; 18:52
Linsey, Albert 12:160
Linsey, Benjamin 1:192
Linsey, C. 21:358
Linsey, F. 12:87; 16:298
Linsey, George 7:32
Linsey, Hiram 23:256
Linsey, J. 11:307
Linsey, James H. 26:43
Linsey, John 8:40; 11:435; 26:169
Linsey, Richard 8:40; 26:169
Linsey, S. 12:83; 16:298
Linsey, W. H. 11:85
Linsey, William A. 8:40; 26:169
Linshore, J. 12:122; 14:26
Linsinbigier, W. R. 1:147
Linskill, Edward 19:255
Linskill, Thomas 14:82
Linsley, Joseph F. 21:257
Linsley, Nelson S. 19:275
Linsley, Wilson S. 9:184
Linsman, Martin 1:50
Linston, Sivan 21:244
Linsuer, W. 16:373
Linsy, William H. 5:42
Lint, Jacob 23:155
Lint, W. S. 13:125
Linten, Noah 26:42
Linter, James 26:43
Lintern, John B. 16:43
Linthcum, G. L. 25:199
Linthicum, G. L. 5:42
Linton, A. R. 23:38
Linton, Albert 15:327; 19:83
Linton, Alfred 9:157
Linton, Charles H. 5:52
Linton, E. 3:120
Linton, Gabe 9:70
Linton, H. B. 20:295
Linton, Ira 23:90
Linton, J. 13:93
Linton, James W 20:295
Linton, James W. 10:124
Linton, John W. 10:124; 20:295
Linton, Leander 20:295
Linton, Levi 11:157
Linton, Luther 9:157
Linton, Luther J. 9:157
Linton, Noah 9:85
Linton, Otho 23:155
Linton, P. 25:199
Linton, Robert 11:419
Linton, S. 1:52
Linton, W. 8:101; 17:459
Linton, Walter 24:153

Linton, William 1:52; 23:250
Lintved, Ole Nelson 21:140
Linty, John R. 22:259
Lintz, Abraham 15:210
Lintz, John 11:155
Lintz, M. C. 25:199
Linviborger, W. H. 14:82
Linville, J. 27:78
Linville, James 14:327
Linway, J. 3:120
Linz, Henry 5:21
Linza, Palmer A. 22:171
Linzen, Frederick W. 21:102
Liofie, Emile 20:295
Lion, Charles 18:43
Lion, Levy 10:163
Lion, Pascal 23:38
Lionhart, Henry 10:65; 20:295
Lions, --- 18:191
Lions, Henry 20:295
Lions, Levy 19:176
Lions, William 17:428
Lipe, A. 13:93
Lipe, Alexander 21:33
Lipe, John 24:23
Lipencott, J. A. 14:190
Lipford, Jesse 21:277
Liphus, James 4:38
Lipomb, W. A. 4:38
Lipp, A. 13:93
Lipp, John U. 4:38
Lippart, --- 26:168
Lippen, H. 9:25; 18:311; 26:105
Lippencott, Thomas 20:98
Lippencott, W. H. 14:190
Lipper, William 14:82
Lippert, Gandret 4:38
Lippet, Nicholas 10:148
Lippincon, S. 11:155
Lippincott, J. N. 14:82
Lippincott, J. S. 22:204
Lippincott, James 17:419; 24:160
Lippith, J. 3:120
Lippman, Francis M. 10:124; 20:295
Lippman, Henry 23:192
Lippolt, Jacob 17:82
Lipps, A. 14:15
Lipps, George C. 21:228
Lippy, Hiram 14:190
Lippy, J. 13:93
Lips, F. 3:120
Lipscomb, --- 14:83
Lipscomb, John H. 22:309

Lipscomb, Simpson 9:222; 18:370
Lipscomb, Thomas 17:180
Lipsett, Thomas 5:21
Lipsey, D. 3:120
Lipsey, John 8:89
Liptrat, Richard 19:176
Liptrot, Richard 10:163
Lircomb, Byron D. 10:163
Lirk, James P. 18:208
Lirnon, William 26:170
Lisabeck, Jack 21:33
Lisater, L. 26:170
Lisbery, Hamilton 22:309
Lisbey, John 8:89
Lisbon, Castor 17:411
Lisbon, Isaac 21:257
Lisbon, J. D. 26:43
Lisby, John 18:208
Lisby, Thomas B. 23:155
Lischer, S. 1:149
Lisco, Rufus 20:31
Lisco, William H. 11:402
Liscom, Charles 12:155
Liscomb, Byron D. 19:176
Liscomb, J. 1:52
Liscomb, J. E. 21:358
Liscomb, J. M. 1:149
Liscomb, John 22:148
Lisenbee, Alfred 17:168
Lisenbee, J. W. 9:55
Lisenby, Allen 8:89
Lisenby, John 23:38
Lish, Alfred 24:23
Lisher, E. 27:74
Lisherness, Austin 21:140
Lisk, Sidney 11:207
Lisk, William 17:149
Lisle, Absolom 21:14
Lisle, George 6:7; 18:112
Lisle, I. D. 11:414
Lisle, W. J. 11:307
Lisles, P. 13:130
Lisless, James 19:83
Lisney, Pomeroy 20:177
Lisonbee, G. 23:39
Lisper, --- 12:169
Lisson, John O. 7:102
Lisson, R. 9:25
Lisspet, Nicholas 18:52
List, Jacob A. 10:124; 20:295
List, L. 18:52
List, Mathias 10:124
List, Matthias 20:295
List, R. C. 1:150
Liste, I. 25:199
Listen, Elisha 23:155
Lister, A. 16:136
Lister, James 23:71
Lister, John 10:65; 20:295

Lister, William H. 18:244; 26:44
Listner, Benjamin 9:100
Liston, David 3:120
Liston, J. D. 18:244
Liston, J. E. 23:39
Lists, S. 1:148
Listy, William L. 16:43
Lisum, Hiram W. 14:190
Lisure, Samuel 3:120
Liswell, S. 3:120
Litch, J. 3:120
Litch, John 22:339
Litch, Tip. P. 20:295
Litch, William 15:210
Litchard, Wallace 19:83
Litchelfelden, Louis 20:295
Litcher, Luke 10:155
Litcher, William 13:66
Litchfield, Charles 7:102
Litchfield, D. W. 11:243
Litchfield, Peter 7:32
Litchfield, R. W. 22:148
Litchfield, Riley W. 22:148
Litchfield, W. G. 9:184
Litchfield, W. S. 19:239
Litchfield, Warren 10:163; 19:176
Lite, C. 1:149
Liter, Daniel 21:123
Literal, Rowland 24:167
Literal, Samuel 21:277
Litewood, James 18:311; 26:105
Lithenburg, John D. 18:397
Litherland, Thomas 7:102; 21:358
Litler, Samuel M. 10:65
Litrell, James A. 22:259
Litschge, Johann 22:281
Litsenberger, Benjamin 21:228
Litsenberger, Francis 21:55
Litson, J. W. 7:68
Litson, W. P. 11:35
Litswood, James 9:25
Littan, Elijah 21:229
Litte, Henry 10:65
Littell, John E. 21:131
Litten, Elijah 21:55
Litten, Milton 4:38
Littenberry, S. 16:208
Litter, Andrew 18:33
Litter, Fulton 14:83
Litteral, Samuel 15:259
Litterle, Joseph 26:125
Litthe, Samuel M. 20:295

Litting, T. 11:219
Littinger, Frank 16:152
Little, A. 4:38
Little, A. S. 14:83
Little, Abel R. 22:431
Little, Albert 19:83
Little, Albert A. 11:192
Little, Alfred 16:208
Little, Ambrose 14:319;
    25:272
Little, Asberry 9:222
Little, Asbery 18:370
Little, Augustus 15:70
Little, B. 3:120
Little, Baxter 18:208
Little, C. 3:120
Little, C. F. 8:51
Little, Charles 13:33;
    14:83
Little, Charles F. 21:73
Little, Charles M. D.
    12:29
Little, Cyrus P. 21:92
Little, D. P. 19:229
Little, Daniel 4:38
Little, Daniel D. 26:42
Little, David S. 21:33, 229
Little, E. D. 3:120
Little, Edward F. 21:358
Little, Edward W. 12:59
Little, Elias 19:83
Little, Emmet 26:169
Little, Emmett 8:40
Little, F. 13:93; 14:15
Little, G. B. 25:323
Little, George 13:33;
    20:23; 22:88, 309;
    21:229
Little, George W. 9:55;
    21:229
Little, H. C. 2:14; 25:51
Little, Henry 9:201;
    20:295
Little, Hiram H. 13:33
Little, I. M. 14:83
Little, Ira 17:46
Little, Ironie 9:121
Little, Irvin 27:76
Little, Isaac 21:131
Little, J. 3:120; 8:51;
    9:146; 11:35;
    12:164; 15:152;
    16:121; 26:169;
    27:75
Little, J. A. 16:208;
    25:199
Little, J. B. 15:294
Little, J. F. 3:120
Little, J. H. 20:295;
    25:323
Little, J. L. 16:78
Little, J. P. 23:114

Little, J. William 17:143
Little, James 11:207;
    13:80; 16:208; 19:83
Little, James D. 24:81
Little, James F. 23:90
Little, James H. 10:65;
    16:43
Little, James P. 8:107
Little, Jared 21:73
Little, Jeremiah 11:36
Little, Jesse B. 12:29
Little, John 7:102; 8:23;
    9:111; 10:124; 17:82;
    18:145, 244; 20:295;
    22:339; 23:99;
    25:199; 26:43
Little, John A. 12:80
Little, John H. 6:31;
    12:166
Little, John M. 15:128
Little, John W. 20:86;
    23:258
Little, Jonathan 11:293
Little, Joseph C. 21:202,
    291
Little, Josiah 16:160
Little, Levi 11:414
Little, M. 3:120; 25:199
Little, Martin 5:22
Little, N. J. 25:50
Little, R. 3:120
Little, Robert 14:190;
    22:259; 25:199
Little, S. 14:190
Little, S. M. 16:121
Little, Samuel 11:207;
    14:257; 17:443;
    24:160
Little, Samuel B. 21:128
Little, Thomas 6:23;
    16:43; 22:520
Little, Timothy 8:89, 114
Little, W. 21:204
Little, W. D. 15:299
Little, W. F. 18:176
Little, W. J. 1:147
Little, W. T. 10:186
Little, William 3:120;
    8:119; 11:35, 219,
    389; 12:29; 17:37;
    22:484; 23:155;
    27:78
Little, William B. 17:37
Little, William D. 11:67;
    16:208
Little, William H. 11:36
Littlebale, John C. 7:8
Littlebrand, Christian
    16:43
Littlebrandt, Christian
    13:33

Littlebrant, Joseph S.
    22:339
Littlefield, --- 17:336
Littlefield, A. 9:146;
    27:75
Littlefield, Albert E. 5:21
Littlefield, Alexander
    21:87
Littlefield, Alonzo 17:99
Littlefield, Augustus
    23:117
Littlefield, C. 3:120;
    25:199
Littlefield, C. H. 15:11
Littlefield, C. L. 23:117
Littlefield, Charles H.
    12:73
Littlefield, Charles M.
    27:77
Littlefield, D. W. 1:98
Littlefield, David M.
    9:121; 27:77
Littlefield, E. 16:208;
    21:358
Littlefield, Elijah 17:15
Littlefield, G. H. 19:83
Littlefield, George W.
    9:214; 21:358
Littlefield, J. D. 11:398
Littlefield, James L. 7:64
Littlefield, Joseph 20:10
Littlefield, L. P. 1:147
Littlefield, Leonard 12:29
Littlefield, Lucien D.
    22:509
Littlefield, Moses 15:11
Littlefield, Thomas 15:109
Littlefield, W. 25:199
Littlefield, W. D. 25:51
Littlefield, William 17:54
Littlehale, E. K. 1:149
Littlehate, J. G. 16:208
Littlejohn, H. S. 3:120
Littlejohn, Jackson 9:25
Littlejohn, L. J. 3:120
Littleman, Abraham H.
    12:29
Littlepage, Allen 24:198
Littler, John 23:39
Littleton, --- 21:167
Littleton, Amos 11:244
Littleton, Fielden 20:10
Littleton, George C. 7:102
Littleton, Joh 26:42
Littleton, John 5:22;
    18:244; 25:199
Littleton, Solomon 15:5
Littleton, T. 3:120
Littleton, William 17:54
Littleton, William M.
    10:124; 20:295

Litton, E. 21:208
Litton, E. M. 16:269
Litton, John 22:259
Litton, K. 10:186
Litton, Philander 17:99
Litton, R. 14:83
Litton, W. 18:176
Litton, Wayne 22:309
Litton, Wesley 21:229
Littrell, James T. 24:59
Littruburgh, John D. 8:73
Litwiter, J. L. 11:36
Litz, Joe 11:67
Litz, Lewis 12:9
Litzinger, Baldus 7:32
Livaing, J. 21:229
Live, W. 20:92
Lively, Daniel S. 22:259
Lively, E. R. 23:39
Lively, Edward 14:190
Lively, G. M. 11:155
Lively, Gallatin 21:277
Lively, James A. 19:23
Lively, L. 18:88
Lively, Lawson 6:13
Lively, Lewis 23:204
Lively, Thomas 9:55
Lively, Tilghman 6:17;
    18:88
Lively, William F. 11:108
Lively, William M.
    17:292
Livenspire, D. E. 11:157
Livergood, Martin H. 7:32
Liverin, George 21:359
Liverman, Lewis 10:163
Livermoore, H. W. 15:39
Livermore, B. 14:83
Livermore, E. W. 22:446
Livermore, Edward 27:74
Livermore, Edwin M.
    22:113
Livermore, H. W. 12:73
Livermore, Henry H.
    15:128
Livermore, Lewis 7:102;
    19:176
Livermore, Ransom 13:33
Livermore, William F.
    1:49
Liverpool, John 12:50
Livers, Leander S. 9:25
Livers, Samuel 22:125
Liverson, George 17:267
Liverston, Brown 11:192
Liverts, George 21:111
Livesey, William H.
    18:145
Livesey, William W. 8:23
Livessay, James 23:185

Livihert, Melvin M.
    21:229
Living, John 15:210
Livingen, John J. 8:107
Livinghard, C. B. 3:120
Livingood, George W.
    21:229
Livingood, John 12:73
Livingood, John P. 20:10
Livingood, Joshua 8:107
Livings, H. 22:41
Livingston, A. 1:149;
    3:120; 27:75
Livingston, Andrew 22:41
Livingston, Anthony
    23:12
Livingston, C. 7:59
Livingston, Charles 8:23;
    18:145; 21:359
Livingston, Duncan
    18:397
Livingston, F. 13:113;
    27:75
Livingston, G. 25:50
Livingston, G. W. 9:44
Livingston, George
    11:108
Livingston, George B.
    20:137
Livingston, Harlon 23:305
Livingston, Henry 13:33;
    21:95
Livingston, J. 1:148, 149;
    13:93; 14:83
Livingston, J. E. 17:504
Livingston, J. H. 3:120
Livingston, J. K. 3:120
Livingston, J. S. 1:51
Livingston, Jacob 12:29
Livingston, Jacob E.
    24:23
Livingston, James 8:23;
    18:145
Livingston, James A. 9:36
Livingston, James D.
    23:71
Livingston, James J.
    17:419
Livingston, John 3:120;
    6:17; 16:43; 22:204
Livingston, John C. 22:42
Livingston, John W. 20:98
Livingston, Lorenzo D.
    10:124; 20:295
Livingston, R. 3:120;
    14:15
Livingston, Richard J.
    22:42
Livingston, Robert 19:321
Livingston, Sedgwick
    22:430

Livingston, Sedwick
    18:220
Livingston, Sylvester
    25:50
Livingston, Thomas G.
    9:184; 19:275
Livingston, William
    15:109, 210; 22:407
Livingstone, Alexander
    15:39
Livington, William W.
    11:276
Livinhagan, F. 1:150
Livoneman, A. 16:208
Lix, Ellas 18:294
Lize, John 19:23
Lizzle, Richard 17:267
Lloid, R. 25:200
Lloyd, Adam 27:77
Lloyd, Albert 21:92
Lloyd, C. M. 21:359
Lloyd, Calvin 10:65;
    20:295
Lloyd, Charles 7:71
Lloyd, D. 24:23
Lloyd, David 22:484
Lloyd, Enoch 12:29
Lloyd, James W. 1:49
Lloyd, Job 7:32
Lloyd, John 14:190
Lloyd, Joseph 20:114
Lloyd, Keerford 21:229
Lloyd, Richard 10:65;
    20:296
Lloyd, Robert 5:22
Lloyd, Samuel 5:42
Lloyd, Thomas 17:387;
    26:169
Lloyd, Thompson P.
    20:114
Lloyd, W. H. 9:55
Lloyd, William B. 9:13
Load, R. L. 11:389
Load, William 18:191
Loafland, Joseph 12:73
Loafman, Edward W.
    17:207
Loake, Isaac A. 5:42
Loan, Ferd 9:184
Loan, Ferdinand 19:275
Loan, J. 1:150
Loar, B. F. 12:29
Loar, H. H. 3:120
Loasey, Richard 22:259
Lob, Emil 19:255
Lob, Lewis 22:167
Lob, Robert 27:157
Lobaw, D. L. 11:244
Lobby, John 21:243
Lobdell, Asbury 9:121
Lobdell, C. 21:111

Lobdell, Daniel 22:281
Lobdell, Isaac M. 13:33;
    16:43
Lobdell, Richard 9:121;
    27:77
Lobdell, Seymore 19:23
Lobdell, T. 1:49
Lober, Daniel 4:38
Lober, William A. 22:42
Loblein, John 22:12
Lobrie, O. 12:73
Lobs, John 11:127
Loby, Charles F. 16:121
Loby, Thomas 9:85
Locard, George 21:123
Locey, J. M. 18:103
Loch, William 18:244;
    26:43
Lochart, Philander 10:65
Lochbain, S. 18:244
Lochbihler, --- 11:307
Loche, James 10:28
Lochember, Frederick
    20:296
Locher, Thomas S. 17:361
Lochman, Charles 18:52
Lochner, M. 3:120
Lochran, H. 12:92; 16:298
Lochrey, A. 3:121
Lochrs, J. 21:111
Lochterhand, E. 1:148
Lock, Aaron 21:149
Lock, Charles 11:402
Lock, D. 18:15
Lock, Elijah 20:98
Lock, Elisha 17:145
Lock, F. 1:52
Lock, H. 21:359
Lock, Henry 22:148
Lock, J. 23:155
Lock, J. C. 25:50
Lock, Jacob 22:88
Lock, James H. 22:125
Lock, John 7:102; 9:36;
    21:359; 26:105
Lock, John F. 10:124;
    20:296
Lock, John L. 22:42
Lock, John W. 17:96
Lock, Josiah 10:124;
    20:296
Lock, Lewis 17:37
Lock, Peter 17:349
Lock, S. 16:373
Lock, Samuel 9:36; 121;
    27:76
Lock, Simon 14:190
Lock, W. 18:15; 27:76
Lock, W. M. 1:149
Lock, William 9:146;
    15:210

Lockard, John 23:155
Lockard, Obadiah 19:83
Lockard, Robert 20:296
Lockard, Samuel 8:23;
    18:145
Lockbain, S. 26:43
Locke, A. B. 12:162
Locke, Albert E. 24:23
Locke, Albert N. 10:163
Locke, Charles W.
    10:173; 19:176
Locke, David E. 22:235
Locke, Hilderman A.
    23:180
Locke, J. 23:204
Locke, J. B. 25:200
Locke, James 11:108;
    19:304
Locke, Jonathan 14:190
Locke, Wesley 12:29
Locke, William 22:309
Lockember, Frederick
    10:124
Locker, Calvin 5:22
Locker, Conrad 3:121
Locker, E. 20:296
Locker, J. 21:33
Locker, Jacob 22:171
Locker, Mounce 20:296
Locker, William L. 23:39
Locket, C. 25:200
Lockett, Charles 5:42
Lockett, Henry 22:309
Lockett, Jacob 7:128
Lockett, James M. 11:187
Locketts, William 12:50
Lockey, L. 16:208
Lockford, Darnes 10:65
Lockhard, J. 3:121
Lockhart, Allen 22:309
Lockhart, James 7:102;
    25:200
Lockhart, John 21:240
Lockhart, Philander
    20:296
Lockhart, Robert 16:121
Lockhart, Samuel 22:204
Lockhart, Thomas D.
    22:339
Lockhead, D. 14:270
Lockiney, B. 16:298
Locking, B. 12:83
Lockington, F. J. 19:83
Locklan, Joel 3:121
Lockland, Secundus
    17:180
Locklayer, William 8:69
Lockley, E. 9:9
Locklin, D. 15:83
Locklin, Dennis 12:73
Locklin, L. A. 11:101

Locklow, George M.
    19:23
Lockman, --- 11:94
Lockman, Alex 12:50
Lockman, Charles 10:150
Lockman, E. E. 19:255
Lockmiller, James 15:57
Lockmine, Herman 7:32
Lockridge, Daniel P.
    21:73
Lockridge, George 11:67
Lockridge, John 22:309
Lockton, William 8:51;
    21:102
Lockwood, --- 25:50
Lockwood, Alfred R.
    17:82
Lockwood, B. F. 20:296
Lockwood, Benjamin F.
    10:65
Lockwood, Charles S.
    17:243
Lockwood, Curtis 23:71
Lockwood, Cyrus 17:425
Lockwood, D. 1:147
Lockwood, Daniel
    17:443; 24:160
Lockwood, David 19:23;
    23:262
Lockwood, Delos 11:389
Lockwood, E. 23:155
Lockwood, F. 25:200
Lockwood, George
    10:163; 21:140
Lockwood, George W.
    11:108
Lockwood, H. 3:121
Lockwood, H. B. 4:38
Lockwood, H. D. 1:149
Lockwood, H. P. 9:184;
    19:272
Lockwood, Henry B.
    21:15
Lockwood, Isaac C. 8:107
Lockwood, J. H. 21:359
Lockwood, J. R. 12:29
Lockwood, James 20:296
Lockwood, James C.
    11:156
Lockwood, James F.
    19:83
Lockwood, James L.
    12:96; 15:360
Lockwood, John 22:407
Lockwood, Jonathan
    14:190
Lockwood, Joseph 20:41
Lockwood, L. D. 1:52
Lockwood, Major F.
    23:108
Lockwood, N. 13:113

Lockwood, O. 13:113
Lockwood, Oscar J. 20:10
Lockwood, P. 15:39
Lockwood, Robert 10:177; 19:176
Lockwood, Samuel N. 21:55
Lockwood, Samuel R. 12:142
Lockwood, Sherman D. 21:15
Lockwood, T. 12:80
Lockwood, W. H. 27:74
Lockwood, William C. 10:205
Lockwook, C. H. 17:292
Locon, Perry 21:359
Locquay, Abraham 15:14
Locus, George M. 9:133
Lodan, Matthew 4:38
Lodd, Joseph F. 4:38
Loddick, L. R. 15:173
Lodds, Daniel 4:38
Lode, John 3:121
Loden, Michael 15:39
Loder, A. 15:210
Loder, George G. 7:32
Loder, James G. 19:23
Loder, John M. 12:155
Loder, W. H. 1:52
Loder, William 19:176
Loder, William J. 22:453
Lodestein, John 23:90
Lodge, Benjamin F. 5:22
Lodge, Isaac 9:121
Lodge, T. 3:121
Lodi, William O. 17:82
Lodiss, H. 3:121
Lodley, R. 14:83
Lodman, Arche 18:311
Lodo, John 19:47
Lodon, J. 1:150
Lodwick, J. W. 18:311; 26:105
Lodzir, Isaac 27:76
Loeb, Emile 9:184
Loecher, Randolf J. 23:155
Loeffler, John I. 17:102
Loeg, J. H. 9:55
Loeker, E. 10:65
Loell, Frederic 24:95
Loeoder, Hiram 18:220
Loeper, James 18:103
Loeps, Frederick 1:50
Loeps, John 7:102; 21:359
Loes, Nicholas 20:296
Loewe, H. 19:255
Loewe, Martin 19:23
Loewe, Nicholas 13:33
Loewer, Henry 24:178

Lofarce, John B. 8:23
Loff, John 15:210
Lofferty, Jesse 23:39
Loffie, F. M. 20:147
Loffin, W. 14:190
Loffingholt, M. 20:296
Loffland, Jacob 16:43
Lofflemann, John 26:169
Lofflin, Albert 13:33
Lofflord, Jacob 13:33
Lofland, Joshua 15:5
Lofler, E. E. 3:121
Loflin, Albert 16:43
Loften, Augustus 18:69
Loften, John G. 25:200
Lofters, H. 3:121
Lofters, M. 3:121
Lofters, Thomas J. 20:296
Loftice, David 22:259
Loftin, Paul 22:309
Loftis, J. 1:149
Loftis, Newton 11:408
Loftus, J. 21:189
Loftus, M. 1:148
Loftus, N. 9:184; 19:245
Loftus, Thomas 11:67
Loftus, Thomas J. 10:65
Loftus, William 11:327; 27:74
Lofty, Richard J. 3:121
Logad, Thomas 8:23
Logae, Philip 12:29
Logan, Alexander 26:170
Logan, Alfred 9:201; 19:291
Logan, B. 3:121
Logan, Baxter K. 21:229
Logan, Benjamin 17:134; 24:198
Logan, Benjamin H. 17:410; 22:125
Logan, Charles 11:156; 19:83; 22:88
Logan, Clinton N. 23:39
Logan, D. 15:329
Logan, D. L. 14:278
Logan, Daniel 14:190
Logan, David L. 23:185
Logan, F. 13:93; 14:15
Logan, F. G. 14:283
Logan, Frank 3:121
Logan, George 8:40; 26:169
Logan, George E. 15:3
Logan, George M. 22:281
Logan, H. 3:121; 19:83
Logan, H. M. 18:424
Logan, Henry 8:23; 18:145; 22:484; 23:71
Logan, Henry Clay 17:203

Logan, J. 13:93
Logan, J. M. 16:43
Logan, Jackson 21:277
Logan, James 7:10, 102; 9:184; 12:64; 13:113; 15:11, 70; 16:121; 19:47; 22:309; 25:286
Logan, James E. 23:99
Logan, James M. 22:503
Logan, James T. 14:190
Logan, John 5:22; 15:57; 17:22; 18:434; 25:200
Logan, John A. 17:326
Logan, John M. 11:36
Logan, John W. 21:359
Logan, Levi 18:88
Logan, Lewis 6:13
Logan, Louis 21:277
Logan, Monroe 9:209
Logan, N. 24:95; 25:200
Logan, Nathan 15:8
Logan, Nelson 8:77
Logan, Newton 13:33
Logan, Oscar 1:191
Logan, Patrick 15:299; 16:208
Logan, Peter 12:29; 22:204
Logan, Reuben 22:42
Logan, Richard 4:38; 21:189
Logan, Robert 1:51; 25:200
Logan, Robert G. 13:33
Logan, Robert J. 22:511
Logan, Rodger 12:57
Logan, S. C. 26:169
Logan, S. D. 16:280
Logan, Samuel W. 11:36
Logan, T. C. 16:43
Logan, Thomas 7:32; 9:240
Logan, Thomas M. 12:62
Logan, Tobias 17:261
Logan, W. 3:121; 17:134; 24:198
Logan, William 18:456, 469
Logan, William E. 16:208
Logan, William S. 8:107
Logane, Ephraim 21:85
Logans, David 11:402
Logen, W. M. 11:265
Logerhart, --- 24:95
Loggins, John L. 18:88
Logguis, John L. 6:17
Login, --- 20:296
Logle, Joseph 9:85; 26:44
Logne, S. 3:121

Logranx, Theophilus 15:17
Logsden, John C. 17:207
Logsden, Rufus J. 22:125
Logsdon, David 18:208
Logsdon, Thomas S. 18:208
Logue, A. 18:52
Logue, David 12:29
Logue, George E. 19:176
Logue, J. A. 15:327; 19:83
Logue, James 19:239
Logue, Jerry 23:291
Logue, John 23:192
Logus, Edward 7:102
Logwood, Louis 22:309
Lohan, Thomas 24:41
Lohill, Martin 18:244; 26:43
Lohman, Andrew 22:204
Lohman, Chr. 1:51
Lohman, E. E. 9:184
Lohman, Henry 10:65; 20:296
Lohman, Jesse 10:124; 20:296
Lohman, John 10:65; 20:296
Lohman, William 10:65
Lohn, Israel 10:65
Lohnayer, --- 3:121
Lohnus, Peter M. 23:39
Lohr, A. 1:51
Lohr, Edward 12:73
Lohr, Frederick 8:23; 18:145
Lohrer, Israel 20:296
Lohrer, Lewis 8:23; 18:145
Lohrer, Vincens 11:156
Lohruss, J. 16:97
Lohse, Julius 12:30
Loibner, John R. 18:145
Loid, M. H. 13:33
Loistan, William 14:190
Loit, Conrad 8:23; 18:145
Loivi, William 25:51
Loker, Curtis 7:102
Loker, E. 3:121
Lokin, G. W. 21:33
Loland, F. 17:149
Lolar, Peter 7:33
Lolenough, John 9:85
Loler, J. 3:121
Lolipper, Henry 6:32
Loll, George 16:365
Loll, John 1:50
Loll, P. 9:55
Loller, Eph 9:40

Loller, Ephraim 18:294; 26:105
Lolley, G. 14:300; 17:475; 27:78
Lolmough, J. 26:42
Lolon, George 10:124
Lolridge, D. P. 15:210
Lolt, Joseph 8:89
Loman, Asa 10:124
Loman, J. 14:83
Loman, James 22:42
Lomas, W. 25:49
Lomax, William 1:50
Lombard, August 1:50
Lombard, B. K. 3:121
Lombard, Charles 12:30
Lombard, Eli 12:30
Lombard, F. O. 25:51
Lombard, George H. 10:153
Lombard, John 16:208; 17:449; 24:174
Lombow, W. 11:16
Lomer, Mathew 7:128
Lomerick, William P. 7:33
Lomey, Timothy 15:210
Lomill, Daniel 9:25
Lomis, --- 18:69
Lomis, Milton 18:145
Lomis, William 26:168
Lomison, Hugh G. 23:192
Lomison, Isaiah 23:12
Lommel, Lewis 8:89
Lomon, George 9:222
Lomping, D. 20:296
Lon, Dennis 6:28
Lonagan, John 22:42
Lonce, B. D. 26:42
Lonce, D. P. 9:85
Loncks, Andrew 9:97
Londay, A. W. 18:112
Londen, John 9:209
Londendeck, N. 3:121
Londey, Edgar 25:49
Londin, H. W. 3:121
Londman, Richard 16:121
London, --- 24:101
London, H. 25:200
London, H. W. 25:200
London, Hiram 5:22
London, Horace M. 9:133
London, J. 10:148
London, John 14:15
London, John W. 22:125
London, Joseph 21:73
London, L. 3:121
London, Luman 27:76
London, S. 11:116
Londsop, Robert 15:210
Londun, John 13:93
Lone, Thomas 15:39

Lone, William 14:190
Lonefield, A. 13:113
Loneler, John 9:115
Loner, --- 22:259
Lonergin, Daniel 25:200
Lonery, George 14:83
Lones, R. 3:121
Lones, William 11:414
Loney, D. 9:154; 27:77
Loney, D. E. 14:83
Loney, Soloman 14:270
Long, --- 14:190, 257; 19:83; 20:181
Long, A. 3:121; 11:244; 18:52
Long, A. D. 20:296
Long, A. J. 20:41
Long, Aaron 7:128
Long, Abram 23:39
Long, Alexander 11:67
Long, Alexander M. 23:155
Long, Alfred H. 23:155
Long, Allen 9:201; 19:292, 304; 20:86
Long, Allen D. 10:65
Long, Amos 11:156
Long, Anderson 22:259
Long, Andrew 10:152; 27:78
Long, Andrew J. 10:124; 18:220; 20:296
Long, Archy 7:128
Long, August 15:39
Long, Augustus 3:121
Long, B. 17:353
Long, B. F. 8:89; 11:276
Long, B. P. 20:296
Long, Bailey P. 10:65
Long, Benjamin 6:17; 18:88
Long, Benjamin F. 17:22, 314
Long, C. C. 3:121
Long, Charles 1:51; 16:152
Long, Charles E. 18:53
Long, Charles M. 15:57
Long, Cleophis 17:46
Long, Colburn 25:50
Long, Conrad 14:190
Long, D. 9:146; 14:190; 15:57
Long, D. M. 1:147; 11:157
Long, Daniel 9:133; 12:73; 27:76
Long, David 14:257
Long, David A. 10:19
Long, David M. 23:155; 27:75

Long, E. 1:94; 2:13; 22:309; 25:49, 52
Long, E. B. 22:484
Long, E. S. 14:83
Long, Edward 10:124; 20:296; 22:339
Long, Eli 25:49
Long, Elias 9:103; 18:340
Long, Ephraim 4:38
Long, Ephraim K. 7:102
Long, F. 11:307
Long, F. M. 10:65
Long, F. W. 20:296
Long, Frederick 22:89
Long, G. P. 18:324
Long, G. W. 10:65; 18:191; 23:155
Long, George 6:17; 11:36; 15:159; 18:88; 22:503
Long, George B. 13:33
Long, H. 11:156
Long, H. E. 25:200
Long, H. G. 12:87; 16:298
Long, H. H. 9:36
Long, H. R. 16:43
Long, Harison 16:121
Long, Harrison 21:55
Long, Harvey M. 23:71
Long, Henry 9:25; 16:43; 17:349; 18:311; 22:309; 26:105
Long, Henry C. 13:33; 19:83
Long, Henry G. 15:316
Long, I. 9:214; 14:190; 18:176; 26:41
Long, Isaac 10:92; 14:242; 20:296; 26:169
Long, Isabel B. 25:200
Long, J. 1:94, 147, 148, 149; 3:121; 5:22; 11:306; 15:263; 21:164, 359; 27:75
Long, J. B. 21:195
Long, J. C. 9:184; 20:89
Long, J. G. 14:83
Long, J. H. 8:51; 9:67
Long, J. K. 6:32; 25:323
Long, J. R. 13:93
Long, J. W. 1:150
Long, Jackson 9:236
Long, Jacob 4:38; 11:36; 12:155; 17:82; 21:140; 22:205; 26:42
Long, James 8:73; 12:73; 13:125; 15:319; 22:259; 25:276
Long, James B. 27:77

Long, James H. 18:33
Long, James L. 22:125
Long, Jeptha 22:167
Long, Jeremiah 9:158
Long, Jesse H. 21:73
Long, Joel 17:309; 22:113
Long, John 3:121; 7:102; 9:55, 85, 103; 11:108, 182; 14:131, 257; 16:121; 17:111; 19:239; 21:74, 277; 23:277
Long, John A. 22:205
Long, John C. 12:155; 22:42
Long, John D. 10:96
Long, John E. 22:42
Long, John H. 22:453; 23:155
Long, John L. 14:190
Long, John M. 11:35; 20:296; 24:112
Long, John S. 4:38
Long, John W. 22:115, 205
Long, Jonathan 3:121
Long, Joseph 14:190; 16:208; 19:318; 21:359; 23:180
Long, Joseph D. 16:280
Long, Joseph L. 23:108
Long, Joshua 17:416
Long, Josiah L. 17:349
Long, L. 3:121; 15:210
Long, Leroy 8:23; 18:145
Long, Levi 9:121; 27:76
Long, Lewis 9:209; 21:55
Long, Lewis K. 9:85; 26:42
Long, Lorenzo D. 23:71
Long, M. 13:93
Long, Mark B. 11:192
Long, Martin 17:82
Long, Michael 16:298
Long, Miles 19:23
Long, Mitchel 12:83
Long, Morris D. 22:204
Long, Moses 16:209
Long, N. 16:209
Long, Nathan S. 10:26
Long, Nicholas 10:124; 13:113; 20:296
Long, Nicholas M. 20:24
Long, Noah 7:128
Long, O. 15:210
Long, P. 3:121; 5:42; 10:96; 25:200
Long, Patrick 25:200
Long, Perry 8:51; 12:30
Long, Peter 17:273; 21:277

Long, Peter D. 22:484
Long, Philip 6:17; 18:88; 20:98
Long, R. 1:52
Long, R. A. 21:167
Long, Ransom 18:244; 26:43
Long, Reuben 10:124; 20:296
Long, Richard 23:12
Long, Richard H. 25:334
Long, Robert 7:59; 10:65; 11:207; 15:279
Long, Robert J. 10:19
Long, Rufus 11:207
Long, S. 7:102; 14:190
Long, S. W. 1:50; 16:280, 298
Long, Sam 25:334
Long, Samuel 8:107; 21:85
Long, Samuel B. 15:334
Long, Samuel R. 24:63
Long, Samuel W. 22:205
Long, Simon 16:43
Long, Solomon 17:510
Long, Stanford 19:289
Long, Stephen 12:155
Long, Stephen H. 6:17
Long, Steven 18:88
Long, T. 1:148
Long, T. J. 11:231
Long, T. M. 15:210
Long, T. S. A. 9:222; 18:370
Long, Thomas 9:25, 159; 17:191; 22:259
Long, Thomas J. 16:3
Long, W. 3:121; 19:279
Long, W. H. 9:25; 21:359
Long, W. P. 11:307
Long, W. W. 15:343; 16:373
Long, Walter B. 23:123
Long, Washburn 9:214; 21:359
Long, William 9:85, 163, 184, 201; 10:65; 14:83, 191; 15:210; 17:134; 20:296; 22:453; 23:256; 24:198; 26:42
Long, William A. 22:125
Long, William H. 11:389
Long, William P. 7:102
Long, William R. 9:235; 18:421
Long, Williamson 11:207
Longacre, James 18:397
Longacre, Josiah 6:7
Longbacker, F. 14:83

Longby, I. 17:292
Longcor, Francis 10:124; 20:296
Longden, J. M. 20:297
Longdo, J. 1:147
Longdorf, H. 26:43
Longdrof, H. 18:244
Longe, C. L. 10:163
Longe, J. 1:150
Longe, Joseph 13:33
Longe, W. A. 19:84
Longecor, Robert 20:18
Longee, J. F. 1:98
Longee, J. L. 14:191
Longee, Lorinzo 15:347
Longelle, Louis 24:67
Longer, James 8:107
Longer, Samuel 13:33
Longer, W. H. 1:52
Longerman, H. 1:149
Longert, Jonas 18:220
Longert, Robert D. 20:98
Longess, Samuel 8:89
Longey, Carl 13:33
Longfellow, --- 9:85
Longfellow, Eben 10:124; 20:297
Longfellow, G. W. 18:340
Longfellow, George 9:103
Longfellow, George E. 10:123; 20:297
Longfellow, James H. 10:65; 20:297
Longfellow, John W. 17:349
Longfellow, Joseph T. 26:42
Longfellow, S. 19:229
Longfellow, Samuel 8:23; 18:145
Longfellow, W. R. 25:200
Longford, James 9:84
Longford, Lewis 24:198
Longham, P. 27:75
Longhernane, Michael 16:9
Longhery, H. 25:50
Longhouse, D. L. 16:209
Longhouse, D. T. 13:66
Longillon, U. R. 5:52
Longinber, H. 8:51
Longkriet, Bruno 10:63
Longland, W. 25:50
Longle, William 3:121
Longley, D. E. 18:33
Longley, Edward 10:19
Longley, G. 3:121
Longley, George W. 19:23
Longley, Henry G. 16:7
Longley, J. 20:133
Longley, James M. 26:125

Longley, Joseph 21:359
Longloss, Gustavus 12:73
Longman, Charles 11:108
Longmire, R. 14:83
Longnare, Ezra 13:33
Longnecker, Henry 25:272
Longnecker, Michael 11:244
Longnecker, William 20:147
Longoere, Joseph 18:112
Longorthy, Irving 11:307
Longrecker, J. 18:191
Longsbury, H. A. 25:49
Longsdorf, George 11:67
Longsdorff, Theodore 13:33
Longsheet, W. F. 14:191
Longshire, L. D. 11:157
Longshore, Jonathan 11:156
Longstaff, Christopher 10:65; 20:297
Longstaff, J. W. 14:191
Longstaff, Thomas 22:281
Longsteth, Philip 10:124; 20:297
Longstreet, James 10:124
Longstreet, W. F. 3:121
Longstreth, W. 1:52
Longstreth, W. D. 22:205
Longstrets, James 20:297
Longton, Patrick 7:128
Longwell, Thaddeus 22:235
Longworth, A. C. 1:147
Longworth, Clement 20:33
Longworth, Jackson 13:33
Longworthy, Sidney A. 17:361
Longyear, Calvin 22:205
Longyear, David 10:19
Longyear, Theodore 10:19
Lonibner, John K. 8:23
Lonis, W. H. H. 11:265
Lonkey, James 1:50
Lonkey, Joseph 10:163; 19:176
Lonks, Alonzo B. 10:163
Lonman, Samuel 12:30
Lonnegan, Patrick 16:88
Lonney, T. 1:52
Lono, F. H. 16:298
Lono, T. H. 12:87
Lonowell, W. H. 11:183
Lonsbury, S. N. 2:14
Lonser, George 11:389
Lonsey, L. 3:121
Lonshore, J. 15:363

Lontrock, Adol's. 1:50
Lontzinhizer, J. 8:51
Lonus, Issacar 13:33
Lonx, Herman 9:231
Lonzie, George 24:101
Looby, Patrick 12:155
Looder, John 8:90
Loodin, A. 11:281
Loogrette, --- 27:79
Look, Gilbert H. 9:16
Look, J. J. 1:49
Look, James 16:97
Look, M. 14:15
Lookard, Robert F. 10:65
Looker, B. 9:55
Looker, J. 25:323
Looker, Joel 22:205
Looker, Rosewell E. 23:192
Looker, T. J. 1:52; 15:27
Looker, Thomas J. 12:73
Looker, William 13:93
Lookey, John E. 21:359
Lookington, Marcellus 18:244; 26:44
Looks, N. B. 20:297
Lookup, Charles 15:343; 16:373
Lookwell, T. 9:55
Loolas, T. 11:219
Looless, J. M. 21:189
Looman, John 23:155
Looman, W. 13:93
Loomar, M. 14:83
Loomas, F. H. 15:57
Loomes, Charles 14:191
Loomes, H. L. 15:299
Loomice, Daniel 26:105
Loomis, Alexander 21:123
Loomis, Alonzo 21:140
Loomis, Amon 11:127
Loomis, Bertrand 21:89
Loomis, C. 5:52; 25:200
Loomis, Chamberlain 12:73
Loomis, Charles R. 21:140
Loomis, Daniel 11:156
Loomis, David 9:237; 26:222
Loomis, E. 19:255
Loomis, Edwin 9:184
Loomis, Elisha 16:98
Loomis, George 11:192; 18:334
Loomis, H. 21:359
Loomis, H. E. 18:285
Loomis, Hart E. 26:135
Loomis, Harvey 11:414
Loomis, Henry 10:124; 20:297

Loomis, Henry N. 16:209
Loomis, Issachari 16:43
Loomis, J. 1:147; 11:307
Loomis, James R. 21:140
Loomis, John 3:121
Loomis, Lloyd A. 9:184
Loomis, Lyman 23:192
Loomis, Lyman C. 7:33
Loomis, Milan 8:23
Loomis, N. C. 9:16
Loomis, Nelson 10:124;
    20:297
Loomis, Ruell B. 23:71
Loomis, S. A. 1:52
Loomis, W. 1:149
Loomis, W. H. 1:52
Loomis, W. W. 10:205
Loomis, William M.
    18:397
Loonai, Charles H. 23:90
Looney, Jeremiah 5:22
Looney, John 27:77
Looney, William H. 13:34
Loonis, C. 15:70
Loonsberry, James 25:200
Loony, John 1:52
Loop, David 23:39
Loop, F. 13:33
Loop, J. W. 13:127
Loop, Mosts 22:407
Loope, M. 13:93
Looper, Alfred 22:205
Looper, E. 3:121
Looper, George 1:51
Loornice, Daniel 18:311
Loos, C. 14:83
Loos, D. 14:83
Loosee, A. J. 15:279
Loosee, Isaac R. 24:53
Looton, F. 26:169
Lootz, Cyrus 16:158
Loovy, C. 3:121
Looy, Japheth 11:156
Lope, John A. 8:23;
    18:145
Loper, A. 14:278
Loper, A. B. 27:74
Loper, Elmer 11:68
Loper, F. R. 4:38
Loper, George W. 23:286
Loper, Gilbert 21:277
Loper, James 18:15
Loper, Lorenzo 10:124
Loper, Luther M. 7:68
Loper, T. 25:49
Lopez, Antony 4:38
Lopez, Francisco 18:426
Lopez, Frank 19:297
Lopez, J. A. 8:121
Lopez, Lorenzo 20:297
Lopley, Isaac 24:95

Lopman, William 7:128;
    12:64
Lopp, G. W. 10:96
Lopp, John 18:311
Lopp, Jon 9:25
Lopp, Louis 9:97
Lopp, Milton P. 22:89
Lopps, A. L. 8:107
Lorah, Samuel 22:484
Lorain, Noah 9:85
Lorall, J. J. 23:304
Loran, Richard 10:96
Loran, William J. 21:74
Lorange, Joseph 11:341
Loranz, N. C. 18:103
Loray, Erin 17:405
Lord, Alexander W. 16:78
Lord, Alvin H. 17:502
Lord, Andrew 16:209
Lord, Andrew J. 23:16
Lord, B. 7:59
Lord, Benjamin 15:70
Lord, C. P. 17:243
Lord, C. W. 9:146; 27:75
Lord, Charles 17:243;
    22:148
Lord, Charles M. 7:102
Lord, Clark 15:327; 19:84
Lord, Cyrus E. 27:78
Lord, D. R. 15:70
Lord, Edson 27:78
Lord, Edward 10:124;
    20:296
Lord, F. 1:148
Lord, Francis J. 13:34;
    16:43
Lord, G. W. 3:121
Lord, George 15:343;
    16:373
Lord, George A. 9:69
Lord, George G. 23:71
Lord, George H. 3:121
Lord, Henry C. 10:163
Lord, J. 1:149; 21:89
Lord, J. M. 13:34; 16:43
Lord, Jacob 1:49; 14:83
Lord, James M. 21:102
Lord, K. 15:343; 16:373
Lord, L. 3:121; 18:33
Lord, Lewis 13:114
Lord, M. 3:121
Lord, P. 15:329; 19:84
Lord, Ralph A. 21:74
Lord, S. R. 3:121
Lord, Samuel 20:24
Lord, Tobias 27:77
Lord, W. 12:87; 16:209
Lord, Wane O. 20:18
Lord, William 1:50; 7:8,
    15; 9:121; 16:298;
    27:77

Lorden, Dennis 23:268
Lords, Joseph F. 22:89
Lore, C. R. 26:212
Lore, John 20:297
Lore, Thompson W. 11:36
Loreber, James 9:184
Lored, F. 19:239
Loree, Alvin 20:189
Loree, G. P. 1:147
Loren, Nero 16:209
Loren, S. 1:148
Lorence, W. E. 20:297
Loreno, Jose R. 18:426
Lorenseler, Wash 9:111
Lorentz, Samuel 15:39
Lorenz, Charles 5:22
Lorenz, Ignatz 22:125
Lorenzo, Alexander
    23:264
Lores, Benjamin 27:78
Lorett, William 26:168
Lorey, A. 17:162
Lorey, Charles M. 22:282
Lorey, George W. 10:124;
    20:297
Lorey, John 24:41
Lorey, Martin 7:128
Lorg, Archilles 26:170
Lorg, D. F. B. 3:121
Lorgan, P. F. 16:373
Lorgrette, L. 14:242
Lorgun, P. M. 15:343
Lorhan, John 22:339
Lorig, Adam 18:294
Lorigan, Daniel 21:74
Lorimer, A. J. 23:39
Lorimer, James 10:19
Lorimer, John C. 21:89
Lorimer, John H. 23:39
Lorin, John 22:259
Lorine, Albert 6:13
Loring, Adam 26:105
Loring, Andrew 16:43
Loring, Corwin H. 8:51;
    21:74
Loring, G. 3:121
Loring, George 20:297
Loring, Horace G. 20:297
Loring, Horace H. 10:124
Loring, James T. 18:397
Loring, John 3:121;
    11:307; 15:109
Loring, John M. 20:24
Loring, Thomas 22:42
Loring, William 22:339
Lorinty, S. H. 11:389
Loris, L. T. 22:309
Lorkin, Alonzo H. 23:39
Lorman, George 18:370
Lorman, Henry 1:50
Lorman, W. 14:15

Lorn, James 12:50
Lornan, Asa 20:297
Lorner, John 16:121
Lorner, Mathew 21:359
Lorony, B. 3:121
Lorran, W. 24:67
Lorris, A. J. 25:200
Lorris, H. A. 5:22
Lorrison, W. H. 22:430
Lorro, John 14:191
Lorsan, C. 3:121
Lorson, D. 14:191
Lorton, F. 8:65
Lorton, H. 25:200
Lorton, Horatio 5:22
Lorton, William 10:124;
    20:297
Lortridge, Eli 25:200
Lortz, Jacob 10:25
Lory, George H. 11:244
Lorzbran, J. 3:121
Losa, Henry 14:191
Losage, S. 13:93
Losdale, Anthony 7:128
Losee, A. J. 25:200
Losee, B. F. 16:209
Losee, Lyman 24:81
Losee, Mark 22:148
Losen, Alex. W. 13:34
Loser, Abram 5:52;
    25:200
Losey, James H. 23:129
Losey, Peter 7:51
Losh, Daniel 23:155
Losh, J. 7:33
Loshin, Lewis 13:80
Loshine, Lewis 16:209
Losne, Emitt 11:414
Loss, F. A. 19:176
Loss, J. E. 1:149
Loss, J. L. 15:17
Lossan, O. 17:323
Lossee, George 17:454;
    24:185
Lossing, Alfred 21:85
Lossing, Jonathan 3:121
Lossman, A. 3:121
Lossman, F. H. 8:121
Losson, David 21:195
Losty, Masses 17:54
Losy, W. 20:155
Lot, J. H. 23:155
Loth, Charles 22:339
Loth, Ernest 22:167
Loth, John 13:114
Lotham, John 14:83
Lothburry, B. B. 14:83
Lothery, James 26:125
Lothope, John 20:297
Lothridge, George 11:207
Lothrop, Jacob H. 9:184

Lothrop, Simon D. 20:31
Lotley, Lewis 24:199
Loton, John B. 23:192
Lotridge, William 8:107
Lott, Charles C. 14:83
Lott, H. 7:33
Lott, Harrison 15:22
Lott, Peter 17:22
Lott, R. 19:239
Lott, Robert 9:184
Lott, Thomas 8:23; 18:146
Lott, William 10:65
Lott, William H. 7:33
Lott, Willis 9:133
Lotta, W. M. 26:168
Lotter, Albert E. 8:107
Lottiham, Jacob 18:112
Lotto, Henry 26:125
Lottz, C. 2:14
Lotz, Adolph 24:67
Lotz, John 10:65; 20:297
Lotz, Peter 21:229
Lotze, Louis 14:191
Louby, O. 3:121
Louch, Charles 22:431
Loucheman, William
    25:50
Louck, J. B. 14:131
Loucks, J. 15:128
Loucks, J. W. 20:126
Loucks, John A. 7:128
Loucks, Joseph 26:125
Loucks, O. D. 1:52
Loucks, Richard 23:283
Loucks, William 27:77
Loucks, William H. 9:121
Loud, Benjamin 15:17
Loud, G. W. 15:39
Loud, George 3:121
Loud, H. 1:149
Loud, Henry 12:142
Loud, Tobias 9:122
Loud, William H. 12:30
Loudan, O. 20:140
Louden, Hiram 11:307
Louden, Ira 17:212
Louden, J. 26:169
Louden, Samuel 3:121
Loudenberg, R. 1:50
Loudenslayer, John 11:67
Loudenstager, David
    20:18
Louder, Charles 19:23
Louder, Charles H. 22:464
Louder, F. M. 9:231
Louder, G. H. 26:126
Louder, Thomas 18:208
Louderbuck, G. 1:149
Loudermich, --- 14:257
Loudermilk, Henry 22:259
Loudner, John 23:71

Loudre, Martin 18:69
Louer, David 17:232
Louer, John 18:294
Louge, C. L. 19:176
Lougee, Lorenzo R.
    15:210
Lougendyke, Hiram 10:19
Lough, A. B. 22:205
Lough, H. 3:121
Lough, I. L. 19:267
Lough, James P. 15:210
Lough, John H. 7:102
Lough, John W. 7:102
Loughery, John 16:121
Loughey, John E. 12:54
Loughhead, J. W. 1:150
Loughlam, P. 9:147
Loughley, Lerr 19:239
Loughlin, Frank H. 25:51
Loughlin, James 25:200
Loughlin, John M. 17:249
Loughry, L. C. 8:23
Loughry, W. 15:70
Lougman, Jacob 23:155
Louis, Bazle M. 24:59
Louis, Bennett 18:191
Louis, C. 3:122
Louis, Charles 7:128
Louis, Evan W. 10:65
Louis, Even W. 20:297
Louis, Gardner 19:23
Louis, H. 3:122
Louis, Henry 17:54
Louis, Isaac 11:276;
    20:297
Louis, J. 3:122
Louis, J. S. 26:222
Louis, James 26:126;
    27:76
Louis, John 13:93
Louis, John W. 7:59
Louis, Phillip 19:283
Louis, T. 9:184
Louis, W. 15:317
Louis, William 17:54
Louis, William S. 5:22
Louis, Willis F. 23:241
Louisiana, Henry 7:128
Loukes, Alonzo B. 19:176
Louks, Nelson B. 10:65
Lounds, Henry 9:133
Lounge, Thomas M. 11:85
Lounnum, H. C. 23:303
Lounsbeck, G. 1:147
Lounsberry, Ephraim
    20:297
Lounsberry, Ephraim E.
    10:124
Lounsberry, George
    24:112
Lounsberry, John 15:210

Lounsberry, John W. 16:43
Lounsberry, Thomas 12:30
Lounsbury, C. 14:300
Lounsbury, James 5:22
Lounsbury, John W. 13:34
Lounsbury, Josuah 9:25
Lourance, C. E. 1:52
Lourcey, W. 27:75
Louress, Andrew 13:34
Louring, Andrew 13:34
Lourmer, T. 1:147
Lourney, Albert 11:307
Louroy, George B. 5:22
Loury, James W. 27:73
Loushore, J. 15:128
Lout, H. 26:126
Louteasloyer, William 13:114
Loutenback, John 21:359
Loutenhiger, John H. 21:74
Louter, Conrad 14:191
Loutermilk, William 18:69
Louth, Peter M. 17:243
Louthan, Hugh D. 23:90
Louthan, Moses 22:431
Louthan, W. H. 19:23
Louthen, John 24:41
Louther, Henry 18:88
Louther, John G. 22:113
Louther, M. D. 9:69
Loutsenhizer, L. D. 4:38
Louven, S. B. 14:83
Loux, Ephraim 21:359
Loux, Herman 20:297
Loux, Reuben 12:30
Lovdis, George W. 20:297
Love, --- 18:244; 26:43
Love, Abraham 8:116
Love, Absalom 11:414
Love, Alexander 10:173; 19:176
Love, Asa L. 22:42
Love, Atwood L. 22:287
Love, Byron 20:176
Love, Charles 18:33
Love, D. 14:83
Love, Daniel 22:309
Love, David 6:25
Love, Easton 25:200
Love, G. 14:191
Love, G. B. 1:150
Love, G. P. 16:373
Love, George 1:52
Love, George W. 21:359
Love, Green 24:101
Love, Hugh D. 22:259
Love, Hugh M. 11:36

Love, I. E. 19:23
Love, J. 3:122; 15:57; 16:209
Love, J. H. 9:55; 12:162
Love, J. S. 17:37
Love, James 12:73; 13:34; 15:14
Love, John 3:122; 10:65; 14:83; 18:370, 426; 23:192
Love, John A. 10:32; 20:297; 22:503
Love, John C. 8:90
Love, John W. 23:114
Love, John W. M. 21:246
Love, Joseph 17:349
Love, M. 1:148; 15:343; 16:373
Love, Talbert 11:207
Love, Thomas 21:277
Love, W. 1:147
Love, Walter 9:25; 18:311; 26:105
Love, William 1:52; 3:122; 8:90; 14:83; 24:101
Love, William J. 17:111
Loveall, A. W. 9:222; 18:370
Loveall, Dutton 11:389
Loveall, Eugenius 22:42
Loveday, William 14:27, 331
Loveffler, Levering 21:359
Lovejoy, A. G. 19:239
Lovejoy, C. 3:122
Lovejoy, C. H. 1:147
Lovejoy, Christopher 7:102
Lovejoy, E. W. 24:81
Lovejoy, Henry S. 15:128
Lovejoy, Jabez F. 8:60; 12:173
Lovejoy, L. B. 7:102
Lovejoy, L. E. 20:297
Lovejoy, Leander 10:65
Lovejoy, Louis 14:191
Lovejoy, W. H. 7:59
Lovejoy, William 22:282
Lovejoy, William P. 13:66; 19:84
Lovel, James 10:124; 20:297
Lovel, John 23:155
Lovel, Lemuel J. 23:277
Lovelace, Daniel 19:23
Lovelace, John W 17:22
Lovelace, Samuel D. 23:123

Lovelady, Allen W. 17:237
Lovelady, Martin J. 22:89
Lovelady, Samuel D. 13:34
Lovelady, William 18:208
Loveland, Edwin L. 13:34
Loveland, J. 1:52
Loveland, John 15:3
Loveland, L. 9:25
Loveland, N. 15:343; 16:373
Loveland, W. C. 21:123
Loveland, William 25:200
Lovelass, --- 14:83
Lovelass, Charles 11:67
Lovelee, Huit 4:38
Loveles, N. 16:280
Loveless, A. 25:200
Loveless, Eli 17:273
Loveless, Joseph B. 22:503
Loveless, L. 17:273
Loveless, Lewis M. 20:189
Loveless, Louis 7:14
Loveless, Nelson 14:300; 17:479; 27:79
Lovelis, George W. 9:231
Lovell, --- 20:88
Lovell, D. D. 14:83
Lovell, David 11:36
Lovell, Eliza O. 26:222
Lovell, H. 13:114; 14:191
Lovell, Isaac 23:108
Lovell, J. W. 25:50
Lovell, James 12:100
Lovell, James M. 9:97; 25:200
Lovell, John B. M. 22:148
Lovell, Lyman 11:287
Lovell, M. 14:83
Lovell, Margaret 26:222
Lovell, Merritt 22:148
Lovell, Peter 11:120
Lovell, Richard 17:361
Lovell, S. S. 9:147
Lovell, Shelton S. 21:229
Lovell, William 10:124; 14:191; 20:297
Lovely, Albert 18:15
Lovely, Francis 3:122
Lovely, John 3:122
Lovely, W. 14:191
Lovender, Joseph 12:30
Lover, A. 1:148
Loverett, C. 27:77
Loveridge, Jerome 24:23
Loverin, Gustavus 21:359
Lovering, C. H. 25:200
Lovering, Charles H. 5:22

Lovering, D. 15:152
Loverl, C. 19:255
Lovers, Thomas 1:51
Lovery, F. 3:122
Loves, T. 21:149
Lovett, A. 3:122
Lovett, A. B. 20:3
Lovett, A. J. 20:3
Lovett, C. 1:147
Lovett, Edward T. 16:133
Lovett, G. G. 1:147
Lovett, J. 1:149; 21:359
Lovett, J. M. 15:128
Lovett, James 12:30
Lovett, John 1:51; 22:353
Lovett, Joseph 21:359
Lovett, Oliver W. 15:26
Lovett, P. 1:103
Lovett, Tony 25:200
Lovett, W. 3:122
Lovett, W. T. 3:122
Lovette, John E. 22:205
Lovie, James 22:464
Lovil, J. 11:287
Lovill, William H. 10:65
Loving, Thomas W. 22:89
Loving, William M. 22:453
Lovington, George 14:83
Lovis, William 16:209
Low, Barry 9:133
Low, D. 25:200
Low, David 5:22
Low, Ephraim 10:65; 20:297
Low, F. 14:191
Low, Francis 20:24
Low, I. 11:244
Low, James 10:65; 20:297; 22:407
Low, James S. 19:23
Low, John 9:227; 10:19; 18:53
Low, John A. 8:65; 26:169
Low, John T. 9:222; 18:370
Low, Joseph C. 10:163
Low, Nathan 21:189
Low, Nathaniel P. 10:163
Low, P. P. 15:210
Low, Parry 27:76
Low, Samuel 7:102
Low, Samuel K. 7:128
Low, Thomas A. 8:65; 26:169
Low, Wiley K. 19:23
Low, Woodman P. 13:34
Low--, G. W. 20:57
Lowall, Gilbert M. 15:128
Lowall, W. H. 25:301

Lowan, James 6:17; 18:88
Lowars, E. 18:176
Lowbert, Blakely S. 21:359
Lowden, Alonzo 12:155
Lowden, Ed 3:122
Lowden, J. 18:53
Lowden, Thomas 8:90
Lowdenback, D. R. 3:122
Lowder, Eber 10:65; 20:297
Lowder, F. M. 20:297
Lowder, Perry 11:67
Lowe, A. 1:52
Lowe, A. L. 7:13
Lowe, Alexander B. 22:205
Lowe, Allice 17:203
Lowe, Alonzo 9:36; 18:294; 26:105
Lowe, Andrew 24:23
Lowe, C. 1:51
Lowe, Christopher C. 9:184
Lowe, David 9:85; 26:41
Lowe, F. 1:148; 3:122; 14:257
Lowe, Francis 14:191
Lowe, Franklin 11:36
Lowe, G. H. 3:122
Lowe, George B. 20:18
Lowe, George L. 9:72
Lowe, George M. 14:191
Lowe, George W. 17:54
Lowe, Henry 1:50
Lowe, Isaac N. 12:62
Lowe, J. 3:122; 8:90; 9:55; 15:211
Lowe, J. H. 14:83
Lowe, J. N. 15:22
Lowe, James 4:38; 12:160; 16:209; 17:203; 27:79
Lowe, James H. 11:219
Lowe, Jeremiah T. 23:71
Lowe, John 3:122; 17:356
Lowe, John F. 21:229
Lowe, John G. 22:503
Lowe, John S. 10:124; 20:297
Lowe, King 4:66
Lowe, L. M. 13:93; 14:15
Lowe, Martin L. 18:208
Lowe, Moses 23:39
Lowe, Oliver 17:134; 24:198
Lowe, P. D. 1:147
Lowe, Peter 11:381; 14:83
Lowe, R. 1:52
Lowe, Robert 11:265
Lowe, Robert F. 23:90

Lowe, S. L. 22:484
Lowe, Samuel 18:220
Lowe, Thomas 26:145
Lowe, V. P. 1:149
Lowe, W. F. 17:149
Lowe, W. G. 3:122
Lowe, W. H. 16:78
Lowe, Wesley 11:36
Lowe, Wil 25:334
Lowe, William 11:287; 17:155; 21:149
Lowe, William W. 17:361
Lowel, Franklin 23:90
Lowell, Bedford 3:122
Lowell, George 3:122
Lowell, George W. 10:19
Lowell, H. L. 22:89
Lowell, Harris 14:83
Lowell, J. J. 25:51
Lowell, J. P. 15:211
Lowell, John 14:191
Lowell, Joseph 3:122; 7:68; 11:35
Lowell, L. M. 14:83
Lowell, Miles W. 9:184
Lowell, O. W. 1:98
Lowell, Omsen 9:85
Lowell, P. 1:148
Lowell, Thomas 25:200
Lowell, W. 9:111
Lowell, W. W. 19:233
Lowell, William H. 7:75; 13:34; 16:43
Lower, C. 14:83
Lower, David 23:72
Lower, F. 23:303
Lower, J. 1:150
Lower, John 11:192; 26:105
Lower, John F. 9:184; 19:267
Lower, Joseph 22:205
Lower, N. G. 3:122
Lower, Patrick 14:191
Lower, R. D. 16:98
Lower, Samuel 10:124; 20:297
Lowering, A. 10:96
Lowers, Andrew J. 17:232
Lowers, C. C. 19:283
Lowers, E. 10:186
Lowers, James 22:205
Lowers, W. 11:314
Lowery, --- 23:314
Lowery, B. 14:83
Lowery, Charles 24:67
Lowery, D. 3:122
Lowery, E. F. 23:155
Lowery, G. M. 21:359
Lowery, H. 19:255
Lowery, J. 14:83; 22:125

Lowery, J. R. 23:155
Lowery, James 22:309
Lowery, James T. 3:122
Lowery, James W. 9:122
Lowery, Joel M. 7:78
Lowery, John L. 12:139
Lowery, John S. 10:124; 20:297
Lowery, L. 21:149
Lowery, Mark 11:94
Lowery, Nelson 23:250
Lowery, Patrick 22:339
Lowery, Robert 23:271
Lowery, S. 24:53
Lowery, Samuel 17:443; 24:160
Lowery, William 11:389
Lowery, William H. 21:131
Lowery, Z. 23:72
Lowes, Josiah E. 23:72
Lowey, Francis 3:122
Lowgester, G. W. 22:148
Lowhead, T. S. 20:85
Lowing, W. W. 8:73
Lowman, F. W. 1:51
Lowman, John G. 17:237
Lowman, John H. 22:431
Lowman, John J. 20:114
Lowman, S. 25:200
Lowman, W. 20:297
Lown, David T. 10:8
Lown, George 20:297
Lown, Nelson 4:38
Lowne, A. J. 16:209
Lowney, W. 1:150
Lownsbory, Banks 4:38
Lowny, John 13:66
Lowra, David 18:370
Lowre, Levi 11:207
Lowrey, A. 11:183
Lowrey, Archibald 22:148
Lowrey, Elkana 13:60
Lowrey, J. W. 9:147
Lowrey, James 2:14; 22:42
Lowrey, John 26:169
Lowrey, John L. 9:72
Lowrey, W. J. 1:150
Lowrie, A. 22:353
Lowring, J. 3:122
Lowry, --- 15:348
Lowry, Albert 9:55
Lowry, Augustus L. 26:41
Lowry, C. W. 11:157
Lowry, Elem 23:155
Lowry, Francis M. 22:125
Lowry, G. 3:122
Lowry, G. W. 16:131
Lowry, George C. 13:114
Lowry, H. 9:184

Lowry, Henry 11:207; 18:220
Lowry, Henry A. 17:37
Lowry, Isaiah 21:33
Lowry, J. 16:374
Lowry, J. C. 25:272
Lowry, J. R. 14:289
Lowry, James 3:122; 11:94
Lowry, James W. 3:122
Lowry, Job 18:244; 26:43
Lowry, John 8:65; 26:42
Lowry, John J. 18:244
Lowry, L. 21:114
Lowry, M. 13:93
Lowry, M. C. 23:155
Lowry, Martin 1:49
Lowry, Patrick 22:89
Lowry, Pleasant 11:207
Lowry, Samuel W. 21:140
Lowry, W. G. 16:121
Lowry, William 8:23
Lowson, Henry 9:184
Lowter, Robert 22:339
Lowth, John 20:193
Lowyd, Thomas 18:146
Loy, Adam 10:124; 20:297
Loy, George 11:155
Loy, John 22:259
Loy, Samuel B. 9:36
Loy, Samuel F. 20:104
Loy, W. B. 3:122
Loyal, D. 1:50
Loyal, S. 25:200
Loyd, A. 1:150
Loyd, B. 11:320; 17:22
Loyd, C. 16:209
Loyd, E. 1:150
Loyd, G. 16:209
Loyd, Housten 9:72
Loyd, J. B. 7:33
Loyd, James 11:243; 18:244; 26:43
Loyd, James M. 10:124; 20:297
Loyd, James W. 22:484
Loyd, John 10:65; 17:92; 20:297
Loyd, John C. 1:49
Loyd, John S. 10:65; 20:298
Loyd, John W. 11:187
Loyd, Joseph 5:42
Loyd, Joseph G. 11:155
Loyd, L. S. 12:83; 16:298
Loyd, Oliver B. 1:49
Loyd, Reuben 4:38
Loyd, S. 3:122
Loyd, Samuel 5:42
Loyd, Simon 24:41

Loyd, Thomas 8:107
Loyd, W. H. 22:484
Loyd, William H. 10:92; 20:298
Loyed, J. 25:201
Loyed, S. 25:201
Loyer, H. 9:184
Loyer, Jacob 22:235
Loyer, Michael 4:38
Loyhon, William 15:343
Loyns, J. 25:201
Loyns, J. A. 25:201
Loyston, I. R. 19:84
Lozar, T. 1:94
Lozier, E. 23:155
Lozier, J. W. 20:137
Lozo, Joseph 13:34
Lozon, Edward 23:260
Lubach, William 20:298
Lubath, William 10:124
Lubenk, George 22:148
Luber, Carl 18:112
Luby, John 10:148; 18:53
Luby, Martin 5:52
Luby, Thomas 16:209
Luca, E. 1:49
Lucah, John 3:122
Lucan, W. O. 14:328
Lucans, Moses W. 4:38
Lucas, A. 24:81
Lucas, A. M. 27:75
Lucas, Abraham 24:9
Lucas, Alfia 8:90
Lucas, Allen 11:307
Lucas, Alonzo W. 12:30
Lucas, Andrew 12:55; 18:220; 26:135
Lucas, Andrew J. 23:72
Lucas, Anthony 6:17; 18:88
Lucas, B. 1:148; 11:244; 16:209
Lucas, B. F. 8:90
Lucas, Benjamin 9:209; 15:70; 18:69
Lucas, C. S. 17:15
Lucas, D. R. 5:52
Lucas, Daniel 10:163; 19:176
Lucas, E. 19:176
Lucas, Edward 22:430
Lucas, Elisha 15:57
Lucas, Elsy 10:124; 20:298
Lucas, Franz 14:191
Lucas, George 13:93; 14:15; 16:86
Lucas, George E. 11:36
Lucas, George L. 9:231; 20:298
Lucas, George M. 27:76

Lucas, George W. 8:65; 22:89, 514; 26:169
Lucas, H. C. P. 20:298
Lucas, H. M. 9:147
Lucas, Henry 21:277
Lucas, Henry D. 17:37
Lucas, Howard 19:176
Lucas, Hugh C. P. 10:65
Lucas, I. 21:123
Lucas, Isaac N. 4:38
Lucas, J. 3:122
Lucas, J. A. 14:83
Lucas, J. D. 23:39
Lucas, James 10:124; 12:122; 13:114; 15:128; 19:23; 22:12, 205
Lucas, James A. 17:96
Lucas, John 8:90; 14:191; 15:211; 24:41
Lucas, John B. 22:407
Lucas, John E. 8:23; 18:146, 220
Lucas, John H. 11:156
Lucas, Joseph 8:107
Lucas, Josiah W. 22:205
Lucas, L. 9:25
Lucas, L. W. 7:102
Lucas, N. 14:83
Lucas, O. 1:150
Lucas, P. 13:66; 19:84
Lucas, Philip 7:128
Lucas, R. N. 15:128, 350
Lucas, Ransom 17:37
Lucas, Reuben N. 22:148
Lucas, Rinatus 23:155
Lucas, Robert 1:191
Lucas, S. 27:76
Lucas, Samuel P. 1:50
Lucas, Sanford L. 11:36
Lucas, Thomas 7:81; 25:301
Lucas, Victory 8:40; 26:169
Lucas, W. 21:111; 25:201
Lucas, W. C. 1:94
Lucas, William 10:65; 17:54; 23:155
Lucas, William H. 22:89
Luccoln, Samuel M. 10:163
Luce, A. 20:57
Luce, Alsbury 16:78
Luce, Augustus 4:38
Luce, B. 11:155
Luce, C. B. 1:148
Luce, C. D. 8:65; 26:169
Luce, Christopher 7:51
Luce, David 12:30
Luce, E. 6:21
Luce, F. 3:122

Luce, G. W. 1:52
Luce, George 8:65
Luce, George F. 1:51
Luce, Henry 1:50
Luce, Jerome 5:52; 25:201
Luce, John T. 9:214; 21:359
Luce, L. P. 9:184; 19:239
Luce, Lyman B. 22:89
Luce, Stephen B. 22:42
Luce, Sullivan 16:78
Luce, Thomas 1:51
Luce, V. 3:122
Luce, W. H. 16:140
Luce, Walter 8:65
Luce, William 11:183
Lucel, --- 26:212
Lucero, Vivian 12:172
Lucet, Richard 23:39
Lucey, James T. 11:156
Luch, J. H. 3:122
Luch, John 7:33
Luchese, Lewis 8:23; 18:146
Luchford, R. 3:122
Luchnich, Edward 15:211
Luchsinger, Jacob 19:327
Lucht, Charles 26:105
Lucia, A. 3:122
Lucia, Sheffield 22:89
Lucial, Ambrose 4:38
Lucid, John 9:122; 27:77
Lucier, J. 3:122
Lucio, --- 12:172
Luck, Edward 17:317
Luck, F. 27:77
Luck, George H. 10:19
Luck, Julius 17:361
Luck, Lewis G. 19:176
Luck, W. 3:122
Luckaloushy, J. 15:39
Luckany, L. J. 2:14; 25:49
Luckara, Samuel 11:182
Lucket, Raphael 11:207
Luckett, George 12:50
Luckey, Jonas C. 9:97
Luckey, T. H. 1:150
Luckey, William 19:84
Luckfried, Henry 18:311
Luckinbeal, Andrew 11:155
Luckinbill, J. 21:74
Luckinbill, Thomas 21:74
Luckitt, C. W. 17:498
Luckman, Fred 27:76
Luckner, J. 16:269
Lucks, William 14:191
Lucky, Charles 12:171
Lucky, Henry H. 17:54
Lucky, James 11:307
Lucky, John P. 9:243

Lucky, William 10:124; 20:298
Lucos, Andrew 18:285
Lucus, B. 3:122
Lucus, James 20:298
Lucus, John 8:114
Lucy, Cornelius 17:37
Lucy, D. 19:256
Lucy, John 14:84
Ludawick, Christopher 22:453
Ludbow, Thomas 21:359
Ludden, S. 15:343; 16:374
Luddington, L. S. 19:23
Luddington, W. W. 9:85
Luddy, Dennis 9:204
Luden, William 15:211
Ludenburg, Charles 18:177
Ludens, Fred 18:15
Luder, --- 15:259
Luderback, S. 19:84
Luders, L. 15:14
Luders, William C. 21:10
Luderson, H. C. 21:33
Ludgate, John 19:23
Ludici, C. 9:67
Ludies, Ludwig 12:73
Ludiking, W. 3:122
Ludington, H. A. 7:33
Ludington, James L. 11:155
Ludington, S. A. 25:201
Ludington, W. W. 26:42
Ludlam, Henry 12:54
Ludlam, Leaming 23:39
Ludlow, Amos P. 22:484
Ludlow, Charles H. 21:10
Ludlow, Frank H. 18:397
Ludlow, O. 21:359
Ludlum, George 7:59
Ludman, George 18:285; 26:135
Ludolph, Louis 18:88
Ludon, Charles 14:191
Ludovice, F. 3:122
Ludres, Frederick 22:407
Ludric, Bane 9:69
Ludwick, C. 14:270
Ludwick, Henry 11:307
Ludwick, J. W. 7:33
Ludwick, Thomas 25:201
Ludwick, V. E. 23:39
Ludwickson, Christian 8:101
Ludwig, Abraham 20:298
Ludwig, Abram 10:124
Ludwig, Albert 13:34
Ludwig, Andreas 24:67
Ludwig, Christopher 1:50

Ludwig, Herman 20:98
Ludwig, John 10:124;
  19:318; 20:298
Ludwig, John W. 11:156
Ludwig, Lorenzo 19:176
Ludwig, M. 15:211
Ludwig, Philip 21:359
Ludwigg, Robert 10:148;
  18:53
Ludwigson, Christian
  17:463; 24:185
Ludy, J. 21:123
Ludy, James M. 24:160
Ludy, W. H. 27:145
Lueck, Daniel 18:413
Luehihoff, Herman 23:256
Luele, George W. 9:85
Luellen, John 26:105
Luellen, Zadoc 10:65
Luellen, Zaduck 20:298
Luener, John 17:500
Luenig, H. 1:149
Luens, L. 18:311
Luff, C. 3:122
Luff, John 9:44
Luff, William 7:128
Luffey, Levi 10:92
Luffman, George 18:33
Luffman, J. 25:201
Lufkin, David H. 13:34
Lufkin, Wade 16:145
Luft, John 26:126
Lugeve, Jackson 18:146
Lugg, J. C. 8:73
Luggel, J. B. 11:35
Luggs, Jesse 26:43
Lughmurger, George
  12:30
Luher, John 8:23; 26:168
Luhm, F. 1:149
Luibern, Charles 11:36
Luid, John 27:78
Luiden, Lucius 11:120
Luidon, H. 25:286
Luidsey, David 12:73
Luigrell, James H. 7:12
Luik, Jacob 9:122
Luins, L. 26:105
Luird, Samuel 12:73
Luke, Addison 17:263
Luke, Albert 7:128
Luke, Earle 24:198
Luke, G. W. 23:155
Luke, Hiram 27:78
Luke, J. 21:74; 25:201;
  27:75
Luke, John 5:42; 21:257
Luke, William 21:149
Lukehart, Christian 15:14
Luken, John H. 11:16
Lukens, Charles 15:109

Lukens, Milton 3:122
Luker, Eli 20:181
Luker, Josiah 22:205
Lukes, C. C. 25:201
Lukes, Cyrus C. 5:22
Lukins, James 16:121
Lukins, Joe 22:484
Lulin, James H. 23:39
Lull, A. 11:288
Lull, Charles E. 10:65;
  20:298
Lull, E. 19:256
Lull, E. P. 16:43
Lull, Edward 9:184
Lull, James W. 13:34
Lull, Julius E. 10:124;
  20:298
Lull, L. W. 24:23
Lull, M. 14:191
Lull, W. K. 18:370
Lull, William R. 9:222
Lullman, John 21:123
Luly, Albert 11:231
Lum, Alfred W. 11:108
Lum, David 12:50
Lum, Jonathan E. 22:162
Lum, Philip 17:282
Lum, W. 1:148
Lum, Wilden 27:78
Lumagett, F. 13:93
Luman, J. A. 9:222;
  18:370
Luman, John 22:12
Lumana, Jean 18:112
Lumazett, F. 14:15
Lumback, Peter 7:33
Lumback, Silas 10:124;
  20:298
Lumbard, Marvin 22:205
Lumbart, Zeph 9:111
Lumbert, Nelson 17:212
Lumberty, Jacob 22:205
Lumby, Samuel 17:82
Lumer, James 16:299
Lumer, Joseph 5:42; 10:10
Lumford, Samuel 21:212
Luming, Aaron 7:33
Lumis, John 10:92;
  20:298
Lumkins, William 17:282
Lumley, John W. 24:23
Lumly, John 7:33
Lummersdorf, Jacob
  17:392
Lummervill, W. 25:201
Lummoman, Benjamin
  11:207
Lummon, J. E. 3:122
Lummons, Samuel 10:124
Lump, Philip 17:111

Lumpkins, David C.
  17:361
Lumpkins, Elias 17:134;
  24:198
Lumpkins, J. H. 3:122
Lumsden, Adolphus A.
  11:424
Lumsden, George L.
  22:162
Lumsden, William 11:265
Lumy, John 9:85
Luna, --- 8:125
Luna, H. C. 15:288
Luna, John 19:321
Lunbach, S. 3:122
Lunceford, William
  17:149
Lunch, Joseph 18:208
Lunch, William 17:416;
  24:153
Lunchbaugh, Lewis
  10:124
Lunchford, Lewis 17:273
Luncom, Charles 9:122
Lund, Adolph 25:323
Lund, Charles 11:414
Lund, E. F. 1:149
Lund, H. C. 16:209
Lund, H. J. 16:160
Lund, J. 1:148
Lund, James 3:122
Lund, Swis 11:192
Lunda, James 17:419
Lunday, James 17:201
Lunday, W. W. 25:51
Lundenback, S. 14:28
Lunderman, William
  22:205
Lundey, J. P. 21:95
Lundey, William A.
  18:278
Lundre, David 15:211
Lundy, J. W. 26:169
Lundy, James 16:43;
  24:160
Lunelang, Fred 11:67
Luney, Ed 3:122
Luney, R. W. 21:164
Lung, Fred 7:102
Lung, G. W. 20:298
Lunger, A. 1:148; 3:122
Lunger, J. B. 25:49
Lunger, Oscar R. 23:123
Lungershaw, William C.
  3:122
Lungford, G. W. 14:84
Lunk, August 18:145
Lunk, Charles 27:79
Lunn, Granderson 24:102
Lunn, John 14:191;
  18:450

Lunn, John S. 25:201
Lunn, Peter P. 18:278
Lunnan, Henry 21:229
Lunnen, Thomas 10:65
Lunney, G. 1:52
Lunno, John 19:283
Lunsford, Darling 22:503
Lunsford, Elisha 17:237,
319
Lunsford, Isaac 17:237
Lunsford, J. W. 1:149
Lunsford, Michael 23:15
Lunt, A. W. 27:74, 78
Lunt, H. W. 9:147
Lunt, James W. 15:334
Lunt, John 11:127
Lunt, P. 1:148
Lunt, W. H. 9:147; 27:74
Luntsford, Enoch 17:308
Luntt, Charles 21:359
Luntz, A. W. 3:122
Luntz, H., Mrs. 26:42
Lupe, William A. 12:73
Luper, John 7:59
Luper, Joseph 22:309
Luplinger, John 5:52
Lupter, Levi 27:79
Lupton, Ellis 9:239
Lupton, Ellis O. 19:337
Lupton, J. D. 24:81
Lupton, Levi 14:242
Lupton, William 20:147
Lurber, Joseph 8:51
Lurch, John 18:311;
26:105
Lurch, Thomas 12:155
Lurchins, R. W. 1:51
Lurcock, E. 3:122
Lurink, Henry 21:10
Luris, Francis 18:311
Lurk, Augustus 1:50
Lurley, Raslow 25:322
Lurmerer, Jacob 9:55
Lurrahs, Charles 21:359
Lurrey, Daniel H. 19:176
Lurry, Edwin 22:464
Lurst, J. M. 14:84
Lurtelotte, R. 1:49
Lurvey, J. H. 1:98
Lusby, Josiah 24:178
Lusby, Robert 8:123
Lusby, William 17:96
Luscomb, Alfred 14:28
Luscomb, S. E. 9:184
Luse, C. K. 24:81
Luser, John 18:146
Lush, Henry 11:156
Lush, Thomas 5:42
Lush, William 10:10
Lushea, Austice 22:42

Lusher, John 11:88
Lusher, William B. 13:114
Lushford, Henry 9:25
Lushly, Josiah 17:451
Lusk, Henry 14:191
Lusk, John 3:122; 16:121
Lusk, T. 25:201
Lusner, S. 20:90
Luspfriend, Henry 26:105
Lussinden, William
11:414
Lust, D. 18:244; 26:43
Lust, Hiram K. 13:34
Lust, John E. 20:147
Lusted, John 21:359
Luster, Addison 22:89
Luster, Charles 23:264
Luster, Hiram 22:42
Luster, James 10:65
Luster, James R. 20:104
Luster, Rufus 22:309
Luster, Spencer 11:187
Luster, Vincent 10:124;
20:298
Luster, W. 3:122
Lutce, Daniel 18:146
Lutch, F. 14:15
Lutch, Frederick 18:146
Lute, George W. 22:113
Lutebeck, C. 24:67
Luten, W. 11:327
Luter, A. W. 17:99
Luter, Lewis 9:237;
26:222
Luters, John 9:97
Lutes, Buford N. 17:282
Lutes, Conrad 22:148
Lutes, Jacob 17:22
Lutes, John 23:155
Lutgen, F. 3:122
Luth, F. 14:15
Lutham, Franklin 10:163
Luther, A. J. 24:58
Luther, Aaron 11:231
Luther, Aaron M. 18:278
Luther, Arthur E. 21:359
Luther, Daniel 20:137;
22:171
Luther, Eugene 17:243
Luther, George 18:69
Luther, George E. 14:191
Luther, George W. 19:176
Luther, Henry Waldo
10:163
Luther, Ira 22:339
Luther, J. 3:123; 21:217;
23:180
Luther, James 17:180
Luther, James F. 27:78
Luther, Jeremiah E.
10:163

Luther, Martin 6:17;
10:124; 18:88;
20:298
Luther, Moses 15:330;
19:84
Luther, Nathaniel 17:155
Luther, U. 11:316
Lutherago, John 27:78
Lutherland, H. 3:123
Lutherland, W. H. 9:55
Luthers, Lafayette 11:116
Luthman, Christian 17:15
Luthrop, C. 1:149
Luthwick, Arnold 22:484
Lutiea, T. 1:52
Lutke, Carl 22:282
Lutkin, David 21:359
Lutler, Charles H. 12:50
Lutman, H. D. 13:66;
19:84
Lutman, Henry 7:33
Lutner, Augustus 11:156
Luton, --- 15:211
Luton, K. P. 9:55
Lutrall, C. 19:176
Lutter, Gilbert J. 12:100
Luttle, J. 3:123
Lutton, E. 1:148
Lutton, William 14:191
Luttrall, Challup 10:173
Luttrell, Haman J. 23:39
Lutts, Elwood 14:191
Lutwell, William E. 9:85
Lutz, Abraham 22:205
Lutz, Adam 12:30
Lutz, Adeline 16:299
Lutz, Charles 2:14; 25:49
Lutz, E. 11:156; 24:81
Lutz, F. 15:14
Lutz, Franklin 12:73
Lutz, Frederic 17:249
Lutz, Henry 17:425
Lutz, Henry S. 23:305
Lutz, J. 16:147; 26:42
Lutz, Jacob 22:205
Lutz, John 3:123; 9:85;
18:112; 22:89
Lutz, Joseph 24:67
Lutz, M. 3:123; 25:50
Lutz, P. M. 3:123
Lutz, Peter 7:8
Lutz, R. W. 14:191
Lutz, Samuel 18:220
Lutz, Scott McD. 22:484
Lutz, William 19:23;
25:49
Lutz, William H. 11:16
Lutzinger, John 12:30
Luvin, Charles 3:123
Lux, J. 21:167
Luxford, Joseph 12:30

Luzader, William 11:67
Luzarder, J. M. 19:84
Luze, Hiram 5:52; 25:201
Lyberger, Harman 25:201
Lyborker, Gilbert 11:109
Lycinger, G. M. 14:191
Lycre, Jackson 26:168
Lydack, Eli K. 13:34
Lyden, Thomas 17:353
Lydick, D. 15:70
Lydick, Smith 14:84
Lydle, Phil 17:180
Lydon, Patrick 19:287
Lydrick, E. 16:209
Lydy, Levi 22:431
Lye, Henry 10:124;
    16:147; 20:298
Lyford, Charles A. 12:122
Lyford, Lawrence 9:184;
    19:234
Lyght, Marion 22:430
Lyke, E. H. 16:209
Lyke, Edward H. 13:76
Lykins, Bailey 20:186
Lykins, Harrison 17:282
Lykins, William 17:282
Lyle, Arthur 10:92
Lyle, Author 20:298
Lyle, Charles 2:14; 25:49
Lyle, David 15:211
Lyle, Peter 4:66
Lyle, Samuel 6:22; 18:88
Lyle, William L. 20:298
Lyler, S. M. 23:303
Lyles, Charles 22:205
Lyles, James 7:128
Lyles, Solomon D. 17:55
Lyman, A. A. 23:155
Lyman, Albert W. 6:32
Lyman, Alfred W. 25:323
Lyman, Charles F. 23:96
Lyman, E. K. 25:201
Lyman, Edward 13:114
Lyman, Edward K. 5:22
Lyman, Edwin W. 17:288
Lyman, Elisha C. 19:176
Lyman, Eurotas C. 21:74
Lyman, F. 1:147
Lyman, G. 8:73
Lyman, H. 21:359
Lyman, H. A. 14:84
Lyman, Henry 10:163;
    19:176
Lyman, I. 23:155
Lyman, J. 3:123; 14:84
Lyman, J. B. 16:209
Lyman, James 25:311
Lyman, M. 1:51
Lyman, O. S. 3:123
Lyman, S. H. 16:43
Lyman, Samuel 19:338

Lyman, W. 14:191, 257
Lyman, W. C. 23:39
Lyman, William 8:23;
    18:146
Lyman, William B. 17:99
Lyman, William H.
    21:111
Lymangrove, J. 18:53
Lyme, Samuel 19:84
Lymem, A. 27:78
Lymons, Owen 16:299
Lymons, R. G. 16:209
Lyn, A. J. 11:243
Lynard, Henry 22:399
Lynaz, Henry D. 20:298
Lynce, Franklin 1:51
Lynch, A. 10:65; 14:84;
    20:298; 21:359
Lynch, A. D. 1:148
Lynch, A. G. 2:14; 25:52
Lynch, Albert F. 11:295
Lynch, Andrew 3:123;
    21:359
Lynch, Andrew J. 24:9
Lynch, Andy 10:173;
    19:176
Lynch, B. 3:123
Lynch, B. F. 26:42
Lynch, Bailey 19:177
Lynch, Barney 10:163
Lynch, Benjamin 18:244;
    26:42
Lynch, Bernerd 7:16
Lynch, Bryant 9:85
Lynch, Charles 1:50;
    20:10; 21:217
Lynch, Christopher 10:19
Lynch, D. 3:123
Lynch, Dennis 8:90;
    22:464
Lynch, Edward 7:33
Lynch, F. 3:123; 20:155;
    21:359
Lynch, F. M. 18:244;
    26:42
Lynch, Frank J. 9:85
Lynch, G. T. 1:148
Lynch, George 7:8; 9:222;
    16:43
Lynch, H. W. 1:51
Lynch, J. 1:51, 147;
    15:294; 16:209;
    18:15; 21:33, 111;
    27:75
Lynch, J. R. 15:17
Lynch, J. W. 17:338
Lynch, James 3:123;
    10:19; 12:30; 13:34;
    14:257; 16:43, 209;
    17:240; 18:69; 19:23;
    21:74; 23:108

Lynch, James D. 24:81
Lynch, James H. 19:256
Lynch, Jasper 22:42
Lynch, John 1:51; 9:85;
    12:30, 73; 13:114;
    14:84, 265; 15:70;
    16:209, 299; 18:208;
    23:155; 25:51
Lynch, John D. 11:94
Lynch, John H. 12:30
Lynch, John R. 21:359
Lynch, Joseph 7:14; 19:23
Lynch, Kate 18:430
Lynch, Levi 21:360
Lynch, Lewis 23:192
Lynch, M. 1:49, 148
Lynch, Mahlen 7:33
Lynch, Martin 1:51; 22:89
Lynch, Mathias 27:77
Lynch, Michael 10:124;
    20:298; 23:290;
    27:75
Lynch, N. J. 3:123
Lynch, Nathias 9:122
Lynch, Nicol 17:253
Lynch, O. 1:150
Lynch, Owen 21:33
Lynch, Patrick 10:19;
    15:39; 16:98; 19:23;
    22:13; 25:323
Lynch, Peter 22:339
Lynch, Samuel 10:124;
    20:298
Lynch, Samuel B. 24:23
Lynch, Simpson 11:94
Lynch, T. J. 2:14
Lynch, Th. 14:300
Lynch, Thomas 10:124;
    13:93; 14:15; 15:299;
    16:43; 17:476;
    20:298; 25:50; 27:79
Lynch, Timothy 14:191
Lynch, V. 3:123
Lynch, W. H. 14:84
Lynch, W. J. 15:291
Lynch, William 8:90;
    9:85; 22:89
Lynch, William A. 22:205
Lynch, William J. 10:124;
    19:84; 20:298
Lynch, William P. 7:102
Lynche, Pat 3:123
Lynchleff, S. H. 19:23
Lynd, J. 1:150
Lynd, William 9:13
Lyndall, William H.
    17:277
Lynde, E. F. 15:211
Lyndell, Stanford 10:65
Lynden, Caleb 10:65
Lynder, C. 19:84

Lynder, Nathaniel 11:35
Lyne, James 6:22
Lynes, Henry D. 10:65
Lynes, James 18:88
Lynn, ---ac R. 20:41
Lynn, A. G. 1:149
Lynn, Alfred 22:464
Lynn, D. F. 13:66
Lynn, David 8:107
Lynn, Edward 25:323
Lynn, Edwin 6:32
Lynn, Ephraim 10:65;
    20:298
Lynn, Granville S. 21:229
Lynn, Harris 18:112
Lynn, I. 18:191
Lynn, J. 1:150
Lynn, J. D. 16:136
Lynn, James H. 21:229
Lynn, James S. 16:121
Lynn, John 18:208
Lynn, John A. 21:33
Lynn, John R. 7:102
Lynn, Lorenzo E. 9:122
Lynn, Owen 8:90
Lynn, S. L. 1:149
Lynn, Samuel N. 18:220
Lynn, Samuel T. 20:18
Lynn, William 17:419;
    24:160
Lynn, Winfield S. 17:82
Lynnier, Farrier 21:277
Lynnier, Samuel 21:277
Lynnier, Washington
    21:277
Lynnville, Preston T.
    20:98
Lyns, N. 11:85
Lyon, A. D. 3:123
Lyon, Albert 1:50; 23:192
Lyon, Alfred 23:155
Lyon, Alfred M. 18:397
Lyon, Andrew J. 21:102
Lyon, B. 10:148
Lyon, B. M. 7:13
Lyon, Burton 11:207
Lyon, Cassius 23:72
Lyon, Charles 3:123;
    11:16; 22:148
Lyon, David 11:156
Lyon, David U. 17:243
Lyon, E. W. 26:169
Lyon, Edmond 15:299
Lyon, Edward L. 10:65
Lyon, Edward T. 20:298
Lyon, George E. 19:23
Lyon, Gilbert 18:112
Lyon, H. 11:307
Lyon, H. C. 14:191
Lyon, H. D. 1:51
Lyon, Henry J. 17:243

Lyon, J. A. 11:331
Lyon, J. E. W. 13:34
Lyon, J. H. 3:123
Lyon, J. R. 19:304
Lyon, James B. 9:111
Lyon, James C. 18:397
Lyon, James L. 2:14
Lyon, James S. 25:51
Lyon, Jerome 11:120
Lyon, John 14:191; 15:39;
    17:207; 20:179;
    25:51
Lyon, John G. 12:57
Lyon, John W. 11:120
Lyon, Jordan 23:289
Lyon, L. 21:208
Lyon, L. L. 3:123
Lyon, Lewis 15:57
Lyon, M. E. 16:280
Lyon, M. S. 5:22; 25:201
Lyon, N. T. 15:303
Lyon, Nathan T. 16:209
Lyon, Nelson L. 22:464
Lyon, O. L. 14:191
Lyon, Orrin J. 25:201
Lyon, P. S. 21:360
Lyon, R. 18:278
Lyon, Ransom P. 9:204
Lyon, S. 24:112
Lyon, S. F. 15:109
Lyon, S. N. 24:81
Lyon, Samuel E. 20:114
Lyon, Seymour 15:343;
    16:374
Lyon, W. D. 1:51
Lyon, William B. 20:298
Lyonans, John G. 24:24
Lyons, A. 14:84
Lyons, Albert 10:19
Lyons, Alfred M. 10:26
Lyons, Augustus 14:191
Lyons, B. 27:75
Lyons, Benj 9:154
Lyons, Benjamin 27:76
Lyons, Benjamin F.
    20:299
Lyons, Benjamin T.
    10:124
Lyons, C. H. 18:311;
    26:105
Lyons, Charles 7:102;
    14:84; 25:272
Lyons, Charles J. 17:361
Lyons, Charles T. 23:155
Lyons, Charles W. 23:242
Lyons, Cornelius 23:129
Lyons, D. 3:123; 5:42;
    21:360
Lyons, D. J. 25:201
Lyons, D. O. 11:307
Lyons, D. W. 1:51

Lyons, Daniel 17:155;
    23:156
Lyons, David 9:85;
    21:360; 22:42
Lyons, E. 3:123; 7:102
Lyons, Edward 8:121;
    10:19
Lyons, Elijah 23:72
Lyons, Frank 9:204
Lyons, Frank E. 17:100
Lyons, G. B. 24:81
Lyons, G. D. 22:205
Lyons, G. L. 1:150
Lyons, George 5:22
Lyons, George R. 17:66
Lyons, George W. 10:124;
    14:84; 20:299
Lyons, H. 20:24
Lyons, Henry 10:92;
    18:244, 245; 26:43,
    44
Lyons, Holly 10:163;
    19:177
Lyons, Hugh 10:65;
    20:299
Lyons, Isaac 8:65; 24:81
Lyons, J. 14:270; 17:149;
    19:239; 23:156
Lyons, J. C. 1:51
Lyons, J. D. L. 26:222
Lyons, J. E. M. 16:43
Lyons, J. M. 22:205
Lyons, J. T. 11:156;
    14:191
Lyons, Jacob 11:156
Lyons, James 6:17; 7:102;
    10:65, 170; 14:191;
    17:504
Lyons, James J. 7:102
Lyons, James M. 5:22
Lyons, Jerome 22:89
Lyons, Jerry 7:128
Lyons, John 8:65, 90;
    9:55; 10:65; 11:265,
    428; 12:9; 13:77;
    14:191; 16:209;
    18:245; 20:10, 35,
    299; 26:43
Lyons, John A. 5:22
Lyons, John B. 17:82
Lyons, Joseph J. 17:55
Lyons, M. 26:42
Lyons, Marcus E. 21:360
Lyons, Martin 1:191
Lyons, Mathew 9:85
Lyons, Michael 3:123;
    25:51
Lyons, Milton M. 22:125
Lyons, Minor 9:55
Lyons, Nathaniel 22:125
Lyons, Newton 24:24

Lyons, Oates 15:128
Lyons, P. 16:209
Lyons, Patrick 18:397
Lyons, Philip 17:38
Lyons, R. 3:123
Lyons, R. H. 17:149
Lyons, R. J. 18:88
Lyons, Richard 9:184;
    13:58; 19:275
Lyons, Robert 18:397
Lyons, Robert J. 6:10
Lyons, T. 25:51
Lyons, Thomas 3:123;
    14:192
Lyons, Thomas G. 1:52
Lyons, Timothy 2:14;
    10:19
Lyons, W. 1:50; 3:123;
    22:205
Lyons, William 3:123;
    11:424; 14:316;
    15:57; 23:123, 156;
    24:183
Lyons, William B. 23:39
Lyser, John M. 11:265
Lyshon, William 3:123
Lysight, John 10:124;
    20:299
Lysinger, George L.
    10:146
Lyson, Benjamin 17:100
Lyster, A. 18:245; 26:43
Lyster, Lewis M. 18:397
Lyter, George 18:88
Lythe, Andrew 9:47
Lythe, James L. 20:299
Lytle, Albert 19:283
Lytle, Andrew 26:126
Lytle, B. F. 1:149
Lytle, Charles M. 11:36
Lytle, Daniel 17:455;
    24:198
Lytle, Emory G. 21:257
Lytle, Garrett 22:125
Lytle, George 11:402
Lytle, J. 20:57
Lytle, James 22:259
Lytle, John 17:425;
    24:178
Lytle, Joseph D. 23:289
Lytle, Lewis 10:124;
    20:299
Lytle, Robert 9:184
Lytle, Rolandus 5:52
Lytle, W. 1:149
Lytle, Walter 20:87
Lyton, H. 22:309
Lyttle, A. 18:370
Lyttle, A. H. 9:222
Lyttle, H. M. 13:34
Lyttle, James F. 10:65

Lyttle, John E. 7:33

M

M'Enerny, Michael 16:82
M---, --- 16:299
M---, A. 17:356; 23:271
M---, A. T. 19:84
M---, B. 17:192
M---, B. F. 11:95; 20:57
M---, Boston 16:209
M---, C. 11:39, 231;
    17:111; 19:84; 20:85;
    21:167; 23:292;
    24:112
M---, C. A. 11:71
M---, C. B. 23:252
M---, C. D. 26:174
M---, C. J. 11:70
M---, C. L. 12:100
M---, C. P. 19:84
M---, C. W. 15:57
M---, D. 10:28
M---, D. H. 23:252
M---, E--- 8:53
M---, E. 23:264
M---, E. H. 15:159
M---, E. J. 21:208
M---, Ellis 18:33
M---, F. 25:311
M---, F. N. 11:308
M---, G. 20:92, 299
M---, G. W. 11:308
M---, George 25:55
M---, George H. 12:142;
    20:299
M---, H. 9:57; 11:245;
    15:217; 18:33, 413;
    19:84; 20:299;
    21:208; 22:353;
    23:252
M---, H. R. 11:308
M---, Herman 15:174
M---, I. 11:415
M---, J--- 11:341
M---, J. 11:245, 309;
    12:166; 14:270;
    18:33, 247; 19:304;
    20:299; 21:167;
    23:245; 24:41, 112;
    25:325; 26:48
M---, J. A. 14:270; 20:155
M---, J. B. 19:183; 20:175
M---, J. D. 11:244
M---, J. E. 21:167
M---, J. H. 11:341
M---, J. L. 25:52
M---, J. M. 10:192;
    18:177; 24:24
M---, J. N. 26:174

M---, J. T. 18:90
M---, J. W. 10:28; 23:264
M---, James 11:220; 18:90
M---, James H. 15:152
M---, James P. 19:24
M---, John 8:53; 13:80;
    19:84
M---, John B. 15:152
M---, John M. 20:179
M---, John P. 25:52
M---, John T. 11:220
M---, Joseph 18:285;
    26:135
M---, L. 14:270; 17:309
M---, L. J. 21:360
M---, M. 11:244, 245;
    17:364; 18:247;
    21:111; 22:353;
    23:99; 24:112; 26:48
M---, M. B. 16:147
M---, M. D. 21:167
M---, M. K. George 8:53
M---, N. 11:246
M---, Nelson 15:320
M---, P. 21:167
M---, P. T. 20:57
M---, P. W. 21:189
M---, R. 12:142; 15:5;
    23:271
M---, R. L. 25:57
M---, S. 15:217; 24:112
M---, S. H. 23:314
M---, S. L. 15:217
M---, S. W. 19:304
M---, T. 15:217
M---, T. A. 24:112
M---, T. F. 17:297
M---, T. O. 11:245
M---, T. S. 14:270; 21:167
M---, Thomas 23:204
M---, W. 11:341, 438;
    16:151; 20:57; 21:33,
    167; 22:353; 26:174
M---, W. E. 20:155
M---, W. F. 16:147
M---, W. H. 17:22
M---, W. J. 20:155
M---, W. W. 23:252
M---, William 15:295;
    23:39, 72
M----, J. A. 22:167
M----, John 22:125
M---ck, Daniel 25:55
Ma---, John 15:214
Ma---, Robert 25:53
Ma---r, John 20:88
Ma--al, Edward 22:205
Maag, John 10:65; 20:299
Maak, A. 20:299
Maak, August 10:65
Maban, Alex 13:34

Mabb, E. 16:209
Mabb, W. L. 25:201
Mabboth, J. T. 18:53
Mabbott, George 9:227
Mabbott, William H. 21:140
Mabee, David 10:163; 19:178
Mabee, George 16:98
Mabee, Lewis 18:53
Maben, L. R. 14:16
Maben, William 13:34
Mabene, L. R. 13:93
Maber, John 19:178
Mabery, John H. 12:73
Mabery, S. M. 12:155
Mabie, A. 9:147
Mabie, Frederick 7:33
Mabie, Hiram C. 22:42
Mabil, A. 27:81
Mable, William 1:60
Mabney, R. G. 14:283
Mabon, Thomas 8:90
Mabry, J. 25:201
Mabry, John 11:266
Mabsy, Edward G. 23:72
Mabury, John 16:299
Mac, James 18:191
Mac, Joseph M. 9:44
Mac, William J. 19:256
Macanes, D. C. 15:306
Macarg, C. 3:123
Macartney, A. 27:81
Maccaffry, Philip 9:159
Maccoy, Benjamin 4:38
MacDavid, James 3:123
Macder, Jacob 11:127
Mace, Adam 10:163; 19:178
Mace, C. H. 16:374
Mace, Calvin 15:212
Mace, E. S. M. 10:124; 20:301
Mace, Edward 7:128; 21:360
Mace, Francis M. 17:149
Mace, George W. 9:147; 27:81
Mace, Isaac 7:102
Mace, J. 4:38; 17:200
Mace, Jefferson 3:123
Mace, Joseph 18:245; 26:47
Mace, Lewis J. 1:53
Mace, William B. 22:89
Macekey, John 10:148
Macelhany, George 26:172
Macer, J. 20:41
Macer, L. 3:123

Macey, C. S. 3:123; 14:195
Macey, Charles 3:123
Macey, Enos 23:90
Macey, W. C. 20:302
Macey, William H. 4:38
MacGee, George W. 17:349
Macguire, William 7:80
Machaby, John 14:195
Machamer, Isaac 5:22
Machamer, J. 25:203
Machamer, John 23:180
Machanic, Joshua 17:441; 24:153
Macharmic, James D. 7:33
Machaway, G. 27:82
Machen, Green 18:245
Machentruz, M. 13:114
Machin, Green 26:49
Machin, Robert 11:109
Machline, Philip 1:55
Machling, K. 15:95
Machner, Henry 1:54
Machtalf, John 23:129
Machter, C. S. 3:123
Macintosh, Jacob 9:122
Mack, --- 10:163
Mack, A. 27:82
Mack, Alexander 9:147
Mack, Christian 8:23; 18:147
Mack, Clark A. 13:34
Mack, Conrad 25:55
Mack, Dandee 9:111
Mack, David 10:170; 22:148
Mack, F. M. 8:23
Mack, Frank 9:122; 27:85
Mack, G. T. 14:242
Mack, Gottleib 24:9
Mack, H. C. 11:389
Mack, Ham 23:286
Mack, J. 3:123; 21:360
Mack, Jacob 22:205
Mack, Jacob H. 10:173; 19:178
Mack, James 11:69; 14:194; 16:45
Mack, James H. 13:58
Mack, John 1:56; 10:65, 125; 13:34; 17:295; 20:303; 22:398; 27:79
Mack, Justus W. 18:278
Mack, M. M. 1:153
Mack, Marson 22:259
Mack, N. 14:86
Mack, Osiman 20:303
Mack, P. H. 23:156
Mack, Pat 4:38

Mack, Peter P. 7:66
Mack, Phillip 23:114
Mack, Richard 10:65; 20:303
Mack, Samuel 7:75; 14:194
Mack, Squire 22:89
Mack, Thomas 4:38; 27:79
Mack, W. 13:93
Mack, William 7:33; 17:395; 20:98; 22:309
Mack, William J. 9:184; 23:283
Mackaboy, E. 15:40
Mackaway, G. 9:154
Mackay, Edward 16:13
Mackay, J. 25:301
Mackay, William 18:270
Mackee, J. 7:78
Mackelay, R. 14:278; 23:72
Mackelhaney, George 8:40
Mackelroy, J. 14:192
Mackelvein, Henry 12:50
Mackeney, Samuel J. 24:175
Mackenhauft, Martin 8:23
Mackensoue, A. 8:51
Macker, Albert 15:213
Macker, J. 9:55
Macker, John 18:192
Mackerel, S. 25:203
Mackerly, A. J. 9:25
Mackero, Michael 19:178
Macket, Emery 17:447
Mackey, A. 1:155
Mackey, A. J. 19:239
Mackey, B. 8:51; 21:33
Mackey, C. 3:123
Mackey, Charles 17:66
Mackey, D. 1:157; 27:81
Mackey, E. 9:147; 25:57; 27:82
Mackey, Emory 14:261
Mackey, F. L. 8:65; 26:173
Mackey, George 18:34, 53
Mackey, Henry 16:209
Mackey, J. 1:151
Mackey, J. C. 1:151; 13:114
Mackey, James 23:156
Mackey, John 22:13, 125
Mackey, Leslie 18:413
Mackey, Michael 1:55; 10:163
Mackey, P. 1:154
Mackey, Perry 6:28

Mackey, Samuel 1:55
Mackey, W. B. 24:214
Mackey, William 13:34;
  17:38, 251; 22:205
Mackie, George 10:163
Mackie, John W. 7:68
Mackin, William 3:123
Mackle, James 12:30
Macklenery, B. C. 16:45
Mackley, Francis 12:30
Macklin, George 4:38
Macklin, John 3:123
Mackly, Alfred 13:66
Mackrall, Samuel 5:42
Mackril, R. 3:123
Mackswaser, --- 3:123
Mackune, Charles 18:397
Maclavey, William 22:13
Maclear, John 22:171
Macleese, A. 25:204
Maclenm, W. 16:209
Maclinlock, W. 26:174
Macomb, H. J. 7:59
Macomb, Samuel M.
  17:70
Macomber, Albert 11:192
Macomber, B. W. 1:157
Macomber, J. G. 14:87
Macomber, John 3:123
Macombs, A. 4:38
Macomy, S. 14:87
Macon, David 17:55
Maconley, J. G. 1:55
Macontosh, Harrison
  11:188
Macothin, J. 22:309
Macready, A. F. 8:90
Mactamore, M. 16:209
Mactavish, H. G. 15:329
Macteller, W. 16:209
Macullock, T. D. 14:87
Macumber, Andrew
  25:204
Macumber, F. 14:193
Macumber, P. B. 27:85
Macumber, Zeno 24:81
Macy, Absalom 22:89
Macy, Allen W. 5:52;
  25:204
Macy, Elisha 17:38
Macy, F. 1:157
Macy, Henry B. 22:432
Macy, Homer 22:89
Macy, John 18:398
Macy, Peter 27:84
Macy, W. Reuben 11:85
Macy, William 20:24
Madale, J. 16:374
Madama, William 23:192
Madans, John 18:192
Madara, Robert 14:195

Madard, H. R. 11:398
Madare, F. 18:371
Madars, Frank 9:222
Madary, D. H. 11:308
Maddan, Frederick 9:13
Maddee, Thomas 14:195
Madden, --- 11:220
Madden, Alfred 8:51
Madden, Amon W. 12:30
Madden, B. 1:57
Madden, C. 3:123
Madden, D. 1:152
Madden, E. 22:42
Madden, F. 3:123; 15:327
Madden, George 22:339
Madden, George W.
  20:305
Madden, I. 8:23
Madden, Jacob 17:499
Madden, James 11:39;
  15:71
Madden, Jeremiah 11:382
Madden, John 5:22;
  9:184; 11:183, 207;
  20:24; 21:360
Madden, L. 3:123
Madden, M. 1:60
Madden, M. B. 22:162
Madden, Michael 10:125;
  20:305
Madden, Nelson 8:23;
  18:147
Madden, Patrick 8:90;
  21:360
Madden, R. 1:151; 8:59
Madden, S. 18:147;
  25:204
Madden, Samuel 3:123
Madden, Sylvester 5:22
Madden, Thomas 16:45
Madden, William 12:73;
  15:40; 22:162;
  23:123
Madden, Wright 9:85;
  23:39; 26:45
Maddens, James 8:90
Maddeon, Thomas M.
  19:330
Madder, John 25:204
Madder, P. 3:123
Madder, Thomas 13:34
Maddex, Charles 21:360
Maddick, Henry 24:24
Maddiegan, Dennis 9:25
Maddigan, Michael
  18:426
Maddin, C. 15:327
Maddin, John 19:239
Maddinglay, Harvey
  10:99
Maddison, C. 14:87

Maddison, E. 18:245
Maddison, Jeffrey 18:245
Maddison, William
  11:208
Maddix, James 22:259
Maddock, G. 1:53
Maddock, Henry 7:16
Maddock, J. 9:31
Maddock, J. W. 3:123
Maddock, William 22:89;
  26:170
Maddocks, C. H. 1:156
Maddors, George H.
  10:66
Maddox, Aaron 14:195
Maddox, Ai 16:133
Maddox, Alfred 10:66;
  20:305
Maddox, D. 1:99
Maddox, George F.
  14:263
Maddox, Henry 21:13
Maddox, I. 14:87
Maddox, J. R. 26:170
Maddox, James 18:33;
  19:47
Maddox, John 9:55
Maddox, Lafayette 11:390
Maddox, Luther 25:56
Maddox, Stephen H.
  22:454
Maddox, William S. 7:102
Maddrel, J. 15:40
Maddrel, James 12:73
Maddren, P. 14:16
Maddron, P. 13:93
Maddux, Alfred 23:39
Maddux, James 23:156
Maddux, Joel 22:205
Maddux, Simeon W.
  20:10
Made, Samuel H. 18:357
Maden, Ben 11:96
Maden, Charles 12:155
Maden, Henry 18:15
Maden, John 18:15
Maden, Samuel 11:122
Mader, Andrew 25:204
Mader, David 4:38
Madera, George 4:38
Maderia, J. 7:68
Maders, W. C. 1:151
Madigan, D. 1:60
Madigan, Dennis 18:311;
  26:106
Madigan, James 22:485
Madigan, M. 12:83;
  16:299; 24:112
Madigan, Michael 13:93
Madigan, Patrick 17:393
Madigan, Thomas 5:52

Madill, Joseph 13:125
Madison, Abner 17:232
Madison, Alfred 9:162;
    27:89
Madison, Andrew 19:84
Madison, Archibald 18:53
Madison, D. 3:123; 14:29
Madison, Darius 12:30
Madison, E. 26:48
Madison, George M. 7:16;
    13:34; 16:45
Madison, H. B. 7:33
Madison, Henry 18:112
Madison, Isaac 6:18;
    18:88
Madison, J. 11:160
Madison, James 9:165;
    10:65; 20:305;
    21:249, 278; 22:309;
    25:204
Madison, James D. 7:51
Madison, Jeffry 26:47
Madison, Jerry 6:29
Madison, John 9:204
Madison, Marias 17:451
Madison, Marion 26:224
Madison, Morris 24:179
Madison, Sampson 21:278
Madison, Samuel 10:19;
    27:87
Madison, Swayne 21:360
Madison, Timothy 12:30
Madison, William 6:18;
    18:88; 21:240, 278;
    27:84, 146
Madison, William H.
    20:10
Madlenor, S. 14:195
Madley, Nathan 26:46
Madley, Samuel 17:393
Madley, Willis 7:128
Madlin, Nathan 6:32
Madlin, William 11:19
Madliner, L. 3:123
Madlock, George 14:263
Madlock, Josiah 7:102
Madnegan, Joseph 3:123
Madoff, S. 15:259
Madole, Adam 11:208
Madole, George 7:59
Madole, I. 15:343
Madon, Martin 22:125
Madow, F. 11:95
Madox, Aaron 9:122;
    27:84
Madox, J. D. 12:162
Madra, James 18:34
Madrall, A. 3:123
Madrid, J. 16:209
Madrid, Steward 21:279
Madson, K. 14:87

Madson, Peter 7:33
Madther, W. H. 23:307
Madvese, J. B. 7:128
Madwell, Pleasant M.
    22:42
Mady, J. P. 14:286
Maear, J. A. 4:38
Maedel, Louis 7:33
Maehler, Henry 24:67
Maeir, William H. 9:85
Maeldon, Charles 6:13
Maeller, Peter 20:305
Maellman, William 11:37
Maergapon, John 8:23
Maeriman, Henry 11:291
Maerz, Jacob N. 17:389
Maf---, James 25:54
Maffatt, W. T. 1:157
Maffatt, William 9:13
Maffit, J. 11:309
Maffitt, James F. 7:102
Mafirma, Charles 11:128
Mafitt, Jasper N. 10:66
Mafumans, Samuel 4:38
Magadorn, John 27:89
Magaha, Joseph 3:123
Magaha, William 22:259
Magan, W. C. 7:68
Magan, William 10:125;
    20:305
Magary, J. 16:209
Magaw, Alex. H. 19:84
Magden, C. M. 22:148
Magden, Charles M.
    22:148
Mage, Heig 11:323
Mage, Lewis 11:209
Magee, Andrew 7:128;
    12:30
Magee, Calvin 7:128
Magee, Egan 9:209
Magee, George W. 4:38
Magee, H. 25:56
Magee, John 4:38;
    22:485; 23:16
Magee, Joseph R. 12:73
Magee, O. W. 9:222
Magee, Oney 4:38
Magee, Patrick 12:30
Magee, Peter 22:497
Magee, Robert 7:128;
    21:131
Magee, William 19:256
Magent, J. 27:88
Mager, Julius 10:66
Mager, Richard F. 15:213
Magerham, A. 2:15
Magerly, J. 1:156
Mageson, J. 3:124
Maggett, Austin 25:205
Maggookin, H. 21:360

Maghan, H. 25:54
Magher, --- 16:374
Magholz, Reinold 1:54
Maghy, William 18:192
Magie, Charles H. 22:408
Magie, John 22:282
Magie, W. S. 26:213
Magill, D. 21:189
Magill, H. P. 3:124
Magill, James 12:30
Magill, Robert 9:184
Magill, Thomas 18:278
Magill, William 12:73
Magines, John E. 12:142
Maginley, J. 9:184
Maginly, J. 19:239
Maginn, John 22:329
Maginnis, Dennis 10:125;
    20:305
Maginnis, J. M. 3:124
Maginnis, John 10:152;
    18:53
Maginnis, Laurence
    12:155
Magley, Christian 21:229
Magley, Hiram 21:360
Magnaghi, Antony 22:503
Magne, George 19:178
Magnemar, --- 14:278;
    23:108
Magner, Felix 9:184;
    19:256
Magner, Jonathan 21:229
Magner, Nathan 26:172
Magnes, Edward 15:40
Magnin, James 10:92
Magnis, Harrison 11:320
Magnord, Heoria 25:55
Magnus, John 21:92
Magoon, Hiram 19:24
Magoon, John B. 17:62
Magoon, O. J. 15:109
Magoon, P. 1:157
Magorel, W. H. 7:51
Magovern, J. 1:152
Magowen, Harrison
    17:237
Magowen, William
    17:319
Magram, J. 3:124
Magrath, G. H. 3:124
Magraw, James C. 22:89
Magraw, Patrick 20:10
Magro, O. W. 18:371
Magrooda, Thomas 5:42
Magruder, Michael 12:50
Magruder, T. 25:205
Magruen, A. 25:52
Mags, V. 23:198
Maguella, John 19:24
Maguire, Bernard 7:33

Maguire, C. L. 1:156
Maguire, Charles 7:33; 12:30
MaGuire, Henry 20:305
Maguire, J. 27:83
MaGuire, James 20:305
Maguire, James M. 9:25
Maguire, John 15:40
Maguire, John H. 12:30
Maguire, Joseph 23:309
Maguire, Lewis 13:114
Maguire, Michael 15:81
Maguire, Patrick 10:9
Maguire, Peter 23:90
Maguire, Ralph 8:90
Maguire, Theodore 10:96
Maguire, Thomas 1:57
Maguire, W. 20:305
Maguire, William 10:66
Maha, --- 19:283
Maha, Nicholas 24:154
Maha, William 7:68
Mahafey, Thomas 11:409
Mahaffe, John 22:433
Mahaffey, John 21:75
Mahaffey, Samuel 23:12
Mahaffey, W. 18:53
Mahaffry, W. H. 10:148
Mahaffy, C. 21:123
Mahaffy, Ham 27:90
Mahaffy, R. 15:71
Mahaffy, S. 19:256
Maham, James 3:124; 9:122
Mahan, A. 17:96
Mahan, A. B. 22:205
Mahan, Charles 20:24
Mahan, E. 3:124; 22:259
Mahan, Ebenezer 23:181
Mahan, Hanson 20:305
Mahan, Hassan 10:92
Mahan, Henry 7:33
Mahan, I. 14:87
Mahan, J. 1:60
Mahan, J. M. 23:181
Mahan, James 22:13; 27:85
Mahan, James F. 20:104
Mahan, James H. 20:35
Mahan, John 15:213
Mahan, John B. 15:213
Mahan, Leonard 19:240
Mahan, Lewis H. 23:156
Mahan, Michael 17:55; 20:10
Mahan, Milton A. 22:89
Mahan, Nicholas 17:441
Mahan, Patrick 19:334
Mahan, S. J. 23:276
Mahan, Samuel D. A. 8:51

Mahan, Thomas 11:70
Mahan, Timothy 17:449
Mahan, Warren 7:102
Mahan, William 9:184
Mahana, Mich 9:147
Mahanah, Nicholas 27:81
Mahaney, Jacob W. 11:277
Mahaney, Jeremiah 20:126
Mahany, John 16:13
Mahappy, John W. 17:393
Mahar, M. 13:34
Mahar, Michael 15:316
Mahar, Patrick 8:23
Mahar, William 13:81; 16:209
Mahargy, William 22:259
Mahay, John 7:51
Mahean, Barney 11:95
Mahen, Daniel 1:55
Mahen, E. 13:93
Maher, Charles 4:38
Maher, Edward 21:75
Maher, Frederick 21:246
Maher, James 10:26
Maher, John 14:195; 15:109; 19:330
Maher, Mary 26:223
Maher, O. Swan 24:95
Maher, P. 3:124; 4:38
Maher, Pat 25:301
Maher, Patrick 7:80
Maher, S. L. 3:124
Mahew, Henry 22:455
Mahew, John 22:432
Mahey, Henry W. 12:30
Mahin, B. 3:124
Mahin, D. 3:124
Mahin, James 24:9
Mahin, John W. 20:24
Mahin, William G. 21:11
Mahison, I. H. 9:147
Mahison, J. H. 27:81
Mahla, Albert 9:209
Mahla, C. 15:213
Mahland, --- 25:56
Mahler, Jacob 10:163
Mahler, John 3:124
Mahler, X. 1:54
Mahlon, Pinkney S. 18:192
Mahn, Moses 9:85
Mahnran, Ebenezer L. 21:56
Mahoir, Theodore 12:83; 16:299
Maholem, George H. 23:72
Maholland, James 21:360
Mahomy, A. J. 11:120

Mahon, A. 4:38
Mahon, C. 3:124
Mahon, Ed 18:88
Mahon, Edward 8:112; 12:30
Mahon, G. 13:93
Mahon, J. F. 24:24
Mahon, James 13:34
Mahon, John 18:421
Mahon, L. 27:81
Mahon, Michael 13:34; 19:84
Mahon, Patrick 8:114; 18:311; 26:106
Mahon, Thomas 3:124; 7:51
Mahon, W. F. 25:205
Mahon, Walter 15:18
Mahon, William 16:45; 19:256
Mahone, J. M. 25:56
Mahone, John M. 2:14
Mahone, John W. 17:232
Mahoney, --- 24:68
Mahoney, B. 9:55
Mahoney, Charles 12:50
Mahoney, Daniel 16:98; 24:67
Mahoney, E. 25:205
Mahoney, Edward 5:22
Mahoney, George W. 10:125; 20:305
Mahoney, James 16:98
Mahoney, John 6:11; 9:184; 15:334
Mahoney, Joseph 22:125
Mahoney, M. M. 11:424
Mahoney, Michael 17:55; 23:181; 25:53
Mahoney, Owen 25:57
Mahoney, P. 1:155
Mahoney, P. I. 12:92
Mahoney, P. J. 14:87; 16:299
Mahoney, Patrick 21:360
Mahoney, R. 14:131; 15:263
Mahoney, Richard 8:126; 17:503
Mahoney, Rudolph 21:360
Mahoney, S. 25:57
Mahoney, Samuel 9:184; 11:424
Mahoney, Thomas 11:37
Mahoney, Timothy 7:9; 8:23; 18:147; 19:24
Mahoney, William 7:13; 8:118; 19:315
Mahoney, William J. 21:360

Mahoney, William R. 24:41
Mahony, Albert 15:159
Mahony, Cornelius 14:195
Mahony, Dennis 10:163
Mahony, J. 19:256
Mahony, L. 14:195
Mahony, R. 14:283
Mahoun, George 8:107
Mahoy, John H. 22:485
Mahr, James 12:30
Mahr, Michael 21:33
Maiberger, George 19:84
Maiburger, George 13:66
Maice, W. P. 17:38
Maicod, James 25:323
Maiden, E. 14:87
Maiden, Thomas 24:81
Maier, J. 14:16
Maier, Lewis 18:34
Maiges, M. 13:114
Maik, F. M. 18:148
Maiken, Jonathan 19:178
Mail, George 22:205
Mailady, Michael 9:184
Mailer, J. R. 3:124
Mailer, Thomas C. 18:371
Mailey, Jonathan R. 21:360
Mailiard, Jaques 8:73
Maillard, E. 14:283
Mailloux, I. 25:273
Mailo, J. 1:157
Main, Amos 18:220
Main, C. M. 13:114
Main, C. P. 15:213
Main, D. W. 26:47
Main, David M. 9:85
Main, F. O. 3:124
Main, G. 13:93; 14:16
Main, George 21:360
Main, Henry 3:124
Main, Isaac 18:398
Main, J. W. 9:237; 26:222
Main, John 19:84
Main, John F. 8:65; 26:173
Main, Mich 18:192
Main, Seymour H. 21:89
Main, W. 9:115
Mainard, Harrison 17:237
Mainard, James R. 17:389
Mainard, William J. 17:55
Mainatt, Thomas B. 15:279
Maine, A. D. 10:66; 20:305
Maine, Amos 13:34; 16:45

Maine, Anson 7:102; 21:360
Maine, C. 1:55; 7:68
Maine, C. W. 25:53
Maine, Daniel 7:102
Maine, David G. 22:89
Maine, G. A. 13:79
Maine, Harrison 22:259
Maine, Job 10:66; 20:305
Maine, John C. 21:56
Maine, Latham H. 25:205
Maine, Marcus 7:128
Maine, Simon 16:131
Maine, William D. 26:46
Maines, Alexander 23:129
Maines, Moses N. 22:174
Maines, Rob 25:205
Maines, W. 19:275
Maines, William 3:124
Mainfold, W. 3:124
Mainhart, E. O. 1:155
Mainhart, F. 3:124
Maining, Edward 15:40
Mainor, A. 14:16
Mains, Eldridge 10:19
Mains, Henry 7:69
Mains, J. C. 10:186; 26:204
Mains, William 9:184
Maintin, G. H. 3:124
Maiorath, August 24:81
Maise, Peter 12:30
Maison, Patrick 19:256
Maison, W. 11:307
Maiss, C. E. 1:55
Maister, Jared 17:425
Maitland, John 10:125
Maitsdort, J. A. 26:48
Maize, Thomas 21:56
Majar, George 19:256
Majo, Monte 17:23
Major, Abraham G. 17:38
Major, Adolphus 7:128
Major, Alexander 22:235
Major, Andrew 17:135; 24:199
Major, Arthur 21:360
Major, Cas 13:93
Major, Charles 25:205
Major, David 10:66
Major, Edmond 6:22
Major, Edward 6:18; 18:88
Major, G. 19:256; 25:276
Major, George 9:184
Major, H. 7:128; 25:205
Major, H. H. 17:273
Major, Henry 5:42; 11:208
Major, J. 27:88
Major, John 13:66; 16:209

Major, Joshua 7:128
Major, L. P. 5:22
Major, Marrion 14:195
Major, Monroe 11:209
Major, S. M. 14:87
Major, Sampson 22:309
Major, T. C. 13:114
Major, Thomas 1:56
Major, Wiley 22:309
Major, William 6:18; 18:88; 23:90
Majors, George T. 8:65
Majors, Isaac R. 22:504
Majors, J. E. 21:111
Majors, Webster H. 7:33
Majors, William R. 22:259
Mak, Michael 15:304
Makemson, Alexander 21:56
Makepeace, N. 1:60
Maker, C. 12:80; 25:205
Maker, Charles 24:9
Makfanbeck, J. 15:310
Makin, W. 3:124
Makin, W. H. 1:153
Mala, Patrick 22:171
Malade, D. 19:84
Malady, M. 4:38
Malady, Michael 9:222; 18:371
Malagin, Z. 23:39
Malalivly, Joseph 11:288
Malaly, P. 3:124
Malan, Dennis 27:80
Malanders, John 9:85
Malanely, William 22:89
Malaney, P. 14:335
Malaney, Thomas 14:87
Malany, D. 4:38
Malany, J. 22:205
Malason, James S. 23:123
Malat, Andrew S. 1:54
Malay, Harrison 11:161
Malb, William L. 5:22
Malbergh, A. 1:59
Malbeth, J. H. 10:180; 18:177
Malby, F. C. 13:114
Malby, George 22:259
Malby, Martin 9:9
Malcolm, David P. 22:486
Malcolm, J. 15:213
Malcolm, J. R. 3:124
Malcolm, S. A. 3:124
Malcolm, W. A. 3:124
Malcolm, Wilmot 19:229
Malcom, A. W. 19:318
Malcom, Brunnias W. 23:243
Malcom, Daniel C. 11:39

Malcom, J. 18:371
Malcom, William M. 21:56
Malcomb, Thomas 15:299; 16:209
Malcon, Henry 4:38
Malcony, J. 16:269
Malcord, James 6:32
Malden, W. 7:102
Maldreth, George 11:209
Maldridge, Francis 19:24
Maldriss, John 3:124
Malehu, Austin 11:17
Malendie, George 19:343
Maler, Jackson 12:50
Maler, James 22:454
Malery, Albert 13:114
Malery, W. B. 11:244
Males, Dan 20:305
Males, Thomas 1:58
Maley, Asa 24:41
Maley, Byron H. 11:288
Maley, E. W. 19:240
Maley, Edward 3:124; 19:178
Maley, James 9:97
Maley, Melvis 18:430
Maley, Patrick 22:42
Maley, Spencer 15:87
Maley, Thomas 22:339
Maley, William 21:229
Malg, J. A. 26:223
Malhoon, D. F. 25:205
Malhorn, James 8:23; 18:148
Malia, Edward 21:11
Malia, Thomas 12:30
Malicoat, James 22:259
Malika, Julius 22:464
Malin, J. A. 24:215
Malin, John G. 22:125
Malindon, Abram 22:453
Malinery, Henry 22:42
Malinney, John 20:305
Maliow, Jesse 25:205
Malish, William T. 11:116
Malkey, D. 3:124
Malkil, James 23:286
Malkin, Cyrus 9:222
Malkin, Cyrus K. 18:371
Malky, G. L. 12:85
Mall, Charles 24:164
Mall, Christopher 11:37
Mall, Isaac 12:30
Mall, J. M. 23:156
Mallady, M. 19:256
Mallaham, Marcus 11:158
Mallard, John 1:54
Mallatt, George W. 17:347
Malleck, M. 3:124

Mallen, J. 16:210
Mallenbre, James 16:140
Maller, L. 10:163; 19:178
Mallery, G. 25:205
Mallery, Henry 15:213
Mallet, C. 1:57
Mallet, George S. 10:164
Mallet, James 20:305
Mallet, Robert 9:133; 27:85
Mallett, George S. 19:178
Mallett, John 18:311; 26:106
Mallett, Levi 22:454
Mallett, M. 1:150
Mallett, T. 19:245
Mallett, W. F. 19:84
Malley, Charles 9:36
Malley, Cornelius 15:303; 16:210
Malley, Garrick 22:433
Malley, Martin O. 11:161
Malley, P. 1:155
Malley, William 8:77
Mallick, Morgan 4:38
Mallin, James A. 1:56
Mallin, Thomas 17:349
Mallinas, William 18:148
Malling, L. 1:156
Malling, Thomas 12:64
Mallinger, Peter 21:103
Mallingly, Bapt 1:57
Mallion, C. 14:87
Mallison, Andreas 23:72
Mallison, J. 1:53
Mallison, Marvin 22:148
Mallo, Manuel 10:125; 20:305
Mallo, W. H. 10:66
Mallock, J. D. 18:15
Mallon, Charles 16:45
Mallon, James 22:42
Mallone, Charles 13:34
Mallone, D. W. 25:205
Mallone, David W. 5:22
Mallone, James W. 22:42
Mallone, John 14:195
Malloney, W. 27:89
Mallony, C. 14:195
Malloon, John 21:360
Mallory, A. B. 23:72
Mallory, Alvah F. 23:156
Mallory, E. 1:54
Mallory, Edward L. 11:288
Mallory, George 5:22
Mallory, George W. 7:102
Mallory, J. 9:227
Mallory, James 7:102; 22:432
Mallory, John 20:10

Mallory, Lorenzo 7:33
Mallory, M. B. 18:53
Mallory, Stephen 1:54
Mallory, T. 4:38
Mallory, William 5:22
Mallot, F. 7:51
Mallot, Victor 7:69
Mallow, James H. 22:167
Mallow, John 7:33
Mallowy, J. C. 11:267
Malloy, James 10:164; 19:179; 21:257, 360
Malloy, John 7:75
Malloy, Levi 19:84
Malloy, Michael 21:360
Malloy, Patrick 12:30
Malloy, Thomas 18:112; 23:241
Malloy, William 15:3; 23:286
Mallroy, Thomas 25:273
Mally, Henry 22:148
Mally, Walter G. 8:23; 18:148
Malman, Thomas 6:32
Malo, Moses 12:83; 16:299
Malody, P. 27:91
Malon, George 7:59
Malon, Harrison 8:107
Malon, I. 21:33
Malon, Isaac H. 12:64; 15:87
Malon, Jesse 5:22
Malon, Pat 3:124
Malon, Samuel S. 21:247
Malon, Thomas 11:245; 21:217
Malona, A. 18:88
Malone, A. 8:73; 19:84
Malone, Alkana 20:137
Malone, Andrew J. 22:504
Malone, Asbury 22:485
Malone, Charles 9:13
Malone, Daniel 10:177; 19:179
Malone, David 10:66; 20:305
Malone, Frank M. 10:125; 20:305
Malone, J. 1:57; 9:55; 14:242; 27:90
Malone, J. M. 11:70
Malone, James 17:212
Malone, James M. 21:103
Malone, John 3:124; 10:164; 12:122; 14:87; 18:112; 19:179
Malone, John D. 12:146
Malone, John H. 8:114

Malone, Joseph 22:259
Malone, L. F. 20:41
Malone, Levi L. 22:125
Malone, M. 1:154
Malone, M. D. 9:161
Malone, Michael 17:353
Malone, Moses 17:181
Malone, P. 11:183; 24:81
Malone, R. J. 3:124
Malone, Richard 13:34
Malone, S. 1:57
Malone, S. B. 3:124
Malone, S. H. 14:87
Malone, Samuel 11:407;
    25:301
Malone, Thomas 8:23;
    11:208; 18:148
Malone, W. 2:15
Malone, William 1:59;
    7:33; 9:243; 15:71;
    18:53; 21:205, 249;
    25:57
Malone, William H.
    22:504
Maloney, --- 8:124
Maloney, A. 3:124
Maloney, B. 3:124
Maloney, Henry C. 10:8
Maloney, J. 1:155; 3:124;
    12:83; 13:93;
    14:195; 16:299;
    21:360
Maloney, Jacob 16:210
Maloney, James 1:55;
    22:42; 23:12
Maloney, John 7:15, 102;
    13:114; 15:129, 166;
    19:222; 21:360;
    23:39; 24:160;
    25:279, 301
Maloney, Joseph 15:14
Maloney, Lawrence 8:59;
    19:272
Maloney, M. 25:301
Maloney, Madison M.
    22:504
Maloney, Martimus O.
    22:205
Maloney, Martin 17:436;
    24:185
Maloney, Michael 7:75;
    15:84; 23:123
Maloney, Nathan H.
    20:110
Maloney, O. 3:124
Maloney, Patrick 10:66;
    20:57, 305
Maloney, Peter 7:59
Maloney, Richard 17:361
Maloney, Thomas 9:16;
    14:195; 19:338

Maloney, Timothy 11:159
Maloney, W. 11:288
Maloney, W. D. 27:89
Maloney, William 25:205
Malony, D. 1:151
Malony, Daniel 7:69
Malony, John 17:460;
    18:421; 22:42
Malony, Thomas 19:84
Maloon, David 7:59
Maloon, H. 15:213
Maloon, Samuel 7:80
Malory, C. M. 4:38
Malory, Ezra 11:128
Malory, M. 1:151
Malory, W. B. 4:38
Malosh, Elijah 22:89
Malott, E. 1:157
Malott, George 21:11
Malott, Theople 24:41
Maloun, William 23:39
Maloy, Andrew 20:18
Maloy, Hugh R. 21:13
Maloy, J. 1:151
Maloy, James 3:124
Maloy, John 18:208, 421
Maloy, John C. 12:167
Maloy, John H. 19:348
Maloy, L. 18:69
Maloy, L. M. 8:51
Maloy, W. G. 20:305
Maloy, William 25:205
Mals, --- 24:112
Malsbray, Asa 3:124
Malsby, F. 3:124
Malsed, J. 9:111
Malsmer, Daniel 22:205
Malson, J. T. 20:41
Maltbie, Elijah 10:19
Maltbie, Eugene 10:173;
    19:179
Maltby, George H. 11:160
Maltby, H. S. 15:213
Maltby, J. 1:60
Maltby, Richard 11:403
Maltebec, Christian
    18:245
Malthey, Charles 11:68
Malthner, E. W. 22:42
Malthouse, J. 14:195
Malthstead, Henry 21:239
Maltman, Calvin 11:109
Maltney, N. 1:158
Malton, Charles 6:13
Maltoon, H. 1:152
Maluin, Alison 22:309
Malvern, Roe 14:195
Malverton, William
    18:245; 26:48
Malvey, Charles 21:360
Mamarr, J. H. 4:39

Mame, G. A. 16:210
Mame, S. 1:58
Mamer, I. 25:205
Mamja, Juan 8:123
Mamming, Leonard T.
    17:38
Mammoth, --- 15:71
Mamon, P. 3:124
Mamott, Joseph 20:108
Mamrton, J. W. 15:353
Man, A. 12:92
Man, George 18:15
Man, James 25:301
Man, John B. 12:30
Man, Patrick 9:184
Man, Sidney A. 25:56
Man, William R. 15:57
Man---, R. 23:156
Manada, J. A. 14:16
Manafoon, John 18:148
Managan, M. 8:52
Managan, W. 15:40
Manahan, A. C. 25:56
Manahan, J. 25:323
Manahan, John 11:38;
    25:323
Manahan, John L. 22:454
Manahan, Robert 9:44
Manahan, Thomas 3:125
Manal, John W. 22:205
Manan, S. 16:210
Manane, George 21:243
Mananville, Fred. K.
    24:24
Manard, C. 21:360
Manas, G. 22:259
Manatt, Alex 20:305
Manay, J. 17:290
Mancaster, John W. 11:69
Manch, Fabrick 12:142
Manch, L. 18:53
Manch, William 20:305
Mancha, John 12:83
Manchester, A. L. 1:58
Manchester, C. B. 15:167
Manchester, C. F. 14:195
Manchester, Dennis
    20:126
Manchester, George
    22:148
Manchester, George L.
    12:122; 15:129
Manchester, Greenleaf N.
    7:102
Manchester, H. 20:155
Manchester, Horace 19:84
Manchester, J. M. 3:125
Manchester, James R.
    9:72
Manchester, Joseph K.
    9:122; 27:85

Manchester, Peter 17:66
Manchester, Thomas
 15:80
Manck, B. F. 23:156
Manck, O. 16:210
Mandee, Casper 15:174
Mandell, James 21:360
Mandell, John 15:23
Manderbeck, M. 16:210
Manderer, F. 1:154
Manderville, D. 13:93
Manderville, Henry
 10:164
Mandervville, John 24:9
Manderville, S. 1:60
Mandeville, C. 1:53
Mandeville, Charles
 23:108
Mandeville, Frank B.
 25:269
Mandeville, H. 19:179
Mandeville, M. 9:184
Mandeville, M. R. 19:256
Mandeville, W. D. 4:39
Mandeville, William
 3:125
Mandexter, James 26:237
Mandigo, Aaron 7:102
Mandigo, H. H. 15:84
Mandlin, Nathan 11:68
Mandrell, Solomon 22:42
Mandway, John 12:30
Maneed, Jacob 21:279
Manel, L. 21:209
Manelt, Charles 9:122
Manen, John 12:85;
 16:299
Maner, H. 11:265
Maner, Leopold 17:321
Maner, Samuel 22:353
Maneral, David 27:86
Manes, A. A. 1:156
Manes, George 21:14
Manes, J. A. 25:205
Manes, Logan 11:19
Maney, James B. 12:172
Maney, John 21:11
Maney, Joseph 7:33
Maney, W. H. 7:102
Manfield, W. 14:242
Mang, H. 11:161
Manga, John 16:71
Mangam, Thomas 14:283
Mangan, D. 1:157
Mangan, David 25:205
Mangan, W. H. 4:39
Mangarder, Mathew 22:42
Mangas, Jos. 19:179
Mangein, W. 3:124
Mangel, David 9:122;
 27:85

Mangen, Alfred 9:209
Mangen, James 3:124
Mangent, M. 17:249
Manger, Abel P. 24:24
Manger, G. 14:87
Manger, John 10:66;
 12:30; 20:305
Manger, L. 1:156
Manger, S. V. 26:172
Manghermer, William H.
 17:38
Mangle, John V. 11:160
Mangle, Joseph 22:205
Mangneau, Toussaint
 21:360
Mangold, Lewis G.
 11:122
Mangold, Peter 12:73;
 15:71
Mangold, W. 1:151
Mangon, Michael 17:253
Mangram, Lewis S. 17:55
Mangs, Jeremiah 7:128
Manguea, Toussaint 7:128
Mangus, Caleb 17:419;
 24:161
Mangus, E. 13:93
Mangus, Eli 11:267
Mangus, James H. 12:54
Manhart, --- 21:75
Manheart, Daniel 22:113
Manher, R. T. 26:47
Manhimsey, John 10:164
Manier, D. W. 20:305
Manier, Samuel 16:374
Manifee, Richard 6:13
Manifer, Richard 18:88
Manifold, H. C. 13:114
Manifold, William C.
 21:75
Manigan, P. 14:87
Manigualt, S. 27:79
Maniham, J. 3:124
Manihugh, Charles
 18:311; 26:106
Manill, Louis 9:122
Maning, John 15:213
Manion, Thomas 11:231
Manir, T. 24:81
Manis, George 22:259
Manis, George W. 17:167;
 22:503
Manis, P. 11:309
Manix, John 22:433
Mank, E. 3:125
Mank, Mathias 17:441;
 24:153
Mankard, John 20:58
Manker, C. A. 7:10
Manker, Lewis 23:72
Manker, Robert T. 9:85

Manker, W. I. 10:66
Mankey, Henry 18:407
Mankham, H. E. 7:59
Mankins, George 11:161
Mankley, Daniel 15:213
Mankose, Willis 18:285;
 26:135
Mankus, Homer 24:62
Manleaf, N. 21:361
Manley, Andrew 25:205
Manley, Bennett 18:53
Manley, Charles 15:129
Manley, Cornelius A.
 17:282
Manley, Elijah 8:51
Manley, Henry 20:305
Manley, J. 3:125
Manley, James 9:133
Manley, James K. 23:156
Manley, Jason W. 22:148
Manley, M. 15:14
Manley, Michael 12:73
Manley, N. F. 5:22;
 25:205
Manley, Richard 11:333
Manley, S. 1:152; 25:205
Manley, Samuel 5:42
Manley, Thomas 16:210
Manley, W. H. 1:152
Manlig, S. 3:125
Manlove, David R. 22:408
Manlove, J. G. 1:57
Manlove, William 23:39
Manly, A. C. 24:89
Manly, Daniel 25:205
Manly, Elijah 21:75
Manly, Frank 25:205
Manly, Henry 10:92
Manly, J. 16:210
Manly, James 27:83
Manly, Orson 9:103
Manly, S. 25:205
Manly, T. 16:98
Manly, Timothy 21:361
Manly, William 9:103;
 14:286; 18:340
Mann, --- 15:40
Mann, A. A. 1:157
Mann, A. D. 10:125;
 20:305
Mann, Alexander 22:89
Mann, Allen 9:133; 27:84
Mann, Amos 22:89
Mann, Andre 22:42
Mann, Andrew 8:90
Mann, Anthony 10:125;
 20:305
Mann, Azro 22:205
Mann, Benjamin 16:374
Mann, Charles A. 8:107
Mann, Conway R. 11:245

Mann, Cyrus 17:164
Mann, D. 7:51
Mann, David 9:25
Mann, Dick 8:40; 26:171
Mann, E. 11:157
Mann, E. H. 15:167
Mann, Edward 18:398
Mann, Essick 8:77
Mann, Fred 9:111
Mann, Frederick 17:100; 25:205
Mann, G. 15:40
Mann, George B. 17:263
Mann, George W. 14:195; 21:128
Mann, H. A. 7:75; 25:301
Mann, Harris 14:88
Mann, Harvey 22:148
Mann, Henry R. 19:256
Mann, Henry S. 17:23
Mann, Horace 9:72
Mann, Ira 10:173; 19:179
Mann, Isaac 18:69
Mann, Isaac B. 21:361
Mann, J. 1:59; 3:124
Mann, J. H. 19:256
Mann, J. J. 1:154
Mann, J. P. 21:33
Mann, James 18:294
Mann, James H. 9:184
Mann, James O. 9:36; 26:107
Mann, Jesse 13:58
Mann, John 13:114; 22:205, 453; 23:114; 24:53
Mann, Joseph 3:124; 8:23
Mann, Joseph W. 26:173
Mann, L. H. 8:73
Mann, Lewis 5:22; 25:205
Mann, Martin 7:83
Mann, N. C. 3:124
Mann, Noyes 22:134
Mann, Oliver P. 10:66; 20:305
Mann, P. 14:88
Mann, Philip 21:361
Mann, R. 24:24
Mann, R. C. 11:37
Mann, Randall 17:181
Mann, Richard 18:469
Mann, Richard F. 20:98
Mann, Robert 18:245; 26:47
Mann, Robert B. 12:30
Mann, S. D. 25:205
Mann, S. H. 26:174
Mann, Samuel 23:156
Mann, T. 1:151
Mann, Theodore 20:147
Mann, Thomas C. 22:89

Mann, Thomas J. 17:237
Mann, W. H. 9:25
Mann, W. W. 20:305
Mann, William 3:124; 15:353; 16:280; 21:361; 24:24
Mann, William A. 18:398
Mann, William O. 8:107
Mann, William R. 12:73
Mann, William T. 8:107
Mann, Williamuth 19:287
Mannay, J. W. 14:88
Mannel, George D. 11:245
Manner, C. 3:125
Manner, Joseph 5:22
Manner, M. 3:125
Manner, M. V. B. 15:213
Mannerd, Samuel 12:122
Mannering, E. 22:287
Mannering, John 5:22
Mannering, John H. 1:56
Mannering, S. 25:205
Manners, J. W. 25:205
Manney, George O. 21:361
Manney, John 22:339
Manney, William T. 18:245
Mannie, W. 14:16; 16:269
Mannin, James F. 17:282
Manning, --- 3:124; 25:273
Manning, A. 1:103; 3:124; 11:231
Manning, A. F. 25:205
Manning, A. J. 21:123
Manning, Abraham 15:87
Manning, B. F. 3:124
Manning, Benjamin 21:361
Manning, Bristol 9:133; 27:85
Manning, C. 13:93
Manning, Carter 17:398
Manning, Charles 10:164; 11:160; 16:98; 18:88
Manning, Cyrus 18:220
Manning, D. 10:148
Manning, Dan A. 21:361
Manning, Daniel 22:339
Manning, Dennis 12:30
Manning, E. F. 19:229
Manning, Edgar F. 15:273
Manning, Edw. F. 9:184
Manning, Elias 7:33; 16:3
Manning, Elias E. 23:72
Manning, Eugene L. 9:244
Manning, F. S. 14:88
Manning, Francis 7:128

Manning, Frank E. 17:361
Manning, G. H. 18:245
Manning, G. N. 26:48
Manning, George 10:66; 20:305
Manning, H. M. 7:75; 25:301
Manning, Hans 7:102
Manning, Harra 17:445
Manning, Harry 6:25
Manning, Harvey M. 24:164
Manning, I. 14:88
Manning, J. 3:124
Manning, J. G. 7:33
Manning, J. H. 11:309; 23:72
Manning, J. W. 7:102
Manning, Jack 22:309
Manning, James 7:102; 12:57; 21:361
Manning, John 8:23; 10:96; 11:403; 13:66; 16:210; 18:148; 22:339; 25:205
Manning, John H. 9:214; 21:361; 22:125
Manning, Joseph 20:126
Manning, Judson 17:66
Manning, Louise 21:361
Manning, Martin 13:34
Manning, P. 1:58
Manning, Patrick 16:86
Manning, S. H. 3:124
Manning, Samuel 9:133
Manning, Samuel A. 20:147
Manning, Thomas 3:124; 8:23; 18:148, 421; 20:193
Manning, W. 3:124
Manning, W. F. 16:210
Manning, William 9:243; 17:102, 111
Manning, William F. 15:304
Manning, William W. 22:433
Manning, Z. 11:396
Mannings, Henry 22:309
Mannis, J. 22:259
Mannis, T. C. 21:361
Mannix, J. 1:156
Mannon, Hugh 12:30
Mannon, J. P. 22:408
Manns, Amos I. 24:41
Mannutt, William 24:182
Manny, Daniel 9:111
Manny, L. M. 4:39
Manny, Philip 9:184

Mannysworth, John P. 12:30
Manon, Richard 17:135; 24:199
Manor, Joseph 25:205
Manor, Joseph M. 18:148
Manor, Walter 11:183
Manosh, J. 1:154
Manrose, David B. 10:96
Mansas, J. S. 17:434
Mansco, John 20:306
Manse, Henry 22:113
Mansel, Guden 7:102
Mansell, Frederick 9:184; 19:275
Mansell, Thomas 8:107
Manser, Frederick 22:148
Mansfiedl, Royal 16:45
Mansfield, A. F. 18:177
Mansfield, A. T. 10:192
Mansfield, Abraham 10:125; 20:306
Mansfield, Albert G. 18:220
Mansfield, Anthony 21:189
Mansfield, Charles 21:361
Mansfield, Charles W. 19:179
Mansfield, D. J. 18:398
Mansfield, D. R. 3:125
Mansfield, Daniel 21:279
Mansfield, David 13:34
Mansfield, E. 14:283
Mansfield, E. P. 14:88
Mansfield, Frank 18:245; 26:49
Mansfield, George 3:125
Mansfield, H. 14:300; 17:478; 27:88
Mansfield, Henry 17:396
Mansfield, J. 3:125; 21:123
Mansfield, J. B. 20:306
Mansfield, J. M. 13:66; 16:210
Mansfield, John 9:214; 14:88; 21:361; 22:89; 25:205
Mansfield, John B. 10:66; 12:30
Mansfield, Joseph H. 10:19
Mansfield, M. 1:152
Mansfield, Patrick 15:174
Mansfield, Richard 27:146
Mansfield, Robert G. 9:222; 18:371
Mansfield, Royal G. 13:34

Mansfield, Solomon 20:193
Mansfield, Stephen 13:34
Mansfield, W. 27:90
Mansfield, W. W. 8:65; 26:171
Mansfield, William 10:173
Mansfield, William H. H. 24:198
Mansfield, William L. 13:34
Manshac, Robert 18:69
Manshey, H. 16:210
Mansion, William 23:108
Mansker, James D. 24:154
Mansker, W. J. 20:306
Mansley, John H. 11:245
Mansol, Stuart 23:309
Manson, E. 11:328
Manson, G. 4:39
Manson, H. B. 21:361
Manson, James 20:306
Manson, James P. 1:57
Manson, John W. 12:30
Manson, Magnus 19:277
Manson, W. 3:125
Manson, W. E. 4:39
Manson, William 18:53
Manspaker, D. 17:92
Mansur, James M. 24:169
Mansur, Michael 22:282
Mantal, James 4:39
Mantaper, C. A. 2:14
Mantaper, C. O. 25:56
Mantece, Cornelius 24:41
Manteeney, George E. 20:306
Mantel, John 21:361
Manter, Daniel F. 22:487
Manter, Francis W. 19:179
Manter, Fred 24:178
Manterich, P. J. 26:49
Mantertich, P. J. 18:245
Manthon, Albion 12:9
Mantle, Oliver 22:235
Mantly, J. M. 3:125
Manton, Henry 10:19
Manton, J. 16:299
Manton, Thomas 9:85
Manton, W. 15:213
Mantooth, Jasper 21:14
Mantor, Emilie M. 19:317
Mantor, Francis W. 10:145
Mantrath, David 17:441; 24:153
Mantwell, H. 19:326
Mantz, P. 3:124
Mantz, W. 13:34; 16:45

Mantzig, --- 9:111
Manuel, Alfred 21:279
Manuel, David M. 17:273
Manuel, G. 25:205
Manuel, George 5:42
Manuel, P. 1:153; 17:181
Manuel, William C. 25:55
Manuel, Wilson 7:128
Manul, William 21:87
Manus, J. 27:146
Manus, William 22:43
Manville, G. W. 10:146
Manville, Irving 9:97
Manwaring, William 3:124
Manwaring, William H. 1:56
Manwarning, S. 5:22
Manwell, George 9:209
Manwilly, J. 3:125
Many, Fred. 8:107
Manzor, George 22:465
Maochynaer, E. 27:81
Maone, Henry 16:45
Maparter, Charles 17:66
Mape, George 3:125
Mapel, Gideon 7:33
Mapell, Henry 18:245
Mapels, James 20:306
Maper, Daniel 15:23
Mapes, Alex. H. 21:33
Mapes, Asbury 26:107
Mapes, Ashbury 9:37
Mapes, C. A. 25:55
Mapes, Charles 22:465
Mapes, E. A. 1:153
Mapes, H. 3:125
Mapes, J. A. 15:279
Mapes, J. J. 17:38
Mapes, John 13:34
Mapes, M. C. 9:222
Mapes, Maded 5:22
Mapes, Mc--- 18:371
Mapes, R. 11:157
Mapes, S. B. 12:62; 15:40
Mapes, Samuel 10:66; 20:306
Mapes, Selah 16:45
Mapes, Wesley 20:10
Mapes, William 12:50
Mapier, I. B. 8:65
Mapill, Henry 26:48
Mapin, Asa 22:309
Mapin, J. A. 11:69
Mapis, Joseph C. 19:179
Mapis, P. 1:151
Maple, Daniel N. 18:192
Maple, J. C. 18:177
Maple, Jacob 9:25
Mapledoram, W. 1:153
Maples, Asbury 18:294

Maples, Austin 22:89
Maples, E. 21:189
Maples, G. J. 22:259
Maples, G. R. J. 22:259
Maples, George C. 17:111
Maples, H. 14:322
Maples, Henry 14:316; 23:185
Maples, James 10:66, 125; 20:306
Maples, James J. 8:65; 26:171
Maples, Joseph 22:309
Maples, Peter 11:209
Mapother, J. 19:85
Mapp, James F. 15:71
Mapp, Levi 4:67
Mappin, David 8:52
Mappin, Robert 11:95
Mappin, Thomas C. 22:89
Mappin, W. 11:244
Mapron, William 4:39
Mapufer, D. L. 18:148
Mara, John 14:88
Mara, Thomas 14:316
Marahar, C. 25:205
Maran, Felix 12:83; 16:300
Maranda, Lafayette 17:38
Marann, James F. 18:208
Maranville, A. 19:240
Maranville, C. L. 23:39
Maranville, Fred A. 24:24
Maranville, Horace 9:185
Marbaugh, J. 3:126
Marberger, J. C. 1:155
Marbeth, Joseph 23:114
Marbeth, Leon 20:126
Marble, Edwin H. 7:16
Marble, G. B. 14:243; 27:91
Marble, G. L. 14:88, 195
Marble, H. A. 21:361
Marble, J. A. 27:86
Marble, J. B. 14:243
Marble, J. H. 22:43
Marble, James A. 22:148
Marbley, John 11:208
Marburger, Samuel 26:126
Marcan, L. 9:111
Marce, --- 25:54
Marcellius, H. 1:54
Marcellus, James 27:87
Marcellus, L. 13:93
Marcer, John 18:245; 26:47
Marcer, Samuel 20:155
Marcey, H. B. 25:205
Marcey, W. 1:151
March, Albert N. 12:73

March, D. 23:156
March, Frederick A. 22:465
March, G. 7:69
March, H. 1:59
March, Isaac 13:34
March, John 17:207, 251; 18:148; 19:85
March, M. 15:213
March, Moses 15:87
March, S. 9:55
March, Sunmer J. 9:103
March, Thomas 11:208
March, W. 14:88; 15:343; 16:374
March, William 16:82; 25:54
March, William B. 17:347
Marchand, Louis 24:108
Marchant, D. C. 23:39
Marchant, N. Y. 15:71
Marchant, S. S. 14:88
Marchant, Wiley B. 10:66
Marchant, William H. 12:54
Marchbanks, Thomas 21:167
Marcher, C. 21:361
Marcher, T. W. 23:156
Marchrises, William 9:122
Marck, Erastus 15:58
Marck, G. 1:151
Marco, George A. 11:266
Marcock, Joseph 1:57
Marcoll, Henry 7:102
Marcote, A. 15:129
Marcott, John 21:114
Marcross, S. B. 16:374
Marcum, Hiram 22:503
Marcum, J. 9:44; 26:126
Marcum, William 17:55
Marcus, General 18:15
Marcus, J. C. 17:364
Marcus, M. 11:245
Marcy, Anthony 24:102
Marcy, C. 26:174
Marcy, C. H. 25:53
Marcy, H. 21:128
Marcy, Hezekiah 20:31
Marcy, J. J. 1:157
Marcy, N. G. 1:152
Marcy, Oscar W. 11:128
Marcy, Sandy 8:40; 26:170
Mardelen, Henry 9:122
Marden, G. C. 3:125
Marden, G. W. 3:125
Marden, J. G. 11:193
Marden, P. P. 21:361
Mardin, Charles 22:43
Mardin, Harvey 27:85

Mardin, J. R. 19:24
Mardin, N. 1:151
Mardis, J. L. 3:126
Mardis, T. 25:205
Mardis, Thomas 5:22
Mardney, A. 8:40
Mardock, Robert 20:306
Mare, W. 16:147
Mareen, James P. 20:86
Maregarver, D. J. 1:99
Mareim, --- 12:172
Marel, Benjamin F. 11:38
Marell, Charles 11:85
Maren, A. C. 19:85
Maren, E. 3:126
Marenus, Nelson 22:282
Mareny, Thomas 9:214
Marer, Henry 23:156
Mareum, Granbery 18:245; 26:49
Mareus, --- 8:124
Marford, Elisha 23:72
Margarite, F. 15:213
Margerman, A. C. 5:52
Margerum, W. S. 19:85
Margeson, W. 1:157
Margeton, Franklin 27:89
Margg, George 7:102
Margison, William 19:179
Margolf, Henry 24:68
Margraves, W. 20:306
Margraves, William 10:66
Marguard, G. 1:103
Marguardt, Peter 11:157
Marguitt, Charles 11:192
Margut, M. 3:126
Marhar, James 9:103
Mariam, William 14:88
Marian, --- 15:174
Mariarie, William 14:195
Marie, Daniel 21:361
Marien, Samuel 25:55
Mariett, H. 3:126
Marihagh, Amos 22:205
Marillius, James 27:89
Marine, William 3:126
Marine, William H. H. 24:53
Mariner, C. E. 1:59
Mariner, John 25:205
Maring, William 22:89
Marion, A. 8:65; 26:173
Marion, Benjamin 8:73
Marion, J. 10:28; 19:304
Marion, J. A. 20:147
Marion, James M. 21:204
Marion, Joseph 21:167
Marion, Peter 4:39
Marion, S. M. 14:195
Marion, Thomas 21:361

Marion, William 21:56;
  27:146
Maris, J. 15:273
Mark, A. H. 18:424
Mark, Charles 26:107
Mark, Christian 18:148
Mark, Daniel 27:87
Mark, G. 19:256
Mark, George 14:283
Mark, Godfrey 9:185
Mark, J. 1:157; 3:126;
  11:309
Mark, John 7:103; 11:245
Mark, John A. 21:140
Mark, M. V. 20:306
Mark, Nathaniel H.
  18:245; 26:49
Mark, November 9:185;
  19:283
Mark, Peter 19:24; 25:334
Mark, S. G. 17:319
Mark, Samuel 25:301
Markam, C. H. 18:371
Markee, J. 25:205
Markel, Abner 11:308
Markel, B. F. 11:267
Markel, Christian 20:306
Markel, Daniel 18:444
Markel, Francis 17:92
Markel, J. 21:189
Markel, Lewis 18:444
Markel, Ringold 15:307;
  19:85
Markel, Samuel 18:444
Markell, E. 4:39
Markell, J. 1:57
Markell, S. 3:126
Marken, Henry 9:237
Markensy, John 15:40
Marker, C. 20:41
Marker, Eli 23:156
Marker, Jacob 8:23;
  26:172
Marker, M. 20:306
Marker, Mathias 17:349;
  23:72
Marker, Michael 10:66
Marker, W. H. 3:126
Marker, William 8:107
Markey, J. J. 25:301
Markey, John 26:45
Markfand, Sylvester 23:90
Markham, Aaron 19:271
Markham, Aaron J. 9:185
Markham, C. H. 9:222
Markham, Charles
  13:130; 20:306
Markham, D. 3:126
Markham, Henry 18:413
Markham, J. 5:52; 16:374;
  25:205

Markham, Norman G.
  22:148
Markham, S. N. 12:155
Markham, Sam D. 24:53
Markham, Willis 19:47
Markhull, Milton 10:66
Markiches, Theodore
  15:167
Markimore, L. 12:9
Markin, John 10:125
Markin, Thomas 17:83
Markin, W. 3:126
Marking, Richard 15:213
Markins, Dennis 23:256
Markins, G. 19:283
Markinson, Thomas H.
  17:451; 24:179
Markison, George 21:279
Markland, Thomas G.
  21:229
Markle, A. F. 14:88
Markle, Charles 12:30
Markle, G. 1:153
Markle, I. H. 9:147
Markle, J. 1:155
Markle, James H. 22:407
Markle, John 1:58
Markle, Lucius 9:25;
  18:320
Marklein, John 16:147
Markley, A. J. 25:323
Markley, Abram 21:189
Markley, C. H. 1:153
Markley, D. V. 15:213
Markley, Francis A.
  11:158
Markley, G. H. 1:157
Markley, Marion 20:58
Markley, Martin 23:156
Markley, Philip 23:305
Markling, John 21:123
Markquart, J. F. 1:152
Marks, --- 16:210
Marks, A. J. 1:156
Marks, Augustus 14:195
Marks, C. B. 14:195
Marks, C. D. 16:210
Marks, Charles 3:126
Marks, D. 14:195
Marks, D. R. 17:249
Marks, Edward 7:13
Marks, Eli T. 17:277
Marks, Elias 24:24
Marks, F. M. 26:46
Marks, Frederick 20:31
Marks, G. 25:206
Marks, George 27:157
Marks, George S. 21:257
Marks, Henry 22:13
Marks, Henry R. 12:30
Marks, Israel 4:39

Marks, J. 11:37
Marks, J. T. 22:339
Marks, James 14:195
Marks, Jeremiah 21:243
Marks, John 18:34;
  20:133, 306; 21:361
Marks, John J. 7:81
Marks, John L. 15:92
Marks, Joseph 21:75
Marks, Joseph H. 12:73;
  15:71
Marks, L. 25:206
Marks, M. A. 4:39
Marks, P. 3:126
Marks, P. G. 7:33
Marks, Peter 16:145
Marks, R. 11:288
Marks, Reuben 15:343
Marks, Robert J. 12:30
Marks, Rubin 16:374
Marks, S. 25:206; 27:87
Marks, Samuel 5:22
Marks, T. K. 9:85
Marks, Vincent 10:208
Marks, W. 13:93
Marks, William 16:98
Marksman, Henry 15:213
Markson, S. W. 16:210
Markwart, John 9:222
Markwell, A. 6:7; 18:112
Markwell, J. N. B. 18:112
Markwell, Milton 20:306
Markworth, John 4:39
Marlain, J. B. 3:126
Marland, C. 27:88
Marland, T. 14:88
Marlenee, Jarret E. 21:75
Marles, J. N. 10:125;
  20:306
Marles, M. 18:177
Marlet, Edward 20:306
Marlett, George B. 12:30
Marlett, Green 20:18
Marlett, I. E. 18:208
Marlett, Levi 20:98
Marlett, Wesley 22:149
Marley, B. H. 18:466
Marley, Charles 19:283
Marley, J. W. 24:24
Marley, John 3:126;
  15:40, 279; 25:206
Marley, M. H. 20:306
Marley, Michael H. 10:66
Marley, William 12:59
Marley, William M. 8:23;
  26:173
Marlin, Henry 22:514
Marlin, John 17:23
Marlin, Newton 18:148
Marlin, Thomas J. 10:180
Marline, Jared B. 12:30

Marling, George 12:64
Marling, Peter 8:23
Marling, Spencer B. 22:432
Marling, Walter B. 22:432
Marlo, Miner 19:85
Marlo, Minner 15:320
Marlock, William 11:109
Marloney, J. 1:103
Marlott, Enoch 22:339
Marlott, James A. 17:143
Marlow, --- 21:361
Marlow, A. 9:69
Marlow, Alexander 8:65
Marlow, Emerson 21:198
Marlow, J. W. 9:25
Marlow, M. 10:186
Marlow, N. 22:484
Marlow, S. 14:88
Marlow, Thomas 17:282, 338
Marlshy, James A. 25:323
Marlton, Isaac 16:210
Marm, William 7:128
Marmaduke, F. 25:301
Marmaduke, Hurmon 7:129
Marmaduke, Thomas 7:78
Marmon, Francis 10:145; 19:179
Marmon, R. 24:81
Marnan, George W. 8:23
Marnathy, George 3:126
Marnell, Joseph 19:24
Marner, C. 18:34
Marner, J. E. 15:213
Marner, T. 1:151
Marnett, H. W. 16:210
Marney, H. 14:88
Marney, Joseph 14:88
Marny, H. B. 5:22
Maron, James 9:85
Marone, Thomas 25:206
Maroney, John 18:294; 22:521
Maroney, Oliver 22:13
Marony, John 9:37; 26:107
Maroon, Charles 14:195
Marooney, Joseph 3:126
Marooney, W. R. 14:88
Marosig, J. C. 14:195
Marour, Lee 16:45
Marp, Alonzo 20:107
Marpla, J. D. 21:123
Marple, J. H. 10:186
Marple, James W. 20:41
Marple, Jefferson 22:125
Marple, S. L. 3:126
Marple, W. H. 8:107
Marplo, H. 22:235

Marquard, F. 4:39
Marquardt, John 21:140
Marquart, Charles 13:34
Marquent, Charles 16:45
Marquet, Sidney 15:355
Marquette, S. 15:311
Marquis, Davis 5:22; 25:206
Marquis, George H. 23:241
Marquis, Joseph 15:294; 16:210
Marquis, William F. 27:85
Marquis, William H. 9:122
Marquison, William 10:153
Marr, Daliel 15:159
Marr, E. D. 11:231
Marr, Isaac 11:281
Marr, James 7:80
Marr, Jefferson 10:99
Marr, John 4:39
Marr, Joseph 15:152
Marr, Nelson 10:66
Marr, Stephen 10:99
Marr, Thomas G. 3:126
Marr, William 19:24
Marr, William C. 22:148
Marrah, Joseph 8:52
Marray, Edward 14:196
Marrell, J. 1:95
Marrell, Ugone M. 16:210
Marrey, William H. 21:361
Marriamd, Thomas 9:122
Marriattey, Dawson 17:233
Marrical, J. 17:203
Marrihue, Valentine 15:350
Marrin, A. C. 12:96
Marring, Nicholas 8:23
Marringill, Lewis 17:55
Marrion, B. F. 9:185
Marriott, T. B. 25:206
Marriotte, G. W. 4:39
Marris, Daniel 23:156
Marrison, Joseph 11:183
Marroll, John 22:339
Marron, David 26:49
Marron, J. 3:126
Marrow, C. J. 9:55
Marrow, Charles 7:12
Marrs, John 7:78; 25:301
Marry, Edward 1:53
Marry, Thomas 11:231
Marry, W. J. 11:95
Mars, Charles 23:114
Mars, H. 1:157
Mars, Henry 18:34

Mars, J. A. 14:195
Mars, John 13:66
Mars, M. 1:152
Mars, Peter 17:450; 24:175
Mars, Thomas 1:58
Marsac, Daniel C. 22:149
Marsden, Joseph 12:9
Marse, John 22:13
Marsey, O. H. 21:361
Marsh, --- 19:85
Marsh, A. 25:206
Marsh, Albert 8:90
Marsh, Albert F. 19:179
Marsh, Albert N. 15:81
Marsh, Alfred H. 22:171
Marsh, Ambrose A. 24:53
Marsh, B. B. 15:40
Marsh, Benjamin 23:181
Marsh, Charles 19:85
Marsh, Charles F. 21:11
Marsh, Christian 17:393
Marsh, Cyrus A. 21:87
Marsh, D. 3:126; 7:33
Marsh, D. D. 25:301
Marsh, Daniel A. 22:43
Marsh, David 23:181
Marsh, Edward N. 13:34
Marsh, Edwin 7:102
Marsh, Edwin C. 23:156
Marsh, Edwin L. 21:75
Marsh, Eli E. 10:125; 20:306
Marsh, Esquire 22:206
Marsh, F. A. S. 25:206
Marsh, F. N. 5:42
Marsh, Francis P. 9:67
Marsh, Francis W. 21:92
Marsh, Frederick 23:192
Marsh, G. H. 20:10
Marsh, G. J. 1:57
Marsh, George 17:496
Marsh, H. H. 1:59
Marsh, Harlow 17:317
Marsh, Harris 11:308
Marsh, Henry 21:279
Marsh, Henry E. 10:164
Marsh, Homer 23:244
Marsh, Ira 3:126
Marsh, Isaac 18:398
Marsh, J. 3:126
Marsh, J. N. 1:59; 13:93; 19:85
Marsh, J. W. 15:71
Marsh, James 18:398; 21:229; 23:12
Marsh, Jeff 4:39
Marsh, John 8:23; 15:336; 16:86; 19:24, 85; 20:98; 21:279
Marsh, John B. 9:7

Marsh, John S. 8:118;
19:315
Marsh, L. H. 7:102
Marsh, M. 25:206
Marsh, Martin 5:22
Marsh, N. 12:92; 16:300
Marsh, Noah D. 21:92
Marsh, O. 1:53
Marsh, O. H. 1:150
Marsh, Oliver 12:30
Marsh, Osker 18:34
Marsh, P. 11:323; 25:206
Marsh, Peter 5:42
Marsh, R. 25:57
Marsh, Samuel 23:90
Marsh, Shubill H. 20:41
Marsh, T. 27:90
Marsh, Thomas W. 7:83;
21:361
Marsh, Tona 22:309
Marsh, Vincent 18:88
Marsh, W. 1:154; 3:126
Marsh, W. H. 4:39
Marsh, W. S. 13:93; 14:16
Marsh, W. W. 1:156;
10:164; 19:179
Marsh, William 20:137
Marsh, William C. 16:98
Marsh, William D. 16:88
Marsh, Z. 1:154
Marshal, Albert A. 19:179
Marshal, G. F. 9:185
Marshal, Leander 19:179
Marshal, Thomas M.
9:237
Marshal, W. 11:37;
18:371
Marshal, Westley 21:149
Marshal, William 11:374
Marshall, --- 1:155;
15:159, 273; 22:309
Marshall, A. 1:55, 58;
3:126
Marshall, A. K. 8:52
Marshall, Alex 20:306
Marshall, Alexander
10:66; 22:309
Marshall, Andrew 9:13
Marshall, Archy 27:146
Marshall, Augustus L.
5:22
Marshall, B. 3:126
Marshall, Ben. W. 24:160
Marshall, Benjamin 23:39
Marshall, Benjamin W.
17:443
Marshall, Beverly W.
17:261
Marshall, Burkley 17:83
Marshall, C. 22:309
Marshall, Calvin 20:137

Marshall, Charles A. 4:39
Marshall, Daniel 11:266;
17:429; 24:187
Marshall, David P. 22:454
Marshall, Douglass 9:185
Marshall, E. 1:152; 9:147;
13:93; 27:81
Marshall, E. F. 3:126;
11:428; 14:88
Marshall, Edward 18:245;
20:10; 26:48
Marshall, Eli 7:78; 25:301
Marshall, Elias J. 23:156
Marshall, Elisha 8:114
Marshall, Emery P.
17:271
Marshall, F. 8:65; 15:309;
25:206; 26:171
Marshall, Frank 24:9
Marshall, G. 1:156; 3:126;
14:300; 17:479;
27:88
Marshall, G. B. 24:68
Marshall, G. F. 19:275
Marshall, G. N. 12:30
Marshall, G. W. 26:170
Marshall, George 10:66;
11:414; 20:306;
22:206, 407
Marshall, George E.
19:256
Marshall, George L.
20:114
Marshall, George W. 8:40;
22:453; 26:171
Marshall, H. 1:153;
15:350; 17:190;
21:164
Marshall, H. E. 3:126
Marshall, H. L. 4:39
Marshall, H. S. 21:361
Marshall, Hamilton
15:129
Marshall, Harvey 4:39
Marshall, Henry 7:102;
8:65; 14:195
Marshall, Herman 22:432
Marshall, Hugh 17:55
Marshall, Ira S. 21:361
Marshall, J. 1:59, 99;
10:28; 13:93; 16:210;
20:41
Marshall, J. A. 14:195
Marshall, J. C. 9:47;
26:142
Marshall, J. D. 23:39
Marshall, J. L. 9:184
Marshall, J. M. 14:283
Marshall, J. O. K. 21:131
Marshall, J. R. 24:81
Marshall, J. T. 12:155

Marshall, Jacob 25:206
Marshall, James 4:67;
13:114; 15:71;
17:181
Marshall, James H. 18:88
Marshall, James M.
20:306
Marshall, James T. 21:86
Marshall, John 9:157,
184; 15:71; 17:400;
21:33; 23:12, 261;
24:167
Marshall, John B. 17:308
Marshall, John L. 16:82
Marshall, John M. 26:170
Marshall, Joseph 9:133,
157; 16:86; 27:84
Marshall, Joseph H. 13:58
Marshall, Joseph M. 10:66
Marshall, L. 1:56; 3:126;
23:117
Marshall, Lavater W.
20:46
Marshall, Levi 9:9; 11:68
Marshall, M. B. 17:292
Marshall, M. F. 25:206
Marshall, M. M. 3:126
Marshall, Major 27:88
Marshall, Martin J. 21:361
Marshall, Michael 7:129
Marshall, Moses F. 5:52
Marshall, N. B. 3:126
Marshall, Nathaniel
9:147; 27:83
Marshall, Nelson 7:129
Marshall, Oliver 24:24
Marshall, Pharaoh 17:135
Marshall, Pharoah 24:200
Marshall, Preston 21:361
Marshall, R. H. 23:39
Marshall, Randall 21:361
Marshall, Robert 4:39;
11:425
Marshall, Robert D. 27:80
Marshall, S. 3:126; 25:55
Marshall, S. L. 19:224
Marshall, S. M. 1:156
Marshall, S. S. 25:53
Marshall, Samuel 8:40;
26:171
Marshall, Samuel J. 22:89
Marshall, Seth 13:34
Marshall, Simeon F.
21:361
Marshall, Smith A. 17:232
Marshall, T. 1:152
Marshall, T. W. 22:485
Marshall, Thomas 1:55;
12:155; 26:222
Marshall, Thomas F.
21:75

Marshall, W. 18:340; 21:361
Marshall, W. H. 25:206
Marshall, W. T. 18:177
Marshall, W. W. 21:56
Marshall, Walter 10:10
Marshall, Washington 23:198
Marshall, William 3:126; 8:90; 9:55, 103, 222; 11:308; 12:50; 14:195, 257; 16:86, 210; 21:189; 22:431
Marshall, William A. 5:22
Marshall, William R. 22:113
Marshall, William T. 10:125, 180; 20:306
Marshall, Willis 24:200
Marshman, George 11:208
Marshman, James 10:125; 20:306
Marshmore, J. 11:308
Marshon, A. 8:73
Marson, B. 1:153
Marson, Daniel 9:185
Marson, David 21:189
Marson, J. 15:84
Marson, John 12:73
Marson, M. 9:185
Marsten, J. 14:88
Marston, A. 3:126; 27:87
Marston, B. 3:126
Marston, David 8:65
Marston, George D. 16:78
Marston, Harvey 22:407
Marston, J. E. 25:206
Marston, Jerome E. 12:80
Marston, John 14:196
Marston, Stephen 10:66; 20:306
Marston, William 3:126
Mart, Joseph 4:39; 12:123
Mart, Martin V. 10:66
Martarion, Fred 26:173
Martechanage, H. 18:88
Marten, James 20:306
Marten, Thomas 26:213
Martenia, David 22:407
Martenia, William W. 22:408
Martens, Frederick 17:361
Marter, O. 10:28
Marter, Robert 19:304
Marterson, James 12:30
Martes, G. S. 27:81
Marteus, A. T. 21:361
Martiason, Fred. 8:23
Martin, --- 8:125; 9:231; 15:109, 152; 16:210; 18:413; 20:306;

Martin, --- 22:353; 23:256; 24:41; 25:334
Martin, A. 3:125; 7:51; 14:88; 17:338; 18:53; 20:306; 21:361
Martin, A. B. 21:85
Martin, A. H. 8:114
Martin, A. J. 3:125; 15:289
Martin, A. P. 25:57
Martin, A. Z. 22:485
Martin, Aaron 4:39
Martin, Absalom 10:66
Martin, Adam B. 10:205
Martin, Addison 9:85
Martin, Adolphus 24:99
Martin, Albert 22:432
Martin, Albert J. 11:159
Martin, Albin D. 4:39
Martin, Alcade A. 17:23
Martin, Alex 1:55
Martin, Alexander 27:79
Martin, Alford 24:41
Martin, Amos 25:206
Martin, Andrew 10:173; 19:179
Martin, Andrew J. 16:210; 22:43; 23:192
Martin, Antonio 19:322
Martin, Armstead 22:309
Martin, Asa L. 22:282
Martin, Asa Wilson 22:43
Martin, Atchison 10:96
Martin, Austin 12:73; 15:5
Martin, B. D. 6:21
Martin, B. E. 16:45
Martin, Bailey 7:102; 21:361
Martin, Benjamin 9:25; 17:249; 18:311; 26:107
Martin, Bryant 22:310
Martin, C. 3:125; 11:157, 308; 16:300; 18:112; 19:85; 21:149; 24:24; 25:57
Martin, C. C. 17:55; 21:361
Martin, C. F. 7:102
Martin, C. H. 12:92; 14:88; 19:240; 21:361
Martin, C. M. 3:125
Martin, C. S. 9:37
Martin, C. W. 16:140
Martin, Caleb 7:102
Martin, Calvin 9:97; 11:209; 22:89
Martin, Carrall 26:223

Martin, Charles 3:125; 9:156, 184, 209; 11:95; 16:121, 210; 19:233; 22:43, 149; 27:88
Martin, Charles H. 23:181
Martin, Christopher 13:34; 22:504
Martin, Clarence 23:39
Martin, Clark 9:69
Martin, Cyrus M. 22:486
Martin, D. 1:154; 3:125; 13:114; 22:259
Martin, D. B. 6:21
Martin, D. H. V. 26:250
Martin, D. R. 17:83
Martin, Daniel 7:33; 8:90; 11:183; 18:245; 21:361; 26:49
Martin, Daniel Z. 27:87
Martin, Darius 18:245; 26:49
Martin, David 11:308; 14:195; 21:361; 22:235
Martin, David B. 21:140
Martin, David E. 12:30
Martin, David N. 22:43
Martin, E. 1:157, 158; 11:341; 13:114; 15:167
Martin, E. A. 3:125
Martin, E. D. 18:88
Martin, E. L. 21:361
Martin, E. M. 24:81
Martin, E. O. 19:24
Martin, Edgar 19:24
Martin, Edmund 9:227; 17:135; 24:199
Martin, Edward 1:58; 4:39; 6:25; 14:195; 15:129; 18:371; 21:279; 22:408; 23:129
Martin, Edwin 4:39
Martin, Edwood 22:206
Martin, Eleazer 11:69
Martin, Eli 22:125
Martin, Elijah 22:43
Martin, Elisha J. 20:18
Martin, Ellis 22:309
Martin, F. 1:56; 11:88, 245; 16:210; 27:81
Martin, F. H. 7:59; 8:65
Martin, F. J. 26:45
Martin, F. K. 10:187
Martin, F. P. 3:125
Martin, Fannie 26:213
Martin, Ferdinand 13:114
Martin, Finley 17:149
Martin, Fleming 7:128

Martin, Francis C. 21:131
Martin, Francis H. 16:88;
   23:72
Martin, Frank 16:210;
   22:206, 310
Martin, Frank C. 25:206
Martin, Fred 25:323
Martin, Frederick 13:34;
   16:45
Martin, G. 1:155; 2:15;
   3:125; 9:97; 10:28;
   13:93; 14:16, 88;
   19:304
Martin, G. A. 9:85; 13:93;
   14:16
Martin, G. B. 11:244
Martin, G. C. 5:52; 14:88
Martin, G. S. 9:147
Martin, G. W. 1:54; 7:59;
   9:85; 26:46
Martin, Gaison 26:45
Martin, George 3:125;
   4:39; 7:33, 102;
   9:103; 10:96;
   11:209; 13:66;
   16:113, 210; 18:340;
   19:47, 85; 20:186;
   23:72; 26:46
Martin, George B. 9:85
Martin, George C. 25:206
Martin, George F. 11:403
Martin, George H. 16:133
Martin, George L. 21:362
Martin, George M. 22:485
Martin, George W. 18:15;
   23:156; 26:171
Martin, Graham 17:23
Martin, Griffin 17:181
Martin, H. 1:60; 8:65;
   11:157; 13:93;
   17:411; 22:43;
   25:206; 26:173
Martin, H. C. 3:125
Martin, H. P. 9:55
Martin, Hamilton 13:34
Martin, Hanson 11:95
Martin, Hardy 11:338
Martin, Harter 19:256
Martin, Henry 1:54; 5:42;
   8:40, 52, 107; 9:122,
   133, 201; 10:125,
   164; 11:128; 14:88;
   15:71, 213; 19:179;
   20:92, 133, 306;
   24:53, 102; 26:171;
   27:83
Martin, Henry C. 23:72
Martin, Henry E. 11:192
Martin, Henry J. 10:125;
   20:307
Martin, Henry S. 7:59

Martin, Hezekiah 11:246;
   17:309
Martin, Horace 9:147
Martin, Hugh 19:179
Martin, Ira 7:33; 10:148;
   16:98; 18:53
Martin, Ira L. 16:78
Martin, Isaac 9:97
Martin, J. 1:153, 157;
   3:125; 8:73; 9:147,
   227; 12:83, 123;
   13:93; 14:195, 196;
   15:129, 273; 17:181;
   18:53, 89, 371;
   19:85; 21:33, 123;
   25:206
Martin, J. A. 24:90;
   25:206
Martin, J. B. 3:125;
   14:196; 18:177;
   20:143; 23:39
Martin, J. D. 15:159
Martin, J. F. 3:125
Martin, J. H. 13:93;
   14:16; 26:171
Martin, J. L. 3:125
Martin, J. T. 16:210
Martin, J. W. 11:246;
   15:288; 16:210
Martin, Jack 18:431;
   27:89
Martin, Jacob 17:83, 159;
   22:309; 23:256
Martin, Jacob W. 10:125;
   20:307
Martin, James 3:125;
   7:83, 128; 9:122,
   231; 10:34, 66, 173;
   11:244; 13:34; 14:16,
   196; 15:174, 213;
   17:23, 447; 19:24,
   179; 20:307; 22:43;
   23:156; 24:185, 200;
   27:86
Martin, James A. 22:43
Martin, James B. 14:196
Martin, James D. 22:259
Martin, James F. 23:72
Martin, James H. 9:97;
   11:70; 17:391
Martin, James M. 16:98;
   24:41, 68
Martin, James R. 17:83
Martin, James S. 20:126
Martin, James T. 17:55;
   20:186
Martin, James W. 10:205;
   14:243
Martin, Jason M. 9:111
Martin, Jefferson P.
   22:504

Martin, Jeremiah 22:89
Martin, Jesse 22:125
Martin, Jesse H. 9:222;
   18:371
Martin, Jesse L. 23:241
Martin, Joel C. 10:206
Martin, John 2:15; 3:125;
   4:39; 5:22; 6:8; 7:33,
   75, 78, 128; 8:40, 52,
   114; 9:44, 67, 85,
   227; 10:125, 205;
   11:208, 293, 308,
   309; 14:88, 196;
   15:214; 16:374;
   17:237, 249; 18:112,
   245, 371; 19:348;
   20:155, 307; 21:56,
   103, 167, 199;
   22:205, 206, 310;
   23:39, 90, 156, 181;
   25:206, 301; 26:46,
   49, 127, 172
Martin, John A. 10:125;
   20:307
Martin, John B. 24:59
Martin, John C. 21:362
Martin, John F. 10:19;
   21:56; 27:87
Martin, John G. 12:155
Martin, John H. 22:43;
   25:54
Martin, John J. 13:34
Martin, John L. 18:371;
   19:179
Martin, John R. 20:190
Martin, John T. 23:268
Martin, John W. 9:157;
   10:125; 11:38;
   20:307; 22:89
Martin, Jose 19:321
Martin, Jose Antonio 9:13
Martin, Joseph 13:93;
   14:88; 17:38, 321,
   449; 22:43, 520;
   24:174
Martin, Joseph C. 20:37
Martin, Joseph E. 17:83
Martin, Joseph M. 16:82;
   22:206
Martin, Joseph W. 27:90
Martin, Josiah 17:23
Martin, L. 1:155; 14:88,
   196, 300; 17:74, 145,
   478; 20:307; 25:206;
   27:88
Martin, L. A. 19:327
Martin, Lafayette 10:66;
   21:229
Martin, Lanson 10:125;
   20:307

Martin, Leander 9:122; 10:125; 20:307; 27:85
Martin, Levi 8:23; 17:257; 18:148
Martin, Levy 5:22
Martin, Lewis 14:89; 16:210
Martin, Lewis G. 7:102
Martin, Louis 22:309
Martin, Luther 11:389; 23:156
Martin, M. 1:157; 3:125; 10:66; 20:307; 23:156
Martin, M. A. 3:125
Martin, M. B. 22:504; 26:212
Martin, Manuel 12:30
Martin, Maurice 21:229
Martin, McClure 10:210
Martin, Michael 10:125; 19:24; 20:307
Martin, Morris 22:310
Martin, Napoleon 22:431
Martin, Nathaniel G. 22:259
Martin, Neil 19:331
Martin, Nephi 26:44
Martin, Nepi 9:86
Martin, Newton T. 8:23
Martin, Noah 11:68
Martin, O. 4:39; 16:211
Martin, O. A. 9:122
Martin, O. H. 27:81
Martin, Oliver 24:102
Martin, Orace A. 27:85
Martin, Orlon 9:25; 18:320
Martin, Owen 22:339
Martin, P. 12:162; 18:34; 23:156
Martin, P. J. 25:206
Martin, Patrick 1:53; 11:39; 14:196; 16:98; 18:34; 19:179; 24:108
Martin, Peter 1:57, 58; 3:125; 17:135; 24:199
Martin, Peter S. 5:22
Martin, Philip A. 26:45
Martin, Phillip 9:86
Martin, Polk 5:52
Martin, Prince 9:133; 27:85
Martin, R. 1:152; 14:16; 16:269; 23:156
Martin, R. C. 8:23; 18:148
Martin, R. H. 25:206
Martin, R. M. 4:39

Martin, R. N. M. 16:45
Martin, R. W. 13:93
Martin, Reuben 10:208
Martin, Richard 17:38, 164; 22:149, 309
Martin, Richard H. 5:22
Martin, Robert 10:66, 125, 205; 17:181; 20:307
Martin, Robert E. 26:172
Martin, Robert H. 20:307
Martin, Robert J. 7:129
Martin, Royal 6:8; 18:103
Martin, Rufus 21:362
Martin, S. 7:65; 11:245; 15:214
Martin, S. C. 20:137; 25:206
Martin, S. D. 2:14
Martin, S. S. 3:125; 25:57
Martin, Sampson A. 22:259
Martin, Samuel 7:78; 9:67, 103, 154; 12:30; 15:259; 18:278; 19:24; 22:514; 23:271; 25:301
Martin, Samuel W. 9:37
Martin, Sandford 6:25
Martin, Sandford T. 20:307
Martin, Sanford S. 10:66
Martin, Silas H. 25:201
Martin, Simpson H. 8:90
Martin, Slater 17:38
Martin, Smith 19:304
Martin, Susan 17:108
Martin, Sylvester 19:24
Martin, T. 3:125; 13:93
Martin, T. E. 14:89
Martin, T. F. 19:179
Martin, T. P. 4:39; 22:206
Martin, T. W. 4:39
Martin, Thomas 9:25, 237; 11:39; 12:30, 55; 13:34, 66; 14:196; 15:174, 289; 16:211; 19:24; 20:143; 21:362; 22:43; 25:53
Martin, Thomas B. 17:55
Martin, Thomas J. 18:177
Martin, Thomas M. 21:229
Martin, Thomas P. 11:245
Martin, Vanburen 11:159
Martin, W. 1:57; 3:125; 14:16; 18:245; 19:179; 21:33, 140; 25:206, 334; 26:49

Martin, W. A. 7:33; 13:93; 14:17
Martin, W. B. 3:125
Martin, W. F. 9:55; 18:112
Martin, W. H. 3:125; 14:89; 15:71, 214; 20:141; 22:485
Martin, W. H. H. 11:266
Martin, W. J. 20:10
Martin, W. J. T. 20:307
Martin, W. K. 22:206
Martin, W. O. 19:24
Martin, W. R. 22:43
Martin, W. T. 1:154
Martin, Welcombe 19:24
Martin, Wiley 18:245; 26:49
Martin, William 3:125; 4:39; 6:32; 7:128; 8:107; 9:55, 86, 133; 10:66, 164; 12:55; 13:93; 14:17; 16:151; 17:39, 249; 18:89, 245; 20:10, 307; 21:230, 362; 22:125; 24:160; 25:55, 323; 26:45, 46, 48; 27:84
Martin, William A. 11:38
Martin, William B. 15:214
Martin, William F. 6:10; 18:208
Martin, William H. 7:33; 8:90; 10:125; 11:38, 70, 128, 389; 12:155; 17:274; 18:220; 20:307
Martin, William L. 9:103
Martin, William M. 7:33
Martin, William P. 22:465
Martin, William T. 10:125; 23:256
Martin, William T. L. 10:66
Martin, Willis B. 22:43
Martin, Wilson 10:19
Martin, Wilson P. 17:419; 24:160
Martin, Zacharias 8:90
Martindale, A. 14:89
Martindale, Benjamin F. 19:179
Martindale, Elisha 11:68
Martindale, Henry 1:53
Martindale, J. H. 10:125; 20:307
Martindale, James M. 11:70
Martindale, L. 25:206
Martindale, Lafayette 21:75

Martindale, Levi 5:22
Martindale, Nelson 18:15
Martindale, S. 10:206
Martindale, Samuel L. 22:43
Martindale, T. B. 23:156
Martindale, Thomas 10:125; 20:307
Martindale, William 14:196
Martine, Horace N. 15:214
Martine, John 15:214
Martine, Valentine 22:353
Martines, George 9:184
Martines, Joseph 24:89
Martingale, --- 26:49
Martingale, F. 27:88
Martingale, T. 14:300; 17:481
Martingall, --- 18:245
Martins, George P. 1:55
Martinson, Andrew 26:47
Martinus, Alfred 21:362
Martison, J. E. 15:109
Martius, Frank 17:267
Martland, John 20:307
Martley, John B. 10:173; 19:179
Martman, William 3:126
Marton, E. E. 24:53
Marton, William 22:89
Marton, William B. 11:109
Marts, G. H. 3:126
Marts, William 20:98
Martt, Isaac M. 22:484
Marturron, Fred 18:148
Martus, Alice 27:87
Marty, L. V. 25:57
Martyler, Philip 16:98
Martyr, S. H. 14:196
Martyrs, S. H. 14:257
Martz, Alonzo 12:57
Martz, Daniel 18:208
Martz, Franklin W. 6:32
Martz, Isaac 22:431
Martz, J. 7:33
Martz, John W. 24:81
Martz, Silas H. 10:125; 20:307
Martz, Sol 18:452
Martzdort, J. A. 18:245
Marun, John 12:73
Marundy, L. 12:83; 16:300
Marvey, And 3:126
Marvilett, Victor 11:425
Marvin, Adolphus 9:184
Marvin, Andrew G. 15:348

Marvin, Andrew L. 23:108
Marvin, Calvin 16:45
Marvin, Edw. H. 7:102
Marvin, Edward N. 21:362
Marvin, G. S. 1:150
Marvin, James 1:53
Marvin, John W. 22:148
Marvin, Lee 13:34
Marvin, Lyman 9:184
Marvin, Robert 4:39
Marvin, S. B. 9:227; 18:371
Marvin, Sylvanus J. 21:33
Marvin, W. 1:156
Marvin, William 9:241
Marvin, William Nelson 18:53
Marvin, William R. 24:53
Marwuet, Sidney 19:85
Marx, George 14:89
Marx, Jacob 20:104
Marxes, James C. 9:55
Mary, Henry 3:126
Marygold, John S. 21:257
Marzauk, Gottlib 7:80
Mas, James A. 11:246
Masblack, R. 14:89
Masch, M. 7:51
Maschmayer, E. 9:147
Masdon, J. D. 1:151
Mase, J. 3:127
Masefen, D. L. 8:24
Maseiam, Cyrus P. 9:13
Masel, John E. 21:33
Masener, J. A. 19:256
Masengale, Richard 17:149
Maser, Frank 22:206
Maser, J. 21:33
Masey, George T. 13:34
Masgau, Thomas 14:196
Mash, Arshaw 9:122; 27:86
Mash, John M. 10:151
Mash, W. G. 23:251
Mash, William 13:76
Mashawer, Dulan 17:135; 24:199
Mashbanks, Alonzo 22:310
Mashby, J. I. 17:201
Masher, D. 5:52
Masher, J. Dallas 12:31
Masher, N. A. 20:307
Masher, S. 13:94
Masher, Simon D. 9:122
Masher, Washington 6:18
Mashier, D. 25:206
Mashley, Charles 9:111

Masier, William R. 24:161
Masiker, George W. 8:24; 18:148
Masin, Samuel 7:129
Maskall, Thomas 22:206
Masker, Jacob 18:148
Maskey, R. 11:120
Maskill, --- 17:496
Masler, J. 3:127
Masley, Brown 24:200
Masley, Charles 23:90
Maslin, Peter 18:148
Maslin, Richard B. S. 20:10
Masmin, Frederick 23:39
Masmon, Nicholas 16:45
Masmore, J. A. 12:73
Masmore, Nicholas 13:34
Mason, --- 16:211; 23:314
Mason, A. 9:185; 13:66, 114; 15:299; 16:211; 19:85, 229
Mason, A. C. 11:160; 14:27
Mason, A. J. 8:107
Mason, A. W. 9:215
Mason, Aaron 10:10
Mason, Aernon 1:53
Mason, Albert 10:125; 20:307
Mason, Alfred 6:25
Mason, Alfred B. 1:54
Mason, Amos 10:66; 20:307
Mason, Amos D. 11:128
Mason, Auguste 8:118
Mason, Augustus 12:170
Mason, Benjamin F. 11:127
Mason, C. 1:151
Mason, C. A. 14:89
Mason, C. W. E. 16:300
Mason, Caleb 4:67
Mason, Charles B. 22:433
Mason, Columbus 21:75
Mason, Cyrus 23:198
Mason, D. 1:153; 4:39; 18:53
Mason, D. S. 12:155
Mason, Daniel 11:69; 19:24
Mason, Darsey 12:155
Mason, David 16:211
Mason, E. 1:155
Mason, Ed 23:39
Mason, Edward 22:509
Mason, Edwin 12:31
Mason, Eli 17:429; 24:185
Mason, Elias 17:181

Mason, Elijah 9:122; 27:84
Mason, Elvin P. 16:45
Mason, Ervin P. 13:34
Mason, F. 1:151; 3:126; 14:89
Mason, Francis 20:151
Mason, Frank 17:398; 20:186
Mason, Frank J. 27:87
Mason, G. 7:33
Mason, G. H. 15:316
Mason, G. W. 25:206
Mason, G. W. E. 12:83
Mason, Gabriel 22:310
Mason, George 1:55; 4:67; 6:18, 29; 10:66, 206; 17:135; 18:89, 245; 20:307; 24:199; 26:49
Mason, George B. 26:46
Mason, George Graham 25:334
Mason, George H. 16:45; 19:85; 22:465
Mason, George R. 12:31; 17:282
Mason, George W. 5:22
Mason, H. 17:181
Mason, H. C. 9:185; 19:240
Mason, H. D. 15:214
Mason, H. H. 1:57; 10:180; 18:177
Mason, Hampton 22:310
Mason, Harrison 17:249
Mason, Henry 1:191; 17:23; 22:310; 23:39; 25:206
Mason, Henry S. 7:59
Mason, Henry W. 22:282
Mason, I. 22:149
Mason, J. 1:152; 3:126; 8:52; 9:55; 16:140; 25:206; 27:82
Mason, J. E. 23:39
Mason, J. G. 3:126; 24:68
Mason, J. H. 1:60; 16:280
Mason, J. M. 1:98
Mason, J. N. 14:89
Mason, J. R. 14:316
Mason, J. S. 4:39
Mason, James 3:126; 9:65, 240; 11:210, 409; 13:34; 15:343; 16:374; 17:181; 19:24; 23:192; 25:273
Mason, James B. 22:509
Mason, James H. 1:53; 23:271

Mason, James M. 11:159
Mason, James S. 8:107
Mason, James W. 21:140
Mason, Jasper 9:185
Mason, Jeremiah 6:18; 18:89
Mason, Jerome B. 18:220
Mason, Joel 7:17
Mason, John 6:25; 7:103, 129; 9:69; 11:208; 12:30, 85; 16:160, 300; 20:10, 31, 307; 22:89; 26:127
Mason, John A. 23:72
Mason, John B. 18:294; 26:107
Mason, John C. 16:211
Mason, John E. 22:524
Mason, John S. 23:156
Mason, Jonathan M. 21:230
Mason, Joseph 5:42
Mason, Joseph W. 1:55
Mason, Julius 6:18; 18:89
Mason, L. 7:69; 14:196, 300; 16:211; 17:476; 27:88
Mason, Leo 21:75
Mason, Lewis 9:201; 27:89
Mason, Lorenzo D. 22:43
Mason, Merril L. 27:87
Mason, N. M. 14:196, 257
Mason, N. R. 18:271
Mason, Nelson B. 10:19
Mason, Noah C. 22:433
Mason, O. A. 15:279; 25:206
Mason, Orin 4:39
Mason, Patrick 9:185
Mason, Paul 10:206
Mason, Peter 3:126; 21:279
Mason, R. J. 9:55
Mason, Riley 10:66; 20:307
Mason, Robert 4:39
Mason, Royal 8:24; 18:148
Mason, Rufus 22:509
Mason, S. 18:34
Mason, S. H. 18:245; 26:48
Mason, Samuel L. 22:206
Mason, Samuel M. 12:50
Mason, Smiley 17:135; 24:199
Mason, T. J. 1:53
Mason, Theodore 15:71
Mason, Thomas 20:114; 24:112

Mason, Thomas A. 27:80
Mason, Thomas B. 3:126
Mason, Thomas C. 10:66; 20:307
Mason, Vincent 15:11
Mason, W. 11:245; 13:94; 15:40; 16:211
Mason, W. B. 25:55
Mason, W. R. 17:203
Mason, William 4:67; 12:73; 14:283; 15:159; 17:181, 498; 19:179; 22:433, 503; 23:104; 24:167
Mason, William A. 6:18
Mason, William B. 23:90
Mason, William C. 23:286
Mason, William H. 18:148
Mason, William M. 9:69
Mason, William N. 20:42
Mason, William W. 8:24
Mason, Willis 22:515
Masoner, Teeter 17:72
Mass, Bennett 18:89
Mass, E. S. 14:243
Mass, Gabriel 21:279
Mass, Henry 10:125; 20:307
Mass, Stephen D. 11:69
Mass, William 7:129; 22:260
Massa, J. 9:55
Massac, F. 22:149
Massac 22:149
Massaker, Ambro 18:324
Massaker, Jacob 17:263
Massaker, John 17:391
Massaler, D. L. 26:172
Masse, A. C. 18:192
Masse, Antoine 21:362
Massee, Abraham 20:307
Massee, Jacob 24:59
Massen, H. L. 3:127
Massena, William W. 20:307
Masser, Abraham 10:66
Masser, Edward 11:109
Masser, George 8:90
Masser, Sam 11:85
Masser, Samuel 11:396
Masser, Valentine 13:114
Masser, William 13:114
Massey, A. 21:362
Massey, Alex 11:69
Massey, David T. 24:68
Massey, F. 14:89
Massey, J. F. 20:58
Massey, James 7:129
Massey, John 13:34; 16:45; 23:185
Massey, R. R. 16:45

Massey, Robert 22:339
Massey, Samuel 17:135; 24:198
Massey, W. F. 3:126
Massey, W. L. 1:151
Massey, William C. 10:66
Masshad, William 15:174
Massie, George 22:206
Massie, Harvie 15:87
Massie, J. C. 3:126
Massie, John T. 22:89
Massie, Peter 7:51
Massingale, Robert H. 16:45
Massinger, Christian 11:157
Massingill, James 10:125; 20:307
Massman, J. W. 11:160
Massman, William W. 10:92
Massmar, M. 10:125; 20:307
Massongale, William 17:215
Massroony, T. 25:206
Massy, A. 15:40
Massy, Henry 22:433
Mast, --- 11:160
Mast, George 23:156
Mast, John 23:181
Mast, Michael 10:164; 19:179
Mast, Valentine 11:159
Mastain, Alva 23:12
Mastaw, T. 1:156
Mastell, Richard E. 13:34
Mastella, Thomas 11:209
Masten, Michael 19:24
Mastenbrook, John 10:125; 20:307
Master, Benjamin 11:307
Master, C. H. 18:34
Master, Charles 14:89
Master, F. 15:214
Master, Henry 14:196
Master, John 25:207
Master, William 9:44; 11:309
Masterd, Samuel 22:89
Masters, Andrew 9:209
Masters, Benjamin 9:25
Masters, Benjamin F. 10:92; 20:307
Masters, Charles 16:140
Masters, Edward 9:25
Masters, Francis M. 23:157
Masters, George 4:39
Masters, Henry 23:100
Masters, J. 3:126; 18:89

Masters, James B. 21:33
Masters, John 8:73; 18:327; 22:149
Masters, John W. 11:389
Masters, Joseph 21:279
Masters, Lewis 6:25
Masters, Michael 15:214
Masters, Richard 18:334; 26:223
Masters, Robert J. 16:300
Masters, Samuel 3:126
Masters, T. 14:243; 27:91
Masters, Walter P. 13:34
Masters, William 3:126; 5:22; 22:206; 25:207
Masterson, E. 3:127
Masterson, Felix 22:339
Masterson, Joel A. 24:161
Masterson, P. 7:51; 25:54
Masterson, Pat 8:24; 18:148
Masterson, Pat. R. 21:362
Masterson, Sylvester J. 24:161
Masterson, Thomas 21:195; 23:100, 181
Mastiden, William 13:94; 14:17
Mastillo, George 22:310
Mastin, John 12:167
Mastin, William 25:55
Mastings, A. F. 7:83
Mastison, --- 18:177
Mastoch, Valentine 22:149
Maston, A. 3:126
Maston, Ferdinand 8:107
Maston, George 23:252
Maston, Henry 27:86
Maston, J. 3:126
Maston, Milton K. 23:72
Maston, Reuben 8:90
Maston, Samuel 3:126
Matbratt, Peter 24:179
Matchell, J. J. 3:127
Matcherly, George W. 19:24
Matchet, G. W. 15:214
Matchett, Edward 16:45
Matchett, Edward N. 13:35
Matchett, J. W. 25:207
Matchett, John W. 5:22
Matchett, Peter E. 21:56
Matchit, Virginois H. 20:108
Matchketh, Gotleib 13:35
Matchum, S. 25:207
Mate, Eli 11:68
Mateer, Alexander L. 20:24

Mateer, John S. 10:164
Matentz, E. 21:189
Mater, J. 1:152
Matews, G. W. 25:207
Mathan, Charles 22:149
Mathaniel, James 11:328
Mathaw, B. 25:57
Mathel, A. 20:58
Mathely, Edward G. 17:55
Mathena, Martin 11:157
Matheney, D. C. 3:127
Matheney, James 20:10
Matheney, N. 3:127
Matheney, V. V. 3:135
Matheney, William H. H. 27:146
Matheny, I. F. 24:81
Matheny, William 11:309
Matheny, William C. 24:24
Matheons, S. S. 18:371
Mather, Ahl 10:66
Mather, Amos 25:207
Mather, B. 23:40
Mather, Darius C. 24:53
Mather, E. R. 7:59
Mather, Ed 26:106
Mather, Ellward 18:311
Mather, Francis W. 23:90
Mather, John H. 24:53
Mather, Lewis 10:92; 20:307
Mather, Nathaniel 9:37
Mather, Spencer 11:109
Mather, Uhl 20:307
Mather, W. 23:40
Mather, William 1:52
Mathern, Charles 7:103
Mathern, William 16:166
Mathers, Asahel A. 20:307
Mathers, John 16:121
Mathers, Samuel 23:72
Mathers, W. 23:157
Matherson, Charles 18:113
Matherson, F. 3:127
Matherson, L. 21:362
Mathes, D. P. 22:353
Mathes, Ira B. 20:308
Matheson, E. H. 3:127
Matheson, Horace 9:185
Mathew, Abraham 14:196
Mathew, C. S. 19:85
Mathew, Daniel P. 22:455
Mathew, David 11:158
Mathew, E. 22:503
Mathew, I. 14:196
Mathew, J. A. 24:53
Mathew, James 15:40
Mathew, John 16:211

Mathew, John P. 27:87
Mathew, Moses R. 27:87
Mathew, R. 11:246
Mathew, Samuel 7:129
Mathew, Thomas C.
    18:148; 26:173
Mathew, W. 2:15
Mathews, --- 25:55
Mathews, A. 1:58; 25:301
Mathews, A. B. 11:341
Mathews, A. C. 11:128
Mathews, Abram 7:78
Mathews, Albert 15:58
Mathews, Alfred 11:390
Mathews, Alfred L.
    21:362
Mathews, Amos 22:310;
    27:84
Mathews, Anderson
    22:504
Mathews, C. H. 19:179
Mathews, C. L. 22:520
Mathews, Charles F.
    17:395
Mathews, Charles H.
    21:362
Mathews, D. C. 20:308
Mathews, Daniel 25:56
Mathews, Daniel C.
    23:100
Mathews, Delenbaugh C.
    10:66
Mathews, Edward 15:214
Mathews, Edward P.
    12:31
Mathews, Emery S. 12:31
Mathews, F. E. 21:362
Mathews, Felix G. 22:125
Mathews, Francis D.
    23:72
Mathews, Francis M.
    8:24; 18:148
Mathews, Frederick 8:114
Mathews, G. B. 25:207
Mathews, George 1:192;
    8:52; 10:148;
    11:209; 12:31;
    18:53; 25:283
Mathews, George W.
    8:24; 9:185; 18:148
Mathews, H. 1:154
Mathews, Henry 11:120;
    17:288
Mathews, Henry C. 1:55
Mathews, Henry W.
    15:214
Mathews, Hor. 19:179
Mathews, I. F. 26:46
Mathews, I. H. 26:46
Mathews, Ira B. 10:66
Mathews, Isaac 6:25

Mathews, Isaac P. 11:85
Mathews, Israiel 18:34
Mathews, J. 1:57; 9:201;
    10:180; 17:155;
    18:177; 26:204
Mathews, J. B. 25:52
Mathews, J. F. 20:147
Mathews, J. G. 9:86;
    15:214
Mathews, J. H. 18:311;
    26:105
Mathews, J. M. 25:55
Mathews, J. P. 24:24
Mathews, Jacob 11:266;
    18:34
Mathews, James 15:214
Mathews, Jasper J. 9:67
Mathews, Jeffrey 22:310
Mathews, John 6:18; 8:24;
    9:111; 13:76; 18:148;
    20:155, 308; 22:43,
    90, 504; 25:53, 323
Mathews, John A. 9:86
Mathews, John W. 24:102
Mathews, Joseph 17:309
Mathews, Joshua S. 13:34
Mathews, Lawrence 25:54
Mathews, Lewis 11:390
Mathews, M. 3:127;
    17:155; 24:81
Mathews, M. F. 2:15
Mathews, N. 8:73
Mathews, Nelson 22:310
Mathews, Noah 16:374
Mathews, O. S. 13:125
Mathews, P. 1:60
Mathews, Patrick 15:129;
    22:310
Mathews, Peter 12:50;
    22:310
Mathews, Randall 11:209
Mathews, Ranson 15:109
Mathews, Reuben 8:90
Mathews, Robert 11:414
Mathews, S. 1:55
Mathews, S. A. 9:163;
    25:323
Mathews, S. J. 3:127;
    23:261
Mathews, S. S. 9:222
Mathews, Samuel 9:122;
    11:267; 18:245;
    21:189; 26:48; 27:86
Mathews, Squire 17:403
Mathews, T. 1:152
Mathews, T. B. 20:308
Mathews, Thomas 10:66;
    11:70; 16:374
Mathews, Thomas C.
    8:24; 17:405

Mathews, W. 9:222;
    18:371
Mathews, W. B. C. 22:43
Mathews, W. C. 3:127
Mathews, W. H. 12:31;
    15:214; 25:52, 207
Mathews, Walter 7:103
Mathews, Wesley 22:149
Mathews, William 1:52;
    7:103; 8:24; 10:66;
    11:210; 18:148;
    20:137, 308; 21:362;
    24:102; 26:173
Mathews, William H.
    5:23; 9:185; 24:41
Mathewson, Alcibiades
    22:149
Mathewson, George
    23:123
Mathewson, H. 7:33
Mathewson, H. A. 14:196
Mathewson, J. 22:310
Mathewson, L. 7:129
Mathias, --- 26:223
Mathias, Allen F. 22:454
Mathias, Frederick
    21:362; 23:286
Mathias, G. W. 11:70
Mathias, Hetzel 12:57
Mathias, John 17:181;
    19:349
Mathias, Jonathan 4:39
Mathias, Lewis 10:173;
    19:179
Mathias, S. 24:112
Mathias, Samuel 17:149
Mathias, T. C. 25:207
Mathias, Thomas 16:45
Mathiason, Claes 23:40
Mathir, N. 16:269
Mathis, J. 14:196
Mathis, John 21:362
Mathison, G. W. 18:340
Mathison, J. 21:362
Mathison, Robert 7:103
Mathison, Thomas
    13:135; 19:347
Mathland, Hugh 5:52
Mathons, Thomas 20:308
Mathor, John D. 20:308
Maths, Amos 17:39
Mathus, D. G. 22:453
Mathwig, Louis 23:267
Mati, H. 11:39
Maticer, Benjamin 9:13
Matier, John 21:360
Matier, John S. 19:179
Matimin, John 17:317
Matinson, Andrew 18:245
Matison, Alf 16:300
Matison, Zaben B. 18:104

Matkin, Samuel G. 18:444
Matkin, William H. 17:47
Matkins, E. 16:211
Matlack, William 17:203
Matler, S. 12:62; 15:92
Matler, Samuel 22:90
Matley, H. 24:199
Matley, John S. 9:97
Matlin, --- 16:158
Matlis, William 1:55
Matlock, H. 25:53
Matlock, Harrison 22:310
Matlock, R. H. 20:308
Matlock, Ransom H.
  10:66
Matlock, Samuel T.
  22:434
Matly, J. 11:439
Matney, William 17:135;
  24:199
Maton, Charles H. 4:67
Matoon, E. H. 16:46
Matoon, R. 22:149
Matoon, Richard D.
  22:149
Matott, A. 1:103
Matox, T. L. 15:214
Matsan, George 14:17
Matsel, P. 13:114
Matsler, A. 16:269
Matson, B. F. 23:157
Matson, Chester 20:308
Matson, Edward 9:185
Matson, George 11:309;
  13:94
Matson, J. W. 22:206
Matson, P. 25:207
Matson, Peter 5:23
Matson, Robert 22:206
Matson, S. W. 16:211
Matson, Thomas 14:196
Matson, William 12:31
Matson, William E. 13:35
Matt, G. 16:211
Matt, Horatio 3:127
Matt, L. 17:155
Matt, Philip 8:24
Mattack, T. 16:374
Mattchien, Frederick
  22:486
Mattebee, Chirinan
  18:245
Matteber, Christian 26:47
Mattebu, Christian 26:48
Matten, --- 11:220
Matten, Thomas C.
  11:116
Matteo, --- 24:24
Matteott, Charles H. 9:237
Matter, John 25:55
Matter, Philman 19:24

Matterson, A. V. 12:80;
  25:207
Matterson, E. H. 7:103
Matterson, Egbert J. 17:23
Matterson, J. 15:330;
  19:85
Matterson, James 8:24;
  18:148
Matterson, Sillman F.
  13:35
Matterson, Stillson 16:46
Matterson, W. P. 22:206
Matteson, A. C. 24:112
Matteson, Albert 1:57
Matteson, Allan 15:129
Matteson, George 21:362
Matteson, George A.
  11:160
Matteson, William 11:192
Mattheinsen, L. 7:12
Mattheney, A. D. 3:127
Matthes, George 6:35
Mattheson, H. 19:256
Matthew, J. 3:127
Matthew, Joseph B. 6:13
Matthews, --- 24:112
Matthews, A. V. 11:390
Matthews, Alfred 22:90
Matthews, C. C. 12:166
Matthews, C. G. 25:323
Matthews, David S. 9:155
Matthews, E. 16:45
Matthews, E. E. 21:189
Matthews, F. M. 3:127
Matthews, Frank 17:506
Matthews, G. S. 18:413
Matthews, G. W. 19:287
Matthews, George 21:75
Matthews, H. 3:127; 7:33
Matthews, Henry G. 10:19
Matthews, Horace 10:177
Matthews, Hubert 14:335
Matthews, Isaac J. 11:277
Matthews, J. 1:59; 14:89;
  16:86; 19:292
Matthews, J. L. 14:89
Matthews, James 16:45;
  17:282; 19:275
Matthews, James H. 9:25
Matthews, James N. 20:98
Matthews, James S. 17:96
Matthews, James W.
  20:58
Matthews, Jesse G. 17:83
Matthews, John 3:127;
  4:39; 6:28; 10:125;
  11:38; 14:89; 18:89
Matthews, John A. 23:90
Matthews, John C. 21:75

Matthews, John W.
  10:125; 20:308; 23:261
Matthews, L. 19:24
Matthews, London 23:291
Matthews, Nathaniel
  21:230
Matthews, Oliver J. 21:75
Matthews, Robert 25:207
Matthews, T. H. 19:24
Matthews, T. N. 14:89
Matthews, Thomas 7:59
Matthews, W. 3:127;
  19:24; 26:126
Matthews, W. J. 21:92
Matthews, William 6:35;
  9:155; 22:90, 260
Matthews, William J.
  21:249
Matthews, William P.
  23:100
Matthews, Z. 23:40
Matthewson, E. 14:89
Matthewson, Erich 9:185
Matthias, A. M. 4:39
Matthias, C. W. 3:127
Matthias, F. 3:127
Matthias, James 3:127
Matthis, Pleasant T. 23:72
Matthison, Alfred 12:92
Matthison, E. 4:39
Matthison, Euch 19:271
Mattice, B. F. 25:283
Mattice, H. C. 3:127
Mattice, M. 25:207
Mattice, S. 25:207
Mattice, Spencer 5:22
Matticks, M. 22:310
Mattie, J. 10:155; 19:179
Mattin, Zet 13:35
Mattinberger, J. 1:155
Matting, D. 14:89
Matting, Zeb 16:46
Mattingley, Robert 10:125
Mattingly, Felix 26:47
Mattingly, John 22:470
Mattingly, Milton 22:454
Mattingly, Robert 20:308
Mattingly, William
  17:261, 282
Mattingly, William B.
  22:453
Mattingsby, T. 17:181
Mattis, Aaron 3:127
Mattis, Albert 19:179
Mattis, Alfred 4:67
Mattis, Daniel 4:39
Mattis, Frederick 12:123
Mattis, John 21:257
Mattis, Levi 19:85
Mattis, Moses 5:22
Mattis, N. 13:94; 14:17

Mattis, Thomas 11:381
Mattison, A. J. 20:126
Mattison, B. 3:127
Mattison, D. 1:58
Mattison, E. C. 1:156
Mattison, E. J. 25:301
Mattison, J. N. 1:58
Mattison, Paul 9:209;
  18:69
Mattison, R. 3:127
Mattix, M. 16:211
Mattixin, C. 16:211
Mattle, Charles 1:55
Mattlebar, G. 16:211
Mattlen, Conrad 9:185;
  19:271
Mattock, G. W. 8:73
Mattock, Hiram 24:41
Mattock, Joseph R.
  18:424
Mattocks, A. J. 23:40
Mattocks, H. 2:15
Mattocks, I. R. 9:234
Mattocks, T. 1:155
Matton, Cornelius W.
  13:35
Matton, J. T. 19:85
Matton, Perry E. 23:181
Mattoon, Bradley 23:108
Mattoon, Charles F.
  26:222
Mattoon, Christopher
  23:108
Mattoon, James 4:39
Mattoon, John 18:148
Mattoon, John F. 8:24
Mattox, Asbery 17:261
Mattox, G. F. 14:89
Mattox, Henry 19:85
Mattox, James 13:35
Mattox, James N. 24:41
Mattox, John 8:24; 18:148
Mattox, Philip 20:308
Mattox, R. F. 16:46
Mattox, Robert 23:279
Mattox, William 8:65
Mattox, William H.
  17:282
Mattrat, Peter 17:451
Mattros, --- 18:177
Matts, William 7:33
Mattson, Jesse G. 10:19
Mattson, Samuel 15:159
Matty, Lewis 4:39
Matueck, Henry 26:44
Maty, Franklin W. 25:323
Matzanke, G. 25:301
Matzdon, A. 27:81
Matzdor, O. 9:147
Maualdi, H. 7:33
Maubash, William 11:69

Mauch, Charles 9:36
Mauch, Jacob 16:121
Maucha, John 16:300
Mauck, T. S. 1:152
Mauck, W. 14:89
Maud, Henry 12:31
Mauder, A. 18:88
Mauer, John 12:31;
  21:140
Mauf, Jacob 15:40
Mauger, John B. 12:31
Maughan, J. W. 10:66
Mauguis, P. 14:257
Mauk, Charles 18:295
Mauk, George 1:58
Mauk, J. 1:56
Maul, R. 15:214
Maulay, I. 15:279
Mauldien, Columbus
  27:86
Mauldore, Columbus
  9:122
Maulker, J. 16:211
Maullar, J. M. 20:147
Maulsburg, William 27:85
Maulsbury, William 9:122
Maulsby, Clark F. 22:90
Maulsby, J. C. 14:89
Maulsby, Mate P. 10:125;
  20:308
Mault, Isaac 9:222
Mault, J. 18:371
Maumcough, T. 14:243
Maun, B. 14:243
Mauney, William P. 26:48
Maunn, --- 18:177
Maunny, L. 22:339
Maunts, W. H. 14:89
Maupaue, John 11:39
Maupin, David D. 21:103
Maurer, D. 1:59
Maurer, H. 1:157
Maurer, John L. 22:43
Maurer, Otto 20:114
Maurer, Robert T. 23:181
Maureyvall, David 9:122
Maurice, L. 4:39
Maurie, W. 13:94
Maurrell, George 18:69
Maurwick, B. 1:56
Maury, J. 21:33
Maury, P. 15:214
Maury, Thomas 19:283
Maury, William 14:89
Mausbargo, Jefferson
  17:213
Mauscoe, John 10:66
Mause, David R. 26:145
Mause, M. 3:127
Mauser, Francis M.
  22:125

Mauson, James 10:66
Mauss, Louis 20:126
Mavahar, Charles 5:23
Mavell, Michael 21:56
Maven, Penball John
  11:160
Maver, John 9:55
Maverson, G. 1:153
Mavin, A. C. 15:360
Mavker, --- 11:95
Mavo, H. K. 15:366
Mavo, J. B. 12:62
Mavree, Peter 8:24
Mawdesley, Robert N.
  21:75
Mawer, George 22:206
Mawes, Lewis 17:55
Mawger, W. A. 14:17
Mawgus, E. 14:17
Mawherter, Robert 22:90
Mawhorter, Robert 22:431
Mawve, Frank 26:50
Max, George 13:80;
  16:211
Max, John 24:81
Maxem, H. C. 3:127
Maxem, Henry 22:149
Maxey, E. 22:43
Maxfield, C. 16:300
Maxfield, Daniel 19:24
Maxfield, David E. 12:73
Maxfield, M. 1:99
Maxfield, Standish 23:108
Maxham, A. E. 7:33
Maxham, Orrin 21:362
Maxim, James 16:46
Maxim, S. 18:15
Maxin, James 13:35
Maxley, Edward 10:96
Maxon, Francis M. 18:398
Maxon, Hunter 27:90
Maxon, J. M. 10:92
Maxon, R. W. 23:157
Maxon, Scuyler A. 19:179
Maxon, William 15:71;
  23:157
Maxsells, Rudolphus 9:37
Maxson, Daniel B. 19:224
Maxson, James A. 21:75
Maxtille, Silal 11:207
Maxum, S. G. 3:127
Maxville, Robert 4:39
Maxville, William 8:24;
  18:149
Maxwell, A. 11:439;
  15:130
Maxwell, Absalom 24:53
Maxwell, Adam P. 12:123
Maxwell, Alex 17:149
Maxwell, Alexander 10:96
Maxwell, Alfred 21:141

Maxwell, Allen 10:66
Maxwell, Amos 9:55
Maxwell, Arthur 12:171
Maxwell, Babey 8:114
Maxwell, Bailey 10:66; 20:308
Maxwell, Bayley 20:308
Maxwell, C. 22:486
Maxwell, Carter 4:67
Maxwell, Charles 23:271
Maxwell, D. 9:55
Maxwell, Ebenezer 9:237; 26:222
Maxwell, Edward W. 19:179
Maxwell, G. 1:153
Maxwell, George W. 22:90
Maxwell, H. A. 1:156
Maxwell, Harman 10:164
Maxwell, Harmon 19:179
Maxwell, Harvey 8:90
Maxwell, Henry 9:133; 27:84
Maxwell, Hudson 16:46
Maxwell, J. 3:127
Maxwell, J. H. 1:157
Maxwell, J. L. 17:326
Maxwell, J. W. 11:245, 246
Maxwell, Jacob C. 12:57
Maxwell, James 10:125; 13:35; 20:308
Maxwell, James I. 10:125
Maxwell, James J. 20:308
Maxwell, James M. 17:83
Maxwell, John 11:95; 21:141; 22:433; 23:157, 198
Maxwell, John C. 22:407
Maxwell, Joseph 19:322
Maxwell, Joseph Y. 7:103
Maxwell, L. E. 16:211
Maxwell, Levi D. 24:41
Maxwell, Lewis 8:52
Maxwell, M. 1:153
Maxwell, Nathan 1:57
Maxwell, P. 1:53; 3:127
Maxwell, R. 25:275
Maxwell, R. J. 22:485
Maxwell, Robert 1:53; 3:127; 25:54
Maxwell, S. 3:127; 9:147; 27:83
Maxwell, S. C. 19:24
Maxwell, S. F. 25:55
Maxwell, S. S. 10:66; 20:308
Maxwell, Samuel 13:35
Maxwell, Silas 19:179
Maxwell, T. G. 26:107

Maxwell, Thomas 9:16
Maxwell, Thomas G. 18:295
Maxwell, Thomas H. 11:69
Maxwell, Thomas J. 9:37
Maxwell, Thomas W. 23:72
Maxwell, W. B. 1:152
Maxwell, W. F. 18:177
Maxwell, W. K. 18:398
Maxwell, William 3:127; 18:53; 22:486; 23:40
Maxwell, William B. 12:155; 23:40
Maxwell, William K. 21:204
Maxwell, William M. 21:75
Maxwell, William R. 18:245; 26:49
May, A. 15:109
May, A. Frederick 25:207
May, A. M. 9:185; 19:240
May, A. N. 10:125; 20:308
May, A. P. 3:127
May, Aaron 22:514
May, Abraham 21:247
May, Abram 22:434
May, Alexander 8:90
May, Alexander B. 21:362
May, Alfred 21:230
May, Alonzo 11:402
May, B. 23:204
May, Benjamin H. 22:90
May, Cary 10:99
May, Charles 18:113
May, Charles W. 23:100
May, D. G. 11:183
May, Daniel 25:55; 26:173
May, David 1:57
May, Dean 14:89
May, Draper 21:75
May, E. M. 24:63
May, Edward 10:66; 13:35; 20:308
May, Edward F. 19:179
May, Franklin 9:55
May, Frederick 8:24
May, George H. 10:146
May, George W. 8:90; 22:90
May, Gilbert 8:41; 26:170
May, H. 23:40
May, H. D. 25:207
May, H. M. 1:59
May, Harrison 23:100
May, Henry 22:310
May, Henry M. 21:141

May, Hiram 10:206; 17:249
May, Isaac M. 9:67; 18:278
May, J. 1:59; 2:15; 9:227; 18:311, 371
May, J. C. 16:211
May, J. H. 17:135
May, J. Z. 9:25
May, James 4:39; 9:185; 16:46; 19:278; 22:454; 27:89
May, James W. 13:35; 14:196; 16:46
May, Jay 26:106
May, John 1:57; 8:65; 9:185; 12:83; 15:309; 16:300; 19:287; 24:81; 25:57, 207
May, John C. 18:359
May, John D. 10:67; 20:24, 308
May, John O. 10:7
May, John S. 19:24
May, John W. 11:160; 13:35
May, L. 19:85
May, LaFayette 17:349
May, Lindsay L. 11:95
May, Louis 14:196
May, M. H. 3:127
May, Marion 17:237
May, Moses 21:230
May, N. 18:69
May, Noah 17:237
May, Ottman 24:72
May, P. 14:283
May, Peter 25:53
May, Pleasant 8:24; 18:149
May, Reece 22:125
May, Rufus 23:271
May, Samuel 1:59; 11:158
May, Thomas 8:24; 11:37; 17:143; 18:149; 26:173
May, Thomas K. 18:149
May, U. R. 14:196
May, W. 1:152; 3:127; 14:283
May, W. B. 17:96
May, W. W. 17:503
May, Washington 25:275
May, West 21:362
May, William 17:274; 19:304; 22:434; 23:157
May, William H. 16:46
Maybee, J. W. 19:179
Maybee, John 25:334
Maybee, Moses 13:35

Maybee, Silas T. 21:75
Mayberg, H. 9:72
Mayberry, Charles 23:72
Mayberry, David 20:308
Mayberry, H. 12:139
Mayberry, J. 1:153
Mayberry, J. B. 15:263
Mayberry, James 11:389;
20:308
Mayberry, James A. 8:24;
18:148
Mayberry, James D. 22:43
Mayberry, James H.
20:186
Mayberry, Pehraim 10:96
Mayberry, Scott 18:192
Mayberry, Thomas 12:50;
22:260
Mayberry, William H.
22:43
Maybery, Benjamin
22:310
Maybery, George A.
21:195
Mayboil, --- 19:85
Maybold, Lewis 17:349
Mayborn, F. 3:127
Mayborn, Frederick 9:86;
26:44
Maybury, Henry 11:95
Maybury, John 5:42
Mayden, William H.
22:465
Maye, Daniel 18:149
Maye, George 8:23
Maye, Henry 11:209
Mayean, James 15:338
Mayee, William M.
22:260
Mayer, A. 3:127; 14:300;
17:473; 27:88
Mayer, Andrew 27:89
Mayer, Aurandes 13:66
Mayer, C. 7:33
Mayer, C. H. 13:114
Mayer, C. T. 11:157
Mayer, Charles 21:189
Mayer, E. Q. 19:85
Mayer, F. 1:155
Mayer, George 13:114;
18:149
Mayer, J. 3:127; 26:174;
27:83
Mayer, J. V. 15:27
Mayer, John 20:18;
25:273
Mayer, Joseph 19:287
Mayer, L. C. 25:52
Mayer, M. 25:56
Mayer, Melville 17:496
Mayer, Moses 2:14

Mayer, Redman 23:181
Mayer, Samuel W. 22:260
Mayer, W. 17:72, 505
Mayer, William 11:415
Mayer, William H. 17:111
Mayers, Hammond 7:103
Mayers, Henry 8:24;
18:149, 208
Mayers, J. 23:256
Mayers, James H. 8:90
Mayers, John 11:389;
26:45
Mayers, Lewis 23:72
Mayers, William 18:177
Mayes, Alex 17:314
Mayes, George W. 9:86
Mayes, James A. 27:86
Mayes, James G. 25:282
Mayes, John 9:86
Mayes, John D. 11:396
Mayes, John H. 23:204
Mayes, Joseph 18:220
Mayes, S. 1:157
Mayes, T. 3:127
Mayes, W. 3:224
Mayes, William H.
10:125; 20:308
Mayfield, Andrew 11:208
Mayfield, Anthony 21:290
Mayfield, H. 14:89
Mayfield, Isaac M. 17:55
Mayfield, J. 21:33
Mayfield, J. S. 14:89
Mayfield, James 10:96;
14:196; 22:503
Mayfield, John 11:266;
18:208
Mayfield, John C. 22:454;
23:157
Mayfield, William 21:195
Mayfield, William F.
24:59
Mayfield, William H.
23:100
Mayfield, William J.
17:353
Mayford, R. S. 9:215;
21:362
Mayhall, George H. 22:43
Mayhall, Samuel 18:208
Mayhan, G. 14:17; 16:269
Mayhear, P. 11:183
Mayheir, David 12:155
Mayhen, Frantes 15:214
Mayhew, A. G. 11:245
Mayhew, Andrew 18:285;
26:135
Mayhew, Charles S. F.
21:116
Mayhew, David 22:149
Mayhew, E. H. 22:206

Mayhew, Ephraim 9:209
Mayhew, G. W. 13:35
Mayhew, J. 3:127
Mayhew, L. 14:196
Mayhew, O. W. 15:343;
16:374
Mayhew, Oliver 7:129
Mayhew, Samuel 9:133;
27:84
Mayhew, Timothy 9:204
Mayhill, Samuel W. 8:90
Mayhood, --- 27:91
Mayhood, J. 14:243
Mayhue, Joseph 13:66;
19:85
Mayhue, Perry G. 10:125;
20:308
Mayhugh, Asa 14:196
Mayhugh, J. W. 16:300
Mayjor, James 9:67
Maylor, Allen H. 7:33
Mayman, P. 16:211
Maymather, Chesley
11:208
Maymen, R. 3:127
Mayn, John 11:220
Maynader, J. A. 13:94
Maynard, A. 1:59; 3:127;
9:154; 27:82
Maynard, Charles 14:196;
22:149
Maynard, D. L. 19:340
Maynard, Dennis 5:52;
25:207
Maynard, Erastus 12:73
Maynard, Frederick 16:86
Maynard, H. H. 11:244
Maynard, Horace J.
25:207
Maynard, J. D. 3:127
Maynard, J. G. 16:211
Maynard, James 17:55
Maynard, John 1:56;
3:127; 22:408
Maynard, Joseph 22:432
Maynard, L. T. 18:334
Maynard, Lewis 11:424
Maynard, Marshall 17:164
Maynard, Robert M.
10:125; 20:308
Maynard, S. 17:358
Maynard, S. H. 12:100
Maynard, Samuel 22:260
Maynard, Stephen 13:114
Maynard, Thomas 12:31;
21:362
Maynard, W. J. 3:127
Maynard, William A. 7:51
Maynard, William F.
24:53
Mayne, Francis 22:340

Mayne, Peter 9:185;
  19:272
Mayne, Philip 18:279
Mayne, Robert 19:25
Mayne, S. 3:127
Mayner, D. 21:103
Mayner, Nathan 8:41
Mayners, John 18:149
Maynes, William H. H. C.
  23:157
Maynold, R. 1:157
Maynus, John 8:24
Mayo, A. H. 3:127
Mayo, C. 1:151; 25:207
Mayo, Charles 5:42
Mayo, D. C. 27:80
Mayo, Emerson 1:58
Mayo, George 11:127
Mayo, H. K. 12:100
Mayo, Henry 16:166
Mayo, J. 11:101
Mayo, J. H. 19:256
Mayo, J. N. 1:56
Mayo, John 19:25
Mayo, John H. 9:185
Mayo, L. K. 1:153
Mayo, Nathaniel 16:86
Mayo, O. 1:155
Mayo, S. A. 19:256
Mayo, S. L. 14:89
Mayo, Samuel A. 9:185
Mayo, William 12:50
Mayo, William C. F.
  23:100
Mayon, Henderson 22:310
Mayon, Jacob 22:310
Mayon, L. 14:257
Mayor, David 20:308
Mayor, J. 1:57; 14:300;
  17:476
Mayor, L. 14:197
Mayor, Levi 16:211
Mayor, S. 1:54
Mayor, William 3:127
Mayors, J. C. 11:37
Mays, A. 22:310
Mays, Albert 22:90
Mays, B. H. 27:80
Mays, D. 14:17
Mays, Daniel 8:24
Mays, Elisha 17:282
Mays, Franklin 24:41
Mays, G. 13:94
Mays, G. W. 21:33
Mays, George T. 24:167
Mays, George W. 10:66
Mays, Henry 27:146
Mays, J. H. 24:199
Mays, James 20:126
Mays, John 14:89; 19:85;
  23:40; 24:24

Mays, John F. 19:85
Mays, Jubal 14:197
Mays, L. 3:127
Mays, Lemuel 14:197
Mays, Philip 17:135;
  24:199
Mays, Thomas 3:127
Mays, V. C. 9:55
Mays, W. H. 14:89
Mays, William 21:362
Mays, William H. 25:288
Mays, William W. 17:237
Mayse, George 26:44
Maysfield, Abram 8:90
Maysman, J. 17:74
Mayson, Jasperson 19:283
Maywater, Charles 9:209
Mayweather, Lafayette
  11:209
Maywood, David 16:98
Maze, J. B. 22:206
Maze, James 3:127
Maze, James A. 9:122
Maze, Willis 21:257
Mazer, Peter 11:309
Mc---, --- 15:70; 19:304
Mc---, G. W. 14:270
Mc---, Henry 19:85
Mc---, J. H. 8:52
Mc---, J. P. 11:341
Mc---, J. W. 18:245;
  26:48
Mc---, Jeremiah 15:299
Mc---, Louis 23:291
Mc---, M. 17:356
Mc---, M. S. 14:270
Mc---, Peter 19:85
Mc---, S. 15:211
Mc---, T. W. 15:174
Mc---, William 11:157;
  22:353
McAbee, Henry 19:275
McAble, Abram 6:29
McAboy, Morris 11:245
McAboy, W. M. 16:98
McAchrane, S. G. 18:398
McAckerly, William W.
  7:33
McAdam, William 16:43
McAdams, Alexander T.
  21:229
McAdams, D. C. 2:14;
  25:52
McAdams, David 8:65
McAdams, G. J. 9:55
McAdams, Henderson
  11:69
McAdams, Henry 19:318
McAdams, J. 21:33
McAdams, James H.
  17:200

McAdams, John 12:31
McAdams, Joseph 8:107
McAdams, Matthew J.
  22:260
McAdams, Samuel 22:90
McAdams, W. D. 9:55
McAdams, W. H. 9:55
McAdams, William 4:39
McAddell, Barney 17:430
McAdder, P. 16:211
McAdell, Barney 24:214
McAdon, J. N. 11:17
McAdoo, Robert 17:160
McAfee, Bird 22:310
McAfee, James 3:128
McAfee, John S. 17:82
McAfee, W. I. 1:54
McAffee, A. G. 16:98
McAffee, Thomas 22:206
McAffee, W. 11:161
McAffey, S. 25:56
McAffey, Samuel 2:14
McAfoos, George W.
  12:31
McAiles, S. F. 15:259
McAlaster, Charles
  12:156
McAlavey, Charles 10:67
McAlbine, A. J. 11:95
McAldian, --- 12:87;
  16:299
McAleer, Edward 25:56
McAlen, Augustine 10:19
McAlester, --- 9:237
McAlexander, J. 1:154
McAlexander, John M.
  21:362
McAlexander, Violet
  26:223
McAlhaton, Patrick 10:19
McAlister, --- 26:222
McAlister, A. 21:198
McAlister, D. P. 1:156
McAlister, David 12:31
McAlister, James 7:14;
  10:67
McAlister, N. 18:53
McAlister, Sims 17:134;
  24:199
McAlister, William 10:67
McAll, C. B. 21:33
McAllen, D. W. 19:25
McAllen, Gilbert 18:34
McAllen, Owen 18:34
McAllion, John 11:266
McAllis, A. 14:192
McAllister, --- 3:127
McAllister, A. P. 3:127
McAllister, Allen 21:277
McAllister, Archibald D.
  21:140

McAllister, D. 15:14, 289
McAllister, Daniel 12:73; 16:211
McAllister, David 16:211
McAllister, E. 14:257
McAllister, Edwin 21:362
McAllister, Francis M. 20:98
McAllister, George 21:277, 278
McAllister, Henry 8:118
McAllister, J. 3:128; 13:125
McAllister, James 20:299
McAllister, James A. 10:125; 20:299
McAllister, John 10:125; 18:327; 20:299; 22:206
McAllister, Joseph 21:362
McAllister, L. S. 21:33
McAllister, Robert 13:35; 17:419
McAllister, Roland 15:166
McAllister, S. 1:95
McAllister, Tipton 22:433
McAllister, W. 1:95; 20:299; 21:362
McAllister, W. B. 3:127
McAllister, William 21:278
McAllister, William L. 22:260
McAlone, John 15:70
McAlpin, Benjamin F. 24:53
McAlpin, George 21:278
McAlpin, Stephen 21:278
McAlpin, Thomas R. 26:223
McAlpine, Arthur 16:152
McAlray, Charles 20:299
McAlton, --- 15:211
McAlvary, James 12:31
McAlvery, William 9:44
McAlvis, Robert 11:266
McAmber, Lawrence 25:201
McAnally, James 10:125; 20:299
McAndlass, G. 1:56
McAndrew, James 20:133
McAndrew, Richard 19:25
McAndy, Thomas 18:146
McAnew, H. 1:95
McAnnally, William 22:125
McAnni, John 5:23
McAnnin, Theodore 7:129

McAnthoney, James 8:24
McAntill, J. 14:283
McAnulty, William 22:521
McArae, J. 25:57
McArdle, Felix 14:192
McArdle, Francis 10:19
McArdle, James 13:35
McArdle, John 23:129
McArdle, P. H. 13:125
McAree, John 8:90
McArlain, John 12:60
McArnold, James 11:415
McArny, J. M. 11:328
McArter, John 17:96
McArthur, Adam J. 22:206
McArthur, Alexander 22:465
McArthur, F. 1:95
McArthur, Franklin 21:362
McArthur, Henry 23:123
McArthur, J. W. 10:148; 18:53
McArthur, John 19:287
McArthur, Michael 11:68
McArthur, Robert 10:125; 20:299
McArthur, Thomas 12:62; 22:486, 514
McArthur, W. 3:128
McArthur, William 17:361
McArtney, William 9:72
McArtris, J. M. 22:465
McAtee, F. 14:257
McAtee, J. H. 14:270
McAtee, M. 3:127
McAttee, J. 15:211
McAuleff, Daniel 21:229
McAuliff, L. 21:209
McAuliffe, James 21:362
McAuliffe, M. 4:39
McAuliffe, Michael 13:114
McAulis, James F. 12:59
McAuly, M. 14:192
McAupneffe, M. 1:58
McAuthor, Thomas 15:70
McAvel, Francis 12:64
McAvoy, J. 13:66; 19:85
McAvoy, Thomas 4:39; 19:177
McAvry, Michael 11:323
McBain, Hough 24:81
McBain, William 19:25
McBaird, Samuel 22:206
McBand, Daniel 11:414
McBane, C. A. 17:102
McBane, J. 26:50

McBane, John 9:86
McBarton, John 10:67; 20:299
McBeady, G. 18:371
McBee, James 22:260
McBee, John 19:331
McBee, Robert 12:142; 20:299
McBee, Thomas 22:260
McBercher, Duncan 11:307
McBeth, J. C. 3:128
McBeth, William H. 22:206
McBird, George W. 18:220
McBourney, R. 7:33
McBoy, Samuel 19:25
McBrahmie, Charles 16:140
McBride, --- 2:15; 3:128; 18:53
McBride, A. 1:56
McBride, A. E. 11:328
McBride, Charles 10:125; 19:25; 20:299
McBride, Comodore 8:99
McBride, Daniel W. 24:68
McBride, David 7:103; 12:147; 19:304
McBride, Devillo D. 23:123
McBride, E. 1:155
McBride, Enos 22:497
McBride, Felix 21:362
McBride, George 22:235
McBride, H. 12:73
McBride, I. 18:430
McBride, Isaac N. 22:90
McBride, J. 3:128; 18:34
McBride, J. D. 4:39
McBride, J. G. 24:81
McBride, J. Q. 1:52
McBride, James 10:211; 16:98; 25:323
McBride, James A. 23:279
McBride, James H. 10:96
McBride, John 5:52; 7:81, 129; 14:192, 236; 22:90; 25:301
McBride, John D. 22:470
McBride, John F. 11:37
McBride, John R. 22:206
McBride, Kelly M. 27:88
McBride, L. 16:211
McBride, L. J. 11:37
McBride, Levi 4:39
McBride, Lewis 16:374
McBride, M. B. 4:39
McBride, Martin 9:133; 27:83

McBride, Mathew 26:171
McBride, Michael 11:308
McBride, Morgan E. 23:72
McBride, Neil 18:146
McBride, Niel 8:24
McBride, P. 14:192
McBride, Pat 3:128
McBride, Patrick 13:35
McBride, R. C. 8:108
McBride, Robert 11:407; 12:123; 15:128; 24:167
McBride, Robert Z. 11:39
McBride, Samuel 20:299; 21:363; 22:433
McBride, Stephen T. 23:241
McBride, T. 20:147
McBride, Thomas 11:160; 25:323
McBride, Thomas B. 20:11
McBride, W. O. 16:211
McBride, William 7:103; 10:9; 13:35; 20:126; 25:52; 27:89
McBride, William G. 22:43
McBride, William I. 24:9
McBride, Wilson 22:125
McBridge, C. L. 9:111
McBridge, I. 14:84
McBrittey, Andrew 18:421
McBroom, H. 25:201
McBroom, William H. 23:157
McBrother, --- 12:168
McBrown, Henry 9:56
McBrun, --- 14:84
McBrunt, M. 14:84
McBryant, Pleasant B. 22:43
McBue, J. 17:337
McC---, --- 21:209
McC---, D. W. 20:299
McC---, E. 9:228
McC---, J. 25:324
McC---, James 20:147
McCabb, Addison B. 17:596
McCabb, O. 19:85
McCabe, Alexander 7:69
McCabe, Alfred 22:43
McCabe, Andrew 18:245; 26:48
McCabe, B. 23:157
McCabe, Barry 12:31
McCabe, Daniel 17:111

McCabe, David 8:101; 17:460; 24:160
McCabe, F. 3:128
McCabe, Francis 19:319
McCabe, G. W. 8:24; 18:146
McCabe, H. 3:128; 22:260
McCabe, Henry 9:185
McCabe, Hiram 21:363
McCabe, Hugh 21:363
McCabe, J. 3:128; 12:80; 25:201
McCabe, J. J. 24:63
McCabe, James 3:128; 7:103; 21:363
McCabe, John 4:39; 14:192; 20:175; 22:162
McCabe, Joseph 10:19
McCabe, Luke 24:24
McCabe, Matthew 8:73
McCabe, Michael 10:164; 14:192; 19:177; 23:12; 25:269
McCabe, P. 3:128
McCabe, Patrick 8:90
McCabe, Peter 3:128; 21:363
McCabe, Robert 11:414; 19:85
McCabe, Terrence 19:316
McCabe, Thomas 1:54; 14:192
McCabe, William 21:195
McCably, James 7:59
McCadden, J. 1:59
McCadden, James 25:311
McCaeb, T. 20:299
McCaferty, Hugh M. 13:114
McCafery, Edward 13:114
McCaffen, Charles 15:70
McCaffer, James 19:85
McCafferty, --- 18:34
McCafferty, C. 15:81
McCafferty, James H. 13:35
McCafferty, Thomas 7:103
McCafferty, W. 3:129
McCaffery, Edward 22:520
McCaffery, H. 15:343
McCaffery, James 4:39
McCaffery, John 24:68
McCaffey, John 17:145
McCaffin, James 15:305
McCaffire, Francis 15:211
McCaffity, W. H. 23:289
McCaffray, Richard 16:374

McCaffrey, Francis 12:31
McCaffrey, H. 16:374
McCaffrey, J. 3:128
McCaffrey, James H. 3:128
McCaffrey, O. 1:155
McCaffry, James 4:40
McCaffy, William R. 17:358
McCahan, C. H. 22:90
McCahan, John F. 24:9
McCahan, Robert 23:90
McCahen, Alexander 8:90
McCaib, T. 10:32
McCaig, J. C. 20:11
McCailin, J. N. 6:32
McCain, Allen 8:24
McCain, Alvan D. 22:260
McCain, Andrew 10:25
McCain, Andrew I. 8:24
McCain, Andrew J. 18:146
McCain, D. 18:245; 26:50
McCain, David A. 20:186
McCain, H. 13:60
McCain, Henry 18:146
McCain, J. A. 23:40
McCain, John 7:103; 11:159; 15:211
McCain, P. 14:243; 21:111
McCain, T. 16:133
McCain, William 10:25
McCaine, W. 21:33
McCair, Charles 14:84
McCalasky, J. E. 3:128
McCaleb, B. 17:441
McCaleb, Marion 24:153
McCalib, Samuel J. 22:260
McCalister, W. H. 3:128
McCall, --- 18:53
McCall, Abner 20:42
McCall, Alonzo 16:121
McCall, Barber 13:66; 19:85
McCall, Barnard 22:340
McCall, D. 22:207
McCall, Daniel 23:309
McCall, David 20:42
McCall, George W. 10:67; 20:299
McCall, Gideon 4:67
McCall, Henry 17:402
McCall, Hugh 15:128
McCall, Isaac 8:41
McCall, J. 9:111
McCall, James 7:129; 9:72; 12:31; 24:99

McCall, John 8:108; 9:25; 16:211; 18:15, 311; 22:340; 26:107
McCall, John S. 16:281
McCall, Joseph M. 11:328
McCall, M. 8:65; 17:155; 26:173
McCall, Nelson 9:165; 13:35
McCall, Patrick 1:55
McCall, Robert 10:10
McCall, Robert H. 9:243
McCall, S. 1:157
McCall, Stephen 5:52; 25:201
McCall, Thomas 3:128; 17:15; 25:273
McCall, W. B. 11:231
McCall, W. W. 21:363
McCall, William 3:128; 5:23
McCall, Z. S. 8:24; 18:146
McCalla, Sandy 21:149
McCalley, D. 15:211
McCalley, George 8:41; 26:171
McCallis, R. F. 19:234
McCallis, Rufus T. 9:185
McCallister, John 24:199
McCallister, Robert W. 20:98
McCallister, Thomas 11:157
McCallister, W. 19:177
McCallock, J. A. 14:283
McCalloy, Augustus 5:23
McCallum, James 1:59; 4:40
McCallum, John 12:31
McCallum, Samuel 14:319
McCallum, Thomas L. 12:31
McCally, Joseph 22:207
McCalory, J. 1:151
McCalpin, James 12:31; 18:191
McCalum, A. 18:191
McCam, James 11:37; 12:142
McCam, John 17:149
McCam, Martin 11:435
McCamb, J. 1:53
McCame, H. 3:128
McCame, Hiram 23:72
McCamel, C. 21:33
McCameron, W. 3:128
McCamm, M. 3:128
McCammerly, John 17:55
McCammeron, E. 13:114

McCammet, James 9:97
McCammon, Alex 20:299
McCammon, Alexander 10:125
McCammon, James 10:67; 20:299
McCamnon, Emory 24:174
McCamonon, Jesse 18:371
McCampbell, D. 3:128
McCampbell, James W. 22:90
McCan, Andrew 11:128
McCan, David 11:70
McCan, J. 13:129
McCan, O. 3:128
McCan, Thomas J. 26:45
McCanaha, John B. 10:125; 20:299
McCanble, Hiram 11:209
McCance, H. H. 20:299
McCance, John M. 17:111
McCandlers, James 22:485
McCandles, John 25:201
McCandles, P. G. 17:162
McCandles, W. W. 11:245
McCandlis, G. 1:155
McCandliss, Samuel D. 24:179
McCane, Charles 14:84
McCane, L. 3:128
McCane, N. 16:211
McCane, Robert 25:201
McCaney, B. 14:16
McCanle, Samuel J. 18:371
McCanles, G. 17:294
McCanley, B. M. 16:269
McCanley, John 11:127
McCanley, John N. 22:470
McCanley, Leonard G. 22:282
McCanley, M. 22:340
McCanley, P. 9:56
McCanley, Robert D. 26:45
McCanley, Tompkins B. 20:299
McCanly, James 21:278
McCann, --- 15:70
McCann, A. 1:156; 3:128; 16:211
McCann, A. (Mrs.) 25:311
McCann, Andrew 15:152; 19:288
McCann, Arthur 9:133
McCann, Austin 16:43
McCann, B. 3:128

McCann, C. 19:256
McCann, C. D. 14:84
McCann, Charles 9:185
McCann, Dennis 21:363
McCann, E. 1:59
McCann, Frank 9:37
McCann, George H. 25:201
McCann, H. 19:240
McCann, H. H. 10:125
McCann, Henry 20:108; 21:278
McCann, Hugh 9:185; 12:59
McCann, Isaac 10:67; 20:299
McCann, J. H. 19:283
McCann, J. N. 25:324
McCann, James 15:211; 19:85; 20:299
McCann, John 3:128; 4:40; 7:103; 8:108; 22:509; 25:269
McCann, John H. 9:185
McCann, Levi S. 22:260; 23:289
McCann, Michael 1:55
McCann, Oliver P. 22:43
McCann, Peter 10:19; 21:363
McCann, Richard 15:211
McCann, Samuel 12:73; 15:81
McCann, Thomas 17:503
McCann, Thomas J. 9:86
McCann, W. 3:128
McCann, W. W. 23:157
McCann, William 7:103; 21:363
McCann, William A. 7:33
McCann, William J. 15:81
McCanna, J. 25:201
McCanna, M. 9:185
McCannauckle, --- 16:299
McCannichie, P. 25:201
McCannis, William 17:96
McCannon, Emery 17:449
McCannon, J. J. 21:363
McCannon, Jesse 21:74
McCannon, William 4:40; 8:24; 18:146
McCanny, Daniel W. 23:279
McCanon, J. N. 7:51
McCans, Alex 20:299
McCansl, A. 20:85
McCant, M. 20:299
McCanton, Riley 17:180
McCany, Charles 14:84
McCany, Edward 12:73
McCaonnard, B. B. 14:84

McCaosland, Robert 18:177
McCape, A. 14:243
McCapon, M. 10:67
McCard, John 4:40
McCarda, Ephraim T. 27:85
McCardell, W. 3:129
McCardle, James 16:43
McCardy, James 7:103; 22:90
McCardy, John 23:108
McCarell, J. B. 23:157
McCarey, L. 16:211
McCargan, W. 10:155; 19:177
McCarger, James 14:84
McCaril, John 21:140
McCarilly, J. 27:86
McCarl, Edward 15:70
McCarl, Jeremiah 17:253
McCarl, John 1:56
McCarlan, John 23:314
McCarlan, William 27:90
McCarle, Joseph 3:128
McCarlee, N. A. 18:53
McCarley, J. C. 26:170
McCarley, John G. 22:485
McCarlin, J. M. 12:166
McCarmack, J. H. 22:340
McCarmal, J. 14:251
McCarman, J. 25:201
McCarman, James 5:23
McCarmell, W. 17:38
McCarmick, Thomas 17:55
McCarnard, Jesse 9:222
McCarney, Thomas 11:402
McCarr, C. D. 19:256
McCarraw, Michael 16:65
McCarrell, James 18:295
McCarrick, J. 1:158
McCarrick, John 23:123
McCarroll, William 15:128
McCarron, J. 3:128
McCarron, James 25:201
McCarron, John 10:67
McCarsland, David 18:146
McCarson, William 9:222; 18:371
McCarston, C. 16:211
McCarston, Edward 26:222
McCart, Albert 18:34
McCart, J. 3:128
McCart, James M. 13:35
McCart, Jeremiah 15:39
McCart, William 3:128

McCartan, James 7:33
McCartan, P. 19:245
McCarter, Alexander 8:24; 18:146
McCarter, Alexander E. 22:90
McCarter, Courtland F. 22:497
McCarter, J. 11:328
McCarter, J. A. 16:211
McCarter, James 3:128
McCarter, John 4:40
McCarter, John L. 23:157
McCarter, W. 3:128
McCarter, William R. 24:89
McCarterchs, --- 14:192
McCarters, C. 2:15
McCartey, D. D. 7:103
McCartey, Thomas L. 10:67
McCarth, Pat 26:50
McCarthen, O. 16:374
McCarther, O. 15:348
McCarthey, J. 11:266; 14:16, 243
McCarthey, John W. 21:229
McCarthy, --- 11:68; 14:84, 329
McCarthy, A. 13:81; 16:211
McCarthy, B. 14:84
McCarthy, Cornelius 20:2
McCarthy, D. 1:158
McCarthy, Daniel 12:83
McCarthy, Dennis 16:98; 20:58
McCarthy, E. 14:84
McCarthy, Eugene 14:192
McCarthy, F. 14:283
McCarthy, Florence 15:273
McCarthy, H. A. 15:312
McCarthy, J. 1:57, 153, 155; 7:51; 13:94; 17:38; 25:201; 27:82, 91
McCarthy, James 7:129; 13:114; 15:70, 303; 16:211; 18:104
McCarthy, Jeremiah 15:279
McCarthy, John 11:245; 14:192; 15:11, 17
McCarthy, John C. 11:109
McCarthy, John D. 22:90
McCarthy, Joseph 7:129
McCarthy, Michael 16:43; 17:55

McCarthy, P. 13:94; 14:84; 15:128
McCarthy, Patrick 9:103; 16:43
McCarthy, Samuel 1:54
McCarthy, T. 14:1
McCarthy, T. L. 18:34
McCarthy, Thomas 26:142
McCarthy, Timothy 7:33; 23:123
McCarthy, William 22:149
McCartie, C. 16:43
McCartin, John 1:56
McCartin, L. 3:129
McCartney, A. 9:147; 15:211
McCartney, F. S. 11:159
McCartney, Francis M. 22:433
McCartney, H. 3:128
McCartney, J. L. 19:177
McCartney, James 11:415
McCartney, John 9:37; 17:243; 19:25
McCartney, Lewis 7:33
McCartney, M. 3:128
McCartney, Robert 18:192; 19:25
McCartney, Sernett 22:149
McCartney, Thomas 7:33
McCartney, Thomas J. 23:72
McCartney, W. A. 26:127
McCartney, William L. 20:299
McCartney, William S. 10:67
McCarty, --- 8:65
McCarty, A. 3:128
McCarty, A. B. 15:343; 16:374
McCarty, Alexander 20:175
McCarty, Amos 22:43
McCarty, Andrew 21:363
McCarty, Barney 14:192
McCarty, Charles 3:128; 16:121
McCarty, Cornelius 22:434
McCarty, D. 3:128; 9:147; 13:125; 15:211; 27:82
McCarty, Daniel 9:72; 16:299; 22:125; 25:52
McCarty, David 20:50

McCarty, Dennis 3:128; 10:164; 13:125; 23:129
McCarty, E. 3:128
McCarty, E. V. 3:128
McCarty, Eugene 17:282
McCarty, F. 3:128
McCarty, Fayette 11:295
McCarty, Felix 22:13
McCarty, Florence 9:240
McCarty, Frank 12:168
McCarty, H. 16:121
McCarty, H. A. 19:85
McCarty, J. 3:128; 9:111; 12:80; 15:39; 16:211; 23:204
McCarty, J. A. 4:40
McCarty, J. H. 11:424; 21:363
McCarty, J. M. 11:69
McCarty, J. S. 23:40
McCarty, Jack 11:207
McCarty, James 3:128; 11:17; 17:389; 18:424; 19:177
McCarty, John 3:128; 4:40; 7:103; 9:16; 11:374; 12:31, 73; 15:39; 16:299; 18:89, 245; 19:330; 20:104; 26:47
McCarty, John V. 22:167
McCarty, John W. 22:90, 485
McCarty, Joseph 17:96
McCarty, M. 27:87
McCarty, Michael 9:13, 185; 19:275; 25:201
McCarty, Miles F. 22:90
McCarty, O. 7:129; 19:256
McCarty, Owen 9:185
McCarty, P. 1:56, 153; 3:128
McCarty, Pat 18:245
McCarty, Patrick 9:185; 13:35; 22:340, 521; 23:40
McCarty, Peter 14:192; 21:164
McCarty, Richard 9:15
McCarty, Robert M. 20:98; 24:41
McCarty, S. 3:128
McCarty, Sam 17:111
McCarty, Samuel 9:111; 22:43
McCarty, T. 12:64; 15:351; 16:374; 22:207
McCarty, T. L. 20:299

McCarty, Terrence 22:521
McCarty, Thomas 9:47; 12:64; 21:363
McCarty, Thomas B. 13:35
McCarty, Timothy 10:19; 12:31
McCarty, W. 27:82
McCarty, William 11:128; 20:104; 22:340
McCarver, A. J. 10:180
McCarver, Green 11:209
McCarver, Joshua 22:260
McCarvey, Thomas 14:335
McCarvin, Arthur 27:84
McCary, G. W. 13:114
McCary, John 16:374
McCasely, O. 7:129
McCasher, William 22:149
McCashland, S. S. 23:40
McCaskey, W. F. 25:201
McCaskey, William F. 5:23
McCasland, John 16:121
McCaslin, Edward 9:237
McCaslin, G. 1:99
McCaslin, George B. 17:251
McCaslin, H. 19:256
McCaslin, Henry 9:185
McCaslin, I. B. 8:24
McCaslin, J. B. 18:146; 26:172
McCaslin, J. N. 25:324
McCaslin, John G. 13:35
McCaslin, M. C. 3:129
McCaslin, Thomas J. 11:39
McCasling, J. 9:56
McCassan, McPheny 22:514
McCassidy, John 23:72
McCasson, James A. 23:157
McCasson, Julius 22:514
McCasson, William D. 22:431
McCatherin, John 22:310
McCatherine, N. 25:201
McCaty, George 17:180
McCaud, J. 3:129
McCaughen, William 22:465
McCaughey, A. F. 23:157
McCaughey, Patrick 23:12
McCaul, F. P. 14:192
McCaul, Thomas 14:319
McCauld, Henry 11:208
McCauley, C. 4:40

McCauley, Charles 27:90
McCauley, Edward 11:246
McCauley, F. 21:363
McCauley, Hugh 18:279
McCauley, J. 18:15; 21:123
McCauley, J. N. 1:153
McCauley, James 5:52; 11:109; 18:104
McCauley, John 7:34; 23:181
McCauley, M. 1:155; 25:324
McCauley, Micajah G. 8:24
McCauley, Michael 6:32
McCauley, S. E. 12:31
McCauley, Samuel J. 9:222
McCauley, Thomas 19:177
McCauley, Thomas J. 10:125; 20:299
McCauley, Tompkins B. 10:125
McCauley, W. 19:85
McCauley, Wilson 12:31
McCaulis, Joseph 22:433
McCaulley, James 12:31
McCaully, James 3:128; 11:183
McCaully, Randall 11:209
McCaully, Robert 25:55
McCauly, Charles P. 23:181
McCauly, G. H. 3:129
McCauly, Robert 13:81
McCausland, David 8:24
McCausland, R. 3:129
McCausland, William E. 12:31
McCauslin, George 22:521
McCausters, Robert 26:213
McCavelley, George 10:99
McCaver, A. J. 18:177
McCavey, Nicholas 22:310
McCavilley, I. 9:147
McCaw, William 16:374; 21:33
McCawdron, Martin 15:91
McCawley, George 25:273
McCawley, J. 1:157
McCawley, W. 3:129
McCawley, William 13:66

McCay, Abner 17:38
McCay, Alex 22:340
McCay, George W. 17:266
McCay, J. 13:94
McCay, J. L. 21:33
McCay, James 11:38
McCay, John 10:125; 23:252
McCay, Joseph 14:16
McCay, W. J. 9:222
McCay, William 18:295
McCay, William A. 22:260
McCe---, P. 23:204
McCea, Philip 22:311
McCeeneky, John 7:81
McCern, William 22:43
McCerrin, James 21:363
McCert, Lawrence 10:164
McChaine, W. 4:40
McCharnan, Hugh 13:35
McCharty, Michael 23:40
McChean, William 1:56
McChesney, J. 1:157
McChesney, James 14:192
McChesney, James B. 12:100
McChesney, R. W. 1:53
McChesney, S. 14:192
McChilson, C. 14:84
McChine, H. 27:81
McChritock, J. 18:34
McChurley, Michael 18:146
McCichand, John 15:366
McCichard, John 12:100
McCidlas, G. W. 9:111
McClabe, Lawrence 16:299
McClain, Alfred 8:112
McClain, C. 9:72
McClain, C. C. 23:157
McClain, Charles 8:108
McClain, D. 26:173
McClain, D. H. 1:153
McClain, Daniel 22:503
McClain, F. M. 26:50
McClain, George 6:22; 22:310
McClain, Henry 6:22
McClain, Isaac F. 8:101
McClain, J. 1:156
McClain, James 22:90
McClain, Jeremiah 8:112
McClain, John 6:22; 10:67; 17:282; 22:310
McClain, John F. 20:11
McClain, Jordan 22:310
McClain, Joseph 14:84

McClain, Josiah B. 18:220
McClain, L. C. 10:206
McClain, Levi 8:112
McClain, Mark 6:22
McClain, Michael 10:125; 20:299
McClain, Neal 22:149
McClain, O. 27:90
McClain, P. M. 3:129
McClain, R. 3:129
McClain, R. T. 14:84
McClain, Robert 20:300; 22:310
McClain, Samuel 11:208
McClain, Steward I. 22:149
McClain, T. M. 18:245
McClain, W. H. 19:325
McClain, William 19:85
McClain, William A. 19:331
McClain, William M. 8:108
McClain, Wyatt C. 22:260
McClaine, Andrew 16:299
McClaine, D. 8:65
McClaine, M. 14:243
McClaine, Samuel 11:68
McClair, George 11:308
McClairn, George 15:70
McClalleen, --- 1:54
McClamarhead, J. 21:363
McClamrock, Thomas 8:90
McClanahan, H. S. 17:282
McClanathan, John 13:35
McClancey, Samuel 12:31
McClane, James 8:65
McClane, John I. 10:125
McClane, John J. 20:300
McClane, Lewis 11:161
McClane, Richard 20:300
McClane, Richard H. 11:158
McClane, Samuel 11:37
McClane, Walter 15:364
McClannahan, William 17:261
McClannahoe, Job 7:129
McClao, --- 14:84
McClare, Anderson J. 22:43
McClare, R. 14:262
McClaren, James 1:54
McClaren, S. 19:245
McClaren, Samuel 19:267
McClarence, John 16:86
McClarey, A. P. 16:121
McClarion, John E. 6:7
McClarkey, T. 25:202
McClarman, Hugh 16:43

McClarney, F. 22:310
McClarr, F. H. 11:185
McClarren, Samuel 9:185
McClary, Adam 10:178
McClary, David 10:126
McClary, J. 3:129
McClary, James 8:24; 26:173
McClary, Lucius C. 9:103
McClary, W. 15:87
McClary, William 3:129; 12:73
McClaskey, James L. 17:426
McClaskey, James W. 21:74
McClasky, James L. 24:179
McClasky, Thomas 8:90
McClason, John 26:223
McClaugh, George 14:85
McClaughlin, H. 4:40
McClaughlin, J. S. 4:40
McClavin, J. C. 18:112
McClaw, Richard 10:67
McClay, James 18:146
McClead, Maddison 20:300
McClead, Madison 10:67
McCleamey, Robert 20:300
McClean, John 24:9
McClean, William C. 22:90
McClearney, Robert 10:126
McClearon, J. 1:153
McCleary, David 20:300
McCleary, Duncan 12:31
McCleary, G. 16:98
McCleary, James 16:152
McCleary, John 16:133
McCleary, John C. 9:134; 27:84
McCleary, M. 8:52
McCleary, Samuel 7:129
McCleary, W. W. 1:57
McCleary, William 17:38; 22:260
McCLeaven, M. 26:173
McCleaven, William 8:24; 18:146
McCleery, John F. 22:408
McCleeskey, --- 18:208
McCleif, William 3:129
McCleland, John 26:222
McClellan, A. G. 26:50
McClellan, Abrin G. 9:86
McClellan, Andrew R. 16:156
McClellan, B. O. 17:166

McClellan, Benjamin
17:46
McClellan, Cornelius 8:90
McClellan, D. 11:308;
14:85
McClellan, David 9:56
McClellan, E. 14:257
McClellan, F. 23:40
McClellan, G. 18:245;
26:48
McClellan, George
11:429; 22:514
McClellan, H. 15:22
McClellan, Hamilton 7:34
McClellan, Harvey 22:90
McClellan, Horatio W.
12:31
McClellan, J. 1:156; 9:56
McClellan, J. C. 1:157
McClellan, J. D. 17:214
McClellan, Jacob H.
20:183
McClellan, James 3:129;
17:66, 134; 19:177;
22:207, 465
McClellan, Joel 9:106
McClellan, John 9:159;
12:162; 21:363
McClellan, John C.
22:207
McClellan, M. 14:85
McClellan, Moses H.
24:59
McClellan, Peter F.
22:167
McClellan, Robert 9:72;
17:46
McClellan, T. L. 9:31
McClellan, Th. R. 1:55
McClellan, Thomas
14:192
McClellan, William 7:34;
16:98; 22:125
McClellan, William H.
9:16
McClelland, Benjamin
17:46
McClelland, Charles A.
20:300
McClelland, D. B. 1:98
McClelland, David 8:90
McClelland, F. G. 26:174
McClelland, Frank D.
22:149
McClelland, George
14:192
McClelland, H. 8:114
McClelland, J. 1:56
McClelland, J. R. 20:300
McClelland, James 24:199

McClelland, James A.
10:67
McClelland, John J. 23:90
McClelland, John R.
10:67
McClelland, L. W. 16:98
McClelland, Th. 14:192
McClelland, Thomas
11:85
McClelland, William C.
10:126; 20:300
McClellen, Fergus 11:309
McClenan, William 20:11
McClenday, John F. 9:222
McClendon, Merriman
17:134; 24:199
McClennan, Charles
7:103
McClennan, Daniel
14:192
McClennan, E. 14:192
McClennan, James 14:192
McClennan, W. 14:192
McClerg, Joseph C.
17:261
McClerman, George
15:314
McClernan, George 19:85
McClery, Daniel 11:128
McCleskey, B. 1:59
McCletchy, Alexander
21:140
McCletchy, Ervin 22:434
McCleutic, --- 14:16
McClevey, J. 21:123
McClew, Patrick 21:363
McClewing, B. 14:85
McClinchy, Hal 12:31
McClincock, M. 13:114
McClindon, J. F. 18:371
McCline, Henry 15:211
McClinthen, Charles S.
M. 17:15
McClintoc, Nap 18:279
McClintock, --- 22:432
McClintock, A. J. 11:265
McClintock, George
22:464
McClintock, Haman
22:433
McClintock, J. 25:202;
27:90
McClintock, J. F. 8:52
McClintock, J. S. 3:129
McClintock, J. W. 13:94
McClintock, James 5:42
McClintock, John 24:24
McClintock, John F.
23:305
McClintock, John T.
21:92

McClintock, L. 1:60
McClintock, M. 23:157
McClintock, Moses 8:90
McClintock, R. 1:56
McClintock, Robert 8:65
McClintock, Thomas
10:173
McClintock, Wares
17:419; 24:161
McClintock, William N.
1:56
McCliss, J. 9:25
McClitchen, E. 18:112
McCloins, George 14:85
McClonahan, Henry
9:209; 18:69
McClone, John 10:67;
20:300
McCloney, J. L. 11:266
McClorg, D. 11:245
McClose, R. 16:211
McCloskey, F. P. 1:54
McCloskey, Francis 13:35
McCloskey, Patrick 7:59
McCloskey, Robert
13:114
McClosky, T. 15:70
McClosky, John 26:212
McClosky, William 17:15
McClosland, G. 13:94
McCloud, A. 3:129;
19:240
McCloud, Alexander
9:185
McCloud, Charles 14:192
McCloud, D. 1:151
McCloud, Daniel 4:40;
5:23; 25:202
McCloud, Henry 10:25
McCloud, Irvin 22:521
McCloud, J. 3:129
McCloud, James F. 7:34
McCloud, Jesse R. 11:389
McCloud, John 3:129
McCloud, Montgomery
11:17
McCloud, N. 25:202
McCloud, P. 9:56
McCloud, Samuel 10:177;
19:177
McClough, Daniel 7:103
McClounts, James 22:207
McClover, J. 10:153;
19:177
McCloy, Harrison 18:146
McCloy, J. 14:85
McCloy, Samuel 21:74
McCloy, William 22:310
McCluchey, Patrick
21:123
McClue, Arthur M. 9:37

McClue, Robertson 19:25
McClue, William 16:133
McCluen, James 9:111
McCluer, Fry 19:349
McCluer, W. E. 25:56
McCluer, William A. 22:433
McClune, James A. 12:31
McClune, Samuel C. 13:35
McClune, William 20:300
McCluney, A. 12:85; 16:299
McClung, B. 14:85
McClung, H. G. 14:85
McClung, P. 14:85
McClung, P. A. 11:183
McClung, W. 21:95
McClure, A. 16:211
McClure, Alva 22:432
McClure, Andrew J. 23:73
McClure, Arthur 18:295; 26:107
McClure, Charles E. 22:503
McClure, Cyrus N. 22:207
McClure, Daniel D. 9:86
McClure, David 23:157
McClure, E. B. 1:151
McClure, E. D. 16:281
McClure, Ephraim 9:244; 19:334
McClure, F. 3:129
McClure, F. M. 23:268
McClure, G. A. 18:245
McClure, H. 13:35
McClure, Hurlburt 11:70
McClure, J. 4:40; 13:66; 21:204
McClure, J. A. 26:50
McClure, J. G. 16:211
McClure, Jacob 11:39
McClure, Jacob M. 17:38
McClure, James 23:157
McClure, James R. 5:23
McClure, John 4:40; 13:35; 20:49; 21:131; 26:45
McClure, John D. 18:209
McClure, John H. 12:59
McClure, John W. 21:102, 131, 214
McClure, John W. B. 24:41
McClure, Joseph L. 17:308
McClure, Lawrence 9:86
McClure, M. 6:32; 25:324
McClure, Norman 16:281
McClure, Peter 3:129

McClure, R. 3:130; 13:76; 26:170
McClure, Richard 8:58; 21:149
McClure, Robert 17:82
McClure, Samuel 19:334; 22:90, 167
McClure, T. H. B. 7:59
McClure, Thomas L. W. 7:34
McClure, Upton 10:126; 20:300
McClure, W. D. 10:210
McClure, W. W. 20:147
McClure, William 9:16; 10:67; 11:389; 17:405; 21:363; 22:125; 26:172
McClure, William F. 11:415
McClure, William T. 17:308
McClurg, --- 3:129
McClurg, Adam 10:151
McClurg, B. 3:129
McClurg, Isaac 24:59
McClurg, James 1:53; 13:35; 14:192
McClurg, Lemuel 9:222; 18:371
McClurg, Manasseh 21:140
McClush, H. 3:130
McClush, J. 19:85
McCluskey, --- 3:129
McCluskey, A. 9:26
McCluskey, Adolph 8:24; 18:146
McCluskey, Charles William 10:67
McCluskey, E. 4:40
McCluskey, Edward 12:31
McCluskey, Gilbert R. 22:125
McCluskey, J. 12:96; 15:166
McCluskey, John 8:59; 13:78; 16:211
McCluskey, Michael 23:157
McCluskey, P. 1:57; 27:81
McCluskey, Patrick 22:311
McCluskey, Paul 14:85
McClusky, A. 26:107
McClusky, Charles M. 20:300
McClusky, Dudley 23:100
McClusky, F. 3:129

McClusky, J. 15:360; 18:311; 25:55
McClusky, James 24:60
McClusky, John 19:347
McClusky, Joseph 21:89
McClusky, Michael 22:207
McClyman, E. 21:102
McClyman, Eugene 21:257
McCoakin, P. 16:212
McCockle, James 21:363
McCofferty, C. 14:192, 257
McCohan, John 5:52
McCole, Daniel 13:35
McColen, Samuel K. 19:25
McColes, Dominick 19:25
McColl, I. 10:67
McColla, J. M. 11:39
McCollam, Henry L. 23:181
McCollard, William T. 18:209
McColleir, J. B. M. 16:43
McColley, A. 25:202
McColley, James W. 19:25
McColley, Joseph 7:34
McColley, Robert 16:212
McColligan, Patrick 3:129
McColliste, John 17:134
McCollister, John W. 23:261
McCollister, W. 25:202
McCollister, William M. 18:146
McCollium, David 14:329
McCollium, J. 14:193
McCollmun, Uri Harris 17:92
McColloch, W. D. 20:300
McColloge, Jos. C. 16:43
McCollom, Amos 10:67
McCollom, Daniel 7:129
McCollom, John 19:177
McCollom, John G. 23:114
McCollon, Alonzo 10:173; 19:177
McCollor, James 11:116
McCollough, A. P. 23:40
McCollough, Fortune 9:134; 27:84
McCollough, J. 1:58; 25:55
McCollough, J. A. 23:40
McCollough, J. F. 15:211
McCollough, J. J. 9:98

McCollough, James
15:211
McCollough, John W.
23:40
McCollough, Joseph
18:89
McCollough, M. R.
18:177
McCollough, Richard
11:207
McCollough, William
17:166; 21:363
McCollum, A. B. 13:35
McCollum, Alexander
24:95
McCollum, Amos 20:300
McCollum, D. 1:60
McCollum, F. G. 17:406
McCollum, G. 4:40
McCollum, Henry R.
16:143
McCollum, Homer 22:149
McCollum, Ira 14:85
McCollum, J. B. 27:79
McCollum, James 17:92
McCollum, John 20:2;
26:138
McCollum, Richard 8:41;
17:72; 26:171
McCollum, Samuel 4:40;
10:126; 20:300
McCollum, T. G. 18:246
McCollum, William
10:126; 20:300
McCollum, William M.
22:260
McColom, Peter 7:103
McColough, Wesley
23:40
McColum, Cyrus S. 23:40
McColum, Joseph W.
11:96
McCom, C. 14:283
McComb, Anthony 8:41;
26:171
McComb, Charles R.
22:149
McComb, D. 7:59
McComb, Henry 12:31
McComb, John 11:71;
19:177
McComb, Joseph 27:90
McComb, Ned 22:514
McComb, R. 3:129
McComb, Uriah A.
23:157
McComb, William 22:90
McComb, William C.
22:206
McCombe, James 21:363

McComber, Charles
14:193
McComber, J. H. 27:80
McComber, William 10:8
McCombs, Addison
11:109
McCombs, Jacob 22:206
McCombs, James 8:41;
17:92; 26:171
McCombs, James W.
21:74
McCombs, Jefferson 8:90
McCombs, John 14:193
McCombs, Robert 12:156
McCombs, Samuel
10:192; 18:177
McCombs, William
18:209
McCommaughey, D.
3:129
McCommell, Robert A.
22:407
McComson, W. 5:52
McComtie, James 9:98
McComus, Martin 21:246
McConaghy, A. 23:181
McConaghy, Abram C.
18:146
McConagle, Thomas
11:308
McConagly, --- 3:129
McConall, --- 19:85
McConall, J. 26:237
McConan, Thomas 9:209
McConaughy, Abram C.
8:24
McConber, John M. 9:185
McCone, John 24:24
McConeghey, Samuel
22:90
McConeghy, John 21:363
McConell, Moses 10:67
McConkey, --- 10:126;
20:300
McConkey, A. L. 3:129
McConkey, Daniel 7:129
McConkey, E. 7:16
McConkey, John 23:157
McConkey, John S.
10:126; 20:300
McConkey, Theodore K.
24:68
McConley, Peter 25:334
McConley, Robert D. 9:86
McConley, S. B. 23:314
McConlin, George W.
10:173
McConn, Alfred 6:25
McConn, Harry 6:32
McConn, William J. 12:62
McConnac, Charles 9:86

McConnac, George 9:86
McConnack, J. 21:164
McConnaha, Jackson 1:53
McConnahay, J. 20:300
McConnaucher, --- 12:92
McConnaughly, S. 14:85
McConnel, Charles H.
11:288
McConnel, E. 11:288
McConnel, J. 19:86
McConnel, J. S. 19:86
McConnel, James 23:40
McConnel, Julius F.
11:266
McConnel, Moses 20:300
McConnel, Nelson C.
9:122
McConnel, Richard
14:236
McConnell, A. 21:123
McConnell, Addison
24:41
McConnell, Alex 20:300
McConnell, Alexander
10:67
McConnell, An's. W. 1:56
McConnell, Bailey 18:209
McConnell, Charles
16:212
McConnell, David
15:211; 24:95
McConnell, E. 3:129
McConnell, F. 7:103
McConnell, F. H. 11:403
McConnell, F. M. 8:24;
18:146
McConnell, Francis
22:485
McConnell, Frank E.
19:268
McConnell, George 16:98
McConnell, H. 21:123
McConnell, Hiram 18:469
McConnell, Horace 7:34
McConnell, J. 2:15;
9:147; 25:52; 27:81
McConnell, J. C. 11:331
McConnell, J. N. 11:309
McConnell, J. W. 1:151
McConnell, James 9:37;
11:419; 12:31; 13:35;
22:206, 340; 23:73
McConnell, James B. 9:86
McConnell, John 9:86;
11:288; 13:35; 16:43;
17:323, 349; 25:202;
26:49
McConnell, John H. 12:9
McConnell, Jonathan
18:34
McConnell, Joseph 25:52

McConnell, L. H. 14:193
McConnell, L. W. 7:103
McConnell, M. 1:54
McConnell, Nelson C. 27:85
McConnell, R. 4:40
McConnell, R. I. 16:44
McConnell, Richard 18:34
McConnell, Robert 11:183; 26:145
McConnell, S. 19:256; 24:215
McConnell, S. C. 24:24
McConnell, Simon 9:185
McConnell, T. W. 25:202
McConnell, Thomas 4:40
McConnell, Thomas W. 5:23
McConnell, W. H. 17:326
McConnell, William 15:81; 23:73
McConnell, William F. 22:206
McConner, Arthur 21:278
McConner, E. 4:40
McConner, J. 3:129
McConner, W. C. 11:308
McConness, Reuben 25:52
McConnichie, Peter 5:23
McConnick, K. 14:193
McConnohay, Jesse 10:67
McConnolley, William 15:87
McConnor, J. R. 4:40
McConomay, A. 16:299
McCont, M. 9:231
McConville, Henry 16:9
McConville, M. 1:153
McConway, --- 21:209
McConway, John 25:202
McCood, James 12:96
McCook, Alexander 7:103
McCook, Jeremiah 14:193
McCook, Michael 22:454
McCook, Robert L. 18:311; 26:107
McCookle, Joseph M. 22:408
McCool, A. B. 1:154
McCool, B. 3:129
McCool, Charles 9:111
McCool, Fletcher 10:67
McCool, Henry 18:398
McCool, J. 18:426
McCool, John 27:80
McCool, Marion 23:241
McCool, Noah 22:464
McCool, Peter 12:31
McCool, William 10:126; 20:300

McCooley, James 17:82
McCoomb, James 4:40
McCooms, J. 1:153
McCoon, A. T. 2:15; 25:57
McCoon, W. T. 20:300
McCoormick, I. 8:24
McCopom, M. 20:300
McCord, --- 3:129
McCord, A. 11:425
McCord, Andrew 10:206
McCord, Charles 9:86
McCord, Cyrus F. 22:432
McCord, Daniel 25:202
McCord, David 20:183
McCord, G. 3:129; 17:180
McCord, H. 3:129
McCord, Hugh 25:56
McCord, J. B. 1:60
McCord, J. G. 3:129
McCord, J. T. 14:319; 25:282
McCord, James M. 21:229
McCord, John 11:390; 25:202
McCord, John T. 17:282
McCord, Perry B. 19:340
McCord, Thomas 17:361
McCord, W. O. 18:53
McCord, William 23:108
McCord, William H. 17:389
McCorder, John 10:67
McCorick, Edward 19:177
McCorkey, James 13:35; 16:44
McCorkle, --- 18:371
McCorkle, -. L. 16:299
McCorkle, Abram S. 23:256
McCorkle, J. E. 15:211
McCorkle, John 17:134; 24:199
McCorkle, Quincy B. 18:220
McCorkle, Robert 21:363
McCorklea, J. H. 15:39
McCorley, John 21:257
McCormac, Alfred G. 20:11
McCormack, Henry 11:267
McCormack, Hugh 22:408
McCormack, J. A. 23:157
McCormack, James 23:40
McCormack, James H. 10:67
McCormack, John 11:37; 20:175; 24:95
McCormack, Joseph 21:74
McCormack, R. 1:154

McCormack, Robert 22:235
McCormack, William 22:340
McCormack, William H. 22:43
McCormic, James E. 22:90
McCormic, Reuben S. 17:288
McCormick, --- 1:152
McCormick, A. 7:34
McCormick, C. 19:177; 26:170
McCormick, Charles 22:431; 26:45
McCormick, Chris 10:9
McCormick, Christian 14:193
McCormick, Daniel 12:31
McCormick, David B. 15:70
McCormick, E. 3:129
McCormick, Edward 18:426
McCormick, Fred 11:159
McCormick, G. 14:283
McCormick, G. W. 12:100; 17:495
McCormick, George 16:299
McCormick, George J. 11:159
McCormick, H. 1:150; 3:129; 17:155
McCormick, I. H. 20:300
McCormick, J. 1:54, 155, 158; 3:129; 4:40; 9:147; 14:193; 15:211; 18:146; 19:256; 27:83
McCormick, J. A. 15:211
McCormick, J. F. 16:98
McCormick, J. J. 10:164; 19:177; 21:363
McCormick, J. M. 9:86
McCormick, J. W. E. 3:129
McCormick, Jacob G. 9:240
McCormick, James 9:69; 15:303; 19:177; 25:202
McCormick, James A. 27:87
McCormick, James E. 18:220
McCormick, James M. 26:45
McCormick, John 8:118; 9:185; 11:85; 14:193;

McCormick, John 18:413; 23:16; 26:171; 27:146
McCormick, John B. 22:407
McCormick, John J. 17:82
McCormick, John R. 18:220
McCormick, K. 14:193
McCormick, Levi 8:90
McCormick, M. 3:129; 13:114; 14:193; 18:398
McCormick, N. 3:129; 21:111
McCormick, P. 3:129; 20:190
McCormick, Pat 27:90
McCormick, Patrick 10:67, 126; 12:64; 14:193; 15:39; 17:482; 20:300; 23:192; 25:55
McCormick, Peter 3:129
McCormick, Philip 7:16
McCormick, R. 3:129; 11:88
McCormick, R. B. 25:202
McCormick, Robert 1:54
McCormick, S. 12:31
McCormick, S. E. 1:153
McCormick, Samuel 11:160
McCormick, T. 1:57; 14:243; 27:91
McCormick, W. 3:129; 14:193
McCormick, W. J. 1:157
McCormick, W. M. 9:56
McCormick, W. P. 3:129
McCormick, William 8:90; 10:177; 11:390; 14:85; 19:177; 24:81
McCormik, James 4:40
McCormish, Ann E. 26:223
McCormish, Mary 26:223
McCormish, S. R. 26:223
McCormmic, James 10:146
McCornbis, --- 14:85
McCorney, Charles R. 15:211
McCornic, John 14:85
McCornish, C. 16:212
McCornish, Eli 8:73
McCornville, Daniel 20:114
McCorpin, John 22:503
McCorran, James 19:25

McCorran, John 19:25
McCorrick, Edward 10:164
McCorry, Hugh 10:67
McCort, James 15:360
McCort, William 16:98
McCorthy, T. 16:212
McCorvin, Peter 23:157
McCorwin, John W. 23:40
McCory, Christopher 11:209
McCory, Hugh 20:300
McCory, Marion 10:187
McCosby, James 22:90
McCosker, J. R. 13:35
McCosking, Robert 17:155
McCoslin, Robert 3:129
McCost, James 19:86
McCostinell, George 11:381
McCough, L. C. 3:129
McCoughel, Charles 16:44
McCoughel, Thomas 13:35
McCoul, --- 25:324
McCoulin, George W. 19:177
McCoullerter, William 8:24
McCound, James 25:324
McCount, Thomas 4:40
McCourtre, Peter 4:40
McCourty, Andrew 24:9
McCouskin, P. 13:127
McCousland, William 22:408
McCovison, George S. 15:299; 16:212
McCowan, G. W. 11:209
McCowan, I. R. 17:292
McCowan, William 9:56
McCowan, William T. 10:67
McCowden, William 26:48
McCowen, Andrew 17:181
McCowen, Elisha 17:38
McCowen, George 13:114
McCowen, John 3:129
McCowl, J. 20:300
McCown, Alexander 16:212
McCown, Henry 25:324
McCown, James 21:217
McCown, John 26:135
McCowry, James 18:146
McCoy, --- 23:268
McCoy, A. 14:85

McCoy, A. C. 15:211
McCoy, Alexander 12:173; 19:86; 25:202
McCoy, Alonzo D. 9:222; 18:371
McCoy, Alonzo G. 16:67
McCoy, August 3:129
McCoy, Charles 20:91
McCoy, Clifton 10:67; 20:300
McCoy, Cornelius 14:85
McCoy, David 8:108; 18:220
McCoy, G. B. 3:129
McCoy, G. N. 16:67
McCoy, G. W. 16:281
McCoy, George 1:60; 9:26
McCoy, George C. 10:67; 20:300
McCoy, Gilbert 5:23
McCoy, H. 11:266
McCoy, H. J. 10:206
McCoy, Harrison 8:24
McCoy, Henry 8:90
McCoy, Henry H. 22:486
McCoy, Isaac 20:98, 133
McCoy, J. 1:151; 3:129; 4:40; 7:34; 9:185
McCoy, J. A. 14:85
McCoy, J. B. 3:129; 14:243; 17:451; 24:179; 27:91
McCoy, J. H. 11:266; 15:211; 26:171
McCoy, J. M. 3:129
McCoy, J. N. 17:257
McCoy, J. S. 9:44; 26:127
McCoy, Jacob M. 26:127
McCoy, James 1:53; 11:69
McCoy, James A. 20:301
McCoy, James H. 11:158
McCoy, James M. 22:90
McCoy, Jeremiah 6:27
McCoy, Jesse C. 12:62; 15:8
McCoy, John 9:185, 240; 10:164; 12:73; 13:114; 14:289; 15:39; 19:86; 21:33
McCoy, John D. H. 22:503
McCoy, John H. 13:35; 19:304
McCoy, John L. 19:177
McCoy, Justice 12:55
McCoy, Leroy S. 23:40
McCoy, Lewis J. 12:156
McCoy, M. 9:185

McCoy, Martin 17:460; 24:160
McCoy, Martin A. 8:108
McCoy, Michael 25:202
McCoy, Nicholas 18:279
McCoy, Q. 1:153
McCoy, R. B. 11:159
McCoy, S. 17:292
McCoy, Samuel 4:40; 11:38
McCoy, Samuel R. 17:317
McCoy, Simon 22:465
McCoy, Sol. B. 11:95
McCoy, Spencer 6:28
McCoy, T. W. 5:23; 25:202
McCoy, Tom 25:334
McCoy, W. 3:129
McCoy, William 7:34; 9:37; 11:158; 13:128; 17:391; 19:268; 26:107
McCoy, William C. 3:129
McCoy, William E. 11:396
McCoy, William H. 12:31
McCoy, William J. 18:371
McCoy, William M. 8:90
McCoy, William R. 19:25
McCracken, A. D. 21:167
McCracken, A. M. 15:70
McCracken, George 7:14
McCracken, Hugh 26:49
McCracken, J. C. 7:34
McCracken, James 11:160
McCracken, Joel 10:92
McCracken, John 4:40; 22:260
McCracken, John W. 7:103
McCracken, Joseph 15:70
McCracken, Otho C. 22:434
McCracken, R. M. 11:157
McCracken, Samuel M. 23:157
McCracken, Thomas 7:66
McCracken, Uriah 16:121
McCracken, W. H. 23:302
McCracken, W. J. 4:40
McCrackin, A. M. 12:73
McCrackin, B. 3:130
McCrackin, John 3:130
McCrackin, R. 11:245
McCracklin, A. 14:193
McCracklin, H. 3:130
McCrade, Owen 11:17
McCrady, William 3:129
McCragin, George 23:198
McCraiken, J. R. 27:82
McCraken, Hugh 18:246

McCram, Felix 16:98
McCrane, W. 14:258
McCrarey, George 11:424; 22:310
McCrary, George 11:336; 19:304
McCrary, J. 11:39
McCrary, John 10:67; 18:89
McCrary, John W. 24:41
McCrary, Julius B. 7:16
McCrary, William 17:38
McCraskin, Reuben B. 22:432
McCraw, L. M. 20:301
McCraw, S. M. 10:67
McCrawley, William 17:389
McCrawwood, William 17:181
McCray, A. 3:130
McCray, J. 3:130
McCray, J. C. 22:91
McCray, John 22:207
McCray, Martin 8:101
McCrea, Bernard 23:40
McCrea, J. 21:363
McCrea, James 7:34
McCrea, R. A. 9:231
McCready, David 19:177
McCready, George 22:235
McCready, J. 11:266
McCready, William 12:57
McCreara, James 15:57
McCreary, G. D. 22:207
McCreary, G. L. 1:152
McCreary, J. 3:130
McCreary, Jacob 21:257
McCreary, James 8:24
McCreary, John 6:22
McCreary, Josh. L. 9:111
McCreary, Peter 7:14
McCreary, William 22:90
McCreary, William N. 10:126; 20:301
McCree, F. 15:129
McCree, S. 21:164
McCreery, Daniel 21:74
McCreery, James 24:53
McCreery, James A. 21:74
McCreery, William H. 20:98
McCreighan, James 14:193
McCreight, A. O. 18:246
McCreight, J. J. 8:65; 26:171
McCreith, A. 3:130
McCrelin, Allen 18:146
McCrery, James P. 20:33
McCreus, Daniel 7:59

McCrevy, Henry 22:408
McCrew, Willis H. 16:299
McCria, Elijah 27:87
McCriden, P. 1:153
McCrillis, Edward 3:130
McCrine, W. 26:49
McCrink, J. 3:130; 27:90
McCrinkeir, J. A. 9:147
McCrisker, James 14:193
McCrite, Allen 8:24
McCrocken, Joel 20:301
McCrocker, E. B. 19:25
McCroclin, Jesse A. 22:90
McCroldrick, Frank 26:223
McCroly, Cyrus 8:73
McCrone, Anthony 23:73
McCrora, John 20:301
McCrosby, Aaron 22:311
McCroskey, J. 11:328
McCroskey, T. W. 23:40
McCross, J. 3:130
McCrossen, John 20:126
McCrosson, L. 1:154
McCrue, Nathan 18:398
McCrum, John 8:90
McCrum, William 10:187
McCruskey, P. 1:53
McCry, Jacob M. 9:44
McCua, Marphu 11:39
McCubbin, D. 15:174
McCubbin, William 22:433
McCubbins, James 17:38
McCubbins, John 13:114
McCubbins, Zach. W. 22:455
McCudden, Samuel 27:146
McCue, --- 12:166
McCue, D. 25:202
McCue, Daniel 5:23
McCue, Edward 13:35
McCue, J. 1:155
McCue, James 14:193; 19:25; 21:11
McCue, M. 25:324
McCue, Michael 4:40
McCue, Peter 8:121
McCue, Thomas 9:13
McCuen, James F. 15:211
McCuisie, A. A. 14:193
McCuite, John 12:83; 16:299
McCul, John 8:126
McCulham, William 26:173
McCulla, William M. 17:265
McCullam, William M. 17:423

McCulleg, J. 14:85
McCullen, --- 3:130
McCullen, Charles H. 11:309
McCullen, Edward 11:403
McCullen, John 10:164
McCuller, I. 14:85
McCuller, S. 3:130
McCulley, John T. 21:74
McCulley, William 7:103; 12:50; 21:198
McCulley, Zachery 9:56
McCullin, Henry 21:278
McCulling, William 22:13
McCulloch, D. J. 18:246
McCulloch, J. 14:193
McCulloch, M. R. 10:180
McCulloch, Robert 12:31
McCulloch, W. D. 10:126
McCulloch, William 9:26
McCullock, D. I. 26:50
McCullock, John A. 22:503
McCullock, Padden 21:363
McCullock, Samuel 22:260
McCullogg, W. D. 4:40
McCullogh, Joseph 6:18
McCullom, A. S. 26:48
McCullom, P. S. 26:49
McCullough, --- 11:341
McCullough, Benajmin 11:415
McCullough, C. 16:212
McCullough, Charles 8:52
McCullough, D. 23:40
McCullough, H. W. 17:411; 22:235
McCullough, Hamilton 12:31
McCullough, Henry 23:271
McCullough, I. 17:292
McCullough, Isaac 7:103
McCullough, J. 3:130; 18:15
McCullough, J. E. 1:153
McCullough, J. J. 10:19
McCullough, J. W. 3:130
McCullough, James 11:159; 21:278
McCullough, James A. 8:52
McCullough, James E. 25:53
McCullough, James H. 7:59; 11:390
McCullough, James N. 24:53

McCullough, James P. 24:53
McCullough, John 13:135; 15:268; 17:83; 19:347; 21:278
McCullough, John A. 17:498; 21:278
McCullough, L. 22:260
McCullough, M. 2:15; 15:129
McCullough, Michael 25:56
McCullough, Robert 7:14
McCullough, Robert E. 22:431
McCullough, Robert F. 23:157
McCullough, S. 3:130
McCullough, Samuel 22:235
McCullough, Samuel G. 12:31
McCullough, Samuel H. 22:408
McCullough, Thomas 22:260
McCullough, Thomas B. 16:121
McCullough, William 8:77; 11:159
McCullough, William R. 23:40
McCulloye, J. C. 13:35
McCullogh, Jacob 15:159
McCullum, A. S. 18:246
McCullum, D. 25:202
McCullum, D. C. 24:81
McCullum, Daniel 21:363
McCullum, Isaac 20:35
McCullum, John C. 27:90
McCullum, M. 21:33
McCullum, Samuel 25:282
McCullum, William 8:24; 18:146
McCullum, William H. 24:173
McCully, B. M. 13:94
McCully, D. 14:270
McCully, J. 10:187; 18:177
McCully, Sam W. 24:53
McCully, Samuel 15:27
McCully, William 11:71
McCumber, Charles 25:55
McCumber, D. 1:59
McCumber, Dallas 20:137
McCumber, J. W. 1:157
McCumber, James W. 23:114

McCumber, John M. 19:257
McCumber, Levi 17:66
McCumber, W. 3:130
McCumsey, Robert 22:465
McCune, --- 21:167; 25:55
McCune, Allen 17:273
McCune, Andrew W. 22:206
McCune, Bernard 12:172
McCune, Charles 3:130
McCune, E. Blakely 15:57
McCune, Edward 11:158
McCune, Henry 8:24
McCune, J. 3:130; 21:363; 24:81
McCune, Jasper 21:257
McCune, John 1:56; 22:206
McCune, John T. 22:206
McCune, Lawrence 26:46
McCune, N. 14:85
McCune, Peter E. 10:67; 20:301
McCune, Robert 3:130
McCune, William 1:56; 23:252
McCuney, E. 14:85
McCunn, Dennis 13:35
McCunning, H. 14:85
McCurd, --- 21:363
McCurdey, Hiram 20:301
McCurdy, A. 25:324
McCurdy, Daniel 10:67
McCurdy, Hiram 10:67
McCurdy, Isaac 15:211
McCurdy, Robert 9:16
McCurdy, Smiley M. 22:90
McCurdy, T. T. 11:267
McCurdy, Thomas J. 23:73
McCurdy, Thomas M. 8:24
McCurdy, V. 1:153
McCure, H. F. 1:60
McCurley, John C. 22:485
McCurley, Michael G. 26:173
McCurn, --- 25:52
McCurry, Henderson 17:335
McCurry, John S. 16:44
McCurten, James 9:72
McCury, William 10:126; 20:301
McCush, --- 15:306
McCush, T. 15:355
McCushard, --- 14:85

McCusker, John K. 16:44
McCussick, E. 13:94
McCutchan, A. 23:157
McCutchan, P. 1:156
McCutchen, Alexander 10:67
McCutchen, Thomas 14:85
McCutcheon, Alex 20:301
McCutcheon, J. 3:130; 7:59
McCutcheon, John H. 22:433
McCutcheon, Lee 18:89
McCutcheon, R. D. 19:25
McCutcheon, Robert G. 10:126; 20:301
McCutcheon, William 15:211; 25:276
McCutchett, Frank 11:209
McCutchin, Berry 22:311
McCutchin, J. B. 18:89
McD---, A. 15:212
McD---, B. 11:266
McDade, J. 9:147
McDade, Jos. 15:294
McDade, Joseph 16:212
McDaid, J. 27:83
McDaid, W. R. 1:95
McDale, R. 3:130
McDale, Thomas 15:273
McDaliel, Solomon 11:208
McDaniel, Andrew J. 22:167
McDaniel, B. 8:52
McDaniel, Bazzel B. 21:257
McDaniel, Bernard 8:24; 18:146
McDaniel, Charles 21:363
McDaniel, D. 21:189
McDaniel, Daniel 13:35; 20:147
McDaniel, Eli K. 11:267
McDaniel, Elisha 17:237
McDaniel, Ezra 17:282
McDaniel, Frank 8:52
McDaniel, George 12:50
McDaniel, George W. 22:260
McDaniel, Henry 23:90
McDaniel, Hugh 22:311
McDaniel, J. 22:207; 26:174
McDaniel, J. W. 20:147; 27:146
McDaniel, James 18:147
McDaniel, James A. 10:126; 20:301
McDaniel, James H. 23:40

McDaniel, Jeremiah 18:147
McDaniel, Joe 7:129
McDaniel, John 9:72; 12:139; 17:349; 25:202
McDaniel, John H. 23:40
McDaniel, John M. 9:70
McDaniel, John S. 22:91
McDaniel, John W. 23:73
McDaniel, M. 15:87; 17:292
McDaniel, Milton 12:73
McDaniel, N. 21:363
McDaniel, Nathan 21:33
McDaniel, P. 11:231
McDaniel, Philip 24:53
McDaniel, Robert 18:246; 26:49
McDaniel, Samuel 10:67; 20:301; 22:43
McDaniel, T. J. 18:398
McDaniel, Thomas 10:67; 11:159
McDaniel, William 13:94; 14:16; 21:189
McDaniel, William M. 10:126; 20:301
McDaniel, Wilson 17:443; 24:160
McDaniels, A. J. 24:112
McDaniels, Albert 22:207
McDaniels, Andrew G. 23:90
McDaniels, C. E. 25:202
McDaniels, Cornelius 5:23
McDaniels, D. M. 12:80
McDaniels, D. W. 25:202
McDaniels, Friend 11:159
McDaniels, Hezekiah 21:34
McDaniels, James 8:24; 17:22
McDaniels, James A. 8:73
McDaniels, James W. 9:16
McDaniels, Jasper 11:308
McDaniels, Jeremiah 8:24
McDaniels, John 5:23; 21:363
McDaniels, Robert 23:291
McDaniels, Thomas 11:39; 13:66; 19:86; 20:301; 27:86
McDaniels, William 10:92; 15:159; 20:301
McDaniold, Alfred 18:371
McDannals, Miguel 6:21
McDannel, Thomas 9:122

McDanney, Jonathan 18:246
McDarley, Augustus 9:185
McDarmold, R. M. 14:85
McDarnel, Thomas 18:177
McDate, P. 25:56
McDaval, Albert S. 9:222
McDavid, J. 3:130
McDavid, Samuel V. 17:261
McDavide, J. 3:130
McDawn, O. E. 11:192
McDay, Caswell 20:176
McDean, C. 14:243
McDeirtha, Hugh 12:73
McDelancey, John 7:103
McDemott, James M. 9:37
McDemott, Michael 27:85
McDenald, Roger 16:148
McDenny, Jonathan 26:47
McDerby, A. 19:272
McDerby, John 12:31
McDerm, J. 10:28; 19:304
McDermatt, John 26:172
McDermit, Henry 11:209
McDermitt, James 2:14
McDermitt, John 25:57
McDermond, George W. 8:90
McDermort, J. 14:85
McDermot, Eliezine 11:208
McDermot, James 12:62; 25:52
McDermot, John 18:177
McDermot, O. 1:153
McDermoth, C. 21:363
McDermott, A. H. 16:44
McDermott, B. 27:80
McDermott, C. 9:215
McDermott, Edward 13:35
McDermott, Francis 12:31
McDermott, H. 3:130
McDermott, J. 1:153; 15:81; 26:107
McDermott, J. M. 3:130
McDermott, James 18:295; 20:114
McDermott, John 1:56; 3:130; 10:67, 145, 180; 13:35; 19:177; 20:301; 22:207
McDermott, Lemuel 13:35
McDermott, M. 19:257, 347; 20:301
McDermott, Matthew 9:185

McDermott, Michael
9:122; 13:135;
21:363
McDermott, Michael A.
12:31
McDermott, N. 12:31
McDermott, O. 1:58
McDermott, P. 3:130
McDermott, Patrick
18:147
McDermott, T. J. 7:34
McDermott, Th. I. 15:70
McDermott, Thomas
16:212
McDermott, William
20:114; 21:229
McDevett, John 3:130
McDevitt, Albert 23:243
McDevitt, D. 16:374
McDevitt, Hugh 15:70
McDevitt, J. 1:153;
23:181
McDevitt, James 15:211;
21:102, 239
McDevitt, Peter 12:31
McDevitt, W. 3:130
McDevitt, William 4:40
McDice, Robert 22:311
McDiegle, James R.
18:371
McDill, J. T. 11:246
McDill, Robert 13:35
McDill, William 3:130
McDings, James 7:103
McDole, Edward O. 12:31
McDole, W. F. 9:56
McDonadl, P. 18:53
McDonal, --- 18:53
McDonal, James 16:44
McDonald, --- 3:130;
11:209; 15:17;
18:444; 26:47
McDonald, A. 1:53, 60;
3:130; 7:34; 19:229;
25:202
McDonald, A. B. 19:240
McDonald, A. C. 23:292
McDonald, A. H. 3:130;
12:123
McDonald, A. J. 21:34
McDonald, Alex. B. 9:185
McDonald, Alexander
8:24; 9:231; 18:147,
192; 22:91, 465
McDonald, Alfred 5:23
McDonald, Alonzo 9:185
McDonald, Andrew 8:41;
26:171
McDonald, Archibald
11:158

McDonald, B. 3:130;
4:40; 8:52; 11:309
McDonald, Benjamin F.
22:408
McDonald, C. 13:94;
14:16; 26:50
McDonald, Casper 12:31
McDonald, Charles
12:168; 21:34;
25:202; 26:224
McDonald, Christopher
16:44
McDonald, Clement
21:195
McDonald, D. 1:155, 157;
7:59; 13:35; 17:500;
20:301
McDonald, D. B. 3:130
McDonald, Daniel 7:9;
9:86; 15:212; 21:363;
22:91; 25:55, 269;
26:50
McDonald, David 9:215;
18:246; 21:363;
26:47
McDonald, Dct. 14:193
McDonald, Donald 10:67,
164; 19:177; 22:465
McDonald, Duncan
17:361; 21:363
McDonald, E. 10:19;
14:85
McDonald, Ed 18:371
McDonald, Ed. A. 11:85
McDonald, Edmond 8:58
McDonald, Edward
16:299; 21:149, 363;
22:239
McDonald, Ennis 7:103
McDonald, F. 15:212
McDonald, Francis 8:120;
9:37; 18:295; 22:43,
125
McDonald, Francis M.
17:389
McDonald, Frank 15:212
McDonald, G. 1:152
McDonald, G. D. 25:279
McDonald, G. W. 14:193
McDonald, George
10:126; 17:15;
20:301; 21:86
McDonald, H. 25:202
McDonald, H. A. 3:130
McDonald, H. H. 14:193
McDonald, Hector 23:305
McDonald, Henry 5:23;
11:159, 160; 16:212
McDonald, I. 17:292;
22:485
McDonald, Israel 21:74

McDonald, J. 1:58, 157;
3:130; 4:40; 11:128;
12:9; 14:85; 15:70;
24:24; 25:202; 27:82
McDonald, J. J. 1:59
McDonald, J. W. 16:212
McDonald, James 3:130;
7:34, 64; 8:121;
10:19, 206; 11:17,
128, 281, 308; 12:31,
156; 13:80; 14:193;
15:166, 212; 16:212;
17:55; 19:25; 20:18;
21:364; 22:91, 407;
23:73; 24:68
McDonald, James H. 9:86;
23:40; 26:45
McDonald, James M.
5:23; 9:13
McDonald, Jane 26:224
McDonald, Jay 10:126;
20:301
McDonald, John 3:130;
7:59; 9:13, 159, 239;
10:67, 126; 12:73;
13:35, 66; 14:193;
15:212, 279; 16:143,
212; 17:149; 18:246;
19:25, 47; 20:301;
21:364; 22:149, 207;
23:40; 24:60; 26:50,
224; 27:80, 87, 90
McDonald, John W.
17:83; 22:207
McDonald, Joseph
11:158; 13:35;
15:129; 20:301
McDonald, Joseph M.
13:130
McDonald, Joseph S.
21:34
McDonald, Josiah 7:34
McDonald, K. 1:60;
13:114
McDonald, L. 14:85
McDonald, Lafayette
11:159
McDonald, Lawrence
14:193
McDonald, M. 1:156;
22:260
McDonald, M. C. 7:103
McDonald, Martin 8:24
McDonald, Michael
11:68; 16:9; 21:257,
364
McDonald, Mike 4:40
McDonald, Nathaniel
8:52; 21:74
McDonald, Nicholas
11:288

McDonald, O. 13:114
McDonald, P. 1:57;
  3:130; 9:147; 16:98;
  25:202; 27:81
McDonald, Patrick 8:90;
  10:164; 16:98;
  19:177; 26:224
McDonald, Perry 12:31
McDonald, Peter 10:67;
  20:301; 21:364
McDonald, R. 3:130;
  21:34; 25:202; 26:50
McDonald, R. B. 9:86
McDonald, Richard 10:67
McDonald, Robert 9:86,
  185; 17:15; 19:257
McDonald, Robert B.
  26:45
McDonald, S. 16:212
McDonald, S. M. 3:130
McDonald, Sam 27:84
McDonald, Samuel 13:35;
  20:190; 26:172
McDonald, Samuel G.
  23:277
McDonald, Stephen 27:89
McDonald, T. 1:60;
  3:130; 25:202
McDonald, T. H. 9:86
McDonald, T. H. M. 9:37
McDonald, Theodore
  21:364
McDonald, Thomas 5:23;
  7:34; 18:15; 20:301;
  22:340
McDonald, Thomas F.
  21:364
McDonald, U. 19:240
McDonald, V. Z. 25:58
McDonald, W. 1:95;
  3:130; 7:103; 9:185;
  11:85; 12:80; 19:25
McDonald, W. M. 11:415
McDonald, W. W. 16:162
McDonald, William 1:56;
  5:23; 8:114; 9:72,
  107; 10:67; 14:85;
  15:212; 20:301;
  22:207; 25:202
McDonald, William H.
  11:309
McDonald, William M.
  22:125
McDonald, William N.
  7:34
McDonald, Wilson 11:208
McDonall, Gedrie 20:301
McDonall, John 17:181
McDonell, G. T. 3:130
McDonly, Patrick 17:254
McDonnald, F. 26:107

McDonnald, George W.
  15:364
McDonnel, --- 11:220
McDonnel, J. 15:343;
  16:374
McDonnell, Charles
  9:185; 19:257
McDonnell, D. 9:56
McDonnell, J. 15:294;
  16:212
McDonnell, J. R. 1:154
McDonnell, John 9:44
McDonnell, Joseph 12:73
McDonnell, M. 16:212
McDonnell, Michael 7:51
McDonnell, P. 1:154
McDonnell, Patrick 9:26;
  11:17; 18:311;
  26:106
McDonnell, Ride 7:129
McDonnell, Samuel 9:134
McDonnell, T. 27:82
McDonnell, Thomas
  21:140
McDonnough, J. 1:151
McDonough, A. A.
  18:246; 26:49
McDonough, J. 21:364
McDonough, Michael
  13:35
McDonough, P. 1:151,
  157
McDonough, Patrick
  22:454
McDonough, R. 1:158
McDonough, T. C. 3:131
McDonough, Thomas
  17:83; 21:257
McDonough, William
  22:91
McDonwell, M. H. 18:340
McDool, J. 10:206
McDormath, Thomas
  13:66
McDougal, Allen 11:17
McDougal, Andrew
  21:229
McDougal, David 17:46
McDougal, Douglass
  19:325
McDougal, Henry 20:301
McDougal, J. 3:130
McDougal, James 15:348
McDougal, John 11:160
McDougal, N. P. 9:69
McDougal, Samuel 4:40
McDougal, W. 1:53
McDougall, Henry 10:67
McDougall, J. 14:85
McDougall, James 16:374
McDougall, John 15:27

McDougall, Stephen
  13:35
McDougall, W. C. 3:130
McDougals, Alexander
  22:171
McDougel, James 10:126;
  20:301
McDoughal, Eli 18:69
McDougherty, C. 7:103
McDover, N. 3:131
McDowall, Daniel 7:34
McDowall, J. 13:94
McDowall, S. M. 11:183
McDowall, W. 21:364
McDowell, --- 12:87;
  16:299
McDowell, A. 22:311
McDowell, Abraham
  17:249
McDowell, Alex 20:301
McDowell, Alexander
  10:126
McDowell, Andrew 13:58
McDowell, B. 25:202
McDowell, Benjamin
  5:23; 21:92
McDowell, C. 16:374
McDowell, Cassel 22:433
McDowell, Curtis 11:39
McDowell, D. L. 7:103
McDowell, David 16:44
McDowell, H. 3:131;
  16:98
McDowell, Henry 13:66
McDowell, Hiram 20:301
McDowell, J. 1:152;
  3:130; 22:485
McDowell, J. A. 14:85
McDowell, J. B. 1:55
McDowell, J. T. 1:58
McDowell, J. W. 1:59
McDowell, James 12:87;
  13:35; 16:299;
  22:260; 23:307
McDowell, James H.
  23:12
McDowell, John 9:122;
  17:155; 19:177;
  27:85
McDowell, Joseph 10:67,
  126; 20:301
McDowell, Levi 22:149
McDowell, Luke 22:207
McDowell, Lyman 14:193
McDowell, M. H. 9:104
McDowell, Peter 22:207
McDowell, R. B. 15:212
McDowell, R. D. 18:34
McDowell, R. V. 7:103
McDowell, Rufus 22:514

McDowell, S. 7:51; 25:202
McDowell, S. W. 25:202
McDowell, Stephen W. 5:23
McDowell, Thomas 15:212
McDowell, Thomas L. 10:67
McDowell, Uriah 23:12
McDowell, W. 16:212
McDowell, William 1:53; 3:130; 10:126; 12:31; 16:44; 20:301
McDowell, William J. 11:183
McDregal, James R. 9:222
McDuff, Frank 23:90
McDuffee, Charles 10:67
McDuffery, William 22:260
McDuffey, James 8:90
McDuffie, John W. 22:433
McDugal, Alfred 19:25
McDuitt, Hugh 15:212
McDungan, James 7:103
McDunn, Louis 25:324
McDurry, R. O. 14:85
McDwire, C. 3:131
McEachman, Donald 22:340
McElderry, D. F. 11:292
McEldridge, Jonathan 17:292
McEldry, J. 17:292
McElfresh, Benjamin 9:44
McElfresh, J. W. 13:94
McElfresh, John 9:44
McElfrit, J. W. 14:16
McElfrush, John 26:126
McElhaney, F. H. 25:273
McElhaney, Lorenzo D. 17:83
McElhany, M. 5:23
McElhany, R. 8:65; 26:173
McElhany, Samuel 19:25
McElharry, M. 25:202
McElheny, Edward B. 17:209
McElheny, J. B. 19:86
McElirsy, H. 17:455; 24:200
McElivian, B. W. 16:44
McEllery, Lewis 7:129
McElligot, R. 16:98
McEllroy, Thomas I. 17:416
McElmury, James S. 9:56
McEloy, J. 13:66

McElrain, J. 3:131
McElrath, Robert 12:59
McElravy, R. B. 19:86
McElroy, --- 19:265
McElroy, A. 1:151, 156; 11:37
McElroy, Daniel 13:35
McElroy, E. 3:131
McElroy, George 15:212
McElroy, Gilaian 8:24
McElroy, Gillim 18:147
McElroy, Green 9:70
McElroy, J. 27:87
McElroy, James 17:504; 21:34, 364; 22:207; 23:123
McElroy, John 3:131; 9:185; 12:123; 15:129; 19:86; 21:74, 128
McElroy, Michael 10:126; 20:301
McElroy, Oliver 7:103
McElroy, Robert 10:126; 20:301
McElroy, S. 22:207
McElroy, T. H. 11:39
McElroy, Terrence 20:114
McElroy, Thomas 25:203
McElroy, W. 17:15
McElroy, William 3:131
McElvain, Green 7:129
McElvane, Jamy 8:77
McElven, Daniel 10:67
McElvery, George 12:73
McElvey, J. 19:86
McElvie, William 21:128
McElwain, C. 1:152
McElwain, M. 20:301
McElwain, Thomas 10:19
McElwee, D. 4:40
McElwee, J. 16:212
McElwin, B. W. 13:35
McElyea, Daniel 20:301
McEnhall, George 19:25
McEntee, John 25:56
McEntee, P. 1:59
McEntee, Patrick 10:19
McEntes, James S. 11:277
McEntire, L. 3:131
McEntire, W. 3:131
McEntire, William 11:245
McEntyre, C. 9:56
McEntyre, Lawson 24:24
McEntyre, Lewis 9:165
McEntyre, Samuel 23:40
McEnvey, Melvin 27:89
McEogle, N. 21:364
McErevin, James 9:231
McErlin, A. 25:203
McErwin, James 20:301

McErwin, John 15:25
McEuckson, Peter 3:131
McEuen, Leander 9:86
McEven, Lorenzo 25:54
McEvers, T. L. 3:131
McEvery, George W. 21:364
McEvery, Thomas 26:223
McEvony, Washington D. 13:35
McEvoy, Edward 7:34
McEvoy, J. 1:57
McEwel, John 11:245
McEwen, Duncan 17:421; 24:164
McEwen, Leander 26:45
McEwen, P. 1:59
McEwing, John 7:129
McEwn, Alex 17:495
McEwn, William 1:52
McF---, George 11:245
McF---, J. D. 15:212
McFadden, A. 1:60; 9:215
McFadden, Amison 8:41
McFadden, Annison 26:171
McFadden, B. 11:266
McFadden, George W. 17:55
McFadden, H. 3:131
McFadden, Hezekiah 23:157
McFadden, Isaac 17:83
McFadden, J. 1:152, 157; 11:157; 14:289
McFadden, James 3:131; 10:67, 126; 20:42, 90, 302
McFadden, John 15:57; 20:126; 27:88
McFadden, L. 1:57; 11:68
McFadden, Martin V. L. 20:302
McFadden, Owen 12:146
McFadden, Thomas 19:25
McFadden, William W. 11:158
McFadder, George 16:212
McFaddin, J. 23:41
McFaddon, Eliha 15:273
McFaden, David 17:336
McFaden, John 12:74
McFague, --- 19:318
McFague, Neal 19:25
McFale, H. 3:131
McFall, A. 17:38
McFall, Andy 17:55
McFall, Dan'l 8:90
McFall, David 18:220; 20:302
McFall, Frank 21:278

McFall, G. W. 3:131; 11:208
McFall, George 17:83
McFall, J. 1:157
McFall, Jacob 15:212
McFall, James 11:277
McFall, James B. 9:185
McFall, James H. 22:433
McFall, Patterson 17:22
McFall, Reuben 20:31
McFall, Robert 12:62; 15:57
McFall, S. F. 8:52
McFall, Samuel T. 21:102
McFall, Thomas J. 10:67; 20:302
McFall, W. J. 20:302
McFall, William I. 10:67
McFaller, M. 13:94
McFalls, Daniel L. 22:260
McFalls, Joel 22:260
McFalls, John 17:167
McFarden, A. 21:364
McFarden, David 25:203
McFarden, Green B. 22:454
McFarlan, Benjamin 22:207
McFarlan, C. 7:59
McFarlan, E. S. 3:131
McFarlan, George N. 22:409
McFarlan, J. 1:155
McFarlan, P. 12:83
McFarlan, Walter 21:364
McFarland, A. 3:131; 4:40; 7:34, 51; 11:439
McFarland, Amos 9:215; 12:83; 16:299
McFarland, Archibald 15:57
McFarland, B. 13:94
McFarland, C. 13:125
McFarland, Charles 19:86
McFarland, David 23:73
McFarland, Dougald 13:36
McFarland, E. M. 11:161
McFarland, Ezra 17:292
McFarland, Frank 8:52; 21:74
McFarland, G. 3:131; 15:279; 25:203
McFarland, H. 3:131
McFarland, H. C. 1:55
McFarland, Harrison 22:486
McFarland, Henry 19:177
McFarland, Ira I. 7:9

McFarland, J. 15:87; 25:203
McFarland, J. C. 24:95
McFarland, Jacob 23:157
McFarland, James 3:131; 17:22; 21:149
McFarland, John 5:23; 17:307; 19:86
McFarland, John D. 13:36; 16:44
McFarland, John H. 21:217
McFarland, Joseph 21:229
McFarland, Marcus 9:44
McFarland, P. 16:299
McFarland, Patrick 9:159
McFarland, R. P. 23:157
McFarland, Roas 18:312; 26:106
McFarland, Robert 11:70
McFarland, Rods 9:26
McFarland, Samuel 16:44
McFarland, Samuel A. 12:31
McFarland, T. 1:58
McFarland, Thomas 10:67; 20:302
McFarland, Thomas W. 23:157
McFarland, Uriah K. 17:460; 24:160
McFarland, W. 3:131; 15:129
McFarland, W. C. 20:302
McFarland, W. K. 8:101
McFarland, William 21:364; 25:203
McFarland, William C. 10:67
McFarlane, Amos 21:364
McFarlane, Peter 21:364
McFarley, James 13:36
McFarley, Peter 18:413
McFarlin, --- 8:65; 15:129
McFarlin, A. 13:76; 14:300; 17:471; 27:88
McFarlin, Alexander 22:282
McFarlin, David 19:25
McFarlin, Henry 16:212
McFarlin, J. 12:62
McFarlin, J. M. 11:187
McFarlin, John 15:109; 25:203
McFarlin, L. 3:131
McFarlin, William A. 23:289
McFarling, O'Connell 21:34

McFarloon, Marcus 26:126
McFarn, James 11:415
McFarney, J. 3:131
McFarren, Albert 4:67
McFarren, Charles 6:13; 12:31
McFarren, G. 9:147; 27:83
McFarren, George 19:177
McFarren, P. L. 20:49
McFarren, T. P. 20:147
McFarris, James 11:70; 12:31
McFatridge, Henry 8:90
McFatridge, Scott 23:73
McFattein, M. 14:16
McFay, John 20:37
McFeathers, John S. 15:129
McFeddan, L. 14:85
McFee, Daniel 13:36; 16:44
McFeeley, D. 19:257
McFeelog, S. R. 14:193
McFeely, Daniel 9:185
McFeeters, John 22:311
McFelidge, J. 20:302
McFell, Asa 9:159
McFern, A. J. 23:157
McFerran, James H. 22:149
McFerrin, J. 13:94
McFersin, Mat 19:86
McFerson, Mathew 15:308
McFessel, George 9:222
McFeters, William 15:212
McFetridge, James 18:220; 22:91
McFetridge, John M. 11:244
McFetters, J. S. 12:123
McFettridge, --- 11:246
McFinley, James 16:44
McFlinn, J. J. 21:34
McForen, William 11:424
McFosh, G. T. 20:140
McFurson, George H. 14:193
McFy, John 22:260
McFyan, John 11:414
McFye, Michael 16:44
McG---, A. A. 12:123
McG---, D. 25:311
McG---, David 15:299
McG---, W. 17:217
McGaffee, William 22:149
McGaffin, John 18:69
McGaha, Isaac 22:504

McGaha, Samuel 22:261
McGahan, James 27:80
McGahey, Andrew S. 22:432
McGahey, George W. 21:229
McGail, Patrick 7:81
McGain, Edward 9:185
McGain, J. 3:131
McGall, George 13:36
McGall, Henry 11:159
McGall, J. 16:212
McGall, James 25:53
McGalley, R. D. 14:85
McGallisbury, J. 14:85
McGamery, F. 14:85
McGamon, Alexander 22:43
McGan, --- 14:85
McGan, J. 3:131
McGangey, B. 14:85
McGann, --- 19:257
McGann, James 13:36
McGany, George 14:85
McGargill, A. 14:193
McGargle, Albert 18:458
McGarit, --- 21:364
McGarley, G. 16:44
McGarr, Daniel 13:36
McGarr, Michael 10:164; 19:177
McGarrak, R. W. 3:131
McGarraty, Francis 7:34
McGarrigul, R. 25:203
McGarry, J. 9:147
McGarry, Peter 23:250
McGarth, Thomas 22:340
McGarthen, John 13:58
McGarvey, Edward 7:14
McGarvey, James A. 21:229
McGarvey, T. 27:82
McGarvey, Thomas 25:54
McGary, George W. 16:133
McGary, J. T. 20:302
McGase, Julia 21:364
McGater, John 24:24
McGath, A. 19:268
McGath, Lewis 8:90
McGaubhey, J. T. 4:40
McGaugey, B. 14:86
McGaugh, John 21:240
McGaughey, D. E. 19:177
McGaughlin, Thomas 7:34
McGaughlin, William 7:34
McGaughy, Alonzo 17:145
McGaughy, D. C. 10:164

McGauley, Thomas 15:212
McGavin, --- 19:318
McGavitt, J. 20:302
McGavitt, James 10:68
McGaw, George 14:86
McGaw, James 22:43
McGaw, John 1:54
McGaw, Martial 18:209
McGaw, W. W. 4:40
McGeary, Bernard 18:112
McGeary, C. 19:86
McGeary, J. 1:156
McGeary, William 18:112
McGebony, D. C. 14:133
McGee, --- 25:53
McGee, A. 3:131; 14:86
McGee, A. C. 7:34
McGee, B. 7:129; 18:209
McGee, Benjamin 9:165; 25:324
McGee, Christian 14:86
McGee, D. 22:149
McGee, Daniel 14:86; 19:349
McGee, E. 8:52
McGee, Elias 21:102
McGee, Francis 18:89
McGee, Fred 17:181
McGee, George A. 10:151, 178
McGee, George F. 13:114
McGee, George W. 22:261
McGee, Green 7:129; 18:285; 26:135
McGee, H. 16:212
McGee, Henry 15:294
McGee, Hugh 2:14
McGee, I. 14:16
McGee, J. 3:131; 13:94; 15:212; 21:102, 189
McGee, James 3:131; 7:34; 13:58; 14:86; 19:177
McGee, James E. 10:92; 20:302
McGee, James F. 22:207
McGee, Jefferson 1:57
McGee, John 4:40; 8:24; 9:237; 11:158; 14:193; 15:57, 91; 18:147, 440; 21:364; 22:340
McGee, John W. 17:96
McGee, Joseph F. 17:314
McGee, Levi 11:320
McGee, P. 18:16
McGee, Patrick 13:36; 22:521

McGee, Peter 17:134; 24:199
McGee, R. 15:39
McGee, Richard 17:295
McGee, Robert 11:207
McGee, Robert W. 8:24; 18:147
McGee, S. 22:311
McGee, Samuel H. 20:186
McGee, Sidney W. 18:398
McGee, Smith 6:18; 18:89
McGee, Stephen 4:40
McGee, T. 1:156; 27:146
McGee, T. H. 23:307
McGee, Thomas 8:24; 10:67; 18:147; 20:302
McGee, W. 13:94; 21:34
McGee, William 3:131; 14:16; 21:217
McGee, William H. 9:185; 19:268; 22:261
McGeehan, William 11:69
McGeen, Daniel 25:283
McGeen, Francis 8:118
McGehan, George 4:40
McGehee, Eli 9:222; 18:371
McGehee, R. 11:267
McGenger, I. 3:131
McGennis, George 10:126; 20:302
McGennis, P. 3:131
McGentry, John 22:43
McGenty, Mathew 18:104
McGeorge, J. 27:146
McGeorge, James 22:44
McGerr, John 21:217
McGery, E. 1:55
McGhaile, --- 25:55
McGhan, Edward 9:111
McGhee, Charles F. 22:261
McGhee, Marshall 20:11
McGibben, Adam C. 24:72
McGibbon, --- 14:321; 23:204
McGibbony, Henry H. 5:23
McGibney, H. 3:131
McGibney, Samuel 25:203
McGien, David 15:70
McGilany, William 22:340
McGilbery, George 9:72
McGileny, John 13:36
McGiles, Isaac 11:291
McGilevery, A. 25:324
McGill, --- 17:214; 27:82

McGill, A. 17:164
McGill, A. A. 15:129
McGill, A. C. 25:54
McGill, A. J. 17:441
McGill, Albert 4:67
McGill, Alexander 23:129
McGill, Alfred 22:311
McGill, Andrew J. 24:153
McGill, B. F. 11:85
McGill, Benjamin 27:79
McGill, C. N. 8:65;
    26:173
McGill, D. 16:98
McGill, F. 17:337
McGill, G. B. 19:25
McGill, G. W. 26:50
McGill, George H. 9:86
McGill, H. C. 11:85
McGill, Henry 22:261
McGill, J. 11:308
McGill, James 24:41
McGill, John 13:94;
    16:44, 212; 17:15;
    22:260
McGill, Joseph 21:34
McGill, M. 27:81
McGill, R. 9:147
McGill, Robert 12:31;
    19:229
McGill, Romaa H. 17:314
McGill, S. 12:96; 19:86
McGill, Silas 22:260
McGill, Squire 9:222;
    18:371
McGill, Thomas J. 11:95
McGill, W. 15:39
McGill, W. J. 22:432
McGill, William 22:261
McGillam, Hiram 22:91
McGillam, Joseph 22:91
McGillan, --- 13:66
McGillan, James 13:36
McGillem, A. J. 11:70
McGillick, Edward
    25:203
McGilligan, Hannah
    26:244
McGillivery, A. 6:32
McGillon, Alex. 8:121
McGillora, A. 16:99
McGilly, Warren 18:147
McGilney, John 16:44
McGilney, Samuel G.
    15:279
McGilton, J. 3:131
McGilton, M. 14:86
McGilvray, James 1:98
McGines, --- 16:299
McGines, J. 14:27
McGinis, Henry 11:160
McGinis, Lemuel 20:126

McGiniss, John C. 21:34
McGinley, D. 19:283
McGinley, Daniel 9:185
McGinley, George 9:222;
    18:371
McGinley, Hugh 9:185;
    19:240
McGinley, I. 14:86
McGinley, John 10:126;
    19:288; 20:302
McGinley, W. M. 18:246
McGinley, Will 26:47
McGinley, William 10:67;
    20:302
McGinn, --- 14:243
McGinn, Adam 8:108
McGinn, T. 3:131
McGinnes, A. 14:86
McGinness, J. 12:96
McGinness, James 18:53
McGinney, William 20:92
McGinniekin, Thomas
    10:164
McGinning, James 20:302
McGinnis, A. 7:34
McGinnis, Absalom
    17:167
McGinnis, Bernard 4:40;
    23:259
McGinnis, Christian
    23:114
McGinnis, Christopher
    9:237; 26:222
McGinnis, Cornell
    10:126; 20:302
McGinnis, E. T. 25:203
McGinnis, Edward 14:193
McGinnis, George 17:55
McGinnis, Hezekiah
    9:185; 19:279
McGinnis, J. 14:86;
    15:360; 16:212
McGinnis, James 7:103;
    10:68; 20:114;
    24:150
McGinnis, Jeremiah
    22:311
McGinnis, John 13:114;
    19:86; 25:203
McGinnis, Joseph 11:389
McGinnis, M. 17:15;
    25:55
McGinnis, P. 4:40
McGinnis, Philip 11:390
McGinnis, Robert 25:203
McGinnis, Samuel 9:56;
    10:19; 25:203
McGinnis, Samuel B.
    10:68; 20:302
McGinnis, William 4:40

McGinnis, William H.
    22:520
McGinnis, Willis F.
    17:207
McGinthy, John 15:11
McGinty, John 10:126;
    20:302
McGinty, Michael 26:126
McGintz, Mike 11:68
McGiony, Thomas 14:193
McGirgan, S. K. 3:131
McGirk, Andrew 22:44
McGirney, M. 27:82
McGirr, Felix J. 11:284
McGirt, Peter 15:292
McGiven, J. 3:131
McGiven, William 3:131
McGivens, J. 3:131
McGivens, Martin 18:246
McGiveran, P. 7:34
McGivin, --- 14:321
McGivinn, Martin 26:50
McGivney, P. 25:203
McGlain, H. 3:131
McGlane, Patrick 22:167
McGlashon, John 22:207
McGlaughlin, John
    10:164
McGlaughlin, John G.
    22:207
McGlaughlin, Thomas
    10:164; 19:177
McGlaund, J. L. 13:114
McGle---, S. 20:42
McGlenny, Samuel 12:31
McGlinchy, John 15:39
McGlinchy, Sarah 4:40
McGlinchy, T. 19:257
McGlinkey, Thomas
    9:186
McGlinnis, Edward J.
    16:86
McGlinskey, John 9:56
McGlintock, William
    24:81
McGlocklin, A. 17:288
McGlocklin, Joseph 13:58
McGloffin, Orin 22:340
McGloney, C. 27:90
McGlooher, Walter 9:104
McGlore, James 17:317
McGloskey, Frederick
    15:91
McGlosson, J. H. 17:55
McGlothem, John 22:125
McGlothlin, John 17:319
McGlothlin, W. L. 20:302
McGlouch, G. T. 15:338
McGloughlin, --- 26:49
McGloughlin, M. J.
    15:353

McGloughlin, Michael 4:40
McGloughlin, Wells 25:324
McGlowry, Andrew J. 16:281
McGlue, Patrick 1:53
McGlue, Samuel 20:50
McGlue, Thomas 3:131
McGluer, John D. 8:90
McGochlin, --- 14:86
McGocken, Henry 7:129
McGof, Alexander 21:364
McGoffey, Otis 12:74
McGoldick, James 7:34
McGome, Daniel 13:77
McGoneygal, R. 3:131
McGonigal, Robert 12:173
McGonigal, William H. 20:24
McGonigil, Bartimeus 20:24
McGoom, M. 15:305
McGooran, Thomas 24:41
McGorman, Michael 7:34
McGorran, W. 9:111
McGothlin, William L. 10:67
McGough, Francis 25:280
McGoven, John 15:212
McGoveny, Thomas 23:157
McGovern, --- 13:36
McGovern, B. 3:131
McGovern, C. 1:152
McGovern, Edward 13:80; 20:302
McGovern, J. 25:203
McGovern, James 16:44
McGovern, John 7:103; 23:41
McGovern, Lorenz 5:23
McGovern, M. 16:212
McGovern, Owen 14:193
McGovern, Thomas 12:173; 22:236
McGovern, William H. 13:36
McGowan, --- 1:154; 15:109
McGowan, A. S. 21:364
McGowan, A. T. 2:14; 25:52, 54
McGowan, Charles 24:53
McGowan, E. 1:59
McGowan, Edward 4:40; 16:212
McGowan, F. 3:131
McGowan, Francis M. 22:44

McGowan, Harrison 17:201
McGowan, J. 1:154; 3:131; 13:94; 20:58
McGowan, James 12:32; 21:115, 212, 364
McGowan, John 3:131; 7:103; 14:86; 20:302; 26:50
McGowan, John K. 20:302
McGowan, M. 7:51
McGowan, Miletus 7:51
McGowan, Owen 27:80
McGowan, Pat 14:335
McGowan, Patrick K. 7:34
McGowan, Samuel 20:302; 21:278; 26:173
McGowan, T. 22:520
McGowan, William 3:131
McGowell, James 22:340
McGowen, --- 18:192
McGowen, J. 3:131
McGowen, J. M. 4:40
McGowen, John 10:126
McGowen, John K. 10:126
McGowen, M. 14:193
McGowen, Michael 15:8
McGowen, Samuel 10:126
McGowen, William 15:80
McGower, George L. 18:69
McGower, William 21:249
McGowin, J. 14:16
McGowin, P. 14:86
McGown, Daniel 23:12
McGown, G. W. 21:364
McGown, Samuel 8:24
McGown, Thomas 17:261
McGowne, J. W. 25:203
McGrade, Terry 13:36
McGrady, James 15:212; 19:86
McGrady, Preston 9:209
McGraft, C. 16:44
McGraft, James 25:203
McGrager, James 4:40
McGrail, Pat 25:301
McGraly, J. 3:131
McGramm, John 8:118
McGran, Francis 5:23
McGrane, John 17:111
McGraph, Michael 7:34
McGrarey, John 9:111
McGrarily, James 8:90
McGrary, John 27:86
McGrath, Andrew 9:185

McGrath, C. 14:86
McGrath, D. 3:131
McGrath, J. 1:155
McGrath, James 7:69; 8:60; 15:3; 21:114
McGrath, Jerry 22:261
McGrath, John 7:34; 17:207; 23:41; 26:223
McGrath, Joseph 16:299
McGrath, L. 15:174; 25:273
McGrath, M. 3:131; 13:114
McGrath, Michael 16:374
McGrath, T. 1:156; 21:123
McGrath, T. A. 25:203
McGrath, T. J. C. 10:25
McGrath, Thomas 7:16; 21:364; 25:283
McGrath, W. F. 14:193
McGratt, John 14:86
McGraven, Thomas 22:340
McGraw, Andrew 27:80
McGraw, Christy 22:287
McGraw, E. 19:283
McGraw, Edward 9:185
McGraw, F. 7:16; 17:361
McGraw, Francis 25:203
McGraw, Frank 25:324
McGraw, J. D. 11:95
McGraw, James 8:52; 23:157
McGraw, Jesse 18:407
McGraw, John 3:131; 8:52; 14:193; 15:263
McGraw, John C. 23:157
McGraw, M. 1:57
McGraw, M. J. 1:56
McGraw, Michael 16:44
McGraw, Moses 11:95
McGraw, Peter 8:90
McGraw, Richard 13:36
McGraw, Squire 9:222; 18:371
McGraw, Thomas 8:24; 18:147, 398
McGraw, William 13:36; 14:194; 22:126
McGray, A. 25:55
McGray, Bernard 16:212
McGray, C. 16:212
McGrayon, James 18:147
McGreary, W. 1:153
McGreen, A. 13:94; 14:16
McGreen, Francis 12:170
McGreen, J. H. 12:87; 16:299
McGreen, Marshal 8:90

McGregor, Alex 9:13
McGregor, D. 1:59
McGregor, D. H. 1:58
McGregor, Dennis 22:311
McGregor, Franklin 14:194
McGregor, H. 1:157
McGregor, J. 1:151
McGregor, J. F. 1:57
McGregor, John 22:455
McGregor, Richard 16:44
McGregor, William 9:227; 10:68; 15:152; 18:371; 20:302
McGregory, --- 11:266
McGregory, Charles 27:89
McGregory, L. 11:307
McGregory, Richard 20:11
McGrenny, James W. 21:364
McGrery, Peter 24:41
McGrew, H. H. 24:215
McGrew, Jefferson 27:87
McGrew, William 16:121
McGriff, Emberson 22:207
McGriffy, Cyrus 21:257
McGrinity, P. 16:148
McGrinley, Mich. 9:44
McGrollick, James 12:59
McGroota, James 1:53
McGroudy, M. 12:83; 16:299
McGrow, Mathew 16:152
McGrowry, Andrew J. 15:353
McGruder, Thomas 21:212
McGrudor, Thomas 21:278
McGrundy, William 4:67
McGrung, James 7:103
McGuany, M. 14:194
McGucken, A. 3:132
McGue, J. 19:86; 26:237
McGue, M. 26:50
McGuegan, Francis 21:364
McGuey, James 24:41
McGuff, A. 25:203
McGuff, Anthony 5:23
McGuff, William 5:23
McGuffin, Samuel F. 20:133
McGugan, George 22:207
McGugan, M. 22:520
McGuggan, Pat 27:80
McGugin, William 22:486
McGuier, Elisha W. 22:91
McGuies, M. 12:92

McGuigan, H. C. 3:132
McGuigean, J. M. 12:74; 15:70
McGuillen, Thomas 14:194
McGuimskin, T. 19:177
McGuineness, A. 10:126
McGuiner, Owen 13:36
McGuiness, A. 20:302
McGuinn, James 13:36
McGuinn, Patrick 22:340
McGuinne, F. 14:265
McGuinnis, A. 3:132
McGuire, --- 1:155; 16:281; 23:204
McGuire, A. 3:132
McGuire, A. B. 18:246; 26:48
McGuire, A. J. 15:212
McGuire, A. L. 15:212
McGuire, Alexander 21:364
McGuire, Archibald 21:199
McGuire, B. 1:152; 10:187; 18:177; 23:123; 25:273
McGuire, B. F. 11:281
McGuire, Barnard 16:299
McGuire, Bernard 10:20; 16:133
McGuire, C. 14:86; 23:41
McGuire, Charles 21:115
McGuire, Charles P. 10:92; 20:302
McGuire, Daniel 7:75; 25:301
McGuire, David 11:38
McGuire, E. 18:246; 26:50
McGuire, Edward 12:32
McGuire, Elizabeth I. 18:192
McGuire, F. 23:157
McGuire, F. W. 1:154
McGuire, Farrell 9:186; 19:257
McGuire, George 19:25
McGuire, Green 11:389
McGuire, H. B. 8:65; 26:173
McGuire, H. W. 21:364
McGuire, Henry 21:364
McGuire, Hugh 7:34; 11:187; 14:194
McGuire, Hughes 12:74
McGuire, J. 1:150, 151; 3:131, 132; 4:40; 9:147; 10:37; 14:194, 263; 20:302; 21:364; 25:203

McGuire, J. A. 2:15; 25:57
McGuire, J. F. 23:41
McGuire, J. P. 10:28; 19:304
McGuire, Jacob 11:389
McGuire, James 10:126; 12:55; 17:23; 20:302; 21:364
McGuire, James G. 21:241
McGuire, James P. 19:330
McGuire, John 3:131; 7:34, 103; 10:10; 13:36; 14:194; 19:316; 21:365; 22:261; 24:68
McGuire, John G. 21:229
McGuire, Jonathan 24:59
McGuire, Joseph 9:56
McGuire, Josiah 22:91, 465
McGuire, M. 3:131; 25:280
McGuire, M. C. 12:74; 15:70
McGuire, Michael 10:19; 12:65; 13:36
McGuire, Nathan 18:209
McGuire, O. 3:132
McGuire, Owen M. 17:207
McGuire, P. 1:59, 152; 3:132
McGuire, Pat 3:131; 14:86
McGuire, Patrick 5:23; 11:159; 12:55; 13:36
McGuire, Peer 18:440
McGuire, Peter 22:340
McGuire, Philip 10:173; 19:177
McGuire, Robert 16:121; 23:12
McGuire, T. A. 22:353
McGuire, Thomas 13:66; 16:212; 18:16, 112, 147; 21:365; 22:520; 24:171; 25:52
McGuire, W. 4:40
McGuire, W. W. 1:58
McGuire, William 14:86; 17:261; 18:421; 21:89, 167; 22:207; 25:301
McGuire, William P. 21:365
McGuirty, B. 14:86
McGuiston, J. 3:132
McGulian, James T. 20:303

McGulley, Michael
15:212
McGullion, James T.
10:68
McGully, Thomas 26:46
McGunder, Israel 21:365
McGunigle, John 15:212
McGunnel, D. 16:212
McGunsky, Eycicle 8:90
McGuny, Barney 13:36
McGuoy, --- 15:14
McGure, Alex 19:25
McGure, Michael 20:58
McGurgene, P. 3:132
McGurk, James 10:20
McGurk, O. 1:151
McGurk, T. 1:59
McGuyer, H. 15:39
McGwinn, James 16:44
McGwinn, John 21:244
McGwinn, Owen 16:44
McGwire, Thomas 17:423
McGyer, Peter 23:204
McHade, J. 9:147
McHaig, B. R. 10:68
McHakill, Thomas 18:147
McHale, George 22:434
McHale, John 20:31;
22:13
McHale, M. 27:87
McHale, Mat 24:68
McHale, Patrick 17:353
McHale, T. 27:81
McHale, William 24:112
McHall, William 17:314
McHalsey, W. J. 9:56
McHalton, John 20:303
McHam, George 6:18
McHamam, B. F. 3:132
McHaney, George 7:34
McHanna, Richard 9:122
McHardy, N. 15:91
McHardy, Norman 12:74
McHarim, W. H. 18:177
McHarn, --- 13:66
McHarne, B. 19:86
McHarty, M. 3:132
McHate, J. 3:131
McHatton, John 10:126
McHaughlin, John 12:74
McHay, George 12:142
McHenry, --- 15:212
McHenry, A. 16:44;
25:203
McHenry, A. J. 26:174
McHenry, Alex. 8:114
McHenry, Alexander
10:20; 22:407
McHenry, Archibald
9:243
McHenry, Charles 13:36

McHenry, G. 1:153;
21:123
McHenry, Gard. M. 8:24
McHenry, George W.
18:147
McHenry, Hiram 22:207
McHenry, J. 21:111
McHenry, James 3:132
McHenry, John 22:44;
23:108
McHenry, John A. 16:44
McHenry, John H. 13:36
McHenry, John W. 10:68;
20:303
McHenry, Joseph 8:41;
26:172
McHenry, M. 9:239
McHenry, P. 9:186
McHenry, R. J. 1:158
McHenry, Seymour 10:68;
20:303
McHenry, W. F. 23:157
McHenry, William
14:194; 18:246;
26:48, 237
McHenry, William M.
23:41
McHiell, Peter 14:86
McHogan, --- 26:223
McHolland, William F.
8:90
McHone, --- 17:498
McHoney, V. 3:132
McHorn, Millington 27:88
McHose, J. 3:132
McHue, Peter 14:86
McHugh, David 22:91
McHugh, Felix 21:365
McHugh, James 11:157;
12:32; 15:212;
20:114
McHugh, John 16:121
McHugh, John P. 11:157
McHugh, Patrick 9:217;
18:104
McHugh, Peter 14:86
McHugh, Robert 22:454
McHugh, S. 1:155
McHugh, T. 1:60
McHugh, Thomas 7:103
McHugh, W. S. 3:132
McHughes, M. 14:86
McHurgue, John 11:95
McHurin, W. H. 10:180
McHy, E. 14:270
McIchalton, G. W. 1:151
McIcott, Amos 11:17
McIlhaney, Robert 23:181
McIlhenny, --- 16:140
McIllroy, George 17:212
McIllroy, Robert 24:200

McIllwraith, J. 25:203
McIllwrath, John 5:23
McIlroy, Robert 11:160
McIlvain, David G.
21:123
McIlvain, Hugh 7:103
McIlvain, J. M. 11:308
McIlvain, John 18:398
McIlvain, Joseph A. 23:73
McIlvain, William 12:65
McIlvaine, Hugh 22:149
McIlvaine, J. 15:353
McIlvaine, James 10:164;
11:109; 19:177
McIlvaine, R. L. 1:156
McIlvaine, Samuel 23:256
McIlvains, William
22:207
McIlvane, J. 16:281
McIlveen, Hugh 5:23
McIlver, H. 25:203
McIlvery, B. 15:8
McIlvin, P. 14:86
McIlwain, John 12:32
McIlwain, William 15:39
McIlwell, John 7:15
McInaidt, W. 21:189
McInary, Pat 11:307
McInch, John 18:69
McInleer, Christopher
13:36; 16:44
McInnes, John 20:303
McInnis, A. Y. 3:132
McInnis, John 10:126
McInorney, J. 1:53
McIntaffer, M. 17:38
McIntash, George 16:121
McIntee, James 19:349
McInter, John 27:80
McIntire, A. J. 9:86
McIntire, Abraham 15:109
McIntire, B. 25:203
McIntire, B. F. 24:24
McIntire, Bishop L.
17:207
McIntire, C. 19:86
McIntire, Charles 25:54
McIntire, D. H. 21:123
McIntire, Daniel 22:432
McIntire, F. S. 27:89
McIntire, George 20:303
McIntire, H. 1:103; 3:132
McIntire, Henry 10:68
McIntire, J. 3:132; 14:86
McIntire, J. A. 4:40
McIntire, James 10:68;
15:212; 20:303
McIntire, John 3:132;
15:212; 19:177
McIntire, John H. 22:261

McIntire, Joseph 10:68; 12:32; 20:303; 25:57
McIntire, Lucretia 26:223
McIntire, N. 14:86; 17:200
McIntire, O. 9:147
McIntire, P. 1:154
McIntire, R. 3:132
McIntire, S. 25:203
McIntire, Sam 21:34
McIntire, T. 14:330
McIntire, Thomas 11:159
McIntire, W. 26:107
McIntire, Washington 26:127
McIntire, Waterman 9:26
McIntire, William 1:54; 18:312
McIntoff, --- 20:303
McIntoff, R. F. 19:25
McIntosh, --- 9:86; 17:326; 18:192, 279; 19:177
McIntosh, A. 21:365
McIntosh, Alexander 14:194; 16:299
McIntosh, Calvin 17:135; 24:200
McIntosh, Charles 14:194
McIntosh, D. 3:132
McIntosh, E. B. 15:212
McIntosh, Edward 8:90
McIntosh, F. A. 11:328
McIntosh, F. J. 17:200
McIntosh, F. M. 12:96
McIntosh, G. M. 14:258
McIntosh, Henry 20:303
McIntosh, I. 14:86
McIntosh, I. F. 24:81
McIntosh, J. 9:56; 15:294; 16:213
McIntosh, Jacob 27:86
McIntosh, James 1:55; 9:16; 20:18; 21:103
McIntosh, John 18:279; 22:340, 408; 26:50
McIntosh, John G. 7:75
McIntosh, Joseph 22:311
McIntosh, L. 1:155; 9:147; 21:74; 27:83
McIntosh, Lachlin L. 15:92
McIntosh, M. M. 17:282
McIntosh, Nathaniel 8:25; 18:147
McIntosh, Taylor 11:68
McIntosh, William 3:132; 10:28; 17:38
McIntosh, William G. 17:273

McInturff, John M. 22:261
McInturiff, C. C. 11:424
McIntush, William 19:304
McIntyre, A. 1:154; 19:275
McIntyre, A. A. 23:302
McIntyre, A. C. 23:157
McIntyre, Aiza 26:44
McIntyre, Alexander 9:186
McIntyre, Arza 9:86
McIntyre, Asbury 22:91
McIntyre, C. L. 16:213
McIntyre, Charles 21:365
McIntyre, D. 9:111; 27:146
McIntyre, Daniel 11:69
McIntyre, David 19:25
McIntyre, David C. 8:119
McIntyre, E. A. B. 21:365
McIntyre, George W. 19:178
McIntyre, H. 22:44
McIntyre, Henry 10:126; 14:194; 20:303
McIntyre, Isaac N. 8:25; 18:147
McIntyre, Isaac T. 21:131
McIntyre, J. 13:36; 25:203
McIntyre, J. H. 26:170
McIntyre, James 14:251; 16:122; 19:178; 22:520
McIntyre, James B. 18:424
McIntyre, James F. 21:365
McIntyre, James G. 22:431
McIntyre, John 1:58; 7:69; 8:91; 10:173; 27:85
McIntyre, John D. 12:156
McIntyre, John J. 13:36; 16:44
McIntyre, Joseph 1:56
McIntyre, L. A. 23:289
McIntyre, Marshall M. 9:100
McIntyre, O. 27:81
McIntyre, P. A. 19:86
McIntyre, Patrick 25:324
McIntyre, Peter 21:365
McIntyre, R. 1:54; 4:40
McIntyre, R. B. 17:55
McIntyre, S. 15:330; 19:86
McIntyre, Sylvester 23:41
McIntyre, Thomas 7:80; 8:91; 25:301

McIntyre, Thomas E. 17:409; 22:44
McIntyre, Thomas G. 24:53
McIntyre, W. 16:213
McIntyre, W. B. 25:203
McIntyre, W. W. 7:34
McIntyre, Washington 9:44
McIntyre, William 5:42; 7:14; 8:91; 22:44
McIroe, John 9:111
McIsaac, Daniel 7:69
McIuroy, Pd. 11:17
McIver, Donald 4:40
McIver, John 8:25; 16:113
McJ---, Thomas 27:79
McJain, Robert 10:68
McJannett, David 12:32
McJenkins, J. S. 13:36
McJoer, John 18:147
McJohn, John 17:111
McK---, --- 17:217; 25:55
McK---, A. 12:142; 20:299
McK---, I. 11:429
McKabe, Pat 4:40
McKahn, John 13:66
McKaig, B. R. 20:303
McKain, William A. 18:34
McKalin, N. 11:161
McKam, George 18:89
McKane, --- 15:273
McKane, G. W. 11:267
McKane, George 5:52
McKane, John 4:41; 11:37
McKann, Henry 16:299
McKanna, J. 15:287
McKanna, M. 19:257
McKanon, James 21:55
McKarrall, William G. 20:11
McKarron, E. M. 3:132
McKarsey, Patrick 9:122
McKaskell, Jacob 21:278
McKaskle, G. W. 19:283
McKay, --- (Mrs. Captain) 18:177
McKay, Alexander 19:178
McKay, Cabe 14:243
McKay, Daniel 13:129
McKay, Daniel J. 6:7
McKay, George 22:431
McKay, Gilbert 20:108
McKay, Henry 16:73
McKay, Hugh 10:174; 19:178
McKay, I. 9:147
McKay, J. 3:132; 15:343; 16:375; 25:203

McKay, J. Q. 1:157
McKay, James 7:64;
  15:17
McKay, James D. 22:487
McKay, John 15:327;
  20:303
McKay, John F. 20:178
McKay, John H. 10:126
McKay, K. 3:132
McKay, M. 1:53
McKay, Morton 17:263
McKay, R. 14:29
McKay, Reuben 16:44
McKay, Robert 10:68;
  15:109; 19:337;
  20:303
McKay, Samuel 22:91
McKay, Thomas 3:132
McKay, Thomas Benton
  18:177
McKay, W. 14:86
McKay, William 7:34;
  27:87
McKe, --- 19:322
McKea, Daniel 22:432
McKeaig, James 13:36
McKealy, --- 27:87
McKean, D. A. 16:148
McKean, George W.
  15:283
McKean, Hiram F. 22:485
McKean, J. W. 18:398;
  26:50
McKean, James W.
  21:239
McKean, John 19:25
McKean, John B. 23:305
McKean, Joseph 1:53
McKean, L. D. 8:25
McKean, Oliver 17:66
McKean, Orville 22:465
McKean, Victor R. 22:44
McKean, William 22:486
McKeand, Samuel 22:432
McKeane, Joseph 24:68
McKearny, Pat 19:86
McKeary, James 16:44
McKeay, G. W. 12:83;
  16:299
McKechnil, William
  15:70
McKee, --- 19:304
McKee, A. 8:124
McKee, Alfred 18:177
McKee, Allen 22:91
McKee, B. 10:28; 19:304
McKee, C. K. 14:243
McKee, Carander 8:108
McKee, Edward P. 12:32
McKee, Fisher 11:309
McKee, G. R. 8:65

McKee, G. W. 18:285;
  26:135
McKee, George H. 11:38
McKee, Henry 22:207;
  23:100
McKee, Homer 8:91
McKee, Isaac 22:207
McKee, J. 1:99; 9:147;
  14:289; 15:213;
  22:486; 23:41, 157
McKee, J. B. 11:69
McKee, J. D. 25:53
McKee, J. M. 8:121
McKee, J. W. 9:16
McKee, James 3:132;
  10:68; 14:87; 20:303;
  27:81
McKee, James T. 17:83
McKee, John 8:25; 17:23;
  20:303; 21:278
McKee, John H. 20:11
McKee, Joseph 11:39
McKee, Marquis 6:21
McKee, Patrick 14:194
McKee, R. G. B. 21:34
McKee, R. J. 22:44
McKee, Robert 10:174
McKee, Robert F. 22:91
McKee, Samuel 14:87,
  194
McKee, Samuel C. 27:80
McKee, W. 15:213
McKee, W. A. 11:308
McKee, William 10:68;
  11:308; 15:289;
  16:213; 20:24, 303;
  22:149
McKee, Wilson A. 23:157
McKeebey, Edward 22:44
McKeehan, S. F. 14:289
McKeehan, Samuel F.
  23:256
McKeel, Ed 27:87
McKeen, Alfred 18:398
McKeen, D. 14:87
McKeen, George W.
  19:86
McKeen, Hiram 8:25
McKeen, John 18:147
McKeen, L. D. 18:147
McKeen, Thomas J. 17:46
McKeenan, P. 21:164
McKeene, E. 23:41
McKeene, J. M. 22:207
McKeeney, B. 25:203
McKeese, Samuel 3:132
McKeevee, James 3:132
McKeever, Alex 12:32
McKeever, E. L. 3:132
McKeever, George 20:137
McKeever, J. 1:154

McKeever, James 1:59
McKeever, John 1:59;
  3:132; 15:70
McKeever, P. 25:203
McKeirman, E. 7:69
McKeiver, K. 25:203
McKelboy, William 21:34
McKeldan, E. 15:14
McKeley, W. 9:56
McKell, William 3:132
McKellar, Albert 15:71
McKellen, B. S. 19:343
McKelley, John 5:23
McKellips, George P.
  16:281
McKellips, John 16:133
McKelpy, Cyrus 7:129
McKelsey, M. 14:87
McKelvey, Charles
  14:194
McKelvey, James 20:155
McKelvey, Jeremiah
  21:55
McKelvey, John 14:194
McKelvey, Joseph 21:217
McKelvey, W. 7:34
McKelvey, William 27:87
McKelvy, James 22:236
McKenday, M. 19:178
McKendricand, Miles
  20:303
McKendrieand, Miles
  10:126
McKendry, A. 9:222;
  18:371
McKendry, William 16:99
McKenery, James 1:55
McKenley, Michael 7:34
McKenly, J. 3:132
McKenly, James 12:9
McKenna, A. 21:365
McKenna, Charles 21:365
McKenna, F. 3:132
McKenna, H. 23:41
McKenna, Henry 1:56
McKenna, J. 3:132
McKenna, James 9:111;
  11:407
McKenna, John 13:36
McKenna, N. 3:132
McKenna, P. 15:343;
  16:375
McKenna, Patrick 16:45
McKenna, William
  15:332; 19:86;
  23:193
McKennedy, --- 18:34
McKennedy, James
  22:311
McKennet, Robert J.
  26:212

McKennett, William 22:44
McKenney, --- 11:341; 13:114
McKenney, A. 4:41
McKenney, Alex 15:213
McKenney, Alonzo F. 9:13
McKenney, Andrew 22:311
McKenney, B. 3:132; 5:42
McKenney, C. 15:287
McKenney, Charles 26:172
McKenney, Crockell 10:126; 20:303
McKenney, Ferris 24:173
McKenney, G. 3:132
McKenney, J. C. 25:203
McKenney, J. H. 27:83
McKenney, J. W. 3:132
McKenney, John 3:132; 15:213
McKenney, Joseph 22:113, 311
McKenney, Patrick 12:61
McKenney, R. 14:87
McKenney, W. M. 15:39
McKenney, William 3:132; 21:103
McKennhan, Isaac 17:96
McKennie, James 18:53
McKennie, Joseph 21:365
McKennie, Patrick 10:20; 13:36
McKennon, George 20:303
McKenny, Alex 9:111
McKenny, Archibald 19:326
McKenny, Charles 16:99
McKenny, D. 21:365
McKenny, H. 18:430
McKenny, J. 4:41
McKenny, James S. 22:162
McKenny, John 16:45; 21:365
McKenny, Pat 4:41
McKenny, Patrick 8:125; 15:322
McKenny, R. 1:52; 13:114
McKenny, Samuel 13:36; 17:462
McKenny, William G. 15:92
McKensey, Henry 17:389
McKensey, John 9:134; 21:365; 27:86
McKensey, N. F. 20:143

McKensia, Andrew 21:365
McKensie, --- 1:152
McKensie, Robert 27:80
McKentosh, F. 19:86
McKenza, J. R. 15:152
McKenzie, --- 1:55
McKenzie, A. 11:101
McKenzie, Alex 11:38
McKenzie, B. 14:243; 20:303
McKenzie, Ballard P. 17:237
McKenzie, Bristol 10:68
McKenzie, Charles 25:55
McKenzie, D. 3:132
McKenzie, Daniel 20:140
McKenzie, Duncan 22:149
McKenzie, George 20:183; 21:257
McKenzie, Hardy T. 16:45
McKenzie, Hector 14:194
McKenzie, John 16:145; 18:220
McKenzie, Joseph 22:44
McKenzie, Lauchlin 11:407
McKenzie, M. 1:53
McKenzie, N. B. 17:237
McKenzie, Nathan F. 18:220
McKenzie, Neal 10:68; 20:303
McKenzie, Patrick 27:85
McKenzie, R. 22:340
McKenzie, R. Harrison 15:92
McKenzie, Samuel 18:220
McKenzie, Thomas 14:194
McKenzie, William 25:53
McKeon, A. H. 8:52
McKeon, E. 1:153
McKeon, Patrick 13:76
McKeon, T. 1:154
McKeoner, S. 3:132
McKeoune, John 19:86
McKeown, G. 4:41
McKeral, James 3:132
McKercher, Marion 10:68
McKercher, Morvin 20:303
McKerchy, J. M. 3:132
McKerma, Richard 27:86
McKerman, William 7:103
McKern, Patrick 16:213
McKernan, F. 1:158
McKernan, Hugh 26:212

McKernan, W. W. 1:54
McKerney, Bernard 21:200
McKeruan, T. 25:278
McKessack, John 7:103
McKethan, J. L. 23:185
McKethrand, J. 16:45
McKettrick, David 21:229
McKewson, George 1:53
McKey, Howard 25:203
McKey, James 5:42
McKey, William 1:57
McKey, William L. 12:32
McKeyen, Boyd 22:91
McKibben, James 8:91
McKibben, L. E. 9:56
McKibben, W. M. 18:53
McKibben, W. R. 24:81
McKibben, William 10:148
McKibbin, --- 18:192
McKibbin, Zebulon 10:126
McKibbon, Bebulon 20:303
McKibbons, William 23:264
McKiben, James L. 23:158
McKid, Thomas 12:156
McKie, Charles W. 7:34
McKie, Robert 19:178
McKien, Hiram 18:147
McKiffe, George 16:213
McKilips, P. 11:390
McKillip, Allen 14:334
McKillip, James M. 22:44
McKillip, John 17:361
McKillips, John 14:87
McKillup, Allen 7:34
McKim, George 22:91
McKim, J. H. 22:207
McKim, Joseph 6:18; 18:89
McKimery, Ambrose 8:91
McKimm, J. 3:132
McKimpson, Aquilla 24:53
McKinatry, Nathaniel 25:54
McKindle, G. 14:258
McKiner, I. N. 19:47
McKinerey, Samuel 8:101
McKinerey, W. A. 15:294
McKinet, Charles 19:86
McKiney, John R. 22:261
McKiney, R. 18:371
McKinlay, William 11:69
McKinley, --- 17:297
McKinley, E. 11:281
McKinley, E. W. 3:132

McKinley, George C. 17:164
McKinley, George S. 20:11
McKinley, J. 3:132
McKinley, James 24:24
McKinley, John 11:38; 22:236
McKinley, Roderick A. 17:38
McKinley, Sevrer 24:89
McKinley, Steven 23:41
McKinley, Wilson A. 21:34
McKinmon, L. J. 17:83
McKinn, Daniel 25:53
McKinna, Bernard 17:55
McKinner, A. 25:203
McKinnestry, N. L. 21:74
McKinney, Alfred 22:514
McKinney, Andrew R. 16:122
McKinney, B. A. 20:126
McKinney, C. 1:151
McKinney, C. H. 14:194
McKinney, C. L. 11:308
McKinney, Charles 8:25; 17:190
McKinney, Cleveland 23:293
McKinney, D. 3:132
McKinney, Ephraim 24:24
McKinney, Felix 11:183
McKinney, G. W. 27:157
McKinney, George T. 23:41
McKinney, Henry 11:70
McKinney, J. 1:153
McKinney, J. M. 11:158
McKinney, James 4:41; 10:9; 17:207; 21:278
McKinney, John 8:25, 52; 10:164; 12:32; 17:167; 21:74
McKinney, John W. 4:41
McKinney, Lewis 13:58
McKinney, Louis 17:181
McKinney, M. 17:96; 23:117
McKinney, Moses 14:194
McKinney, Nathan L. 21:74
McKinney, Nicholas H. 22:282
McKinney, P. 1:158
McKinney, Peter 21:278
McKinney, R. 9:222; 17:181
McKinney, R. A. 20:126

McKinney, Robert 10:126; 20:303
McKinney, Samuel 7:69
McKinney, Stephen H. 22:454
McKinney, T. 9:56
McKinney, Thomas J. 21:13
McKinney, W. 1:150
McKinney, W. A. 16:213
McKinney, William 8:52, 65; 10:68; 17:55, 96; 20:303; 24:214; 26:170
McKinney, William D. 16:143
McKinney, William E. 9:104
McKinney, Wyatt 17:181
McKinney Fry, W. H. 1:54
McKinnif, John C. 5:42
McKinnis, Haley 17:207
McKinnis, Thomas J. 23:100
McKinnon, D. W. 10:68; 20:303
McKinnon, Daniel 9:111
McKinnon, John T. 7:34
McKinnon, Theophelus 20:303
McKinnon, Theophilus 10:126
McKinny, Alexander 5:42
McKinny, Harman 15:22
McKinny, J. 3:132; 16:213
McKinny, John 19:178
McKinsay, John 3:132
McKinsey, David 9:26; 10:96; 18:312; 26:107
McKinsey, George 9:56; 22:91
McKinsey, Harmon 21:209
McKinsey, John 12:93; 16:299; 18:147; 22:91; 24:42
McKinsey, Resin R. 23:73
McKinsey, Robert 21:229
McKinsey, Thomas 22:431
McKinsey, W. 1:153; 23:266
McKinster, John 12:54
McKinstrey, R. 9:147
McKinstry, A. 15:351; 16:375
McKinstry, Horace L. 27:146

McKinstry, Hugh 20:42
McKinstry, Jerome B. 21:257
McKinstry, M. 3:132
McKinstry, R. 27:83
McKinstry, S. P. 9:147; 27:81
McKinstry, V. B. 14:87
McKintz, John 21:365
McKinzey, John 21:229
McKinzie, Charles 17:361
McKinzie, James T. 15:57
McKinzie, Joseph 22:311
McKinzie, W. 21:365
McKipney, William 25:280
McKirahan, James H. 23:158
McKiss, J. 1:59
McKissick, John 3:132
McKissick, Phillip 16:213
McKissick, William 6:32
McKissick, William K. 11:69
McKissick, Willis 11:208
McKissock, R. 25:203
McKissock, Robert 5:23
McKisson, A. J. 17:361
McKisson, B. 17:356
McKisson, David 9:240
McKitchen, Lee 6:13
McKitrick, William 15:57
McKittrick, Ludlow 22:91
McKitzmiller, J. 7:51
McKlavey, W. 22:311
McKlem, C. J. 2:14; 25:57
McKlesky, Owen 22:149
McKliff, W. 9:70
McKlip, J. 18:312; 26:107
McKnabb, Horton 23:256
McKnabe, Charles 5:23
McKnee, John 14:300; 17:474; 27:88
McKneely, John 20:181
McKnight, A. 21:204
McKnight, Alexander 22:91
McKnight, B. 3:132
McKnight, Benjamin 10:68; 20:303
McKnight, Daniel L. 23:100
McKnight, E. 16:136
McKnight, Francis 27:90
McKnight, Frank 9:72
McKnight, G. 10:28; 19:304
McKnight, H. 3:132; 11:307; 18:89
McKnight, Henry L. 22:431

McKnight, Hiram 6:21
McKnight, Israel 22:486
McKnight, J. 3:132;
  12:62; 15:71;
  21:365; 22:91
McKnight, J. E. 3:132
McKnight, Jake 8:41;
  26:171
McKnight, James 10:68;
  15:71; 20:303
McKnight, James A.
  27:87
McKnight, John 12:32;
  18:220
McKnight, Julius 12:50
McKnight, Lawrence
  21:55
McKnight, Louisa L.
  25:311
McKnight, M. 20:303
McKnight, Madison
  17:356
McKnight, Martin 10:68
McKnight, R. 11:328
McKnight, Richard 11:69
McKnight, Robert 9:231;
  20:303
McKnight, Robert J.
  18:295
McKnight, Samuel 22:311
McKnight, William
  22:207
McKnott, Thomas 10:68
McKnough, Thomas
  20:303
McKnown, --- 25:287
McKon, James 3:133
McKon, John 3:132
McKone, William 20:303
McKonkey, --- 8:119
McKonn, Gibbs 10:126
McKonnay, John 27:80
McKordon, Wiley 11:209
McKorkle, John 8:52
McKoun, J. V. 27:88
McKown, Gibbs 20:303
McKown, Henry 23:158
McKown, J. V. 14:300;
  17:473
McKown, John 18:285
McKoy, Chestnut 12:32
McKoy, Silas 19:86
McKratch, William 9:209
McKrea, J. C. 22:91
McKrustie, Charles
  15:330
McKua, M. 1:155
McKue, Martin 3:133
McKuen, John 10:126;
  14:87; 20:303
McKuhn, John 16:213

McKumey, John W.
  16:122
McKummins, Henry
  23:181
McKune, S. H. 9:147
McKusick, William
  25:324
McKussick, E. 14:16
McL---, J. N. 27:81
McLachlin, P. 15:39
McLacklan, Millis 9:163
McLafferty, B. 1:58
McLain, Aaron 11:389
McLain, Andy 22:311
McLain, C. 12:9
McLain, Daniel M.
  23:290
McLain, David 17:252
McLain, Ferguson 22:91
McLain, Garret 11:160
McLain, George 8:41;
  10:151; 26:171
McLain, Hugh 9:44;
  26:126
McLain, Isaac F. 17:463
McLain, J. 25:203
McLain, J. A. 20:58
McLain, J. H. 23:100
McLain, J. R. 1:154
McLain, James 9:186;
  22:44
McLain, John 11:266;
  18:89
McLain, John W. 22:44
Mclain, Peter 16:375
McLain, Peter 26:174
McLain, Robert 17:393
McLain, Stephen E.
  22:261
McLain, Thomas 23:301
McLain, Thomas H.
  11:424
McLain, W. H. 11:328
McLain, William 18:89
McLain, William L.
  21:189
McLain, Zachariah 22:44
McLaine, Brice B. 25:56
McLaine, H. C. 3:133
McLaine, Henry 5:42
McLaine, J. E. 25:203
McLaine, Thomas 3:133
McLair, Charles 21:365
McLalan, E. 1:154
McLam, W. 1:151
McLamas, J. 3:133
McLamick, Michael 26:47
McLand, Pleasant 21:278
McLane, --- 10:177
McLane, Alonzo 22:91
McLane, C. G. 26:171

McLane, Carroll 21:189
McLane, Edward 11:109
McLane, George 9:104
McLane, Gilbert 12:57
McLane, H. 16:213
McLane, J. 19:275
McLane, J. A. 23:41
McLane, J. J. 27:82
McLane, James 14:194;
  16:213
McLane, John 12:31;
  25:203
McLane, Joshua 11:396
McLane, Lewis 18:16
McLane, Peter 8:73
McLane, R. 17:181
McLane, Samuel 22:465
McLane, T. 3:133
McLane, W. 19:86
McLane, William 14:194;
  22:44
McLane, William G.
  9:122; 27:86
McLane, William H.
  11:396
McLanehan, Calvin 17:38
McLanhan, Charles
  25:204
McLanlin, J. C. 12:32
McLard, J. 10:126; 20:304
McLaren, A. 25:204
McLaren, Angus 5:23
McLaren, B. 3:133
McLaren, John B. 17:83
McLaren, William 1:59
McLargin, Joseph 22:207
McLaskey, --- 1:152
McLaskey, Thomas 5:42
McLaubin, Charles 3:133
McLauchen, Robert
  15:213
McLauchlin, Caleb S.
  12:32
McLauchlin, James 12:32
McLaughlan, William
  26:106
McLaughlin, --- 10:68;
  15:285; 16:65
McLaughlin, A. 1:59;
  17:92; 19:304
McLaughlin, A. J. 9:26;
  18:312; 26:107
McLaughlin, B. 1:156;
  3:133; 19:240;
  23:158
McLaughlin, Barlay
  18:177
McLaughlin, Benjamin
  10:20
McLaughlin, Benson
  9:186

McLaughlin, Burley 10:187
McLaughlin, C. H. 13:114
McLaughlin, Charles 15:279; 19:178; 25:204
McLaughlin, Charles P. 15:159
McLaughlin, Cyrus A. 16:281
McLaughlin, Daniel 22:207
McLaughlin, David T. 23:158
McLaughlin, E. 3:133
McLaughlin, Eugene 16:86
McLaughlin, Everett R. 10:126; 20:304
McLaughlin, G. 24:214
McLaughlin, G. A. 16:213
McLaughlin, George 4:41
McLaughlin, H. 22:236
McLaughlin, Henry 22:408
McLaughlin, Herbert 7:103
McLaughlin, Hugh 26:171
McLaughlin, J. 1:58, 152, 155; 3:133; 8:52; 9:111, 147; 10:28; 11:101; 12:162; 15:5, 71; 16:213; 19:86, 229, 304; 25:324
McLaughlin, J. H. 4:41
McLaughlin, J. W. 22:207
McLaughlin, James 1:57; 3:133; 7:34; 9:186; 12:74; 15:18; 21:365; 22:149; 25:204
McLaughlin, Jeremiah 25:58
McLaughlin, John 5:23; 6:32; 9:107; 11:231, 389; 17:237; 20:114; 21:11, 74, 229; 22:261, 340; 23:16; 25:204
McLaughlin, John H. 15:71
McLaughlin, M. 24:24
McLaughlin, M. J. 16:281
McLaughlin, Michael 11:183; 22:91
McLaughlin, O. 15:312
McLaughlin, P. 1:54; 9:111; 15:159
McLaughlin, Patrick D. 23:181
McLaughlin, Peter 23:41

McLaughlin, R. 4:41
McLaughlin, Robert 8:25; 14:301; 15:8; 17:23, 476; 18:147; 27:88
McLaughlin, S. 22:207
McLaughlin, T. 1:153; 19:25; 27:82
McLaughlin, T. A. 19:240
McLaughlin, T. J. 19:229
McLaughlin, T. P. 1:58
McLaughlin, Thomas 9:186; 13:36; 19:25; 21:365
McLaughlin, W. 19:229
McLaughlin, W. W. 23:158
McLaughlin, William 1:55; 9:26; 13:114; 18:69, 312, 398; 20:183; 21:365
McLaughlin, William H. 8:25; 18:147
McLauren, J. 14:87
McLaury, J. N. 9:147
McLaury, James T. 27:86
McLaury, John M. 9:147
McLawery, Ed 18:398
McLay, James 8:25; 12:65; 18:147
McLay, Robert 18:112
McLead, M. 21:365
McLean, A. G. 3:133
McLean, Alex. 8:41
McLean, Alexander 26:171
McLean, Daniel 21:365
McLean, Fred 27:89
McLean, George 18:89
McLean, H. N. 17:200
McLean, Hector 9:147
McLean, Henry 18:89
McLean, J. 13:94
McLean, J. A. 23:41
McLean, Jacob 27:146
McLean, James 11:70; 21:365; 23:123
McLean, James K. 10:126
McLean, John C. 10:151, 178
McLean, L. D. 8:25; 18:147
McLean, Martin 25:288
McLean, Neil 4:41
McLean, Noah 21:365
McLean, P. 3:133
McLean, Peter 7:129
McLean, R. 3:133
McLean, Robert 21:123
McLean, Robert H. 17:83
McLean, Thomas 7:129

McLean, William 1:54; 3:133; 23:41
McLean, Wright 21:245
McLearian, Berry 21:278
McLearn, John 16:375
McLeary, William 11:389
McLeavin, J. 7:103
McLeece, Niel 20:114
McLeelan, J. C. 7:72
McLees, Josiah 12:74
McLeish, David 22:485
McLeiter, John 7:103
McLelan, William 16:45
McLeland, C. E. 19:229
McLeland, T. J. 21:34
McLellan, George O. 16:375
McLellan, Hugh 15:129
McLellan, Isaac 25:54
McLellan, J. 1:155
McLellan, James 6:28
McLellan, Joseph 6:28
McLellan, Miles 25:204
McLellan, Robert 13:66
McLellan, William 13:36
McLelland, H. R. 21:34
McLelland, J. 11:71
McLellen, C. B. 9:186
McLellen, James 7:17
McLellen, Robert 16:213
McLemore, Joseph 4:41
McLemore, M. B. 14:316
McLenahan, William 10:126; 20:304
McLenan, Roderick 23:267
McLennan, Norman 9:204
McLennard, Frank E. 9:186
McLeod, A. 12:123; 15:129
McLeod, Alex R. 20:304
McLeod, Alexander 24:95
McLeod, Alexander R. 10:126
McLeod, Allison 20:193
McLeod, George 27:89
McLeod, Ira N. 20:151
McLeod, J. 1:58
McLeod, N. 1:156
McLeod, P. 1:154
McLeod, Roderick 21:365
McLeod, W. H. 18:34
McLeon, James 25:204
McLermean, Andrew J. 10:148
McLernican, A. J. 18:53
McLeroy, A. F. 1:54
McLewain, Thomas 20:186
McLin, Benjamin 3:133

McLin, Joshua 22:431
McLind, R. 15:109
McLinn, Isaac F. 24:178
McLley, R. 4:41
McLoan, James H. 20:304
McLolo, Israel 9:165
McLong, James F. 9:122
McLoom, James 13:114
McLoon, Patrick 21:365
McLooney, Ezra 20:138
McLoren, Alexander
  16:45
McLorens, --- 3:133
McLoskey, Caleb 13:129
McLoughlin, Abraham
  12:32
McLoughlin, B. 3:133
McLoughlin, J. 3:133
McLowden, William
  18:246
McLure, --- 21:123
McLutyrd, James 20:85
McM---, J. 25:311
McM---, T. T. 20:84
McMabran, John 12:74
McMack, P. 26:50
McMackin, John 10:126;
  20:304
McMahan, --- 27:81
McMahan, D. 11:101;
  20:58
McMahan, Hugh 10:126
McMahan, James 17:451;
  22:503; 24:179
McMahan, John 22:261
McMahan, M. 14:87;
  17:436; 24:187
McMahan, Mathew F.
  23:158
McMahan, P. 14:87
McMahan, Patrick 15:40
McMahan, Peter 19:178
McMahan, Ralph 17:443;
  24:161
McMahan, Robert 11:408
McMahan, Thomas
  12:156
McMahan, William
  11:328
McMahan, William A.
  20:46
McMahen, Hugh 20:304
McMahern, Samuel
  26:172
McMahon, --- 9:147;
  15:159; 16:13;
  25:288
McMahon, Andrew 7:129;
  18:434
McMahon, B. J. 26:172
McMahon, Bernard 23:41

McMahon, C. L. 3:133
McMahon, E. 15:343;
  16:122, 375
McMahon, Edward 1:58;
  13:36
McMahon, J. 1:55; 4:41;
  23:108
McMahon, James 3:133;
  11:192, 193; 15:213;
  18:104
McMahon, John 10:126;
  15:40; 17:353;
  20:304; 22:13; 24:68
McMahon, Joseph 10:206
McMahon, M. 1:151;
  3:133
McMahon, Michael 13:36
McMahon, N. S. 26:173
McMahon, Owen 24:24
McMahon, P. 1:56, 154;
  8:65; 18:112; 26:171
McMahon, Patrick 1:56;
  9:13; 22:340, 432
McMahon, Peter 10:164;
  16:122
McMahon, Thomas 9:44;
  23:193
McMahon, Timothy
  24:175
McMahon, W. S. 8:65
McMahon, William
  14:194
McMahu, James D.
  11:159
McMaik, P. 18:246
McMain, R. 8:52
McMains, Andrew J.
  23:73
McMains, J. 12:162
McMains, Joseph 8:25
McMakin, Alexander
  17:243
McMaldowry, James 4:41
McMamama, Thomas
  27:85
McMan, Martin 24:68
McMamaman, Henry
  19:25
McManaman, J. 5:23
McManamy, J. P. 25:204
McManary, John P. 5:23
McManers, Mary 26:212
McManes, J. 3:133
McManey, J. 13:94;
  14:278
McManey, Morris 14:194
McManie, F. M. 11:85
McManimus, Peter 16:148
McManis, L. 23:41
McManis, Michael 11:95
McManis, O. J. 23:41

McMann, --- 9:240
McMann, G. B. 11:95
McMann, Harland 7:16
McMann, J. 1:151
McMann, James 22:44
McMann, John 13:114
McMann, M. 1:56; 13:66;
  19:87
McMann, Thomas 15:213;
  19:178
McMann, W. 3:133
McMann, William 10:68;
  20:304
McMannaman, J. 1:53
McMannas, --- 13:36
McMannay, Robert 22:44
McManners, Charles 4:41
McMannis, G. 14:87
McMannis, John 22:91
McMannis, Joseph 18:147
McMannis, R. 16:360a
McManns, A. 7:34
McManns, John 16:213
McMannus, --- 7:63
McMannus, F. 15:213
McMannus, S. 4:41
McMannus, William
  25:311
McManouray, --- 9:112
McManter, John F. 8:108
McManus, F. 15:213
McManus, H. H. 17:393
McManus, James 11:95;
  16:122
McManus, John 7:52;
  13:81; 23:90
McManus, John W. 9:100
McManus, Michael 24:81,
  95
McManus, Mitchell 27:87
McManus, Samuel 3:133
McManus, Thomas 9:186;
  19:257
McManus, William
  11:161; 25:204
McMara, M. 13:94; 14:16;
  16:269
McMara, Patrick 16:99
McMarley, George 19:240
McMarley, William
  18:147
McMarly, George 9:186
McMarn, Daniel 13:114
McMarty, L. B. 26:174
McMary, A. 24:200
McMaspy, S. 13:125
McMaster, C. 18:89
McMaster, G. 1:155
McMaster, George 15:87
McMaster, J. 15:213
McMaster, John 5:23

McMaster, S. 1:155
McMaster, Thomas 5:23
McMasters, J. 16:213
McMasters, John 21:365
McMath, A. C. 9:13
McMath, Robert W. 20:108
McMathews, --- 22:340
McMathews, Francis 26:173
McMay, John 21:278
McMeade, Ezra 7:34
McMeal, John 17:83
McMeans, James 22:497
McMeans, L. 27:89
McMecken, Isaac 9:70
McMeehan, F. 14:265
McMeekin, I. 9:69
McMeene, R. 22:485
McMellan, Legrand 22:207
McMellin, Mitchell 17:232
McMellon, John C. 12:142
McMelon, John 20:11
McMenamen, James 22:340
McMenomy, Arthur 19:178
McMesse, Henry 25:280
McMichael, Amos L. 23:91
McMichael, Edward 5:23
McMichael, G. W. 11:419
McMichael, John 10:68; 20:304; 21:74, 365
McMichael, Joseph 10:126; 20:304
McMichael, Samuel 17:261
McMichael, William 9:86; 23:91; 26:46
McMichel, Hugh 24:24
McMichel, J. H. 4:41
McMilan, J. 8:25
McMilan, Samuel 22:464
McMillan, --- 11:406
McMillan, Albert 26:50
McMillan, Alfred 8:125; 12:61
McMillan, Charles 19:178; 20:304
McMillan, E. F. 17:155
McMillan, Isaac 10:68; 20:304
McMillan, J. A. 3:133
McMillan, John 14:243; 22:44, 207
McMillan, John H. 20:99
McMillan, John O. 17:419

McMillan, Malcom 18:295
McMillan, Malcomb 26:107
McMillan, Manley 12:168
McMillan, Morris 23:158
McMillan, Samuel 7:52; 17:509
McMillan, W. G. 14:87
McMillan, W. J. 14:87
McMillen, A. S. 15:129
McMillen, Adam 21:56
McMillen, Alexander 11:209
McMillen, B. G. 15:364
McMillen, Chancey 10:68; 20:304
McMillen, Charles 10:177
McMillen, David 21:123
McMillen, E. 11:109
McMillen, G. C. 17:292
McMillen, George 7:64
McMillen, George L. 23:41
McMillen, Harvey M. 17:92
McMillen, Henry 7:34
McMillen, J. 18:147
McMillen, J. C. 10:68; 20:304
McMillen, J. C. W. 11:424
McMillen, James 3:133; 17:282; 19:178
McMillen, John 4:41; 11:88, 381; 23:158; 24:160; 27:90
McMillen, John D. 23:158
McMillen, John M. 11:160
McMillen, Joseph 11:328
McMillen, Malcomb 9:37
McMillen, Markins A. 9:72
McMillen, Neal 27:79
McMillen, R. 19:87
McMillen, R. H. 20:147
McMillen, Stafford 23:158
McMillen, William 4:41; 11:328; 20:304
McMillen, William H. 22:91; 23:158
McMillenus, J. F. 9:147
McMiller, Charles 10:126
McMiller, Clark 12:55
McMiller, Cyrus 12:9
McMiller, Jeff. O. 19:25
McMiller, Jonathan 21:229

McMillian, Robert S. 20:126
McMillin, --- 21:167
McMillin, William S. 20:126
McMillinix, Charles 12:32
McMillon, J. F. 3:133
McMillon, John C. 20:304
McMillonos, J. F. 27:81
McMillun, John 8:91
McMiltey, Patrick 15:213
McMinans, P. 7:59
McMinds, W. A. 11:390
McMinds, William W. 21:92
McMinen, S. 19:87
McMinimy, William 22:431
McMinin, S. 15:330
McMinn, G. W. 17:145
McMinnis, James H. 25:334
McMinnis, Kate K. 25:334
McMitchell, Samuel 14:283
McMollan, J. 1:58
McMonagle, Hugh 15:27
McMonagle, James 5:52
McMonghe, James 25:204
McMonk, John 20:151
McMontgomery, John 18:246
McMoor, John 10:68; 20:304
McMoore, Hubbard 18:147
McMorris, Joseph 27:87
McMorris, M. 1:151
McMorrow, John 9:222
McMramy, Hugh 18:192
McMull, James 25:324
McMullan, J. B. 1:153
McMullan, James 3:133
McMullan, John W. 17:23
McMullen, Alexander J. 15:71
McMullen, Amos R. 17:349
McMullen, B. 25:204
McMullen, C. 9:112; 25:204
McMullen, Charles 5:23
McMullen, Daniel 13:36; 16:45
McMullen, G. 8:77
McMullen, I. 24:99
McMullen, John 13:36; 22:208; 23:41
McMullen, John A. 7:34
McMullen, Joseph 16:45

McMullen, L. S. 8:52
McMullen, Leslie 21:140
McMullen, M. 12:100
McMullen, Michael
    18:430
McMullen, Peter 9:112,
    186
McMullen, Poseph A.
    15:279
McMullen, Robert 11:159
McMullen, S. 15:213
McMullen, Thomas 4:41
McMullen, W. W. 3:133
McMullen, William
    22:236
McMullen, Willis 10:68
McMuller, James M.
    13:114
McMullin, Andrew
    11:389
McMullin, F. C. 20:58
McMullin, H. C. 7:34
McMullin, James 14:194
McMullin, Joseph A.
    25:204
McMulto, J. 25:324
McMunint, J. A. 13:66
McMurbie, William G.
    9:37
McMurphy, James 20:114
McMurphy, John 9:86
McMurphy, Lewis 22:282
McMurphy, P. 14:87
McMurray, George 3:133
McMurray, J. 10:187;
    18:177
McMurray, John 14:319;
    25:276
McMurray, Robert 10:34;
    26:223
McMurray, Samuel 4:41;
    8:25; 18:147
McMurray, William J.
    20:304
McMurrey, Andrew B.
    12:156
McMurrin, William 3:133
McMurrow, John 18:371
McMurry, I. C. 24:112
McMurry, John 21:278
McMurry, Samuel 22:261
McMurry, William J.
    10:126
McMurtree, W. G. 26:107
McMurtrie, W. G. 18:295
McMurtry, M. M. 20:304
McMurty, Marion M.
    10:68
McMury, H. B. 23:204
McMustro, William P.
    9:37

McN---, J. 16:113
McNab, C. 25:204
McNab, James 20:18;
    21:365
McNab, John 21:365
McNabb, David 22:261
McNabb, J. 4:41; 27:82
McNabb, James E. 24:42
McNabb, John 20:99
McNabb, Joseph 11:415
McNair, A. 22:485
McNair, C. L. 8:52
McNair, Caleb K. 10:68;
    20:304
McNair, Charles L. 21:74
McNair, George 7:129
McNair, Peter 18:327
McNair, Robert 20:108
McNaley, Peter 13:129
McNaley, Thomas D.
    10:68
McNalley, J. 7:34
McNalley, Peter 23:129
McNally, Andrew 14:195
McNally, Daniel 9:186;
    19:233
McNally, J. 1:154
McNally, John 21:257
McNally, Martin 15:109
McNally, Patrick 19:322
McNally, R. 15:18
McNally, Thomas 8:25;
    18:147
McNally, William 23:41
McNaly, A. 14:195
McNamar, Jacob 26:126
McNamara, Charles
    18:147; 22:44
McNamara, Ephraim
    11:266
McNamara, J. 13:114
McNamara, James 21:365
McNamara, John 15:129;
    23:41
McNamara, M. 1:155;
    19:87; 25:204
McNamara, Martin 23:158
McNamara, Michael
    12:32; 13:135;
    19:347; 22:520
McNamara, P. 1:158;
    3:133; 25:204
McNamara, Patrick 5:23;
    15:213; 25:204
McNamara, T. 1:157
McNamara, Thomas 13:36
McNamara, William 5:23;
    25:204
McNamard, Michael
    19:327
McNamarra, Charles 8:25

McNamary, James 15:152
McNamba, D. 11:161
McNamee, J. 4:41
McNamee, Marston
    20:304
McNamy, R. 3:133
McNamy, T. C. 20:304
McNanamy, Samuel
    11:160
McNanamy, Samuel E.
    7:34
McNanney, James 18:421
McNanny, John 12:170
McNarry, Owen 8:60
McNary, A. 17:455
McNary, Dennis 10:206
McNary, George 22:470
McNary, Jay 22:520
McNary, Joseph 11:336
McNary, M. 22:311
McNasser, Peter 23:123
McNatt, Amplis G. 9:222
McNatt, Andrew 5:23
McNatt, Hezekiah K.
    21:131
McNatt, Thomas R.
    21:131
McNaugh, P. 24:113
McNaughton, A. W. 15:57
McNaughton, Alex. E.
    21:257
McNaughton, David 1:55
McNaughton, Duncan
    21:243
McNauma, Michael
    9:163; 25:324
McNaury, Hugh 19:178
McNeal, A. 22:486
McNeal, Alexander
    14:195
McNeal, Amos 22:432
McNeal, Bristoe 7:129
McNeal, David 9:165
McNeal, Dover 27:84
McNeal, E. R. 7:69
McNeal, F. 15:213
McNeal, George H.
    25:204
McNeal, Hugh 17:423;
    24:173
McNeal, Isaac 22:91
McNeal, Israel C. 24:160
McNeal, J. 7:34; 9:86
McNeal, J. B. 14:289;
    23:41
McNeal, James 14:87
McNeal, James G. 21:75
McNeal, John H. 22:44
McNeal, Livingston
    18:147
McNeal, Mathew 19:25

McNeal, P. 25:204
McNeal, Patrick 15:80
McNeal, Porter 20:42
McNeal, S. L. 13:94
McNeal, Samuel 17:181
McNeal, Thomas 9:86;
  17:429; 18:89;
  24:185
McNeal, William 4:41;
  18:413; 20:183
McNeal, William H. H.
  8:52; 21:75
McNealey, W. 3:133
McNealy, F. 17:96
McNealy, J. J. 19:25
McNealy, W. H. 19:25
McNear, D. 27:84
McNear, Simon 11:37
McNear, Thomas 27:79
McNear, William 11:96
McNeay, John 25:204
McNee, Alexander 23:104
McNeeley, John D. 9:98
McNeely, --- 20:175
McNeely, E. 1:58
McNeely, Henry 24:42
McNeely, M. 17:498
McNeely, Philip 22:340
McNeely, Stephen 23:193
McNeely, Thomas 6:10
McNeely, W. 14:283
McNees, Abner 22:261
McNeese, S. 17:191
McNeff, M. 13:78; 16:213
McNeice, Samuel 1:55
McNeice, William 10:126
McNeigh, William 17:249
McNeil, --- 26:174
McNeil, A. I. 26:107
McNeil, A. Orran 17:47
McNeil, Amos 11:157
McNeil, Andrew J. 18:295
McNeil, Bristow 21:365
McNeil, C. 23:264
McNeil, Cobb 9:165
McNeil, Dorer 9:134
McNeil, Edward 4:41
McNeil, Ephraim 12:32
McNeil, Finley 9:98
McNeil, G. 27:83
McNeil, George H. 5:23
McNeil, H. T. 20:304
McNeil, Hannibal 21:278
McNeil, J. W. 3:133
McNeil, James 8:25;
  18:147; 22:149
McNeil, John 7:129; 8:60;
  12:173
McNeil, Joshua S. 19:338
McNeil, M. 20:304
McNeil, Malcolm 10:68

McNeil, Milton 12:156
McNeil, O. 14:87
McNeil, Owen 12:170
McNeil, Patrick 5:23
McNeil, Perry 20:108
McNeil, Ramsey 4:67
McNeil, VanNess 22:471
McNeil, W. H. 16:375
McNeil, William 16:122;
  22:167
McNeil, William N.
  12:156
McNeiley, James 3:133
McNeill, C. 3:133
McNeilly, J. 2:15; 25:52
McNeir, D. 9:134
McNelley, Ephraim 17:38
McNellis, Francis 10:20
McNelly, G. W. 26:222
McNelly, Henry 8:41
McNelly, J. 20:42
McNelly, Patrick 8:118
McNelly, W. B. 19:87
McNellys, T. 4:41
McNeman, Jacob 9:44
McNerley, Henry 26:171
McNert, Lyman A. 17:38
McNesbitt, W. 1:151
McNess, A. P. 2:15; 25:57
McNess, Mathew 7:34
McNett, A. J. 25:204
McNett, Anson 4:41
McNett, Auplin G. 18:371
McNett, Benjamin 7:16
McNew, Carleton 20:304
McNew, Carlton 10:92
McNew, Henry 6:8;
  10:126; 18:112;
  20:304
McNew, Mark 7:103
McNewman, J. S. 11:381
McNial, I. 26:46
McNial, Samuel A. 11:39
McNichol, A. 1:154
McNichols, J. 22:44
McNickle, Robert 7:63
McNicol, Duncan 20:35
McNiece, William 20:304
McNiel, Abraham 20:92
McNiel, Andrew 9:37
McNiel, G. 9:147
McNiel, James B. 20:114
McNiel, R. W. 1:56
McNight, L. G. 8:52
McNight, Robert J. 9:37
McNilse, J. H. 3:133
McNinney, Arthur 7:34
McNish, J. 16:140
McNitt, B. 9:56
McNitt, Horace 22:149
McNitt, J. B. 20:151

McNomont, Elijah 4:41
McNorth, G. S. 1:154
McNorton, A. W. 12:74
McNorton, D. 4:41
McNorton, J. 9:186
McNown, John 20:193
McNown, Robert 10:210
McNuir, David 22:44
McNult, William 14:87
McNultey, John 20:304
McNulty, --- 15:263;
  22:521
McNulty, C. 19:87
McNulty, D. 1:60
McNulty, E. 15:315
McNulty, Eugene 15:213
McNulty, Francis 9:86;
  26:46
McNulty, George 26:174
McNulty, J. 6:32; 9:147;
  27:81
McNulty, J. D. S. 1:54
McNulty, J. R. 1:151
McNulty, James 7:59;
  19:26
McNulty, John 10:68
McNulty, M. 20:304
McNulty, Michael 10:68
McNulty, P. 23:158
McNulty, Patrick 23:12
McNulty, Peter 10:127;
  20:304
McNulty, Thomas 23:104
McNurlen, John T. 25:204
McNurtney, Michael
  23:73
McNut, Samuel 17:107
McNutt, J. 1:58
McNutt, J. H. 21:34
McNutt, John 16:122
McNutt, John H. 13:36
McNutt, Oscar H. 22:433
McNutty, --- 3:133
McNutty, William M.
  22:261
McOawn, F. 27:79
McOlister, Isaac 15:213
McOmber, J. 9:147
McOmber, John M.
  11:109
McOmbre, J. 27:83
McOreen, J. R. 15:174
McOrtar, J. C. 21:167
McOune, J. C. 14:283
McOwen, B. 16:45
McOwen, Barnard 13:36
McPage, --- 1:151
McPark, W. W. 17:108
McPeak, George 22:485
McPeak, Hugh 10:164;
  19:178

McPeak, J. 22:208
McPeak, John B. 17:211
McPeak, L. 12:32
McPeck, H. P. 3:133
McPelston, John 10:127; 20:305
McPhail, Enos 24:24
McPhail, H. C. 4:41
McPhail, W. H. 8:52
McPhail, William 11:109
McPharson, Daniel 18:192
McPharson, John 21:365
McPhedridge, J. H. 9:222; 18:372
McPhee, John 19:87
McPheeters, Thomas J. 20:115
McPheeton, Samuel 13:36
McPheison, John L. 9:86
McPheonan, Hiram 17:135; 24:200
McPherran, J. 1:155
McPherson, --- 12:168; 15:355
McPherson, A. 22:311
McPherson, Aaron 10:177; 19:178
McPherson, Alexander 17:402
McPherson, Angus 22:149
McPherson, Aptner 21:278
McPherson, Austin T. 10:127; 20:305
McPherson, Charles 15:94; 21:365
McPherson, D. 1:152; 3:133
McPherson, Daniel H. 12:32
McPherson, George 13:36; 21:34
McPherson, H. A. 19:87
McPherson, Henry 22:311
McPherson, Henry C. 21:229
McPherson, J. F. 20:27
McPherson, J. H. R. 11:424
McPherson, James 1:59
McPherson, James W. 22:91
McPherson, Jesse 17:162
McPherson, John 7:59; 8:101; 9:162; 11:244; 12:32; 17:463; 21:34; 24:178
McPherson, John B. 11:389

McPherson, Leander 21:229
McPherson, Mathew 11:267
McPherson, Napoleon 21:206
McPherson, Peter 22:282
McPherson, Phinley 15:23
McPherson, Samuel I. 26:145
McPherson, Thomas 24:42
McPherson, W. W. 9:56
McPherson, William 3:133
McPherson, William L. 22:208
McPherson, Wright 7:69
McPhertus, C. 22:524
McPheter, Alexander 25:204
McPheters, William H. 25:53
McPhetis, Warren A. 15:11
McPhsil, John 11:328
McPhurson, Alex. 8:108
McPintler, Frank 11:122
McPowell, James 20:24
McPown, John 16:213
McPugh, John 16:45
McQuaade, Henry 14:336
McQuade, Barney 23:123
McQuade, F. 27:82
McQuade, Felix 18:438, 440
McQuade, H. 9:147; 27:81
McQuade, I. C. 8:119
McQuade, John 12:65
McQuade, P. 9:147
McQuade, Smith 10:174; 19:178
McQuade, Thomas 12:65; 15:40
McQuade, William 16:299
McQuaid, George P. 17:23
McQuaid, Robert H. 22:465
McQuaide, Charles 21:365
McQuany, Michael 14:195
McQuarn, John 22:261
McQuart, Lewis 24:200
McQuary, Charles 20:305
McQuay, W. H. 4:41
McQueen, --- 12:156
McQueen, Calvin 22:91
McQueen, E. 13:114

McQueen, J. 4:41; 18:53; 21:366
McQueen, James 12:74; 15:40
McQueen, Jesse 17:232
McQueen, John 17:237, 282
McQueen, Michael 17:243
McQueen, William 17:55
McQueen, Z. 10:68
McQueens, Godfrey F. 22:261
McQueeny, W. 3:133
McQuen, William A. 8:118
McQuerrie, A. 7:103
McQuestion, Clinton 15:18
McQuestion, Jerome B. 9:7
McQuestion, Samuel 9:8
McQuigg, John 9:56
McQuigly, John 3:133
McQuillan, Lewis 9:26
McQuillan, W. H. 4:41
McQuillen, A. 3:133
McQuillen, Frank 9:147
McQuillen, John 17:319; 25:52
McQuillen, M. 9:215
McQuillen, Richard 15:109
McQuillin, J. 2:15
McQuilly, Jerry 9:209
McQuinlan, M. 21:366
McQuinn, J. 14:87
McQuinn, John 13:115
McQuinn, Theodore 21:366
McQuinnan, Paul 23:193
McQuinty, James 18:426
McQuister, Alexander 22:408
McQuister, George W. 22:353
McQuistern, David 22:236
McQuistion, L. H. 13:125
McQuiston, William 15:213
McQune, A. 1:152
McRae, Alex. 8:121
McRae, C. 1:152
McRae, Christopher 8:120
McRae, Daniel 19:178
McRae, Duncan H. 20:18
McRamara, M. 27:82
McRath, J. 3:133
McRay, --- 15:351
McRay, Daniel 11:69

McRay, John H. 20:305
McRay, P. 15:213
McRay, W. W. 20:177
McRay, William 15:57
McRea, R. A. 20:301
McReady, G. 9:228
McReddy, --- 15:174
McRee, C. R. 27:91
McRevar, James 12:171
McRey, --- 15:355
McReynolds, Antony
    10:146
McReynolds, Edw. 11:209
McReynolds, John 16:45
McReynolds, Lewis
    11:209
McReynolds, Peter 17:38
McReynolds, Robert
    21:56, 257
McReynolds, W. T.
    18:177
McRight, John H. 24:81
McRiley, Daniel 16:45
McRiley, Samuel 16:45
McRill, J. L. 23:158
McRinney, William S.
    12:156
McRitchie, George R.
    23:158
McRiver, J. B. 20:305
McRoberts, H. 5:52
McRoberts, Hugh R.
    23:158
McRoberts, John 18:464
McRoberts, Robert 20:31
McRorey, James 10:127
McRorie, William 17:496
McRory, James 20:305
McRoy, J. 1:154
McRoy, William 11:70
McRuine, T. J. 25:204
McRunnels, --- 26:50
McRunnels, John 18:246
McSane, --- 19:178
McSay, Eli 25:324
McSellen, H. C. 21:195
McShaffren, W. 15:159
McShane, B. 3:133
McShane, Daniel 22:13
McShane, James 22:149
McShane, W. 25:204
McShane, William 5:23
McShea, John 21:366
McShedd, Frank 9:186
McSheery, William 10:20
McSher---, John 23:181
McSherry, Bernard
    21:366
McSherry, Hiram B. 17:55
McSherry, James 5:52
McShinn, F. 15:259

McShirley, W. 13:114
McShore, H. 9:147
McSill, Peter 18:192
McSirley, James 10:127;
    20:305
McSkerber, William
    16:213
McSline, B. P. 11:389
McSnigley, David 11:183
McSockley, James 25:269
McSorley, G. W. 3:133
McSorley, Joe 25:204
McSorly, D. 3:133
McSoul, John 21:366
McSpadden, John 22:261
McSpadden, S. 1:60
McSpadding, William
    3:133
McSparin, Lilburn W.
    21:34
McStarnie, Henry 17:83
McStone, Henry 1:53
McStowell, W. 9:186
McSweeney, John 18:460
McSweeney, Michael
    13:36
McSweeting, Daniel 7:103
McSwiggin, John 12:32
McTagart, M. S. 13:66
McTaggort, M. 19:87
McTammany, Francis
    18:89
McTammey, B. 14:87
McTarrish, C. 19:178
McTarvish, H. J. 19:87
McTash, James 11:157
McTauge, D. 4:41
McTeer, Harvey 21:34
McTeer, William 25:334
McTerren, G. 14:16
McThompson, Allen
    17:149
McThompson, W. 25:57
McThompson, William
    2:15
McThorton, James L.
    18:147
McTier, J. 3:133
McTierman, J. 7:34
McTigue, T. 1:151
McTyle, Michael 13:36
McUmber, L. R. 22:149
McUne, William 7:103
McUnis, Alfred 22:261
McUtcher, C. D. 15:129
McVagh, J. 1:157
McVain, James 14:87
McVannan, C. B. 19:26
McVaugh, J. 1:59
McVaugh, J. H. 14:27
McVaugh, N. 11:39

McVay, Edward 11:266
McVay, Ira 12:59
McVay, John 14:87;
    17:111
McVay, M. 1:156
McVay, M. D. L. 11:320
McVay, W. 22:497
McVay, William 11:95
McVean, Collins C.
    23:193
McVean, D. J. 1:59
McVee, James 19:343
McVeigh, --- 19:87
McVeigh, Charles 25:56
McVeigh, J. 12:96;
    15:360
McVeigh, James 21:366
McVery, --- 10:211
McVery, John 15:71
McVety, William 12:74;
    15:40
McVey, --- 10:153
McVey, Daniel 13:36
McVey, Darius 23:73
McVey, James 18:192
McVey, John 10:20;
    20:99
McVey, R. 3:133
McVey, Thomas 21:56
McVey, William 9:234;
    16:133; 18:430
McViay, John 5:52
McVicar, Clay 9:122;
    27:86
McVicar, James 15:152
McVicar, Robert 27:89
McVicars, Robert 9:162
McVickar, William 16:45
McVicker, Daniel 22:407
McVicker, John 22:44
McVicker, Moses 11:95
McVicker, W. 17:38
McVickers, Alpheas
    16:152
McVitty, Joseph 11:183
McWade, James 14:195
McWade, Robert 15:307;
    19:87
McWair, --- 17:254
McWalten, Charles H.
    9:44
McWatt, Joseph 8:91
McWethey, Bates 22:149
McWharton, Charles
    26:127
McWharton, H. 21:366
McWhinney, Thomas
    23:108
McWhinney, William H.
    15:263
McWhister, A. F. 22:261

McWhister, M. Q. 9:56
McWhorter, James S. 8:25
McWhorter, John 23:252
McWhorter, Thomas 24:24
McWhorton, James S. 26:173
McWhorton, William 20:11
McWillan, A. S. 12:123
McWilliams, Alex 12:32
McWilliams, B. 1:56
McWilliams, C. 16:213
McWilliams, Charles A. 23:73
McWilliams, David 23:158
McWilliams, Elijah 23:41
McWilliams, Franklin 21:229
McWilliams, George 18:434
McWilliams, H. 3:133
McWilliams, H. H. 21:95
McWilliams, J. G. 1:57
McWilliams, Jerry 17:181
McWilliams, John 9:86; 26:50
McWilliams, N. 9:67
McWilliams, R. N. 20:193
McWilliams, T. 12:100
McWilliams, Warren 15:109
McWilliams, William 7:59; 10:68; 17:232; 18:413; 20:305
McWillian, J. S. 14:131
McWilson, --- 3:133
McWilson, L. 18:452
McWithey, R. 14:195
McWithey, William 22:149
McWitkin, N. 16:122
McWyan, --- 14:87
McWyner, I. 14:87
Me---, John 15:215
Mea---er, Jacob 23:123
Meabe, William 22:261
Meace, S. E. 10:68; 20:308
Meach, A. J. 3:134
Meach, Fayeth 8:25
Meach, Nicholas 14:197
Meach, William 23:73
Meachain, Eldridge F 15:58
Meacham, E. 17:473
Meacham, John 7:14; 11:292
Meacham, Orbin C. 11:38

Meachan, E. 14:301; 27:88
Meacher, H. 12:147
Meacher, Henry 19:304
Meachim, J. D. 15:214
Meachum, J. H. 1:60
Meachum, Peter 21:195
Mead, --- 15:214
Mead, A. J. 24:81
Mead, Almond 21:141
Mead, Andrew 21:366
Mead, Andrew J. 1:53
Mead, Angil P. 9:186
Mead, C. A. 23:41
Mead, C. M. 11:39
Mead, Charles 9:98
Mead, Charles E. 16:82; 19:87
Mead, Charles S. 11:403
Mead, D. 1:156
Mead, D. H. 13:115
Mead, E. 1:153
Mead, Ebenezer 10:20
Mead, Edward 15:40
Mead, Edwin R. 18:220
Mead, Fay 11:109
Mead, Fletcher 9:122
Mead, Francis 13:58
Mead, Fred 20:308
Mead, Frederick 10:127
Mead, G. 3:134
Mead, George 4:41; 8:52; 21:92
Mead, George M. D. 21:114
Mead, George W. 16:375; 22:162
Mead, H. C. 19:257
Mead, H. G. 3:134
Mead, Henry 12:32
Mead, Henry R. 19:26
Mead, Henry W. 9:186; 11:158; 19:257
Mead, Hiram 23:158
Mead, Hyronimus 21:128
Mead, Ira S. 7:34
Mead, J. 1:156; 13:94
Mead, J. H. 4:41; 16:99
Mead, Jacob 10:127; 20:308
Mead, Jacob R. 17:405
Mead, James 18:89
Mead, James M. 21:257
Mead, John 1:55; 17:356; 22:150
Mead, John N. 11:109
Mead, Joseph 16:213
Mead, L. 1:153; 10:148; 18:53
Mead, Levi 23:41
Mead, Levi H. 23:41

Mead, Lyman 15:279; 25:207
Mead, Michael E. 8:25
Mead, Nathaniel C. 22:150
Mead, P. 3:133
Mead, Philip 21:34
Mead, Ransom 21:257
Mead, S. S. 1:156
Mead, Samuel 21:257
Mead, Stephen 11:128
Mead, Sylvester 10:127; 20:309
Mead, T. S. 1:155
Mead, Thomas J. 22:91
Mead, W. 19:180
Mead, Well 15:214
Mead, William 9:134; 25:279; 27:84
Mead, William A. 21:366
Mead, William H. 19:26
Mead, Zacheus 22:150
Meaddors, Gamalien 17:23
Meade, D. 11:220
Meade, Ephraim 12:32
Meade, Fletcher 27:86
Meade, G. 1:56
Meade, H. W. 11:157
Meade, Hiram 10:127; 20:309
Meade, Horace 25:207
Meade, James E. 5:23
Meade, John 13:127; 17:39
Meade, L. 14:89
Meade, Luther 24:95
Meade, M. W. 11:39
Meade, Michael E. 18:149
Meade, Samuel 18:113
Meade, Thomas 10:164; 19:180
Meader, A. L. 25:301
Meader, Francis G. 19:229
Meader, George Thomas 26:223
Meader, J. H. 1:153
Meader, John 17:405
Meader, Stephen H. 13:36
Meader, W. F. 15:366
Meades, R. 10:28; 19:304
Meadley, Paul 23:271
Meadon, Charles S. 25:207
Meador, Charles E. 27:79
Meador, H. H. 18:372
Meador, Herman H. 9:222
Meador, Iradill 9:222; 18:372
Meador, Marvin P. 21:34

Meador, W. F. 12:100
Meadore, Craig 21:86
Meadors, John 11:341
Meadow, B. F. 9:227;
18:372
Meadow, Francis W.
18:372
Meadow, James A. 8:52
Meadow, John 3:133
Meadowcroft, George R.
9:104
Meadows, Andrew 22:311
Meadows, D. 14:322
Meadows, David 23:73
Meadows, F. 27:82
Meadows, Francis W.
9:223
Meadows, Hosea 20:309
Meadows, Isaac 17:282
Meadows, John W.
22:504
Meadows, R. 18:113
Meadows, Robert 13:76
Meadows, Taylor 11:396
Meadows, Thomas 9:37;
18:295; 26:107
Meadows, W. L. 3:224;
17:505
Meadows, William
17:282; 19:180
Meagher, Daniel 19:87;
23:12
Meagher, John 13:36
Meagher, S. 19:180
Meagher, T. 4:41; 21:164
Meagher, William 22:340
Meagles, Edward 27:89
Meahan, John 25:207
Meaher, Daniel 15:313
Meains, E. M. 18:285
Meak, Enoch M. 23:158
Meaker, E. H. 3:134
Meal, John 3:134
Mealey, E. 1:154
Mealey, James 22:44
Mealier, Abner 22:174
Mealins, Stephen 25:207
Meals, Samuel 20:46
Mealy, S. G. 15:214
Meamy, P. 19:257
Mean, William 9:44;
26:126
Meaning, William H. 9:86
Meanor, James F. 23:158
Meanor, Robert 8:119
Means, A. O. 15:343;
16:375
Means, C. 19:87
Means, David J. 23:114
Means, Dennis 7:129
Means, George 11:208

Means, Henry W. 15:71
Means, Ira 21:366
Means, Isaac 22:311
Means, James 15:18
Means, James M. 22:487
Means, John 11:160;
15:14
Means, John W. 21:257
Means, Peter 21:279
Means, T. 1:54
Means, Thomas 20:309
Means, William 11:37
Meany, John 21:366
Meare, J. H. 3:134
Meares, George 4:41
Mearklin, William 10:68;
20:309
Mearman, Charles 10:127;
20:309
Mears, Edwin 9:98
Mears, F. A. 21:366
Mears, G. 19:240
Mears, George W. 18:398
Mears, Griffin 20:309
Mears, H. 1:156
Mears, Isam 20:309
Mears, Isom 10:68
Mears, James M. 16:75
Mears, Rufus 14:197
Mears, W. F. 23:204
Mearshorn, J. 14:283
Mearson, William 7:103
Mease, Christopher
23:181
Measels, Haywood 10:170
Measey, Peter 9:134
Measles, Hayward 19:180
Measles, James 3:134
Meater, E. 1:154
Meath, Fayette 18:149
Mebbill, A. B. 11:245
Mec, William 3:134
Mecalaix, Alexander
14:197
Mecay, John S. 24:81
Mechael, --- 15:14
Mechan, John A. 22:208
Mechel, R. 9:243
Mecher, Henry 9:157
Mechin, Edward P. 10:68
Mechum, George 27:88
Meck, C. W. 26:49
Meck, J. 3:134
Meck, Robert 3:134
Meckback, --- 15:94
Mecker, --- 14:331
Meckle, S. 1:156
Meckler, J. 1:154
Meckley, G. 19:87
Mecon, Marion M. 7:103
Mecum, William 13:36

Medara, C. E. 20:309
Medard, C. E. 10:37
Medaris, James A. 22:91
Medcaff, D. 21:34
Medcalf, Benedict 17:55
Medcalf, Charles 11:95
Medcalf, Frederick 9:122
Medcalf, Oliver 3:134
Meddah, George 21:366
Meddah, James 21:366
Meddaugh, C. 1:54
Meddaugh, Jonathan
17:161
Medden, Clark D. 7:103
Medden, George W.
10:127
Medder, J. 16:269
Meddlers, Lawrence J.
21:366
Medearis, John W. 21:103
Medergron, James 16:213
Medernacy, Mathew
11:20
Medford, Albert 16:46
Medford, J. 11:39
Medham, John 14:89
Medlam, F. 3:134
Medlen, George W.
22:167
Medler, Joseph 25:54
Medler, N. 3:134
Medley, Adison 10:127;
20:309
Medley, E. 22:311
Medley, Henry 10:99
Medley, J. A. 27:83
Medley, J. H. 9:147
Medley, Lawrence W.
10:8
Medlicut, John 22:236
Medlin, Francis 16:46
Medlin, George W. 20:46
Medlin, William A.
10:127; 20:309
Medlock, Daniel 20:143
Medlock, David E.
10:127; 20:309
Medlock, Nelson 8:77
Medlock, Reuben 11:409
Medock, George 4:41
Medor, Daniel 22:503
Medows, David 14:316
Medows, Hosea 10:68
Medows, John A. 15:87
Medows, Robert 16:213
Medrew, W. 3:134
Medster, Isaac 26:46
Medura, Esham 7:129
Medus, Isaac 7:129
Mee, George 11:424
Mee, P. 14:89

Mee, Thomas 3:224; 17:505
Mee, William 1:55
Mee, William R. 22:454
Meece, Henry F. 17:149
Meech, C. K. 15:109
Meechan, Thomas 1:55
Meed, Ebenezer 20:147
Meed, J. 14:17
Meed, James W. 14:197
Meed, Mich 14:197
Meed, Riley 17:237
Meeds, Lorenzo 8:118
Meedville, Joseph 14:197
Meegan, James 14:89
Meegers, David 14:336
Meehan, Charles 18:413
Meehan, John 5:23; 14:236
Meehan, Samuel B. 1:56
Meehan, William 1:53
Meehe, James 11:414
Meehen, Robert 14:89
Meeher, --- 25:54
Meek, --- 23:314
Meek, A. J. 9:26; 18:312; 26:105
Meek, C. W. 18:246
Meek, Charles 12:54
Meek, David 3:134
Meek, Gideon 11:159
Meek, John 18:246; 26:49
Meek, Robert 23:41
Meek, Robert N. 23:73
Meek, Samuel 10:92; 20:309; 23:73
Meek, William A. 11:157
Meeke, E. 14:89
Meeken, Peter B. 5:23
Meeker, B. 13:66; 19:87
Meeker, Benjamin F. 22:208
Meeker, Charles 18:34
Meeker, Charles H. 7:34
Meeker, Charles S. 9:13
Meeker, D. 1:60
Meeker, David B. 23:91
Meeker, Glove L. 18:372
Meeker, H. C. 4:41
Meeker, James 8:117
Meeker, Joseph 8:91
Meeker, Lorenzo D. 22:167
Meeker, Moses C. 23:73
Meeker, O. 15:214
Meeker, Thomas V. 9:161
Meeker, Thomas W. 14:327
Meeker, VanBuren 22:208
Meeker, Zenas 18:330
Meekin, P. B. 25:207

Meeking, John 7:81
Meeks, --- 17:237
Meeks, David J. 19:26
Meeks, John 22:208, 454
Meeks, L. M. 20:309
Meeks, Lorenzo M. 10:68
Meeks, Matthew 21:230
Meel, --- 25:286
Meelen, Abraham 26:170
Meelen, William W. 18:285
Meels, Charles 5:52
Meenan, Edward 23:100
Meer, Jose 27:80
Meese, J. 21:34
Meese, James L. 14:197
Meesel, H. 11:308
Meesinger, Isaac 23:41
Meetey, J. O. 11:128
Meff, William O. 9:186
Mefford, Abraham 21:34
Mefford, J. 3:134
Megan, Albert 12:32
Megan, I. 14:197
Megan, Michael 27:90
Megarah, J. S. 1:153
Megarga, Joseph 19:26
Megay, James 5:42
Megee, William 9:186
Megel, A. W. 20:309
Megent, J. 14:301; 17:476
Meger, I. 14:197
Megermider, Joseph 18:149
Megett, Nathan W. 10:68
Megey, J. 25:207
Meghan, R. 13:94
Megin, Mack 18:246; 26:48
Meginny, J. 4:41
Megonigal, A. 1:57
Megram, W. H. 3:134
Megrureden, Joseph 8:25
Mehaffey, J. 7:52
Mehaffey, William 11:246
Mehaffy, J. M. 3:134
Mehan, B. 3:134
Mehan, J. 18:34
Mehan, Leonard 9:186
Mehan, W. 1:157
Mehen, Ellis 1:55
Mehen, John 11:157
Meherly, John 22:91
Mehihop, Henry 5:23
Mehl, George 6:32; 25:324
Mehler, Augustus 10:68; 20:309
Mehlhop, H. 25:207
Mehn, J. 1:58
Mehoffey, D. D. 13:77

Mehoffner, J. 26:47
Mehoney, S. 2:14
Meichling, L. 26:46
Meidenhouser, Jacob 5:53
Meier, A. J. 24:59
Meier, Gustave F. 11:128
Meier, J. 13:94
Meier, John 24:68
Meier, K. 23:158
Meiering, Joseph 21:123
Meighan, William 23:16
Meigs, Abner G. 24:25
Meigs, Henry E. 24:95
Meigs, John H. 13:36
Meigs, M. 21:366
Meikleson, Andrew 6:23
Meilander, John 23:181
Meiller, John 22:208
Meily, Addison 11:183
Meily, George E. 24:25
Mein, John 14:89
Mein, W. 3:134
Meine, William S. 10:20
Meinechoen, H. 20:309
Meins, M. B. 21:366
Meinseig, J. 10:187
Meinshatt, A. 23:158
Meir, Michael 21:257
Meirs, Jacob 9:56
Meirs, William 14:197
Meis, Albert 19:180
Meise, C. 16:375
Meisee, Abram B. 22:433
Meisee, Nathan 22:433
Meisenhelden, N. 27:88
Meisfen, William 19:180
Meisinhelder, N. 14:301; 17:478
Meisner, Adam 8:52
Meisner, C. 14:89
Meissner, Herman 16:375
Meister, C. 1:59
Meister, Henry 17:83
Meitsinger, J. 11:278
Meitz, E. 9:112
Meitz, W. 4:41
Meitzler, Francis 13:36
Mekell, G. 11:39
Mekey, Joseph 18:398
Mekly, U. A. 7:59
Melaeast, Charles 19:26
Melan, John 9:243
Melancon, Philip 21:366
Melane, Carroll 21:217
Melansen, Philip 7:129
Melay, James 8:52
Melber, Leo 19:87
Melchen, James 16:99
Melcher, Andrew 8:52
Melcher, Edward 12:32
Melcher, F. 16:280

Melcher, Frederick 15:353; 16:280
Melchior, Marienne 21:366
Meldour, Morris 21:366
Meldower, D. 3:134
Melen, John 18:312
Melendy, L. 1:60
Melendy, Wesley 9:122
Meler, Conrad 18:407
Melesten, Edene 19:180
Melette, Huson W. 14:197
Meley, Michael 23:41
Meley, Washington J. 13:60
Melhen, Henry 20:87
Melhollen, Charles 10:127; 20:309
Melhose, George 18:209
Melich, J. P. 20:179
Melick, Lyman 17:321
Melick, Thomas 10:127; 20:309
Melie, Joseph O. 5:23
Melin, A. 3:134
Melinger, C. 16:213
Melins, W. 3:134
Meliza, Barry 10:68
Meliza, David 21:75
Melizor, B. 20:309
Melkin, James 12:32
Mell, Fred 19:87
Mell, John R. 22:44
Mell, William 7:52
Mellan, J. M. 13:81
Mellar, W. 1:157
Mellard, J. 14:197
Mellen, Abraham 8:41
Mellen, Franklin H. 22:408
Mellen, H. F. 1:95
Mellen, Henry W. 21:257
Mellen, James 8:25; 18:149; 26:170
Mellen, John 15:327
Mellen, Joseph 23:158
Mellen, Proctor 5:23
Mellen, Sidney 15:18
Mellen, William A. 15:336
Meller, Samson 17:361
Mellers, G. P. 26:45
Mellett, Calvin 21:230
Mellinger, Benedict 12:156
Mellinger, Charles 13:125
Mellinger, John H. 3:134
Mellinger, Manuel 22:434
Mellinger, W. 1:151
Mellis, J. W. 21:366
Mellis, James 23:73

Mellis, John 16:213
Melliver, John S. 12:59
Mellon, Frederick 23:123
Mellon, Henry 21:243
Mellon, J. 1:154
Mellon, M. 16:213
Mellon, William 23:286
Mellot, Frederick 15:71
Mellotte, Seymour H. 21:366
Melman, Carlos 12:74
Melman, Charles 15:27
Melody, E. N. 7:34
Melody, P. 14:243
Melofen, Edene 10:177
Melofen, William 10:177
Melon, William H. 11:39
Melond, William M. C. 11:407
Melondey, Wesley 27:85
Melone, Henry 13:36
Melonson, J. 7:52
Melott, E. 25:57
Melott, Edward E. 23:73
Melott, Norris E. 22:91
Melott, William Stephen 20:99
Meloy, J. H. 23:41
Meloy, Lemuel M. 21:103
Melsom, M. 1:156
Melson, David 8:65
Melson, John 8:25
Melstaff, C. 3:134
Melt, Enos F. 9:26; 18:312; 26:107
Meltenberger, M. 3:134
Melton, Aaron B. 21:34
Melton, Albin 22:91
Melton, D. 25:207
Melton, E. H. 9:243
Melton, G. 17:506
Melton, James 10:92; 20:309
Melton, James F. 22:261
Melton, John 20:138
Melton, Joseph 4:41
Melton, Joseph L. 17:274
Melton, L. B. 21:34
Melton, Reuben O. 20:18
Melton, Robert 13:36
Melton, Thomas 9:56
Melton, V. H. 23:307
Melton, W. M. 3:134
Melton, William 15:8
Meltor, Frederick 9:98
Melveeny, Matthew 9:15
Melville, --- 13:36; 16:46
Melville, George 22:311
Melville, James 4:41
Melville, William 18:69
Melvin, A. P. 14:197

Melvin, Charles I. 10:68; 20:309
Melvin, E. 10:32; 20:309
Melvin, Enos P. 22:465
Melvin, F. 11:333
Melvin, George P. 21:257
Melvin, J. A. 1:99
Melvin, J. C. 1:156
Melvin, J. H. 22:208
Melvin, James R. 22:91
Melvin, John B. 21:366
Melvin, L. 3:134
Melvin, Oscar B. 24:95
Melvin, S. K. 16:280
Melvin, Wallace J. 20:99
Melvin, Wilmot 9:186
Memack, O. G. 11:70
Memen, J. N. 15:214
Memezt, W. 3:134
Meminn, Frank 23:41
Mempel, H. 9:147
Memphil, A. 27:80
Menaghan, J. 1:53
Menard, Henry 16:300
Menard, J. 21:204
Menard, John L. 1:53
Menard, Joseph A. 22:407
Mench, C. 3:134
Mench, John 5:24
Mencher, C. 21:366
Mencsh, William 19:180
Mendall, William 8:91
Mendarez, --- 19:322
Menday, David 9:165
Mende, James B. 23:193
Mendell, --- 10:164
Mendell, Dennis 17:459; 24:153
Mendell, Ira 10:68
Mendell, Lucien 10:127; 20:309
Mendell, Noah E. 9:100
Mendenall, W. S. 21:34
Mendenhall, George 24:62
Mendenhall, J. B. 12:142
Mendenhall, Jacob D. 20:309
Mendenhall, John 24:42
Mendenhall, John T. 23:91
Mendenhall, Jona 12:32
Mendenhall, K. 14:316; 322
Mendenhall, Kelita 23:73
Mender, A. L. 7:75
Mender, Frank 21:201
Menderhall, Diamond 8:99
Mendill, Ira 20:309
Mendin, Decatur 22:44

Mendle, Dennis 8:101
Mendlestein, M. 1:55
Mendlick, Rudolph 1:55
Mendro, Alexander 9:134
Mendrum, George 22:524
MeNeal, D. 1:151
Menear, L. B. 3:134
Menedill, C. 13:94
Menels, James 26:172
Menepee, Henry 20:35
Mener, J. G. 3:134
Menex, J. 3:134
Meng, Philip 13:36
Meng, Phillip 16:46
Mengall, R. 14:89
Menger, N. 14:89
Menger, Wi. A. 13:94
Mengerdorf, Peter 9:26
Mengill, Peter 10:164;
    19:180
Mengt, Wi. 14:197
Menhall, Aaron 11:267
Menhardt, J. 14:89
Menia, John 13:36
Meniller, D. 7:34
Meniman, Frank 14:289
Menk, J. 14:90
Menk, W. 3:134
Menkelberg, Henry
    15:294
Menklebery, Henry
    16:213
Menlford, John 8:25
Mennan, W. H. 9:26
Menner, Jacob 3:134
Mennett, William R.
    22:407
Mennin, John 17:215
Menning, Oscar 9:44
Menning, William H.
    26:46
Mennings, Peter 17:72
Mennon, Herman 14:197
Menon, Charles 18:34
Menor, E. 1:158
Menorast, John 12:32
Menoth, G. 1:56
Menrise, J. 18:312
Mensburger, William 1:53
Mensch, Charles M. 10:20
Menses, George W.
    11:245
Mensie, Charles 9:44
Mensing, Adolph G. E.
    18:89
Mensing, Reinhardin
    26:223
Mensing, Siegfred 26:223
Mensinger, George
    21:366
Menson, D. 17:55

Mensten, Alfred 25:286
Mensur, Samuel 22:208
Mentague, B. 17:292
Menter, George H.
    10:127; 20:309
Mentha, James 15:353
Mentle, Frederick 21:230
Mentle, G. 3:134
Mentmeyer, Charles
    26:171
Mentor, Henry 13:115
Mentor, Robert H. 20:115
Mentry, Henry 21:366
Mentsminger, I. 11:69
Mentz, E. B. 10:68;
    20:310
Mentz, Kaspar 20:309
Mentz, Kasper 10:68
Mentz, Margaret 26:223
Mentz, Maria 18:427
Mentz, Stephen 14:236
Mentzer, John B. 13:36
Menure, Frederick 13:127
Menyman, Lashing 9:165
Menza, Thomas A. 11:39
Menzel, Ernest 7:34
Menzie, A. 3:134
Menzie, Charles 26:126
Mepp, W. 21:195
Meranda, J. L. 26:173
Merandi, D. F. 11:160
Meranes, Joseph 9:44
Merarity, John 22:340
Meravy, James 11:161
Mercan, David 9:13
Mercer, A. F. 23:158
Mercer, A. T. 24:82
Mercer, Alfred 18:89
Mercer, B. J. 5:43
Mercer, Cyrus 10:68;
    20:309
Mercer, Daniel 15:214
Mercer, E. A. 22:208
Mercer, Francis 23:158
Mercer, George 10:68;
    12:74; 15:71; 20:309
Mercer, H. F. 11:161
Mercer, Hamilton 9:86
Mercer, J. 1:154
Mercer, J. D. 19:87
Mercer, J. E. 10:192
Mercer, J. M. 13:115
Mercer, James 22:261
Mercer, James B. 19:26
Mercer, James P. 12:59
Mercer, John 3:134;
    9:122; 12:156;
    14:197, 258; 21:75;
    27:86
Mercer, John J. 20:309
Mercer, John L. 10:92

Mercer, Joseph H. 22:113
Mercer, L. 23:41
Mercer, Levi J. 15:87
Mercer, Mahlon H. 24:42
Mercer, R. U. 23:158
Mercer, R. W. 23:41
Mercer, Simon 22:13
Mercer, T. J. 23:158
Mercer, Thomas 15:214
Mercer, William 1:54
Mercer, William A. 10:68
Mercer, Wilson S. 22:208;
    23:158
Mercerner, Charles 3:134
Merchant, A. 1:153
Merchant, Aaron 21:257
Merchant, D. 20:147
Merchant, David D. 23:91
Merchant, F. 22:464
Merchant, Francis 22:464
Merchant, G. S. 13:115
Merchant, George E.
    25:275
Merchant, John 21:230
Merchant, N. Y. 12:74
Merchant, W. 7:35
Merchant, W. H. 9:215
Merchant, Wiley B.
    20:309
Merchant, William 3:134;
    21:366
Mercheiser, --- 25:53
Mercher, B. F. 25:207
Mercugat, C. A. 14:90
Merd, A. 17:282
Meredeth, J. S. 1:58
Meredeth, Taylor 21:230
Meredink, John M. 22:509
Meredith, A. 14:90
Meredith, A. J. 22:126
Meredith, Albert 22:311
Meredith, C. 18:34
Meredith, Charles 7:103
Meredith, Daniel F.
    22:486
Meredith, E. 11:188
Meredith, Henry 5:43
Meredith, J. 22:340
Meredith, J. C. 9:56;
    11:157
Meredith, J. S. 11:160
Meredith, James 22:408;
    25:324
Meredith, John 6:32;
    21:366
Meredith, New 22:208
Meredith, Oswald 13:37
Meredith, R. 14:90
Meredith, S. 1:150
Meredith, Samuel H.
    18:220

Meredith, Thomas 7:103
Meredith, W. F. 9:56
Merefield, D. M. 16:140
Merehead, J. 22:485
Merenas, J. G. 10:146;
  14:197
Merer, A. C. 9:223;
  18:372
Merer, Gilbert 9:186
Merette, Alpheus 14:197
Merford, Richard 26:222
Mergenthal, E. F. 14:197
Merghan, Charles 14:197
Merhun, John 8:73
Merical, Abraham 22:113
Merical, James 23:193
Merical, John G. 22:162
Merick, Henry 19:87
Mericle, Amos 9:72
Mericle, P. 1:153
Mericle, T. 1:154
Merideth, Jerry A. 10:127
Merideth, John 11:267
Merideth, Silas J. 22:432
Meridith, H. 25:207
Meridlat, Lewis 11:70
Meridy, Howell 17:196
Meriels, H. 12:74
Merill, S. A. 9:147
Merill, William 9:147
Merimond, C. 14:90
Merion, J. W. 14:197
Meriot, John 12:32
Merit, Byron 1:55
Merithew, A. S. 1:151
Meritt, C. 1:153
Meritz, C. 17:307
Merkan, Charles 4:41
Merkel, Anton 24:68
Merkel, Peter 3:134
Merking, Henry 11:246
Merkins, John 12:32
Merkle, Anton 26:223
Merkle, Christian 10:68
Merkle, J. 3:134
Merlateam, John 7:104
Merlin, Robert 11:389
Merling, Henry 10:127;
  20:309
Merman, W. H. 18:312;
  26:106
Mernach, P. 25:207
Merndoff, W. 1:95
Merner, C. 3:134
Merner, William 26:173
Merness, H. C. 25:57
Mernhein, James 7:35
Mernit, C. H. 3:134
Mero, Frederick 21:141
Merober, T. 7:65
Meron, J. 15:8

Merpary, Calvin 16:375
Merple, Robert 22:311
Merreis, E. A. 17:471
Merrel, Henry 18:209
Merrell, R. D. 9:186
Merrell, S. A. 27:83
Merrer, J. E. 18:177
Merrett, George H. 10:145
Merrett, S. T. 26:107
Merriam, Adolphus
  19:288
Merriam, Christ 11:158
Merriam, Enos M. 20:115
Merriam, H. R. 19:224
Merriam, John 16:78
Merriam, W. 1:154
Merriam, W. M. 3:134
Merrian, William S. 20:24
Merrical, N. 1:95
Merrick, A. H. 11:109
Merrick, Alfred 16:213
Merrick, Charles E.
  17:263
Merrick, D. 12:32
Merrick, David 9:106
Merrick, George 9:243
Merrick, J. 1:154
Merrick, John 13:37
Merrick, John D. 9:122
Merrick, Loyd 6:25
Merrick, M. H. 7:75;
  25:301
Merrick, Moses 12:54
Merrick, S. 13:94
Merrick, Squire 18:89
Merrick, Thomas 11:39;
  15:214
Merrick, W. L. 19:275
Merrideth, M. T. 22:454
Merridey, --- (Mrs.) 27:85
Merrie, William 7:129
Merrien, Patrick 13:37
Merrifield, Aquilla 10:68
Merrifield, Horace 22:465
Merrifield, John 25:207
Merrifield, L. 25:301
Merrifield, Samuel 13:37
Merrifield, W. C. 19:286
Merrihew, Orville 14:301;
  17:476
Merrihue, Orrilla 27:88
Merrihue, Valentine
  15:130
Merril, B. J. 3:134
Merril, J. F. 7:75
Merril, William 8:65
Merrill, A. C. 1:54; 4:41
Merrill, A. D. 1:55;
  11:245
Merrill, A. G. 10:206
Merrill, Almon 9:112

Merrill, Anthony 21:279
Merrill, Benjamin 11:101;
  14:197
Merrill, C. 3:134
Merrill, C. G. 20:151
Merrill, C. H. 19:26
Merrill, Charles C. 22:282
Merrill, D. C. 1:53
Merrill, D. W. 21:366
Merrill, Daniel 13:37
Merrill, David W. 7:59
Merrill, Dennis H. 14:197
Merrill, Edwin 23:123
Merrill, Eli 4:41
Merrill, Eugene 19:180
Merrill, Eugene C. 10:164
Merrill, Ezra A. 19:26
Merrill, Frank 21:196
Merrill, Fred 15:215
Merrill, G. C. 15:40
Merrill, G. E. 25:57
Merrill, G. R. 25:56
Merrill, George H. 20:24
Merrill, George W. 9:26;
  21:366
Merrill, H. 3:134
Merrill, H. M. 23:41
Merrill, H. P. 15:215
Merrill, Harlen J. 10:20
Merrill, Henry C. 11:68
Merrill, J. 25:207
Merrill, J. B. 9:147; 27:82
Merrill, J. H. 11:157
Merrill, J. P. 4:41
Merrill, J. T. 21:167
Merrill, J. W. 1:157
Merrill, James 8:41;
  10:177; 11:69;
  21:230; 26:171
Merrill, James A. 19:87
Merrill, James H. 1:57
Merrill, James N. 23:96
Merrill, James P. 9:186;
  19:275
Merrill, John 2:15; 5:23;
  7:103; 8:58; 21:149,
  209; 23:41; 25:57
Merrill, John B. 22:282
Merrill, John L. 7:59
Merrill, Johnson L.
  11:333
Merrill, Joseph 1:56
Merrill, Joseph W. 13:36
Merrill, Lewis 27:86
Merrill, Lewis A. 20:309
Merrill, Louis 14:197
Merrill, Louis A. 10:68
Merrill, M. E. 10:187
Merrill, Marshall 7:104
Merrill, Martin S. 23:73
Merrill, Miner 13:36

Merrill, Pat 22:261
Merrill, R. D. 19:240
Merrill, Reuben G. 18:398
Merrill, S. B. 3:134
Merrill, S. H. 11:403
Merrill, Samuel 17:181
Merrill, Stephen 19:26
Merrill, Tobe 21:279
Merrill, W. 27:81
Merrill, W. A. 1:53
Merrill, W. C. 1:57
Merrill, W. H. 1:156
Merrill, W. S. 19:180
Merrill, William 9:106;
  18:335
Merrill, William P. 15:215
Merrills, James 20:309
Merrils, John 13:37
Merriman, Allen 17:349
Merriman, Campbell
  12:32
Merriman, Daniel 9:237
Merriman, E. 9:56
Merriman, Edwin 22:208
Merriman, George 10:127;
  20:309
Merriman, George M.
  11:414
Merriman, H. R. 9:186
Merriman, Hiram 8:91
Merriman, J. 1:153
Merriman, J. W. 21:241
Merriman, Joseph 17:39
Merriman, L. 25:207
Merriman, Lester 15:279
Merriman, Thomas 21:89
Merriman, Thomas T.
  20:18
Merriman, W. H. 9:243
Merriman, W. R. 11:37
Merriman, William 24:53
Merrimel, J. 9:26
Merrimu, J. 26:105
Merrin, John 16:213
Merrin, R. L. 20:309
Merrin, Richard S. 10:68
Merrinen, Daniel 26:222
Merriniout, George 9:134
Merriocather, J. 9:56
Merrion, Charles F.
  22:150
Merrion, John 11:192
Merris, Gardner S. 21:75
Merris, William Edward
  15:58
Merrit, James 19:180
Merrit, Joseph 9:122
Merrit, William 20:42
Merrith, J. 11:187
Merritt, --- 15:215
Merritt, A. G. 14:197

Merritt, Alex 4:41
Merritt, Alfred 13:58
Merritt, Andrew J. 22:44
Merritt, Asa G. 16:213
Merritt, B. 21:209
Merritt, Bardon 27:80
Merritt, C. B. 1:98
Merritt, E. D. 25:57
Merritt, E. R. 5:23
Merritt, Edmund F. 22:44
Merritt, F. 3:134
Merritt, Francis M. 22:91
Merritt, George 13:115;
  17:190
Merritt, George H. 19:180
Merritt, Griffin 7:129
Merritt, H. D. 3:134
Merritt, Henry 22:311
Merritt, Isham 22:515
Merritt, Jacob 22:311
Merritt, James 13:130
Merritt, John W. 17:201
Merritt, Joseph P. 27:86
Merritt, Kiger 7:129
Merritt, L. 10:153; 19:180
Merritt, Luther 22:150
Merritt, Mends 22:311
Merritt, Morris 8:52
Merritt, N. 11:109
Merritt, Pat. A. 7:104
Merritt, R. 1:153
Merritt, R. D. 15:40
Merritt, Richard L. 21:89
Merritt, Robert 10:148;
  18:53
Merritt, Samuel T. 9:37;
  18:295
Merritt, Seth 23:117
Merritt, Simeon 17:135;
  24:199
Merritt, W. J. 19:87
Merritt, William 17:288
Merritt, William F. 17:83
Merritt, William J. 15:320
Merritts, I. 18:113
Merritts, M. 3:134
Merriwall, Hiram 18:327
Merrman, John 9:67
Merrnes, P. 14:266
Merron, George W.
  22:408
Merron, Patrick 16:46
Merrow, J. 1:151
Merrow, Joseph 21:366
Merrow, Timothy 12:32
Merroy, J. 14:17
Merry, George 21:141
Merry, H. H. 8:73
Merry, J. 3:135
Merry, Mack D. 22:44
Merryfield, F. A. 14:197

Merryfield, James 21:367
Merryfield, R. 14:90
Merryfield, W. M. 9:56
Merryman, David 20:138
Merryman, Henry L.
  21:56
Merryman, Henry M.
  21:75
Merryweather, H. C.
  14:236; 18:34
Mers--, William F. 25:55
Mersacre, L. 18:53
Mersells, John W. 18:398
Merserve, J. M. 3:134
Mersey, Marshal 13:66
Mersey, Marshall 16:213
Mershan, Mahlon 12:9
Mershon, Andrew A.
  22:91
Merson, George 13:115
Merson, Martin 11:192
Merson, P. 19:275
Mert, Frederick 15:215
Merthesheimer, Fred
  18:312
Merthisheimer, Fred
  26:106
Mertin, Charles 11:109
Mertley, Joseph 9:186
Merton, B. 18:177
Merton, Ernest 19:26
Merton, G. 25:53
Merton, G. H. 3:134
Mertrin, Henry 13:115
Merts, C. 3:134
Merty, Conrad H. 13:37
Merty, Hubert 20:309
Mertz, Charles 1:55
Mertz, Hubert 10:127
Merur, Mike H. 26:46
Merv, Fred. R. 8:52
Mervale, Anthony 16:133
Mervill, Harwood W.
  13:66
Mervine, C. B. 18:35
Merwin, A. 3:134
Merwin, George 24:62
Merwin, Lyman 19:257
Merwin, Thomas E.
  22:408
Meryment, George 27:83
Merz, F. 3:134
Merz, F. M. 3:134
Merzy, John 19:180
Mesdale, W. 19:180
Meseroe, D. E. 16:46
Meseroe, Daniel E. 13:37
Meseroe, James 14:197
Mesery, William H.
  12:142
Meshun, John C. 12:32

Mesick, A. 15:327; 19:87
Mesitt, D. 21:56
Mesler, G. T. 1:54
Mesler, H. G. 7:35
Mesly, Thomas 22:208
Mesmer, Benjamin 7:104
Mesmer, Michael 4:41
Mesmore, D. 11:308
Mesmore, William 12:74
Mesnard, Eri 23:158
Mesner, Jacob 27:81
Mess, John 14:237
Messac, Levi 15:40
Messbright, J. A. 21:367
Messcroe, George 9:122
Messele, Val 3:135
Messell, John 12:9
Messelman, M. R. 27:83
Messena, A. 7:104
Messenger, Charles 4:41;
    25:207
Messenger, G. 1:60
Messenger, Gotlib 4:41
Messenger, H. M. 3:135
Messenger, Irah 25:56
Messenger, John F.
    18:398
Messenger, John S.
    18:398
Messer, Benedict 18:295;
    26:107
Messer, Benjamin 11:320
Messer, Elijah R. 21:115
Messer, Fifield H. 5:23
Messer, G. 13:94
Messer, George 11:381
Messer, H. M. 11:407
Messer, J. T. 15:299
Messer, James 22:340
Messer, John 17:83;
    18:192; 20:42
Messer, Neklaus 24:82
Messer, Suget 7:52
Messer, Thomas 22:208
Messer, Tim 13:115
Messer, V. 16:213
Messer, William 3:135
Messeray, Frederick P.
    17:347
Messerby, Gottlieb 11:159
Messerre, George 27:86
Messerschmidt, Louis
    10:69
Messersmith, J. W. 9:148;
    27:82
Messersmith, Louis
    20:309
Messerve, Alonzo 9:215
Messerve, L. B. 1:59
Messey, M. 3:135
Messic, Shirley 17:282

Messick, A. W. 10:69;
    20:309
Messick, David H. 21:217
Messick, E. T. 13:115
Messick, Nathan S.
    16:145
Messick, William A.
    14:197
Messine, Alonzo 21:367
Messing, B. 14:197
Messing, F. 3:135
Messinger, A. 3:135
Messinger, Elias 14:90
Messinger, J. H. 1:56
Messinger, Jacob 9:112
Messinger, M. C. 11:157
Messinger, N. 3:135
Messinger, Nicholas
    22:91
Messinger, P. B. 11:323
Messinger, W. H. 23:158
Messinger, William B.
    11:160
Messinger, William F.
    19:87
Messir, C. K. 3:135
Messir, F. 3:135
Messler, Vincent 11:37
Messleton, Bela C. 9:98
Messmaker, Ambrose
    8:114
Messnal, John 11:68
Messner, J. 9:147
Messner, Philip 17:251
Messon, P. 1:158
Messor, Benedict 9:37
Messter, John R. 21:230
Messters, E. 3:135
Messur, Felix 17:274
Mestella, George 7:35
Mester, Ferdinand 18:149
Mestor, Modena 12:170
Metcal, M. 25:56
Metcalf, A. 3:135; 26:50
Metcalf, A. B. 14:90
Metcalf, Charles 9:56
Metcalf, D. 15:294
Metcalf, Daniel 9:162;
    27:89
Metcalf, David 16:213
Metcalf, F. 27:79
Metcalf, Frank 5:43
Metcalf, Franklin 17:111
Metcalf, G. 13:130
Metcalf, George 17:314
Metcalf, George F. 16:375
Metcalf, Homer 10:20
Metcalf, Horatio N. 22:91
Metcalf, Isaac 14:197;
    21:75
Metcalf, J. 13:81; 16:213

Metcalf, Jacob 10:155
Metcalf, James 7:104;
    10:127; 20:309
Metcalf, James W.
    17:410; 22:126
Metcalf, John 10:28;
    13:125; 19:304
Metcalf, John W. 16:88
Metcalf, Jonathan 21:367
Metcalf, Milo R. 3:135
Metcalf, O. S. 22:340
Metcalf, Pliney L. 11:295
Metcalf, S. 14:131;
    15:215
Metcalf, S. A. 18:53
Metcalf, T. 16:213
Metcalf, W. 13:129
Metcalf, William 8:91;
    11:415
Metcalf, Zebulon 9:104
Metcalf, Zekel 9:209
Metcap, F. 25:207
Meterline, George 15:14
Metheney, Elias 4:41
Metheny, Simeon 17:292
Methery, B. F. 21:189
Methinia, William 9:239
Metlack, Henry 13:37;
    16:46
Metler, Charles W. 11:323
Metlock, N. 4:41
Metlock, T. 24:25
Meton, Lewis B. 21:249
Metre, Moses Van 17:135
Metrer, Thomas 9:56
Mets, Charles 17:39
Metsher, Isaac C. 9:98
Metsker, Abram 18:221
Metsker, Samuel 15:58
Mettee, George 21:230
Metter, Henry T. 16:213
Metters, William 14:197
Metterton, E. E. 21:190
Mettey, Alexander 20:310
Mettler, Phillip 7:52
Metts, Isaac 7:35
Metts, Thomas J. 23:100
Metts, William 10:164;
    19:87, 180
Metty, Alexander 10:69
Metty, J. 1:157
Metuf, Joseph 27:87
Metz, Elias 10:206
Metz, George 1:56, 58;
    13:66; 19:87
Metz, Henry 5:53
Metz, J. H. 1:154
Metz, John 16:122
Metz, Josiah 21:230
Metz, Theodore 20:24
Metzcer, Daniel 11:85

Metzel, Alexander 18:335
Metzel, F. 1:151
Metzer, Augustus 19:325
Metzer, Davis 10:69; 20:310
Metzgar, John T. 15:215
Metzger, Adolph 19:330
Metzger, D. 1:158
Metzger, David 22:485
Metzger, Eli N. 17:419
Metzger, Frank 12:32
Metzger, Frederick 22:353
Metzger, S. 1:156
Metzger, William 19:283
Metzinger, Charles 15:40
Metzinger, H. 14:90
Metzinger, P. 25:207
Metzish, --- 19:180
Metzker, Andrew 1:55
Metzker, George 20:179
Metzker, Isaac 23:158
Metzler, C. 27:89
Metzner, John 8:25; 18:149
Meulin, M. 1:58
Meur, Henry 6:21
Meurer, John 15:40
Meusch, William 10:164
Meushower, J. 27:89
Mevans, John 17:55
Mevi, C. 3:135
Mevit, Levi J. 12:74
Mewhaw, R. 14:17
Mewhirter, J. 20:148
Mews, H. D. 27:79
Mexey, John A. 8:108
Mexwell, G. 16:213
Meyare, Lewis 26:126
Meydam, Antoin 22:150
Meyencke, James F. 11:71
Meyer, Adolph 13:115
Meyer, Andrew 21:230
Meyer, Anthony 26:46
Meyer, Anton 20:155
Meyer, August 21:190, 217; 23:16
Meyer, Augustus 20:138
Meyer, C. 17:432; 25:207
Meyer, Charles 9:104; 27:90
Meyer, Christ 10:69; 20:310
Meyer, Christian 22:44
Meyer, Conrad 17:23
Meyer, Dominick 18:312; 26:105
Meyer, E. 1:60; 19:257
Meyer, F. 1:156
Meyer, Frank 25:207
Meyer, Fred 20:148

Meyer, Frederick 16:133; 21:257
Meyer, G. 18:246
Meyer, G. A. 16:75
Meyer, George 12:146; 17:164; 18:149
Meyer, H. 3:135
Meyer, H. H. 8:52; 21:35
Meyer, Hend'k. 1:56
Meyer, Henry 9:37; 18:295; 23:123; 26:107; 27:85
Meyer, Isaac 20:310
Meyer, J. 1:153, 157; 3:135; 8:73; 18:113; 26:174; 27:79
Meyer, J. H. 16:46; 21:190
Meyer, Jacob 11:159
Meyer, James 20:310
Meyer, John 11:220; 21:230; 26:172
Meyer, John R. 16:133
Meyer, Joseph 24:179
Meyer, Leon 10:96
Meyer, Leopold 10:69
Meyer, M. 1:155
Meyer, Nicholas 10:92; 27:85
Meyer, Nichols 9:122
Meyer, P. P. 21:367
Meyer, Philip 19:87
Meyer, S. 25:56
Meyer, Samuel 2:14
Meyer, William 10:127; 13:66; 17:419; 20:310; 23:158; 24:25
Meyerhoff, Herman 23:91
Meyerkord, Christian 10:127; 20:310
Meyers, A. 9:56
Meyers, A. J. 25:207
Meyers, Abraham 16:213
Meyers, Alfred 20:310
Meyers, Antonio D. 15:40
Meyers, C. J. 23:41; 25:53
Meyers, Charles 7:16; 10:164; 13:80; 15:40; 16:213; 22:150; 23:129
Meyers, Chauncy 8:91
Meyers, Christian 20:310
Meyers, Christian B. 10:127
Meyers, Daniel L. 17:419
Meyers, Elisha E. 25:288
Meyers, F. 24:25
Meyers, Frederick 18:113; 26:172
Meyers, G. 1:158

Meyers, G. W. 13:37
Meyers, George 8:25, 59; 9:98; 10:99, 127; 12:32; 20:310
Meyers, George H. 15:285; 19:87
Meyers, George P. 21:367
Meyers, Hamilton 9:134
Meyers, Hammond 21:367
Meyers, Henry 18:312
Meyers, Henry P. 1:53
Meyers, J. 1:152, 158; 3:135; 12:9; 16:213
Meyers, J. A. 17:292
Meyers, J. E. 25:52
Meyers, J. K. 3:135
Meyers, J. M. 13:115
Meyers, Jacob 8:25; 15:215
Meyers, James 9:37; 10:69; 18:295; 26:107
Meyers, John 9:26; 24:68
Meyers, John Z. 18:324
Meyers, Joseph 9:122; 27:86
Meyers, Lewis 20:310
Meyers, Lorenzo 23:129
Meyers, M. 22:208
Meyers, Samuel 12:32
Meyers, Thomas 7:52
Meyers, Vanderline 10:69
Meyers, W. 3:135
Meyers, William 3:135; 9:209; 16:214
Meyers, William B. 9:26
Meyett, F. 1:152
Meyett, J. F. 8:73
Meyette, J. F. 26:174
Meyler, P. 4:41
Meylr, George 13:115
Meyordirk, J. 1:152
Meyrs, Jacob 19:87
Meyrus, Jacob 18:149
Mezzey, George W. 17:159
Mi---, John 13:80
Miame, James 18:192
Mibbon, Daniel 15:40
Micar, W. 3:135
Mice, Pacol 9:201
Micha, L. 3:135
Michael, --- 3:135; 16:151
Michael, A. 23:159
Michael, Alex 22:311
Michael, Andrew 22:126
Michael, George W. 8:99
Michael, Harrison 22:92
Michael, Harvey 22:433
Michael, Henry H. 9:223; 18:372

Michael, Hiram L. 18:89
Michael, Isaac 22:45
Michael, Isaiah 22:45
Michael, J. W. 23:41
Michael, Jacob 11:192, 309
Michael, Jacob A. 24:95
Michael, John 9:231; 20:18, 310
Michael, Joseph 9:26
Michael, Leonard 23:124
Michael, Lewis 20:99
Michael, Mary 19:180
Michael, Nelson 22:92
Michael, Nicholas 11:116
Michael, Peter 22:311
Michael, S. 3:135; 11:68; 25:208
Michael, Samuel J. 22:92
Michael, Sylvanus C. 16:46
Michael, Sylvester 20:99
Michael, Theo. R. 24:53
Michael, Tobias 13:115
Michael, Willis A. 10:174
Michaels, Andrew 9:86; 26:45
Michaels, Charles 8:59; 19:277
Michaels, Daniel 23:100
Michaels, H. 14:17
Michaels, J. 13:94
Michaels, J. H. 23:41
Michaels, J. S. 9:186
Michaels, James 21:103
Michaels, O. 9:86
Michaels, Robert 16:122
Michaels, Samuel 5:24
Michaels, Zina 7:69
Michall, John 11:323
Michall, R. 13:94
Micham, Edward P. 20:310
Micham, O. 14:17
Michause, John H. 21:103
Michcal, Ariel 17:55
Michel, I. W. 21:35
Michel, J. 3:135
Michel, John 14:283
Michel, R. 1:58
Michel, Robert F. 8:91
Michelfelder, George 13:115
Michell, H. 16:300
Michell, Hugh 16:300
Michell, John B. 1:55
Michell, Thomas 26:107
Michell, Wilbur 14:197
Michello, W. 3:135
Michels, G. 14:17
Michels, Robert 23:41

Michen, Charles 7:35
Michen, Felix 21:279
Michenham, Lewis 11:333
Micheure, John 10:69
Michey, Samuel D. 23:193
Michiel, Q. 12:85
Michler, C. 21:367
Michling, Levi 9:86
Michly, Eli 14:197
Michner, Daniel 21:35
Michner, Ezra T. 21:124
Michner, H. C. 14:197
Mick, Charles W. 21:35
Mick, F. 1:157
Mick, Henry 11:85
Mick, Hiram 8:91
Mick, J. 23:181
Mick, James 15:152
Mick, John 20:42
Mick, Peter 17:23
Mick, Solomon 10:127; 20:310
Mick, William H. 21:217
Mickales, F. 3:135
Mickambee, Thomas 8:114
Mickee, Joseph 22:45
Mickel, William A. 13:37
Mickell, J. 25:208
Mickell, Thomas 8:25
Mickelson, Henry 14:197
Mickens, John 5:43
Mickerson, D. 13:94
Mickett, Thomas 26:173
Mickey, Ellis 22:45
Mickey, Greenburg 21:230
Mickey, Jacob 7:63
Mickey, James 12:32
Mickey, Robert 13:115
Mickey, W. E. 1:154
Mickey, William H. 23:91
Mickilitz, T. 11:333
Micking, J. 25:208
Mickish, Otto 13:37
Mickle, Clark 7:59
Mickle, G. 16:122
Mickle, John D. 22:45
Mickle, Philip 7:104; 21:367
Mickle, Robert 22:432
Mickleham, R. 9:122
Mickleman, R. 27:86
Mickles, Henry H. 22:261
Mickles, J. 1:155
Mickleson, Charles 21:35
Mickley, Dudley 4:67
Mickling, Jacob 11:324
Micknite, Hiram 26:47
Mickols, Jackson 21:212

Micks, J. W. 13:80
Micks, James 9:86
Micks, Jordon 24:102
Micksell, N. 22:486
Mictman, A. 3:135
Middaugh, B. 4:41
Middaugh, J. 1:152
Middaugh, John L. 22:150
Middaugh, M. D. 12:172
Middaugh, Steward D. 13:37
Middaugh, U. H. 12:156
Midden, James 19:180
Middendorf, John G. 22:45
Middlebrook, Lewis W. 10:127; 20:310
Middleburg, William 7:104
Middleton, Alex 9:231; 20:310
Middleton, Archibald B. 23:159
Middleton, Asahel D. 20:310
Middleton, Asheal D. 10:127
Middleton, C. J. 22:208
Middleton, C. W. 27:81
Middleton, Charles 19:297
Middleton, Daniel 9:134; 27:83
Middleton, Dudley R. 20:187
Middleton, E. 11:267
Middleton, E. W. 9:148
Middleton, G. 13:94; 21:35
Middleton, G. C. 8:65
Middleton, G. E. 26:173
Middleton, G. W. 11:245
Middleton, George W. 22:454
Middleton, Green 8:65
Middleton, H. 22:311
Middleton, H. P. 16:46
Middleton, Henry 9:134; 27:84
Middleton, J. A. 17:70
Middleton, J. W. 14:17
Middleton, John 11:293; 19:349
Middleton, Joseph 7:129; 9:134; 11:160; 27:83, 85
Middleton, Lawrence 9:67
Middleton, March 11:208
Middleton, Peter 20:179
Middleton, S. 27:90

Middleton, Samuel 9:209; 21:92
Middleton, Simon 9:154
Middleton, T. 21:149
Middleton, Thomas 21:279
Middleton, Tobias 8:41; 26:171
Middleton, W. R. 11:323
Middleton, Will 20:310
Middleton, William 10:92; 17:402
Middleton, William G. 11:37
Middleworth, B. 12:156
Middough, John 22:434
Middugh, Stewart D. 16:46
Middy, William J. 21:367
Mider, A. S. 8:52
Midfer, Samuel 14:236
Midgett, Silas 8:25; 18:149
Midway, John 1:58
Midway, William 9:201; 19:283
Midz, J. 3:135
Mie, Pacol 19:283
Miedford, Samuel 18:35
Mienor, T. 21:367
Mienshaen, Henry 10:69
Mier, Frederick 10:127; 20:310
Mier, Henri 20:143
Mier, Henry 18:54
Mier, John 21:35
Miers, Charles 18:35; 27:79
Miers, Hawthorn 25:324
Miers, James 7:35
Miers, John 11:308
Miers, Lewis 9:86
Miers, Moses 20:126
Miers, Thomas 11:341
Mieser, B. F. 23:204
Miexon, John 25:208
Miffard, J. 18:246
Miffin, Martin 26:50
Miffler, G. 25:208
Mifflin, William 3:135
Miffling, I. H. 9:231
Miffling, J. H. 20:310
Miggett, William 25:208
Might, John 25:208
Might, Silas 21:279
Migill, J. 3:135
Migner, H. 3:135
Migney, James 22:13
Miheeler, E. R. 16:375
Mihier, G. S. 15:215
Mihilotzy, Geza 11:37

Mihour, J. 3:135
Mik-ke-marter 25:334
Mike, Emile 18:312; 26:107
Mike, Samuel M. 12:50
Mikeal, A. 14:90
Mikel, Lewis 17:349
Mikell, John 7:35
Mikesell, Jeremiah W. 5:24
Mikesell, Solomon 20:141
Mikkelsen, Ole 20:115
Mikkelson, H. 12:162
Mikle, --- 14:90
Mil---, G. W. 15:295
Mil---, M. W. 23:73
Milam, J. 14:90; 19:304
Milam, L. W. 23:42
Milan, B. 9:148; 27:81
Milan, J. 10:29
Milan, John 19:326
Miland, F. J. 3:137
Miland, John 3:137
Milbaugh, D. 8:65
Milburn, D. H. 11:37
Milburn, Daniel 12:65
Milburn, David C. 22:45
Milburn, E. 16:214
Milburn, George E. 7:104; 13:37
Milburn, J. 3:137
Milburn, John 11:38
Milburn, William 9:237; 26:222
Milburne, William L. 22:503
Milcan, T. M. 16:269
Milcher, William 3:137
Milcox, E. B. 21:124
Milde, Thure 21:11
Milden, A. 5:56
Milden, C. 12:123; 15:130
Mildinger, Peter 9:201
Mildram, John 21:367
Mile, Christopher 22:208
Mileet, S. M. 25:53
Milehan, H. 1:154
Mileisn, J. 24:25
Milen, John 3:135
Miler, D. 1:54
Miler, Ezekiel 10:69
Miler, Wilson H. 10:69
Miles, --- 17:353; 26:213; 27:82
Miles, A. 18:149
Miles, B. 11:341
Miles, Belcher B. 23:256
Miles, Benjamin F. 24:42
Miles, C. S. 3:135
Miles, Charles Henry 23:100

Miles, Charles L. 25:54
Miles, Chester 23:181
Miles, D. 10:127; 20:310
Miles, David 20:176
Miles, Davis 14:197
Miles, Dixon S. 25:334
Miles, E. 17:23
Miles, Edward 9:209; 18:69
Miles, Edwin 18:246; 26:48
Miles, F. H. 1:152
Miles, G. 14:289; 23:159
Miles, G. W. 16:269
Miles, George 25:208
Miles, Green 7:129
Miles, Griswold 17:39
Miles, H. 8:25
Miles, H. H. 19:26
Miles, Henry 9:86; 26:45
Miles, Herman 23:73
Miles, Isaac D. 9:122
Miles, J. 16:214; 24:25; 25:208
Miles, J. H. 25:208
Miles, J. J. 20:115
Miles, J. M. 17:145
Miles, James 13:37; 19:87; 22:45
Miles, James L. 19:26
Miles, James M. 11:415
Miles, James W. 13:37; 22:485
Miles, Jerry 22:312
Miles, John 5:43; 7:35; 9:67, 209; 13:115; 20:181; 22:45
Miles, John B. 15:316; 19:87
Miles, John W. 24:59
Miles, Josiah 21:367
Miles, Lewis 3:135; 22:92
Miles, Linden R. 12:32
Miles, M. G. 11:415
Miles, M. J. 3:135
Miles, Martin 8:73
Miles, Morgan D. 22:126
Miles, Newell W. 12:83; 16:300
Miles, Noah 22:453
Miles, O. 17:83
Miles, Orlando 12:74
Miles, R. 19:245
Miles, Reuben 9:186
Miles, Samuel 3:135; 16:214
Miles, Spencer S. 23:193
Miles, Stephen N. 11:389
Miles, T. F. 1:54
Miles, T. J. 15:41
Miles, W. 22:209

Miles, W. C. 17:411; 22:353
Miles, W. T. 9:72; 14:335
Miles, W. W. 10:69; 20:310
Miles, Wilford 17:39
Miles, William 11:209; 13:37; 19:180; 22:209
Miles, William F. 7:35; 21:56
Miles, William H. 22:261
Miles, Willis 17:135; 24:199
Milesah, L. 14:197
Miley, G. W. 16:151
Miley, George 22:45
Miley, James 24:95
Miley, Martin 23:193
Miley, Peter I. 10:69
Miley, Peter J. 20:310
Milfoard, Joseph 7:35
Milford, George 6:18; 18:89
Milford, Henry 9:26
Milford, J. 26:48
Milford, W. 13:115
Milfordt, Carl 19:180
Milhaupt, A. 1:60
Milhausen, Henry H. P. 23:91
Milhouse, Joseph 27:79
Milican, Wilburn 22:115
Milihan, Christian 16:46
Miliman, Frank 17:181
Miling, John 9:231
Militz, Fred 12:169
Milk, George 9:186
Milke, John 1:57
Milke, William 23:193
Milkes, C. H. 14:90
Milkins, J. M. 24:53
Milkowsky, Andreas 24:95
Milkson, Andrew 9:26
Mill, Aaron 8:91
Mill, David 10:29; 19:304
Mill, James H. 11:415
Mill, Randolph 24:95
Millage, Ira 7:129; 21:367
Millain, William 7:104
Millan, Archibald M. 15:71
Millan, Burton 16:375
Millard, A. 16:214
Millard, G. B. 25:324
Millard, George H. 7:104
Millard, Henry 21:230
Millard, Isaac 14:197
Millard, J. 25:208

Millard, J. M. 8:25; 18:149
Millard, J. T. 1:95
Millard, James E. 8:114, 117
Millard, John B. 22:92
Millard, John J. 16:46
Millard, Joseph 5:24
Millard, M. 14:17
Millard, Michael D. 12:33
Millard, Mordicai 8:91
Millard, P. S. 3:137
Millard, R. 1:57
Millard, Samuel 20:126
Millard, Samuel P. 1:56
Millard, T. L. 10:69; 20:310
Millard, Therone D. 27:85
Millard, W. D. 16:122
Millard, Wellington H. 17:361
Millard, William 9:186; 16:99
Millaway, James M. 21:131
Milled, James E. 15:174
Milledge, James 22:92
Milledge, Robert 12:57
Millen, Andrew M. 17:283
Millen, Daniel 3:135
Millen, G. W. 23:108
Millen, Isaac 21:35
Millen, J. A. 26:170
Millen, Jacob 23:193
Millen, James 8:91; 18:327
Millen, Jesse 17:209
Millen, John H. 16:375
Millen, John M. 18:209
Millen, Patrick 14:243; 27:90
Millen, R. 11:37
Millen, William A. 19:87
Millenden, J. J. 9:112
Millener, S. P. 20:310
Millens, Adam 3:135
Millens, G. 17:347
Miller, --- 1:53, 57; 14:243; 16:375; 18:177, 192, 246; 19:87, 180; 20:92; 21:367; 23:204; 24:102, 200; 25:54; 26:47, 237
Miller, A. 1:56, 60, 153; 3:135, 136; 8:99; 10:29, 148; 11:157, 161; 12:50; 13:115; 14:90; 15:41, 268; 18:35, 54, 149;

Miller, A. 19:26, 304; 24:62; 26:172
Miller, A. B. 10:69; 20:310
Miller, A. D. 19:240
Miller, A. D. C. 25:208
Miller, A. G. 1:153
Miller, A. J. 9:56
Miller, A. L. 1:151
Miller, A. M. 13:94; 18:398
Miller, A. N. 2:15
Miller, A. S. 15:215
Miller, A. T. 15:313
Miller, A. W. 3:136; 17:433; 25:52
Miller, Aaron 8:108; 15:71
Miller, Aaron F. 11:70
Miller, Aaron I. 22:150
Miller, Abner 24:153
Miller, Abraham 12:9; 22:208, 261
Miller, Adam 9:148; 10:127; 17:181; 20:310; 27:83
Miller, Adam S. 21:103
Miller, Albert 9:70; 10:69; 20:310
Miller, Albra 10:69; 20:310
Miller, Alex 13:66; 19:87
Miller, Alexander 7:129; 12:74; 17:83, 135; 23:193; 24:199
Miller, Alexander W. 24:164
Miller, Alfred 4:42; 20:310
Miller, Alonri 19:257
Miller, Alonzo 9:186; 10:69; 12:156; 20:311
Miller, Amos G. 9:98
Miller, Andrew 9:186; 10:20, 127; 11:159; 14:198; 16:133, 143; 20:311; 22:92; 24:90
Miller, Andrew H. 22:524
Miller, Andrew J. 10:10; 11:68; 22:126
Miller, Anson B. 21:367
Miller, Arthur F. 22:208
Miller, Arthur W. 17:288
Miller, Aug. J. 17:92
Miller, Aug. P. 14:327
Miller, August 21:204; 23:12; 24:9
Miller, Augustus 21:367
Miller, Augustus P. 9:161
Miller, Augustus R. 4:42

Miller, Austin 8:108; 10:69; 20:311
Miller, B. 1:99; 15:215; 26:48
Miller, B. F. 14:90
Miller, B. G. 27:83
Miller, B. J. 9:148
Miller, Balts 19:87
Miller, Bassie 21:291
Miller, Benjamin 4:67; 17:135; 21:367; 22:434; 24:199
Miller, Benjamin E. 21:75
Miller, Benjamin F. 11:85; 23:91
Miller, Benjamin T. 12:32
Miller, Brock 16:214
Miller, Bryant 25:54
Miller, C. 1:60, 99, 150, 155; 3:136; 7:59; 11:85; 14:90; 16:148, 300
Miller, C. A. 1:154; 12:156
Miller, C. H. 1:98; 3:136; 11:308; 16:375
Miller, C. J. 3:136; 16:375; 20:311
Miller, C. K. 24:25
Miller, C. L. 15:323; 19:87
Miller, C. S. 15:152
Miller, C. W. 1:154; 3:136
Miller, Caleb 13:37
Miller, Calvin 26:173
Miller, Calvin S. 8:73
Miller, Casper W. 23:256
Miller, Cecil 22:162
Miller, Charles 3:135; 7:35; 9:37, 56, 186; 10:127, 164; 13:37, 115; 14:90, 236; 15:27; 16:122; 19:180, 257, 318; 20:11, 311; 22:433; 24:42; 25:55
Miller, Charles A. 5:24; 7:52; 25:208
Miller, Charles B. 3:136
Miller, Charles E. 8:25; 18:149; 22:92
Miller, Charles H. 5:24; 11:38
Miller, Charles J. 15:344
Miller, Charles K. 17:47
Miller, Charles L. 18:35
Miller, Charles M. 11:38; 15:215
Miller, Charles P. 1:55
Miller, Charles S. 22:485

Miller, Charles W. 23:159; 27:87
Miller, Christ 19:321
Miller, Christ. Columbus 26:213
Miller, Christian 10:20, 164; 19:180; 22:486; 23:129
Miller, Christian R. 17:349
Miller, Christopher 16:141
Miller, Christopher J. 10:69
Miller, Collins 21:367
Miller, Columbus 24:113
Miller, Conrad 8:25; 10:206; 11:38; 12:32; 18:149; 20:126
Miller, Cyrus 20:126
Miller, D. 1:152, 154; 3:136; 7:69; 17:66; 22:353; 25:208; 26:174
Miller, D. A. 9:26; 18:312; 26:105
Miller, D. B. 15:364; 19:87
Miller, D. D. 11:309; 22:486
Miller, D. M. 1:57; 4:42; 18:192
Miller, D. T. 21:190
Miller, Daniel 5:43; 9:26, 44, 56; 11:245; 18:312, 421; 26:106; 27:80, 85
Miller, Daniel H. 9:122; 25:53
Miller, Daniel P. 12:74; 15:41
Miller, Daniel W. 18:221
Miller, David 7:35; 9:86; 10:96; 11:308; 15:130; 26:46
Miller, David A. 1:58
Miller, David B. 23:181
Miller, David G. 23:73
Miller, David L. 23:159
Miller, David M. 23:286
Miller, Delos E. 21:257
Miller, Demmie 26:172
Miller, Don Carlos 8:65; 26:171
Miller, Donmo 18:149
Miller, Donumce 8:25
Miller, E. 3:136, 137; 7:104; 9:215; 21:367
Miller, E. A. 22:208
Miller, E. B. 16:99

Miller, E. D. 9:186; 25:284
Miller, E. H. 23:159
Miller, Easby 20:311
Miller, Ebenezer 6:27
Miller, Edmond 11:208
Miller, Edw. 1:53
Miller, Edw. F. 15:41
Miller, Edward 5:43; 10:69; 15:41, 215; 17:135; 20:133, 311; 23:42; 24:199; 25:208
Miller, Edward A. 10:164
Miller, Eli 12:32; 17:39; 20:155
Miller, Elias 8:65; 26:171
Miller, Elihu B. 17:326
Miller, Elijah 10:127; 20:311
Miller, Elisha 22:353
Miller, Elisha P. 17:83
Miller, Elman H. 8:73
Miller, Emil F. 12:65
Miller, Englehart 23:12
Miller, Enles 7:129
Miller, Enoch 10:174; 19:180; 23:159
Miller, Enos 12:156
Miller, Ephraim 22:171
Miller, Ernest 7:59
Miller, Ezekiel 20:311
Miller, Ezra M. 23:42
Miller, F. 1:150, 151, 152, 155, 156; 2:14; 3:135, 136, 137; 7:69; 14:283; 17:502
Miller, F. B. 3:137
Miller, F. D. 3:136
Miller, F. H. 12:93
Miller, F. I. 20:311
Miller, F. J. 15:215; 17:274
Miller, F. M. 9:231; 20:311
Miller, F. P. 4:42
Miller, Felix 8:52; 21:124
Miller, Ferdinand 9:122; 23:159; 27:85
Miller, Francis 24:42
Miller, Frank 7:71, 104; 9:134; 10:174; 11:403; 19:180; 20:311; 23:42, 73; 27:84
Miller, Frank I. 10:69
Miller, Franklin 17:419; 24:160
Miller, Fred 19:87; 20:311; 21:367; 25:208

Miller, Fred. 15:325
Miller, Frederick 9:86,
    244; 10:69, 127;
    13:115; 14:198;
    20:311; 22:236, 282;
    26:45
Miller, Frederick W.
    22:45
Miller, G. 1:153; 3:136;
    10:29; 11:70;
    14:243; 15:344;
    16:375; 23:42;
    25:208
Miller, G. A. 3:136; 25:53
Miller, G. H. 14:131;
    15:259
Miller, G. L. 15:215
Miller, G. M. 9:56
Miller, G. N. 5:24; 25:208
Miller, G. P. 16:214
Miller, G. R. 19:87
Miller, G. W. 8:91;
    15:215; 21:367;
    25:324
Miller, Gabriel P. 23:42
Miller, George 3:136;
    4:38, 42; 7:52; 8:108,
    114; 9:26; 11:128,
    403; 12:32, 156;
    13:66; 15:71, 215;
    16:214; 17:39, 232,
    336; 18:312, 324;
    19:180; 21:204, 279;
    22:208, 311, 341;
    25:57; 26:49, 106,
    172
Miller, George B. 19:26
Miller, George D. 19:87
Miller, George F. 11:109
Miller, George H. 16:141
Miller, George I. 12:156
Miller, George M. 22:113
Miller, George W. 1:57;
    4:42; 6:32; 7:35;
    9:56, 186; 11:183;
    12:32; 14:90;
    19:268; 22:167
Miller, George W. C.
    21:239
Miller, Gilbert 17:135;
    24:199
Miller, Gillis 12:50
Miller, Gilman 5:24
Miller, Grayman 9:209
Miller, H. 1:60, 95, 150;
    3:136, 137; 5:43;
    8:25; 11:245, 281;
    13:94; 14:17, 270,
    283; 16:131; 19:257;
    21:35, 103, 204;
    25:208; 26:170

Miller, H. A. 14:17;
    22:341
Miller, H. C. 15:160
Miller, H. E. 15:215
Miller, H. H. 23:42
Miller, H. P. 13:94; 14:17
Miller, H. W. 3:136;
    14:90; 22:208
Miller, Hamilton 9:86;
    26:46
Miller, Hammond 14:198
Miller, Harman 13:58;
    19:180
Miller, Harmon 23:42
Miller, Harrison 9:26;
    12:74
Miller, Harry 14:198
Miller, Harvey A. 10:127;
    20:311
Miller, Haz'l. 1:54
Miller, Hennison 10:164
Miller, Henry 3:135; 4:42;
    6:18, 25; 7:129; 8:77;
    9:104, 186, 209;
    10:177; 11:17, 425;
    12:32, 59; 13:66;
    14:198; 16:99, 214,
    300; 17:39, 135, 181;
    18:89; 19:180; 20:11;
    21:56, 230, 243, 367;
    22:45, 312, 523;
    24:199; 25:208, 269;
    27:87
Miller, Henry A. 21:35
Miller, Henry B. 21:56
Miller, Henry F. 7:104
Miller, Henry L. 22:208
Miller, Henry T. 24:99
Miller, Henry V. 10:69;
    20:311; 25:55
Miller, Herald 13:37
Miller, Herman 7:35, 104
Miller, Hiram 13:66;
    19:88
Miller, Horace 17:263
Miller, Howard 18:320;
    26:172
Miller, Hudson 21:367
Miller, Hugh 7:83
Miller, Huron 20:311
Miller, I. 1:59; 25:208
Miller, I. R. 24:25
Miller, I. S. 19:277
Miller, Ira P. 20:193
Miller, Isa 26:213
Miller, Isaac 7:35; 8:91;
    9:26; 10:127; 11:157;
    14:198; 17:83;
    18:312; 20:311;
    22:454, 503; 23:73;
    25:208; 26:106

Miller, Isaac C. 10:92;
    20:311
Miller, Isaac F. 20:18
Miller, Isaac N. 17:249
Miller, Isaac S. 9:186
Miller, Isaiah 9:112
Miller, J. 1:56, 60, 154,
    156; 2:15; 3:135,
    136, 137; 4:42; 7:59;
    9:148; 10:29; 11:70;
    12:83, 93; 13:94,
    103; 14:90, 198, 316,
    322; 15:152, 344;
    16:269, 300, 375;
    18:89, 246, 312, 372;
    19:304; 20:179;
    21:167; 22:487;
    23:12, 159, 268;
    25:208; 26:47, 50,
    106; 27:81, 82, 83
Miller, J. A. 1:95, 150;
    14:90; 16:214;
    20:155
Miller, J. A. E. 18:69
Miller, J. B. 14:90
Miller, J. C. 1:155; 15:71
Miller, J. D. 5:24; 9:56;
    25:208
Miller, J. E. 3:135;
    10:127; 12:146;
    20:311; 26:222
Miller, J. F. 1:98, 152;
    11:328; 21:367
Miller, J. G. 6:32; 12:166;
    25:324; 26:174
Miller, J. H. 1:54, 99;
    3:135; 10:69; 11:328;
    13:125; 15:41; 16:46,
    375; 20:311; 27:90
Miller, J. J. 20:311
Miller, J. M. 1:150, 154;
    3:136; 17:449;
    23:204
Miller, J. O. 3:135;
    25:208
Miller, J. P. 4:42; 7:52
Miller, J. S. 7:65; 11:309
Miller, J. T. 11:37; 13:127
Miller, J. W. 3:136;
    12:142; 20:311;
    23:42
Miller, J. W. M. 21:124
Miller, Jack 18:69
Miller, Jackson 11:331;
    25:208
Miller, Jacob 1:54; 3:136,
    137; 4:42; 7:35; 8:41,
    108; 9:37, 44, 223;
    10:127, 145; 11:68,
    157, 160, 161; 12:80;
    15:215, 348; 16:375;

Miller, Jacob 17:167, 237; 18:295; 19:181; 20:311; 21:14, 367; 26:107, 126, 127, 170
Miller, Jacob D. 8:25
Miller, Jacob F. 11:158
Miller, Jacob H. 14:335
Miller, Jacob J. 22:92
Miller, Jacob L. 18:149
Miller, Jacob N. 15:71
Miller, Jacob S. 18:440
Miller, Jacob V. 11:68
Miller, Jacob W. 22:433
Miller, James 1:57; 8:108, 114; 9:10, 122, 165; 11:157, 159, 425; 12:162; 13:37, 115; 14:301; 17:100, 261, 335, 471, 506; 18:117, 246; 21:75, 141, 202; 22:236, 434; 23:124, 276; 24:53; 25:55; 26:49; 27:85, 88
Miller, James A. 7:35
Miller, James B. 11:85; 17:83; 20:11
Miller, James C. 24:25
Miller, James F. 17:445; 24:167; 26:45
Miller, James G. 26:47
Miller, James J. 8:25; 18:149
Miller, James K. 22:261
Miller, James M. 8:101; 22:45; 24:174
Miller, James M. W. 22:167
Miller, James P. 9:86
Miller, James S. 21:95
Miller, James T. 23:181; 24:42
Miller, James W. 10:69; 20:311
Miller, Jasper 10:69; 20:311
Miller, Jefferson H. 21:124
Miller, Jeremiah 12:74; 15:71, 130
Miller, Jeremiah Brown 18:113
Miller, Jesse 11:425; 20:134; 22:208; 24:25
Miller, Joel 27:80
Miller, Joel P. 10:69; 20:311
Miller, Johann 16:214

Miller, John 1:55, 56, 58; 2:14; 3:135, 136; 4:42; 5:24; 6:10, 32; 7:59, 63, 104; 8:65, 91, 101; 9:26, 161, 186, 231; 10:127, 164; 11:159, 309; 12:32, 65, 74, 83, 156; 13:37, 115; 14:17, 90; 15:41, 58, 152, 174, 215; 16:300; 18:246, 312, 340; 19:26, 88, 181, 268, 271, 331; 20:311; 21:75; 22:92, 311, 486; 23:12, 42, 73, 129, 159, 307; 24:82, 113; 25:57, 208, 273, 286, 324; 26:48, 106, 107, 174; 27:89
Miller, John A. 3:136; 12:32; 13:94; 15:344; 25:208
Miller, John B. 22:45, 208
Miller, John C. 23:42, 100; 25:273
Miller, John D. 11:37; 14:198
Miller, John E. 20:126
Miller, John F. 8:25, 101; 15:215; 17:460; 18:149; 22:208, 465; 24:160
Miller, John G. 17:277, 323
Miller, John H. 14:90; 16:214; 17:23, 443; 18:372; 22:150; 24:160
Miller, John J. 14:198; 22:45; 24:108
Miller, John L. 3:136
Miller, John M. 10:20; 23:114
Miller, John N. 15:58; 17:416; 21:124; 24:153
Miller, John R. 11:128
Miller, John V. 22:167
Miller, John W. 8:25; 10:164; 11:158, 381; 17:243; 18:149; 19:181; 21:75; 23:42; 24:42, 53
Miller, Johnson 21:75
Miller, Jona 27:91
Miller, Jona. 14:243
Miller, Jonathan 22:487
Miller, Jonathan P. 17:207

Miller, Joseph 3:135; 4:42; 5:24; 7:104; 10:99, 148; 11:341; 13:37; 17:181; 18:54; 22:45, 236; 25:287; 26:127
Miller, Joseph B. 21:243
Miller, Joseph H. 22:261
Miller, Joseph M. 22:126
Miller, Joseph S. 12:55
Miller, Joseph W. 22:208
Miller, Joshua 9:44; 22:311; 26:126
Miller, Josiah 10:127; 20:311; 23:159
Miller, L. 1:156; 3:136; 4:42; 9:186; 11:39; 12:83; 16:300; 19:257; 20:150; 24:25
Miller, L. A. J. 16:214
Miller, L. B. 9:186; 19:257
Miller, L. C. 23:159
Miller, L. G. 17:155
Miller, L. H. 19:181
Miller, L. L. 15:174
Miller, L. S. 2:14; 3:136
Miller, Laban 11:328
Miller, Lafayette 22:311
Miller, Lawrence 4:41
Miller, Lemuel B. 17:83
Miller, Leonard 9:112
Miller, Levi 13:37; 17:181, 451; 24:179
Miller, Levi A. 19:181
Miller, Levy A. 10:164
Miller, Lewis 4:41, 42; 9:31, 44; 10:69; 15:130; 24:200; 26:126
Miller, Lewis H. 23:73
Miller, Lillie Viola 26:223
Miller, Lottie 18:35
Miller, Louis 20:311
Miller, Louis G. 22:208
Miller, Lucas 22:514
Miller, Luke 22:208
Miller, Lyman S. 24:82
Miller, M. 1:56; 2:15; 3:135, 136; 14:131; 15:328; 25:52; 26:46
Miller, M. B. 13:115
Miller, M. H. 17:393; 21:367
Miller, M. R. 15:130
Miller, M. S. 15:259
Miller, M. W. 17:39
Miller, Mac 3:136
Miller, Madison J. 23:91
Miller, Madison L. 10:206

Miller, Manasses 9:86
Miller, Mark C. 21:367
Miller, Mark S. 22:261
Miller, Marshall 9:44
Miller, Martin 6:29; 9:67; 18:279
Miller, Martin J. 23:73
Miller, Martin M. 22:432
Miller, Martin U. 22:92
Miller, Mat 22:453
Miller, Mathew 17:23
Miller, Mathew W. 23:159
Miller, Mathias 8:25; 18:149
Miller, Meeker 15:95
Miller, Michael 9:122, 134; 17:292; 27:84, 85
Miller, Michael I. 22:485
Miller, Milburn 7:35
Miller, Miligan C. 23:42
Miller, Milo 1:53
Miller, Milton 11:266; 14:198
Miller, Milton D. 21:75
Miller, Mordecai 23:286
Miller, Morgan 17:243
Miller, Morgan H. 20:49
Miller, Morris A. 22:150
Miller, Morrison 8:52
Miller, Moses 4:42; 8:52; 9:217; 16:122; 18:104
Miller, Mynor 25:56
Miller, N. 1:157; 20:311; 21:367; 25:209
Miller, N. W. 3:136
Miller, Nathan 15:304; 16:214
Miller, Nathaniel A. 11:246
Miller, Nelson 5:43; 10:174; 19:181; 22:282
Miller, Newton H. 23:302
Miller, Nicholas 10:69; 17:111; 21:190; 22:341
Miller, Nicholas A. 9:223; 18:372
Miller, Noah 8:91
Miller, Norman 18:285; 26:135
Miller, O. 1:156; 3:135; 15:353; 21:367
Miller, O. C. 14:17
Miller, O. E. 13:94
Miller, Obediah 17:349
Miller, Oliver H. 23:91
Miller, Oswald 13:37

Miller, Owen 17:181
Miller, P. 1:59; 11:161, 309; 13:115; 14:243; 21:56; 25:273, 334; 27:90
Miller, P. T. 13:115
Miller, Parson O. 13:115
Miller, Paul 11:70; 27:87
Miller, Penrose 19:88
Miller, Peter 4:42; 7:104; 11:320; 12:50; 15:109, 215; 16:214; 20:148; 21:128; 22:208; 24:113; 25:209; 27:89
Miller, Peter M. 14:301; 17:474; 27:88
Miller, Philip 9:26; 10:127; 11:309; 17:83; 18:312; 20:311; 21:56; 23:159; 26:106
Miller, Pierout 11:209
Miller, Pierson 27:90
Miller, Quincy 22:311
Miller, R. 3:136; 9:56; 14:131, 198; 24:25; 25:209
Miller, R. A. 10:20
Miller, R. B. 15:263; 19:88
Miller, R. G. 12:123; 15:130
Miller, R. L. 14:90
Miller, Reuben 9:56; 16:122; 22:92
Miller, Richard 16:122; 22:45
Miller, Robert 5:24; 7:129; 9:72; 12:9, 50; 19:26, 88; 22:485; 23:12
Miller, Robert A. 8:118; 27:87
Miller, Robert H. 11:69
Miller, Robert I. 17:39
Miller, Robert L. 24:53
Miller, Robert R. 8:25; 18:149
Miller, Rufus 17:167
Miller, S. 3:136; 5:24; 10:148; 11:127, 219, 309; 18:54, 192, 246; 21:56; 23:159; 26:49
Miller, S. A. 11:69; 14:90; 15:153; 26:45; 27:157
Miller, S. B. 12:156
Miller, S. G. 20:179
Miller, S. H. 14:90, 131; 15:263

Miller, S. K. 15:215
Miller, S. L. 3:136
Miller, S. P. 10:69
Miller, S. R. 9:26; 18:312; 26:106
Miller, S. T. 1:56
Miller, S. W. 22:13
Miller, Salathiel L. 22:92
Miller, Salsbury 10:127; 20:311
Miller, Samuel 3:136; 7:104; 8:91; 9:26; 10:29; 11:209; 12:32, 74; 14:198; 15:41, 71; 17:15, 162, 274, 501; 19:88, 304; 20:99; 21:56, 367; 22:45, 521
Miller, Samuel B. 1:55; 11:161; 22:13, 92
Miller, Samuel C. 7:104
Miller, Saul 10:127; 20:311
Miller, Shepard 26:47
Miller, Silas A. 16:148
Miller, Silas F. 23:286
Miller, Silas H. 10:164
Miller, Silas W. 15:215
Miller, Simon P. 20:134
Miller, Smith 7:35
Miller, Solomon B. 7:16
Miller, Spencer 18:246; 26:48
Miller, Sweden 4:42
Miller, T. 1:152, 156; 3:135; 14:91; 16:122; 18:35
Miller, T. C. 25:288
Miller, T. D. 17:497
Miller, T. M. 20:58
Miller, T. P. 16:300
Miller, T. S. 11:307
Miller, Terissa 22:353
Miller, Theo 9:56
Miller, Theodore 15:215
Miller, Thomas 8:65; 11:328; 12:156; 17:83, 406; 20:42; 22:408
Miller, Thomas A. 22:261
Miller, Thomas B. 25:209
Miller, Thomas J. 20:126; 22:504
Miller, Thomas S. 7:104
Miller, Thuron 10:69
Miller, Tobias 18:54
Miller, U. W. 22:92
Miller, Valentine 20:27; 21:124
Miller, Volney 25:209

Miller, W. 2:15; 3:136, 137; 9:56, 186; 10:29; 11:267; 14:198, 289; 16:214; 17:135; 19:229, 257, 283, 304; 20:141; 21:367; 25:52, 209

Miller, W. A. 19:229; 21:141

Miller, W. C. 3:135, 136

Miller, W. E. 21:367

Miller, W. H. 3:135; 9:67; 15:71; 16:46; 19:88, 245; 20:311; 22:485; 23:159

Miller, W. I. 17:471

Miller, W. J. 4:42; 14:301; 27:88

Miller, W. N. 11:161

Miller, W. R. 19:257

Miller, W. S. 11:267

Miller, W. Scott 23:73

Miller, W. T. 11:246

Miller, W. W. 13:115; 27:84

Miller, Wallace G. 21:56

Miller, Walter F. 23:73

Miller, Graywam 8:41; 26:171

Miller, Washington 3:136; 17:249

Miller, Wesley F. 16:148

Miller, Wilford 11:266; 15:153

Miller, William 1:58; 3:136; 5:24, 53; 7:35, 104; 9:122, 186, 231; 10:9, 20; 11:69, 158, 231, 295, 382; 12:57, 164; 13:37, 94, 115; 14:17, 91, 198; 15:87, 215; 16:46, 99, 133; 17:39, 55, 83, 164, 181; 18:221, 279; 19:181, 240, 279; 20:311; 21:56, 367; 22:13, 45, 115, 126, 150, 341, 485; 23:73, 159; 24:25; 25:55, 209; 27:86

Miller, William A. 10:127; 20:311

Miller, William B. 15:290; 16:214; 22:465

Miller, William C. 11:246; 15:215; 22:92

Miller, William H. 6:11; 9:44, 69; 12:74; 13:37; 17:47, 356;

Miller, William H. 23:159; 26:127

Miller, William Henry 12:32

Miller, William J. 22:408; 24:42

Miller, William L. 16:122; 22:92

Miller, William M. 8:25; 18:35, 149

Miller, William P. 12:55

Miller, William R. 9:186

Miller, William S. 17:314; 23:256

Miller, William T. 12:32

Miller, William W. 9:134

Miller, Willis 11:209

Miller, Wilson 16:122

Millerd, James E. 18:330

Millerman, G. 3:137

Milleroy, S. H. 12:87; 16:300

Millers, P. O. 14:91

Milles, I. 17:295

Milles, Samuel 11:69

Millet, C. 25:209

Millet, G. C. 10:146

Millet, Graywam 18:69

Millet, H. C. 9:186

Millett, Clark 5:24

Millett, E. 7:75; 25:301

Millett, George C. 14:198

Millett, H. 9:67

Millett, H. C. 19:240

Millett, H. W. 14:198

Millett, John H. 14:198

Millett, Joseph 24:68

Millett, Lawrence 20:108

Millett, Sam. W. 24:173

Millett, William E. 9:215

Millhamp, Frederick 15:328

Millhan, Henry 24:72

Millhoff, Charles 15:71

Millholen, Perry 22:113

Millholland, Cyrus 21:257

Millhollen, Solomon 9:98

Millholm, Hugh 22:45

Millhound, R. 3:137

Millhouse, H. 11:220

Millhouse, Israel 22:312

Milliam, A. 17:39

Millian, F. 14:91

Milliard, James E. 8:91

Milliard, L. J. 17:111

Millican, C. W. 9:56

Millican, Joseph 22:524

Millican, W. W. 3:137

Millick, Samuel 22:92

Milligan, Albert S. 20:126

Milligan, Allen 22:45

Milligan, C. W. 15:303

Milligan, Daniel 21:367

Milligan, E. (Mrs.) 1:53

Milligan, J. 3:137; 11:414; 14:91

Milligan, J. D. 1:60; 21:163

Milligan, James M. 20:3

Milligan, James W. 23:241

Milligan, Jeptha 15:71

Milligan, John 17:321

Milligan, John M. 22:236

Milligan, M. 9:31

Milligan, M. G. 24:82

Milligan, Owen W. 16:214

Milligan, Peter 7:35

Milligan, Robert 13:37

Milligan, S. M. 18:54

Milligan, Samuel 10:148

Milligan, W. K. 22:261

Milligan, W. M. 1:53

Milligan, William 21:75

Millihan, Christian 13:37

Millikan, I. 17:292

Milliken, Alexander J. 23:250

Milliken, Fred 18:271

Milliken, M. B. 15:25

Milliken, M. S. 21:367

Milliken, Samuel 11:341

Milliken, William 12:33

Millikin, J. W. 8:65

Milliman, Euginir 12:33

Milliman, H. C. 25:209

Milliman, John B. 18:221

Milliman, Warren O. 18:221

Millin, Thomas D. 9:123

Milliner, George 22:487

Milliner, R. 20:87

Milling, John 20:312

Millinger, Collin 11:159

Millington, J. 3:137

Millington, L. 20:148

Millington, O. 20:148

Millins, Lewis 17:135

Milliot, P. 3:137

Millisack, W. B. 7:13

Millison, Isaac 23:256

Milliway, Martin 17:453; 24:184

Millkoff, Jonathan 12:33

Milller, R. 16:214

Millman, Herman 16:300

Millon, Charles H. 11:158

Millon, William H. 17:353

Millong, James 10:69

Millons, John 10:174; 19:181
Millony, James 20:312
Mills, A. 3:137; 14:91; 21:35; 25:209
Mills, A. C. 11:157
Mills, A. E. 12:32
Mills, A. W. 1:60
Mills, Aaron 17:456; 24:214
Mills, Abraham 16:375
Mills, Adam 13:94; 23:42
Mills, Albion B. 16:78
Mills, Alexander 16:122; 22:209
Mills, Alonzo B. 15:215
Mills, Andrew 10:127; 20:312
Mills, Augustus L. 27:83
Mills, B. F. 23:42
Mills, B. H. 16:375
Mills, Benjamin 10:92; 20:312
Mills, Burrell 20:126
Mills, C. A. 1:154
Mills, Charles 18:295, 427; 26:107
Mills, Charles S. 10:164; 19:181
Mills, Con 27:89
Mills, D. P. 1:95
Mills, David 9:122; 11:159, 389; 27:86
Mills, David W. 24:68
Mills, E. 15:160; 16:300
Mills, Edward A. 12:54
Mills, Edward M. 10:10
Mills, Edwin H. 20:183
Mills, Eli 8:25; 9:26; 18:149; 20:24
Mills, Elijah 15:344
Mills, F. 1:58; 3:137; 20:11
Mills, Fessenden M. 16:78
Mills, Floyd 7:71
Mills, Frederick 16:166
Mills, G. 15:41; 25:209
Mills, G. G. 25:301
Mills, G. H. 1:58
Mills, G. W. 1:152; 3:137
Mills, George 4:42; 5:43; 12:170; 24:25
Mills, George E. 7:75
Mills, George W. 8:99; 19:349
Mills, Gilbert 16:46
Mills, H. 1:155
Mills, H. F. 25:209
Mills, H. J. 12:32
Mills, Harris M. 15:167
Mills, Heeny 10:96

Mills, Herman 9:122
Mills, Hiram A. 7:104
Mills, I. R. 24:214
Mills, Isaac 17:455; 24:200
Mills, J. 9:148; 12:142; 19:229, 240; 20:312; 25:209; 27:83
Mills, J. D. 1:154
Mills, J. H. 1:58; 18:35
Mills, J. J. 3:137
Mills, J. W. 1:157
Mills, Jack 9:134; 27:84
Mills, James 9:138; 11:39; 14:283; 16:46; 17:72, 419
Mills, James A. 24:161
Mills, James D. 24:25
Mills, James G. 22:45
Mills, James H. 7:83; 21:367
Mills, James R. 21:230
Mills, James T. 17:55
Mills, Jeremiah 27:146
Mills, John 3:137; 5:53; 9:186; 12:32; 14:198; 16:300; 17:181, 326, 391; 18:247; 22:126; 24:42, 59; 25:209; 26:48
Mills, John A. 9:104
Mills, John E. 22:470
Mills, John G. 25:271
Mills, John H. 10:127; 20:312; 21:103; 25:56
Mills, John M. 21:56
Mills, Joseph 3:137; 5:43
Mills, L. C. 19:181
Mills, Leander D. 23:124
Mills, Leonard 18:89
Mills, Lewis 22:113
Mills, Louis P. 10:69; 20:312
Mills, M. 3:137; 14:91; 15:174
Mills, M. H. 25:209
Mills, Martin 22:126
Mills, McStanton 21:35
Mills, Milton 3:137; 22:312
Mills, N. 1:154; 3:137
Mills, N. W. 10:26
Mills, Noah M. 18:398
Mills, Noah W. 22:431
Mills, O. 23:159
Mills, Orlando P. 17:314
Mills, Oscar A. 24:62
Mills, Peter 20:193
Mills, Philo T. 20:108
Mills, Potter J. 22:261

Mills, R. 7:35; 13:94; 15:153
Mills, Robert J. 24:68
Mills, S. 3:137
Mills, Sam 21:279
Mills, Samuel G. 9:231; 20:312
Mills, Silas E. 20:24
Mills, Stephen 21:13
Mills, Sylvester 12:59
Mills, T. 14:198
Mills, Thomas 4:42; 26:138
Mills, Thomas Ab. 15:81
Mills, Thomas B. 12:74
Mills, Thomas C. 10:69; 20:312
Mills, Thomas F. 17:55
Mills, Thomas H. 11:324
Mills, Thomas J. 21:56
Mills, W. 18:69
Mills, W. H. 9:186
Mills, W. H. H. 18:247; 26:47
Mills, Washington 24:167
Mills, William 3:137; 5:53; 8:91; 11:157; 17:83; 22:45
Mills, William D. 12:32
Mills, William H. 21:75; 22:45
Mills, William M. 25:324
Mills, William R. 8:25; 18:149; 23:277
Mills, William T. 7:35
Mills, William V. 17:237
Mills, Z. W. 7:104
Mills, Zabin 1:58
Millsap, J. M. 9:227; 18:372
Millsap, L. 14:258
Millslagle, Robert 22:113
Millson, William G. 22:409
Millspaugh, Fred 3:137
Millspaugh, J. 1:59
Millspaugh, Thomas A. 17:500
Millum, Jacob 11:37
Milmine, E. 1:158
Milne, Harvey 6:14
Milne, John 3:135; 21:75
Milne, William 1:56
Milner, Asa H. 22:209
Milner, C. 1:152
Milner, George 22:487
Milner, George W. 14:198
Milner, James M. 17:459
Milner, John B. 24:25
Milner, W. M. 21:167
Milner, William 17:388

Milnes, Joseph 18:398
Milo, George 1:53
Milon, W. H. 26:135
Milotta, Charles 14:91
Milrer, W. 24:199
Milrick, William 22:341
Milrier, James M. 24:150
Milroy, Edwin R. 22:92
Mils, E. F. 1:152
Milsker, J. 3:137
Milson, John 18:149
Milsops, Joseph 8:25;
   18:149
Milster, Harvey A. 24:68
Miltabercer, Jacob 9:56
Milter, R. 1:151
Milton, A. 1:155
Milton, Ben'n. H. 22:261
Milton, C. 3:137
Milton, C. A. 26:47
Milton, Calvin 17:55
Milton, Daniel 5:24
Milton, David 18:89
Milton, Edward 7:129;
   21:367
Milton, F. 26:47
Milton, Franklin 10:69;
   20:312
Milton, G. 1:156; 23:42
Milton, J. S. 26:46
Milton, J. W. 13:125
Milton, James 12:160;
   18:247; 26:49
Milton, John 4:42; 9:26;
   11:68; 12:123;
   14:26; 15:363;
   21:367; 22:312
Milton, John A. 17:317
Milton, Marion C. 17:23
Milton, Pleasant 11:328
Milton, Samuel 17:39;
   24:68
Milton, Smith 9:186
Milton, Solomon 7:129
Milton, T. T. 14:319;
   25:288
Milton, Valsey 7:129
Milton, W. 22:45
Milton, W. A. 21:14
Milton, William 7:78;
   25:301
Milton, William T. 17:353
Miltonburger, John W.
   22:486
Miltz, Fred. 8:60
Miltze, J. 21:201
Milue, Harvey 18:89
Milum, James 3:137;
   25:209
Milun, Adam 7:59
Milwig, P. 12:123

Milyon, Paul 9:209
Mim, George 19:181
Mimick, William 15:290
Mimm, Levi 15:167
Mimm, W. 25:209
Mimmes, Walenstein
   23:73
Mimmick, Levi 8:52
Mimms, George 10:155
Mimms, John T. 14:263
Mimms, Maybery 22:312
Mims, Alber 24:102
Mims, David S. 9:37
Minard, David 11:38
Minard, Hiram 13:58
Minard, J. H. 21:124
Minard, Stephen 11:245
Mince, F. 3:137
Mince, Major 11:424
Minch, Clark 25:209
Minchan, Robert 19:26
Minchin, F. 14:91
Mincy, J. 20:85
Mind, D. 3:137
Minder, Ben D. K. 22:353
Minder, Charles A.
   23:129
Mindler, Peter 3:137
Mindrup, William 22:45
Mindson, Lewis 12:156
Mine, Casper 20:134
Mine, John M. 3:137
Minear, Charles T. 22:485
Minear, Lycurgus 18:398
Minedill, C. 14:17
Minehall, Martin L.
   23:114
Minehart, Charles 12:33
Minehart, Henry 10:69
Mineharth, Adam 11:390
Mineheart, Andrew
   20:312
Miner, Andrew J. 23:159
Miner, Charles E. 16:141
Miner, Charles N. 13:37
Miner, Charles W. 16:46
Miner, Christopher 1:56
Miner, D. 20:175
Miner, Daniel L. 7:104
Miner, E. A. 7:75; 25:301
Miner, George 8:120;
   17:441; 24:153
Miner, George A. 14:236
Miner, Gunis 17:495
Miner, H. 20:312
Miner, Henry 13:58
Miner, Hiram 10:69
Miner, Isaac 16:214;
   21:257
Miner, J. 19:88; 25:209
Miner, J. E. 1:158

Miner, J. G. 20:103
Miner, Jacob A. 11:245
Miner, Jasper J. 20:312
Miner, Jasper L. 10:69
Miner, John 9:70; 18:54,
   149
Miner, John N. 21:75
Miner, Leander P. 18:221;
   22:432
Miner, Lorenzo H. 22:465
Miner, Marvin 21:368
Miner, Moses 22:433
Miner, P. 19:305
Miner, Richard 11:209
Miner, Robert S. 10:69
Miner, S. 3:137; 18:177
Miner, S. P. 15:268
Miner, Scipio 10:99
Miner, T. W. 23:314
Miner, Thomas 4:42;
   10:69; 20:312
Miner, W. 1:154
Miner, William 10:69
Miner, William Charles
   16:137
Miner, William R. 22:45
Miner, William W. 9:186;
   19:271
Minert, Philip 21:368
Mines, J. J. 16:214
Mines, Jacob 15:291
Mines, Lewis 26:46
Minese, George 22:514
Miney, Henry 17:398
Miney, John 22:261
Minfield, W. 21:124
Ming, David 13:37
Ming, W. H. E. 20:148
Mingen, C. H. 4:42
Mingens, C. 21:103
Minger, Cyrus A. 19:88
   18:54
Minger, Henry 10:149;
   18:54
Minger, Henry E. 10:69;
   20:312
Mingett, Matthias 9:56
Mingg, John 7:138
Mingle, George 4:42
Mingo, Charles J. 22:150
Mingo, H. J. 9:134; 27:84
Mingo, John 14:91;
   17:419
Mingus, Marcus 7:52
Minhart, Fred 4:42
Minherber, B. F. 22:236
Minhouse, William
   21:246
Minic, Josiah 15:364
Minicar, Nelson 24:42
Minice, Elias 23:12
Minick, H. 1:55

Minick, William 16:214; 24:42
Minicks, James K. 22:126
Minie, Josiah 19:88
Minier, Joseph 17:309
Minimeck, William 21:368
Minix, John 22:126
Mink, H. 3:137
Mink, H. J. 19:229
Mink, Henry J. 9:186
Mink, John H. 9:26; 18:312; 26:107
Minke, Henry 19:26
Minkie, Herman 22:92
Minkle, Edward 18:398
Minkler, --- 16:281
Minkler, Thomas 10:174; 19:181
Minklinn, Brafear 11:128
Minks, George 11:425
Minks, John F. 17:39
Minks, John W. 17:261
Minks, Thomas P. 22:126
Minley, Charles 10:170
Minmire, Charles 11:381
Minn, H. C. 26:174
Minn, J. W. 11:281
Minn, Joseph 13:37
Minn, Washington 5:24
Minnahan, Timothy 15:273
Minnard, Charles 25:324
Minne, Elmore 15:349
Minnear, Thomas 11:69
Minnehan, D. J. 1:99
Minneke, Henry 22:113
Minner, P. 10:29
Minners, Joseph 16:46
Minnes, Joseph 13:37
Minney, Charles 8:91
Minnick, --- 15:215
Minnick, B. 1:155
Minnick, Henry 11:389
Minnick, John 8:91; 20:312
Minnick, Levi 21:141
Minnick, Stephen E. 17:361
Minnie, Elmne 16:375
Minnier, J. 15:344; 16:375
Minnies, Ed 25:301
Minnies, Edward 7:81
Minniman, R. C. 12:9
Minnin, T. C. 11:109
Minning, J. 18:177
Minnis, Noble 8:66
Minns, G. 15:215
Minogue, J. 1:152

Minor, --- 20:28
Minor, A. 13:94
Minor, A. C. 12:156
Minor, B. F. 21:35
Minor, Frank 15:215
Minor, G. W. 15:215
Minor, George 18:35
Minor, George C. 11:288
Minor, H. C. 8:73
Minor, H. D. 12:80; 25:209
Minor, Henry 7:104; 17:398
Minor, Hiram M. 22:45
Minor, J. D. 1:54
Minor, James G. 17:361
Minor, John 10:149; 11:277; 16:300; 19:88
Minor, John C. 1:54
Minor, John L. 25:209
Minor, John T. 23:243
Minor, Joseph 11:374; 21:92
Minor, M. L. 20:58
Minor, Orson 19:88
Minor, Peter C. 7:104
Minor, Robert S. 20:312
Minor, S. 10:192
Minor, S. P. 14:131
Minor, Theo 20:312
Minor, Theodore 10:69
Minor, W. 17:181
Minor, William F. 21:35
Minor, William R. 17:39
Minor, Wilson S. 20:193
Minot, Charles 4:42
Minott, James K. 11:209
Minphy, George 25:286
Mins, John R. 19:26
Minsall, Robert F. 20:99
Minsbeger, J. 1:154
Minser, D. 1:59
Minson, A. H. 23:293
Minster, D. H. 25:209
Minster, David H. 5:24
Minten, Jesse 10:96
Minter, E. 10:148
Mintgay, J. 10:155; 19:181
Minthorns, D. C. 1:58
Mintline, David 1:55
Minton, --- 19:88
Minton, Henry 23:193
Minton, Jacob 9:123
Minton, Jacob D. 27:86
Minton, John 19:181; 20:58
Minton, John G. 22:92
Minton, Josiah 7:129
Minton, Marten 19:88

Minton, Nathan W. 11:39
Minton, Robert 20:28
Minton, Robert W. 10:174; 19:181
Minton, Samuel A. 22:236
Minton, Thomas J. 19:181
Minton, William 8:52
Mintzer, A. 14:301; 17:479
Mintzinberger, C. 14:91
Mintzu, A. 27:88
Minus, H. 15:299
Minx, William 11:281
Minyart, J. M. 17:149
Mioch, John 14:289
Mipes, J. 3:137
Miracle, Albert 16:99
Mirce, D. L. 25:54
Mircer, J. D. 15:329
Miricle, H. 15:71
Mirnitch, William 14:266
Miron, John 22:261
Mirrick, John 7:71
Mirvall, John A. 18:35
Miscal, R. 14:198
Mischler, C. 7:83
Mise, Allen 24:160
Mise, Sylvester 8:25
Misel, P. 17:155
Miser, D. F. 22:486
Miser, G. 11:309
Mishe, Paul 10:206
Mishler, George 15:174
Mishler, Jacob 20:183
Mishler, John 24:42
Mishler, P. B. 1:155
Mishler, Silas 12:33
Mishner, A. 13:115
Misho, James 12:33
Mishurel, Henry 13:37
Misiner, P. 1:53
Misinger, D. 13:94
Miskal, M. 17:111
Misler, F. A. 14:198
Mismer, A. K. 7:35
Misner, Adam 21:56
Misner, Christopher 17:23
Misner, John 3:137
Misner, Lewis 22:209
Misner, N. 17:23
Misner, W. 1:59
Misner, W. B. 9:69
Misplay, Edward 17:441; 24:153
Mispley, Lewis 10:127; 20:312
Missen, Joshua 15:215
Misser, Isaac 17:207
Misser, Philip 10:145
Missinger, C. 3:137
Mistfall, John 9:186

Miston, J. W. 27:86
Mistort, W. H. 14:91
Mitan, John J. 14:198
Mitch, Jacob 25:209
Mitchal, George 9:223
Mitchald, George 18:372
Mitcham, O. 13:94
Mitcham, William A. 22:209
Mitcheal, O. M. 9:123
Mitchel, A. J. 4:42
Mitchel, Albert 11:309
Mitchel, C. 21:35
Mitchel, C. K. 19:181
Mitchel, Dewitt C. 23:73
Mitchel, George W. 11:328
Mitchel, Henry 13:115
Mitchel, J. 1:151; 13:115; 25:209
Mitchel, James 18:399; 26:107
Mitchel, John 9:237
Mitchel, John G. 18:399
Mitchel, John P. 11:208
Mitchel, Ora B. 19:181
Mitchel, R. G. 12:156
Mitchel, Richard 9:237
Mitchel, Steward 15:167
Mitchel, T. 19:305
Mitchel, Z. F. 23:42
Mitchell, --- 3:138; 11:69; 25:53
Mitchell, A. C. 7:35
Mitchell, A. E. 4:42; 9:56
Mitchell, A. R. 14:91
Mitchell, A. W. 11:37
Mitchell, Aaron 20:148; 25:209
Mitchell, Aaron P. 24:53
Mitchell, Adam 14:198; 22:45
Mitchell, Albert 7:104; 22:433
Mitchell, Alexander 23:124
Mitchell, Alfred 13:37
Mitchell, Allen 9:134, 157; 22:282; 27:84
Mitchell, Allen T. 14:319; 25:275
Mitchell, Alry 14:198
Mitchell, Andrew 11:85
Mitchell, Auburn 5:24
Mitchell, B. 21:149
Mitchell, Benjamin 13:37
Mitchell, Beverly 7:129
Mitchell, Burton 22:485
Mitchell, C. 3:137; 13:115
Mitchell, C. B. 21:368

Mitchell, C. F. 11:245; 18:69
Mitchell, C. R. 7:104
Mitchell, Charles 9:86; 21:368; 25:209; 26:46
Mitchell, Coleman 22:45
Mitchell, D. D. 21:35
Mitchell, D. H. 24:25
Mitchell, D. J. 1:58
Mitchell, David 7:104; 10:20; 11:159; 24:42; 26:46
Mitchell, David W. 17:361
Mitchell, E. B. 18:192
Mitchell, E. G. 20:3
Mitchell, E. W. 1:155
Mitchell, Edgar H. 8:108
Mitchell, Edward 16:214; 19:88; 22:312
Mitchell, Edward B. 12:168
Mitchell, Elery B. 22:407
Mitchell, Elijah 11:95
Mitchell, Emmet 22:432
Mitchell, Eugene 11:159
Mitchell, F. A. 17:23
Mitchell, F. M. 20:3
Mitchell, Franklin 17:237; 22:262
Mitchell, Fred. 8:73
Mitchell, Frederick 1:57
Mitchell, G. 1:157; 14:91; 16:214
Mitchell, G. K. 14:17
Mitchell, G. R. 13:94
Mitchell, G. W. 16:214
Mitchell, George 4:42; 12:123; 15:130, 215; 17:181, 243; 20:126; 21:279
Mitchell, George O. 20:11
Mitchell, George R. 22:13
Mitchell, George W. 17:277
Mitchell, H. 1:157; 9:56; 12:87; 14:91; 15:344; 16:214, 375; 17:181; 19:257
Mitchell, H. H. 1:58
Mitchell, H. J. 14:198
Mitchell, H. K. 1:155
Mitchell, Henry 9:186; 13:37; 17:181; 18:89; 22:209, 262
Mitchell, Henry H. 9:104
Mitchell, Hiram 10:127; 20:312; 22:92
Mitchell, I. B. 9:231
Mitchell, Ira 18:209

Mitchell, Isaac 2:14
Mitchell, Isaac N. 13:37
Mitchell, J. 1:58, 59, 153; 3:137; 9:154; 12:83; 13:94; 14:198; 16:214, 300; 21:111; 25:57; 27:82
Mitchell, J. B. 20:312
Mitchell, J. C. 1:53
Mitchell, J. D. 1:58; 3:138
Mitchell, J. H. 3:137
Mitchell, J. J. 3:137
Mitchell, J. L. 5:24; 25:209
Mitchell, J. P. 3:138; 15:215
Mitchell, J. S. 18:35
Mitchell, J. W. 11:267; 16:46; 17:416; 19:26; 21:368
Mitchell, Jaberry 23:100
Mitchell, Jacob 16:133; 18:372; 22:92
Mitchell, Jacob J. 22:486
Mitchell, Jacob M. 21:246
Mitchell, James 3:137; 5:43; 7:35, 82; 8:41, 66; 9:26, 37, 98; 10:69, 127, 206; 11:266; 14:199, 258; 17:181; 18:295, 312; 20:183, 312; 21:141, 368; 22:312; 23:252; 24:71; 26:106, 172
Mitchell, James A. 11:414
Mitchell, James F. 15:130
Mitchell, James H. 2:14; 9:72; 21:35
Mitchell, James K. P. 18:177; 23:73
Mitchell, James W. 17:233
Mitchell, Jeremiah 12:51
Mitchell, Joe 9:209
Mitchell, Joel D. 22:341
Mitchell, John 3:137, 138; 5:24; 9:244; 10:164, 206; 11:85, 161; 12:168; 18:89; 19:181; 20:42; 22:262, 312; 25:209; 26:145
Mitchell, John C. 10:206
Mitchell, John D. 3:137
Mitchell, John G. 8:91
Mitchell, John L. 22:484; 23:73
Mitchell, John N. 26:222
Mitchell, John P. 23:241
Mitchell, John S. 10:69; 20:312

Mitchell, Johnson 23:159
Mitchell, Jones 11:425
Mitchell, Joseph 3:137;
    7:129; 9:134, 156;
    13:115; 15:11; 27:84
Mitchell, Joseph F.
    11:187
Mitchell, Joseph P. 23:73
Mitchell, Joshua 13:37;
    16:46
Mitchell, Julius 15:215
Mitchell, Lafayette
    10:127; 20:312
Mitchell, Lemuel L. 23:73
Mitchell, Leonard 21:368
Mitchell, Louis 10:127;
    20:312
Mitchell, Luke 1:191
Mitchell, M. D. 1:58
Mitchell, M. L. 11:68
Mitchell, Mason 18:69
Mitchell, Mathew 9:26;
    26:106
Mitchell, Matthew 18:312
Mitchell, N. 1:155; 9:201
Mitchell, N. J. 14:258
Mitchell, N. R. 1:154
Mitchell, Newell S.
    21:206
Mitchell, Newton A.
    20:11
Mitchell, Ora B. 10:164
Mitchell, Orin J. 22:45
Mitchell, Perry 10:69;
    20:312; 22:431
Mitchell, Peter 21:279
Mitchell, Peter G. 12:33
Mitchell, Phelig 12:33
Mitchell, Phelix 21:279
Mitchell, R. 1:58; 11:85;
    21:150
Mitchell, R. C. 3:137
Mitchell, R. M. 1:54;
    3:137
Mitchell, Ransom 17:261
Mitchell, Reuben 10:127;
    17:217; 20:312
Mitchell, Richaed 26:223
Mitchell, Richard E.
    10:69; 20:312
Mitchell, Robert 6:9;
    7:129; 17:237;
    18:104, 279
Mitchell, Robert H.
    11:424
Mitchell, Russell 4:42;
    26:50
Mitchell, S. 1:154;
    16:300; 22:524;
    25:209
Mitchell, S. B. 10:153

Mitchell, S. D. 11:71
Mitchell, S. W. 8:66
Mitchell, Samuel 5:43;
    12:65; 15:71, 81;
    18:417; 26:223
Mitchell, Samuel W.
    21:196
Mitchell, Sandy 7:129
Mitchell, Sanford B.
    19:181
Mitchell, Silas 19:292
Mitchell, Solomon A.
    11:116
Mitchell, Spencer A.
    20:27
Mitchell, Sullivan B.
    7:104
Mitchell, Sylvanus D.
    13:37
Mitchell, T. 1:156
Mitchell, T. H. 4:42
Mitchell, T. S. 12:140;
    20:313
Mitchell, Theodore 10:92;
    20:313
Mitchell, Thomas 9:37;
    12:123; 13:115;
    15:130; 17:181, 398;
    18:149, 295; 21:258,
    368; 22:431
Mitchell, Thomas W.
    22:341
Mitchell, W. A. 11:95;
    19:181, 229
Mitchell, W. C. 3:137
Mitchell, W. F. 23:256
Mitchell, W. G. 24:25
Mitchell, W. H. 3:137;
    4:42; 18:69
Mitchell, W. J. 1:154
Mitchell, W. R. G. 25:276
Mitchell, W. W. 17:453
Mitchell, Wade 27:84
Mitchell, Ward 9:134
Mitchell, William 7:9;
    8:25, 73; 13:37;
    16:47; 17:39, 102;
    18:149; 22:431;
    23:159
Mitchell, William A.
    22:92
Mitchell, William B.
    21:368
Mitchell, William E.
    17:283
Mitchell, William H.
    9:204
Mitchell, William L.
    10:164; 16:47;
    19:181

Mitchell, William P.
    17:361
Mitchell, William S.
    18:335
Mitchell, William W.
    24:183
Mitchell, Wright 7:129
Mitchell, Z. 14:91
Mitchem, A. 3:137
Mitchem, James B. 22:92
Mitcherson, H. 22:312
Mitcherson, James 22:312
Mitcheson, Thomas
    16:281
Mitchiner, H. 3:138
Mitchison, Green 18:247;
    26:48
Mitchle, Henry A. 22:150
Mitchoff, M. 1:53
Miteliman, John 18:113
Mites, G. M. 13:115
Mitger, Abraham 27:88
Mitheny, Aaron 22:341
Mitt, Henry F. 16:214
Mitt, John 22:408
Mittance, L. 3:138
Mitte, Z. 15:130
Mitten, David 20:148
Mittens, G. W. 14:278
Mitter, O. 16:281
Mitterman, John 13:115
Mittias, Wilson 18:335
Mitting, Elmer 24:171
Mitting, Luther 4:42
Mitts, Aaron 11:109
Mitts, Jesse B. 11:85
Mitts, Jesse M. 11:85
Mitts, Morgan V. 21:141
Mitz, J. 1:156
Mitz, John 22:92
Mitz, Samuel 11:160
Mitzel, M. 1:151
Mitzger, Andrew 22:209
Mitzger, William W.
    9:186
Mitzner, S. E. 9:227
Mix, Collins 7:130
Mix, Cranson 4:42
Mix, Eben 17:419
Mix, Franklin 10:69;
    20:313
Mix, Henry 22:171
Mix, Joel 15:41
Mix, Mary Eliza 25:334
Mix, Theodore M. 26:223
Mix, Thomas 21:368
Mixen, Richard 16:47
Mixer, C. D. 1:54
Mixer, D. J. 14:199
Mixer, Daniel 22:45
Mixer, J. 1:152

Mixer, John 21:230
Mixil, L. B. 3:138
Mixon, Abraham 27:84
Mixon, Abram 9:134
Mixon, J. E. 25:301
Mixon, J. J. 7:78
Mixon, Silas 7:78
Mixon, Solomon 7:78
Mixter, J. L. 3:138
Mize, J. 20:58
Mize, John P. 9:69
Mize, Joseph 17:496
Mize, Sylvester 18:149
Mize, William 22:92
Mizenbeck, John G. 20:177
Mizinfebler, Frank 11:120
Mizner, S. E. 18:372
Mizner, W. 3:138
Moaderly, George 15:290
Moak, Charles 1:57
Moakler, Francis J. 11:128
Moan, James 3:138
Moan, L. B. 1:54
Moar, Thomas 10:69
Moarty, James 19:88
Moas, A. 11:439
Moas, G. 11:439
Moat, A. 13:94; 14:17
Moat, Charles 15:41
Moat, James 19:181
Moate, Adam 20:313
Moate, Gume 10:177
Moaten, R. C. 26:172
Moats, Allen S. 22:209
Moats, Christopher V. 17:453; 24:183
Moats, Josiah 17:92
Mobberly, J. B. 14:131
Mobberly, W. H. 25:209
Mobberly, William H. 5:24
Mobech, S. 26:45
Moberly, Ed 19:47
Moberly, Elhanan W. 22:92
Mobins, John G. 22:454
Mobley, Aaron F. 22:486
Mobley, Frank 22:514
Mobley, G. 14:199, 258
Mobley, George 14:91
Mobley, Grandville 22:126
Mobley, J. R. 21:35
Mobley, James 22:341
Mobley, James W. 17:402
Mobley, John 22:209
Mobley, Louis 21:368
Mobley, Milton 17:433; 24:160

Mobley, Sampson 22:312
Mobley, Solomon 22:262
Mobley, Stephen 17:398
Moburgh, Charles P. 23:256
Mocar, Michael 10:149; 18:54
Mock, A. 15:312; 19:88
Mock, Able 20:90
Mock, Adam 24:42
Mock, G. T. 25:301
Mock, George W. 22:92
Mock, J. M. 15:215
Mock, Josiah B. 7:35
Mock, Malachi 9:123
Mock, Malichi 27:85
Mock, Tobias 13:37
Mock, Valentine 23:42
Mock, William 25:53
Mock, William H. 22:126
Mockabbee, Randall 17:267
Mockbee, Thomas 12:148
Mockenhaupt, Martin 18:149
Mockland, Thomas 17:181
Mockler, William 1:57
Mockson, D. T. 5:24
Mod, Willy 11:281
Moddle, James 11:208
Mode, David 20:313
Mode, Samuel 11:341
Moden, Isaac 16:214
Moderey, John 13:37
Moderhaser, Daniel 20:313
Modesitt, W. 14:17
Modger, A. 3:138
Modier, Chris 26:106
Modis, John 21:368
Modiselt, W. 13:94
Modlay, Peter 12:51
Modler, John 17:135; 24:199
Modley, Nathan 9:95
Modlin, Davis 11:328
Modlin, Nathaniel 25:324
Modling, John H. 22:432
Moe, Hiram W. 18:279
Moe, Jens Olsen 21:206
Moe, John 3:138
Moe, Ole G. 24:95
Moe, Perry 6:21; 18:89
Moebins, W. M. 21:124
Moeller, Chris 18:312
Moeller, Peter 10:127
Moench, John C. 20:187
Moenning, Albert 15:23
Moerder, Ferdinand 17:277

Moetig, John 25:301
Moffat, Henry B. 22:92
Moffat, J. 3:138
Moffat, J. S. A. 1:53
Moffat, James 24:68
Moffatt, Aquilla 22:408
Moffatt, Henry 21:368
Moffatt, James 22:520
Moffatt, Owen 12:33
Moffatt, R. C. 22:45
Moffatt, Thomas 7:104
Moffatt, William 12:33; 13:37
Moffell, Dillon 9:86
Moffet, Andrew J. 10:127
Moffet, Sip 18:90
Moffet, Warren 21:103
Moffett, T. 1:156
Moffett, W. 11:95
Moffey, Alfred 20:313
Moffit, Aaron 4:42
Moffit, J. W. 11:95
Moffit, James 24:178
Moffit, Jasper N. 20:313
Moffit, John 8:66; 11:208
Moffit, John J. 6:11
Moffit, O. J. 8:66
Moffit, Thomas 3:138
Moffit, Wilberne 18:149
Moffitt, William 8:25
Moffitt, Aaron 13:37
Moffitt, Charles 1:54
Moffitt, Dillon 26:45
Moffitt, Eber C. 22:150
Moffitt, Ephraim 22:433
Moffitt, Henry 17:400
Moffitt, J. M. 14:91
Moffitt, J. S. 1:157
Moffitt, James 8:101; 17:463
Moffitt, John 22:150
Moffitt, Joseph L. 23:74
Moffitt, Robert 9:86; 26:44
Mogden, Pleasant 18:149
Moger, Charles W. 13:37
Mogher, Michael 15:215
Mogin, Patrick 9:26
Moglocklin, Thomas 17:15
Mohan, M. 1:150
Mohany, William 15:215
Mohel, Hiram 1:54
Moherlin, Francis 22:287
Moherly, John L. 22:485
Mohi, John R. 1:53
Mohl, J. 18:90
Mohler, A. 1:95
Mohman, Fred 9:240
Mohn, Jacob 20:184
Mohn, Sylvester 7:35

Moholland, Samuel 8:25; 18:150
Mohon, Patrick 9:26
Mohorn, Robert 24:89
Mohorter, Charles 22:465
Mohr, David 22:45
Mohr, J. R. 3:138
Mohr, Joseph 22:167
Mohr, T. E. 1:54
Mohts, G. 19:88
Mohukern, Albert 5:24
Moilan, Martin 22:520
Moine, Marcus 21:368
Moinehan, Peter 15:109
Moir, Alex 17:181
Mojean, Rudolf 20:313
Mojean, Rudolph 10:128
Mokate, Mathias 7:52
Mokes, R. 3:138
Molair, Jasper 26:172
Moland, B. 3:138
Moland, William T. 8:25
Molar, John 9:37
Molar, Patrick 18:150
Molash, F. 3:138
Molch, James 22:485
Molden, David 14:199
Molden, Dennis 22:45
Molden, James T. 22:486
Moldenhower, Ernst 22:45
Molebash, Joseph 22:209
Moler, Austin 8:25; 18:150
Moler, Francis 14:91
Moler, William 21:246
Moles, Christopher C. 22:126
Moles, J. 16:148
Moles, Jacob M. 20:24
Molesburg, Allen R. 22:150
Molesworth, Thomas L. 20:138
Moletar, Leonard 10:69
Moleton, P. 1:153
Moley, Thomas 15:216
Moline, Thomas S. 17:55
Molineaux, J. W. 16:122
Molins, Juan 15:216
Moliton, Peter 10:128; 20:313
Molk, O. 14:91
Moll, Charles 17:421
Moll, Frederick 9:106
Moll, Harvey 20:31
Moll, Henry 9:73
Moll, John 20:126
Moll, Walter 1:55
Mollard, P. 1:157
Mollart, Ralph 9:86

Molle, Lucius 18:54
Molle---, George 20:179
Moller, Philip 20:127
Moller, Walter 12:142
Mollerberg, Thomas 17:23
Mollett, J. 9:26
Mollett, Thomas 9:186
Molley, G. 8:66
Mollicott, J. M. 12:166
Mollin, A. 15:41
Mollin, Thomas 25:324
Mollins, D. 22:514
Molloy, Gilham 26:171
Molloy, Patrick 12:33
Molloy, William 26:174
Molloy, Wilson M. 16:99
Mollzie, James 10:34
Molne, Lewis M. 11:320
Molod, M. 14:91
Molone, A. 26:174
Moloney, James 6:9
Moloney, John 8:101
Moloy, A. 1:60
Moloy, Michael 16:99
Molson, Samuel 4:67
Molt, John 14:199
Moltier, C. 1:151
Molton, Thomas 24:113
Molton, W. H. 11:245
Moltor, Paul 17:111
Moltrie, --- 15:94
Molty, Edward 26:47
Moltz, Charles 14:199
Moltzer, George 1:53
Molumby, J. 25:301
Molunds, William B. 18:150
Momaney, Albert A. 22:45
Momen, Maurice 22:514
Momson, J. 9:86
Momson, W. H. 9:86
Mon, S. 17:111
Monaban, Robert 26:126
Monagan, James 10:8
Monagar, Fred 18:35
Monaghan, --- 3:138
Monaghan, John 22:341
Monaghan, M. 1:154
Monaghan, Owen 23:114
Monaghan, P. 20:148
Monaghan, Thomas I. 10:69
Monague, John 18:285; 26:135
Monahan, James 13:37
Monahan, Lawrence 12:33
Monahan, P. 3:138; 20:148
Monahan, Thomas 19:181
Monarty, E. 11:220

Monce, Squire 17:100
Monce, William A. 22:92
Monck, Hans Peter 13:37
Monck, James A. 13:37
Moncraft, Hugh 9:26; 18:312; 26:106
Moncreef, J. H. 11:220
Mond, James 8:26
Mond, W. 14:199, 258
Monda, Thomas 25:209
Monday, Charles H. 20:104
Monday, G. W. 3:138
Monday, James 6:13
Monday, James W. 21:89
Monday, John 7:35; 12:51
Monday, Joseph 21:368
Monday, Pleasant 23:303
Mondebaugh, Samuel J. 17:314
Mondon, L. 27:83
Mondon, Zemeriah 9:86
Mondone, Nelson 13:58; 16:47
Mondorf, D. 24:82
Monds, James 18:150
Moneau, James 26:45
Moneger, William 22:485
Moneghan, Owen 11:159
Monehan, --- 11:96
Monehan, John 23:266
Moner, P. C. 10:20
Monery, J. 25:209
Monett, G. T. B. 15:58
Monette, H. 1:155
Moneure, James 9:86
Money, Aaron 6:18
Money, Charles 7:130
Money, George 18:324
Money, George B. 12:33
Money, H. 14:91
Money, H. F. 3:138
Money, Howell 11:409
Money, J. S. 25:209
Money, James 10:164
Money, James T. 5:43
Money, Lafayette 18:247
Money, W. H. 17:292
Moneyreach, J. 21:368
Monford, J. H. 8:52
Mong, W. 14:283
Mong, William 16:300
Mongar, Julien 18:35
Mongavin, Frank 23:74
Mongby, D. 3:138
Monger, Joseph 17:443; 24:161
Monger, O. V. 1:152
Mongham, W. 7:52
Monghan, J. A. 20:313
Mongomery, H. 15:58

Mongon, Lewis 14:199
Mongrunary, James 9:134
Mongs, Joseph 17:149
Monhoun, Andrew 8:26
Monical, J. 3:138
Moniear, William M. 12:172
Monighan, Daniel 20:108
Monihan, J. 3:138
Monill, G. E. 2:15
Monin, Thomas 17:167
Moninger, John F. 18:54
Monisay, James 22:167
Monison, John 18:313
Monison, Richard 18:313
Monk, Cumming G. 20:313
Monk, Cummings 10:69
Monk, E. 27:81
Monk, Eli 17:274
Monk, Eugene 9:148
Monk, Henry 12:96; 15:360; 19:88
Monk, J. M. 10:69; 20:313
Monk, M. 1:53
Monk, Robert S. 22:431
Monk, Samuel P. 21:35
Monk, William 8:25
Monkhon, A. 25:209
Monkman, J. 15:344
Monks, Isaac 21:204
Monks, J. J. 14:301; 17:476; 27:88
Monks, John 26:45
Monks, Joseph B. 8:25; 18:150
Monks, W. 15:216
Monks, William 18:150
Monland, J. 19:181
Monloch, Edward 27:146
Monnett, P. 1:54
Monnett, William 17:315
Monoca, J. 25:209
Monohan, Daniel 18:113
Monohan, David 22:433
Monohan, Dennis 12:33
Monohan, J. 1:155
Monohan, Patrick 9:243; 19:326
Monohon, William 21:75
Monor, William J. 24:25
Monroe, A. 3:138; 9:148; 27:83
Monroe, A. G. 21:368
Monroe, A. J. 13:115; 18:104
Monroe, Albert 14:199; 17:135; 24:199
Monroe, Alonzo F. 9:123
Monroe, Alpheus 9:201

Monroe, Asa S. 20:108
Monroe, B. 1:153
Monroe, B. C. 25:52
Monroe, C. 25:209
Monroe, C. C. 23:42
Monroe, C. K. 5:43
Monroe, Casper 20:313
Monroe, Charles 23:74
Monroe, Charles E. 10:164
Monroe, Charles H. 9:148
Monroe, Charles M. 27:81
Monroe, Cooper 10:128
Monroe, D. 1:60; 3:138
Monroe, D. C. 18:399
Monroe, Edward 23:108
Monroe, Edward E. 14:199
Monroe, Ephraim J. 13:37
Monroe, Felix 21:124; 22:45
Monroe, Francis 18:35
Monroe, Frank 17:265
Monroe, G. 17:191
Monroe, G. H. 13:95
Monroe, George 21:368
Monroe, George A. 5:24; 24:95
Monroe, George B. 21:368
Monroe, George O. 21:117
Monroe, George W. 9:67; 18:279
Monroe, H. B. 25:209
Monroe, H. J. 3:138
Monroe, Henry 7:130; 20:313; 21:230
Monroe, Henry C. 24:42
Monroe, J. 3:138; 10:29; 14:91; 19:305; 25:52
Monroe, J. C. 16:65
Monroe, J. R. 3:138
Monroe, Jackson 10:208
Monroe, James 2:14; 7:130; 9:209; 10:128; 13:115; 15:41; 16:214; 19:26; 20:85, 313; 22:150; 25:209
Monroe, James M. 10:128; 20:313
Monroe, James T. 21:56
Monroe, John 3:138; 22:13
Monroe, John K. 16:375
Monroe, L. 3:138
Monroe, M. 1:153; 13:37
Monroe, M. V. 12:33
Monroe, Manly 12:33
Monroe, Martin 9:47; 26:126

Monroe, Mitchell 21:368
Monroe, Nelson 27:89
Monroe, Oliver 9:210
Monroe, Peter 17:135; 24:199
Monroe, Phillip 19:292
Monroe, R. E. 4:42
Monroe, Robert S. 15:355; 19:88
Monroe, Sanford 9:26; 18:313; 26:106
Monroe, T. H. 14:17
Monroe, T. K. 13:95
Monroe, W. 21:368
Monroe, William 1:59; 8:121; 22:92
Monroe, William C. 15:216
Monrokan, Peter 14:199
Monroney, George W. 22:46
Monrow, G. W. 9:223
Mons, John 18:421
Mons, Philip 14:301
Monschitz, J. 3:138
Monsen, J. F. 3:138
Monser, F. K. 14:237
Monser, H. A. 18:54
Monsh, B. B. 15:216
Monsher, E. N. 25:209
Monshover, M. 4:42
Monsier, Alfred 23:309
Monsieure, Anthony 18:150
Monsiers, Anthony 8:25
Monson, A. 8:25
Monson, C. L. 15:8
Monson, Charles H. 19:88
Monson, Edmund 4:42
Monson, George 3:138
Monson, Imbret 8:25; 18:150
Monson, John 23:159
Monson, William 3:138
Monsur, H. A. 10:149
Monsure, G. 27:82
Monta, Henry 3:138
Montag, George 3:138
Montagin, Thomas 12:33
Montague, A. 27:82
Montague, A. J. 1:151
Montague, Aaron 22:312
Montague, Alfred 22:13
Montague, Daniel 22:312
Montague, Francis 8:26; 18:150
Montague, George C. 23:193
Montague, George M. 21:89

Montague, H. 9:148;
22:312
Montague, J. R. 19:181
Montague, John 17:249
Montague, P. F. 23:253
Montague, R. 25:209
Montague, Robert 22:514
Montague, Thomas
17:400
Montaney, Norman G.
20:115
Montange, Joseph 16:122
Montania, W. 1:99
Montargue, William 18:35
Monte, Adam 10:69
Monteeney, George E.
10:69
Montegan, P. 3:138
Monteilto, G. A. 9:86
Monteith, --- 3:138
Monteith, G. A. 26:45
Monteith, J. 2:15; 25:52
Monteith, John 9:26
Monteith, John W. 21:368
Monteith, Thomas 15:130
Monteith, W. 12:96
Montel, Daniel W. 23:256
Montel, Fred 21:209
Montenay, J. 3:138
Monter, William 25:210
Montfort, H. 1:156
Montgarner, F. 14:289
Montge, Robert 5:43
Montgomery, --- 23:42
Montgomery, A. 5:24;
17:253; 25:210
Montgomery, Abram
22:236
Montgomery, Alexander
22:150
Montgomery, B. 17:135;
24:199
Montgomery, B. A.
10:206
Montgomery, B. F. 15:27
Montgomery, Benjamin
12:74
Montgomery, C. 3:138;
13:128
Montgomery, C. H. 12:33,
142; 20:313
Montgomery, C. T. 3:138
Montgomery, Charles
9:26; 11:208, 209;
15:130; 18:247, 313;
22:209; 26:48, 106
Montgomery, Charles S.
16:75
Montgomery, Cornelius
18:279
Montgomery, D. 21:35

Montgomery, David
17:39; 23:42
Montgomery, Eli 9:86;
26:44
Montgomery, F. 14:266
Montgomery, F. H.
12:123
Montgomery, Francis
19:331
Montgomery, G. H. 1:57
Montgomery, G. W. 1:157
Montgomery, George
7:130; 11:95; 12:123;
15:216
Montgomery, George C.
22:341
Montgomery, George T.
11:309
Montgomery, George W.
12:33
Montgomery, Gilmore S.
22:236
Montgomery, H. 18:295
Montgomery, Hamson
9:37
Montgomery, Harr 26:107
Montgomery, Hugh 12:62;
17:447; 24:171
Montgomery, I. 18:113;
25:276
Montgomery, Isaac 11:70
Montgomery, J. 3:138;
8:52; 9:223; 13:95;
14:17, 91; 17:111,
308; 18:372; 21:75
Montgomery, J. A. 24:25
Montgomery, J. F. 25:210
Montgomery, J. H. 14:27,
91; 15:216; 23:293;
24:25
Montgomery, J. M.
21:368
Montgomery, J. N. 26:173
Montgomery, J. P. 4:42
Montgomery, James 8:25,
91; 12:33; 14:91;
16:99; 18:150, 327;
19:47; 27:84
Montgomery, James H.
17:23
Montgomery, James R.
17:111, 347
Montgomery, James W.
11:69
Montgomery, Jefferson
22:432
Montgomery, Jesse
11:245
Montgomery, John 6:10;
9:204; 11:157, 209,
389; 12:51; 14:91;

Montgomery, John
21:368; 22:312, 408;
23:42, 100
Montgomery, John A.
23:74
Montgomery, John H.
22:209
Montgomery, John J.
22:167
Montgomery, John M.
26:48
Montgomery, John S.
23:42
Montgomery, John V.
8:25; 18:150
Montgomery, John W.
8:91; 27:80
Montgomery, Joseph
22:45; 23:74
Montgomery, Josimpson
21:103
Montgomery, L. 8:52
Montgomery, L. B.
12:149; 26:222
Montgomery, L. N.
11:267
Montgomery, Lewis
20:399
Montgomery, M. N.
18:209
Montgomery, Maldon
6:18
Montgomery, Marion I.
12:33
Montgomery, Marshall
22:433
Montgomery, Martin
14:199
Montgomery, Mathew
22:236
Montgomery, McCalin
11:159
Montgomery, Molden
18:90
Montgomery, Nathaniel
23:42
Montgomery, O. A. 3:138
Montgomery, Patrick
11:16
Montgomery, Philip 7:35
Montgomery, Prettyman J.
22:45
Montgomery, R. 1:53;
3:138; 21:111
Montgomery, R. E.
10:128; 20:313
Montgomery, R. S. 1:57
Montgomery, Richard
11:38
Montgomery, Ritchey
22:45

Montgomery, S. 17:181; 23:181
Montgomery, Samuel 1:191
Montgomery, Samuel L. 21:75
Montgomery, Silas H. 10:128; 20:313
Montgomery, T. 15:41; 25:210
Montgomery, T. A. 1:157
Montgomery, T. H. 15:130
Montgomery, T. N. 8:25
Montgomery, Theophilus 17:419
Montgomery, Thomas 4:42; 15:41; 17:135; 24:199
Montgomery, W. 3:138; 7:130; 19:88
Montgomery, W. A. 3:138
Montgomery, Washington 10:99
Montgomery, William 3:138; 9:134; 14:199; 16:47; 20:127; 23:288; 27:85
Montgomery, William A. 17:257
Montgomery, William F. 14:199
Montgomery, Young 7:75
Monticue, J. W. 9:56
Montieth, W. 15:360
Montjoy, T. 3:138
Montjoy, Thomas 20:155
Montjoy, William 7:130
Monton, Charles T. 19:181
Monton, Joseph 18:466
Montray, Gilford 22:46
Montromery, T. A. 18:150
Montrose, G. H. 3:138
Montroy, Moses 25:210
Monts, Andrew 17:39
Monts, Eli D. 8:91
Monts, James 18:35
Monty, J. 23:74
Montz, John 14:91
Montz, W. H. 7:59
Monville, James 17:83, 356
Mood, H. 25:210
Mood, Samuel 17:257
Mooden, Alexander 7:130
Moodey, Emanuel 9:56
Moodey, H. H. 9:112
Moody, A. 1:153
Moody, Absalom 20:24

Moody, Anista 11:37
Moody, B. L. 20:92
Moody, C. A. 14:91
Moody, C. R. 3:139
Moody, Charles 25:210
Moody, Charles F. 12:59
Moody, Clinton 9:67; 18:279
Moody, David N. 21:258
Moody, E. 12:83
Moody, E. A. 5:24
Moody, Edward 1:58; 21:258
Moody, G. 15:344; 16:375
Moody, G. C. 21:124
Moody, G. T. 1:156
Moody, Garrett 11:208
Moody, H. C. 13:38
Moody, Harrison 20:187
Moody, Henry C. 10:20; 16:3, 47
Moody, J. 1:154
Moody, J. L. 9:67; 18:279
Moody, James 8:108; 9:112; 11:207; 12:33; 18:192; 19:88
Moody, James D. 11:245
Moody, James W. 5:24; 25:210
Moody, John 8:41; 14:199; 19:47; 21:184, 214; 26:49
Moody, Joseph 7:130; 10:128; 18:69
Moody, Joseph N. 20:313
Moody, Judson L. 9:37
Moody, L. C. 1:58
Moody, M. 1:95
Moody, Mark P. 17:167
Moody, Martin 11:38
Moody, Myron 8:91
Moody, Otis 11:37
Moody, Peter 21:368
Moody, Peter S. 14:199
Moody, Phineas 13:38
Moody, R. 1:60; 16:141
Moody, R. W. 3:139
Moody, Robert 11:309
Moody, S. 1:152
Moody, S. C. 18:279
Moody, S. W. 21:198
Moody, Samuel 18:90; 23:251
Moody, Solon D. 24:82
Moody, Swain 18:209
Moody, Thomas 3:139; 20:313
Moody, Thomas G. 21:368
Moody, W. 25:301
Moody, W. F. 7:59

Moody, W. H. 20:155
Moody, W. S. 22:209
Moody, William 7:75; 19:47
Moody, William H. 8:26; 18:150
Moog, N. 20:313
Moog, Nicholas 10:70
Mook, John 9:87
Moolsey, --- 20:155
Mooman, Thomas 17:393
Moon, A. J. 22:486
Moon, Aaron 10:128; 20:313
Moon, Benjamin F. 13:38
Moon, C. 1:157
Moon, C. W. 8:66; 9:148
Moon, Charles 14:199
Moon, Charles W. 21:141
Moon, Cornelius 22:46
Moon, David 22:262
Moon, Dennis 21:212, 279
Moon, E. 14:289
Moon, Edward 12:33
Moon, Elias 23:91
Moon, George 6:9
Moon, George W. 22:209
Moon, H. 22:312
Moon, Henry 11:109
Moon, J. 3:139; 20:19
Moon, J. G. 14:199, 258
Moon, J. H. 12:91; 16:301
Moon, James E. 25:210
Moon, James H. 9:123
Moon, John 3:139; 22:503
Moon, John D. 20:31
Moon, John W. 24:42
Moon, Joseph 12:33
Moon, Joseph T. 22:262
Moon, Lafayette 23:193
Moon, Levi L. 15:338
Moon, Nathaniel 4:42
Moon, Oliver F. 24:25
Moon, Samuel 10:70; 20:313
Moon, Thomas 9:231; 20:313; 24:200
Moon, W. H. 19:305
Moon, W. W. 9:104
Moon, William 9:223; 13:38; 18:372
Moon, William H. 22:150
Moon, Zachariah 9:237; 18:413
Moonan, Theodore 7:104
Moone, Barney 25:287
Moonehan, William A. 22:262
Mooney, --- 12:33

Mooney, Albert 10:164; 19:181
Mooney, Berriard 24:9
Mooney, Charles 25:325
Mooney, Charles A. 17:288
Mooney, D. 1:155
Mooney, Daniel C. 13:38
Mooney, E. 21:95
Mooney, Edward 16:86; 17:471; 27:88
Mooney, Felix 9:204
Mooney, Francis M. 22:93
Mooney, G. R. 9:56
Mooney, H. 14:91
Mooney, Isaac 22:262
Mooney, J. 3:139; 13:95; 14:17, 91; 25:52
Mooney, J. S. 1:57
Mooney, J. W. 25:210
Mooney, Jacob 12:140; 20:313
Mooney, James 3:139; 13:38; 19:181; 21:111; 23:181; 24:9
Mooney, John 14:91; 16:281
Mooney, Joseph B. 7:35
Mooney, Lafayette 26:47
Mooney, M. 1:153
Mooney, Michael 21:258
Mooney, P. 3:139
Mooney, Patrick 3:139
Mooney, R. 15:216
Mooney, R. L. 23:42
Mooney, T. 3:139
Mooney, T. J. 7:35
Mooney, Thomas 3:139; 7:104; 11:328; 15:167
Mooney, W. F. 17:479
Moonghane, Thomas J. 20:313
Moonlight, Annie 26:223
Moonly, Aaron 18:90
Moont, Thomas 25:325
Moony, Edward 14:301
Moony, W. F. 14:301
Moonyon, L. K. 14:91
Moor, A. 10:128
Moor, D. D. 3:139
Moor, E. C. 14:301
Moor, George 22:433
Moor, Hugh B. 20:187
Moor, James 10:69
Moor, Martin 10:69
Moor, Thomas 17:455
Moor, W. 11:308
Moor, W. H. 10:29
Moor, William 10:128; 18:16

Mooray, Thomas 7:138
Moore, --- 8:119, 121; 10:187; 18:177; 20:313; 21:190
Moore, A. 1:59, 155; 3:139; 11:85; 12:80; 14:91, 199; 20:313; 25:210
Moore, A. C. 1:59
Moore, A. J. 10:128; 11:38; 15:322; 19:88; 20:313
Moore, A. M. 9:104
Moore, A. P. 3:139; 15:109
Moore, A. T. 16:214
Moore, A. V. 10:128; 20:313
Moore, Aaron 22:262
Moore, Aaron J. 7:130
Moore, Abraham 10:69; 15:216; 20:313
Moore, Abram 22:341
Moore, Albert 7:75; 25:301
Moore, Alexander 10:9, 128; 16:141; 20:313; 21:240, 279
Moore, Alexander J. 21:103
Moore, Allen 22:312
Moore, Allen H. 22:209
Moore, Allen W. 11:68
Moore, Alonzo 11:309
Moore, Alvin C. 23:91
Moore, Amos 13:37; 18:247; 26:49
Moore, Andrew 8:66; 15:167; 16:86
Moore, Andrew J. 22:126, 524
Moore, Andrew S. 23:241
Moore, Anson 19:26
Moore, Anton 9:210
Moore, Ara 3:139
Moore, Archie 18:90
Moore, Armstead 21:103
Moore, Arnold 17:135; 24:199
Moore, Augustus 10:96
Moore, Augustus C. 22:282
Moore, B. 16:375
Moore, B. F. 22:262
Moore, Barnabas B. 12:9
Moore, Barney M. 23:74
Moore, Bartholomew 23:74
Moore, Benjamin 18:150
Moore, Benjamin A. 8:26

Moore, Benjamin F. 16:47; 24:174
Moore, Bernel 9:201
Moore, Brown 10:170
Moore, Bryant 18:35
Moore, Burrell 19:292
Moore, C. 1:59; 3:139; 19:305; 21:368; 22:312
Moore, C. A. 3:139
Moore, C. C. 3:139; 6:25; 11:37; 14:243
Moore, C. D. 17:213
Moore, C. F. 17:495
Moore, C. H. 3:139
Moore, C. J. 4:42
Moore, C. R. 1:55
Moore, C. W. 26:171; 27:86
Moore, Calvin W. 15:216
Moore, Camp 9:112
Moore, Carroll 23:42
Moore, Charles 3:138; 6:18; 13:37; 15:71, 303; 16:215; 17:55; 18:90; 19:26; 21:279; 23:204
Moore, Charles A. 16:80
Moore, Charles C. 21:75
Moore, Charles D. 21:76
Moore, Charles E. 12:33; 18:335; 25:210
Moore, Charles H. 6:21; 7:52
Moore, Charles M. 11:37
Moore, Charles T. 12:51
Moore, Charles W. 3:139
Moore, Chauncey 11:288
Moore, Cornelius 9:204
Moore, D. 14:91
Moore, D. P. 13:95; 14:17
Moore, Daniel 11:95; 13:115; 22:408
Moore, Daniel C. 19:297
Moore, Daniel T. 10:70
Moore, Daniel W. 19:26
Moore, David 7:64, 104; 14:301; 17:476
Moore, David E. 22:46
Moore, Dearastus T. 22:408
Moore, Dennis 1:52
Moore, Dick 27:146
Moore, Doctor 6:28
Moore, Dominique 17:243
Moore, E. 4:42; 13:95; 14:266; 16:141; 26:45; 27:83
Moore, E. C. 17:39, 476; 27:146
Moore, E. G. 14:199

Moore, E. H. 15:216
Moore, E. M. 19:240
Moore, E. S. 27:82
Moore, E. W. 12:123;
15:130
Moore, Ebenezer 10:128;
20:313
Moore, Edward 9:26, 47,
87; 21:212
Moore, Edward A. 13:37
Moore, Edward C. 11:157
Moore, Edward F. 8:114
Moore, Edward H.
10:151, 178
Moore, Edward P. 12:9
Moore, Egbert 22:312
Moore, Eland 11:320
Moore, Eli L. 24:25
Moore, Elijah 11:70
Moore, Elijah V. 9:101
Moore, Ephraim 7:130;
11:38
Moore, Ephraim J. 16:47
Moore, Erastus 20:11;
21:258
Moore, F. 11:37; 13:95;
14:17, 91, 199;
15:41; 22:514
Moore, F. H. 3:139
Moore, Francis 12:74
Moore, Francis M. 17:23
Moore, Frank 3:139;
9:156; 21:368
Moore, Franklin 9:87
Moore, Frederick 19:26
Moore, Frederick A.
22:167
Moore, G. 1:154; 3:139;
13:95; 14:17
Moore, G. C. 17:23; 25:54
Moore, G. F. 1:157;
9:223; 18:372
Moore, G. J. 15:279;
25:210
Moore, G. T. 25:53
Moore, G. W. 10:128;
13:37; 20:313
Moore, Gabriel E. 16:47
Moore, George 1:192;
5:53; 9:70, 87, 134;
14:199; 16:215;
17:447; 18:90, 221;
21:368; 23:159, 309;
24:53, 167; 26:44;
27:80, 84
Moore, George C. 10:70;
20:313
Moore, George L. 5:24;
13:37; 16:47;
17:451; 24:179

Moore, George M. 13:37;
14:199
Moore, George N. 26:107
Moore, George P. 10:10
Moore, George R. 24:53
Moore, George W. 4:42;
9:37; 15:216; 16:47;
17:100; 18:295;
20:11; 22:434;
24:171; 25:210
Moore, Green 11:209
Moore, Greenvillle 23:42
Moore, Guy 7:69
Moore, H. 9:26, 56;
16:99; 19:88; 21:209;
25:54
Moore, H. C. 13:95;
14:17; 15:71; 22:209
Moore, H. Hampton 26:49
Moore, H. T. 11:68
Moore, Hampton 18:247
Moore, Harmon 23:108
Moore, Harrison T.
18:221
Moore, Harvey 24:25
Moore, Henry 7:130;
8:66; 11:209, 281;
15:216; 17:510;
18:313; 19:47;
21:249, 368; 26:106,
213
Moore, Henry C. 13:37
Moore, Henry F. 9:106
Moore, Henry R. 22:13
Moore, Hiram 13:115
Moore, Hiram B. 21:369
Moore, Horner 7:35
Moore, Hubbard M. 8:26;
26:173
Moore, Ira 19:88; 23:74
Moore, Ira W. 21:369
Moore, Isaac 12:74;
15:71; 18:247;
21:369; 22:262;
26:49
Moore, Isaac W. 22:433
Moore, Israel E. 11:277
Moore, J. 1:53, 153, 156;
2:14; 3:139; 7:52;
11:309; 14:92, 199;
18:247; 22:312;
25:54; 26:46, 49;
27:80
Moore, J. B. 9:56; 25:210
Moore, J. C. 1:53; 14:92,
199
Moore, J. D. 3:139
Moore, J. F. 18:90
Moore, J. G. 9:112
Moore, J. J. 14:92
Moore, J. K. 25:210

Moore, J. L. 9:223;
18:372
Moore, J. M. 11:209
Moore, J. N. 14:92
Moore, J. P. 11:307
Moore, J. R. 25:302
Moore, J. S. 15:329;
19:88
Moore, J. W. 1:151;
8:101; 9:87; 15:216
Moore, Jackson 12:33
Moore, Jacob 17:83;
22:209; 26:47
Moore, Jacob I. 21:76
Moore, James 1:57; 3:138,
139; 7:104; 9:73;
10:20, 70, 177, 206;
13:128; 14:91, 283;
16:47; 17:56; 19:181;
20:313; 21:369;
22:93, 126, 209, 341;
23:159; 24:42; 26:46,
212
Moore, James A. 9:87;
17:39; 22:485
Moore, James C. 5:24;
22:433; 24:25
Moore, James F. 21:217;
27:87
Moore, James H. 8:101;
17:460; 18:295;
21:57; 22:503;
23:159; 24:160;
26:107; 27:86
Moore, James K. 8:66;
26:170
Moore, James L. 23:42
Moore, James M. 8:26;
18:150; 21:13;
22:209, 455
Moore, James O. 11:403
Moore, James R. 7:80;
10:128; 20:313
Moore, James S. 17:100
Moore, James T. 11:158
Moore, James W. 7:59;
10:128; 20:313;
24:25; 26:45
Moore, Jeremiah 18:192
Moore, Jesse 10:70
Moore, Jesse F. 22:46
Moore, Jesse W. 22:262
Moore, Job 1:191
Moore, John 1:53, 54;
3:139; 4:42; 7:35,
104, 130; 8:66, 108;
9:87, 210, 231; 10:9,
128; 11:160, 193;
12:33; 14:91, 92,
316, 322; 15:109;
16:47;

Roll of Honor Index

Moore, John 17:23, 135, 249; 18:69; 20:193, 314; 21:369; 22:13, 93, 150, 312; 23:159; 24:9, 25, 199; 26:46, 173
Moore, John A. 23:241
Moore, John C. 12:33; 17:358
Moore, John F. 16:86; 17:283
Moore, John G. 18:469
Moore, John H. 5:24; 12:33; 15:174; 21:35; 23:74, 159; 24:160
Moore, John J. 6:10; 7:130; 11:39; 22:454
Moore, John L. 19:240
Moore, John T. 23:159
Moore, John W. 1:55; 10:128; 17:315, 460; 20:46, 314; 21:230; 24:160
Moore, Jonathan 11:244
Moore, Jonathan G. 20:24
Moore, Joseph 12:62; 15:71; 17:56; 21:369; 22:262; 23:91, 159
Moore, Joseph C. 25:210
Moore, Joseph H. 22:209
Moore, Joseph M. 15:92
Moore, Joshua 16:215
Moore, Joshua G. 24:53
Moore, Josiah 15:80; 17:182
Moore, Julian P. 10:20
Moore, Kaund 11:209
Moore, L. 24:82
Moore, L. D. 13:95
Moore, L. G. 7:35
Moore, L. R. 5:43; 13:37; 16:47
Moore, Lemuel 19:181
Moore, Levi 17:135; 20:86; 21:369; 24:199
Moore, Lewis 11:37; 17:400
Moore, Lewis D. 12:123
Moore, Lewis H. 21:76
Moore, Limerick 11:209
Moore, Luther 10:164; 19:181
Moore, Lyndolph M. 21:11
Moore, M. 1:58; 3:138, 139; 6:32; 7:104; 25:325
Moore, M. G. 3:139

Moore, M. I. 14:92
Moore, M. J. 3:139
Moore, M. L. 18:69
Moore, M. P. 7:59
Moore, M. R. 17:149
Moore, M. W. 9:26
Moore, Madison 11:209
Moore, Mahel 24:113
Moore, Marion D. 17:237
Moore, Marshall 22:93; 24:102
Moore, Martin 1:55; 3:138; 19:181; 20:314
Moore, Martin L. 9:223; 18:372; 22:209
Moore, Martin V. 15:216
Moore, McK. G. 25:210
Moore, Michael 21:369; 22:432
Moore, Michael S. 9:37
Moore, Morris 14:199
Moore, Moses 11:208; 17:398; 21:279
Moore, N. 13:95; 22:353
Moore, N. W. 9:223; 18:372
Moore, Nathan B. 23:91
Moore, Nelson 22:93
Moore, Nicholas 17:387
Moore, Nimrod 17:56
Moore, O. 14:199
Moore, Oliver 14:199
Moore, Oliver P. 12:156
Moore, Orlando L. 16:47
Moore, Orlando M. 13:37
Moore, Ormstead 17:135; 24:199
Moore, Oscar 21:369
Moore, Oscar A. 9:7
Moore, Ozro 16:133
Moore, P. 3:139; 14:92; 25:210; 26:46
Moore, P. A. J. 22:167
Moore, P. Z. 18:421
Moore, Patrick 15:279; 25:210
Moore, Peray 18:399
Moore, Perry T. 23:74
Moore, Peter 3:138; 5:43
Moore, Peter S. 21:141
Moore, Philip 14:199
Moore, Prine 9:87
Moore, Q. 22:312
Moore, R. 17:143, 432
Moore, R. A. 3:139
Moore, R. B. 25:210
Moore, R. C. 4:42
Moore, R. F. 3:139
Moore, R. N. 14:92
Moore, R. S. 21:124

Moore, Richard 11:208; 15:41; 24:200
Moore, Robert 13:66; 17:100; 18:221; 19:88; 20:108; 21:150, 279; 24:153
Moore, Robert A. 11:183
Moore, Robert S. 22:407
Moore, Roderick 17:456; 24:214
Moore, Roland H. 15:109
Moore, Rufus 12:59
Moore, Russell B. 22:520
Moore, S. 3:139; 17:182; 19:181
Moore, S. L. 1:153
Moore, S. M. 17:23
Moore, S. W. 24:113
Moore, Samuel 6:32; 9:157; 10:128; 11:37; 17:39, 449; 19:26, 88; 20:314; 21:131, 279; 23:309; 24:174
Moore, Seth 10:20
Moore, Shadrack 17:398
Moore, Sheldire 12:74
Moore, Simeon 4:67; 22:398
Moore, Simon 1:191
Moore, Simon H. 21:230
Moore, Sinclair 7:104
Moore, Smith 22:515
Moore, Solomon W. 20:138
Moore, Spencer 17:182
Moore, Stephen 8:108; 22:431
Moore, Stephen H. 12:65
Moore, Sylvester 11:390
Moore, T. 3:139; 14:243; 26:45
Moore, T. B. 9:235; 21:369
Moore, T. H. 3:138; 24:113
Moore, T. J. 1:59; 14:92
Moore, T. John 22:209
Moore, T. S. 15:72
Moore, Theodore W. 23:193
Moore, Thomas 3:139; 7:71, 84, 130; 8:26, 116; 9:73; 10:34; 11:157; 13:115; 18:150, 192, 427; 20:314; 21:369; 22:312, 454; 23:114, 307; 24:82; 25:210; 26:223
Moore, Thomas E. 12:96; 15:360

Moore, Thomas J. 3:138; 4:42
Moore, Thomas K. 19:26
Moore, Thomas R. 19:268
Moore, Timothy 21:57; 22:150
Moore, Timothy R. 22:46
Moore, Truman P. 23:109
Moore, W. 20:58; 21:124; 25:210; 26:45, 173
Moore, W. A. 22:209
Moore, W. B. 9:112
Moore, W. C. 3:139
Moore, W. H. 3:138; 4:42; 11:291; 15:72
Moore, W. M. 18:321
Moore, W. P. 3:139
Moore, W. R. 8:73; 26:173
Moore, W. S. 3:139; 9:56
Moore, W. W. 23:307; 25:210
Moore, Warren 15:216
Moore, Washington 18:427
Moore, Washington P. 7:52
Moore, Wesley 26:170
Moore, Wiley 9:87
Moore, William 3:139; 5:24; 8:26, 66; 9:56, 87; 10:20, 149; 11:69; 13:115; 15:87; 16:145, 215; 17:72, 191, 237, 243, 274; 18:54, 150, 372, 413; 19:26, 47; 20:314; 21:103, 369; 22:150; 23:159; 24:62; 25:55; 26:171
Moore, William A. 17:426; 24:179
Moore, William C. 12:142; 20:314
Moore, William D. 22:209, 407
Moore, William E. 9:123; 27:85
Moore, William F. 23:74
Moore, William H. 1:59; 9:234; 12:74
Moore, William H. H. 8:114; 11:158; 18:324
Moore, William J. 9:223; 11:323; 21:230, 369; 22:46
Moore, William L. 9:87
Moore, William M. 9:186
Moore, William N. 5:24; 25:210

Moore, William P. 16:47
Moore, William W. 20:19
Moore, Wilson 22:514
Moore, Zebulon 18:421
Moorehart, Columbus 17:83
Moorehead, Israel 9:73
Moorehead, J. 25:210
Moorehead, James A. 21:76
Moorehead, John 13:95
Moorehead, Philip 11:68
Moorehead, Robert 22:209
Moorehead, Thomas 25:325
Moorehead, William L. 22:236
Moorehouse, Andrew 18:150
Moorehouse, C. 16:375
Moorehouse, D. J. 16:215
Moorehouse, Gil 13:115
Moorehouse, J. 25:210
Moorehouse, M. 14:199
Moorehouse, Oscar I. 11:85
Mooreland, Beniah 9:37
Mooreland, W. F. 14:199
Moores, J. N. 15:109
Moores, James W. 9:87
Moores, Louis D. 15:130
Moorey, --- 9:112
Moorfleet, Moses 21:279
Moorhead, --- 26:223
Moorhead, J. B. 22:209
Moorhead, J. M. 20:314
Moorhead, William 20:314
Moorhead, William J. 26:223
Moorheat, --- 15:259
Moorhouse, Ava 1:56
Moorhouse, Gabriel 17:66
Mooris, William 3:139
Moorland, Wesley 20:24
Moorman, John 26:173
Moorman, Stephen 13:38
Moorman, W. A. 20:42
Moors, John 21:369
Moorse, J. 16:215
Moosbrock, Bartholomew 11:295
Moose, David 19:88
Moose, F. 14:92
Moose, J. 16:215
Moose, Lewis 27:146
Moot, William 25:210
Mooter, John 21:85
Moothland, Hugh 5:53
Mooton, John 20:314

Moots, Daniel L. 25:281
Mope, --- 23:314
Mopes, L. 9:56
Mophin, J. H. 21:111
Mopley, Alfred 10:70
Moplin, John 12:51
Moppins, Jesse 17:135; 24:199
Mops, Jehu 22:431
Mor---, S. L. 19:89
Mora, Charles 18:35
Mora, H. 1:154
Morad, Peter 13:38
Morales, Jesus 7:104; 21:369
Moram, M. 11:161
Moran, --- 8:124
Moran, A. 9:240; 25:57
Moran, Allen 18:247; 26:50
Moran, Anthony 2:14
Moran, C. 19:229
Moran, Charles 9:67, 134; 27:84
Moran, D. 1:151; 16:281
Moran, D. G. 3:141
Moran, Daniel 1:55; 13:82; 16:215
Moran, Edward 10:20
Moran, Edwards 23:13
Moran, F. 3:141
Moran, Francis 1:53
Moran, G. 14:243; 16:148
Moran, George 15:18
Moran, H. 1:152
Moran, J. 3:141; 9:148; 19:240; 27:82
Moran, J. E. 9:148; 27:83
Moran, J. H. 21:111
Moran, James 7:59; 17:160, 401; 21:369
Moran, James F. 8:91
Moran, James P. 17:232
Moran, Jesse 10:70; 20:314
Moran, John 1:57; 4:43; 7:81; 9:187; 14:199; 15:41; 19:26, 240; 23:13; 25:302
Moran, L. S. 14:278; 23:185
Moran, M. 1:155
Moran, M. J. 3:141
Moran, Martin 19:288
Moran, Mich 14:199
Moran, Michael 21:35
Moran, P. 14:199
Moran, Patrick 10:20; 12:33; 15:216
Moran, Peter 1:54; 16:47
Moran, Philip 13:38

Moran, T. 1:155
Moran, T. H. 21:209, 279
Moran, Thomas 3:141
Moran, Tom 23:42
Morander, J. A. 9:187
Morandeville, D. 25:55
Morane, Luke 11:95
Morang, Joseph 21:369
Morange, I. 9:148
Morange, J. 27:83
Morant, M. 3:141
Moras, P. 25:53
Moraset, John 13:38
Morash, Peter 23:109
Moray, Phillip 16:47
Morbett, Philip 17:320
Morbley, John 17:182
Morbly, B. 3:141
Morbly, J. 1:156
Morcan, John 8:114
Morcan, W. P. 15:216
Morcartz, J. 3:141
Morce, John 27:90
Morcey, George 8:114
Morcott, Oliver 26:223
Morcotte, Oliver 9:237
Mordan, J. 18:54
Mordney, A. 26:172
Mordock, Robert 10:70
Mordy, John 26:171
More, --- 11:231; 18:340
More, A. 11:71
More, A. B. 11:37
More, Aaron 15:216
More, Amos 9:210
More, Benjamin F. 24:25
More, David 27:89
More, E. C. 27:88
More, Francis 15:87
More, J. W. 26:171
More, James H. 7:9
More, John 4:42; 9:13;
    13:38; 15:58
More, John H. 3:141
More, John O. 10:20
More, Latty 10:26
More, Robert 4:42
More, Stephen 16:47
More, T. 27:90
More, T. R. 18:54
More, Thomas 15:216
More, W. L. 15:130
More, William 18:54;
    19:222; 27:88
More, William R. 27:146
Moree, Elbert S. 22:504
Moree, J. K. 14:199
Moree, John 11:415
Morefield, Mitchel 18:16
Morehart, J. 10:146

Morehead, George W.
    18:340
Morehead, J. 3:140;
    9:201; 18:54; 19:292
Morehead, J. M. 13:132
Morehead, James C. 20:24
Morehead, Jefferson
    21:230
Morehead, John 21:128
Morehead, Major 9:204
Morehead, Ovil 22:353
Morehead, Robert 15:41
Morehead, Spencer 8:91
Morehead, Thomas 6:32;
    17:111
Morehead, William 10:70
Morehead, Y. 16:215
Moreheart, And. L.
    23:159
Morehouse, Benjamin
    11:208
Morehouse, Charles
    20:181; 21:35
Morehouse, Ernst 15:216
Morehouse, John 22:209
Morehouse, Joshua
    11:403
Morehouse, Richard T.
    11:116
Morel, J. P. 13:115
Morel, M. E. 18:177
Moreland, B. 18:295
Moreland, Benaiah 26:107
Moreland, C. L. G. 18:431
Moreland, Charles 19:27
Moreland, H. 3:140;
    9:148
Moreland, J. D. 14:258
Moreland, J. S. 3:140
Moreland, James 10:128;
    20:314
Moreland, Jesse G. 22:93
Moreland, John 26:172
Moreland, Josiah 8:26;
    18:150
Moreland, S. L. G. 9:234;
    10:211
Moreland, Thomas 11:109
Moreland, William
    11:424; 17:39
Morelane, A. 27:83
Morell, --- 15:216
Morell, A. 3:141
Morell, John 13:38; 16:47
Morell, Peter 26:212
Morelock, George 9:223
Morelock, John B. 7:35;
    26:174
Moren, D. O. 17:308
Moren, T. 1:152
Moren, William 22:341

Morena, H. 3:141
Moreno, Juan J. 18:427
Morer, Adam J. 22:93
Mores, B. F. 1:98
Mores, Joseph D. 7:59
Mores, W. W. 19:89
Mores, William H. 11:128
Moreton, G. 18:407
Morey, Albert 23:159
Morey, Benjamin 11:109
Morey, Charles 19:181
Morey, Charles C. 19:89
Morey, Charles H. 25:210
Morey, D. 21:111
Morey, D. B. 10:20
Morey, Edward 25:210
Morey, Ephraim 23:159
Morey, G. H. 13:66
Morey, Ira 13:38
Morey, James H. 10:164;
    19:181
Morey, Joseph K. 18:399
Morey, Sylvester 9:104
Morey, T. B. 25:54
Morey, W. 13:95; 14:17
Morey, W. S. 19:257
Morey, William 1:53;
    27:87
Morey, William S. 9:187
Morey, William W. 7:63
Morfett, Casp 1:56
Morffett, A. 18:113
Morfit, Russell 25:302
Morfitt, Russell 7:81
Morflet, Robert 7:130
Morfon, R. 23:282
Morford, Charles H. 23:74
Morford, E. W. 21:369
Morford, G. 14:92
Morford, Richard 9:237
Morg, William 12:93
Morgan, --- 15:216;
    18:35; 27:91
Morgan, A. 1:155, 157;
    21:150
Morgan, A. C. 10:29;
    19:305
Morgan, A. J. 20:42
Morgan, A. L. 2:14; 25:53
Morgan, Aaron 23:159
Morgan, Alex 17:309
Morgan, Alex. H. 15:321
Morgan, Alexander
    22:454
Morgan, Alfred 13:38
Morgan, Almond P.
    25:282
Morgan, Augustus 21:217
Morgan, B. A. 9:223;
    18:372

Morgan, B. F. 9:44; 21:141; 26:127
Morgan, Benjamin 24:82
Morgan, Benjamin F. 21:245; 22:282
Morgan, Byron E. 17:23
Morgan, C. 3:140; 27:89
Morgan, C. H. 3:140; 13:130
Morgan, C. W. 15:353
Morgan, Carl O. 10:128; 20:314
Morgan, Carlos 10:165; 19:181
Morgan, Charles 3:140; 9:148; 12:142; 16:215; 17:56; 18:202; 19:89; 20:314; 23:200; 26:213; 27:83
Morgan, Charles W. 22:209
Morgan, Clarence P. 10:165
Morgan, Cunnagin 22:262
Morgan, Cyrus 22:446
Morgan, D. 15:23; 18:372; 25:210
Morgan, D. C. 14:92
Morgan, Daniel 12:62; 17:283; 22:113; 27:146
Morgan, Daniel B. 21:57
Morgan, Daniel T. 19:27
Morgan, Daniel V. B. 7:35
Morgan, David 9:215; 15:279; 21:369
Morgan, David B 15:58
Morgan, David L. 24:113
Morgan, David R. 8:108
Morgan, David W. 7:104
Morgan, Dennis 11:39
Morgan, Dudley 5:43
Morgan, E. 3:140; 16:215; 27:89
Morgan, E. A. 19:89
Morgan, E. J. 3:140
Morgan, E. W. 11:187
Morgan, Edward 19:27; 22:150
Morgan, Edward W. 21:141
Morgan, Eli 21:258
Morgan, Elijah 22:407
Morgan, Elisha 10:10
Morgan, Enoch 11:333
Morgan, Enoch E. 22:486
Morgan, Ephraim 17:100

Morgan, Evan 9:26; 17:315; 18:313; 26:107
Morgan, Evan J. 23:193
Morgan, F. 3:140
Morgan, F. C. 7:35
Morgan, Franklin 21:279; 22:113
Morgan, Fred. 22:312
Morgan, G. 4:43; 25:210
Morgan, G. W. 1:157
Morgan, George 8:41; 14:199; 17:238; 21:369; 26:46, 170
Morgan, George C. 23:74
Morgan, George H. 23:100
Morgan, George J. 17:167
Morgan, George N. 22:262
Morgan, George T. 8:91
Morgan, H. 14:266
Morgan, H. D. 25:210
Morgan, H. O. 15:351; 16:375
Morgan, H. S. 3:224
Morgan, H. T. 12:83
Morgan, Hamilton 12:65; 15:72
Morgan, Henry 22:151
Morgan, Henry S. 17:505
Morgan, Henry T. 23:159
Morgan, Hiram 14:289; 23:42
Morgan, Hugh 11:38
Morgan, Isaac 17:135; 24:199
Morgan, Isaac N. 23:74
Morgan, Israel H. 22:46
Morgan, J. 1:155; 3:140; 16:99; 25:210
Morgan, J. A. 16:47
Morgan, J. B. 6:23
Morgan, J. C. 3:140
Morgan, J. H. 11:109; 20:314
Morgan, J. O. 14:17
Morgan, J. S. 22:209
Morgan, J. V. 12:162
Morgan, Jacob 25:211
Morgan, James 7:64; 11:95; 19:27; 22:150, 504
Morgan, James H. 17:238
Morgan, Jefferson 22:93
Morgan, John 5:24; 7:35; 8:108; 9:134; 10:10, 152; 14:199; 17:39; 18:346; 21:369; 22:115, 353; 23:250; 25:53, 211; 27:83

Morgan, John B. 8:26; 18:150; 22:168
Morgan, John C. 8:26; 9:104; 18:150
Morgan, John D. 22:509
Morgan, John F. 17:215; 23:42
Morgan, John G. 7:35
Morgan, John O. 19:27
Morgan, John R. 11:389
Morgan, John S. 8:52; 21:103
Morgan, John T. 23:279
Morgan, John W. 5:24; 11:95; 17:261
Morgan, Jonathan 25:57
Morgan, Joseph 7:130; 12:65; 19:181; 22:353, 434
Morgan, Joseph H. 8:26; 18:150
Morgan, Judson 23:13
Morgan, L. 14:243; 17:135; 24:198
Morgan, L. P. 25:211
Morgan, L. R. 15:312; 19:89
Morgan, Lafayette 23:256
Morgan, Lemuel 18:90
Morgan, Levy 13:38
Morgan, M. 3:140
Morgan, M. C. 10:70; 20:314
Morgan, M. D. 22:485
Morgan, M. L. 7:81; 13:115; 25:302
Morgan, M. R. 26:223
Morgan, Manless 8:41; 26:172
Morgan, Mansfield 20:11
Morgan, Merrick 22:282
Morgan, Miles 10:174; 19:182
Morgan, Morton N. 12:142
Morgan, N. 17:432
Morgan, Nathan 20:58
Morgan, Nathaniel 24:150
Morgan, O. 1:56
Morgan, O. P. 15:216
Morgan, Orson 23:42
Morgan, Pat 3:140; 4:43
Morgan, Patrick 13:38; 18:313; 26:106
Morgan, R. O. 3:140
Morgan, Richard 9:56; 18:202; 26:212
Morgan, Robert 9:187; 19:271
Morgan, Robert P. 15:3
Morgan, Robert T. 1:55

Morgan, Robert W. 9:13
Morgan, Rufus 17:151
Morgan, Rumsay 24:68
Morgan, S. 13:95; 16:269;
22:262
Morgan, S. S. C. 18:177
Morgan, Samuel 9:26;
12:51; 18:313;
26:106
Morgan, Silas 21:241
Morgan, Simeon J. 10:20
Morgan, Stephen 17:409;
22:46
Morgan, Sylvanus 7:81;
25:302
Morgan, T. 13:95
Morgan, T. A. 26:212
Morgan, T. S. 22:353
Morgan, Thomas 1:55;
11:246; 20:193;
23:181
Morgan, Thomas D. 9:223
Morgan, U. A. 15:312
Morgan, W. 1:154
Morgan, W. B. 27:80
Morgan, W. C. 25:54
Morgan, W. D. 11:328
Morgan, W. G. 7:104
Morgan, W. H. 9:244;
21:204
Morgan, W. W. 11:267
Morgan, Walker 22:312
Morgan, Walter 14:199
Morgan, Watson P. 7:35
Morgan, Wilbrier B.
12:33
Morgan, William 8:26,
91; 10:70; 14:92;
16:99; 17:358;
18:150, 221; 19:330;
20:314; 21:279;
23:309
Morgan, William Alonzo
17:73
Morgan, William B. 9:243
Morgan, William D.
11:331
Morgan, William H.
18:221; 23:181
Morgan, William S. 9:87
Morgan, William T.
22:126
Morgan, William W.
11:403; 22:93
Morgar, William 15:216
Morgraff, William 3:141
Morgret, Martin S. 10:145
Morgrett, A. 1:158
Morgrett, Martin L.
19:182

Morgridge, William
10:128; 20:314
Morher, C. M. 18:324
Morhouse, G. W. 22:341
Morian, N. 1:60
Moriarey, T. 13:95
Moriarity, Daniel 21:11
Moriarty, John 10:10;
19:89; 23:74
Moriarty, P. S. 25:52
Moriarty, Phil. S. 2:14
Moriarty, Thomas 12:59
Moriartz, Thomas 16:154
Moriaty, F. 14:199
Moriaty, T. A. 9:112
Morical, Thomas 17:257
Moricay, Patrick 21:369
Moriday, David 25:325
Moril, W. A. 16:154
Morin, Edward 27:89
Morine, John H. 11:95
Moring, Alfred 26:174
Moring, S. 22:341
Moris, Henry 27:85
Moris, P. R. 24:25
Morison, Edwin 11:128;
19:182
Morison, P. J. 19:89
Morison, Thom 24:183
Morit, Joseph 3:140
Mority, H. 21:201
Mority, James 21:201
Moritz, Augustus 4:43
Moritz, Daniel 21:57
Moritz, Joseph 19:257
Moritze, A. 3:141
Morjarty, P. 13:95
Morland, J. 3:140
Morland, J. J. 19:89
Morland, Thomas 2:15
Morlang, Charles 19:89
Morley, Edward 13:115
Morley, H. 3:140
Morley, H. M. 26:174
Morley, Harmon O. R.
22:282
Morley, John 12:65;
22:150
Morley, M. 1:157
Morley, William 14:199
Morley, William H.
11:424
Morlock, George 18:372
Morlock, John B. 8:74
Morman, Henry 16:215
Morman, S. 16:215
Mormesis, Jerry 11:208
Mormon, Mortimer W.
17:209
Mormon, Robert 21:279
Mormun, William 7:130

Morn, M. W. 25:58
Morner, F. 9:187
Morney, Joseph 15:167
Morney, W. F. 27:88
Mornin, Isaiah 24:199
Mornson, J. 15:216
Moron, Henry 20:187
Moron, James 26:45
Moroney, J. 21:111
Morong, C. 9:187
Morony, Thomas 11:38
Morphen, J. W. 3:141
Morphy, Cornelius 9:187;
19:240
Morphy, William 25:302
Morps, Francis 14:199
Morral, T. B. 12:156
Morran, John 15:216
Morran, Patrick 15:160
Morre, Daniel T. 20:314
Morreite, David 23:309
Morrel, A. 27:90
Morrel, E. 24:68
Morrell, A. 1:153; 21:35;
26:45
Morrell, Asa 7:104
Morrell, Austin 25:54
Morrell, Charles E. 27:86
Morrell, George W.
20:314
Morrell, H. J. 19:182
Morrell, J. 19:89
Morrell, J. B. 1:151
Morrell, James C. 13:38
Morrell, Joseph 25:211
Morrell, Joseph W. 16:47
Morrell, M. 11:160
Morrell, M. C. 14:200
Morrell, Martin V. 23:74
Morrell, Orlin 21:117
Morrell, T. G. 16:375
Morrell, Thomas G. 7:9
Morrell, William 9:240;
16:375; 22:168
Morren, Hector 23:159
Morren, Thomas 7:35
Morressey, J. 2:14
Morrey, Robert C. 10:128;
20:314
Morrey, S. L. 15:333
Morriacy, T. 14:17
Morrick, Charles W.
18:54
Morriess, William T.
23:43
Morrigan, Edward 10:9
Morril, Charles 18:150
Morrile, C. W. 9:87
Morrill, C. --- 25:311
Morrill, A. 8:52
Morrill, Abraham 9:87

Morrill, Americus D. 9:227; 18:372
Morrill, Charles 8:26
Morrill, Daniel 4:43
Morrill, E. 14:200
Morrill, G. F. 16:215
Morrill, George T. 15:336
Morrill, George W. 10:70, 128; 11:116; 20:314
Morrill, J. F. 8:52
Morrill, James 13:38
Morrill, P. W. 25:55
Morrill, Robert 8:26; 18:150
Morrill, W. B. 25:211
Morrill, William B. 5:24
Morrill, Winslow A. 12:59
Morrille, William 4:43
Morris, --- 2:14; 15:216; 25:53, 56
Morris, A. 1:57; 11:381; 14:200; 20:314; 25:211
Morris, A. C. 13:95; 14:17
Morris, A. G. 3:140
Morris, A. J. 9:148; 27:81
Morris, A. T. 3:140
Morris, Abraham 22:209
Morris, Absalom 10:70
Morris, Albert 10:70; 20:314; 22:209
Morris, Alexander 22:150, 465
Morris, Alfred 11:159; 18:399
Morris, Allen 18:399
Morris, Allen O. 22:454
Morris, Alonzo 14:200
Morris, Andrew 11:159
Morris, Appollo 14:200
Morris, Augustus 5:43; 8:74
Morris, B. 11:69
Morris, B. B. 8:59; 9:104; 19:277
Morris, B. F. 20:103
Morris, B. I. 11:429
Morris, Baxter 25:211
Morris, Ben B. 17:451
Morris, Benjamin 10:128; 12:51; 20:314
Morris, C. 11:414; 25:211
Morris, C. D. 18:372
Morris, C. E. 3:140
Morris, C. H. 27:89
Morris, C. S. 1:157
Morris, Calvin 3:140
Morris, Carmleus D. 9:223

Morris, Charles O. 17:15
Morris, Claiborne H. 24:42
Morris, Cornelius 9:210
Morris, Cornelius G. 14:200
Morris, D. 1:153, 158; 3:140
Morris, Daniel B. 23:314
Morris, Daniel R. 11:68
Morris, Daniel T. 8:91
Morris, David 12:51; 17:182; 18:70; 19:325; 21:231; 22:209, 282, 454
Morris, Dous 7:35
Morris, E. 3:140; 23:43
Morris, E. A. 27:90
Morris, E. J. 3:140
Morris, Edgar 26:213
Morris, Edward 14:200; 25:211
Morris, Edwin 1:54
Morris, Eli 21:57
Morris, Elijah 21:124; 23:289
Morris, Elijsha 22:93
Morris, Elisha 10:177; 19:182
Morris, Emery C. 11:20
Morris, F. M. 11:95
Morris, Francis 4:42; 12:51
Morris, Francis M. 17:61
Morris, Francis N. 16:65
Morris, Francis W. 17:356
Morris, G. 3:140; 22:209; 27:79
Morris, G. I. 3:140
Morris, G. W. 19:229
Morris, George 1:54; 4:42; 9:201; 10:128; 11:414; 19:89, 292; 20:314; 25:54
Morris, George H. 12:59
Morris, George N. 18:70
Morris, George W. 9:187; 12:51; 22:126
Morris, Ghalse 10:206
Morris, Greaves D. 10:96
Morris, H. 1:151; 3:140; 21:86; 26:49
Morris, H. A. 1:99
Morris, H. D. 14:278; 23:105
Morris, H. S. 3:140
Morris, Henry 8:41; 9:87; 14:200; 26:171
Morris, Henry E. 20:184
Morris, Hiram 17:317; 27:90

Morris, Holland 23:100
Morris, Isaac 9:87, 210; 26:44
Morris, J. 1:98, 157; 3:140; 9:112; 12:54; 15:94; 18:372; 21:35; 25:211
Morris, J. A. 3:140
Morris, J. A. J. 26:223
Morris, J. B. 4:42; 16:269
Morris, J. C. 8:52; 14:92; 18:409
Morris, J. E. 16:65
Morris, J. F. 20:148; 21:35
Morris, J. H. 2:15; 9:154, 223; 25:211; 27:82
Morris, J. K. P. 1:152
Morris, J. M. 3:140; 12:156; 18:372
Morris, J. P. 20:315
Morris, J. W. 20:315
Morris, Jack 22:514
Morris, Jacob 1:55; 17:39; 22:485
Morris, James 3:140; 6:32; 8:74; 10:70, 128; 12:33; 15:316; 16:47; 17:23, 182; 20:314; 25:325
Morris, James F. 8:108
Morris, James H. 10:128; 12:33; 20:314; 25:211
Morris, James K. 10:128; 20:314
Morris, James M. 1:53; 21:217
Morris, James M. B. 14:200
Morris, James R. 21:217
Morris, James S. 12:33
Morris, Jason H. 9:87; 26:44
Morris, Jeremiah P. 10:70
Morris, Jerome 9:134; 27:84
Morris, Jesse 7:130
Morris, John 3:140; 9:44, 57; 10:128; 12:74; 17:39, 149; 18:279; 20:315; 21:217, 369; 22:93, 262, 433; 26:126
Morris, John C. 18:35; 22:93
Morris, John F. 17:56
Morris, John H. 11:70
Morris, John J. 17:56
Morris, John M. 22:150

Morris, John Owen
21:116
Morris, John S. 16:47
Morris, John T. 22:434
Morris, John W. 11:255
Morris, Joseph 7:130;
10:128; 11:382, 389;
15:295; 16:215;
19:331; 20:315
Morris, Joseph W. 10:70
Morris, Joshua 5:43; 8:66
Morris, L. 1:155, 156;
15:216
Morris, L. R. 3:140
Morris, Lafayette 26:126
Morris, Laurence 19:182
Morris, Lawrence 10:164
Morris, Leander 22:93
Morris, Levi 4:42
Morris, Lewis 13:38;
16:47
Morris, M. 3:140; 14:92
Morris, M. L. 27:81
Morris, M. P. 22:398
Morris, Martin 18:247;
26:49
Morris, Matson 23:74
Morris, Matthew 22:312
Morris, Michael 11:127
Morris, N. C. 27:90
Morris, N. J. 17:23
Morris, N. N. 8:73
Morris, N. Y. 14:92
Morris, Neal 10:70
Morris, Nell 20:315
Morris, Nelson 10:70;
18:247; 20:315;
26:49
Morris, Otis 4:42
Morris, P. 14:92; 16:122
Morris, Patrick 9:187
Morris, Peter 25:211
Morris, Philip 6:25; 27:89
Morris, Quiller 22:454
Morris, R. 3:140; 11:69;
14:200; 18:247;
26:49; 27:80
Morris, R. C. L. 20:140
Morris, R. H. 14:301;
17:481; 27:89
Morris, Redmond 1:54
Morris, Richard 13:115;
14:92
Morris, Robert 10:128;
14:92, 283; 20:315
Morris, Robert J. 16:47
Morris, Roswell 11:209
Morris, Rufus 11:159
Morris, S. 8:59; 11:68;
19:288; 21:131;
23:43

Morris, S. C. 18:70
Morris, S. P. 18:192
Morris, Samuel 10:128;
20:315; 22:126
Morris, Sidney A. 10:70
Morris, Sidney G. 11:116
Morris, Solomon 21:103
Morris, Stephen 9:123;
11:128; 21:247;
22:312; 27:85
Morris, Stockley 5:43
Morris, Stokel 25:211
Morris, T. 3:140; 9:123;
27:79
Morris, T. A. 3:140
Morris, T. E. 22:126
Morris, T. H. 20:193
Morris, Thomas 10:128;
20:315
Morris, Thomas C. 17:389
Morris, Thomas F. 7:60
Morris, Thomas L. 7:35
Morris, W. B. 23:277
Morris, W. C. 14:92;
27:90
Morris, W. D. 20:315
Morris, W. H. 14:92;
25:56
Morris, William 3:140;
4:43; 7:52; 9:73, 134,
237; 10:96; 11:266,
278, 428; 12:98;
13:38, 115; 14:333;
15:357; 16:47, 281;
17:83; 23:306;
26:222; 27:79, 83, 87
Morris, William C. 8:91;
18:150; 20:11
Morris, William D. 10:70
Morris, William H.
12:156
Morris, William J. 24:42
Morris, William W.
22:454
Morris, Y. G. 16:215
Morrisay, Alexander 9:98
Morrisey, D. 1:57
Morrisey, J. 25:53
Morrisey, James 1:57;
7:35, 52
Morrisey, John 22:150;
25:53
Morrisey, Thomas 13:38
Morrisey, Thomas J.
25:269
Morrison, --- 9:187;
11:246; 17:294;
18:192
Morrison, A. 1:152;
21:124

Morrison, Abraham C.
7:35
Morrison, Albert 20:315;
23:74
Morrison, Alfred 17:398
Morrison, Amos 22:209
Morrison, Andrew 15:311,
355; 19:89; 24:95
Morrison, Andrew D.
24:42
Morrison, Augus 16:47
Morrison, Benjamin
12:100
Morrison, Benjamin F.
19:268
Morrison, C. 12:56
Morrison, C. D. 19:257
Morrison, Calvin 17:395
Morrison, Charles 13:115;
26:212
Morrison, Charles C.
21:369
Morrison, Charles H.
14:200
Morrison, D. 19:265
Morrison, Daniel 9:187;
13:66; 16:215; 24:62
Morrison, Daniel H. 13:38
Morrison, David 1:54;
24:102
Morrison, David R.
18:413
Morrison, Dick 9:31
Morrison, E. 14:92
Morrison, Edward 15:355
Morrison, Edwin 10:155
Morrison, Ellis 7:104
Morrison, Emerson 11:70
Morrison, F. 1:156
Morrison, Frank 3:139
Morrison, G. W. 11:157
Morrison, George 11:245;
15:216; 22:150
Morrison, Gilford C.
21:131
Morrison, H. 3:140;
17:182
Morrison, Harry 26:145
Morrison, Henry 8:108;
11:68; 23:159
Morrison, Henry F.
11:101
Morrison, Hiram 22:433
Morrison, J. 3:139, 140;
4:43; 11:328; 21:111;
25:211; 26:47
Morrison, J. C. 25:311
Morrison, J. D. 1:57
Morrison, J. H. 3:140;
25:211
Morrison, J. J. 1:56

Morrison, J. P. 25:211
Morrison, J. W. 11:157
Morrison, James 5:53;
 10:164; 11:390;
 13:115; 18:247;
 19:182; 20:33; 22:93,
 341; 25:211; 26:47,
 48
Morrison, James A. 11:38;
 12:33; 27:86
Morrison, Jerry 22:453
Morrison, Job 6:7; 18:113
Morrison, John 1:53;
 2:14; 5:24; 9:26,
 187; 10:9, 164;
 11:71; 16:151;
 17:349; 18:247;
 19:182, 265; 21:369;
 25:56, 269; 26:49,
 105
Morrison, John M.
 10:128; 20:315
Morrison, John R. 11:69
Morrison, John W.
 10:128; 20:315
Morrison, Joseph 19:182
Morrison, Joseph P.
 17:451; 24:179
Morrison, Joseph S.
 22:453
Morrison, L. 22:262
Morrison, Leland 11:69
Morrison, M. 9:87; 10:70;
 20:315
Morrison, Marcus 17:317
Morrison, Matthias
 21:117
Morrison, Miles V.
 17:349
Morrison, O. P. 3:139
Morrison, P. 18:16
Morrison, Peter 7:130;
 13:38; 16:47
Morrison, R. 18:424;
 25:57; 27:87
Morrison, Reuben 6:28
Morrison, Richard 5:24;
 9:134; 26:106; 27:83
Morrison, Robert 16:122,
 148
Morrison, Robert C. 9:13
Morrison, S. 1:154; 13:95;
 14:17
Morrison, S. B. 11:245
Morrison, S. H. 7:60
Morrison, Samuel 20:42,
 115
Morrison, T. 1:60
Morrison, T. E. 15:131
Morrison, T. W. 13:115

Morrison, Thomas
 17:453; 18:413;
 22:46; 23:193
Morrison, Thomas E.
 21:217
Morrison, Thomas L. 9:87
Morrison, Thomas S.
 21:201; 26:45
Morrison, Thomas W.
 22:93
Morrison, W. 3:139, 140;
 24:53
Morrison, W. A. 18:54
Morrison, W. H. 17:249
Morrison, W. J. 15:333
Morrison, W. R. 15:110
Morrison, William 7:35;
 22:453; 23:159;
 24:178
Morrison, William A.
 21:258
Morrison, William E. L.
 5:43
Morrison, William F.
 17:426
Morrison, William H.
 23:43; 24:53; 26:46
Morrison, William J.
 22:126
Morriss, James 19:89
Morriss, Thomas 16:301
Morrissey, J. 11:101
Morrissey, James 4:43
Morrissey, John 25:287
Morrissey, T. 4:43
Morroe, James 9:69
Morrow, Abram 17:401
Morrow, Alex 18:407;
 20:315
Morrow, Alexander 10:70
Morrow, Alpheus 9:187
Morrow, Charles O.
 14:200
Morrow, David 18:247
Morrow, Eugene 20:35
Morrow, G. W. 18:372
Morrow, George 12:33;
 19:27; 21:369
Morrow, H. H. 17:210
Morrow, Henry 10:20;
 21:124
Morrow, Henry F. 9:123;
 27:86
Morrow, J. 3:140
Morrow, J. C. 3:140
Morrow, J. R. 4:43
Morrow, James 16:122;
 20:42; 24:184
Morrow, James W. 23:91
Morrow, John 1:55;
 12:33; 18:247; 26:47

Morrow, John F. 8:26;
 18:150
Morrow, Levi P. 10:70;
 20:315
Morrow, M. 1:152
Morrow, M. K. 11:157
Morrow, Milton P.
 10:128; 20:315;
 21:231
Morrow, P. S. 1:56
Morrow, Randolph 18:192
Morrow, Richard 7:104
Morrow, S. 23:204
Morrow, S. T. 21:204
Morrow, Samuel 7:35
Morrow, Thomas E. 24:82
Morrow, W. C. 18:192
Morrow, W. H. 12:156;
 19:182
Morrow, W. M. 23:314
Morrow, William T.
 15:88; 22:93
Morrsion, James H.
 15:279
Morry, Jacob E. 5:24
Morsch, M. 1:157
Morsden, Minor J. 20:91
Morse, A. B. 21:369
Morse, A. R. 12:9
Morse, Adolph 9:159
Morse, Albert 7:35;
 22:150
Morse, Anthony 18:247;
 20:193; 26:49
Morse, B. 1:158; 15:344
Morse, B. C. 27:82
Morse, B. S. 19:222
Morse, C. 16:215
Morse, C. B. 9:148
Morse, Carlos J. 13:38
Morse, Charles 1:56;
 16:82
Morse, Charles E. 19:89
Morse, Charles J. 16:47
Morse, Charles W. 12:33
Morse, Chester B. 21:369
Morse, Chester G. 26:223
Morse, Cyrus W. 6:21
Morse, D. G. 19:89
Morse, D. M. 21:369
Morse, D. S. 21:35
Morse, Daniel 15:160;
 25:52
Morse, David 12:74;
 14:200; 15:72;
 17:182
Morse, David A. 1:56
Morse, David S. 15:160
Morse, E. 14:200; 15:216
Morse, E. C. 19:27
Morse, E. K. 1:55

Morse, E. L. 17:159
Morse, Edward A. 21:239
Morse, Edwin 11:414
Morse, Francis W. 24:9
Morse, Frank 11:120
Morse, G. B. 1:153
Morse, G. W. 7:104
Morse, George 17:83, 288
Morse, George B. 7:35
Morse, George J. 25:52
Morse, H. 1:152
Morse, H. L. 18:54
Morse, Henry 17:398;
    25:211
Morse, Henry E. 15:344;
    16:375
Morse, Horace 10:164;
    19:182
Morse, I. 19:229
Morse, Ira R. 12:33
Morse, Isaac 9:187; 15:84
Morse, J. 3:140; 14:200;
    21:35
Morse, J. A. 25:211
Morse, J. B. 16:99
Morse, J. H. 1:60
Morse, J. J. 13:115
Morse, J. J. B. 14:92
Morse, J. M. 7:104
Morse, Jacob 15:360;
    19:89
Morse, Jacob A. 5:43
Morse, James 13:38
Morse, James E. 11:20
Morse, Jasper 10:70;
    20:315
Morse, Jedediah 22:93
Morse, Jerome B. 10:151,
    178
Morse, Jerry 18:16
Morse, Joel F. 12:74;
    15:72
Morse, John 16:215
Morse, John T. 27:146
Morse, Joseph 5:43; 9:44;
    22:150; 26:126
Morse, Lewis 23:286
Morse, Lorenzo 23:124
Morse, Lorenzo L. 8:74
Morse, Lucian 26:127
Morse, M. H. 1:151
Morse, M. S. 1:57
Morse, M. W. 9:215;
    21:369; 24:82
Morse, Miles E. 1:57
Morse, Moses 16:215
Morse, N. E. 15:41
Morse, Newell 10:70
Morse, Newill 20:315
Morse, P. O. 1:59
Morse, Peter 9:100

Morse, S. C. 19:240
Morse, S. G. 9:187
Morse, S. S. 4:43
Morse, S. U. 17:463
Morse, S. W. 8:101
Morse, Samuel R. 8:91
Morse, Seymour 7:104
Morse, Sidney S. 17:243
Morse, Silas 15:110
Morse, Sylvester 24:178
Morse, Uriah 6:21
Morse, W. 3:140; 9:187;
    14:200; 19:229
Morse, W. H. 1:155
Morse, W. P. 1:59
Morse, W. S. 11:320
Morse, William 4:43;
    12:74; 14:258, 289;
    23:43; 27:89
Morse, William H. 12:33
Morse, William M. 15:58;
    19:240
Morsell, C. E. 4:43
Morses, Benjamin 21:369
Morsey, M. F. 21:369
Morsey, P. C. 22:262
Morshart, A. J. 24:82
Morsoll, Henry 9:104
Mort, B. 23:204
Mort, Lewis 7:35
Mortar, T. E. 11:309
Morte, Coba 16:215
Morten, Robert 10:128
Mortenson, H. 10:128;
    20:315
Mortes, John S. 7:130
Mortibor, Alfred 21:141
Mortimer, Albert 22:341
Mortimer, Alonzo 10:164;
    19:182
Mortimer, Daniel 9:134;
    27:84
Mortimer, Henry 22:520
Mortimer, John 14:200;
    19:334
Mortimer, L. 3:141
Mortimer, Theodore
    21:243
Mortimer, Thomas
    19:182; 21:89
Mortimer, William 3:141
Mortimer, William S.
    22:236
Mortimore, David 20:11
Mortimore, S. B. 23:160
Mortin, Antonio 12:170
Mortledge, --- 19:297
Morton, A. B. 16:215
Morton, A. I. H. 21:35
Morton, A. J. N. 21:196
Morton, Albert E. 20:24

Morton, Alexander 7:60;
    22:209
Morton, Amos 9:123;
    27:86
Morton, Ashbell 7:35
Morton, Ashley 21:279
Morton, B. H. 18:417
Morton, Benjamin 13:58;
    17:398
Morton, Bryant 3:139
Morton, C. 14:92
Morton, Caleb A. 17:83
Morton, Charles 3:139
Morton, Charles H. 9:187
Morton, Chester L. 12:33
Morton, D. 1:150
Morton, D. H. 1:151
Morton, Daniel 9:165;
    22:262; 25:325
Morton, Daniel B. 22:46
Morton, Darius 1:56
Morton, David J. 20:19
Morton, Dick 19:292
Morton, E. D. 7:69
Morton, E. N. 21:369
Morton, E. P. 14:301;
    17:473; 27:89
Morton, Ed. F. 19:240
Morton, Edward L. 17:15
Morton, F. 10:206; 18:285
Morton, Frank 5:24;
    21:369
Morton, Fuller 19:182
Morton, G. 16:215
Morton, G. H. 3:139
Morton, George 7:104;
    11:335; 13:115;
    17:135; 24:199;
    25:54
Morton, George W. 6:23
Morton, H. F. 16:99
Morton, Harvey 5:24;
    25:211
Morton, Henry 3:139;
    4:67; 22:46
Morton, Henry C. 9:87;
    24:25
Morton, Ira H. 8:26
Morton, J. 3:139; 13:95;
    14:92; 23:159
Morton, J. B. 3:139
Morton, J. D. 12:33
Morton, J. H. 9:163
Morton, J. O. 15:363
Morton, James 27:87
Morton, James A. 20:148
Morton, James G. 10:206
Morton, Jerome 1:57
Morton, Jerry 17:135;
    24:200

Morton, John 1:54; 7:35; 9:98; 13:38; 18:90; 20:108; 22:312; 23:309
Morton, John H. 18:150
Morton, Jonathan 18:399
Morton, Lewis B. 17:83
Morton, Marcus 9:26; 18:313; 26:106
Morton, Morris 11:17
Morton, N. 14:258
Morton, Nathaniel H. 17:261
Morton, Noah C. 15:72
Morton, Noah E. 12:65
Morton, Pleasant 22:126
Morton, Q. T. 14:92
Morton, R. 4:43; 22:209
Morton, Robert 20:315
Morton, S. 3:139
Morton, Samuel 19:47
Morton, Seymour W. 7:104
Morton, Sidney 16:215
Morton, Sketchley 9:148
Morton, T. 24:90; 26:135
Morton, T. J. 7:104
Morton, Thomas 16:71; 18:413
Morton, Thomas B. 23:43
Morton, Thomas D. 22:209
Morton, Thomas G. 19:27
Morton, Thomas L. 19:27
Morton, W. 14:92
Morton, W. F. 8:52
Morton, W. H. 20:315
Morton, Wenzel 8:118
Morton, William 9:37; 14:266; 17:238
Morton, William G. 18:150
Morton, William H. 8:26; 9:231; 11:188; 26:173
Morton, William P. 9:187
Mortro, Henry 26:47
Morts, Daniel 9:44
Mortursur, M. 21:92
Mortus, P. 3:141
Morvens, Louis 18:427
Morwin, Isaiah 17:135
Mosback, Michael 10:165; 19:182
Mosbey, Chester 5:43
Mosbey, Thomas 9:165
Mosbrier, P. 14:92
Mosby, C. 25:211
Mosby, Collin 22:312
Mosby, Harvey 17:182
Mosby, Henry 27:146

Mosby, Jesse 23:256
Mosby, John M. 22:46
Mosby, Samuel 7:130
Moscar, Mosier 13:127
Moscher, P. A. 4:43
Moschutt, M. 1:58
Mose, John 21:279
Mosecraft, J. 22:408
Moseler, A. 13:115
Moseley, --- 9:57
Moseley, John 20:193
Moseley, King Herod 10:206
Mosell, William 10:20
Mosely, Addison 12:74
Mosely, B. F. 14:289
Mosely, Bemi 27:86
Mosely, Daniel 20:50
Mosely, Edmund 7:130
Mosely, G. W. 26:174
Mosely, Griffin 18:16
Mosely, Henry 22:312
Mosely, Jefferson 11:37
Mosely, John 10:20
Mosely, K. T. 14:266
Mosely, Richard 25:54
Moser, --- 15:174; 18:54
Moser, Christian 13:38; 19:27
Moser, Daniel 12:59
Moser, Elias 23:256
Moser, Frank 20:11
Moser, G. 12:83; 16:301
Moser, G. W. 1:152
Moser, Hiram 18:113
Moser, J. Peter 23:114
Moser, John 3:141; 20:193; 22:46
Moser, Lewis 4:43
Moser, Louis 10:128; 20:315
Moser, Martin F. 13:38
Moser, S. 3:141
Moser, W. 1:151; 16:301
Moser, William 23:43
Moserip, W. S. 5:24
Moseripe, W. S. 25:211
Moses, A. 3:141
Moses, Alexander 14:200
Moses, Alonzo D. 10:165
Moses, Asa L. 22:209
Moses, Augustus 9:201
Moses, Benjamin 7:130
Moses, C. 3:141
Moses, E. S. 27:91
Moses, Edward 17:391
Moses, George W. 8:91
Moses, Henry 20:104
Moses, J. 25:211
Moses, J. L. 15:338
Moses, Jacob 14:200

Moses, James 21:279; 23:271
Moses, John 19:240
Moses, John T. 9:187
Moses, L. 3:141
Moses, Michael 11:39
Moses, Peter 12:33
Moses, Philip 15:217
Moses, Robert 11:281
Moses, Robert R. 15:18
Moses, S. F. 17:436; 24:187
Moses, Silas 7:35
Moses, Thornton 9:210
Moses, W. 3:141
Moses, William 27:146
Mosesport, Joseph 8:26; 18:150
Mosey, A. 3:141
Mosey, P. 14:200
Mosgrove, George V. 15:88
Mosher, Aaron 13:38
Mosher, Asa W. 23:109
Mosher, C. E. 25:211
Mosher, C. M. 1:58
Mosher, Charles 9:237; 12:33; 26:222
Mosher, Charles E. 25:211
Mosher, Charles F. 25:211
Mosher, David 21:76
Mosher, E. 3:141; 22:46
Mosher, F. 1:156
Mosher, F. B. 4:43
Mosher, F. George 7:60
Mosher, H. E. 14:243
Mosher, Horace J. 22:465
Mosher, Howard C. 9:187
Mosher, I. 8:52
Mosher, Ira J. 19:325
Mosher, J. D. 7:83
Mosher, J. F. 15:217
Mosher, J. M. 1:59
Mosher, James H. 20:315
Mosher, Jonathan 13:38
Mosher, Michael D. 22:465
Mosher, Nathaniel 25:55
Mosher, Newton A. 10:70
Mosher, Samuel D. 24:25
Mosher, Simon D. 27:85
Mosher, T. 1:99
Mosher, Willard O. 21:258
Mosherton, A. 1:152
Moshia, L. 1:156
Moshief, Lewis 19:234
Mosier, A. 1:103; 14:93
Mosier, Benjamin 20:42
Mosier, David 15:217

Mosier, E. 3:141
Mosier, Elias N. 5:24
Mosier, Frank 11:403
Mosier, G. 1:158
Mosier, Henry 4:43
Mosier, Isaac 13:95
Mosier, J. 9:187; 19:257
Mosier, J. H. 9:26
Mosier, Jacob C. 9:26
Mosier, James 7:104;
    18:247; 26:47
Mosier, John 22:433
Mosier, John W. 17:201
Mosier, L. 11:266
Mosier, L. M. 1:152
Mosier, M. W. 3:141
Mosier, Peter 22:407
Mosier, S. A. 15:153
Mosier, Steward 12:62
Mosier, Stewart 15:92
Mosier, T. C. 21:369
Mosier, W. 12:91
Mosier, W. R. 7:13
Mosier, Warren 17:361
Mosier, William 5:24;
    25:211
Mosier, William R.
    17:419
Moslander, Daniel A.
    17:23
Moslander, Joseph 11:38
Mosley, C. 25:211
Mosley, C. W. 16:215
Mosley, Francis 11:309
Mosley, G. W. 8:74
Mosley, Henry 11:266
Mosley, John 11:409
Mosley, Matthew 23:291
Mosley, Winston 10:208
Mosner, John 1:58
Moss, Albert 4:43
Moss, Alonzo J. 23:74
Moss, Boss S. 22:209
Moss, C. F. 1:155
Moss, Charles 7:35
Moss, Dallas 19:292
Moss, Daniel 4:43
Moss, David 15:304
Moss, E. 3:141
Moss, E. L. 14:243
Moss, Enoch 14:200
Moss, Frederick 14:200
Moss, G. 17:191
Moss, G. S. 16:99
Moss, G. W. 23:43
Moss, George 9:95; 26:44
Moss, George W. 21:103
Moss, Griffy 11:95
Moss, H. 14:93
Moss, H. M. 1:154

Moss, H. T. 12:93; 14:93;
    16:301
Moss, Harry 18:247
Moss, Henry 18:247;
    26:48, 49
Moss, J. 15:167; 20:42
Moss, J. L. 9:223; 18:372
Moss, Jacob 12:96
Moss, Jacob W. 23:43
Moss, James 15:72
Moss, James B. 10:128;
    20:315
Moss, Jeff 18:247; 26:49
Moss, John 15:174;
    17:356
Moss, Joll 16:215
Moss, Leonard 23:271
Moss, Linzy B. 22:126
Moss, M. 9:57
Moss, M. J. 15:330; 19:89
Moss, Martin 1:57
Moss, P. B. 23:267
Moss, Peter 12:51
Moss, Preston 22:312
Moss, S. M. 26:237
Moss, Thomas 19:330
Moss, W. N. 14:93
Moss, W. S. 3:141
Moss, William 1:54;
    3:141; 15:217
Moss, William E. 7:104
Moss, William J. 8:66
Moss, William L. 8:91
Moss, William S. 18:209
Mossbrook, John M.
    17:395
Mosser, Frederick 24:25
Mossier, Thomas R.
    10:128; 20:315
Mossit, Peter 11:183
Mosskamp, Joseph A.
    22:13
Mossler, A. 14:200, 258
Mossman, John C. 22:93
Most, Oratio 4:43
Mostin, M. 14:93
Motag, Wellington 16:47
Mote, John 23:74
Mote, John R. 11:390
Motes, Ely 15:217
Motfer, Mil 24:82
Mother, Gre--- 24:200
Motherbaugh, Jesse O.
    24:68
Motherspaw, Thomas
    22:408
Mothey, Benjamin 17:393
Moths, Henry 17:388
Motler, Walter 20:315
Motley, H. 17:135
Motley, Lewis 17:136

Motley, O. J. 16:281
Motley, Perry J. 22:455
Motley, Reuben 17:261
Motley, Thomas 16:141
Motloin, Jeremiah N.
    22:504
Motog, Wellington 13:58
Motpier, William 18:221
Motshler, A. 13:95
Motsinger, John J. 24:25
Motsinger, Levi 21:201
Motsinger, Ransum P.
    24:99
Mott, A. 19:89
Mott, B. 23:204
Mott, Charles 1:54;
    11:159
Mott, Daniel E. 14:200
Mott, E. 1:151
Mott, Edmund L. 20:193
Mott, F. 13:115
Mott, Frederick N. 22:487
Mott, George 14:200;
    23:160
Mott, George D. 25:211
Mott, George E. 7:52
Mott, George H. 15:5
Mott, George W. 21:57
Mott, Henry 17:92
Mott, J. 1:158; 11:308;
    13:38; 26:47
Mott, J. Milton 12:74;
    15:94
Mott, James 9:87
Mott, Joel 9:57
Mott, John 1:56; 8:115;
    11:120; 18:324
Mott, Malon A. 23:74
Mott, Martin 2:14; 25:56
Mott, Richard 4:67
Mott, Samuel 14:200
Mott, Samuel J. 22:151
Mott, Sheridan E. 22:432
Mott, Stephen 24:82
Mott, Sylvanus 13:38
Mott, Sylvester 21:369
Mott, T. C. 19:182
Mott, W. C. 1:155
Mottay, --- 15:217
Motter, John 17:83
Mottern, William S.
    16:147
Mottier, C. M. 9:26
Motts, C. 3:141
Motwilder, Peter 21:231
Motz, G. L. 1:56
Motz, J. 14:200
Motzer, John 4:43
Mou, James E. 22:433
Moucey, G. 14:93
Moughan, Michael 15:72

Moul, G. A. 15:153
Moulard, C. 14:301;
  17:479
Moulden, James R. 11:69
Moulden, William 3:141
Moulden, William H.
  23:74
Moulder, J. 10:180;
  18:177
Moulder, J. M. 19:268
Moulder, John 15:217
Moulder, L. 14:200
Moulder, Valentine 8:91
Moulder, Valentine P.
  10:128; 20:315
Moulder, William 16:301
Mouldon, Michael 24:42
Moule, Henry A. 13:38
Moulock, Joseph 11:96
Moultay, James H. 21:103
Moulteal, W. 19:89
Moulter, John M. 9:187
Moulthroop, Horace
  16:47
Moulthrop, Evelyn E.
  23:16
Moulthrop, Horace 13:38
Moulthrop, Leroy 20:24
Moulton, Adam 9:98
Moulton, Arthur 10:165
Moulton, C. A. 7:104
Moulton, Charles F.
  19:182
Moulton, Charles N.
  10:165
Moulton, D. 1:57
Moulton, Daniel 10:165;
  19:27, 182
Moulton, H. 3:141;
  14:200
Moulton, J. A. 19:182
Moulton, James 16:215
Moulton, John 10:70;
  20:315
Moulton, John F. 22:464
Moulton, L. S. 14:243;
  27:91
Moulton, Orrin 22:162
Moulton, S. 1:152
Moulton, Samuel 17:136;
  24:199
Moulton, Thomas L.
  7:104
Moulton, William H.
  13:38
Moultrope, Charles 9:57
Moun, A. McK. 15:344;
  16:375
Mounce, William 10:128;
  20:315
Moune, Dingee 27:80

Mounee, Maholan 9:223
Mount, Francis 22:210
Mount, George F. 16:17
Mount, Henry 13:38
Mount, J. H. 11:328
Mount, J. W. 24:25
Mount, James T. 23:91
Mount, John 10:70;
  20:315
Mount, John B. 25:56
Mount, Joseph L. 23:129
Mount, L. W. 14:29
Mount, M. 20:315
Mount, Nathaniel A.
  21:76
Mount, Newton 23:43
Mount, Samuel V. 16:17
Mount, Taylor 17:111
Mount, Thomas 6:32
Mount, William 23:43
Mount, William D. 22:209
Mountain, Benjamin
  17:70
Mountain, H. H. 16:375
Mountain, R. D. 22:497
Mountain, William S.
  7:36
Mountaine, Sylvester
  11:309
Mounts, --- 22:210
Mounts, David K. 23:286
Mounts, Henry N. 23:160
Mounts, Samuel 10:70;
  20:315
Mountz, Eli 22:93
Mountz, Joseph E. 22:93
Mountz, R. 3:141
Mountz, S. I. 11:419
Mour, W. H. 18:372
Mourand, Wilson 27:79
Mourey, William 11:309
Mourne, Thomas 9:37
Mourning, I. W. 17:271
Moury, Jesse A. 11:158
Mous, Philip 17:478
Mouse, Alexander 7:69
Mouse, Archibald 11:159
Mouser, Casper 15:58
Mouser, D. H. 21:124
Mouser, George W.
  17:426
Mouser, Michael 10:128;
  20:315
Mouser, William F. 20:28
Mousley, William T. 1:59
Moust, J. 4:43
Mouthia, J. 27:80
Movean, J. A. 18:247;
  26:49
Moverholtz, Henry 13:38
Movers, E. E. 21:369

Movey, J. 25:312
Movney, J. 14:201
Movr, John 14:201
Mow, Edward H. 7:16
Mow, J. 15:217
Mowber, Aaron 13:58
Mowberry, John C.
  18:150
Mowbry, C. 16:215
Mowder, George W. 9:57
Mowe, James S. 12:156
Mowen, T. 19:89
Mower, A. C. 16:215
Mower, Albion P. 7:104
Mower, Alexander 22:46
Mower, Augustus B.
  21:258
Mower, Henry 13:115
Mower, Jacob 15:72;
  18:35
Mower, Josiah 22:210
Mower, L. 1:152
Mower, Philip A. 12:33
Mower, Richard 20:399
Mower, William 3:141
Mowers, Carl 8:26;
  18:151
Mowers, Eleazer J. 23:124
Mowers, H. 9:112
Mowery, Charles 21:369
Mowery, David 20:148
Mowery, John B. 16:156
Mowery, Samuel 16:133;
  22:93
Mowery, William 18:151
Mowfield, A. 20:315
Mowin, T. 15:315
Mowland, Samuel 11:209
Mowle, Richard W.
  9:235; 18:421
Mown, --- 2:15; 25:57
Mowrey, Cyrus 22:210
Mowrey, Forey 9:157
Mowry, A. 1:103
Mowry, Austin 9:163
Mowry, D. 1:57
Mowry, Edward 12:9
Mowry, Elisha 25:54
Mowry, George W.
  20:138; 21:196
Mowry, J. B. 20:58
Mowry, John 3:141;
  22:353
Mowry, M. B. 27:81
Mowry, M. T. 18:247;
  26:48
Mowry, Oliver 22:151
Mowry, T. 14:201
Mowry, W. 11:128
Mowry, William 8:26
Mowry, William J. 15:217

Moxer, Moses P. 26:44
Moxley, Charles W.
  20:187
Moxley, Lewis 9:70
Moxley, Walter 22:313
Moxton, Oscar 14:201
Moyden, Sack 10:187
Moydon, Pleasant 8:25
Moye, Henry 9:123
Moyer, A. 7:69
Moyer, Abram 22:210
Moyer, Amandes 16:215
Moyer, Charles 1:59
Moyer, D. 20:148
Moyer, F. S. 1:152
Moyer, George 1:58;
  16:122
Moyer, Henry 19:89
Moyer, I. 9:148
Moyer, Isaac 10:70
Moyer, J. 1:154
Moyer, J. C. 25:57
Moyer, J. P. 9:112
Moyer, John 3:141; 9:123;
  12:33; 22:210; 27:85
Moyer, John H. 21:11
Moyer, John N. 22:236
Moyer, Joseph 10:128;
  20:315; 21:164
Moyer, M. 22:486
Moyer, N. H. 17:84
Moyer, Nathaniel 1:56
Moyer, Oliver 14:201
Moyer, P. L. 23:181
Moyer, S. S. 2:14
Moyer, Samuel 22:210
Moyer, Sidney A. 22:485
Moyer, Thomas 3:141
Moyer, W. 3:141
Moyer, W. H. 25:325
Moyer, William M. 3:141
Moyers, William 22:113
Moyey, James 19:182
Moylan, Richard 16:375
Moyle, Allen 17:72
Moyn, Richard 10:149;
  18:54
Moyr, E. 12:9
Moyse, R. 7:52
Mozena, William M.
  22:353
Mozier, --- 15:131
Mozier, Charles 11:109
Mozier, Ebenezer 22:236
Mozier, John 9:210
Muag, C. 3:141
Muarty, J. 11:96
Mubern, Moses 21:279
Mucargham, Thomas
  10:96
Mucddy, R. S. 16:215

Muchler, H. 26:223
Muchler, James S. 12:55
Muchmore, E. D. 14:17
Muchmore, G. 1:55
Muchmore, Stephen
  22:113
Muchmore, William H.
  24:53
Muck, David 20:35
Muck, Emille 17:406
Muck, G. N. 14:243
Muck, G. W. 27:91
Muck, John 20:315
Muckeig, G. L. 14:93
Muckel, W. 13:95
Muckell, A. 14:18
Mucker, Zenas 8:91
Muckle, David 21:370
Muckler, W. 22:13
Mudar, I. 14:201
Mudd, E. W. 21:370
Muddlesworth, A. 1:152
Mudge, Henry 10:20
Mudge, Leander 8:108
Mudgell, E. H. 9:87
Mudgett, E. H. 26:46
Mudgett, George 9:204
Mudley, H. 25:211
Mudy, Tyler 25:211
Muee, William A. 17:315
Mueler, A. 19:89
Mueller, Adam J. 17:353
Mueller, Casper 18:313
Mueller, Charles 17:395
Mueller, Francis 19:27
Mueller, Fred 11:158
Mueller, H. 4:43
Mueller, Henry 18:104
Mueller, John 8:26
Mueller, Louis 23:114
Mueller, Robert 23:193
Muer, J. 1:59
Muer, J. N. 26:173
Muerro, William 18:113
Muett, William 21:370
Mufflemann, S. 26:174
Muffly, John 10:128;
  20:315
Muffy, John 5:53
Mugg, William G. 11:109
Muggins, John 18:279
Mugunin, M. 21:57
Muham, James 11:37
Muher, Washington
  12:156
Muhlbach, G. 18:295
Muhlbach, Gottlob 26:107
Muhlback, Gotleb 9:37
Muhn, Ludovick 18:324
Muhtray, --- 18:431
Muick, V. C. 1:55

Muid, W. H. 2:14; 25:57
Muihr, Robert 22:313
Muir, George 17:419
Muir, Sandy 22:515
Muir, Thomas 9:123
Muir, Thomas A. 27:79
Muir, William F. 23:260
Muirheid, Iven 22:433
Mukel, Benjamin 17:92
Mukings, Richard 7:36
Muky, A. 23:241
Mulalley, T. 1:157
Mulandore, Charles 21:35
Mulanphy, George 18:340
Mulanthy, George 9:104
Mulasky, E. 3:142
Mulberry, Charles 18:151
Mulberry, J. 11:439
Mulbery, Charles 8:26
Mulbry, Isaac 8:66
Mulburger, S. 1:153
Mulby, Lewis 5:43
Mulcahy, W. 3:142
Mulcahy, William 13:38
Mulche, John 10:70
Mulchi, John 20:315
Mulchy, J. 3:141
Mulchy, J. A. 3:141
Mulcohy, D. D. 3:142
Mulculey, Philip 20:315
Mulculy, Philip 10:128
Muldaney, M. 3:142
Muldniger, P. 19:283
Muldoon, J. 3:142
Muldoon, Thomas 9:13
Muldoon, William 19:327
Muleaux, Thomas 15:217
Muleback, C. 4:43
Mulenix, Leroy 11:159
Mulenna, --- 11:193
Muler, Erasmus 10:70
Muler, John 9:104
Mulford, --- 13:66
Mulford, Albert 13:38
Mulford, C. C. 4:43
Mulford, John 18:151
Mulford, Joseph 10:70;
  20:315
Mulford, Samuel 20:90
Mulford, W. R. 3:141
Mulgrave, James 3:142
Mulgrove, Edward 22:151
Mulhall, Peter 3:141
Mulharon, J. 22:210
Mulhenheim, A. 1:154
Mulheren, Alex 22:313
Mulhern, C. 3:142
Mulhill, John 12:168
Mulhive, James 16:301
Mulholand, James 16:215
Mulholany, J. 15:299

Mulholer, S. M. 19:278
Mulhollan, J. 1:158
Mulholland, Daniel 9:26, 187; 10:70; 18:313; 19:257; 20:316; 26:106
Mulholland, George 14:201
Mulholland, J. 3:141
Mulholland, J. P. 26:105
Mulholland, John P. 9:26; 18:313
Mulholland, S. M. 9:187
Mulican, F. N. 13:95
Muligan, J. 3:141
Muligan, Patrick 25:211
Mulikein, Richard 22:46
Mulinex, Jacob 17:405
Mulinex, Walter 4:43
Mulish, A. 3:142
Mulison, David C. 13:38
Mulkey, A. 1:153
Mulkey, G. L. 16:301
Mulkey, Phillip 14:316
Mulkey, Simon 9:87
Mulkey, W. E. 1:59
Mulkey, W. L. 14:93
Mulkin, James 11:69
Mulkin, William 20:31
Mulkins, Charles 1:55
Mulkins, Henry 12:33
Mulkins, Willard 21:76
Mull, C. 1:158
Mull, Cornelius 22:313
Mull, Dallas B. 24:89
Mull, George H. 18:221
Mull, J. H. 16:47
Mull, Samuel 22:46
Mullahey, John 25:334
Mullaly, John 24:95
Mullaly, P. 18:424
Mullanox, A. C. 3:141
Mullany, Nicholas 27:87
Mullany, Thomas 21:370
Mullar, Peter 19:283
Mullarky, John A. 23:43
Mullegan, John 19:27
Mullegan, T. H. 16:148
Mullen, --- 16:215; 21:370
Mullen, A. 3:141
Mullen, A. Z. 9:57
Mullen, Aaron K. 7:104
Mullen, Alexander 22:126
Mullen, Archibald 23:181
Mullen, B. 1:56; 17:192
Mullen, Barney 8:26; 18:151
Mullen, Charles 7:104; 26:172
Mullen, Daniel 9:13

Mullen, Dominick 12:33
Mullen, E. C. 1:155
Mullen, Edward 19:182
Mullen, Emile 15:41
Mullen, Enne 18:70
Mullen, F. H. 5:53
Mullen, G. W. 14:93
Mullen, George J. 25:56
Mullen, Gotfin 18:151
Mullen, Gotfind 8:26
Mullen, H. 1:156
Mullen, J. 1:59; 3:141; 4:43; 21:370; 23:43; 27:82
Mullen, J. A. 25:302
Mullen, J. B. 15:8
Mullen, J. C. 26:173
Mullen, J. F. 7:75
Mullen, James 3:141; 10:20; 11:328; 14:201; 20:316
Mullen, James H. 16:99
Mullen, James R. 12:65
Mullen, John 8:91; 12:33; 15:174, 348; 16:375; 17:15
Mullen, John J. 22:174
Mullen, Matthew 21:76
Mullen, Michael 8:26
Mullen, N. B. 1:59
Mullen, P. 3:141; 15:110
Mullen, Patrick 5:53; 15:217
Mullen, R. W. 15:72
Mullen, Robert 15:217; 21:57
Mullen, Samuel 23:91
Mullen, Samuel D. 19:27
Mullen, T. 1:98
Mullen, Thomas 9:73; 20:316
Mullen, W. A. 27:90
Mullen, W. T. 10:96
Mullen, William A. 21:231
Mullen, William W. 11:69
Mullenax, J. 9:57
Mullender, William 15:27
Mullenhorn, --- 26:48
Mullenhorn, J. 18:247
Mullenn, James 10:128
Mullens, Ben F. 17:453
Muller, --- 13:66
Muller, Baltaser 22:172
Muller, Casper 9:26; 26:106
Muller, Charles 21:118
Muller, Charles L. 9:104
Muller, Claude 7:60
Muller, Emial 12:74
Muller, Erasmus 20:316

Muller, Ernest 4:43
Muller, Felix 7:60
Muller, Frederick 27:146
Muller, George 11:295
Muller, Gustave 21:35
Muller, Henry 21:231
Muller, J. L. 23:283
Muller, John 18:151
Muller, John R. 17:39
Muller, John S. 26:222
Muller, M. J. 21:370
Muller, Melchior 21:118
Muller, Mich 27:80
Muller, Philip 9:123
Muller, W. 19:89; 25:211
Muller, William 5:53
Muller, William F. 11:95
Mullerkey, C. 1:156
Mullett, C. 1:158
Mullett, Charles 7:36
Mullett, W. A. 1:151
Mullett, William 21:163
Mullettt, Jacob 11:320
Mulley, --- 19:89
Mullholand, G. 7:36
Mullholland, Ebbert 27:87
Mullica, P. 4:43
Mullican, T. M. 14:18
Mullick, C. 9:148; 27:83
Mulligan, A. J. 17:249
Mulligan, Bryant 26:223
Mulligan, Dennis 17:160
Mulligan, Edward 13:38
Mulligan, G. 1:56
Mulligan, George H. 16:11
Mulligan, J. 3:141; 12:83; 16:301; 27:80
Mulligan, J. W. H. 1:60
Mulligan, James 15:284; 19:89; 25:56
Mulligan, James S. 16:11
Mulligan, John 18:427
Mulligan, John W. 19:325
Mulligan, P. 9:148; 25:211
Mulligan, Patrick 5:24; 8:108; 13:66; 19:89
Mulligan, Thomas 19:182; 22:172
Mulligan, Wilkerson 24:53
Mulligan, William H. 7:130
Mullighan, P. 27:83
Mulliken, J. W. 26:171
Mullin, Charles 3:141
Mullin, Harrison 11:209
Mullin, Israel 4:67
Mullin, J. 3:141
Mullin, J. B. 22:504

Mullin, J. W. 21:370
Mullin, James 14:201;
  21:370
Mullin, Joel 22:432
Mullin, John 7:60; 11:71;
  22:210
Mullin, John S. 11:277
Mullin, Michael 16:122;
  18:151
Mullin, P. 26:171
Mullin, Patrick 25:269
Mullin, Samuel 8:26;
  18:151
Mullin, T. 18:193
Mullinan, E. B. 11:120
Mullinaux, Richard
  26:213
Mullinex, David 22:434
Mullings, W. 3:142
Mullington, C. 3:141
Mullinick, J. 22:210
Mullinix, E. K. 16:301
Mullinox, H. 14:93
Mullins, Ben 22:341
Mullins, Ben. F. 24:183
Mullins, Charles H. 11:95
Mullins, Cyrus D. 20:316
Mullins, David 22:313
Mullins, Esebius 17:70
Mullins, F. 8:124
Mullins, H. 12:146
Mullins, I. R. 25:282
Mullins, J. R. 14:319
Mullins, John 21:370;
  22:262
Mullins, Lewis 24:198
Mullins, Martin 22:126
Mullins, P. 8:66; 13:95
Mullins, Pat 18:151, 409
Mullins, Pat. 8:26
Mullins, Robert A. 23:74
Mullins, Samuel 21:35
Mullins, Thomas J.
  17:283
Mullins, W. 14:301;
  17:471; 27:89
Mullins, W. W. 3:224
Mullins, Wesley 22:262
Mullins, Wesley W.
  17:499
Mullins, William 8:26
Mullinx, B. R. 1:59
Mullis, Richard 9:26
Mulliss, George 19:27
Mullock, Nelson 21:280
Mullony, Thomas 15:41
Mullory, H. 16:215
Mulloy, E. 1:60
Mulloy, J. 1:156
Mulloy, John 22:341
Mulloy, William 1:59

Mully, Lewis 25:211
Mulnic, Gideon 17:249
Muloey, Michael 19:27
Mulone, J. 1:59
Mulqueen, Patrick 22:46
Mulrooney, William 9:8
Mulse, William R. 21:231
Mulstey, Pete 10:70
Mulstey, Peter 20:316
Multer, J. E. 18:54
Multonburg, John 20:35
Mulvane, Daniel 19:182
Mulvaney, Thomas
  20:138
Mulvany, Henry 20:19
Mulvany, T. 3:141
Mulverhill, T. 12:123
Mulverhill, Timothy
  15:131
Mulvey, Bernard 16:88
Mulvey, F. 14:201
Mulvihill, William A.
  18:70
Muly, Levi A. 22:210
Mumbach, Phillip 25:211
Mumbert, J. 1:59
Mumblehead, Charles
  22:262
Mumblehead, David
  22:262
Mumbrue, Sylvester
  11:109
Mumdorf, Henry 7:105
Mumford, Hezekiah
  10:170
Mumford, James 9:239;
  22:113; 26:222
Mumford, John W. 10:70
Mumford, P. 16:215
Mumford, Samuel 15:5
Mummert, Jeremiah
  16:164
Mumphry, Charles 17:400
Mumpleasant, W. M.
  7:105
Mumuret, Joseph 13:127
Mun, Charles F. 12:33
Mun, David 17:338
Munady, James 18:90
Munager, W. 3:142
Munaker, James D.
  17:416
Munay, Andrew D.
  10:165
Munay, F. 18:431
Munay, Nelson 18:90
Munce, James 6:10
Munce, John A. 8:108
Muncey, Henry 25:56
Munch, --- (Mrs.) 26:223
Munch, Christian 3:142

Munch, H. D. 9:37
Munch, J. 3:142
Munch, Peter 14:201
Munch, Philip 23:160
Munchaum, George
  17:249
Munchuan, H. 16:215
Munck, J. 16:215
Muncy, Enoch 11:95
Mund---y, P. H. 20:316
Mundall, John 25:53
Mundall, Lewis 10:70
Munday, Benjamin
  26:145
Munday, Charles 22:313
Munday, Daniel 6:25
Munday, Enoch F. 22:454
Munday, James H. 22:453
Munday, William H.
  21:241
Mundel, August 1:57
Mundel, Josephus 22:93
Mundell, Lewis 20:316
Mundell, Samuel 26:223
Mundell, Thomas B. 5:53;
  25:211
Munder, L. 9:154
Munderback, Sherman
  21:118
Mundey, George W. 9:87
Mundie, A. H. 1:155
Mundle, Solomon 10:70;
  20:316
Mundoff, John P. 12:74;
  15:72
Mundro, Alexander 27:84
Mundroff, Henry 21:370
Mundt, A. 10:128; 20:316
Mundy, Cornelius 13:38
Mundy, I. 11:341
Mundy, J. 17:337
Mundy, James 11:39;
  17:190
Mundy, John F. 23:181
Mundy, L. H. 9:57
Mundy, L. P. 18:16
Mundy, P. 1:152
Mune, George 11:193
Munea, John 17:277
Munell, John L. 22:210
Munell, William 8:108
Munenmainer, M. 25:211
Munett, G. F. B. 12:62
Muney, William 9:187
Munford, Alex. M. 17:39
Munford, C. 12:83;
  16:301
Munford, Charles 6:25;
  21:370
Munford, J. 21:35

Munford, Thomas B. 23:114
Mung, P. 3:142
Mungar, Edwin 23:109
Mungarin, Andrew 22:93
Munge, Henry 24:175
Munger, Amos D. 17:361
Munger, D. 3:142
Munger, F. 9:148; 27:82
Munger, Frank 20:31
Munger, Horatio 10:8
Munger, J. K. 1:58
Munger, James 9:204
Munger, John 17:84
Munger, John L. 24:95
Munger, M. W. 22:282
Munger, Milo 22:487
Munger, S. B. 23:43
Mungezea, H. J. 4:43
Mungo, E. M. 19:27
Mungo, W. H. 7:130
Munier, Samuel 15:344
Munion, James 11:158
Munis, J. 1:54
Munk, Jacob 21:246
Munks, William 8:66; 26:170
Munman, John 12:33
Munn, Alvin T. 3:142
Munn, C. D. 16:47
Munn, Charles 3:142; 20:193
Munn, E. N. 26:46
Munn, Edward M. 9:87
Munn, Henry 7:16
Munn, J. D. 17:84
Munn, John 22:454
Munn, Nelson 17:162
Munn, W. 1:155
Munnah, John 17:405
Munner, J. H. 14:133
Munning, D. 18:54
Munns, Henry R. 23:193
Munroe, --- 27:146
Munroe, A. J. 3:142
Munroe, Benjamin C. 2:14
Munroe, Caleb 19:27; 22:486
Munroe, Charles E. 19:182
Munroe, Felix 21:205
Munroe, Hector 22:46
Munroe, Henry 10:70
Munroe, J. 3:142
Munroe, J. W. 14:201
Munroe, Jack 9:165
Munroe, James 17:203; 22:13
Munroe, James A. 20:25
Munroe, John 22:341

Munroe, John F. 11:69
Munroe, Mitchell 7:130
Munroe, S. 19:257
Munroe, Sam 9:187
Munroe, W. M. 1:156
Munroe, William 1:58
Muns, Jeremiah 9:187; 19:271
Munsay, Calvin 21:370
Munseay, Heaster M. 20:316
Munsel, W. 19:182
Munsell, A. 1:53
Munsell, Otis D. 25:53
Munsell, Thomas 17:393
Munsen, James M. 9:123
Munsen, William 16:122
Munsey, George F. 16:47
Munsey, H. D. 4:43
Munsey, Heaster M. 10:128
Munsey, James C. 23:74
Munsey, John 17:337
Munsey, Richard 17:238
Munshower, Isaac 24:9
Munson, A. 18:151; 20:316
Munson, A. Enon 15:360
Munson, Aenas 19:89
Munson, Amasa 10:70
Munson, B. G. 17:213
Munson, Benjamin 13:125
Munson, C. 11:245
Munson, Charles 22:465
Munson, Charles H. 17:67
Munson, Charles L. 12:74
Munson, Christian 23:193
Munson, Edward 23:43
Munson, Emory 10:177
Munson, Eneas 12:96
Munson, F. 25:211
Munson, Frederick 5:43
Munson, H. C. 3:142
Munson, J. 19:229
Munson, J. F. 7:9
Munson, J. H. 7:52
Munson, J. R. 14:201
Munson, James M. 27:85
Munson, John 9:13
Munson, M. 1:54
Munson, Marcus 19:27
Munson, Melvin 17:67
Munson, Newton 23:193
Munson, P. H. 10:128; 20:316
Munson, S. 11:246
Munson, Thomas 22:210
Munster, Anthony 4:43
Munster, Michael 15:319; 19:89

Munsterman, August 23:124
Munsterman, William 23:124
Munsun, F. E. 16:99
Munter, R. S. H. 18:193
Muntore, J. 3:142
Munts, Lewis 26:107
Muntz, John 15:84
Muntz, Lewis 9:37; 18:295
Munwanay, J. A. 27:82
Munyon, John 24:95
Munyun, Thomas P. 12:33
Munz, C. 12:142
Munzer, C. F. 1:53
Muper, Samuel 11:37
Mur, T. J. 24:113
Murat, Lewis R. 11:38
Muratt, Edward 23:43
Muray, Adam C. 13:66
Murce, L. 3:142
Murch, Daniel 7:105
Murch, M. 19:229
Murch, William 3:142
Murchant, W. R. 18:193
Murcher, H. 20:127
Murchert, C. 3:142
Murchinson, D. 3:143
Murchison, J. B. 25:325
Murchler, Charles 11:183
Murchman, E. D. 13:95
Murdick, Edwin S. 7:36
Murdick, Warren 11:159
Murdoch, Harrison 19:278
Murdoch, Thomas R. 6:9
Murdock, A. 23:43
Murdock, A. B. 3:143
Murdock, A. J. 12:156
Murdock, A. L. 5:24; 25:211
Murdock, A. R. 12:156
Murdock, Aaron 7:130
Murdock, Benjamin 7:130
Murdock, Calvin A. 16:166
Murdock, D. A. 9:223; 18:373
Murdock, Daniel 20:108
Murdock, Eli 22:341
Murdock, Elijah 22:484
Murdock, George J. 1:57
Murdock, H. 27:80
Murdock, Henry 7:130
Murdock, J. 15:344
Murdock, J. G. 16:47
Murdock, James 24:89
Murdock, John 14:201; 17:354
Murdock, Lewis 9:187
Murdock, O. 24:82

Murdock, Sp'n. 1:56
Murdock, Washington 10:96
Murdock, William 22:46
Murdore, T. 18:90
Murdough, J. 16:376
Murdraugh, F. S. 9:67
Murduff, W. 13:95
Murduff, W. F. 14:18
Mure, Douty A. 20:103
Murehant, C. H. 19:222
Mureon, R. D. 21:35
Murey, John 18:373
Murfin, John H. 24:179
Murfin, John N. 17:426
Murfin, Nathaniel 24:82
Murford, A. 3:142
Murgent, H. J. 14:93
Murgie, A. 3:143
Muric, B. 14:243
Murill, Howard 19:89
Murittis, T. 1:155
Murk, J. 15:41
Murkes, Andrew 11:209
Murldath, B. H. 25:56
Murldth, B. H. 2:14
Murlett, Jacob F. 22:210
Murley, Walter 22:236
Murlien, T. M. 4:43
Murlin, McKendree 22:484
Murlit, James 3:142
Murnan, Barney 14:201
Murnan, John 25:269
Murnann, Timothy 22:17
Murney, M. 3:142
Murney, Willington 27:89
Murphey, Gideon 20:316
Murphey, James A. 6:32
Murphey, James W. 20:316
Murphey, Michael 7:60
Murphey, Peter 18:35
Murphin, John W. 8:91
Murphy, --- 11:95; 15:41, 160; 18:35; 19:182
Murphy, A. 3:142; 8:41; 12:9; 13:95; 14:18, 201; 25:212; 26:171
Murphy, Anderson 17:23
Murphy, Andrew 22:93
Murphy, Anthony 9:98
Murphy, Arthur 16:86
Murphy, Benjamin F. 22:46
Murphy, Burtley 22:126
Murphy, C. 3:142
Murphy, C. F. 11:183
Murphy, Charles 17:56; 22:151
Murphy, Charles D. 5:24

Murphy, Charles S. 22:210
Murphy, Clinton 12:33
Murphy, Cornelius 22:126
Murphy, D. 1:57, 60; 3:142; 9:148; 13:95; 27:81
Murphy, Daniel 3:142; 4:43; 7:52; 13:38; 19:334; 21:141; 22:236
Murphy, Daniel H. 15:110
Murphy, David A. 9:37
Murphy, Dennis 10:165; 16:301; 19:182
Murphy, Dennis J. 11:37
Murphy, Dwight 22:172
Murphy, E. 1:156; 12:167; 14:93; 19:348
Murphy, E. H. 13:115
Murphy, E. W. 9:87; 26:47
Murphy, Edward 8:26; 9:237; 12:55; 18:151; 21:11; 23:160; 26:222
Murphy, Elias 17:182
Murphy, Enoch E. 16:47
Murphy, F. 1:156; 3:142; 12:33
Murphy, F. A. 15:217
Murphy, F. M. 11:158
Murphy, Ferry 24:108
Murphy, Ford 22:93
Murphy, Francis 7:105
Murphy, Frank 24:72
Murphy, Frank M. 12:51
Murphy, G. 17:435
Murphy, George 7:130; 9:187; 11:158; 19:257; 24:178
Murphy, George F. 20:33
Murphy, Gideon 10:70
Murphy, H. 13:127
Murphy, Henry 8:26; 17:136; 18:151; 24:200
Murphy, Henry W. F. 10:149; 18:54
Murphy, Hiram 21:231
Murphy, Hugh 16:99, 215; 19:330
Murphy, Isiah 1:53
Murphy, J. 1:60, 150, 151, 152, 156; 3:142; 8:121; 13:76, 95; 14:18, 93, 201; 15:217; 16:99, 215, 269; 18:247; 25:53; 26:47, 173

Murphy, J. A. 1:59; 13:115; 16:216
Murphy, J. C. 21:124
Murphy, J. D. 25:57
Murphy, J. H. 24:25
Murphy, J. J. 16:71
Murphy, J. M. 13:38
Murphy, J. W. 7:36; 9:57; 18:209; 22:210
Murphy, James 7:36, 69; 8:26; 9:187; 11:38; 12:168; 13:38; 14:93; 15:348; 16:148, 215, 376; 17:67; 18:35, 151; 19:183, 257; 21:35, 141, 370; 22:151, 341; 23:160; 24:9; 26:172, 213; 27:146
Murphy, James D. 15:18
Murphy, James G. 8:91
Murphy, James J. 20:190
Murphy, James P. 12:74; 17:323
Murphy, James W. 10:70
Murphy, Jeff 27:89
Murphy, Jer 1:56
Murphy, Jere 18:54
Murphy, Jeremiah 10:149, 206; 15:217
Murphy, Jerry 2:14
Murphy, John 1:55; 3:142; 4:43; 6:35; 7:12; 8:26, 52; 9:26, 187; 10:8, 128; 11:158; 12:33, 156; 13:38; 14:201; 15:26; 16:216, 301; 18:70, 151, 313; 19:27, 183, 257; 20:316; 21:370; 22:93, 162, 341; 23:13, 43; 24:42, 72; 25:212, 325; 26:106, 170; 27:146
Murphy, John C. 24:25
Murphy, John G. 19:89
Murphy, John H. 11:396; 20:110
Murphy, John J. 22:433
Murphy, John W. 8:91; 19:324; 21:243; 23:43
Murphy, Joseph 7:36
Murphy, Joseph P. 11:307
Murphy, L. 15:344; 16:376; 25:212
Murphy, L. R. 15:217
Murphy, Lawrence 8:26; 18:151
Murphy, Leonard 7:105

Murphy, Levi 17:433; 24:160
Murphy, Lewis 15:279
Murphy, M. 3:142; 9:148; 25:212; 27:81
Murphy, M. J. 3:142; 15:110
Murphy, Marmaduke 21:131
Murphy, Martin V. 12:34
Murphy, Mathew 22:46
Murphy, Michael 7:36; 10:20; 11:94; 12:33; 13:38; 15:41; 17:56; 22:13, 46; 23:193
Murphy, Monroe 20:316
Murphy, Morgan 9:87; 26:45
Murphy, Morris 22:46
Murphy, Moses 21:258
Murphy, Munroe 10:70
Murphy, Nugent 7:105
Murphy, Olmstead 22:313
Murphy, P. 1:58, 59, 60, 158; 2:15; 3:142; 11:281, 341; 15:72; 25:57, 288; 26:47
Murphy, P. O. 19:89
Murphy, Patrick 7:36; 9:87; 10:165; 11:183; 12:83, 96; 13:115; 15:14, 361; 16:301; 19:89, 183; 23:13, 160; 24:25; 27:90
Murphy, Payton 11:95
Murphy, Preston 14:319; 25:273
Murphy, R. 3:142; 25:52
Murphy, R. J. 19:183
Murphy, R. R. 11:187
Murphy, Robert 2:15; 11:158; 16:216; 17:23; 27:79
Murphy, Robert F. 22:503
Murphy, Robert M. 24:113
Murphy, Rufus 11:328
Murphy, Samuel 18:151; 19:89; 25:212
Murphy, Shadrach 4:67
Murphy, Silas 8:91
Murphy, Simeon V. 22:46
Murphy, T. 14:93; 25:212
Murphy, T. C. 25:212
Murphy, Thomas 7:36; 8:26; 9:227; 14:93, 201; 15:41; 16:99; 17:353; 18:151, 373; 19:27, 337; 25:56; 27:80, 87

Murphy, Thomas C. 5:24
Murphy, Thomas H. 9:157
Murphy, Thomas J. 22:151
Murphy, Thomas John 26:212
Murphy, Timothy 22:93
Murphy, W. 1:157; 2:15; 3:142; 16:270
Murphy, W. H. 9:57
Murphy, W. S. 3:142
Murphy, War 27:89
Murphy, Wesley 13:38; 17:203
Murphy, William 2:15; 6:11; 7:80; 10:128; 11:281; 12:162; 16:99; 17:108, 283; 20:316; 21:35, 76, 116; 22:341; 23:266; 24:82; 25:52, 57
Murphy, William H. 18:113, 193; 24:25
Murphy, William J. 7:60
Murphy, William M. 3:142; 23:91
Murr, C. 4:43
Murra, Iram 11:38
Murran, George W. 18:151
Murrance, William 17:100
Murray, --- 9:69; 12:168; 18:178; 21:370
Murray, A. 12:156; 17:436; 24:182
Murray, A. K. 9:223
Murray, A. M. 17:494
Murray, A. R. 18:373
Murray, A. T. 10:128; 20:316
Murray, Abner 11:245
Murray, Adam Cowan 19:89
Murray, Alexander 11:109
Murray, Alfred 17:238
Murray, Andrew 6:32; 25:325
Murray, Arthur 19:27
Murray, B. 1:151; 9:148; 10:187; 18:178; 27:81
Murray, Beverly 13:58
Murray, C. 17:432; 19:241
Murray, Charles 9:187, 204; 11:95; 17:84; 21:370; 24:153
Murray, Charles H. 21:124
Murray, Cyrus 21:35, 231
Murray, D. 7:52

Murray, Daniel 13:38; 17:136
Murray, David 1:55; 11:389
Murray, David P. 22:162
Murray, David W. 22:126
Murray, Donald 21:231
Murray, Duncan 27:88
Murray, E. 3:142
Murray, E. W. 26:174
Murray, Edward F. 12:34
Murray, Exaver 21:76
Murray, Frank 22:46; 27:79
Murray, G. 14:301; 17:471; 27:88
Murray, Gabriel 9:134; 27:85
Murray, George 5:43; 27:79
Murray, George W. 7:130
Murray, Gilbert 14:201
Murray, H. 1:154, 156
Murray, Hardy P. 16:86
Murray, Henry 7:36; 12:51, 123; 15:131
Murray, Hulett 8:26
Murray, Isaac 5:43
Murray, J. 3:142; 9:148; 11:69; 15:217; 20:134; 27:80, 81
Murray, J. B. 1:58; 24:113
Murray, J. I. D. 15:217
Murray, J. J. 3:142
Murray, J. R. 8:52
Murray, Jackson 22:341
Murray, Jacob 23:302
Murray, James 3:142; 8:26, 41; 9:87, 187; 15:41; 19:89, 257; 22:46; 26:172
Murray, James H. 8:26; 11:267; 18:151; 26:172
Murray, Jefferson 9:134; 27:83
Murray, John 3:142; 7:81; 8:26, 74; 9:223; 11:382; 12:74; 16:47, 301; 17:84, 92; 18:151, 247, 270; 19:288; 21:280; 25:302; 26:47, 173
Murray, John B. 21:103
Murray, John C. 22:341
Murray, John F. 9:134; 27:84
Murray, John J. 22:262
Murray, John N. 11:69
Murray, John R. 22:151

Murray, John W. 11:158;
25:334
Murray, Joseph 4:43;
14:201; 19:183
Murray, Joseph H.
10:149; 18:54
Murray, L. 1:152
Murray, Leander 11:70
Murray, Lorenzo 9:187;
19:257
Murray, Luftus L. 22:210
Murray, M. 1:59, 153;
23:124; 27:82
Murray, M. A. 25:212
Murray, Martin 15:217;
19:275
Murray, Michael 1:57;
10:128; 12:65; 15:41,
95; 20:316; 21:11,
35; 23:124; 26:45
Murray, N. 26:47
Murray, Nichols 9:87
Murray, Otto C. 12:74;
15:14
Murray, P. 19:241
Murray, Patrick 8:74;
9:187; 10:96;
21:370; 22:151
Murray, Peter 23:129
Murray, Philip 17:182
Murray, R. 9:123
Murray, Robert 10:70;
13:77; 20:316
Murray, S. H. 21:35
Murray, Seth W. 23:74
Murray, Stephen 25:212
Murray, T. 1:58, 99
Murray, T. A. 21:370
Murray, T. B. 10:70
Murray, T. J. 20:316
Murray, Thomas 3:142;
9:201; 12:55; 14:93,
201; 21:35
Murray, Thomas H. 5:43
Murray, Thomas S.
22:126
Murray, Timothy 1:55
Murray, Uriah 1:55
Murray, W. 3:142;
19:245, 257
Murray, W. C. 1:151
Murray, W. M. 10:180;
18:178
Murray, W. R. 8:74;
11:265
Murray, William 6:28;
9:187; 14:93, 316;
15:18; 18:113;
21:164; 22:93;
24:167; 25:212

Murray, William H.
13:38; 16:47
Murray, William L. 9:13
Murray, William P.
22:486
Murray, Willis 7:130
Murrell, Chilton A.
17:283
Murrell, H. J. 12:34
Murrell, Henry 8:99
Murrell, Joseph 12:34
Murrell, Samuel W. 18:35
Murrell, Truman 7:105
Murrey, James 4:43
Murrey, Michael M. 5:24
Murrey, T. 27:146
Murrey, T. H. 25:212
Murrick, B. 27:90
Murrill, A. P. 25:325
Murrill, R. H. 17:167
Murrin, A. 13:116
Murrin, A. B. 14:322
Murrin, Augustine B.
23:185
Murring, Nicholas 18:151
Murrish, Moses 21:258
Murry, A. 3:142; 14:93;
20:141
Murry, Charles 19:257
Murry, Edward 14:201
Murry, Frank 12:34;
26:172
Murry, G. 25:212
Murry, G. W. 11:245
Murry, George 4:43; 8:66;
18:70
Murry, H. J. 4:43
Murry, Hallett 18:151
Murry, Irane 25:212
Murry, J. 24:26
Murry, J. D. 11:266
Murry, J. W. 25:278
Murry, Jacob B. 23:160
Murry, James 14:201;
18:151; 26:45
Murry, John 3:142;
18:373; 23:114;
24:99; 27:87
Murry, John A. 11:187
Murry, Joseph 17:349
Murry, Leander E. 23:266
Murry, Louis 14:201
Murry, M. 3:142; 14:278
Murry, Marcus D. 17:47
Murry, Melvin 15:88
Murry, Michael 9:87;
16:48
Murry, Mungo 1:55
Murry, N. F. 15:217
Murry, Nicholas 11:328
Murry, P. 15:217

Murry, Patrick 14:93;
20:11; 23:91
Murry, R. 27:85
Murry, Rank 11:109
Murry, Robert 27:89
Murry, S. 18:35
Murry, Thomas 16:148;
19:27
Murry, Timothy 20:27
Murry, W. 16:216; 26:173
Murry, William 5:24;
12:142; 16:216;
23:260
Murry, William R. 9:157;
26:174
Murser, Peter 18:151
Murssell, Truman 21:370
Mursturr, William 14:93
Murswick, Charles 23:74
Murtall, E. 1:157
Murtay, --- 11:70
Murth, C. R. 13:66
Murtha, James 16:281
Murtle, John 4:43
Murton, John 27:146
Murvny, John 3:142
Murvy, J. 3:142
Murwin, Calvin 13:38
Musbaucher, Michael
18:151
Musbeck, C. 24:82
Musbucher, Michael 8:26
Muse, George 4:43
Muse, P. M. 7:36
Muse, R. J. 9:57
Musel, Richard 22:313
Muselman, D. 14:201
Muselman, J. 3:143
Muselman, S. 8:74
Musgrane, P. 16:216
Musgrave, Benjamin T.
8:52; 21:76
Musgrave, Daniel S.
17:317
Musgrave, P. 13:76
Musgraves, J. 26:48
Musgrove, A. 22:210
Musgrove, B. 12:156
Musgrove, George 11:38
Musgrove, J. 22:93; 24:25
Musgrove, J. W. 22:13
Musgrove, Jeremiah
18:178
Musgrove, John A. 19:268
Musgrove, John G. 13:38
Musgrove, M. H. 22:485
Musgrove, William H.
8:74
Mush, Thomas 15:41
Mushbrush, William
13:128

Mushell, John 13:116
Musher, S. 16:270
Musher, W. 18:90
Mushlitz, W. 1:152
Mushrush, George W. 19:183
Music, James 20:316
Music, Philip 25:53
Musick, Daniel 15:72
Musick, Giles 23:109
Musin, James 3:143
Musk, E. 12:74; 15:84
Musket, G. 3:143
Muskey, G. L. 14:283
Muskop, Jacob 17:419; 24:160
Musler, Henry 20:316
Musley, Henry 5:43
Muslin, Peter 26:172
Muspratt, George 22:151
Musrole, William 11:403
Musselman, J. 15:344; 16:376
Musselman, John S. 21:76
Musselman, W. 22:353
Musselschmidt, Fried 24:68
Musser, A. 14:93
Musser, Charles 26:145
Musser, D. 3:143
Musser, Edward 17:321
Musser, George 18:209
Musser, John 3:143; 9:98
Musser, L. 8:53
Musser, Philip 19:183
Musser, Samuel L. 22:93
Musser, W. H. 19:183
Musser, William 23:160
Mussey, George 15:11
Mussingo, M. 3:143
Mussleman, M. R. 9:148
Musson, Alonzo 17:39
Musson, John 22:93
Musson, Thomas G. 20:108
Mussot, Clode 17:100
Mussue, Robert 9:210
Mussulman, Daniel F. 23:91
Mustan, Ward 23:289
Mustard, John 1:58
Muster, Seth S. 11:70
Musy, George 26:45
Mutchler, T. 1:54
Muth, C. 20:115
Muth, Phillip 18:151
Mutler, John E. 10:152
Mutt, William 6:23
Mutter, Joseph 21:370
Mutting, Justice S. 12:55
Mutton, John Y. 8:101

Mutun, David 25:212
Mutzebaugh, Jacob 24:9
Mutzebaugher, Jacob 24:9
Muxum, C. 1:95
Muyers, W. H. 9:87
Muzzey, John B. 12:34
Muzzey, Pliny D. 11:335
Muzzy, Emory C. 4:43
Muzzy, Frank 7:81; 25:302
Myally, H. 9:112
Mycoff, H. P. 17:503
Myenderse, Reuben 18:151
Myer, A. 1:151
Myer, Alexander 16:301
Myer, Anton 17:416; 24:154
Myer, C. 24:153
Myer, Charles 7:60
Myer, Chri's. 1:56
Myer, E. 9:187
Myer, Eliazer 26:47
Myer, F. 14:93
Myer, F. W. 26:50
Myer, Frederick 10:174; 19:183
Myer, Gilbert 16:99
Myer, Gotlieb 11:266
Myer, H. 3:143
Myer, Henry 4:43; 20:176
Myer, J. 3:143; 14:93, 278; 19:183; 23:124, 181
Myer, J. F. 24:113
Myer, John 25:212
Myer, Joseph 21:103
Myer, L. 3:143
Myer, Leopold 20:316
Myer, M. 3:143
Myer, Michael 8:53
Myer, Nicholas 20:316
Myer, P. 14:93
Myer, R. 1:98
Myer, R. R. 15:160
Myer, Robert 21:103
Myer, William F. 17:39
Myerch, H. D. 26:45
Myeres, Israel 23:160
Myeres, Samuel C. 23:160
Myerkoffet, Michael 18:70
Myerly, Israel 10:129; 20:316
Myers, --- 14:26, 201, 322; 17:15; 18:193; 23:204
Myers, A. 1:157; 3:143; 13:95; 14:93; 15:131
Myers, A. J. 18:90
Myers, Abraham 19:47

Myers, Abraham J. 5:24
Myers, Abram 6:29; 22:485; 24:26
Myers, Adam 6:7
Myers, Addison 10:70; 20:316
Myers, Albinus G. 14:201
Myers, Alfred 10:129
Myers, Alfred W. 21:370
Myers, Andrew 6:10; 16:134
Myers, Andrew B. 7:52
Myers, Andrew C. 22:151
Myers, Andrew J. 17:356
Myers, Anthony 9:165; 13:135; 17:450; 19:347; 24:175
Myers, Benjamin 17:39
Myers, Benjamin F. 10:70; 20:316
Myers, C. 11:307; 24:68; 25:212
Myers, C. C. 17:167
Myers, C. H. 3:143
Myers, C. P. 9:148; 27:83
Myers, Carol 9:57
Myers, Ch. H. 21:35
Myers, Charles 3:143; 5:56; 7:75; 12:83; 14:201; 16:301; 18:35; 19:183
Myers, Charles T. 24:68
Myers, Chauncey 8:115
Myers, Christopher 22:93
Myers, D. 3:143
Myers, D. C. 22:210
Myers, D. G. 3:143
Myers, D. H. 9:148; 27:80
Myers, Daniel 13:125; 16:166
Myers, Daniel L. 24:161
Myers, Daniel M. 20:25
Myers, Daniel T. 22:432
Myers, David 7:36; 11:415; 14:201; 17:39; 24:82
Myers, David A. 17:84
Myers, David F. L. 22:262
Myers, David S. 17:277
Myers, E. 3:143; 19:288; 21:111
Myers, E. J. 24:26
Myers, E. S. 15:217
Myers, Edwin 24:53
Myers, Eleanor 9:87
Myers, Eli 12:59
Myers, Elias B. 9:237
Myers, Elisha 20:316; 22:151
Myers, F. 3:143; 17:496
Myers, Frank 11:37; 22:13

Myers, Franklin 7:60; 16:122; 22:93
Myers, Fred 14:93, 283; 22:353
Myers, Frederick 16:301; 22:210
Myers, G. 1:155; 3:143; 5:56; 14:93; 22:210; 23:160; 26:47
Myers, G. S. 16:376
Myers, G. W. 16:48
Myers, George 7:130; 11:70; 17:249; 19:272; 20:99, 316; 21:370; 23:160, 293
Myers, George F. 17:349
Myers, Godfrey 12:162
Myers, H. 1:59, 157; 3:143; 15:217; 16:216; 21:36, 124; 24:82
Myers, H. G. 13:127
Myers, H. J. 1:151
Myers, H. L. 3:143
Myers, H. P. 23:160
Myers, Hamilton 27:85
Myers, Henry 1:54; 7:105; 8:91; 11:284; 15:217; 16:301; 17:434; 18:16; 23:100; 24:171; 26:106
Myers, Henry B. 25:271
Myers, Henry D. C. 7:36
Myers, Herman 13:38
Myers, Hiram S. 10:20
Myers, Homer 22:465
Myers, Isaac C. 11:68
Myers, J. 1:157; 3:143; 9:57; 11:109; 12:80, 93, 163; 16:122, 216, 301; 19:244; 21:124; 25:212
Myers, J. A. 3:143; 20:317
Myers, J. B. 22:210; 24:26
Myers, J. E. 2:15
Myers, J. H. 23:43; 25:54
Myers, J. J. 9:37; 20:25
Myers, J. M. 11:160; 14:93
Myers, J. P. 15:131
Myers, J. R. 3:143
Myers, J. T. 19:89
Myers, J. W. 1:57; 14:133
Myers, Jacob 11:68, 69; 14:93; 17:39; 20:317; 21:36, 76; 24:108
Myers, Jacob L. 10:129; 20:317

Myers, James 1:58; 7:105; 11:281; 15:299; 16:216; 21:370; 22:174, 236, 262
Myers, James A. 19:89; 23:43
Myers, James H. 17:39
Myers, James W. 14:201
Myers, Jeremiah 16:134
Myers, Jerome 13:38
Myers, Jerry 17:136; 21:370; 24:68, 200
Myers, John 1:54; 3:143; 8:53, 91; 9:87, 187; 11:128, 183; 12:62; 14:201; 15:81, 92; 17:84, 398; 18:247, 313; 19:257; 21:164; 22:210; 26:45, 47, 105
Myers, John A. 10:70
Myers, John C. 11:37
Myers, John D. 10:70; 20:317
Myers, John F. 8:115
Myers, John I. 21:36
Myers, John M. 11:187; 15:88
Myers, John N. 17:84
Myers, John S. 22:434
Myers, John W. 23:160
Myers, Jonathan 7:60; 18:178
Myers, Jonathan M. 10:187
Myers, Jonathan S. 22:126
Myers, Joseph 1:53; 3:143; 8:108; 13:116; 17:350, 451; 18:399
Myers, Joseph R. 20:25
Myers, Julius 19:347
Myers, L. 3:143; 11:159
Myers, L. D. 9:187
Myers, L. H. 3:143
Myers, L. S. 3:143
Myers, Lander 19:89
Myers, Lawson 21:370
Myers, Levi 22:486
Myers, Lewis 10:129; 12:34
Myers, M. 3:143; 14:289; 20:317; 21:111; 23:43
Myers, Manson 22:313
Myers, Marcus L. 17:461; 24:164
Myers, Marion 22:46
Myers, Marshall 9:210
Myers, Mart 24:200
Myers, Martin 17:455
Myers, Martin C. 23:109

Myers, Mary 27:83
Myers, Meredith P. 23:91
Myers, Michael 10:70
Myers, N. 17:347; 25:212
Myers, Nathan B. 11:69
Myers, Nelson 5:43
Myers, Nicholas 11:389
Myers, Noah 3:143
Myers, O. 25:302
Myers, Oliver 17:292
Myers, Orin 15:323
Myers, Orrin 19:89
Myers, Orson 11:109
Myers, P. 3:143; 13:95; 14:93; 23:160
Myers, Peter 3:143; 9:210, 231; 13:38, 116; 18:193; 20:317; 23:74
Myers, Philip B. 23:91
Myers, Philo 21:370
Myers, R. 18:90
Myers, R. D. 3:143
Myers, R. H. 6:21
Myers, R. T. 16:99
Myers, Reuben 7:36
Myers, Richard 17:182, 496
Myers, Robert 22:262
Myers, Rufus T. 17:39
Myers, Russell M. 7:130
Myers, S. 3:143; 14:93; 24:82; 25:57
Myers, S. A. 1:158; 11:85; 21:124
Myers, S. D. 19:234
Myers, Samuel 3:143; 9:44; 12:34; 22:433; 25:334; 26:126
Myers, Samuel H. 14:201
Myers, Sanford W. 23:74
Myers, Simon 17:39
Myers, Stephen 17:441; 24:153
Myers, T. 22:520
Myers, T. M. 16:216
Myers, T. W. 10:70
Myers, Thomas 10:174; 12:54; 19:183; 21:370; 22:313, 408
Myers, Thomas W. 9:87
Myers, V. 20:317
Myers, W. 25:57
Myers, W. H. 17:23, 327; 23:160
Myers, W. J. 3:143
Myers, W. N. 26:45
Myers, W. S. 1:56
Myers, Walter S. 17:277
Myers, Wesley 9:231

Myers, William 1:54;
4:43; 7:130; 8:66;
9:187, 243; 10:70;
11:403; 13:116;
14:93; 16:134;
19:265; 20:99;
22:151
Myers, William A. 6:22;
18:90
Myers, William H. 1:57;
8:115; 11:414;
16:123; 22:210
Myers, William L. 16:156
Myers, William N. 8:115
Myers, William W.
18:324; 22:486
Myette, Antoine 26:172
Mygatt, Orlando C.
21:258
Myhoff, T. C. 1:53
Mylan, Thomas 24:150
Myldoon, Arthur 7:105
Myleim, James F. 21:244
Myles, Eli 27:146
Myles, M. M. C. 4:43
Mylin, C. W. 15:217
Mylon, John 4:43
Mylott, Patrick 10:129;
20:317
Mymer, Frederick 11:317
Mynahan, Jerry 7:10
Mynderse, Reuben 8:26
Mynerd, Norman 13:38;
16:48
Mynnick, Sim. V. 1:56
Myor, John 20:317
Myracle, C. 3:143
Myracle, I. P. 17:481
Myracle, J. P. 27:88
Myraele, J. P. 14:301
Myrdot, E. B. 27:90
Myre, E. 11:193
Myre, Nicholas 23:160
Myres, --- 15:81
Myres, A. 14:18
Myres, Elias B. 26:223
Myres, George 5:55;
22:454
Myres, Jasper 20:99
Myres, John 3:143
Myres, Marcus L. 8:101
Myres, P. 14:18
Myres, Wesley 20:317
Myrick, C. P. 13:66;
16:216
Myrick, G. P. 25:212
Myrick, H. D. 9:87
Myrick, John 12:156
Myrick, Peter 7:16
Myrick, William 18:399
Myron, John 8:91

Myron, Thomas 20:11
Myrse, Elisha 10:129
Mysel, John 20:317
Mystatt, Russell 22:262

N

N---, A. J. 17:217
N---, B. E. 14:270
N---, B. N. 26:224
N---, C. 10:29; 19:305
N---, C. T. 12:86
N---, C. W. 23:43
N---, D. 17:364; 20:317
N---, D. H. 10:32
N---, D. L. 25:59
N---, E. 11:341
N---, E. R. 20:181
N---, G. 11:247; 17:364
N---, G. W. 23:253
N---, George W. 9:57
N---, H. 17:364
N---, H. D. 11:293
N---, J--- 11:220
N---, J. 17:111, 254;
24:113
N---, J. B. 11:220; 24:113
N---, J. C. 26:175
N---, J. D. 17:347
N---, N. M. 17:217
N---, N. Y. 25:212
N---, P. 18:413
N---, R. 22:354
N---, S. 11:309
N---, T. 15:218
N---, T. H. 18:178
N---, W. 20:58, 92, 155;
21:167; 23:245
N---, W. J. 27:91
N---, W. S. 25:58
N---, W. T. 11:341
N---, William 20:317
N---, William H. 11:341
Naas, Anton 23:160
Naas, Frederick 17:39
Naber, William 21:190
Nabracong, O. D. 20:90
Nabriel, D. 15:217
Naby, James 22:313
Nace, Harrison 3:143
Nace, Josiah 15:72
Nack, Reuben P. 8:91
Nacy, J. 2:15
Nacy, John 25:58
Nado, Joseph 11:281
Nafey, George S. 13:38
Nage, Horace 13:38
Nagel, Karl 1:61
Nagel, Samuel 15:344;
16:376

Nagelen, Joseph 10:70
Naggels, Joseph 20:317
Naggles, Joseph 10:70
Naghton, Michael 9:57
Nagle, C. 3:143
Nagle, Daniel 24:59
Nagle, E. 1:159
Nagle, Edward B. 12:34
Nagle, F. 12:98
Nagle, Frederick 15:357;
16:281
Nagle, G. 1:60
Nagle, George 11:162
Nagle, Henry 23:160
Nagle, Jacob 12:34; 14:93
Nagle, James 7:16; 14:201
Nagle, James C. 22:13
Nagle, John 9:112; 27:147
Nagle, Leverett C. 12:34
Nagle, Patrick 21:370
Nagle, Richard 18:113
Nagle, W. 1:159; 16:216
Nagle, W. F. 22:354
Nagle, W. H. 1:158
Nagle, W. J. 19:27
Naglen, Joseph 20:317
Naglor, George 11:246
Nagot, John 27:91
Nahler, Christian 1:60
Nahorn, William 25:59
Nail, J. 27:91
Nail, John 10:70
Nail, John L. 23:74
Nail, Thomas A. 20:155
Nailer, James 20:317
Nailer, John 10:70
Nailer, Thomas C. 9:223
Nailles, Charles 17:244
Nailor, George 18:407
Nailor, J. 15:217
Nailor, Jacob 9:37;
18:295; 26:108
Nailor, James 10:129
Nailor, John 20:317
Nailor, N. A. 16:216
Nair, Ephraim W. 10:208
Nairn, James 24:113
Nairy, Michael 11:39
Naison, Moses 21:212
Naive, Christian 22:113
Naker, Faust 19:27
Nakup, Daniel 16:48
Nale, J. 1:99
Nale, John A. 1:61
Nalen, L. 25:212
Nales, L. F. 2:15
Naley, George 16:48
Nall, J. M. 11:267
Nall, James P. 22:127
Nalley, S. 11:96
Nalley, Sebastian 20:99

Nallman, A. 3:143
Nalls, G. W. 13:95
Nally, James 13:95
Nally, Owen 13:39; 16:48
Nalon, Edward 16:301
Nalpeus, John 19:283
Name, James 25:212
Names, Hiram 24:54
Names, Robert 17:361
Namie, Francis J. 24:9
Nance, A. 9:187
Nance, Alexander 8:53
Nance, Charles 4:67
Nance, Dabney 17:283
Nance, David 20:317
Nance, George 17:136;
    22:313; 24:200
Nance, Lewis 10:99
Nance, P. T. 19:279
Nance, Robert 17:443;
    24:161
Nance, Samuel 11:210
Nance, Simon 13:39
Nance, Thomas 10:70;
    20:317; 22:313
Nance, William 12:166
Nance, William S. 10:206
Nancer, Morton 13:116
Nancy, David 10:129
Nanday, Frank 13:116
Nane, S. 17:182
Naney, J. M. 1:159
Nangle, M. T. 13:125
Nanhan, James 12:156
Nanhor, David 22:504
Nanny, John W. 17:84
Nanson, John 11:425;
    18:35
Nansweather, J. 22:313
Naorote, F. 17:435
Nape, John 19:27
Napier, Charles T. 21:11
Napier, Hascal 17:149
Napier, John 11:390
Napier, Richard 11:71
Napledd, James 11:128
Napoleon, Charles 22:313
Napp, Augustus 13:39
Napper, Fonroe 20:99
Napper, Wash 7:130
Napsuman, N. 22:46
Narboe, Peter 4:43
Narcott, Henry D. 22:151
Narcross, Joseph D. 16:48
Nardin, Jacob 7:83
Nare, George 19:275
Nare, James 12:83
Narigan, William 11:161
Nark, John 8:108
Narman, James A. 9:223
Narney, Jacob W. 19:27

Narnguey, M. V. 22:487
Narracong, David S.
    23:193
Narricon, J. W. 14:93
Narrilligan, J. 27:92
Narry, Harry 9:210
Narsh, James N. B. 23:114
Narson, John 5:24
Nartire, Alonzo 3:143
Nary, Dennis 22:282
Nascoll, Frederick 14:201
Naser, Sebastian 22:172
Nash, A. J. 9:27; 18:313;
    26:108
Nash, Abraham 23:281
Nash, Albert 20:115
Nash, Alfred 10:129;
    20:317
Nash, Andrew J. 22:434
Nash, Asahael 22:487
Nash, Ayor W. 11:309
Nash, B. E. 14:283
Nash, C. D. 3:143
Nash, Caleb 7:36
Nash, Carl 8:108
Nash, Charles 3:143;
    18:35
Nash, Coleman 9:98
Nash, Cornelius 9:134;
    27:92
Nash, Daniel T. 19:90
Nash, David 16:99
Nash, E. 14:301; 17:476
Nash, Ed. 27:92
Nash, Elisha 22:515
Nash, F. 1:60
Nash, Francis J. 12:74;
    15:18
Nash, Frank 15:217;
    19:27
Nash, George H. 15:217
Nash, George W. 9:187;
    17:209; 19:257
Nash, H. C. 22:13
Nash, Henry 4:67; 9:165
Nash, Isaac A. 25:58
Nash, Isaac N. 13:116
Nash, J. A. 1:158
Nash, J. B. 1:159
Nash, J. E. 13:67
Nash, J. H. 21:370
Nash, J. W. 11:415
Nash, James M. 11:188
Nash, Jarvis 21:370
Nash, Jeremiah 21:57;
    24:42
Nash, John 18:270;
    21:190; 22:93
Nash, John D. 10:92;
    20:317
Nash, Jonathan 20:317

Nash, Jonathan W. 20:115
Nash, L. 14:93
Nash, Lemuel Y. 17:347
Nash, Martin 4:43
Nash, O. 13:39
Nash, O. W. 11:246
Nash, P. C. 16:48
Nash, P. F. 19:90
Nash, R. W. 1:158
Nash, Reuben 21:371
Nash, Richard 10:129;
    20:317
Nash, Richard T. 23:256
Nash, Robert 21:258
Nash, Samuel D. 8:26
Nash, Sylvester S. 20:42
Nash, William 11:246;
    20:42; 22:210
Nash, William D. 9:187
Nash, William H. 13:39
Nashborn, E. F. 11:293
Nashen, Edward 3:144
Nashot, Edward 13:116
Nasin, Christian 15:95
Nasin, Gustavus 25:325
Naslund, G. 21:92
Nason, B. 27:91
Nason, C. H. 1:159; 3:144
Nason, George W. 13:39
Nason, Hiram T. 9:13
Nason, J. 1:158
Nason, Lavis C. 11:193
Nason, Moses 21:150
Nason, Royal T. 19:27
Nason, S. H. 1:158
Nason, T. 11:267
Nassau, Gustavus 6:32
Nasseger, G. 21:111
Nasser, Henry 8:108
Nassie, Eli 3:144
Nast, George 17:263
Nast, Nathaniel 19:183
Nast, W. D. 19:229
Nastrang, C. 3:144
Natalie, Joseph 10:70
Natall, Joseph 20:317
Natch, Joe 20:148
Nathan, A. 22:313
Nathan, E. 17:15
Nathan, Molley 21:280
Nathan, W. 12:34
Nathaniel, --- 9:223
Nathaniel, Benjamin
    9:210
Nathans, G. W. 16:216
Nathans, S. 2:15
Nathans, Simeon 25:58
Nathland, Gabriel 9:223
Nation, Enoch 7:105
Nation, James R. 22:210
Nation, Joel 17:15

Nation, William Wallace 18:221
Nations, Charles M. 10:129; 20:317
Nations, James H. 22:262
Natisham, Joseph 8:53
Natland, Gabriel 18:373
Natson, George 15:288
Natt, --- 26:174
Natt, David E. 24:54
Nattin, Robert 8:26; 18:151
Natting, Edgar J. 21:76
Nattinham, Phillip 18:113
Nattisheim, Joseph 21:141
Natzke, William 13:39
Nauchrick, William H. 12:62
Naughan, Jacob 10:71; 20:317
Naughlin, D. 7:52
Naughton, James 11:162
Naughton, Martin 24:69
Naughton, Thomas 17:67
Naughton, William H. 17:67; 22:465
Naumann, A. 25:212
Naundeorf, H. 19:257
Naunemaker, John 16:216
Nausbaum, L. 14:94
Nausbaum, W. H. 1:159
Nauser, R. 1:61
Navarre, A. 3:144
Navarre, Tousant 8:91
Nave, Charles 16:301
Nave, D. W. 9:237; 26:224
Nave, Joel D. 11:425
Nave, Joel E. 22:504
Navel, Michael 1:61
Naver, Charles 13:39
Naviel, John 22:341
Naville, Michael J. 21:57
Navilligan, J. 14:301; 17:476
Navoo, G. 3:144
Nay, H. 13:95
Nay, Solomon 11:277
Nayers, Isaac 11:40
Nayham, Henry 6:32
Nayhan, Henry 25:325
Nayler, Henry P. 8:66; 26:175
Naylor, Charles 21:371; 22:93
Naylor, Edward 9:204
Naylor, G. A. 3:144
Naylor, H. 13:60
Naylor, J. 16:216
Naylor, James 8:91
Naylor, John 7:52

Naylor, John C. 23:286
Naylor, L. 17:192
Naylor, R. A. 11:161
Naylor, R. N. 11:161
Naylor, S. 3:144
Naylor, W. 15:259
Naylor, William 9:187; 19:268
Naylor, William T. 15:131
Nays, J. T. 13:67
Nays, John T. 19:90
Nayson, J. 25:212
NcCord, Ephraim T. 9:122
Nea, Francis 19:241
Neable, Henry 22:487
Neace, Philip 22:262
Neach, Joel 18:151
Neack, J. E. 1:60
Neagle, Wilson 12:34
Neagle, Woodford 18:247; 26:51
Neahi, W. 18:54
Neal, --- 21:371
Neal, A. M. 1:99
Neal, A. P. 3:144
Neal, Albert J. 22:497
Neal, Alexander C. 18:247; 26:51
Neal, Alfred B. 11:390
Neal, Amos 22:93
Neal, Arthur 13:39; 16:48
Neal, B. M. 9:237
Neal, Benjamin 17:136; 24:200
Neal, C. 14:289; 19:183; 23:74
Neal, C. K. 27:147
Neal, C. L. 25:282
Neal, Charles 20:84
Neal, Chester 23:309
Neal, Christopher 10:165; 18:221
Neal, Daniel O. C. 17:201
Neal, David 12:34; 22:210
Neal, David A. 24:26
Neal, E. H. 13:95
Neal, Edward 17:92
Neal, Forman 16:69
Neal, G. 22:210
Neal, George W. 8:26; 17:190; 18:151; 20:25
Neal, H. B. 25:58
Neal, H. G. B. 22:262
Neal, Henry 8:41; 20:140; 26:175
Neal, Henry O. 17:23
Neal, J. 1:159
Neal, J. B. 9:57
Neal, J. H. 10:187; 18:178

Neal, J. K. 25:212
Neal, J. L. 12:96
Neal, J. N. 23:43
Neal, J. P. 25:212
Neal, J. R. 14:94
Neal, J. S. 17:167
Neal, J. V. 12:74; 15:58
Neal, James 4:67; 8:74; 14:94; 17:182
Neal, James H. 13:39
Neal, James K. 5:25
Neal, James T. 16:79
Neal, John 3:144; 21:95; 22:151; 25:212
Neal, John T. 18:247; 26:51
Neal, Joseph 1:61; 3:144; 22:515; 23:91
Neal, Moses M. 22:93
Neal, Perry 22:313
Neal, Peter 27:92
Neal, Philey 21:190
Neal, R. M. 26:224
Neal, Robert 13:39; 23:277
Neal, S. 13:95
Neal, Simon 16:216
Neal, T. H. 21:36
Neal, Thomas 21:103
Neal, W. 17:111
Neal, Warren I. 24:54
Neal, William 17:283
Neal, William A. 11:71
Neale, Benjamin 22:313
Neale, P. 25:212
Neale, William 13:116
Neales, James B. 17:277
Nealey, Isaac 4:67
Nealey, J. 3:144
Nealis, James 21:57
Neals, Enos J. 13:39; 16:48
Neals, John 5:25; 25:212
Nealy, B. 11:415
Nealy, B. F. 13:95
Nealy, Charles 16:216
Nealy, H. S. 21:371
Nealy, J. M. 17:163
Nealy, John 22:487
Nealy, William A. 17:249
Neam, J. 26:51
Neam, John 9:87
Near, Charles 25:212
Near, Charles H. 5:24
Near, Charles R. 4:43
Near, Frederick 21:57
Near, George H. 12:34
Near, Joseph 4:43
Near, S. 12:9
Nearan, Henry 17:15
Nearing, H. S. 19:27

Nearry, Barton 18:104
Neary, E. C. 18:54
Nease, Charles 11:429
Nease, Henry R. 24:161
Nease, John 17:96
Nease, Paul V. 17:167
Neason, --- 19:90
Neason, John 15:41
Neason, William F. 8:126
Neatherton, Henry H. 8:26
Neattles, John 9:134
Neave, Paul 18:313;
  26:108
Neaville, Henry B. 15:92
Nebb, M. B. 18:70
Nebell, John 19:27
Neberry, Frank W. 20:317
Nebers, Sampson 9:87
Nebers, Simon 26:50
Nebin, John 20:87
Nebles, James 9:37
Nebsmith, William V.
  4:43
Nechuer, J. J. 18:113
Neck, N. 3:144
Necker, John 20:11
Necker, Joseph 9:13
Neckley, B. W. 3:144
Neclout, W. 3:144
Necomber, George 19:90
Nedden, J. 3:144
Neddi, Hubert 1:61
Neddo, Joseph 11:288
Nedham, T. 11:71
Nedleton, Judson 11:309
Nedron, Jacob 15:72
Nedrow, Joseph 22:13
Nedry, William S. 11:161
Nedwells, W. 14:94
Nee, Batthayer 21:371
Nee, Henry 14:201
Need, John 24:42
Needam, G. W. 16:301
Needam, Peter 9:148
Needegh, Abraham
  18:221
Needham, Austin 23:43
Needham, C. B. 19:257
Needham, C. C. 12:164
Needham, C. W. 4:44;
  12:93
Needham, Caleb 8:53;
  21:103
Needham, Charles B.
  9:187
Needham, G. A. 3:144
Needham, G. E. 9:215;
  21:371
Needham, G. W. 14:94
Needham, J. H. 19:27
Needham, L. H. 3:144

Needham, M. 21:205
Needham, Robert 17:39
Needham, T. 3:144
Needham, W. A. 7:105
Needham, William 10:20;
  22:398, 434
Needler, Lewis 11:390
Needs, Jacob 18:295
Needs, Joshua 26:108
Neefas, John 21:371
Neehans, W. 7:52
Neel, Daniel 10:129;
  20:317
Neel, J. E. M. 17:444
Neel, Jac. W. 17:217
Neelan, Peter 27:91
Neelan, William P. 12:156
Neeley, D. 23:160
Neeley, David 22:46
Neeley, John H. 20:11
Neeley, John W. C. 21:76
Neeley, Robert 8:108
Neely, Daniel 11:17
Neely, David 17:419;
  23:181
Neely, H. 23:43
Neely, Henry C. 23:91
Neely, Hugh L. 20:110
Neely, J. 23:160
Neely, J. S. 22:262
Neely, J. W. 13:95
Neely, James 14:94
Neely, James R. 17:84
Neely, John 21:371
Neely, John H. 17:167
Neely, John L. 23:100
Neely, Joseph 19:27
Neely, Joseph N. 8:53
Neely, Oscar J. 10:165
Neely, W. H. 17:444;
  24:161
Neely, William 10:129;
  20:317; 24:113;
  26:174
Neeosum, M. 24:26
Neeper, James 12:65
Neer, Henry 17:67
Neer, Lewis 20:179
Neer, M. 11:309
Nees, Albert 9:187
Nees, E. 20:317
Nees, Ezekiel 10:71
Neese, John 21:217
Neese, John S. 22:434
Neese, Martin V. R. 17:84
Neeser, Henry 10:129
Neeshan, George 9:123
Neeson, Jasper 1:61
Nefeor, Jacob 19:258
Neff, A. 1:159
Neff, A. S. 14:330

Neff, Anthony 25:59
Neff, B. 3:144
Neff, Christian 27:92
Neff, D. 1:159
Neff, H. 14:94
Neff, Isaac 26:127
Neff, J. 3:144
Neff, J. R. 23:43
Neff, Jackson 20:58
Neff, James 20:148
Neff, James W. 7:105
Neff, John 4:44; 26:50
Neff, John L. 17:84
Neff, Lewis A. 25:212
Neff, Martin 9:87
Neff, N. 11:320
Neff, Russell 11:309
Neff, Salem 23:43
Neff, W. J. 27:91
Neff, W. R. 11:403
Neff, William 3:144;
  11:39; 23:100
Nefler, Jacob 9:187
Nefley, --- 20:85
Nega, John 8:26; 18:151
Neggett, Frank 14:94
Negle, Thomas 9:123;
  27:92
Negley, George 15:88
Negley, H. 13:95
Negley, Ross 20:45
Neglinfin, Thomas 16:216
Negres, J. F. 18:313;
  26:108
Negus, --- 15:41
Negus, John T. 24:82
Neher, A. M. 1:159
Neher, Charles 3:144
Nehmey, Christian 24:173
Neib, H. C. 14:270
Neibergal, Lewis W.
  15:14
Neibergall, Lewis W.
  12:62
Neiblin, N. 22:210
Neibour, Samuel 21:190
Neice, Howard 21:76
Neice, Thompson 4:44
Neice, William 19:349
Neich, J. 16:216
Neiclugh, David 21:231
Neida, Charles S. 22:46
Neidenhauser, J. 25:212
Neider, F. 24:113
Neider, John 8:91
Neiderhauser, Daniel
  10:71
Neidfeldt, Herman 10:71;
  20:317
Neidick, Frederick W.
  11:161

Neidy, Abraham 22:93
Neidy, Lorenzo 19:27
Neieber, Christopher 26:51
Neierburg, Michael 10:129
Neife, George 1:61
Neiffer, W. T. 22:210
Neigh, Charles S. 9:87; 26:51
Neighbaar, N. 3:144
Neighbor, Alonzo W. 20:25
Neighbor, C. 9:87
Neighbor, E. 12:162
Neighbor, M. 18:178
Neighbor, R. 18:399
Neighborgal, John L. 22:211
Neighborn, J. 23:43
Neighbors, A. 3:144
Neighbors, Elijah 10:71; 20:317
Neighbors, John 9:87; 26:50
Neighbors, Joseph 22:113
Neighbors, William 8:91
Neighbour, J. 3:144
Neighbours, J. 25:212
Neihl, Conran 4:44
Neihouse, H. 1:159
Neihouse, William 17:353
Neil, Alamson 9:104
Neil, Alanson 18:340
Neil, C. 1:159
Neil, C. L. 14:316
Neil, Calvin 22:455
Neil, Daniel 11:415
Neil, Douglas 9:227; 18:373
Neil, F. O. 1:61
Neil, George 25:212
Neil, H. 3:144; 14:286
Neil, H. O. 18:373
Neil, Henry 14:286
Neil, Hiram 21:36
Neil, J. 17:478
Neil, J. L. 15:361
Neil, James H. 16:48
Neil, John 18:209; 21:280
Neil, John A. 10:71; 20:317
Neil, John F. 21:371
Neil, John O. 15:321
Neil, M. 14:131; 16:281
Neil, Samuel D. 22:236
Neil, Simon 7:36
Neil, Thomas 10:29; 19:305; 26:175
Neil, William 1:60
Neile, James 27:91

Neiler, John 14:243
Neiles, William J. 5:25
Neill, Charles 14:266
Neill, John K. 12:51
Neills, W. J. 25:213
Neilor, George 10:20
Neils, Charles B. 4:44
Neils, John 8:53
Neils, Johnson W. 4:44
Neilson, H. Nels 20:115
Neilson, Ole 27:147
Neily, A. 1:159
Neily, Jack 18:16
Neily, John 11:161
Neiman, A. F. 15:131
Neiman, J. F. 15:131
Neiman, John A. 7:69
Neimeister, John 10:20
Nein, Arus 22:341
Neiphaus, Gerhard 23:193
Neir, J. 3:144
Neire, August 25:280
Neirs, Dewitt 8:53
Neis, George 20:317
Neisch, H. R. 14:243
Neise, J. 3:144
Neise, Reuben 10:20
Neiske, Henry 20:58
Neiswanger, Edwin 18:452
Neithhammer, J. 3:144
Neitly, Samuel 3:144
Neitsert, Andrew 21:371
Neitzch, Rudolph 21:76
Neitzel, Leonhardt 23:91
Neiw, P. 13:95
Neiwold, Theodore 22:47
Nelder, S. 3:144
Neler, Martin 20:319
Nelfinger, Frederick 21:36
Nelham, Charles 21:212
Nelis, Lafferty 1:61
Nelison, W. 20:58
Nelkenstock, Henry 4:44
Nell, Edward B. 22:409
Nell, Henry O. 9:163
Nell, J. 17:478
Nell, John 8:91
Nell, Philip 17:100
Nelles, Henry 20:11
Nellis, F. 14:322
Nellis, Ferdinand 14:316; 23:124
Nellis, George P. 9:87
Nellis, James 1:61; 17:450
Nellis, James B. 24:175
Nellis, Nelson 7:36
Nellis, William 15:287; 19:90
Nellis, William G. 16:216
Nellish, George 12:34

Nelly, August 26:174
Nelmes, Henry 14:202
Nelms, Samuel 15:217
Nelovis, James 13:116
Nelsa, William 14:243
Nelson, --- 7:8; 23:198; 26:175
Nelson, A. 3:144; 9:57; 13:67; 14:18; 26:51
Nelson, A. P. 17:111
Nelson, Aaron 18:35
Nelson, Abraham 8:26; 18:151
Nelson, Abram 17:296
Nelson, Adam C. 18:151
Nelson, Alexander C. 18:399
Nelson, Alexander M. 17:97
Nelson, Alfred 11:210
Nelson, Allen 9:87
Nelson, Allen B. 27:147
Nelson, Amos 8:41
Nelson, Andrew 16:86; 22:151
Nelson, Arnold 11:396
Nelson, August 18:427
Nelson, Augustus 16:148
Nelson, B. 3:144; 24:200
Nelson, B. F. 9:57
Nelson, B. H. 10:29
Nelson, Bank 7:36
Nelson, Benjamin 8:26; 17:252; 18:151
Nelson, Birney 21:280
Nelson, C. 1:159; 12:162; 14:202
Nelson, C. H. 21:103
Nelson, Carter 15:316; 19:90
Nelson, Charles 7:36; 10:174; 19:183
Nelson, Christ'r (Dalager) 19:344
Nelson, Christian 27:92
Nelson, Christian C. 7:105
Nelson, Cyrus 23:256
Nelson, D. H. C. 1:159
Nelson, Daniel 9:210; 22:313
Nelson, Darius H. C. 9:7
Nelson, David 10:71; 20:317; 22:93
Nelson, David P. 22:263
Nelson, E. 1:159; 18:325, 332; 22:313; 23:309
Nelson, Ebenezer 22:47
Nelson, Edward 22:282
Nelson, Edwin 10:129; 20:317

Nelson, Elias 10:71; 20:317
Nelson, Emery 8:115
Nelson, Enoch 17:23
Nelson, Erick 12:156
Nelson, F. 3:144
Nelson, F. A. 16:216
Nelson, F. W. 17:39
Nelson, Francis 22:151
Nelson, Francis M. 22:151
Nelson, Frank 7:130; 19:90
Nelson, Frederick 17:436; 24:186
Nelson, G. 3:144; 9:243
Nelson, G. W. 9:98; 10:187; 18:178, 279
Nelson, George 8:53; 9:210; 20:11; 21:150, 371
Nelson, George M. 22:211
Nelson, George W. 12:156; 18:399; 22:47
Nelson, Greenbury 8:91
Nelson, H. 14:94; 16:216; 20:58
Nelson, H. R. 19:183
Nelson, Helge 22:282
Nelson, Henry 9:87, 210; 17:182; 18:70; 22:515; 25:213; 26:50
Nelson, Hiram 17:447; 24:171
Nelson, Hodges 8:41; 26:175
Nelson, Horatio 19:183
Nelson, Hugh 11:161
Nelson, I. H. 26:51
Nelson, J. 1:61, 159; 3:144; 9:87; 10:29; 19:90, 305, 326; 25:213
Nelson, J. B. 11:288
Nelson, J. G. 1:61
Nelson, J. H. 3:144; 11:267; 18:247
Nelson, J. M. 11:246
Nelson, J. T. 1:158
Nelson, Jacob 4:44; 10:165; 19:183
Nelson, James 9:87, 134, 239; 10:99; 14:94; 26:224; 27:92
Nelson, James A. 3:144; 21:131
Nelson, James H. 23:74
Nelson, James M. 18:35
Nelson, James R. 9:57
Nelson, James T. 11:161

Nelson, James W. 22:211
Nelson, Jesse 20:317
Nelson, Jesse I. 10:71
Nelson, John 3:144, 224; 5:43; 7:130; 8:108; 9:67, 87; 11:96; 16:216; 17:337; 22:211, 341; 25:213; 26:50
Nelson, John B. 18:399
Nelson, John C. 9:87
Nelson, John E. 11:128
Nelson, John H. 11:415
Nelson, John J. 7:105
Nelson, John L. 17:499
Nelson, John S. 20:175
Nelson, John W. 23:115
Nelson, Joseph 11:267; 17:23; 21:280; 23:193
Nelson, Joseph L. 22:93
Nelson, Josiah 7:105
Nelson, K. 3:144
Nelson, L. 17:286
Nelson, L. D. 21:371
Nelson, L. S. 10:129; 20:317
Nelson, Lafayette 1:60
Nelson, Lewis 17:361; 23:193
Nelson, Lors 11:193
Nelson, Louis A. 19:27
Nelson, Marion 9:44; 26:127
Nelson, Marshal 11:210
Nelson, Martin 12:34
Nelson, Matthew J. 21:76
Nelson, Miles 17:23
Nelson, Milton A. 10:71
Nelson, Moses B. 10:153; 19:183
Nelson, N. 8:26; 11:333; 17:257; 18:151
Nelson, Nathaniel F. 22:263
Nelson, Neil 10:129; 20:318
Nelson, Nelce 20:33
Nelson, Nels L. 17:347
Nelson, Newton 23:181
Nelson, Nicholas G. 8:26; 18:151
Nelson, Nichols 18:247; 26:51
Nelson, Noah 25:213
Nelson, O. 13:95; 19:326; 25:213
Nelson, O. P. 14:301; 17:471; 27:92
Nelson, Odem C. 8:26
Nelson, Ola 22:151

Nelson, P. 18:193; 25:213
Nelson, Patten 5:43
Nelson, Perry B. 19:268
Nelson, Perry T. 9:187
Nelson, Peter 5:25; 9:243; 20:115
Nelson, Pleasant 11:210
Nelson, R. 22:313
Nelson, R. C. 22:162
Nelson, R. D. 10:71; 20:318
Nelson, R. G. 15:217
Nelson, R. H. 1:61
Nelson, Reuben W. 20:11
Nelson, Robert 9:156; 12:100; 15:366
Nelson, Roderick 10:20
Nelson, S. C. 10:29; 19:305
Nelson, Samuel 9:27; 14:202; 18:313; 21:36; 26:108
Nelson, Samuel N. 17:441
Nelson, Samuel R. 7:64
Nelson, Silas 14:94
Nelson, Swain 21:92
Nelson, T. R. 19:27
Nelson, Thomas 3:144; 4:67; 20:115; 22:47, 263; 25:213
Nelson, V. C. 21:36
Nelson, W. C. 7:52
Nelson, W. F. 12:87
Nelson, W. H. 3:144; 25:213
Nelson, W. M. 11:341
Nelson, W. S. 14:94; 18:285; 26:135
Nelson, W. T. 16:301
Nelson, Wallace 11:267
Nelson, Wallace T. 20:318
Nelson, Weste 8:26
Nelson, Wiley B. 26:50
Nelson, William 3:144; 7:130; 8:91; 11:40; 17:253; 18:247; 22:47, 434; 26:51
Nelson, William A. 12:65; 15:92
Nelson, William C. 22:168
Nelson, William F. 23:74
Nelson, William H. 11:71
Nelson, William R. 9:155
Nelson, William Y. 23:75
Nelson, Winslow 10:165
Nelson, Wisle 18:151
Nelty, Isaac 16:301
Nely, William 9:159
Nemee, John M. 21:128
Nemiers, Peter 26:51

Nemitz, Reinhold 23:193
Nengle, H. 17:40
Nenley, George 25:213
Nentzel, J. T. 21:36
Nepekis, George 16:376
Nephan, R. B. 16:216
Nephen, R. B. 13:81
Nephew, Alvin 17:244
Nephuy, Edward 16:216
Nepple, T. 9:187; 19:258
Nerd, John 8:91
Nere, Stephen 8:41
Nere, Theodore 15:174
Nerg, Thomas M. 8:108
Nerils, Robert 19:90
Nerison, Torger 24:95
Nero, Fred 4:44
Nero, Jacob 4:44
Nerpehult, William 7:36
Nerville, S. 3:144
Nervin, Charles 19:90
Nes, M. J. 23:256
Nesbent, George 21:150
Nesbeth, Jeffrey 9:134
Nesbit, Curtis 8:77
Nesbit, J. 11:267, 310
Nesbit, James 15:72
Nesbit, James R. 11:109
Nesbit, Jeffrey 27:92
Nesbit, John W. 7:105
Nesbit, Mathew 25:58
Nesbit, Sharper 9:134
Nesbitt, Hugh 23:160
Nesbitt, Lucas 20:108
Nesbitt, Noble 23:193
Nesmith, J. B. 22:263
Ness, Robert 12:74; 15:72
Ness, Samuel 8:108
Ness, William 13:39
Nessel, Edward 22:162
Nesselroder, P. J. 11:161
Nesser, Henry 20:317
Nest, Willis M. 19:27
Nester, George 10:96
Nester, James A. 9:223
Nestle, Franklin 22:151
Neston, John 11:39
Nestor, John 15:217
Nestor, Samuel 18:285;
    26:135
Neswenter, B. J. 21:124
Net, Fred 19:183
Netchman, W. 14:94
Neter, Frederick 12:74
Nethamer, L. 1:60
Nethercoth, I. 21:128
Netherton, Henry W.
    18:152
Netler, Joseph 6:22
Nette, C. 2:15
Nette, J. 25:312

Netter, James H. 13:39
Netter, John 17:398
Netting, Henry 20:178
Nettle, Charles 25:58
Nettle, George W. 24:42
Nettles, C. C. 21:371
Nettles, John 27:92
Nettleton, --- 21:371
Nettleton, Herman 17:263
Nettleton, R. E. 12:34
Nettleton, Samuel 10:10
Nettleton, W. P. 8:74;
    26:175
Netts, James 16:216
Neubah, Frederic 17:56
Neuberger, J. W. 17:155
Neuburg, Michael 20:318
Neugenberger, A. 14:94
Neugent, Dennis 10:20
Neuman, D. 1:159
Neumonn, E. 14:243
Neupang, Augustus 10:71
Neuters, G. 3:144
Neutuney, Christian
    17:448
Nevarre, Alex J. 9:37
Neve, Stephen 26:174
Nevegold, J. 2:15
Nevegold, J. B. 25:59
Nevelle, J. 27:91
Nevellis, O. 22:341
Nevells, Denton 8:41;
    26:174
Nevels, Robert 22:313
Nevenhizer, C. A. 7:64
Never, Silas 7:36
Nevil, Harrison 21:57
Nevil, Isaac A. 24:54
Nevil, James 26:108
Nevil, Thomas 11:396
Nevill, H. R. 21:124
Nevill, James 18:295
Neville, G. W. 11:39
Neville, H. J. 13:39
Neville, Henry C. 11:267
Neville, J. 1:159
Neville, James 17:152
Neville, John 9:187;
    12:51; 19:224
Neville, P. W. 1:61
Neville, Robert 13:39
Neville, T. 1:61
Neville, Thomas G. 1:61
Nevils, Allen 22:263
Nevin, Edwin 9:223
Nevin, J. A. 20:153
Nevin, Thomas 12:74;
    15:41
Nevins, Charles 15:285
Nevins, Edward S. 24:59
Nevins, Edwin 18:373

Nevins, Elias 11:39
Nevins, George 16:69
Nevins, J. 1:61
Nevins, Manlius V.
    23:100
Nevins, Patrick 14:202
Nevins, William 23:160
Nevitt, John J. 23:100
New, C. 16:270
New, George W. 3:144
New, Richard 12:59
New, V. N. 15:344
New, V. W. 16:376
New, William T. 21:95
Newall, D. 25:213
Newall, F. 1:99
Newall, G. W. 12:123
Newall, Jacob 22:47
Newall, N. 6:32
Newark, John 8:92
Newark, Timothy 8:92,
    115
Newbacker, Marshall
    24:108
Newberg, Frank W.
    10:129
Newberg, John 24:69
Newberger, C. 19:258
Newberger, Christopher
    9:187
Newberger, Jacob 19:27
Newberger, M. 3:144
Newbern, Andrew 18:16
Newberry, Andrew 22:263
Newberry, C. E. 14:266,
    289
Newberry, Charles 23:124
Newberry, Charles H.
    24:54
Newberry, Daniel 22:211
Newberry, Daniel W.
    22:434
Newberry, Eddy 17:244
Newberry, George 5:25
Newberry, H. 25:213
Newberry, Henry 5:25
Newberry, Hiram 10:71;
    20:187, 318
Newberry, J. 7:36
Newberry, James 20:110
Newberry, John C. 8:26
Newberry, L. S. 14:94
Newberry, N. 7:75, 78;
    25:302
Newberry, N. P. 24:213
Newberry, Oscar 22:47
Newberry, Robert 9:231;
    20:318
Newberry, Russell 8:92
Newberry, S. 9:57
Newberry, Samuel 22:127

Newberry, William 3:144
Newbert, Eugene 13:116
Newbert, James 7:75
Newbert, Neville A. 15:11
Newbery, George 11:288
Newbit, A. 25:302
Newbit, Andrew 7:75
Newbold, Joseph 10:71;
    20:318
Newbold, William 18:221
Newbort, T. W. 14:94
Newbradt, Frank 18:248;
    26:51
Newburg, H. 3:144
Newburg, John 3:144
Newburg, Lewis 15:41
Newburg, Richard M.
    21:258
Newburg, Warren H.
    22:465
Newburn, J. 21:111
Newbury, C. E. 23:160
Newbury, Charles W.
    11:109
Newbury, G. O. 25:213
Newbury, H. 19:183
Newbury, James 3:144
Newbury, S. H. 10:165
Newbury, Samuel 11:39
Newby, G. 16:216
Newby, George 13:58
Newby, J. H. 10:96
Newby, John 9:187;
    19:268
Newby, Joseph 17:337
Newby, L. 11:71
Newby, N. B. 26:175
Newby, Nathan 8:66
Newby, Robert 10:129;
    20:318
Newby, T. E. 21:111
Newby, W. 25:213
Newby, William 5:43;
    13:58
Newby, William C. 22:94
Newby, William H. 20:99
Newcom, T. 16:216
Newcomb, B. 13:39
Newcomb, B. C. 21:371
Newcomb, C. O. 18:70
Newcomb, Charles R.
    20:115
Newcomb, Daniel W.
    19:183
Newcomb, Edward H.
    23:160
Newcomb, G. 25:213
Newcomb, George 3:144;
    10:71; 20:318
Newcomb, Henry A.
    14:202

Newcomb, Hiram 11:161
Newcomb, J. P. 25:213
Newcomb, John 21:371;
    24:42
Newcomb, Joseph 10:129;
    20:318
Newcomb, Joseph H.
    22:487
Newcomb, L. H. 13:95
Newcomb, L. P. 16:270
Newcomb, Lafayette
    17:238
Newcomb, Lucius 24:54
Newcomb, Moses 17:67
Newcomb, R. 22:211
Newcomb, S. A. 27:91
Newcomb, Samuel 21:231
Newcomb, Seth P. 13:39;
    16:48
Newcomb, Thomas
    18:285; 26:135
Newcomb, Thomas B.
    19:27
Newcomb, W. B. 15:92
Newcomb, W. H. H.
    11:267
Newcomb, W. O. 4:44
Newcomb, William 9:27;
    22:263
Newcomb, William B.
    12:74
Newcomb, Winfield
    25:213
Newcomber, George
    13:67
Newcome, Abram 10:20
Newcome, George 5:25
Newcome, Henry 19:47
Newcome, J. B. 21:36
Newcome, John E. 3:144
Newcome, S. 3:144
Newcomer, B. F. 23:75
Newcomer, Henry 9:187
Newcomer, Jacob 13:80
Newcomer, John 3:144
Newcross, Joseph 15:131
Newel, Edward 5:43
Newel, John 5:43
Newell, --- 20:11
Newell, B. A. 16:281
Newell, Brayton 22:509
Newell, C. D. 9:240
Newell, C. W. 17:416;
    24:154
Newell, Charles C. 14:202
Newell, Charles L. 10:71;
    20:318
Newell, D. K. 18:279
Newell, David 5:25;
    10:129; 20:318
Newell, E. 25:213

Newell, E. C. 24:42
Newell, E. H. 25:213
Newell, G. S. 3:145
Newell, G. W. 15:131
Newell, George H. 25:278
Newell, George M. 18:151
Newell, George W. 8:27;
    13:39; 16:48
Newell, H. G. 16:48
Newell, Harvey H. 17:244
Newell, Hewitt 11:246
Newell, J. 25:213
Newell, John 13:67; 19:90
Newell, John H. 24:95
Newell, Joseph 12:170
Newell, Joseph J. 8:118
Newell, L. 3:145
Newell, L. M. 1:61
Newell, Lemuel E. 21:231
Newell, Loran D. 15:41
Newell, M. 11:71; 21:371;
    22:313
Newell, N. 13:95; 25:325
Newell, N. B. 24:54
Newell, Nathaniel 4:44
Newell, Perry 19:27
Newell, Robert T. 16:79
Newell, S. C. 21:36
Newell, Samuel 7:105;
    17:182
Newell, Thomas E. 23:43
Newell, Thomas J. 15:58
Newell, W. 17:182
Newell, Washington 10:71
Newell, William 20:318
Newell, William J. 25:58
Newfang, Augustus
    20:318
Newfort, I. A. 26:51
Newgart, Joseph 7:60
Newhall, Charles 8:53
Newhall, E. 14:301;
    17:473; 27:92
Newham, Jasper 18:340
Newhick, Jacob 19:229
Newhoff, William 6:32;
    25:325
Newhouse, Charles 8:27;
    18:152
Newhouse, George W.
    22:93
Newhouse, Ion 10:129
Newhouse, J. E. 11:161
Newhouse, Jacob 27:92
Newhouse, Jonathan
    20:318
Newhouse, William 19:90
Newist, John 16:301
Newitt, George 5:43
Newkirk, Clem 3:145
Newkirk, Francis 18:335

Newkirk, Harrison 17:277
Newkirk, J. C. 11:310
Newkirk, J. P. 1:61
Newkirk, Jacob 9:187;
    22:151
Newkirk, James H. 21:196
Newkirk, John W. 23:75
Newkirk, O. 1:61
Newkirk, Peter 13:116
Newkirk, Tunis D. 24:95
Newkirk, William 20:99
Newlan, H. 3:145
Newlan, William 20:42
Newland, A. L. 7:36
Newland, Alex 22:515
Newland, Alfred M. 13:39
Newland, Aquilla 12:169
Newland, Arch 26:108
Newland, Archibald 9:27;
    18:313
Newland, B. 18:221
Newland, Daniel R. 9:87
Newland, Edward 24:54
Newland, Hiram F.
    23:193
Newland, James D.
    21:103
Newland, Jesse 11:210
Newland, John 8:26;
    18:152; 20:184
Newland, John W. 11:415
Newland, S. M. 19:233
Newland, S. W. 18:90
Newland, W. L. 22:47
Newley, E. 3:145
Newley, James M. 18:193
Newley, W. 25:213
Newlin, Edward 22:313
Newlin, H. 14:94
Newlin, J. 18:466
Newlin, J. R. 11:267
Newlin, John K. 11:255
Newlin, Rose 20:58
Newlin, T. 11:247
Newlin, William H. 10:71;
    20:318
Newling, J. T. 15:131
Newling, John 11:341
Newly, J. 22:47
Newly, Nathan S. 24:42
Newly, Townsend 24:42
Newman, --- 15:217
Newman, A. 3:145; 11:40;
    13:95
Newman, Abraham 12:59
Newman, Adelbert 7:105
Newman, Allen 16:160
Newman, Andrew J. 1:60
Newman, August 11:116
Newman, B. F. 11:128

Newman, Benjamin 7:69;
    9:201
Newman, Bird 22:263
Newman, Caleb W. 17:56
Newman, Carl 12:156
Newman, Charles 14:94;
    23:115
Newman, Charles A.
    22:113
Newman, Conrad 11:161
Newman, D. C. 9:223
Newman, D. D. 18:373
Newman, Daniel 8:26;
    15:344; 18:152
Newman, David 16:376
Newman, David M. 8:123
Newman, E. 11:310;
    15:259
Newman, E. H. 9:87
Newman, E. W. 26:51
Newman, Egbert 12:83;
    16:301
Newman, F. C. 13:67;
    16:216
Newman, Francis 15:41
Newman, Francis M.
    15:217
Newman, G. 1:159;
    25:213
Newman, G. A. 17:445
Newman, George 7:36,
    105; 13:39; 19:183;
    21:371
Newman, George H.
    10:177
Newman, George P.
    24:164
Newman, Harvey 18:279
Newman, Henry 7:105
Newman, J. 1:61; 11:246;
    25:275; 26:224
Newman, J. A. 3:145
Newman, J. F. 19:90
Newman, J. H. 22:236
Newman, J. L. 11:267
Newman, J. S. 9:223
Newman, J. W. 20:181;
    23:43
Newman, James 11:390;
    17:454; 24:186
Newman, James R. 14:202
Newman, Jerome W.
    26:127
Newman, Jesse 3:145
Newman, John 12:34;
    14:202; 17:361;
    18:279
Newman, John L. 22:487
Newman, Jonas 15:217
Newman, Lewis 11:403;
    21:150

Newman, Mathew 8:26;
    18:152
Newman, Morris 25:58
Newman, N. 10:96
Newman, N. G. 8:26;
    18:152
Newman, Nicholas 24:43;
    26:175
Newman, O. P. 1:159
Newman, P. 16:99
Newman, Peter 13:39
Newman, Pinkney A.
    22:47
Newman, R. 11:246;
    25:213
Newman, R. C. 21:190
Newman, Richard 18:313;
    26:108
Newman, S. 14:94, 202;
    18:373
Newman, Samuel 17:84
Newman, T. 1:158
Newman, T. D. 22:211
Newman, Thomas 25:59
Newman, W. 22:354
Newman, W. J. 9:57
Newman, William 5:43;
    14:283; 16:216;
    20:318; 22:409;
    24:63
Newman, William J.
    24:82
Newmans, J. M. F. 1:159
Newmaster, C. 14:202
Newnon, Munroe 22:263
Newnoun, E. 27:92
Newport, --- 23:204
Newport, B. 3:145
Newport, Bonne 9:210
Newport, Calvin 23:266
Newport, Fitz Henry
    10:25
Newport, James P. 23:75
Newport, John A. 9:87
Newport, Paul 18:248;
    26:51
Newport, William 8:53
News, C. 7:52
News, Josiah 11:161
Newsam, George W.
    17:347
Newshan, George 10:20
Newsman, Benjamin
    19:283
Newsock, William 11:161
Newsom, John M. 22:151
Newsom, Peter 21:150
Newsom, Samuel 7:130
Newsom, W. M. 7:105
Newsome, I. 5:43
Newsome, J. 25:213

Newsome, Jesse 26:174
Newson, Daniel 22:465
Newson, J. 22:487
Newson, James 21:371
Newson, James W. 22:151
Newson, Jesse 8:41
Newson, Samuel 21:371
Newson, T. K. 1:159
Newson, Thomas 22:487
Newston, John S. 21:103
Newton, --- 22:354; 26:51
Newton, A. 3:145; 7:13
Newton, A. C. 18:460
Newton, A. M. 21:371
Newton, Abraham J.
  22:263
Newton, Albert A. 10:71
Newton, Alvin A. 20:318
Newton, Andrew J.
  17:283
Newton, Angelo A. 9:27;
  18:313; 26:108
Newton, Butler 22:47
Newton, C. 3:145
Newton, C. W. 3:145
Newton, Calvin 24:113
Newton, Cyrus 22:313
Newton, D. 1:61; 18:193
Newton, Daniel W.
  20:127
Newton, Doggett 19:27
Newton, E. S. 25:302
Newton, Ebenezer 20:193
Newton, Edgar 7:80
Newton, Edward 4:44
Newton, Elias 22:127
Newton, Elijah 22:263
Newton, Everal 12:74
Newton, F. 1:158
Newton, Ferris 14:202
Newton, G. T. 16:376
Newton, George 12:74;
  15:41; 19:28
Newton, George H. 8:108
Newton, Henry 1:61;
  9:67; 21:371; 25:58,
  213
Newton, Hiram 7:130
Newton, Isaac 10:174;
  11:210; 18:35;
  19:183; 24:95
Newton, Isaac W. 11:71
Newton, J. 1:158; 13:95;
  14:18
Newton, J. D. 18:313
Newton, J. E. 14:94
Newton, J. H. 2:15
Newton, J. J. 25:213
Newton, James 10:71,
  129; 17:47; 20:318
Newton, James B. 11:20

Newton, Jerome 5:25
Newton, Jesse 22:341
Newton, John 13:129;
  22:263; 24:102
Newton, John A. 17:97
Newton, John H. 23:75
Newton, John L. 13:39
Newton, Joseph 4:44;
  7:60; 16:123
Newton, Joseph B. 22:127
Newton, Joseph H. 25:59
Newton, L. 8:41; 26:175
Newton, L. C. 3:145
Newton, Milton 17:423
Newton, Milton A. 24:171
Newton, Moses W. 4:44
Newton, Nathan 20:141
Newton, Orvil A. 4:44
Newton, Orville 13:39
Newton, Paul 17:506
Newton, R. J. 3:145
Newton, Robert 7:105
Newton, S. D. 26:108
Newton, Samuel D. 3:145
Newton, Samuel G.
  22:263
Newton, Silas 22:115
Newton, Sylvester 15:351;
  16:376
Newton, T. 15:41
Newton, Thomas 8:92
Newton, Thomas J. 11:71
Newton, W. 17:155;
  18:35; 25:213
Newton, W. D. 25:284
Newton, Warner 12:74
Newton, William 3:145;
  11:288; 17:182
Newton, William A. 12:34
Newton, William H.
  17:207; 19:90
Newton, Zinar 18:271
Newtown, G. F. 15:344
Newzell, Augustus 12:34
Ney, Adam 24:95
Ney, Francis 9:187
Ney, George W. 4:44
Ney, Jeremiah 18:90
Neye, George 17:388
Neyenhouse, W. 20:155
Neyhart, D. 9:148; 27:91
Neyman, N. L. 23:160
Neymit, A. 14:258
Niapoad, --- 25:58
Nibdit, Albert 22:313
Nibert, Francis 4:44
Nibling, Abraham 17:56
Niblo, D. H. 15:217
Niblo, John W. 24:89
Nicandson, Doctor
  17:455; 24:200

Nice, E. T. 25:58
Nice, Jacob 3:145
Nice, John H. 1:61
Nice, Joseph C. 21:57
Nice, Ozro 23:256
Nicely, --- 3:224
Nicely, A. 17:505
Nicely, A. M. 14:202
Nicely, Abraham 21:57
Nicely, Albert T. 22:211
Nicely, F. 3:145
Nicely, George 23:181
Nicely, Pryor 22:263
Nicely, William A. 23:75
Nicewater, G. 14:94
Nichel, C. F. 26:108
Nicheles, Abraham 22:94
Nichlson, W. 27:91
Nichol, B. H. 10:129
Nicholans, George 12:83
Nicholas, --- 18:35
Nicholas, A. 7:36; 14:202
Nicholas, A. J. 9:123
Nicholas, Alanson 19:28
Nicholas, Andrew 7:105
Nicholas, C. 25:213
Nicholas, C. P. 24:113
Nicholas, Charles 7:36,
  105
Nicholas, Charles L.
  16:48
Nicholas, David 18:295
Nicholas, E. 7:36; 25:213
Nicholas, Edward C.
  11:40
Nicholas, Fred 9:187
Nicholas, Frederick
  19:283
Nicholas, Henry 6:13;
  17:400
Nicholas, Henry V.
  22:127
Nicholas, Isaac 12:142
Nicholas, J. 11:161
Nicholas, Jackson 18:152
Nicholas, James 1:61;
  23:279
Nicholas, James D. 7:36
Nicholas, James J. 20:190
Nicholas, John 20:318
Nicholas, John M. 17:261
Nicholas, John W. 22:434
Nicholas, Joseph 21:196
Nicholas, Joseph A.
  22:127
Nicholas, Lemuel N.
  13:58
Nicholas, Lewis 23:185
Nicholas, Mark 11:183
Nicholas, Martin 9:239
Nicholas, Otis 7:105

Nicholas, P. 14:131
Nicholas, R. 1:158
Nicholas, S. 25:213
Nicholas, Saul 6:13
Nicholas, Thomas 10:129; 18:70; 20:318
Nicholas, Thornton 21:150
Nicholas, William 5:25
Nicholass, --- 4:44
Nicholay, William 4:44
Nicholds, H. 8:53
Nicholds, John 3:145
Nicholds, John G. 18:178
Nicholis, B. 1:159
Nicholis, Q. H. 15:361
Nicholls, Frederick 12:51
Nicholls, W. 18:399
Nicholls, W. H. 12:123
Nichols, --- 11:193; 15:131
Nichols, A. 3:145; 15:217; 21:371
Nichols, A. B. 9:87; 16:217
Nichols, A. D. 9:57
Nichols, A. F. 26:237
Nichols, A. N. 22:47
Nichols, A. S. 3:145; 16:217; 17:152
Nichols, Adolph 13:116
Nichols, Adoniram J. 27:92
Nichols, Albert 21:371; 22:434
Nichols, Albert H. 11:116
Nichols, Alvar A. 13:39
Nichols, Alver. A. 16:48
Nichols, Amos 22:434
Nichols, Andrew J. 18:248; 26:51
Nichols, B. 1:158
Nichols, B. F. 25:213
Nichols, B. W. 14:283
Nichols, Benjamin 10:177; 13:39; 19:183
Nichols, Benjamin F. 22:94
Nichols, Byson 18:248; 26:51
Nichols, C. 3:145; 12:9; 15:218; 23:185
Nichols, Calhill 9:27
Nichols, Charles 4:44; 7:105; 8:41; 22:47
Nichols, Charles E. 1:61
Nichols, Charles H. 4:44; 17:419; 22:151; 24:161
Nichols, Charles L. 13:39

Nichols, Christopher 8:27; 18:152
Nichols, Columbus 4:67
Nichols, D. 5:43; 20:11; 25:213
Nichols, D. J. 22:211
Nichols, Daniel 9:37
Nichols, David 11:17; 26:108
Nichols, David D. 8:101; 17:459; 24:154
Nichols, Dwight 21:36
Nichols, E. 14:94
Nichols, Edmund R. 22:151
Nichols, Edward 8:108
Nichols, Edwin 23:43
Nichols, Ezra 11:109
Nichols, Ezra W. 23:109
Nichols, F. 16:217
Nichols, F. E. 3:145
Nichols, Francis 13:67; 19:90
Nichols, Fred A. 16:143
Nichols, Frederick E. 15:58
Nichols, G. 1:159
Nichols, G. H. 14:94
Nichols, G. W. 5:53; 9:73
Nichols, George 1:61; 9:112; 15:26; 17:398; 21:111; 22:313
Nichols, George E. 9:87
Nichols, George F. 22:465
Nichols, George P. 20:318
Nichols, George W. 10:20; 24:26
Nichols, H. 1:159; 3:145; 16:270
Nichols, H. R. 2:15; 25:58
Nichols, H. S. 13:125
Nichols, H. W. 16:99
Nichols, Harmon S. 19:183
Nichols, Henry 9:112; 18:209; 22:211
Nichols, Henry H. 7:60
Nichols, Henry P. 19:183
Nichols, Hudson 21:141
Nichols, Hunt 17:182
Nichols, I. 25:213
Nichols, Isaac 5:43; 20:318
Nichols, Isaac N. 17:361
Nichols, J. 1:61, 159; 3:145; 11:246; 14:270; 16:217; 20:42, 87; 25:213
Nichols, J. E. 7:78; 14:283; 25:302

Nichols, J. H. 17:456; 24:150
Nichols, J. J. 9:27; 18:313; 25:213; 26:108
Nichols, J. R. 19:258
Nichols, J. S. 19:258
Nichols, Jackson 8:27
Nichols, Jacob C. 19:90
Nichols, James 9:13; 11:71; 13:39; 16:217; 17:162; 22:94, 236
Nichols, James D. 10:71; 20:318
Nichols, James R. 9:187
Nichols, Jasper 22:434
Nichols, Jeremiah 11:17
Nichols, Jesse B. 19:28
Nichols, John 6:18; 7:130; 10:32; 17:182; 18:90; 22:94; 25:213
Nichols, John B. 12:34
Nichols, John F. 19:183
Nichols, John G. 10:187
Nichols, John L. 11:390; 20:318
Nichols, John R. 5:25
Nichols, Joseph 7:69; 17:361
Nichols, Joseph J. 5:25
Nichols, Joseph T. 20:2
Nichols, Joseph W. 8:27; 18:152
Nichols, Josiah 23:293
Nichols, L. C. 3:145
Nichols, L. D. 3:145
Nichols, L. H. 12:96
Nichols, LeRoy L. 7:80
Nichols, Leroy L. 25:302
Nichols, Lewis 10:71; 15:218; 20:318
Nichols, M. 3:145; 11:291
Nichols, M. B. 15:218
Nichols, M. W. 22:211
Nichols, Mackencia 7:105
Nichols, Major H. 5:25
Nichols, Marshal 8:92
Nichols, Martin 21:57
Nichols, Moses 9:98; 15:153
Nichols, N. P. 23:43
Nichols, Nat 17:159
Nichols, O. K. 13:95; 14:18
Nichols, O. M. 26:108
Nichols, Orlando 9:37
Nichols, Patrick 22:263
Nichols, Peter 27:92
Nichols, R. 3:145
Nichols, R. H. 8:53
Nichols, Richard 18:434

Nichols, S. 1:159; 14:94;
    25:58, 213
Nichols, S. A. 10:92;
    20:318
Nichols, S. H. 19:90
Nichols, Samuel 7:36;
    17:136; 18:90;
    24:200; 25:286
Nichols, Simon L. 9:223;
    18:373
Nichols, Stephen 8:27;
    18:152
Nichols, Strother 20:27
Nichols, T. 15:263
Nichols, T. B. 1:158
Nichols, Theopilus M.
    11:40
Nichols, Thomas 12:156
Nichols, Thomas S. 13:60
Nichols, Thomas Y.
    22:127
Nichols, Truman 20:11
Nichols, W. 3:145;
    19:258; 25:213
Nichols, W. C. 15:363
Nichols, W. G. 23:43
Nichols, W. H. 11:120;
    14:26
Nichols, W. J. 1:158;
    3:145
Nichols, William 3:145;
    8:27; 9:187, 237;
    10:71, 174; 11:193,
    415; 17:182; 18:152;
    19:183; 20:318;
    21:371; 22:211
Nichols, William A.
    22:341
Nichols, William G.
    26:224
Nichols, William H.
    15:131; 18:193;
    22:94
Nichols, William P. 8:27;
    18:152
Nichols, Willis 10:208
Nicholson, --- 8:74
Nicholson, A. 14:18
Nicholson, Alonzo 22:211
Nicholson, Archibald
    12:51
Nicholson, B. 3:145
Nicholson, C. W. 27:92
Nicholson, Charles 22:409
Nicholson, Daniel 11:390
Nicholson, E. 3:145
Nicholson, E. W. 12:156
Nicholson, F. M. 11:96
Nicholson, Francis A.
    22:47

Nicholson, Francis M.
    15:18
Nicholson, G. 1:158
Nicholson, G. B. 8:66
Nicholson, George 10:96;
    16:99
Nicholson, George A.
    21:231
Nicholson, H. 16:217
Nicholson, J. 1:158, 159
Nicholson, J. H. 22:211
Nicholson, J. W. 27:91
Nicholson, Jacob 7:105
Nicholson, James 13:39;
    23:302
Nicholson, James B.
    20:31
Nicholson, Jesse 10:71;
    20:318
Nicholson, John 3:145;
    4:67
Nicholson, John M.
    22:504
Nicholson, Joshua F.
    22:47
Nicholson, M. H. 8:53
Nicholson, M. M. 21:36
Nicholson, R. H. 3:145
Nicholson, T. P. 9:227;
    18:373
Nicholson, Thomas
    21:239
Nicholson, W. 1:61;
    22:162
Nicholson, William 10:71;
    20:319; 23:280
Nicholson, William B.
    9:187; 19:272
Nicholson, William T.
    18:221
Nicholus, George 16:301
Nick, Christian 22:487
Nick, Jacob 20:99
Nick, John 13:39
Nickart, John W. 7:36
Nickel, B. 12:9
Nickel, C. F. 18:313
Nickel, J. 11:309
Nickelas, Daniel C.
    14:202
Nickell, Robert A. 24:54
Nickels, Henry 16:145
Nickels, Howard 16:217
Nickels, John 16:99
Nickelson, Thomas 21:57
Nickens, J. W. 21:36
Nickerman, Casper 9:148;
    27:91
Nickerson, A. 25:58
Nickerson, Alden 11:267
Nickerson, D. 1:158, 159

Nickerson, D. C. 3:145
Nickerson, David R.
    21:92
Nickerson, E. J. 13:95
Nickerson, E. W. 1:60
Nickerson, J. H. 1:159
Nickerson, J. T. 1:159
Nickerson, J. W. 26:51
Nickerson, John 9:123
Nickerson, John W. 9:87
Nickerson, L. E. 11:71
Nickerson, N. J. 1:61
Nickerson, Ruel 16:79
Nickerson, W. 14:94
Nickerson, W. R. 1:159
Nickerson, William
    19:183
Nickerson, William J.
    9:87
Nickey, Granburry B.
    21:231
Nickey, Samuel 3:145
Nicklas, R. 22:211
Nickle, A. 12:162
Nickle, C. 3:145
Nickle, Henry F. 21:86
Nicklebacker, N. J. 21:371
Nickleson, Ephraim 22:94
Nicknite, Hiram 9:87
Nickolds, Stephen 22:409
Nickols, F. C. 15:218
Nickols, George 20:88
Nickolson, A. 13:95
Nickolson, G. 14:202
Nickolson, Henry 24:200
Nickolson, Neil 11:210
Nickolson, William 24:26
Nicks, John 25:334
Nickson, J. 1:159
Nickson, William 14:202
Nickum, E. 10:129;
    20:319
Nicodemus, J. B. 1:159
Nicodemus, M. 17:97
Nicol, B. H. 20:318
Nicol, Henry 23:160
Nicolai, Gatth 11:39
Nicolson, I. 3:145
Nicord, Hy 4:44
Nidey, William 25:59
Nidget, Samuel 6:25
Niece, Conrad 4:44
Niece, George 27:92
Niederbroker, F. 23:96
Niel, C. 27:91
Niel, James L. 19:90
Niel, John F. 7:69
Niel, Livingston M. 8:27
Niel, Pleasant 21:240
Niel, Thomas 14:202
Nield, John 22:341

Nielson, E. 19:258
Nielson, Haaken 21:258
Nielson, Hans 20:115
Nielson, Isaac 14:94
Nielson, Jacob 21:76, 258
Nielson, John 20:115
Nieman, Henry 24:161
Nieman, Jacob 6:10
Nieman, John 22:94
Niemeyer, John 20:127
Niemyer, Frederick C. 23:43
Nierhoff, Friedrich 23:100
Nieuman, Henry 17:422
Nieurst, John 22:94
Niffin, D. 2:15
Niffong, D. E. 17:24
Nifing, William F. 17:24
Nigele, B. 1:159
Niggins, Joseph 15:218
Nigh, Otho W. 11:320
Nigh, S. C. 24:26
Night, George M. 10:129; 20:319
Night, H. C. 14:202
Night, Nathaniel P. 22:211
Nightengale, Syke 27:92
Nightingale, B. 9:154; 27:91
Nightingale, Charles R. 27:92
Nightingale, Joseph 11:17
Nightingale, Robert H. 23:13
Nightingale, Syke 9:134
Nightshade, Alex 9:210
Nightuire, Abraham 20:35
Niglefind, H. 15:299
Nigurs, J. 9:27
Nihars, Daniel 12:34
Nihart, C. 10:149; 18:54
Nihart, Simon P. 20:19
Nihiser, D. 1:159
Nihiser, Joseph 11:161
Nihoff, William 1:61
Nike, William 21:76
Nikon, George W. 22:211
Nilan, Martin 27:92
Nilan, Thomas 13:39; 16:48
Niland, H. 3:145
Niland, J. 1:159
Nile, John 9:188
Nile, M. 14:270
Niler, Martin 10:71
Niles, A. 9:148; 18:193
Niles, A. P. 9:188; 19:275
Niles, Albert 11:403
Niles, Amasee 27:91
Niles, B. 9:188; 19:241

Niles, Edward W. 15:153
Niles, Franklin F. 8:108
Niles, Garnett 11:382
Niles, George 9:123; 27:92
Niles, George W. 13:39
Niles, H. 15:329; 19:90
Niles, Harris 27:91
Niles, J. A. 19:245
Niles, John 16:217
Niles, Miles F. 11:267
Niles, N. 25:58
Niles, Oscar L. 17:244
Niles, Philo 1:61
Niles, Porter S. 25:213
Niles, Reuben S. 23:280
Niles, S. B. 16:376
Niles, Simeon B. 22:282
Niles, Thomas A. 24:61
Niles, William 12:34; 27:147
Niles, Zenias 22:151
Nill, J. 27:92
Nillard, J. 19:90
Nilson, A. 11:231
Nilson, E. 17:100
Nilson, Lars 22:282
Nilson, Nils 22:509; 23:117
Nim, Thomas 21:280
Niman, John D. 20:127
Nimmer, Edmund 9:157
Nimmo, George 27:91
Nimmo, Richard 21:141
Nimms, William L. 21:76
Nims, DeWitt 21:258
Nims, Frank 22:282
Nims, Leonard B. 17:361
Nimshall, R. 3:145
Nimton, Martin 13:67
Ninbey, J. 18:35
Nincent, J. B. 16:86
Nincy, H. 1:159
Ninder, W. H. 14:243
Nine, John E. 9:16
Nine, Joseph 3:145
Ninehouse, D. W. 20:319
Nines, Otho 9:210
Ninings, Elisha 19:47
Ninmess, John 27:91
Ninnehouse, Charles M. 10:129
Ninno, George S. 9:123
Nipe, John W. 4:44
Niper, Henry 21:116
Nippard, H. C. 1:158
Nipple, J. H. 19:28
Nipps, Adam 14:202
Nirk, Isaac 11:161
Nirsch, Jacob 22:211
Nisber, Henry 8:74

Nisbet, Harrison 10:165
Nisbet, Robert 22:409
Nisbet, Thomas 15:259
Nisbett, Harrison 19:183
Nisley, John 22:94
Nisson, Theodore 24:9
Nite, T. 21:150
Nitigle, F. B. 14:94
Nitras, Charles 14:95
Nits, John 21:280
Nitschelm, Charles 11:161
Nittle, William 15:218
Nitz, W. M. 18:54
Nitzer, S. 14:95
Nivans, Harvey 17:258
Niver, Edward 3:145
Niver, H. 2:15; 25:58
Niver, H. C. 7:36
Niver, Jacob 27:91
Nivily, N. B. 9:112
Nivins, J. S. 12:156
Nivison, George 21:57
Nix, C. 3:145; 11:333
Nix, E. H. 27:91
Nix, Garvin 22:47
Nix, George 4:44
Nix, Jacob A. 16:48
Nix, John 14:95, 266; 18:193; 23:129
Nix, Leroy 21:371
Nix, M. E. (Mrs.) 27:92
Nix, Marion 22:47
Nix, Neroy 21:371
Nixe, Angevine 13:39
Nixon, --- 19:297
Nixon, Alfred J. 22:13
Nixon, Benjamin F. 5:25
Nixon, C. 14:301; 17:469; 27:92
Nixon, Elias 25:302
Nixon, George 11:71; 16:134; 18:346
Nixon, George W. 10:71; 20:319
Nixon, Harvey M. 22:94
Nixon, Henderson 9:157
Nixon, Isabella L. S. 26:224
Nixon, Jesse B. 19:28
Nixon, John 8:59; 19:277; 20:127; 26:224
Nixon, John S. 4:44
Nixon, Jonas 10:25
Nixon, M. 8:53
Nixon, Martin 10:129; 20:319
Nixon, N. 23:43
Nixon, Owen 9:112
Nixon, R. I. 1:60
Nixon, S. 23:43
Nixon, Silas 17:232

Nixon, Sol 25:302
Nixon, W. H. 1:159
Nixon, W. J. 23:43
Nixon, William 1:61;
    16:162; 20:99; 23:43
Nixson, B. F. 25:213
Nixson, Israel 19:28
Nixton, Jacob 14:202
Nizzle, Augustus 23:124
Nnug, Nick 11:40
Noack, D. 1:158
Noah, James 17:182
Noah, John 7:130
Noah, M. 14:95
Noah, R. B. 18:55
Noah, S. 17:292
Noak, M. 9:112
Noaker, Jeremiah 9:112
Noakes, David 25:214
Noakes, Hiram 22:47
Noakes, Samuel 21:371
Noakes, William 23:43
Noal, J. 15:72
Noark, Frederick 24:26
Noarkes, George 13:39
Noarse, Thomas 15:72
Nobeck, Antony 9:87
Nobert, A. 9:210
Noblah, Barnhart 22:47
Noble, A. 25:58
Noble, Alfred 17:182;
    21:217
Noble, Arza 11:193
Noble, August 9:27;
    26:108
Noble, B. H. 7:105
Noble, Benjamin F.
    22:341
Noble, C. 1:159
Noble, C. B. 9:87
Noble, Carlton V. 21:206
Noble, David 3:145;
    18:313; 20:88;
    26:108
Noble, Eugene C. 17:354
Noble, Frank 9:27;
    18:313; 26:108
Noble, Gary L. 15:15
Noble, George B. 22:211
Noble, H. 1:158; 11:310
Noble, H. C. 18:35
Noble, Harvey 12:74;
    15:41
Noble, Henry 6:18; 18:90
Noble, Hezekiah G.
    22:168
Noble, Israel A. 23:160
Noble, J. 3:145
Noble, J. B. 9:27; 18:313;
    26:108
Noble, J. G. 11:246

Noble, J. W. 17:56
Noble, Jacob 23:43
Noble, James 15:58;
    22:211
Noble, James S. 8:27;
    18:152
Noble, John 19:28
Noble, John D. 16:136
Noble, John W. 9:237
Noble, Lewis 11:161
Noble, Louis J. 21:36
Noble, M. 16:376
Noble, Nathan 9:223;
    18:373
Noble, Oliver R. 24:26
Noble, Reuben 10:165;
    19:183
Noble, Samuel 12:74
Noble, Samuel D. 17:238,
    261
Noble, Samuel G. 9:188
Noble, T. 13:95; 14:18
Noble, Thomas 3:145;
    15:218
Noble, W. 8:77; 26:175
Noble, Wilbur 13:39
Noble, William 15:58;
    18:193; 21:231;
    22:47
Noble, William A. 4:44
Noble, William L. 16:48
Nobles, A. 25:214
Nobles, Alexander 5:25
Nobles, Calvin 4:44
Nobles, E. 3:145
Nobles, G. A. 25:58
Nobles, John 12:65; 15:58
Nobles, Joseph W. 26:224
Nobles, K. 14:202
Nobles, Lester 16:217
Nobles, Mary 16:71
Nobles, William H. 12:34
Noblet, Charles 8:92
Noblet, Franklin 18:209
Noblet, John 22:263
Noblet, Thomas 21:231
Noblet, William 8:108
Nobley, Charles 22:515
Noblin, Robert S. 22:504
Noblitt, Benjamin F.
    10:129; 20:319
Nobt, --- 8:41
Noca, John 6:25
Noch, W. H. H. 15:72
Nockton, T. H. 7:105
Nodine, William 14:202
Nodlin, William 17:40
Noe, A. 21:36
Noe, B. F. 17:149
Noe, Hiram F. 20:99
Noe, M. 3:145; 17:435

Noe, Mathias 24:179
Noe, Stamen 24:161
Noe, Wesley 11:109
Noe, William 8:22
Noe, William A. 10:129;
    20:319
Noe, William L. 22:127
Noedler, August 10:129;
    20:319
Noel, A. 10:29; 19:305
Noel, Abraham R. 10:71
Noel, Abram R. 20:319
Noel, Emul 1:60
Noel, George 21:231;
    22:521
Noel, Ira W. 11:246
Noel, J. W. 23:314
Noel, James 11:96
Noel, John 18:248; 26:51
Noel, John H. 22:434
Noel, Mashak 24:54
Noel, W. T. 12:156
Noel, William 23:256
Noelan, John 18:279
Noell, Scott E. 18:178
Noels, William 20:99
Noenlinger, C. 14:95
Noff, Levi 7:52
Noffsinger, Emanuel
    22:211
Noffsinger, James 24:54
Nog, A. 18:70
Noggle, G. W. 23:160
Noggle, John O. 8:74
Noggle, Milton 19:90
Noggle, Nelson 21:57
Noggle, W. N. 1:159
Nogle, William F. 22:434
Noice, George M. 9:44;
    26:127
Noil, R. H. C. 8:74
Noise, A. 13:116
Noise, Charles 14:283
Noise, L. 14:329
Nok-has-se-marrah 25:334
Noke, Richard P. L.
    17:283
Nokes, Abram 17:56
Nokes, Martin 15:41
Nokes, Samuel 9:215
Nokes, William 11:267
Nolan, --- 18:16
Nolan, A. 14:202
Nolan, A. I. 26:127
Nolan, Andrew 14:258
Nolan, Cornelius 9:37;
    18:295; 26:108
Nolan, D. 16:217
Nolan, Daniel 21:371
Nolan, Dennis 26:213
Nolan, Edward 8:66

Nolan, Eugene 11:161
Nolan, H. J. 13:39
Nolan, Henry 9:37;
    10:209; 18:295;
    26:108
Nolan, J. 1:158; 11:162;
    15:348
Nolan, J. M. 19:28
Nolan, James 8:27, 121;
    13:39; 14:202;
    16:301; 18:152;
    22:47, 263, 487
Nolan, James D. 20:87
Nolan, James F. 12:83;
    16:301; 17:40
Nolan, Jeremiah 19:322
Nolan, John 4:44; 8:27;
    12:57; 16:99, 281;
    18:152, 427; 21:76
Nolan, L. 13:95
Nolan, Lawrence 21:371
Nolan, M. 3:145; 12:87;
    14:95; 16:301
Nolan, Maria 18:193
Nolan, Martin 23:44
Nolan, Michael 9:37;
    14:202; 18:295;
    21:141
Nolan, Michel 26:108
Nolan, Mosen 12:34
Nolan, N. J. 1:99
Nolan, P. 7:36
Nolan, Patrick 3:145
Nolan, Peter 25:214
Nolan, Sampson 24:43
Nolan, T. 1:95, 159; 25:58
Nolan, Thomas 1:61;
    7:36; 13:95; 17:151;
    21:87; 23:115
Nolan, Thomas D. 22:409
Nolan, V. 16:376
Nolan, William 15:174
Nolan, William J. 20:99
Noland, --- 12:74
Noland, Barry 20:49
Noland, David 13:116;
    22:94
Noland, Enoch 11:162
Noland, G. 11:396
Noland, G. W. 11:267
Noland, H. 17:182
Noland, John 14:202;
    23:104
Noland, John B. 22:94
Noland, Joseph 22:521
Noland, Justus 17:162
Noland, Leroy 15:218
Noland, M. 1:61
Noland, Thomas 22:47
Nolcu, Patrick 19:183
Nolder, Robert W. 4:44

Nolding, Nelson 21:71
Nole, Benjamin 18:90
Nole, George 16:99
Nole, Jacob 15:218
Nolee, Lucius 10:149
Nolen, George 10:25
Nolen, Henry 12:34
Nolen, Robert 22:313
Nolenger, --- 12:86;
    16:301
Noles, George 9:73
Noles, John E. 22:127
Noles, Jonathan 9:123
Noles, Seth F. 24:26
Nolet, Watson 18:90
Nolf, J. 1:159
Nolf, Robert 22:487;
    24:82
Nolfinger, William 22:47
Nolin, B. 17:182
Noll, Benjamin 6:13
Noll, Edward 6:18; 18:90
Noll, Henry 20:99
Noll, I. 1:61
Noll, Peter 27:92
Noll, Thomas E. 17:393
Noll, William 5:25;
    15:160
Nolles, A. S. 14:95
Nolles, B. P. 14:95
Nolles, C. 14:95
Nolles, H. 14:95
Nolles, N. 14:95
Nolly, P. G. 23:289
Nolmouth, O. 11:281
Nolon, William 24:26
Nolow, Thomas 14:18
Nolt, August 11:96
Nolt, William H. 21:258
Nolte, August 18:313
Nolte, F. 1:158
Nolte, Lebrecht 4:44
Nolton, A. W. 1:158
Nolton, Adam 12:34
Nolton, H. 3:145
Nolton, Richard 27:92
Nontham, O. F. 3:145
Nonweiler, Philip 23:75
Noock, Gutl'a 1:61
Nood, William 18:70
Nooker, David 5:25
Nooland, E. A. 21:124
Noon, Elbert 17:502
Noon, J. 8:66; 26:175
Noon, J. C. 1:158
Noon, Joseph D. 21:36
Noon, P. 12:91; 16:301;
    19:258
Noon, T. 15:88
Noon, Thomas 22:94
Noonan, D. 1:61

Noonan, Dennis 27:91
Noonan, E. 3:145
Noonan, Francis 12:74
Noonan, James 25:214
Noonan, Jeremiah 7:63
Noonan, John 24:58;
    27:91
Noonan, Michael 17:56
Noonan, N. 27:91
Noonan, Patrick 13:39;
    21:371
Noonan, W. 1:159
Noones, G. H. 3:145
Noorony, W. H. 3:146
Noptel, R. D. 11:341
Norance, Joseph 22:211
Noras, Robert 15:218
Norauss, Alfred 15:353
Norbrock, J. 8:53
Norcross, Alfred 16:281
Norcross, Chauncey
    19:183
Norcross, Frederick
    22:283
Norcross, G. W. 1:158
Norcross, George J. 9:162
Norcross, Joseph D. 13:39
Norcross, Levi 22:434
Norcross, T. F. 7:36
Norcus, Shepard 17:495
Nordboe, Jacob J. 21:258
Norden, John 9:67
Nordike, Solomon 26:127
Nordwoods, A. 14:244
Nordyke, Erastus H. 23:91
Nordyke, Solomon 9:44
Norfield, Warren 3:146
Norfles, Peter 21:371
Norflet, M. 22:313
Norflet, Robert 21:371
Norfolk, J. 1:159
Norfow, William 15:88
Norgan, John L. 1:60
Norgis, Calvin 12:34
Norick, Samuel 20:319
Noricoud, Israel 15:92
Noriot, Francis 24:176
Noris, John 22:409
Norland, H. P. (Mrs.)
    18:193
Norman, Alex 17:136
Norman, Alexander
    24:200
Norman, Benjamin 10:71;
    20:319
Norman, Charles H. 4:44
Norman, E. 3:146; 14:202
Norman, Eli H. 8:92
Norman, F. 19:258
Norman, Frank 17:136;
    24:200

Norman, Frederick 9:188
Norman, G. 20:319
Norman, G. L. 3:146
Norman, George 19:28
Norman, H. 3:146; 5:56;
	25:214
Norman, Henry 22:263,
	504
Norman, J. 3:146; 22:211
Norman, James 3:146;
	9:57
Norman, James A. 18:373
Norman, Jeff 22:263
Norman, John 6:18;
	9:112; 13:39; 18:90
Norman, Jonathan F.
	22:47
Norman, Joseph 10:71;
	20:319
Norman, L. 25:214
Norman, Mathew 8:27;
	18:152
Norman, Nelson 11:210
Norman, Peter 22:282
Norman, Richard 5:43;
	10:99; 21:280
Norman, Rudolph 19:28
Norman, S. M. 21:36
Norman, W. 25:214
Norman, W. G. 27:91
Norman, W. H. 1:158
Norman, William 22:263
Norman, William H. 8:92
Norman, William L.
	22:341
Normand, Victor 8:27;
	18:152
Normandy, T. 14:316
Normason, Ernest 4:44
Normdorf, H. 9:188
Normon, Aug 1:61
Norocon, Israel 12:62
Norr, Conrad 7:36
Norracong, Charles W.
	20:91
Norrich, Samuel 10:71
Norrick, Henry 22:94
Norrick, J. G. 22:487
Norries, John 25:214
Norrigen, C. 25:58
Norris, A. B. 22:287
Norris, A. G. 18:70
Norris, A. R. 3:146
Norris, A. S. 16:141
Norris, Alex 9:27; 13:58
Norris, Alexander 18:313;
	26:108
Norris, Almon N. 23:242
Norris, Andrew 6:18;
	18:90; 21:371
Norris, Andrew B. 22:465

Norris, Andrew J. 10:129;
	20:319
Norris, Aug 18:399
Norris, Augustus 19:47
Norris, Bradford D.
	24:179
Norris, C. C. 22:47
Norris, C. J. 11:267
Norris, C. W. 11:309
Norris, Charles 13:39;
	21:280
Norris, Charles L. 11:40
Norris, Clarence 3:146
Norris, Clark 5:25
Norris, Clayton 21:371
Norris, Daniel 22:13
Norris, E. Y. 3:146
Norris, Edward 21:280
Norris, Elias A. 16:99
Norris, Elijah H. 4:44
Norris, F. 17:72
Norris, F. D. 25:214
Norris, F. W. 7:105
Norris, G. 9:123
Norris, George S. 17:263
Norris, George W. 21:13;
	23:160
Norris, Herman 22:398
Norris, Horace 16:48
Norris, Isaac 17:56
Norris, J. B. 13:95; 14:18
Norris, J. C. 18:104
Norris, Jeremiah 21:124
Norris, Jesse 21:371
Norris, John 9:223; 11:96;
	12:83; 16:301; 19:47;
	20:127; 22:341;
	27:92
Norris, John A. C. 11:71
Norris, John B. 9:188
Norris, John D. 10:129;
	17:356; 20:319
Norris, John G. 8:108
Norris, John J. 22:455
Norris, John W. 22:434,
	487
Norris, Jonathan 17:419
Norris, Jonathan L.
	24:161
Norris, Joseph C. 14:202
Norris, Levi 10:71;
	20:319
Norris, M. J. 11:310
Norris, N. L. 4:44
Norris, Peter H. 21:141
Norris, Philip 21:13
Norris, R. H. 21:371
Norris, Robert 12:51
Norris, Samuel 22:354
Norris, Thomas 3:146;
	22:263

Norris, Trustworthy
	10:165; 19:184
Norris, Valentine 22:515
Norris, W. 3:146; 13:135;
	19:347
Norris, William 10:71,
	129; 20:319; 22:127;
	24:82; 26:224
Norris, William C. 8:27
Norris, William H. 1:60
Norris, William N. 16:99
Norson, M. E. 11:309
Nort, John D. 24:59
North, A. J. 11:161
North, C. 1:61; 17:436;
	19:90; 24:182
North, C. D. 8:27; 18:152
North, Charles A. 9:88
North, Chester 24:171
North, Christian 23:160
North, E. 16:217; 18:55
North, Edwin B. 9:210
North, Ferdinand 9:204
North, Frederick 9:37
North, G. 1:61; 13:116
North, G. F. 17:84
North, George 19:183;
	24:108
North, I. 14:95
North, Irving 22:94
North, J. W. 16:301
North, Jacob 3:146
North, James 12:93;
	16:301
North, John 1:61; 16:217
North, Joseph 17:149;
	26:224
North, Joshua 9:237
North, Nath 10:151, 178
North, Nathaniel 10:165;
	19:183
North, P. P. 1:158
North, S. S. 3:146
North, Seneca 8:92
North, Shister 17:456
North, T. R. 25:214
North, Thomas R. 5:25
North, W. 11:162
North, William H. 22:287
North, Zachariah 17:40
Northam, S. R. 3:146
Northcoust, William
	20:319
Northcraft, J. 3:146
Northcut, John 22:313
Northerland, Marion
	22:94
Northern, Eson 9:134;
	27:92
Northern, George 21:371
Northern, R. H. 20:319

Northern, Stephen 17:238
Northern, William 11:17
Northing, John 16:48
Northington, Ed 19:183
Northington, Richard
   22:313
Northrop, --- 25:214
Northrop, A. 14:95
Northrop, Alons 27:92
Northrop, Alvus 9:134
Northrop, Andrew H.
   12:34
Northrop, Angus T. 20:49
Northrop, D. B. 10:129;
   20:319
Northrop, David 3:146
Northrop, F. E. 16:123
Northrop, Freeman G.
   22:465
Northrop, G. W. 9:44;
   26:175
Northrop, George 5:25
Northrop, George W.
   22:211
Northrop, H. 9:237
Northrop, H. G. 22:465
Northrop, J. 1:60, 159;
   11:246
Northrop, J. B. 14:301;
   17:476; 27:92
Northrop, James R. 9:44;
   26:127
Northrop, John 24:9
Northrop, Samuel 17:70
Northrop, Thomas 20:319
Northrop, William B.
   13:39
Northrop, William C.
   10:71
Northrope, S. H. 18:313;
   26:108
Northross, A. D. 15:72
Northross, G. H. 26:127
Northross, Sherman
   18:117
Northroup, William C.
   5:25
Northrup, A. L. 22:282
Northrup, E. 3:146
Northrup, H. 26:224
Northrup, Homer C.
   12:156
Northrup, J. 1:158
Northrup, John 1:60;
   3:146
Northrup, Lemuel 10:92
Northrup, Lewis 13:39
Northrup, Samuel 20:319
Northrup, V. 3:146
Northrup, W. C. 25:214
Northrup, W. E. 3:146

Northrup, William B.
   16:48
Northrup, William H.
   20:148
Northup, W. C. 20:319
Northway, Clement L.
   23:193
Northway, Edward C.
   7:36
Northway, Francis M.
   24:26
Northway, George F.
   21:231
Northway, Joseph 13:116
Northway, William J.
   11:71
Nortman, --- 20:148
Norton, --- 26:175
Norton, A. 14:203
Norton, A. F. 25:214
Norton, A. P. 25:59
Norton, Alfred 22:263
Norton, Andrew 21:141
Norton, B. 10:165; 19:183
Norton, B. F. 1:61
Norton, B. W. 7:75;
   25:302
Norton, Benjamin 1:61
Norton, Benjamin F.
   17:320
Norton, Bird 22:113
Norton, Cato 25:325
Norton, Charles 7:36;
   18:427
Norton, Charles C. 20:11
Norton, Conrad 11:246
Norton, David 15:72
Norton, David M. 9:188;
   19:258
Norton, E. 1:159; 3:146;
   10:149; 18:55;
   21:371
Norton, Edmund 13:39
Norton, Ellsworth H.
   15:131
Norton, F. F. 3:146
Norton, Frank 9:88
Norton, G. 16:217
Norton, George 9:148;
   20:31; 27:91
Norton, George H. 17:288
Norton, George W. 17:24
Norton, H. 11:246
Norton, H. C. 20:141
Norton, Henry 11:40;
   14:203
Norton, Henry D. 17:506
Norton, I. 8:74
Norton, I. D. 25:284
Norton, J. 3:146
Norton, J. C. 14:258

Norton, J. G. 27:91
Norton, J. H. 17:155;
   25:325
Norton, J. L. 1:158; 25:58
Norton, Jacob 23:124
Norton, James 10:180;
   13:67; 14:203;
   18:178, 248; 22:521;
   26:51, 204; 27:92
Norton, James A. 11:39;
   18:152
Norton, James B. 19:90
Norton, Jerome A. 24:95
Norton, John 1:191; 6:18;
   16:99; 17:40; 20:31
Norton, John F. 4:44
Norton, John M. 19:283
Norton, John W. 8:108
Norton, Joseph 25:58, 214
Norton, Lawrence 10:165;
   19:183
Norton, Lewis 19:28
Norton, Loring 22:211
Norton, M. A. 3:146
Norton, Matthew 5:53
Norton, Morral 9:112
Norton, Nicholas 14:316
Norton, Nore C. 16:48
Norton, Patrick 1:61
Norton, Perham 9:188
Norton, Peter 14:203
Norton, R. 10:187
Norton, Robert 10:99
Norton, Russell 8:92
Norton, Samuel 17:476;
   22:470; 27:92
Norton, T. W. 15:344;
   16:376
Norton, Thomas 25:58
Norton, W. C. 18:104
Norton, Washington
   12:169
Norton, Watson 22:465
Norton, William 1:60, 61;
   21:372; 22:409;
   25:214
Norvell, George M.
   17:263
Norvell, H. 21:150
Norville, Henry 9:231;
   20:319
Norwood, E. F. 3:146
Norwood, Edward 12:34;
   22:94
Norwood, Ewing 17:267
Norwood, G. 1:158
Norwood, G. H. 1:158
Norwood, G. W. 19:283
Norwood, Giles 21:212
Norwood, J. 1:61; 14:203;
   27:92

Norwood, Joseph J. 16:48
Norwood, Orson B. 21:89
Norwood, W. 21:372
Norwood, William 3:146
Nose, J. 18:35
Nose, Stephen B. 4:44
Nosker, Jacob 12:156
Nosler, James 18:399
Nosler, William L. 18:399
Nossman, G. 3:146
Nostrand, G. W. 14:203
Nostrand, Nat 19:184
Nostrand, Nathaniel
    10:174
Notan, Thomas 22:341
Notchine, J. 7:36
Note, E. 14:289; 23:75
Note, Elijah 21:57
Note, John 3:146
Noteman, Charles 20:99
Notestein, William 23:264
Notestine, William F.
    22:470
Notgrasst, William 11:210
Nother, E. 14:203, 258
Nothing, John 16:141
Nothingham, P. S. 1:61
Nott, Charles A. 11:419
Nott, J. 3:146
Nott, James A. 8:27;
    18:152
Nott, John K. 22:47
Nott, Justis 25:214
Nott, S. A. 3:146
Nott, William 20:179
Nottage, J. L. 3:146
Notter, Andrew 17:405
Notter, Edward 14:203
Notting, Ebnor A. 17:447
Notting, H. 5:25
Notting, Jerome 5:25
Nottingham, George
    7:130; 21:372
Nottingham, James 17:274
Nottingham, Oscar H.
    22:151
Notton, N. F. 17:292
Nought, William 19:28
Nouman, John 4:44
Noun, Guniene 17:401
Noune, William H. 15:330
Nours, Erwin 15:58
Nourse, Allen N. 4:44
Nourse, George W.
    25:214
Nourse, Luther 9:73
Nourse, Walker 17:136;
    24:200
Nourse, Wilson 18:279
Nova, Caesar 7:130
Nova, Vincent 7:130

Novel, A. 14:95
Novooty, G. 1:159
Novus, Marcus L. 15:218
Nowe, Henry 4:44
Nowell, Henry 16:48
NoWell, Jacob 9:243
Nowell, John A. W.
    23:160
Nowis, J. B. 19:258
Nowlan, John 21:372
Nowlan, William 7:105
Nowland, L. 14:18
Nowlen, Peyton S. 22:94
Nowles, J. 21:36
Nowles, Thomas T. 8:27
Nowlet, Norman 18:209
Nowlin, F. 1:61
Nowling, Frederick S.
    21:57
Nowls, James 21:239
Nowls, Thomas T. 18:152
Nown, M. 22:313
Nox, William M. 22:455
Noxton, W. A. 21:372
Noy, Edward 19:28
Noyce, Erick 21:372
Noycy, James 10:174
Noyes, A. T. 16:217
Noyes, Abirial 21:167
Noyes, Alva H. 11:333
Noyes, C. H. 14:270
Noyes, Charles H. 13:39;
    22:283
Noyes, Daniel T. 20:115
Noyes, E. D. 25:214
Noyes, Edwrd E. 10:20
Noyes, F. W. 1:60
Noyes, Frank 14:203
Noyes, G. M. 19:258
Noyes, George A. 16:5
Noyes, George M. 9:188
Noyes, George S. 16:79
Noyes, George W. 21:258
Noyes, Harvey 22:465
Noyes, Henry 9:210
Noyes, J. 19:305
Noyes, J. H. 1:159
Noyes, J. W. 21:372
Noyes, James E. 3:146
Noyes, John 13:116
Noyes, Nathaniel 9:188;
    19:241
Noyes, O. 1:159
Noyet, Francis 17:84
Noyt, George 18:152
Nuady, George 22:263
Nubia, William 5:43
Nubie, Cisco 6:26
Nuble, M. 15:344
Nuby, William 22:515
Nucer, James 3:146

Nudder, William 9:204;
    18:70
Nuehman, G. 1:158
Nufer, C. 7:52
Nuff, Peter 8:74
Nuff, V. 3:146
Nuff, William 16:217
Nuffer, George 5:25
Nuffer, Jacob F. 21:141
Nugan, John 16:217
Nugen, Christopher
    22:434
Nugent, Augustus 21:196
Nugent, E. 26:175
Nugent, Edward 8:74
Nugent, F. 19:258
Nugent, Felix 9:188
Nugent, George W.
    19:330
Nugent, Jacob 22:236
Nugent, James 26:127
Nugent, Jasper 12:74;
    15:8
Nugent, John 1:61; 5:25;
    7:130; 8:53; 25:214
Nugent, M. 7:105
Nugent, Michael 10:20
Nugent, Pat 18:90
Nugent, Patrick 25:269
Nugent, T. 1:61; 3:146
Nugent, Thomas 7:105;
    15:110; 17:350
Nugent, William H.
    22:283
Nugler, Thomas 17:422
Nugles, Charles E. 19:90
Nuguener, Martin 21:226
Nuhn, C. 23:44
Nuih, S. 25:214
Nuley, Jacob 9:73
Nulf, P. 1:158
Nulf, William 13:67
Null, F. 9:112
Null, James S. 20:319
Null, John 19:28
Null, John H. 20:19
Null, N. 11:40
Null, William 25:214
Null, William W. 17:84
Nuller, Hiram 17:263
Nuller, John 15:295
Nully, C. 3:146
Nully, Sandford 24:26
Nult, Henry A. 24:26
Nulty, John 12:75; 15:18
Numan, J. H. 14:133
Numan, John 12:34
Numan, Lewis 8:58
Numbers, William S.
    23:305
Numen, A. B. 14:316

Nunabar, Harmon 10:129
Nunaber, Harmon 20:319
Nunamacher, J. 1:159
Nunamacker, E. G. 9:223
Nunamaker, E. G. 18:373
Nundley, John 21:280
Nunemaker, Thomas 9:27
Nunemaker, William 11:183
Nunenmainer, --- 5:53
Nuneviller, Samuel G. 23:13
Nungent, Martin 18:209
Nunham, S. 16:217
Nunn, Amos 11:210
Nunn, B. 19:305
Nunn, Draper 16:217
Nunn, Jarvis 4:44
Nunn, John 9:217; 21:372
Nunn, R. 10:29
Nunn, William 8:77
Nunnaley, Benjamin F. 22:455
Nunnaley, James A. 22:127
Nunnaly, Andrew J. 17:207
Nunnaly, E. P. 20:187
Nunnaly, Nelson W. 20:104
Nunneaker, Hy 4:44
Nunnely, H. J. 17:238
Nunnemaker, George 24:179
Nunnemaker, John 13:67
Nunson, Emory 19:182
Nunson, Lyman F. 19:182
Nuphu, James 15:72
Nupper, W. H. 3:146
Nure, J. 14:203
Nurls, John W. 7:36
Nurse, H. W. 3:146
Nusbaum, Albert 18:113
Nuslem, Weslam 9:188
Nuslen, Weslam 19:283
Nuson, William H. 18:399
Nuss, Jacob 15:72
Nussbaum, Benjamin F. 24:54
Nutcher, Frederick 19:184
Nute, George F. 4:44
Nute, John W. 7:36; 14:335
Nute, Joseph 19:90
Nutsler, August 22:211
Nutson, Halmer 8:53
Nutt, Francis M. 21:76
Nutt, H. D. 8:27
Nutt, Henry W. 15:167
Nutt, J. H. 24:99
Nutt, J. Q. A. M. 23:75

Nutt, M. 3:146
Nutt, William 17:452; 21:76
Nutter, David 23:161
Nutter, G. A. 19:288
Nutter, George A. 9:188
Nutter, Henry F. 13:67
Nutter, Hickman 22:211
Nutter, Lewis 13:39
Nutter, R. A. 25:58
Nutting, A. 1:159
Nutting, Charles E. 10:20
Nutting, G. H. 1:158
Nutting, H. 25:214
Nutting, Henry C. 22:465
Nutting, Jonas 7:60
Nuttle, H. 17:292
Nutton, J. C. 11:128
Nuzen, G. 7:36
Nyburg, Erick 20:319
Nyce, Hiram S. 10:20
Nycum, J. 1:158
Nyder, Reuben 14:203
Nye, A. C. 23:44
Nye, Abram 9:112
Nye, Adam 13:39
Nye, Austin 22:283
Nye, C. 9:148; 27:91
Nye, Daniel 23:161
Nye, E. A. 2:15
Nye, E. G. 18:16
Nye, Edgar A. 25:58
Nye, Edward 19:184
Nye, Elisha B. 22:211
Nye, F. 1:158
Nye, Henry 9:231; 20:319
Nye, Isaac 4:44
Nye, Jonathan 19:184
Nye, Josiah T. 1:61
Nye, Mellin 7:105
Nye, Mellire 21:372
Nye, Mortimer L. 11:161
Nye, Nelson 14:283
Nye, Selam 15:327
Nye, Sidney 4:44
Nye, Warren W. 7:105
Nye, William B. 11:333
Nye, William P. 5:53; 25:214
Nye, William T. 19:241
Nyhart, Jacob 11:415
Nyhart, William H. 20:49
Nyman, A. B. 14:95
Nymschull, A. 18:152
Nyneschull, A. 8:27
Nyroop, W. 26:175
Nyrop, W. 12:164
Nys, T. M. 19:90
Nysoaner, David 8:27
Nysse, John 22:151

O

O'Bannon, William 3:146
O'Barre, --- 16:148
O'Branigan, Thomas 8:118; 19:315
O'Brannon, Yelverton 8:121
O'Brian, --- 11:310
O'Brian, Anthony 20:115
O'Brian, F. 14:95
O'Brian, G. 14:203
O'Brian, Henry 22:521
O'Brian, John 16:99; 25:214
O'Brian, M. 14:95; 15:174
O'Brian, Martin 14:203
O'Brian, Patrick 11:40; 25:214
O'Brian, Peter 8:101
O'Brian, T. 18:55
O'Brian, Thomas 7:12
O'Brian, Tim 26:51
O'Brian, Timothy 11:293
O'Brien, A. 9:112
O'Brien, Abraham 12:9
O'Brien, Austin 3:146
O'Brien, Barney 23:100
O'Brien, Charles 3:146; 7:130; 9:234; 10:211; 19:319
O'Brien, Charles M. 8:124
O'Brien, Cornelius 11:40
O'Brien, D. 1:61; 3:146; 4:44; 13:95
O'Brien, Daniel 11:40; 18:55; 21:372
O'Brien, Dennis 21:372; 22:342; 23:13
O'Brien, E. 1:160
O'Brien, Edward 7:63; 11:40, 162, 247; 22:509
O'Brien, Enoch 6:32; 25:325
O'Brien, Felix 1:62; 19:324
O'Brien, Frank 18:152
O'Brien, George 9:13
O'Brien, Henry 9:188; 14:203; 19:241, 340
O'Brien, J. 3:146; 11:231; 12:9; 14:203, 258; 15:218; 16:99; 21:111; 22:13; 27:93
O'Brien, J. C. 20:319
O'Brien, J. O. 13:116
O'Brien, James 8:121; 11:162; 12:34, 62, 75, 83; 15:42;

O'Brien, James 18:424; 21:243, 372; 26:150
O'Brien, James H. 24:26
O'Brien, Jeremiah 21:372
O'Brien, John 9:148, 204; 10:71; 12:34; 13:39, 135; 15:41; 16:48; 18:113, 413; 19:28, 347; 20:42, 319; 21:372; 22:94, 151; 24:113, 179
O'Brien, Joseph 11:323; 13:116; 21:372; 26:52
O'Brien, Lawrence H. 23:262
O'Brien, M. 19:258; 25:59
O'Brien, Martin 12:34
O'Brien, McLain 26:51
O'Brien, Michael 9:112, 188; 10:20; 13:135; 16:217; 19:347; 27:93
O'Brien, Miles 10:206
O'Brien, P. 3:146
O'Brien, Patrick 4:44; 6:9; 7:105; 8:92; 11:17; 12:75; 14:203; 15:42; 18:35; 22:151, 409; 27:93
O'Brien, Peter 7:105
O'Brien, Richard 24:10
O'Brien, S. 1:160; 3:146
O'Brien, T. 19:90
O'Brien, Terrence 20:115
O'Brien, Thomas 5:25; 12:65; 13:125; 14:203; 15:42; 18:113; 21:15, 372; 23:13
O'Brien, Timothy 25:284
O'Brien, W. 3:146; 13:130
O'Brien, W. H. 3:146
O'Brien, W. O. 3:147
O'Brien, William 10:165; 13:39; 14:203; 15:218; 19:184, 322; 20:319; 23:161
O'Brien, William C. 18:113
O'briene, James 16:301
O'Brine, Daniel 9:215; 17:456
O'Brine, Dennis 9:138
O'Brine, Frank 8:27
O'Brine, J. 14:95
O'Brine, James 9:155; 16:376
O'Brine, John 10:129; 14:95
O'Brine, John E. 23:161

O'Brine, Patrick 16:301
O'Bryan, John 6:32
O'Bryan, P. 16:123
O'Bryan, Patrick 21:372
O'Bryan, Peter 17:461
O'Bryan, Walter 20:190
O'Bryant, George 3:147
O'Bryant, John 23:75
O'Bryen, Dennis 20:187
O'Bryen, John 18:35
O'Bryne, Patrick 17:353
O'Bryon, Patrick 25:214
O'Callachan, Michael 18:104
O'Callihan, E. 19:288
O'Carrall, John A. 12:34
O'Carrol, S. E. 9:158
O'Carroll, T. 3:147
O'Cellan, H. O. 21:164
O'Cole, C. 12:156
O'Conell, Martin 23:44
O'Coner, Dennis 15:42
O'Connel, John 15:42
O'Connel, Thomas 27:93
O'Connell, Daniel 12:59; 25:214
O'Connell, J. 1:160; 3:147
O'Connell, J. J. 3:147; 19:184
O'Connell, James 10:174; 19:184; 22:47
O'Connell, Jerry 10:174
O'Connell, John 11:267; 12:34; 17:292
O'Connell, Joseph 22:151
O'Connell, M. 3:147
O'Connell, Martin 23:75
O'Connell, Patrick 1:61
O'Connell, Robert 22:342
O'Connell, Thomas 3:147
O'Connell, Timothy 23:16
O'Connell, William 3:147; 10:174; 19:184
O'Conner, Daniel 10:129
O'Conner, Dennis 13:39
O'Conner, E. 14:95
O'Conner, Edward J. 12:34
O'Conner, H. 21:36
O'Conner, Hugh 12:156
O'Conner, John 7:105
O'Conner, M. 13:95
O'Conner, Michael 13:39
O'Conner, N. 15:58
O'Conner, Patrick 13:39; 18:152; 21:231; 23:75
O'Conner, Thomas 18:279; 22:151, 435
O'Conners, Charles 24:69

O'Conners, Timothy 22:354
O'Connor, --- 3:147; 19:90
O'Connor, Arthur 9:188
O'Connor, Charles 14:203
O'Connor, D. 1:159
O'Connor, Daniel 20:319
O'Connor, David 20:179
O'Connor, Edward 18:113; 22:342
O'Connor, F. 3:147
O'Connor, George 21:372
O'Connor, H. 3:147
O'Connor, J. 1:160; 25:214
O'Connor, James 24:95
O'Connor, John 11:71; 14:203; 16:301; 21:372
O'Connor, M. 1:159, 160; 3:147; 12:9; 14:18; 25:302
O'Connor, Martin 7:52
O'Connor, Michael 20:193; 21:372
O'Connor, P. 1:160; 3:147; 16:376
O'Connor, P. A. 19:258
O'Connor, Patrick 8:27; 10:20; 16:48
O'Connor, Patrick J. 16:123
O'Connor, R. 12:9
O'Connor, R. I. A. 11:40
O'Connor, Richard 8:27; 26:175
O'Connor, Shadrack 23:161
O'Connor, T. 1:160
O'Connor, Thomas 3:147; 7:52; 20:49
O'Connor, William 3:147; 4:44; 8:66; 21:372
O'Conor, Thomas 13:116
O'Creily, Felix 19:184
O'Criely, Felix 10:165
O'Daniel, Casabianca 23:44
O'Daniel, J. 14:95
O'Daniel, J. H. 3:147
O'Daniels, Thomas B. 17:389
O'Dean, Thomas 3:147
O'Deay, Timothy 20:319
O'Dell, E. 3:147
O'Dell, Henry 4:44
O'Dell, J. M. 26:175
O'Dell, Patrick 7:63
O'Dill, James 10:71
O'Dillans, William 3:147

O'Doherty, Roderick 23:115
O'Donald, Hugh 27:93
O'Donald, Jeremiah 9:215
O'Donald, William 23:75
O'Donn, Frank 18:70
O'Donnel, E. 25:215
O'Donnel, James 14:95
O'Donnel, Michael 25:215
O'Donnel, P. 14:18
O'Donneld, James A. 22:127
O'Donnell, --- 12:100
O'Donnell, A. 3:147
O'Donnell, C. 1:160; 22:342
O'Donnell, Charles 26:224
O'Donnell, Constantine 12:34
O'Donnell, Cornelius 9:240; 12:34
O'Donnell, George 8:27; 18:152
O'Donnell, H. 9:148; 27:93
O'Donnell, Hugh 12:34; 27:93
O'Donnell, James 7:105
O'Donnell, Jeremiah 21:372
O'Donnell, John 12:34; 21:11, 372; 22:151
O'Donnell, Joseph 18:421; 22:47
O'Donnell, Michael 23:161
O'Donnell, Nicholas 18:421
O'Donnell, P. 13:95; 18:413
O'Donnell, Philip 21:373
O'Donnell, Thomas 7:105; 19:91; 21:373
O'Donnell, W. 3:147
O'Donnell, William 25:215
O'Donnelly, B. 20:127
O'Donohoe, Peter 21:118
O'Dougherty, J. 3:147
O'Dowd, James 15:81
O'Dyne, W. E. 12:93
O'Fair, John 27:147
O'Farrell, F. 23:283
O'Farrell, H. V. 11:71
O'Felt, P. 26:175
O'Flaherty, William 26:175
O'Gaff, Lindsay 13:39
O'Gara, John 1:62
O'Garra, Michael 19:330
O'Gill, Thomas 25:59

O'Gorman, J. 14:95
O'Grady, John 23:109
O'Grady, M. 1:160
O'Grady, T. 25:215
O'Hagen, M. P. 4:45
O'Haley, W. 14:333
O'Hana, James 24:82
O'Hanlin, Daniel 27:93
O'Hara, --- 15:58; 26:224
O'Hara, Daniel 16:100
O'Hara, Edward 15:218
O'Hara, J. 2:15
O'Hara, James 15:42
O'Hara, John 3:147; 25:59
O'Hara, Martin 20:127
O'Hara, Michael 3:147; 13:39
O'Hara, P. 17:111
O'Hara, Patrick 20:115
O'Haran, Patrick 7:69
O'Hare, Francis 9:237
O'Hare, James 24:95
O'Hare, John 15:131
O'Hare, William 12:59; 17:24
O'Harra, James 11:17
O'Heath, Dennis 12:34
O'Helleran, P. 14:95
O'Hinger, James 3:147
O'Holland, William 6:10
O'Horn, John 18:327
O'Kane, Daniel 12:34
O'Kane, George 12:34
O'Kay, P. 14:203
O'Kay, Peter 3:147
O'Keef, James 4:45
O'Keefe, C. 3:147
O'Keefe, Edward 21:243
O'Keefe, J. 1:160
O'Keefe, John 12:75
O'Keefe, Luke 12:173
O'Keefe, M. 3:147
O'Keefe, Owen 14:203
O'Keefe, Patrick 16:86; 17:402
O'Keefe, Timothy 25:215
O'Keehe, George 18:373
O'Kurn, D. 13:67
O'Larry, Daniel 17:361
O'Larry, Pat 18:152
O'Lary, D. 1:62
O'lary, Pat 26:175
O'Laughlin, Dennis 22:162
O'laughlin, Michael 22:466
O'Leary, Cornelius 9:188
O'Leary, Daniel 22:354
O'Leary, J. O. 3:147
O'Leary, William 1:62
O'Lina, R. 3:147

O'Malley, Pat 20:321
O'Malley, Patrick 10:71
O'Mara, Michael 22:47
O'Maron, M. 14:95
O'Marra, M. 19:324
O'Mera, James 21:93
O'Mura, James 3:148
O'Neal, Bryant J. 22:455
O'Neal, Daniel 10:71; 12:75
O'Neal, Edwin 10:152; 18:55
O'Neal, George 25:215
O'Neal, H. 21:373
O'Neal, Hanibal 8:41
O'Neal, Henry 7:36; 25:215
O'Neal, Isaac 20:321
O'Neal, Isaac C. 11:415
O'Neal, J. D. 19:305
O'Neal, James 19:288; 23:115; 25:59
O'Neal, John 12:65; 14:301; 15:23; 17:84, 469; 19:322; 21:243; 22:47
O'Neal, Michael 9:67; 10:72; 16:160
O'Neal, Oliver 19:28
O'Neal, P. 9:148
O'Neal, Patrick 12:65; 15:42; 19:28
O'Neal, Peter 8:74
O'Neal, Samuel 15:23
O'Neal, Terrence 17:74
O'Neal, Thomas 10:71; 11:390; 24:179; 27:147
O'Neal, Thomas J. 22:521
O'Neal, William 5:25; 9:57; 19:286
O'Neale, Daniel 15:42
O'Neale, John 15:42
O'Neil, C. 14:316
O'Neil, Charles 3:148
O'Neil, D. 3:148, 224; 17:495
O'Neil, Edward 7:131
O'Neil, Emanuel 7:105
O'Neil, F. 23:282
O'Neil, F. T. 23:44
O'Neil, Felix 7:105; 21:373; 27:93
O'Neil, Francis 15:110
O'Neil, Frank 17:56; 21:11, 373
O'Neil, George M. 9:37
O'Neil, Hannibal 26:175
O'Neil, Henry 5:25; 9:159; 11:162; 14:203; 27:93

O'Neil, Isaac 9:231
O'Neil, J. 3:148; 14:203
O'Neil, J. M. 3:148
O'Neil, J. N. 14:203
O'Neil, James 9:161; 13:40; 16:123, 141, 217
O'Neil, James E. 18:36
O'Neil, Jerome 20:31
O'Neil, John 4:45; 9:161; 14:95; 16:301; 21:373; 23:271; 27:93, 94
O'Neil, John H. 19:318
O'Neil, John M. 22:504
O'Neil, Lester A. 16:217
O'Neil, Martin 21:373
O'Neil, Michael 4:45; 7:105; 9:16, 231; 10:129; 18:279; 20:321; 21:231; 22:487; 25:215
O'Neil, P. 27:93
O'Neil, Pat 26:175
O'Neil, Patrick 9:16; 21:373
O'Neil, Peter 21:36; 27:93
O'Neil, Thomas 3:148; 7:130; 16:9; 17:451
O'Neil, Thomas N. 7:16
O'Neil, Timothy 10:20
O'Neil, W. 25:215
O'Neil, Wallace 10:170
O'Neil, William 1:62; 7:105
O'Neil, William F. 25:273
O'Neil, William H. 9:16
O'Neill, Alex 12:34
O'Neill, Edmund 20:104
O'Neill, Freeman 11:210
O'Neill, George 24:10
O'Neill, Jacob 25:302
O'Neill, James 17:315
O'Neill, John 14:327
O'Neill, Michael 12:34; 14:95
O'Neill, Pat 25:302
O'Neill, Patrick 12:34
O'Nela, Thomas 20:321
O'Nial, John 14:95
O'Niel, B. 19:91
O'Niel, John 13:40; 19:91
O'Niel, P. 1:159, 160
O'Niel, Pat 19:91
O'Niel, Patrick 7:52, 81
O'Niell, P. 1:160
O'Pear, John 21:373
O'Pease, S. 3:148
O'Ragan, William 21:259
O'Rea, Augustus 19:278
O'Reagan, D. O. 3:148

O'Rear, Marquis 27:93
O'Reilly, P. 1:160
O'Reilly, Patrick 14:203
O'Reilly, Philip 3:148
O'Reilly, Thomas 3:148
O'Reily, Henry B. 16:75
O'Riley, Cornelius 9:148
O'Riley, Franklin 17:100
O'Riley, James 24:26
O'Riley, Michael 26:175
O'Riley, Patrick 19:28
O'Riley, Thomas 12:75
O'Roake, Charles 3:148
O'Roake, P. 25:215
O'Roark, George W. 22:127
O'Rouark, P. 19:241
O'Rourke, J. 15:218
O'Rourke, John 10:72; 20:321
O'Rourke, M. 1:160
O'Rourke, Patrick 9:188
O'S---, J. M. 20:155
O'Shaute, John 25:59
O'Shea, D. 1:159
O'Shea, John 9:188
O'Shea, W. 2:15
O'Shea, William 25:59
O'Sullivan, Daniel 16:9
O'Sullivan, Jeremiah 15:353; 23:241
O'Sullivan, John 13:96
O'Sullivan, Patrick 7:105; 23:161
O'Sury, Lewis 12:87
O'Teal, M. 9:57
O'Tool, Michael 1:62
O'Tool, Patrick 21:111
O---, --- 23:280
O---, A. 11:231; 22:354; 23:204
O---, A. A. 20:319
O---, D. R. 11:162
O---, E. Mc. 18:373
O---, H. 21:209
O---, I. R. 25:273
O---, J. 11:247; 23:204; 24:113
O---, J. C. 21:209
O---, J. D. 24:113
O---, J. F. 24:113
O---, J. T. H. 23:245
O---, John C. 15:219
O---, L. F. B. 17:356
O---, O. 19:185
O---, P. 11:341
O---, P. M. 25:59
O---, R. L. 21:209
O---, S. O. 11:247
O---, T. M. 24:113
O---, W. P. 17:365

O---rey, J. W. 23:204
O-sa-she-yar-holi 25:334
O-sa-si-ka 13:67; 19:91
O-stah 25:334
Oadds, Casper 19:28
Oage, L. 23:44
Oah-chan-ho-lar-tuchee 25:334
Oak, John 18:209
Oakes, A. 9:188
Oakes, Alexander 17:155
Oakes, Amos 22:341
Oakes, David 22:455
Oakes, Ebenezer 21:372
Oakes, G. H. 1:62
Oakes, H. 14:18
Oakes, J. 15:344; 16:376
Oakes, J. H. 19:184
Oakes, John W. 24:26
Oakes, Robert 18:248; 26:51
Oakes, Samuel E. 4:44
Oakes, T. 9:98
Oakes, Thomas 13:67; 16:217
Oakleaf, Philip 25:59
Oakley, Alfred 22:313
Oakley, Charles N. 10:174; 19:184
Oakley, D. M. 14:301; 17:472; 27:93
Oakley, Daniel 9:27; 18:313; 26:108
Oakley, G. 22:313
Oakley, Gilbert 4:44
Oakley, H. A. 26:51
Oakley, J. 1:160
Oakley, James 9:112; 10:129; 20:319
Oakley, Kay 22:515
Oakley, Patrick 15:41
Oakley, William D. 16:7
Oakly, William H. 5:25
Oakman, John 22:94
Oaks, A. S. 13:95
Oaks, Adin 19:241
Oaks, Charles 15:11
Oaks, D. B. 1:61
Oaks, D. H. 24:26
Oaks, George 25:280; 27:147
Oaks, H. 13:95
Oaks, Isaac 22:263
Oaks, James C. 25:325
Oaks, Jeremiah 11:425
Oaks, John 21:103
Oaks, John S. 10:25
Oaks, Robert 17:403
Oaks, Theodore 26:237
Oaks, Thomas 8:99
Oaks, William 8:108

Oaky, George 16:217
Oales, Andrew 12:34
Oalesby, W. P. 16:270
Oaley, Martin 10:96
Oamly, Francis 26:175
Oammeron, Smison 8:92
Oamsberry, Minor 9:188
Oar, Arthur 22:263
Oard, Jonathan 19:184
Oassell, Christopher 8:92
Oasting, William 23:75
Oaten, Stephen 23:44
Oates, J. W. 27:93
Oates, John A. 9:188;
  19:229
Oates, S. 9:215; 21:372
Oathant, D. 3:146
Oathout, Daniel 19:28
Oatly, W. H. 25:214
Oatman, Albert 22:211
Oatridge, Richard 18:413;
  26:224
Oats, Abraham 10:170
Oats, Arch 21:372
Oats, Benjamin 17:136;
  24:200
Oats, Henry 22:515
Oats, Isaac 24:201
Oats, John 20:58
Oats, M. 14:95
Oats, Mark 19:47
Oats, Riley 6:22
Oats, Thomas 22:515
Oats, Virgil 7:130
Oats, William 25:214
Obarr, William H. 23:44
Obarra, Daniel 11:267
Obbett, M. 1:160
Obdom, H. G. 1:61
Obells, William 18:104
Obenour, Frederick
  23:286
Ober, Oliver 9:88; 26:51
Ober, R. 21:111
Ober, W. B. 14:95
Oberer, John Jacob 10:71;
  20:319
Oberg, A. 9:148
Oberg, John 10:129;
  20:319
Oberley, F. A. 5:25
Oberlin, C. C. 10:71
Oberlin, John 17:162, 426
Oberlin, Orlando 20:184
Oberly, C. 13:116
Oberly, Christian 19:330
Oberly, F. A. 25:214
Oberly, H. 18:373
Oberly, William 15:290;
  16:217
Oberman, John H. 17:24

Obermeyer, A. 11:40
Obermeyer, Anton 11:40
Obernayer, C. S. 9:148
Oberriller, Henry 20:187
Oberst, Antonis 22:354
Oberstreet, James 9:231
Obert, Charles 15:218
Obert, E. A. 19:90
Obevere, O. B. 3:146
Obhoff, Peter 10:25
Obile, W. 2:15
Obile, William 25:59
Obitt, John 10:71
Obleness, W. 1:159
Obliger, J. 18:313; 26:108
Oblinger, Francis M.
  23:161
Oblinger, Frederick
  22:211
Oblinger, G. 1:62
Oblinger, J. 9:27
Obmonf, Edward 9:37
Obrecht, Jacob 26:51
Obrest, G. F. 21:164
Obrien, Edward 23:44
Obrien, Enoch 23:256
Obrigant, James 21:57
Obrihan, Henry H. 24:54
Obrine, Dennis 23:44
Obson, O. 9:188
Obson, Ole 19:275
Ocden, D. 15:218
Och, S. 3:147
Ocha, Joseph 22:151
Ocheltree, L. F. 1:160
Ocherlin, John 13:95
Ochester, A. 3:147
Ochiltree, Andrew 17:201
Ochiltrie, John 20:25
Ochlart, Christian 8:92
Ochle, F. 3:147
Ochley, William 3:147
Ochner, C. 1:160
Ochreline, J. 14:18
Ochsner, Frederick 13:39
Ockerberg, Halver 22:162
Ockerhauser, Fred 23:161
Ockerman, Joseph A.
  22:127
Ockhard, W. 3:147
Ocle, Joseph 26:224
Ocobock, George 9:67
Ocruard, M. 14:95
Octeal, Michael 14:203
Oda, Andrew 8:53
Odam, J. 9:57
Odare, S. S. 16:123
Odden, Theodore W.
  19:28
Odeay, Timothy 10:129
Odekirk, Joseph A. 7:105

Odele, Zephania 21:57
Odell, Ben F. 17:416
Odell, C. F. 19:184
Odell, Charles W. 10:71;
  20:320
Odell, Evan 20:320
Odell, Evan A. 10:71
Odell, Gilbert 22:151
Odell, Horace D. 22:435
Odell, I. C. 18:70
Odell, I. M. 8:27
Odell, J. H. 24:95
Odell, J. S. 25:214
Odell, James 20:320
Odell, Jeremiah 22:94
Odell, John B. 10:71;
  20:320
Odell, John E. 11:295
Odell, John S. 5:25
Odell, Jonas 22:435
Odell, Josiah 10:20
Odell, Laroy E. 24:26
Odell, Lewis 23:314
Odell, M. C. 19:258
Odell, Milton 11:295
Odell, N. 20:134
Odell, Robert 10:206
Odell, Samuel 20:320
Odell, Samuel H. 10:71
Odell, Tobias M. 23:75
Odell, W. J. 5:25
Odell, W. T. 25:214
Odell, William 9:134;
  10:206; 14:203;
  21:13, 246; 27:93
Odell, Wilson A. 11:296
Odells, Ephraim 27:94
Odelway, Joel 11:403
Oden, Albert 22:313
Oden, Alfred 21:372
Oden, Andrew J. 22:263
Oden, G. 25:215
Oden, George 5:43
Oden, J. 22:313
Oden, Jesse 22:313
Oden, Sylvester 27:94
Oden, William 7:105
Oden, William D. 11:331
Odenbaugh, H. 15:72
Odenwald, Michael 10:71
Odenwall, M. 20:320
Oder, George W. 17:249
Oderick, Frederick 21:372
Odeveh, Joseph A. 21:372
Odey, Madison 22:313
Odgen, Andrew 17:462
Odgen, W. H. 18:399
Odikirk, J. 1:160
Odingee, Henry 16:217
Odis, Louis 22:211
Odle, Henry 7:52

Odle, Isaac 27:93
Odleston, Peter 7:36
Odom, Aaron 7:105
Odom, John 3:147
Odom, T. J. 9:112
Odom, W. 3:147
Odom, Willis G. 21:103
Odum, Elias 24:102
Odum, James 16:217
Odum, John 9:243
Oehre, John P. 7:105
Oelsehlager, J. C. 25:215
Oemichen, Reinhold
  18:248
Oemichen, Reinkold
  26:51
Oeng, I. 11:40
Oeth, John 14:203
Offeback, Zed 3:147
Offed, Edward 11:210
Offenlogh, J. C. 22:211
Offet, Gabriel 17:24
Offord, John 16:217
Offord, R. 16:217
Offutt, Franklin 17:416
Ogal, Simeon 22:263
Ogan, A. E. 23:124
Ogan, Charles 8:27
Ogan, James K. 10:129;
  20:320
Ogan, Levi 16:217
Ogan, M. D. 19:327
Ogar, A. E. 14:278
Ogbern, J. 25:215
Ogborn, Henry 11:267
Ogborn, Isaiah 8:92
Ogburn, H. C. 1:160
Ogburn, J. 13:96; 14:18
Ogden, A. 1:62
Ogden, Andrew 8:101;
  24:173
Ogden, Burgin 21:76
Ogden, Charles W. 11:267
Ogden, D. O. 20:42
Ogden, David 9:188;
  19:271
Ogden, E. 20:320
Ogden, E. S. 3:147
Ogden, Eli 11:120
Ogden, Eugene 4:44
Ogden, G. 15:218
Ogden, George 1:62;
  22:151
Ogden, George E. 11:277
Ogden, Giles 21:57
Ogden, Henry H. 22:466
Ogden, Hiram 11:288;
  22:466
Ogden, Israel 8:92
Ogden, J. 7:36; 13:96;
  27:93

Ogden, J. M. 1:160
Ogden, James 22:47
Ogden, John 4:44; 9:37;
  14:203, 258
Ogden, John H. 13:39
Ogden, Nelson 27:147
Ogden, Oliver 4:44
Ogden, Orville 8:115
Ogden, P. L. 7:36
Ogden, Robbin 9:165
Ogden, Robert 9:134;
  27:93
Ogden, Stephen 9:165;
  11:390
Ogden, T. 18:373
Ogden, Thomas 24:26
Ogden, Walter A. 17:100
Ogden, William 12:34;
  17:263
Ogdetree, John T. 18:152
Ogee, Samuel 13:39
Ogeese, Charles 21:373
Ogelen, William 21:124
Oger, P. 25:215
Oger, Peter 5:25
Ogestand, John 25:286
Ogg, John G. 4:45
Oggden, Harrison 23:271
Ogglesby, Martin 11:247
Ogilby, O. 14:289
Ogla, J. H. 13:39
Ogle, Abraham B. 23:44
Ogle, B. F. 26:51
Ogle, B. P. 18:248
Ogle, Benjamin 6:14
Ogle, Benjamin F. 10:129;
  20:320
Ogle, F. Clay 17:361
Ogle, G. M. 11:329
Ogle, Jacob 25:215
Ogle, John 7:105; 21:76
Ogle, L. 11:310; 14:203
Ogle, Orin W. 8:92
Ogle, P. 22:263
Ogle, Preston 17:167
Ogle, Thomas 10:129;
  14:203; 20:320
Ogle, William 22:211
Ogleive, Marion 24:150
Oglesby, David 3:147
Oglesby, G. 7:130
Oglesby, N. J. 21:190
Oglesby, William 11:267
Oglesby, Willis S. 20:127
Oglesee, Ortemian O. 9:44
Oglesman, Charles 16:217
Ogletree, B. F. 19:28
Ogletree, John F. 8:27
Oglevie, Art. O. 26:127
Oglevie, O. 23:161
Oglevie, William B. 20:19

Ogline, Sol 25:59
Oglorn, Albert 12:34
Ogusby, V. 22:313
Ohard, D. 11:268
Oharo, Anthony 15:160
Ohatt, Charles 10:71
Ohea, Dennis 6:32
Ohemer, G. 9:57
Ohia, Dennis 25:325
Ohiel, Cyrus 18:70
Ohissey, William 17:390
Ohl, Henry 22:236
Ohlan, Michael 7:9
Ohlhnes, H. 19:91
Ohlinger, Loren 26:127
Ohlinger, Lorin 9:44
Ohlman, Lewis 20:37
Ohlmstead, William B.
  10:71
Ohlsen, Henry 9:123;
  27:93
Ohlson, Peter 10:71;
  20:320
Ohmart, M. J. 12:156
Ohmart, Samuel 22:211
Ohngemack, John 10:165
Ohrt, Charles 20:320
Ohrus, John 21:243
Ohughemack, --- 19:184
Oiler, Benjamin F. 21:231
Oiler, H. 22:211
Oiler, Samuel 3:147
Oilese, William 17:97
Oiley, Peter 10:71
Ok-la-bis-ge-hajo 25:334
OKeefe, Daniel 21:373
Oker, William H. 17:40
Okes, Samuel C. 6:32
Okland, William 21:141
Okones, Peter 25:325
Olafsom, Hilge 18:248
Olahan, A. 3:147
Olar, John 21:76
Olas, Leo W. 22:151
Olasm, Peter 18:335
Olason, M. 12:93; 16:301
Olasson, Hilge 26:51
Olbram, Ephraim 26:127
Olckar, W. 1:160
Olcoats, J. 11:310
Olcon, William 8:74
Olcott, Edward 14:95
Olcott, G. 15:218
Olcott, George 13:39
Olcott, Herman 12:75
Olcott, William 14:203
Old, Ira C. 8:115
Oldacre, Harrison 9:70
Oldacre, William 17:56
Oldaker, McKendrick B.
  20:320

Oldaker, McKendrie B. 10:129
Olden, Samuel A. 16:217
Oldenburg, Fred 23:44
Oldendalph, H. 26:127
Oldendalph, Henry 9:44
Older, Joseph 25:215
Older, W. M. 3:147
Olderfield, J. R. 3:147
Olderham, Thomas 22:435
Oldfield, E. D. 22:47
Oldfield, G. 1:62
Oldfield, George 10:71; 20:320
Oldfield, John 22:47; 23:75; 25:215
Oldfield, Reuben 11:310
Oldfield, Thomas 22:466
Oldfield, William 23:161
Oldham, Anthony 17:398
Oldham, C. 22:127
Oldham, Chester 22:515
Oldham, D. 17:182
Oldham, George R. 24:43
Oldham, J. 1:62
Oldham, J. R. 18:16
Oldham, James 11:277
Oldham, John S. 19:184
Oldham, L. K. 22:342
Oldham, Michael 9:123
Oldham, R. W. 9:112
Oldham, Samuel G. 21:76
Oldham, T. 18:70
Olding, Carl 25:59
Oldman, Charles 11:310
Oldman, John 21:373
Oldmixon, Jane 25:312
Oldrich, John 7:105
Oldridge, John 21:131
Oldridge, Lewis 23:286
Oldriets, James 14:95
Olds, Adolph 9:27
Olds, Arson W. 15:42
Olds, George W. 22:435, 465
Olds, John A. 22:151
Olds, Joseph E. 22:211
Olds, Lewis C. 19:184
Olds, Lewis G. 10:145
Olds, M. R. 10:153; 19:184
Olds, Martin 19:241
Olds, Oliver H. 8:92
Olds, Oney 18:373
Olds, Orison W. 12:75
Olds, Phil'm. 22:455
Olds, Samuel 11:162
Olds, Samuel F. 15:110
Olds, T. B. 8:53
Olds, Thomas 22:94; 23:161

Olds, Thomas C. 22:342
Olds, William 23:75
Olds, William D. 22:466
Oldson, Gilbert 9:231; 20:320
Oldston, Lewis 11:40
Oldswager, I. 15:218
Oldum, Michael 27:93
Ole, Anderson 12:162
Ole, Lewis 11:116
Oleason, John 9:240
Olehue, George 10:129; 20:320
Olemyre, Phi 27:94
Olen, Alexander 21:258
Olen, C. 17:290
Olendick, J. 27:93
Olenger, William 14:203
Olenhimez, Albert 13:40
Olenhinze, Albert 16:48
Olens, Charles 4:45
Olenstead, Theodore 8:27
Olepy, G. P. 11:40
Oler, A. 11:310
Olerry, A. 3:147
Olerry, W. 27:93
Olery, A. 27:93
Oles, J. 1:160
Olesan, Jacob 18:279
Oleson, Abraham 25:215
Oleson, Andrew 18:295; 24:96; 26:108
Oleson, Anthony 10:129; 20:320
Oleson, Christopher 8:27; 18:152
Oleson, E. 9:69, 104
Oleson, Ever 20:115
Oleson, George 18:248
Oleson, Gulick 21:76
Oleson, Herman 21:76
Oleson, Iver 22:162
Oleson, J. 9:67
Oleson, John 9:104; 15:92; 17:323; 20:115
Oleson, Nelson 22:151
Oleson, Nelus 20:175
Oleson, Ole 11:193; 17:361; 20:49; 23:44, 193
Oleson, Ole B. 21:258
Oleson, Oley D. 20:11
Oleson, P. 17:501
Oleson, Peter 11:116; 20:320
Oleson, Swarte 11:116
Olessen, John 18:340
Olevia, P. D. 16:48
Olf, Eli 1:62
Olf, John 12:96

Olfield, W. 15:218
Olgee, Constantine 5:53
Olham, Fletcher 21:373
Oliba, A. 16:376
Olier, William H. 9:88
Oliffe, George 13:40
Oliger, Mary 9:223
Olillig, John 11:193
Olin, Asa 1:62
Olin, Dillworth 21:258
Olin, Henry 13:116
Olin, Uriel P. 15:92
Olinger, Anthony 23:75
Olinger, Daniel 17:419; 22:487
Olinger, E. 3:147
Olinger, J. 3:147
Olinger, John 3:147
Olinger, John I. 21:239
Olinger, Josiah 21:77
Olinson, Olis 7:105
Olinsted, Edward 25:279
Oliphant, D. H. 1:62
Olis, Oney 9:223
Olison, George 26:51
Olison, Iver 11:293
Olison, Joseph 11:210
Olivan, Peter 4:45
Oliver, --- 25:59
Oliver, A. 3:147
Oliver, A. E. 19:229
Oliver, Abner E. 18:209
Oliver, Abraham 17:136; 24:200
Oliver, Abram E. 8:92
Oliver, Alonzo 23:75
Oliver, Bonaparte 7:130
Oliver, Bryant O. 10:129; 20:320
Oliver, Caffy 19:184
Oliver, Charles 16:376
Oliver, Clauson 7:52
Oliver, Cuffy 10:177
Oliver, D. 9:67
Oliver, David 9:215; 21:373
Oliver, David C. 20:138
Oliver, Dick 21:373
Oliver, E. T. 10:71; 20:320
Oliver, Edward 21:36
Oliver, Franklin 7:130; 19:28
Oliver, George 7:69, 130; 11:162
Oliver, H. 10:187; 15:58; 18:178
Oliver, H. H. 3:147
Oliver, Henry 4:45; 7:130; 9:148; 12:75; 17:398; 27:93

Oliver, Hiram 4:45
Oliver, I. 1:62
Oliver, J. 3:147; 21:36
Oliver, J. H. 1:62
Oliver, J. S. 9:57
Oliver, J. W. 17:149
Oliver, James 7:36, 130;
13:40; 25:325
Oliver, James J. 23:283
Oliver, James M. 23:161
Oliver, James W. 19:28
Oliver, Jesse 22:263
Oliver, John 1:62; 3:147;
6:18; 8:66; 18:91;
23:161; 26:175
Oliver, John A. 15:81
Oliver, John E. 20:99
Oliver, Joseph 6:18; 18:91
Oliver, Joseph M. 11:390
Oliver, L. 3:147
Oliver, L. W. 13:96
Oliver, Levi 12:34; 21:57;
26:127
Oliver, Levi T. 21:87
Oliver, Loring C. 16:79
Oliver, M. P. 9:243
Oliver, Martin V. 10:7
Oliver, Michael 17:283
Oliver, N. C. 19:91
Oliver, Nathan B. 20:193
Oliver, Nicholas 9:104;
18:340
Oliver, R. William 11:183
Oliver, Ralf 4:45
Oliver, Robert 13:40;
22:13, 487
Oliver, S. 21:36, 209, 373
Oliver, S. E. 3:147
Oliver, Samuel 17:111;
21:280; 22:94;
25:215
Oliver, Samuel B. 10:71
Oliver, Samuel P. 20:320
Oliver, Sylvester I. 17:390
Oliver, Sylvester O.
10:145; 19:184
Oliver, Thomas 10:71;
20:320
Oliver, W. 3:147
Oliver, W. A. 1:160
Oliver, W. H. 7:130;
19:91
Oliver, W. J. 20:320
Oliver, Walter J. 10:129;
20:320
Oliver, William 13:116;
18:431; 22:313;
23:161
Oliver, William F. 21:36
Oliver, William I. 10:71
Olives, Pablo 12:172

Olldach, Henry 19:343
Ollendick, Joseph 9:148
Oller, Adam J. 23:100
Oller, Matthew 8:66
Ollery, John 21:373
Olley, Peter 20:320
Ollin, Allen 27:147
Ollinger, Bartholomew
21:245
Ollinger, R. M. 10:129;
20:320
Olliphant, James W.
17:203
Ollis, Andrew A. 9:123
Ollis, George 23:44
Ollison, Burn 21:373
Olliver, Charles 15:344
Olliver, Joseph A. 21:280
Olliver, L. W. 14:18
Olliver, Paul 21:280
Ollman, John 4:45
Ollman, William 3:147
Olm, Martin F. 24:96
Olmnon, Joseph 20:187
Olmon, George 15:8
Olmon, H. 3:148
Olmore, Henslon 9:204
Olmstead, --- 25:59
Olmstead, Calvin M.
23:103
Olmstead, Charles 13:40;
16:48
Olmstead, Charles F.
21:258
Olmstead, D. H. 7:83
Olmstead, Daniel 1:62;
21:373; 22:151
Olmstead, Dictor 8:41
Olmstead, Doctor 26:175
Olmstead, Edward 10:20
Olmstead, F. 15:218
Olmstead, F. D. 17:67
Olmstead, F. H. 3:148
Olmstead, G. 9:112
Olmstead, G. W. 7:36
Olmstead, George W.
27:93
Olmstead, James 11:415
Olmstead, John D. 8:108
Olmstead, Morris M.
22:151
Olmstead, Philo 13:40
Olmstead, S. M. 7:105
Olmstead, Theodore
18:152
Olmstead, William 7:36
Olmsted, Addison 17:350
Olmsted, J. 27:93
Olmsted, Josiah G. 9:73
Olmsted, Oscar 10:165
Olmsted, Tilton 20:58

Olmsted, W. B. 20:320
Olmstene, G. W. 23:277
Olney, Adam 17:391
Olney, F. 20:148
Olney, G. W. 3:148
Olney, Lewis S. S. 18:35
Olney, M. 21:373
Olney, S. 20:320
Olney, Sylvanus 10:71
Olomer, B. 24:96
Olran, Oliver 11:85
Olsen, Amund 22:283
Olsen, Anam 13:40
Olsen, Andrew 23:44
Olsen, Andrew P. 10:20
Olsen, C. 11:193; 21:111
Olsen, Charles 22:283
Olsen, Christian 9:88
Olsen, G. 17:143
Olsen, Gottried 17:429;
24:186
Olsen, Hendrick 21:141
Olsen, James 21:141
Olsen, O. W. 14:286
Olsen, Ole 9:88; 21:258
Olsen, S. L. 11:247
Olsen, Syver 21:258
Olsen, Thomas 22:283
Olsen, William 21:373
Olsion, L. 14:18
Olson, A. 22:162
Olson, Albert 11:427;
21:258
Olson, Andrew 12:156
Olson, Christian 26:51
Olson, D. 12:162
Olson, George 11:128,
210
Olson, Gunder 10:129;
20:320
Olson, Irer 11:193
Olson, J. 3:148
Olson, John 10:71;
14:203; 20:320;
22:342
Olson, Julius O. 10:129;
20:320
Olson, Neils 10:71;
20:321; 22:94
Olson, Nels 20:115
Olson, Nelson 12:156
Olson, O. 3:148
Olson, Ole 11:193;
20:115; 26:51
Olson, Olia 24:10
Olson, P. 11:193
Olson, R. 11:335
Olson, Samuel 14:203
Olson, Thomas 11:333

Olson, William 9:27; 18:55, 313; 26:108
Olsrewoki, Chrs. 17:456
Olston, M. 3:148
Olstrom, Nicholas P. 10:129; 20:321
Olszewski, Charles 24:154
Olt, Frederick 11:96
Oltis, H. 3:148
Oltman, Gerhard 12:59
Olto, John 20:321
Oltz, Daniel 25:215
Olvany, Patrick 16:100
Olverson, Lewis 18:55
Olvey, William 20:99
Olwell, Thomas 18:16
Olwine, A. 15:218
Oman, H. 24:26
Oman, Hardell 9:134
Oman, Henry 16:217
Oman, Joshua 17:84
Oman, Moses A. 22:211
Omandy, Paul 1:61
Omar, Hardee 27:93
Omas, John 15:218
Omat, M. 3:148
Omelie, Joseph 25:215
Omer, John 14:95
Omer, L. 14:95
Omerie, D. J. 3:148
Omly, George 26:52
Omsley, W. J. 3:148
Omurg, G. H. 21:124
Onat, Loyal S. 10:165
Onderdonk, H. H. 20:193
Onderdonk, Leonard F. 23:129
Onderdonk, Marvin 12:34
Onderhick, William 9:123
Onderkirk, J. 25:215
Onderkirk, William 27:93
Oneal, D. W. 9:88; 26:51
Oneal, Daniel 20:321
Oneal, Michael 20:321
Onemitt, Barney 11:390
Onevenoir, Theobold 4:45
Oney, Harry 4:45
Ong--, --- 20:58
Onian, M. F. 24:26
Onich, Robert 26:51
Onicks, Thomas 10:165
Oniel, Patrick 15:306
Onimette, C. 25:215
Onison, John 22:342
Onley, Frank 18:36
Onnbego, W. 10:29
Onnis, James 15:316; 19:91
Onsley, Thomas 11:210
Onstead, George H. 21:243

Onstolt, Jacob 14:203
Onter, George W. 20:321
Ontey, William F. 14:236
Onweller, William 13:125
Ooley, G. A. 1:160
Ooly, W. P. 18:193
Oor, William 23:204
Oot, John 22:211
Opal, August 8:101; 17:459
Opedike, Lyman 21:206
Open, E. 2:15; 25:59
Openaska, Marcelus 11:267
Openchain, James 23:75
Openchain, Jehu 22:94
Oper, L. 3:148
Operle, Louis 23:284
Ophir, Henry 16:134
Opockley, Thomas 5:53
Oppe, Charles 11:71
Oppenkussky, Gottleib 17:56
Opperman, August 11:129
Opperman, Morris 22:342
Oppey, William D. 20:321
Oppey, William T. 10:129
Opplinger, Frity 11:110
Oppy, Christopher 23:161
Opt, Harvey F. 11:162
Orahood, Aaron 21:57
Orahood, Jasper 20:321
Orall, Henry 22:313
Oram, Ira W. 19:184
Oram, John 11:333
Orange, J. M. 17:149
Orange, Million 24:201
Orange, Thomas 8:101; 17:461; 24:161
Orasaby, William 8:27
Orbaugh, George H. 11:162
Orbin, J. 1:160
Orcham, Sylvester 20:85
Orchard, Thomas 17:416
Orchard, William 17:353
Orcoth, F. 25:215
Orcott, A. 15:42
Orcott, Charles H. 25:215
Orcott, F. 5:53
Orcott, George 12:62
Orcott, George D. 17:454; 24:186
Orcott, Joseph 10:129
Orcott, Josiah 20:321
Orcott, Newell 11:310
Orcutt, A. E. 1:160; 17:152
Orcutt, C. 3:148
Orcutt, Charles E. 14:319; 25:276

Orcutt, Charles W. 17:317
Orcutt, Cyrus 24:96
Orcutt, George 15:23
Orcutt, J. E. 1:160
Orcutt, M. M. 9:188
Orcutt, P. E. 20:321
Orcutt, Peter E. 10:72
Orcutt, William 19:91
Ord, C. T. 11:193
Ord, Isaac 10:206
Ordell, L. 9:188; 19:258
Ordewy, Benjamin 12:65
Ordhood, Jasper 10:130
Ordlip, Frank 15:160
Ordman, C. A. 18:36
Ordman, Frederick 20:115
Ordner, John 15:131
Ordung, John 9:188
Ordway, Adson 22:342
Ordway, Benjamin P. 15:92
Ordway, Eli 15:23
Ordway, Hiram 23:161
Ordway, J. H. 17:160
Ordway, James 24:62
Ordway, John W. 22:509
Ordway, Louis 12:34
Ordway, N. H. 22:487
Ordway, Nathaniel 10:165; 19:184
Ordway, W. 23:44
Ordy, R. 11:162
Ore, Ambrose M. 23:185
Ore, James I. 21:131
Ore, John 5:25
Orear, J. D. 20:19
Orear, John D. 20:28
Orear, W. 20:19
Orein, Oscar 23:291
Orelli, R. 1:160
Orendorff, William 14:203
Oretman, G. W. 11:247
Orf, C. 17:436
Orf---, Casper 24:182
Orfa, John B. 16:376
Orford, --- 16:302
Orford, James 10:155; 19:184
Orford, William 15:218
Orfort, William 15:218
Orful, Joseph 10:165; 19:184
Organ, G. A. 25:59
Organ, J. E. 14:95
Organ, John R. 23:161
Organ, M. 1:160
Orger, I. M. 19:184
Orgun, Patrick 15:218
Oriat, S. 9:112
Oriatt, David W. 17:451

Oricks, Thomas 19:184
Orien, Leonard H. 22:409
Orientil, C. 25:59
Origon, J. A. 17:155
Orill, Oliver 22:435
Orin, G. W. 1:61
Orion, John 20:155
Orison, A. 17:156
Orke, Clemen 11:40
Orland, M. D. 20:321
Orland, Martin 10:72
Orlemann, J. 1:160
Orley, William W. 7:36
Orliff, H. I. 19:28
Orlin, Jasper 8:92
Orlopp, Franz 4:36
Orm, Charles 18:104
Orm, Christopher 23:91
Orman, A. 13:132
Ormby, C. 13:96
Orment, W. T. 19:316
Ormesby, W. 13:67
Ormeton, William 16:217
Ormick, John L. 11:310
Ormiston, George H. 7:60
Ormley, Patrick 21:190
Ormsbee, C. 5:53; 25:215
Ormsbee, G. D. 4:45
Ormsbee, John 9:204
Ormsburg, William 25:59
Ormsby, Adin 17:392
Ormsby, C. 24:26
Ormsby, Daniel O. 7:36
Ormsby, George 15:218
Ormsby, James 13:40
Ormsby, Jesse H. 20:321
Ormsby, John P. 14:203
Ormsby, M. 19:241
Ormsby, Martin P. 20:184
Ormsby, Robert 21:231
Ormsby, Rowland L. 16:100
Ormsby, W. 19:91
Ormsby, William 14:203
Orn, Nelson H. 22:435
Ornduff, Andrew 6:13
Orne, G. W. 25:302
Orne, J. R. 13:116
Ornell, Gordon 9:201
Orner, Robert 14:204
Orness, P. 19:283
Orng, J. 23:253
Ornich, Robert 9:88
Ornly, George 18:248
Ornsby, William 18:152
Oroark, James 26:51
Oron, Daniel B. 22:211
Orpen, Harry 11:162
Orr, --- 25:59
Orr, A. 3:148
Orr, A. S. 11:162

Orr, Alasion 8:115
Orr, Ansel 16:49
Orr, Ansenl 13:40
Orr, Arthur 17:84
Orr, C. P. 14:95
Orr, Calvin 8:27; 18:152
Orr, D. G. 2:15
Orr, Elias 14:204
Orr, Eugene 13:116
Orr, George M. 23:44
Orr, George W. 11:310
Orr, H. 18:248; 26:52
Orr, H. C. 20:134
Orr, Harrison 10:72; 20:321
Orr, Isaac M. 15:218
Orr, J. 1:160
Orr, J. H. 16:217
Orr, J. J. 1:160
Orr, James 17:395
Orr, James H. 10:130; 20:321
Orr, John 11:85, 310; 20:138; 25:215
Orr, John C. 17:297
Orr, John T. 8:27; 18:153
Orr, Lott 25:215
Orr, P. 10:29; 19:305
Orr, Peter 21:11
Orr, R. R. 12:34
Orr, Robert 10:130; 20:321
Orr, S. W. 12:156
Orr, Sample 10:130; 20:321
Orr, Samuel 22:354
Orr, Sylvester 12:156
Orr, Thomas H. 11:96
Orr, W. 1:160; 26:108
Orr, W. L. 8:66
Orr, Westfield 23:309
Orr, William 9:27; 16:123; 18:313; 21:89; 23:44, 91, 204
Orr, William A. 7:105
Orr, William D. 23:124
Orr, William H. 23:109
Orr, William S. 23:91
Orrall, James 22:13
Orrand, Lewis 21:150
Orrell, Ira 13:116
Orren, Evan F. 13:40
Orren, Robert 25:284
Orri, John B. 21:259
Orrice, G. A. 9:112
Orrick, John C. 8:27
Orrin, Benjamin 22:94
Orris, Giles 1:61
Orris, Peter 10:72; 20:321
Orris, William 17:84
Orrison, George 3:148

Orrison, W. W. 22:211
Orritt, E. H. 1:62
Orrumsmith, William 10:92
Orsay, Samuel G. 14:204
Orsburn, H. 23:15
Orsch, Jacob 23:264
Orsini, Charles 21:11
Orsinsky, Oloff 10:130; 20:321
Orsmond, Thomas 21:259
Orson, Samuel 9:44
Ort, Christian 9:188; 19:258
Ort, H. K. 1:160
Ort, Henry 22:94
Ortell, Christian 11:71
Ortell, E. 25:215
Ortell, George 18:335
Ortell, J. 13:116
Ortell, M. 3:148; 14:204
Orten, Aaron 21:280
Orten, R. 17:56
Orth, J. 21:373
Orth, Lewis 23:13
Orthon, J. 1:108
Ortis, Harrison 9:134; 27:93
Ortley, Patrick 12:65
Ortner, Henry 22:152
Ortner, J. C. 1:160
Ortney, David F. 10:130; 20:321
Orton, H. C. 3:148
Orton, Herman 27:147
Orton, Isaac 22:47
Orton, J. K. 9:98
Orton, James E. 11:40
Orton, Jordon 7:71
Orton, Marquis W. 20:31
Orton, S. H. 2:15; 25:59
Orton, Thomas E. 23:193
Orton, W. J. 15:219
Orton, William D. 20:58
Ortree, Jason 11:210
Orts, Eliflet 9:148
Orvis, Alonzo H. 17:244
Orwell, George T. 19:288
Orwick, John 4:45
Orwig, J. B. 3:148
Orwig, John C. 4:45
Orwig, S. W. 3:148
Orwin, John H. 4:45
Orwin, S. V. B. 3:148
Osark, E. A. 11:281
Osberg, Paul 20:115
Osbern, J. 11:109
Osborn, --- 15:92; 16:281
Osborn, A. J. 8:108
Osborn, Alfred C. 23:124
Osborn, Alvanon 17:40

Osborn, Andrew 11:71; 19:28
Osborn, Aug. M. 15:219
Osborn, B. C. 9:88
Osborn, B. F. 7:36
Osborn, C. 25:215; 26:175
Osborn, C. A. 27:94
Osborn, C. P. 20:42
Osborn, Cahoun C. 8:92
Osborn, Charles 20:99
Osborn, Charles D. 15:92
Osborn, Charles M. 17:441; 24:154
Osborn, Chauncy 23:193
Osborn, Daniel S. 10:130; 20:321
Osborn, David 22:487
Osborn, E. 3:148; 8:66; 27:93
Osborn, E. W. 13:96
Osborn, Edgar 10:72; 20:321
Osborn, Edward 22:435
Osborn, Edwin 9:188
Osborn, Elijah 26:175
Osborn, Enoch 14:316
Osborn, Ephriam 17:233
Osborn, Eugene F. 17:474
Osborn, F. 12:100; 21:124
Osborn, F. L. 3:148
Osborn, F. M. 21:150
Osborn, Francis A. 16:123
Osborn, G. A. 8:66; 26:175
Osborn, G. G. 11:403
Osborn, G. W. 1:159
Osborn, George H. 9:38
Osborn, George I. 4:45
Osborn, George W. 8:53
Osborn, H. M. 23:161
Osborn, Haywood T. 10:130; 20:321
Osborn, Henry 22:314
Osborn, Hiram 7:52
Osborn, J. 3:148; 11:231; 21:111
Osborn, J. L. 3:148
Osborn, J. S. 16:123
Osborn, J. W. 3:148
Osborn, James 11:247; 18:373; 21:77; 23:282
Osborn, James H. 25:215
Osborn, Jesse 11:390
Osborn, Job E. 18:70
Osborn, John 13:116; 14:95; 21:231; 22:435; 23:161; 24:161
Osborn, John C. 17:56

Osborn, John M. 22:212
Osborn, John N. 20:190
Osborn, John W. 10:72; 20:321
Osborn, Joseph 23:271; 25:59
Osborn, L. F. 1:159
Osborn, L. W. 15:299
Osborn, Lewis 16:217
Osborn, Marion 8:92
Osborn, Moses O. 21:116
Osborn, N. 11:267
Osborn, N. W. 23:256
Osborn, Nathan 10:130; 20:321
Osborn, P. 26:224
Osborn, Ralph 9:44; 26:127
Osborn, Robert R. 11:162
Osborn, S. 3:148
Osborn, Samuel 10:20
Osborn, Scipio 22:314
Osborn, Scott 6:22
Osborn, Solomon 8:74
Osborn, Stephen M. 4:45
Osborn, Sylvanus 17:308
Osborn, Thomas 3:148
Osborn, Thomas J. 21:231
Osborn, W. 3:148
Osborn, W. P. 20:321
Osborn, W. T. V. 9:13
Osborn, Watson C. 24:96
Osborn, William 7:105; 11:390; 23:286
Osborn, William B. 9:188
Osborn, William E. 24:215
Osborn, William H. 9:16; 24:82
Osborn, William P. 10:72; 20:184
Osborne, A. J. 3:148
Osborne, Adam 23:75
Osborne, Barzillai 23:75
Osborne, C. A. 14:244
Osborne, Charles 1:61
Osborne, D. 13:129
Osborne, Daniel 21:373
Osborne, E. 1:160; 3:148; 19:258
Osborne, Edward 13:116
Osborne, Enoch 23:100
Osborne, Ephraim 17:445; 24:167
Osborne, F. M. 21:184
Osborne, Frederick 10:165; 19:184
Osborne, G. J. 13:116
Osborne, Hiram M. 20:99
Osborne, Horace 18:327
Osborne, Isaac F. 22:471

Osborne, J. 25:273, 286
Osborne, J. M. 3:148
Osborne, James 11:40; 21:231
Osborne, James H. 14:204
Osborne, Jeremiah 22:263
Osborne, John 10:165; 17:419; 19:184; 22:263
Osborne, John R. 22:94
Osborne, L. R. 25:215
Osborne, Martin 14:204
Osborne, P. E. 1:62
Osborne, Paul 4:45
Osborne, Peter 7:131
Osborne, Philip 14:131
Osborne, R. H. 3:148
Osborne, R. W. 1:62
Osborne, Robert 20:49
Osborne, S. 22:263
Osborne, S. D. 1:62
Osborne, S. R. 3:148
Osborne, Samuel 19:184
Osborne, Thomas 21:196
Osborne, W. 13:96
Osborne, W. F. 17:149
Osborne, W. H. 1:160
Osborne, William H. 25:59
Osbourn, Scott 18:91
Osbourn, W. W. 13:116
Osbourne, George W. 12:51
Osburn, --- 23:204
Osburn, Curtis 5:25
Osburn, D. C. 25:215
Osburn, David C. 5:25
Osburn, E. W. 14:18
Osburn, Enos 22:94
Osburn, Eugene 27:94
Osburn, George C. 15:219
Osburn, J. H. 27:94
Osburn, James H. 5:25
Osburn, Leonard R. 5:25
Osburn, Samuel L. 27:93
Osburn, Stephen 15:219
Osburn, W. 14:18; 16:217
Osburn, William 23:161
Oscar, John 9:201
Osccwalse, David 25:59
Oscott, James 16:217
Oscudder, B. 25:59
Oscutt, J. 3:148
Osenbough, J. R. 15:219
Osenbreck, Francis A. 22:212
Osgood, --- 23:305
Osgood, Abner W. 9:123; 27:93
Osgood, Alma C. 7:36
Osgood, Andrew E. 16:82

Osgood, Asahel 25:59
Osgood, C. S. 14:95
Osgood, Charles 10:20
Osgood, David 14:204
Osgood, E. R. 14:96
Osgood, Ed. C. 19:91
Osgood, Edward B.
   10:130; 20:321
Osgood, Edward C.
   15:306
Osgood, Enos W. 17:67
Osgood, Frederick 15:351
Osgood, G. H. 1:160
Osgood, George H. 12:9
Osgood, H. T. 17:309
Osgood, Harry 9:104
Osgood, J. 16:270
Osgood, J. W. 25:325
Osgood, James D. 21:259
Osgood, John N. 5:25;
   25:215
Osgood, L. H. 21:373
Osgood, Nelson 27:147
Osgood, T. D. 1:62
Osgood, T. H. 9:215
Osgood, Thomas J. 12:9
Osgood, Uriah 7:36
Osgood, William 19:184
Osham, Frederic 11:110
Oshoncoly, Michael
   14:204
Osien, L. 13:96
Osier, Charles 24:96
Osier, Joseph 13:40;
   19:185
Osier, Peter 7:36
Osierheart, Peter 19:258
Osing, A. 11:128
Osisler, --- 14:96
Oskins, Alexander 20:99
Oslage, Jacob H. 24:43
Oslin, Peter 23:104
Oslon, Soren 21:141
Osman, Calvin 22:152
Osman, G. 26:51
Osman, George 9:88;
   16:123
Osman, J. C. 1:160
Osman, W. B. 15:365;
   19:91
Osmanson, Ole 12:62
Osmer, Aaron 22:212
Osmer, Charles A. 24:26
Osmon, A. 3:148
Osmond, Henry 11:71
Osmond, James F. 7:14
Osmondson, O. 23:193
Osmondson, Ole 20:152
Osmonson, Ole 15:92
Osmus, J. 3:148
Osralt, Frederick 1:62

Oss, --- 3:148
Ossam, Smith William
   20:321
Ossankop, Henry 10:130
Ossaukope, Henry 20:321
Ossiday, Stephen 8:92
Osslen, Andrew 8:27;
   18:153
Ost, Adam 13:96
Ost, John 19:28
Ost, John P. 7:105
Osteen, Elisha 23:304
Osteen, William G. 22:47
Osten, A. B. 17:500
Ostenhal, G. 3:148
Ostenhoudt, B. S. 3:148
Oster, E. H. 11:162
Oster, George 22:127
Oster, Phil 1:62
Osterdock, Anthony 11:71
Osterhaut, George 1:62
Osterhoudt, C. E. 1:62
Osterhouse, John 14:204
Osterhout, C. C. 26:175
Osterhout, Cornelius B.
   21:259
Osterhout, D. D. 9:148
Osterhout, Gideon 22:172
Osterhout, L. B. 20:321
Osterhout, W. 7:36
Osterkang, Gert 17:211
Osterlag, John 11:193
Osterland, Gastof 24:171
Osterland, Gustavus
   17:447
Osterman, A. 13:96; 14:18
Osterman, Joseph 24:26
Osterman, T. 22:409
Osterstuck, William 3:148
Ostin, Alfred 3:148
Ostrand, Henrick 21:93
Ostrand, Henry 15:219
Ostrande, Edward 9:27
Ostrander, --- 19:28
Ostrander, Benjamin
   13:116
Ostrander, C. 25:59
Ostrander, E. W. 3:148
Ostrander, Garrett 12:34
Ostrander, H. L. 19:28
Ostrander, Henry 20:108
Ostrander, J. 3:149
Ostrander, J. H. 3:149
Ostrander, John W. 24:26
Ostrander, P. 25:59
Ostrander, Sydney 7:52
Ostrander, William 7:60
Ostrander, William J. 5:25
Ostrands, Edward 18:313;
   26:108
Ostre, P. 1:160

Ostrom, J. 1:160; 21:190
Ostrom, Thomas J. 13:40
Ostron, Williard 27:93
Ostrum, Miller 9:148
Ostrum, Peter 20:190
Ostwald, Herman 21:93,
   246
Oswald, A. B. 24:82
Oswald, Benjamin 13:116
Oswald, Edward 17:251
Oswald, George 22:172
Oswald, Henry 9:27
Oswald, Herman 26:175
Oswald, Jacob 22:487
Oswald, Joseph 24:26
Oswald, Philip 23:115
Oswald, Silas 27:94
Oswald, Stephen 3:149
Oswalds, David W.
   11:162
Oswalt, Daniel 22:94
Oswalt, Henry 18:313;
   26:108
Oswalt, Michael 22:47
Osward, Fred 9:240
Oswold, Fred 19:316
Oswold, James T. 19:91
Osworth, John E. 16:302
Oswottle, John E. 12:87
Otely, Robert 12:75
Otey, Jordan 23:100
Otey, O. S. 3:149
Othmond, Charles 12:34
Otinger, George 22:263
Otinger, William 14:204
Otis, A. D. 1:62
Otis, Amos 16:100
Otis, Andrew A. 27:93
Otis, H. G. 5:25; 25:215
Otis, Harrison 22:127
Otis, J. D. 15:299; 16:217
Otis, Jacob B. 20:143
Otis, James E. 10:165
Otis, John 3:149; 13:40;
   18:399
Otis, John A. 23:193
Otis, Josiah L. 9:7
Otis, Oral 1:62
Otis, R. S. 22:287
Otis, Raymond 9:13
Otis, Washington 24:215
Otis, William 12:34
Otley, George 23:75
Otman, M. 21:373
Oto, Joseph 7:131
Otom, Timothy 15:219
Ott, A. D. 15:110
Ott, Alfred 20:19
Ott, Bernhard 23:193
Ott, C. 3:149
Ott, D. 25:215

Ott, Feidlus 20:58
Ott, Gustavus 26:51
Ott, H. 20:321
Ott, Jack 14:204
Ott, Jacob 19:185
Ott, John 1:62; 3:149;
 13:40; 20:127
Ott, Michael 1:62
Ottaway, S. 22:314
Otte, William 10:72
Otten, Heinrich 15:72
Ottenger, Lewis 11:425
Otter, William 17:56
Otterman, Charles 22:497
Otterson, Robert 16:152
Ottherton, James 26:175
Ottinger, Emanuel 24:184
Ottinger, J. 3:149
Ottinger, Philip 22:263
Ottis, Samuel B. 9:123
Ottison, A. 13:116
Ottmans, Joseph 11:281
Otto, Anton 4:45
Otto, August 19:91;
 26:237
Otto, Augustus 23:241
Otto, Charles 3:149; 20:27
Otto, D. 16:302
Otto, Emanuel 12:34
Otto, F. 11:40
Otto, G. 14:204
Otto, H. 11:310
Otto, Harkin 1:62
Otto, Henry 9:112
Otto, Herman 20:35
Otto, J. 2:15
Otto, John 3:149; 14:96,
 204
Otto, John A. 12:123;
 15:131
Otto, Joseph 9:44; 12:9;
 26:127
Otto, Joseph B. 1:62
Otto, Justis 25:215
Otto, Valentine 8:120
Otto, William 17:67;
 20:321
Ottoe, Daniel 23:305
Ottoe, David 14:333
Otton, J. L. 3:149
Ottoness, William 18:427
Ottoway, Spencer 22:314
Otts, Martin 16:49
Ottway, D. 3:149
Otwell, Benjamin 8:41
Otwell, Berry 26:175
Otwell, James 10:206
Otwell, Obid 21:36
Otwell, W. H. 9:57
Oty, Henry 15:58
Ouctiener, Edward 15:219

Ouderkirk, Charles 19:185
Ougheltree, Alexander
 22:465
Oulaugh, William 9:37
Ould, Leonard 16:49
Ould, Thomas 16:49
Oulf, John 19:91
Oulner, Philip 9:188
Ounbego, W. 19:305
Ounrake, Frank 9:44
Ouns, John D. 11:40
Ounsbury, W. 2:15
Our, Michael 22:47
Ousley, Adam 16:217
Ousley, Noah 18:399
Ousterhaws, Samuel
 11:403
Ousterhout, Louis P.
 10:72
Ousterhout, O. D. 27:93
Outcelt, John W. 22:435
Outen, Wilson 22:455
Outer, George W. 10:72
Outhaut, D. 14:204
Outland, B. F. 20:59
Outland, Milton 13:40
Outlaw, Daniel 19:292
Outlay, Hays 22:314
Outman, William B. 4:45
Outwater, John W. 15:27
Outwater, Simeon 23:124
Ovendorf, Richard 17:136
Ovenon, Simon 10:72
Overacker, Ralph 22:47
Overall, C. 11:231
Overall, Calvin 11:338
Overall, Isaac 11:210
Overall, James 1:62
Overall, Newson 20:46
Overbaugh, James P.
 19:91
Overbeck, William 20:321
Overbee, Herman 22:487
Overbury, Frederick
 23:100
Overby, John 17:56
Overby, Richard A. 9:188;
 19:277
Overcoat, F. H. 22:504
Overdeer, H. 24:82
Overder, D. C. 15:72
Overen, S. 20:321
Overfelt, John 14:270
Overfelt, Robert 16:49
Overgains, Fred 7:105
Overhalser, Andrew T.
 22:504
Overhalt, John P. 21:125
Overhard, Benjamin 8:115
Overhart, William 11:320
Overheiser, W. B. 21:373

Overholser, Charles
 25:215
Overholt, L. 25:215
Overholt, William 16:134
Overholts, Joseph 22:329
Overholyer, James 5:53
Overhulson, Samuel
 11:247
Overhultzer, H. 23:124
Overleigh, Albert 7:36
Overlightner, J. 24:82
Overlock, A. 10:149
Overlock, Christopher
 4:45
Overlock, E. 7:37
Overloff, I. 14:204
Overloff, J. 14:258
Overly, H. 9:227
Overly, Wilfred 11:162
Overman, C. J. 8:92
Overman, Daniel 22:47
Overman, Elijah 11:320
Overman, Frank 18:36
Overman, Henry 20:19
Overman, Hugh 18:248;
 26:51
Overman, Jeremiah W.
 20:321
Overman, John 9:231;
 20:321; 23:302
Overman, John W. 22:435
Overman, Levi 8:92
Overman, Uriah 10:72;
 20:322
Overman, W. A. 17:40
Overman, W. R. 7:105
Overmeyer, T. J. 27:93
Overmohle, Jasper 11:96
Overmyer, John R. 21:77
Overmyer, Philip 7:37
Overmyre, F. J. 3:149
Overny, --- 19:28
Overpaugh, James 10:20
Oversbe, A. 18:55
Oversbine, William
 22:455
Oversheet, R. A. 10:72
Overson, Linzey 22:94
Overson, T. 1:160
Oversteret, T. D. 25:302
Overstrant, J. J. 11:281
Overstreat, R. O. 20:322
Overstreet, Alfred 22:314
Overstreet, Fayette 19:319
Overstreet, Henry 21:280
Overstreet, J. 25:215
Overstreet, James 20:140
Overstreet, Thomas J.
 21:231
Overstreet, William
 22:127

Overstreet, William C. 17:72
Overstrut, Isaac 18:91
Overthur, William 14:204
Overton, Alfred 22:263
Overton, David 9:98
Overton, George 7:81; 18:209; 25:302
Overton, George W. 11:193
Overton, Granville 8:92
Overton, J. 5:56; 25:215
Overton, J. S. 3:149
Overton, Jeremiah 24:43
Overton, John W. 21:57
Overton, Joseph 17:47
Overton, Lewis 8:92
Overton, Percer 22:127
Overton, Reuben E. 11:71
Overton, Richard 10:174; 19:185
Overton, Squire 20:187
Overton, Stephen 9:98
Overton, Thomas 6:27; 11:210
Overton, William 23:242
Overwell, G. H. 3:149
Overy, J. H. 21:125
Oviatt, David W. 24:179
Oviatt, Samuel J. 24:82
Owan, Christian 27:94
Owanze, M. Ayres 14:204
Owen, A. 3:149; 7:52; 21:190; 23:44
Owen, A. S. 14:96
Owen, Alex 11:220
Owen, Allen 8:41; 26:175
Owen, Andrew 8:66
Owen, Benjamin 9:38; 18:295; 26:108
Owen, Charles 9:27; 14:96; 18:313; 26:108
Owen, Charles M. 24:96
Owen, Charles R. 9:123; 27:92
Owen, Daniel 8:53
Owen, Edward 22:13, 342
Owen, Eli J. 11:162
Owen, Elijah G. 20:184
Owen, Evan T. 16:49
Owen, F. J. 26:175
Owen, Fallen 23:286
Owen, Felix 22:515
Owen, Francis 20:86
Owen, Francis M. 10:130; 20:322
Owen, Frank F. 8:27
Owen, G. H. 3:149
Owen, George 17:136; 24:200

Owen, H. C. 23:44
Owen, Henry C. 21:206
Owen, Henry O. 21:291
Owen, I. 18:178
Owen, Ira 8:92
Owen, Isaiah 21:150
Owen, J. 10:180
Owen, J. A. 18:36
Owen, J. M. 1:160
Owen, James 20:11
Owen, James F. 18:153
Owen, Jeremiah 4:45
Owen, John 9:57
Owen, John B. 16:152
Owen, John F. 7:106; 21:373
Owen, John H. 22:466
Owen, John J. 20:322
Owen, John W. 10:72; 20:322
Owen, Kiah 20:134
Owen, L. Loudaman 17:321
Owen, Mark C. 17:361
Owen, Martin H. 1:61
Owen, Moses 8:53
Owen, Napoleon 20:35
Owen, Peter E. 23:193
Owen, Richard 25:216
Owen, Richard C. 24:43
Owen, Robert C. 22:47
Owen, Robert S. 17:56
Owen, Rodman 12:34
Owen, S. G. 12:156
Owen, T. 14:96
Owen, T. J. 8:27; 18:153
Owen, Thomas S. 7:52
Owen, W. C. 22:354
Owen, W. E. 14:301; 17:481; 27:93
Owen, W. H. H. 9:44
Owen, Warren 15:219
Owen, Warren M. 12:35
Owen, William 3:149; 17:361
Owen, William H. 16:49
Owen, William L. 10:72; 20:322
Owen, William P. 9:38
Owen, Winchester D. 23:286
Owendorf, Richard 24:201
Owens, --- 12:168; 16:217
Owens, A. 16:281
Owens, A. P. 16:49
Owens, B. Nathaniel 15:110
Owens, B. R. 1:160
Owens, Benjamin 11:425; 22:314

Owens, C. 3:149; 16:376
Owens, C. J. 23:314
Owens, Charles 12:34
Owens, Clark 22:314
Owens, D. C. 10:96
Owens, D. D. 15:349; 16:376
Owens, Daniel J. 19:28
Owens, E. 3:149; 13:40; 20:322
Owens, Edward 1:62; 3:149
Owens, Edward C. 24:82
Owens, Edward W. 9:98; 13:40
Owens, Elias 18:209
Owens, Francis 21:141
Owens, G. H. 1:99
Owens, George 7:16; 9:134; 11:390; 23:75; 24:201; 27:93
Owens, George W. 21:103
Owens, Gilford 10:130; 20:322
Owens, Henry 18:248; 26:51
Owens, Israel 27:147
Owens, J. 14:258
Owens, J. F. 14:96
Owens, J. H. 15:153
Owens, Jacob 22:95
Owens, James 5:25; 7:60, 71; 12:35; 20:322
Owens, James E. 24:69
Owens, James O. 24:201
Owens, Jeremiah 17:420
Owens, John 8:92; 12:168; 13:40; 16:134; 17:24; 20:127, 399; 21:95, 373; 22:263, 435
Owens, John J. 10:130
Owens, John T. 21:11
Owens, John W. 17:111
Owens, Joseph 9:27; 17:24
Owens, L. B. 8:53
Owens, Lewis 9:134; 21:280; 27:93
Owens, Louis E. 21:141
Owens, Mary 20:155
Owens, Mathew 8:92
Owens, N. 15:344
Owens, Nelson 9:157, 204
Owens, O. H. 3:149
Owens, Obadiah 11:40
Owens, Orinsteel 22:314
Owens, Owen 10:165; 18:248; 19:185; 26:51
Owens, P. 16:100; 21:373

P

Owens, P. V. 11:310
Owens, Peter R. 20:103
Owens, R. 17:143
Owens, Randolph 7:106
Owens, Richard 11:210;
    22:521
Owens, Robert 20:181;
    22:212
Owens, Samuel 10:165;
    18:16, 36; 19:185
Owens, T. 14:289; 23:13
Owens, T. W. 9:231
Owens, Thomas 4:45;
    14:266; 17:136;
    24:200
Owens, Thomas R. 22:487
Owens, W. 3:149; 16:376;
    22:13
Owens, W. M. 10:29
Owens, W. W. 17:164
Owens, William 8:108;
    9:165; 11:247; 17:40,
    136; 20:322; 21:190;
    22:127; 24:201
Owens, William H. 20:19
Owens, William N.
    19:305
Owens, William R. 20:104
Owens, Williams 21:205;
    23:314
Ower, D. 21:36
Ower, E. 11:247
Owery, Henry 16:49
Owingo, Jackson 24:201
Owings, Jackson 17:136
Owins, D. 23:268
Owlett, A. 17:184
Owlson, --- 24:88
Owria, J. 21:111
Owry, Henry 13:40
Owsley, James 17:283
Owsley, Thomas 17:182
Owyer, T. 18:16
Oxendine, J. P. 11:331
Oxendine, Wilson 20:322
Oxenfals, William 14:335
Oxenrider, Elias 24:54
Oxford, --- 16:123
Oxford, Elias 1:61
Oxford, William J. 22:342
Oxindine, Wilson 10:72
Oxley, Eli H. 21:103
Oxley, Jeremiah 24:83
Oxley, Robert 3:149
Oyan, Charles 18:153
Oyer, A. S. 1:160
Oyler, John S. 7:37
Oystem, Edward 4:45
Oziah, George W. 17:232

P---, --- 11:247; 24:69
P---, A. 17:217; 19:305
P---, A. W. 21:209
P---, B. B. 11:247
P---, C. 17:217; 18:374;
    23:266
P---, Charles 25:216
P---, Chimens 22:354
P---, D. 20:322
P---, D. R. 20:59
P---, D. S. 17:356
P---, E. A. M. 25:61
P---, E. F. 20:92
P---, E. H. 25:60
P---, E. P. 11:232
P---, F. 26:177
P---, F. D. 18:178
P---, F. F. 20:59
P---, G. R. 11:248
P---, G. W. 8:54; 20:155
P---, George 18:36
P---, H. 11:333; 13:67;
    18:249; 26:55
P---, H. C. 25:60
P---, H. M. 19:188
P---, H. P. 11:120
P---, H. W. 17:218
P---, I. 17:297; 18:178
P---, I. A. 11:247
P---, J. 9:215; 17:365;
    24:113; 25:60; 27:99
P---, J. A. 12:100
P---, J. C. 11:438
P---, J. D. 20:322
P---, J. F. 16:302
P---, J. J. 12:148
P---, J. M. 15:160
P---, J. N. 9:228; 18:374;
    21:209
P---, J. S. 11:341; 22:263
P---, J. T. 11:341
P---, J. W. 17:217; 24:113
P---, James 25:216
P---, John 15:18
P---, K. H. 16:100
P---, L. 11:220; 20:322;
    23:204
P---, L. E. 21:36
P---, Ler-- A. 25:60
P---, M. E. 26:177
P---, P. S. 11:116
P---, Peter 8:54
P---, R. 18:178, 249;
    26:55; 27:99
P---, R. T. 24:113
P---, R. W. 19:305
P---, S. 15:153; 17:218;
    21:167

P---, Samuel 13:67
P---, St--- Fran-- 25:61
P---, T. L. 20:59
P---, Thomas 23:198
P---, W. 11:247; 17:217;
    18:374; 21:167, 209;
    23:75
P---, W. H. 20:59
P---, W. K. 25:61
P---, W. S. 16:218; 22:354
P---er, W. S. 17:283
P---g, Jacob 15:221
Pabi, Joseph 23:44
Pabor, W. E. 15:160
Pabst, Charles 10:72;
    20:322
Pacay, John 14:96
Pace, A. J. 21:13
Pace, Alisha C. 20:322
Pace, Calvin A. 16:218
Pace, Elisha 10:72
Pace, J. 3:149
Pace, J. F. 3:149
Pace, Joseph C. 12:162
Pace, Samuel 16:218
Pace, Simon P. 26:127
Pace, T. 22:212
Pace, William 8:53
Pace, William H. 21:77
Pacey, James 22:488
Pacey, William 10:72;
    20:322
Pachon, Francis 7:106
Pack, Eli 19:48
Pack, J. G. 13:96
Pack, Jerry 22:263
Pack, John R. 21:373
Pack, William 23:101
Packard, A. H. 1:160
Packard, Abel F. 10:21
Packard, Alex 27:97
Packard, Belton 9:88;
    26:54
Packard, C. H. 8:27
Packard, Charles E. 10:72;
    20:322
Packard, Charles F.
    21:373
Packard, Dwight 20:127
Packard, E. 1:161
Packard, Frederick M.
    18:313; 26:109
Packard, George 14:96
Packard, George R. 13:40
Packard, Hart H. 12:83;
    16:302
Packard, Hiram 14:328
Packard, Homer D.
    11:164
Packard, Horace 10:165

Packard, Horace C. 19:185
Packard, Ira 27:99
Packard, Isaac 10:72; 20:322
Packard, Isaiah 9:161
Packard, J. B. 21:373
Packard, J. W. 13:67
Packard, J. Wesley 16:218
Packard, Jacob 20:152
Packard, Leverene 20:99
Packard, Lucian N. 7:37
Packard, Luther 19:185
Packard, Lyman 14:204
Packard, M. 1:162; 3:149
Packard, M. G. 3:149
Packard, M. M. 3:149
Packard, Makinza 9:107
Packard, Marcus 7:37
Packard, N. F. 1:163
Packard, Noah F. 22:95
Packard, O. 1:162
Packard, P. 12:96
Packard, Philip 19:29
Packard, T. E. 22:283
Packard, W. W. 9:188
Packart, W. W. 19:241
Packer, C. E. 19:241
Packer, Charles W. 18:313
Packer, Daniel 22:95
Packer, George 17:84
Packer, Henry 14:204
Packer, John 22:436
Packer, John W. 11:110
Packer, Nate 21:280
Packer, P. 23:161
Packer, Perry G. 19:331
Packer, S. B. 3:149
Packer, States 14:204
Packerd, M. 9:123
Packerson, Lenoir D. 11:110
Packery, L. 26:176
Packett, C. 3:149
Packett, T. C. 3:149
Packham, J. S. 9:188; 19:241
Packingham, S. 14:96
Packoard, C. 14:96
Packson, Harvey 7:37
Packwood, William 10:72; 20:322
Pacy, James 18:313; 26:109
Pacy, Thomas 18:55
Padams, James P. 9:123
Padden, John 21:280
Paddin, Aaron 17:182
Paddleford, C. 1:164
Paddleford, F. 1:162

Paddleford, Samuel S. 20:115
Paddock, Alex 17:317
Paddock, D. S. 1:160
Paddock, D. W. 3:149
Paddock, E. R. 13:40
Paddock, Ebenezer 18:209
Paddock, George 20:190
Paddock, H. 25:61
Paddock, Harry 5:43
Paddock, J. 1:161
Paddock, Jefferson 21:217
Paddock, Levi 7:16
Paddock, Richard 5:25; 25:216
Paddock, S. 21:36
Paddock, Theodore A. 4:45
Paddock, William 1:63; 7:131
Paddon, Henry 22:521
Paddy, Isaac M. 9:227; 18:373
Paden, Cyrus 8:66
Paden, Francis H. 21:11
Paden, Thomas W. 15:219
Paden, W. 1:161
Paden, William 7:131
Padfrey, Sylvester 3:149
Padget, Henry 11:72
Padget, Jacob M. 17:350
Padget, John N. 22:263
Padget, Palace 22:314
Padget, Theophilus 17:56
Padget, William 11:41
Padgett, Caleb H. 22:435
Padgett, G. W. 19:268
Padgett, H. W. 9:188
Padgett, John W. 22:263
Padgett, Robert W. 17:350
Padgett, Thomas 16:148
Padgett, William 22:95
Padgham, R. 15:313
Padgit, Benedict A. 8:92
Padon, C. 3:149
Padon, John 21:280
Pafelin, Fred 16:49
Paff, B. 11:391
Paff, Charles 14:316
Paffenberger, Joseph 8:92
Paffitt, Benjamin 9:223
Pagatt, Robert 22:314
Page, A. 16:218
Page, A. A. 21:36
Page, A. G. 12:75; 15:84
Page, A. L. 10:21
Page, A. O. 13:67
Page, Abrm 11:220
Page, Adolph 13:67; 19:91
Page, Albert 15:219

Page, Albert B. 7:106
Page, Albion O. 16:218
Page, Alva B. 24:96
Page, Amb 1:64
Page, B. M. 1:160
Page, Billy 21:373
Page, Brandon 11:281
Page, C. 11:231; 21:373
Page, C. M. 25:280
Page, Camp S. 18:464
Page, Charles 5:25; 19:185; 20:25; 25:216
Page, Charles E. 21:373
Page, Charles H. 23:103
Page, Charles W. 21:373
Page, Columbia 9:159
Page, D. 14:96
Page, David 11:72; 13:40; 17:136; 19:29; 24:201
Page, David H. 21:373
Page, E. 3:149; 7:106
Page, E. D. 9:227; 18:373
Page, E. V. 7:106
Page, Edward 19:323
Page, Erastus W. 23:109
Page, Eugene 21:103
Page, F. F. 21:89
Page, G. 16:218
Page, G. S. 12:163
Page, G. W. 14:18
Page, George 14:204
Page, George A. 9:88; 26:53
Page, George W. 21:373, 374
Page, H. T. 15:84
Page, Harrison 20:115
Page, Henry L. 12:35
Page, Ira E. 12:75; 15:26
Page, Isaac 14:204; 25:216
Page, J. 3:149; 12:162
Page, J. A. W. 18:409
Page, J. C. 8:53
Page, J. E. 3:149; 15:219
Page, J. G. 2:16; 25:61
Page, J. J. 20:156
Page, J. R. 24:26
Page, J. W. 13:96
Page, James 4:45; 8:101; 17:463; 23:286; 24:179
Page, James H. 11:41
Page, James L. 12:75
Page, Jesse F. 10:72; 20:322
Page, John 6:26; 9:88; 11:211; 21:89; 22:152; 26:52

Page, John B. 23:75
Page, John H. 8:27; 18:153
Page, John Q. 18:399
Page, Joseph 22:342
Page, L. 1:64; 3:149
Page, Laurence 10:72
Page, Lawrence 20:322
Page, Levi 25:216
Page, Lewis 4:45; 9:223; 18:373
Page, Luther 10:174; 19:185
Page, Marion 10:72; 20:322
Page, N. F. 11:341
Page, Nelson 21:374
Page, Nicholas 23:277
Page, O. D. 3:149
Page, Orrin F. 21:77
Page, Orwin 20:184
Page, Pony 8:27; 18:153
Page, Samuel 17:182; 27:99
Page, Stephen 25:216
Page, T. 23:44; 27:94
Page, Theodore 16:49
Page, Thomas D. 11:72
Page, Thomas L. 13:40
Page, Tunis 4:45
Page, W. 5:53; 17:149
Page, W. B. 11:288
Page, W. H. H. 15:42
Page, W. S. 1:162
Page, Walter 22:314
Page, Warner 21:141
Page, Wash 17:182
Page, Wesley S. 21:37
Page, William 3:149; 9:134; 11:391; 23:277; 25:216; 27:97
Page, William H. H. 12:75
Page, William S. 12:75
Pagefall, Max 15:42
Pagely, Lewis 22:47
Pagendkopf, H. 7:37
Pages, James 9:188
Pages, Moses P. 16:49
Paget, John 21:196
Pagett, Mead R. 21:259
Pagnard, Luther 10:130; 20:322
Pagnett, Joseph 15:279
Pagnett, Joseph M. 22:342
Pagon, J. C. 9:123
Pahel, A. 1:163
Pahlman, H. C. 12:87
Pahud, E. 11:41
Pai---, S. F. 20:59
Paige, Charles L. 23:44

Paige, F. S. 25:216
Paige, James 15:42
Paigs, Michael 8:27
Pailor, John 8:101
Pailsipher, N. 18:399
Pain, Adam 9:188
Pain, Alden 19:289
Pain, C. 8:27
Pain, J. H. 26:53
Pain, Malos 9:210
Pain, Michael 25:216
Pain, Ransour 11:288
Pain, Robert 8:27
Pain, Thomas 21:374
Pain, William 23:161
Painard, John 26:127
Paince, John M. 9:123
Paine, --- 18:355
Paine, A. B. 18:36
Paine, A. J. 1:62
Paine, Aaron 21:212
Paine, Alfred 11:211
Paine, Alvin E. 11:163
Paine, Ambrose 16:100
Paine, C. W. 8:115
Paine, Charles 21:212; 25:216
Paine, Chauncey B. 22:152
Paine, D. 22:354
Paine, Daniel 9:134; 27:96
Paine, E. 10:152
Paine, E. A. 8:27; 18:153
Paine, E. A. J. 1:95
Paine, Ebenezer 13:40
Paine, Francis 18:399
Paine, G. H. 12:9
Paine, George 14:335
Paine, H. H. 9:188; 19:229
Paine, Horace 7:131
Paine, I. R. 18:178
Paine, J. H. 9:88
Paine, J. R. 10:180
Paine, Jacob R. 10:130; 20:322
Paine, James E. 13:116
Paine, James F. 13:40
Paine, John 9:44; 25:216; 26:128
Paine, L. E. 1:162; 9:163
Paine, L. T. 26:176
Paine, M. 3:149
Paine, Oloff D. 9:98
Paine, Robert 11:429
Paine, Rufus 24:179
Paine, S. 3:149; 25:216
Paine, Samuel 8:74; 26:176
Paine, Steward 25:216

Paine, Sumner 16:86
Paine, T. 14:96
Paine, Taylor 7:106
Paine, Uriah 17:274
Paine, W. A. 19:326
Paine, William 7:131; 11:101, 129; 14:329; 21:374; 22:212
Paine, William H. 17:97; 25:216
Pains, Richard 20:322
Painsett, Lacey 12:75
Painster, John 23:104
Painter, --- 23:200
Painter, A. 9:27; 18:321
Painter, Ash 1:64
Painter, C. 3:149
Painter, Christopher C. 23:75
Painter, Daniel 17:216
Painter, F. 8:74
Painter, George 24:99
Painter, H. 3:149
Painter, H. C. 11:73
Painter, J. 23:161
Painter, J. G. 3:149
Painter, Jacob 20:322; 22:505
Painter, James 9:201; 19:283; 22:487
Painter, John 22:314
Painter, Michael 25:62
Painter, N. 22:212
Painter, S. 3:149
Painter, Samuel H. 14:204
Painter, Suel 18:295
Painter, Thomas D. 15:286; 19:91
Painter, W. M. C. 20:322
Painter, W. P. 3:149
Painter, William 11:110; 15:331; 24:43
Pair, Benjamin 21:280
Paishalls, George E. 22:236
Paisley, A. G. 3:149
Paisley, Charles 17:192
Paisley, F. 3:149
Paisley, James E. 9:123; 27:97
Paisley, John 8:27; 18:153
Paisley, W. 3:149
Pait, Stephen 17:319
Pake, James B. 9:88
Pakham, J. C. 3:149
Palby, John 10:21
Palden, Adam R. 10:174; 19:185
Paleman, H. 16:270
Palen, George 23:305
Palerm, G. 18:36

Pales, A. 15:42
Palfreeman, Edward 11:311
Palfrey, --- 21:374
Palfrey, F. O. 1:64
Palgas, Charles 8:27
Palgers, Charles 18:153
Palimtorey, William H. 15:331
Palimtory, W. H. 19:91
Palinn, Henry 27:99
Pall, A. M. 11:311
Pall, I. 11:211
Pall, James 25:216
Pall, W. 14:204
Pallack, Samuel 23:241
Palladay, Andrew 9:16
Pallen, Charles 21:247
Pallesson, Clark 15:174
Pallett, Edward 8:92
Pallett, Henry 18:70
Pallett, Theodore 20:138
Pallette, D. 3:149
Pallrix, W. 18:193
Pally, John 19:29
Pally, S. C. 3:149
Palm, David 11:403; 22:48
Palm, Joseph 8:66
Palm, W. H. 7:106; 21:374
Palmaseer, A. 14:204
Palmateer, George R. 10:21
Palmateer, J. 25:216
Palmater, A. 19:91
Palmater, H. 15:351
Palmater, John A. 21:77
Palmater, P. 25:216
Palmathier, O. 19:258
Palmatier, Abraham 1:63
Palmatier, Oliver 9:188
Palmatier, William 23:109
Palmer, A. 3:149; 11:288; 23:118
Palmer, A. A. 26:54
Palmer, A. M. 19:185
Palmer, A. W. 9:188; 11:129
Palmer, Alanson 22:212
Palmer, Albert 26:176
Palmer, Alexander 22:95
Palmer, Alonzo B. 9:27
Palmer, Alphonzo 21:231; 24:71
Palmer, Andrew 17:395; 24:96
Palmer, Andrew B. 11:163
Palmer, Anson 12:35
Palmer, Arthur D. 11:164

Palmer, Asa 14:204
Palmer, Benjamin 22:95; 26:128
Palmer, C. B. 21:374
Palmer, C. F. 1:160
Palmer, Charles 4:45; 13:40; 14:204; 16:376; 17:24; 18:285; 25:216; 26:135
Palmer, Charles G. 10:146
Palmer, Charles H. 16:302
Palmer, Charles S. 17:100
Palmer, Charles W. 7:106
Palmer, Christopher 22:152
Palmer, D. 1:65; 3:150; 5:53; 25:216
Palmer, D. H. 1:65
Palmer, D. M. 1:62
Palmer, D. P. 3:150
Palmer, D. W. 22:342
Palmer, Daniel 16:134; 17:321
Palmer, David 9:188; 19:258
Palmer, David C. 19:29
Palmer, David D. 21:77
Palmer, Davis W. 8:115
Palmer, E. 1:99, 162; 3:150; 19:279; 25:216, 302; 26:237
Palmer, E. G. 2:16
Palmer, E. J. 9:188; 19:233
Palmer, E. S. 25:62
Palmer, Edward 18:104
Palmer, Edwin 5:25
Palmer, Elias 10:72
Palmer, Elijah 15:110
Palmer, Elisha 20:322
Palmer, English 10:130
Palmer, Esil 4:45
Palmer, F. 14:204
Palmer, F. G. 3:150
Palmer, F. M. 22:212
Palmer, Frank 22:113
Palmer, Frederick R. 23:241
Palmer, G. B. 1:65
Palmer, G. S. 1:65
Palmer, George 4:67; 7:131; 11:247; 15:23; 19:185
Palmer, George C. 21:374
Palmer, George H. 22:152
Palmer, George L. 18:279
Palmer, George W. 12:35; 22:521
Palmer, Granville C. 21:259

Palmer, H. 17:435; 24:179
Palmer, H. J. 15:219
Palmer, H. W. 9:88
Palmer, Harris J. 11:162
Palmer, Henri 12:93; 16:302
Palmer, Henry B. 10:130; 20:190, 322
Palmer, Henry M. 4:45
Palmer, Henry W. 12:51
Palmer, Hiram 14:316; 17:274
Palmer, Horatio R. 24:96
Palmer, Isaac 10:130; 20:322
Palmer, J. 3:150; 21:190
Palmer, J. B. 11:193
Palmer, J. C. 7:131; 20:323
Palmer, J. D. 1:65
Palmer, J. G. 10:72
Palmer, J. H. 25:216
Palmer, J. O. J. 3:150
Palmer, J. R. 8:53
Palmer, J. W. 9:188; 19:258
Palmer, Jackson 22:524
Palmer, Jacob 22:488
Palmer, James 11:72; 13:40; 15:219; 17:274
Palmer, James D. 20:42
Palmer, James M. 21:103
Palmer, James R. 10:72; 20:323
Palmer, James W. 10:25
Palmer, Jared C. 20:323
Palmer, Jason 21:141
Palmer, Jefferson 7:131
Palmer, John 4:45; 10:72; 17:433; 24:161
Palmer, John H. 5:25
Palmer, John L. 15:23
Palmer, John N. 22:95
Palmer, Joseph 8:53; 21:231
Palmer, Josiah 22:95
Palmer, L. B. 1:161
Palmer, L. H. 3:150
Palmer, L. M. 13:116
Palmer, Leonard 21:374
Palmer, Levi O. 7:131
Palmer, Lory 7:37
Palmer, Luman 23:267
Palmer, M. 1:163; 7:106; 16:49; 20:35
Palmer, M. A. 1:99
Palmer, M. H. 18:399
Palmer, Mason 16:141
Palmer, Mendelburt 13:40

Palmer, Milton 17:136; 23:280; 24:201
Palmer, Milton B. 18:91
Palmer, Morgan 18:70
Palmer, Moses 25:216
Palmer, Myrack 21:374
Palmer, N. W. 19:245
Palmer, Nathaniel 12:35
Palmer, Nicholas 23:124
Palmer, Oliver 8:115; 10:21; 13:40; 18:295
Palmer, Orien 9:38; 26:109
Palmer, Orville 11:164
Palmer, P. 3:150
Palmer, P. H. 3:150
Palmer, Perry M. 22:436
Palmer, R. 11:162
Palmer, R. F. 9:148; 27:98
Palmer, R. J. 21:125
Palmer, Richard 9:201
Palmer, Robert A. 14:204
Palmer, Robert P. 21:57
Palmer, Rufus 17:136; 24:201
Palmer, S. 3:150
Palmer, S. E. 8:108
Palmer, S. S. 20:33; 22:212
Palmer, Samuel 8:41; 17:136; 24:201
Palmer, Smith 21:374
Palmer, Stephen H. 16:80
Palmer, Stephen W. 8:92
Palmer, T. 3:150
Palmer, T. B. 1:160
Palmer, Theodore 22:212
Palmer, Thomas 12:75; 15:18
Palmer, Thomas J. 7:106
Palmer, Thomas P. W. 13:40
Palmer, Thomas R. 11:72
Palmer, Titus 21:280
Palmer, Uriah 16:143
Palmer, W. 3:150; 17:499; 19:258
Palmer, W. E. 3:150
Palmer, W. H. 26:52
Palmer, W. H. H. 27:97
Palmer, W. L. 22:488
Palmer, Walter C. 20:190
Palmer, William 1:64; 9:188; 10:72; 20:323; 21:374; 24:69; 27:95
Palmer, William A. 21:15
Palmer, William C. 10:174; 19:185
Palmer, William F. 10:153

Palmer, William H. 4:45; 7:138; 10:145; 19:185; 25:216
Palmer, William H. H. 9:123
Palmer, William K. 26:53
Palmer, William N. 17:84
Palmer, William S. 8:27; 18:153
Palmer, Willis 11:288
Palmerlee, Stephen 11:117
Palmerly, J. 3:150
Palmerson, J. B. 13:40
Palmerston, Charles 15:348
Palmerton, B. 25:280
Palmerton, James L. 13:116
Palmerton, William S. 15:58
Palmeter, Allen 13:40; 16:49
Palmeter, H. 16:376
Palmiter, J. W. 1:161
Palmiter, Jason L. 7:37
Palmiter, R. 3:150
Palmry, George 1:65
Palsey, J. Perry 12:156
Palsey, N. H. 8:74
Palsey, P. 16:376
Palsgrove, G. W. 15:131
Palsgrove, H. E. 20:104
Palsgrove, S. D. 1:95
Palsgrove, William H. 10:97
Palston, A. 11:310
Palston, D. 16:218
Palten, Alfred 22:515
Paltmore, James 18:153
Paltz, Abraham 9:104
Palver, Henry C. 21:37
Pamann, James C. 17:416
Pammer, Thomas 14:244
Pampe, Charles 25:325
Pamperin, William 3:150
Pamphrey, Alfred 10:130
Pamphrey, Edward 20:323
Pamps, Leonard 21:103
Pams, W. 14:96
Pamter, Jacob 10:130
Pan, W. 21:111
Panborn, Charles 14:205
Pancake, A. J. 21:125
Pancake, Joseph C. 17:347
Panche, Sinclair 18:70
Pancoast, Franklin 11:443
Pandle, F. A. 10:149
Pane, J. 11:247
Panea, Bascom 19:241

Panes, Henry 27:98
Panevell, W. H. 15:219
Paney, John W. 22:212
Pangborn, Cyrus 10:130; 20:323
Pangborn, Hewlet C. 21:77
Pangborn, J. F. 7:37
Pangborn, James 25:216
Pangburn, Charles 26:128
Pangburn, James H. 1:62
Pangcorn, A. L. 25:216
Panic, Henry 19:185
Panice, T. 25:216
Paniel, J. W. 21:190
Panier, J. M. 3:150
Paniton, Thomas E. 11:71
Pankey, A. J. 3:150
Pankey, F. M. 14:316
Pankour, Frederick 11:193
Pankow, L. 12:164
Panley, Ira 10:72
Panley, John S. 24:167
Panmore, J. 7:37
Pannan, L. 3:150
Pannel, Charles 12:167
Pannell, Frank 4:67
Pannell, William 22:263
Pannier, Fred 11:163
Panning, C. 8:74; 26:177
Panolt, Otto 10:149
Panquette, L. 14:244
Panstle, Austin 13:67
Pant, Colley 9:88
Pant, F. 14:96
Panter, R. 3:150
Panter, Samuel 23:115
Panter, W. M. C. 10:72
Panters, J. B. 11:310
Panthurst, M. 11:311
Panties, A. F. 3:150
Pantlow, David S. 24:63
Panton, --- 26:224
Panton, Alice C. 26:224
Panza, Richard 18:91
Pape, James H. 27:99
Pape, Solomon 22:314
Papelle, J. L. 21:57
Papford, Jesse 8:99
Papieman, Joseph 11:415
Papin, E. 11:288
Papler, Green 16:218
Pappert, Nicholas 11:116
Pappino, Franklin G. 5:25
Papple, D. 3:150
Papps, Aug 15:219
Paquet, Nicholas 16:100
Paquett, Joseph 25:216
Paquiner, Tripley 7:52
Parack, William 8:27
Paradan, Michael 11:120

Paradice, J. 14:278
Paradise, A. 23:109
Parbs, Carl 23:193
Parce, Lucien 21:141
Parceley, William K. 20:11
Parcell, A. E. 11:73
Parcell, J. J. 25:216
Parcher, E. P. 11:292
Parchman, Albert 8:41; 26:175
Parchman, Gilbert 21:280
Parcker, --- 25:60
Pardee, Edmund W. 22:466
Pardee, George M. 24:62
Pardee, Mahlon J. 16:100
Pardee, Marcus 15:92
Pardee, Milton S. 4:45
Pardee, O. 9:148
Parden, E. H. 3:150
Parder, George A. 22:409
Parder, John A. 22:409
Parder, Leonard 17:263
Pardier, Wasaledo 10:206
Pardoe, R. J. 15:72
Pardue, Noah 27:97
Pardue, O. 27:96
Pardue, William H. 21:231
Pardum, Leander 22:95
Pardy, E. 3:150
Pare, David J. 20:36
Pare, John 9:201
Pare, Redin D. 22:95
Pare, Robert J. 22:127
Paregen, A. C. 17:336
Parent, --- 18:36
Parent, Peter 21:374
Parent, Samuel 25:288
Parent, Stewart 16:113
Parey, W. 3:150
Parfit, Isaac 9:123
Pargess, James 19:258
Parham, Albert 21:280
Parham, Baker 22:264
Parham, L. H. 7:37
Parham, Rufus 22:264
Parham, T. B. 25:302
Parhosa, --- 10:206
Parich, J. 11:439
Parides, L. 3:150
Parie, Edmond A. 10:165
Paris, Alfred 18:373
Paris, F. 3:150
Paris, G. W. 10:72
Paris, George S. 10:72; 20:323
Paris, J. 1:160
Paris, James S. 23:44
Paris, John S. W. 22:127

Paris, N. 24:113
Paris, S. 3:150
Paris, Thomas M. 22:436
Parish, Anderson 7:131
Parish, Ant 1:64
Parish, C. 3:150
Parish, C. E. 27:95
Parish, C. M. 11:438
Parish, David S. 8:92
Parish, E. 1:162
Parish, Elijah 26:177
Parish, George 11:162
Parish, George P. 4:45
Parish, Henry 18:36, 248; 26:53
Parish, J. 20:179
Parish, J. A. 3:150
Parish, J. M. 16:49
Parish, J. N. 11:96
Parish, James 7:131; 10:209; 18:407; 19:29; 27:99
Parish, Jonathan 11:41
Parish, Joseph 8:53
Parish, Lewis 11:193
Parish, Madison 22:515
Parish, Orin 24:179
Parish, Owen 22:152
Parish, R. B. 25:216
Parish, Rufus F. 14:205
Parish, Thomas M. 11:96
Parish, Thomas P. 23:75
Parish, Walter 22:152
Parish, William 17:40
Parish, William C. 15:5
Parish, William O. 23:277
Parish, William T. 18:153; 22:264
Parist, H. C. 22:515
Pariun, A. 18:178
Park, A. 15:219
Park, A. F. 23:193
Park, A. J. 11:415
Park, A. S. 12:35
Park, Alfred 24:54
Park, B. B. 11:403
Park, Charles 18:153
Park, D. 13:96; 14:18
Park, David 10:72; 20:323
Park, Edward A. 4:45
Park, Henry M. 5:26
Park, Isaac N. 23:280
Park, J. 3:150; 15:160; 21:37
Park, J. M. 14:205
Park, J. V. 11:248
Park, James 1:62; 7:37
Park, Jerry 20:323
Park, John 7:37; 9:123; 11:72; 25:216
Park, John D. 5:44

Park, Joseph 22:212
Park, L. 16:218; 25:217
Park, L. A. 15:219
Park, L. H. 14:96
Park, L. R. 11:310
Park, Leander 18:399
Park, Nicholas 16:49
Park, Peter 14:205
Park, R. J. 8:53
Park, R. S. 23:44
Park, Robert F. 22:488
Park, Roderick J. 21:141
Park, Ruel 24:69
Park, Thomas 25:217
Park, Timothy S. 22:127
Park, W. B. 9:189; 19:271
Park, W. C. 13:96
Park, W. D. 18:70
Park, William 16:152; 19:29; 20:323; 25:60
Parkam, E. 16:218
Parkam, Jesse R. 26:175
Parkan, W. 3:150
Parkard, C. H. 18:153
Parke, Aaron G. 20:31
Parke, Franklin 22:488
Parke, George 16:302
Parke, J. 3:150
Parke, Jerry 9:231
Parke, John 27:97
Parke, Stewart 1:64
Parke, Thomas 5:53
Parke, W. J. D. 1:64
Parke, William 9:231
Parkelson, Perry 8:53
Parkenson, George 11:397
Parkenstraus, William 9:27
Parker, --- 10:130; 15:8; 18:248; 19:91; 20:323; 26:55
Parker, A. 1:163; 3:150; 13:103; 14:19; 16:49, 270; 18:91; 22:212; 23:75, 161
Parker, A. G. W. 22:95
Parker, A. M. 1:162
Parker, A. P. 18:55
Parker, A. S. 21:37
Parker, A. T. 9:189
Parker, A. V. 19:233
Parker, Albert 9:162; 27:99
Parker, Albert P. 10:152
Parker, Alex 20:323
Parker, Alexander 10:72; 21:280
Parker, Alfred N. 22:95
Parker, Allan 8:115
Parker, Allen 18:324
Parker, Alvin 22:162

Parker, Amariah 17:420; 24:161
Parker, Amos 21:374
Parker, Andrew 1:64
Parker, Arthur W. 21:374
Parker, Asbury 18:444
Parker, B. C. 3:150
Parker, B. F. 1:163; 11:96
Parker, Bailey 17:338
Parker, Benjamin 19:48
Parker, Benjamin C. 9:188
Parker, Bradley 19:29
Parker, Brooks 22:314
Parker, C. 12:87; 16:302
Parker, C. F. 16:49
Parker, C. H. 9:189; 13:40; 19:241
Parker, C. W. 1:162; 18:16; 23:75
Parker, Caleb 21:374
Parker, Calvin 22:505
Parker, Charles 12:75; 15:27; 24:202
Parker, Charles A. 23:44
Parker, Charles E. 9:188
Parker, Charles H. 9:188
Parker, Charles L. 5:26; 25:217
Parker, Charles S. 17:495
Parker, Charles W. 9:27; 26:109
Parker, Christian 26:138
Parker, Christopher 21:231
Parker, Cornelius W. 9:123
Parker, D. 3:150
Parker, D. M. 25:217
Parker, Danford 16:134
Parker, Daniel 7:131; 24:43
Parker, Daniel C. 10:153
Parker, Daniel E. 23:109
Parker, David 16:218; 21:247, 374
Parker, David M. 5:25
Parker, Dennard 6:26
Parker, Dennis M. 21:374
Parker, Dexter F. 16:8
Parker, E. 3:150; 5:26; 9:189
Parker, E. D. 9:88; 26:52
Parker, E. L. 19:91
Parker, Easone 22:127
Parker, Edgar F. 9:98
Parker, Edward 19:305
Parker, Edward A. 7:37
Parker, Elias 9:88
Parker, Elijah 8:27; 10:180; 18:178
Parker, Elisha 15:131

Parker, Ellis 26:52
Parker, Emer 22:152
Parker, English 18:153
Parker, Enoch T. 21:116, 280
Parker, Erastus 19:185
Parker, F. 1:163; 3:150; 8:66; 26:176
Parker, F. I. 9:189
Parker, F. M. 18:321; 25:217
Parker, Fletcher 20:323
Parker, Francis J. 19:275
Parker, Francis L. 19:29
Parker, Frank 13:96; 19:185
Parker, Frank N. 24:96
Parker, Franklin 4:67
Parker, Fred 25:276
Parker, Fred. W. 19:91
Parker, G. 5:56; 9:148; 25:217; 27:96
Parker, G. A. H. 17:159
Parker, G. E. 7:106
Parker, G. F. 12:35
Parker, G. W. 19:29, 258
Parker, Gale 16:218
Parker, George 5:43; 7:37; 9:134, 240; 10:130; 12:9; 13:40; 16:49, 218; 19:29; 20:323; 25:288, 325; 27:96
Parker, George D. 17:84
Parker, George N. 9:188
Parker, George W. 17:136; 21:77; 22:48; 24:201
Parker, Grant 22:314
Parker, H. 13:40
Parker, H. A. 19:241
Parker, H. H. 9:237; 26:224
Parker, H. J. 11:101
Parker, Harvey 9:210
Parker, Haynes G. 22:152
Parker, Henry 9:134, 210; 16:218; 18:434; 22:162, 283; 27:94
Parker, Henry A. 9:188
Parker, Henry J. 11:277
Parker, Herman R. 22:436
Parker, Hollis M. 12:59
Parker, I. 14:205
Parker, Ira D. 13:40
Parker, Isaac 9:188; 11:329; 19:283; 27:96
Parker, Isaac J. 18:444
Parker, Isaac N. 12:75
Parker, Israel 9:134; 23:198

Parker, J. 1:161, 162; 3:150; 7:37; 12:96; 15:361; 18:36; 19:91; 21:374; 25:217; 26:204
Parker, J. A. 5:26
Parker, J. B. 1:161
Parker, J. E. 9:189; 15:311, 355; 19:91, 271
Parker, J. H. 9:237
Parker, J. K. 1:163; 13:96
Parker, J. M. 3:150
Parker, J. N. 15:58
Parker, J. R. 8:53; 18:55; 21:37; 25:217
Parker, J. T. 21:150
Parker, J. W. 11:310; 15:219
Parker, Jacob 11:268
Parker, James 5:43; 6:28; 9:210; 10:72; 11:311; 12:96; 13:40; 15:361; 16:49; 17:283; 18:70, 421; 19:29, 91; 20:323; 21:89; 25:287; 27:98
Parker, James A. 21:201, 291
Parker, James H. 17:203; 20:99
Parker, James M. 4:45; 12:142
Parker, Jasper 22:515
Parker, Jeremiah 12:172
Parker, Jesse 10:130; 21:374; 22:95
Parker, Jessie 20:323
Parker, John 6:26; 9:13, 210; 10:72; 14:258, 331; 19:268; 20:156, 323; 21:37; 22:212
Parker, John A. 11:403; 15:72; 18:285; 26:135
Parker, John C. 21:374
Parker, John F. 22:264
Parker, John L. 23:241
Parker, John M. 12:75
Parker, John M. W. E. 22:455
Parker, John N. 13:40
Parker, John R. 5:26
Parker, John S. 21:57
Parker, John T. 17:40
Parker, John V. 20:11
Parker, Jonah 7:78; 25:302
Parker, Jose 17:56
Parker, Joseph 8:41; 16:218; 21:103, 281;

Parker, Joseph 23:75, 161; 26:53, 177
Parker, Joshua E. 8:108
Parker, Kno. 8:92
Parker, L. 13:125; 15:344; 16:376; 17:149; 20:323; 21:103; 22:13
Parker, L. C. 14:284
Parker, Leonard 10:72
Parker, Leonard C. 4:45
Parker, Leroy 22:152
Parker, Lewis 4:45, 67; 9:201; 17:261; 21:374; 22:314
Parker, Lit 4:67
Parker, Lorenzo 5:26
Parker, Louis 19:258, 283
Parker, Luther M. 27:99
Parker, M. 1:162; 14:96, 205; 16:218
Parker, Marion 21:374
Parker, Matthew 21:281
Parker, Michael 22:264
Parker, Miron 15:219
Parker, Mitchell 22:95
Parker, Moses 20:11
Parker, Myron 9:188
Parker, N. 1:160
Parker, Nathan 13:40
Parker, Nathan O. 22:95
Parker, Nelson 21:213
Parker, Nether 13:58
Parker, Oliver 10:165
Parker, P. 15:309; 16:218; 18:16
Parker, P. S. 9:189; 19:234
Parker, Paris 9:215; 21:374
Parker, Patrick 11:41
Parker, Philip 22:264
Parker, Prentiss P. 7:106
Parker, R. 13:103; 14:278; 16:218, 270; 17:290; 21:37; 23:44
Parker, R. B. 22:212
Parker, R. F. 27:94
Parker, R. H . 9:223
Parker, R. H. 22:152
Parker, R. Leroy 18:313; 26:109
Parker, Ralph 10:21
Parker, Ralph W. 23:104
Parker, Richard 4:45; 7:131; 9:188; 10:177; 14:205; 19:185, 283; 23:75
Parker, Richard T. 22:264
Parker, Robert 13:58

Parker, S. 1:63, 65; 3:150; 27:94
Parker, S. B. 3:150
Parker, S. E. 21:37
Parker, Samuel 8:53; 11:110; 14:205; 15:320; 19:91
Parker, Samuel A. 20:187
Parker, Samuel H. 20:90
Parker, Samuel M. 17:210
Parker, Scott 8:58
Parker, Simon 7:16
Parker, Stanton 8:53
Parker, Stephen S. 4:45
Parker, Stephen T. 10:130; 20:323
Parker, T. 13:96; 14:19; 19:268; 20:148; 22:342; 25:279
Parker, T. C. 11:333
Parker, T. H. 25:62
Parker, T. M. 23:44
Parker, Thomas 9:188; 10:165; 11:211, 268; 14:96, 301; 17:476; 19:185; 22:515; 23:300; 24:43; 27:100
Parker, Thomas W. 4:45
Parker, Townsend 26:177
Parker, W. 3:150; 11:110; 14:289; 20:323; 23:194
Parker, W. A. 3:150
Parker, W. C. 23:44
Parker, W. E. 3:150
Parker, W. F. 17:323
Parker, W. H. 1:95; 18:399; 27:95
Parker, Warren 1:64; 15:219
Parker, Washington 10:72
Parker, Wilburn 22:264
Parker, Wiley 3:224; 17:505
Parker, William 7:37; 8:66; 9:44, 188, 210; 10:130; 11:211; 12:157, 166; 17:56, 136, 283; 18:70; 19:283; 20:323; 21:281, 374; 22:342, 409, 515; 23:161; 24:201; 25:325; 26:127
Parker, William C. 22:13
Parker, William E. 20:193
Parker, William G. 7:37
Parker, William H. 9:188; 18:248; 19:258; 26:55

Parker, William M. 22:212
Parker, William S. 10:92; 20:323
Parker, William T. 17:203
Parker, William V. 19:258
Parker, Willis 18:248; 26:54
Parker, Z. 3:150
Parkerson, Frank 21:281
Parkerson, J. B. 19:245
Parkerson, Joseph b. 9:189
Parkes, James E. 25:217
Parkes, John F. 10:97
Parkes, Samuel 10:130
Parkes, William 22:152
Parkey, A. 11:281
Parkey, Lewis 9:189
Parkey, Peter 22:127
Parkfield, L. 1:162
Parkham, A. W. 18:248; 26:53
Parkham, E. 9:69
Parkham, William D. 21:259
Parkham, William M. 16:218
Parkhill, James 27:94
Parkhurst, A. H. 21:374
Parkhurst, C. D. 14:205
Parkhurst, Charles A. 25:62
Parkhurst, Charles M. 24:27
Parkhurst, D. 15:219
Parkhurst, D. E. 14:96
Parkhurst, Edward 21:374; 22:409
Parkhurst, Elisha W. 21:77
Parkhurst, Eugene D. C. 27:94
Parkhurst, F. 3:150
Parkhurst, H. 7:37
Parkhurst, Henry V. 11:247
Parkhurst, Hiram 10:165
Parkhurst, Jay J. 20:31
Parkhurst, John S. 10:165
Parkhurst, L. J. 15:160
Parkhurst, S. 20:86
Parkhurst, Samuel 21:374
Parkhurst, Truman 12:35
Parkhurst, W. 21:374
Parkhurst, W. L. 3:150
Parkhurst, Washington 23:75
Parkin, H. 14:205, 258
Parkington, James 21:374
Parkins, Charles 10:72

Parkins, H. W. 16:218
Parkins, J. H. 16:86
Parkins, John R. 17:156
Parkins, Joseph 10:92;
  20:323
Parkins, Ondaniel 19:185
Parkins, Storey 14:205
Parkins, W. P. 11:71
Parkins, William 7:37
Parkinson, A. 3:150
Parkinson, Daniel 10:174
Parkinson, F. B. 18:153
Parkinson, George 14:96
Parkinson, J. 16:218
Parkinson, James 13:40
Parkinson, James H. 12:35
Parkinson, John 23:109
Parkinson, Oliver 22:354
Parkinson, T. B. 8:27
Parkinson, T. H. 20:179
Parkinson, Valentine
  21:37
Parkinson, William
  20:127
Parkis, Francis 9:134;
  27:96
Parkley, James M. 22:409
Parkman, A. L. 9:69
Parkman, August 9:98
Parkman, Thomas 18:248;
  26:54
Parks, --- 10:165; 19:185
Parks, A. J. 24:26
Parks, A. W. 1:163
Parks, Abram 11:211;
  19:292
Parks, Alanson 18:248;
  26:54
Parks, Alfred 9:98
Parks, Benjamin A. 14:1
Parks, Bird 10:99
Parks, Carlos 13:40
Parks, Charles 17:156,
  183; 22:236
Parks, Charles R. 24:54
Parks, D. 8:66; 26:176
Parks, Daniel 17:267
Parks, E. F. 3:150
Parks, Edward 4:45; 12:55
Parks, Edwin 22:436
Parks, F. 3:150
Parks, F. M. 9:27
Parks, Francis M. 22:455
Parks, G. 25:217
Parks, G. F. 1:162
Parks, G. H. 7:52
Parks, George 4:45; 5:44;
  11:247; 22:48
Parks, George E. 18:36
Parks, George W. 10:72;
  20:323

Parks, H. 14:96
Parks, H. H. 6:21
Parks, Henry 16:218
Parks, Henry H. 23:103
Parks, Henry P. 22:409
Parks, Holsey E. 23:161
Parks, Hoyt R. 13:40
Parks, I. 14:205
Parks, Isaac 20:175
Parks, J. 1:162; 9:57;
  16:376; 25:217
Parks, J. D. 25:217
Parks, J. H. 14:96
Parks, J. L. 11:438
Parks, J. W. 3:150
Parks, James 16:123;
  20:87, 190
Parks, James M. 20:323
Parks, Jesse 17:84
Parks, John 8:118; 9:156;
  10:165; 13:58;
  19:185; 21:85, 281;
  23:44
Parks, John B. 23:104
Parks, John E. 18:209
Parks, John S. 10:72;
  20:323
Parks, Joseph 5:43; 12:57
Parks, L. L. 15:263
Parks, Laban 10:72
Parks, Lawrence 23:75
Parks, Levi 23:91
Parks, Logan W. 7:106
Parks, M. 1:163
Parks, M. P. 9:238;
  26:224
Parks, Melvin 17:447;
  24:171
Parks, Moses 8:118
Parks, Orron L. 26:52
Parks, Orson L. 9:88
Parks, Oscar F. 9:210
Parks, P. L. 14:131
Parks, R. 7:37; 11:188
Parks, R. J. 14:205
Parks, R. T. 3:151
Parks, Raisin 8:53
Parks, Robert 9:112
Parks, S. 1:163
Parks, S. B. 11:72
Parks, Sabin 20:323
Parks, Samuel 8:108;
  10:72; 20:323
Parks, Simeon 17:156
Parks, Simpson 20:138
Parks, Solomon F. 11:17
Parks, T. J. 8:53
Parks, Thomas J. 21:77
Parks, V. 3:151
Parks, W. 1:162; 3:151
Parks, W. H. 8:115

Parks, Wesley 22:48
Parks, William 1:63;
  7:106; 14:205;
  17:215; 19:91;
  21:374; 25:61
Parks, William F. 11:163
Parks, William G. 23:44
Parks, William H. 24:26
Parks, William R. 10:130;
  20:323
Parks, William S. 25:62
Parkson, John G. 11:220
Parkson, Melvin 8:92
Parkson, Thomas 8:108
Parl, Edwin 16:145
Parlen, A. 10:187
Parletts, William H.
  21:375
Parley, J. L. 27:100
Parliament, J. 16:113
Parlton, William T.
  22:436
Parly, E. 25:60
Parm, Abram 4:67
Parm, James 22:314
Parmahip, William 7:37
Parmalee, W. N. 15:355
Parmalee, Watson 4:45
Parman, J. W. 10:97
Parman, William 9:27
Parmateer, E. 25:217
Parmater, W. 20:156
Parmatier, Henry 8:92
Parmatur, Elias 5:26
Parmbarker, John 10:72
Parmelee, Henry H. 12:35
Parmelee, L. T. 23:161
Parmelee, U. W. 15:308
Parmelee, W. N. 19:91
Parmeler, R. G. 19:29
Parmelle, J. 1:64
Parmenter, Aden 17:350
Parmenter, Andrew H.
  17:361
Parmenter, Charles 15:219
Parmenter, Eugene
  10:130; 20:323
Parmenter, G. 1:63
Parmenter, John 12:35
Parmenter, M. M. 17:100
Parmenter, Rufus A. 7:75
Parmenter, Russell B.
  22:152
Parmenter, Stephen H.
  12:55
Parmer, --- 25:61
Parmer, Ben 7:131
Parmer, E. 1:95
Parmer, George N. 22:436
Parmer, Green 11:188
Parmer, Henry 17:274

Parmer, J. 11:295
Parmer, J. M. 8:53
Parmer, James S. 10:130;
    20:323
Parmer, R. J. 23:44
Parmer, W. T. 19:29
Parmer, W. W. 20:323
Parmer, William H. 5:26
Parmer, William W. 10:72
Parmeter, A. 15:23
Parmeter, Frank F. 13:40
Parmeter, J. 1:164
Parmeter, Jonas 12:57
Parmeter, R. A. 25:302
Parmety, Robert 25:217
Parmilee, C. M. 19:245
Parmington, Horace
    10:130; 20:323
Parmlee, C. 3:151
Parmly, A. 1:163
Parmor, E. 3:151
Parn, F. W. 13:67
Parnell, James 10:206
Parnell, James R. 10:72
Parney, --- 4:45
Parnham, Reuben 21:37
Paroin, Charles G. 23:45
Paronto, John 9:67
Parpit, Isaac 27:97
Parpner, W. 1:163
Parr, A. H. 1:161
Parr, A. W. 25:217
Parr, Daniel 5:25; 25:217
Parr, David R. 20:25
Parr, H. C. 11:164
Parr, Huston 8:92
Parr, John 10:72; 20:323;
    24:96
Parr, John A. 10:130;
    20:323
Parr, John B. 18:178
Parr, Loremus 24:54
Parr, M. D. 20:42
Parr, M. L. 12:166;
    25:325
Parr, R. 19:29
Parrack, William 18:153
Parrant, W. 11:248
Parrell, George 21:167
Parrent, J. E. 11:86
Parrent, R. 15:336
Parret, --- 20:46
Parrett, Martin 8:92
Parrett, William 27:95
Parrick, Thomas 5:44
Parrine, Joseph 14:205
Parris, A. W. 12:35
Parris, C. S. 9:148; 27:95
Parris, Elijah 17:24
Parris, George W. 22:127

Parris, Henry 14:301;
    17:481
Parris, J. M. 12:35
Parris, Jesse 8:27; 18:153
Parris, John 26:176
Parris, R. 11:415
Parris, Thomas G. 22:455
Parris, W. 25:217
Parrish, D. 3:151
Parrish, Elliott 21:77
Parrish, George 13:128;
    21:375
Parrish, George W. 8:27;
    18:153
Parrish, Henry B. 17:47
Parrish, Isaac 11:163
Parrish, J. 21:190
Parrish, James 9:161;
    11:396
Parrish, Jasper 17:426
Parrish, Jesse 20:323
Parrish, John 11:41
Parrish, John S. 11:320
Parrish, Joseph M. 17:162
Parrish, Lyman 12:35
Parrish, Monroe 21:167
Parrish, N. C. 1:95
Parrish, Nathaniel C.
    22:152
Parrish, R. J. 25:312
Parrish, S. S. 25:312
Parrish, Samuel R. 22:212
Parrish, T. 3:151
Parrish, T. J. 23:277
Parrish, Taylor 21:231
Parrish, Thomas 18:16,
    113
Parrish, W. H. 1:164
Parrish, W. J. 25:302
Parrish, W. L. 22:342
Parrish, William I. 8:27
Parrish, William T. 17:40
Parriss, Alfred 9:223
Parrister, John 14:278
Parrit, L. M. 11:71
Parrot, Amos 21:231
Parrot, J. 21:37
Parrot, Welsey 21:231
Parrot, William L. 22:264
Parrott, David W. 22:435
Parrott, E. 17:40
Parrott, Elias 10:29;
    19:305
Parrott, F. 1:163
Parrott, George W. 17:233
Parrott, Henry T. 19:229
Parrott, J. 9:57; 14:266
Parrott, John 9:27; 26:146
Parrott, John W. 22:435
Parrott, William R. 20:187
Parrum, Thomas 21:281

Parry, Charles T. 15:268
Parry, Isaac W. 12:123
Parschall, J. M. 3:151
Parsel, D. H. 10:130;
    20:323
Parsell, Melvin 7:37
Parsell, Peter 22:212
Parshall, A. G. 19:185
Parshall, A. M. 8:53
Parshall, Anderson G.
    10:174
Parshall, Timothy 9:27;
    18:321
Parshell, Alexis M.
    21:141
Parsley, Asberry 23:101
Parsley, John 8:118
Parsley, W. 17:162
Parslow, F. 18:16
Parslow, Jacob 1:63
Parsner, E. 13:116
Parsner, H. D. 18:209
Parsners, T. S. 16:218
Parson, A. 1:99
Parson, Cyrus 23:161
Parson, E. 12:75
Parson, E. F. 22:505
Parson, Henry F. 15:82
Parson, J. T. 3:151
Parson, L. 12:83
Parson, L. C. 19:91
Parson, S. 9:154
Parson, T. 16:270
Parson, W. D. 3:151
Parson, W. J. 15:327
Parson, W. W. 1:162
Parsonage, William 7:81;
    25:302
Parsons, --- 24:26
Parsons, A. D. 7:37
Parsons, Adam C. 22:264
Parsons, Benjamin M.
    4:45
Parsons, C. 11:288; 13:96
Parsons, C. L. 9:148
Parsons, C. S. 27:98
Parsons, Charles 17:288;
    20:134
Parsons, Charles A.
    11:110
Parsons, D. 8:66
Parsons, Daniel 11:165
Parsons, David 25:61;
    26:177
Parsons, E. 15:219;
    21:111, 375; 26:53
Parsons, E. C. 9:188;
    19:241
Parsons, E. M. 15:84
Parsons, E. S. 13:67
Parsons, Elisha 21:241

Parsons, Enoch 17:56
Parsons, Fred 10:130
Parsons, Frederick 20:323
Parsons, G. 3:151; 25:217
Parsons, G. H. 1:163
Parsons, George 4:45;
    5:25; 7:131; 15:219
Parsons, George W.
    17:283; 21:196
Parsons, H. 4:46
Parsons, H. C. 5:25;
    25:217
Parsons, H. D. 1:65
Parsons, Harry L. 19:185
Parsons, Harvey L. 10:165
Parsons, Hatson 12:157
Parsons, Henry 12:65;
    15:58
Parsons, Hiram 4:45;
    18:295; 26:109
Parsons, Hiram H. 9:38
Parsons, Howard 23:314
Parsons, Isaac 10:72;
    20:324
Parsons, J. 19:241
Parsons, J. F. 1:161
Parsons, J. L. 2:16; 25:60
Parsons, J. M. 22:48
Parsons, J. O. 9:148;
    27:95
Parsons, J. W. 3:151
Parsons, James 14:205;
    15:219
Parsons, James H. 21:375
Parsons, James J. 22:127
Parsons, Jeremiah 14:205;
    21:104
Parsons, John 5:25; 7:52;
    9:188; 19:185, 233
Parsons, John L. 23:75
Parsons, John O. 14:334
Parsons, John U. 18:469
Parsons, John W. 17:323
Parsons, Joseph M.
    22:436
Parsons, Julius L. 16:218
Parsons, L. 16:302
Parsons, Lewis 21:281
Parsons, Louden 12:65
Parsons, Louder 15:5
Parsons, Luther B. 9:16
Parsons, Michael 25:217
Parsons, P. 23:265
Parsons, Pope 21:281
Parsons, Prescott W.
    10:165
Parsons, R. 1:163
Parsons, Ralph E. A. 8:92
Parsons, Robert 25:217
Parsons, Robert B. 17:201
Parsons, S. 11:165; 27:96

Parsons, S. C. 15:316
Parsons, S. S. 21:111
Parsons, Samuel 12:57;
    22:127
Parsons, Silas 11:86
Parsons, Solomon 16:7
Parsons, Stephen 10:180;
    18:178; 21:375
Parsons, T. 18:248; 26:53
Parsons, T. B. 1:62
Parsons, Thomas 17:238
Parsons, W. 3:151
Parsons, W. C. 1:63
Parsons, W. D. 17:265
Parsons, W. E. 26:138
Parsons, Washington
    15:219
Parsons, William 14:205;
    21:375
Parsons, William D.
    23:286
Parsons, William H. 4:45
Parsons, William J. 19:91
Parsons, William T. 15:72
Parsons, Withrop 21:375
Part, George H. 27:94
Partagle, F. J. M. P.
    27:100
Partchey, A. G. 21:131
Partee, Alexander 23:271
Partee, J. 23:161
Partee, John E. 9:38;
    18:295; 26:109
Partell, J. 14:96
Partell, Owen 7:78
Partelow, B. 1:95
Parter, A. G. 22:212
Parter, George W. 12:9
Parter, James M. 11:164
Parter, John W. 11:163
Parter, Silas 10:21
Parth, Julius 19:29
Parthen, William 11:72
Partillo, Leonard 11:288
Partin, Andrews 17:203
Partin, D. R. 3:151
Partin, J. John 22:264
Partin, James W. 16:49
Partin, R. N. 22:13
Partington, James 16:100
Partis, J. R. 3:151
Partlen, H. P. 22:212
Partlon, A. J. 22:212
Partney, James S. 20:42
Partney, W. A. 26:176
Parton, E. H. 17:40
Parton, J. T. 24:27
Partridge, C. 25:60
Partridge, Cyrus W.
    18:279
Partridge, Fred. S. 27:94

Partridge, G. 2:16
Partridge, George 15:84
Partridge, George H.
    17:70
Partridge, George V.
    9:123; 27:97
Partridge, H. L. 21:112
Partridge, H. W. 11:163
Partridge, J. A. 1:65
Partridge, J. T. 15:110
Partridge, J. W. 3:151
Partridge, Leander 23:124
Partridge, Robert H. 24:43
Partridge, T. J. 13:116
Partridge, W. J. 3:151
Partridge, William 13:40
Parts, Peter 10:130;
    20:324
Partton, Israel 22:212
Partz, H. 14:96
Paruatier, William A.
    27:99
Parunta, John 18:279
Parvel, William 15:219
Parvillier, A. 16:377
Parvis, H. P. 1:163
Parvis, William H. 23:280
Parwell, Alexander 9:210
Pary, J. 16:218
Pasca, S. E. 5:26
Pascal, David 18:248;
    26:53
Pascal, Henry 11:210
Pascall, James 11:211
Pascall, Richard 17:136;
    24:201
Paschal, Charles 9:98
Paschal, D. C. 25:217
Paschal, David 7:131
Paschal, E. 3:151
Paschal, John 22:48
Paschal, M. C. 18:399
Pasco, Edward 17:423;
    24:215
Pasco, J. M. 3:151
Pasco, Milo 10:165;
    19:185
Pascol, J. 17:40
Paseley, Thomas M. 10:72
Paselin, Frederick 13:40
Pasely, Thomas M. 20:324
Paseron, Nicholas 19:29
Pasey, B. 1:63
Pasey, James 21:37
Pasha, Antoine 13:40
Pashby, John 3:151
Paskeleos, John 18:178
Paskill, Charles 16:49
Pasley, D. B. 20:324
Pasley, H. 11:247
Pasley, I. B. 9:231

Pasley, J. 21:37
Pasley, Joseph 8:41; 26:177
Pasmer, William 14:301; 17:477
Passage, Hiram 13:67; 14:205; 16:218
Passage, James 10:130; 20:324
Passenger, Charles E. 11:41
Passins, George W. 21:231
Passmer, T. G. 15:174
Passmore, H. 27:99
Passmore, M. 17:72
Passmore, W. A. 22:488
Passon, Jessie 19:48
Passons, John W. 22:127
Past, Marcus A. 16:153
Paster, J. W. 13:96
Paster, W. H. 11:390
Pasters, Christopher 22:95
Pastil, Joseph 22:283
Pastings, George 14:96
Pastles, John 12:35
Paston, I. 14:96
Paston, Philip 24:202
Pastorus, William 5:26
Pasuro, William 27:98
Pat, Conway 26:176
Patch, A. 1:64
Patch, Anson 15:219
Patch, Daniel 9:123; 27:97
Patch, Eugene 4:46
Patch, Horace D. 20:115
Patch, John 3:151; 23:103
Patch, L. 19:241
Patch, L. J. 9:189
Patch, Peter 8:27; 18:153
Patch, Stephen 7:60
Patch, William H. 21:375
Patch, William L. 21:104
Patchard, Asa 21:190
Patchen, A. 19:185
Patcher, Charles F. 21:375
Patchin, A. 10:145
Patchin, B. 22:212
Patchin, Calvin H. 20:33
Patchin, David 22:283
Patchin, J. 24:212
Patchin, L. T. 22:488
Patco, William 14:96
Pate, Amos 8:77
Pate, Benjamin 8:41; 26:177
Pate, George W. 17:40
Pate, H. 9:57
Pate, J. R. 11:268
Pate, John 22:455

Pate, John W. 22:48, 455
Pate, Joseph 10:72; 20:324
Pate, R. 7:75; 25:302
Pate, Richard 21:375
Pate, S. 27:98
Pate, William 15:174
Pate, William H. 22:127
Patel, William E. 12:35
Patell, Owen 25:302
Pateman, Henry 13:96
Patent, Samuel 1:63
Patent, T. 3:151
Patent, William 12:59; 16:154
Pater, Calvin 9:88
Paterich, John 26:109
Paterson, Albert 18:248
Paterson, Alex 4:67
Paterson, Charles 11:72
Paterson, D. 9:223
Paterson, G. W. 3:151
Paterson, George 14:205; 27:98
Paterson, James H. 4:67
Paterson, John 26:52
Paterson, Lewis 24:186
Paterson, W. 27:96
Pates, William 8:92
Patey, --- 22:314
Pathreef, James D. 23:115
Pathwell, J. W. 20:43
Patlet, A. 13:116
Patley, William 14:284
Patmer, W. K. 9:88
Patmor, Francis R. 7:106
Patnaud, Charles 7:106
Patnot, P. 1:162
Paton, Samuel 22:435
Patram, Peter 21:57
Patrick, Albert A. 10:21
Patrick, Alfred 22:264
Patrick, Alonzo 7:52
Patrick, Bennet 7:75
Patrick, C. E. 1:161
Patrick, Canfield 11:120
Patrick, Charles 18:413
Patrick, D. D. 25:217
Patrick, Dennis 21:150, 213
Patrick, E. F. 9:88
Patrick, Elijah F. 26:53
Patrick, Elisha G. 23:256
Patrick, F. 3:151; 13:96; 22:264
Patrick, Freeman 4:67
Patrick, G. W. 1:163
Patrick, G. W. E. 8:74
Patrick, George 21:57
Patrick, Gus W. 17:40
Patrick, H. 25:217

Patrick, J. 22:314; 27:99
Patrick, J. B. 1:163
Patrick, J. H. 11:40
Patrick, J. I. 12:162
Patrick, James 6:18; 12:164; 18:91
Patrick, John 9:38; 14:97; 18:295; 22:264
Patrick, John B. 10:149; 18:55
Patrick, John G. 9:88
Patrick, John J. 7:37
Patrick, John M. 24:167
Patrick, John W. 22:95
Patrick, L. 14:97
Patrick, Lewis 16:219; 17:238
Patrick, Linus A. 23:161
Patrick, M. 22:521
Patrick, Marshal 24:201
Patrick, Marshall 17:455
Patrick, Martin 11:163
Patrick, Michael D. 13:40; 16:49
Patrick, Miles 21:150
Patrick, Mores C. 23:45
Patrick, P. 9:148; 27:96
Patrick, Robert J. 9:38
Patrick, Thomas C. 23:101
Patrick, William 21:13
Patrick, Willis 22:127
Patridge, Manly 17:162
Patridge, William H. 7:69
Patrill, Sylvester 23:16
Patry, J. 3:151
Patshey, J. 3:151
Patsons, James C. 22:504
Patt, J. C. 11:220
Pattee, Calvin 26:52
Pattee, Elias J. 22:152
Patten, A. 12:80; 14:301
Patten, A. H. 19:29
Patten, A. L. 1:163
Patten, Albert 12:59
Patten, Andrew 22:314
Patten, Asa 15:167
Patten, Azro 11:117
Patten, E. 19:229
Patten, Edward E. 19:29
Patten, F. 5:53; 27:98
Patten, G. 1:162
Patten, George 22:314
Patten, George H. 22:212
Patten, H. C. 9:223; 14:19; 18:373
Patten, Henry 26:204
Patten, Isaac 14:205; 21:196
Patten, J. H. 14:96

Patten, J. W. 12:157; 16:49
Patten, James A. 8:92
Patten, James R. 11:329
Patten, John 11:193; 22:212
Patten, John H. 10:130; 20:324
Patten, Joshua W. 23:13
Patten, Lorenzo 20:324
Patten, M. 14:97
Patten, Otis 23:161
Patten, Richmond 21:281
Patten, S. 11:336
Patten, T. 14:301
Patten, W. 3:151
Patten, William 12:157
Patten, William H. 7:37
Patten, Z. M. 12:86
Pattenburg, P. 15:361
Pattengill, John F. 9:189
Patter, --- 10:192
Patter, Charles 10:21; 19:338
Patter, Cyrus 18:153
Patter, Frank 21:375
Patter, Harvey 15:279; 25:217
Patter, Jackson 21:217
Patter, Jepthat 11:188
Patter, Phillip 11:247
Patter, William H. 22:505
Patter, Wilson 24:62
Pattern, Samuel 4:45
Pattern, William 26:177
Patterson, A. 1:63; 16:218; 18:55; 20:59; 27:94
Patterson, A. B. 19:326
Patterson, A. G. 13:96; 14:19
Patterson, Aaron 17:111; 22:409; 26:146
Patterson, Abraham 20:324
Patterson, Abram 10:72
Patterson, Albert 26:54
Patterson, Albert C. 17:156
Patterson, Alex 4:67
Patterson, Alexander 11:310; 12:35; 22:48; 23:305
Patterson, Alexander F. 9:31
Patterson, Almond G. 22:95
Patterson, Ambrose 17:244
Patterson, Anderson 17:183

Patterson, Andio 25:217
Patterson, Andrew 12:75; 15:23
Patterson, Archibald S. 22:455
Patterson, B. 9:201
Patterson, Barnum 19:292
Patterson, Benjamin 16:49
Patterson, Buck 6:18; 18:91
Patterson, C. 14:97; 25:217
Patterson, C. W. 10:130; 20:324
Patterson, Carson 22:314
Patterson, Charles 7:106; 15:27
Patterson, Charles V. 23:109
Patterson, Colonel 22:342
Patterson, D. 16:218
Patterson, D. B. 10:192; 18:178
Patterson, D. K. 18:373
Patterson, D. L. 1:63
Patterson, D. M. 11:165
Patterson, David 8:92; 13:40
Patterson, David A. 14:316
Patterson, E. 3:151; 17:97
Patterson, E. R. 11:419
Patterson, Easom 9:98
Patterson, Edmond 23:271
Patterson, Edward 23:129
Patterson, Eliakum 22:95
Patterson, Ellis 23:289
Patterson, Erastus 17:67
Patterson, F. 3:151; 14:97; 15:72
Patterson, Fis. 17:97
Patterson, Friely 21:281
Patterson, Fritz 13:40; 16:49
Patterson, G. 14:289
Patterson, G. E. 10:130; 20:324
Patterson, G. W. 22:504; 23:45; 26:53
Patterson, Gardner 14:205
Patterson, George 6:18; 8:27; 9:112; 14:301; 17:477; 18:91, 153; 23:109
Patterson, George W. 8:92; 17:444; 24:161
Patterson, Grant 9:162
Patterson, H. 1:65; 3:151; 15:285; 19:91; 22:212
Patterson, H. V. G. 10:187

Patterson, H. W. 3:151
Patterson, Henry 10:165; 19:185; 20:140
Patterson, Henry C. 11:164
Patterson, Henry K. 22:48
Patterson, Henson 22:264
Patterson, I. P. 21:125
Patterson, I. S. 12:164
Patterson, Isaac 22:314
Patterson, J. 1:160, 161; 3:151; 10:187; 11:268; 14:278, 284; 18:178; 23:161; 24:96; 25:217
Patterson, J. A. 3:151
Patterson, J. B. 9:243
Patterson, J. D. 25:302
Patterson, J. H. 3:151; 18:55
Patterson, J. M. 15:219
Patterson, J. P. 1:163; 19:29
Patterson, J. R. 18:55
Patterson, J. S. 26:176
Patterson, J. T. 3:151; 9:57
Patterson, James 5:26; 8:27; 9:27; 10:72, 130; 11:71; 13:40; 17:136; 19:259; 20:324; 22:95; 23:75; 24:43
Patterson, James C. 11:41
Patterson, James D. 10:72; 20:324
Patterson, James M. 22:488; 24:54
Patterson, James R. 7:106
Patterson, Jerry 24:202
Patterson, Jesse 22:48
Patterson, Joel 22:264
Patterson, John 7:37; 9:57; 11:311; 14:97, 205; 15:42; 16:160; 17:24; 18:321; 21:77; 22:264, 435; 26:176
Patterson, John B. 17:238
Patterson, John D. 17:97
Patterson, John L. 4:45
Patterson, John M. 11:396
Patterson, John W. 2:16
Patterson, Jordan 17:183
Patterson, Joseph 24:201
Patterson, Joseph H. 11:72
Patterson, Josiah 23:244
Patterson, Julius 9:210
Patterson, Junius C. 21:77
Patterson, L. R. 11:73
Patterson, Lyman 9:88
Patterson, M. 14:97

Patterson, Matthew 6:10
Patterson, Miller H. C. 11:163
Patterson, Milton 17:136; 24:201
Patterson, N. 3:151; 14:205; 16:49
Patterson, N. A. 16:281
Patterson, N. S. 3:151
Patterson, Nathan 8:41; 26:177
Patterson, Nelson 14:205
Patterson, O. 22:212
Patterson, O. J. 15:287
Patterson, Ole 22:48
Patterson, Oliver 19:91
Patterson, P. 4:45
Patterson, P. N. 1:64
Patterson, Peter 17:136; 20:25; 24:201
Patterson, R. 1:163; 3:151; 23:161
Patterson, R. M. 9:57
Patterson, Richardson 12:35
Patterson, Robert 12:35, 75
Patterson, Robert F. 22:95
Patterson, Robert G. 9:123; 27:97
Patterson, S. 1:62; 3:151; 14:244; 15:312; 19:91; 26:52
Patterson, S. B. 23:45
Patterson, S. C. 17:265
Patterson, S. H. 13:67; 19:91
Patterson, S. M. 14:97
Patterson, Samuel 8:53; 9:134; 15:219; 17:444; 22:436; 23:181; 27:97
Patterson, Simon J. 7:131
Patterson, Simon P. 21:375
Patterson, Stephen 22:48
Patterson, T. 3:151
Patterson, Thomas 7:52; 8:108; 9:210; 10:8, 72; 18:70; 20:324
Patterson, Van Renssalaer 21:231
Patterson, W. 1:160; 9:57, 148; 26:176
Patterson, W. A. C. 8:27; 18:153
Patterson, W. D. 3:151; 22:264
Patterson, W. K. 9:73
Patterson, Warren K. 23:45

Patterson, Wesley 8:69
Patterson, William 8:66; 11:41, 329; 12:35; 14:97; 17:183; 20:99; 22:95, 283, 314; 26:145
Patterson, William B. 22:212
Patterson, William M. 22:212
Patterson, William S. 23:45
Patterson, Wilson 10:130; 20:324
Pattes, A. 25:217
Patteson, R. R. 9:112
Pattice, W. 1:163
Pattin, C. J. 16:141
Pattin, H. W. 3:151
Pattingal, Stephen P. 22:466
Pattinger, John 14:205
Pattison, D. G. 13:96
Pattison, Henry A. 7:52
Pattison, James W. 21:77
Pattison, John 16:148
Pattison, Thomas 12:54
Pattison, William 24:113
Pattit, J. S. 3:151
Pattle, Alonzo D. 1:62
Pattle, W. F. 18:16
Patton, A. 17:479; 25:217; 27:98
Patton, Aaron 23:280
Patton, Abram 22:264
Patton, Adam 21:150
Patton, Alexander 21:190
Patton, Charles A. 12:35
Patton, Christopher 17:261
Patton, Cyrus 19:91; 22:48
Patton, D. 14:97
Patton, David 18:248; 22:314; 26:54
Patton, David C. 22:48
Patton, E. M. 11:96
Patton, Emory 9:189
Patton, F. 25:217
Patton, F. R. 21:209
Patton, Frank 11:211
Patton, G. W. 9:112
Patton, George 7:131; 14:205; 24:202
Patton, H. 1:99; 14:97; 16:219
Patton, H. C. 13:96
Patton, Henry 22:314
Patton, J. 11:165; 17:162
Patton, J. T. 18:55
Patton, J. W. 13:40

Patton, Jefferson 11:211
Patton, John 22:436
Patton, Joseph 9:27; 18:314; 26:109
Patton, Joseph F. 18:399
Patton, Joseph S. 18:104
Patton, L. F. 21:245
Patton, L. J. 21:95
Patton, L. S. 7:37
Patton, Lorenzo 10:72
Patton, M. 14:97
Patton, Marshall W. 22:283
Patton, N. J. 21:190
Patton, Nelson 22:314, 515
Patton, Robert A. 5:26
Patton, Robert R. 21:57
Patton, S. 21:37; 22:314
Patton, S. O. 13:67
Patton, Samuel 16:302; 22:521
Patton, T. 17:479; 18:55
Patton, T. J. 11:443; 20:134
Patton, Thomas 7:60; 11:73
Patton, William 10:130; 16:148; 18:91; 20:324; 21:217
Patton, William H. 17:207
Patton, William S. 8:92
Patton, Z. M. 16:302
Pattorf, John 9:88; 26:52
Pattrick, Boardman 21:141
Pattridge, J. 15:110
Pattsuheimer, William 12:75
Patty, H. 14:97
Patty, James 9:189; 19:271
Patty, R. N. 9:123
Patty, William 23:45
Patzer, Edward 10:206
Patzrick, A. 8:74
Pauch, William 14:205
Pauff, John N. 17:203
Paugburn, A. L. 5:25
Paugh, Evan D. 16:49
Paugh, J. J. 14:97
Paugh, John 16:100
Paugh, Peter 8:108
Paugh, William 1:65
Paughburn, S. 3:151
Paul, --- 3:151
Paul, A. 27:96
Paul, Abraham 14:244; 27:100
Paul, Adam 7:37
Paul, Alexander 21:259

Paul, Allen D. 6:21
Paul, Arthur H. 21:57
Paul, Azariah 9:148
Paul, Bertrand 19:29
Paul, Blake 21:375
Paul, C. 8:27; 18:153
Paul, C. A. 12:157
Paul, Charles D. 20:11
Paul, Edmes 22:409
Paul, Edward 18:91;
   21:141
Paul, Edward A. 6:18
Paul, Erastus L. 21:217
Paul, Frank 18:464
Paul, George C. 22:455
Paul, George R. 1:63
Paul, George W. 4:46
Paul, Isaac T. 4:67
Paul, J. 8:74
Paul, J. C. 3:151
Paul, J. H. 1:65
Paul, Jacob 14:205; 20:90
Paul, John 9:44; 13:96;
   22:314
Paul, John G. 10:73;
   20:324
Paul, John W. 21:77
Paul, Joseph 10:130;
   20:324
Paul, Joshua 9:38
Paul, Lewis 22:314;
   23:271
Paul, Nelson 21:375
Paul, Peter 12:9
Paul, S. B. 12:93; 16:302
Paul, S. H. 21:190
Paul, S. M. 19:259
Paul, Samuel 9:189;
   19:286
Paul, Samuel H. 7:106
Paul, Samuel M. 9:189
Paul, Spencer 7:131
Paul, Sylvester 8:92, 115
Paul, Thomas E. 22:48
Paul, Walter 10:165;
   19:185
Paul, William 23:45
Paul, William H. 9:38
Pauldin, H. A. 19:91
Paulding, H. A. 26:237
Paule, S. B. 14:97
Paules, John 13:40
Pauley, Ira 20:324
Pauley, James B. 17:24
Pauley, William 10:73;
   20:324
Pauley, William L. 20:138
Paulin, Ernest 21:141
Pauling, Nathan 24:71
Paulison, Isaac N. 10:130;
   20:324

Paulkinhor, J. J. 11:411
Paull, R. 23:45
Paulman, William 8:74;
   26:176
Paulmire, S. 1:163
Paulson, Ethan A. 22:95
Paulson, G. 13:96
Paulson, George 24:102
Paulson, John 18:113
Paulus, Jacob 18:117
Paulus, Jacob M. 17:40
Paulus, Urins 22:212
Paumal, A. 21:37
Paumetier, J. 15:42
Paunbacker, John 20:324
Paup, G. W. 25:62
Paupord, H. 1:163
Pausa, S. 8:53
Paush, John 17:40
Paush, Theodore C.
   16:100
Paustle, Austin 19:91
Pavall, Charles 20:324
Pavatt, Conero 20:324
Pavener, C. 9:38
Pavent, David 1:63
Paver, Jacob 14:205
Pavis, Richard 9:231
Pavott, Corners 10:130
Pavy, Charles 15:219
Pavy, Isaac W. 15:131
Pavy, R. 16:136
Paw, J. 14:97
Pawl, E. 14:97
Pawlett, David 26:138
Pawley, Robert 10:21
Pawson, Andrew 9:47;
   26:142
Pawt, William B. 22:264
Paxon, Benjamin W.
   18:221
Paxon, Isaac 14:205
Paxon, Joseph 7:37
Paxon, S. 25:217
Paxon, Samuel 5:44
Paxon, William 15:131
Paxson, William L.
   21:231
Paxton, C. 25:60
Paxton, James G. 11:163
Paxton, Justus 23:161
Paxton, P. W. 22:487
Paxton, Thomas 22:488
Paxton, William 10:73;
   11:73; 20:324
Pay, John 21:375
Payan, Charles E. 21:375
Paye, James 11:110
Payer, A. L. 26:52
Payer, L. 9:149
Paym, Gilson 21:281

Payn, A. L. 9:88
Payne, A. 4:46
Payne, A. G. 10:29
Payne, Alfred H. 22:212
Payne, Ambrose 24:171
Payne, B. F. 18:113
Payne, B. W. 26:53
Payne, Benjamin 17:56
Payne, C. B. 14:322;
   23:161
Payne, C. E. 17:100
Payne, Charles 21:112
Payne, Charles E. 4:46
Payne, Charles J. 20:138
Payne, Corydon B. 14:316
Payne, D. J. 11:311
Payne, Daniel 19:29
Payne, David J. 6:10
Payne, Delos 12:35
Payne, E. 14:289; 18:55;
   23:204
Payne, E. J. 19:29
Payne, Edward 17:244
Payne, Eugene 9:215;
   21:375
Payne, F. 19:185
Payne, Frank 17:183
Payne, Franklin 19:330
Payne, G. 1:63
Payne, G. A. 3:151
Payne, G. D. 9:57, 112
Payne, G. M. 22:264
Payne, George 5:44;
   10:130; 13:40;
   20:324; 25:217
Payne, George M. 22:264;
   23:161
Payne, Gibson 21:281
Payne, H. 16:377
Payne, H. C. 13:96; 14:19
Payne, H. F. 14:131
Payne, Henry 11:211
Payne, Henry M. 10:21
Payne, Hudson 17:244
Payne, I. 22:515
Payne, Ira 11:41
Payne, Isaiah 17:40
Payne, J. 3:151; 15:153;
   22:515
Payne, J. G. 17:168, 183
Payne, J. H. 1:62; 9:57
Payne, Jackson 15:268
Payne, Jacob 27:94
Payne, James 4:67;
   17:420; 24:161
Payne, James L. 21:125
Payne, Jefferson 17:152
Payne, Jesse C. 11:443
Payne, John 10:130;
   20:324; 23:45

Payne, John M. 10:130; 20:324
Payne, John N. 27:97
Payne, Jonathan 27:94
Payne, Joseph 3:224; 17:501
Payne, Joseph W. 11:390
Payne, Leander C. 20:31
Payne, Leonidas 9:27
Payne, Lewis 1:192; 18:16; 21:231; 24:167
Payne, M. 17:183
Payne, Marcellis 22:95
Payne, Nathan S. 11:164
Payne, Nathaniel 21:104
Payne, O. P. 5:26
Payne, O. W. 26:52
Payne, Oliver 21:281
Payne, R. H. 3:151
Payne, Reuben 17:183; 21:281
Payne, Rufus 17:451
Payne, S. 17:183
Payne, S. B. 20:325
Payne, Samuel 10:73; 20:324; 26:146
Payne, Samuel B. 22:409
Payne, Stephen 22:315
Payne, Susbury 5:44
Payne, Thadeus M. 20:175
Payne, W. 1:163; 26:109
Payne, W. A. 3:151; 21:375
Payne, William 1:62; 9:27; 16:377; 17:183; 18:314; 21:281, 375; 22:455; 26:109
Payne, William C. 11:288
Payne, William E. 22:95
Payne, William H. 5:26
Payne, William L. 22:127
Payne, William M. 14:97
Payne, Windsor 17:263
Paynier, E. 23:204
Paynile, E. 14:289
Payns, E. C. 22:152
Paynter, William 19:91
Paysant, Lewis 12:75
Payson, Lewis B. 10:73; 20:325
Payson, Orin 9:88
Payson, Samuel 12:169
Payson, William 9:88
Payten, Jefferson 12:160
Payton, A. L. 15:58
Payton, A. M. 20:325
Payton, Alonzo L. 17:401
Payton, B. 22:314

Payton, C. H. 8:27; 18:153
Payton, Charles 17:183
Payton, Charles A. 25:217
Payton, Elias I. 8:27
Payton, Elias J. 18:153
Payton, J. H. 11:292
Payton, R. E. 11:85
Payton, Richard 24:201
Payton, Silas 11:247
Paytor, Henry E. 10:130; 20:325
Payzant, Lewis 15:18
Paz, Richard 15:132
Pazey, Joseph 13:40
Pazly, Joseph 16:49
Pchlee, E. 1:161
Pe---, J. 20:138
Pe-to-zo-onqutte, --- 19:92
Pe-to-zo-ouvquitte, --- 13:67
Pea, Abram 21:57
Pea, Daniel M. 19:305
Pea, Hiram Hunter 19:305
Peabody, A. S. 9:215; 21:375
Peabody, Anson 9:38
Peabody, D. 25:217
Peabody, Elias 20:25
Peabody, Francis 10:165
Peabody, Horace 9:189; 19:233
Peabody, J. 25:217
Peabody, J. H. H. 9:149
Peabody, John P. 22:213
Peabody, Joseph B. 17:361
Peabody, L. E. 21:375
Peabody, Miles T. 4:46
Peabody, Nathan 10:73; 20:325
Peabody, Nelson 14:205
Peabody, Nicholas 9:189; 19:241
Peabody, Samuel 15:299; 16:219
Peabody, T. S. 3:151
Peabody, W. T. 3:151
Peabody, William 12:75
Peabody, Winfield 4:46
Peace, David 10:73; 20:325
Peach, --- 15:132
Peach, F. J. 9:112
Peach, George 16:281; 19:92
Peach, James 15:320
Peach, Richard 17:283
Peacher, C. 3:151
Peaches, N. 13:67

Peaches, Nippies 19:92
Peachrist, Peter D. 17:265
Peachy, Aaron 22:152
Peachy, Noah 19:29
Peack, F. N. 13:96
Peacoat, L. C. 15:327
Peacock, A. S. 8:108
Peacock, Amos 9:88; 26:52
Peacock, George 22:48
Peacock, Isaac 13:40; 16:49
Peacock, Jonah 9:38
Peacock, Josiah 23:91
Peacock, R. H. 11:334
Peacock, Robert 23:161
Peacock, S. L. 15:299; 16:219
Peacock, Thomas 1:63
Peacock, William 9:237; 26:224
Peadrick, J. S. 25:217
Peaffenretch, I. 8:101
Peaft, Henry 15:361; 19:92
Peahl, William 9:106
Peak, Benjamin 23:161
Peak, Gilbert 8:53; 21:259
Peak, J. 1:162
Peak, James W. 23:75
Peak, John 14:97
Peak, John T. 17:410; 22:127
Peak, Samuel 17:444; 24:161
Peak, W. H. 10:149; 18:55
Peak, William G. 12:35
Peake, Levi M. 22:264
Peake, R. 22:95
Peake, W. N. 19:29
Peake, William 17:100
Peaker, Henry 25:217
Peaking, C. 16:302
Peakring, C. 12:87
Peaks, Francis 10:174
Peaks, Frank 19:185
Peaks, Simpson 23:251
Peal, Bartley 10:170
Peal, Daniel H. 23:75
Peal, Henry T. 9:134
Peal, Partney 9:223
Peal, Pastneney 18:373
Pealch, Fred 1:64
Pealer, John M. 22:213
Pealer, Oliver 23:161
Pealer, Oscar 14:205
Peales, Oscar 14:205
Pealey, James 7:69
Peall, William 22:172
Peant, H. 15:219
Peany, L. M. 21:375

Pear, Dennis J. 21:57
Pearce, --- 5:53; 18:285; 26:135
Pearce, A. 1:161
Pearce, Arthur 13:40
Pearce, Charles 7:60
Pearce, Clem 23:289
Pearce, Edward 22:152
Pearce, Ermin 12:62
Pearce, George 18:373
Pearce, George C. 9:227
Pearce, H. 3:151
Pearce, J. 24:43
Pearce, J. H. 26:177
Pearce, James 1:63; 12:62
Pearce, James J. 9:44
Pearce, James W. 22:264
Pearce, John 10:130; 20:325
Pearce, Joseph R. 12:59
Pearce, L. D. 20:43
Pearce, Nathan D. 11:164
Pearce, S. 9:88
Pearce, Swift 23:115
Pearce, Thomas 11:341
Pearce, W. 1:163
Pearce, William 10:97; 21:281
Pearce, William H. 21:231; 26:52
Pearce, William R. 17:56
Pearcy, David C. 10:73
Pearcy, Samuel 18:153
Pearl, Albert U. 17:24
Pearl, J. 10:150; 18:55; 21:37
Pearl, Moses 21:281
Pearl, S. 1:161
Pearl, Squire L. 25:217
Pearl, Tom 7:131
Pearlday, Hiram 21:375
Pearler, Shrive 21:375
Pearley, Charles C. 19:92
Pearley, S. A. 9:88
Pearman, John 22:342
Pearnell, J. 3:151
Pearsal, J. H. 15:291
Pearsall, E. W. 1:161
Pearsall, J. H. 16:219
Pearsall, John B. 17:391
Pearsall, Lewis 21:375
Pearse, Elijah C. 12:35
Pearse, Henry 15:23
Pearse, Richard A. 22:283
Pearse, Robert C. 1:64
Pearsell, Dexter 21:243
Pearsins, William E. 12:35
Pearsol, Jacob 10:145; 19:185
Pearsoll, Leonidas 16:49

Pearson, Alber 26:54
Pearson, B. 25:325
Pearson, Barepas 6:32
Pearson, Bartholomew 10:73
Pearson, Clem H. 25:325
Pearson, F. 7:69
Pearson, George 10:146
Pearson, Granville 22:435
Pearson, H. 17:434
Pearson, H. C. 22:488
Pearson, Hiram 24:169
Pearson, Isaac 10:73; 20:325; 23:286
Pearson, J. 10:97
Pearson, James 21:281
Pearson, James M. 22:264
Pearson, Jeremiah 11:72
Pearson, Jesse 22:409
Pearson, John 8:27; 10:165; 11:72; 12:35; 15:285; 19:92; 21:231
Pearson, John J. 22:95; 23:45
Pearson, John L. D. 22:95
Pearson, John W. 15:167; 24:108
Pearson, Joshua 18:373
Pearson, L. 1:162; 19:259
Pearson, L. A. 18:91
Pearson, L. D. 19:29
Pearson, Leonard 6:10
Pearson, Luke 9:189
Pearson, M. 13:96
Pearson, N. D. 1:99
Pearson, Randolph 27:99
Pearson, Robert 20:127
Pearson, S. C. 3:151
Pearson, S. W. 14:263
Pearson, Thomas 17:15; 22:435
Pearson, Thomas C. 22:488
Pearson, W. A. 9:57
Pearson, William 10:130; 11:71; 13:116; 15:58; 16:219; 20:325; 22:95
Pearsons, F. 11:293
Pearsons, H. H. 25:61
Pearsons, Joshua 9:223
Pearsons, K. 15:132
Pearsons, William 25:61
Peas, Freeman 18:70
Peas, Henry 13:116
Peasdall, James 22:264
Pease, Andrew 9:73
Pease, Ashbel 1:63
Pease, Byron A. 23:162
Pease, C. 16:141

Pease, C. G. 18:344
Pease, Erastus B. 15:174
Pease, Frank A. 1:64
Pease, G. E. 3:151
Pease, Gaston 21:77
Pease, H. 1:95
Pease, Henry 14:205
Pease, Isser 13:116
Pease, J. H. 1:99
Pease, James 1:62; 14:205
Pease, John 16:49
Pease, Jonathan 13:40
Pease, Marcus A. 21:259
Pease, Martin 3:152
Pease, N. 14:97
Pease, N. A. 13:67
Pease, Nathaniel 14:97
Pease, Oliver 1:64
Pease, Oliver D. 20:193
Pease, Samuel B. 27:99
Pease, Sylvester 21:141
Pease, Thomas G. 16:219
Pease, W. 1:164; 21:375
Pease, William 10:130; 20:325
Pease, William C. 1:63
Peaseley, Philander S. 10:145
Peasler, Alpheus 10:21
Peasley, Francis 10:73
Peasley, Frank 20:325; 25:302
Peasley, Frank W. 7:76
Peasley, H. 15:174; 25:217
Peasley, Hiram 5:26
Peasley, J. 3:152
Peasley, J. H. 14:97
Peasley, J. L. 13:116
Peasley, James 10:145; 19:185
Peasley, Joseph 23:109
Peasley, Philander S. 19:185
Peasley, Silas 10:73; 20:325
Peasley, Thomas 22:515
Peasley, Tim 25:217
Peasley, Timothy 15:279
Peasley, William C. 23:91
Peasly, R. 1:162
Peasly, W. C. 1:64
Peassell, Andrew 15:174
Peaster, Jacob 1:62
Peat, Thomas 24:27
Peatfield, Joseph S. 10:165; 19:185
Peatrea, A. 27:95
Peats, John A. 15:73
Peatt, C. H. 23:205
Peavey, Hollis S. 13:40

Peavey, Joseph P. 27:95
Peavey, Samuel 8:28
Peavy, Joshua 22:515
Pebbels, L. 17:84
Pebbles, J. K. 14:284
Pebles, Thad 19:185
Pebowith, Robert H. 8:92
Pecant, L. C. 19:92
Peck, --- 24:171; 25:62
Peck, A. 3:152
Peck, A. A. 1:162
Peck, A. J. 8:118
Peck, A. T. 8:53
Peck, Alfred 13:41;
    22:152, 213
Peck, Aloy E. 23:241
Peck, Alpheus 7:69
Peck, Anderson 22:315
Peck, Andrew 9:189;
    19:245
Peck, Andrew J. 1:65;
    23:13
Peck, B. F. 25:302
Peck, B. S. 9:149
Peck, C. 14:301; 17:477;
    27:100
Peck, C. V. 11:41
Peck, C. W. 3:152
Peck, Calvin 17:420;
    24:179
Peck, Chancey C. 20:325
Peck, Chancey J. 10:73
Peck, Charles 10:10;
    18:399
Peck, Charles N. 24:27
Peck, D. D. 8:66
Peck, D. N. 11:165
Peck, D. R. 19:245
Peck, David 18:36
Peck, E. A. 9:149; 27:96
Peck, E. F. 4:46
Peck, E. S. 9:112
Peck, E. W. 8:92
Peck, Edward C. 8:108
Peck, Emery G. 26:146
Peck, Erwin 11:247
Peck, F. W. 9:27; 18:314;
    26:109
Peck, Frederick 20:325
Peck, Freeman 9:104;
    18:340
Peck, George 9:156;
    21:131
Peck, George M. 21:77
Peck, H. 13:96; 14:19;
    25:218; 27:100
Peck, H. E. 14:301;
    17:470
Peck, H. H. 13:67; 19:92
Peck, H. S. 9:240
Peck, Henry C. 21:85

Peck, Henry H. 15:348;
    16:377
Peck, Horace 18:314;
    26:109
Peck, Horace M. 21:77
Peck, Howard B. 11:268
Peck, Ira E. 14:270
Peck, Isaac 13:76; 24:83
Peck, J. 1:162
Peck, J. E. 14:284
Peck, J. G. 3:152; 16:270
Peck, J. H. 3:152
Peck, J. P. H. 8:28
Peck, James 19:92
Peck, James A. 4:46
Peck, James E. 19:185
Peck, Jared 17:158
Peck, Jay 13:41; 16:49
Peck, John 11:391; 13:41
Peck, John H. 26:146
Peck, John T. 21:259
Peck, Joseph 8:92
Peck, Joseph F. 1:63
Peck, L. 8:115
Peck, L. J. 13:125
Peck, Lewis 12:35
Peck, M. K. 15:88
Peck, Martin H. 8:92
Peck, Martin K. 12:75
Peck, O. 1:161
Peck, Orange 10:8
Peck, Orin E. 21:104
Peck, Philo H. 16:86
Peck, R. 8:28; 18:153
Peck, R. H. 11:72
Peck, Robert 11:425
Peck, Robert F. 17:405
Peck, S. 1:65; 14:284;
    25:218
Peck, Samuel A. 5:26
Peck, Stephen 7:52
Peck, T. P. H. 18:153
Peck, W. 25:218
Peck, W. H. 11:73
Peck, Walter 20:325
Peck, William 9:13, 189;
    11:17; 15:286; 19:92;
    20:12; 21:375;
    22:342
Peck, William F. 18:399
Peck, William H. 1:63
Peck, William M. C.
    22:95
Peck, William N. 16:145
Peck, William O. 22:236
Peck, Zachariah 20:325
Peckengpaugh, Aden H.
    22:95
Peckens, Philip 16:123
Pecket, Alfred 11:71
Peckham, A. J. 4:46

Peckham, A. P. 3:152
Peckham, Adelbert 15:110
Peckham, C. W. 12:75
Peckham, H. I. 15:219
Peckham, Henry 13:41
Peckham, James W. 4:46
Peckham, Leir 18:340
Peckham, P. 1:65
Peckham, William 22:113
Peckhart, Conrad 22:342
Peckinpanck, J. H. 11:397
Peckinpaugh, William J.
    17:56
Peckins, L. 3:152
Peckover, Charles H.
    10:73; 20:325
Pecks, David 14:236
Peco, W. 15:58
Pecof, P. G. 16:377
Peddie, J. 1:162
Peddle, Joseph 23:103
Pedego, N. E. 22:521
Peden, Freeman 11:390
Pedenger, Edward 16:219
Pederson, Peder 22:283
Pedigo, John H. 20:187
Pedigo, S. 17:217
Pedigo, Squire W. 22:48
Pedri, Conrad 8:28;
    18:153
Pedrick, William D.
    19:185
Pedro, A. 25:218
Peds, Francis 3:152
Pee, Richard 24:201
Peeber, V. D. 26:53
Peeber, Van D. 9:88
Peebles, David W. 22:283
Peebles, E. J. 11:311
Peebles, G. F. 14:19
Peebles, J. B. 11:247
Peebles, Thaddeus 10:174
Peebles, W. S. 18:248
Peechey, P. 15:132
Peeck, C. 3:152
Peecks, H. 11:247
Peed, F. M. 8:53
Peed, Isaac 22:127
Peed, James O. 11:268
Peed, R. 3:152
Peede, Francis M. 21:57
Peede, Washington
    21:231
Peeden, John 23:302
Peeham, P. R. 8:115
Peek, F. S. 27:95
Peek, Horace 9:27
Peek, James 13:67
Peek, John 17:84
Peek, Joseph 11:96
Peek, W. 5:53

Peek, Zachariah 10:130
Peekey, William 21:375
Peekham, G. T. 11:101
Peekin, Anthony 21:281
Peel, Anderson 21:281
Peel, F. A. 13:135; 19:347
Peel, George W. 24:10
Peel, Henry 17:97
Peel, J. 23:45
Peel, Jesse L. 22:264
Peel, Robert 25:334
Peel, W. 17:97
Peel, William H. H.
    21:231
Peel, William S. 11:72
Peeler, Henry 20:193
Peeler, J. E. 9:88
Peeler, J. H. 25:218
Peeler, John H. 5:26
Peels, G. 14:97
Peen, George 15:73
Peenson, William H. 8:92
Peeps, William 17:451
Peer, Abraham 23:45
Peer, Henry 21:375
Peer, John A. 12:35
Peer, Nat 9:210
Peer, T. 3:152
Peer, W. C. 13:116
Peer, William 23:162, 173
Peerpont, S. 25:273
Peers, James A. 20:140
Peerson, William 21:375
Peery, William 13:41
Peet, Charles D. 23:264
Peet, George B. 9:123
Peet, George K. 27:97
Peet, John S. 16:219
Peet, Lansing 11:129
Peete, A. 3:152
Peeter, H. M. 3:152
Pefester, Henry 11:164
Peffer, John G. 16:377
Peffer, Joseph 20:99
Peforge, William 24:27
Peget, Levi 13:116
Pegg, James A. 18:209;
    23:307
Peggs, Samuel 22:213
Peggy, James A. 8:92
Pegler, George 22:152
Pegram, J. E. 16:49
Pegran, W. 3:152
Pegue, Emanuel 22:315
Peibles, W. S. 26:54
Peifer, G. 15:132
Peifer, Levi J. 12:35
Peiffer, John W. 17:283
Peiffer, Mathew 11:278
Peiffer, Peter 15:336
Peigh, Isaac H. 9:123

Peigh, Samuel 20:325
Peigh, Simon 12:35
Peikert, Charles 1:64
Peilding, James 18:66
Peine, J. 7:52
Peirce, B. B. 14:97
Peirce, Delos 7:106
Peirce, Edward B. 27:98
Peirce, Edward D. 9:123
Peirce, F. A. 1:161
Peirce, George A. 10:165
Peirce, Henry D. 20:325
Peirce, Hiram 20:325
Peirce, Joseph 9:189
Peirce, Lambert 9:123
Peirce, R. F. 20:325
Peirce, T. W. 9:57
Peirce, William 25:218
Peird, James 24:202
Peirie, Dominick 15:219
Peirson, Albert 18:248
Peirson, B. 20:325
Peirson, Daniel 9:123
Peirson, John 9:189
Peirum, Aaron 21:375
Peisdale, William 16:100
Peitzsch, Carl F. 4:46
Pek, Alonzo 19:92
Pekins, G. W. 3:152
Pelan, R. F. 25:62
Pelcott, Ezra F. 8:92
Pele, Z. 9:149
Pelein, Alex 24:54
Pelfry, John 4:46
Pelham, Henry 25:218
Pelham, Levi 14:205
Pelham, Wallace 21:375
Pelham, William C.
    22:409
Pelitt, George 4:46
Pelkey, E. 23:162
Pelkey, Joseph 23:13
Pell, James L. 15:290;
    16:219
Pell, Jeff 23:268
Pell, John 8:28; 18:153
Pell, William 20:3
Pell, William H. H. 8:53
Pellet, Philip 26:54
Pellett, Ed 3:152
Pellner, E. 5:26; 25:218
Pellom, William B.
    11:311
Pellott, James 24:58
Pells, David 19:92
Pelman, Samuel 19:92
Pelnoyer, James 11:71
Pelock, J. 1:163
Pelon, Ch. 20:141
Pelow, John 18:36
Pels, Barney 10:73

Pelson, David L. 9:98
Pelson, Peter 15:219
Pelston, B. 26:176
Pelt, Mason 20:325
Pelton, A. 3:152
Pelton, Albert 13:116
Pelton, Benjamin 23:162
Pelton, Charles N. 14:205
Pelton, David L. 22:152
Pelton, Grosvenor 17:162
Pelton, H. P. 23:162
Pelton, Hiram B. 10:206
Pelton, James 17:84
Pelton, James E. 15:344;
    16:377
Pelton, James H. 22:505
Pelton, N. 14:97
Pelton, W. M. 16:281
Pelton, William 21:168
Pelty, James 8:92
Peltz, Conrad 4:46
Pember, Dennis J. 17:84
Pember, Francis L. 21:259
Pember, Frederic 11:163
Pember, James 17:393
Pember, Merritt C. 7:106
Pembertn, T. 10:206
Pemberton, Elijah 22:488
Pemberton, George 19:92
Pemberton, George G.
    22:213
Pemberton, Henry 10:92;
    18:113; 20:325
Pemberton, J. 8:66
Pemberton, J. C. 10:206
Pemberton, J. D. 9:57
Pemberton, J. M. 18:55
Pemberton, James H.
    21:77
Pemberton, Spencer 7:131
Pemberton, T. 11:292
Pembleton, H. W. 1:163
Pembroke, --- 15:167
Pemcy, W. 3:152
Pemery, O. 15:219
Pemington, Horace 1:63
Pempres, Preston 19:92
Pempres, T. 15:316
Pen, C. 3:152
Pen, Norton 18:421
Pen, R. 3:152
Penabton, J. 3:152
Penage, William S. 13:67
Penago, Milton 27:98
Penapacher, Alnon 11:268
Penas, Charles 9:163
Penat, A. 3:152
Pence, Abraham 22:127
Pence, E. 14:97
Pence, Edward 7:37
Pence, G. 3:152

Pence, Noah 22:95
Pence, P. 26:176
Pence, Sampson 10:174;
19:185
Pence, Samuel 21:125
Pence, W. S. 11:73
Pencer, Cyrus 15:73
Pencer, Jerome 10:206
Pencil, George 20:325
Pencil, Solomon 15:320;
19:92
Pencock, George 14:286
Pendall, Benjamin D. 7:69
Pendall, J. 14:97
Pendar, Thomas 14:205
Pendegrast, William M.
22:264
Pendegrast, William
18:340
Pendele, J. W. 9:88
Pendell, G. 8:108
Pendell, Oscar L. 20:12
Pendell, Stephen 10:130;
20:325
Pender, Dawson 21:150
Pender, John 22:435
Pender, L. R. 1:164
Pender, O. S. 25:62
Pender, William 21:375
Pender, Wright B. 24:27
Pendergass, P. 9:223
Pendergast, James 14:205
Pendergraft, T. T. 13:132
Pendergras, J. 21:164
Pendergrass, --- 9:135
Pendergrass, A. A. 26:52
Pendergrass, Edward
19:29
Pendergrass, I. 14:205
Pendergrass, J. 14:258
Pendergrass, James
23:251
Pendergrass, Lewis 27:97
Pendergrass, Louis 9:135
Pendergrass, M. 19:241
Pendergrass, Michael
9:189
Pendergrass, N. A. 9:88
Pendergrass, Nero 27:98
Pendergrass, P. 18:373
Pendergrass, Robert
26:213
Pendergrast, Edward
14:206
Pendergrast, George W.
23:101
Pendergrast, J. 27:98
Penderson, S. 22:504
Pendhamer, George 13:41
Pendill, Thomas C. 8:92
Pendlan, Charles 21:77

Pendle, F. A. 18:55
Pendle, J. W. 26:52
Pendle, Philip 12:54
Pendle, Stephen R. 19:186
Pendlebury, Henry 27:94
Pendleton, A. 16:219;
26:53
Pendleton, Albert 9:88
Pendleton, Benjamin
11:211
Pendleton, Frank 12:83;
16:302
Pendleton, Henry C. 20:25
Pendleton, Israel 8:115
Pendleton, James H.
16:141
Pendleton, John 17:72;
23:162
Pendleton, John B. 11:415
Pendleton, Lewis 24:102
Pendleton, Samuel 5:26;
11:163
Pendleton, Thomas E.
7:37
Pendleton, W. 3:152;
27:98
Pendleton, William
14:301; 17:471
Pendleton, William B. C.
17:24
Pendleton, William I.
20:31
Pendleton, Zachariah
10:130; 20:325
Pendorf, Frederick M.
5:26
Pendricks, James H.
22:127
Pendruf, J. M. 25:218
Pendry, William 20:325
Penecomph, Archibald
22:264
Penel, Jacob 17:40
Penell, Arminias 18:153
Pener, F. 27:100
Peneryl, Eli 7:37
Penestock, H. 11:41
Penfield, --- 23:291
Penfield, F. 23:45
Penfield, George 10:73;
20:325
Penfield, H. L. 26:53
Penfield, Nathan E. 8:28;
18:153
Penfield, S. M. 20:141
Penfold, James 20:190
Pengery, Thomas 15:219
Pengra, Orrin G. 17:444;
24:161
Penhallow, F. P. 21:375
Penhallow, P. 19:305

Penham, E. H. 21:375
Penhamer, George 16:49
Penhollow, P. 10:29
Penick, David 18:248;
26:53
Penick, Frederick M.
21:37
Penick, Jared 10:177;
19:186
Penick, Ned 17:137;
24:201
Penick, T. J. 7:52
Penicks, G. 1:164
Penington, Henry 9:57
Penington, Preston 17:389
Penix, J. 3:152
Penix, W. 7:37
Penkerton, William
14:206
Penlan, A. 11:86
Penland, John 11:268
Penland, Joseph 23:109
Penley, Joseph 23:103
Penlis, N. 15:299
Penlrs, Nehemiah 16:219
Penman, James R. F.
11:323
Penman, R. T. 11:341
Penn, A. L. 22:354
Penn, C. 8:27
Penn, Caleb 17:183
Penn, Carl 20:152
Penn, Charles 18:153
Penn, Edmund 18:221
Penn, Elizur C. 7:63
Penn, G. 26:54
Penn, George 9:88; 21:13
Penn, George P. 16:377
Penn, H. N. 3:152
Penn, J. 3:152; 7:60
Penn, James T. 17:238
Penn, John 17:84; 22:509
Penn, Joseph 11:320
Penn, Louis 25:218
Penn, Peter 12:35
Penn, R. W. 1:164
Penn, Robert 8:27
Penn, Sanford 21:375
Penn, W. 22:354
Penn, W. F. 1:163
Penn, Watt 9:166
Penn, William R. 21:77
Penna, Nichols 18:91
Pennauk, G. 1:99
Pennel, F. 16:219
Pennel, Fred 13:76
Pennell, Americu 8:28
Pennell, Delos 24:171
Pennell, E. W. 1:161
Pennell, George 12:59
Pennell, H. 27:95

Pennell, Henry 8:92
Pennell, James 16:49
Pennell, Samuel 11:310
Pennell, Wesley H.
26:177
Penneman, James M. 7:60
Penner, Francis 10:131;
20:325
Penner, J. 14:289; 23:205
Penner, James D. 23:75
Pennery, J. B. 15:110
Penney, James 1:62
Penney, L. R. 1:64
Penney, Warren 9:98
Pennick, O. 1:63
Penniman, F. W. 11:101
Penniman, George 10:165
Pennin, Hosea 7:16
Penning, Harmon 4:46
Pennington, Benjamin
17:353
Pennington, C. 17:183
Pennington, C. L. 14:97
Pennington, Francis M.
8:92
Pennington, G. 3:152
Pennington, George
9:189; 19:259; 23:75
Pennington, George B.
22:435
Pennington, Isaac 8:108
Pennington, J. 26:213
Pennington, J. C. 1:65
Pennington, James 7:71;
8:92
Pennington, Jo. W. 21:37
Pennington, Joel 23:286
Pennington, Joel H.
22:213
Pennington, John 11:129
Pennington, L. L. 23:162
Pennington, M. 21:150
Pennington, R. A. 3:152
Pennington, S. W. 25:218
Pennington, Simeon
18:407
Pennington, Thomas
14:206
Pennington, William
21:104
Pennington, Z. K. 9:57
Pennix, G. 17:253
Pennock, Ira 20:108
Pennock, Jacob 15:58
Pennock, John 26:109
Pennoyer, Benjamin
10:73; 20:325
Pennuck, Elijah 19:186
Penny, A. 3:152
Penny, Andrew 4:46
Penny, B. 24:27

Penny, Calvin 9:88; 26:54
Penny, Christopher
22:213
Penny, D. 20:156
Penny, Edward 19:277
Penny, G. 1:162
Penny, Isaac 11:311
Penny, J. 3:152; 19:241
Penny, J. H. 14:206
Penny, James 9:189
Penny, Leander 22:213
Penny, Morris 23:45
Penny, Oliver F. 22:409
Penny, Richard 21:77
Penny, Robert 22:315
Penny, Silas 10:73;
20:325
Penny, Sylvester 9:38
Penny, Walter 7:106
Penny, William 10:131;
12:35; 17:495;
20:325
Penny, William G. 8:28;
18:153
Pennyann, J. 14:206
Pennybacker, Isaac I.
17:167
Pennyman, Charles C.
11:427
Peno, Henry 19:29
Peno, J. 19:259
Penolt, O. 18:55
Penoyar, Ira 16:100
Penoyar, John C. 23:289
Penred, Samuel 22:213
Penrith, J. 23:118
Penrock, John 18:295
Penrod, James 11:164
Penrod, John F. 11:164
Penrod, Tobias 11:311
Penrod, William 8:92
Penrose, Clement B.
16:71
Penrose, John S. 23:162
Penrose, Robert F. 22:48
Penrose, W. H. 21:190
Penroy, --- 22:524
Penry, Henry 19:92
Penry, Lewis F. 21:232
Pensano, J. 14:206
Pense, Alfred 9:237;
26:224
Pense, Wesley 22:213
Pensel, T. 1:63
Penstock, A. 3:152
Pent, P. 14:97
Pentecost, W. G. 3:152
Penticuff, Hanston 17:319
Penticuff, John 21:86
Penticupp, Levi 8:108
Pentis, Jacob J. 9:189

Pentland, W. 13:96
Pentlar, John C. 22:172
Pentler, J. H. 25:218
Pentling, Edward C.
17:356
Penton, Mathias P. 22:409
Penton, William J. B.
22:48
Pentz, John 1:64
Pentz, William A. 22:435
Penwell, James 22:152
Penwell, Thomas 4:46
Peny, A. B. 3:152
Peo, James 3:152
People, N. 11:415
People, Robert M. 4:46
Peoples, --- 20:179
Peoples, Abel 23:162
Peoples, Abraham 17:57
Peoples, Alexander 7:37;
22:48
Peoples, George F. 17:40
Peoples, James 17:84
Peoples, James D. 22:48
Peoples, James J. 11:415
Peoples, Jonathan 17:24
Peoples, R. 18:248; 26:55
Peoples, T. N. 11:72
Peoples, William 21:213
Peper, F. 25:312
Peper, H. L. 19:187
Pepler, Charles 10:21
Pepoon, B. 2:16
Pepoon, Lawrence C.
12:35
Pepoon, P. 25:60
Peppard, William 22:95
Peppardine, William S.
12:157
Peppards, James 12:157
Peppenhaum, Henry 7:52
Pepper, Albert A. 22:455
Pepper, D. 6:32; 25:325
Pepper, Erwin 9:112
Pepper, Heinrich 23:162
Pepper, J. M. 12:83;
16:302
Pepper, James 7:131;
23:291
Pepper, James A. 21:232
Pepper, Joseph B. 9:123
Pepper, M. 2:16; 25:62
Pepper, Nathaniel 15:42
Pepper, Samuel 22:455
Pepper, Stepheno 10:73
Pepper, T. H. 11:281
Pepperdine, Thomas
20:12
Pepperman, Charles W.
12:35
Pepperman, J. 1:63

Pepperman, John 15:110
Peppers, George 10:177;
    19:186
Peppers, Joseph B. 27:97
Peppers, William 24:179
Peppinger, H. 1:63
Peppinger, Simon 10:73
Peppinger, Simon R.
    20:325
Pepworth, J. 14:206
Pequette, F. 3:152
Perahouse, J. J. 7:37
Perastrine, Trogett 8:28
Perat, W. 18:407
Perath, George 19:316
Percary, James 8:66
Percefield, John 17:283
Perceful, David L. 17:283
Percell, Bryson 20:325
Percell, C. 14:97
Percell, Thomas 11:17
Percell, William 6:9
Percelly, Stephen 10:174
Percer, James L. 11:129
Percey, George A. 22:283
Percey, John M. 20:143
Perchard, Thomas W.
    20:325
Percifield, George 18:221
Perciner, Joseph 21:37
Percival, A. E. 2:16; 25:62
Percival, G. E. 16:281
Percival, R. 17:494
Percival, Whitman 19:29
Percry, James M. 9:189
Percury, James 26:176
Percy, David C. 20:325
Percy, G. 25:218
Percy, Howard 10:73;
    20:325
Percy, J. M. 19:259
Percy, Jacob 4:46
Percy, James R. 23:162
Percy, Leonard 4:67
Perdan, Benjamin 6:26
Perden, H. 14:97
Perden, King C. 17:203
Perdew, George 17:207
Perdew, Nathan 19:92
Perdin, J. 25:218
Perdue, Casear 25:60
Perdue, George L. 17:207
Perdue, George W. 24:43
Perdue, Henry H. 22:127
Perdue, J. 9:149; 27:95
Perdue, James W. 9:98
Perdue, Noah 9:135
Perdue, Rufus 21:196
Perdue, William 22:436
Perego, J. 3:152
Perego, W. 3:152

Perely, Ephraim 26:177
Perenoyer, E. 19:29
Peres, --- 19:323
Perey, G. 19:92
Perfect, Edwin R. 20:148
Perfin, Aug 17:447
Perforce, Garrett 7:106
Perged, J. 9:149
Perger, Franz 1:63
Perggay, N. 19:92
Perham, Warren 17:244
Periam, Joseph 16:145
Perick, W. C. 16:270
Pericle, J. 3:152
Perig, Robert 17:24
Perigo, Romey 23:75
Perigo, Warren I. 12:35
Perin, C. H. 8:66; 26:176
Perin, H. 16:219
Perine, Abram 13:116
Perine, David S. 11:164
Perine, Enoch 1:64
Perine, George R. 11:268
Perine, W. E. 20:152
Perino, W. 14:97
Perio, John 9:189
Perish, Benjamin 10:174;
    19:186
Perish, David C. 22:409
Perishal, Herman 10:149
Perishol, Herman 18:55
Perisles, W. 11:248
Periste, William H. 12:65;
    15:73
Perk, Frederick 10:73
Perk, J. G. 15:132
Perke, Christian 6:8
Perkey, David 23:306
Perkey, Elijah P. 22:172
Perkin, L. D. 13:116
Perkins, --- 10:187;
    18:178; 20:43;
    26:213
Perkins, A. A. 18:36
Perkins, A. C. 9:57
Perkins, A. E. 3:152
Perkins, A. H. 3:152
Perkins, A. N. 19:29
Perkins, A. W. 1:161
Perkins, Abijah 7:37
Perkins, Absalom 9:135;
    27:96
Perkins, Addison 21:118;
    22:315
Perkins, Almond 10:92;
    20:325
Perkins, Alvin 11:311
Perkins, Ami 11:129
Perkins, Anthony 21:281
Perkins, Arthur J. 10:21
Perkins, Asa E. 9:7

Perkins, Augustus 21:281
Perkins, Benjamin 18:248;
    26:54
Perkins, C. 25:273
Perkins, C. H. W. 26:52
Perkins, C. R. 1:161
Perkins, C. S. 16:219
Perkins, Calvin M. 11:101
Perkins, Calvin S. 13:67
Perkins, Charles 8:58;
    10:10; 22:152;
    23:162
Perkins, Charles C. 1:63
Perkins, Charles F. 21:375
Perkins, Charles W. 9:88
Perkins, Columbus 9:73
Perkins, D. 3:152; 7:52;
    15:299
Perkins, D. B. 1:99
Perkins, D. F. 15:287;
    19:92
Perkins, Daniel 10:73;
    16:219; 20:325;
    27:99
Perkins, David 7:131;
    9:240
Perkins, Delos 9:104
Perkins, Demsey 17:183
Perkins, E. 1:163; 8:74;
    25:218
Perkins, E. B. 1:64
Perkins, E. F. 8:118
Perkins, Edward 5:44
Perkins, Edwin F. 4:46
Perkins, Edwin J. 19:186
Perkins, Elby 17:57
Perkins, Eli 22:315
Perkins, Elikins 6:26
Perkins, Ezra C. 20:325
Perkins, Ezra H. 10:131
Perkins, F. 14:206, 258
Perkins, F. O. 19:229
Perkins, Freeman 14:335
Perkins, G. W. 1:65;
    11:97
Perkins, George E. 21:259
Perkins, George S. 12:157
Perkins, H. 14:97
Perkins, H. E. H. 11:278
Perkins, H. G. 19:229
Perkins, H. J. 16:219
Perkins, H. L. 1:65
Perkins, H. S. 8:108
Perkins, Hanson C. 4:46
Perkins, Henry 9:123,
    160; 27:97
Perkins, Henry D. 18:249;
    26:53
Perkins, Henry W. 9:9
Perkins, Hiram 21:232
Perkins, Holloway 26:176

Perkins, Horatio G. 19:29
Perkins, I. 1:65
Perkins, I. B. 26:55
Perkins, I. H. 26:224
Perkins, Isaac 17:85
Perkins, Isaiah 1:63
Perkins, Ithamer 22:436
Perkins, J. 4:46; 13:96; 20:326
Perkins, J. A. 3:152; 8:53; 21:37
Perkins, J. G. 22:488
Perkins, J. H. 1:99, 161; 7:60
Perkins, J. P. 3:152
Perkins, J. R. 1:64
Perkins, J. V. 1:162
Perkins, J. W. 17:145; 18:36
Perkins, Jackson 8:41
Perkins, Jackstead 26:177
Perkins, James 1:62; 10:73, 131; 11:222; 15:299; 16:219; 20:326; 22:48
Perkins, James A. 12:35
Perkins, Jefferson 22:127
Perkins, Jeremiah B. 9:88
Perkins, Joel 17:238
Perkins, John 8:41; 9:27; 14:97, 206; 18:314; 21:37; 22:127; 26:109, 177
Perkins, John E. 23:45
Perkins, John H. 4:46
Perkins, Joseph 15:268
Perkins, Joseph W. 17:288
Perkins, L. 10:210; 14:258; 25:218
Perkins, L. L. 26:177
Perkins, Leonard 27:99
Perkins, Leonidas 22:488
Perkins, Lewis 22:264
Perkins, Lewis K. 27:95
Perkins, Lewis L. 12:35
Perkins, Lizzie 26:213
Perkins, Lucien L. 8:74
Perkins, M. H. 14:97
Perkins, Manuel E. 8:53
Perkins, Martin J. H. 13:41
Perkins, Melvin A. 19:29
Perkins, Moses 20:326
Perkins, N. 3:152; 26:53
Perkins, N. D. 11:41
Perkins, Nathan 9:88; 21:281
Perkins, Nelson 17:137; 24:201
Perkins, Norris C. 20:115
Perkins, O. 1:64

Perkins, O. W. 15:11
Perkins, Oliver 22:152
Perkins, Orrin W. 12:75
Perkins, P. D. 1:161
Perkins, P. G. 15:174
Perkins, P. P. 24:113
Perkins, Paul 17:211
Perkins, Reuben J. 21:104
Perkins, Robinson 11:391
Perkins, S. A. 9:189
Perkins, S. O. 14:206
Perkins, Seth 19:29
Perkins, Stephen 10:177
Perkins, Steven 19:186
Perkins, T. 3:152
Perkins, T. J. 2:15; 19:222
Perkins, Thomas 1:64; 5:53; 7:131; 8:53; 9:204; 14:206; 18:270; 22:48; 25:218
Perkins, Thomas B. 13:41
Perkins, Thomas N. 21:77
Perkins, Tobias 23:91
Perkins, Truman 7:37
Perkins, W. 1:163; 14:236; 23:115
Perkins, W. B. 2:16; 3:152
Perkins, W. H. 15:167; 26:52
Perkins, W. L. 7:37
Perkins, W. R. 25:62
Perkins, Wash 11:211
Perkins, Washington 24:102
Perkins, Wesley 11:73
Perkins, William 12:57; 21:232; 22:264, 315; 24:54
Perkins, William F. 21:77
Perkins, William G. 24:54
Perkins, William H. 23:241
Perkins, William J. 5:26; 25:218
Perkins, Wilson 9:215
Perkinson, --- 1:163
Perkinson, B. 22:315
Perkinson, Carter 27:147
Perkinson, Robert H. 19:29
Perkis, Samuel 7:106
Perkiss, J. L. 21:375
Perkiss, Wilson 21:375
Perkisson, William 8:93
Perkizer, U. 15:219
Perkman, C. 1:161
Perkum, H. P. 8:74
Perky, D. 3:152
Perky, L. 11:165
Perlay, S. A. 26:52

Perle, A. 14:244
Perle, Abraham 14:244
Perle, John 7:37
Perler, J. E. 26:52
Perley, J. L. 14:244
Perlte, Isaac 11:96
Perly, David S. 20:156
Permell, Edward 26:224
Permenter, D. 1:62
Permick, George W. 2:16
Pernell, Edward D. 9:237
Pernell, John 22:315
Pernstine, Trogett 18:153
Perny, J. F. 22:48
Pero, Alexander 19:297
Pero, George 8:115
Pero, James 9:210; 18:70
Pero, John 13:58
Pero, Joseph 16:219
Pero, Peter 7:106
Pero, William M. 17:102
Perod, Joseph 13:67
Perona, Bernard 10:131; 20:326
Perow, Benjamin 13:41
Perr, George H. 21:375
Perrego, H. A. 25:218
Perrett, J. R. 22:399
Perrey, E. R. 14:97
Perrey, Thomas C. 14:97
Perriber, Jared T. 25:61
Perrick, Elijah 10:174
Perridan, Henry 21:376
Perridge, Sanford 19:92
Perrig, James 11:164
Perrigan, Thomas 25:303
Perrige, C. W. 14:206
Perriger, Levi 6:18; 18:91
Perrigo, Henry A. 5:26
Perrigo, Herbert 23:194
Perrigo, Oliver P. 4:46
Perrigo, Simeon 23:109
Perrigo, W. 23:45
Perrill, E. R. 26:54
Perriman, Levi 24:102
Perrin, Albert 14:206
Perrin, Almer 25:218
Perrin, Harvey 18:407
Perrin, James M. 23:162
Perrin, John 9:189; 19:259
Perrin, N. 3:152
Perrin, Oscar 22:213
Perrin, S. R. 23:289
Perrin, Thomas G. 17:70
Perrin, W. 25:218
Perrin, William 5:26
Perrine, Alfred 19:186
Perrine, C. D. 11:164
Perrine, Charles 23:109
Perrine, G. 3:152

Perrine, George W. 22:213
Perrine, J. 9:189; 14:97
Perrine, James B. 11:96
Perrine, James C. 11:163; 16:143
Perrine, Joseph H. 4:46
Perrine, Lewis 8:121
Perrine, Richard 25:62
Perrine, Spafford 19:186
Perrine, William T. 17:210
Perring, Cornelius H. 23:76
Perrington, Charles 24:71
Perrinton, Thomas 14:236
Perrish, Dick 17:137; 24:201
Perrish, John P. 25:218
Perro, Julius 15:132
Perry, --- 11:220
Perry, A. 3:152; 19:283
Perry, A. C. 10:73; 20:326
Perry, A. D. 1:162
Perry, A. E. 25:62
Perry, A. F. 15:110
Perry, Abel M. 4:46
Perry, Abner 9:210; 18:70
Perry, Abraham 21:125
Perry, Adams 22:435
Perry, Albert 12:157
Perry, Albert J. 9:88
Perry, Albert R. 1:63
Perry, Albert W. 13:41; 16:49
Perry, Alexander 21:281
Perry, Amos 21:376
Perry, Anderson 9:189
Perry, Andrew 13:116
Perry, Asel 19:29
Perry, Augustus 18:270
Perry, B. 1:162; 5:44; 21:150; 25:218
Perry, C. A. 19:186
Perry, C. F. 9:149
Perry, C. M. 27:95
Perry, C. S. 17:156
Perry, C. W. 26:177
Perry, Cariden W. 8:74
Perry, Chandler F. 16:79
Perry, Charles 11:164; 15:18, 153
Perry, Charles A. 9:57
Perry, Charles H. 4:46
Perry, Charles W. 22:409
Perry, Clark C. 4:46
Perry, Columbia J. 26:225
Perry, Cyrus A. 19:186
Perry, D. A. 5:26; 25:218
Perry, D. H. 12:87; 16:302

Perry, D. L. 11:341
Perry, Daniel 25:60; 26:177
Perry, Daniel W. 21:376
Perry, David 21:77; 22:14, 48, 152
Perry, David E. 11:255
Perry, E. 1:162
Perry, E. R. 7:37
Perry, Edward 8:59; 14:206
Perry, Eli B. 19:229
Perry, Elias 4:46; 22:515
Perry, Elijah 21:77
Perry, Ephraim J. D. 21:259
Perry, F. 1:162
Perry, F. M. 11:248; 23:162
Perry, F. W. 9:149
Perry, Filay 19:283
Perry, Finley 9:201
Perry, Frank 11:391
Perry, G. 3:152
Perry, G. E. 7:60
Perry, G. W. 14:97
Perry, George 8:66; 20:193; 24:27
Perry, George A. 19:29
Perry, George D. 13:67; 19:92
Perry, George W. 14:206; 20:2
Perry, H. 3:152
Perry, H. H. 4:46; 16:49
Perry, H. W. 9:149; 27:95
Perry, Hale 22:48
Perry, Henry 1:63
Perry, Henry A. 21:376
Perry, J. 3:152; 16:219; 24:27
Perry, J. A. 25:218
Perry, J. C. 19:92
Perry, J. F. 19:259
Perry, J. L. 1:99
Perry, Jacob 8:77
Perry, James 1:65; 15:220
Perry, James A. 12:35
Perry, James H. 10:97
Perry, James M. 19:186; 22:436
Perry, James R. 22:435
Perry, Jefferson T. 19:29
Perry, Jesse 11:188
Perry, Joe 9:57
Perry, John 4:46; 8:28; 10:73; 13:67; 15:220; 16:219; 18:55, 153; 19:92; 20:326; 21:190, 376; 25:62, 218

Perry, John D. 16:88
Perry, John E. 5:53; 10:21
Perry, John F. 9:189
Perry, Jonathan 11:73
Perry, Joseph 7:37
Perry, L. 12:75; 14:97; 15:8
Perry, L. B. 21:37
Perry, L. S. 1:64
Perry, Lander 17:156
Perry, Leander 12:83; 16:302
Perry, M. 3:152
Perry, M. A. 26:55
Perry, M. C. 14:98
Perry, M. J. 1:99
Perry, M. R. 19:259
Perry, Martin 7:37
Perry, Marvin L. 22:48
Perry, Mathew 27:98
Perry, Mitchell 18:221
Perry, Mordecai 18:221
Perry, Mordicia 24:43
Perry, Moses 18:91
Perry, N. 3:153
Perry, N. E. 16:49
Perry, Nathan 26:176
Perry, Nathaniel 10:73; 20:326
Perry, Nelson 18:249; 26:54
Perry, Niel A. 20:152
Perry, Nimrod 22:48
Perry, O. 1:164; 21:37
Perry, O. E. 1:160
Perry, O. H. 22:213
Perry, Philip 9:104
Perry, Philips 18:340
Perry, Ransom 7:131
Perry, Reuben J. 17:156
Perry, Robert 8:28; 18:153
Perry, S. 22:213, 504
Perry, S. B. 22:487
Perry, S. G. 19:29
Perry, S. H. 15:220
Perry, S. M. 3:153
Perry, Sampson 13:41
Perry, Samuel 9:135; 18:249, 413; 27:96
Perry, Samuel C. 9:27
Perry, Series 10:10
Perry, Simon 12:51
Perry, Smith 9:210
Perry, T. 1:163; 3:153; 16:377
Perry, T. A. 21:376
Perry, T. W. 27:95
Perry, Thomas 13:58; 23:287; 25:218
Perry, Thomas N. 17:238

Perry, Thornton 23:13
Perry, Tim 15:73
Perry, Timothy 12:75
Perry, Valentine 14:206
Perry, W. 1:161; 3:153;
    4:46; 9:57; 11:73
Perry, W. H. 1:161
Perry, W. J. 1:162
Perry, W. R. 9:189
Perry, W. S. 1:65, 95
Perry, Wesley 9:88; 26:54
Perry, William 3:153;
    8:58; 10:174; 16:49;
    17:504; 19:186;
    21:150; 22:265;
    27:94
Perry, William C. 11:72
Perry, William H. 15:5;
    21:104
Perry, William L. 10:73
Perry, William S. 21:77
Perryer, J. 27:96
Perrygold, G. 1:161
Perryman, Alexander
    8:28; 18:153
Perryman, James 7:8
Perryman, William A.
    21:104
Persales, George 13:116
Persell, C. E. 18:55
Perset, Edward 22:152
Pershin, C. W. 23:45
Persil, F. 3:153
Persinger, Isaiah 24:43
Persinger, Moses B. 8:93
Persley, Gael 11:210
Person, Henry 21:281
Person, J. 14:98
Person, T. 13:96
Person, William 11:163
Personell, James 18:221
Personeous, William J.
    23:124
Personett, John 11:122
Personius, Oliver R. 22:48
Personius, Zachariah 4:46
Persons, A. 1:63
Persons, Alex 16:49
Persons, Alexander 13:41
Persons, Irvin M. 15:132
Persons, L. B. 24:27
Persons, Uriah 11:333
Persons, W. 25:61
Persons, W. B. 3:153
Pertee, John E. 16:49
Perteison, Samuel 10:73
Pertel, Thomas 25:218
Perterson, Christopher
    10:73
Perth, Rudolph 23:261
Pertit, Thomas 5:53

Pertle, Jessee R. 23:115
Pervere, Russell M. 24:61
Perview, E. 18:91
Pervis, James 17:57;
    22:455
Pervis, John A. 5:26
Pervis, Levi 15:333
Pervis, Lewis 19:92
Pervis, T. 3:153
Pery, Samuel 26:54
Perynce, Henry 8:116
Perz, William 21:11
Perzifull, Z. T. 18:178
Pesch, Peter 10:73;
    20:326
Pesgrove, Riley 17:24
Pesha, Lewis 19:305
Peshtel, William 4:46
Peske, Christian 18:113
Pess, M. T. 3:153
Pesso, T. A. 11:164
Pestana, Daniel 9:98
Pete, Elijah 13:41
Pete, Lorin L. 1:64
Petec, Rothins 19:186
Petell, Henry W. 12:35
Petelle, F. 15:300
Petello, F. 16:219
Peter, A. 11:247; 14:206
Peter, Alexander 14:98
Peter, Dunbart 24:202
Peter, E. M. 15:353
Peter, John 19:292;
    22:315
Peter, Louis 13:41
Peter, Lucy 15:220
Peter, Philip 25:325
Peter, Simon 7:131;
    10:99; 21:281;
    22:435
Peter, Thomas 17:24
Peterbaugh, John 22:152
Peterch, Paul 8:108
Peterie, John N. 20:326
Peterin, John A. 10:73
Peterkop, --- 15:94
Peterman, Charles 7:106
Peterman, D. P. 23:45
Peterman, Jacob D. 12:35
Peterman, Randolph 13:41
Peterman, William 21:232
Peters, Alf 25:303
Peters, Alfred 7:80
Peters, Amos 15:220
Peters, Andrew J. 9:135;
    23:13; 27:96
Peters, C. 9:149; 11:248;
    27:96
Peters, C. J. 11:164
Peters, Caleb 13:41

Peters, Carlos B. 10:73;
    20:326
Peters, Charles 7:106;
    20:99; 21:376
Peters, Charles K. 23:76
Peters, Cornelius 4:46
Peters, D. P. 1:162
Peters, Dennis 1:62
Peters, E. 9:149; 27:96
Peters, Edward 5:53;
    22:487
Peters, Essex 11:336
Peters, F. 3:153; 15:313
Peters, Frank 9:157, 189;
    19:275
Peters, Franklin 4:46
Peters, G. E. 25:218
Peters, George E. 5:44
Peters, Gerhard 18:399
Peters, H. 1:161; 3:153
Peters, H. A. 7:65
Peters, Harrison 8:116
Peters, Heinrich 21:141
Peters, Henry 8:93;
    21:376; 23:241;
    24:69
Peters, Henry S. 17:420;
    24:161
Peters, I. 11:73
Peters, Idea F. 22:48
Peters, Isaac 10:131;
    20:326
Peters, J. 3:153; 9:189;
    14:244; 19:259
Peters, J. W. 17:338
Peters, Jacob 21:77
Peters, James 18:16;
    25:286
Peters, Jason 16:219
Peters, Jefferson A. 17:85
Peters, Johan 21:77
Peters, John 6:21; 9:201;
    11:110; 12:65, 75;
    13:41; 15:8, 73;
    20:115; 22:95, 213;
    23:291; 25:61
Peters, John A. 19:29
Peters, John H. 23:101
Peters, John P. 22:48
Peters, John R. 15:8
Peters, John S. 17:393
Peters, Joseph 4:67;
    11:41; 22:342
Peters, Lewis 23:162
Peters, Malcom B. 21:376
Peters, Michael 19:29
Peters, Monroe 11:165
Peters, Morrison 25:218
Peters, P. 19:92
Peters, Philip 6:32
Peters, Randolph 18:440

Peters, Reuben 12:51
Peters, Richard D. 19:186
Peters, Robert 21:281
Peters, S. 13:81; 16:219
Peters, Samuel 7:131;
　10:155; 19:186
Peters, Shadrack 23:271
Peters, Simon 11:163
Peters, Stephen W. 20:28
Peters, T. 1:64
Peters, Thomas 1:63;
　21:376
Peters, Van 24:27
Peters, W. C. 21:37
Peters, Wiley 22:315
Peters, William 10:174;
　16:219; 20:326;
　23:194
Peters, William A. 22:95
Peters, William E. 23:185
Peters, William F. 8:93
Peters, William H. 1:63
Peters, William W. 19:186
Petersburg, D. 18:249;
　26:53
Petersburg, George
　21:201
Petersen, --- 15:42
Peterson, --- 9:201
Peterson, A. 3:153; 13:96;
　14:19; 19:259;
　25:279
Peterson, Abraham 22:113
Peterson, Adam 22:48;
　27:95
Peterson, Alexander 9:189
Peterson, Alfred 9:189
Peterson, Andrew 7:106;
　17:295; 22:342;
　27:95
Peterson, Arnold 6:18;
　18:91
Peterson, Aspian 22:49
Peterson, August 12:157;
　25:218
Peterson, Benjamin 13:41
Peterson, Borre 17:100
Peterson, C. 3:153;
　20:326; 23:45
Peterson, Carey 11:211
Peterson, Chalmon 24:83
Peterson, Charles 11:288;
　19:186; 23:243
Peterson, Charles F. 9:8
Peterson, Charles M.
　23:91
Peterson, Christopher
　23:13
Peterson, Claus 17:317
Peterson, Cornelius
　18:407

Peterson, Daniel 23:194
Peterson, David 21:376;
　24:83
Peterson, E. 11:292;
　12:163
Peterson, F. 3:153
Peterson, F. E. 17:70
Peterson, Falif 8:74
Peterson, Folloff 26:177
Peterson, Francis 10:131;
　20:326
Peterson, Frank 12:35
Peterson, Franklin 25:62
Peterson, Fred 11:41
Peterson, G. 3:153
Peterson, G. L. 22:213
Peterson, Garrett D.
　17:283
Peterson, H. 3:153; 25:61
Peterson, Henry 11:311;
　21:213
Peterson, Herman 11:193
Peterson, Hiram 17:317
Peterson, I. H. 24:83
Peterson, J. 3:153;
　19:241; 21:376;
　25:218
Peterson, J. A. 23:118
Peterson, J. B. 3:153
Peterson, J. P. 23:45
Peterson, J. S. 9:115
Peterson, Jacob 8:93;
　22:113
Peterson, James 4:46;
　10:131; 17:315, 405;
　20:326
Peterson, Janes 9:189
Peterson, John 7:106;
　9:88, 189, 240;
　22:342; 27:147
Peterson, John A. 27:99
Peterson, John B. 22:342
Peterson, John F. 20:326
Peterson, John H. 6:26
Peterson, John M. 11:71
Peterson, John P. 22:95
Peterson, Knud 22:283
Peterson, Knudt 20:326
Peterson, Kudt 10:73
Peterson, L. 1:161
Peterson, Lewis 22:283
Peterson, Lewis W.
　17:454
Peterson, Magnus 10:131;
　20:326
Peterson, Moses 10:165
Peterson, N. B. 19:283
Peterson, Narve 22:509
Peterson, Nelson 9:189
Peterson, O. 9:227;
　11:334; 18:373

Peterson, Ole 8:53;
　21:259; 22:162
Peterson, Oli 22:49
Peterson, P. 3:153
Peterson, Peter 9:135;
　10:97; 14:206; 22:95;
　27:97
Peterson, Peter J. 21:200
Peterson, Ralph 10:174;
　19:186
Peterson, Robert L.
　11:188
Peterson, S. 3:153
Peterson, Samuel 11:232
Peterson, Sidney G.
　13:130
Peterson, Sidney R. 12:35
Peterson, T. 1:62
Peterson, Thomas 17:40;
　22:436
Peterson, W. 1:163;
　11:268; 18:91; 23:45
Peterson, W. C. 23:45
Peterson, W. H. 25:61
Peterson, Warren D.
　22:265
Peterson, William 9:135;
　10:131; 16:50;
　20:326; 22:436;
　25:62; 27:97
Peterson, William B. 6:26
Peterson, William S.
　20:134; 22:95
Peterson, William T.
　21:77
Petery, W. H. 25:218
Peterzick, Henry 4:46
Petet, C. 16:377
Petffer, Peter 19:92
Petherbridge, George
　21:243
Pethord, G. 19:92
Pethtel, H. 1:161
Petibone, John 20:326
Petie, Oliver 27:147
Petigrew, Bennett 22:521
Petijean, Joseph L. 11:72
Petingal, Nathaniel 19:241
Petingill, John F. 19:233
Petisch, Theodore 25:280
Petison, Theodore 12:35
Petit, Francis M. 26:224
Petit, Solomon 24:72
Petitt, Alex 25:303
Petitt, Isaac M. 11:443
Petlit, Fred 13:67
Peto, --- 23:205
Peto, David 8:53
Peto, Edward 16:100
Peto, Joseph 8:53
Petoe, P. 23:293

Petraw, Charles 11:247
Petre, Jacob 8:28
Petree, David 21:232
Petree, Rufus 10:21
Petrey, G. 11:163
Petrie, A. 15:220
Petrie, G. C. 1:64
Petrie, J. 3:153
Petrie, Jacob 23:194
Petrie, L. N. 19:259
Petrie, M. D. 17:156
Petrie, Robert A. 27:94
Petrie, Seth 22:152
Petril, E. M. 16:281
Petristy, H. 3:153
Petro, Lewis 7:37
Petroy, --- 1:161
Petrugal, Nathaniel 9:189
Petry, Nick 27:99
Petsey, F. 14:336
Petson, D. 25:279
Petsor, F. 7:37
Pett, Joseph 9:189
Pett, Mason 10:73
Pett, W. 25:218
Pettay, James F. 22:95
Pettay, John 10:131;
    20:326
Pette, Joseph 12:162
Pette, Valentine 18:209
Pettebone, W. 13:96;
    14:258
Pettee, Rotheus 10:165
Pettegal, Sim 15:175
Pettel, George 23:45
Pettengill, A. 1:161
Pettengill, A. J. 12:9
Pettengill, James A. 13:41
Pettengill, O. C. 23:45
Petteplace, C. H. 19:186
Petter, A. 23:205
Petter, Frederick 19:92
Petterman, Henry 19:186
Petters, J. 11:248
Petterson, A. 3:153
Petterson, C. 25:60
Petterson, Samuel 20:326
Pettes, Henry C. 7:131
Pettes, John W. 22:152
Pettet, John L. 21:245
Petteys, John 18:16
Pettibone, C. S. 2:16
Pettibone, E. 14:98
Pettibone, E. E. 3:153
Pettibone, F. A. 9:124;
    27:94
Pettibone, J. H. 21:93
Pettibone, J. M. 8:53
Pettibone, John 10:73
Pettibone, L. 19:186
Pettibone, R. 21:37

Pettick, George W. 9:57
Petticks, J. M. 11:277
Pettie, C. 3:153
Pettie, George C. 17:448;
    24:173
Pettiford, R. C. 22:315
Pettigg, Hix 22:505
Pettigrew, Henry 21:150
Pettigrew, J. H. 7:52
Pettijohn, Edward 12:93
Pettijohn, Elias 17:24
Pettijohn, J. 3:153
Pettijohn, O. P. 21:376
Pettijohn, S. W. 3:153
Pettijohn, William 9:189;
    19:278
Pettinger, George 16:141
Pettinger, William 26:54
Pettingill, Asa 16:100
Pettingill, Charles 11:110
Pettingill, J. M. 17:159
Pettingill, James 22:466
Pettingill, James A. 16:50
Pettingill, Roswell 22:466
Pettingill, W. 1:163
Pettis, A. B. 14:98
Pettis, Egbert L. 22:265
Pettis, F. 14:19
Pettis, Frank 22:315
Pettis, G. H. 11:311
Pettis, Hiram 7:106
Pettis, John 11:210
Pettis, L. P. 3:153
Pettis, Osborne 22:315
Pettis, Plinny 22:466
Pettis, Robert N. 21:77
Pettis, T. 13:96
Pettis, W. 22:342
Pettis, William 21:246
Pettishfish, A. J. 11:40
Pettit, Abraham 22:152
Pettit, Alexander 7:81
Pettit, Byron 21:77
Pettit, David 5:26
Pettit, E. 14:98
Pettit, Francis M. 9:237
Pettit, G. 21:37
Pettit, J. 1:163; 3:153
Pettit, John 19:186; 22:95;
    26:213
Pettit, Joseph 4:46
Pettit, Joseph A. 21:259
Pettit, Lorenzo N. 13:41
Pettit, Moses M. 13:128
Pettit, Philip 18:249
Pettit, T. W. 22:213
Pettitt, John 10:165
Pettitt, M. E. 18:399
Petton, Dewitt C. 13:127
Petton, Henry 15:300
Petton, William 18:16

Pettry, William H. 5:26
Pettsley, William 9:189
Pettus, James H. 17:350
Pettus, William 3:153
Petty, A. J. 18:314;
    26:108
Petty, Allen 9:243
Petty, Augustus 20:176
Petty, Charles 7:131
Petty, Charles H. 18:221
Petty, Edward 13:58
Petty, Hiram A. 14:98
Petty, James 18:209;
    21:37
Petty, Joel 22:95
Petty, John 15:220
Petty, Joseph 21:376
Petty, Reuben 11:403
Petty, Rufus R. 7:106
Petty, Sampson 22:127
Petty, Samuel 9:88;
    22:409; 26:52
Petty, William 9:237;
    10:73; 20:326
Petty, William A. 22:265
Petty, William E. 10:21
Pettybone, Malcolm G.
    12:35
Pettyjohn, Edward 16:302
Pettyjohn, Mark 22:409
Pettys, Franklin 4:46
Pettys, J. W. 14:98
Pettys, Luther 8:59;
    19:272
Pettys, Zenas B. 10:206
Petus, A. 19:259
Petwick, James 11:40
Petwick, John 4:46
Petzer, Cyrus 21:376
Petzer, H. 1:162
Peuse, --- 9:156
Pew, Christopher 22:168
Pew, David 18:249; 26:54
Pew, E. B. 1:160
Pew, Edward 22:435
Pew, J. W. 1:162
Pew, Thomas 11:403
Pew, William 12:75
Pewin, H. A. 3:153
Pewterlaugh, John 15:220
Pexley, Frederick A.
    22:49
Pexson, Benjamin W.
    23:256
Pey, John De 26:109
Peyle, James 11:164
Peyton, A. L. 12:75
Peyton, Alexander 22:49
Peyton, Benjamin F. 8:28;
    18:154
Peyton, Charles 11:211

Peyton, Fletcher 24:59
Peyton, J. 25:303
Peyton, J. W. 25:62
Peyton, Jackson 24:202
Peyton, James 7:78
Peyton, Lewis 19:29
Peyton, Nathan 14:206
Peyton, Perry 22:488
Peyton, Washington 17:137; 24:201
Peyton, William 27:95
Pfaff, William 26:146
Pfahl, William 11:163
Pfalsgraft, Charles 27:99
Pfatzer, Joseph 22:455
Pfeaster, J. 1:162
Pfeifer, Frank 16:50
Pfeifer, Frederick 15:23
Pfeifer, John 7:37
Pfeifer, Lewis 12:123; 15:132
Pfeifer, Peter 21:37
Pfeiffer, Augustus 15:42
Pfeiffer, James 16:100
Pfeifle, Frederick 20:31
Pfeinning, Fred 21:376
Pfeister, Caspar 12:123
Pfemming, Fred 7:106
Pferffer, F. W. 19:92
Pferris, William 7:106
Pfiefer, Peter 8:53
Pfifer, J. 1:163
Pfinest, John 9:27
Pfinist, John 26:109
Pfister, Carper 21:104
Pfister, Castor 15:132
Pfister, H. 1:161
Pfister, Samuel 11:120
Pflechtroper, John 8:28
Pflitchtroper, John 18:154
Pfluger, Edwin 5:26
Pfranzman, Henry 20:140
Pfrimmer, Henry C. 24:27
Pfuist, John 18:314
Pfuller, Joseph 13:41
Pfunder, John 12:9
Phagan, Sanford 13:41
Phail, William 21:376
Phalen, David 24:61
Phalen, Henry 7:106
Phalon, John 16:219
Pharett, Joseph 16:100
Pharis, Martin 27:147
Pharis, N. 27:147
Pharr, E. F. 14:284
Pharrett, William 3:153
Pharris, James H. 22:127
Pharris, Vanburen 22:455
Phasant, James 4:46
Phatt, G. W. 11:310
Phaunt, Lewis 20:43

Phay, M. 3:153
Phay, William 14:206
Pheanix, Joseph 18:16
Phebus, Jesse 11:72
Pheelan, S. 25:218
Phegley, Thomas 24:96
Pheifer, Frederick 12:75
Phelan, Jacob 13:67
Phelan, John 17:362; 22:455
Phelan, Patrick 7:15
Phelan, T. 15:220
Phelan, William 11:183
Phellen, Albert 22:315
Phelon, W. H. 25:275
Phelp, G. M. 14:301; 17:475
Phelp, H. W. 3:153
Phelp, M. 3:153
Phelp, W. H. 1:164
Phelphs, Lysander F. 21:104
Phelphs, William 21:104
Phelps, --- 16:377; 18:178; 25:61
Phelps, A. 8:66
Phelps, A. E. 19:241
Phelps, Albert 18:249; 19:93; 26:54
Phelps, Alva B. 15:220
Phelps, Amos G. 22:49
Phelps, Andy 17:183
Phelps, Arthur 26:176
Phelps, Austin 12:35
Phelps, C. 25:61
Phelps, Charles 16:141; 17:244; 26:127
Phelps, Charles J. 22:509
Phelps, Charles S. 7:106
Phelps, Daniel 9:244
Phelps, David 16:50
Phelps, Delbert 21:142
Phelps, E. A. 1:161
Phelps, E. S. 14:206
Phelps, Elisha 24:90
Phelps, Enoch 12:35
Phelps, F. M. 3:153
Phelps, Frederick 16:100
Phelps, G. K. 17:85
Phelps, Gamer 19:93
Phelps, George 7:60; 11:335; 17:137
Phelps, George W. 18:346
Phelps, H. 14:206
Phelps, Henry 10:131; 19:186; 20:326
Phelps, Horace 8:115
Phelps, Hugh 14:98
Phelps, J. A. 1:162
Phelps, J. F. 1:162
Phelps, James 7:106

Phelps, James H. 19:186
Phelps, James L. 1:62
Phelps, James M. 17:57
Phelps, Jerrymirah 20:326
Phelps, John 8:66; 17:24, 137, 503; 24:201; 26:176
Phelps, John A. 21:376
Phelps, John C. 22:409
Phelps, Jonathan H. 1:64
Phelps, Joseph 13:41
Phelps, L. 21:37
Phelps, Leven 17:209
Phelps, Lewis 21:291
Phelps, Lloyd 12:55
Phelps, Lorenzo D. 11:403
Phelps, Louis G. 10:21
Phelps, Lyman D. 13:41
Phelps, M. F. 3:153
Phelps, Mandeville 7:14
Phelps, Martin 6:14; 18:91
Phelps, Oliver W. 24:96
Phelps, Otis 15:132
Phelps, Peter S. 12:59
Phelps, Phillip J. 17:353
Phelps, Pliny J. 20:115
Phelps, R. 17:162
Phelps, R. E. 9:189
Phelps, R. S. 9:223
Phelps, Ransom 22:49
Phelps, Robert W. 8:53; 21:37
Phelps, S. D. 13:116
Phelps, S. H. 13:96; 14:19; 17:473; 27:98
Phelps, T. H. 14:301
Phelps, Thomas C. 21:77
Phelps, W. 3:153
Phelps, W. E. 3:153
Phelps, W. H. 3:153; 27:98
Phelps, W. S. 18:373
Phelps, William 7:131; 9:189; 19:259; 22:49
Phelps, William H. 7:60
Phelps, William R. 23:124
Phelson, Phels 11:333
Phemister, William J. 23:45
Phenderson, J. 16:270
Phenegan, John 21:116
Phenegar, Jacob 23:162
Phenil, Michael 7:37
Phenis, B. 19:93
Phenix, A. N. 3:153
Pherrin, S. B. 15:220
Pherson, J. 11:403
Pherson, James 14:206
Pherson, John H. 22:96

Pheshels, Joseph 18:249
Pheshler, Joseph 26:53
Phestplace, Eli 10:131
Phetridge, M. M. 9:231;
　20:326
Phetteplace, George H.
　10:165
Phetterplace, Augustus E.
　10:21
Phettyplace, Eli 20:327
Phias, James B. 16:377
Phibbs, J. 22:265
Phibrook, Peter W. 27:99
Phiefer, Anton 4:46
Phierson, Richard 9:157
Phifer, James W. 9:16
Phifer, John 21:37
Phifer, Joseph 10:174;
　18:16; 19:186
Philan, Thomas 14:98
Philbey, G. 20:326
Philbrick, David 9:13
Philbrick, Frederick B.
　4:46
Philbrick, J. L. N. 25:62
Philbrick, J. N. L. 2:16
Philbrick, J. R. 1:64
Philbrick, J. W. 15:287;
　19:93
Philbrick, M. P. 7:76;
　25:303
Philbrick, Philander 12:35
Philbrick, Preston 9:7
Philbrick, R. 5:26
Philbrick, S. W. 9:38
Philbrook, F. 3:153
Philbrook, J. D. 27:95
Philbrook, Joel H. 22:213
Philbrook, John H. 27:97
Philbrooks, W. W. 1:64
Phile, C. 13:96; 14:19
Philgonicerker, William
　19:259
Philherton, I. 17:500
Philip, Granville 26:177
Philips, --- 1:63; 13:116;
　24:96
Philips, A. 15:220;
　18:249; 19:186;
　26:53
Philips, Adam 19:338
Philips, Allen 10:131
Philips, Benjamin 20:59
Philips, C. J. 15:361
Philips, C. M. 9:16
Philips, C. W. 18:55
Philips, Charles D. 17:156
Philips, Chester 19:93
Philips, D. 24:113
Philips, David 20:327;
　26:52

Philips, E. A. 27:95
Philips, Erastus 13:116
Philips, G. 1:63
Philips, G. W. 1:161
Philips, George 15:220;
　21:376
Philips, George A. 20:327
Philips, H. 19:93
Philips, H. G. 13:125
Philips, Henry 15:351
Philips, Henry C. 7:83
Philips, Isaac A. 27:95
Philips, J. 7:78; 16:219;
　23:115; 26:55
Philips, J. C. 13:116
Philips, J. H. 26:176
Philips, J. P. 27:95
Philips, James 1:64; 9:69
Philips, Jesse 21:201
Philips, John 11:183
Philips, John K. 16:100
Philips, Joseph 7:80;
　25:303
Philips, Lee 11:41
Philips, M. 15:344
Philips, M. E. 27:99
Philips, M. N. 1:161
Philips, Milford B. 19:186
Philips, Perry 15:290
Philips, Peter 19:93;
　26:176
Philips, Richard 18:249;
　26:53
Philips, Salathiel M.
　20:326
Philips, Smith 19:30
Philips, T. A. 15:279
Philips, Thomas 27:100
Philips, Truman 10:97
Philips, W. 27:95
Philips, William 22:14;
　24:113
Philips, Zarornatt 18:154
Philipson, G. 13:125
Phillabaum, Daniel
　23:280
Phillan, Bernard 25:219
Phillbrook, A. 3:153
Phillbrook, J. E. 3:153
Philler, Martin 22:315
Phillip, H. J. 1:63
Phillip, Hiram 14:206
Phillip, Peter 15:319
Phillipard, Andrew 11:41
Phillipot, D. 9:201
Phillipp, Felix 8:121
Phillippi, John 10:165
Phillippin, Henry 16:377
Phillipps, Harrison 8:118
Phillippy, William 11:183

Phillips, --- 9:27; 11:162;
　19:323; 25:61;
　26:176
Phillips, A. 1:161, 163;
　3:153; 4:46; 15:329;
　25:219
Phillips, A. W. 1:63; 9:57;
　14:206
Phillips, Adam 10:165;
　19:186
Phillips, Albert A. 4:46
Phillips, Alexander 13:41
Phillips, Alfred 21:281
Phillips, Allen 20:326
Phillips, Amos 8:77
Phillips, Amos H. 21:77
Phillips, Andrew J. 17:57
Phillips, Ausumus 23:76
Phillips, B. 1:65; 13:96;
　14:19; 19:259
Phillips, B. B. 3:153
Phillips, B. H. 13:96
Phillips, Barney 9:189
Phillips, Benjamin 21:281
Phillips, Birt. S. 20:327
Phillips, Bradford 20:49
Phillips, Burt. S. 10:73
Phillips, C. 3:153; 18:16
Phillips, C. C. 17:249
Phillips, C. J. 12:96;
　19:93
Phillips, C. W. 10:149
Phillips, Calvin 22:505
Phillips, Carl 11:193
Phillips, Charles 9:201;
　19:283; 21:125;
　22:315; 25:219
Phillips, Charles E. 10:21
Phillips, Chester 15:289
Phillips, Columbus 7:37
Phillips, Cornelius 8:28;
　18:154
Phillips, Crockett 22:128
Phillips, Cyrenus 12:96
Phillips, D. 25:62
Phillips, D. B. 11:329
Phillips, D. O. 17:435
Phillips, Daniel 8:53;
　21:125
Phillips, David 6:10;
　10:131; 11:403;
　12:35; 18:113
Phillips, David F. 21:77
Phillips, David L. 16:281
Phillips, David O. 24:179
Phillips, David T. 20:12
Phillips, DeWitt C. 8:101
Phillips, Dewitt C.
　17:462; 24:171
Phillips, Dock 11:211

Phillips, E. 11:425;
21:376; 27:98
Phillips, E. C. 1:161
Phillips, E. J. 4:46; 25:334
Phillips, E. P. 14:302;
17:472
Phillips, E. R. 27:98
Phillips, E. W. 16:50
Phillips, Edgar 7:60
Phillips, Edgar A. 15:59
Phillips, Edmond A. 4:46
Phillips, Edward 23:162
Phillips, Eli 22:435
Phillips, Elijah 21:259
Phillips, Eliphalet 4:46
Phillips, Elizur 4:46
Phillips, Ellis 22:315
Phillips, F. 3:153; 13:96
Phillips, Frank 17:57
Phillips, Franklin 8:28;
18:154
Phillips, Freeman F. 9:100
Phillips, G. 9:57; 25:219
Phillips, G. A. 3:153
Phillips, G. D. 9:149
Phillips, G. J. 25:219
Phillips, G. M. 27:98
Phillips, G. W. 8:66;
14:19; 19:186
Phillips, George 10:131;
11:41, 222; 19:330;
20:327; 21:376;
22:113; 23:13
Phillips, George A. 10:73
Phillips, George E.
13:135; 19:347
Phillips, George H. 1:64
Phillips, George I. 15:279
Phillips, George S. 7:37;
22:96
Phillips, George W. 7:52;
8:93; 10:206; 17:40
Phillips, Granville 8:41
Phillips, H. 1:162, 163;
3:153; 13:96
Phillips, H. B. 15:110
Phillips, H. M. 11:382
Phillips, Henry 8:41;
18:399; 22:96;
26:177
Phillips, Henry B. 22:283
Phillips, Henry C. 21:376
Phillips, Henry E. 7:37
Phillips, Henry G. 8:93
Phillips, Henry W. 23:45
Phillips, Hiram O. 7:106
Phillips, I. 14:206
Phillips, I. M. 11:41
Phillips, Ira H. 10:73;
20:327
Phillips, Ira N. 22:213

Phillips, Isaac 8:93;
22:128
Phillips, Isaiah 24:83
Phillips, J. 3:153; 7:37,
52; 20:87, 156;
21:125
Phillips, J. B. 11:41
Phillips, J. Corwin 17:362
Phillips, J. E. 14:98
Phillips, J. H. 1:65; 8:66
Phillips, J. J. 3:154; 9:57;
14:286
Phillips, J. K. 12:75;
15:12
Phillips, J. N. 1:65; 9:57
Phillips, J. P. 9:149
Phillips, J. W. 3:154;
13:103; 25:219
Phillips, Jabis 17:503
Phillips, James 7:131;
8:93; 10:153; 11:163,
268; 13:41; 18:249;
19:186; 20:31;
21:281; 25:303;
26:54
Phillips, James P. 22:435
Phillips, Jay 7:106
Phillips, Jeremiah 9:189;
19:279
Phillips, John 4:46; 7:37,
106; 8:28; 11:164,
333; 14:98; 18:154;
19:187; 22:213, 315
Phillips, John C. 11:163
Phillips, John H. 16:100
Phillips, John M. 9:101
Phillips, John P. 4:46
Phillips, John R. 11:248
Phillips, John W. 7:37;
21:232; 23:181
Phillips, Jonathan 17:97;
22:524
Phillips, Joseph 8:74;
21:57; 27:95
Phillips, Joseph E. 22:265
Phillips, Josiah 21:376
Phillips, L. D. 9:13
Phillips, L. M. 3:154
Phillips, Levi 12:35
Phillips, Lorenzo 25:60
Phillips, Louis 7:131
Phillips, M. 1:65, 162,
164; 14:98, 251;
16:377
Phillips, M. B. 11:41
Phillips, Martin 17:57
Phillips, Melvin 22:342
Phillips, Michael 8:93
Phillips, Morris 7:131
Phillips, Moses 9:112
Phillips, Moses J. 22:455

Phillips, Mulford B.
10:165
Phillips, N. 3:224
Phillips, N. A. 25:219
Phillips, N. Byron 15:132
Phillips, Nathan 22:342
Phillips, Nathaniel
17:505; 22:504
Phillips, Ned 21:281
Phillips, Nelson 24:27
Phillips, Newman A.
9:189
Phillips, Norris 19:30
Phillips, O. 1:162
Phillips, O. B. 17:249
Phillips, Owen 8:109
Phillips, P. 3:154
Phillips, Patrick 19:30
Phillips, Perry 16:219
Phillips, Peter 8:66;
11:247; 12:35; 20:43
Phillips, R. 1:163; 3:154
Phillips, R. L. 18:373
Phillips, R. R. 14:244;
27:100
Phillips, Reuben 9:123;
27:97
Phillips, Richard 11:163,
211; 16:50, 219
Phillips, Richard W. 4:46
Phillips, Robert N. 22:265
Phillips, S. 7:52; 15:73
Phillips, S. G. 3:154
Phillips, S. J. 9:57; 12:157
Phillips, S. L. 1:62
Phillips, Salathiel M.
10:131
Phillips, Samuel 11:211;
17:265
Phillips, Samuel M. 4:46
Phillips, Seymore C.
20:327
Phillips, Seymour C.
10:73
Phillips, Shadrach 13:41
Phillips, Shadrick 16:50
Phillips, Shelton F.
21:190
Phillips, Simeon 13:41
Phillips, Spencer E. 4:46
Phillips, T. 3:154
Phillips, T. A. 8:53;
25:219
Phillips, T. B. 21:376
Phillips, T. D. 27:95
Phillips, T. F. 25:61
Phillips, T. M. 11:248
Phillips, T. N. 14:98
Phillips, Theo 25:219
Phillips, Theodore 5:26

Phillips, Thomas 1:64;
    8:28; 10:131;
    11:329; 17:238;
    18:154; 20:327;
    22:128
Phillips, Thomas J. 22:213
Phillips, W. 1:65, 161;
    3:154; 14:98; 21:14
Phillips, W. H. 4:46; 9:88
Phillips, W. L. 1:163
Phillips, W. O. 14:98
Phillips, W. R. 9:98
Phillips, W. T. 26:127
Phillips, Ward 11:247
Phillips, Warren 27:98
Phillips, William 1:65;
    6:13; 7:64; 9:223;
    10:73, 131; 11:72;
    16:219; 17:252;
    18:373; 20:326, 327;
    24:43, 83; 25:219
Phillips, William B.
    21:243
Phillips, William H.
    19:187; 22:265;
    26:52
Phillips, William H. H.
    20:327
Phillips, William H. N.
    10:131
Phillips, William R. 8:93;
    17:252
Phillips, William T. 7:106
Phillips, Willie 7:106
Phillips, Wilson 7:106;
    21:376
Phillips, Zackanah 8:28
Phillis, Jacob 22:213
Philmore, R. H. 1:192
Philo, Avery 12:157
Philo, Edward 23:45
Philo, George W. 22:213
Philo, H. 1:163
Philogomcorker, William
    9:189
Philoo, Russell G. 20:127
Philow, Alexander 22:153
Philper, A. J. 11:248
Philpot, Aaron 11:211
Philpot, C. P. 3:154
Philpot, D. 18:91
Philpot, Dock 19:292
Philps, Albert 15:316
Philtrook, J. B. 9:149
Phine, August 21:376
Phineas, John 22:466
Phineas, Peter 21:376
Phiney, Patrick 13:116
Phinly, Edward 19:187
Phinney, Charles C.
    21:376

Phinney, Charles H. 7:83
Phinney, F. 1:161
Phinney, George 18:91
Phinney, George W.
    21:376
Phinney, J. 23:162
Phinney, James A. 4:46
Phinney, Jesse 8:53
Phippen, A. 18:55
Phippen, Abraham 10:152
Phippen, G. 13:116
Phippen, Myron A.
    10:165
Phipps, A. 3:154
Phipps, Benjamin 19:30
Phipps, C. C. 23:101
Phipps, David 8:102;
    17:461; 24:161
Phipps, Edward 4:46
Phipps, F. 21:168
Phipps, George F. 20:31
Phipps, H. B. 3:154
Phipps, H. H. 1:163
Phipps, J. 1:162
Phipps, J. H. 3:154
Phipps, J. W. 21:376
Phipps, John 16:50
Phipps, John H. 21:37
Phipps, Joseph 7:69;
    20:12
Phipps, Lerenas 15:361
Phipps, M. M. 3:154
Phipps, Ralph 14:206
Phipps, Robert 1:63
Phipps, Thomas 19:305
Phipps, Willis O. 24:54
Phips, S. 19:93
Phisterer, David 25:284
Phite, George 11:210
Phlagga, Julius 20:148
Phleger, Abraham 12:35
Phlilips, Jeremiah 10:73
Phlug, G. 1:65
Phoenix, Lewis 1:192
Pholman, August H.
    22:342
Phonax, J. 16:219
Phopard, Solomon 18:279
Phott, Peter 17:40
Phoyt, George 18:16
Phrice, George 11:129
Phumphrey, P. 24:83
Phy, J. S. 20:138
Phyfe, J. 4:46
Phyle, Benjamin A.
    21:376
Piaber, Sherrod 7:131
Piatt, David 23:244
Piatt, Solomon 11:163
Piatt, W. H. 11:268
Piatt, Walton 26:128

Piatt, William 20:127
Picard, Charles A. 12:55
Picard, Richard 9:98
Pice, Gogswell 25:61
Pichard, J. 7:60
Pichtell, Simon 11:164
Pick, A. 14:98
Pick, Chauncey 1:63
Pick, George 8:54
Pick, M. P. 11:247
Pick, R. S. 27:95
Pickabaugh, J. K. 12:75
Pickard, J. L. 6:13
Pickard, John 8:93;
    10:131; 20:327
Pickard, John E. 12:75
Pickard, W. 14:98
Pickard, W. J. 11:248
Pickard, William 22:49
Picke, Christ 24:43
Pickel, Henry W. 17:199
Pickell, D. 1:162
Pickels, Henry 9:27
Pickena, S. 20:127
Pickenpaugh, Jonathan
    17:85
Pickens, A. D. 18:36
Pickens, Albert A. 24:27
Pickens, Bradford 7:76;
    25:303
Pickens, C. 14:98
Pickens, J. W. 11:268
Pickens, John 4:47
Pickens, Samuel 24:161
Pickens, Sandy 11:211
Pickens, W. 14:98
Pickenson, Charles 11:41
Pickeral, William 17:85
Pickerd, M. 11:164
Pickerel, Alexander W.
    22:96
Pickerell, Daniel 17:57
Pickerell, John W. 17:350
Pickering, Charles 14:206
Pickering, E. 3:154
Pickering, George 24:54
Pickering, Greenly H.
    23:76
Pickering, H. 14:98
Pickering, Henry A. 22:96
Pickering, Jacob 21:248
Pickering, James 20:36
Pickering, John 11:311;
    17:47
Pickering, Joseph 15:73
Pickering, M. 24:54
Pickert, Alonzo 19:259
Pickery, John 5:44
Picket, A. V. 18:36
Picket, C. W. 1:163
Picket, F. B. 3:154

Picket, Henry 10:131; 20:327
Picket, J. 20:43
Picket, J. C. 3:154
Picket, James C. 8:109
Picket, James F. 25:284
Picket, Peter 21:281
Picket, Thomas 12:75; 15:18
Picket, Walter 19:93
Pickett, Amos 11:391
Pickett, B. 1:64; 8:54; 21:168
Pickett, Benjamin F. 15:220
Pickett, E. 15:220
Pickett, E. R. 19:187
Pickett, Elliot R. 10:166
Pickett, Ephriam 19:30
Pickett, Frank 21:281
Pickett, G. B. 17:162
Pickett, George 21:376
Pickett, Ira J. 22:49
Pickett, J. 14:322
Pickett, J. A. 7:37
Pickett, J. D. 18:249; 26:53
Pickett, J. E. 14:98
Pickett, J. R. R. 8:28; 18:154
Pickett, James D. 15:88
Pickett, James R. 22:168
Pickett, John I. 21:93
Pickett, Johnson 11:41
Pickett, Leonard 18:221
Pickett, N. 1:161
Pickett, Nathan 17:277
Pickett, O. 1:65
Pickett, Parson M. 22:265
Pickett, Patrick 9:149
Pickett, T. E. 1:63
Pickett, Virgil 17:350
Pickett, Walter 15:286
Pickett, William 18:279
Pickfire, C. 1:163
Pickham, John 1:64
Pickham, S. F. 24:113
Picking, Gerhart 10:131; 20:327
Pickle, Henry 18:314; 26:109
Pickle, Jacob 1:62
Pickle, Ubrick 23:129
Pickle, William H. 24:27
Pickler, John 20:12
Pickmill, George W. 4:47
Picknell, Wilber G. 26:53
Picksley, Benjamin 7:83
Picor, Nelson 17:24
Picott, M. 18:16
Picquard, Emele 13:41

Picquard, George 13:41
Pictol, Philip 21:232
Pidcock, J. B. 10:131; 20:327
Pie, Olive 19:30
Pieae, Peter O. 11:41
Piece, J. 16:302
Piedman, H. 25:219
Pieper, August 24:171
Pier, A. 3:154
Pier, Horace 15:132, 350
Pier, Sylvanus 18:70
Pier---, A. K. 25:61
Pierce, --- 25:63
Pierce, A. 3:154; 15:73
Pierce, A. F. 25:62
Pierce, Abel 19:30
Pierce, Abraham 11:223; 22:153
Pierce, Albert 14:206
Pierce, Albert C. 10:131; 20:327
Pierce, Albert M. 20:327
Pierce, Alfonzo 14:207
Pierce, Allen 15:348
Pierce, Allen P. 16:377
Pierce, Andrew 22:96, 342
Pierce, Andrew J. 22:505
Pierce, Asa 11:247
Pierce, C. 3:154; 18:36
Pierce, C. H. 16:86
Pierce, C. R. 1:161
Pierce, C. W. 1:99; 14:98
Pierce, Calvin C. 10:73; 20:327
Pierce, Charles J. 10:21
Pierce, Clark 23:162
Pierce, Clinton D. 19:93
Pierce, Cornelius 22:49
Pierce, D. 17:159
Pierce, Daniel 21:116
Pierce, David 11:97; 20:148
Pierce, David H. 19:30
Pierce, Delos 8:115
Pierce, E. 7:72; 18:249; 26:53
Pierce, E. P. 13:117
Pierce, Elbert S. 22:505
Pierce, Eli 7:60; 23:162
Pierce, Elizur 4:47
Pierce, Erastus 9:73
Pierce, Erwin 15:92
Pierce, Eugene 10:21
Pierce, Ezra 11:162
Pierce, F. 9:149; 27:95
Pierce, F. M. 19:332
Pierce, Frank 8:74; 26:177
Pierce, Franklin 6:18; 18:91; 22:49, 283

Pierce, Frederick H. 22:49
Pierce, G. E. 1:161
Pierce, George 15:160; 22:14, 315; 23:45
Pierce, George A. 19:187
Pierce, George H. 23:45
Pierce, George W. 11:162, 403; 22:172, 435; 25:62
Pierce, Granville 21:377
Pierce, H. 3:154; 9:112; 16:302
Pierce, H. H. 17:111
Pierce, H. L. 12:87; 14:98
Pierce, H. M. 1:64; 19:187
Pierce, Henry 7:52, 76, 78; 10:131; 13:41; 14:207; 20:327; 25:303
Pierce, Henry A. 10:166
Pierce, Henry D. 10:131
Pierce, Henry F. 22:96
Pierce, Henry H. 13:41
Pierce, Hiram 10:73; 15:92
Pierce, I. 11:281
Pierce, I. K. 19:30
Pierce, Ira 13:67; 16:219
Pierce, Isaac 24:174
Pierce, Isaac A. 10:166
Pierce, Israel 27:97
Pierce, J. 3:154; 12:87, 162; 13:96; 24:69
Pierce, J. A. 1:99
Pierce, J. C. 11:164
Pierce, J. H. 3:154; 13:67
Pierce, J. M. 1:164
Pierce, J. S. 7:52
Pierce, J. W. 9:27
Pierce, Jacob 11:391
Pierce, Jacob A. 11:41
Pierce, James 8:28; 10:131; 14:19; 15:18; 18:153; 19:187; 20:327; 22:213, 466
Pierce, James A. 7:106
Pierce, James B. 22:505
Pierce, James F. 10:149; 18:55
Pierce, James H. 16:377
Pierce, James M. 16:141; 22:466
Pierce, James T. 13:41
Pierce, Jeremiah A. 13:41
Pierce, Jh. 19:93
Pierce, John 1:63; 7:81, 106; 11:391; 15:110; 22:128; 25:303
Pierce, John B. 22:49
Pierce, John C. 15:220

Pierce, John F. 9:112
Pierce, John W. 11:247; 16:134
Pierce, Joseph 22:315
Pierce, Joseph J. 26:128
Pierce, L. 26:53
Pierce, L. C. 27:95
Pierce, L. J. 10:166; 19:187
Pierce, Lambert 27:97
Pierce, Larniston 9:88
Pierce, Leander 9:16
Pierce, Lewis C. 9:149
Pierce, Lobon 17:288
Pierce, M. 7:37; 20:327
Pierce, M. B. 18:279
Pierce, Martin 10:73; 11:320
Pierce, Matthias 12:157
Pierce, Michael 22:342
Pierce, Montraville L. 21:131
Pierce, Moses 9:88; 26:52
Pierce, N. W. 1:64
Pierce, Nathan M. 24:69
Pierce, Nathan S. 13:41
Pierce, O. W. 1:163
Pierce, P. 14:98
Pierce, R. F. 10:73
Pierce, R. W. 15:220
Pierce, Richard 17:213
Pierce, Robert 22:505; 23:162
Pierce, Rufus D. 22:213
Pierce, S. 2:16; 25:60; 26:54
Pierce, S. G. 19:187
Pierce, S. S. 14:98
Pierce, S. W. 1:161
Pierce, T. M. 1:161
Pierce, Thomas 13:67; 19:93
Pierce, Thomas J. 22:409
Pierce, Thomas M. 9:27
Pierce, Timothy 21:142
Pierce, W. 1:64, 162; 3:154
Pierce, W. B. 3:154
Pierce, W. H. 9:88; 23:45
Pierce, W. J. 27:95
Pierce, W. T. 23:277
Pierce, William 5:53
Pierce, William A. 15:273
Pierce, William B. 21:77
Pierce, William D. 10:21
Pierce, William G. 21:77
Pierce, William H. 21:87
Pierce, William M. 16:82
Pierce, William P. 10:73
Pierce, William S. 16:3
Pierce, Willis S. 8:93

Piercefield, John 15:59
Piercel, L. 11:268
Piercy, Jasper 18:424
Pierden, Charles 3:154
Pierdy, J. 10:29
Pierdy, J. T. 19:305
Pierman, David B. 21:57
Pierpont, Horace 9:189; 19:245
Pierre, Fordule 9:210
Pierre, Isaac 7:82
Piers, Michael 18:193
Piers, Thomas 20:134
Piersall, Lewis A. 24:54
Piersall, William H. 23:45
Piersoll, S. 1:162
Pierson, A. 3:154
Pierson, Abram 18:154
Pierson, Ambrose 8:28
Pierson, Amos 18:113
Pierson, C. 25:219
Pierson, C. D. 13:96
Pierson, Charles 5:44
Pierson, D. 3:154
Pierson, D. A. 22:521
Pierson, D. W. 25:219
Pierson, Daniel 27:97
Pierson, E. B. 13:117
Pierson, G. 14:284
Pierson, G. D. 14:19
Pierson, George 1:64; 16:377; 21:281
Pierson, Henry 21:281; 22:213, 515
Pierson, J. 3:154; 19:259
Pierson, J. R. 11:268
Pierson, James 1:192
Pierson, John 4:47; 14:207; 18:154
Pierson, John I. 11:247
Pierson, Joseph 12:54
Pierson, Joseph M. 14:207
Pierson, Lewis 22:487
Pierson, Morris 26:127
Pierson, Nathan H. 15:300
Pierson, Nathon H. 16:219
Pierson, R. 3:154
Pierson, Randolph 9:162
Pierson, Robert 21:150, 213
Pierson, S. D. 14:207
Pierson, S. S. 1:62
Pierson, Samuel 18:249; 26:54
Pierson, T. 14:19
Pierson, W. 1:163; 25:61
Pierson, W. M. 1:65
Pierson, William 9:217; 15:290
Pierson, William H. 21:77

Piert, Samuel L. 17:85
Piert, William 17:356
Piery, John E. 25:219
Pierzall, William 10:73
Pieson, W. J. 25:219
Piett, C. 23:304
Pifer, Augustus 14:207
Pifer, F. 3:154
Pifer, Frederick 14:98
Pifer, Henry 19:187
Pifer, M. 3:154
Pifer, William 22:213
Pifers, Hiram 27:99
Piffer, G. 3:154
Piffer, Hilbert 17:85
Piffer, J. 3:154
Piffer, S. 25:60
Pigeon, Charles 15:348
Pigery, C. F. 16:219
Pigg, Allen 11:72
Pigg, Samuel Henry 22:49
Piggah, Joseph 15:357; 16:281
Piggat, Joseph 12:98
Piggery, C. F. 13:67
Piggott, J. 1:161
Pigham, W. P. 19:93
Pigman, R. 13:96
Pigman, William 17:238
Pigon, James 23:250
Pigott, George 21:11
Pigott, J. 3:154
Pigry, J. 25:219
Pikartz, Peter 20:152
Pike, A. G. 23:45
Pike, A. M. 1:162
Pike, Addison 21:281
Pike, Albert 21:37
Pike, B. H. 3:154
Pike, David 18:36
Pike, Eli 19:187
Pike, G. W. 1:65
Pike, George 9:215; 21:377
Pike, George H. 12:75; 15:18
Pike, Henry 4:47
Pike, Henry D. 23:162
Pike, Horace A. 18:71
Pike, Huston M. 18:279
Pike, Irving 16:50
Pike, Irwin 13:41
Pike, J. 1:162
Pike, J. W. 9:189
Pike, Jacob 7:37
Pike, Jacob M. 21:131
Pike, Jefferson H. 9:123; 27:97
Pike, Jeremiah 10:131; 20:327
Pike, John 13:125; 14:98

Pike, Martin 10:10
Pike, N. H. 18:178
Pike, N. N. 3:154
Pike, Oliver 22:213
Pike, R. 19:93
Pike, Richard 10:131;
   20:327
Pike, S. 23:162
Pike, S. M. 23:45
Pike, Samuel 17:393
Pike, Samuel F. 22:128
Pike, T. 10:145; 19:187
Pike, Theodore 21:377
Pike, Titus A. 1:64
Pike, Tristram 22:96
Pike, W. H. 10:187;
   12:96; 15:361; 19:93
Pike, William 3:154; 4:47
Pikehart, D. 15:220
Piker, W. E. 19:241
Pikes, P. 9:201; 19:292
Pilant, Robert 10:131;
   20:327
Pilbean, Edward 22:466
Pilbury, J. 12:80; 25:219
Pilch, John N. 1:62
Pilcher, Thomas F. 23:244
Pilchet, George 14:331
Pilcurt, J. 14:98
Pile, Alfred 22:409
Pile, Asa 22:128
Pile, C. 15:220
Pile, J. 27:95
Pile, J. D. 25:219
Pile, John 22:504
Pile, Jonathan D. 5:26
Pile, Thomas 17:207
Pile, Wilson 3:154
Pilenger, Smith 15:42
Piles, Absolem 23:162
Piles, Isaac 15:88
Piles, James 22:265
Piles, John W. 17:111
Piles, Peter 15:220
Piles, R. 25:219
Piles, W. 25:219
Piles, William 4:47
Pilgrim, Anthony 27:98
Pilgrim, John 21:377
Pilham, W. L. 21:57
Pilkenton, Archibald
   26:53
Pilkerton, Archibald 9:88
Pilkerton, John 3:224
Pilkerton, William 10:131
Pilkington, John 23:129
Pillar, Hugh 22:505
Pillarte, J. 21:37
Pilling, J. B. 19:241
Pilling, Joseph 7:60
Pillman, Caspar 22:49

Pillow, Armstrong 7:131
Pillow, George 22:315
Pillow, Isom 22:315
Pillow, Thomas 22:315
Pillsbury, A. J. 3:154
Pillsbury, E. G. 23:194
Pillsbury, Edmond H.
   25:219
Pillsbury, Millard 10:174
Pillsbury, Milliard 19:187
Pillsinger, E. G. 16:50
Pilney, G. H. 1:161
Pilot, James 3:154
Pilsbury, F. 3:154
Pilson, Charles 23:124
Pilsuk, F. 3:154
Pilton, Edgar A. 22:153
Pilton, W. C. 9:112
Pimble, A. 3:154
Pimpland, C. B. 12:75
Pin, Hatt 18:422
Pinch, Harry 7:37
Pinchrim, Waldo 7:52
Pinchton, John W. 11:73
Pinckhard, William G.
   13:60
Pinckney, George 21:377
Pinckney, Harry 27:96
Pinckney, S. 16:219
Pinckston, John 13:132;
   20:327
Pincomb, William 20:108
Pinder, Perry S. 22:213
Pinder, William 14:207
Pindergrass, Edgar 20:327
Pindle, Lagore 10:73
Pine, A. B. 7:37
Pine, Albert 22:515
Pine, C. W. 18:324
Pine, Daniel 21:104
Pine, Edward L. 22:488
Pine, John 16:148
Pine, William 13:41
Pinegar, James P. 22:49
Pineo, J. D. 1:63
Piner, J. 3:154
Piner, R. 25:219
Piner, Richard 5:44
Piner, S. 25:219
Pinert, F. 3:154
Ping, Daniel 20:184
Ping, James 24:43
Ping, R. 15:344; 16:377;
   17:192
Ping, W. A. 22:49
Ping, William 21:232
Pingay, Isaac 9:189
Pinger, Enos 17:405
Pinglet, John H. 9:223
Pinglett, John 18:373
Pingree, J. M. 1:162

Pingrey, Isaac 19:268
Pingue, J. S. 20:327
Pinick, John 20:115
Pinick, William 19:323
Pining, J. L. 9:69
Pinion, John 3:154
Pink, John 12:100
Pink, N. 25:219
Pinkard, F. T. H. Julius
   10:34
Pinkard, Wood 8:41;
   26:177
Pinke, C. 19:259
Pinke, Christian 9:189
Pinkert, Joseph 10:73;
   20:327
Pinkerton, Amelia L.
   20:127
Pinkerton, Edward 18:104
Pinkerton, George 7:106
Pinkerton, J. A. 5:26
Pinkerton, J. G. 9:98
Pinkerton, James 21:198
Pinkerton, John 25:219
Pinkerton, L. 22:213
Pinkerton, W. H. 8:28;
   18:154; 21:377
Pinkerton, William 22:96
Pinkerton, William H.
   22:113
Pinkerton, William R.
   22:49
Pinkeston, E. J. 1:164
Pinkett, J. 25:219
Pinkett, Joshua 5:44
Pinkham, --- 9:189;
   19:241
Pinkham, Cyrus C. 16:281
Pinkham, E. 9:163
Pinkham, F. 1:64
Pinkham, George W.
   13:41
Pinkham, H. B. 1:161
Pinkham, I. 25:303
Pinkham, J. 7:76; 25:219
Pinkham, J. T. 1:162
Pinkham, M. W. 3:154
Pinkham, Miles 19:187
Pinkham, Otis W. 25:61
Pinkham, W. 16:219
Pinkham, William M.
   15:300
Pinkhiser, J. 27:98
Pinkhorn, George 11:295
Pinkin, Charles 15:12
Pinkine, Jesse 11:211
Pinkles, August 11:288
Pinkley, Emanuel 27:147
Pinkley, J. 3:154
Pinkner, George 10:73;
   20:327

Pinkney, Henry 9:135
Pinkney, James 13:41
Pinkney, John 21:377
Pinkney, John C. 21:93
Pinkney, William 21:377
Pinksten, Marion 21:77
Pinkston, John 17:168
Pinkston, Squire 17:402
Pinkston, William 22:128
Pinkton, William 10:73
Pinky, Alexander 8:109
Pinnegan, Joseph 22:168
Pinnell, --- 21:209
Pinnell, Thomas C. 21:232
Pinneo, G. M. 17:290
Pinneo, Matthias D. 21:77
Pinner, James 12:75
Pinner, Samuel 15:42
Pinnert, Issac B. 16:50
Pinney, Wilson S. 21:232
Pino, W. H. 1:62
Pinsnick, John A. J. 21:57
Pinson, Harrison 22:265
Pinson, J. W. 21:377
Pinsow, J. 16:219
Pinter, Robert 17:447
Pinther, Fred 4:47
Pintler, J. H. 15:279
Pinto, John 16:50
Pinton, J. H. 18:91
Pionkonosky, Frederick H. 7:38
Piott, James H. 17:167
Pipe, George 27:96
Pipe, T. W. 14:244; 27:100
Piper, A. 14:258
Piper, A. M. 15:153
Piper, C. 3:154
Piper, C. H. 25:303
Piper, Charles 9:189; 19:259
Piper, Charles E. 7:106
Piper, D. 9:215; 21:377
Piper, E. A. 3:154
Piper, Eli 17:183
Piper, F. 3:154
Piper, Francis S. 21:115
Piper, George H. 7:80; 21:104
Piper, J. E. 7:64
Piper, J. R. 7:53
Piper, J. W. 14:244
Piper, Jacob 4:47
Piper, James 22:315
Piper, James F. 11:41
Piper, James P. H. 24:43
Piper, James T. 8:109
Piper, Jeremiah 9:57

Piper, John 6:28; 10:131; 20:327; 22:49, 213; 23:45
Piper, Jonas 24:96
Piper, Joseph 9:98, 135; 15:220; 27:97
Piper, L. 9:27; 18:314; 26:109
Piper, Martin V. B. 17:85
Piper, N. A. 9:189; 19:234
Piper, Orwin 9:112
Piper, Perry C. 15:220
Piper, S. W. 16:219
Piper, Samuel 22:409
Piper, T. 3:154
Piper, Thomas 27:95
Piper, Thomas M. 8:28; 18:154
Piper, W. H. 16:100
Piper, William 19:187; 21:377
Pipher, Samuel 23:302
Pipinbring, G. 3:154
Pipkin, David P. 11:96
Pipkin, Haly D. 18:193
Pipkin, L. R. 11:96
Pipkin, M. Smith 20:187
Pipkins, Peter 21:281
Pipkins, William 16:219
Pippin, E. 25:219
Pippin, Selvanis 20:327
Pippin, Sylvanus 10:131
Pippinger, Henry 22:213
Pipps, P. 14:99
Piquette, F. 14:207
Piret, Byard W. 10:131; 20:327
Pirkenson, Richard 15:132
Pirmus, Lewis 26:177
Piro, L. 11:268
Piro, Leevis 9:210
Piro, Lewis 18:71
Piron, Frederick 14:207
Piror, William 24:171
Pirtle, John M. 26:176
Piscull, F. B. 3:154
Pisel, John C. 23:91
Pisher, P. 9:149; 27:96
Pishon, John 25:312
Pishoock, Jerry 24:202
Pisor, D. Washington 7:60
Pistate, David 20:327
Pistole, David 10:73
Pistole, T. J. 23:253
Pistorious, W. 25:219
Pitanista, --- 19:343
Pitchard, J. E. 15:12
Pitcher, Allen 18:178
Pitcher, Amos 15:220
Pitcher, Dewitt C. 13:117
Pitcher, E. 3:154

Pitcher, Ela F. 7:106
Pitcher, Gales 26:109
Pitcher, George 4:47
Pitcher, Giles 9:38
Pitcher, H. M. 12:96; 15:361; 19:93
Pitcher, H. T. 14:207
Pitcher, Henry 9:13; 15:175
Pitcher, J. 9:112; 19:229
Pitcher, James 27:147
Pitcher, Joseph 1:64; 17:111
Pitcher, Julius 18:296
Pitcher, Lasty 7:131
Pitcher, Nathaniel 8:118
Pitcher, Reuben 10:131; 20:327
Pitcher, S. 25:219
Pitchers, H. M. 14:27
Pitchert, George 14:27
Pitchett, Hen. 19:187
Pitcock, James F. 20:187
Pitcock, L. J. 11:97
Pitcock, Richard 17:207
Pitcock, Richard H. 17:411; 22:524
Pitcock, Thomas 17:207
Pithord, G. 13:67
Pitiman, Lewis 17:137; 24:201
Pitman, Andrew J. 23:76
Pitman, Charles F. 9:8
Pitman, David 10:73; 17:183
Pitman, Elijah 24:69
Pitman, Israel W. 9:189
Pitman, J. 3:154
Pitman, J. H. 7:60
Pitman, James 9:231; 17:183; 20:327
Pitman, James G. 8:28; 18:154
Pitman, Morris 10:97
Pitman, Robert 17:315
Pitman, S. 1:62
Pitman, Stephen 19:316
Pitman, Warrior 7:106
Pitman, William 7:106; 10:131; 20:327
Pitman, William H. 24:43
Pitmann, Michael 18:154
Pitney, Henry 10:97
Pitro, Jacob 18:154
Pits, Andrew 23:291
Pitsinger, William 13:41
Pitsley, J. 1:99
Pitsworth, J. 9:57
Pitt, Alfred 10:9
Pitt, C. F. 14:207
Pitt, G. W. 21:150

Pitt, George W. 10:73; 20:327
Pitt, Isaac 8:28
Pitt, Philip 13:41
Pittard, James M. 19:30
Pittard, William T. 21:196
Pittengell, Roswell 11:288
Pittenger, Reuben 23:76
Pitters, H. 18:36
Pittinger, A. 1:163
Pittinger, William 9:88
Pittington, Jackson 17:249
Pittman, Baird D. 22:49
Pittman, C. 21:150
Pittman, D. 20:327
Pittman, Edwin 12:157
Pittman, I. N. 19:268
Pittman, James 22:354
Pittman, John 22:265
Pittman, L. 18:249
Pittman, Louis 17:183
Pittman, Micajah P. 17:57
Pittman, Mosely 14:316
Pittman, R. D. 22:49
Pittman, S. 26:53
Pittock, Frank 18:36
Pitts, --- 10:180; 18:178
Pitts, Albert H. 22:96
Pitts, Alexander 9:123; 27:98
Pitts, Andrew 11:268
Pitts, C. 25:219
Pitts, Cyrus 5:44
Pitts, David 8:74
Pitts, Elijah 13:41
Pitts, F. T. 20:327
Pitts, Foster 14:266
Pitts, G. 3:155
Pitts, George 22:315
Pitts, George W. 22:49
Pitts, Isaac 9:123; 18:154; 27:97
Pitts, J. 3:155
Pitts, J. A. 1:65
Pitts, J. F. 1:65
Pitts, J. P. 11:188
Pitts, Jacob 22:343
Pitts, James M. 4:47; 22:49
Pitts, Joel B. 19:30
Pitts, John 11:129; 15:220; 22:16
Pitts, John S. 24:43
Pitts, John W. 6:18; 18:91
Pitts, Riley 14:207
Pitts, Robert 19:48; 23:13
Pitts, Stewart 18:91
Pittsford, Timothy H. 11:17
Pittsley, E. 15:304; 16:219

Pittsley, G. W. 11:333
Pittsley, Henry 13:41
Pittsley, William 19:241
Pityrick, A. 26:176
Pitzer, Adam 23:162
Pitzhart, Gustave 22:343
Pivant, A. 3:155
Pixler, Jackson 23:162
Pixler, Robert P. 21:104
Pixley, Benjamin F. 21:377
Pixley, C. J. 10:73
Pixley, John 23:45
Pixley, L. W. 12:9
Pixley, Oscar 14:207
Pixley, Thomas 23:109
Pixoy, F. A. 25:62
Pizer, William 20:138
Pizir, Samuel 9:112
Place, A. 1:65
Place, A. J. 17:165
Place, Albert E. 18:314
Place, Alfred E. 9:27; 26:109
Place, B. F. T. 15:220
Place, E. 3:155
Place, Eugene H. 18:346
Place, H. 1:163
Place, H. P. 25:219
Place, J. H. 14:207
Place, J. K. 3:155
Place, J. R. 12:9
Place, J. S. 9:149; 27:98
Place, J. W. 27:94
Place, L. 25:325
Place, Lester 6:32
Place, Mathew 22:153
Place, Morgan 4:47
Place, Morris E. 21:58
Place, Robert 16:50
Place, S. 3:155
Place, Summer 16:50
Placeway, George 4:47
Placket, Edw. 10:131
Placket, Edward 20:327
Plafford, Henry 17:459
Plagder, James B. 4:47
Plager, Frederick 6:32
Plain, J. V. 19:275
Plain, John W. 9:190
Plain, Morris W. 22:488
Plainhoff, George L. 9:190
Plaint, William 3:155
Plaintiffe, G. W. 8:54
Plaisted, A. T. 17:403
Plaisted, Albert D. 22:96
Plaiton, Frederick 19:259
Plana, Barthelemy 8:60
Plana, Bartholomew 12:169

Plane, --- 19:187
Planet, Julius 8:93
Planey, Henry 22:488
Plangington, J. H. 5:26
Plank, Christ 20:327
Plank, Christian 10:73
Plank, George 13:116
Plank, George D. 16:115
Plank, George L. 23:194
Plank, John 21:232
Plank, John A. 12:57
Plankey, Conrad 9:88
Plankinton, J. H. 25:219
Plannery, H. 3:155
Plans, Didrick 8:109
Plant, C. 1:65
Plant, G. C. 16:86
Plant, Henry 7:63
Plant, Joseph 18:36
Plant, Mitchel L. 19:93
Plant, Peter 18:71
Plant, Samuel 27:99
Plant, T. 1:64
Planter, John 14:207
Planter, W. H. 16:50
Plantey, Frank 21:37
Plantinburg, P. 19:93
Plants, John V. 11:129
Plantz, J. 10:210
Plaom, Adam 14:207
Plappert, W. 1:163
Plase, M. W. 6:21
Plasley, John 25:219
Plasmire, A. 3:155
Plass, E. 4:47
Plass, H. 3:155
Plass, Hamilton 1:62
Plass, J. N. 14:244
Plass, John H. 19:30
Plass, Samuel 1:62
Plass, Seth 9:190
Plaster, Marcellus 21:377
Plaster, William 6:23
Plasters, James 17:24
Plasters, John 10:73; 20:328
Plate, C. C. 9:189
Plath, George 11:403
Platner, J. 15:110
Platner, S. 1:163
Platner, William 10:131; 20:328
Platner, William H. 13:41
Plato, S. 25:219
Plato, Samuel 5:44
Platt, --- 16:100; 27:94
Platt, Alfred Z. 22:128
Platt, B. N. 8:93
Platt, Benjamin 21:232
Platt, David S. 15:23
Platt, Delop 15:110

Platt, Dwight 4:47
Platt, Emanuel 9:44;
  26:127
Platt, F. 16:100
Platt, G. H. 19:245
Platt, Ganno 19:187
Platt, Gano 10:174
Platt, George 1:64; 24:83
Platt, George H. 9:190
Platt, H. 1:64
Platt, James 9:123;
  21:377; 27:97
Platt, John 14:99
Platt, John J. 7:14
Platt, Joseph 18:36;
  22:409
Platt, O. S. 16:113
Platt, R. 3:155
Platt, Robert 9:112
Platt, Robert L. 16:123
Platt, S. 23:162; 25:219
Platt, Samuel 9:190
Platt, Sanford 5:26
Platt, Sylvester C. 13:41;
  16:50
Platt, W. 14:99
Platt, William 24:43
Platt, William M. 16:219
Plattenburg, P. 14:27
Plattenbury, P. 12:96
Platter, C. 22:213
Platter, Harvey C. 22:96
Platter, Lewis N. 21:377
Platton, Jacob 22:487
Platts, Edward M. 25:60
Platts, N. 19:245
Platts, Nelson 11:41
Platygraff, Jacob 22:455
Plavey, Lyford I. 18:346
Plavis, William 6:21
Playfoot, David B. 17:427
Playford, Henry 8:102;
  24:150
Playley, D. 14:19
Playtor, George 21:259
Plazer, Fred 25:325
Pleasant, Eddie R. 18:221
Pleasant, George H. 13:41
Pleasant, I. 14:207
Pleasant, John 9:210
Pleasant, Major 7:131
Pleasant, Samuel 21:377
Pleasant, William S.
  25:219
Pleasure, Octave 23:194
Plechet, L. 16:220
Pledger, Wiley 11:211
Pleggett, Adam 6:18;
  18:91
Pleich, Christian 10:131;
  20:328

Pleiffer, Frank 13:41
Plemmons, Perry G.
  21:104
Plemos, W. C. 16:50
Plenby, Alfred 11:210
Plenby, David 7:106
Plerth, John 13:67
Pleson, Oley 9:234
Pleson, Taloff 8:74
Pletcher, John 23:162
Pleter, Lindsey 27:147
Pletheplace, W. 14:19
Plett, S. 19:245
Plews, Lewis B. 1:63
Plice, S. L. 26:109
Plimer, A. S. A. 25:62
Plimpton, Edgar G. 7:16
Plinky, Conrad 26:52
Plomtreault, A. R. A.
  10:97
Ploof, Peter 5:26
Plook, G. 21:377
Ploor, Henry 22:96
Ploss, Peter 15:42
Ploss, Wheeler 15:73
Plotner, James D. 10:166
Plotner, Samuel 13:41
Plotnet, James D. 19:187
Plott, A. 14:99
Plotts, T. T. 22:236
Plough, Ephraim 1:64
Plough, Silas 7:106
Ploughe, J. W. 3:155
Plouman, James 5:26
Plovex, P. 25:219
Plow, Henry 13:117
Plowman, J. 25:219
Plowman, William 13:117
Pluch, Frederick 9:123
Pluck, G. A. 14:99
Pluck, J. 1:163
Plude, John 3:155
Plugh, Mary Jane 18:193
Plugh, W. H. 1:63
Plum, A. 3:155
Plum, Charles 20:115
Plum, Edward 13:41
Plum, Eugene 22:96
Plum, Harier 13:96
Plum, J. 27:96
Plum, James 3:155
Plum, M. 21:377
Plum, S. M. 11:333
Plum, W. B. 11:247
Plumas, William 14:99
Plumb, Adam 20:138
Plumb, David 9:190;
  19:259
Plumb, Henry 20:99
Plumb, J. 1:162
Plumb, Lafayette 12:157

Plumb, M. 1:64
Plumb, William 4:47
Plumber, Anderson
  11:210
Plumber, P. D. 17:315
Plumber, Thomas H. 9:88
Plumbly, J. 14:99
Plume, Henry 15:132
Plumen, Frederick 18:340
Plumer, A. 3:155
Plumer, E. D. 3:155
Plumer, J. L. 15:357;
  16:281
Plumer, John H. 5:26
Plumer, T. J. 27:157
Plumhoff, George L.
  19:271
Plummer, A. 2:16
Plummer, A. C. 1:161
Plummer, A. J. 7:106
Plummer, A. P. 1:163
Plummer, Abram 22:237
Plummer, Alfred 7:106;
  8:93
Plummer, Amzi S. 13:41
Plummer, Anzil T. 16:50
Plummer, B. 14:99
Plummer, Charles 13:41;
  15:319; 19:93
Plummer, Clement 14:207
Plummer, D. R. 4:47
Plummer, D. W. 18:221
Plummer, David 8:28;
  18:154
Plummer, E. J. 16:80
Plummer, Edward 19:187
Plummer, Edward C.
  10:166
Plummer, Enoch 24:83
Plummer, George 7:106
Plummer, George C.
  22:162
Plummer, George M.
  13:41
Plummer, George W.
  21:377
Plummer, J. 3:155
Plummer, J. J. 12:98
Plummer, J. L. 13:41
Plummer, J. T. 23:162
Plummer, J. W. 25:219
Plummer, Jefferson L.
  7:53
Plummer, Joseph 7:38
Plummer, Keil B. 10:92
Plummer, M. 16:220
Plummer, Richard B.
  20:328
Plummer, Robinson W.
  7:14
Plummer, Samuel 14:207

Plummer, Simon B. 7:106
Plummer, T. H. 21:377
Plummer, William 8:93;
 11:41; 18:399
Plummet, Leander M.
 9:190
Plumney, Amos J. 12:9
Plump, F. 13:96
Plumstead, W. 25:312
Plumsted, T. 19:93
Plumteaux, William R.
 13:41; 16:50
Plunk, Daniel 26:54
Plunk, David 9:88
Plunk, Peter 21:131
Plunkat, G. 14:19
Plunket, G. 13:96
Plunket, M. 3:155
Plunkett, Bernard 18:36
Plunkett, Dominick 12:54
Plunkett, J. 3:155
Plunn, John 24:102
Plupher, J. 18:373
Plyatt, Q. 26:54
Plyatt, Z. 18:249
Plyffer, Gustar 7:63
Plyly, Daniel 13:96
Plymale, James 23:101
Plyman, William 3:155
Plymer, John 4:47
Plyner, S. 3:155
Plyning, W. 3:155
Pneuman, W. H. 27:97
Po---, Benson 19:93
Poake, Henry 20:328
Poart, James B. 20:12
Poast, William 4:47
Poat, Thomas 7:81
Pobin, Simon 10:74
Pobin, Timean 20:328
Pochler, I. 8:66
Pochlo, H. 15:220
Pock, James 26:177
Pocket, C. 13:117
Pocket, J. 1:104
Pocks, George 7:131
Podelsky, A. 7:53
Podges, S. 3:155
Podgett, William T.
 17:283
Podroff, D. 3:155
Poe, A. 17:217
Poe, A. G. 17:441; 24:154
Poe, Andrew A. 23:162
Poe, Anthony 17:149
Poe, Austin 17:207
Poe, George 22:487
Poe, George A. 23:287
Poe, Isaac 21:259
Poe, James D. 10:131;
 20:328

Poe, John 19:305
Poe, John J. 14:207
Poe, L. G. 23:45
Poe, Melanethon 27:99
Poe, N. 22:515
Poe, Oliver C. 17:57
Poe, Richard 17:137
Poe, Thomas 16:65
Poe, Thomas D. 25:60
Poe, W. A. 20:328
Poe, William A. 10:74
Poe, William F. M.
 17:207
Poe, Zachariah 10:131;
 20:328
Poelblkt, William 19:275
Poeples, J. G. 17:283
Poeplin, J. 26:176
Poetsch, John 27:99
Pof, George 17:57
Poff, A. M. 17:40
Poff, Charles 16:220
Poff, S. 27:96
Poff, William H. 21:232
Pogg, --- 11:73
Pogue, George 7:131
Pogue, Jackson 9:223;
 18:373
Pogue, Robert 15:132
Pohamsis, John 14:207
Pohl, Frederick 15:73
Pohl, Henry 9:240
Pohlin, Charles 14:99
Pohlman, B. 25:219
Pohlman, H. A. 7:84;
 21:377
Pohlman, H. C. 16:302
Pohlman, Hans 7:106
Pohlmine, Jacob 7:106
Poidex, Rudolph 20:328
Poindek, Rudolph 10:131
Poinder, T. 3:155
Poindexter, Moses
 17:137; 24:201
Poindexter, Partial 11:188
Poindexter, R. 17:183;
 22:315
Poinnan, C. F. 25:220
Poinrose, S. 21:377
Poinsett, Joseph 24:43
Point, John 17:40
Pointdexter, James H.
 8:74
Pointer, --- 11:310
Pointer, Alfred 7:131
Pointer, George 11:336
Pointer, Henson 22:315
Pointer, James S. 21:14
Pointer, John 9:210; 18:71
Pointer, Samuel 9:38;
 26:109

Pointer, W. 11:281
Points, J. 20:36
Poisins, D. 26:176
Poistian, J. 3:155
Poke, Jim 21:281
Poke, Peter 5:44
Poke, William A. 9:88
Poker, R. H. 18:373
Polan, Thomas J. 4:47
Poland, A. 25:220
Poland, A. D. 10:131;
 20:328
Poland, Amos 22:213
Poland, Erin D. 4:47
Poland, Henry G. 22:265
Poland, Isaiah 17:356
Poland, J. L. 8:66
Poland, Jacob 1:63
Poland, James C. 11:73
Poland, Lewis O. 4:47
Poland, Wesley 11:310
Polard, John 4:47
Polaski, Edward 13:41
Polaskie, Edward 16:50
Pole, Gabriel P. 15:59
Pole, T. B. 17:499
Poleman, H. 3:155; 13:96
Poleman, Philip 18:434
Polen, James 26:175
Polen, W. D. 12:100
Polfton, Thomas 20:328
Polger, M. 3:155
Polhames, John 6:26
Polhamus, John 7:38;
 11:110
Polhamus, Levi 24:27
Polhemer, Abel B. 17:67
Polheumus, J. 1:64
Poliet, Narcice 20:328
Poling, William 11:164
Polininius, H. 20:328
Polite, Narcisse 10:74
Poliver, George W.
 16:220
Poliver, Martin 3:224
Polk, Daniel W. 22:96
Polk, Eliza 21:213
Polk, Ezra 21:281
Polk, F. E. 20:127
Polk, Frank 21:281
Polk, George 17:137;
 24:201
Polk, Henry C. 21:232
Polk, James 5:26; 8:69
Polk, James K. 6:18; 8:28,
 41; 18:91, 154; 22:96
Polk, Leander 10:174;
 19:187
Polk, N. Q. 11:163
Polk, S. H. 8:109
Polk, W. J. 17:265

Polk, William H. 22:96
Polk, William J. 12:51
Polkanus, Robert E. 10:206
Polker, Lewis 6:11
Polks, Lewis 18:113
Pollack, W. J. 15:42
Polland, George 22:283
Polland, H. 21:377
Polland, John 3:155; 13:41
Polland, R. 19:259
Polland, Royal S. 18:314
Pollard, A. 5:26; 15:344; 16:377; 25:220
Pollard, Albert 17:362
Pollard, B. 14:99
Pollard, Bershall 7:106
Pollard, Caesar 6:26
Pollard, Caswell 7:106
Pollard, Charles 15:303; 16:220
Pollard, D. 25:220
Pollard, Elisha 22:435
Pollard, Emmery 25:220
Pollard, F. 3:155
Pollard, G. W. 16:50
Pollard, Hartwell 22:315
Pollard, Humphrey 22:265
Pollard, I. 17:271
Pollard, J. H. 1:161
Pollard, Jerry 7:131
Pollard, John 16:50; 17:183; 24:69
Pollard, L. 22:315
Pollard, Madison B. 23:257
Pollard, Moses 9:223; 18:373
Pollard, P. J. 9:73
Pollard, R. 22:343
Pollard, Royal S. 9:27; 26:109
Pollard, S. 11:96
Pollard, T. T. 15:330; 19:93
Pollard, Thomas 16:220
Pollard, W. P. 19:229, 241
Pollard, William 21:281, 377
Pollart, Henry 17:183
Polle, C. 3:155
Polle, G. 3:155
Pollett, Henry 18:71
Polley, E. A. 25:220
Polley, H. W. 19:187
Polley, J. C. 10:74
Polley, James M. 11:73
Polley, John H. 18:91
Polley, Norton W. 10:166

Polley, Orrin D. 24:96
Polley, Peter G. 10:74
Polley, T. H. 19:229
Polley, V. A. 25:220
Pollick, John 11:72
Pollin, W. F. 11:311
Pollin, William 5:26
Polling, C. E. 21:377
Polling, Eugene 24:27
Polling, Jefferson 24:43
Pollman, William 15:15
Pollock, --- 19:93
Pollock, A. 2:16; 25:62
Pollock, A. D. 22:487
Pollock, Charles T. 20:115
Pollock, E. 8:93
Pollock, Ephraim 7:60
Pollock, Fred 20:328
Pollock, Frederick 10:74
Pollock, James 18:113; 23:162; 27:99
Pollock, Jimerson 22:213
Pollock, Joe 18:113
Pollock, John 8:122; 11:281
Pollock, Orlando 10:166; 19:187
Pollock, Quincin 26:53
Pollock, R. 3:155
Pollock, R. W. 18:249; 26:53
Pollock, Robert 4:47; 10:97
Pollock, Silas 4:47
Pollock, T. C. 15:344
Pollock, T. G. 16:377
Pollock, T. R. 23:45
Pollock, Thomas 7:16
Pollock, W. K. 19:187
Pollock, W. V. 11:164
Pollock, William E. 16:134
Pollocks, George W. 9:88
Pollon, Samuel B. 15:42
Pollord, William P. 9:190
Pollowy, P. 25:220
Polls, Percival M. 15:160
Polluck, --- 15:315
Polly, George 9:38
Polly, Ira A. 23:283
Polly, J. 3:155
Polly, Thomas A. 4:47
Polly, W. B. 9:104
Poloman, H. 14:19
Polsgrove, D. 13:129
Polshon, F. B. 3:155
Polsom, Wesley 11:268
Polson, Robert S. 20:99
Polston, Joseph 17:57

Polston, William T. 23:185
Polyard, L. 13:129
Pombram, John 18:279
Pomell, Peter 15:334; 19:93
Pomeroy, Carlos 23:260
Pomeroy, D. B. 1:162
Pomeroy, David H. 15:220
Pomeroy, Edward 11:163
Pomeroy, George Y. 13:67
Pomeroy, Henry 11:40; 18:427
Pomeroy, J. S. 16:123
Pomeroy, J. W. 1:161
Pomeroy, John 3:155; 10:131; 20:328
Pomeroy, Oscar J. 17:264
Pomeroy, R. B. 7:53
Pomeroy, Richard 24:27
Pomeroy, Titus 12:35
Pomeroy, Uriah 20:328
Pomeroy, William 11:110; 13:41; 18:36
Pomery, Sewell 21:377
Pomoroy, Fenton J. 7:76
Pompey, C. 3:155
Pomroy, C. 3:155
Pomroy, F. J. 25:303
Pomroy, George W. 20:190
Pomroy, O. K. 18:71
Pomroy, William M. 25:62
Pon, Peter D. 18:218
Pon---h, L. F. 20:148
Ponas, Benjamin 11:281
Poncher, W. 25:220
Ponchot, D. 8:66
Pond, --- 14:207
Pond, Ambrose 19:30
Pond, B. F. 14:266, 289; 22:172; 23:162
Pond, C. 3:155
Pond, C. K. 10:131; 20:328
Pond, D. 12:123
Pond, D. A. 7:38
Pond, Edwin F. 13:41
Pond, George 17:183
Pond, Henry 11:183
Pond, John F. 22:435
Pond, Joseph 10:131
Pond, Josiah 20:328
Pond, L. N. 11:129
Pond, Loyal S. 7:107
Pond, M. 17:420
Pond, Simeon 21:142
Pond, Truman 17:67

Pond, W. J. 19:233
Pond, William J. 9:190
Ponder, Franklin 27:97
Ponder, J. 14:289; 23:205
Ponds, Simeon 8:54
Ponds, William 24:102
Ponet, James H. 7:69
Ponner, O. C. 1:99
Ponottar, C. 14:19
Ponsford, John D. 17:70
Pontey, John 22:96
Ponties, G. 3:155
Pontieux, William 14:244
Pontious, B. F. 16:134
Pontis, Jacob I. 19:259
Pontius, Isaac 20:99
Pontius, Samuel 17:496
Pontius, Solomon 20:25
Ponto, O. 1:64
Pontras, Charles 15:220
Pontze, Thomas 8:28;
     18:154
Pontzlaine, Henry 7:53
Pontzler, J. 1:65
Pooh, I. B. 26:52
Pooke, W. 16:100
Pool, A. 14:99
Pool, Andrew J. 11:72
Pool, Asby C. 22:14
Pool, C. 1:95
Pool, C. E. 3:155
Pool, Charles 22:96
Pool, Edward 17:103
Pool, Edward R. 14:207
Pool, F. 14:99; 19:305
Pool, Francis 17:347
Pool, George F. 22:409
Pool, H. A. 25:60
Pool, Hanson 3:155
Pool, Ira 15:333
Pool, Israel P. 22:96
Pool, J. 14:99
Pool, J. H. 13:96
Pool, Jacob 17:420;
     24:161
Pool, James 22:435
Pool, James D. 22:265
Pool, John 17:420; 21:190
Pool, John H. 12:35
Pool, M. A. 17:167
Pool, M. F. 8:66
Pool, M. M. 1:99
Pool, Nathan 22:505
Pool, R. 14:99
Pool, R. W. 8:28; 18:154
Pool, Richard 1:64
Pool, Samuel 1:64;
     21:282; 25:325
Pool, Sanford D. 17:57
Pool, Thomas 10:131;
     20:328; 25:303

Pool, William 8:28;
     12:157; 17:57;
     18:154; 21:377
Pool, William R. 22:49
Poolar, G. 14:99
Poole, A. M. 6:9; 18:104
Poole, David 10:74;
     20:328
Poole, E. 14:99
Poole, E. G. 15:18
Poole, George 1:64;
     15:327; 19:93
Poole, George W. 11:391
Poole, Ira 19:93
Poole, J. F. 15:220
Poole, J. H. 14:19
Poole, J. W. 1:64
Poole, James E. 13:41
Poole, John 9:190; 12:35;
     19:241
Poole, John W. 17:496
Poole, Joseph H. 17:57
Poole, Josiah 13:41
Poole, Nathan 8:93
Poole, R. K. 1:99
Poole, Reazin 23:163
Poole, T. J. 11:415
Poole, William 7:107
Poole, Winfield S. 13:42;
     16:50
Pooler, G. 7:76; 25:303
Pooler, H. H. 18:193
Pooler, John M. 25:61
Pooley, Samuel 5:53
Pooley, William 23:45
Pools, M. 23:205
Poor, A. M. 3:155
Poor, Benjamin F. 17:433
Poor, F. 26:54
Poor, Frederick 9:88
Poor, George W. 11:268
Poor, H. A. 2:16
Poor, Henry 7:53; 10:187;
     18:179
Poor, J. 14:207
Poor, John W. 16:50
Poor, Richard 17:283
Poor, William 17:24
Poor, William L. 11:248
Poore, George W. 10:131;
     20:328
Poore, S. 3:155
Poores, C. 14:284
Poorman, Amos W.
     22:153
Poorman, David 22:435
Poorman, George H.
     11:17
Poormans, William
     11:382
Poorshot, L. 23:163

Poovoce, J. 27:95
Pope, C. H. 24:83
Pope, Camp S. 10:211
Pope, Charles 10:131;
     19:316; 20:328
Pope, Charles L. 22:96
Pope, D. M. 11:73
Pope, David 9:135; 27:96
Pope, David E. 19:30
Pope, Don 26:54
Pope, Dow 18:249
Pope, E. 7:38
Pope, F. 3:155
Pope, Francis C. 12:35
Pope, Frank 3:155
Pope, G. W. 1:162
Pope, George 12:162
Pope, George W. 10:99
Pope, H. F. 25:62
Pope, H. G. 9:58
Pope, Henry 20:49
Pope, J. C. 25:61, 325
Pope, J. T. 3:155
Pope, James 9:210; 24:27
Pope, John A. 20:90
Pope, Lewis D. 11:71
Pope, Matthias D. 4:47
Pope, P. P. 5:26; 25:220
Pope, Peter S. 8:93
Pope, Philander 22:96
Pope, S. 18:36; 21:196
Pope, Samuel 21:78
Pope, Squire 17:232
Pope, Thomas 10:74;
     20:328; 27:99
Pope, W. North 13:125
Pope, Wiley 22:49
Pope, William 10:74;
     13:42; 16:50; 20:328
Pope, William M. 10:74;
     20:328
Pope, Z. 17:257
Popejoy, Alex 20:328
Popejoy, Alexander
     10:131
Popence, A. G. 23:45
Popham, James H. B.
     15:220
Popjoy, William 18:249;
     26:54
Pople, Smith 11:129
Poplin, Elisha 22:49
Poplin, William 17:350
Poplinham, H. 14:99
Poplowski, Armfri 9:237
Popner, William 4:47
Popp, Godfrey 25:220
Popp, J. E. 3:155
Popper, --- 18:16
Poppey, John 20:184
Poppin, Frank 3:155

Popple, --- 19:187
Popple, Albert 7:38
Popple, Alonzo 26:53
Popple, Arville 12:75
Popple, N. G. 3:155
Popple, O. 15:42
Poppleton, B. H. 23:91
Poppleton, S. D. 15:220
Popplewell, Flint 17:207
Poppsino, F. G. 25:220
Poppy, E. A. 16:220
Poquet, M. 1:64
Porchockway, George 9:223; 18:374
Pordung, John 19:283
Pore, Amos 19:30
Porenbough, E. C. 18:36
Porince, A. F. 18:36
Porisby, N. 14:131
Pork, John 19:259
Porker, J. H. 18:413
Porney, A. 13:96
Porr, George 15:42
Porsel, Francis M. 22:96
Porsel, Robert 12:36
Porset, Joseph 7:107
Porsonett, John 21:377
Porsonl, Samuel 3:155
Port, A. C. 21:377
Port, George H. 9:123
Port, George W. 22:488
Port, O. K. 23:45
Porteans, James 19:187
Portell, David 23:115
Portell, John 8:74
Portell, Patrick 26:176
Porteninius, Herman 10:74
Porter, --- 15:3, 221; 18:193
Porter, A. 11:165; 20:176
Porter, A. J. 23:163
Porter, A. W. 25:220
Porter, Abijah E. 8:93
Porter, Abraham 25:61
Porter, Adam 11:129
Porter, Alex 12:35
Porter, Alexander I. 26:146
Porter, Alexander M. 17:24
Porter, Alpha 19:229
Porter, Anthony 8:41; 26:175
Porter, B. 1:162; 14:99
Porter, B. F. 3:155
Porter, B. M. 21:377
Porter, Bela W. 10:74
Porter, Benjamin D. 21:104
Porter, C. E. 7:76; 25:303

Porter, C. L. 19:259
Porter, C. S. 1:162
Porter, C. W. 5:26
Porter, Charles 9:104; 18:340
Porter, Charles H. 8:28; 18:154; 23:76
Porter, Charles J. 23:163
Porter, Curtis L. 9:190
Porter, D. 3:155; 7:65; 14:316
Porter, Dan. S. 19:187
Porter, Daniel 10:131; 20:328; 22:96, 315
Porter, Daniel S. 10:166
Porter, David H. 4:47
Porter, David V. 26:52
Porter, Dempray 8:99
Porter, E. 20:59
Porter, E. A. 12:35
Porter, E. R. 22:107
Porter, Edward 10:166; 19:93, 187
Porter, Edward L. 12:75
Porter, Edward R. 12:36
Porter, Elias D. 27:99
Porter, Elry 20:115
Porter, Ewing 24:27
Porter, Ezekiel 22:96
Porter, F. 14:99
Porter, F. B. 4:47
Porter, F. E. 7:38
Porter, Frederick 22:14
Porter, G. 3:155
Porter, G. H. 1:161
Porter, G. W. 14:302; 17:478; 27:98
Porter, Gachhill 27:94
Porter, Gallehill 9:135
Porter, George 17:111; 18:249; 26:54
Porter, George A. 14:99
Porter, George W. 7:38; 11:72; 20:115
Porter, Gideon B. 4:47
Porter, Green 22:505
Porter, H. 22:343
Porter, H. C. 18:36
Porter, H. H. 20:148
Porter, H. M. 12:123; 15:133
Porter, H. S. 4:47
Porter, Henry 12:36; 17:190; 21:282; 23:13
Porter, Isaac 8:115
Porter, J. 3:155; 9:238; 13:96; 14:19, 99; 17:183
Porter, J. A. 21:125
Porter, J. C. 1:63

Porter, J. D. 22:354
Porter, J. F. 3:155; 27:96
Porter, J. H. 26:52
Porter, J. T. 1:161; 9:149
Porter, J. W. 7:38
Porter, Jacob 13:42
Porter, James 9:58; 12:35; 17:97; 22:466; 27:95
Porter, James A. 10:212
Porter, James G. 8:93
Porter, James J. 21:239
Porter, Jerry 17:137; 24:201
Porter, John 7:107; 9:88; 11:163; 12:75; 15:5; 16:148; 21:377; 22:96; 23:277; 26:53; 27:99
Porter, John A. 23:76
Porter, John C. 18:193; 25:325
Porter, John E. 19:30
Porter, John F. 23:163
Porter, John H. 8:109; 9:88
Porter, John M. 22:497
Porter, John T. 6:32
Porter, John W. 12:51
Porter, Joseph 13:58
Porter, Juransom 5:56
Porter, L. 3:155; 22:315; 23:271
Porter, L. B. 25:220
Porter, Lester H. 21:259
Porter, M. 23:76
Porter, M. B. 7:107
Porter, Martin M. 8:115
Porter, Mary E. 26:213
Porter, Moses 16:220; 21:282
Porter, N. Y. 14:99
Porter, Nathan 27:94
Porter, Newton 6:26; 10:131; 20:328
Porter, Oscar G. 20:27
Porter, P. 20:328
Porter, Perry J. 17:499
Porter, Pleasant 24:102
Porter, R. 1:164
Porter, Reason 22:315
Porter, Rice M. 22:96
Porter, Richard 4:47; 12:51
Porter, Robert H. 18:193
Porter, Robert L. 11:277
Porter, S. 3:155
Porter, S. H. 1:95
Porter, S. J. 20:43
Porter, S. L. 20:134
Porter, S. M. 27:95

Porter, Samuel 8:74; 10:99; 21:282
Porter, Samuel M. 7:38
Porter, Sirenius 21:58
Porter, Stanton 21:232
Porter, Stephen 8:41
Porter, T. F. 25:220
Porter, Theodore 12:35; 18:221
Porter, Thomas 9:98; 20:59; 26:128
Porter, Thomas T. 5:26
Porter, Virginia T. 26:224
Porter, W. 1:161; 3:155; 9:69, 149; 16:220; 27:96
Porter, W. C. 1:64; 3:156
Porter, W. H. 1:99
Porter, W. K. 1:65
Porter, W. M. 17:92; 21:58
Porter, W. W. 8:54; 11:41
Porter, William 4:47; 12:123; 14:131; 15:133; 17:261, 356; 22:487
Porter, William A. 22:96
Porter, William H. 11:163
Porter, William M. 4:47
Porter, William R. 8:28; 18:154; 22:315
Porter, William T. 4:47
Porter, Williams 9:210
Porter, Winfield 21:78
Porterfield, A. D. 26:127
Porterfield, J. 3:156
Porterfield, J. K. 3:156
Porterfield, James F. N. 22:265
Porterfield, Samuel 7:38
Porterfield, William 10:25, 74; 20:328
Porterlage, M. 3:156
Portes, Thomas 20:31
Portil, J. 1:161
Portland, Samuel 13:58
Portlong, Dennis 15:289; 19:93
Portman, G. E. 22:466
Portman, H. 14:207
Portman, Nicholas 22:521
Portney, H. 14:131
Porton, Dilda 10:131; 20:329
Portor, H. 15:153
Portor, Henry 15:160
Portor, Thomas 9:44
Ports, John 17:15
Ports, John S. 23:163
Portwine, George 25:62
Portwood, J. 21:37

Pose, W. W. 13:117
Posey, Benjamin N. 17:233
Posey, Edmond 10:177
Posey, Edmund 19:187
Posey, Edward 4:67
Posey, I. 14:99
Posey, Joseph 11:96
Posey, Pleasant 18:413
Posey, Stephen 18:17
Posley, Samuel 25:220
Poslin, W. P. 3:156
Possatt, M. 7:53
Posset, Thomas W. 4:47
Possum, J. F. 8:66
Post, A. 3:156
Post, A. N. 16:100
Post, Albert 9:237; 26:224
Post, Anson B. 9:223
Post, Austin B. 18:374
Post, C. 3:156
Post, C. J. 3:156
Post, C. S. 1:162
Post, Charles B. 18:221; 27:99
Post, Charles W. 18:279
Post, David 15:110
Post, E. 15:221
Post, Ezra W. 20:115
Post, Fred. D. 19:93
Post, G. 3:156
Post, Garrett O. 20:193
Post, George A. 23:181
Post, George C. 20:190
Post, H. 14:99
Post, H. E. 3:156
Post, Harvey 20:190
Post, Henry 17:156
Post, J. 1:65; 3:156
Post, J. A. 3:156
Post, J. J. 7:38
Post, J. M. 20:148
Post, J. P. 15:42
Post, James 15:304; 16:220; 18:55
Post, John C. 8:28; 18:154
Post, Joseph 11:41; 22:213
Post, L. 25:220
Post, Levi 5:26
Post, Lewis F. 15:221
Post, Lewis R. 11:110
Post, Oliver R. 23:16
Post, Philip 4:47
Post, R. 18:279
Post, R. L. 3:156
Post, Thaddeus W. 7:38
Post, Thomas S. 18:324
Post, W. 15:221
Post, W. H. 11:122
Postan, Albert 10:99

Postan, Nathaniel 11:210
Poster, Eli 12:160
Poster, George 9:44; 10:99; 26:127
Poster, Hiram 10:99
Poster, J. W. 14:19; 16:270
Poster, Joseph 22:315
Poster, William A. 12:162
Postler, John 22:237
Postlewait, John J. 23:91
Postlewait, Joseph 19:334
Poston, Argyle A. 22:96
Poston, W. D. 18:249; 26:54
Potache, A. 3:156
Potasse, Paul 24:108
Poth, Jacob 18:209
Potiger, David R. 25:63
Potoff, Jacob 18:424
Potree, Anthony 11:163
Potrin, William 11:129
Pott, A. 21:377
Pott, J. 3:156
Pott, Jonathan 20:187
Pott, Samuel 3:156
Pott, W. 21:377
Potten, C. H. 15:167
Potten, J. S. 16:302
Pottenheimer, --- 15:18
Potter, --- 18:179
Potter, A. 2:16; 25:59
Potter, A. J. 1:160
Potter, A. V. 20:148
Potter, Albert W. 23:124
Potter, Andrew 19:187
Potter, Anson L. 18:314; 26:108
Potter, Arthur 12:36
Potter, B. F. 16:281
Potter, Benjamin 23:260
Potter, Benjamin H. 17:167
Potter, Benson 15:334
Potter, C. 8:93; 25:220
Potter, C. H. 1:161
Potter, C. M. 15:175
Potter, Charles 5:44
Potter, Charles H. 21:377
Potter, Charles R. 23:194
Potter, Cyrus 8:28
Potter, D. 16:220
Potter, D. F. 15:160
Potter, D. H. 9:223
Potter, D. R. 10:131; 20:329
Potter, D. S. 17:67
Potter, David H. 18:374
Potter, Drown 16:377
Potter, E. A. 16:100
Potter, Ed 11:220

Potter, Edgar 4:47
Potter, Edward 6:13;
    22:343
Potter, F. 2:16
Potter, F. B. 1:161
Potter, F. G. 15:295
Potter, F. T. 16:220
Potter, Francis A. 10:74;
    20:329
Potter, Frank 25:63
Potter, Fred 19:259
Potter, Frederick 9:190
Potter, G. H. 16:220
Potter, G. W. 15:153
Potter, George 5:26
Potter, George E. 11:193
Potter, Gideon 24:54
Potter, Gordon H. 4:47
Potter, H. 3:156; 15:175
Potter, H. B. 11:403
Potter, Henry 20:156
Potter, Henry C. 13:42;
    23:91
Potter, Henry L. 27:147
Potter, Hiram E. 14:207
Potter, Horace B. 7:107
Potter, I. 14:99
Potter, J. 1:65; 25:220
Potter, J. B. 11:403
Potter, J. L. 5:26; 25:220
Potter, J. P. 11:425
Potter, J. S. 12:87
Potter, James 1:64;
    11:211; 14:207
Potter, James H. 13:42
Potter, James T. 11:281
Potter, Jasper 20:127
Potter, Jeremiah 8:93
Potter, Jesse 22:49, 488
Potter, Job 1:63
Potter, John 4:47; 5:44;
    11:164; 13:96;
    14:207; 15:348;
    21:190; 22:466
Potter, John A. 5:26
Potter, John T. 5:26
Potter, Joseph 8:74;
    10:29; 19:305;
    22:172
Potter, Joshua 22:14
Potter, Joshua D. 11:41
Potter, L. 1:64; 12:83;
    16:302; 21:377
Potter, L. F. 10:74; 20:329
Potter, Levi 23:163
Potter, Lucius C. 20:115
Potter, Luther 1:63
Potter, Lyman 22:213
Potter, M. G. 18:249;
    26:53
Potter, Martin 8:54

Potter, Merrett 13:42
Potter, Merritt 16:50
Potter, N. 21:191
Potter, Noadiah 10:174
Potter, Nodiah 19:187
Potter, O. 13:117
Potter, Orland 11:117
Potter, R. 14:99
Potter, R. R. 1:164
Potter, Robert 11:268;
    22:49
Potter, Roil 14:99
Potter, Roswell H. 24:88
Potter, S. 16:153; 27:99
Potter, S. D. 3:156
Potter, S. O. 19:93
Potter, Sam 20:141
Potter, Samuel 3:156;
    9:161; 14:328; 25:61
Potter, Sires 22:49
Potter, T. A. 1:164
Potter, T. B. 12:100;
    15:366
Potter, T. C. 20:12
Potter, T. J. 22:49
Potter, Theron 22:435
Potter, Thomas 10:21;
    17:264
Potter, Thomas E. 11:163
Potter, W. D. 7:107
Potter, W. F. 17:92
Potter, W. H. 1:65; 3:156
Potter, W. M. 15:259
Potter, Walter 16:162
Potter, Walter A. 19:187
Potter, William 12:51;
    13:117; 17:320;
    22:213; 25:334
Potter, William D. 23:76
Potter, William H. 13:42
Potter, William W.
    22:153; 25:61
Potterfield, S. 9:58
Potters, George 25:61
Pottery, Calvin 16:123
Pottet, A. E. 3:156
Pottinger, Samuel 11:41
Pottle, T. C. 21:377
Pottler, B. F. 15:353
Pottore, Jacob 9:234
Pottorff, Marion 8:109
Pottowatami, --- 18:155
Pottowatamie, --- 8:28
Pottruff, John 17:67
Potts, Abraham 9:201
Potts, Alfred 21:58;
    22:213
Potts, Alfred D. 17:40
Potts, B. 14:302; 17:479;
    27:98
Potts, Benjamin 25:220

Potts, Charles 27:97
Potts, D. W. 8:54
Potts, Dave R. 18:55
Potts, David 17:447;
    24:171
Potts, David W. 21:78
Potts, E. 3:156
Potts, Edward 20:33
Potts, F. A. 25:60
Potts, Henry 15:295;
    16:220; 22:315
Potts, Henry D. 17:283
Potts, I. J. 22:213
Potts, J. 1:161; 3:156;
    9:149; 27:95
Potts, J. E. 4:47
Potts, J. P. 8:54
Potts, Jacob 11:72
Potts, James 3:156
Potts, James A. 7:38;
    14:335
Potts, James T. 22:128
Potts, John L. 17:317
Potts, Jonathan 18:399
Potts, Jonathan P. 21:78
Potts, Joshua 20:127
Potts, Norman 15:133
Potts, Stoner 24:43
Potts, Thomas 22:497
Potts, Thomas R. 22:168
Potts, Tyrell 11:211
Potts, William 7:38;
    11:391; 14:205;
    22:49, 213; 23:76
Pouch, S. A. 16:270
Pouche, Sinclair 18:71
Poucher, Abraham 4:47
Poucher, William 5:26
Pouder, Franklin 9:123
Pough, J. 1:163
Pough, Thomas 15:268
Pough, William 15:268
Pouke, Henry 10:74
Poulice, George W. 3:156
Poulin, Henry 7:107
Poulsoe, John R. 11:73
Poulson, G. 14:19
Poulston, John 23:46
Poulton, Henry 3:156
Poulton, M. R. 23:163
Pound, Joseph 24:27
Pound, T. 7:72
Pound, W. 26:109
Pound, Walter W. 18:193
Pound, William 9:27;
    18:314
Pounder, Ezekiel 9:98
Pounders, J. 3:156
Pounds, Amos 9:124;
    27:97
Poundston, Jacob 19:187

Poundstone, Jacob 10:177
Pouroy, Uriah 10:74
Poustler, H. 13:96
Povely, Ephraim 8:41
Povermire, Levi 11:163
Powars, J. G. 13:67
Powcetti, Joseph G. 25:287
Powder, John 23:163
Powderly, W. H. 26:177
Powel, John 11:333
Powel, Joseph R. 15:153
Powel, Thomas P. 13:117
Powell, A. 1:162; 3:156; 14:99; 15:15
Powell, A. N. 3:156
Powell, A. T. 3:156
Powell, Abraham 12:75; 23:163
Powell, Amos 16:302; 22:214
Powell, Andrew 8:74; 21:37
Powell, Anthony 21:213
Powell, B. 9:58
Powell, B. F. 1:162
Powell, Benjamin 22:509
Powell, Charles 7:9; 13:42; 21:377
Powell, Christopher 17:85
Powell, D. 3:156; 5:26
Powell, D. B. 18:279
Powell, D. C. 22:113
Powell, David 14:207
Powell, David H. 8:109
Powell, E. 13:96
Powell, E. A. 25:61
Powell, E. J. 1:163
Powell, Elias 14:19
Powell, Elias E. 17:203
Powell, Elijah A. 11:72
Powell, Elisha 9:98
Powell, F. 3:156; 27:94
Powell, G. 3:156; 9:190
Powell, G. B. 26:176
Powell, George 6:13; 8:112; 9:67; 14:207; 18:279
Powell, George B. 24:54
Powell, George W. 22:96; 26:53
Powell, H. 1:65; 3:156
Powell, H. A. 16:50
Powell, H. J. 21:37
Powell, H. T. 18:154
Powell, Henry 7:78; 15:111; 17:441; 18:209; 22:265; 24:154; 25:303
Powell, Henry C. 20:329
Powell, I. 23:163

Powell, Isaac C. 23:91
Powell, Isaiah 20:108
Powell, J. 3:156; 9:154; 16:220; 27:96
Powell, J. A. 18:193
Powell, J. C. 17:92
Powell, J. T. 1:162
Powell, James 11:425; 14:289, 290; 16:50; 23:182; 27:98
Powell, James L. 10:74
Powell, Jefferson 6:35
Powell, Jerry 11:96
Powell, Joel T. 22:96
Powell, John 4:47; 5:26; 9:135; 11:72, 163; 14:99; 16:141; 17:424; 18:179; 22:237; 23:205; 24:175; 25:60, 63, 220; 26:127; 27:96
Powell, John C. 17:24; 23:260
Powell, John J. 17:308
Powell, John M. 10:131; 20:329
Powell, Jonathan 21:104
Powell, Joseph 11:86; 22:488; 23:76
Powell, Julius 18:249
Powell, Kelso 17:213
Powell, L. 25:220
Powell, Levi 4:47
Powell, Lewis 5:44; 17:455; 24:201
Powell, Lewis A. 20:25
Powell, Luther 21:196
Powell, Mathew 8:28; 18:154
Powell, McNeal 22:265
Powell, Miner 11:415
Powell, Noah 6:23
Powell, R. 21:150
Powell, R. C. 25:277
Powell, R. F. 16:270
Powell, R. H. 25:220
Powell, Reas 21:282
Powell, Richard T. 23:182
Powell, Richmond 22:515
Powell, Robert 11:281
Powell, Robert W. 10:97
Powell, Roland 21:78
Powell, Russel T. 13:42
Powell, Russell G. 16:50
Powell, S. 11:326; 16:220
Powell, S. H. 8:28; 18:154
Powell, S. L. 18:91
Powell, Samuel 17:137; 19:30; 24:201; 25:220
Powell, Scott 22:315

Powell, Solomon 10:131; 20:329
Powell, Squires 7:38
Powell, Swanson 6:21
Powell, T. 3:156; 17:183; 19:283
Powell, T. B. 1:64
Powell, Thomas 1:64; 8:28; 10:74; 12:51; 15:221; 16:50; 17:40; 18:154; 20:329; 21:377
Powell, Thomas J. 11:281
Powell, Thomas W. 8:93
Powell, W. 8:102; 24:113
Powell, W. E. 11:247
Powell, Walter 9:73
Powell, William 3:156; 4:47; 7:131; 8:74; 10:74; 11:129; 13:42; 16:50; 20:329; 22:435; 23:309
Powell, William G. 20:329; 22:214
Powell, William H. 8:54; 15:221; 21:232; 22:497
Powell, William L. 20:329
Powell, William R. 17:453; 22:128; 24:184
Powell, William S. 9:231
Powell, Willoughby 17:461; 24:161
Powells, David O. 4:47
Powellson, C. F. 3:156
Powelt, John M. 22:96
Power, C. W. 21:377
Power, E. 21:104
Power, Edward 12:36
Power, Frederick 7:60
Power, George L. 21:377
Power, Isaac H. 23:91
Power, John 8:115
Power, John W. C. 23:76
Power, Mathew 18:221
Power, Michael 27:94
Power, Patrick 11:268
Power, Reuben 16:141
Power, Robert B. 18:221
Power, W. H. 16:51
Power, W. W. 21:378
Power, William 9:104, 210; 18:340
Powerless, August 21:259
Powers, Anderson 11:72
Powers, Andrew 22:214
Powers, Andrew J. 21:58
Powers, Ashael 8:109
Powers, B. 3:156; 11:41

Powers, Ben 17:137; 24:201
Powers, Benjamin 20:134; 21:142
Powers, C. F. 19:259
Powers, C. J. S. 11:20
Powers, Cannady W. 22:455
Powers, Charles 16:88
Powers, Charles B. 9:7
Powers, Charles F. 9:190; 19:259
Powers, Charles R. 13:42
Powers, Cromwell C. 22:97
Powers, Darwin 17:244
Powers, David 7:38
Powers, David W. 23:76
Powers, Dred 25:220
Powers, E. 8:54
Powers, Earl 15:8
Powers, Ed 18:154
Powers, Ed. 8:28
Powers, Edwin 19:30
Powers, Ephraim 10:166; 19:187
Powers, F. 14:302; 17:481; 27:98
Powers, F. E. 20:138
Powers, F. R. 22:466
Powers, Francis 4:47; 22:128
Powers, Frank 10:151
Powers, Frank L. 13:42
Powers, G. H. 9:38; 18:296; 26:109
Powers, G. L. 21:378
Powers, George 1:64
Powers, George R. 14:99
Powers, Gilbert F. 17:244
Powers, H. 3:156; 9:27; 17:292; 18:314; 25:220; 26:109
Powers, H. D. 19:233
Powers, H. M. 3:156
Powers, Harvey D. 9:190
Powers, Henry C. 10:131
Powers, Henry D. 27:99
Powers, Henry W. 19:30
Powers, Hiram E. 17:402
Powers, I. 14:330
Powers, J. 1:163; 3:156; 11:101, 232; 14:99; 17:192; 19:265, 268
Powers, J. F. 8:54
Powers, J. T. F. 15:221
Powers, J. W. 19:275
Powers, James 11:72; 14:207; 17:57; 18:427; 20:28; 22:49, 162

Powers, James F. 21:78
Powers, James G. 19:93
Powers, James M. 21:191
Powers, Jasper 9:190
Powers, John 1:63; 8:28; 9:190; 11:101; 18:154; 19:241; 21:245; 23:13; 27:98
Powers, John A. 22:14
Powers, John B. 21:378; 24:96
Powers, John C. 7:107
Powers, John E. 8:93
Powers, John S. 23:46
Powers, John W. 9:190
Powers, Joseph 9:190
Powers, Joshua 9:7
Powers, Julius E. 18:209
Powers, L. 1:99; 20:329
Powers, L. J. 9:67
Powers, Leander 10:74
Powers, Lester 18:209
Powers, Lewis 6:35
Powers, Lewis R. 27:97
Powers, Louis R. 9:124
Powers, M. 13:96
Powers, M. H. 9:27, 89; 26:52
Powers, M. J. 13:117
Powers, Michael 10:166; 19:187
Powers, N. 20:329
Powers, Nathan 15:23
Powers, Newman 10:74
Powers, O. A. 18:179
Powers, O. R. 10:192
Powers, Oliver 22:214
Powers, Oren 26:177
Powers, Oscar 8:28; 18:154
Powers, P. 3:156
Powers, Patrick 11:89; 14:207; 23:266
Powers, Peter C. 21:78
Powers, R. 3:156
Powers, Randall 9:190
Powers, Richard J. 20:115
Powers, Robert 7:131; 21:378; 22:214
Powers, Robert O. 20:36
Powers, Rush W. 22:97
Powers, Samuel 22:128
Powers, Samuel H. 22:153
Powers, Samuel K. 21:78
Powers, Samuel P. 8:109
Powers, Stephen 21:282
Powers, T. 1:163
Powers, T. J. 9:149
Powers, Thomas 4:47; 7:76; 19:30; 21:37;

Powers, Thomas 22:128, 343; 25:220; 27:95
Powers, Timothy 11:164
Powers, W. 25:62; 27:96
Powers, W. H. 13:42
Powers, William 10:74; 13:42; 20:329; 25:220
Powers, William A. 12:59
Powers, William F. 12:123
Powers, William H. 9:31, 124; 17:261
Powers, William O. 10:21
Powert, Charles R. 16:51
Powill, Julius 26:54
Powitt, J. 14:266
Powl, I. 23:46
Powl, Samuel 15:279
Powler, Charles 13:42; 16:51
Powler, S. 21:378
Powles, W. H. 1:99
Powless, D. 21:37
Pownall, Charles J. 10:166
Pownall, Isaac W. 22:97
Pownell, H. T. 8:28
Pox, Francis E. 10:131; 20:329
Pox, William 7:131
Poxter, Stephen 26:177
Poyant, S. 25:220
Poyer, Amos D. 19:93
Poyle, John F. 4:67
Poylley, Peter G. 20:329
Poyner, George 22:488
Poynter, Wallace 7:131
Poyntz, Benjamin 4:47
Pr---, Edward R. 15:167
Pradeen, C. 16:220
Prader, G. 22:515
Prader, Unias 7:131
Praf, Thomas 18:249
Prafist, George 13:117
Praft, Thomas 26:53
Prag, Sam 24:54
Prahm, John 22:343
Praish, Miller 27:99
Prales, Edward 9:27
Pralhon, E. 22:49
Prall, David 23:76
Prall, John 25:61
Prall, Novenden 9:89
Pram, John 17:183
Pramer, L. 1:163
Pramiar, David 26:146
Pranty, George A. 15:263
Prapst, A. M. 22:214
Prarrer, Baram 9:190
Prary, O. 19:241

Prary, Oscar 9:190
Prasley, W. S. 14:19
Prat, Daniel 3:156
Prat, M. 27:94
Pratchard, J. 11:311
Prate, J. 18:249; 26:54
Prater, Archibald 10:132; 20:329
Prater, D. 14:99; 21:37
Prater, Davis 22:265
Prater, Dick 11:211
Prater, George W. 20:329
Prather, A. B. 8:28; 18:155
Prather, B. B. 7:53
Prather, Benjamin D. 22:214
Prather, Dellet C. 22:455
Prather, George W. 10:74
Prather, J. A. 22:488
Prather, James M. 20:99
Prather, Less 17:137; 24:201
Prather, M. 9:223; 18:374
Prather, Pleasant 18:399
Prathers, E. L. 25:220
Prathers, Green 17:183
Pratler, Morrison 7:131
Prato, John 25:220
Pratt, --- 21:168
Pratt, A. J. 12:157
Pratt, A. M. 3:156
Pratt, A. W. 11:247
Pratt, Aaron J. 10:166; 19:187
Pratt, Abraham 23:92
Pratt, Abram 11:320
Pratt, Albert E. 9:8
Pratt, Alexander 23:76
Pratt, Arnold 10:206
Pratt, Austin 15:221
Pratt, B. F. 3:156
Pratt, Bernard 12:170
Pratt, C. 7:53
Pratt, C. B. 3:156
Pratt, C. E. 1:163
Pratt, C. P. 15:327
Pratt, C. S. 11:96
Pratt, Charles 23:205
Pratt, Charles A. 7:60
Pratt, D. 1:161
Pratt, D. W. 3:156
Pratt, Dean J. 11:41
Pratt, E. B. 23:46
Pratt, E. C. 14:99
Pratt, Edward 25:221
Pratt, Edward A. 7:107
Pratt, Edward L. 27:147
Pratt, Ezra 10:132; 20:329
Pratt, Ezra B. 23:46
Pratt, F. 3:156

Pratt, Fred J. 9:190
Pratt, Frederick 11:17; 14:207
Pratt, G. 21:150
Pratt, G. B. 3:156
Pratt, G. F. 1:162
Pratt, G. W. M. 11:86
Pratt, George 12:100; 15:348, 366; 23:129
Pratt, George W. 22:214
Pratt, Gordon 21:378
Pratt, Gustavus 1:62
Pratt, H. 3:156; 15:111
Pratt, H. L. 14:99
Pratt, H. S. 1:65
Pratt, H. T. 9:58
Pratt, Harrison 22:49
Pratt, Harrison W. 16:8
Pratt, Henry 19:292
Pratt, Henry D. 10:74; 20:329
Pratt, Homer A. 8:109
Pratt, I. R. 15:353
Pratt, Ingraham 22:237
Pratt, Ira I. 19:259
Pratt, Isaac 9:135; 17:145; 27:97
Pratt, Isaac J. 21:38
Pratt, J. 3:156
Pratt, J. C. 21:38
Pratt, J. F. 3:156
Pratt, J. G. 20:329
Pratt, J. H. 27:99
Pratt, J. M. 16:377
Pratt, J. R. 16:281; 20:92
Pratt, James 11:222; 17:402
Pratt, James G. 9:223; 18:374
Pratt, John 9:112; 23:13
Pratt, John G. 10:74
Pratt, John H. 20:329
Pratt, John L. 22:214
Pratt, John M. 22:172
Pratt, John S. 15:221
Pratt, John W. 11:183
Pratt, Joseph 8:41; 21:378
Pratt, Joseph H. 23:16
Pratt, L. 3:156; 11:163
Pratt, Louis B. 19:347
Pratt, Louis D. 13:135
Pratt, Luther C. 21:89
Pratt, M. 21:378
Pratt, M. A. 8:93
Pratt, M. S. 20:49
Pratt, Marshall 20:127
Pratt, Martin 9:44
Pratt, Miles G. 9:240
Pratt, Milton 27:98
Pratt, N. E. 9:58
Pratt, Nathan L. 11:110

Pratt, Nathan W. 12:157
Pratt, Oliver N. 12:75
Pratt, Oliver P. 15:12
Pratt, P. 3:156
Pratt, R. C. 25:221
Pratt, Reuben O. 5:26
Pratt, S. 25:221
Pratt, S. E. 16:377
Pratt, S. F. 15:345
Pratt, S. H. 22:214
Pratt, Sidney E. 18:399
Pratt, Silas 13:42
Pratt, T. 1:162
Pratt, Thomas 1:64; 16:51; 23:76
Pratt, W. 3:157; 10:206; 21:131
Pratt, Wheeler 17:441; 24:154
Pratt, William 14:244; 21:245, 378; 27:100
Pratt, William H. 11:71; 17:286
Pratt, Zimri 21:89
Pratton, D. W. 22:343
Prave, Albert 27:99
Prawdcicke, F. 1:162
Pray, Daniel 22:49
Pray, Dennison P. 13:42; 16:51
Pray, Dudley 8:102; 17:463; 24:186
Pray, Edward W. 12:36
Pray, F. 9:149; 27:95
Pray, G. C. 18:36
Pray, George W. 21:205
Pray, H. F. 26:54
Pray, Henry F. 9:89
Pray, I. F. 23:163
Pray, J. 9:149; 27:96
Pray, James H. 12:36
Pray, John 20:12
Pray, Paris L. 22:153
Pray, R. 9:149; 27:98
Prayn, Charles T. 24:54
Praynard, J. P. 19:93
Pre, D. 11:163
Preacher, Breno 15:361
Preacher, Bruns 12:96
Preacher, Brunt 19:93
Pream, H. 3:157
Preat, A. C. 11:79
Prebble, Orrin 13:42
Prebble, Sydney 9:190
Preble, C. 13:96; 14:19
Preble, Francis M. 8:93
Preble, George D. H. 20:43
Preble, Orwin 16:51
Preche, J. 19:259
Preddish, W. 10:187

Preddy, Charles 19:187
Predeman, Thomas
    25:221
Predmon, W. G. 14:259
Predmore, Charles B.
    17:244
Predmorn, I. 20:59
Predon, James 18:17
Predong, John 7:131
Pree, Daniel M. 11:193
Preebles, George 19:30
Preebles, W. R. 24:27
Preecs, Hiram J. 11:397
Preeman, Charles 13:80
Preer, W. 21:150
Pregmore, Charles 11:211
Preifer, Emil 16:123
Preis, August 24:96
Preist, J. A. 20:329
Preithing, George F.
    22:214
Prekett, F. 3:157
Prelman, Frederick 1:63
Preman, Charles 16:220
Premer, Frederick 21:58
Premo, Donett 25:277
Prendergrast, R. G.
    15:221
Prenderman, Esau 9:201
Prent, Abner 17:239
Prent, Fleman 17:239
Prentice, A. 26:176
Prentice, B. 23:46
Prentice, Charles 9:215
Prentice, Francis 4:47
Prentice, G. 26:176
Prentice, George 17:15
Prentice, Henry 5:26
Prentice, Henry H. 22:436
Prentice, J. W. 3:157
Prentice, Loraine 11:129
Prentice, Myron 13:42
Prentice, Otheniel 17:233
Prentice, S. R. 25:221
Prentice, S. T. 10:21
Prentice, Sidney 19:30
Prentice, Sidney R. 5:26
Prentice, Simeon 13:42
Prentice, Thomas 13:42
Prentice, Thomas D.
    9:240
Prentice, W. 21:38
Prentice, William 11:73;
    18:55
Prentis, Isaiah L. 12:9
Prentis, Philip 20:127
Prentiss, Alonzo 21:85
Prentiss, Benjamin 23:46
Prentiss, Charles 21:378
Prentiss, George 27:97
Prentiss, Irwin 8:93

Prentiss, John 7:131
Prentiss, Louis 9:210
Prentiss, M. S. 1:95
Prentiss, M. W. 1:160
Prentiss, Samuel 22:515
Prentiss, Samuel M.
    22:163
Prentiss, Samuel W. 7:38
Prentiss, William 10:149
Prerley, E. M. 9:190
Presbay, W. H. 19:234
Presbrey, Charles A.
    11:335
Presby, W. L. 15:287
Presby, William H. 9:190
Prescott, A. 16:220
Prescott, A. H. 9:112,
    149; 27:95
Prescott, C. 3:157; 14:207
Prescott, C. S. 1:63
Prescott, Charles H. 4:47;
    7:9
Prescott, Daniel 13:67
Prescott, David 16:220
Prescott, George W. 20:49
Prescott, H. H. 10:166
Prescott, H. L. 1:99
Prescott, J. 27:96
Prescott, J. P. 9:149;
    27:95
Prescott, Jerrie S. 18:314;
    26:109
Prescott, Jerry S. 9:27
Prescott, John C. 11:397
Prescott, Lucius L. 10:166
Prescott, Lythe C. 13:42
Prescott, O. 9:67
Prescott, T. J. 1:161
Prescott, William 13:117
Prescy, Dovestein 21:378
Preser, William 16:113
Presgrove, George W.
    22:409
Presham, J. A. 3:157
Presho, Alex 24:54
Presho, Robert J. 23:163
Presho, Warren 22:97
Presinger, Moses C.
    18:209
Presler, Samuel 22:214
Presley, Anderson 10:132;
    20:329
Presley, G. 13:96
Presley, J. R. 12:157
Presley, Jeremiah 11:425
Presley, John A. 7:107
Presley, M. B. 1:65
Presley, McKinsey 20:329
Presley, Morgan 13:97
Presley, T. P. 8:54
Presley, W. 13:97

Presley, William 8:66;
    11:425
Presnell, Andrew 13:42
Presnell, Joshua 20:104
Presnell, William H.
    21:232
Presner, John 4:47
Preso, T. 3:157
Preson, A. C. 11:41
Press, Albert 23:266
Press, George 22:115
Press, George S. 19:187
Press, James 27:94
Presse, Joel 18:296;
    26:109
Pressel, D. 21:131
Presselman, C. 3:157
Pressen, George 25:221
Presser, J. 3:157
Pressey, Charles M. 15:12
Pressey, Charles O. 22:97
Pressey, W. W. 17:71
Pressing, H. 21:104
Pressley, C. M. 19:283
Pressley, G. 14:19
Pressley, R. L. 11:40
Pressman, Jacob 10:74
Pressnell, G. 17:97
Pressnell, Isaac 17:97
Presson, J. 21:38
Presten, Joshua 14:236
Presterback, Peter 13:42
Prestice, William 12:157
Prestige, James M. 23:76
Prestly, W. S. 13:97
Presto, George 25:221
Prestoff, William 17:24
Preston, A. A. 1:161
Preston, B. W. 17:183
Preston, Benjamin K. 7:38
Preston, C. 3:157
Preston, C. E. 9:215;
    21:378
Preston, C. W. 14:99
Preston, Charles 22:509
Preston, D. 15:133
Preston, D. M. 1:63
Preston, Dennis 6:18;
    18:91
Preston, E. L. 11:129
Preston, Edwin 19:30
Preston, F. 3:157
Preston, Francis 12:36
Preston, G. C. 9:149
Preston, G. E. 27:96
Preston, G. W. 18:37;
    21:125
Preston, George 18:193
Preston, George F.
    12:167; 19:348;
    22:466

Preston, H. G. 3:157
Preston, H. H. 1:161
Preston, Henry 7:131
Preston, Hezekiah 22:214
Preston, I. 14:207
Preston, J. 3:157
Preston, J. M. 14:207
Preston, Jacob 18:37
Preston, James 19:30
Preston, James A. 7:38
Preston, James H. 23:163
Preston, James R. 21:217
Preston, Joe 7:131
Preston, John 3:157; 6:28;
    8:41; 11:415; 26:177
Preston, John F. 11:41
Preston, John R. 17:24
Preston, John T. 8:115
Preston, John W. 22:237
Preston, Joseph 9:201;
    19:284
Preston, Levi 10:132;
    20:329
Preston, M. 13:77
Preston, M. T. 7:38
Preston, Morgan 17:283
Preston, Neville 4:47
Preston, O. H. 5:53;
    25:221
Preston, Otis 9:190;
    19:241
Preston, Perry 17:244
Preston, Peter H. 21:259
Preston, R. 14:99
Preston, R. L. 14:302;
    17:481; 27:98
Preston, Sam. W. 17:238
Preston, Samuel 11:193
Preston, Sidney 13:42
Preston, Theodore 4:47
Preston, W. 3:157
Preston, Wesley 12:157
Preston, William 7:131;
    20:116; 27:98, 147
Prestwood, E. 16:51
Prether, George 9:237
Pretor, H. 16:302
Pretsinger, Solomon
    17:356
Prett, H. M. 1:99
Prett, J. K. 3:157
Prettenbucker, G. 1:162
Prettylief, H. 15:133
Prettyman, D. H. 17:315
Prettyman, George 11:117
Prettyman, J. P. 10:74
Prettyman, John 9:73
Prettyman, P. 25:221
Prettyman, Percy 5:26
Pretz, D. 14:259
Preussler, August 21:259

Prevey, Franklin 20:194
Prevo, D. H. 18:335
Prevoe, Thomas F. 22:435
Prevost, Joseph G. 22:14
Prewett, David J. 23:302
Prewett, George 17:183
Prewett, H. 1:64
Prewett, Isaac 27:147
Prewett, Meredith H.
    17:57
Prewick, Charles 9:210
Prewit, Sanford 17:267
Prewit, W. 25:221
Prewitt, --- 17:283
Prewitt, Albert 17:283
Prewitt, James R. 17:40
Prewitt, Thomas 23:101
Prewitt, William 11:20
Prewster, Anson 19:187
Prey, Hamilton 8:66
Preyer, Henry 18:104
Preysley, Gardner A.
    11:117
Priatt, I. 14:99
Pribble, S. L. 19:229
Price, --- 15:221
Price, A. 1:63, 65
Price, A. J. 1:162; 14:207
Price, A. R. 7:38
Price, Abraham 9:9
Price, Adam 22:315
Price, Albert 17:441;
    24:154
Price, Albert M. 10:132
Price, Alison 18:209
Price, Alson 8:93
Price, Anderson 22:315
Price, Andrew I. 10:74
Price, Anthony 13:42;
    17:444; 24:161
Price, Armstead 8:41;
    26:177
Price, Augustus 20:12
Price, B. D. 24:83
Price, Bailey 17:137;
    24:201
Price, Barky 3:224
Price, Barry 17:503
Price, Bassie 12:160
Price, Benjamin 22:315
Price, C. 13:80; 16:220
Price, Caleb 21:378
Price, Caline N. 21:131
Price, Charles 14:207;
    22:515
Price, Charles E. 11:162
Price, Chauncey 15:42
Price, Clinton 12:51
Price, Cyrus 11:117
Price, D. 1:163; 3:157
Price, D. W. 17:274

Price, Daniel 8:28;
    14:207; 18:155
Price, David 8:102;
    14:207; 17:461;
    22:265; 24:161
Price, David A. 4:47;
    17:416
Price, David D. 22:97
Price, David M. 23:76
Price, E. 11:247; 18:249;
    23:46; 26:53
Price, Ed 3:157
Price, Edward 9:190;
    19:279
Price, Edward L. 19:332
Price, Ephraim 26:177
Price, Eugene C. 25:221
Price, F. 1:163
Price, F. H. 15:73
Price, F. M. 10:74
Price, Fay 18:409
Price, Francis M. 17:24
Price, Francis S. 9:157
Price, Frank 7:38
Price, G. 3:157; 8:54;
    22:49; 27:94
Price, G. B. 11:311
Price, Gabriel 7:53
Price, George A. 11:72
Price, George D. 22:315
Price, George G. 22:446
Price, George L. 11:403
Price, George P. 22:488
Price, George W. 5:26;
    22:265
Price, Gilmore 21:78
Price, H. 1:163; 11:268;
    12:87; 14:99; 25:221
Price, Harry 17:183
Price, Harvey 26:52
Price, Henry 9:89, 124;
    11:17; 20:329; 27:97
Price, Henry C. 11:88
Price, Henry V. 13:42
Price, Hiram 21:232
Price, Hugh 5:26
Price, I. G. 15:221
Price, Isaac 10:177;
    19:187
Price, Isaac H. 14:207
Price, Isaac N. 22:128
Price, Isaiah C. 20:127
Price, Israel A. 23:257
Price, J. 3:157; 7:53; 9:27;
    11:163, 247; 14:259;
    20:134
Price, J. B. 9:89; 11:391
Price, J. D. 14:99
Price, J. H. 1:160
Price, J. J. 20:329
Price, J. L. 25:221

Price, J. M. 3:157; 11:247
Price, James 7:107; 9:135;
    10:74; 11:211; 17:41,
    183; 18:314; 20:329;
    26:109, 138; 27:99
Price, James D. 20:99
Price, James E. 7:107;
    22:214; 25:221
Price, Jefferson 22:128
Price, Jerome 26:127
Price, John 1:63; 8:28;
    9:13; 11:164, 248;
    15:59, 221; 16:220;
    17:137, 398; 18:155;
    20:31; 21:131, 232;
    22:237; 24:201, 202
Price, John E. 27:97
Price, John H. 7:107;
    23:287
Price, John M. 20:12
Price, John R. 23:76
Price, John W. 14:99;
    17:24
Price, Joseph 1:63;
    17:449; 20:105;
    24:174
Price, Joseph B. 24:90
Price, Joseph H. 27:97
Price, Joseph T. 23:46
Price, Joshua 17:57
Price, L. B. 23:163
Price, Latimer 10:132;
    20:329
Price, Lemuel 22:214
Price, Lewis 8:41; 26:177
Price, M. C. 20:143
Price, Martin 22:343
Price, Melchert H. 24:43
Price, Michael 23:92
Price, N. 17:145
Price, Napoleon B. 22:265
Price, Nathaniel 7:53
Price, Nelson 3:157
Price, O. 3:157
Price, Orlando 21:205
Price, P. H. 9:58
Price, P. W. 16:86
Price, Parrat 15:42
Price, Perrie K. 27:97
Price, Peter 24:96
Price, Peter L. 10:74;
    20:329
Price, R. S. 16:113
Price, Ransler 9:73
Price, Ray E. 27:99
Price, Reed M. 1:63
Price, Richard 22:509
Price, Robert 8:66;
    11:310; 17:137;
    24:201
Price, S. 25:61

Price, S. L. 9:38; 18:296
Price, S. W. 12:83;
    16:302; 27:95
Price, Samuel 4:48;
    22:153
Price, Samuel E. 9:135
Price, Samuel L. 23:76
Price, Sewall B. 27:98
Price, Sewell B. 9:124
Price, Simon P. 23:306
Price, Solomon 26:128
Price, Spencer 17:111
Price, Stephen 9:73
Price, Sylvester 12:75;
    15:59; 17:209
Price, T. 21:378
Price, Taylor 17:183
Price, Theo 9:67
Price, Thomas 5:44; 8:28;
    18:155; 19:48
Price, Thomas B. 23:13
Price, Thomas D. 21:38
Price, Thomas G. 11:86
Price, Thomas P. 15:42
Price, Thomas S. 15:133
Price, Urias 5:44
Price, V. V. 14:319;
    25:276
Price, W. 11:247
Price, W. A. 15:279;
    25:221
Price, W. H. 14:99;
    25:221
Price, W. P. 20:329
Price, W. T. 11:96
Price, Wiley 22:265
Price, William 1:63, 65;
    6:32; 8:93; 10:74;
    11:162; 16:302;
    21:378; 22:168;
    27:99
Price, William B. 16:3;
    17:85
Price, William G. 22:128
Price, William H. 4:48
Price, Wilson 20:329
Pricer, C. B. 22:214
Prichard, --- 8:120
Prichard, Albert 27:96
Prichard, Charles 11:163
Prichard, J. 14:100
Prichard, J. F. 8:66
Prichard, James 9:27;
    18:314; 26:109
Prichard, James F. 18:374
Prichard, W. H. 22:237
Prichard, William 12:170
Prichard, William S.
    13:42
Prichitt, John M. 11:425
Prichman, J. 21:125

Pricht, F. 3:157
Prick, Benjamin 19:259
Prickart, Alonzo 9:190
Pricket, Joseph A. 16:220
Prickett, I. 14:100
Prickett, Isaac P. 10:132;
    20:329
Prickett, Jacob 18:422
Prickett, Nicholas 9:27
Prickett, R. 23:314
Prickett, William 23:129
Priddy, C. W. 20:90
Pride, Benjamin 11:211
Pride, H. 1:163
Pride, Harburd 11:268
Pride, Leonard 13:117
Pride, Thomas 12:36
Pridgen, J. O. 16:51
Pridhard, George W.
    26:109
Pridhardt, George W.
    18:314
Pridmore, Alfred 22:435
Pridmore, George 7:138
Pridy, James 17:151;
    18:249; 26:54
Prie, James 22:14
Prieder, Charles 24:96
Priek, Benjamin 9:190
Prier, J. 8:54
Prier, Thomas 22:515
Pries, Henry 10:74
Priest, --- 18:37
Priest, A. 24:83
Priest, Alfred 24:179
Priest, George 9:89
Priest, Henry A. 7:107
Priest, Henry L. 25:221
Priest, Isaac N. 9:27;
    18:321
Priest, James H. 22:97
Priest, John 11:162; 23:46
Priest, L. C. 14:270, 284
Priest, Lewis C. 17:497
Priest, Samuel 21:104
Priest, Silas P. 21:125
Priest, Timothy 10:132;
    20:329
Priest, W. 3:157; 13:97
Priest, W. E. 11:96
Priest, William 14:19
Priest, William D. 22:49
Priest, William H. 26:52
Priester, S. 15:94
Priestley, William 12:36
Priestly, D. 23:163
Prifer, Charles 1:65
Priggs, G. R. 7:38
Prilk, Frank 4:47
Prill, C. 14:100
Prill, Jacob 17:449

Prill, John W. 20:43
Prim, D. 3:157
Prim, William 17:509
Prime, Charles 13:58; 16:51
Prime, Gelo 21:282
Prime, J. H. 16:145
Prime, L. 3:157
Prime, Wes. F. 1:63
Prime, William 10:132; 20:329
Primer, John 20:329
Primer, Peter 10:206
Primm, Lewis 8:41
Primmer, --- 17:196
Primmer, John 10:74
Primo, Paul 10:132; 20:329
Primrose, J. W. 26:128
Prin, W. H. 3:157
Prina, George 9:113
Prince, A. 17:183
Prince, A. C. 7:60
Prince, Alexander 13:58
Prince, August 11:164
Prince, Charles E. 10:132; 20:329
Prince, Christopher 20:127
Prince, Edmund 7:131
Prince, Eldridge 8:93
Prince, Ephriam 8:74
Prince, G. W. 8:74
Prince, George W. 27:94
Prince, Henry 15:273; 17:455; 24:201
Prince, Henry L. 19:30
Prince, Henry M. 17:315
Prince, Israel N. 9:231; 20:329
Prince, J. A. 27:96
Prince, John A. 21:13
Prince, Joseph 25:221
Prince, Lakin B. 22:97
Prince, Liman 22:97
Prince, Peter 24:201
Prince, Stephen 22:343
Prince, William 27:95
Prince, William C. 22:97
Prince, William H. 10:166
Princeton, A. 17:274
Princeton, Reuben 13:58
Prind, W. P. 18:179
Prindiville, M. 3:157
Prindle, Harrison 22:97
Prindle, James W. 22:214
Prindle, Logan 20:330
Prindle, Richard 23:109
Prindle, W. A. 1:163
Pringel, B. J. 21:191
Pringele, --- 26:213

Pringle, Albert 14:208
Pringle, Andrew 23:194
Pringle, C. 25:221
Pringle, J. 15:221
Pringle, John 22:49
Pringle, N. 1:63
Pringle, Nelson 21:78
Pringle, Robert 21:378
Pringle, T. W. 3:157
Pringle, W. 11:268
Pringle, William 3:157; 13:42; 18:155; 24:83
Pringle, William M. 22:97
Pringo, Michael 18:155
Prink, J. 3:157
Prinkley, H. 25:221
Printer, William H. 21:38
Printers, Taylor 4:47
Printis, George 9:124
Printz, Henry C. 11:183
Printz, Isaac 24:54
Printz, J. 14:208
Printz, Newton 24:54
Prinzinger, John 11:248
Prior, Alfred 4:48
Prior, Charles L. 8:28
Prior, E. A. 18:155
Prior, E. O. 8:28
Prior, Earl W. 13:67
Prior, Early W. 19:93
Prior, Edgar 8:28; 18:155
Prior, Edwin C. 23:277
Prior, George 19:188; 25:61, 221
Prior, George D. 23:46
Prior, J. H. 20:330
Prior, James H. 23:280
Prior, Louis 12:51
Prior, M. 3:157
Prior, William 13:42; 25:60
Prire, James 19:305
Prisgrove, W. D. 9:89
Prisin, E. T. 3:157
Prisington, Robert 17:497
Prisken, S. 14:100
Prisley, G. 14:19
Prison, C. 14:100
Prison, I. 14:208
Prist, Alfred 8:102; 17:463
Pristey, James 25:334
Pritchard, --- 27:100
Pritchard, Albert 9:135
Pritchard, Allen 9:237; 26:224
Pritchard, C. 25:62
Pritchard, Christopher 15:221
Pritchard, Edward 16:131; 22:435

Pritchard, G. B. 14:208
Pritchard, G. W. 9:27
Pritchard, Harrison 10:132; 20:330
Pritchard, J. 3:157; 14:208
Pritchard, J. H. 9:239; 16:220
Pritchard, James 12:123; 15:133
Pritchard, James T. 9:228
Pritchard, John 4:47; 22:49
Pritchard, S. C. 14:244
Pritchard, Thomas W. 10:74
Pritchard, William H. 23:124
Pritchard, William S. 16:51
Pritchatt, W. 22:115
Pritchell, J. 3:157
Pritchell, O. C. 14:100
Pritcher, Allen 10:180
Pritcher, C. B. 15:43
Pritcherd, S. E. 14:244
Pritchett, C. G. 20:134
Pritchett, David 18:193
Pritchett, Henry 9:44
Pritchett, James M. 21:259
Pritchett, John L. 21:378
Pritchett, Monroe S. 23:115
Pritchett, W. J. 21:191
Priterline, Joseph 14:208
Prithen, Marion 9:237
Prithers, Miriam 26:224
Prittchert, Henry 26:127
Pritz, D. 14:208
Private, No. 96 25:60
Privel, W. B. 18:399
Privitt, Miles 17:203
Prizel, J. 21:191
Prizzie, J. 15:319
Prizzle, Boey 18:374
Pro---, J. 12:100
Probasco, John 17:277
Proberting, Louis 9:89
Probertney, Louis 26:52
Probsden, --- 15:43
Probsfield, Antonio 10:132; 20:330
Probsfield, Justice 20:330
Probsfield, Justus 10:74
Probst, Leist 18:340
Probt, Jesse 10:149
Probt, Joseph 26:177
Probus, Jeremiah 11:391
Prock, James 22:128
Prockett, Nicholas 18:321
Procter, George 15:73

Procton, Henry 19:188
Proctor, Alanson 7:107
Proctor, Alfred 11:163
Proctor, Byron 22:214
Proctor, C. W. 10:21
Proctor, Charles 21:378
Proctor, E. 19:230
Proctor, E. B. 11:310
Proctor, E. M. 19:230
Proctor, Eli 16:220
Proctor, Elijah H. 9:190
Proctor, G. 9:190
Proctor, George 12:157
Proctor, H. A. 7:76
Proctor, H. H. 25:303
Proctor, H. J. W. 20:148
Proctor, Henry 10:166
Proctor, Hiram H. 13:42
Proctor, J. 1:164
Proctor, James 11:129;
    25:334
Proctor, Jay 8:74
Proctor, Joel M. 23:76
Proctor, John 17:506
Proctor, Joseph J. 24:161
Proctor, M. 9:154; 27:96
Proctor, M. D. 22:265;
    25:221
Proctor, Moses D. 5:26
Proctor, N. R. 21:378
Proctor, R. 15:221
Proctor, Reuben 22:505
Proctor, T. B. 23:46
Proctor, Thomas 9:89;
    26:52
Proctor, Thomas D. 16:51
Proctor, W. 13:97
Proctor, W. H. 20:330
Proctor, William 4:48;
    10:21; 15:221;
    23:163
Procumire, David 9:38
Prodistant, E. 21:112
Prody, Henry 16:220
Profance, Uriah 18:209
Proffett, J. 3:157
Proffit, Harman H. 17:410
Proffitt, Benjamin 18:374
Proffitt, Harman H.
    22:455
Profitt, James 11:329
Profuter, O. B. 26:176
Promley, George 9:210
Pronty, John G. 11:129
Prooenase, Alexis 25:286
Proper, Elias 11:163
Proper, George W. 9:44;
    26:128
Proper, Gilbert 19:188
Proper, Jacob M. 17:244

Proper, Nelson 25:221
Propern, Nelson 15:279
Properts, F. 14:208
Propes, Joshua D. 17:57
Propes, William T. 17:57
Prophalter, Joseph P.
    24:27
Prophet, James 20:330
Prophet, James A. 13:132
Prophet, James N. 7:38
Prophet, Moses 25:286
Prophrey, J. 15:305
Propps, John A. 21:196
Propsey, J. 9:67
Propst, John 22:214
Proro, Henry 20:127
Prosner, James 11:110
Pross, Jacob 16:377
Pross, Peter 22:49
Prossan, H. 11:415
Prosser, Anthony 21:201
Prosser, C. E. 16:281
Prosser, Cyrus B. 17:85
Prosser, Holden L. 24:54
Prosser, Isaac 17:41
Prosser, James 24:27
Prosser, L. E. 15:353
Prosser, Philip 20:141
Prosser, Thomas 13:117
Prosser, William 12:51
Prothers, Richard 13:117
Prothers, W. 16:220
Protsman, H. J. 22:214
Prott, Jesse 18:55
Protzman, Frank E. 9:38
Protzman, Isaac 26:146
Protzman, James E.
    18:296; 26:109
Proud, Anthony 22:97
Proud, S. F. 19:93
Proudfit, David 12:36
Proudfit, F. M. 2:15;
    25:62
Proudfoot, Francis 14:100
Proudford, Manuel 7:131
Proudy, C. 4:48
Prough, Daniel 1:63
Prough, John M. 22:214
Prouse, L. A. 22:128
Prouse, P. F. 3:157
Prout, A. T. 25:221
Prout, Alfred 10:8
Prout, Elias H. 22:153
Prout, J. H. 8:66; 26:176
Prout, J. R. 13:97; 14:19
Prout, Orrin T. 5:27
Prout, Sylvester 19:93
Prout, Titus M. 9:13
Prout, William 6:18;
    18:91
Prout, William H. 22:466

Proutly, Robert 12:83
Proutty, Robert 16:302
Prouty, Addison 10:153;
    19:188
Prouty, Alfred 1:63
Prouty, Christian 17:321
Prouty, E. 1:65
Prouty, G. A. 14:131
Prouty, Harmon 21:243
Prouty, J. 12:162
Prouty, John F. 15:221
Prouty, Orson 23:109
Prouty, Samuel 23:76
Prouty, Sidney S. 16:87
Prouty, Warren C. 22:283
Prouty, William 3:157
Provance, William A.
    21:104
Provard, Jacob 10:132;
    20:330
Provence, John 15:221
Province, Thomas J. 22:49
Provo, George 15:88
Provo, Herman 9:231;
    20:330
Provo, James T. 17:444;
    24:161
Provost, Andrew 21:217
Provost, Charles E. 7:38
Provost, James 25:221
Provost, Joseph 5:26
Provost, Stephen 7:131
Provost, Thomas 21:85
Prow, A. 25:221
Prow, Antonio 5:26
Prow, Charles R. 23:46
Prow, G. W. 25:60
Prow, John 3:157
Prow, Robert 17:308
Prowell, Oliver 7:107
Prowman, S. H. 3:157
Prowse, Richard 21:38
Prucker, Thomas B.
    18:179
Prudam, Jack 9:210
Prude, Moses Evans
    21:104
Prudeman, Esau 19:292
Pruden, Alexander S. 8:28
Prudenea, George 16:220
Prudhomme, Alfred
    10:132; 20:330
Prudhomme, Alwood
    21:378
Prudhomme, C. 19:292
Prudom, John 7:131
Prudon, William 23:266
Prudy, Daniel H. 16:88
Prudy, I. L. 17:477
Prudy, J. 19:93
Prueman, Jacob 18:113

Pruet, F. 7:38
Pruet, J. M. 3:157
Pruet, Thomas W. 17:347
Pruett, H. C. 3:157;
22:265
Pruett, J. 20:36
Pruett, Levi 11:268
Pruett, P. 21:142
Pruett, William 14:100
Pruile, W. H. 3:157
Pruit, Caleb 26:53
Pruitt, D. S. 17:163
Pruitt, George W. 20:19
Pruitt, John 24:43
Pruitt, Louis 17:183
Pruitt, Marion 21:38
Pruitt, Sanders 21:282
Pruitt, Walter 5:44
Prulman, L. W. 11:164
Prunell, Solomon 12:51
Pruner, Henry 9:190
Pruner, Royal B. 9:38
Prunis, George W. 9:38
Prusell, Clement 8:93
Pruser, H. 3:157
Pruther, Nathan 21:217
Pruval, Pelar 13:117
Pruyn, H. F. 2:16; 25:62
Pry, J. 11:41
Pry, L. 3:157
Pryer, Adaminin 24:27
Pryer, Henry 26:53
Pryer, P. H. 11:163
Pryer, W. 1:164
Pryer, William 15:221
Pryle, George D. 19:93
Pryon, Charles L. 18:155
Pryor, --- 18:374
Pryor, Charles 8:41;
26:177
Pryor, David 7:66; 14:208
Pryor, Edward 22:153
Pryor, Francis 23:46
Pryor, Frederick 7:107;
13:117
Pryor, Frisby 21:378
Pryor, George S. 22:283
Pryor, Henry 18:249
Pryor, Houston 11:210
Pryor, J. 11:329
Pryor, J. H. 10:74
Pryor, J. W. 14:208
Pryor, James 10:177;
19:188
Pryor, James M. 10:132;
20:330
Pryor, Jasper 17:85
Pryor, John N. 22:265
Pryor, John W. 17:67
Pryor, Leander 17:183
Pryor, Minor 11:164

Pryor, Moses 9:223
Pryor, Orville 18:324
Pryor, Robert 14:208
Pryor, T. 1:161
Pryor, Thomas J. 15:221
Pryor, William 3:157;
11:248
Pryor, William A. 16:141
Pryunt, Hampton 20:187
Pte, Cant 15:345; 16:377
Ptomy, Isaac F. 23:46
Puch, B. 26:176
Puch, John 3:157
Pucher, Fred 3:157
Puck, B. 8:66
Puck, Henry 10:132;
20:330
Pucket, William H. H.
20:43
Puckett, --- 1:62
Puckett, Henry 10:206;
17:315
Puckett, John 20:12
Puckett, Levi 19:30
Puckett, M. F. 25:221
Puckett, S. H. 1:65
Puckett, Stephen C.
23:101
Puckett, Thomas B.
10:180
Puckett, Wilson 6:13
Puckett, Zachariah 21:58
Pucketts, R. R. 17:252
Puckney, John 7:107
Puderbauch, Ezra 13:42
Puderlauch, Ezra 16:51
Pudon, Melvey 21:282
Pudrum, James W. 22:487
Pues, Fred. W. 19:327
Puff, C. H. 25:60
Puff, George 9:124
Puff, J. 3:157
Puffenberg, Abraham
13:42
Puffenroth, John 17:463;
24:186
Puffer, Charles H. 4:48
Puffer, E. D. 3:157
Puffer, George 18:249;
26:53
Puffer, Horace 22:214
Puffer, Jabez G. 11:163
Puffer, John 7:60; 14:1
Puffer, John W. 17:362
Puffer, Joseph 16:88
Puffer, Michael 7:38
Puffinberger, I. 15:221
Puget, Benedic 18:209
Pugh, A. 3:157; 14:259;
25:221
Pugh, Alfred 7:16

Pugh, Benjamin F. 22:435
Pugh, David H. 21:142
Pugh, E. F. 23:163
Pugh, E. H. 25:221
Pugh, Eli 16:51
Pugh, Elsey 21:378
Pugh, George W. 17:451;
21:13; 24:179
Pugh, H. R. 18:249; 26:55
Pugh, Isaac H. 27:97
Pugh, J. W. B. 26:177
Pugh, Jesse H. 21:378
Pugh, John 9:135; 18:209;
27:97
Pugh, John A. 9:44;
26:127
Pugh, John M. 13:42;
23:163
Pugh, Josephus N. 17:274
Pugh, L. 3:157
Pugh, Levi 14:208
Pugh, Robert 7:53
Pugh, Sampson M. 1:63
Pugh, Samuel 10:132;
11:329
Pugh, T. S. 20:59
Pugh, Thomas 13:117
Pugh, W. J. 21:209, 217
Pugh, W. R. 11:41
Pugh, Wesley 17:405
Pugh, William 13:117;
17:41; 18:285; 21:38;
22:50; 26:135
Pugsley, Edward 21:38
Puiner, Samuel 5:44
Puky, Lewis 12:157
Pulasky, John 22:265
Pulcher, Lewis 17:264
Pulcur, H. A. 15:221
Puley, Daniel 3:157
Pulier, Mark D. 19:30
Pulis, Reuben E. 21:104
Pulk, Henry 13:42
Pulk, James R. 25:221
Pullam, John W. 17:307
Pulleam, Garlh 15:221
Pullem, Jesse 22:505
Pullem, Thomas 22:214
Pullen, Charles H. 5:27;
25:221
Pullen, F. M. 16:377
Pullen, George W. 21:378
Pullen, Harrison 16:79
Pullen, Lewis A. 11:163
Pullen, W. 25:221
Pullen, William 17:420
Pullen, William H. 11:72
Pullers, U. 3:157
Pullet, Henry 25:221
Pulley, David W. 22:50
Pulley, John E. 11:129

Pulliam, Isaiah 17:57
Pullian, J. 3:157
Pullian, William 3:157
Pullin, S. 3:157
Pulling, A. C. 1:163
Pulling, Adam 24:27
Pullings, Samuel 23:163
Pullins, Marion 20:43
Pullins, Sidney 9:204
Pullis, James 7:60
Pullitt, Henry 5:44
Pullium, J. 22:354
Pullium, William H. 23:92
Pullman, George 3:157
Pullman, John H. 4:48
Pullman, Pascal A. 23:109
Pullman, Zachariah
  11:268
Pullock, J. 25:221
Pullum, Samuel L. 17:350
Pulmur, James 11:193
Pulsfort, William 23:101
Pulsifer, Moses 25:269
Pulsipher, William 22:153
Pults, George W. 17:207
Pultz, A. L. 18:279
Pulver, Chester 17:85
Pulver, John N. 17:463;
  24:186
Pulver, William 18:17
Pulver, William B. 25:221
Pumell, John 8:28; 21:213
Pumer, H. 9:149
Pummell, Thomas 25:303
Pummill, Nelson 23:287
Pumphery, Caleb 24:55
Pumphrey, Reason W.
  21:58
Pumphry, William 15:221
Pumpkin, James S. 10:206
Pumplin, William L. H.
  24:96
Pumroy, C. E. 11:110
Punby, J. C. 14:100
Punch, F. 14:284
Punch, John 13:42
Punches, Daniel 23:46
Pundy, A. 17:183
Punell, John H. 8:109
Punell, Thomas 7:78
Punn, A. 3:158
Punt, Patrick M. 13:42;
  16:51
Punt---, G. L. 12:100
Puny, J. 3:158
Puple, Stephen 19:188
Pupp, George 27:97
Purance, Uriah 8:93
Purce, G. W. 14:100
Purce, Thomas P. 12:36
Purcel, Thomas H. 18:91

Purcell, --- 15:221
Purcell, A. H. 17:217
Purcell, A. P. 7:53
Purcell, Bruce R. 23:92
Purcell, Byron 10:74
Purcell, E. D. 1:63
Purcell, Edward 8:28;
  18:155
Purcell, F. W. 1:64
Purcell, Freeman 20:175
Purcell, Henry P. 10:21
Purcell, J. 3:158; 14:19
Purcell, J. H. 20:127
Purcell, J. P. 21:58
Purcell, J. R. 3:158
Purcell, John 10:97
Purcell, M. C. 18:221
Purcell, Michael 17:15
Purcell, O. H. 9:58
Purcell, P. 7:53
Purcell, Patrick 12:36
Purcell, Peter 6:21
Purcell, Philip 6:21
Purcell, Simon 7:107
Purcell, T. 21:378
Purcell, Thadeus C. 23:92
Purcell, Thomas 6:21;
  22:409
Purcell, Weldon P. 22:97
Purcell, William 18:91
Purcell, William H. 23:76
Purcey, James 21:378
Purdam, Abraham 22:50
Purdam, O. 22:50
Purdee, J. 3:158
Purdell, C. R. 7:38
Purden, Charles B. 13:67
Purdie, D. R. 21:142
Purdin, Francis A. 11:163
Purdin, Jefferson 5:44
Purdon, D. 17:183
Purdue, B. B. 21:168
Purdue, Henry 9:73
Purdum, M. 22:488
Purdy, --- 17:196
Purdy, Daniel 14:100
Purdy, G. 17:137; 24:201
Purdy, George 16:141
Purdy, H. 16:123
Purdy, H. G. 25:60
Purdy, Henry I. 22:50
Purdy, J. 13:97; 14:19
Purdy, J. C. 9:89; 26:53
Purdy, J. L. 14:302
Purdy, J. W. 1:161
Purdy, James 6:32; 25:325
Purdy, John 9:89; 13:42;
  17:244, 495; 23:244
Purdy, John W. 8:118;
  11:110; 12:170

Purdy, Lewis 10:74;
  20:330
Purdy, Lotan 17:71
Purdy, M. 3:158
Purdy, Noble 12:36
Purdy, Ransler 11:110
Purdy, S. L. 27:99
Purdy, Stephen 17:283
Purey, James 7:107
Purfield, H. L. 18:249
Purg, Henry 18:314;
  26:109
Purington, C. H. 17:315
Puritan, O. 3:158
Purkey, Jacob 3:158
Purkins, O. C. 10:132;
  20:330
Purkins, Patrick 15:111
Purmo, Antonio 9:58
Purnel, James R. 20:330
Purnell, Albert 21:378
Purnell, Caleb 10:155;
  19:188
Purnell, Henry 5:44
Purnell, James 7:38; 13:42
Purnell, John 7:53; 18:155
Purnell, Louis 7:131;
  21:378
Purnell, Middleton M.
  24:43
Purnell, Samuel 1:63
Purnell, W. E. 15:345
Purnell, William 16:220
Purnell, William E.
  16:377
Purnell, William H. 18:91
Purney, Jacob B. 15:12
Purney, Samuel 9:45
Puros, Lewis 15:305
Purple, Sheffield 17:294
Purpus, Leopold 20:12
Purqua, J. S. 10:74
Purr, Joseph 14:100
Purraman, William H.
  9:124
Purrell, John 21:282
Purrell, Richard 15:175
Purrington, Samuel W.
  5:44
Purris, John A. 15:345
Purse, Daniel L. 11:163
Pursel, Joshua 16:100
Pursell, E. 13:97
Pursely, John M. 20:175
Pursley, W. B. 3:158
Purson, Aaron 11:110
Purson, Henry 21:282
Purson, James C. 11:17
Purt, Elbert 9:190
Purt, T. W. 9:224
Purtee, John 24:83

Purthe, Samuel 5:53
Purtle, S. 3:158
Purveyor, J. 18:249; 26:53
Purvis, Abraham 10:132; 20:330
Purvis, John 24:69
Pury, Frank 18:37
Puryne, James S. 16:123
Puse, William 21:78
Pusey, James 3:158
Push, Mike 7:38
Pushor, Albert 7:107
Pusley, John 26:54
Pusley, W. S. 16:270
Pusley, Zachary 12:36
Puspher, Theodore 11:310
Pusse, Joel 9:38
Pussler, Henry 8:93
Pustle, John 9:98
Put---, W. O. 21:209
Puter, John 15:221
Putman, D. S. 25:62
Putman, G. L. 16:220
Putman, H. R. 15:167
Putman, James 19:30
Putman, Richard 16:221
Putman, Thomas J. 16:221
Putman, William 10:132; 20:330
Putnam, A. 18:71
Putnam, A. S. 25:221
Putnam, C. 1:164
Putnam, C. H. 14:100
Putnam, D. G. 3:158
Putnam, David 21:217
Putnam, G. 6:11; 18:113
Putnam, George 11:41
Putnam, H. D. 9:190
Putnam, H. F. 27:96
Putnam, H. H. 9:58
Putnam, Hartley 16:17
Putnam, Isaac 4:48
Putnam, Israel 16:51
Putnam, J. 1:65; 21:38; 25:61
Putnam, J. D. 20:152
Putnam, Jeremiah K. 12:36
Putnam, John H. 10:154
Putnam, Judson 21:38
Putnam, L. 1:162; 3:158
Putnam, Lyman 13:117
Putnam, Nathaniel 4:48
Putnam, O. 1:63; 3:158
Putnam, O. D. 1:161
Putnam, Oliver 22:265
Putnam, Orville 16:17
Putnam, Philip 27:99
Putnam, Ransom 20:116
Putnam, Sanford 11:210
Putnam, Spencer 23:92

Putnam, Strod S. 9:16
Putnam, T. J. 15:295
Putnam, Theodore P. 19:332
Putnam, Thomas A. 8:93
Putnam, Tonson 7:132
Putnam, W. D. 19:233
Putnam, Walter 18:71
Putnam, William 5:27; 12:75; 24:161
Putname, W. 15:43
Putney, C. 27:94
Putney, J. M. 15:334; 19:94
Putney, Loyall M. M. 11:193
Putney, S. L. 15:327; 19:94
Putney, Zadock S. 23:194
Putt, Franklin 15:167
Puttoch, J. 12:80
Putts, C. 12:93; 16:302
Putts, William 5:44
Putz, Joseph 23:124
Puyear, Felix 23:282
Pwevis, John A. 16:377
Pyatt, James W. 11:71
Pyatt, M. 3:158; 18:193
Pycraft, Francis 11:415
Pye, George 9:135
Pye, Joshua 12:157
Pye, R. 1:161
Pye, Thornton 23:198
Pye, Watts A. 7:9
Pye, William 7:38, 53
Pyeatt, Christopher C. 24:55
Pyeatt, Robert 11:163
Pyeerson, George 16:302
Pyers, Isaac 3:158
Pyfer, Joseph 18:272
Pygail, George F. 9:190
Pygall, George F. 19:275
Pygold, Thomas W. 21:259
Pyke, George T. 22:436
Pyke, Lafayette H. 11:41
Pyle, A. J. 16:51
Pyle, A. L. 13:117
Pyle, Calvin 10:132; 20:330
Pyle, John W. 22:435
Pyle, L. A. 1:162
Pyle, P. S. 20:330
Pyle, Socrates 10:74
Pyle, T. E. 4:48
Pyle, Wiley 20:99
Pyles, Eli 22:487
Pyles, Jeremiah 1:63
Pyne, Stephen H. 19:188
Pyne, William 4:48

Q

Q---, C. 23:129
Q---, F. 15:3
Qu-mdnil-n, C. 14:100
Quackenbush, --- 3:158
Quackenbush, Alfred 4:48
Quackenbush, C. 21:378
Quackenbush, Columbus 7:107
Quackenbush, George 14:208
Quackenbush, J. P. 16:221
Quackenbush, John G. 16:51
Quackenbush, L. 23:163
Quackenbush, Lewis B. 12:100
Quackenbush, M. 11:288
Quackenbush, P. 1:164
Quackenbush, T. 9:27
Quackenbush, Thomas 18:314; 26:109
Quade, Alfred 14:208
Quade, M. 3:158
Quadlin, Solomon 21:259
Quagle, Ashley 22:214
Quail, Harvey C. 4:48
Quaintance, George 22:214
Quaintance, Thomas 22:436
Quaintance, W. 20:43
Qualles, Joseph 11:211
Qualls, R. W. 9:58
Quam, William 19:48
Quanley, M. 16:221
Quann, Peter 26:177
Quanney, Isaac 25:281
Quant, C. 15:111
Quantry, William 21:378
Quarles, J. H. 25:221
Quarles, Prior 22:455
Quarter, Nelson 13:117
Quarterman, William 21:11
Quartersby, George 14:330
Quartillew, Charles 12:59
Quary, G. 1:65
Quash, Daniel 18:91
Quatta, J. 3:158
Quay, G. W. 15:221
Quay, John 12:51
Quay, Saldon P. 14:302; 17:469
Quay, Saldon R. 27:100
Quay, William H. 22:153
Queen, Benjamin W. 25:284

Queen, C. K. 25:221
Queen, Charles H. 5:44
Queen, Forrest 17:162
Queen, G. 25:221
Queen, George 5:44
Queen, Hiram 18:400
Queen, James 21:14
Queen, James M. 17:317
Queen, Jasper 22:214
Queen, Reuben 10:92;
 20:330
Queen, S. C. 10:132;
 20:330
Queen, Taphta F. 13:60
Queen, W. R. 23:46
Queenan, Farrell 23:13
Queene, Joseph 15:8
Quellen, George A. 4:48
Quen, T. 16:221
Quentpflacht, P. 21:112
Queor, J. 25:221
Querk, Jeremiah 10:74
Querner, Christian 11:165
Querry, F. 13:117
Querry, Humphrey 14:208
Querter, John H. 24:202
Quhal, Conrad 5:27;
 25:222
Quick, Albert 12:36
Quick, Amos M. 25:222
Quick, B. 5:44
Quick, David 17:450
Quick, Dewitt 24:175
Quick, E. 1:65
Quick, George 22:153
Quick, I. 17:293
Quick, I. A. 11:415
Quick, J. 1:164
Quick, J. W. V. 9:98
Quick, Jackson 21:112
Quick, James 7:107
Quick, John 1:65; 22:343
Quick, John A. 17:233
Quick, Lewis 5:53; 17:67
Quick, Michael 10:166
Quick, O. 25:222
Quick, O. T. 7:107
Quick, P. 1:164
Quick, Sidney 18:279
Quick, Stebbins 22:436
Quick, W. 10:187
Quick, William 11:129;
 15:221
Quick, William J. 10:174
Quick, Z. 25:222
Quickle, Elias G. 8:93
Quickley, Patrick 20:330
Quicksall, Thomas 22:214
Quiday, J. H. 10:150
Quidley, Mary J. 19:188
Quier, Jacob 11:129

Quigal, Michael 13:67
Quigg, William 6:10;
 18:91
Quiggins, J. J. 21:378
Quiggle, O. F. 17:503
Quiggs, James 22:436
Quigle, M. 16:221
Quigley, Barney 1:65;
 13:125
Quigley, Edward 9:190;
 19:271
Quigley, J. 3:158; 9:149;
 27:100
Quigley, J. A. 20:43
Quigley, James 10:21
Quigley, Jasper 11:341
Quigley, John 11:73;
 12:65; 15:95, 330;
 19:94
Quigley, John V. 17:350
Quigley, Joseph 27:100
Quigley, Joseph B. 7:69
Quigley, Martin 9:45;
 26:128
Quigley, Mathew 8:93
Quigley, Patrick 4:48;
 5:27; 10:74
Quigley, Philip 9:45;
 23:182
Quigley, R. 1:65
Quigley, Thomas 27:100
Quigley, Thomas R. 17:85
Quigley, W. J. 9:149;
 27:100
Quigley, Wesley 9:38;
 18:296; 26:109
Quigly, Edward 15:5
Quigly, James 11:165
Quilbran, H. H. 16:270
Quilk, Richard 26:128
Quill, M. 25:222
Quill, Matthew 5:44
Quill, R. 3:158
Quillan, Edward 12:51
Quillan, William 17:238
Quilleman, George 22:455
Quillen, C. 19:268
Quillen, Elias H. 4:67
Quilliams, James D.
 22:172
Quillian, E. 13:97
Quillin, J. 3:158
Quilman, Isaac 13:58
Quilty, J. 1:164
Quim, Thomas 9:27
Quiman, R. S. 18:249;
 26:55
Quimbey, A. 1:65
Quimby, A. W. 25:222
Quimby, Charles 23:194;
 25:222

Quimby, D. 9:149
Quimby, David 27:100
Quimby, George W.
 22:214
Quimby, J. S. 19:94
Quimby, M. P. 27:100
Quimby, Matthew 21:78
Quimet, Camille 5:27
Quimsby, M. T. 9:124
Quin, Barney 10:21
Quin, Bartholomew 10:21
Quin, Edmund 19:30
Quin, Richard 10:21
Quinback, J. 3:158
Quinby, F. 13:97
Quince, --- 27:100
Quince, Charles C. 18:71
Quince, Robert 25:222
Quincy, John 17:406
Quindley, B. F. 9:149;
 27:100
Quine, John R. 14:262
Quiner, J. 16:221
Quiner, James 13:42
Quingle, Robert W. 17:24
Quinis, Thomas 9:38
Quinkle, James 18:440
Quinlan, James 9:190;
 19:259
Quinlan, John 7:38
Quinlan, M. 3:158
Quinlan, Morris 11:165
Quinlan, Patrick 3:158
Quinlen, Josephus 9:190
Quinley, F. 14:19
Quinley, Henry S. 21:378
Quinley, John 9:160
Quinley, P. 15:43
Quinley, Thomas 14:208
Quinlin, D. G. 14:244;
 27:100
Quinlin, Patrick 16:87
Quinlivin, John 10:74
Quinn, A. 1:164
Quinn, Arthur 22:214
Quinn, Asa 9:45; 26:128
Quinn, Barney 4:48
Quinn, Bernard 10:9
Quinn, Charles 7:38
Quinn, Charles A. 15:26
Quinn, D. 1:164
Quinn, E. 1:65; 25:222
Quinn, Edson 3:158
Quinn, Edward 5:27;
 25:222
Quinn, Edward W. 22:97
Quinn, F. 3:158
Quinn, Felix 5:27; 10:132;
 20:330
Quinn, Francis 17:398
Quinn, Frank 19:188

Quinn, George 14:208
Quinn, George W. 22:50
Quinn, H. 14:100
Quinn, Henry 1:65; 12:36; 24:43
Quinn, Hugh 18:155
Quinn, J. 1:164; 13:97; 16:123
Quinn, J. J. 27:100
Quinn, James 3:158; 8:28, 54; 9:45; 12:65; 14:100, 289; 15:8; 16:51; 17:25; 18:155, 413; 22:50, 128, 343; 23:109; 26:128
Quinn, James F. 15:73
Quinn, John 7:107; 9:113; 11:232; 12:36; 14:100; 16:377; 19:330; 22:436; 23:163
Quinn, John H. 22:214
Quinn, Joseph 14:208
Quinn, Joseph C. 20:180
Quinn, Luke 9:13
Quinn, M. 1:164; 25:222
Quinn, Michael 5:27; 7:107; 14:208; 21:379; 24:10
Quinn, Oliver B. 4:48
Quinn, Owen 27:100
Quinn, P. 3:158; 13:125; 14:100; 25:222
Quinn, Patrick 15:73; 25:222
Quinn, Paul W. 21:232
Quinn, Peter 12:36; 22:214
Quinn, R. 25:222
Quinn, Richard 26:213
Quinn, S. B. 11:232
Quinn, Stephen W. 21:104
Quinn, Thomas 9:190; 19:316; 22:128; 24:72
Quinn, William 7:38; 9:190; 12:36; 19:234; 21:58
Quinnell, L. 17:434
Quinnell, Lewis 24:173
Quinnell, Thomas 21:93
Quinnett, E. 5:27
Quinnetto, Alexander 18:340
Quinney, Paul W. 23:194
Quinnin, Joseph 16:221
Quint, C. P. 1:65
Quint, F. 15:345
Quint, Joseph 9:113
Quint, L. 16:377

Quint, M. 16:79
Quintan, W. H. 15:303
Quintrell, A. G. 19:94
Quinty, Patrick 21:379
Quinty, William H. 21:379
Quinyard, W. 1:65
Quirk, F. 1:65
Quirk, Jer 20:330
Quirk, John 1:65; 10:132; 14:100; 20:330
Quirk, M. J. 3:158
Quirk, Mary W. 16:303
Quirk, Michael 19:188
Quirk, Oliver 1:65
Quirk, Richard 17:321
Quirk, Thomas 18:434; 25:222
Quirk, W. 18:179
Quirk, William 9:45
Quirk, William J. 19:188
Quisby, Henry 26:128
Quishenberry, J. 18:446
Quisick, James 18:427
Quistin, F. 13:97
Quistorff, F. 1:65
Quitley, P. 14:100
Quitzguard, Ludwig 11:17
Quivey, Daniel 26:204
Quivy, D. T. 10:180
Qulley, J. 25:222
Qumethe, Alex 9:104
Quoin, John 23:46
Quonn, J. H. 25:222
Quonn, James 5:44
Quown, Robert L. 19:94
Qurny, R. S. 27:100
Qusor, Joseph 5:27

R

R---, --- 19:305
R---, A. 11:342; 20:330; 25:63
R---, A. D. 17:335
R---, A. E. 11:248
R---, A. F. 11:342; 24:27
R---, A. H. V. 20:177
R---, A. R. 11:73
R---, B. 11:248; 21:150; 24:69, 114
R---, C. 20:330
R---, C. H. 18:251
R---, C. W. 10:187; 18:179; 20:43
R---, D. 19:305; 20:156
R---, D. M. 23:253
R---, D. S. 17:217
R---, D. W. 24:27

R---, E. 20:59, 156; 21:125; 26:179
R---, E. A. 10:192
R---, E. B. 17:219
R---, E. F. 20:36
R---, E. G. 24:83
R---, E. L. 22:354
R---, E. M. 11:341
R---, E. S. 21:78, 168
R---, F. 9:215; 14:270; 20:156; 23:46
R---, F. M. 15:263
R---, G. 11:248; 24:167; 25:63
R---, G. F. 22:354
R---, G. S. E. 23:268
R---, G. W. 23:314
R---, George 18:17
R---, H. 11:249, 342; 15:268; 16:113; 21:379; 23:205, 259, 264
R---, H. L. 15:259
R---, J. 15:59, 224; 16:378; 17:326; 18:37, 251; 23:205, 287; 24:215; 26:57
R---, J. A. 24:113
R---, J. B. 23:92
R---, J. C. 21:209
R---, J. F. 23:245
R---, J. G. 15:268
R---, J. P. 11:342
R---, James 17:58, 416; 25:65
R---, James B. 15:224
R---, John 16:221; 23:205
R---, John J. 15:73
R---, Joshua 23:205
R---, L. 11:248; 24:114; 26:58
R---, L. F. 11:220
R---, M. 11:416; 25:63
R---, M. E. 15:224
R---, M. L. 20:330
R---, Martin 9:58
R---, P. 20:181; 22:354
R---, P. Y. G. 18:179
R---, Peter 23:291
R---, R. 12:142; 20:330; 25:222
R---, Re--- 11:166
R---, Robert 11:342
R---, S. 12:147; 19:191, 305
R---, S. T. 16:234
R---, S. W. 25:65
R---, T. 18:251; 19:305; 26:58
R---, T. C. 17:326
R---, T. H. B. 20:59

R---, T. M. 24:113
R---, T. P. 20:156
R---, Thomas 11:311
R---, U. 20:59
R---, W. 10:37; 11:249;
  20:156, 330; 25:312
R---, W. B. 19:97
R---, W. C. 15:73
R---, W. F. 11:342
R---, W. G. 11:342
R---, W. H. 8:55; 27:147
R---, W. M. 26:179
R---, Z. B. 23:205
R---hae, Robert 15:224
R---s, John 23:76
R---yon, John 13:80
R., C. H. 26:56
R., T. P. 15:167
Raab, F. 13:97
Raab, John 21:38
Raab, Ladislaus 20:116
Raap, T. 14:19
Raasner, Daniel 23:163
Raatz, Hermann 4:48
Rab, William George
  11:184
Raban, James 9:89
Rabb, Andrew 18:210
Rabb, F. 12:87; 16:303
Rabb, Henry K. 9:124
Rabb, John 11:320
Rabberts, Frank 8:99
Rabbitt, --- 25:334
Rabbitt, E. C. 11:120
Rabe, Fred 24:69
Raber, August 16:134
Raber, J. H. 26:237
Raber, William H. 22:237
Rabern, George 3:158
Rabody, David 5:27
Rabold, Augustus 22:153
Rabosd, Henry 15:313
Raboss, Henry 19:94
Rabsman, H. 19:188
Rabsman, Henry 10:166
Raburn, Garland E.
  22:456
Raburn, James 22:214
Raburn, Joel J. 22:456
Raby, Daniel 10:74
Raccoon, Jackson 22:97
Race, Enos 12:157
Race, G. W. 13:117
Race, George 5:27;
  25:222
Race, J. M. 23:115
Race, James 24:154
Race, Jasper 10:74;
  20:330
Race, Newton W. 10:206
Race, S. 21:38

Race, Sidney J. 4:48
Race, William T. 22:128
Racey, Giles 15:84
Racey, H. B. 10:29
Racey, John 6:9; 18:270
Racha, M. 7:76
Racharter, Christian
  23:163
Rachel, Ambrose 17:25
Rachel, Joseph 21:93
Rachell, Eli 21:379
Racher, Reuben 18:249
Racher, Reubi 26:57
Rachun, Frederick 15:336
Racine, Benjamin 22:97
Racine, Henry 21:217
Racine, P. 3:158
Raciof, Narcisse 20:331
Raciot, Narcisse 10:132
Rack, Christian 15:279
Rack, William 8:74
Rackann, Samuel S. 21:63
Rackcliffe, Nathaniel 7:38
Racke, George 7:38
Rackerly, --- 25:65
Rackerman, P. 15:361
Rackett, George 10:166
Rackistars, William
  26:111
Rackmyer, A. 5:27
Rackmyre, A. 25:222
Rackwell, T. C. 14:100
Racraft, J. R. 23:182
Racy, John T. 10:97
Racy, M. A. 11:311
Racy, William G. 10:97
Radabaugh, W. H. 3:158
Radabaugh, William
  23:163
Radcliff, --- 11:234
Radcliff, Albert 18:324
Radcliff, Benjamin 13:42
Radcliff, Cyrus 7:107
Radcliff, Henry 20:99
Radcliff, J. 8:54; 21:78
Radcliff, James 13:42
Radcliff, James W. 17:232
Radcliff, Oliver P. 17:277
Radcliff, R. 17:149
Radcliff, William 13:42
Radcliffe, Benjamin 16:51
Radcliffe, James H. 15:12
Radcliffe, Randolph 12:36
Raddiker, Cornelius
  11:129
Raddiker, Daniel 5:27
Raddle, J. 22:410
Raden, August 12:65
Raden, C. W. 16:100
Rader, A. G. 22:265
Rader, Adam 9:113

Rader, Andrew S. 22:265
Rader, Clan 22:489
Rader, Daniel 23:185
Rader, Eli R. 23:46
Rader, George 17:85;
  24:43
Rader, Hiram 23:163
Rader, James B. 22:215
Rader, John George
  21:142
Rader, Nicholas 23:163
Rades, Wesley 17:296
Radford, --- 15:221
Radford, Albert 22:316
Radford, Daniel 17:207
Radford, George E. 7:107
Radford, J. L. 23:46
Radford, Robert 22:316
Radford, W. L. 23:46
Radford, William 3:158
Radh, Joseph 9:89
Radican, B. 25:222
Radigan, P. 23:118
Radiker, Dick 10:132;
  20:331
Radings, William 21:201
Radish, Peter 17:401
Radley, E. C. 13:42
Radley, E. S. 25:284
Radolph, Andrew 9:16
Radour, Henry 12:51
Radtke, Emil 12:36
Radtke, William 17:362
Radtze, William 4:48
Radway, William 22:410
Rady, P. 16:221
Rady, Patrick 16:303;
  25:222
Rae, James 1:66
Raeff, J. 3:158
Raegner, L. 7:76; 25:303
Rael, Salvador 8:124
Raenback, Mathew 20:127
Raeper, Frederick 1:68
Raeppel, George 17:25
Raer, A. 17:85
Raetchner, J. 16:100
Rafe, Andrew 13:42
Rafee, --- 11:269
Raferty, John 10:177;
  19:188
Raff, William 11:73
Raffan, George 22:437
Raffell, Louis 7:132
Raffenberger, William H.
  12:57
Raffensperger, D. T. 1:68
Rafferty, Edward 5:27
Rafferty, F. 13:67; 16:221
Rafferty, F. O. 1:69
Rafferty, J. O. 3:158

Rafferty, M. 3:158
Rafferty, P. 3:158; 14:100
Rafferty, T. 3:158
Rafferty, Thomas 14:208
Raffey, M. 25:222
Rafford, James O. 15:12
Raffter, A. M. 21:379
Rafter, M. 1:69
Rafter, William 12:36
Raftery, M. 1:168
Rafty, Edward 11:409
Ragan, Bazil 14:208
Ragan, C. 3:158
Ragan, D. 18:55
Ragan, George 17:274
Ragan, George W. 10:92; 20:331
Ragan, Irvin H. 23:76
Ragan, Isaac J. 22:265
Ragan, J. 1:165; 3:158; 19:259
Ragan, J. A. 10:132; 14:100; 20:331
Ragan, J. H. 14:278
Ragan, James 14:100; 23:264
Ragan, John 3:158
Ragan, John C. 22:97
Ragan, M. 12:9
Ragan, Maurice 5:27
Ragan, Michael 14:208
Ragan, Munroe 23:271
Ragan, Patrick 22:172
Ragan, R. D. 14:100
Ragan, S. J. 14:208
Ragan, W. N. 14:278; 23:104
Ragan, William P. 8:54
Ragdon, Daniel 11:211
Rager, David 12:75; 15:73
Rager, George C. 12:36
Rager, Israel 12:36
Rager, John 22:489
Ragin, Daniel 13:42
Ragin, Franklin 21:232
Ragin, P. 11:129
Raglan, A. D. 21:38
Raglan, Nathan 24:102
Raglin, George 11:211
Raglin, J. J. 11:281
Ragner, Theodore 12:75
Ragoon, Robert 8:109
Ragsdale, A. 11:269
Ragsdale, A. G. 18:155
Ragsdale, Albert 7:107; 21:379
Ragsdale, Alfred 8:54; 21:58
Ragsdale, Dalan 8:54
Ragsdale, Gabriel L. 20:25

Ragsdale, James 8:66
Ragsdale, Squire 7:132
Rah, Christian 21:196
Raher, Michael 9:27; 18:314; 26:110
Rahla, Jacob 10:132; 20:331
Rahlfs, George 25:222
Rahm, Adolph 10:132; 20:331
Rahm, C. 1:166
Rahmstine, John 19:94
Rahn, Jacob 18:413
Rahyer, Frank 13:42; 16:51
Raiborn, Galem 17:203
Raiche, Oliver 26:55
Raiclo, Oliver 9:89
Raider, Richard M. 13:42
Raiger, Anton 18:113
Rail, Calvin 21:232
Rail, R. J. 22:521
Railborne, Thomas H. 22:128
Railey, C. 1:165
Railey, Patrick 10:74; 20:331
Railing, Martin 21:232
Railspeak, Enoch 4:48
Railton, W. 1:165
Raimer, Willis 19:94
Raimor, A. J. 25:312
Rain, Horace 7:132
Rain, Lawrence 23:46
Rain, P. F. 3:158
Rain, Thomas 27:104
Rainbolt, Nelson 24:43
Raine, Andrew 24:184
Rainer, George 5:44
Rainer, M. C. 19:188
Rainer, Mahlon G. 10:174
Rainer, N. 27:100
Rainer, William 13:97; 14:19
Raines, Aaron 26:128
Raines, E. 24:167
Raines, Franklin 10:74
Raines, George 10:74
Raines, J. S. 1:168
Raines, J. W. 8:67
Raines, James 10:92; 22:265
Raines, Jefferson 11:74
Raines, John 13:67; 19:94; 20:85
Rainey, J. W. 15:59
Rainey, James 9:38; 16:51
Rainey, John 20:19; 22:343
Rainey, John W. 12:75
Rainey, Joseph 9:124

Rainey, Robert R. 17:274
Rainey, Scott 11:211
Rainhard, John 5:27
Rainhart, H. 25:64
Rainhart, John 25:222
Rainheart, A. 13:97
Rainier, Joseph G. 20:19
Rains, Anderson P. 17:453
Rains, Cyrus K. 25:64
Rains, Franklin 20:331
Rains, G. D. 3:158
Rains, George 10:74; 20:331
Rains, George W. 17:444; 24:161
Rains, Henry 17:277
Rains, J. W. 26:179
Rains, James 20:331
Rains, James A. 17:238
Rains, Joab 23:287
Rains, John 10:149; 18:55
Rains, John C. 11:42
Rains, John D. 25:63
Rains, N. W. 11:409
Rains, Reuben 12:75; 15:95
Rains, Thomas 17:337
Rains, William 3:158; 11:329
Rainsboth, --- 19:297
Rainsford, Samuel 20:331
Rainshaw, William S. 27:103
Rainson, E. 20:331
Rainsuga, H. 14:208
Rainwater, A. 3:158
Rainwater, John 22:50
Rainwater, R. 7:38
Rainwater, W. E. 10:206
Rairden, Ansel 7:107
Rairdon, John H. 21:379
Rairi, Lawrence 23:46
Rairidon, John 22:215
Raisby, S. 11:382
Raisell, Jacob 12:166
Raisen, R. 25:222
Raiser, A. 3:158
Raiser, Henry 11:193
Raiser, L. 25:66
Raiser, Lorenzo 2:16
Raish, Jacob 16:100
Raisin, Richard 5:44
Raison, M. 9:201
Raison, Masel 19:292
Raison, Robert 23:205
Raister, Catharina 26:225
Raitsboch, George B. 18:249
Raitsbock, George B. 26:56

Raitzel, Samuel 19:188
Raizen, John 9:190
Rake, Godfrey 20:331
Rake, Henry 17:85
Raker, L. 3:158
Rakes, W. 25:222
Rakes, Wesley 16:134
Rakes, William 3:158
Rakle, F. 14:100
Rako, Godfrey 10:92
Rakutz, Fritz 21:142
Ralbren, Benjamin 21:282
Ralburn, Samuel E. 21:379
Raleigh, A. 3:158
Raleigh, O'Keeney 20:331
Raleigh, R. W. 8:54; 21:168
Raley, Daniel 20:331
Raley, George W. 20:88
Raley, H. 3:159
Raliford, D. 7:38
Ralile, S. G. 26:179
Raling, Eli 17:441
Ralinger, J. 3:159
Rall, W. 25:64
Ralley, Thomas 21:282
Rallison, J. D. 16:221
Rallston, William 17:162
Rallstone, George W. 4:48
Ralmstine, John 15:323
Ralph, --- 26:179
Ralph, A. 16:101
Ralph, A. O. 1:166
Ralph, Alfred 17:391
Ralph, Christopher M. 20:12
Ralph, G. 3:158
Ralph, George W. 17:362
Ralph, Henry 8:28; 12:36, 172
Ralph, J. 22:456
Ralph, J. F. 3:158
Ralph, J. H. 14:259
Ralph, James 8:28; 18:155
Ralph, Lawrence 9:124
Ralph, R. D. 11:165
Ralph, Thomas 10:166; 13:42
Ralph, W. E. 15:221
Ralph, William 24:203
Ralph, William H. 21:15
Ralphlrill, --- 15:153
Ralstein, D. B. 9:28
Ralstin, William T. 11:74
Ralston, Alexander 8:54
Ralston, Anderson 23:92
Ralston, Arthur C. 20:12
Ralston, D. M. 7:38
Ralston, J. 17:25
Ralston, J. M. 3:159; 7:53

Ralston, John 22:410
Ralston, Joseph 22:488
Ralston, Samuel 22:265
Ralston, W. C. 14:19
Ralston, W. J. 3:158
Ralston, W. S. 12:148
Ralston, William 17:85
Raltan, W. 1:164
Ram, Dennis 6:26
Rambeau, Ralph 22:163
Rambo, B. F. 1:166
Rambo, Calvin 23:163
Rambo, Hassel 20:138
Rambo, Joel 11:336
Rambo, N. 1:168
Ramboe, Barton 21:379
Rambol, W. F. 19:268
Rambolt, Joseph 9:38
Rambolt, V. 17:323
Rambour, Charles 17:85
Rameler, Israel 21:243
Ramenska, Joseph 22:343
Ramer, David 1:67
Ramer, Jacob F. 14:208
Ramer, Martin S. 12:59
Ramer, W. C. 3:159
Ramer, William 15:338
Rames, Aaron 9:47
Rames, Henry 9:89
Ramey, Alfred 17:308; 22:455
Ramey, Daniel S. 22:456
Ramey, J. T. 16:221
Ramey, James 11:97
Ramey, Logan C. 17:308
Ramey, Pleasant S. 24:43
Ramey, Thaddeus W. 10:74
Ramey, William H. 8:120
Ramford, Josiah 13:42
Ramier, William 11:97
Ramil, Robert 11:193
Ramir, J. W. 24:154
Ramler, Isaac 10:174
Ramley, John 17:238
Ramley, Robert W. 11:97
Ramley, S. 25:222
Rammant, J. 14:100
Rammerig, M. 14:100
Ramon, Osna 21:379
Rampher, George 24:27
Rampthen, William 16:143
Ramsaier, Christian 22:467
Ramsay, E. 19:188
Ramsay, H. 12:87, 123
Ramsay, Hiram 3:159
Ramsay, Isaac 3:159
Ramsay, Isaiah 4:48
Ramsay, J. C. 3:159

Ramsay, J. D. 3:159
Ramsay, Joseph 11:232
Ramsay, Michael 17:257
Ramsay, Robert 3:159
Ramsay, Samuel 21:11
Ramsay, Thomas 4:48; 21:78
Ramsay, W. 3:159; 27:101
Ramsay, W. M. 11:188
Ramsay, William 3:159; 17:25
Ramsay, William S. 21:379
Ramsberger, John 22:97
Ramsbotham, Simeon 19:30
Ramsdale, James B. 13:42
Ramsdale, John P. 16:51
Ramsdall, A. 1:167
Ramsdall, P. 14:101
Ramsdell, --- 10:166; 19:188
Ramsdell, H. 1:68
Ramsdell, J. D. 9:149
Ramsdell, J. S. 25:222
Ramsdell, John P. 13:42
Ramsdell, P. 1:68
Ramsdell, William H. 21:142
Ramsey, A. B. 3:159
Ramsey, Alex 25:303
Ramsey, Alexander 7:76
Ramsey, Allen 21:232
Ramsey, Ben 17:315
Ramsey, Berry 21:86
Ramsey, Bloomfield 25:269
Ramsey, C. H. 1:68
Ramsey, Champion 17:111
Ramsey, D. R. 16:221
Ramsey, Daniel 17:416, 447; 24:171
Ramsey, Daniel A. 12:36
Ramsey, David 17:41, 277
Ramsey, David A. 8:93
Ramsey, Edward 7:132; 19:30
Ramsey, Elijah 10:174; 11:167; 22:265
Ramsey, G. 1:95
Ramsey, G. W. 16:303
Ramsey, George 7:132
Ramsey, Greenburry 22:215
Ramsey, H. 16:303
Ramsey, Harrison 17:315
Ramsey, Henry 15:133
Ramsey, Hiram 22:50
Ramsey, J. 3:159; 18:113
Ramsey, J. T. 15:305

Ramsey, J. W. 17:25
Ramsey, James 8:67;
    11:74; 17:315; 19:31
Ramsey, James A. 22:438
Ramsey, James B. 26:179
Ramsey, John 6:10; 8:93;
    13:42; 19:94; 22:265
Ramsey, John P. 7:107
Ramsey, John S. 1:68;
    11:17
Ramsey, Joseph 21:282
Ramsey, M. G. 14:208
Ramsey, Merrill 22:437
Ramsey, R. 3:159;
    11:311; 23:314
Ramsey, Robert E.
    10:132; 20:331
Ramsey, Robert F. 22:97
Ramsey, S. J. 23:76
Ramsey, Solomon 7:132
Ramsey, T. 8:54
Ramsey, T. A. 16:221
Ramsey, T. J. 3:159
Ramsey, Thaddeus W.
    20:331
Ramsey, Thomas B. 9:28
Ramsey, Thomas J. 22:50
Ramsey, W. E. 22:215
Ramsey, W. G. 14:101
Ramsey, W. H. 1:99
Ramsey, W. S. 17:167;
    18:400
Ramsey, W. W. 9:58
Ramsey, William 3:159;
    21:78
Ramsey, William D. 21:38
Ramsey, William F.
    22:497
Ramsey, William H. 12:36
Ramsey, William T.
    20:103
Ramsey, William W.
    17:353
Ramsford, Samuel 10:74
Ramshear, B. 22:316
Ramsirrer, W. H. 17:85
Ramson, Christian 22:172
Ramson, George 9:210
Ramson, William 17:25
Ramstead, H. 3:159
Ramy, John C. 8:93
Ramy, William 9:89
Ran, Ferdinand 22:215
Ran, Ira 11:43
Ran, John 12:36
Ran, L. 7:38
Ranal, E. F. 27:105
Ranard, Manuel 23:182
Ranay, Martin 4:48
Ranbaugh, William 5:27
Ranboff, William 16:377

Ranch, David 14:208
Ranch, J. 3:159; 11:391
Ranch, Jacob I. 16:134
Ranch, W. W. 19:31
Ranchausen, August
    13:42
Rancl, Willard 15:320
Rancliff, J. W. 13:97
Rancoach, George 14:287
Rancom, Joseph 19:188
Rancorn, Joseph 10:166
Rancy, --- 15:73
Rancy, C. H. 11:194
Rand, --- 27:101
Rand, Bedford L. 4:48
Rand, Charles E. 7:107
Rand, E. C. 21:379
Rand, F. W. 17:160
Rand, H. 3:159
Rand, I. 15:361
Rand, J. 3:159; 12:96;
    19:94
Rand, Jeremiah B. 9:67
Rand, John T. 9:124
Rand, Lewis 21:168
Rand, Louis 17:451;
    24:179
Rand, M. W. 10:74;
    20:331
Rand, Moses W. 13:42
Rand, Royal 16:79
Rand, W. 19:94
Rand, W. W. 16:101
Rand, William 19:94
Randal, D. 16:377
Randal, D. A. 27:106
Randal, J. A. 8:54
Randal, M. S. 15:43
Randal, Marion 17:277
Randal, Oscar P. 23:163
Randal, Tilman 11:249
Randal, W. W. 25:222
Randal, William 11:212;
    17:277
Randall, --- 20:87
Randall, A. B. 3:159
Randall, A. D. 21:38
Randall, Abner E. 13:58
Randall, Alfred A. 22:153
Randall, Arthur L. 10:21
Randall, B. 1:99
Randall, C. E. 9:124
Randall, C. F. 3:159
Randall, C. N. 27:102
Randall, C. W. 9:149
Randall, Charles 10:149;
    18:55; 23:109
Randall, Charles E.
    16:281
Randall, Charles F. 5:27
Randall, Charles W. 22:50

Randall, Cyrus 25:222
Randall, D. 15:345
Randall, Daniel C. 17:159
Randall, Daniel S. 20:152
Randall, Deforest 21:38
Randall, Demster 26:178
Randall, E. 21:164
Randall, E. F. 14:302;
    17:473
Randall, E. N. 26:111
Randall, Edgar 21:282
Randall, Edgar A. 22:97
Randall, Edmond 17:183
Randall, Edw. F. 9:38
Randall, Edw. N. 9:38
Randall, Edward L.
    18:296
Randall, Eldridge G. 6:21
Randall, Elie 11:269
Randall, Elwood 10:132;
    20:331
Randall, Emanuel 9:210
Randall, Enoch 10:74;
    20:331
Randall, Eugene 7:38
Randall, F. A. 18:296
Randall, Ferdinand R.
    17:57
Randall, G. 1:166
Randall, G. P. 15:221
Randall, George 25:66
Randall, George H.
    22:505
Randall, George W.
    22:410
Randall, Grisham G.
    11:129
Randall, H. 11:129
Randall, H. D. 3:159
Randall, Henry 21:282
Randall, Hiram C. 17:57
Randall, Holliday A.
    18:222
Randall, J. 3:159
Randall, J. E. 24:27
Randall, J. F. 18:17
Randall, J. H. 15:73;
    25:222
Randall, J. L. 27:102
Randall, James 10:132;
    20:331; 21:78
Randall, James A. 3:159
Randall, James S. 22:467
Randall, Jedediah 9:190
Randall, Jeremiah 22:50
Randall, John 3:159;
    14:101; 21:282
Randall, John A. 24:27
Randall, John E. 9:28;
    18:314; 26:110
Randall, John M. 9:210

Randall, Joseph 17:152
Randall, Josiah 13:42;
  16:51
Randall, L. 13:126;
  16:221
Randall, L. C. 2:16
Randall, Lloyd 9:89
Randall, Louis 21:282
Randall, Louis A. 22:153
Randall, Loyd 26:55
Randall, Luther 14:209
Randall, Moses 12:36
Randall, P. 25:279
Randall, P. D. 3:159
Randall, R. 21:151
Randall, Robert 5:44;
  21:151, 282
Randall, S. 11:269; 20:85
Randall, S. G. 23:118
Randall, Samuel 19:332
Randall, Sandy 19:297
Randall, Selaw 25:222
Randall, Stephen C.
  20:331
Randall, T. A. 9:38
Randall, Tasman 21:282
Randall, Thomas 10:74;
  11:212; 20:331;
  21:38, 282
Randall, W. 1:165
Randall, W. F. 16:303
Randall, Watson 16:303
Randall, Whiten 21:282
Randall, William 9:190;
  10:132, 152; 18:55;
  21:282; 25:222
Randall, William F. 12:83
Randall, William H.
  12:100
Randall, Zopher 22:215
Randals, Charles 15:361
Randaw, M. A. J. 22:265
Rande, W. 15:305
Randebust, J. W. 15:357
Randel, E. 16:221
Randel, E. L. 26:110
Randel, Holliday 22:438
Randel, Peter 9:89
Randel, Theodore P.
  24:69
Randell, E. 14:101
Randell, H. 3:159
Randell, John 13:42
Randell, M. S. 12:75
Randell, R. 16:221
Randell, R. H. 14:209
Randell, Watson 12:83
Randenshold, Thurs
  19:188
Randgardner, James 3:159
Randle, Charles 12:96

Randle, Peter 26:58
Randle, Thomas 8:54
Randle, Thomas L. 11:89
Randle, W. F. 9:190
Randle, William 9:231;
  20:331
Randleman, H. J. 16:51
Randles, Charles 19:94
Randol, Richard H.
  22:128
Randolf, John 11:404
Randolf, William 5:44
Randoll, D. A. 14:244
Randolph, --- 3:159;
  9:124; 21:151
Randolph, A. F. 14:209
Randolph, Andrew J.
  21:38
Randolph, Archy 11:211
Randolph, D. N. 8:67;
  26:179
Randolph, D. Taylor
  13:58
Randolph, David A. 22:97
Randolph, Edw. L. 9:38
Randolph, Edward 9:190;
  19:289
Randolph, Frank 18:422
Randolph, George 7:132
Randolph, H. 24:27
Randolph, J. A. 10:210
Randolph, J. C. 10:92;
  20:331
Randolph, J. U. 14:316
Randolph, J. W. 12:98;
  14:316
Randolph, James 1:66;
  21:78
Randolph, James W.
  22:471
Randolph, John 7:38, 132;
  11:269; 18:71; 24:27
Randolph, John H. 11:42
Randolph, Lemuel A.
  13:42
Randolph, Nathaniel
  10:92; 20:331
Randolph, Nelson 8:115
Randolph, O. 1:167
Randolph, O. G. 23:46
Randolph, Patrick 6:18;
  18:91
Randolph, Robert 25:286
Randolph, Samuel 11:42
Randolph, T. I. 10:74
Randolph, T. J. 20:331
Randolph, W. 12:166;
  25:223
Randolph, William 7:107
Randon, John W. 7:107

Rands, James 14:320;
  25:284
Randsbottom, D. 19:31
Randsbottom, R. D.
  11:167
Rane, G. H. 25:223
Rane, John 22:505
Rane, Thomas 9:190
Raneipher, Andrew H.
  21:78
Raner, W. J. 9:58
Ranerd, C. H. 15:43
Raners, C. 15:221
Ranevell, L. 11:342
Raney, A. 3:159
Raney, A. K. 3:159
Raney, Albert 11:86
Raney, B. 18:374
Raney, Bery 9:224
Raney, James 18:193
Raney, Jesse 20:331
Raney, Joseph 27:103
Raney, Lester 3:159
Raney, N. B. Walls
  20:331
Raney, Samuel T. 23:92
Rang, A. 14:244
Range, --- 27:106
Range, I. 14:209
Range, James 14:259
Range, Joe J. 22:265
Range, Richard 21:282
Range, S. P. 19:188
Ranger, E. J. 19:31
Ranger, Franklin 21:142
Ranger, O. 12:36
Ranghart, John 3:159
Ranghmen, G. 3:159
Rangott, A. 25:65
Rangsley, A. 14:279
Ranier, J. W. 17:432
Ranier, James J. 21:78
Ranier, William 11:311
Ranion, Albert 18:222
Rank, F. 14:284
Rank, George F. 10:74;
  20:331
Rank, Henry 22:438
Ranker, J. F. 1:166
Rankin, Alex 16:221
Rankin, Anthony 17:97
Rankin, D. 17:315
Rankin, Ed. F. 19:230
Rankin, Edw. F. 9:190
Rankin, G. F. 25:303
Rankin, Gabriel 22:215
Rankin, George 23:271
Rankin, George A. 7:76
Rankin, Isaac 20:85, 331
Rankin, J. 8:54
Rankin, J. C. 20:43

Rankin, J. H. 3:159
Rankin, Jacob 17:398
Rankin, James 1:68
Rankin, John 18:249;
26:57; 27:101
Rankin, Luther 23:46
Rankin, R. 14:302;
17:481; 27:105
Rankin, Robert 7:132
Rankin, S. S. 9:58
Rankin, T. R. M. 4:48
Rankin, William 2:16;
8:28; 11:42; 17:183;
18:155; 19:31; 25:66
Rankin, William A. 22:50,
437
Rankin, William H.
20:105
Rankin, William J. 22:505
Rankins, Anthony M.
22:265
Rankins, George 8:109
Rankins, Isaiah 22:50
Rankins, John 23:13
Rankins, John W. 10:97
Rankins, M. A. 3:159
Rankins, Oliver 14:316
Rankins, W. B. 18:193
Rankins, William 20:43
Ranley, S. E. 15:43
Ranly, --- 15:43
Ranmsbager, H. 25:223
Rann, Thomas 13:42
Ranner, James T. 17:201
Ranney, E. 2:16; 25:63
Ranney, Edward G.
16:134
Ranney, Homer C. 17:295
Ranney, J. J. 17:143
Ranney, Robert R. 7:16
Ranno, --- 11:269
Ranny, R. S. 9:89
Ransar, Even 11:193
Ransbottom, H. 25:223
Ransbotton, Henry 5:27
Ransel, D. A. 14:244
Ransel, E. T. 25:65
Ransford, B. 1:67
Ransh, Thomas K. 23:92
Ranshaw, George J.
20:331
Ransher, George 21:379
Ransier, F. 1:167
Ransire, Solomon 20:331
Ranslar, J. 15:43
Ransom, --- 18:280
Ransom, A. 11:211
Ransom, B. H. 21:379
Ransom, Berry 8:109
Ransom, David 20:12
Ransom, David L. 23:260

Ransom, Edw. T. 10:132
Ransom, Edward 20:331
Ransom, Francis W. 11:73
Ransom, G. C. 17:100
Ransom, George P.
22:237
Ransom, George W. 3:159
Ransom, H. 3:159
Ransom, Ives 22:153
Ransom, J. 3:159; 15:82
Ransom, J. H. 16:51
Ransom, John 9:38
Ransom, Joseph 11:232
Ransom, Lucian 18:249
Ransom, N. W. 21:379
Ransom, Obediah 23:101
Ransom, W. 13:97
Ransom, W. H. 1:166
Ransome, Lewis 27:104
Ransome, R. 25:223
Ranson, G. 1:69
Ranson, H. P. 11:43
Ranson, John 17:288
Ranson, Nathan 17:238
Ranson, Richard 17:416;
24:154
Ranstead, Leonard H.
22:97
Ranthburn, Horace 9:190
Rantles, J. 3:159
Ranzy, John 9:135;
27:102
Rape, Samuel M. 16:51
Rape, Vance 9:201
Rape, William 9:28;
18:314; 26:110
Raper, David 8:74
Raper, John 8:93; 17:444;
24:162
Raper, S. H. 24:83
Raper, William 20:148
Rapke, Adolph 17:450
Rapke, Henry 18:155
Raplee, Anson A. 10:21
Rapp, A. E. 3:159
Rapp, D. 1:69
Rapp, D. C. 3:159
Rapp, David 11:166
Rapp, Edward 12:57
Rapp, G. 17:156
Rapp, H. 3:159
Rapp, J. 11:121
Rapp, Jacob 19:31
Rapp, John 5:27; 25:223
Rapp, Joseph 9:113
Rapp, L. 12:96; 15:361;
19:94
Rapp, Lewis 10:75;
20:331
Rapp, Thomas J. 19:31
Rapp, William G. 11:74

Rappelbee, J. 11:311
Rapperill, John J. 15:221
Rapplogel, Daniel 19:31
Rapps, Daniel 11:289
Rapsie, H. 16:221
Rar---, Henry 15:221
Rarason, Jeff 24:179
Rarch, F. A. 20:181
Rarden, James 11:120
Rardin, J. F. 11:391
Rardon, John 20:331
Rarekes, H. 1:167
Rarey, C. P. 23:46
Rarey, H. B. 19:305
Rarey, James 18:296
Rarick, C. R. 16:51
Rarick, George T. 13:67
Rariden, James E. 22:97
Rariden, Michael 16:79
Rarig, George 11:269
Rarisch, John 9:16
Rarkertrans, William
18:314
Rarnold, Robert 18:374
Raro, Martin 18:250;
26:57
Rarr, M. L. 6:33
Rarret, H. H. 16:141
Rarrey, James 26:111
Rarrick, Jacob 19:31
Rarsbottom, A. F. 3:159
Rarse, Ernst 18:340
Rasaler, J. 1:70
Rasbeck, C. 1:166
Rasbeck, George 16:221
Rasberry, J. J. 24:27
Rasburg, Thomas J.
21:214
Rasch, W. 1:168
Rasche, Frank 10:8
Rase, P. 18:37
Raser, Cyrus S. 21:38
Rash, Ernest 22:168
Rash, J. M. 25:223
Rash, Meldon 19:288
Rasham, James 22:265
Rashaw, Benjamin 22:466
Rashel, Joseph 8:54
Rashly, Solomon 17:451;
24:179
Rasica, E. 15:43
Rasich, Joseph 21:241
Rasler, D. 18:17
Rasley, Anthony 15:221
Rasmanen, Peter 22:343
Rasmason, M. 20:331
Rasmason, Masker 10:75
Rasnewson, Rasmer
22:128
Raspberry, T. 24:69
Rassen, William 18:424

Rasser, Fred. 8:109
Rassett, Martin 17:41
Rassett, W. D. 27:105
Rasseu, William H. 9:241
Rassian, Jean 21:93
Rassmusson, A. 3:159
Rasson, A. 3:159
Rast, William R. 16:51
Rasten, G. 11:249
Rastifer, John 3:159
Rasy, Pierre A. 20:331
Rasy, Piery A. 10:132
Ratchford, W. H. 7:38
Ratchford, William 10:75;
    20:331
Ratcliff, A. 22:316
Ratcliff, Benjamin B.
    22:50
Ratcliff, Henry 21:196
Ratcliff, J. 3:159
Ratcliff, Jacob 22:128
Ratcliff, James 10:75
Ratcliff, John 10:75;
    20:331
Ratcliff, Linton 4:67
Ratcliff, M. 13:97; 14:19
Ratcliff, Moses 20:331
Ratcliff, N. 5:44
Ratcliff, Reuben 17:353
Ratcliff, Thomas 10:75;
    20:332
Ratcliffe, --- 15:268
Ratcliffe, James N. 22:265
Ratcliffe, John M. 24:55
Rateben, John 12:157
Ratell, Paul 17:244
Rater, Andrew 22:437
Rates, Joshua 11:212
Rates, Robert 17:151
Ratey, David 2:16
Ratfield, Robert 17:267
Rath, Chester 15:92
Rath, James 19:188
Rath, John P. 11:167
Rath, S. 14:101
Rathan, Jacob 11:248
Rathaway, Charles 14:209
Rathbane, Hiram 22:410
Rathbern, Henry 26:55
Rathbone, B. 3:159
Rathbone, Ebenezer
    22:153
Rathbone, George 24:27
Rathbone, Reuben 22:153
Rathbone, W. J. 22:215
Rathborne, William H. H.
    20:332
Rathbun, A. 25:223
Rathbun, Benjamin
    23:163
Rathbun, L. W. 1:68

Rathbun, M. 20:175
Rathburgh, W. W. 23:194
Rathburn, Alvah 5:27
Rathburn, David 21:142
Rathburn, E. 1:164
Rathburn, E. K. 9:89
Rathburn, G. 1:166
Rathburn, H. 17:293;
    19:241
Rathburn, J. 3:159
Rathburn, James A. 13:42
Rathburn, John N. 8:54;
    21:104
Rathburn, K. 3:159
Rathburn, M. S. 19:188
Rathburn, Mathew 10:174
Rathburn, Nathan 17:395
Rathburn, Samuel 12:36
Rathburne, J. L. 7:38
Rathcock, Todd 6:22
Rathemea, George 4:48
Rathers, George 22:515
Rathfon, Samuel 24:55
Rathful, Joel H. 4:48
Rathorford, J. 21:38
Rathwell, George W.
    17:57
Raticam, William 14:317
Ratican, John 21:58
Ratier, William 14:322;
    23:205
Ratigan, T. 14:101
Ratiman, W. 9:113
Rating, George 15:286
Ratler, Charles 24:162
Ratliff, J. W. 21:38
Ratliff, John 23:101
Ratliff, P. H. 16:221
Ratliff, Thomas 24:167
Ratliff, William 24:167
Ratlings, George 24:203
Ratlioff, N. 25:223
Ratly, David 25:66
Ratroff, Thomas 22:50
Ratskins, Martin 9:73
Ratsline, Hayward 8:93
Rattan, Robert N. 7:63
Rattenboom, Joseph 3:159
Rattera, Thomas I. 9:235
Ratteree, Thomas J.
    18:422
Rattery, J. 1:69
Rattery, John 3:159
Rattich, J. 7:53
Rattiean, John 22:343
Rattier, J. 26:179
Rattle, William 21:379
Rattleinggoard, Chris
    25:335
Rattler, Charles 17:420
Rau, John W. 1:69

Rau, Valentine 24:179
Rauard, Manuel 23:182
Raub, Isaac P. 11:165
Raub, S. 14:101
Raub, T. W. 23:46
Raudellhaw, --- 8:77
Rauf, Charles 12:36
Raugh, A. 1:68
Raugh, Valentine 12:36
Raulston, David 12:36
Raulston, Thomas H.
    22:50
Raunders, John A. 18:155
Rauner, S. 1:69
Rauppe, William 18:71
Raurey, F. J. 1:66
Raus, Matthew 20:28
Rauschenberger, Julius
    23:194
Raush, J. 23:163
Raush, John 24:27
Rautley, H. 25:63
Ravell, J. 22:215
Ravelle, John 13:117
Raven, J. K. 14:209
Ravenhoist, Frederick
    15:221
Ravens, H. 1:69
Raves, Jackson 5:44
Ravine, Amil 7:38
Ravlin, O. F. 25:303
Raw, A. 1:168
Raw, Henry 16:141
Raw, James W. 20:332
Raw, John 18:114
Rawalt, John 21:38
Rawcleff, J. W. 14:19
Rawden, E. 13:97
Rawdon, James 16:9
Rawhauser, Jesse 13:43;
    16:51
Rawin, Hanibal 22:316
Rawin, R. 22:316
Rawles, Joseph G. 11:249
Rawley, --- 24:179
Rawley, Frederick 22:437
Rawley, John 21:379
Rawley, John F. 2:16
Rawley, Otto 21:379
Rawley, Robert 12:36
Rawley, Samuel F. 21:232
Rawley, William 1:67;
    4:48
Rawlin, Orland F. 7:80
Rawling, Daniel B. 10:92;
    20:332
Rawling, Robert 7:38
Rawlings, Elijah D.
    24:154
Rawlings, G. S. 3:159
Rawlings, J. R. 17:149

Rawlings, J. W. 3:159
Rawlings, S. 3:159
Rawlins, Henry C. 10:97
Rawlins, J. T. 14:209
Rawlins, R. W. 19:31
Rawll, Sandy 22:524
Rawlston, J. 18:250;
    26:57
Rawlston, Samuel 22:265
Rawlston, W. C. 13:97
Rawson, --- 18:280
Rawson, A. S. 13:67
Rawson, Asa 21:232
Rawson, Charles 11:74;
    18:434
Rawson, Daniel 19:31
Rawson, Harvey S. 16:221
Rawson, Jefferson 17:426
Rawson, John 10:75;
    20:332
Rawson, L. F. 27:104
Rawson, L. W. 13:67;
    19:94
Rawson, Orlando 8:93
Rawson, Oscar 1:67
Rawson, P. 1:164
Rawson, Thomas 10:75;
    20:332
Raxdon, Z. F. 9:89
Ray, --- 10:192
Ray, A. 3:160
Ray, A. J. 16:51
Ray, Alfred E. 17:428;
    24:184
Ray, Alfred M. 12:54
Ray, Allan 14:101
Ray, Amos 22:283
Ray, Andrew 19:305
Ray, B. F. 14:209
Ray, Benjamin 11:73
Ray, C. 3:160; 18:37
Ray, C. L. 25:63
Ray, Charles 1:191; 5:44;
    23:109
Ray, Clement 9:210;
    18:71
Ray, Daniel 7:76; 25:303
Ray, David 9:28
Ray, David S. 10:170
Ray, Davis 22:316
Ray, Dewitt 16:221
Ray, E. 5:44; 25:223
Ray, E. L. 11:75
Ray, Edwin R. 10:154
Ray, Elijah 11:120; 12:36
Ray, F. 22:329
Ray, Felix G. 23:46
Ray, Frank 22:50
Ray, G. W. 9:89; 15:221;
    26:55
Ray, George 9:157; 11:42

Ray, George B. 26:179
Ray, George W. 10:149;
    17:200, 203; 18:55;
    22:113
Ray, Harvey M. 23:46
Ray, Henry 9:239; 17:137;
    24:202; 26:225
Ray, Henry L. 23:76
Ray, I. 14:101
Ray, I. B. 12:164
Ray, J. 3:160; 25:223
Ray, J. B. 26:179
Ray, J. C. 27:102
Ray, J. C. O. T. 11:339
Ray, J. H. 16:221
Ray, J. M. 14:19; 24:27
Ray, J. N. 13:97
Ray, J. T. 16:221
Ray, Jackson 11:42, 212
Ray, Jacob 17:137;
    24:202
Ray, Jacob S. 21:78
Ray, James 6:18; 9:104;
    11:43; 13:43; 16:134;
    18:91; 19:31; 23:182
Ray, James B. 23:46
Ray, James H. 25:65
Ray, James M. 22:266
Ray, James R. 3:160;
    9:224; 18:374
Ray, James T. 23:76
Ray, James W. 10:75
Ray, Jerry 6:13; 18:91;
    26:56
Ray, Joab 20:43
Ray, Joel O. 20:100
Ray, John 1:66; 5:44;
    20:184; 21:131;
    22:466; 23:13
Ray, John B. 7:38
Ray, John C. 9:149
Ray, John H. 10:132
Ray, John J. 24:43
Ray, John P. 19:31
Ray, John W. 24:162
Ray, John W. C. 17:420
Ray, Jonathan 21:58
Ray, Jonathan H. 20:332
Ray, Joseph 20:25
Ray, Joseph B. 7:16
Ray, L. A. 11:397
Ray, L. T. 9:210
Ray, Lafayette 27:147
Ray, Leonard 19:268
Ray, Lewis 25:325
Ray, Lucian 11:269
Ray, M. 14:209
Ray, Madison 15:73
Ray, Milan E. 19:275
Ray, Miller A. 22:436
Ray, Milton E. 9:190

Ray, N. 11:281
Ray, O. R. 9:224; 18:374
Ray, Orrin 15:23
Ray, Pendleton Q. 23:101
Ray, Philo 11:165
Ray, R. S. 3:160
Ray, Ralph 17:137, 139;
    24:202
Ray, Reuben 21:379
Ray, Richard 23:46
Ray, S. 14:101, 287, 289;
    23:96
Ray, Samuel 13:97; 23:46;
    24:102; 25:269
Ray, Samuel O. 22:283
Ray, Simon 17:190, 398
Ray, Stephen 11:435
Ray, T. C. W. 19:94
Ray, T. E. 1:67
Ray, W. B. 13:67
Ray, W. G. 11:269;
    14:133
Ray, W. H. 12:36; 21:38
Ray, W. J. 14:320
Ray, Washington 22:343
Ray, William 1:67; 3:159;
    7:78; 8:126; 9:135;
    19:31; 22:97; 25:303;
    27:147
Ray, William A. 22:97
Ray, William E. 24:184
Ray, William F. 11:311
Ray, William H. 16:113
Ray, Willie S. 11:121
Rayal, Morris J. 9:215
Rayan, James 10:166;
    19:188
Raybern, Andrew 18:155
Rayborn, A. 23:205
Rayborn, Enoch L. 11:249
Rayborn, Samuel 17:252
Raybour, A. 14:279
Raybourn, David T. 23:76
Raybuck, David R.
    20:100, 134
Raybur, H. 15:43
Rayburn, A. 14:322;
    23:46
Rayburn, Alfred D.
    14:317
Rayburn, Andrew I. 8:28
Rayburn, Caleb 8:93
Rayburn, John 20:100
Rayburn, Mack 19:31
Raycort, E. 14:209
Rayder, James 11:311
Rayer, David 2:16
Rayer, Mathew 7:63
Rayes, J. M. 12:172
Rayes, L. A. 1:69
Rayfield, William 11:248

Rayl, F. 3:160
Rayl, Harman 18:222
Rayle, Thomas 22:489
Rayle, William 26:177
Raylon, Thomas 20:84
Rayman, A. 18:55
Rayman, H. 14:20
Rayman, Henry W. 9:89
Raymer, Andrew 14:209
Raymer, H. 22:354
Raymer, John 26:58
Raymond, Albert 9:106
Raymond, Alfred A.
    17:389
Raymond, Alonzo 7:107
Raymond, B. 9:154;
    27:102
Raymond, Benjamin D.
    6:28
Raymond, Bringham
    24:27
Raymond, C. 3:224;
    17:500
Raymond, C. E. 14:209;
    25:303
Raymond, Chauncy E.
    7:80
Raymond, E. D. 21:379
Raymond, Edgar 17:452;
    24:182
Raymond, Elias 21:142
Raymond, Ernest 21:232
Raymond, F. 14:209
Raymond, F. W. 12:36
Raymond, Francis 14:101;
    19:330
Raymond, George 13:43
Raymond, George W.
    9:16
Raymond, H. 6:33; 13:97;
    25:326
Raymond, Henry 12:62;
    15:92
Raymond, Henry L.
    23:109
Raymond, Horne 21:379
Raymond, Isaac 16:221
Raymond, Israel 22:283
Raymond, J. E. 18:37;
    21:379
Raymond, J. G. 9:149;
    27:101
Raymond, Jeremiah 11:17
Raymond, John 7:107
Raymond, Juno 22:237
Raymond, Lewis 11:75
Raymond, Livius 20:180
Raymond, Moses 27:148
Raymond, N. 25:65
Raymond, R. F. 7:107
Raymond, S. 13:117

Raymond, S. J. 23:243
Raymond, Thomas 11:86
Raymond, V. 16:221
Raymond, W. D. 1:165
Raymond, W. H. 16:221
Raymond, Walker 14:209
Raymond, Walter 4:48;
    16:221
Raymond, William 7:38;
    14:334; 16:101
Raymond, William M.
    22:437
Raymor, Lam 1:66
Raymor, Noah 11:75
Raymore, George 21:379
Raymore, Lindsay L.
    12:36
Rayn, James 17:428
Raynard, F. 3:160
Rayner, M. 14:259
Raynes, G. B. 7:38
Raynold, Charles 21:379
Raynold, Christian 21:379
Raynold, William 21:379
Raynolds, A. 14:20
Raynolds, Cyrus R.
    17:354
Raynolds, F. 3:160
Raynolds, H. T. 17:435
Raynolds, J. 14:20
Raynolds, Z. T. 15:345
Raynor, Calvin 13:43
Raynor, E. 13:67; 19:94
Raynor, Henry 13:43;
    16:51
Raynor, Louis 3:160
Raynor, M. 14:209
Raynor, W. 1:165
Raynor, W. H. 8:29;
    18:155
Raynor, William I. 21:125
Rayo, John 4:48
Raypole, Isaac 8:93
Rays, B. F. 11:269
Rays, Charles 11:167
Rays, Levi L. 13:117
Rays, Marion 21:191, 291
Raysdale, A. G. 8:28
Rayser, John J. 19:31
Rayshaw, George I. 10:75
Rayson, Thomas 20:194
Rayster, T. 14:101
Rayward, James 12:36
Raz, William 27:103
Raze, John 12:36
Razel, Right 22:343
Razer, Welmington
    22:456
Razette, V. 1:164
Razey, Hiram 9:106;
    18:335

Razier, A. 27:101
Razmay, Henry M. 26:55
Rd---, G. C. 18:17
Re---, E. 21:209
Rea, Albert W. 17:25
Rea, Charles 25:223
Rea, Charles W. 22:50
Rea, D. M. 15:345
Rea, Donegan 9:89
Rea, Henry 23:163
Rea, J. W. 18:56
Rea, John 11:165
Rea, John K. 4:48
Rea, Knox 9:224; 18:374
Rea, W. H. 26:55
Rea, William G. 22:215
Rea, William H. 9:89
Reaba, John 10:132;
    20:332
Reach, Valentine 8:29
Read, A. 15:221; 23:309
Read, A. J. 14:289; 23:47
Read, Abner 9:190
Read, Alex 19:188;
    23:198
Read, Anson E. 18:374
Read, Asa R. 19:31
Read, Birdville 11:404
Read, Charles 1:68;
    15:111
Read, David 8:54
Read, Elvin 27:105
Read, Franklin 10:75;
    20:332
Read, G. H. 3:160
Read, George 10:21
Read, George A. 11:404
Read, George W. 10:132;
    20:332; 21:233
Read, Henry J. 9:190
Read, Hiram Rufus
    25:335
Read, J. 25:223
Read, J. A. 11:248
Read, Jacob S. 6:33
Read, John 9:124; 20:12
Read, Jonathan 17:426
Read, Joseph 9:38
Read, Melvin 11:404
Read, O. 10:149
Read, P. 11:43
Read, P. S. 25:326
Read, Preston A. 18:155
Read, S. S. 9:124
Read, Samuel B. 23:47
Read, Samuel W. 20:36
Read, Silas 22:128
Read, Stephen S. 21:247
Read, W. 7:38
Read, William 5:27;
    15:222; 25:223

Reade, Abel 22:410
Readen, Michael 25:223
Reader, Isaac 17:356
Reader, Isaac N. 17:232
Reader, J. 11:75
Reader, Jacob 9:45
Reader, James A. 23:185
Reader, James O. 27:104
Reader, John 15:88
Reader, John R. 9:9
Reader, Marion J. 20:127
Reader, Spencer 21:282
Reader, Walter V. 11:42
Reader, William 17:362
Reader, William H. A. 22:237
Readern, Patrick 12:157
Readers, Samuel 22:316
Reading, Aaron 22:97
Reading, C. 25:223
Reading, Frank 7:107
Reading, Henry 22:343
Reading, M. 24:83
Reading, Mathew 24:114
Reading, Samuel 10:132; 20:332
Readle, James A. 9:224; 18:374
Readman, H. T. 14:101
Readman, J. 1:69
Readman, William 3:160
Readmore, E. 18:374
Readmore, Edward 9:224
Ready, Albert 20:127
Ready, Charles 9:124
Ready, Charles W. 14:209
Ready, J. C. 1:66
Ready, James 5:27
Ready, James G. 24:43
Ready, Michael 7:81; 14:209
Ready, Nathaniel 11:211
Reafasall, Henry 14:209
Reafeldt, Frederick 19:332
Reagan, Daniel 4:48
Reagan, George W. 3:160
Reagan, J. 1:167
Reagan, James 21:379
Reagan, John 25:326; 27:105
Reagan, Michael 25:223
Reagan, P. S. 21:95
Reagan, W. H. 20:140
Reagan, William S. 7:60
Reager, Joseph 25:223
Reagles, G. M. 16:101
Reagles, Lawrence 4:48
Reagsden, John 23:101
Reagy, J. F. 19:259

Reahard, J. 18:314; 26:110
Reahard, William C. 25:280
Reahine, Frank 18:440
Reahm, Th. 21:38
Reaire, John 18:155
Reak, R. M. 17:294
Reaker, Andrew 17:353
Reaker, J. 22:316
Reaky, John 17:162
Real, Ferdinand 13:127
Real, James 12:51
Realer, William F. 17:402
Reales, Edward 26:110
Reals, F. M. 9:58
Reals, Henry 1:68
Ream, D. L. 11:73
Ream, Frank 22:489
Ream, J. J. 11:74
Ream, J. P. 1:95
Ream, John 7:60
Ream, John P. 17:274
Ream, N. O. 10:75
Ream, Samuel 20:89
Reamer, Henry 19:31
Reamer, J. C. 19:94
Reamer, Jesse 21:58
Reamer, William 13:43; 21:196
Reamond, John 19:94
Reams, J. 1:167; 24:83
Reams, J. L. 16:221
Reams, James F. 20:59
Reams, James M. 22:343
Reams, Joseph 22:237
Reams, Oscar F. 4:48
Reams, Solomon 11:167
Reams, William Perry 22:14
Reams, Zephaniah 22:153
Reamy, J. H. 3:160
Reandon, J. 18:250; 26:57
Reanvy, E. 21:168
Reap, N. 1:164
Reaper, Joseph P. 8:93
Rearadon, P. A. 18:400
Reardon, D. 3:160
Reardon, Edward 25:326
Reardon, J. J. 18:250
Reardon, James A. 1:67
Reardon, Jeremiah 10:21
Reardon, Jerry 26:179
Reardon, John 11:167; 12:168
Reardon, Michael 15:222
Reardon, Patrick 21:379
Reardon, T. 15:365
Reardon, Theodore 5:27
Reardon, Timothy 9:67
Reardon, William 25:223

Rearne, J. 19:259
Rearnon, James 20:116
Reary, J. 19:94
Reary, James 14:101
Rease, Jacob 3:160
Rease, John 9:224; 11:167; 18:374
Rease, Norman A. 16:221
Reasen, James 18:56
Reaser, Nelson 16:123
Reasler, A. 16:377
Reasley, --- 11:248
Reason, Charles R. 9:135
Reason, G. W. 25:275
Reason, George 27:101
Reason, Isaac 9:190
Reason, Joshua 10:132
Reason, Robert S. 17:25
Reason, Thompson 8:59
Reason, W. F. 12:147
Reasoner, Hiram 10:75
Reasoner, John W. 21:78
Reasoner, Thomas 23:163
Reasor, John W. 20:19
Reasor, Joshua 20:332
Reaster, A. 15:345
Reater, M. 13:67
Reater, Mority 19:94
Reatherford, Alexander R. 22:266
Reaussau, C. H. 2:16
Reaut, Warme 9:58
Reavard, William 17:416
Reave, I. W. 15:222
Reavers, James 21:239
Reaves, C. T. 10:180; 18:179
Reaves, J. W. 17:336
Reaves, James A. 17:57
Reaves, John V. 8:74
Reaves, M. 3:160
Reaves, Samuel 11:212
Reaves, Uel 23:268
Reaves, William 15:133
Reavis, J. J. 21:13
Reavis, Robert R. 22:266
Reawem, William 18:193
Reay, Ch. 15:43
Reay, Charles E. 22:14
Reay, Peter 11:165
Reayse, William H. 13:43
Rebe, B. L. 20:43
Rebel, Fred 20:332
Rebel, Frederick 10:75
Rebel, Johann 20:127
Reber, F. 17:200
Reber, J. B. 14:209
Rebern, E. 9:58
Rebley, R. 25:303
Rebout, William 15:300
Reburan, I. 14:209

Recalt, S. 3:160
Recand, John 12:93
Rece, D. M. 16:377
Rece, E. F. 1:164
Recholter, George 22:237
Reckard, J. 1:165
Recker, --- 14:209
Recker, Benjamin 4:48
Recker, Christian 9:73
Recker, W. B. 21:78
Reckes, John B. 15:259
Reckhow, J. 3:160
Reckler, Joseph 23:124
Reckless, James 12:51
Recklighter, Lewis 11:212
Reckman, F. H. 8:74;
    26:179
Record, G. 25:223
Record, James E. 4:48
Record, Martin V. 23:76
Record, Russell L. 17:350
Records, C. 19:259
Records, William H.
    25:64
Recsterer, L. 1:69
Rectchter, Augustus 5:53
Rectemwald, Jacob
    22:467
Recton, Nathan 11:75
Rector, --- 18:179
Rector, Almier 10:75
Rector, Benjamin 9:104;
    18:340
Rector, Charles 20:116,
    332
Rector, Charles J. 22:168
Rector, David 17:353
Rector, Frank W. 22:215
Rector, George 17:41
Rector, George W. 16:67
Rector, James 19:31
Rector, John W. 24:27
Rector, Simon 8:93
Rector, Walter H. 22:437
Recure, John 8:29
Red, Andrew 10:21
Red, George 22:215
Red, Henry 22:316
Red, James 9:113
Red, John 11:42
Red River Stigger 25:335
Red---, J. R. 23:205
Redabaugh, Chan 22:50
Redan, J. 14:20
Redan, John 16:221
Redant, Christian 11:117
Redburn, Ellis 23:47
Redburn, John 17:274
Redclough, O. 11:249
Redd, C. 3:160
Redd, Franklin 11:167

Redden, H. R. 18:250
Redden, J. 3:160
Redden, Joseph 17:274
Redden, Luther 12:51
Redder, G. 3:160
Redderman, Lewis 9:190
Reddick, --- 18:37
Reddick, A. 1:68
Reddick, Frank 25:223
Reddick, Harvey 21:379
Reddick, J. M. 17:41
Reddick, Jack 21:282
Reddick, Lawson 22:215
Reddick, M. W. 15:175
Reddick, Newton 6:26
Reddick, Samuel 7:65
Reddick, W. P. 18:179
Reddick, William 22:316
Reddin, James 1:66
Redding, Abraham 4:67
Redding, G. W. 21:125
Redding, George 10:166
Redding, George W.
    24:27
Redding, J. 19:259
Redding, J. F. 20:134
Redding, Jacob 12:51
Redding, James 9:190
Redding, James F. 20:332
Redding, John 22:215
Redding, John L. 21:233
Redding, L. M. 19:48
Redding, M. D. 18:193
Redding, Rufus 17:428;
    24:184
Redding, William H.
    22:97
Reddington, W. B. 20:332
Reddish, Marquis L.
    20:105
Reddix, James 16:51
Reddo, D. V. 3:160
Reddy, Thomas 23:76
Redeemer, David 27:147
Redell, P. 15:273
Redell, Ransom 16:303
Reden, Barney J. 21:131
Reden, D. 16:377
Redenour, J. 15:133
Reder, C. 3:160
Reder, J. 13:97
Reder, John 22:410
Rederick, William 19:271
Redfan, John W. 20:332
Redfare, John W. 9:231
Redfaren, W. A. 11:438
Redfern, --- 15:222
Redfern, Francis 23:47
Redferrin, Aaron W.
    22:50
Redferrin, Berry 22:50

Redfield, --- 10:166
Redfield, G. C. 20:134
Redfield, I. M. 10:75
Redfield, J. M. 20:332
Redfield, L. W. 9:149;
    27:101
Redfield, Orange S.
    17:423
Redfield, Orin S. 24:173
Redfield, S. T. 14:101
Redfield, Wilils 19:188
Redford, John 22:266
Redford, Nathaniel H.
    22:50
Redford, Pat 16:377
Redforn, Joseph 21:38
Redfu, J. H. 11:248
Redgers, W. G. 17:162
Redhead, J. 1:166
Redhead, J. B. 11:403
Redheffer, Benjamin 7:14
Redick, R. 1:167
Redick, Royal 22:283
Redig, John 11:184
Reding, Alfred 21:233
Reding, Cornelius 5:44
Reding, George W.
    22:410
Reding, Joseph F. 9:231
Redinger, F. 26:138
Redinger, Ferdinand
    23:163
Redingler, Benjamin
    13:117
Redington, J. P. 15:26
Redington, James L. 10:21
Redington, William B.
    10:75
Redley, Charles 22:316
Redlon, Almon H. 7:107
Redman, Alvis C. 23:185
Redman, C. 15:222
Redman, C. E. 21:217
Redman, C. W. 8:67
Redman, Cornelius
    22:456
Redman, David R. 22:215
Redman, G. 10:132;
    20:332
Redman, George W.
    17:85, 137; 24:202
Redman, Henry 11:42
Redman, J. 3:160; 15:361;
    19:94
Redman, J. F. 9:28;
    18:314; 26:110
Redman, James 12:36
Redman, John M. 22:14
Redman, Louis 19:259
Redman, Moses 11:391
Redman, N. E. 3:160

Redman, Robert 11:74;
    24:203
Redman, Robert B. 24:28
Redman, S. 17:183
Redman, S. C. 16:51
Redman, S. G. 23:163
Redman, Samuel 8:54
Redman, Sylvester 23:163
Redman, Thomas 14:209;
    18:400
Redman, Thomas C. 10:21
Redman, Thomas J.
    17:353
Redman, W. R. 3:160
Redmann, Frank 23:163
Redmen, J. 12:96
Redment, John 3:160
Redmire, H. 3:160
Redmond, A. 25:223
Redmond, C. N. 26:179
Redmond, D. 11:232
Redmond, J. 3:160
Redmond, James 9:113;
    22:14
Redmond, John 10:166;
    15:300, 327; 16:221;
    19:188
Redmond, M. 15:222
Redmond, P. 14:209
Redmond, Robert 11:111;
    22:437
Redmond, William Perry
    17:203
Redmore, Spalding 9:237;
    26:225
Redna, T. I. 8:29
Redneck, J. E. 15:259
Redner, Henry C. 23:307
Rednock, J. E. 14:131
Rednower, Louis 12:36
Rednowers, George W.
    17:97
Redo, Louis 21:379
Redpath, Robert 12:36
Redpey, Alfred J. 7:38
Redrick, Bolson 9:156
Redrick, G. H. 16:136
Redrick, Harrison 16:221
Redrow, William 16:113
Redsell, Bradford 15:167
Redson, Charles R.
    27:102
Redson, Fred 4:48
Redson, Stephen 15:351;
    16:377
Redsure, L. 19:94
Reducer, Jacob 11:110
Redun, T. J. 18:155
Redwick, Harvey 7:132
Redwood, W. 5:53
Redwood, William 25:223

Redy, John 19:31
Redyard, A. 3:160
Reeb, A. 1:95
Reeb, Henry 13:43
Reebe, Henry 24:96
Reeber, James B. 14:209
Reece, Amer 23:163
Reece, B. 25:223
Reece, C. 20:181
Reece, Frank 22:343
Reece, Henry 17:453;
    24:184
Reece, Hubbard W.
    22:456
Reece, Jeremiah 24:83
Reece, John 25:276
Reece, John H. 22:215
Reece, Martin 17:238
Reece, Matthew D. 22:436
Reece, Philip 18:92
Reece, William H. 20:332
Reech, John 15:43
Reed, --- 8:54; 18:193;
    26:179
Reed, A. 1:66; 3:160;
    17:295
Reed, A. A. 14:101
Reed, A. C. 1:69
Reed, A. J. 21:379
Reed, A. M. 13:97; 14:20
Reed, A. R. 3:160
Reed, Aaron 9:135;
    23:163
Reed, Abner H. 15:160
Reed, Abraham 10:132;
    20:332
Reed, Albert 21:243;
    22:437
Reed, Alexander 21:125
Reed, Alexander N. 15:94
Reed, Alfred 22:97;
    27:104
Reed, Alfred M. 21:379
Reed, Allan 14:101
Reed, Alonzo 7:107
Reed, Ambrose 15:167
Reed, Amos 21:233
Reed, Amos B. 8:109
Reed, Amos W. 22:215
Reed, Andrew 12:9
Reed, Andrew J. 12:55;
    22:436
Reed, Andrew T. 8:109
Reed, Angus N. 22:409
Reed, Anson E. 9:224
Reed, Asa 15:12
Reed, B. G. 14:101
Reed, B. Miles 11:398
Reed, Bailey 17:274
Reed, Benjamin 5:44
Reed, Benjamin S. 20:105

Reed, Burrell 22:456
Reed, Byron M. 23:76
Reed, C. 3:160; 8:109;
    11:73, 232
Reed, C. B. 12:75; 15:82
Reed, C. F. 9:149; 27:102
Reed, C. H. 16:87; 24:83
Reed, C. O. 13:126
Reed, Charles 3:160;
    9:158; 10:93; 11:403;
    12:36, 96; 13:43;
    14:302; 15:361;
    17:477; 18:37, 250;
    20:332; 22:153;
    25:223; 26:56;
    27:105
Reed, Charles H. 20:25;
    25:223
Reed, Charles P. 4:48
Reed, Chester S. 13:43
Reed, Clark 23:47
Reed, Clark C. 10:92;
    20:332
Reed, Cyrus 11:42
Reed, D. 3:160; 7:38;
    11:42; 14:302;
    17:478; 26:55;
    27:105
Reed, D. C. 14:209
Reed, D. W. 3:160
Reed, Daniel 1:68; 22:505
Reed, David 11:167;
    13:43; 14:209;
    16:101; 18:407
Reed, David A. 15:133
Reed, David B. 14:317,
    322; 23:15
Reed, David E. 7:107
Reed, Degaffin 16:221
Reed, Delos 19:330
Reed, E. 1:67; 21:379
Reed, E. C. 4:48; 14:279
Reed, Eben 23:194
Reed, Edward 14:209;
    17:405; 18:91
Reed, Edwin 1:67; 9:161
Reed, Elbridge 9:69
Reed, Elias 20:19
Reed, Elias M. 24:55
Reed, Emory 6:18; 18:92
Reed, Eugene 13:68
Reed, Ewell 10:97
Reed, F. 13:97
Reed, F. H. 22:14
Reed, F. K. 3:160
Reed, F. M. 21:168;
    22:489; 23:257
Reed, F. R. 3:160
Reed, F. W. 21:379
Reed, Francis 12:36;
    16:160; 20:127

Reed, Frank A. 9:106
Reed, Franklin 9:58; 10:132; 20:332
Reed, Frederick 1:67
Reed, G. H. 23:163
Reed, G. I. 16:221
Reed, G. W. 3:160
Reed, George 4:48; 7:132; 8:29; 9:190; 10:75; 11:111; 14:101, 209; 16:221; 17:183; 18:155, 179; 19:259; 20:332; 22:237
Reed, George C. 9:161; 27:105
Reed, George L. 9:67; 16:221; 18:280; 21:142
Reed, George O. 25:223
Reed, George W. 10:75; 18:37; 22:128
Reed, H. 14:209; 25:223, 284
Reed, H. A. 13:126
Reed, H. G. 9:89; 26:56
Reed, H. H. 3:160
Reed, H. J. 20:156
Reed, H. M. 15:222
Reed, Harman 3:224
Reed, Harmon 17:503
Reed, Harrison 22:97
Reed, Harvey 13:117
Reed, Henry 4:48; 5:27; 10:75; 18:250; 20:332; 22:97, 316; 26:58, 179
Reed, Henry J. 19:271
Reed, Henry L. 22:50
Reed, Henry S. 11:75
Reed, Herbert 26:177
Reed, Hines 13:43
Reed, Hiram 21:58
Reed, Hiram A. 15:153
Reed, Horace 22:316
Reed, Howard 14:209
Reed, I. W. 12:157
Reed, Irwin 21:125
Reed, Isaac 22:437
Reed, Isam 17:398
Reed, J. 1:67; 3:160; 9:58; 13:117; 15:27, 259; 17:293; 18:56; 24:83; 25:66, 223
Reed, J. B. 15:133
Reed, J. C. 15:73; 22:115
Reed, J. F. 22:215
Reed, J. H. 1:164; 7:38
Reed, J. J. 1:70; 9:227; 12:75; 15:18; 18:374; 25:223
Reed, J. L. W. 24:83

Reed, J. M. 3:160; 25:288
Reed, J. R. 1:166; 17:151
Reed, J. S. 1:166; 13:68
Reed, J. W. 1:164
Reed, Jacob L. 11:166
Reed, Jahiel 10:132; 20:332
Reed, James 10:149; 11:167; 12:75; 13:58; 15:43; 17:184; 18:56; 19:94; 22:50, 266; 24:83
Reed, James C. 14:209
Reed, James J. 21:142
Reed, James L. 23:194
Reed, James M. 10:132; 20:332
Reed, James R. 19:94
Reed, Jeremiah 19:31
Reed, Jeremiah N. 13:43; 16:51
Reed, Jeseuh 15:222
Reed, Jesse 5:44
Reed, Joel 13:43
Reed, John 1:66; 3:160; 7:53; 8:74, 93; 9:15, 45, 201; 10:21; 16:221; 17:238; 18:56; 19:292; 21:233; 22:14, 168, 489; 23:277; 26:128
Reed, John C. 3:160
Reed, John E. 22:50
Reed, John J. 5:27; 9:89, 98; 26:55
Reed, John O. 24:154
Reed, John P. 26:55
Reed, John S. 14:101; 22:266
Reed, John W. 1:68; 11:74; 22:438
Reed, Jonathan 19:222
Reed, Jonathan P. 9:89
Reed, Joseph 5:27; 7:38; 11:188; 15:111; 16:221; 18:92; 22:266, 466; 26:178, 179
Reed, Joseph A. 24:69
Reed, Joseph W. 4:48
Reed, L. 11:73; 14:209
Reed, Leonard 25:223
Reed, Leverett 11:166
Reed, Levi 18:250; 22:489; 26:58
Reed, Lewis 17:215
Reed, Lewis W. 11:75
Reed, Luard 10:132
Reed, M. 1:66
Reed, M. H. 18:37
Reed, M. T. 20:87

Reed, Manuel 21:104
Reed, Marcus M. 7:84; 21:379
Reed, Martin 9:237; 22:153; 26:225
Reed, Martin R. 15:222
Reed, Mathias 10:132
Reed, Matthias 20:332
Reed, Melvin 10:132
Reed, Melvin H. 20:333
Reed, Monroe F. 13:43
Reed, Moses D. 7:53
Reed, N. M. 13:117
Reed, Nathaniel 12:36; 21:151
Reed, Nicholas 11:86
Reed, Noah 17:184
Reed, Norman A. 16:222
Reed, O. 18:56
Reed, O. H. 11:289
Reed, Oliver 17:137, 433; 24:162, 202
Reed, Oliver H. P. 24:55
Reed, Otis 10:75, 210; 20:333
Reed, P. W. 1:165
Reed, Perry 17:47
Reed, Peter 1:69; 19:94
Reed, Philander C. 11:42
Reed, Preston A. 8:29
Reed, R. 3:160
Reed, R. B. 14:101
Reed, R. J. 11:42
Reed, Richard 6:26; 11:212; 23:77
Reed, Robert 14:101; 20:127; 23:77, 163
Reed, S. 16:377; 18:250; 26:57
Reed, S. G. 3:160
Reed, S. S. 9:113, 124; 19:188
Reed, Samuel 3:160; 4:48; 12:36; 16:222; 18:17; 19:31; 22:237
Reed, Samuel D. 4:48
Reed, Samuel G. 8:29; 18:155
Reed, Samuel S. 17:85
Reed, Seaborn 8:29
Reed, Shelbourne C. 19:347
Reed, Shellowrne C. 13:135
Reed, Silas 7:60; 15:279; 25:223
Reed, Silas L. 15:18
Reed, Starling B. 22:215
Reed, Stephen W. 17:41
Reed, Suard 20:332
Reed, Sylvester 17:184

Reed, T. 15:279; 25:223
Reed, T. B. 1:66
Reed, T. E. 11:167
Reed, Theodore 8:93
Reed, Thomas 5:44;
    10:174; 11:165;
    15:222; 17:41, 267;
    19:188; 22:266, 410
Reed, Thomas A. 22:215
Reed, Thomas H. 20:25
Reed, Thomas J. 18:155
Reed, Thomas P. 3:160
Reed, Thurston 17:57
Reed, Timothy 7:38
Reed, W. 1:164; 3:160;
    14:209; 18:179;
    20:333; 21:379
Reed, W. B. 20:59
Reed, W. D. 3:160;
    17:433
Reed, W. F. 8:54; 11:269;
    17:489
Reed, W. H. 21:379
Reed, W. H. H. 1:164
Reed, W. J. 14:101
Reed, W. L. 11:249
Reed, W. R. 21:217
Reed, W. S. 3:160
Reed, Warren 22:97
Reed, Warren S. 4:48
Reed, Washington F.
    21:58
Reed, Webster 9:201
Reed, William 7:132;
    8:42, 67; 10:75, 192;
    11:289; 12:36;
    17:137; 18:92, 114,
    340; 22:489; 23:164,
    309; 25:64; 26:178
Reed, William A. 10:21;
    16:51
Reed, William Alex 13:43
Reed, William B. 21:104,
    380
Reed, William D. 24:161
Reed, William H. 10:132;
    11:101; 14:209;
    16:281
Reed, William H. H. 4:48
Reed, William P. 24:55
Reed, William R. 9:124;
    27:102
Reed, William S. 14:209
Reed, William T. 22:153
Reed, Williams 24:202
Reed, Williard H. 9:124;
    27:104
Reed, Willis 24:161
Reed, Wilson 21:213
Reed, Winfield S. 23:77
Reede, C. J. 1:167

Reede, E. 1:165
Reede, E. W. 25:65
Reede, G. 14:20
Reede, Henry 24:96
Reede, Thomas I. 8:29
Reede, William 17:393
Reeder, A. D. 9:190;
    19:271
Reeder, Aaron 18:296;
    26:110
Reeder, Allen B. 17:85
Reeder, Charles 16:51
Reeder, David 12:157
Reeder, E. C. 25:223
Reeder, Elijah 14:302;
    17:474
Reeder, Evan C. 5:27
Reeder, Facrider 11:391
Reeder, George 7:132
Reeder, George O. 22:215
Reeder, Henry Barton
    22:489
Reeder, J. H. 11:249;
    17:92
Reeder, Jacob 22:498
Reeder, Jeremiah 18:296
Reeder, Joseph W. 23:164
Reeder, Levi 23:164
Reeder, Lewis J. 12:75
Reeder, Robert 17:445
Reeder, Robert F. 24:164
Reeder, Zachariah 9:38
Reeder, Zacheriah 26:111
Reeders, Frank 22:516
Reedey, George 17:25
Reedey, Joseph 22:50
Reedman, M. 4:48
Reeds, William 15:222
Reedy, Daniel W. 18:400
Reedy, George 19:31
Reedy, J. 1:167
Reedy, James P. 22:410
Reedy, Joseph 12:157
Reedy, L. D. 3:161
Reedy, Michael 15:73
Reedy, Nathaniel 9:28
Reedy, Thomas A. 16:154
Reedy, William 13:43,
    126; 14:209
Reefe, John 25:288
Reefsnyder, John 4:48
Reegan, Daniel 27:104
Reegard, R. 14:101
Reeghard, William 13:117
Reehl, C. 19:275
Reek, Charles 9:106
Reek, Herbert 25:65
Reel, James 22:50
Reel, John D. 24:28
Reel, Oliver P. 22:113
Reel, William 22:97

Reelhom, Jesse 17:321
Reeling, J. 3:161
Reelingson, T. 9:58
Reelly, Patrick 8:29
Reels, L. 25:326
Reem, A. 3:161
Reem, Colvin 10:32
Reeman, J. 16:148
Reemer, Stephen 10:75
Reen, Adam 16:281
Reender, Eddert 17:288
Reenders, Eddert 22:467
Reenes, Moses 11:329
Reeres, J. N. 19:31
Rees, Amos F. 7:38
Rees, George L. 24:55
Rees, J. 1:166
Rees, John 13:43
Rees, Joseph 22:97
Rees, R. M. 27:102
Rees, Thomas 3:161;
    21:93; 25:65
Rees, William 11:86, 391;
    12:36
Rees, William B. 10:93
Rees, William M. 23:47
Reese, --- 6:26; 18:374
Reese, A. 3:161
Reese, A. B. 25:223
Reese, A. L. 9:89
Reese, A. W. 19:332
Reese, Adolphus 18:427
Reese, Alexander 22:237
Reese, Alfred 21:380
Reese, Amos 7:107
Reese, Amos B. 5:27
Reese, August 12:59
Reese, Benjamin 22:343
Reese, Burel 9:224
Reese, Charles 9:231;
    19:94
Reese, Charles G. 22:471
Reese, Christian 9:89;
    26:55
Reese, D. 3:161; 23:164
Reese, Daniel 22:316
Reese, Daniel A. 10:132;
    20:333
Reese, David 12:36
Reese, David J. 23:194
Reese, Griffith 17:92
Reese, Harloid P. 16:51
Reese, Harlow P. 13:43
Reese, Henry 7:107;
    21:380; 22:237;
    23:164
Reese, Hiram 25:66
Reese, J. 21:209; 25:63,
    223
Reese, J. A. 27:101
Reese, J. E. 16:222

Reese, J. H. 17:92
Reese, Jacob 17:25
Reese, James 1:68; 18:37; 26:128
Reese, James H. 11:269
Reese, Jesse 10:132; 20:333
Reese, John 5:27; 9:239; 26:225
Reese, John A. 22:437
Reese, Joseph 10:155
Reese, Levi 11:42
Reese, Martin 25:273
Reese, Nelson 22:316
Reese, O. 3:161
Reese, R. 3:161
Reese, Richard 20:43
Reese, S. 3:161; 18:37
Reese, S. F. 14:236
Reese, Samuel W. 16:51
Reese, T. J. 9:237; 26:225
Reese, Theodore 18:210
Reese, Thomas 9:67; 13:43; 18:280
Reese, W. H. 17:393
Reese, William 3:161; 8:93; 9:38; 11:184; 16:222; 18:296; 22:50; 26:111
Reese, William A. 22:266
Reese, William B. 20:333
Reese, Winchester 9:210; 18:71
Reeser, David M. 15:287
Reeser, Jacob 14:101
Reeser, James A. 9:58
Reeser, Samuel 20:31
Reesler, G. 14:209
Reesock, --- 24:96
Reesoe, Edward 18:296
Reeson, T. H. 14:209
Reeson, William 8:29
Reespath, Johnston 11:167
Reeve, A. J. 20:179
Reeve, Alfred 7:107
Reeve, C. D. S. 20:333
Reeve, Cephas 12:157
Reeve, G. 3:161
Reeve, James B. 21:78
Reeve, James M. 20:108
Reeves, A. 3:161; 11:165; 12:157
Reeves, A. G. 21:112
Reeves, A. P. 23:253
Reeves, Burrell 11:74
Reeves, C. S. 13:97
Reeves, C. W. 12:157
Reeves, Charles 21:142
Reeves, Christopher 22:215

Reeves, Clark 8:54; 21:78
Reeves, Daniel F. 18:374
Reeves, E. 3:160
Reeves, Edwin B. 17:201
Reeves, Elishen 11:97
Reeves, Francis M. 9:190; 19:271
Reeves, Gates 21:151
Reeves, George 22:163
Reeves, George W. 3:160; 17:238
Reeves, H. 1:66
Reeves, H. C. 12:157
Reeves, Hackless 8:42; 26:178
Reeves, Hazel S. 11:73
Reeves, Henry 8:67; 26:178
Reeves, Henry B. 13:43
Reeves, Isaac 21:283
Reeves, J. 3:161
Reeves, Jackson 9:45
Reeves, Jesse 22:266
Reeves, Jesse S. 23:185
Reeves, John 3:160; 10:166; 18:285; 19:188; 23:47; 26:135
Reeves, John A. 13:43; 24:55
Reeves, John H. 11:166; 23:92, 164
Reeves, John M. 8:109
Reeves, John V. 26:179
Reeves, John W. 10:132; 20:333
Reeves, Jonathan 18:335
Reeves, Jordan 9:106
Reeves, Lewis 17:416; 21:283; 24:154
Reeves, Lorenzo 9:58
Reeves, Morris 13:43; 16:51
Reeves, Mos L. 9:89
Reeves, S. 14:244
Reeves, S. I. 3:161
Reeves, S. S. 23:304
Reeves, Sanders 16:51
Reeves, T. 3:160
Reeves, Thomas 22:153
Reeves, W. 1:164
Reeves, W. J. 7:38
Reeves, W. L. 26:110
Reeves, Washington 11:211
Reeves, William 1:67; 3:161; 16:222
Reeves, William G. 15:353; 16:281
Reeves, William L. 9:28; 18:314

Reeves, William S. 12:60
Reeves, William T. 17:402
Reevis, S. 26:58
Refenburg, George 26:57
Reff, Peter 25:223
Refferner, C. 1:167
Regal, T. H. 14:101
Regan, A. 19:94
Regan, B. 14:209
Regan, Bart 25:303
Regan, Cornelius 13:43
Regan, D. 9:149
Regan, Edward 12:36
Regan, F. G. 22:215
Regan, James K. 20:100
Regan, James M. 11:220
Regan, John 8:75; 9:163; 11:311
Regan, John O. 12:36
Regan, M. 10:206; 15:295
Regan, Matthew 26:248
Regan, P. 1:166; 14:101
Regan, P. I. 9:149
Regan, P. J. 27:102
Regan, Patrick 9:190
Regan, Peter M. 16:51
Regan, T. 1:66
Regan, Thomas 7:60; 14:209
Regan, W. 11:334
Regan, W. M. 14:328
Regan, W. W. 11:255
Regan, William 9:161; 14:209
Regard, Jacob 21:104
Regart, John 3:161
Regas, Reuben 14:210
Regeleyer, J. 1:167
Regenbogen, John 23:92
Reger, E. 25:63
Reger, E. C. 25:63
Reger, E. E. 2:16
Reger, J. F. 15:167
Reggs, William 8:29
Regia, Levi 12:36
Register, Archibald F. 17:410; 22:456
Register, B. M. 1:165
Register, Seth 22:97
Register, T. P. 16:377
Reglin, Reinhardt 20:333
Reglin, Reinhart 10:75
Regman, P. 3:161
Regner, M. 20:149
Regusly, James 26:57
Regusty, James 18:250
Rehart, Joseph 13:117
Rehbock, F. 17:25
Rehl, J. 14:101
Rehling, H. 1:69

Rehling, J. D. 24:83
Rehm, Christopher 24:114
Rehm, F. 15:133
Rehmann, David 23:115
Rehmel, Jonathan W. 11:74
Rehnl, Eincle 17:283
Rehr, Henry 18:250
Rehse, August 10:132; 20:333
Rehu, W. 3:161
Rei, J. 3:161
Reib, Henry 16:52
Reibeff, John 20:333
Reiboff, John 10:75
Reibs, Jacob 11:165
Reic, T. 18:179
Reice, John 7:107
Reice, Judge 8:54
Reich, Augustus 19:260
Reich, Henry 16:222
Reichain, Jacob 13:68
Reichard, Franklin 22:97
Reichard, George 20:12
Reichards, John 20:333
Reichart, George 22:215
Reichart, J. 15:8
Reichart, Jacob 10:132
Reichart, Samuel 27:103
Reiche, Charles F. W. 21:142
Reichenbach, C. 20:127
Reichert, Daniel 23:13
Reichert, Francis 10:132
Reichert, Samuel 9:124
Reichter, B. 15:222
Reichter, Herman 4:49
Reickenberger, H. 18:400
Reicle, L. R. 2:16
Reid, Alexander 18:104
Reid, Andrew J. 7:107
Reid, Arthur 4:48
Reid, B. F. 17:41
Reid, Clayborn 17:238
Reid, D. 15:111
Reid, D. A. 12:123
Reid, David 4:68; 14:317
Reid, Elwin 14:328
Reid, Eugene 16:222
Reid, F. 14:20
Reid, G. 3:161
Reid, G. W. 16:222
Reid, George 10:187; 25:223
Reid, George W. 14:237
Reid, H. 1:66; 25:326
Reid, Henry S. 11:111; 20:31
Reid, I. 3:161
Reid, Isaac 14:336
Reid, J. 13:97

Reid, J. C. 14:244
Reid, James 7:107; 24:28
Reid, James E. 10:21
Reid, James M. 20:143
Reid, Jesse D. 17:85
Reid, John F. 23:277
Reid, John O. 17:416
Reid, Lewis 17:252
Reid, Nathaniel 21:184
Reid, Nelson 17:321
Reid, Ohio B. 18:104
Reid, R. B. 14:101
Reid, Robert 10:21
Reid, Robert K. 3:161
Reid, Thomas 15:153
Reid, Thomas B. 10:75; 20:333
Reid, W. J. 3:161
Reid, William 26:178; 27:100
Reid, William H. 4:48; 17:244
Reid, William J. 17:25
Reiddel, Philip 11:120
Reide, Aaron 27:103
Reidel, F. 14:131
Reidenger, Thomas 17:41
Reidenour, Isaac 22:489
Reider, Albert 21:128
Reider, Charles 24:96
Reider, H. 3:161
Reider, H. W. 25:64
Reider, J. P. 8:54
Reidie, Elijah 27:105
Reief, Henry 1:68
Reiele, S. 25:67
Reif, Augustus 17:410; 22:215
Reif, J. 15:73
Reif, John 1:66
Reif, John F. 10:133
Reiff, Charles 7:78
Reiff, J. B. 3:161
Reifsnyder, M. 25:224
Reifsnyder, W. 1:69
Reifstack, Frederick 21:142
Reigele, Faibob 15:167
Reiger, John 3:161
Reiger, Theodore 12:36
Reiggs, A. 11:248
Reighe, Charles T. W. 8:54
Reigley, C. 1:164
Reigling, Charles 21:128
Reigs, D. 14:101
Reihardt, George 10:75; 20:333
Reiker, Henry 3:161
Reiker, John 11:311
Reiker, William 21:168

Reikert, Francis 20:333
Reile, Adam 10:75; 20:333
Reiley, --- 21:168
Reiley, James 16:303
Reiley, James O. 1:67; 15:222
Reiley, John 11:329
Reiley, Michael 22:521
Reiley, Peter 12:36
Reiley, T. 18:92
Reiley, William I. 10:75
Reilley, Bernard 11:111
Reilley, James 8:122
Reilley, John 16:148; 19:305
Reilley, Thomas 27:147
Reilley, William O. 22:153
Reilly, B. 1:164
Reilly, George 18:92
Reilly, J. 3:161
Reilly, John 10:29; 23:194
Reilly, Joseph T. 22:14
Reilly, P. O. 3:161
Reilly, T. 1:164
Reilly, William S. 21:380
Reily, M. 1:69
Reily, Patrick 18:155
Reily, Thomas 3:161
Reim, Otto 9:8
Reiman, Charles 13:117
Reimel, John 16:123
Reimel, M. 14:101
Reimenschneider, William 18:155
Reimert, Andrew 26:128
Reimuly, Lewis 17:447
Rein, Gethart 18:440
Rein, J. 1:166
Rein, Joseph 15:300
Reinar, George 26:58
Reine, R. 3:161
Reiner, William 15:222
Reinerhart, Morgan 7:38
Reinfls, Johann 21:233
Reinge, Edmund A. 12:76
Reinhard, John 12:57
Reinhardt, Charles 21:142
Reinhardt, Fred 20:333
Reinhardt, Gust 22:409
Reinhardt, James 14:210
Reinhardt, O. R. 27:147
Reinhart, Andrew 7:107
Reinhart, Frederick 10:75
Reinhart, John J. 9:158
Reinhart, Lewis B. 10:75
Reinhart, W. P. 25:66
Reinhart, William 12:123
Reinhart, Z. 14:262, 263
Reinhert, Lewis B. 20:333

Reinich, Jacob 17:160
Reinick, Shirk 16:303
Reinick, Winfield 12:36
Reinoehl, George H.
 17:85
Reinold, John 15:111
Reinolds, Charles A.
 7:107
Reins, Cale 11:232
Reins, S. R. 23:303
Reinzer, Martin 20:12
Reirdan, W. 9:149
Reis, Charles 23:261
Reis, Henry 15:167
Reis, J. C. 11:120
Reis, Josephus 23:13
Reisch, Charles 13:43
Reisch, Daniel W. 10:75
Reisch, Enos 22:488
Reisch, Fr. 23:205
Reischman, Jacob 15:59
Reise, Herman R. 21:259
Reisel, John 14:210
Reisenbeigler, M. 18:56
Reiser, --- 25:63
Reiser, W. 9:28
Reish, Daniel W. 20:333
Reisin, Orville B. 24:43
Reisman, P. 14:210
Reison, M. 18:314
Reison, Peter 20:175
Reison, William 18:155
Reisor, M. 26:111
Reisser, Frederick 26:55
Reist, Jacob 22:498
Reister, George 4:48
Reister, Philip 9:98
Reitel, John F. 22:497
Reiter, Frank 21:207
Reiter, Henry 10:75;
 20:333
Reiter, Peter 10:75;
 20:333
Reith, Charles 15:111
Reither, Henry 17:85
Reitlins, W. 10:149
Reitnor, William 14:210
Reitter, G. 3:161
Reity, Albert 11:403
Reitz, George 15:153
Reitz, P. 1:69
Reives, J. 1:167
Rekenberger, Asa 26:128
Relation, Joseph C. 13:43
Relf, John F. 20:333
Religha, M. 1:67
Rellold, Charles B. 14:328
Relly, Elisa 6:27
Relly, John 25:303
Reln, A. 3:161
Rels, Camnuron 15:338

Relue, Joseph D. 23:164
Relyea, H. 1:165
Relyea, Jos. W. 15:222
Relyea, L. 1:68
Relyea, L. T. 1:165
Relyea, Louis 22:283
Remalia, Reuben 17:85
Remcles, Joseph 18:314
Remear, Charles 20:333
Remele, D. 1:166
Remeles, Joseph 26:110
Remer, Charles 10:75
Remer, Christian 8:109
Remer, James 14:101
Remer, William 10:29
Remers, I. 3:161
Remick, --- 25:67
Remick, A. 8:74
Remick, Charles H. 2:16
Remick, George W. 25:63
Remick, M. F. 1:68
Remick, Prescott 15:18
Remick, S. S. 19:230
Remig, Henry H. 21:79
Remincer, Frederick 15:73
Reminger, Jacob 6:23
Reminger, John 14:210
Remington, A. J. 1:66
Remington, Allen 15:327
Remington, Alva 18:296
Remington, Charles
 25:224
Remington, D. E. 12:9
Remington, Francis V.
 18:210
Remington, George 15:84
Remington, J. B. 10:187
Remington, James 18:210
Remington, John 22:50
Remington, Lucius 20:333
Remington, M. 21:191
Remington, M. D. 12:157
Remington, Marcus
 21:259
Remington, Oliver 20:100
Remington, Orange
 16:222
Remington, Silas 22:153
Remington, Stephen 9:190
Remington, Thomas F.
 15:3
Remley, Anthony 20:108
Remley, Elias F. 21:78
Remley, J. 21:246
Remley, Lycurgus 24:55
Remm, Charles A. 25:224
Remmer, Rudolph 7:38
Remmick, W. P. 18:400
Remmington, Alva 26:110
Remmington, F. A.
 15:361

Remmington, S. 19:260
Remmington, T. M. 19:94
Remney, C. F. 11:166
Remon, Ebenezer 9:89
Remore, M. 1:165
Remorn, A. J. 3:161
Remort, Randolf 27:103
Remp, Manford 9:89
Rempert, Peter 13:117
Rempher, B. 1:66
Rempholtz, J. 21:380
Rempmir, Frederick
 16:101
Remprow, D. 21:380
Rempster, Francis 13:43
Remt-h-coe, John 19:189
Remuel, L. 11:165
Remy, B. 14:101
Remy, J. 22:316
Remy, J. N. 25:312
Remy, John 3:161
Ren, J. 14:101
Ren, T. J. 22:316
Renack, James 19:31
Renaldo, E. 2:16
Renamer, W. H. 3:161
Renard, Antoine 6:14
Renback, C. 3:161
Renbottam, George 13:43
Renbottom, George 16:52
Rence, J. 12:100; 15:366
Rench, John 26:129
Rench, Joseph 18:179
Renchart, Andrew 9:58
Renchen, Francis A.
 22:128
Rencon, John 20:4
Rendall, David 16:52
Rendall, Job A. 21:142
Rendell, George 18:250;
 26:57
Render, Charles 21:380
Render, Daniel 17:151
Rendig, C. H. 3:161
Rendinghourt, T. 14:101
Rendler, Christopher
 18:155
Rendools, J. H. 16:123
Rendrick, Eli 22:515
Rends, Tony 18:250;
 26:57
Rene, Simon 12:171
Renebarger, John 20:45
Renegal, George 19:95
Reneker, George 18:92
Rener, Christopher 22:215
Reneroe, J. 22:266
Reney, H. (Mrs.) 18:427
Renfrew, S. R. 15:222
Renfrew, Samuel C. 9:191
Renfro, John J. 24:43

Renfro, William J. 10:133; 20:333
Renfron, James H. 17:57
Rengel, John 14:336
Rengler, Frederick 20:335
Renglet, Joseph 25:224
Renia, J. 1:104
Renick, A. 22:489
Renier, A. 1:165
Renier, George 9:89
Renier, John 21:380
Reniker, Daniel 9:89
Reniker, Daniel F. 21:233
Renil, Valentine 18:155
Reninger, Daniel 9:124
Renington, I. B. 18:179
Renington, Lucius 10:133
Renio, G. H. 1:165
Renirn, D. C. 7:60
Renkand, K. 1:68
Renkel, W. 8:54
Renkel, William 21:104
Renn, Christian 25:224
Rennan, Henry 11:73
Rennard, Edward 9:89
Rennard, John 9:89
Renne, Leroy 20:194
Rennecker, Abraham 23:264
Rennecker, C. F. 20:36
Rennels, Goul 11:404
Renner, C. R. 1:166
Renner, Israel 22:14
Renner, Jacob P. 22:354
Renner, James 8:93
Renner, John 22:97, 438
Renner, L. H. 19:230
Renner, Uriah 9:98
Renner, William 19:305
Rennerd, Levi 14:101
Rennert, Andrew 9:45
Rennett, Louis 26:213
Renney, J. B. 15:345
Renney, J. W. 7:53
Renney, James B. 16:377
Rennick, Henry 14:210
Renniger, Daniel 27:100
Renning, Charles 8:93
Rennington, F. A. 12:96
Renny, James M. 22:14
Renny, S. 13:43
Reno, Harrison 10:133; 20:333
Reno, John 9:58
Reno, N. 27:105
Reno, Thomas 8:54
Renoad, John F. 22:50
Renolds, Charles R. 14:210
Renolds, R. N. 15:303
Renols, Peter 18:17

Renon, M. 1:167
Renselair, C. M. 3:161
Renseler, H. 3:161
Rensell, Joseph 7:60
Renshal, William 6:35
Renshan, Albert 26:57
Renshaw, Albert 18:250
Renshaw, Alex. D. 21:380
Renshaw, B. F. 20:333
Renshaw, Benjamin F. 10:75
Renshaw, H. G. 3:161
Renshaw, William S. 14:210
Rensine, Miles 13:117
Renson, William 11:43
Rensso, J. W. M. 21:217
Rent, I. 14:210
Rentch, John 6:33
Rentch, Lewis 8:93
Renter, Christ 17:111
Rentleff, John 19:95
Rentter, H. J. 8:120
Renty, Detrick 19:95
Rentz, Jacob 22:215
Rentz, M. 23:164
Rentz, Patrick 15:323
Rentzenbrink, William 1:68
Renwick, A. W. 9:113
Renwick, William 22:343
Renyer, Michael 21:58
Renz, Fred 20:333
Renz, Frederick 10:75
Renz, John W. 20:25
Renzie, A. M. 9:149
Reoles, Edward 18:314
Reoner, Stephen 20:333
Reord, J. 15:73
Repan, A. 3:161
Repay, Dublin 7:132
Reper, James 13:68
Reper, Joseph 19:95
Repford, P. B. 8:67
Repler, Daniel 16:222
Repman, L. 21:142
Repp, George 21:380
Repp, Isaac 22:215
Repp, James 3:161
Reprogle, Leonard 7:107
Rerick, John P. 10:133; 20:333
Rerlmann, Membard 8:29
Rernard, J. 11:122
Res, John 10:75
Resch, Victor 15:43
Rese, John 21:283
Reseker, William 7:53
Resen, Henry 15:3
Resenlark, W. D. 16:52
Reser, Jacob 15:59

Reser, Levi 11:73
Reshaw, John 7:132
Resider, C. 14:210, 259
Resig, Lawrence 17:283
Resin, Thomas 14:210
Resinbach, Charles 14:270
Resir, Frederick 9:89
Resk, Charles 19:265
Resler, John 12:37
Resley, A. 17:217
Resling, J. C. 15:88
Resner, Dial 11:97
Resner, Henry 16:52
Resner, Hiram D. 20:333
Resole, J. 19:241
Respick, J. 19:95
Respick, John 13:68
Ressigner, J. 22:521
Ressique, James 22:509
Ressler, E. J. 23:92
Ressor, Edward 26:111
Ressor, Elwood 9:38
Rest, John 9:38; 18:296; 26:111
Rest, Samuel W. 11:391
Restine, Jeremiah A. 11:403
Reston, Elijah L. 13:43
Reston, Josiah 11:75
Result, J. 21:104
Ret, George 3:161
Ret, H. 17:347
Retalick, Francis 13:117
Retchey, L. 9:73
Retchman, Jacob 13:43
Retenour, William 11:311
Reter, Feter 14:210
Retger, Andrew 24:96
Reto, J. Q. 17:217
Retsmiller, Samuel 21:233
Retterford, J. H. 2:16
Rettock, F. 21:125
Retz, Otti 18:210
Retzer, Joseph 22:163
Reubart, R. M. 18:56
Reuben, Albert 19:289
Reuben, Alexander 9:211
Reuben, Henry 4:49
Reuben, James 11:188
Reuben, John 26:178
Reuben, Lewis 4:49
Reubens, John 8:42
Reubin, Lewis 19:189
Reuble, Valentine 23:109
Reublin, John 11:166
Reubsane, Henry 17:41
Reufrow, Samuel C. 19:278
Reufs, Archibald 11:425
Reugenberger, M. 23:205

Reuguer, P. 14:101
Reuhlin, George 19:265
Reule, Martin 24:62
Reutch, James 25:326
Reuter, Franz 23:194
Reuter, Henry 21:93
Reuther, Anton 19:275
Reutter, P. 1:69
Revan, Peter C. 13:43
Revard, Estach 22:467
Reve, H. S. 3:161
Revelle, John W. 23:77
Rever, Fred 4:49
Rever, Jacob 15:73
Rever, P. S. 14:20
Reveran, Lewis 11:86
Reves, --- 23:307
Reves, John 8:67
Revett, Charles 23:271
Revill, Nicholas 22:172
Revilmeyer, F. 25:224
Revingirth, C. F. 9:191
Revis, Benona S. 15:222
Revis, James N. 21:58
Rew, Charles 19:275
Rew, H. G. 21:38
Rewdle, Joseph 19:189
Rewet, H. 3:161
Rewm, John P. 22:467
Rex, Cornelius 17:85
Rex, Frank 21:283
Rex, George E. 5:27;
    25:224
Rex, I. G. 24:28
Rex, J. W. 3:161
Rex, Nathan 21:38
Rexecker, F. G. 18:56
Rexfor, Russell 27:101
Rexford, F. B. 26:179
Rexford, H. M. 9:149
Rexford, Horatio N.
    27:101
Rexford, John 22:153
Rexoot, S. 11:97
Rexroad, Aloftus 15:88
Rey, Bolla 24:154
Rey, Rolla 17:432
Rey, S. 14:20
Reyburn, Madison 20:138
Reyer, Isaac 22:153
Reyers, Valentine 22:237
Reyholts, W. T. 19:95
Reynard, John 17:321
Reynard, Solomon 22:97
Reynard, Timothy 22:97
Reynear, I. F. 15:27
Reyner, Charles 4:49
Reynodl, Hugh 11:167
Reynods, J. 15:160
Reynold, Charles 19:189
Reynold, William 9:166

Reynolds, --- 15:43
Reynolds, A. 13:97;
    17:293
Reynolds, A. F. 22:410
Reynolds, A. J. 1:68;
    19:245; 21:380
Reynolds, A. M. 25:224
Reynolds, A. P. 9:191
Reynolds, Able 11:334
Reynolds, Albert S.
    22:489
Reynolds, Alex 17:184
Reynolds, Alfred 22:316
Reynolds, Alfred H. 18:92
Reynolds, Allen 9:224;
    18:374
Reynolds, Alsop C.
    21:259
Reynolds, Andrew J.
    22:153
Reynolds, Asa 4:49;
    15:222
Reynolds, B. 1:166;
    9:224; 10:29; 14:266;
    19:305
Reynolds, B. F. 9:58
Reynolds, Bernard 11:220
Reynolds, C. H. 17:156
Reynolds, Charles 9:215;
    10:174
Reynolds, Charles A.
    21:380
Reynolds, Charles H.
    17:264
Reynolds, Charles W.
    16:222
Reynolds, Christian 9:215
Reynolds, Cornelius 17:97
Reynolds, D. 3:162
Reynolds, D. M. 14:101;
    19:189
Reynolds, Daniel L.
    16:303
Reynolds, Daniel M.
    10:166
Reynolds, David 7:39;
    10:75; 18:374;
    20:333
Reynolds, E. 1:165;
    3:162; 25:65
Reynolds, Ebner 7:39
Reynolds, Edmond 22:521
Reynolds, Edward 3:161;
    22:128
Reynolds, Edward R.
    20:100
Reynolds, Elliott 10:166;
    19:189
Reynolds, Emmor 15:73
Reynolds, Ephraim
    10:133; 20:333

Reynolds, F. 15:160;
    22:354
Reynolds, F. M. 17:428;
    23:277
Reynolds, F. S. 3:161
Reynolds, Franklin 12:37
Reynolds, Fred. M.
    19:323
Reynolds, G. 9:149;
    15:167; 16:222;
    27:102
Reynolds, G. F. 1:165;
    14:101
Reynolds, G. H. 13:117;
    19:189
Reynolds, Garrett 10:166
Reynolds, George 11:289;
    21:58, 199; 22:316
Reynolds, George J. 21:93
Reynolds, George T. 8:54
Reynolds, George W.
    9:104; 10:133;
    20:333; 22:410, 489
Reynolds, Green W.
    17:295
Reynolds, Griffin 22:98
Reynolds, H. 18:374;
    25:66
Reynolds, H. C. 17:210
Reynolds, H. F. 22:215
Reynolds, H. H. 12:76
Reynolds, H. K. 21:380
Reynolds, H. M. 20:333
Reynolds, Henry 2:16;
    3:161; 8:29; 9:28;
    18:155, 314; 22:410;
    23:251; 24:43;
    26:110, 179
Reynolds, Henry C.
    21:233
Reynolds, Henry S. 21:38
Reynolds, Herman M.
    10:75
Reynolds, Hiram 22:437
Reynolds, Hiram F.
    21:380; 24:175
Reynolds, Holly 12:55
Reynolds, Hudson 24:55
Reynolds, I. 26:56
Reynolds, I. J. 3:161
Reynolds, Ira M. 21:118
Reynolds, Isaac 14:237
Reynolds, Isaac B. 20:127
Reynolds, J. 1:165, 167;
    3:161; 9:89; 11:282;
    13:97; 14:210, 259;
    15:312; 18:37; 19:95;
    21:125; 24:28
Reynolds, J. D. 1:69
Reynolds, J. E. 25:224

Reynolds, J. F. 10:133;
20:333
Reynolds, J. G. 12:162
Reynolds, J. H. 1:66
Reynolds, J. L. 20:59
Reynolds, J. N. 25:65
Reynolds, J. P. 17:420
Reynolds, J. T. 17:265
Reynolds, J. W. 17:441
Reynolds, Jacob 11:42
Reynolds, James 11:289;
13:43; 18:400;
22:237; 24:83;
25:224
Reynolds, James E. 8:102;
17:461; 24:161
Reynolds, James R.
22:266
Reynolds, James W.
24:154
Reynolds, Jeremiah
22:489
Reynolds, Jerome B.
22:153
Reynolds, John 4:49;
9:135; 10:166;
11:329; 17:184;
19:189; 22:266, 437;
27:103
Reynolds, John C. 10:170
Reynolds, John E. 5:27
Reynolds, John F. 10:75;
20:333
Reynolds, John J. 1:67
Reynolds, John S. 23:164
Reynolds, John W. 4:49;
17:57
Reynolds, Joseph 4:49;
12:55; 15:316;
18:440; 22:354, 515
Reynolds, Joseph P.
24:162
Reynolds, L. 25:303
Reynolds, Lemuel 7:76
Reynolds, Leonard 7:69
Reynolds, Lewis 11:336
Reynolds, Lyman B.
21:196
Reynolds, M. 8:29;
15:222; 17:184;
18:155
Reynolds, M. C. 8:29
Reynolds, Marcus 10:166
Reynolds, Marcus L.
19:189
Reynolds, Marquis D. H.
24:96
Reynolds, Martin 16:303
Reynolds, Michael 22:98
Reynolds, N. A. 3:161
Reynolds, N. H. 11:269

Reynolds, Nathan 7:132
Reynolds, Nathaniel S.
22:153
Reynolds, Noah W. 8:109
Reynolds, O. 3:161; 7:39
Reynolds, O. S. 3:161
Reynolds, Ochland 7:39
Reynolds, P. 1:166
Reynolds, Pat 23:47
Reynolds, Patrick 13:43;
21:380; 22:343
Reynolds, Peter 21:380
Reynolds, Philip 7:107
Reynolds, R. 19:95
Reynolds, Ranson N.
16:222
Reynolds, Reuben F.
10:166; 19:189
Reynolds, Richard 13:43
Reynolds, Robert 11:110;
21:380
Reynolds, S. 1:165; 8:77
Reynolds, S. B. 8:54
Reynolds, S. F. 15:43
Reynolds, S. G. 17:41
Reynolds, S. M. 7:60
Reynolds, S. W. 9:149;
27:101
Reynolds, Samuel 3:162
Reynolds, Samuel L.
24:184
Reynolds, Solomon
23:291
Reynolds, Solomon B.
21:78
Reynolds, T. 1:67; 22:316
Reynolds, T. C. 16:377
Reynolds, Thaddeus
16:101
Reynolds, Theodore
11:110
Reynolds, Thomas 9:28;
10:133; 18:315;
20:333; 22:97;
26:110
Reynolds, Thomas A.
22:97
Reynolds, Thomas E.
21:131
Reynolds, Vilas 19:189
Reynolds, W. 2:16; 3:161;
10:187; 15:222;
18:179; 20:333;
25:64
Reynolds, W. C. 14:210
Reynolds, W. D. 11:232
Reynolds, W. E. 1:165
Reynolds, W. F. M.
10:187; 26:204
Reynolds, W. H. 1:165;
11:43

Reynolds, W. J. 19:95
Reynolds, W. L. 15:23
Reynolds, W. P. 14:101
Reynolds, W. W. 9:89;
26:56
Reynolds, Westley 21:380
Reynolds, Willard 23:261
Reynolds, William 3:161;
4:49; 9:89, 215;
10:75; 11:97; 15:222;
16:123, 148; 19:245;
20:333; 21:205;
22:98, 128, 237;
25:66; 26:56, 138
Reynolds, William G.
23:124
Reynolds, William H.
15:349; 16:378;
23:115
Reynolds, William L.
9:155
Reynolds, William R.
10:97
Reynolds, Wilson 22:215
Reynolds, Zimri P. 20:25
Reynor, James 12:37
Rhea, Charles E. 10:145;
19:189
Rhea, David G. 22:266
Rhea, J. T. 8:54
Rhea, M. V. 9:58
Rhea, William 17:315
Rheahard, J. 9:28
Rhebean, Frank 17:25
Rhedd, M. 22:316
Rheden, Jacob 19:95
Rhedenkizer, H. 18:250
Rhedinkrizer, H. 26:57
Rhehorst, John B. 20:116
Rheil, John 8:126
Rheimschnider, J. W.
15:222
Rheiner, Joseph 10:75;
20:333
Rheinhard, Ernst 15:222
Rheinhart, Aug 11:43
Rheinhart, Elias 7:39
Rheinhart, James 24:150
Rhen, F. 12:123
Rhenebault, R. H. 3:162
Rhetin, W. 3:162
Rhider, A. W. 14:101
Rhiel, William 23:164
Rhimes, A. 3:162
Rhine, Cornelius 22:50
Rhine, G. W. 1:68
Rhine, George 3:162
Rhinebolt, I. 3:162
Rhinehart, Charles 16:134
Rhinehart, D. 3:162;
14:20

Rhinehart, J. 3:162; 7:39
Rhinehart, J. C. 23:293
Rhinehart, L. 13:97
Rhinehart, O. P. 27:147
Rhinehart, P. 13:97
Rhinehart, Philip 22:437
Rhinehart, William M.
    23:77
Rhineholt, James 19:31
Rhines, W. R. 20:334
Rhines, William H. 10:75
Rhinesmith, James H.
    21:39
Rhinesmith, Lyman 10:75
Rhittenhouse, Charles
    14:102
Rhoades, --- 18:71
Rhoades, A. 24:43
Rhoades, C. 19:241
Rhoades, Charles H.
    10:166
Rhoades, Daniel 10:133
Rhoades, Haskel 10:133;
    20:334
Rhoades, Henry 16:101
Rhoades, J. W. 20:334
Rhoades, James 8:54
Rhoades, M. 11:42
Rhoades, Samuel 10:166
Rhoads, Daniel 20:334;
    26:128
Rhoads, Jacob 21:114
Rhoads, John 8:93
Rhoads, Lincoln 19:230
Rhoads, M. L. 18:222
Rhoads, Phil. M. 21:241
Rhoads, Samuel F. 8:93
Rhoads, W. 17:434
Rhoads, William 22:410
Rhoads, William W.
    22:456
Rhobards, Charles 8:42;
    26:178
Rhod, Philip W. 10:212
Rhoda, D. 26:225
Rhoda, Frederick 15:43
Rhode, C. G. 7:39
Rhode, J. H. 13:126
Rhodebaugh, John 14:210
Rhodeham, Jacob 11:75
Rhodeman, Adam 8:74
Rhodenback, Thomas
    14:210
Rhodes, A. 3:162; 11:269;
    13:117; 21:380
Rhodes, Alexander 5:27;
    17:238
Rhodes, Alvin D. 10:8
Rhodes, Anson 10:133;
    20:334

Rhodes, Augustus M.
    8:29; 18:155
Rhodes, B. 14:330; 17:92
Rhodes, Ben 17:249
Rhodes, C. 13:79; 15:18;
    21:112; 25:224
Rhodes, Calvin 22:98
Rhodes, Charles 12:76
Rhodes, Charles H.
    19:189
Rhodes, Christopher
    9:191
Rhodes, Dwight 21:380
Rhodes, E. 1:69
Rhodes, E. D. 21:198
Rhodes, Edward 14:302;
    17:473; 27:105
Rhodes, Eli 9:45
Rhodes, Ernest 18:155
Rhodes, F. 3:162
Rhodes, F. M. 11:166
Rhodes, Franklin 14:210
Rhodes, G. 1:66; 13:97
Rhodes, G. W. 23:47
Rhodes, George 22:437
Rhodes, George W.
    15:222; 20:25
Rhodes, H. 7:39; 8:54, 74;
    26:179
Rhodes, Henry 18:56;
    21:58, 380
Rhodes, Hiram 21:259
Rhodes, Ira D. 9:28
Rhodes, Ira O. 18:315;
    26:110
Rhodes, Isaac 16:166
Rhodes, J. 14:102;
    15:268; 16:123
Rhodes, J. L. 15:222
Rhodes, J. W. 16:223
Rhodes, James L. 15:222
Rhodes, James M. 20:334
Rhodes, James W. 11:43
Rhodes, Jason O. 19:95
Rhodes, Jesse 24:89
Rhodes, John 9:28, 67;
    11:249; 18:315;
    22:237, 488; 24:203;
    26:111
Rhodes, John C. 10:75;
    20:334
Rhodes, John M. 17:67
Rhodes, John T. 4:49
Rhodes, John Thomas
    10:133; 20:334
Rhodes, Jonathan 26:178
Rhodes, Joseph 27:104
Rhodes, Lincoln 9:191
Rhodes, Milton F. 22:438
Rhodes, Monroe 9:224;
    18:374

Rhodes, Moses 22:316
Rhodes, O. D. 14:302;
    17:474; 27:105
Rhodes, O. M. 15:222
Rhodes, Peter 15:88
Rhodes, Phelix 11:211
Rhodes, R. 14:102
Rhodes, Ransom 10:133;
    20:334
Rhodes, Reuben 21:380
Rhodes, Riley 6:13
Rhodes, Robert R. 21:58
Rhodes, S. 23:109
Rhodes, Samuel 19:189
Rhodes, Samuel C. 23:13
Rhodes, Scott 14:210
Rhodes, Solomon 22:98
Rhodes, Thomas 26:213
Rhodes, U. 17:500
Rhodes, W. 17:293;
    24:215
Rhodes, W. M. 15:345;
    16:378
Rhodes, Warren W. 7:60
Rhodes, William 21:78;
    22:266; 23:164;
    25:224
Rhodes, William H.
    22:521
Rhodes, William J. 23:164
Rhodes, Z. 14:29
Rhodewalt, J. 1:69
Rhodimer, A. 14:210
Rhoe, James F. 21:142
Rhoe, Thomas J. 26:213
Rhoman, George H.
    14:210
Rhone, G. W. 26:110
Rhone, George W. 9:28
Rhone, Job 15:73
Rhone, John R. 22:266
Rhone, Joshua 6:26
Rhorig, Peter 10:75
Rhost, Christian 27:101
Rhoton, Jacob W. 22:456
Rhoton, John 23:47
Rhoton, John J. 17:57
Rhrads, Charles 8:93
Rhudy, H. 16:223
Rhute, W. 1:104
Rhyan, Fred. 8:109
Rhyan, John M. 17:249
Rhylander, Edward
    23:194
Rhymus, Asa H. 26:58
Rhyne, J. 13:97; 14:20
Ri---gon, John B. 25:65
Rial, A. 27:102
Rial, Henry 10:133;
    20:334
Rial, James 12:51

Riards, Martin 22:266
Rias, G. 20:149
Ribala, Charles R. 27:105
Ribble, C. 25:224
Ribble, Conrad 5:27
Ribble, Cornelius 1:66
Ribble, Henry 6:21
Ribble, William 11:323
Ribbs, G. 23:314
Riberon, Isabella 27:102
Ribert, John 13:43; 16:52
Ribius, Ira 4:49
Riboe, Charles 1:67
Ribolds, Charles B. 9:161
Ribolds, John 11:166
Ribsam, J. 1:165
Rica, Theo. R. 12:37
Rically, Antoine 17:244
Ricard, J. 25:224
Ricard, J. H. 21:13
Ricards, George C. 24:96
Ricardson, Charles 21:380
Riccor, L. 16:222
Rice, --- 11:429; 15:133, 222; 18:193; 21:85
Rice, A. 3:162; 21:39
Rice, A. C. 25:224
Rice, A. D. 1:165
Rice, A. L. 23:47
Rice, A. P. 11:43
Rice, Abner 11:110
Rice, Addison 17:264
Rice, Albert 4:49
Rice, Alexander 18:92; 21:93
Rice, Andrew 18:250; 26:57
Rice, Anson P. 22:283
Rice, Anthony L. 13:43
Rice, Archy S. 22:436
Rice, Austin S. 8:109
Rice, Austin W. 17:249
Rice, Benjamin 23:271
Rice, Benjamin F. 11:391; 17:25
Rice, Bennett 18:250; 26:57
Rice, Bird C. 9:224; 18:374
Rice, C. 1:66, 164; 11:220, 249, 269; 14:102; 27:106
Rice, C. A. G. 3:162
Rice, C. H. 1:165
Rice, Charles 8:67; 14:244; 15:43; 17:85; 19:31; 22:266
Rice, Charles W. 8:109
Rice, Christian 14:102
Rice, D. E. 12:162
Rice, D. H. 24:83

Rice, D. L. 14:244; 27:106
Rice, Daniel S. 8:29
Rice, David S. 18:155; 26:177
Rice, E. 3:162; 10:187; 16:270
Rice, E. D. 1:67
Rice, E. E. 25:63
Rice, E. H. 10:210
Rice, E. J. 25:66
Rice, E. L. 25:63
Rice, E. O. 13:126
Rice, E. R. 22:50
Rice, Edson 10:133; 20:334
Rice, Edward W. 15:82
Rice, Eli 23:16
Rice, Ephraim F. 7:39
Rice, F. 3:162; 21:380; 22:316
Rice, F. D. 3:162
Rice, F. M. 20:334
Rice, F. W. 3:162
Rice, Fielding 15:222
Rice, Francis 10:133; 17:393; 20:334
Rice, Francis J. 18:280
Rice, Frank 18:250; 26:57
Rice, Frederick 9:191; 19:260; 25:273
Rice, G. B. 9:28
Rice, George 4:49; 5:53; 18:250; 26:57
Rice, George F. 1:67
Rice, George L. 12:83; 16:303
Rice, George M. 8:109
Rice, George W. 10:75; 18:250; 20:12, 334; 26:57
Rice, Green B. 18:315; 26:109
Rice, Griffith T. 21:259
Rice, H. C. 1:166
Rice, H. E. 1:167
Rice, H. F. 18:422
Rice, H. M. 3:162
Rice, H. P. 18:271; 24:28
Rice, Harrison 22:51
Rice, Harvey 17:249; 22:51
Rice, Henry 13:43; 15:222; 16:52
Rice, Henry L. 7:107
Rice, Henry S. 10:166
Rice, Howard 4:49
Rice, I. A. 11:425
Rice, Isaac 11:409
Rice, Isaac N. 8:29; 18:155

Rice, Isaiah 12:162
Rice, J. 3:162; 14:259; 18:37; 22:316
Rice, J. A. 1:167; 25:224
Rice, J. E. 25:63
Rice, J. H. 1:66
Rice, J. L. 11:438
Rice, J. N. 24:83
Rice, J. R. 19:31
Rice, J. S. 16:87; 23:261
Rice, J. W. 11:397; 21:205
Rice, Jackson 12:37; 18:250; 20:25; 26:56
Rice, Jacob 10:145; 14:210; 15:73; 19:189; 21:191
Rice, James 3:162; 9:135; 13:43; 16:123; 24:69
Rice, James B. 15:222
Rice, James E. 24:55
Rice, James H. 22:437; 24:168
Rice, James L. 18:92
Rice, James M. 16:222; 17:420
Rice, James S. 6:10
Rice, Jasper N. 22:266
Rice, Jerome 9:45
Rice, Jesse 16:282
Rice, John 2:16; 7:39; 8:93; 9:58; 12:37; 14:102; 17:424; 21:283, 380; 22:51; 24:83, 174; 25:63, 326
Rice, John C. 20:100
Rice, John E. 18:250; 21:241; 26:56
Rice, John M. 17:261
Rice, John P. 20:138
Rice, John R. 23:47
Rice, John W. 18:222
Rice, Joseph 9:191; 10:166; 19:189, 279; 23:77
Rice, Joseph R. 8:93
Rice, Josiah 12:51
Rice, L. 1:165
Rice, L. G. 11:86
Rice, Levi 22:215
Rice, Lewis 4:49; 11:120
Rice, Louis 17:184
Rice, Luther 7:17
Rice, Lyman R. 9:13
Rice, M. 12:96; 14:102; 15:361; 19:95
Rice, Marion 9:89
Rice, Myron 22:215
Rice, Napoleon B. 22:456
Rice, Norton 22:153

Rice, O. A. 25:65
Rice, Onesimus A. 27:104
Rice, Orson E. 7:69
Rice, Oscar 21:380
Rice, Owen 10:21; 16:222
Rice, P. 11:281
Rice, P. A. 14:102
Rice, P. L. 20:334
Rice, P. S. 9:231
Rice, Quartas N. 21:39
Rice, R. 9:149; 27:102
Rice, R. B. 9:69
Rice, R. E. 14:102
Rice, Richard M. 18:315; 26:110
Rice, Robert 17:184
Rice, Robert C. 18:400
Rice, S. 12:86; 16:303
Rice, S. E. 25:63
Rice, S. W. 9:149
Rice, Sampson 9:135; 27:102
Rice, Samuel 3:162; 11:269; 14:102; 17:57; 22:51
Rice, Samuel B. 9:13; 17:41
Rice, Samuel E. 2:16
Rice, Samuel L. 25:224
Rice, Seth 5:27
Rice, Sexton 9:135
Rice, Sextus 27:103
Rice, Silas 11:211; 21:233
Rice, Squires 8:115
Rice, T. 25:224
Rice, T. C. 19:31
Rice, Thomas 3:162; 9:237; 14:210; 15:350; 16:222; 18:250; 19:323; 25:224; 26:57
Rice, Thomas A. 24:69
Rice, Thomas H. 16:134
Rice, W. C. 1:167
Rice, W. G. 23:47
Rice, W. H. 1:167
Rice, W. T. 11:43
Rice, Walter 17:67
Rice, William 9:73; 11:397; 14:302; 15:59, 133; 17:57, 472; 18:250; 26:56, 57; 27:105
Rice, William C. 23:101
Rice, William D. 24:55
Rice, William F. 24:28
Rice, William H. 4:49
Rice, William M. 22:128
Rice, William R. 21:58
Rice, William T. 20:19
Rice, William W. 11:42

Rice, Wilson 9:135; 27:103
Rice, Zura 11:42
Ricecoop, J. W. 17:294
Ricer, Isaac 10:76; 20:334
Rich, --- 15:8
Rich, A. 1:168; 3:162; 26:178
Rich, A. A. 1:167
Rich, Amos 23:287
Rich, Andrew J. 18:400
Rich, Augustus 9:191
Rich, Bela 25:224
Rich, Benjamin E. 18:37
Rich, C. 3:162
Rich, Calvin 17:420; 24:161
Rich, Charles L. 17:57
Rich, David 9:89; 17:441; 26:56
Rich, David C. 12:60
Rich, E. H. 1:167; 11:42
Rich, Eli 12:37
Rich, Elias 4:49
Rich, F. 15:223
Rich, Gardner L. 7:108
Rich, George 22:153
Rich, George H. 4:49
Rich, Golden 11:269
Rich, H. 1:165, 166; 26:213
Rich, Harrison 16:378
Rich, Henry 10:210
Rich, Henry B. 26:225
Rich, Hiram 26:225
Rich, Isaiah 21:39
Rich, J. 3:162; 16:123
Rich, J. F. J. 11:415
Rich, J. L. 9:149
Rich, Joel 22:51
Rich, John 14:244; 15:223; 16:160; 22:410
Rich, Joseph 13:43
Rich, L. 1:166
Rich, L. H. 1:95
Rich, Lewis M. 23:109
Rich, M. 14:102
Rich, Medara E. 26:225
Rich, Nathan 13:68; 21:380
Rich, P. 23:47
Rich, Peter 13:43
Rich, Reuben D. 21:87
Rich, S. 15:268
Rich, Samuel 3:162
Rich, Stephen 8:54
Rich, T. D. 3:162
Rich, T. L. 27:102
Rich, Thomas C. 9:89; 26:55

Rich, W. 1:95
Rich, W. A. 14:102
Rich, William 9:58; 18:296; 26:110
Rich---, --- 15:160
Richabaugh, J. H. 15:59
Richard, --- 12:37
Richard, A. 3:163
Richard, Alex 13:68
Richard, B. S. 11:312
Richard, Benjamin 17:347
Richard, Carl 20:190
Richard, Charles 13:68; 19:95
Richard, Charles L. 20:334
Richard, D. 24:203
Richard, George 11:165
Richard, H. 3:163
Richard, Henry 13:58
Richard, Hugh 17:429
Richard, J. 14:102
Richard, J. B. 20:334
Richard, J. H. 13:117
Richard, J. M. 10:29
Richard, Jacob 16:222
Richard, James 7:39; 22:437
Richard, Jeremiah 5:44
Richard, Jesse 22:266
Richard, John 22:438
Richard, John E. 6:33
Richard, John O. 9:45
Richard, Lines D. 19:95
Richard, N. 12:166
Richard, R. 15:288
Richard, Thomas 23:267
Richard, W. H. H. 13:68
Richards, --- 8:109; 17:214; 19:95
Richards, A. 3:163; 16:222
Richards, A. T. 26:128
Richards, A. V. 3:163
Richards, Abijah 18:400
Richards, Amer 12:37
Richards, Amos 7:39
Richards, Arthur B. 9:191; 19:275
Richards, August 4:49
Richards, B. B. 10:21; 13:43; 16:52
Richards, Benjamin 10:206
Richards, Benjamin D. 12:37
Richards, Byron 10:166; 19:189
Richards, C. 23:47; 25:224

Richards, C. D. 13:68; 19:95
Richards, C. E. 23:92
Richards, C. W. 1:69
Richards, Charles 10:133; 17:398; 20:2, 334
Richards, Charles A. 8:29; 18:155
Richards, Charles B. 12:157
Richards, Charles E. 23:306
Richards, Charles H. V. 16:5
Richards, Charles L. 10:75
Richards, Charles S. 25:65
Richards, Chesley 10:133; 20:334
Richards, Clark 20:19
Richards, D. 3:163
Richards, D. A. 1:167
Richards, Daniel 24:154
Richards, David 18:37
Richards, David W. 22:129
Richards, E. 1:165; 3:163; 19:189
Richards, E. C. 24:28
Richards, E. O. 16:303
Richards, E. T. 11:166
Richards, Edward 6:9; 18:104
Richards, Elias F. 7:17
Richards, Elijah C. 23:164
Richards, Eliza 9:70
Richards, G. 1:166; 3:162, 163
Richards, G. H. 16:52
Richards, G. L. 3:162
Richards, G. W. 25:284
Richards, George 8:112; 10:206; 16:134; 18:250; 26:57
Richards, George C. 23:194
Richards, George F. 7:53
Richards, George W. 17:41
Richards, Green 8:77
Richards, H. 3:162
Richards, Henry 21:151; 23:271
Richards, Henry C. 11:220; 21:233
Richards, Hiram 17:112
Richards, I. T. 14:102
Richards, Isaac 16:134
Richards, Israel F. 7:107
Richards, J. 1:165; 3:163; 13:97; 14:20; 25:63

Richards, J. B. 17:41
Richards, J. E. 7:76; 12:157; 25:303
Richards, J. H. 4:49; 14:210
Richards, J. J. 18:56
Richards, J. L. 8:119
Richards, J. M. 1:104; 19:306
Richards, J. W. 9:58
Richards, James 7:14; 9:45; 17:67; 22:489; 26:128
Richards, James D. 23:164
Richards, James F. 17:67
Richards, James H. 11:97
Richards, Jasper N. 24:83
Richards, Jeptha 11:166
Richards, John 1:67; 3:163; 7:39, 132; 9:191; 10:75, 133; 11:382; 17:85; 19:275; 20:334; 25:326; 27:103
Richards, John A. 24:55
Richards, John B. 10:75
Richards, John F. 11:42
Richards, John G. 16:222
Richards, John J. 10:152
Richards, John O. 4:49
Richards, John R. 11:43
Richards, John T. 17:25
Richards, Joseph 3:162; 15:223; 19:305; 23:164
Richards, Josiah 21:78
Richards, Josiah W. 20:100
Richards, L. 25:66
Richards, L. D. 15:284
Richards, L. J. 11:101
Richards, Lewis C. 23:164
Richards, M. J. 3:163
Richards, Milton 22:98
Richards, N. 25:326
Richards, N. D. 10:133; 20:334
Richards, Nathan 17:317
Richards, Nicholas 4:49
Richards, Oliver 4:49
Richards, Oscar 7:107
Richards, P. M. 14:102
Richards, Paul 8:109
Richards, Peter 25:326
Richards, R. 12:93; 16:303; 24:83
Richards, R. H. 22:98
Richards, S. 22:51; 25:224
Richards, Samuel 9:135; 12:37; 27:103

Richards, Stephen 14:302; 17:470; 27:105
Richards, T. 16:222; 17:294
Richards, T. E. 14:102
Richards, T. W. 1:167
Richards, Theodore 3:163
Richards, Thomas 10:133; 11:249, 382; 15:43; 20:334; 23:164
Richards, Thomas Z. 24:43
Richards, V. C. 1:70
Richards, W. 1:165; 9:149; 27:104
Richards, W. F. 20:334; 25:64
Richards, W. H. 14:210; 17:85
Richards, W. R. 3:162
Richards, W. W. 1:67
Richards, William 1:68; 11:336; 23:194; 25:284
Richards, William C. 11:312
Richards, William F. 10:93
Richards, William J. 9:28
Richards, William W. 22:455
Richardsen, T. F. 18:374
Richardson, --- 3:162; 11:311; 15:94; 17:326, 365
Richardson, A. 1:68, 164; 3:162; 15:223, 300
Richardson, A. K. 12:51
Richardson, A. M. 22:215
Richardson, Alex. 8:93
Richardson, Alfred C. 19:241
Richardson, Almon 10:75; 20:334
Richardson, Andrew 24:203
Richardson, B. 17:184
Richardson, B. F. 10:133; 20:334
Richardson, B. M. 1:165
Richardson, Barnard 6:9
Richardson, Bernard 18:104
Richardson, Boston 9:135; 27:103
Richardson, C. 3:162; 26:178
Richardson, C. S. 3:162; 20:59
Richardson, Calvin 8:42; 26:178

Richardson, Cassius
17:149
Richardson, Chancey
27:104
Richardson, Charles 17:25
Richardson, Chauncey
9:124
Richardson, Cornelius
8:42
Richardson, D. 3:162;
13:117; 14:102;
25:63
Richardson, D. S. 11:293;
22:163
Richardson, D. T. 3:162
Richardson, Daniel 2:16;
9:45, 104; 17:215
Richardson, Daniel J.
15:59
Richardson, David
11:425; 24:28;
26:128
Richardson, David D.
22:266
Richardson, Dexter 10:21
Richardson, Doctor
18:413
Richardson, E. 3:162;
14:210; 21:380
Richardson, E. A. 18:179
Richardson, E. H. 1:167
Richardson, E. M. 26:179
Richardson, E. O. 25:224
Richardson, Eben L.
10:166; 19:189
Richardson, Edward 6:33;
11:282; 25:326
Richardson, Edwin 13:43
Richardson, Edwin O.
5:27
Richardson, Edwin T.
4:49
Richardson, Elisha A.
22:98
Richardson, Elkins 6:26
Richardson, Ephraim
10:133; 20:334
Richardson, F. 1:167;
3:162
Richardson, F. M. 22:266
Richardson, F. W. 21:380
Richardson, Frank 8:42;
26:178
Richardson, Frederick
16:222; 17:317
Richardson, G. 3:162
Richardson, G. C. 1:67;
11:99
Richardson, G. H. 18:92
Richardson, G. N. 1:95

Richardson, G. W. 1:66;
20:176
Richardson, George
9:135; 14:210;
17:410; 18:250;
22:129; 23:164;
26:57; 27:103
Richardson, George C.
12:76
Richardson, George H.
6:18; 13:43
Richardson, George N.
23:164
Richardson, George P.
15:84
Richardson, Gilbert
11:166
Richardson, Gustavus
12:37
Richardson, H. 3:162;
14:284; 19:241
Richardson, H. B. 22:266
Richardson, H. M. 3:162
Richardson, H. Thomas
21:105
Richardson, Harman
22:51
Richardson, Harvey 23:77
Richardson, Henry 7:132;
16:52
Richardson, Henry J.
18:222
Richardson, Henry T.
10:133; 20:334
Richardson, Holland
20:334
Richardson, Howard
10:75; 20:334
Richardson, I. 13:117;
15:223
Richardson, Isaac 10:75;
20:334; 22:51
Richardson, J. 1:68;
3:162; 11:73; 19:222;
21:380; 25:224;
27:102
Richardson, J. A. 14:102;
21:93
Richardson, J. B. 17:213;
18:17
Richardson, J. C. 21:191
Richardson, J. H. 10:29;
19:306
Richardson, J. K. 3:162
Richardson, J. M. 9:215;
22:215
Richardson, J. P. 13:97
Richardson, J. W. 20:335
Richardson, Jacob 8:42;
26:178

Richardson, James 1:192;
5:27; 10:133; 13:97;
17:441; 18:156;
20:127, 335; 21:259;
22:316; 24:154
Richardson, James B.
5:27; 17:283
Richardson, James D.
21:380
Richardson, James J.
18:156
Richardson, James T. 8:29
Richardson, James W.
10:75
Richardson, Jasper 23:77
Richardson, Jerry 17:184
Richardson, Jesse C.
21:105
Richardson, Joel A.
27:101
Richardson, Joel H. 9:149
Richardson, John 3:162;
4:49; 5:53; 10:133,
177; 13:43; 16:52,
123; 17:137, 149,
207; 19:189; 20:335;
23:77; 24:202
Richardson, John A.
21:245
Richardson, John H. 12:55
Richardson, John J.
10:145; 19:189
Richardson, John L. 17:57
Richardson, John S. 4:49
Richardson, John W.
17:72
Richardson, Jonathan H.
25:280
Richardson, Joseph 7:107;
18:424
Richardson, Josiah
10:133; 20:335
Richardson, L. 3:162;
15:319; 19:95
Richardson, L. G. 13:43
Richardson, L. J. 9:28;
18:315; 26:110
Richardson, Leonard
21:380
Richardson, Lewis 23:272
Richardson, Littleton
21:381
Richardson, Louis 22:316
Richardson, M. 3:162;
13:43; 15:223;
19:189
Richardson, M. B. 3:162;
14:210
Richardson, Mack 9:70
Richardson, Mathew
7:107

Richardson, Milton 10:21
Richardson, Moses C.
10:206
Richardson, N. H. 18:193
Richardson, Orland H.
11:111
Richardson, Orson F.
15:12
Richardson, P. 16:222
Richardson, Parish 18:37
Richardson, Peace 8:42;
26:178
Richardson, Philip 22:153
Richardson, Plenty 9:135;
27:103
Richardson, Preston
9:135; 27:103
Richardson, Prince 7:132
Richardson, R. 3:162;
11:269
Richardson, Richard 6:18;
18:92
Richardson, Robert 9:158;
15:223; 17:283;
22:51
Richardson, Robert M.
16:52
Richardson, S. 19:230,
242
Richardson, S. K. 11:101
Richardson, S. M. 25:65
Richardson, S. P. 3:162
Richardson, S. S. 1:165
Richardson, Samuel 7:39,
132; 21:131
Richardson, Samuel I.
7:107
Richardson, Sanford
21:283
Richardson, Shep 23:47
Richardson, Silas 9:191
Richardson, Solomon
9:210; 15:325;
18:71; 19:95
Richardson, Stella 20:59
Richardson, T. 1:66, 104
Richardson, T. F. 9:227
Richardson, T. H. 21:112
Richardson, Theodore
10:21
Richardson, Thomas
14:210; 16:222;
17:184; 23:261
Richardson, Thomas E.
7:107
Richardson, Thomas H.
26:58
Richardson, Thomas M.
21:291
Richardson, Thomas R.
10:133; 20:335

Richardson, Tolson
22:172
Richardson, Truman B.
12:37
Richardson, W. 3:162;
22:354
Richardson, W. A. 11:75,
86
Richardson, W. H. 9:58;
20:335
Richardson, W. M. 3:162
Richardson, W. T. 14:102
Richardson, William 1:69;
8:54, 67; 9:135;
10:133; 12:51;
14:102; 15:43, 338,
355; 17:41, 244, 261;
19:48; 20:335; 22:51,
98, 153; 26:179;
27:103
Richardson, William A.
22:456
Richardson, William B.
22:456
Richardson, William G.
21:78
Richardson, William H.
10:75; 23:77; 25:224;
27:101
Richardson, William J.
18:400; 24:161
Richardson, William J. C.
17:420
Richardson, William O.
22:129
Richardson, William P.
15:59
Richardson, William T.
18:400
Richardson, Williamson
22:446
Richardson, Zachary
21:381
Richardville, Gabriel
20:19
Richart, Jacob 20:335
Richart, John 10:133;
20:335
Riche, Daniel 12:37
Riche, Joseph 3:163
Riche, Nathan 16:222
Richel, D. 1:67
Richenbauch, George
17:71
Richenbauch, P. 1:164
Richer, Charles 19:31
Richer, Daniel B. 9:98
Richer, Hiram 12:37
Richer, Jefferson 11:167
Richers, Charles 15:345;
16:378

Richerson, James 8:29
Richerson, Samuel
21:233; 22:215
Richert, Albert 11:212
Richert, William 24:69
Richeson, Alfred E. 9:191
Richeson, Caleb C.
10:133; 20:335
Richeson, Henry 13:43
Richesson, Jonathan 8:94
Richey, Andrew 20:25
Richey, Elera P. 21:196
Richey, H. 23:47
Richey, J. W. 8:54
Richey, James E. 8:29
Richey, James L. 22:237
Richey, John 17:244;
22:266
Richey, John A. 22:455
Richey, John W. 21:93
Richey, R. 3:163
Richey, Stephen 12:37;
14:317
Richey, Thomas 11:312
Richfield, William 5:44
Richie, Aaron 6:18
Richie, George W. 21:105
Richie, H. 3:163
Richie, Henrie 9:38
Richie, Henry 18:296
Richie, J. 1:166; 19:95
Richie, James 22:438
Richie, John G. 19:95
Richie, Lucius 22:215
Richie, Martin 26:225
Richie, Milo 11:165
Richie, Moses 23:291
Richie, R. 1:68
Richie, R. H. 14:259
Richie, Samuel 17:41
Richie, William B. 11:74
Richinson, Jacob 18:340
Richison, James M.
20:105
Richistine, C. 3:163
Richland, B. 16:270
Richle, John 23:164
Richle, Joseph 27:101
Richler, Jeremiah 9:160
Richman, Benjamin F.
22:215
Richman, Christian
22:215
Richman, David 4:49
Richman, Finley 9:135
Richman, J. 19:189
Richmayer, Conrad
20:127
Richmer, David 18:400
Richmeyer, Abraham
17:423

Richmeyer, Frank 8:118
Richmon, George 4:49
Richmond, A. 21:381
Richmond, Albert 16:222
Richmond, Arthur 14:211
Richmond, B. 3:163;
22:316
Richmond, Bart 7:39
Richmond, C. F. 1:67
Richmond, E. 9:158
Richmond, Edwin B.
10:75
Richmond, Frank 23:164
Richmond, G. 1:68
Richmond, H. 9:113;
11:293
Richmond, Henry H.
25:64
Richmond, J. 1:164;
14:284
Richmond, J. E. 5:27;
25:224
Richmond, J. P. 18:114
Richmond, J. R. 18:114
Richmond, J. S. W.
27:105
Richmond, James 7:132
Richmond, John 22:128
Richmond, John R. 6:10
Richmond, Joshua 16:136
Richmond, M. 14:284
Richmond, P. S. 1:66
Richmond, Patterson 8:94
Richmond, Peter 14:211
Richmond, Robert 12:157
Richmond, Sanford 17:92
Richmond, Steward 8:67
Richmond, T. 1:165
Richmond, Timothy 7:39
Richmond, W. G. 26:56
Richmond, William C.
22:266
Richmond, William W.
11:165
Richnin, Jeremiah 9:89
Richorson, Henry 9:191
Richpeter, A. 3:162
Richs, David 17:72
Richsnider, William
15:300
Richson, I. 14:211
Richter, Frank 11:129
Richter, Gaston 18:315
Richter, Gustave 26:110
Richter, Julius 23:164
Richter, Lewis 15:223
Richter, Thomas J. 10:25
Richtor, Frederick 20:335
Richtuger, P. 14:102
Richwood, Albert 15:336
Richy, L. 22:215

Richy, William C. 9:38
Rick, Charles 22:466
Rick, Erastus 21:381
Rick, F. B. 19:284
Rick, Royal V. 22:437
Rick, T. B. 9:191
Rick, W. R. 17:469;
27:105
Rick, William 14:211
Rick, William R. 14:302
Rickabaugh, John 17:461;
24:164
Rickabaugh, Perry 21:79
Rickabaugh, Wilson 20:25
Rickard, A. J. 1:165
Rickard, A. L. 23:164
Rickard, F. 19:260
Rickard, Frank 9:191
Rickard, Giles 13:117
Rickard, Noah 24:43
Rickards, J. 16:303
Rickards, Lital 22:129
Rickards, N. 1:167
Rickart, N. 19:189
Rickbaugh, John 8:102
Rickel, Adam H. 21:58
Rickel, Robert 3:162
Rickelson, H. 16:222
Ricker, Algernon O. 7:107
Ricker, Benjamin I. 12:37
Ricker, E. C. 25:65
Ricker, Frederick 9:113
Ricker, George 23:185
Ricker, George H. 7:39
Ricker, Henry 15:223
Ricker, Henry J. 4:49
Ricker, Henry S. 13:80
Ricker, J. A. 11:101
Ricker, Jacob 20:138
Ricker, Jerry F. 4:49
Ricker, John H. 13:43
Ricker, Julius A. 1:67
Ricker, L. B. 14:211
Ricker, M. 3:162; 19:230
Ricker, Moses 9:191
Ricker, S. L. 9:163
Ricker, W. B. 21:199
Ricker, William 3:162
Rickerd, Thomas 3:162
Rickerhoff, J. 8:74
Rickerman, Albert 9:191
Rickerman, C. M. 10:187
Rickers, Henry 8:29;
18:156
Rickers, J. 18:250; 26:57
Rickers, P. 23:47
Rickerson, Agin 11:165
Rickerson, S. N. 10:25
Rickert, George J. 21:39
Rickert, James 25:224
Rickert, M. 19:260

Rickes, J. 14:102
Ricket, Francis 14:211
Ricket, Robert 23:164
Ricketh, Lafayette 11:391
Rickets, Allen 17:57
Rickets, Frank 18:222
Rickets, George 9:231
Rickets, John 18:179;
20:335
Rickets, Joseph 17:137
Rickets, Samuel 17:444
Rickets, William A. 20:87
Ricketson, James 9:89
Rickett, Emanuel 18:92
Rickett, George 15:300
Rickett, H. 16:222
Rickett, Johnson T. 22:98
Rickett, Lewis 12:37
Rickett, W. 16:303
Ricketts, E. E. 9:204
Ricketts, George 20:335
Ricketts, John 10:75
Ricketts, Joseph 24:202
Ricketts, M. 21:112
Ricketts, S. 12:162
Ricketts, Thomas J.
17:261
Rickey, E. 13:97; 14:20
Rickey, Francis 7:65
Rickey, George W. 8:99
Rickey, Henry 17:421
Rickey, John H. 23:164
Rickey, Joseph 21:381
Rickey, Murat 7:39
Rickey, William 13:43;
16:52
Rickitson, James 26:55
Rickle, Murvin 9:124
Rickler, Felix 20:190
Rickler, Peter 20:190
Rickley, John 11:249;
12:37
Rickman, Finley 27:102
Rickman, Henry 13:43
Rickman, John 19:260
Rickman, Joseph 22:316
Rickman, W. 7:39
Rickmeyer, Frank 19:315
Rickner, John 23:264
Rickney, Joseph 26:204
Ricks, G. W. 8:42; 26:178
Ricks, Harry 17:137;
24:202
Ricks, I. J. 12:164
Ricks, Joseph 9:89; 26:56
Ricks, Philip 7:78
Ricks, Phillip 25:303
Ricks, Richard J. 17:41
Ricks, Stephen 9:135
Ricksick, August 22:51
Rickson, Andrew E. 26:56

Rickson, Henry 13:58
Rickstead, C. O. 10:133;
  20:335
Rickwite, L. B. 16:303
Ricky, Henry 24:164
Ricor, Charles 27:104
Ricord, Charles 9:191
Ricord, Lemuel 4:49
Ricord, Lewis 22:343
Rictor, Charles 3:163
Rictor, G. L. 25:224
Rictout, Charles 9:135
Ridan, Thomas 10:166;
  19:189
Ridden, Orgure 21:381
Ridder, C. T. 16:148
Ridder, Edward 7:39
Ridder, James A. 9:113
Riddick, George 16:222
Riddle, A. 1:168; 6:33
Riddle, Abraham I. 22:51
Riddle, Adam 8:74
Riddle, B. 1:166
Riddle, Benjamin 23:13
Riddle, Charles 7:53
Riddle, Charles P. 22:51
Riddle, Edwin C. 7:108
Riddle, F. 3:163; 14:131
Riddle, G. 14:102
Riddle, Isaac 7:108;
  10:133; 11:97;
  20:335
Riddle, J. 11:311
Riddle, J. H. 3:163
Riddle, Jackson 18:193
Riddle, James F. 15:88
Riddle, James M. 22:456
Riddle, John 7:132; 19:48
Riddle, Jones B. 10:180
Riddle, Joseph 10:76
Riddle, L. 17:326
Riddle, Lewis 10:76;
  20:335
Riddle, Pyrus 7:132
Riddle, R. 25:326
Riddle, Robert 3:224;
  17:505
Riddle, Roderick J.
  22:153
Riddle, Thomas E. 22:509
Riddle, Thomas J. 24:44
Riddle, William 10:93;
  20:335
Riddler, L. W. 16:222
Riddleton, A. 18:92
Riddon, Arguse 7:132
Riddon, N. 3:163
Riddy, Daniel 18:156
Ride, William L. 4:49
Rideaway, J. 9:149
Rideff, Thomas 9:28

Ridemour, Andrew 24:44
Ridenour, Benjamin
  22:215
Ridenour, Ephraim 23:164
Ridenour, H. 11:269
Ridenour, J. 12:123
Ridenour, James M.
  22:410
Ridenour, John D. 20:127
Ridenour, S. 1:167
Rideout, C. 1:167
Rideout, Edward 9:10
Rideout, Hugh G. 23:103
Rideout, Thomas T. 16:79
Rider, --- 19:95
Rider, A. R. 20:156
Rider, Aaron M. 9:38
Rider, Barnard L. 22:466
Rider, C. 17:67
Rider, D. B. 19:260
Rider, Daniel B. 9:191
Rider, David 8:67; 17:288
Rider, E. 3:163
Rider, E. H. 12:157
Rider, Edwin 12:76
Rider, Elijah C. 20:28
Rider, Erwin 20:152
Rider, Henry 9:7; 17:41;
  22:129
Rider, J. M. 15:223
Rider, J. S. 16:141
Rider, J. W. 10:76; 20:335
Rider, Jacob 11:120;
  26:128
Rider, John 14:102;
  15:361
Rider, Leonard 22:98
Rider, Mark 19:95
Rider, Richard P. 20:141
Rider, S. 1:165
Rider, S. B. 22:237
Rider, T. 14:102
Rider, W. 1:164
Rider, W. A. 1:166; 3:163
Rider, W. C. 11:166
Rider, W. J. 23:314
Rider, W. S. 18:400
Rider, Walker N. 27:105
Rider, Walter V. 14:302;
  17:477
Rider, Wiley 11:212
Riderback, Alexander
  17:315
Ridfield, W. J. E. 7:108
Ridge, Dav 12:93
Ridge, J. 21:39
Ridge, John 17:57
Ridgedorff, J. 26:179
Ridgeley, Charles 24:83
Ridgeley, F. W. G. 22:489
Ridgeley, J. 12:80

Ridgely, J. 25:224
Ridgely, J. H. 20:43
Ridgeway, Francis S.
  22:216
Ridgeway, G. 1:69
Ridgeway, George 21:79
Ridgeway, Henry 13:43;
  16:52
Ridgeway, J. 27:102
Ridgeway, James 13:43;
  18:400
Ridgeway, John 3:163;
  17:137; 24:202
Ridgeway, O. B. 27:100
Ridgis, Abraham 8:29
Ridgley, L. 1:99
Ridgway, Antrim 21:11
Ridgway, C. 8:58; 21:151
Ridgway, John 7:108
Ridgway, Massom
  18:222; 21:233
Ridgway, R. S. 25:63
Ridgway, Thomas 9:113
Ridick, H. 27:101
Riding, George 1:66
Ridinger, William J.
  21:196
Ridle, George 20:335
Ridle, John 10:76
Ridlen, Samuel 23:77
Ridler, H. A. 3:163
Ridley, A. C. 3:163
Ridley, J. D. 15:355
Ridley, John 21:283
Ridley, Joseph 17:274
Ridley, Mathew 11:188
Ridley, Robert 27:105
Ridley, Willis 22:505
Ridline, John C. 11:17
Ridlon, Almon H. 21:381
Ridlon, James 3:163
Ridly, Patrick 9:124
Ridneer, William 17:479
Ridner, William 14:302
Ridnerr, William 27:105
Ridney, J. 1:167
Ridnour, George 22:215
Ridnour, William 10:97
Ridout, Charles 27:102
Ridout, Eben 25:65
Ridout, Edward 10:76;
  20:335
Ridout, J. 7:39
Ridout, James K. 4:68
Ridwell, --- 17:497
Riebe, Ferdinand 15:92
Riechel, Frederick 20:335
Riecor, L. 13:117
Ried, --- 21:79
Ried, Frank 14:20
Ried, James D. 24:28

Ried, Joseph R. 12:36
Ried, William A. 9:38
Riefenduck, G. W. 13:117
Riefenrath, Charles 23:194
Rieff, R. 3:163
Riegelroth, John 20:100
Rieger, Frantz 24:10
Rieger, Fred 18:315
Riegle, J. 1:165
Riehr, Henry 26:57
Riel, Daniel 15:223
Rield, James C. 11:167
Rieley, Patrick 16:303
Rieley, Peter 17:15
Rielly, P. 3:163
Riels, J. C. 14:102
Riely, B. 1:66
Riely, Benjamin 18:250
Riely, James 18:37; 27:100
Riely, John 9:191
Riemal, John 15:92
Rieman, Ernst 22:216
Rieman, Theo. F. 23:92
Riemel, John 12:62
Rien, Charles 11:97
Rien, David C. 22:216
Riephoff, Henry 24:55
Rierden, John 24:58
Rierden, Patrick 26:178
Rierdon, M. D. 3:163
Rierner, Charles 24:83
Rierodon, J. 14:102
Rierson, J. W. 16:223
Ries, --- 24:114
Ries, George J. 15:111
Ries, H. 25:65
Riesdon, W. 27:101
Riesner, Charles 4:49
Riess, John 15:300
Riester, Alfred L. 12:76
Rietmiller, John G. 19:95
Rieves, Jessie L. 26:213
Rieves, T. E. 16:270
Rife, Carter 17:398
Rifenberger, H. H. 15:73
Rifenburg, C. 1:69
Rifert, W. E. 11:73
Riff, J. 11:167
Riffle, Jesse 10:177
Riffle, Jessie 19:189
Riffle, S. G. 3:163
Riffle, Thomas 21:105
Riffle, William 17:15
Riffutt, Emanuel L. 7:39
Rifle, A. 25:224
Rifle, Andrew J. 5:27
Rifleburg, Peter 19:260
Rigan, R. 14:102
Rigby, A. C. 9:113

Rigby, J. 25:224
Rigby, J. C. 14:103
Rigby, John 14:211; 16:73
Rigby, W. R. 19:189
Rigby, William 5:44
Rigdon, Alfred J. 22:98
Rigdon, W. W. 11:97
Rigeer, Joseph 5:27
Rigel, P. 11:220
Riger, J. 1:167
Riger, John W. W. 19:31
Rigford, Charles 25:224
Rigg, Dav 16:303
Rigg, James 4:49
Rigg, Merida 20:108
Rigg, Thomas 20:108
Riggans, Gilbert 22:316
Riggen, N. D. 14:317
Riggens, R. A. 22:437
Rigger, Amos 23:182
Riggin, James L. 22:489
Riggins, John H. 17:112
Riggins, Starling 22:98
Riggle, D. J. 13:97; 14:20
Riggle, H. H. 20:43
Riggle, James 17:249
Riggle, Jesse 21:142
Riggle, M. 22:216
Riggle, Thomas 12:76; 15:59
Rigglesworth, C. W. 26:110
Rigglesworth, Charles 9:28
Rigglesworth, Charles W. 18:315
Riggs, A. 16:52
Riggs, A. L. 14:20
Riggs, A. T. 13:97
Riggs, Amos 9:135; 27:103
Riggs, Anderson 21:233
Riggs, B. 7:53
Riggs, B. A. 23:303
Riggs, C. F. 19:95
Riggs, C. H. 14:244; 27:106
Riggs, Charles A. 19:189
Riggs, Charles T. 18:444
Riggs, E. 1:165
Riggs, Ezra 22:98
Riggs, Frank 9:28
Riggs, G. T. 10:76
Riggs, George 11:19
Riggs, George C. 7:53
Riggs, George W. 16:52; 23:115
Riggs, H. 3:163
Riggs, J. 3:163
Riggs, J. A. 24:28
Riggs, Jack 22:515

Riggs, James A. 22:266
Riggs, John 9:124; 17:274; 22:129; 27:104
Riggs, John A. 22:129
Riggs, John D. 23:115
Riggs, John W. 17:207
Riggs, K. M. 3:163
Riggs, L. 3:163
Riggs, Lawson P. 26:55
Riggs, M. 16:151
Riggs, Oscar 26:57
Riggs, Peter 1:68
Riggs, R. H. 11:248
Riggs, Robert 4:49; 10:76; 20:335
Riggs, Samuel 17:441
Riggs, Samuel T. 24:154
Riggs, Silas 10:76; 20:335
Riggs, W. B. 20:92
Riggs, Washington 10:76
Riggs, William 8:29; 18:156; 22:410
Riggson, Edward 5:44
Right, B. M. 18:179
Right, C. N. 17:200
Right, Ephraim L. 15:111
Right, Harrison 10:76; 20:335
Right, John 17:25
Right, R. 18:56
Right, Samuel H. 13:117
Rightington, W. B. 7:39
Rightlinger, A. 14:103
Rightman, A. 26:179
Rightmaster, A. 8:67
Rightmire, Samuel 1:67
Rightmon, William 9:45
Rightner, George 19:31
Rightnire, Edward 10:21
Rightoner, George W. 27:104
Riglar, William 17:444; 24:162
Rigleman, Charles 19:31
Rigler, John 20:335
Rigler, P. 1:168
Rigler, W. H. 3:163
Rigley, Ervin 13:43
Rigley, I. 26:56
Rigley, James 15:167
Rigley, John 18:56
Rigley, T. 1:166
Rigly, Joseph 25:275
Rignette, Heinrich 21:259
Rigney, Charles 3:163
Rigot, John 23:255
Rigs, J. M. 15:223
Rigs, William J. 11:75
Rigsby, N. L. 11:248
Rigsby, N. S. 10:133

Rigsby, U. S. 20:335
Rigsby, W. A. 14:103
Rigur, Samuel 22:488
Rihe, Thomas 22:343
Rike, Eugene 22:489
Rike, Eugene E. 26:146
Rike, John L. 4:49
Riker, Abram H. 9:16
Riker, L. D. 17:67
Riker, Martin 9:191
Rikle, Merven 27:104
Riland, Joseph 11:403
Riland, Thomas W.
    18:222
Rilchon, John 26:56
Rile, John 23:115
Rile, William 9:244
Riles, M. 22:317
Riley, --- 16:113
Riley, A. W. 12:142
Riley, Abel W. 11:166
Riley, B. 1:166
Riley, Barney 23:253
Riley, Bazil G. 11:311
Riley, Benjamin 26:57
Riley, Benjamin F. 7:108
Riley, Bernard 9:191;
    10:133; 19:260;
    20:335
Riley, C. 25:224; 27:101
Riley, C. F. 14:302;
    17:473; 27:105
Riley, C. O. 9:149; 27:101
Riley, C. W. 12:157
Riley, Charles 3:163;
    6:28; 9:149; 11:74;
    12:37; 13:117;
    17:184; 19:334;
    22:153
Riley, Cornelius 5:27
Riley, D. 12:9; 21:125;
    23:164
Riley, D. E. 23:77
Riley, Daniel 8:109
Riley, David V. 15:23
Riley, E. 15:43
Riley, E. M. 8:67
Riley, Edward 9:124;
    17:41; 19:95;
    22:521; 27:103
Riley, Edward T. 18:114
Riley, F. 21:381
Riley, Frank 19:48
Riley, George 4:49; 6:18;
    18:56; 23:101, 309
Riley, George M. 14:211
Riley, H. 11:282; 21:381;
    27:102
Riley, H. J. 3:163
Riley, H. W. 20:335

Riley, Henry 14:211;
    18:222
Riley, Hugh 4:49; 10:76;
    20:335
Riley, I. 14:211
Riley, I. M. 3:163
Riley, Irwin 19:189
Riley, Isaac 22:437
Riley, Israel 6:13
Riley, J. 1:167; 3:163;
    11:166; 21:381;
    25:224, 303
Riley, J. F. 1:167
Riley, J. L. 1:66
Riley, J. M. 9:191; 19:268
Riley, J. O. 25:279
Riley, J. S. 1:69
Riley, Jacob 6:10; 18:114
Riley, James 4:49; 8:54;
    9:47, 67; 10:166,
    174; 11:211; 14:211,
    237; 15:153; 18:114;
    19:31, 189, 288, 349;
    26:128; 27:101, 104
Riley, Jerome 23:13
Riley, Joel A. 22:129
Riley, John 1:67; 3:163;
    4:49; 5:27, 53; 6:18;
    9:28, 45; 10:76, 133;
    12:37; 15:18; 16:101,
    378; 18:92, 193, 440;
    19:31; 20:335;
    21:118, 233, 381;
    23:77; 25:67; 26:128;
    27:148
Riley, John A. 22:51
Riley, John H. 20:335
Riley, John S. 17:265
Riley, Joseph 5:44
Riley, Joseph J. 27:101
Riley, Joshua 21:233
Riley, L. M. 26:179
Riley, Lano O. 4:49
Riley, Lawrence 10:166;
    19:189
Riley, Lewis 17:317
Riley, M. 1:68, 95, 166;
    3:163; 14:211, 289;
    19:189; 23:47
Riley, M. E. 23:302
Riley, M. O. 15:223
Riley, Mathers 19:189
Riley, Mathew 21:381
Riley, Mathias 23:164
Riley, Michael 1:66;
    9:204; 10:166; 13:43;
    15:279; 16:101, 223;
    17:57; 25:224
Riley, Michael O. 8:29
Riley, Miles 3:163
Riley, Nathan 21:191

Riley, O. 14:211
Riley, O. Michael 18:156
Riley, Oliver 17:57
Riley, Orrison D. 24:179
Riley, Orson B. 17:426
Riley, P. 1:69, 167
Riley, Patrick 1:68; 4:49;
    14:211; 15:223;
    18:114; 21:381;
    22:14, 398; 25:67;
    27:104
Riley, Peter 7:108;
    14:211; 20:335;
    22:343; 25:287
Riley, R. 3:163
Riley, Ransom 17:203
Riley, Richard 21:112
Riley, Robert 7:132
Riley, S. 10:133; 20:335
Riley, Samuel C. 22:216;
    23:182
Riley, T. 21:39
Riley, T. C. 15:18; 20:156
Riley, Tate 23:309
Riley, Terence 9:224
Riley, Terrence 18:374
Riley, Theodore 23:47
Riley, Thomas 1:68; 2:16;
    9:73; 12:76; 13:117;
    24:114; 25:66;
    27:101
Riley, Thomas F. 23:129
Riley, Thomas S. 21:233
Riley, Valentine 21:381
Riley, W. A. 11:74
Riley, W. H. 21:381;
    25:225
Riley, W. I. 20:335
Riley, W. M. 3:163
Riley, Walter 22:316
Riley, William 6:13; 9:14,
    149; 13:117; 14:211;
    16:223; 17:283;
    18:37; 20:12; 21:58,
    112; 27:101
Riley, William F. 22:283
Riley, William H. 5:27;
    21:233; 22:14
Riley, Zachariah C.
    23:194
Riling, J. 19:260
Rill, F. 25:225
Rill, G. 18:56
Rill, H. H. 20:156
Rill, Henry 9:13
Rille, J. 24:83
Riller, Frederick 8:54
Rillford, C. F. 14:284
Rillhatt, J. B. 16:303
Rilo, Henry 21:199
Rilpley, W. R. 25:225

Riltch, Jacob 15:43
Rilwen, C. 3:163
Rily, Thomas 14:335
Rily, W. 18:179
Rima, G. H. 1:165
Rimbro, John 22:317
Rimenschneider, William
  8:29
Rimer, George W. 17:249
Rimer, John 17:25
Rimer, L. 3:163
Rimes, W. W. 20:179
Rimlehn, George W.
  9:191
Rimner, H. 7:39
Rimpell, John F. 15:321
Rimple, George H. 15:43
Rimple, I. 14:103
Rimppell, John F. 19:95
Rimsen, C. 3:163
Rin, Primus 27:101
Rinal, Henry M. 21:191
Rinard, Abraham 15:9
Rinard, Harrison 22:343
Rinboldt, P. 16:101
Rind, Charles 18:250;
  26:57
Rinde, Erie H. 21:93
Rinde, J. 14:289; 23:47
Rinders, George 13:117
Rindhart, J. 8:74
Rindley, Benjamin 18:280
Rine, C. L. 18:179
Rine, Daniel 8:54
Rine, Henson 22:216
Rine, Michael 11:194
Rine, W. D. 18:413
Rine, William L. 22:216
Rinebolt, Daniel 10:187
Rinecar, Thomas 23:257
Rinehan, E. W. 11:166
Rinehardt, J. N. 10:133
Rinehart, Allen S. 22:129
Rinehart, Arthur I. 12:37
Rinehart, D. 13:117
Rinehart, E. 23:164
Rinehart, Henry 22:398
Rinehart, J. 25:65
Rinehart, J. H. 20:335
Rinehart, James R. 11:165
Rinehart, John C. 21:105
Rinehart, L. 14:20
Rinehart, Preston A.
  10:133; 20:335
Rinehart, Samuel 7:53
Rineland, George W.
  21:259
Riner, Henry S. 16:223
Riner, Philips 13:68
Rines, E. 9:113
Rinesmith, Lyman 20:335

Ring, A. S. 22:410
Ring, Albert S. 21:381
Ring, Alfred 8:60
Ring, Charles H. 15:12
Ring, Franklin 18:375
Ring, George L. I. 9:124
Ring, George L. J. 27:104
Ring, Henry 9:201;
  19:292
Ring, Henry T. 22:51
Ring, Jacob 10:76
Ring, James 23:77
Ring, James W. 9:215;
  21:381
Ring, John 21:381
Ring, Michael 19:95;
  23:182
Ring, Robert 18:250;
  26:56
Ring, S. L. 14:211
Ring, William 21:259
Ring, William H. 23:257
Ringe, Henry 23:16
Ringe, J. 1:69
Ringelbeck, Edwin 24:114
Ringer, George W. 15:357
Ringer, H. C. 7:39
Ringer, Henry 14:211
Ringer, J. 1:164
Ringer, J. C. 13:97
Ringer, J. K. 3:164
Ringer, Jacob 7:65
Ringer, John 23:164
Ringer, Otto 12:37
Ringer, W. 1:166; 15:223
Ringersoll, F. 9:106
Ringert, Andreas 21:105
Ringgold, J. 3:164
Ringgold, Mathias 15:43
Ringham, Francis 18:114
Ringhoff, Henry 24:72
Ringle, David 7:132
Ringleb, A. 16:282
Ringler, Henry 25:65
Ringler, Jacob 19:95
Ringles, Frederick 10:133
Ringley, Nick 17:85
Ringlond, Robert 18:321
Ringman, George 15:133
Ringold, G. 18:17
Ringold, James 22:317
Ringold, John 12:51;
  14:302; 17:471;
  27:105
Ringold, Thomas 15:285
Ringrose, James 4:49
Ringsland, A. H. 3:163
Ringwalt, Charles 20:184
Ringwalt, F. J. 3:163
Ringwood, James 10:76;
  20:335

Ringwood, R. 3:164
Rinhart, Christian 4:49
Rini, Ceves 21:381
Rinice, A. 1:68
Rink, B. 1:167
Rink, David 22:438
Rink, Henry 25:225
Rink, Vile 18:71
Rinke, Anthony 11:193
Rinker, A. 7:39
Rinker, Elias 18:56
Rinker, F. P. 3:163
Rinker, G. W. 18:193
Rinker, John H. 20:134
Rinker, Levi 23:47
Rinkle, George 3:164
Rinks, John 18:280
Rinn, Joseph 20:335
Rinncer, William 14:302
Rinner, E. E. 14:211, 259
Rinner, J. C. 3:164
Rinner, Margaret A.
  26:225
Rinney, Isaac 5:27
Rinniker, Frederick
  17:392
Rinter, Henry WL 18:280
Riolo, Henry 16:141
Rion, John 20:28
Riordan, Mathew 10:174
Riordan, Matt 19:189
Riordan, William 7:39
Riordon, Michael 14:211
Riordon, William 15:43
Riosser, Henry 11:269
Riper, P. H. 3:164
Ripher, Charles 26:55
Ripler, Samuel W. 13:117
Ripley, Alvara 22:410
Ripley, B. L. 9:191
Ripley, B. S. 19:242
Ripley, C. A. 1:99
Ripley, C. L. 25:225
Ripley, Charles A. 23:92
Ripley, D. K. 9:149;
  27:102
Ripley, Dwight 11:398
Ripley, E. J. 1:68
Ripley, Edward 15:286;
  19:95
Ripley, F. A. 3:164
Ripley, Henry W. 7:108
Ripley, J. 3:164
Ripley, J. W. P. 17:159
Ripley, John 9:45; 26:128
Ripley, John R. 27:147
Ripley, L. 16:378
Ripley, Laurie 8:54
Ripley, Levi D. 15:88
Ripley, Lewis H. 20:336
Ripley, Lewis N. 10:76

Ripley, M. F. 3:164
Ripley, Robert 7:76;
    25:303
Ripley, Robert M. 18:400
Ripley, S. L. 10:133;
    20:336
Ripley, Samuel D. 14:211
Ripley, Smith 9:38;
    22:509
Ripley, T. 21:125
Ripley, Thomas 22:317
Ripp, W. 3:164
Ripperdan, James 24:96
Ripperdon, Harlon 20:134
Rippert, William 9:67
Rippeth, William J.
    22:489
Rippetoe, J. M. 11:329
Rippey, John A. 23:77
Ripple, John 22:129
Rippon, William 3:164
Rippy, Granville 22:456
Rippy, Henry 9:28
Riptka, John 25:64
Rirard, M. 25:67
Ris, John 20:336
Risbey, Langdon 10:180
Risbon, Isaac 27:105
Risdon, George M. 11:42
Risdy, Thomas 18:156
Rise, Tillford 17:268
Riseck, R. 3:164
Risedolph, George H.
    13:43
Riser, Ellis 8:94
Riser, G. 15:223
Riser, L. 17:293
Risey, L. 17:283
Rish, B. F. 18:71
Rish, J. 1:165
Risher, R. J. 7:108
Risher, R. S. 21:381
Risher, W. G. 1:166
Rishor, I. 14:211
Risin, S. J. 9:45
Rising, C. 3:164
Rising, George C. 9:38
Rising, R. 9:113
Risinger, A. 14:302;
    17:471
Risinger, J. 16:223
Risinger, Joseph 4:49
Risinger, Solomon 20:127
Risinger, William 17:420;
    24:162
Risinor, William 6:18;
    18:92
Risk, Charles 9:191
Riskine, Henry 13:43
Rislay, E. 3:164
Risler, George 14:103

Risley, C. W. 3:164
Risley, George 5:27
Risley, George W. 3:164
Risley, Harrison 11:75
Risley, J. 3:164
Risley, Samuel 17:41
Risling, Samuel 23:241
Risling, W. 12:93
Risling, William 16:303
Risner, J. 14:259
Rison, S. I. 26:128
Risor, J. H. 21:58
Rissbrick, Theodore
    15:273
Risser, H. 20:149
Risser, Martin 22:489
Rissinger, J. 27:105
Rissler, Michael 9:191
Ristan, J. 25:66
Riste, F. E. 17:156
Rister, A. J. 16:223
Rister, James B. 16:113
Riston, G. F. 16:75
Riston, Kingston 26:178
Ritch, George 12:62;
    15:59
Ritchards, Fitzgerald
    12:173
Ritchell, F. 25:65
Ritcher, E. 7:53
Ritcher, F. 3:164
Ritcher, John J. 14:211
Ritchey, Charles 23:13
Ritchey, David 17:232
Ritchey, H. S. 1:66
Ritchey, J. 11:311; 13:97
Ritchey, Samuel 17:249
Ritchey, Stephen 10:76;
    20:336
Ritchfield, W. 25:225
Ritchie, A. 14:103
Ritchie, Aaron 18:92
Ritchie, Albert 19:337
Ritchie, C. F. 27:101
Ritchie, D. 15:223
Ritchie, E. 19:230
Ritchie, Edward F. 12:37
Ritchie, Elisha 9:191
Ritchie, G. E. 13:117
Ritchie, George 22:98
Ritchie, H. 27:101
Ritchie, Henry 26:110
Ritchie, Hugh 21:381
Ritchie, Jacob 5:27
Ritchie, John 11:289;
    15:330
Ritchie, Johnson 22:456
Ritchie, Robert 19:337
Ritchie, Thomas 11:183
Ritchie, W. 1:69
Ritchie, William 23:47

Ritchson, J. 14:259
Ritenbugen, Asa 9:45
Ritenhouse, Tyler 14:211
Riter, George H. 15:73
Riter, James V. 27:147
Riter, John 3:164
Riter, M. 19:95
Rith, J. 1:167
Rith, Samuel 9:14
Rither, L. 1:168
Rithoe, John 22:343
Ritman, Michael 26:177
Ritner, Isaac N. 8:29
Ritner, Philip 1:68
Ritney, N. 25:326
Ritsell, Samuel 12:157
Ritsen, Mathew 16:52
Ritsom, J. 2:16
Ritson, S. 3:164
Ritt, Louis 25:281
Rittal, I. S. 14:103
Rittenboro, Thomas B.
    17:495
Rittenhouse, William
    13:97
Rittenhouse, Wilson
    11:342
Ritter, --- 15:43
Ritter, A. F. 15:223
Ritter, Abram C. 20:85
Ritter, Albert 18:315;
    26:110
Ritter, Ashbury 21:233
Ritter, August 8:29;
    18:156
Ritter, B. B. 3:164
Ritter, Benjamin 3:164;
    22:317
Ritter, C. L. 11:282
Ritter, Charles 22:51
Ritter, Christopher 4:49
Ritter, D. 3:164; 15:223
Ritter, Daniel 11:167;
    15:223
Ritter, Elias 8:94
Ritter, Emanuel 10:76;
    20:336
Ritter, F. 1:69
Ritter, Frederick 21:105
Ritter, George 21:233
Ritter, George W. 10:133;
    20:336
Ritter, Henry 3:164;
    11:184
Ritter, Henry A. 18:156
Ritter, Henry N. 8:29
Ritter, Hugh 11:289
Ritter, J. 13:68; 14:289;
    15:43
Ritter, Jacob 17:85
Ritter, James 8:94; 9:160

Ritter, Jeremiah 23:164
Ritter, John 3:164; 8:94;
 11:212, 391; 13:117;
 22:98
Ritter, Julius 24:69
Ritter, Levi 11:166
Ritter, Morris 2:16; 25:66
Ritter, Otto 23:124
Ritter, Samuel 17:92
Ritter, W. 11:73
Ritter, W. C. 17:97
Ritter, W. H. 14:103;
 26:179
Ritter, William 15:59;
 17:388; 21:245
Ritterback, Joseph 19:271
Ritterbush, Charles 13:43
Ritterman, James 3:164
Rittigan, J. 1:164
Rittle, M. 14:103
Rittman, A. 1:167
Ritton, John 14:103
Rittor, Aaron 9:58
Rittweger, George E.
 22:398
Ritynitillin, John 3:164
Ritz, Henry 22:489
Ritz, Jacob 16:223
Ritz, Peter 24:83
Ritz, Rocco 6:18; 18:92
Ritzel, Jacob 14:211
Ritzeler, George A. 3:164
Ritzer, James 20:19
Ritzers, J. 12:162
Ritzmann, George 22:98
Ritzon, Mathew 13:43
Ritzpatrick, D. 17:33
Rivard, Eustache 11:111
Rivard, Joseph 10:206
Rivard, Peter P. 12:123;
 15:133
Rivelle, J. T. 25:225
Rivenburg, C. F. 19:275
River, David 22:437
River, William W. 7:108
Rivers, Alfrod 7:69
Rivers, Arthur M. 14:211
Rivers, D. 10:34
Rivers, H. 23:272
Rivers, Herman 23:272
Rivers, I. 15:43
Rivers, Isaac 12:76
Rivers, J. 15:133
Rivers, J. B. 25:225
Rivers, John 12:123
Rivers, John R. 20:100
Rivers, Thomas 21:381
Rives, I. W. 26:58
Rives, Jacob 20:175
Rivet, O. 9:191; 19:284
Rivir, Jacob 22:98

Rivis, John P. 22:505
Rivlar, D. G. 17:350
Rix, George 17:315
Rix, H. 14:103
Rix, Q. H. 16:303
Rix, Q. M. 12:86
Rix, Warren 15:223
Rix, William 3:164;
 11:166
Rixilrond, S. 11:281
Rixley, William 21:381
Rixon, Rolen 19:95
Rixwell, A. 14:103
Rizer, Charles 12:62
Rizer, William H. 21:381
Rizzee, K. 19:95
Rmehbolt, Daniel 18:179
Rnvenn, M. 11:288
Ro---ger, D. 15:223
Roabagrand, L. 18:250;
 26:58
Roach, A. 3:164
Roach, Abner M. 24:83
Roach, Absalom 17:57
Roach, Albert 9:240
Roach, Alex 19:31
Roach, Alfred 17:190
Roach, Austin 21:283
Roach, Calvin 26:128
Roach, Charles 3:164;
 9:89
Roach, Charles E. 7:39
Roach, David 16:223;
 23:253
Roach, E. 16:223
Roach, F. 3:164
Roach, Frank 7:132
Roach, Franklin 11:74
Roach, H. 18:156
Roach, H. W. 21:381
Roach, J. 3:164; 14:103;
 25:225
Roach, J. C. 27:102
Roach, J. W. 3:164
Roach, James 15:300;
 17:15; 21:381; 25:63,
 64
Roach, James H. 2:16
Roach, John 9:124;
 10:180; 13:97; 14:20;
 16:223; 18:179;
 21:381; 27:100
Roach, John C. 17:167
Roach, John M. 22:437
Roach, Joseph A. 16:79
Roach, Lorenzo D. 22:98
Roach, M. 1:165; 11:293
Roach, Margaret 27:102
Roach, Mary 27:104
Roach, Maurice 17:112

Roach, Michael 8:122;
 13:44; 16:282
Roach, N. 18:56
Roach, N. G. 9:160
Roach, Needham 21:218
Roach, Nelson 23:194
Roach, Patrick 23:101
Roach, R. A. 25:66
Roach, Robert 21:283
Roach, Robert A. 2:16
Roach, S. 11:167; 14:103;
 25:312
Roach, Simeon Y. 17:207
Roach, T. 21:381
Roach, Thomas 17:509
Roach, W. D. 27:102
Roach, William 5:27;
 12:37; 22:153;
 25:225; 27:147
Road, --- 18:37
Road, Hildeburtus 25:65
Roadds, R. R. 18:179
Roads, A. 16:223
Roads, C. A. 15:43
Roads, Frederick 3:164
Roads, John 18:179
Roads, John G. 10:180
Roads, John J. 17:137;
 24:202
Roads, R. R. 10:180
Roahr, Charles 22:216
Roak, Josiah 14:317
Roaks, Albert A. 17:433;
 24:167
Roaks, George B. 12:76
Roaler, Solomon 11:282
Roan, Charles 23:268
Roan, Emanuel 9:210;
 18:71
Roan, Henry 9:38
Roan, Jacob 22:317
Roan, P. 11:312; 14:211
Roan, Patrick 14:211
Roan, Richard B. 22:98
Roan, Robert 21:218
Roan, Thomas 25:64
Roan, William 11:404;
 14:211
Roar, Frank 4:49
Roark, Ephraim 22:505
Roark, J. H. 18:315;
 26:109
Roark, James 24:69
Roark, John 15:82
Roark, Patrick 19:189
Roark, Samuel 1:68
Roark, Thomas 24:114
Roarke, William 11:425
Roarty, Joseph 11:74
Roasar, P. 1:68
Roat, F. 11:97

Roat, J. 3:164
Roath, C. 23:164
Roats, Milton 11:269
Roatt, J. 14:20
Rob, Andre 17:62
Rob, Ira 23:280
Robard, Charles 9:58
Robarge, Joseph 23:194
Robarge, Peter 11:120
Robart, William 20:336
Robatan, Joseph 15:223
Robb, A. W. 22:488
Robb, C. 7:69
Robb, George H. 17:57
Robb, Henry 17:184
Robb, Isaiah 23:165
Robb, James 23:92
Robb, James M. 8:102;
    17:459; 24:154
Robb, James S. 10:180
Robb, Jonathan 12:55
Robb, Joseph 12:37
Robb, Joseph S. 18:179
Robb, Lizzie 24:28
Robb, Mathew A. 24:55
Robb, Matthew 25:225
Robb, Maxwell 22:98
Robb, Oliver 20:336
Robb, Robert 11:212
Robb, Sebastin 19:31
Robb, Stephen D. 20:128
Robb, William 9:89;
    26:55
Robberger, P. 3:165
Robbert, William 10:76
Robberts, Isaac 17:57
Robbin, Isaac 17:424
Robbin, J. W. 21:381
Robbin, William 18:156
Robbins, --- 15:5
Robbins, A. 3:164
Robbins, A. A. 20:33
Robbins, A. S. 23:47
Robbins, Aaron 1:66;
    21:142
Robbins, Alvin D. 10:146
Robbins, Ambrose
    10:133; 20:336
Robbins, Andrew 22:216
Robbins, Asa 25:303
Robbins, B. C. 1:166
Robbins, B. F. 15:295
Robbins, Bartholomew
    8:94
Robbins, C. 19:234
Robbins, C. H. 15:18
Robbins, Charles 8:29
Robbins, Charles L.
    18:400
Robbins, Charles W.
    17:112

Robbins, Clark 9:191
Robbins, D. B. 3:164;
    18:222
Robbins, D. C. 19:242
Robbins, D. P. 23:47
Robbins, E. 25:225
Robbins, E. C. D. 24:102
Robbins, Egbert W.
    13:68; 16:223
Robbins, Elliott H. 4:49
Robbins, Ephraim W.
    22:51
Robbins, F. 14:289
Robbins, F. J. 16:223
Robbins, Francis M. 22:98
Robbins, Francis P. 22:98
Robbins, Frank S. 23:104
Robbins, G. 3:164
Robbins, George 1:68;
    22:51
Robbins, H. 1:69; 11:269;
    12:162
Robbins, H. A. 25:225
Robbins, H. M. 23:47
Robbins, H. T. 22:489
Robbins, Harvey M.
    22:154
Robbins, Henry 21:93
Robbins, Henry P. 20:59
Robbins, Isaac 11:167
Robbins, J. 1:166
Robbins, J. B. 1:164
Robbins, J. L. 16:223
Robbins, J. W. 15:223;
    17:495
Robbins, James 16:79;
    23:194
Robbins, James H. 18:222
Robbins, John 7:108;
    10:93; 14:211; 23:77;
    25:66
Robbins, John A. 1:69;
    12:37
Robbins, John F. 9:191;
    19:271
Robbins, John Q. A. 12:37
Robbins, Joseph 12:37
Robbins, Joshua 8:94
Robbins, L. C. 23:165
Robbins, Lemuel 13:44
Robbins, Lindsay L. 12:37
Robbins, Lionel E. 21:259
Robbins, M. 19:95
Robbins, Mathew 9:124
Robbins, Moses 12:37
Robbins, Nathan 7:108;
    27:104
Robbins, Nathan N. 24:88
Robbins, Noah 12:54
Robbins, P. 25:225
Robbins, Peter 5:28

Robbins, R. 3:164; 27:105
Robbins, R. R. 13:44;
    19:260
Robbins, Ralph D. 9:124
Robbins, Ralph G. 27:103
Robbins, Richard R. 9:191
Robbins, Robert J. 15:82
Robbins, Rufus 12:37
Robbins, Samuel 16:52
Robbins, Samuel C.
    22:410
Robbins, Sylvester 12:76
Robbins, Syms 13:117
Robbins, V. 1:68
Robbins, W. 3:164;
    15:175
Robbins, W. H. 9:191;
    19:242
Robbins, W. S. 20:336
Robbins, William 1:69;
    8:29; 10:76; 20:336;
    22:343
Robbins, William N.
    13:117
Robbinson, Charles R.
    18:400
Robbinson, William
    16:223
Robbinson, William W.
    18:400
Robbs, John 18:37
Robbt, S. 12:88
Robbzin, Isaac 7:39
Robe, Bennet 11:74
Robe, James T. 11:75
Robe, W. 26:179
Robe, William 12:87;
    16:303
Robeck, Fritz 14:211
Robeck, William 23:242
Robenult, John 23:266
Robenult, Zachariah 12:37
Rober, H. 11:416
Rober, H. L. 19:31
Rober, J. B. 24:102
Rober, John 17:41
Rober---, George 23:77
Roberg, F. 3:165
Roberge, Nelson 22:163
Roberson, C. A. 3:165
Roberson, David M.
    18:222
Roberson, H. 9:224;
    25:225
Roberson, Israel 15:223
Roberson, J. 1:165
Roberson, James 22:266
Roberson, James W.
    20:134
Roberson, John 13:58
Roberson, John N. 22:456

Roberson, Johnson 23:257
Roberson, Joseph E.
23:16
Roberson, M. E. 9:224
Roberson, N. E. 18:375
Roberson, P. 14:26
Roberson, R. 18:375
Roberson, W. T. 18:222
Roberson, William 16:303
Robert, C. H. 25:225
Robert, Humphrey 7:132
Robert, J. G. 3:165
Robert, John 11:166;
16:223
Robert, John B. 1:67
Robert, L. H. 21:381
Roberts, --- 12:80;
15:223; 17:297, 482,
509; 18:413; 27:106
Roberts, A. 3:165;
16:223; 17:156;
19:189; 21:39
Roberts, A. B. 1:69; 8:115
Roberts, A. G. 11:329
Roberts, A. J. 11:249
Roberts, Aaron 17:167
Roberts, Albert 10:76
Roberts, Albert M. 23:277
Roberts, Albert W. 13:44
Roberts, Allen 22:436
Roberts, Andrew 3:165
Roberts, Andrew P. 24:60
Roberts, Arnold R. 21:142
Roberts, August 9:231;
20:336
Roberts, Austin 7:60
Roberts, B. 18:56; 21:112
Roberts, B. F. 12:157
Roberts, B. S. 9:215
Roberts, Benjamin 8:54;
10:152; 14:211;
21:381
Roberts, Benjamin F. 9:58
Roberts, Benjamin H.
21:105
Roberts, Byron 15:223
Roberts, C. 9:231; 22:317;
25:225
Roberts, C. W. 18:222
Roberts, Caleb 23:165
Roberts, Chancey 10:76
Roberts, Charles 3:165;
9:135; 19:306;
20:88; 22:14; 27:102
Roberts, Charles F.
18:400
Roberts, Charles H. 5:44;
12:37; 16:88
Roberts, Charles P. 1:67
Roberts, Charles W.
22:437

Roberts, Chauncey 20:336
Roberts, Conrad 17:25
Roberts, Cornelius 22:456
Roberts, D. B. 11:294
Roberts, D. C. 20:59;
23:47
Roberts, D. S. 21:381
Roberts, Daniel 9:45;
12:96; 19:95
Roberts, David 11:391;
13:60; 25:63
Roberts, Delivan E. 21:79
Roberts, Dennis 7:108
Roberts, E. 11:311
Roberts, E. B. 16:101
Roberts, E. P. 10:133;
20:336
Roberts, E. V. 1:66
Roberts, E. W. 9:58
Roberts, Eakin J. 22:98
Roberts, Eben 9:191
Roberts, Ed 3:165
Roberts, Edgar G. 22:509
Roberts, Edward 10:133;
20:336
Roberts, Edward A.
11:110
Roberts, Edward C. 13:44;
16:52
Roberts, Edwin F. 25:65
Roberts, Eli 18:400
Roberts, Elijah 8:94;
25:225
Roberts, Elijah P. 19:31
Roberts, Elwin 19:230
Roberts, Ephraim 27:105
Roberts, F. 21:112
Roberts, Flavius J. 21:79
Roberts, Frank 23:304
Roberts, Franklin 22:113
Roberts, G. 1:69
Roberts, G. J. 7:69
Roberts, G. N. 17:112
Roberts, G. W. 7:108;
17:156; 21:381;
22:51; 23:304; 25:67
Roberts, George 4:50;
9:38, 100, 191;
13:44; 17:137;
18:296; 23:243;
24:202; 26:111
Roberts, George C. 10:76
Roberts, George J. 7:69
Roberts, George W.
11:166, 403
Roberts, Griffith 18:346
Roberts, H. 1:69; 3:165;
11:73; 14:284;
16:101; 21:39
Roberts, H. M. 19:224;
25:225

Roberts, H. W. 16:101;
24:28
Roberts, Harrison 23:272
Roberts, Harry 9:135
Roberts, Heal 11:415
Roberts, Henry 13:60;
22:317; 25:225;
27:103
Roberts, Henry B. 13:58
Roberts, Henry C. 17:57
Roberts, Henry T. 8:94
Roberts, Hiram 22:266
Roberts, Hyland 4:68
Roberts, I. 14:103
Roberts, I. H. 3:165
Roberts, Isaac 4:50; 9:98;
17:184; 23:291
Roberts, Isaac N. 19:189
Roberts, Iver 20:108
Roberts, J. 1:165, 166,
167; 3:165; 12:162;
14:103, 289; 16:223;
18:71; 22:317;
26:179
Roberts, J. A. 22:489
Roberts, J. C. 14:302;
17:479; 25:225;
27:105
Roberts, J. E. 11:86
Roberts, J. G. 3:165
Roberts, J. H. 1:166; 9:58
Roberts, J. J. 7:60
Roberts, J. K. 8:75
Roberts, J. M. 3:165
Roberts, J. O. 3:165
Roberts, J. S. 25:65, 225
Roberts, J. W. 9:113;
17:283
Roberts, Jacob 19:31;
22:317
Roberts, James 9:191;
10:76, 133; 12:37;
17:399; 19:189;
20:47, 128, 336;
22:51; 23:165
Roberts, James H. 17:207
Roberts, James M. 10:21;
17:72
Roberts, James N. 23:92
Roberts, James P. 21:79
Roberts, James T. 5:45
Roberts, James W.
11:222; 18:222
Roberts, Jesse 20:25
Roberts, Jesse W. 9:89
Roberts, Joel 22:129
Roberts, John 1:69; 3:165;
6:26; 7:10, 53; 8:29;
9:58, 124, 231;
11:409, 425; 12:172;
13:44; 14:211;

Roberts, John 15:223; 16:141; 17:283; 18:156; 19:48; 20:149, 336; 21:283; 22:51; 23:47, 185; 24:10; 27:103, 106
Roberts, John A. W. 16:52
Roberts, John B. 22:216
Roberts, John D. 16:303; 23:92
Roberts, John F. 4:50
Roberts, John H. 15:223
Roberts, John J. 4:50
Roberts, John M. 9:237; 16:52; 22:266
Roberts, John Q. A. 22:113
Roberts, John R. 22:98, 469
Roberts, John S. 8:29; 9:28; 18:156, 315; 26:110
Roberts, John W. 8:94
Roberts, Johnsey 15:88
Roberts, Jonas 19:260
Roberts, Jordan 7:132
Roberts, Joseph 19:95; 20:43; 22:317
Roberts, Joseph A. 22:51
Roberts, Josiah 23:96
Roberts, Kennon 17:253
Roberts, L. 3:165; 24:96
Roberts, L. A. 20:149
Roberts, L. H. 7:84
Roberts, Lambert 21:381
Roberts, Lester 11:74
Roberts, Levi M. 23:92
Roberts, Lipman 27:105
Roberts, Lovett 9:45
Roberts, Lyman 20:12
Roberts, M. 14:103
Roberts, M. A. 14:103
Roberts, M. D. 23:15
Roberts, M. G. 14:302; 17:471; 27:105
Roberts, M. J. 8:54
Roberts, Martin 11:425
Roberts, Miles 14:211
Roberts, Moses 13:68; 19:95
Roberts, Napoleon B. 23:115
Roberts, Nelson 16:223
Roberts, Newman 21:218
Roberts, Obediah L. 8:29; 18:156
Roberts, Oliver B. 18:114
Roberts, Owen R. 6:8
Roberts, P. 12:9
Roberts, Paul 8:109; 15:361

Roberts, Peter 6:26; 8:42; 9:113; 15:73; 25:65; 26:178
Roberts, Prince 22:317
Roberts, R. 3:165; 17:137; 20:336; 24:202
Roberts, Reese W. 12:37
Roberts, Richard 9:224; 17:238; 25:225
Roberts, Richard W. 1:66
Roberts, Richards 18:375
Roberts, Robert 21:283; 22:489
Roberts, Robert D. 20:116
Roberts, Robert W. 22:436
Roberts, Robinson 10:76
Roberts, Russell 8:75; 11:166; 26:179
Roberts, S. 7:39; 11:269; 14:211
Roberts, S. A. 14:211
Roberts, S. F. 14:266
Roberts, Samuel 7:132
Roberts, Samuel A. 16:303
Roberts, Sebastian L. 24:44
Roberts, Seren 11:110
Roberts, Smassey 20:336
Roberts, Sparks C. 12:37
Roberts, Squire 23:101
Roberts, Swasey 10:76
Roberts, T. 21:112; 25:225
Roberts, T. W. 27:147
Roberts, Theodore F. 23:77
Roberts, Thomas 5:44; 9:38; 18:296; 20:134; 22:98, 216; 26:111
Roberts, Thomas C. 8:54; 21:39
Roberts, Thomas H. 4:50
Roberts, Thomas I. 10:76
Roberts, Thomas J. 20:336; 21:116
Roberts, Tillman 21:381
Roberts, Vincent 12:37; 17:137; 24:202
Roberts, W. 1:165; 9:58; 22:343; 25:225
Roberts, W. G. 24:83; 25:64
Roberts, W. H. 11:193; 26:178
Roberts, W. R. 4:50
Roberts, W. S. 19:284
Roberts, W. W. 3:165
Roberts, Warden 13:44; 16:52

Roberts, Wesley 17:156
Roberts, Wilford 17:274
Roberts, William 5:44; 7:108; 9:135; 11:409; 12:37; 17:25, 151, 156, 204; 21:191; 22:317; 27:103
Roberts, William A. 18:400
Roberts, William D. 16:52
Roberts, William G. 21:381
Roberts, William H. 8:29; 11:167, 249; 15:88; 18:156
Roberts, William J. 27:147
Roberts, William P. 10:210
Roberts, William R. 17:315
Robertson, --- 1:68; 23:268
Robertson, A. 19:48; 22:216
Robertson, Aaron P. 21:79
Robertson, Albert 22:489
Robertson, Alex 20:336
Robertson, Alexander 10:76
Robertson, Anderson 11:212
Robertson, Arie P. 22:98
Robertson, Calvin 22:153
Robertson, Charles 21:381; 22:437
Robertson, Charles S. 24:28
Robertson, Clark J. 22:172
Robertson, D. 7:39
Robertson, David 9:73; 12:37
Robertson, Edmund 19:31
Robertson, Edward J. 17:72
Robertson, Elbert 23:185
Robertson, Elisha 8:109
Robertson, Finlay O. 22:283
Robertson, Francis J. 11:74
Robertson, G. 13:97; 14:20
Robertson, G. H. 9:89; 26:58
Robertson, G. W. 25:303
Robertson, Gaston 13:58
Robertson, George 1:66; 11:17; 14:244; 22:153; 27:106

Robertson, George W. 10:25
Robertson, H. 3:165; 10:76; 26:179
Robertson, H. C. 9:150; 27:101
Robertson, Harry 20:336
Robertson, Henry C. 22:51
Robertson, Hugh 5:27
Robertson, Isaac B. 17:97
Robertson, J. 1:95; 18:193
Robertson, J. A. 16:223
Robertson, J. C. 3:165; 25:225
Robertson, J. F. 11:73
Robertson, J. P. 21:39
Robertson, James 9:237; 11:382; 18:37; 20:336; 21:381; 22:317; 26:56, 225
Robertson, James L. 17:315
Robertson, James M. 20:47
Robertson, Jeremiah 12:160
Robertson, John 3:165; 11:166; 17:184; 22:51, 489; 24:203; 27:105
Robertson, John H. 22:129
Robertson, John J. 20:88
Robertson, John T. 10:133; 20:336
Robertson, John W. 22:51
Robertson, Joseph 3:165; 13:58; 16:52
Robertson, Joseph E. 20:100
Robertson, Joseph T. 12:157
Robertson, Joshua 18:193
Robertson, L. 25:225
Robertson, Lemon 22:524
Robertson, Matthew 17:420
Robertson, P. 16:223
Robertson, R. 3:165
Robertson, Robert 17:85; 27:105
Robertson, Russell P. 23:77
Robertson, Samuel 13:97; 22:98, 129; 23:264
Robertson, Samuel S. 24:55
Robertson, Silas 10:99
Robertson, Squire 24:167

Robertson, Stephen B. 14:211
Robertson, T. 13:97; 14:20
Robertson, Thomas 22:98
Robertson, Thomas B. O. 11:277
Robertson, Thomas P. 8:54
Robertson, Thornton 5:45
Robertson, W. 27:101
Robertson, W. A. 1:67
Robertson, W. H. 3:165
Robertson, W. M. 3:165
Robertson, W. N. 16:223
Robertson, William 8:29; 12:37; 18:156, 400; 21:382; 27:105
Robertson, William C. 18:375
Robertson, William E. 9:224
Robertson, William G. 22:266
Robertson, William H. 5:45
Robertson, William M. 18:400
Robertson, Zimmerman 19:32
Robeson, A. S. 21:168
Robeson, J. S. 27:147
Robey, Andrew F. 24:44
Robey, Ebenezer 17:58
Robey, Notley N. 22:437
Robey, Samuel 10:99
Robey, William H. 23:13
Robie, C. 1:165
Robie, Frank 23:164
Robie, John 21:115
Robin, --- 25:335
Robin, Augustus 7:69
Robin, Robert 11:212
Robinagle, R. 11:323
Robinet, R. J. 24:28
Robinet, Thomas J. 18:251; 26:56
Robinett, Amon 11:311
Robinett, Benjamin 7:60
Robinett, H. C. 21:382
Robinette, Jesse 10:133
Robinhold, Louis M. 2:16
Robinhood, Adam 22:14
Robinnett, Jesse 20:336
Robins, A. 3:164
Robins, Alvin D. 19:189
Robins, Asa 7:76
Robins, B. F. 16:223
Robins, C. S. 17:271
Robins, Charles 18:156; 21:382

Robins, D. G. W. 18:179
Robins, Daniel E. 17:25
Robins, Eli 10:76
Robins, Elisha 5:28
Robins, Elizar 11:117
Robins, Francis 9:89
Robins, Francis W. 26:56
Robins, G. E. 1:99
Robins, George 1:67; 3:164
Robins, H. 21:382; 26:56
Robins, H. H. 1:95
Robins, Henry 10:166; 19:189
Robins, Hiram 9:89
Robins, Isaac 22:129
Robins, J. 3:164; 14:259, 289
Robins, J. W. 17:441
Robins, James 17:283
Robins, John 14:266; 20:336
Robins, John W. 24:154
Robins, Joseph 6:23
Robins, L. 3:164
Robins, L. J. 18:92
Robins, Levi 17:41
Robins, N. A. 14:103
Robins, P. C. 3:164
Robins, R. R. 11:382
Robins, Richard 9:161
Robins, Samuel 19:32
Robins, Tennessee 8:109
Robins, Timothy 14:212
Robins, W. B. 18:251; 26:56
Robins, William 8:109; 17:253
Robins, William R. 21:132
Robins, Willis 4:68
Robinson, --- 2:17; 3:164; 9:89; 18:194; 23:47, 205; 25:64, 65, 66
Robinson, A. 1:69; 3:164, 165; 12:83; 14:331; 16:223, 303; 25:225; 26:56
Robinson, A. D. 8:94
Robinson, A. G. 21:382
Robinson, A. H. 18:37
Robinson, A. O. 25:303
Robinson, A. S. 14:103
Robinson, Aaron 9:89
Robinson, Adam 5:45
Robinson, Albert 9:210; 11:415, 425; 17:184
Robinson, Alex 27:103
Robinson, Alexander 7:47; 9:135, 215
Robinson, Alfred 21:283

Robinson, Alfred B. 21:95
Robinson, Alphonso N.
    23:194
Robinson, Anamar 7:132
Robinson, Andrew
    14:103; 17:362
Robinson, Andrew I.
    25:275
Robinson, B. 12:96
Robinson, B. F. 7:108;
    19:95
Robinson, B. H. 27:101
Robinson, B. T. 17:41
Robinson, Ben 26:55
Robinson, Ben. F. 23:241
Robinson, Benjamin
    7:132; 9:95; 22:317
Robinson, Benjamin L.
    22:51
Robinson, C. 1:69, 164,
    165; 7:39; 21:112;
    23:101; 27:157
Robinson, C. George
    20:43
Robinson, C. H. 13:126;
    21:382
Robinson, C. J. 3:165
Robinson, C. L. 1:166
Robinson, C. N. 27:104
Robinson, C. W. 3:164;
    9:124
Robinson, Calin 19:190
Robinson, Calvin 20:12
Robinson, Carter 18:251;
    26:57
Robinson, Charles 9:240;
    11:129; 12:96;
    15:153, 361; 17:184,
    264; 19:95; 20:31;
    21:118, 283; 22:216;
    27:101
Robinson, Charles J.
    25:65
Robinson, Christopher
    4:49
Robinson, Clayton 21:382
Robinson, Cook 11:165
Robinson, Cooper 5:53
Robinson, Cyrus B.
    22:283
Robinson, Cyrus D.
    22:283
Robinson, D. 3:165;
    20:85; 25:66
Robinson, D. F. 1:67
Robinson, D. P. 21:168
Robinson, D. W. 1:165
Robinson, Daniel 7:108,
    132; 18:92; 26:110
Robinson, Daniel S. 9:38;
    18:296

Robinson, David 6:18, 27;
    7:108; 8:42; 11:249,
    416; 21:382; 26:178
Robinson, David H.
    10:133
Robinson, David P.
    21:233
Robinson, Delano 4:49
Robinson, Demison 24:44
Robinson, E. 9:158;
    11:73; 21:382;
    25:303
Robinson, E. B. 1:167
Robinson, E. H. 3:165
Robinson, E. M. 26:178
Robinson, E. P. 19:32
Robinson, Edgar 10:177;
    19:190
Robinson, Edmond 4:50
Robinson, Edmund
    17:420
Robinson, Edward 6:18;
    7:132; 12:37; 13:44;
    18:92; 19:95; 21:283
Robinson, Edward S.
    24:83
Robinson, Edwin 21:382
Robinson, Edwin F.
    17:410; 22:129
Robinson, Elbert F.
    23:185
Robinson, Elisha 8:29;
    18:156
Robinson, Enert 7:39
Robinson, Enos 12:37
Robinson, F. 1:99; 13:97;
    14:103; 15:111
Robinson, F. A. 11:404
Robinson, F. H. 19:32
Robinson, Fate 19:292
Robinson, Francis 19:32;
    20:176
Robinson, Frank 18:340
Robinson, Frank B. 13:44
Robinson, Franklin 9:104;
    23:124
Robinson, G. 1:69; 7:39;
    15:223
Robinson, G. E. 25:64
Robinson, G. G. 1:68
Robinson, G. H. 7:60;
    9:113
Robinson, G. W. 26:179
Robinson, Gabriel 12:160
Robinson, Gage 17:268
Robinson, Gain D. 4:50
Robinson, George 1:67;
    6:28; 7:132; 9:224;
    11:211, 212, 289;
    12:51, 76; 14:103;

Robinson, George 15:43,
    321; 18:375; 19:95;
    22:216, 317
Robinson, George C.
    10:174; 19:190
Robinson, George F.
    20:336
Robinson, George G.
    23:92
Robinson, George L. B.
    27:105
Robinson, George T.
    10:76
Robinson, George W.
    4:49
Robinson, Goss 21:283
Robinson, Green B.
    22:129
Robinson, H. 3:165; 9:58;
    15:300; 17:15; 24:55
Robinson, H. B. 3:165
Robinson, H. C. 3:164
Robinson, H. H. 3:164
Robinson, H. N. 10:166;
    19:190
Robinson, H. S. 9:28
Robinson, Harris 21:382
Robinson, Harrison 9:104
Robinson, Harry W. 11:42
Robinson, Henry 6:18, 22;
    11:212; 18:92;
    19:190; 21:142, 283;
    23:92
Robinson, Henry F.
    27:101
Robinson, Henry P.
    23:101
Robinson, Henry R.
    22:509
Robinson, Higgins N.
    17:85
Robinson, Horace J.
    11:111
Robinson, Hugh 10:133;
    20:336
Robinson, Hutsler 12:51
Robinson, I. 9:239;
    14:103
Robinson, I. H. 18:407
Robinson, I. L. 11:249
Robinson, Ira 25:225
Robinson, Isaac 3:164;
    6:26; 9:135; 10:76,
    177; 19:190; 20:336;
    21:105; 27:103
Robinson, Isaac N. 12:37
Robinson, Israer 21:283
Robinson, J. 1:66, 68, 69,
    70, 167; 3:165; 7:69;
    8:78; 9:191; 11:75;
    13:97; 14:103;

Robinson, J. 15:3, 295; 16:52, 136, 223; 17:184, 326, 471; 18:375; 19:95, 260; 21:39; 25:225, 280, 326; 26:225; 27:106
Robinson, J. A. 21:125; 22:216
Robinson, J. B. 3:165; 15:223; 25:225
Robinson, J. C. 21:39
Robinson, J. E. 21:39; 23:47
Robinson, J. H. 15:300
Robinson, J. J. 1:67, 167; 23:293
Robinson, J. M. 9:58; 18:315; 26:111
Robinson, J. N. 5:27; 25:225
Robinson, J. P. 12:123
Robinson, J. R. 13:68; 16:223; 19:32
Robinson, J. S. 11:269
Robinson, J. W. 3:165; 17:452; 24:182
Robinson, J. W. B. 21:382
Robinson, Jacob 3:164; 10:76; 19:292; 20:336
Robinson, Jacob H. 10:133; 20:337
Robinson, Jacob M. 5:45
Robinson, James 1:67; 5:45; 7:39; 9:101, 156, 210, 224; 10:76, 177; 11:167; 12:9; 13:44; 14:212, 317; 15:23, 223; 16:52; 17:58; 19:190; 20:337; 21:89
Robinson, James A. 9:38; 18:296; 26:110
Robinson, James C. 22:51
Robinson, James E. 1:67
Robinson, James F. 10:76; 11:73; 20:337
Robinson, James H. 21:89
Robinson, James M. 3:164
Robinson, James S. 21:142
Robinson, James W. 8:67; 22:505
Robinson, Jesse 24:28
Robinson, John 1:68; 3:165; 7:39, 76; 10:76, 97, 133; 11:165, 167, 391; 12:37, 51; 18:222, 296, 375; 20:337; 22:51, 216, 267;

Robinson, John 23:194; 25:66, 303; 26:111; 27:101
Robinson, John A. 11:89
Robinson, John B. 4:49; 15:279; 21:93
Robinson, John H. 4:49; 18:37; 21:382; 22:154
Robinson, John L. 11:212
Robinson, John M. 13:60; 20:134
Robinson, John R. 14:212
Robinson, John W. 9:38; 18:296; 26:110, 111
Robinson, Johnson 15:167; 20:100
Robinson, Joseph 4:49; 12:76; 16:223; 17:405; 19:32; 22:51, 437
Robinson, Joseph H. 4:50
Robinson, Joseph J. 23:47
Robinson, Josiah P. 15:133
Robinson, Josiah R. 11:166
Robinson, L. 14:103; 25:225
Robinson, L. B. 14:212
Robinson, L. L. 7:12
Robinson, L. M. 9:224
Robinson, L. P. 11:282
Robinson, L. W. 18:375
Robinson, Lemon 21:283
Robinson, Levi M. 21:382
Robinson, Lewis 8:115; 24:203
Robinson, Lewis M. 8:29
Robinson, Louis 21:283
Robinson, Louis M. 18:156
Robinson, Ludivio 16:303
Robinson, M. 11:75; 25:284
Robinson, Marcellus 10:99
Robinson, Marion 17:149; 20:12
Robinson, Mark E. 15:88
Robinson, Martin B. 12:142
Robinson, Marvin 19:190
Robinson, Mary 25:312
Robinson, Maskell E. 21:116
Robinson, Mathew 21:382
Robinson, Maur 25:225
Robinson, Melvin C. 7:108
Robinson, Milton 17:184

Robinson, Monroe 22:343; 23:309
Robinson, Moses W. 13:44
Robinson, Myron S. 11:110
Robinson, N. 9:113; 21:382
Robinson, Nathan 9:89, 135; 26:55; 27:103
Robinson, Nathan D. 20:31
Robinson, Nelson 15:43
Robinson, Newton 19:48
Robinson, Noah 27:103
Robinson, Noah L. 9:124
Robinson, O. 9:113; 17:184; 25:312
Robinson, P. 16:223; 21:112
Robinson, Peter 16:148; 22:317
Robinson, Philip 9:201; 19:292
Robinson, Pleasant 22:505
Robinson, Preston 8:42; 26:178
Robinson, R. 3:164, 165; 12:87; 13:44; 14:103, 212; 15:361; 16:303; 19:96; 25:225
Robinson, R. A. 7:39, 132
Robinson, R. E. 21:382
Robinson, R. E. K. 4:50
Robinson, R. F. 14:103
Robinson, R. W. 8:67
Robinson, Renick 9:135
Robinson, Reuben 25:269
Robinson, Richard P. 25:64
Robinson, Robert 16:123; 22:51, 317
Robinson, Robert H. 18:92
Robinson, Rufus 15:43
Robinson, Russell 18:37
Robinson, S. 7:78; 17:145; 24:28; 25:303
Robinson, S. E. 12:37
Robinson, S. L. 22:216
Robinson, S. M. 1:166
Robinson, S. R. 14:27
Robinson, Samuel 5:27; 9:158, 210; 10:133; 11:391; 19:32; 20:337; 23:13; 24:44
Robinson, Samuel W. 22:266
Robinson, Sanford 11:167

Robinson, Scott 21:382
Robinson, Sherman S. 16:87
Robinson, Silas 9:9
Robinson, Simon 22:317; 25:286
Robinson, Sylvester 13:44
Robinson, T. 1:168; 19:96, 260; 25:225; 27:102
Robinson, T. C. 16:52
Robinson, T. F. 25:225
Robinson, Theodore 9:191
Robinson, Theodore F. 5:27
Robinson, Thomas 4:49; 6:18; 9:124, 135; 11:407; 17:184; 18:92; 21:259; 23:165; 25:225; 26:55; 27:103, 147
Robinson, Timothy 12:37
Robinson, Tussen 25:326
Robinson, Uriah 19:32
Robinson, Urick 27:103
Robinson, Varras H. 7:132
Robinson, W. 1:68, 166; 9:113; 26:56
Robinson, W. B. 25:225
Robinson, W. F. 15:223
Robinson, W. H. 11:222; 22:216; 25:226; 26:128
Robinson, W. M. 3:165
Robinson, W. O. 4:50
Robinson, W. R. 3:164
Robinson, W. T. 22:216
Robinson, W. V. 12:37
Robinson, Walter S. 22:489
Robinson, Wattie 25:335
Robinson, Wiley 9:89; 26:55
Robinson, William 1:67; 3:164; 7:60, 108; 8:29; 9:9, 210; 11:184, 338; 12:37, 51, 87; 13:44; 14:103; 15:268, 313, 355; 17:199, 424, 497; 18:156; 19:96; 21:382; 22:267, 524; 24:69, 174; 27:100
Robinson, William D. 9:45
Robinson, William F. 17:25; 20:187; 25:64

Robinson, William H. 17:423; 21:382; 23:109; 24:171
Robinson, William M. 13:44
Robinson, Willis 10:99
Robinson, Winfield S. 17:85
Robinson, Winslow A. 22:456
Robinson, Young 9:135; 27:104
Robinson, Z. R. 19:32
Robison, Alexander 17:261
Robison, Amos 23:77
Robison, David H. 20:337
Robison, Edward S. 15:88
Robison, F. 3:165
Robison, George R. 23:115
Robison, Henry 17:85
Robison, I. 3:165
Robison, J. C. 3:165
Robison, Jeremiah A. 22:456
Robison, L. 3:165
Robison, Richard 17:399
Robison, S. 24:83
Robison, Samuel 20:337
Robison, Thomas 21:283
Robison, Thomas J. 22:129
Robison, William A. 22:410
Roble, D. 24:44
Roblett, George 9:73
Roblyer, J. 1:166
Robneth, Lawson C. 16:52
Robnett, John 22:317
Robnett, William 22:343
Robothane, Thomas 15:43
Robowin, J. N. 20:36
Robshaw, Samuel 7:108
Robshaw, Simon 21:382
Robsin, John 1:69
Robson, Allen 12:97
Robson, J. W. 1:99
Robson, Thomas 22:51
Robston, Robert J. 9:224
Robuck, Aaron 21:205
Robuck, David 9:38
Robuck, Fred 18:156
Robum, A. 14:290
Robust, William 1:67
Roby, Abraham 24:55
Roby, Daniel 20:128
Roby, H. C. 12:157
Roby, Isaac 22:317
Roby, Isaac W. 23:77

Roby, J. 9:149; 27:102
Roby, John 15:88; 17:452
Roby, John T. 22:98
Roby, John W. 24:182
Roby, S. H. 11:194
Roby, W. C. 14:266
Roby, Walter S. 9:149
Roch, J. 7:39
Roch, James 12:83; 16:303
Roch, S. 15:223
Roch, Uriah 10:76
Rocha, M. 25:303
Rochauskey, --- 5:53
Roche, Edward 16:87
Roche, J. 1:167
Roche, Michael 8:126
Roche, Owen 23:242
Rochell, H. 18:56
Rochell, John 3:165
Rochen, Gustave 11:120
Rochester, James 10:76
Rochford, William 23:165
Rochler, Thomas 9:161
Rochlett, J. H. 24:83
Rochm, William 22:216
Rochner, Frederick 16:223
Rochow, Henry 19:275
Rock, Andrew 22:521
Rock, David 26:213
Rock, Edward 19:96
Rock, George 22:216
Rock, Henderson 16:223
Rock, Henry 25:65
Rock, I. E. 3:165
Rock, James F. 4:50
Rock, James S. 12:37
Rock, Jordan 18:92
Rock, Jules 7:132
Rock, Q. 26:178
Rock, Thomas 19:260; 22:51
Rock, Uriah 20:337
Rock, Willard 12:37
Rock, William 23:314
Rockamier, George 11:311
Rockbuck, L. 14:103
Rocke, F. 3:165
Rocker, Edward 12:169
Rocker, Samuel 9:113
Rocket, George 19:190
Rocket, J. 11:311
Rockett, Richard 25:226
Rockett, W. 12:93
Rockey, John 23:165
Rockey, John W. 11:232
Rockey, Leonard 22:237
Rockfellow, A. 18:407
Rockfellow, R. E. 3:165

Rockford, --- 16:148
Rockford, T. 13:97
Rockhill, Andrew 22:98
Rockhill, Jasper N. 20:19
Rockhold, William H.
21:39
Rockinfield, O. P. 11:311
Rockingfield, George L.
10:76; 20:337
Rocklebank, N. C. 15:111
Rockley, John 22:267
Rockliff, Samuel 14:212
Rockliffe, John S. 15:167
Rocknell, J. A. 25:226
Rockstadt, Fred 4:50
Rockstang, John A. 18:37
Rockstead, J. M. 11:42
Rockton, M. L. B. 15:338
Rockweil, Amos 10:76
Rockwell, --- 9:191
Rockwell, A. 3:165
Rockwell, A. G. 20:337
Rockwell, Albert I. 10:76
Rockwell, Alvin W. 12:76
Rockwell, Amos 20:337
Rockwell, Charles 24:28
Rockwell, Charles W.
10:76; 20:337
Rockwell, D. 20:134
Rockwell, D. B. 11:312
Rockwell, Daniel 15:43
Rockwell, Edward 25:275
Rockwell, Edward C. 7:39
Rockwell, Evi 20:19
Rockwell, Francis 10:21
Rockwell, Frederick O.
23:241
Rockwell, George 15:111
Rockwell, Henry 21:142
Rockwell, James 19:318
Rockwell, John 22:216
Rockwell, Joseph 4:50
Rockwell, Joseph E. 22:14
Rockwell, M. C. 3:165
Rockwell, Milo 1:66
Rockwell, P. 15:82
Rockwell, R. A. 15:279;
25:226
Rockwell, Samuel C.
12:37
Rockwell, Thomas
10:133; 20:337
Rockwell, W. 24:44
Rockwell, W. H. 3:165
Rockwell, William 15:291
Rockwill, Samuel R. 4:50
Rockwood, C. A. 1:164
Rockwood, Calvin A.
16:7
Rockwood, Daniel 10:76;
20:337

Rockwood, E. 1:66
Rockwood, H. 9:106;
18:335; 25:226
Rockwood, J. J. 20:194
Rockwood, Jasen 20:337
Rockwood, Jason 10:93;
21:259
Rockwood, John B.
10:166; 19:190
Rockwood, John D.
22:154
Rockwood, W. D. 12:157
Rockyfellow, H. 3:165
Rocourt, J. 1:168
Rodd, E. R. 13:68
Rodda, N. T. 25:226
Rodda, Nicholas D. 5:28
Rodden, James A. 8:29
Rodden, Jonathan U.
22:51
Rodden, M. L. 13:44
Rodden, M. S. 16:52
Rodden, William 15:43
Rodder, B. D. 10:29
Rodderman, W. 19:190
Rodderman, William
10:166
Roddy, Edward 22:267
Roddy, Francis 22:14
Roddy, J. 21:58
Roddy, Terrance 13:44
Rodecker, Adam 15:268
Rodeffer, David 22:436
Rodeget, Jacob 12:65;
15:95
Rodel, Henry 5:28
Rodel, Philip 7:81
Rodell, H. 25:226
Rodeloff, George 16:101
Rodem, R. W. 11:75
Roden, B. D. 19:306
Roden, James A. 18:156
Roden, Jesse 11:19
Rodenberger, N. 3:165
Rodenberger, Samuel
15:153
Rodenburgh, W. 15:73
Rodenburgh, William
12:76
Rodener, Peter 20:337
Roder, C. 1:68
Roder, George 12:173
Roder, John 12:37
Roder, John H. 12:100
Roder, Philip 13:44
Roder, Phillip 16:52
Roder, W. I. 3:166
Roderack, Todd 18:92
Roderick, Harmon 21:58
Roderick, Henry 22:283
Roderick, Jasper 22:410

Roderick, Perry 22:409
Roderick, William 9:191
Roderigo, Lewis 26:110
Roderigo, Louis 18:315
Roderpher, W. H. H.
21:218
Roders, Charles 17:137;
24:202
Rodes, --- 2:16
Rodes, F. 3:165
Rodes, Henry 18:37
Rodes, James 3:165
Rodes, Joel 17:15
Rodes, S. 25:66
Rodevoult, Arnold 20:12
Rodewoner, Peter 10:76
Rodey, J. A. 21:382
Rodge, Orville 26:58
Rodger, Adolph 10:76;
20:337
Rodger, Hiram 17:447;
24:171
Rodger, Orville 9:89
Rodgers, A. 1:165; 9:89;
15:43, 259
Rodgers, A. D. 1:68
Rodgers, Achilles 11:74
Rodgers, Albert 18:422
Rodgers, Alexander 22:98
Rodgers, Anthony 17:25
Rodgers, Asa 12:157
Rodgers, Aster 9:124
Rodgers, Astor 27:103
Rodgers, B. 3:165
Rodgers, B. F. 1:67
Rodgers, Benjamin
22:267
Rodgers, C. 8:54
Rodgers, C. H. 17:307
Rodgers, C. M. 23:165
Rodgers, C. T. 11:166
Rodgers, Charles 8:117;
18:330
Rodgers, Charles H.
13:97; 25:66
Rodgers, D. 1:166
Rodgers, D. A. 4:50
Rodgers, David 8:54
Rodgers, Edmund 19:190
Rodgers, Edward 9:161
Rodgers, Elias 17:41
Rodgers, Elijah F. 4:50
Rodgers, F. 3:165; 12:37
Rodgers, Franklin 22:51
Rodgers, G. A. 17:25
Rodgers, G. H. 7:39
Rodgers, George 4:50;
7:53; 18:400; 24:202
Rodgers, George F.
19:190

Rodgers, George H. 18:222
Rodgers, George L. 22:154
Rodgers, H. 8:69; 18:375
Rodgers, H. H. 25:226
Rodgers, H. M. 22:51
Rodgers, Harper 22:99
Rodgers, Henry 9:224; 22:14; 24:202
Rodgers, Henry C. 5:45
Rodgers, Henry H. 11:188
Rodgers, Hiram 11:111
Rodgers, Horace 4:50
Rodgers, I. J. 25:226
Rodgers, Ira G. 25:226
Rodgers, Isaac 9:166
Rodgers, J. 7:39
Rodgers, J. C. 17:167; 22:51
Rodgers, J. E. 1:167
Rodgers, J. G. 5:28; 11:282
Rodgers, J. R. 18:375
Rodgers, James 4:50; 7:108; 17:149, 283; 21:58; 24:114
Rodgers, James M. 21:79
Rodgers, James W. 18:17
Rodgers, Job 26:56
Rodgers, John 4:50; 10:133, 206; 11:404; 12:157; 19:190; 20:337; 22:436, 455; 23:92, 165
Rodgers, John H. 22:98
Rodgers, John S. 7:39
Rodgers, John W. 19:190
Rodgers, Joseph 23:115
Rodgers, Joseph E. 4:50
Rodgers, Joseph F. 22:410
Rodgers, Jourdon 17:167
Rodgers, L. 3:165
Rodgers, L. W. 22:51
Rodgers, Lamb 7:132
Rodgers, Lewis J. 27:104
Rodgers, M. 25:335
Rodgers, M. C. 1:69
Rodgers, Mack 24:102
Rodgers, Michel 4:50
Rodgers, N. 1:168
Rodgers, Nelson 21:283
Rodgers, Newell 10:76; 20:337
Rodgers, O. 3:165; 24:84
Rodgers, Orville 11:117
Rodgers, Owen 16:52
Rodgers, R. 14:320; 25:282
Rodgers, R. G. 25:66
Rodgers, R. T. 25:63

Rodgers, Reading 1:67
Rodgers, Richard 10:76; 20:337
Rodgers, Robert 11:212; 22:154
Rodgers, Robert C. 20:179
Rodgers, S. 23:13
Rodgers, S. J. 21:105
Rodgers, Samuel 15:3
Rodgers, Stephen B. 7:39
Rodgers, Thomas 10:206; 21:128
Rodgers, Thomas B. 22:267
Rodgers, Thomas M. 10:133
Rodgers, Thomas S. 18:202
Rodgers, Thomas T. 20:12
Rodgers, W. 3:165; 9:243; 16:223; 25:66
Rodgers, W. D. 14:103
Rodgers, W. F. 12:157
Rodgers, W. G. 11:248
Rodgers, W. H. 15:43
Rodgers, W. J. 1:166; 21:39; 27:101
Rodgers, Warner M. 23:165
Rodgers, William 7:39, 53; 8:109; 9:224; 11:167; 18:375; 20:337; 21:39; 22:14, 216; 27:102
Rodgers, William A. 4:50
Rodgers, William H. H. 1:67
Rodgers, William M. 22:505
Rodgers, William R. 4:50; 9:58
Rodgway, J. 25:66
Rodgway, John 2:16
Rodhes, George 18:37
Rodicker, C. 25:326
Rodicker, Christian 6:33
Rodiger, John 8:118; 19:315
Rodiheffer, William 26:55
Rodihiffer, William 9:89
Rodimer, William H. 20:128
Rodinburg, L. P. 9:98
Roding, George 14:103; 18:92
Rodlander, C. 10:29; 19:306
Rodman, B. 9:28
Rodman, Erasmus E. 24:96

Rodman, George 17:250
Rodman, J. 14:302; 17:477; 27:105
Rodman, James T. 21:233
Rodman, Jefferson 11:269
Rodman, Thomas 14:212
Rodmand, --- 13:68
Rodmond, Allen 8:75
Rodney, A. 15:273
Rodney, Adam 23:129
Rodney, George 6:13
Rodney, George W. 10:133; 20:337
Rodney, Hugh 26:56
Rodolph, Henry 11:391
Rods, John 12:76
Rodt, John 1:67
Rodt, Simon 3:165
Rodwick, J. 1:167
Rodwill, D. D. 23:282
Roe, A. H. 5:28
Roe, A. J. 9:58
Roe, B. F. 11:249
Roe, Benjamin H. 24:89
Roe, C. 1:167; 13:97; 14:20
Roe, Claikim 21:382
Roe, Clarkson 7:132
Roe, Edward 19:190; 22:51
Roe, Frilden 11:97
Roe, G. L. 23:277
Roe, H. 15:295
Roe, Hartley 16:223
Roe, Henry 17:319
Roe, J. 14:103
Roe, J. F. 8:75; 26:179
Roe, J. W. 11:97
Roe, James M. 23:280
Roe, John 10:29; 15:43; 18:114
Roe, John M. 24:102
Roe, Jonas M. 12:37
Roe, Joseph 10:207
Roe, L. G. 16:378
Roe, M. 14:270
Roe, Martin 16:101
Roe, T. 13:97
Roe, W. I. 25:282
Roe, W. J. 14:320; 23:47
Roe, William 3:166; 20:337
Roe, William C. 22:216
Roebring, F. 21:205
Roechell, Hiram 24:28
Roedel, Frederick 21:142
Roeder, Nicholas 11:193
Roee, John 14:103
Roegae, William 18:37
Roehin, Henry 9:191
Roel, Frederick 7:108

Roel, William 15:223
Roelch, Frederick 11:334
Roemer, Nicholas 14:212
Roen, R. 13:117
Roen, Zacharias 25:63
Roenspier, Fred 9:231;
    20:337
Roepke, Adolph 24:176
Roesener, C. 1:69
Roessler, Frederick
    10:134; 20:337
Roether, J. P. 22:489
Roethlisberger, Ulrich
    21:259
Roeybaugh, Charles
    15:268
Rofburn, W. 3:166
Roferty, John 3:166
Roff, Crawford 10:93;
    20:337
Roff, John 12:162
Roff, L. 16:223
Roff, Oliver 10:76
Roff, W. 1:165
Roffey, M. 5:54
Roffey, W. H. 5:53;
    25:226
Roffler, Christ 26:213
Roffman, W. H. 17:293
Rofter, J. 1:166
Rogan, C. 3:166
Rogan, Columbia 11:212
Rogan, J. 25:63
Rogan, M. 16:223
Rogan, Patrick 12:9
Rogatt, C. 1:69
Rogel, C. 1:165
Rogensack, John 20:143
Roger, --- 18:375
Roger, Abel H. 7:108
Roger, Albert 13:44
Roger, Hamilton S. 4:50
Roger, John 10:149;
    16:378
Roger, John L. 3:166
Roger, L. 3:166
Roger, Leo 11:416
Roger, Peter 8:94
Roger, Samuel 4:50
Rogers, --- 9:90; 11:232;
    17:509
Rogers, A. 3:166; 10:154;
    15:153; 16:223
Rogers, A. G. 3:166
Rogers, Abbott 8:42;
    26:178
Rogers, Abe 7:108
Rogers, Albert 16:53
Rogers, Amos 12:51
Rogers, And 25:304

Rogers, Andrew 7:78;
    12:37; 22:343
Rogers, Arnold 22:456
Rogers, Asa B. 22:154
Rogers, Augustus 13:44;
    16:53; 23:124
Rogers, Benjamin 21:39,
    382
Rogers, Berry 21:283
Rogers, C. 3:166; 15:223
Rogers, Carlos 19:96
Rogers, Catharine 16:71
Rogers, Charles 8:94;
    15:311; 22:343;
    23:258
Rogers, Charles E. 21:382
Rogers, Charles H. 14:20
Rogers, Charles S. 1:69
Rogers, Cyrus 22:216
Rogers, Cyrus A. 19:230
Rogers, D. F. 25:226
Rogers, Daniel 8:120
Rogers, David 12:37
Rogers, David C. 21:79
Rogers, David K. 8:29;
    18:156
Rogers, David S. 22:267
Rogers, Dean 25:226
Rogers, Dennis 25:304
Rogers, Dyer 16:82
Rogers, E. 27:105
Rogers, E. P. 1:164
Rogers, Eben 22:168
Rogers, Edson C. 5:28
Rogers, Edward 10:154;
    14:328; 19:190;
    23:13
Rogers, Eli M. 9:237
Rogers, Elijah 24:215
Rogers, Elisha S. 20:36
Rogers, Ephraim G. 13:44
Rogers, Ernest 9:241
Rogers, Ezra J. 11:289
Rogers, F. 25:326
Rogers, Frederick 1:68
Rogers, G. 3:166
Rogers, G. S. 11:281
Rogers, G. W. 1:69;
    11:269; 14:263;
    20:59; 23:118
Rogers, Gaslen R. 22:154
Rogers, George 3:166;
    10:134; 13:44; 16:53;
    17:137; 18:92;
    20:337
Rogers, George E. 15:111
Rogers, George F. 10:166
Rogers, George S. 12:37
Rogers, George W.
    20:108; 22:436, 438
Rogers, Gilbert N. 23:194

Rogers, Gordon 17:100
Rogers, Green 18:251
Rogers, Greer 26:57
Rogers, Gustavus 8:109
Rogers, H. 11:73; 16:148
Rogers, H. C. 1:69; 3:166
Rogers, H. J. 3:166
Rogers, Harrison 18:341
Rogers, Harvey 17:244
Rogers, Henry 3:166;
    9:16; 13:80; 17:137;
    18:71
Rogers, Henry F. 19:32
Rogers, Henry G. 20:128
Rogers, Hugh S. 13:44
Rogers, Hugh Y. 22:437
Rogers, Isaac 7:108
Rogers, J. 1:166; 20:59
Rogers, J. H. 13:68; 19:96
Rogers, J. R. 9:224;
    14:302; 17:479
Rogers, J. T. 17:323
Rogers, J. W. 1:166
Rogers, Jacob 9:90;
    22:283
Rogers, James 3:166;
    10:29; 14:212;
    19:306; 21:382;
    23:77
Rogers, James A. 22:437
Rogers, James B. 16:53
Rogers, James C. 23:47
Rogers, James L. 18:37
Rogers, James M. 8:29;
    18:156
Rogers, Job 10:97
Rogers, John 8:42; 9:240;
    11:75; 14:212;
    15:223; 17:97;
    18:251; 20:36;
    21:382; 24:84; 26:57,
    178
Rogers, John A. 8:29;
    18:156
Rogers, John C. 26:179
Rogers, John F. 15:175
Rogers, John J. 22:129
Rogers, John L. S. 21:132
Rogers, John O. 9:90
Rogers, John R. 12:37;
    24:55
Rogers, John S. 22:267
Rogers, John W. 10:134;
    16:223; 20:337
Rogers, Joseph 8:109;
    18:222; 19:96;
    20:100
Rogers, Joseph A. 8:109
Rogers, Joseph F. 1:66
Rogers, Joshua 11:165
Rogers, L. 23:77

Rogers, L. H. 12:96;
  15:361; 19:96
Rogers, L. M. 25:226
Rogers, Leander L. 24:99
Rogers, Levanson 12:38
Rogers, Levi 6:35
Rogers, Lewis N. 25:65
Rogers, M. 3:166; 17:432
Rogers, M. A. 22:283
Rogers, M. C. 25:65
Rogers, Major I. 21:218
Rogers, Mason 10:166;
  19:190
Rogers, Mills 24:84
Rogers, Milton 17:58
Rogers, Miner 22:317
Rogers, Minor B. 24:154
Rogers, Morgan 11:277
Rogers, N. 14:212, 259;
  21:11
Rogers, Nicholas 13:44
Rogers, O. S. 3:166
Rogers, Oscar A. 7:108
Rogers, Owen 13:44
Rogers, P. R. 27:105
Rogers, R. 1:165; 17:156
Rogers, R. C. 20:3
Rogers, R. T. 2:16
Rogers, Ramon 7:108
Rogers, Raymond 13:44
Rogers, Remis 15:23
Rogers, Robert 8:42;
  23:194; 26:178
Rogers, Robert F. 23:77
Rogers, Robert R. 23:77
Rogers, S. 1:166; 16:224;
  25:64
Rogers, S. B. 13:97
Rogers, Samuel 16:224;
  17:58; 23:205
Rogers, Samuel C. 15:300
Rogers, Sandford 13:44
Rogers, Sanford J. 16:53
Rogers, Silas 3:166
Rogers, Stephen 8:42;
  21:246, 382; 26:178
Rogers, T. 3:166; 14:290;
  16:378; 23:47
Rogers, T. B. 21:382
Rogers, Thomas 3:166;
  12:37; 14:212, 266;
  21:112
Rogers, Thomas B.
  22:129
Rogers, Thomas E. 21:79
Rogers, Thomas M.
  20:337
Rogers, Tony 8:78
Rogers, W. 2:16; 3:166;
  14:263
Rogers, W. B. 17:58

Rogers, W. F. 19:96
Rogers, W. J. 16:378
Rogers, William 1:66;
  3:166; 8:29; 10:76;
  11:212; 13:68, 117;
  14:212; 18:156, 222;
  19:96
Rogers, William A. 9:191;
  19:268; 21:39
Rogers, William B.
  18:280
Rogers, William C. 25:64
Rogers, William H. 12:76;
  14:212; 17:58
Rogers, William M. 23:47
Rogers, William P. 9:17
Rogers, William W. 15:43
Rogers, Willis W. 22:168
Rogerson, J. 1:164
Roggers, William 24:28
Roggers, William B.
  17:58
Roghop, John 14:103
Roghus, James 14:266
Rogier, Melsior 21:233
Rogman, --- 3:166
Rogue, Horace 9:28;
  26:111
Rogurman, B. 16:224
Roh, George 7:39
Rohan, Jacob 15:319
Rohbuck, Fred. 8:29
Rohde, Ernest 8:29
Roher, Augustus 1:66
Roher, E. 22:216
Roher, Frederick 1:67
Roher, James 19:96
Roherberry, Henry G.
  22:438
Roheson, F. G. 11:86
Rohier, E. C. 14:317
Rohis, John 24:44
Rohl, Conrad 18:114
Rohlan, Nicholas 22:99
Rohm, Martin 22:354
Rohmiler, Andrew 11:166
Rohn, E. 14:103
Rohn, Henry 11:167
Rohn, John M. 4:50
Rohnmiller, John 18:56
Roholon, John 18:315
Roholor, John 26:109
Rohr, Charles 1:68
Rohr, Peter 1:67
Rohrer, Christian 9:69
Rohrer, D. F. 22:489
Rohrer, H. M. 25:226
Rohrer, Henry M. 5:28
Rohrier, Michael 9:38
Rohrig, Martin 12:57

Rohrin, Michael 18:296;
  26:110
Rohrs, Martin 8:122
Rohue, George W. 18:315
Rohwir, Charles 1:68
Roice, C. C. 22:438
Roice, Frank 20:181
Roice, James 27:103
Roies, William 16:303
Roiler, J. 23:287
Roise, J. 11:269
Roise, Thomas H. 17:25
Roke, C. 25:312
Roke, H. 19:96
Roker, Daniel 4:50
Rolack, J. 3:166
Rolan, John 24:28
Roland, --- 25:65
Roland, August 9:98
Roland, B. F. 2:17; 25:66
Roland, Charles 16:53;
  17:250
Roland, G. W. 9:154;
  27:102
Roland, Harmon 21:382
Roland, Isaac D. 5:54
Roland, J. B. 9:90; 26:57
Roland, J. G. 23:47
Roland, J. H. 14:212
Roland, J. W. 19:32
Roland, Jack 9:211
Roland, John 3:166;
  14:212; 19:288
Roland, L. C. 26:58
Roland, Luther C. 9:90
Roland, Michael 9:98
Roland, Thomas 8:78;
  26:179
Roland, W. C. 7:53
Roland, William R.
  22:456
Rolbt, S. 16:303
Roldder, J. G. 16:53
Rolde, Henry 10:134;
  20:337
Rolens, L. 11:188
Rolf, Benjamin 17:244
Rolf, Darwin 13:68; 19:96
Rolf, O. 19:260
Rolf, Oscar 9:191
Rolf, William 9:224;
  18:375
Rolf, William H. 9:104
Rolfe, --- 20:59
Rolfe, A. V. 9:58
Rolfe, D. B. 1:165
Rolfe, G. 1:167
Rolfe, R. C. 18:422
Rolfe, Samuel B. 20:33
Rolfe, Stephen 9:124;
  27:100

Rolfe, T. 1:165
Rolfe, William M. 22:283
Rolff, James S. 20:337
Rolfing, Conrad 8:94
Rolie, Bennett T. 11:73
Rolin, Burl S. 23:115
Rolin, Charles 9:38
Rolin, George 9:90
Rolin, W. S. 25:226
Rolins, R. 24:175
Rolins, Samuel 9:98
Rolison, C. D. 1:166
Roll, A. 21:196
Roll, A. C. 3:166
Roll, D. 11:397
Roll, Jackson 26:129
Roll, James S. 10:134
Roll, John 10:210
Roll, Jonas W. 23:242
Roll, Nath 17:447; 24:171
Roll, Thomas J. 11:167
Roll, William 22:129
Rolla, Clemla 21:383
Rolla, E. J. 3:166
Rolla, J. 14:212
Rolla, Jonathan 8:94
Rolla, Peter 19:96
Rollan, A. 8:54
Rollan, C. H. 20:156
Rolland, Henry F. 10:134;
    20:337
Rolland, J. 3:166
Rollardson, F. 13:97
Rolle, M. 3:166
Rolle, Martin 13:44
Rollen, Savage 12:169
Roller, Charles 18:296;
    26:111
Roller, Dominick 18:114
Roller, F. 14:131; 15:263
Roller, J. 14:259
Roller, John 23:280
Roller, W. 22:317
Rollerd, W. 23:109
Rolleston, William
    15:303; 16:224
Rolley, Alphonse 11:75
Rolley, James 5:54;
    25:226
Rolley, Oliver G. 4:50
Rolley, William 10:134;
    20:337
Rollin, C. 9:191
Rollin, Edward 22:456
Rollin, Elias 8:109
Rollin, Joseph 17:295
Rollin, William 7:132
Rolling, Daniel 25:65
Rollingsmer, J. 9:58
Rollins, Adolphus 13:44
Rollins, Amos P. 7:39

Rollins, C. 1:66
Rollins, Calvin 21:283
Rollins, Charles 14:103;
    22:317
Rollins, Charles H. 25:226
Rollins, D. 22:317
Rollins, Daniel W. 10:187
Rollins, E. F. 12:60
Rollins, Edward B. 16:87
Rollins, Franklin A.
    16:154
Rollins, G. 18:56
Rollins, George A. 19:96
Rollins, Henry 9:211;
    17:399; 18:431;
    22:99
Rollins, J. 25:226
Rollins, J. C. 15:345;
    16:378
Rollins, James B. 22:51
Rollins, John 5:45
Rollins, John H. 22:51
Rollins, Joseph 10:76;
    20:337
Rollins, M. F. 8:54
Rollins, Michel 11:415
Rollins, Millard F. 21:79
Rollins, Moses 11:391
Rollins, N. B. 23:205
Rollins, N. H. 21:383
Rollins, Robert E. 23:77
Rollins, S. 15:9
Rollins, Stephen 20:105
Rollins, Stephen A. 11:74
Rollins, Sylvester 15:9
Rollins, Thomas 16:53
Rollins, Tucker 22:317
Rollinson, J. 1:67
Rollison, J. 16:224
Rollison, Mordecai
    22:437
Rollison, Richard 22:505
Rolliston, George 16:166
Rollman, John 21:151
Rollman, William 12:76
Rollo, J. P. 1:167
Rolloff, John 3:166
Rolloson, Jacob 5:28
Rolls, Aaron 20:337
Rolls, Amos 17:67
Rolls, Charles 11:129
Rollston, Joseph 22:216
Rolly, J. H. 15:223
Rolly, John 21:233
Rolly, Willis 8:112
Rolman, Robert 4:50
Rolo, T. C. 9:231
Rolof, William 22:283
Roloff, J. 12:123
Rolott, John T. H. 11:165
Rolph, E. T. 11:249

Rolph, Henry 18:156
Rolph, Laurence 27:104
Rolplir, Nelson 15:279
Rolson, J. 3:166
Rolson, Smith 13:44
Rolston, Charles 26:138
Rolston, James 11:167;
    21:233
Rolston, James E. 7:39
Rolston, John 15:223
Rolston, John B. 21:196
Rolston, Robert 18:375
Roltenstetter, Simon
    21:259
Rolth, David 11:311
Roltson, William 16:224
Rolu, Evan 23:194
Romain, I. 3:166
Romaine, John 11:165
Roman, I. 20:43
Roman, J. C. 19:96
Roman, J. F. 9:45
Roman, John 3:166; 20:19
Roman, Patrick 11:42
Roman, Thomas 18:37
Romando, Raffaele
    15:111
Romany, C. 14:103
Romar, Peter 21:105
Romberg, Lars. O. 20:25
Romberger, William
    11:120
Rome, --- 25:63
Rome, R. 3:166; 14:212
Rome, Samuel C. 4:50
Romeis, Joseph 22:113
Romeni, Phillipe 12:170
Romer, J. P. 1:165
Romer, Jacob 17:71
Romer, T. 3:166
Romere, Samuel 7:132
Romero, Jose Maria 8:124
Romers, Alex 9:211
Romes, Henry 21:11
Romey, J. 13:97
Romey, William C.
    18:400
Romick, David 10:76;
    20:337
Romick, Samuel 1:67
Romig, Hiram 17:435;
    24:179
Romig, Oliver 18:71
Romigh, Alex. B. 10:166;
    19:190
Romigh, George 17:92
Romigh, Jacob 22:237
Romin, John 8:75
Romine, Daniel 17:25
Romine, Ebenezer 22:438
Romine, George 22:216

Romine, John 8:58; 10:134; 20:337
Romine, Levi 7:39; 23:165
Romine, W. H. 7:39
Romine, William T. 21:39
Romines, David R. 21:132
Romines, John 26:179
Roming, Franklin 15:73
Rominger, R. 16:53
Romm, Alonzo 9:237
Rommell, Augustus 17:210
Romney, --- 16:378
Romney, G. P. 14:103
Rompel, William 21:383
Romrick, William 14:104
Romsey, Elkand 17:295
Romtree, William H. 9:31
Romy, T. J. 3:166
Ron, John 6:10
Ronabuno, Frank 18:37
Ronan, John 13:68
Ronark, Thomas H. 12:55
Ronaw, P. 1:166
Ronbust, Joseph 24:84
Ronco, John 21:87
Rond, C. M. 16:303
Rondbush, Daniel 3:166
Ronde, Samuel 18:251
Rone, Henry 18:194
Rone, J. 27:105
Rone, J. W. 16:303
Rone, John M. 11:101
Rone, Perry 13:127
Rone, Thomas 19:265
Rone, William 4:50
Roner, Samuel 12:38
Ronet, J. 13:97
Roney, Absalom 10:76; 20:337
Roney, B. 14:104
Roney, Hamilton 22:14
Roney, J. H. 10:76
Roney, James 22:99
Roney, John N. 20:337
Roney, Napoleon 11:111
Roney, Patrick 17:274
Roney, Samuel I. 8:30
Roney, Thomas H. 21:233
Rong, C. 17:15
Ronk, James 12:38
Ronley, Charles 3:166; 15:5
Ronling, J. 16:270
Ronn, James 15:223
Ronn, M. 3:166
Ronsbury, T. 18:251
Ronsey, William 3:166
Rontree, Marcus L. 20:13
Ronu, David F. 18:156

Rooch, A. J. 9:243
Rooch, B. 17:137; 24:202
Rood, Almaron M. 15:133
Rood, C. 3:166
Rood, E. C. 11:255
Rood, E. H. 19:96
Rood, Gresham 11:73
Rood, H. M. 18:251; 26:58
Rood, I. C. C. 20:337
Rood, J. E. 13:126
Rood, James 25:326
Rood, LeGrand 3:166
Rood, Morton 19:190
Rood, Ole C. 10:134
Rood, Osborne C. 17:163
Rood, Silas M. 7:17
Rood, Timothy 9:45; 26:128
Rood, William 12:38; 20:149
Roode, Addison I. 23:77
Roodrick, Daniel A. 27:105
Roods, B. S. 26:225
Rooer, I. 3:166
Roof, Barton 19:190
Roof, Burton 10:174
Roof, George 8:94
Roof, John C. 22:14
Roof, Samuel 21:39
Roof, William 8:109
Roofe, Jacob 19:96
Roohr, Henry F. L. 24:96
Rook, G. 3:166
Rook, Gilmore P. 13:44
Rook, J. C. 14:290; 23:182
Rook, Jeddiah 20:337
Rook, Jedediah 10:134
Rook, John 17:238; 24:28
Rook, R. 23:205
Rook, Richard 17:209
Rook, T. 9:90
Rook, William 7:53
Rooker, McKindey 22:437
Rooker, Thomas 10:76
Rooker, William A. 9:191; 19:268
Rookey, Edward 7:53
Rookfelon, A. 10:207
Rooks, C. W. 20:59
Rooks, G. B. 15:59
Rooks, George W. 10:21
Rooks, H. 3:166
Rooks, Isaac 7:76; 25:304
Rooks, J. C. 18:179
Rooks, J. T. 1:69
Rooks, James 24:114
Rooks, John 11:167

Rookstool, Adam 21:58
Room, Andrew M. 15:133
Rooms, --- 11:248
Roon, Henry 26:110
Roon, Valentine 18:156
Rooney, Hugh 7:39
Rooney, J. 1:66, 167
Rooney, James 19:32
Rooney, John 3:166; 22:99
Rooney, Kate 18:441
Rooney, L. 15:291; 16:224
Rooney, M. 3:166
Rooney, Mark 3:166
Rooney, Michael 15:15; 25:226
Rooney, Owen 21:383
Rooney, P. 3:166
Rooney, P. D. 1:66
Rooney, Patrick 19:330
Rooney, Peter 7:132; 23:250
Rooney, Thomas 18:271; 22:343
Rooney, Timothy 23:125
Roop, Gibson 17:274
Roop, Jacob 10:134; 20:338
Roop, Samuel 14:212
Roope, Jacob 15:310
Roope, M. 1:166
Roorda, Henry 20:25
Roork, Martin 7:60
Roos, C. R. 16:224
Roos, John M. 22:154
Roos, Simon 9:90
Roosa, Jacob 22:489
Roosa, John C. 4:50
Roosa, Stodard H. 20:190
Roose, Fred 12:157
Rooss, S. A. 20:43
Root, A. 20:338
Root, A. W. 3:166
Root, Albert 18:353
Root, Amos C. 12:38
Root, Augustus 24:97
Root, Charles 16:101; 18:157
Root, Charles K. 4:50
Root, Clinton L. 9:98
Root, Cyrus S. 19:32
Root, D. 3:166
Root, Daniel 22:456
Root, Emerson 20:152
Root, Emmerson 20:194
Root, G. 4:50
Root, George 14:104; 18:351
Root, H. 9:150
Root, Harvey 25:226

Root, Henry 27:101
Root, Hiram 22:154
Root, J. W. 17:149
Root, Jacob 16:282
Root, James 20:141;
    22:163
Root, James D. 22:216
Root, Jerome B. 4:50
Root, John R. 22:237
Root, Joseph W. 21:260
Root, L. P. 19:242
Root, Leander W. 9:124
Root, Levi P. 9:191
Root, M. H. 22:283
Root, M. L. 7:39
Root, Marcus 13:44
Root, Morgan J. 17:100
Root, Moses J. 18:400
Root, Nathan 10:134;
    20:338
Root, Nathaniel 8:29;
    18:157
Root, Newton 22:14
Root, Oscar M. 17:74
Root, P. F. 9:150; 27:102
Root, Peter 14:104
Root, R. 1:69; 11:312
Root, Rodney H. 11:74
Root, Rosewell 9:14
Root, S. R. 13:117
Root, Samuel E. 17:362
Root, T. B. 19:326
Root, W. A. 20:338
Root, William 18:194
Root, William A. 10:76
Roote, N. 17:156
Rooter, Joseph 7:8
Rooth, Fred 4:50
Roothman, H. W. 13:97
Roots, William 3:166
Roott, John 12:9
Rope, A. R. 3:166
Rope, H. P. 9:73
Roper, Benton A. 21:15
Roper, C. 22:14
Roper, Elijah 22:267
Roper, Frank 9:135;
    27:102
Roper, H. 3:166
Roper, J. C. 8:75
Roper, James M. 23:47
Roper, John 13:58
Roper, Preston 22:505
Roper, S. T. 24:10
Roper, Washington 9:166
Roper, William 8:67
Ropertson, Peter 26:213
Ropier, John 10:29;
    19:306
Ropke, C. 14:104
Ropp, John 24:84

Ropponecker, S. 9:239
Rorabaugh, Daniel W.
    23:92
Roray, John 12:38
Rorcik, John 18:157
Rorden, Martin 22:51
Rorer, Ernest 9:14
Rorick, Amos H. 4:50
Rorick, John 8:29
Rorig, Lewis 22:99
Rorka, James O. 22:343
Rorke, I. H. 9:28
Rorman, Samuel 18:222
Rorobough, George
    25:226
Roroford, Samuel 22:317
Rorrell, George E. 19:32
Rorrick, D. J. 10:154
Rorthig, A. 1:166
Rorty, John 1:69
Ros, J. R. 21:39
Rosa, Benjamin J. 25:64
Rosa, Daniel 4:50
Rosa, George R. 10:76;
    20:338
Rosa, Richard 23:125
Rosa, William R. 1:67
Rosberg, Nels P. 18:157
Rosberry, Niles P. 8:29
Rosburgh, William 11:391
Rosch, Joseph H. 3:167
Roscoe, Boardman 13:44
Roscoph, Frank 22:217
Rose, --- 15:111
Rose, A. 3:167; 18:37,
    375; 22:489
Rose, A. H. 14:212
Rose, A. M. 13:118
Rose, A. P. 1:167
Rose, Aaron 21:39
Rose, Abram 10:21
Rose, Albert P. 21:89
Rose, Alexander 17:350
Rose, Anderson 6:18
Rose, Andrew 9:224
Rose, Anson 15:345
Rose, Asa 9:135
Rose, Augus 21:39
Rose, Augustus 11:129
Rose, Auson 16:378
Rose, B. 3:167; 23:165
Rose, Benjamin 9:98;
    11:111
Rose, Benjamin F. 23:77
Rose, C. F. 9:232; 20:338
Rose, Chancy 17:320
Rose, Chapman 13:44
Rose, Charles 1:67; 7:108;
    11:212; 12:60;
    15:345; 16:378;
    18:462

Rose, Charles B. 20:31
Rose, Charles E. 21:105
Rose, D. 14:212, 259;
    18:251; 26:56
Rose, Daniel H. 17:156
Rose, Dennis 20:142
Rose, E. E. 11:165
Rose, E. F. 16:224
Rose, Edward 17:420
Rose, Elijah 22:267
Rose, Eugene F. 22:154
Rose, G. 25:226
Rose, G. S. 1:164; 17:441
Rose, George 5:28;
    13:118
Rose, George H. 23:253
Rose, George W. 10:151,
    178; 17:145; 24:44
Rose, H. 16:101; 25:63
Rose, H. C. 19:230
Rose, Henry 10:76;
    18:251; 19:32;
    20:338; 21:58; 26:56
Rose, Henry D. 5:28
Rose, Hiram 8:94
Rose, Horace 2:16
Rose, J. 11:89, 129
Rose, J. A. 25:282
Rose, J. D. 10:76; 20:338
Rose, J. G. 22:129
Rose, J. P. 8:54
Rose, J. W. 25:226
Rose, Jacob 17:211
Rose, Jacob A. 11:42
Rose, Jacob H. 12:38
Rose, James 10:134;
    13:44; 17:441;
    20:338
Rose, James H. 17:67
Rose, James P. 20:338;
    21:79
Rose, Jerry 23:101
Rose, John 3:167; 7:39;
    8:109; 10:76; 17:67,
    97; 20:338; 25:226,
    326
Rose, John A. 14:104
Rose, John C. 21:233
Rose, John F. 24:28
Rose, John F. S. 10:21
Rose, John H. 9:135;
    27:103
Rose, John Q. 7:39
Rose, John V. 11:43
Rose, John W. 5:28
Rose, Joseph 21:383
Rose, Levi 13:44
Rose, Lewis M. 21:233
Rose, M. L. 3:167
Rose, Mason 11:111
Rose, N. 21:105

Rose, Nathaniel 8:55
Rose, Ora 27:103
Rose, Oramel 11:111
Rose, Orson 17:25
Rose, Othaner 9:232;
   20:338
Rose, Othanor 20:338
Rose, P. 16:224
Rose, P. G. 11:294
Rose, Peter 22:99
Rose, Philip 21:79
Rose, R. C. 3:167
Rose, Robert 14:212;
   19:32
Rose, Russell C. 17:238
Rose, S. 1:99
Rose, S. C. 11:165
Rose, S. R. 15:303
Rose, Samuel 10:134;
   20:338
Rose, Samuel B. 12:76;
   15:28
Rose, Samuel R. 16:224
Rose, Simon 11:73
Rose, T. 1:166
Rose, T. E. 16:224
Rose, T. K. 18:157
Rose, T. R. 8:29
Rose, Theodore 18:37
Rose, Thomas 12:38
Rose, Thomas H. 8:29;
   18:157
Rose, Thompson 23:165
Rose, Uriah G. 8:94
Rose, Van Shultz 12:38
Rose, Vernon A. 17:434;
   24:171
Rose, W. 1:166; 9:69;
   11:120; 15:224
Rose, W. B. 11:74
Rose, W. H. 21:89
Rose, W. J. 24:84
Rose, W. L. 11:268
Rose, Warren 13:44;
   16:53
Rose, William 9:38;
   11:42; 15:15;
   17:315; 18:285, 296;
   23:77; 26:110, 135
Rose, William E. 18:251;
   22:172; 26:57
Rose, William H. 8:55;
   21:79, 218
Rose, William P. 17:85
Rose, William S. 12:38
Roseberg, John 12:100
Roseberry, James B.
   22:437
Roseberry, John W. 22:99
Roseberry, Lemuel 23:77
Rosebery, John 15:366

Rosebill, Charles 16:101
Roseboom, Garrett L.
   16:82
Roseborough, C. 7:108
Rosebraugh, Samuel
   22:437
Rosebrook, George N.
   17:391
Rosebrooke, --- 9:191
Rosebrooks, --- 19:275
Rosebrough, James M.
   24:55
Rosebrough, Squire A.
   20:128
Roseburg, Henry 3:167
Rosebush, Hiram 25:65
Rosebush, N. 21:383
Rosecrans, Charles T.
   21:79
Rosecrans, L. E. 3:167
Rosecranz, Harvey 4:50
Rosegie, S. 15:43
Roseglant, E. G. 22:467
Rosegrant, H. C. 16:101
Roseham, John 4:50
Roseher, Joseph 10:10
Rosehill, Sebastian 7:108
Rosel, Isaac 18:114
Rosel, Jonathan 22:99
Rosel, William 11:42
Rosell, J. 19:96
Rosell, John 13:44
Rosell, William 16:224
Roseman, J. F. 26:129
Roseman, James 18:194
Roseman, Martin 18:251
Roseman, P. 17:156
Roseman, Philip 20:338
Rosemon, Carl 21:383
Rosenbalm, George P.
   20:151
Rosenbark, George H.
   22:466
Rosenbaugh, Andrew W.
   22:438
Rosenbaugh, J. S. 22:398
Rosenbaugh, John G.
   22:398
Rosenbaum, --- 15:273
Rosenbaum, Alex 11:249
Rosenbaum, Arnold
   23:195
Rosenbaum, William
   24:28
Rosenbeck, W. B. 13:44
Rosenberg, Samuel S.
   1:66
Rosenberger, A. 1:66
Rosenberger, H. 4:50
Rosenberger, Jacob F.
   11:74

Rosenberger, John A.
   10:134; 20:338
Rosenberger, Joseph
   24:44
Rosenberry, G. 14:104
Rosenberry, J. 14:284
Rosenbery, E. 19:96
Rosenborough, Samuel
   18:315; 26:111
Rosenbower, William
   8:94
Rosenbrook, William
   11:269
Rosenbrough, Samuel
   9:28
Rosenburg, A. 1:167
Rosenburg, Andrew J.
   12:7
Rosenburg, Charles
   19:190
Rosenburg, E. 15:307
Rosenburg, H. 3:167
Rosenburg, Jacob 14:212
Rosencrans, Edward 5:54
Rosencrans, Frank 7:108
Rosencrans, H. 3:167
Rosencrans, Jesse 18:37
Rosencrants, John 22:99
Rosencrantz, Amaza E.
   23:165
Rosencrantz, S. C. 14:104
Rosencranz, Caleb 23:47
Rosendale, Charles
   23:165
Rosendoff, J. 15:44
Rosendorf, John 12:62
Rosenfelder, Alexander
   17:393
Rosenfield, John 8:75
Rosengrant, Henry 7:108
Rosenguest, John 14:212
Rosenkoetter, Henry
   20:36
Rosenkrans, C. 8:55
Rosenkrans, S. E. 11:289
Rosenow, Carl 7:108
Rosenpaugh, J. 3:167
Rosensteel, Christian
   23:77
Rosenstraus, Seligman
   13:44
Rosenstrom, A. 13:79
Rosenstrone, And. 16:224
Rosenthal, D. 9:191;
   19:260
Roser, Edward P. 13:44
Roserear, Richard 20:13
Rosesh, Jacob 24:84
Rosevauls, Edw. 25:226
Rosh, John M. 11:75

Roshnikoff, Edward 18:114
Roshwell, C. F. 14:212
Rosier, Joseph 21:59
Rosier, Robert 19:48
Rosier, Valentine 19:292
Rosinberger, John 3:167
Rosinbury, T. 26:56
Rosincrantz, C. 20:338
Rosingnoll, Louis 19:317
Rosino, --- 19:260
Rosino, R. 25:226
Rosinower, G. 23:165
Rositer, Charles 16:75
Rosley, Race 16:224
Rosling, John 22:172
Rosmer, Frank 3:167
Rosmey, Thomas C. 1:66
Rosmund, G. 14:266
Rosner, G. 14:290
Rosq, William 20:13
Ross, --- 3:166; 11:165; 15:133, 224; 17:509; 18:375
Ross, A. 3:167; 15:224; 17:338; 21:125, 151
Ross, A. E. 14:290; 23:77
Ross, A. H. 9:28
Ross, A. J. 1:167
Ross, Albert 21:283
Ross, Alexander 1:67; 19:288
Ross, Allen H. 21:283
Ross, Amos M. 7:53
Ross, Anderson 18:92; 22:317
Ross, Andrew I. 8:29
Ross, Andrew J. 18:157
Ross, Andrew S. 22:216
Ross, Arthur E. 14:290; 23:77
Ross, B. 21:383
Ross, B. F. 18:37
Ross, B. H. 11:416
Ross, Benjamin 27:104
Ross, Benjamin W. 1:68
Ross, Byron 18:280
Ross, Byron C. 19:32
Ross, C. 3:167; 9:241
Ross, C. B. 9:28; 18:315; 26:111
Ross, C. E. 1:68
Ross, Charles 11:166, 212; 14:266; 17:112
Ross, Charles F. 21:39
Ross, Charles W. 16:82
Ross, Christopher 18:444
Ross, Cutter 17:234
Ross, D. 3:167
Ross, D. H. 25:226

Ross, Daniel 7:108; 11:415
Ross, Daniel D. 21:383
Ross, Daniel P. 11:75
Ross, David 3:167; 9:38; 18:296; 21:283; 22:216; 26:128
Ross, E. 23:205
Ross, E. F. 3:166
Ross, E. W. 10:76; 20:338
Ross, Ebenezer E. 1:67
Ross, Edward 25:67
Ross, Edwin 8:118; 9:124; 27:104
Ross, Elijah J. 11:416
Ross, Elmer L. 16:134
Ross, Enoch 23:47
Ross, F. 14:28
Ross, Francis M. 22:437
Ross, G. 3:167; 14:302; 17:482; 27:105
Ross, G. B. 22:505
Ross, G. D. 22:343
Ross, G. M. 22:267
Ross, G. W. 22:216
Ross, George 9:191; 25:335
Ross, George D. 16:378
Ross, George F. 8:75
Ross, George S. 24:154
Ross, George W. 12:38; 17:162; 21:260
Ross, Gifford 17:184
Ross, Gilbert 18:270
Ross, H. A. 10:192; 18:179
Ross, H. E. 3:167
Ross, Hampton 22:267
Ross, Henry 7:132; 11:165
Ross, Hugh 15:133
Ross, Iovory 12:38
Ross, Ira W. 16:101
Ross, Isaac 11:312
Ross, J. 1:66, 69; 3:167; 9:150; 12:38; 15:345; 16:378; 27:101
Ross, J. A. 14:320
Ross, J. B. 14:104
Ross, J. C. 1:166; 7:39, 108
Ross, J. D. 17:432
Ross, J. E. 12:157
Ross, J. H. 3:167
Ross, J. S. 7:53
Ross, J. W. 3:167
Ross, Jacob 7:132; 15:44
Ross, James 3:167; 5:28; 8:67, 78; 11:74, 110; 17:162, 265; 21:243
Ross, James C. 24:154

Ross, James E. 15:160
Ross, James G. 22:99
Ross, James M. 9:28; 18:315; 26:110
Ross, James W. 22:437
Ross, James W. B. 12:147; 19:306
Ross, John 1:66, 67, 69; 3:167; 8:29; 11:166; 14:212; 15:59; 16:224; 17:455; 18:157, 194; 20:28, 49; 24:202; 25:226
Ross, John A. 20:176
Ross, John F. 8:29, 94; 10:134; 18:157; 20:338
Ross, John W. 10:134; 14:320; 18:92; 20:338
Ross, Joseph 3:166; 14:104; 26:225
Ross, Joseph A. 20:138
Ross, Joseph W. 15:365; 19:96
Ross, Joshua B. 22:52
Ross, Josiah 9:38
Ross, L. 1:166; 14:104
Ross, L. C. 22:52
Ross, L. O. 21:39
Ross, Levi 10:97; 11:211
Ross, Lewis 22:317
Ross, Lorz 1:66
Ross, M. 11:311, 329; 21:196
Ross, Marion 23:264
Ross, Martha Ann 26:225
Ross, Miles 23:47
Ross, N. B. 23:77
Ross, Nathaniel 21:260
Ross, Nelson 4:50
Ross, Noah 16:224
Ross, Oliver 21:383
Ross, Otto 18:114
Ross, Owen 8:115
Ross, Peter 7:39; 9:28; 18:315; 26:110
Ross, Philip 9:211
Ross, R. 5:54; 15:5; 25:63, 226
Ross, Rich 19:48
Ross, Richard 12:76, 157
Ross, Robert 9:211; 18:251, 441; 22:52; 26:57
Ross, Robert E. 11:73
Ross, S. 13:130; 19:96
Ross, Samuel 15:365; 18:251; 19:190; 26:58
Ross, Samuel J. 7:39

Ross, Simon 11:75; 18:251; 26:57
Ross, Stephen C. 7:60
Ross, T. 11:75
Ross, Thomas 3:167; 6:18; 13:44; 14:104; 16:53; 18:92
Ross, Thomas J. 10:77
Ross, Thomas S. 20:338
Ross, Thomas W. 7:108
Ross, W. 22:129
Ross, W. A. 1:168; 8:55
Ross, W. C. 11:425
Ross, W. H. 20:190; 26:109
Ross, Wash 24:202
Ross, Washington 6:18; 17:455; 18:92
Ross, William 11:165; 13:44; 19:96; 20:13; 23:48, 77, 165, 182; 24:203
Ross, William A. 17:25; 22:99
Ross, William C. 22:505
Ross, William H. 12:51; 23:101
Ross, William H. O. 25:278
Ross, William J. 11:248; 13:44
Ross, William M. 4:50; 18:315
Ross, Wilmot 21:383
Rossa, H. 1:165
Rossack, William 14:212
Rossandre, E. H. 21:383
Rosseau, P. 21:383
Rossell, Frank 14:104
Rosselle, Daniel 9:213
Rossellit, J. 11:165
Rossenstrauss, Seligmann 16:53
Rosser, Charles 21:383
Rosser, James 9:191
Rosser, John 11:42; 22:317
Rosser, John F. 15:224
Rosser, Lewis 3:167
Rossett, W. D. 14:302; 17:481
Rossian, Jean 8:55
Rossian, John 12:65
Rossiter, David B. 7:108
Rossiter, S. H. 9:191
Rossiter, W. B. 22:217
Rosskelley, J. 9:224
Rossman, Frederick 18:157
Rossman, Philip 10:77; 20:338

Rossmann, Frederick 8:29
Rossoloss, G. W. G. 23:307
Rosson, Charles 3:167
Rosson, Joseph C. 23:165
Rosswell, Joseph 18:157
Rostan, Roman S. 26:225
Rostel, --- 15:323; 19:96
Roster, Abraham 22:317
Roster, Romans 9:237
Roston, Kingston 8:42
Rostt, Benj 9:124
Roswell, Archy 8:42
Roswell, J. 3:167
Roswell, John 8:29; 18:157
Roswell, Joseph 8:29
Roswell, Levi 8:55
Roswell, William R. 22:154
Rot, Arie 17:67
Rotchin, J. S. 21:201
Rote, James 20:13
Roter, Ferdinand 21:191
Rotes, P. 21:383
Rotgep, J. 11:312
Rotger, Henry 10:93
Roth, A. 1:167; 11:403
Roth, C. 3:167
Roth, Charles 20:31; 22:343
Roth, Francis 18:114
Roth, Frederick 1:68
Roth, Henry 12:38; 14:104
Roth, J. 14:303; 17:474; 27:105
Roth, Jacob 8:94; 23:165
Roth, James 9:113
Roth, John 15:316; 19:96
Roth, Leonard 8:109
Roth, Lewis 3:167
Roth, Milton 18:38
Roth, Nathaniel 4:50
Roth, Peter 11:166
Roth, Reuben 9:124; 27:103
Roth, Rosanna 26:225
Roth, W. D. 7:39
Roth, William 12:38
Rotham, H. 15:224
Rothbone, William H. H. 10:93
Rothburn, Oliver 11:193
Rothcabe, H. 14:284
Rothelitz, August 25:269
Rothell, M. 3:167
Rothencicher, Fred 20:338
Rotheneicker, Frederick 10:134
Rotherick, Julius 18:210

Rothgan, Christ 20:338
Rothgan, Christian 10:134
Rothie, A. L. 23:195
Rothingslife, J. 15:353
Rothlingshefer, J. 16:282
Rothman, William 21:383
Rothmann, Andreas 4:50
Rothrack, William H. 22:52
Rothrock, Christian 11:74
Rothrock, H. 1:165
Rothrock, James 22:237
Rothrock, Peter 22:52
Rothrock, William 7:39
Rothschilds, Louis 19:96
Rothshild, S. 8:122
Rothwell, J. W. 14:284
Rothwell, Jacob 10:149
Rothwell, John 2:16
Rothwell, John W. 14:270
Rothwell, Joseph 18:56
Rothwiler, Charles 11:382
Rotin, William 11:425
Rotter, Charles 17:85
Rotter, G. 16:270
Rotterman, Henry 9:191
Rottger, Henry 20:338
Rottman, P. 1:166
Rottstein, G. 9:150; 27:104
Rou, Eliza 27:104
Roubadean, M. 11:129
Roubleman, John 15:327; 19:96
Roubotham, R. 3:167
Rouby, W. H. 14:290
Rouch, F. 13:44
Rouch, H. 8:30
Rouch, Henry 13:44
Rouch, J. B. 11:329
Rouch, James 11:397
Rouch, John 14:213
Rouch, Nathan 13:44
Rouch, Philip 6:14; 18:93
Rouch, Ralph 22:217
Rouche, F. 16:53
Roudal, F. A. 26:110
Roudebush, Joseph 20:43
Rouf, Joseph 21:199
Rouff, Martin 13:118
Rougan, William 26:178
Rouge, Horace 18:315
Rouge, William 3:167
Rough, Charles 14:213
Rough, D. 9:90; 26:55
Rougher, A. R. 18:251; 26:57
Roughly, Harrison 9:124
Rought, Abraham 14:237
Rought, F. 17:495

Rought, Squire 17:137; 24:202
Roughton, Thomas 27:147
Rouin, P. 14:104
Rouk, H. 21:383
Roulson, Lewis 17:41
Roulston, W. H. H. 22:267
Roun, George 18:38
Roun, Joseph 22:515
Rouna, George W. 18:400
Rouncevell, E. G. 3:167
Rouncivel, E. G. 14:213
Round, Daniel 14:104
Round, E. 13:44
Round, Hiram J. 7:40
Roundabush, H. B. 3:167
Roundebrish, J. W. 16:282
Roundey, G. P. 16:87
Rounding, John 20:128
Rounds, --- 18:194
Rounds, C. 19:230
Rounds, Chester 20:338
Rounds, D. H. 16:53
Rounds, David 16:141
Rounds, E. S. 22:343
Rounds, Franklin 21:260
Rounds, George W. 12:162
Rounds, John 25:64
Rounds, Philip J. 13:44
Rounds, W. 1:164
Rounds, William 14:213
Roundton, J. M. 8:67
Roundtree, B. 8:99
Roundtree, J. N. 26:179
Roundville, Benjamin 22:163
Rounsavily, Isaac 16:378
Roura, Christopher 20:338
Rourdink, Garret W. 21:142
Rourk, Ferrell 21:196
Rourk, J. 3:167
Rourk, M. 1:166
Rourk, Patrick 10:166
Rourk, Thomas 19:332
Rourka, Christopher 10:134
Rourke, Michael 1:66; 7:108; 17:362
Rourke, Patrick 19:190
Rourke, Peter 11:74; 25:326
Rourke, T. 1:167
Rourke, Thomas 9:191; 23:195
Rourse, Joseph 4:50

Rousch, John 9:191; 10:134; 19:260
Rousch, Peter 3:167
Rouse, --- 1:67
Rouse, Alonzo 11:110
Rouse, Amos 22:99
Rouse, Anthony D. 22:283
Rouse, Benjamin 13:44
Rouse, Burditt C. 11:249
Rouse, Charles A. 16:141
Rouse, Charles S. 17:410; 22:129
Rouse, D. W. 13:44
Rouse, Edwin G. 18:346
Rouse, F. 1:69
Rouse, F. B. 8:75
Rouse, George 25:286
Rouse, Horace E. 10:134; 20:338
Rouse, James E. 15:348; 16:378
Rouse, James H. 20:25
Rouse, L. 1:95
Rouse, Levi H. 9:191; 19:271
Rouse, N. 25:66
Rouse, Philip 22:99
Rouse, Richard 9:135; 27:103
Rouse, T. 1:164
Rouse, Thomas S. 26:179
Rouse, W. B. 22:217
Rouse, W. C. 25:227
Rouse, W. D. 1:69
Rouse, W. S. 16:143
Rouse, Wilber C. 5:28
Rouse, William H. 23:185
Rouse, William N. 10:134; 20:338
Rouse, William T. 23:77
Rouseau, Mat 18:194
Rousells, D. 21:383
Rouser, George W. 26:146
Rouser, John 16:224
Rouser, Martin 11:311
Rousey, J. 23:48
Rousey, Reuben 15:224
Roush, Isaac S. 21:233
Roush, J. 14:279
Roush, John 20:338; 24:90
Roush, William 16:224
Roushe, E. J. 23:165
Roussean, R. R. 25:304
Rousseau, Augustus 20:116
Roussell, Forin 21:383
Rouste, Daniel F. 17:393
Rouston, D. A. 22:489
Rout, Charles 8:30

Rout, Sincon 7:17
Route, James W. Th. Dr. 24:114
Routh, Armsted S. 20:100
Routh, Daniel 8:102; 17:463
Routh, James L. 20:134
Routon, Alex 24:174
Routs, William 17:184
Routsh, Christopher 4:50
Routt, A. 20:43
Routt, Daniel J. 24:179
Roux, J. L. 7:40
Roux, Peter 16:378
Rove, O. A. 26:178
Roveing, Alex 12:38
Rovel, Aaron M. 25:227
Rovel, Henry 17:274
Rovell, Charles 13:118
Rovels, Philip 25:304
Rovenstine, Albert 22:438
Rover, Julius 17:495
Rovey, F. 16:148
Rovig, Henry 8:55
Roving, Henry H. 21:79
Roving, J. 3:167
Row, Absalom 17:41
Row, Ferdinand P. 20:177
Row, George 12:60
Row, H. E. 25:227
Row, Jackson 9:45
Row, James 22:456
Row, John 5:45; 6:8; 22:456
Row, John P. 27:104
Row, L. C. 27:104
Row, Lewis 14:266, 290
Row, Louis 23:13
Row, Reuben 22:237
Row, W. J. 3:167
Row, William 17:41
Rowan, A. H. 21:191
Rowan, James 15:111
Rowan, Nathan 9:224
Rowan, Robert 8:30; 18:157
Rowan, Thomas 18:400
Rowand, George 16:123
Rowbinson, James B. 24:44
Rowbotham, E. 1:67
Rowden, Henry 6:33
Rowden, John 9:73
Rowden, Joshua C. 24:69
Rowden, W. A. 18:251
Rowden, William 3:167
Rowden, William A. 26:57
Rowdenbush, Samuel 19:190
Rowder, Alex 17:424

Rowdon, E. 14:20
Rowdy, Thomas 10:97
Rowe, A. 3:167
Rowe, A. G. 5:28
Rowe, A. H. 25:227
Rowe, A. J. 1:166
Rowe, Able 11:391
Rowe, Adolphus 13:135;
   19:347
Rowe, Alexander D. 4:50
Rowe, Alfred 13:68;
   19:96; 22:267
Rowe, Asa 3:167
Rowe, B. 12:86; 16:303
Rowe, Benjamin 22:317
Rowe, Benjamin E. 25:66
Rowe, Benjamin F.
   22:437
Rowe, C. 14:104
Rowe, C. H. 13:98
Rowe, Charles 17:395
Rowe, Cicero 18:222
Rowe, Columbus 21:246
Rowe, D. 14:104
Rowe, E. 3:167; 7:69
Rowe, Edward 19:190
Rowe, Egbert 10:21
Rowe, Frank 8:94
Rowe, G. A. 25:65
Rowe, George 17:62
Rowe, George F. 23:277
Rowe, George W. 25:227
Rowe, Gilbert 12:38
Rowe, Gilbert E. 18:251;
   26:57
Rowe, H. 1:165; 14:104
Rowe, H. M. 19:275;
   25:63
Rowe, Henry 1:66, 69
Rowe, Henry M. 2:16
Rowe, Herbert M. 9:191
Rowe, J. 14:303; 17:479;
   25:227
Rowe, J. F. 8:55; 9:90
Rowe, J. K. 13:118
Rowe, J. M. 14:213, 284
Rowe, J. T. 26:57
Rowe, James 12:38;
   23:266
Rowe, James F. 24:55
Rowe, John 14:104; 19:96
Rowe, John C. 19:32;
   24:114
Rowe, John H. D. 21:143
Rowe, John M. 13:44
Rowe, John N. 16:53
Rowe, John P. 19:32
Rowe, Joshua A. 17:58
Rowe, L. 3:167
Rowe, L. M. 22:168
Rowe, Leonard S. 9:14

Rowe, Nathaniel 4:50
Rowe, O. 17:184
Rowe, Oramandel 7:108
Rowe, R. 21:383
Rowe, R. D. 9:124;
   27:104
Rowe, R. W. 15:300;
   16:224
Rowe, R. Willis 23:92
Rowe, Rice 21:79
Rowe, S. 14:266
Rowe, Shade 18:251;
   26:57
Rowe, Stephen 9:124
Rowe, Valentine 17:451
Rowe, William 6:18;
   10:77; 18:93; 20:338
Rowe, Z. 14:104
Roweke, I. 3:167
Rowel, ---s 20:13
Rowel, A. G. 18:157
Rowel, L. N. 3:167
Rowell, A. G. 8:30
Rowell, A. J. 21:383
Rowell, Abram 25:227
Rowell, Adbbt 1:67
Rowell, C. D. 19:96
Rowell, Chauncey 13:44
Rowell, Corydon 21:383
Rowell, David 7:108
Rowell, E. W. 25:64
Rowell, Edwin 14:213
Rowell, Enas S. 13:44
Rowell, Enos S. 16:53
Rowell, George 14:213
Rowell, I. E. 3:167
Rowell, James 14:289,
   290; 23:182
Rowell, Reuben 4:50
Rowell, Rives 21:283
Rowell, William H.
   22:217
Rowen, Andrew 16:224
Rowen, H. 14:213
Rowen, Harrison 14:104
Rowen, John 17:350
Rowenbush, Samuel
   10:146
Rowens, Joseph 4:50
Rower, J. 20:43
Roweroft, Thomas 19:190
Rowes, H. 7:69
Rowg, J. W. 14:290;
   23:77
Rowl, William W. 12:157
Rowland, B. 3:167
Rowland, Dewitt G.
   21:260
Rowland, F. M. 20:339
Rowland, G. 19:260

Rowland, George 9:191;
   10:77; 20:339
Rowland, George N.
   25:227
Rowland, George W.
   12:60
Rowland, I. D. 25:227
Rowland, J. W. 23:109
Rowland, James 11:289
Rowland, James W. 24:28
Rowland, John H. 10:21
Rowland, Joseph 9:124;
   27:103
Rowland, M. 3:167
Rowland, Miles 14:213
Rowland, Patrick 22:437
Rowland, R. D. 20:339
Rowland, Richard D.
   10:77
Rowland, Robert 13:44;
   16:53; 22:14
Rowland, Stephen 15:224
Rowland, Thomas J.
   17:315
Rowland, Thomas M.
   10:77
Rowland, Thomas R.
   22:52
Rowland, W. W. 22:489
Rowland, William 4:50;
   11:129, 165; 15:73
Rowles, A. 1:167
Rowles, E. B. 23:165
Rowles, Lacy J. 11:86
Rowlett, Charles 17:168
Rowlett, John 20:100
Rowlett, W. F. 10:97
Rowlett, W. J. 8:124
Rowley, A. 1:164
Rowley, C. F. 1:68
Rowley, Charles H. 24:10
Rowley, Charles W.
   22:410
Rowley, E. 13:118
Rowley, G. 9:69
Rowley, George 22:284
Rowley, Gideon 25:64
Rowley, H. 20:59
Rowley, J. R. 1:69
Rowley, J. T. 25:66
Rowley, James M. 10:166
Rowley, James W. 1:66
Rowley, John C. 23:92
Rowley, Lester 21:243
Rowley, Mathew 23:92
Rowley, Perry S. 20:108
Rowley, Reuben 21:39
Rowley, Shubael G.
   22:284
Rowley, Spencer H. 7:108
Rowley, Volney S. 22:113

Rowley, Willard 17:67
Rowley, William 25:227
Rowley, William H. 21:383
Rowling, John 22:154
Rowlings, T. 3:167
Rowlins, E. 13:118
Rowlop, Henry 15:224
Rowls, Augusta 18:407
Rowls, John 20:149
Rowlson, John J. 4:50
Rowly, Spencer A. 21:383
Rowman, Thomas 19:321
Rowne, A. C. 19:97
Rownells, Benjamin 21:249
Rowry, Samuel J. 18:157
Rows, Edward 17:319
Rowsen, J. W. 20:339
Rowsen, R. 18:38
Rowser, A. 3:167
Rowser, Spencer 5:45
Rowson, J. W. 10:134
Rowves, C. T. 18:179
Roy, Alexander R. 23:251
Roy, Daniel R. 21:383
Roy, Elijah 6:18; 18:93
Roy, George B. 12:164
Roy, Gilbert 15:175
Roy, H. 4:68
Roy, Jones W. 20:105
Roy, Joseph 7:132
Roy, Joshua 17:207
Roy, Oliver 15:333
Roy, Peter E. 16:141
Roy, William J. 17:207
Royal, B. 1:165
Royal, J. 22:217
Royal, J. J. 1:167
Royal, John M. 15:224
Royal, Maurice G. 21:383
Royal, William F. 12:38
Royal, William H. 16:53
Royan, Leonard 5:54; 25:227
Royar, Thomas H. 14:303
Royce, Charles B. 16:224
Royce, Chauncey 22:410
Royce, E. 14:213
Royce, Francis L. 23:125
Royce, George E. 15:25
Royce, Joel W. 20:19
Royce, John W. 11:391
Royce, O. F. 12:38
Royd, George R. 24:13
Royds, J. 23:48
Royer, Daniel 21:59
Royer, Franklin A. 23:92
Royer, George 22:237
Royer, John 18:56
Royer, Peter 18:210

Royer, W. 14:290
Royer, W. H. 9:113
Royer, William A. 4:50
Royers, Hamilton 25:227
Royley, Irvin 16:53
Royn, John 14:213
Roynton, O. T. 7:87
Roys, D. W. 14:20
Roys, E. J. 23:13
Royster, R. A. 20:43
Royston, William F. 23:109
Roz, I. 23:293
Rozell, James 1:66
Rozelle, Joshua C. 22:154
Rozenburg, Jacob 19:330
Rozier, Elijah 9:135; 27:103
Ruapp, Neeson P. 11:129
Ruarke, Benjamin 18:375
Ruave, Stephen R. 12:38
Rubal, John 14:213
Rubards, William O. 22:455
Rubb, Johnson 17:41
Rubber, B. 1:166
Rubber, Samuel 9:191; 19:289
Rubbins, J. 16:123
Rubble, Lewis 21:105
Rube, Chauncey S. 22:284
Rubedean, S. 25:66
Rubedean, Samuel 2:16
Ruben, J. T. 2:16
Rubenister, C. 14:290
Rubenstein, Christian 23:195
Ruber, Charles 21:89
Rubert, J. F. 7:13
Rubert, J. T. 25:66
Rubert, W. 23:195
Ruberts, H. B. 3:167
Rubey, W. 10:29; 19:306
Rubia, Charles 4:50
Rubin, --- 15:44
Rubin, Lewis 10:145
Rubin, Samuel 19:32
Rubinet, James A. 15:44
Rubinson, H. 3:167
Ruble, A. 27:102
Ruble, Charles E. 23:266
Ruble, David L. 22:267
Ruble, David R. 22:217
Ruble, G. H. 14:104
Ruble, Henry 8:55
Ruble, Leander 3:167
Ruble, N. 9:150
Rubley, B. 13:98
Rubner, A. 7:69
Rubon, J. T. 9:58
Rubottum, John 11:249

Rubrecht, Samuel 14:213
Rubust, Henry 9:90
Ruby, Anthony 18:427
Ruby, Benjamin 17:362
Ruby, James H. 15:133
Ruby, John 20:100
Ruby, Joseph H. 18:400
Ruby, Levias 23:277
Ruby, Martin B. 23:92
Ruby, Michael 25:304
Ruby, Robert F. 10:166; 19:190
Ruby, William 17:239; 21:233
Ruby, William H. 10:134; 20:339
Ruce, John L. 1:69
Ruch, Silas 15:361
Ruchel, Paul 7:132
Ruchelve, W. 25:227
Ruck, Frank W. 20:36
Ruck, John 1:67
Ruckas, H. R. 9:237
Ruckel, John 23:165
Ruckener, Lawrence 24:174
Ruckenfelder, Frederick 22:217
Rucker, Charles 18:93
Rucker, D. H. (Mrs.) 25:335
Rucker, George 24:203
Rucker, George A. 17:350
Rucker, H. 9:201; 19:292
Rucker, Isaac 22:456
Rucker, J. 12:96; 15:361; 19:97
Rucker, John 20:339; 24:188
Rucker, John E. 8:30; 18:157
Rucker, Julius 22:129; 23:272
Rucker, Levi 22:113
Rucker, Randal 22:317
Rucker, Richard 22:515
Rucker, William M. 24:84
Ruckers, R. H. 26:225
Ruckerts, P. 1:167
Ruckle, John 20:184
Ruckman, G. M. 18:179
Ruckman, Henry 20:339
Ruckman, John L. 24:55
Ruckner, Lawrence 17:449
Ruckston, John 18:413
Rucktassel, John 26:225
Rud, J. 3:167
Rud, Seborn 18:157
Rudar, Charles 16:224
Rudd, Bradley 25:64

Rudd, Erastus 3:167
Rudd, John 22:317
Rudd, T. 3:167
Rudd, William 17:244
Ruddell, Sylvester 22:52
Rudder, Finnery 8:75
Rudder, George 14:104
Ruddick, George 13:77
Ruddin, C. 3:168
Ruddle, F. 26:179
Ruddle, William K. 20:36
Ruddlidge, Henry 11:211
Ruddy, S. L. 12:38
Rude, Alex 20:339
Rude, Alexander 10:77
Rude, Ch. 20:149
Rude, Charles 20:19
Rude, Gilbert L. 24:28
Rude, James 24:28
Rude, L. 24:84
Rude, William H. 23:77
Rudel, Enos G. 25:67
Rudell, Daniel 7:40
Rudenborough, William 10:207
Ruder, Charles 7:108
Ruder, George 22:168
Rudesill, D. 1:167
Rudesill, Samuel 7:132
Rudey, J. B. 12:76
Rudg, Franklin 9:227
Rudge, George 17:164
Rudge, Lewis H. 1:69
Rudibough, B. F. 9:28
Rudibush, B. F. 18:315; 26:111
Rudicil, A. 24:84
Rudig, A. 18:56
Rudin, John W. 17:85
Rudisil, Musser J. 15:73
Rudisill, A. B. 22:217
Rudisill, S. 1:165
Rudler, L. 22:237
Rudler, William 3:168
Rudolph, Asper 22:113
Rudolph, Enna E. 7:69
Rudolph, H. M. 23:48
Rudolph, I. 15:224
Rudolph, J. 24:84
Rudolph, Joseph 10:21
Rudolph, Nelson 18:324
Rudolph, S. 3:168
Rudolph, Thomas 18:315; 26:110
Rudunt, Howard 22:437
Rudwick, --- 19:97
Rudy, Alfred 19:32
Rudy, Cyrus T. 23:287
Rudy, E. T. 3:167
Rudy, Henry 22:52
Rudy, J. 3:168

Rudy, J. P. 15:73
Rudy, John 22:343
Rudy, William J. 23:129
Rudyard, John 20:100
Rue, Carl. F. A. 20:89
Rue, E. 27:105
Rue, Henry 20:339
Rue, John 16:114
Rue, Newton C. 3:168
Rue, W. H. 14:213; 15:345; 16:378
Rueben, Albert 9:191
Rueben, Jacob 14:213
Rueff, I. 3:168
Ruepke, Henry 8:30
Rueton, Anton 21:143
Rufall, H. 26:55
Rufers, Moore 14:284
Ruff, Augustus 21:39
Ruff, C. 10:155; 19:190
Ruff, D. 27:101
Ruff, Frederick 21:39
Ruff, H. 1:68
Ruff, Henry 7:17; 21:93
Ruff, James 1:69
Ruff, John 1:67; 8:30; 10:155; 18:157; 19:190
Ruff, Lewis F. 22:217
Ruff, S. F. 17:284
Ruff, William H. 10:134; 20:339
Ruffell, Samuel 13:44
Ruffener, S. 25:227
Ruffin, William 19:97
Ruffle, --- 9:191; 19:260
Ruffner, James 22:344
Ruffner, Samuel 5:28
Ruffus, L. V. 23:282
Rufinburg, G. 26:55
Rufly, Harrison 27:103
Rufner, Christian 17:85
Rufol, Henry 9:90
Rug, George 22:317
Rug, J. 1:167
Rugan, John 17:416; 24:161
Rugan, Patrick 19:233
Ruger, August 11:165
Ruger, Ellis 15:224
Ruger, William 22:317
Rugg, Adam J. 12:38
Rugg, C. A. 12:157
Rugg, G. 22:317
Rugg, Miles O. 9:90
Rugg, Miles Q. 26:55
Rugg, N. 13:118
Rugg, Nelson B. 21:383
Rugg, Samuel 22:344
Rugg, Van Buren 20:25
Ruggiman, John 16:303

Ruggins, J. 21:85
Ruggles, Alfred 23:48
Ruggles, D. C. 13:98
Ruggles, G. M. 11:220
Ruggles, I. W. 8:30
Ruggles, J. W. 18:157
Ruggles, John M. 25:66
Ruggles, Key 14:104
Ruggles, O. 3:168
Ruggles, S. 12:76; 16:303
Ruggles, S. K. 1:167
Ruggles, S. T. 23:282
Ruggles, Stephen 9:215
Rugh, W. I. 3:168
Rugherford, Henry 19:48
Rugle, William 8:30
Rugler, S. 15:73
Rugles, S---el 12:88
Rugles, Theodore 14:213
Rugley, Charles P. 21:383
Rugsby, Ira 21:383
Rugsby, Isaac 8:94
Ruhe, S. B. 1:166
Ruhm, J. 16:224
Ruhm, Peter 11:167
Ruke, Daniel 7:40
Ruke, William 8:30; 18:157
Rukes, John 19:48
Rukke, Sever 10:134; 20:339
Ruland, Nelson A. 7:108
Rule, Adam 8:30
Rule, Lewis 19:292
Rule, Randolph 22:52
Rule, T. A. 3:224; 17:497
Rulebaugh, M. 15:44
Ruleff, Andrew 17:244
Ruler, Adam 18:157
Ruley, George P. 15:224
Ruley, John T. 18:210
Ruley, John W. 11:165
Ruley, Thomas 19:32
Rulidge, Robert 17:428
Rulker, Benjamin 19:48
Rull, Charles 16:141
Rull, E. S. 17:427
Rulliford, Peter 22:317
Rulon, R. 21:168
Rulon, Robert 21:233
Rum, Joseph 10:77
Rumage, C. B. 9:232
Rumage, C. R. 20:339
Rumage, William 17:253
Ruman, William 25:227
Rumbaly, D. 1:166
Rumbaugh, D. H. 15:175
Rumbaugh, Jeremiah 23:165
Rumbaugh, Peter 17:92
Rumbell, J. P. 8:122

Rumbergh, J. H. 26:128
Rumberkert, Samuel 25:66
Rumberlee, Jacob 17:426
Rumble, Henry 8:30
Rumble, Isaac 11:75
Rumble, J. 13:98; 14:20
Rumble, William 24:62
Rumblehardt, William 19:288
Rumbold, Joseph 18:296; 26:111
Rumels, John 14:317
Rumer, Jacob 17:41
Rumery, John B. 23:287
Rumford, Joseph D. 23:280
Rumings, Emory C. 13:44
Rumion, G. 13:98
Rummber, Robert 16:224
Rummel, Fred 20:37
Rummel, Joseph 23:165
Rummel, W. 11:311
Rummell, E. 13:98
Rummell, Fred 25:227
Rummell, John 9:38
Rummels, Jacob A. 26:109
Rummer, L. 3:168
Rummerfield, William 10:134; 20:339
Rummers, M. 14:104
Rummington, Allen 19:97
Rumney, G. H. 1:99
Rumohr, John 22:154
Rumple, Jacob 10:134; 15:9; 20:339
Rumple, James T. 11:74
Rumrill, E. 25:227
Rums, James 8:109
Rumsdell, John I. 12:38
Rumsey, C. O. 9:45; 26:128
Rumsey, Daniel 24:154
Rumsey, George 4:50
Rumsey, J. 16:53
Rumsey, James E. 11:86
Rumsey, Jeremiah W. 13:44
Rumsey, N. 7:40
Rumsey, R. D. 9:192
Runbaugh, John H. 9:45
Runcamber, M. 26:55
Runcannon, --- 9:90
Runchinson, Joel 18:194
Rundberg, Ole 17:100
Rundell, Eben 17:25
Rundell, George 19:190
Rundell, J. 19:191
Rundell, James 15:224

Rundell, Joshua 10:146; 19:191
Rundell, Marshall H. 10:21
Rundio, F. 23:165
Rundio, Robert H. 20:141
Rundy, Hollis 10:77; 20:339
Runeliro, R. H. 20:190
Runels, C. B. 24:28
Runels, John 3:168
Runett, F. 22:52
Runey, I. 3:168
Rung, Jacob 20:339
Runga, Fritz 21:260
Rungan, Henry 19:97
Rungeon, John H. 24:89
Rungett, G. R. 9:45
Rungon, G. S. 12:76
Rungon, S. Z. 19:97
Runion, J. G. 11:329
Runion, John 8:94
Runisdale, J. H. 14:104
Runishaw, William 9:124
Runk, William G. 18:210
Runkell, Will 2:16
Runkle, Andrew 15:73
Runkle, John A. 3:168
Runkle, S. D. 14:20
Runkle, W. 25:67
Runn, G. 14:104
Runnel, Charles 19:348
Runnell, David 18:210
Runnell, Levi 18:157
Runnells, J. 16:224
Runnels, George 17:25
Runnels, H. E. 1:68
Runnels, J. 14:322; 23:48
Runnels, Jacob A. 18:315
Runnels, James 22:14
Runnels, John 25:64
Runnels, Richard 22:129
Runnels, S. E. 15:345; 16:378
Runner, Charles 1:66
Runningan, R. D. 11:311
Runnings, Emery C. 16:53
Runnion, Freeman 17:41
Runnion, Samuel B. 21:143
Runnyon, Reuben A. 22:99
Runon, E. 26:55
Runsey, G. 14:213
Runsey, George 14:259
Runtang, Herman 26:111
Runtauz, Herman 18:315
Runte, John 8:109
Runtson, E. H. 8:109
Runuges, Jefferson 3:168
Runyan, Alfred 21:383

Runyan, David N. 23:77
Runyan, George W. 24:84
Runyan, Harrison 4:50
Runyan, Harrison A. 26:55
Runyan, Jonathan 18:222
Runyan, William 21:383
Runyn, T. J. 9:58
Runyon, Jonathan 10:77
Runyon, S. L. 13:68
Ruoff, John 17:213
Ruone, Patrick 11:75
Rup, William 8:94
Rupard, John H. 22:129
Rupe, Benjamin 8:94
Rupe, James M. 21:59
Rupe, S. 1:166
Rupell, Hiram 21:233
Rupell, W. 16:224
Rupert, Adam 1:67
Rupert, Amos 10:21
Rupert, Amos P. 8:94
Rupert, Bernard 14:213
Rupert, D. W. 22:437
Rupert, Daniel 22:217
Rupert, E. 12:123
Rupert, F. 3:168
Rupert, F. A. T. 22:217
Rupert, Frederick R. 12:55
Rupert, G. W. 16:224
Rupert, George 5:28
Rupert, Hiram 4:51
Rupert, J. K. 5:54; 25:227
Rupert, James H. 13:133; 20:339
Rupert, John 9:45; 12:38; 14:105
Rupert, P. 1:165
Rupert, William 10:77
Ruperts, P. 17:500
Ruperts, S. 17:500
Rupertson, Roland 18:194
Ruple, Charles E. 20:100
Ruple, Joseph W. 20:13
Rupp, C. 25:66
Rupp, J. W. 19:260
Rupp, John W. 9:192
Rupp, Reuben 4:50
Rupp, William 23:165
Ruppenthall, H. 25:227
Ruppenthall, Henry 5:28
Rupper, Daniel 24:44
Ruppert, Gunther 11:374
Rupright, John 22:217
Ruput, William 20:339
Ruron, G. 14:20
Rurtz, Tobias 4:51
Ruryan, Alfred 7:108
Rusby, Charles 7:40
Rusby, J. 3:168

Ruscel, James H. 23:165
Rusch, Jacob 10:77
Rusco, Albert 15:323;
  19:97
Ruscoe, C. 3:168
Ruscoe, T. 1:167
Ruse, A. L. 26:56
Ruse, John 17:239
Ruse, L. A. 24:84
Ruse, W. 14:105
Ruse, W. I. 3:168
Ruseau, --- 15:224
Rusell, Peter 25:65
Rusey, C. 22:217
Rush, A. 15:323
Rush, B. 1:69
Rush, D. 3:168
Rush, Dan 18:56
Rush, Edmund 21:383
Rush, Edward 10:166;
  19:191
Rush, Ephraim 1:191
Rush, F. M. 25:227
Rush, Francis M. 5:28
Rush, Frank N. 9:124
Rush, Frank W. 27:103
Rush, Franz 18:426
Rush, George 12:76; 15:9
Rush, Henry 9:192
Rush, Isaac S. 13:45;
  16:53
Rush, Jacob 9:113; 27:104
Rush, Jacob M. 21:59
Rush, John 3:168; 15:224
Rush, John F. 11:193
Rush, John S. 22:52
Rush, John W. 23:48
Rush, Joseph 3:168
Rush, L. 22:489
Rush, L. S. 1:67
Rush, Lawrence 14:336
Rush, Levi 16:101
Rush, Marion 22:410
Rush, Richard W. 16:101
Rush, S. 3:168
Rush, S. D. 10:22
Rush, Solomon S. 22:99
Rush, Stephen L. 7:40
Rush, T. 1:166
Rush, Tidell 17:317
Rush, W. 23:48
Rush, William 10:93;
  20:339
Rush, William P. 17:315
Rusha, H. 19:260
Rushe, F. 25:326
Rushen, William G.
  22:267
Rusher, Henry 22:217
Rusher, James 19:32
Rushing, --- 16:53

Rushing, L. T. 25:227
Rushing, M. G. 26:56
Rushing, Theodore B.
  17:58
Rushling, F. 1:165
Rushlong, F. 1:164
Rushton, Rupes 10:77
Rushworth, J. 12:123;
  15:134
Rusk, C. D. Alston 20:59
Rusk, James 22:489
Rusk, James A. 21:79
Rusk, James W. 24:44
Rusk, John 3:168; 13:118
Rusk, Nyal B. 17:25
Rusk, Robert R. 27:100
Rusle, C. P. 22:354
Rusler, G. 14:259
Ruslick, John 11:193
Rusling, W. R. 3:168
Russ, A. 13:68; 16:224
Russ, C. 27:101
Russ, Caleb 22:129
Russ, G. A. 27:106
Russ, George W. 13:44
Russ, H. 1:167
Russ, H. J. 1:165
Russ, J. 13:98
Russ, James A. 22:489
Russ, James B. 21:383
Russ, John 15:44
Russ, William 18:210,
  330
Russam, George 7:40
Russel, Alonzo 25:227
Russel, Benjamin S. 15:5
Russel, C. H. 1:67
Russel, Charles 19:191
Russel, D. 15:153
Russel, F. 15:316; 19:306
Russel, George F. 27:104
Russel, Hiram 19:191
Russel, J. 1:67
Russel, James 22:52
Russel, L. 1:68
Russel, Mark H. 26:213
Russel, Nathaniel 15:44
Russel, Theodore F.
  10:166
Russel, William 15:351;
  24:10
Russell, --- 1:165; 8:125;
  19:297, 321
Russell, A. 1:68; 16:53
Russell, A. I. 22:489
Russell, A. M. 4:51
Russell, A. P. 3:168
Russell, A. W. 23:77
Russell, Aaron 11:282
Russell, Abram 8:94
Russell, Albert L. 23:48

Russell, Alex 11:129
Russell, Allen 17:167
Russell, Alonzo 5:54
Russell, Archibald 25:227
Russell, Archy 22:15;
  26:178
Russell, Asa M. 20:109
Russell, B. 18:56; 21:59
Russell, Benjamin F.
  12:76
Russell, Benjamin W.
  7:40
Russell, Benton 22:489
Russell, C. 1:69
Russell, C. A. 18:251;
  26:57
Russell, C. G. 1:68;
  20:141
Russell, C. H. 12:169
Russell, Charles 1:66;
  10:134; 16:224;
  20:339; 23:304
Russell, Charles E. 22:466
Russell, Charles H. 8:60
Russell, Christopher 7:40
Russell, Clark H. 19:32
Russell, Colby 21:112
Russell, Convers 19:316
Russell, Cyrus H. 17:426
Russell, D. 7:53
Russell, Daniel 10:77;
  20:109
Russell, David 8:42;
  15:321; 26:178
Russell, David D. 19:97
Russell, David F. 24:28
Russell, David M. 23:77
Russell, Decatur 22:172
Russell, Deland 15:287
Russell, Delano 19:97
Russell, E. 3:168
Russell, E. H. 14:213
Russell, E. R. 23:165
Russell, Ed. S. 17:86
Russell, Edward 10:134;
  20:339; 21:260;
  25:65
Russell, Elmise S. 8:94
Russell, Emons 22:154
Russell, Enos M. 21:79
Russell, Erastus 8:99
Russell, F. 3:168; 11:166
Russell, F. C. 14:213
Russell, F. M. 22:267;
  24:28; 26:58
Russell, F. W. 14:105
Russell, Fletcher 19:97
Russell, Francis J. 8:94
Russell, Francis M. 8:94
Russell, Frank 15:224
Russell, Frank M. 22:217

Russell, Franklin 11:165
Russell, G. 17:293
Russell, G. A. 3:168
Russell, G. H. 9:192;
19:260
Russell, G. N. 27:104
Russell, G. S. 1:167
Russell, G. W. 9:150;
17:71; 22:217
Russell, George 4:51;
9:113; 11:212, 269;
13:45; 14:213;
16:225; 24:44
Russell, George A. 21:383
Russell, George B. 21:241
Russell, George W. 23:78
Russell, Granville 10:77;
20:339
Russell, H. 21:383
Russell, H. F. B. 21:115
Russell, H. H. 22:318
Russell, H. R. 22:217
Russell, Harmon C.
11:111
Russell, Henry 7:40;
13:68; 16:224
Russell, Henry A. 17:315
Russell, Hiram J. 22:52
Russell, Horace 27:147
Russell, I. 9:232
Russell, Isaac S. 23:78
Russell, Isaiah 21:383
Russell, J. 1:68, 165, 166;
3:168; 7:60; 10:29,
37; 11:97; 14:105;
19:97; 20:339;
25:227
Russell, J. C. 17:338
Russell, J. F. 1:167
Russell, J. G. 3:168
Russell, J. H. 23:289
Russell, J. J. 11:269
Russell, J. S. 3:168
Russell, J. T. 14:105
Russell, Jack 21:283
Russell, Jacob 3:168;
9:113, 204; 17:97
Russell, Jam 21:39
Russell, James 3:168;
9:135; 13:45;
14:213; 15:345;
16:378; 17:184;
21:89; 23:118;
27:103
Russell, James A. 22:267
Russell, James B. 11:74;
12:157
Russell, James H. 11:86
Russell, James J. 22:267
Russell, James R. 14:213
Russell, James U. 1:69

Russell, James V. 20:143
Russell, Jasper 10:134;
20:339
Russell, Jesse 21:39
Russell, John 4:68; 7:132;
8:30; 10:177; 14:213;
18:71, 157; 19:191;
22:217; 25:227
Russell, John H. 15:175
Russell, John M. 22:489
Russell, John Rice 17:319
Russell, John S. 22:217
Russell, John T. 17:58
Russell, John W. 1:66
Russell, Joseph 27:100
Russell, Joseph M. 5:28
Russell, Josiah 26:128
Russell, L. J. 13:118
Russell, L. M. 21:383
Russell, L. T. 3:168
Russell, Latan 22:344
Russell, Leonard M. 7:108
Russell, Levi 8:30
Russell, Lewis 13:118
Russell, Lewis Jackson
10:134; 20:339
Russell, Luther 22:467
Russell, Luther A. 22:52
Russell, M. 7:60; 22:354;
25:227
Russell, M. L. 14:266
Russell, M. M. 26:55
Russell, Marcell 15:224
Russell, Martin 5:28
Russell, Mathew 15:309;
19:97
Russell, McDaniel 11:425
Russell, Michael 10:134;
12:38; 20:339;
21:383
Russell, Michael G.
17:207
Russell, Milton 10:77;
20:339
Russell, Moses 8:109
Russell, Myron C. 9:156
Russell, N. A. 14:105
Russell, N. H. 12:51
Russell, Nelson 22:317,
318; 25:286
Russell, Noel 22:99
Russell, O. 22:317
Russell, O. H. P. 14:105
Russell, Otis H. 11:111
Russell, P. 9:58; 21:125
Russell, Peter 3:168
Russell, Pompey 18:251;
26:56
Russell, R. 3:168; 7:40;
17:327; 21:383

Russell, R. R. 13:98;
14:20
Russell, R. T. 9:115
Russell, Ransom B.
16:148
Russell, Robert 1:66
Russell, Robert A. 20:116
Russell, Robert L. 11:75
Russell, Roden 8:75
Russell, Ruthven 22:410
Russell, S. 14:279; 23:109
Russell, S. A. 3:168
Russell, S. H. 25:227
Russell, S. S. 1:67
Russell, S. W. 1:66
Russell, Samuel 4:51;
8:42; 11:75, 212,
312; 13:45; 26:178
Russell, Samuel H. 20:103
Russell, Samuel N. 20:100
Russell, Solomon M.
24:97
Russell, Stephen 4:51
Russell, T. 3:168; 5:54;
9:150; 25:227;
27:102
Russell, T. H. 1:67
Russell, Theodore F.
19:191
Russell, Thomas 7:8;
8:30; 9:45, 113;
10:77, 211; 19:32;
20:339; 22:505;
24:28; 26:129
Russell, Tuman 20:339
Russell, Tureman 4:51
Russell, W. 1:167;
16:270; 17:149;
18:56
Russell, W. B. 7:108
Russell, W. C. 8:109
Russell, W. D. 11:42, 407
Russell, W. F. 22:489
Russell, W. H. 3:168
Russell, W. J. 24:99
Russell, Wallace 9:202;
19:292
Russell, William 1:68;
4:51; 5:28; 7:108;
8:42; 9:192; 10:77;
11:220; 12:62; 13:45;
14:105; 15:59;
16:378; 17:41, 58,
112, 420; 22:99, 318,
466; 25:227; 26:178
Russell, William E. 17:58
Russer, Alfred 17:184
Russer, Samuel 7:53
Russet, Joseph 10:134;
20:339
Russett, John 21:239

Russin, Asa 11:391
Russin, Duff 15:134
Russle, J. 22:16
Russman, Jacob 8:94
Russmose, E. 3:168
Russon, William 7:40
Russum, James F. 26:179
Rust, Andrew J. 12:76
Rust, Andrew P. 15:9
Rust, J. Y. 7:53
Rust, James 15:224
Rust, John 17:58
Rust, R. 1:66
Rust, Samuel 11:289
Rust, Thomas 10:134;
    20:339
Ruste, Christian 21:260
Ruster, R. 3:168
Ruster, William 14:105
Rustin, F. 25:227
Rustin, Floyd 5:45
Rustin, John M. 6:13
Rustin, T. M. 18:93
Ruston, George B. 9:28;
    18:315; 26:110
Ruston, Henry 22:437
Rutan, E. B. 3:168
Rutan, James W. 21:116
Rutan, John 4:51; 23:92
Rutan, Warren 9:17
Ruter, C. 24:114
Ruterstine, George 23:165
Rutford, John 18:194
Rutgen, W. 3:168
Ruth, A. M. 21:79
Ruth, B. S. 3:168
Ruth, D. A. 9:150
Ruth, D. N. 27:101
Ruth, F. 3:168
Ruth, George 11:86
Ruth, H. A. 23:302
Ruth, Hiram 2:17; 25:64
Ruth, J. 14:105
Ruth, John 19:328
Ruth, Patrick 16:225
Ruth, Richard 17:424;
    24:175
Ruth, S. 25:66
Ruth, Samuel 2:16
Ruth, William A. 9:192;
    19:268
Ruther, Aaron 9:192
Ruther, Anthony 22:168
Ruther, J. 3:168
Ruther, John G. 5:28
Ruther, R. 2:16; 25:63
Ruther, William 11:89
Rutherbun, Marion
    17:265
Rutherford, --- 26:213
Rutherford, A. J. 23:48

Rutherford, C. H. 9:90;
    26:56
Rutherford, D. 17:25
Rutherford, D. W. 1:68
Rutherford, F. S. 13:60
Rutherford, G. 21:59
Rutherford, G. J. 21:39
Rutherford, George R.
    9:124; 27:104
Rutherford, H. 25:63
Rutherford, J. T. 8:122
Rutherford, James 10:77;
    20:339
Rutherford, John 10:77;
    17:416; 20:339;
    24:154
Rutherford, John C. 22:52
Rutherford, Mark 20:13
Rutherford, R. 22:318
Rutherford, Richard
    22:318
Rutherford, Robert 4:51
Rutherford, S. D. 1:66
Rutherford, William
    9:237; 26:225
Rutherford, Witham 9:58
Ruthers, R. 23:205
Ruthers, S. 23:115
Ruthersford, Royal 24:28
Ruthfan, J. 3:168
Ruthwell, E. 1:167
Ruthwiler, Peter 25:64
Rutland, --- 9:211
Rutland, Benjamin 7:132
Rutledge, Andrew 16:65
Rutledge, Isaac 7:40
Rutledge, J. H. 26:57
Rutledge, James 20:339
Rutledge, John N. 11:74
Rutledge, John O. 10:77
Rutledge, L. 14:105
Rutledge, Miner B.
    22:267
Rutledge, Silas T. 8:109
Rutledge, T. 1:164
Rutledge, Thomas 22:470
Rutledge, William J.
    11:89
Rutler, Benjamin 8:115
Rutler, W. 1:166
Rutley, James 16:225
Rutlidge, J. H. 18:251
Rutlidge, James 9:232
Rutlidge, Samuel 22:217
Rutly, James 15:300
Rutner, Hiram D. 8:94
Rutoff, Jacob 3:168
Rutorn, S. 1:166
Rutry, Elsworth 9:192
Rutt, George 22:437
Rutt, H. D. 18:157

Rutt, John 22:52
Ruttan, Joseph 11:166
Rutter, Anthony E. 13:45
Rutter, C. H. 15:224
Rutter, E. 11:89
Rutter, Hugh 17:250
Rutter, Isaac B. 13:45
Rutter, J. 1:165; 13:98
Rutter, James M. 17:250
Rutter, James S. 16:123
Rutter, Jim 14:105
Rutter, John 10:77;
    20:339
Rutter, John R. 14:213
Rutter, Martin L. 21:233
Rutter, P. H. 20:25
Rutter, W. 14:284
Rutter, William 11:97
Rutter, William C. 19:191
Rutterford, John 21:383
Rutters, Isaac 19:97
Ruttige, Robert R. 24:184
Ruttle, G. 13:118
Ruttle, J. R. 20:59
Ruttledge, James 18:38
Rutty, A. 1:167
Ruty, John 3:168
Ruussell, Martin M. 9:90
Ruvis, Moses L. 26:55
Ruxton, A. 1:68
Ruxton, J. 1:167
Ruy, --- 18:179
Ry, A. O. G. A. 17:293
Ryall, John 11:335
Ryall, William C. 1:68
Ryan, --- 7:63
Ryan, A. 1:69; 26:55
Ryan, A. H. 12:157
Ryan, A. S. 21:384
Ryan, Anderson 9:90
Ryan, Andrew 7:60
Ryan, Anthony 21:384
Ryan, B. 14:27
Ryan, Benjamin 10:77;
    20:339
Ryan, C. 1:66; 21:384;
    26:178
Ryan, C. P. 3:168; 21:384
Ryan, Charles 3:168
Ryan, Charles E. 8:30
Ryan, Cornelius 14:213
Ryan, Cornelius A. 10:22
Ryan, D. 3:168
Ryan, Daniel 18:413;
    21:384
Ryan, David 1:67
Ryan, Dennis 9:113;
    12:93; 14:213
Ryan, Edward 10:77;
    11:122; 14:213;
    20:13, 339

Ryan, Felix 11:391
Ryan, G. A. 14:27
Ryan, George 4:51; 24:44
Ryan, H. 20:339
Ryan, H. W. 15:312
Ryan, Henry 22:466, 467
Ryan, Hugh 10:77; 14:213
Ryan, J. 3:168; 9:150;
    22:163; 27:101
Ryan, J. C. 1:68
Ryan, J. S. 13:98
Ryan, James 5:28; 7:108;
    10:77; 15:44;
    19:330; 20:339;
    21:384; 23:48;
    24:184; 25:227
Ryan, John 3:168; 4:51;
    6:18; 7:40, 108;
    10:174; 13:45;
    16:114; 17:41;
    18:93; 19:32, 191;
    21:11, 384; 22:99,
    172; 23:125, 205;
    24:72; 25:288
Ryan, John W. 9:106
Ryan, M. 1:69, 166;
    3:168; 22:217, 521;
    25:64
Ryan, Martin 1:68; 2:16;
    3:168
Ryan, Martin V. 17:92
Ryan, Mathew 21:384
Ryan, Michael 1:66; 7:40;
    8:30; 10:166;
    16:101; 18:157;
    19:191; 21:11;
    22:217; 23:195;
    25:227
Ryan, Moses 16:378
Ryan, P. 8:55; 25:227
Ryan, P. J. 21:168
Ryan, Pat 22:344
Ryan, Patrick 5:28;
    10:166; 11:193;
    16:53, 114; 17:502;
    19:191; 21:105;
    22:344, 509; 24:28;
    25:65
Ryan, Patrick H. 4:51
Ryan, Perlemon 11:167
Ryan, Peter 10:77;
    20:340; 22:154
Ryan, Peter W. 13:45
Ryan, Richard 5:54;
    19:191; 25:227
Ryan, Robert 14:213
Ryan, Samuel 26:225
Ryan, Simon 11:167
Ryan, T. 1:166

Ryan, Thomas 1:68;
    12:173; 18:56; 23:48,
    92
Ryan, Thomas L. 11:42
Ryan, Timothy 21:384;
    25:64
Ryan, W. 3:168
Ryan, Wallace 18:56
Ryan, William 3:168;
    9:38, 113; 10:166;
    21:39; 22:505;
    23:253; 27:101
Ryans, J. 21:384
Ryans, John 13:118
Ryant, C. H. 1:165
Ryatt, E. L. 15:134
Rybes, Thomas 18:194
Rychmyer, Peter 14:105
Ryckman, P. 9:150;
    27:101
Ryckman, Ransom 20:340
Ryckman, S. 1:69
Ryder, A. C. 1:165
Ryder, Benjamin 7:53
Ryder, Charles 18:93
Ryder, J. F. 11:129
Ryder, James 17:253
Ryder, John 12:96; 19:97
Ryder, Nicholas 4:51
Ryder, Patrick 25:63
Ryder, T. N. 16:225
Ryder, V. B. 11:425
Ryders, J. W. 18:157
Rye, Charles 1:66
Rye, Henry 8:78
Rye, W. L. 22:129
Ryekman, Ranson 10:134
Ryen, Charles E. 18:157
Ryen, James 21:384
Ryen, John E. 12:62
Ryer, C. 1:166
Ryer, Charles 13:45
Ryer, R. 14:213
Ryer, Thomas 19:191
Ryerly, J. W. 8:109
Ryerson, A. 25:64
Ryerson, Austin W. 7:108
Ryerson, H. O. 2:16
Ryerson, John 17:502
Ryerson, Peter M. 22:471
Ryesdale, T. 1:66
Ryeson, G. W. 15:300
Ryeson, George W.
    16:225
Ryhert, Peter T. 11:110
Ryker, Hyram 10:77
Ryker, Hysen 20:340
Rykman, V. W. 20:134
Ryland, --- 11:74
Ryle, Hogan 11:212
Ryley, Owen 1:68

Ryman, J. 18:56
Ryman, John 17:399
Rynders, I. W. 8:30
Rynders, James H. 24:55
Ryne, Dennis 16:303
Ryne, George A. 15:263
Ryne, I. M. 3:169
Rynearson, D. C. 23:48
Rynedollar, William 3:169
Rynehart, Henry 10:134;
    20:340
Ryner, Jacob 12:9
Rynolds, David 9:224
Rynolds, Henry 24:69
Rynolds, W. J. 15:321
Ryon, H. W. 19:97
Ryon, I. 3:169
Ryon, J. 3:169
Ryon, James 15:160
Ryon, Martin 15:44
Ryon, Owen 3:169
Ryon, W. 3:169
Ryouch, John 3:169
Ryse, F. 18:157
Ryson, John 3:169
Ryther, Henry A. 15:335
Ryther, Solon 10:134;
    20:340
Ryther, William F. 25:65

S

S---, --- 10:29; 15:167;
    27:118
S---, ---one 24:114
S---, A. 11:121; 19:197;
    24:114
S---, A. B. 14:271
S---, A. W. 21:384
S---, Aaron 26:237
S---, Alonzo 18:38
S---, B. 15:333; 20:156;
    21:384; 23:205, 314
S---, B. B. 11:87
S---, B. S. 27:108
S---, B. W. 15:333
S---, C. 11:249; 17:356;
    25:68; 27:106
S---, C. B. 11:232
S---, C. D. 19:286
S---, C. E. 23:48
S---, C. H. 17:217
S---, C. J. 17:350
S---, Caleb 20:156
S---, Charles 18:38
S---, D. 13:68; 17:356;
    18:179; 20:92
S---, D. D. 11:221
S---, D. P. 11:221
S---, D. W. 15:9; 20:340

S---, E. 17:213, 217; 19:32; 20:59; 24:114
S---, E. D. 19:288
S---, E. R. 27:107
S---, E. W. 11:314
S---, F. 15:231; 17:365
S---, F. C. 20:340
S---, F. M. 12:142; 20:181
S---, F. M. S. 26:226
S---, F. W. 23:314
S---, Frank 16:225
S---, G. C. 15:231
S---, G. M. 16:123
S---, G. W. 15:231; 20:59; 23:264
S---, George 20:13
S---, H. 11:251; 18:38; 19:197; 23:283; 26:184
S---, H. C. 26:184
S---, H. E. 8:56
S---, H. H. 25:227
S---, H. S. 19:32
S---, Herman 15:153
S---, I. C. J. 18:179
S---, J. 8:68; 10:29; 12:142; 18:255; 19:197, 286; 20:59, 340; 21:59, 209; 23:205; 24:114; 25:227, 312; 26:62, 184
S---, J. A. 11:98
S---, J. C. 21:209
S---, J. D. 23:205
S---, J. E. 8:56
S---, J. F. 15:175; 17:497
S---, J. H. 11:250
S---, J. M. 10:32; 17:217; 20:340; 25:73
S---, J. R. 10:193; 20:156; 26:204
S---, J. S. 17:217
S---, J. T. 14:271; 15:231
S---, J. W. 18:377
S---, Jacob 11:314
S---, James A. 17:254
S---, James F. 25:68
S---, James K. 20:59
S---, John 19:306; 24:215
S---, K. 20:340
S---, L. 20:92
S---, L. A. 20:13; 25:312
S---, L. B. 15:59
S---, L. D. H. 23:245
S---, L. H. 24:114
S---, L. W. 18:71
S---, M. 23:48, 205
S---, M. H. 19:197
S---, M. S. 20:340
S---, N. V. 11:270

S---, O. 17:254
S---, P--- 7:80
S---, Phillips 16:225
S---, R. 8:56; 17:498; 25:312
S---, R. B. 17:93, 217
S---, S. 2:18; 22:355; 25:227
S---, S. C. 17:68
S---, S. D. 20:156
S---, S. L. 25:73
S---, S. S. 25:228, 304
S---, T. 11:220, 251; 14:271; 15:59; 21:209; 22:354; 23:205; 24:215; 25:67
S---, T. A. 11:249
S---, T. G. 11:271
S---, T. J. 11:221; 26:184
S---, T. W. 18:377
S---, U. T. 11:323
S---, V. 15:73
S---, V. J. 20:340
S---, W. 10:193; 11:271, 282; 15:231; 18:38, 179, 255; 20:93, 340; 21:209; 23:253; 25:68; 26:62
S---, W. A. 11:342; 24:114
S---, W. D. 21:209
S---, W. F. 19:197; 23:245
S---, W. H. 21:209
S---, W. H. H. 20:88
S---, W. L. 13:130; 20:59; 21:209
S---, W. M. 20:156
S---, W. R. 25:71
S---, W. S. 23:302
S---, William 20:59, 340
S---, Y. H. 16:380
S----, H. Y. D. 22:267
S----, J. 22:129
S----, J. L. 22:267
S---eary, Daniel 25:240
S---in, --- 24:29
S---ore, James 23:182
S---per, Colt 20:128
S---r, G. 24:44
S--ore, James 23:182
Sa---, S. 19:192
Sa-wan-nok-keh 25:335
Saage, Frederick 26:61
Saathoff, Harry 20:340
Sabal, Henry 11:382
Sabaston, W. 16:225
Sabbitt, R. 18:95
Sabiens, W. B. 7:108
Sabin, Alonzo 3:224; 17:503

Sabin, D. C. 22:217
Sabin, David P. 9:192
Sabin, Downey 9:192
Sabin, Elica C. 10:178
Sabin, G. M. 17:159
Sabin, James 23:165
Sabin, John W. 10:134; 20:340
Sabin, O. W. 11:75
Sabin, Peter H. 18:341
Sabin, Thodor 17:213
Sabin, W. 15:264
Sabine, Charles D. 9:124; 27:113
Sabine, D. N. 21:384
Sabine, E. F. 11:45
Sabine, Elica C. 10:151
Sabine, I. 19:275
Sabine, Orvilla 22:467
Sabine, Peter H. 9:104
Sabine, William 20:152
Sabines, Ed 3:169
Sabins, Emery 22:99
Sabins, Francis 4:51
Sabins, I. 15:224
Sabins, James A. 9:98
Sabor, John 13:45
Saborech, Jefferson 23:307
Sabrmama, E. K. S. 9:192
Sabrooks, Thomas J. 24:44
Sabulk, John 21:384
Sachs, Henry 13:45
Sack, Charles 11:171
Sackell, John A. 22:99
Sackenberger, John 17:429
Sacket, Jonathan 6:7
Sacket, L. H. 8:75
Sacket, R. F. 1:75
Sackett, Charles W. 14:271
Sackett, Edwin H. 22:510
Sackett, H. N. 17:67
Sackett, Isaac 4:51
Sackett, J. 3:169
Sackett, Jacob 11:111
Sackett, John 8:67
Sackett, John H. 22:52
Sackett, John J. 10:22
Sackett, L. H. 26:183
Sackett, Reuben T. 21:384
Sackett, S. 14:284
Sackett, S. L. 9:150; 27:107
Sackett, William P. 23:78
Sackett, Wright 23:92
Sackhimer, George F. 4:51

Sackhouse, Samuel 6:18; 18:93
Sackitt, R. S. 3:169
Sackley, L. W. 16:378
Sackner, Jacob C. 1:71
Sackrider, Abraham 22:99
Sackrider, John 22:52
Sacks, D. 1:176
Sacks, J. 27:118
Sacks, Peter 12:60
Sackun, Marcus 8:94
Sackvasson, J. E. 21:384
Sacmie, Maccus 8:115
Saco, John 9:124; 27:113
Saddle, James 18:93
Saddler, Charles 26:183
Saddler, David 18:157
Saddler, Henry 21:384
Saddler, James 6:19
Saddler, John 19:191
Saddler, Rup. J. 16:87
Saddoris, Elias 27:115
Sadler, David 8:30
Sadler, George N. 22:154
Sadler, H. P. 1:172
Sadler, J. B. 1:100
Sadler, J. L. 9:38
Sadler, J. W. 17:97
Sadler, Jacob 11:87
Sadler, John 11:392
Sadler, Leonard 17:58
Sadler, M. 3:169
Sadler, Robert P. 22:129
Sadler, Samuel G. 22:267
Sadler, Thomas 11:169
Sadler, William H. 23:195
Sadley, J. F. 15:160
Sadley, M. 3:169
Sadvenson, S. 13:68
Sadwin, George 8:55
Sae, J. M. 27:109
Saemke, G. 1:173
Saenger, Fred 24:99
Safely, John W. 10:134; 20:340
Safely, Socrates T. 23:93
Saffel, D. 15:268
Saffel, Johnson 8:42
Saffle, J. 3:169
Saffley, John T. 23:48
Saffner, Charles 20:109
Safford, Edwin 22:467
Safford, H. 18:409
Safford, H. T. 15:111
Safford, John 11:392
Safford, L. B. 8:67
Safford, Legrand 26:180
Safford, Olvier 20:59
Safford, P. J. 3:169
Safford, Philip 9:90; 26:59

Safford, Thomas L. 17:288
Saffrons, George 22:457
Safley, Robert 24:55
Safly, Alex 22:516
Safra, John 7:108
Sage, Agnes S. 18:441
Sage, Com. P. 22:52
Sage, Gardner B. 24:180
Sage, J. B. 17:426
Sage, James 17:86
Sage, James A. 18:222
Sage, John 22:52
Sage, Malcolm S. 8:55
Sage, Marion 22:439
Sage, Oran 14:213
Sage, Park 21:384
Sage, Patrick 21:384
Sage, Revilo 7:108
Sage, Robert F. 23:78
Sage, Samuel 10:210
Sage, Stephen L. 22:52
Sage, Thomas 7:78; 25:304
Sage, Thomas S. 17:244
Sage, Walter 19:191
Sage, Westley 21:39
Sage, William H. 21:79
Sage, William W. 20:128
Sager, H. 17:297
Sager, J. 1:99
Sager, Jackson P. 23:165
Sager, John 16:136
Sager, M. M. 19:191
Sager, Samuel 10:134; 20:340
Sager, W. 1:175
Saggert, Reuben 4:51
Saggs, Daniel 8:42
Saggs, James 8:42
Sagher, J. 25:228
Sagle, John H. 7:63
Sagor, Daniel 1:74
Sahlhut, H. 9:58
Sahmams, Eries K. E. 19:260
Saibel, John 22:440
Saibles, D. B. 21:39
Saichell, J. M. 18:251; 26:62
Saidley, Abraham 11:391
Saile, G. 22:217
Sailer, Robert 4:51
Sailes, A. H. 21:39
Sailing, Frederick 7:40
Sailon, William H. 9:45
Sailor, A. 13:98
Sailor, David 14:213
Sailor, Emanias 21:79
Sailor, George 22:217
Sailor, Henry W. 21:79

Sailor, J. 11:313
Sailor, J. M. 22:505
Sailor, Jacob 7:60
Sailor, James 17:163
Sailor, Jesse 22:217
Sailor, R. F. 22:99
Sailor, S. W. 7:69
Sailor, Samuel 23:165
Sailors, Robert F. 22:99
Sails, A. D. 3:169
Sails, C. 14:105
Sails, Franklin 9:166
Sailsmer, C. 11:98
Sain, Francis 9:90
Sain, George W. 16:144
Saint, C. 14:105
Saint, John Abijah C. 25:228
Saint, Julian Emile 21:384
Saint, Richard H. 7:132
Saint Clair, P. 14:21
Sair, Daniel 12:157
Sair, T. 25:228
Sair, Thomas 5:28
Sairl, Francis 8:94
Sairp, Christian 18:157
Saiter, J. J. 2:17
Sake, John 21:283
Sakemiller, Andrew 23:165
Sakes, Isaac 15:88
Saklen, P. 1:74
Saladee, John W. 22:492
Salamayde, J. 25:304
Salanting, James 27:119
Salar, A. S. 22:490
Salazar, --- 8:124
Salck, Fred 18:251; 26:61
Salcor, John 16:53
Sale, George W. 10:134; 20:340
Sale, James G. 22:440
Sale, John 25:73
Sale, John L. 17:145
Sale, Thomas 3:169
Sale, William A. 16:53
Sale, William H. H. 10:134; 20:340
Salee, A. S. 9:227
Salent, Harrison 11:329
Saler, George W. 17:86
Sales, B. A. 9:73
Sales, John W. 24:29
Sales, Thomas 16:225
Sales, W. H. 21:39
Sales, William 27:115
Salesbury, J. Y. M. 1:169
Salesbury, John 8:30; 18:157
Salesbury, John P. 22:217
Salesbury, R. E. 15:44

Salesby, John 26:182
Salesman, Con 1:73
Saley, Charles 18:285
Saley, J. S. 16:270
Salfeeder, John C. 20:31
Salfrage, Charles Q. 23:185
Saliday, William 8:94
Saliers, Riley 9:243
Saling, J. 18:194
Salisberry, Thompson J. 24:44
Salisberry, W. I. 10:134
Salisburg, S. 9:98
Salisbury, --- 14:105
Salisbury, D. 22:217
Salisbury, E. 3:169
Salisbury, James O. 10:97; 18:400
Salisbury, Jeremiah 9:14
Salisbury, N. B. 15:224
Salisbury, R. 12:62
Salisbury, T. 23:264
Salisbury, W. A. 1:174
Salisbury, W. J. 20:340
Salisbury, William 4:51; 14:213
Salisbury, William A. 15:44
Salisbury, Winslow J. 25:326
Salkald, D. 9:58
Sall, William H. 15:74
Sallan, John L. 23:287
Sallas, --- 19:97
Sallee, A. S. 18:375
Sallee, George 3:169
Sallee, W. 23:48
Sallefield, E. 14:105
Sallengers, Henry 9:243
Sallent, John 22:267
Sallerfield, Young 8:42
Salley, W. R. 13:98
Sallidine, E. 3:169
Sallie, Moses 21:384
Salling, John 11:425
Sallsburry, James 20:340
Sally, Patrick 19:349
Sallyanis, S. 17:101
Sallybaugh, F. 9:150
Salman, G. W. 7:108
Salmand, P. 3:169
Salmar, David 8:94
Salmon, Edward 11:171
Salmon, J. A. 17:420
Salmon, J. D. 25:69
Salmon, John 10:77; 20:340
Salmon, S. 15:44
Salmon, Thomas 18:56

Salmon, William 10:134; 20:340
Salmond, W. 1:175
Salmonds, R. 17:58
Salmons, E. C. 1:174
Saloman, William 9:192
Salome, Theodore 13:45
Salomon, John 9:202
Salone, Theodore 16:53
Salpaugh, Beckman 21:384
Salsberry, Francis 9:224; 18:375
Salsberry, John 11:404
Salsbur, J. 3:169
Salsbury, Eli 17:266
Salsbury, George 10:8
Salsbury, H. 3:169
Salsbury, Horace 25:228
Salsbury, J. 9:115
Salsbury, J. L. 11:251
Salsbury, James 10:77
Salsbury, John 8:55; 16:101
Salsbury, John F. 21:79
Salser, T. 14:105
Salsgiver, D. Y. 19:97
Salt, John 23:195
Salter, A. W. 25:281
Salter, Charles 18:93
Salter, E. 17:192
Salter, G. 25:228
Salter, George 5:45; 12:51
Salter, George H. 14:266
Salter, J. 22:492
Salter, J. C. 19:191
Salter, John 25:286
Salter, John H. 1:73
Salter, Joseph 22:99
Salter, Josiah 11:392
Salter, Marshall 17:218
Salter, Oscar 12:76
Salter, P. 25:228
Salter, W. C. 19:191
Salterback, Andrew 24:55
Salterburg, Christian 8:30
Salters, George 17:67
Salters, J. 23:165
Salterville, A. 14:213
Saltis, William 6:33
Saltmarsh, S. 23:48
Saltmarsh, Stephen 17:507
Saltonstall, R. 19:244
Salts, Cornelius 22:217
Salts, H. C. 14:213
Salts, W. C. 3:169
Saltsbaugh, F. 11:312
Saltsman, J. 10:149; 18:57
Saltz, William 7:53
Salverson, H. 18:57

Saly, Charles 26:135
Salyards, N. B. 13:118
Salyer, S. 1:78
Salyers, Isaac 21:105
Salyers, William 24:44
Salyers, Zachariah 17:402
Salzberger, R. 1:77
Salzman, John 4:51
Sam, --- 11:323
Samaris, W. 12:100
Samber, Daniel 19:191
Sambo, William 21:384
Samdall, J. H. 9:192
Same, Joseph 7:78; 25:304
Samedert, C. P. 21:384
Samercux, J. R. 14:21
Samers, William 9:58
Sames, George 10:77; 20:340
Samet, W. 3:169
Samiller, Andrew 16:134
Samington, --- 25:335
Samis, Henry 22:52
Samis, Samuel I. 18:346
Samlett, --- 3:169
Samm, William 11:121
Sammand, George 22:318
Sammel, Gunsaulus 9:124
Sammerskill, Samuel 19:306
Sammies, John 13:45
Sammis, Alcott 16:53
Sammis, C. A. 9:150; 27:110
Sammis, F. E. 27:108
Sammis, John 16:53
Sammis, T. E. 9:150
Sammon, Daniel 9:192
Sammon, David 19:260
Sammonds, A. 3:169
Sammons, B. 3:169
Sammons, Benjamin 12:51
Sammons, Gilbert 25:280
Sammons, Jacob 15:111
Samms, Josiah 18:413
Samon, E. 14:105
Samon, L. A. 3:169
Samora, Juan 6:8
Samper, C. 24:155
Samper, H. 17:432
Sampere, J. F. 7:13
Sampeter, Francis W. 9:104
Sample, Andrewville 22:439
Sample, Cyrus 12:38
Sample, E. 14:105
Sample, Edmund 25:228

Sample, G. H. 15:330; 19:97
Sample, George 11:78
Sample, J. 25:228
Sample, John 4:51; 10:77; 20:340
Sample, John J. 20:43
Sample, Joseph 7:132
Sample, Milton 23:195
Sample, Robert 11:44
Sample, W. H. 20:340
Sample, William H. 10:77
Samples, Gilbert 22:267
Samples, Joseph A. 22:457
Samples, Reuben 22:267
Samprich, John 19:32
Sampson, Alfred H. 20:187
Sampson, Andrew 10:177; 24:29
Sampson, B. 13:45
Sampson, C. 3:169
Sampson, Charles 5:45; 14:213; 25:228
Sampson, Charles E. 9:192
Sampson, Colonel 12:51
Sampson, E. 3:169; 19:242
Sampson, F. 14:105
Sampson, F. H. 18:251; 26:63
Sampson, Flarbin 21:283
Sampson, G. B. 1:70
Sampson, G. F. 19:233
Sampson, George T. 9:243
Sampson, George W. 16:7
Sampson, H. 1:77; 27:109
Sampson, Harvey 7:132
Sampson, Henry 9:161; 14:261; 21:384
Sampson, I. R. 14:105
Sampson, J. 1:173; 3:169; 13:118
Sampson, J. C. 14:251
Sampson, J. E. 8:67
Sampson, J. F. 26:183
Sampson, J. W. 1:75
Sampson, James G. 21:384
Sampson, Japhet W. 7:40
Sampson, John R. 3:169
Sampson, Joseph 19:191
Sampson, K. 27:119
Sampson, L. A. 16:378
Sampson, Levi 10:77
Sampson, O. 9:192
Sampson, P. 21:125
Sampson, Peter 16:53
Sampson, R. 14:245

Sampson, Robert 14:213
Sampson, S. A. 15:345
Sampson, Samuel 5:45
Sampson, Samuel O. 21:207
Sampson, Simon P. 8:30; 18:157
Sampson, T. W. 11:98
Sampson, Thomas 17:184; 21:260
Sampson, Vinton 15:23
Sampson, W. 27:115
Sampson, W. H. 4:51
Sampson, W. J. 23:165
Sampson, William 10:134; 16:225; 20:340; 23:101
Sampstor, John 11:397
Samro, Frederick 9:124
Samrous, Abner 20:340
Sams, Frederick 9:135; 27:111
Sams, G. 1:173
Sams, H. S. 13:126
Sams, John 12:9
Sams, Lafayette 11:251
Sams, Noah 11:167
Sams, Simeon 9:224
Sams, Simon 18:375
Samse, William 3:169
Samson, Andrew 19:191
Samson, C. E. 19:260
Samson, G. F. 9:192
Samson, H. 24:114
Samson, Henry 9:150
Samson, John B. 8:30; 26:182
Samson, L. B. 14:213
Samson, M. 15:175
Samson, Vinton 12:65
Samson, Willis 18:251; 26:64
Samster, Jacob 14:213
Samuel, --- 9:58; 13:77; 25:326
Samuel, David D. 9:39
Samuel, G. H. 23:302
Samuel, Henry 9:104
Samuel, Isaac 18:251; 26:64
Samuel, J. H. 15:111
Samuel, J. M. 26:183
Samuel, Shaw 21:384
Samuel, W. B. 10:97
Samuels, C. P. 7:65
Samuels, George D. 22:99
Samuels, Henry 6:19; 8:30; 18:157
Samuels, J. M. 8:75; 11:43

Samuels, Richard 9:202; 19:284
Samuels, William 18:93
Sanafer, Alick 24:203
Sanbo, E. 16:378
Sanborn, A. E. 12:157
Sanborn, A. F. 27:111
Sanborn, A. J. 25:68
Sanborn, Andrew J. 2:17
Sanborn, Daniel 7:53
Sanborn, Edgar 4:51
Sanborn, George 5:54
Sanborn, George F. 13:118
Sanborn, H. B. 1:171
Sanborn, Israel 17:254
Sanborn, J. 17:86
Sanborn, J. H. 10:22
Sanborn, J. O. 27:108
Sanborn, James 8:55
Sanborn, Jeremiah 25:228
Sanborn, Joseph 21:143
Sanborn, Levi H. 24:29
Sanborn, Lorenzo L. 9:244
Sanborn, R. 22:509
Sanborn, S. E. 16:282
Sanborn, Samuel 8:94; 9:113
Sanborn, T. 17:435; 24:180
Sanborn, W. 3:169
Sanborne, J. O. 9:150
Sanborne, O. F. 9:150
Sanborne, T. 3:169
Sanbourn, L. W. 25:228
Sanbourn, T. 25:228
Sanboyan, C. H. 1:95
Sanburn, Asa J. 4:51
Sanburn, D. 5:28
Sanburn, Elias 11:117
Sanburn, H. 3:169, 170
Sanburn, W. 18:194
Sanburn, William H. 12:54
Sanchers, M. 3:170
Sanches, Francesco 22:411
Sanchez, Joseph 21:384
Sancicu, Francis 10:77
Sand, Daniel 8:94
Sand, John 22:510
Sand, Philip 20:128
Sand, William 3:169
Sandage, Greenbury 24:44
Sandagreen, Allen 16:53
Sandal, J. H. 19:234
Sandall, Christian 14:271
Sandall, Samuel C. 11:194
Sandals, W. H. 20:43
Sandbach, Joseph 23:13

Sandberg, Hans P. 24:29
Sandberg, James 10:134; 20:340
Sandberg, John 16:53
Sandborn, E. E. 19:191
Sandborn, Edward 11:76
Sandborn, J. 10:154; 19:191
Sandbringer, J. C. 8:67
Sandefer, Isaac 21:233
Sandefur, Joseph 20:105
Sander, Bernt 20:116
Sander, Charles 3:169
Sander, E. 14:105
Sander, George H. 9:45
Sander, John 22:217
Sanderdale, D. 8:109
Sanderland, J. 1:173
Sanderline, Isaac 7:53
Sanders, A. 7:108; 13:98; 17:41
Sanders, Aaron 22:99
Sanders, Andrew 13:45; 24:102
Sanders, August 23:78
Sanders, Augustus 9:124; 22:470; 27:114
Sanders, B. 3:169
Sanders, Benjamin A. 17:112
Sanders, C. L. 7:60
Sanders, C. W. 19:33
Sanders, Carlton 16:101
Sanders, Charles 3:169; 7:132; 21:384; 23:306
Sanders, Charles F. 8:109; 18:114
Sanders, D. 1:168; 3:169
Sanders, Daniel 13:45
Sanders, David 17:399
Sanders, Dred B. 17:350
Sanders, E. M. 25:228
Sanders, Ed. D. 4:51
Sanders, Edward 8:94
Sanders, Elijah 22:318
Sanders, Elwood 22:411
Sanders, Francis A. 11:392
Sanders, Francis M. 17:201
Sanders, Frederick 21:384
Sanders, George 1:75; 16:225; 21:151, 385; 22:318
Sanders, George P. 1:74
Sanders, George S. 9:192
Sanders, George V. 19:275
Sanders, H. 17:184; 22:318

Sanders, H. D. 18:431
Sanders, H. W. 5:28
Sanders, Harvey 13:45
Sanders, Henry 12:9; 16:101
Sanders, Henry C. 25:228
Sanders, Henry F. 19:191
Sanders, Henry O. 4:51
Sanders, Henry T. 10:167
Sanders, Henry W. 17:58
Sanders, Holten 19:191
Sanders, Holton 10:167
Sanders, Horace 18:346
Sanders, I. C. 10:134
Sanders, Irven D. 9:224
Sanders, Irvin D. 18:375
Sanders, Isaac 9:211
Sanders, Isaac P. 22:267
Sanders, J. 3:169; 4:51; 8:75
Sanders, J. C. 20:341
Sanders, J. M. 22:492
Sanders, J. N. 2:17; 25:68
Sanders, J. T. 3:169
Sanders, J. W. 25:72
Sanders, Jackson 10:99
Sanders, Jacob 8:75, 99; 26:181
Sanders, James 1:71; 9:113, 135; 21:283, 385; 22:318; 27:115
Sanders, James A. 17:261
Sanders, James H. 9:232
Sanders, James S. 22:440
Sanders, Jesse 21:233
Sanders, Jesse E. 21:132
Sanders, Joel 26:225
Sanders, John 7:61; 10:77, 134; 14:214; 15:224; 16:225; 18:251; 19:191; 20:341; 21:115; 22:217; 23:101; 25:228; 26:64
Sanders, John A. 9:90; 22:457; 26:182
Sanders, John C. 22:129
Sanders, John L. 10:174; 19:191
Sanders, John W. 19:338
Sanders, L. 7:40
Sanders, L. B. 15:224
Sanders, Levi 21:385
Sanders, Lyman 10:207
Sanders, M. 1:176
Sanders, Nathan F. 16:53
Sanders, Ned 8:67
Sanders, Newton 8:30; 18:157
Sanders, Oliver 25:228
Sanders, Orange 17:184

Sanders, Oscar N. 18:280
Sanders, P. 4:51; 14:105
Sanders, P. A. 1:170
Sanders, P. T. 24:155
Sanders, Pompey 9:135
Sanders, R. 9:90; 14:214; 27:115
Sanders, R. J. 9:90
Sanders, Richard 23:93; 24:162
Sanders, Richard J. 17:274; 22:457
Sanders, Robert 21:199; 22:52
Sanders, S. 12:162; 21:385; 25:68
Sanders, S. B. 10:77
Sanders, S. H. 8:75
Sanders, S. J. 8:55
Sanders, Simon 2:17
Sanders, Solomon H. 21:249
Sanders, Stephen 15:134
Sanders, Sylvester 7:40; 13:118
Sanders, Theo 9:124
Sanders, Theodore 27:114
Sanders, Thomas 19:191; 22:318
Sanders, Thomas J. 7:108; 11:294
Sanders, Timothy 9:39; 18:296; 26:112
Sanders, W. 18:93; 22:217
Sanders, W. D. 20:341
Sanders, W. H. 10:29; 19:306; 22:217, 457
Sanders, Wallace 17:400
Sanders, Wiley 27:148
Sanders, Will 12:93
Sanders, Willey T. 26:226
Sanders, William 17:41, 137; 18:222; 24:204
Sanders, William E. 8:30; 18:157
Sanders, William P. 23:250
Sanders, William R. 26:59
Sanders, William W. 22:99
Sanders, Willie 6:13
Sanders, Z. S. 18:210
Sanders, Zachariah F. 8:94
Sanders, Zeph's 1:74
Sanderson, Andrew J. 20:19
Sanderson, C. M. 25:72
Sanderson, C. R. M. 2:17
Sanderson, Carl 8:109
Sanderson, F. A. 23:165

Sanderson, Flora C. 26:226
Sanderson, George 18:321
Sanderson, H. 3:169
Sanderson, Harrison 18:93
Sanderson, J. 14:245; 27:119
Sanderson, James 17:250
Sanderson, John A. 21:13
Sanderson, Joseph 1:72
Sanderson, Josh. W. 16:53
Sanderson, Joshua W. 13:45
Sanderson, K. 20:341
Sanderson, Kurdt 10:77
Sanderson, L. 17:67
Sanderson, O. 18:280
Sanderson, R. H. 23:48
Sanderson, Sam 11:168
Sanderson, T. M. 8:55
Sanderson, Theo 17:447
Sanderson, Theodore 24:172
Sanderson, Thomas H. 21:93
Sanderson, Timothy 11:117
Sandey, John A. 8:30
Sandfer, William 17:58
Sandford, A. 14:214
Sandford, Benjamin 11:169
Sandford, Charles 4:51
Sandford, Charles W. 23:48
Sandford, David B. 23:125
Sandford, Derby 21:385
Sandford, Eliphalet 23:195
Sandford, George W. 10:22
Sandford, Isaac N. 21:385
Sandford, John 3:169; 22:267
Sandford, M. B. 1:170
Sandford, Stephen 21:385
Sandford, Stephen H. 19:191
Sandford, William 9:192
Sandillio, H. 20:341
Sandker, Rudolph 23:115
Sandler, L. 3:170
Sandlin, Jacob 24:186
Sandlin, James 17:447
Sandlin, Lewis 24:60
Sandlorn, Mayer I. 12:38
Sandman, Dias. K. 7:61
Sandoval, Antonia 18:427
Sandowski, Frank 7:69
Sandrich, Willis 21:283

Sandridge, James 8:94
Sands, Charles G. 24:69
Sands, Daniel 21:105
Sands, Ephraim 12:38
Sands, Francis M. 8:94
Sands, G. W. 3:170
Sands, George 16:225
Sands, George M. 17:86
Sands, Henry 6:19; 18:93
Sands, Ira P. 23:195
Sands, Isaac 22:267
Sands, J. B. 27:119
Sands, James 21:191, 246
Sands, John W. 22:506
Sands, Joshua 11:169
Sands, Marion 10:77; 20:341
Sands, Nicholas B. 13:45
Sands, S. 1:174, 176
Sands, Samuel 15:224
Sands, Thomas 18:38
Sands, William 1:74; 17:41
Sands, William E. 21:112
Sands, William S. 22:99
Sands---, --- 25:67
Sandson, Jesse 17:185
Sandts, Louis 19:33
Sanduida, James 18:210
Sandusky, Charles 17:399
Sandusky, G. 3:224; 17:505
Sandusky, Joseph J. 22:267
Sandusky, Samuel 11:397
Sandwich, J. 3:170
Sandwich, Joel 22:267
Sandwick, Charles 14:336
Sandy, Alexander 25:228
Sandy, Edwin 9:28
Sandy, J. 14:105
Sandy, John 11:44
Sandy, Joseph 13:45
Sane, Andrew J. 21:85
Sane, Joseph 3:169
Saner, John 22:237
Sanerheber, James 17:42
Sanerteig, John 10:134
Sanfagan, Rini 16:53
Sanfagen, Rim 13:45
Sanford, --- 15:74
Sanford, A. H. 12:38
Sanford, Aaron 8:30
Sanford, Arsen 18:157
Sanford, B. F. 23:48
Sanford, C. 3:169
Sanford, C. F. 1:169
Sanford, Charles 13:45; 21:39
Sanford, Charles B. 1:73

Sanford, David C. 9:90; 26:59
Sanford, Edwin 15:295; 16:225
Sanford, G. E. 1:175
Sanford, George B. 22:344
Sanford, George W. 22:457
Sanford, H. G. 24:29
Sanford, Henry 14:214
Sanford, J. D. 3:169
Sanford, J. E. 1:169
Sanford, J. O. 3:169
Sanford, James 7:108; 13:45; 22:344
Sanford, James W. 8:30; 18:157
Sanford, Joseph 20:128; 21:218
Sanford, L. 12:38; 14:259
Sanford, Lewis 22:412
Sanford, Lewis A. 16:153
Sanford, Lou 22:267
Sanford, O. A. 11:86
Sanford, O. W. 15:94
Sanford, Oliver 9:14
Sanford, Peter 22:344
Sanford, Robbins 15:44
Sanford, Samuel 21:95
Sanford, Thomas 9:58
Sanford, Varnum 17:400
Sanford, W. O. 25:69
Sanford, Walter T. 18:71
Sanford, Willard 19:33
Sanford, William 8:42; 26:180
Sang, Albert U. 13:45
Sangdale, A. 2:18
Sange, J. H. 14:263
Sangel, M. 7:53
Sanger, G. H. 17:435
Sanger, George H. 24:175
Sanger, W. H. 22:411
Sangleton, Richard 9:154
Sanglin, J. 3:169
Sangston, G. W. 10:77; 20:341
Sangston, N. H. 3:169
Sangton, M. H. 14:105
Sanguerdore, Peter 10:149
Sangurdore, Peter 18:57
Sanhammer, L. 18:424
Sanifer, Alick 17:137
Sanitt, P. 23:48
Sank, Charles 10:134
Sank, Robert 25:326
Sanker, Aloysius 25:228
Sankey, John 22:344
Sankey, R. 22:217
Sanks, Daniel 11:269

Sanks, Reason K. 21:59
Sanlay, E. 3:170
Sanley, Aaron 7:53
Sanlor, John 17:335
Sann, George 14:105
Sann, John 14:105
Sannemen, E. 1:73
Sannin, David 14:214
Sanno, Fred 27:113
Sannoe, George 9:124;
    27:113
Sannot, --- 3:169
Sannys, C. 3:169
Sanonie, Charles 7:40
Sanpierre, James H.
    22:441
Sanquinont, N. 20:184
Sansausa, Caterius 22:344
Sansbach, George W.
    22:99
Sanson, O. 21:39
Santee, Benjamine 19:306
Santee, N. 25:228
Santeen, Alexander 10:77
Santel, C. 11:250
Santer, Joseph 22:510
Santers, E. D. 18:280
Santh, William H. 19:191
Santhany, J. 1:77
Santrand, E. J. 20:175
Sants, Charles 1:73
Santser, John 24:114
Santum, Francis 16:87
Santun, Alex 20:341
Sanvord, V. 14:214
Sany, P. 1:78
Sape, John 14:105
Saper, Frank 24:203
Saper, George 17:156
Saph, --- 14:266
Sapham, Amos 13:45
Sapho, Madison 23:198
Sapley, Sancho 9:135;
    27:113
Sapp, A. J. 3:170
Sapp, B. 3:170
Sapp, B. B. 11:97
Sapp, B. J. 27:115
Sapp, C. 25:228
Sapp, Francis M. 16:53
Sapp, Isaac 16:225
Sapp, J. L. 22:355
Sapp, James H. 22:129
Sapp, John W. 22:411
Sapp, Logan 20:187
Sapp, Peter 22:129
Sapp, W. H. 3:170
Sappel, Henry 11:173
Sapper, I. 3:170
Sapper, John S. 12:38
Sappinfield, Henry 17:274

Sappington, Amos 15:224
Sappington, George
    21:283
Sappington, Robert 21:59
Sapwell, Thomas A.
    23:109
Saquish, John H. 12:38
Saragens, Edmund 14:214
Sarathfield, W. 5:45
Saratt, Stephen 26:65
Sarbar, John 18:222
Sard, Peter 16:53
Sarf, Henry 3:170
Sarfos, T. 1:169
Sargeant, C. F. 18:344
Sargeant, H. P. 25:228
Sargeant, Henry A. 17:25
Sargeant, J. 1:174
Sargeant, J. C. 3:170
Sargeant, M. 3:170
Sargeant, Samuel 18:355
Sargeant, W. 7:61
Sargeant, W. A. 27:110
Sargeant, William 9:98
Sargent, Aaron 7:69
Sargent, Albert 5:28
Sargent, Andrew 8:94
Sargent, C. H. 1:75
Sargent, C. R. 1:71
Sargent, Charles 14:214;
    22:318
Sargent, Charles A.
    21:260
Sargent, Cyrus M. 7:65
Sargent, D. H. 22:490
Sargent, E. P. 21:385
Sargent, Edward 21:191
Sargent, George P. 19:332
Sargent, George W.
    15:224
Sargent, Gustavus 15:92
Sargent, H. 9:113
Sargent, Henry 18:297;
    26:113
Sargent, Henry R. 9:39
Sargent, Hiram N. 18:210
Sargent, J. O. 22:412
Sargent, J. W. 27:148
Sargent, John 1:70;
    22:318; 27:107
Sargent, Joseph A. 7:40
Sargent, Lewis 7:108
Sargent, Lewis J. 20:341
Sargent, Lewis P. 10:77
Sargent, Lyman 12:140
Sargent, M. 13:126
Sargent, Moses C. 2:17
Sargent, N. F. 16:225
Sargent, Orrin 19:97
Sargent, Samuel P. 12:172
Sargent, T. 26:61

Sargent, Theodore 9:90
Sargent, Thomas 23:253
Sargent, W. H. 22:509
Sargent, W. J. 26:183
Sargent, William 7:69;
    15:295; 16:225;
    20:59
Sargent, William D. 15:88
Sargeson, George 14:214
Sarine, Jacob 22:172
Sarine, Samuel H. 13:45
Sark, L. C. 11:87
Sarle, Fernando R. 26:225
Sarles, Henry C. 7:63
Sarles, John 11:113
Sarles, Owen W. 27:115
Sarles, Soloman 19:191
Sarles, William H. 4:51
Sarlis, James 10:170
Sarlls, Marcus 8:102;
    17:459
Sarns, Joseph 26:226
Sarogdee, Alonzo M.
    19:191
Sarper, James E. 8:94
Sarratt, Loveless 21:283
Sarrels, Hale 11:44
Sarrett, James 3:170
Sarrington, P. C. 25:228
Sarsen, F. 18:251; 26:62
Sartain, Lewis J. 10:134;
    20:341
Sartell, John D. 22:510
Sartell, L. 3:170
Sarter, J. J. 25:67
Sarter, John R. 22:438
Sarters, John F. 22:168
Sarth, Stephen 9:90
Sarthmait, H. 25:228
Sarthward, Archey 9:135
Sartin, Alfred 17:208
Sartin, J. L. 17:411;
    22:524
Sartin, Jefferson G.
    17:207
Sartion, A. J. 11:329
Sartroff, S. C. 1:75
Sartull, William 12:38
Sartwell, Henry D. 10:77
Sartwill, Henry B. 20:341
Sarven, Aaron 17:239
Sarver, F. 15:74
Sarver, Henry G. 20:341
Sarver, Jacob 9:237;
    26:225
Sarver, John 23:48
Sarver, Lynus T. 17:92
Sarver, William 22:318
Sarver, William H. 17:25
Sarvis, G. R. 23:48
Sas---, J. T. 26:184

Sascra, James 10:174; 19:191
Sasebe, Thomas M. 20:341
Sash, Philip 11:392
Sashes, Gustavus 15:167
Sass, Frederick M. 27:148
Sassaman, Henry 12:38
Sassaman, N. 1:70
Sassamann, I. 25:228
Sassare, W. 27:109
Sasse, Charles W. 12:38
Sasse, William 23:195
Sasser, Alex 13:118
Sasserman, John 13:118
Sassin, Lewis I. 5:28
Sasson, --- 17:353
Sasten, James 20:341
Saster, Joseph 10:77
Satchel, Hubert 13:127
Satchell, William W. 10:93; 20:341
Satee, Lawrence 12:76; 15:23
Sater, George H. 10:134; 20:341
Sater, T. W. 18:210
Saterfield, A. 16:131
Saterfield, Greenville 22:99
Saterla, N. 10:77; 20:341
Saterlee, Bolonay 20:341
Saterlie, Bolney 10:77
Sathmarsh, Samuel 8:115
Sathy, J. 7:61
Satlack, R. M. 12:63
Satler, H. 1:174
Saton, Peter 8:30; 26:183
Satru, M. 27:109
Satterbury, Christian 18:157
Satterden, Roswell 9:192
Satterfield, Alex. 8:42
Satterfield, Anthony 18:251; 26:63
Satterfield, Edley 22:267
Satterfield, Eli 19:33
Satterfield, G. A. 16:53
Satterfield, J. 22:267
Satterfield, J. C. 23:205
Satterfield, Jasper 22:267
Satterfield, Lew 17:337
Satterfield, Young 26:182
Satterlee, George 14:214
Satterlee, H. W. 26:58
Satterler, Marcus 11:404
Satterlie, Henry 9:90
Satterly, Charles L. 22:172
Satterly, H. 3:170
Satterly, Peter 11:342

Satterly, R. W. 18:315; 26:112
Satters, J. 1:100
Satterswhait, A. 3:170
Sattin, G. 16:270
Sattle, Alexander 10:134
Sattler, Lewis 21:385
Sattles, Jacob W. 15:167
Satton, John W. 13:45
Sattsman, J. 11:282
Satty, Z. 14:105
Saturlee, C. 25:70
Satvertch, J. 14:214
Satz, J. 7:61
Sauburn, G. B. 3:170
Sauceman, --- 1:168
Sauceman, James 22:267
Saucers, Joseph 27:112
Saucier, Randolph 7:109
Saudelin, Hardin 10:77
Sauder, John 20:341
Sauderland, Joseph 20:341
Sauders, --- 19:97
Sauer, C. B. 27:116
Sauer, George 25:228
Sauer, Philip 10:77; 20:341
Sauerman, John 23:48
Sauers, Francis M. 21:125
Sauertig, John 20:341
Sauerwine, Panel 12:57
Saughessey, John 3:170
Saughton, H. 16:303
Sauk, Charles 20:341
Sauk, Robert 6:33
Saul, E. 27:106
Saul, George 22:344
Saul, Henry 8:94
Saul, Lewis 15:44
Saul, William 15:175
Sauls, J. 14:105
Sauls, P. 23:48
Saulsberry, Moses G. 22:217
Saulsbery, Edward 11:43
Saulsbury, E. J. 1:169
Saulsbury, Henry 21:385
Saulsbury, Horace 8:30; 18:157
Saulsbury, N. 15:59
Saulspaugh, J. K. 16:101
Saulter, Andrew 14:214
Saum, Simon 17:451
Saum, Simon P. 24:180
Saums, John A. 1:75
Saunder, L. C. 1:171
Saunder, William 18:413
Saunders, A. 14:21; 15:225; 22:52
Saunders, A. B. 9:150

Saunders, A. F. 15:287; 19:97
Saunders, B. 15:225
Saunders, Bartlett 7:40
Saunders, C. G. 14:105
Saunders, Charles 7:109
Saunders, Clem 17:185
Saunders, D. 9:192; 19:260
Saunders, E. D. 9:67
Saunders, F. 3:170
Saunders, F. H. 18:57
Saunders, G. W. 11:168
Saunders, George 11:170; 15:225; 19:33
Saunders, George A. 20:105
Saunders, George H. 22:129
Saunders, H. B. 20:341
Saunders, Isaac N. 12:157
Saunders, J. 1:168
Saunders, J. E. 14:105
Saunders, J. F. 14:284
Saunders, J. H. 20:341
Saunders, J. J. 1:78
Saunders, J. R. 11:45
Saunders, J. W. 10:77; 11:169
Saunders, Jacob 17:268
Saunders, James 9:215; 11:43; 21:385; 27:111
Saunders, James A. 17:319
Saunders, James B. 13:58
Saunders, James H. 20:341
Saunders, James T. 10:77
Saunders, Jarvis T. 20:341
Saunders, Joel 9:237; 10:174
Saunders, John 22:318
Saunders, John R. 11:392
Saunders, John W. 23:109; 26:226
Saunders, K. 20:341
Saunders, L. 17:185
Saunders, Levi 23:78
Saunders, Luther 11:313
Saunders, M. 21:112
Saunders, Nathan F. 13:45
Saunders, Ned 26:181
Saunders, P. 7:40
Saunders, P. T. 17:433
Saunders, Philip 5:54
Saunders, R. 14:105
Saunders, Richard 23:241
Saunders, Robert 21:112
Saunders, Robert W. 24:97

Saunders, S. 10:77; 20:341
Saunders, Silas 25:69
Saunders, W. P. 11:282
Saunders, W. S. 10:77; 20:341
Saunders, Warren 25:304
Saunders, Wetheridge 10:77
Saunders, Wiley T. 9:237
Saunders, Will 16:304
Saunter, William B. 14:214
Sauppe, E. 23:165
Saur, A. 15:44
Saur, Andrew 12:76
Saur, R. 25:326
Saure, Charles 12:83
Saures, Angel 1:73
Saurs, W. 15:44
Saury, C. 14:245
Sausley, Elias 18:222
Sauter, Louis 25:69
Sauth, William H. 10:146
Sautler, F. 1:76
Sautor, Marcus 18:104
Sautwell, Thomas 16:304
Sauver, Jacob 18:158
Sauwarayssaris, P. G. 20:128
Savage, A. 13:103; 14:21, 105; 16:270; 22:163
Savage, Alexander R. 23:93
Savage, Asahel 21:105
Savage, Braxton 16:53
Savage, Christy P. 17:261
Savage, Daniel 10:187
Savage, E. 25:228
Savage, Edward 17:86
Savage, Edward D. 24:171
Savage, Erwin D. 17:447
Savage, George 11:416; 13:45
Savage, Henry 7:109; 22:344; 26:65
Savage, Hiram 10:167; 19:191
Savage, Horace 13:45
Savage, J. W. 23:48
Savage, James 19:33
Savage, John A. 18:335
Savage, Leonard 14:214
Savage, M. 1:75
Savage, Newman A. 21:385
Savage, P. 11:232; 14:105
Savage, Patrick 11:17; 14:214
Savage, R. 15:314

Savage, Ruben 19:97
Savage, S. N. 22:344
Savage, Thomas 5:28; 13:118; 17:185; 25:228
Savage, Thomas M. 16:123
Savage, V. 18:93
Savage, W. B. 14:105
Savage, W. T. 20:43
Savage, William 11:404; 15:111
Savage, William M. 7:109
Savely, A. 20:149
Savetgot, Julius 22:99
Savige, J. 21:39
Savill, John 22:99
Saville, James R. 15:337; 16:225
Saville, William F. 12:76
Savillon, John 11:43
Savin, J. H. 3:170
Savory, Charles 7:109; 26:146
Savourey, J. H. 16:378
Savoy, John 21:218
Savoy, William P. 15:5
Savy, A. J. 11:167
Saw, Joseph 25:228
Saw, William 17:416
Saw-nee-see 25:335
Saward, William M. 19:191
Sawback, Michael 8:30
Sawber, J. D. 15:44
Sawders, Horace 11:250
Sawdey, A. J. 19:260
Sawdey, Edwin 18:315; 26:112, 113
Sawdy, Andrew J. 9:192
Sawdy, Lyman L. 20:25
Sawdy, Rufus 23:241
Saweaur, Jacob 4:51
Sawer, Anthony 16:378
Sawer, James 6:33
Sawer, James T. 7:109
Sawer, R. 10:149; 18:57
Sawhill, A. J. 15:59
Sawhill, Alexander 12:76
Sawin, B. 3:170
Sawin, D. H. 10:77
Sawlbrig, H. 16:225
Sawly, J. 8:67
Sawney, Lawrence 11:323
Sawney, William 3:170
Sawtell, George F. 2:17; 25:73
Sawtell, Levi L. 22:217
Sawtell, Lewis 22:522
Sawtell, Solomon N. 17:73

Sawtell, William 16:87
Sawtelle, Charles P. 23:125
Sawtelle, Henry A. 4:51
Sawtelle, Walter H. 7:69
Sawyer, A. 22:318
Sawyer, A. F. 14:105
Sawyer, A. T. 21:385
Sawyer, Adam 9:28; 18:321
Sawyer, Alonzo T. 21:385
Sawyer, Andrew 24:108
Sawyer, B. H. 21:385
Sawyer, B. J. 19:191
Sawyer, C. M. 9:58
Sawyer, Charles 5:45
Sawyer, Crocket 22:411
Sawyer, D. 1:172; 11:250
Sawyer, Daniel 17:426
Sawyer, Daniel B. 9:14
Sawyer, David M. 1:73
Sawyer, E. 9:192
Sawyer, E. A. 1:75
Sawyer, Enos 3:170
Sawyer, Ephraim 25:304
Sawyer, Ezra 20:341
Sawyer, G. 25:228
Sawyer, George 5:28; 9:45; 18:17
Sawyer, George A. 19:33
Sawyer, George E. 9:150
Sawyer, George E. H. 27:111
Sawyer, George P. 4:51
Sawyer, George T. 8:30; 18:158
Sawyer, George W. 24:55; 25:71
Sawyer, Hamilton 18:71
Sawyer, Harman 10:167
Sawyer, Henry 11:167
Sawyer, Henry G. 10:77
Sawyer, Herman 19:192
Sawyer, Hugh S. 17:61
Sawyer, Isaac 4:51
Sawyer, J. 3:170; 6:33; 14:105; 25:326
Sawyer, J. D. 3:170; 15:92
Sawyer, J. H. 11:334
Sawyer, J. M. 3:170
Sawyer, J. T. 25:70
Sawyer, James 25:326
Sawyer, John 1:70; 3:170; 11:213; 16:225
Sawyer, John J. 22:129
Sawyer, John P. 22:284
Sawyer, Joseph 9:115; 14:214
Sawyer, Joseph L. 12:54
Sawyer, Joseph W. 23:14
Sawyer, Louis E. 25:70

Sawyer, Norman R. 24:10
Sawyer, Ozro 10:77
Sawyer, Peter 12:38
Sawyer, Peter E. 21:260
Sawyer, R. A. 16:54
Sawyer, R. C. 14:303;
 17:478; 27:117
Sawyer, Reuben G. 13:45
Sawyer, S. F. 3:170
Sawyer, Samuel 8:67;
 26:183
Sawyer, T. F. 1:74
Sawyer, Theodore 23:165
Sawyer, Thomas 12:38;
 17:86
Sawyer, Thomas D. 25:70
Sawyer, W. 1:170
Sawyer, W. M. 17:42
Sawyer, Ward 17:244
Sawyer, Warren 26:65
Sawyer, William B. 16:54
Sawyer, William H. 12:38
Sawyer, William M.
 13:118
Sawyer, Wilson 17:67
Sawyers, C. 25:228
Sawyers, Daniel C. 23:257
Sawyers, George 11:169
Sawyers, R. W. 25:228
Sawyers, Romanzo 11:404
Sawyers, William 11:416
Saxaman, Jacob 21:385
Saxberry, Lewis 9:67
Saxe, Edward 20:194
Saxe, Ferdinand 24:71
Saxman, J. 14:303
Saxmen, J. 17:481; 27:117
Saxon, J. 1:176
Saxon, William J. 22:438
Saxton, Charles A. 15:74
Saxton, Ebenezer 17:25
Saxton, G. A. 1:172
Saxton, Holly E. 24:10
Saxton, John 9:136;
 21:218; 27:112
Saxton, Joseph 8:55
Saxton, Lafayette 17:239
Saxton, Norris W. 20:194
Saxton, Oliver 21:233
Saxton, R. 7:53
Saxton, R. W. 15:111
Saxton, Samuel 10:167;
 19:192
Saxton, W. R. 9:67
Saxty, F. 1:100
Say, Henry 19:33
Say, J. R. 3:170
Say, William E. 26:181
Saychorn, D. 10:29;
 19:306
Sayer, A. 1:171

Sayer, George 16:225
Sayer, George W. 15:304
Sayer, Harry B. 17:67
Sayer, Henry W. 4:51
Sayer, J. 8:75
Sayer, J. S. 22:217
Sayer, John L. 26:182
Sayer, L. 1:171; 23:165;
 27:109
Sayer, M. M. 10:145
Sayer, T. 22:52
Sayer, W. S. N. 21:385
Sayer, William 25:273
Sayers, A. H. 9:90; 26:58
Sayers, Abraham 18:93
Sayers, Albert 8:30
Sayers, Alfred 9:211
Sayers, Amos 15:134
Sayers, B. 11:250
Sayers, B. F. 8:55
Sayers, Castilian 21:385
Sayers, Charles 9:204
Sayers, G. D. 3:170
Sayers, H. A. 25:228
Sayers, Henry 11:172
Sayers, James 18:38
Sayers, James L. 8:78
Sayers, John 10:134;
 20:341; 26:129
Sayers, John L. 8:30
Sayers, R. A. 1:75
Sayers, Russell 17:67
Sayers, Sullivan 12:54
Sayers, Sutherlan 23:289
Sayers, V. J. 15:345
Sayers, W. 3:170
Sayler, John A. 22:52
Sayler, Simon B. 23:78
Sayles, A. 3:170
Sayles, C. A. 13:118
Sayles, D. 18:375
Sayles, Darius 9:224
Sayles, Levi 15:225
Sayles, Lyman M. 21:385
Sayles, Mordecai 10:77
Sayles, Mordecan 20:341
Sayles, Moses M. 11:44
Sayles, Nathaniel 20:13
Sayles, Oscar 11:43
Sayles, R. 25:228
Sayles, Rolurs 5:45
Sayles, Thomas 7:14
Saylor, --- 18:272
Saylor, C. M. 3:170
Saylor, Henry 17:27
Saylor, J. 14:290; 23:96
Saylor, N. B. 11:313
Saylor, Peter 11:342
Saylor, Samuel 23:165
Saylor, Theodore 16:123
Saylor, William 13:118

Saylors, A. 22:267
Saylors, John T. 9:98
Sayls, H. 1:169
Sayman, Joseph 15:287
Saymell, William D. 9:45
Saynard, J. S. 25:228
Sayne, James M. 4:51
Sayne, Nathan 10:134
Sayre, --- 15:225
Sayre, Elijah P. 1:70
Sayre, H. A. 12:123
Sayre, J. 26:183
Sayre, Nathan 20:341
Sayre, Nicholas 3:170
Sayre, Preston H. 14:214
Sayre, W. A. 25:273
Sayrel, C. M. 8:30
Sayres, Albert 18:158
Sayres, J. W. 1:175
Sayres, John L. 18:158
Sayres, Lewis 14:335
Sayrl, C. M. 18:158
Sayrs, H. F. 15:134
Sayward, J. 1:170
Saywood, James 10:77;
 20:341
Scaber, John 5:45
Scadden, W. 25:68
Scaff, John 1:73
Scaffer, H. 14:214
Scagel, D. E. 19:97
Scaggs, B. 17:185
Scaggs, F. M. 17:167
Scaggs, Henry C. 22:267
Scaggs, John 8:30;
 17:499; 18:158
Scalds, Samuel 22:318
Scale, Thomas 21:93
Scales, Allen 4:51
Scales, Augustus 21:385
Scales, I. T. 26:59
Scales, Iveson T. 9:90
Scales, Johiel 11:111
Scales, John 21:283
Scales, Neil 3:170
Scales, Ransom 17:137;
 24:203
Scales, Samuel 17:42
Scales, William B. 8:59
Scalf, Greenburry 17:204
Scally, Peter 17:15
Scalp, Jesse 22:267
Scaly, John 17:353
Scamerhorn, Abram
 27:112
Scammen, C. 1:173
Scan, Frederic 17:86
Scanck, J. 20:156
Scandler, J. 3:170
Scanlan, --- 26:111
Scanlan, J. 1:169

Scanlan, James 24:97
Scanlan, John 4:51
Scanlan, M. H. 15:290
Scanlan, Ml. H. 16:225
Scanlan, Simon 22:154
Scanland, George 14:284
Scanland, John 6:9;
　18:104
Scanlen, John 10:167;
　19:192
Scanlin, John 14:214
Scanlon, --- 18:315
Scanlon, J. 13:68
Scanlon, James 25:229
Scanlon, John 12:38;
　13:45; 19:97
Scanlon, P. 1:75
Scanlon, Patrick 19:318
Scannell, J. D. 3:170
Scannell, John M. 23:129
Scannell, Patrick 16:87
Scannoll, George 13:45;
　16:54
Scantin, G. 22:15
Scantin, M. T. C. 7:40
Scanton, F. J. D. 5:54;
　25:229
Scarberry, J. 1:172
Scarberry, O. 3:170
Scarboro, Robert 3:170
Scarborough, Charles
　17:15
Scarborough, J. A. 18:158
Scarborough, S. 14:214
Scarborough, S. N. 3:170
Scarborough, Thomas P.
　22:267
Scarborough, Zachariah
　12:76
Scarbory, Z. 15:59
Scarbourough, I. A. 8:30
Scarbro, William 17:58
Scarbrough, William 4:51
Scarburry, Edmund 24:69
Scard, Lones 3:170
Scare, George 15:225
Scare, H. 15:160
Scarf, C. W. 25:68
Scarf, George W. 2:17
Scarff, F. 3:170
Scarlet, Frederick 16:54
Scarlett, A. D. 23:257
Scarlett, Frederick 13:45
Scarlett, George 1:73
Scarlett, James 3:170;
　14:317
Scarlott, Richard 5:28
Scarper, Joseph 14:214
Scates, J. 22:318
Scates, Thomas 8:30;
　18:158

Scauthing, G. 14:271
Scaville, William F. 15:5
Scearce, John 8:94
Scearl, Lucian 19:97
Sceisten, Obadiah 20:341
Scenavaple, Michael
　18:210
Sceple, H. 14:105
Scerror, Jacob 8:94
Sceyers, Joseph 21:168
Scfuro, John 15:345
Sch---, Franz G. 17:293
Schabberhar, Charles
　26:182
Schaber, John 25:229
Schach, Jacob 23:165
Schachter, David 23:48
Schack, Clement 16:54
Schack, Frederick 21:93
Schack, J. 9:150
Schackley, George 13:58
Schad, John 8:30; 18:158;
　26:182
Schade, John 19:261
Schadel, Joseph 25:70
Schadenberg, C. 21:39
Schader, John 7:109
Schadle, John 15:153
Schaedler, William 24:69
Schaefer, John 14:214
Schaefer, William F.
　19:284
Schaeffer, August 25:229
Schaeffer, Christian
　20:341
Schaeffer, T. 11:194
Schaefler, Henry 26:237
Schaen, Jacob 21:233
Schafer, Charles 21:385
Schafer, Conrad 13:68
Schafer, Edward 10:78
Schafer, Ernest 9:224
Schafer, Frederick 22:490
Schafer, G. C. 15:295
Schafer, George 11:289
Schafer, I. C. 3:170
Schafer, I. H. 3:170
Schafer, J. H. 3:170
Schafer, M. 5:28; 18:93
Schafer, P. 3:170
Schafer, W. 13:98
Schaff, A. 27:157
Schaff, John 19:276
Schaff, S. M. 16:54
Schaffer, A. 7:53
Schaffer, Adam 4:51
Schaffer, Anton 17:86
Schaffer, C. 14:105;
　16:225
Schaffer, Charles 15:300
Schaffer, Christian 13:45

Schaffer, Frederick 14:214
Schaffer, George 4:51
Schaffer, H. 1:175
Schaffer, J. 1:74
Schaffer, Jacob 13:118
Schaffer, M. 16:225
Schaffer, M. V. 5:28
Schaffer, W. 15:44
Schaffer, William 10:167;
　25:229
Schaffin, W. 1:170
Schaffle, C. D. 14:106
Schaffner, Benjamin
　11:44
Schaffner, Henry 9:14
Schaftee, Christian 12:76
Schaggs, William H.
　22:129
Schalchof, Henry 10:78
Schalenberg, C. 21:385
Schaler, John 7:40
Schalk, Adam 1:73
Schall, H. 19:246
Schall, Hendrick 9:192
Schallard, Thomas 22:521
Schalls, John 25:270
Schalls, Joseph 12:38
Schalor, S. 14:214
Schambacker, Henry
　20:341
Schambackor, G. W.
　13:46
Schambeck, F. 23:48
Schameberg, Alex 9:58
Schamerhorn, Abram
　9:136
Schamill, D. 1:171
Schammell, John 23:280
Schanck, Alfred 12:38
Schanck, David H. 10:134
Schanck, T. 24:114
Schaner, Charles 15:225
Schaner, F. 1:172
Schanerte, Joseph 20:341
Schanett, --- 12:162
Schanian, C. 25:229
Schank, David H. 20:341
Schank, Henry 10:78
Schank, John 7:78
Schank, John D. 23:48
Schank, Sebastian 8:30
Schanlon, John 9:124;
　27:113
Schaper, Edward 20:342
Schapfinger, Charles 7:40
Schapher, I. 3:170
Schapp, B. 7:109
Schapp, John 14:214
Schardien, A. 15:9
Schare, Francis 7:109;
　21:385

Scharf, Paul 19:33
Scharff, F. 19:97
Schark, Sibastian 18:158
Scharlott, John 15:59
Scharlott, R. 25:229
Scharmaker, W. H. 12:51
Scharrell, F. M. 17:405
Schartzman, John 8:30
Schass, John 13:45
Schatki, Englebert 18:114
Schatt, R. 25:67
Schatt, Theodore 3:170
Schatts, John W. 26:60
Schaub, Dethelm 18:114
Schaub, Frank 17:42
Schaub, Henry 16:54
Schauber, Emil 9:14
Schauer, Martin 23:118
Schauerbe, Joseph 10:135
Schauf, Jacob 20:342
Schauman, August 7:109
Schaunce, G. W. 23:48
Schaup, H. 25:229
Schaup, Henry 5:28
Schaurty, F. 14:106
Schaver, Samuel 12:60
Schaver, William 20:342
Schaw, Cameron 25:229
Schawb, Michael 18:179
Schawell, Peter 24:180
Schaysless, W. 3:170
Schbetcing, Fred 20:343
Schcutle, James George 19:343
Schear, W. 3:170
Scheaver, James F. 11:130
Scheck, B. 3:170
Scheck, Gottliet 8:30
Scheer, T. B. 21:385
Scheets, D. 1:172
Scheffer, G. 7:40
Schegg, George 22:411
Scheible, John 12:55
Scheidenmantel, Fred 9:17
Scheider, John 3:170
Scheidorn, Louis 1:74
Scheifer, George 12:123; 14:26; 15:363
Scheinaman, Charles 10:135
Scheinamon, Charles 20:342
Scheinbier, R. 20:342
Scheinheiter, Frederick 21:93
Scheiver, Peter J. 7:61
Scheivester, Mathias 16:144
Schekley, D. C. 25:229

Scheley, William W. 9:224
Schell, C. H. 13:68
Schell, E. 9:192
Schell, Eugene M. 22:440
Schell, John 23:125
Schell, William 7:109
Schellenger, W. S. 21:40
Scheller, George 11:112
Scheller, Henry 14:237
Scheller, J. J. 25:229
Scheller, Jacob 1:72
Schelling, Fred 4:51
Schelling, T. 1:175
Schelton, Clark 9:58
Schemack, August 7:109
Schemerman, John 7:109
Schemeter, S. 1:71
Schemhl, M. 1:175
Schemiphon, Stephen 18:38
Schemmerhorn, G. W. 1:77
Schemmerhorn, Henry 9:192
Schemp, John M. 5:28
Schemph, M. 3:170
Schenafalt, C. 1:77
Schenafiel, Jared 23:166
Schenbury, C. 1:176
Schench, Christian 18:38
Schenck, C. A. 11:77
Schenck, Carroll 14:214
Schenck, Charles 9:192
Schenck, Charles M. 9:192
Schenck, Ezekiel O. 24:29
Schenck, Goutlieb 18:158
Schenck, Herman 19:192
Schenck, Human 10:145
Schenck, J. 27:108
Schenck, John 17:86; 21:385
Schenck, Joseph 24:29
Schenck, Mathias 18:158
Schenck, Otto 19:97
Schenck, Philip 10:78
Schenck, W. 20:87
Schenck, William 9:124
Schenck, William L. 27:114
Schenck, Wright 17:74
Schendalman, John 11:313
Schenealchof, H. 20:342
Scheneh, Mathias 8:30
Schenell, Charles 27:119
Schenemyer, C. 14:106
Schenendecker, F. 22:217
Schenezier, John 9:90
Schenizel, John 26:59

Schenk, Charles 19:261
Schenk, E. 9:69
Schenk, Gabriel 14:214
Schenk, Joseph 7:109
Schenk, Moses 9:162
Schenk, Otto 13:68
Schenk, Philip 20:342
Schenk, William F. 10:78
Schenke, Frederick 8:30
Schent, John H. 9:28
Scheone, F. 23:48
Scheppers, Jacob 22:154
Scher, --- 16:225
Scherard, P. 25:70
Scherber, S. 21:385
Scherchal, Ludwig 23:166
Scherckengust, S. C. 18:71
Scherer, Augustus 19:33
Scherer, Henry 1:73
Scherer, John 14:106
Scheringer, August 11:194
Scherk, Christian 3:170
Schermehorn, Jacob E. 17:433; 24:162
Schermerhorn, George 22:439
Schermerhorn, H. 19:261
Schermerhorn, J. G. 23:195
Schermerhorn, Joseph B. 13:118
Schermerhorn, T. 21:385
Schermerhorn, Walter G. 20:31
Scherrer, William 19:97
Scherwarhorn, H. 3:170
Scherzinger, Napoleon 20:2
Scheseiger, F. 9:28
Scheumann, G. 1:175
Scheyer, W. 7:61
Schible, Andras 23:125
Schicel, Harrison 22:491
Schick, Adam 17:58
Schick, Anton 22:457
Schick, E. 23:48
Schick, Henry 23:166
Schick, J. 1:170
Schiebe, Lewis 23:115
Schieblin, George 11:271
Schiefer, J. S. 13:98
Schiegel, August 10:78
Schiel, Frederick 22:15
Schiels, Frederick 14:284
Schieu, Christian 8:55
Schieu, George 8:55
Schifert, Jacob 3:170
Schiffer, H. 3:171

Schiffmacher, Theodore 12:76
Schifftner, C. 20:43
Schigel, John 22:267
Schik, Simon 23:125
Schike, D. 1:170
Schike, Frederick 24:69
Schiles, H. 15:225
Schiling, S. 16:225
Schilinger, Simeon 5:55
Schill, Lambert 11:76
Schill, P. 19:242
Schiller, Jacob 7:61; 18:401
Schilling, E. 1:78
Schilling, Henry 4:52
Schilling, William 21:385; 22:154
Schillingberger, Jonas 4:52
Schilman, Theodore 10:167
Schiltmeier, Charles E. 11:392
Schimanker, Frederick 17:403
Schimber, Reinhold 19:33
Schime, Jacob 19:97
Schimer, Jacob 13:68
Schimler, Nick 27:118
Schimmel, Anthony 23:166
Schimmell, Elias B. 22:467
Schimpf, Louis 9:58
Schimplin, B. 22:218
Schin, --- 15:268
Schindler, B. F. 8:30; 18:158
Schine, F. B. 7:61
Schinertman, --- 18:179
Schinetter, H. 19:97
Schingshang, Z. 11:97
Schipper, John 23:101
Schirmaster, B. 3:171
Schirmer, F. 9:150
Schirnt, Henry 20:342
Schissler, Abraham 21:385
Schittenger, John 21:260
Schivinghamer, R. S. 25:70
Schlaback, Joseph H. 9:99
Schlad, Patrick 23:303
Schladen, T. 9:150
Schlae, Adam 21:385
Schlaffi, N. 1:175
Schlafter, Christian 15:12
Schlagel, Frederick 24:114
Schlagheck, H. 7:40

Schlaich, John 15:44
Schlake, Henry 24:55
Schlandroff, William 23:78
Schlapp, Henry 23:306
Schlater, Austin 23:49
Schlatter, Hector L. 10:211
Schlawson, F. deWitt 12:38
Schleassor, J. J. 3:171
Schleber, Peter 10:167
Schlecht, Benjamin F. 23:129
Schlechter, Frank 23:118
Schlecter, I. 24:114
Schlecting, Frederick 10:135
Schlee, C. Fred 9:90
Schlee, Christian 7:109
Schlegel, Charles 21:79
Schlegel, Fred 26:59
Schlegel, Gustave 11:130
Schlehline, John 22:154
Schlehr, P. J. 16:15
Schleider, Jacob 25:67
Schleider, T. 27:110
Schleiffer, Frederick 21:385
Schleiffer, John 9:150
Schlenitzanner, F. 15:74
Schlenker, J. 20:342; 23:49
Schlenstedt, Frederick 23:195
Schlesser, C. 9:67
Schlesser, Conrad 18:280
Schlette, Conrad 1:73
Schlewbaugh, C. 3:171
Schlicher, D. 23:166
Schlichler, Jacob 15:82
Schlichter, J. A. 1:172
Schlick, F. J. 14:214
Schlicker, Jacob 12:38
Schliff, C. 13:118
Schlimmer, William 21:385
Schliner, Simon 16:304
Schlingarmann, C. 1:72
Schlinger, Ernst 23:115
Schlinsog, Gootlieb 20:194
Schlitter, Casper 13:45
Schlitter, Fritz 4:52
Schlitzberger, Louis 7:109
Schloer, C. 21:125
Schlof, Anchor 22:237
Schlosser, Felix 11:282
Schlosser, Henry 21:105
Schlosser, J. 3:171
Schlosser, John 15:59

Schlosser, W. H. 1:174
Schlotman, F. 16:304
Schlotterback, J. 1:175
Schlotterer, F. 1:76
Schlottman, Henry 16:54
Schlucher, John 20:190
Schluckenbier, Frederick 17:395
Schlueki, Jared 8:30
Schlusser, Max 23:14
Schlutner, C. 20:36
Schmabel, Francis 9:202
Schmake, John 3:171
Schmal, Andrew 3:171
Schmaley, J. 3:171
Schmalstick, C. 25:229
Schmaltzried, F. 1:76
Schmatz, A. 3:171
Schmeager, A. 3:171
Schmeckenberger, J. M. 25:74
Schmedler, P. 1:174
Schmeiser, C. 1:77
Schmertzer, P. 1:71
Schmiat, John 21:385
Schmid, John 19:288
Schmidinger, Isaac 11:97
Schmidle, John 22:218
Schmidle, S. R. 3:171
Schmidt, --- 11:313; 15:44
Schmidt, A. 18:324
Schmidt, Adam 17:72
Schmidt, Anton 11:75
Schmidt, Benjamin 22:439
Schmidt, Casper 11:313
Schmidt, Charles 16:148
Schmidt, Daniel 12:100
Schmidt, Dominick 18:413
Schmidt, E. 15:74
Schmidt, F. 1:77; 9:90
Schmidt, Ferdinand 21:385
Schmidt, Francis 19:33
Schmidt, Frank 10:78; 11:129
Schmidt, Fred 9:28; 18:315
Schmidt, Frederick 1:70; 26:111
Schmidt, G. 9:150; 20:342; 27:108
Schmidt, George 16:54; 20:33; 21:105; 23:78
Schmidt, George S. 17:350
Schmidt, Gustav 26:182
Schmidt, H. 1:175; 9:150; 27:110
Schmidt, Harman 10:135

Schmidt, Harmon 20:342
Schmidt, Henry 10:135;
  17:353; 20:13;
  21:105, 260; 23:14
Schmidt, Herman 21:79
Schmidt, Hermann
  18:114; 24:97
Schmidt, I. 14:106
Schmidt, J. 14:106
Schmidt, J. F. 11:313
Schmidt, Jacob 15:320;
  19:97; 22:129
Schmidt, James 11:334
Schmidt, John 11:282;
  13:45; 15:225;
  17:86; 18:315; 23:78,
  195; 26:130
Schmidt, John Casper
  12:38
Schmidt, Joseph A. 9:192
Schmidt, Julius 15:82
Schmidt, Lewis 8:94;
  10:135, 167; 20:342
Schmidt, M. 9:224;
  18:375
Schmidt, Martin 25:70
Schmidt, O. 15:225
Schmidt, Samuel 11:277
Schmidt, Theo. 26:111
Schmidt, Theodore 18:315
Schmidt, W. 16:225
Schmidt, Wilhelm 23:93
Schmidt, William 1:73;
  21:246; 22:457
Schmidth, C. 18:57
Schmidth, Friedz 22:52
Schmidth, Lemuel 16:225
Schmiemann, Henry 23:93
Schmindler, Mac 4:51
Schmit, Julius 12:76
Schmith, J. K. 18:251;
  26:64
Schmitl, J. 1:176
Schmitt, Aaron 11:184
Schmitt, George 8:30;
  11:221; 18:158
Schmitt, Joseph A. 19:284
Schmitt, P. 11:98
Schmitt, Peter 8:30;
  18:158
Schmitter, Jacob 20:36
Schmittlar, John 9:113
Schmity, William 14:106
Schmitz, Henry 27:148
Schmitz, John 22:168
Schmitz, Paul 9:69
Schmmidt, Lewis 18:210
Schmoker, Frederick
  22:113
Schmon, Rudolph 19:33
Schnabel, F. 19:284

Schnable, John 22:287
Schnabley, J. 3:171
Schnack, William 22:99
Schnagel, Frederick
  21:385
Schnal, J. 11:270
Schnank, Daniel 15:74
Schnapp, Conrad 13:45
Schnarr, R. 3:171
Schnauber, Philip 13:45
Schnebly, W. B. 23:166
Schneck, Mabury 15:82
Schneckenberger, J. 2:18
Schneder, C. 1:175
Schnee, T. F. 11:334
Schneider, A. A. 1:77
Schneider, Andrew
  11:121
Schneider, Anton 10:78;
  20:342
Schneider, B. 20:342
Schneider, B. F. 8:30
Schneider, Bernard 10:78
Schneider, C. 12:93;
  16:304
Schneider, Charles 3:171
Schneider, Christian 10:78
Schneider, Conrad 8:30;
  18:158
Schneider, E. 8:30;
  18:158; 26:182
Schneider, George 9:39;
  18:297; 24:179;
  26:113
Schneider, Henry 8:30;
  9:192; 18:158
Schneider, Jacob 9:39
Schneider, Job 22:52
Schneider, John 13:45;
  23:166
Schneider, Joseph 4:51
Schneider, N. 2:18; 25:67
Schneider, Nicholas
  9:192; 14:335;
  23:195
Schneider, P. 25:229
Schneider, Peter 18:158;
  21:118
Schneider, Peter H.
  19:317
Schneider, S. A. 3:171
Schneider, T. 1:170
Schneider, Valentine
  19:97
Schneider, W. 1:173
Schneider, William
  11:121; 15:111;
  22:99
Schneidthoist, Henry
  10:135

Schneidthorst, Henry
  20:342
Schnell, C. 14:245
Schnell, Conrad 15:28
Schnell, Frank 11:314
Schnell, Henry 22:287
Schnell, Peter 5:45
Schnell, V. 9:113
Schnere, Hiram 15:225
Schnevinger, Joseph
  22:344
Schnider, Bernard 19:316
Schnider, F. 24:84
Schnider, Isreal 17:266
Schnider, J. 3:171
Schnider, John 19:33
Schnidez, Christopher
  15:225
Schnidler, J. 3:171
Schniedt, L. S. 7:53
Schnier, John 22:470
Schnister, Theodore 4:51
Schnitz, K. 18:422
Schnnick, A. 18:38
Schnoder, --- 15:345;
  16:378
Schnoler, C. 3:171
Schnooke, A. 21:125
Schnoor, Peter 20:342
Schoat, D. R. 3:171
Schock, Clement 13:45
Schock, William 11:170
Schocking, F. T. 3:171
Schockton, Benjamin
  16:225
Schodee, Jacob 8:115
Schoe, Wendel 21:93
Schoeder, William 17:25
Schoeffel, Peter M.
  21:385
Schoefield, George S.
  11:292
Schoeler, Jacob 18:324
Schoen, Frederick 9:99
Schoenbehler, James
  14:215
Schoenstein, Alex 10:135
Schoepfle, Wilhelm 22:99
Schofeld, L. M. 12:143
Schofer, Conrad 19:97
Schofer, Martin 18:93
Schoff, Jacob 16:225
Schoff, John 5:28; 9:192
Schoff, P. 25:229
Schoff, Philip 12:80
Schoffer, M. 16:225
Schoffler, Peter 15:225
Schoffman, I. 25:280
Schofield, --- 19:97
Schofield, A. F. 22:129

Schofield, Benjamin 25:74
Schofield, C. 3:171
Schofield, Charles 22:471
Schofield, Cornelius 13:45
Schofield, Elisha 17:429
Schofield, Francis 18:341
Schofield, G. 9:28
Schofield, Henry M. 15:3
Schofield, I. F. 9:234
Schofield, J. 3:171; 18:424
Schofield, J. S. 8:94
Schofield, J. T. 2:18
Schofield, James 9:90
Schofield, L. O. 9:124; 27:114
Schofield, Oscar 8:94, 117
Schofield, Theo 27:106
Schofield, William 27:114
Schoh, John W. H. 22:411
Schohum, Franklin 21:40
Schola, R. 14:106
Scholar, Walter 21:385
Schold, David 10:180; 18:179
Scholenderger, A. J. 8:55
Scholes, W. S. 15:12
Scholey, George M. 9:67
Scholittz, Levi 12:38
Scholl, Adam 14:214
Scholl, C. H. 16:225
Scholl, Henry 12:38
Scholl, I. P. 18:71
Scholl, John 3:171
Scholl, Simon B. 12:38
Schollar, James 24:29
Scholom, Albert 8:109
Scholt, John 20:342
Scholts, John 15:44
Scholtz, K. 11:75
Scholz, Adolph 19:97
Schom, C. Augustus 14:237
Schomber, John 3:171
Schomhurst, George 22:457
Schon, Andrew 26:112
Schonerman, E. P. 22:521
Schonert, Charles 4:51
Schonheiter, F. 8:55
Schoning, Anton 11:75
Schonk, John 15:134
Schonk, Martin B. 11:251
Schonwald, Richard 20:2
Schoolcraft, Benjamin 27:148
Schoolcraft, D. 1:173
Schoolcraft, John J. 7:17
Schoolcraft, W. H. 25:229

Schoolder, Abraham 26:60
Schooleight, George 14:215
Schooler, Abraham 9:90
Schooler, Alexander 17:268
Schooler, David 17:138; 24:204
Schooler, Samuel 11:194
Schooler, William A. 20:100
Schoolers, Thomas 25:229
Schooley, E. M. 26:181
Schooley, Ezra 22:492
Schooley, Jacob 10:135; 20:342
Schooley, James 17:388
Schooley, Richard 8:94
Schooley, V. A. 26:182
Schooling, Joseph 8:55; 21:79
Schooling, William L. 8:55
Schoolnel, H. 9:192
Schooly, E. M. 8:75
Schoomaker, A. 20:342
Schoomaker, M. 25:229
Schoomar, Peter 20:342
Schoonmaker, Frank 13:45
Schoonmaker, George 11:45
Schoonmaker, H. E. 13:45
Schoonmeyer, Philip 22:439
Schoonover, A. 25:326
Schoonover, Charles 22:492
Schoonover, Henry 11:75
Schoonover, J. 1:71
Schoonover, James W. 22:218
Schoonover, Thomas 23:125
Schoonover, William 21:40
Schoop, J. 25:229
Schooppe, W. H. 1:171
Schoot, John 25:229
Schopp, Martin 9:28
Schopp, Peter 13:45
Schoppe, A. 13:98
Schopper, C. H. 11:45
Schops, A. 1:171
Schopstain, John 17:353
Schorg, Michael 14:215
Schorge, George 23:49
Schorty, Lutz 5:54
Schortz, Nathan 1:70
Schott, J. 7:40

Schott, Jacob 8:109
Schott, John 10:93, 135; 20:342
Schottsman, F. 3:171
Schoulebee, Jacob 4:51
Schoulter, Jacob 18:158
Schoultz, John 7:109
Schous, Harvey 13:45
Schouse, J. A. 21:385
Schouten, Jeremiah 7:109
Schoveland, Michael 20:128
Schow, Andrew 18:315
Schowl, C. 25:229
Schoyan, Fred 4:51
Schoyer, Andrew 20:342
Schoyers, George 7:76
Schrack, David 19:192
Schrader, --- 18:407
Schrader, Charles 11:130
Schrader, Fred 20:342
Schrader, Frederick 7:109; 10:78
Schrader, H. 19:261
Schrader, Samuel E. 16:54
Schrader, W. 14:245
Schradley, Samuel 14:334
Schraid, Andrew 9:28
Schram, H. 16:134
Schram, Jacob 23:166
Schram, Philip 23:14
Schrambling, A. 22:467
Schramm, Frederick 17:25
Schrand, W. 14:245; 27:119
Schrank, H. 9:150
Schrank, J. 27:110
Schranth, George 20:33
Schraw, Levi 17:393
Schrceongest, Simeon 12:76
Schreck, Jacob 21:233
Schrecongost, S. 15:74
Schreener, George 12:54
Schreener, T. 14:285
Schrefler, John 17:214
Schreiber, A. 1:169
Schreiber, F. 16:304
Schreimer, E. M. 14:106
Schreiner, F. 25:229
Schreiner, Nobert 20:342
Schreivar, E. M. 14:106
Schreive, Henry 20:342
Schremp, H. 25:229
Schrevener, C. 1:71
Schrey, --- 15:44
Schreyer, William 16:54
Schrian, Martin 4:51
Schriber, Jacob 23:14
Schrick, A. 3:171
Schrick, William 18:441

Schriden, D. 3:171
Schrider, W. 17:293
Schriekler, Mathew 15:225
Schrieman, Ernest 17:112
Schrilraw, Mich'l 22:218
Schrimer, F. 27:110
Schrimp, H. 15:225
Schrind, Gottleib 10:78
Schriner, David 12:38
Schriner, J. 3:171
Schriner, Julius 11:78
Schriner, Michael 24:180
Schritzel, L. 19:284
Schritzmeyer, John 22:284
Schriver, William Y. 10:135
Schrivner, William 3:171
Schrnocher, --- 13:77
Schroatz, P. 1:174
Schrober, John 12:38
Schrock, G. W. 7:109
Schrock, John 11:416
Schrodelsecker, M. 22:99
Schroder, C. 9:150
Schroder, F. 3:171
Schroder, G. 3:171
Schroder, H. 1:172
Schroder, Henry 27:107
Schroder, J. 12:9
Schroder, J. H. 25:276
Schroeder, C. 27:109
Schroeder, Charles 7:40
Schroeder, Emil 19:97
Schroeder, Fred 20:342
Schroeder, Frederick 10:78
Schroeder, H. 14:106
Schroeder, Henry 19:192
Schroeder, John 19:192
Schroeder, William 19:33
Schroeter, Francis J. 13:45
Schroetesser, J. 3:171
Schroffenberger, P. 11:169
Schromerer, James H. 11:44
Schroth, John 11:417
Schrotie, C. H. 21:207
Schrouder, Joseph 25:229
Schrurey, Frederick 22:168
Schryers, George 25:304
Schryick, John 8:94
Schu, William 19:318
Schualby, Fritz 8:75
Schuard, --- 16:225
Schuart, George 19:97
Schuban, C. 1:76
Schuber, George 13:45

Schubert, Benjamin 9:106
Schubert, Herman 11:112
Schubert, William 9:224; 18:375
Schuchart, I. 9:150
Schuchart, J. 27:108
Schuchman, Francis 26:225
Schuck, Christian C. 23:281
Schuck, Frederick 22:217
Schuckman, G. 22:218
Schuele, Christian 20:143
Schuette, William 21:105
Schufele, Jacob 13:45
Schugard, --- 13:68
Schughman, Francis 9:238
Schuh, Phillip 3:171
Schuhmacker, Christian 20:105
Schuke, Frederick 18:158
Schule, John 17:15
Schulenkamp, Henry 15:59
Schuler, Conrad 16:101
Schuler, Cornelius 5:28
Schuler, H. 24:63
Schuler, N. J. 9:228; 18:375
Schuler, Peter P. 12:38
Schuler, William 12:51
Schules, Madison 23:166
Schull, Jacob 12:38
Schuller, John S. 25:229
Schully, C. 5:54
Schult, Jacob 24:55
Schulte, Charles 8:75; 26:181
Schulthaers, J. 1:170
Schultz, --- 18:341
Schultz, A. 25:229
Schultz, Amos 26:113
Schultz, Andrew 5:28
Schultz, Arthur P. 22:440
Schultz, Augustus 18:413
Schultz, C. 13:68
Schultz, C. J. 3:171
Schultz, Carl 22:411
Schultz, Charles 10:79; 14:106
Schultz, Christ 24:173
Schultz, Christian 19:97
Schultz, David 11:407
Schultz, Ernst 24:97
Schultz, F. 3:171
Schultz, Frantz 22:154
Schultz, Fred 18:93; 26:130
Schultz, Frederick 9:104; 19:33; 24:97; 25:229

Schultz, Henry 1:72; 15:74; 26:113
Schultz, Jacob 23:195
Schultz, John 13:45
Schultz, John C. 23:182
Schultz, Nicholas 4:51
Schultz, Xavior 20:105
Schultze, P. 9:67
Schultzenback, Edw. 10:135
Schultzer, Frederick 1:72
Schulumaker, Charles 20:36
Schulz, Charles 19:261
Schulz, John 10:78
Schulze, Frederick 16:15
Schumacher, Frederick 17:362
Schumacher, Rinhart 11:392
Schumacker, Karl 21:116
Schumaker, H. 9:150
Schumaker, John 20:342
Schumaker, William H. 21:260
Schuman, August 21:385
Schuman, W. 15:225
Schumann, George 1:70
Schumann, Nicholas 20:342
Schumann, Paul 21:105
Schumate, Jehu 15:225
Schumm, Heinrich 21:233
Schumm, Henry 14:215
Schumm, John 14:215
Schumne, William 16:101
Schumper, George 22:268
Schums, J. 3:171
Schun, I. 3:171
Schun, J. 3:171
Schunk, Joseph 3:171
Schupp, B. 21:385
Schurburn, F. 1:72
Schurch, John 22:217
Schurchman, Fred 27:116
Schure, William 10:77
Schureman, Daniel 9:224
Schurick, A. 12:83; 16:304
Schurle, J. 23:166
Schurmishan, E. 20:342
Schurr, William 20:342
Schurtz, W. 3:171
Schurtz, William 18:251
Schurwickharoth, Frederick 11:397
Schurzman, Carl 7:109
Schuster, Christian 4:51
Schuster, John 8:30; 18:158
Schuster, Nicholas 12:76

Schuster, William 22:168
Schutt, Christopher 17:25
Schutt, Joseph 22:440
Schutt, S. 1:95
Schutt, W. 1:171
Schutters, S. 3:171
Schuttle, August 7:53
Schutz, C. G. 26:183
Schutzenback, Edward 20:342
Schutzer, W. H. 13:126
Schuyler, A. 25:229
Schuyler, Adam 22:498
Schuyler, Augustus 5:28
Schuyler, Henry 21:59
Schuyler, M. 19:97
Schuyler, Thomas 17:100
Schuyler, W. S. 1:170
Schwaab, Peter 11:130
Schwaarck, George 21:79
Schwab, Andrew 21:386
Schwab, C. 23:49
Schwab, Frederick 8:102; 17:459; 24:155
Schwab, Gottlieb 18:312
Schwab, Henry 13:45
Schwab, M. 10:207
Schwab, Michael A. 10:193
Schwab, Paul 18:158
Schwabb, Adolphus 16:225
Schwal, D. 1:70
Schwal, William J. 9:28
Schwandt, August 7:109
Schwank, George 20:343
Schwantes, August 22:284
Schwap, L. 13:118
Schware, F. 3:171
Schwarley, W. S. 19:98
Schwarteout, Charles 15:225
Schwartwalder, A. 11:76
Schwartz, Adolph 23:78
Schwartz, C. 2:18
Schwartz, Charles 7:109
Schwartz, Charles A. 4:51
Schwartz, Christian 10:22
Schwartz, Frederick 23:78
Schwartz, Henry 22:218
Schwartz, John 4:51
Schwartz, L. 1:174
Schwartz, Tilghman 9:125; 27:113
Schwartz, William 1:74; 4:51; 12:97; 15:361
Schwauger, James 9:45
Schwefeling, Fritz 22:168
Schweigert, George 23:49
Schweikart, M. 11:168
Schwein, John 20:105

Schweitzer, G. 1:70
Schweitzer, George 19:244
Schweitzer, K. 1:174
Schweitzer, S. 15:59
Schwenk, C. W. 19:265
Schwenoler, H. 9:28
Schwerin, H. 15:44
Schwester, Frank 7:40
Schwill, Gollfred 26:112
Schwind, Charles 18:315; 26:111
Schwind, John 9:162
Schwind, L. J. 13:45
Schwindler, T. C. 3:171
Schwinn, C. G. 23:261
Schwitzer, Samuel 12:76
Schwope, Gotlieb 22:115
Schworthy, S. 25:229
Schwortz, George 22:168
Schwyhart, J. 24:29
Schyler, J. W. 3:171
Scidle, Simon 22:99
Scied, Henry 17:409; 22:99
Sciefert, C. 12:157
Scifer, George 16:282
Scilch, J. 10:207
Scilley, F. 1:77
Scimgert, J. 3:171
Scip, Jacob 17:452
Scipe, Jacob 24:182
Sciple, Christian 8:30; 18:158
Scirbner, Elmer 15:9
Scirvin, Jacob C. 21:59
Scism, W. H. 25:229
Scism, William 20:25
Scisson, John O. 21:386
Scitaz, Victor 3:171
Scitts, W. 14:21
Scitzman, John 18:158
Sciver, A. C. 12:157
Sclocum, C. A. 3:171
Sclocum, E. B. 11:78
Sclotman, F. 12:88
Sclwab, Paul 8:30
Scobee, J. W. 20:343
Scobee, Stephen 20:187
Scobell, John M. 19:33
Scobie, Charles 11:312
Scoby, Austin 21:283
Scochensperger, William 23:109
Scoff, M. 16:225
Scofield, C. 1:71
Scofield, David F. 22:441
Scofield, E. 18:57
Scofield, Elisha 24:186
Scofield, Francis 9:104
Scofield, H. E. 4:52

Scofield, J. 16:379
Scofield, James 26:60
Scofield, John 8:109
Scofield, L. 1:170
Scofield, L. B. 21:386
Scofield, Oscar 18:330
Scofield, S. 16:225
Scofield, Theo. C. 9:125
Scofield, William 9:125
Scoflet, T. 16:225
Scoggins, J. F. 11:249
Scogman, Gustavus 11:45
Scoles, Erastus 22:411
Scoleton, J. 3:172
Scolley, Edwin R. 23:109
Sconard, --- 15:44
Sconde, Frederick 6:33
Sconlon, John 16:54
Sconover, Andrew J. 27:115
Scontain, Abram W. 24:29
Scooley, Thomas 21:386
Scooliey, John 27:114
Scoolley, John 9:125
Scorbey, L. A. H. 3:172
Scorce, William 7:40
Scorey, G. 14:215, 259
Scot, C. D. 27:118
Scot, Jacob 27:116
Scot, Samuel 27:118
Scotfield, W. 25:229
Scott, --- 9:232; 15:225; 25:70; 26:62
Scott, A. 3:171; 14:215; 15:225; 27:109
Scott, A. B. 21:386
Scott, A. L. 1:175
Scott, A. M. 15:225
Scott, A. W. 12:86; 16:304; 21:59
Scott, Aaron 23:49
Scott, Abraham 18:93
Scott, Adam 4:52
Scott, Albert 9:136; 27:111
Scott, Albert C. 22:438
Scott, Alex 7:40; 17:185; 18:297; 20:343; 23:166
Scott, Alexander 7:69; 9:39; 10:78; 22:100, 218; 26:113
Scott, Alexander J. 20:128
Scott, Alfred 17:185
Scott, Allen 3:171
Scott, Allen D. 27:119
Scott, Allen G. 22:100
Scott, Andrew 8:94; 17:138, 251; 21:93; 24:203
Scott, Andrew J. 17:250

Scott, Archibald 21:40
Scott, B. 3:171; 25:229
Scott, B. E. 24:29
Scott, B. F. 23:166
Scott, Benjamin 5:45;
    26:146
Scott, Benjamin F. 10:93;
    18:210; 20:343
Scott, Blair 3:171
Scott, C. 1:175
Scott, C. B. 17:424
Scott, C. D. 13:98; 17:471
Scott, C. E. 18:71
Scott, C. G. 1:70
Scott, C. J. 22:218
Scott, C. S. 13:98
Scott, Caldwell B. 24:174
Scott, Caleb 16:225;
    19:318
Scott, Calvin 20:343
Scott, Charles 10:22;
    11:417; 14:215;
    19:33, 48; 22:344,
    440
Scott, Charles F. 10:93;
    21:260
Scott, Charles H. 11:284;
    19:33; 26:181
Scott, Charles L. 11:77
Scott, Charles P. 22:52
Scott, Charles W. 11:45
Scott, Cornelius 7:132
Scott, Crow 20:105
Scott, D. 3:171; 14:21;
    20:177; 21:112
Scott, D. R. 14:245;
    27:119
Scott, D. V. 7:40
Scott, Daniel 4:52
Scott, Daniel B. 23:125
Scott, David 17:268;
    25:229
Scott, David W. 10:135;
    20:343
Scott, Dennis 24:29
Scott, Doc 26:180
Scott, Dock 8:42
Scott, E. 25:229; 27:110
Scott, E. G. 3:171
Scott, E. J. 23:49
Scott, E. K. 9:17
Scott, E. M. 13:118
Scott, E. P. 22:218
Scott, Edmund 23:78
Scott, Edwin 17:347
Scott, Eldridge 9:150
Scott, Eli 5:45; 17:185
Scott, Elias 22:100
Scott, Elias M. 23:280
Scott, Elijah 8:42; 21:283
Scott, Elisha 7:40

Scott, Elisha B. 13:45
Scott, Emanuel 12:158
Scott, F. 8:67; 13:118;
    18:251; 26:61, 183
Scott, F. B. 27:107
Scott, F. H. 23:166
Scott, Felix 11:391
Scott, Francis 4:52
Scott, Francis N. 21:386
Scott, Frank 8:42; 26:182
Scott, G. 18:434
Scott, G. D. 9:113
Scott, G. G. 7:40
Scott, G. W. 23:78
Scott, Gabriel 18:251;
    26:63
Scott, General 7:133;
    17:185
Scott, George 4:52; 7:109;
    8:75; 10:174, 209;
    11:130; 15:84;
    17:185; 18:413;
    19:48, 192; 21:386
Scott, George A. 18:38
Scott, George B. 22:218
Scott, George D. 5:28;
    25:229
Scott, George E. 18:401
Scott, George F. 22:411;
    23:93
Scott, George L. 22:154
Scott, George M. 12:65
Scott, George N. 15:5
Scott, George W. 3:171;
    9:45; 26:129
Scott, George W. H. 12:38
Scott, Gordon 22:52
Scott, Gorham R. 4:52
Scott, Gustavus A. 22:284
Scott, H. 1:75; 3:171;
    15:9; 18:38; 25:72,
    229
Scott, H. J. 3:171
Scott, H. W. 13:77
Scott, Hamilton 23:93
Scott, Harris 9:31; 18:315;
    26:112
Scott, Harrison 20:128
Scott, Harrison P. 24:69
Scott, Harvey 5:28
Scott, Harvey E. 23:78
Scott, Henderson M.
    10:211
Scott, Henry 6:19, 26;
    8:42; 10:78, 99;
    13:45; 16:54; 18:93;
    20:343; 22:318;
    26:129, 180
Scott, Henry C. 23:166
Scott, Henry D. 25:229
Scott, Henry W. 11:77

Scott, Hiram 7:109; 22:52
Scott, Hobert H. 21:233
Scott, Howard 6:33;
    25:326
Scott, Hugh 22:440
Scott, Ira 1:70
Scott, Irwin 11:213
Scott, Isaac 9:45; 11:213
Scott, Isaac H. 16:141
Scott, Isaiah R. 11:417
Scott, J. 1:170, 174;
    11:312; 14:106;
    18:251; 21:59;
    22:505; 23:195;
    25:312; 26:63
Scott, J. A. 14:271, 284
Scott, J. C. 3:171
Scott, J. E. 19:306
Scott, J. H. 3:171; 22:268
Scott, J. J. 20:156
Scott, J. L. 7:109; 14:106;
    19:98
Scott, J. M. 8:102;
    23:166; 25:229
Scott, J. N. 10:29
Scott, J. S. 2:18
Scott, J. W. 19:306
Scott, Jack 25:286
Scott, Jacob 7:40; 8:55;
    10:135; 20:343;
    21:125
Scott, Jacob M. 20:19
Scott, James 1:70; 7:132;
    10:78; 11:45; 12:38;
    13:58; 18:38, 210,
    375; 20:343; 21:386;
    25:69
Scott, James A. 21:59
Scott, James B. 8:30;
    18:158
Scott, James C. 22:268
Scott, James D. 23:280
Scott, James H. 3:171;
    23:166
Scott, James M. 9:125,
    224; 23:277; 27:114
Scott, James P. 24:60
Scott, James R. 22:100
Scott, James W. 22:99;
    23:78
Scott, Jasper 10:78
Scott, Jasper H. 22:129
Scott, Jasper P. 22:52
Scott, Jerry 9:202
Scott, Jerry G. 7:12
Scott, Jesse 7:133; 10:29;
    19:306; 25:229
Scott, Jesse D. 17:277,
    297
Scott, John 3:171; 4:52;
    7:40, 109; 10:99;

Scott, John 11:45, 312, 313; 13:45, 118; 16:225; 17:86, 160, 185, 192; 18:38; 19:33, 297, 327; 21:386; 22:524; 23:78, 264; 24:29, 69; 26:63; 27:115, 148
Scott, John A. 22:100
Scott, John B. 23:251
Scott, John D. 11:270; 22:53
Scott, John G. 9:90
Scott, John H. 8:67; 9:125; 26:183; 27:114
Scott, John J. 1:71; 20:25
Scott, John M. 22:439
Scott, John P. 9:227
Scott, John R. 6:19; 7:132; 18:93, 375
Scott, John S. 22:100
Scott, John T. 21:79
Scott, John W. 9:224; 16:144; 18:375
Scott, Jonathan 21:143
Scott, Jonney 18:251
Scott, Joseph 10:78; 11:170; 13:68; 14:215; 15:88; 19:48, 98; 20:343; 23:49; 25:229
Scott, Joshua 19:48
Scott, Joshua G. 17:284
Scott, L. 15:225
Scott, L. J. 11:312
Scott, L. W. 21:386
Scott, Lambert 22:129
Scott, Leander M. 8:94
Scott, Lewis 8:42; 9:136; 12:158; 26:180; 27:112, 119
Scott, Lewis G. 21:386
Scott, Louis 21:207
Scott, Lovell 7:133
Scott, Lucius 4:52
Scott, Madison C. 11:76
Scott, Mark 12:76; 15:59
Scott, Martin L. 16:131
Scott, Michael 22:129
Scott, Milton E. 9:90
Scott, N. 8:58; 21:151
Scott, Nab 17:185
Scott, Nathan 11:397
Scott, Newton 22:163
Scott, O. 1:70; 3:172; 18:252; 26:64
Scott, Oliver P. 22:99
Scott, P. 13:68
Scott, P. C. 3:172

Scott, Patrick 8:42; 19:98; 26:180
Scott, Perry 22:318
Scott, Peter 18:280
Scott, Peter H. 12:38
Scott, Philander 21:386; 24:215
Scott, Philip W. 10:93; 20:343
Scott, R. 1:172; 3:172; 9:150; 25:304
Scott, R. D. 3:172
Scott, R. F. 15:167
Scott, R. H. 26:237
Scott, R. J. 10:180; 11:329; 18:179
Scott, R. S. 7:78
Scott, R. W. 19:98
Scott, Richard 13:58; 23:49
Scott, Richard H. 6:19; 18:93
Scott, Robert 4:52; 9:28; 13:45; 14:106; 16:282; 17:145; 18:315; 19:48, 284; 21:143; 26:111; 27:108
Scott, Roberts 9:202
Scott, S. 11:172; 20:152
Scott, S. C. 16:225
Scott, S. E. 3:172
Scott, S. F. 2:18; 25:67
Scott, S. I. 1:77
Scott, S. J. 1:73
Scott, S. L. 19:261
Scott, S. N. 11:250
Scott, S. S. 26:183
Scott, Samuel 4:52; 13:58; 17:150
Scott, Samuel D. 20:187
Scott, Samuel I. 10:78
Scott, Samuel J. 20:343
Scott, Samuel M. 9:125; 11:313; 27:114
Scott, Samuel W. 8:31; 18:158
Scott, Selic 18:71
Scott, Smith 17:210
Scott, Solomon 8:55
Scott, Stephen L. 9:192
Scott, Sterling 18:435
Scott, T. 1:175; 14:106
Scott, T. G. 19:33
Scott, T. J. 8:75
Scott, T. M. 15:268
Scott, Theodore 18:104
Scott, Thomas 9:136; 10:150; 12:98; 18:57; 20:43; 22:344; 27:111

Scott, Thomas J. 26:181
Scott, Thornton 9:90
Scott, Thurston 26:59
Scott, W. 1:173; 9:45; 15:225; 16:225; 17:67, 185, 451; 24:180; 26:129
Scott, W. B. 18:17
Scott, W. C. 1:169
Scott, W. F. 8:75
Scott, W. G. 20:343
Scott, W. H. 3:172
Scott, W. M. 11:312; 22:268
Scott, W. O. 14:106
Scott, W. W. 3:172; 12:38; 14:106; 16:101; 23:303
Scott, Walter 7:132; 11:171; 17:103
Scott, Walter P. 23:195
Scott, Walter R. 17:401
Scott, Walter W. 17:391
Scott, Wash 27:148
Scott, Wesley 7:40; 14:215
Scott, William 3:172; 7:109; 8:30, 67, 100; 9:14, 99, 211, 224; 10:22, 93; 11:111; 12:163; 14:271, 284; 15:225; 16:379; 17:192, 503; 18:158, 375; 19:48; 20:343; 21:59, 118, 386; 22:318; 23:182, 257; 26:60, 61, 146, 183
Scott, William A. 1:75
Scott, William B. 22:516
Scott, William C. 10:78
Scott, William D. 21:79
Scott, William E. 17:156
Scott, William G. 11:404
Scott, William H. 11:112, 171; 18:413; 21:260
Scott, William J. 21:260
Scott, William S. 12:162
Scott, William T. 26:181
Scott, William W. 18:401
Scott, Willis O. 24:99
Scott, Wilton 26:58
Scott, Winfield 10:177; 19:192; 21:283
Scott, Z. 3:172
Scott, Zachariah S. 7:109
Scotta, John 16:226
Scotten, Charles 20:343
Scotten, Ebenezer C. 21:234
Scotten, John P. 22:268
Scotter, Charles 10:78

Scotthorn, George 7:109
Scottin, Frank 18:93
Scoughton, George W. 20:13
Scout, C. Pitts 11:221
Scout, Dansey 11:221
Scout, Isaac 1:71
Scoval, Orange 10:78
Scovall, Lewis 22:53
Scovall, Orange 20:343
Scoves, William 15:300
Scovey, Henry 11:212
Scovie, J. H. 3:172
Scovil, Charles M. 4:52
Scovil, H. 1:71
Scovil, M. 19:192
Scovill, Asa 17:426
Scovill, Martin S. 24:63
Scoville, A. H. 1:171
Scoville, A. O. 1:170
Scoville, Edward R. 12:38
Scoville, James H. 14:215
Scoville, Martin L. 20:33
Scoville, Nelson 20:181
Scoville, W. W. 12:38
Scovocal, Alonzo 13:45
Scrabb, James 22:53
Scrader, John C. 9:99
Scrafford, Robert 8:120
Scram, J. R. 1:168
Scrambling, J. 15:225
Scramling, Peter 14:215
Scranger, James 26:129
Scranser, J. 1:77
Scranton, Emero 17:244
Scranton, Henry 22:53
Scranton, James 18:280
Scranton, James H. 14:215
Scranton, Jeremiah 4:52
Scranton, L. 1:75
Scranton, Oswald 18:114
Scranton, T. M. 1:75
Scranton, William 11:329
Scratch, S. 1:172
Scraw, D. 11:313
Scrawfield, Pat 22:344
Screna, H. 3:172
Screntler, H. 8:122
Screob, Jacob 7:109
Screven, J. 19:306
Screwmand, G. 27:119
Scribenner, J. B. 1:100
Scriber, Charles E. 10:10
Scribner, Charles H. 8:94
Scribner, George W. 8:31; 18:158
Scribner, Jackson 21:386
Scribner, M. S. 1:169
Scridagunt, George 14:106

Scrieg, Thomas 18:71
Scriger, M. 25:326
Scrimpgher, Joel 24:184
Scrimpsher, Jacob 17:453
Scrip, D. 18:464
Scripp, Charles 9:90
Scripps, John M. 11:405
Scripter, C. E. 3:172
Scriptun, John W. 11:76
Scritchfield, W. 3:172
Scriven, John 19:288
Scrivener, J. S. 19:33
Scrivener, William M. 20:105
Scrivenor, J. 1:171
Scrlack, Jared 18:158
Scrluetter, H. 15:333
Scroggins, Charles 17:92
Scroggins, Jerry 25:304
Scroggins, John 17:192
Scroggins, Joshua 18:93
Scroggins, Lafath 19:293
Scroggins, Lafayette 9:202
Scroggins, Robert 21:59
Scroggins, W. 25:230
Scroggins, Walter 5:45
Scroggs, J. H. 10:135; 20:343
Scroggs, John 15:225
Scroggs, William P. 9:136; 27:112
Scrogin, George W. 22:100
Scrogin, Harrison H. 22:439
Scrole, John 1:72
Scrone, J. S. 14:303; 17:471; 27:117
Scroth, John 12:38
Scrowl, James 1:70
Scruggs, Anthony 11:336
Scruggs, George 22:318
Scruggs, Kesic 23:291
Scruggs, Larkin 22:318
Scruggs, Mans. D. 21:239
Scruggs, Robert 21:218
Scruggs, Thomas 22:344
Scruggs, Wesley 22:318
Scrugs, W. W. 19:33
Scruten, E. F. 25:230
Scruthly, J. W. 12:158
Scrutton, John B. 14:215
Scrutton, W. C. 1:77
Scubben, Jon 10:135
Scubben, Jonathan 20:343
Scuckler, James 20:343
Scudder, B. O. 2:18
Scudder, Charles 7:109
Scudder, D. C. 11:249
Scudder, Dorsey 22:439

Scudder, F. 1:95
Scudder, G. P. 16:304
Scudder, J. 1:175
Scudder, Lewis 11:77
Scudder, S. 16:226
Scudder, Silas H. 7:40
Scudder, W. 2:18
Scudder, W. S. 14:106
Scuh, John 7:109
Scull, James 25:70
Scull, Mark 12:38
Scull, Newton 9:58
Scullcy, Richard 16:79
Scullen, Patrick 15:74
Sculler, H. 27:107
Sculley, J. 16:226
Sculley, Thomas 27:107
Scullion, Barney 18:315; 26:112
Scully, Andrew W. 16:164
Scully, Edward 17:42
Scully, J. 15:295
Scully, John 7:109; 22:100; 24:114
Scully, Thomas 4:52
Scully, William 1:74
Scult, James 25:230
Scurlock, Samuel 20:343
Scurry, J. 1:172
Scutchel, John D. 11:417
Scutliff, Robert 12:100; 15:366
Scutly, Dennis 9:125
Scuyer, N. 3:172
Scybert, Jacob 15:74
Scyler, Christ 21:40
Scyoc, Smith V. 17:92
Scythel, Hans 8:31; 18:158
Se---, T. 20:156
Se-nop-pe 25:335
Seabauer, Martin 17:86
Seabert, Joseph 14:215
Seabole, Charles 7:63
Seabom, William 20:343
Seaborn, George 21:205
Seaborn, Robert 21:386
Seaborn, W. 18:252
Seabourn, W. 26:64
Seabrecht, Henry 17:58
Seabrook, --- 25:230
Seabrook, March 27:106
Seabrook, Peter 9:154
Seabrook, Phillis 27:115
Seaburn, Achilles 17:42
Seaburn, G. H. 17:58
Seabury, Robert 17:138; 24:203
Seacat, Montgomery 21:234

Seacord, John 10:78; 20:343
Seacord, R. D. 12:39
Seadbeaten, J. H. 3:172
Seadin, Wilford N. 22:154
Seaford, Dennis 14:215
Seafoze, Ira 15:225
Seagan, C. W. 23:47
Seager, George W. 17:454; 24:186
Seager, J. C. 9:163
Seager, S. S. 13:118
Seager, William T. 23:166
Seagirt, Charles 10:135; 20:343
Seagle, Tobias 14:215
Seagler, Philip 7:61
Seago, Joseph 20:343
Seagraves, W. A. 8:31
Seagur, Wesley R. 10:22
Seahlegel, Henry 14:215
Seahouse, C. 1:104
Seakins, N. T. 25:304
Seal, George W. 19:98
Seal, H. 14:106
Seal, J. L. 21:386
Seal, Joseph 22:521
Seal, T. J. 24:84
Sealer, Charles 1:75
Sealer, Z. W. S. 25:230
Seales, George P. 10:97
Seales, J. 14:106
Seales, William 10:78
Sealing, Henry 10:78; 20:343
Sealock, Benjamin F. 17:86
Sealock, S. F. 26:111
Seals, Benjamin 7:133
Seals, H. 21:386
Seals, John 3:172
Seals, N. 7:109
Seals, William 17:239; 20:343
Seaman, A. 3:172; 27:118
Seaman, Ezra 21:386
Seaman, Isaac 9:237
Seaman, Isaac M. 26:226
Seaman, J. 13:118
Seaman, J. D. 13:68; 19:98
Seaman, J. S. 14:215
Seaman, John 22:441
Seaman, M. 3:172
Seaman, R. 1:172
Seaman, Rufus W. 13:46
Seaman, Tillman H. 22:100
Seaman, W. 12:9
Seaman, W. D. 1:173
Seaman, W. O. 23:115

Seaman, William 21:79
Seamans, Alfred 4:52
Seamard, Jackson 17:389
Seamen, Frederick 22:168
Seames, John A. 6:33
Seamon, M. 17:289
Seamons, William H. 10:135; 20:343
Seamster, William 23:78
Seandon, Thomas 11:251
Seanians, G. 14:215
Seanion, Thomas 17:353
Seanland, James 17:293
Sear, C. 3:172
Sear, David M. 25:72
Sear, Henry 11:185
Search, Christopher 3:172
Search, Henry 3:172
Search, Luther 19:98
Search, William H. 10:135; 20:343
Searchman, H. 13:118
Searcy, Daniel 21:241
Searett, F. 14:322; 23:78
Searfass, A. J. 1:176
Searfoos, John 20:100
Seargeant, P. H. 17:193
Searight, John T. 22:237
Searkrist, O. 22:237
Searl, Duan 11:314
Searle, David N. 13:46
Searle, George M. 19:246
Searle, Henry B. 10:174; 19:192
Searle, Henry P. 10:7
Searle, J. R. 3:172
Searle, John E. 19:33
Searle, Julius F. 9:14
Searle, William 7:53
Searles, Addison 11:168
Searles, Alfred 9:45
Searles, Alfred D. 26:129
Searles, Alonzo 14:237
Searles, C. M. 19:230
Searles, David N. 16:54
Searles, E. S. 9:90
Searles, Erens 19:192
Searles, George M. 9:192
Searles, George R. 9:90
Searles, Griffin 23:125
Searles, H. M. 4:52
Searles, Henry 27:116
Searles, Joseph 16:54
Searles, Joseph H. 13:46
Searles, Lewis 13:46
Searles, Oscar 25:304
Searles, Sylvester 19:98
Searles, William H. 1:71
Searless, C. W. 9:192
Searls, G. K. 26:60
Searls, Henry 12:39

Searls, Oscar 7:76
Searls, Parry 19:192
Sears, --- 19:306
Sears, Adam 26:61
Sears, Allen 11:404
Sears, Alvin 17:156
Sears, Benjamin 7:69
Sears, C. 11:169
Sears, C. E. 1:173
Sears, Charles 19:192
Sears, Charles H. 19:192
Sears, Daniel 15:345; 16:379; 22:53
Sears, David 11:392
Sears, E. 17:185
Sears, Edmund H. 25:70
Sears, Edwin 7:109
Sears, Eli 15:23
Sears, Elias 19:33
Sears, Frank 25:230
Sears, Frederick C. 22:218
Sears, George S. 22:467
Sears, H. C. 23:303
Sears, Henry 5:28
Sears, Hiram 15:225
Sears, Ivor 11:76
Sears, J. 3:172
Sears, James 4:52; 11:170; 15:23
Sears, Jerome 12:39
Sears, John 27:115
Sears, John A. 25:326
Sears, Joseph 11:342
Sears, Martin 13:45; 22:100
Sears, P. 20:343
Sears, Pearson 10:78
Sears, Peter 25:230
Sears, Reddick 25:230
Sears, Richard W. 20:43
Sears, Robert 16:54
Sears, S. S. 16:226
Sears, Samuel 3:172
Sears, Sylvester 22:53
Sears, T. 3:172
Sears, Urban 15:18
Sears, W. 11:172
Sears, W. A. 19:98
Sears, William A. 12:97; 15:361
Seary, --- 17:192
Seaserhodly, S. 14:215
Seasholtz, George W. 21:234
Seater, W. 23:93
Seater, William W. 23:93
Seathoff, Harry 10:135
Seaton, Alex. W. 10:135; 20:343
Seaton, Edward S. 17:362
Seaton, Enoch G. 22:100

Seaton, Franklin 17:449
Seaton, Henry 22:218
Seaton, James 11:404
Seaton, James C. 21:105
Seaton, James W. 20:28
Seaton, John A. 20:25
Seaton, John L. 19:48
Seaton, John T. 22:491
Seaton, Joseph 9:104
Seaton, M. A. 14:215
Seaton, Marritt R. 11:404
Seaton, Robert 22:511
Seaton, Robert B. 22:411
Seaton, T. B. 3:172
Seaton, W. S. 23:264
Seaton, William 1:78
Seaton, William D. 11:45
Seatt, Jacob 24:204
Seavel, B. 1:71
Seavel, J. S. 21:191
Seaver, A. M. 1:174
Seaver, John 23:115
Seaver, John H. 8:75;
   26:181
Seaver, M. Cutter 9:8
Seavers, Richard 16:87
Seavery, C. H. 17:336
Seavey, C. L. 15:225
Seavey, C. N. 1:73
Seavey, Charles 24:55
Seavey, F. H. 7:76;
   25:304
Seavey, J. O. 17:159
Seavolt, J. W. 25:230
Seavolt, Levi 23:166
Seawell, William 26:182
Seawolt, George W. 5:28
Seay, James W. 21:59
Seay, John P. 11:97
Seay, Thomas 11:435
Seay, William 22:516
Seayfoot, William 16:226
Sebald, H. 16:226
Seban, Samuel 9:90
Sebast, Johnson 14:215
Sebastian, Dread 21:213
Sebastian, J. W. 3:172
Sebastian, N. P. 12:143
Sebbett, J. 16:379
Sebbitt, J. 15:345
Seber, William 15:225
Seberger, F. 3:172
Sebern, Samuel 26:59
Sebers, S. 1:173
Sebins, Charles 14:106
Sebins, Oscar 4:52
Sebring, Abraham 17:447
Sebring, Abram 24:171
Sebring, John 15:160
Sebring, Peter 24:29
Sebring, Thomas 16:101

Seburn, Samuel H. 11:45
Sebut, S. 19:261
Secafe, Ira 20:343
Secap, Ira 10:135
Secaur, John L. 22:218
Secco, O. L. 25:304
Secear, B. 14:251
Sechler, Ashel 22:154
Sechler, Charles P. 20:43
Sechoves, Thomas 13:80
Sechrist, David 12:60
Sechrist, Jacob 22:100
Sechrist, John H. 22:440
Seclar, A. N. 22:154
Seco, Orrin L. 7:76
Secom, William 26:130
Secomb, P. C. 15:225
Second, James D. 8:115
Secor, Gabriel 19:33
Secor, Isaac 20:109
Secor, William H. 19:33
Secord, James S. 25:71
Secore, Chr. C. 10:22
Secose, G. W. 16:101
Secresh, Daniel 18:159
Secresh, James 18:159
Secrest, Daniel 8:31
Secrest, Ira W. 22:100
Secrest, James 8:31
Secrest, James C. 17:42
Secrest, Parker 22:100
Secris, David C. 10:135
Secrist, Aaron 21:40
Secrist, David C. 20:343
Secrist, John 22:130
Secrist, William 9:90
Secroe, John 11:409
Secryst, Cornelius 17:58
Sedam, J. 14:106
Sedbetter, Ward 16:54
Sedchling, J. 15:307
Seddeker, Samuel 14:215
Seddeley, Stephens 7:61
Seddennymer, Augustus
   8:100
Sedford, Marcy M. 26:213
Sedgewick, William W.
   21:386
Sedgler, H. 12:10
Sedgwick, Barney A.
   10:78
Sedgwick, E. B. 4:52
Sedgwick, R. 9:192;
   19:261
Sedling, J. 19:98
Sedo, Charles 20:343
Sedore, E. 16:226
Sedrow, Greenbury 9:107
Seds, Charles 10:78
Sedulis, P. J. 2:18
Sedwick, B. A. 20:343

See, A. 3:172
See, A. M. 7:40
See, Daniel D. 22:154
See, John H. 27:115
See, L. 3:172
See, Parum 11:213
See, Peter 23:125
See, S. 3:172
Seeb, George 15:111
Seebasteen, Emanuel
   23:287
Seeber, Jacob 13:46
Seeberger, Antone 19:323
Seebert, Albert W. 17:25
Seebert, H. C. 3:172
Seebil, August 3:172
Seebold, Castor 12:39
Seech, Andrew 24:69
Seecker, Conrad 8:31
Seeds, O. M. 12:158
Seegar, Jacob 9:204
Seegenhein, J. 25:230
Seekell, J. H. 12:39
Seeker, W. H. 1:74
Seeking, Nathan T. 7:76
Seel, William 12:158
Seeland, Leonard 12:76
Seelay, James W. 22:467
Seeley, A. 24:114
Seeley, Austin 12:39
Seeley, C. H. 3:172
Seeley, Charles 3:172
Seeley, Charles D. 19:224
Seeley, David 18:444
Seeley, E. M. 14:335
Seeley, Eli D. 9:14
Seeley, Emery D. 10:135;
   20:343
Seeley, H. 3:172
Seeley, Henry 1:73; 9:150
Seeley, J. C. 9:244
Seeley, James 17:67
Seeley, M. M. 1:76
Seeley, Norman 3:172
Seeley, P. 12:123
Seeley, Philmore 15:134
Seeley, Pitt 21:234
Seeley, Whitman 12:63
Seeley, William 22:441
Seeley, William H. 21:40
Seeling, George H. 25:230
Seeling, P. 15:111
Seely, A. J. 3:172
Seely, Abel 12:158
Seely, C. B. 3:172
Seely, Ferdinand 21:201
Seely, H. 27:110
Seely, Ira 10:22
Seely, J. B. 21:125
Seely, J. R. 21:116
Seely, James L. 22:492

Seely, John 9:125; 27:113
Seely, John R. 21:239
Seely, Lewis P. 20:343
Seely, W. W. 7:40
Seely, William 14:303;
    17:477; 27:116
Seeman, George 15:365
Seemann, John P. 23:195
Seemen, J. B. 15:9
Seemreese, John A.
    17:112
Seeney, B. L. 20:343
Seeney, Barton L. 10:78
Seeney, D. 23:268
Seeney, William T.
    14:215
Seer, William 14:106
Seeridge, R. D. 9:227
Seery, John 7:84
Sees, Samuel 8:31
Seete, P. 16:226
Seeter, Moses 17:138;
    24:204
Seeton, R. M. 3:172
Seevers, A. F. 23:49
Seevey, Benjamin F.
    13:46
Seevy, A. J. 21:386
Seevy, M. 21:386
Seffi---, --- 24:69
Sefreid, John 20:343
Sefried, John 10:135
Sefton, Samuel 17:456;
    24:169
Segal, H. 25:230
Segar, Abram 22:218
Segar, C. 22:218
Segar, Charles 3:172
Segar, E. B. 9:192
Segar, J. 11:45
Segar, J. D. 1:174
Segar, Mathias 1:76
Segars, Edward 3:172
Seger, William A. 17:503
Seggers, James R. 22:130
Segin, C. 3:172
Segmore, A. 14:215
Segmore, Frank 11:112
Segner, E. 23:280
Segner, E. B. 9:192
Segner, Ed. B. 19:268
Sego, Albert 20:156
Sego, Charles 20:156
Sego, Solomon 21:79
Segouin, J. 1:171
Segraves, Charles 25:71
Segraves, Reuben 19:192
Segraze, Edward 23:195
Segur, Edward B. 19:268
Segur, Henry 20:25
Segwick, William 7:84

Sehl, John 4:52
Seial, J. 7:53
Seian, M. S. 5:28
Seiber, C. 1:169
Seiber, J. 16:231
Seiberg, William 10:135
Seiberlich, William P.
    24:55
Seiberlick, J. 25:230
Seibert, Anthony G.
    23:166
Seibert, Henry 10:78;
    20:343
Seibert, Jacob 12:76
Seibert, John C. 24:60
Seibert, P. 1:171
Seibert, Peter 20:344
Seibert, William 20:344;
    22:440; 24:84
Seic, Malay 16:304
Seic, Maley 12:88
Seick, Frederick 23:281
Seickle, --- 11:342
Seidel, Erhard 23:78
Seidel, G. A. 1:73
Seidell, Benno 23:166
Seidenfure, George
    20:134
Seiderer, John 20:128
Seidle, Henry 21:125
Seidle, James A. 9:125;
    27:114
Seidlitz, H. 1:176
Seidman, Frederick
    22:284
Seidt, A. 14:106
Seiely, E. M. 9:150
Seif, B. W. 21:386
Seifert, Alexander 23:78
Seifert, Fred 27:118
Seifert, John 20:43
Seiffert, M. 2:17
Seifker, L. 10:29; 19:306
Seifman, M. 26:65
Seifold, Jonathan 23:78
Seifres, William L. 21:105
Seifried, Matthias 4:52
Seig, Edward M. 10:78;
    20:344
Seigal, Charles 27:117
Seigal, Charles W. 11:184
Seigar, S. S. 16:226
Seigee, George 11:314
Seigel, Charles 14:303;
    17:477, 480
Seigel, Louis 17:356;
    21:105
Seiger, Charles 22:398
Seiger, J. M. 25:68
Seigerd, C. P. 15:44
Seigfred, H. 24:63

Seigfreid, Levi 24:84
Seigle, Benjamin 17:58
Seigle, C. A. 1:172
Seigle, Charles 27:117
Seigle, G. 1:170
Seigle, Peter 13:126
Seigle, Philip 12:39
Seigler, George 3:172;
    4:52
Seigler, John R. 3:172
Seigler, William 25:129
Seigment, Constance
    19:33
Seigmond, Antoni 26:59
Seignor, Charles J. 24:172
Seigrist, Charles 21:105
Seijiner, L. F. 11:171
Seikel, E. B. 23:166
Seikora, Franta 19:340
Seiler, A. 10:167; 19:192
Seiler, William 22:218
Seimer, Herman 21:40
Seimerman, A. 13:118
Sein, John 9:99
Seine, John F. 9:58
Seined, F. 12:65
Seip, George 14:215;
    16:123
Seiper, Henry 25:326
Seir, Joseph 23:129
Seirface, Martin L. 8:109
Seirney, Henry 21:386
Seites, Nicholas 19:33
Seitez, A. 16:270
Seitz, A. 15:225
Seitz, Jacob 17:405
Seitzer, John W. 11:375
Seiver, Oliver 8:31;
    18:159
Seizer, Samuel 17:266
Seizer, Walter 9:45
Sekinger, Joseph 17:86
Selah, Isaac H. 24:29
Selam, Edward 27:111
Seland, Cashmere 15:225
Seland, Frank 4:52
Selb, Jacob 3:172
Selbender, W. 19:98
Selbey, Garret 16:131
Selby, A. 1:174
Selby, Alexander 7:133
Selby, E. C. 10:29
Selby, George W. 20:344
Selby, Isaac N. 24:29
Selby, James S. 11:312
Selby, John 13:46
Selby, Meredith 15:88
Selby, W. 27:115
Selby, W. B. 1:176
Selcher, J. 1:175
Selcrate, Mathias 23:205

Selden, H. R. 8:125
Selder, William H. 17:86
Seldomridge, G. 1:174
Seldon, --- 9:227
Seldon, Andrew 22:412
Seldon, Robert 18:93
Seldon, T. 14:106
Selerel, C. 3:172
Selery, Samuel 21:218
Seley, J. 14:21
Seley, J. S. 13:98
Self, Alexander A. 21:105
Self, Allen 22:16
Self, David W. 22:268
Self, George W. 8:31;
    18:159; 22:100
Self, Henry 22:440
Self, James H. 11:289
Self, John E. 22:154
Self, M. D. 22:268
Self, M. G. 22:268
Self, William 23:78
Self, William D. 22:439
Self---, --- 17:168
Selfing, J. M. 18:252
Selfkin, Charles F. 21:386
Selger, Seymour 21:386
Selig, Ernest 10:135;
    20:344
Selin, Charles 18:159
Seline, George 22:154
Selip, Frederick 19:33
Selkins, Lear 10:211
Selkirk, J. F. 3:172
Sell, Adam 3:172
Sell, Christopher 10:135
Sell, Christopher W.
    20:344
Sell, Dan 18:466
Sell, Franklin 1:74
Sell, Isham 21:40
Sell, John S. 10:146;
    19:192
Sell, Louis D. 9:101
Sell, McCoy 17:497
Sell, Michael 18:38
Sell, Russell B. 9:192;
    19:261
Sell, Samuel 22:100
Sellard, D. M. 1:173
Sellars, I. 18:180
Sellars, J. 10:193
Sellars, Winyard 20:344
Sellay, Abraham 21:284
Selleck, George A. 19:33
Sellegg, Edwin 20:103
Sellen, Ephraim 21:209
Sellen, Michael 7:109
Sellentine, M. 3:173
Seller, Christian 11:251
Seller, E. 14:106

Seller, John N. 17:232
Seller, Joseph 17:26
Sellers, --- 7:76; 25:304
Sellers, Adolphus 5:54
Sellers, Benjamin F.
    22:130
Sellers, Brigham 8:31
Sellers, Canaan 11:391
Sellers, Charles M. 21:79
Sellers, Frederick 12:39
Sellers, G. S. 12:100;
    15:348
Sellers, George H. 12:158
Sellers, George W. 20:84
Sellers, H. 3:172
Sellers, Hustin 8:78
Sellers, J. 25:230
Sellers, J. I. 21:201
Sellers, Jacob 22:491
Sellers, James 15:74;
    24:44
Sellers, James D. 23:93
Sellers, James M. 21:95
Sellers, James W. 22:268
Sellers, John W. 8:31;
    18:159
Sellers, Joshua 11:417
Sellers, Julius 9:162
Sellers, Minyard 10:135
Sellers, R. 25:230
Sellers, Robert 5:28
Sellers, S. 21:386
Sellers, Thomas 13:118
Sellers, W. H. 11:75;
    20:43
Sellers, William 3:172;
    22:318
Selles, John 5:45
Selley, E. C. 19:306
Selley, Thomas 3:172
Sellick, David 7:40
Sellick, George B. 21:386
Sellick, J. B. 25:304
Sellick, Jonathan 7:80
Sellick, Lewis 20:13
Sellis, C. 1:171
Sellman, Denton G.
    22:218
Sellman, J. 12:162
Sells, D. C. 14:259
Sells, John 3:172
Sells, Joseph 20:149
Sells, L. 14:290; 23:93
Sells, L. S. 23:166
Sells, Sampson 8:69
Sells, Samuel 17:204
Sells, W. 3:172
Selly, George W. 5:54
Selly, Isaac 11:75
Selm, Antoine 21:386
Selman, H. 18:431

Selog, George 24:29
Selove, G. G. 15:313
Selover, David V. 1:74
Selp, Samuel E. 8:109
Selper, A. 1:171
Selrick, J. 16:304
Selson, H. 3:173
Seltish, Joseph 9:45
Seltzer, Frederick 1:71
Seltzman, W. H. 25:275
Selun, Edward 9:136
Selva, Manuel 19:98
Selvey, J. D. 17:167
Selvidge, R. D. 18:375
Selwood, Charles 14:215
Selyer, John P. 23:78
Sem, John 1:72
Semans, Frank 20:19
Semden, James 13:118
Semer, William 15:175
Semes, George 18:252
Semes, I. V. 15:225
Semington, George
    14:215
Semington, William
    20:344
Semins, Green 17:455
Semling, A. 1:76
Semmes, J. H. 17:501
Semmes, Robert 3:173
Semmo, O. 24:102
Semo, H. 1:170
Semon, William 16:54
Semonton, S. 25:72
Semorson, J. 15:153
Semple, D. 25:72
Semple, John 27:106
Sempler, Benjamin B.
    7:14
Sempleten, T. M. 8:67
Semyn, Peter 22:154
Senard, J. 16:134
Senate, William 20:344
Senbury, R. J. 14:215
Sendbene, N. H. 21:386
Sendbrear, Edward 21:386
Senderman, Christopher
    11:97
Sendlewick, George
    11:269
Sendner, Philip 15:82
Sends, A. V. 15:74
Seneca, J. 16:226
Seng, John 22:168
Sengenate, Adolph 25:70
Senger, William 26:213
Sengravre, William A.
    18:159
Senierill, Columbus
    10:135
Seniomin, Samuel 24:69

Senior, U. H. 18:180
Senior, W. H. 10:187
Senks, J. 11:439
Senksen, John 8:31; 18:159
Senles, Berbels 18:180
Senley, George W. 17:42
Senn, William 19:98
Senna, D. B. 19:98
Senna, Jacob 11:170
Sennant, R. M. 11:97
Sennard, W. H. 18:375
Sennart, Conrad 22:218
Sennet, David 15:112
Sennet, Philip 21:85
Sennett, Lolace 21:151
Sennett, William 10:78
Senny, Henry C. 16:54
Senod, Daniel 11:77
Senoir, John 23:166
Senont, Charles 14:107
Senry, David 13:118
Sensabaugh, Andrew 23:78
Sensick, J. 1:168
Sensily, John 11:404
Senslumyer, Robert 16:123
Sentance, J. 13:98
Senter, Henry 18:252; 26:63
Senter, James 7:109
Senter, William 11:111; 24:29
Sentern, J. 3:173
Seoback, J. 13:126
Sephas, John 11:213
Sepley, Jacob 9:39
Sepp, Philip 17:15
Seppeirs, W. H. 9:192
Seppenfeldt, Henry 9:125
Sepper, S. 13:98
Seppy, Anthony 22:100
Septer, David 8:109
Septer, George 24:44
Seque-yah 25:335
Seran, A. 14:107
Seraphine, Calvin 9:39
Seraw, T. R. 27:109
Serbels, Augustus 9:192
Serber, George A. 4:52
Serby, W. 1:175
Serch, Luther 15:319
Sercy, Edward 18:93
Serders, J. S. 3:173
Serene, R. B. 3:173
Serens, John W. 18:252; 26:63
Sererson, C. 9:150
Sereton, J. 11:329

Serewees, Charles H. 18:341
Serey, Elijah 11:409
Serfried, C. 11:185
Serg, Amos 24:99
Sergante, William 23:282
Sergeant, A. S. 14:21
Sergeant, Jeremiah 17:232
Sergeant, John B. 21:386
Sergeant, L. 3:173
Sergeant, M. J. 8:67
Sergeant, Sidney H. 4:52
Sergeant, W. H. 1:170; 9:150; 25:69
Sergent, C. 11:375
Sergent, J. 16:270; 25:72
Sergent, John E. 22:130
Sergent, Lyman 20:344
Sergeon, Joseph 17:86
Sergerst, J. C. 23:96
Sergeson, William 23:166
Sergg, Pet 11:43
Sergo, Joseph 10:78
Seright, James A. 24:55
Serim, William H. 5:28
Serine, Orrin 9:14
Sering, I. 21:40
Seriven, John 9:192
Serks, William H. 4:52
Serles, Edward 4:52
Serlin, Charles 8:31
Serman, Thomas 23:167
Sern, C. 3:173
Serofer, Cornelius 15:279
Serom, George H. 13:46
Serost, Charles 14:107
Serpain, Calvin 18:297
Serphin, Calvin 26:112
Serrals, Matthew T. 22:100
Serrel, Jesse 22:100
Serrels, Andrew B. 17:42
Serriatt, John 7:109
Serrill, John 8:67
Serrock, John R. 22:412
Serry, John 21:386
Sersey, Anderson 17:399
Serus, Levi M. 8:94
Seruscon, Henry 13:46
Serusion, Henry 16:54
Serva, Clemente 8:124
Servant, Richard 25:230
Service, S. 25:230
Service, Thomas 2:17; 25:73
Servier, N. 18:180
Serviere, H. 3:173
Serviess, George B. 13:46
Servine, James 13:46
Servitt, W. H. 15:225
Seseman, Henry 11:43

Sesler, J. 18:57
Seson, O. B. 3:173
Session, Albert 22:329
Session, G. O. 2:17; 25:73
Sessions, J. F. 9:150
Sessions, James A. 10:167
Sessions, Jarius A. 19:192
Sessions, Nathan C. 11:111
Sessions, O. O. 7:109
Sessler, E. 16:282
Sessler, J. B. 26:183
Sessons, H. 1:176
Sester, John A. 27:116
Sestt, Joseph L. 20:178
Setch, George 13:127
Setchel, D. W. 24:69
Setchell, Frank 25:230
Setcher, Joseph 22:355
Setchler, George 16:140
Setchmiller, Valentine 11:78
Seter, W. H. H. 15:112
Seth, A. 12:88; 16:304
Setlers, Brigham 18:159
Setley, K. A. 14:107
Seton, C. R. 21:387
Seton, Joseph E. 18:341
Setscott, F. E. 7:62
Setten, James 10:93
Setter, Anderson 25:230
Setter, John L. 21:260
Setter, William 26:60
Setters, George H. 3:173
Setters, John 5:28
Settle, Alex 20:344
Settle, Enoch 23:110
Settle, John 7:61
Settle, Joseph H. 23:101
Settler, Henry 3:173
Settles, John W. 22:15
Setzer, Harrison 4:52
Setzer, M. 13:68
Setzer, Michael 19:98
Setzer, P. W. 11:314
Setzler, T. 15:15
Seuft, Rudolph 15:44
Seurlock, Samuel 10:135
Seuser, Peter 25:230
Sevan, William 21:284
Sevanders, Alfred 13:98
Sevart, Jeremiah 11:427
Seveir, William G. 17:215
Sevenson, Benjamin A. 12:51
Sever, H. 18:252; 26:63
Sever, Manuel 15:321
Sever, Philip 13:46
Sever, Phillip 16:54
Sever, S. N. 15:9
Severance, Albert 14:215

Severance, Augustus 14:107
Severance, Clarence 12:158
Severance, E. M. 21:387
Severance, Edwin 12:39
Severance, L. 9:113
Severance, S. 15:44
Severance, W. E. 7:61
Severanes, William 25:230
Severe, David 15:259; 20:344
Severe, Eli J. 17:67
Severe, H. B. 8:75
Severe, J. 1:169
Severe, Lyman 8:75; 26:181
Severence, T. 1:173
Severman, A. H. 12:39
Severn, C. 3:173
Severs, Brent 21:387
Severs, Henry F. 17:42
Severs, Lemuel 11:417
Severs, Levi M. 18:327
Severs, R. D. 15:225
Severson, Leslie F. 13:46
Severson, Ole 11:117; 20:116; 27:115
Severy, --- 9:192; 19:289
Severy, Levi 9:202
Sevester, Henry 21:105
Sevey, A. H. 1:71
Sevey, John 18:252
Sevier, J. R. 8:67
Sevier, James Richard 26:183
Sevier, R. 3:173
Seviere, H. 10:187
Sevill, E. J. 16:226
Seville, A. 15:225
Seville, John 22:318
Sevills, Kelby 9:192
Sevin, John 13:46
Seviney, Charles 22:457
Sevins, Leopold 9:99
Sevnin, John 9:99
Sevoice, Squire 5:28
Sevrns, Elbt. 21:40
Sevton, Madison S. 8:31
Sevulter, M. 15:74
Sewall, Frank 11:77
Seward, --- 13:46; 16:226
Seward, Albert 6:19; 18:93
Seward, B. 16:226
Seward, Charles 11:392
Seward, E. 12:98
Seward, Eli 16:282
Seward, F. T. 9:227; 18:375

Seward, G. 11:250
Seward, G. H. 3:173
Seward, Henry A. 9:14
Seward, Houston 11:336
Seward, Isaac 17:150
Seward, J. H. 22:130
Seward, J. S. 5:28
Seward, John 25:230
Seward, John B. 18:401
Seward, Letser 24:29
Seward, O. 3:173
Seward, R. 3:173
Seward, Robert W. 22:114
Seward, T. R. 12:100
Seward, W. C. 14:215
Seward, William H. 13:46
Sewart, William 11:184
Sewass, Lorenzo 8:94
Sewell, A. R. 18:222
Sewell, Aaron R. 11:249
Sewell, Charles 7:133; 9:211
Sewell, Cyrum 12:39
Sewell, David 14:215
Sewell, E. J. 13:68
Sewell, Eli 10:207
Sewell, Henry 25:67
Sewell, Ira B. 18:159
Sewell, J. H. 9:224; 18:375
Sewell, John 17:150
Sewell, Joseph 18:194
Sewell, Joseph S. 23:264
Sewell, Peter 22:440
Sewell, Reuben 1:72
Sewell, Samuel S. 25:304
Sewell, Stephen W. 22:53
Sewer, Perry 11:172
Sewers, L. 14:107
Sewerton, Henry 8:55
Sewood, Richard 17:138; 24:203
Sewter, John 4:52
Sex, Henry 26:60
Sexon, Carroll S. 21:234
Sexon, David P. 17:42
Sexton, --- 18:355
Sexton, Alexander F. 22:130
Sexton, Archibald 10:97
Sexton, C. 11:289
Sexton, D. 25:230
Sexton, Dennis 4:52
Sexton, E. 1:170; 14:107; 18:93
Sexton, Eli 17:86
Sexton, F. 21:199
Sexton, Franklin 24:174
Sexton, H. 14:107
Sexton, Henry W. 22:268
Sexton, Isaac 11:87

Sexton, J. R. M. 9:58
Sexton, James 17:42, 150; 24:168
Sexton, James W. 22:53, 130
Sexton, Julius C. 1:73
Sexton, Madison S. 18:159
Sexton, Michael F. 21:387
Sexton, Norris W. 9:104
Sexton, T. 1:170
Sexton, Wiley H. 22:130
Seybald, Moses F. 20:344
Seyberd, Josephus 15:44
Seybert, A. J. 3:173
Seybert, Samuel 22:53
Seybold, David 12:76; 15:74
Seybold, H. 14:322; 23:78
Seybold, Moses F. 10:135
Seybold, Samuel 7:109
Seybolds, Benjamin F. 17:42
Seyelkin, Otto 8:126
Seyer, E. 19:288
Seyers, William H. 11:172
Seyfers, John 15:74
Seyfong, Andrew 22:100
Seyfort, John 12:65
Seyler, W. L. 23:49
Seymore, C. 14:107
Seymore, George C. 26:237
Seymore, J. C. 1:70
Seymore, J. D. 20:156
Seymore, Jaret 4:52
Seymore, Thomas 16:115
Seymour, A. B. 14:215
Seymour, Aaron 3:173
Seymour, C. A. 8:31; 18:159
Seymour, Charles 8:31; 18:159; 25:288
Seymour, E. 1:77; 14:215
Seymour, Edward S. 17:16
Seymour, Elijah 20:116
Seymour, Ezra A. 17:454; 24:186
Seymour, F. 3:173; 19:306
Seymour, F. P. 19:242
Seymour, Franklin B. 24:44
Seymour, Fred 9:192
Seymour, G. 22:491
Seymour, G. W. 21:112
Seymour, Garrett 22:218
Seymour, George 22:398
Seymour, George B. 15:44
Seymour, H. 3:173

Seymour, J. H. 1:76
Seymour, James 22:318
Seymour, Jerome B.
20:109
Seymour, John 6:28;
20:116
Seymour, John L. 9:192;
19:246
Seymour, Joseph 13:46;
14:215
Seymour, L. 12:123;
15:134
Seymour, M. J. 15:345;
16:379
Seymour, Mortimer H.
21:105
Seymour, P. 25:230
Seymour, Robert 13:46;
16:54
Seymour, S. 14:107
Seymour, Starks 10:78
Seymour, Stephen 25:69
Seymour, Thomas 27:148
Seymour, William 9:211;
20:100
Seymour, William C.
19:98
Seymour, William F.
23:16
Seymour, William H.
15:225
Seymour, William S.
18:469
Seymours, Amos W.
22:100
Sh---, Moses 9:215
Sh---, William 27:107
Sha---, --- 22:53
Shabino, Joseph 25:284
Shack, J. R. 12:158
Shack, L. 14:107
Shackelford, S. 3:173
Shackels, John 16:226
Shacker, J. 11:270
Shackett, Ferdinand 24:44
Shackhouse, V. F. 5:29
Shackleford, Charles
23:101
Shackleford, Eugene L.
17:72
Shackleford, W. 15:88
Shackles, --- 20:181
Shackley, Charles 6:19;
18:93
Shackley, Elias J. 11:404
Shad, Ambrose 9:106
Shad, Richard 25:230
Shad, W. D. 25:70
Shadbott, D. 17:100
Shaddaker, Christopher
23:195

Shadden, John 20:344
Shadden, Kelly 9:224
Shadden, Septimus 22:168
Shaddock, Alvin 14:215
Shaddock, C. 18:17
Shaddoick, L. H. 25:230
Shaddon, John 10:78
Shade, Daniel 24:29
Shade, Isaac 17:86
Shade, J. 1:171
Shade, Joseph 20:109
Shade, Philip 6:26
Shadem, Kelly 18:375
Shades, James D. 14:215
Shades, John I. 17:396
Shadinger, W. J. 27:107
Shadley, Franklin 11:77
Shadmann, W. 20:149
Shadow, John 13:46
Shadowens, Thomas W. F.
17:58
Shadrach, Joseph 6:19
Shadrach, P. G. 23:264
Shadrack, Joseph 18:93
Shadrock, Edward 16:11
Shadwick, J. 1:173
Shadwick, L. M. 18:458
Shae, G. W. 3:173
Shae, Patrick 3:173
Shaefer, Joseph 21:125
Shaeffer, Christian 10:134
Shafer, --- 11:323
Shafer, A. 14:107
Shafer, A. D. 15:225
Shafer, Benjamin 24:162
Shafer, Charles 13:46;
15:264
Shafer, Cornelius 25:230
Shafer, Daniel 3:173;
22:439
Shafer, David 25:230
Shafer, Ernst 18:375
Shafer, Frank 21:40
Shafer, G. 11:121
Shafer, G. P. 26:61
Shafer, George 23:110
Shafer, George L. 22:100
Shafer, George W. 23:93
Shafer, H. S. 11:312
Shafer, Henry 4:52;
25:230
Shafer, J. 1:175, 176;
14:107
Shafer, J. B. 13:98
Shafer, J. V. 14:21
Shafer, Jacob B. 10:25
Shafer, Jessee N. 20:134
Shafer, John 9:90; 22:100
Shafer, John A. 8:94
Shafer, John F. 18:297;
26:112

Shafer, John P. 9:39
Shafer, L. E. 21:40
Shafer, Noah 10:78
Shafer, Noble 24:84
Shafer, P. 14:107; 27:148
Shafer, S. 3:173
Shafer, Samuel 11:44
Shafer, Samuel M.
18:297; 26:113
Shafer, Stephen 14:215
Shafer, Thomas 21:199
Shafer, Thomas J. 21:40
Shafer, W. 3:173; 13:98;
14:21
Shafer, William 10:78;
19:222; 22:440
Shafer, William F. 9:192
Shafer, William H. 20:19
Shaferberger, --- 17:16
Shaferty, J. 16:226
Shafeur, Benjamin F.
22:163
Shaff, William 11:112;
12:39
Shaffe, William 15:134
Shaffel, Peter 21:387
Shaffer, --- 15:44, 259
Shaffer, A. M. 27:107
Shaffer, Adam 21:234
Shaffer, Alexander 23:287
Shaffer, Alfred 21:239
Shaffer, Benjamin F.
23:257
Shaffer, Burke D. 20:184
Shaffer, C. 9:113; 14:131
Shaffer, Caleb H. 27:107
Shaffer, Ch. 21:40
Shaffer, Charles 4:52;
11:173
Shaffer, Christian 16:54
Shaffer, Cyrus 22:114
Shaffer, D. 1:176
Shaffer, Daniel 14:215
Shaffer, Eli 15:26
Shaffer, Elias 11:169
Shaffer, Emary 12:39
Shaffer, Enos 10:135;
20:344
Shaffer, Ephraim 23:93
Shaffer, Frank 16:134
Shaffer, Frederick L.
22:284
Shaffer, G. 14:131
Shaffer, George 11:416;
16:101
Shaffer, George A. 22:284
Shaffer, George H. 13:118
Shaffer, George S. 12:57
Shaffer, George U. 13:118
Shaffer, George W.
17:145

Shaffer, H. 3:173; 14:259; 22:218
Shaffer, H. F. 12:164; 26:181
Shaffer, I. 3:173
Shaffer, Israel 10:175
Shaffer, J. 1:174; 3:173
Shaffer, J. P. 1:172
Shaffer, J. S. 21:40
Shaffer, Jacob 17:67; 18:210
Shaffer, James 17:426
Shaffer, Jewitt 25:73
Shaffer, John 4:52; 12:39; 17:86; 21:59; 25:69
Shaffer, John M. 20:128
Shaffer, John V. F. 22:412
Shaffer, John W. 10:78; 20:344
Shaffer, Joseph 7:40; 11:425; 21:143
Shaffer, Josiah 11:171
Shaffer, L. A. 1:70
Shaffer, Levi H. 20:19, 184
Shaffer, Levi N. 20:134
Shaffer, Lewis 13:46
Shaffer, M. 3:173
Shaffer, Morris R. 23:101
Shaffer, N. 22:218
Shaffer, Noah 20:344
Shaffer, Peter 3:173; 10:135; 20:344
Shaffer, Philip 11:77; 23:166
Shaffer, R. N. 4:52
Shaffer, Russell B. 24:55
Shaffer, S. 23:205
Shaffer, Samuel M. 9:39
Shaffer, Sebastian 1:71
Shaffer, T. G. 11:78
Shaffer, Terham 17:347
Shaffer, Theodore 1:70
Shaffer, Valentine 21:89
Shaffer, W. 15:225; 22:268
Shaffer, William 13:118; 16:153; 19:192; 20:344; 23:78; 25:230
Shaffer, William J. 25:273
Shafferd, James S. 22:218
Shaffin, Michael 12:10
Shafflin, James 18:159
Shaffner, J. 1:78, 176; 21:125
Shafford, Louis 14:216
Shafford, T. 14:107
Shafford, William H. 11:169
Shaffstall, M. 22:218

Shafler, C. 1:74
Shafner, Albert B. 10:78; 20:344
Shafner, John 17:26
Shafner, Joseph 18:270
Shafstall, Henry 17:410
Shafter, Albert 25:326
Shafter, Frank 22:168
Shaftnetzel, Charles 26:130
Shaggath, John 11:392
Shaggs, I. P. 3:224
Shagle, Ephraim S. 20:27
Shagwagger, A. 9:17
Shah, John 18:252; 26:62
Shahan, John 14:216
Shahan, W. 21:168
Shaiffer, August 12:158
Shailer, William A. 23:205
Shain, Ambrose 23:101
Shairer, Daniel 11:77
Shairs, Edwin 24:172
Shaits, Benjamin 11:313
Shake, William J. 22:457
Shakelden, William 19:33
Shakely, Solomon N. 19:98
Shakeshaft, George 10:22
Shakles, L. 23:166
Shalenbarger, --- 20:156
Shales, Daniel S. 7:40
Shales, William H. 14:107
Shaley, Amos 14:216
Shaling, Jacob 18:297; 26:112
Shalk, John 15:3
Shall, --- 12:100
Shall, John 14:237; 25:230
Shaller, --- 25:67
Shaller, John 13:46
Shalley, Paul 22:237
Shalling, Jacob 9:39
Shallow, J. 27:107
Shallow, Joseph 9:125
Shallu, Pernam 15:363
Shalmadine, John 20:59
Shalmon, John A. 24:55
Shaltell, John 19:192
Shalter, R. 1:176
Shaltwod, David 8:115
Shaltz, F. 14:21
Sham, William A. 12:170
Sham, William E. 12:170
Shamahan, T. 9:59
Shamaway, J. W. 16:270
Shambacker, George W. 16:54
Shambaugh, Charles 22:491

Shambaugh, Edward 23:200
Shamberry, James 9:136
Shambers, W. 14:303; 17:469; 27:116
Shambler, C. W. 11:425
Shamblin, A. 11:314
Shambs, Joseph 24:108
Shambury, James 27:112
Shamer, W. E. 10:135; 20:344
Shamlstick, Charles 5:29
Shamlur, Frank 11:213
Shammack, J. 3:173
Shamon, A. 14:107
Shamon, D. R. 7:109
Shamon, F. 5:54
Shamon, John 6:10
Shamon, S. A. 10:207
Shamp, Aaron 26:129
Shampine, P. 7:69
Shampoor, Samuel 9:90
Shamrock, Page 22:319
Shan, A. 15:226
Shan, F. F. 3:173
Shan, F. G. 23:293
Shan, Morris 18:114
Shana, Hugh 15:336; 19:98
Shanahan, --- 12:83
Shanahan, A. 16:304
Shanahan, Daniel 19:192
Shanahan, Edward 22:237
Shanahan, John 15:226
Shanahan, M. 7:40
Shanahan, Thomas 16:141
Shanahan, W. 3:173
Shanahon, Patrick 19:288
Shanberger, William 15:353
Shancel, George 23:110
Shand, C. 1:169
Shand, John W. 11:44
Shandvin, J. C. 24:89
Shane, Charles N. 10:135; 20:344
Shane, Cornelius 10:135; 20:344
Shane, G. W. 21:125
Shane, James 22:490
Shane, James E. 22:130
Shane, John 14:216
Shane, Joseph 14:216
Shane, L. 14:29
Shane, O. M. 20:149
Shane, Richard M. 23:101
Shane, Stanley 22:490
Shane, W. J. 17:250
Shanen, John 15:226
Shaner, A. Q. 9:160
Shaner, C. 1:74

Shaner, Francis A. 22:130
Shaner, H. S. 24:84
Shaner, John 1:77; 11:44
Shanes, Joseph 14:216
Shaney, Patrick 15:226
Shang, D. 3:178
Shanger, Lewis 1:74
Shango, Hango 18:414
Shangs, William 7:109
Shanibin, Isiah 15:226
Shanir, Findley M. 22:237
Shank, A. 1:77; 3:173
Shank, Amos 4:52
Shank, Charles W. 19:98
Shank, David 26:129
Shank, Isaac 17:422;
    24:168
Shank, J. 15:153
Shank, J. D. 5:29
Shank, J. H. 14:317, 322
Shank, James 19:192;
    22:440
Shank, James H. 23:166
Shank, John 7:40; 11:98;
    25:304
Shank, John A. B. 23:101
Shank, Joseph W. 17:86
Shank, Martin 21:234
Shank, William 14:216
Shankamer, W. 1:169
Shanke, Louis W. 20:138
Shankle, Isaac 23:166
Shankley, John 14:107
Shanklin, David 17:503
Shanklin, Flem 17:185
Shanklin, J. 13:98; 14:21
Shanks, Asbury M.
    22:268
Shanks, Christian 20:13
Shanks, Daniel 11:416
Shanks, David 9:45
Shanks, Elbert F. 22:268
Shanks, Elzy B. 20:128
Shanks, G. 11:169
Shanks, Henry 19:98
Shanks, J. D. 25:230
Shanks, James W. 22:411
Shanks, John 8:55
Shanks, Joseph 22:268
Shanks, Peter 10:78;
    20:344
Shanks, Philo 20:344
Shanks, Richard 17:388
Shanks, Robert 11:97
Shanks, S. 14:107
Shanks, William 1:78
Shanks, William S. 3:173
Shanley, Barney 23:125
Shanley, Henry 22:319
Shanley, James 7:53
Shanlon, William 7:72

Shanly, John 10:167
Shann, --- 12:97; 15:361
Shann, Fred 13:118
Shannahan, Dan 10:145
Shannahar, P. 1:173
Shanner, A. M. 21:40
Shanner, Jacob 5:29
Shanner, S. P. 12:60
Shannessy, James 24:29
Shannessy, John 4:52
Shannessy, Michael
    12:97; 15:361
Shannesy, Mike 19:98
Shannon, Alex 4:52
Shannon, Andrew 11:271
Shannon, Barney 4:52
Shannon, Charles 3:173;
    15:226
Shannon, Claton 5:29
Shannon, D. R. 21:387
Shannon, Daniel H. 23:93
Shannon, E. 3:173
Shannon, F. 25:230
Shannon, Frank 22:319
Shannon, George 20:100
Shannon, George E 4:52
Shannon, George S.
    22:218
Shannon, H. 15:74
Shannon, H. N. 1:75
Shannon, Henderson
    12:76
Shannon, Henry 4:52
Shannon, Isaac 10:78;
    25:231
Shannon, J. 18:114
Shannon, J. H. 1:74
Shannon, J. S. 11:282
Shannon, Jacob 22:218
Shannon, James 15:59;
    21:205; 22:100
Shannon, James B. 10:78
Shannon, James M. 9:90;
    26:59
Shannon, John 3:173;
    4:52; 17:138; 24:203
Shannon, John H. 10:10
Shannon, John J. 8:95
Shannon, John S. 1:73
Shannon, N. F. 27:109
Shannon, P. 16:379
Shannon, Patrick 19:330
Shannon, Peter 27:148
Shannon, R. G. 18:57
Shannon, Robert 22:218
Shannon, Samuel 23:166;
    26:65
Shannon, Thomas 22:467;
    23:244
Shannon, W. F. 9:150
Shannon, W. H. 26:181

Shannon, Wiley 22:319
Shannon, William 4:52;
    8:95; 9:136; 11:98;
    23:166
Shannon, William B.
    21:239; 23:166
Shannon, William C.
    27:106
Shannonhouse, J. 25:231
Shanny, Patrick N. 4:52
Shanon, Franklin 5:28
Shanon, I. B. 20:344
Shanon, Isaac 20:344
Shanon, W. I. 23:49
Shanon, William 11:417
Shanpoo, Joseph 27:115
Shanran, William 27:112
Shansbaugh, F. 14:290
Shanton, F. 17:293
Shantz, George I. 23:166
Shanver, Jacob 26:182
Shape, F. 3:173
Shapley, Roderic 22:218
Shaplin, Jacob 19:33
Shappard, J. 13:98
Shappe, George P. 21:245
Shappy, Louis 24:97
Sharaletter, Nicholas 8:95
Sharda, August F. 22:284
Shardrach, G. H. 3:173
Share, Organ 9:45
Shared, Nelson 21:284
Sharer, C. M. G. 10:151
Sharer, H. 20:344
Sharer, John F. 25:73
Sharer, Owen D. 19:192
Sharer, William 18:93
Sharers, Mathew 27:111
Shares, William M. 7:17
Sharfaphy, John 26:65
Sharits, J. W. 22:268
Shark, --- 16:226
Shark, Andrew 13:118
Shark, D. M. 1:175
Shark, J. 18:252; 26:63
Shark, James 3:173;
    10:167
Shark, William B. 8:95
Shark, William J. 25:231
Sharke, George 22:410
Sharkey, A. 1:77
Sharkey, James 14:216
Sharkey, Michael 19:330
Sharkey, Moses 21:213
Sharkey, P. 1:170
Sharkey, Patrick 19:192
Sharkey, S. 24:29
Sharkley, William D.
    20:43
Sharks, J. W. 3:173
Sharle, Thomas 20:344

Sharley, J. 1:100
Sharlow, Joseph 27:114
Sharlow, Peter 7:109
Sharocross, Briston 11:18
Sharp, --- 15:300
Sharp, A. 3:173; 12:164; 20:344
Sharp, A. N. 25:231
Sharp, A. W. 14:107
Sharp, Aaron 9:45
Sharp, Abner 9:99
Sharp, Abram 10:78
Sharp, Alexander 25:286
Sharp, Almyron L. 22:154
Sharp, Andrew 22:318
Sharp, Basil 19:48
Sharp, Benjamin 17:42, 499
Sharp, Benjamin F. 21:234
Sharp, Calvin 9:59
Sharp, Charles 7:109; 9:136; 22:318; 23:78; 27:112
Sharp, Charles N. 13:46
Sharp, Cyrus 11:392
Sharp, D. H. 12:123
Sharp, Daniel 15:44
Sharp, Daniel C. 10:78
Sharp, Daniel H. 15:134
Sharp, E. A. E. 22:130
Sharp, E. D. T. 3:173
Sharp, E. W. 13:80
Sharp, Edward 22:100
Sharp, Egbert 21:387
Sharp, Elijah 22:319
Sharp, Elmer 6:23
Sharp, Elmere 18:93
Sharp, F. 18:114
Sharp, Franklin 17:93
Sharp, G. 7:40
Sharp, G. M. 23:185
Sharp, G. O. 1:174
Sharp, George 13:118
Sharp, George B. 22:439
Sharp, George E. 9:28; 18:315; 26:112
Sharp, George W. 16:54; 20:27, 138
Sharp, H. 14:107
Sharp, H. A. 14:216
Sharp, H. J. 21:112
Sharp, Harden 10:167
Sharp, Henry 9:28; 12:60; 18:315; 22:101; 26:112
Sharp, Henry R. 23:110
Sharp, Hugh A. 11:282
Sharp, Isaac 22:100
Sharp, J. 2:17; 12:93; 16:304

Sharp, J. F. 25:231
Sharp, J. L. 14:21; 16:271
Sharp, J. W. 3:173
Sharp, Jack 7:133
Sharp, James 17:138; 22:100; 24:203
Sharp, James S. 11:77
Sharp, Jeremiah F. 15:88
Sharp, John 4:52; 10:175; 11:329; 12:39; 18:252; 19:192; 22:218, 318; 23:101, 291; 25:68; 26:62, 64
Sharp, John B. 4:52
Sharp, John C. 23:78
Sharp, John F. 22:100
Sharp, John M. 23:78
Sharp, John T. 5:29
Sharp, John W. 11:270
Sharp, Joseph 7:69; 18:375
Sharp, Josiah 9:224
Sharp, Judson 9:136; 27:112
Sharp, M. 13:98
Sharp, M. L. 14:271
Sharp, Morris 18:114
Sharp, Moses 21:151
Sharp, Nicholas T. 4:52
Sharp, O. M. 3:173
Sharp, Peter 14:216
Sharp, S. 16:226
Sharp, S. M. 20:344
Sharp, Samuel 10:151, 178
Sharp, Samuel H. 22:53
Sharp, Simeon 22:268
Sharp, Stephen G. 22:101
Sharp, Stinson W. 23:302
Sharp, T. 18:252; 26:62
Sharp, T. C. 19:98
Sharp, T. M. 12:143
Sharp, T. S. 3:173
Sharp, Theodore W. 9:14
Sharp, Thomas 10:78; 20:345
Sharp, W. 1:171; 23:167
Sharp, W. H. 7:109
Sharp, W. S. 17:496
Sharp, Washington 16:54
Sharp, Westley 22:319
Sharp, William 1:74; 12:171; 22:100; 23:78, 182
Sharp, William D. 20:345
Sharp, William F. 11:426
Sharp, William H. 5:29; 13:46; 17:284; 25:231
Sharp, William M. 18:469
Sharp, William W. 27:107

Sharp, Wilson 9:150
Sharpe, D. C. 20:345
Sharpe, Daniel J. 20:345
Sharpe, George 13:58; 16:54
Sharpe, Harden 19:192
Sharpe, J. 11:329
Sharpe, Jesse W. 17:58
Sharpe, John W. 11:289
Sharpe, Joshua 16:54
Sharpe, Josiah 13:58
Sharpe, T. 11:251; 22:154
Sharpe, Thomas 11:255; 20:345
Sharpe, W. 7:40
Sharpe, William 26:63
Sharpe, William A. 22:268
Sharpe, William H. 18:252
Sharpley, George 3:173
Sharpley, Henry 23:49
Sharpley, T. 21:112
Sharpneck, William 22:53
Sharps, Daniel I. 10:78
Sharpstein, Charles 19:192
Sharpstien, C. 9:150
Sharpstien, G. 27:109
Sharpteen, Charles 10:167
Sharpton, Daniel 22:16
Sharpton, Joel 11:19
Sharr, E. A. 10:135
Sharr, George 9:95
Sharrah, Edward 25:231
Sharrow, A. 16:304
Sharrow, J. 12:84
Sharrp, Moses 18:297
Sharruck, Richard 15:226
Sharves, S. H. 14:107
Shary, James 16:379
Shas---, --- 19:192
Shasangs, H. 12:76
Shasdor, T. 7:40
Shaser, G. 11:313
Shasner, Jacob 17:160
Shasteen, Peter 22:218
Shastine, Joseph 8:95
Shastol, William 12:51
Shatatr, W. 14:107
Shatche, H. 21:387
Shater, S. L. 13:126
Shatler, William 14:259
Shatless, David 7:109
Shatt, I. 3:173
Shattee, Henry 9:90
Shattick, D. 14:216
Shattleroe, Eli 4:52
Shattleron, David 8:95
Shatto, Daniel 23:182
Shatto, David 1:73

Shatto, William 14:317;
 23:167
Shattock, J. F. B. 16:226
Shattock, William H.
 10:22
Shatton, J. A. 3:173
Shattoo, William 14:322
Shattrick, B. 8:55
Shatts, John 10:78
Shattuck, A. B. 9:7
Shattuck, Albert 7:40
Shattuck, Arad 19:192
Shattuck, Benjamin F.
 21:79
Shattuck, E. 25:231
Shattuck, H. H. 21:387
Shattuck, Henry K.
 25:231
Shattuck, Ira 1:71
Shattuck, L. W. 13:127
Shattuck, Nathaniel 12:39
Shattuck, R. 15:226
Shattuck, S. 11:313
Shatzford, George 13:46
Shaub, A. 18:57
Shaub, Augustus 17:93
Shaub, F. 3:173
Shaub, Samuel 22:53
Shaube, Max 10:135;
 20:345
Shaue, Asa F. 14:216
Shauefelt, Josiah 22:100
Shaughanassy, M. 25:304
Shaughnasey, J. 12:76
Shaughnasy, --- 15:82
Shaughnesny, T. 14:290
Shaughnessy, George
 23:195
Shaughnessy, J. 3:173
Shaughuassy, Michael
 7:80
Shaulis, Andrew 4:52
Shaull, John 22:344
Shaum, --- 19:98
Shaum, M. 15:361
Shaup, S. H. 12:158
Shautz, I. 3:173
Shave, Martin 16:54
Shaver, A. 25:231
Shaver, Aaron A. 17:97
Shaver, Benjamin F.
 11:392
Shaver, Benjamin W.
 20:194
Shaver, Charles 12:65;
 15:74
Shaver, E. 1:168, 176
Shaver, F. 3:173
Shaver, George W.
 10:135; 20:345
Shaver, Jacob 8:31

Shaver, James 17:317
Shaver, John H. 21:260
Shaver, Levi 23:125
Shaver, Merritt C. 10:22
Shaver, Solomon 9:243
Shaver, William 16:54
Shaverly, A. 9:31
Shavers, Mathew 9:136
Shavoness, T. 14:107
Shavry, A. J. 12:39
Shaw, --- 16:226; 17:509
Shaw, A. 10:180; 11:271;
 18:180
Shaw, A. A. 11:391
Shaw, Abner A. 20:345
Shaw, Adam 16:101
Shaw, Albert 22:439
Shaw, Albert A. 17:426
Shaw, Alexander 3:173
Shaw, Andrew 1:70;
 3:174; 22:516
Shaw, Andrew J. 11:171
Shaw, Antonie 20:345
Shaw, Arthur G. 16:226
Shaw, Augustus 9:113
Shaw, Austin 10:78
Shaw, B. 12:158
Shaw, Benjamin 12:39
Shaw, Bernard 27:107
Shaw, Binri 24:180
Shaw, C. 19:242
Shaw, C. A. 20:345
Shaw, C. C. 26:130
Shaw, C. L. 3:174
Shaw, Caleb 5:45
Shaw, Camerson 5:45
Shaw, Charles 9:192;
 24:84
Shaw, Charles E. 15:324
Shaw, Charles F. 19:98
Shaw, Charles W. 8:31;
 18:159; 26:184
Shaw, D. 15:259; 19:193
Shaw, D. M. 17:204
Shaw, Daniel W. 7:84;
 21:387
Shaw, David 21:284
Shaw, E. A. 15:167
Shaw, E. H. 1:171
Shaw, Edward P. 9:28;
 18:315; 26:111
Shaw, Enoch 14:216
Shaw, Eugene 7:109;
 21:387
Shaw, F. A. 5:28; 20:44;
 25:231
Shaw, F. N. 3:174
Shaw, Forrester H. 11:117
Shaw, George 15:226;
 25:280; 26:60
Shaw, George B. 24:29

Shaw, George E. 10:22
Shaw, George W. 3:174;
 4:52; 7:53; 10:175;
 19:193; 21:59
Shaw, H. 1:168; 11:78;
 17:290
Shaw, H. G. O. 22:344
Shaw, Harvey 13:118
Shaw, Henry 7:133; 8:95,
 120; 17:67; 22:130;
 25:231
Shaw, Henry D. 23:78
Shaw, Horace 4:52
Shaw, Hugh 16:54
Shaw, I. 15:226
Shaw, I. V. 23:49
Shaw, Isaac 8:95; 9:136;
 27:112
Shaw, J. 1:70, 176; 3:173;
 14:216, 337; 19:193
Shaw, J. A. 16:226
Shaw, J. C. 23:185
Shaw, J. F. 1:75
Shaw, J. H. 9:154
Shaw, J. H. D. 9:156
Shaw, J. J. 8:67
Shaw, J. M. 25:231
Shaw, J. P. 11:392
Shaw, Jackson M. C.
 11:416
Shaw, James 10:78;
 11:271; 12:158;
 13:46; 14:216; 16:55,
 226; 17:100; 20:345;
 21:387
Shaw, James A. 12:76;
 17:86
Shaw, James F. 23:243
Shaw, James P. 11:271
Shaw, James W. 24:29
Shaw, Joe D. 14:131
Shaw, John 1:70, 73, 76;
 9:150; 11:121, 426;
 14:259; 18:38;
 21:112; 22:130;
 27:108
Shaw, John A. 19:33;
 22:100
Shaw, John J. 17:207
Shaw, John M. 5:28
Shaw, John W. 1:74; 5:28;
 18:401
Shaw, Joseph 3:174;
 13:118
Shaw, Joseph C. 5:28
Shaw, Joseph E. 10:22
Shaw, Joseph H. 23:79
Shaw, Joshua 7:40
Shaw, Jotham 17:448
Shaw, Jothan 24:173
Shaw, Julius C. 8:125

Shaw, L. D. 26:182
Shaw, L. H. 23:185
Shaw, Levi 18:252; 26:63
Shaw, Louis 20:59
Shaw, M. 1:172; 3:174
Shaw, Marcus 12:39
Shaw, Marvin E. 13:46
Shaw, Mathew 11:130
Shaw, Milford N. 7:109
Shaw, Milton 7:53
Shaw, Milton N. 21:387
Shaw, Moses 14:216; 17:26
Shaw, N. W. 13:118
Shaw, O. 1:171
Shaw, Oliver 21:40
Shaw, Organ 26:129
Shaw, Perry 21:387
Shaw, Peter 7:133; 21:387
Shaw, R. E. 1:77
Shaw, R. W. 18:252; 26:63
Shaw, Richard 11:77
Shaw, Richard B. 17:158
Shaw, Robert 5:28; 12:57; 14:216
Shaw, Ross W. 22:53
Shaw, S. 9:150; 18:57; 27:108
Shaw, S. H. 15:153
Shaw, S. N. 9:99
Shaw, Samuel 7:133; 9:192; 19:230
Shaw, Stephen 19:33
Shaw, T. 1:175
Shaw, T. J. 3:174
Shaw, T. W. 19:33
Shaw, Theo. W. 20:345
Shaw, Theodore W. 10:78
Shaw, Thomas 1:77; 15:134; 23:110; 27:107
Shaw, Thomas F. 11:295
Shaw, W. 1:174; 3:173, 174
Shaw, W. B. 22:492
Shaw, W. N. 1:174
Shaw, W. R. 3:174
Shaw, W. W. 3:174
Shaw, William 7:40; 9:104, 202; 12:39; 16:282; 17:97, 250; 19:284; 21:168; 22:319; 23:93; 24:29; 27:106, 149
Shaw, William B. 4:52; 12:76; 15:12
Shaw, William C. 17:471; 27:117
Shaw, William E. 8:55
Shaw, William F. 21:143

Shaw, William H. 12:39
Shaw, Zemry 11:271
Shaw, Zinsi 17:426
Shawalter, Edward 9:125
Shawalter, Edward R. 27:114
Shawandt, Auguste 21:387
Shawback, Edward 3:174
Shawen, Madison 22:268
Shawers, J. 21:40
Shawgr, John 16:226
Shawis, Samuel 18:285
Shawl, Newell B. 10:135; 20:345
Shawley, David 4:52
Shawley, J. 1:172
Shawley, James 14:259
Shawley, Lewis P. 10:78
Shawp, Moses 26:112
Shawpan, J. 2:18
Shaws, H. 15:226
Shawsen, D. 9:45
Shawson, Andrew 11:406
Shawson, James 10:135
Shawton, A. B. 27:115
Shawver, Reuben 23:166
Shay, A. H. 3:174
Shay, B. 15:167
Shay, D. 3:174
Shay, Daniel 1:71
Shay, Daniel R. 13:46
Shay, Ebenezer B. 22:155
Shay, G. W. 14:216
Shay, George 19:98
Shay, Henry 17:347
Shay, I. 3:174
Shay, I. D. 16:282
Shay, Isaac 12:56
Shay, J. 14:216; 19:246
Shay, J. D. 15:353
Shay, James 17:58
Shay, John 3:174; 22:237, 498
Shay, John A. 10:22; 15:319; 19:98
Shay, Martin 11:76; 22:521
Shay, Michael 15:45
Shay, P. D. 15:353; 16:282
Shay, Richard 22:344
Shay, T. 21:40
Shay, Thomas 15:226; 25:287; 27:118
Shay, Timothy 10:135; 20:345
Shayer, James E. 21:387
Shayer, Lester 21:218
Shayres, George 15:226
Shays, George E. 24:29

Shcorer, J. 18:71
She, P. 9:150
Shea, A. B. 1:170
Shea, D. 1:170
Shea, Daniel 25:312
Shea, Daniel O. 10:78; 20:345
Shea, Dennis 9:192; 19:261
Shea, E. 1:169
Shea, H. 14:107
Shea, James M. 16:123
Shea, John 3:174; 9:90, 192; 10:207; 13:46; 21:11; 26:61
Shea, John O. 19:261
Shea, M. 11:251
Shea, Martin 25:231
Shea, Michael 25:231
Shea, P. 27:109
Shea, Patrick 4:53; 23:304
Shea, Patrick J. 27:148
Shea, Robert 16:304
Shea, Samuel B. 16:79
Shea, T. 1:168
Shea, Thomas 13:46; 22:130, 355
Shea, Thomas E. 8:120; 19:340
Shea, W. 16:101
Shea, William H. 20:59
Sheaborn, Elisha 22:16
Sheadle, W. J. 25:231
Sheafer, Daniel 21:125
Sheafer, Francis M. 23:241
Sheaham, H. H. 18:280
Shealer, George 14:216
Sheals, J. 15:112
Sheals, William B. 11:250
Shean, Timothy 13:46
Shean, William 25:231
Shear, A. L. 24:171
Shear, C. 1:76
Shear, E. A. 14:216
Shear, George B. 4:53
Sheara, William 22:101
Sheard, Eli 18:57
Shearer, Andrew 8:55
Shearer, Azor 15:112
Shearer, B. 11:86
Shearer, Frederick 22:101
Shearer, G. W. 7:109; 21:59
Shearer, George 17:393
Shearer, George M. 11:86
Shearer, Henry 15:226
Shearer, Henry H. 11:87
Shearer, J. M. 11:97
Shearer, James 11:392
Shearer, John 11:45

Shearer, Jonathan E. 23:288
Shearer, Joseph 11:17
Shearer, Peter 6:33
Shearer, Simeon 22:114
Shearer, Thomas 23:277
Shearon, John 19:319
Shears, Allen 5:45
Shears, G. M. 9:59
Shears, George A. 22:53
Shears, J. S. 3:174
Shears, John M. 11:76
Shears, Minard C. 11:314
Shears, S. W. 15:226
Sheator, F. 17:497
Sheats, Andrew J. 24:168
Sheats, William B. 11:331
Sheaven, --- 18:194
Sheaver, Benjamin 14:216
Sheaver, D. 1:176
Sheaver, David 13:46
Sheaver, John George 21:112
Sheble, John 13:118
Shebo, Joseph 27:115
Sheck, F. 1:172
Sheckle, William J. 4:53
Sheckler, Daniel 5:29
Shecks, William 10:79
Shectt, Jacob 8:60
Shed, E. 15:323
Shed, Erwin 19:98
Shed, L. 15:59
Shed, Thomas 4:53
Shed, W. H. 19:242
Shedaker, John 12:39
Shedalie, John C. 11:172
Shedd, C. R. 22:163
Shedd, George E. 24:55
Shedd, John 9:192
Shedel, G. A. 4:52
Shedeler, Simeon 11:170
Sheder, Andrew T. 16:55
Shedey, William W. 18:375
Shedle, G. 3:174
Shedrick, John 22:268
Shedron, Henry M. 22:498
Shedron, P. 15:74
Shedron, Peter 12:76
Sheean, Cornelius 7:53
Sheean, Michael 21:89
Sheean, William 1:73
Sheeds, William H. 10:135
Sheefer, Jacob 10:135; 20:345
Sheehan, Daniel 21:387; 22:101, 521
Sheehan, E. 1:77

Sheehan, Genett 4:53
Sheehan, John 1:73; 14:216; 23:125
Sheehan, M. 12:97
Sheehan, Timothy 19:193
Sheehand, Louis K. 22:219
Sheehay, John 18:159
Sheehey, John 8:31
Sheehy, William 11:416
Sheeks, William 20:345
Sheelenberger, S. 14:216
Sheeler, A. 1:74
Sheeley, Frank 9:211
Sheeley, Henry C. 18:210
Sheeley, Joseph 22:219
Sheelket, --- 18:223
Sheen, --- 11:282
Sheen, John 14:216; 19:98
Sheen, Patrick 21:105
Sheenan, Dennis J. 21:387
Sheendoller, H. 1:72
Sheene, James R. 4:53
Sheepan, Joseph 16:55
Sheer, George 11:117
Sheeran, A. 1:174
Sheerber, R. 13:46
Sheerer, James S. 24:44
Sheerer, John A. 20:138
Sheerer, Joseph 13:46
Sheerer, Paul A. 22:498
Sheet, Hiram 9:163
Sheeter, C. H. 14:107
Sheets, A. 21:40
Sheets, Christian 13:68; 19:98
Sheets, E. 3:174; 13:98
Sheets, Foster C. 19:98
Sheets, Fred 16:141
Sheets, H. P. 22:355
Sheets, I. 17:433
Sheets, Israel 24:162
Sheets, J. M. 11:250
Sheets, J. W. 23:167
Sheets, John 11:169; 17:201; 21:184
Sheets, John A. 22:219
Sheets, John C. 22:411
Sheets, John J. 22:268
Sheets, John S. 16:115
Sheets, Joseph 10:135; 20:345
Sheets, Oscar 17:185
Sheets, P. 16:101
Sheets, R. 21:163
Sheets, S. 8:75; 26:181
Sheets, T. E. 16:148
Sheets, Thomas 15:134
Sheets, W. 3:174
Sheets, William 25:270
Sheevers, W. 1:173

Sheey, John 21:40
Sheeyn, H. 16:160
Shefelt, Louis 14:216
Sheff, M. 20:345
Sheffee, Jerome 7:109
Sheffee, Joseph 7:109
Sheffer, D. H. 11:221
Sheffer, George 25:73
Sheffer, Henry F. 20:345
Sheffer, Israel 19:193
Sheffer, J. B. 15:259
Sheffer, James M. 21:79
Sheffer, John F. 15:18
Sheffer, Loyd 17:308
Sheffer, Peter 17:250
Sheffield, Albert P. 23:195
Sheffield, G. R. 1:72
Sheffield, George T. 23:241
Sheffield, I. S. 18:210
Sheffield, J. 14:107; 25:231
Sheffield, John 10:79; 20:345
Sheffield, John W. 22:268
Sheffield, Siamon 13:118
Sheffield, W. H. 25:69
Sheffield, William 13:118
Sheffler, Daniel 6:23
Sheffler, W. 3:174
Shefflet, Hillory 11:168
Shefford, S. 14:107
Sheffrey, John 21:218
Shefler, Henry H. 10:135
Sheflin, Frederick 14:216
Shegle, Jacob 15:226
Shehan, James 3:174
Shehan, John 16:136
Shehan, N. 23:118
Shehe, Michael 8:95
Shehoney, D. 11:251
Sheiat, Henry 6:23
Sheider, John 11:89
Sheihan, C. 21:164
Sheik, Jacob 16:114
Sheil, Orlando 1:72
Sheilds, A. H. 9:59
Sheilds, Francis 10:9
Sheilds, J. M. 7:133
Sheilds, John 10:22
Sheilds, John D. 7:133
Sheilds, Nero 7:133
Sheilds, Philip 12:39
Sheilds, Robert 11:212
Sheilds, Silas 14:290; 23:115
Sheiter, Edward 5:29
Sheithaner, N. 1:75
Shekel, W. 7:40
Shel, Albert 16:304

Shelan, Luther 8:75
Shelba, Charles 16:379
Shelbe, Nicholas 1:75
Shelbern, Hans J. 18:375
Shelberry, Perry E. 16:55
Shelborn, Curtis P. 9:90; 26:61
Shelburne, Hans J. 9:224
Shelburne, J. 14:259
Shelby, Anderson 8:42; 26:180
Shelby, Asa W. 4:53
Shelby, Belle 9:70
Shelby, Frederick 18:159
Shelby, Henry 11:213
Shelby, J. 21:191
Shelby, James M. 22:53
Shelby, Jesse 7:133
Shelby, John 11:313
Shelby, John W. 4:53; 21:79
Shelby, Joseph 15:74
Shelby, P. 21:151
Shelby, Samuel 21:40
Shelby, Thomas 8:31; 18:159; 26:182
Shelby, William 21:196
Shelchwell, Leroy P. 19:33
Sheld, Charles 4:52
Shelden, John 19:99
Shelden, Remer 12:158
Sheldon, --- 9:163
Sheldon, A. G. 24:84
Sheldon, Austin 15:112
Sheldon, Benjamin F. 9:150; 27:110
Sheldon, C. 1:77, 173
Sheldon, C. S. 1:170
Sheldon, Charles 7:109
Sheldon, D. 1:174
Sheldon, Daniel 18:464
Sheldon, Erwin A. 11:289
Sheldon, Francis 12:39
Sheldon, G. 13:118; 15:353; 16:282
Sheldon, G. W. 16:149
Sheldon, George J. 20:116
Sheldon, H. 3:174; 14:107
Sheldon, H. S. 3:174
Sheldon, H. W. 18:427
Sheldon, Henry 10:167; 18:341; 19:193
Sheldon, Horace F. 23:49
Sheldon, James 8:31; 18:159
Sheldon, John 4:53; 9:90; 12:39; 19:99; 26:58
Sheldon, Joseph D. 15:226
Sheldon, Lyman 1:73

Sheldon, M. 3:174; 24:84
Sheldon, Miles C. 24:174
Sheldon, O. 13:98
Sheldon, Orlando 22:155
Sheldon, Robert 26:59
Sheldon, S. 19:261
Sheldon, Samuel 9:192
Sheldon, T. 2:17; 19:261; 25:67
Sheldon, Thomas 9:28, 192; 18:315; 22:101; 26:112
Sheldon, W. 3:174
Sheldon, William 22:168, 219
Sheldon, William S. 19:33
Sheldon, Y. 3:174; 14:216
Sheler, Henry 18:93
Shelf, A. J. 12:143
Shelfer, Jacob 5:29
Sheling, G. W. 18:57
Shelker, E. 16:304
Shell, A. E. 19:99
Shell, A. J. 20:345
Shell, Alexander 11:111
Shell, Andrew D. 22:219
Shell, Charles 4:53
Shell, David 15:74
Shell, George 19:193
Shell, Henry 24:44
Shell, J. 11:129; 23:268
Shell, J. S. 15:88
Shell, James L. 11:320
Shell, John 10:79; 20:345; 27:116
Shell, John W. 20:116
Shell, L. 24:44
Shell, Simon 22:219
Shell, W. 13:98; 25:231
Shell, William 3:174; 13:58; 21:387
Shell, William A. 22:268
Shellay, Thomas 18:159
Shellcott, J. 18:252; 26:63
Shelledy, Carson 22:412
Shellenberger, August 21:93
Shellenberger, Samuel 12:39
Sheller, Jacob 14:237
Sheller, John J. 5:29
Shelley, A. E. 25:73
Shelley, C. G. 13:118
Shelley, E. J. 27:106
Shelley, J. 11:168; 22:355
Shelley, John 11:168
Shelley, N. 1:76
Shelley, Oliver 11:76
Shelley, Phineas 23:79
Shelley, William C. 22:268

Shellhammer, Abram 24:29
Shellhon, John 15:74
Shellhorn, Gustav 18:114
Shellhorn, John 23:167
Shellhouse, Isaac 22:492
Shellhouse, John 11:171
Shelling, Francis 20:103
Shelling, George 19:193
Shelling, Lewis 26:182
Shellingsburg, S. C. 13:98
Shellington, William 11:271
Shellits, R. 3:174
Shellmire, --- 15:134
Shellon, W. 11:429
Shellsworth, Samuel 16:55
Shellum, D. 14:216
Shelly, --- 18:38
Shelly, Abram 19:343
Shelly, Adam 17:185
Shelly, B. 3:174
Shelly, C. 16:226
Shelly, Charles 17:185
Shelly, G. W. 25:231
Shelly, George 14:217
Shelly, Jacob 22:441
Shelly, Jacob N. 23:79
Shelly, James 10:135; 20:345
Shelman, Harrison 22:355
Shelnnel, John S. 11:184
Shelp, William 25:72
Shelshouser, John 27:116
Shelter, Adam 10:79
Shelter, Charles A. 12:60
Shelter, E. 25:231
Shelter, John W. 11:170
Shelter, Mat 11:77
Sheltock, A. 14:107
Shelton, --- 12:88; 16:304
Shelton, Alexander 26:65
Shelton, B. S. 11:188
Shelton, G. M. S. 9:99
Shelton, George 25:304
Shelton, George T. 21:79
Shelton, George W. 11:282
Shelton, H. 8:55; 21:105
Shelton, Henry 9:202; 19:293
Shelton, J. 21:40
Shelton, J. D. M. 22:268
Shelton, J. H. 18:252; 26:62
Shelton, James 8:109; 17:150
Shelton, Joseph 7:109
Shelton, Larkin L. 10:135; 20:345

Shelton, Lewis 7:109
Shelton, M. C. 17:434
Shelton, Madison 21:291
Shelton, R. 14:107
Shelton, Richard S.
    17:428; 24:184
Shelton, Robert 21:284
Shelton, Samuel R. 22:53
Shelton, Stephen F. 20:36
Shelton, Stephen J. 22:53
Shelton, Turner 21:284
Shelton, William 14:107;
    20:187
Shelton, William G.
    22:268
Shelton, William T.
    22:268
Shemaker, P. 3:174
Sheman, Owen 20:345
Shemeld, A. 14:217
Shemele, Nelson 7:40
Shemia, William H.
    18:252
Shemp, John 12:65; 15:45
Shen, Michael 11:44
Shenalt, Dodson 17:185
Shenan, J. H. 2:17
Shenan, Thomas 8:31;
    18:159
Shenblin, Lawson 4:53
Shenden, James 14:107
Shendon, John 12:39
Sheneker, B. 12:93
Sheneler, B. 16:304
Shenenberger, Reuben
    23:49
Shenhouse, Solomon S.
    15:226
Shenid, Wiley 9:136
Shenid, Wyley 27:111
Shenk, A. 15:160
Shenkel, John 14:217
Shenkle, Antone 10:135
Shenkle, Antoni 20:345
Shenkler, B. 14:107
Shenlaub, Christopher
    23:167
Shenneman, Michael
    17:42
Shenor, N. 27:107
Sheny, A. 19:99
Sheobalds, Manuel 6:19
Sheobold, Julius 18:316
Sheos, Allen 25:231
Sheother, G. W. 19:261
Shepard, --- 20:179
Shepard, A. 26:183
Shepard, Allen R. 10:167;
    19:193
Shepard, Anderson 17:47
Shepard, B. C. 23:167

Shepard, Barney 12:158
Shepard, C. 17:296
Shepard, Charles 13:127
Shepard, D. 15:160
Shepard, Daniel 20:184
Shepard, David 12:60
Shepard, E. B. 22:168
Shepard, Edward R.
    22:284
Shepard, George 20:109
Shepard, H. W. 22:218
Shepard, Henry A. 8:118
Shepard, J. H. 3:174
Shepard, J. N. 18:252;
    26:63
Shepard, John 14:107;
    15:15; 20:128; 23:49
Shepard, John D. 24:154
Shepard, John F. 27:116
Shepard, John J. 17:264
Shepard, John T. 14:303;
    17:470
Shepard, John W. 11:382
Shepard, N. 18:180
Shepard, Oliver 18:93
Shepard, Parley 11:112
Shepard, Pleasant 22:101
Shepard, R. C. 26:129
Shepard, Thomas H.
    17:67
Shepard, W. C. 23:167
Shepards, G. 1:176
Shepardson, Charles
    10:167; 19:193
Shepardson, L. 3:174
Shepardson, Mark 15:226
Shepardson, W. 26:60
Sheperd, Aaron 21:168
Sheperdson, George 23:49
Sheperdson, O. H. 19:242
Shepfield, T. 16:226
Shephard, A. 16:226
Shephard, Abraham P.
    23:93
Shephard, Alex 20:345
Shephard, B. 5:29
Shephard, D. G. 27:108
Shephard, David 20:345
Shephard, Eli 15:5
Shephard, Ephraim R.
    10:135
Shephard, G. Y. 16:226
Shephard, George 10:135;
    20:345
Shephard, Henry 22:441
Shephard, Henry H.
    11:282
Shephard, Hezekiah 15:88
Shephard, J. 16:226
Shephard, J. M. 15:167
Shephard, James D. 5:29

Shephard, John A. 23:79
Shephard, John W.
    10:135; 20:345
Shephard, L. H. 17:112
Shephard, Ned 22:319
Shephard, Nelson 12:39
Shephard, Oliver P.
    20:345
Shephard, William
    10:209; 17:42
Shepheard, Robert 8:95
Shepherd, A. 12:164
Shepherd, Abraham
    18:401
Shepherd, Alexander
    10:78
Shepherd, Andr 18:401
Shepherd, Andrew 11:249
Shepherd, B. R. 24:84
Shepherd, Benjamin F.
    10:135; 20:345
Shepherd, Charles 25:286
Shepherd, Charles W.
    14:217
Shepherd, D. 1:174
Shepherd, D. O. 11:416
Shepherd, David 10:79
Shepherd, Ed. M. 11:76
Shepherd, Fielding 17:150
Shepherd, H. D. 9:243
Shepherd, H. W. 23:167
Shepherd, Isah M. 23:79
Shepherd, J. B. 23:167;
    26:226
Shepherd, J. W. 26:130
Shepherd, Jacob 22:218
Shepherd, James 1:73;
    23:93
Shepherd, James M.
    21:234
Shepherd, Jeremiah 16:55
Shepherd, Jesse D. 21:234
Shepherd, John 16:226
Shepherd, John A. 22:53
Shepherd, Mathew 20:345
Shepherd, Matthew 10:79
Shepherd, Morrill 9:204
Shepherd, Oliver P. 10:79
Shepherd, Orin 16:101
Shepherd, Peter 19:273
Shepherd, Richard 9:211
Shepherd, Thomas 11:213
Shepherd, Thomas C. D.
    10:135; 20:345
Shepherd, William 21:125
Shepherdson, Simon 4:53
Shephony, H. 15:45
Sheplee, Isaac 14:107
Shepler, --- 15:363
Shepler, J. P. 23:264
Sheples, --- 19:99

Shepley, C. H. 18:280
Shepley, Elijah 24:44
Shepley, G. T. 19:99
Shepley, George 13:46
Shepley, J. 13:98
Shepley, James B. 8:95
Shepley, James M. 22:398
Shepley, L. C. 14:107
Shepley, N. 22:344
Shepord, Henry 13:118
Shepp, Michael 10:79
Sheppard, --- 22:355
Sheppard, A. 3:174;
    14:107
Sheppard, Alonzo 7:40
Sheppard, B. 4:53
Sheppard, B. H. 25:231
Sheppard, Benjamin
    21:387
Sheppard, C. 3:174;
    25:231
Sheppard, Cyrus N. 22:53
Sheppard, D. 14:107
Sheppard, D. G. 9:150
Sheppard, Daniel 11:111
Sheppard, Dexter E.
    21:387
Sheppard, E. 3:174;
    14:107
Sheppard, Ephraim R.
    20:345
Sheppard, G. W. 21:387
Sheppard, George 10:78;
    18:424
Sheppard, George F.
    13:46
Sheppard, H. 1:175;
    19:193
Sheppard, H. B. 1:169
Sheppard, H. H. 9:90
Sheppard, Henry 9:192;
    19:261
Sheppard, I. 15:226
Sheppard, Isaac 21:249
Sheppard, J. 1:168; 14:21;
    27:106
Sheppard, J. G. 1:169
Sheppard, J. M. 8:75
Sheppard, James 11:271;
    22:411
Sheppard, James B. 7:40
Sheppard, James H.
    20:100
Sheppard, Jared L. 19:193
Sheppard, Jeremiah 13:46
Sheppard, Joel T. 22:268
Sheppard, John 3:174;
    7:40; 23:49
Sheppard, John P. 17:245
Sheppard, Joseph 22:218;
    26:182; 27:107

Sheppard, L. A. 22:268
Sheppard, Lartin T.
    22:268
Sheppard, Louis 25:286
Sheppard, Luther 8:122
Sheppard, M. 1:169
Sheppard, Miles 4:68
Sheppard, N. 9:224;
    18:375
Sheppard, N. K. 17:67
Sheppard, Nathaniel 4:53
Sheppard, Nelson 14:217;
    20:27
Sheppard, Oliver 1:74;
    6:19
Sheppard, Peter 9:193
Sheppard, R. 19:99
Sheppard, Robert 14:107
Sheppard, S. 1:175
Sheppard, S. L. 14:108
Sheppard, Samuel 18:93
Sheppard, Samuel Turner
    9:238
Sheppard, Solomon K.
    20:128
Sheppard, T. 14:108
Sheppard, T. L. 3:174
Sheppard, T. W. 13:98;
    14:21
Sheppard, W. 1:175;
    12:10
Sheppard, W. A. 10:149;
    18:57
Sheppard, W. H. 3:174
Sheppard, William 1:71;
    8:109; 23:79
Sheppard, William C.
    24:162
Sheppard, William Y.
    8:95
Shepperd, H. 21:40
Shepperd, Henry 7:133;
    22:101
Shepperd, I. V. 23:49
Shepperd, J. 22:268;
    24:29
Shepperd, Nelson 7:133
Shepperd, Samuel Turner
    26:226
Shepperd, W. C. 17:420
Sheppey, Frank 27:119
Sheppler, Peter 20:13
Sheppord, John 17:416
Sher---, --- 15:300
Sherad, John M. 21:79
Sherall, Amos 8:67
Sheran, W. 23:205
Sheran, William J. 10:207
Sherban, William 19:338
Sherbert, Gotlieb 3:174
Sherbondy, C. 25:71

Sherbondy, E. 18:252
Sherbondy, Ezra 26:62
Sherbourne, R. 19:99
Sherbrooke, G. G. 24:63
Sherbudd, B. 1:168
Sherburn, R. 15:361
Sherburn, William L.
    9:192; 19:261
Sherburne, R. 12:97
Sherburne, William G.
    22:509
Sherdock, Mathew 7:61
Sherdon, Peter 22:268
Sherend, T. H. 22:268
Sherer, A. 14:131; 15:259
Sherer, George 15:226
Sherer, Henry 1:71
Sherer, John A. 4:53
Sherer, Julius C. 22:457
Sherer, Lyman 15:226
Sheres, W. A. N. 15:28
Sheres, William 12:76
Sherevis, Thomas F.
    15:226
Sherew, C. B. 14:29
Sherey, David 7:63
Sherg, M. H. 7:40
Sherger, Durade 7:41
Sherick, James 8:95
Sherick, John A. 19:33
Sheridan, --- 1:171
Sheridan, A. 9:90
Sheridan, A. M. 9:241
Sheridan, Andrew 13:46
Sheridan, F. 14:217
Sheridan, George W.
    12:39
Sheridan, H. 25:231
Sheridan, Ingersol B.
    18:316
Sheridan, J. 1:175; 3:174
Sheridan, J. B. 26:111
Sheridan, James 11:184;
    16:379; 26:181
Sheridan, Jesse 22:468
Sheridan, John 13:46, 76;
    17:477
Sheridan, Joseph 17:387
Sheridan, Josiah B.
    11:112
Sheridan, Lawrence 10:22
Sheridan, M. 3:174
Sheridan, M. P. 21:387
Sheridan, Mathew 19:193
Sheridan, Pat 16:227
Sheridan, Patrick 8:118;
    11:130; 13:76; 19:33,
    315
Sheridan, Philip 17:393
Sheridan, Richard 11:44;
    16:101

Sheridan, S. 22:319
Sheridan, Thomas 18:159, 280
Sheridan, William 23:115
Sheriden, A. M. 19:316
Sheriden, John 27:118
Sheriff, Edward A. 21:143
Sheriff, J. F. 18:57
Sheriff, William H. 20:13
Sherill, Aram E. 22:412
Sherim, John 20:13
Sherk, Henry 24:108
Sherk, W. M. 7:109
Sherkliff, Simeon 27:116
Sherley, Edward J. 22:101
Sherley, Jasper 8:95
Sherley, John 3:174
Sherley, Nathan 9:70
Sherley, Nichols 8:110
Sherley, W. A. 11:221
Sherlick, N. T. 10:135
Sherlock, Christopher 10:135; 20:345
Sherlock, Lafayette 17:74
Sherlock, N. T. 20:345
Sherlock, Thomas 15:112
Sherly, Robert 24:29
Sherman, --- 11:213; 15:45; 18:17
Sherman, A. 1:169; 11:249
Sherman, A. A. 11:313
Sherman, A. C. 16:227
Sherman, A. F. 21:387
Sherman, A. G. 11:289
Sherman, Abel 8:31; 18:159
Sherman, Alfred 26:226
Sherman, B. 8:31
Sherman, B. B. 14:217
Sherman, B. F. 16:134
Sherman, Benjamin 12:39
Sherman, Benson 21:387
Sherman, C. D. 25:231
Sherman, Caleb D. 5:29
Sherman, Charles 10:135; 18:114; 20:346; 21:387
Sherman, Charles J. 19:33
Sherman, Charles R. 22:344
Sherman, D. P. 1:171
Sherman, Daniel M. 10:79; 20:346
Sherman, David 24:84
Sherman, Dexter A. 20:19
Sherman, E. 14:108
Sherman, E. C. 26:60
Sherman, Edw. 10:135
Sherman, Edward 17:289; 25:72

Sherman, Edward W. 20:346
Sherman, Elisha 13:46
Sherman, F. 3:174; 20:346
Sherman, F. B. 14:1
Sherman, F. I. 10:135
Sherman, Francis 21:93
Sherman, Frank 23:79
Sherman, G. 19:261
Sherman, George 9:192; 11:270; 22:441; 23:110; 25:231
Sherman, George S. 22:510
Sherman, George W. 5:29
Sherman, H. 1:78
Sherman, H. C. 22:492
Sherman, H. H. 18:401
Sherman, Harbred 27:112
Sherman, Hardbread 9:136
Sherman, Henry 1:73; 12:39; 16:379
Sherman, Henry H. 19:34
Sherman, Henry S. 10:136; 20:346
Sherman, Hiram 15:226; 20:109
Sherman, I. 3:174
Sherman, Ira 15:74
Sherman, J. 1:169, 171
Sherman, J. A. 7:109
Sherman, James 4:53; 5:29; 11:89, 271; 16:227; 25:231
Sherman, Jirah 11:289
Sherman, John 8:95; 10:79; 14:108; 17:264; 20:346
Sherman, John B. 19:193
Sherman, John G. 19:34
Sherman, John W. 3:174
Sherman, Joseph 3:174
Sherman, Joseph F. 7:109
Sherman, Leonard 22:219
Sherman, Levi 22:53
Sherman, Levi B. 7:41
Sherman, Levy 18:38
Sherman, M. 19:99
Sherman, M. J. 1:173
Sherman, Marling 10:97
Sherman, Martin 7:133
Sherman, Miles R. 21:246
Sherman, Moses 15:74
Sherman, Moses D. 22:15
Sherman, Myron 13:118
Sherman, N. C. 18:252; 26:63
Sherman, Oliver P. 21:260
Sherman, Orin 10:79
Sherman, P. H. 3:174

Sherman, Palmer 22:284
Sherman, Powell 9:125; 27:115
Sherman, Robert 10:155
Sherman, Robert C. 21:387
Sherman, Roger 21:387
Sherman, Rollin S. 22:517
Sherman, S. 1:168
Sherman, S. C. 15:167
Sherman, S. L. 15:300
Sherman, S. S. 26:61
Sherman, Seymour M. 10:167
Sherman, Silas B. 15:112
Sherman, Thomas 9:14
Sherman, Thomas B. 7:61
Sherman, W. 3:174
Sherman, W. A. H. 1:74
Sherman, W. F. 14:303; 17:472
Sherman, W. H. 1:73
Sherman, W. O. 23:167
Sherman, W. T. 27:117
Sherman, William 5:29; 9:136; 10:79; 20:346; 25:231; 27:112
Sherman, William H. 20:190; 24:55
Sherman, William M. 22:467
Sherman, William R. 9:99
Shermasten, A. 8:67
Shermerhorn, Frank 12:39
Shermerhorn, George S. 12:39
Shermin, Daniel 25:70
Shermond, Daniel 20:346
Shern, John 15:337
Shernbrand, John G. 20:44
Shero, F. M. 19:261
Sherod, J. B. 27:118
Sheron, T. 25:231
Sherquest, C. F. 26:64
Sherquist, C. F. 18:252
Sherrall, Mack 22:319
Sherrall, Thomas M. 22:457
Sherran, Joseph 16:123
Sherrard, C. E. 9:90
Sherrard, David 9:90
Sherrell, Bayler H. 22:130
Sherrell, Jefferson 22:458
Sherrell, William W. 22:457
Sherren, James 23:16
Sherrer, George 15:264
Sherrer, L. 14:108
Sherrey, James 9:192
Sherrick, William 20:178

Sherridan, B. 1:74
Sherridan, Charles 14:217
Sherridan, Thomas 8:31
Sherrif, J. F. 10:149
Sherriff, William 12:39
Sherrill, Lewis 17:42
Sherrill, Robert O. 21:85
Sherrington, William 11:76
Sherrod, L. R. 15:290; 16:227
Sherrod, Thomas 10:207
Sherrod, William 8:31; 18:159
Sherron, Joseph 22:219
Sherrow, J. 1:175
Sherrow, W. J. 18:407
Sherry, Christopher 13:118
Sherry, George 19:34
Sherry, Henry E. 24:55
Sherry, J. 19:261; 20:44
Sherry, James 10:25
Sherry, M. S. 15:336
Sherry, Patrick 22:344
Sherry, R. 1:77
Sherry, R. F. 23:276
Sherry, W. 24:29
Sherry, William O. 20:19
Shershell, N. 22:219
Sherus, Laben 15:59
Sherver, F. 3:174
Sherver, W. 1:71
Sherweell, W. 1:74
Sherwin, Abner 17:244
Sherwin, W. 1:169
Sherwood, A. 14:217
Sherwood, Aaron 17:362; 26:129
Sherwood, Amos 9:45
Sherwood, Anson 17:68
Sherwood, B. 25:231
Sherwood, Benjamin 5:29
Sherwood, C. H. 3:174
Sherwood, Charles 12:84; 16:304
Sherwood, Charles E. 10:167
Sherwood, D. 3:174
Sherwood, Daniel 10:79; 18:17; 22:101
Sherwood, Dover 21:284
Sherwood, E. 16:227
Sherwood, Enos 16:227
Sherwood, G. 14:108
Sherwood, George 23:14
Sherwood, George B. 26:226
Sherwood, Gilbert F. 19:34

Sherwood, H. 14:290; 23:205
Sherwood, Henry 8:31
Sherwood, J. 13:98; 21:191
Sherwood, J. B. 1:173
Sherwood, J. E. 3:174
Sherwood, J. F. 3:174
Sherwood, James 8:75; 23:282
Sherwood, Jason 12:39
Sherwood, John 15:226; 17:245
Sherwood, L. D. 11:334
Sherwood, L. S. 16:227
Sherwood, M. 1:71
Sherwood, M. M. 11:184
Sherwood, Morgan 22:172
Sherwood, Norman 23:195
Sherwood, Ogden 21:260
Sherwood, Orson 7:17
Sherwood, P. 3:174; 18:57
Sherwood, R. 25:231
Sherwood, Robert 19:34
Sherwood, S. 11:250
Sherwood, W. 12:93
Sherwood, W. H. 21:387
Sherwood, W. P. 11:130
Sherwood, Wash. 8:67
Sherwood, Washington 26:180
Sherwood, William 4:52; 11:171
Sherwood, Winfield S. 21:79
Shesler, Charles 14:217
Shesrer, Peter 25:326
Shester, Albert 7:41
Shetland, Lei 9:113
Shetler, Jacob 18:38
Shetley, A. E. 2:18
Shetterly, Andrew 24:162
Shettle, Joseph 9:59
Shettle, Oliver J. 20:105
Sheubenacy, Nap 4:52
Sheultry, Cornelius 22:457
Sheusfeldt, Jacob 8:95
Sheuter, Henry W. 22:163
Sheve, William 15:74
Shevelier, Peter 27:116
Shever, Edward 17:315
Shever, H. 3:174
Shevers, Henry 14:108
Sheverts, J. 14:217
Shew, Barton 10:79; 20:346
Shew, John G. 17:234

Sheward, Perry 20:19
Shewell, D. Benville 10:22
Shewell, Zachariah 10:79; 20:346
Shewmaker, James M. 10:79
Shey, W. T. 19:99
Shiader, C. 21:40
Shiber, George H. 17:158
Shible, G. 22:168
Shibley, Charles 14:217
Shibley, G. W. 14:108
Shibley, James 10:187
Shick, Amos 22:237
Shickles, J. 19:286
Shider, --- 15:300; 16:227
Shider, Captain 9:125
Shiding, Francis 20:346
Shidler, George 3:174
Shidler, John 17:258; 22:438
Shidler, Joseph 22:101
Shidly, Willis 17:449
Shidnig, Francis 10:136
Shiefer, J. T. 14:21
Shiel, A. 11:249
Shields, A. 1:74; 22:491
Shields, Adam 1:71
Shields, Alfred 11:76; 17:420; 24:162
Shields, Ambrose 17:138; 24:203
Shields, Benjamin 1:70
Shields, C. 27:107
Shields, Charles 7:41
Shields, David 22:269
Shields, E. 5:45; 25:231
Shields, Edwards 11:169
Shields, Eli 23:49
Shields, Franc 16:55
Shields, G. 14:108
Shields, George 3:174; 18:210; 21:234
Shields, H. 12:80; 25:231
Shields, Hugh 23:130
Shields, J. 3:175; 25:231
Shields, J. A. 3:175
Shields, J. J. 13:46; 25:231
Shields, J. M. 12:158
Shields, Jacob 17:97; 22:53
Shields, Jacob R. 9:237; 26:226
Shields, James 4:53; 16:304; 20:128; 24:97
Shields, James C. 11:323
Shields, James I. 21:85

Shields, John 4:53; 13:46; 17:93; 18:441
Shields, John D. 22:237
Shields, John J. 5:29
Shields, Joseph 24:84
Shields, Joshua 9:69
Shields, L. 10:210; 16:227
Shields, Lewis W. 8:95
Shields, Madison 20:346
Shields, Mathew 22:344
Shields, Michael 11:173; 22:344
Shields, Oliver 20:345
Shields, Patrick 13:46
Shields, Peter 18:17
Shields, R. 3:175
Shields, Richard 3:174
Shields, Robert 11:86; 16:101; 22:101
Shields, S. S. 14:108
Shields, T. 11:86
Shields, Thomas 13:46; 16:123
Shields, W. 19:99
Shields, William 14:217; 16:227; 22:101; 24:69
Shields, William B. 22:521
Shields, William H. 7:41; 17:239; 20:345; 24:55
Shields, William H. H. 22:438
Shields, William S. 8:95
Shields, Wyatt 9:158
Shields, Zachariah 17:410; 22:456
Shieler, Dan 14:108
Shienbrier, R. 9:232
Shietas, J. 3:175
Shiffbower, William 21:86
Shiffen, Peter 9:125
Shiffer, A. G. 13:118
Shiffer, George H. 17:93
Shiffer, John F. 12:76
Shiffer, Peter 27:113
Shiffert, Reuben 24:55
Shifflet, John 18:297
Shifflett, John 26:113
Shifflit, A. 14:108
Shiffmaker, Theodore 15:45
Shiflet, John 17:97
Shigley, T. W. 3:175
Shikler, James 9:202
Shikles, John S. 20:89
Shilady, Eugene N. 8:110
Shilard, M. 16:227
Shilbur, C. 10:187

Shilden, C. 14:108
Shilds, Lawrence 15:300
Shiley, William B. 9:28
Shilg, Charles 24:29
Shilker, P. 23:49
Shill, Arthur 16:304
Shill, G. W. 9:99
Shillborn, John 18:280
Shillenby, John B. 19:99
Shiller, --- 25:68
Shilley, A. 11:313
Shilley, W. 2:17
Shilley, William 25:73
Shilliday, John 12:39
Shillinberger, Urian 8:115
Shilling, Ferdinand 15:300
Shilling, J. 23:167
Shilling, J. B. 11:269
Shilling, James 14:217
Shilling, John 11:130; 15:19
Shilling, John M. 12:39
Shilling, William 3:175
Shillinly, J. B. 15:331
Shilser, John F. 9:45
Shilton, --- 14:217
Shilton, Alexander 18:252
Shilton, Clements 3:175
Shiltz, F. 13:98
Shiltz, Farrington 14:217
Shiltz, John 11:234
Shilvan, Henry 18:93
Shily, S. 14:217
Shim, I. 3:175
Shiman, Aaron 12:76
Shimer, John 20:19
Shimfelt, James 15:74
Shimkwiler, Jacob 11:404
Shimla, William H. 26:64
Shimmel, Willie 26:226
Shimmerhorn, Richard 17:208
Shimpff, Ernest 26:225
Shimple, Ernest 9:238
Shin, Robert M. 8:110
Shinall, P. 25:231
Shinalt, Amos 26:59
Shinan, J. H. 25:68
Shinault, --- 16:304
Shinbein, C. 19:261
Shindler, A. 21:105
Shindler, John 3:175
Shindler, O. 16:304
Shindler, Ollis 12:93
Shindler, W. 2:17
Shine, Thomas 4:53
Shine, William 23:125
Shineborne, J. 3:175
Shinefelt, Jacob 18:210
Shiner, C. C. 2:17

Shiner, Charles 21:260
Shiner, David L. 24:55
Shiner, John 14:131
Shiner, Nero 22:319
Shiner, T. 17:86
Shinerman, Samuel 20:346
Shingle, D. 3:175
Shingle, David 15:153
Shingle, G. 14:108
Shingle, George W. 19:99
Shingle, Washington 15:226
Shingler, John J. 22:130
Shingleton, Thomas 17:42
Shink, James 3:175
Shinke, William 8:75
Shinkel, I. 11:173
Shinkes, H. 9:224
Shinkle, H. 18:375
Shinkle, J. T. 18:71
Shinkle, Marion 20:138
Shinkle, Peter W. 22:219
Shinkle, T. W. 19:99
Shinley, B. F. 9:39
Shinley, T. S. 27:109
Shinn, H. C. 23:49
Shinn, N. C. 15:226
Shinn, Silas N. 22:101
Shinneman, H. H. 26:58
Shinney, J. H. 16:271
Shinrock, J. 1:76
Shintes, G. 12:88; 16:304
Ship, Bristol 22:319
Ship, Emanuel 11:392
Ship, George 21:213, 284
Ship, William 17:42
Shipard, --- 15:45
Shipard, G. Y. 13:118
Shipe, Milton 22:269
Shipler, Harvey 11:251
Shipler, Jacob 12:97; 15:361
Shipley, C. W. 20:346
Shipley, Charles E. 10:136; 20:346
Shipley, D. M. 23:49
Shipley, Daniel 9:224; 18:376
Shipley, David 11:426
Shipley, Ephraim 24:29
Shipley, Equilar 10:136
Shipley, Equiller 20:346
Shipley, George 17:289
Shipley, J. L. 14:108
Shipley, J. W. 25:73
Shipley, James A. 1:70
Shipley, John 8:31; 18:159; 22:344
Shipley, John A. 11:167
Shipley, L. D. 1:76

Shipley, Roland P. 10:79
Shipley, Rolland P.
  20:346
Shipley, Thomas 13:98
Shipley, W. 3:175
Shipley, W. H. 9:224;
  18:376
Shipley, William 21:59
Shiplin, Philip 16:134
Shiplon, D. S. 21:79
Shipman, A. 1:172
Shipman, Alex 17:167
Shipman, Charles B.
  23:93
Shipman, Clinton W.
  15:226
Shipman, G. M. 11:314
Shipman, G. W. 1:176
Shipman, Henry 22:155
Shipman, Jacob 9:193;
  19:261
Shipman, Jerome B. 21:79
Shipman, Levi F. 17:315
Shipman, M. D. 15:226
Shipman, Moses 2:17
Shipman, Nath. 14:217
Shipman, P. M. 15:226,
  347
Shipman, R. 14:108
Shipman, T. J. 22:505
Shipman, W. 1:71
Shipman, William 23:79
Shipman, William H.
  20:346
Shipman, William W.
  10:79
Shipmann, M. 25:67
Shipner, Richard 11:45
Shipp, Isaac 17:353
Shipp, James 9:136;
  27:111
Shippee, Z. E. 8:31
Shippeon, Daniel 16:227
Shipper, M. 19:34
Shippey, F. 3:175
Shippey, Franklin W. 9:14
Shipple, John 3:175
Shipple, N. 1:169
Shipple, Z. E. 18:159
Shippler, Jacob 19:99
Shipps, D. M. 17:192
Shippy, Asa A. 4:53
Shippy, George 17:434;
  24:172
Shippy, Willis O. 13:46
Ships, John M. 11:271
Shira, William 11:169
Shirar, Lewis 11:416
Shircliff, James T. 24:44
Shire, W. C. 5:54
Shireley, Philip 8:95

Shirer, G. H. 3:175
Shiri, Isaac 26:213
Shirk, A. H. 24:84
Shirk, Alfred 17:423;
  24:172
Shirk, Bird 4:53
Shirk, Casper 21:387
Shirk, Edward H. 9:125;
  27:113
Shirk, Edwin P. 20:13
Shirk, George 22:441
Shirk, J. W. 23:167
Shirk, James M. 11:169
Shirk, M. B. 3:175
Shirk, Solomon 16:124
Shirket, --- 11:188
Shirkson, James N.
  26:181
Shirky, Hugh 20:143
Shirl, Benjamin 22:53
Shirley, A. 23:245
Shirley, C. 19:230
Shirley, Charles H. 7:109
Shirley, D. 14:108
Shirley, Henry 3:175
Shirley, Horace L. 10:136;
  20:346
Shirley, Isham 26:183
Shirley, J. B. 11:98
Shirley, Jacob E. 20:100
Shirley, John 1:77; 6:19;
  18:93
Shirley, P. 3:175
Shirley, Robert 14:217
Shirley, S. A. 2:18
Shirley, W. B. 26:111
Shirley, William 4:68
Shirley, William B.
  18:316
Shirling, E. 24:55
Shirlly, Wallace 4:53
Shirlock, John 11:171
Shirlock, R. 3:175
Shirls, W. S. 9:59
Shirmon, O. J. 20:346
Shirt, P. 3:175
Shirther, George M. 9:193
Shirtle, George 1:75
Shirtler, A. P. 11:313
Shirts, Edmund 20:109
Shirts, William 11:170
Shirwood, F. 3:175
Shisler, J. M. 23:182
Shisler, Noah 16:227
Shislon, J. A. 17:284
Shisser, Jacob 23:79
Shissler, William C. 1:72
Shith, Thomas 17:445
Shitler, C. A. 3:175
Shivar, B. F. 14:217
Shiveley, H. 24:84

Shively, A. C. 11:313
Shively, Jacob 22:219
Shively, John C. 22:130
Shiven, William 19:34
Shiver, Harley W. 17:26
Shiver, Henry 11:184
Shiver, L. 3:175
Shiverick, Andrew F.
  21:260
Shiverly, K. 11:98
Shivers, Henry 18:252;
  26:63
Shivers, William 10:136;
  20:346
Shives, Joshua 11:425
Shives, W. 15:134
Shivly, --- 11:294
Shizer, Daniel 12:39
Shleep, Jake 11:171
Shlegel, August 20:346
Shlegel, M. 19:332
Shlissler, J. 14:217
Shlonaker, George W.
  22:491
Shlorff, Michael D. 24:29
Shlote, C. 1:174
Shlott, Henry 10:79;
  20:346
Shmkwin, Peter 22:344
Shnander, Jo 23:268
Shneeler, B. 11:439
Shneider, James 9:158
Shnell, E. 25:67
Shnell, Edwin 2:17
Shnell, William 9:113
Shnied, Charles 24:114
Shoaf, Wesley H. 10:93
Shoafstrall, Daniel 11:314
Shoals, --- 14:217
Shoals, Frederick 10:136;
  20:346
Shoals, Henry 19:34
Shoap, Wesley H. 20:346
Shoarod, Charles 17:474
Shoart, James 11:425
Shoat, Benjamin 10:136;
  20:346
Shoate, James 23:272
Shobe, Henry 23:79
Shobe, J. 17:138; 24:203
Shober, Gideon 17:213
Shock, --- 11:250
Shock, A. 13:98
Shock, Andrew 10:167;
  19:193
Shock, William 4:53
Shockback, William
  14:108
Shocke, Jeremiah 20:13
Shockeuse, James J.
  11:251

Shockey, J. B. 22:490
Shockey, John 15:175
Shockey, M. 23:264
Shockey, Sam. W. 23:167
Shockey, William L. 10:136
Shockin, William 19:99
Shockincey, William 15:306
Shockley, A. 25:231
Shockley, Aaron 5:29
Shockley, Abram 11:416
Shockley, Asberry 10:136; 20:346
Shockley, George W. 11:397
Shockley, Samuel I. 10:79
Shockley, T. A. 11:86
Shockley, W. F. 7:110
Shockley, W. T. 21:387
Shockley, William L. 20:346
Shockly, Eli 16:227
Shoddeik, M. 1:76
Shodden, J. 11:121
Shoe, David 12:123; 15:134
Shoe, Peter 23:49
Shoeder, C. J. 1:74
Shoefner, John 17:261
Shoemake, George 17:208
Shoemake, James M. 20:346
Shoemake, William 11:97
Shoemaker, --- 15:226
Shoemaker, A. 13:46
Shoemaker, A. G. 17:245
Shoemaker, Absolom 23:287
Shoemaker, Albert 11:277
Shoemaker, Andrew B. 22:130
Shoemaker, Andrew J. 22:15
Shoemaker, Benjamin 13:46
Shoemaker, C. 3:175; 14:217
Shoemaker, Charles 11:169; 25:335
Shoemaker, D. 14:108
Shoemaker, E. 1:76
Shoemaker, E. R. 1:76
Shoemaker, E. S. 11:313
Shoemaker, E. W. 3:175
Shoemaker, Frank 18:114; 21:112
Shoemaker, Franklin M. 17:362
Shoemaker, G. W. 1:73

Shoemaker, George 15:227
Shoemaker, George H. 23:167
Shoemaker, George W. 11:44
Shoemaker, Grafton 11:43
Shoemaker, Granville 6:26
Shoemaker, Henry 8:75; 21:80; 22:168
Shoemaker, Isaac F. 10:167; 19:193
Shoemaker, J. 3:175; 13:118
Shoemaker, J. A. 11:270
Shoemaker, Jacob L. 8:95
Shoemaker, Jesse J. 9:193; 19:284
Shoemaker, John 9:59; 10:136, 154; 17:451; 18:252; 19:193; 20:346; 22:411; 24:180; 26:65
Shoemaker, John C. 8:110
Shoemaker, John M. 10:79; 20:346
Shoemaker, Joshua 25:68
Shoemaker, Luke 22:219
Shoemaker, M. 1:172; 3:175
Shoemaker, Michael 10:136; 20:347
Shoemaker, Michael H. 24:44
Shoemaker, Nathan 23:195
Shoemaker, Ph. 8:122
Shoemaker, R. 17:161
Shoemaker, Robert 8:95
Shoemaker, S. 11:185; 16:124
Shoemaker, Samuel 17:86
Shoemaker, Samuel O. 6:33
Shoemaker, Solomon 7:110
Shoemaker, Stephen 19:338
Shoemaker, Theodore 18:252; 26:62
Shoemaker, W. 23:167
Shoemaker, W. P. 11:251
Shoemaker, William 10:136; 15:74; 20:347; 22:130
Shoeman, P. 1:168
Shoen, Israel 25:231
Shoen, John G. 16:75
Shoeneck, J. 1:171
Shoenfolt, J. 25:231

Shoenfolt, Joseph 5:29
Shoening, Francis 22:237
Shoers, J. 1:172
Shoewalter, S. 14:108
Shoff, Frank 22:155
Shoffer, John 22:490
Shoffer, M. V. 25:231
Shofford, Wilbur F. 23:167
Shoffstal, J. 15:310; 19:99
Shoflar, Henry 14:217
Shofstall, Henry 22:219
Shohn, Marcus 15:227
Shohon, --- 8:55
Shohoney, William W. 17:26
Sholder, Ed 3:175
Sholder, J. 9:59
Sholer, H. W. 10:97
Sholes, Christopher H. 23:79
Sholes, Henry 22:219
Sholes, John 16:141
Sholes, William 6:26; 24:97
Sholey, John 20:19
Sholl, J. P. 3:175
Sholl, Samuel S. 20:13
Shollan, A. 1:168
Sholt, John 25:327
Sholte, Joseph 20:347
Sholts, G. 14:108
Sholts, W. 18:38
Sholtz, --- 24:29
Sholtz, Ernest 7:110
Sholtz, Gustav 17:253
Sholwalter, J. 1:170
Sholy, Ernest 21:387
Shomaker, Samuel O. 25:327
Shoman, J. 1:175
Shoman, Solomon 22:219
Shomas, G. F. 18:376
Shomberger, G. W. 14:108
Shomburg, H. 1:75
Shomers, John 14:108
Shonack, --- 14:108
Shonall, John 3:175
Shonassey, Thomas 23:14
Shonberger, William 16:282
Shonchoff, Henry 14:217
Shond, Charles 12:88; 16:304
Shone, Noah 25:70
Shoneburg, Daniel 23:49
Shoner, Frederick 16:124
Shoner, Thomas 22:491
Shonewitz, Anthony 12:39

Shong, John 16:304
Shong, Joseph 17:93
Shong, L. 3:175
Shonleber, Lewis 15:279
Shonlip, John A. 18:114
Shonlon, Michael 18:270
Shonoer, O. 20:347
Shoob, Jacob 4:53
Shook, --- 22:269
Shook, C. H. 25:327
Shook, E. M. 26:213
Shook, F. 19:193
Shook, H. 3:175
Shook, Henry 20:347;
     22:101
Shook, J. C. 11:78
Shook, J. H. 9:163
Shook, James A. 24:29
Shook, James F. 22:219
Shook, Jerome 16:141
Shook, John 12:39; 20:44
Shook, John W. 9:39;
     22:439
Shook, Lewis E. 17:420
Shook, N. A. 3:175
Shook, R. 22:219
Shook, W. 12:147; 19:306
Shook, W. A. 1:169
Shooke, George 15:19
Shoollin, Cornelius 25:69
Shoomaker, M. 1:74
Shooner, Peter 10:79
Shoonhaven, John 17:74
Shoonover, George
     21:105
Shoop, G. 3:175
Shoop, George 13:68;
     16:227
Shoop, J. 1:172
Shoop, J. B. 3:175
Shoop, Jacob 3:175
Shoop, Nicholas 4:53
Shoop, W. 3:175
Shoop, William 1:73
Shoorad, Charles 27:117
Shoot, --- 11:426
Shoot, J. L. 25:232
Shoots, William 3:175
Shop, Henry 8:100; 23:49
Shoper, A. J. 13:98; 14:21
Shophause, J. B. 25:232
Shopner, Henry H. 17:239
Shoppeurst, Henry 7:110
Shore, F. 15:349
Shore, Henry 10:167
Shore, Henry A. 19:193
Shore, J. F. 14:108
Shore, J. H. 27:109
Shore, J. J. 3:175
Shore, O. D. 11:439
Shore, Samuel 22:53

Shore, Thompson M.
     17:315
Shore, William L. 16:55
Shoredon, Henry 5:45
Shoreley, Henry C. 8:95
Shores, Frank 24:29
Shores, James 9:211;
     18:71
Shores, John 7:110; 23:49
Shores, Lewis 15:284;
     19:99
Shores, P. P. 15:227
Shores, Rufus A. 22:101
Shores, W. A. N. 12:76
Shores, William 18:401
Shoret, Augustin 21:93
Shorey, Appleton 14:217
Shorey, B. F. 1:171
Shorey, Ed 3:175
Shorey, Edmond 25:232
Shorey, F. 1:171
Shorey, Horace F. 12:39
Shorey, S. 1:76
Shorey, William 21:387
Shork, Isaac 24:154
Shork, L. F. 3:175
Shork, William 4:68
Shorkey, C. M. 22:219
Shorley, J. H. 1:100
Shorlo, Thomas 9:232
Shorm, Max 19:34
Shorman, Charles W.
     15:227
Shorman, Moses 16:55
Shorp, A. H. 3:175
Shorp, Robert M. 15:227
Shorpler, Harvey 7:17
Shorrey, Valentine M.
     12:39
Shorrod, Charles 14:303
Shorry, Richard 4:53
Short, --- 17:509
Short, Alfred 12:51;
     17:399
Short, Charles 11:289
Short, Cornelius 11:342
Short, D. 1:176
Short, Daniel 15:227
Short, Edward 19:193
Short, Elijah 14:217
Short, F. 1:175
Short, Francis M. 17:58
Short, Freeman 11:111
Short, G. 12:100
Short, George 8:55
Short, George W. 21:260
Short, H. 23:280
Short, Henry 17:447;
     24:171
Short, Isaac 17:416

Short, J. 1:172; 3:175;
     14:108
Short, J. W. 15:335;
     19:99; 26:181
Short, James 3:175; 8:95;
     22:440
Short, James F. 18:252;
     26:64
Short, James H. 15:88
Short, James W. 23:101
Short, John 9:73; 10:175;
     19:193; 25:72
Short, John D. 22:53
Short, John F. 7:110
Short, John S. 10:79;
     20:347
Short, L. 9:150; 27:108
Short, L. C. 3:175
Short, L. H. 3:175
Short, L. J. 20:93
Short, M. 3:175
Short, Michael 4:68
Short, Michael P. 27:113
Short, Michel P. 9:125
Short, Newton A. 7:109
Short, Pat 3:175
Short, Patrick 22:344
Short, Peter 7:78; 15:89;
     25:304
Short, Phillip 16:227
Short, Rile 24:44
Short, Robert 16:55;
     22:355
Short, Stephen 9:59
Short, Thomas 14:217
Short, Tipton 22:439
Short, W. 1:176
Short, W. D. 10:79
Short, Washington 21:143
Short, William 1:74;
     10:22, 79; 20:347;
     22:319, 411
Short, William A. 18:252;
     26:62
Short, William S. 22:101
Shortee, Benjamin 22:457
Shortee, William 8:116
Shortell, Edward 10:167
Shorten, Orange 9:99
Shorten, Robert 26:179
Shorter, C. 10:155;
     19:193
Shorter, Clinton 18:93
Shorter, Joseph 9:238;
     26:226
Shorter, Robert 8:42
Shortes, Samuel 19:99
Shortley, Robert 3:175
Shortman, J. 3:175
Shorton, A. 3:175

Shortridge, George 10:136; 20:347
Shorts, --- 14:217
Shorts, C. 3:175
Shorts, Casper 9:90; 26:61
Shorts, G. H. 25:232
Shorts, James 15:227
Shorts, Levi 9:59
Shorts, P. S. 22:491
Shorts, Samuel 15:285
Shorty, G. O. 8:67
Shostey, William 14:317
Shotes, C. H. 17:159
Shotliff, J. 3:175
Shott, Anthony 4:53; 11:171
Shott, D. 14:21
Shott, John W. 9:90
Shottenkirk, William H. 10:136; 20:347
Shotter, Henry 26:59
Shotterly, Andrew 17:420
Shottle, Horace 9:193
Shotts, E. 11:43
Shotts, Henry S. 6:21
Shotwell, F. R. 9:243
Shotwell, George 9:125; 27:113
Shotwell, J. 15:227
Shotwell, James 10:136; 20:347
Shoub, S. H. 16:153
Shoufler, William R. 21:40
Shough, D. A. 19:306
Shough, S. 14:217, 259
Shoulder, E. 3:175; 6:33; 25:327
Shoulders, Henry 22:101
Shoulders, Jacob 19:34
Shoulders, Samuel S. 23:79
Shoulebet, E. W. 25:232
Shoulers, Edward H. 4:53
Shouley, Michael 5:29
Shoull, G. B. 10:149; 18:57
Shoup, Henry 20:100; 23:167
Shoup, J. 1:77
Shoup, Joel 22:101
Shoup, Nathan 4:53
Shoup, Nicholas 7:110
Shoup, S. 3:175
Shoup, W. D. 24:29
Shoupe, W. 11:172
Shouse, Harvey V. 10:79
Shouse, Henry 20:128
Shouse, Isaac H. 22:412, 438
Shoush, James 11:397

Shouston, Thomas 18:252
Shout, Jesse A. 11:271
Shout, Job B. 20:135
Shove, F. 16:379
Shove, J. M. 13:118
Shove, Jacob 4:53
Shove, Martin 13:46
Shove, W. H. 13:118
Shover, David 17:102
Shover, Robert 21:199
Shoves, John 10:97
Show, J. 3:175
Show, J. F. 24:180
Show, Joseph L. 20:116
Show, L. 13:98
Show, Lewis G. 11:323
Show, William 12:164
Showalter, C. 16:136
Showalter, David H. 21:125
Showalter, John H. 22:238
Showatter, F. F. 11:78
Showe, P. 3:175
Showecy, M. 11:121
Shower, C. 3:175
Shower, Isaac 22:155
Shower, O. 10:79
Shower, Reuben 8:31; 18:159
Showerman, W. J. 19:261
Showerman, W. R. 9:193
Showerman, William 23:110
Showers, Alfred 11:78
Showers, Daniel 25:69
Showers, Elisha B. 17:362
Showers, John H. 10:136; 18:223; 20:347
Showers, William 25:71
Showers, William S. 15:227
Showis, Samuel 26:135
Showler, Elijah 18:376
Showlter, Jacob 8:31
Showlter, W. 1:173
Showman, Moses 13:58
Showman, William 13:46
Shown, Alber 18:114
Showston, Thomas 26:64
Shoyer, Josiah 22:101
Shrader, George 11:78; 14:217
Shrader, Henry 9:193
Shrader, Isaac 13:118
Shrader, J. T. 1:173
Shrader, William 22:219, 269
Shrake, Edward M. 11:249
Shran, George S. 15:19
Shran, John J. 26:183

Shraner, C. M. G. 10:178
Shratker, Henry 10:149; 18:57
Shre---, Jacob H. 16:227
Shreb, John 17:86
Shreck, August 22:219
Shreeve, Charles 23:49
Shreeves, E. 15:259
Shreeves, Lemuel 9:90
Shreff, John 9:73
Shreffer, Jacob 22:238
Shreffler, Joseph 22:219
Shreiber, Henry 10:93
Shrelons, F. H. 9:59
Shreve, Amos 23:49
Shreve, David H. 22:53
Shreve, Franklin M. 22:101
Shreve, Harry B. 7:41
Shreve, John H. 10:136; 20:347
Shrever, W. H. 20:143
Shrew, Levi 19:34
Shrewder, Michael 4:53
Shrewsberry, S. 8:102
Shrewsberry, Samuel 24:155
Shrewsbery, S. 17:459
Shrewsbury, Samuel 24:29
Shrieng, J. 1:168
Shrier, L. 11:406
Shrieves, J. W. 14:21
Shrigley, H. 3:176
Shriner, A. 24:84
Shriner, B. 1:176
Shriner, J. S. 20:19
Shriner, W. 13:46
Shriney, Michael 15:45
Shrinier, Michael 17:426
Shrinkley, Thomas 17:138; 24:204
Shritzel, Lewis 9:202
Shrive, Alex. 16:227
Shrively, E. S. 3:176
Shriver, Adam G. 23:167
Shriver, B. 3:176; 15:310; 19:99
Shriver, E. C. 22:219
Shriver, E. J. 22:219
Shriver, Ellis 11:168
Shriver, George 3:176
Shriver, H. 3:176
Shriver, J. 1:170; 20:85
Shriver, J. E. 11:313
Shriver, J. W. 13:98
Shriver, James M. 8:95; 18:330
Shriver, Philip 23:167
Shriver, W. 11:313

Shriver, William Y. 20:347
Shrivers, J. 9:59
Shrizer, Peter 7:41
Shroap, W. H. 22:219
Shroeder, Con 20:347
Shroeder, E. 1:75
Shroeder, Mat 18:57
Shroeder, William 3:176
Shrojer, John 26:226
Shrok, H. A. 9:193
Shronk, Joseph 15:5
Shrook, John 8:115; 18:324
Shrope, David P. 24:10
Shropshire, Major 17:185
Shroud, William 8:110
Shrouder, Conrad 10:79
Shrouds, J. 3:176
Shroudy, C. 18:38
Shroup, Francis M. 9:39
Shrout, --- 15:227
Shrow, Thomas 5:29
Shroyer, Andrew 10:79
Shroyer, Leonard 4:53
Shroyer, Samuel 23:167
Shrukes, H. 22:355
Shrulder, Henry 22:319
Shrum, Jacob 7:110
Shrum, John W. 24:29
Shrum, William 20:347
Shrumf, Moses 9:39
Shrumgost, A. 3:176
Shryer, Sidney B. 17:497
Shuan, M. 15:361; 19:99
Shuart, B. K. 19:261
Shuatliff, H. H. 17:309
Shuback, F. G. 7:41
Shubard, Joseph 11:426
Shuber, Daniel 22:269
Shuber, Joseph 10:79; 20:347
Shubers, Daniel P. 26:61
Shubert, Benjamin 18:335
Shubert, John 22:219
Shubert, K. 3:176
Shubert, Nicholas 9:8
Shubet, G. 11:43
Shubet, Reuben 11:171
Shubick, W. 1:174
Shuburne, Daniel 23:93
Shuburne, S. 14:108
Shucarl, Joseph 15:227
Shuck, --- 22:269
Shuck, Charles 20:128
Shuck, David M. 24:56
Shuck, F. 1:175
Shuck, Hatrick 22:319
Shuck, J. 1:175
Shuck, S. 9:28; 11:168

Shuck, Samuel 10:79; 20:347
Shuck, Stephen M. 10:136; 20:347
Shuder, G. 26:130
Shuder, John W. 21:128
Shudle, Andrew 11:323
Shudler, John 14:108
Shue, Michael 12:76
Shuecraft, Frank 23:49
Shuenk, J. 16:379
Shuer, James 22:319
Shuer, L. G. 18:325
Shuey, Amos 7:53
Shuey, Antheus 15:227
Shufeldt, T. 21:168
Shufele, Jacob 16:55
Shufelt, O. 1:78
Shufelt, R. 1:172
Shufelt, William 19:193
Shufelt, William H. 5:29
Shufer, A. 1:95
Shufett, W. H. 25:232
Shuff, Andrew C. 23:14
Shuff, Clara 15:227
Shuff, Jacob 15:300
Shuff, James 22:219
Shuff, John 22:219
Shuffelbarger, Simon 10:97
Shuffield, Moses 11:78
Shufflebarger, Elias 22:53
Shufflet, Samuel 21:387
Shuffleton, J. 3:176
Shufflin, James 8:31
Shufnes, William 13:46
Shufshay, Samuel 27:106
Shughart, Isaac 20:149
Shuhart, Ernest 16:144
Shuk, Daniel 16:114
Shuke, Robert F. 8:95
Shukes, John 15:135
Shular, William 11:270
Shulder, Jacob 1:73
Shule, D. M. 14:108
Shule, Fred 7:110
Shule, John 20:347
Shulee, Christopher C. 10:79
Shuler, Andrew T. 13:46
Shuler, C. 25:232
Shuler, Charles 3:176
Shuler, Daniel M. 16:55
Shuler, Edward 11:171
Shuler, George 13:46
Shuler, William 11:416
Shull, Charles 20:13
Shull, E. F. 18:252; 26:63
Shull, James B. 10:193
Shull, John S. 22:440; 23:101

Shull, S. 25:232
Shull, Sherman 5:29
Shull, William Y. 22:440
Shulley, Joseph 15:227
Shult, Eli 23:167
Shult, Henry 21:246
Shult, J. 12:88; 16:304
Shult, M. D. 23:49
Shulte, A. M. 3:176
Shulte, D. A. 18:57
Shulte, Martin H. 23:115
Shulters, W. S. 4:53
Shulties, Nicholaus 23:49
Shulting, Mary 16:71
Shultis, Isaac E. 25:72
Shults, Auguste 9:238
Shults, Carl 20:347
Shults, Christopher 12:39
Shults, George 3:176; 21:116
Shults, J. S. 11:329
Shults, Jacob 12:169
Shults, John 3:176; 20:347
Shults, Nelson 12:100
Shults, P. D. 3:176
Shults, W. 19:193
Shulty, Charles 19:99
Shulty, Henry 19:99
Shulty, Marion H. 26:226
Shultz, --- 16:227
Shultz, A. 13:98; 23:245
Shultz, Amos 9:39; 18:297
Shultz, Ananias 22:219
Shultz, Augustus M. 7:110
Shultz, B. 5:54; 25:232
Shultz, C. 1:75; 15:74, 310; 16:227; 25:232
Shultz, Carl 10:136
Shultz, Charles 12:76
Shultz, Christ 10:79
Shultz, Christian 17:100
Shultz, Christy 11:45
Shultz, Deidrich 22:53
Shultz, Edward 11:121
Shultz, Erwin 11:169
Shultz, F. 3:176
Shultz, F. E. 5:29
Shultz, Ferdinand 7:53
Shultz, G. B. 14:217
Shultz, H. H. 1:174; 3:176
Shultz, Harvey 23:167
Shultz, Henry 9:39; 13:46; 15:316; 18:297
Shultz, I. 19:261
Shultz, Isaiah 13:98
Shultz, J. 1:174; 9:193; 13:81; 16:227
Shultz, J. G. 8:75

Shultz, J. M. 26:63
Shultz, Jesse 8:31; 18:159
Shultz, John 3:176; 8:75;
    16:55; 18:316;
    23:167; 26:112
Shultz, John C. 23:182
Shultz, John R. 11:45
Shultz, John W. 11:45
Shultz, Melvin 23:101
Shultz, P. 1:76, 78
Shultz, Peter 13:119;
    22:491
Shultz, Thomas 25:71
Shultz, V. 11:169
Shultz, W. M. 23:264
Shultz, William 1:72;
    14:217; 16:124;
    17:42; 22:441;
    25:327
Shultz, William E. 11:184
Shultz, William T. 22:219
Shultze, H. 13:119
Shultzs, Christ 20:347
Shultzs, John 20:347
Shuly, William 16:101
Shulz, Frederick 8:31
Shum, Daniel 22:219
Shuma, Benjamin 25:327
Shumacher, Frederick
    18:335
Shumake, Asa 17:58
Shumaker, --- 18:431
Shumaker, B. F. 22:219
Shumaker, H. 27:111
Shumaker, Orlando
    22:491
Shumaker, Richmond W.
    17:86
Shumaker, William H.
    22:491
Shuman, B. 18:159
Shuman, C. 19:276
Shuman, Christian 9:193;
    10:136; 20:347
Shuman, Conrad 8:120
Shuman, D. 15:227
Shuman, F. 9:193; 19:242
Shuman, Henry 15:28;
    27:118
Shuman, James 25:232
Shuman, James Y. 10:25
Shuman, John 11:270
Shuman, John F. 16:79
Shuman, Joseph 4:53
Shuman, Joshua 22:219
Shuman, S. F. 25:232
Shuman, T. H. 20:347
Shuman, William E. 10:25
Shumard, G. 14:245
Shumard, Jacob 22:491
Shumard, William 17:353

Shumare, John D. 10:167
Shumat, M. 8:31; 18:159
Shumat, Mark 11:409
Shumate, C. 15:89
Shumate, Isaac 11:45
Shumate, Parkerson
    17:162
Shumb, John 11:20
Shumdeher, George
    16:102
Shume, Conrad T. 27:119
Shumer, John 15:273
Shumichen, W. 14:303;
    17:473
Shumm, John P. 22:439
Shumo, Benjamin 9:166
Shumoray, S. G. 15:259
Shump, Thomas 19:34
Shumway, Allison 21:387
Shumway, Charles 13:119
Shumway, Francis 20:49
Shumway, G. H. 1:170
Shumway, George 19:99
Shumway, Gilbert 19:34
Shumway, J. W. 13:98
Shumway, Lawrence
    22:219
Shumway, Philo 7:110
Shumway, William 3:176
Shun, L. 25:232
Shuneburg, Mary I.
    15:227
Shuneld, F. 11:184
Shuneman, H. 9:90
Shunghrae, John 11:392
Shunk, A. 10:149
Shunk, C. W. 13:68
Shunk, Henry 11:251
Shunk, Isaac 21:105
Shunk, J. 15:345
Shunk, S. H. 3:176
Shunk, William 15:227
Shunleworth, W. 14:109
Shunn, William 10:79
Shuntenberger, --- 9:232
Shup, John 12:39
Shupe, Denis 23:49
Shupe, F. 19:193
Shupe, George 23:167
Shupe, J. 1:174
Shupe, Jacob 22:219
Shupe, Michael 22:219
Shupe, Tillman 23:79
Shupe, William 15:9
Shuper, James 11:78
Shur, J. 21:387
Shur, Richard 11:184
Shure, J. P. 3:176
Shureman, Samuel 10:79
Shurhan, Joseph 13:46
Shurland, Theodore 7:41

Shurles, Henry 16:55
Shurley, Charles M. 24:45
Shurley, G. W. 8:95
Shurley, John 8:69
Shurley, Willis 24:174
Shurling, George W.
    10:149
Shurman, Vol 22:168
Shurman, William H.
    24:29
Shurman, William T.
    18:210
Shurmand, G. 14:245
Shurp, J. L. 13:98
Shurtiff, W. D. 1:170
Shurtleff, Hyrcanus 10:79
Shurtleff, O. C. 17:71
Shurtliff, F. 1:74
Shurtliff, H. B. 17:250
Shurtliff, J. 3:176
Shurtliff, J. H. 17:250
Shurts, William W. 22:53
Shurtz, John 9:28
Shurtz, William 26:62
Shusburger, John 18:210
Shuschel, Charles 16:227
Shuseman, Daniel 18:376
Shushel, Charles 15:300
Shusnevay, G. B. 13:68
Shuster, --- 3:176
Shuster, F. 3:176
Shuster, J. 18:252; 26:64
Shuster, N. 15:45
Shuster, Samuel 4:53
Shute, D. 10:22
Shute, Dexter B. 10:187
Shute, J. 1:169
Shute, Major 22:155
Shuter, J. W. 25:232
Shuter, James 19:99
Shuter, William 9:160
Shuterman, J. 27:117
Shutes, James 21:85
Shuth, John 6:26
Shutier, Joseph 26:64
Shutir, Joseph 18:253
Shutlepp, H. 20:347
Shutler, Daniel 18:316
Shutler, David 9:28
Shutlock, John B. 27:106
Shutoof, John W. 19:34
Shutsman, J. 14:303;
    17:477
Shutt, Henry 26:63
Shutt, James M. 17:163
Shutt, John W. 5:29
Shutt, Mark 1:71
Shutt, W. 17:478; 27:117
Shutt, William 14:303
Shuttar, Andrew 22:15
Shutter, Daniel 26:111

Shutter, Daniel B. 9:90
Shutter, J. 3:176
Shuttler, Julius 18:104
Shuttlesworth, William 15:227
Shutts, Benjamin 24:84
Shutts, C. 3:176
Shutts, Charles 20:347
Shutts, Chris 17:448
Shutts, Dexter B. 18:180
Shutts, F. E. 25:232
Shutts, Nelson 15:366
Shutts, William 13:46
Shuty, John 3:176
Shutz, C. 3:176
Shutz, John 24:180
Shutzford, George 16:55
Shuward, --- 26:213
Shuward, Doctor 18:202
Shuyter, Sylvester 19:34
Shy, Alexander R. 22:130
Shyeanner, S. 15:227
Shyland, W. A. 10:150
Shyler, George 15:45
Shyler, Peter F. 24:30
Shyrock, John 20:347
Siah, Eugene 9:211
Siar, James 7:110
Siark, Richard 11:213
Siars, --- 14:109
Sias, Solomon 25:232
Sias, W. W. 4:53
Sibald, R. F. 1:173
Sibbald, George 7:41
Sibbard, Henry L. 8:95
Sibbets, George A. 12:39
Sibbett, Francis L. M. 17:350
Sibbett, Oliver P. 13:46
Sibble, J. 1:100
Sibble, W. 3:176
Sibert, Adam 14:303; 17:472; 27:117
Sibert, Charles 13:119
Sibert, H. 20:156
Sibert, John 26:59
Sibert, John A. 21:59
Sibert, John H. 18:316; 26:111
Sibert, Matthew 17:504
Sibert, Simon 9:193
Siberts, Peter 22:219
Sibery, John 1:71
Sible, J. 1:169
Sibley, J. E. 3:176
Sibley, John 17:393
Sibley, John H. 7:110
Sibley, Maria Louisa 18:194
Sibley, Samuel 22:319
Sibley, William 21:387

Sibold, Albert 20:347
Sibold, Robert 10:136
Sibra, William 19:193
Sibrel, John 21:234
Siceloff, F. 26:183
Siceloff, T. 8:67
Sicely, Amos A. 17:416
Sick, Alexander P. 11:188
Sick, Conrad 18:38
Sick, Emil 19:99
Sick, Emit 15:334
Sick, K. 3:176
Sickafus, William 21:40
Sickel, B. 27:118
Sickeler, John 17:86
Sickels, C. Van 12:162
Sickeneas, H. 18:104
Sickenger, Andrew 20:31
Sickle, Rodney 8:42; 26:180
Sickle, William 22:344
Sickler, Daniel 13:127
Sickler, E. 3:176
Sickler, John 14:237
Sickles, A. 3:176
Sickles, Charles 15:112; 23:195
Sickles, Dallas 15:45
Sickles, Daniel 3:176/
Sickles, J. 3:176
Sickles, J. S. 25:232
Sickles, James S. 5:29
Sickles, M. 3:176
Sickles, O. T. 14:217
Sickles, Van 12:65
Sickles, W. 9:113; 20:347
Sickles, Watson 10:79
Sickman, S. 1:77
Sico, M. 14:109
Sicott, William 11:289
Sidale, Harvey 27:116
Siddel, J. 15:319
Siddell, G. 3:176
Sidebottom, William L. 11:76
Sidelinker, O. A. 1:169
Sidell, Peter 21:213
Sidell, Robert 13:46
Sidell, William 23:167
Sidels, J. 19:99
Sidelston, David 11:282
Siden, J. F. 21:387
Siden, R. A. 26:181
Sidendorf, George 18:210
Sidener, Samuel T. 25:71
Siders, Ja--- 21:40
Sides, David 11:271; 17:86
Sides, E. W. 25:69
Sides, Eli 13:131; 20:347
Sides, G. 3:176

Sides, Joseph 19:34
Sides, Pirkley S. 16:227
Sides, Samuel F. 22:53
Sides, William H. 6:23
Sides, William O. 19:242
Sidler, J. A. 13:98
Sidles, J. W. 22:490
Sidley, Israel 14:317
Sidmore, Franklin 13:46
Sidnam, Abram 22:155
Sidney, Charles 17:185
Sidney, Emeline 23:276
Sidney, Henry 9:211
Sidney, James 4:53
Sidney, William N. 17:138; 24:203
Sidnor, C. 13:98
Sidold, A. 11:172
Sidon, August 9:193
Sieald, A. 11:184
Siebbel, Michael 9:106
Siebelis, Herman 21:118
Sieberlich, Julius 5:29
Siebert, Adam W. 11:184
Siebert, August 9:155
Siebert, J. M. 11:323
Siebert, John 20:143
Siebert, Peter 10:79
Sieberts, Edward 15:273
Siebkin, Max 27:108
Siebles, A. 19:261
Siebrecht, G. S. 15:301
Siebs, John 23:115
Siecle, John 18:376
Siedaft, Isaac 10:8
Siefert, Adam 24:84
Siefert, Michael 22:169
Sieffert, M. 25:73
Siefinan, Mike 9:90
Sieford, Laurence 11:77
Siegal, Conrad 27:116
Siegel, Heugo 5:29
Siegel, William 9:244
Siegle, Charles 14:109
Siegle, G. 18:38
Siegmalt, Antonie 9:239
Siehe, Frederick 22:172
Siemer, Frederick 23:167
Sieter, Henry 11:129
Sifers, John W. 23:79
Sifert, Elijah 25:232
Sifert, Theodore 22:219
Siff, M. 16:227
Siffle, H. 3:176
Siffley, A. 15:227
Sifford, John M. 21:143
Sifislags, Lewis 20:347
Siflet, James 22:101
Siford, J. 18:57
Sig--, W. R. 22:355
Sigafoose, Jacob 24:56

Sigafose, William 22:219
Sigars, Albert 20:100; 23:257
Sigepoor, A. 22:155
Sigford, G. H. 3:176
Sigg, P. 11:43
Sigglecon, William 8:31; 18:159
Sight, John 15:227
Sights, Frederick 23:280
Sigler, Daniel A. 19:193
Sigler, Frederick 23:167
Sigler, Henry 23:125
Sigler, Michael 7:41; 18:114
Sigler, P. 13:98
Sigley, James 13:59
Sigley, P. 14:21
Sigling, John M. 22:219
Sigman, Charles 7:61
Sigman, J. 11:250
Sigman, Presly 22:490
Sigmond, Jacob 23:182
Sigmore, Clairborne 22:269
Signal, J. 15:327
Signal, James 19:99
Signer, William C. 22:101
Signers, F. C. 7:110
Signor, Charles J. 17:447
Signor, Ed 17:250
Signor, John 9:125; 27:114
Sigo, A. 20:179
Sigwall, --- 3:176
Siher, William H. 16:227
Sikes, Arthur 4:53
Sikes, George 21:284
Sikes, George L. 17:68
Sikes, John 17:420; 24:162
Sikes, Newton 21:284
Sikes, R. 20:179
Sikes, S. A. 22:521
Sikes, William D. 10:79; 20:347
Sikkilrot, John 20:86
Silar, John 9:90; 26:59
Silas, Benjamin C. 22:269
Silas, John 11:405
Silas, John W. 14:337
Silas, Joseph D. 11:172
Silas, Robert 6:19; 18:94
Silaway, A. D. 1:171
Silbaugh, J. 18:38
Silber, --- 14:109
Silber, George 17:447; 24:171
Silburn, William 22:101
Silcham, Cyrus D. 18:324
Silcott, L. W. 7:41

Silcox, E. 14:109
Silcox, J. 14:109
Silcox, William 10:79
Silden, D. M. 26:129
Silence, David T. 17:86
Silence, George W. 20:138
Silence, James L. 17:444; 24:162
Siler, F. 14:303; 17:477; 27:117
Siler, J. M. 25:232
Siler, Jacob 22:510
Siler, John 22:219
Siler, William 18:414
Silfing, J. M. 26:64
Silin, Jacob 15:167
Silk, Alfred 12:123; 15:135
Silk, Ed 11:173
Silk, Joseph H. 11:18
Silk, Patrick 10:167; 19:193
Silken, Henry 22:491
Silkwood, H. M. 3:176
Silkwood, Solomon 10:79; 20:347
Sill, James 3:176; 8:95
Sillaer, George 8:112
Sillars, Donald 19:193
Sillcox, William 20:347
Sillers, David 11:170
Sillers, Joseph 24:114
Sillers, Thomas 17:185
Silley, Allen 21:191
Silley, Benjamin F. 4:53
Silley, M. W. 4:53
Sillis, William 18:194
Sillivan, T. 3:176
Silliway, John 9:150
Sillman, Henry 10:207
Sillman, Jeremiah 13:47; 16:55
Sillman, Jerry 17:185
Sillon, Hugh 25:232
Sillotron, Will 11:314
Sills, Hugh R. 22:53
Sills, Jonathan 23:167
Sills, William E. 23:167
Sillsby, Phi. O. 13:47
Silly, F. 13:98
Silon, John 13:47
Siloras, W. H. 3:176
Siloway, J. 27:110
Silrey, David 3:176
Silrins, H. E. 19:34
Silsbee, James A. 23:125
Silsbey, William 10:8
Silsbury, Charles M. 4:53
Silsby, Amandus 11:194
Silsby, Burtus 9:99

Silsby, Charles 21:387
Silsby, H. M. 13:119
Silsby, Morris 12:158
Silsby, Philo O. 16:55
Silter, John 3:176
Siltger, D. 3:176
Silva, Antonio 21:387
Silvens, William 7:41
Silver, A. 15:345; 16:379
Silver, G. 14:109
Silver, George 23:288
Silver, John 19:261
Silver, John J. 9:238
Silver, M. 2:17
Silver, Manuel 19:99
Silver, Monroe 20:116
Silver, Samuel 19:99, 100
Silver, Samuel F. 19:230
Silver, T. 1:173
Silver, W. H. 11:170
Silverjohn, J. 26:225
Silvermail, J. F. 19:261
Silvermail, John L. 9:193
Silverman, John 13:119
Silvernail, Charles 27:116
Silvernall, J. 11:130
Silvers, J. 18:57
Silvers, J. W. 25:232
Silvers, John S. 17:208
Silvers, Jordan 4:53
Silvers, Thomas B. 18:223
Silvers, W. H. 15:301
Silvers, Walter 11:112
Silvertooth, Fremont 22:319
Silvery, J. 14:109
Silvester, G. 14:109
Silvey, John 9:193
Silvis, L. J. 25:72
Silvis, P. 15:227
Silwood, Silas A. 16:55
Silwood, Silas H. 13:59
Sim, --- 18:17
Sim, Edmund A. 15:59
Sim, James B. 20:128
Sim, John 9:99
Sim---y, John 11:194
Simail, Benjamin J. 14:317
Siman, J. F. 14:109
Siman, J. N. 7:110
Siman, R. A. 17:308
Simans, Benjamin 9:136
Simar, Anson E. 24:164
Simar, Stephen O. 24:164
Simarl, B. A. 14:322
Simarl, Benjamin A. 23:115
Simed, F. 15:45
Simeon, G. 14:109
Simer, Anselo 17:445

Simer, Stephen 17:445
Simerill, Columbus
  20:347
Simerly, G. W. 3:176
Simerly, Henry 11:329
Simerson, Dubois 22:284
Simerson, John E. 24:97
Simes, G. W. 7:133
Simes, James 11:409
Simes, Lewis W. 24:69
Simes, Moses 18:38
Simins, Thomas A. 17:284
Siminton, J. W. 14:109
Simis, George 26:63
Simkins, Barrilla 7:41
Simkins, David 4:53
Simkins, James D. 18:57
Simkins, S. 7:69
Simkins, Smith 27:116
Simlot, Philip 21:105
Simm, --- 16:304
Simm, A. S. 24:30
Simmean, Daniel 9:125
Simmel, L. 22:220
Simmen, Henry 22:492
Simmerback, Charles
  17:284
Simmerly, G. 14:263
Simmerly, J. 14:263
Simmerman, M. 1:72
Simmerman, Winter 24:30
Simmers, J. K. 1:175
Simmerson, James 8:31;
  18:159
Simmes, Henry 18:71
Simmington, William
  10:79
Simmond, J. C. 25:232
Simmond, S. P. 3:176
Simmonds, --- 10:29;
  19:306
Simmonds, D. 19:193
Simmonds, E. 3:176
Simmonds, Eli 18:38
Simmonds, George W.
  23:79
Simmonds, J. F. 18:424
Simmonds, John 24:84
Simmonds, Jonathan
  19:193
Simmonds, Joseph R.
  17:245
Simmonds, N. W. 20:87
Simmonds, S. 1:71
Simmonds, Samuel T.
  15:264
Simmonds, T. J. 18:180
Simmonds, W. J. 10:29;
  19:306
Simmonds, Walter D.
  17:26

Simmonds, William
  12:169
Simmons, --- 12:76;
  19:99; 20:128
Simmons, A. 1:71; 3:176;
  7:110; 14:109
Simmons, A. D. 10:167
Simmons, A. G. 11:43
Simmons, Alexander
  21:41
Simmons, Alexander C.
  22:269
Simmons, Andrew 17:399
Simmons, Andrew J. 7:61
Simmons, Armsted 22:269
Simmons, B. 16:55;
  18:38; 22:319
Simmons, Benjamin
  9:136, 211; 22:457;
  27:111, 112
Simmons, C. 17:185
Simmons, C. G. 3:176
Simmons, Caleb 18:316;
  26:113
Simmons, Charles 4:53
Simmons, Charles F.
  19:34
Simmons, Christian B.
  24:30
Simmons, Christopher C.
  7:110
Simmons, Clark 17:185
Simmons, D. 10:154
Simmons, D. A. 19:193
Simmons, Dan'l S. 22:457
Simmons, Daniel 6:35
Simmons, E. 3:176
Simmons, E. C. 20:347
Simmons, Enoch C. 10:79
Simmons, Eph 7:84
Simmons, Ephraim
  10:136; 20:347
Simmons, F. 14:217, 259;
  23:127
Simmons, F. A. 11:382
Simmons, Francis 21:59;
  22:220
Simmons, Frank 16:55
Simmons, Franklin 9:104
Simmons, G. 22:163
Simmons, G. F. 16:82
Simmons, G. T. 3:176
Simmons, George 18:38;
  20:109; 22:319
Simmons, H. 13:130;
  18:104; 27:106
Simmons, H. C. 1:77
Simmons, Henry 9:193;
  19:261
Simmons, Henry S. 17:26
Simmons, Horace 13:47

Simmons, Ira 18:94
Simmons, Isaac 9:136,
  156; 27:111
Simmons, J. 1:73, 173;
  3:176; 9:28; 11:250,
  277; 14:109
Simmons, J. A. 12:76
Simmons, J. E. 13:68
Simmons, J. F. 7:61
Simmons, J. H. 25:232
Simmons, J. J. 1:175
Simmons, J. R. C. 12:167;
  19:348
Simmons, J. W. 9:150;
  10:136; 20:347;
  24:84; 27:108
Simmons, Jacob 22:524
Simmons, James 12:52;
  15:227; 17:185;
  27:118
Simmons, James C. 10:93;
  20:347
Simmons, James M. 17:97
Simmons, James W.
  21:105
Simmons, January 9:136;
  27:112
Simmons, Jay 24:56
Simmons, Jefferson 9:224;
  18:376
Simmons, Jeremiah
  13:119
Simmons, Joel 10:93;
  20:347
Simmons, John 3:176;
  10:25; 21:388
Simmons, John A. 13:119;
  15:15
Simmons, John J. 23:167
Simmons, John P. 22:130
Simmons, Johnson R.
  22:220
Simmons, Joseph 9:155;
  13:119
Simmons, Josephus
  16:102
Simmons, L. 1:171
Simmons, Lamback 17:59
Simmons, Levi 10:79;
  19:34; 20:348
Simmons, Lewis 8:42;
  26:180
Simmons, Luther L. 22:53
Simmons, M. A. 3:177
Simmons, Moses 18:115
Simmons, Moulton 8:95
Simmons, Nicholas 10:97
Simmons, O. 23:167
Simmons, P. 25:232
Simmons, P. C. 1:75
Simmons, Paris 27:106

Simmons, Patrick 15:345
Simmons, Peter W. 10:79
Simmons, Reddie 6:19;
    18:94
Simmons, Richard 9:136;
    27:111
Simmons, Robert 8:59;
    19:277; 21:234
Simmons, S. 1:169, 172;
    5:45
Simmons, S. W. 14:109
Simmons, Samuel 17:87
Simmons, Stephen 22:53
Simmons, T. H. 10:93
Simmons, T. J. 10:187
Simmons, Thomas 11:97;
    21:59
Simmons, W. 17:97;
    22:53; 23:49
Simmons, W. D. 3:177
Simmons, W. H. 11:329
Simmons, Walter 23:272
Simmons, William 4:53;
    8:42; 10:9, 79;
    16:136; 21:284;
    26:182
Simmons, William A.
    17:42
Simmons, William H.
    4:53; 11:45
Simmons, William S.
    20:31
Simmons, Williamson W.
    22:53
Simmons, Y. 14:279
Simmonson, Andrew
    21:260
Simmos, James 20:100
Simms, Albert 17:185
Simms, Andrew 11:168
Simms, Archibald 23:49
Simms, Beverly 12:76
Simms, C. 17:204
Simms, D. 24:155
Simms, E. C. 11:168
Simms, Elliott 22:269
Simms, G. N. 12:158
Simms, G. R. 17:156
Simms, George 3:176;
    11:213
Simms, Henry 9:211
Simms, Hiram B. 18:401
Simms, J. F. 11:173
Simms, J. S. 1:100
Simms, Jerome B. 22:439
Simms, John 7:133;
    19:297
Simms, John W. 6:35
Simms, London 9:211
Simms, Oliver 24:84
Simms, Redding 22:269

Simms, Robert J. 14:217
Simms, S. 3:176
Simms, W. F. 18:253
Simms, W. J. 26:63
Simms, Washington 7:133
Simms, William 1:77
Simms, William J. 17:234
Simon, --- 25:68
Simon, Albert 11:169
Simon, Daniel W. 11:312
Simon, George 17:87
Simon, H. 3:177
Simon, Jacob 11:97;
    12:76
Simon, John 11:130;
    20:348
Simon, Michael 17:42
Simon, Peter 23:261
Simon, S. H. 13:47
Simon, Samuel 19:48
Simon, Smith 10:167
Simon, T. Fitz 27:148
Simon, V. 11:250
Simonbow, Thomas 4:53
Simond, G. 1:174
Simond, J. 16:102
Simond, Lemuel M. 13:47
Simondinger, B. 3:177
Simonds, Charles 20:116
Simonds, E. . 15:353
Simonds, E. M. 16:282
Simonds, G. B. 2:18
Simonds, J. 14:245
Simonds, James 19:34
Simonds, John 11:270;
    22:412
Simonds, Joseph 1:76
Simonds, L. W. 27:107
Simonds, Levi 22:319
Simonds, M. J. 11:43
Simonds, Riley E. 12:39
Simonds, W. 27:106
Simonds, W. R. 23:49
Simonds, William H.
    10:22
Simonette, Samuel 22:438
Simons, A. 3:177
Simons, Alanson 22:155
Simons, B. 25:73
Simons, C. 22:219
Simons, C. E. 3:177
Simons, Daniel 4:53
Simons, Edward 15:324;
    19:99
Simons, Enis 22:53
Simons, F. 16:227
Simons, F. H. 20:348
Simons, G. W. 1:173
Simons, George 7:133;
    22:172; 25:74

Simons, George W.
    26:138
Simons, Green 24:204
Simons, H. 11:439
Simons, H. L. 3:177
Simons, H. S. 16:227
Simons, Henry 18:210;
    19:48
Simons, Henry M. 4:53
Simons, Hiram 21:59
Simons, I. 3:177
Simons, Ira A. 13:79;
    16:227
Simons, J. 10:167;
    14:109; 16:227;
    19:193
Simons, J. E. 19:99
Simons, J. L. 12:10
Simons, James 11:232
Simons, James H. 5:45;
    11:249
Simons, John 11:111;
    19:99; 25:232
Simons, John L. 21:93,
    218
Simons, Joseph 24:204
Simons, L. 3:177
Simons, Levi 11:18
Simons, Lineas 9:73
Simons, Loring 11:323
Simons, M. 14:109
Simons, Mingo 27:118
Simons, Moulton 18:210
Simons, N. E. 19:99
Simons, Nathan E. 11:188
Simons, Nixon 17:42
Simons, P. W. 20:348
Simons, Perry 11:212
Simons, Peter 1:72
Simons, Phineas A.
    15:279
Simons, Richard 13:119
Simons, S. A. 18:17
Simons, Samuel 22:220
Simons, Simon 26:135
Simons, Solomon 17:42
Simons, Stephen 22:155
Simons, T. V. 14:109
Simons, Taylor 11:213
Simons, W. H. 3:177
Simons, W. J. 19:34
Simons, William 4:53
Simonson, George 18:280
Simonson, Hans 16:145
Simonson, Isaac 25:273
Simonson, J. 16:124
Simonson, Jay 22:468
Simonson, Stephen 13:47
Simont, Jacob 11:170
Simont, William F. 9:17
Simore, Jacob 15:82

Simous, S. S. 4:53
Simpkerson, G. G. 22:220
Simpkins, George W.
   11:169
Simpkins, James 12:65;
   15:92
Simpkins, John 21:143
Simpkins, S. P. 9:91;
   26:59
Simpkins, Thomas 3:177
Simpkins, Wayne 11:168
Simpkins, William T.
   12:39
Simple, R. 27:109
Simpson, --- 15:74;
   16:379
Simpson, A. 20:175
Simpson, A. H. 16:227
Simpson, A. J. 11:112;
   22:355
Simpson, Alexander
   17:72; 18:376
Simpson, Andrew J.
   20:105; 22:467
Simpson, Austin 8:75
Simpson, B. 8:58; 14:21;
   21:151; 25:232
Simpson, Baxton 17:218
Simpson, Benjamin
   11:213
Simpson, C. 3:177;
   25:232
Simpson, C. A. 7:110
Simpson, C. W. 15:227
Simpson, Canolonel 11:45
Simpson, Charles 22:101,
   220
Simpson, Charles H.
   22:172
Simpson, Charles W. 7:41
Simpson, Crockett 5:45
Simpson, D. 3:177
Simpson, D. O. 3:177
Simpson, D. W. 25:232
Simpson, Daniel 10:79
Simpson, David 24:102;
   25:327
Simpson, E. P. 3:177
Simpson, Ebenezer P.
   17:239
Simpson, Edward 20:157;
   26:181
Simpson, Elias 22:114
Simpson, Ernest 16:88
Simpson, F. D. 1:170
Simpson, F. M. 7:110
Simpson, Francis 7:110
Simpson, Franklin 17:208
Simpson, G. 27:119
Simpson, G. M. 21:388

Simpson, George 1:72;
   5:45; 9:28; 18:316;
   21:105; 22:467;
   23:79; 24:56; 26:112
Simpson, George A. 15:74
Simpson, George D.
   20:100
Simpson, George W.
   11:171
Simpson, Glanville 7:110
Simpson, H. 26:58
Simpson, Henry 8:110;
   17:71, 185
Simpson, Henry C. 22:130
Simpson, Henry J. 11:130
Simpson, Hiram 9:91
Simpson, I. 26:60
Simpson, J. 1:173; 3:177;
   12:84; 13:98; 14:109,
   217; 15:264; 16:304;
   25:232; 27:109
Simpson, J. A. 8:67;
   26:183
Simpson, J. B. 9:39;
   21:388
Simpson, J. C. 14:109
Simpson, J. H. 14:217
Simpson, J. M. 1:169
Simpson, J. P. 3:177
Simpson, Jackson B.
   20:13
Simpson, Jacob 9:69
Simpson, James 5:45;
   7:15; 9:91, 113;
   12:52; 15:45; 17:185;
   21:115; 25:232
Simpson, James A. 14:27
Simpson, James D. 7:14
Simpson, James W.
   22:130
Simpson, Jeremiah 10:32;
   20:348
Simpson, John 6:19;
   9:163, 232; 10:79,
   136; 12:39; 17:97;
   18:94, 407; 20:33,
   348; 21:388; 22:220;
   25:69
Simpson, John D. 21:95
Simpson, John F. 17:284
Simpson, John H. 23:79
Simpson, John L. 19:193
Simpson, John W. 11:404
Simpson, Joseph 7:133;
   8:95; 12:76; 25:327
Simpson, Joseph D. 16:79
Simpson, Joseph V.
   18:297; 26:112
Simpson, Joseph W.
   10:136; 20:348
Simpson, L. C. 25:74

Simpson, M. 13:47
Simpson, M. P. 8:55
Simpson, Mary 16:55
Simpson, Meredith 21:125
Simpson, Moses 7:133;
   18:401; 22:319
Simpson, O. 13:119
Simpson, P. 1:174; 25:232
Simpson, P. A. 27:148
Simpson, Peter 9:136;
   10:136; 20:175, 348;
   22:524; 27:111
Simpson, Pompey 5:45
Simpson, R. 1:75
Simpson, R. B. 11:270
Simpson, R. M. 11:397
Simpson, Reuben 10:99
Simpson, Richard 16:55;
   24:204
Simpson, Robert 14:109;
   21:41; 22:319
Simpson, S. W. 23:49
Simpson, Samuel W.
   11:112
Simpson, Saunders 17:185
Simpson, Solomon 17:87
Simpson, T. 3:177
Simpson, T. J. 23:167
Simpson, Thomas 10:79;
   20:348; 22:269, 284;
   23:195; 24:45;
   25:232
Simpson, Ulric 27:148
Simpson, W. 14:217
Simpson, W. A. 11:255;
   17:145, 213
Simpson, W. J. 3:177
Simpson, Walter 14:217
Simpson, Washington
   27:156
Simpson, William 3:177;
   8:67; 11:101; 13:68,
   119; 15:227; 16:15,
   124
Simpson, William H.
   23:167
Simpson, William M.
   8:110; 22:457
Simpson, William R.
   23:79
Simpson, William T.
   17:353
Simpter, J. H. 1:74
Simrell, H. 1:173
Sims, A. 11:313
Sims, Andrew J. 22:53
Sims, Archibald 16:227
Sims, B. 3:177
Sims, Beverly 15:9
Sims, D. 17:433
Sims, David L. 12:100

Sims, Edward 12:51
Sims, Eleazer 22:516
Sims, G. 16:227
Sims, George W. 22:220
Sims, Henry 13:119
Sims, J. 11:167
Sims, Jackson 22:319
Sims, James 11:76; 17:449
Sims, James E. 10:136; 20:348
Sims, James W. 22:467
Sims, Jerome 25:67
Sims, Jesse 4:53
Sims, John 1:70; 17:268; 21:388; 22:269
Sims, John F. 17:59
Sims, John I. 11:397
Sims, John M. 22:440
Sims, John W. 22:53
Sims, Jos. 22:220
Sims, Joseph 7:17
Sims, M. 18:57
Sims, N. R. 22:411
Sims, P. M. 25:232
Sims, Preston 8:75
Sims, S. 3:177; 11:169
Sims, Thomas 12:52
Sims, W. 16:227
Sims, W. C. 22:220
Sims, Wesley 11:419
Sims, William 3:177; 14:109; 25:232
Sims, William H. 22:101
Sims, William M. 22:53
Simson, Francis 17:26
Simson, Lewis 24:204
Simsubaugh, James 9:73
Simvay, P. 3:177
Sin--, P. N. 22:355
Sinber, Daniel 22:412
Sincil, M. T. 7:41
Sinclair, A. 3:177
Sinclair, A. W. 1:169
Sinclair, Benjamin F. 22:169
Sinclair, Charles 25:273
Sinclair, Charles W. 24:45
Sinclair, D. 1:170
Sinclair, David 15:227
Sinclair, F. 21:41
Sinclair, Francis 9:17
Sinclair, George 17:289
Sinclair, George D. 22:155
Sinclair, James 25:70, 288
Sinclair, John 21:205
Sinclair, John B. 22:17
Sinclair, Lewis B. 20:140
Sinclair, Maggie 27:115

Sinclair, Stacy 8:31; 18:159
Sinclair, W. H. 15:112; 27:116
Sinclare, Archibald 18:17
Sincock, Thomas 23:49
Sincoke, Andrew J. 24:45
Sincox, William H. 21:260
Sincox, William S. 13:68
Sindel, Michael 21:41
Sindell, Leonard 11:172
Sinder, Henry 17:42
Sinder, S. 22:490
Sinderwood, Aaron M. 22:506
Sindle, Peter 20:348
Sindrick, Frederick 16:55
Sine, A. C. 17:338
Sineath, J. D. 25:232
Siner, David G. 21:199
Siner, W. L. 1:174
Sinerber, Marcus 19:34
Sines, Charles W. 22:101
Sines, Henry M. 10:136
Sines, Henry R. 22:101
Sines, Isaac 16:305; 24:30
Sines, Robert J. A. 22:220
Sines, William H. 23:306
Sinet, H. C. 1:175
Sing, Henry 9:45; 26:129
Sing, Isaiah 14:317
Sing, Peter 1:76
Singer, Augustus 12:60
Singer, Charles 1:72
Singer, D. 7:65
Singer, David B. 22:238
Singer, France 1:73
Singer, H. 21:112
Singer, Henry E. 11:323
Singer, J. 3:177; 17:150; 23:302
Singer, J. A. 12:76
Singer, L. 19:261
Singer, Lambert 9:193
Singer, Lewis 6:33; 25:327
Singer, Samuel 17:284
Singer, William H. 4:53; 22:220
Singerson, W. P. 11:168
Singher, E. 11:313
Singhous, N. 22:220
Singhurn, Luther 23:79
Single, --- 23:49
Single, Charles A. 11:121
Singles, Isaac T. 11:184
Singletary, Cyrus 17:87
Singleton, Abney 11:282
Singleton, Amos 20:36

Singleton, Benjamin 11:271; 22:101
Singleton, Charles 19:323; 27:118
Singleton, Dennis 26:65
Singleton, E. T. 18:316; 26:113
Singleton, G. T. 9:28
Singleton, George 22:319
Singleton, Homer 9:162
Singleton, James 8:31; 9:232; 18:159; 20:348; 23:79
Singleton, John 8:31
Singleton, Josiah 10:79; 20:348
Singleton, L. 7:53
Singleton, Luke 9:162
Singleton, M. 9:202
Singleton, Mac 19:284
Singleton, R. 27:119
Singleton, Richard 9:155; 24:97
Singleton, Samuel 25:286
Singleton, Thomas 25:233
Singleton, Thomas J. 17:284
Singleton, W. C. 9:59
Singleton, William 4:53; 13:47; 23:272; 26:183
Singleton, William F. 24:114
Singleton, William S. 9:67; 18:280
Singley, F. 12:10
Sings, C. B. 26:184
Sinhart, John 7:41
Sinictse, P. P. 7:61
Siniff, Charles 26:60
Sinitz, Nicholas 7:53
Sink, Andrew J. 23:79
Sink, F. 19:99
Sink, Solomon 13:47
Sinkletter, William 12:39
Sinkney, J. 21:199
Sinks, Abraham T. 22:53
Sinley, O. 20:348
Sinleyside, J. S. 15:166
Sinn, Sylvester 13:127
Sinn, Theobald 21:105
Sinn, William R. 15:227
Sinne, Samuel 15:316
Sinnean, Daniel 27:113
Sinnet, John A. 11:169
Sinnett, A. R. 21:41
Sinnett, George R. 23:195
Sinnett, Hiram 21:143
Sinnett, James W. 12:39
Sinonaman, John 8:31

Sinsanberler, W. W. 25:233
Sinsay, D. 14:217
Sinsebaugh, Cyrus 24:85
Sinsel, William 17:87
Sinski, Casimiry 25:327
Sinson, John 4:53
Sinter, J. 27:108
Sinting, J. 14:21
Sinton, Archibald G. 22:53
Sintser, Samuel 11:97
Sinville, W. H. 22:491
Siomon, John 10:136
Sions, Edward 18:324
Siounk, L. 13:47
Sipe, F. 3:177
Sipe, J. 3:177
Sipe, Jacob 1:75
Sipe, James 13:80
Sipe, James S. 16:227
Sipe, John A. 22:439
Sipe, Levi 12:60
Sipe, Oscar 14:218
Sipe, P. 18:17
Sipe, S. 14:21
Siperly, R. H. 17:323
Sipes, Jacob 24:45
Sipes, John 8:95; 21:132
Sipes, Nathaniel 20:140
Sipes, Pleasant 21:234
Sipes, Richard 20:348
Sipher, James W. 22:220
Sipher, Levi 17:74
Siple, Cleris R. 12:60
Siple, L. H. 19:306
Siple, William D. 23:167
Sippel, Charles 1:76
Sippins, David 11:213
Sipple, J. 1:173
Sipple, J. L. 7:78; 25:304
Sipple, James 3:177
Sipples, John A. 24:168
Sippy, Nelson G. 21:196
Siprell, James E. 10:22
Sips, Richard 10:136
Sipsey, John 18:210
Sirbirt, F. 3:177
Sircho, Alonzo 20:190
Sircy, J. A. 11:97
Sire, Dorson 19:284
Sire, Joseph 21:388
Sirels, James 14:303; 17:471
Sires, Alex. S. 11:86
Sirgent, James 13:98
Sirles, James H. 23:101
Sirley, Solomon 11:77
Sirlott, James 23:49
Sirly, F. 23:167
Sirman, John A. 21:388

Sisan, Eli 17:42
Siscle, Henry 5:45
Sisco, Calvin 18:223
Sisco, E. F. 13:126; 16:227
Sisco, G. 14:109
Sisco, Harrison 25:233
Sisco, John G. 22:114
Sisco, T. 14:109
Sisco, Zachariah 11:416
Sisk, Alfred P. 22:269
Sisk, G. W. 10:136; 20:348
Sisk, J. 26:225
Sisler, J. 2:18; 25:73
Sisler, Joseph V. 16:145
Sisler, Obadiah 10:79
Sisler, William 12:39
Sisley, John 6:33
Sison, F. P. 18:57
Sison, Henry 11:130
Sissel, John S. 9:224
Sissen, Randall 18:316
Sissirus, J. F. 27:108
Sisson, C. W. 8:55
Sisson, Charles S. 3:177
Sisson, Charles W. 21:80
Sisson, D. S. 1:74
Sisson, George K. 22:101
Sisson, H. 15:112; 19:261
Sisson, Henry 9:193
Sisson, J. 3:177
Sisson, James 3:177; 26:213
Sisson, John W. 17:356
Sisson, Loren 10:136; 20:348
Sisson, P. V. 3:177
Sisson, Philo F. 21:143
Sisson, Randle 26:112
Sist, Lucian 10:152
Sister, George M. 20:348
Sisty, William L. 13:47
Siswell, S. 14:218
Sitany, Christ 24:72
Siter, Andrew 20:85
Sites, Adam 11:314
Sites, George 8:75; 10:167; 19:193
Sites, John 8:67
Sites, Joseph 21:205
Sith, H. 19:99
Sith, W. A. 11:111
Sitiky, Frederick 11:249
Sitler, G. W. 23:50
Sits, Charles 16:141
Sittan, James 20:348
Sitton, Elijah 21:291
Sitton, Henry 9:91
Sitton, Prospect M. 21:105

Sitts, George 17:68
Sittzer, Walter 7:110
Situs, John 13:47
Sitze, B. 11:194
Sitzler, S. 17:436; 24:184
Siute, David 11:87
Sivallon, Charles 9:232
Sivan, T. B. 14:21
Sivargyat, M. 14:109
Sivarts, Levi S. 21:388
Siveat, Stephen 23:314
Sivels, S. W. 11:329
Siver, Charles 22:172
Siver, George 17:423
Siver, Jacob 8:95
Siverley, Harry 1:72
Siverly, F. 14:218
Siverly, George 22:319
Sivernail, Amos H. 17:86
Sivers, J. 16:227
Sivers, James 13:47
Sivers, William 19:34
Siverson, Kund 27:114
Siverts, William B. 20:36
Sivertson, Amon 8:31
Sivetson, P. 9:125
Sivil, J. 21:168
Sivisher, John 19:99
Siwone, Simon 18:285
Six, Elias 9:39
Six, Ellas 26:113
Six, James 13:47
Six, T. H. 14:109
Six, W. 1:174
Sixberg, Adam 9:204
Sixburg, H. 7:110
Sixton, M. 18:341
Sizamore, Daniel 17:261
Sizeman, S. 3:177
Sizemore, Charles J. 10:136; 20:348
Sizemore, Owen 17:59
Sizemore, S. T. 10:79; 20:348
Sizer, Abram F. 23:287
Sizer, Albert M. 9:193
Sizer, Fielding 11:167
Sizer, Nelson W. 17:87
Sizer, Royal 18:57
Sizire, A. M. 19:246
Skaggs, Andrew J. 23:79
Skaggs, Bird W. H. 17:59
Skaggs, Francis M. 10:136; 20:348
Skaggs, Ikuer 12:147
Skaggs, Jefferson 17:59
Skaggs, Jenken 22:130
Skaggs, M. 1:174
Skaggs, Miner 19:306
Skaggs, Solomon 13:60
Skaggs, William S. 17:59

Skall, J. 3:177
Skanlan, John 14:218
Skate, James 22:319
Skeddy, G. 3:177
Skeeler, George 18:316;
  26:111
Skeeles, William 19:193
Skeels, Asberry 22:220
Skeels, David 13:119
Skeels, Nelson 23:167
Skeels, William 10:175
Skeels, William N. 22:411
Skeen, James R. 22:101
Skeen, John F. 9:224
Skeen, John T. 18:376
Skeen, Wilson D. 21:234
Skeer, Alfred 21:284
Skeetup, Justus 7:110
Skeever, Leonidas 22:492
Skeggs, Coleman 9:73
Skeggs, George W. 11:98
Skehan, William 9:125;
  27:114
Skeily, T. 3:177
Skein, M. 22:269
Skeiton, R. T. 24:114
Skeling, William H.
  22:490
Skell, C. W. 3:177
Skellie, Robert W. 23:125
Skellinger, J. C. 1:168
Skellings, I. 15:227
Skells, E. 14:21
Skells, W. 3:177
Skelly, A. 23:50
Skelly, Andrew 23:50
Skelly, Hiram 22:220
Skelly, Peter 23:167
Skelly, William G. 13:47
Skelton, Alexander 16:55
Skelton, Columbus 9:243
Skelton, G. T. 1:173
Skelton, J. 17:350
Skelton, James R. 11:76
Skelton, John 26:182
Skelton, Joseph 11:112
Skelton, Josiah 18:159
Skelton, Samuel H. 7:41
Skelton, William 10:167;
  19:193
Skelton, Zachariah 22:101
Skene, George 20:157
Skene, William H. 16:3
Skensell, D. 14:218
Skepper, Silas 9:193
Skerrett, George H.
  18:253; 26:62
Skerritt, Nicholas 9:193
Skidmore, Asa C. 18:223
Skidmore, D. H. 18:401
Skidmore, John T. 21:41

Skidmore, Robert 12:39
Skieller, H. 9:150
Skiff, James 21:284
Skiff, John M. 20:139
Skiff, S. M. 25:233
Skiff, S. N. 15:279
Skiffington, James 12:39
Skiles, Riley A. 23:284
Skiles, Robert F. 12:39
Skiles, William 14:109;
  22:345
Skill, Arthur 12:88
Skillen, Adam 18:194
Skillinger, George 26:138
Skillinger, P. H. 1:168
Skillinger, Stephen 8:95
Skillington, G. 3:177
Skillington, John A. 4:53
Skillman, John 1:70
Skillman, Joseph 7:41
Skillman, W. F. 22:344
Skilly, J. 19:261
Skilly, John 9:193
Skilman, Theodore 19:193
Skilman, Wesley 26:61
Skilton, John 10:145;
  19:193
Skilton, Josiah 8:31
Skimer, E. 12:162
Skimmons, W. 18:39
Skinkle, H. 18:376
Skinkle, Harry 9:224
Skinkle, Thomas L.
  21:105
Skinn, W. R. 14:259
Skinner, --- 3:177; 17:16
Skinner, Alex 11:77
Skinner, Alva 23:195
Skinner, Amos 22:155
Skinner, Andrew 21:388
Skinner, Ansel 22:284
Skinner, Asahel 21:11
Skinner, August A.
  22:101
Skinner, B. I. 11:98
Skinner, C. 10:29; 19:306;
  26:61
Skinner, C. H. 1:77
Skinner, C. M. 20:348
Skinner, C. P. 1:170
Skinner, Charles 20:348
Skinner, Charles Barton
  17:284
Skinner, Charles F.
  22:101
Skinner, Charles N. 21:80
Skinner, Darvin E. 15:167
Skinner, David 10:79;
  17:394; 20:348
Skinner, Eli C. 25:68
Skinner, F. A. 3:177

Skinner, Fred. B. 15:227
Skinner, G. F. 1:76
Skinner, George 7:133;
  9:8; 12:39
Skinner, Gilbert 19:48,
  193
Skinner, H. 3:177; 9:125;
  11:271; 14:218
Skinner, H. A. 9:104
Skinner, Harrison 17:347
Skinner, Hezel 27:113
Skinner, Isaac 15:227
Skinner, Isaiah 18:401
Skinner, J. 1:168; 13:98;
  14:21; 18:450; 24:85;
  25:233
Skinner, J. A. 3:177
Skinner, J. B. 27:109
Skinner, J. G. 13:127
Skinner, J. M. 16:141
Skinner, J. R. 25:304
Skinner, James 18:253;
  26:64
Skinner, James A. 17:245
Skinner, James W. 11:334
Skinner, John 10:79;
  17:389
Skinner, John B. 8:95
Skinner, John L. 21:59
Skinner, John S. 1:76
Skinner, Joseph 11:87;
  13:47; 15:167
Skinner, Joshua 10:79;
  20:348
Skinner, Judson 21:59
Skinner, L. 3:177
Skinner, Lipman B.
  23:167
Skinner, Luther 4:53
Skinner, M. H. 14:218;
  16:227
Skinner, Myron 11:77
Skinner, N. D. 7:41
Skinner, N. F. 15:227
Skinner, N. N. 1:170
Skinner, N. R. 14:218
Skinner, Orlander 21:234
Skinner, R. 25:233
Skinner, R. P. 22:355
Skinner, Renselair W.
  22:468
Skinner, Robert 21:388
Skinner, Russell P. 22:458
Skinner, S. A. 26:61
Skinner, S. O. 3:177
Skinner, Samuel R. 9:91
Skinner, Sidney S. 16:102
Skinner, W. 26:146
Skinner, William 3:177;
  9:28; 13:98; 14:21
Skinner, William B. 24:45

Skinning, B. P. 19:34
Skinnington, J. 9:113
Skiovianski, M. T. 14:218
Skipler, O. A. 18:253;
26:64
Skipper, James L. 18:94
Skipper, Samuel 25:233
Skipper, Silas 19:284
Skipton, Jackson 18:401
Skipton, James A. 18:401
Skirm, William 25:70
Skirvin, John 24:30
Skiss, Moses 9:125;
27:112
Skite, George W. 1:72
Skiver, J. 3:177
Skjelds, Ole Nelson
21:260
Skools, --- 18:431
Skowden, Allen 22:457
Skowden, George 22:130
Sktoe, A. M. 21:41
Skully, Denis 27:114
Skully, T. 15:23
Skunpshire, David 11:188
Skye, W. 1:169
Sl---, J. 11:221
Slaaten, Nils N. 22:284
Slack, C. 19:99
Slack, Charles 22:319
Slack, Charles D. 12:77;
15:84
Slack, Christopher R.
21:59
Slack, D. 25:233
Slack, D. B. 7:41
Slack, David 5:29
Slack, E. 27:110
Slack, Edwin 9:155
Slack, G. 15:322
Slack, George 14:218
Slack, Henry 26:129
Slack, Hiram 22:155
Slack, J. 1:71
Slack, J. A. 18:253; 26:62
Slack, James 16:227;
17:87
Slack, James W. 11:172
Slack, R. B. 11:172
Slack, Randolph 23:101
Slack, William 15:45
Slack, William M. 11:171
Slacker, John 4:53
Slackford, George 23:167
Sladdard, J. S. 2:17
Slade, E. 3:177
Slade, Edwin E. 1:74
Slade, F. 15:3
Slade, Frederick 12:77
Slade, H. 25:71
Slade, Henry 13:119

Slade, Jesse 7:110
Slade, John 18:414
Slade, M. C. 9:150
Slade, N. C. 27:108
Slade, Samuel 22:491
Slader, F. 3:177
Slader, G. C. 18:253;
26:62
Slaffer, Hector 21:284
Slafter, A. 11:404
Slafter, Albert 16:141
Slagel, Frank M. 18:210
Slaght, C. 1:168
Slaglane, --- 15:175
Slagle, Alfred 10:22
Slagle, D. W. 15:227
Slagle, Franklin 21:234
Slagle, J. R. 14:317
Slagle, John 22:163
Slahe, E. 25:73
Slain, R. 12:54
Slale, J. R. 14:322
Slamel, Peter 10:80
Slamner, John A. 22:441
Slamson, Reuben 12:39
Slanager, F. 1:172
Slander, Edwin A. 14:109
Slaner, Anthony 7:61
Slanson, D. S. 14:303
Slanter, --- 10:193
Slantower, --- 15:227
Slanucline, W. 27:117
Slapel, William 23:168,
173
Slarett, A. 26:59
Slark, H. 16:305
Slash, Henry 9:45
Slasher, E. 13:98; 14:21
Slasher, Elijah 17:42
Slasinger, Herman 17:59
Slasleman, M. 27:116
Slasser, Noiah 18:159
Slasser, Uriah 8:31
Slat, Phelan 16:227
Slate, A. F. 19:326
Slate, Charles S. 12:39
Slate, Isaac A. 13:47
Slate, J. F. 9:243
Slate, J. R. 23:168
Slate, L. L. 20:348
Slate, Robert H. 24:10
Slate, T. 23:15
Slate, W. 12:97
Slate, William 21:191
Slaten, Francis 20:348
Slater, --- 17:144
Slater, A. J. 20:47
Slater, Albert H. 7:110
Slater, Alonzo 1:71
Slater, Charles 3:177

Slater, Daniel 7:81;
25:304
Slater, E. B. 9:59
Slater, Ed 3:177
Slater, Edward 7:110
Slater, Garrett 20:36
Slater, George 14:109;
22:345
Slater, George D. 21:388
Slater, Hiram 10:79;
11:112; 20:190
Slater, J. 1:169, 171; 2:18;
15:6; 18:71; 25:67
Slater, J. L. 17:289; 22:54
Slater, James 14:218
Slater, James H. 1:73
Slater, John 3:177; 7:84;
15:168; 16:227;
21:388; 22:238;
24:162
Slater, John H. 4:53
Slater, John J. 17:232
Slater, Major 11:112
Slater, Marcus 21:59
Slater, Mathew 18:94
Slater, P. 1:169
Slater, Peter 21:388
Slater, R. 3:177; 9:59, 91
Slater, Robert 14:218
Slater, Samuel 14:218;
22:220
Slater, Samuel W. 17:239
Slater, Seymour S. 22:411
Slater, Thomas 10:79
Slater, W. 26:183
Slater, Walter 5:54
Slater, William 8:67;
22:155
Slater, William H. 9:91;
17:323; 26:59
Slater, William W. 23:280
Slaterly, B. W. 9:28
Slaterly, C. D. 13:119
Slatery, J. 14:218
Slates, William L. 12:39
Slatherty, T. 1:173
Slation, Sumner F. 22:130
Slatler, Henry 1:73
Slatman, Joseph 20:349
Slator, William 9:232
Slatt, George 1:71
Slatt, Lionel L. 10:80
Slatten, Andr 18:401
Slatten, Andrew 10:26
Slatten, James A. 20:13
Slatter, B. 1:76
Slatter, Peter 9:150
Slatterback, James 25:327
Slatterback, John H. 6:33
Slatterback, Joseph 6:33
Slatteri, J. 21:41

Slatterly, A. H. 20:152
Slatterly, P. 1:74
Slattery, Daniel 9:17
Slattery, J. 1:95
Slattery, J. D. 16:102
Slattery, Jessie 16:227
Slattery, John 17:403
Slattery, P. 15:45
Slattery, Patrick 12:77
Slattery, Tim 22:345
Slattery, W. 15:327;
    19:99, 194
Slattry, John 13:47
Slaugh, Abraham 21:234
Slaugh, James 12:39
Slaughenhouss, Levi
    19:34
Slaughter, B. W. 16:228
Slaughter, Benjamin 8:42;
    26:180
Slaughter, D. 14:109
Slaughter, E. 1:73
Slaughter, F. 22:319
Slaughter, George 10:79;
    20:349
Slaughter, Henry 7:133
Slaughter, J. 14:109;
    20:149
Slaughter, J. C. 9:104
Slaughter, J. L. 9:91;
    26:61
Slaughter, Joseph 22:114
Slaughter, Lewis 22:101
Slaughter, Nicholas 19:48
Slaughter, S. 17:185
Slaughter, Samuel 8:78
Slaughter, Selim 16:55
Slaughter, Solomon 7:133
Slaughter, Taylor 4:54
Slaughter, Thomas 5:45
Slaughter, W. A. 23:167
Slaughter, W. H. 2:17
Slaughter, William 8:95
Slaughter, William H.
    25:70
Slaughterback, B. 3:177
Slausan, D. S. 17:470
Slausher, August 1:75
Slauter, T. 25:233
Slavach, Benjamin 16:124
Slaven, James 11:407
Slaven, John E. 12:54
Slaven, P. 1:171
Slavens, James 13:129
Slavey, John 26:62
Slavin, H. 17:16
Slawson, D. S. 27:117
Slawson, J. 14:109
Slawson, J. N. 4:54
Slawson, James 20:349;
    27:107

Slawson, Oscar 21:85
Slawter, W. H. 15:319
Slay, James 22:284
Slay, T. 10:180; 18:180
Slayhill, J. 9:31
Slayian, James G. 20:349
Slaymakey, J. S. 18:401
Slayman, J. 21:126
Slayton, James G. 9:232
Slayton, James S. 22:490
Slayton, Morris 17:289
Slayton, R. H. 27:116
Slayton, William J. 17:68
Sleade, G. H. 7:41
Sleagle, Elias 11:45
Slean, W. C. 2:17; 25:73
Slearns, W. 16:305
Sleattry, John 16:55
Sleavens, William H.
    10:80
Sleck, R. 9:193
Sledge, Egber N. 21:284
Slee, C. 25:233
Slee, Christian 5:29
Slee, Cook 19:194
Slee, Cork 10:167
Slee, R. 3:177
Sleege, Richard 20:399
Sleek, Hezekiah 14:218
Sleek, Rudolph 16:228
Sleep, Samuel 24:97
Sleepe, William C. 11:392
Sleeper, B. 13:47
Sleeper, Charles 21:59
Sleeper, George 13:47;
    16:55
Sleeper, George G. 14:218
Sleeper, Henry 4:54
Sleeper, John B. 16:55
Sleeper, O. F. 25:233
Sleeper, Oscar F. 5:29
Sleeper, R. 16:228
Sleers, I. 15:59
Sleete, George 17:308
Sleeth, James 10:136;
    20:349
Sleetman, Thomas 12:40
Sleezer, F. J. 17:42
Slegel, M. 27:110
Sleibock, D. R. 14:218
Sleighpaugh, H. 13:47
Sleight, C. 3:178
Sleight, G. G. 21:388
Sleight, J. 21:112
Sleighter, --- 18:180
Sleigle, M. 9:150
Sleim, Robert 15:112
Sleinbeck, Francis J.
    23:125
Sleine, John 18:159

Sleish, Benjamin F.
    10:136
Slem, J. J. 13:127
Slemmer, Henry 10:80;
    20:349
Slemson, William 13:47
Slenaker, C. 10:29;
    19:306
Sleralt, James 9:45
Slesser, H. 14:303;
    17:480; 27:117
Slewallen, Jacob 13:47
Sleybaugh, Joseph 22:510
Sleyers, John 25:233
Slicer, Joseph 26:181
Slick, Francis R. 19:261
Slick, John 13:119
Slick, P. 3:178
Slicker, J. 3:178
Slicker, Rufus 1:71
Slicter, Uriah 19:34
Slicton, Andrew 8:120
Slidell, J. 17:478
Slidell, John 14:303;
    27:117
Slidell, Joseph 24:69
Slider, Jesse 22:439
Slider, Wesley 12:77; 15:9
Sliderlee, J. 25:74
Sliea, Thomas 22:130
Sligh, Robert 16:141
Slight, C. F. 17:42
Slight, H. 7:41
Slight, Jeremiah 12:39
Slighter, William 8:55
Slighton, I. F. 8:31
Slighton, J. T. 18:159
Slimer, Henry 14:109
Slimm, M. 13:98; 14:21
Slimon, Charles 11:221
Slimp, W. 3:178
Sline, John 8:31; 16:305
Slinger, A. E. 3:178
Slinger, Oliver 9:193;
    19:271
Slingerland, D. 17:434;
    24:172
Slingerland, H. 1:170
Slingerland, W. H. 1:76
Slingerlaw, John 3:178
Slingrous, R. 14:109
Slinker, J. W. 17:308
Slinker, Lewis R. 22:457
Sliron, Albert 21:239
Slish, Benjamin F. 20:349
Slite, William 26:129
Sliter, Adelbert L. 7:110
Sliter, Erwin 14:218
Sliter, G. 9:193; 19:261
Sliter, H. R. 9:193
Sliter, W. R. 19:261

Slith, A. W. 14:109
Slitroill, William 13:119
Slitt, John 26:61
Slitzer, G. 3:178
Slivens, C. 3:178
Sloab, Melanthon 7:17
Sloan, --- 10:175; 14:322;
　23:206
Sloan, Abner 7:110
Sloan, Arthur 11:130
Sloan, B. K. 17:112
Sloan, Charles F. 10:93
Sloan, Daniel 11:111
Sloan, David 10:167;
　15:327; 19:100, 193
Sloan, David A. 23:79
Sloan, E. P. 23:168
Sloan, Edward S. 20:349
Sloan, Edwin S. 9:232
Sloan, George 1:75;
　13:68; 18:39; 19:194
Sloan, George B. 4:54
Sloan, Granville H.
　24:204
Sloan, Harvey 21:234
Sloan, Hugh 10:207
Sloan, I. 3:178
Sloan, I. M. 3:178
Sloan, J. 13:126; 14:237
Sloan, J. P. 9:67; 18:280
Sloan, Jacob W. 21:234
Sloan, James 9:39;
　21:213, 218
Sloan, John 23:168;
　27:114
Sloan, John A. 21:197
Sloan, John B. 12:40
Sloan, John H. 24:69
Sloan, Josiah 11:313
Sloan, L. 3:178
Sloan, Miles 26:226
Sloan, Milton 9:163;
　25:327
Sloan, P. 3:178
Sloan, Richard 15:227
Sloan, S. 3:178; 22:355
Sloan, Samuel 10:170;
　19:194
Sloan, W. J. 2:17
Sloan, W. W. 26:184
Sloan, William 4:54;
　15:227; 22:130
Sloan, William H. 1:70
Sloan, Y. 13:98
Sloane, Frederick 22:130
Sloane, M. 14:109
Sloane, William 15:284;
　19:100
Sloat, D. 3:178
Sloat, E. 3:178
Sloat, Edward A. 23:261

Sloat, G. W. 3:178
Sloat, J. I. 26:226
Sloat, John 16:102
Sloat, Louis 14:218
Sloat, Samuel 23:110
Sloat, William 3:178
Sloats, F. 3:178
Slocan, J. B. 19:325
Slock, H. 12:93
Slocker, C. B. 14:218
Slockholmes, John 20:349
Slocum, C. H. 22:155
Slocum, C. S. 1:70
Slocum, Charles H.
　22:155
Slocum, Edward 13:47
Slocum, G. 1:174
Slocum, George 12:40
Slocum, George T. 3:178
Slocum, Henry 8:95; 9:14,
　136; 27:111
Slocum, J. H. 2:18; 25:73
Slocum, J. M. 1:77
Slocum, James W. 17:87
Slocum, John 16:228
Slocum, Lester 10:93;
　20:349
Slocum, Lloyd 4:54
Slocum, Louis 14:218
Slocum, M. L. 19:224
Slocum, Martin H. 24:56
Slocum, Martin W. 9:202
Slocum, Reuben 27:148
Slocum, Samuel 21:151,
　284
Slocum, Theodore 7:110
Slocum, W. 1:174
Slocum, William 13:135;
　19:347
Slocum, Zina B. 21:243
Slograt, Martin 16:149
Sloman, Robert 14:218
Slomfer, E. 16:271
Slomhecks, J. D. 3:178
Slone, John 9:125
Slong, James 19:100
Sloniker, George W.
　23:280
Slonniker, John 22:54
Slony, Francis 8:110
Sloon, George 14:109
Sloops, W. H. 9:243
Sloover, A. 3:178
Sloper, Myron J. 10:80
Slosher, H. 3:178
Sloss, Charles 9:211
Slote, George 14:109
Slote, P. P. 13:68
Sloter, S. 11:168
Sloth, Oliver 8:95
Slothouse, Henry 13:47

Slottberg, Christopher E.
　9:106
Slottenberg, Hans 20:349
Slough, A. 15:9
Slough, Abraham 12:77
Slough, Adam 8:55
Slough, E. B. 3:178
Slough, Frank 18:422
Slough, W. H. 9:91
Slough, William H. 26:61
Sloughton, J. B. 4:54
Sloup, H. 3:178
Sloup, J. 3:178
Sloute, James 12:77
Sloven, John 16:102
Slover, A. W. 3:178
Slover, Joel 17:441
Slow, George 19:100
Slow, Sylvester 4:54
Slow, William 22:441
Slow, William E. 24:45
Slowe, L. 21:41
Slowen, Robert 19:100
Slowley, Lewis P. 20:349
Slowman, Christian
　22:155
Slowman, Francis 20:349
Slowmand, Francis
　10:136
Slowns, T. F. 20:139
Slowood, C. 14:109
Slowron, M. 14:109
Sloy, J. M. 21:113
Slucker, T. E. 8:95
Sluckey, Thomas 8:95
Sluder, J. M. 11:97
Slufrew, B. W. 16:55
Slufrio, B. W. 13:47
Slumon, Isaac H. A.
　19:324
Slumsford, James 18:71
Slunner, Joseph L. 9:28
Slurd, J. 22:269
Slurgis, Daniel 19:34
Slusher, Calvin 10:80
Slusher, David 22:101
Slusher, George 8:31
Slusher, George T. 18:159
Slusher, James 17:201
Slusher, M. 12:147;
　19:307
Sluss, George 22:54
Sluss, John L. 22:54
Slusse, J. 11:250
Slusser, James 11:250
Slusser, Robert 21:41
Slusser, Thomas 23:168
Slusten, Calvin 20:349
Sluster, Leander C. 13:47;
　16:55
Slutz, Carrie 21:151

Sluvellan, Jacob 16:55
Sluyter, Alonzo 13:127
Sly, Cornelius 18:280
Sly, F. 3:178
Sly, F. C. 15:227
Sly, H. 14:266, 267
Sly, H. J. 15:112
Sly, Henry 12:97; 15:361; 19:100
Sly, J. D. 22:220
Sly, J. W. 17:307
Sly, Moses 21:388
Sly, Vincent F. 1:76
Sly, William 10:136; 13:119; 20:349
Slyke, Henry 11:173
Slyming, F. 10:149; 18:57
Slyoff, H. 3:178
Slypes, R. 12:93
Slyter, William T. 21:143
Slytes, Charles 19:194
Slythe, George W. 20:101
Smaatzried, C. 27:107
Smackem, A. 27:109
Smackire, Abram 9:155
Smades, W. 3:178
Smail, W. 21:126
Smalain, Ransom B. 8:95
Smalhood, Stephen 18:94
Small, --- 2:17; 15:227; 25:68
Small, Abraham K. 12:40
Small, Alexander 11:212
Small, B. 25:233
Small, Benjamin F. 19:34
Small, C. C. 15:112
Small, C. E. 14:110
Small, Charles 21:284
Small, Charles M. 4:54
Small, Daniel 13:47
Small, David 9:232; 21:388
Small, E. A. 8:67; 26:183
Small, Edward 12:65; 21:388
Small, Frederick 21:234
Small, G. R. 19:234
Small, George R. 9:193
Small, H. 3:178
Small, H. L. 9:244
Small, Henry 1:192
Small, Henry J. 9:136; 21:143
Small, Henry John 27:112
Small, Henry S. 16:79
Small, Hughs 4:54
Small, I. 3:178
Small, J. A. 25:67
Small, J. F. 1:170
Small, J. J. 2:18
Small, Jackson 8:95

Small, James 7:110
Small, James W. 23:50
Small, Jerome P. 15:227
Small, John 16:149; 19:194; 21:93; 22:155
Small, John P. 12:40
Small, Joseph 13:47; 16:55
Small, L. C. 14:218
Small, Michael 9:125; 27:114
Small, O. D. 21:388
Small, Oscar D. 9:215
Small, Ozra 23:93
Small, Peter 17:426; 23:168
Small, Reuben 15:301; 16:228
Small, Robert 19:347
Small, S. 3:178
Small, Samuel 27:118
Small, T. 13:98
Small, T. J. 21:388
Small, Thomas 22:319; 27:107
Small, Timothy 9:212
Small, Waner 14:218
Small, William 1:77, 78; 14:218; 18:285; 26:135
Small, William H. 16:228
Small, William P. 12:40
Small, William R. 23:93
Smallen, Glenn 20:47
Smalley, A. C. 8:55
Smalley, Abner 23:168
Smalley, Alexander C. 21:261
Smalley, Daniel 7:110
Smalley, Frazier F. 24:62
Smalley, George 3:178; 25:233
Smalley, H. B. 8:75
Smalley, J. 22:345
Smalley, J. A. 22:220
Smalley, J. F. 1:77
Smalley, James 11:289
Smalley, John 10:22; 11:312
Smalley, Nathan B. 9:193; 19:261
Smalley, Reuben 18:223
Smalley, Robert N. 9:104
Smalley, S. 3:178
Smalley, S. S. 3:178
Smalley, S. W. 1:70
Smalley, Samuel C. 8:95
Smalley, Theron M. 21:261
Smalley, Thomas 16:228

Smalley, William 22:492
Smallford, E. 13:98
Smalling, George W. 27:114
Smalling, I. 19:261
Smalling, Isaac 9:193
Smalling, William D. 20:47
Smallman, John 11:416
Smallman, S. H. 22:269
Smallmann, J. W. 3:178
Smallridge, A. 14:110
Smallwood, C. 3:178
Smallwood, Eli 24:45
Smallwood, Elijah 21:132
Smallwood, Elisha 10:80; 20:349
Smallwood, Henry 9:162
Smallwood, J. 22:355
Smallwood, J. M. 11:329
Smallwood, Lawson H. 20:28
Smallwood, Levi 24:60
Smallwood, Madison 25:270
Smallwood, Martin V. 22:457
Smallwood, Thomas 11:112
Smallwood, W. 22:355
Smallwood, W. B. 1:174
Smallwood, William 22:54
Smally, Allen G. 24:30
Smally, J. H. 3:178
Smaltz, John 17:497
Smaltz, L. 3:178
Smaple, George F. 24:44
Smart, A. 10:151, 178
Smart, Adam 18:431
Smart, Charles 17:399
Smart, Charles A. 8:55; 21:126
Smart, Charles H. 21:218
Smart, D. 21:388
Smart, Daniel 19:344
Smart, G. 7:76; 25:304
Smart, George 8:110; 11:213; 21:59
Smart, Henry 25:233
Smart, Hugh 10:93
Smart, J. A. 24:102
Smart, J. W. 10:80; 20:349
Smart, Jackson 27:112
Smart, James C. 19:100
Smart, John 12:171
Smart, John C. 15:227
Smart, John W. 10:80; 20:349
Smart, Joseph T. 14:218

Smart, Joshua 24:204
Smart, Levi 17:268
Smart, M. T. 27:109
Smart, Robert 21:388
Smart, W. H. 7:76; 25:304
Smartley, Solon 9:193
Smartz, Solon 19:284
Smash, Christian 4:54
Smash, Isaac E. 7:110
Smathel, George 19:100
Smatts, John 1:72
Smay, Albert 16:228
Smays, David 3:178
Smayzer, M. 20:349
Smazer, Mallum 10:80
Smead, John 19:35
Smead, L. 3:178
Smeales, Alex 13:47
Smearbauch, L. 8:55
Smearer, George 17:59
Smearpoch, Lawrence
  21:261
Smeck, Marbur 12:77
Smedley, Dallas 17:156
Smedley, J. 1:77
Smedley, Richard 21:218
Smeedes, Isaac 21:388
Smeidle, Adolphus 11:78
Smelcer, Abraham J.
  20:349
Smelcer, William 18:401
Smelear, John C. 13:47
Smell, Daniel 15:227
Smell, L. D. 16:228
Smelledge, Charles B.
  10:22
Smelling, George W.
  9:125
Smelling, James K. Polk
  22:269
Smelser, Adam 11:19
Smelser, Charles W.
  23:168
Smelser, John 11:392
Smelt, Powell 25:72
Smelter, Noah 9:67
Smeltzer, J. 1:75; 25:233
Smeltzer, Milton 22:101
Smelzer, James F. 9:150
Smerick, Prucilla 15:228
Smettrer, John 15:279
Smetzer, C. F. 16:149
Smice, David 7:61
Smice, W. 3:178
Smich, Alonzo 20:349
Smich, Isaac 21:80
Smick, Alonzo 10:136
Smickel, G. 1:74
Smiddy, G. G. 17:297
Smiddy, Reuben 17:167
Smidey, E. 3:178

Smidt, Carsten N. 17:26
Smidt, Frank 20:349
Smidt, George 8:110;
  13:48
Smidt, Jacob 17:42
Smidt, S. 11:130
Smidts, Michael 17:26
Smike, Jacob 15:228
Smilcer, Abraham H.
  10:136
Smile, William F. 11:171
Smiler, Samuel 8:75
Smiley, A. 18:407
Smiley, A. P. 15:135
Smiley, Amos 21:388
Smiley, C. C. 2:18
Smiley, D. 1:175
Smiley, David 12:40
Smiley, E. M. 23:168
Smiley, F. 14:218
Smiley, George 14:110
Smiley, George W. 24:56
Smiley, Hiram 22:155
Smiley, Jesse 18:376
Smiley, John 9:151;
  17:420; 22:221;
  24:162
Smiley, John A. 6:19;
  18:94
Smiley, John J. 11:397
Smiley, John T. 20:44
Smiley, Jonathan A.
  17:266
Smiley, M. 15:228
Smiley, S. H. 11:44
Smiley, Thaddeus 22:320
Smiley, William 18:17;
  21:80
Smilk, Simon 24:204
Smilley, --- 3:178
Smilley, Charles C. 25:73
Smily, John 27:110
Smiter, George 22:439
Smith, --- 1:71; 10:180;
  11:168, 417; 12:170;
  14:111, 218, 322;
  15:135; 17:213, 499,
  509; 18:17, 39, 71,
  180; 19:100, 297;
  22:355, 467; 23:206;
  26:61
Smith, ---os 24:114
Smith, A. 1:172, 174;
  2:18; 3:178; 7:41;
  9:150; 12:84, 93;
  14:110, 219, 285;
  15:84; 16:282, 305;
  17:185; 18:17; 20:44;
  21:388; 23:50; 25:73,
  233, 273

Smith, A. A. 9:113;
  21:388
Smith, A. B. 8:55; 14:263;
  27:118
Smith, A. C. 3:178; 9:99;
  18:57; 20:175, 179;
  21:202, 291; 22:522
Smith, A. D. 8:55
Smith, A. E. 1:75; 7:133;
  14:110
Smith, A. G. 15:112
Smith, A. H. 3:178;
  12:143; 13:68;
  19:100; 20:349;
  21:388; 22:130;
  25:233
Smith, A. J. 1:174; 3:178;
  10:80; 12:158; 13:98;
  20:349
Smith, A. K. 13:98
Smith, A. L. 17:165;
  18:253; 26:62
Smith, A. M. 1:173; 9:99;
  18:71
Smith, A. P. 1:172; 13:48
Smith, A. R. 18:253;
  26:64
Smith, A. T. 9:29; 21:164
Smith, Aaron 9:136, 232;
  17:185; 20:349;
  27:112
Smith, Aaron C. 11:271
Smith, Aaron G. 19:34
Smith, Aaron H. 5:29
Smith, Abraham 17:162;
  18:401; 22:220
Smith, Abraham J. 22:131
Smith, Abram 21:234
Smith, Abram W. 8:95
Smith, Adam 8:95; 23:168
Smith, Adam B. 21:106
Smith, Adam W. 22:440
Smith, Addis E. 17:293
Smith, Addison 17:138,
  145; 24:204
Smith, Adelbert 12:77;
  15:82
Smith, Adventure 21:261
Smith, Alba B. 20:109
Smith, Albert 2:17; 4:54;
  7:133; 8:75, 110;
  9:67, 125, 193, 211;
  12:100; 13:68;
  15:348, 366; 16:141,
  282; 17:72; 19:100;
  22:221; 25:287;
  27:112, 114, 119
Smith, Albert C. 9:91;
  22:284; 26:59
Smith, Albert D. 27:107
Smith, Albert E. 4:54

Smith, Albert G. 4:54
Smith, Albert H. 7:84; 26:181
Smith, Alex A. 17:204
Smith, Alex. M. 22:490
Smith, Alexander 7:133; 8:42, 55; 10:80; 11:213, 270; 12:77; 19:330; 22:269; 26:180
Smith, Alford 22:54
Smith, Alfred 17:185; 19:261; 22:115, 522; 23:309; 25:233; 27:109, 148
Smith, Alfred C. 19:340
Smith, Alfred L. 10:136; 20:349
Smith, Alfred N. 22:467
Smith, Allen 3:178; 8:32; 18:159; 22:269
Smith, Allen H. 13:48
Smith, Almon 20:49
Smith, Alonzo 11:194; 16:55; 27:108
Smith, Alturna C. 22:172
Smith, Alva 10:80; 20:190, 349; 24:180
Smith, Alva S. 10:136
Smith, Alvah S. 20:349
Smith, Alvin 21:93
Smith, Alvin W. 18:210
Smith, Alvrado 23:287
Smith, Americus P. 17:362
Smith, Ami 22:54
Smith, Ami M. 25:69
Smith, Amos 7:110; 11:270; 13:119; 23:168
Smith, Amos A. 14:271; 23:79
Smith, Amos C. 1:72
Smith, Amos F. 9:14
Smith, Anderson 17:185; 22:102
Smith, Anderson C. 13:47
Smith, Andrew 3:178; 9:39; 17:353; 18:94, 297; 19:100; 21:95; 22:173, 345; 24:97; 25:69; 26:112
Smith, Andrew C. 16:162
Smith, Andrew F. 22:284
Smith, Andrew J. 11:213
Smith, Andrew J. P. 21:248
Smith, Andrew W. 15:74
Smith, Anson 17:501
Smith, Anthony 7:41; 14:335; 18:194

Smith, Anthony H. 10:22
Smith, Anton G. 15:168
Smith, Arbey 22:155
Smith, Archibald 1:72
Smith, Arras A. 20:349
Smith, Arthur 14:218
Smith, Asa 13:76; 14:219; 16:228; 17:449; 24:174
Smith, Asa S. 23:79
Smith, Augustus 13:59; 23:93
Smith, Aurelius C. S. 5:29
Smith, Austin 22:439
Smith, B. 3:178; 13:48, 98, 99; 16:55; 17:185; 20:349; 21:113
Smith, B. A. 18:39
Smith, B. C. 7:111; 25:312
Smith, B. F. 11:45; 12:40; 14:21; 21:191
Smith, B. H. 9:59
Smith, B. M. 7:41
Smith, B. N. 3:178
Smith, B. P. 9:59
Smith, B. S. 13:99
Smith, B. W. 9:193; 19:271
Smith, Barney 8:75; 21:41; 23:168
Smith, Bartlett 21:388
Smith, Benjamin 4:54; 8:42; 9:136; 10:80; 13:48, 59; 18:39; 20:139, 349; 22:320; 26:180; 27:111
Smith, Benjamin Beady 4:54
Smith, Benjamin E. 1:70
Smith, Benjamin F. 9:99; 22:54
Smith, Benjamin H. 17:93
Smith, Benjamin P. 1:75
Smith, Benjamin R. 15:345; 16:379
Smith, Bentley J. 14:110
Smith, Bernard 3:178; 10:22
Smith, Bethuel 21:261
Smith, Bird 10:80; 20:349
Smith, Bishop 17:167
Smith, Bishop B. 21:388
Smith, Briton 9:91
Smith, Brittan 26:59
Smith, Bund 10:80
Smith, Buris 21:41
Smith, Burr W. 13:48
Smith, Burrell 8:42; 26:180

Smith, Burris W. 23:168
Smith, Butler 25:327
Smith, Buttler 9:166
Smith, Byron D. 15:228
Smith, C. 1:76, 168, 173, 174; 3:179; 7:41; 12:166; 14:110, 219, 259; 15:337; 16:379; 18:407; 19:100; 21:164; 22:220; 23:50
Smith, C. A. 1:173; 3:179; 14:219, 259; 23:50
Smith, C. B. 1:99; 3:179; 19:194
Smith, C. C. 25:233
Smith, C. D. 10:136
Smith, C. E. 3:179; 25:233; 27:115
Smith, C. F. 18:253; 26:64; 27:107
Smith, C. H. 1:168; 10:80; 16:305; 20:349; 25:233
Smith, C. J. 1:169; 15:314
Smith, C. K. 19:242
Smith, C. L. 20:349; 21:388; 25:71
Smith, C. M. 25:233
Smith, C. O. C. 1:76
Smith, C. P. 1:70
Smith, C. R. 15:135
Smith, C. R. G. 25:304
Smith, C. S. 1:75, 172; 9:91; 12:123; 14:303; 15:135; 17:473; 21:388; 25:71; 27:117
Smith, C. W. 1:78; 3:179; 12:77; 17:362; 22:238; 27:107
Smith, Cabe 5:45
Smith, Cacine 9:136; 27:111
Smith, Cal 21:388
Smith, Caleb 17:399
Smith, Calvin 10:180; 18:180
Smith, Calvin J. 8:95
Smith, Calvin L. 22:220
Smith, Cammel 25:286
Smith, Carter 9:211
Smith, Cephus 22:319
Smith, Chancy H. 9:125
Smith, Charles 1:76, 191; 3:179; 6:27; 7:76, 110, 133; 9:91, 125, 211; 10:22, 136, 151; 11:17, 184, 213, 404; 12:40, 52; 13:48, 59, 119; 14:110, 219;

Smith, Charles 15:75, 82, 228, 288; 16:228; 17:68, 394, 455; 19:100; 20:349; 21:143; 22:221, 320; 24:204; 25:72, 304; 26:60; 27:111
Smith, Charles A. 21:388; 22:54, 411
Smith, Charles D. 10:80; 11:289; 20:349
Smith, Charles E. 5:45; 17:68
Smith, Charles F. 21:11, 389; 22:155
Smith, Charles H. 5:29; 17:208; 22:467; 24:45; 25:71
Smith, Charles J. 18:253; 26:63
Smith, Charles L. 9:59; 11:172
Smith, Charles M. 5:29
Smith, Charles N. 10:207
Smith, Charles O. 9:125
Smith, Charles R. 10:80; 12:77; 15:23; 20:349
Smith, Charles R. C. 7:76
Smith, Charles W. 5:29; 7:110; 8:118; 11:171; 14:219; 17:26; 21:143; 24:56; 25:233
Smith, Chauncey 14:219; 22:173
Smith, Chauncy H. 27:113
Smith, Chester 16:102; 21:59
Smith, Christian 10:80; 13:135; 19:347; 20:349
Smith, Christopher 7:110; 11:77; 21:389
Smith, Christopher C. 10:136; 20:349
Smith, Christopher K. 9:193
Smith, Clarence R. 1:73
Smith, Clark H. 23:50
Smith, Clarkson 13:119
Smith, Cline 15:228
Smith, Columbus 17:264
Smith, Commodore P. 24:70
Smith, Conrad 3:179
Smith, Constantine 22:457
Smith, Cornelius 10:167
Smith, Cornelius F. 11:18
Smith, Creed 10:136; 20:349
Smith, Crocket C. 23:185

Smith, Cyrus 7:41; 11:393; 22:220
Smith, Cyrus B. 21:389
Smith, Cyrus W. 22:163
Smith, D. 1:77, 169, 174, 176; 2:18; 3:179; 7:41; 14:219, 279, 303; 16:102, 228; 17:481; 18:376; 25:74; 27:117
Smith, D. A. 7:41; 23:93
Smith, D. B. 8:67
Smith, D. G. 15:228
Smith, D. H. 3:179; 10:187; 18:180; 20:3
Smith, D. L. 7:61
Smith, D. M. 11:77
Smith, D. N. 15:112
Smith, D. O. 1:170
Smith, D. P. 9:59
Smith, D. R. 11:43
Smith, D. W. 23:250
Smith, Daniel 1:70; 4:54; 8:67; 9:233; 10:210; 11:213, 342; 13:68; 14:110; 15:228; 16:102; 17:138; 21:389; 22:102; 24:203; 26:180, 183
Smith, Daniel B. 12:40
Smith, Daniel G. 4:54; 20:350
Smith, Daniel H. 7:111
Smith, Daniel J. 7:63
Smith, Daniel K. 21:197
Smith, Daniel O. 7:80; 25:304
Smith, Daniel S. 7:111
Smith, Daniel V. 9:45
Smith, Darius C. 8:55
Smith, David 1:70, 74; 4:54; 10:93; 14:219, 317, 322; 15:301, 309; 17:43; 18:17; 19:100; 20:44, 350; 21:85, 126; 22:15, 221, 468; 23:50, 309; 24:85
Smith, David C. 4:54; 13:48
Smith, David D. 7:41
Smith, David G. 10:80
Smith, David H. 9:99
Smith, David L. 10:136; 20:350
Smith, David M. 22:221; 23:50
Smith, David N. 9:39; 18:297; 26:113
Smith, David P. 23:241
Smith, David W. 10:22

Smith, Delos C. 21:261
Smith, Denmark 4:54
Smith, Dennis 6:9; 17:406; 18:105
Smith, Dennis R. 22:439
Smith, Dexter 23:104
Smith, Doctor 7:133
Smith, Douglass 21:389
Smith, Duke 7:133
Smith, Duncan 7:111
Smith, Dunion 9:224
Smith, Durvis 7:110
Smith, E. 1:71, 74, 78, 170, 172, 176; 3:179; 7:41, 69; 10:187; 11:270; 13:99, 103; 14:110, 219; 15:345; 16:271, 379; 17:218, 357; 18:180; 19:261; 24:108, 115; 25:233
Smith, E. A. 10:193; 18:180
Smith, E. B. 13:119; 15:288; 16:228
Smith, E. C. 23:303
Smith, E. D. 22:345
Smith, E. E. 3:179
Smith, E. F. 7:41; 10:210
Smith, E. G. 26:181
Smith, E. H. 10:149; 12:86; 13:131; 14:110; 15:160, 228; 16:305; 18:57
Smith, E. Hamilton 8:55
Smith, E. K. 15:168
Smith, E. M. 1:70; 3:179; 26:60
Smith, E. R. 8:115; 25:233; 27:107
Smith, E. S. 15:175
Smith, E. W. 4:54; 11:111, 251; 25:74
Smith, Eben 12:84; 16:305
Smith, Ebenezer 5:29
Smith, Ebenezer H. 22:131
Smith, Ed 17:138, 185; 24:204
Smith, Edgar 4:54
Smith, Edmond 8:42
Smith, Edmond J. 4:54
Smith, Edom Allen 21:80
Smith, Edw. F. 9:104
Smith, Edward 1:72; 3:179; 4:54; 7:110; 8:32, 55; 9:9, 91, 99; 17:297; 18:159, 341; 19:194; 21:151, 284; 23:182; 26:58, 180
Smith, Edward A. 24:97

Smith, Edward C. 21:143
Smith, Edward L. 10:149;
13:47; 18:57
Smith, Edward M. 9:91
Smith, Edward N. 22:102
Smith, Edward S. 22:54,
412
Smith, Edwin 17:138;
24:203
Smith, Edwin R. 5:29
Smith, Edwin S. 7:17
Smith, Egbert J. 11:111
Smith, Eleazer 11:112
Smith, Eli 8:31; 18:160
Smith, Elias 23:110
Smith, Elias D. 27:106
Smith, Elias J. 17:350
Smith, Elias W. 17:87
Smith, Eliazer 22:54
Smith, Elieum M. 14:219
Smith, Elijah 8:69, 95;
10:167; 11:336, 426;
24:30; 26:180
Smith, Elisha 11:77;
12:40; 17:275;
23:291
Smith, Elizar B. 10:136
Smith, Elizur B. 20:350
Smith, Ellridge 21:389
Smith, Elva A. 9:193;
19:233
Smith, Emerson L. 23:195
Smith, Emery N. 9:155
Smith, Emery W. 13:48
Smith, Emmanuel 17:145
Smith, Emmet D. 19:194
Smith, Enoch 9:136;
27:112
Smith, Enos 22:54;
23:182
Smith, Enos W. 13:119;
22:411
Smith, Ephraim 11:76;
22:115
Smith, Ephraim A. 22:438
Smith, Ernest 22:169
Smith, Erson H. 16:142
Smith, Esquire 11:336;
22:490
Smith, Eugene 9:125;
27:114
Smith, Eugene O. 7:110
Smith, Ewing 21:41
Smith, Ezra 5:29, 54;
10:80; 20:350
Smith, Ezra P. 24:45
Smith, F. 1:169, 170;
2:17, 18; 3:179;
5:45; 8:55; 13:119;
15:23; 16:124, 379;
20:180; 21:389;

Smith, F. 25:73, 74, 233;
26:183
Smith, F. A. 9:244
Smith, F. B. 15:301;
20:175
Smith, F. C. 25:304
Smith, F. D. 1:171
Smith, F. E. 12:40; 13:99
Smith, F. F. 13:119
Smith, F. H. 9:243
Smith, F. H. C. 9:193
Smith, F. I. 17:389
Smith, F. J. 9:59
Smith, F. L. 25:69
Smith, F. M. 10:136;
17:156, 192; 20:350
Smith, F. R. 1:171; 3:179
Smith, F. W. 8:31;
16:136; 18:160;
26:182
Smith, Fernando 22:130
Smith, Finley 18:341
Smith, Fistus 22:319
Smith, Fitch C. 7:80
Smith, Flavius I. 10:136
Smith, Flavius J. 20:350
Smith, Francis 7:111;
8:67; 13:119; 15:160;
20:157; 21:389;
22:155, 498; 23:195
Smith, Francis E. 13:48
Smith, Francis L. 12:40
Smith, Francis M. 21:241;
22:102, 411; 23:168
Smith, Francis W. 8:95
Smith, Frank 1:72; 3:179;
9:91; 12:65; 15:59,
303; 16:228; 21:151,
218, 389; 23:50;
26:59
Smith, Frank C. 9:193
Smith, Frank D. 19:194
Smith, Frank E. 19:276
Smith, Frank H. 9:125;
27:113
Smith, Frank L. 16:228
Smith, Frank M. 22:221
Smith, Frank R. 22:155
Smith, Frank W. 8:31;
18:160
Smith, Franklin 9:45, 113;
10:99; 15:9; 26:129
Smith, Franklin A. 21:128
Smith, Franklin T. 11:313
Smith, Freak 7:61
Smith, Fred 7:133;
12:166; 13:135;
18:253; 19:100, 347;
23:50, 110; 26:62
Smith, Fred. 8:69

Smith, Frederick 7:41;
11:45; 17:138;
22:506; 24:204;
25:233
Smith, Frederick E. 7:69
Smith, Freeman 5:29
Smith, Friday 22:319
Smith, G. 1:168; 3:179;
12:158; 13:119;
15:345; 16:228;
19:100; 21:95;
23:242, 308; 25:233,
327
Smith, G. A. 3:179
Smith, G. B. 12:84;
16:305
Smith, G. C. 1:173; 3:179;
19:194; 23:251
Smith, G. D. 14:110, 317,
322; 16:79; 23:125
Smith, G. F. 1:172;
21:389
Smith, G. H. 1:169; 3:179;
11:112; 14:219;
15:324; 19:100
Smith, G. L. 14:110
Smith, G. M. 1:76; 17:156
Smith, G. N. 17:160
Smith, G. O. 1:100
Smith, G. R. 3:179;
15:345
Smith, G. S. 1:168;
11:289
Smith, G. T. 26:61
Smith, G. W. 1:70, 77;
3:179; 10:180;
13:119; 14:110;
18:180; 21:261, 389;
23:168, 257, 287;
25:233; 27:118
Smith, Gabriel 7:133
Smith, Galloway 7:41
Smith, Garrett 5:45;
10:80; 20:350
Smith, Garritt 9:193
Smith, Geardus 11:404
Smith, Gee C. 1:75
Smith, George 1:72;
3:179; 4:54; 5:29;
6:33; 7:17, 84, 110;
8:78; 9:193; 10:80,
145, 167; 11:44, 282,
312, 329, 336; 12:40,
52, 56, 158; 14:110,
219; 15:273; 16:149;
17:59, 87, 138, 293;
18:39, 115, 253;
19:100, 194; 20:350;
21:41, 132, 151, 249,
261, 284, 389;
22:355, 516;

Smith, George 23:168, 182; 24:203, 204; 25:233, 289, 327; 26:61, 64
Smith, George A. 21:234
Smith, George A. W. 22:221
Smith, George B. 12:158
Smith, George C. 11:43
Smith, George D. 4:54; 10:136; 20:350
Smith, George E. 9:14, 125; 15:353; 16:102, 282; 21:389; 27:113
Smith, George G. 25:68
Smith, George H. 9:193; 13:47; 21:15; 27:148
Smith, George K. 22:490
Smith, George L. 7:41; 22:490
Smith, George M. 1:75; 9:91; 24:30
Smith, George N. 15:301; 16:228; 22:220
Smith, George R. 10:167; 18:223; 19:194; 21:389
Smith, George S. 16:102
Smith, George V. 11:312
Smith, George W. 5:29; 7:41; 8:95; 9:125; 12:77; 15:301; 16:228; 17:250; 18:253; 20:350; 21:126, 389; 22:54, 155, 220, 441, 467, 492; 23:283; 24:30, 213; 26:61; 27:113, 148
Smith, Ghas. W. 7:65
Smith, Gilbert 7:110; 19:293
Smith, Giles H. 7:41
Smith, Granville 21:284; 22:505
Smith, Granville H. 15:19
Smith, Grayson 9:136; 27:111
Smith, Green 10:209; 22:319, 457
Smith, Griffin L. 20:116
Smith, H. 1:71, 77, 168, 171, 176; 2:18; 3:179, 180; 5:29; 9:59, 91; 11:173; 12:57, 97; 13:99; 14:21, 219; 15:112, 135, 295, 361; 16:228; 20:157; 21:113; 22:221, 319;

Smith, H. 25:67, 233, 234; 26:61; 27:107
Smith, H. A. 9:113; 14:21, 110
Smith, H. B. 1:174; 3:179
Smith, H. C. 1:172; 8:31; 17:59; 18:160; 27:119
Smith, H. D. 21:41
Smith, H. E. 1:75, 169
Smith, H. F. 9:232; 10:80; 14:110; 18:253; 20:350; 25:72; 26:64
Smith, H. G. 18:316
Smith, H. H. 3:179; 18:280
Smith, H. I. 15:228
Smith, H. L. 7:41
Smith, H. M. 13:119
Smith, H. P. 1:78; 11:98
Smith, H. T. 14:110
Smith, H. V. 9:193; 19:230
Smith, H. W. 3:180; 11:171; 14:110
Smith, H. Y. 26:112
Smith, Hamilton 10:136; 20:350
Smith, Hamilton C. 11:77
Smith, Hamilton E. 21:80
Smith, Hanaril 19:100
Smith, Hardy 17:59
Smith, Harlan 17:138; 24:203
Smith, Harman 21:106
Smith, Harmon J. 11:17
Smith, Harrison 7:133; 11:392; 21:389
Smith, Harry 18:280; 22:320
Smith, Harvey 1:73; 4:54; 14:219
Smith, Harvey Y. 24:60
Smith, Henchel H. 22:411
Smith, Hendall T. 10:22
Smith, Henry 1:73; 3:179; 4:54, 68; 5:29, 45; 6:27; 7:41, 110; 8:42, 58, 95; 9:59, 193, 202, 238; 10:22, 167, 177; 11:76, 249, 404; 12:40, 77; 13:47, 119; 14:219; 15:92, 228, 309; 16:55, 228; 17:59, 185, 284, 448; 18:341; 19:100, 194, 276, 293; 20:13, 128, 350; 21:106, 151, 191, 213, 284; 22:102, 319, 345, 411; 23:79;

Smith, Henry 24:30, 173; 25:67, 69, 234; 26:180, 214, 225; 27:118
Smith, Henry A. 11:416
Smith, Henry C. 10:80; 20:350; 22:269
Smith, Henry Clay 17:410; 22:456
Smith, Henry D. 21:106; 22:15
Smith, Henry E. 1:72
Smith, Henry F. 10:136; 20:350; 22:284
Smith, Henry G. 11:45, 398
Smith, Henry H. 16:82; 18:223; 19:34; 22:221; 23:168
Smith, Henry J. 16:154
Smith, Henry L. 11:212; 12:171; 21:389
Smith, Henry M. 7:41
Smith, Henry O. 20:25
Smith, Henry R. 10:80; 20:350
Smith, Henry T. 13:47
Smith, Herbert 19:34
Smith, Herman 13:47
Smith, Hezekiah 15:45
Smith, Hillery 1:192
Smith, Hiram 8:31; 11:43; 18:160
Smith, Hiram A. J. 12:40
Smith, Hiram E. 24:97
Smith, Hiram T. 4:54
Smith, Holles 12:40
Smith, Hollis R. 12:100
Smith, Homer W. 11:111
Smith, Horace 3:179; 10:209; 13:48; 19:35
Smith, Howard B. 9:91
Smith, Hugh 4:54
Smith, Hulit 12:40
Smith, Humphrey 8:31; 18:160; 25:71
Smith, I. 3:180; 14:219; 15:228; 23:308; 25:234
Smith, I. A. 14:219; 15:228
Smith, I. C. 3:180; 20:350
Smith, I. J. 11:313
Smith, I. M. 1:77
Smith, I. S. 16:55
Smith, I. W. 8:31
Smith, Ira 10:149; 18:57
Smith, Ira C. 20:135
Smith, Ira H. 8:55; 21:261
Smith, Ira W. 22:54
Smith, Irwin 19:318

Smith, Isaac 4:54; 5:29, 45; 6:19; 8:32, 110; 9:163; 10:175; 11:169, 426; 13:47; 17:326; 18:94, 160; 19:194; 21:284; 23:125; 25:327
Smith, Isaac A. 11:188
Smith, Isaac B. 11:77
Smith, Isaac E. 17:350
Smith, Isaac H. 7:111; 10:136; 11:121; 20:350
Smith, Isaac M. 9:238; 20:25; 23:79; 26:225
Smith, Isaac N. 23:115
Smith, Isaac W. 10:80; 20:350
Smith, Isaiah 4:54; 9:244; 22:220
Smith, Isham 9:159; 21:213
Smith, Isom 21:151
Smith, J. 1:71, 74, 76, 99, 169, 170, 171, 172, 173, 174, 175; 3:180, 181; 7:61; 8:59; 9:150, 155; 10:29; 11:78, 172, 270; 12:123; 13:99, 126; 14:110, 111, 333; 15:45, 135, 309, 312, 319; 16:102, 228; 17:112; 18:94, 253; 19:100, 246, 277, 307; 21:41, 113, 389; 23:50, 245; 24:45, 85; 25:69, 234; 26:63; 27:109, 110
Smith, J. A. 1:174; 3:180, 181; 15:45; 16:55, 305; 19:100; 27:106
Smith, J. A. D. 23:206
Smith, J. B. 1:175; 3:180; 6:19; 7:41; 8:55; 14:111; 17:159; 18:94
Smith, J. C. 1:77; 3:180; 10:80; 13:47; 20:350; 25:70, 74
Smith, J. C. P. 17:307
Smith, J. D. 1:71; 3:181; 5:29; 17:290; 25:234
Smith, J. E. 3:180
Smith, J. F. 1:176; 3:181; 20:90; 23:314
Smith, J. G. 1:170; 7:41
Smith, J. H. 1:96; 3:180; 6:33; 9:59, 91, 113; 11:250, 342; 12:80; 15:75; 16:55;

Smith, J. H. 18:253; 21:205; 22:457; 25:234, 327; 26:63
Smith, J. Henry 22:221
Smith, J. J. 1:170; 4:54; 13:129; 14:285
Smith, J. K. 11:172; 18:253; 25:234; 26:63
Smith, J. L. 1:173; 14:111
Smith, J. M. 1:168, 169; 7:41; 10:136; 14:219; 17:162; 20:47, 350; 23:291; 24:30; 25:335; 26:58
Smith, J. N. 11:271; 14:219
Smith, J. P. 3:180; 14:111; 19:261; 21:41
Smith, J. R. 9:59; 18:270; 21:41; 22:220; 23:272
Smith, J. S. 20:180; 25:234
Smith, J. T. 9:91; 25:305; 26:61
Smith, J. W. 1:75, 78, 169; 3:180; 9:193; 17:43; 18:160; 19:194, 246, 261; 21:41; 22:221; 23:50
Smith, Jackson 3:180; 8:42; 26:180
Smith, Jackson W. 1:71
Smith, Jacob 1:72; 3:180; 6:13; 7:133; 8:95; 9:9, 29, 39, 193, 204; 10:136, 167; 13:47; 18:253, 297, 316, 344; 19:273; 20:350; 21:197; 22:457; 26:62, 113
Smith, Jacob A. 16:55; 19:194
Smith, Jacob D. 23:168
Smith, Jacob F. 12:40
Smith, Jacob H. 13:47
Smith, Jacob J. 17:317
Smith, James 1:74, 75, 191; 3:180, 181; 4:54, 68; 6:26; 7:41, 66, 78, 84, 110, 133; 9:29, 106, 136, 160, 193, 204, 211; 10:80, 136; 11:18, 77, 213, 271, 419; 12:158; 13:47, 99, 119; 14:21, 219, 237, 259; 15:135, 153, 228, 259, 303;

Smith, James 16:228, 305; 17:43, 138, 185, 218, 264; 18:39, 94, 115, 194, 223, 316, 422, 431; 19:100, 194; 20:3, 25, 90, 177, 350, 351; 21:85, 191, 205, 245, 284, 389; 22:345, 411; 24:60, 204; 25:234, 287, 305, 312; 26:111; 27:107, 112, 118
Smith, James A. 7:41; 10:22, 34; 12:77; 14:219; 15:75; 17:43, 162, 362; 23:168, 308
Smith, James C. 4:54; 10:80; 24:10
Smith, James D. 6:19; 25:71
Smith, James E. 17:26; 21:143
Smith, James F. 4:54; 12:40; 17:72
Smith, James G. 25:234
Smith, James H . 17:317
Smith, James H. 10:93, 137; 13:47; 17:208, 497; 20:351; 22:54, 131; 23:182
Smith, James I. 11:173; 24:97
Smith, James J. 9:193; 19:242; 23:264
Smith, James L. 10:137; 20:351
Smith, James M. 10:80, 97; 12:158; 17:43, 87, 321; 18:253; 20:105, 351; 21:80; 22:269; 26:62, 146
Smith, James Money 17:43
Smith, James P. 22:269; 25:70
Smith, James R. 14:219
Smith, James S. 12:158; 22:102
Smith, James T. 21:59
Smith, James U. 10:137
Smith, James W. 4:54; 10:137; 17:239; 19:194; 20:351; 23:79; 24:203
Smith, Japhet B. 22:54
Smith, Japtha 11:426
Smith, Jasper 17:426; 24:180
Smith, Jeff 17:150
Smith, Jefferson 27:111

Smith, Jefferson I. 14:271
Smith, Jehial 15:280;
   25:234
Smith, Jeremiah 9:125;
   10:22, 137; 15:228;
   18:280; 20:351;
   21:87, 389; 22:221,
   491; 25:234; 27:113
Smith, Jerome L. 17:357
Smith, Jerry 8:42; 9:202;
   19:293; 21:389;
   25:234; 26:180
Smith, Jesse 16:136;
   21:59, 143; 22:220;
   25:234
Smith, Jesse F. 21:143
Smith, Jesse M. 22:412
Smith, Jessie William
   26:214
Smith, Jo. 8:42
Smith, Joe 26:180
Smith, Joel 3:180
Smith, Joel C. 11:44
Smith, Joel J. 16:82
Smith, John 1:71, 72, 73,
   77; 3:180, 181, 224;
   4:54, 68; 5:29, 45;
   7:17, 41, 61, 65, 69,
   110, 133; 8:32, 95,
   110; 9:14, 136, 166,
   193, 202, 224, 238;
   10:8, 22, 93, 137,
   149, 150, 167; 11:17,
   43, 77, 121, 168,
   170, 184, 417, 435;
   12:40, 52, 77, 84,
   158, 169; 13:47, 99,
   119; 14:27, 110, 133,
   219, 259, 331; 15:45,
   228, 301, 320, 329;
   16:102, 114, 228,
   305; 17:16, 43, 87,
   112, 138, 150, 156,
   185, 245, 289, 391,
   447, 451, 499; 18:57,
   71, 94, 105, 115,
   160, 194, 211, 376;
   19:35, 48, 100, 101,
   194, 284, 293, 332;
   20:190, 351; 21:89,
   93, 113, 205, 261,
   389; 22:114, 221,
   238, 269, 319, 320,
   345, 398; 23:50, 130,
   168, 182, 195, 302;
   24:115, 172, 203;
   25:69, 71, 234, 312;
   26:60, 61, 225
Smith, John A. 10:152;
   11:18, 284; 12:40;
   13:119; 14:29;

Smith, John A. 17:420;
   18:57; 21:389; 22:54,
   102, 269; 23:50, 185;
   24:162
Smith, John B. 3:180;
   7:41; 8:95; 13:47;
   16:55; 17:284;
   21:218; 27:118
Smith, John C. 4:54; 9:59;
   17:163; 23:110;
   24:45, 115
Smith, John D. 14:219
Smith, John E. 21:59
Smith, John F. 3:180;
   8:95; 9:73; 10:22;
   11:398; 16:305;
   17:315; 19:35;
   22:131; 23:195
Smith, John G. 12:171
Smith, John H. 4:54; 8:55,
   95; 10:137; 11:171;
   14:219; 19:49;
   20:139, 149, 351;
   22:54; 23:79, 185;
   24:180
Smith, John H. J. 11:86
Smith, John J. 1:75;
   3:180; 8:75; 11:334;
   19:35; 20:128;
   21:115
Smith, John K. 5:29
Smith, John L. 17:112;
   23:79
Smith, John M. 3:180;
   9:29; 17:87; 18:316;
   23:50; 24:69; 26:113;
   27:109
Smith, John N. 21:389
Smith, John P. 1:72; 21:80
Smith, John Peter 9:193
Smith, John Q. 18:280
Smith, John R. 1:72;
   11:77; 12:40; 17:43,
   365; 22:102
Smith, John S. 4:54; 9:91,
   125; 17:232; 25:234;
   27:114
Smith, John T. 18:253;
   22:102; 26:62
Smith, John W. 3:180;
   4:54; 8:32; 11:77;
   15:23; 18:160;
   22:102, 220, 491,
   505
Smith, John Z. 9:224;
   18:376
Smith, Johnson 27:148
Smith, Jonas 22:221
Smith, Jonathan 7:41;
   9:73; 11:112; 19:35
Smith, Jonathan E. 11:130

Smith, Joseph 1:73, 74;
   3:180; 4:54; 7:110;
   9:193; 10:80; 11:170,
   213, 382; 15:228;
   16:228; 17:186;
   19:101, 338; 20:351;
   21:389; 22:54, 102,
   221; 23:168, 310;
   25:67, 270, 305
Smith, Joseph A. 15:320;
   22:54
Smith, Joseph G. 7:41
Smith, Joseph H. 5:45
Smith, Joseph P. 7:17
Smith, Joseph R. 15:337;
   16:229; 19:35; 21:41;
   22:54
Smith, Joseph S. 7:110
Smith, Joseph W. 23:110
Smith, Joseph Willard
   23:283
Smith, Joshua 5:29;
   11:78; 15:45; 17:138;
   19:101; 24:204
Smith, Joshua S. 4:54
Smith, Josiah 17:167;
   19:35; 23:93
Smith, Julius 6:9; 18:105;
   23:110
Smith, Julius P. 24:30
Smith, Justice 24:30
Smith, Justin E. 9:29;
   18:321
Smith, K. 3:181
Smith, Kingsbury 22:492
Smith, L. 1:171, 172, 176;
   3:181; 14:290;
   19:284; 23:50, 206;
   24:30; 25:69
Smith, L. A. 3:181;
   15:228
Smith, L. C. 1:168
Smith, L. D. 18:253;
   26:62
Smith, L. E. 11:391
Smith, L. F. 3:181
Smith, L. L. 21:41
Smith, L. O. 19:101
Smith, L. R. 1:75
Smith, L. S. 3:181; 18:444
Smith, L. W. 2:17;
   21:126; 25:73
Smith, Laban 4:54
Smith, Lafayette 17:266;
   19:297; 24:30
Smith, LaFayette 25:234
Smith, Landell T. 10:167;
   19:194
Smith, Landon 11:250
Smith, Lawrence 6:26;
   13:47; 21:389

Smith, Lee 7:133
Smith, Lent A. 7:111
Smith, Leonard A. 9:125;
    27:113, 114
Smith, Leonard B. 22:102
Smith, Leonard J. 7:41
Smith, Leroy J. 23:168
Smith, Levi 3:181; 8:115;
    12:55; 15:306;
    19:101; 20:128;
    22:345; 23:79;
    24:212
Smith, Levi L. 12:40
Smith, Levias 1:73
Smith, Lewis 4:54; 7:133;
    8:78; 9:104, 193;
    10:137; 12:54;
    13:59; 18:401;
    19:35; 20:177, 351;
    21:389; 22:320;
    24:204; 25:71
Smith, Lewis D. 20:351
Smith, Lewis N. 17:210
Smith, Lewis T. 10:80
Smith, Lorenzo 1:71
Smith, Louis 13:48;
    14:219; 22:319
Smith, Louis C. 23:101
Smith, Loyal 15:84
Smith, Lucas 11:129;
    12:40
Smith, Lucius P. 17:138;
    24:203
Smith, Luther 12:40
Smith, Luther M. 7:41;
    9:7
Smith, Luther N. 8:31;
    18:160
Smith, Luther T. 7:41
Smith, Lyman 13:48;
    25:69
Smith, Lyman D. 21:261
Smith, M. 1:176; 3:181;
    9:99, 150; 11:168,
    170; 13:99; 14:111,
    219, 220; 18:39;
    19:242; 21:389;
    25:234; 26:61;
    27:108, 110
Smith, M. A. 19:194
Smith, M. B. 14:111
Smith, M. D. 3:181; 8:55;
    13:68; 14:245;
    16:229
Smith, M. H. 23:50
Smith, M. J. 22:269
Smith, M. M. 20:351
Smith, M. O. 7:111;
    23:168
Smith, M. R. 12:158;
    25:72

Smith, M. S. 19:224
Smith, M. V. 23:50
Smith, M. V. B. 25:234
Smith, M. W. 1:76
Smith, Madison 1:192
Smith, Mahlen 10:80
Smith, Major 16:55
Smith, Malachi 7:111
Smith, Maplan 20:351
Smith, Mardin 19:230
Smith, Marion 11:417;
    18:253; 26:62
Smith, Marion D. 21:80
Smith, Marshal J. 23:168
Smith, Marshall 4:54;
    13:119
Smith, Marshall M. 10:80
Smith, Martin 3:181;
    24:30
Smith, Martin G. 11:393
Smith, Martin V. 17:47;
    19:35
Smith, Martin V. B.
    21:243
Smith, Marvin 10:22
Smith, Mason C. 3:181
Smith, Mathew 10:80;
    16:124; 17:157;
    20:351; 22:15;
    27:117
Smith, Mathias 9:91;
    24:45
Smith, Matthew 4:54;
    17:16
Smith, McDonald 10:80
Smith, McKendric 12:40
Smith, Menley 22:319
Smith, Merret A. 21:80
Smith, Merton L. 15:28
Smith, Michael 5:45;
    9:193; 15:3; 17:16,
    150; 19:318, 319;
    23:79
Smith, Michael G. 23:79
Smith, Michael K. 4:54
Smith, Michael S. 19:297
Smith, Miles 17:451;
    24:180
Smith, Milton 9:163;
    19:242; 22:102;
    24:45
Smith, Milton C. 9:17
Smith, Milton J. 10:22
Smith, Mitchell 11:172
Smith, Mo--- 15:228
Smith, Monroe 8:95, 115;
    10:175; 19:194
Smith, Montellon 12:40
Smith, Morris 21:284
Smith, Mortimer 18:71
Smith, Mortimer C. 22:54

Smith, Moses 9:136;
    14:220; 22:220, 320;
    27:112
Smith, Moses S. 9:193
Smith, Myron 8:31;
    18:160
Smith, N. 1:100, 169;
    3:181; 10:29; 11:312;
    14:111; 15:112;
    16:229; 17:68; 18:39;
    27:109
Smith, N. A. 25:234
Smith, N. B. 9:151
Smith, N. H. 3:181; 8:55;
    9:31
Smith, N. I. 11:313
Smith, N. J. 1:74; 15:153;
    20:157
Smith, N. N. 23:168
Smith, N. P. 3:181;
    14:111
Smith, Napoleon 21:284
Smith, Nathan 13:48, 119;
    14:220; 17:480;
    22:155
Smith, Nathan C. 19:194
Smith, Nathan D. 16:56
Smith, Nathan H. 9:39;
    13:47
Smith, Nathan J. 24:45
Smith, Nathaniel 11:75;
    18:17
Smith, Nathaniel C.
    19:101
Smith, Nathaniel H.
    21:143
Smith, Naughford D.
    22:457
Smith, Nehemiah 7:110
Smith, Nelson 4:68;
    22:155
Smith, Nelson A. 5:45
Smith, Nelson C. 8:125
Smith, Nelson G. 19:321
Smith, Newell R. 19:194
Smith, Newton 21:218;
    22:131
Smith, Nicholas 4:54;
    7:41; 22:457
Smith, Noah 9:193;
    17:150; 19:265
Smith, Noah L. 24:56
Smith, Norman 11:289
Smith, Norman W. 18:280
Smith, O. 1:76, 172; 2:17;
    3:181; 16:229;
    23:168; 25:73, 234
Smith, O. C. 3:181;
    11:101
Smith, O. F. 22:220
Smith, O. K. 14:21

Smith, O. L. 26:59
Smith, O. M. 9:39
Smith, O. R. 25:234
Smith, O. T. 18:17
Smith, Oakley 14:111
Smith, Ohio 9:29
Smith, Oliver 5:45; 14:220
Smith, Oliver P. 12:40
Smith, Orange S. 10:80; 20:351
Smith, Orlando 15:228
Smith, Orrin A. 22:467
Smith, Oscar 1:70; 11:97; 20:31
Smith, Oscar D. 9:45; 26:129
Smith, Othelon 9:59
Smith, Owen 7:41; 18:271; 21:389
Smith, P H. 10:80
Smith, P. 1:169, 174; 3:181; 5:45; 9:113; 10:80; 11:121; 12:10; 13:99; 14:21, 330; 19:261; 20:149, 351; 25:234, 235
Smith, P. A. 1:169; 14:333
Smith, P. B. 27:106
Smith, P. H. 1:75; 20:351
Smith, P. J. 14:220; 17:266
Smith, P. S. 7:78; 25:305
Smith, Pat. H. 21:389
Smith, Patent 16:305
Smith, Patrick 8:67, 122; 9:193; 19:101, 284; 22:54, 345; 23:16
Smith, Patrick D. 19:330
Smith, Patrick H. 19:330
Smith, Paul A. 12:40
Smith, Paul H. 23:79
Smith, Paxton 20:116
Smith, Perley 21:389
Smith, Perry 20:101
Smith, Peter 5:29; 6:8; 9:29, 39, 99, 156, 193; 11:312; 12:40; 14:111; 17:186; 18:115, 280, 297, 321; 19:49; 21:59, 389; 26:112
Smith, Peter B. 11:43
Smith, Peter M. 19:334
Smith, Peyton 22:101
Smith, Philip 1:77; 7:133; 11:170; 12:77; 15:75; 17:26, 315; 21:390
Smith, Philip R. 19:35

Smith, Philip S. 22:101
Smith, Pleasant 17:43, 208
Smith, Powell 9:14
Smith, Purley E. 22:284
Smith, R. 1:71, 173, 174; 10:150; 11:168; 12:88, 158; 13:103, 119; 16:271; 17:192; 18:57; 21:390
Smith, R. C. 3:181
Smith, R. E. 1:72
Smith, R. F. 3:181
Smith, R. J. 2:17; 14:111; 17:162; 25:68
Smith, R. K. 10:207
Smith, R. M. 1:170
Smith, R. P. 25:235
Smith, R. R. 12:88; 14:111; 16:305
Smith, Randall 21:284
Smith, Ransom 10:137; 11:213; 20:351
Smith, Recompence 23:283
Smith, Reider H. 18:223
Smith, Reuben 7:133; 12:40; 22:54, 446
Smith, Reuben J. 22:102
Smith, Richard 7:111; 9:125; 10:180; 11:172; 12:40; 17:204; 18:17, 180; 21:285; 27:112, 114
Smith, Richard B. 22:411
Smith, Richard C. 21:390
Smith, Richard S. 20:181
Smith, Riley 22:345
Smith, Robert 5:45; 7:63; 9:91, 99; 10:80, 137; 11:43, 75, 130, 220; 12:65; 13:48, 126; 15:75, 95; 17:43, 138, 186, 250; 18:253; 20:351; 22:131; 24:203; 26:59, 64, 146
Smith, Robert B. 23:182
Smith, Robert D. 1:72; 23:168
Smith, Robert F. 10:22
Smith, Robert K. 17:444; 24:162
Smith, Robert T. 22:155
Smith, Rockwell H. 27:148
Smith, Rose W. 17:250
Smith, Rush 22:54
Smith, S. 1:169, 171, 173, 174; 3:181; 8:75; 9:136; 10:80;

Smith, S. 12:123, 162; 14:26, 111; 15:112, 135, 363; 19:268; 20:141, 351; 23:168; 24:56; 25:235; 27:111
Smith, S. A. 3:181; 9:31; 14:259; 15:112; 16:102; 18:376
Smith, S. B. 10:80; 20:128, 351
Smith, S. C. 1:100; 19:269
Smith, S. D. 1:95; 18:253; 26:63
Smith, S. E. 26:59
Smith, S. F. 14:111
Smith, S. M. 3:181; 18:57; 22:490
Smith, S. P. 1:170; 3:181; 14:285; 20:351
Smith, S. R. 13:119
Smith, S. S. 11:188; 15:301; 16:229
Smith, S. V. 14:220
Smith, S. W. 3:181; 11:270; 27:108
Smith, Sam 17:138; 24:203
Smith, Samuel 1:72; 5:45; 8:32, 42, 95; 9:91, 104, 115, 136; 10:137, 167; 12:56; 13:48, 68; 14:111; 16:229; 17:26, 138, 277, 426; 18:39, 160; 19:194; 20:135, 351; 21:11, 59; 22:102, 284, 355; 23:168; 24:108, 203; 26:59, 182; 27:107, 112
Smith, Samuel A. 12:40; 27:116
Smith, Samuel B. 17:43
Smith, Samuel D. 14:220; 20:184
Smith, Samuel E. 3:181; 9:91; 24:180
Smith, Samuel G. 25:235
Smith, Samuel H. 22:102; 24:114
Smith, Samuel K. 14:220
Smith, Samuel M. 1:75
Smith, Samuel R. 7:111
Smith, Samuel S. 1:73; 19:35
Smith, Samuel T. 11:76
Smith, Samuel W. 9:125; 10:97; 22:155; 27:113
Smith, Sanford 9:211

Smith, Seldom 26:226
Smith, Seldon 9:238
Smith, Septimus T. 10:167
Smith, Sessa. P. 20:19
Smith, Sibian 11:77
Smith, Sidney 7:110; 18:253; 26:65
Smith, Sidney C. 10:137; 20:351
Smith, Sidney J. 19:195
Smith, Sidney M. 22:441
Smith, Silas A. 9:224
Smith, Silas W. 21:207
Smith, Simon 1:74; 6:26; 19:195; 23:93, 125
Smith, Simon J. 14:220
Smith, Simpson 15:59
Smith, Simson 13:48

Smith, Solomon 5:45; 6:28; 9:193; 17:43; 21:86, 285; 22:490
Smith, Solomon B. 10:22
Smith, Solomon C. 9:193
Smith, Solomon W. 23:168
Smith, Squire 22:320
Smith, Stephen 4:54; 7:133; 9:136; 13:47; 14:220; 18:253; 21:285; 26:62; 27:111
Smith, Stephen B. 15:45
Smith, Stephen D. 21:191
Smith, Stephen F. 7:111
Smith, Stephen M. 9:14
Smith, Stepney 8:42; 26:180
Smith, Steven M. F. 12:158
Smith, Sylo 17:451; 24:180
Smith, Sylvester 15:321; 19:101; 22:102
Smith, T. 1:176; 2:18; 3:181; 7:111; 11:289; 15:228; 16:229; 17:218; 23:14; 24:115; 25:235
Smith, T. A. 3:181
Smith, T. B. 7:111
Smith, T. C. 9:59; 18:253; 26:64
Smith, T. E. B. 19:101
Smith, T. F. 25:68
Smith, T. H. 3:181
Smith, T. R. 1:70
Smith, T. S. 7:41; 14:111; 25:67

Smith, Taffy 9:136; 27:111
Smith, Theodore 9:45; 21:390; 26:129
Smith, Theodore R. 22:101
Smith, Theodore V. 10:175; 19:195
Smith, Theron 7:133
Smith, Theron A. 22:102
Smith, Thomas 1:73; 3:181; 4:54; 5:29, 45, 54; 6:26; 7:41, 61, 111, 133; 8:78; 9:8, 136; 10:137; 11:172, 188, 336; 12:40; 13:47, 68, 119; 14:245, 303, 320; 15:45; 16:56, 102, 229; 17:167, 429, 481; 18:341; 19:101, 318, 320, 323; 20:25, 116, 351; 21:261, 390; 22:54, 221, 319, 345, 516; 23:14; 25:67, 235, 289; 26:181; 27:112, 117, 119
Smith, Thomas B. 24:85
Smith, Thomas E. 9:225; 13:99; 18:376
Smith, Thomas G. 13:47
Smith, Thomas H. 11:45; 24:164
Smith, Thomas J. 11:45; 17:59; 23:115
Smith, Thomas L. 10:137; 20:351
Smith, Thomas N. 24:56
Smith, Thomas R. 12:100
Smith, Thomas S. 24:45
Smith, Thomas W. 11:45; 21:132
Smith, Tilston D. 13:47
Smith, Tilton D. 16:56
Smith, Tim 15:75
Smith, Timothy A. 9:125; 27:113
Smith, Tom 8:42; 26:180
Smith, U. 17:357; 25:235
Smith, Upton 5:45
Smith, V. 3:181
Smith, Vanburen 17:410; 22:130
Smith, Victory J. 21:261
Smith, Vilas 25:235
Smith, Volney 14:220
Smith, W. 1:72, 76, 77, 169, 170, 171, 174; 3:181, 182; 8:55; 9:224; 11:270;

Smith, W. 12:123; 14:21, 220, 259, 279, 303; 15:135, 175; 17:474; 18:17, 39, 376; 19:101; 20:175, 180; 21:151; 23:50, 182; 25:235; 26:135; 27:108, 117
Smith, W. A. 1:174, 175; 3:182; 24:115; 25:280
Smith, W. B. 3:182; 10:29; 19:35, 307
Smith, W. C. 10:137; 18:72; 20:351; 21:126, 132; 26:129
Smith, W. E. 7:61; 15:6
Smith, W. E. L. 17:232
Smith, W. F. 1:170
Smith, W. G. 1:174; 17:72; 23:206; 25:235
Smith, W. H. 1:168, 170; 3:181, 182; 4:54; 7:111, 133; 9:113; 11:342; 15:9, 168, 175; 16:282; 17:59, 293; 18:115; 19:101, 307; 25:235
Smith, W. H. H. 7:42; 17:150
Smith, W. J. 14:111; 16:379
Smith, W. K. 14:220
Smith, W. L. 9:150; 11:269; 25:235; 27:110
Smith, W. M. 7:111; 17:218; 25:235
Smith, W. N. 23:168
Smith, W. O. 9:45
Smith, W. P. 8:31; 18:280; 20:149
Smith, W. R. 16:56; 19:35; 20:351; 24:85
Smith, W. S. 1:175; 14:220; 20:351
Smith, W. T. 25:235
Smith, W. V. 15:264
Smith, W. W. 3:181; 11:282; 13:99; 14:111
Smith, Walter 14:220; 23:195; 25:235
Smith, Walter W. 16:9
Smith, Warren 10:177; 19:195
Smith, Washington 10:137; 11:213; 20:351; 24:10
Smith, Wesley 16:136

Smith, Westfield 13:119
Smith, Wheeler 7:110
Smith, Wheeler J. 22:155
Smith, Wiley 22:524
Smith, William 1:71, 72, 74, 76, 77; 3:181, 182; 4:54; 5:29; 6:13, 26; 7:41, 54, 110, 133; 8:96, 110; 9:59, 136; 10:80, 93, 137; 11:169, 170, 171, 221, 323, 397, 404; 12:40, 57, 100; 13:47, 59, 81, 99, 119; 14:111, 220, 317; 15:75, 135, 161, 175, 228, 330, 361, 366; 16:56, 229, 282; 17:16, 208, 319, 416, 426, 444; 18:39, 94, 194, 211, 285; 19:101; 20:13, 85, 101, 149, 351; 21:41, 80, 126, 213, 390; 22:15, 130, 155, 284, 345, 440, 457, 491; 23:50, 110, 277, 310; 24:45, 102, 162, 180; 25:73, 235; 27:112, 118
Smith, William A. 3:182; 12:97; 13:47; 16:56; 17:152; 21:390; 22:516
Smith, William B. 17:26; 21:390; 25:235
Smith, William C. 13:47; 24:45
Smith, William D. 16:5; 21:390; 23:79
Smith, William E. 1:72, 77; 14:220; 22:269
Smith, William F. 1:70; 23:104
Smith, William G. 26:60
Smith, William H. 1:75; 3:182; 5:29; 7:42; 9:14; 10:80; 11:295; 13:47; 14:220; 16:79, 124; 17:239; 20:36, 351, 352; 21:80, 234, 390; 22:102, 284, 345, 439; 24:45
Smith, William J. 10:80; 11:130; 15:345; 19:195; 20:352; 22:269, 345
Smith, William K. 22:220
Smith, William L. 20:101
Smith, William M. 11:251; 12:63;

Smith, William M. 15:23; 16:229; 18:160; 22:102; 26:58
Smith, William Mitchell 8:32
Smith, William N. 13:47; 22:221
Smith, William P. 7:133; 10:146; 18:160; 19:195
Smith, William R. 10:80; 11:171; 12:40; 17:169, 250, 284; 22:221; 23:50
Smith, William S. 10:80
Smith, William T. 1:71; 14:220; 20:352
Smith, William W. 20:129; 22:54
Smith, William Y. 10:80
Smith, William Z. 25:235
Smith, Willis 8:32; 11:130; 18:160
Smith, Wilson 8:96; 22:54; 26:60
Smith, Winfield 12:148
Smith, Woodby 14:111
Smith, Wyatt T. 20:88
Smith, Z. 12:123
Smith, Zemerick 16:56
Smith, Zephaniah 10:137; 20:352
Smith, Zimri 10:137; 20:352
Smitherly, George S. 5:30
Smithers, --- 21:168
Smithers, A. 15:135, 350
Smithers, Andrew 11:76
Smithers, Edwin R. 5:29
Smithers, Elias 23:50
Smithers, G. 13:68; 19:101
Smithers, H. 1:74
Smithers, James 19:195
Smithers, James M. 10:175
Smithers, St. Clair 27:115
Smithers, William 5:30
Smithers, William L. 17:250
Smithers, William M. 9:91
Smithey, J. 24:85
Smithgall, David 25:71
Smithing, Joseph 10:93; 20:352
Smithis, G. J. 22:54
Smithley, G. F. 25:235
Smithline, Andrew 23:287
Smithpeter, Eli 3:182
Smiths, W. J. 10:154
Smithson, E. M. 15:228

Smithson, G. 12:84; 16:305
Smithson, H. N. 8:31; 18:160
Smithson, J. D. 11:76
Smithwick, Elias 9:17
Smithy, Franklin H. 23:110
Smitson, Charles 25:71
Smitson, Peter 17:239
Smitten, John 27:111
Smittenberg, A. M. 2:18
Smittle, Fritz 16:124
Smitzer, J. F. 27:110
Smitzer, Jacob H. 9:91
Smizer, D. 8:67
Smizer, Samuel 17:138; 24:204
Smkth, E. A. 13:99
Smoadley, W. H. 20:352
Smoat, James 1:77
Smock, A. 3:182
Smock, Byron E. 19:262
Smock, D. D. 26:182
Smock, David W. 22:439
Smock, John R. 22:102
Smock, Oscar 4:54
Smock, W. I. 8:32
Smock, W. J. 18:160
Smock, William H. 22:440
Smok, Mathias 17:447
Smoke, Absalom 21:390
Smoke, G. W. 21:390
Smoke, H. B. 3:182
Smoke, Mathias P. 24:171
Smoke, Orville M. 17:100
Smolser, Henry L. 10:137; 20:352
Smoot, James P. 22:131
Smoot, Marshall 19:49
Smootheley, James S. 4:54
Smothers, Green B. 17:239
Smothers, John 8:42; 22:457; 26:180
Smothers, M. L. 23:168
Smots, Jacob 15:228
Smout, Charles 10:80; 20:352
Smuck, James 11:18
Smuger, Charles 27:118
Smuk, Ephraim 17:277
Smulley, John 3:182
Smurchick, V. 1:75
Smurphet, John 27:113
Smurrh, A. 11:112
Smutland, E. M. 8:115
Smuty, William H. 5:30
Smutz, H. W. 25:235

Smyhart, Jacob 11:89
Smyth, Henry M. 4:55
Smyth, James 3:182
Smyth, John S. 5:30
Smyth, Joseph 22:284
Smyth, P. 15:112
Smyth, Thomas A. 7:15
Smyth, W. 1:171
Smythe, William 10:167; 19:195
Smythman, Alfred 22:102
Smytre, W. 21:106
Snachamer, Isaac 24:180
Snaclout, John 22:345
Snader, F. 9:59
Snadgrass, William 8:55
Snafford, James M. 9:91
Snailer, Frederic 17:87
Snance, William 18:407
Snany, Timothy 8:110
Snapp, G. W. 23:310
Snapp, Joseph T. 22:131
Snapp, S. 17:297
Snapp, William 11:282
Snare, Henry M. 1:76
Snaringer, D. O. 11:97
Snarty, John 3:182
Snaser, Joseph 19:271
Snauk, Frank 11:169
Snavely, J. K. 11:314
Snavely, Jacob 22:411
Snavely, L. C. 18:57
Snazer, Joseph 9:193
Snead, --- 20:175
Snead, Harrison 15:333; 19:101
Snead, James 16:229
Snead, Thomas 7:133
Snead, U. 22:269
Snealey, John 18:211
Snearly, Hiram 9:227
Sneck, L. 15:228
Snedeker, N. 18:401
Snedeker, W. M. 22:221
Sneden, Silas 25:235
Sneder, Jacob 13:48
Snederker, Isaac 13:48
Snedgeon, A. J. 3:182
Snediker, Albert 21:126
Snedker, J. B. 15:153
Sneebecker, Joseph 16:102
Sneed, C. 17:436; 24:187
Sneed, George 22:320
Sneed, J. L. 22:269
Sneed, J. M. 24:60
Sneed, Louis 7:133
Sneed, Sylvester H. 21:246
Sneederker, William 25:235

Sneek, Lewis 13:68
Sneetzlander, J. N. 18:39
Sneff, Daniel B. 11:271
Sneider, E. 14:220
Sneider, George 6:23; 13:48
Sneider, J. 9:151
Sneider, Martin 14:220
Sneider, William R. 14:220
Sneidiker, William 11:170
Sneil, Charles 17:362
Snelgrove, Solomon 17:157
Snell, A. E. 19:101
Snell, Charles D. 1:72
Snell, Chauncey 16:102
Snell, Cyrus 4:55
Snell, Daniel 18:17
Snell, Francis 4:55
Snell, Franklin B. 17:93
Snell, Henry 21:41
Snell, Isaac 7:133
Snell, J. 25:235
Snell, J. H. 17:26
Snell, Jerome 5:30
Snell, John 9:204; 17:47
Snell, John A. 4:55
Snell, Joseph 22:221
Snell, L. D. 15:295
Snell, Lannon 4:55
Snell, M. 24:99
Snell, N. T. 1:170
Snell, O. B. 1:173
Snell, S. Walter 11:172
Snell, Sam 15:153
Snell, Samuel S. 7:76
Snell, W. 10:29; 19:307
Snell, W. H. 25:73
Snell, W. S. 19:101
Snell, William 4:55; 12:40; 22:54
Snelling, Samuel 18:194
Snelling, William 26:60
Snelling, William W. 10:22
Snelson, J. 3:182
Snelyen, Jonathan 6:23
Snend, A. 15:301
Snerhenberger, John 12:77
Snerling, Samuel 27:118
Snether, Bridgeman 22:221
Snetzler, Joseph 22:490
Snick, W. R. 7:111
Snickel, Doffiel 22:284
Snider, --- 14:220; 17:284
Snider, Charles 17:416; 24:155
Snider, Chauncey 18:280

Snider, D. 1:168; 3:182; 25:235
Snider, Eber 22:155
Snider, G. 14:220, 259
Snider, G. F. S. 14:21
Snider, George 11:271; 21:390; 22:398
Snider, Godfrey 10:80
Snider, H. 14:111
Snider, Henry 9:91; 23:169; 26:59
Snider, J. 1:175; 3:182; 13:99; 14:21; 24:63; 27:110
Snider, J. K. 11:439
Snider, J. N. 11:269
Snider, Jackson 10:80
Snider, Jacob 11:314; 14:220; 20:84; 22:155
Snider, James 3:182
Snider, John 3:182; 18:376; 22:491
Snider, John H. 19:101
Snider, Lewis 18:57
Snider, Luther 23:79
Snider, M. 14:111
Snider, Matthias 20:116
Snider, Morgan 22:54
Snider, Moses 22:439
Snider, Nicholas 26:181
Snider, Reuben 21:234
Snider, S. 1:171; 3:182
Snider, S. S. 13:99
Snider, Samuel 8:55
Snider, Solomon 23:169
Snider, Thomas 9:70
Snider, Thomas N. 10:80; 20:352
Snider, W. H. H. 26:183
Snider, W. W. 11:43
Snider, William 20:352
Snider, William F. 18:376
Snider, William Marion 17:350
Snidle, Peter 10:137
Snidrock, Frederick 13:48
Sniere, C. 3:182
Sniff, A. B. 24:85
Sniffen, S. 1:75
Snigir, Samuel 11:78
Sniles, S. 22:320
Snillenbarger, F. 3:182
Snilling, William 9:91
Snipps, G. 14:220
Snirmers, Robert 13:119
Snitham, William 5:30
Snitzlen, Joseph 19:35
Sniveley, Andrew 10:80; 20:352

Sniveley, George H. 17:472
Sniveley, Henson 6:19
Sniveley, Jacob A. 24:85
Snively, Abraham 20:399; 22:345
Snively, Ezra 11:76
Snively, Henson 18:94
Snobe, John 11:171
Snoddy, Harvey M. 21:390
Snoddy, Henry 10:137; 20:352
Snoddy, Quinn 26:61
Snoddy, Thomas S. 14:221
Snoder, Israel 18:115
Snoder, Sylvester 16:229
Snoderly, George 26:129
Snoderly, Lewis 11:77
Snodger, --- 14:262
Snodgrass, Ambrose 7:61
Snodgrass, B. F. 22:345
Snodgrass, C. C. 18:105
Snodgrass, C. F. 23:169
Snodgrass, Franklin 20:44
Snodgrass, G. W. 11:45
Snodgrass, Gibson 17:59
Snodgrass, H. 16:229
Snodgrass, Henry M. 12:40
Snodgrass, Isaac 21:41
Snodgrass, Jackson 11:44
Snodgrass, James L. 15:75
Snodgrass, John 8:96; 22:55
Snodgrass, John W. 10:137; 20:105, 352
Snodgrass, Joseph W. 11:43
Snodgrass, Newton 11:426
Snodgrass, R. 21:41
Snodgrass, R. P. 3:182
Snodgrass, Ralph 10:81; 20:352
Snodgrass, Robert S. 23:79
Snodgrass, T. 26:182
Snodgrass, William 22:320
Snodney, John 22:269
Snody, James 9:211
Snofe, F. M. 21:199
Snofford, James 24:45
Snoody, George 25:69
Snook, A. 13:119; 14:21
Snook, Abraham 24:62
Snook, C. H. 1:171
Snook, G. 11:313
Snook, J. 18:39

Snook, J. S. 24:85
Snook, James M. 22:221
Snook, John 14:221
Snook, Lewis 16:229
Snook, Mathew J. 22:522
Snook, R. A. 11:111
Snooke, A. 13:99
Snooks, A. W. 12:40
Snooks, John 8:110
Snooks, John Milton 8:110
Snooks, Peter 9:202; 19:293
Snooks, Samuel N. 9:125; 27:114
Snooks, W. 3:182
Snope, George 7:61
Snope, W. H. 22:398
Snorel, Philip 18:39
Snorer, Edwin 7:42
Snores, Buss 1:73
Snother, M. N. 8:55
Snottgrass, John 14:111
Snover, George W. 22:345
Snover, Jacob 21:116
Snover, S. C. 3:182
Snow, --- 18:180; 21:247
Snow, A. B. 9:227; 18:376
Snow, Alfred J. 12:77; 15:19
Snow, Amasa 16:65
Snow, Andrew 22:238
Snow, Barney 19:35
Snow, Benjamin 10:137; 20:352
Snow, C. 18:17
Snow, Caleb E. 23:185
Snow, Charles 21:390
Snow, Charles C. 4:55
Snow, Charles H. 1:76
Snow, D. 1:173; 8:55; 25:235
Snow, Delbert 21:143
Snow, E. 22:355
Snow, E. A. 1:174
Snow, E. T. 19:35
Snow, Edwin A. 17:449; 24:174
Snow, Eli 22:131
Snow, F. 13:99; 14:21
Snow, Frank 12:40; 19:101
Snow, G. 10:29
Snow, G. E. 13:68
Snow, George 15:229; 22:320
Snow, George C. 19:101
Snow, George M. 17:100
Snow, H. O. 1:168
Snow, Henry A. 4:55

Snow, Henry P. 22:221
Snow, Isaac 10:137; 18:39; 20:352
Snow, J. 3:182; 5:54; 15:45; 25:235
Snow, J. B. 12:143
Snow, J. P. 20:352
Snow, James 11:77
Snow, James F. 22:102
Snow, James O. 7:111
Snow, James S. 18:376
Snow, James T. 9:225
Snow, Jesse L. 16:56
Snow, John 8:115; 9:113; 12:77, 143; 20:13; 23:115
Snow, John L. 15:75
Snow, John W. 10:81; 20:352
Snow, L. L. 20:59
Snow, Larkin F. 22:269
Snow, Levi 3:182
Snow, Lorenzo S. 27:107
Snow, Lucius J. 21:390
Snow, McDonald 22:457
Snow, Nelson H. 17:152
Snow, Nicholas 7:42
Snow, Oscar 1:70; 9:29
Snow, Peter 11:46
Snow, Phillon 13:48
Snow, Phillow 16:56
Snow, Reed 11:76
Snow, S. 1:169
Snow, S. A. 19:101
Snow, S. C. 15:75
Snow, Samuel 17:266, 395
Snow, Samuel C. 12:77
Snow, Theodore 20:129
Snow, W. 3:182; 13:68; 19:101
Snow, W. J. C. 21:390
Snow, Wilbin F. 12:40
Snow, William 15:229; 22:320; 25:289
Snowberger, Amos 19:195
Snowberger, David 13:48; 16:56
Snowberger, T. 1:172
Snowdale, T. 3:182
Snowden, Andrew 12:173
Snowden, Daniel E. 20:129
Snowden, Edward 23:241
Snowden, I. 23:169
Snowden, J. A. A. 27:115
Snowden, John 26:213
Snowden, Joseph 6:19; 18:94
Snowden, M. 16:229
Snowden, Mores 21:151

Snowden, Moses 8:58
Snowden, P. 25:235
Snowden, Peter 5:45
Snowden, Polly 27:109
Snowden, Samuel 13:59
Snowden, Sanford 22:320
Snowden, Thomas 20:25
Snowden, William 8:78
Snowder, Peter 23:303
Snowman, Thomas 9:193; 19:230
Snurley, Hiram 18:376
Snybliss, Sanford 21:390
Snydam, Edward W. 22:521
Snydam, J. G. 25:235
Snyden, William 1:73
Snyder, --- 16:56; 20:352
Snyder, A. 3:182; 20:44; 25:235
Snyder, A. A. 15:229
Snyder, A. C. 15:292
Snyder, A. J. 25:235
Snyder, A. M. 12:40; 16:229
Snyder, Abram 22:221; 23:79
Snyder, Adam 4:55; 8:96; 16:134; 17:201
Snyder, Albert 25:70
Snyder, Augustus 22:55
Snyder, B. 3:182; 27:118
Snyder, Burnett 14:220
Snyder, C. 13:119; 14:111
Snyder, Calvin 9:193; 19:269
Snyder, Charles 5:30
Snyder, Charles V. 7:61
Snyder, Christian 25:68
Snyder, D. 1:100; 23:169; 27:119
Snyder, D. S. 25:72
Snyder, Daniel 5:30; 8:96; 14:111
Snyder, Daniel L. 4:55
Snyder, Darias 10:167
Snyder, Darius 19:195
Snyder, David 15:89, 229
Snyder, David M. 17:234
Snyder, E. 3:182; 27:119
Snyder, E. F. 23:253
Snyder, Edwin R 15:92
Snyder, F. 14:111; 18:57; 19:347
Snyder, Finley 19:35
Snyder, Francis 4:55
Snyder, Frank 17:210
Snyder, Franklin 13:48
Snyder, Fred 12:158
Snyder, Frederick 14:111; 23:257

Snyder, G. 13:135; 22:491; 25:235
Snyder, G. T. 1:100
Snyder, George 4:55; 17:74, 337, 451; 20:352; 21:234; 25:71
Snyder, George H. 2:17; 10:22
Snyder, George W. 17:164
Snyder, H. 10:29; 11:121; 19:307; 21:126
Snyder, H. E. 5:30; 25:235
Snyder, H. M. 3:182
Snyder, Hand 11:392
Snyder, Harland 22:221
Snyder, Henry 2:17; 11:323; 12:40; 14:220; 21:285; 22:155; 25:69; 27:148
Snyder, Herman 7:111
Snyder, I. 15:229
Snyder, Ira 9:113
Snyder, Isaac 11:77; 21:106; 23:269; 24:204
Snyder, J. 1:76, 171; 3:182; 9:151; 18:446; 27:110
Snyder, J. A. 3:182
Snyder, J. G. 14:111
Snyder, J. H. 17:200
Snyder, J. J. 11:76
Snyder, J. K. 1:77
Snyder, J. M. 23:206
Snyder, J. V. 27:148
Snyder, Jac 1:74
Snyder, Jackson 20:352
Snyder, Jacob 1:70; 5:54; 8:96; 15:19; 25:235
Snyder, James 7:42; 20:109
Snyder, James D. 11:77
Snyder, James L. 19:343
Snyder, James P. 8:32; 18:160
Snyder, Jefferson O. 5:54
Snyder, John 5:45; 7:42, 111; 9:91, 113, 228; 11:169; 14:111, 221; 21:93; 23:14; 25:305; 26:59; 27:115
Snyder, John D. 23:169
Snyder, John E. 9:99
Snyder, John G. 26:129
Snyder, John H. 4:55; 16:158
Snyder, John M. 12:10
Snyder, John O. 9:45

Snyder, John S. 9:125; 27:113
Snyder, John Van Metre 21:80
Snyder, John W. 7:61
Snyder, Jonathan 11:112
Snyder, Joseph 7:111; 10:137; 17:87; 20:352; 23:259
Snyder, Joseph C. 17:245
Snyder, Joseph D. 22:441
Snyder, Josiah 7:42; 22:102
Snyder, Kingsley N. 7:42
Snyder, L. 1:76; 3:182; 23:264
Snyder, Lafred 8:96
Snyder, Levi 17:452; 24:182
Snyder, Lewis 3:182; 10:149
Snyder, Louis 17:394
Snyder, M. 1:174; 3:182
Snyder, M. S. 3:182
Snyder, Martin 18:39
Snyder, Milton 9:125; 27:113
Snyder, N. 19:262
Snyder, Nathan 11:75
Snyder, Nelson 13:135; 17:186
Snyder, Nicholas 1:73
Snyder, O. 11:44
Snyder, O. N. 14:237
Snyder, O. W. 25:71
Snyder, Owen 18:39
Snyder, P. 1:170, 175
Snyder, P. S. 11:440
Snyder, Peter 11:78; 17:87; 22:173
Snyder, Philip 22:467
Snyder, Phineas S. 23:241
Snyder, R. 1:169; 16:102
Snyder, Reuben 22:55
Snyder, Rudolph 9:59; 23:169
Snyder, Rufus S. 10:167; 19:195
Snyder, S. 1:169; 2:17; 13:79; 14:112; 25:74
Snyder, S. H. 1:172
Snyder, Samuel 7:111; 18:316; 22:221, 411; 23:288; 26:112
Snyder, Samuel C. 21:234
Snyder, Samuel H. 22:102
Snyder, Samuel S. 12:40
Snyder, Sebastian 21:390
Snyder, Simon 22:221, 238

Snyder, Solomon 22:491; 24:30
Snyder, T. 9:113
Snyder, Thomas 3:182
Snyder, Thomas A. 20:352
Snyder, Thomas H. 10:137
Snyder, Thomas P. 17:59
Snyder, Tyler J. 16:102
Snyder, W. 1:95; 11:313; 13:119
Snyder, W. A. 24:85
Snyder, W. H. 11:97; 13:119
Snyder, W. H. H. 8:67
Snyder, W. J. 11:111
Snyder, W. L. 1:76
Snyder, Walter S. 15:229
Snyder, Wash 18:253; 26:64, 65
Snyder, Wilbur 4:55
Snyder, Willard B. 7:65
Snyder, William 3:182; 7:133; 9:10; 11:44, 168; 14:303; 15:45, 135; 17:480; 19:35; 21:126; 22:102, 221; 25:305; 27:117
Snyder, William H. 13:48; 22:221
Snyder, William H. H. 23:79
Snyder, William J. 12:40
Snyder, William L. 12:40
Snyder, William M. 12:40
Snyder, Wilson 19:347
Soales, B. R. 14:337
Soals, J. R. 2:17
Soaper, S. 2:17; 25:69
Soaphdraf, Hans 18:253; 26:63
Soards, William 14:221
Sobdell, Eli 10:22
Sober, S. 11:313
Soble, Martin 13:127
Soby, William 9:151
Sockum, A. 3:182
Sodd, Norman 11:184
Sodder, --- 26:184
Sodder, J. 25:235
Sodders, --- 8:75
Soden, Abraham 11:391
Soden, Brown 17:399
Soden, John 1:73
Soder, Charles 12:123; 15:135
Soder, Charles W. 13:48; 16:56
Sodestrom, Andrew 21:80
Sodon, Peter 14:112

Soe, Andrew 5:30
Soellig, Robert 19:195
Soers, Alcock 25:235
Soesman, F. A. 1:170
Sofera, D. 11:391
Soffel, Johnson 26:182
Sofield, A. J. 16:124, 153
Sogers, J. C. 14:112
Soggs, Henry 13:59
Sohisher, Martin 23:206
Sohn, N. 23:118
Sohnle, John P. 10:81
Sohr, Peter 22:221
Sohruind, John 27:119
Sol, A. 25:235
Solberger, William 1:72
Solbrig, Herman 13:119
Solcom, Z. B. 21:168
Solders, Francis 12:40
Soldier, --- 19:195
Soldier, Indian 18:160, 316
Sole, J. H. 11:168
Soleday, W. H. 1:172
Soler, D. 1:76
Soles, H. 1:172
Soles, Jeduther 22:510
Soles, William 11:289
Solesby, Charles W. 20:352
Soliday, J. 1:170
Sollars, Samuel 17:405
Soller, R. E. A. 16:56
Sollers, Levi D. 19:35
Sollers, S. 1:169
Solley, W. R. 14:21
Solliday, John 18:58
Sollinoge, C. 3:182
Sollins, Franklin 19:35
Solmes, F. W. 12:162
Solnave, Charles D. 22:345
Soloman, E. G. 15:319
Soloman, M. 25:236
Soloman, Tobias 10:137
Solomon, A. F. 11:173
Solomon, B. H. 11:426
Solomon, E. 12:80; 25:236
Solomon, E. C. 17:43
Solomon, Eugene 7:133
Solomon, H. 14:112
Solomon, Henry 11:121
Solomon, J. 23:314
Solomon, J. L. 14:112
Solomon, John 19:284
Solomon, L. E. 11:391
Solomon, Lewis 16:102
Solomon, M. 11:250
Solomon, Tobias 20:352

Solomon, William 9:204; 19:269; 23:272
Solomonson, Sivon 10:137; 20:352
Solsberg, W. 9:67
Solsberg, William 18:281
Solsbury, A. J. 1:78
Solsen, O. 1:174
Solsworth, William 10:81
Solton, Aaron 23:257
Soltzer, G. 1:77
Soltzer, John 1:73
Solverson, Peter 7:42
Somer, R. M. 18:58
Somer, R. N. 10:149
Somercamp, E. N. 16:124
Somerdike, Jacob W. 17:93
Somerfield, W. 3:183
Somerman, August 22:284
Somers, Ambrose 22:102
Somers, Charles 15:113
Somers, F. 3:183
Somers, Fred 15:345; 16:379
Somers, George 19:101
Somers, George W. 27:107
Somers, H. 13:99
Somers, Harrison 13:59
Somers, J. 1:175
Somers, James M. 10:175
Somers, John 3:182; 17:93
Somers, P. 3:182
Somers, Sials 10:137
Somers, Silas 20:352
Somers, W. 14:21
Somers, W. C. 24:63
Somers, W. R. 27:119
Somerville, George H. 22:345
Somerville, J. 11:269
Somerville, J. W. 15:229
Somerville, Jack 27:112, 113
Somerville, James 16:87
Somerville, Joseph 21:390; 22:345
Somerville, S. B. 7:54
Somerville, Solomon 21:285
Somerville, William 17:433; 24:155
Somes, George B. 19:195
Somes, I. 11:342
Somle, S. P. 25:236
Sommer, Eben 16:56
Sommer, John 18:160
Sommer, Michael 17:462
Sommermuir, H. 13:126

Sommers, Benton 25:236
Sommers, Eber 13:48
Sommers, Edward 27:112
Sommers, George 9:99;
  18:39
Sommers, James 18:39
Sommers, John 8:32;
  12:168
Sommers, Levi 16:229
Sommers, Michael 8:102;
  24:175
Sommers, Onas 12:40
Sommers, Thomas 14:245
Sommers, W. 3:183
Sommers, W. R. 14:245
Sommers, William 8:118
Sommersett, Peter 9:104
Sommersett, T. 14:112
Sommerville, Thomas
  8:42; 26:180
Sommerville, William
  5:45
Soms, C. 3:182
Son, Christian 23:253
Son, John S. 22:355
Son, R. R. W. 8:56
Sona, Matthias 12:40
Sonday, William 7:111
Sondell, Charles 7:9
Sonden, James 11:17
Sondeniker, Jacob 15:280
Sonder, S. 3:183
Sondericker, Jacob 25:236
Sonders, John 18:211
Sone, Peter 10:149; 18:58
Sonea, N. 26:59
Soners, W. 14:21
Sones, James R. 12:40
Song, Howard E. 5:30
Songer, A. J. 24:30
Songer, Thomas B.
  10:137
Songless, Gustavus 15:23
Sonnenwald, A. 1:77
Sonnett, T. W. 14:112
Sonnvine, William 13:126
Sonslynn, John H. 8:32
Sontag, David 4:55
Sonten, M. 9:155
Sontine, --- 10:81
Sonton, M. 11:269
Soogh, Peter 7:80
Sools, F. F. 8:96
Soolsby, Charles W.
  10:81
Soon, W. R. 17:505
Soots, David 21:235
Sooy, J. 1:172
Sooy, Samuel K. 1:77
Sope, Calvin 3:183
Soper, A. J. 16:271

Soper, Charles 22:155
Soper, Charles D. 10:167;
  19:195
Soper, Edward 22:284
Soper, Edwin 16:229
Soper, Frank 17:138
Soper, George W. 12:60
Soper, J. H. 16:229
Soper, Joel 1:74
Soper, John T. 7:63
Soper, P. 3:183
Soper, Reuben 12:40
Soper, Roland 11:111
Soper, S. E. 18:39
Soper, S. H. 14:221
Soper, William 13:119;
  26:129
Soper, William E. 13:119
Sophat, L. 25:236
Sopher, Alex. 16:229
Sopher, Asa 23:50
Sopher, J. D. 20:149
Sopher, James 3:183
Sopher, S. 3:183
Sopher, W. H. 23:169
Sopman, William 15:75
Sopp, C. 5:54
Sopper, H. A. 1:75
Sopser, Andrew 23:93
Sorait, H. Clay 27:118
Sorbear, Samuel 16:229
Sorber, Frederick 23:182
Sorber, Mager 16:124
Sorber, P. 1:168
Sorbie, George B. 22:489
Sord, William 3:183
Sorebear, Samuel 15:290
Sorebee, John E. 22:269
Soreilee, J. 19:101
Sorenson, Peter 22:284
Sorey, John 14:112
Sorg, A. 3:183
Sorg, F. Augustus 15:229
Sorg, John 23:79
Sorg, William 22:169
Sorick, Franz 14:221
Soriefier, A. 11:269
Soringers, P. 14:112
Sorinland, J. 14:112
Sork, Peter 18:39
Sornchoff, Henry 14:221
Sorrel, James 18:160
Sorrell, J. W. 9:91; 26:60
Sorrell, James 8:32
Sorrell, John 22:131
Sorrell, Moses 18:115
Sorrells, P. 18:253; 26:62
Sorrels, James 17:87
Sorrels, Marquis 24:154
Sorrick, Adam 22:221
Sorry, Adam 9:39

Sorry, Reuben 8:96
Sortell, J. 1:173
Sorter, John D. 7:17
Sorton, James 9:91; 26:60
Sortore, Samuel 25:67
Sosebe, Thomas M. 10:81
Sossa, A. L. 11:323
Soster, R. 15:229
Sothman, John 10:137;
  20:353
Sothoron, J. F. 17:426
Sott, J. 14:112
Sotter, I. M. 3:183
Sotter, John 5:45
Sottle, Warren 8:32
Sotts, H. A. 10:22
Souble, Arthur 4:55
Soucks, D. 15:229
Souder, Jacob D. 21:80
Souder, T. B. 21:390
Souders, Chris 14:221
Souders, G. 1:172
Soug, Franklin 12:40
Souger, George W. 22:55
Souger, Thomas B.
  20:352
Souh, Peter 17:102
Souhwick, Clark 9:125
Soukil, Philip 9:17
Soule, Alexander V.
  25:289
Soule, Charles 17:474;
  18:105; 27:118
Soule, David 23:79
Soule, G. A. 1:175
Soule, Harvey 1:70
Soule, Henry G. 12:162
Soule, J. B. 25:68
Soule, J. W. 15:23
Soule, John B. 23:195
Soule, John W. 12:77
Soule, Martin 10:137
Soule, Preston 13:48
Soule, Silas S. 8:120
Soule, Warren 18:160
Soule, William 21:87
Souler, Francis 7:111
Soules, Charles 6:9; 24:62
Soules, H. B. 1:171
Soules, J. M. 1:171
Soules, James H. 22:467
Soules, Thomas 11:112
Souley, Martin 20:353
Soulignie, Prident 7:111
Soull, Daniel 15:153
Souls, J. H. 3:183
Soult, Harry 17:245
Souly, A. G. 14:267
Sour, John 23:125
Sour, Joseph 17:16
Sourbeck, George 3:183

Sourbeer, J. E. 14:221
Sourbur, J. E. 3:183
Sourett, Thomas L. 21:390
Sours, Jacob C. 15:229
Sous, O. 14:221
Sousicee, F. 20:352
Souslinn, John W. 18:160
Souter, C. 3:183
Souter, Thomas 23:93
South, Archibald 23:80
South, Archibald M. 10:137; 20:353
South, D. 21:41
South, E. 11:251
South, George 26:225
South, James 11:184
South, Nathaniel F. 22:102
South, Peter 3:183
South, Richard 7:42
South, T. B. 22:55
Southall, Addison 22:516
Southand, Walter 16:379
Southard, D. 14:22
Southard, Daniel 14:221
Southard, Eugene F. 10:81; 20:352
Southard, George 9:29; 18:316; 26:112
Southard, H. 3:183; 13:99
Southard, John 23:280
Southard, Joseph 11:391; 17:245
Southard, Leonard A. 23:306
Southard, Levi 20:149
Southard, Matthew 3:183
Southard, Stephen M. 7:111
Souther, Henry 3:183
Souther, Lenas 13:48
Southerd, N. 16:102
Southerland, C. 14:221
Southerland, George M. 11:425
Southerland, John 10:137
Southerland, Philip 2:17
Southerland, W. 11:188
Southerlin, J. 16:271
Southerlin, Sidney 17:215
Southern, John 21:241
Southern, Robert 22:440
Southers, David 22:320
Southers, Frankling 23:302
Southers, John 11:416
Southers, Samuel M. 22:492
Southers, William 22:320
Southerton, John 21:59

Southerworth, Charles H. 11:112
Southgate, John A. 19:49
Southland, A. 11:438
Southland, L. 9:67
Southland, Walter 15:351
Southmayd, John 15:331
Southus, T. 23:303
Southward, Archy 27:111
Southward, Lewis H. 4:55
Southward, N. O. 9:104
Southward, W. A. 3:183
Southwell, Jesse 20:32
Southwell, William 22:114
Southwick, Albert 22:468
Southwick, C. C. 11:313
Southwick, Charles E. 10:137; 20:353
Southwick, Clark 27:114
Southwick, Dewitt 10:81; 20:353
Southwick, Elmar G. 10:167
Southwick, Guy 16:124
Southwick, J. W. 8:56
Southwick, Joseph W. 11:112
Southwick, P. 14:112
Southwick, W. B. 16:229
Southwick, W. H. S. 4:55
Southwick, William H. 10:167; 19:195
Southwick, William P. 21:143
Southworth, Chester O. 20:353
Southworth, Chester V. 10:137
Southworth, E. 1:76
Southworth, E. B. 20:13
Southworth, Ezra 9:39; 18:297; 26:113
Southworth, H. C. 8:120
Southworth, J. 3:183
Southworth, John 3:183
Southworth, Nelson 15:319; 19:101
Southworth, Otis 16:142
Southworth, R. 3:183
Southworth, Reuben 12:40
Southworth, Wallace 22:411
Southworth, William A. 21:390
Southworth, William H. 21:80
Southworth, William O. 7:111
Soutime, --- 20:353

Soutmayd, John 19:101
Soves, Martin 16:229
Sowalter, Martin 12:77
Sowards, Henry J. 17:87
Sowards, James 17:87
Sowards, William W. 15:89
Sowash, C. 11:168
Sowden, W. H. 1:169
Sowder, Jacob 17:162
Sowders, Thomas 20:353
Sowders, Thomas J. 10:81
Sowenson, Seven 8:110
Sower, Cyrus 9:104
Sower, D. E. 16:379
Sowers, Alva A. 22:102
Sowers, C. 22:221
Sowers, Francis M. 21:205
Sowers, Franklin 21:59
Sowers, Henry 11:323
Sowers, John 17:405; 22:238
Sowers, S. Meredith 8:96
Sowers, W. 11:314
Sowers, W. A. 11:314
Sowers, W. L. 23:50
Sowers, William 12:77; 20:103
Sowle, D. P. 5:54
Sowler, Elijah 9:225
Sowles, L. 19:195
Sowls, J. 14:245
Sowls, Lucius H. 17:323
Sowman, Jesse 22:522
Sowsdown, A. J. 22:55
Soyers, John 21:201
Sozer, William 11:404
Sp---wn, John 21:168
Spaan, Heinrich 22:284
Space, W. 1:100
Space, William H. 21:390
Spacht, Michael J. 1:71
Spacious, James 16:114
Spade, David 7:42
Spade, Jerry 4:55
Spade, S. 14:112
Spade, W. C. C. 25:69
Spade, William 22:438
Spades, Winslow 10:177; 19:195
Spadinger, Fidell 24:45
Spadle, John 22:491
Spadlin, T. 22:524
Spafford, Andrew J. 10:137; 20:353
Spafford, E. D. 20:194
Spafford, George 17:426
Spafford, George F. 24:180
Spafford, H. S. 21:126

Spafford, John 24:115
Spafford, P. A. 9:193
Spafford, R. Amos 19:242
Spafford, Sid'ny 1:75
Spafford, William 22:284, 467
Spaher, George 5:54
Spahr, C. H. 22:221
Spahr, Henry 24:45
Spahr, Madison 22:221
Spaht, B. 20:44
Spain, David R. 15:59
Spain, Eli A. 8:75
Spain, Hamilton 21:41
Spain, Jacob 11:416
Spain, Jesse 11:77
Spain, John E. 22:491
Spain, Michael 5:54
Spain, Milton 20:25
Spain, Moses 21:41
Spain, Peter D. 13:48
Spain, Richard 3:183
Spain, Samuel 7:42
Spain, Thomas 3:183
Spake, George 12:77
Spalburgh, E. 1:78
Spalding, Abner 15:229
Spalding, Aeny S. 19:297
Spalding, Asa B. 17:357
Spalding, Edward J. 8:96
Spalding, G. 12:123
Spalding, G. H. 14:290; 23:110
Spalding, G. M. 15:168
Spalding, G. T. 7:111
Spalding, G. W. 7:111
Spalding, George H. 15:353
Spalding, George W. 19:307
Spalding, H. 3:183
Spalding, J. 3:183
Spalding, James 20:49
Spalding, John 16:229
Spalding, Josiah 10:81
Spalding, L. M. 25:71
Spalding, T. R. 1:71
Spalding, William 3:183; 7:111; 8:96
Spalks, M. W. 16:305
Spall, Samuel 22:412, 438
Spaller, Bernam 14:26
Spame, George W. 18:160
Span, Hampton 27:113
Spaneer, John 14:112
Spaner, Christian 8:32
Spangabier, Chris 17:416
Spangenberg, Christian 24:154
Spangenberg, William 25:70

Spanger, John 21:390
Spangle, Moses 8:96
Spangler, --- 2:17; 15:259; 25:68
Spangler, A. 3:183; 14:112
Spangler, Abraham 17:93
Spangler, Annanias 4:55
Spangler, Benjamin 10:81; 20:353
Spangler, C. C. 19:195
Spangler, Christopher C. 10:175
Spangler, Edward 4:55
Spangler, George 11:184
Spangler, H. J. 3:183
Spangler, J. 23:169
Spangler, J. J. 23:251
Spangler, Jacob 22:155
Spangler, James 17:93
Spangler, John 18:427
Spangler, John G. 17:112
Spangler, L. O. 9:99
Spangler, Maz 5:30
Spangler, Philip 11:314
Spangler, R. 2:17
Spangler, William 7:42
Spanhigh, --- 22:155
Spaniel, George 11:250
Spankenburgh, George 14:221
Spanker, John C. 22:498
Spankey, W. 14:22
Spankey, W. H. 16:271
Spann, Christian 17:68
Spann, Hanston 9:136
Spann, Harris 9:136; 27:112
Spann, W. W. 21:41
Spann, William T. 17:204
Spannuth, Charles 10:137; 20:353
Spanogle, Mathlow 5:30
Spar, H. 3:183
Sparenberg, Henry 26:112
Sparenburg, Henry 18:316
Spargeon, John 14:221
Spargo, Samuel 12:41
Spargo, William 12:60
Spark, David 15:75
Spark, G. 3:183
Spark, Jacob O. 15:229
Spark, Louis 22:320
Spark, W. 26:213
Sparkes, James 26:183
Sparkes, William 10:187
Sparkhall, George 7:42
Sparkles, --- 18:194
Sparks, --- 17:268
Sparks, Addison 10:97
Sparks, Allen 11:97

Sparks, Andrew 14:331
Sparks, Charles B. 10:137; 20:353
Sparks, Cornelius L. 23:125
Sparks, Cyrus L. 7:42
Sparks, Daniel 23:115
Sparks, E. 3:183
Sparks, Eli 7:111
Sparks, Ellery E. 23:93
Sparks, F. M. 7:42
Sparks, Field 10:81; 20:190
Sparks, George 16:229; 27:116
Sparks, George W. 9:125; 27:114
Sparks, Henry C. 17:353
Sparks, I. 7:71
Sparks, J. 1:172
Sparks, J. P. 15:168; 25:73
Sparks, J. T. 2:17
Sparks, James 8:67; 22:103; 23:115
Sparks, James W. 11:334
Sparks, John 13:68; 18:58; 25:68
Sparks, John C. 21:80
Sparks, John W. 11:342; 21:59
Sparks, L. D. 3:183
Sparks, L. L. 11:172
Sparks, M. F. 3:183
Sparks, Milo 18:180
Sparks, Morris 21:191
Sparks, P. 1:73
Sparks, Preston 17:43
Sparks, R. D. 11:221
Sparks, Reuben 24:168
Sparks, Samuel E. 11:77
Sparks, Stephen 20:187
Sparks, Thomas 25:236
Sparks, Thomas H. 18:401
Sparks, W. L. 20:353
Sparks, William 18:253; 26:63
Sparks, William L. 10:81
Sparks, William R. 21:235
Sparkson, George B. 11:194
Sparling, Andrew 10:137
Sparling, Peter 1:73
Sparner, George W. 26:182
Sparr, Philip 11:194
Sparr, Wilson 25:236
Sparring, T. 3:183
Sparron, A. 13:119
Sparrow, Ebenezer E. 17:317

Sparrow, Henry 22:457
Sparrow, J. 14:112
Sparrow, Jacob 13:48
Sparrow, James C. 20:187
Sparrowgrass, Isaac T. 13:59
Sparry, N. 11:172
Spartin, Levi 12:158
Sparting, William 12:158
Spates, Joseph 22:320
Spathoey, John 18:297
Spatholy, John 26:113
Spatks, M. W. 12:84
Spatta, John 21:60
Spaulding, A. 9:151; 27:110
Spaulding, A. D. 15:319; 19:101
Spaulding, A. F. 8:115
Spaulding, Abbott 21:41
Spaulding, Alb. L. 21:390
Spaulding, Albert F. 8:96; 18:327
Spaulding, C. 1:75
Spaulding, C. H. 26:181
Spaulding, Charles N. 21:390
Spaulding, D. 1:168
Spaulding, E. A. 11:169
Spaulding, E. E. 8:56
Spaulding, E. J. 20:157
Spaulding, Edward 18:211
Spaulding, Edward M. 22:468
Spaulding, Edwin D. 20:109
Spaulding, Eugene 4:55
Spaulding, F. 3:183
Spaulding, F. A. 15:229
Spaulding, F. C. 3:183
Spaulding, Freeman 22:490
Spaulding, George H. 16:282
Spaulding, Giles G. 8:32; 18:160
Spaulding, H. 1:75, 173
Spaulding, H. D. 7:54
Spaulding, Henry D. 27:148
Spaulding, Hy. A. 14:112
Spaulding, J. 3:183; 14:112
Spaulding, J. E. 14:112
Spaulding, James 3:183
Spaulding, James C. 23:80
Spaulding, James R. 10:22
Spaulding, John 21:261; 24:30
Spaulding, Joseph 26:61

Spaulding, Joseph B. 20:36
Spaulding, Josiah 20:353
Spaulding, L. 1:72
Spaulding, Lyman 11:171
Spaulding, N. D. 12:40
Spaulding, O. H. 13:48
Spaulding, Page 13:48
Spaulding, R. E. 19:276
Spaulding, Robert E. 9:194
Spaulding, S. 14:112, 221
Spaulding, S. A. 27:108
Spaulding, S. H. 9:151
Spaulding, Thomas 22:490
Spaulding, W. H. 12:10
Spaulding, Warren 12:158
Spaulding, Wisley 12:40
Spaulter, F. J. 19:101
Spaulter, S. J. 15:329
Spaur, Christian 18:160
Spaur, Robert 10:81; 20:353
Spaw, George 11:78
Spawn, Solomon 8:67
Speace, J. E. 25:236
Spead, Henry 4:55
Spead, O. B. 19:195
Speadle, W. J. 12:80
Speak, James 6:19; 18:94
Speaker, H. 3:183
Speaker, Jacob B. 11:167
Speakman, Alex 4:55
Speakman, Thomas 9:29; 18:316; 26:111
Speakman, W. J. 22:221
Speaks, Joseph 13:59
Speaks, W. F. 11:169
Speane, Johnson 4:55
Spear, C. 1:170
Spear, C. E. 26:65
Spear, Carlos 21:261
Spear, Charles E. 9:91
Spear, Charles W. 10:167; 19:195
Spear, Corn's. 1:72
Spear, E. C. 9:29; 18:316; 26:112
Spear, Edmund 12:41
Spear, Edw. A. 14:221
Spear, Edwin 21:133
Spear, G. 17:138; 24:204
Spear, Green 26:60
Spear, Greenville O. 21:41
Spear, J. B. 20:36, 176
Spear, J. S. 14:303; 27:117
Spear, John 4:55; 15:113
Spear, John G. 23:50
Spear, John J. 17:264

Spear, John S. 17:350
Spear, Joseph 21:235
Spear, Robert 18:444
Spear, Samuel 7:70; 11:171
Spear, Thomas 13:119
Spear, Thomas M. 10:22
Spear, W. 1:78
Spear, W. G. 18:160, 161
Spear, W. I. 14:112
Spear, Willard H. 23:125
Spear, William 7:42
Spear, William A. 25:305
Spear, William F. 15:12
Spearague, William T. 18:160
Speare, Washington 19:49
Speares, L. M. 14:317
Spearing, W. E. 7:111
Speark, I. S. 17:472
Spearman, Caezar 21:285
Spearman, George 22:345
Spearman, H. 10:187
Spears, A. 1:170
Spears, Alfred 11:392
Spears, Alvin 14:290; 23:110
Spears, Daniel 7:61
Spears, Edwin 17:447
Spears, Enos 20:129
Spears, F. W. 15:229
Spears, George 9:59; 17:186
Spears, H. E. 15:345
Spears, J. 3:183; 14:112
Spears, J. K. 23:50
Spears, Jacob 21:143
Spears, James 20:353
Spears, John 11:167
Spears, John D. 24:97
Spears, L. 1:172
Spears, Louis 17:275
Spears, Martin 15:229
Spears, Morgan S. 11:98
Spears, R. 21:41
Spears, S. 11:189
Spears, Samuel 17:167
Spears, Samuel H. 23:169
Spears, T. 9:59
Spears, Thomas 11:98
Spears, Thomas H. 17:261
Spears, Thomas J. 17:239
Spears, W. 12:147; 19:307
Spears, W. E. 16:379
Spears, W. G. 8:32
Spears, W. M. 3:183
Spears, William 11:97
Speas, A. W. 1:95
Speas, Gotlieb 15:229
Spease, Louis 1:72
Spease, T. 1:76

Speays, Thomas 16:229
Specht, Austin 8:110
Specht, George H. 11:271
Specht, John A. 14:221
Specht, Michael 17:347
Speck, Augustus 3:183
Speck, Francis B. 11:44
Speck, M. 14:112
Speck, Oliver 3:183
Speck, William 1:70; 7:54
Speckman, John 7:70;
23:195
Speckman, W. M. 21:126
Spect, F. 14:22
Speddling, W. H. 19:35
Speed, Eliphalet I. 10:137
Speed, Eliphalet J. 20:353
Speed, H. 9:241
Speed, Henry 15:229, 338
Speed, J. 12:163
Speed, John W. 19:195
Speede, Thomas H.
14:112
Speegall, C. K. 22:16
Speel, Thomas 12:77
Speelman, Fred 14:221
Speelman, Joseph 22:492
Speen, Nelson 16:229
Speener, Hyman 15:229
Speer, Daniel 12:41
Speer, G. 21:191
Speer, William A. 7:78
Speer, William H. 21:60
Speerman, A. 19:195
Speers, Allen 17:139;
24:204
Speers, Jesse 21:201
Speers, Otto 4:55
Speers, W. 15:45
Speers, W. H. 23:50
Spees, L. H. 12:93;
16:305
Spehr, Albert 24:85
Speicher, B. 1:78
Speicker, Moses 9:125;
27:113
Speigelmoire, G. A. 12:57
Speigles, William 4:55
Speiker, Josiah 12:77
Speileder, Charles 19:35
Speiler, Frederick 4:55
Speilman, Jonathan
11:169
Spein, August 12:60
Speir, Robert 14:221
Speisberger, Charles
16:102
Speit, F. 13:99
Spelburgh, William 13:48
Spell, R. C. 9:161;
14:328; 27:119

Spellburg, Henry 17:213
Spellburgh, William 10:22
Spelling, Eli 8:110
Spelling, George 10:175
Spellman, Abraham
10:81; 20:353
Spellman, Albert 23:169
Spellman, D. 9:59
Spellman, Ed 17:186
Spellman, J. 3:183
Spellman, Jacob 6:9
Spellman, Patrick 21:41
Spellman, Stephen 22:320
Spellman, T. H. 7:42
Spellman, Thomas
10:167, 175
Spellman, William 15:59
Spellmard, Jeremiah 7:42
Spells, Peter 11:76
Spelman, F. 18:115
Spelman, Thomas 19:195
Spelman, William 24:30
Spence, David 3:183;
17:357
Spence, E. L. 26:182
Spence, Elisha 21:285
Spence, George W. 7:54
Spence, J. 20:60; 22:320
Spence, J. S. 21:106
Spence, James 23:182
Spence, John 11:397
Spence, John F. 21:151
Spence, Joseph 18:17
Spence, Levi 3:183
Spence, William 14:112;
16:229; 17:284
Spencer, --- 11:342;
19:101; 26:226
Spencer, A. 3:183; 19:284
Spencer, A. A. 1:175
Spencer, A. H. 15:280;
25:236
Spencer, A. S. 21:93
Spencer, Albert 13:119
Spencer, Albert S. 21:245
Spencer, Alfred 8:56;
21:106
Spencer, Alonzo B.
21:391
Spencer, Anderson 22:320
Spencer, Andrew 10:81;
20:353
Spencer, Andrew J.
17:293
Spencer, Archibald
22:285
Spencer, Arza B. 17:444;
24:162
Spencer, Austin 9:194
Spencer, B. H. 19:271
Spencer, Bartley 23:101

Spencer, C. 25:236
Spencer, Charles 4:55;
7:42; 22:55
Spencer, Charles H.
21:235
Spencer, Charles R. 4:55
Spencer, Charles W.
24:30
Spencer, Cornelius 17:495
Spencer, Cyrus 13:48
Spencer, Daniel 9:194;
17:284; 19:277;
21:391
Spencer, Darwin 20:139
Spencer, David H. 15:229
Spencer, David P. 22:441
Spencer, Davis 17:43
Spencer, Dempsey 26:180
Spencer, Dempsy 8:42
Spencer, DeWitt C.
17:362
Spencer, E. 13:119; 21:41
Spencer, E. S. 26:237
Spencer, Edson 27:113
Spencer, Elias 25:236
Spencer, Elijah 17:43
Spencer, Elmer 21:243
Spencer, Elston 17:232
Spencer, Ererebus 14:221
Spencer, F. M. 14:221,
259
Spencer, Francis M. 10:81
Spencer, Frank 24:102
Spencer, G. 2:17; 18:253;
25:73, 236; 26:64
Spencer, G. D. 15:345;
16:379
Spencer, G. M. 1:175
Spencer, G. R. 25:280
Spencer, G. W. 15:229
Spencer, George 3:183;
5:30; 12:54
Spencer, George E.
11:168
Spencer, George S.
14:221
Spencer, George W. 8:32
Spencer, H. 13:99; 14:221
Spencer, H. H. 9:125;
27:106
Spencer, H. K. 12:100
Spencer, Harrison 15:12
Spencer, Hiram 11:270
Spencer, Isaac L. 9:194
Spencer, Israel 22:345
Spencer, J. 15:259;
19:269
Spencer, J. A. 25:236
Spencer, J. B. 27:119
Spencer, J. C. 25:236
Spencer, J. G. 17:264

Spencer, J. H. 3:183; 16:229
Spencer, J. L. 1:173
Spencer, J. O. 19:101
Spencer, J. W. 10:137; 20:353
Spencer, James 4:55; 6:33; 20:187; 22:355; 25:327
Spencer, Jason 1:72
Spencer, Jerome B. 18:407
Spencer, John 3:183; 9:39, 194; 10:22; 11:111; 12:10; 19:49; 23:169, 185; 25:236
Spencer, John B. 9:161
Spencer, John C. 10:93; 17:362; 20:353
Spencer, John M. 11:382
Spencer, John P. 11:111
Spencer, John S. 5:30; 21:235; 25:236
Spencer, John T. 10:211; 18:456
Spencer, Joseph 9:73; 22:155
Spencer, Joseph O. 15:335
Spencer, Judson A. 15:280
Spencer, L. 2:18; 16:229; 17:284
Spencer, Lewis 13:48
Spencer, Louis 25:69
Spencer, Lucius 15:229
Spencer, M. 3:183; 21:391
Spencer, Madison 17:441; 24:155
Spencer, Martin A. 8:32
Spencer, Michael 1:72
Spencer, Mustin A. 18:161
Spencer, N. 25:236
Spencer, N. G. 23:264
Spencer, Noah 5:46
Spencer, R. 19:246
Spencer, R. A. 9:151
Spencer, Ransom H. 9:194
Spencer, Raymond 24:72
Spencer, Reuben A. 27:108
Spencer, Richard 8:56
Spencer, Richard A. 9:14
Spencer, S. 1:168; 11:416; 18:94; 23:51; 27:107
Spencer, S. M. 3:183
Spencer, Samuel 6:10; 8:102; 13:119;

Spencer, Samuel 17:157, 463; 19:195; 24:180
Spencer, Samuel G. 16:102
Spencer, T. M. 20:353
Spencer, Tennet R. 12:41
Spencer, Theodore 18:253; 26:63
Spencer, Thomas 9:9; 15:229; 18:335; 22:221, 510, 522; 23:125
Spencer, U. 14:221
Spencer, W. 10:137; 18:94; 20:353; 25:236
Spencer, W. H. 14:290; 19:276; 21:391
Spencer, W. H. G. 14:267
Spencer, Wash 6:13
Spencer, William 5:46; 9:99; 10:81; 16:114; 18:211; 20:353; 21:205; 22:491; 23:284
Spencer, William H. 10:137; 20:353; 22:345
Spencer, William H. J. 23:80
Spencer, William N. 22:491
Spencer, William W. 12:41
Spences, Wallis C. 20:143
Spencey, W. H. 23:51
Spend, Adam 14:221
Spendlow, W. C. 15:259
Spenerlow, W. C. 14:131
Spenks, William 18:180
Spenlock, Humphrey 11:89
Spense, Adam 1:76
Spense, D. F. 26:182
Spenser, David 1:72
Spensly, William 26:58
Spensor, Edson 9:125
Sperceful, John 17:59
Sperey, Charles 8:32
Sperick, George O. 15:59
Sperin, John 18:281
Spermer, John 5:30
Sperry, A. 3:183
Sperry, A. A. 25:72
Sperry, Arthur 11:289
Sperry, C. A. 1:170
Sperry, Calvin 17:168
Sperry, Columbus 21:241
Sperry, David 23:80
Sperry, E. 13:99
Sperry, E. S. 13:48

Sperry, Henry 10:167; 20:129
Sperry, Henry S. 19:195
Sperry, Ira E. 16:82
Sperry, Isaac J. 16:134
Sperry, J. 11:173
Sperry, John 22:345
Sperry, Joseph E. 17:68
Sperry, Judson 25:70
Sperry, M. H. 21:41
Sperry, O. M. 11:44
Sperry, S. 22:490
Spertz, Joseph 9:151
Spess, James 1:73
Spessard, Andrew 11:213
Spetnaget, --- 11:312
Spettor, G. W. 5:30; 25:236
Spevey, Charles 18:161
Sphon, Henry 7:42
Spicer, Albert D. 13:48
Spicer, D. 1:78; 11:87
Spicer, Daniel H. 4:55
Spicer, Edgar L. 22:55
Spicer, Edwin 21:80
Spicer, Elijah 10:22
Spicer, F. 19:262
Spicer, Frank 16:379
Spicer, Franklin 9:194
Spicer, G. 25:236
Spicer, Henry 10:137; 20:353
Spicer, I. R. 8:32
Spicer, J. 23:51
Spicer, J. M. 9:113
Spicer, J. R. 18:161
Spicer, John 23:169
Spicer, John L. 18:297; 26:113
Spicer, John M. 20:129
Spicer, Joseph 11:313
Spicer, Merritt A. 20:129
Spicer, Michael 7:111
Spicer, Oscar A. 15:45
Spicer, Philip R. 15:5
Spicer, R. A. 9:59
Spicer, Samuel B. 13:48
Spicer, Solomon 20:129
Spicer, W. 3:183
Spicer, William 15:229; 22:412
Spicher, Joseph 11:289
Spichiger, John 21:41
Spicht, Perry 19:293
Spickelmire, Thomas H. 21:80
Spickeman, William 22:285
Spickerman, S. 1:76
Spickleman, David 8:96

Spicks, Bernard 12:77; 15:82
Spiddle, Wilson 5:30
Spidell, W. 25:236
Spiegle, Fritz 23:51
Spiel, Henry 15:75
Spieler, Alden 5:30
Spielman, David 15:135
Spiels, Alexander 22:320
Spier, E. 8:56
Spiers, Granvil 17:234
Spiers, Henry 5:30
Spies, James M. 27:115
Spies, M. 12:77
Spiess, Jacob 20:13
Spiffen, Henry 6:27
Spigelmire, Emanuel 10:137; 20:353
Spigemer, S. 16:229
Spiggs, George 4:68
Spigle, F. 3:183
Spike, Charles 22:285
Spiker, A. 24:30
Spiker, Christopher 22:238
Spiker, J. 3:184; 15:45
Spiker, S. 14:303; 17:478; 27:117
Spiker, William L. 21:42
Spilet, William S. 22:155
Spilker, Henry 22:439
Spilkey, Edward 7:111
Spillane, J. 16:73
Spillard, John 19:101
Spiller, A. 25:236
Spiller, F. K. 16:229
Spiller, George H. 18:17
Spiller, J. B. 21:42
Spiller, J. F. 19:35
Spillers, D. 7:84
Spillhorn, John 9:67
Spillman, George 26:61
Spillman, Jacob 18:105
Spillman, James 18:427; 23:169
Spillman, Jeremiah 10:81
Spillman, John 3:183
Spillman, John H. 22:131
Spillman, O. F. 3:183
Spillman, Thomas 22:221
Spilman, Daniel 12:41, 123
Spinck, J. M. 15:45
Spindler, Clark 21:80
Spindler, John 23:169
Spindler, W. 3:184
Spindler, W. H. 23:169
Spindler, William 25:73
Spindlew, W. C. 14:131
Spine, William J. 11:113
Spiner, G. 14:112

Spiner, I. 14:221
Spiner, Nicholas 16:379
Spinerman, James 22:320
Spiney, Thomas G. 19:279
Spingteen, S. 16:229
Spink, Charles 23:51
Spink, J. 3:184
Spink, William 7:42
Spinks, Charles 7:76
Spinks, John 9:95; 26:60
Spinna, Lewis 10:137; 20:353
Spinner, Alex 13:48
Spinner, Jeremiah 19:35
Spinner, M. 7:42
Spinner, Michael 21:42
Spinnetta, John C. 17:68
Spinney, A. J. 25:305
Spinney, Alphonso L. 9:125
Spinney, Alphonzo L. 27:113
Spinney, R. F. 9:151; 27:108
Spinning, --- 14:290
Spinning, Perlee 26:146
Spinsley, William 9:91
Spipes, James M. 9:125
Spiranney, L. 14:22
Spires, Henderson 17:139; 24:203
Spires, John 10:151, 178
Spires, William 27:118
Spirey, George 22:221
Spirley, George H. 14:303
Spirry, Lucius 24:115
Spitewood, Daniel 9:136
Spitler, Israel 22:55
Spitler, John 9:125; 27:114
Spitler, S. 22:491
Spitler, Solomon 23:169
Spitnall, J. 22:221
Spits, Carl 23:80
Spitser, J. 22:269
Spittenwood, Daniel 27:111
Spitter, Isaiah 15:59
Spityken, John 9:91
Spitz, Albert 16:102
Spitz, Benjamin H. 11:43
Spitz, Joseph 27:110
Spitz, Leonard 10:81
Spitzer, J. 23:195
Spitzfater, A. 3:184
Spitziker, J. 26:61
Spivey, David 17:97
Spivney, L. 13:99
Splain, Samuel B. 16:56
Splawn, Hobber 11:121
Spleen, Michael 7:61

Splege, Thomas C. 22:269
Splitstone, Levi 23:287
Spoenaman, Henry 8:32
Spoenamann, Henry 18:161
Spofford, Levi C. 8:110
Spoh, Abraham 11:334
Spohn, Levi 22:439
Spohr, Jacob L. 11:271
Spohr, John 26:65
Spokely, D. 1:77
Spokely, Latus 26:64
Spokley, Latus 18:253
Spolle, Henry 13:48
Sponagle, Jacob 10:81
Sponburg, S. 3:184
Sponcelar, G. 14:221
Sponcelar, George 3:184
Sponer, Lyman 27:116
Sponigel, Jacob 20:353
Sponmore, John H. 21:42
Sponsler, James A. 20:2
Spoole, Henry 16:56
Spoole, Linden 18:180
Spooler, Jacob 21:235
Spoon, A. J. 14:112
Spoon, J. T. 25:305
Spoon, Jacob E. 11:282
Spoon, James 3:184
Spoon, John 21:15
Spoon, Joseph D. 22:221
Spoon, Tickwith 23:198
Spoon, W. G. 9:232
Spoon, William G. 20:353
Spooner, Albert 12:41
Spooner, Asa P. 22:345
Spooner, C. S. 3:184
Spooner, Charles W. 7:42
Spooner, F. 3:184
Spooner, H. M. 10:22
Spooner, L. L. 18:401
Spooner, Luther 27:107
Spooner, S. O. 9:113
Spooner, U. 3:184
Spoonheimer, J. 1:173
Spoonway, --- 11:222
Spoor, George J. 13:48
Spoor, Stephen H. 26:181
Spoor, Wallace 22:509
Spoor, William M. 22:471
Spoore, W. C. 3:184
Spore, Henry 25:236
Sporker, Lucius B. 15:161
Sport, Isaac 12:52
Sporter, C. 15:301
Sporter, William 4:55
Sportridge, Roon H. 22:222
Sports, Jeremiah 12:41
Sportsman, Nelson 7:133
Sposer, J. 1:170

Spoteashe, L. 13:119
Spothe, Andrew 15:23
Spotswood, Richard E. 21:197
Spotts, Adam 22:439
Spotts, Edmund 18:194
Spotts, Franklin 17:47
Spotts, Phillip 15:75
Spoudle, C. 3:184
Spoul, E. 3:184
Spoul, John 12:57
Spouse, Harvey B. 20:353
Spouse, William 9:39
Spradlin, Elliott 17:150
Spradlin, John M. 23:101
Spradlin, Pleasant 17:284
Spradling, James 20:105
Spradling, R. H. 11:249
Spraeth, Adolph 22:222
Spragan, J. P. 14:112
Spragan, L. 14:112
Sprage, George 15:84
Spragg, Charles 24:56
Spragg, E. 20:60
Spragg, Edw. 27:107
Spragg, L. F. 1:72
Spraggins, Hiram 21:391
Spraggins, Milton 17:350
Spraggins, William K. 17:284
Sprague, --- 10:167
Sprague, A. J. 12:41
Sprague, A. W. 14:245
Sprague, Abner L. 1:72
Sprague, Allen 8:120
Sprague, Allen H. 16:79
Sprague, Andrew A. 23:169
Sprague, Andrews 4:55
Sprague, B. 3:184
Sprague, B. D. 13:48
Sprague, C. A. 20:152
Sprague, D. 19:262
Sprague, Daniel 8:102
Sprague, Daniel G. 17:461; 24:162
Sprague, David 9:194
Sprague, Delos 13:48
Sprague, DeWitt C. 26:58
Sprague, Edgar A. 17:68
Sprague, Edwin H. 3:184
Sprague, F. 27:108
Sprague, Franklin 9:151
Sprague, Frederick A. 12:41; 16:160
Sprague, G. 13:99
Sprague, George 3:184
Sprague, George H. 4:55
Sprague, George Washington 16:102

Sprague, H. 13:99; 14:22; 16:229; 23:51
Sprague, H. B. 3:184; 7:54
Sprague, H. L. 1:171
Sprague, Henry M. 17:87
Sprague, Ira 5:30
Sprague, J. 3:184; 12:97; 13:99; 15:361; 19:101; 21:391
Sprague, J. E. 27:119
Sprague, James 10:145; 19:195; 21:143
Sprague, James D. 11:45
Sprague, John 8:32; 9:211; 12:93; 18:161
Sprague, John C. 23:306
Sprague, Jonathan 9:73
Sprague, L. 14:221, 259
Sprague, L. H. 9:29
Sprague, Lewis B. 12:41
Sprague, M. 20:353
Sprague, M. C. 18:297; 26:113
Sprague, M. W. 27:119
Sprague, Marshall 12:60
Sprague, Martin 16:229
Sprague, Martin P. 8:96
Sprague, O. 1:171
Sprague, P. 16:271
Sprague, P. M. 22:491
Sprague, Perry 24:85
Sprague, Reuben 18:281
Sprague, Samuel 22:55
Sprague, T. 1:78; 4:55
Sprague, T. S. 25:305
Sprague, Theo. S. 7:76
Sprague, Thomas 15:229
Sprague, W. 3:184
Sprague, W. C. 16:379
Sprague, W. L. 3:184
Sprague, William 10:81; 18:462
Sprague, William J. 22:155
Sprague, William T. 8:32
Spraht, H. 1:76
Spraig, James 25:236
Spraight, C. 13:99
Spraight, E. 16:271
Sprang, Jacob 19:101
Spranger, F. 11:194
Sprangler, George 21:197
Spranks, George 15:301
Spratberry, John 20:353
Spratbery, John 10:137
Spratholy, John 9:39
Spratt, A. D. 14:221
Spratt, A. G. 20:140
Spratt, H. C. 21:391

Spratt, James 9:194; 19:262
Spratt, James H. 17:261
Spratt, Robert 11:213
Sprauge, George W. 18:211
Sprauge, John 16:305
Spray, A. A. 26:59
Spray, Barrett 17:43
Spray, J. 9:59
Spray, Joseph 8:126
Spray, T. 9:59
Sprecher, D. 18:94
Sprecher, Nathan 4:55
Spreese, John V. 19:195
Spregelholder, John 13:48
Spressard, John 17:26
Spricker, Cyrus 13:119
Sprig, James A. 3:184
Sprigg, Nelson G. 10:81; 20:353
Spriggs, Aaron 6:35
Spriggs, Enoch 17:317
Spriggs, G. A. 14:221
Spriggs, Nathaniel 17:445; 24:164
Spriggs, T. 15:229
Spriggs, William 22:320
Sprigle, A. A. 18:253
Sprigle, B. 12:77; 15:75
Sprill, Bailey 10:167
Spring, C. 19:101
Spring, David E. 19:101
Spring, George 22:222
Spring, Heman J. 24:97
Spring, Henry G. 13:48
Spring, J. 14:113
Spring, James 13:48
Spring, John 12:63
Spring, John A. 15:84
Spring, John W. 8:110
Spring, Joseph 25:236
Spring, M. 1:176; 18:194
Spring, O. 14:29
Spring, Samuel 23:278
Spring, William D. 22:55
Spring, William H. 16:80
Spring, William P. 19:349
Springelmyer, J. 13:120
Springer, A. 9:67
Springer, Anthony 22:238
Springer, B. F. 23:287
Springer, Benjamin 21:191
Springer, C. 15:45; 23:169
Springer, C. B. 25:236
Springer, C. C. 15:229
Springer, Cathormas 7:42
Springer, Charles B. 5:54

Springer, Charles H. 27:116
Springer, Chester D. 22:222
Springer, D. M. 17:112
Springer, Dennis 21:391
Springer, Dermis 7:133
Springer, E. 1:73
Springer, G. 18:409
Springer, G. A. 11:45
Springer, G. W. 1:95
Springer, George 14:221
Springer, George W. 22:131
Springer, Greg 23:283
Springer, H. W. 3:184
Springer, Henry 19:101; 22:438
Springer, J. 3:184
Springer, J. M. 18:39
Springer, James 11:313
Springer, John 3:184; 7:111; 8:32; 17:503; 18:161; 25:73
Springer, John M. 22:510
Springer, John S. 21:235
Springer, Lander 18:316
Springer, Leander 9:29; 26:111
Springer, Leonard 11:417
Springer, Levi 9:39; 18:297; 26:113
Springer, Lewis 24:56
Springer, M. 3:184
Springer, Marion 22:441
Springer, N. 24:85
Springer, Paul 21:391
Springer, Philip 9:39; 18:297; 26:113
Springer, Richard 8:110
Springer, Robert W. 11:250
Springer, S. 1:173
Springer, Th. W. 14:221
Springer, Thomas E. 9:194
Springer, Uriah 22:411
Springer, William 23:261
Springfield, D. B. 1:173
Springle, A. A. 26:63
Springsted, Aug's J. 22:285
Springsteel, John J. 27:110
Springsteel, Wilber 19:101
Springsteen, Calvin B. 21:143
Springstein, J. J. 9:151
Springstid, Wilbur 13:69
Springston, Alex. I. 9:158

Springston, Granville 10:167; 19:195
Springston, J. 10:207
Sprink, A. 3:184
Sprinker, P. J. 7:61
Sprinkle, A. 1:77
Sprinkle, Benjamin F. 12:10
Sprinkle, Conrad 11:416
Sprinkle, Henry 7:65
Sprinks, C. 25:305
Spriss, H. 25:236
Sprisser, Michael 10:22
Sprivey, Isaac 7:133
Sproeil, W. A. 9:194
Sproeil, William A. 19:262
Sproll, Lendru 10:180
Spronce, Elijah 24:115
Sprong, William H. 22:412, 439
Spronglenburg, F. 25:236
Spronse, W. D. 23:51
Sprougleburgh, Francis 5:30
Sproul, A. 13:120
Sproul, John D. 11:407
Sproul, Thomas S. 23:93
Sproules, F. J. 16:56
Sprouls, Cyrus 10:22
Sprouse, A. 3:184
Sprouse, G. 21:113
Sprouse, R. H. 8:67; 26:183
Sprouse, W. 3:184
Sprouse, William 18:297; 26:113
Sprouse, William G. 17:26
Sprout, A. 3:184
Sprowks, J. 8:67
Sprowl, John R. 11:76
Sprowl, Sylvester 11:168
Sprowls, J. 1:168
Sprowls, John 26:183
Sprows, B. 11:89
Sprows, John H. 20:60
Spruel, Stephen 12:52
Spruger, Michael I. 10:81
Spruger, W. 20:353
Spruil, Baily 19:195
Sprum, Newton J. 17:410; 22:131
Spruse, Charles 7:133
Spry, A. A. 9:91
Spry, F. M. 22:269
Spry, John 22:438
Spry, Joseph T. 26:226
Spuir, William 12:41
Spulburg, --- 16:56
Spulding, O. K. 16:56
Spuller, Bernam 12:124

Spulma, T. 19:195
Spunell, E. S. 17:26
Spunger, Shadrach 11:76
Spunkey, W. H. 13:99
Spur, Simon 20:187
Spurgeon, A. 21:42
Spurgeon, E. 14:113
Spurgeon, Elias 13:48
Spurgeon, G. M. 17:43
Spurgeon, Jeremiah 17:239
Spurgeon, John 14:113, 320; 25:282
Spurgeon, Samuel P. 22:269
Spurgeon, Solomon D. 25:275
Spurgeon, W. H. 11:44
Spurgeon, William 10:97
Spurkman, W. M. 22:345
Spurling, Andrew 20:353
Spurling, E. H. 7:72
Spurling, George 10:81; 20:353
Spurling, Samuel 17:139; 24:203
Spurlock, --- 3:184
Spurlock, Francis 22:269
Spurlock, H. 10:150; 18:58
Spurlock, James H. 22:269
Spurlock, John 21:205; 22:506
Spurney, A. J. 7:76
Spurr, Abram 22:222
Spurr, Charles E. 7:15
Spurr, John 7:111
Spurr, Thomas Jefferson 16:8
Spurrier, W. A. 18:401
Spurry, William 22:440
Spuybay, James 22:222
Spybuck, James 11:314
Squares, Daniel 14:221
Squares, George R. 9:151
Squares, Samuel 3:184
Squer, Harvey 13:69
Squers, Harvey 19:101
Squers, Peter 19:101
Squiers, Atlin 9:39
Squiers, Eli 18:223
Squill, William 26:225
Squimer, P. 25:236
Squins, H. W. 14:113
Squint, Henry 14:113
Squire, A. C. 18:253; 26:64
Squire, Edwin S. 17:317
Squire, G. W. 21:42
Squire, Joseph W. 4:55

Squires, Adam E. 18:297
Squires, Adine 26:113
Squires, Alfred W. 22:467
Squires, Ambrose 10:81;
    20:353
Squires, Charles 26:58
Squires, Daniel 6:26
Squires, Dewitt 1:70
Squires, Ethan E. 8:115
Squires, F. 1:72
Squires, George 14:221
Squires, George R. 27:110
Squires, H. 25:236
Squires, Harlan A. 24:97
Squires, Henry 27:115
Squires, James B. 22:55
Squires, John W. 14:221
Squires, Joseph 21:143
Squires, L. J. 16:145
Squires, Leonard 4:55
Squires, Orrin 22:222
Squires, P. S. 20:176
Squires, S. 1:74; 27:106
Squires, Samuel 18:281
Squires, Samuel C. 11:289
Squires, Thomas 3:184
Squires, Thomas B. 8:32;
    18:161
Squires, Uriah 10:81;
    20:353
Squires, William 9:194;
    19:262
Squires, William A.
    10:81; 20:353
Squires, William H.
    21:118
Squirles, Jacob 15:75
Squisser, P. 15:280
Squyers, Platt J. 20:184
Srafer, J. 22:55
Sreene, James 15:349
Sregenheim, John 5:30
Sremble, W. 11:282
Srigen, W. A. 18:39
Srisa, Peter 13:120
Sriver, James M. 8:117
Srong, A. J. 20:149
Srong, B. F. 15:175
Sroufe, A. 3:184
Sroufe, I. 20:353
Srumphet, John 9:125
Sryde, Alexander 9:65
St---, --- 23:80
St---, D. 25:327
St---, W. 15:231
St---ck--e, Henry 25:71
St. Ammen, Augustus C.
    18:324
St. Anthony, Henry
    10:167

St. Armand, Augustus
    19:191
St. Armond, Augustus
    10:167
St. Clair, A. 7:42; 17:145
St. Clair, A. T. 2:17;
    25:68
St. Clair, Barney 8:42;
    26:180
St. Clair, Benjamin 3:185
St. Clair, Elkins 17:239
St. Clair, Henry 18:105;
    19:32
St. Clair, Ira 17:41
St. Clair, James 10:137;
    20:354
St. Clair, Jerome 11:112
St. Clair, John 9:91; 10:8;
    11:78; 22:222; 26:59
St. Clair, Joseph 10:137;
    20:354
St. Clair, Levi 18:194
St. Clair, Nicholas H.
    19:337
St. Clair, Otis P. 10:81
St. Clair, P. 13:99
St. Clair, R. 1:174
St. Clair, Reuben 22:103
St. Clair, Samuel 24:85
St. Clair, Thomas 10:81;
    20:354
St. Clair, William 20:44;
    22:222
St. Clare, George 12:41
St. Clare, J. 14:260
St. Dane, James 19:191
St. Dennis, James 7:42
St. Dennis, L. 3:185
St. Dons, Idron 11:294
St. George, Oliver 9:91
St. George, P. 7:42
St. George, W. 8:75
St. John, --- 19:318
St. John, A. 3:186; 14:114
St. John, Albert 8:32;
    18:157; 20:101
St. John, Campbell 11:329
St. John, Charles 5:46
St. John, Edwin G. 21:143
St. John, Ferdinand
    20:116
St. John, James 25:327
St. John, John 6:33; 12:41
St. John, L. 10:177;
    19:191
St. John, Luther 4:56
St. John, Pharoah 17:265
St. John, Reuben 22:467
St. John, Roselle 21:260
St. John, Thomas 7:42
St. John, William 23:257

St. Johns, John 1:73
St. Johns, L. D. 1:175
St. Jones, T. A. 14:114
St. Julien, Emile 7:134
St. Luke, Joseph 9:241
St. Martin, Joseph 9:202;
    19:284
St. Peter, F. 3:188
St. Peters, J. 25:305
St. Peters, Joseph 7:80
St. Pierre, Xavier 24:31
St. R---, George W.
    10:187
Staats, Alexander G.
    10:137
Staats, Daniel W. 19:195
Staats, I. I. 14:221
Staber, Peter 18:161
Stable, Edward 12:172
Stable, Lewis 10:81
Stabler, J. 11:130
Stabler, O. L. 4:55
Stabler, Peter 8:32
Stables, York 9:204
Stablock, Joseph P. 25:71
Stacer, P. 6:33
Stacey, D. 12:167
Stacey, Dwight 23:195
Stacey, James 10:180;
    18:180
Stacey, John 18:180;
    20:354
Stacey, Joseph 22:114
Stacey, L. L. 9:225
Stacey, Michael E. 15:80
Stacey, Pleasant M. 7:111
Stacey, S. S. 13:49
Stach, Adolph 19:288
Stachers, Francis W. 7:42
Stachle, H. F. 11:249
Stack, E. H. 21:391
Stack, F. L. 18:17
Stack, G. W. L. 16:229
Stack, H. 27:111
Stack, James 4:55
Stack, John 8:32; 10:81
Stack, Morris 19:35
Stack, Samuel B. 25:312
Stack, Thomas 10:81;
    20:354
Stack, William 7:42
Stack, William E. 1:77
Stacker, Christian 10:93;
    20:354
Stackford, G. 9:113
Stackhouse, Daniel 7:134
Stackhouse, David 8:96
Stackhouse, H. 11:168
Stackhouse, John 22:222
Stackhouse, L. 13:99;
    14:22

Stackhouse, S. W. 13:49
Stackhouse, William B.
    12:54
Stackpole, Alex 7:42
Stackpole, Eugene 13:49
Stackpole, James B.
    22:238
Stackpole, Thomas 22:222
Stackpole, William
    14:113
Stacks, Israel 22:285
Stacks, J. C. A. 9:59
Stacks, Moses A. 22:285
Stacks, Robert 17:353
Staco, P. 25:327
Stacy, Alexander 23:110
Stacy, E. 15:113
Stacy, E. W. 2:17; 25:68
Stacy, Emery 17:293
Stacy, G. L. 1:170
Stacy, George L. 11:220
Stacy, George Malcomb
    22:55
Stacy, H. 14:113
Stacy, J. S. 12:77
Stacy, John 3:184; 9:232
Stacy, John S. 15:12
Stacy, L. L. 18:376
Stacy, S. F. 16:56
Stacy, T. 7:70
Stacy, William 18:211
Stacy, William E. 17:59
Staddard, R. 15:175
Stader, John A. 17:284
Stading, J. F. 14:22
Stadlebruer, J. 27:106
Stadler, J. 3:184
Stadler, John 19:35
Stadler, John W. 6:33
Stadlin, Charles W. 25:72
Stadter, J. B. 11:130
Staecifer, Daniel 12:57
Staeetman, --- 16:305
Staffer, David 11:270
Staffer, E. 18:58
Stafford, A. 1:169
Stafford, Aaron 4:55
Stafford, Abner 4:55
Stafford, Andrew J.
    10:137; 20:354
Stafford, Charles 1:72;
    19:35
Stafford, David 22:467
Stafford, Edmond D.
    10:81; 20:354
Stafford, F. W. 5:30
Stafford, Frank 14:221
Stafford, George 13:120;
    24:204
Stafford, Harve 12:147
Stafford, Harvey 19:307

Stafford, Henry 22:222
Stafford, I. 1:74
Stafford, Isaac 27:148
Stafford, J. 25:236
Stafford, J. A. 1:173
Stafford, J. H. 20:85
Stafford, J. L. 14:290
Stafford, J. W. 3:184
Stafford, Jacob 19:49
Stafford, James 5:30;
    20:354
Stafford, James H. 20:26
Stafford, John 3:184; 8:96
Stafford, John W. 21:60
Stafford, Joseph 9:91;
    19:35
Stafford, Judson A.
    17:264
Stafford, L. 14:221
Stafford, Lewis B. 21:241
Stafford, M. 25:237
Stafford, Martin V. 5:30
Stafford, P. E. 8:110
Stafford, Rhodes 12:41
Stafford, Richard 21:391
Stafford, Robert 24:45
Stafford, Rufus 21:261
Stafford, Russell A. 7:111;
    21:391
Stafford, S. 3:184; 15:89
Stafford, S. S. 14:267
Stafford, Samuel 14:221
Stafford, Samuel S.
    22:510
Stafford, Sanford A.
    18:341
Stafford, Stanforth J.
    9:104
Stafford, Stephen 10:81;
    11:213; 20:354
Stafford, Stephen S. 23:14
Stafford, Sylvester 17:284
Stafford, T. W. 25:237
Stafford, Thomas O.
    11:249
Stafford, W. 3:184; 23:51
Stafford, W. G. 20:36
Stafford, William 3:184;
    22:285
Staffur, H. 10:149
Staflin, J. B. 15:301
Stagall, Jesse 17:186
Stagdall, Elias 17:43
Stage, Albert 7:42
Stage, David 11:112
Stage, Elijah 12:57
Stage, George H. 8:96
Stage, Henry A. 22:103
Stage, L. 1:174
Stage, Silas B. 11:130
Stage, William 13:48

Stagen, Thomas 13:48
Stagers, James 14:221
Stagg, C. 14:221
Stagg, William 3:184;
    20:116
Staggenburg, Henry
    22:131
Stagger, Vincent 11:170
Staggs, Edward 9:91
Staggs, Edward W. 26:58
Staggs, Jeremiah 17:239
Staggs, John 10:81;
    20:354
Staggs, Jonathan 11:393
Staggs, Joseph 22:270
Staggs, William P. 17:239
Stagle, Charles 19:334
Stagley, Martin L. 17:347
Stagman, Henry 19:35
Stagner, Daniel 5:46
Stagner, G. W. 25:305
Stagoner, Ephraim D.
    9:47
Stagowait, Edward 10:81;
    20:354
Stags, H. 20:354
Stags, Hiram 10:81
Stahel, John C. 20:149
Stahl, A. 2:18
Stahl, Aug--- 25:72
Stahl, Charles 27:148
Stahl, E. 2:17
Stahl, F. F. 11:43
Stahl, George 13:120
Stahl, Hartman 4:55
Stahl, J. 1:171; 24:85
Stahl, Jacob 13:48
Stahl, Joel 22:491
Stahl, John 22:173
Stahl, John F. 24:97
Stahl, Joseph 10:137;
    20:354
Stahl, Nicholas 22:491
Stahl, Philip 23:169
Stahl, Samuel 22:222
Stahl, W. B. 23:51
Stahl, William 14:222;
    15:75; 19:35; 23:110
Stahler, D. 3:184
Stahler, S. 3:184
Stahll, John A. 19:35
Stahll, U. 1:173
Stahlnicker, James W.
    17:253
Stahr, Adam 10:81;
    20:354
Stailer, N. W. 23:169
Stailey, F. G. 17:204
Stain, G. W. 3:184
Stainbrook, David 16:124
Stainer, Peter 9:73

Stainforth, Thomas 20:49
Staing, Joseph M. 11:416
Staingardt, John F. 9:194
Stainmets, Christian 7:42
Stair, Franklin 23:169
Stairs, J. M. 23:169
Stakeim, James P. 7:42
Staker, Human 19:278
Stakey, H. 9:194
Stalard, G. 3:184
Stalbird, Loring 17:159
Stalcup, Mathias W. 23:93
Stalder, E. P. 3:184
Stale, John A. 1:71
Stale, Sydenham 19:35
Stalee, O. 15:59
Stalee, William B. 13:48
Staley, A. 20:354
Staley, A. B. 18:469
Staley, A. S. 18:407
Staley, Daniel 22:491
Staley, E. J. 17:293
Staley, Frank 16:102
Staley, Frederick 24:30
Staley, G. W. 3:184
Staley, Hiram 22:270
Staley, J. H. 16:379
Staley, John 9:91; 17:26;
    21:261; 27:116
Staley, Josiah 7:54
Staley, Stephen G. 13:48
Staley, Thomas 20:354
Staley, William H. 17:87
Stalhoult, A. 3:184
Staliper, J. 22:222
Stalkbridge, Thomas
    18:435
Stalker, G. W. 16:124
Stalker, George 10:81;
    20:354
Stalker, John 12:41;
    19:195
Stalker, William 14:222
Stall, A. 11:45; 27:119
Stall, Ferdinan 15:229
Stall, H. 14:113
Stall, John 17:68; 21:191;
    22:55
Stall, Minie B. 26:226
Stall, Philetus 22:173
Stall, S. 15:229
Stall, Samuel 3:184;
    15:319; 19:101
Stallard, D. W. 23:169
Stallard, L. N. 18:376
Stallary, C. 14:113
Stallcup, S. P. 22:490
Stallen, Christ 18:161
Staller, Christ. 8:32
Staller, W. 16:229
Staller, William 21:42

Stalley, J. W. 27:110
Stalley, S. 11:269
Stalline, J. W. 22:490
Stallins, Thomas A.
    17:319
Stallion, J. F. 17:59
Stallman, Andrew 17:441;
    24:155
Stallman, G. W. 13:126
Stallman, Harrison 23:182
Stallman, John 17:362
Stallman, Solomon 24:56
Stallman, William 9:91;
    26:60
Stallsworth, A. J. 20:87
Stallup, E. 16:136
Stalrey, John 21:391
Stalter, Peter 27:110
Staltman, L. H. 11:173
Staly, J. 11:271; 26:61
Staly, Thomas 10:137
Stam, Eben W. 8:75
Stam, Edward 9:241
Stambaugh, Samuel
    22:467
Stamber, C. 1:169
Stamberger, James 26:138
Stambo, Frederick 22:103
Stamer, Joshua 10:81
Stamfield, Christian
    11:169
Staminback, Henry 20:354
Stamm, George 22:491
Stamm, H. H. 16:379
Stamm, J. M. 9:59
Stamm, William D. 24:30
Stamm, William S. 16:124
Stammback, Henry 10:137
Stamost, Henry 19:284
Stamp, C. 14:133
Stamp, Columb 18:58
Stamp, Columbus 10:149
Stamp, George W. 22:498
Stamp, J. D. 1:74
Stamp, John 3:184;
    11:112; 18:297;
    26:112
Stamp, John J. 24:45
Stamp, L. A. 15:229
Stamp, Philip 1:73
Stamp, S. 1:77
Stamp, W. 7:43
Stamper, Crocket 17:112
Stamper, H. 14:222
Stamper, John 11:270
Stamper, Jonathan D.
    9:194; 19:269
Stamps, James 21:168
Stamps, Richard 17:186
Stamps, Thomas 17:453;
    24:184

Stamson, James M. 16:56
Stamtuary, Ressing M.
    8:110
Stan, Benjamin 16:56
Stan, Charles B. 16:229
Stan, S. 9:151
Stan, William B. 10:81
Stanage, J. 20:354
Stanard, E. P. 15:3
Stanard, Ezra R. 12:77
Stanard, Thomas 18:297
Stanard, William F.
    23:287
Stanbaugh, D. 11:45
Stanber, Joseph 16:15
Stanberg, August 11:172
Stanberg, J. S. 18:281
Stanberg, William 20:26
Stanberry, James F.
    22:131
Stanbery, B. B. 13:69
Stanbrook, Thomas 11:20
Stanbury, James 12:54
Stanbury, Samuel 18:194
Stanby, Emil 19:195
Stance, Joseph 27:116
Stanch, Andrew 7:61
Stanch, Gonleib 13:48
Stanch, Gotlieb 16:56
Stanchfield, Benjamin A.
    13:69
Stanchfield, Solomon
    21:42
Stanchley, William 3:185
Stancliff, A. B. 3:185
Stancliff, James 22:439
Standacher, George
    21:191
Standacher, Philip 22:457
Standafer, James 22:55
Standard, D. 19:195
Standard, DeForest
    10:167
Standard, Howard 21:391
Standard, Thomas 9:39
Standcher, L. 25:73
Standeep, J. 9:151
Standefer, Job 8:32
Standeper, Job 18:161
Standerd, Thomas 26:112
Standfield, J. M. 9:238
Standforth, Osborn 23:169
Standiford, Aquilla
    23:169
Standiford, E. E. 23:169
Standiford, Milton 9:238
Standinger, I. 18:180
Standinger, J. 10:193
Standinger, William
    23:115
Standish, --- 19:297

Standish, A. 16:379
Standish, E. 5:30; 25:236
Standish, M. 3:185
Standley, A. D. 25:69
Standley, H. J. 9:228
Standley, John R. 10:81
Standling, R. 25:237
Standly, Samuel 10:137;
  20:354
Standrat, Sanford 18:254
Standridge, William J.
  22:270
Standstone, J. J. 7:13
Standt, S. 1:172
Standup, J. 27:109
Standwich, William
  20:101
Staner, Casper 10:175
Staner, M. J. 3:185
Stanett, John 10:81
Stanfield, George W.
  21:80
Stanfield, J. M. 26:225
Stanfield, Jackson 22:320
Stanfield, John 18:223;
  21:235; 22:516
Stanfield, Martin 22:169
Stanfield, Samuel 10:137;
  20:354
Stanfield, W. 11:194
Stanfill, F. L. 23:289
Stanford, F. S. 9:17
Stanford, Isaac F. 6:21
Stanford, J. W. 12:124;
  15:135
Stanford, James 9:45
Stanford, James H. P.
  13:49
Stanford, John 26:130
Stanford, L. 11:250
Stanford, P. W. 3:185
Stanford, Perry 11:44
Stanford, R. 15:345;
  16:379
Stanford, Richard 15:45;
  22:355
Stanforth, Peyton 11:321
Stang, Benjamin 10:81
Stang, Frederick 24:97
Stangel, Joseph 4:55
Stanhop, W. 9:151
Stanhope, George 19:230
Stanhope, J. M. 1:78
Stanhope, W. 27:108
Stanhope, W. H. 3:185
Staniford, William 18:270
Staniker, Thomas N.
  22:222
Staning, G. W. 3:185
Stanislaus, J. 1:175
Stank, William 22:345

Stankamp, William
  25:327
Stankemp, William 6:33
Stanlege, Henry 21:218
Stanley, A. W. 25:237
Stanley, Abner H. 10:137;
  20:354
Stanley, Abraham 11:89
Stanley, Adolphus 7:111
Stanley, Alfred H. 7:42
Stanley, Amos 9:91
Stanley, Antonio 12:41
Stanley, B. 21:191
Stanley, C. 25:275
Stanley, C. O. 3:184
Stanley, Charles 20:19,
  184
Stanley, Daniel 21:285
Stanley, E. 11:234; 23:51
Stanley, Edmund 7:134
Stanley, Edward 14:329
Stanley, Elias 24:30
Stanley, F. 1:78
Stanley, F. M. 23:308
Stanley, F. P. 10:149;
  18:58
Stanley, Frank 8:42;
  26:180
Stanley, Fred 16:230
Stanley, Frederick 13:69
Stanley, George 11:87;
  15:12; 17:509;
  23:116
Stanley, George W.
  10:138; 20:354;
  22:155
Stanley, H. 19:102
Stanley, H. J. 18:376
Stanley, H. Moses 9:17
Stanley, Harrison 25:237
Stanley, Henry 9:136
Stanley, Hezekiah 19:35
Stanley, Hyman 26:130
Stanley, I. 18:180
Stanley, Isaac 19:195
Stanley, J. 9:59; 10:180;
  12:124; 13:99; 14:22,
  132; 15:135; 17:43
Stanley, J. C. 3:184
Stanley, J. M. 9:59
Stanley, J. S. 11:78
Stanley, J. W. 9:151;
  26:63
Stanley, James 12:77;
  21:80; 25:72
Stanley, Jethro 13:49
Stanley, John 3:184; 4:55;
  8:67; 16:230; 22:285
Stanley, John W. 8:96
Stanley, Joseph 25:237
Stanley, Kirkey 26:226

Stanley, L. 14:222;
  18:254; 26:62
Stanley, Lewis 22:285
Stanley, Logan 9:225;
  18:376
Stanley, Louis 20:3
Stanley, M. 14:113, 333;
  16:102
Stanley, Mary 25:305
Stanley, Melvin 22:468
Stanley, Moses 22:115
Stanley, N. L. 20:354
Stanley, Nathan 8:96
Stanley, O. H. 12:164;
  26:181
Stanley, Reuben F. 22:155
Stanley, Richard 14:222
Stanley, Richmond 7:134
Stanley, Robert 10:138;
  20:19, 354
Stanley, S. 11:78
Stanley, Sargent 14:222
Stanley, Solomon 18:281
Stanley, Stillman G.
  9:215; 21:391
Stanley, Sylvester 17:451;
  24:180
Stanley, Thomas B. 23:80
Stanley, Thomas E.
  22:439
Stanley, W. 11:269
Stanley, W. H. 8:75
Stanley, W. S. 11:249
Stanley, Wakefield 22:470
Stanley, Walter H. 4:55
Stanley, Wesley B. 24:45
Stanley, William 3:184;
  17:250; 19:35;
  25:237
Stanley, William A.
  22:270
Stanley, William H.
  23:51; 26:181
Stanly, Henry 27:111
Stanly, J. W. 18:254
Stanly, Jethro 16:56
Stanly, William 11:255
Stanmore, J. 16:230
Stannard, A. D. 12:41
Stannard, George 4:55
Stannard, Henry R.
  20:354
Stannard, John 1:73
Stannard, Wellington
  23:195
Stannett, J. R. 21:205
Stansberry, A. 3:184
Stansberry, Aril 17:43
Stansberry, Jacob 10:81;
  20:354
Stansbery, George 16:379

Stansborough, James 13:49
Stansburg, John F. 23:51
Stansbury, E. 3:184
Stansbury, George 15:345
Stansbury, Howard 9:104
Stansbury, J. M. 8:56
Stansbury, Joseph M. 21:80
Stansbury, S. 14:222
Stansell, C. 11:440
Stansfield, H. 3:184
Stanson, S. 16:379
Stant, G. 19:284
Stant, John 8:110
Stant, William 5:30
Stanter, David 8:42
Stanton, A. 16:102; 25:74
Stanton, A. B. 13:77; 16:230
Stanton, Aaron 4:55
Stanton, Abram 8:96
Stanton, Alexander 17:139; 24:203
Stanton, C. 3:185
Stanton, C. B. 1:77
Stanton, C. E. 11:78
Stanton, Chancey W. 15:23
Stanton, Charles 25:237
Stanton, David 12:52; 26:180
Stanton, Francis E. 17:289
Stanton, Frank 4:68
Stanton, Frank W. 21:391
Stanton, G. 5:54
Stanton, George W. 22:270
Stanton, H. D. 17:451
Stanton, H. H. 3:184
Stanton, Henry 16:230
Stanton, Horatio D. 24:180
Stanton, J. 3:185
Stanton, James 16:149; 22:156, 285
Stanton, James W. 12:124; 15:135
Stanton, John 1:192; 14:222; 22:270; 23:201; 27:148
Stanton, John W. 7:134
Stanton, Joseph 22:524
Stanton, Joseph P. 21:11
Stanton, King 9:166
Stanton, L. 22:222
Stanton, L. H. 3:184
Stanton, Lyman 21:89
Stanton, M. V. 13:81; 16:230
Stanton, Martin B. 12:158

Stanton, N. 13:120
Stanton, R. 3:185
Stanton, Reuben 7:42
Stanton, Roswell 21:93
Stanton, S. 25:237
Stanton, S. F. 11:405
Stanton, Simon B. 22:131
Stanton, Thomas 19:327; 22:156
Stanton, W. 1:170; 3:224
Stanton, W. A. 14:113
Stanton, Willard L. 13:49
Stanton, Willard S. 16:56
Stanton, William 1:74; 17:353, 505; 18:72; 22:270
Stanton, William H. 25:72
Stanton, William T. 11:76
Stantt, John M. 11:419
Stanturf, S. 18:376
Stanturf, Samuel 9:225
Stanwell, B. 10:149; 18:58
Stanwell, Charles 22:467
Stanwood, G. F. 1:170
Stapies, F. 17:239
Staple, --- 25:68
Staple, Anderson 7:133
Staple, Holman 12:41
Staple, Squire 25:237
Staple, Thomas 11:429
Staples, A. 14:263
Staples, A. A. V. 12:56
Staples, Albert 4:55; 15:135; 17:245
Staples, C. W. 19:230
Staples, E. F. 1:175
Staples, George D. 13:48
Staples, J. 13:99
Staples, J. D. 10:81; 20:354
Staples, J. H. 1:70
Staples, James M. 21:106
Staples, Joshua 24:30
Staples, Lucius 16:87
Staples, Nuvel E. 11:170
Staples, Orlando 13:48
Staples, W. 19:230
Staples, W. L. 25:70
Stapleton, Edward 12:146
Stapleton, Granville 10:81
Stapleton, J. 15:113
Stapleton, Jacob 21:205
Stapleton, Joseph 9:211
Stapleton, M. G. 1:175
Stapleton, Patrick 20:13
Stapleton, S. 18:254; 26:63
Stapleton, William 20:89
Stapleton, William H. 23:51

Stapp, Charles 11:194
Stapp, D. W. 10:138; 20:354
Stapp, John J. 22:457
Stapp, Milton 9:225; 18:376
Star, B. W. 15:229
Star, C. 3:185
Star, G. 15:45
Star, Gillis 25:305
Star, J. 1:100
Starback, E. 20:60
Starbind, George 22:345
Starbird, A. C. 1:104
Starbird, F. W. 25:305
Starbird, J. W. 1:74
Starbrick, T. 3:185
Starbuck, D. 9:225
Starbuck, Darius 18:376
Starbuck, Eurias 7:42
Starbuck, John 27:116
Starbuck, John C. 10:81
Starbuck, Samuel P. 10:138; 20:355
Starbuck, William P. 20:194
Starbusk, John P. 20:355
Stare, Andrew J. 22:131
Stares, Warren E. 27:116
Starhoof, Frederick 12:143
Starhoop, Fred 20:355
Stark, A. 9:59; 21:391
Stark, A. D. 16:56
Stark, Adams 9:91
Stark, Amos 4:55
Stark, Anthony 16:124
Stark, Arthur J. 11:289
Stark, B. F. 9:194
Stark, Benjamin F. 17:59; 19:269
Stark, Charles 19:102
Stark, Charles M. 23:93
Stark, Daniel 7:111
Stark, David 10:207
Stark, E. 20:157
Stark, F. 3:185
Stark, George W. 11:45
Stark, H. 9:151
Stark, H. B. 13:48
Stark, Henry 16:134
Stark, J. D. 3:185
Stark, J. H. 3:185
Stark, Jacob 8:115; 13:48
Stark, James 18:115
Stark, Jerome 21:391
Stark, Jesse 21:151
Stark, John 3:185; 18:161
Stark, John B. 23:169
Stark, John H. 14:222
Stark, John W. 21:60

Stark, Joseph 14:113
Stark, Joseph M. P. 22:238
Stark, M. S. 3:185; 14:222
Stark, Nathan 7:61
Stark, Oliver H. 12:56
Stark, Peter 17:353
Stark, R. 24:70
Stark, R. J. 21:42
Stark, S. 3:185
Stark, T. 11:97
Starke, Charles W. 19:49
Starke, Joseph 24:70
Starke, Joshua 8:42; 26:179
Starker, Clinton L. 9:17
Starker, James 10:93
Starker, Joseph 4:55
Starker, W. F. 11:323
Starkerson, --- 1:174
Starkes, William M. 22:355
Starkey, A. H. 25:237
Starkey, Abel 25:68
Starkey, B. 7:13
Starkey, B. F. 14:22; 16:271
Starkey, C. 26:181
Starkey, C. M. 1:169
Starkey, Charles D. 19:195
Starkey, F. 1:76
Starkey, Hugh 17:59
Starkey, J. 3:185
Starkey, Joel W. 8:32; 18:161
Starkey, John 9:225; 18:376; 21:235
Starkey, John B. 17:284
Starkey, John W. 7:42
Starkey, Nelson 23:51
Starkey, Stacy 21:60
Starkey, W. 1:168
Starkey, W. A. 12:158
Starkey, W. M. 19:230
Starkey, William 12:158
Starkey, William H. 22:222
Starkins, Gotleib 22:55
Starkle, J. M. 15:361
Starkley, Charles 11:86
Starkley, J. 7:111
Starkpole, W. 17:433
Starks, Alfred 11:111
Starks, Barnett 22:103
Starks, C. 23:169
Starks, Charles 7:134
Starks, Danforth 23:110
Starks, Draper 17:186
Starks, Ethan D. 22:468
Starks, J. 23:51

Starks, James C. 22:55
Starks, John 10:177; 19:195
Starks, M. 1:77
Starks, Oliver C. 22:467
Starks, Sydney 6:19
Starks, Thomas 16:230
Starks, W. 1:168
Starks, William W. 22:511
Starkson, S. 13:99
Starkson, William 14:22
Starkweather, E. 24:85
Starkweather, E. M. 3:185
Starkweather, J. 2:18; 25:69
Starkweather, L. 3:185
Starkweather, W. 12:93; 16:305
Starky, E. 8:75
Starky, John 17:43
Starlack, Alexander 8:96
Starlen, Henry 18:94
Starlin, G. H. 22:222
Starlin, William 20:151
Starling, C. C. 23:269
Starling, D. S. Denard 15:350
Starling, Joe 17:139; 24:203
Starling, Robert 24:204
Starling, William 22:270
Starmer, George 22:505
Starner, Daniel 13:48
Starner, Frederick 17:321
Starner, J. 1:176
Starner, Joshua 20:355
Starner, Solomon E. 7:42
Starner, William 23:169
Starnes, James 11:425
Starnes, James T. 21:197
Starns, Peter 13:60
Staroith, A. 9:91
Starpley, J. 21:42
Starr, B. 25:237
Starr, Benjamin 13:48
Starr, C. C. 1:175
Starr, C. F. 3:185
Starr, Charles 14:320; 25:282
Starr, D. 3:185
Starr, E. 3:185
Starr, Elisha E. 22:103
Starr, Francis H. 17:503
Starr, G. W. 11:98
Starr, H. 18:39
Starr, Henry 9:99
Starr, Hiram 7:12
Starr, Isaac H. 9:99
Starr, J. H. 11:170
Starr, Jesse 26:63
Starr, Jessee 18:254

Starr, John 22:103
Starr, John L. 23:169
Starr, John S. 23:116
Starr, John T. 17:59
Starr, Lewis 22:222
Starr, Long 25:335
Starr, N. 3:185
Starr, Robert 19:102
Starr, S. 27:108
Starr, S. C. 14:320; 25:281
Starr, Thomas 22:169
Starr, William 15:229; 18:316; 26:112
Starr, Wilson 18:407
Starr, Zachariah 18:223
Starret, William 11:76
Starret, William F. 22:490
Starrett, Andrew J. 9:14
Starrett, H. C. 23:169
Starrett, J. 3:185
Starrett, John 17:43
Starrett, William 20:355
Starrost, Henry 9:194
Starrs, Aretus 21:247
Starrs, Charles 9:14
Starrs, Robert 7:111
Starry, Benjamin 20:355
Starry, James H. 15:229
Start, Edwin J. 20:191
Start, Thomas 7:134; 14:222
Starting, Edmund 21:89
Starton, William 21:391
Starts, Hugh 22:55
Starver, Casper 19:195
Starweather, H. 16:230
Starweather, James 22:270
Stasey, Peter 4:55
Stasson, Henry 22:163
Statalman, Joseph 19:35
State, W. 15:361; 19:102
Statea, Isaac 19:102
Staten, Joseph 10:138; 20:355
Staten, M. 16:56
Staten, Samuel T. 17:261
Staten, William 23:80
States, Alf. G. 20:13
States, D. 23:51
States, Daniel W. 11:312
States, John G. 11:312
Statesman, John 6:19; 18:94
Statfield, David 17:261
Statford, George J. 23:206
Stathers, William 16:379
Statia, William A. 22:411
Statler, C. 10:180
Statler, Erastus 24:97
Statler, Nelson 4:55

Statley, I. M. 11:393
Statman, H. 1:173
Staton, John T. 22:103
Staton, Thomas 11:270
Staton, William 8:32;
18:161
Statt, I. S. 21:168
Statt, J. W. 9:151
Statt, John W. 22:103
Statting, F. 26:59
Statts, Alexander 22:498
Statts, Alexander Y.
20:354
Statts, Charles E. 21:391
Statts, David W. 10:145
Statts, J. 26:59
Statzer, C. S. 12:84;
16:305
Staub, John 7:42; 18:431
Staubird, F. W. 7:76
Staubs, George C. 4:55
Stauder, C. 1:74
Staufer, Samuel R. 22:103
Stauff, J. 3:185
Stauffer, George W.
13:120
Stauffer, J. 3:185
Stauffer, Peter B. 23:182
Stauffer, Samuel H.
22:103
Stauley, Amos 26:59
Stauley, Nathan L. 10:81
Staumer, J. 23:169
Staung, Jonas 19:35
Staunton, E. W. 9:238
Staunton, Harry 15:259
Staunton, John F. 19:102
Staut, James H. 9:91
Staut, William 9:91;
25:237
Stauts, Peter 22:238
Stavens, George 5:46
Stavens, Samuel 23:264
Stavers, William 9:91
Stavner, Ethan 21:290
Stawter, William H.
19:102
Stayer, Daniel 22:156
Stayman, Joseph 19:102
Stayner, James E. 19:102
Staynor, D. 25:237
Staysa, J. 13:76
Staytens, John B. 11:282
Ste, Daniel 18:211
Ste---, H. 16:305
Stead, A. P. 19:262
Stead, J. 3:185; 14:113
Stead, James W. 5:30;
25:237
Stead, Joseph 15:229
Stead, William 12:54

Steadman, A. 18:254;
26:62
Steadman, F. M. 14:113
Steadman, George E.
11:111
Steadman, Hiram 9:105
Steadman, John 16:379;
25:335
Steadman, John H. 16:230
Steadman, L. D. 3:185
Steadman, S. 3:185
Steadman, W. 3:185
Steadman, W. C. 9:59
Steadman, William 19:224
Steadson, W. 3:185
Steadwell, George 1:74
Steagle, Andrew 24:30
Steale, J. 1:170
Steally, J. C. 11:167
Steam, --- 18:195
Steam, A. C. 18:194
Steamer, F. 3:185
Steamer, Francis 8:123
Steams, John 4:56
Steamwoko, J. 25:237
Steamworks, Jeremiah
5:30
Steanboard, Robert S.
18:281
Steaphens, P. I. 18:180
Stearer, W. S. 25:69
Stearkweather, Charles W.
5:30
Stearman, William H.
11:397
Stearn, Michael 17:449;
24:174
Stearn, O. S. 14:222, 260
Stearnes, --- 19:102
Stearnes, J. 16:230
Stearnes, John 19:35
Stearnes, O. B. 8:67
Stearnes, W. 9:151
Stearnes, W. H. 1:71
Stearnes, Warren 16:230
Stearnes, William 21:143
Stearns, --- 6:9; 15:363
Stearns, Albert M. 19:102
Stearns, Alva J. 18:281
Stearns, Anthony 13:135
Stearns, C. W. 8:75
Stearns, Charles 27:110
Stearns, Charles E. 7:112
Stearns, Charles W. 17:87
Stearns, Cyrus 22:55
Stearns, D. M. 9:243
Stearns, D. W. 18:281
Stearns, Dan 7:112
Stearns, E. K. 3:185
Stearns, Franklin 17:289
Stearns, Frederic 11:194

Stearns, G. W. 1:172;
26:184
Stearns, George 12:41
Stearns, George T. 16:1
Stearns, Henry 25:71
Stearns, J. 18:105
Stearns, John 13:126
Stearns, John M. 21:80
Stearns, Justus C. 20:33
Stearns, Leonard 22:468
Stearns, Lyman K. 9:14
Stearns, N. 27:109
Stearns, Nathaniel D.
14:222
Stearns, Philander F.
23:80
Stearns, S. 15:315
Stearns, Seb 15:45
Stearns, Thomas J. 22:55
Stearns, Thomas R. 8:56
Stearns, W. 12:84
Stears, D. C. 19:102
Steavens, Pleasant 18:195
Steavens, W. H. 20:355
Stebbens, David 22:222
Stebber, John A. 12:77
Stebbing, John M. 20:26
Stebbins, A. 14:222
Stebbins, Abraham F.
17:26
Stebbins, Benjamin J.
22:55
Stebbins, Charles E. 5:30
Stebbins, Charles F.
22:156
Stebbins, Consider H.
22:510
Stebbins, Cuyler 23:169
Stebbins, Edward M.
12:41
Stebbins, F. R. 10:22
Stebbins, H. 3:185
Stebbins, J. S. 19:242
Stebbins, James S. 9:194;
19:242
Stebbins, L. J. 11:111
Stebbins, Oliver 11:112
Stebbins, V. W. 7:61
Stebbins, W. B. 19:242
Stebbins, W. D. 1:172
Stebbins, W. W. 13:49
Stebbins, William 21:42
Steben, Joe 10:211;
18:456
Steber, William E. 4:56
Stebins, Henry 12:77
Stebins, Z. 3:185
Stebler, J. A. 15:89
Stebs, H. 11:294
Steckel, Henry 23:170
Stecker, Franz 13:80

Steckler, Gilbert 15:45
Steckner, Tranez 16:230
Stecy, Theodore F. 10:22
Stedding, J. F. 13:99
Steddings, G. 16:230
Stedena, John 13:69
Stedge, P. M. 1:176
Stedham, Jacob 7:134
Stedhouse, Jacob 21:391
Stedman, Alfred 15:259
Stedman, C. 14:113; 21:168
Stedman, Charles H. 13:49
Stedman, E. S. 14:222
Stedman, George 11:112
Stedman, Hiram 18:341
Stedman, John 8:75; 9:194; 19:273
Stedman, Oscar 7:112
Stedman, W. 12:93; 16:305
Stedman, William 4:56; 9:194; 14:113
Stedoman, Leiow 16:144
Steebleen, Mishael 19:279
Steeby, John 17:321
Steede, Edward 12:173
Steedman, William 10:138; 20:355
Steeglesmond, Anton 9:90
Steekans, William 4:56
Steel, --- 11:172
Steel, A. 1:100
Steel, Abraham 3:185
Steel, Allen 1:71
Steel, Andy 17:186
Steel, Arthur 15:319
Steel, Benedict 12:143
Steel, Bub 15:229
Steel, C. 2:18
Steel, Charles 25:67
Steel, Charles W. 16:79
Steel, D. 2:17; 25:67
Steel, Dallas E. 20:355
Steel, E. 3:185
Steel, F. 23:169
Steel, F. S. 23:170
Steel, Frank 17:507
Steel, Frederick H. A. 11:184
Steel, G. 14:113
Steel, G. B. 9:91
Steel, George H. 12:41
Steel, H. 3:185
Steel, H. C. 9:194
Steel, H. O. 9:91
Steel, Henry 22:222
Steel, Isaac 11:77; 18:223
Steel, J. H. 7:61; 11:77
Steel, J. S. 3:185

Steel, James 20:355
Steel, James A. 18:105
Steel, John 9:91; 12:52; 15:229; 21:207; 26:61
Steel, John H. 11:213; 12:77; 15:60, 229
Steel, John L. 11:86
Steel, John S. 11:397
Steel, Luke 12:52
Steel, M. 10:187; 18:180
Steel, Nathaniel 22:169
Steel, Newton 22:345
Steel, O. D. 11:329
Steel, Osmer 1:72
Steel, P. 17:139; 24:203
Steel, R. 14:113
Steel, S. A. 22:222
Steel, S. B. 1:176
Steel, Samuel 12:60
Steel, Thomas 22:516
Steel, Thomas C. 1:71
Steel, Thompson 7:66
Steel, W. C. B. 13:120
Steel, W. H. 16:230
Steel, William 9:136; 14:22
Steel, William I. 18:401
Steel, Z. T. 25:70
Steele, --- 11:294
Steele, ---erly B. 25:72
Steele, Alfred P. 16:56
Steele, Andrew J. 10:138; 20:355
Steele, Arthur 19:102
Steele, Austin 9:46
Steele, Bazele 9:39
Steele, Benedict 20:355
Steele, Dallas E. 10:82
Steele, Daniel 16:305
Steele, David 10:99
Steele, Edwin D. 9:244
Steele, Frederick S. 17:239
Steele, G. 25:237
Steele, G. S. 1:172
Steele, George 3:185; 5:46; 8:32; 18:161
Steele, George W. 22:103
Steele, H. C. 19:242
Steele, Hamilton 22:320
Steele, Henrich 26:181
Steele, Ishmael 7:15
Steele, J. 3:185
Steele, J. M. C. 1:173
Steele, J. N. 20:13
Steele, J. R. 1:168
Steele, James 10:8, 82; 11:404; 18:94
Steele, James M. 3:185; 22:103, 470

Steele, James P. 24:56
Steele, James W. 22:270
Steele, John 17:495; 22:320; 26:146
Steele, John A. 18:223
Steele, John V. 22:457
Steele, Joseph 21:391
Steele, Josiah 23:14
Steele, L. 14:222
Steele, L. W. 25:237
Steele, Lampert W. 5:30
Steele, Luke 8:43; 26:180
Steele, Mack 22:320
Steele, Myers F. 9:194; 19:262
Steele, N. A. 9:59
Steele, Nelson 8:32; 18:161
Steele, Philander 9:67; 18:281
Steele, Samuel 3:185; 9:39; 21:235
Steele, Samuel W. 24:60
Steele, W. 1:173; 13:99
Steele, William 13:120; 20:101; 21:60; 22:103; 23:170; 27:111
Steele, William M. 24:30
Steeley, G. W. 10:138; 20:355
Steeley, James J. 10:82; 20:355
Steelman, William P. 22:103
Steely, John 14:222
Steely, Reuben 21:391
Steely, S. 16:56
Steemer, Oswold 25:70
Steen, Ephraim 20:355
Steen, Hugh S. 17:87
Steen, J. F. 15:229
Steen, J. S. 11:382
Steen, Thomas W. 22:222
Steeples, Henry 10:82; 20:355
Steepry, W. 16:230
Steer, S. 23:206
Steere, John F. 17:252
Steers, Isaac 12:77
Steers, William P. 23:93
Steese, Alfred P. 13:49
Steese, F. F. 3:185
Steese, William 12:139
Steesey, Peter 8:32
Steet, Henry 11:122
Steety, Reuben 8:110
Steeve, Ephraim 10:138
Stefar, Frank 13:49
Steff, Frank 12:158
Steffen, J. 1:176

Steffen, Michael 23:169
Steffeson, Michael 20:116
Steffey, Aaron 22:223
Stegamiller, William F. 23:80
Steger, Arthur 22:320
Stegles, W. 14:22
Stegman, John 21:93
Stegmeyer, Lewis 1:74
Stegner, Frederick W. 23:51
Stegoll, J. 3:185
Steibe, Albert 13:49
Steidenger, George 22:355
Steier, Gerhard 22:103
Steiff, John 3:185
Steiger, Henry 13:49
Steiger, Jacob 11:18
Steiger, John 21:126; 23:169
Steigler, Clement V. 9:125; 27:113
Steih, Jacob 22:173
Steil, William 19:49
Steilbein, Caspar 9:194
Steiling, C. 15:229
Steimle, John 9:17
Stein, --- 17:402
Stein, Andrew 10:149; 18:58
Stein, August 16:154
Stein, Charles 9:194; 14:320; 19:262; 25:284
Stein, David D. 23:14
Stein, E. 1:74
Stein, Edward 16:379
Stein, George 23:182
Stein, Ilgen 7:42
Stein, J. 3:185; 21:106, 391; 23:51
Stein, Jacob 8:32; 18:161
Stein, John B. 16:230
Stein, M. D. 20:355
Stein, Mary 26:226
Stein, Moses 9:29
Stein, T. 9:113
Steinard, Thomas 10:82; 20:355
Steinbach, F. 14:267
Steinback, John 21:285
Steinback, Michael 15:45
Steinbarger, Alex 21:391
Steinbeck, John 19:195
Steinberg, Julius 4:56
Steinberger, S. 5:54
Steinberger, William 16:56
Steinberry, Andrew 10:82

Steinbrayer, Alexander 7:112
Steinbrook, A. 3:185
Steinbrook, Charles 17:26
Steinburg, Andrew 20:355
Steinburg, Banker V. 19:102
Steinburgh, George 12:169
Steinchl, William 14:267
Steine, Lewis 18:115
Steine, Peter 23:169
Steineman, George 11:121
Steineman, Robert 22:411
Steiner, C. 3:185; 17:503
Steiner, Edwin 15:135
Steiner, Garrett 15:89
Steiner, Henry 9:114
Steiner, Joseph 17:16
Steiner, Nicholas 7:42
Steiner, R. 15:45
Steiner, S. 8:59
Steiner, S. P. 1:175
Steiner, Samuel 24:85
Steinhawes, J. 3:185
Steinhege, Ernest 24:70
Steinhilber, George 21:199
Steinhilber, M. 11:76
Steinhilner, B. 14:222
Steinhoff, A. 3:185
Steinhoff, F. 1:76
Steinhour, William A. 1:70
Steinhurgh, E. 1:71
Steininger, F. 24:70
Steinkraus, Carl 22:163
Steinlein, William 19:36
Steinman, Henry 9:91; 26:59
Steinman, John 20:13
Steinmehl, William 23:80
Steinmetz, Joseph 25:237
Steinmetz, Peter 24:31
Steinmetz, W. H. 15:75
Steinmitzer, Samuel 10:34
Steinneff, Gottleib 12:41
Steinour, D. 19:102
Steins, Robert 24:103
Steins, William 16:57
Steinson, L. 17:101
Steinson, Niles 17:101
Steinwick, Adolph 13:49
Steiple, John 15:230
Steister, J. 25:237
Steitsman, John 14:222
Steitz, Lewis 22:15
Steiver, John 14:222
Steiwhower, Nelson P. 5:30
Stekle, J. M. 12:97

Steles, Lewis 25:237
Steley, John 9:67
Stelker, William 1:78
Stell, J. M. 26:181
Stell, J. W. 27:119
Stell, James 9:91; 19:36; 26:65
Stella, J. F. 3:185
Stelle, A. 3:185
Stelle, F. 3:185
Steller, Henry 17:401
Steller, Isaac 15:324; 19:102
Stellwell, Clark 15:45
Stelrocht, D. 3:186
Stelzer, Charles 23:170
Stelzer, Philip 18:316
Stem, Max 25:237
Stem, W. 1:170
Stem, Wayne 11:184
Stembrock, George 17:87
Stemes, I. B. 8:67
Stemmang, C. 1:171
Stemmer, D. 14:245
Stemmett, J. 3:186
Stemmuhd, --- 14:290
Stemper, Henry 11:98
Stempferd, J. 1:176
Stemple, A. G. 4:56
Stemrich, John 24:85
Stemshoren, Fred 17:210
Stemson, William 16:57
Stenard, William H. 17:26
Stenbeck, F. F. 14:290
Stenchel, William I. 12:56
Stened, Frederic 11:170
Stener, Martin 22:222
Stengel, John 8:32
Stenger, J. 1:174
Stenkal, Fred 11:98
Stenks, J. 19:307
Stenner, John 15:321
Stennett, David 8:32; 18:161
Stennett, Mason 25:327
Stensher, John 20:36
Stensley, D. 3:186
Stensley, James 25:286
Stenson, James 9:238
Stenton, Andrew 21:391
Stentt, James 26:129
Stenur, Jacob 17:59
Stenyett, William W. 18:254; 26:63
Steorns, Frank 4:56
Step, Carlo B. 17:204
Step, I. 17:275
Stepen, Gross 5:54
Stepens, Edward 5:54
Stepenson, James S. 8:75
Stepes, R. 14:113

Stephen, Baker 8:110
Stephen, David 11:406
Stephen, Samuel 17:209
Stephen, William 18:211
Stephen, William C. 12:41
Stephens, A. 14:113, 285;
    16:230; 27:108
Stephens, A. B. 17:497
Stephens, Aaron H.
    22:458
Stephens, Abijah A. 24:31
Stephens, Albert E.
    22:345
Stephens, Albert M. 9:194
Stephens, Alexander
    22:457
Stephens, Alfred M. 22:55
Stephens, Alonzo P.
    23:261
Stephens, Andrew 22:490
Stephens, Andrew R.
    17:26
Stephens, Anthony 18:316
Stephens, Atkinson 9:202;
    19:293
Stephens, B. 12:93;
    14:113, 290; 16:305;
    23:51
Stephens, B. E. 8:110
Stephens, B. H. 3:186
Stephens, Benjamin 7:12;
    14:267
Stephens, Burrece 20:129
Stephens, C. 23:201
Stephens, C. D. 5:30
Stephens, C. H. 16:230
Stephens, C. P. 3:186
Stephens, Charles 17:362
Stephens, Charles E.
    9:125
Stephens, D. C. 18:195
Stephens, D. P. 1:176
Stephens, D. T. 25:237
Stephens, Daniel 21:11
Stephens, Daniel C.
    22:222
Stephens, David 10:81;
    11:392; 20:355
Stephens, David D. 5:30
Stephens, E. 15:295;
    27:107
Stephens, E. N. 21:391
Stephens, Ed 1:74
Stephens, Edward 23:110
Stephens, Elisha 22:131
Stephens, F. N. 16:57
Stephens, Francis M.
    10:81; 20:355
Stephens, Frank 11:313;
    22:345
Stephens, Frederick 7:42

Stephens, G. 1:171;
    14:113
Stephens, G. A. 1:100
Stephens, G. H. 25:237
Stephens, G. W. 23:245
Stephens, George 4:68;
    9:194; 17:239;
    19:102, 230; 20:191
Stephens, George H. 6:14;
    20:129
Stephens, George M.
    22:55
Stephens, Goit 10:138
Stephens, H. 11:282;
    23:282
Stephens, H. S. 13:49
Stephens, Harrison 19:36
Stephens, Henry 16:305;
    27:108
Stephens, Henry A. 9:17
Stephens, Henry C. 20:28,
    105
Stephens, Henry S. 12:63
Stephens, Hiram 22:438;
    24:45
Stephens, I. 14:222
Stephens, J. 1:171;
    11:249; 19:102;
    27:110
Stephens, J. A. 1:77;
    10:81; 14:113;
    20:355; 23:170
Stephens, J. B. 26:60
Stephens, J. F. 3:186
Stephens, J. H. 22:169
Stephens, J. W. 11:184;
    20:191; 25:305
Stephens, Jacob 23:269;
    24:213
Stephens, James 8:110;
    10:81; 20:355;
    22:490
Stephens, James P. 20:13
Stephens, Jerrold 10:97
Stephens, John 7:42;
    10:81; 12:41; 14:113;
    20:116, 355; 23:51;
    24:162
Stephens, John D. 17:261
Stephens, John H. 24:30
Stephens, John N. 22:441
Stephens, John R. 17:308
Stephens, John S. 11:255
Stephens, Joshua 22:156
Stephens, L. 19:195;
    25:237
Stephens, Levi 21:391
Stephens, Leyman 20:109
Stephens, Lyman W.
    10:168

Stephens, M. 16:230;
    18:376; 22:521
Stephens, Mackner 7:111
Stephens, Mason 4:68
Stephens, Mathew 24:45
Stephens, Morgan 9:225
Stephens, N. 1:76
Stephens, N. C. 13:120
Stephens, Nathan 10:138;
    20:355
Stephens, Noah 11:270
Stephens, O. 16:230
Stephens, P. J. 26:204
Stephens, Palmer 23:266
Stephens, Peter 12:77
Stephens, Philip 13:80
Stephens, Provost 21:391
Stephens, R. S. 8:56
Stephens, Ransom S.
    9:163
Stephens, Robert 8:96
Stephens, S. 20:355;
    22:270
Stephens, S. J. W. 12:84;
    16:305
Stephens, Scott 17:250
Stephens, Sherman B.
    8:110
Stephens, Silas 7:134
Stephens, T. 14:113
Stephens, The. 11:45
Stephens, Thomas 16:305;
    17:72, 455; 24:204
Stephens, Thomas J.
    26:129
Stephens, Thomas T.
    22:103
Stephens, Townsend
    21:391
Stephens, Uriah 22:467
Stephens, W. 17:433;
    21:132
Stephens, W. H. 26:129
Stephens, W. H. (Mrs.)
    24:10
Stephens, W. L. 23:51
Stephens, W. S. 12:88;
    16:305
Stephens, Webster 22:156
Stephens, William 9:194,
    211, 232; 11:312;
    20:19, 355; 21:191;
    24:168
Stephens, William C.
    22:55
Stephens, William H.
    24:10
Stephens, William S.
    12:41
Stephens, William T.
    10:138; 20:355

Stephens, William W. 9:45
Stephens, Wilson 22:131
Stephens, Zachariah 11:170
Stephensn, W. 1:78
Stephenson, --- 27:110
Stephenson, A. 22:222
Stephenson, A. T. 11:170
Stephenson, Alex 20:355
Stephenson, Alexander 10:82
Stephenson, Allen 19:49
Stephenson, Charles 7:42; 21:93
Stephenson, E. B. 1:70
Stephenson, Edwin 13:120
Stephenson, Emma 23:198
Stephenson, Felix F. 22:506
Stephenson, Frank 22:321
Stephenson, G. N. 17:59
Stephenson, George 7:42; 20:13; 23:306; 26:214
Stephenson, H. 9:194
Stephenson, Harvey 9:232
Stephenson, Hugh 10:138; 20:355
Stephenson, Isaac 5:46
Stephenson, J. 1:74, 170; 3:186; 7:12; 22:222; 25:237
Stephenson, J. L. 17:162
Stephenson, James 14:222; 18:161; 20:101; 21:106; 22:439; 26:181
Stephenson, James B. 11:271
Stephenson, Jim 21:285
Stephenson, Joel E. 22:131
Stephenson, John 14:222
Stephenson, Joseph 7:78
Stephenson, Joseph B. 23:80
Stephenson, Joseph M. 13:132
Stephenson, Josiah W. 17:59
Stephenson, L. 11:251
Stephenson, Lafayette 9:91
Stephenson, Martin 9:136
Stephenson, Patrick 8:96
Stephenson, Paul 10:193; 18:180
Stephenson, Philip 14:222

Stephenson, R. 14:222
Stephenson, R. W. 19:36
Stephenson, Robert 14:237
Stephenson, Robert B. 22:169
Stephenson, Smith 23:170
Stephenson, Thomas 17:43; 24:182
Stephenson, W. R. 24:115
Stephenson, W. W. 21:106
Stephenson, William 8:96; 10:138; 17:26, 43; 20:157, 355; 25:237
Stephenson, William A. 17:284
Stephenson, William P. 22:103
Stephey, David 19:102
Stephony, Harmount 12:77
Stephy, W. H. 14:113
Steple, Anderson 21:391
Stepler, George L. 15:230
Stepler, Jacob 11:314
Stepler, William 9:194
Steples, Charles E. 1:75
Stepleton, I. 15:230
Stepleton, Squire 22:103
Stepp, George 18:254
Stepp, Gin 26:63
Stepp, Preston 3:186
Stepp, Riley 17:239
Steppenger, John 23:125
Steppick, Paul 10:175; 19:196
Steptel, Peter 12:52
Steraus, S. C. 7:42
Sterems, Charles 10:168
Sterenbeger, C. M. 1:74
Sterens, John 14:260
Sterhenson, J. C. 9:59
Steries, Andrew 21:391
Sterimeby, W. H. 12:77
Sterkmdier, John M. 9:138
Sterling, -enard 15:135
Sterling, A. 26:60
Sterling, Charles 23:51
Sterling, David 21:151
Sterling, E. D. 19:196
Sterling, E. E. 1:172
Sterling, Frank 7:134
Sterling, Frederick 25:269
Sterling, G. 16:230
Sterling, J. 12:124; 14:303; 15:136; 17:477
Sterling, James A. 16:305
Sterling, James D. 21:235

Sterling, James P. 9:125; 27:114
Sterling, Jesse 17:43
Sterling, John H. 23:130
Sterling, John W. 9:158
Sterling, Josiah 20:3
Sterling, Robert 20:129
Sterling, Robert L. 1:73
Sterling, Thaddeus 4:56
Sterling, Thomas 7:112
Sterling, Victor 18:72
Sterling, William 12:52; 23:110
Sterm, William 15:45
Sterman, John F. 9:99
Sterms, H. C. 23:170
Stern, Charles 25:270
Stern, George 4:56
Stern, H. A. 1:173
Stern, P. 1:174
Sternbargh, William J. 22:468
Sternberg, --- 20:3
Sternberg, Addison 16:379
Sternberg, Jordan 21:151
Sternberry, William 15:92
Sternburg, George W. 8:60
Sterner, David 17:43
Sterner, J. 21:113
Sternes, Charles 9:151
Sternes, H. 14:222, 260
Sternes, John 14:222
Sternhofer, A. 1:168
Sternholt, William 3:186
Sterns, --- 19:102
Sterns, Augustus 13:69
Sterns, C. E. 1:74
Sterns, Edgar H. 21:80
Sterns, George M. 8:110
Sterns, James B. 10:82; 20:355
Sternt, L. 21:391
Sterpent, Leonard 18:115
Sterporet, Leonard 6:8
Sterr, N. B. 1:74
Sterree, A. 25:68
Sterrel, J. C. 22:156
Sterrell, John R. 18:321
Sterret, Oliver 12:65
Sterrett, J. M. 20:129
Sterrick, William 16:57
Sterrill, Robert 8:56
Sterrinck, Peter 4:56
Sterrit, W. F. 21:391
Sterritt, A. 16:160
Sterritt, C. 1:170
Sterritt, Edward 17:139; 24:203
Sterritt, John 9:29

Sterry, Phineas B. 9:194
Sterting, J. 27:117
Sterword, Isaac 11:397
Stesey, Peter 18:161
Stesraeb, William H.
    8:110
Stessenger, Charles
    15:136
Steth, C. 7:42
Stetler, Charles 21:391
Stetler, Daniel 19:36
Stetler, H. 1:75
Stetler, J. 20:149
Stetler, Thomas I. 17:357
Stetler, William W.
    10:138; 20:355
Stetson, --- 11:249
Stetson, Ambrose 8:110
Stetson, C. G. 25:284
Stetson, David 21:391
Stetson, G. G. 18:349
Stetson, George F. 4:56
Stetson, M. W. 4:56
Stetson, N. B. 19:242
Stett, James 3:186
Stettison, Gilbert 7:112
Stetzer, Philip 9:29
Stetzler, C. 12:10
Steuben, Joseph 10:22
Steuben, W. H. 18:39
Steurmer, Heinrich 21:60
Steuss, W. 1:172
Stevans, E. 1:76
Steven, Frederic 17:59
Steven, H. N. 1:171
Steven, William 4:56
Stevens, --- 15:45; 19:297
Stevens, A. 3:186; 9:151;
    12:63; 19:276;
    21:391
Stevens, A. M. 19:273
Stevens, Abraham 10:93
Stevens, Abraham V.
    22:410
Stevens, Albion H. 22:55
Stevens, Alfred 15:19
Stevens, Allen 22:156
Stevens, Almon 11:171
Stevens, Alonzo 9:194
Stevens, Alvah G. 22:55
Stevens, Amos 4:55
Stevens, Andrew 27:118
Stevens, Andrew J. 7:54
Stevens, Anson 22:156
Stevens, Anthony 19:347
Stevens, August 19:102
Stevens, B. 16:379
Stevens, Benjamin 6:7;
    13:49; 16:57

Stevens, C. 9:151; 14:260;
    18:94; 19:242; 27:108
Stevens, C. D. 25:237
Stevens, C. E. 15:311
Stevens, C. L. 9:59
Stevens, C. P. 1:77
Stevens, C. S. F. 16:57
Stevens, C. V. 11:130
Stevens, C. W. 21:391
Stevens, Carleton 10:146
Stevens, Charles 9:194;
    13:128; 19:196
Stevens, Charles C.
    21:391
Stevens, Charles F.
    27:113
Stevens, Charles H. 4:55;
    7:111; 22:174
Stevens, Clarence H. 10:8
Stevens, Colonel I. 22:467
Stevens, Cornelius 6:21
Stevens, Crit. 20:355
Stevens, D. 15:312;
    19:102
Stevens, Daniel B. 11:45
Stevens, Daniel L. 20:13
Stevens, David 21:218
Stevens, David B. 1:74
Stevens, Durand D.
    10:138; 20:355
Stevens, E. 1:173, 175;
    3:186; 9:151
Stevens, E. B. 27:109
Stevens, E. W. 3:186;
    7:111
Stevens, Edmund 22:439
Stevens, Edward 17:102;
    19:293
Stevens, Edward F.
    25:237
Stevens, Edwin F. 22:498
Stevens, Eldridge S. 7:111
Stevens, Everett L. 9:7
Stevens, F. 25:237
Stevens, F. M. 13:99
Stevens, F. W. 21:392
Stevens, Franklin W.
    13:49
Stevens, Frederick 9:194
Stevens, G. 25:237
Stevens, G. C. 13:133;
    20:355
Stevens, G. W. 1:76;
    3:186; 13:120;
    16:142; 17:159
Stevens, George 9:91;
    21:285; 22:321;
    25:237
Stevens, George B. 4:55
Stevens, George E. 12:77;
    15:45; 18:72

Stevens, George F. 7:54
Stevens, George H. 12:10;
    16:144
Stevens, George W. 7:42;
    20:355
Stevens, Gustavus A.
    24:97
Stevens, H. D. 11:194
Stevens, H. G. 20:355
Stevens, H. M. 11:342
Stevens, Harrison 17:167
Stevens, Henderson
    16:230
Stevens, Henry 3:186;
    7:134; 9:39, 151;
    16:57; 18:297; 21:80;
    22:222; 23:125, 269;
    25:237; 26:113
Stevens, Henry B. 10:81
Stevens, Henry C. 21:191
Stevens, Henry H. 13:49
Stevens, Henry J. 8:96
Stevens, Henry S. 15:3
Stevens, Hiram 4:55
Stevens, Horace 6:19;
    18:94; 19:196
Stevens, Howard S.
    23:170
Stevens, I. M. 21:95
Stevens, Isaac 21:243
Stevens, J. 1:95, 96;
    9:155; 25:237
Stevens, J. H. 1:169;
    25:71
Stevens, J. M. 16:142
Stevens, J. P. 1:172
Stevens, J. W. 20:355
Stevens, Jacob 5:30;
    12:65; 15:75
Stevens, James 7:54; 9:91,
    125; 11:112; 14:113;
    20:355; 27:114
Stevens, Joel 7:42
Stevens, John 7:65, 111;
    9:243; 13:49; 18:272
Stevens, John L. 17:422
Stevens, John S. 3:186
Stevens, John W. 7:111;
    10:81; 17:420
Stevens, Jonas 20:26
Stevens, Joseph 22:320
Stevens, Joseph H. 11:44
Stevens, L. 3:186; 25:305
Stevens, L. D. 25:237
Stevens, L. W. 1:172
Stevens, Lander 4:56
Stevens, Lemon B. 23:170
Stevens, Leonard 21:261
Stevens, Levi 7:78
Stevens, Lorenzo 21:126

Stevens, Lyman W. 19:196
Stevens, M. 1:74; 15:295
Stevens, M. A. 10:81; 25:69
Stevens, M. V. 20:356
Stevens, Manly 27:106
Stevens, Marcus F. 10:138
Stevens, Martus L. 20:356
Stevens, Michael C. 17:209
Stevens, Mildun 7:111
Stevens, N. 3:186
Stevens, Nelson 13:69; 19:102, 196
Stevens, O. 16:87
Stevens, O. A. 19:262
Stevens, O. S. 1:75
Stevens, Oliver A. 9:194
Stevens, Owen 21:80, 191
Stevens, P. L. 3:186
Stevens, Patrick 27:112
Stevens, Peter C. 15:45
Stevens, R. 3:186
Stevens, R. B. 21:191
Stevens, R. L. 1:104
Stevens, Ranson 15:136
Stevens, Reuben 25:70
Stevens, Ross B. 10:138; 20:356
Stevens, Royal S. A. 22:156
Stevens, Rozel 22:222
Stevens, S. 3:186; 10:82; 19:102
Stevens, S. G. 3:186
Stevens, Samuel 11:112; 21:80; 25:69; 26:129; 27:148
Stevens, Stanford 22:55
Stevens, T. W. 7:111
Stevens, Thomas 3:186; 10:22; 22:222, 355
Stevens, Thomas H. 12:60
Stevens, Thomas J. 9:45
Stevens, V. 7:70
Stevens, Virgil 11:417
Stevens, W. 3:186; 16:230; 25:237
Stevens, W. B. 4:56
Stevens, W. C. 12:158
Stevens, W. H. 1:173; 7:42; 15:75
Stevens, W. L. 14:222
Stevens, W. M. 19:262
Stevens, W. S. 14:113; 27:148
Stevens, William 6:28; 10:81, 93; 13:49; 17:43; 19:262; 20:356; 22:173; 27:116

Stevens, William H. 10:138; 13:49; 20:356
Stevens, William I. 18:281
Stevens, William T. 10:22; 21:115
Stevensburg, Jerry 17:399
Stevenson, --- 7:15; 9:151; 10:168; 25:281
Stevenson, Abur 11:213
Stevenson, Alexander 10:82
Stevenson, Andrew 21:235
Stevenson, Anglo S. 17:405
Stevenson, Cornelius 9:136; 27:112
Stevenson, D. 3:186; 13:126
Stevenson, Dallas 12:52
Stevenson, David 12:52; 17:97
Stevenson, Edward 21:285
Stevenson, F. 19:262
Stevenson, Frank 13:49; 16:57
Stevenson, Frs. M. 17:43
Stevenson, George 13:126
Stevenson, Gilbert 17:59
Stevenson, Harvey 20:356
Stevenson, Horace 10:175
Stevenson, I. N. 23:51
Stevenson, Ily 11:271
Stevenson, Increase 10:175
Stevenson, Incriese 19:196
Stevenson, Isaac A. 10:138; 20:356
Stevenson, J. 9:151; 25:305; 27:110
Stevenson, J. H. 22:270
Stevenson, Jacob 17:250; 19:49
Stevenson, James 4:56; 7:42; 8:32; 23:130
Stevenson, James B. 16:230
Stevenson, James J. 15:45
Stevenson, James M. 18:254; 26:64
Stevenson, James P. 13:69
Stevenson, James S. 12:41
Stevenson, John 3:186; 16:57; 17:388; 18:94
Stevenson, John S. 10:82; 20:356

Stevenson, Joseph 11:416; 24:30
Stevenson, L. 26:60
Stevenson, L. I. 22:490
Stevenson, Lewis 4:56
Stevenson, M. 9:114
Stevenson, M. D. B. 22:492
Stevenson, Martin 27:115
Stevenson, O. 9:67; 18:254; 26:64
Stevenson, Oliver 18:281
Stevenson, P. 16:102
Stevenson, Peter 17:186
Stevenson, R. 18:94
Stevenson, R. M. 7:134
Stevenson, R. S. 15:93
Stevenson, Reuben 9:46; 26:130
Stevenson, Robert W. 21:15
Stevenson, S. 11:168; 16:230
Stevenson, S. V. 19:36
Stevenson, Samuel 8:102; 11:289; 17:461; 24:162
Stevenson, Samuel W. 19:36
Stevenson, T. 1:170; 11:342
Stevenson, Thomas 17:452; 19:307; 25:67
Stevenson, W. 3:186
Stevenson, W. H. 17:420; 24:162
Stevenson, William 1:76; 3:186; 7:111; 11:184, 277; 12:41; 19:49, 196; 22:439
Stevenson, William A. 10:138; 20:356
Stevenson, William E. 9:91
Stevenson, William M. 12:41; 22:156
Stever, Franklin 4:56
Stever, L. 23:169
Stever, Mathew 10:138; 20:356
Stever, Robert W. 1:73
Steves, Charles I. 15:230
Steves, Richard 12:10
Steveson, --- 15:45
Stevins, H. 15:3
Stevor, N. 9:151
Steward, --- 12:98; 13:76
Steward, A. 14:260; 17:186
Steward, A. C. 25:237

Steward, Alexander
  17:403
Steward, Alvin 21:191
Steward, Blamis 13:59
Steward, C. 1:173; 3:186;
  10:29; 19:307;
  25:237
Steward, C. S. 3:186
Steward, Charles 15:60;
  18:377
Steward, Clark 21:143
Steward, D. 21:126
Steward, E. 5:46; 25:237
Steward, Ed 27:111
Steward, Edward 24:103
Steward, F. 3:186
Steward, F. A. 18:58
Steward, F. M. 19:102
Steward, G. 3:186
Steward, George 3:186;
  7:134; 20:33
Steward, George W.
  7:134; 8:96; 27:111
Steward, H. 13:99; 14:22
Steward, H. H. 19:265
Steward, Harris H. 9:194
Steward, Isaac 13:59
Steward, J. 1:168; 3:186
Steward, J. D. 23:51
Steward, J. H. 25:237
Steward, J. L. 18:39
Steward, James 12:41;
  19:102, 284; 22:321;
  27:111
Steward, Jeremiah 22:15
Steward, John 5:46; 8:96
Steward, John T. 25:238
Steward, Jonas 21:239
Steward, Joseph 25:238
Steward, Joshua 27:111
Steward, Leander 8:100
Steward, M. 25:238
Steward, Morrow 10:82
Steward, Robert 12:52
Steward, Rufus B. 8:96
Steward, S. 11:75
Steward, Stephen M. 9:91
Steward, W. 18:422
Steward, W. D. 21:42
Steward, W. V. 3:186
Steward, William 7:82;
  9:166; 11:271;
  12:52; 21:199; 24:30
Steward, William F.
  22:321
Steward, Zephaniah 12:52
Stewarf, Joseph 25:69
Stewart, --- 8:125; 15:15,
  338
Stewart, A. 1:169; 14:223
Stewart, A. J. 21:392

Stewart, A. M. 21:392
Stewart, Abraham 23:170
Stewart, Albert 19:307
Stewart, Alex 8:32;
  11:173
Stewart, Alexander
  11:171; 18:161
Stewart, Alfred 4:56
Stewart, Alva F. 23:257
Stewart, Amos C. 11:296
Stewart, Andrew 8:42;
  22:270; 26:182
Stewart, Armstrong
  11:313
Stewart, B. C. 1:176
Stewart, Benjamin F.
  17:150
Stewart, Beserly 19:49
Stewart, Beverly 8:43;
  26:180
Stewart, Bradley K. 9:194
Stewart, C. 1:76, 171;
  5:54; 7:61; 12:84;
  16:305
Stewart, C. A. 3:186
Stewart, C. H. 9:126;
  27:115
Stewart, C. W. 10:138;
  20:356
Stewart, Cajor 22:103
Stewart, Chandler 21:392
Stewart, Charles 7:61,
  111; 10:175; 12:158;
  19:196; 21:218
Stewart, Charles C.
  14:303; 17:474;
  27:116
Stewart, Charles E. 1:71
Stewart, Charles P. 9:225;
  18:377
Stewart, Clark 22:15, 173
Stewart, Coleman 6:19;
  18:94
Stewart, Collins B. 20:13
Stewart, Columbus 5:30
Stewart, D. 14:290;
  23:170
Stewart, D. J. 21:392
Stewart, Daniel 6:10;
  10:138; 18:94;
  20:356
Stewart, Daniel A. 19:36
Stewart, Daniel T. 17:350
Stewart, David 10:93;
  11:213; 15:9; 22:156;
  23:125
Stewart, David H. 7:112;
  21:392
Stewart, Dennis 18:94
Stewart, E. 3:186; 25:238
Stewart, E. A. 1:76

Stewart, E. B. 3:186
Stewart, E. W. 3:186;
  7:111
Stewart, Eddie 20:356
Stewart, Edward 9:136;
  13:120
Stewart, Edwin 16:305
Stewart, Elias 22:169
Stewart, Elijah 7:112;
  17:151; 21:392
Stewart, Elish 17:308
Stewart, Elisha 9:194
Stewart, Emma Carrie
  20:157
Stewart, Ephram 15:89
Stewart, Ezekiel W. 7:111
Stewart, F. 14:113; 19:262
Stewart, F. M. 15:310
Stewart, Frank 7:134;
  15:60
Stewart, Franklin 9:194;
  13:135; 15:314;
  19:102, 347
Stewart, G. 7:54; 10:29
Stewart, G. L. 14:113
Stewart, G. M. 8:56;
  20:129
Stewart, G. W. 9:151;
  27:108
Stewart, George 4:56;
  6:26; 9:194; 13:120;
  16:124, 153; 17:399;
  19:307; 21:285
Stewart, George M. 21:80
Stewart, George W. 9:136;
  16:153
Stewart, H. 13:99; 14:22
Stewart, H. A. 14:113
Stewart, H. B. 4:56;
  22:345
Stewart, H. V. 25:71
Stewart, H. Y. 2:17
Stewart, Hamilton 14:223
Stewart, Henry 1:72;
  13:59; 15:345;
  16:379; 17:357;
  18:39, 195, 281;
  19:323; 21:285
Stewart, Hezekiah 15:230
Stewart, Hugh 18:346
Stewart, Isaac H. 9:136;
  27:112
Stewart, J. 1:72, 175;
  3:186; 7:42; 11:169,
  173; 14:113, 260;
  15:153, 345; 16:230,
  379; 19:244; 20:149;
  25:238
Stewart, J. B. 3:186;
  14:223
Stewart, J. C. 13:69

Stewart, J. E. 9:151;
12:10; 27:108
Stewart, J. F. 17:426;
22:287; 24:180
Stewart, J. H. 5:54; 7:42
Stewart, J. M. 14:113
Stewart, J. N. 1:169; 5:30
Stewart, J. P. 23:51
Stewart, J. W. 3:186
Stewart, Jackson 4:56;
24:115
Stewart, Jacob 11:43;
22:411
Stewart, James 1:71; 6:19;
7:70; 8:75; 9:59, 69,
105, 136, 194;
11:130; 15:230, 284;
16:7; 17:317; 18:95,
223; 20:191; 22:103;
23:51
Stewart, James H. 8:32;
11:397; 18:161
Stewart, James R. 20:129
Stewart, James S. 21:132;
22:55
Stewart, James W. 17:424;
24:175
Stewart, Jarvis W. 19:196
Stewart, Jerome 22:285
Stewart, Jerry M. 23:51
Stewart, John 1:71, 72,
75; 3:186; 7:134;
8:122; 9:194; 10:151,
178; 11:167; 12:97;
14:113; 15:362;
17:43; 18:281;
19:102; 20:177;
21:81, 392; 24:108;
25:238
Stewart, John A. 9:29;
18:316; 22:491;
23:287; 26:111;
27:116
Stewart, John B. 11:172
Stewart, John C. 19:102;
23:169
Stewart, John E. 9:151
Stewart, John H. 22:131,
156
Stewart, John J. 17:43;
22:114, 524
Stewart, John L. 22:55
Stewart, John M. 8:32;
18:161
Stewart, John P. 8:32;
20:13
Stewart, John R. 12:41
Stewart, John S. 3:186
Stewart, John W. 17:295;
23:51, 278

Stewart, Joseph 7:54;
9:126; 10:97; 22:103
Stewart, Joseph H. 2:17
Stewart, Joseph P. 18:161
Stewart, Joshua 9:136
Stewart, L. D. 5:30;
25:238
Stewart, Lawrence 4:68
Stewart, Lee H. 26:181
Stewart, Levi 16:230
Stewart, Littleton 5:46
Stewart, Lyman 27:117
Stewart, Lyman L.
14:303; 17:472
Stewart, M. 5:46
Stewart, M. B. 17:504
Stewart, Manassa 17:474
Stewart, Manassah 14:303
Stewart, Marshall 18:72
Stewart, Martin 7:112
Stewart, Martin V. 20:109
Stewart, Marvin 18:377
Stewart, Matthew 6:23
Stewart, Michael 7:134
Stewart, Morrow 20:356
Stewart, N. 19:102
Stewart, N. J. 18:95
Stewart, N. M. 7:111
Stewart, O. F. 3:186
Stewart, O. L. 1:171
Stewart, Oliver R. 13:80;
16:230
Stewart, Orlando 17:347
Stewart, Otis 9:225;
18:377
Stewart, Peter 3:186; 8:75
Stewart, Philemon P.
22:103
Stewart, Phillip 17:495
Stewart, Pleasant 22:440
Stewart, R. 1:74; 15:230
Stewart, R. H. 3:186
Stewart, R. J. 23:169
Stewart, R. L. 14:260;
20:356
Stewart, R. S. 13:120
Stewart, Richard 7:134;
23:110
Stewart, Robert 8:32;
9:73; 11:19, 221;
13:49; 17:43, 93;
18:161; 25:238
Stewart, Robert B. 23:287
Stewart, Robert L. 10:82;
11:19, 221
Stewart, S. 15:301;
16:230; 25:238
Stewart, S. B. 16:124
Stewart, S. H. 27:118
Stewart, S. T. F. 18:72

Stewart, Samuel 7:112;
8:96; 17:43; 22:103
Stewart, Samuel J. 17:72
Stewart, Samuel T. 15:75
Stewart, Solomon 22:55
Stewart, Stanley 15:230
Stewart, Stephen 8:96
Stewart, T. 1:172
Stewart, T. C. 11:173
Stewart, T. L. 11:169
Stewart, T. T. 21:42
Stewart, Theodore 16:131
Stewart, Thomas 7:42;
9:136; 11:169;
19:349; 22:222;
27:111
Stewart, Thomas F.
22:114
Stewart, Thomas G.
20:129
Stewart, Thomas H.
23:101
Stewart, Thomas J. 17:261
Stewart, Thomas P. 11:75
Stewart, Thomas R. 10:82
Stewart, W. 1:175; 7:42;
11:329; 14:113;
15:357; 16:282;
17:150; 19:277;
25:238
Stewart, W. A. 3:186;
20:356
Stewart, W. H. 14:223
Stewart, W. J. 6:8;
23:170; 26:182
Stewart, W. R. 6:8
Stewart, W. T. 9:65
Stewart, Watson 22:270
Stewart, William 9:194,
234; 10:23, 82, 138,
211; 11:77; 12:158;
17:59, 451; 18:431;
20:356; 22:222;
23:93; 25:327
Stewart, William A.
10:82; 20:356;
24:179
Stewart, William C.
20:157
Stewart, William E.
21:235
Stewart, William F.
11:277; 13:49; 16:57
Stewart, William H.
22:103; 23:116
Stewart, William J. 18:115
Stewart, William M.
16:103; 17:204;
20:356
Stewart, William N. 10:82

Stewart, William R. 18:115
Stewart, Willis 4:56
Stewer, Herman 20:36
Stewfield, J. 17:97
Sthler, Anton 25:72
Sthroe, Daniel 20:356
Sthrole, Daniel 10:82
Stiarlout, Addison 18:161
Stibbs, W. 3:186
Stiber, David 15:354
Stice, J. E. 14:113
Stich, Henry 1:76
Stichel, William 15:161
Stichfield, C. 14:223
Stichlo, Peter 18:254
Stichter, G. 14:223
Stick, Francis 7:112
Stick, John 11:169
Stick, T. 1:176
Stickdant, David 8:96
Stickel, B. S. 12:162
Stickel, Joseph 27:116
Stickel, L. P. 7:42
Stickel, Schimp 4:56
Stickens, W. A. 7:112
Stickeny, William C. 15:12
Stickert, J. 14:22
Stickforth, John 18:115
Stickland, A. 1:75
Stickland, J. Z. 9:59
Stickle, --- 16:230
Stickle, Christian 7:112
Stickle, Frederick W. 22:55
Stickle, John A. 8:56
Stickleman, John 23:80
Sticklep, James 16:136
Stickler, Daniel 15:230
Stickler, H. 17:433
Stickler, Harrison 24:155
Stickler, Jacob 9:39
Stickler, Mathias 21:392
Stickler, S. 14:113
Stickler, Silas 11:169
Stickles, E. 3:187; 11:249
Stickles, E. J. 10:149; 18:58
Stickley, Alfred 9:202
Stickley, C. 3:186
Stickley, Samuel 14:113
Sticklin, Thomas 10:30
Sticklin, W. 10:30; 11:250
Sticklo, Peter 26:61
Stickner, Allen G. 26:111
Stickner, Allen J. 18:316
Stickner, William 9:126
Stickney, --- 9:194; 19:242

Stickney, David W. 19:196
Stickney, F. B. 1:73
Stickney, James P. 10:97
Stickney, Joseph 24:204
Stickney, Mose W. 12:41
Stickney, S. M. 17:68
Stickney, Thomas 21:392
Sticknor, William 27:114
Stid, Isaac 22:223
Stid, J. 1:172
Stidd, Alexander 12:158
Stidd, David 11:320
Stidell, William 14:113
Stidham, F. H. 7:42
Stidham, Joseph K. 7:15
Stidman, Oliver 22:439
Stiedman, Charles H. 16:57
Stiel, A. 26:213
Stiels, J. B. 14:114
Stien, Albert 18:335
Stien Stra, Dirk 21:143
Stiener, Jacob 22:131
Stiener, John 18:115
Stienheout, John 25:335
Stienman, Barnhart 22:55
Stier, Christian 16:144
Stierhof, George W. 22:398
Stiers, Andrew G. 22:439
Stiers, J. H. 22:223
Stiers, John 11:313
Stiers, William N. 11:171
Stiff, A. 25:238
Stiff, Alfred 5:46
Stiff, David D. 22:156
Stiff, George 25:238
Stiff, George C. 21:392
Stiff, Micajah 23:102
Stiff, William H. 23:243
Stiffenhaden, C. 25:238
Stiffenhoden, C. 5:30
Stiffer, Edward 8:67
Stiffers, R. 3:187
Stiffey, F. 21:42
Stiffey, W. B. 14:113
Stiffey, William A. 22:223
Stiffin, August 23:51
Stiffler, John R. 22:223
Stiffler, William J. 3:187
Stiffy, Robert L. 20:356
Stiflen, Edward 26:183
Stifler, H. 1:171
Stifler, Philip 17:87
Stifner, C. W. 11:87
Stigall, George 17:186
Stigall, John 11:44
Stigell, John 18:161
Stiger, C. S. 22:223
Stigerman, William 12:63

Stigler, S. 1:176
Stigman, John 12:63; 15:93
Stikel, D. 3:187
Stiker, G. H. 24:31
Stile, Harper 26:61
Stiles, A. 13:99
Stiles, Alonzo 9:39; 18:297; 26:112
Stiles, Daniel M. 10:93; 20:356
Stiles, E. R. 1:176
Stiles, Ed 17:441
Stiles, Edgar G. 24:155
Stiles, Elijah H. 10:93; 20:356
Stiles, F. 15:346
Stiles, F. C. 16:379
Stiles, G. 1:173
Stiles, G. D. 9:194
Stiles, George 26:181
Stiles, George W. 3:187; 15:75
Stiles, Henry C. 20:149
Stiles, Homer 20:32
Stiles, Isaac 12:88; 16:305
Stiles, J. 14:114
Stiles, J. M. 25:67
Stiles, Jacob 16:115
Stiles, John 18:377
Stiles, Joseph 21:205
Stiles, Joshua L. 24:56
Stiles, L. 13:49
Stiles, M. D. 11:270
Stiles, Margaret 26:226
Stiles, R. R. 18:377
Stiles, Robert R. 9:225
Stiles, S. B. 9:194; 19:230
Stiles, Samuel 4:56
Stiles, Stephen 18:401
Stiles, T. A. 13:120
Stiles, Warner 11:112
Stiles, Warren 22:467
Stiles, William 9:67; 18:105, 281
Stiles, William S. 6:9
Stiles, William W. 17:210
Still, Arnold 10:187; 18:180
Still, Charles B. 23:80
Still, D. 3:187
Still, George 9:99; 12:52; 14:223
Still, Isaac 16:57
Still, Isaiah 20:101
Still, J. 25:238
Still, Jerry 5:46
Still, John 9:92; 14:223; 21:392
Still, Samuel 14:223; 17:315

Still, Tobias 16:57
Still, W. H. 1:70
Still, William 11:405; 20:356
Stiller, John 1:72
Stiller, Robert 22:55
Stillhamer, William 19:102
Stilling, A. 9:92
Stilling, Hanson 16:57
Stillings, George M. 12:100
Stillman, A. 9:194; 19:262
Stillman, C. D. 1:175
Stillman, F. W. 21:392
Stillman, Henderson 25:327
Stillman, John H. 12:52
Stills, Samuel 16:103
Stillson, Amos H. 13:49
Stillson, George W. 7:42
Stillwater, --- 15:230
Stillwell, A. C. 21:392
Stillwell, Amos 10:82
Stillwell, Barnett 11:194
Stillwell, C. 16:231
Stillwell, Charles W. 21:235
Stillwell, D. H. 11:296
Stillwell, Hattan 20:105
Stillwell, Henry M. 5:30
Stillwell, J. 14:271
Stillwell, J. F. 1:173
Stillwell, J. H. 3:187
Stillwell, James 12:10, 41
Stillwell, James B. 11:44
Stillwell, John 3:187; 14:285
Stillwell, L. D. 3:187
Stillwell, O. A. 13:120
Stillwell, Stephen M. 17:59
Stillwell, Thomas 21:81
Stillwell, W. 1:95; 16:231
Stillwell, W. M. 10:187
Stillwell, William 24:45
Stillwell, William W. 10:168
Stillwill, W. M. 18:180
Stilman, Henry 13:120
Stilmers, T. J. 10:212
Stilnecker, Tilman 10:212
Stilnell, Amos 20:356
Stilson, --- 13:80; 16:231
Stilson, A. 1:75
Stilson, Harris 23:110
Stilson, J. 12:162
Stilson, Joseph 9:194
Stilson, Lyman 20:194
Stilson, Samuel 12:41
Stilson, Thomas 26:60

Stilton, T. 13:99
Stilts, Isaac 22:55
Stilts, W. 17:59
Stiltson, Lawrence 9:105
Stiltz, Martin 8:96
Stilwell, Clark 12:77
Stilwell, Cornelius 23:125
Stilwell, H. W. 25:238
Stilwell, Martin 18:254; 26:63
Stilwell, W. H. 25:238
Stilwell, William W. 19:196
Stilzle, Alonzo F. 23:170
Stimmeretz, G. 7:54
Stimour, Solomon 12:41
Stimp, David M. 22:506
Stimpson, Albert R. 1:72
Stimpson, F. E. 1:168
Stimpson, Th. 21:42
Stimpson, William M. 22:439
Stimson, James 26:225
Stinbacker, J. 1:168
Stince, E. 1:76
Stinchcomb, E. C. 14:223
Stinchfield, A. W. 4:56
Stinchfield, C. A. 21:392
Stinchfield, Daniel 20:19
Stindts, Frans 25:327
Stine, --- 20:89
Stine, A. 3:187
Stine, C. 3:187
Stine, Charles 12:60
Stine, David 10:82; 20:356
Stine, F. 1:77
Stine, Jacob 7:43
Stine, Jacob C. 22:156
Stine, John 3:187; 11:117; 15:320; 19:103
Stine, Joseph 8:32; 18:161
Stine, P. 3:187
Stine, Philip L. 17:68
Stine, S. L. 3:187
Stine, Samuel 20:116
Stine, Thomas 3:187
Stine, W. 11:271; 25:327
Stine, William H. 18:211
Stineback, Peter 22:103
Stinebaugh, Lewis 12:41
Stinebreaker, James K. 8:96
Stinech, John 7:134
Stinecker, S. S. 15:230
Stineford, Amos 4:56
Stinehour, W. N. P. 25:238
Stiner, Bazel 11:121
Stiner, Gotlieb 3:224
Stiner, Henry J. 22:492

Stiner, J. 1:175
Stiner, John 3:187
Stiner, W. H. 3:224
Stiner, William H. 17:505
Stines, David 22:270
Stines, H. 1:171; 3:187
Stines, Henry 16:231
Stines, J. H. 15:295
Stines, Thomas P. 21:42
Stinese, J. H. 16:231
Stiney, Charles 15:168
Stingel, James 7:112
Stinger, Frank 11:213
Stinges, Willie 26:226
Stingwood, J. 16:231
Stininger, J. D. 19:103
Stinit, D. 3:187
Stinkamp, F. 11:250
Stinkland, S. B. 1:168
Stinkle, William 22:103
Stinler, N. 11:172
Stinman, Melcher 18:161
Stinmann, Melcher 8:32
Stinner, John 19:103
Stinnett, Hugh 8:32; 18:161
Stinnett, John 22:345
Stinnett, Reuben 23:102
Stinnett, William 10:82; 20:356
Stinocker, Charles 7:112
Stinor, John 20:356
Stinset, B. 18:254; 26:63
Stinson, --- 8:96
Stinson, A. 25:238
Stinson, A. H. 5:30
Stinson, Ambrose N. 22:131
Stinson, D. 21:106
Stinson, D. G. 25:312
Stinson, E. 8:67; 26:183
Stinson, Edward 16:153
Stinson, Eugene 21:143
Stinson, F. J. 14:335
Stinson, Gilbert 7:134
Stinson, Harrel 17:59
Stinson, Harvey 22:457
Stinson, Isaac 21:143
Stinson, John 8:96; 15:230; 18:223
Stinson, N. A. 21:168
Stinson, Roland 17:59
Stinson, Thomas 19:49; 22:321
Stinson, W. W. 9:194
Stinson, Warren B. 15:230
Stinson, William 9:7; 14:223; 22:55
Stint, G. T. 9:92
Stintz, John I. 11:170
Stipe, Andrew W. 11:270

Stipe, James 11:271
Stipe, Pleasant 23:80
Stipes, Reuben 16:305
Stipes, Thomas 7:112
Stipes, William 17:261
Stires, A. 20:149
Stires, D. 23:206
Stires, John 21:128
Stirgan, H. W. 21:60
Stirk, W. I. 12:158
Stirling, F. M. 14:114
Stirling, Joseph 9:73
Stirling, Southey 16:131
Stitch, --- 12:41
Stiteler, C. B. 11:17
Stiter, Drp. 20:129
Stites, John T. 24:70
Stith, Gabriel B. 11:171
Stith, Samuel 13:59
Stitson, Thomas 9:92
Stitt, Amos 22:441
Stittinberger, J. 3:187
Stittwell, S. 3:187
Stivens, Robert 12:158
Stiver, A. 1:168
Stiver, Ambrose W.
    10:175
Stiver, David 16:282
Stiver, J. 3:187
Stiver, W. W. 18:39
Stivers, Abraham 20:356
Stivers, Abram 22:238
Stivers, Amb. W. 19:196
Stivers, George 11:313;
    18:223
Stivers, J. 25:238
Stivers, Jackson 5:46
Stivers, John G. 22:411
Stivers, R. 3:187
Stizer, S. 1:168
Stnaford, Hiram 12:56
Stoaks, Adam T. 23:125
Stoan, D. 11:314
Stoar, O. 25:238
Stoarn, William J. 18:161
Stoat, John 8:68
Stobaugh, Ananias 10:82
Stobaugh, Thomas W.
    8:32
Stobbs, W. 8:56; 21:42
Stobbs, W. W. 3:187
Stobel, C. S. 7:61
Stoble, E. L. 11:169
Stobray, John 7:112
Stobunght, Thomas W.
    18:161
Stoby, Edward 21:392
Stocer, J. 25:238
Stochas, Areustas 8:56
Stock, Abram 11:168

Stock, Christian 10:23;
    11:130; 12:41
Stock, David 23:51
Stock, H. 24:215
Stock, H. C. 14:114
Stock, Herman J. 16:57
Stock, J. 12:88
Stock, John 12:41
Stock, M. 25:327
Stock, Samuel 20:93
Stockbridge, C. H. 27:106
Stockbridge, J. T. 1:174
Stockdale, Benjamin M.
    11:170
Stockdale, William 9:92;
    11:169
Stockdale, William F.
    11:392
Stockdell, Jacob 7:61
Stocken, D. 8:75
Stocker, C. B. 14:259
Stocker, Charles 23:51
Stocker, Jacob 15:280
Stocker, John F. 21:392
Stocker, Josiah 7:112
Stocker, S. 3:187
Stocker, William 11:213
Stockesvery, I. 20:357
Stocket, Samuel 9:17
Stockham, William
    11:314
Stockhart, George 27:115
Stockhausen, Charles
    12:41
Stockhoff, G. 3:187
Stockholms, John 10:138
Stockhouse, D. 3:187
Stockin, Edward H.
    17:362
Stocking, Gilbert M.
    20:357
Stocking, Gilbert U.
    10:138
Stocking, James 6:10
Stocking, R. 1:174
Stockinger, John W.
    21:197
Stockinger, Samuel
    20:101
Stockings, J. 18:95
Stockle, Christopher
    25:238
Stockle, David 13:120
Stockle, John 5:30;
    25:238
Stockley, E. W. 19:196
Stockley, John 25:238
Stockling, William H.
    15:327
Stockman, Jesse 21:392

Stockman, John W.
    16:131
Stockman, L. M. 3:187
Stockman, W. H. 27:117
Stockman, William H.
    14:303; 17:481
Stocks, John 20:357
Stocks, William A. 8:68
Stockstill, William 23:251
Stockston, S. A. 20:357
Stockstone, J. D. 14:114
Stockton, A. L. 15:113
Stockton, Benjamin
    18:414
Stockton, E. D. 9:92;
    26:61
Stockton, F. J. 8:67
Stockton, J. D. 14:114
Stockton, James A. 10:138
Stockton, James M.
    20:357
Stockton, James P. 22:131
Stockton, John 16:124
Stockton, John C. 20:33
Stockton, L. K. 10:180
Stockton, L. W. 18:180
Stockton, Louis C. 23:257
Stockton, M. 21:113
Stockton, Robert 22:55
Stockton, S. 24:31
Stockton, S. A. 10:82
Stockton, T. J. 26:183
Stockton, Thomas 17:326
Stockton, William H.
    19:103
Stockweather, T. 18:58
Stockwell, A. 3:187
Stockwell, C. E. 1:78
Stockwell, C. H. 3:187;
    7:112
Stockwell, Charles 21:392
Stockwell, D. 14:114
Stockwell, Edward G.
    21:106
Stockwell, H. 1:72
Stockwell, L. 1:175
Stockwell, M. 12:54
Stockwell, Norman P.
    22:156
Stockwell, Orville L. 4:56
Stockwell, Simeon 12:158
Stockwell, Solomon 9:29;
    18:316; 26:112
Stockwell, William 9:194;
    11:168; 19:242
Stockwish, Henry 22:103
Stocton, Samuel 16:114
Stocze, Henry 16:57
Stodard, Solomon 17:239
Stodardy, Elisha 22:131
Stodart, M. 21:106

Stodart, Samuel 16:160
Stoddard, Asa M. 23:196
Stoddard, Charles 16:57
Stoddard, D. 25:69
Stoddard, D. W. 10:82;
  20:357
Stoddard, Daniel 16:87
Stoddard, Ed 11:121
Stoddard, Francis A.
  14:114
Stoddard, Freeman B.
  17:410; 22:156
Stoddard, H. 17:362
Stoddard, H. A. 25:74
Stoddard, Haverley A.
  2:17
Stoddard, Henry 9:126;
  27:114
Stoddard, J. 3:187
Stoddard, John 14:223
Stoddard, John F. 21:392
Stoddard, L. H. 14:223
Stoddard, Marshall
  22:103, 441
Stoddard, Milton 22:55
Stoddard, Ralph 17:245
Stoddard, S. 3:187
Stoddard, S. A. 23:51
Stoddard, S. M. 13:120
Stoddard, W. 1:170;
  18:254; 26:62
Stoddard, W. H. 1:176;
  27:115
Stoddard, William 9:160
Stoddard, William E.
  23:170
Stoddard, William J.
  9:194
Stoddart, Charles W.
  13:49
Stoddart, Orlando 16:57
Stoddart, W. S. 19:230
Stoddel, Eugene 4:56
Stodden, P. E. 15:75
Stodder, W. J. 2:18
Stodder, W. P. 25:73
Stodgehill, John 23:80
Stodghill, John S. 22:131
Stodgill, Samuel 24:162
Stodler, F. 3:187
Stodord, Samuel 12:41
Stodtard, Orlando 13:49
Stoe, S. L. 17:295
Stoeber, Gottleib 20:357
Stoeker, Carlos 12:77
Stoen, Gustavus 16:305
Stofacker, F. 3:187
Stofer, Abner 23:93
Stofer, George 22:223
Stofer, Jacob W. 21:205
Stofer, L. 3:187

Stoffield, Ray A. 16:231
Stoffil, Peter 11:194
Stofford, William T.
  17:277
Stofle, John 20:357
Stofor, John 17:16
Stogdell, William C.
  11:270
Stogel, H. R. 7:54
Stogerwald, J. A. 3:187
Stogsdill, A. 21:209
Stogsdill, Elias 22:440
Stohlen, John 11:171
Stohr, M. 1:169
Stoke, C. T. 14:114
Stokely, Catharine 27:115
Stokely, E. A. M. 27:115
Stokely, E. W. 21:201
Stokely, L. J. 27:115
Stokely, S. 27:115
Stoker, C. 22:223
Stoker, John T. 22:55
Stoker, L. 22:321
Stoker, William R. 22:223
Stokers, Archibald 21:392
Stokes, A. G. 25:238
Stokes, A. L. 24:108
Stokes, Abram J. 19:36
Stokes, Alfred 18:431
Stokes, B. B. 16:57
Stokes, C. W. 9:59
Stokes, Charles 8:56
Stokes, David 1:192
Stokes, Edward W.
  24:180
Stokes, Elisha 9:46;
  26:129
Stokes, G. 14:223
Stokes, George E. 9:17
Stokes, George M. 8:110
Stokes, Gustavus 11:170
Stokes, H. 14:285
Stokes, Handy 7:134
Stokes, Henry 1:192;
  9:29; 18:316; 26:113
Stokes, J. 21:42
Stokes, J. N. 21:42
Stokes, J. W. 22:16
Stokes, Jacob 8:110
Stokes, James 25:238
Stokes, James E. 17:59
Stokes, James M. 21:60
Stokes, John 1:72; 10:82;
  20:357
Stokes, Joseph H. 23:14
Stokes, Macklin 7:134
Stokes, Matt 25:72
Stokes, Nathan W. 23:284
Stokes, Nelson 25:286
Stokes, Oakley 5:30
Stokes, P. 17:139

Stokes, Patrick A. 17:444;
  24:162
Stokes, Peter 24:204
Stokes, Robert T. 10:82;
  20:357
Stokes, Sim 18:254; 26:64
Stokes, T. R. 22:321
Stokes, W. 1:171
Stokes, W. H. 27:107
Stokes, William C. 11:169
Stokes, William T.
  10:138; 20:357
Stokes, Willis P. 23:284
Stokesberry, John W.
  10:138; 20:357
Stokesbery, J. 11:251
Stokesbury, J. 8:56
Stokesverry, James 10:82
Stokey, William 7:43
Stole, Carle 18:161
Stolenberg, Hans 10:82
Stoley, George 14:303;
  27:117
Stolger, John 15:230
Stolger, Stephen 21:81
Stoling, W. 19:286
Stoll, A. 1:173
Stoll, Charles 27:116
Stoll, Frederick 15:60
Stoll, H. 21:126
Stoll, Joseph 11:75
Stoll, Otto 17:26
Stoll, S. W. 12:100
Stoll, Samuel 15:95
Stolla, Frederick 10:138
Stollard, L. N. 9:225
Stollard, William N.
  22:411
Stollcap, Virgil 20:139
Stolle, Carl 8:32
Stoller, Frederick 10:138;
  20:357
Stollers, I. 26:62
Stollers, J. 18:254
Stolls, William 17:186
Stolta, Frederick 20:357
Stolte, Charles 18:444
Stolte, Fred 14:114
Stoltenberg, Nicholas
  20:357
Stoltz, G. 25:327
Stoltz, George 21:126
Stoltz, H. C. 24:31
Stoltz, Jacob 26:146
Stolworth, William
  20:357
Stoly, George 17:472
Stolz, B. 3:187
Stolz, D. 3:187
Stolzer, Stephen 8:56
Stomas, N. 15:168

Stomfer, E. 13:99
Stomm, H. 1:76
Ston, John 18:17
Stonate, Mason 6:33
Stoncifer, E. 14:22
Stone, --- 9:59; 10:168; 15:273
Stone, A. 15:346; 16:380
Stone, A. G. 12:41; 20:37
Stone, A. M. 22:270
Stone, Aaron A. 9:126; 27:113
Stone, Addison J. 13:49
Stone, Alfred L. 23:93
Stone, Andrew J. 8:115
Stone, B. 1:78, 169
Stone, Benjamin 16:231
Stone, Benjamin D. 20:187
Stone, Benjamin V. 4:56
Stone, Benoni 21:126; 23:170
Stone, C. 14:223; 27:109
Stone, C. A. 19:276
Stone, C. H. 13:99; 14:22
Stone, C. M. 18:58
Stone, Charles 13:49; 14:260; 21:392; 25:327
Stone, Charles A. 21:392
Stone, Charles H. 19:36
Stone, Charles W. 12:41
Stone, Cyruc C. 22:440
Stone, D. 11:168
Stone, D. B. 19:242
Stone, D. H. 1:78
Stone, Daniel 4:56
Stone, Daniel B. 9:194
Stone, Dennis 22:321
Stone, E. A. 11:313
Stone, E. J. 24:85
Stone, E. V. 16:380
Stone, Eben B. 10:138
Stone, Ed. 16:103
Stone, Edward 15:80; 21:392
Stone, Emerson 9:194; 19:276
Stone, F. 15:346; 16:380
Stone, F. P. 3:187; 14:223
Stone, Frank 18:281
Stone, Franklin 14:223
Stone, G. 14:114
Stone, G. E. 1:170
Stone, G. H. 9:194; 19:242
Stone, G. P. 16:57
Stone, G. S. 1:76
Stone, George 9:46, 92; 11:416; 16:231; 20:175

Stone, George B. 9:73
Stone, George E. 8:32; 18:161; 26:59
Stone, George W. 22:15
Stone, H. 1:77; 5:30; 14:114
Stone, H. H. 1:173
Stone, H. J. 23:280
Stone, Henry 8:96
Stone, Henry L. 23:125
Stone, Henry T. 3:187
Stone, Henry W. 23:257
Stone, Henson 8:100
Stone, Hiram 26:129
Stone, Hiram L. 23:196
Stone, Hubert 19:103
Stone, Irvin 6:8
Stone, Irwin 18:115
Stone, Isaac 13:120
Stone, J. 1:171, 173; 7:112; 15:19; 16:231; 21:42, 209
Stone, J. A. 1:77
Stone, J. B. 27:119
Stone, J. M. 21:392
Stone, J. N. 16:57
Stone, J. P. 11:168
Stone, J. W. 16:57; 20:152
Stone, Jacob C. 4:56
Stone, James 4:56; 11:392, 416
Stone, James A. 3:187; 22:223
Stone, James C. 17:218
Stone, James H. 11:250
Stone, James W. 13:49; 20:357
Stone, Joel 10:138
Stone, John 6:35; 12:77; 13:120; 15:113, 230; 21:392; 25:327
Stone, John A. 3:187
Stone, John C. 10:97
Stone, John Q. 17:239
Stone, Joseph 19:196
Stone, Joseph G. 1:70
Stone, Joseph H. 4:56
Stone, Joseph W. 10:82
Stone, L. 3:187; 7:43; 16:103
Stone, L. S. 11:113; 15:362
Stone, Levi 19:36
Stone, Lewis H. 4:56
Stone, Madison 22:270
Stone, Marble F. 24:85
Stone, Martin 27:148
Stone, Milton 10:138; 16:231; 20:357
Stone, N. R. 26:225

Stone, O. F. 14:285
Stone, Osne 4:56
Stone, P. 14:114
Stone, Peter 11:336; 19:323
Stone, Philander 16:103
Stone, R. 9:194; 19:271
Stone, R. F. 22:223
Stone, R. S. 15:113
Stone, Reuben 21:132
Stone, Rice 17:399
Stone, Richard E. 17:289
Stone, Robert 13:49; 16:57; 17:186; 22:55
Stone, Roderick 8:122
Stone, S. 12:124; 14:114; 16:231; 21:392
Stone, S. C. 24:31
Stone, S. D. 8:56
Stone, S. F. 25:67
Stone, S. L. 19:103
Stone, Samuel 3:187; 6:19; 7:43; 10:138; 18:95; 20:357
Stone, Sidney S. 22:492
Stone, Solomon 10:138; 11:213; 20:357
Stone, Stephen 8:32
Stone, Stern 18:161
Stone, Sylvanus 9:92; 26:59
Stone, T. 15:280; 25:238
Stone, T. J. 18:254; 26:62
Stone, Tato 7:134
Stone, Thomas 2:17; 25:73
Stone, Thomas F. 23:185
Stone, Thomas I. 8:32
Stone, Thomas J. 18:161
Stone, Vanrensaller W. 10:138
Stone, Vanrunsaller W. 20:357
Stone, Vincent 22:439
Stone, W. 1:172; 9:114; 14:114; 25:68
Stone, W. B. 20:357
Stone, W. D. 18:254; 26:63
Stone, W. F. 3:187
Stone, W. G. 17:435
Stone, W. H. 14:245
Stone, W. J. 1:170
Stone, Walter 13:49
Stone, Wesley 26:226
Stone, William 5:30; 12:41; 21:392; 25:70
Stone, William B. 10:138
Stone, William E. 21:392
Stone, William F. 10:23
Stone, William G. 24:180

Stone, William H. 10:168; 22:131
Stone, Wilson B. 10:23
Stoneback, F. 25:67
Stonebarger, Charles 7:112
Stonebarger, Charles L. 21:392
Stoneberger, Caper 12:41
Stoneberger, George W. 9:101
Stonebraker, William 13:69
Stonebreaker, Frederick 15:230
Stonebreaker, John 8:96
Stonebrook, John 13:49
Stonebrook, Joseph 9:92; 26:58
Stonebrook, R. 1:171
Stonebuck, F. 2:17
Stonebumer, Josiah 5:30
Stoneburner, Isaac 10:138; 20:357
Stoneburner, James S. 7:43
Stoneburner, John F. 22:223
Stoneburner, S. S. 11:342
Stoneking, Lewis 10:138; 20:357
Stoneking, Washington 9:46; 26:130
Stoneman, --- 1:104
Stoneman, E. W. 16:380
Stoneman, J. W. 1:75
Stoneman, Joseph N. 20:44
Stoneman, P. 23:170
Stoneman, William 15:230; 17:429; 24:186
Stonemetz, William 25:70
Stoner, Alexis 14:223
Stoner, Andrew 22:439
Stoner, C. 23:170
Stoner, D. 18:58; 22:516
Stoner, Daniel 22:103
Stoner, Decatur 22:223
Stoner, Egerton 9:204
Stoner, Elias 11:213
Stoner, G. W. 21:164
Stoner, George 25:72; 26:129
Stoner, H. G. W. 1:77
Stoner, J. 1:169
Stoner, James 11:222
Stoner, John H. 21:235
Stoner, John S. 17:43
Stoner, Michael 23:182
Stoner, Philip 7:61

Stoner, Samuel J. 11:111
Stoner, Thomas J. 23:93
Stoner, William 11:77
Stoner, William A. 23:80
Stoner, William B. L. 22:491
Stoner, William H. 22:131
Stoner, William K. 23:170
Stonerook, David 4:56
Stones, T. 3:187
Stones, Thomas 14:114
Stonesifer, Josiah 13:49
Stoney, Garnett 16:231
Stoneycipher, Samuel 1:74
Stongatle, George 14:223
Stonham, M. 1:75
Stonic, William 1:70
Stonking, J. A. 15:60
Stonmont, William 13:49
Stonte, M. 25:327
Stood, John 2:17; 25:73
Stook, John H. 22:439
Stookel, F. L. 16:231
Stookey, William E. 4:56
Stookey, William R. 23:80
Stookley, John H. 1:73
Stooks, James 5:54
Stooks, Peter 9:136; 27:112
Stooks, S. 14:114
Stooks, William 19:49
Stoole, John 26:59
Stooley, Franklin 8:43
Stools, John 9:92
Stoom, James A. 11:250
Stoop, Francis 25:281
Stooples, J. 16:231
Stoops, H. 1:172
Stoops, John 4:56
Stoops, Pleasant 17:296
Stoops, William N. 18:223
Stoops, William W. 23:170
Stoothoof, William 5:30·
Stop, Trussant 21:393
Stop, Walter 25:335
Stoper, M. 20:357
Stopes, S. W. 3:187
Stophine, Anthony 26:113
Stopper, John 23:125
Stopper, Sebastian 15:19
Stopper, William 3:187
Stopples, A. 14:114
Stopps, W. H. 9:151
Stops, John G. 12:158
Storbell, M. 18:95
Storch, C. 14:114
Storck, Herman J. 13:49
Store, John 21:393

Storell, J. B. 8:56
Storer, G. 1:70
Storer, J. 9:151
Storer, J. W. 11:45
Storer, John 19:36
Storer, S. S. 12:97
Storer, William 17:87; 25:238
Storer, William D. 22:467
Stores, William 16:231
Storey, A. H. 21:393
Storey, F. 14:114
Storey, James 23:51
Storey, Jay 9:105
Storey, John 7:65
Storey, John D. 9:29
Storey, John M. 9:105
Storey, N. R. 25:305
Storey, William 26:111
Storie, N. C. 11:426
Storil, C. N. 19:103
Storing, A. 3:187
Stork, A. 12:10
Stork, J. 19:103
Stork, Jos. 8:110
Stork, Lawrence 22:223
Storkley, Jesse 7:134
Storkman, Frederic 17:72
Storksbury, S. 11:188
Storm, A. 10:149; 18:58
Storm, David 25:238
Storm, E. 3:187
Storm, Francis A. 21:235
Storm, Harvey 6:19; 18:95
Storm, Henry 15:93
Storm, I. 3:187
Storm, J. M. 23:170
Storm, James 4:56
Storm, John 10:138; 20:357
Storm, John A. 18:223
Storm, Joseph 12:84
Storm, L. 21:393
Storm, S. M. 3:187
Stormbaugh, Martin 21:85
Storme, Peter 15:367
Stormes, A. N. 3:187
Stormes, Charles H. 11:130
Stormes, H. 8:75
Stormes, J. B. 9:136
Stormout, William 16:57
Storms, David 4:56
Storms, George L. 27:111
Storms, H. 26:181
Storms, Peter 10:9
Storms, S. E. 25:238
Stornes, William 15:314; 19:103
Storre, B. H. 1:71
Storrs, A. 21:118

Storrs, Daniel C. 5:30
Storrs, H. H. 21:393
Storts, James W. 7:43
Story, Andrew J. 20:14
Story, David 12:41
Story, E. 1:169
Story, Frederick S. 22:491
Story, George 27:119
Story, George W. 21:243
Story, H. W. 23:125
Story, Henry 18:39
Story, I. 18:341
Story, Isaac S. 10:23
Story, J. N. 21:42
Story, James 11:393
Story, John 11:44; 17:71;
    18:341; 22:345
Story, John D. 18:316;
    26:113
Story, John O. 19:196
Story, Marcus P. 22:55
Story, Nelson A. 14:335
Story, R. A. 25:67
Story, Robert 18:414
Story, Rolin G. 22:56
Story, S. 21:199
Story, Squire A. 21:235
Story, T. B. 25:74
Story, William 9:29;
    13:49; 16:57;
    18:316; 22:103
Story, William B. 21:114
Story, William P. 22:506
Story, William W. 16:153
Stosberg, Gottlieb 10:138
Stoser, Junatoz 13:49
Stoss, John B. 19:334
Stotler, H. H. 1:75
Stotler, Henry 17:388
Stotler, John O. 22:223
Stots, John 3:187
Stots, John L. 11:78
Stott, E. 23:51
Stott, Isaac 22:238
Stott, Joseph 5:30; 25:238
Stott, S. W. 15:367
Stott, Thomas 1:75
Stott, William 16:380
Stottard, J. 1:77
Stottard, John 16:124
Stottenberg, Nicholas
    10:138
Stotts, Benjamin 23:253
Stotts, David L. 7:112
Stotts, Francis A. 22:169
Stotts, Mayze 22:103
Stouber, Joseph 4:56
Stoubley, Godfill 10:82
Stoubly, Godfill 20:357
Stoud, M. 17:143
Stouder, John F. 21:393

Stouder, Moses 1:71
Stoudt, E. L. 13:120
Stoudt, Gideon 15:355
Stouffer, J. E. 13:120
Stouffer, Peter 18:195
Stouffer, William 10:25
Stough, --- 14:114
Stough, Horner 17:43
Stough, I. S. 15:230
Stough, J. H. 11:417
Stough, Joseph 11:312
Stough, S. E. 22:223
Stoughton, Andrew 4:56
Stoughton, Benjamin F.
    17:47
Stoup, David 16:124
Stous, M. H. 18:195
Stous, Walter 1:73
Stout, --- 2:18; 3:187;
    15:264
Stout, A. 17:43
Stout, A. I. 8:32
Stout, A. J. 18:161
Stout, Algernon 27:148
Stout, Ambrose 22:103
Stout, Benjamin F. 19:196
Stout, C. 10:30
Stout, Charles 3:187;
    9:239; 19:338
Stout, D. B. 13:120
Stout, Daniel 11:171
Stout, David D. 3:224;
    17:505
Stout, E. W. 10:82;
    20:357
Stout, Edward R. 9:211
Stout, Elias 24:180
Stout, Ephraim 21:106
Stout, F. B. 5:46
Stout, Felix 24:85
Stout, Franklin 10:138;
    20:357
Stout, G. H. 12:97
Stout, G. N. 19:103
Stout, George 10:82;
    20:357
Stout, George K. 22:223
Stout, George W. 23:80
Stout, H. 3:187
Stout, H. H. 25:73
Stout, Harrison 25:238
Stout, Henry 18:195;
    19:196
Stout, Ira 22:103
Stout, Irvin K. 22:270
Stout, Isaac 17:87
Stout, Isah 10:138
Stout, Isaiah 12:57;
    17:399; 20:357
Stout, J. 1:169
Stout, J. H. 1:171

Stout, J. L. 26:225
Stout, Jacob 20:37, 116
Stout, Jacob W. 22:270
Stout, James 13:59; 15:23
Stout, James A. 26:60
Stout, James W. 20:357
Stout, Joel 20:357
Stout, John 3:187; 18:39,
    458; 20:357; 23:80;
    26:146
Stout, John C. 21:42
Stout, John J. 18:161
Stout, John W. 11:188
Stout, Johnson 7:43
Stout, Joseph 23:280
Stout, Joshua W. 10:82
Stout, Josiah 9:59
Stout, L. 1:176; 3:187
Stout, Lewis 12:41
Stout, Loyd 8:96
Stout, M. 16:103
Stout, N. L. 9:238
Stout, Oliver B. 11:392
Stout, P. 15:75
Stout, Peter 8:75
Stout, Ralph E. 20:32
Stout, Richard 6:19; 18:95
Stout, Samuel 7:112
Stout, Solomon 20:101
Stout, T. D. 25:238
Stout, Thomas 4:56;
    17:186
Stout, Thomas F. 22:56
Stout, W. H. 27:117
Stout, W. R. 17:482
Stout, W. W. 23:170
Stout, Willard 21:393
Stout, William 9:126;
    22:439; 27:113
Stout, William E. 11:188
Stout, William H. 14:303;
    21:261
Stout, William L. 22:103
Stout, William P. 22:103
Stout, Zebedee 22:223
Stout, Zeville 7:43
Stoutenburg, William C.
    12:41
Stouts, Samson 3:187
Stoutsebarger, George
    22:238
Stoval, C. A. 12:97
Stovall, David P. 9:194
Stovall, George W. 17:59
Stovall, I. B. 21:42
Stovall, J. William 11:121
Stovall, Jerry 22:516
Stovall, Obadiah 9:194
Stovall, Samuel 20:50
Stove, Thomas 24:103
Stoveale, O. 19:284

Stoveall, David J. 19:284
Stoveall, L. F. 19:230
Stovell, C. A. 15:362
Stovell, Charles 16:231
Stovell, W. 26:181
Stovene, Anthony 9:29
Stover, A. 3:188
Stover, Andrew N. 13:49
Stover, Andrew W. 16:57
Stover, C. L. 17:295
Stover, David 11:416
Stover, Elisha B. 24:70
Stover, G. 17:435
Stover, G. O. 20:44
Stover, George 13:49
Stover, George R. 24:180
Stover, George W. 23:14
Stover, J. 1:168
Stover, J. F. 27:110
Stover, Joel 24:155
Stover, John 3:187; 11:78;
    13:49
Stover, John H. 23:51
Stover, John W. 24:85
Stover, L. 11:251
Stover, Matthew 21:235
Stover, Obediah 22:287
Stover, Oliver 14:223
Stover, S. 22:223
Stover, S. D. 1:71
Stover, Thomas F. 21:393
Stover, William 26:61
Stover, William M. 23:93
Stover, William R. 11:194
Stovers, David 11:312
Stow, Austin 7:54
Stow, C. W. 12:158
Stow, Charles M. 9:244
Stow, David B. 10:138;
    20:357
Stow, G. W. 3:188
Stow, George 3:188
Stow, John 7:43
Stow, Robertson 8:32;
    18:161
Stowall, C. K. 7:112
Stowall, H. 21:164
Stowall, M. A. 24:31
Stowall, Thomas 22:516
Stowars, William 19:278
Stowder, W. Q. 17:204
Stowe, A. 3:188
Stowe, Durand W. 19:196
Stowe, G. 19:196
Stowe, G. F. 14:114
Stowe, George 25:70
Stowe, H. 25:238
Stowe, J. 25:275
Stowe, John B. 21:143
Stowe, R. 27:109
Stowe, Walter 27:113

Stowe, Walter W. 9:126
Stowe, William H. 21:261
Stowell, Asa W. 9:14
Stowell, B. H. 23:51
Stowell, Byron S. 13:49
Stowell, Charles 21:81
Stowell, Eugene N.
    22:163
Stowell, F. M. 16:103
Stowell, Frank L. 4:56
Stowell, G. W. 21:393
Stowell, George 24:97
Stowell, George D. 19:103
Stowell, H. 25:239
Stowell, H. G. 21:393
Stowell, H. H. 11:220
Stowell, Harvey 5:30
Stowell, Ira 19:196
Stowell, John 13:99;
    16:103
Stowell, L. M. 17:499
Stowell, Marshall 4:56
Stowell, Meyron E. 25:74
Stowell, N. J. 19:262
Stowell, R. G. 25:279
Stowell, William 16:231
Stowell, Wilson M. 9:194;
    19:262
Stower, E. N. 18:72
Stower, H. 1:172
Stower, Henry M. 19:36
Stower, J. 3:188
Stowers, Andrew 17:275
Stowers, R. W. 9:68
Stowers, Samuel 4:68
Stowers, Stephen 11:77
Stowers, William 9:194
Stowley, Franklin 26:180
Stows, Charles W. 21:393
Stowtenger, Jo 16:103
Stoy, Eli H. 22:223
Stoy, Franklin 22:223
Stoyden, Joseph 8:32
Stoyer, William 15:89
Stoyton, Lewis 18:180
Strabel, William 4:56
Strachan, D. 1:169
Stracher, L. 25:327
Stracke, Charles 21:126
Strackengast, Lewis
    22:492
Strackhouse, Robert
    12:146
Strackpole, William
    24:155
Strad, George 15:310;
    19:103
Stradburg, Andrew 22:163
Straddon, David B. 23:51
Strader, James 7:112
Strader, John A. 22:131

Strader, Peter W. 20:187
Stradey, John 18:254;
    26:64
Stradler, J. W. 25:327
Stradley, J. W. 1:77
Stradley, W. S. 8:59
Stradling, Thomas 12:41
Strael, Daniel 22:223
Stragen, Thomas 16:57
Straham, H. 15:327;
    19:103
Strahan, Simon 8:33
Strahl, Edward 21:393
Straight, Jacob 11:172
Straight, John B. 16:144
Straight, L. L. 11:45
Straight, Luther W. 17:68
Straight, Thomas 25:239
Straight, William G.
    22:467
Straile, John G. 11:416
Strailey, F. 25:239
Strailey, Frederick 5:30
Strain, Adam 10:138;
    20:357
Strain, C. 23:182
Strain, David S. 22:441
Strain, E. F. 11:392
Strain, H. P. 18:254;
    26:62
Strain, Harvey 21:191
Strain, J. 3:188
Strain, James 22:56
Strain, S. 15:113
Strain, Scott S. 11:313
Strain, T. P. 8:56
Strain, Thomas J. 9:68
Strainch, Michael 15:230
Strait, Cyrus L. 9:105
Strait, F. 25:239
Strait, Frank 5:30
Strait, H. 9:155; 24:85;
    27:110
Strait, Harvey T. 22:223
Strait, James 23:310
Strait, Jerome 22:156
Strait, William 10:146;
    19:196
Strait, Zepemiah 7:43
Straitner, Henry 6:13
Straits, L. J. 18:39
Straka, A. 13:69
Strakel, Ludwig 22:223
Strale, J. 3:188
Straley, David B. 22:270
Straley, George 11:171
Straley, J. 10:187
Straley, Lewis 22:103
Straley, W. J. 22:223
Stralford, Claudius 8:96
Straly, John 25:239

Stram, J. M. 11:171
Stram, William I. 8:32
Stramber, William 16:231
Stramer, John 18:317;
    26:111
Stramp, William R. 7:43
Stran, H. A. 26:183
Stran, L. D. 26:65
Stranage, I. 10:138
Stranbell, L. 3:188
Strand, F. 13:99
Strand, I. 18:180
Strand, John 3:188;
    12:158
Strand, N. S. 8:75
Strand, Ole E. 21:93
Strand, R. A. 21:106
Strand, Thomas 12:158
Strander, A. 3:188
Strandial, Sanford 26:64
Straney, John 14:303;
    17:471; 27:117
Strang, Daniel 10:23
Strang, Gabriel 19:103
Strang, Jacob 12:41
Strang, Samuel F. 20:357
Strange, Aaron 23:170;
    27:115
Strange, C. H. 14:223
Strange, Elisha 21:235
Strange, George 23:102;
    27:116
Strange, Isaac 23:51
Strange, James 17:168
Strange, Jesse 22:458
Strange, John A. 10:138;
    20:357
Strange, M. 13:99
Strange, M. A. 17:72
Strange, P. 25:239
Strange, W. F. 14:114
Strange, William 8:68
Strangel, John 19:196
Stranger, E. F. 4:56
Stranger, John 7:112
Strangler, Thomas 18:422
Strann, Edw. J. 8:96
Stranthers, Robert 18:181
Stranton, Aaron 10:138;
    20:357
Strap, George 27:115
Strap, Henry 4:68
Strap, James H. 21:60
Strap, John 14:223
Straper, Ludion 6:33
Strapp, Jacob 8:102
Strasburg, W. 1:171
Strassburg, --- 14:267
Stratdler, T. 1:170
Strather, John H. 10:93
Strathern, James H. 10:8

Stratheron, John 4:56
Strathers, Joseph 15:230
Strathouse, Gust 11:173
Stratman, C. 14:223
Straton, George W.
    11:189
Strats, S. L. 18:341
Stratten, S. 7:78
Stratton, --- 20:85
Stratton, A. 1:172
Stratton, Adelbert 5:30
Stratton, Alfred 13:49
Stratton, B. F. 9:194
Stratton, C. 15:301
Stratton, C. F. 18:58
Stratton, Charles 3:188;
    20:26
Stratton, Clinton 16:231
Stratton, D. B. 3:188
Stratton, Darius 21:393
Stratton, E. 3:188; 25:239
Stratton, Edward 5:46;
    18:72
Stratton, Enos J. 9:17
Stratton, Eugene W. 16:8
Stratton, Ezra 8:102;
    17:463; 24:180
Stratton, George F. 13:49
Stratton, George O. 24:97
Stratton, Henry 24:45
Stratton, Isaac 23:170
Stratton, J. 1:176
Stratton, J. A. 14:114
Stratton, J. H. 3:188
Stratton, J. J. 5:30; 25:239
Stratton, J. L. 3:188
Stratton, J. M. 1:72
Stratton, John 7:134;
    11:172; 16:103
Stratton, Joseph J. 20:135
Stratton, Julius 17:73
Stratton, Landa 9:211
Stratton, Levi 9:225;
    18:377
Stratton, Lewis 11:277;
    18:223
Stratton, M. C. 12:97;
    15:362
Stratton, R. 8:75
Stratton, S. 25:305
Stratton, S. C. 14:223, 260
Stratton, Stephen A.
    21:235
Stratton, Thomas 19:36
Stratton, Walter 13:49
Stratton, William 18:17
Stratton, William A.
    22:411
Stratton, William H. 21:60
Stratum, M. C. 19:103
Straty, William 27:118

Straub, Adam 17:429
Straub, C. A. 3:188
Straub, John 20:32
Straub, Sylvester 7:66
Strauble, Abraham 20:20
Strauges, W. 1:70
Straugler, --- 9:235
Straule, J. S. 22:440
Straume, James 3:188
Straurberman, Henry
    22:457
Straus, Edward 20:357
Straus, Elijah 17:186
Straus, James 17:186
Straus, Myer 15:230
Straus, Zach 17:186
Strausbaugh, F. 23:182
Strausburg, A. 21:126
Strausburg, William
    22:223
Strausburgh, Daniel 10:82
Strause, George 23:264
Strause, William J. 16:124
Strauser, J. 1:176
Strauss, H. 1:76
Strauss, Henry W. 10:138;
    20:358
Strauss, J. 21:393
Straut, J. 25:239
Strauther, Efica 27:111
Strauthouse, H. 7:43
Strautter, Effica 9:136
Straw, Emanuel 4:56
Straw, G. 14:114
Straw, Giles 7:80
Straw, J. Baker 21:393
Straw, L. D. 9:92
Straw, Sylvester 22:285
Straw, William 10:168;
    19:196
Strawberger, Andrew 4:56
Strawbridge, George 4:56
Strawbridge, Israel 9:126;
    27:113
Strawbridge, S. 14:322
Strawbridge, Samuel
    23:170
Strawcutter, D. W. 1:70
Strawer, George 17:426
Strawhicker, John 10:93
Strawmat, Reuben E.
    10:138; 20:358
Strawsbaugh, B. A. 12:10
Strawsbaugh, Henry 22:56
Strawsbury, D. 20:358
Strawser, D. 26:129
Strawser, George W.
    24:180
Strawyick, J. W. 25:71
Straxdall, Benjamin
    20:358

Stray, Vandermark 20:109
Strayer, E. 1:176
Strayer, Ira 10:93
Strayer, Isaiah 20:358
Strayer, J. C. 22:223
Strayer, James 8:56
Strayer, Jesse 9:46
Strayer, Louis 22:491
Strayer, N. 1:175
Strayler, Andrew 23:170
Strayline, G. 7:61
Strayman, H. 1:171
Strayn, Samuel 23:170
Strayns, Samuel 14:290
Streaker, James 21:213
Strech, Francis M. 9:99
Streckey, B. F. 13:99
Stredson, Henry H. 9:105
Streeby, H. 23:170
Streel, Philip 11:270
Streep, M. 15:113
Street, Aaron 10:168;
    19:196
Street, Charles C. 22:223
Street, David R. 17:139;
    24:203
Street, Elias S. 17:426
Street, G. F. 27:109
Street, H. C. 21:393
Street, Jacob 13:49; 16:57
Street, James 9:69; 16:231
Street, John J. 3:188
Street, Joseph 24:45
Street, L. H. 23:170
Street, Lawrence 10:82;
    20:358
Street, M. 21:113
Street, M. S. 11:277
Street, Nathan 22:411
Street, Ned 22:321
Street, P. S. 16:57
Street, Samuel 17:239;
    22:506
Street, Sigel 21:205
Street, Thomas 22:270
Street, Wesley 17:186
Street, William 10:168;
    19:196; 21:60
Streete, Jacob 8:32;
    18:161
Streeter, A. S. 9:126
Streeter, Charles 12:41;
    15:113
Streeter, D. 1:176
Streeter, H. 19:103
Streeter, H. S. 27:106
Streeter, J. 3:188
Streeter, James 25:270
Streeter, L. 13:69
Streeter, Lorenzo 19:103

Streeter, Marshall S.
    19:36
Streeter, S. 1:76
Streetes, G. 10:138
Streetinwater, Fredelin
    13:99
Streetman, J. 3:188
Streets, G. 20:358
Streets, George 9:136;
    27:115
Streets, J. T. 14:22
Streets, James D. 22:441
Streets, T. 23:170
Streets, W. 25:239
Streets, William 5:46
Streiber, William 10:82
Streich, August 21:261
Streicher, Peter 23:118
Streif, John 22:490
Streight, A. 7:112
Streight, J. 1:175
Streight, Lewis 3:188
Streighter, Louis 9:211
Streightiff, J. 1:75
Streightiff, Jacob 16:57
Streightliff, Jacob 13:49
Streit, Christian 4:56
Strek, J. 16:305
Strell, Philip 22:441
Stremple, C. 17:338
Strena, H. A. 8:68
Strenor, John 9:29
Streper, M. 3:188
Stress, Samuel 15:301
Stressner, John 12:41
Stretch, J. 3:188
Stretch, William M.
    20:184
Strever, J. B. 7:43
Strevis, John R. 15:230
Strewsbury, R. 3:176
Stribbling, John C. 24:56
Stribley, Wall 22:103
Stribling, Bradford 22:103
Stribling, James W. 24:45
Stribling, John 22:321
Stribling, T. 11:270
Stribling, William 9:158
Striby, Amos 10:168
Strickard, Joshua 8:96
Stricker, J. 3:188
Stricker, J. W. 3:188
Stricker, Joseph 12:41
Stricker, Silas H. 24:97
Stricker, William H. 23:51
Strickert, J. 13:99
Strickey, Peter 18:115
Strickland, Alexander
    11:213
Strickland, B. 9:195

Strickland, Benjamin
    20:14
Strickland, Charles 8:96;
    22:468
Strickland, D. 14:245;
    27:119
Strickland, George 19:36
Strickland, George G.
    10:23
Strickland, Harvey M.
    17:347
Strickland, Henry 8:68
Strickland, Henry E. 15:3
Strickland, J. D. 1:70
Strickland, J. R. 17:482;
    27:117
Strickland, Jacob 24:90
Strickland, James 8:110;
    22:321
Strickland, James M. 8:76
Strickland, John 17:163;
    20:356
Strickland, John W.
    23:269
Strickland, L. 14:22
Strickland, Levi G. 16:149
Strickland, Lewis 10:82;
    20:358
Strickland, P. 16:231;
    25:239
Strickland, Robert 7:134
Strickland, S. 11:425
Strickland, Thomas 3:188
Strickland, W. R. 25:239
Strickland, Walter 9:39;
    18:297; 26:113
Strickland, Wayne 27:118
Strickland, William D.
    8:96
Strickler, Benjamin
    22:131
Strickler, Henry 26:183
Strickler, J. H. 22:56
Strickler, John M. 22:223
Strickler, Robert H. 24:31
Strickles, Edwin 7:134
Strickley, Alfred 19:284
Strickley, J. 11:78
Strickley, John 18:285;
    26:135
Stricklin, C. C. 8:33
Stricklin, James L. 21:249
Stricklin, Jasper M. 23:51
Stricklin, P. 21:126
Stricklin, W. J. 11:438
Strickner, Allen J. 9:29
Strickner, J. 3:188
Strickwater, James 11:130
Stridley, E. B. 11:270
Strie, William 25:327
Strieber, William 20:358

Strief, Andrew 22:492
Strieklank, J. 13:99
Striffin, H. 3:188
Strike, Francis 10:138; 20:358
Strike, G. 15:306
Strike, James 6:19; 18:95
Strikel, J. M. 19:103
Striker, E. 14:114
Striker, F. 3:188
Striker, Fred 11:184
Striker, J. 16:231
Striker, Jacob 18:297; 26:112
Striker, James D. 9:232; 20:358
Striker, William 13:49
Striley, S. G. 14:114
Strills, John 15:230
Strimp, Martin V. 12:41
String, Frank 23:306
String, John 25:269
Stringer, C. 3:188
Stringer, F. K. 1:169
Stringer, Frank R. 8:120
Stringer, James 8:32; 18:161; 22:506
Stringer, Michael 15:46
Stringer, R. 17:102
Stringer, S. 22:270
Stringer, Thomas 11:271
Stringer, William 15:153
Stringfellow, J. G. 14:223
Stringfellow, J. W. 25:72
Stringfield, V. R. 14:115
Stringham, Henry 22:156
Strip, W. 3:188
Striplin, T. 17:284
Stripling, F. K. 20:129
Stripling, Thomas 11:392
Stripp, A. 1:77
Stripp, A. V. 7:43
Stritick, R. 14:115
Strito, William 11:173
Stritt, John 20:44
Stritt, Ludwig 4:56
Strittmaker, Joseph 18:195
Stroap, Henry 20:44
Stroba, J. J. 20:60
Strobach, George 27:114
Strobaugh, William F. 22:131
Strobel, Frank 26:182
Strobel, George 17:87
Strobel, John 12:41; 17:74
Strobere, Henry 20:37
Strobie, J. 27:118
Stroble, J. 16:124
Strobridge, George 16:103
Strobridge, L. 1:168

Strobridge, Oliver 9:92; 26:58
Strock, A. F. 16:124
Strock, Isaac 11:171
Strock, Levi 22:223
Strock, Sampson 20:101
Strockadall, Benjamin 10:93
Strocker, George 3:188
Strode, Charles R. 17:59
Strof, Joseph C. 10:138
Strofe, Jerome 10:139; 20:358
Strofe, Joseph C. 20:358
Strofies, Andrew J. 20:358
Stroger, W. 14:291
Stroghen, William 14:267
Strohback, George 9:126
Strohm, John 19:103
Strohm, John H. 9:126; 27:113
Strohn, John 13:69
Strohue, Jacob 26:60
Stroker, Henry 22:345
Strom, A. 3:188
Stroman, Absalom 16:57
Stroman, F. 15:230
Stroman, Martin 22:411
Strombley, Morris 8:115
Strome, Peter 12:100
Stroms, John 16:305
Stronberg, Charles 21:393
Strond, F. 14:22
Strond, John I. 8:33
Strong, A. M. 15:230
Strong, Abner 22:223
Strong, Andrew 20:109
Strong, Asahel 17:264
Strong, Ashur T. 17:245
Strong, B. P. 1:78
Strong, Brainard E. 17:347
Strong, Cassius M. 8:96
Strong, Charles 18:58
Strong, D. A. 13:120
Strong, E. 16:103
Strong, E. M. 3:188
Strong, Edmond 9:215
Strong, Edward 11:417; 21:393
Strong, Francis A. 8:56
Strong, G. W. 16:103; 25:239
Strong, George 14:245
Strong, George W. 5:30
Strong, Green 18:254; 26:65
Strong, H. 3:188; 14:279; 23:185
Strong, H. B. 17:449

Strong, Harrison B. 24:174
Strong, Harry 10:139
Strong, Harvey P. 20:358
Strong, Hayden W. 17:239
Strong, Henry 22:156
Strong, Hiram 26:146
Strong, Isaac 24:85
Strong, J. 1:171; 11:439; 19:103
Strong, J. C. 10:139; 20:358
Strong, James 9:204; 19:286
Strong, James C. 22:321
Strong, Jasper 26:129
Strong, Joseph 9:46
Strong, Joseph W. 10:23
Strong, Kitt 7:134
Strong, L. 3:188
Strong, M. B. 8:96
Strong, Philamon B. 19:36
Strong, R. 9:46; 11:282; 26:129
Strong, S. H. 10:82; 20:358
Strong, Samuel 18:401
Strong, Samuel T. 10:82
Strong, Smith 14:115
Strong, W. 7:65
Strong, William 16:115; 26:58
Strong, William H. 21:393
Stroop, J. 12:80
Stroop, R. 1:172
Stropes, Andrew J. 10:139
Stroser, J. 13:120
Strotham, James 21:393
Strothers, George 13:49
Strouce, N. J. 8:68
Stroud, Barnett M. 22:440
Stroud, Caleb 9:92
Stroud, Charles A. 21:13
Stroud, Edward 18:254; 26:63
Stroud, George 10:139; 20:109, 358
Stroud, Greenbury 9:92
Stroud, Henry 23:51
Stroud, J. 2:17; 25:67
Stroud, James 9:195
Stroud, L. C. 23:52
Stroud, Maddock T. 21:42
Stroud, R. A. 7:54
Stroud, Thomas 10:175; 19:196
Stroud, W. 24:99
Stroud, William 20:358
Strough, Ira V. 7:43
Strought, R. H. 1:169

Stroup, A. 9:232; 20:358
Stroup, Cornelius 11:171
Stroup, Milton 17:151
Stroup, Russell 9:155
Stroup, S. 3:188
Stroup, William 7:54
Stroupe, Benjamin 8:43;
   26:182
Strous, Addison J. 10:23
Strous, Henry 18:254
Strous, John 17:157
Strous, O. P. 18:39
Strouse, D. 14:303;
   27:117
Strouse, George 8:33;
   18:162
Strouse, I. I. 8:33
Strouse, J. J. 18:162
Strouse, Jacob F. 16:153
Strouse, William P.
   21:235
Strousick, Edward 7:112
Strouss, D. 17:480
Strout, A. 13:99
Strout, E. 12:77; 15:12
Strout, G. H. 15:362
Strout, J. 12:84; 16:306
Strout, Lucas 12:77; 15:28
Strout, S. W. 25:239
Strout, Samuel 7:43
Strout, W. 11:255
Strow, Peter 22:103
Strown, J. H. 23:52
Strown, Moses 21:60
Strows, Henry 26:64
Stroyan, William 23:52
Stroyer, J. 1:174
Stroyer, James M. 21:235
Stru, William 6:33
Strubel, Daniel W. 21:197
Struben, D. 16:158
Struble, George 23:170
Struble, Lucus 16:135
Struchean, F. E. 3:188
Struck, William C. 7:70
Strucker, J. 26:183
Struckland, H. 16:57
Strudeback, H. 8:68
Struder, William 13:69
Struen, John 16:231
Struen, Paul 1:72
Struler, William 19:103
Strults, J. G. 13:99
Strum, Daniel 24:203
Strum, G. B. 16:57
Strunce, D. 3:188
Strunck, J. 1:78
Strune, Surron 18:162
Strunk, Henry 22:438
Strunk, J. 15:295; 16:231
Strunk, J. L. 16:380

Strunk, James 12:41
Strunk, Jasper 22:131
Strunk, Samuel 19:320
Strunterman, John 9:73
Strupp, Jacob 17:463;
   24:186
Strurer, George 9:73
Strut, Sand 24:204
Struter, Danford 7:61
Struter, H. 13:69
Struthers, Robert 10:187
Strutter, F. 3:188
Strutts, George 7:112
Strutts, L. J. 18:39
Strutzman, N. 1:168
Struwatter, E. 16:271
Struyer, Jesse 26:129
Stryden, Joseph 18:162
Stryker, John 13:69
Stuard, Charles 13:49
Stuard, E. 14:223
Stuard, J. 10:187
Stuart, --- 25:69; 26:226
Stuart, Andrew J. 17:59
Stuart, D. F. 14:223
Stuart, Eddie 10:82
Stuart, Edward 11:392
Stuart, Henry 7:134
Stuart, J. 21:197
Stuart, J. B. 23:52
Stuart, J. N. 25:239
Stuart, J. W. 9:228;
   18:377
Stuart, John 17:495
Stuart, Jones Z. 17:101
Stuart, Joseph 27:113
Stuart, Julius 14:223
Stuart, Marshall 9:211
Stuart, Martin 13:49
Stuart, Nathan 8:118
Stuart, Rufus 25:239
Stuart, T. 25:70, 72
Stuart, Thomas J. 17:101
Stuart, W. L. 16:103
Stuart, Willey 26:226
Stuart, William 17:59
Stuart, William J. 17:112
Stuarte, Sanford 19:103
Stubanus, Andreas
   17:454; 24:186
Stubb, H. 15:75
Stubben, Thomas 17:284
Stubbins, Robert 21:393
Stubblefield, --- 26:213
Stubblefield, Archibald J.
   22:56
Stubblefield, Charles
   22:15
Stubblefield, James 9:211;
   18:223; 21:197
Stubbs, Allen 21:235

Stubbs, Charles 15:230
Stubbs, D. M. 1:73
Stubbs, George 7:61
Stubbs, H. S. 16:57
Stubbs, Henry S. 13:49
Stubbs, Isaac 21:126
Stubbs, J. 3:188
Stubbs, Jacob 9:92
Stubbs, James 10:8
Stubbs, John 9:195;
   19:271
Stubbs, Joseph A. 15:230
Stubbs, Lewis 22:223
Stubbs, Miles H. 26:183
Stubbs, Nathaniel 7:43
Stubbs, Silas B. 10:93;
   20:358
Stubbs, Sylvester 10:139;
   20:358
Stubbs, Thomas 22:103,
   441, 498
Stubbs, W. 3:188
Stubbs, Wesley K. 19:36
Stubbs, William 8:33;
   18:162
Stubbs, William A.
   23:170
Stubel, Levi H. 21:197
Stuben, Jacob 22:223
Stubens, J. C. 18:39
Stuber, Stephen 22:223
Stubfield, James 21:106
Stubleen, Michael 9:195
Stubs, L. 27:109
Stuby, Gus 23:52
Stucat, Manassa 27:117
Stuchal, Samuel 17:93
Stuchel, Henry 15:75
Stuck, Caray 19:103
Stuck, Christian 7:43
Stuck, Eli 3:188
Stuck, H. M. 3:188
Stuck, Henry 22:56
Stuck, J. O. 19:265
Stuck, John 15:230
Stuck, L. H. 3:188
Stuck, William 22:56
Stucker, J. 8:68
Stucker, J. F. 8:68
Stucker, S. 8:96
Stuckey, H. 1:173
Stuckey, H. G. 25:239
Stuckey, Henry 24:31
Stuckey, I. C. 12:158
Stuckey, Jacob 21:42
Stuckey, John W. 22:104
Stuckey, L. E. 21:393
Stuckey, W. 9:114
Stuckgish, H. 14:115
Stucklasser, A. 21:393
Stucklier, C. G. 18:162

Stucky, Job 23:52
Stude, Jacob 10:82; 20:358
Studebaker, Henry 26:181
Studer, Frederick 22:15
Studer, J. 9:46
Studhum, Simpson H. 11:43
Studivan, S. 22:223
Studivant, James D. 15:230
Studley, D. B. 1:175
Studley, David F. 24:31
Studley, Edward 19:196
Studley, S. W. 9:114
Studobacher, Andrew 17:43
Studor, Thomas 17:87
Studt, Abraham 9:59
Studt, Henry 27:157
Studtman, Aug. 15:286
Study, Francis A. 8:110; 22:441
Study, Samuel 22:104
Stueker, G. W. 21:151
Stuffer, J. 1:95
Stuffey, Eli 24:180
Stufflebeam, George 23:257
Stufflebeam, John 22:169
Stufft, William 10:146
Stuffy, W. 17:297
Stuft, M. 1:176
Stuft, William 19:196
Stuges, Morrell 18:72
Stugo, A. O. 19:317
Stuhl, Adam 9:39; 18:297; 26:113
Stukey, John 19:36
Stule, Austin 26:129
Stuley, J. H. 15:346
Stull, Adam 23:170
Stull, Daniel 22:56
Stull, F. 12:164; 26:181
Stull, G. 3:188
Stull, G. E. 3:188
Stull, G. W. 22:15
Stull, Isiah 25:239
Stull, J. P. 5:30
Stull, James 15:230
Stull, Joshua 13:49
Stull, Michael 3:188; 22:491
Stull, S. S. 23:280
Stull, W. H. 13:69
Stuller, C. 18:181
Stuller, D. 1:76
Stulls, Charles 27:106
Stulman, John B. 19:196
Stults, Henry 19:36
Stults, John 5:46

Stults, P. 3:188
Stultz, C. M. 20:358
Stultz, F. M. 22:223
Stultz, J. 1:71
Stultz, J. M. 18:254
Stultz, John 12:41; 22:103
Stuly, Abram 10:23
Stum, Daniel 19:36
Stum, William H. 10:82
Stumber, John J. 10:97
Stumf, John 9:39
Stumm, H. H. 15:346
Stump, A. 3:188
Stump, Aaron 7:112
Stump, C. E. 15:46
Stump, Daniel 9:202; 19:284
Stump, Ephraim 17:433; 24:162
Stump, Frank 9:59
Stump, Henry 24:168
Stump, Henry E. 11:171
Stump, J. A. 14:115
Stump, John 22:104; 26:129
Stump, Johnson 22:491
Stump, Joseph 10:82
Stump, L. 13:99
Stump, Leonard 8:110
Stump, Nathan 10:207
Stump, S. 1:96
Stump, W. 3:188
Stump, William 14:303; 17:472; 27:117
Stump, William J. 11:77
Stumpf, Joseph 20:358
Stumpf, Lewis 3:188
Stumps, J. 3:188
Stundall, F. 14:115
Stundifund, John 16:380
Stundish, Charles H. 21:241
Stunkard, Miles 20:101
Stunkard, R. W. 1:70
Stunly, F. 25:239
Stunnett, --- 3:188
Stuns, Samuel F. 12:41
Stuplet, Philip 18:39
Stupplebeau, William H. H. 22:169
Sturam, John 17:43
Sturdebank, G. 3:178
Sturdevant, H. 1:74
Sturdevant, H. B. 12:158
Sturdevant, James 24:45
Sturdevant, Levi 22:104
Sturdevant, M. O. 15:230
Sturdevant, O. E. 1:75
Sturdevant, Russell O. 12:41
Sturdevant, Sanford 26:65

Sturdevant, W. 3:188
Sturdewant, W. 3:188
Sturdivan, Charles 15:46
Sturdivant, Sanford 18:254
Sturdivant, William 25:305
Sturge, George 8:33; 18:162
Sturgel, James 21:393
Sturgeon, R. 1:77
Sturgeon, William F. 8:96
Sturgeon, William H. 21:60, 235
Sturges, Alfred 5:30
Sturges, G. W. 15:346; 16:380
Sturges, Joseph A. 10:168
Sturges, Robert C. 17:59
Sturges, William F. 25:289
Sturgess, Edward 12:77
Sturgess, Joseph A. 19:197
Sturgess, Nathan 14:223
Sturgess, W. A. 3:188
Sturgill, James 13:129
Sturgis, A. 25:239
Sturgis, Albert 11:111
Sturgis, Edward 25:70
Sturgis, Thomas M. 8:96
Sturgis, William 17:26
Sturgis, William F. 17:284
Sturgiss, George 7:43
Sturgiss, W. T. 3:188
Sturgon, W. H. 26:183
Sturgus, J. 12:10
Sturling, A. 1:77
Sturling, Denton 20:129
Sturm, Daniel 17:139
Sturm, Gottfried 21:261
Sturm, Thornton T. 24:45
Sturm, William H. 20:358
Sturman, I. O. 18:181
Sturman, J. O. 10:193
Sturme, Burel 9:225
Sturn, E. E. 3:188
Sturne, Burel 18:377
Sturnes, W. 4:56
Sturnman, L. 19:103
Sturns, Oscar R. 7:70
Sturnt, D. 25:276
Sturon, Nelson 14:335
Sturrick, William 13:49
Sturtevant, Christian 11:130
Sturtevant, Creighton 13:49
Sturtevant, George W. 9:8
Sturtevant, Isaiah J. 6:10
Sturtevant, L. P. 7:43

Sturtevant, Thomas D. 4:56
Sturtevant, William 7:81
Sturtevean, L. A. 13:120
Sturtiphant, James 7:43
Sturtz, D. G. 21:126
Sturtz, Michael 8:33; 18:162
Sturtz, Solomon 24:56
Stute, James 6:19
Stuterant, Vallnor 6:33
Stuterill, John 11:43
Stutevant, L. 12:84; 16:306
Stutevant, V. 25:327
Stutie, W. 19:103
Stutler, J. N. 3:189
Stutler, William 17:394
Stutliff, Albert B. 22:56
Stutliff, Henry S. 12:52
Stutney, Augustus 24:88
Stuts, John 21:393
Stuttles, William 9:92
Stutton, John 21:393
Stutton, Lewis 22:104
Stutts, George 21:393; 22:223
Stutz, J. 25:239
Stutz, Jacob 5:30
Stutzel, Lewis 17:421
Stutzman, Albert 20:86
Stutzman, David 11:271
Stutzman, I. 24:70
Stutzman, P. 3:189
Stveoze, Henry 13:49
Stweet, John H. 27:107
Styck, Jacob O. 9:195
Styer, J. R. 15:168
Styles, A. A. 20:157
Styles, A. B. 3:189
Styles, Harper 9:92
Styles, I. N. 3:189
Styles, J. L. 25:71
Styles, John 9:225
Styles, John F. 9:92
Styles, John P. 21:393
Styles, N. 1:173
Styner, Jacob 25:72
Stype, Joseph 4:56
Stypes, S. M. 7:43
Styre, Christian 19:103
Styres, T. 9:59
Styron, Simon 10:168; 19:197
Styron, William 4:56
Stythe, James 18:254; 26:62
Suager, William S. 22:223
Suano, C. F. 1:174
Suart, Daniel E. 14:115
Suartz, Benjamin 19:36

Suartz, Charles 19:36
Suatsil, Francis 11:425
Subbs, Milor H. 8:76
Suber, A. F. 22:223
Subert, Mathew 1:71
Subert, Washington G. 10:93
Subke, Michael 18:95
Subkeman, Henry 12:41
Subkin, Max 9:151
Sublet, L. F. 21:393
Sublett, Reuben 6:13
Subois, Charles 6:23
Subra, John 23:196
Suburn, M. S. 3:170
Subzie, Charles 18:58
Such, J. C. 18:39
Suchin, Calvin 5:54
Sucht, T. 3:189
Suck, Michael 1:72
Sucker, Burnt 1:72
Sucker, Conrad 18:162
Sucker, James A. 9:195
Suckforth, Charles A. 7:112
Suckler, John H. 7:43
Sucklist, Frederick 4:56
Suckmauer, Fred 9:126
Sudard, Eli 15:357
Sudbeck, J. 1:175
Suddaby, Isaac 23:93
Suddard, Thomas I. 24:10
Suddarth, Henry 17:445
Suddarth, Henry J. 24:168
Suddarth, John W. 22:131
Sudden, C. F. 22:56
Sudden, Robert 11:111
Sudder, William H. 12:42
Sudderth, Mach 22:131
Suddeth, James 22:131
Suddith, Joseph 21:60
Sudendorf, George 8:96
Suder, Casper 10:139; 20:358
Sudith, J. 9:243
Sudler, H. K. 13:99
Sudlowe, William M. 17:357
Sudwick, P. 7:112
Sue, August 25:284
Suedere, John 19:197
Suel, Ames 20:32
Suels, James 27:117
Suene, Albert 18:39
Suerman, John 15:231
Suert, W. 14:115
Suess, Jacob 9:14
Suet, J. B. 9:59
Suet, John 14:115
Sueter, Martin 22:104
Suethen, John 21:234

Suetors, John R. 22:491
Suey, Ibsen 19:279
Suffecal, S. 3:189
Suffer, Jacob 8:96
Sufferage, E. 13:99
Suffery, Peter 10:139; 20:358
Suffett, W. I. 15:231
Suffield, James 17:43
Suffield, James K. 22:441
Suffle, James 21:113
Suffolk, Newell 1:71
Suffolk, Owen 12:77; 15:46
Suffrage, D. 14:115
Suffrage, E. 14:22
Suffrage, J. 14:22
Suffrige, J. 13:99
Suffrin, John 21:393
Sufleberger, Gordon 9:59
Sugars, Emanuel 22:238
Sugbern, J. 3:189
Sugbert, James S. 3:189
Sugg, J. R. 22:270
Sugget, Thomas 16:142
Suggs, Daniel 26:182
Suggs, James 26:180
Suggs, Jessee 18:254
Suggs, John 17:186
Suggs, L. B. 9:243
Sugher, F. 11:334
Sugill, Daniel 22:56
Sugland, Adolphus 13:49
Sugler, Benjamin 11:184
Sugler, George 14:267
Suhager, Robert 15:80
Suhr, Frederick 23:116
Suimey, J. 23:303
Suines, Sidney C. 18:324
Suit, H. M. 14:287
Suit, Ralph 8:76
Suiter, A. 1:73
Suiter, Andrew 11:170
Suiter, F. 15:231
Suiter, J. 9:151
Suiter, William 1:70
Suitor, Abraham 11:117
Suitor, Alfred 22:56
Suits, Alford 21:235
Sukell, William H. 22:156
Sukins, Frederick B. 17:405
Sukow, Lewis 9:17
Sulavan, John 15:46
Sulavan, P. 9:59
Sules, J. B. 3:189
Suley, E. M. 27:107
Sulger, James 12:42
Sulgroof, A. 16:136
Sulidon, Samuel 17:444; 24:162

Sulivan, J. 16:271
Sulivan, James D. 17:59
Sulivan, Jeremiah 11:77
Sulivan, John 9:241;
    19:293
Sulivan, P. 12:158
Sulken, --- 15:136
Sulkert, --- 12:124; 14:26;
    15:364
Sullen, Treman 12:158
Sullenander, Similan
    20:358
Sullender, Simon 10:93
Sullenger, Romulus
    10:139; 20:359
Sullenmyers, William
    18:211
Sullens, Jesse 22:56
Sullers, James 10:139;
    20:359
Sullevian, D. 3:189
Sullinger, J. 9:92; 26:59
Sullins, Joseph G. 9:68
Sullins, Josiah M. 21:106
Sullins, W. 21:209
Sullivan, --- 4:57; 16:149;
    22:505
Sullivan, A. H. 20:358
Sullivan, Amos 7:43
Sullivan, Barney 9:29
Sullivan, Bartholomew
    23:116
Sullivan, C. 8:56; 9:195;
    19:242
Sullivan, Charles 8:43;
    22:104; 26:180
Sullivan, Cornelius 7:43;
    21:261
Sullivan, D. 3:189; 11:45;
    14:115; 19:276;
    25:71
Sullivan, D. C. 14:115
Sullivan, D. M. 18:181
Sullivan, D. R. 11:101
Sullivan, D. W. 10:187
Sullivan, Daniel 7:43;
    9:195; 21:393;
    22:346; 27:118
Sullivan, David J. 4:57
Sullivan, Dennis 10:187;
    13:120; 14:223;
    15:319; 18:181;
    19:103, 197; 21:393;
    24:70
Sullivan, E. 15:231
Sullivan, E. G. 19:103
Sullivan, Edward 3:189;
    7:43
Sullivan, Eugene 17:87,
    430

Sullivan, F. 7:43; 8:122;
    25:239
Sullivan, F. J. 15:295
Sullivan, Frank P. 19:330
Sullivan, G. 21:126, 168;
    27:109
Sullivan, George 19:36;
    23:80
Sullivan, H. C. 18:271
Sullivan, Henry 18:115
Sullivan, I. 14:223
Sullivan, Isaac 11:97
Sullivan, Isaac N. 20:187
Sullivan, J. 1:77, 168,
    172; 2:18; 3:189;
    7:61; 12:162; 14:115,
    303; 15:295; 16:231;
    17:471; 19:197;
    21:393; 23:52; 25:67,
    239; 27:109, 117
Sullivan, J. A. 12:158
Sullivan, J. F. 19:103
Sullivan, J. O. 27:109
Sullivan, Jaffrey 21:393
Sullivan, James 1:70;
    4:57; 7:13; 8:76;
    10:23; 13:50; 16:57;
    19:197; 22:410;
    26:181
Sullivan, James A. 23:110
Sullivan, James D. 22:346
Sullivan, James H. 19:197
Sullivan, Jefferson 21:235
Sullivan, Jeremiah 15:75;
    22:441
Sullivan, Jeremiah O.
    16:282
Sullivan, Jermiah 24:97
Sullivan, Jerry 1:70; 7:43;
    23:170
Sullivan, John 1:71, 72;
    3:189; 4:57; 6:8;
    8:33, 76; 9:9, 92,
    202; 10:139; 12:42,
    65; 13:50; 15:15;
    16:282; 17:108, 426;
    18:115, 162, 281;
    19:36; 20:359; 21:87,
    393; 24:31; 25:71;
    27:107
Sullivan, John B. 21:106
Sullivan, John D. 1:72
Sullivan, John E. 23:52
Sullivan, John P. 21:393
Sullivan, John W. 19:36
Sullivan, Joseph 11:425
Sullivan, Lawrence
    23:125
Sullivan, M. 3:189; 5:31;
    11:232; 14:115, 223;

Sullivan M. 16:231;
    19:197; 25:239
Sullivan, M. J. 27:109
Sullivan, M. O. 1:168
Sullivan, M. R. 19:36
Sullivan, Manoah 17:201,
    317
Sullivan, Marcus O.
    20:101
Sullivan, Michael 1:70;
    7:54; 8:68; 14:223;
    16:231; 17:43;
    22:131, 238, 346;
    23:196
Sullivan, Michael M.
    21:394
Sullivan, Michael O.
    21:81
Sullivan, Morris 22:492
Sullivan, Moses 22:439
Sullivan, O. J. 9:151
Sullivan, Otho 25:72
Sullivan, P. 3:189;
    15:231; 24:85
Sullivan, P. O. 3:189
Sullivan, Pat 26:182
Sullivan, Pat. 8:33
Sullivan, Patrick 3:189;
    6:14; 11:44; 16:103;
    18:95, 115, 254;
    19:197; 21:143;
    22:346; 24:10; 26:61
Sullivan, Patrick O.
    21:394
Sullivan, Peter 17:250
Sullivan, Philip 12:168
Sullivan, R. 14:115
Sullivan, R. W. 13:120
Sullivan, Reuben L.
    23:102
Sullivan, Richard 27:118
Sullivan, Robert 18:162
Sullivan, S. R. 11:314
Sullivan, Samuel 15:19;
    17:284; 22:321
Sullivan, T. 3:189; 25:239
Sullivan, T. J. 16:231
Sullivan, T. T. 12:149
Sullivan, Thomas 8:68;
    9:211; 11:269; 13:50;
    14:131; 15:264;
    19:36; 26:183;
    27:115
Sullivan, Thomas L.
    17:350
Sullivan, Tim 13:120
Sullivan, Timothy 18:17;
    21:191; 22:285
Sullivan, Timothy B.
    18:281
Sullivan, W. 3:189

Sullivan, W. J. 11:121
Sullivan, W. P. 8:56
Sullivan, W. T. 22:15
Sullivan, Wesley 7:112
Sullivan, William 8:56,
    96; 13:50; 15:75,
    346; 16:57, 380;
    23:80
Sullivan, William J.
    26:226
Sullivan, William P.
    21:106; 22:505
Sullivan, William W.
    23:280
Sullivan, Willis 7:70
Sullivan, Z. B. 9:59
Sullivan, Zenus A. 22:56
Sullock, Dewer 21:394
Sullon, Charles 17:428
Sullon, Nelson 17:428
Sullvan, M. 15:161
Sullyards, B. F. 9:126
Sullyards, Benjamin F.
    27:114
Sulson, Joseph A. 20:129
Sulsor, John B. 22:223
Sultliff, H. V. 1:73
Sulton, George W. 8:96
Sulton, H. K. 23:171
Sulton, John 14:115
Sulton, O. 3:189
Sultzbaugh, F. 27:110
Suly, Benjamin 22:104
Suly, T. B. 15:23
Sulzer, Jacob 20:14
Sulzie, Charles 10:149
Suman, Aaron 15:46
Suman, John 8:96
Sumay, Joel 10:82;
    20:359
Sumer, J. P. 17:59
Sumer, Theodore 4:57
Sumerlot, V. E. 11:75
Sumers, H. 11:169
Summa, David J. 20:359
Summa, Frederick 8:96
Summer, Benjamin
    16:231
Summer, Charles 22:285
Summer, Dempsey 16:231
Summer, George 14:115
Summer, Gootleb 11:270
Summer, H. 3:189
Summer, Henry 24:162
Summer, Isam 23:198
Summer, J. 1:75; 12:86;
    16:306
Summer, Joseph 14:115
Summer, Luther G.
    12:158
Summer, Peter 18:341

Summer, Rufus 12:57
Summer, S. 11:45
Summer, W. H. 18:162
Summerell, James 13:50
Summerfield, William
    21:113
Summerland, Henry
    11:169
Summerlott, John 23:264
Summerly, John 11:45
Summerman, John 18:162
Summers, A. 14:285
Summers, Alex 11:313
Summers, C. 11:43
Summers, C. A. 23:52
Summers, Charles L.
    22:104
Summers, David 11:417;
    22:411
Summers, E. M. 15:231
Summers, Edward 9:136
Summers, Elijah 10:82;
    20:359
Summers, Elijah E.
    17:112
Summers, Francis M.
    22:104
Summers, G. 17:290
Summers, G. W. 1:172
Summers, George 21:285
Summers, Gilbert 18:254;
    26:64
Summers, H. 16:271
Summers, H. F. 1:78
Summers, Harrison
    22:131
Summers, Harvey 24:31
Summers, Henry 17:60;
    22:321
Summers, J. 1:172, 174;
    14:115; 25:239
Summers, J. M. 1:176
Summers, J. W. 1:70
Summers, James E.
    10:139; 20:359
Summers, John 24:97
Summers, John H. 18:409
Summers, John S. 13:50
Summers, John W. 4:57
Summers, Joseph 5:31;
    6:19; 18:95
Summers, Jourdan H.
    24:31
Summers, King 18:254;
    26:63
Summers, Levi 15:303
Summers, Lewis 24:56
Summers, Lyons 10:82
Summers, M. 9:92;
    15:113; 26:65
Summers, Marion 21:202

Summers, Mathias 22:104
Summers, Moses 4:57
Summers, N. 14:223
Summers, Noah 22:506
Summers, Perry 23:171
Summers, Riley 11:43
Summers, Robert 1:75
Summers, S. W. 14:115
Summers, Samuel 8:68
Summers, T. M. 24:31
Summers, Theodore 4:57
Summers, Thomas 27:119
Summers, Thornton
    18:254
Summers, W. 3:189;
    9:114; 21:113;
    22:104
Summers, W. H. 3:189
Summers, William 8:68;
    14:223; 21:42;
    22:270; 26:184
Summers, William E.
    18:58
Summerskill, Samuel
    10:30
Summerson, N. 27:109
Summert, Jeremiah C.
    17:350
Summerville, A. 14:304;
    17:480; 27:117
Summerville, H. A. 22:56
Summerville, H. P. 9:59
Summerville, J. 1:173
Summerville, J. H. 24:31
Summerville, Jack 9:136
Summerville, James
    22:104
Summerville, L. 11:172
Summerville, W. 14:260
Summerville, William H.
    17:275
Summervolt, V. 3:189
Summet, W. R. 12:77
Summiski, E. W. 10:168
Summons, C. A. 14:115
Summons, Franklin
    18:341
Sumna, Myre 21:199
Sumner, A. P. 15:82
Sumner, Anthony W.
    22:56
Sumner, Charles 21:394
Sumner, E. C. 15:153
Sumner, Eugene 17:62
Sumner, George 21:235
Sumner, Herman 19:288
Sumner, J. 14:115
Sumner, J. B. 2:18
Sumner, James 17:26
Sumner, John W. 10:23
Sumner, Joseph A. 21:143

Sumner, Josiah 10:82; 20:359
Sumner, Lewis 12:77
Sumner, Lewis J. 15:82
Sumner, Lucas 1:70
Sumner, N. 11:289
Sumner, Rosemore 21:60
Sumner, S. W. 15:84
Sumner, Samuel 23:93
Sumner, Samuel W. 12:77
Sumner, W. H. 8:33
Sumner, William 13:99; 14:115
Sumners, C. S. 1:172
Sumners, George F. 19:103
Sumners, Thornton 26:63
Sumons, William 20:359
Sumpter, A. T. 10:187; 18:181
Sumpter, Andrew J. 17:60
Sumpter, William 27:111
Sumptur, William 24:31
Sumser, J. 3:189
Sumter, Robert A. 20:47
Sumter, William 9:136
Sunain, F. 9:151
Sunan, S. F. 1:75
Sunbay, George 7:61
Sunby, George G. 14:1
Sunday, Jacob C. 11:44
Sunday, Peter 20:32
Sundbury, Gustave 10:82
Sundell, Charles J. 21:93
Sundels, John 20:129
Sunderland, A. 18:254; 26:62
Sunderland, Cosmo 23:171
Sunderland, D. W. 25:71
Sunderland, Henry 23:171
Sunderland, J. R. 7:112
Sunderland, Joseph 10:82
Sunderland, Joseph W. 7:65
Sunderland, Lemuel 10:93; 20:359
Sunderland, Thomas 10:139
Sunderland, Thomas J. 20:359
Sunderland, W. 21:394
Sunderlien, E. 3:189
Sunderlin, J. 25:72
Sunderman, Henry 23:80
Sundermarker, Henry 11:170
Sunders, Pompey 27:111
Sundrille, Andrin 15:231
Suneler, P. 19:49
Suneral, G. R. 27:109

Sunguist, John 20:359
Suniddley, W. 3:189
Sunier, G. S. 3:189
Sunken, George 20:129
Sunman, Henry P. 8:110
Sunn, Hyman 9:195
Sunnydecker, J. L. 12:42
Sunpoon, B. 16:271
Sunratt, Mason 12:167
Sunshine, Frederick 12:42
Supler, E. 14:115
Suppes, S. E. 3:189
Supple, C. M. 3:189
Supplee, George 15:75
Supplee, William 21:42
Suppo, Charles 21:213
Supprise, J. 19:103
Supry, Edward 10:82; 20:359
Surat, J. B. 11:312
Surben, J. 8:56
Surber, John 13:120
Surber, Joseph 21:106
Surber, W. G. 20:359
Surcoxes, Joseph 9:238
Surcoxis, Joseph 26:226
Surdam, I. W. 25:239
Surey, George 19:103
Surface, J. 13:99
Surgis, John W. 22:104
Suriag, J. 23:80
Surk, Charles 18:317; 26:112
Surkelow, R. 12:158
Surles, Anthony 11:86
Surls, A. D. 11:169
Surls, Francis 9:29; 26:112
Surminski, E. W. 19:197
Surplus, --- 3:189
Surprise, J. 15:331
Surra, John M. 11:44
Surran, John 18:211
Surrey, J. 21:81
Surrill, Dennis 11:171
Surrine, David 18:401
Surrine, John 17:68
Surry, J. 23:171
Surry, Lewis O. 16:306
Surtees, George 22:56
Surtyman, H. 16:231
Survant, Charles 23:125
Susears, Frederick 3:189
Susong, Talbert L. 22:270
Susor, Moses H. 7:54
Sut, Henry 11:171
Sutberry, C. 21:151
Sutch, O. L. 9:92
Sutcliff, B. 3:189
Suteliff, T. 11:45
Suter, B. F. 3:190

Suter, Jacob 1:73
Suter, James D. 11:76
Suter, Sevier 23:250
Suter, W. W. 25:69
Suters, Benjamin F. 10:25
Sutfin, Parley 20:116
Sutgen, F. 3:190
Suthard, William 16:57
Sutheland, John G. 27:148
Suther, Amos 4:57
Suther, J. 21:191
Sutherland, A. 13:130
Sutherland, Andrew 21:200
Sutherland, B. 17:266
Sutherland, Bailey 17:353
Sutherland, D. C. 26:59
Sutherland, Demetrius I. 9:92
Sutherland, F. 10:149
Sutherland, F. J. 10:82; 20:359
Sutherland, Francis 9:9
Sutherland, George 10:139; 20:359
Sutherland, Gilbert M. 17:68
Sutherland, Isidore 18:181
Sutherland, J. 3:189; 14:22; 18:58
Sutherland, J. E. 3:189
Sutherland, J. W. 1:76
Sutherland, Jacob 20:85
Sutherland, James 10:97; 21:394
Sutherland, James B. 22:411
Sutherland, James M. 19:36
Sutherland, James T. 23:196
Sutherland, Jeptha D. 17:239
Sutherland, John 20:359
Sutherland, John J. 21:143
Sutherland, John K. 23:171
Sutherland, Mason M. 7:43
Sutherland, Michael 13:50
Sutherland, N. 14:115
Sutherland, P. 25:73
Sutherland, S. 23:52
Sutherland, Samuel 8:120
Sutherland, Solomon 10:139; 20:359
Sutherland, Webster 7:54
Sutherland, William 13:50; 17:319
Sutherlin, J. C. 13:99
Sutherlin, James 17:284

Sutherly, H. B. 14:115
Suthers, --- 22:270
Suthers, James 22:223
Suthers, John 17:186
Suthers, Matand 26:59
Suthers, Munroe 22:321
Suthers, Thomas 23:14
Suthphar, H. W. 3:190
Suthphu, M. C. 9:238
Suthron, J. H. 3:190
Sutire, J. 1:74
Sutker, G. 1:73
Sutleff, Friend 9:163
Sutleff, George 18:281
Sutleff, Isaac 8:56
Sutler, Alexander 12:52
Sutler, J. C. 15:231
Sutler, J. J. 23:245
Sutler, Joseph 11:404
Sutler, William 1:75
Sutley, --- 2:18
Sutley, Alex 23:171
Sutley, John 25:73
Sutlif, David L. 15:75
Sutliff, Able 11:250
Sutliff, E. 3:190
Sutliff, W. J. 16:103
Sutliffe, J. G. 1:168
Sutly, William 14:115
Suton, Peter 11:98
Sutor, R. 24:85
Sutorius, William 21:116
Sutphen, Alfred W. 21:116
Sutphen, Anson 22:56
Sutphin, M. C. 26:226
Sutphin, T. 16:114
Sutrouns, William H. 23:80
Sutten, Charles 8:76
Sutten, Redmond 25:286
Sutten, William 25:239
Sutter, Benjamin 22:56
Sutter, Frank 21:394
Sutter, G. 13:100; 14:260
Sutter, J. 1:173
Sutter, Jacob 14:223
Sutter, Joseph 16:142
Sutter, Lucien 17:429
Sutter, Lucius 24:186
Sutter, Nicholas 15:93
Sutter, Theophilus 22:169
Sutter, Valentine 19:197
Sutterfield, Alex 26:180
Suttle, Cleveland 18:211
Suttle, Harvey 11:17
Suttle, Jacob 25:239
Suttle, John N. 8:110
Suttle, William 22:355
Suttlelymer, M. 12:42
Suttler, Peter J. 18:341

Suttler, William 26:59
Suttles, A. M. 27:109
Suttles, Anderson 5:46
Sutton, --- 18:181
Sutton, A. 1:174; 14:115
Sutton, A. J. 15:231
Sutton, Aaron 21:143
Sutton, Able 5:46
Sutton, Albert 26:61
Sutton, Alfred 17:60; 23:272
Sutton, Alonzo 9:225; 18:377
Sutton, Alvin C. 22:270
Sutton, Andrew 3:189
Sutton, Armstead 17:44
Sutton, Benjamin 9:241; 12:52
Sutton, Benjamin E. 22:56
Sutton, C. 23:52; 24:31
Sutton, Charles 27:113
Sutton, Charles B. 15:231
Sutton, Charles C. 25:239
Sutton, Charles E. 13:50; 16:57
Sutton, Charles H. 11:405
Sutton, Charles M. 24:184
Sutton, Clark 25:239
Sutton, D. 3:189
Sutton, E. L. 21:191
Sutton, E. M. 13:100
Sutton, Edward 10:82; 17:362; 20:359
Sutton, Edwin 8:59; 19:273
Sutton, Elbert 9:92
Sutton, Elisha N. 24:184
Sutton, Eugene 17:68
Sutton, F. 23:52
Sutton, Frederick 9:8
Sutton, George 11:75; 15:301; 16:231
Sutton, George W. 22:491
Sutton, Green 17:26
Sutton, H. 3:189
Sutton, Henry 11:329; 22:321; 26:60
Sutton, J. 3:189; 12:80; 14:115; 25:239
Sutton, J. H. 1:170; 9:29
Sutton, J. Peter 15:362
Sutton, J. R. 1:172
Sutton, J. W. 11:282
Sutton, Jacob 9:29; 18:317; 26:112
Sutton, James 4:68; 5:46; 11:397; 17:44
Sutton, John 3:189; 10:139; 20:359; 22:104
Sutton, John D. 21:60

Sutton, John E. 21:261
Sutton, John T. 15:231; 17:264
Sutton, John W. 15:231
Sutton, Jones 7:70
Sutton, L. 7:54; 14:115
Sutton, Lewis 1:191
Sutton, Louis 22:131
Sutton, M. 3:189
Sutton, M. H. 16:231
Sutton, Peter F. 19:103
Sutton, Peter J. 12:97
Sutton, Philetus 18:341
Sutton, Philip 18:297
Sutton, Philip E. 9:39; 26:112
Sutton, Powell 10:82; 20:359
Sutton, R. E. 22:270
Sutton, Rezin 21:81
Sutton, S. 3:189
Sutton, Simon 25:70
Sutton, T. 3:189
Sutton, T. M. 11:426
Sutton, Theodore W. 23:110
Sutton, Thomas 3:189, 224; 17:505
Sutton, Thomas J. 21:106; 22:270
Sutton, Thomas P. 22:169
Sutton, W. H. 26:181
Sutton, W. L. 7:43
Sutton, W. W. 16:380
Sutton, William 1:72; 11:382; 14:131; 15:307; 16:231; 17:201; 19:103; 20:157, 359; 22:156
Sutton, William E. 21:60
Sutton, William H. 17:461; 24:162
Sutton, William M. 8:102
Suttury, Charles 21:285
Sutz, Herman 17:213
Sutzer, J. 18:58
Sutzer, John 10:153
Sutzin, Henry B. 21:81
Suver, Hezekiah 11:171
Suvilin, John 11:173
Suwet, Henry 13:131
Suydam, C. R. 4:57
Suydam, H. 1:72
Suydam, Jac. G. 5:31
Svoun, Lambert 22:270
Sw---, Larry 11:270
Swab, George 19:103
Swabb, John 9:46; 26:129
Swachamer, Isaac 17:452
Swackhamer, Alden H. 12:42

Swackhamer, Jacob 16:135
Swaddle, William C. 22:468
Swader, Frank 22:399
Swadling, Charles 11:111
Swafford, A. P. 17:97
Swafford, Alfred 11:426
Swafford, Charles 14:317
Swafford, Howard 20:47; 21:86
Swafford, James M. 23:52
Swafford, John L. 24:45
Swafford, William 11:188
Swaford, James M. 26:60
Swager, M. 3:190
Swager, Uriah 8:96
Swagerty, James 22:270
Swaggart, John 14:223
Swagger, H. 3:190
Swaggers, Joseph 19:197
Swaggert, Robert 20:359
Swaidler, S. 9:195
Swail, William C. 12:42
Swain, A. 22:270
Swain, Alexander 11:130
Swain, Benjamin F. 24:71
Swain, C. 3:190
Swain, Charles P. 9:126
Swain, Christopher 10:139; 20:359
Swain, D. 3:190
Swain, D. H. 20:359
Swain, Ezra 22:521
Swain, F. C. 17:159
Swain, G. M. 19:262
Swain, George E. 17:421
Swain, George F. 24:162
Swain, George M. 9:195
Swain, Isaiah 9:92
Swain, J. 14:115; 26:61
Swain, J. W. 3:190; 25:327
Swain, John 9:99
Swain, Joshua A. 26:146
Swain, Luther J. 13:50
Swain, Martin 23:258
Swain, Peter 12:42
Swain, Sampson 23:171
Swain, Samuel R. 10:8
Swain, W. T. 1:176
Swain, William 14:115; 24:56
Swainbank, S. 11:232
Swaine, C. 12:163
Swaine, Charles P. 27:106
Swaine, J. W. 16:271
Swaine, Samuel H. 16:57
Swaine, William T. 7:43
Swainey, E. 3:190
Swains, E. G. 15:113

Swaitz, Emory 11:44
Swaize, J. 13:100
Swale, Robert 13:135
Swaley, George 16:57
Swall, Isaac 22:104
Swallow, Charles 20:359
Swallow, Harrison T. 24:56
Swallow, James W. 22:224
Swallows, William J. 7:70
Swalt, Simeon O. 16:58
Swambly, C. 17:365
Swamer, A. 20:359
Swamock, Edward 15:354
Swampton, H. 17:186
Swamrell, John 10:168
Swan, B. F. 22:169
Swan, Charles 14:223
Swan, D. 1:171
Swan, David K. 22:224
Swan, Edward 19:36
Swan, F. 3:190
Swan, G. 19:307
Swan, G. W. 14:223
Swan, George W. 14:115; 22:56, 411
Swan, H. 9:92; 26:61
Swan, H. B. 3:190
Swan, Henry 10:168; 19:197; 27:148
Swan, James 27:148
Swan, James C. 8:33; 18:162
Swan, James Q. 15:46
Swan, John 3:190; 10:82; 15:285; 17:68; 19:103; 20:359; 25:73
Swan, Jonas 23:118
Swan, Levi 18:281
Swan, Moses 9:137; 27:111
Swan, N. C. 1:172
Swan, O. 25:273
Swan, Perry 11:329
Swan, Porter H. 15:136
Swan, R. 14:115, 304; 27:117
Swan, Samuel 8:96
Swan, Solomon 23:171
Swan, V. B. 13:100
Swan, W. D. 22:56
Swan, William 16:231; 17:71; 21:197
Swan, William W. 21:143
Swancent, J. 3:190
Swander, Aaron 23:171
Swanders, A. 14:22
Swane, J. 18:422

Swaney, George W. 17:357
Swaney, Hugh 23:171
Swaney, Luther 10:82; 20:359
Swaney, T. 19:262
Swang, F. 26:60
Swanger, Adam 23:250
Swanger, G. N. 26:60
Swanger, George W. 9:92
Swanger, Ira J. 23:171
Swanger, W. H. 17:87
Swanger, William 11:417
Swangeuser, G. W. 15:60
Swango, James 8:33; 26:182
Swangsner, G. W. 12:63
Swank, Daniel L. 24:180
Swank, Ephraim 23:171
Swank, James F. 18:401
Swank, James O. 18:401
Swank, Nathan E. 17:250
Swank, P. 23:171
Swank, William 11:78
Swann, J. 21:205
Swann, William H. 17:362
Swanner, Albert 10:82
Swanner, John 22:505
Swanson, August 20:33
Swanson, E. 11:194
Swanson, H. 11:45
Swanson, John 11:382; 21:93; 23:52
Swanson, John W. 17:213
Swanson, Joseph 22:321
Swanson, Nils 9:17
Swanson, P. 3:190
Swanson, Rasmus 22:163
Swanson, Reuben 11:426
Swanstrome, Charles F. 12:42
Swanwick, Edward 16:282
Swap, Buchus 11:213
Swap, George 9:29; 15:313
Swape, Allison 12:42
Swape, Peter J. 12:42
Swappoes, P. B. 3:190
Swarer, L. 1:76
Swarm, Joseph 11:170
Swarney, H. W. 14:115
Swarson, Siver 18:162
Swarson, Tharston 10:139; 20:359
Swart, A. W. 16:103
Swart, E. 11:43
Swart, J. 26:61
Swart, Jeremiah 7:112; 21:394
Swart, John 8:96

Swart, John A. 13:50; 16:58
Swart, John T. 9:126; 27:114
Swart, M. M. 3:190
Swart, William M. 22:285
Swarte, H. B. 2:17
Swarthon, George 25:70
Swarthort, G. H. 16:306
Swarthort, G. W. 12:84
Swarthout, Charles A. 23:125
Swarthout, J. 26:181
Swarthout, James V. 9:126; 27:113
Swarthout, O. 23:52
Swarthwood, Dewitt 23:287
Swartiwent, Calvin L. 19:197
Swartkash, C. 3:190
Swartout, Addison 8:33
Swarts, D. G. 8:33
Swarts, E. 3:190; 14:223; 20:149
Swarts, F. 20:157
Swarts, H. 27:115
Swarts, Jacob 22:104
Swarts, P. 3:190
Swarts, William 21:241
Swartsell, David 22:224
Swartwood, Jacob 9:241
Swartwort, A. 22:224
Swartwoudt, Chauncey 20:359
Swartwoudt, Chauncy 10:139
Swartz, --- 27:119
Swartz, A. 3:190; 19:285
Swartz, Abram 4:57
Swartz, D. 1:174
Swartz, D. G. 18:162
Swartz, F. 11:172
Swartz, Frederick 15:15
Swartz, G. 16:231
Swartz, George 3:190
Swartz, H. 1:78
Swartz, H. C. 8:56
Swartz, Henry 11:271, 321; 12:42
Swartz, J. 1:175
Swartz, Jacob 22:224
Swartz, John 11:250
Swartz, John G. 19:103
Swartz, Jones 21:235
Swartz, Joseph 8:33; 18:162
Swartz, M. 3:190
Swartz, W. 1:173
Swartz, Wesley 23:306

Swartz, William 7:112; 8:56; 12:60; 17:26
Swartz, Winfield T. 17:503
Swartzfager, J. F. 1:175
Swartzlander, Adam 15:75
Swartzs, David 20:359
Swartzweller, Adam 17:44
Swasey, A. 13:120
Swathwood, Jonathan 20:20
Swatman, Benjamin F. 21:81
Swatswalter, Asa 22:104
Swatz, Jacob 8:97
Swayer, J. 3:190
Swayman, G. 16:380
Swayne, George 25:72
Swayney, P. 3:190
Swazy, Henry 27:116
Sweager, J. 13:128
Sweaney, John J. 24:45
Sweaney, L. 14:304; 17:482
Sweany, Jacob 21:197
Sweany, John 14:22
Swear, Henry 18:211
Swearegen, Abram 11:382
Swearengen, William 17:60
Swearer, Daniel 1:74
Swearer, G. 3:190
Swearingen, William 10:139
Swearinger, Austin R. 22:457
Swearinger, J. G. 27:107
Swearinger, Simon P. 22:104
Swearinger, William 20:359
Swearington, Thomas 11:77
Swears, Charles 6:19; 18:95
Sweasey, Shannon 17:362
Sweat, Augusta C. 21:169
Sweat, Blaisdell 27:113
Sweat, Christopher C. 17:93
Sweat, Daniel C. 22:438
Sweat, Isabella 21:169
Sweat, John 1:75
Sweat, Sylvester 9:232
Sweat, William J. 10:168
Sweatland, E. 11:129
Swecker, A. 20:14
Sweede, A. 13:120
Sweedie, Thomas 13:50
Sweeds, Louis 21:94
Sween, T. A. H. 22:104

Sweeney, Adam 26:60
Sweeney, D. 13:100
Sweeney, David 18:255; 26:62
Sweeney, E. 9:68
Sweeney, Edward 13:50
Sweeney, G. 23:253
Sweeney, George 1:76
Sweeney, H. 18:401
Sweeney, Henry 27:107
Sweeney, J. 1:170, 171; 9:151; 25:71; 27:108
Sweeney, James 3:190; 10:23
Sweeney, John 1:71; 7:43; 13:100; 14:115, 260; 18:414; 21:394; 23:171
Sweeney, Joseph 14:115
Sweeney, M. 1:71; 3:190
Sweeney, Martin 11:194
Sweeney, Michael 4:57
Sweeney, O. 14:317
Sweeney, Owen 19:197
Sweeney, P. 18:105
Sweeney, Rufus 21:191
Sweeney, Thomas 9:195; 12:65
Sweeney, W. H. 14:304; 27:117
Sweeney, W. P. 3:190
Sweeney, William 10:145; 12:42; 13:50; 19:197; 20:175
Sweeney, William C. 4:57
Sweeny, Adam 9:92
Sweeny, Andrew 13:127
Sweeny, D. 3:190
Sweeny, Daniel 14:223
Sweeny, Edward 16:58
Sweeny, George 11:213
Sweeny, Henry 3:190
Sweeny, Henry C. 21:42
Sweeny, James 11:173
Sweeny, John 4:57; 14:224
Sweeny, Lysander 22:440
Sweeny, M. 21:42
Sweeny, Newton 11:392
Sweeny, Patrick 10:23
Sweeny, Samuel 3:190
Sweeny, Thomas 19:262
Sweeny, W. H. 17:481
Sweeny, William 12:42
Sweeny, Win. J. 11:101
Sweep, Marshall B. 21:144
Sweet, --- 25:68
Sweet, A. W. 25:74
Sweet, Alfred B. 7:112; 21:394

Sweet, Amos G. 16:124
Sweet, Andrew J. 25:72
Sweet, B. F. 3:190
Sweet, Caleb 14:116
Sweet, Calvin 19:197
Sweet, Charles 22:346
Sweet, Charles B. 24:171
Sweet, Charles T. 11:313
Sweet, D. C. 11:250
Sweet, Delos 21:81
Sweet, E. 3:190; 15:75
Sweet, Edward R. 17:71
Sweet, Elias C. 4:57
Sweet, Eugene 16:231
Sweet, G. E. 1:99
Sweet, G. W. 17:68
Sweet, George 10:149;
  23:93; 25:239
Sweet, George W. 4:57;
  23:52
Sweet, H. 3:190; 12:10
Sweet, H. E. 14:116
Sweet, H. F. 21:42
Sweet, H. M. 14:116
Sweet, Henry 10:139;
  17:87; 20:359
Sweet, J. 7:70; 24:85;
  27:109
Sweet, James 1:75; 13:50;
  16:58; 21:43
Sweet, James H. 8:110
Sweet, Joel 27:115
Sweet, John 8:33; 18:162;
  23:125
Sweet, John A. 19:197
Sweet, John L. 21:132
Sweet, John S. 9:151;
  27:111
Sweet, Joseph 22:440
Sweet, Kyler 13:50
Sweet, L. 3:190
Sweet, L. H. 1:176
Sweet, M. 3:190
Sweet, Menzo 24:56
Sweet, Moses 22:321
Sweet, R. 17:502
Sweet, Reuben 22:285
Sweet, Rufus 8:115;
  18:324
Sweet, S. 9:151
Sweet, S. H. 9:151;
  27:108
Sweet, Samuel 27:108
Sweet, Thomas 11:169
Sweet, Timothy 22:156
Sweet, W. H. 18:17
Sweet, W. R. 1:173
Sweet, William 3:190;
  18:255; 19:197;
  25:239, 312; 26:64
Sweet, Zenas 22:156

Sweetapple, J. B. 25:239
Sweetapple, William
  10:82; 20:359
Sweeth, Nelson S. 12:42
Sweetland, A. 1:168
Sweetland, L. P. 14:224
Sweetland, Lyman 26:146
Sweetland, Reuben
  11:250
Sweetman, Henry 15:46
Sweetman, James 14:260
Sweetman, John P. 11:130
Sweetman, Simon D.
  20:359
Sweetman, Siom D.
  10:139
Sweetner, George 9:151;
  27:110
Sweets, David 8:97
Sweetser, Edward 1:73
Sweetser, John W. 22:285
Sweett, George 18:58
Sweetwood, Daniel 12:42
Sweetwood, L. 1:174
Sweezee, John J. 23:102
Sweezy, Bayliss 22:468
Sweezy, Joseph 7:134
Sweiderfritz, Henry 17:27
Sweidhart, David 11:184
Sweig, Alfred 8:43;
  26:182
Sweigart, James 17:208
Sweill, Isaac 17:58
Sweinhart, Peter 19:36
Sweister, Theodore 16:58
Sweitser, P. 3:190
Sweitt, Barnsdell 9:126
Sweitzer, George 9:195
Sweitzer, M. 3:190
Sweitzer, Sylvanus M.
  11:194
Swekett, Lewis 17:445;
  24:168
Swelling, Thomas 8:56
Swells, Hiram 18:255;
  26:64
Swendell, Henry 6:26
Swendensky, M. 24:56
Sweney, F. 16:103
Sweney, L. 27:117
Sweney, Thomas 23:171
Sweney, William 18:162
Swengood, John E. 12:42
Swenk, A. 3:190
Swenk, Jacob 19:103
Swenk, Peter 20:90
Swenney, J. 2:17
Swenson, E. 11:194
Swenson, Kittell 22:285
Swenson, Swen 8:33
Sweringen, L. G. 24:31

Swerner, Jacob H. 3:190
Swertson, Anderson
  18:162
Swerzy, Charles 4:57
Swetland, William L.
  24:97
Swetrer, James C. 8:110
Swett, John 11:171
Swett, W. 25:72
Swezey, Moses 22:346
Swicher, J. J. 12:97
Swick, J. H. 17:157
Swick, John 22:491
Swick, Martin 4:57;
  22:492
Swick, William R. 21:394
Swicker, John 21:394
Swiffert, S. 24:97
Swift, --- 18:195; 26:184
Swift, A. 14:224
Swift, A. B. 19:224
Swift, Byron S. 7:72;
  26:183
Swift, C. 25:239
Swift, Charles 17:27
Swift, Charles M. 5:31
Swift, D. 25:305
Swift, D. W. 5:31; 25:239
Swift, Dean 11:321;
  16:103
Swift, E. B. 12:77; 15:46
Swift, E. J. 1:172
Swift, Edgar W. 20:139
Swift, Edward Cuyler
  26:226
Swift, F. M. 14:116
Swift, G. C. 13:69; 16:231
Swift, George 27:115
Swift, George H. 1:76
Swift, George J. 19:307
Swift, Henry 21:285
Swift, Henry M. 20:139
Swift, J. 3:190; 14:116
Swift, J. W. 13:81; 16:232
Swift, Jabez N. 13:69
Swift, James A. 24:45
Swift, John 11:168;
  13:120; 25:73
Swift, John W. 10:139;
  20:359
Swift, Joseph 18:377
Swift, Legrande 22:467
Swift, Martin 22:131
Swift, Mary Ellen 18:195
Swift, Michael 4:57
Swift, N. J. 9:195
Swift, Peleg 19:103
Swift, Peter 21:285
Swift, R. 23:52
Swift, Richard 11:77
Swift, Ross B. 22:467

Swift, William H. 22:114
Swigar, George W. 17:68
Swiger, Arnisha 22:104
Swiger, E. M. 1:176
Swiger, George 24:171
Swigert, John 17:284
Swigert, Peter 21:394
Swiggart, James W.
   11:334
Swiggitt, N. P. 20:143
Swighart, William 22:56
Swigork, J. 1:170
Swihart, Gabriel 23:80
Swihart, Milton M. 21:60
Swillinger, Peter 12:56
Swills, Kelly 19:278
Swim, W. L. 17:44
Swin, A. H. 21:13
Swin, Jacob 8:115
Swincrer, J. 21:43
Swindell, Andrew J.
   11:213
Swindell, John 22:104
Swindle, Charles 20:101
Swindle, Gibbs 10:154;
   19:197
Swindler, George W.
   21:60
Swindles, Robert 4:57
Swineck, John 21:394
Swinehart, J. W. 3:190
Swinehart, Lewis 18:72
Swineson, Christian
   21:144
Swiney, B. B. 14:116
Swiney, John 20:359
Swiney, R. T. 21:394
Swinford, Richard M.
   24:56
Swing, E. M. 22:506
Swing, William 17:275
Swinger, George C.
   20:116
Swinger, Jesse 23:80
Swinger, John 19:103
Swingle, Henry 7:112
Swingle, John M. L. 7:70
Swingleton, John 18:162
Swink, J. 14:29
Swink, L. 16:58
Swink, Nelson 21:285
Swink, W. W. 20:359
Swink, William H. 24:31
Swinney, Charles 17:351
Swinney, J. M. 3:190
Swinney, John 10:93
Swinney, Mich'l. 22:457
Swinney, Robert H.
   22:132
Swinohart, Jonathan 10:93
Swinson, Howell 24:97

Swinton, Ola 11:111
Swinton, Peter 9:137;
   27:112
Swinton, W. 1:71
Swintz, W. A. 7:43
Swisher, Abraham 22:104
Swisher, G. 25:239
Swisher, George 5:31
Swisher, Henry 9:39;
   26:113
Swisher, J. L. 21:126
Swisher, James W. 8:33;
   15:89; 18:162
Swisher, John 12:42
Swisher, John G. 22:224
Swisher, John J. 15:362
Swisher, Josiah 23:284
Swisher, Manassah 8:97
Swisher, Phileman 22:398
Swisher, Stephen 22:224
Swisher, W. B. 8:68
Swisher, W. L. 26:181
Swisher, William M.
   22:490
Swiskord, Joshua 18:211
Swiss, --- 12:170
Swister, W. H. 9:126
Swiston, A. 27:109
Switser, Alex 11:97
Switzer, George 14:116;
   22:104
Switzer, George F. 7:54
Switzer, Granville 12:60
Switzer, J. 1:175; 3:190
Switzer, Jacob H. 26:60
Switzer, John 12:63;
   15:75
Switzer, John M. 24:31
Switzer, John T. 26:129
Switzer, L. 3:190
Swivel, J. 9:59
Swiveley, George H.
   27:117
Swivley, Isaac 17:163
Swofford, J. P. 19:103
Swofford, N. 22:321
Swofford, W. C. 8:68;
   26:183
Swong, F. 9:92
Swoop, B. F. 22:56
Swoop, George W. 18:181
Swoop, T. P. 16:124
Swoops, --- 17:501
Swoops, J. 14:285
Swop, George 18:317
Swope, Alfred 25:239
Swope, George 26:111
Swope, Jonathan 21:235
Swope, William H. 22:224
Sword, David 5:31
Sword, M. D. 22:457

Sword, Zac 24:204
Sworden, Harvey 23:171
Swords, Elisha 20:101
Swords, Hugh H. 23:288
Sworm, J. 3:190
Swortz, John G. 13:69
Swoth, John 9:92
Swoveland, William 3:190
Swoyer, John B. 24:56
Swungo, James 18:162
Swyman, G. 15:346
Syatt, Lorenzo D. 21:108
Sybold, H. 14:317
Sybraly, Charles C. 8:97
Sydenstricker, S. H. 17:87
Syders, William I. 22:104
Sydes, R. 17:139; 24:203
Sydmer, Joseph 20:129
Syender, F. 3:190
Syers, W. 1:71
Syfrits, Chris 18:401
Sykes, Alfred 21:151, 285
Sykes, Enoch 13:69;
   16:232
Sykes, George 13:50;
   21:285
Sykes, J. 27:109
Sykes, J. E. 23:171
Sykes, John 26:58
Sykes, Joseph 15:231;
   19:37
Sykes, Lewis 11:194
Sykes, Major 21:285
Sykes, Norris 21:285
Sykes, Oliver 21:285
Sykes, Robert 21:151, 285
Sykes, W. E. 1:168
Sylburd, Henry 18:211
Sylers, S. 3:190
Syles, David G. 25:239
Syliay, L. 18:115
Syling, Lewis 6:10
Sylocy, Peter 22:271
Sylor, P. 1:77
Sylva, B. A. 10:212
Sylvan, J. J. 3:190
Sylvester, A. 14:245;
   25:240
Sylvester, A. T. 9:195;
   19:230
Sylvester, Alfred 19:104
Sylvester, D. 3:190;
   15:346; 16:380
Sylvester, E. 3:190
Sylvester, F. M. 17:167
Sylvester, George 16:136
Sylvester, H. 15:280
Sylvester, J. 3:190
Sylvester, J. Q. A. 25:240
Sylvester, Robert 25:69
Sylvester, Silas 13:50

Sylvester, Silas A. 15:231
Sylvester, W. T. 9:114
Sylvester, Y. 14:224
Sylvester, Z. F. 18:181
Sylvester, Z. T. 10:187
Sylvestine, Anthony 25:286
Sylvia, G. 1:169
Sym, Henry 10:139; 20:360
Symer, Albert A. C. 13:50
Symes, Albert A. C. 16:58
Symes, John 21:151
Symington, Daniel 16:380
Symington, H. 11:17
Syminister, Eli 15:367
Syminster, Eli 12:100
Symmerman, H. 25:240
Symmonds, John 11:172
Symmons, Virgil 9:14
Symonds, A. 1:174
Symonds, Charles L. 22:56
Symonds, G. 17:245
Symonds, J. L. 24:31
Symonds, James W. 9:234
Symonds, L. Charles 17:409
Symonds, Lamon R. 16:58
Symonds, R. H. 18:72
Symons, Jasper N. 22:132
Symons, Joel 18:223
Symons, Shadrick 10:139
Symons, Shadrock 20:360
Symoure, Oscar 5:31
Sympson, B. 13:100
Sympson, F. M. 9:70
Syms, James 10:139; 20:360
Syms, S. 25:240
Syms, William 21:394
Synthia, John 11:171
Syphers, N. L. 21:394
Syphonese, Charles 21:394
Syples, Kuney 23:102
Syre, John 12:158
Syre, William 8:97
Syres, Abraham 12:52
Syse, Roswell 20:360
Sytle, John 15:231
Syungland, John 22:346
Syverson, Knud 21:261
Sywassink, B. W. 1:175
Syze, Boswell 10:82

T

T---, --- 12:147; 25:74
T---, A. A. 15:75

T---, B. 10:188; 17:218; 23:314
T---, B. J. 17:365
T---, B. R. 20:178
T---, B. T. 10:188
T---, B. W. 17:93
T---, C. 11:46
T---, D. 24:115
T---, D. E. 14:271
T---, D. R. 21:169
T---, E. 20:60
T---, E. H. 18:422
T---, E. M. 18:181
T---, E. N. 15:233
T---, E. S. 18:377
T---, E. W. C. 23:306
T---, F. 12:143; 15:95
T---, G. 14:271; 17:157; 26:185
T---, G. B. 23:314
T---, G. R. M. A. 17:357
T---, G. W. 15:46
T---, George O. 25:74
T---, H. 18:377; 23:269
T---, H. M. S. 24:70
T---, I. B. 18:181
T---, I. L. 16:114
T---, J. 15:46; 18:39; 20:360; 22:355; 24:115; 25:75
T---, J. C. 26:185
T---, J. E. L. 23:314
T---, J. H. 23:245
T---, J. K. 26:185
T---, J. M. 20:60
T---, J. N. 17:351; 21:169
T---, J. P. 20:157
T---, J. W. 23:278; 24:115
T---, John P. 20:360
T---, L. B. 25:75
T---, L. C. 14:271
T---, L. K. 15:153
T---, M. 20:60; 25:305
T---, M. C. 26:214
T---, N. 25:328
T---, N. C. 16:306
T---, Nicholas 11:342
T---, P. M. 20:181
T---, P. W. 14:271
T---, R. 12:167; 25:74, 328
T---, R. C. 22:355
T---, R. S. 23:206
T---, R. W. 25:75
T---, S. 27:122
T---, Silas 15:295
T---, T. 11:397; 18:427; 20:360; 21:209
T---, T. A. 18:377
T---, T. L. 21:169
T---, T. R. 17:365

T---, T. S. H. 12:143
T---, U. C. 17:357
T---, V--- B--- 26:66
T---, V. B. 18:256
T---, V. W. 12:100
T---, W. 11:314; 12:100; 17:338; 19:307; 25:305
T---, W. B. 21:169
T---, W. S. 9:228
T---, W. T. 25:305
T---d-, G. 11:343
T--oll, John 22:441
Ta---or, Israel S. 25:76
Taaney, Charles T. 9:99
Tabal, Frederick 18:162
Tabb, Allen 17:186
Tabeason, M. 14:116
Taber, A. G. 25:74
Taber, Alden 17:289
Taber, C. H. 7:43
Taber, Granville 24:45
Taber, Halbut 8:115
Taber, J. 3:191
Taber, Jesse 22:56
Taber, John 12:140
Taber, L. 1:177
Taber, S. 18:58
Taber, S. C. 27:121
Taber, S. H. 14:22
Taber, Samuel 10:153
Taber, Silas 3:191
Taber, William 21:15
Taber, William D. 17:275
Tabert, J. H. 18:255; 26:66
Tabias, Asheel 16:232
Tabin, James 3:191
Tabor, B. 3:191
Tabor, E. S. 7:43
Tabor, Gardiner 21:15
Tabor, Henry 12:42
Tabor, James A. 23:102
Tabor, John 20:360
Tabor, John T. 17:208
Tabor, S. C. 9:151
Tabor, S. H. 13:100
Tabor, William S. 15:136
Tabors, E. 8:76
Tabott, James 20:360
Taboy, Benjamin 14:224
Tabscot, J. 25:240
Tabst, Fred 26:184
Tacey, Frank 22:156
Tacey, George 22:173
Tack, Abraham 8:97
Tack, Charles 8:33; 26:184
Tackelbury, Charles W. 12:158
Tackerberry, I. 19:197

Tacket, George 20:3
Tacket, Philip 22:271
Tackett, J. 9:59
Tackett, John 14:285
Tackett, John W. 24:31
Tackett, T. 17:336
Tackett, W. 23:253
Tackett, Warren 22:522
Tackett, William 21:43;
22:56
Tackington, William
26:184
Tacklebury, George
13:120
Tackswell, J. 17:60
Tacler, David 22:224
Tadale, Alfred 18:72
Tadden, Joseph E. 22:163
Tade, John T. 23:102
Tadlock, Edward 6:19;
18:95
Tadman, W. P. 14:22
Taef, H. 2:18
Taeslor, G. 14:224
Tafel, H. C. 16:124
Tafel, Hugo 17:213
Taff, Ansell H. 1:79
Taff, George 7:43
Taff, J. M. 12:143; 20:360
Taff, John 1:78
Taff, Moses 7:61
Taffe, John 8:33
Taffee, James B. 26:227
Taffey, J. S. 23:116
Taffilmire, Charles 8:76
Taffinger, Joseph 13:50
Taffle, James B. 9:238
Taffner, Samuel 14:224
Tafield, T. 15:365
Taft, --- 27:123
Taft, A. C. 8:97
Taft, Benjamin 14:224
Taft, Bennona 19:197
Taft, Edward 15:46
Taft, Francis H. 10:23
Taft, J. B. 11:131
Taft, James B. 23:125
Taft, James W. 16:124
Taft, John 7:15
Taft, Joshua 15:349
Taft, Josiah 16:380
Taft, Thomas 14:116
Taft, Timothy F. 23:16
Tafts, J. T. 12:10
Tafts, William B. 18:281
Tage, James 12:168
Taggard, Arch 25:240
Taggart, Albert R. 7:112
Taggart, Alexander 23:14
Taggart, George 4:57
Taggart, J. 14:285

Taggart, James 21:394
Taggart, S. D. 9:114
Taggart, William 10:97
Taggart, William A.
22:399
Taggarty, Jackson 3:191
Taggert, Charles 8:115
Taggert, James 19:37
Taggert, John 3:191
Tagne, Henry 25:240
Tague, J. T. 11:330
Tague, James B. 17:201
Tague, Parker 3:191
Tahbenmerkle, C. 16:271
Tail, Wendell 9:195
Tailor, C. 8:110
Tailor, John 13:120
Tailor, William 5:46
Tainter, David 9:195;
19:271
Tair, James E. 9:114
Tait, E. L. 14:287
Tait, Granville 11:214
Tait, Henry H. 15:93
Tait, J. 25:75
Tait, James M. 18:72
Tait, Joseph 13:120
Tait, Tipton 22:104
Tait, William 12:42
Take, Henry 9:211
Takerly, T. 13:100
Takey, Harvey 7:17
Tal-e-peo-sa 25:335
Talan, Patrick 3:191
Talbert, Addison 23:171
Talbert, Alfred B. 22:412
Talbert, Benjamin 24:56
Talbert, Elijah 11:393
Talbert, George P. 12:81
Talbert, J. 22:56
Talbert, J. A. 6:9
Talbert, J. B. 4:57
Talbert, J. P. 25:240
Talbert, James M. 10:139
Talbert, John 7:112
Talbert, Lawrence 17:139;
24:205
Talbert, P. 18:95
Talbert, R. 3:191
Talbert, Thomas J. 7:112
Talbert, William 11:79
Talbert, William D. 7:112
Talbet, J. A. 18:105
Talborn, Henry 17:186
Talbot, B. P. 11:117
Talbot, C. 11:271
Talbot, Charles 12:168
Talbot, E. R. 25:286
Talbot, George 7:78;
25:305

Talbot, Henry 18:255;
26:67
Talbot, Henry T. 11:46
Talbot, J. 1:80
Talbot, James 10:93;
12:158
Talbot, James B. 10:168
Talbot, John 21:394
Talbot, Jonathan 11:79
Talbot, L. 16:380
Talbot, Nicholas 8:56
Talbot, T. J. 23:171
Talbot, Thomas C. 21:394
Talbot, William 8:33
Talbot, William H. 1:79
Talboth, George 18:435
Talbott, Greenby 24:45
Talbott, James M. 20:360
Talbott, John 7:17
Talbott, Joseph 1:79
Talbott, Nicholas R.
21:235
Talbott, Philip 6:13
Talbott, Samuel 14:285
Talbott, W. H. 15:93
Talbott, William 18:162
Talbott, William T.
22:104
Talboys, Robert V. 23:93
Talcott, Ebenezer C.
13:50
Talcott, Ezra T. 18:211
Talcott, Joseph 24:62
Talden, I. 26:67
Talden, J. 18:255
Talent, Henry 22:506
Talent, L. 1:178
Taler, F. M. 26:65
Taler, Henry 16:232
Talf---, H. 25:76
Talifero, Claiborne 23:14
Talk, A. 14:116
Talkington, William 8:33;
17:87
Tall, P. 14:285
Talleckson, Talleck
20:117
Talleman, Frank 17:320
Tallent, George G. 22:271
Tallent, William C.
21:106
Taller, William 17:186
Tallerday, Marshall A.
17:321
Tallett, Zander 18:162
Talley, Allen 11:79
Talley, B. W. 14:116
Talley, Benjamin R.
23:266
Talley, Charles T. P.
17:167

Talley, Henderson 23:291
Talley, John 11:426
Talley, Joseph W. 11:189
Talley, P. 13:100
Talley, Stephen J. 22:271
Talley, T. 1:80
Talley, T. L. 22:412
Talley, Willis 23:80
Tallhamer, Jonas 23:14
Tallifaro, Hardin 22:104
Tallmadge, David 9:126
Tallmadge, Grier 18:353
Tallmage, T. 9:151
Tallman, Alexis W. 23:196
Tallman, C. H. 6:33
Tallman, George 23:171
Tallon, Martin 15:320; 19:104
Tallor, Alfred 15:231
Talls, Daniels 16:232
Tallus, Thomas 23:80
Tallust, William 18:270
Tally, Richard 23:289
Tally, Robertson 8:33; 18:162
Tally, William 11:426; 17:275
Talmadce, Augustus 15:303
Talmadge, Augustus 16:232
Talmadge, David 27:122
Talmadge, Gier 5:54
Talmage, Edgar L. 21:81
Talmage, Fred 27:120
Talmage, G. 1:79
Talman, A. 3:191
Talman, G. W. 11:417
Talman, Marcus 17:152
Talman, Robert 11:315
Talman, Truston C. 12:42
Talman, Ulysses S. 23:52
Talman, W. C. 3:191
Talmon, D. 14:224
Taloday, Henry 23:183
Talson, Riley 26:184
Talsott, Chauncey H. 11:443
Talte, John W. 8:68
Tamahill, James 20:360
Tambach, Joseph Mak 19:104
Tambar, John 9:68
Tame, O. J. 21:245
Taminsky, Antonio 11:46
Tamlinson, Philo 15:161
Tamm, August 10:139
Tamm, John 27:122
Tamnor, J. 14:116
Tamore, Albert 22:355

Tampered, C. 14:304
Tampied, C. 17:474
Tampir, C. 27:123
Tampkins, J. A. 14:260
Tamsett, W. T. 19:269
Tamsey, Oscar G. 17:41
Tanahil, James 10:93
Tanar, Horace 9:195
Tanbitz, Frank 21:11
Tanbrick, A. 3:191
Tancred, M. 3:191
Tanderburk, Abel E. 20:360
Tandorf, --- 14:116
Tandy, Albert 22:321
Tandy, George 22:321
Tanebling, G. H. 1:179
Taner, Sandy 7:134
Tanery, Liney 18:211
Taney, James 25:240
Tanfield, Harriet K. 26:244
Tangerhan, Charles 18:281
Tanguary, William J. 22:442
Tank, George N. 15:268
Tankersby, C. A. 11:18
Tanksley, George 22:104
Tankwood, James 7:134
Tann, L. 16:232
Tannamaker, --- 26:185
Tannehill, Alpheus 10:139; 20:360
Tannehill, Hugh H. 21:235
Tannehill, Martin B. V. 10:83
Tannehill, Winnian 24:56
Tanner, --- 22:355
Tanner, A. 3:191
Tanner, A. V. 13:100
Tanner, Alva C. 23:94
Tanner, August 20:360
Tanner, Charles E. 10:83; 20:360
Tanner, D. 1:78, 177
Tanner, D. F. 27:120
Tanner, David 25:240
Tanner, Emanuel 8:100
Tanner, Fred. F. 19:104
Tanner, Frederick 14:224
Tanner, G. 1:78
Tanner, G. F. 1:178
Tanner, George W. E. 17:204
Tanner, H. 18:424
Tanner, Henry 25:75
Tanner, Hiram 18:255; 26:67
Tanner, Ira 1:79

Tanner, J. 1:177; 3:191; 19:104
Tanner, J. B. 3:191
Tanner, J. E. 23:171
Tanner, J. H. 20:32
Tanner, Jackson 24:168
Tanner, John 14:224; 27:119
Tanner, John F. 22:522
Tanner, John L. 22:238
Tanner, Joseph 16:232
Tanner, Judson L. 4:57
Tanner, L. M. 1:179
Tanner, M. 3:191
Tanner, M. L. 11:79
Tanner, O. M. 25:75
Tanner, T. 27:120
Tanner, T. C. 18:335
Tanner, Thomas 9:151
Tanner, W. P. 1:176
Tanner, William 9:195; 19:271
Tanner, William W. 11:417
Tanney, Patrick 19:320
Tannier, Frederick 8:68
Tannihill, Henry 7:13
Tanning, Edward M. 25:75
Tannoff, John 10:23
Tanns, W. D. 21:43
Tanschirit, Ed 3:191
Tanson, R. 14:267
Tant, Andrew J. 23:302
Tantlinger, J. M. 1:179
Tantlinger, John S. 20:184
Tanton, M. 13:100
Tapan, Samuel P. 22:442
Tape, William 22:224
Tapering, D. M. 9:60
Tapes, W. T. 14:116
Tapescott, Charles 11:417
Tapl, F. 12:88; 16:306
Taples, William H. 9:126
Tapless, William H. 27:122
Tapley, George S. 15:60
Tapley, John 23:52
Tapley, Monroe 11:336
Taplin, Amos W. 11:292
Taplin, Charles H. 13:50
Taplin, James 20:101
Taplin, Osman P. 15:93
Tapner, M. A. 22:224
Tapp, George 3:191
Tapp, George W. 26:184
Tapp, Thomas 11:409; 18:95
Tappan, Charles 19:197
Tappan, Christopher 20:360

Tappan, George 20:117
Tappan, James A. 10:139; 20:360
Tappan, William E. 4:57
Tappe, John 18:162
Tappen, Moses 11:131
Tapper, George 15:5
Tapper, William 21:95
Tappin, M. 26:65
Tappin, Martin 9:92
Tapping, John 15:93
Tappins, Edward 12:42
Tapsico, Jacob 5:46
Tar, Washington 25:75
Tarbell, J. 25:305
Tarbell, Joel D. 10:23
Tarbell, L. J. 27:120
Tarbell, T. I. 9:151
Tarbell, W. S. 15:354; 16:282
Tarbert, F. H. 21:394
Tarbet, J. M. 26:185
Tarblee, Josiah 7:79
Tarbor, Albert E. 16:144
Tarbox, A. D. 23:171
Tarbox, C. H. 14:224
Tarbox, C. P. 1:177
Tarbox, Chandler 21:394
Tarbox, D. Brainerd 15:94
Tarbox, George H. 15:3
Tarbox, H. 16:282
Tarbox, William S. 7:70
Tarbrick, --- 14:116
Tarbull, John E. 8:56
Tarbush, Nelson 22:321
Tarbutton, Reuben S. 22:271
Tarby, John 7:134; 21:394
Tardam, William 22:321
Tardley, A. C. 23:253
Tardy, James A. 22:56
Tarentine, M. F. 22:271
Tarey, L. 3:191
Targat, Frank 15:231
Targendon, Isaac 22:321
Targer, P. L. 15:93
Targer, Peter L. 12:63
Targle, Patrick 26:184
Tarham, W. J. 16:271
Tarin, --- 19:323
Tarin, Manuel 19:320
Tarkington, William 18:162
Tarlbut, Alfred 7:134
Tarler, John E. 14:224
Tarlton, J. T. 9:29
Tarlton, John H. 9:238
Tarlton, John N. 26:227
Tarlton, T. W. 10:212
Tarman, Edward 1:80
Tarnage, Henry 26:65

Tarnage, Oliver 4:57
Tarner, Jack 18:407
Tarner, Nancy Jane 18:407
Tarnes, John 14:224
Taro, Richard 7:134
Taroy, Benjamin F. 12:65
Tarpenning, Lewis 10:83; 20:360
Tarpenning, S. 13:50
Tarplar, Richard 25:240
Tarpley, John 21:218
Tarr, Hamilton J. 23:94
Tarr, John F. 1:79
Tarr, S. Y. 14:116
Tarrer, John 20:3
Tarry, William 11:214
Tart, Aken 21:394
Tart, John 16:232
Tartare, R. H. 9:60
Tarton, J. W. 1:179
Tarvis, G. W. 3:191
Tarwater, Alex 23:314
Tarwater, Jesse 21:285
Tarwater, William D. 9:225; 18:377
Tascoe, J. 13:100
Tasdale, M. E. 7:61
Taser, Albert 18:162
Tash, Jesse 22:56
Tash, T. 1:177
Tasier, George J. 8:56
Tasker, Adolphus 16:58
Tasker, C. B. 1:78
Tasker, Edward L. 9:126
Tasker, R. 1:177
Tasker, William 1:80
Taskill, C. F. 21:394
Tasquinn, J. B. 25:284
Tassay, P. 1:80
Tasser, Albert 8:33
Tasser, Edward 17:16
Tassler, C. B. 1:177
Tate, A. 7:43; 9:151; 27:120
Tate, D. 25:240
Tate, F. 1:79
Tate, Francis M. 21:106
Tate, George 26:214
Tate, George H. 10:168; 19:197
Tate, H. C. 16:232
Tate, Henry 26:214
Tate, Isaac 7:134
Tate, J. 1:178; 9:225; 13:100; 18:377; 21:43
Tate, J. E. 13:100
Tate, James 16:232

Tate, John 18:401; 20:129; 21:60, 285; 22:271
Tate, John R. 8:33; 18:162; 26:67
Tate, Joseph 21:285
Tate, Joshua 11:46
Tate, Leander 21:285
Tate, Lorenzo 10:139; 20:360
Tate, N. F. 21:394
Tate, R. E. 8:68; 26:185
Tate, Robert 11:393; 23:307
Tate, Samuel 18:195
Tate, Silas 21:285
Tate, Thomas 12:124; 15:136
Tate, W. 12:100
Tate, W. H. 9:225; 18:377
Tate, Wesley 22:321
Tate, William 9:211
Tate, William A. 23:52
Tate, William C. 9:105
Tate, William I. 12:42
Tatem, William 19:37
Tatern, S. R. 25:240
Tathe, C. 12:93
Tatlock, Abram 20:20
Tatlom, J. W. 9:238
Tatlow, J. W. 26:227
Tatlow, Thomas 21:81
Tatman, Isaac 22:224
Tatman, W. P. 13:100
Tatnam, Putnam 12:42
Tator, Henry 5:54
Tatro, J. B. 9:151; 27:120
Tatro, Joseph 15:354; 16:283
Tatro, L. 3:191
Tatt, Fostin 21:394
Tattee, C. 16:306
Tatten, James 4:57
Tattersall, James 7:63
Tatterson, John 4:68
Tattra, Alfred 3:191
Tatum, James 9:225; 18:377
Tatune, J. 3:191
Taturn, Josephus 22:458
Taub, Charles 18:211
Taube, F. 1:179
Taunt, Stephen 23:196
Taunter, E. 14:116
Tauraw, William H. 13:50
Tausend, Robert 14:22
Tauven, W. 24:72
Tavvial, Inor C. 9:29
Tawah, Antoine 9:126
Tawer, John 21:394
Tawham, J. 18:255; 26:67

Tawlis, Calvin 24:31
Taws, Charles 10:168;
    19:197
Tawsley, James 13:50
Tawson, Eugene 15:365
Taxtaler, F. G. 11:131
Tay, Honis 26:184
Tay, S. W. 15:364
Tayler, A. 7:76
Tayler, William H. 7:76
Taylor, --- 11:98, 342;
    13:50; 15:23, 75,
    136; 17:357; 18:40;
    20:44; 27:123
Taylor, A. 3:191; 11:221;
    25:305; 27:123
Taylor, A. B. 3:191;
    14:263
Taylor, A. J. 23:52; 24:31
Taylor, A. L. 3:191
Taylor, A. O. 11:173
Taylor, A. S. 11:87
Taylor, Abram 18:40
Taylor, Addison 23:272
Taylor, Albert 14:237;
    18:40; 20:184
Taylor, Albert P. 23:171
Taylor, Alexander 9:105
Taylor, Alfred 4:57;
    18:255; 26:66
Taylor, Alfred J. 10:23
Taylor, Allen 22:458
Taylor, Alonzo M. 4:57
Taylor, Amy 18:40
Taylor, Anderson 10:83;
    20:360
Taylor, Andrew 8:78;
    10:139; 20:360;
    26:184
Taylor, Andrew J. 22:224
Taylor, Ansel G. 25:240
Taylor, Asher F. 17:421
Taylor, Augustus 7:112
Taylor, Austin 9:215
Taylor, Authur S. 18:401
Taylor, B. 1:80; 10:150;
    14:224, 260; 18:58;
    25:240
Taylor, B. C. 10:23;
    13:100
Taylor, B. E. 14:23;
    16:306
Taylor, Ball 7:134
Taylor, Benjamin 4:57;
    5:46; 9:105; 11:174;
    13:50; 16:58; 17:208,
    277; 18:341
Taylor, Bennet 19:197
Taylor, Bennett 10:168
Taylor, Bob 6:22
Taylor, Boon 22:321

Taylor, Burl 23:272
Taylor, Byron 13:69;
    16:232
Taylor, C. 3:191; 12:63;
    13:126; 15:231;
    19:246
Taylor, C. B. 3:191;
    16:232
Taylor, C. F. 25:240
Taylor, C. M. 4:57
Taylor, C. W. 3:224;
    17:504
Taylor, Caleb 7:134
Taylor, Calvin 22:224
Taylor, Certer 22:105
Taylor, Charles 5:54;
    9:160, 195, 232;
    12:42; 15:82, 113,
    287; 17:44; 18:95;
    19:37, 104, 197;
    20:360; 21:394;
    22:224; 23:52, 287;
    25:240; 27:123
Taylor, Charles A. 10:23;
    17:421; 22:156
Taylor, Charles E. 9:126
Taylor, Charles H. 19:197;
    27:122
Taylor, Charles L. 24:97
Taylor, Charles M. 19:330
Taylor, Charles P. 23:102
Taylor, Charles W. 16:80
Taylor, Christopher
    11:321
Taylor, Cicero S. 22:156
Taylor, Clayborn 27:121
Taylor, Clayborne 9:137
Taylor, Clayton 15:9
Taylor, Clingman 10:83;
    20:360
Taylor, D. 1:80; 3:191;
    9:202; 19:293
Taylor, D. L. 17:44
Taylor, D. R. 25:240
Taylor, Daniel 7:54;
    17:399; 21:394;
    22:412
Taylor, Daniel S. 7:54
Taylor, Daniel W. 21:163
Taylor, David 1:79; 9:137;
    12:42; 15:60; 17:139;
    20:149; 21:87;
    24:205; 27:121
Taylor, David H. 22:132
Taylor, Degrove 22:156
Taylor, Dillon W. 13:50
Taylor, Dilton W. 16:58
Taylor, Doctor 23:289
Taylor, Dwight 27:123
Taylor, E. 1:177; 3:191;
    9:228; 11:272;

Taylor, E. 14:263, 291;
    17:186; 18:377;
    23:171; 25:240;
    27:120
Taylor, E. F. 15:46
Taylor, E. M. 5:31;
    27:156
Taylor, E. R. 1:80
Taylor, E. V. 1:178
Taylor, Ebenezer L. 17:87
Taylor, Ed 7:134
Taylor, Edmond 11:214
Taylor, Edmund 21:285
Taylor, Edward 9:211;
    11:101; 12:52;
    14:116; 18:115;
    21:395; 23:265
Taylor, Edward B. 9:126;
    27:122
Taylor, Edwin D. 20:152
Taylor, Elbert E. 10:139;
    20:360
Taylor, Eli 22:56
Taylor, Eli C. 12:42
Taylor, Elias 5:46; 11:277
Taylor, Elijah 20:47
Taylor, Elijah L. 11:426
Taylor, Elisha 20:360
Taylor, Ellis C. 4:57
Taylor, Elmore 11:131;
    18:286; 26:135
Taylor, Emerson S.
    22:271
Taylor, Emmanuel 22:173
Taylor, Emory B. 22:57
Taylor, Ephraim 21:395
Taylor, Essex 7:134
Taylor, Eugene B. 10:139;
    20:360
Taylor, F. 1:176; 14:116;
    18:58, 195
Taylor, F. M. 17:275
Taylor, Fir'n. 1:79
Taylor, Francis C. 21:95
Taylor, Francis M. 18:401
Taylor, Frank 1:78;
    10:177; 19:197
Taylor, Fred 16:283
Taylor, Frederick 19:37
Taylor, Frederick B. 24:97
Taylor, G. 3:191; 11:251;
    14:285; 24:85
Taylor, G. A. 3:191; 23:52
Taylor, G. P. 15:231
Taylor, G. W. 7:43; 11:46;
    16:232; 21:207
Taylor, General 7:134;
    9:211
Taylor, George 4:57; 8:68;
    9:166; 10:30, 97;
    11:46, 174;

Taylor, George 13:50, 59; 14:116, 224; 15:333; 16:232; 17:44, 87, 289; 18:414; 19:104; 21:60, 395; 22:441; 25:240
Taylor, George F. 8:115; 22:271
Taylor, George H. 26:130
Taylor, George W. 1:78; 13:50; 16:58; 22:442, 458
Taylor, Gerard 27:123
Taylor, Green 8:68
Taylor, Gus 8:78
Taylor, H. 1:79; 3:191; 18:17; 25:75; 27:121
Taylor, H. C. 3:191; 14:245; 27:123
Taylor, H. P. 19:37
Taylor, H. W. 1:80; 20:140
Taylor, Harris 9:211
Taylor, Harrison 17:444; 21:285; 24:163
Taylor, Henry 7:61; 9:60; 11:417; 12:42; 13:50; 17:27, 139; 19:37; 20:101; 21:132; 22:321; 24:205
Taylor, Henry B. 21:395
Taylor, Henry C. 17:239
Taylor, Henry M. 10:23; 22:468
Taylor, Henry S. 27:119
Taylor, Hesley 9:105
Taylor, Hiram 17:410; 22:224
Taylor, Hiram T. 12:42
Taylor, I. H. 19:49
Taylor, I. I. 18:211
Taylor, Isaac 8:58; 11:46; 12:42; 13:50; 17:101; 21:106
Taylor, J. 1:80, 96, 100, 177, 178, 179; 3:191; 13:100; 14:23; 16:271; 27:120, 123
Taylor, J. A. 18:72
Taylor, J. B. 1:178
Taylor, J. C. 9:60; 20:135, 360
Taylor, J. D. 25:74
Taylor, J. F. 3:191; 9:225; 11:334; 17:204; 18:377
Taylor, J. G. 20:44
Taylor, J. H. 12:158
Taylor, J. L. 10:32; 20:360

Taylor, J. M. 3:191; 11:342; 14:116
Taylor, J. N. 23:206
Taylor, J. P. 22:493
Taylor, J. R. 1:177; 14:23; 20:60
Taylor, J. S. 26:185
Taylor, J. W. 1:179; 3:191; 7:70; 9:60; 13:100; 14:116; 23:171
Taylor, J. W. A. 25:240
Taylor, Jackson 25:240
Taylor, Jacob 9:205
Taylor, Jacob C. 10:83
Taylor, James 6:19; 9:39, 92; 10:83; 12:77, 93, 167; 14:116, 331; 15:75; 17:186, 253; 18:95, 105, 341, 377; 20:26, 361; 21:285, 395; 22:104, 132, 271, 321; 26:114
Taylor, James B. 7:54; 8:110; 10:83; 20:361; 24:45
Taylor, James C. 18:401; 20:26
Taylor, James E. 4:57
Taylor, James H. 9:105, 126; 26:66; 27:122
Taylor, James J. 9:126; 27:122
Taylor, James L. 26:226
Taylor, James M. 9:228; 11:289, 314; 18:281; 19:104; 22:173; 24:56; 25:327
Taylor, James N. 8:33; 18:162
Taylor, James P. 21:43
Taylor, James T. 23:80
Taylor, James W. 10:23; 21:81; 23:171
Taylor, James Z. 11:79
Taylor, Jarrett 22:132
Taylor, Jarvis 15:3
Taylor, Jasper 11:214
Taylor, Jeremiah 9:17; 22:224
Taylor, Jerry 1:192
Taylor, Jesse 8:56; 17:232
Taylor, Jessie 16:232
Taylor, John 1:78; 4:57; 7:134; 9:29, 99, 195; 10:83, 139; 14:267; 15:9, 60, 153; 16:58, 80; 17:416; 18:115, 317; 19:233, 271, 286, 320; 20:361; 21:43, 144; 23:307;

Taylor, John 24:70, 155; 25:335; 26:65, 113, 184; 27:123
Taylor, John B. 17:27; 22:104
Taylor, John C. 9:29; 18:317; 26:113
Taylor, John E. 12:42
Taylor, John G. 4:57; 17:60
Taylor, John H. 16:380; 19:37
Taylor, John L. 25:240
Taylor, John M. 6:7; 24:46, 85
Taylor, John N. 9:92
Taylor, John P. 11:113
Taylor, John R. 22:271
Taylor, John W. 4:57; 10:139; 11:87; 18:202; 20:361; 23:80; 24:85; 26:66, 214
Taylor, John Y. 22:57
Taylor, Johnson 12:42
Taylor, Johnson R. 22:132
Taylor, Jonathan 22:132
Taylor, Joseph 7:70; 9:60; 11:289; 12:52, 97; 13:50; 14:224; 15:362; 17:16; 19:104; 21:395; 22:132, 271; 23:283; 24:168
Taylor, Joseph C. 22:105
Taylor, Joseph S. 17:351
Taylor, Joseph W. 16:58
Taylor, K. 21:151
Taylor, L. 14:116; 18:58; 22:224
Taylor, L. P. 17:275
Taylor, L. W. 10:83; 20:361
Taylor, Lander C. 14:320; 25:282
Taylor, Lee 19:293
Taylor, Leonard 9:195; 19:269
Taylor, Leroy 8:97
Taylor, Levi 11:113; 21:285
Taylor, Lewis 8:112; 17:186; 21:285
Taylor, Lewis B. 10:23
Taylor, Lindsey 7:112
Taylor, Lorenzo P. M. 5:54
Taylor, Lucius 20:109
Taylor, Lum 22:524
Taylor, Luther H. 11:321
Taylor, Luther N. 21:81

Taylor, M. 5:31; 12:143; 14:224; 20:28; 22:224, 321
Taylor, M. D. 3:191
Taylor, M. P. 14:224
Taylor, M. V. L. 11:342
Taylor, Madison 17:44
Taylor, Mahlon 8:68
Taylor, Marcell 17:187
Taylor, Marcus M. 22:412
Taylor, Mark 24:85
Taylor, Mathew F. 22:458
Taylor, Melvin 21:43
Taylor, Moses 7:43; 10:146
Taylor, N. 3:191
Taylor, N. P. 3:191
Taylor, Nathaniel 22:224
Taylor, Newberry 10:155; 19:197
Taylor, Norman 9:14
Taylor, O. 1:79; 19:104
Taylor, O. C. 25:75
Taylor, O. M. 1:178
Taylor, Oliver 10:83; 20:361; 22:57
Taylor, Orrin 25:240
Taylor, Orrin L. 16:58
Taylor, Orrin S. 13:50
Taylor, P. M. 9:92; 26:65
Taylor, Pardov D. 22:156
Taylor, Perry 16:135
Taylor, Peter 3:191
Taylor, Philip 22:105
Taylor, Phoenix 12:52
Taylor, Pleasant 9:60
Taylor, Polion 22:321
Taylor, R 9:60
Taylor, R. 1:80, 178; 3:191; 14:116
Taylor, R. B. 14:116
Taylor, R. C. 18:181
Taylor, R. H. 3:191; 24:115
Taylor, R. J. 1:177
Taylor, R. P. 1:79; 7:43
Taylor, R. S. 14:116
Taylor, Redic 22:57
Taylor, Reub 24:205
Taylor, Reuben 10:177; 17:455
Taylor, Richard 10:207
Taylor, Richard E. 19:307
Taylor, Richard N. 17:454; 24:186
Taylor, Richmond 22:321
Taylor, Robert 6:33; 7:112; 9:195; 10:139; 17:139, 151; 18:95, 255, 401; 19:262; 20:361;

Taylor, Robert 21:285; 24:205; 25:240, 270, 327; 26:66
Taylor, Robert E. 22:346
Taylor, Robert H. 11:79
Taylor, Roland 16:80
Taylor, Roma 7:134
Taylor, Rub 19:197
Taylor, Rufus K. 18:414
Taylor, S. 1:178, 179; 9:60; 16:125; 17:284; 27:122
Taylor, S. B. 3:191
Taylor, S. C. 1:177
Taylor, S. G. 18:40
Taylor, S. H. 15:46
Taylor, S. P. 7:112; 23:15; 25:240
Taylor, Sally H. 25:312
Taylor, Samuel 1:79, 80; 12:54, 77; 16:306; 19:321; 21:395; 22:132, 169; 24:46, 103
Taylor, Samuel A. 23:196
Taylor, Samuel H. 20:101
Taylor, Samuel W. 11:405
Taylor, Sanders 26:114
Taylor, Sandy 7:134; 18:40
Taylor, Sanford 21:81
Taylor, Saunders 18:297
Taylor, Seth C. 25:76
Taylor, Silas 22:321
Taylor, Sim 7:134
Taylor, Simon 9:60
Taylor, Simon F. 10:23
Taylor, Simpson 22:321
Taylor, Smith 9:137; 27:121
Taylor, Spencer 17:268; 25:240
Taylor, Stephen 9:162; 23:110; 24:103; 26:184
Taylor, T. 1:178; 3:191; 9:151; 11:78; 13:129; 23:52; 25:75; 27:120
Taylor, T. B. 3:191
Taylor, T. D. 1:79
Taylor, T. H. 21:201
Taylor, T. S. 14:116
Taylor, T. W. 17:309; 23:52
Taylor, Theodore C. 22:224
Taylor, Thomas 1:79; 9:29, 92, 151; 10:139; 12:42; 13:100;

Taylor, Thomas 17:93, 139, 498; 22:104; 24:205; 26:65; 27:122
Taylor, Thomas C. 12:42
Taylor, Thomas G. 22:57
Taylor, Thomas George 22:412
Taylor, Thomas J. 18:255; 26:66
Taylor, Thomas L. 1:79; 8:56; 11:98
Taylor, Turner 24:45
Taylor, Udell S. 21:81
Taylor, Van Cook 11:174
Taylor, W. 3:192; 14:224; 16:232; 18:255; 26:66
Taylor, W. C. 1:80
Taylor, W. D. 13:126
Taylor, W. E. 24:85
Taylor, W. F. H. 18:317
Taylor, W. G. 13:100
Taylor, W. H. 3:192; 9:73, 137; 20:60; 24:163; 27:121
Taylor, W. H. H. 8:56
Taylor, W. K. 9:73; 14:117
Taylor, W. M. 8:110; 14:260
Taylor, W. W. 3:192; 14:117
Taylor, Walter 16:232
Taylor, Walter D. 23:94
Taylor, Washington 19:297
Taylor, Washington L. 15:46
Taylor, Watson 15:60
Taylor, Wesley 16:232
Taylor, William 4:57; 6:22; 7:43, 76, 112; 9:46, 205, 211; 10:149; 11:393; 12:164; 13:120; 14:267; 15:231; 16:232; 17:44, 145, 284, 399; 18:58, 95; 21:235; 22:57, 115, 224, 271, 321; 25:240, 286, 305; 26:185
Taylor, William A. 5:46; 20:14; 23:16; 25:273, 276
Taylor, William B. 10:83; 18:281; 20:361
Taylor, William C. 15:75; 20:187
Taylor, William F. 20:129

Taylor, William F. H. 26:114
Taylor, William H. 7:43; 9:29; 10:139; 12:65; 13:59; 14:335; 17:289; 18:401; 20:361
Taylor, William J. 22:224
Taylor, William K. 21:395
Taylor, William L. 1:79
Taylor, William M. 20:194
Taylor, William S. 22:105
Taylor, William W. 7:84; 13:69; 21:395
Taylor, Winston 21:285
Taylor, Worthy S. 9:39
Taylor, Z. 16:232; 22:321
Taylor, Zach 9:211; 17:187
Taylor, Zachariah 17:139; 24:205
Taylor, Zack 18:72
Tayne, John 11:189
Tayner, George A. 15:231
Tayrill, O. A. 25:305
Taytler, J. 14:304; 17:480
Tazzel, J. 25:240
Tchestiter, T. 10:139; 20:361
Teabe, Noah 17:245
Teabean, F. 8:56
Teabo, Joseph 17:320
Teabout, Jacob H. 7:134
Teach, J. 21:126
Teach, J. W. 17:44
Teachner, Thaddeus 20:14
Tead, C. E. 15:280
Teadaman, C. J. 7:43
Teagarden, L. D. 9:39; 26:114
Teagel, Thomas H. 17:112
Teagerden, L. D. 18:297
Teague, Francis 8:97; 18:211
Teague, J. 10:207
Teague, James 15:354; 22:271
Teague, James S. 23:280
Teague, Nathaniel 18:162
Teague, Richard 7:134
Teague, Rufus H. 13:50
Teague, William 22:105
Teahan, John 8:122
Teal, Ferguson 21:81
Teal, Frank 20:135
Teal, Richard 23:110
Teal, T. 20:175
Teal, W. 27:157
Teal, Webster H. 20:37
Teamans, W. A. 8:68

Teaple, Edward 8:76
Tearn, H. 21:395
Tearney, James 7:112
Tearney, Thomas 10:168; 19:197
Tearwelliger, S. M. 1:80
Teary, John P. 12:42
Teas, Adam J. 22:105
Teas, Trevanion H. 20:139
Teasdale, John 14:285
Teasdale, Joseph 22:285
Tease, George N. 20:129
Teask, Eugene T. 19:332
Teat, J. B. 10:207
Teater, Isaac 12:42
Teater, W. 19:262
Teates, William 9:195
Teath, William 15:231
Teatka, John M. 15:175
Teats, J. F. 23:118
Teats, John A. 12:77
Teats, Thomas 22:132
Teazel, George W. 22:493
Tebarg, Joseph 15:168
Tebedeaux, George 8:56
Tebis, H. 19:307
Tebo, Lewis W. 1:80
Tebo---, Jacob 20:60
Tebor, T. S. 4:57
Tebs, A. 25:75
TeCamp, Gerrett J. 21:144
Techner, James R. 17:44
Tedball, J. W. 17:44
Tedd, John 25:75
Tedder, Elisha 10:83
Tedford, A. H. 10:93
Tedford, J. A. 11:251
Tedford, John E. 22:105
Tedford, M. 22:321
Tedford, Robert A. 23:94
Tedley, Joseph 25:240
Tedron, A. H. 22:224
Tedros, Charles K. 9:92
Teed, C. E. 25:241
Teed, Truman 24:97
Teed, W. M. 16:380
Teedgarden, Joseph 10:139
Teegarden, James 22:493
Teegarden, Joseph 20:361
Teegorden, Simon 12:163
Teel, J. H. 27:121
Teel, Moses 22:105
Teel, Noel 9:70
Teeland, James 27:120
Teele, S. H. 9:151
Teems, Andrew J. 22:224
Teeple, Isaac 24:85
Teeple, Pelham 10:139
Teeple, Pellum 20:361

Teeple, Samuel 17:421; 24:163
Teeple, W. 18:58
Teeser, J. 21:81
Teete, Nicholas 9:211
Teeter, C. 14:224, 260
Teeter, Frank 21:261
Teeter, James 24:155
Teeter, Joseph 17:441
Teeter, Marion 22:132
Teeter, P. R. 18:460
Teeter, Philip F. 20:101
Teeter, Walter 21:60
Teeter, Williams 22:132
Teeters, William 18:163
Teetres, William 8:33
Teets, Henry 24:85
Teetsell, James H. 4:57
Teetus, Charles 20:361
Tefensee, John 6:10
Teffee, A. 23:302
Tefft, J. 20:361
Tefft, John 20:14
Tefft, John Q. 10:139; 20:361
Tefinsea, --- 18:95
Tefro, C. P. 23:306
Teft---, --- 15:295
Tegarden, Abraham 23:80
Tegardin, J. M. 25:76
Tegardner, W. A. 9:225; 18:377
Teguhan, Francis 26:184
Tehan, John 4:57
Teichmann, Ernst 19:104
Teiman, John 10:32
Teinmour, I. 22:224
Teionter, James M. 26:67
Teir, Gerhard 21:106
Teison, Howard 20:361
Teitch, H. 1:80
Teitorntor, James M. 18:255
Teits, Charles 10:83
Teives, August 23:196
Teizell, J. H. 26:66
Tekentroup, Henry 18:407
Tekling, Louis 21:106
Telenor, S. 17:250
Telford, Charles H. 9:151
Telkins, W. C. 20:14
Tell, Swan 21:43
Tell, William 3:192
Teller, John 17:87
Teller, Nicholas 22:132
Teller, Pierne 12:77
Teller, Pierre 15:46
Teller, S. 21:395
Teller, William 21:144
Telley, M. M. 9:60
Telly, J. 16:232

Telts, William S. 21:239
Telyea, M. 13:126
TeMaat, Jan. H. 21:261
Temer, F. 1:81
Temer, M. 21:43
Temerson, Oscar 12:77
Temke, Fritz 22:285
Temmins, W. J. 12:88
Tempelman, James A.
14:271
Temple, Andrew 15:324;
19:104
Temple, Augustus W.
21:106
Temple, David 24:31
Temple, E. H. 10:83;
20:361
Temple, F. 2:18
Temple, Frank 18:115
Temple, Franklin 6:10
Temple, Fred 17:139;
24:205
Temple, H. 25:74
Temple, H. Randol 18:95
Temple, H. S. 9:195;
19:262
Temple, Henry 24:85
Temple, J. 3:192; 16:306
Temple, J. L. 15:93
Temple, James 11:251
Temple, James M. 23:282
Temple, John 11:79;
22:224
Temple, Joseph 10:83;
14:224; 20:361
Temple, W. M. 23:265
Temple, William 6:8
Temple, William H.
17:208
Temple, William W.
21:106
Templeman, J. H. 14:285
Templer, James A. 21:113
Templer, W. M. 9:60
Temples, Ephraim 9:92
Templeton, E. 11:79
Templeton, F. M. 26:185
Templeton, G. W. 3:192
Templeton, George 8:33;
18:163
Templeton, H. B. 16:58
Templeton, J. 9:151;
17:150; 27:120
Templeton, James 21:197
Templeton, John 22:271
Templeton, John A. 12:42
Templeton, John F. P.
21:197
Templeton, L. C. 20:361
Templeton, Lewis C.
10:83

Templeton, Robert H.
23:196
Templeton, T. P. 1:178
Templeton, W. 17:421
Templeton, W. H. 3:192
Templeton, Warren
24:163
Templeton, Wesley
11:397
Templeton, William M.
11:426
Templin, John 18:163;
26:184
Temps, Henry W. 13:135
Tenant, A. 5:31; 25:241
Tenant, E. A. 25:241
Tenant, George 19:104
Tenant, J. L. 18:163
Tenant, S. R. 25:241
Tenant, Samuel R. 5:31
Tenary, T. M. 21:43
Tenbridge, John W. 5:31
Tenbroeck, William H.
25:74
Tencellent, Charles 9:126;
27:122
Tench, Joseph 14:117
Tender, Jeremiah W.
9:195
Tendrow, John 14:118
Tene, George A. 22:346
Tenell, George C. 10:175
Tenell, George W. 16:283
Tenell, Thomas M. 17:293
Tenesh, Charles 24:31
Tenett, A. C. 11:87
Teneych, M. 3:192
TenEyck, Barnett 24:186
TenEyck, Charles H.
13:59
Teneyck, David 21:81
TenEyck, J. T. 18:95
Teneyck, Joseph 9:137
TenEyck, Joseph 27:121
TenEyck, T. 6:19
TenEyke, Henry 4:57
Tenholt, --- 12:88
Tenike, Anthony 16:58
Tenis, Charles 11:323
Tenison, Benjamin F.
10:139
Tenison, J. 15:23
Tenke, Anthony 13:59
Tenmey, Perkins 9:73
Tennant, Alex 19:37
Tennant, Dallas P. 16:380
Tennant, George 15:311
Tennant, I. L. 8:33
Tennant, James 20:117
Tennel, Samuel 18:286
Tennell, Samuel 26:135

Tenney, Moses E. 16:380
Tenney, Nelson M.
22:285
Tenney, Theodore 19:104
Tenney, W. W. 1:100
Tenneyok, John 15:75
Tennin, Warren 18:255;
26:67
Tennis, F. S. 20:44
Tennis, J. 11:271
Tennis, James 15:60
Tennis, John 17:421;
22:57; 24:163
Tennison, Benjamin F.
20:361
Tennison, H. 18:255;
26:67
Tennison, W. C. 21:209
Tennstedt, Chris 26:130
Tenny, Charles 21:395
Tenny, David 24:97
Tenny, H. A. 25:241
Tenny, Henry C. 13:50
Tenny, L. E. 21:395
Tenny, Moses E. 15:351
Tenorio, Carlos 8:125
Tenqslin, John 8:33
Tenry, George G. 14:267
Tensdell, T. H. 3:192
Tenseler, M. 1:178
Tensey, John 7:134
Teny, E. 16:271
Teny, Thomas 18:163
Teoheva, Jeremiah 17:214
Tepin, John 11:195
Tepler, John 26:130
Tepps, Lewis 8:115
Terbeest, James 21:261
Terby, Green W. 12:159
Terel, --- 27:123
Terhine, A. A. 25:75
Terhorn, Samuel T.
17:150
Terhune, Abraham B. 5:31
Terich, --- 25:75
Teris, H. 10:30
Terley, William 22:516
Terman, Joseph S. 19:37
Termane, George 4:57
Termmins, W. J. 16:306
Terney, J. 14:117
Terney, James 25:241
Terney, William 3:192
Terpen, David S. 8:33
Terpin, David S. 18:163
Terple, Henry B. 8:97
Terpox, Charles F. 4:57
Terraron, Alexander 7:134
Terrell, --- 14:335
Terrell, Clarence 7:43

Terrell, Cone 21:246
Terrell, D. F. 14:23
Terrell, David J. 21:395
Terrell, F. O. 21:395
Terrell, Henry W. 20:14
Terrell, Herman 8:115
Terrell, James 16:283; 25:76
Terrell, James A. 8:97
Terrell, Jesse 9:225
Terrell, John 9:202
Terrell, Joseph H. 22:132
Terrell, Robert 17:60
Terrell, Thomas S. 21:235
Terrell, William B. 7:112
Terrey, Thomas T. 18:255
Terrick, Hill P. 12:100
Terril, L. B. 11:113
Terril, R. E. 18:255
Terrileger, A. 9:195
Terrill, A. J. 1:80
Terrill, Benton T. 7:112
Terrill, D. F. 13:100
Terrill, Edward 20:361
Terrill, Eli 9:225; 18:377
Terrill, Elliot 8:76
Terrill, George 22:516
Terrill, George H. 17:163
Terrill, Isaac 17:137, 139; 24:202
Terrill, John 23:94
Terrill, John T. 19:37
Terrill, O. A. 7:76
Terrill, Samuel E. 22:224
Terris, Charles 12:42
Terris, Edgar 12:42
Terris, J. 17:362
Territt, John 5:46
Terrold, T. M. 17:297
Terrwilliger, William 17:27
Terry, --- 17:112
Terry, A. A. 25:241
Terry, A. B. 14:224
Terry, Aaron 3:192
Terry, Aaron A. 5:31
Terry, Abram 21:395
Terry, Amos 14:117
Terry, B. F. 10:168
Terry, Barney F. 24:99
Terry, C. H. 12:42
Terry, Calvin 20:94
Terry, Charles 9:202
Terry, D. 3:192; 14:117
Terry, David 18:321; 21:114
Terry, David I. 12:42
Terry, E. E. 21:132
Terry, E. K. 16:380
Terry, Eliah M. 14:23
Terry, Ellias E. 21:247

Terry, Fayette 14:224
Terry, Frank L. 26:65
Terry, G. J. 14:291
Terry, George 14:224; 21:81
Terry, H. 10:30; 19:307
Terry, Hines M. 23:280
Terry, I. 21:43
Terry, J. 11:46, 314
Terry, J. C. 22:492
Terry, J. T. 21:395
Terry, James 25:241
Terry, James T. 8:33; 18:163
Terry, Joel 9:195; 19:265
Terry, John 3:192; 10:83; 21:169, 395; 27:122
Terry, John N. 22:443
Terry, L. 25:241
Terry, Leander 5:46
Terry, Noran 20:361
Terry, Norin 10:83
Terry, Orlan E. 13:50
Terry, Oscar 22:156
Terry, P. 9:126; 21:151; 25:328
Terry, Philip 6:33
Terry, R. 20:44
Terry, Reuben S. 8:97
Terry, S. 13:100; 17:433
Terry, S. H. 2:18
Terry, Seymour 24:155
Terry, Thomas 8:33
Terry, Thomas T. 26:66
Terry, W. 15:231
Terry, W. P. 14:317, 322
Terry, W. R. 21:60
Terry, W. T. 12:171
Terry, William 3:192; 21:169
Terry, William P. 23:185
Terry, Wilson 22:492
Terrygarling, C. 14:237
Tersdell, H. 14:271
Terwak, Antrim 27:122
Terwillager, A. 19:262
Terwillager, C. W. 19:262
Terwilleger, I. W. 15:231
Terwilliger, B. 15:168
Terwilliger, B. C. 3:192
Terwilliger, C. M. 1:178
Terwilliger, J. W. 27:121
Terwilliger, Jesse 25:76
Terwilliger, Nathaniel 22:156
Terwillinger, M. 1:79
Tery, V. B. 16:232
Tes, John 11:221
Tesler, Hiram 22:271
Tesory, Alfred 24:205

Tesrean, Charles 10:83; 20:361
Tessell, Richard 7:112
Tessin, Frederick 23:196
Test, Daniel W. 20:20
Test, J. 21:43
Test, Miles H. 21:235
Tester, Harrison 22:271
Tester, U. C. 13:100
Tester, W. C. 14:23
Teter, John H. 11:173
Tetherly, George 7:80
Tetley, Daniel 19:262
Tetrick, E. P. 1:80
Tetrick, J. 11:78
Tetter, Jacob 8:68
Tetterman, W. 7:61
Tetworth, T. 16:103
Teveling, William 11:315
Tevis, Lloyd 26:130
Tevis, Melauchton 21:235
Tew, M. D. 16:58
Tew, Richard 25:241
Tewell, Franklin 22:458
Tewell, Henderson 21:395
Tewell, John 22:458
Tewey, J. 3:192
Tewgan, H. 1:177
Tewgwe, John 18:195
Tewkes, J. W. 19:104
Tewksberry, Isaac N. 20:141
Tews, Charles 19:37
Tews, John 18:341
Texter, J. 2:18
Texter, James 25:74
Textor, Amos 1:78
Teyner, C. 26:214
Th---, T. C. 17:218
Thabald, David 13:120
Thackay, S. 14:117
Thacker, Alias C. 11:174
Thacker, Isaac 22:346
Thacker, J. R. 14:304; 17:481; 27:123
Thacker, James 7:17
Thacker, John C. 11:121
Thacker, M. 26:204
Thackerberry, J. 10:154
Thades, --- 17:285
Thaer, Hiram C. 4:57
Thaers, Joseph 4:57
Thaggart, J. B. 16:232
Thair, W. 3:192
Thalheim, Henry 16:232
Thame, John 21:235
Thamer, Daniel 14:224
Than, E. F. 17:496
Thanason, Walter H. 19:269
Thaner, J. 25:241

Thaney, Ml. 15:113
Thangherty, J. S. 11:251
Tharber, Lewis D. 9:39
Tharp, Giles 21:81
Tharp, H. A. 23:52
Tharp, Isaac 22:516
Tharp, Jason 22:224
Tharp, Jefferson P. 24:56
Tharp, John A. 23:116
Tharp, Richard 24:205
Tharpe, John A. 23:196
Tharpe, William H. 21:60
Thartel, E. 18:255
Thatcher, Bert 1:79
Thatcher, Charles 16:149;
  23:52
Thatcher, David 9:39;
  18:297; 20:184;
  26:114
Thatcher, E. H. 3:192
Thatcher, Eugene Q.
  23:126
Thatcher, G. B. 1:177
Thatcher, J. 3:192;
  13:100; 14:224
Thatcher, J. F. 1:177
Thatcher, J. P. 3:192
Thatcher, John E. 11:173
Thatcher, M. 11:79
Thatcher, R. 3:192
Thatcher, Thomas 11:382
Thatcher, W. 1:80, 177
Thatcher, William 14:225;
  17:16; 24:46
Thatcher, William C. 1:80
Thatcher, William W.
  12:42
Thatford, S. H. 1:79
Thaurnhonef, Frank 7:112
Thausbury, U. C. 3:192
Thaw, B. J. A. 1:178
Thaway, H. H. 17:139
Thawoy, H. H. 24:205
Thawton, R. 4:57
Thaxton, F. M. 9:60
Thaxton, J. M. 27:122
Thaxton, Levi 17:394
Thaxton, Sampson 23:52
Thayer, Albert W. 19:37
Thayer, Amos 9:39;
  18:297; 26:114
Thayer, Benjamin D. 16:8
Thayer, Chandler 24:56
Thayer, Charles 16:142
Thayer, D. 3:192; 14:225
Thayer, D. A. 9:151
Thayer, Daniel B. 10:23
Thayer, Daniel K. 19:37
Thayer, Fordyce 17:450;
  24:175

Thayer, Francis A. 8:33;
  18:163
Thayer, Frank B. 23:196
Thayer, G. 3:192
Thayer, George W. 11:405
Thayer, H. H. 1:80
Thayer, Horace P. 12:77;
  15:82
Thayer, J. 3:192
Thayer, J. D. 8:60
Thayer, J. F. 26:185
Thayer, James D. 12:171
Thayer, James H. 23:196
Thayer, John 9:29;
  18:317; 26:113
Thayer, Leonidas 17:351
Thayer, Lester 21:192
Thayer, Milo 10:8
Thayer, N. A. 16:103
Thayer, N. H. 5:31
Thayer, Napoleon B.
  23:80
Thayer, Neal 6:26
Thayer, Nelson L. 14:225
Thayer, R. H. 21:395
Thayer, Richard 7:112;
  21:395
Thayer, S. 25:241
Thayer, Samuel 22:224
Thayer, Stephen 20:361
Thayer, T. M. 14:117
Thayer, W. 18:58
Thayer, W. T. 14:304;
  17:473; 27:123
Thayer, Will T. 13:60
Thayers, I. J. 24:85
Thayre, Stephen 10:83
The---, W. H. 18:40
Theabald, Jacob 13:120
Theasant, J. 14:225
Thedy, Frank 13:50
Theede, Carston 23:116
Theek, George 20:191
Theelbrook, D. C. 21:395
Thees, Nicholas 11:232
Thein, Herman 25:241
Thein, Stephen 21:94
Their, A. F. 3:192
Theirs, J. F. 10:187;
  18:181
Theison, John 11:251
Thelan, John P. 16:142
Thelen, Nicholas 23:116
Theller, W. H. 16:271
Theman, Frederick
  10:139; 20:361
Thement, James 17:157
Themer, Charles L.
  22:412
Themes, Augustus 17:321
Thenback, Otto 3:192

Theobald, Henry 24:85
Theobald, J. 9:29
Theobalt, Christopher
  7:112
Theobold, H. I. 26:113
Theobold, Heinrich Jacob
  18:317
Theobold, Julius 26:114
Thermain, F. 25:74
Therman, A. 22:516
Therman, Pleasant 18:163
Therman, Robert 19:197
Therner, C. L. 18:271
Theroux, Peter 15:349
Therrett, John 11:405
Therroll, Aaron 11:336
Thery, William 8:110
Thesang, H. 15:82
Thetare, Judus 16:149
Theurer, Philip 22:57
Thewer, Henry 12:42
Thibadeau, Joseph 11:405
Thibault, Aug. 16:58
Thibault, Isaac 13:50
Thibbery, Ernest 21:395
Thickens, F. B. 1:79
Thickson, Josiah 22:443
Thiel, Emie 4:57
Thiele, Charles 17:405;
  18:317
Thiele, H. 22:224; 25:75
Thielman, Henry 10:23
Thielson, Gustav 23:250
Thierman, F. 2:18
Thies, Lewis 10:139;
  20:361
Thies, Thomas 15:231
Thiesen, John C. 23:116
Thietaull, John 17:27
Thifts, Charles C. 24:31
Thilack, H. 1:177
Thilbeaux, P. 1:177
Thilker, Henry 24:46
Thilman, F. 9:69
Thimbly, George 19:197
Thime, R. A. 3:192
Thiner, Christian 4:57
Thinglemick, William
  7:112
Thinnis, Augustus 10:83;
  20:361
Thirlway, J. 1:179
Thirmin, H. 21:192
Thirse, Allen 21:285
Thirsten, H. 25:241
Thirston, Albert P. 12:159
Thisen, Mathias 23:126
Thiser, E. 14:117
Thiss, Charles 23:52
Thistlewood, J. 3:192
Thitacer, C. H. 23:253

Thite, --- 23:14
Thlor, Casper 21:248
Thoams, Loyd 24:205
Thockmorton, J. B. 18:466
Thods, --- 18:40
Thoen, Hanson P. 23:196
Thoene, Henry 23:102
Thole, H. H. W. 1:79
Tholheim, Henry 13:69
Tholler, W. H. 14:23
Tholmeyer, --- 9:39
Thom, David 19:262
Thom, E. 3:192
Thom, M. V. B. 7:113
Thom, William 16:306
Thom--, E. 20:157
Thoma, Charles 17:60
Thoman, Max. A. 16:103
Thomas, --- 16:306; 18:377; 21:132, 285; 25:75, 273; 27:123
Thomas, A. 1:79, 177; 3:192; 18:95
Thomas, A. B. 25:305
Thomas, A. L. 16:232
Thomas, A. T. 1:100
Thomas, Aaron 10:99; 12:146; 23:171
Thomas, Abram 11:382; 22:322
Thomas, Albert 9:211; 12:159; 18:72; 22:105
Thomas, Alexander 22:322
Thomas, Alfred B. 17:395
Thomas, Alfred M. 21:395
Thomas, Alonzo I. 15:231
Thomas, Anderson 9:211
Thomas, Andrew 9:29; 18:255; 22:322; 26:67
Thomas, Asa 14:237; 18:40
Thomas, Augustus 13:120
Thomas, B. P. 15:113
Thomas, Bannah 22:442
Thomas, Benjamin 13:128; 18:105, 324; 23:94
Thomas, Benjamin F. 22:442
Thomas, C. 8:56; 12:163; 22:493
Thomas, C. C. 11:195
Thomas, C. E. 21:395
Thomas, C. H. 15:327; 16:232
Thomas, C. M. 1:178; 9:211

Thomas, C. Thomas 17:208
Thomas, Captain 7:134
Thomas, Charles 1:191, 193; 4:58; 6:19; 12:52; 13:59; 14:225; 15:290; 16:232; 18:95, 211; 19:197; 23:196
Thomas, Charles F. 9:39; 18:297; 26:114
Thomas, Charles H. 19:104
Thomas, Charlotte 26:227
Thomas, Chesley E. 20:14
Thomas, Chockly W. 22:443
Thomas, Christian 13:59
Thomas, Christopher 19:104
Thomas, Colonel 21:286
Thomas, D. 21:126
Thomas, Dan 17:187
Thomas, Dan'l L. 22:506
Thomas, Daniel 4:68; 9:46; 26:130
Thomas, Daniel T. 19:231
Thomas, Dav 18:195
Thomas, David 10:139; 20:361; 21:201
Thomas, David P. 22:441
Thomas, Davis M. 5:31
Thomas, Dennis 21:395
Thomas, E. 1:178; 3:192; 17:163; 24:31
Thomas, E. B. 25:276
Thomas, E. C. 9:92; 26:67
Thomas, E. E. 21:126
Thomas, E. H. 18:255; 26:66
Thomas, E. L. 15:231
Thomas, E. S. 9:151; 27:121
Thomas, Edward 7:61; 20:361
Thomas, Edward P. 22:443
Thomas, Edwin H. 20:129
Thomas, Eli 4:58
Thomas, Elias 10:83; 20:361
Thomas, Elliott 25:286
Thomas, Enoch 10:207; 17:87
Thomas, Ensley 22:271
Thomas, Erasmus 9:8
Thomas, Eugene M. 26:146
Thomas, Evans 22:458
Thomas, Ezra 14:322; 22:156; 23:94

Thomas, F. 3:192; 11:46; 16:380
Thomas, F. A. 25:241
Thomas, F. J. 1:177
Thomas, F. M. 16:232
Thomas, Fayette 21:286
Thomas, Francis 11:113
Thomas, Francis M. 22:238
Thomas, Frank 8:97
Thomas, Franklin 9:46; 21:235; 26:130
Thomas, Fred. E. 19:197
Thomas, Frederick 25:335
Thomas, Frederick E. 10:168
Thomas, Friend 11:214
Thomas, G. 1:177; 11:315; 16:232, 233; 22:271; 25:241
Thomas, G. C. 1:178
Thomas, G. F. 9:225
Thomas, G. J. 21:395
Thomas, G. M. 1:80
Thomas, Garuthy 16:306
Thomas, George 1:78; 5:46; 10:23; 11:251; 14:117; 15:84, 231; 17:426; 18:40; 19:49; 21:43, 395; 22:57; 24:181
Thomas, George F. 23:171
Thomas, George H. 9:92, 99
Thomas, George N. 11:46
Thomas, George P. 19:37
Thomas, George R. 22:105
Thomas, George S. 13:50
Thomas, George W. 22:285; 26:227
Thomas, Gideon 8:33; 18:163
Thomas, Gilbert 19:37; 22:322
Thomas, Gilbert L. 20:117
Thomas, H. 1:80; 3:192; 9:195; 15:46; 16:283; 19:104; 22:225
Thomas, H. B. 24:70
Thomas, H. D. 3:192; 9:232; 20:361
Thomas, H. L. 1:178
Thomas, H. S. 16:125
Thomas, Harris 26:66
Thomas, Harrison 18:255; 26:67
Thomas, Harry 20:14
Thomas, Harvey 24:205
Thomas, Henry 1:191; 7:134; 8:78; 10:83;

Thomas, Henry 11:393;
   12:52; 14:225;
   15:231; 16:233;
   17:87, 318; 19:49;
   20:50, 361; 21:81,
   395; 24:108; 27:121
Thomas, Henry C. 7:43
Thomas, Henry E. 20:109
Thomas, Henry L. 13:69;
   20:152
Thomas, Henry W. 22:271
Thomas, Henshai C. 16:79
Thomas, Hiram 17:139;
   24:205
Thomas, Hiram S. 10:139;
   20:361
Thomas, Hiram W. 22:442
Thomas, Hudson 11:417
Thomas, I. 11:174; 20:93
Thomas, I. L. 11:174
Thomas, Ira 7:17
Thomas, Irvin W. 22:412
Thomas, Isaac 11:173,
   283; 22:322
Thomas, Isaac B. 26:146
Thomas, Isaiah 18:95
Thomas, J. 1:80, 178, 179;
   3:192; 13:100, 126;
   14:117, 333; 18:115;
   22:157, 238, 322;
   23:52, 307; 25:241
Thomas, J. A. 3:192;
   14:260
Thomas, J. B. 16:103;
   17:87
Thomas, J. C. 11:79
Thomas, J. F. 13:100
Thomas, J. H. 1:177;
   3:192; 23:52; 25:241
Thomas, J. J. 20:361
Thomas, J. K. 1:78
Thomas, J. L. 1:100;
   13:69
Thomas, J. M. 23:171
Thomas, J. O. 22:225
Thomas, J. P. 22:225
Thomas, J. R. 21:43
Thomas, J. S. 1:78, 178
Thomas, J. W. 3:192;
   13:135; 15:113;
   16:58; 19:347;
   23:171; 24:85
Thomas, J. Y. 14:245;
   27:124
Thomas, Jacob 25:241
Thomas, James 1:80;
   7:134; 13:120;
   14:117; 15:301;
   17:187; 20:361;
   21:395; 22:442;
   26:66

Thomas, James B. 22:57
Thomas, James H. 5:46;
   18:469; 26:146
Thomas, James O. 21:60
Thomas, James R. 21:291
Thomas, Jasper 11:417
Thomas, Jeffry 7:134
Thomas, Jentry 11:79
Thomas, Jerry 17:187;
   19:323
Thomas, Jesse 24:60
Thomas, Joel L. 15:161;
   22:169
Thomas, John 4:58; 6:26;
   8:97; 9:14, 46, 60;
   11:174, 214; 12:42,
   52; 13:50, 69, 100;
   15:15; 16:58, 233;
   17:187, 395; 18:72,
   95, 377; 21:395;
   22:57, 105, 173, 322,
   346; 25:241; 26:130
Thomas, John B. 9:68;
   18:281
Thomas, John C. 7:13
Thomas, John E. 9:126;
   27:122
Thomas, John H. 8:68;
   12:52; 17:285, 297;
   20:361; 21:144, 246
Thomas, John M. 11:393
Thomas, John N. 7:43;
   11:79
Thomas, John P. 1:79
Thomas, John R. 24:46
Thomas, John W. 21:261
Thomas, Jonathan J. 10:83
Thomas, Joseph 6:10;
   7:134; 8:33; 13:120;
   16:233; 18:163;
   22:271
Thomas, Joseph D. 19:330
Thomas, Josiah 10:168
Thomas, Josiah E. 17:427
Thomas, Killis 18:255;
   26:67
Thomas, L. 1:179; 5:31;
   7:43; 9:65; 13:100;
   18:469; 21:151;
   25:241
Thomas, L. D. 11:79
Thomas, L. F. 1:80
Thomas, Lemon 22:346
Thomas, Lemuel 21:213
Thomas, Levi 22:238
Thomas, Lewis 17:44;
   21:395
Thomas, Louis 17:187;
   21:286
Thomas, Loyd 17:139
Thomas, Luther 9:195

Thomas, M. 3:192; 9:202;
   14:271; 18:72, 95
Thomas, Marion 19:37
Thomas, Martin 8:33;
   9:211; 11:283; 18:72,
   163
Thomas, Martin K. 22:493
Thomas, Mary 18:195
Thomas, Mary E. 25:312
Thomas, Mathias 18:341
Thomas, Matthew 6:19
Thomas, Michael 15:324;
   19:104
Thomas, Milton 10:83;
   20:361
Thomas, Morgan 22:225
Thomas, Morris 7:17
Thomas, N. 14:245
Thomas, Nap'n. Bonap't.
   9:151
Thomas, Nathaniel 21:395
Thomas, Nicholas 19:297
Thomas, Norris 9:211;
   18:72
Thomas, Oliver 7:134;
   13:127
Thomas, Oliver C. 22:105
Thomas, Oliver W. 21:261
Thomas, Peter 10:93;
   20:361; 22:105
Thomas, R. 1:179;
   13:103; 14:23;
   18:105; 25:241
Thomas, R. E. 21:395
Thomas, R. M. 18:58
Thomas, R. S. 20:44
Thomas, R. W. 10:175;
   19:198
Thomas, Real 10:23
Thomas, Richard 5:31, 46;
   7:134; 21:395;
   27:120
Thomas, Richard B.
   27:120
Thomas, Richmond
   15:175
Thomas, Riston 4:68
Thomas, Robert 7:15;
   8:116; 9:29; 10:139;
   16:58; 18:40, 324;
   20:362; 24:205
Thomas, Robert J. 11:195
Thomas, Robert S. 22:442
Thomas, Ross 16:103
Thomas, Rufus 10:34
Thomas, S. 3:192; 7:54,
   61; 11:46, 251;
   13:100; 17:187;
   21:43; 25:241
Thomas, S. A. 1:178

Thomas, S. C. 5:31; 25:241
Thomas, S. H. 26:66
Thomas, S. O. 21:126
Thomas, S. W. 22:493
Thomas, Sam 21:286
Thomas, Samuel 4:58; 7:134; 13:50; 15:231, 346; 16:233, 380; 17:456; 19:49; 22:322; 24:213
Thomas, Samuel E. 22:458
Thomas, Samuel M. 17:62
Thomas, Silas E. 21:235
Thomas, Stephen 5:31
Thomas, Stephen H. 9:92; 13:50
Thomas, Stephen M. 16:58
Thomas, Sylvester 22:458
Thomas, Sylvester W. 24:56
Thomas, T. B. 21:43
Thomas, T. F. 14:23
Thomas, T. J. 11:79; 21:43
Thomas, T. P. 23:171
Thomas, T. W. 19:104
Thomas, Tabor J. 23:52
Thomas, Theodore B. 4:58
Thomas, Thomas 12:42; 22:322, 346
Thomas, Thomas G. 11:419
Thomas, Thomas W. 11:194
Thomas, Thompson 10:139; 20:362
Thomas, Thurston 16:103; 23:52
Thomas, Tiler 22:346
Thomas, W. 1:178; 3:192; 9:155; 21:151; 27:121
Thomas, W. A. 12:159
Thomas, W. B. 3:192; 11:314
Thomas, W. C. 9:151; 27:120
Thomas, W. E. 3:192
Thomas, W. F. 18:195
Thomas, W. H. 3:192; 9:29; 13:100; 18:401; 19:307
Thomas, W. J. 15:295
Thomas, W. L. 18:40
Thomas, W. M. 26:185
Thomas, W. M. C. 20:129
Thomas, W. O. 27:123

Thomas, W. R. 3:192
Thomas, W. S. 1:177
Thomas, Walter 9:39; 18:297; 26:114
Thomas, Warren 13:50
Thomas, Washington 18:255; 26:67
Thomas, Wesley 18:95
Thomas, Wesley E. 22:442
Thomas, Will 21:286
Thomas, William 5:54; 6:19, 28; 8:68; 11:214, 405; 13:50, 100; 14:23, 225; 16:58, 125; 17:97; 18:95, 255, 414; 19:49; 21:213, 249; 22:492; 23:81; 24:103; 25:241, 289; 26:66
Thomas, William A. 8:56
Thomas, William B. 7:112
Thomas, William D. 15:303; 23:171
Thomas, William G. 16:233
Thomas, William H. 23:185
Thomas, William I. 23:53
Thomas, William J. 16:233
Thomas, William M. 12:159; 20:135
Thomas, William P. 20:109; 21:144
Thomas, William R. 22:443
Thomas, Willis 17:139; 24:205
Thomas, Zenas 11:405
Thomaset, Lars 20:117
Thomason, G. 25:241
Thomason, George 5:46
Thomason, George T. 23:102
Thomason, T. 1:177
Thomason, W. W. 9:195
Thomber, John 16:58
Thomburg, --- 16:233
Thomburg, T. 27:119
Thomelson, David 21:60
Thomeraft, David 18:297
Thomey, Martin 20:191
Thomhill, Green 10:99
Thomington, H. R. 18:402
Thomison, David 10:83; 20:362
Thomison, Lanedy 11:46
Thomlinson, E. J. 25:241
Thomlinson, G. L. 5:31

Thomlinson, John H. 8:33
Thomlinson, Thomas 26:130
Thomm, William 10:154; 19:198
Thommas, James 15:9
Thomnau, James O. 9:46
Thompkins, A. C. 21:43
Thompkins, James K. 9:68
Thompkins, Jerry 21:286
Thompkins, John 11:131
Thompkins, P. 25:241
Thompkins, William 18:58
Thompsen, Edwin 27:122
Thompson, --- 10:37; 11:174; 12:168; 19:349; 20:362
Thompson, A. 1:80, 179; 3:193; 9:69, 92; 10:187; 14:117, 225, 245; 15:346; 16:233, 380; 18:181; 21:151, 395; 23:196; 24:115; 25:76; 26:65; 27:124
Thompson, A. B. 3:193; 22:238
Thompson, A. C. 9:195; 19:262
Thompson, A. E. 16:233
Thompson, A. J. 10:83; 21:395
Thompson, A. L. 12:77; 15:12
Thompson, A. M. 14:117
Thompson, A. W. 1:178; 7:113
Thompson, Aaron 10:168; 19:198
Thompson, Abner 13:50
Thompson, Abraham 23:272
Thompson, Abram P. 20:14
Thompson, Albert 9:195; 13:59; 17:264
Thompson, Alex. E. 25:75
Thompson, Alex. P. 10:83
Thompson, Alexander 22:321; 23:278; 27:123
Thompson, Alfred 8:43; 26:184
Thompson, Allen 10:139; 17:139; 20:362; 24:205
Thompson, Amos 21:395
Thompson, Amos A. 11:46
Thompson, Andrew 13:50; 21:192

Thompson, Andrew T. 7:17; 21:261
Thompson, Archibald 24:215
Thompson, Arthur W. 22:442
Thompson, Augustus 21:246
Thompson, Austin 8:56
Thompson, B. 3:193; 26:65
Thompson, B. F. 19:198
Thompson, B. H. 24:115
Thompson, Bartley 24:205
Thompson, Benjamin 9:211; 18:72
Thompson, Benjamin F. 13:50
Thompson, Benjamin G. 23:126
Thompson, Byron 10:83; 20:362
Thompson, C. 1:177; 3:193; 5:46; 12:84; 14:225; 16:306; 21:113; 25:241; 27:119
Thompson, C. A. 13:50; 15:357; 16:283
Thompson, C. C. 1:178
Thompson, C. E. 21:127
Thompson, C. H. 7:113; 21:396
Thompson, C. N. 11:174
Thompson, C. O. 10:93; 13:126; 20:362
Thompson, C. P. 9:195
Thompson, C. R. 11:407
Thompson, C. S. 9:105
Thompson, C. W. 3:193; 14:117; 25:76
Thompson, Calvin 11:393
Thompson, Chaly 20:117
Thompson, Charles 4:57; 6:7, 35; 7:10; 16:233; 18:40, 195; 22:322
Thompson, Charles D. 22:458
Thompson, Charles F. 10:23
Thompson, Charles H. 8:110; 14:225; 20:117
Thompson, Charles W. 8:33; 18:163; 23:14
Thompson, Clement 14:291
Thompson, Cornelius 7:134; 16:58

Thompson, Crawford 7:65
Thompson, Cyrus 5:46; 11:294; 20:90
Thompson, D. 1:177; 3:193; 11:255; 14:237; 15:232, 362; 19:104
Thompson, D. D. 3:193
Thompson, D. R. 8:56
Thompson, D. W. 1:179; 26:130
Thompson, Daniel 9:92
Thompson, Daniel W. 9:46
Thompson, David 8:33; 12:52; 17:139; 18:163; 24:205
Thompson, David A. 20:101
Thompson, Dennis 18:95
Thompson, Duncan 11:173
Thompson, E. 1:177; 11:251; 18:40; 23:53
Thompson, E. A. 1:177
Thompson, E. H. 25:273
Thompson, E. J. 19:37
Thompson, E. T. 11:405
Thompson, Ebenezer 24:181
Thompson, Ebo 17:452
Thompson, Ed 11:194; 17:264
Thompson, Edgar 9:105
Thompson, Edmond 20:362
Thompson, Edmund 7:135; 10:83
Thompson, Edward 4:57; 9:46, 205; 11:405
Thompson, Edwin 7:43; 9:161; 14:328; 18:115
Thompson, Edwin J. 10:23
Thompson, Eldridge G. 16:103
Thompson, Eli S. 11:382
Thompson, Elijah F. 12:159
Thompson, Ellis 27:122
Thompson, Elmore M. 11:18
Thompson, Ely 16:233
Thompson, Ennu 11:417
Thompson, Enos 11:329
Thompson, Erastus 10:23
Thompson, F. 1:80; 3:193; 9:238; 16:233; 17:496; 18:414; 24:85

Thompson, F. A. 19:263
Thompson, F. A. B. 3:193
Thompson, F. M. 14:260
Thompson, Ferris W. 6:21
Thompson, Franc 17:447
Thompson, Francis 24:31, 172
Thompson, Francis O. 21:81
Thompson, Frank 8:43; 18:435; 21:261; 26:184
Thompson, Frank C. 19:104
Thompson, Frank L. 7:113
Thompson, G. 1:80, 178; 3:193; 16:233; 19:231, 243; 21:113
Thompson, G. G. 3:193
Thompson, G. W. 1:79; 7:113
Thompson, Gabriel B. 4:57
Thompson, George 4:68; 5:31, 46; 7:113, 135; 8:110; 9:195, 238; 10:168; 13:120; 14:304; 17:44, 261, 315, 477; 19:198; 22:321; 24:56; 25:241; 26:227; 27:120, 123
Thompson, George B. 22:346
Thompson, George H. 16:135
Thompson, George H. G. 25:75
Thompson, George J. 19:104
Thompson, George R. 22:442
Thompson, George S. 11:79
Thompson, George W. 22:271; 26:130
Thompson, George W. A. 17:357
Thompson, Gideon 9:60
Thompson, H. 3:193; 7:43; 11:131, 232; 13:129; 14:117, 245; 16:103; 21:396; 23:171; 25:241; 26:66; 27:123
Thompson, H. A. 9:195
Thompson, H. B. 22:346
Thompson, H. C. 11:46
Thompson, H. E. 18:401

Thompson, H. F. 16:58; 21:396; 23:171; 25:328

Thompson, H. N. 19:104

Thompson, H. P. 13:129

Thompson, H. R. 17:210

Thompson, H. V. 13:69

Thompson, Harvey 22:510

Thompson, Haynie 17:62

Thompson, Henry 4:57; 5:31; 6:23; 7:71; 11:214; 13:120; 16:233; 17:60; 19:104; 21:43; 22:225; 26:67

Thompson, Henry B. 21:43

Thompson, Henry R. 23:183

Thompson, Hillard 9:137

Thompson, Hilliard 27:121

Thompson, Howard 23:81

Thompson, Hughes C. 14:225

Thompson, I. 26:67

Thompson, I. L. 13:120

Thompson, I. M. 15:232

Thompson, I. N. 24:57

Thompson, I. W. 25:277

Thompson, Ichmael 19:293

Thompson, Ira P. 21:144

Thompson, Isaac 7:113; 10:187; 18:181

Thompson, Isaac C. 7:43

Thompson, Isaac O. 21:127

Thompson, Isaiah 10:139; 20:362

Thompson, Ishmael 9:202

Thompson, Israel 20:399

Thompson, J. 1:79, 80, 178, 179; 3:193; 11:174; 12:84; 14:117, 133, 225, 304; 16:233, 306; 17:357, 480; 18:40, 255; 20:44; 21:43; 22:493; 24:115; 25:74, 241, 328; 27:123

Thompson, J. A. 9:151; 11:173; 14:117; 15:153; 16:103

Thompson, J. B. 15:161; 24:31

Thompson, J. Benson 20:143

Thompson, J. C. 7:76; 25:305

Thompson, J. D. 1:80; 14:328; 25:328

Thompson, J. E. 12:84; 16:306

Thompson, J. H. 11:79; 14:245; 25:241

Thompson, J. J. 24:108

Thompson, J. M. 3:193; 19:104, 243, 334; 20:149

Thompson, J. P. 15:232

Thompson, J. R. 1:80; 23:171

Thompson, J. S. 3:193; 14:117, 225

Thompson, J. T. 14:117; 15:232; 18:402; 25:241

Thompson, J. W. 25:241

Thompson, Jacob 10:83; 20:362

Thompson, James 6:33; 7:54, 112; 8:110; 9:105; 10:99, 155, 175; 11:173, 214, 272, 397; 12:52, 167; 13:120; 14:271; 16:58; 17:87, 159; 18:115, 211, 255; 19:198; 20:135; 21:235, 396; 23:53, 171; 24:99; 25:328; 26:66

Thompson, James A. 11:79; 20:117; 21:235; 23:14

Thompson, James B. 22:271

Thompson, James C. 20:117

Thompson, James E. 22:105

Thompson, James F. 8:110; 21:239

Thompson, James L. 17:250

Thompson, James M. 20:149

Thompson, James W. 8:97; 10:139; 20:362; 22:458; 24:46

Thompson, Jeremiah 7:135; 11:173

Thompson, Jesse 9:211; 17:208, 411; 22:524

Thompson, Jesse H. 20:20

Thompson, Job 21:396

Thompson, John 1:79; 4:57, 58, 68; 5:31; 6:19; 7:135; 8:33; 9:69;

Thompson, John 11:79, 89, 213, 283; 12:168; 13:50; 15:46, 310; 16:58; 17:27; 18:72, 95, 163, 402; 19:49, 104, 330; 20:33, 101; 21:43, 81, 396; 22:15, 105; 23:81; 25:75; 26:67

Thompson, John C. 12:42

Thompson, John Ed. 20:129

Thompson, John F. 9:137

Thompson, John H. 7:43; 10:83; 13:50

Thompson, John M. 22:443

Thompson, John N. 4:57; 22:225

Thompson, John P. 10:139; 20:362

Thompson, John R. 23:171

Thompson, John S. 8:110

Thompson, John W. 8:120; 17:60; 19:37

Thompson, Johnson 5:31

Thompson, Joseph 5:46; 6:22; 8:33; 9:211; 12:167; 18:72, 95, 163, 255; 19:348; 20:178; 21:261, 286; 23:171; 26:66, 67

Thompson, Joseph C. 10:83; 20:362

Thompson, Joseph D. 11:294

Thompson, Joseph G. 25:241

Thompson, Joseph H. 21:396

Thompson, Joseph L. 23:257

Thompson, Joseph S. 22:114

Thompson, Josephus 8:97

Thompson, Joshua 11:214; 22:443; 23:94

Thompson, L. 1:178; 16:380

Thompson, L. D. 9:195; 19:263

Thompson, L. L. 19:37

Thompson, L. M. 14:317, 322

Thompson, Lafayette 20:362

Thompson, Lawson 18:181

Thompson, Leonid M.
23:185
Thompson, Levi 7:112;
21:113; 22:225;
23:259
Thompson, Lewis 12:42;
15:316; 19:104;
21:261
Thompson, Lorenzo D.
22:105
Thompson, M. 3:193;
10:149; 14:245, 330;
18:59; 25:75, 242
Thompson, M. C. 3:193
Thompson, M. H. 9:29
Thompson, M. J. 13:120;
20:103
Thompson, M. S. C. 18:40
Thompson, M. W. 3:193
Thompson, Marcus 8:97
Thompson, Mark 10:139;
20:362
Thompson, Marshall
10:83
Thompson, Marshall W.
20:362
Thompson, Martin 9:225;
18:377
Thompson, Martin V.
10:83
Thompson, Mills 17:27
Thompson, Milton 5:31;
7:112
Thompson, Mose 18:255;
26:67
Thompson, Moses B.
20:94
Thompson, N. 25:242
Thompson, Nathaniel
12:42; 17:88
Thompson, Nathaniel P.
21:81
Thompson, Nelson 5:31;
9:126; 27:122
Thompson, Nelson B.
24:86
Thompson, Nye 22:225
Thompson, O. 12:159;
14:225
Thompson, O. M. 18:40
Thompson, O. W. William
24:31
Thompson, Ole 21:144;
25:284
Thompson, Oley P.
16:151
Thompson, Orin 12:54
Thompson, Otha 22:57
Thompson, Otis 4:57
Thompson, Owen 22:322

Thompson, P. 1:177;
3:193
Thompson, P. G. 11:330
Thompson, P. H. 20:135
Thompson, P. I. 25:273
Thompson, P. J. 14:320
Thompson, Patrick 9:195;
19:263
Thompson, Perry 21:261
Thompson, Peter 5:46;
12:52; 22:285;
24:205
Thompson, Peter M.
11:117
Thompson, Philetus
22:157
Thompson, Philip 7:10;
19:49; 22:225
Thompson, Pompey
22:322
Thompson, R. 1:177, 178;
3:193; 12:147;
14:260; 15:232;
19:307
Thompson, R. D. 20:362
Thompson, R. J. 25:242
Thompson, R. M. 8:56;
21:169
Thompson, Ransom T.
19:198
Thompson, Rease 11:214
Thompson, Reason
19:273
Thompson, Reese B.
27:123
Thompson, Richard
9:195; 19:243;
21:286
Thompson, Richard M.
23:102
Thompson, Richard W.
11:174
Thompson, Robert 4:68;
9:105; 10:139; 13:59;
15:232; 16:125;
20:362; 22:346;
24:46
Thompson, Robert C.
24:56
Thompson, Robert J. 5:46;
22:225
Thompson, Robert S.
23:81
Thompson, Robert T.
14:225
Thompson, Royal D.
10:83
Thompson, Rufus 22:321
Thompson, Rufus D.
16:82

Thompson, Russell W.
21:132
Thompson, S. 1:179;
3:193; 11:173; 12:97;
14:225; 25:242
Thompson, S. C. 18:40
Thompson, S. D. 1:177;
21:396
Thompson, S. E. 18:341
Thompson, S. H. 25:75
Thompson, Sam 17:293
Thompson, Sampson
22:493
Thompson, Samuel 5:31;
7:135; 9:166; 10:155;
11:251; 16:58; 18:40,
255; 19:37, 198;
21:396; 22:157, 346;
26:66
Thompson, Samuel C.
20:139
Thompson, Samuel D.
10:83; 20:362
Thompson, Samuel N.
11:278
Thompson, Samuel R.
22:271
Thompson, Sarah 17:218
Thompson, Sever 7:43;
23:196
Thompson, Silas 18:255
Thompson, Silas C.
22:225
Thompson, Silas W. 16:59
Thompson, Simon 9:211
Thompson, Simon C.
10:23
Thompson, Smith 19:37
Thompson, Sol. W.
21:205
Thompson, Spear 18:255;
26:67
Thompson, Stephen 9:29;
11:426; 18:72
Thompson, Stephens
26:113
Thompson, Sumner 9:8
Thompson, Syver 12:159
Thompson, T. 3:193
Thompson, T. D. 14:117
Thompson, T. H. 21:60
Thompson, T. M. 1:177
Thompson, T. W. 18:95
Thompson, Target 10:139
Thompson, Thomas 4:57;
5:31; 7:43; 9:137,
195; 10:139; 11:426;
13:50; 14:117;
17:421; 20:14, 32,
88, 362; 21:43, 245;

Thompson, Thomas 22:322; 24:31; 27:121

Thompson, Thomas A. 18:255; 26:66; 27:121

Thompson, Thomas B. 9:92

Thompson, Thomas W. 9:105

Thompson, Turner 24:205

Thompson, V. B. 3:193

Thompson, Vanrensaler 9:39

Thompson, W. 1:80, 100, 176, 177, 178, 179; 3:193; 4:57; 9:114; 11:314; 14:117, 225; 15:264; 17:293; 21:218; 25:242

Thompson, W. A. 1:176; 3:193; 16:306

Thompson, W. B. 2:18; 7:54; 8:110; 14:225; 25:74

Thompson, W. C. 1:176; 22:225, 346; 23:53

Thompson, W. D. 3:193; 20:135; 21:396; 22:225; 23:53; 25:75

Thompson, W. E. 13:80

Thompson, W. F. 3:193

Thompson, W. H. 1:177; 11:79; 15:232

Thompson, W. J. 14:304; 27:123

Thompson, W. L. G. 18:223

Thompson, W. M. 11:271; 17:432

Thompson, W. P. 24:31

Thompson, W. S. 15:232

Thompson, W. W. 3:193; 18:422

Thompson, Wallace 17:239

Thompson, Walter 7:54

Thompson, Wellington 18:441

Thompson, William 5:46; 7:113, 135; 8:33, 97, 110; 10:23, 139, 140; 11:393; 12:77, 78, 159; 13:50; 14:27, 117, 225; 15:60, 76, 136, 175, 232; 16:233; 17:232, 239; 18:163, 223, 435; 20:44, 362; 21:107, 235, 396; 22:57, 105, 225, 271, 322, 346;

Thompson, William 23:53; 24:97, 103; 25:242; 27:119

Thompson, William A. 22:57

Thompson, William A. C. 20:184

Thompson, William B. 9:68, 100; 18:281; 22:57, 493

Thompson, William C. 17:102

Thompson, William H. 4:68; 19:198; 20:117; 23:81, 94

Thompson, William H. H. 21:236

Thompson, William J. 17:481

Thompson, William L. 18:163

Thompson, William M. 24:150

Thompson, William McK. 22:132

Thompson, William S. 8:33; 11:98; 16:233

Thompson, William T. 11:131

Thompson, William W. 10:168; 18:223

Thompson, Yaney 22:321

Thompson, Young 10:140; 20:362

Thompton, James 13:50

Thoms, Andrew 18:317; 26:113

Thoms, G. 1:177

Thoms, Thomas 9:99

Thomsen, August 23:94

Thomsley, Joseph 11:173

Thomson, Alfred 15:231

Thomson, Archibald 17:439

Thomson, Cornelius 13:50

Thomson, Evory 15:231

Thomson, John 18:255

Thomson, John F. 27:121

Thomson, Rufus 16:103

Thomson, Target 20:362

Thomson, Thomas W. 18:341

Thomson, William A. 15:231

Thonan, Peter 10:140

Thor, Thomas J. 18:195

Thorey, David 19:330

Thorin, Joseph 21:81

Thorington, Stephen C. 10:140; 20:362

Thorison, Carl 8:33

Thork, J. 11:251

Thorn, Albert S. 17:264

Thorn, Andrew 12:42; 16:160

Thorn, Benjamin 7:43

Thorn, Benjamin E. 8:97

Thorn, David M. 11:46

Thorn, E. 2:18; 25:76

Thorn, George 25:242

Thorn, George W. 16:233

Thorn, H. T. 3:193

Thorn, Henry B. 17:391

Thorn, Henry C. 15:89

Thorn, Ira G. 22:105

Thorn, Isaac 24:31

Thorn, Isaac W. 12:78; 15:60

Thorn, J. 3:193; 12:88

Thorn, James 18:402

Thorn, John 13:100; 14:23

Thorn, John G. 21:261

Thorn, Julius 9:14

Thorn, Martin V. B. 21:396

Thorn, P. C. 3:193

Thorn, R. W. 15:259

Thorn, S. 17:93

Thorn, Stanley 17:157

Thorn, Thaddeus 22:105

Thorn, W. W. 13:50

Thorn, William 4:58; 7:65; 9:99; 12:86

Thorn, William S. 25:76

Thornal, William 22:105

Thornberry, L. 25:242

Thornberry, Thornton 17:27

Thornborough, J. 1:177

Thornbrow, George 9:238; 26:227

Thornburg, --- 11:174

Thornburg, Addin D. 21:207

Thornburg, John C. 20:101

Thornburg, L. 11:79

Thornburg, W. B. 24:86

Thornburg, Wesley 9:46

Thornburg, William 10:83

Thornbury, B. 3:193

Thornbury, Isaac 8:110

Thornbury, Lewis 5:31

Thorncraft, David 9:39

Thorncroft, David 26:114

Thorndicke, George E. 4:58

Thorndie, --- 3:193

Thorndike, J. E. 19:231

Thorndike, John E. 9:195

Thorndyke, J. F. 4:58

Thorne, Edward F. 23:94

Thorne, Henry 12:160
Thorne, John 24:31
Thorne, W. 25:242
Thorne, William H. 17:427
Thornely, N. D. 22:492
Thorner, James 17:139; 24:205
Thorneycroft, Henry 22:15
Thornhill, J. W. 18:464
Thornhill, Jesse L. 22:458
Thornhill, Reuben 4:68
Thornison, Carl 18:163
Thornley, Frank 22:157
Thornley, G. 14:117
Thornley, Thomas 22:225
Thornop, Horace 12:63
Thornop, Horance 15:93
Thornsburg, John 12:159
Thornton, --- 19:104
Thornton, A. 25:242
Thornton, Abram 9:126; 27:122
Thornton, B. 8:33; 12:86; 18:163
Thornton, C. W. H. 19:37
Thornton, Calvin 22:225
Thornton, Charles 9:162
Thornton, Charles A. 15:232
Thornton, Charles B. 9:105
Thornton, Charles D. 18:341
Thornton, Charles H. 11:393; 23:110
Thornton, Clem 17:187
Thornton, D. 14:117; 16:306
Thornton, D. G. 10:207
Thornton, D. M. 12:97; 15:362; 19:105
Thornton, David 17:27
Thornton, Doctor G. 18:407
Thornton, Edwin R. 24:97
Thornton, George 10:145; 19:198
Thornton, Green 24:103
Thornton, H. 21:43
Thornton, H. H. 11:271
Thornton, Harry 13:50
Thornton, Henry 16:59
Thornton, Henry W. 8:97
Thornton, J. 3:193; 15:60
Thornton, J. W. 23:53
Thornton, James 9:243; 12:78; 16:59
Thornton, James R. 19:105

Thornton, John 9:99; 15:329; 19:105
Thornton, John A. 22:225
Thornton, John G. 13:51; 16:59
Thornton, John W. 21:261
Thornton, L. 25:242
Thornton, Lewis 5:46
Thornton, M. V. 22:355
Thornton, Mathew 17:268
Thornton, Nathaniel 10:140; 20:362; 27:156
Thornton, P. 14:225
Thornton, Patrick 19:37
Thornton, Perry 11:121
Thornton, R. 4:58
Thornton, Richard 13:60
Thornton, Richard D. 20:187
Thornton, Robert 8:43; 26:184
Thornton, S. A. 3:193
Thornton, S. F. 25:242
Thornton, S. T. 5:46
Thornton, Samuel 9:202; 19:293
Thornton, Samuel E. 20:26
Thornton, Stephen 17:444; 24:163
Thornton, T. J. 21:169
Thornton, Thomas 6:19; 10:83; 18:95; 20:362
Thornton, W. 9:60
Thornton, Wesley 18:255; 26:67
Thornton, William 21:286
Thornton, William A. 17:315
Thornton, William M. 10:140; 20:362
Thorp, A. B. 14:225
Thorp, A. J. 23:102
Thorp, Abner 14:225
Thorp, Andrew 20:14
Thorp, B. W. 26:146
Thorp, C. 1:100
Thorp, D. 3:193
Thorp, Elevan C. 11:79
Thorp, Eli 18:59
Thorp, Elias 12:78
Thorp, Francis 16:306
Thorp, Franklin 8:97
Thorp, G. 14:117
Thorp, George B 22:441
Thorp, George M. 13:50
Thorp, Henry 23:126
Thorp, J. 3:193
Thorp, James 27:123
Thorp, James B. 10:83

Thorp, James P. 20:14
Thorp, Jerry 21:249
Thorp, John 15:335; 27:122
Thorp, John W. 1:80; 12:42; 20:117
Thorp, L. 3:194
Thorp, L. R. 27:120
Thorp, N. 12:97; 27:121
Thorp, Richard 17:139
Thorp, Rodolph C. 22:132
Thorp, Samuel 9:73; 13:50
Thorp, Silas 17:27
Thorp, Simeon B. 20:27
Thorp, William 8:110; 9:92; 14:117; 20:101; 26:65
Thorp, William H. 24:97
Thorpe, Amos 17:27
Thorpe, Elish 16:233
Thorpe, Francis 12:93
Thorpe, H. 3:194
Thorpe, Hiram 1:78; 22:225
Thorpe, James B. 20:362
Thorpe, L. R. 9:151
Thorpe, N. 15:362
Thorpe, Nelson 9:151
Thorpe, Robert 17:187
Thorpe, S. S. 3:194
Thorpe, Samuel 10:23
Thorpe, W. C. 3:194
Thorpe, William 8:76
Thorrington, J. 14:117
Thorsburg, G. W. 14:117
Thorson, Edward H. 22:57
Thorson, John 23:53
Thorson, P. 3:194
Thorstinson, Thomas 20:117
Thorston, S. T. 1:100
Thorter, William 18:324
Thorton, Henry 21:201
Thorward, John C. 15:168
Thorwood, Henry 18:163
Thoshier, D. 25:242
Thosten, Gilbert 21:261
Thoulan, Pirrie 21:107
Thoundhurst, Frederick 19:37
Thoup, M. J. 9:92
Thowher, John 13:51
Thracey, M. 14:117
Thrackhill, L. 14:117
Thrackmorton, C. 1:80
Thrailkill, Elijah E. 21:236
Thrailkill, Henry 22:225
Thrailtell, David 27:123
Thraket, Oscar 17:399

Thrall, Aaron 11:232
Thrall, B. 21:396
Thrall, Chauncy T. 22:57
Thrall, George N. 16:59
Thrall, George W. 13:51
Thrall, J. 19:246
Thrall, James 15:232
Thrall, W. G. 14:117
Thralls, George 8:33
Thralls, William L. 23:53
Thranson, Ola 10:140;
  20:363
Thrapp, M. E. 22:492
Thrasher, Anty 25:74
Thrasher, Asel S. 22:157
Thrasher, Ben. F. 24:31
Thrasher, H. A. 14:117
Thrasher, John B. 22:442
Thrasher, John S. 11:46
Thrasher, Joseph 17:44
Thrasher, Nathaniel 21:88
Thrasher, Nelson 12:78
Thrasher, O. T. 19:198
Thrasher, Ray H. 22:157
Thrasher, Thompson O. T.
  22:132
Thrasher, William H.
  9:92; 26:66
Three, John 16:306
Threet, Samuel 22:322
Threfal, Robert 7:113
Threlkeld, --- 20:93
Threnikill, Joshua 17:44
Thresh, G. 3:194
Thresher, Elbridge D.
  19:105
Thret, Albert 21:286
Throal, H. 21:127
Throckmorton, Absalom
  22:493
Throckmorton, L. 22:225
Throckmorton, Samuel
  17:187
Throckmorton, Winfield
  11:382
Throll, Charles 21:205
Throm, William 7:43
Thromon, James 26:130
Thronson, Knud 23:94
Thronton, M. 27:120
Throop, Orange 11:271
Throp, Benjamin 21:60
Throp, James 14:304;
  17:480
Thrope, L. L. 19:224
Througate, D. 1:79
Thrower, Robert W.
  19:198
Thrulls, George 18:163
Thrumdren, Torben
  27:123

Thrus, N. 14:117
Thrush, J. M. 15:232
Thrush, John 23:278
Thrush, William A. 20:94
Thruston, W. P. 7:43
Thuck, T. 3:194
Thulan, J. 3:194
Thule, Charles 26:113
Thullard, J. L. 14:260
Thumb, W. 25:273
Thumil, Peter 17:187
Thumon, William 22:271
Thurber, D. 3:194
Thurber, H. 15:113
Thurbur, Silas 22:225
Thureton, Hiram 18:163
Thurlach, Charles 16:142
Thurley, Adam 14:225
Thurlow, Charles 13:51
Thurlow, Daniel 8:33;
  18:163
Thurlow, Isaac 15:93
Thurlow, W. 13:100
Thurman, Berry 17:285
Thurman, David 8:97
Thurman, F. C. 9:232
Thurman, Frank 20:363
Thurman, H. C. 1:179
Thurman, J. 3:194
Thurman, James 11:426;
  17:27
Thurman, M. B. 27:121
Thurman, Parker 9:70
Thurman, Pleasant 8:33
Thurman, Squire 8:97
Thurman, Wayne 22:105
Thurman, Wiley O. 17:60
Thurmer, D. A. 9:152
Thurn, Frederick 17:101
Thurner, Jacob 19:198
Thurs, James A. 23:284
Thurselings, William 9:29
Thurston, A. D. 1:179
Thurston, A. J. 1:177;
  22:346
Thurston, A. M. 14:225
Thurston, C. C. 3:194
Thurston, D. 17:309
Thurston, Daniel 17:363
Thurston, Deloss 21:107
Thurston, F. C. 21:396
Thurston, Frank L. 21:396
Thurston, G. 1:177
Thurston, G. M. 3:194;
  11:174
Thurston, George 25:242
Thurston, George H. 5:31
Thurston, H. A. 25:242
Thurston, H. H. 20:32
Thurston, H. L. 1:178
Thurston, Henry 5:31, 46

Thurston, Hiram 8:33
Thurston, James 24:46
Thurston, Jesse 24:205
Thurston, John 12:84;
  16:306
Thurston, L. D. 1:80
Thurston, Mathias 24:70
Thurston, N. E. 3:194
Thurston, Noah 8:78
Thurston, Peter C. 22:285
Thurston, Quincy F. 13:51
Thurston, S. 16:233
Thurston, Silas E. 16:142
Thurston, T. J. 4:58
Thurston, Thomas 9:202;
  19:198
Thurston, Thomas M.
  8:110; 10:168
Thurston, William A.
  22:105
Thurston, William B.
  22:157
Thurstrong, L. 1:177
Thurtell, E. 26:67
Thurtin, Charles 19:198
Thuston, Thomas 19:293
Thutford, John 8:33;
  18:163
Thuton, W. W. 9:60
Thwing, H. S. 1:177
Thyer, F. 8:97; 18:327
Thyer, Peter 8:56
Tiado, John 9:238; 26:227
Tianmons, James H.
  17:201
Tibb, Daniel 21:286
Tibbals, Emanuel 6:19;
  18:95
Tibbels, H. 3:194
Tibbels, William 3:194
Tibbens, James B. 21:396
Tibberts, William H.
  20:129
Tibbes, John 4:58
Tibbet, A. 3:194
Tibbet, E. D. 11:79
Tibbet, James 16:306
Tibbet, William 18:377
Tibbeth, W. H. 5:46
Tibbeths, T. 1:80
Tibbets, J. E. 1:80
Tibbets, J. H. 13:100
Tibbets, Nathaniel 12:42
Tibbets, Nathaniel W.
  4:58
Tibbets, W. B. 1:79
Tibbets, W. C. 9:152
Tibbett, F. A. 15:232
Tibbett, R. 14:117
Tibbett, William 9:228

Tibbetts, B. F. 7:76;
25:305
Tibbetts, Henry 19:198
Tibbetts, Hiram 20:117
Tibbetts, Isaac 13:51
Tibbetts, Isaiah P. 9:195
Tibbetts, J. 2:18; 19:243;
25:76
Tibbetts, J. W. 25:242
Tibbetts, John 16:283
Tibbetts, L. M. 25:305
Tibbetts, Sumner 10:23
Tibbetts, W. B. 1:179
Tibbetts, William 16:3;
25:75
Tibbetts, William H.
13:69; 16:233;
22:105
Tibbit, George 18:402
Tibbits, H. 15:154
Tibbits, John 7:18
Tibbits, John W. 5:31
Tibbitts, Isaac 16:59
Tibbitts, J. 1:177
Tibbitts, J. N. 14:23
Tibbitts, James 9:195
Tibbitts, L. M. 7:80
Tibbitts, M. S. 17:245
Tibbitts, Spencer 7:54
Tibbitts, W. 1:176
Tibbitts, Waldo 22:285
Tibbs, A. 18:255; 26:67
Tibbs, Benson 9:92
Tibbs, George 22:132
Tibbs, James 17:151;
22:57
Tibbs, L. 25:242
Tibbs, Levi 25:242
Tibbs, Milton 17:399
Tibbs, Silas 25:242
Tibbs, Washington 21:396
Tibbutt, Robert W. 23:81
Tibets, D. M. 13:126
Tibetts, Warren C. 27:120
Tiblet, J. 14:245
Tiblet, James 27:123
Tice, A. D. 16:103
Tice, Berry 8:115
Tice, Charles W. 15:46
Tice, G. H. 15:175
Tice, J. P. 11:417
Tice, James 4:58; 15:232
Tice, John 16:136
Tice, Jonathan 12:78;
15:28
Tice, Joseph M. 17:44
Tice, Levi 17:27
Tice, M. 12:81
Tice, N. 25:242
Tice, R. 25:75
Tice, S. J. 3:194

Tichark, Henry 9:195
Tichenor, Charles H.
22:468
Tichenor, G. D. 1:178
Tichl, Jacob 11:315
Tichler, Lewis 16:380
Tichmond, John 19:37
Tichnor, Nathaniel A.
22:114
Tichnor, William 9:29
Tickenor, Irvan 1:79
Tickle, W. H. 21:192
Tickner, William 15:75
Ticknor, H. 18:18
Ticknor, Horace 23:53
Ticknor, John 25:242
Ticknor, William E.
17:423
Tidaback, H. C. 14:304;
17:477; 27:123
Tidall, James 17:27
Tidball, B. 15:232
Tidd, Charles A. 25:242
Tidd, Joseph H. 24:155
Tidd, L. C. 14:317, 322;
23:110
Tidd, Moses 22:225
Tidd, R. 9:152; 27:121
Tidd, Shelbourn H.
22:157
Tidd, W. P. 1:177
Tidman, A. 27:121
Tidman, Andrew 9:155
Tidmarsh, John 13:120
Tidwell, Clark 16:59
Tidwell, F. 3:194
Tidwell, J. W. 3:194
Tidwell, John 8:33;
18:163; 20:47
Tidwell, Silas 10:83
Tidwell, Wyatt N. 21:43
Tiedemann, Ehlert 22:285
Tiedman, C. 27:120
Tiefield, Royal 18:377
Tiehe, J. A. 13:69
Tielow, A. 19:263
Tieman, John 20:363
Tieman, Peter 18:163
Tiement, Richard 7:135
Tiemeyer, Herman 22:105
Tiemper, Henry W.
19:347
Tiems, Daniel 19:37
Tienney, M. 1:79
Tierants, J. 11:334
Tiereney, James 25:242
Tiernan, Patrick 1:78
Tiernan, Thomas 21:144
Tiernay, George B. 19:347
Tiernay, W. 3:194
Tierney, D. 12:78

Tierney, George B. 13:135
Tierney, James 18:427
Tierney, Patrick 20:135
Tierney, Richard 13:51;
16:59
Tierney, William 19:105
Tierrell, James 18:427
Tierule, Charles 10:8
Ties, John B. 18:255
Ties, John V. 26:67
Tifaney, H. 1:80
Tiff, Thomas 13:120
Tiffany, C. 14:131;
15:264
Tiffany, Cornelius 13:51
Tiffany, H. A. 3:194
Tiffany, J. 7:70
Tiffany, James 12:42
Tiffany, John 17:363
Tiffany, Lewis R. 22:442
Tiffay, Tobias T. 21:218
Tiffe, Benjamin 18:195
Tiffets, W. 25:242
Tifford, Charles 17:399
Tifft, J. 12:143
Tifft, J. L. 1:80
Tifft, Linas C. 1:79
Tifield, G. 16:233
Tifield, Royal 9:225
Tift, H. 3:194
Tift, J. W. 25:284
Tift, L. M. 12:159
Tifton, F. M. 1:100
Tige, J. A. 27:119
Tighe, Charles 11:323
Tighe, John A. 19:105
Tighe, Patrick 9:195;
16:149; 19:243
Tighe, Philip 9:195
Tighe, Phillip 19:263
Tigler, John 14:225
Tilbe, John 24:31
Tilbets, W. H. 11:342
Tilburry, N. 24:86
Tilbury, G. 23:53
Tilbury, P. 16:103
Tilden, A. 3:194
Tilden, Bradley 21:261
Tilden, F. 16:233
Tilden, William O. 20:109
Tilet, James 1:80
Tiley, M. 20:363
Tilford, B. 17:187
Tilford, David L. 9:225
Tilford, George 22:322
Tilford, J. 16:233
Tilford, James 8:33;
9:225; 18:163, 377
Tilford, Jesse W. 22:443
Tilkil, John 18:255
Tilkin, John 26:67

Till, Absalom 9:137; 27:121
Till, Barman 10:170; 19:198
Till, George W. 8:33; 18:163
Till, John 9:137; 25:305; 27:121
Till, John A. 9:126; 27:122
Till, Wendell 19:263
Tillapaugh, G. W. 1:177
Tillatson, J. 17:16
Tilldeman, C. 9:152
Tiller, A. 14:225
Tiller, Abraham 14:117
Tiller, Hiram 22:285
Tillery, A. C. 7:113
Tillery, Isaac 17:60
Tillery, Mordecai 22:506
Tillery, P. F. 9:60
Tillery, Thomas A. 21:236
Tillerz, Alfred 17:44
Tilles, Washington 7:113
Tilleton, C. L. 21:396
Tillett, Charles 23:171
Tilletts, George W. 19:37
Tilley, Albert 18:435
Tilley, G. W. 9:232
Tilley, H. 25:242
Tilley, Henry 5:31
Tilley, James E. 12:78
Tilley, John 23:172
Tilley, John J. 17:351
Tilley, Martin 10:83
Tilley, William 11:173; 16:59
Tilley, William M. 22:105
Tillford, David L. 18:377
Tillford, James 1:79
Tillie, Andrew 11:79
Tillingash, Charles E. 19:198
Tillinghast, Charles E. 10:154
Tillinghast, W. D. 16:11
Tillinghast, William H. 13:51
Tillirge, N. 14:245
Tillirge, W. 27:123
Tillitson, A. P. 3:194
Tillman, A. 23:53
Tillman, H. 16:233
Tillman, Jerry 25:242
Tillman, Josiah 9:92
Tillman, Leander D. 11:315
Tillman, Robert 6:23
Tillman, Willis 7:135
Tillo, R. C. 1:179
Tillor, G. W. 3:194

Tillostan, Charles 5:31
Tilloston, Robert 16:380
Tillotsen, Charles 15:46
Tillotson, Albert 22:157
Tillotson, C. G. 25:242
Tillotson, Calvin 11:113
Tillotson, Charles A. 17:47
Tillotson, E. H. 11:174
Tillotson, James 10:155
Tillotson, P. D. 10:83; 20:363
Tillotson, Robert 15:346
Tillotson, Thaddeus 22:15
Tillotson, W. H. 5:31; 25:242
Tillotson, William 16:136
Tillottson, S. C. 22:285
Tills, E. 25:242
Tills, Edward 5:31
Tillson, Charles E. 3:194
Tillson, Sylvester 7:70
Tillson, William T. 15:136
Tilly, James E. 15:60
Tilman, Benjamin 22:322
Tilman, Frank 6:13
Tilman, Lender 6:26
Tilman, Oliver 10:83; 20:363
Tilson, Ezra J. 7:66
Tilson, H. H. 8:68
Tilson, Jesse 22:346
Tilson, Lewis 10:140
Tilson, Samuel E. 22:271
Tilt, George 3:224; 17:500
Tilt, M. 3:194
Tiltan, N. M. 3:194
Tilte, H. 14:245; 27:123
Tilton, --- 27:119
Tilton, A. E. 18:377
Tilton, D. B. 3:194
Tilton, David 14:117
Tilton, E. 23:53
Tilton, F. H. 27:120
Tilton, George 1:79
Tilton, H. 3:194
Tilton, Hazer 12:168
Tilton, J. 3:194; 14:118; 19:233
Tilton, J. B. 17:157
Tilton, L. G. 3:194
Tilton, R. C. 7:43
Tilton, Robert 23:81
Tilton, T. H. 9:152
Tilton, Timothy 13:51
Tilton, William 18:195
Tilton, William H. 22:225
Tilton, William L. 22:493
Timasson, James 21:396
Timball, William 3:194
Timbell, A. 15:232

Timberian, J. 24:70
Timberlain, James 4:58
Timberlake, Henry E. 11:314
Timberlake, J. 9:152
Timberlake, R. B. 9:195; 19:231
Timberlake, T. 16:59; 27:120
Timberlick, Lewis 11:173
Timberman, Charles 21:116
Timbers, Charles 15:75
Timefroth, A. 15:307
Times, Irvin 24:174
Timins, Erwin 17:449
Timlan, G. F. 1:177
Timlin, John 15:136
Timm, Edward 11:342
Timm, James 3:194
Timmale, Samuel 7:113
Timmay, Frank 12:42
Timmel, John 22:441
Timmeny, O. 21:128
Timmerman, A. 23:53
Timmerman, Henry 23:130
Timmish, --- 3:194
Timmons, Catlin 9:92
Timmons, Catline 26:65
Timmons, Cyrus 27:156
Timmons, John 7:15
Timmons, Leonard 9:239
Timmons, M. 7:43
Timmons, O. P. 21:396
Timmons, Patrick 10:23
Timmons, Purnell 17:321
Timmons, Robert 17:44
Timmons, Thomas M. 20:101
Timms, Irvin 24:174
Timms, J. F. 1:177
Timothy, C. 26:184
Tims, William 19:273
Tin, John 9:158
Tinbrook, V. 10:23
Tincate, Frank 18:115
Tinch, Edward 19:49
Tincher, James H. 22:105
Tincher, William R. 10:188
Tindall, Alfred M. 22:412
Tindall, Henry 9:211; 18:72
Tindall, Henry F. 16:59
Tindall, J. A. 11:251
Tindall, James 17:27
Tindall, Joseph 15:136
Tindall, L. 11:251
Tindall, Robert V. 23:172
Tindall, William 3:194

Tindel, C. 3:194
Tindel, F. 15:175
Tindell, Peter 16:59
Tinder, J. W. 19:269
Tinder, N. 15:9
Tinder, Nathan 12:63
Tindle, E. 3:194
Tindle, Peter L. 16:59
Tine, John 21:192
Tinell, Jefferson 9:73
Tiner, J. W. 3:194
Tiner, Tiles 7:113
Tiner, William N. 11:294
Tines, B. F. 4:58
Tingay, W. 3:194
Tingee, Annasies H. 18:18
Tingle, Albert 12:52
Tingle, John J. 17:44
Tingle, Joseph 22:346
Tingle, Shadrick 8:33
Tingle, Shadwick 18:163
Tingley, Richard 10:177
Tinhot, --- 16:306
Tinineger, J. T. S. 15:323
Tining, T. 16:271
Tinis, David 3:194
Tinkam, Samuel A.
    20:117
Tinker, A. J. 1:179
Tinker, Charles 19:198
Tinker, Charles M. 18:407
Tinker, Clarence 15:232
Tinker, Eli 11:426
Tinker, Eugene O. 18:281
Tinker, G. M. 21:396
Tinker, George E. 11:46
Tinker, Harvey 8:115;
    18:324
Tinker, J. 13:100; 14:23
Tinker, J. E. 20:141
Tinker, J. W. 20:14
Tinker, James 3:194
Tinker, M. 20:90
Tinker, Milan T. 4:58
Tinker, William 22:225;
    25:76
Tinkham, Andrew 22:441,
    493
Tinkham, Charles 27:122
Tinkham, E. W. 10:140;
    20:363
Tinkham, H. A. 18:72
Tinkham, J. 14:23
Tinkham, J. M. 1:178
Tinkham, J. W. 1:80
Tinkham, W.,1:79
Tinkle, Jeremiah F.
    21:236
Tinklepaugh, Edward
    Lewis 17:289
Tinklepaugh, S. 1:178

Tinkler, F. 21:43
Tinkler, Jesse 20:101
Tinks, John 10:83
Tinkum, Leroy 4:58
Tinlayson, Henry 16:59
Tinler, W. 3:194
Tinley, A. 18:435
Tinn, Henry 9:158
Tinner, James N. 21:43
Tinney, Alexander 23:53
Tinney, Charles 15:349;
    16:381
Tinney, John W. 4:58
Tinnins, Frederick 20:105
Tinolson, --- 21:396
Tinsdale, --- 3:194
Tinsdale, Charles H.
    10:23
Tinsier, Harris 26:67
Tinsler, Harris 18:256
Tinsley, Benjamin F.
    20:187
Tinsley, Charles E. 22:458
Tinsley, George N. 22:132
Tinsley, Jeremiah B.
    23:102
Tinsley, Joseph P. 22:132
Tinsley, Thomas 1:80
Tinsly, Delany H. 21:86
Tinsman, Andrew J.
    11:315
Tinsman, Henry 22:238
Tinth, Michael 7:70
Tipner, August 8:33;
    18:163
Tippeny, William 3:194
Tipper, George A. 14:225
Tipper, J. H. 10:83
Tippets, George D. 5:31;
    25:242
Tippett, Joseph 10:83;
    20:363
Tippett, William 14:225
Tippie, J. 24:86
Tippie, J. H. 20:363
Tippin, Isaac F. 10:83;
    20:363
Tippin, W. 21:60
Tipping, William 20:91
Tippins, W. 21:169
Tipple, Ben 9:105
Tipple, Edgar 14:225
Tipton, B. 21:43
Tipton, B. F. 2:18; 25:75
Tipton, Benjamin 10:140;
    17:167; 20:363
Tipton, Charles 11:409
Tipton, E. 21:200
Tipton, George H. 9:29
Tipton, George W.
    17:201; 25:328

Tipton, H. 11:173
Tipton, Isaac H. 17:27
Tipton, J. B. 11:131
Tipton, John W. 17:399;
    22:225
Tipton, Jonathan 11:409
Tipton, Joseph M. 23:266
Tipton, Lucas 17:293
Tipton, Newton 22:271
Tipton, Samuel 17:72;
    20:44; 22:271; 23:81
Tipton, Solomon 7:113
Tipton, Spencer 11:330
Tipton, Thomas 9:202
Tipton, Vincent 8:110
Tipton, W. H. 3:194
Tipton, William 14:225
Tirelesse, Emilie 18:441
Tirely, D. 15:46
Tirey, John B. 20:101
Tirny, S. W. 3:194
Tirpp, George 9:137
Tirrell, Allen 17:101
Tirrey, Robert 11:405
Tisch, Charles 25:242
Tischer, --- 27:123
Tisdale, E. F. 3:194
Tisdale, Peter I. 17:277
Tisdall, Thomas 9:105
Tisdell, J. 24:31
Tisen, Evan 22:225
Tiser, L. 3:194
Tishant, Hannibal 4:58
Tisnell, R. C. 19:37
Titan, M. 1:179
Titcom, C. Leonard
    14:225
Titcomb, Calvin 19:231
Titcomb, Charles 7:113
Titcomb, John H. 1:79
Titcomb, Joseph 17:403
Titcomb, Otis M. 12:163
Tite, W. F. 3:194
Titelson, James 19:198
Titer, P. 21:199
Titerick, H. 25:281
Tites, Mark 26:214
Tithroe, Isaac 7:113
Title, Hox 9:239; 26:227
Titlett, Michael 10:83
Titon, John 14:225
Tits, P. 3:194
Titson, Lewis 20:363
Titsworth, David 25:76
Tittil, George 3:194
Tittiworth, Jacob 7:135
Tittle, Lawrence 15:232
Tittle, Michael 20:363
Titu, Daniel A. 23:196
Titus, A. C. 21:396
Titus, Albert E. 25:328

Titus, Clark J. 19:198
Titus, D. 1:177, 179
Titus, Daniel N. 19:198
Titus, David S. 13:51;
  16:59
Titus, Dewitt 8:97; 18:327
Titus, George B. 22:493
Titus, Graham M. 21:396
Titus, Harvey 22:105
Titus, J. M. 24:31
Titus, Jacob H. 23:278
Titus, James 18:256;
  19:105; 26:67
Titus, Joseph 15:319
Titus, Joshua 17:157
Titus, L. J. 1:80
Titus, Lowry 23:183
Titus, M. I. 5:31
Titus, Orlando 22:468
Titus, P. D. 25:76
Titus, Peter 11:79
Titus, R. H. 1:178
Titus, Samuel 1:79
Titus, Stephen 18:223
Titus, W. 3:194
Titus, W. W. 22:492
Titus, William R. 9:9
Titwell, William 21:95
Tives, C. 3:194
Tivining, A. 5:31
Tivis, Bensen 26:65
Tivoller, Fritz 9:202
Tivyman, W. 26:185
Tjostleson, Erick 23:196
Toadvin, Peter 27:121
Toadvine, Peter 9:137
Toal, William 3:194
Toaner, L. 3:194
Tobaugh, --- 15:280
Tobby, Iron 9:137
Tobe, Ferdinand 24:86
Tobeman, John 20:363
Toben, Thomas 18:441
Tober, T. 25:76
Tober, W. J. 22:15
Tobey, George W. 1:79
Tobey, Henry 17:93
Tobey, Jere 18:59
Tobey, Joseph A. 7:17
Tobey, Stephen 21:396
Tobey, Teney 11:214
Tobias, --- 19:231
Tobias, A. 3:194; 13:69;
  14:225
Tobias, C. L. 4:58
Tobias, Henry 8:76
Tobias, Henry B. 14:304;
  17:482; 27:123
Tobias, J. 13:69; 19:105
Tobias, James 17:44
Tobias, John 9:114

Tobias, N. M. 14:118
Tobias, S. 7:79; 25:305
Tobias, William 12:52
Tobias, William H. 22:442
Tobies, Ezra 9:137
Tobin, --- 25:76
Tobin, A. 15:259
Tobin, Ezra 27:121
Tobin, James 9:68; 21:396
Tobin, James E. 4:58
Tobin, John 12:42;
  18:105; 21:396
Tobin, Michael 13:51
Tobin, Patrick 21:11
Tobin, Stephen 21:396
Tobin, Thomas 4:58;
  9:195; 19:263
Tobin, William 19:37;
  22:271
Tobine, Charles 19:323
Tobine, T. 3:194
Tobine, William B. 12:42
Tobins, --- 23:196
Toblet, James 12:93
Tobr, Aug 17:214
Tobst, Frederick 8:33
Toby, C. N. 14:225
Toby, Irom 27:121
Toby, J. 7:65
Toby, Jeremiah 10:149
Toby, William 14:225
Toda, C. 14:118
Todd, Anderson 7:135
Todd, Byron R. 25:242
Todd, Calvin 11:417
Todd, Charles 10:210
Todd, Charles S. 11:443
Todd, Christopher 11:173
Todd, D. E. 8:56
Todd, David 17:139;
  22:157; 24:205
Todd, David E. 19:198;
  21:94
Todd, David W. 22:132
Todd, Doctrin E. 19:198
Todd, Doctrine E. 10:168
Todd, Edmond D. 9:14
Todd, F. 14:29
Todd, H. J. 25:76
Todd, Henry 9:14;
  13:128; 24:32
Todd, Ira 1:78
Todd, J. 14:118; 23:53;
  25:242
Todd, J. A. 22:225
Todd, J. M. 25:243
Todd, J. P. 1:178
Todd, J. T. 8:110
Todd, J. W. 22:225
Todd, Jacob R. 10:140;
  20:363

Todd, James 9:205;
  10:140; 11:78; 18:72;
  21:61; 22:173
Todd, John 10:83; 17:441;
  20:363
Todd, John A. 23:172
Todd, John W. 21:236
Todd, Jordan 7:135
Todd, L. Frank 17:309
Todd, L. H. 7:135
Todd, Lavens 20:363
Todd, M. B. 13:100, 103;
  14:23
Todd, M. H. 23:183
Todd, Micajah 21:236
Todd, R. F. 23:53
Todd, S. A. 14:118
Todd, Samuel 20:399
Todd, T. 3:194
Todd, Theodore 25:243
Todd, Thomas 1:79; 4:58;
  17:187; 18:211
Todd, W. 14:118; 16:233
Todd, W. C. 12:146;
  15:310; 19:105
Todd, Walter 27:123
Todd, Wesley 9:195;
  19:269
Todd, William 3:194;
  9:92; 10:140; 20:363;
  23:81, 257; 24:10
Todd, William H. 14:118;
  26:65
Todd, William T. 17:27
Todde, John 21:396
Toddy, Daniel W. 4:58
Toddy, Miles J. 17:60
Tode, Dulleff 20:363
Tode, Dutlef 10:140
Todell, Jacob 7:44
Todford, A. H. 20:363
Todgner, Joseph 26:65
Tody, George 4:58
Tody, William 18:40
Toe, Loyd Vitta 11:98
Toedt, H. 3:195
Toeker, James H. 6:33
Toffer, J. 3:195
Toffinger, Joseph W.
  23:81
Togener, S. A. 9:60
Toges, James 26:66
Togle, Peter 21:286
Tohen, Thomas P. 25:328
Tohesherr, S. 27:157
Tohl, Richard 23:269
Tol, A. A. 27:123
Tol-mar-fix-e-co 25:335
Tolan, B. 3:195
Tolan, Hiram C. 12:42

Toland, Daniel 9:195; 19:279
Toland, John 21:127
Toland, John W. 24:86
Toland, W. B. K. 23:53
Toland, W. J. 21:127
Tolbert, --- 17:498
Tolbert, I. V. 11:427
Tolbert, J. C. 27:120
Tolbert, James 17:399
Tolbert, John 18:95
Tolbert, R. 8:56; 21:169
Tolbert, Tyrus 17:351
Tolbert, W. E. 23:172
Tolbey, Berry 22:105
Tolby, Edward 13:120
Tolcott, Carrie 1:80
Told, Jackson 9:105
Tole, John 11:46
Toleman, A. P. 7:113
Tolen, J. 21:43
Toler, Bluford 22:132
Toler, Calvin 24:32
Toler, John L. 23:94
Tolerson, R. D. 8:33
Tolett, George 25:75
Tolins, D. 19:263
Tolivar, Aaron 22:322
Toliver, C. 17:187
Toliver, J. D. 22:322
Toliver, John H. 18:402
Tolk, John 19:332
Toll, Frederick 17:112
Tolldy, William 25:76
Tolle, F. H. 6:33; 25:328
Tolle, Moses C. 24:70
Tolle, William A. 8:111
Tolleman, C. H. 25:328
Toller, Frederick 22:271
Tollersen, Knud 24:97
Tolles, Frederick 10:23
Tolley, D. 3:195
Tolley, Edward 5:31
Tolley, P. 14:23
Tollickson, S. 11:194
Tollier, Davis 17:455; 24:205
Tollinver, S. 25:243
Tolliver, A. J. 17:97
Tolliver, Martin 17:505
Tolliver, Silas 5:46
Tollman, Richard M. J. 27:123
Tolls, Cicero 16:103
Tolls, John 18:95
Tolman, French 17:139
Tolman, H. 15:23
Tolman, J. 2:18
Tolman, J. A. 25:74
Tolmes, David 9:195
Tolmie, J. G. 16:381

Tolmon, Moses B. 7:70
Tolsom, Enoch 18:95
Tolson, James C. 17:60
Tolt, Joseph 21:127
Tom, William 20:101; 21:236
Tom--, --- 26:185
Toman, John 15:113
Tomason, Henry 10:83; 20:363
Tomb, Closier 22:412
Tomberlin, Toliver M. 22:271
Tombinson, Robert 3:195
Tomblin, Edward 14:225
Tombs, B. 9:60
Tombs, C. W. 15:232
Tombs, G. H. 25:243
Tombs, George H. 5:31
Tombs, John W. 12:42
Tombs, Levi 25:243
Tombs, Richard 18:95
Tomelson, Joseph 11:79
Tomelson, Robert 26:214
Tomer, Albert 17:250
Tomerson, Joel 20:60
Tomkins, S. C. 19:263
Tomkins, Samuel 19:263
Tomlanson, William 4:58
Tomlin, A. 3:195
Tomlin, George 4:58; 21:286
Tomlin, Harvey 17:285
Tomlin, Izra 18:40
Tomlin, Mathew 18:256; 26:66
Tomlin, W. J. 22:225
Tomlinson, --- 17:351
Tomlinson, A. 9:195
Tomlinson, Aaron 4:58
Tomlinson, Alexander 21:192
Tomlinson, Asbury 19:278
Tomlinson, C. 20:191
Tomlinson, Charles L. 9:101
Tomlinson, Daniel 17:351
Tomlinson, G. 25:243
Tomlinson, George N. 23:16
Tomlinson, Henry 10:93; 20:363
Tomlinson, J. 10:188
Tomlinson, J. M. 11:79; 22:225
Tomlinson, S. 3:195
Tomlinson, Silas 4:58
Tomlinson, Thomas 9:46
Tomlinson, W. F. 3:195
Tomma, John 3:195

Tommy, --- 18:181
Tommy, C. C. 25:243
Tompey, Richard 21:396
Tompinson, Turner C. 17:264
Tompkins, --- 10:168
Tompkins, A. 1:177
Tompkins, A. J. 26:227
Tompkins, Alfred 15:321; 19:105
Tompkins, Amos S. 10:93; 20:363
Tompkins, Andrew 20:129
Tompkins, B. P. 1:80
Tompkins, C. 1:80
Tompkins, Charles 13:120
Tompkins, Cyrus F. 22:105
Tompkins, Daniel 19:105
Tompkins, G. 25:243
Tompkins, G. W. 11:251
Tompkins, George 18:402; 22:157; 23:81
Tompkins, Henry 7:54; 9:211
Tompkins, J. 3:195
Tompkins, J. B. 3:195
Tompkins, J. C. 24:63
Tompkins, J. M. 2:18
Tompkins, John 9:14; 10:140; 20:363
Tompkins, John R. 1:79
Tompkins, Joseph 17:139; 24:205
Tompkins, L. G. 9:195
Tompkins, Levi 21:118
Tompkins, Moses 11:173
Tompkins, N. M. 16:59
Tompkins, N. R. 3:195
Tompkins, Samuel 9:195
Tompkins, Silas W. 13:51
Tompkins, Solomon 7:135
Tompkins, W. 1:177
Tompkins, W. J. 12:149
Tompkins, Wesley 13:51
Tompkins, William 22:57
Tompkinson, J. 1:78
Tompson, A. J. 20:363
Tompson, Elis 19:37
Tompson, Silas 26:67
Tompson, Stephen 18:317
Tompson, Sylvester 19:37
Tompson, T. 3:195
Tompson, William 3:195
Toms, A. 24:86
Tomson, James 25:76
Tomson, T. H. 12:88; 16:306
Tomson, W. 8:56

Tomson, William 19:286
Tonar, Finley 22:225
Tonay, A. 18:96
Tonby, Richard B. 10:83
Tonels, H. E. 15:280
Toner, James 23:183
Toner, Martin 22:412
Toner, Michael 25:243
Toner, Peter 3:195
Toner, Robert 22:441
Tonera, William 23:172
Toney, C. B. 14:285
Toney, Dudley 18:256
Toney, Lacy 22:516
Toney, R. 22:322
Toney, Richard 17:187;
    22:322
Toney, Samuel A. 20:90
Toney, William 19:49
Tonga, Arnada 6:11
Tongue, Benjamin 17:68
Tonkinson, Stephen 4:58
Tonnan, Samuel 19:37
Tonner, William 26:214
Tonney, Domenick 14:225
Tonston, Alexander
    21:213
Tonston, H. 9:105
Tonston, Ulronsic 21:286
Tont, James W. 22:441
Tony, George 8:115
Tood, Eugene H. 9:205
Tood, James 20:363
Toofoot, John 10:168;
    19:198
Toogood, John 17:139;
    24:205
Toohal, John 7:44
Toohey, M. 11:174
Toohouse, Henry 22:57
Tooker, J. W. 19:198
Tooker, James P. 7:17
Tooker, John 7:113
Tooker, William H. 9:92
Tookey, Thomas C.
    21:396
Tookieson, T. 9:243
Tool, Cyrus 23:183
Tool, J. 14:118
Tool, Michael 19:332
Tool, P. 11:343; 14:23
Tool, Sol 7:10
Tool, Thomas 15:168
Tool, Ulysus 18:40
Toole, John 23:126
Toole, Lawrence O.
    19:340
Toole, Martin 23:81
Toole, Mathew 10:140;
    20:363
Toole, P. 13:100

Toole, Van Buren 14:337
Toole, W. 27:120
Toole, William 22:346
Tooles, John A. 18:163
Tooley, A. J. 1:177
Tooley, Abram B. 22:458
Tooley, G. W. 3:195
Tooley, Horace H. 23:126
Tooley, James 11:121
Tooley, John 13:69;
    16:233; 17:208
Tooley, Joshua 20:105
Tooley, Michael 3:195
Tooley, Solomon 18:256;
    26:67
Tooley, W. K. 3:195
Tooly, J. J. 11:282
Tooman, Patrick 25:243
Toombs, A. S. 23:259
Toombs, Benjamin F.
    22:132
Toombs, James 23:282
Toomey, J. 1:178
Toomey, J. T. 3:195
Toomey, James 23:104
Toomey, Michael 23:14
Toomey, Patrick 10:168;
    19:198
Toomy, Henry 19:105
Toomy, William 4:58
Toon, David 23:302
Toon, Demetrius 22:105
Toon, N. 18:181
Toon, V. 10:188
Toon, William H. 21:61
Tooney, Edmund 22:346
Tooney, M. 16:233
Tooney, Sylvester 25:243
Tooper, William 11:393
Toops, Fletcher 20:363
Toops, William 10:83;
    20:363
Toorleves, John A. 8:33
Toorney, Thomas 22:346
Toosot, Owe-wit 7:13
Toot, O. 22:225
Toot, W. 1:177
Tootel, John 19:263
Tootell, William 1:80
Toothacre, J. 3:195
Toothaker, Ira D. 5:31
Toothaker, J. D. 25:243
Toothaker, W. 16:233
Toothman, William 12:10
Tootil, Frederick 4:58
Tope, A. 1:179
Topfrass, James 26:227
Topher, W. 15:136
Topher, William 12:124
Topka, H. 9:68
Topley, George W. 19:105

Topling, Robert 17:16
Topman, Milton 17:187
Topp, A. 3:195
Toppas, James 9:238
Topper, Jacob 22:57
Topper, Jonathan 10:83;
    20:363
Topper, William 17:357
Toppie, Henry 22:442
Topping, Amasa 16:103
Topping, M. D. 18:223
Topping, William 18:223
Topping, William A. J.
    22:57
Topps, Fletcher 10:83
Topser, E. 1:178
Topsom, M. 10:150
Topson, M. 18:59
Toptine, Augustus 24:56
Toptine, James C. 23:196
Toralinson, J. 18:181
Toranto, George 4:58
Torbert, Hugh 1:79; 7:15
Torbert, William H. 4:58
Torbet, John N. 23:206
Torbett, Samuel 21:261
Torck, Anthony 19:105
Torden, Albert 22:442
Toren, Jackson 26:184
Torepson, Turner 18:40
Torey, V. Y. 14:118
Torgenson, Aslack 18:341
Torgerson, Anders 21:144
Torgerson, Ole 24:97
Torgeson, Haslick 9:105
Tork, M. 25:243
Torles, Ulysses 14:237
Tormer, I. 24:10
Tormey, John 18:96
Torr, Albert 9:205
Torr, William H. 10:83
Torre, Daniel 20:50
Torrell, Robert 9:195
Torrence, A. 11:174
Torrence, Adam 24:32
Torrence, B. 3:195
Torrence, George A.
    11:87
Torrence, H. A. 1:178
Torrence, J. H. 9:60
Torrence, John 27:156
Torrence, Joseph 21:397
Torrence, Wilbur E. 10:83
Torres, Santiago 8:124
Torres, T. 19:318
Torrey, Charles 27:123
Torrey, Charles L. 20:129
Torrey, Edw. F. 1:79
Torrey, George D. 20:141
Torrey, George E. 1:79
Torrey, Jack 21:397

Torrey, John 15:333
Torrey, Lewis 10:207
Torrey, N. 15:331
Torrey, Naaman 17:297
Torrey, Nathan 1:79;
   19:105
Torrey, William H. 23:196
Torrin, --- 2:18
Torrins, Joseph 12:42
Torry, C. S. 3:195
Torry, G. J. 23:171
Torry, George 8:97
Torston, Niles 18:341
Torton, Joseph 8:76
Toryand, Lewis 22:516
Toser, William 13:51
Tosh, Robert 20:109
Toshier, D. 5:54
Tost, Ezra C. 8:111
Toten, Isaac 13:128
Toten, J. 14:260
Totman, E. M. 18:256;
   26:67
Totman, Irving I. 10:175
Totman, Irwing 19:198
Tottel, William 4:58
Totten, Edwin H. 11:417
Totten, John 16:80
Totten, P. F. 26:184
Totten, Samuel F. 23:172
Totten, W. H. 21:199;
   25:305
Totten, William 7:76
Totton, Jonas 23:302
Touart, Mary 25:312
Toughley, Patrick 9:195
Touhey, Patrick 19:276
Toule, O. H. 20:175
Touley, John 14:225
Touley, Michael 12:171
Toullinger, Benjamin
   11:271
Touney, David 22:442
Touney, J. M. 3:195
Tounier, A. 2:18
Touns, J. H. 1:79
Tounsend, J. 13:100
Tounsend, Robert 13:100
Tounsson, M. 18:181
Toup, L. E. 11:292
Toupee, David 20:149
Touperay, Alexander
   18:72
Tourgee, Alonzo 25:75
Tourjee, George B.
   17:327
Tourney, F. 14:225, 260
Tourney, M. 14:226
Tourney, P. 14:226
Tournley, H. 18:96
Tournson, Thomas 15:12

Tourtelot, Lewis J. 10:83
Tourtlott, J. A. 19:276
Tousche, Joseph 8:97
Touse, D. 17:275
Touse, Doe 16:306
Tousey, Charles 19:105
Tousey, Jack 7:135
Tousis, Edward 22:346
Tousley, A. H. 9:195
Tousley, Andrew 23:172
Tousley, Arie 22:157
Tousley, C. W. 11:173
Tousley, H. H. 21:397
Tousley, Stoel A. 20:194
Tousley, William H.
   20:194
Toustner, J. 7:61
Touston, Alexander
   21:151
Tout, William H. 22:442
Touver, James H. 15:76
Touz, James 21:397
Tover, T. 2:18
Tovey, John 1:78
Tovy, William 1:79
Tow, William R. 21:61
Towd, Henry 18:195
Towdry, Michael 9:196
Towe, C. 23:314
Towe, Nicholas 25:275
Towell, James H. 18:435
Towell, W. H. 25:275
Tower, C. A. 1:80
Tower, George 11:289
Tower, H. 5:31; 25:243
Tower, H. S. 1:78
Tower, James 17:285
Tower, Mathew 22:442
Tower, Robert B. 22:105
Tower, Timothy 27:123
Tower, W. W. 23:53
Tower, William 4:58;
   17:68
Towers, Albert 4:58
Towers, George 14:226
Towers, John 5:54;
   25:243
Towers, Leo P. 17:88
Towers, P. C. 15:232
Towers, Thomas 21:116
Towers, V. 23:314
Towers, William H. 4:58
Towesley, Amos H.
   19:263
Towesley, Ebenezer 13:51
Towilliger, B. 9:152
Towl, Henry 5:31
Towle, Clark J. 9:105
Towle, D. W. 9:152
Towle, Ezra 15:12
Towle, G. B. L. 9:152

Towle, Henry M. 21:261
Towle, Mark S. 14:226
Towle, P. W. 1:96
Towle, V. B. L. 27:120
Towles, Frederick 15:76
Towles, John 6:22
Towles, Richard 6:22
Towley, C. 3:195
Towley, M. 19:263
Towman, S. 10:150; 18:59
Town, Arthur D. 9:39
Town, C. W. 27:120
Town, Charles 17:44
Town, David 9:195
Town, Enoch L. 13:51
Town, H. 1:178
Town, J. 22:355
Town, James E. 11:113
Town, James G. 21:144
Town, John 15:232
Town, Leonard 20:33
Town, Newell 8:97
Town, Ormand 13:120
Town, Richard M. 25:243
Town, Stephen H. 7:113
Towne, A. 9:114
Towne, A. C. 27:120
Towne, A. E. 9:196;
   19:243
Towne, Arch. C. 9:152
Towne, Arthur 26:114
Towne, Arthur D. 18:298
Towne, C. W. 9:152
Towne, John G. 18:402
Towne, Sylvester 22:510
Towne, T. 19:198
Towner, Francis S. 23:172
Towner, S. S. 7:113
Towner, Walter 26:138
Townes, C. L. 1:178
Towney, --- 23:287
Towney, D. 1:79
Towney, Marshall H.
   13:128
Towney, Robert 6:13
Townley, --- 7:113
Townley, Harrison 6:13
Townley, William 10:23
Townley, William H.
   10:83
Townly, J. J. 3:195
Towns, A. 14:118
Towns, A. M. 14:226
Towns, Ezra L. 17:157
Towns, George 26:184
Towns, J. J. 1:178
Towns, Norman 25:243
Towns, W. 1:178
Townsand, H. M. 18:377
Townsand, R. 1:79
Townschid, --- 26:185

Townsdy, E. M. 3:195
Townsend, A. 14:226
Townsend, A. G. 25:305
Townsend, A. R. 16:103
Townsend, Albert 12:43
Townsend, Alvin 7:61
Townsend, B. F. 11:315
Townsend, C. 3:195; 23:172
Townsend, Charles H. 10:84; 20:363
Townsend, D. 3:195; 22:322
Townsend, Daniel 22:516
Townsend, E. 1:177; 15:329; 19:105
Townsend, E. L. 25:75
Townsend, Ed 17:139; 24:205
Townsend, Edward 22:57; 25:75
Townsend, Eli 10:140; 20:363
Townsend, Enoch D. 25:243
Townsend, F. 3:195
Townsend, G. 25:243
Townsend, G. B. 17:494
Townsend, G. H. 1:78
Townsend, G. W. 15:76
Townsend, George 5:31; 9:99; 12:43; 23:14
Townsend, George W. 22:15
Townsend, H. 19:263
Townsend, H. M. 9:228; 25:243
Townsend, Henry 22:57
Townsend, Henry L. S. 22:105
Townsend, Henry W. 22:442
Townsend, Ira 11:213
Townsend, Isaac S. 22:442
Townsend, J. 1:177; 3:195; 14:23
Townsend, J. S. 11:174
Townsend, James 7:135; 21:397; 23:265
Townsend, James J. 20:135
Townsend, James M. 24:46
Townsend, John 9:60
Townsend, John H. 25:75
Townsend, L. 3:195
Townsend, L. D. 11:315
Townsend, Lafayette 11:405
Townsend, Luther 7:17

Townsend, M. 10:193; 21:397
Townsend, M. S. 6:33; 25:328
Townsend, Milton 10:193; 18:181
Townsend, N. 16:125
Townsend, R. 11:113; 20:363
Townsend, Reuben 10:84; 22:132
Townsend, Richard H. 16:114
Townsend, Robert 11:409
Townsend, S. 9:92; 26:65
Townsend, S. B. 7:113
Townsend, Samuel 7:135
Townsend, Sidney 15:303; 16:233
Townsend, T. A. 25:328
Townsend, Thomas 10:207
Townsend, W. 3:195; 16:233
Townsend, W. A. 1:178
Townsend, William 1:79; 9:92; 10:140; 16:59; 20:363; 26:67
Townsend, William S. 12:42
Townsend, Y. M. 3:195
Townsent, William 13:51
Townser, Arthur 14:226
Townsley, Henry 9:238; 17:139; 24:205; 26:227
Townsley, John 10:188
Townsley, Justice 9:68
Townsley, Justus 18:281
Townsley, Lafayette 21:132
Townsley, William 24:60
Townsley, William H. 20:363
Towry, Isaac 23:293
Towry, John 23:293
Towsend, Albert G. 7:80
Towsend, Elijah 16:381
Towsend, Elisha 10:93
Towser, T. 1:80
Towsley, Hiram 17:68
Towsley, James 16:59
Towsly, P. J. 14:226
Toy, Edward 5:31
Toy, H. 25:243
Toy, Henry 5:31
Toy, J. 3:195
Toy, John 4:58
Toyan, Anderson 25:243
Toye, Henry M. 25:76
Toye, William 25:74

Toyle, Daniel 13:120
Toyle, Joseph 7:135
Toysley, William F. 4:58
Tozer, T. D. 20:157
Tozer, W. 1:177
Tozer, Warren 23:53
Tozier, J. 1:178
Tozier, James 19:198
Tozier, M. 25:243
Tozier, W. N. 25:328
Tozzle, Jacob 5:46
Traby, D. 20:181
Trace, C. 13:69
Trace, J. 3:195
Trace, J. H. 21:127
Tracey, A. 9:29
Tracey, Alfred A. 7:44
Tracey, Benjamin 12:43
Tracey, Daniel 10:23
Tracey, E. B. 9:158
Tracey, F. M. 1:78
Tracey, Francis 20:363
Tracey, Henry 23:81
Tracey, Henry M. 19:37
Tracey, Hugh 9:29
Tracey, I. R. 19:37
Tracey, J. 14:118
Tracey, James 9:39
Tracey, John 9:39; 10:84; 12:43; 14:226; 15:314; 19:105; 20:363; 26:114
Tracey, M. 15:46
Tracey, Michael 9:196
Tracey, Orin C. 19:37
Tracey, Orlando 26:227
Tracey, P. F. 7:44
Tracey, Pat 20:363
Tracey, Patrick 10:84
Tracey, Philip 16:135
Tracey, R. 12:124
Tracey, Robert 7:113
Tracey, Timothy 20:363
Track, Joseph 13:51; 16:59
Track, M. C. 21:397
Tracy, Albert 24:103
Tracy, Alf 11:174
Tracy, Charles H. 22:225
Tracy, Christopher 10:168
Tracy, D. 3:195
Tracy, David P. 11:315
Tracy, David W. 11:174
Tracy, Elisha 22:157
Tracy, Evan 9:92
Tracy, Francis 10:140; 21:85, 118
Tracy, Fred. 16:233
Tracy, G. W. 1:178
Tracy, George 13:126; 22:346

Tracy, George H. 25:270
Tracy, Grisby 22:441
Tracy, H. 24:32
Tracy, Henry L. 22:157
Tracy, Hugh 18:317;
26:114
Tracy, Ira W. 23:196
Tracy, J. 1:178; 3:195;
18:59
Tracy, James 18:298;
26:114
Tracy, John 1:79; 18:298;
19:105; 21:199;
22:522
Tracy, John W. 22:493
Tracy, Levi 19:105
Tracy, M. 15:232; 19:231
Tracy, Marion J. 21:397
Tracy, Martin 17:27
Tracy, Orlando 9:238
Tracy, Pat 3:195
Tracy, Patrick 1:79
Tracy, Phineas 21:397
Tracy, Pleasant 11:174
Tracy, R. 15:136
Tracy, Spencer 18:72
Tracy, Thomas 9:8;
11:174
Tracy, Timothy 10:140
Tracy, W. H. 26:237
Tracy, William A. 8:97
Tracy, William H. 22:57
Trader, E. M. 26:146
Trader, William 21:236
Traff, John 25:75
Trafford, John 11:393
Traffton, H. M. 9:152
Trafings, Levi 18:211
Trafton, C. C. 1:178
Trafton, Edwin D. 5:31
Trafton, H. M. 27:120
Trafton, Harrison 9:215
Trafton, James E. 9:126;
27:122
Trafton, John 9:196;
19:231
Trafton, O. 1:176
Tragausiel, William P.
19:37
Tragel, Charles 14:118
Trager, C. 1:179
Tragzare, James E. 14:226
Trahern, S. T. 13:120
Trahn, Joseph H. 18:163
Trail, B. 13:103
Trail, B. S. 14:23; 16:271
Trail, James 6:35
Trail, John T. 21:61
Trail, N. 15:60
Trail, Nathan 18:441
Trail, Nathan B. 12:78

Trail, Noah 12:78
Trailey, Herman 22:516
Trailor, Thomas 9:166
Train, A. 21:397
Train, C. 20:89
Train, Henry 15:301
Train, J. D. 12:43
Train, S. H. 12:163
Train, Samuel 22:493
Train, Spencer M. 16:144
Trainer, Alex 21:397
Trainer, Barney 20:117
Trainer, Charles 15:232;
19:105
Trainer, J. 25:243
Trainer, M. 3:195
Trainer, Michael 4:58
Trainer, P. 16:103
Trainer, Philip 10:140;
20:363
Trainer, Robert 3:195
Trainer, Thomas 22:105
Trainor, Charles 15:327
Trainor, George 20:129
Trainor, James 21:291
Trainor, Patrick 15:46
Trains, Robert E. 18:181
Trairs, Dickey A. 20:14
Traiton, William 16:59
Tralter, Amos 22:271
Trame, W. H. 27:156
Trammel, John 17:505
Tran, A. 25:277
Tranch, Robert 26:184
Tranchet, N. 15:232
Traney, Lawrence 9:196
Trann, Herbrand G.
22:285
Trant, George 7:44
Trant, John 10:84
Trantvelter, E. 1:179
Tranum, Benjamin F.
17:60
Trap, John 14:118
Traphagan, Harrison
21:243
Trapman, William 20:117
Trapp, Andrew M. 23:172
Trapp, Oliver 22:57
Trapp, Reuben 18:211
Trash, G. K. 3:195
Trash, Martin N. 5:31
Trash, S. 3:195
Trask, Albert 10:168;
19:199
Trask, Alfred 13:51
Trask, C. W. 21:397
Trask, Charles 16:233;
21:397
Trask, Charles A. 9:152;
16:87

Trask, Dexter 10:168;
19:199
Trask, Edgar 18:40
Trask, Henry N. 19:199
Trask, J. J. 3:195
Trask, Joseph 10:140;
20:364
Trask, M. N. 25:243
Trask, Warren 17:434
Trask, William 22:468
Trasn, O. 9:215
Trass, Alexander 10:140;
20:364
Trasy, G. W. 14:226
Tratchter, John 20:364
Trather, J. M. 8:76
Tratler, J. M. 8:76
Traty, John F. 11:393
Traub, William 1:78
Traufler, John 13:51
Traugh, W. 1:177
Traughbaugh, H. 22:271
Traut, John 20:364
Traut, Matthias 20:101
Traut, William 9:14
Trautman, I. V. 1:79
Trautman, J. 3:195
Trautwine, J. 1:178
Traux, Albert 1:80
Traux, G. 25:243
Travas, T. 14:23
Travel, George W. 12:43
Traveller, William 9:196
Traver, David 22:346
Traver, Elbert 16:103
Traver, Frederick F. 23:53
Traver, James 11:113
Traver, L. 25:243
Traver, Thomas G. 23:126
Travere, George 22:468
Travern, W. 3:195
Travers, A. W. 21:113
Travers, B. 14:226
Travers, Francis 15:136
Travers, H. 14:260
Travers, J. M. 12:78
Travers, Jacob 22:15
Travers, James G. 22:157
Travers, John 16:233
Travers, Milford S. 4:58
Travers, S. 1:179; 25:243
Travers, Thomas 11:131
Traverse, J. 1:176
Traverse, John 10:8
Traverse, Sylvanus 11:131
Traverse, William 8:76
Traverst, William 14:226
Traves, Ulysses 24:32
Travier, Larkin 18:115
Travilion, Emezara 21:113
Travis, A. N. 18:59

Travis, Abram 22:15
Travis, Boley 19:293
Travis, Charles 25:328
Travis, Charles S. 9:163
Travis, David 9:73
Travis, G. 3:195
Travis, H. C. 3:195
Travis, Harvey M. 22:57
Travis, Henry C. 23:172
Travis, Isaac A. 18:281
Travis, J. 9:152; 13:100;
    21:397; 27:121
Travis, James 5:31; 17:88;
    25:243
Travis, James B. 21:244
Travis, James E. 23:278
Travis, James P. 21:81
Travis, Joel 17:88
Travis, John 14:226;
    18:271
Travis, Joseph W. 23:94
Travis, Logan 17:187
Travis, Morrison 10:209
Travis, R. E. 10:180
Travis, Sacket 11:296
Travis, Samuel 5:46
Travis, Smith 16:233
Travis, T. 3:195
Travis, Theodore 19:199
Travis, Tilghman 17:44
Travis, William 9:211;
    22:225
Travis, William H. 22:468
Travis, William J. 10:140;
    20:364
Travoc, --- 16:283
Travus, George 14:118
Trawlwein, J. 23:172
Traworth, F. 3:195
Traxler, E. G. 1:178
Traxler, George C. 14:226
Traxler, I. J. 16:59
Traxler, John W. 10:93
Tray, Henry 7:135
Tray, John 12:57
Tray, N. 19:37
Tray, Norvell L. 4:58
Trayer, John 17:16
Traylor, John E. 17:277
Traylor, T. J. 8:97
Traylor, William 26:130
Trayner, J. 3:195
Traynor, Charles 16:87
Traynor, James 21:202
Treadaway, William 17:60
Treadway, C. H. 25:243
Treadway, Charles U.
    5:46
Treadway, David W.
    22:132

Treadway, Edwin S.
    11:405
Treadway, J. H. 3:195
Treadway, James A. 8:33;
    18:163
Treadway, Martin L.
    22:57
Treadway, Martin V.
    11:221
Treadwell, Andrew
    24:103
Treadwell, Charles 9:137;
    27:121
Treadwell, Heyward
    27:121
Treadwell, Josiah 11:79
Treadwell, Nathan C.
    12:78
Treadwell, Nathaniel C.
    15:19
Treames, P. J. 14:320
Treanor, James 1:79
Treas, Albert 10:140;
    20:364
Treas, Andrew J. 21:132
Treasher, William 19:285
Treat, --- 20:178
Treat, A. C. 11:79
Treat, E. J. 20:364
Treat, H. 27:120
Treat, James M. 4:58
Treat, Siral 18:163
Treat, Sivul 8:34
Treat, W. S. 15:136
Treaton, E. M. 5:31
Treaver, Henry 11:113
Treback, N. 22:458
Treban, Elijah 12:43
Trebault, Augustus 12:43
Treble, Alex 17:192
Treble, Allen B. 10:84
Treble, J. A. 21:107
Treble, Joel R. 22:271
Trecy, John 14:118
Tredmore, F. H. 15:316
Tree, Frank 19:286
Tree, William P. 22:225
Treece, William 23:172
Treedocks, A. J. 14:23
Treege, C. 15:136
Treehope, John 22:346
Treel, H. B. 1:100
Treel, James 12:43
Treeland, J. 9:152
Treelock, P. S. 15:232
Treeman, William H.
    12:43
Treen, John 15:19
Treep, Joseph 17:145
Trees, John 13:121
Trees, Nathan 7:135

Treese, H. 9:152; 27:120
Treese, Jacob F. 12:43
Trefeethin, T. G. 16:381
Trefethin, T. G. 15:346
Trefts, John 27:156
Tregler, Jacob 18:286
Treible, Peter A. 1:79
Treibley, Henry 15:349
Treida, Henry 21:61
Treinay, Hugh 17:112
Treinor, John 10:140;
    20:364
Treixler, Henry 18:211
Treleven, Daniel 21:262
Trell, J. A. 19:243
Tremain, J. R. 15:76
Tremaine, George W. 7:54
Treman, John 14:226
Trembley, W. 21:397
Trembly, J. E. 11:78
Trembly, O. W. 16:283
Trembly, Wesley S. 23:53
Tremer, Jacob 8:111
Tremers, G. 5:31
Tremon, John 11:417
Tremont, L. 7:135
Trempert, A. 23:53
Tren, Charles 10:140
Trenary, Samuel J. 11:46
Trenber, John 12:159
Trendwell, C. E. 25:75
Treneller, Matthias 22:132
Trenert, G. 25:243
Trenery, Thomas L.
    10:84; 20:364
Trenkle, J. 19:231
Trenmer, Jacob 13:121
Trenor, N. 3:195
Trent, Allen 11:426
Trent, C. 14:23; 16:271
Trent, Calvin 17:208
Trent, Freeling 22:271
Trent, G. 13:100
Trent, George 1:78; 21:61
Trent, M. 1:179
Trent, R. 22:271
Trent, Robert 17:97
Trent, Westly 18:195
Trent, Wilburn 22:132
Trent, William A. 10:84;
    20:364
Trent, Z. 1:178
Trenthan, Robert J.
    21:107
Trentner, Phillip 18:59
Trenyser, Isaac 13:127
Treon, Franklin 15:76
Trepler, George C. 15:76
Tres, H. W. 12:86; 16:306
Trescott, Samuel 3:195
Trescott, Solan A. 19:315

Tresenriter, Hamilton 22:442
Tresker, --- 19:323
Tresler, H. W. 3:195
Treslett, M. C. 26:227
Trespan, P. 3:195
Tressel, William 22:441
Tresser, Charles 11:131
Tressler, A. W. 14:118
Tressler, George M. 22:225
Tressler, J. G. 11:46
Tresswell, S. 21:397
Tresszan, James 9:99
Trester, Simon 22:458
Trestgate, Joseph 12:65
Trestur, O. F. 12:65
Treswell, Lewis 7:135
Trethian, Edward 18:256
Tretzler, William 4:58
Trevathan, J. 25:243
Trevett, Roseor 9:161
Trevitt, R. 27:122
Trevohit, John 18:195
Trevour, John 15:232
Trew, Anthony 17:88
Trew, Charles 20:364
Trew, John 15:232
Trewarcy, George H. 1:79
Trewick, Jesse 21:397
Trewitt, Elias 24:60
Trewsdell, H. S. 25:243
Trexler, James H. 15:232
Treyo, Aaron 22:105
Tribb, William B. 15:46
Tribble, B. F. 9:60
Tribble, Benjamin F. 9:232
Tribble, George 17:187
Tribble, Harrison 6:19
Tribble, Harry 17:187
Tribble, John 13:60
Tribble, William 21:236
Tribby, A. 14:304; 17:478; 27:123
Triben, John H. 9:92
Triby, J. W. 11:271
Trice, Daniel B. 11:46
Trice, Henry 24:205
Trice, John 19:323
Trice, R. N. 15:175
Trice, William 25:328
Trickett, I. J. 23:308
Trickett, J. 14:333
Trickett, William 11:343
Trickey, Joseph 4:58
Trickey, Joseph M. 23:290
Trickey, Robert 24:163
Trickle, William 20:364
Trickler, F. 16:381

Tricot, John B. 21:262
Triddy, W. A. 25:277
Tride, Grand 26:184
Tridgman, John 9:92
Tridline, Harrison 19:37
Triebel, Robert 9:126; 27:122
Triece, John W. 25:74
Tried, Grand 8:43
Triekle, William 10:140
Triemer, A. 1:178
Trifel, Christopher 12:43
Triffit, A. C. 1:176
Triffit, G. W. 1:177
Triflinger, John W. 23:172
Trigey, Archibald 19:37
Trigg, Philip 7:66
Trigg, William H. 8:97
Triggs, Eli 22:225
Trilg, Daniel 14:226
Triller, G. P. 10:140; 20:364
Trillman, F. 18:95
Trim, Theodore 9:29; 18:317; 26:113
Trim, William 22:322
Trimbach, Stanislaus 23:116
Trimball, J. K. 14:118
Trimble, A. 17:293
Trimble, Alexander 17:363
Trimble, D. A. 3:195
Trimble, Emanuel 20:364
Trimble, Francis 11:174
Trimble, Francis M. 22:271
Trimble, Henry 7:135
Trimble, J. 1:178
Trimble, J. W. 21:127
Trimble, John 9:92; 12:43; 20:149; 23:172; 26:65
Trimble, John R. 23:81
Trimble, Lewis G. 23:53
Trimble, R. 25:243
Trimble, W. N. 11:78
Trimble, William 9:92
Trimble, Wilson 11:214
Trimbley, Frank 9:92
Trimblin, Philip 6:10
Trimbly, F. 26:65
Trimbly, George 10:168
Trimm, Ephraim 22:157
Trimmer, Thomas 22:225
Trimmer, William 3:195
Trin, Homer 4:58
Trine, James P. 19:332
Tring, Charles 9:126
Trinker, Joseph 19:199

Trinkle, John B. 20:20
Trinkle, Martin 11:79
Trinkle, William 11:393
Trinkler, Joseph 10:168
Trinn, E. 3:195
Trion, E. 22:468
Trip, E. 16:142
Trip, E. S. 18:181
Trip, S. 21:127
Triplet, Humphrey 11:79
Triplet, O. 8:68
Triplet, Samuel 21:61
Triplett, Barrett 22:441
Triplett, Frederick C. 17:351
Triplett, J. 7:82; 25:305
Triplett, M. C. 18:469
Tripley, William 26:214
Tripp, A. 16:233; 19:263; 27:123
Tripp, A. J. 20:364
Tripp, A. W. 20:364
Tripp, Albert W. 10:84; 21:236
Tripp, Alfred F. 22:468
Tripp, Anthony 9:196
Tripp, Augustine 16:233
Tripp, C. 15:46
Tripp, Charles 12:78
Tripp, E. G. 15:362
Tripp, E. S. 10:193
Tripp, G. W. 21:43
Tripp, George 27:121
Tripp, H. 1:178
Tripp, Hermond 10:178
Tripp, Horace 8:34; 18:163
Tripp, I. N. 16:59
Tripp, Ilemond 10:151
Tripp, Ira 3:195
Tripp, J. H. 21:397
Tripp, J. N. 13:51
Tripp, J. O. 1:178
Tripp, J. P. 15:319
Tripp, J. T. 19:105
Tripp, J. W. 1:177
Tripp, James H. 22:157
Tripp, James S. 21:61
Tripp, Jeremiah 10:23
Tripp, John 1:80; 7:44
Tripp, Marcus B. C. 24:46
Tripp, Marion N. 4:58
Tripp, Moses B. 27:122
Tripp, O. S. 3:196
Tripp, Robert 8:97
Tripp, Samuel B. 15:161
Tripp, Simon 14:226
Tripp, Stephen J. 10:140; 20:364
Tripp, Truman 10:175; 19:199

Tripp, Virgil 11:405
Tripp, W. F. 1:80
Tripp, William 13:59;
  14:226
Tripp, William H. 21:239
Trippe, Athaniel 8:118
Trippe, Othaniel 19:315
Tripple, N. L. 16:233
Tripplett, Sylvester 24:46
Trippo, Andrew 7:113
Trisdel, Chester P. 22:105
Trisket, Charles 16:125
Trisler, John 1:80
Trisler, Joseph 17:421;
  24:163
Trislett, George 17:68
Tristy, J. N. 10:30
Tristy, Jn. 19:307
Triterline, Joseph 14:226
Triterpo, George 20:101
Trithian, Edward 26:67
Tritten, Stephen 14:271
Tritton, J. W. 22:355
Tritton, S. 17:506
Tritton, T. 14:285
Trober, George W. 9:152
Trobery, Gustavus 13:51
Trobridge, A. B. 25:74
Trobridge, E. 1:79
Trobridge, S. 3:196
Troby, Samuel 17:16
Trocker, Edmund 8:100
Trockmorton, John C.
  22:272
Trockter, John 10:84
Trodd, H. 25:76
Trodgner, J. 26:66
Trodwell, Robert 18:223
Troeger, Conrad 10:140;
  20:364
Troel, Thomas 12:159
Troey, F. J. 19:231
Trofakten, E. A. 27:156
Trogur, Peter 8:56
Troh, H. 2:18; 25:76
Trohler, George 15:60
Troler, Harrison 8:58
Troley, Hanson 21:152
Troller, Isaiah 22:271
Trols, Olson 22:163
Trombley, A. K. J. 7:113
Tromlee, Thomas 15:301;
  16:234
Tromp, J. 16:306
Trompter, F. 3:196
Tron, E. 22:225
Tronch, Nicholas 11:173
Tronda, E. R. 10:23
Tronnent, George W.
  10:23
Tronson, C. 14:267

Tronson, G. 20:49
Trontman, A. 3:196
Trontner, Calvin E. 4:58
Troolock, James 9:73
Troop, Adam 11:173
Troop, Frank 11:338
Troop, James 21:397
Troop, O. W. 22:225
Troop, William H. 12:43
Troops, Samuel 22:322
Troove, Randolph 20:129
Trope, M. N. 19:105
Tropp, W. N. 11:315
Troro, D. 22:105
Trossler, Mitchell 23:172
Trostle, L. 25:75
Trot, Isaac C. 9:196
Troth, Fred 7:135
Trother, William 9:92
Trotler, James L. 10:140
Trott, G. 15:15
Trotter, A. H. 11:329
Trotter, Aleck 21:397
Trotter, Anderson 21:286
Trotter, Dudley 21:286
Trotter, Edward 21:286
Trotter, G. W. 11:329
Trotter, Horace 17:187
Trotter, Isaac 17:187
Trotter, J. 21:13
Trotter, James 11:329
Trotter, James L. 20:364
Trotter, Jeremiah 23:81
Trotter, John 6:21, 35;
  18:96
Trotter, Joseph F. 23:172
Trotter, P. L. 25:243
Trotter, Peter E. 10:23
Trotter, Weston 17:187
Trotter, William 26:65
Trotvine, John 22:226
Troucin, Joseph 22:441
Trougtman, M. M. 25:243
Troup, Douglas 20:50
Troup, Edward 24:32
Troup, Harry 22:442
Troup, Paul 9:93; 26:66
Troup, Simon 15:76, 95
Trousdale, Alfred N.
  21:262
Trout, Alexander 16:234
Trout, C. 11:214
Trout, Dixon H. 21:209
Trout, E. 3:196
Trout, George 23:53
Trout, Isaac 11:214
Trout, Jacob 9:93; 26:65
Trout, Jacob H. 7:65
Trout, John G. 7:44
Trout, John O. 16:59

Trout, John W. 19:105;
  22:57
Trout, Philip 16:234
Trout, W. D. 1:179
Trouten, S. 21:397
Troutman, Daniel 10:140;
  20:364
Troutman, E. 11:440
Troutman, James A.
  17:285
Troutman, M. 14:226
Troutman, William H.
  22:412
Troutte, A. B. 20:364
Trover, Fred 27:120
Trover, George W. 27:120
Trover, James 20:14
Troville, Paul J. 9:39
Troville, Shipley 8:56
Trovills, Shepley 21:43
Trow, Charles 15:26
Trow, Josiah 15:26
Trow, W. G. 11:195
Trowbridge, Charles
  10:140; 20:364
Trowbridge, Enoch 17:27
Trowbridge, Firman 9:196
Trowbridge, Freeman
  19:276
Trowbridge, George W.
  7:44
Trowbridge, J. 20:141
Trowbridge, James 11:393
Trowbridge, John 15:12;
  20:109
Trowbridge, L. 3:196
Trowell, Martin 5:46
Trowell, Z. B. 2:18
Trowner, George 18:96
Trownfitter, Elmore
  11:194
Trows, Benjamin 10:84;
  20:364
Trowton, R. 17:187
Troxee, William 16:234
Troxel, T. W. 23:253
Troxell, A. 15:232
Troxell, Aaron 9:101
Troxell, S. O. 23:53
Troxell, William 17:88
Troxtall, Hiram 17:204
Troxter, J. W. 20:364
Troy, D. H. 7:44
Troy, F. J. 9:196
Troy, J. 3:196
Troy, Jeremiah 13:69;
  19:105
Troy, Martin 9:93
Troy, Morris 10:84;
  20:364
Troyman, W. 8:68

Troyson, Cassius 9:137
Truair, Orange M. 10:168
Truall, Charles 14:337
Truan, Mesheck 8:100
Truax, Isaac 22:15
Truax, Jacob 13:51
Truax, John 11:272
Truax, Martin 23:110
Truax, Thomas 4:58
Truax, William 13:51; 16:59
Truax, William I. 10:140
Truax, William J. 20:364
Trubble, Samuel 17:258
Trube, Franklin 15:60
Trube, John 23:287
Trubel, Frank 9:152
Truber, Joel 11:173
Truble, John A. 14:226
Trubone, R. S. 3:196
Truby, Henry 13:51
Truby, Richard B. 20:364
Trucher, W. R. 18:181
Truchuss, Charles 7:44
Truck, L. 27:123
Truckey, Narcisus 22:105
Trucks, Joseph 18:163
Trude, Edwin 1:78
Trudell, Alfred 16:103
Trudell, F. 1:177
Trudell, Frank 7:113
Truden, John 17:387
Trudge, J. 11:289
Trudgeon, John 11:251
True, B. E. 16:125
True, Benjamin 12:43
True, Charles 11:131
True, Charles C. 4:58
True, D. C. 12:124
True, Darwin J. 17:239
True, George W. 10:140; 17:389; 20:364
True, J. D. S. 25:243
True, James D. S. 5:31
True, John 18:441
True, Joseph E. 22:285
True, Luther 26:65
True, Milan J. 21:236
True, Orange M. 19:199
True, Robert 20:93
True, Smith 11:289
True, Thomas 8:34; 18:163
True, Tuther 9:93
True, W. 11:334
True, Wesley 24:57
True, William H. 4:58
Trueax, David 9:126; 27:122
Trueberg, E. 3:196
Trueble, Frank 27:120

Trueblood, Elijah 20:364
Trueblood, Isaac J. 23:81
Trueblood, James P. 22:105
Trueblood, John 23:81, 280
Trueblood, Jonathan 23:14
Trueblood, O. Q. 20:176
Trueblood, Samuel 24:46
Trueblood, William 22:105
Truebridge, J. W. 25:243
Truebswasser, J. 26:65
Trueby, D. M. 20:149
Truehill, Joseph 7:135
Truel, Amos 14:226
Truell, Z. B. 25:76
Truelock, A. J. 13:100
Truelove, Solomon 8:43; 26:184
Trueman, R. 3:196
Trueman, Stephen G. 8:97
Truesdale, C. B. 1:179
Truesdale, Hobert 17:213
Truesdale, John 17:101
Truesdale, John K. 9:99
Truesdale, N. J. 3:196
Truesdale, Samuel 22:157
Truesdale, William E. 10:23
Truesdall, Silden S. 23:172
Truesdell, G. W. 10:188
Truesdell, I. W. 18:181
Truesdell, LeE. 4:58
Truesdell, Martin 9:14
Truesdell, Seth 13:51
Truesoil, Gilbert 9:241
Truet, George 22:412
Truett, E. 23:206
Truett, William 11:272
Trueworthy, George S. 21:397
Truex, J. P. 1:177
Trufant, Edwin F. 16:87
Trufitt, H. P. 2:18
Truford, David 22:493
Truilt, John 9:93
Truitt, Daniel 19:323
Truitt, Henry 10:140; 20:364
Truitt, J. 23:206
Truitt, Samuel H. 22:132
Trukell, A. 18:40
Truland, Hiram 23:130
Trulett, James R. 22:106
Trull, Willard 22:106
Trull, William 22:458
Trullinger, Francis M. 23:81

Trulock, Parker M. 22:106
Truly, John 22:506
Truman, A. C. 1:80
Truman, Asa 8:111
Truman, Charles 25:75
Truman, David 26:113
Truman, E. W. 3:196
Truman, George 14:118
Truman, H. 1:178
Truman, Henry 18:96, 256; 26:66
Truman, J. 3:196
Truman, James W. 8:111
Truman, L. H. 3:196
Truman, Robert 15:89
Truman, Samuel 15:89
Truman, Thomas T. 20:109
Trumball, Oliver 17:427
Trumbell, Albert 4:58
Trumbell, James 9:126
Trumble, Emanuel 10:140
Trumble, G. W. 5:31
Trumble, James 10:9; 14:317
Trumble, Mark R. 27:122
Trumble, S. 1:80
Trumble, S. C. 11:117
Trumble, William 17:363
Trumblett, P. 17:506
Trumblood, Elijah 10:84
Trumbo, John J. 17:60
Trumbower, Franklin J. 17:93
Trumbull, Austin 10:168; 19:199
Trumbull, C. E. 10:84; 20:365
Trumbull, Charles W. 19:105
Trumbull, Dwight S. 11:18
Trumbull, H. 3:196
Trumbull, Israel 20:365
Trumbull, James 27:122
Trumbull, L. A. 11:18
Trumbull, Oliver 24:180
Trumbull, P. 22:442
Trumbull, Smith 4:58
Trummell, Richard 22:355
Trump, Charles 15:76
Trump, David 11:174
Trump, Henry 17:192
Trump, J. 23:172
Trump, J. B. 11:174
Trump, John 25:76, 243
Trump, John M. 22:226
Trump, Philip 22:446
Trumpp, E. 3:196
Trumpy, William S. 26:227

Trumty, J. 14:118
Trun, F. 13:100
Trun, P. 14:10, 23
Trundleman, Charles 18:211
Trunnell, William H. 22:412
Trupe, Charles E. 1:80
Trurodt, Henry 18:211
Truscutt, W. M. 3:196
Trusdale, H. L. 25:243
Truse, Leslie 10:140; 20:365
Trusel, Solomon 22:493
Trusell, T. W. 9:60
Trusey, J. 14:118
Trush, Joseph 21:236
Trusler, John 13:100
Trusles, John 14:23
Truslon, James 15:89
Truss, A. 25:244
Truss, Armand 5:46
Trussel, David 25:75
Trussell, George E. 9:215
Trussell, H. J. 10:140; 20:365
Trussell, William C. 22:106
Trussely, George A. 21:397
Trussler, Phillip I. 7:63
Trust, Alexander 9:60
Trust, Caleb 10:177; 19:199
Trust, D. 9:152; 27:121
Trustin, Simon 22:524
Trusty, Elihu 23:259
Trusty, George M. 22:132
Trusty, John 10:30; 17:208; 19:307
Trusty, Samuel 10:177; 19:199
Trusty, Spencer 5:46
Trusty, W. 25:244
Trusty, William 5:46; 10:140; 20:365
Trute, John 24:32
Truther, L. 23:183
Trutner, Philip 10:150
Truttman, Louis 20:14
Trutz, Louis 14:271
Truxall, C. 1:177
Truxall, Homer 17:88
Truxton, Talbot 6:11
Truzillo, Hestor 8:124
Try, George 14:118
Try, H. 7:44
Try, James H. 11:321
Tryan, Nathan 19:37
Tryer, Charles 16:59
Tryling, W. 15:367

Trym, Joseph B. 13:127
Tryman, H. 22:226
Tryon, Aaron 11:321
Tryon, Jeremiah 21:236
Tryon, Silas S. 13:121
Tryon, William B. 12:78; 15:46
Tryson, Cassius 27:121
Tryson, George 16:234
Tschan, F. 1:178
Tschappal, David 26:130
Tschudy, Nathan D. 22:115
Tualey, John A. 17:88
Tub, Malvin 13:51; 16:59
Tubas, Ole 22:285
Tubb, L. E. 2:18
Tubbin, Oscar M. 4:58
Tubbs, A. 14:226
Tubbs, Alfred S. 17:321
Tubbs, Almon H. 20:109
Tubbs, C. 23:53
Tubbs, Charles 18:223
Tubbs, Clark 27:123
Tubbs, Daniel 21:262
Tubbs, E. 3:196
Tubbs, E. A. 12:43
Tubbs, E. C. 18:341
Tubbs, Edward F. 15:232
Tubbs, Egbert B. 23:110
Tubbs, Elias 13:121
Tubbs, George R. 5:32; 25:244
Tubbs, H. 1:78
Tubbs, Isaac 19:38
Tubbs, J. 25:244
Tubbs, J. R. 10:9
Tubbs, John 1:78
Tubbs, Joseph 5:32
Tubbs, L. D. 9:93; 26:66
Tubbs, L. E. 25:76
Tubbs, Leander 9:40
Tubbs, Orrin 25:244
Tubbs, P. 3:196
Tubbs, R. S. 17:88
Tubbs, Seth 19:38
Tubbs, Sinclair 18:298; 26:114
Tubbs, W. H. 3:196
Tubbs, William 21:205, 249
Tubey, Daniel 17:108
Tubman, Alex 19:199
Tubman, Alexander 10:177
Tuck, F. A. 13:131
Tuck, Harvey 20:365
Tuck, Henry 10:84
Tuck, James 8:76
Tuck, W. M. 22:346
Tucker, --- 3:196; 20:60

Tucker, A. 14:226
Tucker, A. H. 21:397
Tucker, A. W. 15:82
Tucker, Aaron 9:163; 25:328
Tucker, Albert 4:58; 12:43
Tucker, Alfred 21:152
Tucker, Andrew J. 7:70
Tucker, Bonaparte 9:126; 27:122
Tucker, Byron 15:303; 16:234
Tucker, C. 14:118
Tucker, C. A. 13:121
Tucker, C. H. 15:280; 25:244
Tucker, C. P. 3:196
Tucker, Charles 9:14; 21:85, 107; 23:81; 25:244
Tucker, Charles E. 9:196; 21:113
Tucker, Charles M. 10:207
Tucker, Charles P. 14:226
Tucker, Charles W. 9:93; 26:66
Tucker, D. 25:244; 27:120
Tucker, D. R. 21:43
Tucker, Dan 25:328
Tucker, Daniel 5:46; 21:13; 23:272
Tucker, E. 3:196; 15:232
Tucker, E. L. 11:113
Tucker, E. M. 21:397
Tucker, Eliza 20:365
Tucker, Elzy 10:93
Tucker, Felix 7:113
Tucker, Francis M. 22:169; 24:32
Tucker, Franck 15:46
Tucker, Frank 9:14; 12:78
Tucker, G. 11:417
Tucker, G. H. 7:61
Tucker, G. N. 14:118
Tucker, G. W. 8:97; 15:233
Tucker, George 10:84; 20:365
Tucker, George D. 24:32
Tucker, Granville 11:315
Tucker, Greenberry 11:417
Tucker, H. 24:86
Tucker, H. C. 27:120
Tucker, H. H. 1:80; 11:79
Tucker, Harris S. 9:40
Tucker, Heber S. 22:132
Tucker, Henry T. 19:38
Tucker, Hiram 10:140; 20:365

Tucker, Hiram P. 9:126; 27:122
Tucker, Hugh 11:272
Tucker, I. H. 8:34
Tucker, Isaac 11:315; 21:286
Tucker, Isaac H. 22:506
Tucker, J. 3:196; 13:100; 14:23; 15:309; 21:397
Tucker, J. A. 3:196
Tucker, J. F. 19:243
Tucker, J. H. 8:68; 26:185
Tucker, J. M. 18:377
Tucker, J. S. 3:196
Tucker, J. W. 9:228; 13:100; 16:271
Tucker, James 7:61; 13:100; 27:122
Tucker, James H. 9:152; 21:236; 25:328; 27:120
Tucker, James M. 21:236
Tucker, Jesse W. 24:32
Tucker, John 9:202; 17:422; 19:293; 23:81, 172; 24:168; 27:121
Tucker, John B. 18:195
Tucker, John E. 20:117
Tucker, John W. 19:49
Tucker, Joseph 16:142; 22:346; 23:53; 25:335
Tucker, L. 3:196; 15:15; 19:105; 21:192
Tucker, L. A. 11:189
Tucker, Levroy 15:233
Tucker, Lewis 25:244
Tucker, M. D. 9:69
Tucker, Malvin 8:97
Tucker, Mark W. 21:397
Tucker, Martin 9:70
Tucker, Masham 11:314
Tucker, Moses 22:322; 23:291
Tucker, N. 21:397
Tucker, N. F. 21:397
Tucker, Nathan 22:57
Tucker, Norman 21:397
Tucker, Oscar 9:244
Tucker, Otis 25:244
Tucker, R. A. 23:53
Tucker, R. B. 15:303
Tucker, Richard 9:162
Tucker, Richard B. 16:234
Tucker, Robert 3:196; 24:46
Tucker, S. 21:43, 107
Tucker, S. H. 18:163
Tucker, Sampson 22:322

Tucker, Samuel 10:207; 11:174
Tucker, Samuel S. 13:121
Tucker, Silas 25:305
Tucker, Simeon 22:322
Tucker, Simon 9:137; 27:121
Tucker, Spotwood 23:102
Tucker, Stephen 7:113; 21:248; 24:181; 27:121
Tucker, T. 20:90; 25:244
Tucker, Thomas 5:46; 10:140; 20:365
Tucker, Thomas O. 4:58
Tucker, W. 1:178, 179; 3:196; 18:409
Tucker, W. H. 15:233
Tucker, Washington 1:79
Tucker, William 9:162; 11:214, 397; 16:234; 21:397; 23:81
Tucker, William A. 11:46; 19:38
Tucker, William H. 17:101; 22:272
Tucker, William P. 10:140; 20:365
Tuckerman, Benjamin 4:58
Tuckerman, George 20:37
Tuckey, Edward C. 11:113
Tuckins, F. A. 20:365
Tucks, John 7:113
Tuckton, T. 18:96
Tuckwell, Thomas 17:506
Tuckwood, George 21:262
Tuctes, George 15:233
Tuder, Davaid B. 22:458
Tuder, David 9:46
Tuder, E. 17:295
Tuder, William W. 7:44
Tudlige, T. 1:176
Tudor, A. B. R. 3:196
Tudor, Edward B. 18:256; 26:66
Tudor, Joseph I. 22:458
Tudor, R. 18:59
Tue, James 4:68
Tueley, A. 14:226
Tuell, John A. 9:196
Tuelskey, F. 22:57
Tuesburgh, Hanson 20:14
Tuesdale, M. 27:119
Tuesdell, J. 18:256; 26:67
Tuesdy, George W. 13:121
Tuesler, --- 15:233
Tuesley, Addeson 23:272
Tuffle, John 17:163

Tuffleman, M. L. 21:144
Tufney, Lot 15:154
Tufoll, A. E. 22:412
Tuft, James 7:65
Tuft, John A. 21:397
Tuft, John D. 5:32
Tufts, J. 3:196
Tufts, Louis A. 12:43
Tufts, William 16:3
Tugend, D. 1:80
Tuggle, David 17:27
Tuggle, Hugh 17:187
Tuggle, James 24:60
Tuggle, Washington 21:286
Tuggle, William H. 11:334
Tugh, Peter 15:259
Tuhappart, Daniel 9:46
Tuisley, James W. 18:377
Tuke, H. W. 25:244
Tuke, Harry W. 15:280
Tulch, C. 15:259
Tuleson, Asa 19:105
Tuley, William 22:106
Tulip, M. 15:346; 16:381
Tull, Charles N. 18:195
Tull, Charles W. 22:443
Tull, D. 3:196
Tull, Ephraim 22:442
Tull, F. B. 12:140
Tull, James 10:140; 20:365
Tull, Thomas 20:20
Tull, W. B. 11:87
Tull, William 10:84
Tullar, H. C. 21:81
Tullass, --- 23:206
Tullba, Nelson 24:175
Tullen, John 17:399
Tuller, Charles 4:59
Tuller, E. 27:121
Tuller, Sidney 4:59
Tullerton, W. 15:233
Tulles, L. B. G. 3:196
Tulley, Charles 16:234
Tulley, David 22:106
Tulley, Frederick W. 23:280
Tulley, J. 1:177
Tulley, T. 13:126
Tulley, T. B. 20:365
Tulley, William C. 21:107
Tullis, Daniel 20:14
Tullis, Samuel A. 10:84; 20:365
Tulliver, Anderson 17:399
Tulloch, M. 16:67
Tullous, William T. 7:113
Tully, George 11:214
Tully, John 8:122

Tully, John M. 22:226
Tully, Joseph 5:32
Tully, M. 15:233
Tully, Patrick 25:244
Tully, Thomas C. 22:441
Tully, W. H. 27:119
Tulp, Emanuel 15:9
Tulton, John T. 17:108
Tumage, Henry 9:93
Tumage, William A. 21:213
Tuman, I. 15:233
Tumbey, J. 1:80
Tumblasser, Felix 10:140; 20:365
Tumbleson, James 11:272
Tumblin, Andrew 23:53
Tumblin, P. H. 18:115
Tumblin, R. G. 20:365
Tumblin, Reuben G. 10:84
Tumblord, B. 3:196
Tumelty, E. 19:263
Tumey, E. 16:137
Tumey, N. 1:80
Tumlivan, John 20:365
Tummerson, O. 15:46
Tumpan, George 9:93
Tumpan, George W. 26:65
Tunchell, Willard 13:79
Tunday, --- 16:306
Tunderback, William 21:218
Tune, Jesse 23:53
Tuner, Samuel 1:79
Tunerholm, S. H. 3:196
Tunerson, William 3:196
Tunert, T. J. 3:196
Tunford, Thomas 11:314
Tung, William 9:196
Tungate, John 22:169
Tungatt, J. 14:226
Tunguet, Josiah 17:150
Tunis, J. 27:122
Tunis, James H. 11:173
Tunis, John E. 25:75
Tunis, Robert 27:122
Tunis, William 22:272
Tunison, Cornelius 17:363
Tunkie, William 15:161
Tunley, S. D. 1:79
Tunnage, George I. 21:286
Tunnage, George W. 21:152
Tunnage, William A. 21:286
Tunnel, Isaac 27:121
Tunnell, David O. 24:32
Tunnell, J. C. 14:285

Tunnell, J. W. 20:365
Tunnell, Josiah 22:169
Tunney, R. L. 25:244
Tunney, Washington 12:78
Tunnicliffe, Moses 26:244
Tunstad, W. 1:178
Tunstall, Thomas T. 24:70
Tunwell, Charles 11:315
Tuomey, John 4:59
Tuono, C. 19:321
Tupin, Artim 16:59
Tuppan, Christopher 10:140
Tupper, A. 1:178
Tupper, Charles 13:121
Tupper, Hanford C. 16:144
Tupper, J. C. 13:69
Tupper, Jonathan 19:38
Tupper, Silas 8:97
Tupper, T. P. 20:129
Tuppin, Charles E. 7:113
Tupple, H. 3:196
Turan, Rufus 22:323
Turbell, Jason 22:163
Turbett, William C. 17:351
Turck, A. 13:126
Turck, Lewis 16:234
Turden, E. T. 3:196
Turell, James 15:354
Turflinger, Benjamin F. 22:441
Turgeon, E. 16:234
Turgle, Patrick 8:43
Turhune, A. B. 25:244
Turk, E. W. 11:131
Turk, H. 3:196
Turk, J. E. 1:79
Turk, Washington 23:206
Turk, William B. 25:284
Turk, William H. 13:51
Turk, William W. 5:32
Turke, Thomas 18:117
Turkle, George 19:327
Turl, George 22:57
Turles, Harry 21:397
Turley, Charles R. 22:442
Turley, Floyd 15:233
Turley, Giles A. 10:84
Turley, Giles J. 20:365
Turley, J. 11:87
Turley, M. 19:199
Turley, McDonald 18:256; 26:67
Turn, David E. 19:263
Turnags, John 9:225
Turnbauch, Jacob 4:59
Turnbaugh, J. C. 21:43
Turnbaugh, J. W. 24:32

Turnbell, Mark B. 9:126
Turnbull, E. 1:178
Turnbull, Henry O. 11:79
Turnbull, John 21:152
Turnbull, Joseph 23:172
Turnbull, Mark 22:493
Turnbull, William 22:442
Turnby, William 9:225
Turner, --- 10:207; 18:181
Turner, A. 3:196; 14:226; 23:206; 24:86; 25:244
Turner, A. P. 19:38
Turner, Aaron 11:174
Turner, Abraham 10:99; 14:227
Turner, Adam 12:43
Turner, Addison 5:46
Turner, Albert 11:214; 20:32
Turner, Alex 4:68
Turner, Alexander 15:15
Turner, Alonzo 17:250; 23:172
Turner, Alonzo W. 17:250
Turner, Andrew 11:375
Turner, Andrew J. 22:506
Turner, Andy 11:214
Turner, Anson 19:286
Turner, Anthony 23:272
Turner, Arthur L. 23:196
Turner, Ashville 21:43
Turner, B. 3:196
Turner, B. F. 6:33; 13:100; 25:328
Turner, Benjamin 16:234; 17:112, 187; 22:443
Turner, Benjamin W. 13:51
Turner, Burton C. 15:84
Turner, Burton J. 20:129
Turner, C. 3:196; 19:246; 21:192
Turner, C. A. 25:74
Turner, C. C. 3:196
Turner, C. H. 13:69; 19:105
Turner, Charles 11:213; 16:234; 18:317; 24:32; 25:328; 26:114
Turner, Charles A. 16:142
Turner, Charles E. 16:234
Turner, Charles H. 22:510
Turner, Charles W. 21:397
Turner, Clifton 17:187
Turner, Cornelius 9:196
Turner, D. 12:143; 15:23; 20:365; 25:244
Turner, D. B. 1:80

Turner, D. S. 9:60; 22:355
Turner, Dan 11:18
Turner, Daniel 12:78;
    21:397
Turner, Daniel B. 20:365
Turner, Daniel H. 22:285
Turner, David 18:317;
    21:286
Turner, David E. 9:196
Turner, Daviel 24:205
Turner, Davis 9:29;
    26:114
Turner, Decker 17:245,
    264
Turner, Dennis 5:46
Turner, E. D. 17:245
Turner, E. L. 14:23
Turner, E. S. 13:100
Turner, Edward 7:61;
    21:286
Turner, Eli 17:449;
    24:174
Turner, Ephraim 18:223
Turner, Eugene 22:157
Turner, F. 1:178; 3:196;
    21:397
Turner, F. M. 11:98
Turner, Francis 22:285
Turner, Francis M. 27:123
Turner, G. A. 18:256;
    26:67
Turner, G. E. 9:152;
    27:121
Turner, G. F. 10:168
Turner, Gabrial 9:47
Turner, Gabriel 26:142
Turner, George 1:79;
    10:99, 140; 16:234;
    18:40; 20:365;
    23:102
Turner, George A. 25:277
Turner, George P. 8:97
Turner, George W. 8:97;
    24:46; 26:237
Turner, H. 3:196; 14:285;
    16:234; 23:53
Turner, Harrison 17:187
Turner, Harrison B. 19:38
Turner, Henry 9:211;
    18:72, 256; 24:103;
    26:67
Turner, Henry B. 23:110
Turner, Henry J. 7:79;
    25:306
Turner, Hiram 14:271
Turner, Isam 18:195
Turner, J. 1:179; 3:196;
    14:118; 24:86;
    25:244
Turner, J. A. 10:84;
    20:365

Turner, J. B. 9:196
Turner, J. H. 15:46;
    17:157, 163; 26:113
Turner, J. J. 17:27
Turner, J. K. 1:177
Turner, J. R. 20:365
Turner, J. S. 1:78; 14:245
Turner, Jackson 16:59
Turner, Jacob 10:168;
    21:286
Turner, James 5:32, 46;
    10:84; 11:79; 17:143,
    187; 18:402; 19:38;
    20:365; 21:286;
    22:322, 323; 23:94
Turner, James A. 5:47
Turner, James H. 9:29;
    18:317; 26:66
Turner, James J. 19:38
Turner, James L. 8:34;
    18:163
Turner, James M. 22:272
Turner, James R. 10:84
Turner, James Simpson
    26:227
Turner, Jasper 10:140;
    20:365
Turner, John 4:59; 5:47;
    10:155, 168; 12:43;
    17:428; 18:96, 195;
    19:199; 20:101;
    22:323; 24:184
Turner, John C. 19:38
Turner, John H. 21:81
Turner, John P. 4:59
Turner, John R. 22:468
Turner, John W. 11:272;
    19:38; 21:133, 236;
    22:441
Turner, Jonathan 22:106
Turner, Joseph 11:443;
    16:1, 234; 21:286;
    22:322
Turner, Joseph N. 17:201
Turner, Larkin 6:8; 17:44
Turner, Laurence 12:43
Turner, Lewis 18:115
Turner, Logan 17:399
Turner, Loudon 22:524
Turner, Louis 18:72
Turner, M. 3:196; 14:118;
    22:272; 25:244
Turner, M. J. 22:106
Turner, Marcus 15:9
Turner, Marion 20:37
Turner, Mark 9:137;
    27:121
Turner, Max 9:202
Turner, Michael 5:32;
    23:307
Turner, Milton 11:113

Turner, N. 7:135; 11:131;
    21:397
Turner, Nathan 21:218
Turner, Nelson 9:60, 213;
    22:322
Turner, O. H. 8:59
Turner, Orson A. 22:57
Turner, Orville 20:117
Turner, Otis 11:289
Turner, P. 9:225; 18:377
Turner, P. H. 15:46
Turner, Peter 17:150
Turner, Philip 12:65
Turner, R. 7:54; 9:232;
    11:173; 20:365
Turner, R. W. 15:15
Turner, Richard 21:15
Turner, Robert 12:43;
    24:46
Turner, Robert H. 12:78
Turner, Robert L. 18:402
Turner, Rufus 11:329
Turner, S. 3:196; 9:196;
    20:365
Turner, S. B. 1:179; 3:196
Turner, S. G. 1:79
Turner, Sackwell 10:84
Turner, Samson 23:172
Turner, Samuel 12:52;
    15:233; 22:458
Turner, Stephen 23:172
Turner, T. 3:196; 9:215
Turner, T. E. 20:44;
    23:315
Turner, T. W. 14:131
Turner, Taylor 22:323
Turner, Terrance 19:38
Turner, Thomas 9:234;
    10:211; 18:431;
    21:95, 192
Turner, Thomas J. 8:97
Turner, Thornton R.
    20:101
Turner, W. 3:196; 9:114,
    152; 25:244; 27:121
Turner, W. A. 3:196
Turner, W. E. 19:231
Turner, W. G. 19:263
Turner, W. H. 9:152;
    14:131, 291; 15:260;
    23:172; 27:121
Turner, W. H. H. 15:9
Turner, W. J. 15:60
Turner, Wesley 22:226
Turner, William 7:113,
    135; 9:126, 241;
    10:140; 11:251;
    18:298; 19:307;
    20:365; 21:397;
    22:106, 516; 25:244;
    26:114; 27:122, 156

Turner, William B. 17:167
Turner, William E. 22:226
Turner, William G. 9:196
Turner, William H. 7:44;
  16:234
Turner, William H. H.
  12:78
Turner, William N. 17:88
Turner, William S. 23:265
Turner, Willis 5:47;
  17:187
Turnetty, Edward 9:196
Turney, Enoch B. 12:78
Turney, H. 12:85; 16:306
Turney, Isaac 19:38
Turney, J. J. 1:179
Turney, James 9:99;
  22:522
Turney, John H. 20:37
Turney, Joseph 26:130
Turney, M. 14:227
Turney, Michael 9:99
Turney, Richard L. 5:32
Turney, Robert W. 9:93
Turney, Samuel 26:130
Turney, Seth 11:213
Turney, U. S. 3:196
Turney, William 10:30
Turngate, J. 14:118
Turnham, William L.
  23:53
Turnimer, W. T. 9:46
Turniper, Joseph 21:397
Turniper, Preston 21:397
Turnits, Henry 7:113
Turnley, J. T. 26:66
Turnley, William 18:377
Turns, U. S. 24:46
Turns, William 17:452;
  24:181
Turnstead, W. G. 14:118
Turntine, --- 22:355
Turpin, Artem 13:51
Turpin, Dick 18:407
Turpin, Ed 18:435
Turpin, James 9:93
Turpin, Joseph 26:67
Turpin, Mart 21:43
Turpin, Robert 10:99
Turpin, S. 14:119
Turpin, Thomas 21:213
Turpin, W. 1:80
Turpin, William 9:100
Turpin, William A.
  22:412
Turpine, I. 1:80
Turquay, James S. 8:97
Turrell, A. 3:196
Turrell, H. 3:196
Turrell, Henderson 7:135
Turrell, Henry 24:182

Turrell, James C. 22:132
Turrey, John 8:102;
  17:463; 24:215
Turrill, George E. 17:245
Turry, Benjamin F. 15:96
Turry, James N. 7:113
Tursily, M. 3:197
Tursley, James W. 9:225
Turtlett, James 9:202
Turton, W. F. 3:197
Turty, Carr 17:187
Tury, Cruit P. 21:287
Tus--, John 26:185
Tusdale, John 14:285
Tusing, Noah 24:57
Tuskin, W. 13:100
Tusles, H. 7:135
Tusley, John 18:256
Tussey, E. D. 3:197
Tussie-c-hoja 25:335
Tutan, Henry 25:244
Tute, R. 1:179
Tuter, J. W. 14:23
Tuteroe, William 22:272
Tuthill, B. 1:78
Tuthill, C. 3:197
Tuthill, J. D. 21:94
Tuthill, Oscar E. 12:60
Tuthill, S. B. 3:197
Tuthill, T. B. 25:74
Tuthill, William S. 21:94
Tutler, Albert 13:121
Tuton, W. 14:23
Tutor, William R. 17:102
Tutt, Andy 17:399
Tutt, John C. 20:101
Tutt, John G. 16:59
Tutt, Robert 10:99
Tuttell, John G. 26:66
Tutter, Lewis 15:320
Tutterson, A. 23:315
Tuttie, E. C. 9:238
Tuttle, --- 16:71
Tuttle, Abner 23:111
Tuttle, Alfred B. 15:175
Tuttle, Alonzo 9:215;
  21:398
Tuttle, Amos 11:417
Tuttle, Benjamin 14:227
Tuttle, Bliss 10:168
Tuttle, C. B. 15:175
Tuttle, C. Frank 27:119
Tuttle, C. S. 3:197
Tuttle, Charles 10:23, 84;
  13:121
Tuttle, Cleveland 8:97
Tuttle, Curtis 23:16
Tuttle, D. L. 3:197
Tuttle, David W. 16:11
Tuttle, E. 14:119
Tuttle, E. C. 26:226

Tuttle, Emery 16:142
Tuttle, F. A. 19:243
Tuttle, F. L. 15:93
Tuttle, Francis A. 9:196
Tuttle, Francis D. 21:236
Tuttle, Franklin N. 12:63
Tuttle, Frederick H.
  22:442
Tuttle, G. W. 17:159
Tuttle, George 24:86
Tuttle, H. M. 27:120
Tuttle, Harrison 7:113;
  21:398
Tuttle, Henry 10:84;
  20:365
Tuttle, J. D. 1:178
Tuttle, J. E. 11:232
Tuttle, J. H. 1:178; 21:207
Tuttle, J. W. 15:233
Tuttle, James F. 22:132
Tuttle, Jerome 22:442
Tuttle, Joel 18:402
Tuttle, L. S. 3:197
Tuttle, Luther 16:59
Tuttle, Martin D. 14:227
Tuttle, Mary Jane 26:227
Tuttle, Moses R. 23:111
Tuttle, R. J. 8:76
Tuttle, S. 1:80; 9:114;
  21:262
Tuttle, S. B. 25:244
Tuttle, S. D. 16:307
Tuttle, Solomon 13:51;
  16:59
Tuttle, Thomas W. 16:87
Tuttle, W. 3:197
Tuttle, William A. 17:285
Tuttle, William C. 22:57
Tuttle, William R. 21:398
Tuttle, Wilmer 20:14
Tuttle, Wilson 4:59
Tutton, Henry 5:47
Tutwell, John J. 9:93
Tuxford, George 11:46
Tuydor, H. 3:197
Tuyler, Emely 13:51
Tuyman, James 9:70
Tuynll, J. 3:197
Twaddle, W. 3:197
Twamley, G. H. 27:121
Twanley, C. H. 9:152
Tway, A. G. 24:86
Twedel, Alexander 9:29
Twedle, Thomas W.
  15:233
Tweed, Alexander 18:317;
  26:113
Tweed, J. 14:119
Tweed, Robert 20:90
Tweedale, J. W. 1:177
Tweedel, Thomas 19:347

Tweedie, Thomas 16:59
Tweedle, John 8:34; 18:163
Tweedle, R. 3:197
Tweedle, Thomas J. 25:244
Tweedy, John 23:172
Tweedy, Richard 14:119
Tweedy, W. S. 8:76
Tweer, B. 3:197
Twell, James 15:365
Twesten, Martin 14:227
Twicals, Thomas 12:139
Twichell, C. S. 1:178
Twichell, Richard 26:67
Twichell, Willard 16:234
Twick, A. 16:234
Twick, L. 14:304; 17:482
Twiddy, Franklin 19:199
Twiford, Henry 11:271
Twiggs, John 12:43
Twiggs, Samuel 9:93; 26:66
Twinam, William 11:98
Twine, Mat 17:187
Twiner, J. 16:234
Twiner, Max 19:293
Twining, A. 25:244
Twining, Aaron 21:144
Twining, Charles 11:417
Twining, Cyrus 20:180
Twining, F. F. 11:131
Twining, Joseph 22:492
Twining, Quincey 8:56
Twining, Stephen 22:347
Twining, Wilson 11:405
Twinings, Eli 11:417
Twinkle, William 12:43
Twinning, John G. 1:79
Twisler, C. 3:197
Twiss, Jason E. 15:3
Twiss, John 14:119
Twissing, Jacob 11:173
Twist, John 14:227
Twist, John H. 19:199
Twitchel, A. J. 1:176
Twitchell, --- 3:197
Twitchell, J. 3:197
Twitchell, John W. 9:93; 26:65
Twitchell, Jonathan 19:105
Twitchell, Samuel R. 12:54
Twitchell, T. S. 14:227
Twitchlen, Richard 18:256
Twitley, Napoleon 9:211
Twogo, Hiram 15:175
Twogood, Reuben 22:157
Twohey, Frank 20:178

Twohey, James 11:79
Twohy, James 24:70
Twoling, Maurice 9:205
Twombley, David 8:116
Twomey, David 19:231
Twyford, Thomas W. 15:321; 19:105
Twyman, Squire 17:139; 24:205
Tyas, George 22:57
Tyas, Paul 21:43
Tybal, Frederick 16:103
Tye, Frederick 11:18
Tye, George W. 10:211; 18:456
Tye, Patrick 11:185
Tye, Warren W. 23:53
Tyes, I. M. 19:38
Tyffe, John 3:197
Tygard, Samuel 21:85
Tygart, William J. 23:94
Tyghe, M. 23:289
Tyle, Edw. 25:244
Tyler, --- 20:93
Tyler, Aaron 16:234
Tyler, Abraham 18:256; 26:66
Tyler, Albert H. 23:111
Tyler, Asa S. 11:251
Tyler, Ashbel B. 20:49
Tyler, Benonia 24:10
Tyler, C. 23:265
Tyler, C. G. 14:119
Tyler, Charles 7:113
Tyler, Charles L. 24:57
Tyler, Corydon 24:57
Tyler, Daniel 21:152, 213
Tyler, David A. 19:38
Tyler, Dock 22:323
Tyler, E. 26:66
Tyler, E. A. 21:219
Tyler, E. B. 3:197
Tyler, E. J. 1:177
Tyler, Edward H. 14:119
Tyler, Edwin 4:59; 15:80
Tyler, Emory H. 16:59
Tyler, Ezra 9:93
Tyler, F. 14:119
Tyler, Ferdinand H. 21:398
Tyler, Francis K. 9:93
Tyler, Frank 17:187
Tyler, G. E. 19:297
Tyler, George 18:96; 19:307
Tyler, Harrison 10:140
Tyler, Harrison M. 20:365
Tyler, Henry 15:175
Tyler, Hiram 21:61
Tyler, Hubbard 22:57
Tyler, Ishiel 8:56

Tyler, J. 1:80; 3:197; 20:3; 22:323
Tyler, J. M. 1:96
Tyler, J. S. 12:164
Tyler, James 13:51; 16:59
Tyler, James H. 23:196
Tyler, Jehiel 21:81
Tyler, Jeremiah F. 9:17
Tyler, John 7:13; 11:214; 15:76; 18:18; 19:49
Tyler, John T. 1:79; 7:44
Tyler, L. 22:323
Tyler, Lemuel 11:87
Tyler, Levi 20:26
Tyler, Martin V. 12:100; 15:348, 367
Tyler, Mason 4:59
Tyler, Moses 3:197
Tyler, Orville 21:262
Tyler, P. 17:139; 24:205
Tyler, R. S. 12:43
Tyler, Richard 8:43; 18:407; 26:184
Tyler, Robert 6:19; 18:96; 22:272
Tyler, Robert W. 11:283
Tyler, S. 2:18; 25:76
Tyler, Samuel 10:97
Tyler, Samuel S. 22:157
Tyler, Sylvestus 12:43
Tyler, Testus G. 11:174
Tyler, Thomas 21:11
Tyler, Thomas M. 22:106
Tyler, Thomas W. 20:365
Tyler, Tobin K. 1:78
Tyler, W. 1:179
Tyler, Washington 17:139; 22:516; 24:205
Tyler, Wiley S. 23:15
Tyler, William 1:78; 21:236; 22:323
Tyler, William A. 22:106
Tyler, William F. 18:281; 22:106
Tylerson, G. 12:88; 16:307
Tylor, John 14:227
Tyman, Ames 4:59
Tymson, Daniel F. 15:46
Tynan, W. M. 8:60
Tyne, Jacob 10:170; 19:199
Tyner, Edw. E. 8:97
Tyner, Richard 8:56
Tynes, Alfred 21:287
Tynes, John 21:287
Tynor, William 23:250
Typer, Andrew 20:129
Tyra, Elijah 22:443
Tyrce, Tim 13:103; 14:23

Tyre, J. 21:192
Tyre, William S. 22:133
Tyree, Jackson W. 11:46
Tyree, Samuel D. 10:140;
20:365
Tyree, William B. 16:59
Tyrell, F. 9:160
Tyrell, Henry 20:365
Tyrell, J. 25:75
Tyrell, J. A. 15:233
Tyrell, L. 1:177
Tyrell, O. 1:177
Tyrell, William 1:78
Tyren, T. 3:197
Tyrey, George W. 10:140;
20:365
Tyroll, Henry 10:140
Tyron, Lewis 21:61
Tyron, Prentiss J. 21:236
Tyron, Riley C. 19:38
Tyrone, Christopher 7:113
Tyrone, D. A. 9:60
Tyrrell, --- 7:44
Tyrrell, Charles 4:59
Tyrrell, Harush A. 10:23
Tyrrell, J. E. 17:27
Tyrrell, John 18:281
Tyrrell, Michael 21:398
Tyrrell, William 19:337
Tyrrell, William B. 12:171
Tyrrell, Willis H. 25:244
Tyson, A. J. 14:227
Tyson, B. P. 16:59
Tyson, E. 9:60
Tyson, E. L. 3:197
Tyson, G. W. 11:46
Tyson, Henry C. 17:261
Tyson, J. 1:100, 178;
14:227
Tyson, J. T. 3:197
Tyson, Jesse 14:227;
15:76
Tyson, John C. 11:79
Tyson, Moses B. 22:442
Tyson, Peter 25:244
Tyson, Tyler 4:59
Tyson, W. T. 16:59
Tyson, William 14:227
Tyson, William L. 16:59
Tyvill, W. H. 1:177

U

U---, L. L. 20:157
Ubbefohde, George S.
11:87
Uber, Charles 3:197
Uber, J. C. 9:114
Ubert, George 5:54;
25:244

Ucher, Henry 15:64
Uchre, S. 3:197
Uchtman, Christopher
10:140; 20:365
Uckley, Martin 17:245
Udall, Luther 11:316
Udel, I. 14:227
Udell, Benjamin 4:59
Udell, E. 1:81
Udell, J. 3:197
Udell, James 6:9; 18:105
Udell, Peter 22:157
Udinger, Joseph 22:272
Udley, George 21:287
Ueary, E. C. 10:153
Uenger, Francis 21:107
Ufer, Henry 24:70
Uffenheimer, M. 1:82
Uffer, Chris 1:81
Ugant, --- 14:119
Uglow, James 9:126
Uhl, Christian C. 16:59
Uhl, Christian G. 13:51
Uhl, F. 9:152; 27:124
Uhl, Henry S. 23:261
Uhl, John 23:257
Uhl, Peter J. 22:157
Uhl, William 10:168
Uhland, F. 9:152; 27:124
Uhle, Samuel 18:272
Uhlrick, Joseph 22:106
Uhrback, B. 1:82
Uhrich, Bowers B. 20:365
Uhrich, John 21:197
Uhrmaker, Ganlieb 8:34
Ukele, Philip 18:317;
26:114
Uland, J. 20:86
Ulantz, Nelson 9:68
Ulbie, --- 12:43
Ulbrick, Frederick 23:53
Ulck, S. P. 9:93
Ulemon, Nichols 9:29
Ulet, E. 9:40
Ulet, Eli 18:298; 26:114
Ulet, James S. 22:226
Ulgea, Jacob 20:191
Ulham, Nathan 21:398
Ulignan, A. 11:175
Uline, L. J. 14:119
Ullman, Adam 11:174
Ullman, P. 1:82
Ulm, Charles W. 20:129
Ulmer, A. 25:76
Ulmer, Andrew 13:69
Ulmer, F. 1:179
Ulmer, G. 16:103
Ulmer, H. 3:197
Ulmer, Jacob 11:46
Ulmer, John 8:34
Ulray, Samuel 17:88

Ulreksam, Charles 19:38
Ulrey, Joseph H. 26:135
Ulric, Thomas 15:316;
19:105
Ulrice, George 1:82
Ulrich, B. F. 16:125
Ulrich, Charles 1:81
Ulrich, Daniel 3:197
Ulrich, George 9:68
Ulrich, John 15:76
Ulrich, Joseph F. 25:328
Ulrich, Martin 5:32
Ulrich, T. 16:307
Ulrich, Thomas 22:157
Ulrick, Bowers B. 10:140
Ulrick, Frederick 15:15
Ulrick, George 10:84;
20:365
Ulrick, John 3:197
Ult, John H. 26:185
Ult, John J. 15:171
Ultard, John 19:105
Ulthman, John 10:8
Ulthmeire, Hermann
22:285
Ults, --- 25:76
Ulty, J. R. 3:197
Ultz, George 11:98
Ulvey, James H. 18:286
Ulvin, A. 3:197
Um Holtz, Isaac 15:306
Umbarger, Christopher C.
27:124
Umbarger, Samuel 19:319
Umbel, N. 14:227
Umberry, Christopher
9:225
Umbree, U. 21:81
Umburg, H. 15:233
Umford, Timothy 22:15
Umgelder, G. 3:197
Umhol, Isaac 19:105
Umlauff, John F. 12:171
Ummah, Solomon 14:227
Ummensetter, Charles
22:106
Umminsetter, Thomas
17:405
Umpherd, S. W. 1:81
Umphill, P. 16:137
Umphrey, John 6:26;
23:172
Umphries, John W.
21:236
Umpieby, Isaac 21:127
Umpshaw, George 17:315
Umpstead, Daniel W.
11:321
Umstead, K. W. 25:76
Umstead, Thomas 9:14
Unberger, J. 1:81

Unberger, Jacob 11:18
Unbrach, John 23:126
Uncapher, W. H. 19:38
Uncel, William 9:60
Unchaper, W. 1:82
Uncles, Benjamin 11:175
Undall, Andrew J. 17:68
Underdown, George
  22:272
Underhill, Arnold 24:98
Underhill, D. 17:293;
  18:59
Underhill, Daniel 10:153
Underhill, Earl 11:46
Underhill, H. 3:197
Underhill, Obed 23:257
Underhill, W. 19:105
Undershover, M. 13:100;
  14:23
Underwider, K. 8:56
Underwood, --- 12:173;
  15:233
Underwood, Allen
  18:266; 26:82
Underwood, B. 3:197
Underwood, C. 24:86
Underwood, Calvin 17:68
Underwood, Charles H.
  22:226
Underwood, Daniel 10:84;
  20:365
Underwood, David B.
  20:139; 21:81
Underwood, Dickson
  17:44
Underwood, E. R. 11:316
Underwood, Ed 17:97
Underwood, Eugene 4:68
Underwood, G. 19:276
Underwood, George 8:56;
  9:196; 21:43
Underwood, George A.
  22:57
Underwood, H. 23:53
Underwood, Henry R.
  10:10
Underwood, I. 26:130
Underwood, Irvin 20:49
Underwood, Isaac 11:121;
  22:323
Underwood, J. 17:448;
  24:173
Underwood, J. N. 21:398
Underwood, J. S. 24:86
Underwood, James 4:59;
  9:93; 17:338; 19:38;
  21:127; 22:493;
  26:82
Underwood, James B.
  22:106
Underwood, Jesse 22:133

Underwood, Joel 17:319
Underwood, John 7:113;
  17:388; 22:114
Underwood, John H.
  17:347
Underwood, L. L. 13:129
Underwood, Manuel
  21:287
Underwood, N. 21:152
Underwood, O. 25:244
Underwood, Oscar 5:32
Underwood, P. 3:197
Underwood, Perry G.
  18:321
Underwood, Perry J. 9:29
Underwood, R. N. 1:179
Underwood, S. 11:331
Underwood, Sampson
  20:187
Underwood, Squire
  21:236
Underwood, T. A. 18:407
Underwood, Thomas
  12:43
Underwood, Thomas A.
  17:60
Underwood, Thomas D.
  10:207
Underwood, Ulson 21:287
Underwood, Uriah 8:97
Underwood, W. R. 1:81
Underwood, Wesley
  18:402
Underwood, William
  16:142
Underwood, William H.
  22:106
Underwood, William J.
  22:522
Underwriter, A. 3:197
Undleburgh, L. N. 3:197
Unel, N. 25:76
Unger, Austin 4:59
Unger, Cyrus 26:130
Unger, Monroe 4:59
Unger, Peter 12:78; 15:9
Unger, William J. 22:285
Ungerer, E. 1:82
Ungley, Martin 26:130
Ungry, Daniel B. 20:184
Unham, S. 13:121
Unisted, Samuel D. 23:94
Univin, Jacob 17:421
Unks, G. W. 1:179
Unmack, John 23:116
Unmich, C. 3:205
Unrah, A. 26:185
Unran, Jurgen 24:57
Unrick, John 22:347
Unruh, Henry 22:58
Unruh, Sylvester D. 22:58

Untue, Jacob 17:318
Unwin, J. 3:205
Unwin, John 24:164
Uoll, M. 3:205
Upchurch, Alvin L.
  17:261
Upchurch, Henry 17:449;
  24:174
Upchurch, John J. 17:239
Upchurch, Stephen A.
  10:140; 20:382
Upcraft, Jesse 7:65; 12:43
Updegraff, George 17:88
Updegraft, J. 10:203
Updegraph, Jerome 21:82
Updegrass, I. 18:181
Updell, J. S. 3:205
Updergraff, George
  21:236
Updike, A. 14:23
Updike, A. B. 18:266;
  26:82
Updike, Foster 23:288
Updike, Isaiah 10:140;
  20:382
Updirke, A. 13:100
Updyke, J. H. 11:382
Upergrow, Elijah 26:82
Upham, A. P. 18:73
Upham, Charles F. 21:12
Upham, E. S. 1:179
Upham, Newell 17:363
Upham, Silas 16:137
Upham, W. I. 5:32
Upkins, A. 3:205
Uplinger, Absalom 22:15
Upman, William 9:233;
  20:382
Upp, C. W. 23:54
Upp, J. M. 20:149
Upper, C. P. 16:234
Uprecker, Frank 8:123
Upright, Benjamin 9:196
Upright, Neal 13:52
Upsal, John 9:93; 26:82
Upshaw, Jonathan 22:272
Upsher, John 11:215
Upshur, William S. S. W.
  G. 12:52
Upson, Hezekiah 21:144
Upson, William 6:26;
  22:468
Uptergraff, Joseph 17:296
Upton, A. F. 11:252
Upton, Ambrose 13:75;
  19:105
Upton, Augustus 1:81
Upton, B. 21:192
Upton, B. F. 12:145;
  20:382
Upton, George 22:157

Upton, Henry P. 11:393
Upton, J. M. 3:205
Upton, John 8:34; 18:164; 19:40
Upton, L. E. 21:398
Upton, Nathan 1:82
Upton, Orrin S. 22:157
Upton, S. B. 12:43
Upton, W. 25:254
Upton, W. A. 26:185
Upton, William 5:47; 11:131
Uptune, Edward 7:135
Upture, George 18:115
Upugrow, Elijah 18:266
Upwright, William 13:121
Urban, Andrew 23:173
Urban, George 20:382
Urban, H. H. 24:86
Urban, William H. 22:226
Urbane, Jacob 1:81
Urbani, H. 12:10
Urbaugh, G. 19:105
Urbego, Clement 7:113
Urbin, Peter 17:405
Ureeland, O. 25:76
Uretting, Albert 16:390
Urick, John 14:227
Urick, M. 27:124
Urigelum, A. 14:121
Urim, Adolphus 9:40
Urim, D. B. 9:40
Urine, David 17:44
Urmston, Jonathan 11:79
Urnas, Peter 22:285
Ursetter, Henry 17:44
Ursrey, Samuel 23:291
Uruh, Samuel 5:32
Urvent, C. 3:205
Urwin, George W. 22:272
Ury, J. C. 23:173
Ury, James 22:226
Use, W. 25:254
Use, William 5:47
Uselton, Samuel 14:227
Usewick, Samuel 17:245
Usher, A. B. 16:103
Usher, Daniel 12:43
Usher, Harrison 25:254
Usher, James 10:23
Usher, John 19:40
Usher, John J. 22:443
Usher, Rias 16:235
Usher, Samuel 3:205
Usher, W. 25:254
Ushler, Stephen 13:121
Usser, Film'n 1:81
Ustard, J. A. 26:82
Ustech, J. Y. 18:266; 26:82
Uster, James A. 18:377

Ustrand, John 9:93
Utee, Jacob 14:227
Uthe, Charles 18:317; 26:114
Uthe, Christopher 24:115
Uther, Charles 22:458
Uthwick, --- 21:82
Utley, Eli 22:157
Utley, James 9:93
Utley, Pascall 21:287
Utley, S. 1:179
Utley, Samuel 21:207
Utley, W. Winchester 22:133
Utley, William 7:44
Utley, William H. 20:49
Utman, Norman C. 13:52
Utsler, David 16:235
Utt, G. 23:54
Utt, John H. 8:68
Utter, A. W. 14:285
Utter, Alfred 12:159
Utter, C. 1:179
Utter, Charles 23:54
Utter, George 8:97
Utter, Joseph 26:82
Utter, Reuben 22:226
Utter, Stephen 3:205
Utter, W. 25:254
Utter, William 3:205; 15:283
Utterback, Albert 18:402
Utterback, James 17:285; 22:15
Utterback, S. 20:382
Utterbank, Tirus 18:223
Utterbock, Sidnor 10:84
Uttley, H. C. 1:81
Utz, Gustavus 17:401
Uyston, C. 16:235

V

V---, A. 20:181; 24:32
V---, B. 24:103
V---, D. 23:269
V---, D. S. 17:365
V---, E. L. 23:278
V---, George W. 19:138
V---, H. F. 15:283
V---, J. 20:382
V---, J. H. 10:203; 22:355; 26:207
V---, J. O. 24:103
V---, L. 23:269
V---, M. 16:115
V---, P. A. 24:70
V---, S. W. 19:138
V---, W. 15:9
V---, W. R. 23:269

Va---, M. 20:82
Vacanbourgh, H. 13:100
Vaccard, Charles M. 21:249
Vacht, John 13:122
Vacon, Austin 19:40
Vactor, David 25:307
Vactor, Henry 25:307
Vaden, Dennis 8:43
Vader, Jacob 22:106
Vaed, Charles 15:50
Vagan, Harman 19:263
Vagle, J. 12:172
Vagne, R. 11:215
Vagngon, C. 12:167
Vahdal, Henry 15:251
Vahl, August 11:47
Vahle, W. M. 9:73
Vaice, J. 18:73
Vaighn, Philip 26:82
Vail, Augustus W. 17:318
Vail, Charles H. 20:194
Vail, Daniel C. 6:33; 25:328
Vail, David C. 17:88
Vail, Edward E. 22:413
Vail, G. B. 3:205
Vail, G. M. 3:205
Vail, G. W. 22:493
Vail, Isaac 17:452; 24:181
Vail, J. A. 9:152
Vail, John A. 27:124
Vail, John L. 3:205
Vail, N. 3:205
Vail, Samuel I. 4:59
Vail, Thomas J. 22:413
Vail, W. 15:171
Vaine, J. 14:227
Vainer, Ralph 16:258
Vainidge, L. A. 11:80
Vakinbrough, F. 14:23
Vakopp, Philip 24:32
Valance, Joseph 9:46
Valance, Robert 15:283; 25:254
Valbly, Edward S. 27:124
Valcot, J. J. 8:68; 26:197
Valdez, Marcelino 8:124
Valdez, Rafael 19:321
Vale, Adrain 14:227
Vale, Charles 10:84; 20:382
Vale, J. B. 7:113
Vale, J. M. 14:227
Vale, John W. 17:434; 24:172
Vale, Silas 1:82
Valencia, Antonio 19:318
Valenee, Henry 23:173
Valenstine, Martin 19:323

Valentine, Albert N. 23:116
Valentine, Alexander 21:114
Valentine, C. 3:205
Valentine, C. W. 14:121
Valentine, Charles H. 18:321
Valentine, D. 12:90; 16:358
Valentine, D. H. 14:121
Valentine, Daniel 20:382; 22:493
Valentine, David 11:47
Valentine, Freeland 9:196; 19:285
Valentine, G. 16:258
Valentine, Henry C. 25:123
Valentine, Isaac 7:135; 10:140; 20:382
Valentine, J. 1:82, 180; 20:382
Valentine, J. B. 9:64
Valentine, Jacob 10:84
Valentine, John 25:123
Valentine, John H. 22:226
Valentine, Joseph 9:212; 18:73
Valentine, Nathan 7:54
Valentine, Nelson 7:135
Valentine, Nicholas 12:43
Valentine, O. J. 20:152
Valentine, S. 14:121
Valentine, Shadrack 1:191
Valentine, Sidney 9:126
Valentine, Silas 11:382
Valentine, Site 14:326
Valentine, Sydney 27:124
Valentine, W. 16:258
Valentine, W. H. 14:121; 19:138; 23:54
Valentine, William 10:84; 20:382; 25:123; 26:131
Valentine, Z. 14:121
Valeska, Debro 25:254
Valez, Philip 18:115
Valier, Vincent 18:422
Valkenberg, William 17:44
Valkenburg, James 19:138
Valkhofen, Charles 17:93
Valkman, Isaac 18:201
Vall, William 15:251
Vallandigham, George W. 24:46
Vallaningham, William 22:15
Vallean, Andrew J. 20:32
Vallean, William 13:52

Valleau, Charles F. 1:82
Valler, David R. 4:59
Vallet, E. D. 19:138
Vallett, E. D. 15:331
Vallett, W. 3:205
Valley, F. 3:205
Valley, Felix 9:126; 14:227; 27:125
Valley, J. R. 9:114
Valley, John 3:205; 12:163
Valley, Paul 8:58
Vallis, J. 3:205
Vallon, Richard H. 17:157
Vallons, D. 25:254
Vally, Adolphus 23:173
Valmer, Anton 11:46
Valmer, John 9:126
Valson, W. A. 21:398
Valter, G. 14:121
Valtier, John 22:355
Valtine, George 21:398
Valton, P. 2:19; 25:122
Valty, Valentine 20:382
Valweller, F. 11:131
Vamerkes, D. 3:205
Vamey, E. C. 16:275
Vamlet, William 11:393
Vammite, C. P. 25:123
Vampelt, C. C. 2:19
Vamver, K. 15:362
Van, C. H. 14:249; 27:125
Van, Daniel 26:197
Van, Frank 9:233; 20:382
Van, Henry 5:47; 10:207
Van, Huston 9:233
Van, Jesse 10:209
Van, Lewis 19:138
Van, R. Calhowe 20:191
Van, Reeves 17:430
Van, Thompson 11:121
Van---, Charles H. 25:123
Van---, H. 25:254
VanAbal, August 25:123
Vanachaughsac, S. E. 19:138
Vanacker, Josiah 22:468
VanAeman, B. C. 21:398
VanAikins, J. 1:82
Vanaisdale, E. 14:23
Vanakin, J. 9:152; 27:124
Vanalkenter, A. B. 9:216
VanAllen, C. 3:205; 27:124
VanAllen, D. 15:252
VanAllen, John 9:40; 24:98
Vanallen, P. 1:83
VanAllen, Samuel 12:52
VanAlstein, Albert 22:285
Vanalstine, C. 3:205

Vanalstine, Charles 17:145
VanAlstine, George H. 22:285
Vanalstine, H. 3:205
Vanalstine, Lewis 15:252
Vanalstine, William 7:113; 17:315
VanAlter, C. H. 19:321
VanAltype, John P. 16:111
VanAlystyne, Henry 5:32
Vanaman, E. A. 21:44
Vanaman, M. 3:205
VanAmburg, Philip 22:58
Vanamer, E. A. 8:57
Vanand, T. 17:112
Vanander, J. 12:97
Vananher, --- 23:304
VanAnken, Alfred 15:252
Vananken, William E. 23:126
VanAnken, M. 1:82
VanAnmann, B. F. 16:60
Vanansdall, Jacob 4:59
Vanante, John 13:76
VanAnthony, Henry 21:287
Vanantwerp, A. 15:50
VanAntwerp, Aaron 21:398
VanAntwerp, Arthur 22:347
VanAntwerp, C. P. 19:263
Vanantwerp, Edward 22:413
VanAntwerp, G. 25:254
VanAntwerp, J. 5:55; 25:254
VanAntwerp, J. W. 21:398
VanAntwerp, James 16:285
Vanardall, A. 11:273
Vanardsdale, E. 13:100
Vanarman, C. E. 14:227
VanArman, J. 3:205
VanArsdale, George B. 13:52
Vanarsdale, Isaac 15:252
Vanarsdale, P. 3:205
Vanarsdale, S. 17:271
VanArsdale, Thomas 13:52; 16:60
Vanarsdale, William 25:123
VanArsdale, William B. 13:52
VanArsdall, W. H. 21:398
Vanarsdall, William M. G. 22:413

Vanasdale, Milton 12:44
Vanasdol, Robert 11:175
Vanasse, Joseph 25:284
Vanast, J. W. 7:113
Vanator, John N. 21:236
Vanatta, Levi 10:84; 20:382
Vanatta, Morgan B. H. 21:262
Vanatta, W. R. 23:54
VanAtten, Joel 13:52
Vanatter, Aaron 11:405
Vanatter, Asa 8:57
Vanatter, T. 1:179
Vanaughken, J. P. 27:124
Vanaughton, J. P. 9:152
Vanausdal, John N. 25:281
Vanausdale, Henry 27:125
Vanausdale, William 27:125
VanBelt, John L. 4:59
Vanbenschoten, G. 1:82
VanBentley, R. 15:93
Vanbergen, Peter 7:135
VanBetheysen, H. 3:205
Vanbibber, William 1:82
VanBlack, M. 19:216
VanBlake, J. 27:125
VanBlarcom, A. H. 4:59
VanBlark, Everett 9:233
Vanbleaugh, W. 21:127
Vanbonton, William 19:216
VanBoskirk, Richard F. 21:82
Vanboyseen, F. 1:180
VanBramer, F. 3:205
Vanbranan, F. 14:227
VanBrant, --- 7:17
VanBrauer, John 21:107
VanBrent, A. J. 22:157
Vanbrickman, J. W. 18:435
Vanbroceand, J. 15:252
VanBrock, Adolphus 22:157
VanBrocklin, Ezekiel 12:43
Vanbruin, W. 14:121
VanBrunt, Benjamin 12:78; 15:28
VanBrunt, Gilbert 17:68
VanBrunt, H. 14:121
VanBrunt, Henry 21:12
VanBrunt, I. 1:82
VanBrunt, Jacob 12:78; 15:28
VanBrunt, John 11:47
Vanbrunt, W. H. 3:205
Vanbry, A. L. 3:206

VanBuren, A. H. 27:124
VanBuren, C. 1:180
VanBuren, Franklin 12:52
VanBuren, Henry 3:205
VanBuren, J. 3:205
VanBuren, J. W. 3:205
VanBuren, M. 16:258
VanBuren, Martin 14:227, 335; 19:293; 22:347
VanBuren, P. 1:83; 16:258
VanBuren, Peter 15:252
VanBuren, Richard B. 21:207
VanBuren, W. H. 3:205
VanBuren, William 9:156
VanBurg, Cornelius 22:443
Vanburt, Martin 27:125
VanBuskirk, Caleb 21:398
VanBuskirk, D. 19:138
VanBuskirk, George 16:150
VanBuskirk, I. 15:78
VanBuskirk, J. W. 18:402
Vanbuskirk, John 17:394
VanBuskirk, John 18:282
Vanbuskirk, W. E. 10:84; 20:382
VanBuskirk, William 16:129
Vanbuskirt, T. 11:316
Vanc---, --- 20:82
Vancam, J. 19:314
VanCamp, E. 7:44
Vancamp, E. 26:82
Vancamp, James 12:159
VanCamp, James 22:106
VanCamp, James A. 23:196
VanCamp, Joseph 11:80
VanCamp, Nelson 25:254
Vancamp, P. 23:173
VanCamp, Robert 11:290
VanCamp, William 11:175
VanCampen, Elijah 12:60
Vancampment, George 3:205
Vancan, I. 10:31
VanCarmel, Eugene 9:106
VanCarnett, James 22:506
VanCase, Nicholas 5:47
VanCass, N. 25:254
Vance, A. 8:43; 26:197
Vance, A. F. 18:266; 26:82
Vance, Aaron 19:285
Vance, Dallas 21:287
Vance, Daniel 17:97
Vance, David G. 11:393

Vance, David W. 17:427; 24:181
Vance, Dewitt C. 14:320
Vance, DeWitt C. 25:281
Vance, George S. 18:317
Vance, George T. 9:30; 26:115
Vance, H. J. 3:205
Vance, Henry 8:43; 26:197
Vance, Isaac A. 10:141; 20:382
Vance, J. A. 14:227
Vance, J. M. 15:267
Vance, Jacob 11:87
Vance, Jacob T. 21:61
Vance, James 27:125
Vance, John 10:141; 11:407; 17:239; 20:382; 24:86; 25:123
Vance, Jos. 19:138
Vance, King 24:103
Vance, P. F. 9:196
Vance, P. L. L. 1:82
Vance, R. 1:180
Vance, Robert C. 24:32
Vance, Robert L. 24:70
Vance, Samuel 19:293; 22:272
Vance, Samuel C. 22:133
Vance, Samuel T. 17:208
Vance, Simeon 16:60
Vance, Thomas 9:14, 64
Vance, W. 11:316
Vance, W. D. 9:114
Vance, W. H. 14:227
Vance, William 16:390; 22:106; 24:90
Vance, William D. 10:141; 20:382
VanCeoe, William 8:34
Vancess, Charles 22:522
Vanche, E. 25:254
Vancher, James 11:47
Vanchoick, W. 15:61
Vanchooter, G. 1:180
Vanchoy, F. 18:387
Vancise, P. J. 1:82
Vanclack, F. 3:205
Vanclake, William 3:205
VanCleaf, Thomas 16:115
Vanclean, George 20:382
VanCleave, John S. 21:82
VanCleaver, George 10:84
Vancleef, John S. 14:227
Vanclerk, E. L. 14:121
Vancleve, John H. 22:106
Vancleve, Thomas 9:93
VanCleve, William 12:43

VanCleve, William H. 22:443
Vancleve, William N. 22:106
Vanclibb, W. M. 14:334
VanClick, S. H. 7:113
VanCoart, Charles 10:8
VanCole, William 18:164
VanConghuct, John 9:158
Vanconsell, Jaques 9:93
Vancoor, David 15:50
VanCoover, Henry 12:43
VanCordon, J. C. 10:150
Vancott, J. M. 25:254
VanCott, Stephen 23:196
Vancotten, William 3:205
Vancount, G. H. 1:100
Vancourt, William 17:68
VanCoy, Jacob 11:80
VanCullen, Aaron 19:216
Vancuman, J. 11:296
VanCuran, John 19:325
Vancuren, Frank A. 21:82
Vancuren, James S. 21:82
Vancyox, George 20:382
Vandam, C. 11:113
VanDaren, Williams 18:98
Vandaverter, George W. 22:226
Vandbeck, W. 1:179
VanDeborgert, Theodore 16:111
Vandebury, Allus 14:227
Vandefeer, --- 16:129
VanDeger, John 23:111
Vandegraft, George 17:60
Vandegrepp, James 21:127
Vandegriff, J. 16:60
Vandeker, K. 14:27
Vandemark, Daniel 11:80
Vandemur, Isaac 20:382
Vandenberg, J. 10:210
Vandenburg, G. W. 11:316
Vandenburg, Volney O. 22:469
Vandenecker, Conrad 7:113
Vandenhoof, John 15:354
VanDenzen, J. 12:139
Vanderanter, William 8:97
Vanderbayden, W. J. 6:21
VanDerbeck, A. 3:205
Vanderbeck, William 13:52; 19:216
Vanderbeek, --- 10:168
Vanderbeek, Art 21:144

Vanderbilt, D. 13:122; 21:61
Vanderbilt, Isaac 14:276
Vanderbilt, J. 3:205; 14:285
Vanderbilt, W. T. 1:180
Vanderbogent, W. 3:205
Vanderbrock, Peter 18:282
Vanderburg, Clark 22:443
Vanderburg, John 13:100
Vanderburge, G. H. 15:171
Vanderburgh, H. S. 25:254
Vanderburgh, Henry 23:54
Vanderburgh, John 8:97
Vanderburgh, N. 24:57
Vandercook, J. D. 4:59
Vandercrook, Thomas 25:273
Vanderenter, --- 16:71
Vanderer, J. M. 19:138
Vandergrate, A. 3:205
Vandergrave, Pleasant 11:426
Vandergriff, Frank M. 22:272
Vandergriff, John 17:151
Vandergriff, Samuel 12:78
Vandergrift, Horatio 15:147
Vandergrift, W. H. 21:44
Vandergruff, S. 15:61
Vanderhauffer, Richard 23:81
Vanderhaust, Henry 7:62
Vanderhide, F. 1:180
Vanderhiden, H. 16:258
Vanderhoe, Peter S. 22:468
Vanderhof, James 3:205
Vanderhoff, J. C. 21:398
Vanderhoff, J. M. 4:59
Vanderhoof, F. 22:157
Vanderhoof, George 27:124
Vanderhoof, Gilbert 22:157
Vanderhoof, John 16:285
Vanderhoof, Orlin 21:262
Vanderhyde, Andre 7:54
Vanderipe, Sidney 20:382
Vanderkarr, Joseph 15:252
Vanderkempt, A. 12:43
Vanderkin, James 27:156
Vanderkoof, A. 23:173
Vanderlyre, Abram 4:59
Vandermaker, Jacob 13:59

Vandermark, B. 15:147, 350
Vandermark, George 18:164
Vandermark, T. W. 12:60
Vandermarker, E. 11:175
Vandermart, S. 14:227
Vandermeer, John 13:52
VanDermolen, R. P. 8:34
Vandermorrel, John 23:94
Vandernook, Peter 23:196
Vanderogan, John 23:54
Vanderough, C. C. 9:196
Vanderpard, Andrew 15:178
Vanderpool, Daniel B. 10:84; 20:382
Vanderpool, F. 3:206
Vanderpool, J. 20:383
Vanderpool, Jeremiah 22:106
Vanderpool, John 13:122
Vanderpool, Josiah 10:84
Vanderpool, Robert 11:397
Vanderpool, S. 16:111
Vanderpool, W. 1:180
Vanderslice, Jones 12:43
Vanderslmen, W. 15:252
Vanderson, E. 19:138
Vanderstow, D. H. 11:253
Vanderveer, A. 3:206
Vanderventer, J. W. 16:390
Vandervere, J. 7:79
Vandervoort, E. H. 13:122
Vandervoort, George W. 22:413
Vandervoorte, Clark 22:157
Vandervoot, Cyrus 10:23
Vandervoot, J. 25:254
Vanderwaker, Lorenzo 12:43
Vanderwalk, G. 14:285
Vanderwalker, George 11:113
Vanderwalker, Hiram 13:52
Vanderwalker, Stanley 7:44
Vanderwarken, G. M. 4:59
Vanderwater, F. R. 27:124
Vanderwater, George 22:157
Vanderworker, Charles H. 22:510
Vanderype, J. 15:252
Vanderzee, Charles 15:351

Vandeusen, John P. 22:58
Vandeusen, S. 19:263
Vandeuzen, James 15:348
VanDeuzen, Nelson 8:76
Vandevanter, Selby 23:94
Vandevart, William H. H.
  12:149
VanDeven, Garrett 9:126
Vandevent, Paul 17:427
Vandeventer, J. W.
  15:346
Vandever, Columbus
  22:493
Vandever, Isaac 24:172
Vandever, James W.
  18:164
Vandevere, G. 25:307
Vandevere, J. 3:206
Vandevere, James W. 8:34
Vandevier, Jacob 23:258
Vandevin, S. W. 15:325
Vandevisse, Sidney
  10:141
Vandewalker, Hiram
  16:60
Vandewater, F. R. 9:152
Vandeweer, J. H. 9:152
VanDewzen, James
  15:367
Vandeze, Charles 16:390
Vandezer, H. 12:139
Vandick, John A. 16:60
VanDicker, F. H. 14:335
VanDiem, A. 26:214
Vandier, W. M. 3:206
Vandike, Erastus 17:69
VanDike, P. 1:180
Vandike, S. 18:387;
  19:138
Vandike, Samuel 17:69
VanDim, A. V. 5:32
Vandine, A. V. 25:254
Vandine, Christopher
  17:45
Vandine, W. H. 8:68
VanDine, W. H. 26:197
Vandiver, Atkins 11:80
Vandiver, Henry 23:54
Vandiver, Jeptha 11:47
Vandiver, John W. 22:458
Vandiver, Milton C.
  18:223
Vandivere, Edwin 20:14
Vandonk, Emanuel 9:137
Vandoosen, Isaac 17:462
VanDoran, Peter 22:157
Vandorn, George 7:79;
  25:307
Vandorn, J. 1:83
Vandoron, Henri 1:82
Vandousen, H. L. 20:141

VanDown, Charles 12:52
VanDozen, G. W. 1:82
VanDreck, William 9:105
VanDreser, Rock 18:270
Vandruff, H. C. 22:493
VanDrum, William H.
  7:135
Vandrusen, J. 14:26
Vandudeslin, --- 16:358
VanDuesan, H. 1:180
VanDugen, H. 3:206
Vandunk, Emanuel
  27:124
VanDurmolen, R. P.
  18:164
Vandusen, Abraham
  10:84
Vandusen, C. 2:19;
  25:123; 26:82
Vandusen, Charles 25:123
Vandusen, Cyrus 9:93
VanDusen, D. 9:196
Vandusen, E. 13:75
Vandusen, Edwin 11:405
VanDusen, George L.
  13:52
VanDusen, H. 19:263
Vandusen, J. 15:364
VanDusen, J. 19:263
VanDusen, John 8:97
Vandusen, John A. 9:73
Vandusen, Johnson C.
  21:61
Vandusen, L. 9:196
VanDusen, Martin 10:207
VanDusen, Morgan 4:59
Vandusen, R. 25:254
VanDusen, S. 19:263
VanDusen, S. L. 1:179
Vandusen, Samuel 9:196
VanDusen, Spencer 12:43
VanDusen, Thusten
  23:196
VanDuser, Amos O.
  23:196
Vandusin, J. 16:259
Vanduslice, A. H. 19:40
VanDuyn, Richard 12:43
Vanduyne, Asa 22:226
VanDuza, Samuel 4:59
Vanduzen, H. 1:180
Vanduzen, J. 14:292
Vanduzen, John 9:196
Vanduzen, R. 27:124
Vanduzer, Morris 20:117
VanDuzon, George 10:24
Vandwin, J. H. 27:124
Vandyk, John 20:383
VanDyke, D. L. 3:206
Vandyke, Daniel 7:44

VanDyke, Edward 16:111
Vandyke, H. C. 22:498
Vandyke, J. 16:111; 24:89
Vandyke, J. W. 16:285
Vandyke, John 3:206;
  10:141
VanDyke, John 13:52
Vandyke, John 17:187
Vandyke, John H. 18:402
Vandyke, John W. 22:522
Vandyke, Mathew 11:405
VanDyke, S. 15:330
Vandyke, Thomas J. 21:82
Vandyke, W. 25:123
Vandyke, W. S. 2:19;
  25:123
Vandyke, William 10:84
Vandyne, Mahlon 9:40;
  26:115
Vandyne, William 20:383
Vane, John 20:131
Vane, R. 14:320; 25:282
VanEaton, Joseph C.
  23:54
Vaneghn, J. 14:260
VanEicken, Gustave 10:23
Vanelkenter, A. B. 21:398
Vaneller, J. 16:390
Vanellor, J. 15:346
Vanelsan, Stephen 25:123
VanEmon, Ira 11:80
Vanennan, Mahon 10:93
Vaneoshil, D. D. 14:249
VanEpps, Everett 8:34;
  18:164
Vanereey, George 8:116
Vanerman, Marion 20:383
Vaness, Charles A. 23:173
VanEss, Peirce B. 25:122
Vanesse, George 22:133
Vanesse, M. 3:206
Vanest, J. H. 3:206
VanEster, A. 3:206
Vanetten, M. 1:83
VanEtten, VanBuren
  22:157
Vaneventor, Edward
  11:80
VanEvery, D. 9:68
VanEvery, George 8:97
Vanevery, N. 25:254
Vanevy, I. 22:226
Vaneyre, George 10:84
VanFleet, H. 3:206
Vanfleet, Judiah H.
  22:157
Vanfleet, Richard 22:58
Vanfleet, T. 13:100
VanFlut, William 23:206
VanForce, G. H. 14:121
Vanfossen, Harry 9:93

VanFrank, David 22:106
Vangaasbeck, William 10:23
Vanganett, William R. 14:227
VanGarden, Sylvester 14:237
VanGartin, L. 25:255
Vangasbeck, H. 1:82
Vangaslick, Thomas 7:135
Vangdon, A. G. 16:259
VanGeesan, James 5:32
Vangelder, Levi B. 22:471
Vangelder, M. C. 21:44
Vangelder, W. 14:121
Vangerden, H. H. 19:216
Vanghyning, George 24:181
VanGiesen, J. H. 1:180
Vangilder, G. A. 14:227
Vangilder, H. 3:206
Vangilder, J. H. 14:227
VanGilder, J. H. 14:260
VanGilder, Rufus 13:52
Vangilder, T. 25:307
VanGorden, J. C. 18:60
VanGorder, J. 25:255
Vangorder, L. 16:111
Vangorder, U. 9:216
Vangordon, Jacob 23:81
VanGordon, James 5:32
Vangordon, John 23:173
VanGordon, M. 25:255
VanGordon, N. 21:398
Vangregan, John 21:12
VanGrenigen, Gotleib 26:131
VanGuilden, Jeremiah 9:30
VanGuilder, George 23:126
Vanguilder, T. 7:80
Vangunby, Calvin 22:413
Vangundy, David 22:226
Vangundy, James 22:226
Vangusen, L. 3:206
Vanhaman, John 10:150
VanHarten, --- 27:125
VanHassor, W. C. 18:201
Vanhatteman, --- 3:206
VanHaughton, J. 3:206
Vanhaun, Andrew 22:226
VanHausen, B. 3:206
Vanhauten, Ira 7:76
VanHauton, Isaac 10:168
VanHee, A. 1:179
VanHer, Charles 12:10
Vanhesseld, Hy 23:94
VanHise, Edward 10:23
Vanhise, John 9:93; 26:82
VanHollen, Ben 17:347

VanHolt, T. 3:206
Vanhonton, I. 25:307
Vanhook, A. 17:187
VanHook, Franklin 21:144
VanHook, J. 1:82
Vanhook, J. M. 3:206
VanHook, J. T. 10:97
Vanhook, John 22:106
Vanhoose, George W. 24:168
Vanhoose, Lewis 7:44
Vanhoosen, Abraham 4:59
Vanhoozel, William 20:383
Vanhoozle, William 10:141
VanHorn, A. 14:251
Vanhorn, Abraham 6:9
VanHorn, Abram 18:105
Vanhorn, B. 1:180
Vanhorn, Benjamin 8:97
Vanhorn, Buren 21:61
VanHorn, Charles 9:99
Vanhorn, Charles C. 20:32
Vanhorn, Clark 19:40
VanHorn, George W. 4:59
Vanhorn, H. 20:383; 27:125
Vanhorn, Hiram 10:84
Vanhorn, J. 2:19; 3:206; 21:61
VanHorn, J. 25:122
Vanhorn, J. B. 8:97
VanHorn, J. B. 8:116; 18:328
VanHorn, Jared 22:158
Vanhorn, John 24:46
Vanhorn, Lafayette 22:493
VanHorn, M. Francis 10:207
Vanhorn, N. H. 1:83
VanHorn, S. 3:206
VanHorn, S. M. 1:96
VanHorn, Samuel 24:57
Vanhorn, T. 1:180
VanHorn, Thomas 10:25
Vanhorn, Uriah 9:161
VanHorn, William 1:82; 17:88
Vanhorn, William 22:226
Vanhorne, A. J. 21:127
VanHorne, Charles 14:328
VanHorne, Thomas B. 10:175
VanHorton, R. H. 21:398
VanHory, Henry 8:34

VanHosen, C. 3:206
Vanhosen, T. 19:263
Vanhosier, Gentry 26:131
VanHosier, Thomas 21:86
Vanhoten, John 11:427
Vanhoughton, Thaddeus C. 21:244
Vanhouse, B. A. 3:206
Vanhousen, A. B. 21:127
Vanhousen, I. B. 23:54
Vanhousten, J. B. 17:450; 24:175
Vanhousten, John 22:158
Vanhouston, Aaron 21:127
VanHouston, J. 25:122
VanHouston, Morris 12:43
VanHouter, M. C. 1:180
Vanhouton, W. 25:307
Vanhovenburgh, Dewitt 1:83
VanHovey, Henry 18:164
VanHoward, Richard 24:62
Vanhozer, Wilson 10:97
Vanhuff, Andrew 22:226
VanHusen, L. 24:32
VanHyming, George 17:427
Vanice, I. 10:153
Vaniper, Martin 11:122
Vanivan, J. 16:259
Vanivars, --- 12:43
Vanke, A. 17:347
Vankeely, Z. 15:252
Vankerk, Henry 7:13
VanKeuren, J. S. 1:180
Vankhausen, Henry 11:397
VanKillich, O. H. 14:121
VanKink, A. 5:55
VanKirk, A. 25:255
VanKirk, G. 3:206
Vankirk, H. 1:83
Vankirk, James 17:45
VanKirk, John 10:84
Vankirk, John 11:175; 20:383
Vankirk, W. 3:206
Vankirk, W. J. 19:40
Vankison, P. 16:259
Vankiver, Alanson 7:113
Vankusen, E. H. 20:194
Vanlack, A. S. 12:90; 16:358
VanLant, G. 15:163
Vanlashet, David 17:439
Vanlassell, Daniel M. 8:97
Vanlaw, John 23:54

Vanlaw, William 22:356
Vanlear, Lucas 11:215
Vanlear, W. 16:275
VanLeer, Edmund 22:325
Vanleer, Edward 22:325
Vanleer, W. 13:103
VanLeiw, Jacob 5:32
Vanlewven, A. B. 1:180
Vanliew, H. B. 23:54
Vanliew, J. 25:255
Vanliew, Jared L. 23:54
VanLiew, Minah 16:69
Vanlim, C. 3:206
Vanlin, Joseph C. 10:84
VanLinten, John 12:43
VanLitrow, L. 1:82
VanLlyke, William S.
   21:398
VanLoan, Peter 4:59
Vanlone, --- 1:83
Vanlone, D. 14:121
VanLoo, Francis 10:25;
   16:60
VanLoran, William
   27:124
Vanlorn, Benjamin F. D.
   15:178
VanLoun, George W.
   19:40
VanLovan, William 9:126
Vanluren, Daniel R.
   12:159
Vanlyle, M. C. 14:227
Vanmaker, F. 3:206
VanMartin, --- 16:259
Vanmater, P. 18:60
Vanmater, Peter 10:153
Vanmeker, H. F. 17:69
Vanmercer, John 10:84;
   20:383
Vanmeter, David J. 21:44
Vanmeter, Erasmus
   22:106
Vanmeter, George 10:84;
   20:383
VanMeter, Henry N. 8:34
VanMeter, Henry W.
   18:164; 26:197
Vanmeter, J. 18:387
Vanmeter, J. H. 11:316
Vanmeter, J. T. 17:326
VanMeter, John 9:225
VanMeter, L. S. 15:252
VanMeter, Morris 23:282
VanMeter, Moses 24:205
VanMeter, Silas 11:215
Vanmeter, William C.
   20:14
Vanmetter, M. 1:82
VanMoulden, William
   9:106

Vann, D. 1:179
Vann, Moses 25:335
Vann, Rufus 8:43
VanNalley, J. M. 3:206
Vannalstine, James 7:44
Vannaman, B. F. 13:52
Vannatta, Benjamin
   17:321
Vannatta, Joseph K.
   10:141; 20:383
Vannatta, Squire H. 7:44
Vannattan, William 7:44
Vannatten, Richard E.
   24:71
Vannatton, John 17:60
Vannee, I. 17:293
Vanneh, W. 1:180
Vannelser, G. W. 25:255
Vannemie, Arsur 18:266
Vannergrift, J. 14:121
Vannert, James C. 13:52
Vanness, Abram W.
   22:158
Vanness, B. 23:54
Vanness, Edwin 20:49
Vanness, H. 1:83
Vanness, John E. 6:21
Vanness, L. J. 25:255
Vanness, P. G. 1:180
VanNess, Pierre 25:122
Vannett, John 9:196
Vannetta, J. 11:175
Vannetten, Francis 19:263
Vannice, Samuel G.
   20:139
Vannice, T. 18:60
VanNolton, Isaac 19:216
VanNorman, Abraham
   13:52
Vannorman, T. 14:121
Vannorman, William 4:59
VanNormon, Seldon
   7:113
VanNorwick, Daniel
   22:15
Vannostrand, George
   14:227
VanNostrand, Lawrence
   22:174
VanNull, W. 1:180
Vanolstine, John 19:40
Vanoman, W. 11:419
Vanonw, W. 1:179
Vanop, Joseph 8:118
VanOran, --- 15:50
Vanorden, Charles 12:44
Vanorden, N. J. 25:255
VanOrden, Peter 21:398
Vanorman, Benjamin
   11:405

VanOrman, Charles
   15:305
Vanorman, Charles
   16:259
VanOrman, James T.
   24:86
VanOrman, John 23:173
Vanorman, Marcus
   20:383
Vanorten, E. 25:281
Vanortwick, William
   23:111
VanOsdal, John 16:60
VanOsdal, Thomas G.
   16:60
Vanosdale, --- 27:125
Vanosdall, Richard 24:57
Vanosdall, S. B. 22:226
VanOsdell, Thomas G.
   13:52
Vanosen, Joseph 3:206
VanOsten, C. 3:206
Vanostrand, --- 13:101
VanOstrand, Isaac 17:424;
   24:175
VanOstrand, J. 14:23
VanOstrand, W. 9:93
Vanostrand, W. 26:82
VanOstrand, William J.
   21:144
Vanote, D. 21:205
Vanour, Andrew J. 22:133
VanOusen, Abraham
   20:383
Vanoute, James 16:259
Vanover, Amos R. 22:458
Vanover, Riley 17:167
Vanover, William 17:167
VanPand, H. P. 15:333
Vanpel, Aaron 18:266
VanPelk, Jacob 16:111
Vanpell, John 17:258
Vanpelt, Cyrus 22:493
VanPelt, Daniel 11:87
VanPelt, John 10:141;
   20:383
Vanpelt, L. 25:255
VanPelt, Lafayette 5:32
Vanpelt, Thomas C. 24:57
VanPelt, William 25:279
Vanpelt, William M.
   21:107
VanPerron, Alexander F.
   20:383
VanPink, C. J. 21:398
VanPiper, Stephen 25:123
VanPluth, Gust 24:32
Vanquirk, S. 3:206
Vanratten, Isiah 22:158
VanReese, Peter 5:55;
   25:255

VanRipan, Maurice 14:227
VanRiper, C. 27:124
VanRiper, J. B. 9:68
Vanriper, John 22:443
VanRisey, Wash 25:123
VanRoss, Marcus 22:516
Vans, Charles 11:47
Vansant, James J. 4:59
Vansberg, H. 20:383
VanSchenck, John 27:124
VanSchenk, John 9:126
Vanschoice, F. 9:225
Vansciever, William 22:15
Vanscooter, H. 25:255
Vanscota, S. 1:82
Vanscott, L. 3:206
Vanscoy, A. 3:206
Vanscoy, William 22:443
Vansdall, J. 14:121
Vansel, J. 16:358
VanShoick, Abram 22:158
Vanshoton, W. A. 3:206
VanSickle, --- 18:448
VanSickle, Charles 22:158
VanSickle, Charles A. 22:443
VanSickle, George 15:252
VanSickle, J. R. 17:69
Vansickle, James 11:405
VanSickle, James 22:443
VanSickle, L. 3:206
VanSickle, Peter 10:97
Vansickle, Peter 13:122
VanSickle, William 22:443
Vansickle, William 22:517
VanSicklen, Theodore C. 23:126
Vansickles, --- 15:50
VanSickles, George 12:43
Vansickles, J. 22:493
Vansicle, George 17:140; 24:205
VanSides, Andrew 25:123
Vansigle, John 21:197
VanSill, Henry 8:116
VanSize, Cornelius 4:59
Vanskierer, Alvard 20:149
VanSkike, Samuel 9:233
Vanskike, Samuel 20:383
Vanskoy, Helm 17:69
Vansky, Isaac 10:141; 20:383
Vansloosin, Isaac 8:102
VanSlycke, Delavan 4:59
VanSnyder, C. 1:180

Vansooter, H. 15:283
Vanstee, A. 18:60
Vanstee, Peter 4:59
Vansteeny, F. 15:50
VanSteinberg, Charles 12:43
Vanstimberg, D. 13:122
VanStyler, F. 14:121
Vansveelan, Tim 7:113
VanSyck, G. W. 20:176
Vansyckles, Abram 8:97
Vant, Daniel 22:272
Vantassall, J. W. 25:255
VanTassel, --- 16:111
Vantassel, B. 1:82
Vantassel, David 24:150
VanTassel, Henry 19:216
VanTassel, J. 15:50
VanTassel, Jerome 20:149
VanTassel, John 13:52; 16:60
VanTassle, Henry 10:168
VanTaush, Frederick 21:398
Vantesson, Robert 15:78
Vantigue, Patrick 12:65
Vantilburg, Thomas 10:141
Vantilburgh, William H. 22:493
Vantill, W. A. 9:30
Vantine, J. H. 24:32
Vantine, William 19:216
Vantique, Patrick 15:78
Vantram, John V. 22:173
Vantree, John 9:225
Vantreese, John 18:387
Vantress, Thomas 22:493
VanTrop, C. H. 25:255
Vantross, Charles H. 5:47
VanTyle, Damenta 13:52
VanTyne, George 18:347
Vanueren, James 8:57
VanValen, C. L. 21:144
VanValkenberg, C. 21:118
Vanvalkenburg, George 7:44
VanValkenburg, George 10:97
Vanvalkenburg, R. 25:255
VanValkenburg, William 9:196
VanValkenburgh, Alfred 11:113
VanValkenburgh, George 11:113
VanValkerby, M. H. 1:82
VanValkinburg, Jacob 7:70

Vanvaltenberg, Benjamin 21:262
VanValtenberg, W. 19:243
VanVann, J. 16:259
VanVelson, P. 1:83
Vanvelzer, J. M. 3:206
VanVenken, Caleb 4:59
Vanverithusa, J. 20:383
VanViah, Albert 9:211
VanVieck, J. M. 21:144
VanVleave, T. 26:82
VanVleck, Dors J. 17:101
VanVleck, George S. 16:60
VanVleek, Charles 11:113
VanVleek, Charles H. 13:52
VanVleek, George S. 13:52
VanVleet, Charles D 22:471
VanVleet, Darius 13:52
VanVleet, Joseph 13:127
Vanvleet, W. 1:83
VanVleet, William 27:125
VanVleit, Charles H. 16:60
VanVleit, Darius 16:60
VanVleit, Delos 7:113
Vanvlick, H. 1:180
VanVliet, Frederick 22:468
VanVoise, H. 14:227
VanVolkenburg, A. S. 16:111
VanVoltenburg, Henry 14:227
Vanvoorhees, Abraham 23:261
Vanvoorhis, A. C. 24:86
Vanvoris, Isaac 23:54
VanVorst, Asa 22:285
Vanvorst, Lawrence 19:40
VanVranken, N. A. 7:113
VanWagener, J. 1:180
Vanwagner, C. 3:206
Vanwagner, G. 1:180
VanWagner, John 11:273
VanWagner, Levi 13:52
VanWagner, W. 1:180
VanWallier, A. 19:40
VanWart, Daniel 21:398
Vanwart, J. A. 7:65
Vanway, Samuel 12:10
VanWee, George 9:105
Vanwer, Henry C. 11:405
Vanwert, E. 7:44
VanWert, Edward 5:32
VanWert, Frank 18:435
VanWert, James C. 16:60

Vanwetchen, H. 1:82
VanWichlen, George 9:156
Vanwick, William 11:405
VanWickie, Walter 14:228
Vanwickle, Ephraim 20:383
VanWie, J. S. 19:216
VanWill, George J. 20:109
VanWinkle, --- 17:421
VanWinkle, Benjamin 9:93
VanWinkle, D. 16:259
VanWinkle, Daniel 13:52
Vanwinkle, Ephraim 10:84
VanWinkle, George 12:43
VanWinkle, Isaac 20:184
Vanwinkle, John B. 22:133
Vanwinkle, Myron H. 16:111
VanWinkle, Paul R. 22:413
VanWinkle, William 8:34; 18:164
VanWirt, Benjamin 16:153
Vanwirt, E. 25:255
VanWormer, Charles 14:228
Vanwormer, Eli S. 11:131
Vanwormer, Francis 11:296
Vanwormer, J. H. 1:180
VanWort, J. L. 18:460
Vanyat, --- 14:121
Vanz, Joseph 22:226
VanZandt, Jacob 7:70
Vanzani, Seth E. 10:93
Vanzant, Garratt 7:54
VanZant, Seth E. 20:383
VanZarl, William 3:206
Vanzen, W. 14:260
VanZile, Stephen S. 20:383
VanZwalawenburg, G. 1:179
Vaple, A. 14:121
Varbende, Adolph 22:58
Vardaman, George W. 21:82
Varden, George 22:58
Vare, Alfred 11:405
Vargaston, John G. 15:147
Vargishon, G. 1:180
Varick, F. 16:390
Varier, Frank 23:81

Varis, J. H. 10:31
Varis, Ross 3:206
Varlem, B. 17:45
Varlett, Y. F. 16:259
Varley, I. 14:249
Varley, John 27:125
Varlin, J. 9:160
Varling, Ludwig 8:97
Varmemie, Oscar 26:82
Varmest, W. H. 13:122
Varn, Hangford D. 16:60
Varnaman, George 17:394
Varnat, B. F. 20:37
Varndale, J. 3:206
Varndell, Charles 13:52
Varneiss, E. L. 14:121
Varnell, York 7:135
Varnenon, William G. 12:163
Varner, Ademe 15:252
Varner, Andrew M. 21:82
Varner, Conrad 23:54
Varner, D. W. 22:493
Varner, F. A. 8:57
Varner, Louis 7:113
Varner, Perley 10:84
Varner, Perly 20:383
Varner, Peter 22:107
Varner, T. L. 3:206
Varnette, E. 19:285
Varney, Aaron 27:124
Varney, C. 3:206
Varney, E. C. 13:101
Varney, H. W. 7:44
Varney, Homer A. 22:15
Varney, Horace 14:228
Varney, James H. 15:171
Varney, John S. 22:115
Varney, John W. 25:255
Varney, Michael 17:394
Varney, Obadiah 10:23
Varney, Richard 16:259
Varnier, E. 14:260
Varnkill, J. 18:115
Varnock, B. T. 21:127
Varnom, Adam 22:58
Varnum, A. 25:255
Varnum, C. P. 14:121, 228
Varnum, D. P. 12:44
Varnum, Hugh 20:383
Varnum, Leroy H. 12:56
Varnum, Rufus B. 21:44
Varnum, Washington 22:325
Varpel, Aaron 26:82
Varray, Jonathan 17:163
Varrel, James M. 10:141; 20:383
Varrid, Enard 8:116
Varuse, Jesse 20:180

Vasburg, Anderson 21:236
Vasburgh, William H. 9:17
Vasd, Charles 12:66
Vase, --- 3:206
Vaser, Jackson 21:213
Vasery, A. C. 15:147
Vashan, John 12:44
Vasion, Lewis 23:14
Vaskuhl, Henry F. W. 17:353
Vasneer, Joseph 13:122
Vass, Charles 23:196
Vass, Christian 20:383
Vass, David R. 9:40
Vass, John 24:186
Vass, Robert A. 22:356, 516
Vassar, C. 12:139
Vasser, C. 15:147
Vasser, Peter 25:255
Vasser, William 10:84
Vassy, William H. 24:98
Vast, B. 25:273
Vastbinder, G. 1:83
Vatan, William H. 24:86
Vatang, C. 13:101
Vatch, V. H. 3:206
Vate, P. S. 25:123
Vatier, J. 3:206
Vatley, J. L. 21:398
Vattaki, C. 5:32
Vaubeck, --- 18:342
Vaug, W. S. 18:73
Vaugh, A. G. 16:60
Vaugh, Albert 7:135
Vaugh, D. D. 21:44
Vaugh, James 9:64
Vaugh, Lysander 17:157
Vaugham, Irad W. 25:255
Vaughan, A. 1:180; 25:123
Vaughan, Beverly K. 15:78
Vaughan, Charles 25:123
Vaughan, Daniel 10:146; 19:216
Vaughan, Enoch W. 11:113
Vaughan, George 14:121
Vaughan, Henry S. 10:175; 19:216
Vaughan, J. 3:206; 9:152
Vaughan, J. C. 20:131
Vaughan, John 8:34; 18:164; 21:192
Vaughan, Joshua 17:261
Vaughan, Richard 15:9
Vaughan, S. 14:228
Vaughan, T. J. 7:44

Vaughan, William 7:44
Vaughen, Moses 18:98
Vaughen, Richard 14:249
Vaughn, Albert 21:398
Vaughn, Albert N.
    10:145; 19:216
Vaughn, Alexander 17:88
Vaughn, Alfred C. 22:272
Vaughn, Alonzo 10:141;
    20:383
Vaughn, Andrew 11:283
Vaughn, Augustine
    17:285
Vaughn, B. 3:206; 22:325
Vaughn, B. W. 25:255
Vaughn, Benjamin 22:325
Vaughn, C. 10:211;
    25:123
Vaughn, Charles 2:19;
    22:516
Vaughn, D. A. 14:251
Vaughn, Damon 9:202
Vaughn, David 22:58
Vaughn, Eli T. 21:15
Vaughn, Elijah 10:141;
    20:383
Vaughn, Freeman 10:141;
    20:383
Vaughn, G. 1:179
Vaughn, George 19:323;
    22:325
Vaughn, Henry C. 10:141;
    20:383
Vaughn, Hiram 9:196
Vaughn, Hiram P. 19:269
Vaughn, Isaac 9:64, 238;
    26:234
Vaughn, Isaac M. 21:82
Vaughn, J. 11:253; 27:124
Vaughn, James 3:206;
    10:141; 18:266;
    20:383; 26:83
Vaughn, James H. 20:15
Vaughn, John 17:239;
    21:262
Vaughn, John D. 23:111
Vaughn, John H. 25:122
Vaughn, Joseph 21:219
Vaughn, Levi W. 20:49
Vaughn, M. S. 17:293
Vaughn, Martin 26:83
Vaughn, Philip 18:266
Vaughn, R. 27:125
Vaughn, R. E. 18:266;
    26:82
Vaughn, S. 14:267
Vaughn, Samuel 22:133
Vaughn, T. B. 25:328
Vaughn, Thomas 9:202;
    10:99; 22:356, 443;
    27:125

Vaughn, W. 10:141;
    20:383
Vaughn, W. D. 19:138
Vaughn, W. H. 3:206
Vaughn, W. W. 20:383
Vaughn, William 10:141;
    20:383
Vaughn, William E.
    11:253
Vaughn, William S.
    17:285
Vaughn, William W.
    10:141
Vaught, Alfred 22:133
Vaught, Andrew Jackson
    26:214
Vaught, G. 27:124
Vaught, George 10:84;
    20:383
Vaught, George W. 10:84;
    20:383
Vaught, Isaac J. 17:410;
    22:133
Vaught, John W. 23:81
Vaught, Michael 23:81
Vaught, S. 1:180
Vaught, William L. 16:60
Vaught, Willis 22:413
Vaugier, Joseph 23:81
Vaulcer, William 16:358
Vaulin, Joseph C. 20:383
Vaulker, John 1:82
Vauloon, F. 16:259
Vaulps, J. W. 23:306
Vault, George 11:426
Vault, Harrison 11:80
Vaun, Henry 18:409
Vaun, J. L. 10:141;
    20:383
Vaun, Rufus 26:197
Vaunce, Peter 17:187
Vauntry, William P.
    22:107
Vaupelt, C. E. 25:122
Vausel, John 12:94
Vaust, G. 12:159
Vauston, Daniel 21:398
Vauters, D. 21:398
Vaux, V. W. 14:333
Vauzile, Stephen S.
    10:141
Vavidlipp, Delos 21:399
Vawanfrink, Andrew
    10:84
Vawrolskenberg, A.
    17:405
Vawters, J. C. 14:317
Vayles, Joseph 20:87
Vazel, James 9:14
Veach, Edward 24:57
Veach, Hezekiah 25:123

Veach, James H. 17:208
Veach, Jesse 3:206
Veach, Joel 8:34; 26:197
Veach, Joseph 11:131
Veach, Newton 9:93
Veach, William 9:40
Veach, William R. 22:133
Veal, Henry 18:223
Veal, Lorenzo D. 21:61
Veal, Newton 26:82
Veal, Thomas 11:80
Vealsky, Frank 22:413
Veasey, James E. 17:351
Veasie, Charles H. 4:59
Veasie, John 1:83
Veatch, James F. 24:32
Veatch, James M. 22:133
Veats, D. 16:259
Veaucont, Alexander 4:59
Veaughn, Joel J. 17:357
Veazie, E. B. 25:123
Veazie, F. 3:206; 14:228
Veazie, William W.
    10:23; 16:5
Veber, H. L. 14:261
Veber, J. 25:255
Veber, John 5:32
Vecter, David 7:79
Vector, Henry 7:79
Vedder, A. 1:180
Vedder, Alvah 17:245
Veedar, Stanley M.
    11:293
Veenschoten, Evert 21:82
Veenshoten, E. 8:57
Veetel, B. 7:54
Vehost, O. H. 3:206
Veighte, W. H. 7:113
Veil, Henry C. 16:285
Veileit, Leander 22:58
Veira, John 10:141;
    20:383
Veirson, William 9:64
Veis, A. 19:263
Veisey, Moses 4:59
Veislett, C. 19:138
Veitch, John W. 22:58
Veith, B. 15:89
Veith, Barnham 12:78
Veith, Jacob 26:234
Veitzert, J. C. 26:82
Velery, Peter 8:76
Veley, Peter 26:197
Velhim, J. W. 8:76
Velie, G. W. 1:180
Velkenburg, H. V. 9:196
Vell, William A. 7:113
Vellan, Andrew 21:262
Vellener, Hiram D. 12:44
Velmar, Augs 1:83
Veloick, J. M. 18:342

Veloick, John M. 9:105
Velsor, A. K. 9:152; 27:124
Velsor, Daniel S. 27:124
Veltman, Alfred 11:290
Velton, Nicholas 11:292
Veltzert, John C. 9:93
Velum, A. 8:57
Velzer, H. 10:141; 20:383
Vemme, John 4:59
Vemon, C. E. 7:65
Venable, Charles 15:78
Venable, Joseph 1:83
Venable, W. L. 9:64
Venable, W. P. 10:146
Venaghn, J. 14:228
Venara, John 23:265
Venatti, S. 1:82
Vencot, L. 3:206
Venden, William H. 18:164
Vender, William 9:196
Vendevant, Paul 24:181
Vendham, Nelson 17:427
Vendicar, E. 1:83
Vendue, O. H. 11:80
Veneble, W. C. 14:228
Venell, William 1:82
Venerable, A. V. 25:307
Venible, F. 17:337
Venil, R. 7:44
Venill, Rufus 1:82
Venmen, H. 12:90; 16:358
Vennessu, John W. 14:228
Venning, Henry 23:54
Vennon, W. 1:180
Vennum, Aurica W. 23:54
Venoes, H. 15:252
Venome, James 3:206
Venon, Joshua 24:57
Vensee, Rosin 21:399
Vensil, William 19:40
Venson, Amos 21:399
Ventirs, John 11:175
Ventler, Charles 3:206
Venton, Nathan 14:228
Ventriss, John H. 21:44
Vercelius, A. S. 1:180
Verden, Isaac 25:277
Verden, William H. 8:34
Verdett, James 22:347
Verdick, James 9:205
Verdier, W. S. 27:124
Verdier, William S. 9:137
Veredenburg, Joseph 24:98
Verena, E. 2:18
Vergenary, --- 16:259
Vergneray, --- 13:81

Vergson, D. D. 1:179
Verhaden, Joseph 22:347
Verhouse, D. 3:206
Verine, Peter 18:73
Verity, John W. 16:87
Verker, Theodore 24:72
Verlan, P. 14:121
Vermett, John 7:54
Vermilion, R. 9:64
Vermilliae, C. 14:121
Vermillion, Charles 17:88; 22:58
Vermillion, Helfrey 15:78
Vermillion, J. 25:255
Vermillion, J. K. 15:89
Vermillion, John K. 12:78
Vermillion, R. R. 23:173
Vermillya, S. A. 9:244
Vermilya, J. C. 1:179
Vermilyea, Peter 7:44
Vernal, --- 8:125
Vernan, Byron 5:32
Verneis, E. 1:180
Vernel, I. 19:321
Verner, Abram 14:228
Verner, H. G. 10:168; 19:216
Verner, J. C. 10:168; 19:216
Verner, Josh 1:82
Verner, W. O. 7:113
Vernes, C. 16:259
Vernia, Joseph 22:158
Vernine, Peter 9:212
Vernity, Stephen 10:168
Vernon, Asa 22:226
Vernon, E. J. 20:117
Vernon, Edward 22:443
Vernon, George W. 17:88
Vernon, Nicholas 18:321
Vernon, S. 3:206
Vernon, W. 10:150
Vernon, William 10:150; 17:447; 18:60; 24:172
Vernot, E. 9:196
Vernum, James 22:506
Verona, A. 14:121
Verplanck, Henry 13:52
Verplank, Henry 10:23
Verrell, Edward 12:60
Verrill, C. 3:206
Verrill, G. D. 1:180
Verrity, Steven S. 19:216
Verrnum, Hiram 14:121
Verronder, Robert 14:121
Verry, Jacob 10:84
Verry, Louis 21:88
Vers, Alexander 21:287
Verschure, P. 17:289
Versey, Edward 6:13

Versey, James 18:73
Vert, Nicholas 22:443
Verterson, John 4:59
Vertz, Andrew 20:194
Verun, Francis E. 1:82
Very, A. A. 15:252
Very, W. 3:207
Vesey, James 9:205
Vesper, C. W. 10:191; 18:184
Vesper, James W. 3:207
Vesper, Ormand S. 10:23
Vesper, S. W. 10:191; 18:184
Vess, Zephania 11:409
Vessel, John 19:40
Vessey, J. C. 15:171
Vest, James 10:141; 20:383
Vest, Job 17:439
Vest, Jonathan 24:150
Vest, McFarland 11:417
Vest, Meredith 9:229; 18:387
Vest, Solomon J. 22:273
Vest, William 22:468
Vest, William R. 20:20
Vestel, Elias M. 22:58
Vester, Albert 22:325
Vester, J. D. 22:468
Vester, Jesse D. 11:290
Vester, Lewis 19:40
Vester, William 14:121
Vesterman, W. 1:179
Vestry, J. W. 20:383
Veter, Frederick 15:50
Veth, J. C. 1:179
Vett, John 10:84
Vette, John 20:384
Vetter, George 19:216
Vetter, J. 3:207
Vetter, Joseph 8:116; 13:52
Vetter, Robert 22:58
Vetze, H. H. 25:123
Veuder, William 19:263
Veun, George 21:82
Vevena, E. 25:122
Vevis, William 14:122
Vexter, J. 1:179
Vial, George W. 9:196
Vial, Lawrence 22:226
Viall, G. M. 19:243
Viallat, John 10:168; 19:216
Vians, Edwin 11:131
Viar, S. 17:188
Viare, Thomas 25:255
Viars, Charles 22:58
Vibbard, George 3:207
Vibbard, Lorz'o 1:82

Vibbard, Seymour 13:52
Vibbert, Hiram 10:84
Viber, J. 18:60
Vibur, J. 10:150
Vice, E. T. 17:102
Vice, George 19:40
Vice, Henry 22:107
Vice, Thomas J. 17:239
Vicelles, Daniel 9:196
Vicellis, Daniel 19:285
Vicker, George 21:236
Vicker, W. 14:28
Vicker, William 14:28
Vickerey, John F. 4:59
Vickers, George 8:57
Vickers, J. J. 24:86
Vickers, James H. 20:384
Vickers, Peter 24:205
Vickers, Thomas 17:262
Vickers, W. H. 4:59
Vickers, William M. 7:44
Vickery, Amanda S. 9:7
Vickery, C. B. 1:180
Vickery, Charles 9:7
Vickery, David G. 7:113
Vickery, Fletcher 22:58
Vickery, Fred 20:384
Vickery, Frederick 10:84
Vickery, G. W. 11:290
Vickery, John H. 1:83
Vickery, Thomas W. 7:70
Vickery, William 3:207
Vicket, Pat 22:169
Vickler, John 22:347
Vickney, James 7:113
Vickroy, Henry J. 22:226
Vicorg, William L. 12:44
Victor, --- 7:62
Victor, Elias 7:79; 25:307
Victor, George 22:325
Victor, Godo 14:228
Victor, H. 3:207; 21:399
Victor, L. 9:152; 27:124
Victor, Louis 21:399
Victory, R. 21:399
Vidett, C. F. 19:243
Vieght, A. 3:207
Viehl, John 14:121
Viel, J. 18:431
Viel, Peter 21:399
Viel, William 3:207
Vield, Leander 1:83
Viene, Isaac 11:380
Vier, Tony 10:141;
    20:384
Vieret, William H. 11:253
Vierson, Abraham C.
    13:52; 16:60
Viess, Samuel 21:205,
    249
Viets, Elliott L. 11:175

Vietter, John 6:33
View, Michael 7:113
View, P. 20:152
Vifield, Augustus 26:197
Vigen, August 13:52
Viger, John H. 18:317
Vigers, J. E. 14:122
Viglen, William 14:228
Vignelle, Louis 15:252
Vignet, J. L. 14:249
Vigor, John H. 9:30;
    26:115
Vigus, Horace B. 23:81
Vila, George 21:399
Viland, Henry 7:135
Vilas, William R. 22:158
Vilbert, Hiram 20:384
Vilcott, Harrison 23:81
Viles, G. G. 19:276
Viles, S. P. 19:231
Viles, Simon P. 9:196
Villafranch, J. 9:152
Villapranch, H. 27:124
Viller, John 25:328
Villicrose, J. 25:328
Villizette, G. 6:14
Vilson, Job 23:269
Vilstrup, Otto 21:118
Vim, Thomas 25:255
Vimmons, Abram 9:137
Vimont, Lewis B. 11:98
Vimpany, Charles 9:196;
    19:271
Vinaker, Jacob 25:328
Vinal, G. 13:101
Vinar, Charles 22:493
Vince, F. 1:180
Vince, Francis 17:88
Vince, John 17:285
Vincen, Cave 18:267;
    26:82
Vincent, A. 20:28
Vincent, Chester 22:468
Vincent, D. I. 13:122
Vincent, E. A. 1:82
Vincent, Eli S. B. 16:150
Vincent, Eugene 7:13
Vincent, G. W. 25:255
Vincent, H. B. 12:159
Vincent, Harness R. 24:86
Vincent, Henry 8:43;
    10:97; 26:197
Vincent, Horace G. 13:52
Vincent, I. 25:273; 26:82
Vincent, Isaac 19:138
Vincent, J. 18:267
Vincent, J. K. 18:60
Vincent, J. R. 10:153
Vincent, J. T. 16:285
Vincent, James 3:207;
    7:44; 24:32

Vincent, Judd 18:60
Vincent, L. 13:101
Vincent, L. D. 3:207
Vincent, L. M. 10:84;
    20:384
Vincent, Levi 5:47
Vincent, Lewis C. 8:34
Vincent, Louis C. 18:164
Vincent, Mial 22:443
Vincent, Newel P. 23:111
Vincent, Nora 21:399
Vincent, P. 1:180
Vincent, R. 3:207; 14:228
Vincent, Shubad 17:423
Vincent, Stephen 21:236
Vincent, Sylvester 22:133
Vincent, Theron G.
    21:262
Vincent, Thomas 13:101;
    23:272
Vincent, Thomas W.
    21:192
Vincent, W. H. 9:93;
    26:82
Vincent, William 23:118
Vincent, William H. 11:47
Vincent, William L.
    22:158
Vincent, Zarchariah
    20:384
Vincomb, William 25:123
Vincounts, A. J. 3:207
VinDrach, J. 9:114
Vine, Curtis 6:19; 18:98
Vine, George 24:205
Vine, Thomas E. 25:255
Vinegar, George
    Washington 4:68
Vinegar, W. 16:259
Viner, H. E. 13:122
Vines, Calvin F. 22:107
Vines, Charles 15:252
Vines, P. 20:384
Vines, Wilbourn 22:273
Vineyard, Doctor 6:23
Vineyard, Enoch F.
    22:506
Vineyard, Harry 12:97
Vineyard, Henry 15:362
Vineyard, Isaiah J. 23:54
Vingard, Henry 19:138
Vingiar, William 10:84
Vingle, A. M. 15:252
Vining, Edwin 22:158
Vining, Francis 8:97
Vining, James L. 15:89
Vining, Robert E. 17:69
Vining, W. H. H. 3:207
Vining, Wilber 22:227
Vinith, Edward 7:62
Vinning, L. 1:180; 16:111

Vinning, Thomas V. 26:131
Vinny, Thomas 11:294
Vinott, Tabien 7:70
Vinsant, G. W. 3:207
Vinslow, A. 19:138
Vinson, Charles 1:82
Vinson, H. 14:122
Vinson, Ira 18:60
Vinson, J. 18:73
Vinson, J. D. 10:84
Vinson, James W. 10:141; 20:384
Vinson, John 17:445; 20:384; 24:168
Vinson, R. C. 15:6
Vinson, William 20:37
Vinson, William J. 16:60
Vintilburg, Thomas 20:384
Vinton, E. C. 15:51
Vinton, J. H. 19:263
Vinton, Jacob 17:444; 24:163
Vinton, John N. 21:399
Vinton, John R. 9:152
Vinton, Samuel 7:44
Vinyard, Henry 7:113
Vinyard, J. L. 14:249; 27:125
Vinyard, J. R. 18:98
Vinyard, Tabah 11:20
Vinyard, W. D. 27:125
Violet, J. 1:180
Virble, Tobias 20:82
Vire, Henry G. 15:354
Virgiar, William 20:384
Virgil, James 19:293
Virgin, Andrew J. 21:199
Virgin, S. T. 23:303
Virgin, W. W. 14:228
Virrill, Anson 13:122
Virtrus, J. 11:98
Virts, R. 3:207
Virtue, David S. 17:321
Virtue, Samuel 11:195
Virus, Frederick 27:125
Visars, Thomas 17:239
Vise, Henry 10:209
Vise, William I. 22:107
Vish, O. 3:207
Visit, M. 19:216
Visley, Thomas 9:202
Vitcher, Joseph 9:196
Vitetoc, James 18:267
Vitiboe, James 26:82
Vitman, Ira P. 7:54
Vitrell, Samuel 17:97
Vitson, James 23:276
Vittam, Giles L. 19:40
Vittum, George S. 16:81

Vittum, James H. 22:227
Vittun, E. W. 3:207
Vivian, John 7:135
Vivier, Edward 22:135
Vlick, Andrew 23:261
Voannah, William 14:122
Vober, Francis 7:70
Vocus, W. D. 22:356
Vodee, T. 3:207
Voden, Dennis 26:197
Vodria, Daniel A. 16:142
Voegeli, Balthasar 22:510
Voegtel, Henry 10:97
Voerling, H. 3:207
Voett, A. 23:315
Vogan, George W. 7:65
Vogan, S. 11:316
Vogel, Ferdinand 18:317; 26:115
Vogel, George 22:58
Vogel, John 9:196; 19:269
Vogel, L. 3:207
Vogelbach, Michael 16:154
Vogenety, A. 16:259
Voght, Albert 8:68
Voght, Charles 13:52
Voght, J. F. 23:173
Vogle, Anton 3:207
Vogle, Ferdinand 9:30
Vogle, Frank 12:44
Vogle, Jacob 3:207
Vogle, John 17:285
Vogle, Joseph 12:44
Vogle, Theodore 9:225; 18:387
Vogle, V. 3:207
Voglear, John 13:52
Voglebaugh, Michael 12:60
Vogler, Alfred 24:72
Vogler, August 14:228
Vogler, D. 11:316
Vogler, Frederick 22:169
Vogler, John 23:54
Vogt, Anton 12:146
Vogt, Frederick 22:347
Vogt, Jacob 23:94
Vogthy, J. 11:316
Vogtt, Charles 19:216
Vogus, H. 18:73
Vogus, J. 1:179
Vohamn, John 18:60
Voight, Edward 11:273
Voight, Ilrias 19:276
Voight, Randolph 8:34
Voigt, William E. 23:54
Voiles, H. 11:80
Voit, F. 3:207
Voit, Randolph 18:165
Voke, John 3:207

Volcart, Nicholas 1:82
Volentine, Daniel 10:141
Volentine, William 24:60
Volger, L. 14:122
Volk, C. 13:101; 16:275
Volk, Ferdinand 9:225
Volk, G. 27:124
Volk, George 4:59
Volke, Edward 1:82
Volkel, George 10:141
Volker, Fred 20:384
Volker, George 20:384
Volkert, Frederick 10:84
Volkes, Ferdinand 18:387
Volkham, Ferdinand 27:124
Vollenburg, H. V. 19:263
Vollenmider, F. 1:100
Vollett, Garrett 13:59
Vollette, Eugene 24:46
Vollkemer, Joseph 10:23
Vollkurln, --- 2:19
Vollman, A. R. 1:83
Vollmer, Christ 18:165
Vollmer, Christ. 8:34
Vollmer, Nicholas 22:510
Volmar, Ernest 11:131
Volmer, John 27:124
Volmore, J. 3:207
Volong, John 24:70
Volsburg, Henry 10:84
Voltair, Prosper 9:212
Volter, George 3:207
Volter, H. 3:207
Voltire, George 7:113
Volton, A. 11:47
Voltz, Abraham 21:236
Voltz, P. 19:138
Vonart, Rodolph 14:228
VonBachelli, Werner 15:94
Vonderan, Joseph 21:262
Vonderhide, B. 19:263
VonDroeben, Edward 22:227
VonDyne, M. 18:298
VonEinsdel, Debveto 19:138
VonGrief, Otto 19:216
VonLettow, Ferdinand 22:15
VonMalesdorf, Henry 14:228
Vonn, Thomas 22:325
Vonns, Richard 19:216
VonOrden, N. 5:32
Vonpenon, Alex F. 10:85
VonSchmidt, B. 19:40
Vonsden, Henry 10:8
VonShilling, Hans 25:328
Vontress, William 24:57

Voodre, Amos 21:399
Voodry, H. C. 15:252
Voor, W. H. 20:384
Voorhans, G. B. 15:301
Voorhees, A. H. 3:207
Voorhees, Daniel 4:59
Voorhees, J. 27:124
Voorhees, J. T. 21:44
Voorhees, Jackson M.
    4:59
Voorhees, James 19:297
Voorhees, Samuel 23:81
Voorhia, George 3:207
Voorhies, --- 11:426
Voorhies, Charles 17:264
Voorhies, Cornelius L.
    17:391
Voorhies, E. 11:131
Voorhies, E. R. 3:207
Voorhies, Harvey P.
    22:107
Voorhies, John 23:126
Voorhies, Julius T. 22:493
Voorhies, Peter 8:116
Voorhies, S. 1:179
Voorhis, L. 14:122
Voors, Edward 11:316
Voose, Chr. 7:71
Voralh, J. 11:253
Vorcaso, Antonio 18:427
Voren, --- 25:123
Vorhees, C. 12:139;
    15:147
Vorhees, C. A. 13:122
Vorhees, James L. 11:175
Vorhees, John 9:212
Vorhees, W. B. 2:19
Vorheese, --- 8:76
Vorheese, O. 8:76
Vorhes, Louis 20:149
Vorhess, Steven 15:164
Vorhies, William B.
    25:123
Voris, A. 24:32
Voris, John 22:107
Voris, John H. 23:173
Voris, Marion 18:223
Vorn, Allen 19:49
Vorney, Isaac 22:356
Vorrey, A. S. 23:54
Vorse, Norton 21:399
Vorter, E. R. 22:107
Vortmier, Victor 23:94
Vorton, James 1:82
Vosburg, A. M. 1:180
Vosburg, Aaron P. 7:113
Vosburg, E. R. 27:124
Vosburg, J. E. 27:124
Vosburg, William 16:129
Vosburgh, Aaron 21:399
Vosburgh, E. R. 9:152

Vosburgh, H. 1:180
Vosburgh, John M.
    22:468
Vosburgh, L. 1:180
Vosburgh, Martin 17:245
Vosburgh, W. H. 1:83
Vosburs, A. 21:44
Vosbury, Crayton S.
    21:61
Voschild, John 26:138
Vose, C. H. 14:249
Vose, Edwin O. 15:252
Voshell, John 9:73
Vosknil, Anthony 21:262
Vosler, Christian 21:107
Vosmer, Henry 1:82
Vosper, --- 19:138
Voss, Christian 10:85
Voss, Henry 10:141;
    20:384
Voss, John 17:454
Voss, John G. 27:125
Voss, William 15:323;
    19:138
Vosse, Jesse 21:399
Vosser, W. 20:384
Vossiller, W. 15:252
Vossler, Jacob 11:417
Vostzh, John 20:101
Votan, Jacob 11:397
Votang, C. 14:23
Vote, W. H. 23:54
Voter, A. J. 1:180
Voucher, E. 5:32
Vouchorn, E. 24:57
Vough, Albert 26:197
Voughd, James 25:123
Voughn, Moses 6:19
Voughn, Robert 7:70
Voughn, William 17:285
Vought, J. C. 1:83
Vought, Samuel 3:207
Vouham, Thomas 19:293
Vouhecker, John 15:252
Vounch, Joseph 14:228
Vouns, Richard 10:177
Vourden, J. B. 22:470
Voustin, S. 20:384
Vouzel, A. 14:228
Vowell, Louis M. 24:163
Vox, William 3:207
Voyenmitz, August
    13:122
Voyles, H. 17:295
Voyt, George 8:34
Vradenburgh, H. L. 7:62
Vredenberg, Clark A.
    22:158
Vredenburg, Joseph 24:62
Vreeland, A. 25:255
Vreeland, Abraham 5:32

Vreyes, S. D. 9:197
Vroman, David 24:98
Vroman, J. J. 11:47
Vroman, Jones B. 11:175
Vroman, W. W. 20:175
Vroom, Samuel 10:85;
    20:384
Vrooman, Henry G.
    22:493
Vrooman, J. H. 1:180
Vrooman, King 27:125
Vudndeslin, --- 12:86
Vulgrave, Calvin 11:87
Vundt, W. H. 19:138
Vungan, George 13:122
Vust, Thompson 14:228

W

W---, --- 10:191; 11:253;
    15:171; 16:358;
    18:184; 22:356;
    26:207
W---, A. 11:221, 253,
    318; 17:333; 25:125
W---, A. D. 19:138
W---, A. H. 8:58
W---, A. M. 10:203
W---, A. S. 25:307
W---, A. W. 25:125
W---, Amos 15:156
W---, B. 20:131
W---, B. D. 20:82
W---, B. F. 8:58; 26:201
W---, B. W. 26:85
W---, C. 9:65; 15:283;
    17:107; 19:314;
    20:50; 21:162;
    22:356; 25:255
W---, D. 15:156; 16:358;
    18:417; 20:135;
    23:253; 25:124
W---, D. C. 20:26; 22:356
W---, D. D. 23:206
W---, D. H. 18:444;
    25:128
W---, Daniel 18:288;
    26:136
W---, E. J. 23:269
W---, E. T. 20:82
W---, Edmond 15:256
W---, F. 16:137; 24:33, 57
W---, F. N. 22:356
W---, F. S. 25:127
W---, F. V. 18:389
W---, Frank M. 15:61
W---, Frederick 24:115
W---, G. 11:222; 18:73;
    20:82; 22:356;
    24:163; 25:126

W---, G. B. 17:343
W---, G. L. 11:283
W---, G. M. 20:181
W---, G. S. 22:356
W---, G. W. 26:201
W---, George 9:65;
  11:290; 16:390;
  20:175; 27:125
W---, H--- 26:237
W---, H. 8:58; 9:65;
  11:317; 12:167;
  23:259; 25:329
W---, H. C. 15:256
W---, H. E. 17:297
W---, H. F. 25:329
W---, H. R. 17:348
W---, H. W. H. 14:276
W---, I. 17:297
W---, J--- 26:85
W---, J. 8:58; 10:31;
  11:82, 179, 254, 275,
  318; 14:276; 17:348,
  365, 503; 18:40, 269;
  19:138; 20:384;
  23:269; 25:126;
  27:125, 134
W---, J. A. 21:169; 27:126
W---, J. B. 18:328
W---, J. D. 17:365
W---, J. E. 8:58; 20:384
W---, J. F. 15:96; 17:365
W---, J. H. 18:389
W---, J. N. 20:82
W---, J. R. 25:274
W---, J. S. 25:125
W---, J. W. 18:422;
  25:314
W---, James 26:85
W---, Jesse 18:269
W---, John M. 15:256
W---, John W. 11:343
W---, Koff 19:272
W---, L. 18:40; 23:315
W---, L. A. 24:115
W---, M. 11:175; 17:194;
  18:409; 20:82
W---, M. T. 23:315
W---, O. 12:145; 20:384
W---, O. O. 19:297
W---, O. T. 18:269
W---, P--- 9:126
W---, P. 17:510; 21:169,
  192; 27:125
W---, P. B. 23:293
W---, P. E. 26:214
W---, R. 22:356; 23:253,
  315
W---, R. B. 21:209
W---, R. E. 20:157
W---, R. H. C. 24:115
W---, R. M. 16:111

W---, R. N. 20:181
W---, S. 20:384; 21:169;
  23:315
W---, S. D. 11:318
W---, S. F. 19:287
W---, S. J. 14:276
W---, T. 14:276; 16:391;
  17:497; 20:135;
  23:302
W---, T. A. 15:256
W---, T. M. 24:115
W---, T. W. 17:254
W---, W. 10:31; 15:256;
  17:213; 18:40;
  19:288; 26:201;
  27:125, 133
W---, W. B. 18:269;
  23:315
W---, W. H. 11:317
W---, W. P. 13:78
W---, W. S. 21:192
W---, W. T. 23:81
W---, W. W. 19:138
W---, William 21:82
W----, Peter S. 22:445
W---ett, George 23:81
W---ins, W. 23:54
W---st, --- 15:178
W---t, Tom 11:48
W., J. 15:156
W., O. T. 26:86
Wa--, Arnold 8:43
Waan, George 4:59
Wacart, R. 3:207
Wacelin, James 6:11
Wacenhurst, Jacob 19:40
Wachtler, August 9:93
Wachtman, Andrew
  22:285
Wacker, George 5:55
Wacker, J. 19:138
Wacker, William 7:82;
  25:307
Wackman, David M.
  20:384
Wacox, William 16:358
Waczeman, John 14:228
Wad, Alonzo W. 11:82
Wadams, M. 16:259
Waddel, David 22:507
Waddel, R. 21:44
Waddell, Cato 21:287
Waddell, George 9:69
Waddell, George W. 9:69
Waddell, J. C. 24:86
Waddell, John H. 7:44
Waddell, Joseph 22:227
Waddell, Luther 22:443
Waddell, Walter 22:58
Waddell, William 23:81
Wadden, Charles 21:399

Waddick, Michael 22:107
Waddill, Henry 23:102
Waddle, A. F. 16:391
Waddle, A. T. 11:179
Waddle, Aaron 11:397
Waddle, B. N. 7:54
Waddle, Columbus 7:135
Waddle, H. 18:267; 26:86
Waddle, Harlan 18:317;
  26:115
Waddle, Harlem 9:30
Waddle, J. 3:207
Waddle, Joseph 17:326
Waddles, J. 23:258
Waddleton, Jesse 11:215
Waddlo, A. F. 15:346
Waddy, Francis P. 24:46
Wade, A. 13:101; 14:23
Wade, A. D. L. 3:207
Wade, A. F. 14:122
Wade, A. K. 18:165
Wade, A. R. 26:200
Wade, Abner 15:301
Wade, Absalom 10:85;
  20:384
Wade, Andrew J. 24:57
Wade, Anthony 15:156
Wade, B. F. 24:33
Wade, Benjamin 22:285
Wade, Berry 27:129
Wade, C. 3:207; 17:69
Wade, C. D. 21:399
Wade, C. H. 13:52
Wade, Charles 7:135;
  10:168; 22:445
Wade, Charles T. 19:216
Wade, D. L. 16:154
Wade, Daniel 19:40
Wade, Dulaney 17:60
Wade, E. 1:184
Wade, E. E. 19:138
Wade, E. P. 14:122
Wade, Edward Thomas
  7:44
Wade, Elijah 22:133
Wade, F. 9:64
Wade, Frank 4:60, 68
Wade, Franklin 9:238;
  26:234
Wade, George 3:207;
  22:107, 506
Wade, George P. 4:59
Wade, Hamilton 21:213
Wade, Henry 26:85
Wade, Henry H. 23:278
Wade, Henry T. 16:87
Wade, Hubert 19:216
Wade, I. 9:152
Wade, J. 27:128
Wade, J. C. 10:85; 20:384
Wade, J. F. 1:185

Wade, J. G. 1:96
Wade, J. N. 16:358
Wade, James 22:325; 27:133
Wade, James M. 17:208
Wade, John 5:32; 7:135; 13:52; 23:173
Wade, John C. 11:82
Wade, John H. 17:240
Wade, John R. 21:107
Wade, Johnson 21:287
Wade, Joseph 21:287
Wade, Joshua 21:399
Wade, Lewis F. 21:399
Wade, Loren 12:44
Wade, M. 3:207
Wade, M. C. 5:32; 9:64
Wade, N. 12:90; 14:122
Wade, N. L. 18:184
Wade, Orin D. 16:142
Wade, Oscar 23:54
Wade, Peter B. 11:223
Wade, Robert 26:131
Wade, Robert D. 11:393
Wade, Roberts 9:46
Wade, S. C. 5:32
Wade, S. E. 25:255
Wade, T. 14:122
Wade, T. E. 1:184
Wade, Thomas 11:82; 21:44, 61
Wade, Thomas B. 8:34; 18:165
Wade, Turner 7:114
Wade, W. 3:207
Wade, W. F. 21:399
Wade, W. H. 12:44; 20:87
Wade, W. L. 10:203
Wade, William 11:87; 14:122; 15:95
Wade, William B. 21:399
Wade, William F. 7:114
Wade, William H. 22:107
Wade, William I. 26:84
Wade, William J. 25:307
Wade, William W. 22:107
Waden, Emma 17:400
Wadenheimer, C. 25:307
Wadenhimer, Charles 7:80
Wader, Charles 21:169
Wadford, George H. 21:287
Wadges, John P. 10:141; 20:384
Wadhaus, William N. 12:44
Wadill, J. 16:259
Wadington, Burl 22:325
Wadkins, Anderson 21:107
Wadkins, Daniel 10:191

Wadkins, David 22:133
Wadkins, E. C. 12:163
Wadkins, Felix 23:291
Wadkins, J. M. 6:26; 17:481; 27:134
Wadkins, James 17:88
Wadkins, Merrill 22:325
Wadkins, Thornton 11:216
Wadkins, W. J. 17:88
Wadkins, Westley 22:325
Wadle, Michael 11:274
Wadle, William 8:68
Wadleigh, E. 13:81; 16:259
Wadleigh, J. 12:139
Wadley, Henry 20:384
Wadley, Herman 10:85
Wadley, William 6:10; 18:116
Wadlin, L. H. 1:181
Wadlington, Anthony 24:103
Wadock, W. 8:68
Wadsworth, Andrew J. 4:59
Wadsworth, B. F. 3:207
Wadsworth, Benjamin 16:60
Wadsworth, Charles 14:228
Wadsworth, David 9:225
Wadsworth, Davis 18:387
Wadsworth, Eli W. 16:60
Wadsworth, Francis 9:197
Wadsworth, J. E. 1:84
Wadsworth, Nois W. 20:384
Wadsworth, Truman H. 23:183
Wadsworth, William 7:114; 9:197
Wadups, Thomas 24:100
Wadworth, James W. 22:227
Wadworth, Samuel 7:62
Waelde, Conrad 16:111
Waer, Alanson 8:111
Waers, John 25:255
Waesie, J. W. 17:251
Waethee, William 15:356
Waffle, Sylvanus 11:48
Waffle, Walter 12:44
Wafford, L. 17:188
Wafield, William J. 24:33
Wagaman, Eli 22:495
Waganer, Philip C. 26:199
Wagener, A. 14:267
Wagener, Frederick 21:107
Wagener, J. 11:179

Wagener, Stephen 21:107
Wagener, Wi. 14:122
Wagenhauser, John 15:156
Wager, Benjamin 8:97
Wager, Charles 11:175
Wager, H. B. 18:165
Wager, James A. 5:32
Wager, M. 1:182
Wager, P. 1:184
Wager, W. B. 26:200
Wagerman, William 4:60
Wagers, W. W. 9:225; 18:387
Wages, Isaac 8:57; 21:107
Wages, John 6:10
Waget, Job 13:78
Waggen, David 22:227
Wagger, John 13:52
Waggle, F. 13:101
Waggoner, A. J. 8:34
Waggoner, B. 21:85
Waggoner, F. M. 19:138
Waggoner, Gabriel 22:107
Waggoner, H. 1:87
Waggoner, Henry 18:223
Waggoner, J. W. 25:255
Waggoner, James W. 15:283
Waggoner, Joel 9:30
Waggoner, John 6:8; 8:34; 18:165; 21:44
Waggoner, John H. 10:141
Waggoner, Joseph 9:93
Waggoner, Lewis D. 20:384
Waggoner, Milton 22:445
Waggoner, Perry 17:45
Waggoner, Wesley 10:141; 20:384
Wagher, P. H. 12:167
Waghn, B. H. 25:328
Waghorst, Henry 11:177
Wagle, John 23:173
Wagman, S. 13:101
Wagner, --- 15:51
Wagner, A. 14:292; 16:111; 23:102
Wagner, A. G. 13:122
Wagner, Andrew 15:252
Wagner, August 20:385
Wagner, C. 3:207; 19:138
Wagner, Charles 13:75, 122; 16:259; 21:399
Wagner, Christol 12:10
Wagner, Christopher 12:44
Wagner, Daniel 21:246
Wagner, David 14:228
Wagner, E. 3:207

Wagner, E. R. 9:197; 19:263
Wagner, Ferdinand 22:169
Wagner, Frank 15:79
Wagner, G. 1:86
Wagner, G. A. 4:60
Wagner, G. F. 21:44
Wagner, G. P. 1:186
Wagner, George 4:60; 9:197; 15:147, 252; 17:394; 19:138, 285; 22:58, 273
Wagner, George E. 23:174
Wagner, George W. 7:44
Wagner, Gustav 24:115
Wagner, H. B. 8:34
Wagner, H. C. 25:278
Wagner, Henry 11:222; 12:44; 14:122, 228; 22:158
Wagner, I. 26:84
Wagner, Israel 8:34; 18:165
Wagner, J. 1:185; 3:207; 11:283
Wagner, Jacob 7:70; 12:44; 13:75, 122; 19:139; 23:116
Wagner, James 10:85; 25:255
Wagner, Jeremiah 22:238
Wagner, John 1:83; 7:44, 62; 9:30, 197; 13:52; 15:51; 17:389; 18:116, 267; 19:263; 22:227; 26:87
Wagner, John M. 11:178
Wagner, Joseph 15:61
Wagner, Joseph A. 10:12
Wagner, Joseph F. 9:225
Wagner, Joseph N. 21:61
Wagner, Julius 20:385
Wagner, Lester 24:98
Wagner, Levi 21:82
Wagner, Lewis 20:385; 21:399
Wagner, M. 3:207
Wagner, Martin 13:126; 16:158
Wagner, Mathew 10:85
Wagner, Michael 7:44
Wagner, Newton 9:99
Wagner, Nicholas 23:287
Wagner, Otto 7:114
Wagner, Peter 9:137
Wagner, Philip 8:68
Wagner, Reuben 11:216
Wagner, Samuel 7:114
Wagner, T. 3:207
Wagner, Thomas E. 19:40

Wagner, Volunteer 18:60
Wagner, W. 13:101; 14:23; 20:45; 21:113
Wagner, William 13:75; 16:145; 19:139
Wagner, William H. 10:168; 19:216
Wagnor, J. 21:44
Wagone, G. L. 11:318
Wagoner, --- 20:385
Wagoner, A. 1:185; 9:46; 26:131
Wagoner, A. J. 18:165
Wagoner, Amon 18:402
Wagoner, August 10:85
Wagoner, C. 1:183
Wagoner, C. E. 24:115
Wagoner, Charles 1:85; 10:85; 20:385
Wagoner, D. M. 22:494
Wagoner, Edmund 17:254
Wagoner, Evan C. 18:402
Wagoner, Frederick 20:47
Wagoner, H. 3:207
Wagoner, Henry A. 22:133
Wagoner, Henry H. 22:459
Wagoner, Isaac 11:216
Wagoner, J. 8:68; 26:200
Wagoner, James 1:85; 9:241; 10:85; 17:240; 20:385
Wagoner, Joel 18:317; 26:115
Wagoner, John 14:228; 17:315; 18:317; 22:347; 26:116
Wagoner, Johnson 26:146
Wagoner, Joseph 23:265
Wagoner, Joseph F. 18:387
Wagoner, Lewis G. 10:85
Wagoner, Logan 17:277
Wagoner, M. 20:385
Wagoner, N. 20:178
Wagoner, Oliver H. 21:61
Wagoner, P. 11:253
Wagoner, Peter 22:286; 27:129
Wagoner, Philip 10:85; 20:385
Wagoner, S. W. 12:146
Wagoner, Thomas 22:325; 23:173
Wagoner, W. A. 11:81
Wagoner, W. C. 17:433; 22:469
Wagoner, William C. 24:164
Wagot, H. 1:84

Wagoun, F. M. 15:323
Wagy, W. A. 22:227
Waha, Washington John 18:342
Wahburn, E. 2:20
Wahbury, E. 25:128
Wahl, Constantine 7:44
Wahl, John 3:207
Wahl, M. 3:207
Wahl, Melchion 21:94
Wahlgrand, Alexander F. 22:58
Wahmock, Y. 23:265
Wahn, Robert 23:55
Wahnemaker, Peter 27:132
Wahola, Matthias 17:45
Waibel, Burnhart 12:145
Waid, Edwin 21:236
Waid, Hubert 10:168
Waid, J. H. 13:127
Waid, Jairns 16:285
Waid, James 11:330
Waid, Warren 20:385
Waid, William B. 12:78
Waid, William J. 7:76
Waidden, D. B. 16:285
Waide, J. 13:122
Waidi, Berry 9:137
Waidle, Christian 8:34; 18:165
Waidler, Benjamin 11:324
Waidler, I. 11:179
Waigel, Christopher 21:399
Waigfield, Alex 22:325
Waight, Charles J. 14:228
Waight, J. 14:122
Waiker, James A. 11:81
Waikley, Frank 8:102
Wail, John 27:133
Wailes, C. N. 3:207
Wailes, William H. 12:78
Wailong, --- 17:501
Waimon, John 22:58
Wain, George 9:197
Waine, James 7:114
Wainer, S. C. 15:252
Wainright, J. J. 9:233
Wainsworth, C. 17:290
Wainteran, E. 17:112
Wainwright, --- 3:207
Wainwright, J. J. 20:385
Wainwright, L. G. 3:208
Wainwright, Nathaniel C. 17:45
Wainwright, Robert 10:24
Wair, Reuben 18:201
Waird, C. William 26:85
Waird, William C. 18:267
Wairright, Jacob 15:252

Waison, T. I. 25:255
Wait, A. 1:183
Wait, B. J. 8:57
Wait, Benjamin 4:60
Wait, Byron 17:69
Wait, C. A. 20:149
Wait, George 11:82; 18:98
Wait, Granville 19:40
Wait, Henry F. 4:60
Wait, J. 16:285
Wait, John 7:44
Wait, L. B. 1:88
Wait, Lewis 27:132
Wait, M. B. 16:259
Wait, M. C. 25:255
Wait, Orrin L. 23:174
Wait, Richard 19:40
Wait, S. 1:181
Wait, Samuel C. 20:32
Wait, Sharezer 23:174
Wait, T. 24:215
Wait, Tracey D. 9:126
Wait, Tracy D. 27:131
Wait, W. 15:51
Wait, W. L. 17:218
Wait, Wash 9:114
Wait, William 25:255
Wait, William H. 18:402
Waite, Fred. K. 19:216
Waite, Frederick 10:168
Waite, G. W. 19:263
Waite, J. W. 9:197
Waite, John 8:111; 25:255
Waite, John W. 22:58
Waite, Joseph 21:61
Waite, Martin 19:40
Waite, William N. 24:168
Waites, Newton 19:40
Waith, C. 1:182
Waithael, E. 9:64
Waitkneight, John 19:139
Waitman, John 20:26
Waitman, Sylvanus 7:70
Waitmon, Lewis 26:131
Waits, A. 14:313
Waits, Jefferson 22:58
Waits, R. 17:481
Waits, William 22:507
Waits, William N. 17:422; 24:168
Wake, Anthony 19:216
Wake, William H. 4:60
Wakefield, --- 19:139
Wakefield, A. 14:228
Wakefield, B. 1:84
Wakefield, Chauncey 23:278
Wakefield, D. 3:208
Wakefield, D. W. 1:182
Wakefield, Elihu 25:329
Wakefield, Elisha 6:33

Wakefield, Enos 10:85; 20:385
Wakefield, Francis M. 10:141; 20:385
Wakefield, Freeman 7:44
Wakefield, H. 14:122
Wakefield, Harvey M. 13:52
Wakefield, Henry 22:325
Wakefield, J. A. 27:132
Wakefield, James 27:156
Wakefield, John 8:111; 21:287
Wakefield, John B. 21:94
Wakefield, Joseph A. 10:185; 18:185
Wakefield, L. 9:64
Wakefield, M. 5:32; 25:255
Wakefield, O. 1:83
Wakefield, R. F. 22:227
Wakefield, T. 26:85
Wakefield, Thomas 9:93
Wakefield, W. 1:185; 23:174
Wakefield, William 20:180
Wakefield, William F. 9:40
Wakefield, William P. 22:169
Wakeland, Henry 21:399
Wakeley, Charles 9:99
Wakeley, Frank 24:186
Wakely, Daniel 19:216
Wakely, Frank 17:463
Wakely, Samuel 15:252
Wakely, Wesley 15:252
Wakeman, H. 1:86
Wakeman, Horace 8:97, 116
Wakeman, I. 26:84
Wakeman, Isaac 17:188
Wakeman, J. 11:175
Wakeman, James H. 25:255
Wakeman, M. 1:185
Wakeman, M. B. 1:88
Wakeman, Orlando 15:252
Wakeman, Reuben 23:197
Wakeman, Samuel 1:85
Waker, A. H. 11:317
Wakerhagen, --- 25:329
Wakes, L. F. 2:19
Wakesfield, J. H. 3:208
Wakins, A. F. 25:127
Wakins, W. P. 6:21
Wakinson, A. J. 9:114
Wakker, S. B. 15:25
Wakle, Martin 15:61

Wakley, S. 3:208
Wakman, Lyons 7:114
Wakotsche, Herman 25:335
Walace, James 18:282
Walaney, William J. 7:114
Walbaer, Andreas 22:495
Walbarn, Elisha 20:385
Walben, J. 27:134
Walborn, A. 9:238
Walborn, William 10:24
Walbran, Elisha 10:85
Walbridge, C. 14:122
Walbridge, Don C. 7:80; 25:307
Walbridge, Edwin 7:84
Walbright, A. E. 24:33
Walburg, Andrew 27:126
Walburn, John 10:141; 20:385
Walburn, Joseph E. 22:107
Walby, Howard 15:51
Walch, --- 17:394
Walch, E. 23:55
Walch, J. 19:139
Walch, J. H. 26:84
Walch, L. C. 11:253
Walch, M. 22:273
Walch, N. C. 12:84; 16:358
Walch, Patrick 22:522
Walch, Patrick E. 14:228
Walch, William 24:86
Walch, William F. 11:185
Walcho, Luman 17:391
Walchold, L. 12:78
Walcort, M. 14:122
Walcott, --- 16:358
Walcott, A. 21:399
Walcott, Daniel H. 23:94
Walcott, G. P. 3:208
Walcott, H. S. 25:124
Walcott, H. T. 2:19
Walcott, Jerome B. 9:105
Walcott, John 27:125
Walcott, L. A. 10:168
Walcott, Martin 21:399
Walcutt, Edward L. 11:117
Walcutt, James L. 17:88
Wald, Bennevill 22:15
Wald, Joseph 18:335
Wald, William H. 9:99
Waldem, Charles 16:60
Walden, Charles 15:51
Walden, E. 21:399
Walden, E. S. 7:114
Walden, Edward N. 9:106
Walden, F. M. 14:285
Walden, G. 25:255

Walden, George 22:133
Walden, H. 21:44
Walden, J. 14:313
Walden, James B. 8:34;
    18:165
Walden, Lebem 8:43
Walden, Lebren 26:199
Walden, Samuel 10:177;
    19:216
Walden, Samuel W.
    21:115
Walden, W. 3:208
Walden, William 10:99
Walder, Adam 22:471
Walder, J. 3:208
Walder, Joseph 21:399
Waldher, James 12:78
Waldie, John 11:49
Waldier, Joseph 15:252
Waldin, F. C. 12:78;
    15:82
Waldin, George 5:47
Waldmeyer, W. 1:184
Waldner, Christopher
    17:27
Waldo, A. 1:83
Waldo, A. E. 1:181
Waldo, George E. 20:194
Waldo, George H. 21:262
Waldo, Ira K. 4:60
Waldo, J. 20:117
Waldo, J. M. 3:208
Waldo, John 26:84
Waldo, L. 25:329
Waldo, Limon 15:252
Waldo, William 9:239;
    26:234
Waldo, William R. 22:493
Waldock, John 12:78
Waldom, James 18:201
Waldon, Anthony B.
    22:59
Waldon, Cassius 24:62
Waldon, I. 17:477
Waldon, J. 1:184
Waldon, John 11:334
Waldon, Kennut 10:150;
    18:60
Waldorf, Albert 4:60
Waldorf, W. 24:86
Waldrain, Edward 18:335
Waldren, D. 13:101
Waldren, Samuel 13:75
Waldress, Pinckney 23:15
Waldron, Charles 13:52
Waldron, Cortland 16:61
Waldron, Courtland 13:52
Waldron, D. 14:23
Waldron, E. 13:122
Waldron, Elias 17:348

Waldron, George H.
    19:231
Waldron, H. 1:180; 3:208
Waldron, Henry 22:325
Waldron, Hubbard 9:197
Waldron, James F. 12:44
Waldron, John 25:124,
    125
Waldron, John L. 27:130
Waldron, Joseph M.
    22:227
Waldron, N. 3:208
Waldron, Reuben 22:107
Waldron, William 23:174
Waldron, William H.
    22:158
Waldrop, Greenbaugh
    11:47
Waldrop, J. H. 9:64
Waldrop, R. S. 23:55
Waldross, John L. 9:126
Waldroup, James K.
    22:507
Waldruff, S. 20:385
Waldruff, Sylvester 10:85
Waldschmidt, P. 17:102
Waldson, Benjamin 7:44
Walduck, John 15:61
Wale, Isaac 24:57
Wale, J. W. 22:227
Wale, James 15:51
Wale, Philip 17:441
Walebmer, Frank 4:60
Walen, Levi P. 22:107
Walensley, M. V. 6:33
Walenstine, Louis 11:296
Walensy, M. V. 25:329
Waler, --- 15:51
Waler, John 15:51
Walers, S. E. 12:159
Wales, A. 13:101
Wales, Colga 22:471
Wales, Ira 11:49
Wales, J. 3:208
Wales, James 5:32;
    25:255
Wales, L. W. 16:391
Wales, Selden D. 16:111
Wales, W. 7:62
Wales, William H. 17:240
Waley, Jacob 11:178
Walf, H. 3:208
Walf, Yost 7:44
Walfers, George 18:201
Walfhope, J. 3:208
Walfinbarger, John
    20:151
Walfington, John 8:98
Walford, Isaac 6:26
Walford, James H. 20:385
Walford, W. 3:208

Walfram, C. 22:227
Walhaught, John 18:165
Walhaupt, John 8:34
Walhom, --- 19:293
Walhorn, A. 26:234
Walis, Jeptha L. 22:273
Walivor, Jacob 11:81
Walk, John H. 8:34;
    18:165
Walk, Samuel 6:19; 18:98
Walk, Theodore 15:309;
    19:139
Walkalong, George 9:100
Walke, R. 16:391
Walkenburg, D. 14:329
Walker, --- 11:131; 15:51;
    18:288; 20:385;
    26:136
Walker, A. 3:208; 14:122,
    229; 15:51; 21:44;
    25:256
Walker, A. E. 23:55
Walker, A. H. 22:444
Walker, A. J. 5:32; 12:159
Walker, A. L. 1:181
Walker, A. O. 15:275
Walker, A. R. 1:86
Walker, Aaron 7:135
Walker, Adelbert 23:102
Walker, Albert 1:83; 5:32;
    11:217; 16:83;
    23:197; 27:125
Walker, Albert B. 17:351
Walker, Alexander 4:60;
    22:273
Walker, Alford 22:445
Walker, Alfred 13:59;
    19:317; 21:287
Walker, Allen J. 25:125
Walker, Ambrose 1:83
Walker, Amos J. 11:82
Walker, Anderson 7:135
Walker, Andrew 9:162;
    20:180
Walker, Asa 10:85;
    20:385
Walker, August 7:135
Walker, Austin 23:55
Walker, B. 16:259
Walker, B. F. 11:253;
    19:40
Walker, B. H. 13:122
Walker, Bart 22:517
Walker, Benjamin 6:26;
    21:213
Walker, Benjamin F.
    11:418; 21:133, 291
Walker, Boyd 9:202;
    19:293
Walker, C. A. 20:385
Walker, C. H. 3:208

Walker, C. M. 12:86;
    14:122; 16:358
Walker, C. P. 20:180
Walker, C. R. 2:19;
    25:127
Walker, C. W. F. 14:122
Walker, Cary 17:188
Walker, Cassen 8:78
Walker, Charles 6:19;
    8:78; 10:85; 18:41,
    98, 267; 19:40;
    20:385; 21:287;
    23:310; 26:85
Walker, Charles E. 20:26
Walker, Charles I. 22:163
Walker, Charles L. 18:73
Walker, Charles S. 8:98
Walker, Christian 10:85
Walker, Clarence 26:87
Walker, Cleb 8:43; 26:198
Walker, Cyrus 11:253
Walker, D. 1:88; 9:64;
    11:274; 14:122;
    24:212
Walker, Dan 16:358
Walker, Daniel 9:70;
    12:94
Walker, David 6:28; 9:64;
    23:94
Walker, E. 3:208; 17:188;
    25:256; 27:127
Walker, E. A. 7:62
Walker, E. D. 27:156
Walker, E. R. 15:82
Walker, Edsel L. 21:399
Walker, Edward 8:57;
    17:188
Walker, Elijah 6:26
Walker, Ellis 4:60
Walker, Enos 9:40
Walker, Ephraim 20:385
Walker, Evans 18:298;
    26:116
Walker, Ezekiel 9:152
Walker, F. 1:104; 15:253
Walker, F. G. 25:256
Walker, Foster 24:86
Walker, Francis G. 13:53;
    16:61
Walker, Francis M. 8:57;
    12:168
Walker, Frank 6:14;
    9:212; 18:98; 21:399
Walker, Frederick 7:114;
    13:52; 21:399
Walker, Frederick N.
    22:158
Walker, G. 3:208; 16:135
Walker, G. A. 25:128
Walker, G. B. 14:122

Walker, G. W. 1:87;
    21:199
Walker, George 1:85;
    7:135; 9:126; 10:97;
    12:84; 14:122;
    16:358; 18:402;
    21:399; 27:131, 133
Walker, George A. 19:41
Walker, George D. 13:52;
    22:158
Walker, George F. 16:17
Walker, George W. 4:31;
    20:37; 23:81
Walker, George Walker
    27:156
Walker, Gideon 26:234
Walker, H. 3:208; 8:76;
    12:145; 20:385;
    25:256; 26:201
Walker, H. A. 22:347
Walker, H. B. 15:317;
    19:139
Walker, H. C. 3:208;
    14:229
Walker, H. H. 1:85
Walker, H. M. 14:122
Walker, Harmon H. 9:244
Walker, Harrison 9:100;
    11:114
Walker, Harry 9:197
Walker, Harvey 19:285
Walker, Henry 5:32;
    8:116; 9:126; 12:44,
    52; 14:229; 16:259;
    18:324; 22:273;
    27:131
Walker, Henry A. 22:227
Walker, Henry H. 13:129
Walker, Herman 22:158
Walker, I. G. 19:279
Walker, Isaac 11:47, 405;
    14:326; 20:177
Walker, Isaac D. 22:238
Walker, Isaac M. 24:98
Walker, J. 1:182; 2:19;
    3:208; 9:155; 11:253;
    15:317; 16:259;
    17:169; 21:399;
    25:256; 27:128
Walker, J. A. 16:129
Walker, J. B. 20:15;
    21:107
Walker, J. C. 9:197; 23:81
Walker, J. C. L. 16:61
Walker, J. E. 15:253;
    27:134
Walker, J. H. 25:256
Walker, J. J. 10:141;
    20:385
Walker, J. N. 7:44

Walker, J. P. 10:141;
    20:385
Walker, J. R. 3:208;
    27:133
Walker, J. V. 11:177
Walker, J. W. 1:181;
    25:256; 27:127
Walker, Jacob 10:141;
    11:317; 18:402;
    20:385
Walker, James 6:19;
    7:114; 8:111; 9:202;
    11:177, 253; 14:122;
    17:140; 18:98;
    20:175, 385; 22:107,
    506; 23:55; 24:207
Walker, James E. 24:71
Walker, James L. 7:13
Walker, James P. 21:61
Walker, James V. 20:194
Walker, James W. 18:223
Walker, Jefferson 9:93;
    22:107
Walker, Jeremiah 11:274
Walker, Jesse 8:43;
    12:159; 26:198
Walker, John 8:34; 9:14,
    99, 197, 212; 10:24,
    141; 11:426, 427;
    12:159; 13:52;
    14:249; 16:129;
    17:16, 394; 18:165;
    19:278; 20:385;
    21:44; 22:273, 347;
    24:10; 25:127, 256;
    26:200; 27:134
Walker, John A. 21:246
Walker, John B. 11:89;
    23:81
Walker, John F. 20:45;
    22:273
Walker, John G. 10:24
Walker, John H. 17:72
Walker, John Jacob
    23:126
Walker, John M. 17:409;
    22:58
Walker, John R. 17:60
Walker, John T. 11:429;
    23:174
Walker, John W. 5:32;
    10:85, 141; 20:385;
    22:495
Walker, Johnson 17:498
Walker, Johnston 19:314
Walker, Jonas B. 22:227
Walker, Joseph 6:28;
    7:114; 9:212; 13:122;
    14:122; 17:216;
    18:267, 409; 20:82,
    90; 21:82; 26:87

Walker, Joseph R. 23:242
Walker, Joseph S. 17:88
Walker, Joseph W. 5:32
Walker, Joshua B. 22:58
Walker, Josiah T. 11:177
Walker, L. 7:13; 18:98;
  25:256
Walker, L. D. 14:27
Walker, Lafayette 23:81
Walker, Larenby 6:21
Walker, Lebanon 10:97
Walker, Lee 16:61
Walker, Leonidas 20:187
Walker, Lewis 4:60;
  7:135; 10:85; 20:45
Walker, Louis 5:32;
  20:385
Walker, M. 1:184; 19:139
Walker, M. C. 3:208
Walker, M. H. 5:47;
  25:256
Walker, M. W. 11:274;
  22:273
Walker, Marion 20:85
Walker, Mathew 22:273
Walker, Milton 7:135;
  11:18
Walker, Moses 9:197;
  15:61
Walker, N. 14:313;
  16:259; 17:214, 470
Walker, Nat 17:188;
  27:156
Walker, Nat. R. 26:136
Walker, Nathaniel R.
  18:288
Walker, Newton 11:189
Walker, Nicholas B.
  11:178
Walker, O. 21:287
Walker, O. F. 9:152
Walker, O. H. 18:41
Walker, Orrin 16:79
Walker, Orville P. 24:33
Walker, Owen 22:494
Walker, P. 1:88, 182, 183;
  7:54; 14:122
Walker, P. B. 11:393
Walker, P. C. 12:44
Walker, P. H. 23:206
Walker, Peter V. 17:245
Walker, Q. K. 22:356
Walker, R. 17:140;
  21:113; 24:206
Walker, R. C. 7:44
Walker, R. D. 1:96;
  25:256
Walker, R. J. 15:329;
  19:349
Walker, Renald J. 19:139

Walker, Richard 6:19;
  17:188; 18:98;
  21:144; 22:348
Walker, Richard R.
  17:285
Walker, Rius R. 20:117
Walker, Robert 1:85;
  4:60, 68; 21:287;
  22:227
Walker, Robert J. 23:82
Walker, Roswell 8:34;
  18:165
Walker, Roswell A.
  25:126
Walker, Rowland 12:44
Walker, Rynear M. 20:26
Walker, S. 14:123;
  19:276; 23:55;
  24:108; 25:256
Walker, S. A. 3:208
Walker, S. C. 9:197;
  19:276
Walker, S. G. 14:285
Walker, S. H. 11:47
Walker, S. T. 11:49
Walker, Samuel 5:47;
  8:34; 12:44; 18:165,
  282; 21:287
Walker, Sidney B. 22:459
Walker, Simon 23:82
Walker, Smith 11:176
Walker, Spencer C. 24:46
Walker, Stephen 9:93;
  26:85
Walker, Sylvester 10:210
Walker, T. 9:64; 21:44;
  25:256
Walker, T. W. 9:152
Walker, Thomas 8:43,
  111; 9:225; 11:405;
  18:387; 22:273, 325;
  26:198
Walker, Thomas J. 22:133
Walker, Thomas S. 7:54
Walker, Thornton 27:156
Walker, Valentine 11:48
Walker, W. 13:101;
  22:58; 25:256;
  27:132
Walker, W. D. 12:81;
  25:256
Walker, W. D. L. 13:60
Walker, W. E. 21:399
Walker, W. H. 1:84; 9:127
Walker, W. J. 11:274
Walker, W. M. 21:13
Walker, W. N. 22:495
Walker, W. R. 11:87
Walker, W. W. 17:399;
  23:315; 25:256
Walker, Walter 11:81

Walker, Wesley 9:197;
  19:263
Walker, Wesley A. 21:44
Walker, William 1:88;
  3:208; 4:60; 7:79;
  8:111; 9:155, 225;
  11:215, 274, 409;
  12:44, 81; 14:229;
  15:85; 17:88, 285;
  18:41, 98, 201, 387;
  19:139; 21:144, 213;
  22:227, 325, 445;
  25:307; 26:85;
  27:156
Walker, William A.
  11:419; 15:156;
  18:267; 23:94; 26:85;
  27:131
Walker, William B.
  22:413, 445
Walker, William H. 9:93;
  17:253; 23:94
Walker, William J. 27:133
Walker, William K. 20:45
Walker, William O.
  22:469
Walker, William T.
  22:413
Walker, William W. 26:83
Walker, Wilson 22:325
Walkerick, S. 9:64
Walkille, C. G. 26:200
Walkin, J. 19:231
Walkin, John 9:197
Walkin, William 25:124
Walkins, W. H. 16:61
Walkins, Wilford 9:93;
  26:83
Walkman, H. 3:208
Walkonk, C. 25:256
Walkup, Christopher
  23:242
Wall, A. 3:208; 9:197
Wall, Adam 21:197
Wall, B. G. 9:114
Wall, C. 15:61
Wall, C. B. 12:139
Wall, C. L. 7:114
Wall, Calvin 9:239
Wall, Charles 11:175;
  15:114
Wall, Chesley N. 23:116
Wall, Clarence 12:78
Wall, David 1:86
Wall, F. A. 21:197
Wall, Fred 16:391
Wall, G. 1:182
Wall, George 1:87
Wall, George W. 22:348
Wall, H. 11:98
Wall, Hurbert 8:98

Wall, J. 3:208
Wall, J. B. 16:259
Wall, J. W. 9:114
Wall, James 1:86; 8:76;
    18:288; 24:169;
    26:136
Wall, James H. 19:139
Wall, Jeremiah 20:109
Wall, Joel 22:107
Wall, John H. 8:76
Wall, Johnson C. 8:34;
    18:165
Wall, Joseph 7:45; 19:323
Wall, Joshua 22:325
Wall, R. 25:123
Wall, R. S. 22:227
Wall, S. J. 25:256
Wall, Thomas 10:210;
    22:158
Wall, W. 19:347
Wall, Washington 22:325
Wall, William 11:317;
    13:135; 17:188;
    23:55
Walla, George 22:107
Walla, John 10:141;
    20:385
Wallace, --- 10:168;
    19:317
Wallace, A. 13:101;
    14:23; 16:111;
    23:55; 25:275
Wallace, A. K. P. 25:127
Wallace, Adam 22:273
Wallace, Albert C. 21:133
Wallace, B. 22:158
Wallace, B. C. R. 18:201
Wallace, B. F. 8:100
Wallace, B. L. 11:393
Wallace, Benjamin 22:158
Wallace, Benjamin F.
    20:2; 22:273
Wallace, Beverly 21:213
Wallace, C. 18:98
Wallace, C. M. 14:24
Wallace, Charles 9:197;
    11:177; 19:217;
    21:82; 22:325
Wallace, Charles F. 20:87
Wallace, Clendennis 6:21
Wallace, D. 16:150
Wallace, D. B. 1:185
Wallace, Daniel 22:227;
    24:98
Wallace, David 25:126
Wallace, E. 18:267; 26:86
Wallace, E. C. 25:125
Wallace, E. L. 12:159
Wallace, Edward 10:94;
    18:117; 20:385;
    22:325

Wallace, Ezra B. 21:115
Wallace, Ezra C. 7:45
Wallace, F. 14:229
Wallace, F. A. 21:237
Wallace, F. W. 1:86
Wallace, Frank 8:57;
    21:169
Wallace, Franklin 22:273
Wallace, G. 8:57
Wallace, George 9:212;
    15:315; 17:285;
    18:267; 19:139;
    22:494; 26:86
Wallace, George C. 4:60
Wallace, George W. 9:69;
    11:175
Wallace, Green 21:287
Wallace, Greenburg 19:49
Wallace, Gustavus 19:139
Wallace, H. 2:19; 3:208;
    9:64; 17:163; 25:124
Wallace, H. C. 14:123
Wallace, H. H. 23:307
Wallace, Harrison 21:162
Wallace, Henry 11:216;
    12:44; 19:293;
    22:347
Wallace, Henry C. 13:53
Wallace, Hiram 21:262
Wallace, Horace E.
    14:313; 17:474;
    27:132
Wallace, Hugh 17:69
Wallace, I. I. 13:122
Wallace, J. 1:183; 27:127
Wallace, J. A. 15:21
Wallace, J. J. 15:320;
    19:139
Wallace, J. N. 20:385
Wallace, J. R. 1:185
Wallace, J. S. 21:399
Wallace, J. W. 1:86;
    22:495
Wallace, Jacob 23:102
Wallace, James 10:85;
    14:123; 16:129;
    20:385
Wallace, James C. 23:111
Wallace, James M. 8:98
Wallace, John 9:73, 161,
    244; 10:145; 11:253;
    13:75; 16:259;
    17:285; 19:41, 217;
    20:175; 22:169, 273;
    23:55; 25:124;
    27:134
Wallace, John A. 12:63
Wallace, John D. 8:34;
    18:165
Wallace, John F. 22:133
Wallace, John H. 21:287

Wallace, John J. 22:133;
    23:55
Wallace, John N. 10:85
Wallace, John P. 9:127;
    27:130
Wallace, John S. 18:98;
    21:197
Wallace, Johnson 5:32
Wallace, Jonathan 5:47
Wallace, Joseph 16:259;
    22:227
Wallace, Joseph H.
    17:391
Wallace, L. 3:208; 11:18;
    21:162
Wallace, Levi 21:44
Wallace, Luther 27:132
Wallace, M. 18:387;
    23:174
Wallace, M. L. 17:289
Wallace, M. W. 11:343
Wallace, Mance 21:287
Wallace, Manual 18:267
Wallace, Manuel 26:86
Wallace, N. 14:123
Wallace, O. 1:86
Wallace, O. F. 15:171
Wallace, Oliver 11:185
Wallace, P. 3:208; 9:64
Wallace, Patrick 19:217
Wallace, Peter 7:135
Wallace, R. 12:84;
    16:259, 358
Wallace, R. H. 23:55
Wallace, Richard 17:240
Wallace, Robert 21:107;
    23:174
Wallace, S. 3:208
Wallace, Samuel 8:118;
    19:315; 21:399;
    22:522
Wallace, Sanford 21:287
Wallace, Scott 17:188
Wallace, Seth 25:256
Wallace, Squire 17:140;
    22:325; 24:206
Wallace, Stephen 8:57
Wallace, Stephen J.
    21:262
Wallace, T. 12:84;
    14:313; 16:358;
    17:491; 27:132
Wallace, Thomas 6:26;
    13:53; 19:139;
    21:237
Wallace, Thomas O. 17:88
Wallace, Ubas 25:126
Wallace, V. J. 20:15
Wallace, Verga 21:287
Wallace, W. 1:88; 13:101

Wallace, W. B. 13:75;
16:259
Wallace, W. C. 19:243
Wallace, W. G. 25:273
Wallace, W. L. 13:122
Wallace, W. William
11:324
Wallace, Walter 19:217
Wallace, Wesley 9:197;
19:271
Wallace, William 4:60;
7:45, 114, 135; 8:43,
98; 9:202, 225;
11:175, 223, 283;
13:53, 122; 14:123;
16:61; 17:188;
18:421; 19:139, 285;
22:107, 325; 26:197
Wallace, William B. 9:40;
18:298; 26:116
Wallace, William C. 9:197
Wallace, William H. 7:45;
11:81; 21:115, 399
Wallace, William N.
13:122
Wallace, William Penn
4:60
Wallace, William R.
11:418; 17:60; 22:15
Wallace, William S.
9:225; 18:387
Wallace, Yancey 9:225;
18:387
Wallach, Edward 18:116
Wallach, Sanford 22:107
Wallack, E. B. 15:253
Wallack, Isaiah 11:177
Wallack, Stephen S. 9:107
Wallam, A. J. 23:174
Wallam, David W. 23:82
Wallar, J. S. 24:86
Wallar, M. K. 3:208
Wallard, Joseph 16:391
Wallard, Robert M.
20:149
Wallcart, O. R. 21:144
Walldorf, Ph. 11:195
Wallen, Campbell P.
22:273
Wallenberg, Charles
20:15
Wallenberg, Francis A.
22:59
Wallenhoss, Christopher
11:178
Waller, Alexander 20:131
Waller, C. 3:208
Waller, Charles H. 22:413
Waller, Daniel P. 10:24
Waller, David 23:315
Waller, E. 14:123

Waller, E. J. 11:274
Waller, Francis H. 22:227
Waller, George 5:32
Waller, Harrison 17:357
Waller, J. 14:229
Waller, John 21:399
Waller, John R. 17:240;
22:15
Waller, N. 14:123
Waller, R. 20:385
Waller, Robert B. 17:60
Waller, Rueben 10:85
Waller, Scott 21:213
Waller, T. 20:150
Waller, William 18:185
Wallermyer, William
14:229
Wallers, William M.
17:395
Walles, Charles 19:231
Wallese, T. 21:107
Walley, Henry 16:259
Walley, J. 16:275
Walley, Jerome A. 9:93
Wallians, A. A. 14:123
Wallice, George J. 7:114
Wallig, James E. 18:165
Wallikeck, J. 16:137
Wallin, John 10:141;
20:385
Walling, Daniel 4:60
Walling, Eli 23:55
Walling, F. E. 9:152
Walling, George 3:208
Walling, James E. 8:34
Walling, T. E. 27:127
Wallingford, Charles A.
7:114
Wallingford, James E.
22:413
Wallingford, W. 8:34;
18:165
Wallingsford, John P.
20:26
Wallis, A. 3:208
Wallis, Ben 21:399
Wallis, C. N. 13:101
Wallis, Calvin 11:114
Wallis, E. B. 16:11
Wallis, F. A. 21:44
Wallis, G. 14:229
Wallis, H. 3:208
Wallis, J. 3:208
Wallis, Patrick 9:127
Wallis, S. J. 25:256
Wallis, W. 3:208
Wallis, William 19:217
Wallison, J. 18:73
Wallker, Wallis 21:287
Wallls, Martin 15:290

Wallmouth, George
18:387
Wallon, Daniel 5:47
Wallraven, Thomas
19:139
Wallravin, Thomas 15:335
Wallrod, James G. 9:127
Walls, Alex 16:166
Walls, Benjamin G. 17:60
Walls, C. 22:325
Walls, Cyrenus 12:166
Walls, Cyrus 19:293
Walls, F. 14:229
Walls, G. H. 7:45; 14:334
Walls, H. F. 12:163
Walls, Henry 22:107
Walls, J. W. 3:208
Walls, John H. 8:98
Walls, Jonathan 9:197;
19:269
Walls, Joseph 7:135
Walls, M. 14:123; 20:180
Walls, Peter 3:208
Walls, Philander 18:224
Walls, Sykes 6:26
Walls, Thomas 17:60
Walls, William T. 4:60;
17:309
Wallts, Jeremiah 27:129
Wallus, William L. 9:31
Wallwork, Alfred 20:91
Wallworth, Daniel S.
10:141; 20:385
Walmar, --- 3:208
Walmer, Joseph 13:75;
19:139
Walmer, Joseph D. 13:122
Walmire, D. 25:256
Walmire, L. 20:150
Walmsley, Jeremiah 26:85
Walmsley, W. 18:60
Walmuth, George 9:228
Waln, John 23:290
Waln, John N. 21:399
Walne, Leonard 5:32
Walner, --- 10:207
Walner, Giles 23:55
Walper, Daniel 11:175
Walrath, Daniel G. 1:85
Walraven, Oliver 8:34;
26:200
Walrich, P. 3:208
Walrod, James G. 27:131
Walrond, Charles 22:459
Walse, Benjamin 27:133
Walser, G. W. 22:227
Walser, John 3:208;
22:107
Walsh, A. 10:85; 20:385
Walsh, Benjamin A. 12:44
Walsh, Benjamin B. 8:116

Walsh, Carimer 19:335
Walsh, Charles B. 25:335
Walsh, Charles D. O. 15:346; 16:391
Walsh, D. 27:128
Walsh, Daniel 20:15
Walsh, David 12:44
Walsh, David E. 19:41
Walsh, Edw. P. 7:114
Walsh, Edwin 14:229
Walsh, F. 25:127
Walsh, J. 2:19; 3:208; 8:57; 12:97; 21:44; 25:124
Walsh, J. C. 27:126
Walsh, J. E. 3:208
Walsh, J. H. 21:107
Walsh, Jacob 12:44; 23:126
Walsh, James 1:84, 86; 3:208; 8:116; 22:133
Walsh, John 10:85; 16:259; 20:385; 21:400; 22:163
Walsh, John M. 9:197; 19:263
Walsh, M. 3:208
Walsh, Mary 16:358
Walsh, Michael 7:70; 12:44; 18:117; 19:343; 22:348; 24:70
Walsh, P. 12:84; 16:358
Walsh, Patrick 9:197; 24:10, 70
Walsh, Peter 25:256
Walsh, Phillip 8:123
Walsh, Richard 21:12, 400; 23:55; 25:256
Walsh, Robert 19:41; 21:287
Walsh, T. 1:185
Walsh, T. E. 11:175
Walsh, Thomas 3:208; 9:73; 18:98; 21:262
Walsh, W. 3:208
Walsh, William 9:14; 11:47; 16:61; 19:288; 25:127; 26:214
Walshe, J. 15:362
Walshe, John 11:18
Walshslayer, L. 20:385
Walsin, M. 20:385
Walstern, William 13:122
Walston, G. 16:259
Walston, William 22:227
Walt, Engebe 22:59
Waltby, M. R. 15:253
Waltch, P. 12:86
Walte, Rudolphe 23:174

Waltemeyer, H. J. 15:79
Waltemyer, H. F. 12:78
Walten, John J. 11:82
Walten, Robert 27:133
Waltenbaugh, Andrew 10:141
Waltenberg, G. 1:183
Waltenmyer, C. 16:259
Waltens, John 12:172
Walter, A. B. 1:86
Walter, A. G. 16:358
Walter, Adam 15:253
Walter, Adolph W. 23:197
Walter, Alexander 15:96
Walter, Augustus 25:256
Walter, C. 13:81; 16:259
Walter, C. W. 1:86
Walter, Carl 17:392
Walter, Charles 8:34; 17:73; 18:73, 165
Walter, Christopher 22:227
Walter, Clarence 18:267
Walter, D. 9:152; 27:128
Walter, David 19:319
Walter, David F. 11:418
Walter, E. 18:267; 26:86
Walter, Edm. 25:256
Walter, F. 1:185; 22:494
Walter, Frederick 16:61
Walter, G. 25:256
Walter, George 18:317; 26:115
Walter, Gotleib 5:32
Walter, Gustavus 8:98
Walter, Henry 9:93; 27:127
Walter, Howard J. 19:41
Walter, I. 3:209
Walter, Isaac 12:52
Walter, J. 1:183; 2:19
Walter, J. H. 1:184
Walter, J. W. 12:97; 17:112
Walter, Jacob 7:45
Walter, James 16:259
Walter, Jasper 20:386
Walter, John 5:55; 14:261; 21:144
Walter, John L. 10:85; 20:386
Walter, L. 20:82
Walter, Lewis 5:32
Walter, Love 22:516
Walter, Manley 25:256
Walter, Miles 9:93
Walter, O. F. 14:335; 27:127
Walter, P. 1:182; 17:188
Walter, R. J. 9:229
Walter, Rufus C. 24:57

Walter, S. P. 3:209
Walter, Saffer 17:409
Walter, Seth E. 22:227
Walter, Steffen 22:59
Walter, T. Are. 11:114
Walter, V. 1:181
Walter, W. 3:208; 18:185
Walter, W. H. 18:41
Walter, William 23:14
Walterbury, George O. 18:60
Walterhouse, E. 3:209
Walterman, W. 15:253; 18:60
Waltermyre, H. 3:209
Walternick, Charles 11:317
Walternure, H. A. 18:387
Walters, A. 11:417; 16:275
Walters, A. J. 12:44
Walters, Aaron 23:111
Walters, Albert 13:52
Walters, Albert H. 19:331
Walters, Alfred S. 22:471
Walters, Andrew 11:427
Walters, Archibald 7:114
Walters, Barkin S. 7:45
Walters, Benjamin 1:191
Walters, Benjamin F. 10:85
Walters, C. 3:209; 16:130
Walters, Charles 9:127
Walters, D. 3:209
Walters, Daniel 22:227
Walters, Daniel G. 10:141
Walters, Daniel N. 22:107
Walters, David 14:229; 17:60
Walters, David G. 20:386
Walters, David W. 23:82
Walters, Drury 7:114
Walters, Elias A. 7:114
Walters, F. 3:209
Walters, Francis 18:105
Walters, Francis M. 21:61
Walters, Frederick 8:34; 18:165; 27:156
Walters, G. 1:181; 9:114
Walters, G. J. 23:174
Walters, G. W. 14:249
Walters, George 7:62; 8:34, 57; 14:1; 21:244
Walters, George A. 10:85; 20:386
Walters, George F. 14:123; 22:107
Walters, Green B. 26:86
Walters, H. 12:94; 25:256; 26:83

Walters, Hanson W. 9:17
Walters, Henry 5:32;
    12:44; 18:60; 21:400
Walters, Horatio 19:139
Walters, J. 1:182, 183,
    185; 3:209; 13:101;
    16:259; 24:86
Walters, J. H. 3:209;
    21:133
Walters, J. W. 21:400
Walters, Jackson 8:111
Walters, Jacob 11:216;
    17:61
Walters, James 7:45;
    11:81; 13:52; 25:256
Walters, James E. 8:34;
    18:165
Walters, James M. 11:274
Walters, James S. 18:267;
    26:85
Walters, Jefferson A.
    9:197
Walters, Jefferson D.
    19:265
Walters, Jerome 12:44
Walters, John 9:40;
    11:176; 12:78;
    17:357; 22:133;
    23:174; 25:125
Walters, John B. 5:32
Walters, John C. 22:227
Walters, Joseph H. 21:248
Walters, L. 1:182; 25:256
Walters, Mathew 20:386
Walters, Michael 9:233
Walters, Nelson 3:209;
    16:142; 21:244
Walters, P. 14:261
Walters, Patrick 13:52
Walters, Peter J. 22:16
Walters, Pleasant C. 21:61
Walters, R. 14:229;
    19:217
Walters, R. B. 25:256
Walters, Reuben 14:123
Walters, Samuel 10:85;
    20:386; 22:413
Walters, T. B. 17:152
Walters, Thomas 8:98
Walters, W. 1:182
Walters, W. A. 19:139
Walters, W. M. 26:139
Walters, Watson B. 20:45
Walters, William 10:85;
    11:178; 12:44;
    13:52; 20:150; 23:55
Walters, William J.
    20:386
Waltes, Jacob F. 22:227
Waltge, Charles 16:11
Walthall, James 18:41

Waltham, J. 18:431
Waltham, John 17:365
Walthbaum, Henry 11:177
Walthbrink, Henry 11:178
Walthe, William 15:338
Walthen, J. 17:353
Walther, J. 15:21
Walther, Philip 7:70
Walthers, Patrick 16:61
Waltman, D. 18:116
Waltman, W. 10:150
Waltmyre, Daniel 5:32
Walto, M. 10:178
Walton, --- 20:175
Walton, A. 3:209; 9:64;
    15:79
Walton, A. B. 11:179
Walton, A. S. 12:10
Walton, Amos L. 10:24
Walton, B. 24:86
Walton, Benjamin 22:325
Walton, Charles M. 13:52
Walton, D. 14:229
Walton, David 8:34;
    18:165
Walton, E. 1:184; 15:253;
    23:55
Walton, E. A. 3:209
Walton, Elisha 12:52
Walton, G. W. 27:135
Walton, George 19:139
Walton, George G. 17:208
Walton, H. 9:64
Walton, Henry 21:192
Walton, Herman 10:85;
    20:386
Walton, Hiram W. 22:444
Walton, I. 23:174
Walton, J. 3:209; 16:111
Walton, J. D. 1:184
Walton, J. W. 15:362;
    19:139
Walton, Jackson 11:98
Walton, Jacob A. 22:59
Walton, James 12:44;
    17:399
Walton, James A. 8:34,
    57; 18:165
Walton, James H. 19:331;
    20:187
Walton, James M. 17:213
Walton, John 4:60;
    10:141; 20:386;
    26:139
Walton, John B. 22:444;
    24:86
Walton, John F. 11:176
Walton, Joseph 14:229
Walton, Levi 24:205
Walton, Marion 10:203
Walton, Matt 21:287

Walton, Miles 1:86
Walton, N. 3:209
Walton, Nathan 22:107
Walton, Polk 17:188
Walton, R. 27:131
Walton, R. G. 21:169
Walton, Riley 18:73
Walton, Robert 10:141;
    18:267; 20:386;
    26:87
Walton, Samuel 17:253
Walton, William 10:141;
    12:44; 20:386
Walton, William H. 5:32;
    22:286; 25:256
Waltons, H. 16:358
Waltos, J. 15:296
Waltrip, James J. 23:102
Waltros, J. 25:256
Waltrout, W. R. 1:184
Walts, Charles 15:147
Walts, Henry 24:70
Walts, Jesse H. 22:107
Walts, John 22:107
Walts, O. F. 25:125
Waltus, J. 15:61
Walty, I. 17:297
Walty, J. 3:209
Waltz, A. 1:86
Waltz, Daniel 13:122
Waltz, George 21:262
Waltz, J. 1:88
Waltz, John 8:98, 116;
    16:259; 18:328;
    21:262
Waltz, L. J. 25:256
Waltz, Lewis J. 5:32
Waltz, M. 3:209
Waltz, O. S. 20:180
Waltz, Samuel 22:413
Waltz, Socrates 10:141
Waltze, Socrates 20:386
Waltzworth, C. 14:124
Walwork, T. 3:209
Walworth, C. 3:209
Walworth, F. W. 18:41
Walwroth, Andrew 20:32
Walz, F. 1:183
Wamack, J. A. 20:85
Wamack, William H.
    22:133
Wambyer, F. 13:122
Wammamaugher, Samuel
    16:61
Wampler, William 17:262
Wampshire, Samuel
    23:183
Wamscott, A. 9:64
Wamsley, A. 9:225;
    18:388
Wamsley, W. 15:346

Wamsley, William 16:391
Wan, Benjamin 20:386
Wan, William 18:165
Wanaker, George 17:188
Wanamacher, Harrison 22:16
Wanatove, J. B. 21:197
Wanbold, H. H. 20:87
Wance, Rich 11:338
Wancel, Lorenzo 24:33
Wandaker, G. 12:97
Wandall, Benjamin 17:69
Wandel, William R. 4:60
Wandell, Jacob 10:24
Wandell, S. 1:86
Wanderer, John 14:267
Wanderlick, G. 14:123
Wanderling, W. H. 11:185
Wandley, John 10:141; 20:386
Wandling, D. 11:383
Wands, Charles 15:51
Wane, Daniel 8:58; 21:162
Wanfrect, Enos 19:139
Wanfred, E. 15:310
Wanger, H. 1:183
Wanger, John 24:73
Wanhoozer, George 17:61
Wanhum, George O. 18:165
Wanie, John A. 20:386
Waning, Stephen 9:137
Wanjchenk, C. 19:276
Wanke, L. 21:207
Wanmuck, Richard 18:165
Wannamaugher, Samuel 13:53
Wanner, --- 16:391
Wanner, F. 27:126
Wano, John A. 10:85
Wans, Samuel 9:46
Wansbraugh, George J. 20:150
Wanser, Logan 22:325
Wanshn, Daniel 18:60
Wanst, Claus 16:358
Wanters, Augustus 23:177
Wanther, W. M. W. 21:44
Wanton, Sarah 27:131
Wants, A. 13:101
Wants, Jacob 12:60
WanWormer, Frank 13:52
Wanzee, Ludwick 21:262
Wanzer, E. 10:85; 20:386
Wanzer, J. R. 17:275
Wanzer, Sidney 18:270
Wap, David 25:257
Wappner, John 14:229
War---, ---r 25:127

War---, W. T. 24:115
Waran, J. 1:88
Warbeck, Anton 19:41
Warbritton, Eli 8:98
Warbritton, William 22:107
Warbritton, William M. 22:444
Warbulton, James 7:114
Warburn, Jesse A. 9:93
Warchonier, William 27:130
Ward, --- 17:365; 19:139; 23:102
Ward, --- (Mrs.) 10:175
Ward, A. 3:209; 14:123; 15:253
Ward, A. F. 16:259
Ward, A. J. 12:159; 15:164
Ward, Aaron 11:216
Ward, Aaron T. 4:60
Ward, Abram R. 20:109
Ward, Albert 27:156
Ward, Alfred 20:26
Ward, Andrew J. 22:227
Ward, Andy 17:188
Ward, Andy J. 11:317
Ward, Apen 21:89
Ward, Archibald 11:82
Ward, Arthur 11:418
Ward, Ashley 22:325
Ward, Augustus 11:274
Ward, B. F. 11:87; 14:285; 15:9
Ward, Ben 11:47
Ward, Benjamin 15:25
Ward, C. 3:209; 15:253
Ward, C. A. B. 21:400
Ward, C. H. 1:182
Ward, Calvin M. 11:82
Ward, Carlos M. 10:169
Ward, Carlos P. 19:217
Ward, Carrol 22:325
Ward, Charles 5:47; 8:35; 18:165; 25:257
Ward, Charles D. 24:71
Ward, Charles O. 9:64
Ward, Chauncey C. 12:44
Ward, D. 3:209; 16:259; 20:386
Ward, D. C. 22:524
Ward, D. W. 18:185
Ward, Damascus 19:41
Ward, Daniel 12:172; 15:332; 19:139
Ward, Darius 1:85
Ward, David 11:18, 48; 15:51; 21:262
Ward, E. 13:122; 14:333
Ward, E. A. 7:62

Ward, E. C. 14:123; 16:358
Ward, E. S. 13:75; 16:260
Ward, E. T. 17:45
Ward, Eaton 11:215
Ward, Ebenezer 7:70
Ward, Edmund 9:212
Ward, Edward 21:287; 25:257
Ward, Elijah G. 23:197
Ward, Elmer H. 11:317
Ward, Emanuel 23:102
Ward, Enos 10:141; 20:386
Ward, Erastus E. 4:60
Ward, F. 16:275
Ward, Francis H. 17:499
Ward, Francis M. 11:317
Ward, Franklin 8:43; 26:198
Ward, Frederick C. 15:79
Ward, G. P. 3:209
Ward, G. W. 3:209; 14:123
Ward, Garwin 22:445
Ward, George 16:8; 21:118; 23:206
Ward, George J. 24:10
Ward, George R. 25:257
Ward, George W. 22:107; 23:94
Ward, Green 23:200
Ward, H. 3:209; 14:123; 16:275; 25:128
Ward, H. B. 14:123
Ward, H. F. 9:64
Ward, Harrison 8:98
Ward, Harvey 11:273
Ward, Henry 19:338; 21:94, 287
Ward, Henry W. 10:141; 20:386
Ward, Hiram 23:197
Ward, I. L. 1:88
Ward, I. S. 17:481
Ward, Ira 3:209
Ward, Isaac 14:123
Ward, Isaac L. 11:334
Ward, Isaac M. 15:147
Ward, J. 1:182; 3:209; 12:78; 14:249; 15:61; 25:257
Ward, J. B. 15:253; 16:391
Ward, J. E. 9:114
Ward, J. F. 1:184; 21:400
Ward, J. H. 2:19; 25:128
Ward, J. P. 20:82
Ward, J. S. 1:181; 14:313; 19:314; 27:132

Ward, Jacob 5:32; 16:391; 22:227
Ward, James 1:88; 5:32; 7:45; 8:35; 9:238; 11:234; 13:53; 18:165; 19:316; 22:59, 273; 23:94; 24:103; 26:234
Ward, James A. 1:86
Ward, James D. 8:68; 26:199
Ward, James M. 11:254; 23:126
Ward, James S. 19:217
Ward, Jerome B. 5:55; 25:257
Ward, Jesse 17:88
Ward, John 1:84; 7:15; 9:64, 158; 12:78; 13:53; 14:123, 229; 15:51; 16:285; 19:41, 49; 21:45; 22:16, 59
Ward, John E. 15:331; 19:139; 21:107
Ward, John H. 20:15
Ward, John L. 11:393
Ward, John M. 20:15
Ward, John S. 19:231
Ward, John W. 7:62; 9:30; 18:317; 22:158; 26:116
Ward, Jona 24:215
Ward, Jonas P. 23:94
Ward, Josephus 9:225; 18:388
Ward, Josiah 9:152; 27:127
Ward, Julius 14:326; 21:45
Ward, L. 11:317
Ward, L. L. 17:232
Ward, Lamson 4:60
Ward, Lansan 20:386
Ward, Laurence 7:114
Ward, Lawson 10:85
Ward, Lester M. 10:141; 20:386
Ward, Levi T. 10:178
Ward, Lewis 1:85
Ward, Louis T. 10:152
Ward, Luke W. 8:98
Ward, Luther H. 11:290
Ward, M. 14:123
Ward, M. H. 1:182
Ward, Martin 6:34; 25:329
Ward, Merris 15:51
Ward, Morgan L. 10:24
Ward, Morris 12:78
Ward, Moses 22:325
Ward, N. 17:69

Ward, N. S. 12:91; 16:358
Ward, Nathaniel 22:469
Ward, Nicholas 26:132
Ward, O. 14:123
Ward, O. K. 3:209
Ward, Oliver 9:100
Ward, Oren 11:87
Ward, Orrin B. 7:114
Ward, P. 3:209
Ward, Pat 10:145
Ward, Patrick 19:217; 22:348
Ward, Peter 9:197; 10:168; 14:276; 17:500; 19:263; 21:127
Ward, Philip 22:510
Ward, Pleasant H. 20:20
Ward, R. A. 7:76; 25:307
Ward, R. S. 3:209
Ward, Randle 25:257
Ward, Ranson 10:141; 20:386
Ward, Raymond 17:61
Ward, Richard 8:35; 18:165
Ward, Richard E. 22:133
Ward, Robert 11:253
Ward, Romeo H. 10:24
Ward, S. 3:209; 17:140; 24:206
Ward, Samuel 4:60; 20:131
Ward, Shelby 6:19, 22; 18:98
Ward, Smith 4:60
Ward, Solomon 23:102
Ward, Stephen 4:60
Ward, Sylvester 11:177
Ward, T. 23:55; 26:83
Ward, T. B. 3:225
Ward, T. H. 17:157
Ward, Thomas 9:93; 10:99; 11:80, 317; 14:229; 17:188; 21:45, 133, 400; 22:459; 25:257
Ward, Thomas J. 17:61; 22:459
Ward, Timothy 9:93; 26:83
Ward, Toply 11:427
Ward, W. 3:209; 12:90; 13:101; 14:24; 16:358; 25:257
Ward, W. A. 3:209
Ward, W. F. 14:123
Ward, W. G. 4:60
Ward, W. H. 7:62; 16:61; 21:13; 25:257
Ward, W. R. 1:181

Ward, W. W. 1:184; 7:45
Ward, Warren 10:141
Ward, Wesley 9:64
Ward, William 5:32; 7:73; 8:35; 9:101, 225, 241; 10:24, 141; 12:159; 13:53, 126; 15:346; 16:391; 18:388; 19:319; 20:386; 21:400; 22:107, 273, 494; 23:55, 174; 24:103; 25:284; 27:125, 129
Ward, William B. 24:33
Ward, William H. 11:405; 20:32; 21:400; 22:16; 23:55
Ward, William H. H. 18:224
Ward, William J. 22:59
Ward, William W. 9:233
Wardecker, Samuel 22:348
Wardel, George W. 8:98
Wardell, C. P. 1:183
Wardell, George A. 13:53
Wardell, J. 1:87
Wardell, J. W. 19:139
Wardell, John 4:60
Wardell, N. B. 14:1
Wardell, Webster 10:24
Warden, Adam 11:216
Warden, Anton E. 25:127
Warden, B. 19:326
Warden, Charles 18:342
Warden, Charles P. 23:243
Warden, Clayton 22:227
Warden, Daniel 9:64
Warden, Erastus S. 13:53
Warden, G. W. 23:174
Warden, H. 3:209
Warden, H. B. 3:209
Warden, J. 13:101; 18:388
Warden, James H. 23:174
Warden, John B. 21:400
Warden, John F. 20:150
Warden, L. 1:181
Warden, R. 14:29
Warden, Robert 11:177
Warden, Stephen S. 14:229
Warden, W. S. 9:93
Warden, William 11:185, 195
Wardenfelt, J. 3:209
Warder, A. J. 9:225
Wardike, S. 16:260
Wardle, Freeman 21:400
Wardler, John 22:227
Wardlow, Mal 21:162

Wardls, W. H. 15:51
Wardman, J. 16:275
Wardman, Thomas
   13:101; 14:24
Wardner, G. 3:209
Wardroler, R. 14:123
Wardrupt, P. W. 18:388
Wardrupts, P. W. 9:225
Wardsworth, F. E. 19:231
Wardsworth, W. 19:243
Wardwell, Emers 15:4
Wardwell, Emerson 12:78
Wardwell, J. H. 1:86
Wardwell, Thomas H.
   12:78
Wardwell, William 19:217
Ware, --- 10:168
Ware, A. H. 16:260
Ware, Alex 10:36
Ware, Alexander 19:314
Ware, Charles 20:87
Ware, D. D. 1:181
Ware, George R. 13:53
Ware, George W. 14:317;
   22:444
Ware, H. H. 13:126
Ware, H. S. 13:53
Ware, Henry A. 27:131
Ware, Henry B. 9:93;
   26:84
Ware, Henry P. 27:132
Ware, Isaac 27:133
Ware, J. B. 3:209
Ware, J. P. 24:70
Ware, J. R. 20:86
Ware, Jacob S. 22:114
Ware, James 6:9; 15:114;
   18:98
Ware, James P. 7:45
Ware, John 23:250
Ware, Levi 21:400
Ware, Lewis 20:386
Ware, Logan 8:43; 26:198
Ware, Marcus 21:94
Ware, Oscar B. 22:286
Ware, Peter 12:44
Ware, R. C. 1:180
Ware, S. D. 14:229
Ware, Sam 26:86
Ware, Samuel 3:209;
   18:267
Ware, Stephen 13:75;
   19:139
Ware, W. W. 12:163
Ware, Wilbert 27:134
Ware, William 9:17;
   20:101
Ware, William F. 21:237
Warefield, James 17:188
Warehaser, George O.
   8:35

Warehouse, Josephus
   18:165
Warehuire, D. 23:95
Wares, David 11:101
Wares, M. B. 10:141;
   20:386
Warfel, David 14:337
Warffender, J. W. 3:209
Warfield, A. W. 10:150;
   18:60
Warfield, Benjamin 17:45
Warfield, C. 14:229
Warfield, E. 12:94;
   14:123
Warfield, G. W. 11:274
Warfield, Gilford 24:33
Warfield, J. L. 5:47;
   25:257
Warfield, Owen B. 19:41
Warfield, P. 9:73; 12:139
Warfield, Richard 21:287;
   22:59
Warfield, W. H. 17:157
Warfield, William H. H.
   20:101
Warfield, William W.
   20:184; 23:55
Warford, A. 21:400
Warford, Joseph 22:227
Warford, Simeon B.
   22:114
Warhurst, Samuel 3:209
Warhurst, W. 1:184
Warick, John 23:82
Warick, N. 14:229
Waring, Charles M.
   21:262
Waring, Q. 25:257
Waring, Thomas 3:209
Waring, Watford 17:452
Waris, John 25:257
Wark, G. F. 15:253
Warker, Mathew 17:251
Warkinger, Sylvester
   22:107
Warle, William H. 11:81
Warlet, S. A. O. 25:257
Warlett, John C. 8:98
Warlett, S. A. E. 5:33
Warley, George 21:61
Warley, Robert 10:175;
   19:217
Warlham, Josephus 8:35
Warling, David 21:237
Warm, W. A. 10:191
Warmack, Richard 8:35
Warmack, Thomas J.
   20:386
Warman, David 26:146
Warman, Edward 15:308
Warman, G. W. 20:45

Warmann, P. 13:75
Warmer, M. F. 20:386
Warmesley, Wesley 20:32
Warmick, Andrew 15:15
Warmon, --- 14:123
Warmstick, F. 25:257
Warn, --- 15:114
Warn, John 17:354
Warn, Mark A. 26:84
Warn, W. R. 18:185
Warnach, C. C. 8:57
Warnach, E. 16:359
Warnach, John E. 24:108
Warnack, E. 12:84
Warnack, Thomas J.
   10:141
Warnake, Benjamin
   11:216
Warne, George N. 25:257
Warnecker, Henry 10:85
Warneka, Henry 20:386
Warnen, Frederick 4:60
Warner, --- 19:323;
   21:197
Warner, A. 3:209
Warner, A. F. 3:209
Warner, A. K. 4:60
Warner, Aaron 17:88
Warner, Abraham A.
   21:400
Warner, Adam 11:179
Warner, Adney 14:229
Warner, Adson 18:417
Warner, Albert 4:60
Warner, Albert O. 23:197
Warner, Andrew 9:159
Warner, B. F. 3:209;
   16:61
Warner, C. H. 20:37
Warner, C. J. 14:267
Warner, C. P. 2:19
Warner, C. S. 3:209;
   14:292
Warner, C. W. 3:209
Warner, Caleb 4:60
Warner, Charles 1:88;
   8:35; 12:78; 18:165,
   409; 19:41
Warner, Charles H. 13:53
Warner, Charles J. 23:55
Warner, Charles R.
   15:253
Warner, Charles S.
   14:292; 23:55
Warner, D. 3:209; 11:318;
   14:285; 16:391
Warner, Daniel 15:61
Warner, David 17:285
Warner, David H. 10:24
Warner, Delos W. 22:469
Warner, E. 3:209; 11:317

Warner, E. L. 1:183
Warner, E. T. 15:321
Warner, Edgar 4:60
Warner, Edgar F. 9:127
Warner, Edmund C. 7:114
Warner, Edward A.
   16:142
Warner, Emery 7:114
Warner, Ethan E. 21:145
Warner, Ezra G. 19:139
Warner, F. 19:263
Warner, F. F. 25:124
Warner, Foster 17:27
Warner, Frank 19:139
Warner, Franklin 7:45
Warner, Frederick D.
   22:413
Warner, G. 25:126
Warner, G. A. 10:141;
   20:386
Warner, G. R. 3:209
Warner, G. W. 11:234;
   15:79
Warner, George 10:141;
   11:48; 12:60
Warner, George E.
   10:141; 20:386
Warner, George W.
   22:443
Warner, H. 3:209
Warner, H. C. 26:199
Warner, Harvey 13:53
Warner, Henry 10:85,
   142; 20:386; 22:494;
   24:73
Warner, Henry T. 10:85;
   20:387
Warner, Hillimas 11:81
Warner, Hiram 24:57
Warner, Horace 11:405
Warner, Horace M.
   10:169; 19:217
Warner, J. 1:184; 3:209,
   210; 9:160; 10:31;
   16:135, 391; 17:432;
   18:267; 19:289;
   20:150; 26:85
Warner, J. F. 19:321
Warner, J. N. 16:111
Warner, J. S. 12:159
Warner, J. W. 20:387
Warner, Jack 17:107
Warner, Jacob 17:210
Warner, James W. 24:33
Warner, Jarvis 14:229
Warner, Jeremiah 23:102
Warner, John 12:52;
   13:122; 21:61;
   22:107; 23:174;
   25:257
Warner, John D. 20:101

Warner, John E. 7:45;
   14:335
Warner, John F. 9:197;
   15:89
Warner, John H. 17:348
Warner, John M. 11:177
Warner, John W. 4:60;
   10:85; 21:237;
   23:183
Warner, Joseph 8:35;
   11:176, 179; 13:53;
   16:61; 17:452;
   18:165; 19:217;
   24:181; 26:200
Warner, Just 16:111
Warner, L. 3:210; 14:229
Warner, L. D. 8:35;
   18:165
Warner, Layman C. 24:73
Warner, Leander 25:257
Warner, Leonard 18:402
Warner, Levi 23:278
Warner, Lewis 15:262
Warner, Loaman 20:387
Warner, Lowman 10:85
Warner, Luther 3:210
Warner, M. 3:210
Warner, M. B. 12:139;
   15:147; 17:45
Warner, M. F. 10:85
Warner, M. S. 19:263
Warner, Marion 11:176
Warner, Mason 23:82
Warner, O. 1:186
Warner, Orange 21:287
Warner, P. 1:184
Warner, P. P. 3:210
Warner, Peter 9:238;
   18:224; 22:443;
   26:234
Warner, Phineas F. 13:53
Warner, R. C. 7:45
Warner, Reuben 20:387
Warner, Robert 10:85;
   20:387
Warner, Robert P. 8:111
Warner, Rudolph 18:21
Warner, S. 3:210
Warner, S. C. 22:227
Warner, S. N. 16:130
Warner, Samuel A. 7:45
Warner, Sherman H.
   13:53
Warner, Silas 21:287
Warner, Simon 23:174
Warner, Solomon L.
   11:185
Warner, Thomas 19:41;
   20:387
Warner, Thomas W.
   23:253

Warner, W. 23:206
Warner, W. B. 19:246
Warner, W. H. 11:131
Warner, W. S. 9:197
Warner, Washington
   11:87
Warner, William 4:60;
   8:35; 9:197; 15:324;
   17:151; 18:98;
   19:139, 264
Warner, William D. 15:89
Warner, William E.
   10:169; 19:217
Warner, William H. 8:98;
   12:44; 22:286
Warner, William R.
   23:261
Warner, Wilson 17:188;
   21:287
Warnermaker, William L.
   13:53
Warnes, Daniel 22:107
Warnfotts, John 18:185
Warnick, Joseph 4:60
Warnick, Samuel 21:61
Warnick, William 1:85;
   12:52
Warnock, Alfred 22:517
Warnock, Archibald
   17:277
Warnock, Daniel 15:114
Warnock, H. 24:33
Warnock, John R. 17:309
Warnock, William 8:35;
   18:165
Warnor, J. A. 5:32
Warple, M. 1:88
Warr, Austin C. 21:262
Warr, Charles S. 21:94
Warr, George 20:387
Warran, Jonathan 14:229
Warrell, --- 9:127
Warrell, C. 3:210
Warrell, J. W. 3:210
Warrell, John M. 20:387
Warren, --- 16:83; 19:139
Warren, A. 3:210; 10:185;
   11:175; 14:123;
   18:185
Warren, Abel 6:21;
   25:127
Warren, Adelbert V.
   23:197
Warren, Alden 7:54
Warren, Alford 18:224
Warren, Alfred H. 22:227
Warren, Alonzo 27:133
Warren, Bartlett 11:255
Warren, Benjamin 13:126
Warren, C. 9:228; 18:388

Warren, C. A. 14:313; 17:472; 27:132
Warren, C. L. 24:33
Warren, Charles 10:168; 17:188; 22:107
Warren, Charles W. 22:107
Warren, D. J. 17:441; 24:155
Warren, D. O. 1:183
Warren, Daniel 7:114
Warren, Daniel S. 22:158
Warren, E. 3:210; 16:260
Warren, E. F. 3:210
Warren, Edward 9:229; 12:44; 14:237
Warren, Edward B. 21:400
Warren, Elijah 17:501
Warren, Ephraim 9:238; 26:234
Warren, Ezra B. 17:69
Warren, F. 7:54; 13:101
Warren, F. D. 23:201
Warren, Francis 9:93
Warren, Francis L. 20:131
Warren, Francis M. 17:200
Warren, G. 1:181; 3:210
Warren, G. B. 9:93
Warren, G. O. 3:210
Warren, G. W. 26:84
Warren, George 4:60; 5:32; 21:400; 23:272; 25:257
Warren, George J. 23:82
Warren, George W. 4:60; 12:44; 23:82
Warren, Gilbert W. 22:286
Warren, Gustavus W. 9:93
Warren, H. 3:210; 13:101; 25:257
Warren, H. S. 1:88
Warren, Harvey E. 17:289
Warren, Henry 1:87; 5:47; 20:387
Warren, Hiram B. 11:179
Warren, I. 20:152; 21:45; 26:84
Warren, Isaac 20:117
Warren, J. 1:86; 2:19; 9:93
Warren, J. B. 1:100
Warren, J. H. 22:273
Warren, J. M. 14:123; 15:178
Warren, J. R. 25:280
Warren, Jacob 22:59
Warren, James 1:88; 21:400

Warren, James A. 24:150
Warren, James C. 22:494
Warren, James K. 23:55
Warren, James W. 7:135; 21:83
Warren, Jeremiah 18:211
Warren, Jerome B. 9:40
Warren, John 17:167; 22:158
Warren, John B. 27:126
Warren, John E. 22:107
Warren, John H. 18:224
Warren, John W. 7:76; 21:400; 25:307
Warren, Jordan 21:162
Warren, Joseph 18:165; 21:219
Warren, Joseph H. 4:60
Warren, Joseph W. 13:80
Warren, Josiah W. 16:260
Warren, L. 3:210
Warren, Lewis 8:35; 18:165
Warren, Lorenzo 27:130
Warren, Louis J. 9:127
Warren, M. A. 21:400
Warren, M. T. 15:253
Warren, Mac 8:58
Warren, Mack 21:162
Warren, Major 23:200
Warren, Manuel 10:99
Warren, Marion M. 17:201
Warren, Marshall E. 5:33
Warren, Michael G. 17:208
Warren, Mill 7:114
Warren, Moses 2:19
Warren, Moses Scott 21:262
Warren, N. G. 14:229
Warren, Nathan 9:197; 19:243
Warren, O. 14:123
Warren, Oisiman 19:217
Warren, Oliver 14:123
Warren, Orinton 9:158
Warren, Orren 18:60
Warren, Orville A. 16:135
Warren, P. 3:210; 16:260
Warren, P. A. G. 21:45
Warren, R. 20:131
Warren, R. V. 9:64
Warren, Richard 8:43, 57; 11:215; 22:107, 173; 26:198
Warren, Richard T. 21:83
Warren, Robert 17:188
Warren, S. 18:98
Warren, S. W. 15:178

Warren, Samuel 12:172; 20:143
Warren, Sanborne 11:216
Warren, T. 1:86
Warren, T. S. 19:41
Warren, Theodore M. 23:126
Warren, Thomas C. 23:243
Warren, Thomas J. 20:187
Warren, W. 7:45; 14:123
Warren, W. G. 10:207
Warren, W. H. 3:210
Warren, W. P. 3:210
Warren, Walter A. 22:445
Warren, William 10:8; 11:99; 15:164; 17:61; 18:165, 282; 19:139; 22:16, 273; 23:116
Warren, William H. 24:215
Warren, William W. 23:197
Warren, Zachariah 20:387
Warrenburg, W. H. 17:427
Warrenburg, William H. 24:181
Warrener, Frederick 27:133
Warrick, G. W. 18:224
Warrick, George W. 22:107
Warrick, James 21:83
Warrick, Jeanda 15:348
Warrick, M. V. B. 11:330
Warrick, W. P. 16:61
Warrick, William 22:59
Warriner, S. P. 1:88
Warriner, William N. 21:262
Warring, Benjamin 11:131
Warring, George E. 25:125
Warring, S. 1:183
Warring, Sampson 27:130
Warring, Stephen 27:130
Warring, W. H. 13:101
Warring, Westford 24:181
Warringter, A. 1:86
Warrington, G. W. 1:83
Warrington, John 8:126
Warrington, Miles 11:177
Warrington, William 11:113
Warrren, George G. 15:61
Warsen, Alexander 10:85
Warsen, Charles W. 20:387
Warshu, Daniel 10:150

Warskinbry, P. 14:329, 332
Warson, Alexander 20:387
Warson, Charles W. 10:85
Wart, C. 3:210
Wart, George 3:210
Wartell, E. 9:46
Warten, J. F. 23:82
Wartenbe, N. 23:174
Warter, John 4:60
Warthan, R. 22:325
Warthen, Carr E. 10:85
Warther, C. E. 20:387
Warthew, James 20:150
Warthing, Charles W. 23:174
Warthley, J. 25:257
Warthrop, --- 15:51
Wartin, John L. 9:225
Wartman, Lewis 9:46
Wartmouth, J. S. 8:76
Warton, J. 16:275
Wartrum, W. A. 21:400
Warts, R. 27:132
Wartuck, J. 3:210
Warver, Franz J. 22:286
Warvil, --- 21:45
Warwick, A. 12:97
Warwick, Calvin 21:237
Warwick, E. 3:210
Warwick, E. M. 25:275
Warwick, Henry 23:265
Warwick, J. 22:227; 25:257
Warwick, Jackson 22:495
Warwick, Jacob 17:321
Warwick, N. 3:210
Warwick, Samuel W. 23:278
Warwick, William 18:402
Warychenk, Charles 9:197
Warzy, A. 17:157
Wasahburn, J. L. 8:57
Wasburn, T. 1:88
Wasbury, Frederick 7:62
Waschall, Harry 18:342
Wasden, William 7:114
Wase, D. 16:260
Wasen, George W. 21:107
Waserum, G. 3:210
Wash, Arnold 26:199
Wash, Daniel D. 18:166
Wash, George 10:85; 20:387
Wash, John M. 10:178
Wash, Josiah 7:54
Wash, W. D. 9:64
Washam, Richard 17:268
Washburn, --- 8:123; 9:93; 26:83

Washburn, A. D. 15:253
Washburn, Adelbert 4:60
Washburn, Benjamin L. 27:126
Washburn, Conrad 19:217
Washburn, D. 9:114; 14:24, 123
Washburn, Daniel 12:78; 15:13
Washburn, David 17:503
Washburn, E. F. 11:292
Washburn, Edwin C. 17:363
Washburn, Eli 23:55
Washburn, F. 3:210
Washburn, F. S. 18:402
Washburn, F. T. 14:123
Washburn, Frank 10:191; 18:185
Washburn, George 12:44
Washburn, George W. 21:145
Washburn, H. 13:101
Washburn, Henry C. 23:111
Washburn, Ira C. 21:237
Washburn, Isaac 8:68; 11:131
Washburn, James M. 17:502
Washburn, Jesse A. 26:83
Washburn, John 22:59, 107
Washburn, John W. 22:443
Washburn, Joseph G. 15:253
Washburn, Julius 9:14
Washburn, L. 13:101; 14:229
Washburn, L. Z. 1:185
Washburn, Luther 9:197; 19:264
Washburn, M. 19:139; 26:84
Washburn, Marcus 9:93
Washburn, Marian 18:211
Washburn, Milton 17:245
Washburn, N. 3:210
Washburn, Oliver 15:283
Washburn, Orison H. 20:33
Washburn, R. H. 3:210
Washburn, Richard 19:217
Washburn, S. 19:246
Washburn, Sam 9:197
Washburn, Samuel W. 17:27
Washburn, W. E. 3:210

Washburn, Wallace 17:289
Washburn, Watson J. 9:216
Washburn, William 11:113; 18:288; 26:136
Washburne, A. 12:94; 14:123; 15:322; 16:359
Washburne, Charles 16:359
Washburne, D. 14:123
Washburne, David L. 16:359
Washburne, Erastus 1:88
Washburne, George W. 24:98
Washburne, I. 14:123
Washburne, Ira 9:152
Washburne, Martin B. 15:13
Washburne, Oliver 25:257
Washburne, Oscar F. 5:33
Washburne, Watson G. 21:400
Washburne, Wiley 17:240
Washburne, William 23:55
Washer, Benjamin 21:400
Washer, Dick 18:267; 26:86
Washer, H. T. 20:387
Washer, Lyman 12:78
Washington, --- 25:335
Washington, A. 5:47; 25:257
Washington, A. Y. 12:44
Washington, Aaron 25:308
Washington, Abram 7:79
Washington, Albert 8:43; 26:200
Washington, Alexander 7:136
Washington, Alford 21:287
Washington, Allen 21:213
Washington, B. 17:400
Washington, Ben 9:202
Washington, Benjamin 19:285
Washington, Charles 13:59
Washington, Clayborn 21:287
Washington, Clayborne 21:213
Washington, D. 25:257
Washington, David 11:216; 23:272

Washington, Dennis 5:47; 17:192
Washington, E. 7:79
Washington, E. G. 9:30
Washington, Elias 9:225
Washington, Ernest 11:217
Washington, F. 25:307
Washington, Fred 6:26
Washington, G. 10:207; 16:260; 21:113; 25:257
Washington, Gabriel 9:137; 27:129
Washington, Geary 9:225
Washington, Gee 22:348
Washington, General 18:267; 26:87
Washington, George 4:60; 5:47; 6:19, 26; 7:135, 136; 8:43, 68, 69, 111, 116; 9:9, 64, 70, 137, 158, 167, 202, 212; 10:99, 209; 11:216, 217; 12:52, 160, 163; 16:260; 17:140, 188, 509; 18:73, 98, 201, 267, 388; 19:285; 21:213, 287, 400; 22:59, 326, 517; 24:207; 25:287, 329; 26:86, 198; 27:129, 130, 156
Washington, George A. 21:287
Washington, H. 18:73; 25:257
Washington, Henry 5:47; 8:43; 17:188; 21:400; 26:200
Washington, Hy 18:73
Washington, Isaac 11:215
Washington, J. 3:210; 18:201; 25:257
Washington, Jacob 9:162
Washington, James 5:47; 12:52; 22:348
Washington, James E. 26:200
Washington, Jenser 14:229
Washington, Jerry 7:136
Washington, John 7:136; 18:98; 21:400
Washington, Jordan 5:47
Washington, Joseph 11:216; 21:400
Washington, Josiah 19:49
Washington, L. 19:49; 25:257

Washington, Lafayette 9:202; 19:293
Washington, Levi 22:108
Washington, Levy 19:323
Washington, Malvin 21:288
Washington, N. 7:136
Washington, O. 16:260
Washington, Palmer 16:260
Washington, Parish 24:103
Washington, Peter 7:136; 12:52
Washington, Philip 25:287; 27:156
Washington, Robert 1:193; 6:26
Washington, S. 9:202
Washington, Samuel 6:26
Washington, Sandy 7:136; 12:52
Washington, Stewart 22:325
Washington, T. 21:113; 25:257
Washington, Thomas 6:19; 8:100; 9:197; 18:98, 267; 19:285; 21:400; 26:87
Washington, William 6:26; 16:260
Washington, Z. 15:253
Washington, Z. J. 22:326
Washlagen, L. 9:233
Washman, George 17:394
Washman, Oscar 15:147
Washman, W. 22:326
Washpuh, Ira 27:129
Wasingle, Samuel 11:217
Waskoff, W. 14:123
Wasmer, J. H. 11:234
Wasner, Mark 1:84
Wason, S. 14:24
Waspis, M. 1:88
Wass, Lewis 9:197
Wass, T. 11:99
Wassenburg, John 22:238
Wasser, John 19:331
Wasser, P. 14:313; 17:477; 27:132
Wasserbach, Daniel C. 27:126
Wassermann, T. 11:317
Wasson, B. E. 21:401
Wasson, David N. 23:95
Wasson, Florence 14:229
Wasson, J. M. 8:68
Wasson, Jacob 14:317
Wasson, John 11:80
Wasson, John A. 21:85

Wasson, John D. 18:224
Wasson, Palmer 22:495
Wasson, S. 13:101
Wasson, Samuel 15:51
Wasson, Samuel B. 20:20
Wasson, Thomas J. 16:137
Wasson, William 11:87
Wasten, Th. 14:229
Waster, D. A. 19:217
Waster, John T. 22:286
Wastrant, John M. 16:111
Wat, --- 10:150; 18:60
Watcher, Henry 9:137
Watcher, John 10:24
Watches, G. 1:84
Watchler, August 26:83
Watchman, S. 5:47
Watchold, L. 15:61
Watchter, J. 3:210
Wate, P. A. 18:21
Wateman, George 9:40
Wateman, J. 9:152
Water, Henry 9:152; 13:122; 27:127
Water, L. 25:257
Water, Warren 13:53
Waterbury, George H. 19:331
Waterbury, J. 27:128
Waterbury, N. J. 19:325
Waterbury, Peter L. 23:126
Waterbury, W. B. 14:123
Waterfield, Edward 19:319
Waterfield, George 22:16
Waterhouse, B. F. 19:231
Waterhouse, F. 13:122
Waterhouse, James E. 24:62
Waterhouse, Michael 23:116
Waterhouse, Miles J. 15:93
Waterhouse, S. J. 19:217
Waterhouse, Samuel 10:169
Waterhouse, W. 3:210
Waterhouse, William D. 23:259
Waterhouse, William H. 22:445
Waterland, John 8:35; 18:166
Waterman, --- 15:275
Waterman, Adin 11:253
Waterman, Adna 17:357
Waterman, Alfred 12:44
Waterman, Arthur S. 13:53

Waterman, Charles 13:75; 19:139; 25:257
Waterman, Charles L. 5:33
Waterman, David 6:10
Waterman, E. 14:229
Waterman, E. D. 16:391
Waterman, E. K. 1:88
Waterman, G. 1:100
Waterman, H. 10:150; 18:60
Waterman, H. C. 8:68
Waterman, Henry D. 11:81
Waterman, J. 1:87; 27:127
Waterman, J. R. 1:182
Waterman, J. W. 9:114
Waterman, James P. 23:197
Waterman, Jeph 24:172
Waterman, Jeptha 17:447
Waterman, John 3:210; 10:94; 11:81; 20:387
Waterman, L. 3:210; 14:229
Waterman, Ralph C. 20:45
Waterman, S. 3:210; 22:227
Waterman, W. 18:60
Waterman, W. J. 20:387
Waterman, Warren 18:282
Waterman, William 11:418
Waterman, William A. 10:85
Waters, --- 3:210; 15:89, 253
Waters, A. 14:24; 15:79
Waters, A. L. 3:210
Waters, Abbey Jane 26:234
Waters, Alexander 4:60
Waters, Asa 8:35; 18:166
Waters, Byron G. 4:60
Waters, Charles 7:136; 11:81; 18:60; 26:214; 27:130
Waters, Charles L. 21:145
Waters, D. 1:182
Waters, D. D. 1:184
Waters, Daniel G. 7:84; 21:401
Waters, Daniel M. 11:82
Waters, David N. 19:217
Waters, E. 11:222
Waters, E. C. 12:163
Waters, Ebner H. 17:112
Waters, Edwin D. 19:217
Waters, Elijah 21:127
Waters, Francis J. 22:443

Waters, Frank 7:114; 9:127
Waters, Freeman 8:116
Waters, G. 11:122; 17:233; 21:401; 27:128
Waters, G. T. 23:55
Waters, George 15:79; 18:166; 21:401
Waters, Green 18:21
Waters, H. 1:184; 16:260; 21:205
Waters, H. C. 1:180
Waters, H. D. 10:175; 19:217
Waters, H. S. 15:61
Waters, Henry 18:317
Waters, Henry A. 9:30; 26:116
Waters, Horace 7:17
Waters, Horatio 15:334
Waters, Isaac E. 21:262
Waters, J. 9:225
Waters, J. C. 16:260
Waters, J. H. 1:180
Waters, James 6:26
Waters, James H. 1:85; 23:82
Waters, James S. 10:142; 20:387
Waters, John 9:30; 12:54; 19:139; 26:138
Waters, John B. 17:45; 25:257
Waters, John H. 10:175; 19:217; 23:82
Waters, John M. 27:133
Waters, Joseph 10:142; 20:387
Waters, Joshua 23:174
Waters, L. F. 25:127
Waters, L. J. 26:199
Waters, Larkin 8:68
Waters, Lewis H. 5:47
Waters, Lucius L. 18:282
Waters, Manly 11:177
Waters, Marada 7:114
Waters, Mareda 21:401
Waters, Moses 21:237
Waters, Oscar 8:43; 26:198
Waters, P. S. 19:41
Waters, Perry 6:13
Waters, R. T. 11:82
Waters, S. J. 18:388
Waters, Samuel 22:227
Waters, Silas 22:348
Waters, Sylvanus C. 15:26
Waters, Thomas 27:133
Waters, William 12:163; 17:188

Waters, William R. 22:414
Waters, William W. 10:154
Waterson, James 1:84
Waterson, R. 7:45
Wates, J. 22:273
Wates, William 3:210
Wather, James 16:260
Watherby, N. J. 14:229
Watherspoon, D. 12:94; 16:359
Wathlech, George 19:41
Wathley, Oliver 5:47
Watier, James C. 21:401
Watkin, Henry 22:326
Watkins, --- 12:172
Watkins, Abraham 21:61
Watkins, Alva 17:27
Watkins, Anderson 22:517
Watkins, Andrew 21:45
Watkins, Atha C. 4:60
Watkins, C. 2:19
Watkins, C. B. 1:87
Watkins, Caesar 22:326
Watkins, Charles 25:127
Watkins, D. J. 21:192
Watkins, D. P. 22:227
Watkins, Daniel 1:192; 4:60
Watkins, Daniel F. 14:317
Watkins, Daniel S. 18:288; 26:136
Watkins, Daniel W. 10:85; 20:387
Watkins, E. 1:185
Watkins, Eli 9:46; 26:131
Watkins, Franck 9:31
Watkins, Frank 18:318; 26:116
Watkins, Frederick 21:244
Watkins, G. 1:89
Watkins, G. C. 3:210
Watkins, George 23:206
Watkins, Henry 11:216; 27:129
Watkins, Henry A. 20:131
Watkins, Hy 4:68
Watkins, Isaac 8:43; 17:293; 21:401; 26:198
Watkins, Isaac A. 10:169
Watkins, J. 3:210; 15:253; 20:157; 21:45
Watkins, J. A. 19:217
Watkins, J. M. 3:210
Watkins, James W. 22:459
Watkins, Jefferson 21:401
Watkins, Jesse 9:127; 27:130

Watkins, John 22:326
Watkins, John H. 4:60
Watkins, John J. 11:418
Watkins, John T. 23:82
Watkins, Joseph 8:35;
    9:162; 18:166
Watkins, Leander 22:326
Watkins, M. 1:89
Watkins, Martin B.
    21:133
Watkins, Paul 7:136
Watkins, Perry 22:158,
    444
Watkins, R. 15:25
Watkins, Reason 11:81
Watkins, Reuben 12:169
Watkins, Richard 12:78;
    23:291
Watkins, Robert 7:54
Watkins, S. 9:65; 22:326
Watkins, S. C. 23:265
Watkins, Samuel 17:98;
    20:117
Watkins, Samuel J.
    18:166
Watkins, Samuel S. 8:35
Watkins, T. 27:126
Watkins, Thomas 22:114,
    326
Watkins, Thomas E.
    10:156; 19:217
Watkins, Volney 22:348
Watkins, W. D. 1:86
Watkins, W. H. 9:197
Watkins, William 6:19;
    8:35; 10:24, 85;
    11:195; 17:399;
    18:99, 166; 20:387;
    21:401
Watkins, William J.
    21:237
Watkins, William W.
    24:33
Watkins, Wilson G. 24:46
Watkinson, D. 19:139
Watley, Alphonso 4:60
Watley, Richard 22:273
Watrick, F. 14:123
Watron, G. 3:210
Watros, James 5:47
Watrous, E. W. 19:139
Watrous, James E. 27:126
Wats, Cyrus 26:131
Wats, D. G. 23:55
Wats, E. 23:259
Watsell, Benjamin 16:61
Watsling, Joseph 10:142;
    20:387
Watson, --- 15:15, 51, 79
Watson, A. 1:88; 15:253;
    25:257

Watson, A. D. 25:126
Watson, A. J. 9:225;
    18:388
Watson, A. P. 1:185
Watson, Abram 11:178
Watson, Albert 23:111;
    24:163
Watson, Alexander 11:47;
    22:158
Watson, Alfred 9:197;
    19:264
Watson, Alfred A. 11:81
Watson, Ananias 8:111
Watson, Andrew J. 20:15
Watson, Anthony 13:53
Watson, Avery L. 11:175
Watson, B. 3:210
Watson, B. F. 15:346;
    16:391
Watson, Benedict 11:113
Watson, C. 3:210; 9:216;
    14:229, 261; 17:403;
    21:401
Watson, C. O. 25:308
Watson, Charles 10:85;
    12:57; 17:240, 388;
    20:387
Watson, Charles A.
    17:363
Watson, Charles O. 7:76
Watson, Christian 24:46
Watson, Colbert R. 15:25
Watson, Daniel 7:45;
    13:53; 25:258
Watson, David 8:112;
    11:82; 17:188
Watson, David M. 22:108
Watson, Durham 10:142;
    20:387
Watson, E. 11:175; 14:29,
    123; 19:264
Watson, E. S. 8:123
Watson, Ebert 17:268
Watson, Edmund 1:83
Watson, Edward 18:267;
    20:109; 25:126;
    26:85
Watson, Edwin R. 22:158
Watson, Eli 12:44
Watson, Eli G. 22:273
Watson, Elvert 17:421
Watson, Evan S. 7:15
Watson, Ezekiel 21:401
Watson, F. F. 3:210
Watson, Ferdinand 21:145
Watson, G. 1:185; 3:210
Watson, G. A. 1:183
Watson, G. F. 1:183
Watson, G. W. 16:260
Watson, George 4:60;
    9:46; 15:287; 17:101;

Watson, George 19:139;
    22:522; 26:131
Watson, George H. 11:81;
    21:45
Watson, H. 3:210; 7:79;
    9:115; 14:229; 24:33;
    25:258
Watson, H. A. 20:86
Watson, Harrison 17:234
Watson, Henry 5:47; 6:27;
    12:146; 16:260;
    18:99; 21:288;
    22:348
Watson, Henry C. 23:82
Watson, Henry G. 17:354
Watson, Hezekiah 7:114
Watson, Hiram 17:461;
    24:163
Watson, Hiram H. 8:102
Watson, Horace 27:129
Watson, Horatio N. 22:59
Watson, Isaac 7:136;
    20:387; 21:288
Watson, J. 1:88, 185, 186;
    3:210; 12:139;
    14:124; 15:147;
    16:130, 260; 19:139,
    217; 21:113, 164;
    22:227; 24:33
Watson, J. A. 25:329
Watson, J. C. 3:210
Watson, J. D. 17:150
Watson, J. G. 23:174
Watson, J. H. 20:139;
    21:205
Watson, J. J. 3:210
Watson, J. S. 13:75;
    16:260
Watson, J. T. 23:174
Watson, James 9:14;
    12:44; 14:320; 15:9;
    16:260; 21:401;
    22:348; 23:95;
    25:273
Watson, James A. 20:37
Watson, James B. 10:85;
    20:387; 21:83
Watson, James F. 4:60
Watson, James L. 22:108
Watson, James P. 7:114
Watson, James R. 22:495
Watson, James S. 22:413
Watson, Jefferson 16:61
Watson, Jesse T. 22:286
Watson, John 1:87; 7:136;
    8:34; 9:137; 11:49;
    12:120; 13:53;
    14:124; 15:253;
    16:260; 18:166, 267,
    444; 21:61;

Watson, John 22:348, 445, 494; 26:86; 27:129
Watson, John A. 27:131
Watson, John H. 9:127; 12:44
Watson, John P. 21:107
Watson, John S. 9:105, 241; 11:405
Watson, Joseph 7:136; 8:43; 9:40, 73; 10:85; 20:109, 387; 21:145; 26:198
Watson, Joseph F. 7:54
Watson, Joseph M. 17:108
Watson, Josiah H. 21:133
Watson, K. C. 12:163
Watson, Levi 20:20
Watson, Lewis B. 5:33
Watson, Louis 21:192
Watson, M. 9:233; 14:229
Watson, Martin W. 20:15
Watson, Memas 21:401
Watson, Michael B. 9:40
Watson, Moses 9:212
Watson, Nathaniel 15:253
Watson, Newton J. 21:83
Watson, Nicholas H. 23:82
Watson, O. 22:108
Watson, Ora D. 13:122
Watson, Orlando 8:57; 21:45
Watson, Orrin J. 25:258
Watson, P. W. 17:71
Watson, Parker S. 22:228
Watson, Peter 21:263
Watson, Peter W. 12:52
Watson, Philip 9:202
Watson, Phillip 19:293
Watson, R. 25:258; 27:126
Watson, R. M. 25:308
Watson, Richard 7:136
Watson, Robert 7:136; 12:44; 15:15, 253; 17:157, 307
Watson, S. 21:162
Watson, S. J. 21:401
Watson, Samuel 4:60; 22:227
Watson, Squire 21:213; 23:55
Watson, T. 3:210
Watson, T. M. 11:405
Watson, Thomas 7:136; 14:124; 18:402; 21:61; 22:326; 25:273
Watson, Thomas A. 12:44
Watson, Thomas J. 11:177

Watson, Timothy 7:114
Watson, W. 1:184; 9:64; 12:84; 14:124, 229, 313; 16:359; 17:477; 27:132
Watson, W. C. 14:326; 23:103
Watson, W. R. 22:356
Watson, W. W. 24:86
Watson, Wesley M. 17:318
Watson, William 3:210; 5:47; 7:114; 9:40; 11:274, 290, 427; 13:53; 16:260; 17:321; 18:298; 21:401; 23:287; 26:117
Watson, William G. 14:317
Watson, William H. 23:258
Watson, William W. 17:277
Watson, Willis 9:202
Watt, --- 9:106
Watt, A. Jackson 11:253
Watt, B. M. 11:179
Watt, Daniel H. 23:174
Watt, E. D. 14:249
Watt, Farlin E. 23:197
Watt, Francis M. 9:30
Watt, George M. 8:111
Watt, H. 3:210
Watt, I. 9:152
Watt, J. W. 23:55
Watt, James 22:445
Watt, James H. 22:59, 228
Watt, John 18:402
Watt, M. 11:429
Watt, W. 25:258
Watt, William M. 10:97
Wattenbaugh, Andrew 20:387
Watter, Lewis 11:317
Watterman, Alfred P. 16:79
Watterman, George 23:55
Watterman, H. C. 26:199
Wattermire, H. A. 9:226
Watters, A. 18:185
Watters, C. 1:181
Watters, Elbert 11:427
Watters, Green B. 18:267
Watters, Lemuel 11:427
Watters, Matthew 10:142
Watters, Michael 20:387
Wattles, J. 14:24
Wattles, John 9:197
Wattles, L. 15:253
Wattley, Wilmer 22:59

Watts, A. J. 3:210
Watts, Anderville 22:59
Watts, Andrew J. 23:197
Watts, Arch 17:188
Watts, B. E. 25:308
Watts, Benjamin 11:47
Watts, C. 3:210
Watts, C. C. 3:210
Watts, C. W. 17:101
Watts, Charles 22:326
Watts, Charles H. 19:41
Watts, D. L. 19:41
Watts, Daniel 13:53
Watts, Dill 17:188
Watts, Elisha 23:259
Watts, Elisha D. 21:107
Watts, Emery 4:68
Watts, George 10:24, 170; 19:217
Watts, George W. 10:85; 20:387
Watts, H. 25:308
Watts, H. H. 26:85
Watts, Harvey 13:53
Watts, Henry 1:193
Watts, Hiram 4:60
Watts, Isaac 11:393
Watts, J. 11:80; 12:94; 16:359; 27:128
Watts, James 8:57; 15:253; 21:107
Watts, James H. 23:55
Watts, James S. 22:108; 23:281
Watts, John 9:93; 11:291; 13:53; 16:61; 21:401; 26:87
Watts, John R. 4:60
Watts, John W. 22:495
Watts, Jonathan M. 23:116
Watts, Joseph A. 22:273
Watts, Martin 18:328
Watts, Oscar F. 2:19
Watts, Q. 26:86
Watts, Reuben 7:45
Watts, Richard 9:212
Watts, Robert 11:131
Watts, S. 14:229, 261
Watts, Samuel 10:97
Watts, Samuel T. 11:177
Watts, T. 3:210; 7:45
Watts, Thomas 6:13; 18:99
Watts, Thomas R. 19:41
Watts, W. 14:124; 21:202
Watts, Washington 11:215
Watts, Wesley 15:85
Watts, William 11:195
Watts, William B. 11:253
Watts, William H. 18:422

Watts, Z. 18:267
Wattson, J. 27:127
Watz, Frederick 21:401
Watz, Jeremiah 9:137
Watzell, W. N. 3:211
Waugh, David 17:315;
   22:59
Waugh, F. 18:267; 26:86
Waugh, G. S. 14:124
Waugh, James H. 22:444
Waugh, John 11:234
Waugh, Luther 18:282
Waugh, W. H. 22:228
Waugh, William 17:27
Waugh, William A.
   18:444
Waugh, William H.
   22:228
Waught, Johnston 11:177
Waugtel, Starling 21:237
Waulis, E. 14:124
Wauls, Hugh 12:44
Waunser, C. 23:55
Waurch, J. 1:183
Wauser, George 7:136
Wauzer, Charles 22:173
Waverly, Frank 22:522
Wawble Wau-kauth-ah,
   (or High Eagle)
   19:326
Wax, John 27:125
Wax, Mathew 25:279
Waxter, J. W. 18:185
Waxwin, Walter A.
   22:443
Waxwood, A. 13:101
Way, A. D. 4:60
Way, A. F. 11:179
Way, Baldwin E. 11:48
Way, Benjamin 16:150
Way, D. L. 20:150
Way, Daniel 5:33; 25:258
Way, David 13:126
Way, F. 3:211
Way, F. L. 14:124
Way, H. C. 3:211
Way, J. 3:211
Way, James 18:402;
   25:314
Way, John T. 21:401
Way, O. H. 19:41
Way, S. S. 19:41
Way, Solomon 4:60
Way, William H. 8:35;
   18:166
Wayant, E. 25:258
Wayburn, Oscar M. 9:93
Waycox, William 12:91
Wayer, J. W. 7:84
Wayes, I. 18:116
Wayland, J. E. 15:114

Wayland, Michael 22:174
Waymack, N. T. 20:93
Wayman, A. G. 22:59
Wayman, J. 11:222
Wayman, James 20:387
Wayman, Peter 13:123
Wayman, W. W. 9:216
Waymin, J. H. 3:211
Waymire, Isaac 8:76
Waymire, James 22:507
Wayne, Francis A. 16:61
Wayne, George 4:60
Wayne, Harden 21:288
Wayne, Isaac 23:174
Wayne, Isaac L. 13:53
Wayne, J. 23:303
Wayne, James 22:273;
   24:169
Wayne, John 16:359
Wayne, John W. 25:258
Wayne, Peter 19:273
Wayne, Thomas T. 21:263
Waynur, F. 1:88
Wayor, G. 16:260
Wayson, B. 24:33
Wayson, S. 24:87
Wayt, Alfred 17:89
Wayt, George W. 11:177
Wayt, Napoleon R.
   17:388
We---, J. E. 24:115
We---, James 25:127
We---, Simon 19:139
We---, William 25:258
Weaber, C. A. 18:342
Weaber, William 12:44
Weachart, E. 23:265
Wead, A. 14:124
Weagley, Eli 22:114
Weahney, F. 1:183
Weakerman, O. T. 19:140
Weakland, William 15:79
Weakley, G. W. 23:308
Weakley, J. 1:181
Weakley, L. 1:183
Weakley, O. B. 15:253
Weaks, Charles 11:234
Weale, Paul 3:211
Wealind, Frederick
   10:142; 20:387
Weamer, G. 20:135
Weams, Isaac 19:41
Weams, William 22:326
Wean, George W. 22:108
Wean, John M. 23:82
Wean, Martin 22:108
Weaner, W. D. 11:176
Weans, Thomas 9:197
Weapper, Charles 3:211
Wear, David 11:185

Wear, David M. 10:142;
   20:387
Wear, George W. 10:85
Wear, Henry A. 9:127
Wear, John 11:330
Wear, John M. 21:192
Wear, Wesley 10:85
Weard, William 20:101
Wearen, S. 20:387
Wearer, Frederick 20:387
Wearer, W. 9:114
Wearmouth, George 23:95
Wearts, Augustus 9:238;
   26:234
Weascot, J. 14:24
Wease, James 8:57; 21:45
Weasenberg, Albert
   10:169; 19:217
Weasett, A. 3:211
Weasner, Frank 13:53
Weasner, William 20:90
Weason, J. 3:211
Weat, James 9:93
Weater, J. H. 14:313;
   17:477; 27:132
Weathens, S. 22:59
Weather, Dellis 17:188
Weatherald, H. W. 3:211
Weatherby, David 4:61
Weatherby, Emily 17:27
Weatherby, Isaac M.
   23:174
Weatherby, J. B. 16:61
Weathercamp, --- 15:288
Weatherford, Daniel L.
   10:85; 20:387
Weatherford, Richard
   11:216
Weatherhead, H. L. 18:73
Weatherhold, Charles
   8:98
Weatherholt, George
   15:79
Weatherholt, Jacob 20:28
Weatherly, C. W. 14:124
Weatherly, Eli 21:288
Weatherly, Frederick
   19:217
Weatherly, Henry 9:93
Weatherly, James 9:137;
   27:129
Weatherold, Oscar 22:108
Weathers, George 12:145
Weathers, J. S. 7:114
Weathers, James E. 20:28
Weathers, John G. 21:401
Weathers, Robert 4:60
Weathers, Solomon 23:82
Weathers, William 9:137;
   17:189; 27:130

Weatherston, Thomas 10:24
Weatherstone, I. 17:189
Weatherton, Henry 11:215, 216
Weatherwax, A. D. 27:126
Weatherwax, J. C. 8:76
Weatman, Frederick 11:177
Weaver, Albert 17:214
Weaver, Alex 3:211
Weaver, Alton 13:53
Weaver, Anderson B. 23:102
Weaver, Andrew 13:128; 21:249
Weaver, B. S. 3:211
Weaver, Benonia 15:80
Weaver, C. A. 9:105
Weaver, C. D. 7:62
Weaver, Caleb 11:290
Weaver, Casper 22:498
Weaver, Charles 1:85, 87; 9:46; 13:75; 23:174; 26:131
Weaver, Cyrus S. 18:224
Weaver, D. 16:359; 25:258
Weaver, Daniel 11:217
Weaver, David 5:33; 22:228; 23:174
Weaver, David C. 10:85; 20:387
Weaver, Dr. 20:131
Weaver, Edward 10:170
Weaver, Elza W. 22:444
Weaver, F. 19:314; 25:308
Weaver, Francis M. 10:142; 17:427; 20:387
Weaver, Frederick 10:85
Weaver, G. 1:89
Weaver, G. H. 25:128
Weaver, G. W. 17:27
Weaver, George 3:211; 23:82
Weaver, George W. 6:21; 22:108
Weaver, H. 3:211
Weaver, H. B. 11:175
Weaver, H. C. 2:19
Weaver, H. E. 18:201
Weaver, Hardin 17:189
Weaver, Harvey C. 17:262
Weaver, Henry 9:212; 11:178; 13:53; 16:61; 17:89; 19:140; 21:83
Weaver, I. 12:159

Weaver, Isaac 14:229
Weaver, J. 2:19; 3:211; 11:114; 16:260; 25:126
Weaver, J. B. 15:79
Weaver, J. H. 11:274
Weaver, J. J. 18:116
Weaver, J. M. 7:114
Weaver, J. U. 22:326
Weaver, Jacob 12:44, 60; 13:53, 78; 14:229; 15:79; 16:260
Weaver, James 3:211
Weaver, James C. 22:459
Weaver, James G. 22:273
Weaver, James H. 23:82
Weaver, James N. 26:131
Weaver, Jesse L. 13:53
Weaver, John 8:35, 98; 9:40, 212; 11:178; 12:139; 14:230, 261; 15:147; 17:354; 18:166, 211, 267, 298; 20:150; 23:259; 24:64; 26:85, 117
Weaver, John B. 4:61
Weaver, John D. 10:175; 19:217
Weaver, John E. 16:137
Weaver, John I. 24:10
Weaver, John M. 19:331
Weaver, John N. 14:230
Weaver, John R. 11:275; 20:387
Weaver, John V. 21:117
Weaver, John W. 11:177; 22:326
Weaver, Jonathan 17:89
Weaver, Joseph 16:260
Weaver, Joshua 15:96
Weaver, L. 16:61
Weaver, Lewis P. 17:61
Weaver, Luther 22:228
Weaver, Lyman H. 9:68
Weaver, M. 1:185; 3:211; 13:123; 19:217
Weaver, M. A. 14:124
Weaver, Marcus D. L. 22:108
Weaver, Martin 9:93; 10:169; 26:83
Weaver, Mathew 17:45
Weaver, Micager 10:185
Weaver, Milton 23:174
Weaver, Minger 18:185
Weaver, Moses 17:140
Weaver, P. 3:225; 13:101; 14:24; 17:505
Weaver, P. W. 15:290
Weaver, Philip A. 19:41
Weaver, Philo B. 19:41

Weaver, R. 19:140
Weaver, Randolph 10:142; 20:387
Weaver, Reuben 1:84
Weaver, Richard 10:155; 19:217; 22:173
Weaver, Rockwell 21:192
Weaver, S. 14:124
Weaver, S. M. 20:45
Weaver, Samuel 11:189; 18:211; 21:61; 22:228; 23:174
Weaver, Samuel G. 24:62
Weaver, Samuel H. 11:81
Weaver, Solomon 10:85
Weaver, Solomon H. 22:108
Weaver, Thomas G. 21:107
Weaver, Truman 22:158
Weaver, W. 14:124
Weaver, W. A. 20:388
Weaver, W. H. 11:274, 290
Weaver, William 6:11; 8:43; 10:99; 11:217; 20:15; 22:16, 506; 23:55; 24:33; 26:198
Weaver, William A. 9:233; 20:139
Weaver, William P. 27:129
Weavy, A. 23:174
Web, John 8:116
Webb, --- 19:323
Webb, Alexander 8:35; 18:166
Webb, Allen 8:35; 18:166
Webb, Andrew W. 17:321
Webb, Brainard 12:44
Webb, C. 1:181
Webb, C. A. 1:87; 22:59
Webb, C. B. 3:211
Webb, Carey C. 21:145
Webb, Charles 22:108
Webb, Charles W. 12:78; 15:13
Webb, Chrisey 11:330
Webb, Christopher 13:59
Webb, Cyrus R. 9:64
Webb, D. 3:211; 23:116
Webb, Daniel 3:211; 17:140; 24:205
Webb, Dennis 8:43; 26:198
Webb, Denton 9:226; 18:388
Webb, Dillard 22:273
Webb, E. 3:211; 14:124; 22:326
Webb, E. B. 9:93

Webb, Edmond 17:455
Webb, Edmund 24:207
Webb, Edward 17:214
Webb, Elijah 10:86;
  20:388
Webb, Eliott 22:493
Webb, F. 18:99
Webb, Francis M. 11:318;
  21:45
Webb, Franklin 25:126
Webb, G. B. 26:84
Webb, George 12:44;
  17:140; 18:41;
  24:206
Webb, George I. 10:142
Webb, George J. 20:388
Webb, George W. 11:318;
  20:15; 27:126
Webb, H. 1:185; 11:179;
  17:192; 19:140
Webb, H. A. 20:45
Webb, Henderson 8:35;
  18:166
Webb, Isaac S. 18:324
Webb, J. 1:88; 3:211;
  11:179; 15:253;
  16:61; 18:267, 388;
  25:125; 26:86
Webb, J. A. 17:112
Webb, J. D. 11:80
Webb, J. H. 12:163
Webb, J. P. 14:124
Webb, J. S. 3:211
Webb, J. W. 14:124
Webb, Jackson 11:217
Webb, Jackson S. 11:330
Webb, Jacob 22:59
Webb, James 11:48
Webb, James C. 12:44
Webb, James F. 22:445
Webb, James N. 18:267;
  26:86
Webb, James W. 17:45;
  22:445
Webb, Jesse C. 22:273
Webb, John 7:114; 9:30;
  11:215; 17:168;
  18:318; 21:197;
  25:126; 26:115
Webb, John E. 9:93
Webb, John H. 17:322
Webb, John P. 14:230
Webb, John R. 17:262
Webb, John W. 7:7; 16:61
Webb, Jonathan 11:177
Webb, Joseph 15:9, 253;
  22:356
Webb, Joseph H. 8:35;
  18:166
Webb, Josiah 7:136
Webb, Lemuel W. 17:363

Webb, Lewis 11:215
Webb, Lewis H. 10:169;
  19:217
Webb, Lorenzo D. 11:331
Webb, M. E. 3:211
Webb, M. F. 27:156
Webb, Mathew 20:388
Webb, Matthew 10:142
Webb, Milton 22:133
Webb, Moses 10:85, 99
Webb, O. R. 1:87
Webb, Oscar 23:55
Webb, Philip 17:89
Webb, R. G. 23:55
Webb, R. O. 25:258
Webb, R. S. 18:267;
  26:87
Webb, Richard 13:123
Webb, Richard H. 7:15
Webb, Robert 3:211
Webb, Robert F. 19:140
Webb, Rod 11:179
Webb, S. G. 9:64
Webb, S. W. 1:83
Webb, Samson 21:288
Webb, Samuel 24:33
Webb, Samuel E. 17:47
Webb, Samuel P. 11:274
Webb, Sanford 16:112
Webb, Sigm. 16:112
Webb, T. 1:182
Webb, T. M. 14:124
Webb, Tobias 17:140;
  24:206
Webb, W. 3:211; 17:89;
  20:45
Webb, W. A. 9:64
Webb, William 9:226;
  14:124, 230; 17:421;
  18:99, 388; 22:158;
  24:163
Webb, William A. 4:61
Webb, William E. 17:61
Webb, William F. 7:7;
  13:53
Webb, William H. 8:111
Webb, William O. 19:246
Webb, William P. 12:44
Webb, Woodbridge 13:53
Webb, Woodbury 10:24
Webb, Wyatt 22:326
Webbcom, L. D. 11:330
Webbe, J. 3:211
Webber, A. K. P. 5:33;
  25:258
Webber, Alexander 8:76
Webber, Amos 1:84
Webber, Asa W. 7:114
Webber, Berchard 10:142
Webber, Berhard H.
  20:388

Webber, C. J. 24:87
Webber, Charles E.
  19:231
Webber, Charles F.
  16:112
Webber, Charles H. 10:24
Webber, Conrad 14:230
Webber, David 15:301;
  16:260
Webber, Frank 7:82;
  25:308
Webber, Franklin 7:80
Webber, Fred 17:429
Webber, G. A. 1:182
Webber, H. S. 13:53;
  16:61
Webber, Henry 6:34;
  15:308; 25:329
Webber, Isaac 15:253
Webber, J. 1:87; 3:211;
  18:185
Webber, John 1:85;
  15:309; 19:140
Webber, John C. 11:47
Webber, John R. 27:133
Webber, Joseph 8:98
Webber, Levi 11:427
Webber, Luther P. 10:169;
  19:217
Webber, M. 19:264
Webber, Matthias 18:342
Webber, Michael 9:197
Webber, O. 3:211
Webber, Peter 12:78;
  23:175
Webber, Randolph 26:116
Webber, Samuel C. 4:61
Webber, Scipi 21:213
Webber, Sebastian 21:85
Webber, William 9:197;
  10:86; 19:272;
  20:388
Webby, John 14:230
Weber, Andrew J. 9:101
Weber, Bernard 23:282
Weber, C. H. 3:211
Weber, Christian 12:44
Weber, F. 9:226; 18:388
Weber, Frank 17:240
Weber, Frederick 11:177
Weber, George 14:237;
  15:93
Weber, Henry 10:86, 142;
  15:356; 20:388;
  22:173; 23:174;
  24:33
Weber, Hiram 12:44
Weber, J. 1:184; 9:114;
  10:185
Weber, Jacob 23:197
Weber, John 4:61; 23:174

Weber, Joseph 9:17
Weber, L. 15:51; 16:359
Weber, Leander J. 13:53
Weber, Lewis 12:78
Weber, Nicholas 22:286
Weber, Peter 15:93
Weber, Philip 11:48
Weber, Pius 4:61
Weber, Randolph 9:40
Weber, Rudolph 18:298
Weber, S. J. 16:61
Weber, Talbert 26:85
Weber, Theodore 11:131
Weber, W. 3:211; 25:258
Weber, William 11:253
Weber, William H. 12:54
Webert, David M. 23:82
Webert, H. 21:401
Webler, James 24:71
Webner, Frederick 27:133
Webourne, B. L. 10:142;
    20:388
Webrick, John H. 3:211
Webs, H. 15:253
Webster, --- 13:75;
    16:359; 19:140
Webster, A. 1:183
Webster, A. C. 3:211;
    17:394
Webster, Aaron 21:401
Webster, Al 25:308
Webster, Albert 7:79
Webster, Andrew 11:216
Webster, Benjamin F.
    18:271
Webster, C. 14:285
Webster, C. L. 19:243
Webster, Charles 4:61;
    15:346; 16:391
Webster, Charles E.
    16:130
Webster, Charles J. 9:152;
    23:55; 27:127
Webster, Charles L. 9:197
Webster, Christopher
    20:131
Webster, D. B. 14:249
Webster, D. P. 27:134
Webster, Daniel 7:79;
    18:267; 21:45;
    25:308; 26:85
Webster, Dennis 22:495
Webster, E. 3:211; 16:260
Webster, E. C. S. 25:271
Webster, Edgar 10:86;
    20:388
Webster, Edmund 18:41
Webster, Edwin 11:195;
    25:258
Webster, Enoch 1:83
Webster, Erastus 23:126

Webster, F. 21:401
Webster, F. O. 14:313;
    17:474; 27:132
Webster, Francis 4:61
Webster, Francis C.
    11:195
Webster, Fred 22:326
Webster, Frederick H.
    9:127
Webster, G. 3:211;
    12:145; 15:328
Webster, George 18:201;
    27:133
Webster, George F.
    11:393
Webster, George P.
    19:140
Webster, H. 1:88; 3:211;
    13:101
Webster, H. A. 16:260
Webster, H. C. 20:82
Webster, H. G. 21:401
Webster, H. J. 19:140
Webster, Harrison 21:237
Webster, Harvey R.
    16:261
Webster, Horace 22:59
Webster, Hugh 11:290
Webster, J. 3:211; 7:62;
    25:126, 258
Webster, J. B. 12:78; 15:4
Webster, J. W. 25:287
Webster, James 3:211;
    7:70; 16:61; 21:239,
    401
Webster, James E. 12:44
Webster, Jason 17:391
Webster, Joel F. 9:93;
    26:84
Webster, John 8:98, 116,
    123; 9:197; 11:273;
    19:279
Webster, John B. 17:245
Webster, John G. 18:105
Webster, Joseph 12:81
Webster, L. 24:87
Webster, L. H. 7:45
Webster, L. L. 17:337;
    18:267; 26:85
Webster, M. D. 5:33
Webster, M. S. 9:30;
    18:318; 26:115
Webster, Mark M. 8:35;
    18:166
Webster, Martin 8:68
Webster, Mary I. 8:35
Webster, Matt 11:317
Webster, Mills A. 16:142
Webster, Moida 22:517
Webster, Monroe 22:59
Webster, Nathaniel 9:7

Webster, Neal J. 18:41
Webster, Newton 17:363
Webster, Robert 9:167
Webster, Samuel 3:211
Webster, Samuel J. 27:133
Webster, Sheldon M.
    8:35; 18:166
Webster, Spencer 20:101
Webster, Stephen 8:43;
    26:198
Webster, Thomas 26:214
Webster, U. A. 13:75
Webster, Ushel 20:388
Webster, W. A. 3:211
Webster, W. D. 1:85
Webster, W. H. 20:388
Webster, W. L. 25:258
Webster, W. S. 9:160
Webster, W. W. 1:182;
    11:291; 19:243
Webster, Walter 21:401
Webster, Wesley R. 5:33
Webster, William 7:136;
    18:41; 22:163; 23:55
Webster, William H.
    10:86; 22:59
Webster, Willis 23:206
Wecever, D. A. 15:253
Wechester, Mathias
    20:388
Wechman, William
    22:348
Wechselberg, William
    17:363
Wechter, Philip 22:16
Weck, William 22:108
Weckbacker, Peter 24:87
Wecker, Adam 14:313
Weckerson, John 21:12
Weckesser, Julius 11:47
Weckle, John G. 26:146
Weckle, Perrie T. 17:251
Weckliff, William 9:70
Wecksilbery, W. C.
    18:335
Wector, Newton 8:111
Wed, G. 11:122
Weddecomb, James
    26:131
Weddel, Pleasant D.
    17:351
Weddell, G. D. 11:283
Wedder, A. C. 3:211
Weddle, Aaron M. 20:37
Weddle, Alven 19:314
Weddle, George H.
    15:253
Weddles, J. 13:101
Wedeler, Benjamin
    11:324
Wedemeyer, F. W. 19:217

Wedemeyer, Henry 22:16
Weden, Alex 22:326
Wederin, Louis 17:387
Wedford, Aaron W. 9:40
Wedfort, Henry A. 13:128
Wedge, James H. 18:99
Wedge, James W. 6:19
Wedge, Robert 9:197;
 19:264
Wedger, Clark 7:15
Wedlin, R. M. 17:323
Wedman, Charles 9:127;
 27:130
Wedmyer, Fred. W.
 10:169
Wedner, Charles 19:140
Weeas, Michael 3:211
Weeb, E. P. 1:183
Weeber, L. 12:94
Weech, I. 25:280
Weed, A. 21:45; 25:258
Weed, A. B. 3:211
Weed, A. S. 14:124
Weed, Alfred 10:169;
 19:217
Weed, Andrew J. 19:41
Weed, Charles 9:8
Weed, D. 15:253
Weed, D. D. 14:124
Weed, Dennis 4:61
Weed, Edward R. 21:401
Weed, Edwin 19:41
Weed, George W. 6:21
Weed, James 7:17
Weed, James A. 17:277
Weed, Joseph C. 11:393
Weed, Lewis 1:86
Weed, Nelson 12:56
Weed, Ramond 15:4
Weed, Raymond 12:78
Weed, Silas 12:159
Weed, Theodore 9:94;
 26:83
Weed, W. C. 21:401
Weed, William 3:211;
 15:156
Weed, William A. 10:24
Weedbeck, Christopher
 15:356
Weeden, B. F. 4:61
Weeden, Frederick 25:278
Weedham, J. H. 24:46
Weedles, J. 14:24
Weedlove, Thomas
 18:166
Weedman, J. 20:86
Weedmer, F. 18:60
Weegan, James 14:230
Week, John 15:362
Week, Manning 27:130

Weeker, Adam 17:478;
 27:132
Weeker, Grove L. 9:228
Weeker, P. G. 23:174
Weeker, Simeon 11:176
Weekey, Anthony 15:253
Weekland, F. 3:211
Weekley, Aaron 15:253
Weekley, George W.
 19:41
Weekley, Gideon F.
 22:133
Weekley, James 15:253
Weekley, James H. 13:53
Weekly, Christie 6:21
Weekly, James H. 16:61
Weekly, John 3:211
Weekoith, Zudwid 26:83
Weeks, --- 27:129
Weeks, A. M. 25:258
Weeks, Andrew M. 5:33
Weeks, Ansel D. 18:402
Weeks, Benjamin 3:211
Weeks, C. 3:211
Weeks, C. F. 15:253
Weeks, Charles 4:61;
 15:25
Weeks, Charles A. 18:116
Weeks, D. 3:211
Weeks, Darwin D. 22:158
Weeks, Ed 11:98
Weeks, Elisha 10:86;
 20:388
Weeks, F. 15:114; 22:326
Weeks, F. A. 1:184
Weeks, Francis 12:44
Weeks, Franklin C. 10:24
Weeks, G. 1:86
Weeks, George 13:75;
 16:261
Weeks, George H. 4:61
Weeks, H. 21:162
Weeks, Hampton 21:288
Weeks, Henry 13:75
Weeks, J. 3:211
Weeks, J. O. 9:152
Weeks, J. R. 25:258
Weeks, J. W. 15:362
Weeks, James 9:70;
 22:173; 23:251
Weeks, John 9:40, 197;
 10:86; 15:301;
 16:261; 19:264;
 20:388; 23:82
Weeks, John M. 14:230
Weeks, Joseph 10:24;
 12:44
Weeks, K. H. 26:200
Weeks, Levi 16:61
Weeks, Lyman G. 21:83
Weeks, Martin 21:197

Weeks, Mathew W.
 11:254
Weeks, Merrett 13:53
Weeks, N. 19:217
Weeks, Nathan 3:211
Weeks, Nathan H. 4:61
Weeks, Nathaniel 13:59
Weeks, O. H. 17:27
Weeks, Othal L. 21:207
Weeks, R. H. 21:401
Weeks, S. 17:296
Weeks, S. N. 9:152
Weeks, S. W. 27:127
Weeks, Stephen M. 23:95
Weeks, Sylvester 10:152,
 178
Weeks, T. M. 12:139
Weeks, Tenn 18:267
Weeks, Tennessee 26:86
Weeks, Theodore G.
 10:26
Weeks, Thomas 7:136;
 14:124
Weeks, Thomas C. 12:10
Weeks, Thomas G. 18:402
Weeks, W. 25:258
Weeks, W. W. 2:19;
 25:128
Weeks, Willard 5:33
Weeksler, Mathias 10:86
Weeland, Abraham 9:30;
 26:115
Weeland, William 16:261
Weelond, Abraham
 18:318
Weels, William J. 16:391
Weems, T. 19:243
Weene, P. 16:115
Weeney, J. S. 18:41
Weese, L. 19:276
Weese, R. H. 26:234
Weese, S. 21:45
Weese, William 3:225;
 17:505
Weesner, W. 17:102
Weeson, J. P. K. 20:93
Weets, R. 14:124
Weff, Moses 20:388
Wegal, Charles 22:469
Wegand, Frank 18:318;
 26:116
Wegelein, J. 18:41
Wegener, Frank 11:334
Wegerman, J. 25:258
Weggan, Joseph C. 9:152
Weghel, E. 11:343
Weghorst, Louis 22:228
Wegle, August 10:142
Wehage, John 14:230
Wehele, Ehrhardt 22:173
Wehester, A. 12:159

Wehner, Henry 9:228; 18:388
Wehrong, Jacob 5:55; 25:258
Weiant, J. 1:183
Weibeck, Charles 25:125
Weibel, Joseph 21:94
Weiber, Charles 3:211
Weiber, Gottlieb 4:61
Weiber, Henry 1:84
Weiber, L. 16:359
Weibert, Charles C. 10:142; 20:388
Weibke, John 13:53; 16:61
Weible, W. H. 1:184
Weichard, Christian 6:8; 18:116
Weichart, W. 1:83
Weicher, Daniel 9:160
Weichsel, Michael 16:15
Weid, Abraham 5:33
Weidabush, Henry 11:81
Weidam, H. 3:211
Weidan, J. 3:212
Weiddeman, Carl 25:125
Weideman, John 26:115
Weider, L. 3:212
Weidermann, James V. 23:126
Weidle, J. 1:182
Weidlick, Rodolph 21:401
Weidman, A. 3:212
Weidman, P. 1:87, 88
Weidman, William H. 19:217
Weidner, E. 18:318; 26:116
Weidner, James 27:132
Weidner, John 16:130
Weidner, M. 1:89
Weigand, John 22:495
Weigel, John 19:264
Weigeld, John F. 17:89
Weigell, George 25:258
Weiger, George 25:126
Weigert, H. 19:264
Weighard, G. H. 17:394
Weight, William 16:112
Weightman, Charles 11:113
Weights, J. B. 23:102
Weigle, John 9:17; 23:175
Weigle, Joseph J. 20:388
Weigler, Andrew 20:50
Weigman, J. W. 3:212
Weiht, Adam 15:114
Weikman, J. 25:127
Weil, Adam 17:251
Weil, Christopher 21:401
Weil, F. 9:114

Weil, John 23:175
Weiland, George 19:140
Weiland, H. 1:183
Weiland, Joseph 22:173
Weilber, John N. 20:388
Weiler, G. F. 1:87
Weiler, J. 1:181
Weilly, Henry 5:33
Weils, Laden 11:131
Weiman, A. F. 12:139
Weiman, F. 11:253
Weiman, George W. 8:98
Weiman, M. 1:181
Weimar, Robert 17:164
Weimer, Benjamin F. 17:213
Weimer, Eugene 21:45
Weimer, P. 15:253
Weimer, Phillis 8:98
Weinacht, Abraham 22:108
Weinant, J. 1:181
Weinberg, William 23:111
Weinboldt, Henry 19:217
Weinborn, John 17:363
Weinch, S. 24:87
Weiner, A. 1:181
Weiner, John 15:61
Weiner, N. 1:183
Weiner, N. J. 17:405
Weingand, G. 11:318
Weingarte, Joseph 19:140
Weingater, James 15:311
Weinhoff, Theodore 4:61
Weinkauf, John August 23:116
Weinman, J. W. 23:175
Weinmann, Philip 19:217
Weinreh, E. 26:87
Weinrich, Wilhelm 4:61
Weinzel, Leopold 4:61
Weinzenreid, Frederick 23:175
Weipert, George 11:195
Weipfler, Sebastian 11:176
Weir, Adam 10:25
Weir, Alexander 21:401
Weir, Allen 14:320; 25:277
Weir, Edward 1:83
Weir, George 10:86; 20:388
Weir, George J. 20:388
Weir, George W. 1:86
Weir, J. K. 23:55
Weir, James 1:83
Weir, John 8:98; 9:233; 10:86; 11:393; 20:388; 25:258
Weir, Joseph 13:123

Weir, Lewis 4:61
Weir, Matthias 21:127
Weir, S. H. 17:168
Weir, Thomas 13:53; 16:61; 18:116; 22:158
Weir, William 9:197; 10:169; 11:122; 19:217
Weir, William J. 23:55
Weir, William T. 21:94
Weirich, Nicholas 23:82
Weirner, C. 19:41
Weirsig, Julius 20:388
Weis, Alexander 11:215
Weis, E. 19:314
Weis, F. 1:183
Weis, H. H. 7:62
Weis, J. G. 14:292
Weis, John G. 23:96
Weis, Robert 12:163
Weisand, Charles 4:61
Weisbecker, John 23:175
Weisbrick, Charles 9:127; 27:131
Weisbrod, F. 3:212
Weise, A. 14:124
Weise, Clause 6:8
Weise, H. C. 18:282
Weise, James 20:143
Weise, John 11:47
Weise, Joseph 10:86
Weisel, Rufus 22:228
Weiseman, C. 1:184
Weisensal, J. C. 16:112
Weiser, A. 15:83
Weiser, Anten 25:126
Weiser, Daniel 25:329
Weiser, George 15:290; 16:261
Weiser, J. 25:123
Weiser, Wilson 23:175
Weishan, M. 1:185
Weishaw, M. 1:185
Weishinger, James E. 18:166
Weiskoff, Peter 23:197
Weisland, Fred 19:218
Weisler, Conrad 11:291
Weisman, Henry 17:27
Weisman, Simon 17:427
Weison, Andrew 11:81
Weiss, --- 25:258
Weiss, A. 1:183
Weiss, Carl Gustave 21:401
Weiss, Casper 17:89
Weiss, E. 10:31
Weiss, Joseph 4:61
Weiss, Joseph H. 5:33
Weiss, Julius 18:105

Weiss, Peter 21:145
Weiss, William 11:185
Weissell, F. 21:61
Weisser, C. 1:87
Weisser, John 2:20
Weissgerber, P. 1:83
Weistein, Felix 14:230
Weister, G. 20:388
Weiter, R. 1:86
Weithurs, A. A. 14:230
Weitman, F. 1:181
Weitman, L. 17:215
Weitt, Stephen 7:114
Weitz, Ludwig 19:218
Weitzel, J. F. 11:47
Weitzer, H. 9:99
Weitzhansen, F. 3:212
Weivle, J. 1:89
Weizel, --- 10:203
Weizenaker, G. 3:212
Wekks, J. W. 19:140
Wekks, John 19:140
Weland, S. M. 9:197
Welant, A. 19:231
Welbanks, William
    25:314
Welber, E. G. 3:212
Welborn, Y. 7:114
Welby, Jacob 13:53
Welby, James 20:131
Welce, John 12:84;
    16:359
Welch, A. 25:284
Welch, A. E. 22:469
Welch, Aaron 22:348
Welch, Adam 1:85
Welch, Alfred 25:258
Welch, Bendon 22:326
Welch, Benjamin 13:53
Welch, Benjamin F.
    18:328
Welch, Byron 16:146
Welch, C. 3:212
Welch, C. H. 27:125
Welch, Caleb 11:99
Welch, Charles 1:85;
    9:127; 27:131
Welch, Charles P. 17:159
Welch, Christie 1:85
Welch, D. 13:101; 14:24
Welch, Daniel 10:86;
    11:48; 12:45, 66;
    15:51; 20:388
Welch, David 16:9;
    21:145
Welch, David E. 26:85
Welch, E. 3:212; 15:115
Welch, E. N. 14:124
Welch, E. R. 16:261
Welch, Edward 12:163
Welch, Edwin 8:98

Welch, Eli M. 22:108
Welch, F. B. 15:290;
    16:261
Welch, Frederick 9:241
Welch, Freeman 23:310
Welch, George 7:62;
    13:123; 14:230
Welch, George M. 22:59
Welch, Gilbert 25:125
Welch, Greely 27:125
Welch, H. 9:152; 23:55
Welch, H. D. 11:87
Welch, H. F. 13:53; 16:61
Welch, H. M. 14:230
Welch, Henry 9:8; 14:124;
    23:126; 27:127
Welch, Hiram 8:35
Welch, Hiram J. 21:145
Welch, Isaac 7:45
Welch, J. 1:85; 3:212;
    10:24; 13:76; 14:24;
    16:261; 22:356;
    27:128
Welch, J. T. 25:258
Welch, J. W. 7:114
Welch, Jacob 23:175
Welch, James 3:212; 9:94;
    13:53; 14:230; 16:61;
    17:319; 20:388;
    22:348, 495; 23:56;
    26:83
Welch, James D. 20:139
Welch, James H. 22:326
Welch, James M. 20:131
Welch, Jeremiah 13:123
Welch, Jerome 22:228
Welch, Jerry 22:16
Welch, John 3:212; 8:98;
    11:317; 12:45; 13:53,
    126, 128; 14:124,
    230; 16:61; 17:108;
    19:41; 22:287
Welch, John G. 14:230
Welch, Joseph 17:45
Welch, Josiah 21:61
Welch, L. 3:212
Welch, Lester L. 23:95
Welch, Lewis 23:304
Welch, M. 11:99; 14:24;
    21:45
Welch, Michael 9:94;
    13:53, 123; 14:230;
    26:83
Welch, Morris 11:185
Welch, Oliver 11:215
Welch, P. 1:184; 15:61;
    17:192; 19:264;
    27:128
Welch, Patrick 9:152;
    12:78; 13:123;
    14:230; 21:401; 22:348

Welch, Philip 14:230
Welch, Phillip 8:98
Welch, R. 1:84, 185
Welch, Reuben 13:53
Welch, Robert 11:253;
    15:147; 21:401;
    26:139
Welch, Robert F. 10:142;
    20:388
Welch, T. 1:88; 9:64
Welch, T. C. 3:212
Welch, Th. 14:230
Welch, Thomas 9:30;
    18:318; 20:117;
    22:59; 26:116
Welch, Thomas S. 15:89
Welch, V. 3:212
Welch, W. 3:212; 12:94;
    16:359
Welch, W. C. 13:101;
    14:24
Welch, W. W. 1:182
Welch, William 8:98;
    11:87; 12:78; 14:125;
    15:51; 16:135;
    17:285; 18:41; 24:46;
    25:258; 27:126
Welch, William J. 7:114;
    21:61
Welch, William M.
    22:493
Welch, William S. 19:140
Welcher, Andrew 21:83
Welcher, Henry 27:130
Welcher, John 19:218
Welcher, Joseph 11:330
Welcher, Lyman 17:210
Welcher, Nelson 19:41
Welchner, Daniel H. 8:98
Welcoe, Albert 7:45
Welcome, E. D. 3:212
Welcome, J. A. 27:126
Welcome, Jerome 14:230
Weld, Gustavus 8:35;
    18:166
Welday, Hiram 13:123
Welde, Theodore C. 4:61
Welden, Charles 16:112
Welden, George W. 10:86
Welden, Henry 10:86
Welden, N. W. 20:388
Welden, Sidney 26:83
Welder, David 4:61
Welder, Lewis C. 8:102
Welder, P. E. 25:258
Welder, Solomon D.
    21:401
Welderson, Charles E.
    14:237
Weldey, Edward M. 9:216
Weldier, D. 1:183

Weldin, Henry 20:388
Weldman, H. G. 1:184
Weldman, U. M. 7:45
Weldon, Alex. D. 21:133
Weldon, Charles 3:212
Weldon, E. 23:206
Weldon, E. J. 14:230
Weldon, Edson 3:212
Weldon, George W. 20:388
Weldon, H. L. 11:317
Weldon, Henry 3:212
Weldon, John 3:212; 14:125; 26:214
Weldon, Mathew W. 20:131
Weldon, Patrick 21:401
Weldor, N. W. 10:86
Weldren, Samuel 19:140
Weldy, Nathan 22:494
Welford, Amos 17:327
Welford, Wolcott 5:55
Welfort, Charles 8:35
Welgong, P. 1:182
Welhause, H. 11:175
Welhillet, Samuel 17:448
Welhoff, John 22:445
Welk, J. 1:88
Welker, Anthony 23:183
Welker, H. B. 1:184
Welker, Isaac 23:116
Welker, John 9:30; 18:318; 26:115
Welker, Samuel C. 23:258
Welking, --- 11:343
Welkins, Frederick 11:87
Welkins, H. J. 17:441
Welkins, Hans J. 24:155
Welkman, J. 2:19
Well, Conrad 11:185
Well, E. C. 3:212
Well, George 16:61
Well, Hiram 14:230
Well, Jeremiah 16:261
Well, Perry 10:207
Wellborn, John 18:201
Wellbrooks, William D. 26:199
Wellcock, Albert 10:86; 20:388
Wellder, C. M. 3:212
Welldon, Patrick 8:125
Welle, Edward 11:132
Wellen, Franklin 11:101
Wellen, J. F. 20:131
Wellens, H. C. 15:9
Wellens, Henry C. 12:78
Weller, Calvin P. 22:469
Weller, Casper 9:94
Weller, Charles 22:286
Weller, D. 3:212; 21:192

Weller, F. L. 18:73
Weller, George 14:27
Weller, George W. 19:140
Weller, Harvey H. 24:98
Weller, Henry 24:10
Weller, J. 1:182; 14:125
Weller, J. P. 22:228
Weller, John 14:237
Weller, L. D. 17:289
Weller, Loyd 23:126
Weller, N. 16:261
Weller, R. 23:56
Weller, Smith 17:294
Weller, Theodore 14:125; 24:71
Weller, Thomas B. 8:111
Weller, William 10:185
Welles, C. K. 3:212
Welles, Charles 10:97
Welles, E. 3:212
Welles, F. W. 14:337
Welles, J. 3:212
Welles, Samuel 9:160
Wellestumph, John H. 21:145
Wellett, J. W. 7:62
Wellhigh, James 16:61
Wellhoener, Bryce T. 20:101
Welling, J. 13:101
Welling, O. M. 15:253
Welling, Raymond 22:228
Wellington, Benjamin 10:9; 21:401
Wellington, C. H. 10:25
Wellington, Charles 23:116
Wellington, Charles H. 16:87
Wellington, Daniel 9:212
Wellington, E. 20:87
Wellington, G. R. 3:212
Wellington, G. W. 3:212; 25:258
Wellington, James 8:43; 26:198
Wellington, John 6:9; 12:45; 18:105
Wellington, L. 13:101
Wellington, M. 1:185
Wellington, S. F. 1:83
Wellington, Samuel B. 10:142; 20:389
Wellington, William T. 9:105
Wellington, Wiltso 7:45
Wellis, B. 14:24
Wellit, S. 3:212
Welliver, Washington 7:114
Wellman, --- 8:125

Wellman, Delaware B. 23:102
Wellman, E. 25:258
Wellman, Edward 5:33
Wellman, H. B. 19:243
Wellman, Joe Tinker 6:22
Wellman, John C. 23:302
Wellman, Joseph 12:57
Wellman, Madison 20:139
Wellman, W. 11:318
Wellman, Wilber F. 16:146
Wellman, William 18:224
Wellmon, John C. R. 13:53
Wellnitz, Ernst 21:263
Wellover, Edward 21:89
Wells, --- 20:389
Wells, A. R. 25:258
Wells, Abraham 15:115
Wells, Albert 1:84; 4:61
Wells, Albert M. 12:56
Wells, Alex 13:59
Wells, Andrew 11:217
Wells, Andrew J. 23:82
Wells, Augustus 6:20; 18:99
Wells, B. 1:181; 22:326
Wells, B. F. 13:123
Wells, Benjamin 17:322
Wells, Bernard 20:117
Wells, C. B. 15:79
Wells, C. G. 20:157
Wells, C. J. 3:212
Wells, Caleb 14:276; 17:501
Wells, Charles 1:85
Wells, Charles F. 20:389
Wells, Charles H. 10:86; 20:389
Wells, Charles S. 27:156
Wells, Charles T. 10:94
Wells, Courtland 11:18
Wells, Cyrennus 26:199
Wells, Cyrus 9:203
Wells, D. 1:184, 185
Wells, D. M. 9:64
Wells, Daniel P. 22:16
Wells, David 17:433; 21:162; 22:326; 24:87, 163
Wells, David E. 22:495
Wells, David W. 24:87
Wells, E. 3:212; 18:267; 22:494; 23:253; 26:86
Wells, E. F. 21:209
Wells, E. K. 1:96
Wells, Edmund 9:212
Wells, Edmund H. 20:2
Wells, Edward H. 22:114

Wells, Elijah 22:108
Wells, Elisha 20:32
Wells, Ellison 14:317
Wells, Erastus 10:86;
 20:389
Wells, Erastus A. 10:142;
 20:389
Wells, Eugene A. 20:131
Wells, F. 3:212; 18:409
Wells, Ferdinand 23:291
Wells, Francis 13:53
Wells, Francis M. 17:405
Wells, Frank 18:441
Wells, Franklin 10:142;
 20:389
Wells, Fred 17:93
Wells, Frederick W. 7:45
Wells, G. A. 3:212
Wells, G. G. 14:285
Wells, Gardner H. 11:291
Wells, George 12:52;
 13:53
Wells, George C. 19:264
Wells, George D. 6:10;
 18:116
Wells, George M. 23:56
Wells, George O. 9:197
Wells, George W. 13:53;
 22:445
Wells, Greenbury 22:108
Wells, H. 16:261
Wells, H. A. 22:494
Wells, H. L. 15:156
Wells, Henry 13:53;
 16:61; 25:258
Wells, Henry C. 9:30
Wells, Henry T. 21:83
Wells, Isaiah 21:145
Wells, Isaiah L. 12:45
Wells, Isam 19:297
Wells, Israel 17:424;
 24:174
Wells, J. 1:88, 96, 181;
 14:125; 25:258
Wells, J. B. 11:283
Wells, J. D. 11:253
Wells, J. H. 5:33
Wells, J. J. 11:417
Wells, J. M. 3:212;
 14:230
Wells, J. R. 5:55
Wells, J. T. 12:166;
 26:199
Wells, J. W. 11:418
Wells, James 5:47; 7:45;
 9:212; 20:389;
 21:401
Wells, James H. 21:145;
 22:59
Wells, James M. 9:197;
 19:231

Wells, Jeff 3:212
Wells, Jeremiah 16:87
Wells, John 9:69; 13:53;
 16:61; 18:41; 21:45;
 22:115; 25:259
Wells, John G. 1:84
Wells, John H. 10:24;
 11:48
Wells, John M. 22:59
Wells, John P. 16:112
Wells, John R. 24:168
Wells, John W. 3:212;
 22:108
Wells, Joseph 10:97;
 22:59, 108
Wells, Julius 7:114
Wells, L. P. 2:19
Wells, L. W. 22:522
Wells, Lee 21:288
Wells, Levi 21:213;
 22:158
Wells, Lorenzo D. 22:108
Wells, M. 14:24; 17:157
Wells, M. W. 9:30;
 18:318; 26:116
Wells, Marcellus W.
 12:45
Wells, Marcus P. 8:111
Wells, Marshall 6:14;
 18:99
Wells, Martin 21:401
Wells, Mathew C. 22:413
Wells, Michael C. 24:71
Wells, N. 14:125
Wells, N. D. 9:197
Wells, N. J. 27:127
Wells, Nathan 22:59
Wells, Nathaniel K. 12:45
Wells, Nelson 13:59
Wells, Nimrod 17:189
Wells, O. E. 1:96
Wells, P. 9:64
Wells, Peter 15:79
Wells, Poney 23:56
Wells, Porter 23:175
Wells, R. 1:184
Wells, R. C. 23:56
Wells, R. M. 22:348;
 27:156
Wells, R. S. 10:94; 20:389
Wells, R. W. 12:172
Wells, Reason 10:86;
 20:389
Wells, Reuben 26:199
Wells, Richard 18:224
Wells, Royall 23:56
Wells, Russell 27:132
Wells, S. 3:212
Wells, S. I. 24:33
Wells, S. P. 13:101
Wells, S. S. 18:99

Wells, Samuel 4:61;
 16:261; 20:131;
 22:326
Wells, Sarah 7:7
Wells, Seymour 15:348;
 16:391
Wells, Simeon R. 22:108
Wells, Stephen 7:114
Wells, Stephen C. 6:11
Wells, Thomas 11:318,
 418; 12:159; 16:285;
 21:288
Wells, Thomas Jefferson
 27:157
Wells, Uriah 17:285
Wells, Uriate T. 23:16
Wells, W. 1:83, 185;
 10:150; 18:61
Wells, W. A. 14:125
Wells, W. H. 1:100; 3:212
Wells, W. J. 9:152;
 25:259
Wells, W. M. 20:180
Wells, Ward S. 21:83
Wells, Waylome C. 9:105
Wells, William 9:137;
 10:86, 169; 12:159;
 19:140; 20:389;
 22:273, 494; 23:82;
 27:129
Wells, William B. 22:108
Wells, William C. 10:86;
 20:389; 22:59
Wells, William D. 20:26
Wells, William E. 22:273
Wells, William H. 24:47
Wells, William P. 9:17
Wells, William R. 20:177;
 23:175
Wells, William W. 19:218
Wells, Z. 9:203
Wells, Zealbor 19:285
Welly, E. W. 21:402
Welm, Peter 16:146
Welman, James T. 4:61
Welman, John L. 17:286
Welman, Thomas 21:402
Welman, William 17:421
Welmer, F. 25:259
Welmon, Newton 13:75
Welner, George 10:169
Welsch, --- 11:317
Welsch, John 7:114
Welsch, Peter 20:131
Welsch, W. 9:152
Welse, G. 23:245
Welser, Adam 27:133
Welser, M. W. 15:178
Welsh, --- 16:130
Welsh, A. 14:125
Welsh, Alone 20:389

Welsh, C. F. 12:139
Welsh, C. H. 9:127
Welsh, Charles 16:160
Welsh, D. 14:125; 16:112
Welsh, Daniel 11:405;
    17:89
Welsh, David 7:45
Welsh, E. 16:153
Welsh, E. M. 14:230
Welsh, E. R. 15:296
Welsh, Edw. 25:259
Welsh, Edward 12:172;
    15:283
Welsh, Edward P. 21:402
Welsh, F. 19:218
Welsh, Frank 3:212
Welsh, G. L. 3:212
Welsh, George 12:44;
    25:259
Welsh, George W. 24:10
Welsh, H. 19:140
Welsh, H. S. 1:86
Welsh, Harper 10:86
Welsh, Hiram 18:166
Welsh, Iray 22:413
Welsh, J. 13:101; 15:147
Welsh, J. C. 9:152;
    27:131
Welsh, J. H. 23:56
Welsh, J. M. 14:335
Welsh, James 4:61; 10:86,
    142; 11:47; 12:54,
    56; 20:389
Welsh, John 4:61; 6:11;
    9:205; 12:45; 14:29,
    125; 18:105
Welsh, John F. 5:33
Welsh, Josiah 14:320;
    25:273
Welsh, L. 3:212
Welsh, M. 13:101
Welsh, M. S. 14:125
Welsh, Morris 12:45
Welsh, Owen W. 7:65
Welsh, P. 14:125; 25:259
Welsh, Patrick 12:44;
    23:102
Welsh, Perry 5:33
Welsh, Peter 14:331
Welsh, Robert 9:216;
    14:337
Welsh, Samuel A. 22:238
Welsh, Susan 22:348
Welsh, Thimothy 14:320
Welsh, Thomas 10:142;
    20:389; 22:522;
    27:131
Welsh, Thomas H. 4:61
Welsh, Timothy 25:273
Welsh, W. 14:125;
    16:275; 27:128

Welsh, William 5:55;
    16:160
Welshe, Haper 20:389
Welsheimer, O. 17:45
Welshouse, Reuben
    22:444
Welshow, Stephen 17:271
Welson, L. H. 14:125
Welt, John W. 23:175
Weltch, Thomas 9:127
Welter, Henry 26:84
Weltick, E. 20:389
Weltick, Ernest 10:86
Weltloff, Gottlieb 10:86
Weltoff, G. 20:389
Welton, Alma 22:158
Welton, Bruce 20:191
Welton, Daniel P. 22:348
Welton, J. A. 13:126
Welton, Jesse 17:101
Welton, Milton J. 21:145
Welton, N. S. 3:212
Welton, S. 15:4
Weltraw, Henry 10:7
Welts, A. 18:41
Welts, Robert 22:522
Welts, William H. 22:522
Welty, David S. 22:286
Welty, Emanuel F. 21:237
Welty, John 21:237
Welty, Samuel F. 17:27
Weltz, Charles E. 25:278
Weltz, David 13:53;
    22:443
Weltz, Ira 3:212
Weltz, J. 21:192
Weltz, John 20:389
Weltz, Joseph 22:59
Welver, Charles 17:245
Wembal, J. 11:283
Wempe, John 11:81
Wemple, A. Zeily 21:263
Wemple, E. 14:230
Wemple, Henry D. W.
    21:118
Wemple, Nelson 12:45
Wempler, Austin 24:168
Wempner, Augustus C.
    10:142; 20:389
Wen, Joshua T. 10:142
Wen, S. 15:253
Wenborn, Thomas 1:85
Wencell, Edward 23:14
Wench, Andrew 8:98
Wench, Asa 21:402
Wend, A. 14:125
Wendal, Adam 17:45
Wendalin, Hoag 20:109
Wendall, Augustus 26:117
Wendall, Charles J. 12:45
Wendall, Elijah 9:30

Wendall, J. 27:129
Wendall, William 11:89
Wendell, Augustus 9:40;
    18:298
Wendell, Clipah 26:116
Wendell, Clipoh 18:318
Wendell, J. 9:152
Wendell, J. J. 14:27;
    15:262
Wendell, James 9:64
Wendell, John C. 10:7
Wendell, John R. 22:108
Wendelschaeffer, Henry
    22:16
Wendenhall, J. A. 18:388
Wenderlin, Hugh 10:142
Wendewhall, J. A. 9:226
Wending, T. 14:125
Wendland, John 21:263
Wendlarby, A. 3:212
Wendle, W. 11:253
Wendler, George 10:86;
    20:389
Wendling, George 4:61
Wendling, Henry 22:228
Wendling, Thomas P.
    12:45
Wendorff, Frederick
    22:286
Wendrich, C. 14:27
Wendrick, James O.
    17:240
Wendsor, Lawrence
    15:254
Wendsworth, Champ
    9:160
Wendt, Charles 4:61;
    9:30; 26:116
Wendt, Frederic 17:101
Wendworth, Robert H.
    5:33
Wenger, Joseph 24:87
Wenger, Reuben 21:219
Wengert, Frederick 15:15
Wenglein, J. 1:184
Wengler, John 26:83
Wengman, Frederick
    20:389
Wengo, S. R. 3:212
Weniger, David 23:56
Weniter, A. 1:100
Wenk, W. B. 14:125
Wenkel, L. 13:123
Wenkoop, George 16:61
Wenlile, E. W. 9:46
Wenman, Arthur 12:45
Wenman, James W. 9:46
Wenn, Solomon 21:402
Wennebrenner, William
    8:98
Wenner, Charles 17:74

Wenner, James 18:318
Wenner, N. 1:184
Wenner, William 17:93
Wenrick, William H. 9:127; 27:130
Wensel, John G. 16:75
Wensel, Robert E. 22:238
Wensel, W. 18:318; 26:115
Wensel, W. J. 10:207
Wensell, William 9:30
Wenst, Henry 21:128
Went, Charles 3:212
Went, Lewis 15:61
Wentgel, Thomas 3:212
Wenthworth, Charles H. 15:13
Wentle, C. 15:254
Wentley, J. 3:212
Wentling, Joseph 3:212
Wentt, Theodore 23:175
Wentworth, A. C. 1:88
Wentworth, Alexander 24:64
Wentworth, Alvin S. 4:61
Wentworth, B. 15:254
Wentworth, Charles 3:212; 10:142; 20:389
Wentworth, David 10:142; 20:389
Wentworth, David W. 19:231
Wentworth, E. 13:123; 15:254; 16:261; 19:140
Wentworth, E. J. 14:262
Wentworth, F. 1:184
Wentworth, Fred 9:152
Wentworth, Frederick 27:127
Wentworth, G. 19:231; 25:259
Wentworth, George 9:197
Wentworth, George A. 10:24
Wentworth, George D. 12:45; 16:160
Wentworth, Grant 5:33
Wentworth, J. 12:78
Wentworth, J. H. 21:402
Wentworth, J. Q. 7:76; 25:308
Wentworth, J. W. 8:76
Wentworth, Jacob 4:61
Wentworth, John 7:70; 16:61
Wentworth, John H. 9:241
Wentworth, Joseph 3:212
Wentworth, L. 3:213
Wentworth, L. D. 27:130

Wentworth, N. 21:402
Wentworth, R. 25:259
Wentworth, S. D. 9:127
Wentworth, Sewell 9:216
Wentworth, W. 14:230
Wentworth, W. H. 1:183
Wenty, Martin 5:33
Wentz, Anthony 4:61
Wentz, Aug 18:402
Wentz, C. 3:213
Wentz, C. K. 27:125
Wentz, Charles 10:86; 20:389
Wentz, Frederick 16:112
Wentz, Isaac 12:57
Wentz, Jacob 14:231
Wentz, James 10:86; 20:389
Wentz, Martin 25:259
Wentzell, John T. 21:219
Wentzer, Samuel B. 4:61
Wenwright, George 23:244
Wenzel, Frank 19:293
Wenzell, Frank 9:203
Weolfe, J. D. 21:127
Wepmore, Crup 8:57
Wepp, Henry 23:175
Weppard, John 22:228
Wepper, C. 14:231
Werak, Anton 18:212
Werchkensist, George 12:78
Werde, William 11:18
Werdin, W. 3:213
Werdner, J. W. 5:33
Werdon, Joseph 22:444
Werds, John 12:97
Were, Archibald 11:132
Wergel, Christopher 7:114
Werhen, Eugene 21:402
Werkis, J. G. 8:57
Werkmeister, George 15:79
Werkmeister, John 4:61
Werley, Abram 18:269
Werline, John P. 23:287
Werlker, Benjamin 22:326
Werls, E. H. 15:79
Wermer, Joseph 26:115
Wermuth, J. 14:231
Werner, A. 1:88
Werner, Albert 18:318; 26:115
Werner, Charles W. 20:117
Werner, F. 17:194
Werner, Frederick 21:107
Werner, George 10:169; 16:154; 19:218; 20:389

Werner, Howard 22:356
Werner, J. 19:314
Werner, John 23:175
Werner, John C. 1:85
Werner, P. 12:81; 25:259
Werner, Samuel 22:108
Wernsing, Fred. G. 23:175
Werper, J. 3:213
Werpert, H. 15:254
Werrich, H. C. 24:87
Wersett, Isaac 22:399
Werst, Joseph 16:130
Werst, Stephen 23:95
Wert, Jonas 4:61
Wert, Sandy 18:41
Wertenberger, Daniel 17:275
Werth, E. 20:389
Werth, Herm 17:310
Werther, J. 21:165
Werting, John 3:213
Wertlew, Rad'p's 1:85
Wertman, David A. 10:98
Wertman, Francis 20:109
Wertman, John L. 25:125
Werts, August 11:397
Werts, D. 17:293
Werts, Louis 3:213
Werts, N. I. 18:298
Werts, N. J. 26:116
Wertsch, C. 1:182
Wertworth, S. W. 8:57
Wertz, Charles 3:213
Wertz, James 3:213
Wertz, John 22:348
Wertz, N. J. 9:40
Wertz, Seymour 23:82
Werzer, Fred 25:308
Wes, David 18:388
Wes, Michael 23:175
Wesbrook, G. W. 16:275
Wesbury, C. 10:211
Wescatt, D. K. 22:522
Wesch, Henry 10:142; 20:389
Wescler, Jacob 21:61
Wesco, T. 26:199
Wescoat, G. W. 16:359
Wescot, G. W. 13:101
Wescot, Isaac 21:45
Wescott, Alvin 9:197; 19:264
Wescott, Bowen 21:12
Wescott, C. 20:389; 22:414
Wescott, Charles 7:82; 15:93
Wescott, Charles A. 11:274
Wescott, Cyrus 16:261
Wescott, David B. 17:252

Wescott, Degualvas
14:231
Wescott, F. A. 19:287
Wescott, Isaiah 7:70
Wescott, John 19:41
Wescott, L. 13:75; 19:140
Wescott, Losbett 16:261
Wescott, Noel B. 7:80
Wescott, R. H. 12:79;
15:51
Wescott, S. 15:301
Wescott, Theodore 25:259
Wesden, Henry 17:189
Wesel, Ira 8:57
Weser, D. 12:167
Weser, Joshua 20:389
Wesgate, N. B. 16:275
Wesgate, N. W. 14:24
Weslake, J. 3:213
Wesler, Adam J. 23:175
Wesler, William R.
25:329
Wesley, --- 25:335
Wesley, Augustus 18:435
Wesley, C. 1:185
Wesley, D. J. 15:254
Wesley, Deley 17:497
Wesley, Edward 8:57
Wesley, F. 1:185
Wesley, Gurry 17:208
Wesley, J. 13:101
Wesley, J. G. 19:244
Wesley, James 10:177;
17:189; 19:49, 218
Wesley, Joe 11:426
Wesley, John 5:33; 6:20;
8:112; 9:212;
11:217; 14:231;
18:99; 19:49, 293;
21:288; 22:524
Wesley, John G. 9:197
Wesley, Jordan 11:82
Wesley, Kindley 11:177
Wesley, Robert T. 17:208
Wesley, S. R. 16:285
Wesley, Thomas 17:189
Wesley, Venerable 16:112
Wesley, W. 9:155; 27:128
Wesley, William 21:402
Wesner, Charles 15:79
Wesner, J. 3:213
Wess, M. 21:86
Wessee, E. S. 17:473
Wessel, Barnard 22:163
Wessel, James 15:164
Wessell, Frederick 10:86
Wesser, George 17:168
Wessie, E. S. 14:313
Wessley, A. 1:181
West, A. 21:45
West, A. J. 11:221; 23:56

West, A. L. 13:126
West, Aaron 19:41
West, Adin 20:32
West, Albert 14:285;
15:61; 17:503
West, Alfred 12:45
West, Arzy 16:112
West, Ashbel W. 23:197
West, Benjamin 22:158
West, Benona B. 11:178
West, C. 11:19
West, C. H. 3:213; 11:114
West, Charles 8:68; 9:40;
11:175; 13:53;
14:231; 15:156
West, Charles E. 18:299;
26:117
West, Christopher 23:82
West, Claus 12:94
West, Clay 12:60
West, Clayborn 22:443
West, Covington O.
22:459
West, D. 15:346; 16:391
West, D. J. 7:76
West, Daniel 7:136;
10:86; 20:389
West, David 22:59, 326
West, Demon A. 25:259
West, E. 3:213; 16:261;
17:189
West, E. M. 22:326
West, Eathan A. 27:132
West, Edw. 1:85
West, Edward 7:136
West, Ervin 20:82
West, F. 3:213; 14:125
West, F. L. 11:113
West, F. W. 11:274
West, Francis 13:123;
16:261
West, Francis A. 8:35;
18:166
West, Frank M. 25:259
West, Freeman 23:102
West, G. 13:101
West, G. W. 14:231
West, George 9:17;
17:286; 25:259;
26:85
West, George H. 20:45
West, George W. 22:286
West, H. 1:87; 3:213;
15:89
West, H. B. 14:249
West, H. C. 24:115
West, H. M. 25:125
West, Hamilton 12:79
West, Harrison 12:52
West, Harry 14:231
West, Harry Boyd 26:234

West, Henry 4:61; 7:136
West, Henry L. 9:127;
27:131
West, Horatio 23:102
West, Hugh S. 12:45
West, I. 10:142
West, I. A. 26:115
West, I. F. 25:275
West, Isaac 5:47; 22:228;
25:259
West, Isaac J. 17:357
West, Isaac N. 8:35;
18:166
West, J. 1:184; 3:213;
9:152; 12:159;
20:175, 389; 23:206
West, J. A. 9:30; 18:318
West, J. B. 25:259
West, J. D. 25:308
West, J. G. 3:213
West, J. H. 8:35; 18:166
West, J. L. 26:199
West, J. M. 1:183
West, J. P. 3:213
West, J. Q. A. 1:85
West, J. W. 10:86;
20:389; 27:128
West, Jacob 11:48
West, James 1:86; 3:213;
7:136; 10:207;
11:397; 13:123;
20:131; 25:335;
26:84
West, James M. 24:33
West, James P. 5:33
West, James S. 9:99
West, James W. 4:61
West, Jasper C. 18:212
West, John 3:213; 17:61;
22:399, 495; 23:304
West, John C. 3:213
West, John D. 22:443
West, John H. 11:284
West, John W. 11:397
West, Joseph 22:59
West, Judson H. 12:45
West, L. 1:181
West, L. W. 9:153
West, Lenox F. 10:10
West, Levi 1:84
West, Lorenzo D. 12:45
West, Lyman 27:133
West, M. 1:183, 185;
3:213
West, M. J. 1:184
West, Manassah 24:33
West, Marcus 23:304
West, Miles 7:45
West, Myron L. 21:263
West, N. 25:259; 27:127
West, N. A. 8:123

West, Nathaniel 5:47
West, Nelson N. 18:342
West, O. M. 1:181
West, Oliver 10:98; 24:33
West, P. H. 3:213
West, Peter 10:86;
    16:112; 20:389
West, R. 13:53
West, R. W. 21:61
West, Recan 22:273
West, Reuben 11:215, 283
West, Robert 7:136
West, S. 9:64; 12:167;
    14:125; 18:388
West, S. D. 11:405
West, S. F. 22:159
West, S. H. 20:47
West, S. N. 3:213
West, Samuel 9:226
West, Samuel P. 23:82
West, Samuel R. 12:147
West, Samuel W. 21:402
West, Santer 1:87
West, Silas B. 27:132
West, Simon 6:34; 25:329
West, Stephen 10:210
West, Sylvanus 8:35;
    18:166
West, T. 16:261; 23:175
West, Thomas 7:136;
    14:313; 17:61, 481;
    21:83; 22:469, 494;
    27:132
West, Thomas A. 8:111
West, Titus L. 4:61
West, Vincent 22:348
West, W. 9:64, 153;
    19:314; 21:13;
    22:326; 23:265
West, W. F. 3:213
West, W. H. 11:47
West, W. H. H. 15:178
West, W. S. 26:85
West, Westley 22:273
West, William 3:213;
    9:30; 10:86; 11:48;
    20:86, 389; 21:45;
    22:495; 23:102
West, William C. 17:45
West, William D. 18:224;
    22:414
West, William H. 8:98;
    22:133; 23:14
West, William J. 22:59
West, William M. 6:34;
    23:116
West, William R. 25:329
West, William S. 18:267
West, William T. 12:57
West, Williamson 21:145
West, Wilson M. 9:105

Westacott, R. 1:86
Westall, Booth 11:418
Westall, James 23:253
Westbrook, A. 1:87
Westbrook, Abner H.
    21:45
Westbrook, B. D. 3:213
Westbrook, Henry 10:142;
    20:389
Westbrook, J. 1:182; 2:19;
    25:128
Westbrook, J. H. 3:213
Westbrook, L. 1:185
Westbrook, R. 19:264
Westbrook, R. L. 3:213
Westbrook, R. M. 19:140
Westbrook, S. 15:254
Westbrook, T. 27:127
Westbrook, William 8:68;
    24:47
Westbrook, Z. 13:101
Westbrooks, --- 17:509
Westbrooks, Richard
    9:197
Westburg, Joseph L.
    21:239
Westcoat, J. 13:101
Westcoat, James 13:54
Westcol, George 16:391
Westcott, A. 14:125
Westcott, C. 25:308
Westcott, David D.
    25:126
Westcott, Get 15:346
Westcott, H. S. 17:333
Westcott, James 16:61
Westcott, Joseph 1:85
Westcott, N. B. 25:308
Westcott, P. R. 14:125
Westcott, W. W. 13:53
Westenbarg, A. J. 22:228
Westenbarger, D. 22:228
Westenbarger, J. 20:150
Westenbarger, John
    22:228
Westenbrook, --- 25:259
Westenham, A. 18:318;
    26:116
Westenhaven, Abe 9:30
Westenhaver, I. E. 24:87
Westenholt, Benjamin
    6:11
Wester, Ferdinand 8:35
Westerbrook, D. 3:213
Westerfield, C. A. 11:318
Westerfield, Cornelius E.
    12:45
Westerfield, P. S. 3:213
Westerfield, W. B. 9:74
Westerfield, W. S. 1:84
Westerland, E. 24:33

Westerler, S. 15:254
Westerly, William H. 5:33
Westerman, Calvin A.
    22:495
Westerman, F. 16:359
Westerman, F. B. 1:181
Westerman, George W.
    15:61
Westerman, John 11:117
Western, J. 14:125
Western, Reuben 22:459
Western, T. B. 13:81
Western, Thomas B.
    16:261
Westerso, Thomas 22:228
Westervelt, --- 10:169;
    19:319
Westervelt, Peter 12:60
Westfall, A. 19:264
Westfall, David 9:226
Westfall, Ed 17:264
Westfall, F. 18:299
Westfall, Fellman 26:116
Westfall, G. W. 23:175
Westfall, George 13:53;
    22:108
Westfall, Greenup J.
    23:103
Westfall, J. 1:184; 3:213
Westfall, J. C. 11:418
Westfall, J. J. 1:180
Westfall, Jacob 4:61
Westfall, Joel 22:228
Westfall, John 3:213
Westfall, John W. 25:280
Westfall, L. 14:125
Westfall, P. 11:175
Westfall, Robert R.
    23:259
Westfall, Tillman 9:40
Westfall, W. M. 9:226
Westfall, W. W. 7:138
Westfall, William 12:45;
    18:388
Westfield, Charles 12:45
Westfield, Edward E.
    9:127; 27:131
Westfield, Reeder 21:219
Westfrap, H. 3:213
Westgate, C. E. 19:218
Westgate, Freeling 20:117
Westgate, N. W. 13:101
Westgate, Warren M.
    11:114
Westgate, William 16:160
Westgte, D. 1:86
Westhand, B. 21:402
Westhis, Bernard 21:402
Westhoff, Gustavus
    12:148; 19:314
Westhouse, A. 20:389

Westiel, C. M. 15:254
Westlake, --- 25:259
Westlake, Albion B. 13:53
Westlake, J. H. 11:418
Westlake, L. 22:228
Westlake, Oscar 16:359
Westlake, Samuel 10:142; 20:389
Westlake, Samuel R. 17:251
Westlake, Thomas J. 17:277
Westland, Jonas 20:15
Westle, A. 13:101
Westle, E. 14:24
Westley, John 17:69; 21:288; 22:506
Westley; Joseph 25:124
Westman, G. W. 24:87
Westman, N. 3:213
Westmeyer, Abe 16:166
Westmoreland, D. L. 9:244
Westmoreland, W. H. 22:273
Westmuller, Conrad 13:54
Weston, --- 3:213
Weston, C. L. 20:389
Weston, Cyrenus L. 10:86
Weston, F. 24:47
Weston, G. 10:31; 19:314
Weston, George 11:117; 14:337
Weston, George E. 19:325
Weston, H. L. 1:181
Weston, Harvey C. 17:289
Weston, Henry 11:317
Weston, J. 18:185
Weston, J. L. 15:51
Weston, J. M. 16:142
Weston, John 1:191; 21:83; 22:59
Weston, John L. 12:79
Weston, John W. 13:123
Weston, Jotham F. 24:71
Weston, L. 3:213
Weston, Lafayette 7:45
Weston, W. C. 11:273
Weston, W. L. 18:41
Weston, W. W. 3:213
Weston, William 9:127; 10:86; 20:389; 27:131
Westover, George 10:7
Westover, Henry 26:132
Westover, J. 3:213
Westover, John 14:125
Westover, L. E. 20:131
Westphal, August 25:335
Westrahan, Charles 10:94
Westred, Jacob 9:94

Westrel, Jacob 26:83
Westrope, Daniel S. 20:131
Westruham, Charles 20:390
Westworth, J. 15:79
Westy, R. 25:259
Wet, H. B. 27:135
Weteger, Jerome 10:169
Wetgger, Jerome 19:218
Wetharm, Henry 11:176
Wethearld, Henry L. 23:82
Wethee, D. 18:21
Wetheral, N. 25:259
Wetherall, W. 1:89
Wetherbee, Delon 10:24
Wetherbee, Edward 10:24
Wetherbee, S. N. 25:126
Wetherby, H. 25:126; 26:84
Wetherby, W. F. 14:231
Wetherby, William H. 25:259
Wethercatt, John 21:248
Wetherel, Asa 5:33
Wetherell, J. W. 11:175
Wetherell, Joseph 22:494
Wetherford, Stephen 22:273
Wetherhoe, C. M. 15:254
Wetherholt, C. 3:213
Wetherill, J. 16:261
Wetherill, W. 16:261
Wethers, A. W. 14:261
Wethers, Henry 4:61
Wethers, Isaac 21:402
Wethers, J. 25:259
Wethers, R. P. 19:41
Wethery, J. R. 25:259
Wethiffer, Adam 21:402
Wethman, A. 14:231
Wetling, Charles E. 20:390
Wetluffer, Adam 7:114
Wetman, Cyrus 12:45
Wetman, Newton 16:261
Wetmer, T. S. 18:41
Wetmore, George 18:41
Wetmore, J. 1:89
Wetmore, Ruel 22:228
Wetmore, Werner 21:402
Wetrel, S. 1:96
Wetry, J. M. 3:213
Wets, Frederic 18:61
Wett, Austin G. 11:82
Wett, George 14:133
Wett, J. F. 3:213
Wette, Henry 7:45
Wettemer, P. 1:88
Wetter, W. H. 3:213

Wetteran, Louis 21:94
Wettereau, Lewis 8:57
Wetterer, Ferdinand 4:61
Wetters, Charles 24:33
Wettseh, Harrison 11:121
Wettus, M. V. 14:125
Wettz, John 10:86
Wetzel, Aaron 15:254
Wetzel, Adam 8:76
Wetzel, Benjamin 13:54
Wetzel, Jacob 14:231
Wetzel, John 11:324
Wetzel, Joseph 18:201
Wetzel, William 9:30
Wetzel, William M. 19:218
Wetzel, William W. 10:146
Wetzell, Thomas J. 17:351
Wever, E. A. 27:156
Wever, Henry C. 25:124
Wever, O. 12:163
Wever, William 18:99
Wever, William P. 9:137
Wevitt, G. 25:259
Wexky, Albert 21:402
Wey, Addison A. 16:61
Wey, Addison H. 13:54
Weyand, William 3:213
Weyburn, Oscar 26:83
Weyerbacker, Henry 27:126
Weygandt, J. A. 23:293
Weygart, E. 7:54
Weygman, Frederick 10:142
Weyhrick, Peter 22:413
Weyman, H. A. 25:329
Weyman, Henry 23:82
Weyman, Hubert 11:47
Weyman, James B. 22:459
Weymer, Abraham G. 9:40
Weymouth, A. D. 7:76; 25:308
Weymouth, Fred A. 13:54
Weymouth, G. S. 15:147
Weymouth, J. 1:182
Weymouth, Orrin 13:54
Weymouth, William 1:84
Weymouth, William P. 25:259
Weyrarck, Thomas J. 23:175
Weyser, Charles W. 16:62
Weysievusky, J. 22:348
Weysser, Charles N. 13:54
Whacer, William 12:66
Whach, John C. 25:259
Whaeton, William 19:41
Whalen, Andrew 17:391

Whalen, David 11:334
Whalen, Dennis 25:125
Whalen, E. 9:127
Whalen, Edward 23:82
Whalen, Elijah 20:187
Whalen, F. H. 7:45
Whalen, H. 3:213
Whalen, James 7:114;
21:402; 22:108, 173
Whalen, John 17:61;
21:94, 291; 22:348
Whalen, M. 3:213; 24:33
Whalen, Michael 17:98
Whalen, Nicholas 21:237
Whalen, P. 1:87, 184
Whalen, Thomas 8:35;
18:166; 22:228, 494
Whalen, W. E. 27:130
Whalen, William 15:51
Whalen, William H.
17:410; 22:159
Whalend, James 14:125
Whaler, George 17:140;
24:206
Whaler, John 25:124
Whales, Joseph A. 21:237
Whales, Thomas 21:200
Whaley, A. H. 10:169
Whaley, Aaron 17:427;
24:181
Whaley, Albert H. 19:218
Whaley, C. H. 1:85
Whaley, Charles 11:113
Whaley, Cyrus E. 11:178
Whaley, Daniel 16:9
Whaley, Francis 4:61
Whaley, G. 1:100
Whaley, G. S. 1:88
Whaley, J. C. 13:101
Whaley, James 27:126
Whaley, Jefferson 17:399
Whaley, Jerry 11:406
Whaley, John 11:253;
22:286
Whaley, John R. 17:61
Whaley, Joseph 11:114
Whaley, Joshua W.
17:318
Whaley, Manfred 10:175;
19:218
Whaley, O. 22:228
Whaley, Pat 18:166
Whaley, Pat. 8:35
Whaley, Peter 7:136
Whaley, Preston 9:100
Whaley, Samuel 17:189
Whaley, Sidney 19:49
Whaley, W. F. 19:140
Whaley, Wash 26:131
Whaley, Washington 9:46
Whaley, West O. 11:330

Whaley, William 8:35;
18:166
Whalin, David 21:244
Whalin, John 8:35; 18:166
Whalin, R. 5:47; 25:259
Whalin, Samuel E. 8:111
Whalin, Samuel H. 17:61
Whalint, Thomas H.
11:406
Whalke, Charles 12:45
Whallay, John 1:83
Whalley, George W.
17:204
Whalon, John 19:41
Whalwick, Sidney 23:56
Whan, Peter H. 6:34
Whang, James 18:99
Whar---, Charles 20:45
Whard, Peter H. 25:329
Wharff, A. F. 19:231
Wharhiel, J. 11:132
Wharmby, Thomas 25:126
Wharry, George 24:73
Wharry, Thomas M. 7:65
Wharton, C. 11:178
Wharton, Cyrus B. 20:26
Wharton, David B. 21:107
Wharton, George 20:45
Wharton, J. 1:183;
13:101; 14:24
Wharton, R. 3:213
Wharton, Samuel 3:213;
22:495
Wharton, William 1:88
What, I. 14:231
Whaters, Joseph 9:64
Whatey, William 15:115
Whatford, Alex. 16:261
Whatley, O. 25:259
Whatley, William B.
21:402
Whatlin, T. 15:346
Whatman, Elijah 22:326
Whatt, George 13:123
Whatten, F. 16:391
Whaum, T. S. 3:213
Whaxter, Benjamin 7:45
Whealan, J. H. 1:87
Whealan, M. 1:184
Whealen, Charles K.
18:402
Whealer, N. S. 15:4
Wheat, A. A. G. 14:125
Wheat, Charles L. 13:54
Wheat, George 14:237
Wheat, J. 3:213
Wheat, J. C. 11:101
Wheat, Jack 17:189
Wheat, Joseph 15:115
Wheat, Pharaoh 17:189
Wheat, Richard 14:125

Wheat, Thompson H. 1:85
Wheat, Watson 25:259
Wheatcraft, Mulah 11:177
Wheaten, John 14:231
Wheater, B. E. 13:101
Wheater, V. E. 14:24
Wheatley, Elias 10:86;
20:390
Wheatley, J. H. 7:54
Wheatley, James 18:267;
19:331; 26:85
Wheatley, Mathew 10:86;
20:390
Wheatley, T. 1:100
Wheatley, William M.
20:101
Wheatly, J. 22:59
Wheaton, A. D. 26:200
Wheaton, Almon 11:176
Wheaton, B. L. 22:348
Wheaton, C. 21:184, 288
Wheaton, Campbell
11:217
Wheaton, H. 17:157
Wheaton, Henry 13:123
Wheaton, Henry F. 12:79
Wheaton, James 1:86
Wheaton, Jasup B. 4:61
Wheaton, Jerome 15:115
Wheaton, Reuben B.
24:73
Wheaton, William 17:293
Wheaton, William B.
10:169; 19:218
Whedling, John A. 24:181
Wheed, George 18:41
Wheelan, D. 8:57
Wheelan, Daniel 25:127
Wheelan, George 16:62
Wheelan, J. 3:213
Wheelan, J. N. O. 22:159
Wheeland, W. P. 1:185
Wheelbarger, F. W. 8:57
Wheeldon, John H.
21:237
Wheeler, --- 18:201
Wheeler, A. 15:25
Wheeler, A. A. 1:83
Wheeler, A. P. 18:61
Wheeler, Aaron H. 22:108
Wheeler, Able A. 20:101
Wheeler, Adam 10:142
Wheeler, Albert 1:86;
11:215; 12:139
Wheeler, Almer H. 22:59
Wheeler, Alonzo 12:79
Wheeler, Amos C. 22:108
Wheeler, Anthony 9:30;
26:116
Wheeler, Archibald 4:61
Wheeler, Augustus 21:219

Wheeler, B. 3:213, 214
Wheeler, B. F. 10:150; 18:61
Wheeler, Barton 22:133
Wheeler, Benjamin 12:45
Wheeler, C. 1:181, 184; 12:94; 14:125; 16:359
Wheeler, C. C. 3:213
Wheeler, C. E. 1:183; 17:233
Wheeler, C. H. 14:317
Wheeler, C. W. 16:261
Wheeler, Calvin 17:445; 24:164
Wheeler, Charles 9:137, 212; 10:154; 18:73; 19:218, 337; 22:159; 27:129
Wheeler, Charles E. 8:35; 18:166
Wheeler, Charles H. 21:402
Wheeler, Cyrus B. 22:159
Wheeler, D. 3:213; 13:123
Wheeler, Daniel 1:85
Wheeler, David 22:326
Wheeler, E. 11:274; 15:346; 16:391; 25:259
Wheeler, E. A. 7:70
Wheeler, E. H. 1:83
Wheeler, Ed 25:308
Wheeler, Edward 9:197
Wheeler, Edwin 15:93
Wheeler, Edwin R. 15:348
Wheeler, Elias 22:444
Wheeler, Enos L. 7:136
Wheeler, Ephraim 17:251
Wheeler, Esau 1:191
Wheeler, Ezekiel 21:197
Wheeler, Ezra 26:85
Wheeler, F. 1:185; 15:254; 19:140
Wheeler, F. E. 5:33
Wheeler, F. F. 25:259
Wheeler, F. N. 14:125; 15:147
Wheeler, F. W. 12:139
Wheeler, Francis 13:54
Wheeler, Francis W. 10:86
Wheeler, Franklin B. 21:263
Wheeler, G. 1:180; 19:140
Wheeler, G. F. 25:259
Wheeler, G. H. 11:81
Wheeler, G. N. 25:259
Wheeler, George 7:76; 13:54; 18:417
Wheeler, George F. 5:33

Wheeler, George N. 5:33
Wheeler, George W. 21:402
Wheeler, Green 7:136
Wheeler, H. 1:87; 13:101; 19:264
Wheeler, H. B. 25:259
Wheeler, Harrison 11:393
Wheeler, Harvey 19:218
Wheeler, Helamiah 9:197
Wheeler, Henry 9:203; 11:216; 19:293; 22:507
Wheeler, Henry F. 20:32
Wheeler, Henry S. 19:41
Wheeler, Horace 12:45
Wheeler, I. 22:228
Wheeler, Isaac 4:61
Wheeler, Isaac L. 7:15
Wheeler, J. 1:87, 183; 2:19; 3:214; 13:101; 14:24
Wheeler, J. C. 13:101; 14:24
Wheeler, J. Carman 7:17
Wheeler, J. D. 9:216; 21:402
Wheeler, J. F. 25:284
Wheeler, J. H. 1:87
Wheeler, J. P. 1:100
Wheeler, J. S. 18:185
Wheeler, James 1:84; 10:86; 11:47; 19:41; 23:56
Wheeler, James A. 27:129
Wheeler, James H. 9:137
Wheeler, James M. D. 20:390
Wheeler, Jeremiah 22:444
Wheeler, Jerome 19:218
Wheeler, Job 17:189
Wheeler, John 1:84; 6:14; 12:66; 13:59; 15:51; 16:62, 391; 18:99, 267; 25:127; 26:87
Wheeler, John B. W. 21:107
Wheeler, John D. 9:127; 10:169; 19:218; 27:131
Wheeler, John F. 10:24
Wheeler, John P. 7:114
Wheeler, John R. 7:70
Wheeler, John W. 23:56
Wheeler, Joseph 1:87; 6:20; 8:43; 18:99; 26:198
Wheeler, Julius T. 9:244
Wheeler, L. 14:125; 25:124

Wheeler, Levi 20:15; 22:59
Wheeler, M. 1:183
Wheeler, Marcus G. 25:125
Wheeler, Marion 11:409
Wheeler, Michael 4:61
Wheeler, Monson 11:296
Wheeler, Morton 22:348
Wheeler, Moses 17:209
Wheeler, N. M. 25:259
Wheeler, N. S. 12:63
Wheeler, N. W. 19:218
Wheeler, Norman 23:111
Wheeler, O. D. 16:285
Wheeler, P. C. 23:118
Wheeler, Peter 4:61
Wheeler, R. 1:84, 180
Wheeler, Richard 11:405
Wheeler, Robert 7:136
Wheeler, S. 11:216
Wheeler, S. C. 1:84
Wheeler, S. N. 15:254
Wheeler, S. T. 11:101
Wheeler, S. W. 14:231
Wheeler, Sidney I. 9:99
Wheeler, Simon 18:267; 26:87
Wheeler, Solomon F. 20:50
Wheeler, Spencer 7:136
Wheeler, Stephen 21:45
Wheeler, Sylvester 13:54
Wheeler, T. 9:153; 27:128
Wheeler, Thomas 11:81; 17:27
Wheeler, U. 5:55
Wheeler, Uriel 5:47
Wheeler, W. 14:231, 261; 21:162; 25:259
Wheeler, W. H. 17:69; 18:41, 271; 21:402; 25:259; 26:200
Wheeler, Warna R. 19:297
Wheeler, Warren 21:402
Wheeler, William 5:33; 10:86; 15:147; 20:390; 22:169
Wheeler, William F. 23:56
Wheeler, William H. 5:47; 24:33
Wheeler, William W. 16:112
Wheeler, Z. 1:182
Wheelock, A. 3:214
Wheelock, Charles W. 20:131
Wheelock, Edgar C. 7:84
Wheelock, Granville 22:159

Wheelock, Harrison 22:114
Wheelock, I. R. W. 26:84
Wheelock, J. 22:348
Wheelock, J. H. 1:84
Wheelock, J. P. W. 9:94
Wheelock, N. B. 1:89
Wheelock, O. 1:100
Wheelock, Orville 4:61
Wheely, J. A. 3:214
Wheerch, Price 24:100
Wheetly, John 22:445
Wheets, George 18:41
Whelan, E. M. 14:279
Whelan, Michael 24:71
Whelan, William 1:88
Wheland, Mike 9:161
Whelen, E. M. 23:111
Wheler, Adam 20:390
Wheley, Owen 7:114
Whelly, Buckner 21:288
Whelmer, J. 17:497
Whelpley, Gilbert H. 21:12
Whelsel, John W. 17:27
Whelton, J. H. 3:214
When, George C. 14:125
Whenerich, William 12:45
Whermour, M. 3:214
Wherritt, George 11:178
Wherry, J. A. 16:62
Whertler, John 14:267
Whesling, Th. 14:231
Whet, A. 3:214
Wheton, Richard B. 8:98
Whetsel, Francis N. 9:137
Whetsel, Richard M. 21:402
Whetsine, J. W. 18:61
Whetstine, John K. 23:82
Whetstone, Abraham 9:30; 18:318
Whetstone, J. 22:228
Whetstone, John 24:181
Whetstone, Thomas 20:45
Whetzel, Hawkins 19:140
Whetzel, J. 19:140
Whibeck, William 18:282
Whicks, N. 3:214
Whidden, George H. 10:24
Whidden, Joseph G. 23:197
Whidden, R. L. 22:494
Whidicre, J. 9:226
Whiet, William D. 9:198
Whig, Richard 25:329
Whigand, Robert 13:54
Whigham, John W. 22:349
Whight, Aaron 12:54

Whight, Th. 14:231
Whilbraie, Charles V. 18:282
Whilden, P. 18:267; 26:86
Whilden, R. 7:45
Whildhead, M. B. 3:214
Whilecotton, Jacob 8:98
Whileman, A. J. 9:40
Whileplummer, Jefferson 20:390
Whiler, Anthony 18:318
Whilff, Frederick 12:169
Whilhoit, Napoleon S. 22:59
Whili, John 14:261
Whili, S. 14:261
Whilian, William 8:57
Whility, George 19:218
Whillhirt, J. 13:102
Whillow, William 9:64
Whilly, E. 24:215
Whilstone, Abram 26:117
Whilton, Isaiah 16:62
Whily, Thomas 11:176
Whimay, John 11:49
Whims, E. 22:327
Whinery, W. W. 18:185
Whinney, W. W. 10:185
Whiny, George 10:87
Whip, Daniel G. 23:175
Whip, Joseph 15:96
Whipiler, F. 25:260
Whipken, Henry 10:87
Whipkey, Cyrus 10:175
Whipkey, P. 15:273
Whipley, Cyrus 19:218
Whipley, Eli 7:45
Whipley, Merritt 11:178
Whipp, C. 3:214
Whipp, George T. 19:218
Whipp, John 23:175
Whippeler, F. 12:81
Whipple, A. 9:241; 15:147
Whipple, A. L. 7:45
Whipple, A. S. 13:54
Whipple, Abel 4:62
Whipple, Alfred 18:116
Whipple, B. A. 19:276
Whipple, Burton A. 9:198
Whipple, Charles 10:87; 20:390
Whipple, D. M. 1:84
Whipple, David 23:126
Whipple, David R. 11:321
Whipple, E. 1:184; 7:62
Whipple, Enoch 7:63
Whipple, F. T. 21:83
Whipple, Freeman T. 21:83
Whipple, G. 3:214

Whipple, George 6:20; 18:99
Whipple, H. 3:214
Whipple, Harlon 23:116
Whipple, J. 3:214
Whipple, Jefferson 8:98
Whipple, John 1:84; 10:169; 13:54; 19:218; 21:61
Whipple, Joseph F. 8:35; 18:166
Whipple, M. 3:214
Whipple, M. V. 6:34
Whipple, M. Van 25:329
Whipple, O. A. 22:109
Whipple, P. C. 3:214
Whipple, Patrick 21:402
Whipple, Porter 23:197
Whipple, R. J. 1:183
Whipple, Samuel B. 11:418
Whipple, Stephen D. 11:427
Whipple, W. 1:180
Whipple, William 14:125; 17:320
Whippo---, J. V. 24:115
Whipsker, Henry 20:390
Whirdlow, John 18:105
Whirley, James 20:390
Whirly, James 10:87
Whirry, George 20:390
Whisenand, Aaron M. 10:87
Whisennand, J. S. F. 23:243
Whislar, William 10:142; 20:390
Whisler, David 15:61
Whisler, James B. 23:82
Whisler, John 22:495
Whisler, L. 27:125
Whisler, Ready 11:177
Whisman, James M. 11:18
Whissenger, Benjamin F. 22:444
Whist, J. 27:128
Whist, John 9:153
Whistler, --- 26:244
Whistler, A. W. 14:131
Whistler, Frank 23:56
Whistler, John 20:131
Whitacer, Hiram 7:73
Whitacker, John 15:15
Whitacker, W. 16:261
Whitacre, Perry 22:229
Whitacre, Preston 17:427; 24:181
Whitaker, --- 3:214
Whitaker, A. 1:100

Whitaker, Alfred G. 15:254
Whitaker, Andrew 11:176
Whitaker, D. 1:185
Whitaker, E. 3:214
Whitaker, E. P. 23:56
Whitaker, Edward W. 7:70
Whitaker, Francis 11:318
Whitaker, George G. 20:20
Whitaker, George W. 22:445
Whitaker, H. 25:308
Whitaker, Harrison 17:266
Whitaker, Henderson L. 23:82
Whitaker, Henry 25:260
Whitaker, Israel 10:87
Whitaker, J. 3:214; 9:40
Whitaker, James 21:402
Whitaker, Jasper 20:20
Whitaker, Jesse W. 22:134
Whitaker, John 18:41; 21:83
Whitaker, John F. 22:60
Whitaker, N. G. 21:45
Whitaker, Nathaniel L. 11:274
Whitaker, Noah 12:159
Whitaker, Olid 8:111
Whitaker, P. 12:163
Whitaker, S. P. 9:127
Whitaker, W. C. 11:443
Whitaker, Wesley M. 22:60
Whitaker, William 11:20
Whitall, John A. 8:125
Whitbeck, J. 3:214
Whitbeck, J. M. 19:140
Whitbeck, Jacob 10:169
Whitbeck, M. 13:102
Whitbeck, Martin 13:123
Whitbeck, Wessel 16:112
Whitberg, L. 21:83
Whitbreck, J. M. 15:313
Whitby, J. R. 9:64
Whitby, R. B. 3:225
Whitby, William 16:135
Whitcher, Charles B. 5:33
Whitcher, Joseph 14:231
Whitcher, Orrill B. 4:62
Whitcher, T. 23:56
Whitcomb, A. 2:19; 25:123
Whitcomb, A. C. 1:86
Whitcomb, A. P. 7:62
Whitcomb, C. W. 2:19
Whitcomb, Culburt 19:41
Whitcomb, E. D. 25:260

Whitcomb, E. E. 8:57; 21:94
Whitcomb, Edgar D. 5:33
Whitcomb, G. 21:402
Whitcomb, George 4:62
Whitcomb, James B. 9:46
Whitcomb, John 14:231
Whitcomb, Lewis J. 22:445
Whitcomb, Lyman 22:109
Whitcomb, Michael 22:109
Whitcomb, N. 15:309; 25:127
Whitcomb, Orrin 22:469
Whitcomb, S. 1:83
Whitcomb, S. E. 1:186
Whitcomb, Shepperd 21:61
Whitcomb, Silas F. 12:45
Whitcomb, Stillman 21:402
Whitcomb, W. H. 18:268; 26:85
Whitcomb, W. J. 1:84
Whitcomb, William 10:24, 87; 20:391
Whitcomb, William P. 21:12
Whitcombe, Stillman 7:115
Whitcombe, T. C. 3:214
Whitcraft, George 10:142; 20:391
Whitcroft, Isaac 10:86
White, --- 18:417; 25:127
White, A. 1:181, 185; 3:214; 7:80; 11:221; 16:261; 17:435; 18:388; 21:45; 22:469; 24:181; 25:308; 27:128
White, A. B. 12:45
White, A. D. 13:75; 20:390
White, A. E. 18:402
White, A. J. 9:64; 15:79
White, A. L. 20:150
White, A. M. 23:56
White, A. P. 27:134
White, A. R. 14:313; 17:472; 27:134
White, A. S. 10:98
White, A. V. 8:57
White, Aaron 18:268; 21:288; 26:85
White, Aaron B. 4:61
White, Abner 22:326
White, Abraham 1:85; 10:170; 15:51

White, Abram 9:137; 27:130
White, Absalom 21:237
White, Alcutt 9:226
White, Alex 9:155
White, Alexander 7:45; 18:268; 26:86
White, Alfred J. 22:133
White, Alonzo 1:84
White, Alton 22:159
White, Alvey 22:159
White, Alvin 23:262
White, Ambrose 17:216
White, Ambrose S. 22:445
White, Andrew 9:198; 10:142; 11:113; 20:390; 21:288; 22:228
White, Andrew J. 4:61
White, Anson 23:197
White, Ariel D. 10:86
White, Asa T. 15:254
White, Ashel 21:402
White, Austin 26:132
White, B. 1:87; 13:123
White, Benjamin 1:86; 12:45; 17:348
White, Benjamin P. 22:108
White, Bernard 12:45
White, Bonnin 20:150
White, Budd 22:327
White, Byron D. 10:24
White, C. 1:185; 3:214; 15:178; 25:260
White, C. H. 14:125
White, C. L. 27:133
White, C. P. 22:348
White, C. U. 22:356
White, Caleb 12:160; 22:108
White, Calvin 10:86; 20:390; 23:14
White, Carleton 18:73
White, Cassander 22:273
White, Charles 9:46; 10:86; 15:324; 19:140; 20:390; 21:88; 22:273, 348; 25:126
White, Charles A. 17:69
White, Charles E. 14:317; 22:413
White, Chase 26:131
White, Clarence 18:402
White, Cyrus L. 12:45
White, D. 3:214; 16:261; 25:260
White, D. B. 10:86; 20:390
White, D. C. 7:45; 20:140

White, D. E. 25:260
White, D. H. 1:86; 18:388
White, D. J. 20:390
White, Danfor K. 22:159
White, Daniel 7:45; 22:60; 24:108
White, Daniel E. 5:33
White, Daniel J. 22:273
White, Daniel W. 11:176
White, Darwin 10:98
White, David 7:136; 21:288; 25:127
White, David D. 17:208
White, David M. 5:33
White, David S. 11:185
White, Dempsey 21:133
White, Dennison 19:49
White, Dever 22:286
White, E. 1:88, 181; 3:214; 19:218; 25:260; 27:127
White, E. B. 17:445
White, E. D. 3:214
White, E. I. 15:254
White, Eben 10:24
White, Edward 5:47; 7:71; 9:197; 10:142; 12:79; 14:320; 15:83; 19:140, 234; 20:390; 23:111; 25:277
White, Edwin 20:117
White, Edwin F. 16:391
White, Edwin J. 22:414
White, Edwin R. 24:164
White, Elias 10:86; 20:390
White, Elijah 23:175; 26:234
White, Elisha 16:62
White, Emery C. 10:24
White, Epaphrod 24:33
White, Everard 13:54
White, F. 25:124
White, F. C. 9:64
White, F. H. 9:229
White, Finley Q. 17:351
White, Frank 23:82
White, Franklin 16:62
White, Fred 26:200
White, Frederick 4:62; 8:43
White, G. 3:214; 11:234
White, G. A. 22:444
White, G. B. 1:85; 13:123
White, G. D. 25:260
White, G. H. 16:150
White, G. M. 1:86
White, G. N. 10:142; 20:390

White, G. W. 9:153; 11:48, 254; 17:295; 25:260; 27:127
White, George 4:68; 5:33; 6:28; 8:35; 14:231, 249; 15:147, 164, 328; 16:261; 18:166; 19:141; 21:402; 22:348; 25:126, 260; 26:200, 214
White, George A. 8:98, 117
White, George B. 4:61
White, George C. 17:16
White, George H. 15:164; 20:26, 50; 22:413
White, George J. 18:282
White, George P. 20:45
White, George U. 19:218
White, George W. 9:94; 11:114; 14:335; 21:45, 402; 22:60, 159
White, Granville C. 17:218
White, Grayson 6:20; 18:99
White, Green 5:47
White, Green B. 27:156
White, H. 1:183; 3:214; 9:155; 16:261; 22:228; 23:183; 25:260; 27:128
White, H. B. 22:356
White, H. C. 1:87; 22:495
White, H. D. 27:131
White, H. F. 1:84
White, H. H. 18:116; 19:243
White, Harrison 12:45; 15:79
White, Harvey 12:79; 21:61
White, Harvey G. 15:10
White, Henry 1:87; 9:137, 158; 10:169; 11:337; 12:79; 14:125; 15:13, 164; 17:107, 140; 19:218; 21:192, 197; 22:327; 24:206; 26:199; 27:129
White, Henry C. 9:74; 16:83
White, Henry E. 1:83
White, Henry F. 12:45; 22:133
White, Henry Kirk 10:86; 20:390
White, Henry P. 4:61
White, Hiram 14:231
White, Hiram H. 9:197

White, Horace 8:43; 26:198
White, Horace H. 6:10
White, Hugh 5:33; 21:288; 25:127
White, I. G. 17:293
White, I. P. 23:175
White, I. R. 26:84
White, Ira 23:56
White, J. 1:100, 185; 2:19; 3:214; 8:98; 9:64, 114; 11:253, 318; 13:54, 101; 14:24; 16:359; 22:413; 25:125, 260
White, J. A. 1:100; 20:117; 26:85
White, J. C. 27:133
White, J. F. 14:125, 231
White, J. G. 1:182
White, J. H. 15:338; 20:176; 21:12
White, J. J. 23:56; 27:125
White, J. M. 3:214; 11:330; 15:61; 21:403
White, J. P. 3:214
White, J. S. 1:85; 18:318; 26:84
White, J. T. 9:30; 26:115
White, J. W. 1:88; 3:214; 6:26; 8:57; 11:283; 13:126; 14:125; 15:156, 171; 23:175
White, Jackson 12:159; 22:273
White, Jacob 17:351
White, Jacob D. 8:35; 18:167
White, James 4:62; 5:33; 8:43; 9:137, 159; 10:142, 175; 11:114, 409; 13:59; 14:231; 15:254, 334; 17:45, 89, 240; 19:41, 141, 218; 20:390; 21:290, 403; 23:16; 24:103, 168; 25:260; 26:198; 27:129
White, James A. 19:41
White, James A. L. 11:81
White, James B. 7:114; 14:125; 21:403
White, James C. 23:83
White, James E. 1:85; 9:17
White, James G. 8:57; 21:83
White, James H. 27:126
White, James J. 14:231

White, James L. 9:94, 156; 10:142; 20:390; 26:83, 84
White, James N. 9:74
White, James P. 22:60
White, James R. 22:133
White, James S. 5:33; 7:45; 22:348; 24:33; 25:260
White, James W. 7:73; 11:48; 17:69; 21:83; 26:200
White, Jarvis 12:45
White, Jason L. 9:127; 27:131
White, Jeff 14:231
White, Jerome 23:272
White, Jerry 5:47; 10:99
White, Jesse 11:337; 16:112
White, Jewett F. 20:15
White, Joe 11:47
White, John 2:20; 4:61; 6:34; 7:12, 45, 54; 10:86, 169; 11:179, 215; 12:94; 13:54; 14:231; 15:254, 328; 16:261, 359; 17:157, 211, 254; 18:409, 427; 19:141, 218; 20:175, 390; 21:237; 22:229; 23:56; 24:207; 25:123, 329
White, John C. 11:394
White, John E. 5:33; 16:130
White, John G. 24:98
White, John H. 9:94
White, John J. 11:80; 15:4; 20:390
White, John L. 10:86; 12:45
White, John M. 21:83; 22:228
White, John N. 10:86; 20:390
White, John O. 21:237
White, John R. 21:237
White, John S. 7:114; 19:41; 26:83
White, John W. 21:107
White, Joseph 10:98; 11:47; 12:52; 14:125; 17:399; 23:175; 25:125
White, Joseph L. 13:59
White, Joseph R. 9:94
White, Joshua 18:41
White, Josiah 11:317
White, Josiah M. 12:79

White, L. 3:214; 11:274; 12:166; 23:83; 26:200
White, L. B. 12:45
White, L. E. 15:148
White, L. S. 3:214
White, Leartes 15:79
White, Lemuel 6:26
White, Leonard 11:131
White, Levi 7:45; 23:83
White, Lewis 15:147; 16:261; 19:49; 23:95; 24:58
White, Lewis B. 25:260
White, Lewis R. 10:142; 20:390
White, Liberty 21:403
White, Luther 7:45
White, M. 3:214; 14:24; 25:260
White, M. J. 12:79; 15:61
White, M. W. 7:45
White, Martin 9:94; 11:216; 18:388
White, Martin E. 9:226; 26:87
White, Martin L. 22:60
White, Mary 17:112
White, Matthew 21:244
White, Michael 4:61; 17:445; 22:60; 24:164
White, Mitchell 23:267
White, Moses 7:136; 11:49; 13:54; 16:62; 20:400
White, Moses E. 13:54
White, N. 10:191; 14:126; 18:185; 22:228
White, Nelson 11:217
White, Nelson D. 17:27
White, O. P. 27:126
White, Orville 13:54
White, Oscar 25:127
White, Oslo F. 21:94
White, P. 3:214; 8:57; 17:189; 21:113; 24:168; 25:260; 26:131
White, P. C. 18:61
White, P. H. 11:317
White, P. M. 15:334; 19:141
White, Patrick 11:81
White, Paul 23:265
White, Perry 10:86; 20:390
White, Peter 19:41; 20:109; 22:109; 23:278

White, Philip 15:254; 27:127
White, Phillip 9:153
White, Pinckney A. 8:98
White, Pliny F. 16:83
White, Powell 8:76
White, R. 1:88; 16:261; 17:510; 19:264; 24:89
White, R. B. 3:214
White, R. D. 9:30
White, R. E. 20:139; 24:115
White, R. M. 3:214; 25:274
White, R. N. 1:182
White, R. O. M. 3:214
White, Ransom 1:85
White, Ransom L. 20:150
White, Reddick 8:43; 26:198
White, Richard 7:45, 136; 9:197; 10:86; 12:98; 16:62, 285; 20:391; 21:403; 22:286
White, Richard D. 15:357
White, Richard S. 17:45
White, Robert 12:52; 15:115; 18:201; 19:218; 22:228, 348
White, Robert B. 20:391; 24:57
White, Russell 17:233
White, S. 3:214; 14:231; 16:261; 21:45; 22:516; 26:83
White, S. A. 3:214
White, S. E. 21:403
White, S. L. 14:29
White, S. P. 1:183
White, Samuel 4:68; 7:136; 9:94; 11:283; 19:41, 218; 23:83
White, Samuel J. 24:57
White, Samuel K. 1:84
White, Samuel L. 1:84
White, Samuel Q. 24:57
White, Samuel T. 12:45
White, Samuel U. 10:169
White, Seth 21:403
White, Shadrach S. 22:286
White, Sharon 4:61
White, Sheton 17:422
White, Shubal C. 23:83
White, Sidney C. 22:133
White, Silas 19:141; 21:403
White, Simon W. 4:61
White, Smith 11:217
White, Stephen 7:54

White, Sylvester 21:237;
    23:103
White, Sylvester D. 10:86;
    20:391
White, T. 2:20; 3:214;
    18:61; 23:56
White, T. B. 1:186
White, T. C. 21:205
White, T. G. 9:153;
    27:127
White, T. J. 2:19; 9:30;
    25:127
White, T. P. 1:88
White, T. P. C. 11:254
White, T. S. 1:87
White, Tho. 8:117
White, Thomas 7:45, 136;
    8:35, 98; 9:226;
    11:235, 294; 13:60;
    18:167, 212, 330,
    388; 19:141; 21:403;
    22:229, 326, 517;
    23:17, 56; 26:199
White, Thomas A. 13:54;
    15:93
White, Thomas B. 24:33
White, Thomas C. 21:237
White, Thomas H. 12:56
White, Thomas J. 22:228
White, Thomas K. 23:175
White, Thomas M. 4:62
White, Thomas S. 15:354
White, Thornton 24:207
White, Valentine 22:443
White, W. 1:184; 3:214,
    215; 11:101; 13:101;
    15:148; 16:261;
    18:424
White, W. A. 9:197;
    18:330; 19:233;
    20:45
White, W. B. 18:201
White, W. C. 9:216;
    15:331; 19:141;
    21:403; 26:214
White, W. F. 17:498
White, W. G. 7:45
White, W. H. 11:98;
    14:249; 27:135
White, W. J. 23:56;
    27:133
White, W. L. 1:183
White, W. M. 3:215
White, W. N. 9:226
White, W. P. 13:101;
    14:24
White, W. Q. 14:313;
    17:473
White, W. T. 14:24
White, W. V. 18:388

White, W. W. 20:391;
    23:175; 27:134
White, W. Y. 13:101
White, Washington 6:20;
    18:99
White, Welro 11:216
White, Wesley C. 10:142;
    20:391
White, Wilbur 13:54
White, William 5:55;
    9:64; 11:47, 81, 82,
    177, 290; 14:231,
    285; 17:441; 18:61;
    19:42, 141, 218;
    21:288, 403; 22:108,
    327; 24:155; 25:125
White, William B. 7:62
White, William C. 1:88;
    7:70; 20:32
White, William D. 19:269
White, William E. 16:62;
    21:237
White, William F. 12:52;
    21:107
White, William H. 21:45,
    197, 403; 24:33
White, William J. 15:156;
    21:403
White, William S. 9:228;
    18:388
White, William W. 10:86;
    22:494
White, Willis 25:260
White, Wilson S. 4:61
White, Winchester 10:7
White, Zephaniah 11:113
Whitebread, Godfrey
    19:347
Whitebred, Godfrey
    13:135
Whitecotlon, John 23:83
Whitecraft, Isaac 20:391
Whitecraft, T. 1:100
Whitecraft, Thomas
    10:86; 20:391
Whited, W. M. 24:57
Whitefeather, W. 18:201
Whitefield, Charles
    21:288
Whitefield, Floyd 21:288
Whitefield, Jackson
    21:288
Whitefoot, E. S. 14:231
Whiteford, J. 16:261
Whitegar, Charles 13:123
Whitehall, George 3:215
Whitehart, C. 16:261
Whitehead, --- 2:20;
    25:128
Whitehead, A. 14:249;
    27:134

Whitehead, A. B. 3:215
Whitehead, A. J. 14:261
Whitehead, Adam W.
    17:233
Whitehead, Alfred 14:231
Whitehead, Alfred B.
    22:459
Whitehead, Amos 17:101
Whitehead, Bristow
    9:137; 27:130
Whitehead, C. W. 1:84
Whitehead, Charles
    22:159
Whitehead, D. T. 25:260
Whitehead, Daniel 17:27
Whitehead, David 22:274
Whitehead, F. F. 9:198;
    19:264
Whitehead, G. 7:136
Whitehead, George H.
    19:219
Whitehead, H. 1:182;
    23:175
Whitehead, Hiram 11:131
Whitehead, J. 1:87; 3:215;
    12:163
Whitehead, J. M. 11:47
Whitehead, John 13:54
Whitehead, Nathan
    10:170; 19:219
Whitehead, Patrick H.
    22:133
Whitehead, R. 1:88;
    25:260
Whitehead, S. A. 9:198;
    19:264
Whitehead, S. P. 11:48
Whitehead, Samuel O.
    10:87
Whitehead, Stephen E.
    21:113
Whitehead, Thomas M.
    22:413
Whitehead, W. 1:183;
    22:327
Whitehead, W. L. 11:427
Whitehead, W. N. 26:200
Whitehead, William 8:68;
    10:87; 13:54; 20:391;
    22:273
Whitehead, William W.
    22:133
Whitehill, C. K. 7:82;
    25:308
Whitehill, H. H. 11:323
Whitehill, Harrison 19:42
Whitehill, P. C. 7:82;
    25:308
Whitehood, C. 17:480
Whitehorn, David A.
    23:83

Whitehouse, Amos
18:268; 26:86
Whitehouse, George
26:199
Whitehouse, J. 11:254;
14:24
Whitehouse, J. L. 24:33
Whitehouse, James A.
17:61
Whitehouse, Joel T.
22:134
Whitehouse, Russell
13:54
Whitehouse, William C.
10:142; 20:391
Whitehuror, J. 13:101
Whitehurst, A. 22:229
Whitehurst, Jordan H.
22:60
Whitekar, W. H. 1:83
Whiteleather, John C.
22:444
Whitelong, William
16:162
Whitely, George 10:169
Whitely, John 22:349
Whitely, Joseph 4:62
Whitely, Samuel 20:391
Whitely, William 22:133
Whiteman, A. M. 3:215
Whiteman, Adam 22:494
Whiteman, Alonzo 7:70
Whiteman, D. 7:70
Whiteman, David 11:317
Whiteman, G. 1:96
Whiteman, G. S. 24:73
Whiteman, George 22:16
Whiteman, H. J. 22:495
Whiteman, J. W. 3:215
Whiteman, Jesse 11:80
Whiteman, Joseph 23:175
Whiteman, Joshua M.
10:142; 20:391
Whiteman, Milton 17:497
Whiteman, R. A. 16:261
Whiteman, Riley 22:273
Whiteman, Tobias 22:16
Whiteman, W. R. 13:75
Whitemarsh, Erasmus
4:62
Whitemarsh, William
8:35; 26:200
Whitemen, J. D. 25:125
Whitemen, W. F. 27:125
Whitemore, Albert 10:142
Whitemore, Amos 4:62
Whitemore, C. 1:185
Whitemore, Harney
22:229
Whitenight, M. 14:24
Whitenmier, Joseph 24:71

Whitenock, W. C. 15:148
Whiteny, James A. 18:299
Whiteon, H. 14:126
Whiteon, R. P. 20:391
Whiteplummer, Jefferson
10:142
Whiteridy, William J. 8:68
Whiters, John 11:292
Whiteside, Isaac 17:189
Whiteside, Thomas
10:208
Whitesides, Thomas E.
11:18
Whitesides, Thomas F.
17:315
Whitesides, W. 21:199
Whiteson, George 20:391
Whitewolth, L. 26:214
Whiteworth, Robert 9:226
Whitfield, --- 25:128
Whitfield, Crocket 21:288
Whitfield, George 21:288
Whitfield, I. 22:327
Whitfield, J. 21:162
Whitfield, Jack 21:288
Whitfield, James 22:327
Whitfield, Jeff 21:288
Whitfield, Manus 21:403
Whitfield, Martin 7:136
Whitfield, Moses 21:288
Whitfield, Samuel 21:289
Whitfield, Shepherd
21:162
Whitfield, Tyler 27:133
Whitfield, William 23:103
Whitfield, Wright 21:289
Whitford, --- 19:141
Whitford, A. L. 1:85
Whitford, Burnett 14:317
Whitford, C. 1:88
Whitford, Dennis W.
20:117
Whitford, Samuel 21:263
Whitford, Thomas 16:150
Whitham, B. 3:215
Whitham, G. W. 21:403
Whitham, George 21:62
Whithead, B. 14:326;
23:95
Whithead, Calvin 23:315
Whithead, Samuel O.
20:391
Whither, E. T. 20:93
Whither, John 21:45
Whithy, John 14:231
Whiticar, John W. 20:102
Whitiker, S. 3:215
Whitimore, S. M. 21:45
Whitin, Joseph 14:231
Whiting, A. 3:215; 25:260
Whiting, A. A. 1:87

Whiting, A. B. 17:477
Whiting, A. R. 14:313
Whiting, Albert P. 5:47
Whiting, Alfred 4:68
Whiting, Alonzo 11:131
Whiting, Andrew 13:54;
16:62
Whiting, C. 21:113;
25:124
Whiting, C. M. 1:184
Whiting, Charles 22:159
Whiting, E. 16:261
Whiting, Ephraim J.
26:200
Whiting, G. 1:96
Whiting, Henry S. 12:45
Whiting, Horace D.
11:113
Whiting, J. 3:215; 11:82
Whiting, J. E. 20:86
Whiting, James R. 11:178
Whiting, Jasper 26:199
Whiting, John 14:231;
16:261
Whiting, M. 3:215
Whiting, Robert 21:263
Whiting, Salem 4:62
Whiting, Samuel A. 11:89
Whiting, Silas 25:287
Whiting, T. H. 25:124
Whiting, Thomas 22:229
Whiting, W. W. 1:100;
11:47
Whitington, H. 15:254
Whitington, Jasper 22:60
Whitington, John 15:83
Whitinhouse, --- 16:275
Whitish, Baston 19:219
Whitker, C. B. 1:181
Whitlach, Henry H. 23:83
Whitlatch, George 14:133
Whitleather, Joseph
11:418
Whitlemore, Vict 1:85
Whitler, Robert 5:33
Whitley, --- 18:212
Whitley, George W.
17:392
Whitley, James F. 8:98
Whitley, John 15:52
Whitley, S. 22:506
Whitley, Samuel 10:87
Whitley, T. 19:219
Whitley, W. 9:64
Whitlock, B. 11:397
Whitlock, Charles A. 8:98
Whitlock, Francis 12:45
Whitlock, G. W. 1:183
Whitlock, George 10:150;
18:61

Whitlock, J. M. 8:125; 12:61
Whitlock, J. W. 23:83
Whitlock, James B. 22:443
Whitlock, James M. 8:76
Whitlock, John L. 19:42
Whitlock, Joseph 16:88
Whitlock, M. 3:215
Whitlock, Obil 22:327
Whitlock, R. C. 12:159
Whitlock, S. 17:157
Whitlock, S. F. 14:279; 23:186
Whitlock, William 14:126; 15:313
Whitlock, William A. 22:274
Whitlock, Woodson 23:103
Whitlook, William 19:141
Whitlow, Joseph 17:140; 24:205
Whitman, --- 20:93
Whitman, Albert 8:111
Whitman, Alex 19:293
Whitman, Alexander 9:203
Whitman, Alexander B. 18:224
Whitman, Assa 15:350
Whitman, C. S. 24:115
Whitman, Charles 11:419; 17:73; 19:42; 22:327
Whitman, Charles E. 13:54
Whitman, Charles H. 12:45; 22:469
Whitman, Claibold 20:152
Whitman, Curtis E. 11:405
Whitman, E. H. 1:89
Whitman, E. J. 13:102
Whitman, G. E. 3:215
Whitman, Guston 11:48
Whitman, Hanson 7:114
Whitman, Henry 8:98
Whitman, J. 14:126
Whitman, J. A. 18:299; 26:116
Whitman, J. M. 22:413; 26:234
Whitman, J. O. 11:80
Whitman, Jasper 12:45
Whitman, John 12:45; 20:184
Whitman, Joseph 20:117
Whitman, L. 13:102
Whitman, Luther R. 11:185
Whitman, Michael 8:111

Whitman, P. 3:215
Whitman, Peter 14:126
Whitman, Philip 19:42
Whitman, Samuel 17:394
Whitman, Sebourn L. 21:133
Whitman, T. 12:120
Whitman, William 12:60
Whitman, William H. 1:85
Whitmarch, Charles 25:123
Whitmarsh, A. M. 9:94
Whitmarsh, C. 2:19
Whitmarsh, D. B. 18:403
Whitmarsh, Lewis 24:115
Whitmer, Daniel 17:93
Whitmer, J. D. 18:41
Whitmer, James P. 22:458
Whitmer, Vanrenseller 9:40
Whitmier, Frederick 7:45
Whitmire, August 7:62
Whitmire, George W. 22:229
Whitmire, Jacob 14:276; 17:497
Whitmoe, David 8:98
Whitmond, C. R. 3:215
Whitmor, H. G. 19:264
Whitmore, A. 11:80
Whitmore, Amos 12:45
Whitmore, Benjamin S. 7:114
Whitmore, C. 3:215
Whitmore, C. A. 20:194
Whitmore, C. B. 3:215
Whitmore, C. M. 10:150
Whitmore, C. W. 18:61
Whitmore, Chancey 11:177
Whitmore, Charles 12:45; 22:159
Whitmore, Daniel 12:45
Whitmore, David 18:212
Whitmore, E. 16:112
Whitmore, Enoch 12:45
Whitmore, Enos 18:73
Whitmore, H. G. 9:198
Whitmore, Harmon W. 27:134
Whitmore, Henry 18:212
Whitmore, I. H. 11:318
Whitmore, J. 3:215; 14:285
Whitmore, J. H. 7:76
Whitmore, J. L. 21:403
Whitmore, J. W. 14:285
Whitmore, John 9:105
Whitmore, Joseph L. 23:103
Whitmore, L. 3:215

Whitmore, Robert 7:114
Whitmore, S. 17:16
Whitmore, Samuel 23:126
Whitmore, Silas A. 22:413
Whitmore, Smith 10:94
Whitmore, Timothy 22:60, 445
Whitmore, Vankenseler 18:299
Whitmore, Vanranselir 26:116
Whitmore, W. D. 23:56
Whitmore, William 8:35; 12:45; 16:112; 18:167
Whitmoyer, D. 13:123
Whitnack, W. P. 14:126
Whitner, J. W. 12:147
Whitner, John 11:393
Whitner, Uriah 17:427
Whitney, --- 13:75
Whitney, A. 3:215
Whitney, A. N. 1:181
Whitney, A. R. 27:133
Whitney, A. S. 25:126
Whitney, Alfred 14:231
Whitney, Alonston 11:117
Whitney, Alonzo 21:207
Whitney, Amos 12:79
Whitney, Anthony 7:136
Whitney, Asaph 27:132
Whitney, B. F. 15:254
Whitney, Benjamin 7:45
Whitney, C. 21:108
Whitney, C. H. 16:150
Whitney, Charles 11:273; 15:254; 21:89
Whitney, Charles B. 16:166
Whitney, Charles H. 10:142; 20:391
Whitney, Charles W. 16:83
Whitney, D. 15:346; 16:391; 23:265
Whitney, Daniel 26:84
Whitney, Darius 4:62
Whitney, David 14:231
Whitney, Douglas 21:94
Whitney, E. 3:215; 16:261; 19:219
Whitney, E. E. 23:175
Whitney, E. L. 1:185
Whitney, Edward 19:42, 49
Whitney, Eli 11:179
Whitney, Emery E. 11:18
Whitney, Epnama G. 8:35
Whitney, Erastus 1:83
Whitney, Ezra 11:177
Whitney, F. 15:254

Whitney, F. D. 1:181
Whitney, G. B. 25:260
Whitney, G. S. 27:132
Whitney, George 7:136
Whitney, George H. 12:45
Whitney, George T. 7:45
Whitney, George W.
    22:109
Whitney, H. 1:183; 18:41;
    27:131
Whitney, H. H. 21:88
Whitney, H. M. 8:68;
    26:199
Whitney, Henry 22:109
Whitney, Henry T. 1:87
Whitney, I. B. 23:56
Whitney, Isaac 15:51
Whitney, Isaac N. 15:61
Whitney, Israel C. 21:403
Whitney, J. 3:215; 23:14
Whitney, J. A. 26:83
Whitney, J. H. 9:40; 11:49
Whitney, J. T. 3:215
Whitney, J. W. 1:84;
    3:215; 19:314
Whitney, Jacob 12:79
Whitney, James A. 9:40;
    26:116
Whitney, John 22:349
Whitney, John A. 9:94
Whitney, John B. 8:116
Whitney, John M. 17:264
Whitney, John O. 21:403
Whitney, Joseph 9:106
Whitney, K. D. 1:86
Whitney, L. J. 1:185
Whitney, Lorain M.
    17:245
Whitney, Luke S. 17:89
Whitney, M. S. 12:163
Whitney, O. 1:88
Whitney, Olando 16:391
Whitney, Palmer 8:111
Whitney, Richard 9:137;
    27:130
Whitney, Roderick B.
    11:132
Whitney, Rouel 17:245
Whitney, Rufus 22:109
Whitney, S. C. 21:403
Whitney, S. G. 21:403
Whitney, S. P. 3:215
Whitney, Samuel 8:123
Whitney, Selden 15:51
Whitney, T. C. 14:231
Whitney, Thomas B.
    13:54
Whitney, W. 3:215;
    15:346; 16:391
Whitney, W. A. 3:215
Whitney, W. H. 16:166

Whitney, William 15:254
Whitney, William A.
    17:240
Whitney, William L. 1:86
Whitney, William R. 4:62
Whitnight, M. 13:102
Whitnight, Valentine
    14:231
Whiton, Frank 15:51
Whitsel, C. 14:231
Whitsel, Francis W.
    27:129
Whitsell, Phil 18:403
Whitsett, L. 7:73
Whitsle, William 20:15
Whitson, Allen 10:208
Whitson, George 10:86
Whitson, Jes 18:201
Whitson, John W. 21:62
Whitson, Joseph 22:444
Whitson, Thomas W.
    11:81
Whitson, W. D. 26:234
Whitson, W. W. 7:45
Whitson, William D.
    9:238
Whitson, Willis 21:197
Whitstine, George W.
    10:150
Whitstone, Adam 21:403
Whitstone, John 17:427
Whitt, John 20:391
Whitt, Meredith 21:202
Whitt, W. 19:141
Whitta, Patrick 17:351
Whittacker, O. 25:127
Whittaker, A. 14:126;
    17:295
Whittaker, Abram L.
    22:494
Whittaker, Allen 22:327
Whittaker, Alphonso
    22:327
Whittaker, B. 26:199
Whittaker, Christopher
    16:62
Whittaker, Clark 4:62
Whittaker, Daniel 10:99
Whittaker, Daniel A.
    18:268
Whittaker, David 17:61
Whittaker, David A. 26:85
Whittaker, Elizabeth
    18:105
Whittaker, Ephraim
    20:400
Whittaker, F. 2:19; 25:128
Whittaker, G. 1:85
Whittaker, Henry 4:62;
    22:327
Whittaker, Howard 10:24

Whittaker, Isaac 22:327
Whittaker, Ismel 20:391
Whittaker, J. M. 11:175;
    25:127
Whittaker, J. P. 10:142;
    20:391; 27:131
Whittaker, James 22:327
Whittaker, John 10:142;
    20:391
Whittaker, John E. 5:33
Whittaker, Joshua 13:54
Whittaker, K. M. 23:56
Whittaker, O. 2:19
Whittaker, Philander
    21:145
Whittaker, R. 19:264
Whittaker, Robert 7:45;
    9:198
Whittaker, Sam 22:517
Whittaker, Samuel 22:327
Whittaker, Thomas
    Russell 18:167
Whittaker, William 8:98;
    11:427
Whittaker, Wilson 21:219
Whittaker, Z. P. 1:184
Whittale, Invie 18:342
Whittamore, --- 11:48
Whittecker, S. B. 4:62
Whitted, Elias 21:83
Whitted, John W. 22:444
Whitted, William T.
    20:102
Whitteman, J. D. 1:85
Whittemore, A. W. 10:24
Whittemore, Albert
    20:391
Whittemore, C. E. 19:231
Whittemore, Hiram 13:54
Whittemore, Ira J. 8:116
Whittemore, J. H. 19:231;
    25:308
Whitten, Charles 4:62
Whitten, Charles F. 13:54
Whitten, Ellis 21:403
Whitten, Francis 11:397
Whitten, G. 15:115
Whitten, George 21:403
Whitten, George W. 4:62
Whitten, Increase Sumner
    21:83
Whitten, J. K. P. 3:215
Whitten, J. L. 8:68;
    19:243; 26:199
Whitten, James M. 22:274
Whitten, John 21:263
Whitten, John W. 23:56
Whitten, Joseph L. 9:198
Whitten, M. C. 21:403
Whitten, M. L. 7:62
Whitten, Thomas 4:62

Whittenberger, Bruce 21:237
Whittenburg, Joseph 9:94
Whittendorn, John 7:62
Whitter, A. A. 9:40
Whitter, Charles 4:62
Whitter, J. C. 14:292
Whitter, R. 25:260
Whitter, William 23:175
Whittere, C. W. 2:19
Whitters, C. L. 13:102
Whittey, Michael 7:115; 21:403
Whittey, Thomas 19:219
Whittfield, Samuel 22:327
Whittie, Richard 25:260
Whittier, A. J. 1:87
Whittier, Austin W. 12:45
Whittier, C. 21:403
Whittier, C. A. 1:180
Whittier, C. H. 1:182
Whittier, C. W. 25:124
Whittier, Charles 9:198; 19:224
Whittier, Daniel 16:62
Whittier, David 13:54
Whittier, E. C. 21:403
Whittier, Henry H. 18:344
Whittier, James 27:133
Whittier, L. P. 9:127; 27:125
Whittier, N. 1:182
Whittier, Ruel 16:87
Whittier, Seboy 11:18
Whittier, W. L. 21:403
Whittiker, D. C. 4:62
Whittiker, William 17:208
Whittim, H. 16:359
Whittimore, Page 10:170; 19:219
Whiting, A. 3:215
Whiting, Ephraim S. 18:167
Whiting, John 18:73
Whittinger, Lazarus 22:109
Whittington, Benjamin R. 7:115
Whittington, J. 21:108
Whittington, R. G. 25:260
Whittington, T. 23:56
Whittington, Thomas 5:33
Whittish, Baston 10:170
Whittle, H. W. 3:215
Whittle, John R. 22:274
Whittle, Joshua 17:289
Whittle, W. C. 3:215
Whittler, B. 7:82; 25:308
Whittlesay, Charles B. 22:494

Whittlesey, James H. 18:288
Whittlesey, Joseph H. 26:136
Whittley, John J. 22:413
Whittly, F. 10:155
Whittmer, P. 12:86
Whittmore, B. 3:215
Whittmore, O. 19:219
Whittmore, Smith 20:391
Whittock, A. H. 11:254
Whittock, Claud M. 11:114
Whittock, D. 1:87
Whittock, J. T. 21:45
Whittock, W. 3:215
Whitton, Asher 22:169
Whitton, B. F. 12:45
Whitton, G. 3:215
Whitton, G. G. 10:24
Whitton, H. 1:181
Whitton, James W. 16:137; 18:268; 26:85
Whitton, John E. 11:178
Whitton, Robert 3:215
Whitton, Thomas L. 7:115
Whittra, Charles 9:241
Whittum, H. 12:94
Whitty, R. B. 17:505
Whitwash, William H. 18:167
Whitworth, H. 21:62
Whitworth, R. A. 25:260
Whitworth, Robert 18:388
Whitworth, Sandford 22:169
Whitworth, W. G. 3:215
Whl, William 19:219
Whleler, O. D. 15:357
Whoberry, Allen S. 17:208
Whoeler, A. 3:213
Wholand, William 19:42
Wholgumuth, Frederick 22:60
Whooten, Linley 21:219
Whortan, Elisha 22:444
Whorton, Charles 11:19
Whorton, J. 27:133
Whorton, W. 2:19
Whright, G. L. 14:126
Whrous, William 9:64
Whrumaker, Ganliet 18:167
Whuma, Stephen 16:62
Whyatt, W. W. 21:199
Whyes, William 6:28
Whylard, W. A. 18:61
Wianeach, T. K. 14:285
Wiant, Solomon 13:54

Wiard, Elijah 20:157
Wiard, Elisha 20:191
Wiatt, Edward 10:142
Wiatt, Edward A. 20:391
Wiatt, Jesse 20:400
Wibben, Winfield 15:21
Wibber, L. 14:126
Wiber, R. 15:254
Wiburn, W. 21:45
Wical, Eugene 15:254
Wiche, J. 3:215
Wichman, Charles 18:99
Wick, A. 1:184; 22:60; 25:128
Wick, I. 1:87
Wick, J. 1:185; 3:215
Wick, John 21:237
Wick, R. C. 3:215
Wick, William 22:229
Wickam, N. B. 18:342
Wickar, Richard 10:142
Wickart, A. 14:24
Wickart, David 17:89
Wickel, Wilson W. 7:45
Wickell, John W. 7:45
Wickels, Gilbert 21:162
Wickenhoffer, H. 25:260
Wickens, James 27:129
Wicker, C. 1:86
Wicker, Charles M. 23:127
Wicker, Edmond 19:219
Wicker, H. T. 11:47
Wicker, J. 21:403
Wicker, Jacob 17:27
Wicker, John 3:215
Wicker, Markus 10:98
Wicker, N. S. 11:47
Wicker, Richard 20:391
Wickerhan, James 11:317
Wickersham, Caleb I. 18:224
Wickersham, Sam. B. 26:86
Wickersham, Samuel B. 18:268
Wickerson, James 12:45
Wickerson, John 27:130
Wickerson, Philip 9:30; 18:318; 26:115
Wickert, A. 13:102
Wickert, Henry 3:215
Wickesberg, A. 1:186
Wicket, Gilbert 8:58
Wickett, T. 19:276
Wickett, Thomas 9:198
Wickey, Carrer 26:199
Wickham, D. 18:61
Wickham, Elijah 21:108
Wickham, G. H. 3:215
Wickham, G. W. 21:45

Wickham, Isaac 13:54; 23:95
Wickham, J. 1:88; 3:215; 20:391
Wickham, J. S. 12:163
Wickham, James T. 9:30
Wickham, James W. 16:112
Wickham, James W. S. 18:318
Wickham, James W. T. 26:117
Wickham, Jeremiah 10:87
Wickham, L. 25:260
Wickham, Philander 11:418
Wickham, William 3:215
Wickham, William C. 17:320
Wickhan, Nathan 22:495
Wickhoff, George 13:54
Wickhorn, R. 14:126
Wickins, James 9:153
Wicklam, H. 11:175
Wicklaw, John 8:57
Wickle, W. A. 16:62
Wicklie, Garrett C. 23:95
Wickliff, James 10:203
Wickliff, P. 16:262
Wickliffe, George 14:231
Wickline, E. 1:182
Wickman, Christopher 22:60
Wickman, Daniel 18:61
Wickner, John W. 11:330
Wickoff, George W. C. 23:130
Wickroff, G. 11:189
Wicks, Alfred 2:19
Wicks, D. 3:215
Wicks, D. R. 22:229
Wicks, Frank 3:215
Wicks, Frank E. 20:117
Wicks, George R. 20:26
Wicks, Hiram 4:62
Wicks, I. H. 11:406
Wicks, J. 14:126
Wicks, J. W. 12:97
Wicks, L. 3:215
Wicks, Orlando 17:363
Wicks, Thomas M. 16:62
Wicks, W. H. 25:260
Wicks, W. M. 21:45
Wicks, William 17:240
Wicks, William H. 5:33
Wicksberg, D. K. 11:195
Wickson, A. B. 23:56
Wickstrum, Olof 20:15
Wickwire, Horace E. 8:35
Wickworth, R. 16:275

Wickwroe, Horace E. 18:167
Wicky, J. 3:215
Wicly, Henry 18:268
Wicson, George S. 21:237
Wicware, Joseph 12:169
Wicware, Thomas 12:169
Widaman, Samuel 22:229
Widby, James F. 22:274
Widden, A. W. 14:231
Widder, W. 3:215
Widdigar, J. 14:313; 17:480; 27:132
Widdle, H. 23:95
Widdows, Daniel 3:215
Widdows, H. 14:285
Widdup, J. 14:126
Wideimer, Henry 4:62
Widel, Elias D. 20:26
Wideman, John 9:30; 18:318
Wideman, William 9:156
Widemier, J. 25:260
Widen, Robert 22:327
Widenbaur, John 21:237
Widener, Cornelius 19:269
Widener, Jacob A. 19:269
Widener, Lee 11:330
Widener, William 20:391
Widentown, Jan 21:403
Wider, N. H. 3:215
Widernax, George 19:42
Widiberg, William A. 7:115
Widige, John 13:75
Widiman, J. B. 8:57
Widley, Joseph 9:167
Widman, Mark 23:116
Widner, George 10:87; 20:391
Widner, John 21:108
Widner, Madison 23:186
Widner, Russell 22:506
Widney, Joseph 22:109
Widney, Joseph B. 22:109
Widock, Samuel 10:87; 20:391
Widoner, William H. 17:277
Widow, L. H. 10:87; 20:391
Widows, H. 17:497
Widy, Henry 26:85
Wiebeck, C. 2:19
Wiechies, Fred. W. 27:126
Wiednor, E. 9:30
Wiegand, --- 15:156
Wieks, R. H. 7:115
Wieks, Thomas M. 13:59

Wiel, Simeon 15:317
Wieland, Charles A. 11:185
Wieland, George 13:75
Wield, Allen 18:41
Wield, Lemages 14:131
Wiele, Leamyes 15:267
Wiellit, N. 12:91
Wien, A. 20:150
Wiener, Joseph 9:30
Wienlapper, John 23:83
Wier, A. 21:45
Wier, A. T. 1:88
Wier, Daniel 6:34
Wier, E. 27:126
Wier, J. 20:37
Wier, James O. 11:47
Wier, John 1:85
Wier, Nelson 12:45
Wier, William 19:264; 22:469
Wier, William T. 22:443
Wiers, P. H. 13:78; 16:262
Wiersig, Julius 10:142
Wies, W. S. 27:127
Wiesa, Joseph 20:391
Wiesburn, --- 11:80
Wiese, Ferdinand 4:62
Wiese, Henry 24:71
Wiese, J. G. 14:267
Wiese, Lewis 27:126
Wiese, Samuel 14:333
Wiess, Wilhelm 11:179
Wiesse, Claus 18:116
Wiessensee, Clemens 16:87
Wiestell, Charles 15:319
Wifel, Ira 8:57
Wifong, Samuel H. 1:85
Wiford, Anthony 11:178
Wigan, M. 3:215
Wigand, Frederick 20:15
Wigele, August 20:391
Wigert, Henry 9:198
Wigg, Thomas T. 13:78
Wiggam, John 22:494
Wiggand, F. 21:45
Wiggand, George 3:215
Wiggans, R. 1:180
Wiggen, Joseph 4:62
Wiggens, Charles 9:127
Wiggens, M. 11:334
Wiggin, A. L. 17:159
Wiggin, Leonard 16:262
Wiggin, N. 3:215
Wiggins, --- 20:20
Wiggins, Alvin H. 17:71
Wiggins, Andrew S. 19:219
Wiggins, C. 7:70

Wiggins, Charles 10:169; 19:219; 27:131
Wiggins, Christian 23:83
Wiggins, D. 3:215; 25:128
Wiggins, David 2:19; 17:27
Wiggins, Elijah 7:136
Wiggins, Emily 26:234
Wiggins, Ezekiel 10:169; 19:219
Wiggins, Francis J. 20:131
Wiggins, G. H. 26:84
Wiggins, G. W. 3:215
Wiggins, George 6:34; 14:126; 18:268; 26:87
Wiggins, George H. 9:94
Wiggins, George W. 7:115; 20:135
Wiggins, Henry 10:210
Wiggins, I. H. 1:85
Wiggins, Isaac 11:179
Wiggins, J. F. 1:86
Wiggins, J. M. 21:45
Wiggins, Jacob H. 17:27
Wiggins, James 3:215; 17:286; 25:260
Wiggins, John B. 22:494
Wiggins, John L. 27:133
Wiggins, Joseph C. 27:129
Wiggins, King 18:212
Wiggins, Leander E. 17:363
Wiggins, M. 16:262
Wiggins, Philips 10:170
Wiggins, Randel 10:177
Wiggins, Randul 19:219
Wiggins, Reuben 22:327
Wiggins, Robert F. 25:260
Wiggins, S. R. 14:126
Wiggins, Samuel 10:87; 20:391
Wiggins, Stephen 10:170
Wiggins, William 18:224; 23:261
Wiggins, Z. C. 16:112
Wigglesworth, H. 16:262
Wiggleworth, Moses S. 3:215
Wiggs, Daniel 22:60, 413
Wiggs, Thomas T. 16:262
Wiggs, W. 15:273
Wigham, Ben 9:212
Wighley, E. 3:215
Wighner, Isaac 9:212
Wight, Charles N. 9:216
Wight, Ogilvie 10:12
Wight, William A. 17:363
Wightman, H. A. 1:87

Wightman, Jacob 22:60
Wightman, James L. 18:417
Wigin, Michael 21:403
Wigins, Charles 16:391
Wigle, John 9:198
Wigley, C. F. 9:64
Wigton, Thomas J. 20:139
Wihaucker, F. 14:126
Wihrley, A. 20:391
Wihrley, Andrews 10:87
Wik, P. 20:151
Wike, A. 3:216
Wike, Isaac 9:127; 27:130
Wike, Jonathan 26:146
Wikel, Alexander 4:62
Wikeson, Robert 24:207
Wikh, John W. 21:403
Wikoff, Thomas C. 18:167
Wil---, James P. 17:286
Wilamon, P. 23:176
Wilan, Peter 12:45
Wiland, J. 1:86
Wilant, Austin 9:198
Wilback, M. 7:62
Wilban, John T. 11:283
Wilber, C. C. 1:86
Wilber, Charles 4:62
Wilber, E. 3:216
Wilber, Edward 17:152
Wilber, Frederick 22:159
Wilber, George W. 1:84
Wilber, H. H. 21:403
Wilber, Henry C. 14:232
Wilber, J. B. 17:309
Wilber, James 25:260
Wilber, James E. 23:258
Wilber, Jesse 8:57
Wilber, John F. 12:46
Wilber, John R. 25:261
Wilber, N. A. 18:388
Wilber, P. C. 16:112
Wilber, Ramsey 18:268; 26:85
Wilber, S. D. 27:129
Wilber, Stephen 13:54
Wilbert, Abner 17:89
Wilbert, Augustus 14:313; 17:471; 27:132
Wilbert, H. E. 25:261
Wilbert, J. 1:184
Wilbertsayers, Eli 11:406
Wilbey, J. 17:365
Wilbier, Thomas E. 23:83
Wilborn, George W. 22:229
Wilborn, Isham 7:136
Wilborn, Payton 10:142; 20:391
Wilborn, Robert 22:60

Wilborn, William 9:65
Wilbowen, Henry 11:176
Wilbur, A. 11:274
Wilbur, Fred. M. 18:403
Wilbur, G. W. 9:17
Wilbur, George W. 20:191
Wilbur, H. F. 9:153
Wilbur, H. P. 24:115
Wilbur, H. T. 27:128
Wilbur, Isaiah S. 19:141
Wilbur, James 1:86
Wilbur, John N. 10:87
Wilbur, L. C. 10:87
Wilbur, Lander 25:128
Wilbur, Leroy 13:75
Wilbur, N. 1:185
Wilbur, Norman 8:116
Wilbur, Orson 21:45
Wilbur, Oscar 1:85
Wilbur, P. 1:185
Wilbur, Philander 12:60
Wilbur, S. D. 9:153
Wilbur, S. G. 1:87
Wilbur, S. P. 20:392
Wilbur, Stephen 16:62
Wilbur, T. H. 12:159
Wilbur, W. 1:182
Wilbur, W. H. 25:126
Wilbura, Gabriel 20:392
Wilburn, --- 14:126
Wilburn, C. 25:261
Wilburn, Flem 18:288
Wilburn, Gabriel 10:87
Wilburn, George 3:216
Wilburn, H. 22:494
Wilburn, Hiram P. 17:391
Wilburn, Jacob A. 17:208
Wilburn, Oliver 8:111
Wilburn, Reuben J. 22:134
Wilburn, Robert 23:56
Wilburn, Simon 26:198
Wilburn, William 6:20; 17:98; 18:99
Wilby, John 13:76
Wilcema, John 4:63
Wilcock, John R. 22:60
Wilcocks, John M. 9:127
Wilcocks, Mycuk 9:74
Wilcocks, Stanton A. 9:127
Wilcomb, Moses J. 22:349
Wilcoss, Levi 11:291
Wilcox, --- 9:161; 15:156
Wilcox, A. 1:86; 20:180
Wilcox, A. B. 25:128
Wilcox, A. S. 10:142; 20:391
Wilcox, Albert 7:62
Wilcox, Alex 19:293

Wilcox, Allen 3:216
Wilcox, Borden 17:351
Wilcox, C. 3:216
Wilcox, C. H. 11:48; 16:11
Wilcox, Charles 11:20; 15:254
Wilcox, Collin 4:63
Wilcox, Crawford 21:289
Wilcox, D. 19:219
Wilcox, D. D. 15:115
Wilcox, D. G. 5:34; 25:261
Wilcox, D. H. 7:54
Wilcox, Daniel 12:79; 15:93
Wilcox, Daniel E. 8:116
Wilcox, David 11:254
Wilcox, David A. 20:50
Wilcox, David W. 23:116
Wilcox, E. 7:54; 12:163; 15:323; 19:141
Wilcox, E. A. 1:185
Wilcox, E. H. 1:183; 23:56
Wilcox, E. M. 18:167
Wilcox, Edmund F. 22:159
Wilcox, Edward 15:156; 17:427; 24:181
Wilcox, Ephraim 17:69
Wilcox, Eugene 19:219
Wilcox, Ezra 22:109
Wilcox, F. E. 3:216
Wilcox, F. S. 19:272
Wilcox, G. A. 11:317
Wilcox, George 3:216; 6:21; 10:169; 19:219
Wilcox, George A. 15:79
Wilcox, George W. 1:86; 12:46; 21:403; 23:17
Wilcox, H. 20:82; 26:84
Wilcox, H. G. 14:126
Wilcox, H. H. 9:64
Wilcox, H. R. 3:216
Wilcox, H. S. 27:134
Wilcox, Haml 1:86
Wilcox, Henry 20:109
Wilcox, Henry C. 9:105; 18:342
Wilcox, Hiram 9:94; 15:79; 23:176
Wilcox, I. H. 14:126
Wilcox, I. L. 19:42
Wilcox, I. M. 11:383
Wilcox, J. 1:182; 3:216; 8:68
Wilcox, J. N. 13:75
Wilcox, J. O. 26:200
Wilcox, J. P. 16:262

Wilcox, J. W. 13:75; 19:141
Wilcox, James 10:87; 11:131; 20:391
Wilcox, James L. 10:87; 20:391
Wilcox, Jasper N. 22:60
Wilcox, Jeffrey H. 10:142; 20:391
Wilcox, John 8:116; 10:175; 14:232; 15:254; 18:324; 19:219
Wilcox, John A. 18:282
Wilcox, John W. 23:176
Wilcox, L. D. 2:20; 25:123
Wilcox, L. E. 18:116
Wilcox, Lewis 20:87
Wilcox, M. 1:84; 22:229, 494
Wilcox, Martin 23:269
Wilcox, Martin L. 23:197
Wilcox, Morton 22:159
Wilcox, Moses 1:84
Wilcox, Noble 1:84
Wilcox, O. 15:115
Wilcox, O. A. 21:145
Wilcox, Oliver P. 23:83
Wilcox, Orville 7:114
Wilcox, Otis S. 15:334; 19:141
Wilcox, P. 13:102
Wilcox, Philip 16:142
Wilcox, Pliney 13:131; 20:391
Wilcox, R. 3:216
Wilcox, Richard 11:176
Wilcox, Robert A. 21:108
Wilcox, Robert B. 10:94; 20:392
Wilcox, S. 19:264
Wilcox, S. F. 9:198
Wilcox, Samuel 9:198; 12:120, 168; 17:262
Wilcox, Seth 13:123
Wilcox, Smith 7:114
Wilcox, Stanton A. 27:131
Wilcox, T. J. 23:56
Wilcox, W. 3:216; 7:70; 13:102; 14:25, 232, 261; 20:45
Wilcox, Warren 13:54; 17:289
Wilcox, Warren W. 8:98
Wilcox, Whitman A. 20:117
Wilcox, Willard P. 15:80

Wilcox, William 7:70; 9:30; 11:290, 435; 12:97; 15:93; 22:274
Wilcox, William B. 26:116
Wilcox, William H. 4:63
Wilcox, William P. 18:318
Wilcox, William S. 15:362; 25:127
Wilcoxen, H. 11:274
Wilcoxen, Walter 17:140; 24:206
Wilcoxson, E. M. 8:36
Wilcoxson, W. 8:68; 26:200
Wilcus, A. 7:73
Wilcus, William T. 11:80
Wilcuts, Calvin 21:237
Wild, Andrew 27:132
Wild, Charles 22:495
Wild, Daniel 23:176
Wild, J. 14:232
Wild, Lemages 14:131
Wild, Peter 10:142; 20:392
Wild, William 23:83
Wilday, Charles 7:45
Wilday, H. 16:262
Wilday, Sylvester 19:42
Wildback, Charles W. 9:198
Wildberger, P. 3:216
Wilde, James S. 1:83
Wilde, John S. 19:324
Wilden, Andrew 11:99
Wilden, John 8:57
Wildens, August 21:403
Wildentome, Gem 7:137
Wilder, A. 14:133
Wilder, Albert 14:232
Wilder, Albert A. 23:56
Wilder, Albert G. 7:17
Wilder, Alfred 22:114
Wilder, B. W. 21:403
Wilder, Charles 7:114
Wilder, Cyrus R. 11:113
Wilder, Edgar 9:137; 27:130
Wilder, Edward B. 4:62
Wilder, Edward M. 21:403
Wilder, Elias D. 22:159
Wilder, George 7:115; 11:317
Wilder, George W. 17:61
Wilder, H. C. 4:62
Wilder, H. S. 3:216
Wilder, Henry 18:41; 22:60
Wilder, Henry C. 14:232

Wilder, Hiram 13:54
Wilder, J. R. 9:198;
19:243
Wilder, Jack 6:13
Wilder, James B. 17:286
Wilder, Joel J. 22:413
Wilder, John 3:216; 18:99
Wilder, John W. 18:349
Wilder, L. 23:57
Wilder, L. E. 3:216
Wilder, L. F. 3:216
Wilder, Leonard 13:54
Wilder, Lewis C. 17:461;
24:168
Wilder, O. A. 1:182
Wilder, R. 21:403
Wilder, Samuel 17:444;
24:163
Wilder, Seth B. 17:28
Wilder, Solomon S. 17:61
Wilder, T. A. 21:145
Wilder, T. J. 9:65
Wilder, Thomas D. 19:42
Wilder, Wallace 19:42
Wilder, William 4:62;
22:506
Wilderman, E. 3:216
Wildermuth, Henry 9:127;
27:131
Wildermuth, John 20:117
Wilders, George 14:126
Wilders, W. 1:185
Wilderson, Charles 18:41
Wilderson, Henry 7:114
Wildey, M. E. 13:75;
19:141
Wildhack, C. W. 19:285
Wildhagan, J. 7:45
Wildham, H. C. 16:262
Wildie, A. 17:271
Wilding, George 15:296;
16:262
Wildish, Charles 8:57
Wildish, Charles W.
21:145
Wildman, Fred 23:175
Wildman, H. H. 7:45
Wildman, Ira 20:153
Wildman, J. 18:73
Wildman, Randolph C.
4:63
Wildman, Thomas 10:88;
20:392
Wildon, James 18:201
Wildridge, James 8:98
Wilds, David 11:419
Wilds, George 18:99
Wilds, Henry O. 23:103
Wilds, J. 3:216
Wilds, John 1:86
Wilds, W. W. 11:427

Wilds, William D. 11:394
Wilds, William L. 10:94;
20:392
Wildsien, Fred 10:88;
20:392
Wildt, E. A. 27:127
Wildt, E. H. 9:153
Wildt, Frederick 25:125
Wildy, Thomas 15:178
Wile, A. 3:216
Wileman, Franklin 22:274
Wileman, Henry 15:89
Wileord, --- 21:45
Wiler, L. 12:94
Wiler, W. 8:57
Wiles, --- 8:57
Wiles, D. K. N. 20:152
Wiles, Jacob 15:15
Wiles, John 17:405
Wiles, Simon 11:321
Wiles, W. H. 22:494
Wilets, A. 10:203
Wiley, --- 15:255
Wiley, A. 3:216; 11:443;
13:102; 14:25
Wiley, A. C. 22:274
Wiley, A. F. 16:391
Wiley, Allen B. 10:143;
20:392
Wiley, Andrew J. 4:62
Wiley, Andrew S. 23:103
Wiley, B. R. 9:198;
19:243
Wiley, Benjamin 18:268;
26:87
Wiley, C. H. 19:233
Wiley, C. M. 1:86
Wiley, Charles 5:33;
9:198; 21:162;
25:261
Wiley, Charles M. 23:116
Wiley, David 21:403
Wiley, David D. 19:42
Wiley, E. Frank 10:24
Wiley, E. T. 3:216
Wiley, Edward J. 15:348
Wiley, Edwin 6:27
Wiley, F. M. 8:57
Wiley, G. 26:84
Wiley, G. S. 25:123
Wiley, George W. 16:80;
22:60
Wiley, H. R. 23:83
Wiley, Hall 22:328
Wiley, I. 14:232
Wiley, J. 3:216; 23:258
Wiley, J. W. 26:200
Wiley, James 5:33; 15:89;
18:185
Wiley, James F. 7:45

Wiley, John 14:261;
16:262; 17:363;
22:229
Wiley, John D. 1:86
Wiley, John M. 11:179
Wiley, Joseph 11:217
Wiley, Keeny 23:186
Wiley, L. 21:404
Wiley, Luke 17:189
Wiley, Mathew 21:404
Wiley, Moses 18:167
Wiley, Nathan 22:328
Wiley, Patrick 21:162
Wiley, Philip P. 7:45
Wiley, Renshaw 21:404
Wiley, Reuben M. 24:34
Wiley, Richard 22:60;
23:272
Wiley, S. M. 25:126
Wiley, Samuel 3:216
Wiley, Susannah 25:261
Wiley, T. 3:216
Wiley, T. M. 18:61
Wiley, Thomas 7:137;
9:94; 26:85
Wiley, Thompson M.
21:145
Wiley, W. 3:216
Wiley, William 7:45;
9:94; 23:173, 175
Wilfert, Charles 18:167
Wilffenback, J. 11:195
Wilfoln, --- 1:182
Wilfong, J. R. 14:25
Wilfony, J. R. 16:275
Wilford, David 11:175
Wilford, Hardy 8:35;
18:167
Wilford, Robert 27:133
Wilfot, Thomas 21:289
Wilgemwood, J. F. 24:87
Wilger, John 23:15
Wilgus, Daniel R. 24:57
Wilgus, I. L. 14:126
Wilgus, Joseph 12:120
Wilhart, Henry 21:202
Wilheek, Philip 10:87
Wilheight, Andrew 22:517
Wilhelm, A. 1:185
Wilhelm, Antonie 24:47
Wilhelm, Benjamin
22:274
Wilhelm, Daniel E. 10:88;
20:392
Wilhelm, Flem 26:136
Wilhelm, G. A. 3:216
Wilhelm, Harvey 17:160
Wilhelm, J. 15:51
Wilhelm, Jacob 12:79
Wilhelm, Thomas 8:98
Wilhet, Collins 25:261

Wilhight, Simeon 11:427
Wilhite, Charles 7:115
Wilhite, J. B. 10:88
Wilhite, Jesse 10:142; 20:392
Wilhite, John P. 18:299; 26:116
Wilhite, Samuel P. 17:150
Wilhite, Volney 17:240
Wilhock, Philip 20:392
Wilhorst, John P. 9:40
Wilhouk, Sebastian 22:169
Wilhouse, Empress 27:130
Wilhouse, Emprus 9:137
Wilhout, Abraham 10:87
Wilhyde, S. 3:216
Wililams, Daniel D. 9:74
Wiliney, C. A. 15:346
Wilke, Jacob 25:261
Wilken, William L. 22:114
Wilkens, W. 14:285
Wilkenson, A. J. 1:182
Wilkenson, Francis M. 22:109
Wilkenson, George 10:142
Wilkenson, Isaiah 22:109
Wilkenson, J. C. 20:392
Wilkenson, John 7:46; 18:99
Wilkenson, John A. 17:394
Wilkenson, Thomas 22:229
Wilkenson, W. 12:84
Wilkenson, William 11:334
Wilker, Edward 22:495
Wilker, William 18:268
Wilkerson, Bayard 16:11
Wilkerson, George 21:289
Wilkerson, Henry M. 24:169
Wilkerson, Isaac F. 11:277
Wilkerson, J. 27:133
Wilkerson, J. W. 16:11
Wilkerson, James 17:286
Wilkerson, Milton 17:357
Wilkerson, Nathaniel 17:444
Wilkerson, Peter 23:83
Wilkerson, Stephen B. 17:461; 24:169
Wilkerson, W. 13:102; 14:25
Wilkerson, Washington 10:177

Wilkerson, William K. 5:34
Wilkes, C. 1:183
Wilkes, George 27:131
Wilkes, Henry 8:58
Wilkes, J. 1:185
Wilkes, J. H. 8:69
Wilkes, James P. 21:133
Wilkes, John 11:99
Wilkes, Nathan 17:430
Wilkes, R. 3:216
Wilkes, S. 3:216
Wilkey, Carter 8:69
Wilkey, Coransey D. 23:266
Wilkey, Edward B. 20:392
Wilkey, Godfrey 19:219
Wilkey, William B. 22:109
Wilkham, A. W. 11:275
Wilkie, Edward B. 10:87
Wilkie, Godfrey 10:175; 19:219
Wilkie, Thomas 1:86
Wilkin, Chester 6:27
Wilkin, E. W. 12:159
Wilkin, James A. 22:229
Wilkin, Jeremiah 11:398
Wilkington, M. L. 5:34
Wilkins, --- 18:201; 26:214
Wilkins, A. 3:216
Wilkins, A. B. 7:80; 25:308
Wilkins, Ambrose 21:404
Wilkins, B. 9:106
Wilkins, C. L. 10:169
Wilkins, Charles W. 23:103
Wilkins, E. P. 21:165
Wilkins, F. 1:184
Wilkins, George 7:136
Wilkins, George W. 10:142; 20:392
Wilkins, Girard 21:404
Wilkins, Hamilton 21:404
Wilkins, Henry 8:111; 14:232
Wilkins, Henry A. 10:169
Wilkins, Hiram 23:95
Wilkins, Ira 7:17
Wilkins, Irwin 1:84
Wilkins, J. 3:216; 25:261
Wilkins, J. B. 15:320
Wilkins, J. C. 25:261
Wilkins, J. J. 7:79; 25:308
Wilkins, J. N. 21:192
Wilkins, J. R. 15:255
Wilkins, J. W. 19:243
Wilkins, James 5:48; 15:51

Wilkins, James D. 23:103
Wilkins, James E. 9:94; 26:87
Wilkins, James W. 9:198
Wilkins, John 1:83; 4:62; 15:171
Wilkins, John W. 22:229
Wilkins, Joseph 4:62; 8:98
Wilkins, Julius 18:167
Wilkins, Julius E. 8:36
Wilkins, L. O. 25:308
Wilkins, Levi P. 23:111
Wilkins, Moses 23:57
Wilkins, Noah 14:232
Wilkins, O. B. 12:46
Wilkins, Oliver P. 17:277
Wilkins, Owen P. 18:212
Wilkins, Philip 23:278
Wilkins, R. 12:159
Wilkins, S. O. 3:216
Wilkins, W. H. 9:94; 26:83
Wilkins, W. S. 14:249
Wilkins, Willard 7:54
Wilkins, William 4:62; 13:79; 16:262
Wilkins, William F. 15:178
Wilkinson, Aaron 22:413
Wilkinson, Albert 11:177
Wilkinson, C. 3:216
Wilkinson, Charles 9:156; 10:8, 87; 20:392; 23:175
Wilkinson, Clarence 22:159
Wilkinson, D. D. 11:418
Wilkinson, D. E. 11:343
Wilkinson, Dark 23:272
Wilkinson, E. 23:253
Wilkinson, Franklin 20:392
Wilkinson, George 7:115; 16:62; 20:392
Wilkinson, George W. 22:495
Wilkinson, Henry 6:20; 16:359; 18:99, 116
Wilkinson, Hi. A. 26:85
Wilkinson, Isaac 9:212
Wilkinson, Isaac H. 26:199
Wilkinson, J. D. 10:87
Wilkinson, J. H. 8:69
Wilkinson, J. N. 3:216
Wilkinson, James 17:140; 21:83; 24:206
Wilkinson, James H. 4:69
Wilkinson, John 6:20; 7:46; 18:99

Wilkinson, John G.
20:150
Wilkinson, John R.
21:145
Wilkinson, Joseph 23:176,
261
Wilkinson, Leonard
17:140; 24:206
Wilkinson, Levi B. 22:60
Wilkinson, Levi N.
12:168
Wilkinson, Lewis 7:70
Wilkinson, Milo 11:176
Wilkinson, Nathaniel
24:163
Wilkinson, P. 19:49
Wilkinson, Phile 19:219
Wilkinson, Philip 9:233;
20:392
Wilkinson, Philo 10:169
Wilkinson, Richard
17:140; 24:206
Wilkinson, S. B. 8:102
Wilkinson, Samuel 11:215
Wilkinson, Thomas 6:20;
18:99; 20:37; 22:274
Wilkinson, Thomas J.
17:69
Wilkinson, W. 3:216
Wilkinson, W. R. 8:69
Wilkinson, Wash. 19:219
Wilkinson, William
11:81; 25:261
Wilkinson, William P.
17:416; 24:155
Wilkison, Samuel 10:175
Wilkison, William 19:219
Wilklin, Myron 10:24
Wilklow, Clinton 22:16
Wilkons, Henry 26:214
Wilks, George 9:127
Wilks, Gustavus 25:126
Wilks, John R. 17:309
Wilks, Martin 9:94; 26:83
Wilks, Nathan 17:423;
24:172
Wilks, Nathaniel 11:338
Wilks, Samuel 15:255
Wilkson, W. 16:359
Wilkson, William 18:268;
26:87
Wilky, John 18:321
Will, --- 11:178
Will, Anthony 16:262
Will, Gustavus 3:216
Will, J. 3:216
Will, John 12:79; 15:51,
255
Will, Joseph 6:34
Will, Philip 24:155
Will, Robert 24:60

Will, Robert G. 11:176
Will, William 18:41
Will, William H. 10:143
Willa, George 11:117
Willaby, H. A. 11:253
Willagan, Henry 10:98
Willard, --- 10:169
Willard, A. 14:126;
20:392
Willard, A. G. 25:127
Willard, Alfred M. 18:167
Willard, Andrew 9:156
Willard, Ch. 14:233
Willard, F. O. 1:181
Willard, Francis 13:55
Willard, Frederic I.
11:406
Willard, Frederick 11:317
Willard, George W.
21:133
Willard, H. K. 1:83
Willard, Henry 9:198
Willard, Horatio B. 4:62
Willard, Hugh A. 22:134
Willard, J. 14:25
Willard, J. B. 20:93
Willard, J. J. 12:97;
15:362
Willard, Jacob 16:13
Willard, James 5:48
Willard, James H. 17:61
Willard, John 7:115;
10:143; 11:47;
20:392; 23:103
Willard, John S. 20:20
Willard, Joseph P. 22:159
Willard, M. 13:102
Willard, Milo 17:363
Willard, Nicholas 22:159
Willard, O. K. 12:46
Willard, O. O. 25:308
Willard, Oliver O. 7:80
Willard, R. H. 18:185
Willard, V. M. 24:33
Willard, W. 3:216
Willard, William 19:264
Willart, Z. 19:234
Willbanks, W. 16:62
Willburn, Simon 8:44
Willcock, Edward 11:215
Willcott, Emerson 13:54
Willcox, John M. 27:130
Willcoxen, B. H. 21:241
Willell, Joseph 13:102
Willema, August 15:148
Willen, William 11:20
Willenmine, James A.
17:322
Willens, W. J. 9:94
Willer, Cornelius S. 23:83
Willer, George D. 15:356

Willer, John 11:175
Willer, Michael 11:317
Willerd, D. F. 18:224
Willers, John A. 15:51
Willershouser, Jacob 7:62
Willes, Jesse R. 8:36
Willes, W. H. 20:392
Willeson, H. 8:68
Willet, Arnold 22:413
Willet, D. 11:81
Willet, E. E. 13:102
Willet, G. F. 27:131
Willet, George F. 9:127
Willet, Isadore 10:87
Willet, John 12:45
Willets, A. 16:262; 18:282
Willets, George W.
22:469
Willets, William 12:45
Willett, Elbert 8:78
Willett, George 21:108
Willett, J. 7:46
Willett, James 17:140;
24:207
Willett, John 22:328
Willett, John P. 13:123
Willett, Joseph 14:25
Willett, Martin 17:189
Willett, Trueman 8:116
Willett, W. 3:216; 21:113
Willett, William 14:232
Willette, Isador 20:392
Willetts, Hugh H. 22:444
Willetts, James 19:264
Willetts, Newton E.
17:264
Willetts, Oliver 25:335
Willetts, Pleasant A.
17:461; 24:163
Willey, Alph'a 1:84
Willey, Alphonso 19:42
Willey, Carlas C. 12:45
Willey, D. H. 3:216;
27:157
Willey, Edward J. 16:391
Willey, Foster W. 22:444
Willey, G. S. 2:19
Willey, G. W. 11:113
Willey, George 14:232
Willey, George A. 10:169
Willey, George H. 9:127;
27:130
Willey, H. 25:261
Willey, H. C. 9:114
Willey, Henry H. 17:73
Willey, Hiram V. 20:139
Willey, I. 17:293
Willey, J. 3:216; 21:404;
25:261
Willey, J. S. 3:216
Willey, James 1:83

Willey, James D. 9:127
Willey, John 18:282
Willey, Joseph 16:262
Wiley, Moses 8:36
Willey, Ottis 25:261
Willey, P. S. 21:192
Willey, R. W. 7:62
Willey, William J. 23:175
Willfing, J. R. 13:102
Willfong, G. 23:57
Willhart, J. 14:25
Willhelm, David B. 17:89
Willhelm, John 23:57
Willhelm, Luther M. 23:103
Willhigh, James 13:55
Willhite, J. B. 20:392
William, --- 12:169; 25:124
William, A. 14:126
William, E. Van 15:15
William, F. 3:216
William, G. 25:261
William, George 3:216
William, Henry 17:192
William, J. F. 14:126
William, James 5:48
William, King Augustus 17:351
William, Orland 3:216
William, W. 16:275
William, W. H. 22:229
Williamburg, Harmon 11:177
Williams, --- 10:203; 11:283; 12:120, 145; 13:75; 15:95, 262; 16:88; 17:336; 18:268; 19:319; 20:392; 21:404; 23:287; 26:86, 214, 234
Williams, A. 1:183, 184; 3:216; 7:79, 115; 14:126, 232; 19:231; 21:45, 404; 22:274, 413; 25:261, 308; 27:127
Williams, A. A. 14:126; 23:176
Williams, A. B. 2:19; 25:127
Williams, A. F. 1:88, 185
Williams, A. G. 14:317; 21:404
Williams, A. J. 5:47; 9:94; 17:189; 20:392; 25:261
Williams, A. L. 10:87
Williams, A. S. 11:255

Williams, A. T. 1:85; 9:153; 15:305; 16:262; 27:127
Williams, Aaron 21:289; 23:83; 27:133
Williams, Aaron W. 21:205
Williams, Abel 17:389
Williams, Abner 23:176
Williams, Abraham 7:137; 8:59; 12:45; 20:37; 23:272
Williams, Abraham H. 4:62
Williams, Abram 14:232
Williams, Adam 5:47; 21:289
Williams, Albert 21:237; 22:327
Williams, Albert H. 22:159
Williams, Albert R. 22:60
Williams, Alden 24:168
Williams, Alex 19:264; 26:198
Williams, Alex. 8:43
Williams, Alexander 7:137; 9:198; 22:327
Williams, Alexander S. 22:229
Williams, Alfred 11:48; 15:255; 17:140; 19:297; 21:404; 22:274; 24:47, 206
Williams, Alfred M. 21:237; 23:116
Williams, Allen 13:55
Williams, Alva 10:169; 19:219
Williams, Ambrose 21:404
Williams, Amos 18:41; 20:400
Williams, Amos P. 11:176
Williams, Amos W. 25:126
Williams, Anderson 9:203, 212; 19:285
Williams, Andrew 7:46; 12:46; 21:289
Williams, Andrew J. 5:48; 23:127
Williams, Andrew P. 22:445
Williams, Andrew S. 11:178
Williams, Andy 9:203; 19:293
Williams, Anson 11:405
Williams, Anthony 7:137; 10:209; 21:289

Williams, Archimedes 8:35
Williams, Arthur 11:178
Williams, Asa 11:47
Williams, Asa W. 17:423; 24:172
Williams, Athmedias 18:167
Williams, Augustus 21:192, 404
Williams, B. 14:126, 232; 17:510; 25:261
Williams, B. E. 23:111
Williams, B. G. 1:84
Williams, B. P. 22:349
Williams, B. S. 15:171
Williams, Ballard P. 22:229
Williams, Benjamin 7:137; 21:404; 22:349
Williams, Benjamin F. 17:45, 73; 21:108
Williams, Bill 11:175
Williams, Blakely 7:137
Williams, Bonaparte 9:203
Williams, Boneparte 19:285
Williams, Boston 21:404
Williams, Brian 21:169
Williams, Briton C. 17:61
Williams, Britton C. 17:286
Williams, Bryan 17:444; 24:163
Williams, Burr 11:290
Williams, C. 1:89, 184; 3:216; 13:76; 16:262, 359; 21:45, 404; 25:261; 26:234
Williams, C. C. 23:293
Williams, C. D. 26:244
Williams, C. F. 1:182
Williams, C. G. 25:261
Williams, C. H. 1:182; 3:216; 11:20; 18:41
Williams, C. J. 14:313; 17:471; 27:131
Williams, C. L. 27:133
Williams, C. M. 15:255
Williams, C. R. 3:216; 20:15
Williams, C. S. 3:216
Williams, C. W. 3:216
Williams, Calvin 9:203; 19:285
Williams, Carrall 26:87
Williams, Carroll 18:268
Williams, Ch. 14:232
Williams, Chancey 16:286

Williams, Charles 1:83, 84, 191; 3:216; 6:26; 7:46, 79, 115, 137; 9:137; 14:335; 17:189, 452; 18:73, 99; 21:404; 22:60; 23:57; 25:261, 308; 27:129
Williams, Charles A. 12:46
Williams, Charles B. 27:133
Williams, Charles C. 10:143
Williams, Charles E. 10:94; 20:392; 23:242
Williams, Charles H. 9:14; 23:127
Williams, Charles L. 24:181
Williams, Charles M. 1:87
Williams, Charles T. 21:113
Williams, Charles W. 8:60
Williams, Christian C. 22:274
Williams, Claburn 21:289
Williams, Clark 15:83
Williams, Clarke 8:98; 21:213
Williams, Clytus 11:321
Williams, Cornelius 21:263
Williams, Cyrenus 7:115
Williams, Cyrus 11:131
Williams, Cyrus W. 21:237
Williams, D. 3:217; 5:33; 11:113; 21:404; 25:261
Williams, D. H. 11:317
Williams, D. T. 1:86
Williams, D. W. 17:297
Williams, Daniel 1:84; 6:26; 9:212; 10:143; 14:237; 19:49; 20:392; 21:13, 404; 22:169; 27:133
Williams, Daniel H. 7:115
Williams, Daniel M. 22:159
Williams, Daniel W. 17:286
Williams, David 7:137; 9:40; 11:215, 426, 427; 12:53; 18:299; 21:113, 289, 404; 22:229; 26:116
Williams, David C. 24:57
Williams, David J. 22:510

Williams, David R. 17:89
Williams, Demeratus 21:263
Williams, Dennis 16:62
Williams, Dick 24:103
Williams, Dotjon 24:207
Williams, Dudley 17:140; 24:206
Williams, E. 3:217; 9:155; 15:255; 16:262; 24:87; 25:261; 26:136; 27:128
Williams, E. E. 1:182
Williams, E. G. 10:24
Williams, E. J. 1:185; 14:261
Williams, E. L. 15:255
Williams, E. M. 16:150
Williams, E. O. 19:219
Williams, E. R. 26:83
Williams, E. S. 11:131
Williams, Ed 3:217
Williams, Ed C. 20:180
Williams, Edmond 18:21
Williams, Edward 5:47, 48; 7:70, 137; 8:36; 9:74; 10:143; 17:286; 18:167, 268; 19:219; 20:392; 21:289; 22:229; 25:261; 26:87
Williams, Edward D. 13:55
Williams, Edward R. 9:94
Williams, Edwin 4:62; 9:137; 27:129
Williams, Eli 19:219
Williams, Elias 4:69; 9:161; 10:208; 14:328; 17:168; 27:134
Williams, Elijah 15:61; 16:166; 22:459
Williams, Elliott W. 18:424
Williams, Emerson 5:33
Williams, Endus 24:207
Williams, Enoch J. 20:117
Williams, Ephraim 18:268; 26:87
Williams, Ev'n 1:87
Williams, Evan 9:106
Williams, F. 3:217; 14:126; 16:262; 19:285; 21:404; 22:229; 25:261; 27:127
Williams, F. M. 21:62
Williams, Faunt 22:517
Williams, Field 5:48
Williams, Flavus 22:493

Williams, Flemin 22:445
Williams, Francis 17:113
Williams, Francis M. 12:168
Williams, Francis O. 17:275
Williams, Frank 6:27; 7:137; 8:98; 9:153, 203, 205; 20:392; 24:87
Williams, Franklin 5:33; 22:327; 26:132
Williams, Fred 3:217
Williams, Fred. G. 21:404
Williams, Frederick 19:42
Williams, G. 5:47; 7:46; 11:114; 13:81; 15:51; 16:262; 19:50; 23:57; 25:261; 26:201
Williams, G. A. 3:217
Williams, G. B. 18:282; 24:115
Williams, G. F. 13:55
Williams, G. H. 21:46
Williams, G. K. 13:123
Williams, G. L. 8:76; 26:200
Williams, G. M. 11:175
Williams, G. N. 11:292
Williams, G. R. C. 5:33; 25:261
Williams, G. W. 3:217; 7:46; 9:226; 16:262; 25:308
Williams, George 1:83; 3:217; 5:33, 48; 7:17, 115, 137; 8:44; 9:46, 47, 162, 217; 10:143, 169; 11:19, 81, 216, 317, 393; 12:45, 53, 79, 173; 13:55; 14:232; 15:62, 346; 16:262, 391; 17:89, 140, 429; 18:99, 116, 330; 19:219; 20:117, 392; 21:289, 404; 22:109; 23:206; 24:186, 207; 25:308; 26:131, 132, 198
Williams, George A. 9:99
Williams, George B. 16:286
Williams, George D. 6:23; 7:115
Williams, George F. 26:200
Williams, George H. 22:229; 25:128
Williams, George M. 10:87; 20:393

Williams, George S.
7:115; 22:229
Williams, George T. 23:83
Williams, George W.
1:85; 7:79; 8:69;
9:14; 10:87; 11:393;
17:28; 18:388; 20:15,
393; 21:13
Williams, Gilbert 23:267
Williams, Granville
21:108
Williams, Green 24:60
Williams, Gustaf 8:36;
18:167
Williams, H. 1:83, 84;
3:217; 5:55; 8:69;
9:155, 203; 15:317;
16:112, 262; 18:99;
19:219; 21:113;
25:261; 27:128
Williams, H. A. 18:268
Williams, H. C. 14:232,
261; 17:211; 18:268;
26:85
Williams, H. D. 3:217
Williams, H. E. 14:126
Williams, H. F. 15:301
Williams, H. J. 13:102
Williams, H. M. 22:493;
24:33
Williams, H. P. 1:181,
186
Williams, H. S. 25:261
Williams, H. W. 14:126
Williams, Hardy 18:61
Williams, Harrison 10:154
Williams, Hector 9:137;
27:129
Williams, Henry 1:191;
4:62; 6:13, 20, 27;
7:79; 8:43; 9:68, 137,
198, 212; 10:25;
11:274; 12:46;
14:232, 320; 16:262,
391; 18:41, 73, 99,
116; 19:243, 293;
21:133, 219, 289,
404; 22:327; 24:103,
207; 25:261, 274,
308; 26:198; 27:129
Williams, Henry C. 12:45
Williams, Henry E. 13:54
Williams, Henry F. 16:262
Williams, Henry H. 10:87;
20:393
Williams, Henry J.
18:268; 26:86
Williams, Henry P. 13:54
Williams, Henry R.
22:109
Williams, Henry W. 12:45

Williams, Henson 22:134
Williams, Herman 7:84;
21:404
Williams, Hiram 11:318
Williams, Hormer 27:130
Williams, Hugh 4:62
Williams, I. 25:280
Williams, I. H. 11:394
Williams, Ira B. 18:185
Williams, Irving 17:348
Williams, Isaac 7:137;
8:111; 9:94, 198,
212; 11:80; 12:159;
14:232; 18:73, 268;
19:285; 22:274;
26:84, 86; 27:134
Williams, Isaac H. 22:229
Williams, Isaac T. 7:54
Williams, Isaiah 21:289
Williams, Isaiah L. 23:57
Williams, J. 1:89, 183;
3:217; 7:79; 9:153;
11:222, 316, 343;
12:79, 84, 159, 163;
13:102, 123; 14:25,
127, 232; 15:51, 62,
115; 16:137, 262,
359; 17:61; 18:424;
20:131; 21:62, 83,
113; 22:327; 24:60;
25:126, 261, 308;
27:126, 127
Williams, J. A. 3:217
Williams, J. B. 3:217;
7:46; 9:114; 20:393
Williams, J. C. 25:261
Williams, J. D. 14:276;
15:255; 17:497;
26:201
Williams, J. G. 9:153;
27:127
Williams, J. H. 1:185;
11:394; 17:163;
25:284
Williams, J. J. 18:99;
21:46; 23:176;
25:261
Williams, J. L. 1:181, 182;
11:254; 21:83
Williams, J. M. 9:65;
15:255; 25:127, 262
Williams, J. N. 3:217
Williams, J. P. 13:54;
17:45; 19:42; 23:83
Williams, J. R. 1:87;
11:394
Williams, J. S. 12:145
Williams, J. T. 1:185;
10:150; 14:285;
18:61

Williams, J. W. 8:57;
18:388; 20:135;
25:262
Williams, Jabez 10:143;
20:393
Williams, Jack 7:8; 9:137;
10:177; 19:219;
27:129
Williams, Jackson 11:217;
27:156
Williams, Jacob 8:36;
9:127; 10:87, 208;
13:129; 18:167;
20:393; 21:289
Williams, Jacob B. 22:109
Williams, James 1:192;
3:217; 4:69; 6:23;
7:115, 137; 8:35, 43,
98; 9:40, 137, 162,
167, 212, 244; 10:87;
11:253, 296; 12:53;
14:127, 232; 15:255;
17:45, 140, 144, 190;
18:105, 167, 268,
299; 19:42, 319;
20:393; 21:162, 405;
23:111, 289; 24:206;
25:127, 262, 329;
26:86, 198; 27:125
Williams, James A. 5:48;
9:198
Williams, James B. 10:94;
20:393; 22:60
Williams, James D.
23:242
Williams, James J. 5:33
Williams, James K. P.
10:87; 20:393
Williams, James L.
22:495; 24:33
Williams, James M.
17:286; 22:229;
23:258
Williams, James P. 9:226;
18:388, 441
Williams, James S.
14:317; 22:446;
24:87
Williams, James T. 22:459
Williams, James W.
25:125; 26:116
Williams, Jared 17:28;
27:130
Williams, Jasher 17:289
Williams, Jefferson M.
13:54
Williams, Jeffrey 21:405
Williams, Jenin 13:55
Williams, Jerome B.
18:224
Williams, Jerry 7:137

Williams, Jesse 11:80; 17:140; 24:207
Williams, Jesse L. 18:224
Williams, Joel 13:102
Williams, Joel N. 23:287
Williams, John 1:83, 192; 3:217; 4:62; 5:33; 7:46, 70, 115, 137; 8:35, 43, 57; 9:40, 105, 213; 10:150, 156, 169, 175; 11:48, 99, 215; 12:10, 46, 79; 13:59, 79, 128; 14:237; 15:287; 16:262, 263; 17:28, 61, 315; 18:21, 41, 61, 116, 167, 268, 299, 321, 342, 422; 19:50, 141, 219; 21:94, 108, 263, 405; 22:229, 274, 327, 524; 23:175, 269; 24:98; 25:127, 262, 289; 26:87, 116, 198; 27:125
Williams, John A. 7:115; 22:159, 413; 23:95; 25:127
Williams, John B. 10:87; 17:405; 21:46
Williams, John C. 10:87; 17:89; 20:393; 23:197; 27:133
Williams, John D. 17:286; 24:98
Williams, John D. B. 17:28
Williams, John E. 23:287
Williams, John H. 5:47; 12:46; 17:164; 20:194; 22:510
Williams, John J. 22:229, 444, 495
Williams, John K. 10:143; 25:128
Williams, John M. 8:36; 9:30; 18:167; 26:199
Williams, John P. 10:143; 20:393; 22:274
Williams, John R. 20:15, 393
Williams, John T. 10:87; 20:393; 22:495
Williams, John W. 8:69, 111; 10:143; 15:89; 20:393; 21:83; 22:109; 24:90
Williams, Johnson 22:229
Williams, Jonathan 11:178

Williams, Jonathan L. 22:274
Williams, Jordan 17:192
Williams, Joseph 9:160; 10:10, 87, 155; 12:53; 13:123; 14:127, 232; 17:45, 89, 354; 18:224; 19:50, 243; 20:15, 393; 21:248, 289; 22:349; 23:57; 25:281; 27:156
Williams, Joseph K. 11:177
Williams, Josiah 21:127
Williams, Julius 21:289
Williams, Justis G. 22:414
Williams, Justus H. 24:98
Williams, Knute 10:143
Williams, Kunte 20:393
Williams, L. 1:182; 3:217; 14:127, 267, 292; 25:262; 26:85
Williams, L. B. 22:60
Williams, L. D. 3:217; 13:54
Williams, L. E. 1:186
Williams, Lafayette 16:263
Williams, Larkins 18:41
Williams, Lawrence 17:164; 22:274
Williams, Leonhardt 24:33
Williams, Leroy R. 15:255
Williams, Levi 11:176
Williams, Lewellyn 20:131
Williams, Lewis 7:137; 8:118; 9:46, 105; 11:215; 17:251, 309; 18:271; 22:327; 23:176
Williams, Lewis P. 11:324
Williams, Lucian 21:405
Williams, Luther H. 11:18; 22:445
Williams, Lyman B. 4:62
Williams, Lymas 21:405
Williams, M. 1:86, 96, 184; 3:217; 14:127; 16:263; 21:85, 405; 25:262
Williams, M. F. 16:263
Williams, M. J. 11:418
Williams, M. L. 11:275
Williams, M. W. 3:217
Williams, Mac 21:405
Williams, Magena 21:405
Williams, Maria 27:131
Williams, Marion 17:240

Williams, Mark 11:419; 21:213
Williams, Mark L. 11:296
Williams, Mat 17:140; 24:206
Williams, Mathew 20:393
Williams, Mathew A. 17:262
Williams, Matthew 10:143
Williams, Med 21:405
Williams, Michael 23:111
Williams, Milton 9:212; 23:83
Williams, Monroe 16:286
Williams, Morgan 24:33
Williams, Morris 5:48
Williams, Moses 7:137; 9:14; 17:140; 24:87
Williams, Myron B. 21:169
Williams, N. 1:87; 7:84; 14:127; 16:263; 21:405
Williams, Nathan 13:59; 18:99
Williams, Nathan L. 23:176
Williams, Nathaniel 11:294
Williams, Nathaniel N. 22:159
Williams, Nathaniel S. 9:40
Williams, Ned 21:289
Williams, Nelson 9:212; 21:289
Williams, Nicholas 14:127
Williams, Norman 21:405
Williams, Normer 9:137
Williams, O. 3:217; 13:102; 14:25, 127
Williams, O. L. 7:54
Williams, Oliver 19:42, 331
Williams, Orange 10:24
Williams, Orville 21:133
Williams, Orville D. 18:224
Williams, Oscar G. 20:393
Williams, Owen G. 10:37
Williams, P. 3:217; 9:69; 14:267; 19:293; 22:327; 25:262; 27:127
Williams, P. A. 12:120
Williams, P. L. 16:359
Williams, P. W. 3:217
Williams, Paris 5:47
Williams, Pascall 22:163
Williams, Perry 8:44; 11:216; 26:199

Williams, Peter 7:137; 9:238; 13:54, 102; 18:116; 22:327

Williams, Peter W. 8:35; 18:167

Williams, Philip 22:274

Williams, Philo 22:229

Williams, Pleasant 8:35; 18:167

Williams, Preston 27:134

Williams, R. 1:85, 182; 5:48; 9:155; 13:102, 103; 15:51; 16:275; 18:73; 22:356, 443, 495; 25:262; 27:128

Williams, R. A. 14:326

Williams, R. F. 16:62

Williams, R. G. 7:46

Williams, R. H. 14:318

Williams, R. L. 12:84

Williams, R. S. 10:87; 20:393

Williams, Randall 17:189

Williams, Ranson 8:78

Williams, Reuben 22:274

Williams, Rich 19:50

Williams, Richard 5:33, 47; 6:20; 7:137; 10:87; 17:422; 18:99; 19:42; 20:393; 21:289; 22:327, 349; 24:168

Williams, Richard W. 17:208

Williams, Riley 9:46; 26:131

Williams, Robert 4:62, 69; 17:140; 21:83, 289; 22:327; 24:206; 25:329; 27:134

Williams, Robert A. 22:109; 23:57

Williams, Robert O. 10:175; 19:219

Williams, Robert P. 22:109

Williams, Rufus B. 20:15

Williams, Rugan N. 23:183

Williams, S. 1:182; 3:217; 7:70; 11:253, 273; 14:127; 16:263; 20:88; 21:405; 22:327; 25:262

Williams, S. B. 25:277

Williams, S. D. 17:61

Williams, S. G. 8:69; 26:200

Williams, S. H. 17:498; 23:57

Williams, S. J. 18:41

Williams, S. K. 18:268; 26:86

Williams, S. M. 3:217

Williams, S. P. 23:175

Williams, S. S. 22:495

Williams, S. W. 1:183; 14:127

Williams, S. W. W. T. 20:187

Williams, Sam 9:212

Williams, Samuel 5:47; 6:20; 7:46, 137; 8:43; 10:87; 11:195; 18:268; 20:393; 21:213, 405; 22:349; 26:87, 198

Williams, Samuel J. 23:83

Williams, Samuel R. 18:224

Williams, Sander 10:94; 20:393

Williams, Shadrack 17:394

Williams, Sharick 10:87

Williams, Sidney 9:212; 16:62

Williams, Silas 8:35, 43; 18:167; 21:405; 22:327; 26:198, 200

Williams, Silas H. 10:24

Williams, Simon 7:137

Williams, Simon W. 17:61

Williams, Smith 13:54

Williams, Solomon 4:62; 7:82; 21:405; 25:262

Williams, Stephen 14:232, 313; 17:140, 189, 491; 21:162; 24:206; 27:133

Williams, Stephen D. 21:62, 197

Williams, Stockley 19:335

Williams, Sudren 11:216

Williams, Sylvester 15:354; 16:286; 27:133

Williams, T. 1:84, 87, 181; 3:217; 9:153; 16:263; 17:140; 19:264; 21:162; 24:73, 206; 25:262; 27:126, 128

Williams, T. G. 3:217; 14:232

Williams, T. H. 14:127

Williams, T. J. 1:184

Williams, T. K. 1:88

Williams, T. L. 18:61

Williams, Tate 22:327

Williams, Taylor 11:178

Williams, Theodore 4:62

Williams, Thomas 1:85; 3:217; 5:47; 7:137; 9:47, 198, 241; 10:87; 11:179; 13:129; 16:263; 17:286; 18:268; 19:141; 20:15, 393; 21:62, 405; 22:16, 327, 349, 445; 23:176; 25:289; 26:87, 132

Williams, Thomas B. 15:335

Williams, Thomas D. 14:331

Williams, Thomas E. 8:98; 17:363

Williams, Thomas W. 11:177

Williams, Timothy 21:237

Williams, Tunis 13:55

Williams, W. 3:217; 11:274; 13:103; 14:127, 233; 15:4; 16:142, 263; 18:403; 22:327; 23:116; 27:125

Williams, W. A. 10:177; 19:219

Williams, W. B. 11:283; 13:102

Williams, W. E. 14:127; 17:266

Williams, W. F. 13:75

Williams, W. G. 26:199

Williams, W. H. 1:180; 4:62; 10:177; 19:219

Williams, W. N. 16:130

Williams, W. Norton 16:135

Williams, W. O. 9:160

Williams, W. P. 14:250; 27:135

Williams, W. R. 8:35; 18:167

Williams, W. T. 26:199

Williams, W. V. 14:25

Williams, W. W. 13:55

Williams, W. Z. 1:87

Williams, Walter 7:76; 21:62

Williams, Warder 4:62

Williams, Warren H. 19:219

Williams, Washington 9:162; 22:327; 27:134

Williams, Wellington 16:62

Williams, Wesley 22:327

Williams, Wesley C. 22:413
Williams, Wesley M. 4:62
Williams, Wezet 12:53
Williams, William 1:85, 87; 5:33, 47; 7:71, 79; 8:69, 76, 98; 10:10, 87; 11:81, 216; 12:46, 54, 79; 13:55; 15:301, 320; 16:135, 263; 17:89, 189; 18:21, 224; 19:141; 20:393; 21:162, 289; 22:327; 23:83, 176; 25:308; 26:198, 199, 201
Williams, William A. 4:62; 9:40; 18:167
Williams, William B. 18:167; 22:60, 413
Williams, William C. 17:417; 21:405; 22:134; 23:83; 24:155
Williams, William G. 9:40
Williams, William H. 10:143; 20:393; 21:86; 22:159; 23:83, 116
Williams, William J. 19:42; 21:62
Williams, William L. 22:356
Williams, William N. 8:36
Williams, William P. 19:42; 21:199; 22:286
Williams, William S. 24:98
Williams, William T. 21:193; 23:103
Williams, William V. 8:35
Williams, William W. 20:135
Williams, Wilson 22:349
Williams, Winfield 9:137
Williams, Wirfield 27:129
Williams, Y. B. 27:132
Williams, York 21:405
Williams, Z. C. 9:127
Williamson, --- 7:115; 13:75; 14:127; 15:273
Williamson, A. 7:137
Williamson, A. C. 11:177
Williamson, A. J. 25:308
Williamson, Albert 15:255
Williamson, Alden 24:168
Williamson, Alex 26:198
Williamson, Alex. 8:44

Williamson, B. 11:179
Williamson, B. F. 11:185
Williamson, C. 14:127
Williamson, C. W. 9:94
Williamson, Charles 15:28
Williamson, D. 3:217
Williamson, E. 9:198; 20:181
Williamson, E. D. 9:198; 19:269
Williamson, Edgar J. 4:62
Williamson, Feliceana 18:99
Williamson, Frank J. 27:132
Williamson, G. 1:184
Williamson, G. W. 22:109
Williamson, George 20:26; 23:57; 24:98
Williamson, George N. 10:87; 20:393
Williamson, H. 12:91; 16:359; 20:393
Williamson, H. F. 10:143; 20:393
Williamson, Henry 1:85; 21:289
Williamson, Henry C. 13:55
Williamson, Hugh 8:98
Williamson, I. 22:349
Williamson, Isaac 12:46
Williamson, J. 3:217; 9:153; 13:132; 19:265; 22:495; 27:128
Williamson, J. H. 1:183; 18:61
Williamson, Jacob 9:198
Williamson, James 10:175; 15:178
Williamson, James K. 22:444
Williamson, John 9:114, 212; 10:87; 11:222; 14:127; 20:393
Williamson, John C. 7:12
Williamson, Joseph 12:46; 19:50
Williamson, Keenus 23:103
Williamson, Lamar 18:388
Williamson, Leonard 17:318
Williamson, Luther C. 21:237
Williamson, M. 20:50
Williamson, Michael 24:71

Williamson, Moody C. 9:127
Williamson, Mooty C. 27:130
Williamson, N. J. 9:40
Williamson, Nathaniel 18:299; 26:116
Williamson, Peter 7:137
Williamson, Philip H. 22:109
Williamson, R. 14:25
Williamson, R. G. 17:315
Williamson, Rufus 23:176
Williamson, S. C. 27:134
Williamson, Samuel 9:138; 27:129
Williamson, Smith 23:176
Williamson, Thomas 18:427
Williamson, Thomas J. 22:274
Williamson, W. 3:217; 21:62
Williamson, William 8:36; 17:28; 18:167
Williamson, William H. 8:102; 17:463; 24:184
Williamson, William J. 26:234
Williamson, William T. 8:57; 11:80
Williamsons, James 19:219
Williard, --- 19:219
Williard, Alfred 8:36
Williard, D. A. 9:40
Williard, Edward 25:281
Williard, George W. 10:24
Williard, John B. 20:131
Williard, Judson 22:494
Williard, Leverett 7:46
Williard, Parkman D. 9:127; 27:130
Williard, William 8:76
Williard, Winslow H. 7:46
Willie, C. H. 14:232
Willie, H. 1:182
Willie, Jacob 24:73
Willie, James 1:86
Willie, W. W. 10:98
Willie, William 12:45
Williford, James H. 20:139
Williford, O. 8:76
Willig, Joseph H. 25:314
Willigan, Th. 14:232
Willigen, M. 26:139
Willimman, E. 19:244
Willingby, Egner 9:153
Willinger, Robert 27:126

Willingham, A. 9:64
Willingham, Harvey 22:517
Willingham, J. W. 19:348
Willingher, John 15:255
Willingmyre, Samuel 23:183
Willington, G. 3:217
Willington, H. 3:217
Willington, L. 14:25
Willinner, David 19:141
Willis, --- 11:113; 25:335
Willis, A. 3:217; 16:275; 23:111
Willis, A. H. 21:405
Willis, A. P. 3:217
Willis, Abel 1:86
Willis, Abram V. 17:316
Willis, Adam 7:115
Willis, Albert 9:138; 27:129
Willis, Andrew 9:226; 18:388
Willis, Aug. P. 14:328
Willis, B. 13:102
Willis, Bech 12:94
Willis, Beck 16:359
Willis, Benjamin 8:44; 10:143; 20:393; 26:199
Willis, C. 3:217; 27:132
Willis, C. H. 25:262
Willis, Charles 11:99; 14:232; 16:263; 25:262
Willis, Charles B. 17:262
Willis, Cornelius 11:338
Willis, D. 11:439
Willis, Daniel H. 15:115
Willis, E. 3:217; 12:84; 16:359
Willis, Edmund 14:232
Willis, Edwin E. 7:13
Willis, Elester 23:111
Willis, Elias 8:44; 26:198
Willis, Ellis 10:177; 19:219
Willis, Emma 27:131
Willis, Eugene G. 22:274
Willis, Ferris 13:123
Willis, Francis E. 23:258
Willis, Francis M. 15:89
Willis, G. 23:57
Willis, G. M. 7:46; 20:141
Willis, George 4:62; 21:405; 24:168
Willis, George W. 15:89; 21:289; 22:60, 493
Willis, H. H. 1:182
Willis, Hamilton 17:150

Willis, Henry 7:136; 9:99; 19:141
Willis, Henry F. 25:262
Willis, Isaac 16:135
Willis, J. 1:100; 3:217; 21:113; 25:262
Willis, J. A. 13:102; 14:25
Willis, J. H. 11:255
Willis, J. J. 10:185; 18:185
Willis, J. P. 3:217
Willis, Jacob 9:94; 23:262; 26:83
Willis, James 3:217; 9:94; 21:83; 26:83
Willis, James D. 7:115; 27:131
Willis, James H. 13:54; 18:403; 21:237
Willis, James P. 16:62
Willis, Jesse P. 18:167
Willis, John 16:150; 17:45, 216, 240; 20:45; 21:405; 23:83; 25:262
Willis, John S. 11:175
Willis, Jonas 10:169
Willis, Jonas P. 19:220
Willis, Joseph 17:351
Willis, L. P. 20:140
Willis, Leander 17:45
Willis, Louis 7:136; 19:220
Willis, M. 3:217; 19:348
Willis, M. C. 21:405
Willis, M. H. 21:405
Willis, Moses 10:208; 18:409
Willis, Nathan 24:33
Willis, Nicholas J. 17:240
Willis, Ozrel 15:51
Willis, Payne 18:268
Willis, Peter 9:198; 19:289
Willis, Robert 6:27; 22:328
Willis, S. 1:88
Willis, S. A. 27:128
Willis, S. F. 21:405
Willis, Samuel 17:140; 24:206
Willis, Sidney 23:200
Willis, Stillman 21:405
Willis, T. 14:267
Willis, Thomas 1:86; 7:136; 18:73
Willis, Thomas C. 9:233; 20:393
Willis, Thomas S. 23:127
Willis, W. B. 14:232
Willis, W. F. 13:75

Willis, Westley 15:255
Willis, William 11:383; 13:128; 14:127; 17:61; 25:262
Willis, William E. 20:191
Willis, William F. 19:141
Willis, William G. 11:273; 21:86
Willis, William H. 10:87
Willis, William T. 20:15
Willis, Zachariah 21:289
Willison, James H. 7:46
Willison, Moses 10:87; 20:393
Willison, Samuel 1:84
Willison, W. 3:217
Willison, William E. 23:15
Willispoon, David 4:62
Willisson, Simeon 11:177
Willit, M. 3:217
Willitt, Pleasant 8:102
Willman, Jehiel 15:10
Willman, John C. 16:62
Willmayer, John 11:121
Willmore, George 24:87
Willmoth, George W. 8:98
Willoby, B. 23:282
Willoby, E. 17:189
Willock, J. J. 19:141
Willorer, J. 1:181
Willough, A. 17:286
Willoughby, Benjamin 17:240
Willoughby, Granville 22:274
Willoughby, H. C. 7:115
Willoughby, James 10:143; 17:421; 20:393
Willoughby, John R. 12:46
Willoughby, Joseph 17:449; 24:174
Willoughby, Nixon 17:286
Willoughby, T. 10:208
Willoughby, William P. 23:83
Willougkley, E. 3:217
Willover, George I. 17:245
Willow, Joshua 11:216
Willow, R. M. 12:172
Willow, Sullivan W. 7:17
Willowby, James 24:163
Willows, Sidney 12:160
Wills, A. 14:25
Wills, C. 14:285
Wills, F. 19:141
Wills, Harrison 23:83

Wills, J. 11:47
Wills, Jacob L. 11:176
Wills, Jesse 16:137
Wills, John 11:122
Wills, John H. 4:69
Wills, John P. 20:152
Wills, M. 13:102
Wills, Payne 26:87
Wills, Ransom 22:328
Wills, Robert 9:17
Wills, S. 3:217
Wills, W. D. 21:113
Wills, W. J. 27:127
Willser, J. 3:217
Willsie, John 20:393
Willson, A. 21:127
Willson, A. S. 24:100
Willson, Aaron 8:98
Willson, Benjamin 22:61
Willson, David W. 27:131
Willson, H. 26:199
Willson, James 21:246
Willson, James J. 20:188
Willson, James M. 22:274
Willson, Mark 21:289
Willson, William 21:289
Willsops, M. D. L. 11:99
Willspaugh, Cornelius S.
    8:111
Willvarst, J. 5:34
Willy, S. H. 19:220
Willyard, Martin 8:98
Wilm, Leonard 22:445
Wilman, Aug 16:112
Wilman, M. W. 21:405
Wilman, Stephen 7:136
Wilmarth, Frederick L.
    14:233
Wilmarth, John Q. 5:34
Wilmarth, Martin V. B.
    20:109
Wilmarth, W. C. 9:64
Wilmath, C. W. 3:217
Wilmer, Alfred 12:53
Wilmer, C. A. 16:391
Wilmer, Charles E.
    17:264
Wilmer, Cornelius 9:198
Wilmer, O. B. 20:393
Wilmington, Oliver C.
    22:445
Wilmont, C. F. 14:313;
    17:471; 27:132
Wilmore, Abraham
    24:207
Wilmore, Edward 12:53
Wilmore, Robert M.
    22:109
Wilmot, George 7:136
Wilmot, John 12:46
Wilmot, Samuel 23:183

Wilmot, Stephen 7:46
Wilmoth, J. 9:69
Wilmott, Walker 7:54
Wilmouth, J. N. 21:405
Wilnor, John 7:35
Wilous, Joseph 15:348
Wilpor, Henry 11:394
Wilrelt, P. W. 11:49
Wils, Levi 23:57
Wilsa, William 27:135
Wilsay, Jacob 4:63
Wilse, Charles H. 25:124
Wilsey, A. 8:57
Wilsey, Abraham 21:145
Wilsey, Cornelius 10:143;
    20:393
Wilsey, E. 1:83
Wilsey, Jacob S. 10:143
Wilsey, Julius C. 15:4
Wilsgrove, H. P. 19:231
Wilsie, George B. 7:46
Wilson, --- 10:169; 11:18,
    290; 16:65; 17:365,
    496; 19:220; 21:133;
    26:200
Wilson, A. 1:84, 89, 182,
    185; 3:217, 218;
    8:68; 9:155; 15:255;
    21:127; 25:123;
    26:199; 27:128
Wilson, A. B. 14:292
Wilson, A. G. 26:234
Wilson, A. J. 1:183;
    9:226; 18:388
Wilson, A. L. 11:275
Wilson, A. N. 1:83
Wilson, A. R. 14:233
Wilson, A. S. 18:185
Wilson, A. W. 18:201
Wilson, Aaron 17:89
Wilson, Aaron W. 22:459
Wilson, Abel F. 20:393
Wilson, Able F. 10:143
Wilson, Abner N. 1:85
Wilson, Abraham 14:233;
    23:272
Wilson, Adam 4:62;
    22:328
Wilson, Admin 21:193
Wilson, Albert 7:136;
    8:36; 18:167; 23:95
Wilson, Albert D. 16:112
Wilson, Albert M. 22:469
Wilson, Alen. J. 18:282
Wilson, Alexander 8:98;
    9:8, 162; 14:127;
    17:141, 351; 24:206;
    27:134
Wilson, Alexander B.
    22:274

Wilson, Alfred 1:88;
    23:310
Wilson, Alice 25:308
Wilson, Allen 8:36
Wilson, Allia 18:167
Wilson, Alonzo O. 11:176
Wilson, Alonzo R. 23:95
Wilson, Amos 11:254;
    23:83
Wilson, Anderson 17:189
Wilson, Andrew 2:20;
    3:218; 14:233;
    21:405; 22:328
Wilson, Andrew D. 7:136
Wilson, Andrew J.
    17:354; 22:229
Wilson, Arthur 17:289
Wilson, Arthur B. 23:15
Wilson, Asa 4:62
Wilson, Augustus 7:136
Wilson, Austin 9:30;
    18:318; 26:116
Wilson, B. 1:180; 3:218;
    17:189; 21:127
Wilson, B. F. 12:160
Wilson, B. H. 19:315
Wilson, B. J. 14:127
Wilson, Ballsor 6:34
Wilson, Benjamin 10:87;
    19:287; 20:393
Wilson, Benjamin S.
    17:497
Wilson, Bonaparte 13:54
Wilson, Buchanan 10:169
Wilson, Buchaw 19:220
Wilson, Buell 22:229
Wilson, Buonaparte 16:62
Wilson, Burney C. 20:191
Wilson, C. 1:87, 88, 185;
    19:264, 326; 25:128
Wilson, C. A. 16:359
Wilson, C. B. 20:131
Wilson, C. E. 22:498
Wilson, C. H. 16:142;
    24:87
Wilson, C. M. 1:181
Wilson, C. O. 16:263
Wilson, C. W. 3:218;
    9:94; 25:262; 26:85
Wilson, Caleb 8:111
Wilson, Calvin 10:143;
    11:290; 20:393
Wilson, Cephus 22:328
Wilson, Chancey 11:82
Wilson, Charles 1:83, 85;
    2:19; 5:34; 7:54;
    13:54, 75; 15:79;
    16:150; 17:189;
    18:268, 427; 19:50,
    141; 22:60; 23:127;
    25:262; 27:134

Wilson, Charles A. 22:274
Wilson, Charles D. 4:62
Wilson, Charles E. 27:126
Wilson, Charles M. 9:64
Wilson, Charles S. 21:405
Wilson, Charles W. 5:48
Wilson, Chester 9:198
Wilson, Chockley 10:87;
  20:393
Wilson, Christopher
  10:94; 20:394
Wilson, Clark 12:160
Wilson, Clark L. 15:148
Wilson, Clen 23:206
Wilson, Cole A. 18:268;
  26:85
Wilson, Cyrus I. 24:47
Wilson, D. 1:88, 184;
  3:218; 13:102
Wilson, D. C. 16:391
Wilson, D. M. 19:317
Wilson, D. S. 1:86
Wilson, Daniel 11:215;
  17:62
Wilson, Daniel F. 17:145
Wilson, David 7:80; 9:30;
  10:208; 16:62, 263;
  17:89; 18:212, 318;
  25:309; 26:117, 199
Wilson, David A. 13:54
Wilson, David C. 17:141;
  24:206
Wilson, David W. 9:127
Wilson, Dearborn S.
  8:116
Wilson, Dempsey 9:203;
  19:285
Wilson, Dewit C. 9:94
Wilson, Douglas 11:215
Wilson, Duncan 11:337
Wilson, E. 1:89; 3:218
Wilson, E. S. 21:199
Wilson, Ebenezer 21:405
Wilson, Edmond I. 9:99
Wilson, Edmund 21:213
Wilson, Edward 13:54;
  22:109, 274
Wilson, Edward E.
  12:139; 15:148
Wilson, Edwin R. 11:195
Wilson, Elias 11:427
Wilson, Elisha B. 20:185
Wilson, Emanuel 26:214
Wilson, Enos P. 15:89
Wilson, Ezekiel 8:126
Wilson, Ezra J. 17:89
Wilson, F. 13:76
Wilson, F. C. 3:218
Wilson, F. F. 17:405
Wilson, F. J. 18:446
Wilson, F. M. 4:62

Wilson, Fanny 21:46
Wilson, Field 7:136
Wilson, Francis 8:112;
  21:405
Wilson, Frank 7:136;
  19:50
Wilson, Fred 18:318;
  26:117
Wilson, Frederick 9:30;
  12:53; 15:4; 25:262
Wilson, G. 3:218; 14:127;
  25:262
Wilson, G. N. 3:218
Wilson, G. P. 23:306
Wilson, G. W. 1:86;
  3:218; 11:343;
  15:115; 22:274
Wilson, George 1:191;
  3:218; 4:62; 5:34;
  6:26; 8:98; 9:162;
  10:170; 11:189;
  14:233; 15:328;
  18:41; 19:141, 220,
  323; 22:328, 493;
  26:87, 214; 27:126
Wilson, George A. 9:226;
  18:389
Wilson, George D. 23:265
Wilson, George E. 11:81;
  25:128
Wilson, George F. 11:179;
  15:164; 17:101
Wilson, George H. 16:62
Wilson, George K. 16:135
Wilson, George L. 22:444
Wilson, George S. 7:46;
  16:62; 23:176
Wilson, George W. 9:99;
  13:54; 16:130;
  17:209, 234; 21:46,
  237
Wilson, Gilbert 9:105
Wilson, Gilfred 25:262
Wilson, Glen 23:206
Wilson, Gordon S. 16:87
Wilson, Green 22:328;
  23:307
Wilson, Gueral 11:217
Wilson, H. 1:181; 2:19;
  3:218; 12:91, 167;
  13:102; 14:285;
  16:359; 19:220;
  20:394; 23:175;
  25:262
Wilson, H. A. 3:218;
  14:127; 27:126
Wilson, H. B. 20:150;
  23:251
Wilson, H. D. 22:469
Wilson, H. H. 1:83
Wilson, H. J. 15:255

Wilson, H. K. 1:88
Wilson, H. R. 1:186;
  17:441
Wilson, H. S. 13:54
Wilson, Hardin 22:517
Wilson, Henry 5:48; 7:70;
  9:203; 10:24, 170;
  12:160, 168; 15:346;
  16:112, 391; 17:69,
  446; 19:293; 22:286;
  24:169; 25:124, 262,
  329; 26:214
Wilson, Henry F. 22:109
Wilson, Henry M. 22:109
Wilson, Henry S. 8:98
Wilson, Herber 12:160
Wilson, Hezehiah 10:87
Wilson, Hezekiah 18:99
Wilson, Hiram H. 1:85
Wilson, Hiram W. 10:143;
  20:394
Wilson, Hopp 17:141;
  24:206
Wilson, Horatio R. 24:155
Wilson, Howard 11:178
Wilson, Hugh 17:113
Wilson, Ira M. 17:289
Wilson, Isaac 5:48; 7:136;
  9:14, 162, 203;
  11:176, 393; 21:405;
  22:114
Wilson, Isaac R. 22:328
Wilson, Isaiah 10:87, 211;
  18:450
Wilson, Israel S. 13:54
Wilson, J. 1:87, 88, 182;
  3:218; 7:70; 9:198,
  226; 11:179; 14:127,
  261; 15:301; 16:263,
  286; 17:435; 18:21,
  389; 19:264; 20:117,
  394; 21:46, 113;
  25:262; 27:126, 134
Wilson, J. A. 1:85
Wilson, J. A. L. 13:123
Wilson, J. B. 1:181;
  3:218; 10:87; 11:49;
  16:112; 19:264;
  20:394
Wilson, J. C. 9:153;
  11:131, 318; 27:127
Wilson, J. D. 11:195
Wilson, J. F. 11:222;
  14:127, 233
Wilson, J. G. 15:79; 23:57
Wilson, J. H. 1:84; 8:57;
  25:262
Wilson, J. H. H. 1:186
Wilson, J. J. 10:98
Wilson, J. K. 14:263;
  27:128

Wilson, J. M. 3:218;
18:269; 20:394;
23:176; 26:85
Wilson, J. N. 3:218; 24:64
Wilson, J. P. 11:397;
12:46; 23:176
Wilson, J. R. 1:84
Wilson, J. S. 10:31;
13:75; 19:315
Wilson, J. T. 9:114; 19:42
Wilson, J. W. 2:19;
11:253, 273; 16:63;
21:202; 23:176;
25:127, 262
Wilson, Jack 18:269;
22:356; 26:86
Wilson, Jacob 23:57
Wilson, James 3:218;
4:62; 5:34; 6:26;
7:46, 62; 8:68, 99;
9:47, 64, 155, 244;
10:87, 143; 11:81,
113, 121, 222; 12:46;
14:233, 313; 15:51;
16:62, 263, 391;
17:233, 477; 18:224,
269, 431, 444;
19:141; 20:15, 28,
394; 21:406; 22:134,
445; 23:269; 24:33,
181; 25:262, 329;
26:86, 132, 199;
27:132
Wilson, James A. 21:62
Wilson, James B. 20:394;
23:176; 25:124
Wilson, James E. 13:54;
16:62
Wilson, James F. 9:198;
19:285; 22:159
Wilson, James H. 22:356
Wilson, James L. 9:94
Wilson, James M. 22:60;
23:83
Wilson, James P. 10:143;
20:152, 394
Wilson, James R. 9:198;
10:143; 11:283;
19:269; 23:83; 24:33
Wilson, James S. 10:87;
20:394; 22:444, 510
Wilson, James W. 8:36;
18:167
Wilson, Jasper 7:136;
21:406
Wilson, Jefferson 24:207
Wilson, Jerry 17:189;
26:87
Wilson, Jesse 11:290
Wilson, Jesse B. 11:82
Wilson, Jethro 22:109

Wilson, John 1:84, 85;
3:218; 4:62; 5:48;
7:46, 136; 8:111,
116; 9:30, 127, 158;
10:87; 11:82, 179,
290; 12:46; 14:127;
15:255, 286; 16:263;
17:16, 45, 251;
18:318, 325, 450;
20:20, 45, 394;
21:46, 406; 22:445;
24:164; 25:125, 262,
271, 281, 314;
26:115; 27:131, 156
Wilson, John C. 7:84;
21:406; 23:57
Wilson, John F. 20:152;
24:87
Wilson, John H. 5:48;
11:82, 274; 15:171;
21:406; 22:274
Wilson, John I. 22:229
Wilson, John J. 11:185
Wilson, John L. 18:224
Wilson, John M. 7:115;
8:112
Wilson, John N. 21:83
Wilson, John O. 9:99;
10:143; 20:394
Wilson, John S. 11:274;
13:81; 16:263;
22:445
Wilson, John T. 11:48
Wilson, John W. 10:87;
13:54; 16:63; 17:69,
351; 20:394; 22:109,
134
Wilson, Johnson 20:188
Wilson, Jordan 6:13
Wilson, Jordon 18:99
Wilson, Joseph 7:46;
9:217; 11:215;
14:233; 15:89;
17:399; 20:105, 188;
22:134; 25:262
Wilson, Joseph C. 11:48
Wilson, Joseph E. 20:131
Wilson, Joseph F. 20:150
Wilson, Joseph H. 4:69
Wilson, Joseph J. 19:141
Wilson, Joseph L. 17:417;
24:155
Wilson, Joseph M. 23:57
Wilson, Joseph R. 24:57
Wilson, Joseph W. 17:319
Wilson, Joshua P. 24:163
Wilson, Josiah 9:226;
18:389
Wilson, Kinsey 9:162
Wilson, L. E. 11:179
Wilson, L. H. 17:189

Wilson, Lacy 25:335
Wilson, Lafayette 4:62
Wilson, Lagrand 21:406
Wilson, Leander 5:34;
21:62
Wilson, Levi 24:103
Wilson, Lewis 8:112;
12:53; 17:264;
26:132
Wilson, Lorenzo D. 7:15
Wilson, Louis 21:406
Wilson, Luke 17:141;
24:206
Wilson, M. 3:218; 9:127;
13:102; 18:201;
27:130
Wilson, M. C. 21:406
Wilson, Manuel 17:336
Wilson, Marcus 24:87
Wilson, Marion 11:427;
24:47
Wilson, Mark L. 5:34
Wilson, Marshal 22:134
Wilson, Marshall 10:143;
20:394
Wilson, Marshall S.
10:143; 20:394
Wilson, Martin 8:68;
16:263; 19:319;
22:229
Wilson, Mat 22:328
Wilson, Mathew 11:131;
23:176
Wilson, Matt 9:106
Wilson, Mattias 18:335
Wilson, McCoy 10:170;
19:220
Wilson, Melville C. 9:212
Wilson, Michael 7:46
Wilson, Miles 7:136;
17:240
Wilson, Milton 22:109
Wilson, Morris R. 20:15
Wilson, Morton I. 8:36
Wilson, Morton J. 18:167
Wilson, Moses 8:36;
18:167; 21:289
Wilson, N. 11:275
Wilson, N. B. 18:185
Wilson, N. J. 14:127
Wilson, Nathan 1:193;
10:31; 17:286;
19:315
Wilson, Nathan G. 22:159
Wilson, Nathaniel 16:63
Wilson, Ned 21:406
Wilson, Nelson 10:100;
12:46
Wilson, Nicholas 11:217
Wilson, Niel 15:289

Wilson, Norman 8:116; 17:245; 19:141
Wilson, Norman D. 1:85
Wilson, O. 14:25; 25:262
Wilson, O. A. 27:135
Wilson, O. H. 14:250
Wilson, O. P. 8:68; 26:200
Wilson, Ole 1:85
Wilson, Oliver 1:84
Wilson, Orange 21:46
Wilson, Oren M. 26:199
Wilson, Orian M. 8:68
Wilson, Orvill M. 15:4
Wilson, Osborn 23:111
Wilson, Oscar 9:138; 27:130
Wilson, Otto 5:34
Wilson, P. 11:175; 14:286; 16:263; 17:141; 23:175; 24:206
Wilson, P. D. 3:218
Wilson, Perry 4:68
Wilson, Perry G. 13:75; 16:263
Wilson, Peter 25:128
Wilson, Peter J. 21:62
Wilson, Peter M. 10:143; 20:394
Wilson, Phelom 23:272
Wilson, Philip 19:50
Wilson, Pleasant 9:238; 26:234
Wilson, Priscilla 26:234
Wilson, Quincy 22:495
Wilson, R. 11:47; 14:261; 15:79; 16:263, 391
Wilson, R. D. 17:358
Wilson, R. E. 11:185
Wilson, R. J. 16:391
Wilson, R. S. 9:153; 27:128
Wilson, R. W. 7:115
Wilson, Raphael 21:214
Wilson, Rech D. 19:42
Wilson, Rech G. 19:42
Wilson, Reuben 4:69
Wilson, Richard 9:105; 14:335
Wilson, Robert 3:218; 9:198; 11:81; 12:57; 16:263; 17:168, 357; 21:197; 22:229, 349, 443; 24:73
Wilson, Robert A. 21:133
Wilson, Robert B. 5:33; 22:274
Wilson, Robert G. 11:18
Wilson, Robert J. 24:47
Wilson, Robert N. 17:61

Wilson, Robert T. 11:189
Wilson, Robert W. 10:87; 20:394; 24:163
Wilson, Ross 17:394
Wilson, Royal L. 19:42
Wilson, S. 1:181, 186; 3:218; 10:191; 11:253; 18:185
Wilson, S. A. 25:263
Wilson, S. B. 25:123
Wilson, S. C. 14:127; 20:153
Wilson, S. F. 13:75
Wilson, S. J. 11:89
Wilson, S. R. 1:182; 14:261
Wilson, S. S. 3:218
Wilson, S. W. 22:109; 23:176
Wilson, Samuel 4:68; 5:33; 6:23; 10:87; 11:99, 393; 18:269, 403; 19:220; 20:394; 21:83; 22:60; 23:272; 24:57, 207; 26:86, 87
Wilson, Samuel E. 12:171
Wilson, Samuel N. 24:155
Wilson, Samuel P. 20:188
Wilson, Samuel R. 24:98
Wilson, Sanford C. 10:143; 20:394
Wilson, Scott C. 22:134
Wilson, Shabro 27:129
Wilson, Shatrow 9:138
Wilson, Silas 10:143; 20:394
Wilson, Stephen 10:175; 17:74
Wilson, Stephen B. 7:46
Wilson, Stephen E. 19:220
Wilson, Sylvanus 27:126
Wilson, T. 11:189; 13:102; 15:275; 16:263; 25:263
Wilson, T. G. 11:87
Wilson, T. I. 12:139
Wilson, T. J. 11:253
Wilson, T. N. 14:127
Wilson, Tad 21:108
Wilson, Taylor 21:197
Wilson, Thomas 5:34; 6:34; 8:68; 9:30, 40, 46, 138; 10:169; 11:18, 278; 12:84; 14:127; 15:171, 349; 16:263, 359, 391; 19:42, 220; 21:237; 22:238, 274, 507, 517; 23:57, 310; 24:57, 98, 207;

Wilson, Thomas 25:274, 329; 26:131; 27:129
Wilson, Thomas A. 11:277
Wilson, Thomas B. 10:87; 20:394
Wilson, Thomas F. 23:103
Wilson, Thomas H. 16:391; 20:139
Wilson, Thomas I. 26:117
Wilson, Thomas J. 24:33
Wilson, Thomas M. 22:109
Wilson, Thomas P. 22:274
Wilson, Thomas S. 21:406
Wilson, Toby 22:328
Wilson, W. 1:100, 181, 182; 3:218; 7:62; 9:153; 10:31; 13:102, 126; 14:25; 15:156; 16:263, 392; 17:45; 18:61; 19:141, 315; 27:128
Wilson, W. A. 9:64; 12:160; 23:265
Wilson, W. B. 17:453; 24:184
Wilson, W. C. 11:48
Wilson, W. D. 16:263
Wilson, W. E. 9:153; 27:127
Wilson, W. H. 14:331; 16:137; 22:522; 27:134
Wilson, W. I. 22:229
Wilson, W. J. 12:150; 20:394; 26:199
Wilson, W. L. 15:156
Wilson, W. M. 23:315
Wilson, W. W. 8:36; 13:75; 18:167
Wilson, Wallace 11:48
Wilson, Wallard 14:233
Wilson, Walter 3:218
Wilson, Warren 13:123
Wilson, Washington 18:41
Wilson, Watson 26:131
Wilson, Wells 20:90
Wilson, Wiley B. 9:94
Wilson, William 3:218; 7:115, 136; 8:99, 100; 9:198; 10:150; 11:82, 292, 419; 12:10, 46, 166; 13:54; 14:29, 233, 335; 15:28, 89, 95, 255, 302; 16:263; 17:363; 18:21, 41, 105, 270; 19:265, 272, 331; 20:191;

Wilson, William 21:289, 406; 22:159; 23:57, 261, 289; 27:134
Wilson, William A. 3:218
Wilson, William B. 9:127; 17:150; 27:131
Wilson, William C. 8:99; 12:46
Wilson, William E. 12:46; 16:88; 19:42; 22:60, 109
Wilson, William F. 26:199
Wilson, William H. 4:62; 6:20; 17:45; 18:99; 19:42
Wilson, William I. 10:143
Wilson, William J. 20:394
Wilson, William M. 17:61
Wilson, William P. 17:233
Wilson, William R. 22:522; 23:57, 103
Wilson, William T. 10:143; 20:394; 23:116; 24:33
Wilson, William W. 8:57; 14:233; 21:83; 22:109; 25:124
Wilson, Willis N. 23:95
Wilson, Wyatt 16:263
Wilson, Yancey 6:26
Wilsoy, H. 14:127
Wilsy, J. M. 10:150
Wilt, Jacob H. 9:127; 27:131
Wilt, James 23:183
Wilt, John 17:89
Wilt, Joseph 15:79; 25:263
Wilt, Louis 15:52
Wilt, Michael 11:177
Wilt, Noah S. 17:168
Wilt, R. 14:286
Wilt, Reuben H. 12:60
Wilten, Hiram 8:102
Wilter, Amos A. 18:299
Wilter, John B. 15:255
Wiltfong, Hiram A. 21:83
Wiltinger, G. 16:286
Wilton, Daniel 9:158; 19:42
Wilton, Richard 17:316
Wilton, W. 10:169; 19:220
Wilton, William M. 1:86
Wiltonberger, Joseph 11:318
Wiltse, Alexander 17:101
Wiltse, Gardner H. 17:101
Wiltsee, Daniel W. 17:157

Wiltshire, A. 14:128
Wiltshire, Gaines 23:176
Wiltss, Alfred 23:206
Wilty, Tyson T. 21:83
Wiltz, Adam W. 25:270
Wiltzer, B. 25:329
Wily, Edward 4:63
Wimberley, William 23:95
Wimberly, Jerry 7:137
Wimbs, Luke 19:42
Wimer, George 22:169; 24:163
Wimer, Reuben 10:143; 20:394
Wimer, Thomas K. 23:183
Wimmer, Ezekiel 17:441; 24:155
Wimmer, Henry 24:34
Wimmer, J. 3:218
Wimple, J. 1:181
Wimple, Thompson 20:15
Wimsett, Harvey 24:163
Win---, A. J. 23:83
Winall, H. C. 22:229
Winan, A. G. 22:159
Winan, F. B. 8:76
Winan, Francis 10:88; 20:394
Winan, Garrick 8:111
Winan, James B. 17:286
Winans, A. 22:230
Winans, Albert 8:36; 18:167
Winans, F. B. 26:201
Winans, George H. 8:116
Winans, George W. 23:176
Winans, Henry C. 22:173
Winans, Samuel 15:115
Winans, Washington 21:406
Winans, Wilton 22:159
Winarer, Washington 7:115
Winback, William 21:406
Winberg, Werner 7:115
Winberger, E. 16:263
Wince, Lewis 16:263
Winch, Clark 5:34
Winchart, J. 19:285
Winchart, John 9:198
Winchel, G. 1:181
Winchel, John L. 3:218
Winchell, Albert 19:272
Winchell, Elias 22:349
Winchell, F. 8:76
Winchell, Fred 26:201
Winchell, George 20:394
Winchell, Harrison 18:212
Winchell, J. 14:279
Winchell, J. J. 19:265

Winchell, John 10:88; 20:394
Winchell, John J. 9:198
Winchell, Lennon 8:36
Winchell, Limeron 26:200
Winchell, P. 23:127
Winchell, Ralph 22:443
Winchell, S. 3:218
Wincheser, Spencer 23:197
Winchester, --- 17:286; 19:141
Winchester, A. J. 21:193
Winchester, Andrew 21:219
Winchester, C. 17:293
Winchester, Charles J. 27:126
Winchester, David 17:253
Winchester, Edwin F. 20:117
Winchester, George 3:218
Winchester, J. D. 3:225; 17:505
Winchester, James 16:263
Winchester, Jonathan 17:240
Winchester, Joseph 15:302
Winchester, Josiah 11:189
Winchester, Labrom 23:176
Winchester, Orson 21:406
Winchester, Owen 18:61
Winchester, R. G. 9:94; 26:83
Winchester, S. 11:440
Winchester, T. 21:46
Winchester, Uriah C. 22:61
Winchester, Washington 9:94; 26:83
Winchester, Wiley 9:203; 19:293
Winchill, George 10:143
Wincin, L. 25:263
Winck, Andrew D. 18:212
Winckle, D. M. 14:318
Wincle, C. 14:128
Wind, Charles 19:141; 27:156
Windall, Henry W. 21:406
Winded, S. 25:263
Windeer, H. S. 16:263
Windel, George 14:233
Winden, Samuel 16:263
Winder, A. 3:218
Winder, George 8:111
Winder, Jacob 12:46
Winder, James M. 15:79
Winder, John M. 17:45

Winder, Mathias 21:406
Winder, P. 3:218
Winders, Arch'd E. 22:443
Winders, D. 20:45
Winders, George D. 22:109
Winders, Joseph R. 18:389
Windgate, C. 3:218
Windinger, John 3:218
Windlar, H. S. 13:123
Windlass, S. 3:218
Windle, George W. 9:30
Windle, Walter 21:108
Windnagee, J. A. 10:208
Windnep, A. 3:218
Windock, C. 15:262
Windolph, John 8:36; 18:167
Windon, Ulrich 12:79
Windon, Uriah 15:62
Windoon, George W. 8:99
Windover, James 15:255
Windows, F. M. 17:61
Windows, Hiram 17:45
Windows, Jacob 9:226
Winds, Francis 19:50
Windsor, Simon 23:281
Windsor, William 15:25
Windsore, Nathaniel 18:99
Windston, J. 26:84
Wine, Eli 13:55
Wine, James 22:328
Wine, John 21:46
Wine, S. 11:254
Wineberey, J. 3:218
Wineberry, G. H. 16:263
Winebrenner, David 22:286
Winebrenner, George M. 23:176
Winebrook, P. 3:218
Winegar, G. 12:10
Winegar, Harvey 22:229
Winegar, Reuben 22:275
Winegar, W. W. 25:263
Winegard, D. 21:406
Winegard, J. 7:115
Winegarden, A. 3:218
Winegarden, A. K. 20:143
Winegarden, A. S. 3:218
Winegarden, John 22:109
Winegardner, L. 3:218
Winegarten, D. C. 1:86
Wineheater, Orrin 9:217
Winehenner, William 18:212
Winehester, Harrison 7:137

Wineingar, Henry W. 17:45
Winekop, Jan 7:137
Wineland, John 13:55
Winell, Charles P. 18:167
Wineman, Rinehart 10:143
Wineman, Robert 22:230
Winemann, Rinehart 20:394
Winemiller, John 3:218
Winer, H. 1:183
Winer, Ira 17:254
Winer, J. 25:125
Winer, Lorenza J. 11:255
Winer, Thomas F. 23:176
Winerman, J. 3:219
Wines, Alex 17:309
Wines, G. E. 13:123
Wines, George 22:229
Wines, H. W. 27:125
Wines, Henry 14:237
Wines, John 7:137
Wines, O. 1:96
Wines, S. 9:226; 18:389
Wines, William 23:176
Winesberger, Morgan 7:62
Winestock, A. 14:292
Winestock, Adam 23:83
Winfield, --- 15:115
Winfield, George 9:68; 15:96
Winfield, I. 9:153
Winfield, J. 27:128
Winfield, J. H. 1:84
Winfield, Jacob 16:263
Winfield, M. M. 7:76; 25:309
Winfield, Thomas 21:289
Winfield, William 19:220
Winfrey, C. M. 8:69; 26:200
Winfrey, Jeremiah 10:98
Winfries, W. S. 3:219
Wing, --- 11:343
Wing, A. 3:219
Wing, Abraham 6:8; 18:116
Wing, C. T. 25:281
Wing, Charles 25:263
Wing, Charles C. 17:417
Wing, Charles J. 22:469
Wing, D. B. 10:143; 20:394
Wing, F. 3:219
Wing, F. N. 25:263
Wing, Frank 10:143; 20:394
Wing, Fred. W. 7:115
Wing, Gideon 20:102

Wing, H. J. 1:182
Wing, Harvey 26:200
Wing, Henry H. 22:469
Wing, Henry O. 15:320; 19:141
Wing, J. J. 27:128
Wing, James 16:264; 18:269; 26:85
Wing, James D. 12:46
Wing, John 1:89; 17:499
Wing, John P. 16:112
Wing, Joseph N. 21:406
Wing, Julian A. 21:406
Wing, Leonard 22:469
Wing, Leonard L. 7:115
Wing, Owen W. 7:115
Wing, Phillip 16:63
Wing, Samuel 23:111
Wing, Seneca L. 22:61
Wing, Thomas A. 7:84; 21:406
Wing, V. B. 8:57; 21:46
Wing, W. 14:128
Wing, W. S. 21:406
Wingard, D. 3:219
Wingate, B. 8:123
Wingate, Chase 16:112
Wingate, David 17:189
Wingate, G. B. 7:46
Wingate, Henry 18:344
Wingate, Lemuel 22:229
Wingate, Lemuel P. 7:115
Wingate, O. 9:114
Wingate, R. 15:255
Wingate, R. H. 25:263
Wingate, Rufus H. 5:34
Wingate, T. H. 16:264
Wingdes, Thomas H. 13:80
Wingell, C. 21:108
Wingent, David 22:61
Winger, Armaund 12:66
Winger, Benjamin F. 22:495
Winger, C. 24:87
Winger, C. W. 12:98
Winger, E. 14:233
Winger, Ezra B. 7:62
Winger, Jacob 10:143; 20:395
Winger, John 14:233
Winger, Urias 21:237
Wingert, Nicholas 12:46
Winget, Andrew 18:269; 26:86
Winget, C. B. 1:182
Winget, Caleb 23:83
Winget, G. 11:317
Winget, Ziba 22:109
Wingett, W. H. 19:43
Wingfield, J. H. 20:82

Wingfield, Martin L. 21:406
Wingfield, Thomas H. 23:57
Wingle, S. S. 18:61
Wingle, Ulrick 20:395
Wingler, Harvey 8:99
Wingler, John 11:80
Wingler, Ulrick 10:88
Wingo, Ransom 25:263
Wingrove, A. 15:319; 19:141
Wings, W. C. 18:185
Wington, Edgar 16:264
Winhall, Albert 9:198
Winhart, James D. 8:36
Wining, David 16:130
Wining, Samuel C. 9:127
Winings, J. 19:141
Wink, J. 25:263
Wink, Lewis 3:219
Wink, William F. 17:354
Winkelman, William 14:233
Winkle, Harman 17:233
Winklebunch, George 13:55
Winkleman, J. 23:265
Winkleman, John 12:10; 21:62
Winklepeck, John 9:226; 22:494
Winklepleck, J. 18:389
Winkler, --- 16:63
Winkler, Augustine 22:109
Winkler, Charles 15:157; 22:61
Winkler, Christopher 11:274
Winkler, G. 17:74
Winkler, Harvey 13:55
Winkler, Henry 7:115; 11:82; 17:45
Winkler, Ignus 22:61
Winkler, J. 19:142
Winkler, James 23:265
Winkler, John W. 20:139
Winkler, T. N. 22:524
Winkles, John 22:275
Winkles, N. 10:31; 19:315
Winklet, T. 3:219
Winkley, Christian 15:354; 16:286
Winkley, F. L. 23:96
Winkley, H. W. 9:153; 27:127
Winkworth, R. 13:102
Winlan, John H. 15:62
Winland, Charles 20:45
Winlei, R. 14:261

Winlei, S. R. 14:261
Winlknight, John 15:321
Winlock, Joshua 22:517
Winman, William 18:282; 26:131
Winn, A. 14:233, 261
Winn, Alfred 9:167; 25:329
Winn, Arthur A. 22:494
Winn, George B. 1:87
Winn, George W. 17:446
Winn, Harrison 21:406
Winn, Hel 26:198
Winn, Hel. 8:44
Winn, I. D. 17:297
Winn, J. 1:185
Winn, J. A. 26:83
Winn, James 3:219; 9:94; 17:286; 23:95; 26:83
Winn, James A. 9:94
Winn, James R. 7:54
Winn, John 11:216; 17:141; 24:206
Winn, John Monroe 24:34
Winn, Joseph 19:323
Winn, L. 12:163
Winn, Leonard M. 21:406
Winn, Michael 4:63; 21:12
Winn, Morris 9:153; 27:129
Winn, P. 3:219
Winn, Samuel 13:55
Winn, T. 1:180
Winn, W. 24:115
Winn, W. H. 9:198; 19:234
Winn, Walker G. 15:51
Winn, William 23:307
Winn, Zachariah 7:137
Winna, Stephen 13:55
Winnans, William 9:46
Winnegan, William S. 16:145
Winnegar, A. A. 1:181
Winnepleck, Samuel 22:229
Winner, Daniel R. 15:283; 25:263
Winner, John F. 4:63
Winner, Joseph 23:176
Winner, Robert H. 22:173
Winner, William A. 25:126
Winners, Lewis 22:159
Winney, Daniel P. 19:220
Winney, G. A. 3:219
Winney, John 2:20
Winney, William 11:429; 26:234
Winnger, Alex 19:315

Winnick, Daniel 14:233
Winnie, E. L. 1:184
Winnie, T. 1:88
Winnie, William 6:13
Winniger, Daniel 8:99
Winniger, W. 14:128
Winning, David M. 3:219
Winningham, J. 3:219
Winningham, James 11:215
Winno, Joseph L. 10:24
Winons, I. H. 13:123
Winoock, Edward 21:62
Winows, J. H. 16:264
Winpfheimer, Max 15:95
Winpigle, J. L. 21:199
Winrich, Henry 17:113
Winsarth, John 26:84
Winsate, John 9:94
Winscheinmer, Charles 21:406
Winscher, F. 1:86
Winscott, Simon R. 17:146
Winser, N. 16:264
Winseth, Alfred 12:46
Winsett, Harvey 17:433
Winsey, Isaac A. 10:146
Winsey, James A. 19:220
Winsford, John W. 7:46
Winsheimer, Henry 21:46
Winship, Calvin E. 21:46
Winship, D. H. 15:26
Winship, H. 25:309
Winship, Horace 7:76
Winship, J. H. 3:219
Winship, James 3:219
Winship, John 19:220
Winship, N. W. 16:112
Winship, Sylvanus A. 16:83
Winsinger, S. 3:219
Winslow, Albert D. 4:63
Winslow, Amos 10:88; 20:395
Winslow, Andrew 4:63
Winslow, Benjamin 22:109
Winslow, C. S. 12:81
Winslow, Charles 4:63
Winslow, E. 3:219; 5:34
Winslow, Edward 9:167; 25:329
Winslow, G. A. 15:255
Winslow, H. 11:317
Winslow, Henry 16:264
Winslow, Ira 22:286
Winslow, Jasper A. 10:169
Winslow, Joel 9:94
Winslow, John W. 11:48

Winslow, L. A. 15:347; 16:392
Winslow, L. D. 25:128
Winslow, N. 1:182
Winslow, N. L. 3:219
Winslow, Nathan 12:46
Winslow, O. S. 25:263
Winslow, S. M. 1:185
Winslow, T. 26:84
Winslow, T. W. 25:263
Winslow, Thomas 9:94
Winslow, Thomas H. 17:213
Winslow, W. 13:102
Winslow, Warren 21:406
Winslow, William H. 22:61
Winson, Elijah 10:100
Winsor, Gersham 10:24
Winsor, J. 3:219; 16:264
Winsor, S. 1:182
Winsor, Sidney 5:48
Winstead, Alexander 11:406
Winstead, C. C. 19:272
Winstead, Riley 7:46
Winsted, C. C. 9:198
Winsteel, H. 22:328
Winstein, Phil 15:255
Winster, H. W. 16:63
Winster, Jacob F. 17:61
Winston, Carter 22:328
Winston, Gabriel 17:141; 24:207
Winston, George D. 17:108
Winston, George W. 11:217
Winston, William 7:46
Winston, Winfield 11:215
Wint, Philip 18:269; 26:86
Winten, Martin 9:167
Winter, A. 16:264
Winter, Andrew 21:46
Winter, Charles 27:126
Winter, Charles N. 19:328
Winter, Christian 17:150
Winter, Christian F. 24:34
Winter, D. R. 26:84
Winter, F. 18:61
Winter, Francis A. 20:26
Winter, Frederick W. 11:195
Winter, G. 3:219
Winter, G. W. 17:69
Winter, George 3:219
Winter, H. 3:219
Winter, H. B. 19:222
Winter, Jacob 24:34

Winter, John 15:328; 19:142
Winter, Lewis 9:46; 26:132
Winter, Peter R. 10:88; 20:395
Winter, R. 14:233
Winter, R. D. 27:125
Winter, Thomas J. 22:159
Winter, Thomas W. 25:263
Winter, W. W. 11:195
Winter, William 19:43
Winteralter, Peter 18:212
Winterhalls, John 15:96
Winterhalter, Leo 8:36; 18:168
Winterlater, Conrad 4:63
Wintermate, Peter K. 22:109
Winternugham, J. 9:30
Winters, Abraham 24:73
Winters, Andrew J. 19:43
Winters, Charles 7:115; 8:99; 10:169; 13:123; 19:220
Winters, Charles E. 12:170
Winters, Charles H. 17:101
Winters, Daniel 10:143; 20:395
Winters, David 18:349
Winters, F. W. 3:219
Winters, Francis 10:88; 20:395
Winters, Frederick 21:46
Winters, G. C. 17:28
Winters, Harvey 15:255
Winters, Henry 12:46
Winters, Isaac 10:146; 19:220
Winters, James O. 20:86
Winters, John 7:115; 22:61; 25:263
Winters, John F. 23:206
Winters, John L. 8:99
Winters, John S. 8:36; 18:168
Winters, Joseph W. 17:89
Winters, Josiah P. 13:55
Winters, Lawrence 25:127
Winters, Merritt 12:46
Winters, Michael 9:127; 25:125; 27:131
Winters, Obediah J. 22:109
Winters, Owen 18:422
Winters, P. 3:219; 15:329; 21:46
Winters, Peter 19:142

Winters, R. D. 9:127
Winters, Richard 8:44; 26:198
Winters, Rodney 5:55
Winters, S. 9:155; 16:264; 27:128
Winters, Samuel 7:62
Winters, Tony 7:137
Winters, W. H. 23:57
Winters, W. S. 2:19; 25:123
Winters, William 3:219; 7:46
Winterscheid, Sullivan 23:57
Winterstein, S. R. 1:87
Winterton, S. 18:460
Wintes, Isaac N. 23:176
Winthe, Ludwig 23:57
Winther, Christian 11:121
Winthrop, H. 21:406
Winton, Horace 23:176
Winton, Jackson 11:217
Winton, James H. 9:226; 18:389
Winton, James N. 22:109
Winton, John A. 19:142
Winton, W. 22:230
Wintringham, Job 18:318; 26:115
Wintzer, Gustave A. 24:87
Winver, John 18:168
Winworth, G. 3:219
Winy, James 3:219
Winzeler, C. 9:153; 27:127
Winzer, Armand 15:21
Wiollett, N. 16:359
Wion, David 18:403
Wion, John 7:62
Wior, Samuel 26:131
Wipf, Albert 11:81
Wipple, C. 14:233
Wipple, Matis 14:233
Wirbaugh, Henry 7:70
Wirchat, James D. 18:168
Wirchill, Linneron 18:168
Wirdman, Paul 15:354
Wire, Henry 20:175
Wire, J. D. 18:73
Wire, John 9:198; 19:272
Wire, William 11:215
Wire, William H. 11:323
Wirebaugh, Nicholas 24:87
Wireman, G. B. 16:130
Wireman, H. L. 17:337
Wireman, John H. 22:445
Wireman, S. F. 1:87
Wires, John 22:444
Wires, William 23:83

Wirick, Peter 11:318
Wirl, E. D. 11:393
Wirley, Conrad 15:148
Wirner, J. C. 25:127
Wirockee, Joseph 19:43
Wirshing, Jacob 23:117
Wirt, A. 1:185
Wirt, David 8:111
Wirt, E. 11:114
Wirt, George W. 17:266
Wirt, John 5:34
Wirt, William 22:230
Wirtehood, C. 14:313;
    27:132
Wirtemberger, Isaac
    11:178
Wirth, Friedrich 22:173
Wirth, John 24:87
Wirthington, William A.
    1:84
Wirts, William W. 21:83
Wirtz, John 17:69
Wisburn, James 17:417
Wiscoe, R. P. H. 11:132
Wiscon, Daniel D. 12:79
Wiscott, Carver 10:88
Wisdom, A. S. 12:166;
    26:199
Wisdom, B. 20:15
Wisdom, Gread 18:201
Wisdom, William 21:289
Wise, A. 12:86; 16:359
Wise, A. B. 15:255
Wise, A. F. 14:286
Wise, Alonzo 17:69
Wise, Anthony 14:233
Wise, Asa 22:230
Wise, B. 1:181; 15:296;
    16:264
Wise, Benjamin F. 12:46
Wise, C. 1:88
Wise, C. D. 20:82
Wise, C. M. 27:133
Wise, C. W. 13:75;
    19:142
Wise, Charles 10:143;
    11:427; 20:395;
    22:239
Wise, D. 19:142
Wise, Daniel 21:145
Wise, Daniel D. 11:290
Wise, David 23:15
Wise, Demas 12:79; 15:62
Wise, E. 23:303
Wise, Edward 11:177
Wise, Edward W. 21:83
Wise, Ely 3:219
Wise, F. B. 9:94
Wise, Frank 15:255
Wise, Franklin 8:99;
    17:405

Wise, G. 1:184
Wise, G. B. 3:219
Wise, G. W. 14:128
Wise, George 17:214
Wise, George S. 16:87
Wise, H. 13:102; 14:128;
    25:263
Wise, Henry 1:83; 5:34;
    12:53; 21:108; 23:57
Wise, Henry O. 21:263
Wise, Hiram 17:163
Wise, Isaac 3:219
Wise, J. A. 1:84
Wise, J. B. 19:265
Wise, J. D. 11:253
Wise, J. J. 22:459
Wise, J. W. 14:128;
    17:189
Wise, Jacob 12:46;
    18:282; 21:117;
    22:110
Wise, James 12:46;
    17:189
Wise, James T. 21:62
Wise, John 1:85; 3:219;
    4:63; 8:57; 9:233;
    21:95
Wise, John A. 23:283
Wise, John R. 17:61
Wise, Joseph 7:137
Wise, Joseph A. 9:40
Wise, Joseph B. 9:198
Wise, Joseph M. 19:43
Wise, Judson 22:275
Wise, Lafayette 17:266
Wise, Lewis 19:220;
    22:230
Wise, Merritt 7:137
Wise, Michael 11:113;
    23:176
Wise, Peter 11:427
Wise, Porter 6:27
Wise, Robert 13:55
Wise, Samuel 21:199;
    23:306
Wise, Samuel L. 7:46
Wise, Samuel T. 22:134
Wise, W. 27:128
Wise, W. H. 5:55; 25:263
Wise, W. L. 20:140
Wise, W. M. 25:277
Wise, W. W. 18:409
Wise, William 15:79
Wise, William H. 8:99
Wisegi1ner, Michael
    11:318
Wisehart, M. 11:179
Wisel, Ezra 10:7
Wisel, Ira 21:145
Wisel, James H. 9:105
Wisel, Joseph H. 18:342

Wisel, M. 3:219
Wiseman, A. 17:157
Wiseman, Abram 8:99
Wiseman, Charles 23:176
Wiseman, E. F. 18:185
Wiseman, Frederick C.
    18:282
Wiseman, G. 14:128
Wiseman, George 20:150;
    25:263
Wiseman, H. H. 19:43
Wiseman, H. W. 12:79;
    15:10
Wiseman, Isaac N. 23:83
Wiseman, J. 1:180
Wiseman, James 9:94;
    26:83
Wiseman, John 22:328
Wiseman, John S. 5:34
Wiseman, R. A. 22:169
Wiseman, Robert 18:435
Wiseman, S. 25:263
Wiseman, T. 1:86
Wiseman, William 9:94;
    26:83
Wiseman, Z. 17:251
Wisemer, H. 3:219
Wisemuller, John 24:34
Wisener, Andrew 22:230
Wiser, A. 22:356
Wiser, Felix 8:99
Wiser, Henry 11:113
Wiser, Hiram 5:34
Wiser, Jacob 9:226;
    18:389
Wiser, John 16:135
Wiser, Madison 22:459
Wiser, N. L. 1:181
Wiser, R. M. 3:219
Wish, Wilson 11:177
Wisham, Anderson 24:103
Wishart, J. D. 1:183
Wishenger, James E. 8:36
Wishepard, Palmer 16:392
Wisher, Henry S. 18:299
Wishmyer, C. E. 16:137
Wishon, Leonard 19:43
Wisinard, A. M. 20:395
Wiskham, James 9:114
Wiskrom, --- 16:359
Wiskron, --- 12:91
Wisler, Solomon 25:127
Wisley, William A. 26:83
Wisman, George 5:34
Wisman, W. S. 23:176
Wisner, Alvin 22:469
Wisner, Anthony B.
    22:159
Wisner, Benjamin C.
    10:88; 20:395
Wisner, E. 27:133

Wisner, H. C. 18:41
Wisner, Hiram B. 10:143;
   20:395
Wisner, J. 3:219
Wisner, Jehiel 22:159
Wisner, John W. 11:176;
   17:69
Wisner, Noah 22:110
Wisner, Richard 11:317;
   22:328
Wisner, Samuel 5:34;
   24:71
Wisner, William 25:263
Wison, L. 25:263
Wisong, William M.
   22:110
Wissa, F. 11:323
Wissel, Fred 20:395
Wissen, J. 18:42
Wissendorff, H. 11:48
Wisser, F. J. 3:219
Wissinger, Harvey B.
   23:95
Wissinger, Jonathan 12:46
Wisston, S. 25:263
Wistaba, Peter 11:185
Wisterman, P. 12:91
Wiston, George 18:21,
   201
Wiston, Nathan S. 12:46
Wisttrell, A. B. 14:131
Wiswell, Charles E. 8:36
Wiswell, James H. 15:62
Wit, T. 23:57
Witaker, John 19:49
Witbeck, Abraham 25:263
Witchcraft, C. 7:115;
   21:406
Witcher, William H.
   17:363
Witchery, William 27:156
Witcholson, Jackson
   11:253
Witcomb, Lermon 25:125
Wite, H. 24:115
Witecop, Jan 21:407
Witeman, George 11:87
With, S. 14:276; 17:500
Withal, C. 13:102; 14:25
Witham, A. 1:182
Witham, A. H. 9:217;
   21:407
Witham, Charles W. 21:83
Witham, E. 9:198; 19:231
Witham, George 18:422
Witham, James A 15:13
Witham, L. M. 16:392
Witham, Morris Oliver
   23:95
Witham, S. 24:34
Withaner, J. 11:131

Withcot, Nelson 11:175
Withcroft, G. 1:86
Withee, Charles 21:145
Withen, Henry 21:407
Withenburg, Charles 8:36
Withenick, A. K. 3:219
Witheral, Benjamin O.
   25:329
Witherapt, J. M. 26:200
Witherde, David 13:55
Withered, Samuel 11:321
Witherel, Levin 6:21
Witherell, Charles 19:297
Witherell, David 16:63
Witherell, G. W. 19:243
Witherell, O. 3:219
Witheright, William 1:88
Withern, S. 18:73
Witherow, Samuel P.
   17:45
Withers, Dick 17:141;
   24:206
Withers, Edward 10:143;
   20:395
Withers, George 12:46
Withers, Isaac 7:115
Withers, J. 18:185
Withers, J. P. 24:34
Withers, Jacob 9:94
Withers, Joshua 5:48
Withers, L. 16:275
Withers, P. 22:399
Withers, William 27:133
Witherspoon, Thomas J.
   18:299; 26:116
Witherspoon, W. P.
   14:128
Witherstay, Henry 11:177
Witherwax, William 1:88
Withford, Jeremiah
   22:169
Withington, Elijah 17:241
Withington, J. 27:126
Withington, M. L. 25:263
Withington, O. 9:65
Withington, William M.
   18:342
Withley, E. 1:181
Withman, J. 14:286
Withneck, James 1:86
Withom, Asa 15:148
Withrow, James 11:253
Withrow, Samuel G.
   11:82
Withu, Clark 11:318
Witled, John 1:85
Witler, Gotleb 20:395
Witly, E. 17:436
Witman, D. 3:219
Witman, J. 1:181

Witman, J. C. 9:30;
   18:318; 26:115
Witman, John H. 22:61
Witman, P. 14:286
Witmer, Christian 20:150
Witmer, M. S. 22:230
Witmore, A. 11:131
Witner, William 7:115;
   21:407
Witrohn, J. H. 20:15
Wits, Charles 11:195
Witsal, Frank 17:102
Witser, John 10:88
Witsin, J. 3:219
Witson, M. C. 26:214
Witt, Alfred 11:383
Witt, Andrew 19:277
Witt, Clarke 16:264
Witt, David 9:238; 26:234
Witt, E. B. 10:208
Witt, E. D. 27:135
Witt, Fred. I. 19:43
Witt, George 19:43
Witt, H. T. 11:318
Witt, J. E. 1:184
Witt, James 8:57
Witt, Jenkins 22:61
Witt, Jeremiah 10:143;
   20:395
Witt, John 19:43; 24:87
Witt, Joseph 24:207
Witt, Reuben P. 21:83
Witt, T. 3:219
Witt, William 8:58; 10:31;
   19:315; 21:162;
   22:275
Witt, William H. 20:395
Wittcome, Joseph 25:309
Witteer, L. S. 2:19
Witten, A. E. 25:277
Witten, Hiram 17:461;
   24:168
Wittenberg, Herman 26:83
Wittenberg, Hiram 9:94
Wittenberg, Marcus 26:84
Wittenburg, Arnold 8:36;
   18:168
Wittenburg, Charles
   18:168
Wittenger, G. 15:354
Witter, Amos A. 26:116
Witter, Gotlieb 10:143
Witter, John E. 22:159
Witter, Robert W. 9:198;
   19:276
Witter, Thomas 24:87
Witters, Benjamin F.
   20:395
Witters, L. C. 14:25
Wittich, P. 23:177
Wittig, Christian 18:389

Wittiker, T. S. 2:19
Witting, Charles E. 10:88
Witting, Christian 9:226
Wittinger, J. 12:79; 15:79
Wittins, Jesse 9:241
Wittle, Ira 12:46
Wittman, Charles 20:395
Wittman, Christian A. 10:143
Wittman, Peter 22:61
Wittmar, Christ A. 20:395
Wittmer, H. 23:177
Wittmer, Henry 21:127
Wittmer, P. 16:359
Witts, Rodolph 11:175
Wittsey, D. 3:219
Wittshire, A. 14:128
Wittup, Bernard 25:125
Witturn, P. 14:128
Witty, Albert 17:189
Witzel, James 23:177
Witzel, P. 23:57
Witzel, Reun 1:83
Witzgall, John 3:219
Witzland, B. 13:102
Witzleo, M. 14:261
Witzler, A. 1:183
Witzler, M. 14:233
Witzman, J. 1:88
Wivey, William E. 17:277
Wixam, Robert 14:128
Wixen, Atwell 14:233
Wixen, Lemuel 20:32
Wixon, A. 1:183
Wixon, B. F. 25:128
Wixon, Daniel D. 15:52
Wixon, Dennis 22:159
Wixon, G. B. 1:88
Wixon, Henry 16:359
Wixtry, Albert 7:115
Wizener, Ab'm. G. 26:117
Wizener, Abraham 18:299
Wleooper, C. 19:265
Wlson, George 24:60
Wo---d, William 24:207
Woasham, W. M. 17:319
Wobecks, D. S. 9:94
Wobley, John 17:254
Wochin, John Frederick 18:224
Woden, Henry 22:328
Woden, John B. 19:142
Woe, William 1:84
Woefkill, Alfred 17:45
Woel, D. 9:30
Woelffu, H. 18:269
Woell, --- 16:112
Woerner, Leopold 20:102
Wofel, Nicholas 18:318
Wogan, John 16:130
Woglen, Samuel 15:52

Woglom, Samuel 12:79
Wogoman, David 23:83
Wogomon, M. 9:65
Wogram, John W. 14:233
Wohlfart, P. S. 1:184
Wohlford, Benjamin F. 21:237
Wohlford, G. 27:156
Wohlrabe, A. 1:186
Wohrman, Henry 22:61
Woising, Samuel C. 27:131
Wol, Lewis 14:250; 27:135
Wol---, M. 17:495
Wolber, Andreas 22:495
Wolburn, Joseph 22:445
Wolcer, L. C. 13:123
Wolcot, --- 12:91
Wolcot, J. 1:181
Wolcot, Owen 14:233
Wolcot, Welford 25:263
Wolcott, --- 14:128
Wolcott, Charles 22:61
Wolcott, David A. 18:318; 26:115
Wolcott, Edward D. 22:159
Wolcott, George L. 21:145
Wolcott, J. 17:157
Wolcott, Joseph M. 17:101
Wold, J. 14:128
Wold, Lara T. 24:57
Wolemb, W. T. 23:315
Wolener, Charles 1:85
Woley, David S. 20:395
Woley, J. E. 1:184
Wolf, --- 1:83; 15:52
Wolf, A. 3:219; 25:125
Wolf, A. C. 19:327
Wolf, A. D. 22:498
Wolf, Abraham 11:113
Wolf, Adam 16:359; 22:445
Wolf, Albert 11:195
Wolf, Alfred 14:233
Wolf, Andrew 19:220
Wolf, Andrew G. 4:63
Wolf, Anthony 12:79
Wolf, Austin M. 17:93
Wolf, B. F. 3:219; 14:128
Wolf, Berry H. 14:128
Wolf, C. 14:233
Wolf, C. A. 7:55
Wolf, Charles A. 27:126
Wolf, Christopher 7:54; 22:163; 25:284
Wolf, Conralius 18:318

Wolf, Cornelius 9:30; 26:115
Wolf, D. 13:102
Wolf, D. E. 8:36
Wolf, D. W. 7:46
Wolf, Daniel 11:114
Wolf, David 7:46; 22:230
Wolf, David R. 17:163
Wolf, F. W. 11:175
Wolf, Frederick 12:60; 23:197
Wolf, G. 1:184
Wolf, George 22:495
Wolf, George A. 9:30
Wolf, George W. 23:269
Wolf, H. 16:264
Wolf, Henry 9:198; 11:47; 15:148
Wolf, Henry C. 22:114
Wolf, Herman 21:407
Wolf, Ignus 22:134
Wolf, J. 10:31; 15:79; 19:315
Wolf, J. W. 23:245
Wolf, Jacob 11:177; 22:134; 23:177
Wolf, Jacob L. 23:177
Wolf, James 9:46; 19:43; 24:71; 26:131
Wolf, James D. 23:95
Wolf, John 9:127; 12:160; 15:255; 18:441; 19:220; 22:230, 239; 25:263; 27:131
Wolf, John K. 26:116
Wolf, John R. 18:318
Wolf, Joseph 9:68; 17:69; 18:282, 417; 20:185
Wolf, Joseph H. 11:177
Wolf, Leonidas H. 10:88; 20:395
Wolf, Levi 9:30; 18:319; 26:115
Wolf, Lewis 14:250
Wolf, Louis 15:292; 19:142
Wolf, Lucian H. 21:83
Wolf, Luman P. 9:46
Wolf, Max 22:230
Wolf, Michael 10:143; 20:395; 22:110
Wolf, Michael J. 24:175
Wolf, N. B. 11:177
Wolf, Nathaniel William 9:69
Wolf, P. 12:94
Wolf, Peter 24:71
Wolf, Philip 5:34
Wolf, Philip H. 11:318
Wolf, Philip M. 20:188
Wolf, R. 7:55

Wolf, S. 18:319; 26:116
Wolf, S. S. 9:31
Wolf, Samuel 3:219; 9:31;
  10:88; 18:321;
  19:142; 20:395;
  23:183
Wolf, Simon 9:94
Wolf, Simon P. 26:131
Wolf, Solomon 15:25
Wolf, Stephen 21:62
Wolf, T. 3:219
Wolf, T. D. 14:250;
  27:134
Wolf, T. J. 8:36
Wolf, Thomas 17:275
Wolf, Thomas C. H.
  19:142
Wolf, W. 1:183, 186;
  3:219
Wolf, Walter S. 11:176
Wolf, William 8:111;
  10:88; 17:316;
  20:152, 395
Wolf, William D. 25:274
Wolfanges, F. 1:88
Wolfe, --- 21:407
Wolfe, C. 3:219
Wolfe, C. C. 9:153
Wolfe, Ch. 14:233
Wolfe, Christian 13:55
Wolfe, D. E. 18:168
Wolfe, E. 1:184; 14:128;
  16:392
Wolfe, F. 3:219
Wolfe, Frederick 3:219;
  7:70
Wolfe, George 8:69
Wolfe, H. T. 16:63
Wolfe, Henry 11:234;
  19:269
Wolfe, Henry F. 15:62
Wolfe, J. 3:219; 13:102
Wolfe, J. D. 3:219; 13:126
Wolfe, J. H. 3:219
Wolfe, John 7:46; 10:175;
  13:55; 17:89
Wolfe, P. 14:128; 16:359
Wolfe, P. N. 8:69
Wolfe, Patrick 22:522
Wolfe, Peter 14:233
Wolfe, Simon 16:359
Wolfe, T. J. 18:168
Wolfe, Thomas 9:153
Wolfe, Thomas E. 27:127
Wolfe, W. 1:185; 14:128
Wolfe, William 7:46, 62
Wolfenbarker, John 17:98
Wolfendin, William 20:15
Wolfer, William 26:199
Wolfernger, Godfrey
  9:198

Wolff, Charles 1:88;
  12:46; 24:57
Wolff, Daniel 22:459
Wolff, G. C. 27:128
Wolff, John 22:230
Wolff, Milton 25:126
Wolffe, George 18:269;
  26:86
Wolffer, H. 15:296
Wolffor, H. 16:264
Wolfgang, Abel 22:61
Wolfield, William 4:63
Wolfinger, A. 25:329
Wolfinger, E. 9:233
Wolford, D. 3:219
Wolford, Francis M.
  17:499
Wolford, George 27:156
Wolford, H. A. 27:132
Wolford, Henry 20:20
Wolford, James M. 22:445
Wolford, John B. 21:108
Wolford, John R. 22:110
Wolford, Joseph 22:230
Wolford, William 11:317;
  19:43; 22:230
Wolfram, A. 3:219
Wolfram, Otto F. 25:263
Wolfran, A. 13:76
Wolfran, Adolphus
  16:264
Wolfrod, William 18:99
Wolfrom, Daniel 1:86
Wolfskill, Jacob 9:68
Wolfus, Henry 4:63
Wolgamott, P. 23:57
Woliver, Henry 21:85
Woll, Gottl'b 1:87
Wollard, John W. 24:100
Wollem, August 20:194
Wollenberger, James M.
  10:143
Wollenburger, James M.
  20:395
Woller, Ferdinand 23:197
Wollet, Michael 8:111
Wolley, James 17:28
Wolman, Henry 27:132
Wolpert, Andrew 17:240
Wolpinger, Godfrey
  19:243
Wolrath, M. 1:84
Wolrkank, Charles 5:34
Wolsey, James F. 22:275
Wolsey, John P. 22:275
Wolsey, S. 19:315
Wolsinger, S. 18:201
Wolson, James 21:407
Woltman, August 21:207
Wolts, M. 10:152
Woltz, John 13:81

Wolven, Andrew 17:245
Wolven, Michael 17:264
Wolvenston, Amzy
  11:131
Wolvert, Charles 16:63
Wolverton, --- 3:219
Wolverton, Alfred 10:143;
  20:395
Wolverton, C. 3:219
Wolverton, Charles 13:55
Wolverton, G. W. 1:180
Wolverton, J. S. 3:220
Wolverton, John V.
  15:273
Wolverton, William
  10:211
Womack, J. H. 25:263
Womack, L. B. 11:121
Womack, William N.
  23:117
Woman, George 14:318
Womber, John 25:263
Womesley, William
  17:163
Womth, J. 25:263
Wonaker, Jonathan
  23:258
Wonard, Columbus M.
  6:21
Wondell, John 12:139;
  15:148
Wonderley, J. K. 27:134
Wonderley, P. S. 27:134
Wonderlin, Hugh 20:395
Wonderly, Charles H.
  15:79
Wonderly, George 16:264
Wonderly, Michael 12:57
Wonders, Allen W.
  10:143; 20:395
Wondt, Charles 18:319
Wonger, Charles 19:50
Wonorad, Patrick 16:359
Wons, James 18:224
Wonsch, Charles 13:55
Wonser, R. 14:333
Wonson, Joseph P. 19:220
Wonton, --- 18:61
Wooberry, H. A. 27:134
Wood, --- 13:55; 14:233;
  18:185; 22:356;
  25:125
Wood, A. 1:84; 3:220;
  13:123; 15:321;
  19:142; 21:407;
  25:263
Wood, A. D. 15:255
Wood, A. G. 23:57
Wood, A. I. 12:160
Wood, A. J. 21:407
Wood, A. L. 3:220

Wood, A. O. 3:220
Wood, A. R. 16:392
Wood, Abel 17:421
Wood, Abner 8:57
Wood, Abraham 17:363;
    21:407; 24:215
Wood, Adam 22:286
Wood, Aden H. 11:316
Wood, Albert 22:61
Wood, Albert J. 7:46
Wood, Albert O. 4:63
Wood, Alexander 21:108
Wood, Alfred 21:46;
    23:111
Wood, Alfred H. 15:26
Wood, Alonzo 9:40;
    17:89; 18:299
Wood, Alonzo D. 25:125
Wood, Alvin 7:79; 25:309
Wood, Anderson 5:48
Wood, Andrew 15:148
Wood, Andrew J. 9:105;
    18:444
Wood, Anthony 5:48
Wood, Asa K. 10:9
Wood, B. F. 9:114
Wood, Benjamin 8:123;
    9:94; 21:133
Wood, Benjamin F.
    11:318; 25:125
Wood, Bishop 1:84
Wood, C. 1:183
Wood, C. B. 9:94; 15:89;
    26:83
Wood, C. E. 16:63
Wood, C. H. 1:184; 7:115
Wood, C. J. 16:264
Wood, C. M. 17:71
Wood, C. W. 13:102;
    14:25, 233
Wood, C. W. H. 11:316
Wood, Calvin 6:20;
    18:100
Wood, Cars. P. 1:85
Wood, Charles 4:63; 7:62;
    14:128, 233; 24:98
Wood, Charles B. 12:79
Wood, Charles C. 22:230
Wood, Charles E. 13:55
Wood, Christopher
    22:275
Wood, D. A. 17:45
Wood, D. C. 8:76
Wood, D. H. 10:191
Wood, Daniel 11:175;
    12:163
Wood, Daniel B. 17:251
Wood, Daniel C. 24:98
Wood, Daniel W. 22:159
Wood, David 8:57
Wood, David E. 18:353

Wood, David L. 22:445
Wood, Dudley 22:328
Wood, Durett L. 17:240
Wood, E. A. 1:84
Wood, E. B. 9:94
Wood, E. C. C. 16:63
Wood, E. D. 26:84
Wood, E. G. 3:220
Wood, E. M. 15:52
Wood, Edmund 22:110
Wood, Edward 9:31;
    15:52; 22:445
Wood, Edward D. 22:328
Wood, Edwin F. 20:15
Wood, Edwin L. 12:56
Wood, Eli 10:143;
    20:131, 395; 21:83
Wood, Elias 21:83
Wood, Elias A. 4:63
Wood, Elijah 8:44; 26:198
Wood, Emery J. 17:113
Wood, Enoch P. 23:197
Wood, Ethiel A. 16:130
Wood, Ezra 10:143;
    20:395
Wood, F. 3:220
Wood, F. B. 1:186
Wood, F. M. 11:189
Wood, Fletcher 19:43
Wood, Francis 23:57
Wood, Francis M. 8:36;
    18:168
Wood, Frank 11:234;
    25:126
Wood, Frank A. 22:61
Wood, Frank D. 15:311,
    356; 19:142
Wood, Franklin F. 17:28
Wood, Frederick 5:48
Wood, G. 1:184, 185;
    15:255
Wood, G. C. 11:132
Wood, G. H. 1:185
Wood, George 4:63;
    12:79, 163; 15:52,
    80; 16:160; 21:407;
    22:110; 25:128
Wood, George E. 11:195
Wood, George H. 17:74
Wood, George T. 5:34
Wood, George W. 7:46;
    16:153; 20:102
Wood, Gideon M. 11:114
Wood, H. 1:100; 3:220;
    13:55, 102; 16:112;
    19:265; 21:46; 23:57;
    25:125, 128
Wood, H. D. 23:57
Wood, H. H. 5:55
Wood, H. S. 1:83
Wood, H. W. 25:263

Wood, Hamilton 26:84
Wood, Harrison 7:137
Wood, Harry A. 21:407
Wood, Henry 12:46;
    14:233; 21:237
Wood, Hiram 5:34;
    22:110
Wood, Hollis 10:88;
    20:395
Wood, I. 9:153
Wood, Icem 21:407
Wood, Ira 12:160; 13:55
Wood, Isaiah 20:102;
    24:98
Wood, J. 1:181, 185;
    3:220; 9:114; 14:128;
    27:129
Wood, J. A. 22:275
Wood, J. B. 1:84; 3:220
Wood, J. E. 1:184; 18:73
Wood, J. G. 19:43
Wood, J. H. 1:181, 182;
    8:69; 26:199
Wood, J. J. 16:130
Wood, J. K. M. 21:237
Wood, J. M. 3:220;
    19:243, 277
Wood, J. S. 3:220
Wood, Jackson 11:291;
    24:163
Wood, Jacob 9:105
Wood, James 5:34; 9:105;
    18:42, 342
Wood, James H. 23:57
Wood, James M. 9:198
Wood, James T. 12:46
Wood, Jerome 22:173
Wood, Jerry 17:141;
    24:206
Wood, Jesse 21:407
Wood, Jesse M. 11:179
Wood, Jewell 21:407
Wood, Joel 13:75; 19:142
Wood, Joel R. 17:307
Wood, John 4:63; 7:115;
    8:57; 9:226; 11:47;
    15:148, 255; 16:112;
    17:73; 18:269, 389;
    19:220, 332; 20:45,
    139, 395; 21:169;
    22:134; 23:127;
    25:263; 26:87
Wood, John A. 22:239
Wood, John A. I. 10:143
Wood, John A. J. 20:395
Wood, John G. 9:105
Wood, John H. 9:138;
    13:55; 23:95
Wood, John L. 22:160
Wood, John R. 22:230

Wood, John W. 8:102, 111; 9:198; 13:55; 17:461; 24:163
Wood, Jonathan 7:115
Wood, Joseph 13:55; 17:354
Wood, Joseph B. 17:363
Wood, Joshua 11:81; 24:206
Wood, Josiah 22:61
Wood, Josiah Q. G. 13:55; 16:63
Wood, L. 1:180, 181; 9:198; 19:233; 27:125
Wood, L. R. 13:123
Wood, L. W. 12:160
Wood, Landsley 23:183
Wood, Levi 7:46
Wood, Lewis 17:394
Wood, Lewis A. 12:46
Wood, M. 3:220
Wood, M. J. 17:69
Wood, Marcus 23:307
Wood, Mason 11:215
Wood, Mathew 17:45
Wood, Miles A. 17:233
Wood, Munson 17:399
Wood, N. 15:52
Wood, Nathan 17:399
Wood, Nelson C. 22:61
Wood, Newton 15:157
Wood, Norman F. 17:316
Wood, Oliver 11:81
Wood, Orville 25:263
Wood, Ozias 21:237
Wood, P. D. 3:220
Wood, Peter 19:220
Wood, Preston 5:48
Wood, R. 1:183
Wood, R. F. 19:265
Wood, R. S. 9:31
Wood, Richard 6:20; 18:100; 22:230
Wood, Ross 9:138
Wood, Rufus 9:198
Wood, Rufus M. 11:330
Wood, S. 3:220; 9:127; 11:113
Wood, S. A. 13:75
Wood, S. L. 9:31
Wood, S. S. 2:19; 10:191; 18:185; 25:127
Wood, S. W. 25:263
Wood, Salmer 22:159
Wood, Samuel 4:63; 7:137; 9:105, 212; 15:296; 16:264; 18:100; 25:329
Wood, Samuel E. 10:143; 20:395

Wood, Samuel R. 18:319; 22:230; 26:116
Wood, Sh'd. 24:207
Wood, Simeon 25:126
Wood, Solomon S. 11:254; 22:61
Wood, Stephen 8:116
Wood, Stephen A. 9:127; 27:131
Wood, T. 1:181; 15:283; 16:113
Wood, T. G. 14:128
Wood, Thaddeus 7:115
Wood, Theodore 9:99
Wood, Thomas 12:10; 13:55; 17:189; 19:142
Wood, Thomas C. 19:43
Wood, Thomas M. 11:393
Wood, W. 1:183; 16:63; 20:82; 23:15
Wood, W. B. 18:389
Wood, W. C. 9:94
Wood, W. F. 7:46
Wood, W. H. 3:220; 9:65; 17:200
Wood, W. J. 1:181; 3:220; 13:55
Wood, W. M. 19:325
Wood, W. W. 9:198; 17:196
Wood, Walter 14:233
Wood, Willard 21:407
Wood, William 1:87; 3:220; 4:69; 5:34; 9:153; 12:160; 13:55; 15:115; 18:73; 19:142; 20:32, 109; 21:83, 84; 23:278; 24:213; 27:129
Wood, William C. 26:84
Wood, William E. 9:226
Wood, William H. 4:63; 5:55; 10:143; 16:63; 19:142; 20:20, 395; 22:61; 25:263
Wood, William J. 9:233; 20:395
Wood, William P. 24:34
Wood, William R. 25:309
Wood, Williams 7:17
Wood, Willis M. 20:109
Wood, Wilson E. 12:46
Wood, Zeb 7:81; 25:309
Wood, Zera W. 8:76
Wood Pecker Joe 25:335
Woodall, James 17:351
Woodall, M. J. 16:63
Woodall, P. H. 22:134
Woodall, Stephen 9:127
Woodall, Steven 27:130

Woodall, W. 11:275
Woodall, W. E. 22:275
Woodard, --- 10:208
Woodard, A. 12:163
Woodard, Albert 23:197
Woodard, Bartholomew F. 20:15
Woodard, Cromwell 22:356
Woodard, E. F. 1:87
Woodard, G. 25:263
Woodard, J. K. 10:185
Woodard, John W. 11:216
Woodard, Joseph 4:63
Woodard, Lawrence 21:46
Woodard, Oscar 1:83
Woodard, W. G. 26:234
Woodard, W. P. 1:87
Woodbar, A. 25:279
Woodbarn, A. G. 14:128
Woodbeck, Christopher 19:142
Woodberry, A. H. 21:407
Woodberry, Charles W. 21:407
Woodberry, Dean J. 4:63
Woodberry, F. A. 8:99
Woodberry, George H. 21:94
Woodberry, William 22:356
Woodbinz, L. S. 11:195
Woodborn, Edward 15:171
Woodbowne, Edwin 4:63
Woodbreck, C. 15:311
Woodbridge, Clancen 26:87
Woodbridge, W. H. 1:84
Woodbridge, W. O. 25:263
Woodbridge, William O. 5:34
Woodburn, A. G. 12:94; 16:360
Woodburn, H. H. 20:139
Woodburn, J. D. 3:220
Woodburn, J. H. 7:115
Woodburn, Jack 19:220
Woodburn, Jackson 10:175
Woodburn, James 10:36
Woodburn, Louis N. 11:81
Woodburn, Robert 4:63
Woodburn, Thomas J. 20:103
Woodburry, S. 14:128
Woodbury, A. 3:220; 25:263
Woodbury, Arad 7:115

Woodbury, B. 3:220
Woodbury, Benjamin 5:34
Woodbury, C. E. 25:309
Woodbury, Charles E. 7:81
Woodbury, Charles M. 13:55
Woodbury, Clement C. 22:495
Woodbury, Emerson 11:274
Woodbury, G. H. 8:57
Woodbury, George S. 10:24
Woodbury, H. A. 14:250
Woodbury, J. 3:220; 11:318
Woodbury, J. C. 17:251
Woodbury, J. H. 2:19; 25:128
Woodbury, J. P. 1:181
Woodbury, John L. 10:169
Woodbury, John S. 19:220
Woodbury, L. 13:102; 14:25
Woodbury, Nathan 10:143; 20:395
Woodbury, Orrin 5:34
Woodbury, William A. 21:238
Woodby, Peter 17:168
Woodcock, Alex 24:155
Woodcock, E. 1:100
Woodcock, George A. 17:89
Woodcock, H. 1:182; 9:158; 14:128
Woodcock, Hiram 4:63
Woodcock, Ira 8:69; 26:200
Woodcock, James 9:94; 15:317; 19:142
Woodcock, James A. 26:84
Woodcock, Joseph 10:143; 20:395
Woodcock, Parrish H. 17:209
Woodcock, R. 3:220; 4:63
Woodcock, Selvy 15:83
Woodcock, Th. 14:233
Woodcock, W. S. 10:191; 18:185
Woodcock, William T. 10:88; 20:395
Woodcox, Alex 17:417
Woodcox, Ira B. 13:55
Woode, Thomas 15:354
Woode, William 18:335

Woodell, T. 14:233
Wooden, G. 9:65
Wooden, John 21:145; 22:275
Wooden, John H. 21:407
Wooden, Levi 10:34; 19:315
Wooden, M. 9:65
Wooden, M. W. 23:265
Wooden, Richard 10:143; 20:395
Wooden, Thomas 23:186
Wooden, William 10:88; 19:43; 22:507
Wooden, William J. 10:143; 18:42; 20:395
Wooder, Edwin 5:34
Wooder, Walter H. 13:55; 16:63
Wooderd, William 4:63
Woodert, C. 10:88
Woodey, J. H. 14:263
Woodey, Joseph 4:63
Woodfall, Richard 25:124
Woodfall, William 22:459
Woodfield, Charles 18:288; 26:136
Woodford, Albert W. 21:84
Woodford, Allen 27:156
Woodford, Byran 15:10
Woodford, H. 25:264
Woodford, Harrison 5:34
Woodford, J. A. 3:220
Woodford, John B. 13:55
Woodford, L. 17:141; 24:206
Woodford, Levi 22:328
Woodford, Levi H. 8:36; 18:168
Woodford, Robert 22:110
Woodfull, William 17:61
Woodfurd, W. A. 24:47
Woodhall, Green 22:328
Woodham, George 12:46
Woodham, W. 1:184
Woodhead, Bernard 12:46
Woodhouse, C. 16:264
Woodhouse, F. C. 1:183
Woodhouse, George 13:55; 16:63
Woodhouse, J. 25:264
Woodhouse, James T. 22:275
Woodhull, D. F. 3:220
Woodin, Oliver 7:79; 25:309
Wooding, Morgan F. 20:194
Wooding, Peter 10:88

Woodington, D. S. 1:86
Woodiongh, William 16:264
Woodland, Austin 18:100
Woodland, C. L. 11:253
Woodland, Nace 21:407
Woodland, Shadrake 13:59
Woodle, A. 11:49
Woodley, --- 27:133
Woodley, A. L. S. 1:185
Woodley, B. 18:61
Woodley, E. 14:128
Woodley, F. J. 15:178
Woodley, J. 12:79
Woodley, R. 10:150
Woodling, J. W. 24:34
Woodling, P. 20:396
Woodman, Albert 9:217; 21:407
Woodman, Barnard 19:43
Woodman, Carl 18:116
Woodman, Charles 7:115
Woodman, Charles W. 21:145
Woodman, E. D. 1:85
Woodman, F. 2:19; 25:127
Woodman, G. C. 25:124
Woodman, J. 12:10; 19:220
Woodman, Jacob B. 20:15
Woodman, James 26:234
Woodman, James C. 15:255
Woodman, James M. 22:230
Woodman, John P. 12:46
Woodman, Larkin E. 17:73
Woodman, Osmore 19:220
Woodman, Robert 17:421; 24:163
Woodman, Silas B. 9:14
Woodman, Thomas 15:336; 19:142
Woodman, Thomas W. 13:55; 16:63
Woodmanest, A. 13:102
Woodmaney, G. 3:220
Woodmansee, Levi J. 22:114
Woodmanser, A. 14:25
Woodmany, A. J. 18:42
Woodmemsey, D. M. 3:220
Woodnard, G. 18:42
Woodraw, Samuel 12:160
Woodren, S. H. 14:128
Woodrich, C. 18:61

Woodrich, Charles 10:150
Woodrich, S. 1:183
Woodridge, Fleming G. 17:61
Woodrie, Miles 17:275
Woodring, --- 15:255
Woodring, Charles 22:349
Woodring, John D. 17:251
Woodrome, John D. 22:413
Woodrow, Thomas 10:143; 20:396
Woodruff, --- 24:87
Woodruff, A. 15:331
Woodruff, A. K. 26:237
Woodruff, A. T. 19:246
Woodruff, Albert 14:233
Woodruff, Ambrose H. 9:99
Woodruff, Archibald 19:142
Woodruff, Byron M. 7:17
Woodruff, C. J. 1:184
Woodruff, Charles 22:328
Woodruff, Edward 7:17
Woodruff, Elias 12:60
Woodruff, Ephraim T. 17:388
Woodruff, F. G. 9:212
Woodruff, Franklin B. 19:43
Woodruff, George 9:203; 19:285
Woodruff, George W. 12:139
Woodruff, H. 3:220; 27:126
Woodruff, Henry 22:230
Woodruff, Hiram 16:130
Woodruff, J. 3:220
Woodruff, J. C. 22:230
Woodruff, J. M. 3:220; 11:317
Woodruff, James A. 17:45
Woodruff, James K. 10:144; 20:396
Woodruff, Jesse 12:46
Woodruff, John 10:144; 19:142, 331; 20:396; 22:134
Woodruff, John N. 17:98
Woodruff, John V. 20:47
Woodruff, L. 18:21
Woodruff, Landon 22:275
Woodruff, M. 18:61
Woodruff, Medad F. 17:89
Woodruff, Richard 7:115
Woodruff, Richard K. 13:59; 16:63

Woodruff, Robert W. B. 22:459
Woodruff, S. 9:153; 27:127
Woodruff, S. F. 1:88
Woodruff, S. G. 1:183
Woodruff, Samuel 8:120
Woodruff, T. 20:150
Woodruff, Truman 17:233
Woodruff, Upton 22:110
Woodruff, W. 18:61
Woodruff, W. D. 3:220
Woodruff, W. S. 1:182
Woodruff, William 21:145; 22:328
Woodruff, William H. 16:150
Woodruff, Wilson 11:321
Woodrun, Lewis 8:99
Woodrup, Bledsoe 22:459
Woods, --- 16:264
Woods, A. F. 13:102; 14:25
Woods, A. G. 11:394, 429; 17:168
Woods, Abraham 7:137
Woods, Alfred 9:138; 27:129
Woods, Allen 22:114
Woods, Barnard 12:46
Woods, Benjamin 11:427
Woods, Burton 18:403
Woods, C. W. 17:293
Woods, Calvin 11:382
Woods, D. 1:87; 14:233; 18:61
Woods, D. P. 14:128
Woods, David 1:85
Woods, David L. 22:413
Woods, E. B. 9:31; 26:115
Woods, F. 3:220; 11:393; 25:264
Woods, G. E. 24:34
Woods, G. G. 21:407
Woods, George 10:88; 20:396; 22:134; 23:177
Woods, George W. 18:224
Woods, H. 3:220; 12:163; 23:177
Woods, Henry 9:198
Woods, Hugh C. 22:110
Woods, Irac C. 18:224
Woods, Isaac 26:198
Woods, J. 14:261, 276; 18:61; 25:264
Woods, J. F. 1:181
Woods, J. G. 1:182
Woods, J. M. 3:220

Woods, Jacob 8:111; 22:328
Woods, James 9:198; 10:88; 11:177, 189, 429; 19:279, 293; 20:396; 21:407; 22:349
Woods, James C. 22:169
Woods, James M. 24:34
Woods, James W. 23:258
Woods, Jesse 8:44
Woods, Job R. 23:269
Woods, John 1:87; 5:34; 7:46; 8:111; 10:88; 12:160; 14:234; 17:424; 18:319; 21:263; 25:264; 26:115
Woods, John A. 11:273
Woods, John B. 16:63
Woods, John F. 23:177
Woods, John L. 20:139
Woods, John O. H. 16:130
Woods, Joseph 9:127; 27:131
Woods, L. 2:19; 25:123
Woods, L. E. 22:286
Woods, Leroy B. 21:407
Woods, O. 15:171
Woods, P. 25:264
Woods, Patrick 21:407
Woods, Peter 23:15
Woods, Playford 16:150
Woods, R. C. 3:220
Woods, Richard 25:264
Woods, Robert C. 9:100
Woods, S. 17:293
Woods, Samuel 10:144; 20:396; 21:162; 23:272
Woods, Seth 18:224
Woods, Sid 12:166; 26:200
Woods, Simon 19:315
Woods, Squire A. 24:34
Woods, Stephen 19:142
Woods, T. 2:19; 25:264
Woods, T. R. 16:130
Woods, Thomas 10:88; 11:406; 16:286; 18:201; 20:396
Woods, Thomas L. 22:115
Woods, W. 13:81; 16:264
Woods, W. C. 20:396
Woods, W. L. 11:253
Woods, W. W. 19:234
Woods, William 9:94; 10:88, 144; 11:114; 20:396; 21:407; 22:230; 23:83

Woods, William C. 12:145
Woods, William S. 11:47
Woodsend, T. 3:220
Woodsick, F. R. 23:307
Woodside, G. 1:87
Woodside, H. 21:46
Woodsides, R. T. 22:356
Woodsides, Robinson S. 22:459
Woodsides, W. J. 3:220
Woodson, Amos 18:269; 26:87
Woodson, Andrew D. 11:426
Woodson, Dasey 6:27
Woodson, George 6:28
Woodson, J. 10:209; 16:264
Woodson, J. J. 25:264
Woodson, James 26:84
Woodson, Jared 17:107
Woodson, Joseph 17:141; 24:206
Woodson, Moses 10:156; 19:220
Woodster, D. M. 25:127
Woodsworth, --- 18:185
Woodtridge, Claucen 18:269
Woodung, W. 2:19
Woodung, William 25:127
Woodvine, A. C. 10:144; 20:396
Woodvy, Charles 11:275
Woodwan, George C. 2:19
Woodward, A. 14:250
Woodward, A. M. 5:34
Woodward, Abner T. 13:123
Woodward, Albert 17:69
Woodward, Alexander 22:328
Woodward, Andrew L. 11:101
Woodward, Augustus A. 9:127
Woodward, Avey 24:34
Woodward, B. 1:185
Woodward, Charles 11:117
Woodward, D. 1:87
Woodward, Daniel B. 10:175
Woodward, David 7:115; 17:152; 21:407
Woodward, David C. 21:15
Woodward, E. 25:309

Woodward, Forest F. 21:89
Woodward, Frank 11:176
Woodward, G. 18:100
Woodward, G. H. 5:34
Woodward, G. W. 3:220
Woodward, George 14:237; 21:407
Woodward, George A. 6:11
Woodward, George T. 21:145
Woodward, H. B. 8:123
Woodward, H. C. 26:85
Woodward, Harry 21:407
Woodward, Henry C. 17:245
Woodward, Henry M. 17:69
Woodward, Hiram B. 12:46
Woodward, Hiram C. 9:94
Woodward, I. W. 12:160
Woodward, J. 3:220; 11:80; 14:128; 25:264; 27:134
Woodward, J. A. 1:87
Woodward, J. G. 16:264
Woodward, J. W. 25:264
Woodward, Jack 21:289
Woodward, Jacob 5:34
Woodward, James 10:144; 22:61
Woodward, James L. 21:84
Woodward, James M. 21:94
Woodward, James W. 17:28
Woodward, John 7:115; 11:274; 12:53; 15:79
Woodward, John A. 10:24
Woodward, John B. 22:445
Woodward, John E. 5:34
Woodward, John H. 7:46
Woodward, Josiah 11:394
Woodward, L. A. 3:220
Woodward, Lorenzo 21:219
Woodward, Oliver 25:309
Woodward, Oscar 16:146
Woodward, P. M. 20:396
Woodward, Robert 23:244
Woodward, Robert M. 10:88
Woodward, S. H. 19:332
Woodward, S. P. 3:220
Woodward, Samuel 8:58
Woodward, Silas 16:264

Woodward, T. 9:153; 25:264; 27:127
Woodward, W. 1:182; 15:255
Woodward, W. A. 3:220
Woodward, W. D. 3:220
Woodward, W. G. 9:238
Woodward, W. H. 18:21
Woodward, W. W. 3:220
Woodworth, Adolphus P. 15:52
Woodworth, Albert 17:452; 24:182
Woodworth, B. 3:220
Woodworth, Charles C. 19:43
Woodworth, D. 15:349
Woodworth, Douglass 12:46
Woodworth, Eben'r F. 22:275
Woodworth, Francis M. 11:81
Woodworth, G. W. 1:184
Woodworth, George 22:469
Woodworth, George L. 11:253
Woodworth, H. C. 23:57
Woodworth, Henry 22:61
Woodworth, J. O. 23:177
Woodworth, Jerome B. 9:106; 18:335
Woodworth, John B. 22:159
Woodworth, Lee 9:241
Woodworth, Marcus M. 17:89
Woodworth, Napoleon 22:286
Woodworth, Norman 12:46
Woodworth, O. 16:392
Woodworth, O. L. 22:414
Woodworth, Rowland P. 17:395
Woodworth, T. 25:264
Woodworth, Watson P. 21:263
Woody, G. 11:283
Woody, G. H. 14:129
Woody, Henderson 6:8; 18:116
Woody, John 4:63
Woody, Joseph 24:163
Woody, Philip 22:110
Woody, Robert 21:239
Woody, Thomas 21:291
Woof, Thomas B. 23:57
Wooff, William 20:396
Woofington, John 18:212

Woofter, Albert 19:43
Wookers, Michael 12:60
Wookorth, Zudwid 9:94
Wool, Alonzo 26:116
Wool, J. B. 20:131
Wool, R. 21:163
Wool, Samuel 17:141; 24:206
Woolace, George 17:189
Woolan, Joseph 15:255
Woolard, Lewis 22:445
Woolbridge, William T. 8:99
Woolcot, L. L. 11:290
Wooldridge, Joseph 21:407
Wooldridge, W. 13:123
Wooldy, Frank 9:160
Wooledge, Truman 12:46
Woolen, S. T. 19:43
Woolen, Thomas P. 23:83
Woolen, W. R. 25:274
Woolenweber, L. 1:87
Woolery, G. 1:180
Woolery, Henry 9:40
Woolery, John 22:110
Woolery, Whorton 22:230
Woolether, Martin 23:287
Wooley, Adam 25:124
Wooley, Benjamin 17:101
Wooley, Carroll 20:396
Wooley, Charles H. 16:264
Wooley, Daniel 22:110
Wooley, David S. 10:88
Wooley, E. 11:175
Wooley, G. W. 10:88; 20:396
Wooley, George 19:43
Wooley, Hiram 10:88
Wooley, J. 9:228; 18:389
Wooley, John 11:80
Wooley, Layton 17:69
Wooley, Samuel 9:17
Wooley, T. 23:254
Wooley, Thomas 17:449; 21:202; 24:174
Woolf, A. M. 1:182
Woolf, Jacob 22:110
Woolf, John W. 17:450
Woolf, Peter 13:123
Woolfe, D. 14:25
Woolfe, J. 14:25
Woolfe, James 12:66
Woolffin, H. 26:85
Woolfinger, E. 20:396
Woolfinger, H. 3:220
Woolfolk, Michael 8:111
Woolford, Isaiah 9:31
Woolford, John N. 17:446; 24:169

Woolford, John W. 24:34
Woolheater, A. 13:123
Woolheiser, F. 1:184
Woolheter, Benjamin 22:110
Wooliver, Miles 21:108
Woolley, H. 20:396
Woolley, J. 3:220
Woolley, J. C. 3:220
Woolley, M. 3:220
Woollums, Alexander 22:61
Woolly, --- 11:274
Woolman, D. F. 1:181
Woolman, E. 11:253
Woolman, H. 3:220
Woolnough, M. 7:55
Woolnough, William 18:325
Woolrick, Grandison 19:285
Woolrick, Grandleson 9:198
Woolridge, Daniel B. 22:134
Woolridge, J. B. 17:210
Woolse, Charles 16:392
Woolsencroft, Edward 23:57
Woolsey, Aaron 4:63
Woolsey, Charles A. 17:69
Woolsey, David 9:65
Woolsey, Francis E. 9:31; 18:319; 26:115
Woolsey, Frank 18:469
Woolsey, J. 3:220; 24:87
Woolsey, Jeremiah 11:216
Woolsey, R. 3:220
Woolsey, S. 10:31
Woolsey, Samuel 9:105
Woolsey, Simon 20:37
Woolsey, William 22:159
Woolsey, William H. 11:48
Woolsey, William J. 11:113
Woolslair, W. H. 3:220
Woolson, Gilbert 18:342
Woolston, Michael 22:399
Woolston, S. P. 3:220
Woolston, William 10:208
Woolum, R. 17:150
Woolums, Milton 11:80
Woolverson, Jackson 21:193
Woolvin, C. C. 11:393
Woolwine, Lewis 10:88
Woolwine, Louis 20:396
Woolworth, Solomon 10:88; 20:396

Woomer, William 22:444
Woorheis, E. 18:185
Woorkman, Rhodes 24:90
Woorman, J. 15:321
Woosley, David 10:144; 20:396; 23:57
Woosley, Elijah 11:81
Wooster, A. 14:129
Wooster, A. M. 2:19
Wooster, Aaron L. 13:55
Wooster, O. B. 25:124
Wooster, Oren 10:169; 19:221
Wooster, P. 1:87
Wooster, S. W. 15:255
Wooster, Thomas 11:317
Wooster, W. S. 15:83
Wooster, William 16:264
Wooston, M. 14:29
Wooteir, J. 25:127
Wooton, J. 21:46
Wooton, John 22:275
Wor---, Oscar 23:206
Worcester, B. F. 7:82; 25:309
Worcester, I. H. 9:153
Worcester, J. Y. 27:134
Word, A. 14:129
Word, Charles 17:141; 24:207
Word, Daniel D. 23:83
Word, H. 23:306
Word, J. R. 14:129
Word, Joshua 17:141
Word, William 9:138
Wordan, J. 19:265
Wordand, H. 3:221
Wordell, G. K. 3:221
Worden, A. 17:500
Worden, Alanson 7:115
Worden, Alexander 19:43
Worden, Amasa P. R. 22:61
Worden, Andrew G. 15:347; 16:392
Worden, C. E. 21:407
Worden, Charles 25:264
Worden, Chester 9:105
Worden, Cyrus 5:34
Worden, David 7:115
Worden, E. 25:264
Worden, Edward C. 12:46
Worden, Edwin 22:160
Worden, F. P. 16:142
Worden, G. B. 10:191
Worden, G. W. 3:221
Worden, George W. 23:111
Worden, H. 1:182
Worden, H. C. 24:34
Worden, Hiram 10:24

Worden, I. B. 18:185
Worden, Ira 12:120;
    15:367
Worden, J. 3:221
Worden, James 8:78
Worden, John 9:198
Worden, John S. 11:114
Worden, L. D. 20:87
Worden, N. F. 21:407
Worden, O. S. 4:63
Worden, P. 17:69
Worden, Peter 19:142
Worden, Schuyler 22:110
Worden, Silas 22:349
Worden, William 21:407;
    22:110
Worden, William R.
    23:197
Wordert, C. 20:396
Wordin, George G.
    11:132
Wordley, J. 15:52
Words, E. B. 18:319
Words, James 21:407
Wordsworth, Noyes W.
    10:88
Wordwell, M. S. 15:115
Worenton, J. H. 3:221
Worhis, John 18:42
Worin, J. M. 15:255
Work, --- 18:73
Work, A. 1:84
Work, A. A. 21:84
Work, Alexander 23:95
Work, Anderson R.
    22:495
Work, B. A. L. 23:265
Work, Elias D. 11:81
Work, George M. 4:63
Work, Isaac L. 22:444
Work, John W. 22:444
Work, L. M. 15:287;
    19:142
Work, Robert 10:144;
    20:396
Worke, John 22:349
Workem, J. H. 20:93
Workheiser, L. 15:255
Workhouse, D. J. 13:123
Workhuser, John 12:46
Working, N. 1:183
Workman, A. 3:221
Workman, A. N. 11:179
Workman, Albert G.
    22:239
Workman, Andrew 10:208
Workman, Benjamin
    22:275
Workman, Cyrus 12:46
Workman, Isaac 9:94

Workman, J. 3:221;
    11:317
Workman, J. W. 21:46
Workman, James 8:36;
    10:144; 18:168;
    20:396
Workman, James H.
    19:323
Workman, James K.
    22:230
Workman, John P.
    10:144; 20:396
Workman, Logan 17:141;
    24:206
Workman, N. 13:129
Workman, Noah 8:36;
    18:168
Workman, Thomas J.
    21:407
Workmuster, H. 1:184
Works, Charles C. 4:63
Works, F. 21:407
Works, T. H. 23:302
Works, William 1:88
Works, William W. 24:34
Workus, E. 10:203
Worland, Richard 1:85
Worland, William 20:188
World, Newton 22:61
Worldrich, William
    11:216
Worldton, Adam 9:100
Worley, --- 11:222
Worley, Aaron 17:323
Worley, Abram 26:86
Worley, Amos E. 22:459
Worley, Brice 11:47
Worley, David 23:177
Worley, Elisha 17:28
Worley, John 7:115;
    21:407
Worley, Julius 25:264
Worley, M. 8:69; 26:199
Worley, P. 23:177
Worley, P. C. 25:309
Worley, Reuben 17:240
Worley, S. 1:181
Worley, Valentine 20:194
Worley, William 18:403;
    23:197; 26:138
Worline, G. 22:495
Worls, D. E. 15:52
Worls, Ludwic 9:100
Worm, Peter 9:160
Wormeldorf, Joseph H.
    21:407
Wormells, Marion 11:321
Wormley, Jeremiah
    18:269
Wormworth, John 13:55
Worner, Andrew 15:79

Worner, Thomas 10:144
Wornick, Alexander 9:114
Wornock, Henry 22:275
Wornstaff, Henry L. 9:40
Wornstaff, R. L. 23:177
Wornys, --- 11:19
Worone, John 22:349
Worp, J. 3:221
Worrell, Floyd N. 22:444
Worrell, Harrison 18:116
Worrell, John 10:144;
    23:127
Worrell, John F. 15:255
Worrell, John W. 17:322
Worrell, Thomas 12:53
Worrill, John T. 23:83
Worringer, John 21:263
Worse, G. C. 21:108
Worsell, Jacob 18:73
Worstab, Charles 10:144
Worstal, Charles 20:396
Worste, James 19:231
Worstel, J. 24:87
Worstell, E. 26:131
Worster, C. B. 3:221
Worster, Charles W. 15:10
Worster, J. M. 10:203
Worster, William 21:238
Worster, William S. 12:79
Wort, Charles D. 22:239
Wort, Jacob 11:99
Wort, Joseph 11:99
Wort, S. W. 17:108
Wort, William 18:225
Worte, J. 3:221
Wortell, H. H. 3:221
Worten, William 10:98
Worter, Frank 8:36;
    18:168
Worter, John 9:94; 26:83
Worth, A. 1:85
Worth, Albert 8:126
Worth, Charles 12:46
Worth, Datus 22:286
Worth, E. 16:264
Worth, E. R. 19:142
Worth, Edmond E. 7:115
Worth, F. 1:88
Worth, F. B. 19:221
Worth, Frederick 12:46
Worth, I. H. 1:85
Worth, I. W. 1:83
Worth, J. 17:145
Worth, J. H. 4:63
Worth, J. W. 17:168;
    27:127
Worth, John L. 1:87
Worth, L. 11:87
Worth, Max 24:98
Worth, S. H. 9:153;
    27:128

Worth, Seth 1:83
Worth, W. W. 12:163
Worth, William 14:234
Worth, William H. 9:205
Worthen, D. 3:221
Worthen, D. J. 22:230
Worthen, George 1:85
Worthen, Harvey 21:407
Worthen, W. 3:221
Worthing, Augustine 7:62
Worthing, Ene. 25:125
Worthing, John 13:55
Worthington, Artis 22:230
Worthington, Charles
    10:177; 19:221
Worthington, D. H.
    22:230
Worthington, David R.
    12:79
Worthington, Edwin R.
    22:230
Worthington, Elias 18:389
Worthington, G. 1:84
Worthington, H. 14:234,
    261
Worthington, Ham 18:116
Worthington, J. 9:69
Worthington, Jefferson
    11:178
Worthington, John
    10:177; 19:221
Worthington, John A.
    23:177
Worthington, John W.
    22:495
Worthington, Josiah 9:9
Worthington, M. 11:253
Worthington, Martin T.
    22:134
Worthington, Reuben
    10:88; 20:396
Worthington, W. 11:397
Worthins, S. F. 3:221
Worthley, Edward 22:61
Worthley, John 5:34
Worthrope, Alex 12:46
Worthy, A. A. 3:221
Worthy, Osborn 24:34
Wortman, Aaron R.
    11:318
Wortman, F. V. 16:392
Wortman, George B.
    22:61
Wortman, J. T. 8:58
Wortman, Jacob 22:230
Wortman, James 21:84
Wortman, Reuben 9:40
Wortman, William 13:78
Worton, Thomas 9:74
Wortz, E. G. 1:185
Worwood, A. 16:275

Wosher, Lewis 9:198
Wosson, William 10:98
Wott, W. M. 14:129
Wotten, J. 3:221
Would, Joseph 3:221
Wouldridge, M. 16:264
Wounell, William 9:127;
    27:131
Wouson, Joseph P. 10:169
Woyer, J. S. 11:317
Wrahgg, D. L. 14:267
Wrallon, Samuel 11:80
Wrankle, Lawrence 13:55;
    16:63
Wray, David C. 23:57
Wray, F. C. 12:97; 15:362
Wray, F. M. 12:145
Wray, G. 1:186
Wray, H. 17:436
Wray, James P. 11:418
Wray, John 20:131
Wray, Samuel 3:221
Wray, T. C. 15:362
Wray, Thomas S. 7:46
Wray, W. 7:55
Wray, W. J. 11:49
Wreay, B. F. 19:142
Wregand, Magnees
    15:157
Wren, F. 8:69; 26:199
Wren, George 12:160
Wren, J. 14:129
Wren, Joshua T. 20:396
Wren, Louis 17:401
Wren, Oliver 12:46
Wren, Richard 7:137
Wren, Timothy 8:36;
    18:168
Wren, Warren 8:36;
    18:168
Wren, William 6:27
Wren, William J. 23:282
Wrenn, J. 13:102
Wrenn, James 16:360
Wrenn, Thomas 1:86
Wrenn, Thomas N. 8:123
Wrestler, John 24:87
Wrettle, S. M. 25:329
Wrider, A. H. 14:250
Wrieran, Peter 16:264
Wries, J. 3:221
Wrigert, M. 11:47
Wriggle, M. A. 12:46
Wright, --- 11:48; 13:102;
    17:45; 19:319;
    23:290
Wright, A. 1:183; 11:275,
    290, 292; 14:129;
    19:142
Wright, A. C. 14:129
Wright, A. G. 16:137

Wright, A. I. 14:234
Wright, A. P. 22:230
Wright, A. W. 1:87
Wright, Aaron 1:84; 21:89
Wright, Aaron C. 11:82
Wright, Abel 11:178
Wright, Albert 14:234;
    19:142; 21:62
Wright, Alexander 21:407
Wright, Alfred W. 20:117
Wright, Allen 17:61
Wright, Almon L. 22:469
Wright, Alonzo 19:43
Wright, Amos 17:28
Wright, Anderson 9:31
Wright, Andrew 8:36;
    18:168; 22:328
Wright, Andrew W.
    17:388
Wright, Anthony 17:189
Wright, Anton 26:234
Wright, Arthur 22:413
Wright, B. 1:181
Wright, B. C. 20:45
Wright, B. M. 26:207
Wright, Benjamin 9:226;
    18:389; 22:134
Wright, Benjamin F.
    11:132; 22:160, 231
Wright, Benjamin N.
    16:83
Wright, C. 3:221; 9:155;
    11:87; 27:128
Wright, C. C. 1:181
Wright, C. E. 3:221
Wright, C. R. 1:183
Wright, C. T. 25:309
Wright, Caleb 8:76
Wright, Calvin S. 24:34
Wright, Carpenter N. 4:63
Wright, Charles 3:221;
    9:205; 11:81; 16:264;
    21:193, 239; 22:349
Wright, Charles D. 22:469
Wright, Charles H. 23:95
Wright, Charles J. 20:86
Wright, Charles N. 21:408
Wright, Charles S. 3:221;
    7:46
Wright, Claudius D. 20:32
Wright, Columbus 17:201
Wright, Columbus F.
    10:144; 20:396
Wright, Cuffee 27:134
Wright, Cyrus 11:405;
    22:160
Wright, D. 3:221; 14:129;
    15:255; 21:86;
    25:264
Wright, Dana 21:248

Wright, Daniel 5:48; 9:138, 212; 27:130
Wright, Daniel F. 18:225
Wright, Daniel H. 11:48
Wright, David 10:98; 14:234; 22:231
Wright, E. 21:408; 25:335
Wright, E. J. 7:76; 13:123; 25:309
Wright, E. L. 15:115; 18:42; 27:126
Wright, E. P. 7:46; 24:115
Wright, Ebenezer 23:197
Wright, Edgar M. 10:24
Wright, Edmond 25:335
Wright, Edward 19:317; 21:289
Wright, Edward O. 18:344
Wright, Edwin F. 17:391
Wright, Eleam P. 23:281
Wright, Eli 8:36; 18:168
Wright, Elihu 4:63
Wright, Elijah 8:36; 18:168
Wright, Elizah 7:46
Wright, Elliott H. 4:63
Wright, Erie T. 17:45
Wright, Ezekiel 7:46
Wright, F. 1:183, 184
Wright, F. S. 11:101
Wright, Francis J. 13:59
Wright, Frank 9:233; 19:142; 20:396
Wright, Franklin G. 22:413
Wright, Frederick R. 21:408
Wright, G. 10:150; 15:10; 18:61; 19:50; 25:264
Wright, G. W. 11:177; 15:283; 25:264
Wright, Garrett 11:393
Wright, George 11:195; 13:123; 14:234; 15:255; 16:265, 286; 18:116; 21:197, 205
Wright, George B. 11:176
Wright, George D. 25:126
Wright, George M. 10:88; 13:123; 20:397
Wright, George W. 1:84; 5:34; 20:26
Wright, Gifford M. 24:57
Wright, Gilbert 1:191
Wright, Gilbert S. 9:199
Wright, Green 7:137
Wright, Green B. 10:98
Wright, H. 16:265
Wright, H. C. 16:63
Wright, H. E. 15:157
Wright, H. S. 13:55

Wright, H. V. 16:63
Wright, Harrison 12:53
Wright, Harvey L. 9:105
Wright, Headwin R. 7:115
Wright, Henry 11:81; 21:219, 289, 290; 25:287; 27:125
Wright, Henry G. 10:88; 20:397
Wright, Henry L. 18:342
Wright, Henry S. 16:63
Wright, Henry V. 13:55
Wright, Henry W. 20:185; 23:84
Wright, Hezekiah J. 23:183
Wright, Hiram 22:413
Wright, Isaac 9:31, 138; 17:316; 20:397; 22:230; 26:116; 27:129
Wright, Isaiah 1:193
Wright, Isham C. 22:134
Wright, Israel 9:199; 18:319
Wright, J. 1:182, 185; 3:221; 7:70; 18:100; 19:142; 22:160; 25:264; 27:127, 134
Wright, J. A. 14:25; 20:20
Wright, J. B. 20:3
Wright, J. C. 3:221; 27:134
Wright, J. D. 11:195
Wright, J. H. 14:129; 21:219
Wright, J. J. 3:221; 13:123
Wright, J. M. 7:62; 25:309
Wright, J. S. 3:221
Wright, J. T. 23:57
Wright, J. W. 3:221; 11:275; 14:234
Wright, Jackson 8:36; 18:168
Wright, Jacob 11:178; 13:59; 15:256; 19:293; 22:61, 445
Wright, James 9:153; 10:169; 14:129; 19:221; 20:150; 21:46, 62, 193; 25:264
Wright, James B. 21:263
Wright, James K. 10:98
Wright, James P. 22:275
Wright, James R. 13:55
Wright, James S. 10:24
Wright, James W. 9:14; 12:46; 23:84
Wright, Jasper 25:264
Wright, Jasper N. 22:134

Wright, Jerial 26:115
Wright, Jerome 7:46; 20:135
Wright, Jesse 7:137
Wright, John 7:115; 9:198, 238; 12:145; 14:129, 234; 16:265; 17:151, 189; 19:221, 243, 319; 22:517; 23:127; 25:264; 26:234
Wright, John A. 22:160
Wright, John Baty 18:212
Wright, John C. 11:82
Wright, John D. 8:111
Wright, John E. 21:145; 22:275
Wright, John H. 16:265
Wright, John J. 13:55
Wright, John L. 11:222
Wright, John P. 20:131
Wright, John S. 22:510
Wright, John W. 18:403; 23:117
Wright, Jonathan 17:289
Wright, Jordan 7:137
Wright, Joseph 5:48; 6:13; 7:46; 9:40, 94; 10:31; 19:315; 25:264; 26:83
Wright, Joseph C. 17:286
Wright, Joseph E. 12:56
Wright, Josh 17:189
Wright, Joshua 21:238
Wright, Josiah A. 21:263
Wright, L. D. 10:88; 20:397; 23:57
Wright, Leman 7:115
Wright, Leonidas 20:32
Wright, Leonidas H. 9:31; 18:321
Wright, Leroy 23:127
Wright, Leveir P. 21:108
Wright, Lewis 9:100; 11:383; 14:250; 18:403; 22:517; 26:131
Wright, Lewis C. 17:45
Wright, Lindsey 7:116
Wright, Lock 9:212
Wright, Lucas 18:299
Wright, Lucus 26:116
Wright, Lyman 23:262
Wright, M. 1:180; 3:221
Wright, M. E. 3:221
Wright, M. F. 8:36; 18:168
Wright, M. L. 11:176
Wright, Malley S. 9:234
Wright, Milton 8:99

Wright, Moses 3:221;
  9:65, 138; 27:130
Wright, N. W. 18:61
Wright, Nathan 9:46
Wright, Nathaniel 14:234
Wright, Nathaniel R.
  17:89
Wright, Nelson D. 20:32
Wright, Nelson J. 1:83
Wright, Newton P. 23:95
Wright, O. J. 14:261
Wright, O. M. 17:245
Wright, Oliver 10:175;
  16:265; 24:103
Wright, P. 1:184; 16:265;
  21:408
Wright, P. M. 22:61
Wright, Parker 17:189
Wright, Paul 21:46
Wright, Perry 11:176;
  26:198
Wright, Pery 8:44
Wright, Philbard S.
  19:269
Wright, Powell O. 10:208
Wright, R. 25:264; 27:125
Wright, R. H. 17:69
Wright, R. S. 9:153
Wright, Reuben 23:111
Wright, Reuben S. 27:129
Wright, Richard 16:265;
  20:37; 21:290
Wright, Robert 11:175;
  23:84
Wright, Robert A. 22:459
Wright, Robert W. 21:46
Wright, Rufus 5:48; 9:40;
  15:52
Wright, S. 1:87, 181;
  11:254, 294; 12:139;
  13:103; 14:25;
  15:148; 16:275;
  21:219; 22:328
Wright, S. G. 8:58
Wright, S. H. 11:330
Wright, S. M. 3:221
Wright, S. S. 13:129
Wright, S. W. 21:408
Wright, Salathiel 22:231
Wright, Sampson 1:192
Wright, Samuel 3:221;
  11:217; 22:414;
  24:103
Wright, Samuel D. 20:93
Wright, Samuel G. 21:88
Wright, Samuel H. 10:88;
  20:397
Wright, Samuel M. 9:100
Wright, Samuel W.
  22:494
Wright, Silas 19:43

Wright, Smith 23:57
Wright, Smith C. 21:108
Wright, Stephen C. 20:37
Wright, Stephen H. 4:69
Wright, Sylvester 13:55
Wright, T. 11:317; 21:113
Wright, T. C. 1:182, 183
Wright, Temple 22:356
Wright, Theodore 14:234
Wright, Thomas 9:203,
  226; 18:389; 19:221,
  285, 332; 22:61, 134
Wright, Thomas J. 23:95
Wright, Thomas W.
  23:127
Wright, W. 1:88; 3:221;
  8:123; 9:46; 12:91;
  16:360; 17:45;
  21:193; 25:125, 264,
  314; 26:131; 27:134
Wright, W. A. 3:221;
  13:102; 14:25;
  15:267
Wright, W. B. 16:265
Wright, W. H. 1:86;
  13:102; 24:100
Wright, W. M. 3:221
Wright, W. R. 25:264
Wright, W. T. 26:83
Wright, W. W. 20:397;
  25:124
Wright, Wade 21:408
Wright, Walker 6:13;
  18:100
Wright, Wesley 21:214
Wright, William 3:225;
  5:34; 8:58; 9:94, 217;
  11:47, 99; 14:129,
  234; 15:256, 332;
  17:316, 498; 18:73,
  225; 20:86; 21:46,
  408; 22:61, 110, 328,
  356; 24:47; 26:84
Wright, William A. 7:46;
  21:84
Wright, William C.
  11:274; 24:71
Wright, William D. B.
  8:99
Wright, William F. 1:85
Wright, William H.
  11:317; 14:234;
  21:84
Wright, William J.
  17:262; 23:58
Wright, William M. 9:94
Wright, William R. 5:48
Wright, William S. 1:84;
  23:95
Wright, William T. 9:95;
  16:5

Wright, William W. 4:63;
  10:88
Wright, William Winfield
  19:143
Wright, Wilson 25:264
Wright, Zach 11:215
Wright, Zachariah 27:132
Wright, Zalmon R. 22:61
Wrighten, W. F. 21:408
Wrightman, P. R. 25:264
Wrightman, Peter R. 5:34
Wrightnower, W. 26:131
Wrights, W. 19:143
Wrightwell, C. 16:265
Wrigle, Joseph J. 10:144
Wrigle, W. 1:182
Wrigley, Charles 17:194
Wrigley, G. 22:230
Wrigley, Miles 17:45
Wrin, John 11:176
Wrinch, John 20:15
Wripperdan, Samuel
  22:110
Wrist, Francis 4:63
Wriston, Joseph 18:105
Writ, G. 25:125
Writh, John 7:55
Writler, W. 21:95
Writsman, J. G. 22:110
Writsman, Peter 22:445
Writswon, Peter 11:275
Writter, Huser 9:14
Writzland, R. 14:25
Wroe, Hiram C. 20:15
Wroe, John 26:146
Wroe, Thomas 26:146
Wrong, C. 25:264
Wroten, D. 3:221
Wroten, S. C. 11:318
Wroth, John 25:264
Wroton, William 20:15
Wrow, Clay 5:48
Wry, George 11:178
Wryling, Michael 11:253
Wucks, Hampton 21:290
Wuder, A. H. 27:134
Wudling, John 17:427
Wuertz, Louis 21:238
Wugle, I. 18:185
Wuldoan, P. 22:349
Wulf, A. 1:185
Wulf, Christian 24:98
Wulf, Christian D. 23:95
Wulff, Frederick 12:169
Wullenburger, C. 1:88
Wulslager, John 3:221
Wunner, Samuel 25:125
Wunplepeck, Joseph
  22:494
Wuorst, Jacob 23:84
Wurmsteidt, Francis 5:34

Wurtz, Ferdinand 21:145
Wust, Carl 21:108
Wyanan, Henry 11:317
Wyand, Daniel F. 5:34
Wyand, Phil 19:143
Wyand, Philip 15:311, 356
Wyandt, D. 25:264
Wyandt, Joseph 12:46
Wyant, Elias 5:34
Wyant, H. 3:221
Wyant, Henry 18:42
Wyant, I. A. 26:131
Wyant, J. 25:274
Wyant, J. A. 9:46
Wyant, James 12:160
Wyath, J. 7:46
Wyath, John B. 8:99
Wyatt, A. H. 12:163
Wyatt, Amos 4:63
Wyatt, G. 1:89
Wyatt, George 18:269; 26:86
Wyatt, H. C. 1:84
Wyatt, Jacob 11:418
Wyatt, James 3:221; 10:98
Wyatt, John 4:63; 17:141; 24:71, 206
Wyatt, John D. 21:197
Wyatt, John W. 7:137
Wyatt, M. 18:389
Wyatt, M. J. 26:199
Wyatt, Philip 25:329
Wyatt, Richard 10:209; 21:62; 25:264
Wyatt, Robert 18:269; 26:87
Wyatt, Samuel 8:69
Wyatt, Samuel C. 15:256
Wyatt, Thomas 11:294; 26:86
Wyatt, W. A. 23:58
Wyatt, William 8:111; 17:169, 192; 22:275
Wyatt, William E. 8:69
Wybe, M. 14:261
Wyble, Jacob 11:178
Wyck, Albert 25:264
Wyckhames, D. D. 3:221
Wyckoff, A. V. 15:164
Wyckoff, D. G. 1:87
Wyckoff, Ephraim 22:61
Wyckoff, James 7:46
Wyckoff, W. 9:199
Wyckoff, William W. 9:31
Wycoff, Burkley B. 10:144; 20:397
Wycoff, Francis 11:222
Wycoff, James 10:88
Wycoff, L. U. 23:207
Wycoff, Thomas C. 8:36

Wycoff, W. 19:272
Wycroff, W. 17:98
Wye, George 5:48; 25:264
Wyer, Charles L. 5:34
Wyer, Peter Daniel 12:160
Wyer, R. 3:221; 14:234
Wyer, William 16:113
Wyess, Edward 23:304
Wyett, A. 18:61
Wyett, J. 3:221
Wyett, James B. 23:307
Wygal, John 25:264
Wygand, Ch. 14:234
Wygant, James 23:84
Wygant, L. A. 9:153
Wygant, Thomas 18:282
Wyken, Daniel J. 7:46
Wyker, W. C. 11:254
Wykes, Charles 22:61
Wykoff, J. 14:129
Wyland, J. N. 8:76
Wyland, L. A. 1:87
Wyland, Simond 1:84
Wylde, Charles 21:197
Wyle, M. 14:234
Wyle, Paul 10:144; 20:397
Wyle, W. 19:143
Wyley, James 18:185
Wyley, William 10:144; 20:397
Wylie, A. 16:275
Wylie, Alexander 9:95; 26:83
Wylie, Hance V. 23:281
Wylie, Harvey H. 21:62
Wylie, J. 19:143
Wyllie, James 13:55
Wyllis, Ralph J. 17:245
Wyllyams, Frederick 18:441
Wymai, Henry 26:198
Wyman, A. 3:221
Wyman, A. H. 20:157
Wyman, Allen H. 21:94
Wyman, Benjamin 13:55
Wyman, Charles E. 23:177
Wyman, Chauncey 19:43
Wyman, Cyrus 25:124
Wyman, D. 19:288
Wyman, Daniel 9:199
Wyman, Don 11:81
Wyman, E. J. 9:105
Wyman, Elijah 9:65
Wyman, F. M. 1:87
Wyman, Frederick 11:324
Wyman, G. H. 1:87
Wyman, George 13:123; 21:263
Wyman, George B. 13:55

Wyman, George H. 14:234
Wyman, H. C. 3:221
Wyman, H. S. 25:309
Wyman, Henry 10:88; 20:397
Wyman, J. 3:221
Wyman, J. E. 16:392
Wyman, James 10:88
Wyman, Joel W. 18:389
Wyman, L. W. 21:408
Wyman, Leroy 19:43
Wyman, P. A. 12:60
Wyman, Thomas 25:265
Wyman, W. 21:408
Wyman, W. H. 14:234
Wyman, W. W. 19:231
Wyman, William 16:65
Wyman, William W. 9:199
Wymar, Homer S. 7:76
Wymbs, Michael 10:9
Wymeb, David 11:178
Wymer, G. G. 20:397
Wymer, George G. 10:88
Wymer, John 15:89
Wymer, W. F. 22:231
Wymore, A. E. S. 8:58
Wymuth, W. P. 5:34
Wynans, J. 3:221
Wyncook, Abram 13:59
Wyncoop, G. 3:221
Wyncoop, T. J. 3:221
Wyne, Henry 8:44
Wyne, James W. 23:258
Wyne, W. E. 3:221
Wynekoop, James A. 22:114
Wyner, Michael 22:239
Wynes, George W. 21:46
Wyngo, James 7:137
Wynings, John 25:265
Wynkook, Wesley 11:176
Wynkook, James 12:47
Wynn, David J. 24:57
Wynn, Edward 19:325
Wynn, H. 3:221
Wynn, J. D. 1:96
Wynn, James 22:444
Wynn, John W. 22:506
Wynn, Nathan G. 12:79
Wynn, Peter 14:234
Wynn, Thomas 7:137
Wynn, W. H. 17:204
Wynn, William 17:145
Wynn, William D. 16:63
Wynne, George W. 24:168
Wynor, John 24:87
Wynsman, F. W. 21:408
Wyon, George 11:324

Wyoskesett, Paul 14:234
Wyre, Edward 27:133
Wyre, N. 10:203; 18:185
Wyrick, C. C. 9:226;
    18:389
Wyrick, Eli 3:221; 17:343
Wyrick, Ephraim 17:46
Wyrick, Henry 15:324
Wyrick, J. M. 22:231
Wyrick, Joshua L. 17:89
Wyrick, William 22:275
Wyrne, J. P. 27:127
Wyrucur, Asa 7:46
Wyse, John 13:123
Wysham, Samuel 6:20;
    18:100
Wyss, John B. 11:277
Wythe, Robert 23:183
Wyzant, Louis A. 27:127
Wyzincke, Casper 7:116

X

Xander, John 22:445
Xayent, Joseph V. 22:414

Y

Y---, G. G. 23:302
Y---, H. 16:392
Y---, J. 17:218
Y---, J. A. 24:115
Y---, P. 15:62
Y---, R. 20:175
Y---, S. 21:169
Yaber, Philip 21:408
Yacht, E. 3:222
Yackall, H. 1:186
Yackjer, John 22:349
Yadd, R. 13:102
Yaden, J. M. 17:150
Yadon, Jacob 22:275
Yaeger, Conrad 1:89
Yageng, F. 14:234
Yager, C. 25:129
Yager, Daniel 6:28
Yager, George 11:217;
    22:231
Yager, George W. 23:258
Yager, J. 16:265
Yager, John 23:265
Yager, W. H. 18:460
Yager, William 23:58;
    25:335
Yaghle, C. 3:222
Yagle, John F. 22:110
Yahner, Albert 22:349
Yairs, Adam 11:254
Yakely, William 10:192

Yakey, A. 21:205
Yakley, William 18:185
Yale, Alfred 14:234
Yallsbrezht, --- 12:47
Yamas, Alex 12:47
Yames, Christian 4:63
Yames, Robert 4:63
Yancey, Ambrose 11:132
Yancey, Christian 11:179
Yancey, J. 11:291
Yancey, John 21:15
Yancey, William 8:44;
    26:201
Yancy, --- 8:111; 23:207
Yancy, Beziah 11:222
Yancy, Charles 17:189
Yancy, Emanuel 21:290
Yancy, John H. 24:34
Yancy, Walter C. 20:131
Yandall, Marcus 18:168
Yandell, W. 18:269; 26:88
Yander, Samuel 22:414
Yandle, William O.
    20:397
Yaney, George 15:256
Yang, Samuel 23:84
Yank, Conrad 19:288
Yank, D. 1:89
Yankee, Henry 22:61
Yankee, John M. 20:397
Yanker, John M. 10:88
Yankessly, S. 14:25
Yankessly, T. 14:25
Yankin, John 14:234
Yankorly, S. 14:25
Yankorly, T. 14:25
Yanksuitch, Windelin
    19:43
Yanslyke, R. B. 1:89
Yanson, H. 1:186
Yant, C. B. 22:356
Yant, Jacob 22:61
Yant, William 19:221
Yantiss, Jonah F. 22:110
Yantz, H. 1:186
Yantz, Henry 22:61
Yantz, I. 18:185
Yantz, J. 10:203
Yaple, Allen 16:135
Yaple, J. 25:265
Yaple, Jeremiah 5:55
Yaple, T. I. 12:57
Yapp, George W. 11:394
Yarber, B. R. 22:507
Yarber, George 21:290
Yarber, Howard 17:150
Yarber, Lewis 9:203;
    19:285
Yarber, Pleasant 17:141;
    24:207
Yarber, Thomas 21:290

Yarber, W. 22:328
Yarbes, A. 17:189
Yarbor, Y. 3:222
Yarborough, James
    22:275
Yarbrough, Jacob 22:349
Yarbrough, M. C. 23:186
Yarder, S. 23:177
Yardley, B. F. 23:177
Yardley, E. 24:87
Yardley, James 25:128
Yardley, William 19:221
Yardly, William 1:89
Yardron, Jerry 27:135
Yardron, Jesse 9:138
Yarger, A. 3:222
Yarger, Henry 22:231
Yarger, Samuel 21:205
Yarger, W. H. 25:128
Yargus, John A. 22:231
Yarham, J. W. 14:25
Yarham, W. J. 13:102
Yarhouse, Jacob 22:231
Yarm, William 20:50
Yarn, James M. 23:255
Yarnall, J. 17:427
Yarnel, Martin R. 11:179
Yarnell, Israel 24:181
Yarnell, J. E. 3:222
Yarnell, Jesse 12:54;
    18:168
Yarnell, Thomas 22:275
Yarnell, V. 15:337;
    16:265
Yarnett, George 14:234
Yarnold, H. 1:89
Yarns, George 18:212
Yarrece, William 14:234
Yarrington, A. 5:34;
    25:265
Yarrington, Horace 7:116
Yaskins, M. D. 17:394
Yast, H. 16:265
Yast, John M. 5:34
Yaten, Jacob 9:226
Yater, Jacob 18:389
Yates, A. 15:79
Yates, Alexander 12:79
Yates, Alexander H.
    22:459
Yates, Amos S. 11:291
Yates, Butler 17:141;
    24:207
Yates, Charles 20:397
Yates, Charles M. 18:269;
    26:87
Yates, Comes 17:61
Yates, Cyrus 13:55; 16:63
Yates, Daniel 6:28
Yates, E. W. 17:157
Yates, Enoch 13:59

Yates, G. W. 7:55
Yates, George H. 11:179
Yates, H. 8:76
Yates, Haskell 10:208
Yates, Henly 17:145
Yates, Henry 10:24
Yates, Ira 18:100; 24:169
Yates, Isaiah 7:137
Yates, Ishmael 23:272
Yates, J. 3:222
Yates, J. F. 17:157
Yates, Jacob 8:44; 26:201
Yates, James 16:265
Yates, James H. 21:113
Yates, Jasper R. 11:394
Yates, John 7:55; 10:88;
    12:172; 20:397;
    23:58, 84
Yates, John W. 17:421;
    22:496
Yates, Joshua 22:275
Yates, Madison 17:421
Yates, Nelson 8:99
Yates, Pake 8:76
Yates, R. 21:408; 23:58
Yates, S. 1:100
Yates, Samuel 8:99, 117;
    18:330
Yates, Thomas 11:179;
    22:349
Yates, W. C. 3:222
Yates, W. J. 11:321
Yates, William 8:69;
    21:290
Yates, William H. 11:99
Yates, William L. 20:20
Yates, William R. 15:26
Yates, Wyatt 18:105
Yatt, Jacob W. 10:88;
    20:397
Yatton, Lucius 5:34
Yaucenn, F. 1:186
Yaughber, Isaac 11:121
Yaulin, E. 11:254
Yaumans, W. C. 11:132
Yaunce, J. 22:356
Yaunt, Henry 22:61
Yauson, Peter 9:114
Yaut, William 10:169
Yaw, Andrew J. 13:55
Yaw, John W. 16:63
Yaw, Jonathan 15:148
Yaw, L. 21:408
Yaw, Wallace 9:14
Yawman, M. 1:186
Yeacer, Ferdinand 19:143
Yeagar, F. 15:331
Yeager, Alexander 26:201
Yeager, Anton 13:55
Yeager, Daniel 18:100
Yeager, F. 1:186

Yeager, F. C. 1:186
Yeager, George 18:168
Yeager, J. 3:222
Yeager, James A. 22:496
Yeager, James C. 23:177
Yeager, James H. 14:234
Yeager, John 3:222; 4:63;
    15:115; 22:239;
    24:98
Yeager, L. 3:222
Yeager, Nicholas 8:69;
    26:201
Yeager, Samuel 3:222
Yeager, William 22:496
Yeager, William G.
    17:351
Yeagle, H. 11:418
Yeagley, George 22:414
Yeakey, John H. 22:110
Yeakley, G. W. 11:275
Year--y, J. 25:265
Yeardley, Albertine 7:116
Yearger, Lewis 16:360a
Yeargin, James A. 23:58
Yearkes, Charles B.
    16:115
Yearley, John 23:95
Yearly, Zeno S. 22:164
Yearsley, G. 25:265
Yearwood, James J.
    10:144; 20:397
Yeasley, --- 10:8
Yeast, Adam 21:127
Yeast, C. 9:155
Yeast, Jacob 7:55
Yeast, P. 27:135
Yeast, R. 3:222
Yeater, William 15:148
Yeates, Isaac D. 7:116
Yeatman, Hooper 19:143
Yeaton, E. M. 25:265
Yeaugur, Lewis 4:63
Yeazel, William 23:84
Yedder, Stephen 16:63
Yehender, Chris 26:132
Yehl, Alfred 14:234
Yeiger, Henry 11:185
Yeisley, Jacob 13:55
Yelden, James 21:46
Yelgler, J. G. 25:265
Yelkin, John 10:88
Yelkon, John J. 20:397
Yelly, Andrew 8:99
Yelton, John J. 24:34
Yelvey, Charles 20:131
Yencer, J. D. 3:222
Yendle, William O. 10:88
Yene, George 18:225
Yenger, A. G. 15:256
Yenter, William 12:139
Yeoman, Ira 22:110

Yeoman, Isaac 18:100
Yeoman, Robert 25:265
Yeoman, Samuel F. G.
    7:70
Yeomand, G. 3:222
Yeomans, Benjamin R.
    20:32
Yeomers, George 25:265
Yeople, J. 14:129
Yeothers, Alfred H. 23:58
Yera, Oliver 13:123
Yerba, Edward 22:495
Yerby, John 7:137
Yerenton, A. 1:89
Yergenson, A. 23:197
Yerger, J. 9:153
Yerger, John 27:135
Yerkes, Leander 22:160
Yerks, Lewis M. 22:469
Yers, L. M. 15:157
Yerton, Thomas 20:141
Yesant, Courraia 20:191
Yessen, A. 3:222
Yest, A. 8:58
Yettaw, L. 25:265
Yetter, C. 14:129
Yetton, Benson 16:265
Yetton, James F. 23:84
Yeuts, E. 14:235
Yewend, Clarendo 24:108
Yewing, Roscoe G.
    16:392
Yewing, W. E. 25:265
Yewman, Henry W.
    15:256
Yheller, W. H. 13:102
Yieldhall, R. 3:222
Yiesley, Jacob 16:63
Yingling, E. 3:222
Yingling, H. A. 14:234
Yingling, John 13:78
Yman, Charles 25:265
Yoakum, Allen 22:61
Yober, David 22:328
Yober, J. 18:269
Yock, C. B. 12:97
Yock, William 17:93
Yockey, James E. 22:231
Yockey, John 7:62
Yockey, Philip 11:179
Yocomb, J. 3:222
Yocomb, W. B. 3:222
Yocombs, H. 3:222
Yocum, D. 3:222
Yocum, Francis M. 24:60
Yocum, J. A. J. 9:65
Yocum, J. P. 11:49
Yocum, Jerome N. 22:231
Yocum, Malon 15:25
Yocum, Silvester 20:181
Yoden, Moses F. 11:179

Yoder, D. F. 25:265
Yoder, Daniel 13:123
Yoder, David 22:446
Yoder, Jacob 21:263
Yoders, J. D. 13:126
Yoeley, S. 1:89
Yoeman, Isaac 6:21
Yoens, James 22:517
Yoerder, Aaron 22:495
Yoffe, --- 24:47
Yoh, Israel 11:275
Yoha, Jacob 17:213
Yoha, William H. 23:177
Yohe, Henry 11:82
Yohe, John H. 22:110
Yohn, H. 15:256
Yohn, Joseph 26:201
Yoho, Peter 12:47
Yoho, Reuben 15:256
Yohon, A. J. 1:96
Yoht, R. 14:25
Yoke, Elisha 5:34
Yoke, Jacob 8:111
Yoke, James W. 22:446
Yokeley, William 22:329
Yoken, John 13:123
Yokers, William 13:76;
    19:143
Yokler, A. J. 26:201
Yokoff, W. 19:287
Yole, Elisha 25:265
Yoler, J. 1:89
Yolk, J. W. 14:234
Yoman, John H. 9:95;
    26:87
Yon, Nelson 18:169
Yond, J. 16:275
Yong, Daniel 19:221
Yonger, Charles 25:265
Yonker, Gotheib 11:185
Yonker, H. 7:46
Yonkes, Anthony 22:16
Yor, John 11:217
Yoran, Sylvester 12:47
Yorber, J. 26:87
York, A. G. 13:102
York, A. L. 9:153; 27:135
York, Aaron 11:114
York, Alfred 14:235
York, Almeron 15:283;
    25:265
York, Alonzo 12:47
York, Andrew J. 22:231
York, B. T. 1:89
York, Balam 17:410;
    22:134
York, Benjamin O. 19:231
York, C. B. 15:362;
    19:143
York, C. F. 9:65
York, C. P. 16:63

York, Charles 3:222;
    11:49
York, Charles F. 13:55
York, Dolos 4:63
York, E. 1:186; 12:85;
    16:360
York, E. A. 1:89
York, Edward 12:79
York, Erastus 5:55
York, G. H. 19:243
York, George 10:154;
    16:265; 19:221
York, George W. 10:88;
    20:397
York, Henry 11:217
York, Henry C. 21:46
York, Hiram C. 4:63
York, Horace J. 4:63
York, Isaac 15:157; 19:43
York, J. C. 1:186
York, J. F. 14:129
York, J. M. 11:49
York, J. W. 25:129
York, James 4:69
York, Jesse O. 11:82
York, John 10:88; 20:397
York, John K. 13:55
York, M. 11:132
York, M. S. 22:275
York, Mill'd. 25:265
York, Morris 19:43
York, Nicholas 9:127;
    27:135
York, Oliver 22:469
York, Orestes J. 18:74
York, P. 1:186
York, P. S. 21:169
York, S. 5:51
York, Sylvester 7:116
York, Thomas J. 17:209
York, W. 5:55
York, W. H. 1:186; 12:79
York, W. W. 17:150
York, Walter E. 19:231
York, William 8:99;
    17:337
York, William A. 8:36;
    21:263
York, William B. 24:47
York, William H. 15:13;
    18:168
York, Zac 20:397
York, Zach 9:233
Yorke, C. 3:222
Yorke, Manuel 22:275
Yorke, Peter 25:284
Yorkey, H. 7:46
Yorkley, N. J. 8:69
Yorlet, H. 7:70
Yorst, F. 10:31
Yorter, David 3:222

Yorton, James 19:143
Yorw, William 18:389
Yost, --- 19:323
Yost, Alex 13:55
Yost, David 22:496
Yost, George 22:160
Yost, Isaac S. 18:74
Yost, John 9:95; 11:318;
    18:100; 26:87
Yost, Nicholas 12:47
Yost, Philip D. 23:183
Yost, William T. 10:88;
    20:397
Yother, James E. 17:343
Yotter, Daniel F. 5:34
You, I. F. 18:74
Youell, W. 11:292
Youels, H. E. 25:265
Youer, Samuel 18:168
Youger, D. 17:189
Youghs, James 18:21
Youmans, Aaron 4:64
Youmans, Jason J. 22:173
Youmans, William H.
    21:145
Younce, C. A. 3:222
Younce, Joseph A. 22:507
Younce, Philip 8:99
Younce, Philip P. 18:116
Yound, David F. 23:95
Young, --- 3:222; 9:199;
    13:76; 15:52; 17:509
Young, A. 3:222; 7:46,
    76; 8:111; 16:265;
    25:265, 309; 27:135
Young, A. B. 3:222
Young, A. H. 26:214
Young, A. M. 14:129;
    19:143
Young, A. N. 13:76
Young, Aaron 19:221
Young, Abiah 22:231
Young, Abraham 21:238
Young, Abram 5:34;
    19:231; 22:329
Young, Adam 8:36;
    10:177; 18:168;
    19:221; 22:231
Young, Albert B. 18:42
Young, Alexander 9:95;
    26:87
Young, Allen 14:235
Young, Amos 7:116
Young, Andrew 21:408
Young, Andrew G. 12:47
Young, Andrew J. 17:213
Young, Antney 11:217
Young, Arthur 10:211;
    18:456
Young, Augustus 23:127

Young, B. F. 8:58;
14:235; 25:128
Young, Barney 17:61
Young, Bella 26:234
Young, Benjamin 22:446
Young, Benjamin C.
22:522
Young, Benjamin D.
22:16
Young, Benjamin S.
15:164
Young, Beverly D. 16:63
Young, Buck 9:212
Young, C. 1:186; 3:222;
9:153; 13:102;
27:135
Young, C. H. 1:89
Young, C. J. 1:186
Young, C. L. 3:222
Young, C. P. 9:153;
27:135
Young, Calvin W. 22:507
Young, Carl 12:10
Young, Charles 15:115;
18:42, 116; 21:84,
290; 22:287, 459
Young, Charles A. 6:20;
18:100
Young, Charles E. 11:82
Young, Charles W. 24:62
Young, Chicken 10:208
Young, Christian 17:28;
21:408; 22:169;
25:265
Young, Clark 13:56
Young, Clemens 22:275
Young, Cornelius 12:47,
79
Young, D. 3:222; 14:235;
15:52
Young, D. J. 16:265
Young, Daniel B. 24:98
Young, Daniel C. 16:63
Young, David 1:89;
8:111; 10:177;
11:407; 12:79; 13:56,
59; 16:63; 17:322,
363, 427; 20:157;
22:231; 24:181
Young, David C. 13:56
Young, David H. 10:88;
11:179
Young, David J. 20:397
Young, David Z. 15:93
Young, Dudley 17:286
Young, E. 3:222
Young, E. C. 1:186
Young, E. H. 20:397
Young, E. O. 11:49
Young, E. W. 3:222
Young, Edson 24:34

Young, Edward 4:64;
7:137; 18:61
Young, Edward C. 13:56
Young, Edward H. 10:89
Young, Edward W. 4:64
Young, Edwin 3:222
Young, Elijah 7:55
Young, Ephraim 21:238
Young, Esquire 10:89;
20:397
Young, Eugene 3:222
Young, Ezra 1:89
Young, F. 1:186
Young, F. B. 3:222
Young, F. D. 1:89
Young, F. E. 20:397
Young, F. H. 11:179
Young, F. M. 14:235;
20:45
Young, F. S. 19:265
Young, Francis 22:496
Young, Franklin E. 10:89
Young, Fred. C. 20:191
Young, Frederick 16:265;
20:2
Young, Freeman 22:160
Young, G. 1:89; 13:80;
27:135
Young, G. A. 1:186
Young, G. H. 14:235
Young, G. I. 23:127
Young, G. W. 1:186;
3:222; 8:58
Young, George 4:63, 64;
11:179, 217; 12:47;
13:123; 14:129;
16:130, 265; 22:329;
25:265
Young, George B. 4:64
Young, George C. 3:222
Young, George F. 10:89;
20:397
Young, George W. 9:14;
10:89; 12:60; 19:43,
221; 20:102, 397;
21:84; 23:272;
25:265; 27:135
Young, Green 18:269;
26:88
Young, H. 1:186; 7:46;
8:58; 9:31; 14:129;
18:319; 26:117
Young, H. A. 15:347
Young, H. C. 23:177
Young, H. E. 9:95; 26:87
Young, H. H. 1:100; 7:62
Young, H. L. 21:408
Young, H. M. 21:113
Young, H. Oscar 4:64
Young, H. S. 21:408
Young, Hanks 11:179

Young, Harrison 14:129;
17:277, 297
Young, Harry G. 10:211
Young, Harvey 15:52
Young, Henry 3:222;
6:20; 7:46; 10:88;
11:132, 383, 429;
12:79; 15:115;
17:323, 406; 18:100;
20:397; 25:265, 287
Young, Henry A. 14:235
Young, Henry C. 10:88;
20:397
Young, Henry M. 22:160
Young, Henry W. 17:89
Young, Hiram 13:56
Young, Hiram N. 12:47
Young, Homer 21:62
Young, I. 15:256
Young, Ira 22:110
Young, Isaac 9:213;
18:269; 19:50;
20:102; 22:275, 414;
26:88
Young, Israel 4:64;
12:139; 15:148
Young, J. 1:186; 3:222;
15:256; 21:408;
23:118; 25:265
Young, J. B. 3:222;
10:192; 11:179;
18:185; 25:129
Young, J. C. 1:89; 3:222;
19:265
Young, J. H. 20:157;
21:205
Young, J. J. 7:84; 13:76;
21:408
Young, J. L. 2:20; 25:128
Young, J. M. 16:153
Young, J. S. 25:265
Young, J. T. 23:255
Young, J. W. 2:20; 3:222;
10:98; 25:128
Young, Jackson 8:78;
19:323
Young, Jacob 1:89; 9:100,
114; 10:89; 11:82;
17:28; 18:61; 22:110,
496; 26:87; 27:135
Young, James 3:222;
4:63; 5:34, 48; 6:20;
7:65; 8:99; 12:79;
15:10; 16:65, 265;
17:141, 150; 18:100,
427; 19:50; 20:26;
21:62, 214; 22:231;
24:207; 25:265;
27:135
Young, James C. 11:275;
22:496

Young, James K. 10:144; 20:397; 22:61
Young, Jasper J. 20:397
Young, Jasper L. 10:88
Young, Jerome 7:55
Young, Jesse 21:163
Young, Jim 22:517
Young, Joel F. 22:231
Young, John 3:222; 7:46; 9:8; 10:144; 11:49, 217; 12:47; 13:59; 14:235; 15:115; 16:63; 17:143; 18:185, 269; 19:288; 20:82, 397; 21:87, 163, 214; 22:160; 25:265; 26:87
Young, John A. 14:235; 22:496
Young, John B. 8:111; 12:47; 21:263
Young, John C. 9:199
Young, John F. 5:55
Young, John G. 13:56
Young, John H. 7:116; 27:135
Young, John J. 1:89; 18:74
Young, John L. 22:446
Young, John M. 9:95
Young, John S. 10:89
Young, John W. 10:175; 19:221; 22:61; 26:248
Young, Jonathan 18:269; 23:281; 26:87
Young, Joseph 8:36; 10:89, 144; 11:217; 16:15; 17:389; 18:168; 20:180, 397; 21:290
Young, Joshua B. 12:47
Young, Joshua C. 21:244
Young, Kine 18:269; 26:88
Young, L. 1:89
Young, L. B. 24:34
Young, L. G. 25:128
Young, L. G. C. 18:403
Young, L. P. 1:89
Young, Lake 22:231
Young, Leonard 1:89
Young, Lewis 17:357
Young, Lewis E. 23:183
Young, Lewis G. C. 18:403
Young, Louis 12:47
Young, Luther 17:47
Young, M. A. 9:153; 14:129; 27:135
Young, M. M. 25:309

Young, M. V. 20:140
Young, Martin 16:145
Young, Math 17:446
Young, Mathew 11:418
Young, Matthew P. 24:169
Young, McCager 20:181
Young, Michael 23:84
Young, Miller 22:110
Young, Milo 13:56
Young, Mitchell 14:318
Young, Moses C. 7:116
Young, N. C. 3:222
Young, Nathan 20:32
Young, Nathan L. 27:135
Young, Nathan S. 9:138
Young, Nelson 10:154; 12:79; 15:13; 19:221
Young, Nicholas 12:79; 15:52
Young, O. 7:76; 14:129; 25:309
Young, Oliver 18:74
Young, Oliver P. 24:60
Young, Orlando 9:228; 18:389
Young, Orson 17:389
Young, Ovid 8:99
Young, Owen N. 9:40
Young, Owen W. 18:299; 26:117
Young, P. 9:153; 27:135
Young, P. S. 9:153; 15:349; 16:392; 27:135
Young, Paris 17:141; 24:207
Young, Peter 9:153; 17:89; 23:111; 27:135
Young, Peter B. 11:275
Young, Philip 11:87; 22:114
Young, Proctor 21:408
Young, R. 9:65; 13:123; 16:265; 17:189; 25:265
Young, R. S. 14:276; 17:498
Young, R. W. 9:100
Young, Reuben 8:78
Young, Richard 11:217; 13:56; 27:135
Young, Richmond A. 9:14
Young, Robert 3:222; 5:48; 14:286; 27:135
Young, Robert M. 22:446
Young, Roger 9:138
Young, Ross 18:269; 26:87

Young, S. 9:155; 11:254; 14:129; 19:143, 265; 27:135
Young, S. B. 14:129
Young, S. D. 3:222; 14:261; 25:265
Young, S. J. 26:207
Young, S. P. 25:309
Young, S. Westley 15:256
Young, Sampson 12:79; 15:10
Young, Samuel 4:69; 15:115; 16:360; 22:62, 349, 414; 23:283
Young, Samuel D. 1:89
Young, Samuel F. 22:459
Young, Samuel H. 10:144; 20:397
Young, Seth 17:444; 24:163
Young, Sheppard 21:290
Young, Silas 11:394, 427
Young, Spencer 22:329
Young, Squire 22:517
Young, Sylvester 21:408
Young, T. M. 18:269; 26:88
Young, T. S. 9:199; 25:265
Young, Theodore 22:498
Young, Thomas 7:81, 116; 9:9; 10:89; 12:47; 14:261; 15:283; 19:50; 20:191, 397; 22:495; 23:177; 25:265, 309; 26:214
Young, Thomas B. 8:36; 18:168
Young, Thomas M. 22:231
Young, Thomas S. 5:34
Young, U. W. 20:82
Young, Uriah 22:496
Young, W. 1:89, 186; 3:222; 9:155; 15:21; 17:218; 19:143; 25:128; 27:135
Young, W. A. 3:222
Young, W. C. 7:47; 20:397; 23:58
Young, W. H. 3:222; 11:283; 19:143; 20:397
Young, W. J. 11:330
Young, W. R. 11:321
Young, Wallace 11:217
Young, Warren 22:62; 27:135
Young, Weadham 12:54

Young, Wilber F. 19:43
Young, Willard A. 9:127
Young, William 1:89;
    4:64; 7:46, 137;
    8:44; 9:95; 10:185;
    11:179; 12:60, 79;
    13:59, 76; 14:235;
    17:246; 18:185, 225,
    269; 19:43, 143;
    21:47; 22:62, 164,
    275, 329; 26:87, 88,
    201
Young, William A.
    15:178
Young, William B. 22:414
Young, William C. 10:88
Young, William D. 4:63
Young, William H. 10:24,
    88; 11:49, 283;
    23:127, 177
Young, William J. 22:62
Young, William L. 16:286
Young, William M. 10:88;
    20:397
Young, William P. 23:177
Young, William W.
    22:110, 469
Young, Williard B.
    27:135
Youngblood, --- 18:21
Youngblood, Archibald
    8:36; 18:168
Youngblood, Jacob 15:62
Youngcloud, CHarles
    4:64
Younger, Francis 17:354
Younger, John 12:97;
    15:362; 19:143
Younger, Joseph 11:429
Youngerman, Daniel
    20:397
Youngerman, G. 22:445
Youngerman, George M.
    24:47
Younginar, Joseph 16:63
Younginker, Leonard
    22:239
Youngk, George 1:89
Youngkin, R. A. 12:47
Younglas, Orick 9:241
Younglove, G. 1:186
Youngman, George
    17:277
Youngs, Charles 3:222
Youngs, J. 11:275
Youngs, James C. 22:160
Youngs, Jeremiah 9:127;
    27:135
Youngs, Jerome C. 22:134
Youngs, John Y. 22:414
Youngs, Samuel 11:49

Youngs, W. 13:76
Youngs, William 17:210;
    19:143
Younk, Joseph 22:496
Younker, S. 3:222
Younker, W. 3:222
Younkin, John 14:235
Younkins, William 11:179
Yount, Jacob 10:144;
    17:113; 20:398
Yount, Joseph O. 23:84
Yount, Raimons 18:42
Your, W. R. 11:99
Yourk, G. W. 1:186
Yourke, William C.
    17:215
Yournams, George 4:64
Yourson, D. C. 1:89
Yous, George 13:56
Youser, Albert N. 17:61
Youst, James 10:144;
    20:398
Yout, George W. 11:195
Yow, J. 1:186
Yow, William 9:226
Yowart, J. R. 9:31
Yowl, Henry 22:275
Yowman, J. 25:265
Yoxen, S. 23:265
Yu--der, Ekie--- 25:128
Yucknell, Z. G. 13:123
Yugler, Jacob 26:136
Yuill, Thomas 1:89
Yule, J. 11:254
Yumans, A. 1:89
Yumroald, Solomon
    18:117
Yundy, H. 17:190
Yuner, Andy 11:179
Yung, Homer 1:89
Yunker, G. 7:47
Yunt, James 22:110
Yupp, George 9:40
Yuterler, W. A. 3:222
Yutzy, John 24:57
Yyke, Henry 24:57

Z

Z---, F. 20:398
Z---, H. C. 26:201
Z---, Henry 18:42
Z---, J. 16:265
Z---, W. 17:333
Zaberbier, Charles 18:169
Zabiowski, John 12:10
Zaboraski, Martin 20:87
Zabraough, P. 14:129
Zachariah, Brior 11:99
Zachary, Peter 17:286

Zackary, Michael 17:204
Zackery, Daniel 22:523
Zackman, Henry 4:64
Zahn, George 13:56
Zahnders, August 12:60
Zaic, P. 3:223
Zailagka, W. 13:102
Zaing, Michael G. 12:160
Zakery, W. 14:129
Zalant, Ch. 24:115
Zalkner, B. C. 12:97
Zaller, John 10:89; 20:398
Zan, Charles 21:263
Zand, Z. J. 9:127; 27:135
Zane, Hiram C. 12:56
Zane, James 22:174
Zane, M. 3:223
Zane, William 3:223
Zane, William C. 26:88
Zaner, E. W. 15:302
Zaner, Erhardt 15:148
Zanger, Sylvester 4:64
Zanise, John 22:414
Zankers, Fred 12:160
Zannier, Jesse 1:89
Zaphan, H. P. 3:223
Zapp, John 17:245
Zareovich, John 13:56
Zarewich, John 16:63
Zarfoss, A. S. 1:89
Zarr, Charles 22:110
Zarr, Francis 22:414
Zarring, G. W. 1:186
Zartman, --- 10:32
Zartman, D. 19:315
Zaung, G. W. N. 12:160
Zbilous, Joseph 13:56
Zbilows, Joseph 16:63
Zeagamyer, Hermann
    22:62
Zeagler, John 9:199
Zeagler, Michael 19:285
Zeak, William A. 22:111
Zearing, Joseph 22:231
Zebb, Henry 7:137
Zeboldt, Samuel E.
    23:177
Zech, Frank 8:36; 18:169
Zech, Jacob 8:36; 18:169
Zeck, George C. 1:89
Zeck, W. J. 3:223
Zeckman, Samuel 16:130
Zedemah, Adolph 4:64
Zeed, Charles 13:128
Zeegles, John 16:265
Zeek, --- 22:357
Zeet, John 16:265
Zefley, Andrew 11:114
Zehnder, Jacob 13:56
Zehner, Francis 11:82
Zehr, Charles 7:116

Zehuder, Jacob 16:63
Zeick, Charles 21:408
Zeigelbaur, Casper 20:398
Zeigellair, Casper 10:89
Zeiger, James M. 18:403
Zeiger, Ludwig 10:89;
  20:398
Zeigle, James C. 24:182
Zeigler, A. 15:256
Zeigler, August 19:288
Zeigler, F. 3:223
Zeigler, Frank 15:362
Zeigler, John A. 13:56
Zeigler, John E. 10:208
Zeigler, Michael 9:199
Zeigler, Moses 27:135
Zeigler, S. F. 1:186
Zeigler, William 2:20
Zeiler, W. 1:186
Zeiner, Ferdinand 4:64
Zeisert, --- 2:20
Zeitz, H. 1:186
Zelhart, G. 13:102
Zeliph, E. 1:186
Zell, Franklin M. 12:47
Zell, J. J. 1:89
Zell, J. W. 12:47
Zellar, W. W. 11:49
Zellars, Asa 11:418
Zeller, A. 25:265
Zeller, A. S. 11:180
Zeller, E. O. 8:58
Zeller, Frank 17:452;
  24:182
Zeller, Jacob 16:265;
  24:57
Zeller, Louis 17:354
Zellhoffer, Michael
  17:101
Zeluff, John M. 21:263
Zemkeller, C. 7:62
Zemmer, Henry 11:49
Zenetto, Arnold 19:221
Zenger, Ernest 22:111
Zengerio, Andrew 11:180
Zengle, Joseph 17:423
Zentemeyer, F. 14:129
Zenze, Andrew 23:84
Zephernick, Alpheus
  22:231
Zerb, J. 1:186
Zergable, Louis 24:71
Zerger, A. 1:186
Zergler, Frand 19:143
Zergler, Frank 12:97
Zerl, S. 3:223
Zerphes, Solomon 22:446
Zerphy, J. 3:223
Zerr, Joseph 22:111
Zerter, G. 3:223
Zetchie, Albert 1:89

Zett, J. 3:223
Zettler, Michael 20:139
Zeune, Charles 23:84
Zeutmeyer, Henry S.
  23:58
Zew, S. A. 25:274
Zickparse, Elias 27:156
Zieger, Loring 8:36;
  18:169
Ziegera, Olts 19:43
Ziegle, James C. 17:452
Zigler, Balder 26:88
Zigler, Daniel 25:129
Zigler, Daniel A. 10:169
Zigler, Jacob 23:177
Zike, J. 17:113
Zike, James W. 22:446
Ziller, D. 14:129
Zilligans, John 11:49
Zillis, L. 19:285
Zillox, William 1:89
Zilsdorf, Fritz 16:145
Zim, Blau 24:207
Zim, Hubert 9:100
Zimelman, P. 20:398
Zimelman, Philip 10:89
Zimer, William 10:208
Zimman, --- 21:408
Zimmans, Alonzo D.
  11:406
Zimmer, C. 1:186; 16:265
Zimmer, Francis 21:408
Zimmer, John 18:225
Zimmer, Joseph 10:89;
  20:398
Zimmer, P. 14:129
Zimmer, Peter 9:233;
  20:398
Zimmer, William 14:250
Zimmerly, A. 14:131
Zimmerly, J. 15:267
Zimmerly, S. 14:131
Zimmerman, --- 9:31;
  18:321; 20:398
Zimmerman, A. 10:89;
  12:60; 20:398
Zimmerman, Adolph
  25:274
Zimmerman, Albert
  19:143
Zimmerman, B. 3:223
Zimmerman, B. F. 1:89
Zimmerman, B. M. 8:69;
  26:201
Zimmerman, Benjamin F.
  24:47
Zimmerman, C. 1:100;
  12:97; 19:143
Zimmerman, Caleb
  20:181

Zimmerman, Charles
  3:223
Zimmerman, D. 14:261;
  16:142, 154
Zimmerman, Elias 4:64
Zimmerman, Franklin A.
  23:15
Zimmerman, Frederick
  11:117
Zimmerman, Fritz 23:117
Zimmerman, G. 1:89, 186;
  15:362; 16:360
Zimmerman, George
  22:231
Zimmerman, George M.
  22:111
Zimmerman, Henry 11:49,
  330
Zimmerman, I. 25:265
Zimmerman, J. 3:223;
  7:62; 14:279; 23:58
Zimmerman, J. B. 22:498
Zimmerman, J. R. 14:235
Zimmerman, Jacob 4:64;
  13:126; 16:130;
  23:177; 26:88
Zimmerman, James
  20:398
Zimmerman, Jesse 13:76
Zimmerman, Jessie
  19:143
Zimmerman, John 22:160
Zimmerman, John F.
  7:116
Zimmerman, Joseph
  10:89; 22:111;
  23:183
Zimmerman, L. H. 20:45
Zimmerman, M. 3:223;
  9:153; 11:294
Zimmerman, Martin
  23:177
Zimmerman, Martin B.
  15:52
Zimmerman, Matthias
  17:503
Zimmerman, Orlando
  23:258
Zimmerman, P. 12:91;
  15:79
Zimmerman, P. S. 16:360
Zimmerman, Peter 7:47;
  11:49; 12:63
Zimmerman, R. M.
  11:324
Zimmerman, S. 25:129
Zimmerman, Samuel W.
  23:177
Zimmerman, T. B. 15:256
Zimmerman, Thomas
  20:150

Zimmerman, W. H. 1:186
Zimmerman, W. W.
   15:115
Zimmermann, G. 14:129
Zimmers, Peter 17:93
Zimmila, John 16:88
Zimmons, Abram 27:135
Zimrick, Fred 11:114
Zin---, Griff 19:143
Zinchelt, George 14:235
Zinck, C. M. 17:322
Zinckenham, J. 14:129
Zincle, Edward 11:132
Zingling, John 16:265
Zink, A. J. 3:223
Zink, George 10:89;
   20:398
Zink, Philip 22:62
Zinke, J. 1:186
Zint, J. J. 3:223
Zipe, M. 14:276; 17:495
Zipperlain, Christopher
   5:55
Zipperlein, C. 25:265
Zirbel, John 7:84
Zirble, John 21:408
Zirby, Daniel 22:239
Zirkaler, August 15:178
Zizbin, Jacob 15:115
Zoast, Morgan 22:446
Zoeller, Charles 10:89

Zoellner, C. 19:276
Zoffi, Frederic 23:104
Zollars, Frank 22:231
Zoller, C. 23:58
Zoller, Edward 19:143
Zoller, F. W. 3:223
Zoller, George 24:10
Zoller, Henry 12:47
Zoller, S. 19:143
Zoller, Stephen 19:143
Zollers, C. 11:439
Zollers, Nathan 9:31
Zollicoffer, Emil 10:144;
   20:398
Zollner, T. 11:406
Zolman, Alfred P. 20:15
Zolman, Elias 22:111
Zonker, David 15:62
Zook, Azariah 1:89
Zook, Hinckley 4:64
Zook, John 22:62
Zook, William N. 23:306
Zootman, Ferdinand 17:89
Zoran, Philip 3:223
Zorge, Samuel 18:288
Zorn, John 1:89
Zornes, George 8:99
Zorns, W. 15:347
Zortman, S. A. 23:58
Zottler, Edward 15:317
Zouldice, John 8:36;
   18:169

Zouver, Ephraim 17:213
Zower, William 16:392
Zowvell, John 16:130
Zschoche, Theodore S.
   4:64
Zubber, John 16:113
Zuber, J. M. 3:223
Zuberbier, Charles 8:36
Zucker, George 22:329
Zug, Albert 25:129
Zuh---, --- 21:209
Zuleney, Joseph 6:34
Zulher, Charles 24:163
Zulkner, B. C. 15:362
Zuluy, James 25:329
Zumalt, Obadiah 22:62
Zumberger, Henry 21:127
Zumwalk, Simon 13:56
Zundle, William 1:89
Zundlock, Ferdinand 4:64
Zunkle, John 21:408
Zupermick, R. 20:45
Zur Megede, William
   20:143
Zurcher, Charles 17:427
Zurpleah, A. 25:265
Zuver, James W. 1:89
Zweifel, Albert 22:62
Zwick, G. I. 12:54
Zwol, Henry 22:469
Zyla, Anthony 22:173